SHAKESPEARE

Twenty-Three Plays
and the Sonnets

SHAKESPEARE

Twenty-Three Plays and the Sonnets

WITH GENERAL INTRODUCTION, SPECIAL INTRODUCTION FOR EACH PLAY, AND NOTES

BY

THOMAS MARC PARROTT

Professor of English, Princeton University

Associate Editors

EDWARD HUBLER

Assistant Professor of English
Princeton University

AND

ROBERT STOCKDALE TELFER

CHARLES SCRIBNER'S SONS

New York · Chicago · Boston
Atlanta · San Francisco · Dallas

PRINTED IN THE UNITED STATES OF AMERICA

H

PREFACE

THE PRESENT COLLECTION of twenty-three of Shakespeare's plays embraces all that are likely to be read in schools and colleges. The sonnets have been included because they throw light upon the personality of the poet-playwright and contribute not a little to the better understanding of the plays.

This text is the result of a very careful study and, where possible, a collation of the original editions. All possible use has been made of the advance in recent years in the determination and interpretation of a genuine text, purified from the arbitrary alterations of earlier editors. Yet the best older editions have been consulted, and generally accepted emendations have been received into the text. Since this edition is meant for use in schools and colleges, the editors have limited the discussion of textual problems to a minimum. Brackets marking, often inconsistently enough, departures from the original do not appear. Old lists of characters, stage-directions, etc., have, so far as possible, been retained, but whatever seemed necessary to a modern understanding has been silently added. The accepted division into acts and scenes has been retained; brief localizations of the action have been added, and, for purpose of reference, the standard line numbering of the Globe Shakespeare has been followed. The editors have deliberately refrained from taking up space and the time of students with discussion of matters in which, as a rule, college students have little interest.

Old spellings, such as *swound* for *swoon,* have been retained and glossed where they preserve an Elizabethan word-form. The old punctuation has been followed except where it would confuse or mislead a modern reader; the loose and easy syntax of the Elizabethans and the fluent rhythm of Shakespeare's dialogue have been too often disturbed in modern editions by a system of logical punctuation. Old elisions and contractions have been preserved where they indicate pronunciation or are needed for the metrical structure of a line. In particular, care has been taken to distinguish in verse between the full *ed* and the elided *'d,* past and participial forms; in prose, however, the full form has been regularly preferred.

The glossary, printed for convenience at the foot of the page, has been prepared for the average undergraduate reader. Repetitions have not been avoided, since it is unlikely that the student will read all the plays in the volume or recall from his reading of one play a definition necessary to his understanding of a later line. Difficult passages have been paraphrased, but elaborate critical and esthetic comment has been purposely avoided. That, we believe, is rather the function of the teacher than the editor. The notes and glosses are in the main the work of Doctor Telfer.

By way of general introduction, *William Shakespeare, A Handbook,* has been reprinted with a few necessary changes and corrections. The special introductions to individual plays are in the main the work of the general editor. Eight of them, which had previously appeared in print, have been revised and shortened for the present work; thirteen have been written specially for this volume. The introduction to *Richard III* is the work of Doctor Telfer; that to *Coriolanus* is by Professor Hubler, who has also written the introduction to the Sonnets.

There has been throughout the preparation of this work collaboration and mutual aid, but the general editor assumes full responsibility for the final form of the text, the notes, and the opinions expressed.

THOMAS M. PARROTT

CONTENTS

SHAKESPEARE

Twenty-Three Plays
and the Sonnets

WILLIAM SHAKESPEARE

General Introduction

I

ENVIRONMENT AND HEREDITY

ENVIRONMENT and heredity do not determine, but they at least condition and influence genius. It is well, therefore, before beginning the study of Shakespeare's life and work to know something of the town in which he was born, the surroundings that gave form and color to his early life, and the parents from whom he sprang.

The little town of Stratford-on-Avon numbered at the time of Shakespeare's birth about two thousand inhabitants. No greater mistake could be made, however, than to liken it to some American village of this size. It had a local history and tradition stretching back almost to pre-historic times. Its name bears testimony to its historic past. A Roman road (*strata via,* Old English *straet*) crossed the Avon (Welsh *afon,* river) by a *ford,* and the combination of Latin, English, and Welsh gives us Stratford-on-Avon. Near this point there was a Roman military post to guard against raids by the Celtic tribes of the great forest of Arden (Celtic *Ard,* great, *Den,* wooded valley; cf. the *Ardennes* of France and Belgium). In Saxon times the district was under the control of the Bishop of Worcester and a monastery near the site of the present church became the nucleus of a little group of houses. At the time of the Norman conquest, the inhabitants, some 150, were apparently all engaged in agriculture. In the reign of Richard I, however, one of the bishops of Worcester transformed the community into a little town by opening streets, laying out building sites, and granting a charter for a weekly market. The Rother, *i.e.* cattle market (Old English *Hreother*) has given its name to a main street in the modern town.

The lovely church of the Holy Trinity, where Shakespeare was baptized and in which he lies buried, owes its present form in the main to the benefactions of John of Stratford, a Stratford priest who rose in the reign of Edward III to be Archbishop of Canterbury and Lord Chancellor of England. He enlarged the old church and founded a chantry to sing masses for the souls of himself, his relatives, and his friends. His nephew, Ralph, Bishop of London, built a stone house near the church for the residence of the chantry priests. This building was called the College of Stratford and the church, under the control of the chantry priests, became known as the Collegiate Church of Stratford. A Warden of the College under Edward IV built the beautiful choir, and a later successor completed the building by constructing the double row of large windows above the nave which now form so conspicuous a feature of the church from without and flood its interior with light. During all these changes the church remained what it still continues, the parish church of the community, the centre of the religious life of Stratford.

Another religious organization developed in the Middle Ages which had an even greater influence on the life of the town, the Guild of the Holy Cross. Originally a simple fraternity for mutual aid and the performance of religious rites and duties, it came to be in the fourteenth and fifteenth centuries, the dominant social and administrative body of the community. It was richly endowed and every citizen of good standing in the town was a member. As the brethren were under vow not to enter into litigation with one another without the consent of its officers, it acquired considerable civil jurisdiction. Its fame spread throughout England; rich merchants in distant cities were among its members, and even a Prince of the blood, Shakespeare's "false, fleeting, perjured Clarence" was glad to enroll himself and his wife, daughter of the Kingmaker Warwick, in the fraternity.[1]

Meanwhile the Guild was giving practical and permanent evidence of its wealth and beneficence. The foundations of its noble chapel were laid by Robert of Stratford, the father of Archbishop John. The chapel itself was enlarged and rebuilt in its present form toward the close of the fifteenth century by Hugh Clopton, a citizen of Stratford, who had made his fortune in London and become Lord Mayor of that city. Clopton also built the stately stone bridge which crosses the Avon to-day and left money for the education of poor boys at Oxford and Cambridge. The Guild was specially interested in education, and early in the fifteenth century it founded a free grammar school for the children of its members. It was at this school, still in existence, that Shakespeare probably received his education.

The sweeping changes of the Reformation profoundly modified the social life of Stratford. The College was suppressed and the building became a private residence, occupied in Shakespeare's day by his friend John Coombe. The Guild was dissolved and its property passed to the Crown. For a period of six or seven years the little town was left almost wholly without means of self-government. In 1553, however, a charter was obtained from Edward VI which remodelled the old Guild into the new Corporation of Stratford.

The property of the Guild, the chapel and guildhall, school-house, almshouse, and real estate in the town, was handed over to the Corporation. The old officers of the Guild, the bailiff, aldermen, chamberlains, and so forth, became municipal officials. The town council, composed of these officers and of ten leading citizens, became the supreme local authority and exercised strict control over the lives and conduct of the citizens. It fixed the price and regulated the quality of ale and bread, prescribed the dress of all inhabitants over six years of age, imposed fines for profanity and non-attendance at church, set refractory citizens in the stocks, and ducked scolding wives in the Avon. Stratford became under the new charter a little self-governing world; but the government lay solely in the hands of a small body, the "free men of the Corporation," order and degree were strictly observed, and the idea of personal liberty so dear to the heart of modern Americans was a thing unknown. Local autonomy and governmental control of private life count for quite as much in differentiating Shakespeare's Stratford from an American village as do the old traditions and monuments in stone that link it to its past. In Shakespeare's day it was a thriving country town, humming with industry, the market-place of a rich farming countryside, and by no means out of touch with London.

Round about Stratford spreads the lovely country of central England, far more heavily wooded in Shakespeare's day than now, but less so then than in former times when, as the saying ran, a squirrel might leap from bough to bough across all Warwickshire. It was, and is, a gently rolling country of plough-land and pastures set off by hedgerows and watered by slow full streams that rise at times to flood their banks. The rich soil and the mild moist climate give rise to a profuse vegetation; the trees are heavy with leafage and the grassy lanes and green meadows gay with flowers in spring and summer. The streams swarm with fish; the air is vocal with the song of thrush, lark, and nightingale, and in Shakespeare's day there were still deer in the woods and boar in the deeper recesses of the forest of Arden. All this wealth of nature lay at Shakespeare's very door; five minutes' walk from his home on Henley Street would take him into the heart of the country, and there is abundant evidence in his plays and poems that Shakespeare knew and loved all the rich and changing aspects of nature that lay about his youth. He is the country-bred poet, as his friend Jonson was the product of the city streets and taverns, and the nature that Shakespeare loved was not the grand, the terrible, nor the stormy nature of the mountains or the sea, but the soft and smiling revelations of beauty of his own English country-side.

One other feature of the country around Stratford is worth noting. It was rich in memories of the Wars of the Roses. Warwick, with its ancient castle, a few hours' walk from Stratford, had been the seat of the Yorkist Kingmaker. Coventry, with its old walls, only a little further distant, had been a Lancastrian stronghold. This epoch of English history, not

[1] The ordinances of the Guild in the reign of Richard II are reprinted in Sidney Lee's *Stratford-on-Avon* and throw much light on the social life of the town.

much further removed from Shakespeare's day than our own Civil War from us, had a peculiar fascination for him. His chronicle plays deal almost exclusively with this period; of earlier English kings and heroes, William the Conqueror, Richard Cœur de Lion, the great Edwards I and III, he has little to say. His great cycle of Histories from Richard II to Richard III deals wholly with the struggle between York and Lancaster, and the lessons that he draws from this struggle, the folly and the wickedness of civil strife, the necessity and blessedness of national unity and civil peace, he was never tired of repeating.

Into Stratford town there came about 1550 the poet's father, John Shakespeare. He belonged to a family, perhaps originally Norman, that had many branches in Warwickshire. Another John Shakespeare, often confused with him, was his fellow citizen, a shoemaker in Stratford. John came of sound yeoman stock; his father, Richard, was a farmer who rented the fifty-acre farm of Asbies from Robert Arden, a rich squire of the neighboring village of Wilmcote. John, however, turned his back upon the farm, and opened a shop in Stratford for the sale of country produce, corn, wool, timber, skins, and so forth, and enrolled himself in the Glovers' guild. His first recorded appearance in Stratford is not exactly to his credit, for in April, 1552, he was fined 12d for failing to remove a dirt heap in front of his house. But in spite of this unpromising beginning John Shakespeare prospered and rose rapidly to be one of the leading citizens of the little town. No doubt his marriage about 1552 to Mary Arden, the daughter of his father's landlord, helped to establish his social position. He bought several houses in the borough, contributed to the relief of sufferers from the plague, and helped to pay the beadle's salary. He took an active part in town affairs and was chosen by his fellow citizens for one office after another. He became first ale-taster, (supervisor of the price and quality of ale and bread offered for sale), then town councillor, chamberlain, (keeper of borough accounts), alderman, and finally in 1568 bailiff or presiding officer of the Corporation. In this capacity he granted licenses to travelling companies of players, the Queen's and Worcester's Men. The year 1568 marks the first recorded appearance of professional actors at Stratford and it is quite likely that William Shakespeare saw his first stage play as a boy of four standing by John's side in the guildhall where these companies performed.

John Shakespeare seems, however, to have failed to retain the honorable position that he had won in the community. His family and his expenses increased rapidly and he seems to have met with financial losses. We hear of vexatious lawsuits and heavy fines. He begins to absent himself from the meetings of the town-council; in 1578 it is recorded that he was unable to pay the weekly sum of fourpence for the relief of the poor expected from every councillor. In the same year he mortgaged and sold outright property that his wife had inherited; finally in 1586 he was deposed from his office as alderman because of his continued absence from council meetings, and in 1592 he was reported as a "recusant," that is, one failing to attend the parish church, and the excuse was given that he feared to be arrested for debt.

Apart from these recorded facts little is known of the poet's father. It is probable that he was in our sense of the word uneducated; indeed it was almost impossible for a country boy in the early sixteenth century to obtain even the rudiments of an education. He probably could read and certainly knew how to keep accounts, but wrote with difficulty and preferred to use the Glovers' trademark as his signature rather than to sign his name. Tradition reports him as "a merry-cheeked old man" talking in his shop about his famous son and asserting that "Will was a good honest fellow but that he (John) durst have cracked a jest with him at any time." He lived to see this "good honest fellow" "the best of the family" [1] as an old account calls him, restore their sinking fortunes, purchase New Place, one of the largest houses in Stratford, and secure for him from the Herald's Office a patent of gentility and the well-known coat of arms.

From his father the poet seems to have inherited his interest in practical affairs, his love of landed property, and above all his sanguine temperament and his love of a good jest.

Shakespeare's mother came from a higher class in society than did his father, that of the landed gentry. Her family, the Ardens, was

[1] An interesting novel by this name, the work of Caroline Oman, gives a lively and on the whole accurate picture of Shakespeare's environment and his life in Stratford and in London.

one of the great clans of Warwickshire. As far back as 1438 a Robert Arden had been sheriff of the county and his descendant, Edward Arden, also once high sheriff, was executed in 1583 for alleged complicity in a Roman Catholic plot against the life of Queen Elizabeth. Mary's father, Robert, a distant relative of the main branch, was well-found in this world's goods. He lived at ease in a large well-furnished house hung with "painted cloths." He was the proud owner of many sheep and cattle and still prouder father of seven daughters. His will shows him a professing Catholic and it is quite possible that Mary adhered in secret to her father's faith. She married John Shakespeare about a year after her father's death, bore him eight children, survived him seven years, and was buried in Stratford churchyard.

Shakespeare's mother, we may well believe, had even less knowledge of letters than his father, but she bequeathed her son two excellent things: a gentle nature and a reverence for the past, the old manners, the old traditions, and the old faith of England. The word "gentle" is almost a stock epithet applied by his contemporaries to William Shakespeare, and in Elizabethan English the word had a more strictly defined meaning than it has with us. It implied race and breeding; a "gentle" man was a gentleman, and there is nothing plainer in Shakespeare's work than his inborn sympathy with refinement, courtesy, and aristocratic charm. He detested the London mob as heartily as any nobleman, and probably nothing in his life gave him greater pleasure than his success in lifting himself out of the despised players' caste and writing himself down "William Shakespeare of Stratford-on-Avon, gentleman." It is worth noting, too, that Shakespeare had nothing of the prejudice partly national, partly religious, against Catholicism which marked so many of his contemporaries. Spenser might symbolize the Roman church in the person of a foul witch; Marlowe introduce the Pope and Cardinals into a scene of gross buffoonery in *Dr. Faustus,* and Dekker entitle an anti-papal play *The Whore of Babylon.* Shakespeare on the other hand has no trace of the Puritan's bitterness or the playwright's readiness to raise a laugh by a jeer at Rome. The figures of priests, friars, cardinals, and bishops that he introduces in his plays are always respectable, sometimes venerable characters, and his references to Catholic doctrines and practices are always reverent. This does not mean that Shakespeare was at heart a Roman Catholic; he lived and died a professing member of the Church of England, and, no doubt, like most Englishmen of his day, felt himself safe in the *via media* that his church marked out for him. Yet the absence in Shakespeare of any trace of religious prejudice in an age of controversy, calumny, and persecution is not a little remarkable, and it is not altogether fanciful to attribute this trait, in part at least, to a filial respect for the faith of his gentle mother.

II
SHAKESPEARE'S YOUTH

Of the early life of Shakespeare at Stratford we have only two recorded facts: the entry of his baptism, and the bond relating to his marriage. Yet we know enough of his environment to be able, in some measure, to reconstruct his early life; and we have ample testimony to his early studies, pursuits, and pastimes in allusions scattered throughout his work. The picture, then, that we may draw of Shakespeare's youth is by no means purely imaginary.

According to the parish register of Stratford, *Gulielmus filius Johannes Shakspere* was baptized on Wednesday, April 26, 1564, the festival of England's patron saint, St. George. The exact day of his birth is unknown; the tradition that he was born on April 23, the day of his death in 1616, is late and unreliable. In those days, however, children were baptized as soon as possible and it is unlikely that William was born before the 21st or 22nd of April. He saw the light in one of the two contiguous houses in Henley Street, probably not in the one now shown as the Birthplace, which did not become John's property till 1575, but in the other, now called the Museum, which John had bought just before his marriage.

William was the oldest surviving child; two girls born before him had died in infancy; but a numerous brood succeeded him, three brothers, Gilbert, Richard, and Edmund, and two sisters Joan and Ann. In Shakespeare's home the strict discipline of the Middle Ages still prevailed. The boy rose early, waited on his parents at table, kept silent in their presence, capped to his elders on the street, and, no doubt, was whipped for any petty fault. Yet his parents must have been proud of their vigorous, handsome eldest son and arranged at the first moment for him to enjoy the education which had been denied to them.

The old Guild school had been transformed by Edward VI in 1553 into the King's New School of Stratford-on-Avon. The salary of the master was fixed at £20 a year, a much higher figure than was usual in Elizabethan schools, and a succession of able scholars conducted the teaching. The school offered free education to all the sons of Stratford citizens, and when we consider John Shakespeare's position in the town it seems incredible that he should have neglected to avail himself of this opportunity for his son. A lively appreciation of the advantages of a classical education was one of the distinguishing characteristics of Elizabethan England, as is shown by the founding of almost as many free schools during the Queen's reign as had been in existence up to her time, and John Shakespeare, town-councillor and bailiff of Stratford, was not the man to deprive his son of such an advantage.

Before William entered the grammar school, however, he must have mastered the alphabet in the horn-book, learned to spell out simple English, and to write in the old-fashioned script which he continued to use all his life.[1]

The curriculum of an Elizabethan grammar school was almost entirely composed of Latin and Latin was the vehicle of instruction, for the end of education was conceived to be the ability to read, speak, and write this common language of scholars. The Latin Grammar of Colet and Lyly had been authorized by royal proclamation as the only textbook to be used in English schools. The rules were written in Latin and the unhappy schoolboy was forced to learn them by heart before he understood the language in which they were written. Along with the study of grammar came exercises in Latin conversation, based on phrase books like the *Sententiae Pueriles,* which the boys also had to learn by heart. The bits of Latin dialogue between the schoolmaster, Holofernes, and the parson in *Love's Labour's Lost* are modelled on such exercises and show how well Shakespeare remembered his early training. Along with these studies came the reading of Latin: *Æsop's Fables* and the *Eclogues* of Baptista Mantuanus, the popular Renaissance poet,—"for style and matter very familiar and grateful to children," says an old schoolmaster; one wonders what the boys thought of Baptista. Holofernes both quotes and praises him. Then came Cicero, the idol of the Renaissance, in his *Epistles, De Officiis, De Amicitia,* and other works. The Latin poets and playwrights, Virgil, Ovid, Terence, Plautus, and the much praised tragedies of Seneca, were also read, usually in selections. Ovid was evidently Shakespeare's favorite; he prefixes a quotation from the *Amores* to his first poem, *Venus and Adonis,* makes innumerable references to the stories of the *Metamorphoses,* and borrows from that poem the name of his fairy queen, Titania.[1]

The question has sometimes been raised whether Shakespeare knew Greek. The masters of the Stratford school in Shakespeare's day were Oxford scholars no doubt qualified to teach Greek, and Jonson's well-known statement that Shakespeare had "small Latin and less Greek" seems to imply that the poet had at least an acquaintance with that language; otherwise Jonson might have written "no Greek." But the question, after all, is idle since there is no reason whatever to believe that Shakespeare read Greek or had any acquaintance with Greek literature—except Plutarch—either in the original or in translations.

[1] The only certain specimens of Shakespeare's handwriting that remain are six signatures of his to various documents—three of them to his last will. It is possible that three pages of the MS. play of *Sir Thomas More* (cf. p. 70) now in the British Museum, are in Shakespeare's hand. The apparent illegibility of his handwriting has led some uninstructed persons to think of him as an illiterate person, but scholars know that his handwriting is the usual old English script taught in all provincial schools in his time. The new Italian script, now current, was only used in the most cultured circles at that time.

[1] An old copy of the *Metamorphoses,* now in the Bodleian, bears on the title-page the abbreviated signature Wm Shre and opposite the signature the entry in a seventeenth-century hand: "This little Booke of Ovid was given to me by W. Hall who sayd it was once Will. Shakesperes, T. N. 1682." The supposed signature is probably a forgery.

With Latin the case is different. What seemed "small Latin" to such a scholar as Jonson would be a very respectable quantity today. A boy must have been dull indeed who could spend six or seven years devoted almost exclusively to the study of Latin for about ten hours [2] a day and yet emerge from the process without a very fair command of the language.

Apart from the Latin classics the only book studied was the Bible in the Geneva version with which Shakespeare's plays show a perfect familiarity. There is some reason, however, to believe that Shakespeare had studied the formal Rhetoric which was taught only in the most advanced forms of such schools.

What may we believe, then, to have been the final result of Shakespeare's schooling? A possible smattering of Greek may be discarded, but he must have had such a knowledge of Latin as enabled him to read the best authors with ease and fluency. More important still was a real mastery of English composition acquired by the constant practice of translating Latin into English and English back into Latin. Along with this went a thorough grasp on the Latin element in the English language; no author could use this with the precision and power that Shakespeare displays unless he had enjoyed a sound classical education.

Even in such a school as Shakespeare's a boy's life was not all work. There were the legal holidays, the holidays granted at the request of a graduate or a patron of the school (Master Slender gets the boys leave to play, *Merry Wives,* IV, i), and the happy hours stolen by the truants. The boyish games with which these hours were filled were well known to Shakespeare and there is frequent mention of them in his works. We have no reason to imagine him a shy, retiring, bookish lad. On the contrary in his youth as in his manhood he must have loved the society of his fellows, and revelled in such games as hide-and-seek and blind-man's buff (the *Hide fox* and the *hoodman-blind* of *Hamlet*), prisoner's base (*Cymbeline,* V, iii, 20), football (*Comedy of Errors,* II, i, 82), and the ninemen's morris (*Midsummer Night's Dream,* II, ii, 98). Like Falstaff in his youth he probably plucked geese, played truant, and whipped the top (*Merry Wives,* V, i, 26), and if he were beaten for his pranks, weighed the pain against the pleasure, shrugged his shoulders, and continued in his ways with the fat Knight's own equanimity. He swam and fished in the Avon and made an early acquaintance with the field sports which seem to have had a decisive influence on his career some time later. In short, as Shakespeare was a man's man in London, we may well believe him to have been a real boy in Stratford.

It was usual then for boys to spend some seven years in the grammar school, and if Shakespeare entered it at the age of seven, he would have been ready to leave in 1578. His first biographer, Rowe, says that Shakespeare's father withdrew him from school at an early age because of his financial difficulties. It is not, however, until 1577 that John's financial difficulties appear in the records and it is hard to see how these would have been lessened by withdrawing his son from school. There were no school bills for John to pay and William could hardly have been a help to him in business before his fourteenth year. It is possible that John's increasing troubles prevented him from sending his son to one of the universities, but whether William lost much thereby is an open question.

Upon leaving school then, about 1578, Shakespeare was probably bound over as apprentice to his father, possibly later, according to an old tradition, to a Stratford butcher. This was the usual, in fact the necessary practice for a boy who was expected to take his father's place in such a town as Stratford. Without passing through an apprenticeship to a recognized craft no one could open a shop, practice a trade, or become a free citizen of the town. No doubt John Shakespeare expected William to take over his business, restore his sinking fortune, and succeed him in his various offices.

It is not likely, however, that William shared his father's expectations. The traditions of his youth at Stratford may be late and uncertain, but they point to a life quite unlike that of the industrious apprentice. The story of his drinking bout with the "sippers" of Bidford and his subsequent night's lodging under a crabtree would hardly have been told about a man whose youth was remembered as one of sobriety and self-restraint. More particularly Shakespeare's familiarity with field sports,

[2] School began in Shakespeare's day at 6 or 7 a. m. and lasted with brief intermissions till 5.30 or 6 p. m.

hawking and hunting, and with the care and training of horse, hawk, and hound, point, like that efficiency in billiards on which Emerson once remarked, to many ill-spent hours in youth. It is hard to exaggerate the significance of this familiarity. Madden, whose *Diary of Master William Silence* is the recognized authority on this matter, comments on Shakespeare's knowledge of the most intimate secrets of woodcraft and falconry and of the nature and disposition of the horse. He notes, moreover, that this knowledge is peculiar to Shakespeare; no such familiarity with field sports and horses appears in the work of any other Elizabethan playwright. Now it is certain that the young Shakespeare, son of a busy Stratford shopkeeper, never owned a hawk, much less a kennel of hounds, and never bestrode a horse, except perhaps a heavy plough horse on some country farm. Nor could he have acquired this familiarity during his busy years in London. It comes from the period of his youth that lies between his schooldays and his departure to London, and points to hours on hours spent in following on foot the chase of stag and hare as practiced by gentlemen about Stratford and to more hours spent in hanging about the stables, mews, and kennels of such a country house as Charlecote in intimate converse with grooms, falconers, and huntsmen, and in loving observation of their charges. Such hours, after all, were not misspent; they have left their traces in delightful passages in his work, but they were not likely to lead to success in business or gladden the heart of an anxious father.

Another pastime which must have delighted young Shakespeare was the drama. Coventry was within walking distance of Stratford and at Coventry some scenes of a famous cycle of miracle plays were annually performed on Corpus Christi day in early summer as late as 1584. Shakespeare may well have seen such a performance more than once and as a boy of eleven he may have gone with his father to see the splendid pageants and masques with which Leicester in 1575 entertained the Queen at Kenilworth some fifteen miles from Stratford. There were, moreover, opportunities for seeing plays at home of which Shakespeare would surely have taken advantage. A travelling company performed at Stratford in 1568 while John Shakespeare was bailiff. They must have given a good report of the little town, for in the seventies and early eighties a number of companies appeared there.[1] It seems more than a guess that the young Shakespeare never missed a chance to attend these performances and that as a boy at Stratford he made his first acquaintance with the crude early work of the Elizabethan drama to which he was destined to contribute its greatest plays.

Shakespeare was hardly more than a boy—not yet nineteen—when he took the most important step in a man's life and married. Such a cloud of controversy has gathered about this marriage and so many inferences have been drawn from it that it seems best simply to state the known facts and leave the inferences to be drawn by the reader.

Shakespeare's bride was Anne, daughter of Richard Hathaway, a farmer at Shottery near Stratford, who died in the summer of 1582. Anne was eight years older than William and apparently quite uneducated. Some months after Richard's death, on November 28, 1582, two friends of his filed a bond with the Bishop of Worcester, in whose diocese the town of Stratford lay, freeing him from all liability if any lawful impediment prevented a marriage between Anne and William Shakespeare. The purpose of this action was to obtain the Bishop's license permitting the couple to marry without the customary delay of a triple asking of the banns in church. Such a delay would have carried them into the Advent season and by the old church law marriage was forbidden from Advent Sunday till about the middle of January. And there was urgent reason for a speedy marriage. The Bishop accordingly granted a license [2] and the young couple were married, not in Stratford, as would have been most natural, but in some unknown church. To Stratford they came, however, and there Anne's child was born and baptized Susanna in Trinity Church on May 26, 1583.

It is an interesting fact that John Shake-

[1] In 1573 Leicester's Men; in 1576 the companies of Warwick and Worcester; in 1577 Leicester's and Worcester's; in 1579 Lord Strange's; in 1580 Derby's; in 1581 Worcester's and Lord Berkeley's.

[2] A license preserved in the Bishop's register dated Nov. 27, 1582, authorizing the marriage of William Shaxpere to Anne Whateley of Temple Grafton. Most scholars believe this to be the license granted to our William and Anne, and explain the discrepancy as due to a clerk's careless copying. On the other hand it may be a license to a quite different pair. The name, William Shakespeare, was not uncommon in the district and Anne Whately of Temple Grafton seems a long remove from Anne Hathaway of Stratford.

speare seems to have taken no part in this marriage. His consent, however, must have been obtained as William was still a minor, and it must have been to his house that William brought his bride, for neither he nor Anne had the means to take a house of their own. John can hardly have approved his son's marriage with a poor girl eight years his elder, and it is unlikely that he had consented to or been aware of a formal betrothal before the filing of the bond, an engagement which some apologists for Shakespeare conjecture to have taken place.

Less than two years after Susanna's birth Anne presented her husband with twins who were baptized Hamnet and Judith in Trinity Church on February 2, 1585. After this there is no record of Shakespeare in Stratford for years to come, and there is reason to believe that shortly after the birth of the twins he left his home, his wife, and his children to seek his fortune in the world.

There has been much idle talk about the married life of Shakespeare. The simple facts are that he left his wife at Stratford—their son, Hamnet, died and was buried there in 1596 and there is no evidence that Anne ever joined her husband in London—that no children were born to them after 1585, that about 1611 he installed his wife and daughters in New Place, the fine house in Stratford that he had bought in 1597, that he joined them there and died in that house in 1616, leaving Anne his "second best bed" in his will.[1]

These facts do not suggest a congenial and happy marriage, but rather a hasty wedding, a brief life together, a long separation, and late in life an amicable reunion. Further than this we have no right to inquire.

Shakespeare's departure from Stratford is by old tradition connected with a poaching affair. His first biographer states that he had robbed a park belonging to Sir Thomas Lucy and was prosecuted by that gentleman so severely that he was forced to fly to London. There is independent and old corroboration of this story and it is so in accord with what we know of Shakespeare's love of sport and the reckless spirit which led to his hasty marriage that we may well accept it as in the main correct. The only question is why such a trivial offence as poaching, punishable at that time by fine and a brief imprisonment, should have driven the culprit into exile. The question, however, is answered when we realize the social position of the two parties in the case. Sir Thomas was the greatest magnate in the neighborhood of Stratford; he was not only a Knight, but a member of Parliament and at one time high sheriff of Warwickshire and Worcestershire. He was interested in preserving game and a rigorous enforcer of the law. When he visited Stratford the Corporation formally entertained him with food and drink at an inn. Shakespeare, on the other hand, though married and the father of three children, may still have been an apprentice, and was certainly a doubtful character; there is no evidence that he had become a free citizen of the town. His father was rapidly losing the high position he had once held, and Shakespeare himself possessed no independent means of support. It is plain that the vindictive wrath of such a personage as Lucy, fanned into flame, the story goes, by a scurrilous ballad which Shakespeare wrote against him, might well render the poet's life at Stratford intolerable.

Another tradition, even older and resting on better authority, comes from a certain William Beeston, whose father, Christopher, had played as a boy in Shakespeare's company. He told the antiquary Aubrey that Shakespeare "understood Latin pretty well: for he had been in his younger years a schoolmaster in the country." This is by no means impossible, for Shakespeare's training in the Guild School would qualify him at least for a subordinate position in a country school. Nor is the report incompatible with the poaching tradition. There is a gap of seven or eight years between the last record of Shakespeare in Stratford and his appearance in London, and it is quite possible that a period of school-teaching intervened between the two. If so, Shakespeare spent this time in all probability in the neighboring country of Gloucester. The names of Shakespeare and Hathaway occur repeatedly in that district, so that William may have found friends and relatives there who would help him to a position in a school, and in one

[1] This bequest and the fact that it was an afterthought interpolated into the first draft of the will have been taken to show Shakespeare's disregard of his wife. This is quite improbable. Mrs. Shakespeare, now over sixty, was apparently regarded as incapable of managing property; she was left in charge of Susanna, who with her husband, Dr. Hall, lived in New Place after Shakespeare's death. The bed, probably the one she had used for years, was bequeathed to her as her own personal property, perhaps at her special request.

of his plays (*2 K. H. IV*) he shows an intimate acquaintance with family names, localities, and local customs of the Cotswold district. A year or two of school-teaching, however, was probably enough for Shakespeare and he began to turn his eyes longingly toward London. It is not at all likely that he thought of taking up a trade there, as his fellow Stratfordian, Richard Field, later the publisher of *Venus and Adonis* and of *Lucrece,* had done. He would have heard reports of the building of theatres, the formation of new companies of actors,[1] perhaps even of the brilliant success of Lyly's courtly comedies and the popular triumph of Kyd's *Spanish Tragedy.* It was no doubt with a view to sharing in the bright future dawning for the English drama as an actor, perhaps as a playwright, that Shakespeare, some time about 1587 or 1588, threw down the schoolmaster's rod, closed his books, and took the road to London.

[1] The Queen's new Company was organized in 1583 and its members were allowed wages and liveries as grooms of the chamber—a privilege accorded many years later to Shakespeare himself.

III

SHAKESPEARE'S LONDON

SHAKESPEARE probably came to London about 1587 or 1588—there is no certainty as to the date—and remained there except for short visits to Stratford for some twenty-five years, that is, all his working life. The life of London, the pursuits and pleasures of the citizens, influenced and colored all his life and work. It was for Londoners that he wrote his poems and produced his plays. The country youth had perforce to adapt himself to an urban environment, but there is nothing to show that he shrank from this adaptation. On the contrary it would seem that he plunged gladly into the tide of London life and swam strongly with the current. He won his success, in part at least, by the truth and beauty with which he reflected in his work the spirit and the color of his new surroundings.

London in Shakespeare's day presented the spectacle of a medieval city bursting its bonds, physical and spiritual, under the stimulus of the Renaissance. It was the one city in England which had come fully under the influence of this movement and it was rapidly concentrating in itself all the life in England that was touched by this new spirit. It was not only the capital of the kingdom, but the centre of its social, commercial, and intellectual life. The Queen held her court at Whitehall in Westminster just outside the city proper, or at Greenwich on the Thames below, or at Richmond or Windsor above London. The road along the Thames from the city to Westminster, the Strand of to-day, was lined with the town-houses of great nobles. The Royal Exchange, built by Sir Thomas Gresham in 1566, was the sole building in England devoted to the meetings of merchants for the transaction of business. The quays along the Thames were crowded with shipping from all parts of the world, for English commerce with East and West was increasing with leaps and bounds, and the customs duties paid at London constituted a substantial part of the royal revenue. Except for the university presses at Oxford and Cambridge all the printers and publishers in England were gathered in London, and it was only in London that theatres for the public performance of the drama were to be found. To this great centre of the kingdom there flowed a steady stream of students from the universities, young gentlemen from the homes of the landed aristocracy, and apprentices from provincial towns like Stratford. London was indeed the heart of England, and in Shakespeare's day this heart was beating high with a full consciousness of its supreme importance.

No greater contrast can well be imagined than that between the huge metropolitan London of today and the city of Shakespeare's time. The Thames, a tidal river, swarming with fish, as yet unpolluted by the refuse of factories on its banks, ran all along the old town. It was crossed by a single bridge, London Bridge, reckoned one of the wonders of the world with its score of arches through which the tide rushed with tremendous force.

The bridge was built up with shops and houses like the Ponte Vecchio at Florence, and defended at its southern end by a tower and gate over which grinned the rotting heads of traitors fixed on spikes. Flocks of swans sailed gracefully upon the river and hundreds of little boats—some two thousand in Shakespeare's day—plied busily up and down stream with cries of "Westward Ho" and "Eastward Ho," serving the same function of transportation as is today performed by the underground railway, the bus, and the taxicab. It is worth noting that coaches were unknown in London streets before 1564, the year of Shakespeare's birth, and wheeled vehicles were still rare in the narrow streets when Shakespeare came to town. The river was the main artery of traffic and served also as a highway for stately pageants and solemn funerals.

The city proper was still surrounded by its mediæval walls describing an arc of over two miles from the Tower in the east, to a brook called the Fleet in the west. The Tower, according to common opinion first built by Julius Cæsar and enlarged from age to age, at once fortress, armory, prison, mint, and menagery for the royal lions, still frowned upon the city. The walls were pierced by gates, closed at the curfew hour, whose names still survive in the London districts of Ludgate, Aldgate, Newgate, the western gate by which Shakespeare entered London, and Bishopsgate. The growing pressure of population, however—London rose from ca. 100,000 at the beginning of Elizabeth's reign to double that number under her successor—had long since pushed the inhabitants outside the circle of the walls. There were almost as many people living in the suburbs, Southwark, Moorfields, and Charing Cross, as in the city. The suburbs, like one or two small districts within the walls, were not under the jurisdiction of the city authorities. They were known as the "liberties" and were not of the best repute; one angry contemporary calls them "dens for adulterers, thieves, murderers, and every mischief-worker." It was in these "liberties" that the first theatres were built.

Within the walls lay the city proper, traversed by a few main crowded thoroughfares intersected at irregular intervals by narrow lanes, unpaved, dark, and dirty. Open sewers ran along them to the river and sanitary conditions were so bad that the city was seldom free from the plague, and during Shakespeare's residence was devastated by terrible epidemics in 1593 and 1603. To modern notions the policing of the city was quite unsatisfactory; there was no police force at all by day, and at night the dim streets were protected only by a volunteer guard, of whose efficiency we may form some idea from Shakespeare's humorous picture of the night watch in *Much Ado*. Yet London in his day seems to have been singularly free from crimes of violence.

The closely crowded houses were built of brick and timber and many private dwellings as well as shops and taverns were distinguished by large hanging signs. Yet there were gardens behind many houses and just without the walls there were open fields where the citizens enjoyed their sports. Gentlemen hawked and hunted where today the buildings of the British Museum cover the ground. It is probable that the Londoners of Shakespeare's time spent many more hours in the open than the citizens of to-day. The shops themselves lay open to the air, their goods exposed for sale on benches protected from the rain by penthouses springing from the main building and projecting over the narrow street.

London was a city of churches; the one hundred and twenty steeples of its parish churches rose toward heaven like a forest of stone. Yet it was by no means a religious city. To this the extraordinary condition of its great cathedral, St. Paul's, bears amazing witness. Shortly before Shakespeare's birth a flash of lightning struck the lofty spire and the fire that followed left only the stone walls standing. The church was promptly rebuilt, all but the spire, but in the years that followed it became quite as much a meeting and lounging place for Londoners as a house of prayer. Divine service was performed daily in the choir, but the transept became a city thoroughfare and the great central aisle, known as Paul's Walk, was a combination of business exchange and city club. Merchants made appointments to meet at this or that pillar and lawyers transacted business there with clients. One pillar was reserved for jobless serving men to post up their qualifications—Falstaff engaged Bardolf in St. Paul's—young gallants strolled up and down to show off their fine clothes, and tailors hung about with tablets to take note of the latest fashions and with tape to measure customers. Penniless adventurers lounged about the tomb known as Duke Humphrey's, waiting for an invitation to dinner or a chance to fasten upon some country gull; courtesans and their attendant squires hunted the place in pursuit of prey. And all the while the solemn liturgy of the church was being chanted in the choir. The service, however, was liable to sudden interruption, for by a local rule, if a gentleman entered the choir with his spurs on during worship, he was subject to a fine which was collected on the spot by the choir boys who left their posts to swarm about him like a flock of white butterflies. Paul's Churchyard—the walled enclosure of the cathedral—and the lanes adjoining were the centre of the book trade—over half of Shakespeare's plays published in his lifetime issued from Paul's Yard, and he must have spent hours at the bookstalls reading some new poem or turning over a book of old tales in search for a plot for a play.

This conversion of the great cathedral to secular uses was characteristic of the spirit of London in Shakespeare's day. The busy, eager, many-colored life of the town, was pre-eminently a worldly life. The old religion had lost its hold upon the people, and Puritanism, though growing ever stronger among the middle classes, had not yet become predominant. If London had a real religion it was that of patriotism. The great city was devotedly loyal to the Queen. There was a fierce outburst of popular wrath when a Catholic posted on the door of the Bishop of London's palace a papal bull, excommunicating and deposing Elizabeth, and it was only appeased by the public execution of the offender in St. Paul's Churchyard. It is worth noting in this connection that Catholics were prosecuted in Elizabeth's reign on civil, not on religious grounds, and that the victims were executed as traitors, not as Catholics; a loyal Catholic was as a rule left unmolested. London merchants joined with the Queen in financing the plundering and colonizing expeditions which challenged the power of Spain in the New World. At the approach of the Armada Elizabeth called on London for fifteen ships and five thousand men; the loyal city promptly offered double the number of both and raised an additional force of ten thousand men to meet a possible invasion. The wealth of the city, due in the main to its commerce, was rapidly increasing and the citizens were well aware that their peace and prosperity rested upon the firm rule and wise policy of the Queen.

London was not only a busy and patriotic city; it was passionately addicted to pleasure. In spite of the attempted restrictions of a Puritan magistracy the spirit of the citizens at large was still that of Merry England. They poured out of the walls on Sundays and holidays to seek their pleasure in the open fields and suburbs, to play at bowls or football, to shoot at the butts, to watch the baiting of bulls and bears, or to see a play in some inn courtyard or theatre.

In the life of pleasure-loving London the taverns played a principal part. Originally mere inns for the reception of travellers, these houses had in Shakespeare's day developed a variety of functions. They served not only as lodging places but as restaurants where a guest might either eat at the host's table, the so-called "ordinary," or order what food he wished served to him in a private room. It was customary for a gentleman visiting a tavern to engage such a room for himself and his friends, male or female, where he might eat and drink, transact business, gamble, or make love, undisturbed except by the entrance of the "drawer"—the waiter—or by the appearance of a band of musicians—"a noise" in Elizabethan English—who wandered from tavern to tavern to offer their services to gentlemen inclined for a little music. Such rooms were distinguished, not by numbers as now-a-days, but by proper names, the Rose, the Angel, the Dolphin, etc., with corresponding signs over the doors and the amount consumed therein was charged up to the room at the central bar—"score a pint of bastard"—a sweet Spanish wine—"in the Half Moon" is the drawer's cry in *I King Henry IV*. In such rooms, where visitors were assured of a certain amount of privacy, groups of friends assembled for social intercourse and so made a beginning of the modern club. We hear, for instance, of the famous group comprising Shakespeare, Jonson, Beaumont, Fletcher, and other wits, poets, and playwrights, who used to meet at the Mermaid tavern, and somewhat later Jonson presided in state over a club which met in the Apollo room of the Devil tavern at Temple Bar. Here the old scholar-poet wrote the club rules in Latin and engraved them in marble over the fireplace and here he formally adopted young wits and poets into "the tribe of Ben."

In the large common room before the bar all sorts and conditions of men assembled to drink a cup of sack, meet a friend, chaff the drawer, and kiss the hostess. Here was the soldier, full of strange oaths, back from the Low Countries, the sailor from the Indies, the traveller from the Continent, the scholar from Oxford or Cambridge, the flat-capped city prentice, and the county squire open-eyed in wonder at strange sights and sounds. The Elizabethan drama, not only of Shakespeare, but particularly of such city playwrights as Jonson, Dekker, and Middleton, is redolent of the London tavern.

There was, moreover, a particular bond between the tavern and the new drama. From early times the inn courtyard had been a common place for dramatic performances. Entered from the street by a single arch through which the carriers led their horses, and surrounded by galleries opening on the adjacent rooms of the inn, the courtyard was easily adapted to a crude sort of theatre. A scaffold projecting into the yard was erected for the stage opposite the entrance and a curtain hung from the gallery over the scaffold gave a backdrop to the actors who entered the stage from their dressing-room in the inn behind the curtain. They could also use, if they wished, a part of the gallery just above the scaffold to represent an upper chamber or the wall of a town. One of the actors stood at the arch to exact the penny entrance fee which admitted the spectator to standing room in the flagged courtyard. Such spectators were the "groundlings" of Shakespeare's plays. Visitors of higher rank, with heavier purses, hired a room in the tavern, sat on stools in the gallery and witnessed the performance at their ease. There were no theatres in or near London till some years after Shakespeare's birth and the natural home of the new drama was the inn courtyard. Performances within the city limits were indeed forbidden by a local ordinance in 1567, but the prohibition, like other prohibitions, was not strictly enforced; plays long continued to be given at such London taverns as the Crosskeys, where Shakespeare himself may have acted, at the Red Bull, and at the Boar's Head which he made immortal as the peculiar habitation of Sir John Falstaff.

Performances at such places were attended by a motley throng of spectators. The dregs of the city, harlots and pickpockets, plied their trade and jostled sober citizens with their wives, while rowdy prentices rubbed elbows with country squires. London citizens delighted in shows of every sort; malicious gossip declared that city wives would sell their honor for a sight of a masque at court. The city fathers presented gorgeous pageants in the streets or on the river on every fit occasion. All this thirst for pleasure in the form of spectacle found a quick gratification in the lively action, the songs and dances, the clownage, the broad-sword combats, and the dumb-shows of the new drama. The rapid building of theatres and the amazing development of the drama in Shakespeare's day show how heartily the city supported this new art. It must not be forgotten that Elizabethan drama was a popular entertainment; it was neither endowed by the state like the Attic drama nor supported by the court as later in France. It appealed directly to and depended mainly upon audiences composed of London citizens.

There were, however, two institutions which exerted a very considerable influence upon the new drama, neither of which were in any sense popular. The first of these was the Inns of Court. These famous London law-schools, through which alone admission to the Bar was possible, were, and still are, something more than law-schools. Dating back to the thirteenth and fourteenth centuries the four great Inns, the Inner and the Middle Temple, Lincoln's Inn, and Gray's, resembled the colleges of Oxford and Cambridge. They required the residence of students within their walls or in subordinate Inns, such as Clement's, Staple's, and Furnivall's, which were attached to them. Their members dined together, summoned to table by the blast of a horn, and attended worship together in their own chapels. The Inns were self-governing bodies, outside the jurisdiction of the city, and ruled by their senior members, the Benchers. Even the King's writ did not run in the precincts of an Inn of Court and a story is told of an unlucky royal messenger who was shaved, ducked, and beaten by the students for venturing within their grounds to serve a warrant on one of them. Membership was strictly limited to the upper classes, for all students were required to be sons of "persons of quality." Many famous Elizabethans were members of these Inns;

Sidney and Bacon belonged to Gray's, Sackville and Beaumont to the Inner Temple, John Donne to Lincoln's Inn. It was customary for a student to retain his membership in his Inn long after he had completed his studies. Bacon, for example, through his long and busy life, retained an active interest in the affairs of Gray's, devised their Court masques, contributed generously to these costly shows, and laid out the lovely gardens of the Inn where his statue now stands. Thus the Inns of Court were social as well as educational institutions. Members had as a matter of course the entry of the royal court. They were taught dancing and courtly manners as well as law and it was not only the privilege, but in a sense the duty, of the Inns to entertain the sovereign with revels, masques, and dramatic performances.

Now the interest of these Inns in the drama of Shakespeare's day was lively and intelligent. Members of the Inns acted in works of their own composition and sometimes called in professional actors on state occasions; *The Comedy of Errors,* for instance, was acted at Gray's in 1594 and *Twelfth Night* at the Middle Temple in 1602. A large proportion of the members came from the universities; all of them had probably received the common classical training of the grammar-schools. It is, therefore, not surprising that they were for the most part admirers of classical drama. Indeed the attempt to domesticate Senecan drama in England was closely connected with the dramatic activities of the Inns of Court. Sackville and Norton led the way with their *Gorboduc,* performed at the Inner Temple in 1562 and later before the Queen at Whitehall. At the same Inn in 1566 Gascoigne and Kinwelmersh produced *Jocasta,* their translation of an Italian version of the *Phoenissae* of Euripides. *Gismond of Salerne,* revised and published as *Tancred and Gismonda,* was written by five members of the Inner Temple and played at Court in 1568. Finally *The Misfortunes of Arthur,* the most purely Senecan of Elizabethan tragedies, was the work of a member of Gray's.

The influence of the Inns of Court upon the new drama must have been profound and lasting. Members of the Inns were constant and enthusiastic supporters of the theatre. They furnished a group of auditors at once appreciative and critical who cared less than the "groundlings" for mere action, jigs, and clowning, but demanded lofty rhetoric, classical allusions, regular structure, and polished verse. They not only attended the theatres but conversed with the playwrights and actors at the tavern and elsewhere. Jonson boasts of his friendship with "divers members of the Inns of Court" and though we have no record of such an intimacy on Shakespeare's part, it is most likely that as a popular playwright and an actor in the best company of his day he must have been well acquainted with the dramatic enthusiasts of the Inns. One can imagine how these gentlemen would urge their views upon the playwrights and it is fairly certain that the classical influence which helped to transform the crude popular drama of the first decades of Elizabeth's reign came in large measure through the Inns of Court.

The second great influence upon the new drama was that of the Court. It is hard for us today to appreciate the extent of this influence upon life in Shakespeare's London. The Queen was, of course, the sole fount of honor; her favor could raise any man to the highest pinnacle of fortune; her wrath could break the proudest noble; and both her favor and wrath were exhibited in most capricious fashion. The Court constantly intervened in private affairs and in the daily business of the city. The Queen apparently thought herself possessed of the power of veto on the marriages of her courtiers; she granted and withdrew trade monopolies by which fortunes were made and lost. Even in the provisioning of the city the Court played a part, for its caterers had the first choice on every shipload of fish or cartload of country supplies that was brought into town.

The Court circle, too, was larger than it is today. It was open, as a matter of course, to all members of the landed gentry who swarmed to London to share in the new life of the realm. It was open at certain times under certain restrictions to the citizens themselves. From time to time the Queen made stately progresses through the city and was feasted by rich merchants or city magistrates. A host of Londoners were in one way or another dependent on the Court, holding minor offices about it, supplying its needs or satisfying its pleasures. Court intrigues, the rise and fall of favorites and factions, were as interesting to the Londoner of Shakespeare's day as local and national politics are to us. The Court certainly influenced the daily life of Shakespeare's London far more intimately and powerfully than it does the London of today.

Now the Court of Elizabeth was not only pleasure-loving, but it found a main source of its pleasure in spectacles, masquing, and the drama. The Queen herself, a true Renaissance sovereign, at once cultured and luxurious, was an ardent lover of such entertainments. She had a special official, the Master of Revels, whose business it was to prepare and supervise all masques and plays at Court and who finally came to exercise the function of licenser and censor of all plays. Through her Privy Council Elizabeth more than once intervened to protect the players from the attacks of the city magistrates. In 1583, for example, when they were waging an aggressive war upon actors and theatres, the Queen selected twelve of the best actors from various organizations to form her own company, the Queen's Servants, and gave them a special license to play in London and in the country. The Children of the Chapel, that is the choir-boys of the Court Chapel, were under her special protection. They began at an early date to present plays at Court and later began giving public performances in a hall in the former monastery of Blackfriars. The Queen helped to pay their expenses, lent her musicians to accompany their performances, outfitted them from her magnificent wardrobe, and seems once at least to have attended a performance at Blackfriars along with her maids of honor.

As a rule, however, when Elizabeth wished to see a play she commanded a performance at Court. We have numerous records of such performances by various companies, but from 1594 on Shakespeare's company was the Queen's favorite. Shakespeare and his fellows appeared at Court every year from 1594 till the Queen's death in 1603, often several times a year. Their popularity was due not only to their ability as actors, but also to the fact that they alone could present Shakespeare's plays. We know that *Love's Labour's Lost, The Comedy of Errors, The Merchant of Venice, King Henry IV*, *King Henry V*, and *Much Ado about Nothing* were acted before Elizabeth, and there is an old tradition that *The Merry Wives of Windsor* was written at her command. The favor that she showed this company was increased rather than diminished under her successor. James took Shakespeare and his fellows under his direct patronage, gave them the title of the King's Servants, and attached them officially to the royal household as grooms of the Chamber. It is even credibly reported that James once wrote Shakespeare a letter with his own royal hand.

As a result of this intimate connection between the Court and the drama, Shakespeare as actor and playwright came into close touch with the aristocracy of England. Some of the great nobles of the day, Stanley, Essex, Southampton, the Pembroke brothers, William and Philip, were among his patrons, acquaintances, and even friends. The public audiences to which he played were almost exclusively masculine, but at Court he saw and met the loveliest, wittiest, and most cultured ladies of the realm. It was from them that he drew such gracious and charming figures as the Princess and her ladies in *Love's Labour's Lost*, Portia, Rosalind, Beatrice, and Imogen; and the influence of the Court is no less noticeable in the dialogue of his plays, in the high-flown style, the conceits, affectations, and sparkling repartee with which his comedies abound. Lacking this connection with the Court, Shakespeare would doubtless have been a great dramatist, but his plays would not have been what they are without the deep and lasting influence to which this connection exposed him.

Enough has been said to show the difference between Shakespeare's London and the environment of his early life in Stratford. He must have felt when he settled down to work in the city as if he had been transported into a brave new world. The rich, busy, pleasure-loving city, the lively, intelligent, and critical gentlemen of the Inns of Court, the royal Court with its circle of splendid nobles and fair women, formed a world of which he could hardly even have dreamed at Stratford. Yet he was quick to recognize that the life of this new world was altogether human. Unlike his Miranda he did not mistake its inhabitants for immortal spirits. He saw, no one more clearly, their affectations, follies, and vices. Yet Shakespeare was a child of the Renaissance and the Renaissance atmosphere which surrounded him for a quarter of a century in London was the very environment needed to bring his genius to its full and splendid flower.

IV

SHAKESPEARE IN LONDON—UNDER ELIZABETH

THERE is no certain record of Shakespeare's life or activities between February, 1585, when the twins, Hamnet and Judith, were baptized in the church at Stratford, and the year 1592, when he was at work as actor and playwright in London, as we know from Robert Greene's attack on him referred to below.

This period from 1585 to 1592 is sometimes spoken of as "the lost years"; some part of it may have been spent as a school-teacher, but to have obtained such a position in London as is shown by Greene's onslaught, he must have been active there for a considerable period. It is a fair guess, but only a guess, that he came to town to seek his fortune about 1587 or in the Armada year of 1588. No doubt he plunged at once into the world of play-acting and play-making. An old tradition that his career in London began by holding horses outside one of the new theatres is hardly credible. It is more likely that he attached himself at once to one of the companies of actors. The parish clerk at Stratford told a visitor in 1693 that Shakespeare was at first received into the play-house as a "serviture," which means that he was engaged by one of the companies to do odd jobs and play minor parts, in other words that he was one of the "hirelings" (see below p. 27). It has long been believed that this company was that of Lord Strange with which we find him associated from 1594 for the rest of his life. Recent scholarship inclines to the view that he joined a company organized under the patronage of Lord Pembroke about the year 1590. There are arguments, not very convincing for either view, and it does not after all make much difference. Of one thing we may be sure, that Shakespeare was both busy and successful in his new career by 1592 when we next hear of him.

In the late summer of 1592 Robert Greene, the brilliant and dissolute poet, playwright, and pamphleteer, lay on his death-bed. In extreme poverty and deserted by his former friends he roused himself to write an autobiographical tract, *Green's Groatsworth of Wit bought with a Million of Repentance* which he hoped to sell for enough to pay his debts. After narrating the rather scandalous life of a certain Roberto, i.e. Greene himself, he closes with a sharp warning to his former friends and fellow playwrights, Marlowe, Peele, and Nashe, to beware of the players who will desert them as they have deserted him. "Yes, trust them not:" he continues, "for there is an upstart crow beautified with our feathers that with his *Tygers heart wrapt in a Players hide* supposes he is as well able to bombast out a blank verse as the best of you: and being an absolute *Johannes fac totum,* is in his owne conceit the onely Shakesscene in a countrey." The phrase, a *Tygers heart,* etc., is parodied from a line in *III K. H. VI* (I, iv, 137), a play perhaps originally by Marlowe, but revised by the young Shakespeare who is directly pointed at in the pun on his name, "Shakes-scene." It is plain that Greene was provoked by the success of Shakespeare both as an actor, "a crow beautified by our feathers," i.e. famous by speaking the poetical lines of Greene and his fellows, and as a rising dramatist able, at least in his own conceit, to write blank verse with the best of them.

The *Groatsworth* was edited for publication by Henry Chettle, an old friend of Greene's, and appeared in print shortly after his death, September 3, 1592. It caused a distinct sensation; Marlowe, who had been accused of atheism, a very dangerous accusation at that day, when even a Unitarian like Kett of Cambridge might be burnt as a heretic, was naturally furious, and Shakespeare, or his friends, seem to have been deeply offended. At any rate pressure was brought to bear on Chettle, who in a preface to his *Kind-Heart's Dream,* entered in the Stationers' Register, December 8, 1592, made a formal apology. Chettle's reference to Shakespeare is so interesting that it deserves to be quoted in full.

After noting that Greene's address to "diverse playmakers is offensively by one or two of them taken" he goes on to say that "With neither of them that take offence was I acquainted, and with one of them [Marlowe, of course] I care not if I never be. The other, whome at that time I did not so much spare, as since I wish I had . . . that I did not, I am as sorry as if the originall fault had beene my fault, because my selfe have seene his demeanor no lesse civill than he exelent in the qualitie he professes [i.e. acting]: Besides divers of worship have reported his uprightnes of dealing, which argues his honesty, and his facetious grace in writting, that aproves his Art."

There are several interesting things to be noted in this statement. Chettle seems to have met Shakespeare for the first time—no doubt in connection with the controversy over Greene's pamphlet—and to have been as much impressed with his "civill demeanor," well-bred manners, as by his ability generally recognized, as an actor. Apparently, moreover, "divers of worship," i.e. noblemen or gentlemen of standing, had testified to Shakespeare's "uprightnes of dealing"—he was too honest to steal another man's work as Greene had insinuated, and to the charm and grace of his writing—he did not need to steal. Evidently Chettle recognized at once that Shakespeare was something better than the "upstart crow, the Johannes fac totum" of Greene's attack.

It seems likely that a combination of circumstances turned Shakespeare in the autumn of 1592 from his work as actor-playwright to a more ambitious undertaking, the effort to establish himself as a true poet. A scandalous riot of apprentices in June, 1592, brought about the closing of all theatres for a period of three months. Before this time had elapsed the plague broke out in London with such severity that the theatres were forced to remain closed, except for a few brief intervals, until the summer of 1594. The chief companies, Pembroke's and Lord Strange's, went on tour in the provinces, but Shakespeare did not accompany either of them. On the contrary he remained in London and devoted himself to the composition of a long poem in the fashionable erotic manner of the time, his *Venus and Adonis*.

Every poet in that day needed a patron; the Elizabethan public might support, after a fashion, a popular playwright; it was quite incapable of buying enough books of verse to keep a poet alive. And so, naturally, Shakespeare looked about for a benefactor. It may be that "divers of worship" suggested to him the name of the Earl of Southampton, young, rich, and extravagant, but in the words of a contemporary "a dear lover and cherisher as well of the lovers of poets as of poets themselves." To him Shakespeare dedicated *Venus and Adonis,* which he called "the first heir of my invention," in a respectful epistle remarkable for the absence of the customary fulsome flattery of Elizabethan dedications.

The little volume, printed by Richard Field, appeared some time in the early summer of 1593 and was sold for the usual price of 6d. It is interesting to note that some years ago a copy was sold in London for £15,000. The work had a phenomenal success; eight editions were published in Shakespeare's lifetime and his rank as one of the leading poets of the day was at once established. From 1593 on there are repeated references to "honey-tongued" Shakespeare and to his popularity especially with young lovers of poetry. More than this the poem seems to have brought Shakespeare into familiar and friendly association with Southampton and the brilliant circle of which the young earl was an ornament. There is a tradition going back to Davenant that Southampton once gave Shakespeare £1,000 "to enable him to go through with a purchase." The figure is probably much exaggerated, but a handsome gift is more than likely.

In January, 1594, during a brief lull in the plague the theatres were re-opened and a minor company, Sussex's Men, presented *Titus Andronicus* at the Rose. Henslowe, the owner of this theatre, marked this play in his account book "ne"—probably meaning that it was played in a new and revised form, and there is some reason to believe that he engaged the popular poet Shakespeare to make this revision.

Shakespeare's revision of *Titus* was probably the product of a few hours withdrawn from a more serious undertaking. This was the composition of a long narrative poem on the story of Lucretia. It may be that the frequent references to the erotic quality of *Venus and Adonis* provoked Shakespeare to attempt a poem on a graver subject. He completed it in the spring of 1594 and published it in the summer of that year. Like *Venus and Adonis* it was dedicated to Southampton, but this time in an epistle that shows the nature of the relation that had grown up between the poet and his patron. "The love I dedicate to your Lordship" wrote Shakespeare "is without end —what I have done is yours; what I have to do is yours; being part in all I have, devoted yours."

Lucrece was at once successful. It never quite attained the popularity of *Venus and Adonis*, but five editions were called for in Shakespeare's lifetime and there was a consensus of opinion that the poet had done well to leave "love's foolish lazy languishment" and turn to a theme that could "please the wiser sort."

It was in these years 1593-94, apparently, that Shakespeare, following again the fashion of the time, began the composition of his sonnets. These were intended for private circulation among his friends; it is possible that some of them were addressed directly to Southampton. But the whole vexed question of the sonnets needs fuller treatment than can be given here. (See below, pp. 73–75.)

With the cessation of the plague in the summer of 1594 the theatres re-opened. Two main companies of actors re-organized—one headed by Alleyn, playing under the patronage of the Lord Admiral; the other formerly Lord Strange's, under that of the Lord Chamberlain. It was to this company that Shakespeare now attached himself, if, indeed, he had not been connected with it before, and with this company he remained as actor and playwright for the rest of his life in London. A warrant for payment of two performances at Court in the Christmas season of 1594 joins Shakespeare's name with those of Kemp, the clown of the company, and Burbage the famous tragedian, and reveals his position as one of the full-fledged members of the company. In 1595-96 we find him living in the Parish of St. Helen's near the theatre where his company was acting. He must have been a very busy man, rehearsing in the morning, acting in the afternoon, and busily engaged in touching up old and writing new plays for his fellows. Most of the older playwrights, Lyly, Greene, Marlowe, Peele, and Kyd, had died or stopped writing by 1594—a group of younger writers had yet to win their spurs upon the stage—and Shakespeare rose rapidly into eminence as the most popular and successful dramatist of the day. The years from 1594 to 1600 must have been among the busiest and happiest of Shakespeare's life.

A couple of interesting documents discovered lately among old court records in London show that in the autumn of 1596 Shakespeare had shifted his lodging from St. Helen's Parish to the Surrey side of the Thames. The one of these that concerns us is a petition by a certain William Wayte, stepson of William Gardiner, Justice of the Peace in Surrey, praying that William Shakespeare, Francis Langley, builder of the Swan Theatre, and others, might be bound over to keep the peace since they had put him in the fear of death. This petition is part of a long wrangle between Gardiner and Langley in which only a few weeks before Langley had filed a similar petition against Gardiner and Wayte. What Shakespeare's part in the quarrel was we do not know, but it is interesting to learn that at one time of his life he is at least alleged to have put the fear of death into a fellow citizen.

These were the years in which he began to amass a quite considerable fortune. The first evidence of this is seen in 1596 when his father at Stratford applied to the Herald's Office for the grant of a coat of arms which would permit him and his son after him to write themselves down as "gentlemen." It is probable that William suggested the application; other members of his company, Phillips, Pope and Burbage, were securing such patents of gentility and Shakespeare was not the man to fall behind in the race. After due consideration and the receipt of the customary fee the Heralds granted John Shakespeare the well-known coat of arms with a falcon shaking a spear—the pun on the name is evident—and the motto *Non sanz droict*.

A more substantial sign of his increasing prosperity appears in his purchase in 1597 of New Place, one of the finest houses in Stratford, originally built by Sir Hugh Clopton, and often spoken of as "the Great House." It had fallen into considerable decay and Shakespeare acquired it for the small sum of £60, but he repaired and restored it till it became one of the glories of the town, surrounded by orchards and gardens and boasting the extreme luxury of ten fireplaces. Fifty years later during the Civil Wars when Queen Henrietta Maria came to Stratford at the head of a Royalist Army, she took up her residence at New Place, then occupied by Shakespeare's daughter Susanna and his grandchild Elizabeth. This was the first of several purchases of landed property that Shakespeare made. As late as 1613 we find him purchasing a dwelling-house in the fashionable quarter of Blackfriars; but New Place was his country home. He seems to have established his wife and daughters there at once—the boy Hamnet had died in 1596—and it was to New Place that he finally retired. One can imagine the sensation in Stratford when it was known that young Shakespeare, who had left the town under a cloud and joined himself to the "roguish players" in London, was now the master of New Place. The re-action of the townsfolk was characteristic; they at once attempted to get Shakespeare to invest more money at Stratford and one of the Stratford Quineys on business and in debt at London tried to borrow £30 of him.

In 1598 Francis Meres, a scholar and clergyman, living at that time in London wrote a book with the high sounding title of *Palladis Tamia: Wits Treasury*. It was in the main a review of English literature from the time of Chaucer and a comparison of English authors with their classical prototypes. He paid particular attention to Shakespeare and after declaring that "the sweete wittie soule of Ovid" lived again in Shakespeare's verse, he went on to speak of his work as dramatist. The passage deserves quotation in full: "As Plautus and Seneca are accounted the best for Comedy and Tragedy among the Latines: so Shakespeare among the English is the most excellent in both kinds for the stage; for Comedy, witnes his *Gentlemen of Verona*, his *Errors*, his *Love labors lost*, his *Love labours wonne*, his *Midsummers night dreame* & his *Merchant of Venice:* for Tragedy, his *Richard the 2. Richard the 3. Henry the 4. King John, Titus Andronicus* and his *Romeo and Juliet*."

There are some interesting facts about this famous list. In the first place out of the twelve plays named only six—*Titus, Richard II, Richard III, Henry IV, Romeo and Juliet* and *Love's Labour's Lost*—had appeared in print when Meres published his book (entered S. R. Sept. 15, 1598). Of these only three, the second editions of *Richard II* and *Richard III* and *Love's Labour's Lost,* bore Shakespeare's name on the title-page. It is plain that Meres must have seen the other six upon the stage, or at least have talked with men who had seen them and that he had been assured that these six as well as the three printed but unsigned plays were the work of "honey-tongued Shakespeare." In other words Meres must have been closely in touch with the world of the theatre in London in 1597–98 and have known what he was writing about.

In the second place there is a curious addition and an interesting omission in this list. No play bearing the name of *Love's Labours Won* has come down to us. It is most unlikely that a play with this title has been lost and it is probable that it was the first name of *All's Well That Ends Well,* later revised, re-named, and printed for the first time in the Folio of 1623. It has also been identified, less probably, with *The Taming of the Shrew*. The omission is that of the trilogy on the reign of Henry VI. (See below, p. 49.) We may assume that if these plays were on the stage when Meres wrote, which is rather doubtful, he did not feel justified in claiming them for Shakespeare. On the other hand, we note that he did so claim *Titus Andronicus* and his testimony may at least assure us that this repulsive tragedy passed for Shakespeare's in Meres' day.

We may assume that Meres meant to give and gave, as far as his knowledge allowed, a complete list of Shakespeare's plays up to the date of his writing, i.e. to the summer of 1598. The list seems complete; there is no extant play by Shakespeare with the possible exceptions of *The Shrew* and the *Henry VI* trilogy which can be dated before this time.

Finally the list throws an interesting light on the character of Shakespeare's work for the theatre up to 1598. Apart from his revision of *Titus* and the early poetic lyric tragedy of *Romeo and Juliet,* it consisted entirely of comedy—Meres lists six plays—and of chronicle plays which Meres groups under tragedy. The chronological order of these plays is discussed below. (pp. 49–55.)

Another interesting proof of Shakespeare's popularity appeared in the following year, 1599, when an enterprising publisher, W. Jaggard, secured a manuscript which included among other poems two of Shakespeare's sonnets, yet unprinted, two others from *Love's Labour's Lost,* and a song from that play. The manuscript was probably a gentleman's commonplace book in which the owner had copied poems printed and unprinted that he had come across. Jaggard had the impudence to label it *The Passionate Pilgrime* and to publish it as by W. Shakespeare. The fraud seems to have been successful, for a second edition appeared some time later—no copy has come to us and the exact date is unknown—and a third in 1612. To this last Jaggard prefixed the statement "newly augmented and corrected. By W. Shakespeare" and added a pair of poetical epistles between Helen and Paris which he lifted from *Troia Britanica,* a poem by Shakespeare's contemporary playwright, Thomas Heywood. Heywood naturally protested vigorously against the theft and in an epistle added to his *Apology for Actors,* 1612, remarked that Shakespeare was "much offended with M. Jaggard that (altogether unknowne to him) presumed to make so bold with his name." This is, I believe, the only bit of evidence we have that Shakespeare ever took offence at the improper use of his name or the piratical publication of his work.

In 1599 a very important change occurred in Shakespeare's fortunes and his relation to his fellow actors which deserves attention. His company, the Chamberlain's Men, had been acting for some years at the Theatre in the suburbs north of London. This building had been erected by James Burbage, father of Shakespeare's friend Richard, in 1576 on ground for which he had taken a twenty-one-year lease. Shortly before its expiration he had attempted to open a new playhouse in the fashionable district of Blackfriars in the very heart of London. The residents of the district entered an emphatic protest and the Privy Council forbade Burbage to proceed with his undertaking. He died in 1597, leaving his troubles to his sons Cuthbert and Richard. Cuthbert, to whom the Theatre had been left by his father's will, tried in vain for a year or more to secure an extension of the lease from Giles Alleyn, the landlord, but in the last days of 1598 he realized that Alleyn not only was determined to refuse, but meant to seize and tear down the building. Thereupon Cuthbert secured the services of a master-builder, tore down the Theatre himself, and transported the material across the Thames to the sporting district of the Bankside where the builder promptly erected a new playhouse for him, the famous Globe Theatre. This must have been a very expensive business and Cuthbert, who seems to have inherited his father's business ability, devised a scheme for financing it which was new in his day and of great importance to the leading players of the company. He formed a stock company consisting of ten shares of which he and Richard took five and invited the actors to subscribe for the remaining half. Five of the company, Shakespeare, Heminges, Phillips, Pope, and Kemp, responded, taking one share each. This little group—the "housekeepers" they were called—along with the Burbage brothers thus became the owners of the Globe which they then leased out to the company on profitable terms. This excellent arrangement secured the loyalty of the chief actors to the company—only one of the housekeepers, Kemp, ever left them—increased their profits, and made it possible to admit in later years deserving actors to this favored inside ring. Henceforth Shakespeare as one of this group enjoyed a triple source of revenue; as a dramatist he was paid for the plays he furnished the company, as an actor he received his proportionate share of the net profits on all plays acted at the Globe, and in addition as a housekeeper, he received a tenth, later somewhat more, of the rent the company paid the owners of the theatre.

The Globe opened probably in the summer of 1599. Jonson's *Every Man out of his Humor* was one of the early productions and it was quickly followed by a group of Shakespeare's comedies, *Much Ado, As You Like It,* and *Twelfth Night.* These are the so-called Joyous Comedies and, as we have seen, there was every reason at this time for Shakespeare to be in the best of spirits. But clouds were beginning to gather.

In the spring of 1599 Essex, a popular hero since his raid on Cadiz, started for Ireland to put down the dangerous Tyrone rebellion. In his company went Shakespeare's friend and patron Southampton. The expedition set out with high hopes which are reflected in a well-known passage in the Chorus to the last act of *Henry V* where Shakespeare pictures Essex returning from Ireland "bringing rebellion broached on his sword" and the Londoners pouring out to welcome him. But the expedition proved a complete failure; instead of crushing Tyrone, Essex made a truce on favorable terms with him and rushed back to England to regain the favor of the Queen which his ill-success had forfeited. In this too he was unsuccessful; he was brought to trial, stripped of his offices, and driven at last to open rebellion. Early in February, 1601, he and Southampton and a group of discontented nobles and gentlemen determined to march into London at the head of an armed force, rouse the city, and seize the person of the Queen. They may even have planned to depose her, for a day or two before the rising some of the conspirators came to the Globe and asked the actors to give a performance of "the play of the deposing and killing of *King Richard II*" with the idea, probably, that the representation of such a precedent would win the sympathy of the audience for their proposed rebellion. The prudent actors demurred but were induced by promise of a special bonus to accede to the request, and accordingly revived the old play on Saturday, February 6, before a house packed by the friends of Essex.

On Sunday the 7th Essex with a body of 200 armed men marched into London and attempted to raise the city. The loyal Londoners, however, were in no mood to join even such a popular hero as Essex. The mad attempt collapsed at once; Essex was arrested, tried and convicted of high treason and, on February 25, beheaded on Tower Hill. Southampton, too, was condemned to death, but the sentence was commuted at the last moment to life imprisonment and he was accordingly confined in the Tower for the remaining years of Elizabeth's reign.

The rebellion and death of Essex ended the glorious period of Elizabeth's reign. "The Queen," it was said, "had no comfort thereafter and the people were wrathful at the death of their favorite. . . . The death of Essex like a melancholy cloud did shade the prospect of her people's affection." And over Shakespeare this cloud must have cast an especial shadow. The sudden and tragic fall of so brilliant a figure as Essex, the danger and long imprisonment of his beloved Southampton, contributed not a little, we may well believe, to the gloomy outlook upon life which shows itself in his work for years to come. It is not without significance that when a chorus of poets burst out in mournful strains at Elizabeth's death, March, 1603, Shakespeare was noticeably silent. His company, in fact, had been involved in the rebellion and one of its oldest and most respected members, Augustine Phillips, was called on to testify at the trial of Essex and Southampton to their innocency in performing *Richard II* at the request of the conspirators. Phillips seems to have cleared his companions of all blame, for no punishment of any kind was inflicted on the company, and Elizabeth actually invited them to play before her on the eve of the execution of Essex. One would like to know what play was acted and in what mood Shakespeare performed before her Majesty.

Another cloud that appeared on the horizon meant less, no doubt, to Shakespeare personally than the ruin of Essex and Southampton, but even more to his company. This was the new and lively competition in the theatrical world thrust upon them by the sudden rise to favor of the Children of the Chapel. Their enterprising manager, Evans, secured permission to give so-called private performances in the hall of Blackfriars where James Burbage had been forbidden to put on plays and which Evans now rented from Richard Burbage. The closed hall was a far more pleasant place in which to sit and watch a play than the open air theatre of the Globe. The Children were well trained and accomplished actors; the music, vocal and instrumental, was excellent, and the high prices charged for admission kept the audience select. A little group of poets and playwrights began selling their works to the Children and before long the whole fashionable world of London was crowding to Blackfriars. That Shakespeare's company suffered from and resented this competition is plain from the well-known passage in Hamlet referring to the "little cyases" [the unfledged birds] that are now the fashion and carry away "Hercules and his load"—the swinging sign of Shakespeare's theatre was, of course, Hercules with the Globe on his shoulders.

This competition was intensified, moreover, by what is known as the "War of the Theatres." Jonson for some reason turned his back on Shakespeare's company which had produced his two *Every Man* plays and began writing for the Children. In the plays they staged for him Jonson indulged not only in general satire, but gave free rein to personal animosities which culminated in his *Poetaster,* 1601, with some very ill-natured slurs on his old friends at the Globe, the "common players." In revenge Shakespeare's company secured the right to present at the Globe *Satiromastix,* a play written by two of Jonson's enemies for the private theatre where the Boys of Pauls were playing. In the play Jonson himself under the name of Horace was brought on the stage, scolded, laughed at, tossed in a blanket, and crowned with nettles instead of the poet's laurel. It is not likely that Shakespeare contributed anything to this abusive performance, but the laughter which it provoked seems to have put an end to the War; and since Shakespeare's company had staged the play, Shakespeare himself was credited with having given that "pestilent fellow," Horace-Jonson, "a purge that made him bewray his credit." That Shakespeare's company had regained their own credit is shown by the fact that they were called on to play before the Queen three times in the Christmas season of 1602. A little over a year later in February, 1603, they played to her at Richmond for the last time. Elizabeth died in March of that year and with the coming of her successor Shakespeare and his company enter upon a new period which deserves special consideration.

V

SHAKESPEARE IN LONDON—UNDER JAMES —LAST YEARS AT STRATFORD

THE death of Elizabeth and the accession of James mark the beginning of a new period in Shakespeare's life.

Much has been said of the personal clumsiness, the pedantry, and the political stupidity of James, but one thing must not be forgotten. He like all the Stuarts was a lover and patron of the arts, and the art that he most loved was that of the theatre. Even in Scotland where the grim elders of the Kirk threatened to excommunicate players and playgoers, he had contrived to enjoy performances by a company of visiting English comedians in 1601, headed by a certain Lawrence Fletcher. James, in fact, seems to have given Fletcher the right to call a company which he led on tour in England in 1602 "His Majesty's Players," and this title may have suggested to James an interesting step that he took immediately upon his arrival in London in May, 1603. He took Shakespeare's company, the Chamberlain's Men, under his own patronage with the name of the King's Men, added his favorite Fletcher to their number, and gave them a patent to play, not only at the Globe, but anywhere else in his "realms and dominions." Each member of the company was granted a small annual salary and in addition received an issue of scarlet cloth to be worn on state occasions as cloak and cap with the royal arms embroidered in gold on the sleeve to mark them as indeed His Majesty's Servants. Furthermore James promoted Shakespeare and his fellows to the honorary rank of Grooms of the Chamber. We may well believe that Shakespeare, already signing himself Gentleman of Stratford-on-Avon, was gratified by these marks of royal favor; probably he was made even happier by the release from imprisonment of his friend and patron, Southampton, which followed shortly after the King's arrival in London.

The gloom that seems to have settled over Shakespeare's mind in the last days of Elizabeth's reign was not lifted by these signs of royal favor. He had already entered into what is known as his tragic period. Even the comedies of this time, *All's Well, Troilus,* and *Measure for Measure,* show a bitter humor far other than the happy mirth of his earlier plays and the shadow deepens as he goes on to write, *Othello, Lear,* and *Macbeth.* The change of tone and temper in his work has been explained by the changing dramatic fashion of the time, shifting from romantic comedy and the chronicle play to realistic satiric comedy and tragedy; but this is hardly a sufficient cause. His change of theme may have been due in part to his unceasing desire to explore new realms of art; a deeper cause, no doubt, was his growing realization of the powers of evil that lay beneath the brilliant surface of Renaissance culture and that were to show themselves in abhorrent forms during the reign of the first Stuart king.

It may have been with the idea of rehearsing at the Globe a play likely to please their learned master when presented at Court that Shakespeare's company some time in 1603 staged Jonson's grave classical tragedy *Sejanus.* The play has a special interest for us because of the fact that Shakespeare himself acted in it, the last play in which we can be certain that he ever played a part. More and more he was devoting himself from this time on to his true work, play-writing, and letting his old business as actor fall to his fellows. Whether the ill success of *Sejanus,* which was hissed off the stage by an angry audience had anything to do with Shakespeare's withdrawal from public performances we cannot say, but it is at least not impossible.

Before the end of May, 1603, the plague had grown so hot in London that all theatres were closed. A vivid account of this visitation of the plague in Dekker's *The Wonderful Year* shows how all that could leave the stricken city fled into the country. The King was forced to postpone his formal entrance into London and Shakespeare's company went on tour in the provinces. On December 2nd they were summoned to play before the King at Wilton, the country seat of the Earl of Pembroke, who according to the dedication of the First Folio "prosecuted" the author of the plays "with so much favour." Later the King shifted his residence to Hampton Court and there between December 26th and February 18th the Company presented six plays, for which they were paid £53. In addition the King gave Burbage £30 "for the mayntenaunce and releife of himselfe and the rest of his company being prohibited to p'sente any playes publiquelie in or neere London . . . till it shall please God to settle the cittie in a more p'fecte health."

By March, 1604, conditions had so far improved that James was able to make his formal entrance into London. There was a grand procession through the city from the Tower to Whitehall and Shakespeare and his fellows received a special grant of red cloth for liveries, though we do not know that they took part in the procession.

On April 9th the London theatres were allowed to open, and Shakespeare's company settled down to their regular spring and summer season at the Globe. *Measure for Measure* and *Othello* seem to have been Shakespeare's offerings at the Globe this year and both of them were presented at Court in November and December of 1604.

In August the Company was called on to assist in the entertainment of the Ambassadors of Spain and Austria who had come to London to negotiate a treaty of peace. They were invited in their capacity of Grooms of the Chamber, not as actors. They certainly did not perform before the Ambassadors and their retinue, few of whom probably understood a word of English. They only served as their official attendants during the Ambassadors' stay of a fortnight or so at Somerset House. The Company was paid the sum of £21 12s for this service and the Spanish Ambassador was very bountiful in his gifts "unto all that attended him." It is possible that Shakespeare received from him at this time the silver-gilt bowl which he left in his will to his daughter Judith, or the sword which he bequeathed to his friend, Thomas Coombe. The rise in favor of the King's Men at Court is shown by the fact that in the holiday season of 1604-5 they were called on for eleven performances at Whitehall as against two by other companies, and of these eleven, eight were plays by Shakespeare. An interesting letter which has come down to us shows that Queen Anne, the pleasure-loving wife of James, was not satisfied with the regular programme at Court, but insisted on having a new play presented to her privately between New Year's and Twelfth Day. There was much running to and fro to fulfill her Majesty's request and at last Burbage, who stated that there was no new play which she had not seen, suggested that she attend a revival of *Love's Labour's Lost* "which for wit and mirth" he said "would please her exceedingly." Accordingly this early work of Shakespeare's, furbished up perhaps for the occasion, was played before the Queen in a nobleman's house in London.

Shakespeare's personal fortune was so largely increased by the popularity of his plays and their frequent performance at Court that in July, 1605, he was able to put through the largest transaction of his life, the purchase of certain fixed rents at Stratford, for the sum of £440, a purchase that turned out very favorably for his heirs.

From about 1602 to 1607 Shakespeare was living in the house of a French refugee, Mountjoy, in the heart of the city. It has recently been discovered that Shakespeare interested himself in the marriage of Mountjoy's only child, Mary, to Mountjoy's apprentice. The marriage led in the end to a law-suit brought by Mary's husband against her father and in 1612 Shakespeare was dragged, against his will no doubt, into the case. Certain questions as to a promised dowry and legacy were put to him to which he returned somewhat inconclusive answers. The case is interesting to us only because the formal interrogatory laid before William Shakespeare of Stratford-upon-Avon, Gentleman, preserves for us one of the half-dozen of his autograph signatures which still remain.

It may have been the family troubles of the Mountjoys that drove Shakespeare away from their house in 1606-7. He seems to have been living on the Bankside in the latter year when his younger brother Edmund, "a player," was buried in St. Saviour's in Southwark, the special church of the actors, "with a forenoon toll of the great bell—20 shillings"—a fee no doubt paid by William.

A happier event had called Shakespeare back to Stratford in the preceding June. In that month his oldest child, Susanna, was married to John Hall, a doctor of good family and skill in his profession—*medicus peritissimus*, the burial register calls him. The Halls settled in a little house, Hall's Croft, not far from Shakespeare's New Place and the doctor became the close friend and medical adviser of Shakespeare in his later years. We know of at least one occasion when he accompanied him to London. The sole child of this marriage, Elizabeth, was born in February, 1608, to become the darling of Shakespeare's last days.

The winter of 1607-8 was the most severe that England had known for years. The Thames was frozen over for weeks and the bitter weather must have had a most discouraging effect upon the audiences of the open-air Globe. This may have had a bearing upon a decision taken in the spring of 1608 which led to important results in the history of the King's Men and had a direct influence upon the later life and work of Shakespeare himself. When James came to the throne, the Children of the Chapel, long a thorn in the side of Shakespeare's company, were taken under royal protection, and given the title of the Children of Her Majesty's Revels. Their manager, however, was indiscreet and ungrateful. In 1605 he produced a lively comedy, *Eastward Ho,* with some pointed satire on the King's countrymen; in this play indeed a boy actor went so far as to mock the King's broad Scotch accent. The royal patronage was withdrawn and the theatre was closed. Evans, however, managed to get it re-opened and the boys continued to act under the title of the Children of Blackfriars. Once more, however, the managers in their efforts to create a sensation over-reached themselves. In 1608 two plays in quick succession gave bitter offence. In one, the name of which is unknown, the King himself was brought on the stage, drinking and swearing; in the other, Chapman's *Conspiracy of Byron,* the French Queen was shown quarrelling with and boxing the ears of her husband's mistress. The French Ambassador entered an energetic protest and King James swore that the children "should never play more but should first beg their bread." Evans saw that the game was up and entered into negotiations with Burbage for the surrender of his lease.

This was a heaven-sent opportunity for the King's Men. Secure now in the royal favor, they could take over an enclosed theatre in the heart of the town where they could produce plays in winter protected from the weather while charging a higher price of admission than was possible at the Globe. Burbage at once formed a syndicate to take over the management. He invited Shakespeare, Condell, Heminges, and Sly of the company to participate, and associated with them his brother Cuthbert and Evans himself. The undertaking proved immensely successful; it was alleged in a law-suit in 1612 that the King's Men got "more in one winter by a thousand pounds than they were used to get on the Bankside." A good share of these profits of course went into Shakespeare's hands.

It reached him in all probability at a most opportune time. The strain on Shakespeare as actor, playwright, and man of business in the last ten years must have been prodigious. There is indeed some reason to believe that about 1608 he suffered some sort of physical breakdown. With the acquisition of the Blackfriars, the enlargement of his company—two able actors from the old Revels Company were added to the King's Men at this time—the engagement of two promising young playwrights—Beaumont and Fletcher—who had already been delighting the Blackfriars audience with their romantic and courtly plays, a period of rest and relaxation began for Shakespeare. He seems to have spent more time at home in Stratford and to have felt less of an obligation to furnish his company with a couple of plays a year as had been his earlier practice. And the plays that he wrote from

1609 on were of a quite different type from the histories and tragedies that had poured from his active brain for a period of years. They have been called "romances"; tragi-comedies would be a better word. It has even been suggested that he was influenced by the work of the young pair of playwrights with whom he was now associated. This is, perhaps, too sweeping an assertion; Beaumont and Fletcher did not invent tragi-comedy. They, Beaumont in particular, learned more from Shakespeare than he from them. But the Blackfriars theatre had specialized in romantic drama; Chapman had written for the children acting there the first play, *The Gentleman Usher,* ca. 1602, that seems a genuine forerunner of the later fully developed tragi-comedy. No doubt when the King's Men began to play to the Blackfriars audience in 1608 or 1609 they felt obliged to offer, in part at least, something of the fare to which their hearers were accustomed; and the Company naturally looked to their fellow, the most popular playwright of the day, to furnish something of this fare. It must have been a great relief to Shakespeare after the storm and stress of *Othello, Lear,* and *Macbeth* to turn to the composition of the plays that mark his last period. He patched up an old popular success in *Pericles,* dramatized a novel by Greene in *The Winter's Tale,* and apparently was willing to furnish a partly written play, *The Two Noble Kinsmen,* for Fletcher to put in shape for production. *The Tempest,* 1611, seems to show that Shakespeare was looking forward to retirement from active life, and after *Henry VIII,* in which he collaborated with Fletcher, he wrote no more. This play was put on at the Globe with great splendor in June, 1613. At the first performance a bit of burning wadding discharged from a small cannon behind the stage set fire to the thatched roof of the galleries; the fire spread downward, and although the audience and actors escaped unhurt—except for one unlucky man whose burning breeches had to be extinguished with a bottle of ale—the famous theatre was burnt to the ground.

Shakespeare may have been in London at the time of this catastrophe. He certainly was there in March, 1613, when he bought a piece of property in Blackfriars; two of his six remaining autograph signatures are on documents connected with this transaction. In the same month he devised an *impresa,* a symbolic device with motto, for the Earl of Rutland to display at a Court tournament. It is interesting to note that Shakespeare's old friend, Burbage, received the same amount, 44 shillings, for painting the device, that Shakespeare did for designing it. A creditable tradition also relates that he coached Lowin of the King's Men in the rôle of Henry in the ill-fated play, a task which would probably keep him in town at least until the first performance.

A heavy assessment was levied on the "housekeepers" of the Globe and the theatre was rebuilt, "the fairest that ever was in England," and ready for the players by June, 1614. Shakespeare probably saw it when he was in London, attended by his son-in-law and physician, Dr. Hall, in November of that year, but by that time the Company would have been playing in their winter house, the Blackfriars. This is Shakespeare's last recorded appearance in London and from this time we must imagine him living quietly in Stratford, the most distinguished and perhaps the wealthiest citizen of the little town.

It is difficult to estimate Shakespeare's income in these last years and still more difficult to appreciate its actual value in purchasing power. The statement of the Stratford vicar, John Ward, ca. 1662, that "he spent at the rate of £1,000, a year" is a wild exaggeration, based no doubt on Stratford gossip. Probably Shakespeare received from all sources less than a quarter of that sum, say £200, which might, perhaps, be worth some $4,000 today. On this income we may be sure that Shakespeare lived well and comfortably in Stratford. He practiced hospitality; the Corporation sent him "a quart of sack and a quart of claret wine" when a preacher was stopping at his house. He worked in his garden and planted the famous mulberry tree that flourished till the middle of the next century when it was cut down by a peevish clergyman. He cultivated friendly relations with various Stratfordians, the Coombes, the Sadlers, Julius Shaw, and others. He must have been disturbed by the slander that was circulated about his daughter Susanna, and still more by the imprudent marriage of Judith. In 1616 she married an old friend of the family, Thomas Quiney, in February, the "closed season," without a special license. Cited and failing to appear before the Church Court to explain their irregular action she and her husband were formally excommunicated. There is some reason to believe that Shakespeare took cognizance of this affair in the alterations made in the will he had already drawn.

According to a tradition preserved by the Vicar of Stratford, "Shakespeare, Drayton and Ben Jonson had a merry meeting and it seems drank too hard for Shakespeare died of a fever there contracted." This meeting must have taken place early in March, 1616, when Jonson was visiting Drayton, then staying with friends near Stratford. We need not believe that Shakespeare was the victim of a wild drinking bout; in his enfeebled health the excitement of such a meeting, late hours, and over-indulgence may well have brought about the attack to which he succumbed. Certainly on the 25th of March, 1616, he sent for his lawyer, Francis Collins, to make certain changes in his will. He arranged for a marriage portion for Judith, cancelled his gift of plate to her in favor of his little grandchild, Elizabeth, left memorial rings to Burbage, Heminges, and Condell, and, in an often discussed interpolation, his "second best bed" to his wife. The probable explanation of this bequest has already been given [p. 8, *n.*].

Shakespeare signed the rewritten sheets of the will in a hand so faltering that he was evidently very ill or quite exhausted; the signatures contrast most unfavorably with the final "by me William Shakespeare" written some weeks before. He lingered on for about a month, died on the 23rd of April, and was buried in the Stratford church. Over his grave is a flagstone with the well-known inscription:

> Good frend for Jesus sake forbeare,
> To digg the dust encloased heare!
> Bleste be ye man y^t^ spares thes stones,
> And curst be he y^t^ moves my bones.

A credible tradition reports that Shakespeare himself composed these lines and ordered them to be carved on his gravestone. The reason for such an action is plain enough. Burial inside the church was a favor highly esteemed at Stratford and elsewhere. As claimants for this favor multiplied and available space diminished, it was customary to dig up the bones of those who had no friends or descendants left to protect them and pitch them into the charnel-house outside the church. This is exactly what happened to the bones of Susanna in 1707 when her grave near her father's was wanted for a fresh occupant. Shakespeare, if we may judge from the grave-diggers' scene in *Hamlet,* had a not unnatural horror of such a fate, and, as a seventeenth-century visitor to Stratford tells us, laid a curse on any who should disturb his repose and composed it in language simple enough to be understood by "clarks and sextons, for the most part a very ignorant sort of people." Whether the tradition is true or not, the inscription has had the desired effect; Shakespeare's grave has never been opened since his death.

Some years after his burial a firm of Dutch tomb-makers in London, the brothers Johnson (originally Janssen) were commissioned to prepare the monument which is still to be seen in the Stratford church. It contains a half-length bust of the poet "in his habit as he lived" in a scarlet doublet—perhaps representing the royal livery of a King's Man—a black gown, and a white collar. The rather heavy face may have been modelled after a death mask; it has been stigmatized as the portrait of a "self-satisfied pork butcher"; but it is the only portrait of Shakespeare—except for the engraving prefixed to the First Folio which seems to be derived from it—that has any claim to authenticity, and we must accept it for what it is worth, remembering always that the Johnsons who made it were architectural designers and not portrait sculptors. It was originally painted, then whitewashed, and repainted in 1861 in the original colors.

The terms of Shakespeare's will seem to show that he had hoped to found a family. Since his only son had died in childhood, all his estate was to go to Susanna and her children. But Susanna's only child, Elizabeth, herself died childless in 1670 and the three sons of Judith had died long before. The descendants of Shakespeare were soon extinct; his heritage was left to the world in his immortal works.

VI

SHAKESPEARE'S COMPANY

APART from the work of the playwright there are three factors to be taken into account in any successful dramatic performance: the actors, the theatre, and the audience. That Shakespeare's plays were successful from the first we have not only contemporary testimony but the fact of their long survival in the English-speaking theatre and their conquest of foreign stages. To what extent did these three factors influence the work of the playwright William Shakespeare? Let us consider first the actors who originally presented his plays.

In the first collected edition of Shakespeare's plays, the Folio of 1623, Heminges and Condell, who furnished the copy for the printers, included on the page just preceding the "catalogue" of the plays a list of "the names of the principall actors in all these plays." There are twenty-six names beginning with that of Shakespeare himself and ending with that of John Rice, who had been Heminges' apprentice in 1607 and had become a regular member of the Company only a few years before the publication of the Folio. These twenty-six were Shakespeare's "fellows" with whom he acted and for whom he wrote.

An Elizabethan company of actors was such a different thing from the group gathered now-a-days for the presentation of a play by the producer that some account of its development and organization seems necessary. The increasing taste for dramatic performances in the late fifteenth and sixteenth centuries led to the formation of little groups of players, five or six in number, with a boy or two for female parts, who wandered about the country, giving shows of various sorts, especially the so-called "moralities" and interludes, in town-halls, inn-yards, or noblemen's houses. These groups were looked on with increasing disfavor by the authorities and were finally included in the famous statute of 1572 as "masterless men" and therefore "rogues and vagabonds." To escape the penalties denounced against such undesirables the actors sought to shelter themselves under the protection of a nobleman by becoming, nominally at least, members of his household. As early as 1559 we find Robert Dudley—later the Earl of Leicester, Elizabeth's first favorite—writing to a fellow nobleman in behalf of "my servants—players of interludes" and requesting his friend's license for them to play in his county of Yorkshire. In 1574 Dudley secured from the Queen a royal "patent" which permitted his "servants" to act in London or elsewhere in spite of local rules to the contrary, on the condition that their plays had been approved by the Master of the Revels. Dudley's example was followed by many other noblemen. The Earls of Worcester, Pembroke, and Warwick, and the great Admiral, Lord Charles Howard, each had his own company. Some of these were more or less permanent bodies; others broke up and re-formed, but until the end of the Queen's reign there were always two or three companies of adult actors under the patronage of a noble lord acting in London, while other less distinguished companies toured the provinces. In 1583 the Queen herself ordered the formation of a company of twelve to be known as the Queen's Company, perhaps by way of demonstrating the royal patronage of the profession as opposed to the ceaseless efforts of the city authorities to prohibit it altogether. This company included among others James Burbage, the father of Shakespeare's friend, and the famous clown, Dick Tarleton. When James came to the throne in 1603, the privilege of retaining a company of actors was withdrawn from the nobility and henceforth till the closing of the theatres in 1642 all companies were under the direct patronage of the King himself and other members of the royal family.

The organization of such a company was somewhat along the lines of a medieval guild. It consisted in the first place of a small and limited number of full members, corresponding to the "masters" in a guild. It is probable that each of them had a more or less definite "line" in the profession; one played clown's parts, another the old man's, a third the young hero, and so on. Some allowance must be made, of course, for the actor's versatility; Burbage, for example, played the young lover Romeo, the villainous Richard III, and the old magician Prospero; but in the main it is probable that each member held fairly closely to his "line."

It is evident, of course, that the small group of members could not possibly, even by doubling, fill all the parts demanded by the average Elizabethan drama. To fill these parts the company hired for a limited time minor actors, corresponding in a way to the "journeymen" of the guild. These were paid the regular wage of a skilled workman, but had no share in the company's profits, and seem rarely to have been admitted into full membership.

The third class in the company was composed of the apprentices. These for the most part were young boys engaged at about the age of ten. Each of them was apprenticed to an individual member who trained him in all the routine of the profession and when he was able to play in public hired him out to the company. All the parts for women in Elizabethan plays were taken by these boys since the actress was unknown to the public stage until after the Restoration. It was possible, though rather unusual, to take on a grown man as an apprentice, and it has been suggested that Shakespeare himself was an apprentice for the usual period of seven years in the company of which he was later a full member. It was, in fact, from these well-trained young actors, boys or youths, that the company was accustomed to add to its membership as vacancies occurred.

The first requisite for such a company, of course, was a place to play in. In the early years of Elizabeth's reign, the actors played for the most part in the inn courtyards of London. Five of such inns were more or less adapted as regular playing-places, but after the building of the first playhouse, the Theatre, 1576, it became of course the desire of every company to find a footing in this or one of the rapidly succeeding theatres. This they did by renting the building for a term from the owner, James Burbage at the Theatre, or Henslowe at the Rose. Rent was paid by allotting to the owner half the admission money charged for seats in the galleries, which naturally cost more than standing room on the ground floor. The balance of the admission money, after expenses had been paid, was divided equally among the full members.

The expenses, however, were by no means limited to the rent; there was the wage to be paid the hired men and the fee to the actor whose apprentice was actually playing. More costly still would be the outlay for properties of all sorts, especially for the gorgeous costumes in which the actors strutted their hour upon the stage. The initial outlay for all such charges was as a rule met by the owner of the theatre who recouped himself by levying on that half of the gallery money which went to the company. When the leading members of Shakespeare's company formed a syndicate (cf. p. 19) to build the Globe and later to lease the Blackfriars, this syndicate took the place of such an owner as Henslowe; its members, the so-called "housekeepers," met all expenses and in return received a larger share of the receipts than their less fortunate fellows.

The Elizabethan company, we see, was a self-governing and self-perpetuating body. It owed, indeed, a certain allegiance to its patron and was liable to be disciplined by royal authority acting through the Master of the Revels for trenching upon forbidden topics—religious or political themes, or offensive personal satire. Apart from this it was free, and it was particularly free in its relation to the poets who furnished it with plays. A dramatist to-day writes his play according to his own best will and judgment; he finds a producer who undertakes to stage it and assembles a company to act the parts. In rehearsal, it is true, lines may be struck out, passages added, and various changes made, but on the whole the play stands or falls according to the author's design. In Elizabethan times, on the other hand, a play was written for a particular company and we know from records still preserved that the company sometimes furnished the book which was to be dramatized or the old play that was to be re-written. The author sketched his plot for the actors, received their approval, read the first couple of acts to them at a tavern after their acting for the day was done, and received an advance payment. He then finished the play, incorporating, no doubt, whatever suggestions the actors offered, wrote out a clean copy which would be sent up to the Master of the Revels for licensing, and received his final payment. At every stage in his work the playwright was conditioned by the company for whom he was writing; he must have a good part for each principal actor, if there were not sufficient parts in the tale he was dramatizing, he must work up a sub-plot which would furnish them. This, by the way, is one of the reasons for the frequent appearance of the sub-plot—sometimes a comic one in a tragic play—in Elizabethan drama. He must so far as possible adapt the characters of this play to the "lines" of the actors who were to perform it. For example, while the comedian Kemp was a member of Shakespeare's company the poet created for him such low comedy rôles as those of Peter, Bottom, and Dogberry. When Kemp's place was taken by the brilliant and witty Armin, Shakespeare furnished his new fellow with such high comedy parts as those of Touchstone and Feste. Perhaps the most striking instance of Shakespeare's consideration of an actor occurs in *King Lear*. In *Othello,* the play immediately preceding this tragedy, there is indeed a part for the Clown (Armin) but it is so short and so slight—indeed is cut out in all modern acting versions—that we may well imagine Armin strongly objecting to so poor a rôle. As if to recompense him Shakespeare introduced into his next play, *King Lear,* the part of the Fool—for which there is no corresponding part in the old source—a role which would at once tax and exhibit all of Armin's quality as an actor.

The boy apprentices in the company were not only carefully trained by their masters but had special parts written for them by the dramatist. Granville-Barker has noted how carefully Shakespeare avoids what we call "sex-appeal" in his boys; they are gay, witty, mocking, at times sentimental, never, except in the case of Cressida, sensuous. When they could sing, Shakespeare exploited their voices as in the roles of Ophelia, Desdemona, and Ariel. In addition to women's parts Shakespeare wrote for the boys the roles of roguish pages, such as those of Moth in *Love's Labour's Lost* and Falstaff's page who carries over into *Henry V*. When Shakespeare wrote *A Midsummer Night's Dream,* there were evidently two boys in the company who differed greatly in size; one of them played Helena, the tall "maypole," the other Hermia, the little "dwarf."

Since Shakespeare never wrote for the Children who played at Blackfriars and Paul's we need not dwell at length upon the constitution of these companies. It is sufficient to say that they were in no sense independent self-governing bodies like a company of adult actors. Their managers had a royal license to impress children for singing and acting which they strained so far as actually at times to kidnap children on the streets of London. The manager supported and trained the boys, produced their plays, which were characterized by an unusual amount of music, vocal and instrumental, and pocketed all the proceeds. The training in these companies was no doubt excellent; when the Children of the Chapel were dissolved in 1608-9, Shakespeare's company took over two of the best young actors; one of them, Nat Field, was to become a rival of Burbage himself as an actor of tragic parts.

The history of the company to which there is good reason, though not positive certainty, to believe that Shakespeare belonged throughout his career may be briefly traced. It began in the first years of the Queen's reign as Lord Leicester's Men. It is possible that Shakespeare became attached to this company shortly after their visit to Stratford in 1587. At Leicester's death in 1588 the principal actors joined a company under the patronage of Ferdinando Stanley, Lord Strange. They acted for a time in 1592 at Henslowe's theatre, the Rose, where they were joined by Edward Alleyn, the leading tragedian of the Admiral's Men. With him they, or most of them, toured the provinces in the plague years of 1592-94. While on tour their patron, Lord Strange, became, in September 1593 by the death of his father, the Earl of Derby, and the Company accordingly took over this new title, and became the Earl of Derby's Men. The new earl, however, lived only till April of 1594, shortly after which the Company secured the patronage of Henry Carey, Queen Elizabeth's cousin, at that time Lord Chamberlain. On his death in 1596 they became the "servants' of his son, George Carey, Lord Hunsdon, and when he succeeded his father as Lord Chamberlain in 1597 they once more regained the title of the Lord Chamberlain's Men. This title they bore until the accession of James who, as we have seen, took them under his direct patronage and they remained the King's Majesty's Servants from 1603 till the closing of the theatres in 1642.

The various names borne by this company appear from time to time in records of their performances and on the title page of published plays. It is well to remember, however, that under these various titles the Company remained essentially the same, adding of course new members and losing old ones by death or resignation, at least from the reorganization as Lord Strange's Men in 1588 to the dissolution of the Company in 1642. All things considered, it was the most stable, the most prosperous, and the most talented of all Elizabethan companies, and its success was due in no small measure to the fact that it early secured and long retained the services of William Shakespeare as its regular playwright.

VII

SHAKESPEARE'S THEATRE

It is a commonplace of criticism that the technique of acting drama is of necessity strongly influenced by the physical conditions of the theatre for which the dramatist writes. The plays of the Greek tragedians, for instance, were written to be represented in vast open air theatres; those of Molière for the small closed "tennis-court" theatre of seventeenth-century France; Ibsen's for the modern "picture-frame" stage. Recent developments in lighting and staging are having a profound effect upon the technique of contemporary drama. Strangely enough, however, it is only in comparatively recent years that this self-evident truth has been taken into account in a consideration of Shakespeare's plays. His first editors divided them into acts and scenes and equipped them with stage-directions and indications of locality in accordance with the practice of the eighteenth-century theatre, a theatre, by the way, different in many important respects from that for which Shakespeare wrote. Modern producers find it difficult, if not impossible, to present his plays in their original form upon the stage of today and are driven to excisions, alterations, and additions to fit them to this Procrustean bed. There is even a tendency at times to find fault with the technique of Shakespeare and his contemporaries because it is not adapted to the modern stage. This is as foolish as it would be to blame Æschylus or Sophocles for writing plays with choral songs and dances, features conspicuously absent in the modern "well-made" play. On the other hand we sometimes hear that if Shakespeare had enjoyed the advantages of the modern theatre, scenery, realistic settings, electric lighting, and so on, he would have made use of them. From this it is supposed to follow that the modern producer is justified in adapting some of Shakespeare's plays to the modern "picture-frame" stage and neglecting those, *Lear* for example, which seem incapable of such adaptation. Certainly if Shakespeare had written for our stage his plays would have been different, but he did not, and to understand his work, at least in its technical aspect, we must know something of the stage for which he wrote.

The patient researches of a group of scholars, based largely upon a contemporary sketch of the Swan, an Elizabethan theatre, the contract for the building of the Fortune, upon stage-directions and other indications in the texts of Elizabethan plays, have dispelled certain misconceptions handed down from the past and enabled us to form a fairly accurate idea of the Elizabethan stage. It is no longer possible to think of it as a bare platform without decoration or properties of any kind. It did not seem poor or bare to contemporaries. There is abundant testimony to the fact that Englishmen and foreigners alike regarded the London theatres of Shakespeare's day as magnificent structures and the stage as admirably equipped. De Witt, the Dutchman who sketched the Swan, mentions their beauty, and Coryat, the famous traveller, remarks that the theatres of Venice were "beggarly and bare in comparison with our stately playhouses in England." So far from the stage being bare it was strewn, like the halls of gentlemen's houses with rushes, or on special occasions covered with matting. Elaborate properties were often brought upon the stage, the chariot, for example, in which Tamburlaine was drawn by captive Kings, the arbor in which Don Horatio was hanged by the neck (see the frontispiece to the 1615 edition of the *Spanish Tragedy*), a fountain with real water, a well-head down which a body could be dropped, trees, possibly pushed up on the stage through a trap, substantial enough for an actor to climb upon them, rocks, mossy banks, shops, beds, thrones, tents, and wayside crosses. The back-stage was hung with arras, sometimes painted in perspective—Henslowe had a "painted cloth" of the City of Rome—sometimes with scenes from the Bible or from classical mythology. In the *Knight of the Burning Pestle* there is an allusion to such a picture which the Citizen's Wife thinks may be "The Confutation of St. Paul," but which her wiser husband calls "Rafe and Lucrece." Extravagant sums were spent upon the actors' costumes. Henslowe, who usually paid about £8 for a play, once laid out £20 upon a single cloak. Garments of silk and satin decked with gold and silver lace, trimmed, cut, and slashed with all the fantasy of Elizabethan tailoring, were the ordinary apparel of the Elizabethan actor. The Puritan opponents of the stage were loud in their denunciation for such extravagance of dress, but it must have added more than a little color to Shakespeare's stage.

Sometimes the actors presented great spectacular shows and gorgeous processions upon the stage. Sir Henry Wotton wrote to a friend in 1613: "The King's players had a new play called *All Is True* [*Henry VIII*]—which was set forth with many extraordinary circumstances of pomp and majesty even to the matting of the stage; the Knights of the Order with their Georges and garters; the Guards with their embroidered coats and the like; sufficient in truth within a while to make greatness very familiar, if not ridiculous." When we add to such spectacles the introduction into Elizabethan plays of elaborate masques, calling at times for the employment of complicated machinery, such as appear, for instance, in *Cymbeline* and *The Tempest*, it is plain that the old notion of the Elizabethan stage as a bare scaffold must be altogether rejected.

Such matters as properties, costumes, and spectacles are, however, non-essential. Of greater importance to the art of the dramatist is the physical structure of the stage itself. On this point there is now a practical agreement among scholars; differences remain only on a few minor details.

The Elizabethan theatre may be regarded as evolving from the inn courtyards which were, long before the first playhouse was built, favorite places for dramatic performances by the old companies of actors.

A description of these courtyards and of their adaptation for dramatic performances has already been given (p. 12).

When James Burbage built the Theatre in 1576 he naturally designed it along the lines of the inn-yards in which he had been accustomed to play. The building had two entrances—one in front for the audience; one in the rear for the actors, musicians, and the personnel of the theatre. Inside the building a rectangular platform projected far out into what was called "the yard"—we know that the stage of the Fortune ran halfway across the "yard," some twenty-seven and a half feet. Here the common herd of spectators, the "groundlings" stood—there were no seats on the ground floor in the old public theatres—in front and on both sides of the stage. Around and above the yard ran three galleries approached by interior stairs and divided into "rooms" or boxes where the better class of spectators who paid an additional price for the accommodation sat more or less comfortably on stools. There was no front curtain and the performance was viewed not from the front alone but from three sides by the spectators in the yard and in the galleries. On this projecting platform the greater part of the action took place. As a rule the playwright made no attempt to localize such action; the platform was, so to speak, neutral ground. It might be any place, outdoors or in, and if the poet wished to designate a locality he wove an allusion to it into the dialogue. "This is the forest of Arden," says Rosalind when the scene has shifted from the Court to the greenwood.

Over a large part of this platform there extended a wooden roof, called "the heavens" or "the shadow," which served partly to protect the actors from bad weather, but primarily to contain the machinery needed to let down on the stage certain properties—"the creaking throne" at which Jonson laughed—or actors impersonating fairies or gods. In the sketch of the Swan we see this "shadow" supported by strong pillars resting on the platform. These, one would suppose, must have interfered with the action, but they could no doubt be used by an actor to conceal himself from others on the stage. We hear once of a pick-purse caught plying his trade in the yard who was hoisted up on the stage and tied to a post for the rest of the performance.

Across the back of the platform ran a wall partly concealed by arras, woven or painted cloth set on frames standing out three feet or so from the wall. This cloth was sometimes painted in perspective, but rarely, if ever, presented a realistic background and certainly was not shifted to denote a change of scene. It served a decorative rather than an illusion-producing purpose. In the narrow space between the arras and the back wall an actor might hide himself, as Polonius does in *Hamlet,* and it was here that Falstaff was found "fast asleep and snorting like a horse" by the Prince and Peto.

Directly behind the back wall, in the centre under the balcony, was a recess, variously known as the "rear-stage" or the "alcove." It was cut off from the front by a "traverse," i.e. a curtain hanging before it. This was drawn back to disclose an action taking place in the rear-stage and pulled over it again at the close of such a scene. This "alcove" was an essential feature of the Elizabethan stage. Since it was concealed from the front by a curtain it could be set beforehand with properties to suggest a definite locality, a scholar's study (*Dr. Faustus*), a lady's bed-chamber (*Cymbeline*), a magician's cell (*Tempest*), or a tomb (*Romeo and Juliet*). An action beginning in this alcove, like the last scene of *Othello,* might be transferred to the front stage—the alcove being too small for the numbers of actors involved—which then became for the time the same locality as that indicated by the setting of the alcove. At the close of such a scene the curtain was drawn and the front stage became again "neutral ground," ready for whatever action the playwright needed. It may be noted here, that the sketch of the Swan shows no trace of this alcove, only a flat back wall of the front stage pierced by two doors. But the existence of such a recess on the Elizabethan stage is quite certain; either the Swan differed from the other theatres of the day in this respect or, which is perhaps more likely, De Witt failed to represent it.

A Drawing of the Swan Theatre in London about 1596.

From the De Witt drawing, the only contemporary picture of an Elizabethan theatre known.

To right and left of the alcove were doors, set flat in the back wall, as in the Swan sketch, or possibly set on the bias, so that actors emerging from them would meet each other in the centre of the stage. These doors connected the stage with the "tiring-room," the modern "green room," from which another entrance was possible through the alcove to the front stage.

Above this rear-stage was the upper-stage, a gallery, slightly projecting over the platform and provided with a curtain by which it could at need be cut off from the view of the audience and like the alcove could be set with properties. This space seems at first to have been occupied by specially favored spectators and was known as "the lord's room"; occasionally the musicians needed for a performance were placed here. Its peculiar value in the presentation of plays, however, was soon realized and it became a positive asset to the playwright. It was used especially to designate a locality above the plane of the main action on the lower stage: the wall of a city from which the defenders could converse with an opponent below, the window, or the balcony of a private house, a high rock, or Cleopatra's monument up to which she and her women draw the dying Antony. This upper-stage was entered as a rule by back stairs from the tiring-room, but it was also possible to reach it from the front by temporary stairs, by a practicable tree set on the main-stage, or by a rope-ladder. It is by such a ladder that Romeo is seen to descend from Juliet's balcony after their wedding-night. In some of the later theatres there seem also to have been boxes over the back doors which could be used at need for the windows of an upper room.

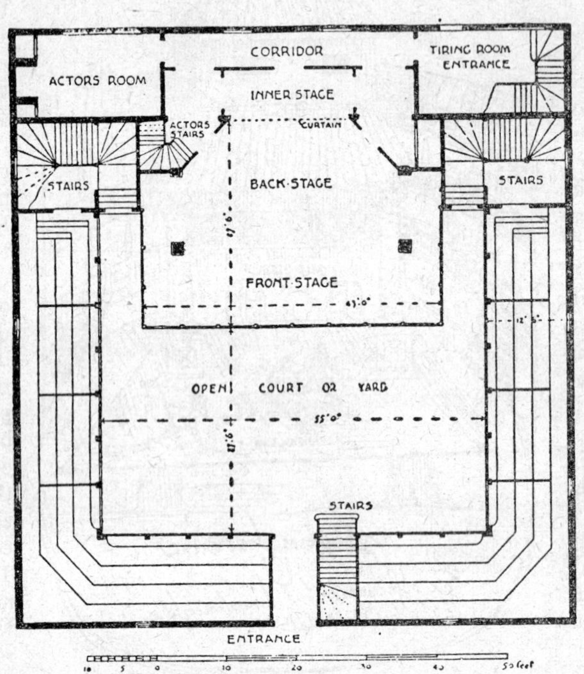

FLOOR PLAN OF THE FORTUNE THEATRE, 1600.

Such was in general the structure of the Elizabethan stage in one of the large public theatres; the Swan seated, De Witt reckons, about three thousand people. There was no essential difference in the so-called "private" theatres. These consisted simply in the adaptation of a hall in a private house for theatrical purposes. The private theatre, like the public, had its uncurtained front stage, its curtained alcove and balcony. The whole space stage, pit, and gallery was under cover, whereas in the public theatre the "yard" was open to the sky and only the galleries and the shadow were roofed with thatch or tile. An upper room or attic served the purpose of the shadow in providing space for the necessary machinery. Performances took place by artificial light and there is reason to believe that the alcove was larger and better lighted. The same plays were produced at public and private theatres, as when Shakespeare's company played both at the Globe and the private Blackfriars; and there is no evidence that any reconstruction of these plays was necessary. The main part of the audience sat on benches on the floor or in the one gallery which sufficed the private theatre. The custom of sitting on a stool upon the stage itself which seems to have originated in public theatres became especially fashionable, and objectionable, in the private houses where a more select audience was ready to pay as much as a shilling extra for such a seat.

The stage, then, for which Shakespeare wrote, consisted of three parts: the front stage, uncurtained and visible from three sides; the rear-stage which could be cut off from public view by a curtain and set with properties; and the balcony, which could also be cut off and disclosed by a curtain hanging before it and withdrawn at need. There was no scenery at all in our sense of the word. The use of set properties to suggest a definite locality was in the main confined to the rear-stage, although at times a bed was thrust out or a throne dropped from the shadow upon the front stage and necessary properties like the caldron in *Macbeth* were raised to the stage and dropped again through traps in the floor. It is quite unlikely that the medieval practice of permanent properties to denote separate and distinct localities upon the same stage was long retained, though there are traces of it, in the public theatres early in Shakespeare's day. Sometimes signboards were hung over the back doors to indicate the place of action, but this naïve device seems soon to have been discontinued.

Over these three stages the action of a play of Shakespeare's flowed smoothly and swiftly without pause for scene-shifting or change of properties. There were, to be sure, brief intermissions, for music, though there was not much of this at the Globe. There is no act division in any of the old texts of Shakespeare which we may imagine to have been printed from his manuscript, so that it is at least doubtful whether he thought of a play as a thing to be composed in the regulation five acts. The word "act," indeed, occurs at times in the old texts to denote the intermission, as when we learn in a stage direction that the lovers in *A Midsummer Night's Dream* "sleep all the act," that is, lie sleeping on the stage throughout the intermission. A bit of action beginning in the alcove might shift to the front stage and vice-versa. Both stages might be occupied at once as when in *Hamlet* the *Mouse-Trap* is presented by the strolling players in the alcove, while Claudius and his court occupy the front stage. Balcony and front stage could be used together, as when Juliet at her window converses with Romeo below in the orchard.

The absence of a front curtain made it impossible for the dramatist to work up to some effective situation on which the curtain falls. Since the greater part of the action took place on the front stage it was incumbent on him to get his characters off at the close of the play. Thus in tragedy dead bodies are [1] dragged or carried off, in *Hamlet* to a funeral march; in comedy the characters often dance off together as at the close of *Much Ado*. In comedy and tragedy alike there is a relaxation of tension before the close, not a swift ending on the highest note with the curtain dropping on the "tableau" beloved by modern playwrights.

Change of place during the play was effected by the simple process of getting all the actors off the stage; the rhymed tags so common in Shakespeare are often a device to mark the end of a scene. When the stage was deserted, it became for a moment no man's land, so to speak, only to become another place with the entrance of a fresh group of actors. In the first act of *Cymbeline,* for example, the scene shifts from Britain to Rome and back again. We know where the scene is laid by the presence of certain actors, not by a scenic background. Decorations and properties were employed to suggest a certain locality rather than to give as on the modern stage a realistic illusion. Shakespeare was not bound by the necessity of fixing every scene in his plays in a definite locality realistically represented on the stage. His stage, in fact, has been well characterized as symbolic or suggestive rather than illusion-producing.

The influence of the physical structure of the Elizabethan stage upon the dramatic technique of Shakespeare has never been quite fully appreciated. Certain aspects of this influence, however, seem fairly clear. In the first place this stage allowed the playwright an almost boundless freedom as to the place of any action; like the writer of scenarios for the cinema, he could shift his scene at will. He could, if he pleased, localize a scene by the use of setting and properties, but he was under no compulsion to do so. We must always remember that the indications of place in modern editions of Shakespeare—"a room in the palace, another room in the same," etc., are the addition of modern editors; there are no such scene-headings in the original texts. The scene-divisions themselves are, for the most part, supplied by modern editors. Shakespeare apparently thought of a play as a continuous whole, interrupted, to be sure, by brief act-pauses for relaxation, but otherwise running an unbroken course; certainly he never dreamed of such breaches of continuity as occur when the attempt is made upon the modern stage to provide each of his short scenes with its appropriate setting. The possibility of swift, continuous action was one of the main gifts of the Elizabethan stage to Shakespeare and his contemporaries.

It was this speed of presentation which made possible the length of Shakespeare's plays as compared with the modern drama. The time allowed for the performance of an Elizabethan play was, as we know from contemporary evidence, about the same as is required today, some two and a half hours. To

[1] Exceptions to this rule occur when death has taken place in the alcove. Thus in *Othello* the bodies of the Moor, Emilia, and Desdemona are on or in the bed in the alcove and at the close of the play are concealed by simply drawing the curtain. In *Romeo and Juliet* the bodies of the lovers within the tomb in the alcove were similarly concealed while the survivors file out in procession.

produce *Hamlet* uncut in its complete form would require today something like six hours. It is probable, indeed, that Shakespeare's plays were originally produced in a somewhat shorter form than that in which they appeared in print; but even in this shorter form they would be too long for a production interrupted by constant pauses for scene-shifting as on the modern picture-frame stage. It seems clear that the speed of performance on the Elizabethan stage gave the dramatist an opportunity of which Shakespeare fully availed himself to get more of the story, the background, and the environment, into his play than is possible to the writer for the stage today.

It is by no means certain, however, that this liberty and speed of action were unalloyed benefits. The liberty tended at times to degenerate into a license which impaired concentration and dramatic power. The forty-two scenes of *Antony and Cleopatra* scattered all over the known Roman world could indeed be represented on Shakespeare's stage as they cannot be on ours, and Shakespeare obtained in this manner a scope and breadth of effect which is lacking in all other dramatic versions of this story. But it is equally clear that the third and fourth acts of *Antony and Cleopatra*, which contain together some twenty-eight scenes, are on the whole the least dramatic of the play. In the last act of *Macbeth*, again, Shakespeare obtained a unique effect by the rapid alternation of short scenes within and without the castle of Dunsinane, an effect impossible of realization on the modern stage. Yet it is undeniable that the last act of *Macbeth* lacks the concentrated dramatic force of the closing scenes of *Lear, Othello,* and *Hamlet.* Of these single scenes of unbroken action that of *Lear* is but a few lines shorter than the whole fifth act of *Macbeth*, while the closing scenes of *Othello* and *Hamlet* are even longer. The great central scene of *Othello*, perhaps the finest single specimen of Shakespeare's dramatic power, is about one-third longer than the last act of *Macbeth*. It would appear, then, that while Shakespeare exploited the opportunities of his stage to the fullest extent, he was led away at times from the highest perfection of his art by the very opportunities presented by his stage.

Other characteristic features of Elizabethan drama are probably due in part to the influence of the Elizabethan stage. It has been remarked by critics from the time of Sidney to the present day that there is something too much of narrative method in Elizabethan drama. This was due in part to medieval tradition, in part to the delight of an unsophisticated audience in the mere story presented; but another cause may be found in the stage itself. Its freedom from fixed locality, the speed of action which it allowed, positively tempted the unwary playwright to compose in something like a narrative form. Many Elizabethan plays are stories in action, a mere sequence of events with little or none of the causal connection which marks true drama. This is especially true of the popular chronicle plays in which the events of a king's reign were presented in chronological order with little care for dramatic sequence. Shakespeare himself is by no means free from this fault; *Henry V*, for example, hardly conforms to strict dramatic requirements, and even *Macbeth*, which approaches the chronicle play more nearly than do the other great tragedies, shows in the first and last acts something of this loose method of narrative technique. A good story, of course, is always popular, a story represented in action doubly so, as is shown by the vogue of the "photo-play," and the Elizabethan stage like the modern cinema afforded special facilities for this style of easy popular dramatic composition. To this cause, too, we may ascribe in part the Elizabethan fashion for double and multiple plots. Shakespeare, indeed, knew how to get genuine dramatic effects of contrast and parallel from the use of minor plots, but in many of his contemporaries the under-plot is a mere device to get in more story and entertain the audience by variety of incident.

Another aspect of the influence of this stage upon Elizabethan drama also calls for notice. In the absence of anything like scenery and the comparative insignificance of properties and setting, the attention of the audience was directed primarily to the action. The elaborate and beautiful stage-settings of today too often divert attention to non-essentials. In Shakespeare's day the play was the thing, not the trappings of the play. Moreover the projection of the stage into the very midst of the yard drew and fastened all eyes upon the actor. He was not separated from his audience as he is today by the orchestra and the proscenium arch. In fact at times the most critical and influential part of his audience sat upon the stage itself. The actor was seen not at a distance, moving like a figure in an animated picture, but in the round, so to speak, in close and intimate relation with his hearers. Words, gestures, facial expression, must all have gone home with a directness and force that is hardly even conceivable today.

This intimate contact of actor and audience gave to the playwright, himself at times like Shakespeare an actor on this stage, an impulse, an inspiration, a lively sense of the reality of his action. Whatever else the Elizabethan drama lacks it abounds in life-like characters, and this is largely due to the fact that the actors were not puppets seen at a distance, but live men moving among their fellows and in close touch with them. How real the action on this stage seemed to unsophisticated hearers may best be realized from the delightful running commentary of the Citizen and his wife in *The Knight of the Burning Pestle.*

There was, to be sure, another side to this intimacy between actor and audience. It gave rise at times to certain tricks that we have discarded today. The soliloquy, whether used as a method of exposition or as a self-revelation of character, was credible upon that stage, but has been generally discarded today. The aside, rather absurd upon the modern stage, was a natural and easy device when the speaker was perhaps nearer to a part of his audience than to his fellow actors. Still worse was the direct appeal to the audience in the form of improvised "gags" against which Hamlet warned the players, a striking proof, by the way, of Shakespeare's dislike of this breach of dramatic illusion. Yet some such "gags" seem to have crept into the text of his plays as it has been handed down to us. A somewhat similar breach of illusion appears in the customary epilogue when a player, still in costume, stepped forward to beg a *plaudite,* punctuating his appeal at times by more or less witty comments on his auditors, as Rosalind does at the close of *As You Like It.* Akin to this last, was the address by a Presenter or Chorus at the beginning or between the acts of a play. Yet we should remember that an Elizabethan audience lacked such an aid to the understanding of a performance as is furnished by our programmes which give the actor's names, sometimes with a bit of characterization, and specify the localities in which the scenes are laid. We need not be too severe on the first author of *Pericles,* who prefaced each act with a speech by Gower as Chorus informing the audience of the present situation and naming the characters about to enter, a naïve device left unchanged by Shakespeare in his revision of the old play.

One last point deserves consideration. The absence of scenery and the prominence of the actor on the Elizabethan stage forced the playwright to rely for his effect primarily upon the spoken word. Now it is a patent fact that Shakespeare's plays, like other Elizabethan dramas, contain much beside pure dramatic dialogue; they are packed with rhetorical, descriptive, and lyrical passages. Something of this redundancy was due to the temper of the times. The Elizabethans, like other Renaissance people, had a very passion for words; they delighted in word-play, puns, conceits, and far-fetched images; in set orations, grandiose tirades, and lyrical interludes. Now the very nature of the Elizabethan stage forced the playwright to appeal to this passion. His stage was comparatively bare; the setting and properties were suggestive only. To create that illusion of reality which is the life of the drama he was forced to address himself to the imagination of his audience—consider Shakespeare's appeal in the choruses of *Henry V*—and he appealed to their imagination through the spoken word. Hence instead of the present stage-picture of Macbeth's castle we have the spoken description of it by Duncan and Banquo, a description packed, by the way, with dramatic irony. It is for a like reason that we get so often in Shakespeare's plays the lovely songs which give tone and atmosphere to a scene. To stir the imagination of his audience the dramatist had first of all to rouse his own and thus he became, by necessity as it were, poet as well as playwright. The Elizabethan drama as a whole is poetic drama because the Elizabethan stage demanded from the playwright the exercise of his poetic imagination. It was by recognizing and complying with this demand that Shakespeare became early in his career a popular playwright, and it is because he rose steadily to even loftier heights of poetic imaginative utterance that he towers over the heads of his contemporaries and remains, in Jonson's noble words "not of an age, but for all time."

VIII

SHAKESPEARE'S AUDIENCE

A THIRD influence on the drama is, of course, the audience for whom the dramatist writes. No other art demands as peremptorily as the drama a prompt and sympathetic response, and in every age the character of the drama has been conditioned by the audience to whom it appealed. The religious drama of Athens, the miracle plays of medieval times, were addressed to hearers of an age of faith; the drama of the golden age of France to a society dominated by the social and political conventions of the period. The Elizabethan drama at once springs from and reflects the Elizabethan age as expressed in the Elizabethan audience.

What was the character of the audience that thronged to Shakespeare's plays at the Theatre and the Globe? A rather unfavorable picture has too often been drawn, reflecting the hostile traits embodied in Puritan denunciations or the objections of the staid city fathers. We are led to think of this audience as composed of the lowest classes of London society, riotous apprentices, courtesans and pickpockets plying their disreputable trades, with perhaps a sprinkling of dissolute court gallants. This is quite wrong. The truth is that Shakespeare's audience was a representation in miniature of Shakespeare's nation, the English people of Elizabeth's day. Apprentices and criminals came to his plays, but so did sober citizens and their wives, so did the flower of Elizabethan gentry and nobility. The students of the universities and members of the Inns of Court were devoted lovers of the drama. We hear from a contemporary witness that in 1599 Shakespeare's patron, Southampton, and his friend Lord Rutland "come not to court" but "pass away the time merely in going to plays every day." We know that scholars and courtiers took notebooks to the theatre with them to jot down jests, epigrams, and poetic phrases that they might use when wooing a mistress. Marston, a satirist of Shakespeare's day, laughs at a gallant who courts Lesbia "from out some new pathetic tragedy"; from his lips

> doth flow
> Naught but pure Juliet and Romeo.

To stigmatize Shakespeare's audience as a recent poet-critic has done, as "those wretched beings who can never be forgiven their share in preventing the greatest poet and dramatist of the world from being the best artist" is to misunderstand both the audience and the dramatist. Shakespeare was himself an Elizabethan; he sympathized with the tastes of his audience and gave them what they wanted; but he was artist enough to give it to them in a form better than they expected.

The Elizabethans, we must remember, were what we could call today "temperamental" people, quick to anger, to laughter, and to tears. They were accustomed to swift and sudden changes of emotion and behavior. Philip Sidney, "the president of noblenesse and chevalree," threatened on mere suspicion to thrust his dagger into his father's faithful secretary. Elizabeth struck her favorite Essex across the face in the council chamber, and Essex with a savage curse laid his hand upon his sword. Yet not long after the Queen sent Essex to Ireland as commander-in-chief with almost regal powers and Essex on his return from his unfortunate campaign burst into the Queen's chamber all stained with travel to find her half-dressed with her hair about her ears. The notion of "decorum" so dear to later ages was unknown to the Elizabethan people as to Elizabethan drama.

What the people wanted in a play was first of all action—serious or comic, but even the serious must be interspersed with comedy. The popular play of *Cambyses,* written about the time of Shakespeare's birth, was printed with a title page describing it as a "lamentable Tragedie mixed full of pleasant mirth." The clown was always the favorite actor; Tarleton was a darling of the public before Alleyn or Burbage rose to fame. It was customary, indeed, to end every performance with a "jig," a comic dance which developed into a rough farce spoken or sung. Shakespeare's early plays have good parts for the comic actor Kemp, another popular idol, and even in his latest there are such rôles as those of the merry rogue Autolycus or the uncouth monster Caliban. In serious action the audience wanted plenty of fighting, armies on the stage, or duels to the death. Every Elizabethan gentleman wore a sword; their retainers walked the street with swords and bucklers. There were frequent street fights, such as Shakespeare showed in *Romeo and Juliet;* frequent single combats, such as that in which Jonson killed his fellow-actor Gabriel Spencer. "Masters of fence" gave exhibitions of their art to crowded houses in the public theatres. We may be sure that Shakespeare's audience watched the rapier duel of Tybalt and Mercutio with keen interest and howled disapproval when the villain slew Mercutio with a foul thrust. Such broadsword fights as those of Hal and Hotspur or Macbeth and Macduff were not the tame affairs that one sees on the stage today, but genuine exhibitions of the art followed with the same keen interest that a crowd today watches a prize-fight. In many ways the Elizabethans were thicker skinned than men of today. Royalty itself delighted in the bloody sports of bull and bear-baiting. Executions were public spectacles, and crowds, women as well as men, gathered to see the savage punishment inflicted on traitors. Such mimic mutilations as we get in the Senecan plays, in the *Spanish Tragedy* and *Titus Andronicus,* could not shock an audience that had witnessed more horrid things at Tyburn. Shakespeare did not stoop as often as some of his contemporaries to gratify the taste of his audience for such sensations, but he had no objection to weaving scenes of physical agony into a play where they were in accord with the theme. He brings in King John dying of poison in the play by that name and in his most powerful tragedy he shows the blinding of Gloucester on the stage—"a blot" on his work, says a Victorian critic, rather a master-stroke showing to what depths of cruelty wicked cowardice can sink.

On the other hand Shakespeare's audience was capable of something better than clownage and bloodshed. For one thing it was intensely patriotic. Satirists might mock at English follies, more especially the English imitation of foreign manners, but the average Elizabethan believed most sincerely that an Englishman was the noblest work of God—*Englishmen for my Money* is the title of a popular play of Shakespeare's time—and that England was the best and noblest of all countries. With this went a keen interest in England's past, an interest which the playwrights gratified with a long roll of chronicle plays stretching from the mythical times of Cymbeline and Lear to the defeat of the Spanish Armada in 1588. Shakespeare contributed something more than his share to this type of play and has done more than most historians to tell the story and fix the characters of certain English kings. The great Marlborough said that he had learned all the English history he knew from Shakespeare. And again Shakespeare did something more than stoop to gratify a taste of his audience; he raised and purified it. There is no such exalted expression of love of country in English, perhaps in any, literature, as that which he puts into the mouth of the dying John of Gaunt. The other and less pleasing side of this patriotism is a rather cheap contempt of foreigners, not so marked in Shakespeare as in many of his contemporaries, but evident enough in his caricature of the French nobles in *Henry V.*

Like most audience in most ages the Elizabethans sometimes came to the theatre to escape from the sordid realities of daily life; they loved tales of chivalry, of magic, of enchanted islands, of witches and fairies. But even in these they liked a touch of the familiar daily life, and so when Shakespeare sent his lovers wandering in the fairy-haunted wood near Athens, he brought in Bottom and his crew, typical English homespuns, to give a note of realism to his fantastic play. For the same reason he introduced the tavern scenes and Shallow in his orchard into the chronicle plays of *I* and *II Henry IV.* On the whole, it seems, Shakespeare cared less than most of his contemporaries for the drama of everyday life. He never wrote such plays as Dekker's *Shoemakers' Holiday* or Jonson's *Bartholomew Fair.* Yet he loved the humors of simple country folk and was never tired of introducing them into his plays whether in comedy, as Dogberry and Verges in *Much Ado* or in tragedy, as the grave-diggers in *Hamlet,* or the clown who brings the asp to Cleopatra. And the language that Shakespeare puts into their mouths is vigorous, realistic, sometimes coarse, like that of the porter in *Macbeth;* there is nothing affected or sentimental about Shakespeare's treatment of common people. It took a German to transform the drunken porter into a pious old watchman chanting a morning hymn.

It is to his intimate knowledge of the common people that we may ascribe in part at least Shakespeare's partiality for broad jests. The Anglo-Saxon male is as a rule chaster in manners than in speech. There is nothing suggestive or veiled about these jests of Shakespeare's; many of them are, fortunately, lost to the average reader of today because of the change in the meaning of words. Some of them, no doubt, are interpolations in the text by a comic actor who once got a laugh by a "wisecrack" and handed it on to his successors in the part. But Shakespeare belonged to a free-spoken age and it is absurd to think of him as lowering himself to get a laugh from the yard when he and his noble friends probably enjoyed the joke as much as the groundlings.

It is another matter with a good deal of Shakespeare's language that offends æsthetic sensibilities of today. Dr. Johnson remarked that a pun had an irresistible attraction for Shakespeare; he indulges in puns at times in quite serious, even tragic passages, especially in his early plays. But the Elizabethans loved word-play of all sorts, and a pun to them was not necessarily comic. Shakespeare was certainly not aiming at a laugh when he made Lady Macbeth pun on "gild" and "guilt." The fact is that the power, the range, the versatility of the English language was only being discovered in Shakespeare's day, and poets, scholars, wits, and courtiers indulged themselves to their hearts' content in taking liberties with their mother tongue. It is to this passion for playing with words that we must ascribe the so-called "conceits" that cluster in the early plays of Shakespeare. Once more, however, Shakespeare is not writing down to his audience, but writing what he and his audience, especially the better part of it, both alike enjoyed.

The songs and musical effects of Shakespeare's plays were written and composed to delight and entertain his audience. The English people before the Puritan revolution were famous singers. At a gentleman's house the music books were brought out after dinner as regularly as cards and bridge-tables would be now, and guests were expected to join the family in singing complicated part-songs. Foreign visitors to Elizabethan theatres were sure to comment on the beauty of the music they heard there. This music, of course, was instrumental as well as vocal, for most Elizabethans played one instrument or another. Citterns hung in every barber shop for the amusement of the waiting customers.

Shakespeare's plays are full of references to the various instruments of his day, the lute, the recorder, the viol de gamba. His kings come on the stage to flourishes, and trumpets announce the entrance of an army. Music is used to wake a sleeper, to lament the dead, to minister, as in *Lear,* to a mind diseased. All this is in perfect accord with the practice of Shakespeare's day, and here as elsewhere Shakespeare shows himself a true Elizabethan.

A word must be said in closing about the poetry of Shakespeare's plays. We wonder sometimes how the groundlings who packed the yard of the Globe could appreciate or even listen patiently to his poetic plays. It has been suggested that his poetry was for the gentlemen and scholars of the boxes as his clowns and combats were for the groundlings. But this, again, is to misunderstand the Elizabethan audience. In the first place it was by old tradition that the drama was written in verse; the miracle plays are composed in rhymed stanzaic metres; the early farces and interludes in the seven-foot doggerel of which traces still remain in some of Shakespeare's early plays; blank verse had been introduced into tragedy by the authors of *Gorboduc* early in Elizabeth's reign and had in Shakespeare's time come to be the recognized medium for dramatic expression. The Elizabethan age has been called "a nest of singing birds," and while this phrase was meant to apply to the lyric poets of the day, it might almost as well characterize the Elizabethan people. They all sang; they all loved poetry of a sort as well as music; the most popular printed works were the broadcast ballads in which contemporary events of all sorts were versified and set to popular tunes. And if this was the case with the common people it was still more so with the better classes. Gentlemen rhymed as naturally and as easily as they sang. The proper way to court a lady was by writing sonnets to her beauty. Orlando was simply following a fashion of the day when he festooned the trees of Arden with poems in praise of Rosalind. We must imagine, then, the Elizabethan audience listening, not merely patiently, but with delight to the long tirades, the high-flown speeches, the lyrical interludes of Shakespeare's plays. The Elizabethans read less and listened more than we do to-day. They appreciated at its full value the sonorous beauty of such a line as

> The multitudinous seas incarnadine.

They picked up to use, or to misuse, as the numerous malapropisms in Shakespeare's comedies show, strange new words that sounded well even if their sense was not quite clear. And this delight in poetry was, so to speak, grist to Shakespeare's mill. He could indulge his poetic fancy to the limit, and sometimes in his early plays, it outran his dramatic powers, knowing that it was addressed to a sympathetic audience. It was for his hearers at the Theatre and at the Globe that Shakespeare wrote Mercutio's description of Queen Mab, the lyric love-making of Romeo and Juliet, the soliloquies of Hamlet, and the tragic outbursts of King Lear. All that is changed today. Our playwrights, even when dealing with tragic themes, are driven by the convention of realism to write common-place words and "language such as men do use," to express even intense emotion in colloquial speech. There has been perhaps quite as much loss as gain.

Properly to appreciate the influence of the audience upon Shakespeare we must always remember that Shakespeare was himself "of his age" as well as "for all time," a true Elizabethan. What seem to us faults and flaws in his works are not there because he consciously wrote down to his audience, but because in taste and tone and temper he was one with them. He wrote to please his hearers and in so doing pleased himself. His friend and critic Ben Jonson with a fine scorn for his hearers wrote to please himself, to gratify his own severe and limited critical standards. As a result Jonson failed to win his audience. Shakespeare was not ignorant of these standards; he probably heard of them often enough from Ben at their meetings in the Mermaid Tavern. He could have observed the unities if he wished; he did so, in fact, in *The Tempest.* Had he written for an audience of scholars and critics he would have written plays of another sort, perhaps such plays as his Hamlet, scholar and critic, praises, when he speaks of one that was "caviare to the general; but . . . an excellent play . . . as wholesome as sweet and by very much more handsome than fine." We can be thankful that he did not. When we consider the work of Shakespeare as a whole, its breadth, its infinite variety, its broad humor, its unrestrained expression of emotion, its unparalleled poetic utterance, we may give some measure of thanks to the audience for which he wrote, which, like the actors who performed his plays and the stage upon which they were represented, contributed to make them what they are.

IX
THE NEW DRAMA

WHEN Shakespeare came to London, he found the acting drama in a vigorous and flourishing condition. It was in the hands of the professional actors protected by the court and supported by a growing popular demand. Playhouses had been built for regular dramatic performances and a group of young poet-playwrights was busily engaged with furnishing the actors with dramas. Their work must have been new and immensely interesting to Shakespeare, who, during his youth in the country, can have seen little or nothing of the new drama which this group was creating. His prentice years as actor and playwright from 1588 to 1593 coincided with a wonderful advance in every line of dramatic activity, and we cannot fully understand his own work, especially his early plays, unless we realize to some extent the nature of the new drama which was then taking shape.

Elizabethan drama is essentially an outgrowth of the religious drama of the Middle Ages, and it is well to remember that this drama was by no means extinct in Shakespeare's day. Miracle plays were acted at Coventry as late as 1584, and we have a record of a religious play in London eight or nine years after Shakespeare's death. Now the outstanding characteristic of this old drama was its frank and homely realism; it strove to represent events and characters of the sacred story in terms of simple everyday English life. This realism struck at times a grim and almost savage note; the playwright of the Passion did not spare Christ a buffet or a pang of pain. On the other hand it might turn into broad farce. When Mrs. Noah boxed her husband's ears, we may be sure that the audience was moved to laughter not by the wit of the words but by the humor of the situation. The characters, too, are real and English; the shepherds of the *Secunda Pastorum* are real shepherds grumbling about the weather and concerned about their sheep. All that there is of dramatic value in the miracle plays comes from the naïve, sincere, and convincing realism. Their technique, simplicity itself, consisted in representing the whole story on the stage.

This homely realism, long accepted as essential in popular drama, was transmitted in an unbroken channel from the miracle plays through the moralities and interludes of the early sixteenth century to the new drama of Shakespeare's day. It was a keen sense of its value as a drawing-card that led Shakespeare's company to call their great spectacular play of *Henry VIII, All Is True.* Titles like the *True Tragedy* and the *True History* abound in Elizabethan drama. So strong, indeed, was the popular demand for realism, so ready to response of the playwrights, that we may fix on this note of realism as the distinguishing mark of one aspect of Elizabethan drama, the native and popular.

In early popular comedy this realism produced a series of lively humorous scenes and incidents rather than complete and well-made plays. The interest of closely complicated and neatly solved intrigue is almost entirely lacking. At best we get a series of dramatized incidents. Such comic scenes often appear at intervals in serious plays. They continue the tradition of the comic interpolations in the miracle plays and beget the convention of the so-called "comic relief," characteristic of Elizabethan as compared with classical drama. The characters of these scenes are drawn almost exclusively from the lower classes; the fun consists in showing them in absurd situations, as when the Vice in *Cambyses,* masquerading as a warrior, with a pot for a helmet and a rake for a spear, is chased off the stage by an old woman with a broom. The humor of early popular comedy was essentially physical, the humor of scuffles, kicks, and pots of water on unsuspecting heads. The popular nature of such scenes and their lasting appeal is shown not only by their constant appearance in later Elizabethan drama—even in the works of Shakespeare—but by their persistence through the farce and fiction of later centuries down to the comic strips and comic films of the present day.

The language of this popular comedy was, of course, plain everyday English. There is a marked absence of the witty, pointed dialogue, of the gay word-play, so frequent in the later comedy. On the contrary there is an over-plus of profanity, a "humor of filth," sinking at times to gross obscenity. The dialogue is for the most part composed in doggerel rhymed verse, and except for occasional songs, there is nothing of the heightening effect of poetry. The note of romance, more particularly what we call the "love interest," is conspicuously absent. It would almost seem as if the old playwrights felt this topic to be taboo.

Of early popular tragedy there is little to be said, for the simple reason that there was very little of it. The old tradition of a realistic presentation of tragic scenes from the Bible had died out and for a considerable period nothing came in to take its place. The crowd preferred boisterous farce to the falls of princes and clamored for the appearance on the stage of the Devil and the Fool. So far as they took an interest in tragic themes, they demanded realism. A tragedy to be popular must present a true story in convincing fashion. The few specimens of early popular tragedy that remain from the time before Kyd and Marlowe might almost be called histories rather than tragedies proper. They fall into two classes: histories of private and of public life. In the first class we find such lost plays as *Murderous Michael* and *The Cruelty of a Step-Mother* presented at Court in 1578 and 1579. Such plays were the direct ancestors of the Elizabethan domestic tragedy like *Arden of Feversham* and *A Woman Killed with Kindness,* plays that bear witness to the popularity of such realism in the very heyday of the romantic drama.

The histories of public life strike the same note. The English chronicle play, to be sure, seems hardly to have appeared before Shakespeare came to London. It sprang into sudden life along with the outburst of patriotic enthusiasm that marked the years just before and after the defeat of the Spanish Armada in 1588. But before this time there were plays dealing with historical events which continue the technique of the miracle plays and anticipate that of the chronicles, that is, a simple succession of scenes in their natural order of time. Those that remain to us deal with themes drawn from classical sources; but their apparent aim is to present an ancient story in as familiar and realistic a style as possible. In *Horestes* a murderer is very properly "hanged from a ladder;" a stage-direction in *Cambyses* reads: "Smite him in the neck with a sword to signify death." These plays are also marked as products of the popular drama by the presence of the Vice and of allegorical figures from the old moralities.

At the opposite pole from this native and popular drama lay another which may be called the classical and academic. It was one of the results of Renaissance humanism and began to appear about the middle of the sixteenth century. Springing from the study of the classical drama in the grammar schools, it was reinforced by the critical dicta of Aristotle and Horace as interpreted by Renaissance commentators. It flourished almost exclusively in such institutions as the grammar schools, the universities, and the Inns of Court where it produced a group of plays designed for cultured audiences. Apparently none of these plays ever attempted to compete on the public stage with the drama in the native tradition. Yet the influence of this academic drama was felt in both comedy and tragedy and it introduced into both elements that had permanent effect in the development of Elizabethan drama.

In comedy the models for this academic drama were the plays of Plautus and Terence and the Italian comedies of the fifteenth and sixteenth centuries, themselves an imitation and elaboration of the Latin dramatists. Perhaps the most important gift of these models to English playwrights was a sense of the significance of plot. From the Latins and their Italian followers English comedy now took over involved intrigues and deft solutions. The division of a play into acts and scenes, adopted from the classical models, assisted the English playwright in an orderly development of the plot. Along with this came the adoption into English comedy of a number of stock characters from the classic models: the worldly wise father, the roistering son, the wily servant, the braggart, and the pedant. Commonplace as these types seem to us, they were a real enrichment of the stock figures of native English comedy, where the Devil and the Vice, plus a pair of rustics, had long been almost the sole representatives of the comic spirit.

In diction as well as in construction and characterization this new comedy represented a great advance over the old. For the doggerel rhyme and coarse language of the native comedy it substituted little by little a polished prose, heightened by witty repartee and wordplay. This too was an imitation of the diction of the Latin playwrights, and the academic character of the new comedy is shown by the fact that most of the specimens that remain are the work of school-masters, university students, and Inns of Court men, written for private performance. It was not until the time of Lyly and his followers in the 1580's that the new comedy appeared upon the public stage. Yet in spite of its academic origin this comedy retained a distinctly English atmosphere, laying its scenes in England and drawing its characters from English life. The little masterpiece of *Ralph Roister Doister* is perhaps the best example of this blending of the classic and native comedy.

In tragedy the influence of classical studies was at first rather different. Whereas in comedy the classic models exerted an immediate and beneficent effect upon the drama, in tragedy we find only a slavish imitation which for a long period seems totally divorced from the native tradition. The reason lies in the gulf which separated popular practice from the classical theory of tragedy. The first consisted in action realistically presented; the second pushed action as far as possible off the stage, reported it by messenger, and stressed primarily the emotions of the *dramatis personae*. The popular practice enlivened a tragic theme with interpolations of "comical mirth;" classical theory rigidly excluded comic scenes and characters from the tragic stage. Popular tragedy either presented familiar English characters as in the murder plays, or attempted to bring distant scenes and characters home to the audience by giving them a familiar English dress. Classical tragedy, on the other hand, chose its themes by preference from the remote legendary or mythological past and threw about them an atmosphere of unreality, of stately aloofness. The ideal was, in Kyd's phrase—

> *Tragoedia cothurnata,* fitting kings,
> Containing matter and not common things.

Where such differences existed there was little chance of a direct influence of the classic model on popular practice, and classical tragedy in English remained for nearly a generation, from the first translation of Seneca in 1559 to *The Misfortunes of Arthur* in 1587, in academic isolation.

The first translation of a Senecan play into English marks the starting point of classical tragedy in English. It was Seneca, not the Greek dramatists, who during the Renaissance served as the pattern of classic tragedy on the Continent as well as in England. This was due, primarily, to the Renaissance mastery of Latin and comparative ignorance of Greek, but also to the fact that the tone and temper of Seneca, "the most modern of the classics and the most romantic of the ancients," were more in accord with the spirit of the Renaissance than were those of the Greek dramatists. There is something cosmopolitan, universal, one might say, in Seneca's discarding the local color and national tradition of his borrowed Greek themes in order to emphasize the tragedy of individual characters, and this treatment appealed with special force to the Renaissance belief in the supreme importance of the individual.

Certain characteristics of Seneca's work exerted a profound influence upon Elizabethan drama. Most obvious of these is his partiality for sensational themes; all his plays deal with adultery, incest, murder, and revenge. Yet Seneca's main interest lies not in the sensational action, but in its reaction upon the emotions of his characters. They are all self-conscious and introspective, and Seneca, crude as much of his work seems to us, is in fact a psychological dramatist. Moreover, the technique of Seneca is simple and regular; he divides his plays into the standard five acts; avoids epic detail in his plot, and concentrates upon the crisis of the action. His rather formal method of construction was much admired in the Renaissance, and many of his dramatic devices: the moralizing chorus, the messenger, the confidant, the ghost crying for revenge, passed over into Elizabethan drama. Finally, Seneca's diction evoked at that time an enthusiastic response which seems almost inexplicable to us. We find him verbose, bombastic, singularly deficient in true dramatic utterance. The Renaissance, however, loved language for its own sake and saw in the elaborate tirades of Seneca the perfect model of dramatic eloquence. Sidney could find no higher praise of the diction of *Gorboduc* than to speak of it as "climbing to the height of Seneca his style."

Seneca's fashion of moralizing comment, also—comment couched in terse and epigrammatic Latin—appealed especially to an age which held that the first function of tragedy was moral and didactic. The *sententiae,* or moral maxims, of Seneca appear again and again in the ethical commonplaces and moral "tags" of Elizabethan drama.

Perhaps the most important contribution of the Senecan school to Elizabethan drama was the adoption of blank verse as the medium of dramatic dialogue. This metre introduced into English poetry by Surrey in his translation of Virgil (published 1557) was employed by the authors of *Gorboduc* (1563) and the success of that play brought about a recognition of this metre as a standard form of tragedy. Simple, flexible, yet dignified, it was recognized at once as far superior to the popular rhymed doggerel, approximating in some degree at least the stately measures of classical tragedy.

There is nothing to show any influence of this Senecan school upon popular drama until the great dramatic outburst of the 1580's. The authors of the new tragedy, Peele, Greene, Marlowe, and Kyd were classical scholars, and it is in their work that we note for the first time a fusion of classical and popular strains.

Even before Shakespeare came to London another tendency had begun to show itself in Elizabethan drama. This may best be described as the romantic impulse. It differs in choice of theme, method of treatment, and manner of expression, alike from native tradition and from classical convention. It is marked by the romantic love of the strange and the mysterious. Instead of representing on the stage familiar scenes and characters of real life, it takes wing to distant lands and times, introduces knights, ladies, and emperors of the East, shifts the scene from England to

Cathay or Arcady, and seeks above all to touch and kindle the imagination. It has the romantic love of the supernatural; it employs the devices of the old romances of chivalry, magicians, enchantments, and strange transformations, and it adds to these the fairies, witches, and ghosts of popular superstition. The ghost, to be sure, appears in Senecan tragedy, but there is a vast difference between the ghost of Tantalus in Seneca's *Thyestes* and the "perturbed spirit" that stalks across the stage in *Hamlet.* The first is a mere piece of machinery to set the plot in action; the second fulfills the same purpose and is, so far, Senecan, but brings with him in addition a chill breath from the other world that gives the true romantic thrill.

Along with this desire for the strange and supernatural there begins to appear in the new drama the romantic passion for beauty. There is little sense of the beautiful in the old popular drama or in the imitations of Seneca, but the new tendency beginning with faltering accents swells gradually into the haunting music of Marlowe and of Shakespeare. It is in Marlowe's *Tamburlaine,* the first English tragedy inspired by this new force, that we get the supreme expression of this passion. Moved beyond his wont by the sorrow and loveliness of his mistress Tamburlaine exclaims:

What is beauty, saith my sufferings, then?
If all the pens that ever poets held
Had fed the feeling of their masters' thoughts
And every sweetness that inspir'd their hearts,
Their minds and muses on admired themes;
If all the heavenly quintessence they still
From their immortal flowers of poesy,
Wherein, as in a mirror, we perceive
The highest reaches of a human wit;
If these had made one poem's period,
And all combined in beauty's worthiness,
Yet should there hover in their restless heads
One thought, one grace, one wonder, at the least,
Which into words no virtue can digest.

A beauty ineffable, beyond all words, was what the romantic poet-dramatists were striving to express.

The development of this new tendency coincides with the amazing outburst of poetry that followed the appearance of Spenser's *Shepheards Calendar* in 1579. Before that date the popular drama was written for the most part in halting rhymed doggerel. After it we catch more and more clearly that "full-mouthed utterance of the early gods" which distinguishes Elizabethan drama from all that went before or followed it in English. The playwrights were quick to learn their art of speech from the poets.

This passion for beauty has all the range and richness of the Renaissance; it finds its food in the world of nature and in the works of man, but most of all in man himself, in his thoughts, his desires, and his emotions. In comedy it attaches itself particularly to the theme of love, a theme absent alike from popular and from classical comedy. In the former it is markedly avoided; in the latter it is often treated with a certain Latin cynicism. It remained for the new romantic comedy to treat this theme at once as a source of mirth and as a thing of beauty. It is a sign of the growing freedom of the Renaissance spirit in Elizabethan England that with the development of the drama the theme that had been shunned by the old medieval tradition came forward in ever-growing grace and beauty until it reached its climax in the romantic comedies of Shakespeare.

Of the first beginnings of romantic tragedy it is impossible to speak precisely because of the scanty material that has survived. In fact it is only by an extension of the term "tragedy," to cover all serious plays, that we can speak of romantic tragedy as existing at all before the time of Kyd and Marlowe. The first plays of this type seem to have been dramatized romances, stories of strange adventure on land and sea. Plays founded on old tales of chivalry seem to have been particularly popular at Court in the 1570's.

As time went on and the spirit of the Renaissance made itself felt in the drama, there is a notable enlargement of the field. Playwrights began to turn for their themes to the tragic stories of the Italian *novelle.* The interest of these tales centres upon individuals and the chief interest of the tragedy based on them tends to concentrate upon the struggle of the individual against the hostile forces of environment or of fate. The characteristic note of the new romantic tragedy is its appeal to sympathy and pity. The old histories and murder plays were satisfied to present an interesting action; the classical tragedies to arouse admiration and horror; but the new tragedy presents the protagonist in a sympathetic light and evokes pity for his fate. Shakespearean tragedy is essentially one of individual character and appeals perhaps more strongly than any other work of man to our human sense of pity, and Shakespearean tragedy springs directly from the romantic drama of his predecessors.

The fusion of these diverse elements, the traditional realistic, the conventional classic, and the new romantic into the fully developed Elizabethan drama was the work of a group of dramatists often known as the "university playwrights." Beginning their attack on the London stage somewhere in the early 1580's they carried it by storm and held the boards for ten years or so until the early 1590's when one by one they dropped out. Shakespeare's debt to them was very great; two or three are in a very special sense his models and masters. They did not, indeed, constitute a school with a formula for the creation of a new type of drama. Each of them was an individual genius and contributed something of his own to the stage; there is a vast difference between the courtly comedies of Lyly and the heroic plays of Marlowe. Yet essentially there is a similarity between them that goes far to unify their work. They were all born poets, makers, inventors; not one of them was content to follow the beaten path. They were all artists in words consciously engaged in devising for the drama a better medium of utterance than it had heretofore possessed. They were all imbued with the spirit of romance, seekers after the strange and lovers of beauty. Furthermore they had all enjoyed a sound classical education which gave them a command of classic sources, an acquaintance with classic models, and an admiration for the polished dialogue of comedy and the stately speech of tragedy in the classical masterpieces. They were, however, loving students rather than slavish imitators of the classics; they borrowed freely from their models, but their borrowings were for the purpose of improving and enriching the popular drama rather than for transforming it into an imitation of the classic.

The explanation of their free handling of the revered classic models may be found in another common bond which unites the members of this group. They were all professional playwrights writing for the public stage at a time when this career offered a man of letters the quickest and the surest reward. But this reward was only to be obtained if their plays were successful upon the stage, and of success or failure the London audience was the final arbiter. To gain their livelihood these playwrights would have been forced even against their will to yield in large measure to the demands of the public. Yet it is more than doubtful if there was any conscious yielding on their part. These men were themselves members of the public for which they wrote; they were men about town, gay Bohemians, haunters of taverns, not cloistered pedants nor refined courtiers. They shared the tastes of their public, but they guided, purified, and elevated these tastes until at last they trained an audience ready to receive and applaud the masterpieces of Shakespeare.

Of this group the work of four men was so individual, their contribution to Elizabethan drama and to the plays of Shakespeare so important that they deserve a brief consideration. John Lyly (1554?-1606), the first and oldest of them, was the creator of a new type of comedy. An Oxford graduate, he became famous in 1579 by his prose novel *Euphues.* The story of this book is a mere peg on which to hang a series of discourses on education, polite behavior, and courtly love. The brilliant, witty, and highly affected style of *Euphues* made a deep impression on the society of the day and actually set a fashion of speech in courtly circles. Sometime in the mid-1580's Lyly turned to the theatre and began writing plays for the Children of Paul's, plays which were first produced in public and later presented at court.

Lyly's plays, as their titles, *Endimion, Sapho, Midas,* show, deal with classic themes, but the characters in these plays are transformed from figures of the classic world into Elizabethan gentlemen and ladies. All the plays deal with love, but it is a graceful, courtly, passionless love, more concerned with apt turn of speech than with attainment. Lyly can construct a deft plot; one of his later plays *Mother Bombie* presents an extremely complicated intrigue after the fashion of Plautus, but his main gift to English comedy was that of dialogue. For the rhymed metres of popular drama he substituted the brilliant balanced manner of speech that *Euphues* had made popular. He rejected altogether the knockabout farce and foul language of the old comedy and taught his hearers to delight in clever repartee and word-play. It is not too much to say that Lyly is the first English dramatist to have some notion of high comedy. Since his plays were presented by children he introduced as a stock character the impudent page who mocked his master and exchanged gay jests with the ladies of the play. Lyly's plays were all the rage in the best circles when Shakespeare came to town, and though Shakespeare never adopted the full-fledged euphuistic style —he even ridicules it in the mouth of Falstaff (*I K. H. IV.* II, iv, 4, 449ff.)—he learned from Lyly the trick of fluent graceful speech, the value of polished prose in comedy, and took over, as in *Love's Labour's Lost,* some of Lyly's characteristic figures, as the braggart soldier and the mocking page.

The influence of Robert Greene (1558-1592) upon later drama was less direct and visible than Lyly's, but, perhaps, more profound. A brilliant and versatile man of letters with something of the mocking-bird's facility of imitation, Greene began his career by writing a series of love stories in Lyly's euphuistic prose. He closed it with a group of pamphlets revealing the sordid side of underworld life in Elizabethan London and another confessing the sins of his own wayward career. In the meantime he had been a popular and prolific writer for the stage. Some of his plays, no doubt, have been lost; two of them are imitations of Marlowe's heroic vein, so extravagant in style that one imagines Greene composing them with his tongue in his cheek. His real contribution to English comedy rests upon two plays, *Friar Bacon and Friar Bungay* (ca. 1589) and *James IV* (ca. 1591). The first of these tells the story of a famous English magician, Friar Bacon. The novel element, however, and the lasting appeal of the play is not in the doings of the wizard but in the love-story of Margaret, the fair Maid of Fressingfield, beloved by the Prince of Wales, herself in love with Lacy, the Prince's friend. When Lacy courts her for the Prince she woos and wins him for herself, is apparently rejected by him later, and is finally re-united to him on the threshold of a convent in one of the most delightful scenes of Elizabethan comedy. Back and forth through the scenes of magic and love-story wander two characters dear to the audience of the day, Ralph the Court Fool, and Miles, Friar Bacon's blundering servant, a development of the mischief-making Vice, who is finally carried off to hell upon a devil's back.

James IV, perhaps Greene's last, and in many ways his best play, was published in 1594 after his death under the title of *The Scottish History of James IV Slain at Flodden,* probably to exploit the contemporary popularity of the chronicle play. It has, however, no basis in history, but is a clever dramatization of an Italian story of romantic love. Greene shifts the scene to Scotland, shows us a Scottish king turning from Dorothea, his chaste and loving wife, to pursue Ida, a fair lady of the court. The queen escapes the murderer who has been hired to despatch her, assumes male disguise, and finally reconciles her penitent husband to her angry father, the king of England.

Greene's contribution to the new comedy is three-fold. He knew better than any of his predecessors how to tell an interesting story in dramatic form; his friend, Nashe, called him a "master of his craft" in plotting plays. And he set these stories in a homely realistic British background while at the same time breathing into them the spirit of romance, a fusion which was to be eminently characteristic of later Elizabethan comedy. Finally, Greene was the first of English playwrights to deal with the theme of romantic love and to centre it about the figures of real, charming, and lovely women. There are no characters in English drama before Greene that can compare with his Margaret, Ida, and Dorothea. It would be absurd to say that Greene taught Shakespeare how to create such characters as Portia, Rosalind, and Imogen, but it is perhaps reasonable to suppose that the success of Greene's plays suggested to Shakespeare the possibility of bringing lovely and beloved women upon the stage whether in their own dress, or like Dorothea and his own Rosalind and Viola in doublet and hose. Greene hated the upstart Shakespeare but the young Shakespeare was not too proud to learn all that he could even from an enemy.

As Lyly and Greene were Shakespeare's forerunners in comedy Kyd and Marlowe open the road for him in tragedy. Of Kyd (1558-1594), the elder of the two, little is known, though much is conjectured. Only one play can be certainly ascribed to him, but that play, *The Spanish Tragedy* (ca. 1584), was the most popular and influential tragedy upon the public stage before Shakespeare came to London, and was revived and revised over and over again during his lifetime. Its success was due to the fact that it represented the fusion of Senecan and popular elements in a play aimed at the London public. It is the story of a father's revenge for his murdered son, a revenge long delayed, in which the father hovers on the brink of madness, and finally accomplished in spite of obstacles and counter-intrigues in a general massacre that heaps the stage with corpses. We have here the Senecan ghost, the Senecan sensationalism, the stately though rather stiff and frigid Senecan blank verse. On the other hand Kyd knew his public too well to keep the action off the stage in Senecan fashion. There is no such thrilling scene in pre-Shakespearean drama as that in which the old father called from his bed at night discovers the body of his murdered son hanging in the arbor where only an hour before the youth had been courting his princely mistress. Kyd was no great master of characterization; the people in his plays resemble somewhat the figures of archaic sculpture; but he tried not altogether without success to make them real and lifelike. The intriguing villain, Lorenzo, in this play is the first of a long line of Machiavellian plotters which culminates in Shakespeare's Iago.

In addition to *The Spanish Tragedy* Kyd wrote, we have good reason, though no definite proof, to believe, the lost play of *Hamlet* on which Shakespeare's masterpiece is founded. If he also wrote, as some critics hold, *Arden of Feversham* he broke fresh ground in the realistic domestic tragedy as well as in the drama of intrigue and revenge. Briefly Kyd's contribution to English tragedy can be summed up in a few words. He gave it a dignity and power unknown before by infusing it with Senecan elements; he was the first of English tragic writers to have some mastery of plotting and intrigue; and his keen sense of the value of a dramatic situation was something new in English literature and was caught up, exploited and brought to perfection by Shakespeare himself in his recast of the lost *Hamlet*.

Christopher Marlowe (1564-1593) the youngest, was also the greatest of these predecessors of Shakespeare, greatest in his influence on the evolving drama, and greatest in his transforming power of poetry. A Cambridge scholar, he left the university in 1584 apparently to undertake some secret service work for the Government. He received his M. A. degree at Cambridge in 1587 and in the same year produced his epoch-making play of *Tamburlaine* upon the London stage with the great actor Alleyn in the title-role. The next six years of his short life were crowded with dramatic and poetic composition. He wrote five plays that we know of (*Tamburlaine, Dr. Faustus, The Jew of Malta, Edward II,* and *The Massacre at Paris*), possibly took part in several others, translated parts of Ovid and Lucan into English verse, and left unfinished the lovely erotic poem, *Hero and Leander*. He seems to have been closely associated with the group of poets and scholars that gathered round Sir Walter Raleigh where he must have read parts of *The Faerie Queene* in manuscript and caught something of the music of Spenser's poetry. He shared too in the popular suspicion of Raleigh's unconventional circle, and was accused, justly or not, of blasphemy and atheism. He was in fact under bond to answer such charges before the Privy Council when he was killed in a tavern brawl. The story that he was killed in a fight over a low woman is a slander invented by Puritan enemies of poetry and drama; there seems reason to suspect that he was put out of the way by a gang of rascals who feared him.

Marlowe's contribution to Elizabethan tragedy may be summed up in three words: Passion, Power, and Poetry. Himself a reckless, passionate nature, he transformed the cold and stiff tragedy of the Senecan school into a fiery presentation of human passion, the passion for power, for knowledge, and for wealth. Furthermore he embodied these passions in superhuman figures, the Scythian Shepherd "scourging kingdoms with his conquering sword," Dr. Faustus selling his soul to hell to obtain a knowledge that shall make him master of the world. Barabas the Jew gloating over the gold and jewels that give him

> Infinite riches in a little room.

With a single exception the plays of Marlowe are one-star plays and this concentration of interest in the single figure of a great protagonist was one of the secrets of his art which he handed down to the young Shakespeare. The single exception to this rule is his historical play *Edward II,* and here too Marlowe was an innovator of genius. Instead of simply reciting in dramatic form the events of a king's reign in chronological order, he so selected, arranged, and altered the facts of history as to transform the chronicle play into a tragedy, foreshadowing such Shakespearean plays as *King John, Richard III,* and *Richard II.* His greatest gift, however, to the drama was his transformation of the stiff monotonous blank verse written by Kyd and his predecessors into the most perfect vehicle for dramatic utterance that English literature has known. It is not too much to say that Marlowe is the first great English poet to write drama, and the effect of his dramatic poetry upon his contemporaries and successors was overpowering. It is interesting to recall the fact that the young Shakespeare must have heard the music of Marlowe's mighty line for the first time after he came to London, that he was fascinated by it and set himself, as we see in his early plays, to imitate it and then to study its powers and possibilities until he came to write such poetry as Marlowe himself never dreamed of. We do not know whether Shakespeare ever met Marlowe face to face; we do know that he admired and followed him and that of all his contemporaries it is Marlowe alone whom Shakespeare honors by allusion and quotation. When Phoebe in *As You Like It* says

> Dead shepherd, now I find thy saw of might,
> Whoever loved that loved not at first sight

the dead shepherd is no other than Christopher Marlowe and the "saw" a quotation from *Hero and Leander.*

Marlowe was cut off in his prime. What he might have accomplished had he lived out his life like Shakespeare no one can say. Certain limitations of his genius are apparent; he had little sense of humor, none of Shakespeare's interest in the whimsicalities of common folk. We cannot imagine him ever creating such a character as Dogberry or writing the gravediggers' scene in *Hamlet.* He had nothing of Shakespeare's sincere patriotism; a Renaissance individualist, his desire of the impossible leaped over the bounds of country. Finally he lacked Shakespeare's profound sense of the moral order of the universe and of man's life in this universe of law. Marlowe is a rebel against order and convention; his sympathy goes out to rebels against and tramplers upon the established order, to such a conqueror as Tamburlaine, to such a defier of God's law as Faustus, even to the desperate revengeful Jew. Marlowe would never have become a Shakespeare, but it is not too much to say that his influence upon the young Shakespeare was greater than that of any other poet or playwright and that without Marlowe there would never have been the William Shakespeare whom we know.

X

SHAKESPEARE'S DEVELOPMENT

Part I

It is plain from what has been said that Shakespeare knew little or nothing of the new drama before he came to London. Nor is there any reason to suppose that he sprang into sudden prominence as a dramatist. Marlowe did so with his first play, but Marlowe was a more precocious genius than Shakespeare and at his death left a body of work far superior to anything that his contemporary Shakespeare had yet achieved. There is good reason to believe that Shakespeare slowly formed himself as a playwright gaining experience as an actor and in the hard school of experience. It is possible in fact to trace his development from somewhat hesitant beginnings to supreme mastery of his art; but to do this we must have a fairly definite knowledge of the chronological order of his plays.

This knowledge has been made possible by the untiring labor of Shakespearean scholars for a century or more. Nothing can be gained from the arrangement of his plays in the first Folio. The editors of that work grouped the plays in classes: Comedies, Histories, and Tragedies. They opened the volume with *The Tempest,* Shakespeare's latest play and one which had never yet been printed, probably in order to stimulate a possible purchaser. They arranged the Histories in the order of their historic time, beginning with *King John* and ending with *Henry VIII.* They inserted *Troilus and Cressida* between the Histories and the Tragedies, uncertain perhaps to which class it belonged; we group it today with the so-called "bitter comedies." There seems to be no reason at all for the Folio's order of the Tragedies which begins with the late *Coriolanus,* follows it with *Titus Andronicus,* certainly very early work, and ends with *Cymbeline,* which we would not call a tragedy.

Scholarly research, however, has given us three kinds of evidence which help to fix with some degree of precision the date of composition of Shakespeare's plays and so to arrange them in approximately chronological order. Approximately only, for while we can be sure that *The Tempest* is a late play and the *Comedy of Errors* an early one, it is by no means certain that such a table as that printed on pp. 97 *ff.* is accurate as regards either the year or the position of any particular play. These three kinds of evidence are known as the external, the internal-external, and the internal. The first of these is the most important and the most satisfactory. It consists of references to Shakespeare's plays by his contemporaries, dates of performances at Court, and the entry of a play in the Stationers' Register for subsequent publication. Thus Francis Meres in his *Palladis Tamia,* entered for publication on September 7, 1598, speaks of Shakespeare with highest praise and lists a dozen of his dramas as examples of his work. It is of course apparent that all the plays he names had been produced on the stage, few of them had been published, when Meres wrote. Conversely, since he seems to have been well acquainted with the stage of his day, it is at least probable that with one exception Shakespeare had not written any other plays than those of this list before the summer of 1598. The exception is the historic trilogy of Henry VI, already discussed (p. 18). Another piece of evidence of this kind is found in the mention by a member of the Middle Temple of a performance of "a play called *Twelve Night*" at a feast in that Inn of Court on February 2, 1602. The Stationers' Register lists sixteen plays by Shakespeare entered for publication in his lifetime beginning with *Titus Andronicus* in 1594 and ending with *Pericles* in 1608. This evidence, however, which only establishes a date before which a play was written, does not cover all the dramas; there is no external evidence at all for *The Taming of the Shrew, All's Well, Coriolanus,* and *Timon of Athens;* and for a number of other plays it is quite uncertain. For these, then, we must depend on evidence of another sort.

Internal-external evidence is furnished by allusions in the plays themselves to events which can be historically dated. The most striking of these is the allusion in one of the choruses of *Henry V* to the campaign of Essex in Ireland and to the confident expectation of his return in triumph. Now Essex set out on this campaign in March, 1599, and returned in anything but triumph (see p. 19) in September. It is plain, therefore, that the chorus, and presumably the play of which it is a part must have been written in the summer of 1599. Few pieces of evidence of this sort, however, are so definite as this. There seems to be an allusion in *A Midsummer Night's Dream* to the rainy summer of 1594; in *King Lear* to the eclipses of sun and moon in 1605; in *Macbeth* to the "equivocation" charged against a Jesuit connected with the Gunpowder Plot. The epilogue to *2 King Henry IV* promises another play to follow which can be identified with *Henry V.* Here belong also the known dates of sources such as North's *Plutarch,* from which Shakespeare drew his material. All these, however, fix only an initial date and show that the play in which they occur was written after the event alluded to; how long after they do not show, although it seems safe to assume that it would not be long after, since allusion of this sort to be understood by the audience would naturally be to recent events. On the whole there is not a large body of such evidence; Shakespeare does not seem to have been in the habit of indulging in topical allusions.

Internal evidence is that derived from the plays themselves, from their subjects, method of treatment, weakness or mastery of dramatic technique, and in particular from the style, the use of language, the employment of prose, the amount of rhyme, and more especially the development in the way of free expression of the prevailing blank verse. This so-called metrical evidence will be discussed later (p. 93); it is sufficient to say here that by combining this internal with the other types of evidence we can at least arrange Shakespeare's plays in periods. It is plain, for example, that the histories, except *Henry VIII,* follow one another through what we call the first and second periods of Shakespeare's career and come to a close with *Henry V;* that the "joyous comedies" belong together about the turn of the century, 1599-1600, and that a long succession of tragedies stretches from *Julius Cæsar* in 1599 to *Coriolanus,* ca. 1608. Within these periods, however, and interrupting the succession of such groups, we find plays of quite another type; the grim tragedy of *Titus Andronicus* (1593-94) falls within the period of the early comedies, and the "bitter comedy" *Measure for Measure* (ca. 1604) interrupts the succession of the tragedies. We must not think of these "periods" of Shakespeare's work as water-tight compartments sharply cut off from one another in which he confined himself to writing only plays of a certain type. They are more like the seasons of the year which melt almost imperceptibly into one another, where in spring we may get a day that recalls winter weather and another that foretells the approach of summer. Yet by a study of these periods and of the plays now by general assent assigned to them it is possible to get a fairly accurate view of Shakespeare's development as a dramatist.

It is usual to divide Shakespeare's work into four periods: the first of apprenticeship ending about 1594, the second of mastery of comedy and history, 1594-1600, the third that of the tragedies and of the "bitter comedies," 1599-1608, and the last, that of the "romances" or tragi-comedies, 1608-1613. It is unsafe to ascribe the changes in theme as some critics have done to changes in Shakespeare's outlook on life; various causes may have influenced him to shift, for example, from history in *Henry V* to tragedy in *Julius Cæsar,* or from tragedy in *Coriolanus* to tragi-comedy in *Cymbeline.* Yet it is by no means impossible as we follow the development of Shakespeare's art to see also a broadening, deepening, and finally a ripening of his conception of human life and his judgment of men's acts and motives.

It is often said that Shakespeare's earliest work was confined to patching up and revising plays by other dramatists. There is little evidence for this and it seems rather unlikely that an apprentice in the art should be asked to revise plays that had already won success upon the stage. We can be certain, however, that the trilogy of *Henry VI* belongs to this early period. The first part was staged by Lord Strange's Men in the spring of 1592. It was immensely successful, particularly because of the scenes which showed the English hero Talbot fighting and dying heroically in the wars in France. Some of these scenes were undoubtedly written by Shakespeare either in collaboration with other authors—Peele and Greene are suggested—or to replace older work. The finest scene of the play, which represents the origin of the Red and the White Rose quarrel, is also his, but seems to have been written later, perhaps about 1598 when the play was revised to bring it into organic connection with the later parts and with *Henry V.* This play was printed for the first time in the Folio, 1623.

The second and third parts of *Henry VI* were originally a two-part play dealing with the Wars of the Roses. They were on the stage in 1592 as is shown by Greene's parody of a line occurring in the third part in his attack of Shakespeare already mentioned. They were published under the titles of the *First Part of the Contention* (1594) and the *True Tragedy of Richard Duke of York* (1595) in an abbreviated and corrupt form on the break-up of the company, Pembroke's, by which they were first performed. There seems some reason to believe that they were the work of Marlowe, perhaps with the assistance of Peele, that they came into the hands of Shakspeare's company, and that their present form, as it appears in the Folio, represents Shakespeare's revision of the lost original. Another theory holds that these two parts are early and original work by Shakespeare alone. If so, he was clearly working under the influence of Marlowe. The inclusion of all three parts in the Folio shows that they were considered by the editors as in their final form the work of Shakespeare. The omission of any mention of them by Meres in his well-known list may be due to the fact that they were withdrawn from the stage during his residence in London in the mid-1590's.

Another play of this early period, *Titus Andronicus,* has been the subject of much debate. It is a Senecan tragedy of closely woven intrigue in the manner of Kyd and apparently very popular on the Elizabethan stage. That in its present form it represents the work or at least the revision of Shakespeare is as certain as anything can be. It is not only included in the Folio, but is mentioned by Meres in 1598.

Its early history, however, is most obscure. A play on the subject of Titus and the Goths was on the stage as early as 1592 as is shown by an allusion in *A Knack to Know a Knave*, a play of that year. In the winter of 1594 Sussex's Men produced a play called by the illiterate Henslowe *Titus & Ondronicus*. He marked it *ne*, which is supposed to mean either a new play or, as in this case, a revision. When the theatres were again closed by the plague, Henslowe sold the play to a printer who brought out a copy of it in this year, 1594. Of this edition, the first of Shakespeare's plays to be printed, only one copy, that in the Folger Library at Washington, still survives. It does not bear his name on the title-page. Later the play passed into the hands of Shakespeare's company and was played by them on various occasions.

Perhaps the simplest explanation of these facts is to assume that an unknown writer, possibly Peele, traces of whose hand abound in *Titus*, was the original author, that Henslowe secured the acting rights and in the plague season of 1593-94 called on the young dramatist Shakespeare, who had recently achieved great success by his poem *Venus and Adonis* (1593) to touch up the play so that it could be produced with a flourish of trumpets as *ne*. It is certain that Shakespeare was in London in 1593-94 busy on his *Lucrece*. He was probably glad to earn an honest penny in a time of deep depression for actors and playwrights by doing an odd job of this sort. Traces of Shakespeare's revising hand are fairly evident in the play; [1] but he apparently left the original framework untouched. Such an explanation agrees with a tradition dating from 1687 that Shakespeare "only gave home master touches to one or two of the principal parts" and it relieves Shakespeare of the responsibility of the crude horrors with which the play abounds.

It is sometimes asserted that *Romeo and Juliet* must have been written as early as 1591 because of an allusion in that play to an earthquake which occurred eleven years before, 1580. If so, it attracted little attention at the time and must have been thoroughly reworked some years later. It may best be considered with the plays of Shakespeare's second period.

It was in the field of comedy that the young Shakespeare learned the technique of his craft, and a trio of comedies of this early period, *The Comedy of Errors, Two Gentlemen of Verona*, and *Love's Labour's Lost*, show him at work experimenting in different types of comedy and practicing construction, characterization, and dramatic expression. Of these three the *Errors* probably comes first. In fact there is some reason to believe it Shakespeare's first unaided and original play. The interesting suggestion has been made that he may have drafted it while still a country school-master, but if so he revised it later from beginning to end, for much of the play is written in Marlovian blank verse which Shakespeare would not have been able to imitate before he came to London. Traces of the old-fashioned doggerel still remain in the dialogue and we are probably not far wrong in dating it ca. 1590. We first hear of a performance during the Christmas Revels at Gray's Inn in 1594, but it was certainly on the boards long before that time; in fact it was probably selected as a play for the Revels because of its fame as a fun-maker.

The *Errors* is a good example of a common Elizabethan practice, the adaptation of classical comedy to the contemporary stage. It is founded upon the *Menaechmi* of Plautus, an amusing comedy dealing with the adventures and mishaps of two indistinguishable twin brothers. In the Plautine play there is only one pair of twins; in Shakespeare's there are two, twin servants as well as twin masters, which, of course, makes the comic confusion more confounded. For this duplication Shakespeare probably drew on another Plautine play the *Amphitryon*.

These classical comedies gave Shakespeare what he needed most at this time, a well-knit plot, ingeniously developed, and neatly solved: the final rally of all the characters and the solution of the mistaken identities in the last scene is a little masterpiece of construction. Yet Shakespeare in this play did much more than imitate or even adapt a classical comedy. The atmosphere of the play, the citizens' houses, the old inns, the merchants doing business on the streets, all is genuinely and realistically Elizabethan England. Moreover, Shakespeare sets this scene against a romantic background drawn from the well-known story of *Apollonius of Tyre*, a tale of the separation of a family by shipwreck, of a father's wanderings in search of a lost wife and child, and of

[1] See my article in *Modern Language Review*, 1915.

the final happy reunion of the family. To this he adds the shadow of tragedy, so often found in his later comedies, by presenting the father, Ægeon, in the first scene under sentence of death, saved at the very end by his recognition as the father of the twins. Finally Shakespeare adds the "love-interest" demanded in a popular play by providing the shrewish wife of one twin with an amiable sister with whom the other twin promptly falls in love.

We look in vain in the *Comedy of Errors* for the characterization and the poetry in which Shakespeare was later to excel. It is essentially an ingenious piece of dramatic construction, far more complex and amusing than its source and lifted above the realm of farce by added touches of love-making and romance.

The *Two Gentlemen of Verona* is a somewhat less successful attempt at a form in which Shakespeare was later to become preeminent, romantic comedy dealing primarily with the theme of love. The rather slight story of two lovers, one constant, the other fickle, of a lady disguised as a page following her faithless lover, of love's crosses and misadventures, crowned at last with a happy ending is somewhat artificial for modern taste, but very much in the fashion of Elizabethan courtly love. Especially shocking to our ideas is the scene where true lover Valentine actually hands over to his faithless but now repentant friend his own beloved Sylvia upon whom that friend has just laid violent hands. Yet this very action is part of the Renaissance creed which rated friendship between man and man far above love between man and woman. Shakespeare himself was once a believer in this creed, traces of which appear again and again in his sonnets—see especially numbers forty and forty-two. He never again allowed himself to end a play in such an unsatisfactory and hurried fashion as he did here, and this huddling up of the conclusion is one of the signs of his immaturity. When he had Plautus to guide him he could manage a capital denouement; working on his own he was less successful. Yet there are certain features in which this play shows an advance upon the *Comedy of Errors.* It pays more attention to characterization; the lovers are well discriminated: Julia, the forsaken lady, anticipates some of the most charming of Shakespeare's later heroines, and the two comic servants, especially Launce with his dog, are capital bits of realistic comedy. The special charm of the play, however, is its poetry. Here in a tale of love the young poet-playwright lets himself go to his heart's content and fills his scenes with passages of lyric beauty. One of the first and loveliest of Shakespeare's songs "Who is Sylvia?" appears here as a serenade. All in all, while the *Two Gentlemen of Verona* is a poorer stage play than the *Comedy of Errors,* it is a play of more promise and points more directly to later triumphs in romantic comedy.

In *Love's Labour's Lost* Shakespeare attempted this time with brilliant success a new type of comedy, one of personal and social satire. The play has come down to us in a revision prepared for presentation at court in the Christmas season of 1597. Signs of this revision are apparent in the text, particularly in Biron's long speech, IV, iii, 289-365, and it is probable that much of the play was carefully rewritten. At any rate it shows a marked advance, if not in construction at least in its outlook on life, over the *Two Gentlemen.* In that play Shakespeare accepted the conventions of courtly love and friendship without question; in this he ridicules the social follies of the day. More especially he laughs at the Elizabethan extravagance of language, at the Renaissance parade of learning, and even at the fashions of courtly love. There is some reason to believe that it was written for a private performance in the plague year of 1593 and that some of the comic characters, Armado, Holofernes, Moth, are caricatures of well-known people of that day. This personal satire is lost to us; what is not lost is Shakespeare's fine, strong common sense. This is embodied in the chief character Biron, the first and one of the best of Shakespeare's witty gentlemen, into whom, no doubt, Shakespeare has put a great deal of himself. It is Biron who recognizes the folly of the vow taken by the king and his comrades to live a life of seclusion devoted to study and to abjure the society of women. It is he who exposes the perjury of his fellows when they yield to the charms of the princess and her ladies and, when his own passion for one of them is revealed, he defends in a burst of eloquence love as the source and fountain of poetry, beauty, and true wisdom. The moral of the whole action is plain enough: men cannot live without women, and if they wish to win their loves they must woo them with simple sincerity. The play is a courtly comedy something in the style of Lyly as is shown by the artificial grouping of the characters, the king and his three lords balanced against the princess and her three ladies. There is little of Lyly's characteristic euphuism, but there is all of Lyly's delight in word-play, puns, conceits, and far-fetched images. It is written for the most part in rhyme, sometimes in artful rhyme-schemes such as alternates and sonnets. Yet around all this courtly extravagance of speech Shakespeare has thrown an atmosphere of rural England. The scene, supposedly in Navarre, is really somewhere in the English countryside. The country parson, school-master, and clown are figures such as Shakespeare knew at home and the fanciful and artificial play ends with a lovely song of spring and winter redolent of the breath of Shakespeare's England. All in all when allowances are made for topical allusions lost to us today and for confusions caused by the revision, *Love's Labour's Lost* remains the most original and the most delightful of Shakespeare's early comedies.

Part II

There is nothing to show that any one of Shakespeare's plays except those already discussed was written before 1594. The great plague of 1593-94 closed the theatres for many months in those years and Shakespeare spent a good part of his time in the composition of two long poems, *Venus and Adonis* and *Lucrece* (see below, p. 71 ff.). He may also have been at work on one or more plays in view of the reopening of the theatres. Certainly with this reopening in the summer of 1594 he resumes his work as a playwright and for the next six years is extremely busy turning out play after play in quick succession.

This second period is the time of his great histories and most brilliant comedies, but these come toward the end of the period. It opens with a group of plays that link it with his earlier work. Of these we may first discuss the early histories.

It is perhaps well to begin with *King John* (ca. 1596), in some ways the least interesting, as it is the least original of Shakespeare's histories. It is a rewriting of an old chronicle play, *The Troublesome Reign of King John*, published in two parts in 1591, but certainly written some years earlier, possibly by Peele. Shakespeare's skill as a playwright is shown by the manner in which he condensed the two parts into one, selecting, omitting, and enlarging as he sees fit; his independence appears by the fact that while he keeps in the main the scenario of his source he disdains to take over any of the dialogue.

Like the other chronicle plays of the day *King John* appeals to the enthusiastic patriotism of the Elizabethan audience. Following old tradition, Shakespeare represents John as a valiant defender of England against France and more especially against the arrogant claims of the Pope, a "sure-fire" hit in Elizabethan days. Yet Shakespeare knew history too well to make King John a hero. As a matter of fact he appears in this play as the villainous murderer, in intent if not in fact, of his little nephew. The true hero of the play is Falconbridge, the bastard son of Richard Cœur de Lion, who avenges his father's death, leads the royal army against foreign invaders and domestic rebels, and rallies the nobles of England around John's innocent successor with the proud words:

Now these her princes are come home again,
Come the three corners of the world in arms,
And we shall shock them. Nought shall make us rue,
If England to itself do rest but true.

There are two interesting omissions in this play; there is no mention of the great event of John's reign, the granting of the Magna Carta; it would not have been prudent, perhaps not even safe, for Shakespeare to show a body of rebellious nobles wresting by force a charter from their king. The second is the excision of an amusing but scandalous scene in his source attacking the morals of nuns and friars; Shakespeare never stoops to win a laugh by abusing his mother's church.

The play is written in rather formal Marlovian blank verse; there is no prose, and little rhyme. Shakespeare is following in the footsteps of Marlowe in his treatment of English history in tragic fashion.

This is even more apparent in the next of the chronicle plays, *Richard III*, probably staged soon after the opening of the theatres in 1594 and possibly written a little earlier. It picks up the thread of English history where Marlowe, if it was he who wrote the *Henry VI* plays *II* and *III* in their first form, had dropped it, and carries the story on to the end of the Wars of the Roses. More than this it centers all the action in Marlowe's own manner about a single figure, Richard Crookback. This character had been sketched by Marlowe in *3 King Henry VI,* but Shakespeare develops, refines, and varies the hero-villain until while still recognizable as one of Marlowe's supermen of the Renaissance, Shakespeare's Richard is more real, more human, and more effective on the stage than any character in Marlowe's plays. Here certainly the disciple has surpassed his master. Six editions of this play were published before 1623. We could ask for no better evidence of its contemporary popularity and we know that the part of Richard was one of Burbage's most successful rôles. From Shakespeare's day until the present the play has held the stage, largely because of the magnificent opportunity it offers for a star in the part of Richard. It must be confessed, however, that the acting version has as a rule been Colley Cibber's revision, (1700), rather than Shakespeare's own play.

Like *King John, Richard III* is written in Marlovian blank verse; there is no better example of Shakespeare's adaptation of Marlowe's style than the opening soliloquy of the play. The verse is rhetorical and declamatory rather than lyrical, and the long tirades and choral lamentations are reminiscent of Senecan influence. On the whole it is a play for the stage rather than for the lover of Shakespeare's poetry.

There is one feature of this play, however, that marks it as characteristically Shakespeare's and represents a distinct advance over Marlowe's and his own earlier work. This is his interpretation in dramatic form of history. To Shakespeare the internecine Wars of the Roses was a period to be looked back upon with horror. He represents this period as culminating in the "cacodemon," Richard, who after trampling on the Red Rose turns in his mad pursuit of power against his own family. Richard rises by slaughter to the throne, only to become a prey to the stings of conscience, to be outwitted and betrayed by his subjects, and finally slain in battle by the founder of the House of Tudor who unites the Roses and brings peace to England. The conception of the Nemesis that pursues the hero-villain, the hatred of civil strife, and the sincere belief in the greatness and unity of England under the Tudors, all this is Shakespeare's contribution to the tragic story of Richard's rise and fall.

By common consent *Richard II* is dated in or near 1595. It is certainly later than *Richard III* and shows Shakespeare diverging still further from the school of Marlowe. There is, to be sure, a certain resemblance between it and Marlowe's *Edward II.* Both plays deal with the tragical fall of a weak but lovable king; but while Marlowe tells the story of the whole reign, Shakespeare concentrates on the last years, the crisis and collapse of Richard. Compared with Marlowe's simple and straightforward presentation of his protagonist, Shakespeare's portrayal of Richard shows a more penetrating and subtler psychology. Edward is overthrown by an outside power, the rebellious barons; Richard is a victim of his own character, his self-indulgence, his rashness, his blindness to the realities of life, and Shakespeare brings out at once the weakness and the charm of Richard by contrasting him with the hard realist, Bolingbroke. It is hardly too much to say that this play foreshadows, however faultily, the later and greater tragedies of Shakespeare.

In the matter of style, too, *Richard II* shows a sense of conscious freedom in the young dramatist. Shakespeare abandons the rhetorical blank verse of Marlowe for a more fluent metre. There is a greater proportion of rhyme in this play than in any of the earlier histories and even the blank verse often has a lyric lilt. Shakespeare indulges in this play, too often for one's taste, in puns, in word-play, and conceits. In short, one feels in reading *Richard II* that the poet has graduated from the school of Marlowe and is now his own master. It is not as good an acting play as *Richard III* but it is more Shakespearean.

The one tragedy of this period, *Romeo and Juliet,* may be dated fairly definitely in its present form in 1596. An unauthorized edition, Q1, appeared in 1597; an authoritative edition, Q2, "corrected and augmented" two years later. Like *Richard II,* with which it has many points of resemblance, *Romeo and Juliet* shows Shakespeare striking out for himself, this time in the field of tragedy. He turns his back on Seneca and the Senecan convention of horrors, and writes the first tragedy in English literature to deal with the theme of romantic love. *Romeo and Juliet* is the work of a poet-playwright who has found a plot into which he can throw all his power and his passion. At times indeed it seems as if the passion of the poet got the better of the playwright's power, as when Shakespeare stops the action to let Mercutio recite the well-known verses on Queen Mab. Yet one has only to compare Shakespeare's play with its source, a long narrative poem by Arthur Brooke (1562), to see how skillfully he adapted the story to the stage. In characterization, too, *Romeo and Juliet* shows an advance over Shakespeare's earlier work; Romeo is at first a sentimentalist like Richard II, but he is ennobled by his love and rises above himself as Richard never does. Juliet is the first and in some ways the most appealing of Shakespeare's tragic heroines; the nurse is his first complete triumph in the realistic presentation of a comic character. Yet the real charm of the play lies neither in its construction nor in its characterization but in its poetry. The theme of young love, pure, passionate, and ill-fated, is given dramatic form with a lyric beauty that is unmatched elsewhere in English literature. *Romeo and Juliet* lacks the depth, the power, the tragic intensity, of the great plays of the third period, and it may well be that Shakespeare, no doubt his own severest critic, felt he was not yet ready to deal competently with great tragic themes. At any rate in spite of the instant success of *Romeo and Juliet* upon the stage and with all lovers of poetry, he turned his back on tragedy and set himself to write a long series of comedies and to complete his group of English histories.

The first comedy of this period, *A Midsummer Night's Dream* (ca. 1595), is Shakespeare's first complete success in the field of romantic comedy. It is a little masterpiece of plot construction; the various threads drawn from diverse sources are deftly woven together into a most delightful pattern. The "enveloping action," the wedding festival of Theseus and Hippolyta, comes from Plutarch by way of Chaucer; the story of the lovers probably from a lost Italian source; Oberon, the fairy king, had appeared in Greene's *James IV;* Puck is a well-known character in English folklore, and Bottom with his crew of rude mechanicals represents Shakespeare's laughing observation of amateur performances in English country towns. It is interesting to note how skillfully Shakespeare has blended in the play the classical, the realistic, and the romantic elements of Elizabethan drama. The setting, Athens, and the main characters are classical in name at least; but more important is the complicated intrigue and the deft solution of an artfully entangled plot. This is a technique that Shakespeare learned from his classic masters, but he has surpassed them in this play. It seems almost needless to call attention to the homely realism of the scenes in which Bottom plays a part. This is genuine English stuff and it is interesting to note that when the theatres were closed these scenes were made into a "droll" and played by touring actors in English towns and villages. In Oberon, Titania, and the magic herbs we have pure matter of romance, and nowhere in literature is there such a union and comic contrast of romance and realism as in the scene where Titania falls in love with Bottom crowned with the ass's head.

The style is a delightful blending of blank verse and rhyme; the blank verse itself, like much of *Romeo and Juliet,* has a lyrical note, and the frequent songs and rhymed speeches of the fairies add to the musical effect. The Bottom scenes are written in vigorous prose which Shakespeare was coming to realize as the true vehicle for realistic comedy. Had Shakespeare written nothing else, his fame as a master of English romantic comedy would have been assured; but he was to go on to even greater work.

The *Merchant of Venice* (ca. 1596-97), again represents an advance in Shakespeare's art and a deepening of his outlook on life. *A Midsummer Night's Dream* is a comedy of fancy; the *Merchant* is a rather serious study of certain aspects of human life, of love and marriage, of the use and abuse of wealth. The idea of a play whose chief character should be a wicked Jew may have been suggested to Shakespeare by the revival in 1594 of Marlowe's *Jew of Malta,* a revival provoked by the outburst of the anti-Semitism that accompanied the execution in that year of the Queen's Jewish physician for alleged high treason. Yet Shakespeare's Shylock is a very different character from Marlowe's Jew, at once more dramatically effective and more truly human than the monster Barabas.

The main plot, the bond entered into by a merchant in order that his young friend may woo and win the lady of Belmont, the forfeiture of the bond, and the delivery of the merchant by the lady disguised as a lawyer, along with the intrigue of the rings, goes back to an Italian *novella* of the fourteenth century. The theme of the caskets, Shakespeare's clever substitution for the somewhat indelicate fashion in which the lover of the *novella* wins the lady, comes from a collection of moral tales, the *Gesta Romanorum*. The Jew's fair daughter who loves a Christian has a counterpart in Marlowe's play. These diverse elements have been combined into a harmonious whole by masterly plot construction. Especially ingenious is the manner in which the tragic threat of the court scene is averted by the wit and wisdom of Portia, and in the last act tragedy is pushed quite into the background by the romance of the lovers and the merry business of the rings in the moonlit garden of Belmont. Actors starring in the part of Shylock who have rung down the curtain with his exit from the courtroom have quite misunderstood the significance of Shakespeare's play.

It is not so much in construction, however, as in characterization that Shakespeare shows his developing mastery. Shylock is in some ways the most complete, rounded, and convincing character that he had yet created; the motivation of his action, the blending of greed. racial antipathy, and personal revenge is admirably rendered. And Shylock's part in the play is admirably balanced by that of Portia, the perfect picture of a great lady of the Renaissance. Shakespeare's transformation of the siren of the *novella* into the heroine of this play is one of his masterpieces of character creation. There is less gay fancy and riotous fun in the *Merchant* than in the earlier comedies, but this lack is more than atoned for by the grave beauty of the verse, the moral earnestness of the central casket scene, and the natural magic of the opening lines of the last act.

It must have been shortly after the *Merchant of Venice* that Shakespeare took up the revision and completion of the trilogy which crowns his series of histories, *Henry IV*, parts *I* and *II*, and *Henry V*. There is some reason to believe that the *Henry IV* plays were written earlier, probably soon after *Richard II*, 1595; it is certain that the fat knight who figures in them was originally called Sir John Oldcastle. The presentation on the stage of the historic Sir John, as a "villainous abominable misleader of youth" naturally provoked an indirect descendant, Lord Cobham, then holding the high office of Lord Chamberlain, and he insisted on a re-baptism of the character. Shakespeare yielded, apologized, indeed, in the epilogue to the second part, and substituted the name of Falstaff, apparently a corruption of Fastolfe, also a historic character who had left no descendant able to enter protest. There is a consensus of opinion that the revised form of the two parts dates in the year 1597-8 and *Henry V* in 1599.

In these plays Shakespeare shakes off definitely and completely the influence of Marlowe. He reverts in fact to an older type of chronicle play where comic scenes are interspersed in the serious matter of history. Following an old tradition which told of the riotous youth of Prince Hal and represented Oldcastle as his companion, Shakespeare created the glorious comic figure which we know as Falstaff. He carries him triumphantly through the first part, and shows his gradual degeneration in the second which closes with his rejection by his old friend, the newly crowned king. It seems plain from the epilogue to the second part that Shakespeare's first intention was to carry him on into the play of *Henry V*, but he thought better of it, feeling no doubt that such a character would be out of place in the epic-heroic play of Henry's war in France. And so all we have of Falstaff in *Henry V* is the humorous-pathetic account of his death-bed babbling of green fields and his passage to "Arthur's bosom."

The serious matter of these plays deals with the last great monarch of medieval England, "the mirror of all Christian kings," Henry V. He is first mentioned in *Richard II* as a wild young reprobate, a thorn in his father's side. We see him in the first part of *Henry IV* as a haunter of taverns and a companion of rioters and purse-takers, yet able to rise to heroic heights at the call of duty. In the second part we see less of him till near the end when he is reconciled with his father on the old king's death-bed, and assumes the crown. The play that bears his name is rather dramatized history than drama proper and is composed of a series of scenes showing Henry as the perfect king, taking wise counsel with his lords, crushing domestic treason, winning the crowning victory of the English wars in France, and finally completing his conquest by wooing and winning Katherine, the French princess. The note of love of country, of pride in England's past, which rings through all the histories of Shakespeare rises to what has been called "a chant of patriotic triumph" in *Henry V*. The enthusiastic nationalism which evokes this note was waning sadly in the last troubled years of Elizabeth's reign and Shakespeare must have felt that he had done all that could be done with the chronicle play and that it was time to turn to other fields. The period of Shakespeare's tragedies follows hard upon the closing of the series of his histories, but before we turn to them we still have a group of comedies to consider.

Shakespeare seems to have found time during his work on the Henry trilogy to write a couple of farce comedies. The first of these, *The Taming of the Shrew,* must be dated at least as late as 1598, since it is not included in Meres' list. It is a rewriting by Shakespeare, apparently with the help of a collaborator, of an old play, *The Taming of a Shrew,* published in 1594. The induction and the scenes dealing with Petruchio and Katherine are Shakespeare's and in his best vein of lively comedy; he follows the scenario of his source fairly closely but completely rewrites the dialogue. The underplot, dealing with the wooing of the shrew's gentle sister, is the work of the collaborator, who, perhaps on Shakespeare's suggestion, lifted the plot from Gascoigne's prose comedy, *The Supposes,* and turned it into such tame flat verse that it seems impossible that Shakespeare could have written it at any time of his life. Yet the two plots are so well woven together that we must assume that Shakespeare planned and directed the whole work. It is an interesting fact that the old play has an epilogue in which the drunken tinker is laid asleep by the ale-house where he had been discovered in the Induction, awakes to fancy that the play he has seen was a dream, and goes home to tame his own shrewish wife. Such an ending seems almost necessary, and the absence of anything corresponding to it in Shakespeare's play is hard to explain. Possibly the manuscript from which the Folio version was printed—there is no earlier text—had lost the last leaf or two in which some such scene was written.

The Taming of the Shrew is not a great play; it is probably a work dashed off in haste by Shakespeare; but it bears witness to his skill in construction, to his sense of fun and farcical situation and, in the Induction, to his loving reminiscence of the country-side about Stratford.

An old tradition tells us that Queen Elizabeth was so delighted with the character of Falstaff that she commanded Shakespeare to write another play about him and to show him in love. It is also said that he wrote the play she ordered, *The Merry Wives of Windsor,* in fourteen days. We need not take this last statement literally, but there is good reason to believe that the play was written at top speed for a performance before the Queen. It may be safely dated late in 1599 after *Henry V* and may be regarded as Shakespeare's apology to Elizabeth for having failed to keep his promise and introduce Sir John in that play.

To show Falstaff in love was beyond the power even of Shakespeare; Falstaff as Shakespeare knew him and drew him in the *Henry IV* plays was incapable of the tender passion. To comply with the royal command, however, he stooped to show his comic hero engaged in amorous pursuit of two merry but honest English wives who confederate together to pretend love to him, arrange to get him ducked in the Thames, well-beaten by a jealous husband, and finally exposed to the derision of the entire company. This is not the old Sir John, master of every situation in which he finds himself, and indeed there is little of the true Falstaff in the character who bears his name in *The Merry Wives* except his exuberant language.

The Merry Wives is the one example in Shakespeare's work of bourgeois comedy, written in the realistic satirical mood which was becoming popular toward the end of the century. Jonson's *Every Man In* and *Every Man Out of His Humour,* both performed by Shakespeare's company, had opened this vein with marked success, and it seems quite likely that Shakespeare writing under pressure tried his hand for once at this type of play. There is no touch of his romantic imagination in it; the slender story of the love of Fenton and Mistress Anne is pushed quite into the background; the fairies of the last scene are not real fairies but children in disguise. Half a dozen characters, the Welsh Parson, and the French Doctor, Corporal Nym, taken over from *Henry V,* and above all the jealous Ford are "humour characters" of the Jonson school. This may be one of the reasons why the play has always been successful on the stage; a "humour character" is an excellent part for an actor, and the combination and contrast of "humours" in this play along with the lively well-planned farcical action gives *The Merry Wives* a dash and vigor that is irresistible on the stage. No one would rank the play, however, among Shakespeare's best comedies; it is a hasty experiment triumphantly carried off, but never repeated. The next comedies that we have to consider are in quite another vein.

A trio of plays sometimes called the Joyous Comedies concludes this period; these are in the order of composition: *Much Ado about Nothing, As You Like It,* and *Twelfth Night.* The first of these, *Much Ado,* can be dated fairly accurately. It is not mentioned by Meres in 1598, and Kemp, who played the part of Dogberry, left the company about the middle of 1599; the play therefore was probably written between the autumn of 1598 and the summer of 1599.

Much Ado is in some ways Shakespeare's comic masterpiece. Founded upon an Italian tale of a slandered lady deserted by her lover and at last reunited to him, it incorporates a bit of genuine English realism in the Dogberry-Verges scenes and adds to this combination the two characters by whom the play really lives, those of Benedick and Beatrice. There is no source known for this couple, nor need one be sought; they are Shakespeare's creation, or rather his re-creation in more perfect form of the reluctant, witty lovers of *Love's Labour's Lost.* Their story is technically the sub-plot, but it is by far the most interesting part of the play and Shakespeare has in fact rearranged the incidents of the main plot so as to bring these lovers together. There is nothing in the Italian tale to compare with the dramatically effective scene in which Claudio, the nominal hero of the play, renounces his bride at the altar and Benedick and Beatrice unite to revenge and vindicate her.

There is less fine poetry in this play than in most of Shakespeare's comedies. On the other hand the comic scenes, whether the stupidities of Dogberry and his mates or the wit-combats of the lovers, are written in his very best prose. It has always been successful on the stage. Just before the closing of the theatres in 1642 a contemporary writer tells us that an appearance of Benedick and Beatrice was sure to pack the house, and most of the famous actors and actresses since Garrick's day have starred in these roles.

As You Like It (probably early 1600), the second of this group, differs as much from its predecessor as one romantic comedy can from another. *Much Ado* is one of the best built of Shakespeare's comedies; *As You Like It* one of the most loosely constructed. Its charm, and it is one of the most delightful of Shakespeare's plays, lies largely in the woodland atmosphere in which the greater part of the action is laid, and not a little in the group of lovable people who meet and make love, or laugh at love's follies under the greenwood tree. It is an adaptation for the stage of a popular romance of the day, Lodge's *Rosalynde* (1590). Lodge's book is a pastoral romance of the type that Sidney's *Arcadia* had introduced into English literature, and Shakespeare's play is in some sense a pastoral drama. Yet Shakespeare, now full master of his art, is by no means inclined to accept the artificialities and false sentiment of the pastoral. Indeed, he ridicules them in the figures of Silvius and Phoebe, the despairing lover and the cold shepherdess of the pastoral. Over against these unreal characters he places such realistic figures as Audrey and William and opposes to their conventional amours the very human love-affair of Orlando and Rosalind. Touchstone's wooing of the rustic Audrey is a frank burlesque of romantic love.

Apart from the atmosphere, largely created by the woodland scenes and the lovely lyrics with which the play abounds, *As You Like It* lives by its characters. Rosalind is to many lovers of Shakespeare the most charming, as in some ways the most modern of his heroines. Touchstone, the first part Shakespeare wrote for his new "fellow" Armin, is the wittiest of his court fools; Jacques, a humour character, is Shakespeare's portrait of the "malcontent" or melancholy cynic, a figure not uncommon in both Elizabethan life and literature as the century drew to an end; and both Touchstone and Jacques are Shakespeare's inventions; there is no trace of them in his source. We may well excuse the careless plotting of the play and its huddled and conventional conclusion for the sake of its poetry and its delightful characters.

Twelfth Night, late in 1600, the last of the trio, is in some ways the most nearly perfect of the three. Less poetical than *As You Like It,* less witty than *Much Ado,* it is a perfect blend of romance and realism. The main plot, the story of the twin brother and sister, with the business of love at cross purposes and mistaken identity, goes back ultimately to an Italian play which had been retold in English prose some twenty years before *Twelfth Night* was written. Shakespeare takes this plot, sets it in Illyria for the purpose of romantic distance, although his Illyria is hardly distinguishable from Elizabethan England, and to keep it from degenerating into mere intrigue or mawkish sentiment surrounds it with background figures of English life, the steward, the jester, the hard-drinking cousin, the foolish suitor, such as might be found in any noble house in England. The romantic plot deals with love in its varied forms, the fanciful sentiment of the Duke, the sudden passion of Olivia, the true and tender passion of Viola. The comic realism turns about the trick played on the presumptuous steward, Malvolio. Perhaps no comedy of Shakespeare exhibits so clearly his mastery of his craft as the way in which he interweaves and complicates these plots and brings them at last together in a most natural and happy solution.

The characterization, too, represents Shakespeare at his best. The characters are not sacrificed to the plot as some of them are in *Much Ado* nor is the plot a mere background for the characters as in *As You Like It.* Viola is perhaps the most lovable of Shakespeare's heroines; Sir Toby, a figure of the family of Falstaff, is nicely adjusted to his surroundings; Sir Andrew is the most hopeless simpleton that Shakespeare ever drew; and Malvolio the perfect picture of the overweening Jack in office. All in all, *Twelfth Night* with its blend of mirth and beauty is Shakespeare's supreme creation in high romantic comedy.

A brief review of this period will show both the character of Shakespeare's work and his great advance in independence and mastery in these crowded years. In his chronicle plays he begins as a disciple of Marlowe, excels his master in *Richard III,* and carries this genre to its highest pitch in the Henry trilogy. In comedy he achieves the first of his masterpieces, *A Midsummer Night's Dream,* his first serious drama, *The Merchant of Venice,* and toward the close his supreme trio of romantic comedies. History and comedy occupy his attention during this period. The tragedy of *Romeo and Juliet,* though enough in itself to make Shakespeare immortal, is the only play of this type between 1594 and 1599.

Part III

The third period is essentially the period of the great tragedies, but it includes a trio of plays usually known as the Bitter Comedies which may first be considered.

The first of these, *All's Well that Ends Well,* is generally thought to be a revision (ca. 1602-3) of an earlier comedy, possibly the *Love's Labour's Won* of Meres' list. It has come down to us in one text, that of the Folio, a text so corrupt and at times so obscure as to suggest that it was printed from a manuscript where passages had been crossed out and rewritten until it was a puzzle to the compositor, as it has been to later editors. Internal evidence, especially the amount of rhyme and the varying style of the blank verse in different parts of the play, go far to support the theory of a revision.

The source of *All's Well* is a story of Boccaccio (*Decameron,* iii, 9) which Shakespeare probably read in an English translation, Painter's *Palace of Pleasure,* 1566. In Boccaccio the story is told to illustrate the constancy in love and the cunning practice by which a woman of comparatively low birth wins a reluctant noble husband. It must have been the character of the woman, Helena in Shakespeare's play, which attracted him to the theme, for there is little else in the story likely to have appealed to him. To exalt her he degrades the ostensible hero, Bertram, even below the corresponding character in the *novella,* and the simple and effective ending of the tale is altered in the play to a tissue of lies, charges, and countercharges that leave a most unpleasant impression on the modern reader. There is none of the laughing humour of Shakespeare's earlier comedies; the Clown is a dull jester, not to be compared with Touchstone or Feste, and Parolles a poor specimen of the *miles gloriosus*. The breath of romance that blows through the earlier comedies has given place to a grave and often bitter wisdom. There seems no better explanation of this strange play than the hypothesis that it is a careless early comedy re-written at a time when Shakespeare's heart was not in his work.

Troilus and Cressida may be dated with some degree of accuracy in 1602. It was entered in the Stationers' Register Feb. 7, 1603, "as it is acted by my Lord Chamberlain's men." A clear allusion to Jonson's *Poetaster* acted in 1601 sets the earliest date. The play was not published until 1609, in which year two editions suddenly appeared. The second contains what is found in no other play of Shakespeare's, an epistle to the reader urging him to buy the book and remarking that this play was "never stal'd with the stage, never clapper-clawed with the palms of the vulgar." If this means anything it means that the play had never been acted, which seems to contradict both the original entry and the statement on the title-page of the first edition that it had been acted at the Globe. It seems certain that the quartos of 1609 were unauthorized; the epistle intimates that "the grand possessors," i.e., Shakespeare's company, would have prevented its publication if they could. Possibly the publishers got hold of a transcript of the play made for a friend of the author after a private performance at Court or one of the Inns of Court.

The play is a strange compound of old and new. It tells the story of the siege of Troy from the point of view of medieval historians and romancers who without exception took the Trojan side against the Greeks; it retells the story of the love of Troilus told long before by Chaucer in perfect form, but here by Shakespeare in the later tradition which had degraded Cressida into a synonym for inconstancy in love; it takes the character of Thersites from Chapman's unfinished translation of Homer and converts him into the most foul-mouthed rogue in all Shakespeare's plays. All in all a strange and mystifying play. So far as the love-story goes it is a comedy of disillusion. Troilus is as true a lover as Romeo, but he loves a wanton and inconstant Cressida instead of a Juliet. On the other hand some of the speeches, especially those of Ulysses, are in Shakespeare's gravest and most thoughtful vein. It is supposed to be a play for the study rather than the stage, but a performance by the Players in New York in 1932 showed an undreamed-of theatrical effectiveness. Possibly the puzzling nature of the play might be explained by the hypothesis that Shakespeare was called on by his company to write a Siege of Troy play to compete with one that was being performed at a rival theatre and that the poet whose mind and heart were busy with his tragedies wrote something that he thought would fill the bill.[1]

Measure for Measure was played at Court on December 26, 1604, and was almost certainly written some time earlier that year when the theatres were opened after the Great Plague of 1603-4. A possible revision for the court performance may account for the difficulties and inconsistencies in the one text preserved, that of the Folio. Like the two preceding plays it is nominally a comedy, but it deals with a tragic theme violently wrested to bring about a happy ending. As Sir Walter Raleigh says, if Shakespeare's fellows asked him for a comedy in his tragic period they got *Measure for Measure*. The source is a tedious two-part play, *Promos and Cassandra*, 1578, by George Whetstone which in turn goes back to an Italian *novella*. The Italian story, based apparently upon some historical incident, tells how a deputy of the Emperor condemned to death a young gentleman for having outraged a virgin. The culprit's sister pleaded for his life and the deputy offered to spare him if the sister would become his mistress. She refused, but finally yielding to her brother's entreaty, consented to sacrifice her honor to save his life. The deputy, however, had her brother executed and sent her the dead body. The lady took her case to the Emperor, who first ordered the deputy to marry her and then condemned him to suffer death. The lady now begs for the life of her new-made husband, which is granted by the Emperor, and the story concludes by saying that they lived happily together. Whetstone altered the story by saving the brother's life who escapes from prison and comes forward at the end to second his sister's plea for her husband's pardon. Shakespeare went a step further in amelio-

[1] A most interesting and suggestive interpretation of this play is given by Wilson Knight in *The Wheel of Fire*.

rating the tragic theme and spared his heroine the necessity of sacrificing her honor. To effect this he substitutes for her at the rendezvous another woman, the former betrothed of the judge, who mistakes her for the sister. It is plain that Shakespeare simply lifted this device from his own *All's Well* where the substitution of the virgin wife for a lady guiltily desired by the husband is an integral and essential part of the story. It is not so here, and the comic device of mistaken identity makes possible a conventional happy ending. It seems as if after the climax of the play when the heroine indignantly repels her brother's plea for life a comedy of intrigue has been superimposed on what had begun as a tragedy; certainly the great scenes of the play are in the earlier, the tragic part. Why Shakespeare did this no one can say; we may guess that when he decided to spare Isabella, he felt bound to provide a way for her escape and adopted the easiest solution. The conclusion in which Angelo is spared to marry his betrothed and Isabella is asked in marriage by the Duke has seldom satisfied lovers of Shakespeare and believers in justice. Yet the play is full of poetry, contains a group of realistic humorous characters, and shows in every scene Shakespeare's profound knowledge of human nature and his genial sympathy with all sorts and conditions of men.[1]

The long roll of the great tragedies opens with *Julius Cæsar*. This play was certainly on the stage in the autumn of 1599, the year of *Henry V*. It is a link-play between the histories and the tragedies, based upon a famous episode, the murder of Cæsar, in Roman history, yet dealing with it in tragic fashion. It has none of the bitterness of the later tragedies, and the grave beauty of the verse is rather that of the second period than of Shakespeare's later style. All this goes to show that the periods of Shakespeare's work are not rigidly defined, but melt imperceptibly one into another. Two at least of Shakespeare's finest comedies follow *Julius Cæsar*.

The direct source of the play was Plutarch's *Lives* in the English translation of Sir Thomas North, 1579, one of Shakespeare's favorite books. Plutarch supplied him not only with the historical facts, but also with an admirable presentation of the leading characters. Sometimes, indeed, Shakespeare turns the very words of North's prose version into his own verse. Yet this is not to say that *Julius Cæsar* lacks originality. Shakespeare selects, arranges, and emphasizes his material; the famous oration by Antony is not found in Plutarch at all, and his suppression of a whole series of events between the death of Cæsar and the battle of Philippi gives a speed and unity to the play that is lacking in the source.

The essential unity of the play is due to the fact that it revolves about the murder of Cæsar and the revenge exacted for his death. Yet Cæsar is not the hero of the play; on the contrary Shakespeare has sometimes been blamed for depicting the greatest man of ancient times as an arrogant, superstitious, and physically feeble despot. He drew some of these traits from his source, but he also followed a Renaissance tradition which depressed the character of Cæsar to exalt that of Brutus. Yet Shakespeare was not unaware of the greatness of "the mightiest Julius" and the last acts of the play show his spirit still powerful and "ranging for revenge."

The true tragic hero of the play is Brutus and it is in his treatment of this figure that Shakespeare shows his developing power and his gradual approach to the protagonists of the later tragedies. Romeo in Shakespeare's first original tragedy is a victim of fate, a "star-crossed lover." Brutus, like Hamlet whom he much resembles, is a victim of his own character. A philosopher, an idealist, he is incapable of seeing things as they are. He undertakes a great action, the freeing of Rome from a tyrant, without realizing the true situation or the probable consequences of the deed. He makes mistake after mistake and finally falls upon his sword a beaten man. Yet his high sense of honor, and his sweetness of temper are such that he never forfeits our sympathy. This was to become Shakespeare's practice in his characterization of his later tragic heroes, even of such a far from honorable murderer as Macbeth.

In *Hamlet* (1600), the second of the great tragedies, Shakespeare definitely abandoned the field of history and devoted all his energies to the reconstruction of a tragic theme. A reconstruction, for strange as it may seem, *Hamlet*, Shakespeare's best known play, is not an original creation.

[1] A suggestive and stimulating appreciation of this play occurs in Knight's *The Wheel of Fire*.

An old play on the subject was on the stage some time in the 1580's; Shakespeare's company played a *Hamlet* in 1594 and again in 1596. Some years later, about the time that revenge plays came into fashion again, Shakespeare undertook to revise this old play. We know that a version bearing his name was on the stage in 1600, since a contemporary writing toward the close of that year says that "Shakespeare's *Lucrece* and his tragedy of *Hamlet Prince of Denmark* have it in them to please the wiser sort." The writer, Gabriel Harvey, must have seen the play or heard of it from a friend, for no version of it had yet appeared in print. In 1603 a printed version was offered for sale to the London public. This is known as the first Quarto, a "stolen and surreptitious" copy. It was advertised with a flourish as written by Shakespeare and played by the King's Men, but it was as a matter of fact an impudent fraud. It seems to rest on the old play partly revised by Shakespeare, along with passages corresponding word for word with his latest revision, these being acting parts spoken by the hired man who perpetrated the theft, and finally on what the thief could remember of parts spoken by his fellow actors. It is hard to believe that such a hodge-podge as this was ever played on the stage.

Shakespeare and his fellows must have been shocked by such an outrage and took prompt pains to set it right. In the plague year of 1603-4 when Shakespeare had time on his hands he set himself to a final revision of the play, which was published in 1604. This is the second Quarto "enlarged" the title-page states "to almost as much again as it was, according to the true and perfect copy." Except for a good many errors in printing and a few deliberate omissions this is the play as Shakespeare conceived it. A third text, that of the Folio, is, apparently, based upon a playhouse version shortened and arranged for acting. Modern editions represent a fusion of the second Quarto and the Folio text.

The story of Hamlet goes back to the Viking age in Denmark. It was first written down by Saxo Grammaticus toward the close of the twelfth century, translated from Saxo's Latin into French about 1582, and shortly after dramatized for the Elizabethan stage, quite possibly by Kyd. The old play is lost but we can form some idea of it from a German play *Der Bestraffte Brudermord* (*Fratricide Punished*) which probably represents an abbreviated and corrupt form of the old play carried to Germany by English actors.

If we can reconstruct the old play from the German version and from what we know of Kyd's method, we shall see that he materially altered the story to fit it for the English stage. He introduced the Ghost crying for revenge—a genuine Senecan note—and in so doing deprived Hamlet of the obvious reason for his feigned madness—self-preservation. Instead of the open slaughter of the old king, as in the story, Kyd devised a secret murder by poison; he used the device of a play within a play as in his *Spanish Tragedy* to force a betrayal of the murderer's guilt; and finally he ended the play by a general massacre in which the hero and his enemies perish together.

Something, at least, like this must have been the outline of the play as it came to Shakespeare's hands. His transformation of the Senecan play of revenge for blood into the *Hamlet* that we know is one of the miracles of genius. He was bound to keep in the main the familiar action and indeed he found it, as the world has found it since, immensely effective on the stage. What he did was to recreate the character of the protagonist. Shakespeare's Hamlet is quite another person than the hero of the old saga or the straightforward revenger of the lost play. He is perhaps the most complex character that Shakespeare ever drew, a prince of the Renaissance,—courtier, soldier, scholar—a disillusioned idealist, a contemplative rather than an active man. It is worth noting that about 1600 Shakespeare had turned away from such men of action as Bolingbroke and Prince Hal and was interesting himself in such characters as the melancholy Jacques, the pessimistic Duke of *Measure for Measure,* and the worldly wise Ulysses. Hamlet is his supreme creation of this type and into the character of Hamlet Shakespeare has put more of himself than into any other figure in all his work. To sum up briefly: others had told the story; Shakespeare created the character of Hamlet, and by this creation solved the dramatic problem that confronted him. It is because Hamlet is what he is that he delays his revenge until the last moment; it is because Hamlet is what he is that the play is perennially effective on the stage—there is no such role in dramatic literature for a great actor—and perennially fascinating in the study.

Othello was played at Court on Nov. 1, 1604, and there can be little doubt that it was written earlier in that year. It follows directly upon *Hamlet* and there is no greater proof of Shakespeare's versatility and independence of formula than the contrast between these plays. *Hamlet* deals in Senecan fashion with the tragic falls of kings and princes; *Othello* is almost a domestic tragedy; no kingdom nor noble house is involved in the catastrophe that overwhelms the Moor and his wife. In *Hamlet* Shakespeare was bound to follow lines already laid down in a popular play; in *Othello* his source was an Italian *novella*. Shakespeare apparently felt himself at liberty to handle this story, probably unknown to most of his audience, in the freest fashion. The original is a brutal tale of sexual jealousy. The raw material of tragedy Shakespeare found there, the chief characters and the main events of his play. His task was to transform a straggling narrative into a compact drama and to lift a sordid story into the realm of high tragedy. This he accomplished with amazing success; no one can realize Shakespeare's magical power of turning dull metal into gold who has not read the original story. Here as nowhere else in this period he relied upon his own power of invention and this did not fail him.

Othello is in many ways Shakespeare's masterpiece of construction in the realm of tragedy. The magnificent opening act, which brings the situation at once before us and stirs our sympathy for the characters, is practically his own invention, and serves as a sort of prologue to the play. After the shift of the scene from Venice to Cyprus the action begins in earnest and rushes on in headlong haste to the final and terrible catastrophe. Here, too, Shakespeare discarded the long drawn-out conclusion of the *novella* and invented a solution—Emilia's loyalty to her murdered mistress and her denunciation of her husband—which dispels the fog of treachery and slander in which the hero had wandered. The action is single as it is swift; there is no double plot as in *Lear;* no postponement of the deed to be done as in *Hamlet*. There are no comic scenes, the poor part of the Clown, probably forced on Shakespeare to make a role for Armin, may be disregarded,. and the play is distinguished by unity of tone as by unity of action.

Of all Shakespeare's tragedies *Othello* is the most realistic; it lacks the element of the supernatural and the mysterious. Yet Shakespeare has transfigured the characters of his source even as he transformed the story. Othello himself is perhaps the most admirable of Shakespeare's tragic heroes, a noble soldier betrayed by the friend he trusted, who after his fall regains our sympathy when he confesses his crime and executes judgment upon himself. Iago is the incarnation of selfish and cynical malignity. It is no doubt significant that Shakespeare gave this mercenary soldier a Spanish name. It was easy for an Elizabethan audience familiar with the cruelties of the Spanish soldiery in the Low Countries and in Mexico to accept Iago as the perfect villain. Desdemona is the most wistful and pathetic of Shakespeare's tragic heroines, and the minor characters all fall naturally into their parts in the play.

The characters and events of *Othello* are the most real and credible in the whole range of Shakespeare's tragedies. Yet about this realistic play there breathes an air of romance. This in the main is due to the extraordinary charm of the poetry. Less profound and meditative than that of *Hamlet,* less impassioned than that of *Lear,* it is flexible enough to carry on easy colloquial conversation, but rises at times, especially in the speeches of Othello, to a singular power and beauty. Something of the romance of Italy and the Orient clings to the tragedy of the Moor of Venice.

King Lear was acted at Court December 26, 1606. It was probably written late in 1605 or early in 1606. It was published in 1608 with Shakespeare's name on the title-page, probably to assure the intending purchaser that this was the genuine play of the master and not another bearing practically the same name which had appeared a few years before. This quarto is one of the worst printing jobs ever turned out by an Elizabethan printer, yet it is invaluable to the student of Shakespeare, since it contains about three hundred lines omitted in the Folio. The Folio text rests upon a manuscript probably revised and shortened for the performance at Court.

The immediate source of the play is the old play of *King Leir,* acted as early as 1594, but not printed till 1605. There is some evidence that Shakespeare had read this play, saw in it good usable material, and set himself to revise it for his stage as he had lately remade the story of *Othello*. The old play presents in rather pleasant tragi-comic form the legend of Lear and his daughters which was first told by Geoffrey of Monmouth in the twelfth century and had been retold by poets and historians ever since. Shakespeare seems to have known various versions of the legend and to have borrowed from them whatever he could use. His one great original stroke was the conversion of the legend into a stupendous tragedy.

King Lear differs from *Othello* as from the other great tragedies in that it contains an under-plot, the story of Gloster and his sons which runs parallel to and is interwoven in the story of Lear and his daughters. This story Shakespeare drew from the most popular romance of his day, Philip Sidney's *Arcadia*. Possibly Shakespeare felt that the legend of Lear alone lacked the element of dramatic action and might as in the old play degenerate into the merely pathetic. By interweaving the Gloster plot he introduced an element of intrigue and counter-action that heightened the interest, and the wicked son of this story becomes the unwitting agent of the ruin of the wicked daughters. Moreover by the duplication of an instance of a child's ingratitude and cruelty he adds credibility to the old tale—one such instance might be exceptional, two are far more convincing—and before we finish *Lear* we feel ourselves transported into a world torn by strife between the powers of good and evil.

Shakespeare gained the effect he wanted by this use of the sub-plot but he lost something as well. *Lear* lacks the unity and concentration of *Othello,* which precedes, or *Macbeth,* which follows it. The action especially toward the close, is excessively complicated; the play in its first form was too long for presentation and was heavily cut even in Shakespeare's day. It was driven from the stage for over a century by the sentimental adaptation of Tate (1681) and is rarely produced in the modern theatre. In fact it has become a commonplace of criticism to say that *Lear* is a great dramatic poem but not a great play. This is a superficial error. The play was acted with success on Shakespeare's stage; that it cannot be presented on the "picture-frame" stage is hardly Shakespeare's fault. It remains for some modern producer capable of exploiting all the resources of the twentieth-century theatre to restore to the stage this most tremendous of Shakespeare's tragedies.

There is something symbolic, awe-inspiring, in *King Lear*. Shakespeare alone of all those who had handled the theme perceived its tragic quality, and in his hands it takes on a universal significance; it becomes a world war on a heroic scale between Evil naked and unashamed and Good, suffering, enduring, and sustaining. In the end the leading figures of the two parties perish in a common catastrophe, an offence against "poetic justice" which has shocked old-fashioned critics, but the storm of evil has blown over and a new world is left purified. Yet symbolic as the play, taken as a whole, seems to be, the characters are real and human. Lear is not a symbol but a king, a father, and a man "more sinned against than sinning." Kent is something more than the faithful servant; Cordelia than the loving daughter. In some ways the most interesting figure is that of the Fool, introduced into high tragedy by Shakespeare in defiance of classical decorum, whose shrewd comments furnish an ironic chorus to the tragic action. All in all it is not too much to say that the play of *King Lear* is the most magnificent example of Shakespeare's tragic genius.

Timon of Athens (ca. 1606) is one of the most puzzling plays in the Shakespeare canon. It first appeared in print in the Folio and there is no evidence that it was ever performed. The elaborate stage-directions, however, show that the play was prepared for a performance and we may guess that it was played a few times, proved a failure, and was withdrawn from the stage. The reason for its failure is plain enough; the play as we have it is, by common consent, only in part the work of Shakespeare. Of the two theories to account for this, (a) that Shakespeare revised the work of an inferior playwright, (b) that Shakespeare left some fragmentary scenes of a play on Timon which were patched up for presentation by an inferior hand, the second seems the more acceptable. It is hard to believe that Shakespeare at the very height of his power turned over to his fellows a revised play so incoherent, inconsistent, and unplayable as this. On the other hand we may well believe that his fellows, finding among his papers some splendid dramatic scenes, felt warranted in having them patched up by one of their working playwrights, perhaps by Middleton, who as we shall see certainly touched up *Macbeth*. At any rate Heminges and Condell felt that there was enough of Shakespeare's work in the play to warrant their including it in the Folio where it appeared in print for the first time. The text is so bad as to suggest that it was printed from a much revised manuscript.

There is no external evidence to fix the date of *Timon*. Internal evidence of metre, style, and temper connects it rather closely with *King Lear*. Perhaps the best guess that we can make is that Shakespeare shortly after his tremendous effort on *Lear* began to write another play in something of the same style, planning to provide Burbage with the rôle of a misanthrope as eloquent in his curses as Lear in his ravings. After writing certain scattered scenes—his hand is plainer in the last acts than in the beginning—he laid it aside. Perhaps he was weary of the task; possibly he realized as he worked on it the undramatic nature of the Timon story. It is an interesting fact that several playwrights at different times in different countries have tried to dramatize this theme and that not one of them has made a good play out of it. For once Shakespeare seems to have erred in his choice of a subject; but he was wise enough to see his mistake and abandon his unfinished work.

The chief source of *Timon* is Plutarch's *Life of Antony*. Some hints were caught also from Lucian's dialogue, *Timon the Misanthrope*, which Shakespeare may have read in translation. An old play written ca. 1600 but not printed till the last century contains the incident of the mock banquet which occurs in no other version of the story. Shakespeare may have seen this play, or even heard of it, and lifted from it this effective bit of business.

It contains some passages of magnificent poetry as the great curse (IV, 1) or Timon's farewell to the world:

> Come not to me again: but say to Athens,
> Timon hath made his everlasting mansion
> Upon the beached verge of the salt flood;
> Who once a day with his embossed froth
> The turbulent surge shall cover.

It would be an interesting task for the young student of Shakespeare to read through this play and mark the passages in which he seems to catch the unmistakable voice of the master of dramatic poetry.[1]

Macbeth can be dated with some degree of certainty in 1606. The subject may have been suggested to Shakespeare by a show presented to King James at Oxford, August 27, 1605, in which three youths dressed as sybils recited some Latin verses containing the old prophecy that Banquo's descendants should be kings. As James claimed descent from Banquo, he was naturally gratified by this performance. It has even been suggested, though without any proof, that the letter James is said to have written Shakespeare contained a request that the poet write a play on this subject.

The text has come down to us only in the Folio version. It is the shortest of all Shakespeare's plays except the *Comedy of Errors* and the confusion and corruption of the text shows that it was printed from a manuscript that had been cut and revised. Unfortunately it was shortened in order to interpolate some spectacular and musical effects; the rôle of Hecate, the songs in III, 5 and IV, 1 and a speech by the first witch in this last scene (ll. 125-132) along with the dance of the witches are interpolations. They are probably the work of Middleton who was writing for Shakespeare's company before the publication of the Folio. The songs in question, mentioned by title in *Macbeth*, appear in full in Middleton's play *The Witch*.

The source of *Macbeth* is Holinshed's *Chronicle* familiar to Shakespeare from the time of his English history plays. Holinshed's account contains the story of the prophecy of the witches to Macbeth and Banquo and various other incidents which Shakespeare uses in the play. For the actual murder of Duncan, however, he turned over a few pages of Holinshed and read the tale of the murder of King Duff by Donwald, a story far more to his purpose than the true account of Duncan's death, since Duncan was killed in battle by Macbeth, whereas Duff was murdered in his sleep by his host and subject acting on the instigation of his wife. It is proof of Shakespeare's now complete freedom of treatment

[1] For a full discussion of the problem of this play see my article in the publications of the British Shakespeare Association, 1923.

that he should have dared to depart so far from historical fact. He would hardly have felt free to do so at an earlier period.

The "supernatural soliciting" of the witches is part of the old story, but Shakespeare has made it an essential feature of the play; the first scene in which the witches prepare to meet Macbeth is his own invention, as is Macbeth's visit to them in the caldron scene. Original with Shakespeare also is the great scene in which the ghost of Banquo rises to appal his murderer at the royal feast. Shakespeare no doubt knew that a play about witches, ghosts and prophecies would please his royal master, but he had more in mind than that. *Macbeth* is essentially the tragedy of a man who wittingly does evil, sells himself to the devil whose servants and representatives are the witches of the play, suffers the agonies of remorse without repentance, and meets his just fate at the hands of the man he had most wronged. The supernatural element is the very atmosphere that pervades *Macbeth* and lends the play its characteristic tone and color.

One gets the impression that *Macbeth* was written in headlong haste by Shakespeare. It shows no such marks of careful revision as does *Hamlet,* nor such evidence of planned construction as *Othello.* The great scenes are in Shakespeare's most splendid style; others scattered through the play are tame and colorless; the long dialogue between Macduff and Malcolm in the fourth act taken almost literally from Holinshed is so dull that one wonders why it was not cut by the first reviser as in all modern performances. The metre shows signs of experimentation with blank verse looking forward to the license Shakespeare allowed himself with this form in later plays. *Macbeth* is the last of the great tragedies, but one feels in reading it after the others that Shakespeare was beginning to weaken; the mental and emotional strain under which he had labored for the past five or six years must have been more than any mortal could endure. We shall see in his later plays that he turned away from tragedy, as about 1599 he had turned away from history; his best work in the tragic field was already done.

Antony and Cleopatra was entered in the Stationers' Register on May 10, 1608, but did not appear in print until its inclusion in the Folio, 1623. There is reason to believe that it was written in 1606 or early in the following year.

There is but one source for the play, Plutarch's *Life of Antony* in North's translation. Shakespeare follows his source more closely than in his former Roman play *Julius Cæsar.* Not only does he at times adopt the very words of North, but the scenario itself, the arrangement and succession of scenes, particularly in the last acts, follows the order of the source. Yet Shakespeare is not slavishly dramatizing a history; again and again when he is versifying North's prose he adds a phrase of his own which glorifies the passage.

In form *Antony and Cleopatra* is a chronicle play. Shakespeare's reversion to this older type of drama shows, we may believe, his inability or unwillingness to concentrate as he had been doing on the harder tasks of tragedy. The play is a magnificent panorama of struggle for power in the Roman world and adds to this the struggle between ambition and love in the breast of one of the two masters of that world. Yet one scene, almost demanded by the theme, that in which Antony should make the tragic decision to return to Cleopatra, Shakespeare never troubled to compose. In his broad treatment with its shifting scenes he gains an effect unparalleled in any other dramatic version of this theme. Shakespeare's Antony is a heroic figure, though not exactly a noble character, and his fall and death followed by the death of the woman who caused his fall lift a chronicle play into the realm of tragedy.

In the matter of characterization Shakespeare concentrated in this play upon these two figures. Apart from them with the exception of Enobarbus, a realist whose ironic commentary recalls at times that of King Lear's Fool, and the clown of the last act, one of Shakespeare's homely country folk introduced rather incongruously into Cleopatra's palace, there is hardly a fully realized man or woman among the many characters who crowd the stage. Here as in the matter of construction we seem to feel a slackening of Shakespeare's powers as a playwright.

The peculiar glory of *Antony and Cleopatra* is its poetry. It is as if Shakespeare renouncing for a time the harder labor of the constructive dramatist had given full rein to the course of his poetic genius. Coleridge characterized it perfectly when he spoke of the "happy valiancy" of the style. Moreover this flow of poetry in *Antony and Cleopatra* is not lyrical as in earlier plays; there is no interruption of the action for the insertion of a little poem as in *Romeo and Juliet;* it is strictly adapted to the dramatic dialogue. It is not too much to say that the verse of *Romeo and Juliet,* like the passion of the lovers, is that of youth; the poetry of *Antony and Cleopatra,* like the passion that dominates its hero, is that of the grown man. It is the veil of poetry, sensuous, glowing, highly figurative, and truly dramatic, which Shakespeare throws over the story of Antony and his mistress that adds glamour and romance to the tale and makes us believe for a moment that for such a love as theirs the world was indeed well lost.

Coriolanus certainly follows *Antony and Cleopatra* and may be dated late in 1608 or early in 1609. It was printed for the first time in the Folio, 1623. Here too Shakespeare found the source of this play in North's *Plutarch,* and as in *Antony and Cleopatra* he followed his source closely, more than once simply versifying the prose of the original. On the other hand he deals more freely with the matter of his source, suppressing, condensing, and arranging to suit his dramatic aims; certain scenes such as those in which the hero reluctantly seeks the "voices" of the people, or withstands the pressure of his family and friends to humble himself to the populace, are Shakespeare's addition to the story. Certain characters, especially that of Menenius, are practically Shakespeare's creation.

There are some aspects of *Coriolanus* that resemble the chronicle play. In the first act there are the alarums and excursions, single combats and pitched battles, of the old histories; but after this prologue Shakespeare sets himself resolutely to molding the narrative into strict dramatic form. He does this by centering the whole action about the person of his hero and by revealing in scene after scene how the character of Coriolanus brings about his inevitable fall. The play has too often been interpreted from a modern point of view and used as a text to proclaim Shakespeare's hatred of democracy. Of democracy in the modern sense of the word Shakespeare could by the nature of things have no conception and therefore could not hate it. As a matter of fact the play might quite as well be interpreted as a dramatic denunciation of the aristocratic temper. Coriolanus is a thorough aristocrat, brave, proud, insolent, incapable of flattery, but capable under pressure, as aristocrats have been since his day, of turning his arms against his country. Like Antony he is a heroic figure, but he is the least amiable of Shakespeare's heroes. He shares with Lear an ungovernable temper, but unlike Lear never learns the folly of his rage, and at the very end it is a last outburst of well-nigh insane anger that precipitates the catastrophe.

Unlike *Antony and Cleopatra* there is little of Shakespeare's finest poetry in this play; he seems here to be subordinating poetic expression to strict and even severe dramatic treatment; rhetoric and eloquence take the place of fancy and imagination. None of Shakespeare's tragedies lacks so completely his characteristic breathings of romance; the atmosphere is realistic, and, except as relieved by touches of humor, cold and hard. *Coriolanus* is Shakespeare's farewell to tragedy; the tragic temper, the sympathy with the tragic hero, the poetic rendering of the tragic theme, are perceptibly waning in this fine play. The time had come for Shakespeare to turn to other fields.

A brief summary of this period may serve to show something of the development of Shakespeare's power as a tragic poet. The bitter comedies of the early years of this period may be disregarded here; they serve only to show how far his mind had swung away from the joyous mirth and gay romance of the earlier work. The series of the tragedies begins calmly and gravely with *Julius Cæsar.* This play, almost as much history as tragedy, is followed by *Hamlet,* Shakespeare's most complex and subtle drama, but one where he was definitely limited by the conditions under which he worked. In *Othello* he attains his full height as a master of his art, in construction, in characterization, and in dramatic expression. *Lear,* less nearly perfect perhaps than *Othello,* is yet a greater work, more universal, more significant, more magnificently tragic. This is the mountain peak. The fragmentary *Timon* shows already something like a collapse; ground is regained in the feverish and unequal tragedy of *Macbeth,* and then the end approaches. *Antony and Cleopatra* and *Coriolanus* close the period, neither of them for all their beauty, eloquence, and power a match for the earlier plays, and with *Pericles* we see the transition to the tragi-comedies of the final period.

Part IV

Pericles, Prince of Tyre (ca. 1607-8) is the play that links the tragic period to that of the comedies. Its date is uncertain. A play called *Pericles* was entered in the Stationers' Register on May 20, 1608. This may be Shakespeare's play but it is more probably an old one of the same name.

It is quite certain that the *Pericles* now included in the Shakespeare canon is his re-writing in part, and only in part, of an older play, possibly by George Wilkins a very minor playwright of the day. In 1608 Wilkins published a prose version of the story, which was advertised as "the true history of the play as it was lately presented." Possibly the explanation is that Wilkins wrote a play with this title for Shakespeare's company, that Shakespeare saw that something more could be made of the theme than the bungling Wilkins had accomplished and so consented to touch it up. He let the first two acts stand almost unchanged, grew interested as he went on, and from the beginning of the third act practically rewrote the whole, though he retained some of the old choruses and dumb shows.

Whether Wilkins was pleased or not we cannot say, but as the play was immensely successful he tried to turn an honest penny by publishing what we should call a "novelized" version. The publisher who had entered *Pericles* in 1608 never printed his version, but in 1609 another bookseller got hold of a "stolen and surreptitious" copy and straightway printed it. It sold so well that he got out a second edition in the same year; a third appeared in 1611, and others followed. The play was not included in the first Folio; probably the editors thought Shakespeare's part in it was too slight to warrant ascribing it to him. It was added to the third Folio, 1664, along with six other plays, none of which have any claim to Shakespearean authorship. Later editors alternately accepted or rejected it. Tennyson once said to a scholar who questioned whether Shakespeare wrote any of it: "Oh, that won't do. He wrote all the part relating to the birth and recovery of Marina and the recovery of Thaisa," and Tennyson's verdict is now generally accepted.

The source of *Pericles* is the medieval legend of *Apollonius of Tyre*, a legend which took on fresh life in the Renaissance with its delight in tales of voyages, shipwrecks, and adventure. The great popularity of the play shows the revived taste of the theatre-going public for romantic drama as the vogue of realistic comedy began to wane. Shakespeare's revision of *Pericles* was his first experiment in this genre and his success may have been one of the reasons that impelled him to devote the few years remaining of his working life to romantic tragi-comedy.

Pericles is a poor enough play; Shakespeare's revision left the absurd meandering construction unchanged. Yet it contains some lovely poetry and the recognition scene between father and daughter (V, i) points in both style and temper to the best work of his last period.

Cymbeline (1609-10) opens the last period of Shakespeare's work. It is a romantic tale dramatized in loose and careless form, dealing in part with the theme of marital jealousy which in *Othello* had furnished matter for tragedy, but handling it in such fashion as to bring about a happy ending. This play resembles Beaumont and Fletcher's *Philaster* and the suggestion has been made that Shakespeare was following a fashion set by these young playwrights. This suggestion has been considered above (p. 24) and need not be discussed here. There is only one text of *Cymbeline*, that of the Folio.

There is a double source for *Cymbeline*, the story of the wager laid by Postumus and its well-nigh fatal consequences, and the pseudo-historic matter of the wars of the Britons and and the Romans. The first of these comes from a tale in the *Decameron* (ii, 9) which itself goes back to a French original, the *Roman de la Violette*. The second comes from Holinshed's account of the legendary kings of early Britain. Shakespeare has cleverly woven these two threads together by making the slandered lady the daughter of a British king and using a British victory over the Romans to bring about the revelation of her innocence. Hints from various other sources have been picked up and worked into the play which interests mainly by its lively and varying action, its surprises, and, indeed, its sensationalism. Like all the plays of this period *Cymbeline* contains a good deal of the spectacular. We have not only scenes at court and pitched battles, but in the last act a masque-like spectacle—"Jupiter descends in thunder and lightning, sitting upon an eagle; he throws a thunderbolt"—which must have taxed the resources of the Globe and Blackfriars.

Cymbeline is not one of the best of Shakespeare's plays, but it contains one of his most lovely characters, Imogen, the perfect wife. It has always been a favorite with poets; Swinburne closes his *Study of Shakespeare* with an impassioned eulogy of this his favorite play, and Tennyson died with his copy of Shakespeare open at a page of *Cymbeline*.

The Winter's Tale can be dated fairly accurately. It was originally licensed by Sir George Buc, who became Master of the Revels in August, 1610, and it was played at Court on November 5, 1611. Somewhere between these dates it must lie, probably early in 1611, since the dance of the satyrs in the fourth act seems an imitation of a similar feature in Jonson's *Masque of Oberon,* performed at Court on January first of that year. The only text is that of the Folio.

The source of this play is Robert Greene's pastoral novel *Pandosto* (1588) reprinted in 1607 as *Dorastus and Fawnia.* This later edition may have come into Shakespeare's hands some time in his last period and suggested to him the composition of a romantic pastoral drama. Shakespeare deals very freely with his source, altering names, changing scenes, and particularly eliminating the death of the slandered queen and the suicide of her remorseful husband. Such tragic incidents he felt were out of keeping with the tone of the play that he was planning. He did not, however, disdain to delight his audience by having a bear chase a minor character and—off-stage—tear him to pieces.

The Winter's Tale is, perhaps, Shakespeare's masterpiece of tragi-comedy. It lacks unity of action, to be sure; there is a gap of sixteen years between the third and the fourth acts, and in the last two the interest shifts from Hermione, supposed dead, to her daughter, Perdita. But the play has all the characteristics of tragi-comedy: intrigue, disguise, suspense, and surprise, and all most dexterously handled. Fault has been found with the causeless jealousy of the king; but to have given him grounds for his suspicion would have been to write *Othello* over again. Leontes is jealous for no other reason than to start the action, and his outbreak of jealousy in the second scene starts it with a rush to the complete surprise of the reader or spectator. In the midst of the delightful scene of the shepherd's festival the revelation of the disguised Polixenes and his denunciation of his son's love for the fair shepherdess give another startling change of tone. The last and best surprise of all is at the very end when the statue of the dead queen comes to life and Hermione descends to embrace her penitent husband and to bless her restored daughter. This scene is wholly Shakespeare's invention; and of its superb effect upon the stage those can testify who have had the good fortune to see the beautiful Mary Anderson in the rôle of Hermione.

Fine characterization, as a rule, is not expected in tragi-comedy where the plot governs the characters; but in this play Shakespeare lavishes his skill upon such figures as the noble queen, the faithful shrew Paulina, the old shepherd, and above all upon Autolycus, the most delightful rogue in literature. One feels that Shakespeare was happy when he wrote *The Winter's Tale;* perhaps part of his happiness came from his return to Stratford. Rural sights and sounds, country folk, and country customs give a pleasant background of realism to a romantic tragi-comedy.

The Tempest cannot have been written before the autumn of 1610 and may date early in 1611. It was performed at Court on November first of that year. It was printed for the first time in the Folio.

The theme of a shipwreck on an enchanted island was certainly suggested to Shakespeare by a series of events that had aroused great interest in London. In June of 1609 a fleet set sail from England for the new colony of Virginia. It was scattered by a storm and the flagship was wrecked on a reef off Bermuda. The crew reached shore safely and spent the winter in what was then known as "the Isle of Devils." They built two small ships and in May, 1610, sailed across to Virginia. In England they had been given up for lost and the news of their escape was hailed with joy. Several accounts of the shipwreck and of the islands appeared late in 1610 which Shakespeare certainly used, as he also seems to have used a manuscript account not printed till after his death. Kipling has made the interesting if fanciful suggestion hat Shakespeare got his information from a drunken sailor of the shipwrecked crew whom he later introduced into the play as Stephano, who swam ashore upon a butt of sack.

No direct source has been found for the main plot of the exiled duke turned magician who gets his enemies into his power by magic only to forgive them, and who marries off his daughter to his chief enemy's son. Shakespeare may have picked up hints for this story from various sources; he has woven them very artfully into a background suggested by the Bermuda voyage.

The Tempest is a unique play; there is nothing quite like it in all the rest of Shakespeare's work. The character of Prospero, especially in his farewell to his art, so strongly suggests the poet-dramatist about to retire from the stage that the whole play has been interpreted as an allegory. This is far from likely, though the temptation to read between the lines is strong indeed. It has been called a masque adapted for the stage, but it is rather a play which includes a formal marriage masque. Alone among Shakespeare's plays it preserves the unities of time—the action lasts about four hours—and place—after the first scene the action is all on the island. It is as if Shakespeare after defying the unities in *The Winter's Tale* amused himself by showing Jonson and other classical critics that he too could obey the classic rules.

Essentially *The Tempest* is what we would call "a good show." It has enough of incident to interest the spectator, with a charming love-story, with characters good and bad, serious and comic, and with plenty of spectacle in the way of songs, dances, hunting dogs, and "quaint devices." The poetry, the serene wisdom, are Shakespeare's additions to the "show," but such a glorious addition as to outweigh at least in a reader's mind all else in the play. It is a drama of forgiveness, of reconciliation, and of peace, a beautiful sunset after the storms of the tragic period.

There are two other plays of this period that are only in part by Shakespeare. The first of these is the spectacular historical pageant, *Henry VIII* [1613]. It is included in the Folio and was long accepted as Shakespeare's own unassisted work. Recent scholarship has proved beyond all reasonable doubt that about half the play was written by Fletcher, at this time succeeding Shakespeare as the chief dramatist for the King's Men. The evidence is internal and rests upon Fletcher's unmistakable stylistic and metrical idiosyncrasies. A comparison of one of his scenes, II, i, for instance, with a Shakespearean scene, II, iv, will show such a difference in diction, rhythm, and treatment of the blank verse as to convince any unprejudiced reader that the scenes are by two authors, and any reader acquainted with Fletcher's style that he is one of them.

Scholars are now generally agreed that Shakespeare wrote I, i, ii; II, iii, iv; III, ii, ll. 1-203; and V, i. Shakespeare starts most of the various themes in this loosely constructed play and Fletcher finishes them. This division, it may be noted, gives Fletcher some of the best known scenes of the play, including Wolsey's famous farewell to greatness, III, ii, ll. 350–372. It has been remarked that if Fletcher wrote the scenes ascribed to him in this play he did better work here than anywhere else. This is quite possible, for he was writing under the influence of Shakespeare and no doubt anxious to put his best foot forward as Shakespeare's successor with the company.

Henry VIII cannot be judged by comparison with any of the earlier histories; strictly speaking, it is less a drama than a succession of scenes dealing with striking events in the king's reign interspersed with a great deal of spectacle. This may be due in part to the manner of the collaboration, in part to the desire of the company to stage a magnificent pageant, for which by the way they charged an unusually high price of admission, one shilling [Prologue 1. 12]. Probably the company begged Shakespeare, now residing at Stratford, to furnish them with a play of this sort, that he consented to write certain scenes, and allowed Fletcher to finish it off. The one character that is his throughout is that of Queen Katherine, and Dr. Johnson's comment "Shakespeare's genius comes in and goes out with Katherine" still holds good.

As a brilliant stage spectacle with several good acting parts *Henry VIII* has held the stage intermittently from Shakespeare's day down to the time of Irving and Beerbohm

Tree; but we can learn little from it as to Shakespeare's art or the point to which it had developed by 1613.

The second of these plays, *The Two Noble Kinsmen* (1613), has a curious history. It was not included in the Folio and did not appear in print until 1634, eighteen years after Shakespeare's death and nine years after that of Fletcher. Both these names appeared upon the title-page of the first edition which advertises the play as "presented at the Black-friars with great applause; written by the memorable worthies of their time; Mr. John Fletcher and Mr. William Shakespeare Gent." In spite of this title-page the play was long regarded as the work of Fletcher and was included in the second Folio (1679) of the Beaumont and Fletcher plays.

It was not until the time of the Romantic critics that voices were raised to defend Shakespeare's share in this play; both Lamb and Coleridge were certain that Shakespeare had a hand in it and for the last hundred years or so there has been a general agreement, though by no means unanimous, that the play represents a collaboration of Shakespeare and Fletcher. Certain scenes—the greater part of Act I, the first scene of Act III, and the magnificent invocations of Act V, i—are unmistakably Shakespeare's; others appear to be his only in part; throughout the play there seem to be signs of Fletcher as the last writer, welding scattered scenes together and writing little patchs of his characteristic verse at the beginning and end of Shakespearean scenes. This may perhaps explain the exclusion of the play from the Folio; Fletcher, then at the height of his popularity, may have consented to surrender his claim to *Henry VIII* on condition that *The Two Noble Kinsmen* should be regarded as essentially his work.

The source of the play is Chaucer's *Knight's Tale.* On the whole the play follows its source rather closely, but, naturally, reshapes the narrative in dramatic form. In spite of some superb poetry by Shakespeare one can hardly say that the authors have improved upon their source. There is an evident intention to transform the tragic tale of Chaucer into a tragi-comedy in the later Elizabethan manner. In particular the death of Arcite and his farewell to Palemon, the climax of Chaucer's poem, is hastily glossed over in the play; the death of a main character was out of place in a tragi-comedy. Yet in spite of alterations, spectacular interpolations, muddled construction, and confused characterization—all due, we may suppose, to Fletcher—the play is pleasant reading and contains many lines of splendid poetry. One can only regret that Shakespeare was unable for one reason or another to complete a play which he evidently began in the best style of his final period.

A bitter controversy has raged in recent years over a play, more especially over one scene of a play, that bears the name of *Sir Thomas More.* It is one of the few original manuscripts of Elizabethan plays that are still preserved and was not printed till 1844. There is no reason to believe that it was ever played and rather good reason why it should not have been. The original author, Anthony Munday, was rash enough to introduce certain scenes dealing with a London riot provoked by the insolence of alien residents. Elizabeth and her councillors were eager to promote the immigration of such industrious craftsmen as French and Flemish Protestants, and quick to suppress any threat directed against them. Accordingly her Master of Revels, Edward Tilney, returned this play when it was sent to him for his license with a sharp warning "Leave out the insurrection wholly and the cause thereof," besides marking various passages for alteration. To have followed his directions would have been to destroy the play, so it was apparently laid aside for some years when a group of writers was called on to revise and write new scenes for it with the hope that this time it might pass the censor.

One hand in the five that contributed the additions has been identified on good authority with that of Shakespeare as preserved in his signatures. This hand contributed one scene so markedly superior in thought and expression to the rest of the play that it was suspected to be the work of Shakespeare long before a study of the handwriting was undertaken. This scene deals with the climax of the riot and contains More's address to the rebels which persuades them to submit. It is hard to believe that any Elizabethan author except Shakespeare was capable at once of such humorous sympathy with an unruly mob and such vigorous insistence on order and authority as this speech shows. If we accept this scene as Shakespeare's, as most scholars are inclined to do, we must imagine him lending a friendly hand to a group of dramatists in an effort to achieve the impossible. For Tilney's orders were not complied with and consequently the play remained unstaged. When it was first written and when the additions were made is quite uncertain. The style and metre of the Shakespearean scene point to a date midway in his second period, ca. 1595-96.

Of the many plays ascribed at various times in whole or in part to Shakespeare there is, with possibly a single exception, none that deserves consideration. This exception, *Edward III,* contains a romantic episode of the wooing of the Countess of Salisbury by the young king, which has some slight resemblance to the style of Shakespeare in his first period, and contains a line,

Lilies that fester smell far worse than weeds.

that appears in one of his sonnets. But his sonnets, as we know, were circulating in manuscript at the time this play appeared, 1596, and it is not impossible that the unknown author simply lifted the line to adorn his play. On the whole the episode in question does not carry with it such conviction of Shakespeare's authorship as does the scene in *Sir Thomas More.*

The last plays mentioned need not be seriously considered in a study of the development of Shakespeare's art. In *Sir Thomas More,* indeed, we seem to catch a glimpse of his mind; in *Henry VIII* we see one of his strong yet pathetic characters; and in *The Two Noble Kinsmen* we find some lofty poetry. But Shakespeare's course as a playwright was run before he agreed to assist his young successor Fletcher in the composition of a couple of plays for the Globe. His last active years had been devoted to the writing, probably at his ease in Stratford and with a certain careless abandon, of the delightful trio of his so-called romances.

XI

THE POEMS AND SONNETS

SHAKESPEARE was a poet before he became a playwright and there was a period in his life when he was better known as the author of his first long poem than of any of his plays. Except for the *Sonnets* his poems are little read nowadays, but no account of Shakespeare's work would be complete without a discussion of his two long narrative poems, so characteristic are they both of the writer and of his age.

Venus and Adonis was entered in the Stationers' Register on April 18, 1593, and published early in that year by Richard Field, like Shakespeare a Stratford boy, who had come to London and set up there as printer and publisher. The first edition is so carefully printed, so free from the errors that mar the early editions of the plays, that there is good reason to believe that Shakespeare read the proof himself, a thing we can be sure he never troubled to do for the plays. There was a good reason for this painstaking care; the poem was to be a gift to a noble lord, the young Earl of Southampton whose favor and patronage Shakespeare was seeking. In the dedication prefixed to the poem Shakespeare apologizes for dedicating his "unpolished lines" to his lordship, calls the poem "the first heir of my invention," and promises, if the work pleases his patron, to honor him "with some graver labour," a promise which he fulfilled a year later in his *Lucrece.* The phrase "first heir of my invention" has sometimes been understood to mean that this poem was the first thing Shakespeare ever wrote, and a pleasant fancy has suggested that he brought it up to town from Stratford. This is most unlikely; *Venus and Adonis* is in the full tide of the fashionable narrative and erotic poetry of the day and full of hints from poems that Shakespeare could have known only after he came to London. It was, however, the first of his writings to be given to the world, and Shakespeare no doubt regarded his plays, especially his early experimental plays, as matter for the stage rather than for the press.

The poem was instantly and immensely successful; a whole series of editions in quarto and octavo form followed the first; there were some sixteen issues before 1640. The references to *Venus and Adonis* in contemporary literature are constant; it became indeed a sort of *vade mecum* for amorous young gentlemen and wanton ladies.

The source of the story is found in Ovid's *Metamorphoses.* Ovid was evidently Shakespeare's favorite Latin poet; he had studied him in school and re-read him not only in the original but in Golding's translation (1567), some lines from which he paraphrases in a famous speech in *The Tempest* (V, i, 33-50). The two Latin lines prefixed as a motto to *Venus and Adonis* come from Ovid's *Amores.* There is no trace in Ovid's version of the reluctant youth wooed by the goddess of love; but elsewhere in Ovid Shakespeare found a story of the passionate wooing of a boy, Hermaphroditus, by a nymph, Salmacis, which he skillfully blended with the Adonis theme. Apparently he picked up suggestions for this fusion from various contemporary poems which represented Adonis coldly rejecting the advances of Venus. Here, as in his plays, it is not so much Shakespeare's power of invention as his skill in combining and transforming his material that compels our admiration.

Venus and Adonis is written in iambic pentameter, rhyming *ababcc,* like the last six lines of a Shakespearean sonnet. This was a common verse form of the day; Spenser had used it in his *Shepheards Calendar,* and Lodge, the author of *Rosalynde,* in a long and rather incoherent erotic poem, *Glaucus and Scylla;* but no poet of the day, not even Spenser, handled it with such ease and grace or shaped it into such a form of beauty.

Like Marlowe's *Hero and Leander,* which Shakespeare must have read in manuscript, *Venus and Adonis* is a narrative poem. The story is well told with a beginning, middle, and end, but it is not the story that makes the poem. The dress in which Shakespeare has clothed the tale is, perhaps, more lovely than the tale itself, and this dress is woven of various threads. We have first what one may call the landscape pieces, a landscape which is that of Shakespeare's England rather than of Greece or the Orient. This landscape is animated with English beasts and birds, the hunted hare, the hunting dogs, the grisly boar, the lark, the nightingale, and fragrant with English flowers. Upon this more or less realistic background are super-imposed the "discourses," the set speeches of Venus and her beloved. Here, too, Shakespeare is writing quite in the fashion of the day, as Lyly did when he used the story of Euphues as a peg on which to hang long discourses of every sort. The set speech, the formal plea, for and against such a topic as love or friendship, seems strange and unreal to us. It was not so to Shakespeare, and it is impossible to deny the grace and eloquence of his "discourses." Finally and most important, we have what may be called the dominant theme of the poem, Beauty, the incarnation of Beauty in the beloved, and the desire to perpetuate beauty by the bodily union of two lovers. This is a characteristic Renaissance conception, but there is nothing like it in the various erotic poems of Shakespeare's day. It is a theme that he made his own and was to treat more fully with greater power and beauty in the *Sonnets.*

A book called *The Ravishment of Lucrece* was entered in the Stationers' Register on May 9, 1594 by Master Harrison who, a month later, bought from Field the copyright of *Venus and Adonis.* He engaged Field to print it and it appeared in 1594 under the simpler title of *Lucrece.* Field did a good printer's job with *Lucrece,* as he had done with the earlier poem, and once more we may believe that Shakespeare read the proof. The second poem, like the first, was dedicated to Southampton.

Lucrece was no doubt the "graver labour" which Shakespeare had promised his friend a year before. It never achieved the signal popularity of *Venus and Adonis,* but something like eight editions were published before 1640, and the wiser sort, as Harvey noted, were pleased to see that the young poet had abandoned erotic poetry to strike a deeper note.

The story of Lucretia, told in Ovid's *Fasti* in verse and in Livy's prose, was well known in the Middle Ages; Chaucer enrolled the heroine among the martyrs of love in his *Legend of Good Women.* All these versions were known to Shakespeare, who used them as he saw fit; from Livy he must have drawn the straightforward historical "Argument" prefixed to the poem.

Lucrece is written in iambic pentameter rhyming *ababbcc*. This is the so-called Rhyme Royal stanza; it should really be known as the Chaucerian, for the old poet had used it again and again, with special power and beauty in his *Troilus*. It had come down to Shakespeare with a tradition of dignity and distinction, a metre "very grave and stately," an Elizabethan critic called it. Shakespeare's contemporary, Samuel Daniel, had used it in his *Complaint of Rosamond* (1592), and it may be that the grave beauty of this work suggested to Shakespeare the use of this stanzaic form.

It is an interesting fact that Shakespeare was at work on this poem at the very time that he was engaged in revising *Titus Andronicus*. There are several points of resemblance between play and poem, particularly in the manner in which a veil of poetry is thrown over a tale of brutal outrage. It is possible, though of course not certain, that the rape of Lavinia in the play suggested to Shakespeare a narrative poem on the famous story of Lucretia.

Like *Venus and Adonis, Lucrece* purports to be a narrative poem, but the narrative is even less essential in this than in the earlier work. Shakespeare omits the interesting incidents of the rivalry between the husbands at camp as to the virtues of their wives at home, and the visit of the lords to Rome with the winning of the wager by Lucretia's husband. At the close of the poem, too, he hurries over the consequences of her suicide, the revolt of the people, and the expulsion of the Tarquins. What interested him was not so much the story, but its emotional values, the struggle in the heart of Sextus between shame and lust, and the bitter anguish of Lucrece after the perpetration of the outrage. These are in their essence dramatic themes belonging rather to tragedy than to narrative poetry; and, as we have already seen, Shakespeare was not yet prepared to handle high themes of tragedy. The situation, the conflicting emotions of Sextus before the deed, are not unlike those of Macbeth before the murder of Duncan, but what a difference in the writer's grasp and power between the diffuse argument pro and con of Sextus and the brief soliloquy of Macbeth, where every word goes home.

Lucrece finds fewer readers today than *Venus and Adonis*. To our minds the poem drags interminably; to appreciate it properly we should strive to put ourselves back in the mood of the Renaissance reader and enjoy with him the "conceits," the *sententiæ*, and the eloquence of the long tirades. It is in these tirades, the long set speeches that correspond to the "discourses" of *Venus and Adonis*, that the poet has expended all his strength, and they abound in lovely single lines as in the apostrophe to Time

> Thou ceaseless lackey to Eternity

who delights

> To feed oblivion with decay of things.

To enjoy *Lucrece* one should read the poem slowly, a little at a time, with an eye open to catch and appreciate at their worth Shakespeare's felicities of diction, felicities that often link it with his supreme lyrical expression in the *Sonnets*.

On May 20, 1609, Thomas Thorpe, a not very reputable publisher, entered in the Stationers' Register a book called "Shakespeares sonnettes." He published it the same year, appending to the sonnets an elegiac poem, *The Lover's Complaint*. We may disregard this last; there is no warrant for ascribing it to Shakespeare except the statement of an unscrupulous publisher.

The text is not too good; there are misprints and evident corruptions, enough to show that Shakespeare had not authorized publication and read the proof as he had done for the poems. There is reason to believe that Thorpe secured various manuscripts in which Shakespeare's sonnets were circulating, arranged them as best he could, and gave them to the world. The book was a "stolen and surreptitious copy"; but we may well be grateful to Thorpe, for without his enterprise we might never have known some of the loveliest sonnets in the English language.

Instead of a dedication by the poet to his patron, Thorpe wrote his own dedication in terms that have puzzled readers ever since: *To the onlie begetter of these insuing sonnets Mr. W. H. all happinesse and that eternity promised by our ever living poet wisheth the well-wishing adventurer in setting forth. T. T.* It is best to take the word "begetter" in the sense of inspirer, that is, the friend who was the inspiration of most of the sonnets. Evidently Thorpe knew, or thought he knew, the identity of the friend whom he addresses as Mr. W. H. and for whom he wishes the immortality of fame that the sonnets so often promise the friend. If Thorpe really knew, it seems a pity that he hid his knowledge behind the mysterious initials. Had he spoken out he would have saved the world of scholarship many volumes of weary controversy.

Thorpe's enterprise in securing and publishing the sonnets was not rewarded. It is interesting to note that while the poems were very successful, the volume of sonnets, so greatly superior as poetry, fell almost dead from the press. No second edition was called for until 1640, when they were included in the volume called *Poems Written by Wil. Shakespeare Gent.*, where they were fortified, so to speak, by the addition of other poems, including the well-known elegy on Shakespeare by the young John Milton. Little interest was shown in them during the late seventeenth and the eighteenth century. Only when students of Shakespeare began to suspect that some passionate secret of his life was concealed in these poems did attention revert to them. Even down to the present there has been more discussion—for the most part futile—of the "mystery of the sonnets" than appreciation of the poetry they contain.

It is harder to date the *Sonnets* than it is to date one of Shakespeare's plays. In fact, it is impossible to fix on a year or two in which they were written, for the simple reason that they seem to have been written over a period of years, three at least, at various times. Probably they may be regarded as occasional verses or verse-letters sent from time to time by Shakespeare to his friend or to his mistress. Yet it is possible to set certain limits within which the greater part of them were in all likelihood composed.

A comparison of the sonnets with the poems and the plays goes to show a large number of correspondences in thought and expression between them and the poems and the plays up to 1594-95; a much smaller number with plays after 1596-97. This internal evidence is strengthened by what we know of the vogue of the sonnet, especially of the sonnet-sequence in the 1590's. In 1591 Sidney's *Astrophel and Stella*, which had been circulating in manuscript, got into print. Sidney's fame, the romantic story enshrined in this sequence, and the beauty of the poetry, gave the work an instant and great success. It set a fashion and all the poetasters and many of the poets of the day broke out in like fashion. Constable, Daniel, Drayton, all composed sonnet-sequences; Spenser's lovely *Amoretti* appeared in 1595. It would be strange if Shakespeare, always responsive to the fashions of the day, had himself not experimented in this form. In fact, we know that he did; his early plays, *Love's Labour's Lost* and *Romeo and Juliet,* contain sonnets, and in 1598 Meres spoke of "mellifluous and honey-tongued Shakespeare witness his . . . sugred sonnets among his private friends." Evidently by 1598 Shakespeare had not only begun to write sonnets but copies of his poems in this form were circulating among his friends, yet not so privately as to escape the notice of the inquiring Meres. It is safe to assume that most of the sonnets were composed somewhere between 1594 and 1598; some, it may be, later; one indeed, number 107, has been thought to allude to the death of Elizabeth in 1603.

Shakespeare followed the fashion, but as usual he followed it in his own way. His sonnets are not a conventional sonnet-sequence; they bear no title, they are not for the most part addressed to a woman, but to a friend, and the conventional lament that mourns an unrequited love is altogether absent. Yet like other sequences of the time, notably those of Sidney and Spenser, Shakespeare's sonnets seem to spring from a personal experience and to imply, though not to tell, a story. Briefly the story seems to be this: the poet has a friend, young, beautiful, of high birth, whom he loves better than himself; he has also a mistress, the so-called Dark Lady, an accomplished and fascinating wanton who at once attracts and repels him; "Two loves I have," he writes in sonnet 144. The woman seduces the friend who betrays the poet, but after a brief period of alienation the poet forgives and rejoins his friend, assured, as a man of the Renaissance would be, that true friendship is a purer, loftier thing than woman's love. Some such story seems, indeed, to be implied, but there are many sonnets that have no relation to it, and to think of Shakespeare's sonnets as written to immortalize this story, if such there were, is quite to misunderstand them.

Assuming that the sonnets imply such a story a natural question arises as to the identity of the friend and of the mistress. To this question various answers have been given. The friend has been identified with Southampton, naturally enough considering the known relation between Shakespeare and his patron. But if the friend was, as seems almost certain, Mr. W. H. of the dedication, he can hardly also be Henry Wriothesley, Earl of Southampton. Again, the friend has been found in William, Lord Herbert, Earl of Pembroke, one of the brothers to whom the First Folio was dedicated. This theory carried with it the notion that the Dark Lady was Mary Fitton, one of the Queen's maids of honor, with whom Herbert is known to have carried on an intrigue. There are, however, very strong arguments against this theory which is now abandoned by most scholars. It is perhaps wiser to renounce any attempt at identification and think of Mr. W. H. simply as a charming young gentleman of good birth who was fortunate enough to win the almost adoring friendship of the poet. As for the lady, the less said of her, perhaps, the better.

It is a relief to turn from such matters to the true, the poetic values of the sonnets. They are written like most sonnets of that age in the English form which Surrey had invented as an equivalent to the Italian sonnet with its division into the octave (eight lines) and sestet (six lines). This English form consists of three quatrains rhyming *abab, cdcd, efef,* and closing with a couplet. This gives a progressive movement, repeating, illustrating, reinforcing the topic, and winding up with a sententious comment in the couplet. The English form may lack the unity of the Italian with its interwoven rhymes and the harmonious correspondence of the sestet to the octave that precedes it. Indeed from the time of Milton English poets for the most part have preferred the Italian form. Yet in the hands of such a poet as Shakespeare the English form reveals undreamed-of qualities of beauty, grace, and dignity.

This is not to say that all the sonnets are of great and equal value; on the contrary, many of them are slight things, occasional verses, too often marred by the Elizabethan fondness for strained conceits. But when the poet is strongly moved he rises to very lofty heights of thought and to such perfection of expression as is matched, if matched at all, only in his own plays. What moves him most and stirs him to such expression is the Renaissance theme of Beauty, beauty revealed in the person of his friend, beauty that irresistibly evokes love, beauty warred upon by Time, love triumphing over the wreckage of Time, and conferring immortality on the beautiful beloved in enduring verse.

Love's not Time's fool, though rosy lips and cheeks
Within his bending sickle's compass come;
Love alters not with his brief hours and weeks,
But bears it out even to the edge of doom.
  If this be error and upon me proved,
  I never writ, nor no man ever loved.

It would be well for the young student to avoid a consecutive reading of the sonnets, especially if undertaken in the vain hope of puzzling out the story. It would be more profitable by far to select a few written in what Tennyson called the deeper vein, read and re-read them, get them by heart, and learn the truth of Shakespeare's words when he spoke of

Beauty making beautiful old rhyme.

In the great sonnets, as nowhere else in his works, we may hear the voice of the supreme master of English poetry opening his heart, revealing his profoundest thoughts and most poignant emotions in accents surer of immortality than the eternity promised to the beloved friend.

XII

THE TEXT OF SHAKESPEARE

THE student who reads a play of Shakespeare's in the usual school or college textbook probably thinks, if he thinks about the matter at all, that he is reading what Shakespeare wrote as certainly as if he were reading a modern play by Shaw or Eugene O'Neill. On the other hand, a student who opens a critical edition of Shakespeare, such as the Furness *Variorum,* is likely to be greatly puzzled by the multitude of readings in the textual notes with their references to quartos, folios, and modern emendations. The truth is that in no single play of Shakespeare's can we be quite sure that we are in every line reading the very words the poet wrote. And the reason for this lies in the methods of the publication of plays in Shakespeare's day, a method which was widely different from that followed by a dramatist of today. Mr. Shaw, for instance, when he is ready to publish a play contracts for its appearance with a publisher, sends him a neatly typed manuscript, receives several sets of proof which he carefully corrects, and finally sees his work given to the world in a printed form as nearly accurate as human ingenuity and care can make it. Things were otherwise in Shakespeare's day.

In the first place, throughout the greater part of Shakespeare's life plays were hardly regarded as literature in the true sense of the word. They were written to be produced on the stage, not for publication. "Comedies," said Marston, Shakespeare's contemporary playwright, "are writ to be spoken, not read." It is true that in the early years of the seventeenth century, owing in part to the excellence of Shakespeare's own works, plays began to rise in estimation, and various authors, Chapman, Jonson, Heywood, and Massinger, began to send their plays to the press with dedications to prospective patrons. Shakespeare, however, never did so, and he was well on in his career before his name appeared on the title-page of any of his plays; *Love's Labour's Lost, Richard II,* and *Richard III* were all published in 1598, the year in which Meres proclaimed the excellence of Shakespeare as poet and playwright, as the work of Shakespeare. Evidently by this time his name had an advertising and commercial value.

The usual practice, as has already been said (page 27), was for a dramatist to sell his play outright to a company of actors. It then became their exclusive property; it was considered distinctly unethical for a writer to re-sell his play to a publisher. After securing a license for performance from the Master of the Revels, making the changes, if any, that he demanded, cutting the manuscript to a proper length for the two-hour limit, and equipping it with the necessary stage-directions, the company entrusted it to their book-keeper, who had it bound up, often in an old bit of vellum, and carefully preserved it among the company's archives.

This final form was the so-called "book of the play," and as a rule the company was most reluctant to allow the publication of this their property. For this there were two reasons: rightly or wrongly they felt that if the public could read a play they would be less likely to come to the theatre to see it. A still stronger reason was that if a play were in print it would be difficult, if not impossible, to prevent another company from acting it in London or on the road. There were at that time no such stringent laws to prevent the infringement of stage copyright as exist today. Nevertheless the public which flocked to see plays on the stage was equally eager to read them in print and as always the demand created the supply. All through Shakespeare's life-time his plays as well as those of his contemporaries kept appearing in print. Finally, in 1616, the year of Shakespeare's death, Jonson set the seal of his great reputation upon the practice of publication by collecting such of his plays as he was willing to own, seeing them through the press, and giving them to the world with the title of *The Works of Benjamin Jonson,* a title, by the way, which elicited a good deal of ridicule at the time, since mere plays were hardly considered to be "works."

There were various ways in which copy for setting up a play in print might come into a publisher's hands. These may be distinguished as legitimate and illegitimate methods. It was, of course, illegitimate for a publisher to print and sell a play without the consent of its owners the actors, but in the absence of copyright laws at that time the owners had no redress. A publisher bent on securing copy might send a stenographer to the theatre to take down the play in shorthand. We know enough of the systems of shorthand in use at that time to be sure that such a report would be very imperfect. In fact, Heywood, one of Shakespeare's contemporaries, remarks of a successful play of his own that

"some by Stenography drew
"The plot: put it in print: (scarce one
word trew:)"

A similar practice would be to send a man or men repeatedly to a play to memorize and report as much of it as possible. This, too, would not be likely to get satisfactory results but would at least produce copy that could be palmed off on the public. Lastly, and this is a method from which we know that Shakespeare suffered, it was possible to bribe one of the hired men of the acting company to transcribe his own carefully written-out part, which would of course be an accurate reproduction of his rôle, and to eke this out by repeating from memory what he had heard his fellow actors recite in rehearsals or public performances. It seems fairly certain that the first editions of *Romeo and Juliet, The Merry Wives, Henry V,* and *Hamlet* rest upon copy obtained in this fashion. After the publication of the first quarto of *Hamlet,* Shakespeare no longer suffered from such piracy; it seems likely that his company detected and discharged the thief.

Such illegitimate methods, however, were exceptional. Most Elizabethan publishers were honest business men, and copy for the great majority of plays published in Shakespeare's lifetime was obtained in perfectly legitimate fashion. When a company broke up, for instance, as Pembroke's Men did in 1594, their play-books might be sold to publishers and the money divided among the needy actors. Similarly, when a company was in straits for money it might dispose of its play-books in this fashion. It is an interesting fact that during and immediately after the great plague years of 1593-94 and 1603-1604 an unusual number of plays issued from the press. Finally a company might consent, however reluctantly, to the publication of an authentic edition of one of their plays to supplant a "stolen and surreptitious" copy. It seems fairly certain that the second editions of *Romeo and Juliet,* and *Hamlet,* for instance, were printed from copy supplied by the actors and published to supplant the badly garbled reports of these plays in the first quartos; the second quarto of *Hamlet,* in fact, carries on the title-page the statement that it is "enlarged to almost as much again as it was, *according to the true and perfect copy.*" It has been suggested also that the first edition of *Lear* rests upon copy supplied the publisher to forestall the appearance of a stolen and garbled version like the first quarto *Hamlet,* which the actors had reason to believe was about to be published.

When an honest publisher got the manuscript of a play his first action was to pay the usual fee of 6d. and enter it on the Stationers' Register. This was the record kept by the corporation of printers and publishers, and an entry therein of intent to publish any book protected or was supposed to protect the entrant from infringement of his right by a fellow member of the corporation. Another purpose of such an entry was to prevent the illicit publication of a play. Roberts, who printed the play-bills for Shakespeare's company, was frequently employed to enter plays that they wished to withhold for the present from publication.

It was not necessary to make such an entry and it is an interesting fact that most stolen plays were published without an entry in the Register. Having thus secured his rights, the publisher turned his copy over to a printer to compose for him. Now the art of printing and of book-making in general was at a rather low ebb in Elizabethan England and plays were cheap books—the usual selling price was 6d. Consequently the printing as a rule was hastily and rather carelessly done. We must remember also that if the compositor was setting up his form from a "book of the play," he was working on copy that had been cut, revised, altered, and emended on its passage from the author's hands to those of the licenser and back again to the prompter, who scribbled stage directions and actors' names in the margin. Even if there had been careful proof reading of the first impression, the result would probably have been far from accurate; but proof reading in an Elizabeth printing shop was notoriously careless. It was a rare exception for an author to read the proof of his plays as Jonson did for the publication of his folio edition. More often some one in the shop had a hasty glance at the sheets as they came from the press, corrected the more obvious blunders, and made the compositor correct his forms. By this time, however, a number of sheets had been struck off and instead of throwing them away and starting afresh, the old misprinted sheets were bound up indiscriminately with the new more or less corrected ones. As a result, it is unusual to find copies of the same edition of a play which correspond exactly. Of the first quarto of *Lear,* one of the worst jobs of printing turned out in Shakespeare's days, some nine or ten copies still survive and not a single one of these even approaches accuracy; every copy has some corrected and some uncorrected sheets, and no two of them correspond. It is not surprising, therefore, that the text of Elizabethan plays is far from representing accurately the words the author wrote.

Sixteen of Shakespeare's plays were published in quarto form during his lifetime and one more, *Othello,* six years after his death just before the appearance of the First Folio. These sixteen are now divided into two classes, the good and the bad quartos. The bad quartos are those which were published without the consent of the actors, copy for which had been obtained by one of the illegitimate methods described above. There are five, perhaps one should say six of these, namely *Romeo and Juliet, The Merry Wives, Henry V, Hamlet,* and *Pericles,* to which we might add *Troilus and Cressida,* although this play was apparently printed from a fairly accurate transcript of Shakespeare's manuscript (cf. page 59 above). The other ten, or eleven, were honestly secured and, as a rule, present a text nearer to Shakespeare's original than that of the Folio version of the play. In fact, it is now known that certain plays in the Folio were printed directly from quarto editions; a word will be said of this hereafter. All these quartos good and bad, except those of *Lear, Troilus,* and *Pericles,* were published before 1603, that is, before Shakespeare's company became the King's Men; after that date they seem to have had influence enough with the Master of the Revels, who now claimed the right to license plays for publication as well as for the stage, to stop the printing of all but these three plays. All his other plays, some nineteen or twenty in number, remained in manuscript in the hands of the Company until 1623, when they appeared in the Folio.

The following table shows the dates of the quarto editions of Shakespeare's plays up to 1623, and also the comparative popularity of the plays.

Titus	1594, 1600, 1611
Richard II	1597, 1598, 1608, 1615
Richard III	1597, 1598, 1602, 1605, 1612, 1622
Romeo and Juliet	1597, 1599, 1609, one undated quarto
I Henry IV	1598, 1599, 1604, 1608, 1613, 1622
Love's Labour's Lost	1598
Merchant of Venice	1600, 1619
Henry V	1600, 1602, 1619
Much Ado	1600
II Henry IV	1600
Midsummer Night's Dream	1600, 1619
Merry Wives	1602, 1619
Hamlet	1603, 1604, 1605, 1611
Lear	1608, 1619
Troilus	1609
Pericles	1609 (two editions), 1611, 1619
Othello	1622

The publication of Jonson's collected plays in the Folio of 1616 may have suggested the collection and publication of the plays of his even more famous contemporary, William Shakespeare, who died in that year. The idea seems to have occurred first about 1619 to an unscrupulous publisher, Thomas Pavier. He owned the copyrights of the corrupt version of *Henry V,* of the *Contention* and the *True Tragedy* (see page 49), of a murder play called *A Yorkshire Tragedy,* which he had published as the work of Shakespeare as far back as 1605, and of a chronicle play, *Sir John Oldcastle,* often confused with Shakespeare's *Henry IV,* where Falstaff, as we have seen, was originally called Oldcastle. In addition to these he picked up copies of the popular *Pericles,* of *The Merchant of Venice* and *A Midsummer Night's Dream,* both long out of print, and secured from the owners the right to reprint the corrupt *Merry Wives* and the one edition of *Lear.* These ten plays he apparently meant to publish in a single volume, offering them to the public as a collection of Shakespeare's plays. He had actually started the printing of the set in quarto form when he was forced to abandon his purpose. Possibly the Company got wind of his scheme and appealed to their patron, Shakespeare's friend, William Lord Herbert, then Lord Chamberlain. In May, 1619, Herbert wrote to the Stationers' Company forbidding the printing of any of the King's Men's plays without their consent. Pavier, however, was unwilling to lose the money he had already spent on the work and proceeded to issue these ten plays in quarto form separately, except for the two *Henry VI* plays, which appeared in one volume under the title of *The Whole Contention,* etc. To cover his traces he gave false dates to a number of the plays, to *Henry V,* that of 1608, to the *Merchant* and *A Midsummer Night's Dream,* 1600 (the date of the original quartos) with the lying statement that they were printed by J. Roberts, dead some years before. On the title-page of his *Lear* he put the name of Butter, the original publisher, and the date 1608. *The Merry Wives* and *Pericles* he dated correctly, 1619. These copies he disposed of separately, but it is known that a number of them were bound up by purchasers into a collected volume, one specimen of which still exists in the Folger Library at Washington. Pavier's trickery and the false dates he placed on various volumes long caused great confusion to Shakespeare's bibliographers, but some clever bibliographical and typographical detective work about 1909 cleared up the whole matter. The various editions dated 1619 in the table on page 78 are those which Pavier published in that year, regardless of the date he set on the title-pages.

It must have been shortly after the breakdown of Pavier's plan of publication, possibly even in consequence of it, that two of Shakespeare's "fellows," Heminges and Condell, resolved to collect and publish all his plays. These two were at this time, 1620, the sole surviving members of the original Globe "housekeepers," special friends of Shakespeare to whom he had in his will left a handsome sum for the purchase of memorial rings. As old members of the Company they probably had little difficulty in securing permission to print from the "play-books" the hitherto unpublished plays, but to secure permission to reprint those already in existence in quarto form involved probably a good deal of bargaining with the owners of the copyrights. To secure these and to finance an expensive undertaking a partnership was formed by Jaggard, printer of play-bills for the King's Men, and Blount, a publisher of some standing who owned the copyrights to *Antony and Cleopatra* and *Pericles,* though he had never published either. Later two other publishers, Smithwick and Aspley, who between them controlled the copyright of six plays, were added to the partnership, and the volume was finally printed at their joint expense.

On November 8, 1623, Blount and Jaggard entered in the Stationers' Register "Master William Shakspeers *Comedyes, Histories* and *Tragedyes,* soe manie of the said copies as are not formerly entred to other men vizt. Comedyes. The Tempest. The two gentlemen of Verona. Measure for Measure. The Comedy of Errors. As you like it. All's well that ends well. Twelfe Night. The winters tale. Histories. The thirde part of Henry ye sixt. Henry the eight. Tragedies. Coriolanus. Timon of Athens. Julius Cæsar. Mackbeth. Anthonie and Cleopatra. Cymbeline."

One or two comments on this list are necessary. The "thirde part of Henry the Sixt" refers to what we now know as the first part; the two *Contention* plays had been entered by Pavier in 1602 as the first and second part of *Henry VI.* It would have been more accurate to speak of the play now entered as a third play introductory to the other two. There is no mention in this list of *King John,* which had neither been entered nor published previously, but this play, as has been shown (page 52), was Shakespeare's re-writing of an old chronicle, and registration was probably considered unnecessary. *The Taming of the Shrew,* also omitted from this list, is a re-writing of *A Shrew* (see page 56) of which Smithwick, one of the Folio syndicate, owned the copyright.

The owners of *Troilus* made so much difficulty in releasing the copyright that it was at first intended to omit this play from the collection; it is not mentioned in the catalogue of plays prefixed to the volume and was apparently crowded in at the last moment between the Histories and the Tragedies. *Pericles,* although owned by Blount, was omitted from the collection, as was the collaborated play, *The Two Noble Kinsmen* (see pages 67 and 70).

The Folio was a rather pretentious volume. It included besides the plays, a short poem by Jonson on the portrait; the well-known Droeshout portrait of Shakespeare, possibly costumed for the part of Old Knowell in Jonson's *Every Man In,* inserted on the title-page after the statement that Shakespeare's Comedies, Histories, and Tragedies are here "published according to the true original copies"; an elaborate dedication to "the most noble and incomparable pair of brethren, William Earl of Pembroke and Philip Earl of Montgomery," signed by Heminges and Condell; an epistle "to the great variety of readers" also signed by Heminges and Condell, but possibly written by Jonson; a long poem "to the memory of my beloved, the author, Mr. William Shakespeare and what he hath left us," by Ben Jonson; a sonnet by Hugh Holland; an elegy by L. Digges; and a short poem by an unknown I. M. Then follows the list of actors' names already referred to (page 26), a catalogue of the several comedies, histories, and tragedies arranged in these three groups, and the plays begin with *The Tempest*.

In the epistle to the readers, Shakespeare's friends state that whereas the public had heretofore been abused by "diverse stolen and surreptitious copies," even these were now offered to view "cured and perfect." These expressions were once thought to be a denunciation of all editions published before the Folio, but it is more likely that the reference was only to the "bad quartos." Modern scholarship has, in fact, demonstrated that various quarto editions were actually sent to Jaggard's printing shop to be used as copy for the Folio. Thus *Love's Labour's Lost, Romeo and Juliet,* and *The Merchant of Venice* were reprinted in the Folio from quarto editions; *Richard II, A Midsummer Night's Dream, I Henry IV, Titus,* and *Much Ado* were printed from quarto copies which had been used in the theatre as prompt books and contained various corrections and marginal notes. For six other plays which had previously been published, *Richard III, II Henry IV, Hamlet, Lear, Troilus,* and *Othello,* Heminges and Condell preferred to rely upon the Company's "play-books," even when, as in the case with *Hamlet,* the quarto presented a fuller and presumably more accurate form. The bad quartos of *Henry V* and *Merry Wives* were naturally rejected, and here as with the twenty unpublished plays they drew upon the "play-books." It is very doubtful whether they actually sent the valuable "play-books" bearing the Master of the Revels license to the printing shop; more likely they arranged to have them transcribed and sent the transcripts to Jaggard. It has been suggested also that the original play-books were lost for certain plays, as we know that of *The Winter's Tale* was in August, 1623, before the Folio was printed and that copy was prepared by "assembling" the actors' parts and so reconstructing the play. The evidence for this view, however, is not very strong.

From what has been said it is plain that the Folio can no longer be regarded as presenting everywhere the exact words of Shakespeare, "absolute in their numbers, as he conceived them," to quote a phrase of the epistle. Shakespeare's fellows, no doubt, did their best, but they were not critical scholars nor expert editors; and the text of the Folio, once regarded with almost superstitious reverence, leaves much to be desired. There are many palpable misprints, some careless omissions of words, phrases and even whole lines. There are evident signs of editing in modernization of spelling and grammar and in a rather inconsistent purging the text of profanity.

When one turns, moreover, from the text to the stage-directions, to exits and entrances, and to division into acts and scenes, the Folio is quite unsatisfactory. It has taken the labor of Shakespearean scholars a couple of centuries and more to restore the text of Shakespeare to something approximately like the "true original," and there is still work to be done. Some account of these labors will be found in a later chapter.

A second Folio, published in 1632, reprinted the first, corrected some obvious misprints, and introduced a number of fresh ones. No other edition appeared until Restoration times, when the Third Folio was issued in 1663. To a second issue of this edition in 1664 there were added a new group of plays; of these *Pericles,* appearing for the first time in a folio collection, alone has any claim to authenticity. The others, *The London Prodigal, Thomas Lord Cromwell, Sir John Oldcastle, The Puritan, A Yorkshire Tragedy,* and *Locrine,* are all spurious, and are no longer found in any edition of Shakespeare. The Fourth and last Folio was printed in 1685. No authority can be attached to any alterations in these later editions, as one folio simply reprints another, making some obvious corrections and introducing new errors. The work of actual editing begins with Rowe's edition in 1709.

XIII

EDITORS AND EDITIONS

THE student of to-day familiar with the text of Shakespeare in the current emended and annotated editions of his plays can have little or no conception of the difficulties which confronted readers of the poet at the close of the seventeenth century. The First Folio was, as has been said, a poor piece of work, abounding in misprints, confused and confusing punctuation, printing verse sometimes as prose and sometimes prose as verse. Every succeeding folio increased the difficulty and confusion by adding to the errors of the first until the text had become a veritable jungle of errors and obscurities. It is no wonder that even such a lover of Shakespeare and such a clear-sighted critic as Dryden complained at times of the difficulty of the poet's style. With the beginning of the eighteenth century the first attempt was made to render his work more generally intelligible. It is probable that the idea of an emended, legible, and popular edition to replace the expensive and unsatisfactory folios occurred first to a famous publisher of the day, the well-known Tonson. He engaged the services of Nicholas Rowe, a practicing and successful playwright, to edit the plays of Shakespeare.

Rowe's work of reform, published first in 1709, was partial and unsatisfactory. He based his text upon the Fourth Folio, the worst of the four, and as a natural result reproduced many of its errors, retaining also the spurious plays which had been added to the text in 1664. He did, however, consult some of the quartos and added to the text passages wanting in all the folios, notably the last soliloquy of Hamlet. His chief work apparently, apart from the correction of obvious errors, was to give a list of dramatis personæ for each play—only eight of such lists appear in the folios—and to divide the plays into acts and scenes. This division he carried out in accordance with the stage practice of his day, a practice quite different from that of the Elizabethans. In the main Rowe's arrangement has prevailed to the present day, often to the bewilderment of the reader as when he split the beginning of the second act of *Romeo and Juliet* into two scenes where Shakespeare evidently meant it to run on without a break. To a second edition of the plays, 1714, Rowe prefixed the first biography of Shakespeare.

Rowe's editions apparently whetted the public appetite for a revised version of Shakespeare, and about 1720 Tonson called on Pope, then at the height of his fame as translator of the *Iliad,* to superintend the publication of a new edition. This appeared in a handsome and expensive form in 1725. Pope discarded the seven plays added to the Third Folio, excluding even *Pericles.* In his preface he professed to have made a careful collation of the old editions, to have put the various readings in the margin, to have explained obsolete words and in general to have "discharged the dull duty of an editor" to the best of his judgment. Unfortunately Pope's judgment as an editor was far below his genius as a poet. He based his text in the main upon Rowe, only occasionally consulted the original copies, constantly altered the text to suit his own conception of propriety of language and regularity of metre, and worst of all cut out many passages which he considered unworthy of Shakespeare, stigmatizing them as interpolations by the actors and relegating them to the foot of the page or omitting them without notice. It seems hardly credible, but it is true, that he treated one of Shakespeare's grandest lines in this fashion, degrading

> "The multitudinous seas incarnadine"

to a footnote and misprinting it even there.

Much had been expected of Pope's work and although he made some ingenious conjectures and occasionally corrected a bit of mangled metre, there was a general sense of disappointment. This found a voice and very emphatic utterance in the year following the appearance of his edition.

In 1726 Lewis Theobald, a first-rate classical scholar, for years a student of Shakespeare and of Elizabethan literature, published a work entitled *Shakespeare Restored, or a specimen of the many errors as well committed as left unamended by Mr. Pope.* About two-thirds of the book was devoted to a rectification of the text of Hamlet; an appendix of some sixty pages contained emendations for most of the other plays. Perhaps the most famous of these was the correction of Mrs. Quickly's phrase in describing the death of Falstaff which was printed in the Folio: "his Nose was as sharpe as a Pen, and a table of greene fields." Pope, who had been puzzled by the last quite unintelligible words, explained them as a stage direction which had crept into the text; a table was wanted for a tavern scene, he said, and Greenfield, the property man, was directed to have one ready. Quite an ingenious guess; unfortunately there never was any such person as Greenfield and directions of this sort never occur in the middle of a scene. Theobald's emendation "and a (*i.e.*, he) babbled of green fields" is so happy that one feels that if Shakespeare did not write the phrase he certainly should have done so. It has been universally received into the text. This is only one of some three hundred of Theobald's corrections and emendations which have been very generally accepted by later editors.

Pope naturally was furious at Theobald's exposure of his incompetence as an editor. He made Theobald, "piddling Tibbald" as he called him, the hero of his first version of the *Dunciad*, 1728, and was never weary of abusing him and crying down his work. Undismayed, however, Theobald proceeded to bring out his own edition in seven volumes in 1734. In spite of the fact that Theobald used Pope's text to print from—a mere concession to convenience—it is with this edition that a real beginning was made of the slow process of correcting the text of Shakespeare. Pope fancied that he was deriding Theobald by calling him The Restorer. It is a title that Theobald might have been proud to claim and he deserves it better than any other editor of Shakespeare. Working as he did without the apparatus of dictionaries, concordances, reprints of old plays and rare books accessible to the student today, he accomplished wonders. Yet the cloud of misrepresentation raised around him by Pope and Pope's disciples was so thick that it is only in late years that his true merit has been recognized. This merit can be stated very briefly: Theobald brought to the restoration of the text of Shakespeare the same diligence in collation, the same wide reading in contemporary literature, and the same reasonable prudence in emendation which heretofore had been practiced in the restoration of a Greek or Latin text; in other words he treated Shakespeare as a true scholar of the Renaissance treated an old classic.

Passing over other eighteenth-century editions we come in 1765 to that of Dr. Johnson. Johnson did little to improve the text, but his explanations of difficult passages remain today among the most convincing of the many that crowd the pages of the *Variorum Shakespeare.* Johnson's contemporary, Capell, made the fullest and most scholarly collation of the various texts that had yet appeared. Unfortunately his clumsy style—Johnson declared that he "gabbled monstrously"—robbed his work of half its value.

Malone's edition, 1790, restored *Pericles* to the plays and added the poems and sonnets which an earlier editor had rejected because, he said, "the strongest Act of Parliament that could be framed would fail to compel readers into their service." Malone's special merit was his knowledge of Elizabethan life and literature; he inaugurated the study of the chronology of Shakespeare's plays, and his tireless researches in Shakespearean lore were included after his death in the so-called *Third Variorum* edited in 1821 by the younger James Boswell.

Few of the many nineteenth-century editions deserve special mention. Little by little the work of correcting and explaining the text of Shakespeare went forward. Knight's once popular editions, 1838-42 and 1842-44, showed a reversion to the letter-worship of the First Folio. J. P. Collier's, 1841-44, work was marked, or rather marred, by perversely ingenious guesses for some of which that erratic scholar sought support by marginal entries, undoubtedly forged, in a copy of F_2. Finally, 1863-66, the *Cambridge Shakespeare* edited by Clark, Glover, and Wright (revised 1891-93 by Wright) appeared with a complete *apparatus criticus* containing all the textual variations and the most significant conjectures of former editors. This edition long remained the standard; its text reprinted in the popular Globe edition and in the well-known *Temple* format, one play to one volume, became, so to speak, the *textus receptus* of Shakespeare.

The *New Variorum,* begun in 1871 by Dr. Howard Furness, continued after his death by his son, now also deceased, and still in progress in the hands of a committee of scholars, started with an eclectic text and later diverged into a reprint of the First Folio. Like the *Cambridge* it contains a complete collation of variants, the best emendations, and a vast number of explanatory notes, good and bad, wise and foolish.

The best single volume texts of Shakespeare are the *Oxford,* edited by W. J. Craig, and the American *Cambridge,* edited by W. A. Neilson. The text of this latter, revised and reprinted in the popular *Tudor* edition, has deservedly attained wide circulation in this country.

For the serious student copies or facsimile reprints of the folios, specifically of the First and of the various quartos, are a prime necessity. There is an accurate reprint of this folio by Booth, 1862-64; another by Halliwell-Phillips, 1876, reproduced in smaller and cheaper form, unfortunately in such minute type as to be almost illegible. The best reproduction is probably that of Sidney Lee, 1902. The *Shakespeare Quarto Facsimiles,* 1880-89, forty-one volumes supervised by Dr. Furnivall, are indispensable, although at times not absolutely accurate. The prefaces to the various volumes contain very valuable textual studies.

Of late years English scholars have devoted much time and pains to bibliographical and paleographical studies. A better knowledge of the ways of Elizabethan printers and the peculiarities of Elizabethan handwriting have suggested many plausible explanations of errors or variants in the old texts. The definitive text of Shakespeare has not yet appeared. There is still room for such an edition as Theobald would have given to the world had he possessed the knowledge and the facilities within easy reach of Shakespearean scholars today.

XIV

SHAKESPEAREAN CRITICISM

Criticism is not, as is too often thought, a process of fault-finding. It is rather a process of discrimination, of sifting faults from merits, of determining the permanent as opposed to the ephemeral in an author's work, and of bringing to light beauties ignored by the casual reader. The progress of Shakespearean criticism, like that of the correction and elucidation of the text, has been slow and gradual. Often it reveals the idiosyncrasy of the critic and the prevailing critical standards of his age quite as much as it does the merits and defects of Shakespeare. Yet it is quite true to say that with a few negligible exceptions all critics of Shakespeare, whatever their personal prejudices, whatever the accepted critical dogmas of their age, have recognized his transcendent greatness. A brief review of the progress of Shakespearean criticism from his own time to our own will make this clear.

There was little or no criticism of Shakespeare in Elizabethan time. The triumphant success of his plays upon the stage found an echo in a chorus of praise from his contemporaries. Only Ben Jonson exercised a certain liberty of expression. When the players mentioned it as an honor to Shakespeare that in his writing, "he never blotted a line," Jonson replied "would that he had blotted a thousand —he flowed with that facility that sometimes it was necessary that he should be stopped." This is genuine criticism. One of the characteristics of Shakespeare's art, like that of the Gothic workman in Ruskin's famous chapter, is the quality of redundance, "the uncalculating bestowal of the wealth of its labor." Yet in his well-known eulogy of Shakespeare prefixed to the First Folio Jonson is lavish of praise. Shakespeare, he says, not only surpassed his contemporaries—Jonson mentions by name Lyly, Kyd, and Marlowe—but challenged comparison with all the work of "insolent Greece or haughty Rome." He goes on to praise not only Shakespeare's truth to nature but the "art" which turned and fashioned his "true-filed lines." And finally his emphatic declaration that Shakespeare "was not of an age, but for all time" was the truest prophecy ever made by a poet-critic of a brother poet.

No age had such difficulty in understanding and appreciating Shakespeare as that of the Restoration. This was due in part to the shocking condition of his text at that time, even more perhaps to changed theatrical conditions and to the prevalence of neo-classical dogmas, especially as applied to the drama. This lack of understanding found its full and final expression in the work of Thomas Rymer, *Tragedies of the Last Age,* 1678, and *Short View of Tragedy,* 1692-93. Rymer has been styled "the worst critic that ever lived," and if the first qualification of a critic is a sympathetic appreciation of his subject, Rymer's bad eminence can hardly be disputed. "There is more meaning and expression," he declares, "in the neighing of a horse or the growling of a mastiff than in Shakespeare's tragical flights." A soldier, he believes, should always be shown as frank and plain-dealing, therefore Shakespeare's Iago is an unnatural monster; "there never was in tragedy, comedy, or nature such a soldier as Iago." Othello is, in short, "a bloody farce." The cause of all this, Rymer, like later critics who have found fault with Shakespeare, discovers in the "illiterate audience, carpenters and cobblers" for whom Shakespeare wrote.

Rymer, however, does not represent his own age; he is the hyper-critic rebuked even by his contemporaries for his excess. A better mirror of Restoration criticism is found in the work of Dryden. He begins, *Essay of Dramatick Poesie,* 1668, by calling Shakespeare "the man who of all modern and perhaps ancient poets, had the largest and most comprehensive soul." That is high praise and its effect is not greatly diminished when Dryden complains of the irregularity of Shakespeare's plots or the extravagance of his diction. We must always remember that Dryden read Shakespeare in the uncorrected folio text and was rightly puzzled and often offended by what he read there. Moreover one of the tasks of the Restoration authors and critics was to purge literature of the characteristic Elizabethan license of excess. In the Restoration adaptations of Shakespeare for the contemporary stage it is interesting to note how often the authors, themselves poets as well as playwrights, shy off in alarm from some fine figurative phrase of Shakespeare's and water it down to a harmless mediocrity. Thus in D'Avenant's *Macbeth* such a magnificent outburst as the Lady's

> "The raven himself is hoarse
> That croaks the fatal entrance of Duncan
> Under my battlements"

becomes

> "There would be music in a raven's voice,
> Which should but croak the entrance of the King
> Under my battlements."

Yet Dryden admits that Shakespeare has often written better than any poet in any language and that he excels in characterization. "We English venerate Shakespeare," he declares, "as the Greeks do Æschylus."

Pope, the typical Augustan, was a better critic than an editor of Shakespeare. The preface to his edition is a better piece of work than the edition itself. Like Dryden, he is open-eyed to what seem Shakespeare's faults, his puns, his "conceits," his extravagance of language, but he is less severe than Dryden in his reprobation; at times attributes them to Shakespeare's condescension to his audience, at times clears him of them by ascribing them not to Shakespeare but to interpolations by the actors. He justifies Shakespeare's violation of the Aristotelian canons by asserting that to judge him by those rules would be "like trying a man by the laws of one country who acted under those of another"—a perfect defence, if indeed defence is needed. Shakespeare's chief excellence is his unequalled perception of nature; his characters "like those in nature are infinitely diversified—every single character in Shakespeare is as much an individual as those in life itself." A poet himself, Pope feels Shakespeare's power over the passions; Shakespeare induces our tears and commands our laughter. In his edition he marked by stars and commas the most "shining passages" and it is gratifying to note that the most "correct" of English poets could respond to the lament of Constance for her lost Arthur and to Prospero's

"We are such stuff
As dreams are made on, and our little life
Is rounded with a sleep."

His final conclusion is that Shakespeare is "justly and universally elevated above all other dramatic writers."

Like Pope, Dr. Johnson, literary dictator of the succeeding age, composed a critical preface for his edition of Shakespeare. It is interesting to note that he considers that Shakespeare "may now begin to assume the dignity of an ancient and claim the privilege of an established fame." Johnson's approach to Shakespeare has been called the method of common sense. The first aim of a poet, he holds, must be to instruct by pleasing and Shakespeare pleases because he holds up "a faithful mirror of manners and of life." Johnson defends the mingling of tragic and comic scenes in Shakespeare's plays, a grave fault according to neoclassical standards, because this "mingled drama" resembles life more nearly than either pure tragedy or comedy. Addison's *Cato* has long been recognized as the masterpiece of "regular" tragedy in English, and Johnson praises its innumerable beauties but adds, what is quite true, that its sentiments "communicate no vibration to the heart," whereas *Othello,* so bitterly denounced by Rymer, is "the offspring of observation impregnated by genius." Johnson is less sensitive than Pope to the poetic beauty of Shakespeare; he denounces Shakespeare's fondness for word-play and conceits; "a quibble," he says, "is the golden apple for which he will always turn aside from his career or stoop from his elevation." He prefers Shakespeare's comedies to his tragedies since "in his tragic scenes there is always something wanting"—one wonders what the Doctor would have added to the death of Lear—whereas "his comedy often surpasses expectation." In the main, Johnson, himself primarily a moralist, applauds Shakespeare as a great, although unconscious, master of morals; it is from Shakespeare's truth to general human nature that "so much instruction is derived." The practical commonsense attitude of Johnson to Shakespeare comes out perhaps most clearly in his advice to the young reader: "notes are often necessary, but they are necessary evils. Let him that is yet unacquainted with the powers of Shakespeare, and who desires to feel the highest pleasure that the drama can give, read every play from the first scene to the last with utter negligence of all his commentators,—let him read on through brightness and obscurity,—let him preserve his comprehension of the dialogue and his interest in the fable (*i.e.,* the story). And when the pleasures of novelty have ceased, let him attempt exactness, and read the commentators." This is advice which might well be printed today at the beginning of every school and college edition of a play of Shakespeare's.

The dawn of a new school of criticism, the romantic, is seen in Morgann's famous essay, 1777, on the character of Falstaff. Its thesis is that Falstaff was neither a coward nor a boaster, but a man of natural courage and alacrity of mind. The whole essay is an elaborate and ingenious paradox, impressionistic rather than judicial. Here is no weighing of Shakespeare's faults against Shakespeare's merits, but an attempt to glorify his creative power by displaying his mastery of character creation. The fault that permeates the essay is Morgann's tendency to consider Falstaff not as a figure in a play but a real character, and to argue from what he says and does and what is said of him to what Morgann calls his "internal character" as distinguished from the impression he makes upon the stage. Yet it was just this impression for which Shakespeare created the character. More and more the tendency grew in the romantic school to forget Shakespeare the dramatist and to think of him as a creator of real characters about whom one could argue as about characters in history.

The romantic school of criticism broke into full flower in the work of Coleridge, Hazlitt, and Lamb. Of these Coleridge is the greatest critic as he is the greatest poet and philosopher. His criticism, preserved in fragmentary form from two series of lectures delivered in 1811–12 and in 1818, is indeed a blend of poetry and philosophy. Like a true philosopher, he seeks to find a unity in the whole of Shakespeare's work and in each play that belongs to the body of that work. Like a true poet he is more keenly sensitive to the beauty of Shakespeare's verse than any preceding critic. He defends Shakespeare against the old charge that he was an "irregular" genius of vast powers but little judgment. One feels indeed in reading Coleridge on Shakespeare that the critic was possessed with the conception that the object of his worship was incapable of error. When something in Shakespeare offended even Coleridge—as the speech of the drunken porter in *Macbeth*—he was inclined to reject it as an interpolation by the actors—a throw-back to the method of Pope. With a growing tendency toward a realistic historic criticism today it is only natural that the extraordinary value of Coleridge's criticism should be slighted or ignored; but it is impossible to read even one of his studies of a play of Shakespeare's without feeling that here was something wholly new, imaginative interpretation of a great work of art, no mere weighing of merits and defects. And much that Coleridge was the first to say has become the commonplace of criticism ever since.

Not much need be said of Lamb in this connection. His *Tales from Shakespeare*, 1807, still a classic, is not criticism, but a rendering into easy prose of the plots of Shakespeare's plays. He was widely read in Elizabethan drama, and his *Specimen of English Dramatic Poets*, an anthology of gems from Shakespeare's contemporaries accompanied by brief notes of genuine critical appreciation, did much to bring back forgotten playwrights to the reading public. His fine essay *On the Tragedies of Shakespeare*, 1810, is his one contribution to Shakespearean criticism. Lamb's point of view is that of the reader and lover of poetry; he holds that Shakespeare's plays are "less calculated for performance on a stage than those of almost any other dramatist whatever. Their distinguishing excellence is a reason why they should be so." This is, as Lamb admits, a paradox. It seems indeed an absurd one; the greatest dramatist of all time, whose plays have held the stage through successive changes of public taste in the centuries since his death, wrote, it would seem, plays unsuitable for acting. The truth is that Lamb's own keen delight in the poetry of Shakespeare left him incapable of realizing the potential dramatic power of the poetry he loved. To render it in public seemed to him to vulgarize it; "Hamlet," he says, "what does he suffer by being dragged forth to give lectures to the crowd—the shy, negligent, retiring Hamlet!" Evidently Hamlet is to Lamb a real person, not a character created by Shakespeare for the sole purpose of being represented in action on the stage.

Hazlitt, whose main body of Shakespearean criticism is preserved in his *Characters of Shakespeare's Plays*, 1817, is in some ways a more useful, as he is a more practical critic than either Lamb or Coleridge. Like them he is an enthusiastic worshipper of Shakespeare and is frank to confess it. "An overstrained enthusiasm is more pardonable with respect to Shakespeare," he says, "than the want of it; for our admiration cannot easily surpass his genius." Like them he is a lover of poetry; he anticipates Arnold in his belief in the high moral value of poetry: "Poetry is an interesting study, for this reason, that it relates to whatever is most interesting in human life. Whoever therefore has a contempt for poetry, has a contempt for himself and humanity." Accordingly the pages of his studies of Shakespeare's characters are packed with quotations chosen for their poetic beauty and dramatic fitness. Yet Hazlitt, though a devotee of the acted drama and an expert dramatic critic, felt like Lamb that Shakespeare was better in the closet than in the theatre; "poetry and the stage do not agree well together." He is not always consistent in this; he praises Mrs. Siddons's performance of Lady Macbeth: "She was tragedy personified," and calls Kean "this celebrated actor and able commentator on Shakespeare (actors are the best commentators on the poets)." Like a true romantic he denounced Johnson's "judicial" criticism of Shakespeare. "Johnson," he says, "was neither a poet nor a judge of poetry"—his "powers of reasoning overlaid his critical susceptibility." It is just this "susceptibility" to the beauty and the grandeur of Shakespeare's poetry that gives to Hazlitt's criticism its peculiar charm, that "gusto" which characterizes all his best prose, and in his criticism as in his other essays, Hazlitt contrives to impart something of his own delight to the reader of his work. "For the reader of today who wishes to read the plays of Shakespeare with unadulterated enjoyment—Hazlitt is a sure guide," says a writer who knows and loves his Hazlitt better than most of us.[1]

The note struck by the Romantics echoes through the nineteenth century until it culminates in the ecstatic rhapsody of Swin-

[1] W. D. Howe, *Cambridge History of English Literature*, Vol. xii, p. 186.

burne, *A Study of Shakespeare,* 1880. Criticism in the old sense ceased; for it we have admiration, applause, almost adoration. A more sober appreciation appears in such a writer as Dowden, *Shakespeare—His Mind and Art,* 1875, where the attempt is made to reveal Shakespeare's personality and his attitude toward the great problems of human life through a study of his plays. Something of the same sort, combined with a subtler psychological analysis of Shakespeare's characters, is found in Bradley's admirable *Shakespearean Tragedy,* 1904. Here after a philosophic æsthetic lecture on the *Substance of Tragedy* there follows an illuminating discussion of construction in Shakespeare's tragedies. This might lead one to believe that Bradley meant to deal with Shakespeare primarily as a dramatist, but the four lectures which follow on the four great tragedies are in the main character studies, often indeed of the most interesting and suggestive sort, but with too little consideration of their prime purpose, that of presentation on the stage. To this book there must be added to complete Bradley's criticism of Shakespeare his lectures on *Antony and Cleopatra, Shakespeare the Man,* and *Shakespeare's Theatre and Audience,* in *Oxford Lectures on Poetry,* 1909, and his study of *Coriolanus* (*British Academy,* 1912).

A natural and necessary reaction from romantic criticism began to appear as far back as the German Rümelin's onslaught on the Shakespeare presented by German professors of æsthetics, *Shakespearean Studies,* 1874. It is current today in such work as Schücking's *Character Problems in Shakespeare's Plays,* 1919, and in the work of Professor Stoll ranging from *Shakespeare Studies,* 1911, to *Art and Artifice in Shakespeare,* 1933. In both of these we find a return to the critical attitude of the eighteenth century with, be it said, a great and striking difference.

Unbounded admiration for the genius of Shakespeare has been replaced by a recognition, at times even an insistence upon, his faults. But these faults are no longer perceived by an application of classical critical standards but rather by what one may call the historic method. Schücking points out with real acumen that Shakespeare's technique is that of Shakespeare's day when modern drama was just emerging from medievalism. He sees Shakespeare combining an extraordinary insight into human nature with an almost naïve technique in the conduct of his plot and an inconsistency in character portrayal. Stoll, who has done real service in forcing a reexamination of romantic eulogies, lays stress on the theatrical conventions of Shakespeare's day; he sees in Falstaff the traditional *miles gloriosus,* in Hamlet the conventional revenger of the tragedy of blood. Both critics denounce the excess of psychological analysis in romantic criticism, and insist that Shakespeare wrote with more regard for the immediate impression of each scene than with an eye to a unified conception of the whole play. One feels at times in reading their work that one is listening to the voice of advocates, of prosecutors even, rather than of judges; their reaction against the indiscriminate eulogy of earlier writers carries them at times to excess. Yet their criticism serves as a valuable corrective to much that has been written in the last hundred years.

Some of the most stimulating contemporary criticism has been written by Granville-Barker (*From Henry V* to *Hamlet—British Academy,* 1925, *Prefaces to Shakespeare,* 1927–37, *Shakespeare's Dramatic Art* in the *Companion to Shakespeare Studies,* 1934). Himself, like Shakespeare, both actor and dramatist, Granville-Barker comes to a study of the plays with other qualifications than those of the academic critic. His special merit is his insistence on the perfect adaptation of Shakespeare's plays to the theatre for which Shakespeare wrote, on the excellence of Shakespeare's dramatic art, on the fact that Shakespeare wrote "not merely plays in poetic form, but something that is essentially and fundamentally poetic drama." It should follow, he holds, in opposition to most romantic critics, that only in the theatre can Shakespeare's plays come to their full life. Only in an ideal theatre perhaps and under the direction of an ideal manager, but Granville-Barker's plea for the actor's part in the interpretation of Shakespeare carries with it profound significance.[1]

[1] The foregoing sketch of Shakespearean criticism is necessarily limited to the history of that genre in English. The student who cares to inform himself as to the work of French and German critics of Shakespeare is referred to the account of Shakespeare's reception on the Continent in J. G. Robertson's chapter in the *Cambridge History of English Literature,* Vol. v, Chap. 12.

XV

SHAKESPEARE ON THE STAGE

So much has been said and written about Shakespeare's plays as literature that it is sometimes forgotten by the student of his work that he was a supremely successful playwright. Of all the brilliant group of dramatists of his day he alone survives in the twentieth century, and there never has been a time in the history of the English-speaking stage when some, at least, of his plays in one form or other were not being presented to the public.

Shakespeare's success was early attained and endured without a break till the closing of the theatres in 1642. From the time that he is known as a member of the Chamberlain's Company, 1594, until the death of Elizabeth, 1603, there is an unbroken succession of plays presented by that organization at Court during the Christmas festivities. Probably most of the plays presented were Shakespeare's; we know certainly that *Love's Labour's Lost* and *Merry Wives* were acted before the Queen, and it is to be presumed that other and better plays had the same honor. Royal favor continued and increased during the reign of James. We find the King's Men presenting ten, twelve, and thirteen plays at Court during the holiday season. Once more we may assume that many of these were Shakespeare's. *King Lear* was played at Court in 1606, *The Tempest* and *Winter's Tale* in 1611. Among the many plays presented during the festivities in honor of the Princess Elizabeth's marriage we find listed *Much Ado, The Tempest, Winter's Tale, I King Henry IV, Othello,* and *Julius Cæsar*. Later, in 1618, *Twelfth Night,* in 1619-20 *Hamlet, Two Noble Kinsmen,* and *II King Henry IV* were played at court.

With the accession of Charles I, 1625, there seems to have been some falling off, but we hear of Court performances of *Richard III, Taming of the Shrew* and *Cymbeline* in 1633-34, and of *Hamlet, Othello* and *Julius Cæsar* in 1636.

Meanwhile the popularity of Shakespeare's plays on the public stage continued undiminished by the rise to favor of new writers. Their drawing power was such that a rival company playing at the Red Bull attempted in 1627 to produce them there; Shakespeare's old friend, Heminges, had to hurry to the Master of Revels and fee him with £5 to secure a prohibition of such a trespass. As late as 1640 Leonard Digges in a copy of verses prefixed to the edition of Shakespeare's *Poems* in that year asserted that it was Shakespeare's plays which kept the King's Men alive, that performances of *King Henry IV,* of *Much Ado,* and of *Twelfth Night* packed the house at Blackfriars when revivals of Jonson's *Volpone* and the *Alchemist* were so scantily attended that the receipts barely covered the cost of production. We can check performance of at least twenty-two of Shakespeare's plays before the closing of the theatres.

During the interregnum, 1642-1660, the Puritan rule forbade the performance of all plays, Shakespeare's or others. We hear of some private and illegal representations of Beaumont and Fletcher plays in this period, but of Shakespeare we have only records of a few "drolls," comic scenes adapted from his plays, such as those of Bottom in *A Midsummer Night's Dream* and the Gravediggers in *Hamlet* which seem to have been played at town and country wakes and fairs. With the Restoration and the reopening of the theatres Shakespeare promptly returned to the stage.

In the first year of Charles II's reign Davenant and Killigrew were granted the sole right to form companies of actors, lease or build theatres, and produce plays. Some rough division of Shakespeare's plays was made between them. Killigrew secured *Othello, Julius Cæsar, Henry IV,* and a couple of comedies; Davenant seems to have had the acting rights of most of the rest. Killigrew was responsible for one most important innovation, the substitution of women actors for the Elizabethan boys. The long roll of famous Shakespearean actresses begins on the Restoration stage with Mrs. Betterton, the lovely Bracegirdle, and the lively Barry. Contemporary records show that the Beaumont and Fletcher plays were more popular with Restoration audiences than those of Shakespeare. Yet Pepys in the ten years covered by his diary attended forty-one performances of twelve of Shakespeare's plays, seeing *Hamlet* five times, *The Tempest* eight times, and *Macbeth* nine times. It is probable indeed that some of these performances were of the scandalous adaptations of Shakespeare which blot the theatrical record of the Restoration. Davenant, in particular, allowed himself the greatest freedom in adapting Shakespeare's plays to the changed taste of his time. As early as 1661 he re-wrote *Measure for Measure* as *The Law Against Lovers,* introducing Benedick and Beatrice from *Much Ado* and creating a singing and dancing part for a little girl whose performance delighted Mr. Pepys. Later on he laid violent hands on *Macbeth,* writing several new scenes and introducing a "divertissement" of dancing and flying witches which Pepys pronounced "a strange perfection in a tragedy." Worst of all he and Dryden converted Shakespeare's lovely *Tempest* into a sort of comic opera which has been called "the worst perversion of Shakespeare in the two-century history of such atrocities." *Romeo and Juliet* was equipped with a happy ending by Howard and for a time it was performed alternately as a tragedy and as a tragi-comedy—an excellent example of "pay your money and take your choice." *Lear,* too, was degraded from the realm of tragedy by Nahum Tate, who in 1681 presented a version which cut out the part of the Fool as violating neo-classic ideas of decorum, made Edgar and Cordelia lovers from the start, and united them in marriage at the close when Lear is happily restored to the throne. It is an unhappy fact that this perversion in more or less modified form held the stage for over a century. It is interesting, however, to note that amid this flood of adaptations such plays as *Hamlet* and *Othello* held the stage in unchanged form, except for certain cuts and unimportant changes in the text. The part of Hamlet in fact was one of the great roles of Betterton, the foremost actor of the time; "Betterton," says Pepys, "did the prince's part beyond imagination." The romantic comedies of Shakespeare, alien as they were to Restoration taste, were for the most part left untouched and seldom performed.

It is easy to blame Restoration managers and playwrights for their mutilations of Shakespeare; it is only fair, however, to recognize the difficulties under which they labored. They appreciated the great dramatic power of Shakespeare and attempted to keep his plays alive upon the stage; yet they knew that in their original form they would not be accepted by a contemporary audience. Some remarks by Pepys are illuminating: *A Midsummer Night's Dream* he called "the most insipid ridiculous play that ever I saw in my life"; *Twelfth Night* is "a silly play," "one of the weakest that ever I saw"; even *Othello* when compared with the new *Adventures of Five Hours* was but "a mean thing." If Shakespeare's plays were to draw, they must be purged of their Elizabethan extravagance of speech; their lack of decorum and disregard of the unities must be remedied, and they must be equipped with spectacle and "divertissement." They were acted at least; our age which reverences the text of Shakespeare sees him all too seldom on the stage.

A change for the better begins to appear about the middle of the eighteenth century. One by one such romantic comedies as *Much Ado, As You Like It,* and *Twelfth Night* came back to the stage. Macklin in 1741 won fame as "the Jew that Shakespeare drew" by acting the *Merchant of Venice* in its original form instead of Lansdowne's travesty, 1701, of that play.

David Garrick, perhaps the greatest of all English actors, was an enthusiastic admirer of Shakespeare. His London début, 1741, was in the part of Richard III, and in the thirty-five years of his stage career he played in or produced no less than twenty-four of Shakespeare's plays in which he himself acted seventeen characters. He was especially successful as Hamlet, as Romeo, and as Lear, but he was also a brilliant comedian; Benedick in *Much Ado* was one of his favorite parts. Contemporary witnesses praise Garrick for the versatility and the vigor of his acting. He discarded the traditional stately declamation of blank verse, and substituted for it a realistic delivery which rose to passionate heights and fell to colloquial discourse in accordance with the significance of the text. He began the work of restoring true Shakespearean versions to the stage; he cleared *Macbeth* of most of Davenant's additions, and removed much of Tate's rubbish from *King Lear*. He was not so far in advance of his age as to discard these traditional versions altogether and he took an actor-manager's liberties with *Romeo and Juliet* and with *Hamlet.* In the former he altered the last scene by having Juliet awake before her lover dies and working up a pas sionate parting scene. It was immensely successful on the stage and persisted well into the next century; in fact it is still retained in the operatic version of this play. His alteration of *Hamlet* was severely criticized by contemporaries and by later writers who had never read it. As a matter of fact it consisted mainly in omitting the Gravediggers' scene and the rôle of Osric, both of which had become in the passage of time almost farcical bits of acting. A unique printed copy of Garrick's version preserved at the Folger Library shows that he restored many lines that earlier versions had dropped and added only enough of his own to fill up the gaps his cut had made. In fact Garrick deserves real praise for refraining on the whole to blend new and alien matter with the text of Shakespeare; nothing that he did compares with the enormity of Tate's adulteration of *King Lear.* Some of Garrick's arrangements of Shakespeare held the stage for many years; his *Catherine and Petruchio,* a genially farcical adaptation of the *Taming of the Shrew,* lingered on till near the end of the last century. Garrick's brilliant career as actor, producer, and adapter of Shakespeare is a milestone in the long journey back to the stage presentation of the plays as Shakespeare wrote them, a journey not yet wholly accomplished; Cibber's travesty of *Richard III* may still be seen upon the boards.

The age of Kemble follows close on that of Garrick and while Kemble as an actor was hardly comparable in range and power with his predecessor, yet as actor-manager and producer he probably did more for Shakespeare on the stage than any one either before or after him. Born in 1757 of a theatrical family he was acting at nineteen, made his début at Drury Lane as Hamlet in 1783, and five years later became manager of that great theatre. In 1803 he transferred his allegiance to the rival house, Covent Garden, which he controlled until his retirement in 1817. Kemble was a devoted lover of Shakespeare. Unlike Garrick he rejected the neo-classic drama of the day and bent every effort to restoring Shakespeare to the stage. He produced at one time or another some twenty-five of his plays, many of which had not been acted for years. He was not content simply to revive old versions of the plays, but himself worked over and produced an acting version of each text. He would hardly be regarded as a purist to-day; he retained much of Tate in his *Lear* and actually introduced passages from Dryden's *All for Love* into his production of *Antony and Cleopatra.* Yet on the whole his influence in purifying the acting versions was for good, and no manager before him paid such careful attention to the setting and costuming of the plays: Garrick had acted Macbeth in the uniform of a British officer and Hamlet in a costume closely resembling that of an eighteenth-century clergyman. Kemble was among the first to make some attempt at historical accuracy both in scenery and costume.

He was aided throughout his life by his great sister Sarah, better known as Mrs. Siddons, perhaps the most famous actress, at least of tragic parts, that ever trod the English stage. She and her brother were supreme in such rôles as Macbeth and his wife, Coriolanus and Volumnia. Mrs. Siddons was the first actress to discard the fashionable hoops and nodding feathers worn by stage heroines of the eighteenth century and to model her costume, especially in classic plays, upon the drapery of antique sculpture.

The genius, combined with the dignity and unblemished character of the Kembles, brother and sister, especially remarkable in the licentious days of the Regency, gave to actors and the stage a position and a recognition unknown since Shakespeare's own day. Their stage career coincides with the period of the romantic critics and both together gave new life to Shakespeare's works. After Coleridge and Hazlitt, after Kemble and Mrs. Siddons, there was no longer a danger that Shakespeare should be considered an "irregular" genius or that his dramas should lie at the mercy of any audacious playwright who aspired to better them.

Edmund Kean, 1787-1833, embodied in his acting the new romantic spirit of the age. He was supreme in passionate and tragic parts; on the stage what Byron was in poetry. To see him act was, Coleridge said: "to read Shakespeare by flashes of lightning." He made his début in 1814 as Shylock and for a brief period the rivalry between him and Kemble ran high until Kean's fervor and intensity eclipsed the somewhat formal and measured impersonations of his predecessor. Contemporary testimony is unanimous as to the overpowering effect of his acting in such rôles as Shylock, Richard, and Massinger's Sir Giles. Unlike

Kemble, he was never a manager or producer. Apart from his acting which, undoubtedly, awoke a new and lively interest in stage performances of Shakespeare, his one great service was in restoring to the acting version the tragic close of *Lear*.

With the passing of the Kembles and of Kean a new era opens. The two great theatres, Drury Lane and Covent Garden, still held their monopoly of so-called legitimate drama. Both houses had been rebuilt and enlarged until the old effects obtained by the intimate relation between actor and audience had become impossible. They began, therefore, to resort to spectacles, to stress the splendor of their presentations of Shakespeare, and to advertise the accuracy of their costuming—Planche's costumes for the protagonists in *King John* and *King Henry IV* were designed after the monumental effigies of these monarchs. Producers halted the action to introduce magnificent processions, crowding the stage with hundreds of people against a scenic background built up with scrupulous regard to historical accuracy. All was in vain, and by 1843 the failure of both theatres to maintain their hold on the public led to the abrogation of their long monopoly of presenting the plays of Shakespeare.

A word must be said in passing, however, on the work of the actor-manager, Macready, at Covent Garden, 1837-39, and at Drury Lane, 1841-43. A hard-working and scrupulous producer rather than an actor of genius, Macready did much to purify the text of the stage versions. Among other changes he finally purged *Lear* of the Edgar-Cordelia rubbish which even Kean had left untouched and brought back the character of the Fool, unseen on the stage since the first performance of Tate's version. Strangely enough, he cast a girl of his company for this role. Macready was, perhaps, the first manager to institute the system of special productions of Shakespeare's plays, redecorating and recasting a pair of them each season and relegating others to so-called "stock" performances. His refusal to allow long-continued runs to these productions was probably responsible for his financial failure. He came to realize, as a later bankrupt manager declared, that "Shakespeare spelled ruin."

With the abrogation of the old patent theatre monopoly a host of new and smaller theatres opened their doors to Shakespeare. A system of visiting "stars" sprang up, distinguished actors, like Macready himself, playing leading parts in various theatres supported as best they could be, by the regular company of the theatre where they played. Two tendencies, however, were strongly marked.

The most interesting of these was that initiated by Samuel Phelps, once an understudy of Macready, who in 1844 took over what was then the little suburban theatre of Sadler's Wells and for nearly twenty years, until 1862, presented there a succession of Shakespearean performances such as had not been seen since the closing of the Globe and the Blackfriars. During his régime he produced all but six of Shakespeare's plays, and four of these, *Titus* and the three parts of *King Henry VI*, were of doubtful authenticity. To these performances he invited a public at what seems to-day incredibly low prices, one shilling for the pit and sixpence for a gallery seat. The long and on the whole successful career of Phelps was rendered possible by his stern discouragement of extravagance in costuming and scenery, by his rigorous training of a small low-salaried stock company, and by his confident reliance on the power of the plays themselves to pack his house. Contemporary criticism of his productions stresses the purity of his texts—he assigned the role of Lear's Fool to a man, not a girl as Macready had done, and replaced the Garrick version of *Romeo and Juliet* by Shakespeare's own—and the harmonious effect of the whole performance. Phelps founded a tradition which continues to this day in London where at his own Sadler's Wells and across the Thames at the "Old Vic" one may still see the plays of Shakespeare presented by a well-trained stock company, adequate and interesting presentations, too, although undistinguished by the acting of famous "stars" or a background of magnificent scenery. And both these houses maintain the Phelps tradition of popular prices.

The other tendency may be briefly characterized as one that preferred pageant to poetry. It found its full expression at the Princess's under the direction of Charles Kean, son of the great actor, for about ten years from 1850. Kean continued and exaggerated the methods of Kemble and Macready; he stressed spectacle and ruthlessly cut and re-arranged the scenes of Shakespeare's plays to fit them into the rigid framework of scenery. Lavish expenditure on productions was combined with loudly proclaimed archæological accuracy of costuming and scenery; picturesque tableaux and processions were introduced wherever possible; in short, Kean attempted not without success to turn the auditors of Shakespeare's poetic drama into spectators of his picturization of Shakespeare's plays. He started the system of long runs; his *Midsummer Night's Dream* ran for one hundred and fifty performances; his spectacular *Richard II* for eighty-five. Kean's principles of production were the direct forerunner of those of Irving and Beerbohm Tree.

Irving's brilliant career as actor-manager at the Lyceum, 1878-98, marks a further development of the system of spectacular production combined with the long run. His *Merchant of Venice* ran for two hundred and fifty consecutive performances; his magnificent pageant of *Henry VIII* for over two hundred. He secured the assistance of such famous painters as Ford Madox Brown and Alma Tadema in his productions of *Lear* and *Cymbeline*. He always asserted his devotion to Shakespeare, and as a matter of fact kept his stage versions fairly free from traditional adulteration, but on the other hand he cut the text at will and shifted scenes about to correspond with the elaborate scenic effects. Irving was not an actor of genius, but he was an incomparable manager and had the happy faculty of assembling and training a body of actors equipped as none has been since his day in acting Shakespearean parts and giving to Shakespearean verse its full significance and musical value. Foremost of these was the lovely and talented Ellen Terry, long Irving's running-mate, playing Portia to his Shylock—probably his best Shakespearean rôle—and Beatrice to his Benedick.

Irving was at his best in so-called "character" parts; he was a comparative failure as Hamlet, Macbeth, and Othello. Perhaps for this reason he often turned aside from Shakespeare to produce such spectacular plays as Wills's adaptation of *Faust*. It is interesting to note that during the first ten years of his management of the Lyceum he produced only six of Shakespeare's plays.

Whatever fault may be found with Irving's program it is not to be denied that he produced Shakespeare, at least in certain plays, with an altogether unprecedented splendor. His productions became a fashionable rage in England and in America as well, on his repeated visits to this country. He was honored as no actor before him had ever been with the dignity of knighthood and from 1895 on appeared on the stage as Sir Henry. Yet the tremendous expense of his productions tended to outrun receipts and in 1898 he was forced to relinquish control of the Lyceum.

Beerbohm Tree, 1853-1917, continued the work of Irving. He became the manager of Her Majesty's Theatre in 1897 just as Irving was leaving the Lyceum and until the outbreak of the World War produced there a long succession of Shakespeare's plays. Less gifted as an actor than Irving, he was equally successful as manager and producer. There was, however, nothing new about his methods. He too engaged great artists to paint his scenic backgrounds; built up elaborate stage-sets, and rearranged the action of the play to fit his scenery. He was specially fond of spectacular processions and tableaux, introducing into *King John*, for instance, a dumb-show of the granting of Magna Carta, an incident which Shakespeare for very good reasons (p. 52) had omitted from his chronicle play. Like Irving, Tree enjoyed a great popular reputation and like Irving he received the honor of knighthood; between them they had made it something more than merely respectable to perform the plays of Shakespeare.

With the turn of the century a reaction against this whole system of spectacular production set in. In 1900 F. R. Benson brought a repertoire troupe to the Lyceum and gave a long succession of Shakespeare's plays with weekly changes of the program, a decided innovation in the time of long runs. He actually produced an uncut *Hamlet* which took six hours or so to play, kindly allowing the audience an hour and a half's intermission for dinner, an experiment repeated in this country at the performances of two of O'Neill's long plays. Benson relied neither on spectacle nor on the drawing power of individual actors but on the plays themselves delivered so far as possible in their pristine purity. This principle governed the production of the Elizabethan Society directed by William Poel, which began to present the plays of Shakespeare and his contemporaries with the minimum of scenery on stages more or less resembling that of

Shakespeare's theatre. Ben Greet carried a company of young and well-trained actors all over England and across the Atlantic, presenting, in the main, comedies, sometimes on quite bare stages, with no inconsiderable success. In the main, this principle, the play rather than the spectacle, the words of Shakespeare rather than the performance of a star, governs the annual presentations of the plays at the Stratford Shakespeare Festival.

The survey of Shakespeare on the stage has been necessarily confined to English productions. There have been great American actors of Shakespeare, notably Edwin Booth, whose Hamlet was a supreme rendition of the role; but there have been few or no American actor-managers to initiate and direct a program of Shakespearean performances. Augustin Daly's career as manager of Daly's Theatre in New York, 1879-99, almost coterminous with that of Irving at the Lyceum, was marked by a succession of brilliant performances of Shakespearean comedies, *Taming of the Shrew, As You Like It,* and *A Midsummer Night's Dream.* Daly was not himself an actor, but he gathered and trained probably the finest company ever assembled in America, including such favorites as Ada Rehan, Maude Adams, and John Drew. There was nothing novel, however, about Daly's productions; they were of the school of Irving with perhaps less stress laid on scenery and more on ensemble acting.

Little can be said of Shakespearean production in the period following the World War. The old spectacular Irving-Tree tradition has gone by the board; occasional revivals waver between a faint imitation of its glories and a half-hearted attempt to introduce a simpler and more realistic style. Neither in England nor America is there to-day, with the possible exception of the Old Vic, a theatre devoted primarily to the production of Shakespeare, nor an actor capable of rendering the greatest comic and tragic Shakespearean characters. " 'Tis true, 'tis pity."

METRICAL STATISTICS

It is improbable that the young student will be much interested in the statistics compiled by investigators of Shakespeare's verse. In accordance with precedent, however, a table of such statistics based upon the work of Fleay, Furnivall, and König is here presented. The student may be warned that the following figures are approximate rather than exact. Counts made by independent investigators differ according to the text used—the *Globe,* for instance, because of its format, gives many more lines of prose than the *Cambridge*—and according to the investigator's subjective interpretation of such phenomena as the "run-on" line and the double, or feminine ending.

In the main, however, the counts come fairly near agreement, and there is substantial concurrence of opinion as to their significance.

A few words in explanation of the following table may not be out of place. The first column shows the total number of lines in a play. It will be noticed that these vary greatly; the early farce, *Comedy of Errors,* shows the lowest figure; *Hamlet,* the largest. It is not likely that these figures represent the exact length of each play as produced on Shakespeare's stage. *Macbeth,* for example, the shortest play after the *Errors,* has been heavily cut in the one text that we have, and it is practically certain that a version of *Hamlet* containing nearly 4,000 lines was never played by Shakespeare's company.

The second column shows the number of prose lines in a play. It will be seen at a glance that the number is low for the early comedies, except for the revised *Love's Labour's Lost,* and early histories; that it increases with the comedies of the second period —*Merry Wives* is almost entirely in prose—and the contemporary histories—the high figures for *II King Henry IV* and *Much Ado* are due to the prominence of the rôles of Falstaff and Benedick and Beatrice in those plays, all of them prose speakers. It falls off considerably in the tragedies and tragi-comedies.

The third column shows the number of blank verse lines in a play, that is, the number of regular five-foot lines in the so-called iambic pentameter. This number naturally varies with the amount of prose and of rhyme present in a play; compare, for example, the low figures for *Love's Labour's Lost* and

TABLE OF METRICAL TESTS APPLIED TO SHAKESPEARE'S PLAYS

Name of Play	No. of Lines	Prose	Blank Verse	5-Foot Rhymes	% Run-on Lines	% Double Endings	% Speech Ending	No. Light & Weak Endings
L. L. L.	2789	1086	579	1028	18.4	7.7	10.0	3
Com. Er.	1778	240	1150	380	12.9	16.6	0.6	0
Two Gent.	2294	409	1510	116	12.4	18.4	5.8	0
Tit. And.	2523	43	2338	144	9.5	8.6	2.5	5
1 Hen. VI	2677	0	2379	314	10.4	8.2	0.5	4
2 Hen. VI	3162	448	2562	122	11.4	13.7	1.1	3
3 Hen. VI	2904	0	2749	155	9.5	13.7	0.9	3
Rich. III	3619	55	3374	170	13.1	19.5	2.9	4
R. & J.	3052	405	2111	486	14.2	8.2	14.9	7
Mids. Dream	2174	441	878	731	13.2	7.3	17.3	1
K. John	2570	0	2403	150	17.7	6.3	12.7	7
Rich. II	2756	0	2107	537	19.9	11.0	7.3	4
Mer. Ven.	2660	673	1896	93	21.5	17.6	22.2	7
Tam. Shrew	2649	516	1971	169	8.1	17.7	3.6	14
1 Hen. IV	3176	1464	1622	84	22.8	5.1	14.2	7
2 Hen. IV	3446	1860	1417	74	21.4	16.3	16.8	1
Much Ado	2826	2106	643	40	19.3	22.9	20.7	2
Hen. V	3380	1531	1678	101	21.8	20.5	18.3	2
Merry Wives	3018	2703	227	69	20.1	27.2	20.5	1
J. C.	2478	165	2241	34	19.3	19.7	20.3	10
A. Y. L. I.	2857	1681	925	71	17.1	25.5	21.6	2
12th Night	2690	1741	763	120	14.7	25.6	36.3	4
T. & C.	3496	1186	2025	196	27.4	23.8	31.3	6
All's Well	2966	1453	1234	280	28.4	29.4	74.4	13
Hamlet	3931	1208	2490	81	23.1	22.6	51.6	8
Meas. Meas.	2821	1134	1574	73	23.0	26.1	51.4	7
Othello	3316	541	2672	86	19.5	28.1	41.4	2
K. Lear	3334	903	2238	74	29.3	28.5	60.9	6
Macbeth	2108	158	1588	118	36.6	26.3	77.2	23
A. & C.	3063	255	2761	42	43.3	26.5	77.5	99
Tim. of Ath.	2373	596	1560	184	32.5	24.7	62.8	30
Coriolanus	3410	829	2521	42	45.9	26.4	79.0	104
Pericles	2398	418	1436	225	18.2	20.2	71.0	82
Cymbeline	3339	638	2585	107	46.0	30.7	85.0	130
Wint. Tale	3075	844	1825	0	37.5	32.9	87.6	100
Tempest	2064	458	1458	2	41.5	35.4	84.5	67
Henry VIII	2822	67	2613	16	46.3	47.3	72.4	84

Merry Wives with the high figures of *Antony and Cleopatra,* where there is little prose and much less rhyme.

The fourth column shows the number of five-foot rhymed lines in a play; songs and four-foot lines, such as those of the speeches of the Witches in *Macbeth,* are excluded from this count. The figures vary greatly. On the whole, however, the early plays show a preponderance of rhyme, except for the early histories written under the influence of Marlowe, such as *King John* and *Richard III*. It is most marked in such lyrically poetic plays as *Romeo and Juliet, A Midsummer Night's Dream* and *Richard II*. The extraordinary number in *All's Well* indicates an early date of composition for that revised play. The excessive figures for *Timon* and *Pericles* are due to the inclusion in those plays of a large amount of non-Shakespearean verse containing much more prose and rhyme than was Shakespeare's custom at that date. In *Winter's Tale* there is no rhyme at all except in the speech of Time as Chorus, and the *Tempest* has only one pair of rhymed lines in the regular dialogue. It is safe to say that there is a progressive abandonment of rhyme, except as a lyrical decoration, as Shakespeare becomes more and more a master of blank verse.

The fifth column shows the percentage of "run-on" lines in the total number of blank verse lines in a play. A "run-on" line is one where both sense and voice are carried forward without pause into the line that follows. It is opposite of the so-called "end-stopped" line.

Thus in such a passage as:

> I am yet
> Unknown to woman, never was foresworn,

The first line is "run-on," the second "end-stopped." A "stop" is not always indicated by punctuation as here. Whenever the sense calls for a pause on the last word of the line, that line is "end-stopped." Naturally the subjective element comes into play here; a pause seems necessary to one reader and not to another. This phenomenon, the running on of one line into another, is a device of Shakespeare's for breaking up the deadly monotony of the old-fashioned blank verse composed line by line as a bricklayer imposes one brick upon another. Even Marlowe, greatest of all the early poet-playwrights, composed in the main in this fashion, and those plays of Shakespeare's written under Marlowe's influence show a small percentage of "run-on" lines as compared with end-stopped: A good example of their style is seen in the opening soliloquy of *Richard III*, where in forty lines there is not a single clear example of a "run-on." With this compare a speech by Prospero (*Tempest* V:33-50), where in seventeen lines there are about a dozen which might well be counted as "run-on." A glance at the table will show how this practice increased with Shakespeare until, in his latest plays from *Macbeth* on, over a third of the lines are "run-on."

The sixth column shows the percentage of the double, or feminine ending. A double ending is one where the line instead of closing with the stressed tenth syllable adds an unstressed one. Thus in such a trio of lines as:

> Is this a dagger that I see before me,
> The handle toward my hand? Come, let me clutch thee.
> I have thee not, and yet I see thee still.

The first two have the double ending, the last the final stressed syllable. The use of the double ending is another device to vary the monotony of the regular blank verse line; a judicious blend of double endings gives great variety and charm to the verse. There is a definite, though by no means regular, increase in the percentage of double endings from the early to the late plays. Such a low figure, 7.3, in *Midsummer Night's Dream* is due to the prevalence of rhyme in that play, since double rhymes are comparatively rare in English. In the tragi-comedies the proportion is about one in three. The excessive figure, 47.3, for *Henry VIII* is due to the amount of verse in that play by Fletcher, for the use of the double-ending became a positive mannerism with that author.

The seventh column shows the percentage of the so-called "speech-ending." Earlier writers of blank verse plays, and Shakespeare in his earlier work, used to make each speech end at the close of a line and begin the next speech by another speaker with a new line. As Shakespeare drew further away from the conventional manner of composition, the line-by-line method, he adopted the device of ending a speech midway in a line and completing the line by the first words of the next speaker. This device tended to give a greater air of realism to the spoken dialogue. A good example appears in *Macbeth* V, iv, a short scene of twenty-one lines where every speech ends in the middle of a line. The table shows Shakespeare's progressive employment of this device. The early *Errors* has only six per cent; in the late tragi-comedies the vast majority of speeches are broken in this fashion.

The last column shows the number of light and weak endings in each play. A light-ending is one where an unstressed word, usually a monosyllable, takes the place of the stressed syllable which closes the normal line. Pronouns, auxiliaries, forms of "to be," and a few others constitute the light-endings. Thus in

> If I say sooth, I must report they were
> As cannons overcharged with double cracks.

The first line has a light-ending; the second is normal. The weak ending is a heightening, so to speak, of the light. The last word in the line in this case is so insignificant as to force the running on of the voice into the next line. In this group we find prepositions and conjunctions; *at, in, to, and, if, or, etc.*

Thus in

He hath been in unusual pleasure and
Sent forth great largesse to your offices.

The first line has a weak ending, the second a normal ending, the stress falling on the tenth syllable.

The trick of light and weak endings, if we may call it so, is a device employed to force *enjambment,* or the running on of line to line. As one might expect, the device is progressively employed. The *Errors* shows no instance of either light or weak endings; light-endings appear for the first time in large numbers in *Macbeth,* many weak endings first in *Antony and Cleopatra.*

So marked is the increase in his work from about 1606 that this feature has been used to date his latest plays; no play containing over twenty of such endings can well have been written before that time. The comparatively small number in *Timon* is due to the large amount of un-Shakespearean matter in that play.

I have spoken several times in the above paragraphs of a metrical phenomenon as a device employed by Shakespeare. This does not imply that he made a conscious use of any or all of these devices; there is no reason to suppose that he determined at any time to employ a greater proportion of double endings or of "run-on" lines. What happened was that, possibly without his being fully aware of it, he moved steadily in his composition of blank verse in his plays from the rigid regular form of his predecessors to a free and far more varied form. The first was well suited to declamation; we can imagine it being spouted by Alleyn in *Tamburlaine* or Burbage in *Richard III.* The latter was better suited to inter-action of characters upon the stage. We may perhaps suppose that Shakespeare's progress toward freedom corresponded with a movement of his company away from declamation to the audience and toward team-play among themselves. Instead of ranting they came to speak the lines "trippingly on the tongue."

From the point of view of metrical characteristics, Shakespeare's work falls into four periods, which do not, however, correspond exactly with the four periods of his development as a dramatist. The first of these, extending to about 1594,[1] is called by D. L. Chambers, upon whose excellent study *The Metre of Macbeth* I have drawn largely in this brief survey, the *Vanity of Rhyme.* It includes such plays as *Love's Labour's Lost, Midsummer Night's Dream, Romeo and Juliet,* and *Richard II.* Early unrhymed plays, such as *Richard III* and *Titus,* also belong here. The second period, *The Balance of Power,* 1594-1600, shows less rhyme, more prose, some increase of double endings and of "run-on" lines. Such plays as *Merchant of Venice, King Henry IV, King Henry V,* and *Julius Cæsar,* and the joyous comedies, belong here. In this period we find "the most even and easy balance of thought and metre." The third period, the *Discordant Weight of Thought,* 1600-1606, shows a still further departure from the normal line; the content of his thought begins to outweigh the poet's facility of expression and we find him breaking up the line, cutting speeches short in midline, using short and broken lines. At his best in this period, Shakespeare rises to his highest pitch of poetic dramatic expression, but sometimes at the cost of ease and grace. The last period, 1607-1613, the *License of Weak Endings,* shows Shakespeare permitting himself a careless freedom unknown before. The sudden appearance of a host of light and weak endings, about the beginning of the period, seems to mark an almost deliberate attempt to shatter the old norm of the line. At times, especially in passages where there is nothing to fire the poet's imagination, the verse is hardly distinguishable from prose. On the other hand, when Shakespeare catches fire in this period there is nothing in his earlier work quite comparable to the "happy valiancy" of *Antony and Cleopatra* or the grave beauty of the *Tempest.*

[1] The dates in this paragraph are only approximate; the periods are not sharply divided, but melt into each other. *Macbeth,* for example, is a link between the third and fourth periods.

CHRONOLOGICAL TABLE

The dates assigned to the plays in the following table are approximate dates of first production. In the main the dates assigned by Chambers (*Elizabethan Stage,* Vol. 3) have been accepted.

The dates of the other literary works, books not plays, are those of publication.

In the dating of Shakespeare's plays the earlier of two possible years is given. Thus a play dating 1594-95 is entered in 1594. If attempts to date a play range over three years the middle date is given here. Thus a play dating 1595-97 is entered under 1596.

Historical Events	*Life and Work of Shakespeare*	*Works of Other Authors*
1553. Lyly born (between Oct., 1553 and Jan. 1554).		
1558. Accession of Elizabeth. Kyd born. Greene born.		
1562.		Norton and Sackville, *Gorboduc.* Brooke, *Romeus and Juliet.*
1564. Marlowe born.	Shakespeare born.	
1566.		Gascoigne, *Supposes.* Painter, *Palace of Pleasure.*
1567.		*Gismond of Salerne.*
1568. First recorded appearance of professional actors at Stratford.		
1572. Massacre of St. Bartholomew.		
1575. Festivities at Kenilworth.		
1576. Erection of first permanent playhouse, Burbage's The Theatre.		
1577. Drake begins circumnavigation of the globe; completed 1580.		
1578.		Holinshed, *Chronicles of England, Scotland, and Ireland.* Lyly, *Euphues, the Anatomy of Wit,* 1578–79. Whetstone, *Promos and Cassandra.*

Historical Events	Life and Work of Shakespeare	Works of Other Authors
1579.		North's translation of Plutarch, *The Sheppeardes Calendar.*
1580.		Montaigne, *Essais.*
1581.		*Tenne Tragedies* of Seneca.
1582.	Shakespeare's marriage.	
1583. Queen's Company formed.	Susanna Shakespeare born	
1584.		Peele, *Araygnement of Paris.* Kyd, *Spanish Tragedie.*
1585.	Shakespeare's twins, Hamnet and Judith, born.	
1585. Death of Phillip Sidney. Star Chamber decree for licensing of the press.		
1587. Execution of Mary Queen of Scots.		Marlowe, *Tamburlaine.*
1588. Defeat of the Spanish Armada. Robert, Earl of Leicester, died. Principal actors of Lord Leicester's Company join Lord Strange's men.	Shakespeare probably in London.	*The Famous Victories of Henry the Fifth.* *The Troublesome Raigne of John.* Marlowe, *Dr. Faustus.* Greene, *Pandosto.* Lyly, *Endimion.*
1589.		Greene, *Friar Bacon and Friar Bungay.* Hakluyt, *Voyages.* Marlowe, *Jew of Malta.*
1590.	*Comedy of Errors*	Lodge, *Rosalynde.* Sidney, *Arcadia.* Spenser, *Faerie Queene* (I-III).
1591.	*Two Gentlemen of Verona.*	Sidney, *Astrophel and Stella.* Greene, *James IV.*
1592. Plague in London. Theatres closed for three months. Death of Greene.	1, 2, 3 *Henry VI.*	Greene, *Groatsworth of Wit.* Marlowe, *Edward II. First part of the Contention, True tragedy of Richard, Duke of York.*
1593. Plague closes theatres. Lord Strange's men become Earl of Derby's Men. Death of Marlowe.	*Venus and Adonis.* *Titus Andronicus.* *Love's Labour's Lost.*	*The True Chronicle.* *History of King Leir.*

Historical Events	*Life and Work of Shakespeare*	*Works of Other Authors*
1594. Plague until summer. The Earl of Derby's Men become the Lord Chamberlain's Men. The Lord Chamberlain's Men at The Theatre; the Lord Admiral's Men at the Rose. Death of Kyd.	*Lucrece.* *Richard III.* Shakespeare member of Chamberlain's Company.	*Edward III.*
1595.	*Midsummer Night's Dream.* *Richard II*	Spenser, *Amoretti.* Sidney, *Defense of Poesy.*
1596. The Cadiz Expedition.	Shakespeare's father applies for grant of coat of arms. Hamnet Shakespeare dies. *Romeo and Juliet.* *Merchant of Venice.* *King John*	Spenser, *Faerie Queene* (IV-VI).
1597. The Islands Voyage.	Shakespeare purchases New Place, Stratford. 1, 2 *Henry IV.*	Bacon, *Essays* (first version).
1598.	*The Taming of the Shrew.* *Much Ado About Nothing.*	Chapman's Translation of the *Iliad* (seven books). Meres, *Palladis Tamia.* Jonson, *Every Man In His Humour.*
1599. Essex in Ireland. Death of Spenser. Lord Chamberlain's Men occupy The Globe.	*Henry V.* *Merry Wives of Windsor.* *Julius Caesar.*	*The Passionate Pilgrim.* Jonson, *Every Man Out of His Humour.*
1600. Alleyn builds Fortune Theatre. Children of Chapel begin playing at Blackfriars.	*As You Like It.* *Twelfth Night.* *Hamlet.*	
1601. Execution of Essex. The War of the Theatres.		Jonson, *The Poetaster.* *The Return from Parnassus,* part II.
1602.	*All's Well That Ends Well.* *Troilus and Cressida.*	
1603. Death of Queen Elizabeth. Accession of James I. The Lord Chamberlain's Men become the King's Majesty's Servants. Plague stops playing.		Florio's Translation of Montaigne's *Essays.* Jonson, *Sejanus.* Heywood, *Woman Killed with Kindness.*
1604. Theatres reopen in April. Treaty of Peace with Spain.	*Measure for Measure.* *Othello.*	

Historical Events	*Life and Work of Shakespeare*	*Works of Other Authors*
1605. Gunpowder Plot.	Shakespeare purchases certain fixed rents at Stratford. *King Lear.*	*Eastward Ho.* Bacon, *Advancement of Learning.*
1606. Statute forbidding the use of the name of the Deity on the stage.	*Timon of Athens.* *Macbeth.*	Jonson, *Volpone.*
1607. The bitter winter of 1607–8.	Susanna Shakespeare marries Dr. John Hall. *Antony and Cleopatra.* *Pericles, Prince of Tyre.*	Beaumont, *The Knight of the Burning Pestle.*
1608. Children of Blackfriars disbanded. Burbage leases the Blackfriars.	*Coriolanus.*	Fletcher, *The Faithful Shepherdess.*
1609. Wreck of The Sea Venture off the Bermudas.	*Cymbeline.* Shakespeare's *Sonnets* published.	Beaumont and Fletcher, *Philaster.* Dekker, *The Gull's Hornbook.*
1611.	*The Winter's Tale.* *The Tempest.*	Authorized version of the Bible. Chapman completes translation of *Iliad.* Beaumont and Fletcher, *King and No King.*
1612. Death of Prince Henry.		Heywood, *Apology for Actors.* Webster, *The White Devil.*
1613. Marriage of Princess Elizabeth. Globe Theatre burnt.	Shakespeare purchases property in Blackfriars, *Henry VIII.* *The Two Noble Kinsmen.*	Webster, *The Duchess of Malfi.*
1614. Globe Theatre rebuilt.		
1616.	Judith Shakespeare marries. Death of Shakespeare.	
1619.		Pavier attempts a collection of Shakespeare's plays.
1623.	First Folio published.	

BIBLIOGRAPHY

The following bibliography makes no pretence to even approximate completeness. It merely suggests a few books, carefully selected, that may prove useful and interesting to the student in connection with the topics discussed in this introduction.

I. GENERAL

Schuecking and Ebisch, *A Shakespearean Bibliography;* 1931. The latest and most satisfactory of the many books of this sort.

Schelling, F. E., *Elizabethan Drama.* 2 Volumes; 1902. The best and fullest history of Elizabethan drama.

Chambers, E. K., *The Elizabethan Stage.* 4 Volumes; 1923. An invaluable reference book with bibliographies complete to date.

Chambers, E. K., *William Shakespeare.* 2 Volumes; 1930. The latest and fullest biography, a book for reference rather than for reading; the second volume reprints important documents.

Harrison and Granville-Barker, *A Companion to Shakespearean Studies;* 1934. A collection of essays of unequal merit, but containing some valuable information and up-to-date bibliographies.

Adams, J. Q., *A Life of William Shakespeare;* 1923. The best and most readable life, containing all that is known or conjectured about the poet and his work.

CHAPTER I

Lee, S., *Stratford-on-Avon;* 1906. The most interesting historical account of Shakespeare's birthplace.

Fripp, E. I., *Shakespeare's Stratford;* 1928. Interesting notes by a Stratford antiquarian.

CHAPTER II

Madden, D. H., *The Diary of Master William Silence;* 1907. The best account of Elizabethan field sports. Interesting and suggestive in connection with Shakespeare's youth at Stratford.

Wilson, J. D., *The Essential Shakespeare;* 1932. A stimulating imaginative reconstruction of Shakespeare's life, particularly interesting in connection with his youth and his London associations.

CHAPTER III

Raleigh, Walter, *Shakespeare's England.* 2 Volumes; 1916. A series of studies containing the fullest account of town and country life in Shakespeare's day.

Harrison, G. B., *England in Shakespeare's Day;* 1928. An anthology of selections from Elizabethan prose and verse describing contemporary manners.

CHAPTERS IV-V

The student is referred to Chambers's *William Shakespeare,* and Adams's *A Life of William Shakespeare.*

CHAPTER VI

Baldwin, T. W., *Organization and Personnel of the Shakespearean Company;* 1927. The standard book on the subject, difficult reading, but invaluable for reference.

Chambers, E. K., *The Elizabethan Stage.* Volume III contains a full account of the Elizabethan companies of actors.

Nungezer, *A Dictionary of Actors . . . before 1642.* A useful reference book.

CHAPTER VII

Chambers, E. K., *The Elizabethan Stage.* Volume II has a full account of Elizabethan theatres; Volume III treats of staging in Shakespeare's day.

Thorndike, A. H., *Shakespeare's Theatre;* 1916. The best single book on the subject.

CHAPTER VIII

Green, J. R., *Short History of the English People;* 1877-80. Book VI, Chapter vii, has a very stimulating account of the tone and temper of the Elizabethans.

Harrison, G. B., *An Elizabethan Journal;* 1928. *A Second Elizabethan Journal;* 1931. *A Last Elizabethan Journal;* 1933.

The three volumes covering the period from 1591 to 1603 present a picture drawn from contemporary sources of Elizabethan life in Shakespeare's day—extremely interesting.

CHAPTER IX

Brooke, Tucker, *Tudor Drama;* 1912. A useful study of the development of English drama from the beginning to Shakespeare.

Symonds, J. A., *Shakespeare's Predecessors;* 1884. Obsolete as history, but packed with stimulating appreciative criticism.

Stuart, D. C., *Development of Dramatic Art;* 1928. Chapters vi to viii contain a valuable account of the development of the medieval into the Elizabethan drama and of the influence of Seneca—a technical study.

CHAPTER X

Baker, G. P., *The Development of Shakespeare as a Dramatist.* Apart from some now discarded notions of the Elizabethan stage, the best single book on the subject.

Dowden, Edward, *Shakespeare—His Mind and Art;* 1880. Old-fashioned, but interesting and suggestive.

CHAPTER XI

Wyndham, George, *The Poems of Shakespeare;* 1898. Perhaps the best edition of the poems and sonnets with an admirable introduction and notes.

Brooke, Tucker, *Shakespeare's Sonnets;* 1936. The best re-arrangement of the sonnets. The notes are full and the introductory essay is always aware of the poetry of the sonnets.

CHAPTER XII

Chambers, E. K., *The Elizabethan Stage.* Volume III has a valuable chapter on the printing of plays.

Pollard, A. W., *Shakespeare's Folios and Quartos;* 1909. *Shakespeare's Fight with the Pirates;* 1920.

These two books lay the foundation for recent bibliographical and textual study of Shakespeare.

CHAPTER XIII

Lounsbury, T., *The Text of Shakespeare;* 1906. A very full account of the work of early editors up to and including Theobald.

McKerrow, R. B., *The Treatment of Shakespeare's Text by His Earlier Editors;* 1933. The latest and most accurate study of the subject, an essay rather than a full discussion.

CHAPTER XIV

Ralli, A., *A History of Shakespearian Criticism.* 2 Volumes; 1932. A useful summary with quotations and paraphrases of Shakespearean criticism from the beginning to the present.

Bradley, A. C., *Shakespearean Tragedy;* 1904. *Oxford Lectures on Poetry;* 1909.

Bradley's criticism of the tragedies is the best of its kind; the second volume contains lectures on *Antony and Cleopatra,* on Falstaff and others.

Granville-Barker, *Prefaces to Shakespeare.* Three series; 1927, 1930, 1937. Very stimulating modern criticism, especially the latest volume devoted to *Hamlet.*

Raleigh, Walter, *Shakespeare (English Men of Letters)*; 1907. Critical rather than biographical, and very good reading.

Schuecking, L. L., *Character Problems in Shakespeare's Plays;* 1922. Modern realistic criticism.

Stoll, E. E., *Shakespeare Studies;* 1927. Like Schuecking, a reaction against the romantic interpretation of Shakespeare.

Smart, J. S., *Shakespeare, Truth and Tradition;* 1928. A valuable and suggestive work.

Lawrence, W. W., *Shakespeare's Problem Comedies;* 1931. The best study of the so-called "Bitter Comedies."

CHAPTER XV

Odell, G. C. D., *Shakespeare from Betterton to Irving.* 2 Volumes; 1921. The best book on Shakespeare on the English stage; delightful reading.

Winter, William, *Shakespeare on the Stage*; 1911. Interesting account of the stage history of some of Shakespeare's plays; valuable records of American theatres and actors.

The Comedy of Errors

Text.—This entertaining farce-comedy, one of the earliest of Shakespeare's plays, was first printed in the Folio of 1623. It was, however, acted on the stage many years before this date. The first record we have of its performance was at a famous "night of errors" in the hall of Gray's Inn December 28, 1594. At this time the lawyers of the Inn were holding their Christmas revels and to supplement them engaged a troupe of players, no doubt Shakespeare's company, to present a play "a *Comedy of Errors* (like to Plautus his *Menechmus*)" to entertain their guests. There is no reason to believe that this was the first performance. In fact it is probable that this play was selected for the occasion because of its previous success upon the public stage, and because of its brevity—it is by far the shortest of Shakespeare's plays, some 1770 lines in all—since it was to be but one feature in an evening of processions, speeches, dancing, and revelling. It is probable that the text as it has come down to us represents a careful revision by the author for this gala performance.

Date.—There is no possibility of determining exactly the date of composition. Probably the best conclusion is to set the date somewhere near 1590 and allow for a revision about 1594. Such a date and such a revision would account for the diversity of style, of which a word must be said later.

Source.—From the time of its first recorded performance it has been recognized that *The Comedy of Errors* was based upon a play by Plautus. As a matter of fact this play, and this alone of Shakespeare's comedies, shows him accepting the academic convention of his time and following Plautus as the recognized master of comedy, another reason for suspecting that this may be his first play. He had, no doubt, read Plautus at school; he had even, perhaps, taught Plautus himself, and seen a Plautine comedy presented by school-boys. It would be natural enough, then, if he wished to recommend his work to a London company, that he should follow the pattern set by Plautus. Something has been said in the General Introduction (p. 41) as to the general influence of Latin comedy on Elizabethan drama; here we may turn at once to the particular Latin play which was the source of this work of Shakespeare's.

This was the *Menaechmi* of Plautus, and a brief sketch of the action of that play will show how deeply Shakespeare is indebted to it.

In the Prologue which introduces the play we are told that a certain man of Syracuse had twin sons so much alike as to be indistinguishable. One of these was stolen from him and brought up as his own child by a man of Epidamnus. The other twin was given the name, Menaechmus, of his lost brother, and when he came to man's estate set out in search of him. After long wandering he came to Epidamnus and here the play proper begins.

The stolen twin, henceforth to be designated as the Citizen to distinguish him from his brother, the Traveller, is now a grown man blessed with riches but cursed with a shrewish wife. We see him coming out of his house swearing at her and announcing his intention of dining with a courtesan, Erotium, to whom he means to give a cloak that he has stolen from his wife. This lively lady welcomes him, accepts the cloak, and sends her cook off to buy provisions for a very special feast for him and his hanger-on Peniculus, the parasite of Latin comedy. The Citizen has some law business to transact and goes off to the forum with Peniculus. As the second act opens the Traveller appears on the scene with his slave, Messenio. The cook, returning from the market, mistakes him for the Citizen, the first of many errors of the play, a mistake at once repeated by Erotium, who bids him in to dinner. Somewhat bewildered but quite ready to get a good meal for nothing, he accepts and follows her in while his slave departs shaking his head at his master's folly. The third act brings Peniculus back from the forum furious because he has lost his patron there and with him the chance of a free meal. He is just in time to see the Traveller coming out from Erotium's licking his lips and bearing on his arm the stolen cloak which the courtesan wants him to carry to the dyer's but which he has every intention of keeping for himself. Peniculus, of course, mistakes him for the Citizen, and after a bitter wrangle runs off to tell the Citizen's wife of her husband's behavior. Before the Traveller leaves the stage Erotium's maid brings him a gold chain, which the Citizen had also stolen from his wife, and bids him take it to the goldsmith's to be enlarged and mended, a stroke of good luck which he thankfully accepts. In the fourth act the Citizen's wife accompanied by Peniculus catches the husband coming back late to the house of Erotium. The wife upbraids him with the theft of the cloak and bids him restore it or never enter her doors again. In despair he begs Erotium to let him have the cloak back, but she quite naturally says that she had given it to him already and a gold chain as well and angrily shuts her door on such an Indian giver. The unlucky man departs to seek counsel from his friends. And now the Traveller re-appears with the cloak and chain upon his arm only to be confronted by the Citizen's wife, who abuses him and whom he abuses in round terms. Her old father appears on the scene to join in the family quarrel; he and the wife both think the Traveller mad to deny, as he of course does, his identity. Out of all patience at last the Traveller feigns madness and raves so wildly that the wife and her father are frightened and depart to get a doctor for him, whereupon he hurries off to find his slave. And now the Citizen coming back runs into the Father and the Doctor who summon help to carry him to the Doctor's for a course of treatment. A scuffle ensues and the Citizen is rescued by Messenio, who appears on the scene and mistakes him for his master, the Traveller. As a reward the slave begs his freedom, which the Citizen readily grants, and departs to have another try for the cloak. When the slave meets his true master, the Traveller denies that he set him free and the slave might have got a beating instead of his freedom, had not the Citizen appeared upon the scene. Now for the first time the brothers are together; the slave brings about a recognition, the errors are explained, and the Citizen professes his readiness to accompany his brother to Syracuse. He will sell all that he has, his wife too, if any one will buy her, and so the play ends with the brothers in each other's arms.

The general likeness of this play to *The Comedy of Errors* is unmistakable, but there is much in the *Errors* that is not in the *Menaechmi,* and for this a second source must be examined. Another play by Plautus, the *Amphitruo,* deals with the old myth of Jupiter's amour with Alcmena. It is not necessary to tell the whole story of this play, but certain incidents which re-appear in the *Errors* may be noted.

In the first place Jupiter visiting Alcmena in the guise of her absent husband, Amphitruo, is accompanied by Mercury in the shape of the husband's slave, Sosia. Mercury plays the part of porter at Alcmena's house, refuses admission to Sosia, claims that he is the real Sosia, and reduces the unhappy slave to a hopeless state of confusion. Later on Mercury as Sosia refuses admission to the husband and asserts that the real Amphitruo is in the house with his wife. The angry husband beats the wretched Sosia who, he thinks, has barred the door upon him and vows revenge on all in the house. The situation is only saved by the self-revelation of Jupiter and his promise that the hero Hercules will be born as the result of his visit to Alcmena.

Evidently the doubling of the servants in the *Errors* comes from this play as well as the best comic situation in the plot when Antipholus of Ephesus is refused admission to his own house.

But there are still other things in Shakespeare's play which are not to be found in either of the Plautine comedies. Chief among these is the so-called enveloping action which opens and which ends the play, the story of Ægeon, father of the twin boys, who had been separated from his wife and one of his sons by ship-wreck, and who had sought for them in vain for many years, only to fall at last into the hands of a hostile prince, the Duke of Ephesus, by whom he is condemned to death. It is with the narrative of Ægeon that the *Errors* begins and it ends with his recognition by his long-lost wife, now an Abbess at Ephesus. It has long been recognized that this story derives from the old medieval tale of Apollonius of Tyre, retold by Gower in the *Confessio Amantis* and put into Elizabethan prose by Lawrence Twine in 1576. It is a story of wandering adventure and romance with a happy ending such as the Elizabethans loved. It was a happy inspiration that led him to surround the rather sordid plots of the *Menaechmi* and the *Amphitruo* with this romantic tale.

There is yet another strand in the intricate plot which, apparently, is Shakespeare's own invention. This is woven around the figure of Luciana, the gentle sister of the jealous wife, and her wooing by the wandering brother. There is, of course, no such figure in the Plautine plays, and it is worth noting that in the scenes which deal with her wooing Shakespeare breaks into a vein of lyric poetry such as appears nowhere else in the play, one which would, indeed, be quite out of place in the comic scenes derived from Plautus.

Such then were the varied materials out of which Shakespeare evolved the complicated, swift-moving, and humorous action of his comedy. The pattern, we may well believe, was of his own devising. It seems unkind as well as uncritical to seek to deprive Shakespeare of all credit for plot-construction in this play and to limit his contribution to a few interpolated and re-written scenes. It is more likely that with the well-articulated framework of Plautus before him he followed in the main the classical design, wove around it a serious action, the Ægeon-Emilia story, which cast a shadow of possible tragedy upon the comic plot—a device that he was to employ again in his later plays—and set in it the pretty, faintly sentimental, theme of the wooing of Luciana.

But Shakespeare did something more than double the errors of Plautus and add a dash of romance to the old farce-comedy. Writing as he did for the public stage and not for an academic audience, he gave the action a realistic and recognizably English background. The Ephesus in which the fantastic errors occur is classic only in name. It is an English sea-port like Shakespeare's London with its harbor and its mart, its inns, the Centaur and the Tiger, its houses distinguished not by numbers in our practical fashion, but by painted signs, the Phoenix where Adriana lives, and the Porpentine which marks the dwelling of the Courtesan. Merchants transact business on the open street, and men are arrested for debt by a sheriff's officer dressed in a suit of buff and carrying a mace, his badge of office. Shakespeare has eliminated the character of the parasite, one unfamiliar to his English audience, and turned the *medicus* of Plautus into an English school-master equipped by his knowledge of Latin to exorcise the demon that possesses a madman. Notably too he has elevated the whole moral tone of the play. The twins of Plautus are rather scurvy fellows; one of them is a frequenter of the harlot's house, the other a lecher and little better than a thief. It is interesting and amusing to note that while the Citizen in the Latin play slips out from his wife's house with a gift for the courtesan, the husband in Shakespeare only visits the wench "pretty and witty, wild, and yet, too, gentle" when his own door is barred upon him by his wife. In like manner the Traveller of Plautus goes off rejoicing with Erotium's chain while his counterpart in Shakespeare offers, like an honest man, to pay for the chain when it is thrust upon him. To put it in a word, Shakespeare's twins are gentlemen; one has been a soldier and saved the Duke's life in battle; the other is a sober, rather melancholy, wanderer who repels the bold advances of the courtesan and makes poetic declarations to a fair gentlewoman. This lady is a character of Shakespeare's own invention and her sister, the jealous, passionate Adriana, is miles removed from the vulgar wrangling wife of Plautus; her jealousy springs from her love, and in the last scene she throws herself at the Duke's feet to retrieve a husband she believes a madman from the Abbess who detains him, so that she may bear him home and be his nurse. The role of the courtesan, so prominent in Plautus, is cut down to a few lines in Shakespeare and a very human touch is added when she runs to tell Adriana of her husband's madness because the ring he had snatched from her, worth forty ducats, is "too much to lose." We may be sure that Shakespeare's audience while they laughed heartily at the farcical happenings of the play were wholly in sympathy with the characters.

A word must be said in passing about the metrical characteristics of the play. About one-half of it is written in blank verse, and it is an interesting fact that certain passages of this verse (especially I, i and V, 282-407) are of a markedly archaic quality compared to the rest of this play. This has been held to indicate the hand of another author than Shakespeare, but these passages may well represent Shakespeare's first attempt at writing in the to him unfamiliar form of blank verse, left untouched when he rewrote the play. About one-fifth of the verse is in rhyme, usually in rhymed pentameter couplets, varied at times by alternating rhymes as in the scene between Luciana and Antipholus (III, ii.). We find also a greater amount of rhymed doggerel in the old fourteeners, the common form of early Elizabethan drama, than in any other play of Shakespeare's except *Love's Labour's Lost*. There is less prose than rhyme, prose limited almost entirely to the comic Dromio scenes.

On the basis of metrical characteristics it seems a fair guess that Shakespeare wrote the play at first in the old doggerel metre varied by pentameter couplets and that a later revision cut out most of the doggerel, added scenes in blank verse, and possibly inserted some jests in prose.

It would be foolish in any final estimate of *The Comedy of Errors* to assign the play a high rank in the body of Shakespeare's work or even to see in it sure promise of his future greatness. One or two points, however, may be made. We find here a marked ability in plot-construction, notably absent in many of the early, and even in some of Shakespeare's later plays. This, of course, is due to Shakespeare's careful study and close following of his Latin original. Again we may note Shakespeare's sense of the theatrically effective situation, due no doubt to his intimate association with the theatre in his apprentice years. The last scene of the *Errors* with its grand rally upon the stage of all the characters in the play and its general happy solution of all the entanglements of the action is particularly successful. Something of the same sort occurs in the last scene of what is in many ways his most perfect comedy, *Twelfth Night*.

There is little in this play to foretell Shakespeare's mastery of characterization. Some slight difference between the characters of the Antipholi may be noted, and Dromio of Syracuse seems a gayer jester than his long-suffering brother of Ephesus. There is a purposed contrast between the domineering Adriana and her gentle sister. Yet it is hardly too much to say that there is not a single fully developed and instantly recognizable human individual in this play, no Bottom, no Nurse, much less a Touchstone or a Falstaff. Nor is there any promise in this play of Shakespeare's magic of poetic expression such as glorifies his later work. Passages of true poetry are few and far between, occurring for the most part in the Luciana scenes. It would almost seem as if the young poet-playwright had sternly repressed the flow of his poetic vein in his concentrated effort to produce a well-planned and theatrically effective comedy. Perhaps the one distinct foreshadowing of Shakespeare's mature genius is to be found in his realization of the tangled thread of tragedy and comedy in the affairs of men. Something of this sort was to appear again and again in Shakespeare's later comedies, notably in such plays as *The Merchant of Venice* and *The Winter's Tale*.

Stage History.—In spite of its well-wrought plot and farcical action *The Comedy of Errors* has never been popular. There are but two records of its performance in Shakespeare's life-time—that of Gray's Inn already referred to, and a later one before King James at Whitehall on December 28, 1604. Nothing is heard of it again until about the middle of the eighteenth century when it appears from time to time. John Philip Kemble prepared an acting version in the early 19th century. It was turned into an opera by Reynolds in 1819 and played in its original form with some success by Phelps at Sadler's Wells. Records show that Squire Bancroft and John Hare acted in it in their early days and it has been a stock piece in the Benson company in this century.

The Folio version, divided into the regular five acts with no intermediate scene division, probably reproduces the setting of the play on a platform in the great hall of Gray's Inn. For scenery all that is needed are three houses to represent the home of Antipholus of Ephesus, the house of the Courtesan, and the Priory. Very likely each of these was designated by an appropriate sign. Characters appear from and enter into these houses, but all the action takes place on the open stage in front of them, which may be regarded as a street in Ephesus. There is, with one exception, no interior action at all, and even this is doubtful. In the first scene of Act III Dromio of Ephesus speaks from within to his brother outside, and a little later on Luce and Adriana, according to modern texts, also speak from within. No doubt when Shakespeare wrote the play for the public theatre the women appeared on the balcony stage, as if entering from the dining-room—cf. II, ii, 209—of the house. It would have been easy for the stage-manager at Gray's Inn or Whitehall to provide an equivalent for this balcony stage at an upper window of the house, so as to allow the women to appear in view and thus avoid confusing the audience by three voices proceeding from unseen characters. A reader to-day would do well to disregard all modern indications of place, such as a *Hall in the Duke's Palace* or *The Mart,* and think of the action as proceeding without interruption, upon an open street in Ephesus.

THE COMEDY OF ERRORS

Dramatis Personæ

Solinus, duke of Ephesus.
Ægeon, a merchant of Syracuse.
Antipholus of Ephesus, } twin brothers, and sons
Antipholus of Syracuse, } to *Ægeon* and *Æmilia.*
Dromio of Ephesus, } twin brothers, and bonds-
Dromio of Syracuse, } men to the two *Antipholuses.*
Balthazar, a merchant.
Angelo, a goldsmith.
First Merchant, friend to *Antipholus* of Syracuse.
Second Merchant, to whom *Angelo* is a debtor.
Pinch, a schoolmaster.

Æmilia, wife to *Ægeon,* an abbess at Ephesus.
Adriana, wife to *Antipholus* of Ephesus.
Luciana, her sister.
Luce, servant to *Adriana.*
A Courtezan.

Jailer, Officers, and other Attendants.

SCENE: *Ephesus.*

All the action takes place on the front stage, supposed a street in Ephesus before the houses of Antipholus and the Courtezan, and the Priory. In III, i, the women appear on the balcony, supposed a window of the house of Antipholus.

ACT I. Scene I. *A hall in the Duke's palace.*

Enter *The Duke of Ephesus, Ægeon the Merchant of Syracuse, Jailer,* and other *Attendants.*

Æge. Proceed, Solinus, to procure my fall,
And by the doom of death end woes and all.
Duke. Merchant of Syracusa, plead no more;
I am not partial to infringe our laws.
The enmity and discord which of late
Sprung from the rancorous outrage of your duke
To merchants, our well-dealing countrymen,
Who, wanting guilders to redeem their lives,
Have seal'd his rigorous statutes with their bloods,
Excludes all pity from our threat'ning looks,
For, since the mortal and intestine jars
'Twixt thy seditious countrymen and us,
It hath in solemn synods been decreed,
Both by the Syracusians and ourselves,
To admit no traffic to our adverse towns.
Nay, more:
If any born at Ephesus be seen
At any Syracusian marts and fairs;
Again, if any Syracusian born
Come to the bay of Ephesus, he dies,
His goods confiscate to the Duke's dispose,
Unless a thousand marks be levied,
To quit the penalty and to ransom him.
Thy substance, valued at the highest rate,
Cannot amount unto a hundred marks;
Therefore by law thou art condemn'd to die.
Æge. Yet this my comfort: when your words are done,
My woes end likewise with the evening sun.
Duke. Well, Syracusian, say in brief the cause
Why thou departed'st from thy native home,
And for what cause thou cam'st to Ephesus.
Æge. A heavier task could not have been impos'd
Than I to speak my griefs unspeakable;
Yet, that the world may witness that my end
Was wrought by nature, not by vile offence,
I 'll utter what my sorrow gives me leave.
In Syracusa was I born, and wed
Unto a woman, happy but for me,
And by me, had not our hap been bad.
With her I liv'd in joy; our wealth increas'd
By prosperous voyages I often made
To Epidamnum, till my factor's death
And the great care of goods at random left
Drew me from kind embracements of my spouse;
From whom my absence was not six months old
Before herself, almost at fainting under
The pleasing punishment that women bear,
Had made provision for her following me,
And soon and safe arrived where I was.
There had she not been long but she became

4. partial, inclined to favor you. **8. guilders,** money. **11. intestine,** civil, fatal. **22. marks,** coins worth 13s. 4d. apiece.

35. nature, natural affection of a father. **42. Epidamnum,** a town in Albania, on the Adriatic. **factor's,** agent's.

A joyful mother of two goodly sons;
And, which was strange, the one so like the other
As could not be distinguish'd but by names.
That very hour, and in the self-same inn,
A meaner woman was delivered
Of such a burden male twins, both alike.
Those, for their parents were exceeding poor,
I bought and brought up to attend my sons.
My wife, not meanly proud of two such boys,
Made daily motions for our home return.
Unwilling I agreed. Alas! too soon
We came aboard.
A league from Epidamnum had we sail'd
Before the always wind-obeying deep
Gave any tragic instance of our harm;
But longer did we not retain much hope;
For what obscured light the heavens did grant
Did but convey unto our fearful minds
A doubtful warrant of immediate death;
Which though myself would gladly have embrac'd,
Yet the incessant weepings of my wife,
Weeping before for what she saw must come,
And piteous plainings of the pretty babes,
That mourn'd for fashion, ignorant what to fear,
Forc'd me to seek delays for them and me.
And this it was, for other means was none:
The sailors sought for safety by our boat,
And left the ship, then sinking-ripe, to us.
My wife, more careful for the latter born,
Had fasten'd him unto a small spare mast,
Such as seafaring men provide for storms.
To him one of the other twins was bound,
Whilst I had been like heedful of the other.
The children thus dispos'd, my wife and I,
Fixing our eyes on whom our care was fix'd,
Fasten'd ourselves at either end the mast;
And floating straight, obedient to the stream,
Was carried towards Corinth, as we thought.
At length the sun, gazing upon the earth,
Dispers'd those vapours that offended us;
And, by the benefit of his wished light,
The seas wax'd calm, and we discovered
Two ships from far making amain to us,
Of Corinth that, of Epidaurus this.
But ere they came,—O, let me say no more!
Gather the sequel by that went before.

Duke. Nay, forward, old man; do not break off so;
For we may pity, though not pardon thee.

Æge. O, had the gods done so, I had not now
Worthily term'd them merciless to us!
For, ere the ships could meet by twice five leagues,
We were encounter'd by a mighty rock;
Which being violently borne upon,
Our helpful ship was splitted in the midst;
So, that, in this unjust divorce of us,
Fortune had left to both of us alike
What to delight in, what to sorrow for.
Her part, poor soul, seeming as burdened
With lesser weight but not with lesser woe,
Was carried with more speed before the wind;
And in our sight they three were taken up
By fishermen of Corinth, as we thought.
At length, another ship had seiz'd on us;
And, knowing whom it was their hap to save,
Gave healthful welcome to their shipwreck'd guests;
And would have reft the fishers of their prey,
Had not their bark been very slow of sail;
And therefore homeward did they bend their course.
Thus have you heard me sever'd from my bliss,
That by misfortunes was my life prolong'd
To tell sad stories of my own mishaps.

Duke. And, for the sake of them thou sorrowest for,
Do me the favour to dilate at full
What hath befallen of them and thee till now.

Æge. My youngest boy, and yet my eldest care,
At eighteen years became inquisitive
After his brother; and importun'd me
That his attendant—so his case was like,
Reft of his brother, but retain'd his name—
Might bear him company in the quest of him;
Whom whilst I labour'd of a love to see,
I hazarded the loss of whom I lov'd.
Five summers have I spent in farthest Greece,
Roaming clean through the bounds of Asia,
And, coasting homeward, came to Ephesus;
Hopeless to find, yet loath to leave unsought
Or that or any place that harbours men.
But here must end the story of my life;
And happy were I in my timely death,
Could all my travels warrant me they live.

Duke. Hapless Ægeon, whom the fates have mark'd
To bear the extremity of dire mishap!
Now, trust me, were it not against our laws,
Against my crown, my oath, my dignity,
Which princes, would they, may not disannul,
My soul should sue as advocate for thee.
But, though thou art adjudged to the death,
And passed sentence may not be recall'd

55. meaner, of lower rank. **56. male,** a pun on mail, baggage. **59. meanly,** moderately. **60. motions,** proposals. **65. instance,** sign, proof. **74. for fashion,** in imitation of others. **78. sinking-ripe,** about to sink. **93. amain,** with all speed. **94. Epidaurus,** town in Argolis, in Greece. **96. that,** what.

104. ship, here the mast (see l. 86). **131. of,** because of. **137. Or . . . or,** either . . . or. **139. timely,** speedy, early. **140. travels,** both "travels" and "travails." **warrant,** furnish evidence that. **145. disannul,** annul.

But to our honour's great disparagement,
Yet I will favour thee in what I can.
Therefore, merchant, I 'll limit thee this day
To seek thy health by beneficial help.
Try all the friends thou hast in Ephesus;
Beg thou, or borrow, to make up the sum,
And live; if no, then thou art doom'd to die.
Jailer, take him to thy custody.

Jail. I will, my lord.

Æge. Hopeless and helpless doth Ægeon wend,
But to procrastinate his lifeless end. *Exeunt.*

Scene II. *The mart.*

Enter *Antipholus of Syracuse, Dromio of Syracuse,* and *First Merchant.*

1. Mer. Therefore give out you are of Epidamnum,
Lest that your goods too soon be confiscate.
This very day a Syracusian merchant
Is apprehended for arrival here;
And, not being able to buy out his life
According to the statute of the town,
Dies ere the weary sun set in the west.
There is your money that I had to keep.

Ant. S. Go bear it to the Centaur, where we host,
And stay there, Dromio, till I come to thee.
Within this hour it will be dinner-time;
Till that, I 'll view the manners of the town,
Peruse the traders, gaze upon the buildings,
And then return and sleep within mine inn,
For with long travel I am stiff and weary.
Get thee away.

Dro. S. Many a man would take you at your word,
And go, indeed, having so good a mean. *Exit.*

Ant. S. A trusty villain, sir, that very oft,
When I am dull with care and melancholy,
Lightens my humour with his merry jests.
What, will you walk with me about the town,
And then go to my inn and dine with me?

1. Mer. I am invited, sir, to certain merchants,
Of whom I hope to make much benefit;
I crave your pardon. Soon, at five o'clock,
Please you, I'll meet with you upon the mart
And afterward consort you till bed-time.
My present business calls me from you now.

Ant. S. Farewell till then. I will go lose myself,
And wander up and down to view the city.

1. Mer. Sir, I commend you to your own content. *Exit.*

Ant. S. He that commends me to mine own content
Commends me to the thing I cannot get.
I to the world am like a drop of water
That in the ocean seeks another drop,
Who, falling there to find his fellow forth,
Unseen, inquisitive, confounds himself.
So I, to find a mother and a brother,
In quest of them, unhappier, lose myself.

Enter *Dromio of Ephesus.*

Here comes the almanac of my true date.
What now? How chance thou art return'd so soon?

Dro. E. Return'd so soon! rather approach'd too late.
The capon burns, the pig falls from the spit,
The clock hath strucken twelve upon the bell;
My mistress made it one upon my cheek;
She is so hot because the meat is cold;
The meat is cold because you come not home;
You come not home because you have no stomach;
You have no stomach having broke your fast;
But we that know what 't is to fast and pray
Are penitent for your default to-day.

Ant. S. Stop in your wind, sir; tell me this, I pray:
Where have you left the money that I gave you?

Dro. E. O,—sixpence, that I had o' Wednesday last
To pay the saddler for my mistress' crupper?
The saddler had it, sir; I kept it not.

Ant. S. I am not in a sportive humour now.
Tell me, and dally not, where is the money?
We being strangers here, how dar'st thou trust
So great a charge from thine own custody?

Dro. E. I pray you, jest, sir, as you sit at dinner.
I from my mistress come to you in post;
If I return, I shall be post indeed,
For she will score your fault upon my pate.
Methinks your maw, like mine, should be your clock
And strike you home without a messenger.

Ant. S. Come, Dromio, come, these jests are out of season;
Reserve them till a merrier hour than this.
Where is the gold I gave in charge to thee?

Dro. E. To me, sir? Why, you gave no gold to me.

Ant. S. Come on, sir knave, have done your foolishness
And tell me how thou hast dispos'd thy charge.

152. health, safety. **159. lifeless end,** end of his life, death; cf. l. 138 above. **Scene ii, 9. host,** lodge. **13. peruse,** observe. **18. mean,** means, money. **21. humour,** disposition. **28. consort,** accompany.

38. confounds, loses. **41. almanac,** Dromio, having been born at the same time as Antipholus, serves as a calendar of his age. **49. stomach,** appetite. **63. post,** haste. **64. post,** post in a tavern used for chalking reckonings.

Dro. E. My charge was but to fetch you from the mart
Home to your house, the Phœnix, sir, to dinner.
My mistress and her sister stays for you.
Ant. S. Now, as I am a Christian, answer me
In what safe place you have bestow'd my money,
Or I shall break that merry sconce of yours
That stands on tricks when I am undispos'd.
Where is the thousand marks thou hadst of me?
Dro. E. I have some marks of yours upon my pate,
Some of my mistress' marks upon my shoulders,
But not a thousand marks between you both.
If I should pay your worship those again,
Perchance you will not bear them patiently.
Ant. S. Thy mistress' marks? What mistress, slave, hast thou?
Dro. E. Your worship's wife, my mistress at the Phœnix;
She that doth fast till you come home to dinner,
And prays that you will hie you home to dinner.
Ant. S. What, wilt thou flout me thus unto my face,
Being forbid? There, take you that, sir knave.
Dro. E. What mean you, sir? For God's sake, hold your hands!
Nay, an you will not, sir, I 'll take my heels.
Exit.
Ant. S. Upon my life, by some device or other
The villain is o'er-raught of all my money.
They say this town is full of cozenage,
As nimble jugglers that deceive the eye,
Dark-working sorcerers that change the mind,
Soul-killing witches that deform the body,
Disguised cheaters, prating mountebanks,
And many such-like liberties of sin.
If it prove so, I will be gone the sooner.
I 'll to the Centaur to go seek this slave;
I greatly fear my money is not safe. *Exit.*

ACT II. Scene I. *The house of Antipholus of Ephesus.*

Enter *Adriana, wife of Antipholus of Ephesus,* with *Luciana, her sister.*

Adr. Neither my husband nor the slave return'd,
That in such haste I sent to seek his master!
Sure, Luciana, it is two o'clock.
Luc. Perhaps some merchant hath invited him
And from the mart he 's somewhere gone to dinner.
Good sister, let us dine and never fret.
A man is master of his liberty.
Time is their master, and when they see time
They 'll go or come; if so, be patient, sister.
Adr. Why should their liberty than ours be more?
Luc. Because their business still lies out o' door.
Adr. Look, when I serve him so, he takes it ill.
Luc. O, know he is the bridle of your will.
Adr. There's none but asses will be bridled so.
Luc. Why, headstrong liberty is lash'd with woe.
There 's nothing situate under heaven's eye
But hath his bound; in earth, in sea, in sky,
The beasts, the fishes, and the winged fowls
Are their males' subjects and at their controls;
Man, more divine, the master of all these,
Lord of the wide world and wild watery seas,
Indu'd with intellectual sense and souls,
Of more preëminence than fish and fowls,
Are masters to their females, and their lords:
Then let your will attend on their accords.
Adr. This servitude makes you to keep unwed.
Luc. Not this, but troubles of the marriage-bed.
Adr. But, were you wedded, you would bear some sway.
Luc. Ere I learn love, I 'll practise to obey.
Adr. How if your husband start some other where?
Luc. Till he come home again, I would forbear.
Adr. Patience unmov'd! no marvel though she pause.
They can be meek that have no other cause.
A wretched soul, bruis'd with adversity,
We bid be quiet, when we hear it cry;
But were we burden'd with like weight of pain,
As much or more we should ourselves complain;

75. Phœnix, sign of Antipholus' house. **79. sconce,** head. **80. stands on,** deals in, plays. **Act. II, Scene i: 11. still,** constantly. **96. o'er-raught,** swindled. **97. cozenage,** cheating. **102. liberties of sin,** licensed offenders. **Act II, Scene i: 33. other cause,** cause to be otherwise.

So thou, that hast no unkind mate to grieve thee,
With urging helpless patience would relieve me;
But, if thou live to see like right bereft,
This fool-begg'd patience in thee will be left.

Luc. Well, I will marry one day, but to try.
Here comes your man; now is your husband nigh.

Enter *Dromio of Ephesus.*

Adr. Say, is your tardy master now at hand?

Dro. E. Nay, he 's at two hands with me, and that my two ears can witness.

Adr. Say, didst thou speak with him? Know'st thou his mind?

Dro. E. Ay, ay, he told his mind upon mine ear.
Beshrew his hand, I scarce could understand it.

Luc. Spake he so doubtfully, thou couldst not feel his meaning?

Dro. E. Nay, he struck so plainly, I could too well feel his blows; and withal so doubtfully that I could scarce understand them.

Adr. But say, I prithee, is he coming home?
It seems he hath great care to please his wife.

Dro. E. Why, mistress, sure my master is horn-mad.

Adr. Horn-mad, thou villain!

Dro. E. I mean not cuckold-mad;
But, sure, he is stark mad.
When I desir'd him to come home to dinner,
He ask'd me for a thousand marks in gold.
"'Tis dinner-time," quoth I; "My gold," quoth he.
"Your meat doth burn," quoth I; "My gold!" quoth he.
"Will you come home?" quoth I; "My gold!" quoth he.
"Where is the thousand marks I gave thee, villain?"
"The pig," quoth I, "is burn'd;" "My gold!" quoth he.
"My mistress, sir," quoth I; "Hang up thy mistress!
I know not thy mistress. Out on thy mistress!"

Luc. Quoth who?

Dro. E. Quoth my master.
"I know," quoth he, "no house, no wife, no mistress."
So that my errand, due unto my tongue,
I thank him, I bare home upon my shoulders;
For, in conclusion, he did beat me there.

Adr. Go back again, thou slave, and fetch him home.

Dro. E. Go back again, and be new beaten home?
For God's sake, send some other messenger.

Adr. Back, slave, or I will break thy pate across.

Dro. E. And he will bless that cross with other beating.
Between you I shall have a holy head.

Adr. Hence, prating peasant! Fetch thy master home.

Dro. E. Am I so round with you as you with me,
That like a football you do spurn me thus?
You spurn me hence, and he will spurn me hither.
If I last in this service, you must case me in leather. *Exit.*

Luc. Fie, how impatience loureth in your face!

Adr. His company must do his minions grace,
Whilst I at home starve for a merry look.
Hath homely age th' alluring beauty took
From my poor cheek? Then he hath wasted it.
Are my discourses dull? Barren my wit?
If voluble and sharp discourse be marr'd,
Unkindness blunts it more than marble hard.
Do their gay vestments his affections bait?
That 's not my fault; he 's master of my state.
What ruins are in me that can be found
By him not ruin'd? Then is he the ground
Of my defeatures. My decayed fair
A sunny look of his would soon repair.
But, too unruly deer, he breaks the pale
And feeds from home; poor I am but his stale.

Luc. Self-harming jealousy! fie, beat it hence!

Adr. Unfeeling fools can with such wrongs dispense.
I know his eye doth homage otherwhere,
Or else what lets it but he would be here?
Sister, you know he promis'd me a chain;
Would that alone, alone he would detain,
So he would keep fair quarter with his bed!
I see the jewel best enamelled

39. helpless, unavailing. **41. fool-begg'd,** so foolish as to qualify you to be "begged" as an idiot—Idiots and the insane were "begged" i.e. put under guardianship by petition. **49. beshrew,** bad luck to. **understand,** stand under. **57. horn-mad,** mad as a horned animal, with a reference to the "horns" of the husband of an unfaithful wife.

82. round, spherical, plain-spoken. **87. minions,** darlings. **95. master of my state,** responsible for my wardrobe. **97. ground,** cause. **98. defeatures,** disfigurements. **fair,** beauty. **100. pale,** fence, fenced area. **101. stale,** stalking horse, dupe. **103. dispense,** put up. **105. lets,** hinders. **107. detain,** withhold. **108. keep fair quarter,** treat fairly. **109ff.** This apparently corrupt passage has been variously explained. The contrast between the easily tarnished enamel and the gold setting which is little affected by handling may apply to Antipholus, whose established reputation is not blasted by infidelity.

Will lose his beauty; and tho' gold bides still
That others touch, yet often touching will
Wear gold; and no man that hath a name,
By falsehood and corruption doth it shame.
Since that my beauty cannot please his eye,
I 'll weep what 's left away, and weeping die.

Luc. How many fond fools serve mad jealousy? *Exeunt.*

Scene II. *The mart.*

Enter *Antipholus of Syracuse.*

Ant. S. The gold I gave to Dromio is laid up
Safe at the Centaur; and the heedful slave
Is wander'd forth, in care to seek me out.
By computation and mine host's report
I could not speak with Dromio since at first
I sent him from the mart. See, here he comes.

Enter *Dromio of Syracuse.*

How now, sir! is your merry humour alter'd?
As you love strokes, so jest with me again.
You know no Centaur? You receiv'd no gold?
Your mistress sent to have me home to dinner?
My house was at the Phœnix? Wast thou mad,
That thus so madly thou didst answer me?

Dro. S. What answer, sir? When spake I such a word?

Ant. S. Even now, even here, not half an hour since.

Dro. S. I did not see you since you sent me hence
Home to the Centaur with the gold you gave me.

Ant. S. Villain, thou didst deny the gold's receipt
And told'st me of a mistress and a dinner;
For which, I hope, thou felt'st I was displeas'd.

Dro. S. I am glad to see you in this merry vein.
What means this jest? I pray you, master, tell me.

Ant. S. Yea, dost thou jeer and flout me in the teeth?
Think'st thou I jest? Hold, take thou that, and that. *Beats Dromio.*

Dro. S. Hold, sir, for God's sake! Now your jest is earnest.
Upon what bargain do you give it me?

Ant. S. Because that I familiarly sometimes
Do use you for my fool and chat with you,
Your sauciness will jest upon my love
And make a common of my serious hours.
When the sun shines let foolish gnats make sport,
But creep in crannies when he hides his beams.
If you will jest with me, know my aspect
And fashion your demeanour to my looks,
Or I will beat this method in your sconce.

Dro. S. Sconce call you it? So you would leave battering, I had rather have it a head. An you use these blows long, I must get a sconce for my head and insconce it too, or else I shall seek my wit in my shoulders. But, I pray, sir, why am I beaten?

Ant. S. Dost thou not know?

Dro. S. Nothing, sir, but that I am beaten.

Ant. S. Shall I tell you why?

Dro. S. Ay, sir, and wherefore; for they say every why hath a wherefore.

Ant. S. Why, first—for flouting me, and then, wherefore,—
For urging it the second time to me.

Dro. S. Was there ever any man thus beaten out of season,
When in the why and the wherefore is neither rhyme nor reason?
Well, sir, I thank you.

Ant. S. Thank me, sir! For what?

Dro. S. Marry, sir, for this something that you gave me for nothing.

Ant. S. I 'll make you amends next, to give you nothing for something. But say, sir, is it dinner-time?

Dro. S. No, sir. I think the meat wants that I have.

Ant. S. In good time, sir; what 's that?

Dro. S. Basting.

Ant. S. Well, sir, then 't will be dry.

Dro. S. If it be, sir, I pray you, eat none of it.

Ant. S. Your reason?

Dro. S. Lest it make you choleric and purchase me another dry basting.

Ant. S. Well, sir, learn to jest in good time. There's a time for all things.

Dro. S. I durst have denied that before you were so choleric.

Ant. S. By what rule, sir?

Dro. S. Marry, sir, by a rule as plain as the plain bald pate of father Time himself.

Ant. S. Let 's hear it.

Dro. S. There 's no time for a man to recover his hair that grows bald by nature.

Ant. S. May he not do it by fine and recovery?

116. **fond,** doting. **Scene ii: 24. earnest,** money paid to confirm a bargain, with a quibble on the meaning "serious." **29. common,** common or public ground.

32. aspect, expression (in astrology, the favorable or unfavorable position and influence of a heavenly body). **34. sconce,** head (in 35, fort; in 38, helmet). **39. seek . . . shoulders,** my head will be pounded down into my shoulders. **58. In good time,** indeed. **63. choleric,** dry meat was supposed to produce choleric, angry temper. **64. dry basting,** severe beating. **74-5. fine and recovery,** legal terms denoting complete ownership.

Dro. S. Yes, to pay a fine for a periwig and recover the lost hair of another man.

Ant. S. Why is Time such a niggard of hair, being, as it is, so plentiful an excrement?

Dro. S. Because it is a blessing that he bestows on beasts; and what he hath scanted men in hair he hath given them in wit.

Ant. S. Why, but there 's many a man hath more hair than wit.

Dro. S. Not a man of those but he hath the wit to lose his hair.

Ant. S. Why, thou didst conclude hairy men plain dealers without wit.

Dro. S. The plainer dealer, the sooner lost; yet he loseth it in a kind of jollity.

Ant. S. For what reason?

Dro. S. For two; and sound ones too.

Ant. S. Nay, not sound, I pray you.

Dro. S. Sure ones then.

Ant. S. Nay, not sure, in a thing falsing.

Dro. S. Certain ones then.

Ant. S. Name them.

Dro. S. The one, to save the money that he spends in tiring; the other, that at dinner they should not drop in his porridge.

Ant. S. You would all this time have proved there is no time for all things.

Dro. S. Marry, and did, sir; namely, e'en no time to recover hair lost by nature.

Ant. S. But your reason was not substantial, why there is no time to recover.

Dro. S. Thus I mend it: Time himself is bald and therefore to the world's end will have bald followers.

Ant. S. I knew 't would be a bald conclusion.—But, soft! who wafts us yonder?

Enter *Adriana* and *Luciana.*

Adr. Ay, ay, Antipholus, look strange and frown,
Some other mistress hath thy sweet aspects;
I am not Adriana, nor thy wife.
The time was once when thou unurg'd wouldst vow
That never words were music to thine ear,
That never object pleasing in thine eye,
That never touch well welcome to thy hand,
That never meat sweet-savour'd in thy taste,
Unless I spake, or look'd, or touch'd, or carv'd to thee.
How comes it now, my husband, O, how comes it,
That thou art then estranged from thyself?
Thyself I call it, being strange to me,
That, undividable, incorporate,
Am better than thy dear self's better part.
Ah, do not tear away thyself from me!
For know, my love, as easy mayst thou fall
A drop of water in the breaking gulf
And take unmingled thence that drop again,
Without addition or diminishing,
As take from me thyself and not me too.
How dearly would it touch thee to the quick
Shouldst thou but hear I were licentious,
And that this body, consecrate to thee,
By ruffian lust should be contaminate!
Wouldst thou not spit at me, and spurn at me,
And hurl the name of husband in my face,
And tear the stain'd skin off my harlot-brow,
And from my false hand cut the wedding-ring
And break it with a deep-divorcing vow?
I know thou canst; and therefore see thou do it.
I am possess'd with an adulterate blot;
My blood is mingled with the crime of lust;
For if we two be one and thou play false,
I do digest the poison of thy flesh,
Being strumpeted by thy contagion.
Keep then fair league and truce with thy true bed;
I live distain'd, thou undishonoured.

Ant. S. Plead you to me, fair dame? I know you not.
In Ephesus I am but two hours old,
As strange unto your town as to your talk;
Who, every word by all my wit being scann'd,
Wants wit in all one word to understand.

Luc. Fie, brother! how the world is chang'd with you!
When were you wont to use my sister thus?
She sent for you by Dromio home to dinner.

Ant. S. By Dromio?

Dro. S. By me?

Adr. By thee; and this thou didst return from him,
That he did buffet thee, and in his blows
Denied my house for his, me for his wife.

Ant. S. Did you converse, sir, with this gentlewoman?
What is the course and drift of your compact?

Dro. S. I, sir? I never saw her till this time.

Ant. S. Villain, thou liest; for even her very words
Didst thou deliver to me on the mart.

Dro. S. I never spake with her in all my life.

Ant. S. How can she thus then call us by our names,
Unless it be by inspiration?

Adr. How ill agrees it with your gravity
To counterfeit thus grossly with your slave,

79. **excrement,** outgrowth. 85ff., references to diseases causing loss of hair. 95. **falsing,** deceptive. 99. **tiring,** dressing the hair. 110. **bald,** foolish. 111. **wafts,** beckons. 120. **carv'd to,** served at the table. 125. **better part,** soul, spirit.

127. **fall,** let fall. 132. **dearly,** keenly. 148. **distain'd,** defiled.

Abetting him to thwart me in my mood!
Be it my wrong you are from me exempt,
But wrong not that wrong with a more contempt.
Come, I will fasten on this sleeve of thine.
Thou art an elm, my husband, I a vine,
Whose weakness married to thy stronger state
Makes me with thy strength to communicate.
If aught possess thee from me, it is dross,
Usurping ivy, brier, or idle moss;
Who, all for want of pruning, with intrusion
Infect thy sap and live on thy confusion.

Ant. S. To me she speaks; she moves me for her theme.
What, was I married to her in my dream?
Or sleep I now and think I hear all this?
What error drives our eyes and ears amiss?
Until I know this sure uncertainty,
I 'll entertain the offer'd fallacy.

Luc. Dromio, go bid the servants spread for dinner.

Dro. S. O, for my beads! I cross me for a sinner.
This is the fairy land. O spite of spites!
We talk with goblins, owls, and sprites.
If we obey them not, this will ensue,
They 'll suck our breath or pinch us black and blue.

Luc. Why prat'st thou to thyself and answer'st not?
Dromio, thou drone, thou snail, thou slug, thou sot!

Dro. S. I am transformed, master, am I not?

Ant. S. I think thou art in mind, and so am I.

Dro. S. Nay, master, both in mind and in my shape.

Ant. S. Thou hast thine own form.

Dro. S. No, I am an ape.

Luc. If thou art chang'd to aught, 't is to an ass.

Dro. S. 'T is true; she rides me and I long for grass.
'T is so, I am an ass; else it could never be
But I should know her as well as she knows me.

Adr. Come, come; no longer will I be a fool,
To put the finger in the eye and weep,
Whilst man and master laughs my woes to scorn.
Come, sir, to dinner. Dromio, keep the gate.
Husband, I'll dine above with you to-day
And shrive you of a thousand idle pranks.
Sirrah, if any ask you for your master,
Say he dines forth and let no creature enter.
Come, sister. Dromio, play the porter well.

Ant. S. Am I in earth, in heaven, or in hell?
Sleeping or waking? Mad or well-advis'd?
Known unto these, and to myself disguis'd!
I 'll say as they say and persever so,
And in this mist at all adventures go.

Dro. S. Master, shall I be porter at the gate?

Adr. Ay; and let none enter, lest I break your pate.

Luc. Come, come, Antipholus, we dine too late. *Exeunt.*

ACT III. Scene I. *Before the house of Antipholus of Ephesus.*

Enter *Antipholus of Ephesus,* his man *Dromio, Angelo,* the goldsmith, and *Balthazar,* the merchant.

Ant. E. Good Signior Angelo, you must excuse us all;
My wife is shrewish when I keep not hours.
Say that I linger'd with you at your shop
To see the making of her carcanet,
And that to-morrow you will bring it home.
But here 's a villain that would face me down
He met me on the mart, and that I beat him
And charg'd him with a thousand marks in gold,
And that I did deny my wife and house.
Thou drunkard, thou, what didst thou mean by this?

Dro. E. Say what you will, sir, but I know what I know.
That you beat me at the mart, I have your hand to show.
If the skin were parchment and the blows you gave were ink,
Your own handwriting would tell you what I think.

Ant. E. I think thou art an ass.

Dro. E. Marry, so it doth appear
By the wrongs I suffer and the blows I bear.
I should kick, being kick'd; and being at that pass,

173. exempt, separated. **179. possess,** keep. **180. idle,** barren. **182. confusion,** ruin. **183. moves,** appeals to. **188. fallacy,** delusion. **190. beads,** rosary. **Act III, Scene i: 4. carcanet,** gold necklace set with jewels. **8. charg'd,** asked him to account for.

206. to . . . weep, behave like a child. **210. shrive,** hear confession and impose penance. **215. well-advis'd,** sane. **218. at all adventures go,** act without knowing what I am doing.

You would keep from my heels and beware of an ass.

Ant. E. You 're sad, Signior Balthazar; pray God our cheer
May answer my good will and your good welcome here.

Bal. I hold your dainties cheap, sir, and your welcome dear.

Ant. E. O, Signior Balthazar, either at flesh or fish,
A table-full of welcome makes scarce one dainty dish.

Bal. Good meat, sir, is common; that every churl affords.

Ant. E. And welcome more common; for that's nothing but words.

Bal. Small cheer and great welcome makes a merry feast.

Ant. E. Ay, to a niggardly host and more sparing guest;
But though my cates be mean, take them in good part;
Better cheer may you have, but not with better heart.
But, soft! my door is lock'd. Go bid them let us in.

Dro. E. Maud, Bridget, Marian, Cicely, Gillian, Ginn!

Dro. S. [*Within.*] Mome, malt-horse, capon, coxcomb, idiot, patch!
Either get thee from the door or sit down at the hatch.
Dost thou conjure for wenches, that thou call'st for such store
When one is one too many? Go get thee from the door.

Dro. E. What patch is made our porter? My master stays in the street.

Dro. S. [*Within.*] Let him walk from whence he came, lest he catch cold on 's feet.

Ant. E. Who talks within there? Ho, open the door!

Dro. S. [*Within.*] Right, sir; I 'll tell you when, an you 'll tell me wherefore.

Ant. E. Wherefore? For my dinner. I have not din'd to-day.

Dro. S. [*Within.*] Nor to-day here you must not, come again when you may.

Ant. E. What art thou that keep'st me out from the house I owe?

Dro. S. [*Within.*] The porter for this time, sir, and my name is Dromio.

Dro. E. O villain! thou hast stolen both mine office and my name.
The one ne'er got me credit, the other mickle blame.
If thou hadst been Dromio to-day in my place,
Thou wouldst have chang'd thy face for an aim, or thy name for an ass.

Enter *Luce* [above].

Luce. [*Above.*] What a coil is there, Dromio? Who are those at the gate?

Dro. E. Let my master in, Luce.

Luce. [*Above.*] Faith, no; he comes too late;
And so tell your master.

Dro. E. O Lord, I must laugh!
Have at you with a proverb—Shall I set in my staff?

Luce. [*Above.*] Have at you with another; that 's—When? Can you tell?

Dro. S. [*Within.*] If thy name be called Luce,—Luce, thou hast answer'd him well.

Ant. E. Do you hear, you minion? You 'll let us in, I hope?

Luce. [*Above.*] I thought to have ask'd you.

Dro. S. [*Within.*] And you said no.

Dro. E. So, come, help: well struck! there was blow for blow.

Ant. E. Thou baggage, let me in.

Luce. [*Above.*] Can you tell for whose sake?

Dro. E. Master, knock the door hard.

Luce. [*Above.*] Let him knock till it ache.

Ant. E. You'll cry for this, minion, if I beat the door down.

Luce. [*Above.*] What needs all that, and a pair of stocks in the town?

Enter *Adriana* [above].

Adr. [*Above.*] Who is that at the door that keeps all this noise?

Dro. S. [*Within.*] By my troth, your town is troubled with unruly boys.

Ant. E. Are you there, wife? You might have come before.

Adr. [*Above.*] Your wife, sir knave! Go, get you from the door.

Dro. E. If you went in pain, master, this knave would go sore.

Ang. Here is neither cheer, sir, nor welcome; we would fain have either.

Bal. In debating which was best, we shall part with neither.

Dro. E. They stand at the door, master; bid them welcome hither.

28. cates, dainties. **31. Gillian,** Juliana. **Ginn,** Jenny (or Joan). **32. Mome,** blockhead. **malt-horse,** brewer's horse. **patch,** fool. **33. hatch,** half-door, wicket. **37. on 's,** on (in) his. **42. owe,** own.

45. mickle, much. **47. an aim,** a butt or mark. His face has been the "aim" of blows and he has been called an ass. **48. coil,** row. **51. set in my staff,** make myself at home. **52. When? Can you tell?** proverbial phrase for evading a question. **67. part,** depart.

Ant. E. There is something in the wind, that we cannot get in.
Dro. E. You would say so, master, if your garments were thin.
Your cake here is warm within; you stand here in the cold.
It would make a man mad as a buck to be so bought and sold.
Ant. E. Go fetch me something; I 'll break ope the gate.
Dro. S. [*Within.*] Break any breaking here, and I 'll break your knave's pate.
Dro. E. A man may break a word with you, sir, and words are but wind,
Ay, and break it in your face, so he break it not behind.
Dro. S. [*Within.*] It seems thou want'st breaking. Out upon thee, hind!
Dro. E. Here 's too much "out upon thee!" I pray thee, let me in.
Dro. S. [*Within.*] Ay, when fowls have no feathers, and fish have no fin.
Ant. E. Well, I 'll break in; go borrow me a crow.
Dro. E. A crow without feather? Master, mean you so?
For a fish without a fin, there 's a fowl without a feather.
If a crow helps us in, sirrah, we 'll pluck a crow together.
Ant. E. Go, get thee gone; fetch me an iron crow.
Bal. Have patience, sir; O, let it not be so!
Herein you war against your reputation
And draw within the compass of suspect
Th' unviolated honour of your wife.
Once this—your long experience of her wisdom,
Her sober virtue, years, and modesty,
Plead on her part some cause to you unknown;
And doubt not, sir, but she will well excuse
Why at this time the doors are made against you.
Be rul'd by me; depart in patience,
And let us to the Tiger all to dinner;
And about evening come yourself alone
To know the reason of this strange restraint.
If by strong hand you offer to break in
Now in the stirring passage of the day,
A vulgar comment will be made of it,
And that supposed by the common rout
Against your yet ungalled estimation
That may with foul intrusion enter in
And dwell upon your grave when you are dead;
For slander lives upon succession,
For ever hous'd where it gets possession.
Ant. E. You have prevail'd. I will depart in quiet,
And, in despite of mirth, mean to be merry.
I know a wench of excellent discourse,
Pretty and witty, wild, and yet too gentle.
There will we dine. This woman that I mean,
My wife—but, I protest, without desert—
Hath oftentimes upbraided me withal.
To her will we to dinner. [*To Angelo.*] Get you home
And fetch the chain; by this I know 't is made.
Bring it, I pray you, to the Porpentine;
For there 's the house. That chain will I bestow—
Be it for nothing but to spite my wife—
Upon mine hostess there. Good sir, make haste.
Since mine own doors refuse to entertain me,
I 'll knock elsewhere, to see if they 'll disdain me.
Ang. I 'll meet you at that place some hour hence.
Ant. E. Do so. This jest shall cost me some expense. *Exeunt.*

Scene II. *The same.*

Enter *Luciana* with *Antipholus of Syracuse.*

Luc. And may it be that you have quite forgot
A husband's office? Shall, Antipholus,
Even in the spring of love, thy love-springs rot?
Shall love, in building, grow so ruinous?
If you did wed my sister for her wealth,
Then for her wealth's sake use her with more kindness;
Or if you like elsewhere, do it by stealth;
Muffle your false love with some show of blindness;
Let not my sister read it in your eye;
Be not thy tongue thy own shame's orator;
Look sweet, speak fair, become disloyalty;
Apparel vice like virtue's harbinger;
Bear a fair presence, though your heart be tainted;
Teach sin the carriage of a holy saint;
Be secret-false. What need she be acquainted?
What simple thief brags of his own attaint?

72. bought and sold, imposed upon. **77. hind,** slave. **80. crow,** crowbar. **83. pluck a crow,** quarrel, settle accounts. **89. Once this,** in short. **93. made,** shut. **95. Tiger,** the sign of a tavern. **99. stirring passage,** busy traffic. **100. vulgar comment,** common talk. **102. ungalled estimation,** unblemished reputation.

105. succession, future, i.e., slander begets slander. **108. in despite of mirth,** though I do not feel merry. **112. without desert,** without my deserving it. **116. the Porpentine,** the sign (a porcupine) of the courtesan's house. **Scene ii: 11. become disloyalty,** make disloyalty becoming to you. **16. attaint,** dishonor.

'T is double wrong to truant with your bed
And let her read it in thy looks at board.
Shame hath a bastard fame, well managed;
Ill deeds is doubled with an evil word.
Alas, poor women! make us but believe,
Being compact of credit, that you love us;
Though others have the arm, show us the sleeve;
We in your motion turn and you may move us.
Then, gentle brother, get you in again;
Comfort my sister, cheer her, call her wife.
'T is holy sport to be a little vain,
When the sweet breath of flattery conquers strife.

Ant. S. Sweet mistress,—what your name is else, I know not,
Nor by what wonder you do hit of mine,—
Less in your knowledge and your grace you show not
Than our earth's wonder, more than earth divine.
Teach me, dear creature, how to think and speak;
Lay open to my earthy-gross conceit,
Smother'd in errors, feeble, shallow, weak,
The folded meaning of your words' deceit.
Against my soul's pure truth why labour you
To make it wander in an unknown field?
Are you a god? Would you create me new?
Transform me then, and to your power I 'll yield.
But if that I am I, then well I know
Your weeping sister is no wife of mine,
Nor to her bed no homage do I owe.
Far more, far more to you do I decline.
O, train me not, sweet mermaid, with thy note,
To drown me in thy sister's flood of tears.
Sing, siren, for thyself, and I will dote;
Spread o'er the silver waves thy golden hairs,
And as a bed I 'll take them and there lie,
And in that glorious supposition think
He gains by death that hath such means to die.
Let Love, being light, be drowned if she sink!

Luc. What, are you mad, that you do reason so?

Ant. S. Not mad, but mated; how, I do not know.

Luc. It is a fault that springeth from your eye.

Ant. S. For gazing on your beams, fair sun, being by.

Luc. Gaze where you should, and that will clear your sight.

Ant. S. As good to wink, sweet love, as look on night.

Luc. Why call you me love? Call my sister so.

Ant. S. Thy sister's sister.

Luc. That 's my sister.

Ant. S. No;
It is thyself, mine own self's better part,
Mine eye's clear eye, my dear heart's dearer heart,
My food, my fortune, and my sweet hope's aim,
My sole earth's heaven, and my heaven's claim.

Luc. All this my sister is, or else should be.

Ant. S. Call thyself sister, sweet, for I am thee.
Thee will I love and with thee lead my life;
Thou hast no husband yet nor I no wife.
Give me thy hand.

Luc. O, soft, sir! hold you still.
I 'll fetch my sister, to get her good will. *Exit.*

Enter *Dromio of Syracuse.*

Ant. S. Why, how now, Dromio! Where runn'st thou so fast?

Dro. S. Do you know me, sir? Am I Dromio? Am I your man? Am I myself?

Ant. S. Thou art Dromio, thou art my man, thou art thyself.

Dro. S. I am an ass, I am a woman's man, and besides myself.

Ant. S. What woman's man, and how besides thyself?

Dro. S. Marry, sir, besides myself, I am due to a woman; one that claims me, one that haunts me, one that will have me.

Ant. S. What claim lays she to thee?

Dro. S. Marry, sir, such claim as you would lay to your horse; and she would have me as a beast: not that, I being a beast, she would have me; but that she, being a very beastly creature, lays claim to me.

Ant. S. What is she?

Dro. S. A very reverend body; ay, such a one as a man may not speak of without he say "Sir-reverence." I have but lean luck in the match, and yet is she a wondrous fat marriage.

Ant. S. How dost thou mean a fat marriage?

22. **compact of credit**, made up of credulity. 27. **vain**, false. 30. **hit of**, guess. 32. **our earth's wonder**, perhaps a complimentary allusion to Queen Elizabeth. 34. **conceit**, understanding. 36. **folded**, hidden. 44. **decline**, incline. 45. **train**, entice. **mermaid**, siren. 52. **light**, a quibble on the sense "wanton." 54. **mated**, bewildered; also, matched with a wife.

56. **being by**, near at hand. 58. **wink**, shut eyes. 64. **sole earth's heaven**, only heaven on earth. **heaven's claim**, claim on heaven hereafter. 93. **"Sir-reverence,"** "save your reverence," an apologetic phrase introducing a remark which might give offence.

Dro. S. Marry, sir, she 's the kitchen wench and all grease; and I know not what use to put her to but to make a lamp of her and run from her by her own light. I warrant, her rags and the tallow in them will burn a Poland winter. If she lives till doomsday, she 'll burn a week longer than the whole world.

Ant. S. What complexion is she of?

Dro. S. Swart, like my shoe, but her face nothing like so clean kept: for why, she sweats; a man may go over shoes in the grime of it.

Ant. S. That 's a fault that water will mend.

Dro. S. No, sir, 't is in grain; Noah's flood could not do it.

Ant. S. What 's her name?

Dro. S. Nell, sir; but her name and three quarters, that 's an ell and three quarters, will not measure her from hip to hip.

Ant. S. Then she bears some breadth?

Dro. S. No longer from head to foot than from hip to hip. She is spherical, like a globe; I could find out countries in her.

Ant. S. In what part of her body stands Ireland?

Dro. S. Marry, sir, in her buttocks; I found it out by the bogs.

Ant. S. Where Scotland?

Dro. S. I found it by the barrenness; hard in the palm of the hand.

Ant. S. Where France?

Dro. S. In her forehead; armed and reverted, making war against her heir.

Ant. S. Where England?

Dro. S. I looked for the chalky cliffs, but I could find no whiteness in them; but I guess it stood in her chin, by the salt rheum that ran between France and it.

Ant. S. Where Spain?

Dro. S. Faith, I saw it not; but I felt it hot in her breath.

Ant. S. Where America, the Indies?

Dro. S. Oh, sir, upon her nose, all o'er embellished with rubies, carbuncles, sapphires, declining their rich aspect to the hot breath of Spain, who sent whole armadoes of caracks to be ballast at her nose.

Ant. S. Where stood Belgia, the Netherlands?

Dro. S. Oh, sir, I did not look so low. To conclude, this drudge, or diviner, laid claim to me; called me Dromio; swore I was assured to her; told me what privy marks I had about me, as, the mark of my shoulder, the mole in my neck, the great wart on my left arm, that I, amazed, ran from her as a witch.
And, I think, if my breast had not been made of faith and my heart of steel,
She had transform'd me to a curtal dog and made me turn i' th' wheel.

Ant. S. Go, hie thee presently post to the road;
An if the wind blow any way from shore,
I will not harbour in this town to-night.
If any bark put forth, come to the mart,
Where I will walk till thou return to me.
If every one knows us and we know none,
'T is time, I think, to trudge, pack, and be gone.

Dro. S. As from a bear a man would run for life,
So fly I from her that would be my wife. *Exit.*

Ant. S. There 's none but witches do inhabit here;
And therefore 't is high time that I were hence.
She that doth call me husband, even my soul
Doth for a wife abhor. But her fair sister,
Possess'd with such a gentle sovereign grace,
Of such enchanting presence and discourse,
Hath almost made me traitor to myself.
But, lest myself be guilty to self-wrong,
I 'll stop mine ears against the mermaid's song.

Enter *Angelo* with the chain.

Ang. Master Antipholus,—
Ant. S. Ay, that's my name.
Ang. I know it well, sir; lo, here 's the chain.
I thought to have ta'en you at the Porpentine;
The chain unfinish'd made me stay thus long.

Ant. S. What is your will that I shall do with this?

Ang. What please yourself, sir; I have made it for you.

Ant. S. Made it for me, sir! I bespoke it not.

Ang. Not once, nor twice, but twenty times you have.
Go home with it and please your wife withal;
And soon at supper-time I 'll visit you
And then receive my money for the chain.

Ant. S. I pray you, sir, receive the money now,
For fear you ne'er see chain nor money more.

Ang. You are a merry man, sir; fare you well. *Exit.*

108. in grain, fast dyed, indelible. **111. Nell,** Shakespeare may have forgotten that he had used the name Luce before. In any case, the name Nell is clearly used here for the sake of the pun that follows. **112. ell,** 45 inches. **125-7. France . . . heir,** from 1589 to 1593 the Catholic League of France fought against Henry of Navarre, the heir to the kingdom. **126-7. reverted,** revolted. **129. cliffs,** teeth. **139. declining,** bending. **140. armadoes of caracks,** fleets of galleons alluding to the Spanish Armada of 1588.

144. diviner, sorceress. **145. assured,** betrothed. **149. that,** so that. **151. curtal,** with docked tail. **wheel,** wheel that turned the spit. **152. presently,** at once. **road,** harbor. **168. to,** of.

Ant. S. What I should think of this, I cannot tell;
But this I think, there 's no man is so vain
That would refuse so fair an offer'd chain.
I see a man here needs not live by shifts,
When in the streets he meets such golden gifts.
I 'll to the mart and there for Dromio stay.
If any ship put out, then straight away. *Exit.*

ACT IV. Scene I. *A public place.*

Enter *Second Merchant, Angelo* the goldsmith, and an *Officer.*

2. Mer. You know since Pentecost the sum is due,
And since I have not much importun'd you;
Nor now I had not, but that I am bound
To Persia and want guilders for my voyage.
Therefore make present satisfaction,
Or I 'll attach you by this officer.

Ang. Even just the sum that I do owe to you
Is growing to me by Antipholus,
And in the instant that I met with you
He had of me a chain. At five o'clock
I shall receive the money for the same.
Pleaseth you walk with me down to his house,
I will discharge my bond and thank you too.

Enter *Antipholus of Ephesus* and *Dromio of Ephesus* from the courtezan's.

Off. That labour may you save; see where he comes.

Ant. E. While I go to the goldsmith's house, go thou
And buy a rope's end; that will I bestow
Among my wife and her confederates,
For locking me out of my doors by day.
But, soft! I see the goldsmith. Get thee gone,
Buy thou a rope and bring it home to me.

Dro. E. I buy a thousand pound a year! I buy a rope! *Exit.*

Ant. E. A man is well holp up that trusts to you.
I promised your presence and the chain,
But neither chain nor goldsmith came to me.
Belike you thought our love would last too long,
If it were chain'd together, and therefore came not.

Ang. Saving your merry humour, here 's the note
How much your chain weighs to the utmost charect,
The fineness of the gold, and chargeful fashion,
Which doth amount to three odd ducats more
Than I stand debted to this gentleman.
I pray you, see him presently discharg'd,
For he is bound to sea and stays but for it.

Ant. E. I am not furnish'd with the present money;
Besides, I have some business in the town.
Good signior, take the stranger to my house;
And with you take the chain, and bid my wife
Disburse the sum on the receipt thereof.
Perchance I will be there as soon as you.

Ang. Then you will bring the chain to her yourself?

Ant. E. No; bear it with you, lest I come not time enough.

Ang. Well, sir, I will. Have you the chain about you?

Ant. E. An if I have not, sir, I hope you have,
Or else you may return without your money.

Ang. Nay, come, I pray you, sir, give me the chain.
Both wind and tide stays for this gentleman,
And I, to blame, have held him here too long.

Ant. E. Good Lord! you use this dalliance to excuse
Your breach of promise to the Porpentine.
I should have chid you for not bringing it,
But, like a shrew, you first begin to brawl.

2 Mer. The hour steals on; I pray you, sir, dispatch.

Ang. You hear how he importunes me;—the chain!

Ant. E. Why, give it to my wife, and fetch your money.

Ang. Come, come, you know I gave it you even now.
Either send the chain or send by me some token.

Ant. E. Fie, now you run this humour out of breath.
Come, where 's the chain? I pray you, let me see it.

---

185. vain, foolish. **Act IV, Scene i: 6. attach,** arrest. **8. growing,** accruing. **16. bestow,** use. **21.** Dromio is as likely to buy a rope as an annuity of a thousand pounds, for the rope would mean a thousand poundings at the hand of his master. **28. charect,** carat.

29. chargeful, expensive. **34. present,** ready. **41. time,** in time. **56. send . . . token,** authorize me by some token to receive the money.

2. Mer. My business cannot brook this dalliance.
Good sir, say whether you 'll answer me or no;
If not, I 'll leave him to the officer.
Ant. E. I answer you! What should I answer you?
Ang. The money that you owe me for the chain.
Ant. E. I owe you none till I receive the chain.
Ang. You know I gave it you half an hour since.
Ant. E. You gave me none; you wrong me much to say so.
Ang. You wrong me more, sir, in denying it.
Consider how it stands upon my credit.
2. Mer. Well, officer, arrest him at my suit.
Off. I do; and charge you in the Duke's name to obey me.
Ang. This touches me in reputation.
Either consent to pay this sum for me
Or I attach you by this officer.
Ant. E. Consent to pay thee that I never had!
Arrest me, foolish fellow, if thou dar'st.
Ang. Here is thy fee; arrest him, officer.
I would not spare my brother in this case,
If he should scorn me so apparently.
Off. I do arrest you, sir: you hear the suit.
Ant. E. I do obey thee till I give thee bail.
But, sirrah, you shall buy this sport as dear
As all the metal in your shop will answer.
Ang. Sir, sir, I shall have law in Ephesus,
To your notorious shame; I doubt it not.

Enter *Dromio of Syracuse* from the bay.

Dro. S. Master, there is a bark of Epidamnum
That stays but till her owner comes aboard,
And then, sir, she bears away. Our fraughtage, sir,
I have convey'd aboard, and I have bought
The oil, the balsamum, and aqua-vitæ.
The ship is in her trim; the merry wind
Blows fair from land; they stay for nought at all
But for their owner, master, and yourself.
Ant. E. How now! a madman? Why, thou peevish sheep,
What ship of Epidamnum stays for me?
Dro. S. A ship you sent me to, to hire waftage.
Ant. E. Thou drunken slave, I sent thee for a rope,
And told thee to what purpose and what end.
Dro. S. You sent me for a rope's end as soon.
You sent me to the bay, sir, for a bark.
Ant. E. I will debate this matter at more leisure,
And teach your ears to list me with more heed.
To Adriana, villain, hie thee straight;
Give her this key, and tell her, in the desk
That 's cover'd o'er with Turkish tapestry
There is a purse of ducats; let her send it.
Tell her I am arrested in the street
And that shall bail me. Hie thee, slave, be gone!
On, officer, to prison till it come.
Exeunt all but Dromio.
Dro. S. To Adriana! That is where we din'd,
Where Dowsabel did claim me for her husband.
She is too big, I hope, for me to compass.
Thither I must, although against my will,
For servants must their masters' minds fulfil.
Exit.

Scene II. *Before the house of Antipholus of Ephesus.*

Enter *Adriana* and *Luciana.*

Adr. Ah, Luciana, did he tempt thee so?
Mightst thou perceive austerely in his eye
That he did plead in earnest? Yea or no?
Look'd he or red or pale, or sad or merrily?
What observation mad'st thou in this case
Of his heart's meteors tilting in his face?
Luc. First he denied you had in him no right.
Adr. He meant he did me none; the more my spite.
Luc. Then swore he that he was a stranger here.
Adr. And true he swore, though yet forsworn he were.
Luc. Then pleaded I for you.
Adr. And what said he?
Luc. That love I begg'd for you he begg'd of me.
Adr. With what persuasion did he tempt thy love?
Luc. With words that in an honest suit might move.
First he did praise my beauty, then my speech.
Adr. Didst speak him fair?
Luc. Have patience, I beseech.

60. **answer,** pay the debt. 68. **stands upon,** concerns. 87. **fraughtage,** freight. 89. **balsamum,** balm. **aqua-vitæ,** ardent spirits. 90. **in her trim,** ready to sail. 93. **peevish,** silly. 95. **waftage,** passage.

110. **Dowsabel,** ironic use of a poetic name for a girl. **Scene ii:** 2. **austerely,** thyself unmoved. 6. **heart's meteors,** changes of color, like luminous appearances in the sky. 8. **spite,** sorrow.

Adr. I cannot, nor I will not, hold me still;
My tongue, though not my heart, shall have his will.
He is deformed, crooked, old, and sere,
Ill-fac'd, worse bodied, shapeless everywhere;
Vicious, ungentle, foolish, blunt, unkind,
Stigmatical in making, worse in mind.
Luc. Who would be jealous then of such a one?
No evil lost is wail'd when it is gone.
Adr. Ah, but I think him better than I say,
And yet would herein others' eyes were worse.
Far from her nest the lapwing cries away.
My heart prays for him, though my tongue do curse.

Enter *Dromio of Syracuse.*

Dro. S. Here! go; the desk, the purse! Sweet, now, make haste.
Luc. How hast thou lost thy breath?
Dro. S. By running fast.
Adr. Where is thy master, Dromio? Is he well?
Dro. S. No, he 's in Tartar limbo, worse than hell.
A devil in an everlasting garment hath him;
One whose hard heart is button'd up with steel;
A fiend, a fury, pitiless and rough;
A wolf, nay, worse, a fellow all in buff;
A back-friend, a shoulder-clapper, one that countermands
The passages of alleys, creeks, and narrow lands,
A hound that runs counter and yet draws dry-foot well;
One that before the judgement carries poor souls to hell.
Adr. Why, man, what is the matter?
Dro. S. I do not know the matter; he is 'rested on the case.
Adr. What, is he arrested? Tell me at whose suit.
Dro. S. I know not at whose suit he is arrested well;
But he 's in a suit of buff which 'rested him, that can I tell.
Will you send him, mistress, redemption, the money in his desk?
Adr. Go fetch it, sister. This I wonder at,
Exit Luciana.
That he, unknown to me, should be in debt.
Tell me, was he arrested on a band?
Dro. S. Not on a band but on a stronger thing,
A chain, a chain! Do you not hear it ring?
Adr. What, the chain?
Dro. S. No, no, the bell; 't is time that I were gone.
It was two ere I left him, and now the clock strikes one.
Adr. The hours come back! That did I never hear.
Dro. S. O, yes; if any hour meet a sergeant, 'a turns back for very fear.
Adr. As if Time were in debt! How fondly dost thou reason!
Dro. S. Time is a very bankrupt and owes more than he 's worth to season.
Nay, he 's a thief too; have you not heard men say,
That Time comes stealing on by night and day?
If 'a be in debt and theft, and a sergeant in the way,
Hath he not reason to turn back an hour in a day?

Re-enter *Luciana.*

Adr. Go, Dromio; there 's the money, bear it straight,
And bring thy master home immediately,
Come, sister; I am press'd down with conceit—
Conceit, my comfort and my injury.
Exeunt.

Scene III. *A public place.*

Enter *Antipholus of Syracuse.*

Ant. S. There 's not a man I meet but doth salute me
As if I were their well-acquainted friend;
And every one doth call me by my name.
Some tender money to me; some invite me;
Some other give me thanks for kindnesses;
Some offer me commodities to buy.
Even now a tailor call'd me in his shop
And show'd me silks that he had bought for me
And therewithal took measure of my body.
Sure, these are but imaginary wiles,
And Lapland sorcerers inhabit here.

22. **Stigmatical,** branded by nature with deformity. **making,** form, body. 29. **Sweet, now,** probably a variant on "good, now" (cf. 4.4.22). 32. **Tartar limbo,** the Tartar or Mohammedan hell, worse than the Christian one. **limbo,** hell (prison). 33. **everlasting garment,** buff or leather coat worn by sergeants or constables. 37. **back-friend,** false friend, with reference to sergeant approaching from behind to make an arrest. **countermands,** forbids. 38. **creeks,** narrow or winding passages. **narrow lands,** possibly lanes, or landing places at the river. 39. **runs counter,** runs backward on the trail, with a reference to "counter" or prison. **draws dry-foot,** tracks game by the scent of the foot.

49-50. **band,** bond; also, chain or leash for a dog. 54. **one,** pun on "on" and "one." 56. **'a,** he (it). 58. **to season,** for the season (a quibble on "time and the season"). 65. **conceit,** imagination, fancies. **Scene iii: 11. Lapland,** Lapland was especially noted for the prevalence of witchcraft.

Enter *Dromio of Syracuse.*

Dro. S. Master, here's the gold you sent me for. What, have you got the picture of old Adam new-apparelled?

Ant. S. What gold is this? What Adam dost thou mean?

Dro. S. Not that Adam that kept the Paradise, but that Adam that keeps the prison; he that goes in the calf's skin that was killed for the Prodigal; he that came behind you, sir, like an evil angel, and bid you forsake your liberty.

Ant. S. I understand thee not.

Dro. S. No? Why, 't is a plain case: he that went, like a bass-viol, in a case of leather; the man, sir, that, when gentlemen are tired, gives them a sob and 'rests them; he, sir, that takes pity on decayed men and gives them suits of durance; he that sets up his rest to do more exploits with his mace than a morris-pike.

Ant. S. What, thou mean'st an officer?

Dro. S. Ay, sir, the sergeant of the band; he that brings any man to answer it that breaks his band; one that thinks a man always going to bed and says, "God give you good rest!"

Ant. S. Well, sir, there rest in your foolery. Is there any ship puts forth to-night? May we be gone?

Dro. S. Why, sir, I brought you word an hour since that the bark Expedition put forth to-night; and then were you hindered by the sergeant, to tarry for the hoy Delay. Here are the angels that you sent for to deliver you.

Ant. S. The fellow is distract, and so am I;
And here we wander in illusions.
Some blessed power deliver us from hence!

Enter a *Courtezan.*

Cour. Well met, well met, Master Antipholus.
I see, sir, you have found the goldsmith now.
Is that the chain you promis'd me to-day?

Ant. S. Satan, avoid! I charge thee tempt me not.

Dro. S. Master, is this Mistress Satan?

Ant. S. It is the devil.

Dro. S. Nay, she is worse, she is the devil's dam, and here she comes in the habit of a light wench; and thereof comes that the wenches say, "God damn me"; that 's as much to say, God make me a light wench. It is written, they appear to men like angels of light; light is an effect of fire, and fire will burn; *ergo,* light wenches will burn. Come not near her.

Cour. Your man and you are marvellous merry, sir.
Will you go with me? We 'll mend our dinner here?

Dro. S. Master, if you do, expect spoon-meat; or bespeak a long spoon.

Ant. S. Why, Dromio?

Dro. S. Marry, he must have a long spoon that must eat with the devil.

Ant. S. Avoid then, fiend! What tell'st thou me of supping?
Thou art, as you are all, a sorceress.
I conjure thee to leave me and be gone.

Cour. Give me the ring of mine you had at dinner,
Or, for my diamond, the chain you promis'd,
And I 'll be gone, sir, and not trouble you.

Dro. S. Some devils ask but the parings of one's nail,
A rush, a hair, a drop of blood, a pin,
A nut, a cherry-stone;
But she, more covetous, would have a chain.
Master, be wise; an if you give it her,
The devil will shake her chain and fright us with it.

Cour. I pray you, sir, my ring, or else the chain.
I hope you do not mean to cheat me so?

Ant. S. Avaunt, thou witch! Come, Dromio, let us go.

Dro. S. Fly pride, says the peacock; mistress, that you know.

Exeunt Antipholus and Dromio.

Cour. Now, out of doubt Antipholus is mad,
Else would he never so demean himself.
A ring he hath of mine worth forty ducats,
And for the same he promis'd me a chain.
Both one and other he denies me now.
The reason that I gather he is mad,
Besides this present instance of his rage,
Is a mad tale he told to-day at dinner,
Of his own doors being shut against his entrance.
Belike his wife, acquainted with his fits,
On purpose shut the doors against his way.
My way is now to hie home to his house,
And tell his wife that, being lunatic,

13ff., the sergeant is "the picture of Old Adam" because he wears a buff or leather jacket and Adam had worn buff of another kind. If the sergeant were engaged in a new legal suit, he would, like Adam, be "new-apparelled." **24. sob,** a quibble upon "sob," a rest given a horse to regain its wind. **26. suits of durance,** prison clothes, with a quibble on ideas of duration and durable cloth. **sets up his rest,** stakes everything. **27. mace,** sergeant's staff of office. **morris-pike,** Moorish pike. **40. hoy,** small vessel. **41. angels,** gold coins worth about ten shillings. **48. avoid,** avaunt. **52. light,** wanton.

54. It is written, cf. 2 Corinthians, xi, 14. **60. mend,** supplement. **81. Fly . . . peacock,** for the dishonest courtezan to accuse a man of stealing is as absurd as for the peacock to bid men shun pride. **83. demean,** behave.

He rush'd into my house and took perforce
My ring away. This course I fittest choose;
For forty ducats is too much to lose. *Exit.*

Scene IV. *A street.*

Enter *Antipholus of Ephesus* with the *Officer*.

Ant. E. Fear me not, man; I will not break away.
I 'll give thee, ere I leave thee, so much money,
To warrant thee, as I am 'rested for.
My wife is in a wayward mood to-day,
And will not lightly trust the messenger.
That I should be attach'd in Ephesus,
I tell you, 't will sound harshly in her ears.

Enter *Dromio of Ephesus* with a rope's-end.

Here comes my man; I think he brings the money.
How now, sir! have you that I sent you for?

Dro. E. Here's that, I warrant you, will pay them all.

Ant. E. But where 's the money?

Dro. E. Why, sir, I gave the money for the rope.

Ant. E. Five hundred ducats, villain, for a rope?

Dro. E. I 'll serve you, sir, five hundred at the rate.

Ant. E. To what end did I bid thee hie thee home?

Dro. E. To a rope's end, sir; and to that end am I returned.

Ant. E. And to that end, sir, I will welcome you. *Beating him.*

Off. Good sir, be patient.

Dro. E. Nay, 't is for me to be patient; I am in adversity.

Off. Good now, hold thy tongue.

Dro. E. Nay, rather persuade him to hold his hands.

Ant. E. Thou whoreson, senseless villain!

Dro. E. I would I were senseless, sir, that I might not feel your blows.

Ant. E. Thou art sensible in nothing but blows, and so is an ass.

Dro. E. I am an ass, indeed; you may prove it by my long ears. I have served him from the hour of my nativity to this instant, and have nothing at his hands for my service but blows. When I am cold, he heats me with beating; when I am warm, he cools me with beating; I am waked with it when I sleep; raised with it when I sit; driven out of doors with it when I go from home; welcomed home with it when I return: nay, I bear it on my shoulders, as a beggar wont her brat; and, I think, when he hath lamed me, I shall beg with it from door to door.

Enter *Adriana, Luciana,* the *Courtezan,* and a Schoolmaster called *Pinch.*

Ant. E. Come, go along; my wife is coming yonder.

Dro. E. Mistress, *respice finem,* respect your end; or rather, to prophesy like the parrot, "beware the rope's-end."

Ant. E. Wilt thou still talk? *Beating him.*

Cour. How say you now? Is not your husband mad?

Adr. His incivility confirms no less.
Good Doctor Pinch, you are a conjurer;
Establish him in his true sense again,
And I will please you what you will demand.

Luc. Alas, how fiery and how sharp he looks!

Cour. Mark how he trembles in his ecstasy!

Pinch. Give me your hand and let me feel your pulse.

Ant. E. There is my hand, and let it feel your ear. *Striking him.*

Pinch. I charge thee, Satan, hous'd within this man,
To yield possession to my holy prayers
And to thy state of darkness hie thee straight.
I conjure thee by all the saints in heaven!

Ant. E. Peace, doting wizard, peace! I am not mad.

Adr. O, that thou wert not, poor distressed soul!

Ant. E. You minion, you, are these your customers?
Did this companion with the saffron face
Revel and feast it at my house to-day,
Whilst upon me the guilty doors were shut
And I denied to enter in my house?

Adr. O husband, God doth know you din'd at home;
Where would you had remain'd until this time,
Free from these slanders and this open shame!

Ant. E. Din'd at home! Thou villain, what sayest thou?

Dro. E. Sir, sooth to say, you did not dine at home.

Ant. E. Were not my doors lock'd up and I shut out?

95. **perforce**, by force. **Scene iv: 22. Good now**, interjectional phrase expressive of entreaty. **28. sensible**, having sense, sensitive. **30. ears**, pun on "ears" and "years."

39. wont, is wont to. **44. respice finem**, consider your end. A common quibble linked the phrase with *respice funem*, "respect the hangman's rope." The context suggests that this latter was a phrase taught to parrots. **50. conjurer**, a schoolmaster who knew Latin was qualified to exorcise spirits. **52. please**, pay. **54. ecstasy**, madness. **63. customers**, guests (in a bad sense). **64. companion**, fellow. **saffron**, yellow.

Dro. E. Perdie, your doors were lock'd and you shut out.
Ant. E. And did not she herself revile me there?
Dro. E. Sans fable, she herself revil'd you there.
Ant. E. Did not her kitchen-maid rail, taunt, and scorn me?
Dro. E. Certes, she did; the kitchen-vestal scorn'd you.
Ant. E. And did not I in rage depart from thence?
Dro. E. In verity you did; my bones bear witness,
That since have felt the vigour of his rage.
Adr. Is 't good to soothe him in these contraries?
Pinch. It is no shame. The fellow finds his vein,
And, yielding to him, humours well his frenzy.
Ant. E. Thou hast suborn'd the goldsmith to arrest me.
Adr. Alas, I sent you money to redeem you,
By Dromio here, who came in haste for it.
Dro. E. Money by me! Heart and good-will you might,
But surely, master, not a rag of money.
Ant. E. Went'st not thou to her for a purse of ducats?
Adr. He came to me and I deliver'd it.
Luc. And I am witness with her that she did.
Dro. E. God and the rope-maker bear me witness
That I was sent for nothing but a rope!
Pinch. Mistress, both man and master is possess'd;
I know it by their pale and deadly looks.
They must be bound and laid in some dark room.
Ant. E. Say, wherefore didst thou lock me forth to-day?
And why dost thou deny the bag of gold?
Adr. I did not, gentle husband, lock thee forth.
Dro. E. And, gentle master, I receiv'd no gold;
But I confess, sir, that we were lock'd out.
Adr. Dissembling villain, thou speak'st false in both.
Ant. E. Dissembling harlot, thou art false in all
And art confederate with a damned pack
To make a loathsome abject scorn of me;
But with these nails I 'll pluck out these false eyes
That would behold in me this shameful sport.

Enter three or four, and offer to bind him. He strives.

Adr. O, bind him, bind him! Let him not come near me.
Pinch. More company! The fiend is strong within him.
Luc. Ay me, poor man, how pale and wan he looks!
Ant. E. What, will you murder me? Thou jailer, thou.
I am thy prisoner. Wilt thou suffer them
To make a rescue?
Off. Masters, let him go.
He is my prisoner, and you shall not have him.
Pinch. Go bind this man, for he is frantic too. *They bind Dromio.*
Adr. What wilt thou do, thou peevish officer?
Hast thou delight to see a wretched man
Do outrage and displeasure to himself?
Off. He is my prisoner; if I let him go,
The debt he owes will be requir'd of me.
Adr. I will discharge thee e'er I go from thee.
Bear me forthwith unto his creditor
And, knowing how the debt grows, I will pay it.
Good master doctor, see him safe convey'd
Home to my house. O most unhappy day!
Ant. E. O most unhappy strumpet!
Dro. E. Master, I am here enter'd in bond for you.
Ant. E. Out on thee, villain! wherefore dost thou mad me?
Dro. E. Will you be bound for nothing?
Be mad, good master; cry "The devil!"
Luc. God help, poor souls, how idly do they talk!
Adr. Go bear him hence. Sister, go you with me.
Say now, whose suit is he arrested at?
Exeunt all but Adriana, Luciana, Officer, and Courtezan.
Off. One Angelo, a goldsmith. Do you know him?
Adr. I know the man. What is the sum he owes?
Off. Two hundred ducats.
Adr. Say, how grows it due?
Off. Due for a chain your husband had of him.
Adr. He did bespeak a chain for me, but had it not.

74. **Perdie,** certainly (corruption of *par Dieu*). 76. **Sans,** without. 78. **kitchen-vestal,** like the vestal virgins, the maid kept the fire burning. 82. **soothe,** humor. 95. **possess'd,** of the devil, mad. 96. **deadly,** deathlike. 97. This was the regular Elizabethan mode of curing insanity.

126. **unhappy,** unlucky (127, miserable). 139. **bespeak,** order.

Cour. When as your husband all in rage to-day
Came to my house and took away my ring—
The ring I saw upon his finger now—
Straight after did I meet him with a chain.

Adr. It may be so, but I did never see it.
Come, jailer, bring me where the goldsmith is.
I long to know the truth hereof at large.

Enter *Antipholus of Syracuse* with his rapier drawn, and *Dromio of Syracuse.*

Luc. God, for thy mercy! they are loose again.

Adr. And come with naked swords. Let 's call more help
To have them bound again.

Off. Away! they 'll kill us.

Exeunt all but Antipholus of Syracuse and Dromio of Syracuse, as fast as may be, frighted.

Ant. S. I see these witches are afraid of swords.

Dro. S. She that would be your wife now ran from you.

Ant. S. Come to the Centaur; fetch our stuff from thence;
I long that we were safe and sound aboard.

Dro. S. Faith, stay here this night; they will surely do us no harm. You saw they speak us fair, give us gold; methinks they are such a gentle nation that, but for the mountain of mad flesh that claims marriage of me, I could find in my heart to stay here still and turn witch.

Ant. S. I will not stay to-night for all the town;
Therefore away, to get our stuff aboard.

Exeunt.

ACT V. SCENE I. *A street before a Priory.*

Enter *Second Merchant* and *Angelo.*

Ang. I am sorry, sir, that I have hinder'd you;
But, I protest, he had the chain of me,
Though most dishonestly he doth deny it.

2. Mer. How is the man esteem'd here in the city?

Ang. Of very reverend reputation, sir,
Of credit infinite, highly belov'd,
Second to none that lives here in the city.
His word might bear my wealth at any time.

2. Mer. Speak softly; yonder, as I think, he walks.

Enter *Antipholus of Syracuse* and *Dromio of Syracuse.*

Ang. 'T is so; and that self chain about his neck
Which he forswore most monstrously to have.
Good sir, draw near to me, I 'll speak to him.
Signior Antipholus, I wonder much
That you would put me to this shame and trouble;
And, not without some scandal to yourself,
With circumstance and oaths so to deny
This chain which now you wear so openly:
Beside the charge, the shame, imprisonment,
You have done wrong to this my honest friend,
Who, but for staying on our controversy,
Had hoisted sail and put to sea to-day.
This chain you had of me; can you deny it?

Ant. S. I think I had; I never did deny it.

2. Mer. Yes, that you did, sir, and forswore it too.

Ant. S. Who heard me to deny it or forswear it?

2. Mer. These ears of mine, thou know'st, did hear thee.
Fie on thee, wretch! 'T is pity that thou liv'st
To walk where any honest men resort.

Ant. S. Thou art a villain to impeach me thus.
I 'll prove mine honour and mine honesty
Against thee presently, if thou dar'st stand.

2. Mer. I dare, and do defy thee for a villain. *They draw.*

Enter *Adriana, Luciana,* the *Courtezan* and others.

Adr. Hold, hurt him not, for God sake! He is mad.
Some get within him; take his sword away.
Bind Dromio too, and bear them to my house.

Dro. S. Run, master, run; for God's sake, take a house!
This is some priory. In, or we are spoil'd!

Exeunt Antipholus and Dromio to the Priory.

Enter the *Lady Abbess.*

Abb. Be quiet, people. Wherefore throng you hither?

Act V, Scene i: 8. His word . . . time, I would lend him my wealth on his mere word. **10. self,** same. **16. circumstance,** particulars.

34. within him, within his guard. **36. take,** take refuge in.

Adr. To fetch my poor distracted husband hence.
Let us come in, that we may bind him fast
And bear him home for his recovery.

Ang. I knew he was not in his perfect wits.

2. Mer. I am sorry now that I did draw on him.

Abb. How long hath this possession held the man?

Adr. This week he hath been heavy, sour, sad,
And much different from the man he was;
But till this afternoon his passion
Ne'er brake into extremity of rage.

Abb. Hath he not lost much wealth by wreck of sea?
Buried some dear friend? Hath not else his eye
Stray'd his affection in unlawful love?
A sin prevailing much in youthful men,
Who give their eyes the liberty of gazing.
Which of these sorrows is he subject to?

Adr. To none of these, except it be the last;
Namely, some love that drew him oft from home.

Abb. You should for that have reprehended him.

Adr. Why, so I did.

Abb. Ay, but not rough enough.

Adr. As roughly as my modesty would let me.

Abb. Haply, in private.

Adr. And in assemblies too.

Abb. Ay, but not enough.

Adr. It was the copy of our conference.
In bed he slept not for my urging it;
At board he fed not for my urging it;
Alone, it was the subject of my theme;
In company I often glanced it;
Still did I tell him it was vile and bad.

Abb. And thereof came it that the man was mad.
The venom clamours of a jealous woman
Poisons more deadly than a mad dog's tooth.
It seems his sleeps were hinder'd by thy railing,
And thereof comes it that his head is light.
Thou say'st his meat was sauc'd with thy upbraidings;
Unquiet meals make ill digestions,
Thereof the raging fire of fever bred;
And what 's a fever but a fit of madness?
Thou say'st his sports were hinder'd by thy brawls:
Sweet recreation barr'd, what doth ensue
But moody and dull melancholy,
Kinsman to grim and comfortless despair,
And at her heels a huge infectious troop
Of pale distemperatures and foes to life?
In food, in sport, and life-preserving rest
To be disturb'd, would mad or man or beast.
The consequence is, then, thy jealous fits
Hath scar'd thy husband from the use of wits.

Luc. She never reprehended him but mildly,
When he demean'd himself rough, rude, and wildly.
Why bear you these rebukes and answer not?

Adr. She did betray me to my own reproof.
Good people, enter and lay hold on him.

Abb. No, not a creature enters in my house.

Adr. Then let your servants bring my husband forth.

Abb. Neither. He took this place for sanctuary,
And it shall privilege him from your hands
Till I have brought him to his wits again,
Or lose my labour in assaying it.

Adr. I will attend my husband, be his nurse,
Diet his sickness, for it is my office,
And will have no attorney but myself;
And therefore let me have him home with me.

Abb. Be patient; for I will not let him stir
Till I have us'd the approved means I have,
With wholesome syrups, drugs, and holy prayers,
To make of him a formal man again.
It is a branch and parcel of mine oath,
A charitable duty of my order.
Therefore depart and leave him here with me.

Adr. I will not hence and leave my husband here;
And ill it doth beseem your holiness
To separate the husband and the wife.

Abb. Be quiet and depart; thou shalt not have him. *Exit.*

Luc. Complain unto the Duke of this indignity.

Adr. Come, go. I will fall prostrate at his feet
And never rise until my tears and prayers
Have won his grace to come in person hither
And take perforce my husband from the abbess.

2. Mer. By this, I think, the dial points at five.
Anon, I 'm sure, the Duke himself in person
Comes this way to the melancholy vale,
The place of death and sorry execution,
Behind the ditches of the abbey here.

Ang. Upon what cause?

44. possession, madness. **51. Stray'd,** led astray. **62. copy,** subject. **66. glanced,** hinted at.

82. distemperatures, disorders. **105. formal,** rational. **106. parcel,** part. **121. sorry,** sad.

2. Mer. To see a reverend Syracusian merchant,
Who put unluckily into this bay
Against the laws and statutes of this town,
Beheaded publicly for his offence.
Ang. See where they come; we will behold his death.
Luc. Kneel to the Duke before he pass the abbey.

Enter *Duke of Ephesus* and *Ægeon* bare-headed, with the Headsman and other Officers.

Duke. Yet once again proclaim it publicly,
If any friend will pay the sum for him,
He shall not die; so much we tender him.
Adr. Justice, most sacred Duke, against the abbess!
Duke. She is a virtuous and a reverend lady;
It cannot be that she hath done thee wrong.
Adr. May it please your grace, Antipholus, my husband,
Who I made lord of me and all I had,
At your important letters,—this ill day
A most outrageous fit of madness took him;
That desperately he hurried through the street,—
With him his bondman, all as mad as he,—
Doing displeasure to the citizens
By rushing in their houses, bearing thence
Rings, jewels, any thing his rage did like.
Once did I get him bound and sent him home,
Whilst to take order for the wrongs I went
That here and there his fury had committed.
Anon, I wot not by what strong escape,
He broke from those that had the guard of him;
And with his mad attendant and himself,
Each one with ireful passion, with drawn swords,
Met us again and, madly bent on us,
Chas'd us away, till, raising of more aid
We came again to bind them. Then they fled
Into this abbey, whither we pursu'd them;
And here the abbess shuts the gates on us,
And will not suffer us to fetch him out,
Nor send him forth that we may bear him hence.
Therefore, most gracious Duke, with thy command
Let him be brought forth and borne hence for help.
Duke. Long since thy husband serv'd me in my wars,
And I to thee engag'd a prince's word,
When thou didst make him master of thy bed,
To do him all the grace and good I could.
Go, some of you, knock at the abbey-gate
And bid the lady abbess come to me.
I will determine this before I stir.

Enter a *Messenger.*

Mess. O mistress, mistress, shift and save yourself!
My master and his man are both broke loose,
Beaten the maids a-row and bound the doctor,
Whose beard they have sing'd off with brands of fire;
And ever, as it blaz'd, they threw on him
Great pails of puddled mire to quench the hair.
My master preaches patience to him and the while
His man with scissors nicks him like a fool,
And sure, unless you send some present help,
Between them they will kill the conjurer.
Adr. Peace, fool! thy master and his man are here,
And that is false thou dost report to us.
Mess. Mistress, upon my life, I tell you true;
I have not breath'd almost since I did see it.
He cries for you, and vows, if he can take you,
To scorch your face and to disfigure you.
Cry within.
Hark, hark! I hear him, mistress. Fly, be gone!
Duke. Come, stand by me; fear nothing. Guard with halberds!
Adr. Ay me, it is my husband! Witness you,
That he is borne about invisible.
Even now we hous'd him in the abbey here;
And now he 's there, past thought of human reason.

Enter *Antipholus of Ephesus* and *Dromio of Ephesus.*

Ant. E. Justice, most gracious Duke, O grant me justice!
Even for the service that long since I did thee,
When I bestrid thee in the wars, and took
Deep scars to save thy life; even for the blood
That then I lost for thee, now grant me justice.
Æge. Unless the fear of death doth make me dote,
I see my son Antipholus and Dromio.
Ant. E. Justice, sweet prince, against that woman there!

132. so much . . . him, so much grace we allow him. **138. important,** urgent, **letters,** Adriana has apparently been the Duke's ward. **146. take order,** take measures to settle. **148. strong,** violent.

170. a-row, one after another. **175,** cuts his hair in odd shapes, like that of a professional fool. **176. present,** immediate. **183. scorch,** score, i.e., slash with a knife. **185. halberds,** weapons combining pikes and axes, usually carried, as here, by guards. **192. bestrid,** stood over (to defend).

She whom thou gav'st to me to be my wife,
That hath abused and dishonoured me
Even in the strength and height of injury!
Beyond imagination is the wrong
That she this day hath shameless thrown on me.

Duke. Discover how, and thou shalt find me just.

Ant. E. This day, great Duke, she shut the doors upon me,
While she with harlots feasted in my house.

Duke. A grievous fault! Say, woman, didst thou so?

Adr. No, my good lord. Myself, he, and my sister
To-day did dine together. So befall my soul
As this is false he burdens me withal!

Luc. Ne'er may I look on day, nor sleep on night,
But she tells to your highness simple truth!

Ang. O perjur'd woman! They are both forsworn.
In this the madman justly chargeth them.

Ant. E. My liege, I am advised what I say,
Neither disturbed with the effect of wine,
Nor heady-rash, provok'd with raging ire,
Albeit my wrongs might make one wiser mad.
This woman lock'd me out this day from dinner.
That goldsmith there, were he not pack'd with her,
Could witness it, for he was with me then;
Who parted with me to go fetch a chain,
Promising to bring it to the Porpentine,
Where Balthazar and I did dine together.
Our dinner done, and he not coming thither,
I went to seek him. In the street I met him
And in his company that gentleman.
There did this perjur'd goldsmith swear me down
That I this day of him receiv'd the chain,
Which, God he knows, I saw not; for the which
He did arrest me with an officer.
I did obey, and sent my peasant home
For certain ducats; he with none return'd.
Then fairly I bespoke the officer
To go in person with me to my house.
By the way we met
My wife, her sister, and a rabble more
Of vile confederates. Along with them
They brought one Pinch, a hungry lean-fac'd villain,
A mere anatomy, a mountebank,
A threadbare juggler and a fortune-teller,
A needy, hollow-ey'd, sharp-looking wretch,
A living dead man. This pernicious slave,
Forsooth, took on him as a conjurer,
And, gazing in mine eyes, feeling my pulse,
And with no face, as 't were, outfacing me,
Cries out, I was possess'd. Then all together
They fell upon me, bound me, bore me thence,
And in a dark and dankish vault at home
There left me and my man, both bound together;
Till, gnawing with my teeth my bonds in sunder,
I gain'd my freedom, and immediately
Ran hither to your grace; whom I beseech
To give me ample satisfaction
For these deep shames and great indignities.

Ang. My lord, in truth, thus far I witness with him,
That he din'd not at home, but was lock'd out.

Duke. But had he such a chain of thee or no?

Ang. He had, my lord; and when he ran in here,
These people saw the chain about his neck.

2. Mer. Besides, I will be sworn these ears of mine
Heard you confess you had the chain of him
After you first forswore it on the mart;
And thereupon I drew my sword on you;
And then you fled into this abbey here,
From whence, I think, you are come by miracle.

Ant. E. I never came within these abbey-walls,
Nor ever didst thou draw thy sword on me.
I never saw the chain, so help me heaven!
And this is false you burden me withal.

Duke. Why, what an intricate impeach is this!
I think you all have drunk of Circe's cup.
If here you hous'd him, here he would have been.
If he were mad, he would not plead so coldly.
You say he din'd at home; the goldsmith here
Denies that saying. Sirrah, what say you?

Dro. E. Sir, he din'd with her there, at the Porpentine.

Cour. He did, and from my finger snatch'd that ring.

Ant. E. 'T is true, my liege, this ring I had of her.

Duke. Saw'st thou him enter at the abbey here?

Cour. As sure, my liege, as I do see your grace.

205. harlots, rascals. **209. burdens,** charges. **210. on day,** during the day. **on night,** at night. **214. am advised,** speak with due deliberation. **219. pack'd,** in league. **231. peasant,** servant. **239. anatomy,** skeleton.

269. impeach, accusation. **270. Circe's cup,** These people seem as irrational as if the potion of Circe had changed them into beasts. **272. coldly,** rationally.

Duke. Why, this is strange. Go call the abbess hither.
I think you are all mated or stark mad.
Exit one to the Abbess.
Æge. Most mighty Duke, vouchsafe me speak a word.
Haply I see a friend will save my life
And pay the sum that may deliver me.
Duke. Speak freely, Syracusian, what thou wilt.
Æge. Is not your name, sir, call'd Antipholus?
And is not that your bondman, Dromio?
Dro. E. Within this hour I was his bondman, sir,
But he, I thank him, gnaw'd in two my cords.
Now am I Dromio and his man unbound.
Æge. I am sure you both of you remember me.
Dro. E. Ourselves we do remember, sir, by you;
For lately we were bound, as you are now.
You are not Pinch's patient, are you, sir?
Æge. Why look you strange on me? You know me well.
Ant. E. I never saw you in my life till now.
Æge. O, grief hath chang'd me since you saw me last,
And careful hours with Time's deformed hand
Have written strange defeatures in my face.
But tell me yet, dost thou not know my voice?
Ant. E. Neither.
Æge. Dromio, nor thou?
Dro. E. No, trust me, sir, nor I.
Æge. I am sure thou dost.
Dro. E. Ay, sir, but I am sure I do not; and whatsoever a man denies, you are now bound to believe him.
Æge. Not know my voice! O time's extremity,
Hast thou so crack'd and splitted my poor tongue
In seven short years, that here my only son
Knows not my feeble key of untun'd cares?
Though now this grained face of mine be hid
In sap-consuming winter's drizzled snow,
And all the conduits of my blood froze up,
Yet hath my night of life some memory.
My wasting lamps some fading glimmer left,
My dull deaf ears a little use to hear.
All these old witnesses—I cannot err—
Tell me thou art my son Antipholus.
Ant. E. I never saw my father in my life.
Æge. But seven years since, in Syracusa, boy,
Thou know'st we parted; but perhaps, my son,
Thou sham'st to acknowledge me in misery.
Ant. E. The Duke and all that know me in the city
Can witness with me that it is not so.
I ne'er saw Syracusa in my life.
Duke. I tell thee, Syracusian, twenty years
Have I been patron to Antipholus,
During which time he ne'er saw Syracusa.
I see thy age and dangers make thee dote.

Re-enter *Abbess,* with *Antipholus of Syracuse* and *Dromio of Syracuse.*

Abb. Most mighty Duke, behold a man much wrong'd. *All gather to see them.*
Adr. I see two husbands, or mine eyes deceive me.
Duke. One of these men is Genius to the other;
And so of these. Which is the natural man,
And which the spirit? Who deciphers them?
Dro. S. I, sir, am Dromio; command him away.
Dro. E. I, sir, am Dromio; pray, let me stay.
Ant. S. Ægeon art thou not? or else his ghost?
Dro. S. O, my old master! Who hath bound him here?
Abb. Whoever bound him, I will loose his bonds
And gain a husband by his liberty.
Speak, old Ægeon, if thou be'st the man
That hadst a wife once call'd Æmilia
That bore thee at a burden two fair sons.
O, if thou be'st the same Ægeon, speak,
And speak unto the same Æmelia!
Æge. If I dream not, thou art Æmilia.
If thou art she, tell me, where is that son
That floated with thee on the fatal raft?
Abb. By men of Epidamnum he and I
And the twin Dromio all were taken up;
But by and by rude fishermen of Corinth
By force took Dromio and my son from them,
And me they left with those of Epidamnum.
What then became of them I cannot tell;
I to this fortune that you see me in.
Duke. Why, here begins his morning story right.
These two Antipholuses, these two so like,
And these two Dromios, one in semblance,—
Besides her urging of her wreck at sea,—
These are the parents to these children.

281. mated, bewildered. **298. careful,** full of cares. **deformed,** deforming. **310.** the weak tone of my voice that is changed by grief. **311. grained,** furrowed. **315. lamps,** eyes.

332. Genius, attendant spirit. **334. deciphers,** distinguishes. **356-361.** In the original these lines of the Duke's speech follow l. 345 and the last line 362 comes after l. 355. There has been cutting and re-arrangement. The text follows the arrangement of all modern editions.

Which accidentally are met together.
Antipholus, thou cam'st from Corinth first?
Ant. S. No, sir, not I; I came from Syracuse.
Duke. Stay, stand apart; I know not which is which.
Ant. E. I came from Corinth, my most gracious lord,—
Dro. E. And I with him.
Ant. E. Brought to this town by that most famous warrior,
Duke Menaphon, your most renowned uncle.
Adr. Which of you two did dine with me to-day?
Ant. S. I, gentle mistress.
Adr. And are not you my husband?
Ant. E. No; I say nay to that.
Ant. S. And so do I, yet did she call me so;
And this fair gentlewoman, her sister here,
Did call me brother. [*To Luc.*] What I told you then,
I hope I shall have leisure to make good;
If this be not a dream I see and hear.
Ang. That is the chain, sir, which you had of me.
Ant. S. I think it be, sir; I deny it not.
Ant. E. And you, sir, for this chain arrested me.
Ang. I think I did, sir; I deny it not.
Adr. I sent you money, sir, to be your bail,
By Dromio; but I think he brought it not.
Dro. E. No, none by me.
Ant. S. This purse of ducats I receiv'd from you
And Dromio my man did bring them me.
I see we still did meet each other's man,
And I was ta'en for him, and he for me,
And thereupon these errors are arose.
Ant. E. These ducats pawn I for my father here.
Duke. It shall not need; thy father hath his life.
Cour. Sir, I must have that diamond from you.
Ant. E. There, take it; and much thanks for my good cheer.
Abb. Renowned Duke, vouchsafe to take the pains
To go with us into the abbey here
And hear at large discoursed all our fortunes;
And all that are assembled in this place,
That by this sympathized one day's error
Have suffer'd wrong, go, keep us company,
And we shall make full satisfaction.
Thirty-three years have I but gone in travail
Of you, my sons; and till this present hour
My heavy burden ne'er delivered.
The Duke, my husband, and my children both,
And you the calendars of their nativity,
Go to a gossips' feast, and joy with me;
After so long grief, such festivity!
Duke. With all my heart, I 'll gossip at this feast.
Exeunt all but the two Dromios and the two brothers.
Dro. S. Master, shall I go fetch your stuff from shipboard?
Ant. E. Dromio, what stuff of mine hast thou embark'd?
Dro. S. Your goods that lay at host, sir, in the Centaur.
Ant. S. He speaks to me. I am your master, Dromio.
Come, go with us; we 'll look to that anon.
Embrace thy brother there; rejoice with him.
Exeunt the two brothers Antipholus.
Dro. S. There is a fat friend at your master's house,
That kitchen'd me for you to-day at dinner;
She now shall be my sister, not my wife.
Dro. E. Methinks you are my glass, and not my brother.
I see by you I am a sweet-fac'd youth.
Will you walk in to see their gossiping?
Dro. S. Not I, sir; you are my elder.
Dro. E. That's a question: how shall we try it?
Dro. S. We 'll draw cuts for the senior; till then lead thou first.
Dro. E. Nay, then, thus:
We came into the world like brother and brother;
And now let 's go hand in hand, not one before another.
Exeunt.

397. sympathized, shared by all. **404. calendars**, cf. n. on 1. 2. 41. **405. gossips'**, baptismal sponsors'. **407. gossip**, take part in, like a gossip. **410. lay at host**, were stored. **415. kitchen'd**, entertained in the kitchen. **422. cuts**, lots.

A Midsummer Night's Dream

A Midsummer Night's Dream is Shakespeare's first undisputed masterpiece, an almost perfect blending of romance and realism, bathed like his moon-lit fairy-haunted wood in a flood of exquisite lyric verse.

Text.—It is fortunate that the text has come down to us in a comparatively perfect form. The first and sole authentic text is that of the First Quarto, the so-called Fisher Quarto of 1600. Another Quarto, bearing on the title-page the same date and the name of Roberts as printer, is now known to be one of the falsely dated imprints of 1619—see Introduction, p. 78. It was printed from a copy of Q_1 and has, of course, no independent authority. The Folio text was printed from a copy of Q_2, apparently from one which had been collated with the prompt-book at the theatre, gathering from it numerous additional stage-directions along with a few obvious corrections in the dialogue and dividing the play into the regulation five acts.

The First Quarto, on the other hand, goes back direct to Shakespeare's original manuscript; probably the "copy" for Fisher's printer was this manuscript prepared for acting by the stage-manager, as is shown by such stage-directions as *Enter the King of Fairies at one door with his train and the Queen at another with hers,* and such emphatic injunctions to the actors as *Lie down* and *Sleep.* It is on the text of Q_1 with the necessary modernization and a few corrections that the present edition is based.

Date.—There has been much discussion as to the date of this play and it is not possible to fix it with any precision. It is first mentioned by Meres in 1598, but it must have been written some years before that date, since it is one of a group of lyric-poetic dramas, *Love's Labour's Lost, Romeo and Juliet,* and *Richard II,* that mark Shakespeare's re-appearance as a practising playwright after the year or two (1593-4) devoted to the composition of his narrative poems—see Introduction, pp. 16-17. There is a fair consensus of opinion that it was written late in 1594 or early in 1595, quite probably to be performed at the festivities attending a noble wedding. Titania's description of the changing seasons (II, i, 81-117) is quite plainly an allusion to the dreadful summer of 1594, marked by storms, floods, and wintry cold. The fear expressed by the rude mechanicals as to the danger of bringing in a lion among ladies seems to be a jest at the prudent substitution of a blackamoor for the originally proposed lion drawing a triumphal car at the christening feast of Prince Henry of Scotland, August 30, 1594. Such a jest would lose its point unless the account of this feast was fresh in the minds of the audience.

To fix the date of composition about 1595 does not, however, exclude the possibility of revision. In fact it seems certain that the play was revised, probably for performance in a public theatre, some time after that date and before it was given to the press. This is clear from the fact that it contains a double ending. The song and dance of the fairies (V, i, 378-429) is an appropriate and lovely close to the private performance. Robin's epilogue, on the other hand, with its apology and appeal for applause, is plainly addressed to a public audience. How far this revision extended it is impossible to say. It is an interesting fact that the speeches of the mischief-making goblin are headed sometimes *Robin* and sometimes *Puck;* in like manner Shakespeare heads some speeches *Oberon,* some *King;* some speeches *Titania,* some *Queen;* some *Bottom,* and some *Clown.* Apparently writing at full speed he headed the speeches in his manuscript with whatever name or title came into his head first, fully assured that the stage-manager would see that they were spoken by the proper actor. The text as it has come down to us preserves the form of presentation at the private performance. There is no balcony scene, and no inner stage. According to a stage-direction in the Folio the Lovers sleep all the Act, *i.e.,* upon the open stage throughout the act-interval between Acts IV and V. In fact they are not awakened till Theseus rouses them with a flourish of horns nearly 150 lines later. Meanwhile Titania and the transformed Bottom come upon the stage, and fall asleep beside the lovers without noticing them. Titania is awakened by Oberon, but Bottom sleeps calmly on through the music, the horns, and speeches until the end of the scene. All this is improbable, not to say fantastic, but we should remember that this is not a comedy written in the first instance for a public performance, but a show composed for a private entertainment where such improbabilities would be overlooked by an audience delighted with the spectacle, the music, and the dancing.

Source.—Properly speaking there is no source for *A Midsummer Night's Dream,* no pattern which Shakespeare followed as he followed Plautus in the *Comedy of Errors.* The pattern of *A Midsummer Night's Dream* is composed of varied threads drawn by Shakespeare from his reading and observations and woven with the utmost skill into the lovely tapestry of his play. The story of Theseus comes partly from Plutarch, more directly from Chaucer's *Knight's Tale,* where Theseus appears as the Duke of Athens just wedded to the Amazon, Hippolyta. The plot of the lovers and the love-charms seems to derive from Montemayor's *Diana,* from which Shakespeare had drawn some details from his *Two Gentlemen* (*ca.* 1591), and also from Gil Popo's continuation of Montemayor's romance. The name of the fairy King, Oberon, comes ultimately from the old French romance *Huon of Bordeaux,* but Shakespeare may as well have lifted it from Greene's play, *James IV* (ca. 1591). Shakespeare took the name of the fairy Queen, Titania, from his favorite poet, Ovid; not, it may be noted, from the Golding translation, but from the original Latin. Puck (properly speaking, *the puck,* or goblin; his proper name is Robin Goodfellow) comes straight from English folk-lore. In contrast to the courtly Oberon and Titania "come from the farthest steep of India," Robin represents the homely English notion of the fairies as good familiar spirits, fond of fun and ready for mischief, but by no means malicious, and always ready to lend a hand in house-hold tasks and bring good luck to the well-deserving. The very names of Titania's attendant elves, Peaseblossom, Cobweb, Moth, and Mustardseed are drawn from an English garden. Like Robin Goodfellow, Bottom and his mates are thoroughly English. The names and occupations of the "hempen-home-spuns" are all good Elizabethan English; in fact their names, with one exception, are significant of their occupations—see note, p. 53. Characteristic of Elizabethan England, too, is the purpose for which they meet, to present a play at the wedding of their sovereign lord. Shakespeare's England from the Queen's Court to the remotest village was drama-mad, and enough of the old tradition of the community play still lingered to embolden anywhere a group of villagers to undertake the presentation of some "most lamentable comedy." Their performances, especially if they were rash enough to attempt a dramatic version of a classic story, were no doubt highly ridiculous to a sophisticated London audience, as is shown by the mocking comments of Theseus and his courtiers on the play of *Pyramus.* More particularly Shakespeare ridicules in this performance the awkward attempt of the amateurs to preserve in contemporary drama the belated realism, in such characters as Wall and Moonshine, of the old miracle plays.

Construction.—It is a commonplace of criticism to praise the construction of *A Midsummer Night's Dream* and to point out how skillfully the various plots are interwoven. Yet such criticism may obscure the real excellence of the play. It tends to picture Shakespeare as a skilled artificer fitting pieces of mosaic into a pre-conceived pattern. This is too artificial a conception; the structure of *Midsummer Night's Dream* is organic rather than mechanical. There are indeed four themes in the play, but they have no independent existence, rather they are parts of a living whole, a romantic comedy with one central action dominated by one controlling idea. The central action, of course, is the story of the lovers; the dominating idea is that of the irrational nature of love, "fancy," the Elizabethans called it, "engender'd in the eyes" and "fed with gazing," presented in its most fantastic form in Titania's dotage on the "translated" Bottom. This is, of course, the conception of love from the standpoint of comedy as opposed to the idea of love as a consuming and purifying passion expressed in the almost contemporary tragedy of *Romeo and Juliet.* Let us see how this action proceeds and how it is controlled by the conception of love as "fancy."

At the very beginning of the play we find Lysander in love with Hermia, who returns his affection. Demetrius, once the lover of Helena, has deserted her for no known cause to woo Hermia, but Helena still follows him with love.

Before long Lysander transfers his affection to Helena so that we have the complete love-chain: Hermia loves Lysander who loves Helena who loves Demetrius who loves Hermia. The chain is broken when Demetrius returns to his first love Helena, and the final solution is attained when Lysander returns to Hermia and we have two happy couples instead of the wrangling four. These changes in the action are brought about by the various love-charms, the juice of "Love-in-idleness"—how characteristic a name!—and that of "Dian's bud," symbols and nothing else, of the irrational character of love. Now these charms are administered by the fairy-king and his servant, Robin Goodfellow, and Oberon's first design is not upon the lovers but upon the Queen with whom he has quarrelled, and it is Robin's love of mischief that equips Bottom with the ass's head and throws him into the arms of the bewitched Titania. Bottom, in turn, has entered the charmed circle of the fairies' domain when he comes with his fellows to rehearse the play to be performed at the wedding of Theseus and Hippolyta, and it is to celebrate this union of their old-time favorites that Oberon and Titania have come to the haunted wood near Athens. This wedding, in fact, serves as the enveloping action with which the play begins and closes, and every action in the play is in one way or another connected with it. The wedding-day is set by Theseus as the date on which he must pass judgment upon Hermia's love-affair; and when the tangled skein of the lovers has been unwound it is along with Theseus that they are married. After Bottom's restoration to human shape he bravely performs the part of Pyramus before the wedded couples, and the fairies who have come to grace the wedding of the Duke remain to bless the triple marriage. We may analyze the play as a botanist dissects a flower, but it is a perfect whole and all its parts are vitally interrelated.

Characterization.—Shakespeare's advance in originality and mastery of dramatic technique over his earlier work is very evident in *A Midsummer Night's Dream.* No less evident is his increasing power of characterization. One has only to compare the fully realized character of Theseus with that of the Duke in *The Comedy of Errors.* Solinus is a rather shadowy figure, a necessary factor in the action, but almost wholly lacking in individuality. Theseus is not only a ruler, but a lover, whose sane and sensible affection for his bride contrasts, as Shakespeare meant it to do, with the fickle passions of the lovers. He is a sportsman breeding hounds "of the Spartan kind" like an English gentleman of Shakespeare's day. A man of action rather than of intellect or passion, he is a little contemptuous of the fine frenzy of the poet, but ready like a courteous prince to endure the "tedious brief scene" offered by his subjects,

> For never anything can come amiss
> When simpleness and duty tender it.

It has been frequently remarked that Shakespeare has done little to characterize the lovers: "Lysander differs in nothing from Demetrius, Helena in nothing but height from Hermia," says one critic. There is a certain truth in this remark, but, on the other hand, it seems plain that this lack of individual characterization was purposely designed. The lovers and their chops and changes present dramatically the conception of love as a fantastic and irrational passion. To have made a Romeo of Lysander or a Troilus of Demetrius would have turned the merry comedy that Shakespeare planned into something like a tragedy. And it is simply untrue that Hermia and Helena differ only by their height. One must be a very careless reader who fails to distinguish between the warm-hearted quick-tempered little Hermia and her sentimental spaniel-like rival in love. Particularly characteristic is Helena's appeal to the men for protection against the threats of physical violence on the part of the maid who "was a vixen when she went to school."

It is in the figure of Bottom, however, that Shakespeare attains supreme mastery. Written as a clown's part designed for Shakespeare's fellow-actor Kemp, Bottom develops in Shakespeare's hands into one of the eternally ridiculous figures of comic literature. He is as near us to-day as he was to the Elizabethans who shook with laughter over his absurdities; the Bottom character, self-conceited, bumptious, and unabashed, endures forever. A central figure in this most fanciful of comedies, there is no shade or trace of romance in Bottom's character. Cast for the part of a lover in a tragedy, he promptly offers to play the part of the lady or the lion and is concerned as to the color of the beard he is to wear. Abandoned by his companions at night in the haunted wood, he sings and jests to show that he is not afraid. Courted by the Queen of Fairyland he has no sense of the glamour and the peril of his situation. On the contrary he accepts the kisses and caresses of his fairy mistress with the utmost complacency and calls for a "bottle of hay" and the music of the tongs and bones. Incongruity is said to be the essence of the comic, and where in all literature is there a finer instance of the incongruous than that most memorable scene when Bottom with his fine large ass's ears, true symbol of his asininity, falls asleep in the arms of the dainty and doting Titania? Bottom is Shakespeare's first fully realized, highly individual, and unmistakably human character.

The Poetry.—After all it is neither the action nor the characterization that lingers in the memory when the lover of Shakespeare thinks of *A Midsummer Night's Dream.* The peculiar charm of this play is the magical music of Shakespeare's verse. If in *The Comedy of Errors* the young playwright sternly repressed his lyric vein in order to achieve a dramatic triumph, here, confident of his success upon the stage, and elated by the extraordinary popularity of *Venus and Adonis,* he gives free rein for the first time to that power of lyric dramatic utterance which was then and is still the special and characteristic mark of Shakespeare's genius. Alike in the dainty rhymed couplets of the lovers' scenes, and the stately blank verse assigned especially to Theseus we recognize the voice of the master. But nowhere is it clearer and more bewitching than in the fairy scenes. The songs seem to have been written for a chorus of children whom Shakespeare was fortunate enough to command for the private performance; but the lyric note rings as unmistakably through the speeches of Oberon, Titania and Robin. It is the fairies, their songs and dances and lyric speeches, that make *A Midsummer Night's Dream* what it is, the most perennially charming of Shakespeare's plays. Deeper passion, graver thought, a more solemn music were yet to come, but in no succeeding play shall we find anything quite like the fresh fascination and liquid lyric of this early comedy.

Stage History. — *A Midsummer Night's Dream* has never been a great success. The title-page of Q_1 states that it had been publicly acted by the Lord Chamberlain's company. Probably Elizabeth attended the private performance and smiled approval of the homage paid to the "fair vestal throned by the west." A performance before King James on New Year's night, 1604, is recorded under the title of "a play of Robin Goodfellow." After the closing of the theatres the humors of Bottom and his mates were detached from the body of the play and given more or less surreptitiously during the Commonwealth. One of these "drolls" *The Merry Conceited Humours of Bottom the Weaver* was published in 1661 and again in 1673. Mr. Pepys attended a revival of the comedy in 1662 and pronounced it "the most insipid ridiculous play that ever I saw." Shakespeare's airy fancy was not to the taste of the sophisticated Restoration, except as an operatic spectacle, in which form it was produced by Betterton, under the title of *The Fairy Queen* with music by Purcell. During the eighteenth century it was frequently cut down to an after-piece or partially presented as an interlude in another play. It was not until well along in the nineteenth century that the play as Shakespeare wrote it returned to the stage. It was given at Covent Garden in 1840 accompanied by Mendelssohn's music. A performance at the Prince's Theatre in 1856 introduced Ellen Terry at the age of eight to the stage in the role of Puck. Later performances include a very beautiful production by Augustin Daly at his New York theatre in 1888 and Granville Barker's in London, 1923, sharply criticized for its fantastic presentation of the fairies, strange creatures with scarlet and gilded faces. Final mention should be made perhaps of the production of the play upon the screen under the direction of Reinhardt—more Reinhardt, it was remarked, than Shakespeare—a show of lovely dance and spectacle, with little of the text remaining and a horrible travesty of the character of Puck.

A MIDSUMMER NIGHT'S DREAM

Dramatis Personæ

Theseus, duke of Athens.
Egeus, father to *Hermia.*
Lysander, betrothed to *Hermia.*
Demetrius, in love with *Hermia.*
Philostrate, master of the revels to *Theseus.*

Quince, a carpenter.
Bottom, a weaver.
Flute, a bellows-mender.
Snout, a tinker.
Snug, a joiner.
Starveling, a tailor.

Hippolyta, queen of the Amazons, betrothed to *Theseus.*
Hermia, daughter to *Egeus,* betrothed to *Lysander.*
Helena, in love with *Demetrius.*

Oberon, king of the fairies.
Titania, queen of the fairies.
Robin Goodfellow, a Puck.
Peaseblossom, *Cobweb,* *Moth,* *Mustardseed,* } fairies.

Other fairies attending their King and Queen.
Attendants on Theseus and Hippolyta.

SCENE: *Athens, and a wood near by.*

ACT I. Scene I. *Athens. The Palace of Theseus.*

Enter *Theseus, Hippolyta, Philostrate,* with others.

The. Now, fair Hippolyta, our nuptial hour
Draws on apace: four happy days bring in
Another moon; but, O, methinks, how slow
This old moon wanes! She lingers my desires,
Like to a step-dame or a dowager
Long withering out a young man's revenue.
Hip. Four days will quickly steep themselves in night;
Four nights will quickly dream away the time;
And then the moon, like to a silver bow
New-bent in heaven, shall behold the night
Of our solemnities.
The. Go, Philostrate,
Stir up the Athenian youth to merriments;
Awake the pert and nimble spirit of mirth;
Turn melancholy forth to funerals;
The pale companion is not for our pomp.
Exit Philostrate.
Hippolyta, I woo'd thee with my sword,
And won thy love, doing thee injuries;
But I will wed thee in another key,
With pomp, with triumph, and with revelling.

Enter *Egeus* and his daughter *Hermia* and *Lysander* and *Demetrius.*

Ege. Happy be Theseus, our renowned Duke!
The. Thanks, good Egeus; what 's the news with thee?
Ege. Full of vexation come I, with complaint
Against my child, my daughter Hermia.
Stand forth, Demetrius. My noble lord,
This man hath my consent to marry her.
Stand forth, Lysander: and, my gracious Duke,
This man hath bewitch'd the bosom of my child.
Thou, thou, Lysander, thou hast given her rhymes,
And interchang'd love-tokens with my child.
Thou hast by moonlight at her window sung
With faining voice verses of faining love,
And stol'n the impression of her fantasy
With bracelets of thy hair, rings, gawds, conceits,
Knacks, trifles, nosegays, sweetmeats,—messengers
Of strong prevailment in unharden'd youth,
With cunning hast thou filch'd my daughter's heart,
Turn'd her obedience, which is due to me,

The names of the "mechanicals" are all but one significant of their trades: Quince means "quoins," wedges of wood; Bottom is the "bottom" or core of a skein of yarn; Snout is the "spout" of a kettle, such as tinkers mended; Snug means "tight-fitting"; the name suits a joiner; Flute would mend the "flutes," pipes, of organs; Starveling fits a tailor, since "it takes nine tailors to make a man."

4. lingers, delays fulfillment of. **5. dowager,** a widow with a dower. **13. pert,** lively. **19. triumph,** public show, festivity.

31. faining, (1) yearning, (2) feigned. **32.** Captured (stamped your image upon) her imagination. **33. gawds,** gewgaws. **conceits,** fancy articles. **34. knacks,** knick-knacks. **35. strong prevailment,** great power.

To stubborn harshness; and, my gracious Duke,
Be it so she will not here before your Grace
Consent to marry with Demetrius,
I beg the ancient privilege of Athens,
As she is mine, I may dispose of her;
Which shall be either to this gentleman
Or to her death, according to our law
Immediately provided in that case.

The. What say you, Hermia? Be advis'd, fair maid.
To you your father should be as a god,
One that compos'd your beauties, yea, and one
To whom you are but as a form in wax
By him imprinted, and within his power
To leave the figure or disfigure it.
Demetrius is a worthy gentleman.

Her. So is Lysander.

The. In himself he is;
But in this kind, wanting your father's voice,
The other must be held the worthier.

Her. I would my father look'd but with my eyes.

The. Rather your eyes must with his judgement look.

Her. I do entreat your Grace to pardon me.
I know not by what power I am made bold,
Nor how it may concern my modesty,
In such a presence here to plead my thoughts;
But I beseech your Grace that I may know
The worst that may befall me in this case,
If I refuse to wed Demetrius.

The. Either to die the death or to abjure
For ever the society of men.
Therefore, fair Hermia, question your desires,
Know of your youth, examine well your blood,
Whether, if you yield not to your father's choice,
You can endure the livery of a nun,
For aye to be in shady cloister mew'd,
To live a barren sister all your life,
Chanting faint hymns to the cold fruitless moon.
Thrice-blessed they that master so their blood
To undergo such maiden pilgrimage;
But earthlier happy is the rose distill'd,
Than that which withering on the virgin thorn
Grows, lives, and dies in single blessedness.

Her. So will I grow, so live, so die, my lord,
Ere I will yield my virgin patent up
Unto his lordship, whose unwished yoke
My soul consents not to give sovereignty.

The. Take time to pause; and, by the next new moon—
The sealing-day betwixt my love and me,
For everlasting bond of fellowship—
Upon that day either prepare to die
For disobedience to your father's will,
Or else to wed Demetrius, as he would,
Or on Diana's altar to protest
For aye austerity and single life.

Dem. Relent, sweet Hermia; and, Lysander, yield
Thy crazed title to my certain right.

Lys. You have her father's love, Demetrius,
Let me have Hermia's; do you marry him.

Ege. Scornful Lysander! true, he hath my love,
And what is mine my love shall render him.
And she is mine, and all my right of her
I do estate unto Demetrius.

Lys. I am, my lord, as well deriv'd as he.
As well possess'd; my love is more than his;
My fortunes every way as fairly rank'd,
If not with vantage, as Demetrius';
And, which is more than all these boasts can be,
I am belov'd of beauteous Hermia.
Why should not I then prosecute my right?
Demetrius, I 'll avouch it to his head,
Made love to Nedar's daughter, Helena,
And won her soul; and she, sweet lady, dotes,
Devoutly dotes, dotes in idolatry,
Upon this spotted and inconstant man.

The. I must confess that I have heard so much,
And with Demetrius thought to have spoke thereof;
But, being over-full of self-affairs,
My mind did lose it. But, Demetrius, come;
And come, Egeus; you shall go with me,
I have some private schooling for you both.
For you, fair Hermia, look you arm yourself
To fit your fancies to your father's will;
Or else the law of Athens yields you up—
Which by no means we may extenuate—
To death, or to a vow of single life.
Come, my Hippolyta; what cheer, my love?
Demetrius and Egeus, go along.
I must employ you in some business
Against our nuptial, and confer with you
Of something nearly that concerns yourselves.

Ege. With duty and desire we follow you.

Exeunt all but Lysander and Hermia.

Lys. How now, my love! why is your cheek so pale?
How chance the roses there do fade so fast?

45. Immediately, expressly. **51. disfigure,** destroy. **54. kind,** respect. **voice,** approval. **60. concern,** befit. **71. mew'd,** confined. **74. blood,** passions. **76. earthlier happy,** happier in this world. **80. patent,** privilege.

89. protest, vow. **92. crazed,** flawed. **98. estate unto,** bestow upon. **100, as well possess'd,** as well off. **106. head,** face. **120. extenuate,** mitigate. **125. Against,** in preparation for. **126. nearly that,** that closely.

Her. Belike for want of rain, which I could well
Beteem them from the tempest of my eyes.
Lys. Ay me! for aught that I could ever read,
Could ever hear by tale or history,
The course of true love never did run smooth;
But, either it was different in blood,—
Her. O cross! too high to be enthrall'd to low.
Lys. Or else misgraffed in respect of years,—
Her. O spite! too old to be engag'd to young.
Lys. Or else it stood upon the choice of friends,—
Her. O hell! to choose love by another's eyes.
Lys. Or, if there were a sympathy in choice,
War, death, or sickness did lay siege to it,
Making it momentany as a sound,
Swift as a shadow, short as any dream,
Brief as the lightning in the collied night,
That, in a spleen, unfolds both heaven and earth,
And ere a man hath power to say "Behold!"
The jaws of darkness do devour it up;
So quick bright things come to confusion.
Her. If then true lovers have been ever cross'd,
It stands as an edict in destiny.
Then let us teach our trial patience,
Because it is a customary cross,
As due to love as thoughts and dreams and sighs,
Wishes and tears, poor fancy's followers.
Lys. A good persuasion; therefore, hear me, Hermia.
I have a widow aunt, a dowager
Of great revenue, and she hath no child.
From Athens is her house remote seven leagues;
And she respects me as her only son.
There, gentle Hermia, may I marry thee;
And to that place the sharp Athenian law
Cannot pursue us. If thou lovest me then,
Steal forth thy father's house to-morrow night;
And in the wood, a league without the town,
Where I did meet thee once with Helena
To do observance to a morn of May,
There will I stay for thee.
Her. My good Lysander!
I swear to thee, by Cupid's strongest bow,
By his best arrow with the golden head,
By the simplicity of Venus' doves,
By that which knitteth souls and prospers loves,
And by that fire which burn'd the Carthage queen,
When the false Troyan under sail was seen,
By all the vows that ever men have broke,
In number more than ever women spoke,
In that same place thou hast appointed me
To-morrow truly will I meet with thee.
Lys. Keep promise, love. Look, here comes Helena.

Enter *Helena.*

Her. God speed fair Helena! Whither away?
Hel. Call you me fair? That fair again unsay.
Demetrius loves your fair, O happy fair!
Your eyes are lode-stars, and your tongue's sweet air
More tuneable than lark to shepherd's ear
When wheat is green, when hawthorn buds appear.
Sickness is catching; O, were favour so,
Yours would I catch, fair Hermia, ere I go;
My ear should catch your voice, my eye your eye,
My tongue should catch your tongue's sweet melody.
Were the world mine, Demetrius being bated,
The rest I 'll give to be to you translated.
O, teach me how you look, and with what art
You sway the motion of Demetrius' heart.
Her. I frown upon him, yet he loves me still.
Hel. O that your frowns would teach my smiles such skill!
Her. I give him curses, yet he gives me love.
Hel. O that my prayers could such affection move!
Her. The more I hate, the more he follows me.
Hel. The more I love, the more he hateth me.
Her. His folly, Helena, is no fault of mine.
Hel. None, but your beauty. Would that fault were mine!

131. **Beteem,** give, pour on. 137. **misgraffed,** ill matched. 143. **momentany,** momentary. 145. **collied,** blackened. 146. **spleen,** fit of passion. 149. **confusion,** ruin. 150. **ever,** always. 152. **teach . . . patience,** teach ourselves patience to endure our trial. 155. **fancy's,** love's. 160. **respects,** regards. 167. To celebrate May Day.

170-74. **By his best arrow with the golden head,** the arrow that kindles love. **the simplicity of Venus' doves,** to the birds of Venus is added a Biblical suggestion, "harmless as doves." **that which knitteth souls and prospers loves,** the girdle of Venus which inspired love. **the Carthage queen,** Dido, deserted by the Trojan Æneas, committed suicide on a funeral pyre. 182. **fair,** beauty. 183. **lode-stars,** guiding stars. 184. **tuneable,** musical. 186. **favour,** physical qualities. 190. **bated,** excepted. 191. **translated,** transformed.

Her. Take comfort; he no more shall see my face;
Lysander and myself will fly this place.
Before the time I did Lysander see,
Seem'd Athens as a paradise to me;
O, then, what graces in my love do dwell,
That he hath turn'd a heaven unto a hell!

Lys. Helen, to you our minds we will unfold.
To-morrow night, when Phœbe doth behold
Her silver visage in the wat'ry glass,
Decking with liquid pearl the bladed grass,
A time that lovers' flights doth still conceal,
Through Athens' gates have we devis'd to steal.

Her. And in the wood, where often you and I
Upon faint primrose-beds were wont to lie,
Emptying our bosoms of their counsel sweet,
There my Lysander and myself shall meet;
And thence from Athens turn away our eyes,
To seek new friends and stranger companies.
Farewell, sweet playfellow: pray thou for us;
And good luck grant thee thy Demetrius!
Keep word, Lysander; we must starve our sight
From lovers' food till morrow deep midnight.

Lys. I will, my Hermia. *Exit Hermia.*
Helena, adieu:
As you on him, Demetrius dote on you!
Exit Lysander.

Hel. How happy some o'er other some can be!
Through Athens I am thought as fair as she.
But what of that? Demetrius thinks not so;
He will not know what all but he do know;
And as he errs, doting on Hermia's eyes,
So I, admiring of his qualities.
Things base and vile, holding no quantity,
Love can transpose to form and dignity.
Love looks not with the eyes but with the mind,
And therefore is wing'd Cupid painted blind.
Nor hath Love's mind of any judgement taste;
Wings and no eyes figure unheedy haste;
And therefore is Love said to be a child,
Because in choice he is so oft beguil'd.
As waggish boys in game themselves forswear,
So the boy Love is perjur'd every where:
For ere Demetrius look'd on Hermia's eyne,
He hail'd down oaths that he was only mine;
And when this hail some heat from Hermia felt,
So he dissolv'd, and showers of oaths did melt.
I will go tell him of fair Hermia's flight;
Then to the wood will he to-morrow night
Pursue her; and for this intelligence
If I have thanks, it is a dear expense.
But herein mean I to enrich my pain,
To have his sight thither and back again.
Exit.

209. **Phœbe**, Diana, the moon. 215. **faint**, pale. 237. **figure**, symbolize. 242. **eyne**, eyes.

Scene II. *Athens. Quince's house.*

Enter *Quince* the Carpenter and *Snug* the Joiner and *Bottom* the Weaver and *Flute* the Bellows-mender and *Snout* the Tinker and *Starveling* the Tailor.

Quin. Is all our company here?

Bot. You were best to call them generally, man by man, according to the scrip.

Quin. Here is the scroll of every man's name, which is thought fit, through all Athens, to play in our interlude before the Duke and the Duchess, on his wedding-day at night.

Bot. First, good Peter Quince, say what the play treats on, then read the names of the actors, and so grow to a point.

Quin. Marry, our play is, *The most lamentable comedy and most cruel death of Pyramus and Thisby.*

Bot. A very good piece of work, I assure you, and a merry. Now, good Peter Quince, call forth your actors by the scroll. Masters, spread yourselves.

Quin. Answer as I call you. Nick Bottom, the weaver.

Bot. Ready. Name what part I am for, and proceed.

Quin. You, Nick Bottom, are set down for Pyramus.

Bot. What is Pyramus? A lover, or a tyrant?

Quin. A lover, that kills himself most gallant for love.

Bot. That will ask some tears in the true performing of it. If I do it, let the audience look to their eyes. I will move storms, I will condole in some measure. To the rest. Yet my chief humour is for a tyrant. I could play Ercles rarely, or a part to tear a cat in, to make all split.

"The raging rocks
And shivering shocks
Shall break the locks
Of prison gates;

248. intelligence, news. **249. dear expense**, a thing that will cost me dear. **Scene ii: 2. generally**, severally (the first of Bottom's malapropisms). **3. scrip**, list. **29. condole**, lament. **31. Ercles**, Hercules, a ranting part in early drama. **tear a cat in**, rant.

And Phibbus' car
Shall shine from far
And make and mar
The foolish Fates."

This was lofty! Now name the rest of the players. This is Ercles' vein, a tyrant's vein; a lover is more condoling.

Quin. Francis Flute, the bellows-mender.

Flu. Here, Peter Quince.

Quin. Flute, you must take Thisby on you.

Flu. What is Thisby? A wandering knight?

Quin. It is the lady that Pyramus must love.

Flu. Nay, faith, let not me play a woman; I have a beard coming.

Quin. That 's all one; you shall play it in a mask, and you may speak as small as you will.

Bot. An I may hide my face, let me play Thisby too. I 'll speak in a monstrous little voice, "Thisne! Thisne! Ah Pyramus, my lover dear! thy Thisby dear, and lady dear!"

Quin. No, no; you must play Pyramus; and, Flute, you Thisby.

Bot. Well, proceed.

Quin. Robin Starveling, the tailor.

Star. Here, Peter Quince.

Quin. Robin Starveling, you must play Thisby's mother. Tom Snout, the tinker.

Snout. Here, Peter Quince.

Quin. You, Pyramus' father; myself, Thisby's father. Snug, the joiner, you, the lion's part; and, I hope, here is a play fitted.

Snug. Have you the lion's part written? Pray you, if it be, give it me, for I am slow of study.

Quin. You may do it extempore, for it is nothing but roaring.

Bot. Let me play the lion too. I will roar, that I will do any man's heart good to hear me. I will roar, that I will make the Duke say, "Let him roar again, let him roar again."

Quin. An you should do it too terribly, you would fright the Duchess and the ladies, that they would shriek; and that were enough to hang us all.

All. That would hang us, every mother's son.

Bot. I grant you, friends, if you should fright the ladies out of their wits, they would have no more discretion but to hang us; but I will aggravate my voice so that I will roar you as gently as any sucking dove; I will roar you an 't were any nightingale.

Quin. You can play no part but Pyramus; for Pyramus is a sweet-faced man; a proper man, as one shall see in a summer's day; a most lovely gentleman-like man: therefore you must needs play Pyramus.

Bot. Well, I will undertake it. What beard were I best to play it in?

Quin. Why, what you will.

Bot. I will discharge it in either your straw-colour beard, your orange-tawny beard, your purple-in-grain beard, or your French-crown-colour beard, your perfect yellow.

Quin. Some of your French crowns have no hair at all, and then you will play bare-faced. But, masters, here are your parts; and I am to entreat you, request you, and desire you, to con them by to-morrow night; and meet me in the palace wood, a mile without the town, by moonlight. There will we rehearse, for if we meet in the city, we shall be dogged with company, and our devices known. In the meantime I will draw a bill of properties, such as our play wants. I pray you, fail me not.

Bot. We will meet; and there we may rehearse most obscenely and courageously. Take pains; be perfect; adieu.

Quin. At the Duke's oak we meet.

Bot. Enough; hold or cut bow-strings.

Exeunt.

ACT II. SCENE I. *A wood near Athens.*

Enter a *Fairy* at one door and *Robin Goodfellow* at another.

Robin. How now, spirit! whither wander you?

Fai. Over hill, over dale,
Thorough bush, thorough brier,
Over park, over pale,
Thorough flood, thorough fire,
I do wander every where,
Swifter than the moon's sphere;
And I serve the fairy Queen,
To dew her orbs upon the green.
The cowslips tall her pensioners be;

37. Phibbus', Phœbus'.

84. aggravate, Bottom means "moderate." **88. proper,** handsome. **95. discharge,** perform. **97. purple-in-grain,** dyed red. **French-crown-colour,** color of a French gold coin. **99-100. Some of your French crowns have no hair at all,** the usual joke about "the French disease" causing loss of hair. **111. obscenely,** Bottom means "obscurely" or "seemly." **114. hold . . . bow-strings,** a phrase from archery, evidently meaning "be sure to be on hand." **Act II, Scene i: 9. orbs,** fairy rings. **10. pensioners,** royal bodyguard.

In their gold coats spots you see;
Those be rubies, fairy favours,
In those freckles live their savours.
I must go seek some dewdrops here
And hang a pearl in every cowslip's ear.
Farewell, thou lob of spirits; I 'll be gone.
Our Queen and all her elves come here anon.

Robin. The King doth keep his revels here to-night;
Take heed the Queen come not within his sight;
For Oberon is passing fell and wrath,
Because that she as her attendant hath
A lovely boy stolen from an Indian king.
She never had so sweet a changeling;
And jealous Oberon would have the child
Knight of his train, to trace the forest wild;
But she perforce withholds the loved boy,
Crowns him with flowers, and makes him all her joy;
And now they never meet in grove or green,
By fountain clear, or spangled starlight sheen,
But they do square, that all their elves for fear
Creep into acorn-cups and hide them there.

Fai. Either I mistake your shape and making quite,
Or else you are that shrewd and knavish sprite
Call'd Robin Goodfellow. Are not you he
That frights the maidens of the villagery;
Skim milk, and sometimes labour in the quern,
And bootless make the breathless housewife churn,
And sometime make the drink to bear no barm,
Mislead night-wanderers, laughing at their harm?
Those that Hobgoblin call you, and sweet Puck,
You do their work, and they shall have good luck.
Are not you he?

Robin. Thou speakest aright;
I am that merry wanderer of the night.
I jest to Oberon and make him smile
When I a fat and bean-fed horse beguile,
Neighing in likeness of a filly foal;
And sometime lurk I in a gossip's bowl,
In very likeness of a roasted crab,
And when she drinks, against her lips I bob
And on her withered dewlap pour the ale.
The wisest aunt, telling the saddest tale,
Sometime for three-foot stool mistaketh me.
Then slip I from her bum, down topples she,
And "tailor" cries, and falls into a cough;
And then the whole quire hold their hips and laugh,
And waxen in their mirth, and neeze, and swear
A merrier hour was never wasted there.
But, room, fairy! here comes Oberon.

Fai. And here my mistress. Would that he were gone!

Enter the King of Fairies *Oberon* at one door with his train; and the Queen *Titania* at another with hers.

Obe. Ill met by moonlight, proud Titania.

Tita. What, jealous Oberon! Fairy, skip hence:
I have forsworn his bed and company.

Obe. Tarry, rash wanton! Am not I thy lord?

Tita. Then I must be thy lady; but I know
When thou hast stol'n away from fairy land,
And in the shape of Corin sat all day,
Playing on pipes of corn and versing love
To amorous Phillida. Why art thou here,
Come from the farthest steep of India?
But that, forsooth, the bouncing Amazon,
Your buskin'd mistress and your warrior love,
To Theseus must be wedded, and you come
To give their bed joy and prosperity.

Obe. How canst thou thus for shame, Titania,
Glance at my credit with Hippolyta,
Knowing I know thy love to Theseus?
Didst thou not lead him through the glimmering night
From Perigenia, whom he ravished?
And make him with fair Ægle break his faith,
With Ariadne, and Antiopa?

Tita. These are the forgeries of jealousy;
And never, since the middle summer's spring,
Met we on hill, in dale, forest or mead,
By paved fountain or by rushy brook,
Or in the beached margent of the sea,
To dance our ringlets to the whistling wind,
But with thy brawls thou hast disturb'd our sport.
Therefore the winds, piping to us in vain,
As in revenge, have suck'd up from the sea
Contagious fogs; which, falling in the land,

16. lob, lout. **20. passing fell and wrath,** very angry and wroth. **23. changeling,** ordinarily a child left behind by fairies as a substitute when they stole a human one; here the stolen child. **30. square,** quarrel. **that,** so that. **36. quern,** handmill. **38. barm,** yeast. **47. gossip's bowl,** the drink of a gossiping woman. **48. crab,** crab-apple, put in liquor. **50. dewlap,** loose skin on an animal's throat. **51. saddest,** most serious.

54. And "tailor" cries, an obscure allusion, perhaps a slang word for thief, the one who stole the stool. **55. quire,** company. **56. waxen,** increase. **neeze,** sneeze. **66. Corin,** common name of lover in pastoral literature. **67. versing love,** making love verses. **68. Phillida,** see Corin. **69. steep,** mountain range. **70. Amazon,** Hippolyta, queen of the Amazons. **71. buskin'd,** wearing buskins, high boots. **75. glance at,** attack indirectly. **78-80. Perigenia . . . Antiopa,** the allusions to women Theseus had loved are taken from the *Life of Theseus* in North's translation of Plutarch. **82. spring,** beginning. **85. in,** on. **margent,** margin. **86. ringlets,** rounds, circular dances.

Hath every pelting river made so proud
That they have overborne their continents.
The ox hath therefore stretch'd his yoke in vain,
The ploughman lost his sweat, and the green corn
Hath rotted ere his youth attain'd a beard.
The fold stands empty in the drowned field,
And crows are fatted with the murrain flock,
The nine men's morris is fill'd up with mud,
And the quaint mazes in the wanton green
For lack of tread are undistinguishable.
The human mortals want their winter cheer;
No night is now with hymn or carol blest;
Therefore the moon, the governess of floods,
Pale in her anger, washes all the air,
That rheumatic diseases do abound.
And thorough this distemperature we see
The seasons alter: hoary-headed frosts
Fall in the fresh lap of the crimson rose,
And on old Hiems' thin and icy crown
An odorous chaplet of sweet summer buds
Is, as in mockery, set; the spring, the summer,
The childing autumn, angry winter, change
Their wonted liveries; and the mazed world,
By their increase, now knows not which is which.
And this same progeny of evils comes
From our debate, from our dissension;
We are their parents and original.

Obe. Do you amend it then; it lies in you.
Why should Titania cross her Oberon?
I do but beg a little changeling boy
To be my henchman.

Tita. Set your heart at rest;
The fairy land buys not the child of me.
His mother was a vot'ress of my order,
And, in the spiced Indian air, by night,
Full often hath she gossip'd by my side,
And sat with me on Neptune's yellow sands,
Marking th' embarked traders on the flood,
When we have laugh'd to see the sails conceive
And grow big-bellied with the wanton wind;
Which she with pretty and with swimming gait
Following, her womb then rich with my young squire,
Would imitate, and sail upon the land
To fetch me trifles, and return again,
As from a voyage, rich with merchandise.
But she, being mortal, of that boy did die;
And for her sake do I rear up her boy,
And for her sake I will not part with him.

Obe. How long within this wood intend you stay?

Tita. Perchance till after Theseus' wedding-day.
If you will patiently dance in our round
And see our moonlight revels, go with us;
If not, shun me, and I will spare your haunts.

Obe. Give me that boy, and I will go with thee.

Tita. Not for thy fairy kingdom. Fairies, away!
We shall chide downright, if I longer stay.

Exit Titania with her train.

Obe. Well, go thy way; thou shalt not from this grove
Till I torment thee for this injury.
My gentle Puck, come hither. Thou remem-b'rest
Since once I sat upon a promontory,
And heard a mermaid on a dolphin's back
Uttering such dulcet and harmonious breath
That the rude sea grew civil at her song,
And certain stars shot madly from their spheres,
To hear the sea-maid's music?

Robin. I remember.

Obe. That very time I saw, but thou couldst not,
Flying between the cold moon and the earth,
Cupid all arm'd. A certain aim he took
At a fair vestal throned by the west,
And loos'd his love-shaft smartly from his bow,
As it should pierce a hundred thousand hearts;
But I might see young Cupid's fiery shaft
Quench'd in the chaste beams of the wat'ry moon
And the imperial votaress passed on,
In maiden meditation, fancy-free.
Yet mark'd I where the bolt of Cupid fell.
It fell upon a little western flower,
Before milk-white, now purple with love's wound,
And maidens call it love-in-idleness.
Fetch me that flower, the herb I shew'd thee once.
The juice of it on sleeping eye-lids laid
Will make or man or woman madly dote
Upon the next live creature that it sees.
Fetch me this herb; and be thou here again
Ere the leviathan can swim a league.

91. pelting, petty. **92. continents,** banks. **97. murrain,** diseased. **98. nine men's morris,** a rustic game played on a square in the turf marked with nine stones. **99. quaint mazes,** intricate figures marked out on the grass. **wanton green,** rich grass. **101. The human mortals want their winter cheer,** the line may mean that people lack their winter sports and festivals because summer has been turned into a sort of winter; the hymns and carols of winter are not heard. **109. Hiems',** God of winter. **112. childing,** fruitful. **113. mazed,** bewildered. **117. original,** source. **121. henchman,** page.

149. Since, when. **158. vestal,** Vestal Virgin, hence virgin. **"A fair vestal throned by the west,"** and **"imperial votaress"** (163), are usually regarded as complimentary allusions to the virgin queen of England, who may have been witnessing the play. **168. love-in-idleness,** pansy.

Robin. I 'll put a girdle round about the earth
In forty minutes. *Exit.*
Obe. Having once this juice,
I 'll watch Titania when she is asleep,
And drop the liquor of it in her eyes.
The next thing then she waking looks upon,
Be it on lion, bear, or wolf, or bull,
On meddling monkey, or on busy ape,
She shall pursue it with the soul of love;
And ere I take this charm from off her sight,
As I can take it with another herb,
I 'll make her render up her page to me.
But who comes here? I am invisible;
And I will overhear their conference.

Enter *Demetrius, Helena* following him.

Dem. I love thee not, therefore pursue me not.
Where is Lysander and fair Hermia?
The one I 'll slay, the other slayeth me.
Thou told'st me they were stolen unto this wood;
And here am I, and wode within this wood,
Because I cannot meet my Hermia.
Hence, get thee gone, and follow me no more.
Hel. You draw me, you hard-hearted adamant;
But yet you draw not iron, for my heart
Is true as steel. Leave you your power to draw,
And I shall have no power to follow you.
Dem. Do I entice you? Do I speak you fair?
Or, rather, do I not in plainest truth
Tell you, I do not, nor I cannot love you?
Hel. And even for that do I love you the more.
I am your spaniel, and, Demetrius,
The more you beat me, I will fawn on you.
Use me but as your spaniel, spurn me, strike me,
Neglect me, lose me; only give me leave,
Unworthy as I am, to follow you.
What worser place can I beg in your love,—
And yet a place of high respect with me,—
Than to be used as you use your dog?
Dem. Tempt not too much the hatred of my spirit,
For I am sick when I do look on thee.
Hel. And I am sick when I look not on you.
Dem. You do impeach your modesty too much,
To leave the city and commit yourself
Into the hands of one that loves you not;
To trust the opportunity of night
And the ill counsel of a desert place
With the rich worth of your virginity.
Hel. Your virtue is my privilege. For that
It is not night when I do see your face,
Therefore I think I am not in the night;
Nor doth this wood lack worlds of company,
For you in my respect are all the world.
Then how can it be said I am alone,
When all the world is here to look on me?
Dem. I 'll run from thee and hide me in the brakes,
And leave thee to the mercy of wild beasts.
Hel. The wildest hath not such a heart as you.
Run when you will, the story shall be chang'd:
Apollo flies, and Daphne holds the chase;
The dove pursues the griffin; the mild hind
Makes speed to catch the tiger; bootless speed,
When cowardice pursues and valour flies.
Dem. I will not stay thy questions; let me go;
Or, if thou follow me, do not believe
But I shall do thee mischief in the wood.
Hel. Ay, in the temple, in the town, the field,
You do me mischief. Fie, Demetrius!
Your wrongs do set a scandal on my sex.
We cannot fight for love, as men may do.
We should be woo'd and were not made to woo. *Exit Demetrius.*
I 'll follow thee and make a heaven of hell,
To die upon the hand I love so well.
Exit Helena.
Obe. Fare thee well, nymph. Ere he do leave this grove,
Thou shalt fly him and he shall seek thy love.

Re-enter *Robin Goodfellow.*

Hast thou the flower there? Welcome, wanderer.
Robin. Ay, there it is.
Obe. I pray thee, give it me.
I know a bank where the wild thyme blows,
Where oxlips and the nodding violet grows,
Quite over-canopied with luscious woodbine,
With sweet musk-roses and with eglantine.
There sleeps Titania sometimes of the night,
Lull'd in these flowers with dances and delight;
And there the snake throws her enamell'd skin,

192. **wode**, mad. 195. **adamant**, loadstone. 214. **impeach**, call in question.

220. **privilege**, protection. 224. **respect**, regard. 231. **Apollo flies, and Daphne holds the chase.** In Ovid. Apollo pursued Daphne; here, the girl pursues the man. 232. **griffin**, fabulous monster, part lion, part eagle. **hind**, female deer. 235. **stay thy questions**, listen to thy talk. 249. **blows**, blooms. 250. **oxlips**, flowers akin to cowslip and primrose. 251. **woodbine**, honeysuckle. 252. **eglantine**, sweetbriar.

Weed wide enough to wrap a fairy in;
And with the juice of this I 'll streak her eyes,
And make her full of hateful fantasies.
Take thou some of it, and seek through this grove.
A sweet Athenian lady is in love
With a disdainful youth: anoint his eyes,
But do it when the next thing he espies
May be the lady. Thou shalt know the man
By the Athenian garments he hath on.
Effect it with some care, that he may prove
More fond on her than she upon her love;
And look thou meet me ere the first cock crow.

Robin. Fear not, my lord, your servant shall do so. *Exeunt.*

Scene II. *Another part of the wood.*

Enter *Titania,* Queen of the Fairies, with her train.

Tita. Come, now a roundel and a fairy song;
Then, for the third part of a minute, hence;
Some to kill cankers in the musk-rose buds,
Some war with rere-mice for their leathern wings
To make my small elves coats, and some keep back
The clamorous owl that nightly hoots and wonders
At our quaint spirits. Sing me now asleep;
Then to your offices and let me rest.

Fairies sing.

1. Fairy.

"You spotted snakes with double tongue,
Thorny hedgehogs, be not seen;
Newts and blind-worms, do no wrong,
Come not near our fairy queen."

Chorus.

"Philomel, with melody
Sing in our sweet lullaby;
Lulla, lulla, lullaby; lulla, lulla, lullaby.
Never harm,
Nor spell nor charm,
Come our lovely lady nigh.
So good night, with lullaby."

1. Fairy.

"Weaving spiders, come not here;
Hence, you long-legg'd spinners, hence!
Beetles black, approach not near;
Worm nor snail, do no offence."

256. Weed, garment. **257. streak,** touch. **266. fond,** doting. **Scene ii: 1. roundel,** dance in a ring. **3. cankers,** canker-worms. **4. rere-mice,** bats. **7. quaint,** dainty. **8. offices,** duties. **11. Newts,** lizards. **blind-worms,** small lizards supposed to be blind. **13. Philomel,** poetic name for the nightingale.

Chorus.

"Philomel, with melody," etc.

2. Fairy. Hence, away! now all is well.
One aloof stand sentinel.

She sleeps. Exeunt Fairies.

Enter *Oberon* and squeezes the flower on *Titania's* eyelids.

Obe. What thou seest when thou dost wake,
Do it for thy true-love take.
Love and languish for his sake.
Be it ounce, or cat, or bear,
Pard, or boar with bristled hair,
In thy eye that shall appear
When thou wak'st, it is thy dear.
Wake when some vile thing is near.

Exit Oberon.

Enter *Lysander* and *Hermia.*

Lys. Fair love, you faint with wandering in the wood;
And to speak troth, I have forgot our way.
We'll rest us, Hermia, if you think it good,
And tarry for the comfort of the day.

Her. Be it so, Lysander. Find you out a bed;
For I upon this bank will rest my head.

Lys. One turf shall serve as pillow for us both;
One heart, one bed, two bosoms and one troth.

Her. Nay, good Lysander; for my sake, my dear,
Lie further off yet; do not lie so near.

Lys. O, take the sense, sweet, of my innocence!
Love takes the meaning in love's conference.
I mean that my heart unto yours is knit
So that but one heart we can make of it;
Two bosoms interchained with an oath;
So then two bosoms and a single troth.
Then by your side no bed-room me deny;
For lying so, Hermia, I do not lie.

Her. Lysander riddles very prettily.
Now much beshrew my manners and my pride,
If Hermia meant to say Lysander lied.
But, gentle friend, for love and courtesy
Lie further off; in humane modesty
Such separation as may well be said
Becomes a virtuous bachelor and a maid,
So far be distant; and, good night, sweet friend.
Thy love ne'er alter till thy sweet life end!

Lys. Amen, amen, to that fair prayer, say I;
And then end life when I end loyalty!
Here is my bed; sleep give thee all his rest!

30. ounce, lynx. **cat,** wildcat. **31. Pard,** leopard. **36. troth,** truth. **42. troth,** love. **57. humane,** courteous.

Her. With half that wish the wisher's eyes be press'd! *They sleep.*

Enter *Robin Goodfellow.*

Robin. Through the forest have I gone,
But Athenian found I none,
On whose eyes I might approve
This flower's force in stirring love.
Night and silence—Who is here?
Weeds of Athens he doth wear!
This is he, my master said,
Despised the Athenian maid;
And here the maiden, sleeping sound,
On the dank and dirty ground.
Pretty soul! she durst not lie
Near this lack-love, this kill-courtesy.
Churl, upon thy eyes I throw
All the power this charm doth owe.
When thou wak'st, let love forbid
Sleep his seat on thy eyelid;
So awake when I am gone,
For I must now to Oberon. *Exit.*

Enter *Demetrius* and *Helena,* running.

Hel. Stay, though thou kill me, sweet Demetrius.
Dem. I charge thee, hence, and do not haunt me thus.
Hel. O, wilt thou darkling leave me? Do not so.
Dem. Stay, on thy peril; I alone will go. *Exit Demetrius.*
Hel. O, I am out of breath in this fond chase!
The more my prayer, the lesser is my grace.
Happy is Hermia, wheresoe'er she lies,
For she hath blessed and attractive eyes.
How came her eyes so bright? Not with salt tears;
If so, my eyes are oftener wash'd than hers.
No, no, I am as ugly as a bear,
For beasts that meet me run away for fear;
Therefore no marvel though Demetrius
Do, as a monster, fly my presence thus.
What wicked and dissembling glass of mine
Made me compare with Hermia's sphery eyne?
But who is here? Lysander! on the ground!
Dead? or asleep? I see no blood, no wound.
Lysander, if you live, good sir, awake.
Lys. [*Awaking.*] And run through fire I will for thy sweet sake.
Transparent Helena! Nature shows art,
That through thy bosom makes me see thy heart.
Where is Demetrius? O, how fit a word
Is that vile name to perish on my sword!
Hel. Do not say so, Lysander; say not so.
What though he love your Hermia? Lord, what though?
Yet Hermia still loves you; then be content.
Lys. Content with Hermia! No; I do repent
The tedious minutes I with her have spent.
Not Hermia but Helena I love.
Who will not change a raven for a dove?
The will of man is by his reason sway'd;
And reason says you are the worthier maid.
Things growing are not ripe until their season,
So I, being young, till now ripe not to reason;
And touching now the point of human skill,
Reason becomes the marshal to my will
And leads me to your eyes, where I o'erlook
Love's stories written in love's richest book.
Hel. Wherefore was I to this keen mockery born?
When at your hands did I deserve this scorn?
Is 't not enough, is 't not enough, young man,
That I did never, no, nor never can,
Deserve a sweet look from Demetrius' eye,
But you must flout my insufficiency?
Good troth, you do me wrong, good sooth you do,
In such disdainful manner me to woo.
But fare you well; perforce I must confess
I thought you lord of more true gentleness.
O, that a lady, of one man refus'd,
Should of another therefore be abus'd! *Exit Helena.*
Lys. She sees not Hermia. Hermia, sleep thou there;
And never mayst thou come Lysander near!
For as a surfeit of the sweetest things
The deepest loathing to the stomach brings,
Or as the heresies that men do leave
Are hated most of those they did deceive,
So thou, my surfeit and my heresy,
Of all be hated, but the most of me!
And, all my powers, address your love and might
To honour Helen and to be her knight. *Exit.*
Her. [*Awaking.*] Help me, Lysander, help me! do thy best
To pluck this crawling serpent from my breast!
Ay me, for pity! what a dream was here!
Lysander, look how I do quake with fear.
Methought a serpent eat my heart away,
And you sat smiling at his cruel prey.

68. approve, prove. **79. owe,** possess. **86. darkling,** in the dark. **89. grace,** good fortune. **99. sphery eyne,** star-like eyes.

118. ripe, grow ripe. **119. point,** height. **skill,** reason, knowledge. **150. prey,** preying.

Lysander! what, remov'd? Lysander! lord!
What, out of hearing? Gone? No sound, no word?
Alack, where are you? Speak, an if you hear;
Speak, of all loves! I swoon almost with fear.
No? then I well perceive you are not nigh;
Either death or you I 'll find immediately.
Exit.

ACT III. Scene I. *The wood. Titania lying asleep.*

Enter the Clowns—*Quince, Snug, Bottom, Flute, Snout,* and *Starveling.*

Bot. Are we all met?

Quin. Pat, pat; and here 's a marvellous convenient place for our rehearsal. This green plot shall be our stage, this hawthorn-brake our tiring-house; and we will do it in action as we will do it before the Duke.

Bot. Peter Quince!

Quin. What say'st thou, bully Bottom?

Bot. There are things in this comedy of Pyramus and Thisby that will never please. First, Pyramus must draw a sword to kill himself, which the ladies cannot abide. How answer you that?

Snout. By 'r lakin, a parlous fear.

Star. I believe we must leave the killing out, when all is done.

Bot. Not a whit! I have a device to make all well. Write me a prologue; and let the prologue seem to say, we will do no harm with our swords and that Pyramus is not killed indeed; and, for the more better assurance, tell them that I Pyramus am not Pyramus, but Bottom the weaver. This will put them out of fear.

Quin. Well, we will have such a prologue; and it shall be written in eight and six.

Bot. No, make it two more; let it be written in eight and eight.

Snout. Will not the ladies be afeard of the lion?

Star. I fear it, I promise you.

Bot. Masters, you ought to consider with yourselves. To bring in—God shield us!—a lion among ladies, is a most dreadful thing; for there is not a more fearful wild-fowl than your lion living; and we ought to look to 't.

Snout. Therefore another prologue must tell he is not a lion.

Bot. Nay, you must name his name, and half his face must be seen through the lion's neck; and he himself must speak through, saying thus, or to the same defect, "Ladies," or "Fair ladies, I would wish you," or "I would request you," or "I would entreat you, not to fear, not to tremble: my life for yours. If you think I come hither as a lion, it were pity of my life. No, I am no such thing; I am a man as other men are!" and there indeed let him name his name, and tell them plainly he is Snug the joiner.

Quin. Well, it shall be so. But there is two hard things; that is, to bring the moonlight into a chamber; for, you know, Pyramus and Thisby meet by moonlight.

Snout. Doth the moon shine that night we play our play?

Bot. A calendar, a calendar! Look in the almanac! Find out moonshine, find out moonshine.

Quin. Yes, it doth shine that night.

Bot. Why, then may you leave a casement of the great chamber window, where we play, open, and the moon may shine in at the casement.

Quin. Ay; or else one must come in with a bush of thorns and a lantern, and say he comes to disfigure, or to present, the person of Moonshine. Then, there is another thing: we must have a wall in the great chamber; for Pyramus and Thisby, says the story, did talk through the chink of a wall.

Snout. You can never bring in a wall. What say you, Bottom?

Bot. Some man or other must present Wall; and let him have some plaster, or some loam, or some rough-cast about him, to signify wall; or let him hold his fingers thus, and through that cranny shall Pyramus and Thisby whisper.

Quin. If that may be, then all is well. Come, sit down, every mother's son, and rehearse your parts. Pyramus, you begin. When you have spoken your speech, enter into that brake. And so every one according to his cue.

Enter *Robin Goodfellow* behind.

Robin. What hempen home-spuns have we swagg'ring here,

Act III, Scene i: 5. tiring-house, dressing-room. **8. bully,** "good old." **14. by r lakin,** by our ladykin, the Virgin Mary. **parlous,** perilous. **25. eight and six,** alternate lines of eight and six syllables. **32. a lion among ladies,** see Introduction, p. 131. **39. defect,** Bottom means "effect."

154. of, for the sake of. **Act III, Scene i: 58. great chamber window,** the great chamber of a Tudor mansion corresponded to the modern drawing-room, and was the natural place for the presentation of plays. **62. disfigure,** Quince means "figure forth."

So near the cradle of the fairy queen?
What, a play toward! I 'll be an auditor;
An actor too perhaps, if I see cause.

Quin. Speak, Pyramus. Thisby, stand forth.

Bot. "Thisby, the flowers of odious savours sweet,"—

Quin. Odours, odours.

Bot. —— "odours savours sweet;
So hath thy breath, my dearest Thisby dear.
But hark, a voice! Stay thou but here awhile,
And by and by I will to thee appear."
Exit Bottom.

Robin. A stranger Pyramus than e'er play'd here. *Exit Robin.*

Flu. Must I speak now?

Quin. Ay, marry, must you; for you must understand he goes but to see a noise that he heard, and is to come again.

Flu. "Most radiant Pyramus, most lily-white of hue,
Of colour like the red rose on triumphant brier,
Most brisky juvenal and eke most lovely Jew,
As true as truest horse that yet would never tire,
I 'll meet thee, Pyramus, at Ninny's tomb."

Quin. "Ninus' tomb," man. Why, you must not speak that yet; that you answer to Pyramus. You speak all your part at once, cues and all. Pyramus enter. Your cue is past; it is, "never tire."

Flu. O,—"As true as truest horse, that yet would never tire."

Re-enter *Robin Goodfellow,* and *Bottom* with the ass's head.

Bot. "If I were, fair Thisby, I were only thine."

Quin. O monstrous! O strange! we are haunted. Pray, masters! fly, masters! Help!
Exeunt all the Clowns.

Robin. I 'll follow you, I 'll lead you about a round,
Through bog, through bush, through brake, through brier.
Sometime a horse I 'll be, sometime a hound,
A hog, a headless bear, sometime a fire;
And neigh, and bark, and grunt, and roar, and burn,
Like horse, hound, hog, bear, fire, at every turn. *Exit Robin.*

Bot. Why do they run away? This is a knavery of them to make me afeard.

Re-enter *Snout.*

Snout. O Bottom, thou art changed! What do I see on thee?

Bot. What do you see? You see an ass-head of your own, do you? *Exit Snout.*

Re-enter *Quince.*

Quin. Bless thee, Bottom! bless thee! thou art translated. *Exit Quince.*

Bot. I see their knavery; this is to make an ass of me, to fright me, if they could. But I will not stir from this place, do what they can. I will walk up and down here, and I will sing, that they shall hear I am not afraid. *Sings.*

"The ousel cock so black of hue,
With orange-tawny bill,
The throstle with his note so true,
The wren with little quill,"—

Tita. [*Awaking.*] What angel wakes me from my flowery bed?

Bot. [*Sings.*]

"The finch, the sparrow, and the lark,
The plain-song cuckoo gray,
Whose note full many a man doth mark,
And dares not answer nay;"—

for, indeed, who would set his wit to so foolish a bird? Who would give a bird the lie, though he cry "cuckoo" never so?

Tita. I pray thee, gentle mortal, sing again,
Mine ear is much enamoured of thy note;
So is mine eye enthralled to thy shape;
And thy fair virtue's force (perforce) doth move me
On the first view to say, to swear, I love thee.

Bot. Methinks, mistress, you should have little reason for that; and yet, to say the truth, reason and love keep little company together now-a-days; the more the pity that some honest neighbours will not make them friends. Nay, I can gleek upon occasion.

Tita. Thou art as wise as thou art beautiful.

Bot. Not so, neither; but if I had wit enough to get out of this wood, I have enough to serve mine own turn.

Tita. Out of this wood do not desire to go;
Thou shalt remain here, whether thou wilt or no.
I am a spirit of no common rate;
The summer still doth tend upon my state;
And I do love thee; therefore, go with me.
I 'll give thee fairies to attend on thee,

81. toward, going forward. **97. brisky juvenal,** brisk young man. **100. Ninus' tomb,** in Ovid's story of Pyramus and Thisbe the lovers used to meet at the tomb of Ninus, founder of ancient Babylon.

122. translated, transformed. **129. ousel,** blackbird. **131. quill,** pipe. **134. plain-song,** singing a simple melody. **135-36. Whose note . . . nay,** the note of the cuckoo resembled "cuckold" and thus fell unpleasantly on the ear of many a husband. **150. gleek** scoff. **158. still,** always.

And they shall fetch thee jewels from the deep,
And sing while thou on pressed flowers dost sleep.
And I will purge thy mortal grossness so
That thou shalt like an airy spirit go.
Peaseblossom! Cobweb! Moth! and Mustardseed!

Enter Four Fairies: *Peaseblossom, Cobweb, Moth,* and *Mustardseed.*

Peas. Ready.
Cob. And I.
Moth. And I.
Mus. And I.
All. Where shall we go?
Tita. Be kind and courteous to this gentleman.
Hop in his walks and gambol in his eyes;
Feed him with apricocks and dewberries,
With purple grapes, green figs, and mulberries;
The honey-bags steal from the humble-bees,
And for night-tapers crop their waxen thighs
And light them at the fiery glow-worm's eyes,
To have my love to bed and to arise;
And pluck the wings from painted butterflies
To fan the moonbeams from his sleeping eyes.
Nod to him, elves, and do him courtesies.
Peas. Hail, mortal!
Cob. Hail!
Moth. Hail!
Mus. Hail!

Bot. I cry your worships mercy, heartily. I beseech your worship's name.

Cob. Cobweb.

Bot. I shall desire you of more acquaintance, good Master Cobweb. If I cut my finger, I shall make bold with you. Your name, honest gentleman?

Peas. Peaseblossom.

Bot. I pray you commend me to Mistress Squash, your mother, and to Master Peascod, your father. Good Master Peaseblossom, I shall desire you of more acquaintance too. Your name, I beseech you, sir?

Mus. Mustardseed.

Bot. Good Master Mustardseed, I know your patience well. That same cowardly, giant-like ox-beef hath devoured many a gentleman of your house. I promise you your kindred hath made my eyes water ere now. I desire you of more acquaintance, good Master Mustardseed.

Tita. Come, wait upon him; lead him to my bower.
The moon methinks looks with a watery eye,
And when she weeps, weeps every little flower,
Lamenting some enforced chastity.
Tie up my love's tongue, bring him silently.
Exeunt.

Scene II. *Another part of the wood.*

Enter *Oberon,* King of the Fairies.

Obe. I wonder if Titania be awak'd;
Then, what it was that next came in her eye,
Which she must dote on in extremity.

Enter *Robin Goodfellow.*

Here comes my messenger. How now, mad spirit!
What night-rule now about this haunted grove?
Robin. My mistress with a monster is in love.
Near to her close and consecrated bower,
While she was in her dull and sleeping hour,
A crew of patches, rude mechanicals,
That work for bread upon Athenian stalls,
Were met together to rehearse a play
Intended for great Theseus' nuptial-day.
The shallowest thickskin of that barren sort,
Who Pyramus presented in their sport,
Forsook his scene and enter'd in a brake.
When I did him at this advantage take,
An ass's nole I fixed on his head.
Anon his Thisby must be answered,
And forth my mimic comes. When they him spy,
As wild geese that the creeping fowler eye,
Or russet-pated choughs, many in sort,
Rising and cawing at the gun's report,
Sever themselves and madly sweep the sky,
So, at his sight, away his fellows fly;
And, at a stump, here o'er and o'er one falls;
He murder cries, and help from Athens calls.
Their sense thus weak, lost with their fears thus strong,
Made senseless things begin to do them wrong;
For briers and thorns at their apparel snatch;
Some sleeves, some hats, from yielders all things catch.
I led them on in this distracted fear,
And left sweet Pyramus translated there;
When in that moment, so it came to pass,
Titania wak'd and straightway lov'd an ass.

191. Squash, unripe pea-pod. **197. patience,** sufferings.

205. enforced, violated. **Scene ii: 3. in extremity,** extremely. **5. night-rule,** diversion for the night. **9. patches,** fools. **13. barren sort,** stupid crew. **17. nole,** head. **19. mimic,** actor. **21. russet-pated choughs,** grey-headed jackdaws. **in sort,** in company.

Obe. This falls out better than I could devise.
But hast thou yet latch'd the Athenian's eyes
With the love-juice, as I did bid thee do?
Robin. I took him sleeping,—that is finish'd too,—
And the Athenian woman by his side;
That, when he wak'd, of force she must be ey'd.

Enter *Demetrius* and *Hermia.*

Obe. Stand close; this is the same Athenian.
Robin. This is the woman, but not this the man.
Dem. O, why rebuke you him that loves you so?
Lay breath so bitter on your bitter foe.
Her. Now I but chide; but I should use thee worse,
For thou, I fear, hast given me cause to curse.
If thou hast slain Lysander in his sleep,
Being o'er shoes in blood, plunge in the deep,
And kill me too.
The sun was not so true unto the day
As he to me: would he have stolen away
From sleeping Hermia? I 'll believe as soon
This whole earth may be bor'd and that the moon
May through the centre creep and so displease
Her brother's noontide with the Antipodes.
It cannot be but thou hast murder'd him;
So should a murderer look, so dead, so grim.
Dem. So should the murdered look, and so should I,
Pierc'd through the heart with your stern cruelty;
Yet you, the murderer, look as bright, as clear,
As yonder Venus in her glimmering sphere.
Her. What 's this to my Lysander? Where is he?
Ah, good Demetrius, wilt thou give him me?
Dem. I had rather give his carcass to my hounds.
Her. Out, dog! out, cur! thou driv'st me past the bounds
Of maiden's patience. Hast thou slain him, then?
Henceforth be never number'd among men!
O, once tell true, tell true, even for my sake!
Durst thou have look'd upon him being awake,
And hast thou kill'd him sleeping? O brave touch!
Could not a worm, an adder, do so much?
An adder did it; for with doubler tongue
Than thine, thou serpent, never adder stung.
Dem. You spend your passion on a mispris'd mood.
I am not guilty of Lysander's blood;
Nor is he dead, for aught that I can tell.
Her. I pray thee, tell me then that he is well.
Dem. An if I could, what should I get therefore?
Her. A privilege never to see me more.
And from thy hated presence part I so:
See me no more, whether he be dead or no.
Exit Hermia.
Dem. There is no following her in this fierce vein;
Here therefore for a while I will remain.
So sorrow's heaviness doth heavier grow
For debt that bankrupt sleep doth sorrow owe;
Which now in some slight measure it will pay,
If for his tender here I make some stay.
Lies down and sleeps.
Obe. What hast thou done? Thou hast mistaken quite
And laid the love-juice on some true-love's sight.
Of thy misprision must perforce ensue
Some true love turn'd and not a false turn'd true.
Robin. Then fate o'er-rules, that, one man holding troth,
A million fail, confounding oath on oath.
Obe. About the wood go swifter than the wind,
And Helena of Athens look thou find.
All fancy-sick she is and pale of cheer
With sighs of love, that cost the fresh blood dear.
By some illusion see thou bring her here.
I 'll charm his eyes against she do appear.
Robin. I go, I go; look how I go,
Swifter than arrow from the Tartar's bow.
Exit Robin.

Obe. Flower of this purple dye,
Hit with Cupid's archery,
Sink in apple of his eye.
When his love he doth espy,
Let her shine as gloriously
As the Venus of the sky.
When thou wak'st, if she be by,
Beg of her for remedy.

Re-enter *Robin Goodfellow.*

Robin. Captain of our fairy band,
Helena is here at hand;
And the youth, mistook by me,
Pleading for a lover's fee.

36. **latch'd,** moistened. 40. **force,** necessity. 57. **dead,** deadly. 70. **touch,** exploit. 71. **worm,** snake.

74. **on a mispris'd mood,** in mistaken anger. 87. **his tender,** sleep's tender or offer. 96. **fancy-sick,** love-sick. **cheer,** face. 97. **with sighs . . . dear,** a sigh was supposed to cost a drop of blood.

Shall we their fond pageant see?
Lord, what fools these mortals be!
Obe. Stand aside. The noise they make
Will cause Demetrius to awake.
Robin. Then will two at once woo one;
That must needs be sport alone.
And those things do best please me
That befall prepost'rously.

Enter *Lysander* and *Helena*.

Lys. Why should you think that I should woo in scorn?
Scorn and derision never come in tears.
Look, when I vow, I weep; and vows so born,
In their nativity all truth appears.
How can these things in me seem scorn to you,
Bearing the badge of faith to prove them true?
Hel. You do advance your cunning more and more.
When truth kills truth, O devilish-holy fray!
These vows are Hermia's; will you give her o'er?
Weigh oath with oath, and you will nothing weigh.
Your vows to her and me, put in two scales,
Will even weigh, and both as light as tales.
Lys. I had no judgement when to her I swore.
Hel. Nor none, in my mind, now you give her o'er.
Lys. Demetrius loves her, and he loves not you.
Dem. [*Awaking.*] O Helen, goddess, nymph, perfect, divine!
To what, my love, shall I compare thine eyne?
Crystal is muddy. O, how ripe in show
Thy lips, those kissing cherries, tempting grow!
That pure congealed white, high Taurus' snow,
Fann'd with the eastern wind, turns to a crow
When thou hold'st up thy hand. O, let me kiss
This princess of pure white, this seal of bliss!
Hel. O spite! O hell! I see you all are bent
To set against me for your merriment.
If you were civil and knew courtesy,
You would not do me thus much injury.
Can you not hate me, as I know you do,
But you must join in souls to mock me too?
If you were men, as men you are in show,
You would not use a gentle lady so;
To vow, and swear, and superpraise my parts,
When I am sure you hate me with your hearts.
You both are rivals, and love Hermia;
And now both rivals, to mock Helena.
A trim exploit, a manly enterprise,
To conjure tears up in a poor maid's eyes
With your derision! None of noble sort
Would so offend a virgin and extort
A poor soul's patience, all to make you sport.
Lys. You are unkind, Demetrius; be not so;
For you love Hermia; this you know I know.
And here, with all good will, with all my heart,
In Hermia's love I yield you up my part;
And yours of Helena to me bequeath,
Whom I do love and will do till my death.
Hel. Never did mockers waste more idle breath.
Dem. Lysander, keep thy Hermia; I will none.
If e'er I lov'd her, all that love is gone.
My heart to her but as guest-wise sojourn'd,
And now to Helen is it home return'd,
There to remain.
Lys. Helen, it is not so.
Dem. Disparage not the faith thou dost not know,
Lest, to thy peril, thou aby it dear.
Look where thy love comes; yonder is thy dear.

Re-enter *Hermia*.

Her. Dark night, that from the eye his function takes,
The ear more quick of apprehension makes;
Wherein it doth impair the seeing sense,
It pays the hearing double recompense.
Thou art not by mine eye, Lysander, found;
Mine ear, I thank it, brought me to thy sound.
But why unkindly didst thou leave me so?
Lys. Why should he stay, whom love doth press to go?
Her. What love could press Lysander from my side?
Lys. Lysander's love, that would not let him bide,
Fair Helena, who more engilds the night
Than all yon fiery oes and eyes of light.
Why seek'st thou me? Could not this make thee know,
The hate I bare thee made me leave thee so?
Her. You speak not as you think. It cannot be.
Hel. Lo, she is one of this confederacy!
Now I perceive they have conjoin'd all three
To fashion this false sport, in spite of me.
Injurious Hermia! most ungrateful maid!
Have you conspir'd, have you with these contriv'd
To bait me with this foul derision?

114. fond pageant, foolish spectacle. **119. sport alone,** unique sport. **121. prepost'rously,** in wrong order. 124-5. Vows born in tears are obviously true. **141. Taurus,** mountain range in Asia Minor.

157. trim, pretty (ironical). **160. extort,** torment. **175. aby,** pay for. **188. oes,** circles. **195. Injurious,** insulting.

Is all the counsel that we two have shar'd,
The sisters' vows, the hours that we have spent,
When we have chid the hasty-footed time
For parting us,—O, is all forgot?
All school-days' friendship, childhood innocence?
We, Hermia, like two artificial gods,
Have with our needles created both one flower,
Both on one sampler, sitting on one cushion,
Both warbling of one song, both in one key,
As if our hands, our sides, voices, and minds,
Had been incorporate. So we grew together,
Like to a double cherry, seeming parted,
But yet an union in partition;
Two lovely berries moulded on one stem;
So, with two seeming bodies, but one heart;
Two of the first, like coats in heraldry,
Due but to one and crowned with one crest.
And will you rend our ancient love asunder,
To join with men in scorning your poor friend!
It is not friendly, 't is not maidenly.
Our sex, as well as I, may chide you for it,
Though I alone do feel the injury.

Her. I am amazed at your passionate words.
I scorn you not; it seems that you scorn me.

Hel. Have you not set Lysander, as in scorn,
To follow me and praise my eyes and face?
And made your other love, Demetrius,
Who even but now did spurn me with his foot,
To call me goddess, nymph, divine and rare,
Precious, celestial? Wherefore speaks he this
To her he hates? And wherefore doth Lysander
Deny your love, so rich within his soul,
And tender me, forsooth, affection,
But by your setting on, by your consent?
What though I be not so in grace as you,
So hung upon with love, so fortunate,
But miserable most, to love unlov'd?
This you should pity rather than despise.

Her. I understand not what you mean by this.

Hel. Ay, do persévér, counterfeit sad looks,
Make mouths upon me when I turn my back.
Wink each at other, hold the sweet jest up;
This sport, well carried, shall be chronicled.
If you have any pity, grace, or manners,
You would not make me such an argument.

203. artificial, skilled in art. **213-4. Two of the first . . . one crest,** *Two of the first,* i.e., *bodies,* like the double coats in heraldry that belong to man and wife as *one person,* but which, like our *single heart,* have but *one crest.* **237. persêver,** persevere. **238. mouths,** faces. **242. argument,** subject for a story.

But fare ye well; 't is partly my own fault,
Which death or absence soon shall remedy.

Lys. Stay, gentle Helena; hear my excuse,
My love, my life, my soul, fair Helena!

Hel. O excellent!

Her. Sweet, do not scorn her so.

Dem. If she cannot entreat, I can compel.

Lys. Thou canst compel no more than she entreat;
Thy threats have no more strength than her weak prayers.
Helen, I love thee; by my life, I do!
I swear by that which I will lose for thee,
To prove him false that says I love thee not.

Dem. I say I love thee more than he can do.

Lys. If thou say so, withdraw, and prove it too.

Dem. Quick, come!

Her. Lysander, whereto tends all this?

Lys. Away, you Ethiope!

Dem. No, no; he will
Seem to break loose. Take on as you would follow,
But yet come not. You are a tame man, go!

Lys. Hang off, thou cat, thou burr! Vile thing, let loose,
Or I will shake thee from me like a serpent!

Her. Why are you grown so rude? What change is this?
Sweet love,—

Lys. Thy love! Out, tawny Tartar, out!
Out, loathed med'cine! O hated potion, hence!

Her. Do you not jest?

Hel. Yes, sooth; and so do you.

Lys. Demetrius, I will keep my word with thee.

Dem. I would I had your bond, for I perceive
A weak bond holds you. I 'll not trust your word.

Lys. What, should I hurt her, strike her, kill her dead?
Although I hate her, I 'll not harm her so.

Her. What, can you do me greater harm than hate?
Hate me! wherefore? O me! what news, my love!
Am not I Hermia? Are not you Lysander?
I am as fair now as I was erewhile.
Since night you lov'd me; yet since night you left me:
Why, then you left me—O, the gods forbid!—
In earnest, shall I say?

Lys. Ay, by my life;
And never did desire to see thee more.
Therefore be out of hope, of question, doubt;
Be certain, nothing truer; 't is no jest
That I do hate thee and love Helena.

Her. O me! you juggler! you canker-blossom!
You thief of love! What, have you come by night
And stol'n my love's heart from him?
Hel. Fine, i' faith!
Have you no modesty, no maiden shame,
No touch of bashfulness? What, will you tear
Impatient answers from my gentle tongue?
Fie, fie! you counterfeit, you puppet, you!
Her. Puppet? Why so? Ay, that way goes the game.
Now I perceive that she hath made compare
Between our statures; she hath urg'd her height;
And with her personage, her tall personage,
Her height, forsooth, she hath prevail'd with him.
And are you grown so high in his esteem,
Because I am so dwarfish and so low?
How low am I, thou painted maypole? Speak,
How low am I? I am not yet so low
But that my nails can reach unto thine eyes.
Hel. I pray you, though you mock me, gentlemen,
Let her not hurt me. I was never curst;
I have no gift at all in shrewishness;
I am a right maid for my cowardice.
Let her not strike me. You perhaps may think,
Because she is something lower than myself,
That I can match her.
Her. Lower! hark, again,
Hel. Good Hermia, do not be so bitter with me.
I evermore did love you, Hermia,
Did ever keep your counsels, never wrong'd you;
Save that, in love unto Demetrius,
I told him of your stealth unto this wood.
He followed you; for love I followed him;
But he hath chid me hence and threaten'd me
To strike me, spurn me, nay, to kill me too.
And now, so you will let me quiet go,
To Athens will I bear my folly back
And follow you no further. Let me go.
You see how simple and how fond I am.
Her. Why, get you gone; who is 't that hinders you?
Hel. A foolish heart, that I leave here behind.
Her. What, with Lysander?
Hel. With Demetrius.
Lys. Be not afraid; she shall not harm thee, Helena.
Dem. No, sir, she shall not, though you take her part.
Hel. O, when she 's angry, she is keen and shrewd!
She was a vixen when she went to school;
And though she be but little, she is fierce.
Her. Little again! Nothing but low and little!
Why will you suffer her to flout me thus?
Let me come to her.
Lys. Get you gone, you dwarf,
You minimus, of hindering knot-grass made;
You bead, you acorn.
Dem. You are too officious
In her behalf that scorns your services.
Let her alone; speak not of Helena;
Take not her part; for if thou dost intend
Never so little show of love to her,
Thou shalt aby it.
Lys. Now she holds me not.
Now follow, if thou dar'st, to try whose right,
Of thine or mine, is most in Helena.
Dem. Follow! Nay, I 'll go with thee, cheek by jowl.
Exeunt Lysander and Demetrius.
Her. You, mistress, all this coil is 'long of you.
Nay, go not back.
Hel. I will not trust you, I,
Nor longer stay in your curst company.
Your hands than mine are quicker for a fray,
My legs are longer though, to run away.
Exit Helena.
Her. I am amaz'd, and know not what to say. *Exit Hermia.*
Obe. This is thy negligence. Still thou mistak'st,
Or else committ'st thy knaveries wilfully.
Robin. Believe me, king of shadows, I mistook.
Did not you tell me I should know the man
By the Athenian garments he had on?
And so far blameless proves my enterprise,
That I have 'nointed an Athenian's eyes;
And so far am I glad it so did sort,
As this their jangling I esteem a sport.
Obe. Thou see'st these lovers seek a place to fight;
Hie therefore, Robin, overcast the night.
The starry welkin cover thou anon
With drooping fog as black as Acheron,
And lead these testy rivals so astray
As one come not within another's way.
Like to Lysander sometime frame thy tongue,
Then stir Demetrius up with bitter wrong;
And sometime rail thou like Demetrius;
And from each other look thou lead them thus,

282. **canker-blossom**, worm that destroys blossoms. 300. **curst**, shrewish. 302. I am a true maiden in fearing violence. 310. **stealth**, stealing away.

323. **shrewd**, sharp-tongued. 329. **minimus**, dwarf. **knot-grass**, an infusion of knot-grass was supposed to stunt growth. 333. **intend**, offer. 339. **coil**, turmoil. **'long**, because. 352. **sort**, turn out. 357. **Acheron**, river in Hades. 361. **wrong**, insults.

Till o'er their brows death-counterfeiting sleep
With leaden legs and batty wings doth creep:
Then crush this herb into Lysander's eye;
Whose liquor hath this virtuous property,
To take from thence all error with his might,
And make his eyeballs roll with wonted sight.
When they next wake, all this derision
Shall seem a dream and fruitless vision;
And back to Athens shall the lovers wend,
With league whose date till death shall never end.
Whiles I in this affair do thee employ,
I 'll to my queen and beg her Indian boy;
And then I will her charmed eye release
From monster's view, and all things shall be peace.

Robin. My fairy lord, this must be done with haste,
For night's swift dragons cut the clouds full fast,
And yonder shines Aurora's harbinger,
At whose approach, ghosts, wandering here and there,
Troop home to churchyards; damned spirits all,
That in crossways and floods have burial,
Already to their wormy beds are gone;
For fear lest day should look their shames upon,
They wilfully themselves exile from light
And must for aye consort with black-brow'd night.

Obe. But we are spirits of another sort.
I with the morning's love have oft made sport,
And, like a forester, the groves may tread,
Even till the eastern gate, all fiery-red,
Opening on Neptune with fair blessed beams,
Turns into yellow gold his salt green streams.
But, notwithstanding, haste, make no delay.
We may effect this business yet ere day.

Exit Oberon.

Robin. Up and down, up and down,
I will lead them up and down.
I am fear'd in field and town.
Goblin, lead them up and down.
Here comes one.

Re-enter *Lysander.*

Lys. Where art thou, proud Demetrius? Speak thou now.

Robin. Here, villain; drawn and ready. Where art thou?

Lys. I will be with thee straight.

Robin. Follow me, then,
To plainer ground.

Exit Lysander, following the voice.

Re-enter *Demetrius.*

Dem. Lysander, speak again!
Thou runaway, thou coward, art thou fled?
Speak! In some bush? Where dost thou hide thy head?

Robin. Thou coward, art thou bragging to the stars,
Telling the bushes that thou look'st for wars,
And wilt not come? Come, recreant; come, thou child,
I 'll whip thee with a rod. He is defil'd
That draws a sword on thee.

Dem. Yea, art thou there?

Robin. Follow my voice. We 'll try no manhood here.

Exeunt Robin and Demetrius.

Re-enter *Lysander.*

Lys. He goes before me and still dares me on.
When I come where he calls, then he is gone.
The villain is much lighter-heel'd than I;
I followed fast, but faster he did fly,
That fallen am I in dark uneven way.
And here will rest me. Come, thou gentle day!

Lies down.

For if but once thou show me thy grey light,
I 'll find Demetrius and revenge this spite.

Sleeps.

Re-enter *Robin Goodfellow* and *Demetrius.*

Robin. Ho, ho, ho! Coward, why com'st thou not?

Dem. Abide me, if thou dar'st; for well I wot
Thou runn'st before me, shifting every place,
And dar'st not stand, nor look me in the face.
Where art thou now?

Robin. Come hither; I am here.

Dem. Nay, then, thou mock'st me. Thou shalt buy this dear,
If ever I thy face by daylight see.
Now, go thy way. Faintness constraineth me
To measure out my length on this cold bed.
By day's approach look to be visited.

Lies down and sleeps.

Re-enter *Helena.*

Hel. O weary night, O long and tedious night,
Abate thy hours! Shine, comforts, from the east,

367. **virtuous,** potent, also, beneficient. 368. **with his might,** by its power. 379. **night's swift dragons,** the dragon team of the goddess of Night. 380. **Aurora's harbinger,** the morning star, forerunner of the dawn. 383. **crossways and floods,** suicides were buried at crossroads; those who were drowned would have no proper burial. 389. **I with the morning's love have oft made sport,** "the morning's love" may be the hunter Cephalus, whom Aurora loved, or Aurora herself. 402. **drawn,** with sword drawn.

422. **wot,** know. 432. **Abate,** shorten.

That I may back to Athens by daylight,
From these that my poor company detest.
And sleep, that sometimes shuts up sorrow's eye,
Steal me awhile from mine own company.
Lies down and sleeps.

Robin. Yet but three? Come one more;
Two of both kinds makes up four.
Here she comes, curst and sad.
Cupid is a knavish lad,
Thus to make poor females mad.

Re-enter *Hermia.*

Her. Never so weary, never so in woe,
Bedabbled with the dew and torn with briers,
I can no further crawl, no further go;
My legs can keep no pace with my desires.
Here will I rest me till the break of day.
Heavens shield Lysander, if they mean a fray! *Lies down and sleeps.*

Robin. On the ground
Sleep sound.
I 'll apply
To your eye,
Gentle lover, remedy.
Squeezing the juice on Lysander's eyes.
When thou wak'st,
Thou tak'st
True delight
In the sight
Of thy former lady's eye;
And the country proverb known,
That every man should take his own,
In your waking shall be shown.
Jack shall have Jill;
Nought shall go ill;
The man shall have his mare again, and all shall be well. *Exit Robin.*

ACT IV. Scene I. *The same.*

Lysander, Demetrius, Helena, and *Hermia,* lying asleep.

Enter *Titania* and the Clown *Bottom; Peaseblossom, Cobweb, Moth, Mustardseed* and other Fairies; *Oberon* behind them unseen.

Tita. Come, sit thee down upon this flowery bed,
While I thy amiable cheeks do coy,
And stick musk-roses in thy sleek smooth head,
And kiss thy fair large ears, my gentle joy.

Bot. Where 's Peaseblossom?

Peas. Ready.

Bot. Scratch my head, Peaseblossom. Where 's Mounsieur Cobweb?

Cob. Ready.

Bot. Mounsieur Cobweb, good mounsieur, get you your weapons in your hand, and kill me a red-hipped humble-bee on the top of a thistle; and, good mounsieur, bring me the honey-bag. Do not fret yourself too much in the action, mounsieur; and, good mounsieur, have a care the honey-bag break not; I would be loath to have you overflown with a honey-bag, signior. Where 's Mounsieur Mustardseed?

Mus. Ready.

Bot. Give me your neaf, Mounsieur Mustardseed. Pray you, leave your curtsie, good mounsieur.

Mus. What 's your will?

Bot. Nothing, good mounsieur, but to help Cavalery Cobweb to scratch. I must to the barber's, mounsieur; for methinks I am marvellous hairy about the face; and I am such a tender ass, if my hair do but tickle me, I must scratch.

Tita. What, wilt thou hear some music, my sweet love?

Bot. I have a reasonable good ear in music. Let 's have the tongs and the bones.

Music. Tongs. Rural music.

Tita. Or say, sweet love, what thou desirest to eat.

Bot. Truly, a peck of provender; I could munch your good dry oats. Methinks I have a great desire to a bottle of hay. Good hay, sweet hay, hath no fellow.

Tita. I have a venturous fairy that shall seek
The squirrel's hoard, and fetch thee new nuts.

Bot. I had rather have a handful or two of dried peas. But, I pray you, let none of your people stir me; I have an exposition of sleep come upon me.

Act IV, Scene i: 2. coy, caress. **20. neaf,** fist.

21. leave your curtsie, put on your hat. **24. Cavalery,** cavaliero, gentleman. **31. the tongs and the bones,** crude musical instruments. **35. bottle,** bundle. **41. exposition of,** Bottom means "disposition to."

Tita. Sleep thou, and I will wind thee in my arms.
Fairies, be gone, and be always away.
Exeunt fairies.
So doth the woodbine the sweet honeysuckle
Gently entwist; the female ivy so
Enrings the barky fingers of the elm.
O, how I love thee! how I dote on thee!
They sleep.

Enter *Robin Goodfellow.*

Obe. [*Advancing.*] Welcome, good Robin. See'st thou this sweet sight?
Her dotage now I do begin to pity;
For, meeting her of late behind the wood,
Seeking sweet favours for this hateful fool,
I did upbraid her and fall out with her.
For she his hairy temples then had rounded
With coronet of fresh and fragrant flowers;
And that same dew, which sometime on the buds
Was wont to swell like round and orient pearls,
Stood now within the pretty flowerets' eyes
Like tears that did their own disgrace bewail.
When I had at my pleasure taunted her
And she in mild terms begg'd my patience,
I then did ask of her her changeling child;
Which straight she gave me, and her fairy sent
To bear him to my bower in fairy land.
And, now I have the boy, I will undo
This hateful imperfection of her eyes;
And, gentle Puck, take this transformed scalp
From off the head of this Athenian swain,
That, he awaking when the other do,
May all to Athens back again repair,
And think no more of this night's accidents
But as the fierce vexation of a dream.
But first I will release the fairy queen.
Touching her eyes.
Be as thou wast wont to be;
See as thou wast wont to see:
Dian's bud o'er Cupid's flower
Hath such force and blessed power.
Now, my Titania; wake you, my sweet queen.

Tita. My Oberon! what visions have I seen!
Methought I was enamour'd of an ass.

Obe. There lies your love.

Tita. How came these things to pass?
O, how mine eyes do loathe his visage now!

Obe. Silence awhile. Robin, take off this head.
Titania, music call; and strike more dead
Than common sleep of all these five the sense

Tita. Music, ho! music, such as charmeth sleep! *Music still.*

Robin. Now, when thou wak'st, with thine own fool's eyes peep.

Obe. Sound, music! Come, my queen, take hands with me,
And rock the ground whereon these sleepers be.
Now thou and I are new in amity
And will to-morrow midnight solemnly
Dance in Duke Theseus' house triumphantly
And bless it to all fair prosperity.
There shall the pairs of faithful lovers be
Wedded, with Theseus, all in jollity.

Robin. Fairy king, attend, and mark;
I do hear the morning lark.

Obe. Then, my queen, in silence sad
Trip we after night's shade.
We the globe can compass soon,
Swifter than the wandering moon.

Tita. Come, my lord, and in our flight
Tell me how it came this night
That I sleeping here was found
With these mortals on the ground.
Exeunt. Wind horns.

Enter *Theseus, Hippolyta, Egeus,* and all his train.

The. Go, one of you, find out the forester,
For now our observation is perform'd,
And since we have the vaward of the day,
My love shall hear the music of my hounds.
Uncouple in the western valley, let them go.
Despatch, I say, and find the forester.
We will, fair queen, up to the mountain's top
And mark the musical confusion
Of hounds and echo in conjunction.

Hip. I was with Hercules and Cadmus once,
When in a wood of Crete they bay'd the bear
With hounds of Sparta. Never did I hear
Such gallant chiding; for, besides the groves,
The skies, the fountains, every region near
Seem'd all one mutual cry. I never heard
So musical a discord, such sweet thunder.

The. My hounds are bred out of the Spartan kind,
So flew'd, so sanded, and their heads are hung
With ears that sweep away the morning dew;
Crook-knee'd, and dew-lapp'd like Thessalian bulls;

45. woodbine, probably an error for "bindweed," i.e., convolvulus. **57. orient,** eastern. **69. other,** others. **72. fierce,** wild. **76. Dian's bud o'er Cupid's flower,** Diana's bud may be the *Agnus Castus,* which according to old herbals was a preservative of chastity.

85. these five, the four lovers and Bottom. **99. sad,** sober. **106. Stage direction: wind,** blow. **108. observation,** May Day rites. **109. vaward,** vanguard, early part. **112. Despatch,** hasten. **119. chiding,** noise. **122. So musical a discord,** Elizabethan huntsmen made a point of assembling a pack of hounds whose cries would be harmonious. **124. flew'd,** with large chaps. **sanded,** of sandy color.

Slow in pursuit, but match'd in mouth like bells,
Each under each. A cry more tuneable
Was never holla'd to, nor cheer'd with horn,
In Crete, in Sparta, nor in Thessaly.
Judge when you hear. But, soft! what nymphs are these?
Ege. My lord, this is my daughter here asleep,
And this, Lysander; this Demetrius is;
This Helena, old Nedar's Helena.
I wonder of their being here together.
The. No doubt they rose up early to observe
The rite of May, and, hearing our intent,
Came here in grace of our solemnity.
But speak, Egeus; is not this the day
That Hermia should give answer of her choice?
Ege. It is, my lord.
The. Go, bid the huntsmen wake them with their horns.

Horns and shout within. Lysander, Demetrius, Helena, and Hermia wake and start up.

Good morrow, friends. Saint Valentine is past;
Begin these wood-birds but to couple now?
Lys. Pardon, my lord.
The. I pray you all, stand up.
I know you two are rival enemies;
How comes this gentle concord in the world,
That hatred is so far from jealousy,
To sleep by hate, and fear no enmity?
Lys. My lord, I shall reply amazedly.
Half sleep, half waking; but as yet, I swear,
I cannot truly say how I came here.
But, as I think,—for truly would I speak,
And now I do bethink me, so it is,—
I came with Hermia hither. Our intent
Was to be gone from Athens, where we might,
Without the peril of the Athenian law—
Ege. Enough, enough, my lord; you have enough.
I beg the law, the law, upon his head.
They would have stolen away; they would, Demetrius,
Thereby to have defeated you and me,
You of your wife, and me of my consent,
Of my consent that she should be your wife.
Dem. My lord, fair Helen told me of their stealth,
Of this their purpose hither to this wood;
And I in fury hither followed them,
Fair Helena in fancy following me.

127. mouth, voice, note. **128. Each under each,** with different notes. **cry,** pack of hounds. **143. Saint Valentine,** on St. Valentine's Day birds were supposed to choose their mates. **156. where,** wherever. **157. Without,** beyond.

But, my good lord, I wot not by what power,—
But by some power it is,—my love to Hermia,
Melted as the snow, seems to me now
As the remembrance of an idle gaud
Which in my childhood I did dote upon;
And all the faith, the virtue of my heart,
The object and the pleasure of mine eye,
Is only Helena. To her, my lord,
Was I betroth'd ere I saw Hermia;
But like a sickness did I loathe this food;
But, as in health, come to my natural taste,
Now I do wish it, love it, long for it,
And will for evermore be true to it.
The. Fair lovers, you are fortunately met;
Of this discourse we more will hear anon.
Egeus, I will overbear your will;
For in the temple, by and by, with us
These couples shall eternally be knit.
And, for the morning now is something worn,
Our purpos'd hunting shall be set aside.
Away with us to Athens; three and three,
We 'll hold a feast in great solemnity.
Come, Hippolyta.

Exeunt Theseus, Hippolyta, Egeus, and train.

Dem. These things seem small and undistinguishable,
Like far-off mountains turned into clouds.
Her. Methinks I see these things with parted eye,
When every thing seems double.
Hel. So methinks;
And I have found Demetrius like a jewel,
Mine own, and not mine own.
Dem. Are you sure that we 're awake? It seems to me
That yet we sleep, we dream. Do not you think
The Duke was here, and bid us follow him?
Her. Yea; and my father.
Hel. And Hippolyta.
Lys. And he did bid us follow to the temple.
Dem. Why, then, we are awake. Let 's follow him;
And by the way let us recount our dreams.
Exeunt the lovers.

Bot. [*Awaking.*] When my cue comes, call me, and I will answer. My next is, "Most fair Pyramus." Heigh-ho! Peter Quince! Flute, the bellows-mender! Snout, the tinker! Starveling! God 's my life, stolen hence, and left me asleep! I have had a most rare vision. I have had a dream, past the wit of man to say what dream it was. Man is but an ass, if he go about to expound this dream. Methought I was—there is no man can tell what.

193. parted eye, eyes not in focus. **211. go about,** try.

Methought I was,—and methought I had,—but man is but a patched fool, if he will offer to say what methought I had. The eye of man hath not heard, the ear of man hath not seen, man's hand is not able to taste, his tongue to conceive, nor his heart to report, what my dream was. I will get Peter Quince to write a ballad of this dream. It shall be called Bottom's Dream, because it hath no bottom; and I will sing it in the latter end of our play, before the Duke; peradventure, to make it the more gracious, I shall sing it at her death. *Exit.*

Scene II. *Athens. Quince's house.*

Enter *Quince, Flute, Snout,* and *Starveling*

Quin. Have you sent to Bottom's house? Is he come home yet?

Star. He cannot be heard of. Out of doubt he is transported.

Flu. If he come not, then the play is marred. It goes not forward, doth it?

Quin. It is not possible. You have not a man in all Athens able to discharge Pyramus but he.

Flu. No, he hath simply the best wit of any handicraft man in Athens.

Snout. Yea, and the best person too; and he is a very paramour for a sweet voice.

Flu. You must say "paragon"; a paramour is, God bless us, a thing of naught.

Enter *Snug* the Joiner.

Snug. Masters, the Duke is coming from the temple, and there is two or three lords and ladies more married. If our sport had gone forward, we had all been made men.

Flu. O sweet bully Bottom! Thus hath he lost sixpence a day during his life; he could not have 'scaped sixpence a day. An the Duke had not given him sixpence a day for playing Pyramus, I 'll be hanged. He would have deserved it. Sixpence a day in Pyramus, or nothing.

Enter *Bottom.*

Bot. Where are these lads? Where are these hearts?

Quin. Bottom! O most courageous day! O most happy hour!

Bot. Masters, I am to discourse wonders, but ask me not what; for if I tell you, I am no true Athenian. I will tell you everything, right as it fell out.

Quin. Let us hear, sweet Bottom.

Bot. Not a word of me. All that I will tell you is, that the Duke hath dined. Get your apparel together, good strings to your beards, new ribbons to your pumps; meet presently at the palace; every man look o'er his part; for the short and the long is, our play is preferred. In any case, let Thisby have clean linen; and let not him that plays the lion pare his nails, for they shall hang out for the lion's claws. And, most dear actors, eat no onions nor garlic, for we are to utter sweet breath; and I do not doubt but to hear them say, it is a sweet comedy. No more words; away! go, away!

Exeunt.

ACT V. Scene I. *Athens. The palace of Theseus.*

Enter *Theseus, Hippolyta,* and *Philostrate,* with Lords and Attendants.

Hip. 'T is strange, my Theseus, that these lovers speak of.
The. More strange than true; I never may believe
These antique fables, nor these fairy toys.
Lovers and madmen have such seething brains,
Such shaping fantasies, that apprehend
More than cool reason ever comprehends.
The lunatic, the lover, and the poet
Are of imagination all compact.
One sees more devils than vast hell can hold;
That is, the madman. The lover, all as frantic,
Sees Helen's beauty in a brow of Egypt.
The poet's eye, in a fine frenzy rolling,
Doth glance from heaven to earth, from earth to heaven;
And as imagination bodies forth
The forms of things unknown, the poet's pen
Turns them to shapes and gives to airy nothing
A local habitation and a name.
Such tricks hath strong imagination,

214. patched, wearing motly. **224. I shall sing it at her death,** Bottom looks forward to rising at the end of the play, to sing his ballad over the body of Thisbe. **Scene ii: 4. transported,** carried off, or, transformed. **14. thing of naught,** wicked thing. **Act V, Scene i: 3. antique,** strange. **toys,** trifles. **5. shaping fantasies,** inventive imagination.

Scene ii: 26. hearts, good fellows. **38. presently,** at once. **40. preferred,** on the preferred list. **Act V, Scene i: 8. compact,** composed. **11.** Sees the beauty of Helen of Troy in the dark face of a gypsy.

That, if it would but apprehend some joy,
It comprehends some bringer of that joy;
Or in the night, imagining some fear,
How easy is a bush suppos'd a bear!
Hip. But all the story of the night told over,
And all their minds transfigur'd so together,
More witnesseth than fancy's images,
And grows to something of great constancy;
But, howsoever, strange and admirable.

Enter the lovers, *Lysander, Demetrius, Hermia,* and *Helena.*

The. Here come the lovers, full of joy and mirth.
Joy, gentle friends! joy and fresh days of love
Accompany your hearts!
Lys. More than to us
Wait in your royal walks, your board, your bed!
The. Come now; what masques, what dances shall we have,
To wear away this long age of three hours
Between our after-supper and bed-time?
Where is our usual manager of mirth?
What revels are in hand? Is there no play
To ease the anguish of a torturing hour?
Call Philostrate.
Phil. Here, mighty Theseus.
The. Say, what abridgement have you for this evening?
What masque? what music? How shall we beguile
The lazy time, if not with some delight?
Phil. There is a brief how many sports are ripe.
Make choice of which your Highness will see first. *Giving a paper.*
The. [*Reads*]. "The battle with the Centaurs, to be sung
By an Athenian eunuch to the harp."
We 'll none of that: that have I told my love,
In glory of my kinsman Hercules.
"The riot of the tipsy Bacchanals,
Tearing the Thracian singer in their rage."
That is an old device; and it was play'd
When I from Thebes came last a conqueror.
"The thrice three Muses mourning for the death
Of Learning, late deceas'd in beggary."
That is some satire, keen and critical,
Not sorting with a nuptial ceremony.
"A tedious brief scene of young Pyramus
And his love Thisbe; very tragical mirth."
Merry and tragical! Tedious and brief!
That is, hot ice and wondrous strange snow.
How shall we find the concord of this discord?
Phil. A play there is, my lord, some ten words long,
Which is as brief as I have known a play;
But by ten words, my lord, it is too long,
Which makes it tedious; for in all the play
There is not one word apt, one player fitted.
And tragical, my noble lord, it is;
For Pyramus therein doth kill himself.
Which, when I saw rehears'd, I must confess,
Made mine eyes water; but more merry tears
The passion of loud laughter never shed.
The. What are they that do play it?
Phil. Hard-handed men that work in Athens here,
Which never labour'd in their minds till now,
And now have toil'd their unbreathed memories
With this same play, against your nuptial.
The. And we will hear it.
Phil. No, my noble lord;
It is not for you. I have heard it over,
And it is nothing, nothing in the world;
Unless you can find sport in their intents,
Extremely stretch'd and conn'd with cruel pain,
To do you service.
The. I will hear that play;
For never anything can be amiss,
When simpleness and duty tender it.
Go, bring them in; and take your places, ladies.
Exit Philostrate.
Hip. I love not to see wretchedness o'ercharged,
And duty in his service perishing.
The. Why, gentle sweet, you shall see no such thing.
Hip. He says they can do nothing in this kind.
The. The kinder we, to give them thanks for nothing.
Our sport shall be to take what they mistake;
And what poor duty cannot do, noble respect
Takes it in might, not merit.
Where I have come, great clerks have purposed
To greet me with premeditated welcomes;
Where I have seen them shiver and look pale,
Make periods in the midst of sentences,
Throttle their practis'd accent in their fears,
And in conclusion dumbly have broke off,
Not paying me a welcome. Trust me, sweet,

25. Is evidence of more than mere imagination. **26. constancy,** certainty. **39. abridgement,** pastime. **42. brief,** schedule. **44. Centaurs,** there was a battle between the Centaurs and the Lapithæ at a wedding, in which Theseus and Hercules took part. **48-9. The tipsy Bacchanals . . . the Thracian singer,** Orpheus, the poet, was torn to pieces by the women followers of Bacchus. **55. sorting with,** befitting.

74. unbreathed, unpracticed. **80. stretch'd,** strained. **92.** Takes the will for the deed. **93. clerks,** scholars. **96. periods,** full stops.

Out of this silence yet I pick'd a welcome;
And in the modesty of fearful duty
I read as much as from the rattling tongue
Of saucy and audacious eloquence.
Love, therefore, and tongue-tied simplicity
In least speak most, to my capacity.

Re-enter *Philostrate.*

Phil. So please your Grace, the Prologue is address'd.
The. Let him approach.
Flourish, trumpets.

Enter *Quince* for the Prologue.

Pro. If we offend, it is with our good will.
That you should think, we come not to offend,
But with good will. To show our simple skill,
That is the true beginning of our end.
Consider then we come but in despite.
We do not come as minding to content you,
Our true intent is. All for your delight
We are not here. That you should here repent you,
The actors are at hand, and by their show
You shall know all that you are like to know.

The. This fellow doth not stand upon points.

Lys. He hath rid his prologue like a rough colt; he knows not the stop. A good moral, my lord: it is not enough to speak, but to speak true.

Hip. Indeed he hath played on this prologue like a child on a recorder; a sound, but not in government.

The. His speech was like a tangled chain; nothing impaired, but all disordered. Who is next?

Enter with a trumpet before them, *Pyramus* and *Thisbe, Wall, Moonshine,* and *Lion.*

Pro. Gentles, perchance you wonder at this show;
But wonder on, till truth make all things plain.
This man is Pyramus, if you would know;
This beauteous lady Thisby is certain.
This man, with lime and rough-cast, doth present
Wall, that vile Wall which did these lovers sunder;
And through Wall's chink, poor souls, they are content
To whisper. At the which let no man wonder.
This man, with lantern, dog, and bush of thorn,
Presenteth Moonshine; for, if you will know,
By moonshine did these lovers think no scorn
To meet at Ninus' tomb, there, there to woo.
This grisly beast, which Lion hight by name,
The trusty Thisby, coming first by night,
Did scare away, or rather did affright;
And, as she fled, her mantle she did fall,
Which Lion vile with bloody mouth did stain.
Anon comes Pyramus, sweet youth and tall,
And finds his trusty Thisby's mantle slain;
Whereat, with blade, with bloody blameful blade,
He bravely broach'd his boiling bloody breast;
And Thisby, tarrying in mulberry shade,
His dagger drew, and died. For all the rest,
Let Lion, Moonshine, Wall, and lovers twain
At large discourse, while here they do remain.
Exeunt all but Wall.

The. I wonder if the lion be to speak.

Dem. No wonder, my lord; one lion may, when many asses do.

Wall. In this same interlude it doth befall
That I, one Snout by name, present a wall;
And such a wall, as I would have you think,
That had in it a crannied hole or chink,
Through which the lovers, Pyramus and Thisby,
Did whisper often very secretly.
This loam, this rough-cast, and this stone doth show
That I am that same wall; the truth is so;
And this the cranny is, right and sinister,
Through which the fearful lovers are to whisper.

The. Would you desire lime and hair to speak better?

Dem. It is the wittiest partition that ever I heard discourse, my lord.

Enter *Pyramus.*

The. Pyramus draws near the wall. Silence!

Pyr. O grim-look'd night! O night with hue so black!
O night, which ever art when day is not!
O night, O night! alack, alack, alack,
I fear my Thisby's promise is forgot!
And thou, O wall, O sweet, O lovely wall,

105. to my capacity, to my (sympathetic) understanding. **106. address'd,** ready. **108ff.,** Quince's perversion of sense by blundering punctuation had a well-known dramatic precedent in *Ralph Roister Doister*. **118.** This fellow "does not care about trifles," and "does not regard punctuation." **119. the stop,** a term in horsemanship. **123. recorder,** instrument resembling a flute. **124. government,** control.

140. hight, is called. **143. fall,** let fall. **145. tall,** handsome. **148. broach'd,** opened, stabbed. **164. sinister,** left. **168. partition,** (1) wall, (2) section of a book.

That stand'st between her father's ground and mine!
Thou wall, O wall, O sweet and lovely wall,
Show me thy chink, to blink through with mine eyne!

Wall holds up his fingers.

Thanks, courteous wall; Jove shield thee well for this!
But what see I? No Thisby do I see.
O wicked wall, through whom I see no bliss!
Curs'd be thy stones for thus deceiving me!

The. The wall, methinks, being sensible, should curse again.

Pyr. No, in truth, sir, he should not. "Deceiving me" is Thisby's cue. She is to enter now, and I am to spy her through the wall. You shall see it will fall pat as I told you. Yonder she comes.

Enter *Thisbe.*

This. O wall, full often hast thou heard my moans,
For parting my fair Pyramus and me!
My cherry lips have often kiss'd thy stones,
Thy stones with lime and hair knit up in thee.

Pyr. I see a voice! Now will I to the chink,
To spy an I can hear my Thisby's face.
Thisby!

This. My love thou art, my love I think.

Pyr. Think what thou wilt, I am thy lover's grace;
And, like Limander, am I trusty still.

This. And I like Helen, till the Fates me kill.

Pyr. Not Shafalus to Procrus was so true.

This. As Shafalus to Procrus, I to you.

Pyr. O, kiss me through the hole of this vile wall!

This. I kiss the wall's hole, not your lips at all.

Pyr. Wilt thou at Ninny's tomb meet me straightway?

This. 'Tide life, 'tide death, I come without delay. *Exeunt Pyramus and Thisbe.*

Wall. Thus have I, Wall, my part discharged so;
And, being done, thus Wall away doth go.

Exit.

The. Now is the mural down between the two neighbours.

Dem. No remedy, my lord, when walls are so wilful to hear without warning.

Hip. This is the silliest stuff that ever I heard.

The. The best in this kind are but shadows; and the worst are no worse, if imagination amend them.

Hip. It must be your imagination then, and not theirs.

The. If we imagine no worse of them than they of themselves, they may pass for excellent men. Here come two noble beasts in, a moon and a lion.

Enter *Lion* and *Moonshine.*

Lion. You, ladies, you, whose gentle hearts do fear
The smallest monstrous mouse that creeps on floor,
May now perchance both quake and tremble here,
When lion rough in wildest rage doth roar.
Then know that I, as Snug the joiner, am
A lion fell, nor else no lion's dam;
For, if I should as lion come in strife
Into this place, 't were pity on my life.

The. A very gentle beast, and of a good conscience.

Dem. The very best at a beast, my lord, that e'er I saw.

Lys. This lion is a very fox for his valour.

The. True; and a goose for his discretion.

Dem. Not so, my lord; for his valour cannot carry his discretion, and the fox carries the goose.

The. His discretion, I am sure, cannot carry his valour; for the goose carries not the fox. It is well; leave it to his discretion, and let us hearken to the moon.

Moon. This lanthorn doth the horned moon present;—

Dem. He should have worn the horns on his head.

The. He is no crescent, and his horns are invisible within the circumference.

Moon. This lanthorn doth the horned moon present;
Myself the man i' th' moon do seem to be.

The. This is the greatest error of all the rest. The man should be put into the lantern. How is it else the man i' th' moon?

Dem. He dares not come there for the candle; for, you see, it is already in snuff.

Hip. I am aweary of this moon. Would he would change!

The. It appears, by his small light of discretion, that he is in the wane; but yet, in courtesy, in all reason, we must stay the time.

183. sensible, capable of perception. **199-200. Limander . . . Helen,** blunders for Leander and Hero. **201. Shafalus . . . Procrus,** Cephalus and Procris. **206. 'Tide . . . death,** whether life or death betide. **209. mural,** wall.

227. lion fell, only as Snug the joiner is he a lion fierce. **242. lanthorn,** lantern. **244-5.** The inevitable joke on the "horns" of the cuckold. **253. for,** because of. **254. in snuff,** offended, and, in need of snuffing.

Lys. Proceed, Moon.

Moon. All that I have to say, is to tell you that the lanthorn is the moon; I, the man in the moon; this thorn-bush, my thorn-bush; and this dog, my dog.

Dem. Why, all these should be in the lanthorn; for all these are in the moon. But, silence! here comes Thisbe.

Enter *Thisbe.*

This. This is old Ninny's tomb. Where is my love?

Lion. [*Roaring.*] Oh—— *Thisbe runs off.*

Dem. Well roared, Lion.

The. Well run, Thisbe.

Hip. Well shone, Moon. Truly, the moon shines with a good grace.

The Lion shakes Thisbe's mantle and exit.

The. Well moused, Lion.

Dem. And then came Pyramus.

Lys. And so the lion vanished.

Enter *Pyramus.*

Pyr. Sweet Moon, I thank thee for thy sunny beams;
I thank thee, Moon, for shining now so bright;
For, by thy gracious, golden, glittering gleams,
I trust to take of truest Thisby sight.
But stay, O spite!
But mark, poor knight,
What dreadful dole is here!
Eyes, do you see?
How can it be?
O dainty duck! O dear!
Thy mantle good,
What, stain'd with blood!
Approach, ye Furies fell!
O Fates, come, come,
Cut thread and thrum;
Quail, crush, conclude and quell!

The. This passion, and the death of a dear friend, would go near to make a man look sad.

Hip. Beshrew my heart, but I pity the man.

Pyr. O wherefore, Nature, didst thou lions frame?
Since lion vile hath here deflower'd my dear;
Which is—no, no—which was the fairest dame
That liv'd, that lov'd, that lik'd, that look'd with cheer.
Come, tears, confound;
Out, sword, and wound
The pap of Pyramus;
Ay, that left pap,
Where heart doth hop. *Stabs himself.*
Thus die I, thus, thus, thus.
Now am I dead,
Now am I fled;
My soul is in the sky.
Tongue, lose thy light;
Moon, take thy flight.
Exit Moonshine.
Now die, die, die, die, die. *Dies.*

Dem. No die, but an ace, for him; for he is but one.

Lys. Less than an ace, man, for he is dead; he is nothing.

The. With the help of a surgeon he might yet recover, and yet prove an ass.

Hip. How chance Moonshine is gone before Thisbe comes back and finds her lover?

Re-enter *Thisbe.*

The. She will find him by starlight. Here she comes; and her passion ends the play.

Hip. Methinks she should not use a long one for such a Pyramus. I hope she will be brief.

Dem. A mote will turn the balance, which Pyramus, which Thisbe, is the better; he for a man, God warrant us; she for a woman, God bless us.

Lys. She hath spied him already with those sweet eyes.

Dem. And thus she means, videlicet:—

This. Asleep, my love?
What, dead, my dove?
O Pyramus, arise!
Speak, speak! Quite dumb?
Dead, dead? A tomb
Must cover thy sweet eyes.
These lily lips,
This cherry nose,
These yellow cowslip cheeks,
Are gone, are gone!
Lovers, make moan.
His eyes were green as leeks.
O Sisters Three,
Come, come to me,
With hands as pale as milk;
Lay them in gore,
Since you have shore
With shears his thread of silk.
Tongue, not a word!
Come, trusty sword;
Come, blade, my breast imbrue;
Stabs herself.

273. **moused,** shaken (as a cat shakes a mouse). 283. **dole,** grief. 289. **fell,** fierce. 291. **thread and thrum,** the warp of a piece of cloth and the loose threads at the end. 292. **Quail,** overpower. **quell,** kill. 299. **cheer,** face.

330. **means,** complains. **videlicet,** as follows. 343. **Sisters Three,** The Fates. 351. **imbrue,** stain with blood.

And, farewell, friends;
Thus, Thisby ends.
Adieu, adieu, adieu. *Dies.*

The. Moonshine and Lion are left to bury the dead.

Dem. Ay, and Wall too.

Bot. [*Starting up.*] No, I assure you; the wall is down that parted their fathers. Will it please you to see the epilogue, or to hear a Bergomask dance between two of our company?

The. No epilogue, I pray you; for your play needs no excuse. Never excuse; for when the players are all dead, there need none to be blamed. Marry, if he that writ it had played Pyramus and hanged himself in Thisbe's garter, it would have been a fine tragedy; and so it is, truly; and very notably discharged. But, come, your Bergomask; let your epilogue alone. *A dance.*

The iron tongue of midnight hath told twelve.
Lovers, to bed; 't is almost fairy time.
I fear we shall out-sleep the coming morn
As much as we this night have overwatch'd.
This palpable-gross play hath well beguil'd
The heavy gait of night. Sweet friends, to bed.
A fortnight hold we this solemnity
In nightly revels and new jollity. *Exeunt.*

Enter *Robin Goodfellow.*

Robin. Now the hungry lion roars,
And the wolf behowls the moon;
Whilst the heavy ploughman snores,
All with weary task fordone.
Now the wasted brands do glow,
Whilst the screech-owl, screeching loud,
Puts the wretch that lies in woe
In remembrance of a shroud.
Now it is the time of night
That the graves, all gaping wide,
Every one lets forth his sprite,
In the church-way paths to glide.
And we fairies, that do run
By the triple Hecate's team
From the presence of the sun,
Following darkness like a dream,
Now are frolic. Not a mouse
Shall disturb this hallowed house.
I am sent with broom before,
To sweep the dust behind the door.

361. Bergomask dance, a rustic dance, named from Bergamo in Italy. **374. palpable-gross,** palpably crude. **381. fordone,** worn out. **391. triple Hecate's team,** Diana was *Triformis,* a goddess of heaven, earth, and hell; as an infernal deity she was called Hecate. Shakespeare pronounced the name as a dissyllable.

Enter *King* and *Queen of Fairies* with all their train.

Obe. Through the house give glimmering light,
By the dead and drowsy fire,
Every elf and fairy sprite
Hop as light as bird from brier;
And this ditty, after me,
Sing, and dance it trippingly.

Tita. First, rehearse your song by rote,
To each word a warbling note.
Hand in hand, with fairy grace,
Will we sing, and bless this place.
Song and dance.

Obe. Now, until the break of day,
Through this house each fairy stray.
To the best bride-bed will we,
Which by us shall blessed be;
And the issue there create
Ever shall be fortunate.
So shall all the couples three
Ever true in loving be;
And the blots of Nature's hand
Shall not in their issue stand;
Never mole, hare-lip, nor scar,
Nor mark prodigious, such as are
Despised in nativity,
Shall upon their children be.
With this field-dew consecrate,
Every fairy take his gait,
And each several chamber bless,
Through this palace, with sweet peace;
And the owner of it blest
Ever shall in safety rest.
Trip away; make no stay;
Meet me all by break of day.
Exeunt all but Robin.

Robin. If we shadows have offended,
Think but this, and all is mended,
That you have but slumber'd here
While these visions did appear.
And this weak and idle theme,
No more yielding but a dream,
Gentles, do not reprehend.
If you pardon, we will mend.
And, as I am an honest Puck,
If we have unearned luck
Now to 'scape the serpent's tongue,
We will make amends ere long;
Else the Puck a liar call.
So, good night unto you all.
Give me your hands, if we be friends,
And Robin shall restore amends.
Exit

419. prodigious, unnatural. **432.** Cf. title of the play. **440. serpent's tongue,** hissing. **444. Give . . . hands,** clap applause.

The Tragedy of Romeo and Juliet

The Bodleian library at Oxford exhibits as one of its peculiar treasures the long-lost and happily recovered copy of the first Folio which it received from the printers in 1623 and chained to a reading shelf for the benefit of the students of that distant day. In this copy one play and one passage in that play was read and re-read until the margin of the page crumbled under the touch of countless eager fingers. The play is *Romeo and Juliet;* the passage is the balcony scene. No other play, no other passage, seems to have appealed so strongly to the college youth of the seventeenth century, and what was true then has remained true ever since. In all the fluctuating phases of taste and judgment in succeeding centuries, *Romeo and Juliet* has survived as the supreme expression of the supreme and characteristic passion of youth, the passion of instinctive, romantic, world-forgetting love. The play is the work of Shakespeare's youth, his first utterance in the field of romantic tragedy, and it has remained ever since the poem best beloved by romantic youth.

Text.—Romeo and Juliet has come down to us in two widely varying forms. The first edition, a quarto, appeared in 1597 announced with a flourish on the title-page as *An Excellent conceited Tragedie of Romeo and Juliet. As it hath been often (with great applause) plaid publiquely, by the right Honourable the L. of Hunsdon his Servants, London, Printed by John Danter.* This is one of the so-called "bad" quartos of Shakespearean bibliography and there is reason to believe that the copy from which it was printed was made up in part from material furnished by a hireling actor, in part from notes taken down at a performance of the play. The publication of this play was an act of piracy, and as might be expected, the First Quarto gives us a short and very corrupt version.

Shakespeare and his fellows were no doubt aggrieved at so wretched a reproduction of his most popular play, and two years later they arranged for an authorized edition. This appeared in 1599 at the shop of a reputable publisher, Cuthbert Burby, and announced itself on the title-page as the true version: *The Most Excellent and lamentable Tragedie of Romeo and Juliet. Newly corrected, augmented, and amended. As it hath been sundry times publiquely acted by the right Honourable the Lord Chamberlaine his Servants.* A Third Quarto, 1609, and a Fourth, undated, reprint the Second Quarto; the Folio text was apparently set up from a copy of the Third.

Date.—Evidence for the date of *Romeo and Juliet,* at least in its present form, is found on the title-page of the First Quarto. We learn there that this play had often been performed "with great applause" by Lord Hunsdon's Servants. Now Shakespeare's company bore this title for a brief period only. Their patron Henry Carey, Lord Chamberlain, died in July, 1596, and they passed at once under the protection of his son George, Lord Hunsdon. On March 17, 1597, however, George succeeded to his father's post as Lord Chamberlain. Hence it follows that *Romeo and Juliet* was acted in the period between July, 1596, and March, 1597, by Lord Hunsdon's Men and thereafter by the Lord Chamberlain's Servants; the company was, of course, the same in both cases. It seems reasonable to conclude, then, that *Romeo and Juliet,* at least in its present form, was composed some time in 1596 and staged in the late Summer of that year.

Source.—The first source of Shakespeare's play is an Italian tale by Luigi da Porto, *ca.* 1530, of two noble lovers of Verona, Romeo and Giulietta. In its main outlines the story is that of Shakespeare's play, except that the lady awakes in the tomb before her husband's death (as in Gounod's opera) and dies herself of a broken heart when he expires. The beautiful and tragic tale of ill-fated love sprang into instant popularity. It was re-told in prose and verse in Italy and later dramatized by Italian, French, and Spanish writers. In 1559 a French author, Boisteau, translated a version he found in the *novelle* of Bandello and altered the catastrophe by deferring Juliet's awakening till after her husband's death; whereupon she stabs herself, as in Bandello's version, with his dagger. It was in this form that the story came to England; a long narrative poem by Arthur Brooke, 1562, and a prose tale in Painter's *Palace of Pleasure,* 1567, are both derived from Boisteau. Shakespeare's play rests directly upon the poem, although, no doubt, he was also acquainted with the prose tale.

Shakespeare's Alterations.—It would take too long to trace in detail Shakespeare's indebtedness to Brooke. It runs throughout the play which, so far as mere plot goes, follows the poem very closely. Sometimes indeed Brooke seems to have suggested the very words of Shakespeare's dialogue. It is more important to note Shakespeare's alterations. In the first place he has greatly compressed the time of the action; in Brooke it extends over nine months, the play begins and ends in the brief space of five days. The rapidity of action thus obtained adds immensely to the intensity and dramatic passion of the story. Throughout the play, moreover, Shakespeare employs stronger motivation and displays a far greater power of character portrayal. It is he who introduces Tybalt recognizing Romeo at Capulet's ball, and the rebuke the young hot-head undergoes there from his uncle leads directly to the duel, the death of Mercutio, his own death, and Romeo's banishment. In Brooke Tybalt is slain in a general street fight of the Montagues and Capulets. The character of the jesting Mercutio, so sharp a contrast to the love-sick Romeo, is Shakespeare's creation from a mere hint in Brooke, and the rough sketch of the Nurse in the poem becomes a masterpiece of comic portraiture in Shakespeare's shaping hands.

Atmosphere.—Shakespeare's greatest and most triumphant change, however, is found in his complete transformation of the tone, the sentiment, the atmosphere of the story. What Brooke thought of this we may learn from the words of his preface: "To this end, good Reader, is this tragical matter written, to describe unto thee a couple of unfortunate lovers, thralling themselves to unhonest desire; neglecting the authority and advice of parents and friends; conferring their principal counsels with drunken gossips and superstitious friars . . . abusing the honourable name of lawful marriage to cloak the shame of stolen contracts; finally by all means of unhonest life hasting to most unhappy death." These be bitter words! Too much of a Puritan to understand or appreciate the fiery passion of the old story, Brooke did not realize that passion like fire can purify as well as destroy. It is true that his bark in the preface is worse than his bite in the poem; there are spots where he shows himself an Elizabethan as well as a Puritan and almost sympathizes with the lovers. But on the whole his tone is condemnatory. He represents Juliet as a "wily wench" who laughs at the trick she plays on her mother when she slips off to marry Romeo and who deliberately sets herself to win the love of Paris that she may assuage the anger of her parents. Romeo, too, has nothing of the sentiment and grace of Shakespeare's hero; in the poem he is a mere mouthpiece of conventional love-longing. Friar Laurence appears in the main as a wise and friendly counsellor, but Brooke's hatred of priests leads him to aver that his cell had served for many an amorous rendezvous in his youth. It is an interesting fact that Brooke sets the feast of Capulet at which the lovers meet in the weary winter nights and the balcony scene a few weeks later. The atmosphere of the fierce Italian summer with its burning days when a man's hand leaps to his sword-hilt and its soft warm nights when the maid melts into her lover's arms—all this fervent atmosphere with which Shakespeare's play is steeped and drenched is Shakespeare's own creation, an incomparable accompaniment to his tale of fervent love. And this love is as pure as it is passionate; there is no trace in Shakespeare of the "unhonest desire" that Brooke found in the story. The love of Shakespeare's Romeo and Juliet is the perfect blending of body and soul.

In the romantic love tragedy of *Romeo and Juliet* Shakespeare produced something entirely new in English drama. Nothing at all resembling it can be found in the work of his predecessors. Shakespeare's inspiration for his treatment of the tale of *Romeo and Juliet* comes not from earlier Elizabethan drama, but from a quite different source. It is a commonplace of criticism that *Romeo and Juliet* is the most lyrical of all his tragedies and the reason for this is plain enough. Shakespeare drew his inspiration here from the full and lovely fountain of Elizabethan lyric. Long before the early drama had shaken off its chains of classic and medieval convention the Elizabethan lyric had reached its freest and highest point and the years immediately preceding the composition of *Romeo and Juliet* were resonant with songs, sonnets, lyrical erotic poems, and tragic tales in verse touched with lyric beauty. It is Shakespeare's peculiar glory that in this play he opened the gates to this lyric fountain and sent its flood sweeping and singing through the stricter lines of the drama. Three well-known lyric forms appear in *Romeo and Juliet:* the sonnet at the meeting of the lovers (I, v, 95-108), the epithalamium in the soliloquy of Juliet before her wedding night (III, ii, 1-31), and the aubade, or dawn-song, when Romeo leaves her on the morning after (III, v, 1-36). To these we might add the elegy embodied in the last speech of Romeo in the tomb (V, iii, 91-120). And it is worth while noting that these lyric poems have been so closely interwoven into the texture of the play that they are not likely to be recognized as such except by the trained eye of the scholar. They are no mere lyrical inserts, like the songs in other plays, but a part of the actual dialogue to which they with countless other passages impart that lilting music which distinguishes *Romeo and Juliet* from any other of Shakespeare's tragedies.

Style.—Shakespeare, we may well believe, attacked the dramatization of Brooke's poem with a fine enthusiasm which shows itself in the lyric rapture of the verse; but no admiration for the charm of Shakespeare's poetry should blind us to the fact that *Romeo and Juliet* is the work of a young poet rather than of the finished dramatist. True, Shakespeare had already mastered the fundamentals of his craft; in construction and characterization there is little fault to be found with this play; but the highest art, that of dramatic dialogue, is only imperfectly and intermittently achieved. Any careful reading of the play discloses the presence of two widely differing styles—not separated, so that we might attribute one to the first draft, the other to a subsequent revision—but inextricably intertangled. One is the style of Shakespeare's earlier plays and poems, marked not only by rhyme, which abounds in this play, but by puns, fantastic "conceits," and all the extravagances of Elizabethan poetry. For much of this we must make some critical allowance. When Romeo describes love as a blend of contrarieties:

O brawling love! O loving hate!
O anything of nothing first create!
O heavy lightness! serious vanity!
Mis-shapen chaos of well-seeming forms!
Feather of lead, bright smoke, cold fire, sick health!

he is using the exact language of the Petrarchian love-lyric of his time. When at a moment of extreme anguish he envies the carrion-fly which may steal "immortal blessing" from his Juliet's lips while he is banished from them:

Flies may do this, but I from this must fly

the execrable pun no doubt pleased the fancy of the day. The absurd notion that if Juliet's eyes changed places with two stars, they would banish night from the heavens, while the stars themselves would be shamed by the brightness of her cheek, is a typical Elizabethan "conceit." And then, immediately after this extravagance come the words in which Romeo utters with perfect simplicity and directness the wish of all lovers of all ages:

O that I were a glove upon that hand
That I might kiss that cheek.

And so the scene runs on with change and interchange of fantastic and realistic speech.

It is an interesting fact that such extravagance of speech occurs as a rule in scenes of high dramatic tension. The loveliest and most memorable passages in the play are those which express a single and simple passion, the balcony scene, the parting of the lovers, Juliet's epithalamium, Romeo's elegy. Here the lyric power of the poet lifts and kindles the dialogue into high dramatic beauty. When it came, however, to expressing the clash of contending emotions within one mind, perhaps the highest and most difficult point in tragic art, Shakespeare's hand seems to have faltered and to have turned to an extravagance of speech which, though it passed well enough in his own day, can hardly veil from us the essential emptiness of the thought behind the words. Shakespeare was, no doubt, his own severest critic, and it may well be that it was his own recognition of this imperfection which led him for some years to renounce the sphere of tragedy for the easier fields of comedy and the chronicle-play. When he returned to tragedy in *Julius Cæsar* and in *Hamlet* he had wholly overcome this weakness and was fully able to give realistic and highly dramatic expression to the conflict of a soul divided against itself. Brutus and the Prince of Denmark never break into the wild extremes so often found in *Romeo and Juliet.*

The Problem of Evil.—There is yet another point of view from which *Romeo and Juliet* appears as a play of Shakespeare's youth, the attitude it reveals toward the presence of evil in the world of human life. The problem of evil, its subtlety and dreadful power, was one with which Shakespeare was to come to close grips in his great tragedies. It is only faintly foreshadowed in *Romeo and Juliet.* Evil here takes the form of the feud; it is incarnate in the person of Tybalt. But this evil is purely external; it affects the hero and heroine only from without. Neither Romeo nor Juliet is so touched with this passion of hate that their love must struggle against it. Each regrets, to be sure, that the loved one is a member of a hostile house, but neither thinks for a moment of renouncing a newborn passion on that account. Romeo and his lady are not brought to tragic ruin by evil as Othello is wrecked, Hamlet driven half mad, and Timon plunged into fierce misanthropy. On the contrary their death is in a sense a triumph: "lovely and pleasant in their lives, in their death they were not divided," and over their dead bodies the evil feud is extinguished. There is no such sense of moral wreckage here as in the later tragedies.

One reason for this, perhaps, is that evil, in this play, is not merely external, but comparatively weak. It is powerless to hinder the meeting of the lovers, or to prevent the mutual confession and the consummation of their love, and it is not the evil force, after all, but a mere accident which prevents their final reunion. It seems clear that in *Romeo and Juliet* Shakespeare was far more interested in love, the good, than in hate, the evil thing. One chapter in the work of a modern author shows how first-hand knowledge outweighs uninterested imaginative conception; the story of a Southern feud in *Huckleberry Finn,* with its brooding atmosphere of suspicion and ruthless anger and its desolating outcome, carries with it a far deeper sense of the evil power of hatred than do all the acts of *Romeo and Juliet.*

A Tragedy of Fate.—There is still one more important aspect in which this play differs from the later tragedies. It is, in essence, a tragedy of fate rather than a tragedy of character. This may seem a heresy; it is part of the accepted critical creed that Shakespeare's tragedies spring from character, that some weakness or some excess in the protagonist is responsible for his tragic fall. Efforts have even been made to force *Romeo and Juliet* into this category and to trace the catastrophe which overtakes the lovers to their excessive passion, their precipitancy, or some other imagined flaw in their natures. But the common sense of the reader revolts against such a dogma; it will not endure the test either of first apprehension or critical examination. What action on the part of Romeo or Juliet can be pointed out as the "tragic guilt" of either? Did they do wrong to fall in love, or to wed in secret? Did Romeo sin in avenging the foul murder of his dear friend? Did Juliet err in risking her life with the sleeping potion to escape a hateful marriage? To ask such questions is to answer them, and the plain fact that at the close of the play both hero and heroine are stronger and finer than at the beginning is in itself an answer. Here is no picture of lives ruined by a tragic fault, rather of characters exalted by ennobling passion.

What, then, is the dominating force of this play? Shakespeare himself has given us the answer when he speaks in the prologue of the "pair of star-cross'd lovers." What is this but to say that they were under the spell of an adverse power which they could neither evade nor resist, in other words Fate. And this inevitable Fate works upon their lives by a series of accidents until it brings them to the fore-ordained catastrophe. It is by chance that Romeo first meets Juliet; it is primarily another's action, Tybalt's murder of Mercutio, that brings about his banishment; it is the determination of her parents that forces Juliet to take the sleeping potion; and finally it is by sheer accident that Romeo fails to learn the plan devised by Friar Laurence for their reunion. Shakespeare seems to have shared the old romantic belief that a jealous fate looked with angry eyes upon true love. The great love stories of the world—Hero and Leander, Antony and Cleopatra, Tristan and Iseult—are all tragedies, and in a sense they are all tragedies of Fate. For the more stress the teller of such tales lays upon the strength and the beauty of their passion, the more impossible it is for him to represent this passion as an evil power that wrecks human life. That is Brooke's view, the Puritan's; it is not Shakespeare's.

The fact, then, that *Romeo and Juliet* is a drama of Fate rather than of character, is in itself enough to separate this play from the later work of Shakespeare in the field of tragedy. It lacks the deep tragic note, the moral earnestness, the sense of awed wonder at the soul of man so mysteriously composed, the pang of pity for a world of men that trample on each other and wreck themselves in vain. Yet we may be glad that Shakespeare did not wait to tell the tale of Romeo and Juliet till he had attained full tragic mastery. What he would have done with it then we can only guess, but it would have been something other than it is. Even Shakespeare could not have recaptured later in life the fine rapture that burns in this play of his youth, nor portrayed in such glowing colors and hymned in such lyric notes the love, at once innocent and passionate, the love that guides the star-cross'd lovers through stormy seas to the restful haven of death in each other's arms.

Stage history.—From its first appearance *Romeo and Juliet* has been one of the most popular of Shakespeare's plays upon the stage. Yet, strangely, there is no record of a performance at Court or elsewhere before the closing of the theatres. It was promptly revived after the Restoration; Pepys saw a performance, March 1st, 1662, and pronounced it "the worst that ever I heard in my life and the worst acted." Yet it is probable that even a better performance would not have pleased him. Mr. Pepys reflects the Restoration taste in the drama and there is little in *Romeo and Juliet* to please the wits of the Restoration. It is characteristic of the period that a minor playwright prepared a version with a happy ending and that this travesty was performed alternately with Shakespeare's play. But worse was to come.

In 1680 Otway lifted bodily some of the loveliest scenes from *Romeo and Juliet* and embodied them in his *Caius Marius,* a drama dealing with the civil wars in republican Rome. Strange as it may seem this incongruous mixture of Roman politics and Renaissance love making drove Shakespeare's play from the boards for half a century or more. Even when Theophilus Cibber brought the true version back to the stage in 1744, he lacked the courage to discard one of Otway's alterations, the denouement in which Juliet awakes before her lover's death. There must be something in this version of the catastrophe peculiarly appealing to the stage-manager, for Garrick retained it in his adaptation of *Romeo and Juliet,* and it still appears to-day in the operatic version.

Such great actors as Kemble and Macready used the Garrick version and it was not until about the middle of the last century that *Romeo and Juliet* came back to the stage in the true Shakespearean form. The credit for this defiance of stage tradition may be accorded to Charlotte Cushman, who further tempted fate by appearing as Romeo, allotting the role of Juliet to her sister Susan. It is pleasant to note that her audacity was duly rewarded; her version—Shakespeare's *Romeo and Juliet*—ran for eighty-four nights, and since then no actor-manager has dared to present the Otway-Garrick conclusion.

During the last hundred years every actress of note has played the part of Juliet, and nearly every great actor that of Romeo. Irving staged the play with great splendor at the Lyceum in 1882 with Ellen Terry as Juliet.

In America, Sothern and Marlowe will long be remembered for repeated performances which were in the true sense of the word a revelation of the poetry and the passion of Shakespeare's play. In recent years Katherine Cornell's inspired interpretation of the part of Juliet quite over-shadowed the role of Romeo. A widely heralded cinematic version was rather picturesque than tragic, but at least it carried the story of the star-cross'd lovers far and wide across this continent.

THE TRAGEDY OF ROMEO AND JULIET

Dramatis Personæ

Escalus, Prince of Verona.
Paris, a young nobleman, kinsman to the Prince.
Montague, } heads of two houses at variance with
Capulet, } each other.
An old man, of the Capulet family.
Romeo, son to *Montague.*
Mercutio, kinsman to the Prince, and friend to *Romeo.*
Benvolio, nephew to *Montague,* and friend to *Romeo.*
Tybalt, nephew to *Lady Capulet.*
Friar Laurence, } Franciscans.
Friar John, }
Balthasar, servant to *Romeo.*
Abraham, servant to *Montague.*
Sampson, } servants to *Capulet.*
Gregory, }
Peter, servant to *Juliet's* nurse.
An Apothecary.
Three Musicians.
Page to Paris; another Page.
An Officer.

Lady Montague, wife to *Montague.*
Lady Capulet, wife to *Capulet.*
Juliet, daughter to *Capulet.*
Nurse to Juliet.
Chorus.

Citizens of Verona; Men and Women, kinsfolk to both houses; Maskers, Guards, Watchmen, and Attendants.

SCENE: *Verona; Mantua.*

Prologue

Enter *Chorus.*

Two households, both alike in dignity,
In fair Verona, where we lay our scene,
From ancient grudge break to new mutiny,
Where civil blood makes civil hands unclean.
From forth the fatal loins of these two foes
A pair of star-cross'd lovers take their life;
Whose misadventur'd piteous overthrows
Doth with their death bury their parents' strife.
The fearful passage of their death-mark'd love,
And the continuance of their parents' rage,
Which, but their children's end, nought could remove,
Is now the two hours' traffic of our stage;
The which if you with patient ears attend,
What here shall miss, our toil shall strive to mend.

ACT I. Scene I. *Verona. A public place.*

Enter *Sampson* and *Gregory,* of the house of Capulet, with swords and bucklers.

Sam. Gregory, on my word, we 'll not carry coals.

Gre. No, for then we should be colliers.

Sam. I mean, an we be in choler, we 'll draw.

Gre. Ay, while you live, draw your neck out of collar.

Sam. I strike quickly, being moved.

Gre. But thou art not quickly moved to strike.

Sam. A dog of the house of Montague moves me.

Gre. To move is to stir, and to be valiant is to stand; therefore, if thou art moved, thou run'st away.

Sam. A dog of that house shall move me to stand: I will take the wall of any man or maid of Montague's.

Gre. That shows thee a weak slave; for the weakest goes to the wall.

6. **star-cross'd,** doomed by malevolent stars. **Act I, Scene i: 2. carry coals,** endure insults. **7. moved,** angered.

9. passage, course. **14. miss,** be wanting. **Act I, Scene i: 15. take the wall,** in the narrow streets of Shakespeare's time the place nearest the wall was freest from filth thrown from above or splashed from the center of the street. It was polite to "give the wall" and insulting to "take the wall" from a stranger or enemy.

Sam. 'T is true; and therefore women, being the weaker vessels, are ever thrust to the wall; therefore I will push Montague's men from the wall, and thrust his maids to the wall.

Gre. The quarrel is between our masters and us their men.

Sam. 'T is all one, I will show myself a tyrant: when I have fought with the men, I will be cruel with the maids; I will cut off their heads.

Gre. The heads of the maids?

Sam. Ay, the heads of the maids, or their maidenheads; take it in what sense thou wilt.

Gre. They must take it in sense that feel it.

Sam. Me they shall feel while I am able to stand; and 't is known I am a pretty piece of flesh.

Gre. 'T is well thou art not fish; if thou hadst, thou hadst been poor John. Draw thy tool; here comes two of the house of Montagues.

Enter two other serving men, *Abraham* and *Balthasar.*

Sam. My naked weapon is out; quarrel, I will back thee.

Gre. How! turn thy back and run?

Sam. Fear me not.

Gre. No, marry; I fear thee!

Sam. Let us take the law of our sides; let them begin.

Gre. I will frown as I pass by, and let them take it as they list.

Sam. Nay, as they dare. I will bite my thumb at them; which is disgrace to them, if they bear it.

Abr. Do you bite your thumb at us, sir?

Sam. I do bite my thumb, sir.

Abr. Do you bite your thumb at us, sir?

Sam. [*Aside to Gre.*] Is the law of our side, if I say ay?

Gre. No.

Sam. No, sir, I do not bite my thumb at you, sir; but I bite my thumb, sir.

Gre. Do you quarrel, sir?

Abr. Quarrel, sir? No, sir.

Sam. But if you do, sir, I am for you: I serve as good a man as you.

Abr. No better.

Sam. Well, sir.

Enter *Benvolio.*

Gre. Say "better"; here comes one of my master's kinsmen.

Sam. Yes, better, sir.

Abr. You lie.

Sam. Draw, if you be men. Gregory, remember thy swashing blow. *They fight.*

Ben. Part, fools!
Put up your swords; you know not what you do. *Beats down their swords.*

Enter *Tybalt.*

Tyb. What, art thou drawn among these heartless hinds?
Turn thee, Benvolio, look upon thy death.

Ben. I do but keep the peace: put up thy sword,
Or manage it to part these men with me.

Tyb. What, drawn, and talk of peace! I hate the word
As I hate hell, all Montagues, and thee.
Have at thee, coward! *They fight.*

Enter three or four *Citizens* and *Officers,* with clubs or partisans.

Off. Clubs, bills, and partisans! Strike! Beat them down!
Down with the Capulets! down with the Montagues!

Enter *Capulet* in his gown, and *Lady Capulet.*

Cap. What noise is this? Give me my long sword, ho!

La. Cap. A crutch, a crutch! why call you for a sword?

Cap. My sword, I say! Old Montague is come,
And flourishes his blade in spite of me.

Enter *Montague* and *Lady Montague.*

Mon. Thou villain Capulet,—Hold me not, let me go.

La. Mon. Thou shalt not stir one foot to seek a foe.

Enter *Prince Escalus* with his train.

Prin. Rebellious subjects, enemies to peace,
Profaners of this neighbour-stained steel,—
Will they not hear?—What, ho! you men, you beasts,
That quench the fire of your pernicious rage
With purple fountains issuing from your veins,
On pain of torture, from those bloody hands

37. **poor John,** salt fish. 48-9. **bite my thumb,** an insulting gesture. 65-6. **one of . . . kinsmen,** Tybalt seen approaching.

80. **Clubs,** a 'prentice cry in London. When this cry was raised, the apprentices would seize their clubs and rush into the streets. A **bill** was a long-handled battle-axe or halberd. A **partisan** was a kind of pike or spear, with a two-edged knife on the end in place of the barbed point. 85. **in spite of,** in defiance of. 89. **neighbour-stained,** stained with neighbor's blood.

Throw your mistemper'd weapons to the ground,
And hear the sentence of your moved prince.
Three civil brawls, bred of an airy word,
By thee, old Capulet, and Montague,
Have thrice disturb'd the quiet of our streets,
And made Verona's ancient citizens
Cast by their grave beseeming ornaments,
To wield old partisans, in hands as old,
Canker'd with peace, to part your canker'd hate:
If ever you disturb our streets again
Your lives shall pay the forfeit of the peace.
For this time, all the rest depart away:
You, Capulet, shall go along with me;
And, Montague, come you this afternoon,
To know our farther pleasure in this case,
To old Free-town, our common judgement-place.
Once more, on pain of death, all men depart.
Exeunt all but Montague, Lady Montague, and Benvolio.

Mon. Who set this ancient quarrel new abroach?
Speak, nephew, were you by when it began?

Ben. Here were the servants of your adversary,
And yours, close fighting ere I did approach:
I drew to part them: in the instant came
The fiery Tybalt, with his sword prepared,
Which, as he breath'd defiance to my ears,
He swung about his head and cut the winds,
Who, nothing hurt withal, hiss'd him in scorn:
While we were interchanging thrusts and blows,
Came more and more and fought on part and part,
Till the Prince came, who parted either part.

La. Mon. O, where is Romeo? Saw you him to-day?
Right glad I am he was not at this fray.

Ben. Madam, an hour before the worshipp'd sun
Peer'd forth the golden window of the east,
A troubled mind drave me to walk abroad;
Where, underneath the grove of sycamore
That westward rooteth from this city side,
So early walking did I see your son:
Towards him I made, but he was ware of me
And stole into the covert of the wood:
I, measuring his affections by my own,
Which then most sought where most might not be found,
Being one too many by my weary self,
Pursued my humour not pursuing his,
And gladly shunn'd who gladly fled from me.

Mon. Many a morning hath he there been seen,
With tears augmenting the fresh morning's dew,
Adding to clouds more clouds with his deep sighs;
But all so soon as the all-cheering sun
Should in the farthest east begin to draw
The shady curtains from Aurora's bed,
Away from light steals home my heavy son,
And private in his chamber pens himself,
Shuts up his windows, locks fair daylight out,
And makes himself an artificial night.
Black and portentous must this humour prove
Unless good counsel may the cause remove.

Ben. My noble uncle, do you know the cause?

Mon. I neither know it nor can learn of him.

Ben. Have you importun'd him by any means?

Mon. Both by myself and many other friends;
But he, his own affections' counsellor,
Is to himself—I will not say how true—
But to himself so secret and so close,
So far from sounding and discovery,
As is the bud bit with an envious worm
Ere he can spread his sweet leaves to the air
Or dedicate his beauty to the sun.
Could we but learn from whence his sorrows grow,
We would as willingly give cure as know.

Enter *Romeo.*

Ben. See, where he comes! So please you, step aside;
I 'll know his grievance, or be much denied.

Mon. I would thou wert so happy by thy stay
To hear true shrift. Come, madam, let 's away. *Exeunt Montague and Lady.*

Ben. Good morrow, cousin.

Rom. Is the day so young?

Ben. But new struck nine.

Rom. Ay me! sad hours seem long.
Was that my father that went hence so fast?

Ben. It was. What sadness lengthens Romeo's hours?

Rom. Not having that which, having, makes them short.

Ben. In love?

Rom. Out—

Ben. Of love?

Rom. Out of her favour, where I am in love.

Ben. Alas, that love, so gentle in his view,

94. mistemper'd, angry, or tempered for evil purpose. **102. canker'd,** (1) withered, (2) malignant. **109. Free-town,** translation of "Villa Franca," in the Italian source. **121. part,** side. **131. ware,** aware. **133. affections,** inclinations.

144. heavy, sad. **158. envious,** malicious. **166. shrift,** confession. **176. view,** appearance.

Should be so tyrannous and rough in proof!
Rom. Alas, that love, whose view is muffled still,
Should, without eyes, see pathways to his will!
Where shall we dine? O me! What fray was here?
Yet tell me not, for I have heard it all.
Here 's much to do with hate, but more with love.
Why, then, O brawling love! O loving hate!
O anything, of nothing first created!
O heavy lightness! serious vanity!
Mis-shapen chaos of well-seeming forms!
Feather of lead, bright smoke, cold fire, sick health!
Still-waking sleep, that is not what it is!
This love feel I, that feel no love in this.
Dost thou not laugh?
Ben. No, coz, I rather weep.
Rom. Good heart, at what?
Ben. At thy good heart's oppression.
Rom. Why, such is love's transgression.
Griefs of mine own lie heavy in my breast,
Which thou wilt propagate, to have it prest
With more of thine: this love that thou hast shown
Doth add more grief to too much of mine own.
Love is a smoke made with the fume of sighs;
Being purg'd, a fire sparkling in lovers' eyes;
Being vex'd, a sea nourish'd with loving tears.
What is it else? A madness most discreet,
A choking gall, and a preserving sweet.
Farewell, my coz.
Ben. Soft! I will go along.
An if you leave me so, you do me wrong.
Rom. Tut, I have left myself; I am not here;
This is not Romeo; he 's some otherwhere.
Ben. Tell me in sadness, who is that you love?
Rom. What, shall I groan and tell thee?
Ben. Groan! why, no;
But sadly tell me who.
Rom. Bid a sick man in sadness make his will,—
Ah, word ill urg'd to one that is so ill!
In sadness, cousin, I do love a woman.
Ben. I aim'd so near, when I suppos'd you lov'd.
Rom. A right good mark-man! And she 's fair I love.
Ben. A right fair mark, fair coz, is soonest hit.
Rom. Well, in that hit you miss: she 'll not be hit
With Cupid's arrow; she hath Dian's wit;
And, in strong proof of chastity well arm'd,
From Love's weak childish bow she lives uncharm'd.
She will not stay the siege of loving terms,
Nor bide the encounter of assailing eyes,
Nor ope her lap to saint-seducing gold.
O, she is rich in beauty; only poor
That, when she dies, with beauty dies her store.
Ben. Then she hath sworn that she will still live chaste?
Rom. She hath, and in that sparing makes huge waste;
For beauty starv'd with her severity
Cuts beauty off from all posterity.
She is too fair, too wise, wisely too fair,
To merit bliss by making me despair:
She hath forsworn to love, and in that vow
Do I live dead that live to tell it now.
Ben. Be rul'd by me; forget to think of her.
Rom. O, teach me how I should forget to think.
Ben. By giving liberty unto thine eyes;
Examine other beauties.
Rom. 'T is the way
To call hers, exquisite, in question more.
These happy masks that kiss fair ladies' brows
Being black puts us in mind they hide the fair;
He that is strucken blind cannot forget
The precious treasure of his eyesight lost;
Show me a mistress that is passing fair,
What doth her beauty serve, but as a note
Where I may read who pass'd that passing fair?
Farewell! Thou canst not teach me to forget.
Ben. I 'll pay that doctrine, or else die in debt. *Exeunt*

Scene II. *A street.*

Enter *Capulet, Paris,* and the Clown, a *Servant.*

Cap. But Montague is bound as well as I,
In penalty alike; and 't is not hard, I think,
For men so old as we to keep the peace.
Par. Of honourable reckoning are you both;
And pity 't is you liv'd at odds so long.

177. proof, experience. 194. to have it, by having it. 198. purg'd, cleared (of smoke). 206. sadness, seriousness.

216. wit, mind (to remain single). 217. proof, armor. 223. store, riches. 225. sparing, abstinence. 226. starv'd, afflicted with want. 236. in question, into discussion. 245. pay that doctrine, give that instruction. Scene ii: 4. reckoning, reputation.

But now, my lord, what say you to my suit?
Cap. But saying o'er what I have said before:
My child is yet a stranger in the world;
She hath not seen the change of fourteen years;
Let two more summers wither in their pride,
Ere we may think her ripe to be a bride.
Par. Younger than she are happy mothers made.
Cap. And too soon marr'd are those so early made.
The earth hath swallowed all my hopes but she,
She is the hopeful lady of my earth;
But woo her, gentle Paris, get her heart,
My will to her consent is but a part;
An she agree, within her scope of choice
Lies my consent and fair according voice.
This night I hold an old accustom'd feast,
Whereto I have invited many a guest,
Such as I love; and you, among the store
One more, most welcome, makes my number more.
At my poor house look to behold this night
Earth-treading stars that make dark heaven light.
Such comfort as do lusty young men feel
When well-apparell'd April on the heel
Of limping winter treads, even such delight
Among fresh female buds shall you this night
Inherit at my house; hear all, all see,
And like her most whose merit most shall be.
Which on more view of, many, mine being one,
May stand in number, though in reck'ning none.
Come, go with me. [*To Servant.*] Go, sirrah, trudge about
Through fair Verona; find those persons out
Whose names are written there, and to them say
My house and welcome on their pleasure stay.
Exeunt Capulet and Paris.

Serv. Find them out whose names are written here! It is written that the shoemaker should meddle with his yard, and the tailor with his last, the fisher with his pencil, and the painter with his nets; but I am sent to find those persons whose names are here writ, and can never find what names the writing person hath here writ. I must to the learned.—In good time.

Enter *Benvolio* and *Romeo.*

Ben. Tut, man, one fire burns out another's burning,
One pain is lessen'd by another's anguish;
Turn giddy, and be holp by backward turning;
One desperate grief cures with another's languish:
Take thou some new infection to thy eye,
And the rank poison of the old will die.
Rom. Your plaintain-leaf is excellent for that.
Ben. For what, I pray thee?
Rom. For your broken shin.
Ben. Why, Romeo, art thou mad?
Rom. Not mad, but bound more than a madman is;
Shut up in prison, kept without my food,
Whipp'd and tormented and—God-den, good fellow.

Serv. God gi' god-den. I pray, sir, can you read?

Rom. Ay, mine own fortune in my misery.

Serv. Perhaps you have learned it without book. But, I pray, can you read anything you see?

Rom. Ay, if I know the letters and the language.

Serv. Ye-say honestly; rest you merry!

Rom. Stay, fellow; I can read. [*Reads.*]

"Signior Martino and his wife and daughters;
County Anselme and his beauteous sisters;
The lady widow of Vitruvio;
Signior Placentio and his lovely nieces;
Mercutio and his brother Valentine;
Mine uncle Capulet, his wife, and daughters;
My fair niece Rosaline; Livia;
Signior Valentio and his cousin Tybalt;
Lucio and the lively Helena."

A fair assembly: whither should they come?
Serv. Up. To supper?
Rom. Whither?
Serv. To our house.
Rom. Whose house?
Serv. My master's.

Rom. Indeed, I should have ask'd you that before.

Serv. Now I 'll tell you without asking. My master is the great rich Capulet; and if you be not of the house of Montagues, I pray, come and crush a cup of wine. Rest you merry! *Exit.*

15. **of my earth,** of my body, cf. Sonnet, 146. 32-3. A disputed passage. It may mean: "On more view of her (the lady of most merit), many other ladies, my daughter being one, may be counted of her company (**may stand in number**) but not of her estimation or value (**reck'ning**)."

57. **God-den,** good evening. 85. **crush a cup,** crack a bottle.

Ben. At this same ancient feast of Capulet's
Sups the fair Rosaline whom thou so loves,
With all the admired beauties of Verona:
Go thither; and, with unattainted eye,
Compare her face with some that I shall show,
And I will make thee think thy swan a crow.

Rom. When the devout religion of mine eye
Maintains such falsehood, then turn tears to fires;
And these, who, often drown'd, could never die,
Transparent heretics, be burnt for liars!
One fairer than my love! The all-seeing sun
Ne'er saw her match since first the world begun.

Ben. Tut, you saw her fair, none else being by,
Herself pois'd with herself in either eye;
But in that crystal scales let there be weigh'd
Your lady's love against some other maid
That I will show you shining at this feast,
And she shall scant show well that now seems best.

Rom. I 'll go along no such sight to be shown,
But to rejoice in splendour of mine own.
Exeunt.

Scene III. *A room in Capulet's house.*

Enter *Lady Capulet* and *Nurse.*

La. Cap. Nurse, where 's my daughter? Call her forth to me.

Nurse. Now, by my maidenhead at twelve years old,
I bade her come. What, lamb! What, lady-bird!
God forbid!—Where's this girl? What, Juliet!

Enter *Juliet.*

Jul. How now! Who calls?

Nurse. Your mother.

Jul. Madam, I am here.
What is your will?

La. Cap. This is the matter.—Nurse, give leave a while,
We must talk in secret.—Nurse, come back again;
I have remember'd me, thou 's hear our counsel.
Thou know'st my daughter 's of a pretty age.

Nurse. Faith, I can tell her age unto an hour.

La. Cap. She 's not fourteen.

Nurse. I 'll lay fourteen of my teeth,—
And yet, to my teen be it spoken, I have but four,—
She 's not fourteen. How long is it now
To Lammas-tide?

La. Cap. A fortnight and odd days.

Nurse. Even or odd, of all days in the year,
Come Lammas-eve at night shall she be fourteen.
Susan and she—God rest all Christian souls!—
Were of an age: well, Susan is with God;
She was too good for me.—But, as I said,
On Lammas-eve at night shall she be fourteen;
That shall she, marry; I remember it well.
'T is since the earthquake now eleven years;
And she was wean'd,—I never shall forget it—
Of all the days of the year, upon that day:
For I had then laid wormwood to my dug,
Sitting in the sun under the dove-house wall;
My lord and you were then at Mantua;—
Nay, I do bear a brain;—but, as I said,
When it did taste the wormwood on the nipple
Of my dug and felt it bitter, pretty fool,
To see it tetchy and fall out with the dug!
"Shake," quoth the dove-house; 't was no need, I trow,
To bid me trudge.
And since that time it is eleven years;
For then she could stand high-lone; nay, by the rood,
She could have run and waddled all about;
For even the day before, she broke her brow;
And then my husband—God be with his soul!
'A was a merry man—took up the child.
"Yea," quoth he, "dost thou fall upon thy face?
Thou wilt fall backward when thou hast more wit;
Wilt thou not, Jule?" and, by my holidam,
The pretty wretch left crying and said, "Ay."
To see, now, how a jest shall come about!
I warrant, an I should live a thousand years,
I never should forget it. "Wilt thou not, Jule?" quoth he;
And, pretty fool, it stinted and said, "Ay."

La. Cap. Enough of this; I pray thee, hold thy peace.

Nurse. Yes, madam; yet I cannot choose but laugh,
To think it should leave crying and say, "Ay."
And yet, I warrant, it had upon it brow
A bump as big as a young cockerel's stone;
A perilous knock; and it cried bitterly:

90. unattainted, unprejudiced. **95. these,** i.e., my eyes. **100. pois'd,** weighed. **Scene iii: 9. thou 's,** thou shalt.

12. lay, wager. **13. teen,** sorrow. **15. Lammas-tide,** August 1st. **32. tetchy,** fretful. **36. rood,** cross. **40. 'A,** he. **48. stinted,** ceased. **52. it,** its.

"Yea," quoth my husband, "fall'st upon thy face?
Thou wilt fall backward when thou comest to age;
Wilt thou not, Jule?" It stinted and said, "Ay."

Jul. And stint thou too, I pray thee, nurse, say I.

Nurse. Peace, I have done. God mark thee to his grace!
Thou wast the prettiest babe that e'er I nurs'd.
An I might live to see thee married once,
I have my wish.

La. Cap. Marry, that "marry" is the very theme
I came to talk of. Tell me, daughter Juliet,
How stands your dispositions to be married?

Jul. It is an honour that I dream not of.

Nurse. An honour! were not I thine only nurse,
I would say thou hadst suck'd wisdom from thy teat.

La. Cap. Well, think of marriage now; younger than you,
Here in Verona, ladies of esteem,
Are made already mothers. By my count,
I was your mother much upon these years
That you are now a maid. Thus then in brief:
The valiant Paris seeks you for his love.

Nurse. A man, young lady! Lady, such a man
As all the world—why, he 's a man of wax.

La. Cap. Verona's summer hath not such a flower.

Nurse. Nay, he 's a flower; in faith, a very flower.

La. Cap. What say you? Can you love the gentleman?
This night you shall behold him at our feast;
Read o'er the volume of young Paris' face
And find delight writ there with beauty's pen;
Examine every married lineament
And see how one another lends content,
And what obscur'd in this fair volume lies
Find written in the margent of his eyes.
This precious book of love, this unbound lover,
To beautify him, only lacks a cover:
The fish lives in the sea, and 't is much pride
For fair without the fair within to hide:
That book in many's eyes doth share the glory,
That in gold clasps locks in the golden story;
So shall you share all that he doth possess,
By having him, making yourself no less.

Nurse. No less! nay, bigger; women grow by men.

La. Cap. Speak briefly, can you like of Paris' love?

Jul. I 'll look to like, if looking liking move;
But no more deep will I endart mine eye
Than your consent gives strength to make it fly.

Enter *Servant.*

Serv. Madam, the guests are come, supper served up, you called, my young lady asked for, the nurse cursed in the pantry, and everything in extremity. I must hence to wait; I beseech you, follow straight. *Exit.*

La. Cap. We follow thee. Juliet, the County stays.

Nurse. Go, girl, seek happy nights to happy days. *Exeunt.*

Scene IV. *A street.*

Enter *Romeo, Mercutio, Benvolio,* with five or six other *Maskers, Torch-bearers.*

Rom. What, shall this speech be spoke for our excuse?
Or shall we on without apology?

Ben. The date is out of such prolixity.
We 'll have no Cupid hoodwink'd with a scarf,
Bearing a Tartar's painted bow of lath,
Scaring the ladies like a crow-keeper;
Nor no without-book prologue, faintly spoke
After the prompter, for our entrance;
But let them measure us by what they will,
We 'll measure them a measure and be gone.

Rom. Give me a torch: I am not for this ambling;
Being but heavy, I will bear the light.

Mer. Nay, gentle Romeo, we must have you dance.

Rom. Not I, believe me: you have dancing shoes
With nimble soles; I have a soul of lead
So stakes me to the ground I cannot move.

Mer. You are a lover; borrow Cupid's wings,
And soar with them above a common bound.

Rom. I am too sore enpierced with his shaft
To soar with his light feathers, and so bound
I cannot bound a pitch above dull woe:
Under love's heavy burden do I sink.

Mer. And, to sink in it, should you burden love;

76. man of wax, perfect as a wax figure. **83. married,** harmonious. **86. margent,** margin. **89. The fish lives in the sea,** the lover is at large, is not yet hooked.

Scene IV: 1. this speech, explained by l. 4 ff. **3. such prolixity** is out of date. **4. hoodwink'd,** blindfolded. **6. crow-keeper,** boy employed to scare crows. **10. measure,** stately dance.

Too great oppression for a tender thing.
Rom. Is love a tender thing? It is too rough,
Too rude, too boisterous, and it pricks like thorn.
Mer. If love be rough with you, be rough with love;
Prick love for pricking, and you beat love down.
Give me a case to put my visage in.
Puts on a mask.
A visor for a visor! what care I
What curious eye doth quote deformities?
Here are the beetle brows shall blush for me.
Ben. Come, knock and enter; and no sooner in,
But every man betake him to his legs.
Rom. A torch for me; let wantons light of heart
Tickle the senseless rushes with their heels,
For I am proverb'd with a grandsire phrase:
I 'll be a candle-holder, and look on.
The game was ne'er so fair, and I am done.
Mer. Tut, dun 's the mouse, the constable's own word.
If thou art Dun, we 'll draw thee from the mire
Of this sir-reverence love, wherein thou stickest
Up to the ears. Come, we burn daylight, ho!
Rom. Nay, that 's not so.
Mer. I mean, sir, in delay
We waste our lights in vain, light lights by day.
Take our good meaning, for our judgement sits
Five times in that ere once in our five wits.
Rom. And we mean well in going to this mask;
But 't is no wit to go.
Mer. Why, may one ask?
Rom. I dream'd a dream to-night.
Mer. And so did I.
Rom. Well, what was yours?
Mer. That dreamers often lie.
Rom. In bed asleep, while they do dream things true.

30. A visor for a visor, a mask for a mask-like face. **31. quote,** note. **36. rushes,** used as floor covering. **37. grandsire phrase,** an ancient saying or proverb. The first that follows is: "A good candle-holder (i.e., onlooker) proves a good gamester." The other is to the effect that he does well who gives over (is done) when the game is the fairest. **40. dun 's the mouse,** the meaning of **"dun 's the mouse"** is not clear. It is generally taken to mean "keep still." **Dun** in the next line (l. 41), however, very evidently means "horse" and refers to the ancient Christmas game "Dun is in the mire," in which Dun, a heavy log, is supposed to be dragged out of the mire by the players. **42. sir-reverence,** a phrase used instead of the proper word for a filthy thing. Mercutio means that love is filthy mire.

Mer. O, then, I see Queen Mab hath been with you.
She is the fairies' midwife, and she comes
In shape no bigger than an agate-stone
On the fore-finger of an alderman,
Drawn with a team of little atomies
Over men's noses as they lie asleep;
Her waggon-spokes made of long spinners' legs,
The cover of the wings of grasshoppers,
Her traces of the smallest spider web,
Her collars of the moonshine's watery beams,
Her whip of cricket's bone, the lash of film,
Her waggoner a small grey-coated gnat,
Not half so big as a round little worm
Prick'd from the lazy finger of a maid:
Her chariot is an empty hazel-nut
Made by the joiner squirrel, or old grub,
Time out o' mind the fairies' coachmakers.
And in this state she gallops night by night
Through lovers' brains, and then they dream of love;
On courtiers' knees, that dream on curtsies straight;
O'er lawyers' fingers, who straight dream on fees;
O'er ladies' lips, who straight on kisses dream,
Which oft the angry Mab with blisters plagues,
Because their breath with sweetmeats tainted are:
Sometime she gallops o'er a courtier's nose,
And then dreams he of smelling out a suit;
And sometime comes she with a tithe-pig's tail
Tickling a parson's nose as 'a lies asleep,
Then he dreams of another benefice:
Sometime she driveth o'er a soldier's neck,
And then dreams he of cutting foreign throats,
Of breaches, ambuscadoes, Spanish blades,
Of healths five fathom deep; and then anon
Drums in his ear, at which he starts and wakes,
And being thus frighted, swears a prayer or two
And sleeps again. This is that very Mab
That plats the manes of horses in the night,
And bakes the elf-locks in foul sluttish hairs,
Which, once untangled, much misfortune bodes:
This is the hag, when maids lie on their backs,
That presses them and learns them first to bear,
Making them women of good carriage:
This is she—
Rom. Peace, peace, Mercutio, peace!
Thou talk'st of nothing.

57. atomies, tiny animals. **59. spinners',** spiders'. **79. tithe-pig's,** pig paid as church dues. **89. plats,** plaits. **90. elf-locks,** tangled hair.

Mer. True, I talk of dreams,
Which are the children of an idle brain,
Begot of nothing but vain fantasy,
Which is as thin of substance as the air
And more inconstant than the wind, who wooes
Even now the frozen bosom of the north,
And, being anger'd, puffs away from thence,
Turning his face to the dew-dropping south.

Ben. This wind you talk of blows us from ourselves;
Supper is done, and we shall come too late.

Rom. I fear, too early; for my mind misgives
Some consequence yet hanging in the stars
Shall bitterly begin his fearful date
With this night's revels, and expire the term
Of a despised life clos'd in my breast
By some vile forfeit of untimely death.
But He that hath the steerage of my course
Direct my sail! On, lusty gentlemen!

Ben. Strike, drum.

They march about the stage and Servingmen come forth with napkins.

Scene V. *A hall in Capulet's house.*

First Serv. Where 's Potpan, that he helps not to take away? He shift a trencher! He scrape a trencher!

Sec. Serv. When good manners shall lie all in one or two men's hands, and they unwashed too, 't is a foul thing.

First Serv. Away with the joint-stools, remove the court-cupboard, look to the plate. Good thou, save me a piece of marchpane; and, as thou loves me, let the porter let in Susan Grindstone and Nell. Anthony and Potpan!

Sec. Serv. Ay, boy, ready.

First Serv. You are looked for and called for, asked for and sought for, in the great chamber.

Third Serv. We cannot be here and there too. Cheerly, boys; be brisk a while, and the longer liver take all. *They retire.*

Enter *Capulet,* with his *Wife, Juliet, Tybalt,* and all the *Guests* meeting the *Maskers.*

Cap. Welcome, gentlemen! Ladies that have their toes
Unplagu'd with corns will walk a bout with you.
Ah, my mistresses, which of you all
Will now deny to dance? She that makes dainty,
She, I 'll swear, hath corns: am I come near ye now?
Welcome, gentlemen! I have seen the day
That I have worn a visor and could tell
A whispering tale in a fair lady's ear,
Such as would please; 't is gone, 't is gone, 't is gone.
You are welcome, gentlemen! Come, musicians, play.

Music plays, and they dance.

A hall, a hall! give room! and foot it, girls.
More light, you knaves; and turn the tables up,
And quench the fire, the room is grown too hot.
Ah, sirrah, this unlook'd-for sport comes well.
Nay, sit, nay, sit, good cousin Capulet,
For you and I are past our dancing days:
How long is 't now since last yourself and I
Were in a mask?

Sec. Cap. By 'r lady, thirty years.

Cap. What, man! 't is not so much, 't is not so much:
'T is since the nuptial of Lucentio,
Come Pentecost as quickly as it will,
Some five and twenty years; and then we mask'd.

Sec. Cap. 'T is more, 't is more. His son is elder, sir;
His son is thirty.

Cap. Will you tell me that?
His son was but a ward two years ago.

Rom. [*To a Serving-man.*] What lady 's that which doth enrich the hand
Of yonder knight?

Serv. I know not, sir.

Rom. O, she doth teach the torches to burn bright!
It seems she hangs upon the cheek of night
As a rich jewel in an Ethiop's ear;
Beauty too rich for use, for earth too dear!
So shows a snowy dove trooping with crows,
As yonder lady o'er her fellows shows.
The measure done, I 'll watch her place of stand,
And, touching hers, make blessed my rude hand.
Did my heart love till now? Forswear it, sight!
For I ne'er saw true beauty till this night.

Tyb. This, by his voice, should be a Montague.
Fetch me my rapier, boy. What! dares the slave
Come hither, cover'd with an antic face,

103. dew-dropping, rainy. **108. date,** time. **109. expire,** conclude. **S. d.:** As the maskers march about, the Servingmen enter and the stage that was the street now becomes a hall in Capulet's house. **Scene v: 7. joint-stools,** folding stools. **8. court-cupboard,** sideboard. **9. marchpane,** cake made of sugar and almonds. **19. walk a bout,** tread a measure in a dance.

28. a hall, make room. **58. antic face,** fantastic mask.

To fleer and scorn at our solemnity?
Now, by the stock and honour of my kin,
To strike him dead I hold it not a sin.
Cap. Why, how now, kinsman! wherefore storm you so?
Tyb. Uncle, this is a Montague, our foe,
A villain that is hither come in spite
To scorn at our solemnity this night.
Cap. Young Romeo is it?
Tyb. 'T is he, that villain Romeo.
Cap. Content thee, gentle coz, let him alone,
'A bears him like a portly gentleman;
And, to say truth, Verona brags of him
To be a virtuous and well-govern'd youth:
I would not for the wealth of all this town
Here in my house do him disparagement;
Therefore be patient, take no note of him;
It is my will, the which if thou respect,
Show a fair presence and put off these frowns,
An ill-beseeming semblance for a feast.
Tyb. It fits, when such a villain is a guest.
I 'll not endure him.
Cap. He shall be endur'd.
What, goodman boy! I say he shall; go to!
Am I the master here, or you? Go to!
You 'll not endure him? God shall mend my soul!
You 'll make a mutiny among my guests!
You will set cock-a-hoop! You 'll be the man!
Tyb. Why, uncle, 't is a shame.
Cap. Go to, go to!
You are a saucy boy. Is 't so, indeed?
This trick may chance to scath you; I know what.
You must contrary me! Marry, 't is time.—
Well said, my hearts!—You are a princox; go!
Be quiet, or—More light, more light!—for shame!
I 'll make you quiet.—What, cheerly, my hearts!
Tyb. Patience perforce with wilful choler meeting
Makes my flesh tremble in their different greeting.
I will withdraw; but this intrusion shall
Now seeming sweet convert to bitt'rest gall. *Exit.*
Rom. [*To Juliet.*] If I profane with my unworthiest hand
This holy shrine, the gentle fine is this:
My lips, two blushing pilgrims, ready stand
To smooth that rough touch with a tender kiss.
Jul. Good pilgrim, you do wrong your hand too much,
Which mannerly devotion shows in this;
For saints have hands that pilgrims' hands do touch,
And palm to palm is holy palmers' kiss.
Rom. Have not saints lips, and holy palmers too?
Jul. Ay, pilgrim, lips that they must use in prayer.
Rom. O, then, dear saint, let lips do what hands do;
They pray, grant thou, lest faith turn to despair.
Jul. Saints do not move, though grant for prayers' sake.
Rom. Then move not, while my prayer's effect I take.
Thus from my lips, by thine, my sin is purg'd.
Kissing her.
Jul. Then have my lips the sin that they have took.
Rom. Sin from my lips? O trespass sweetly urg'd!
Give me my sin again. *Kissing her again.*
Jul. You kiss by th' book.
Nurse. Madam, your mother craves a word with you.
Rom. What is her mother?
Nurse. Marry, bachelor,
Her mother is the lady of the house,
And a good lady, and a wise and virtuous.
I nurs'd her daughter, that you talk'd withal;
I tell you, he that can lay hold of her
Shall have the chinks.
Rom. Is she a Capulet?
O dear account! my life is my foe's debt.
Ben. Away, be gone; the sport is at the best.
Rom. Ay, so I fear; the more is my unrest.
Cap. Nay, gentlemen, prepare not to be gone;
We have a trifling foolish banquet towards.
Is it e'en so? Why, then, I thank you all;
I thank you, honest gentlemen; good-night.
More torches here! Come on then, let 's to bed.
Ah, sirrah, by my fay, it waxes late;
I 'll to my rest.
All but Juliet and Nurse begin to go out.
Jul. Come hither, nurse. What is yond gentleman?
Nurse. The son and heir of old Tiberio.
Jul. What 's he that now is going out of door?

59. fleer, sneer. **65. solemnity**, feast. **68. portly**, well-bred. **79. goodman**, familiar term of address. **83. cock-a-hoop**, everything in disorder. **88. princox**, saucy boy. **95-108.** This passage is in the Shakespearean sonnet form. A second, beginning at l. 109 is interrupted by the Nurse at l. 113.

102. palmers', pilgrims'. **119. chinks**, money. **120. my life is my foe's debt**, this means that his life—since to live he must have Juliet—is in the power of his foe Capulet. **124. banquet**, a dessert of fruit, wine, and sweetmeats. **towards**, just coming.

Nurse. Marry, that, I think, be young Petruchio.
Jul. What 's he that follows there, that would not dance?
Nurse. I know not.
Jul. Go, ask his name.—If he be married,
My grave is like to be my wedding-bed.
Nurse. His name is Romeo, and a Montague;
The only son of your great enemy.
Jul. My only love sprung from my only hate!
Too early seen unknown, and known too late!
Prodigious birth of love it is to me
That I must love a loathed enemy.
Nurse. What 's this? what 's this?
Jul. A rhyme I learn'd even now
Of one I danc'd withal.
One calls within, "Juliet."
Nurse. Anon, anon!
Come, let 's away; the strangers all are gone.
Exeunt.

Act II

Enter *Chorus.*

Chor. Now old Desire doth in his death-bed lie,
And young Affection gapes to be his heir;
That fair for which love groan'd for and would die,
With tender Juliet match'd, is now not fair.
Now Romeo is belov'd and loves again,
Alike bewitched by the charm of looks,
But to his foe suppos'd he must complain,
And she steal love's sweet bait from fearful hooks:
Being held a foe, he may not have access
To breathe such vows as lovers use to swear;
And she as much in love, her means much less
To meet her new-beloved anywhere:
But passion lends them power, time means, to meet,
Temp'ring extremities with extreme sweet.
Exit.

Scene I. *A lane by the wall of Capulet's orchard.*

Enter *Romeo,* alone.

Rom. Can I go forward when my heart is here?
Turn back, dull earth, and find thy centre out.
He climbs the wall, and leaps down within it.

Enter *Benvolio* with *Mercutio.*

Ben. Romeo! my cousin Romeo! Romeo!
Mer. He is wise;
And, on my life, hath stol'n him home to bed.
Ben. He ran this way, and leap'd this orchard wall.
Call, good Mercutio.
Mer. Nay, I 'll conjure too.
Romeo! humours! madman! passion! lover!
Appear thou in the likeness of a sigh!
Speak but one rhyme, and I am satisfied;
Cry but "Ay me!" pronounce but "love" and "love";
Speak to my gossip Venus one fair word,
One nick-name for her purblind son and heir,
Young Adam Cupid, he that shot so trim,
When King Cophetua lov'd the beggar-maid!
He heareth not, he stirreth not, he moveth not;
The ape is dead, and I must conjure him.
I conjure thee by Rosaline's bright eyes,
By her high forehead and her scarlet lip,
By her fine foot, straight leg, and quivering thigh,
And the demesnes that there adjacent lie,
That in thy likeness thou appear to us!
Ben. An if he hear thee, thou wilt anger him.
Mer. This cannot anger him; 't would anger him
To raise a spirit in his mistress' circle,
Of some strange nature, letting it there stand
Till she had laid it and conjured it down.
That were some spite; my invocation

Act II, Scene i: 2. dull earth, i.e., his body. **S. d.:** This is a modern stage direction. The original editions have none here. It is plain that Romeo simply walked across the stage and hid himself. After the departure of his friends he came forward again and the action continues. Note that the first line of Scene ii rhymes with the last line of Scene i.

142. Prodigious, portentous. **Act II, Scene i: 11. gossip,** friend. **13-14. Adam,** Adam Bell, the famous archer of the ballads. The name became proverbial for skill in archery. Cf. *Much Ado* 1. 1. 261. The remainder no doubt refers to a stanza from the ballad of "King Cophetua and the Beggar-Maid":

"The blinded boy that shoots so trim
From heaven down did hie,
He drew a dart and shot at him,
In place where he did lie!"

27. spite, vexation.

Is fair and honest; in his mistress' name
I conjure only but to raise up him.
Ben. Come, he hath hid himself among these trees,
To be consorted with the humorous night:
Blind is his love and best befits the dark.
Mer. If Love be blind, Love cannot hit the mark.
Now will he sit under a medlar tree,
And wish his mistress were that kind of fruit
As maids call medlars, when they laugh alone.
O, Romeo, that she were, O, that she were
An open *et cetera*, thou a poperin pear!
Romeo, good-night; I 'll to my truckle-bed;
This field-bed is too cold for me to sleep.
Come, shall we go?
Ben. Go, then; for 't is in vain
To seek him here that means not to be found.
Exeunt Benvolio and Mercutio.

Scene II. *Capulet's orchard.*

Romeo advances.

Rom. He jests at scars that never felt a wound.

Enter *Juliet* above.

But, soft! what light through yonder window breaks?
It is the east, and Juliet is the sun.
Arise, fair sun, and kill the envious moon,
Who is already sick and pale with grief
That thou, her maid, art far more fair than she:
Be not her maid, since she is envious;
Her vestal livery is but sick and green,
And none but fools do wear it; cast it off.
It is my lady, O, it is my love!
O, that she knew she were!
She speaks, yet she says nothing; what of that?
Her eye discourses; I will answer it.—
I am too bold, 't is not to me she speaks:
Two of the fairest stars in all the heaven,
Having some business, do entreat her eyes
To twinkle in their spheres till they return.
What if her eyes were there, they in her head?
The brightness of her cheek would shame those stars,
As daylight doth a lamp; her eyes in heaven
Would through the airy region stream so bright
That birds would sing and think it were not night.
See, how she leans her cheek upon her hand!
O, that I were a glove upon that hand,
That I might touch that cheek!
Jul. Ay me!
Rom. She speaks!
O, speak again, bright angel! for thou art
As glorious to this night, being o'er my head,
As is a winged messenger of heaven
Unto the white-upturned wond'ring eyes
Of mortals that fall back to gaze on him
When he bestrides the lazy-pacing clouds
And sails upon the bosom of the air.
Jul. O Romeo, Romeo! wherefore art thou Romeo?
Deny thy father and refuse thy name;
Or, if you wilt not, be but sworn my love,
And I 'll no longer be a Capulet.
Rom. Shall I hear more, or shall I speak at this?
Jul. 'T is but thy name that is my enemy;
Thou art thyself, though not a Montague.
What 's Montague? It is nor hand, nor foot,
Nor arm, nor face, nor any other part
Belonging to a man. O, be some other name!
What 's in a name? That which we call a rose
By any other word would smell as sweet;
So Romeo would, were he not Romeo call'd,
Retain that dear perfection which he owes
Without that title. Romeo, doff thy name,
And for thy name which is no part of thee
Take all myself.
Rom. I take thee at thy word.
Call me but love, and I 'll be new baptiz'd;
Henceforth I never will be Romeo.
Jul. What man art thou that thus bescreen'd in night
So stumblest on my counsel?
Rom. By a name
I know not how to tell thee who I am:
My name, dear saint, is hateful to myself,
Because it is an enemy to thee;
Had I it written, I would tear the word.
Jul. My ears have yet not drunk a hundred words
Of thy tongue's uttering, yet I know the sound.
Art thou not Romeo and a Montague?
Rom. Neither, fair maid, if either thee dislike.
Jul. How cam'st thou hither, tell me, and wherefore?
The orchard walls are high and hard to climb,
And the place death, considering who thou art,
If any of my kinsmen find thee here.

31. consorted with, in company with. **humorous**, damp. **39. truckle-bed**, small bed. **Scene ii: 2. S. d.:** There is no stage direction here in the old editions, but it is plain that Juliet comes out here on the balcony of Shakespeare's stage. **5. sick,** of a sickly hue.

46. owes, possesses. **49.** At this point Romeo advances to the balcony and addresses Juliet. **61. dislike,** displease.

Rom. With love's light wings did I o'er-perch these walls;
For stony limits cannot hold love out,
And what love can do that dares love attempt;
Therefore thy kinsmen are no stop to me.
Jul. If they do see thee, they will murder thee.
Rom. Alack, there lies more peril in thine eye
Than twenty of their swords! Look thou but sweet,
And I am proof against their enmity.
Jul. I would not for the world they saw thee here.
Rom. I have night's cloak to hide me from their eyes;
And but thou love me, let them find me here:
My life were better ended by their hate,
Than death prorogued, wanting of thy love.
Jul. By whose direction found'st thou out this place?
Rom. By Love, that first did prompt me to inquire;
He lent me counsel and I lent him eyes.
I am no pilot; yet, wert thou as far
As that vast shore wash'd with the farthest sea,
I should adventure for such merchandise.
Jul. Thou know'st the mask of night is on my face,
Else would a maiden blush bepaint my cheek
For that which thou hast heard me speak to-night.
Fain would I dwell on form, fain, fain deny
What I have spoke; but farewell compliment!
Dost thou love me? I know thou wilt say "Ay,"
And I will take thy word; yet, if thou swear'st,
Thou mayst prove false: at lovers' perjuries,
They say, Jove laughs. O gentle Romeo,
If thou dost love, pronounce it faithfully;
Or if thou think'st I am too quickly won,
I 'll frown and be perverse and say thee nay,
So thou wilt woo; but else, not for the world.
In truth, fair Montague, I am too fond,
And therefore thou mayst think my 'haviour light;
But trust me, gentleman, I 'll prove more true
Than those that have more cunning to be strange.
I should have been more strange, I must confess,
But that thou overheard'st, ere I was ware,
My true love's passion; therefore pardon me,
And not impute this yielding to light love,
Which the dark night hath so discovered.
Rom. Lady, by yonder blessed moon I swear
That tips with silver all these fruit-tree tops—
Jul. O, swear not by the moon, th' inconstant moon,
That monthly changes in her circled orb,
Lest that thy love prove likewise variable.
Rom. What shall I swear by?
Jul. Do not swear at all;
Or, if thou wilt, swear by thy gracious self,
Which is the god of my idolatry,
And I 'll believe thee.
Rom. If my heart's dear love—
Jul. Well, do not swear. Although I joy in thee,
I have no joy of this contract to-night;
It is too rash, too unadvis'd, too sudden,
Too like the lightning, which doth cease to be
Ere one can say "it lightens." Sweet, good night!
This bud of love, by summer's ripening breath,
May prove a beauteous flower when next we meet.
Good-night, good-night! as sweet repose and rest
Come to thy heart as that within my breast!
Rom. O, wilt thou leave me so unsatisfied?
Jul. What satisfaction canst thou have to-night?
Rom. Th' exchange of thy love's faithful vow for mine.
Jul. I gave thee mine before thou didst request it;
And yet I would it were to give again.
Rom. Wouldst thou withdraw it? For what purpose, love?
Jul. But to be frank, and give it thee again.
And yet I wish but for the thing I have:
My bounty is as boundless as the sea,
My love as deep; the more I give to thee,
The more I have, for both are infinite.
Nurse calls within.
I hear some noise within; dear love, adieu!
Anon, good nurse! Sweet Montague, be true.
Stay but a little, I will come again. *Exit.*
Rom. O blessed, blessed night! I am afeard,
Being in night, all this is but a dream,
Too flattering-sweet to be substantial.

Re-enter *Juliet,* above.

Jul. Three words, dear Romeo, and good-night indeed.
If that thy bent of love be honourable,
Thy purpose marriage, send me word to-morrow,

66. **o'erperch,** fly over. 78. **prorogued,** postponed. 89. **compliment,** ceremony.

131. **frank,** generous. 143. **bent,** inclination.

By one that I 'll procure to come to thee,
Where and what time thou wilt perform the rite;
And all my fortunes at thy foot I 'll lay
And follow thee my lord throughout the world.

Nurse. [*Within.*] Madam!

Jul. I come, anon.—But if thou meanest not well,
I do beseech thee—

Nurse. [*Within.*] Madam.

Jul. By and by, I come:—
To cease thy suit, and leave me to my grief.
To-morrow will I send.

Rom. So thrive my soul—

Jul. A thousand times good-night! *Exit.*

Rom. A thousand times the worse, to want thy light.
Love goes toward love, as schoolboys from their books,
But love from love, toward school with heavy looks. *Retiring.*

Re-enter *Juliet,* above.

Jul. Hist! Romeo, hist! O, for a falc'ner's voice,
To lure this tassel-gentle back again!
Bondage is hoarse, and may not speak aloud;
Else would I tear the cave where Echo lies,
And make her airy tongue more hoarse than mine,
With repetition of my Romeo's name.
Romeo!

Rom. It is my soul, that calls upon my name.
How silver-sweet sound lovers' tongues by night,
Like softest music to attending ears!

Jul. Romeo!

Rom. My dear?

Jul. What o'clock to-morrow
Shall I send to thee?

Rom. By the hour of nine.

Jul. I will not fail; 't is twenty year till then.
I have forgot why I did call thee back.

Rom. Let me stand here till thou remember it.

Jul. I shall forget, to have thee still stand there,
Rememb'ring how I love thy company.

Rom. And I 'll still stay, to have thee still forget,
Forgetting any other home but this.

Jul. 'T is almost morning, I would have thee gone;
And yet no farther than a wanton's bird;
That lets it hop a little from her hand,
Like a poor prisoner in his twisted gyves,
And with a silk thread plucks it back again,
So loving-jealous of his liberty.

Rom. I would I were thy bird.

Jul. Sweet, so would I;
Yet I should kill thee with much cherishing.
Good-night, good-night! Parting is such sweet sorrow,
That I shall say good-night till it be morrow. *Exit.*

Rom. Sleep dwell upon thine eyes, peace in thy breast!
Would I were sleep and peace, so sweet to rest!
Hence will I to my ghostly father's cell,
His help to crave, and my dear hap to tell. *Exit.*

Scene III. *Friar Laurence's cell.*

Enter *Friar Laurence,* alone, with a basket.

Fri. L. The grey-ey'd morn smiles on the frowning night,
Chequ'ring the eastern clouds with streaks of light,
And flecked darkness like a drunkard reels
From forth day's path and Titan's fiery wheels:
Now, ere the sun advance his burning eye,
The day to cheer and night's dank dew to dry,
I must up-fill this osier cage of ours
With baleful weeds and precious-juiced flowers.
The earth, that 's nature's mother, is her tomb;
What is her burying grave, that is her womb;
And from her womb children of divers kind
We sucking on her natural bosom find,
Many for many virtues excellent,
None but for some, and yet all different.
O, mickle is the powerful grace that lies
In plants, herbs, stones, and their true qualities;
For nought so vile that on the earth doth live
But to the earth some special good doth give,
Nor aught so good but, strain'd from that fair use,
Revolts from true birth, stumbling on abuse.
Virtue itself turns vice, being misapplied;
And vice sometime 's by action dignified.
Within the infant rind of this weak flower
Poison hath residence and medicine power;
For this, being smelt, with that part cheers each part;

160. **tassel-gentle**, tiercel gentle, i.e., male hawk.

180. **gyves**, fetters. 189. **ghostly**, spiritual. 190. **dear hap**, good fortune. **Scene iii:** 7. **osier cage**, willow basket. 15. **mickle**, much. 25. **that part**, the odor.

Being tasted, slays all senses with the heart.
Two such opposed kings encamp them still
In man as well as herbs, grace and rude will;
And where the worser is predominant,
Full soon the canker death eats up that plant.

Enter *Romeo*.

Rom. Good morrow, father.
Fri. L. *Benedicite!*
What early tongue so sweet saluteth me?
Young son, it argues a distempered head
So soon to bid good morrow to thy bed:
Care keeps his watch in every old man's eye,
And where care lodges, sleep will never lie;
But where unbruised youth with unstuff'd brain
Doth couch his limbs, there golden sleep doth reign;
Therefore thy earliness doth me assure
Thou art up-rous'd with some distemp'rature;
Or if not so, then here I hit it right,
Our Romeo hath not been in bed to-night.
Rom. That last is true; the sweeter rest was mine.
Fri. L. God pardon sin! Wast thou with Rosaline?
Rom. With Rosaline, my ghostly father? No!
I have forgot that name, and that name 's woe.
Fri. L. That 's my good son; but where hast thou been, then?
Rom. I 'll tell thee, ere thou ask it me again.
I have been feasting with mine enemy,
Where on a sudden one hath wounded me,
That 's by me wounded; both our remedies
Within thy help and holy physic lies.
I bear no hatred, blessed man, for, lo,
My intercession likewise steads my foe.
Fri. L. Be plain, good son, and homely in thy drift;
Riddling confession finds but riddling shrift.
Rom. Then plainly know my heart's dear love is set
On the fair daughter of rich Capulet.
As mine on hers, so hers is set on mine;
And all combin'd, save what thou must combine
By holy marriage. When and where and how
We met, we woo'd, and made exchange of vow,
I 'll tell thee as we pass; but this I pray,
That thou consent to marry us to-day.
Fri. L. Holy Saint Francis, what a change is here!
Is Rosaline, that thou didst love so dear,
So soon forsaken? Young men's love then lies
Not truly in their hearts, but in their eyes.
Jesu Maria, what a deal of brine
Hath wash'd thy sallow cheeks for Rosaline!
How much salt water thrown away in waste,
To season love, that of it doth not taste!
The sun not yet thy sighs from heaven clears,
Thy old groans yet ringing in mine ancient ears;
Lo, here upon thy cheek the stain doth sit
Of an old tear that is not wash'd off yet.
If e'er thou wast thyself and these woes thine,
Thou and these woes were all for Rosaline.
And art thou chang'd? Pronounce this sentence then:
Women may fall, when there 's no strength in men.
Rom. Thou chid'st me oft for loving Rosaline.
Fri. L. For doting, not for loving, pupil mine.
Rom. And bad'st me bury love.
Fri. L. Not in a grave,
To lay one in, another out to have.
Rom. I pray thee, chide me not. Her I love now
Doth grace for grace and love for love allow;
The other did not so.
Fri. L. O, she knew well
Thy love did read by rote that could not spell.
But come, young waverer, come, go with me,
In one respect I 'll thy assistant be;
For this alliance may so happy prove,
To turn your households' rancour to pure love.
Rom. O, let us hence; I stand on sudden haste.
Fri. L. Wisely and slow; they stumble that run fast. *Exeunt.*

Scene IV. *A street.*

Enter *Benvolio* and *Mercutio*.

Mer. Where the devil should this Romeo be? Came he not home to-night?

Ben. Not to his father's; I spoke with his man.

Mer. Ah, that same pale hard-hearted wench, that Rosaline,
Torments him so, that he will sure run mad.

Ben. Tybalt, the kinsman of old Capulet,
Hath sent a letter to his father's house.

Mer. A challenge, on my life.

Ben. Romeo will answer it.

Mer. Any man that can write may answer a letter.

Ben. Nay, he will answer the letter's master, how he dares, being dared.

Mer. Alas, poor Romeo! he is already

28. grace, divine grace. **30. canker**, canker-worm. **33. distempered**, diseased. **52. physic**, healing art. **54. steads**, aids. **56. shrift**, absolution.

88. rote, memory. **93. stand on**, insist on. **Scene iv: 12. dared**, challenged.

dead; stabbed with a white wench's black eye; run through the ear with a love song; the very pin of his heart cleft with the blind bow-boy's butt-shaft: and is he a man to encounter Tybalt?

Ben. Why, what is Tybalt?

Mer. More than prince of cats. O, he 's the courageous captain of compliments: he fights as you sing prick-song; keeps time, distance, and proportion; he rests his minim rests, one, two, and the third in your bosom: the very butcher of a silk button; a duellist, a duellist; a gentleman of the very first house, of the first and second cause. Ah, the immortal *passado!* the *punto reverso!* the *hai!*

Ben. The what?

Mer. The pox of such antic, lisping, affecting fantasticoes; these new tuners of accent! "By Jesu, a very good blade! a very tall man! a very good whore!" Why, is not this a lamentable thing, grandsire, that we should be thus afflicted with these strange flies, these fashionmongers, these *pardona-mi's,* who stand so much on the new form, that they cannot sit at ease on the old bench? O, their bones, their bones!

Enter *Romeo.*

Ben. Here comes Romeo, here comes Romeo.

Mer. Without his roe, like a dried herring: O flesh, flesh, how art thou fishified! Now is he for the numbers that Petrarch flowed in: Laura to his lady was a kitchen-wench, marry, she had a better love to be-rhyme her; Dido a dowdy; Cleopatra a gipsy; Helen and Hero hildings and harlots; Thisbe, a grey eye or so, but not to the purpose. Signior Romeo, *bonjour!* There 's a French salutation to your French slop. You gave us the counterfeit fairly last night.

Rom. Good morrow to you both. What counterfeit did I give you?

Mer. The slip, sir, the slip; can you not conceive?

Rom. Pardon, good Mercutio, my business was great; and in such a case as mine a man may strain courtesy.

Mer. That 's as much as to say, such a case as yours constrains a man to bow in the hams.

Rom. Meaning, to curtsy.

Mer. Thou hast most kindly hit it.

Rom. A most courteous exposition.

Mer. Nay, I am the very pink of courtesy.

Rom. Pink for flower.

Mer. Right.

Rom. Why, then is my pump well flowered.

Mer. Sure wit! Follow me this jest now till thou hast worn out thy pump, that, when the single sole of it is worn, the jest may remain, after the wearing, solely singular.

Rom. O single-soled jest, solely singular for the singleness!

Mer. Come between us, good Benvolio; my wits faint.

Rom. Switch and spurs, switch and spurs; or I 'll cry a match.

Mer. Nay, if our wits run the wild-goose chase, I am done, for thou hast more of the wild-goose in one of thy wits than, I am sure, I have in my whole five. Was I with you there for the goose?

Rom. Thou wast never with me for anything when thou wast not there for the goose.

Mer. I will bite thee by the ear for that jest.

Rom. Nay, good goose, bite not.

Mer. Thy wit is a very bitter sweeting; it is a most sharp sauce.

Rom. And is it not, then, well served in to a sweet goose?

Mer. O, here 's a wit of cheveril, that stretches from an inch narrow to an ell broad!

Rom. I stretch it out for that word "broad"; which added to the goose, proves thee far and wide a broad goose.

Mer. Why, is not this better now than groaning for love? Now art thou sociable, now art thou Romeo, now art thou what thou art, by art as well as by nature; for this drivelling love is like a great natural, that runs lolling up and down to hide his bauble in a hole.

Ben. Stop there, stop there.

Mer. Thou desir'st me to stop in my tale against the hair.

Ben. Thou wouldst else have made thy tale large.

Mer. O, thou art deceived; I would have made it short; for I was come to the whole

15. **pin,** center of a target. 16. **butt-shaft,** blunt arrow for target shooting. 19. **prince of cats,** Tibert or Tibalt is the name of the cat in the old story of "Reynard the Fox." 21. **prick-song,** music sung by notes. 22. **proportion,** rhythm. **minim,** short note. 25. **first house,** best school of fencing. 26. **first and second cause,** recognized reasons for quarrel. 27. *passado,* etc., technical fencing terms for thrusts. 31. **tall,** brave. 35. *pardona-mi's,* people affecting foreign terms. 36. **form,** (1) fashion, (2) bench. 37. **bones,** pun on *bons.* 39. **without his roe,** in this pun Romeo =**Roe** (fish roe) and **me O** (a sigh). Nothing but the sigh is left. 44. **hildings,** worthless persons. 47. **slop,** large breeches. **counterfeit,** counterfeit coins were called "slips."

64. **pump well flowered,** this, and what follows, is an extreme example of the Elizabethan punning play on words. **To pink** in fencing is to touch or stab an opponent with the point of the rapier. Romeo's pumps are evidently "pinked" or perforated with holes in a flowered design. 69. **single-soled,** contemptible. 70. **singleness,** triviality. 85. **sweeting,** a sweet apple. 87. **cheveril,** kid leather. 88. **ell,** 45 inches. 96. **natural,** idiot. 100. **against the hair,** against the grain.

depth of my tale, and meant, indeed, to occupy the argument no longer.

Rom. Here 's goodly gear!

Enter *Nurse* and her man *Peter.*

A sail, a sail!

Mer. Two, two; a shirt and a smock.

Nurse. Peter!

Peter. Anon!

Nurse. My fan, Peter.

Mer. Good Peter, to hide her face; for her fan 's the fairer face.

Nurse. God ye good morrow, gentlemen.

Mer. God ye good den, fair gentlewoman.

Nurse. Is it good den?

Mer. 'T is no less, I tell ye; for the bawdy hand of the dial is now upon the prick of noon.

Nurse. Out upon you! what a man are you!

Rom. One, gentlewoman, that God hath made for himself to mar.

Nurse. By my troth, it is well said; "for himself to mar," quoth 'a! Gentlemen, can any of you tell me where I may find the young Romeo?

Rom. I can tell you; but young Romeo will be older when you have found him than he was when you sought him. I am the youngest of that name, for fault of a worse.

Nurse. You say well.

Mer. Yea, is the worst well? Very well took, i' faith; wisely, wisely.

Nurse. If you be he, sir, I desire some confidence with you.

Ben. She will indite him to some supper.

Mer. A bawd, a bawd, a bawd! So ho!

Rom. What hast thou found?

Mer. No hare, sir; unless a hare, sir, in a lenten pie, that is something stale and hoar ere it be spent. *Sings.*

"An old hare hoar,
And an old hare hoar,
Is very good meat in Lent;
But a hare that is hoar
Is too much for a score,
When it hoars ere it be spent."

Romeo, will you come to your father's? We 'll to dinner thither.

Rom. I will follow you.

Mer. Farewell, ancient lady; farewell, [*singing*] "lady, lady, lady."

Exeunt Mercutio and Benvolio.

Nurse. I pray you, sir, what saucy merchant was this, that was so full of his ropery?

Rom. A gentleman, nurse, that loves to hear himself talk, and will speak more in a minute than he will stand to in a month.

Nurse. An 'a speak anything against me, I 'll take him down, an 'a were lustier than he is, and twenty such Jacks; and if I cannot, I 'll find those that shall. Scurvy knave! I am none of his flirt-gills; I am none of his skains-mates.—And thou must stand by too, and suffer every knave to use me at his pleasure?

Peter. I saw no man use you at his pleasure; if I had, my weapon should quickly have been out. I warrant you, I dare draw as soon as another man, if I see occasion in a good quarrel, and the law on my side.

Nurse. Now, afore God, I am so vexed, that every part about me quivers. Scurvy knave! Pray you, sir, a word: and as I told you, my young lady bid me inquire you out; what she bid me say, I will keep to myself: but first let me tell ye, if ye should lead her into a fool's paradise, as they say, it were a very gross kind of behaviour, as they say; for the gentlewoman is young, and, therefore, if you should deal double with her, truly it were an ill thing to be offered to any gentlewoman, and very weak dealing.

Rom. Nurse, commend me to thy lady and mistress. I protest unto thee—

Nurse. Good heart, and, i' faith, I will tell her as much. Lord, Lord, she will be a joyful woman.

Rom. What wilt thou tell her, nurse? Thou dost not mark me.

Nurse. I will tell her, sir, that you do protest; which, as I take it, is a gentlemanlike offer.

Rom. Bid her devise
Some means to come to shrift this afternoon;
And there she shall at Friar Laurence' cell
Be shriv'd and married. Here is for thy pains.

Nurse. No, truly, sir; not a penny.

Rom. Go to; I say you shall.

Nurse. This afternoon, sir? Well, she shall be there.

Rom. And stay, good nurse;—behind the abbey wall
Within this hour my man shall be with thee,
And bring thee cords made like a tackled stair;
Which to the high top-gallant of my joy
Must be my convoy in the secret night.
Farewell; be trusty, and I 'll quit thy pains.
Farewell; commend me to thy mistress.

107. gear, matter. **134. confidence,** she means "conference." **135. indite,** conscious mistake for "invite." **136. So ho!,** the hunter's cry when he sights a hare. **153. ropery, roguery.**

160. Jacks, saucy fellows. **162. flirt-gills,** flirting women. **162-3. skains-mates,** (meaning uncertain) probably "ruffians." **201. tackled stair,** rope ladder. **203. convoy,** conveyance. **204. quit,** requite.

Nurse. Now God in heaven bless thee! Hark you, sir.
Rom. What say'st thou, my dear nurse?
Nurse. Is your man secret? Did you ne'er hear say,
"Two may keep counsel, putting one away"?
Rom. I warrant thee, my man 's as true as steel.

Nurse. Well, sir; my mistress is the sweetest lady—Lord, Lord! when 't was a little prating thing,—O, there is a nobleman in town, one Paris, that would fain lay knife aboard; but she, good soul, had as lief see a toad, a very toad, as see him. I anger her sometimes and tell her that Paris is the properer man; but, I 'll warrant you, when I say so, she looks as pale as any clout in the versal world. Doth not rosemary and Romeo begin both with a letter?

Rom. Ay, nurse; what of that? Both with an R.

Nurse. Ah, mocker! that 's the dog's name. R is for the—No; I know it begins with some other letter—and she hath the prettiest sententious of it, of you and rosemary, that it would do you good to hear it.

Rom. Commend me to thy lady.

Nurse. Ay, a thousand times. [*Exit Romeo.*] Peter!

Pet. Anon!

Nurse. Before, and apace. *Exeunt.*

Scene V. *Capulet's orchard.*

Enter *Juliet.*

Jul. The clock struck nine when I did send the nurse;
In half an hour she promis'd to return.
Perchance she cannot meet him: that 's not so.
O, she is lame! Love's heralds should be thoughts,
Which ten times faster glides than the sun's beams
Driving back shadows over louring hills.
Therefore do nimble-pinion'd doves draw Love,
And therefore hath the wind-swift Cupid wings.
Now is the sun upon the highmost hill
Of this day's journey, and from nine till twelve
Is three long hours, yet she is not come.
Had she affections and warm youthful blood,
She would be as swift in motion as a ball;
My words would bandy her to my sweet love,
And his to me;
But old folks, many, feign as they were dead;
Unwieldy, slow, heavy and pale as lead.

Enter *Nurse* and *Peter.*

O God, she comes! O honey nurse, what news?
Hast thou met with him? Send thy man away.
Nurse. Peter, stay at the gate.
Exit Peter.
Jul. Now, good sweet nurse,—O Lord, why lookest thou sad?
Though news be sad, yet tell them merrily;
If good, thou sham'st the music of sweet news
By playing it to me with so sour a face.
Nurse. I am a-weary, give me leave a while.
Fie, how my bones ache! What a jaunce have I had!
Jul. I would thou hadst my bones, and I thy news.
Nay, come, I pray thee, speak; good, good nurse, speak.
Nurse. Jesu, what haste! Can you not stay a while?
Do you not see that I am out of breath?
Jul. How art thou out of breath, when thou hast breath
To say to me that thou art out of breath?
The excuse that thou dost make in this delay
Is longer than the tale thou dost excuse.
Is thy news good, or bad? Answer to that;
Say either, and I 'll stay the circumstance.
Let me be satisfied, is 't good or bad?

Nurse. Well, you have made a simple choice; you know not how to choose a man. Romeo! no, not he; though his face be better than any man's, yet his leg excels all men's; and for a hand, and a foot, and a body, though they be not to be talked on, yet they are past compare. He is not the flower of courtesy, but, I 'll warrant him, as gentle as a lamb. Go thy ways, wench; serve God. What, have you dined at home?

Jul. No, no! But all this did I know before.
What says he of our marriage? What of that?
Nurse. Lord, how my head aches! What a head have I!
It beats as it would fall in twenty pieces.
My back o' t' other side,—O, my back, my back!
Beshrew your heart for sending me about
To catch my death with jauncing up and down!
Jul. I' faith, I am sorry that thou art not well.

217. properer, handsomer. **219. clout,** rag. **versal,** universal. **222-3. R . . . that's the dog's name,** R was commonly called the dog's letter. The Nurse means that Romeo's name cannot begin with that ugly letter. **225-6. sententious,** used for "sentences," i.e., proverbs. **Scene v: 14. bandy,** toss.

26. jaunce, jaunt. **36. stay the circumstance,** wait for the details.

Sweet, sweet, sweet nurse, tell me, what says my love?
Nurse. Your love says, like an honest gentleman, and a courteous, and a kind, and a handsome, and, I warrant, a virtuous,—Where is your mother?
Jul. Where is my mother? why, she is within;
Where should she be? How oddly thou repliest!
"Your love says, like an honest gentleman,
'Where is your mother?'"
Nurse. O God's lady dear!
Are you so hot? Marry, come up, I trow;
Is this the poultice for my aching bones?
Henceforward do your messages yourself.
Jul. Here 's such a coil!—Come, what says Romeo?
Nurse. Have you got leave to go to shrift to-day?
Jul. I have.
Nurse. Then hie you hence to Friar Laurence' cell;
There stays a husband to make you a wife:
Now comes the wanton blood up in your cheeks,
They 'll be in scarlet straight at any news.
Hie you to church; I must another way,
To fetch a ladder, by the which your love
Must climb a bird's nest soon when it is dark.
I am the drudge and toil in your delight,
But you shall bear the burden soon at night.
Go; I 'll to dinner; hie you to the cell.
Jul. Hie to high fortune! Honest nurse, farewell. *Exeunt.*

Scene VI. *Friar Laurence's cell.*

Enter *Friar Laurence* and *Romeo.*

Fri. L. So smile the heavens upon this holy act,
That after hours with sorrow chide us not!
Rom. Amen, amen! but come what sorrow can,
It cannot countervail the exchange of joy
That one short minute gives me in her sight.
Do thou but close our hands with holy words,
Then love-devouring Death do what he dare;
It is enough I may but call her mine.
Fri. L. These violent delights have violent ends,
And in their triumph die, like fire and powder,
Which as they kiss consume. The sweetest honey
Is loathsome in his own deliciousness
And in the taste confounds the appetite;
Therefore love moderately; long love doth so;
Too swift arrives as tardy as too slow.

Enter *Juliet.*

Here comes the lady. O, so light a foot
Will ne'er wear out the everlasting flint.
A lover may bestride the gossamer
That idles in the wanton summer air,
And yet not fall; so light is vanity.
Jul. Good even to my ghostly confessor.
Fri. L. Romeo shall thank thee, daughter, for us both.
Jul. As much to him, else is his thanks too much.
Rom. Ah, Juliet, if the measure of thy joy
Be heap'd like mine and that thy skill be more
To blazon it, then sweeten with thy breath
This neighbour air, and let rich music's tongue
Unfold the imagin'd happiness that both
Receive in either by this dear encounter.
Jul. Conceit, more rich in matter than in words,
Brags of his substance, not of ornament:
They are but beggars that can count their worth;
But my true love is grown to such excess
I cannot sum up sum of half my wealth.
Fri. L. Come, come with me, and we will make short work;
For, by your leaves, you shall not stay alone
Till Holy Church incorporate two in one.
Exeunt.

ACT III. Scene I. *A public place.*

Enter *Mercutio, Benvolio,* and men.

Ben. I pray thee, good Mercutio, let 's retire:
The day is hot, the Capulets abroad,
And, if we meet, we shall not scape a brawl,
For now, these hot days, is the mad blood stirring.
Mer. Thou art like one of these fellows that, when he enters the confines of a tavern,

67. coil, fuss.

Act II, Scene vi: 4. countervail, equal. 18. gossamer, spider-web. 26. blazon, proclaim. 30. conceit, imagination.

claps me his sword upon the table and says, "God send me no need of thee!" and by the operation of the second cup draws him on the drawer, when indeed there is no need.

Ben. Am I like such a fellow?

Mer. Come, come, thou art as hot a Jack in thy mood as any in Italy, and as soon moved to be moody, and as soon moody to be moved.

Ben. And what to?

Mer. Nay, an there were two such, we should have none shortly, for one would kill the other. Thou! why, thou wilt quarrel with a man that hath a hair more, or a hair less, in his beard, than thou hast. Thou wilt quarrel with a man for cracking nuts, having no other reason but because thou hast hazel eyes. What eye but such an eye would spy out such a quarrel? Thy head is as full of quarrels as an egg is full of meat, and yet thy head hath been beaten as addle as an egg for quarrelling. Thou hast quarrelled with a man for coughing in the street, because he hath wakened thy dog that hath lain asleep in the sun. Didst thou not fall out with a tailor for wearing his new doublet before Easter? with another, for tying his new shoes with old riband? And yet thou wilt tutor me for quarrelling!

Ben. An I were so apt to quarrel as thou art, any man should buy the fee-simple of my life for an hour and a quarter.

Mer. The fee-simple! O simple!

Enter *Tybalt, Petruchio,* and others.

Ben. By my head, here comes the Capulets.

Mer. By my heel, I care not.

Tyb. Follow me close, for I will speak to them.
Gentlemen, good den; a word with one of you.

Mer. And but one word with one of us? Couple it with something; make it a word and a blow.

Tyb. You shall find me apt enough to that, sir, an you will give occasion.

Mer. Could you not take some occasion without giving?

Tyb. Mercutio, thou consortest with Romeo,—

Mer. Consort! what, dost thou make us minstrels? An thou make minstrels of us, look to hear nothing but discords. Here 's my fiddle-stick; here 's that shall make you dance. 'Zounds, consort!

Ben. We talk here in the public haunt of men:
Either withdraw unto some private place,
Or reason coldly of your grievances,
Or else depart; here all eyes gaze on us.

Mer. Men's eyes were made to look, and let them gaze;
I will not budge for no man's pleasure, I.

Enter *Romeo.*

Tyb. Well, peace be with you, sir; here comes my man.

Mer. But I 'll be hang'd, sir, if he wear your livery.
Marry, go before to field, he 'll be your follower;
Your worship in that sense may call him "man."

Tyb. Romeo, the love I bear thee can afford
No better term than this: thou art a villain.

Rom. Tybalt, the reason that I have to love thee
Doth much excuse the appertaining rage
To such a greeting. Villain am I none;
Therefore farewell; I see thou know'st me not.

Tyb. Boy, this shall not excuse the injuries
That thou hast done me; therefore turn and draw.

Rom. I do protest I never injured thee,
But love thee better than thou canst devise
Till thou shalt know the reason of my love;
And so, good Capulet,—which name I tender
As dearly as mine own,—be satisfied.

Mer. O calm, dishonourable, vile submission!
Alla stoccata carries it away. *Draws.*
Tybalt, you rat-catcher, will you walk?

Tyb. What wouldst thou have with me?

Mer. Good king of cats, nothing but one of your nine lives; that I mean to make bold withal, and, as you shall use me hereafter, dry-beat the rest of the eight. Will you pluck your sword out of his pilcher by the ears? Make haste, lest mine be about your ears ere it be out.

Tyb. I am for you. *Drawing.*

Rom. Gentle Mercutio, put thy rapier up.

Mer. Come, sir, your *passado. They fight.*

Rom. Draw, Benvolio; beat down their weapons.
Gentlemen, for shame, forbear this outrage!
Tybalt, Mercutio, the Prince expressly hath
Forbid this bandying in Verona streets.
Hold, Tybalt! Good Mercutio!

10. drawer, waiter. **14. moody,** angry. **35. fee-simple,** absolute ownership. **37. S. d.: Petruchio,** cf. 1. 5. 134 above. **49. Consort,** (1) keep company with, (2) band of musicians.

74. tender, hold. **77.** *Alla stoccata,* a thrust, here figuratively of Tybalt. **82-3. dry-beat,** to beat without drawing blood. **84. pilcher,** scabbard.

Tybalt under Romeo's arm thrusts Mercutio in, and flies with the other Capulets.

Mer. I am hurt.
A plague o' both your houses! I am sped.
Is he gone, and hath nothing?
Ben. What, art thou hurt?
Mer. Ay, ay, a scratch, a scratch; marry, 't is enough.
Where is my page? Go, villain, fetch a surgeon. *Exit Page.*
Rom. Courage, man; the hurt cannot be much.

Mer. No, 't is not so deep as a well, nor so wide as a church-door; but 't is enough, 't will serve: ask for me to-morrow, and you shall find me a grave man. I am peppered, I warrant, for this world. A plague o' both your houses! 'Zounds, a dog, a rat, a mouse, a cat, to scratch a man to death! a braggart, a rogue, a villain, that fights by the book of arithmetic! Why the devil came you between us? I was hurt under your arm.

Rom. I thought all for the best.
Mer. Help me into some house, Benvolio,
Or I shall faint. A plague o' both your houses!
They have made worms' meat of me. I have it,
And soundly too. Your houses!
Exeunt Mercutio and Benvolio.
Rom. This gentleman, the Prince's near ally,
My very friend, hath got his mortal hurt
In my behalf; my reputation stain'd
With Tybalt's slander,—Tybalt, that an hour
Hath been my cousin! O sweet Juliet,
Thy beauty hath made me effeminate
And in my temper soften'd valour's steel!

Re-enter *Benvolio.*

Ben. O Romeo, Romeo, brave Mercutio's dead!
That gallant spirit hath aspir'd the clouds.
Which too untimely here did scorn the earth.
Rom. This day's black fate on moe days doth depend;
This but begins the woe others must end.
Ben. Here comes the furious Tybalt back again.

Re-enter *Tybalt.*

Rom. Alive, in triumph! and Mercutio slain!
Away to heaven, respective lenity,
And fire-ey'd fury be my conduct now!
Now, Tybalt, take the villain back again,
That late thou gav'st me; for Mercutio's soul
Is but a little way above our heads,
Staying for thine to keep him company.
Either thou, or I, or both, must go with him.
Tyb. Thou, wretched boy, that didst consort him here,
Shalt with him hence.
Rom. This shall determine that.
They fight; Tybalt falls.
Ben. Romeo, away, be gone!
The citizens are up, and Tybalt slain.
Stand not amaz'd; the Prince will doom thee death
If thou art taken. Hence, be gone, away!
Rom. O, I am fortune's fool!
Ben. Why dost thou stay?
Exit Romeo.

Enter *Citizens.*

First Cit. Which way ran he that kill'd Mercutio?
Tybalt, that murderer, which way ran he?
Ben. There lies that Tybalt.
First Cit. Up, sir, go with me;
I charge thee in the Prince's name, obey.

Enter *Prince, Old Montague, Capulet, their Wives,* and all.

Prin. Where are the vile beginners of this fray?
Ben. O noble Prince, I can discover all
The unlucky manage of this fatal brawl:
There lies the man, slain by young Romeo,
That slew thy kinsman, brave Mercutio.
La. Cap. Tybalt, my cousin! O my brother's child!
O Prince! O cousin! husband! O, the blood is spilt
Of my dear kinsman! Prince, as thou art true,
For blood of ours, shed blood of Montague.
O cousin, cousin!
Prin. Benvolio, who began this bloody fray?
Ben. Tybalt, here slain, whom Romeo's hand did slay!
Romeo that spoke him fair, bid him bethink
How nice the quarrel was, and urg'd withal
Your high displeasure; all this uttered
With gentle breath, calm look, knees humbly bow'd,
Could not take truce with the unruly spleen
Of Tybalt deaf to peace, but that he tilts
With piercing steel at bold Mercutio's breast,
Who, all as hot, turns deadly point to point,
And, with a martial scorn, with one hand beats
Cold death aside, and with the other sends
It back to Tybalt, whose dexterity
Retorts it. Romeo he cries aloud,

94. sped, done for. **122. aspir'd,** attained. **124. moe,** more. **128. respective,** considerate. **129. conduct,** guide. **147. discover,** reveal. **159. nice,** trivial. **162. take truce,** make peace.

"Hold, friends! friends, part!" and, swifter than his tongue,
His agile arm beats down their fatal points,
And 'twixt them rushes; underneath whose arm
An envious thrust from Tybalt hit the life
Of stout Mercutio, and then Tybalt fled;
But by and by comes back to Romeo,
Who had but newly entertain'd revenge,
And to 't they go like lightning, for, ere I
Could draw to part them, was stout Tybalt slain,
And, as he fell, did Romeo turn and fly.
This is the truth, or let Benvolio die.

La. Cap. He is a kinsman to the Montague;
Affection makes him false; he speaks not true.
Some twenty of them fought in this black strife,
And all those twenty could but kill one life.
I beg for justice, which thou, Prince, must give;
Romeo slew Tybalt, Romeo must not live.

Prin. Romeo slew him, he slew Mercutio;
Who now the price of his dear blood doth owe?

Mon. Not Romeo, Prince, he was Mercutio's friend;
His fault concludes but what the law should end,
The life of Tybalt.

Prin. And for that offence
Immediately we do exile him hence:
I have an interest in your hate's proceeding,
My blood for your rude brawls doth lie a-bleeding;
But I 'll amerce you with so strong a fine
That you shall all repent the loss of mine.
I will be deaf to pleading and excuses;
Nor tears nor prayers shall purchase out abuses;
Therefore use none. Let Romeo hence in haste,
Else, when he 's found, that hour is his last.
Bear hence this body and attend our will.
Mercy but murders, pardoning those that kill.
Exeunt.

Scene II. *Capulet's orchard.*

Enter *Juliet,* alone.

Jul. Gallop apace, you fiery-footed steeds,
Towards Phœbus' lodging; such a waggoner
As Phaethon would whip you to the west,
And bring in cloudy night immediately.
Spread thy close curtain, love-performing night,
That runaway's eyes may wink; and, Romeo,
Leap to these arms, untalk'd of and unseen.
Lovers can see to do their amorous rites,
By their own beauties; or, if love be blind,
It best agrees with night. Come, civil night,
Thou sober-suited matron, all in black,
And learn me how to lose a winning match,
Play'd for a pair of stainless maidenhoods.
Hood my unmann'd blood, bating in my cheeks,
With thy black mantle; till strange love grow bold,
Think true love acted, simple modesty.
Come, night; come, Romeo; come, thou day in night;
For thou wilt lie upon the wings of night,
Whiter than new snow on a raven's back.
Come, gentle night, come, loving, black-brow'd night,
Give me my Romeo; and, when he shall die,
Take him and cut him out in little stars,
And he will make the face of heaven so fine
That all the world will be in love with night,
And pay no worship to the garish sun.
O, I have bought the mansion of a love,
But not possess'd it, and, though I am sold,
Not yet enjoy'd: so tedious is this day
As is the night before some festival
To an impatient child that hath new robes
And may not wear them. O, here comes my nurse,

Enter *Nurse,* with cords.

And she brings news; and every tongue that speaks
But Romeo's name speaks heavenly eloquence.
Now, nurse, what news? What hast thou there? The cords
That Romeo bid thee fetch?

Nurse. Ay, ay, the cords.
Throws them down.

Jul. Ay me! what news? Why dost thou wring thy hands?

Nurse. Ah, well-a-day! he 's dead, he 's dead, he 's dead!
We are undone, lady, we are undone!
Alack the day! he 's gone, he 's kill'd, he 's dead!

Jul. Can heaven be so envious?

Nurse. Romeo can,
Though heaven cannot. O Romeo, Romeo!
Who ever would have thought it? Romeo!

173. envious, malicious. **195. amerce,** punish by fine.

Scene ii: 6. That runaway's eyes, this is one of the most disputed passages in Shakespeare. There are dozens of interpretations, but one that seems to harmonize with the context as well as any is that **runaway's** refers to the sun, perhaps with a reference to Phaethon, and that when his eyes close (wink) the night will come and cover the lovers. **10. civil,** grave. **14. Hood** (blindfold), **unmann'd** (untamed), **bating** (fluttering): terms in falconry.

Jul. What devil art thou, that dost torment me thus?
This torture should be roar'd in dismal hell.
Hath Romeo slain himself? Say thou but ay,
And that bare vowel *"I"* shall poison more
Than the death-darting eye of cockatrice:
I am not I, if there be such an ay;
Or those eyes shut, that makes thee answer ay.
If he be slain, say ay; or if not, no.
Brief sounds determine of my weal or woe.

Nurse. I saw the wound, I saw it with mine eyes,—
God save the mark!—here on his manly breast:
A piteous corse, a bloody piteous corse!
Pale, pale as ashes, all bedaub'd in blood,
All in gore-blood; I swounded at the sight.

Jul. O, break, my heart! poor bankrupt, break at once!
To prison, eyes, ne'er look on liberty!
Vile earth, to earth resign; end motion here;
And thou and Romeo press one heavy bier!

Nurse. O Tybalt, Tybalt, the best friend I had!
O courteous Tybalt! honest gentleman!
That ever I should live to see thee dead!

Jul. What storm is this that blows so contrary?
Is Romeo slaughter'd, and is Tybalt dead?
My dearest cousin, and my dearer lord?
Then, dreadful trumpet, sound the general doom!
For who is living, if those two are gone?

Nurse. Tybalt is gone, and Romeo banished;
Romeo that kill'd him, he is banished.

Jul. O God! did Romeo's hand shed Tybalt's blood?

Nurse. It did, it did; alas the day, it did!

Jul. O serpent heart, hid with a flow'ring face!
Did ever dragon keep so fair a cave?
Beautiful tyrant! fiend angelical!
Dove-feather'd raven! wolvish ravenous lamb!
Despised substance of divinest show!
Just opposite to what thou justly seem'st,
A damned saint, an honourable villain!
O nature, what hadst thou to do in hell,
When thou didst bower the spirit of a fiend
In mortal paradise of such sweet flesh?
Was ever book containing such vile matter
So fairly bound? O, that deceit should dwell
In such a gorgeous palace!

Nurse. There 's no trust,
No faith, no honesty in men; all perjur'd,
All forsworn, all naught, all dissemblers.
Ah, where 's my man? Give me some *aqua vitæ;*
These griefs, these woes, these sorrows make me old.
Shame come to Romeo!

Jul. Blister'd be thy tongue
For such a wish! he was not born to shame.
Upon his brow shame is asham'd to sit;
For 't is a throne where honour may be crown'd
Sole monarch of the universal earth.
O, what a beast was I to chide at him!

Nurse. Will you speak well of him that kill'd your cousin?

Jul. Shall I speak ill of him that is my husband?
Ah, poor my lord, what tongue shall smooth thy name,
When I, thy three-hours wife, have mangled it?
But wherefore, villain, didst thou kill my cousin?
That villain cousin would have kill'd my husband.
Back, foolish tears, back to your native spring;
Your tributary drops belong to woe,
Which you, mistaking, offer up to joy.
My husband lives, that Tybalt would have slain;
And Tybalt's dead, that would have slain my husband.
All this is comfort; wherefore weep I then?
Some word there was, worser than Tybalt's death,
That murder'd me; I would forget it fain;
But, O, it presses to my memory
Like damned guilty deeds to sinners' minds:
"Tybalt is dead, and Romeo—banished."
That "banished," that one word "banished,"
Hath slain ten thousand Tybalts. Tybalt's death
Was woe enough, if it had ended there;
Or, if sour woe delights in fellowship
And needly will be rank'd with other griefs,
Why follow'd not, when she said, "Tybalt 's dead,"
Thy father, or thy mother, nay, or both,
Which modern lamentation might have mov'd?
But with a rear-ward following Tybalt's death,
"Romeo is banished," to speak that word,
Is father, mother, Tybalt, Romeo, Juliet,
All slain, all dead. "Romeo is banished!"
There is no end, no limit, measure, bound,
In that word's death; no words can that woe sound.
Where is my father and my mother, nurse?

47. **cockatrice**, fabulous animal, supposed to kill with a glance. 56. **gore-blood**, clotted blood. 59. **Vile earth**, wretched body. **resign**, yield.

88. *aqua vitæ*, brandy. 117. **needly**, of necessity. 120. **modern**, ordinary.

Nurse. Weeping and wailing over Tybalt's corse.
Will you go to them? I will bring you thither.
Jul. Wash they his wounds with tears? Mine shall be spent,
When theirs are dry, for Romeo's banishment.
Take up those cords. Poor ropes, you are beguil'd,
Both you and I, for Romeo is exil'd:
He made you for a highway to my bed,
But I, a maid, die maiden-widowed.
Come, cords, come, nurse; I 'll to my wedding-bed;
And death, not Romeo, take my maidenhead!
Nurse. Hie to your chamber. I 'll find Romeo
To comfort you; I wot well where he is.
Hark ye, your Romeo will be here at night.
I 'll to him; he is hid at Laurence' cell.
Jul. O, find him! Give this ring to my true knight,
And bid him come to take his last farewell.
Exeunt.

Scene III. *Friar Laurence's cell.*

Enter *Friar Laurence.*

Fri. L. Romeo, come forth; come forth, thou fearful man:
Affliction is enamour'd of thy parts,
And thou art wedded to calamity.

Enter *Romeo.*

Rom. Father, what news? What is the Prince's doom?
What sorrow craves acquaintance at my hand,
That I yet know not?
Fri. L. Too familiar
Is my dear son with such sour company.
I bring thee tidings of the Prince's doom.
Rom. What less than dooms-day is the Prince's doom?
Fri. L. A gentler judgement vanish'd from his lips,
Not body's death, but body's banishment.
Rom. Ha, banishment! Be merciful, say death;
For exile hath more terror in his look,
Much more than death. Do not say banishment!
Fri. L. Here from Verona art thou banished.
Be patient, for the world is broad and wide.
Rom. There is no world without Verona walls,
But purgatory, torture, hell itself.
Hence banished is banish'd from the world.
And world's exile is death; then "banished"
Is death mis-term'd: calling death "banishment,"
Thou cut'st my head off with a golden axe,
And smilest upon the stroke that murders me.
Fri. L. O deadly sin! O rude unthankfulness!
Thy fault our law calls death; but the kind Prince,
Taking thy part, hath rush'd aside the law,
And turn'd that black word death to banishment.
This is dear mercy, and thou seest it not.
Rom. 'T is torture, and not mercy. Heaven is here,
Where Juliet lives; and every cat and dog
And little mouse, every unworthy thing,
Live here in heaven and may look on her;
But Romeo may not. More validity,
More honourable state, more courtship lives
In carrion-flies than Romeo; they may seize
On the white wonder of dear Juliet's hand
And steal immortal blessing from her lips,
Who, even in pure and vestal modesty,
Still blush, as thinking their own kisses sin;
But Romeo may not; he is banished.
This may flies do, when I from this must fly;
They are free men, but I am banished:
And say'st thou yet that exile is not death?
Hadst thou no poison mix'd, no sharp-ground knife,
No sudden mean of death, though ne'er so mean,
But "banished" to kill me?—"Banished"?
O friar, the damned use that word in hell;
Howlings attend it. How hast thou the heart,
Being a divine, a ghostly confessor,
A sin-absolver, and my friend profess'd,
To mangle me with that word "banished"?
Fri. L. Thou fond mad man, hear me a little speak.
Rom. O, thou wilt speak again of banishment.
Fri. L. I 'll give thee armour to keep off that word;
Adversity's sweet milk, philosophy,
To comfort thee, though thou art banished.
Rom. Yet "banished"? Hang up philosophy!
Unless philosophy can make a Juliet,
Displant a town, reverse a prince's doom,
It helps not, it prevails not. Talk no more.
Fri. L. O, then I see that madmen have no ears.
Rom. How should they, when that wise men have no eyes?

10. vanish'd, issued.

26. rush'd, brushed. **33. validity,** worth. **45. mean,** means. **so mean,** so base. **52. fond,** foolish

Fri. L. Let me dispute with thee of thy estate.
Rom. Thou canst not speak of that thou dost not feel.
Wert thou as young as I, Juliet thy love,
An hour but married, Tybalt murdered,
Doting like me and like me banished,
Then mightst thou speak, then mightst thou tear thy hair,
And fall upon the ground, as I do now,
Taking the measure of an unmade grave.
Knocking within.
Fri. L. Arise; one knocks: good Romeo, hide thyself.
Rom. Not I; unless the breath of heart-sick groans,
Mist-like, infold me from the search of eyes.
Knocking.
Fri. L. Hark, how they knock! Who 's there? Romeo, arise;
Thou wilt be taken—Stay a while!—Stand up; *Knocking.*
Run to my study.—By and by!—God's will,
What simpleness is this!—I come, I come!
Knocking.
Who knocks so hard? Whence come you? What 's your will?

Enter *Nurse.*

Nurse. Let me come in, and you shall know my errand:
I come from Lady Juliet.
Fri. L. Welcome, then.
Nurse. O holy friar, O, tell me, holy friar,
Where is my lady's lord, where 's Romeo?
Fri. L. There on the ground, with his own tears made drunk.
Nurse. O, he is even in my mistress' case,
Just in her case! O woeful sympathy!
Piteous predicament! Even so lies she,
Blubb'ring and weeping, weeping and blubb'ring.
Stand up, stand up; stand, an you be a man.
For Juliet's sake, for her sake, rise and stand,
Why should you fall into so deep an O?
Rom. Nurse!
Nurse. Ah sir! ah sir! Death 's the end of all.
Rom. Spakest thou of Juliet? How is it with her?
Doth she not think me an old murderer,
Now I have stain'd the childhood of our joy
With blood remov'd but little from her own?
Where is she? and how doth she? and what says
My conceal'd lady to our cancell'd love?
Nurse. O, she says nothing, sir, but weeps and weeps;
And now falls on her bed; and then starts up,
And Tybalt calls; and then on Romeo cries,
And then down falls again.
Rom. As if that name,
Shot from the deadly level of a gun,
Did murder her, as that name's cursed hand
Murder'd her kinsman. O, tell me, friar, tell me,
In what vile part of this anatomy
Doth my name lodge? Tell me, that I may sack
The hateful mansion.
He offers to stab himself, and the Nurse snatches the dagger away.
Fri. L. Hold thy desperate hand!
Art thou a man? Thy form cries out thou art;
Thy tears are womanish; thy wild acts denote
The unreasonable fury of a beast.
Unseemly woman in a seeming man,
And ill-beseeming beast in seeming both,
Thou hast amaz'd me! By my holy order,
I thought thy disposition better temper'd.
Hast thou slain Tybalt? Wilt thou slay thyself,
And slay thy lady that in thy life lives,
By doing damned hate upon thyself?
Why rail'st thou on thy birth, the heaven, and earth?
Since birth, and heaven, and earth, all three do meet
In thee at once, which thou at once wouldst lose.
Fie, fie, thou sham'st thy shape, thy love, thy wit;
Which, like a usurer, abound'st in all,
And usest none in that true use indeed
Which should bedeck thy shape, thy love, thy wit.
Thy noble shape is but a form of wax,
Digressing from the valour of a man;
Thy dear love sworn but hollow perjury,
Killing that love which thou hast vow'd to cherish;
Thy wit, that ornament to shape and love,
Mis-shapen in the conduct of them both,
Like powder in a skilless soldier's flask,
Is set a-fire by thine own ignorance,
And thou dismember'd with thine own defence.
What, rouse thee, man! thy Juliet is alive,
For whose dear sake thou wast but lately dead:
There art thou happy. Tybalt would kill thee,
But thou slewest Tybalt: there art thou happy.
The law that threaten'd death becomes thy friend
And turns it to exile: there art thou happy.

63. dispute, reason. **estate,** condition. **90. O,** groan. **98. conceal'd,** secretly married.

103. level, aim. **123. Which,** who. **127. Digressing,** deviating. **134. defence,** means of defence.

A pack of blessings light upon thy back;
Happiness courts thee in his best array;
But, like a misbehav'd and sullen wench,
Thou pouts upon thy fortune and thy love:
Take heed, take heed, for such die miserable.
Go, get thee to thy love, as was decreed;
Ascend her chamber; hence! and comfort her.
But look thou stay not till the watch be set,
For then thou canst not pass to Mantua,
Where thou shalt live till we can find a time
To blaze your marriage, reconcile your friends,
Beg pardon of the Prince, and call thee back
With twenty hundred thousand times more joy
Than thou went'st forth in lamentation.
Go before, nurse; commend me to thy lady;
And bid her hasten all the house to bed,
Which heavy sorrow makes them apt unto.
Romeo is coming.

Nurse. O Lord, I could have stay'd here all the night
To hear good counsel. O, what learning is!
My lord, I 'll tell my lady you will come.

Rom. Do so, and bid my sweet prepare to chide.

Nurse offers to go in, and turns again.

Nurse. Here, sir, a ring she bid me give you, sir.
Hie you, make haste, for it grows very late.

Rom. How well my comfort is reviv'd by this! *Exit Nurse.*

Fri. L. Go hence; good-night; and here stands all your state:
Either be gone before the watch be set,
Or by the break of day disguis'd from hence.
Sojourn in Mantua; I 'll find out your man,
And he shall signify from time to time
Every good hap to you that chances here:
Give me thy hand; 't is late. Farewell; good-night.

Rom. But that a joy past joy calls out on me,
It were a grief, so brief to part with thee.
Farewell. *Exeunt.*

Scene IV. *A room in Capulet's house.*

Enter old *Capulet, his Wife,* and *Paris.*

Cap. Things have fallen out, sir, so unluckily
That we have had no time to move our daughter:
Look you, she lov'd her kinsman Tybalt dearly,
And so did I. Well, we were born to die.
'T is very late, she 'll not come down to-night;
I promise you, but for your company,
I would have been a-bed an hour ago.

Par. These times of woe afford no times to woo.
Madam, good-night; commend me to your daughter.

La. Cap. I will, and know her mind early to-morrow;
To-night she 's mewed up to her heaviness.

Paris offers to go in and Capulet calls him again.

Cap. Sir Paris, I will make a desperate tender
Of my child's love: I think she will be rul'd
In all respects by me; nay, more, I doubt it not.
Wife, go you to her ere you go to bed;
Acquaint her here of my son Paris' love;
And bid her—mark you me—on Wednesday next—
But, soft! what day is this?

Par. Monday, my lord.

Cap. Monday! ha, ha! Well, Wednesday is too soon,
O' Thursday let it be,—o' Thursday, tell her,
She shall be married to this noble earl.
Will you be ready? Do you like this haste?
We 'll keep no great ado,—a friend or two;
For, hark you, Tybalt being slain so late,
It may be thought we held him carelessly,
Being our kinsman, if we revel much;
Therefore we 'll have some half a dozen friends,
And there an end. But what say you to Thursday?

Par. My lord, I would that Thursday were to-morrow.

Cap. Well, get you gone; o' Thursday be it, then.
Go you to Juliet ere you go to bed;
Prepare her, wife, against this wedding-day.
Farewell, my lord. Light to my chamber, ho!
Afore me! it is so very late that we
May call it early by and by. Good-night.
Exeunt.

Scene V. *Capulet's orchard.*

Enter *Romeo* and *Juliet,* aloft.

Jul. Wilt thou be gone? it is not yet near day:
It was the nightingale, and not the lark,
That pierc'd the fearful hollow of thine ear;
Nightly she sings on yond pomegranate-tree.
Believe me, love, it was the nightingale.

148. watch, guard. **151. blaze,** announce. **166. and . . . state,** this is the state of your affairs. **174. brief,** briefly.

Scene iv: 11. mewed up, shut up. **12. desperate tender,** bold offer. **Scene v: S. d.: aloft,** on the stage balcony.

Rom. It was the lark, the herald of the morn,
No nightingale: look, love, what envious streaks
Do lace the severing clouds in yonder east:
Night's candles are burnt out, and jocund day
Stands tiptoe on the misty mountain tops:
I must be gone and live, or stay and die.
Jul. Yond light is not day-light, I know it, I;
It is some meteor that the sun exhales,
To be to thee this night a torch-bearer,
And light thee on thy way to Mantua;
Therefore stay yet; thou need'st not to be gone.
Rom. Let me be ta'en, let me be put to death;
I am content, so thou wilt have it so.
I 'll say yon grey is not the morning's eye,
'T is but the pale reflex of Cynthia's brow;
Nor that is not the lark, whose notes do beat
The vaulty heaven so high above our heads:
I have more care to stay than will to go:
Come, death, and welcome! Juliet wills it so.
How is 't, my soul? Let 's talk; it is not day.
Jul. It is, it is! Hie hence, be gone, away!
It is the lark that sings so out of tune,
Straining harsh discords and unpleasing sharps.
Some say the lark makes sweet division;
This does not so, for she divideth us.
Some say the lark and loathed toad change eyes;
O, now I would they had chang'd voices too!
Since arm from arm that voice doth us affray,
Hunting thee hence with hunt's-up to the day.
O, now be gone; more light and light it grows.
Rom. More light and light; more dark and dark our woes!

Enter *Nurse*

Nurse. Madam!
Jul. Nurse?
Nurse. Your lady mother is coming to your chamber:
The day is broke; be wary, look about.
Exit.
Jul. Then, window, let day in, and let life out.
Rom. Farewell, farewell! One kiss, and I 'll descend. *He goeth down.*
Jul. Art thou gone so? Love, lord, ay, husband, friend!
I must hear from thee every day in the hour,
For in a minute there are many days:
O, by this count I shall be much in years
Ere I again behold my Romeo!
Rom. Farewell!
I will omit no opportunity
That may convey my greetings, love, to thee.
Jul. O think'st thou we shall ever meet again?
Rom. I doubt it not; and all these woes shall serve
For sweet discourses in our times to come.
Jul. O God, I have an ill-divining soul!
Methinks I see thee, now thou art below,
As one dead in the bottom of a tomb.
Either my eyesight fails, or thou look'st pale.
Rom. And trust me, love, in my eye so do you;
Dry sorrow drinks our blood. Adieu, adieu!
Exit.
Jul. O Fortune, Fortune! all men call thee fickle;
If thou art fickle, what dost thou with him
That is renown'd for faith? Be fickle, Fortune;
For then, I hope, thou wilt not keep him long,
But send him back.

Enter *Lady Capulet.*

La. Cap. Ho, daughter! are you up?
Jul. Who is 't that calls? It is my lady mother.
Is she not down so late, or up so early?
What unaccustom'd cause procures her hither?
La. Cap. Why, how now, Juliet?
Jul. Madam, I am not well.
La. Cap. Evermore weeping for your cousin's death?
What, wilt thou wash him from his grave with tears?
An if thou couldst, thou couldst not make him live;
Therefore, have done: some grief shows much of love,
But much of grief shows still some want of wit.
Jul. Yet let me weep for such a feeling loss.
La. Cap. So shall you feel the loss, but not the friend
Which you weep for.
Jul. Feeling so the loss,
I cannot choose but ever weep the friend.
La. Cap. Well, girl, thou weep'st not so much for his death,
As that the villain lives which slaughter'd him.

20. reflex, reflected light. **23. care,** desire. **28. sharps,** high notes. **29. division,** melody. **33. affray,** frighten. **34. hunt's-up,** song to arouse hunters. **42. He goeth down,** this old s. d. shows that Romeo descended from the balcony to the front stage, probably by the rope-ladder (cords, cf. 3. 2. 34). His last farewell is spoken from the front stage to Juliet on the balcony.

54. ill-divining, evil-foreboding. **59. Dry sorrow,** grief and sighing were popularly supposed to exhaust the blood and make one pale. **64.** An old s. d. at this point reads: *She goeth down from the window.* This probably means that Juliet descended from the balcony to meet her mother in the inner stage which would be the "chamber" of l. 39. **67. down,** in bed. **75. feeling,** affecting.

Jul. What villain, madam?
La. Cap. That same villain, Romeo.
Jul. [*Aside.*] Villain and he be many miles asunder.—
God pardon him! I do, with all my heart;
And yet no man like he doth grieve my heart.
La. Cap. That is, because the traitor murderer lives.
Jul. Ay, madam, from the reach of these my hands:
Would none but I might venge my cousin's death!
La. Cap. We will have vengeance for it, fear thou not;
Then weep no more. I 'll send to one in Mantua,
Where that same banish'd runagate doth live,
Shall give him such an unaccustom'd dram,
That he shall soon keep Tybalt company;
And then, I hope, thou wilt be satisfied.
Jul. Indeed, I never shall be satisfied
With Romeo, till I behold him—dead—
Is my poor heart, so for a kinsman vex'd.
Madam, if you could find out but a man
To bear a poison, I would temper it
That Romeo should, upon receipt thereof,
Soon sleep in quiet. O, how my heart abhors
To hear him nam'd, and cannot come to him,
To wreak the love I bore my cousin Tybalt
Upon his body that hath slaughter'd him!
La. Cap. Find thou the means, and I 'll find such a man.
But now I 'll tell thee joyful tidings, girl.
Jul. And joy comes well in such a needy time.
What are they, beseech your ladyship?
La. Cap. Well, well, thou hast a careful father, child;
One who, to put thee from thy heaviness,
Hath sorted out a sudden day of joy,
That thou expects not nor I look'd not for.
Jul. Madam, in happy time, what day is that?
La. Cap. Marry, my child, early next Thursday morn,
The gallant, young, and noble gentleman,
The County Paris, at Saint Peter's Church,
Shall happily make thee there a joyful bride.
Jul. Now, by Saint Peter's Church and Peter too,
He shall not make me there a joyful bride.
I wonder at this haste; that I must wed
Ere he that should be husband comes to woo.
I pray you, tell my lord and father, madam,
I will not marry yet; and, when I do, I swear,
It shall be Romeo, whom you know I hate,
Rather than Paris. These are news indeed!
La. Cap. Here comes your father; tell him so yourself,
And see how he will take it at your hands.

Enter *Capulet* and *Nurse.*

Cap. When the sun sets, the air doth drizzle dew;
But for the sunset of my brother's son
It rains downright.
How now! a conduit, girl? What, still in tears?
Evermore show'ring? In one little body
Thou counterfeits a bark, a sea, a wind:
For still thy eyes, which I may call the sea,
Do ebb and flow with tears; the bark thy body is,
Sailing in this salt flood; the winds, thy sighs;
Who, raging with thy tears, and they with them,
Without a sudden calm, will overset
Thy tempest-tossed body. How now, wife!
Have you delivered to her our decree?
La. Cap. Ay, sir; but she will none, she gives you thanks.
I would the fool were married to her grave!
Cap. Soft! take me with you, take me with you, wife.
How! will she none? Doth she not give us thanks?
Is she not proud? Doth she not count her blest,
Unworthy as she is, that we have wrought
So worthy a gentleman to be her bride?
Jul. Not proud, you have; but thankful that you have.
Proud can I never be of what I hate;
But thankful even for hate, that is meant love.
Cap. How, how, how, how, chop-logic? What is this?
"Proud," and "I thank you," and "I thank you not;"
And yet "not proud." Mistress minion, you,
Thank me no thankings, nor proud me no prouds,
But fettle your fine joints 'gainst Thursday next,
To go with Paris to Saint Peter's Church,
Or I will drag thee on a hurdle thither.
Out, you green-sickness carrion! Out, you baggage!
You tallow-face!
La. Cap. Fie, fie! what, are you mad?

95. **dead,** can be taken either with what precedes, "Romeo," or what follows, "my poor heart." 98. **temper,** mix. 112. **in happy time,** very well.

130. **conduit,** water-pipe. 142. **take me with you,** let me understand you. 146. **bride,** sometimes used in Shakespeare's day for bridegroom. 150. **chop-logic,** reasoner, sophist. 152. **minion,** spoilt favorite. 154. **fettle,** prepare. 156. **hurdle,** sledge to carry criminals to execution. 157. **green-sickness,** a kind of anemia.

Jul. Good father, I beseech you on my knees,
Hear me with patience but to speak a word.
Cap. Hang thee, young baggage! disobedient wretch!
I tell thee what: get thee to church o' Thursday,
Or never after look me in the face.
Speak not, reply not, do not answer me!
My fingers itch. Wife, we scarce thought us blest
That God had lent us but this only child;
But now I see this one is one too much,
And that we have a curse in having her.
Out on her, hilding!
Nurse. God in heaven bless her!
You are to blame, my lord, to rate her so.
Cap. And why, my lady wisdom? Hold your tongue,
Good prudence; smatter with your gossips, go.
Nurse. I speak no treason.
Cap. O, God ye god-den.
Nurse. May not one speak?
Cap. Peace, you mumbling fool!
Utter your gravity o'er a gossip's bowl;
For here we need it not.
La. Cap. You are too hot.
Cap. God's bread! it makes me mad.
Day, night, hour, tide, time, work, play,
Alone, in company, still my care hath been
To have her match'd; and having now provided
A gentleman of noble parentage,
Of fair demesnes, youthful and nobly train'd,
Stuff'd, as they say, with honourable parts,
Proportion'd as one's thought would wish a man;
And then to have a wretched puling fool,
A whining mammet, in her fortune's tender
To answer, "I 'll not wed; I cannot love,
I am too young; I pray you, pardon me."
But, an you will not wed, I 'll pardon you.
Graze where you will, you shall not house with me.
Look to 't, think on 't, I do not use to jest.
Thursday is near; lay hand on heart, advise.
An you be mine, I 'll give you to my friend;
An you be not, hang, beg, starve, die in the streets,
For, by my soul, I 'll ne'er acknowledge thee.
Nor what is mine shall never do thee good.
Trust to 't, bethink you; I 'll not be forsworn.
Exit.
Jul. Is there no pity sitting in the clouds,
That sees into the bottom of my grief?
O, sweet my mother, cast me not away!
Delay this marriage for a month, a week;
Or, if you do not, make the bridal bed
In that dim monument where Tybalt lies.
La. Cap. Talk not to me, for I 'll not speak a word.
Do as thou wilt, for I have done with thee.
Exit.
Jul. O God!—O nurse, how shall this be prevented?
My husband is on earth, my faith in heaven;
How shall that faith return again to earth,
Unless that husband send it me from heaven
By leaving earth? Comfort me, counsel me!
Alack, alack, that heaven should practise stratagems
Upon so soft a subject as myself!
What say'st thou? Hast thou not a word of joy?
Some comfort, nurse.
Nurse. Faith, here it is.
Romeo is banish'd; and all the world to nothing,
That he dares ne'er come back to challenge you;
Or, if he do, it needs must be by stealth.
Then, since the case so stands as now it doth,
I think it best you married with the County.
O, he 's a lovely gentleman!
Romeo 's a dishclout to him: an eagle, madam,
Hath not so green, so quick, so fair an eye
As Paris hath. Beshrew my very heart,
I think you are happy in this second match,
For it excels your first; or if it did not,
Your first is dead; or 't were as good he were,
As living here and you no use of him.
Jul. Speak'st thou this from thy heart?
Nurse. And from my soul too; else beshrew them both.
Jul. Amen!
Nurse. What?
Jul. Well, thou hast comforted me marvellous much.
Go in; and tell my lady I am gone,
Having displeas'd my father, to Laurence' cell,
To make confession and to be absolv'd.
Nurse. Marry, I will; and this is wisely done.
Exit.
Jul. Ancient damnation! O most wicked fiend!
Is it more sin to wish me thus forsworn,
Or to dispraise my lord with that same tongue
Which she hath prais'd him with above compare
So many thousand times? Go, counsellor;
Thou and my bosom henceforth shall be twain.
I 'll to the friar, to know his remedy;
If all else fail, myself have power to die.
Exit.

170. rate, berate. **172. smatter,** chatter. **182. demesnes,** estates. **186. mammet,** doll. **in her fortune's tender,** when good fortune offers.

207. faith, plighted troth.

ACT IV. Scene I. *Friar Laurence's cell.*

Enter *Friar Laurence* and *Paris*.

Fri. L. On Thursday, sir? The time is very short.
Par. My father Capulet will have it so;
And I am nothing slow to slack his haste.
Fri. L. You say you do not know the lady's mind?
Uneven is the course, I like it not.
Par. Immoderately she weeps for Tybalt's death,
And therefore have I little talk of love,
For Venus smiles not in a house of tears.
Now, sir, her father counts it dangerous
That she do give her sorrow so much sway,
And in his wisdom hastes our marriage
To stop the inundation of her tears;
Which, too much minded by herself alone,
May be put from her by society.
Now do you know the reason of this haste.
Fri. L. [*Aside.*] I would I knew not why it should be slow'd.
Look, sir, here comes the lady toward my cell.

Enter *Juliet*.

Par. Happily met, my lady and my wife!
Jul. That may be, sir, when I may be a wife.
Par. That may be must be, love, on Thursday next.
Jul. What must be shall be.
Fri. L. That 's a certain text.
Par. Come you to make confession to this father?
Jul. To answer that, I should confess to you.
Par. Do not deny to him that you love me.
Jul. I will confess to you that I love him.
Par. So will ye, I am sure, that you love me.
Jul. If I do so, it will be of more price,
Being spoke behind your back, than to your face.
Par. Poor soul, thy face is much abus'd with tears.
Jul. The tears have got small victory by that,
For it was bad enough before their spite.
Par. Thou wrong'st it, more than tears, with that report.
Jul. That is no slander, sir, which is a truth;
And what I spake, I spake it to my face.
Par. Thy face is mine, and thou hast slander'd it.
Jul. It may be so, for it is not mine own.
Are you at leisure, holy father, now;
Or shall I come to you at evening mass?
Fri. L. My leisure serves me, pensive daughter, now.
My lord, we must entreat the time alone.
Par. God shield I should disturb devotion!
Juliet, on Thursday early will I rouse ye;
Till then, adieu; and keep this holy kiss. *Exit.*
Jul. O, shut the door! and when thou hast done so,
Come weep with me, past hope, past care, past help!
Fri. L. Ah, Juliet, I already know thy grief;
It strains me past the compass of my wits:
I hear thou must, and nothing may prorogue it,
On Thursday next be married to this County.
Jul. Tell me not, friar, that thou hearest of this,
Unless thou tell me how I may prevent it:
If in thy wisdom thou canst give no help,
Do thou but call my resolution wise,
And with this knife I 'll help it presently.
God join'd my heart and Romeo's, thou our hands;
And ere this hand, by thee to Romeo's seal'd,
Shall be the label to another deed,
Or my true heart with treacherous revolt
Turn to another, this shall slay them both:
Therefore, out of thy long-experienc'd time,
Give me some present counsel, or, behold,
'Twixt my extremes and me this bloody knife
Shall play the umpire, arbitrating that
Which the commission of thy years and art
Could to no issue of true honour bring.
Be not so long to speak; I long to die
If what thou speak'st speak not of remedy.
Fri. L. Hold, daughter! I do spy a kind of hope,
Which craves as desperate an execution
As that is desperate which we would prevent.
If, rather than to marry County Paris,
Thou hast the strength of will to slay thyself,
Then is it likely thou wilt undertake
A thing like death to chide away this shame,
That cop'st with Death himself to scape from it;
And, if thou dar'st, I 'll give thee remedy.
Jul. O, bid me leap, rather than marry Paris,
From off the battlements of any tower,

5. Uneven, irregular.

57. label, slip or string to which seal was attached. **64. commission,** authority. **74. chide,** drive. **75. cop'st,** meetest.

Or walk in thievish ways, or bid me lurk
Where serpents are; chain me with roaring bears,
Or shut me nightly in a charnel-house,
O'er-cover'd quite with dead men's rattling bones,
With reeky shanks and yellow chapless skulls;
Or bid me go into a new-made grave
And hide me with a dead man in his shroud,—
Things that, to hear them told, have made me tremble;
And I will do it without fear or doubt,
To live an unstain'd wife to my sweet love.

Fri. L. Hold, then: go home, be merry, give consent
To marry Paris. Wednesday is to-morrow.
To-morrow night look that thou lie alone;
Let not the nurse lie with thee in thy chamber:
Take thou this vial, being then in bed,
And this distilling liquor drink thou off;
When presently through all thy veins shall run
A cold and drowsy humour; for no pulse
Shall keep his native progress, but surcease;
No warmth, no breath, shall testify thou livest;
The roses in thy lips and cheeks shall fade
To paly ashes, thy eyes' windows fall,
Like death, when he shuts up the day of life;
Each part, depriv'd of supple government,
Shall, stiff and stark and cold, appear like death:
And in this borrowed likeness of shrunk death
Thou shalt continue two and forty hours,
And then awake as from a pleasant sleep.
Now, when the bridegroom in the morning comes
To rouse thee from thy bed, there art thou dead:
Then, as the manner of our country is,
In thy best robes uncover'd on the bier
Thou shall be borne to that same ancient vault
Where all the kindred of the Capulets lie.
In the mean time, against thou shalt awake,
Shall Romeo by my letters know our drift,
And hither shall he come; and he and I
Will watch thy waking, and that very night
Shall Romeo bear thee hence to Mantua.
And this shall free thee from this present shame:
If no inconstant toy, nor womanish fear,
Abate thy valour in the acting it.

Jul. Give me, give me! O, tell not me of fear!

Fri. L. Hold; get you gone, be strong and prosperous
In this resolve. I 'll send a friar with speed
To Mantua, with my letters to thy lord.

Jul. Love give me strength! and strength shall help afford.
Farewell, dear father! *Exeunt.*

Scene II. *Hall in Capulet's house.*

Enter *Father Capulet, Mother, Nurse,* and *Serving-men,* two or three.

Cap. So many guests invite as here are writ. *Exit a Servant.*
Sirrah, go hire me twenty cunning cooks.

Serv. You shall have none ill, sir; for I 'll try if they can lick their fingers.

Cap. How canst thou try them so?

Serv. Marry, sir, 't is an ill cook that cannot lick his own fingers; therefore he that cannot lick his fingers goes not with me.

Cap. Go, be gone. *Exit Servant.*
We shall be much unfurnish'd for this time.
What, is my daughter gone to Friar Laurence?

Nurse. Ay, forsooth.

Cap. Well, he may chance to do some good on her:
A peevish self-will'd harlotry it is.

Enter *Juliet.*

Nurse. See where she comes from shrift with merry look.

Cap. How now, my headstrong! where have you been gadding?

Jul. Where I have learn'd me to repent the sin
Of disobedient opposition
To you and your behests, and am enjoin'd
By holy Laurence to fall prostrate here,
And beg your pardon. Pardon, I beseech you!
Henceforward I am ever rul'd by you.

Cap. Send for the County; go tell him of this:
I 'll have this knot knit up to-morrow morning.

Jul. I met the youthful lord at Laurence' cell;
And gave him what becomed love I might,
Not stepping o'er the bounds of modesty.

Cap. Why, I am glad on 't; this is well; stand up.
This is as 't should be. Let me see the County;
Ay, marry, go, I say, and fetch him hither.
Now, afore God! this reverend holy friar,
All our whole city is much bound to him.

Jul. Nurse, will you go with me into my closet,
To help me sort such needful ornaments
As you think fit to furnish me to-morrow?

79. **thievish**, full of thieves. 81. **charnel-house**, vault where bones are stored. 83. **reeky**, reeking. **chapless**, jawless. 94. **distilling**, distilled. 96. **humour**, fluid. 119. **toy**, whim.

14. **harlotry**, wench. 26. **becomed**, fitting.

La. Cap. No, not till Thursday; there is time enough.
Cap. Go, nurse, go with her; we 'll to church to-morrow.
Exeunt Juliet and Nurse.
La. Cap. We shall be short in our provision;
'T is now near night.
Cap. Tush, I will stir about,
And all things shall be well, I warrant thee, wife;
Go thou to Juliet, help to deck up her.
I 'll not to bed to-night; let me alone;
I 'll play the housewife for this once. What, ho!
They are all forth. Well, I will walk myself
To County Paris, to prepare up him
Against to-morrow. My heart is wondrous light,
Since this same wayward girl is so reclaim'd.
Exeunt.

Scene III. *Juliet's chamber.*

Enter *Juliet* and *Nurse.*

Jul. Ay, those attires are best; but, gentle nurse,
I pray thee, leave me to myself to-night;
For I have need of many orisons
To move the heavens to smile upon my state,
Which, well thou know'st, is cross and full of sin.

Enter *Mother.*

La. Cap. What, are you busy, ho? Need you my help?
Jul. No, madam; we have cull'd such necessaries
As are behoveful for our state to-morrow.
So please you, let me now be left alone,
And let the nurse this night sit up with you;
For, I am sure, you have your hands full all,
In this so sudden business.
La. Cap. Good-night.
Get thee to bed, and rest; for thou hast need.
Exeunt Mother and Nurse.
Jul. Farewell! God knows when we shall meet again.
I have a faint cold fear thrills through my veins,
That almost freezes up the heat of life.
I 'll call them back again to comfort me.
Nurse!—What should she do here?
My dismal scene I needs must act alone.
Come, vial.
What if this mixture do not work at all?
Shall I be married then to-morrow morning?
No, no; this shall forbid it. Lie thou there.
Laying down her dagger.
What if it be a poison, which the friar
Subtly hath minister'd to have me dead,
Lest in this marriage he should be dishonour'd,
Because he married me before to Romeo?
I fear it is; and yet, methinks, it should not,
For he hath still been tried a holy man.
How if, when I am laid into the tomb,
I wake before the time that Romeo
Come to redeem me? There 's a fearful point!
Shall I not then be stifled in the vaults,
To whose foul mouth no healthsome air breathes in,
And there die strangled ere my Romeo comes?
Or, if I live, is it not very like,
The horrible conceit of death and night,
Together with the terror of the place,—
As in a vault, an ancient receptacle,
Where, for this many hundred years, the bones
Of all my buried ancestors are pack'd;
Where bloody Tybalt, yet but green in earth,
Lies fest'ring in his shroud; where, as they say,
At some hours in the night spirits resort;—
Alack, alack, is it not like that I,
So early waking, what with loathsome smells,
And shrieks like mandrakes' torn out of the earth,
That living mortals, hearing them, run mad;—
O, if I wake, shall I not be distraught,
Environed with all these hideous fears,
And madly play with my forefathers' joints,
And pluck the mangled Tybalt from his shroud,
And, in this rage, with some great kinsman's bone
As with a club, dash out my desperate brains?
O, look! methinks I see my cousin's ghost
Seeking out Romeo, that did spit his body
Upon a rapier's point. Stay, Tybalt, stay!
Romeo, I come! This do I drink to thee.
She falls upon her bed, within the curtains.

Scene IV. *Hall in Capulet's house.*

Enter *Lady of the House* and *Nurse.*

La. Cap. Hold, take these keys, and fetch more spices, nurse.
Nurse. They call for dates and quinces in the pastry.

Scene iii: 5. cross, perverse.

29. tried, proved. 37. conceit, idea. 47. shrieks like mandrakes', the mandrake root, which somewhat resembles the human figure, was supposed to shriek when pulled from the ground and to drive the hearer insane. 58. s. d.: This old stage direction shows that Juliet fell on a bed behind the curtains which cut off the back stage. They were then drawn and the next scene was acted in front till line 28 when the Nurse draws the curtains open and finds Juliet on the bed. Scene iv: 2. pastry, pastry room.

Enter *Old Capulet*.

Cap. Come, stir, stir, stir! the second cock hath crow'd,
The curfew-bell hath rung, 't is three o'clock.
Look to the bak'd meats, good Angelica;
Spare not for cost.

Nurse. Go, you cot-quean, go.
Get you to bed. Faith, you 'll be sick to-morrow
For this night's watching.

Cap. No, not a whit! What! I have watch'd ere now
All night for lesser cause, and ne'er been sick.

La. Cap. Ay, you have been a mouse-hunt in your time;
But I will watch you from such watching now.

Exeunt Lady and Nurse.

Cap. A jealous-hood, a jealous-hood!

Enter three or four *Serving-men,* with spits, logs, and baskets.

Now, fellow,
What 's there?

Serv. Things for the cook, sir; but I know not what.

Cap. Make haste, make haste.

Exit First Servant.

Sirrah, fetch drier logs:
Call Peter, he will show thee where they are.

Serv. I have a head, sir, that will find out logs,
And never trouble Peter for the matter. *Exit.*

Cap. Mass, and well said; a merry whoreson, ha!
Thou shalt be logger-head. Good faith, 't is day. *Play music.*
The County will be here with music straight,
For so he said he would. I hear him near.
Nurse! Wife! What, ho! What, nurse, I say!

Re-enter *Nurse*.

Go waken Juliet, go and trim her up;
I 'll go and chat with Paris. Hie, make haste,
Make haste; the bridegroom he is come already.
Make haste, I say. *Exeunt.*

Scene V. *Juliet's chamber.*

Enter *Nurse*.

Nurse. Mistress, what, mistress! Juliet!—Fast, I warrant her, she.—
Why, lamb! why, lady! fie, you slug-a-bed!
Why, love, I say, madam! sweetheart! why, bride!
What, not a word? You take your pennyworths now;
Sleep for a week; for the next night, I warrant,
The County Paris hath set up his rest
That you shall rest but little. God forgive me!
Marry, and amen. How sound is she asleep!
I needs must wake her. Madam, madam, madam!
Ay, let the County take you in your bed;
He 'll fright you up, i' faith. Will it not be?
What, dress'd, and in your clothes! and down again!
I must needs wake you. Lady! lady! lady!
Alas, alas! Help, help! my lady 's dead!
O, well-a-day, that ever I was born!
Some *aqua vitæ,* ho! My lord! my lady!

Enter *Lady Capulet*.

La. Cap. What noise is here?

Nurse. O lamentable day!

La. Cap. What is the matter?

Nurse Look, look! O heavy day!

La. Cap. O me, O me! My child, my only life,
Revive, look up, or I will die with thee!
Help, help! Call help.

Enter *Capulet*.

Cap. For shame, bring Juliet forth; her lord is come.

Nurse. She 's dead, deceas'd, she 's dead; alack the day!

La. Cap. Alack the day, she 's dead, she 's dead, she 's dead!

Cap. Ha! let me see her. Out, alas! she 's cold;
Her blood is settled, and her joints are stiff;
Life and these lips have long been separated.
Death lies on her like an untimely frost
Upon the sweetest flower of all the field.

Nurse. O lamentable day!

La. Cap. O woeful time!

Cap. Death, that hath ta'en her hence to make me wail,
Ties up my tongue, and will not let me speak.

Enter *Friar Laurence* and *Paris,* with *Musicians.*

Fri. L. Come, is the bride ready to go to church?

Cap. Ready to go, but never to return.
O son! the night before thy wedding-day

6. cot-quean, used derisively of man playing the housewife. **11. a mouse-hunt,** a philanderer. **13. jealous-hood,** jealous person. **20. logger-head,** blockhead. **Scene v: 1. Fast,** fast asleep.

4. pennyworths, money's worth. **6. set up his rest,** a term from the game of primero meaning to stake his all on a set of cards. **Cf. 5, 3, 110** and note *Henry V*, 2, 1, 17.

Hath Death lain with thy wife. See there she lies,
Flower as she was, deflowered by him.
Death is my son-in-law, Death is my heir;
My daughter he hath wedded. I will die
And leave him all; life, living, all is Death's.

Par. Have I thought long to see this morning's face
And doth it give me such a sight as this?

La. Cap. Accurs'd, unhappy, wretched, hateful day!
Most miserable hour that e'er time saw
In lasting labour of his pilgrimage!
But one, poor one, one poor and loving child,
But one thing to rejoice and solace in,
And cruel Death hath catch'd it from my sight!

Nurse. O woe! O woeful, woeful, woeful day!
Most lamentable day, most woeful day,
That ever, ever, I did yet behold!
O day! O day! O day! O hateful day!
Never was seen so black a day as this.
O woeful day, O woeful day!

Par. Beguil'd, divorced, wronged, spited, slain!
Most detestable Death, by thee beguil'd,
By cruel cruel thee quite overthrown!
O love! O life! not life, but love in death!

Cap. Despis'd, distressed, hated, martyr'd, kill'd!
Uncomfortable time, why cam'st thou now
To murder, murder our solemnity?
O child! O child! my soul, and not my child!
Dead art thou! Alack! my child is dead;
And with my child my joys are buried.

Fri. L. Peace, ho, for shame! Confusion's cure lives not
In these confusions. Heaven and yourself
Had part in this fair maid; now heaven hath all,
And all the better is it for the maid:
Your part in her you could not keep from death,
But heaven keeps his part in eternal life.
The most you sought was her promotion,
For 't was your heaven she should be advanc'd;
And weep ye now, seeing she is advanc'd
Above the clouds, as high as heaven itself?
O, in this love, you love your child so ill,
That you run mad, seeing that she is well:
She 's not well married that lives married long;
But she 's best married that dies married young.
Dry up your tears, and stick your rosemary
On this fair corse; and, as the custom is,
In all her best array bear her to church;
For though fond nature bids us all lament,
Yet nature's tears are reason's merriment.

Cap. All things that we ordained festival,
Turn from their office to black funeral;
Our instruments to melancholy bells,
Our wedding cheer to a sad burial feast,
Our solemn hymns to sullen dirges change,
Our bridal flowers serve for a buried corse,
And all things change them to the contrary.

Fri. L. Sir, go you in; and, madam, go with him;
And go, Sir Paris; every one prepare
To follow this fair corse unto her grave.
The heavens do lour upon you for some ill;
Move them no more by crossing their high will.

Exeunt Capulet, Lady Capulet, Paris, and Friar.

First Mus. Faith, we may put up our pipes, and be gone.

Nurse. Honest good fellows, ah, put up, put up;
For, well you know, this is a pitiful case.

Exit.

First Mus. Ay, by my troth, the case may be amended.

Enter *Peter.*

Pet. Musicians, O, musicians, "Heart's ease, Heart's ease!" O, an you will have me live, play "Heart's ease."

First Mus. Why "Heart's ease"?

Pet. O, musicians, because my heart itself plays "My heart is full of woe." O, play me some merry dump to comfort me.

First Mus. Not a dump we; 't is no time to play now.

Pet. You will not, then?

First Mus. No.

Pet. I will then give it you soundly.

First Mus. What will you give us?

Pet. No money, on my faith, but the gleek; I will give you the minstrel.

First Mus. Then will I give you the serving-creature.

Pet. Then will I lay the serving-creature's dagger on your pate. I will carry no crotchets; I 'll *re* you, I 'll *fa* you. Do you note me?

First Mus. An you *re* us and *fa* us, you note us.

Sec. Mus. Pray you, put up your dagger, and put out your wit.

Pet. Then have at you with my wit! I will

41. thought long, longed. **79. rosemary,** an evergreen used at funerals as a symbol of immortality.

83. Sober reason ridicules the tears that nature bids us shed. **108. dump,** mournful tune. **115. gleek,** mock, gibe. **120. carry,** bear, endure. **crotchets,** (1) quarter-notes, (2) whims. **124. put out,** (1) extinguish, (2) use.

dry-beat you with an iron wit, and put up my iron dagger. Answer me like men:

"When griping grief the heart doth wound,
And doleful dumps the mind oppress,
Then music with her silver sound"—

why "silver sound"? Why "music with her silver sound"? What say you, Simon Catling?

First Mus. Marry, sir, because silver hath a sweet sound.

Pet. Prates! What say you, Hugh Rebeck?

Sec. Mus. I say "silver sound," because musicians sound for silver.

Pet. Prates too! What say you, James Soundpost?

Third Mus. Faith, I know not what to say.

Pet. O, I cry you mercy; you are the singer. I will say for you. It is "music with her silver sound," because musicians have no gold for sounding:

"Then music with her silver sound
With speedy help doth lend redress."

Exit.

First Mus. What a pestilent knave is this same!

Sec. Mus. Hang him, Jack! Come, we 'll in here, tarry for the mourners, and stay dinner. *Exeunt.*

ACT V. SCENE I. *Mantua. A street.*

Enter *Romeo.*

Rom. If I may trust the flattering truth of sleep,
My dreams presage some joyful news at hand:
My bosom's lord sits lightly in his throne,
And all this day an unaccustom'd spirit
Lifts me above the ground with cheerful thoughts.
I dreamt my lady came and found me dead
(Strange dream, that gives a dead man leave to think!)
And breath'd such life with kisses in my lips,
That I reviv'd, and was an emperor.
Ah me! how sweet is love itself possess'd,
When but love's shadows are so rich in joy!

Enter *Balthasar,* his man, booted.

News from Verona!—How now, Balthasar!
Dost thou not bring me letters from the friar?
How doth my lady? Is my father well?
How fares my Juliet? that I ask again;
For nothing can be ill, if she be well.

Bal. Then she is well, and nothing can be ill.
Her body sleeps in Capel's monument,
And her immortal part with angels lives.
I saw her laid low in her kindred's vault,
And presently took post to tell it you:
O, pardon me for bringing these ill news,
Since you did leave it for my office, sir.

Rom. Is it even so? Then I defy you, stars!
Thou know'st my lodging; get me ink and paper,
And hire post-horses; I will hence to-night.

Bal. I do beseech you, sir, have patience.
Your looks are pale and wild, and do import
Some misadventure.

Rom. Tush, thou art deceiv'd:
Leave me, and do the thing I bid thee do.
Hast thou no letters to me from the friar?

Bal. No, my good lord.

Rom. No matter; get thee gone
And hire those horses; I 'll be with thee straight. *Exit Balthasar.*
Well, Juliet, I will lie with thee to-night.
Let 's see for means. O mischief, thou art swift
To enter in the thoughts of desperate men!
I do remember an apothecary,—
And hereabouts 'a dwells,—which late I noted
In tatter'd weeds, with overwhelming brows,
Culling of simples; meagre were his looks,
Sharp misery had worn him to the bones:
And in his needy shop a tortoise hung,
An alligator stuff'd, and other skins
Of ill-shap'd fishes; and about his shelves
A beggarly account of empty boxes,
Green earthen pots, bladders and musty seeds,
Remnants of packthread and old cakes of roses,
Were thinly scattered to make up a show.
Noting this penury, to myself I said,
"An if a man did need a poison now,

132. Catling, catgut lute string. The names of all the musicians mentioned have reference to musical instruments. **Rebeck**, l. 135, was the name of a three-stringed violin; and **Soundpost**, l. 139, the post on the inside of a viol instrument directly under the "bridge." **135. Prates**, either a noun=nonsense, or a form of "pratest." **Act V, Scene i: 3. bosom's lord**, heart. **18. monument**, burial vault. **21. took post**, traveled by post-horses.

142. singer, as he can't "say," but only sing, Peter says for him. **Act. V, Scene i: 39. weeds**, clothing. **overwhelming**, over-hanging. **40. simples**, medicinal herbs. **45. beggarly account**, meagre store.

Whose sale is present death in Mantua,
Here lives a caitiff wretch would sell it him."
O, this same thought did but forerun my need;
And this same needy man must sell it me.
As I remember, this should be the house.
Being holiday, the beggar's shop is shut.
What, ho! apothecary!

Enter *Apothecary*.

Ap. Who calls so loud?
Rom. Come hither, man. I see that thou art poor;
Hold, there is forty ducats. Let me have
A dram of poison, such soon-speeding gear
As will disperse itself through all the veins
That the life-weary taker may fall dead,
And that the trunk may be discharg'd of breath
As violently as hasty powder fir'd
Doth hurry from the fatal cannon's womb.
Ap. Such mortal drugs I have; but Mantua's law
Is death to any he that utters them.
Rom. Art thou so bare and full of wretchedness,
And fear'st to die? Famine is in thy cheeks,
Need and oppression starveth in thy eyes,
Contempt and beggary hangs upon thy back;
The world is not thy friend nor the world's law;
The world affords no law to make thee rich;
Then be not poor, but break it, and take this.
Ap. My poverty, but not my will, consents.
Rom. I pay thy poverty, and not thy will.
Ap. Put this in any liquid thing you will,
And drink it off; and, if you had the strength
Of twenty men, it would dispatch you straight.
Rom. There is thy gold, worse poison to men's souls,
Doing more murder in this loathsome world,
Than these poor compounds that thou mayst not sell.
I sell thee poison; thou hast sold me none.
Farewell! Buy food, and get thyself in flesh.
Come, cordial and not poison, go with me
To Juliet's grave; for there must I use thee.
Exeunt.

Scene II. *Verona. Friar Laurence's cell.*

Enter *Friar John.*

Fri. J. Holy Franciscan friar! brother, ho!

Enter *Friar Laurence.*

Fri. L. This same should be the voice of Friar John.
Welcome from Mantua! What says Romeo?
Or, if his mind be writ, give me his letter.
Fri. J. Going to find a bare-foot brother out,
One of our order, to associate me,
Here in this city visiting the sick,
And finding him, the searchers of the town,
Suspecting that we both were in a house
Where the infectious pestilence did reign,
Seal'd up the doors, and would not let us forth;
So that my speed to Mantua there was stay'd.
Fri. L. Who bare my letter, then, to Romeo?
Fri. J. I could not send it,—here it is again,—
Nor get a messenger to bring it thee,
So fearful were they of infection.
Fri. L. Unhappy fortune! By my brotherhood,
The letter was not nice but full of charge
Of dear import, and the neglecting it
May do much danger. Friar John, go hence;
Get me an iron crow, and bring it straight
Unto my cell.
Fri. J. Brother, I 'll go and bring it thee.
Exit.
Fri. L. Now must I to the monument alone;
Within this three hours will fair Juliet wake.
She will beshrew me much that Romeo
Hath had no notice of these accidents;
But I will write again to Mantua,
And keep her at my cell till Romeo come;
Poor living corse, clos'd in a dead man's tomb! *Exit.*

Scene III. *A churchyard; in it a tomb belonging to the Capulets.*

Enter *Paris,* and his *Page* with flowers and sweet water and a torch.

Par. Give me thy torch, boy; hence, and stand aloof.
Yet put it out, for I would not be seen.
Under yond yew-trees lay thee all along,
Holding thine ear close to the hollow ground;
So shall no foot upon the churchyard tread,
Being loose, unfirm, with digging up of graves,
But thou shalt hear it: whistle then to me,
As signal that thou hearest something approach.
Give me those flowers. Do as I bid thee, go.
Page. [*Aside.*] I am almost afraid to stand alone

60. **gear**, stuff. 67. **utters**, sells.

Scene ii: 8. **searchers**, sanitary police. 18. **charge**, importance. 21. **crow**, crowbar. 26. **beshrew**, blame.
Scene iii: S. d. **sweet water**, perfumed water. 3. **all along**, prone.

Here in the churchyard; yet I will adventure. *Retires.*

Paris strews the tomb with flowers.

Par. Sweet flower, with flowers thy bridal bed I strew,—
O woe! thy canopy is dust and stones—
Which with sweet water nightly I will dew,
Or, wanting that, with tears distill'd by moans.
The obsequies that I for thee will keep
Nightly shall be to strew thy grave and weep.

The Page whistles.

The boy gives warning something doth approach.
What cursed foot wanders this way to-night,
To cross my obsequies and true love's rite?
What, with a torch! Muffle me, night, a while.

Retires.

Enter *Romeo* and *Balthasar,* with a torch, a mattock, and a crow of iron.

Rom. Give me that mattock and the wrenching iron.
Hold, take this letter; early in the morning
See thou deliver it to my lord and father.
Give me the light: upon thy life, I charge thee,
Whate'er thou hear'st or seest, stand all aloof,
And do not interrupt me in my course.
Why I descend into this bed of death,
Is partly to behold my lady's face;
But chiefly to take thence from her dead finger
A precious ring, a ring that I must use
In dear employment; therefore hence, be gone:
But if thou, jealous, dost return to pry
In what I farther shall intend to do,
By heaven, I will tear thee joint by joint
And strew this hungry churchyard with thy limbs:
The time and my intents are savage-wild,
More fierce and more inexorable far
Than empty tigers or the roaring sea.

Bal. I will be gone, sir, and not trouble ye.

Rom. So shalt thou show me friendship. Take thou that;
Live, and be prosperous; and farewell, good fellow.

Bal. [*Aside.*] For all this same, I 'll hide me hereabout.
His looks I fear, and his intents I doubt.

Retires.

Rom. Thou detestable maw, thou womb of death,
Gorg'd with the dearest morsel of the earth,
Thus I enforce thy rotten jaws to open,
And, in despite, I 'll cram thee with more food! *Opens the tomb.*

Par. This is that banish'd haughty Montague,
That murder'd my love's cousin, with which grief,
It is supposed, the fair creature died;
And here is come to do some villainous shame
To the dead bodies: I will apprehend him.

Comes forward.

Stop thy unhallowed toil, vile Montague!
Can vengeance be pursued further than death?
Condemned villain, I do apprehend thee.
Obey, and go with me; for thou must die.

Rom. I must indeed; and therefore came I hither.
Good gentle youth, tempt not a desperate man;
Fly hence, and leave me; think upon these gone,
Let them affright thee. I beseech thee, youth,
Put not another sin upon my head,
By urging me to fury: O, be gone!
By heaven, I love thee better than myself;
For I come hither arm'd against myself:
Stay not, be gone; live, and hereafter say
A madman's mercy bid thee run away.

Par. I do defy thy conjurations,
And apprehend thee for a felon here.

Rom. Wilt thou provoke me? Then have at thee, boy! *They fight.*

Page. O Lord, they fight! I will go call the watch. *Exit.*

Par. O, I am slain! [*Falls.*] If thou be merciful,
Open the tomb, lay me with Juliet. *Dies.*

Rom. In faith, I will. Let me peruse this face:
Mercutio's kinsman, noble County Paris!
What said my man, when my betossed soul
Did not attend him as we rode? I think
He told me Paris should have married Juliet.
Said he not so? Or did I dream it so?
Or am I mad, hearing him talk of Juliet,
To think it was so? O, give me thy hand,
One writ with me in sour misfortune's book!
I 'll bury thee in a triumphant grave.
A grave? O, no! a lantern, slaughter'd youth,
For here lies Juliet, and her beauty makes
This vault a feasting presence full of light.
Death, lie thou there, by a dead man interr'd.

Laying Paris in the tomb.

How oft when men are at the point of death
Have they been merry! which their keepers call
A lightning before death. O, how may I

33. **jealous,** suspicious.

68. **conjurations,** entreaties. 84. **lantern,** a windowed turret. 86. **presence,** presence-chamber. 89. **keepers,** nurses.

Call this a lightning? O my love! my wife!
Death, that hath suck'd the honey of thy breath,
Hath had no power yet upon thy beauty.
Thou art not conquer'd; beauty's ensign yet
Is crimson in thy lips and in thy cheeks,
And death's pale flag is not advanced there.
Tybalt, liest thou there in thy bloody sheet?
O, what more favour can I do to thee,
Than with that hand that cut thy youth in twain
To sunder his that was thine enemy?
Forgive me, cousin! Ah, dear Juliet,
Why art thou yet so fair? Shall I believe
That unsubstantial Death is amorous,
And that the lean abhorred monster keeps
Thee here in dark to be his paramour?
For fear of that, I still will stay with thee,
And never from this palace of dim night
Depart again: here, here will I remain
With worms that are thy chamber-maids; O, here
Will I set up my everlasting rest,
And shake the yoke of inauspicious stars
From this world-wearied flesh. Eyes, look your last!
Arms, take your last embrace! and, lips, O you
The doors of breath, seal with a righteous kiss
A dateless bargain to engrossing death!
Come, bitter conduct, come, unsavoury guide!
Thou desperate pilot, now at once run on
The dashing rocks thy sea-sick weary bark!
Here 's to my love! [*Drinks.*] O true apothecary!
Thy drugs are quick. Thus with a kiss I die.
Dies.

Enter *Friar Laurence,* with lantern, crow, and spade.

Fri. L. Saint Francis be my speed! how oft to-night
Have my old feet stumbled at graves! Who 's there?
Bal. Here 's one, a friend, and one that knows you well.
Fri. L. Bliss be upon you! Tell me, good my friend,
What torch is yond, that vainly lends his light
To grubs and eyeless skulls? As I discern,
It burneth in the Capels' monument.
Bal. It doth so, holy sir; and there 's my master,
One that you love.
Fri. L. Who is it?
Bal. Romeo.
Fri. L. How long hath he been there?
Bal. Full half an hour.
Fri. L. Go with me to the vault.
Bal. I dare not, sir.
My master knows not but I am gone hence;
And fearfully did menace me with death
If I did stay to look on his intents.
Fri. L. Stay, then; I 'll go alone. Fear comes upon me:
O, much I fear some ill unthrifty thing.
Bal. As I did sleep under this yew-tree here,
I dreamt my master and another fought,
And that my master slew him.
Fri. L. Romeo!
Friar stoops and looks on the blood and weapons.
Alack, alack, what blood is this, which stains
The stony entrance of this sepulchre?
What mean these masterless and gory swords
To lie discolour'd by this place of peace?
Enters the tomb.
Romeo! O, pale! Who else? What, Paris too?
And steep'd in blood? Ah, what an unkind hour
Is guilty of this lamentable chance!
The lady stirs. *Juliet rises.*
Jul. O comfortable friar! where is my lord?
I do remember well where I should be,
And there I am. Where is my Romeo?
Noise within.
Fri. L. I hear some noise. Lady, come from that nest
Of death, contagion, and unnatural sleep.
A greater power than we can contradict
Hath thwarted our intents. Come, come away:
Thy husband in thy bosom there lies dead;
And Paris too: come, I 'll dispose of thee
Among a sisterhood of holy nuns.
Stay not to question, for the watch is coming;
Come, go, good Juliet [*Noise again*], I dare no longer stay.
Exit Friar Laurence.
Jul. Go, get thee hence, for I will not away.
What 's here? A cup, clos'd in my true love's hand?
Poison, I see, hath been his timeless end.
O churl! drunk all, and left no friendly drop
To help me after? I will kiss thy lips;
Haply some poison yet doth hang on them,
To make me die with a restorative.
Thy lips are warm.

Enter *Watch,* with the *Page* of Paris.

First Watch. Lead, boy; which way?

115. dateless, everlasting. **engrossing,** monopolizing. **122. stumbled at graves,** this was considered a bad omen.

136. unthrifty, unfortunate. **148. comfortable,** comforting. **162. timeless,** untimely.

Jul. Yea, noise? Then I 'll be brief. O happy dagger!
Snatching Romeo's dagger.
This is thy sheath; [*Stabs herself*] there rust, and let me die.
Dies.

Page. This is the place; there, where the torch doth burn.

First Watch. The ground is bloody; search about the churchyard.
Go, some of you, whoe'er you find attach.
Exeunt some.
Pitiful sight! here lies the County slain;
And Juliet bleeding, warm, and newly dead,
Who here hath lain this two days buried.
Go, tell the Prince; run to the Capulets;
Raise up the Montagues; some others search.
Exeunt others.
We see the ground whereon these woes do lie;
But the true ground of all these piteous woes
We cannot without circumstance descry.

Re-enter some of the *Watch,* with *Balthasar.*

Sec. Watch. Here 's Romeo's man; we found him in the churchyard.

First Watch. Hold him in safety till the Prince come hither.

Re-enter another *Watchman,* with *Friar Laurence.*

Third Watch. Here is a friar, that trembles, sighs, and weeps.
We took this mattock and this spade from him,
As he was coming from this churchyard side.

First Watch. A great suspicion: stay the friar too.

Enter the *Prince* and *Attendants.*

Prince. What misadventure is so early up,
That calls our person from our morning rest?

Enter *Capulet* and his *Wife,* and others.

Cap. What should it be, that they so shriek abroad?

La. Cap. Oh! the people in the street cry Romeo,
Some Juliet, and some Paris; and all run,
With open outcry, toward our monument.

Prince. What fear is this which startles in our ears?

First Watch. Sovereign, here lies the County Paris slain;
And Romeo dead; and Juliet, dead before,
Warm and new kill'd.

Prince. Search, seek, and know how this foul murder comes.

First Watch. Here is a friar, and slaughter'd Romeo's man,
With instruments upon them, fit to open
These dead men's tombs.

Cap. O heavens! O wife, look how our daughter bleeds!
This dagger hath mista'en,—for, lo, his house
Is empty on the back of Montague,—
And is mis-sheathed in my daughter's bosom!

La. Cap. O me! this sight of death is as a bell,
That warns my old age to a sepulchre.

Enter *Montague* and others.

Prince. Come, Montague; for thou art early up,
To see thy son and heir more early down.

Mon. Alas, my liege, my wife is dead to-night;
Grief of my son's exile hath stopp'd her breath.
What further woe conspires against mine age?

Prince. Look, and thou shalt see.

Mon. O thou untaught! what manners is in this,
To press before thy father to a grave?

Prince. Seal up the mouth of outrage for a while,
Till we can clear these ambiguities,
And know their spring, their head, their true descent;
And then will I be general of your woes,
And lead you even to death: meantime forbear,
And let mischance be slave to patience.
Bring forth the parties of suspicion.

Fri. L. I am the greatest, able to do least,
Yet most suspected, as the time and place
Doth make against me, of this direful murder;
And here I stand, both to impeach and purge
Myself condemned and myself excus'd.

Prince. Then say at once what thou dost know in this.

Fri. L. I will be brief, for my short date of breath
Is not so long as is a tedious tale.
Romeo, there dead, was husband to that Juliet;
And she, there dead, that Romeo's faithful wife:
I married them; and their stol'n marriage-day
Was Tybalt's dooms-day, whose untimely death
Banish'd the new-made bridegroom from this city,
For whom, and not for Tybalt, Juliet pin'd.

173. attach, arrest.

203. house, scabbard. **207. warns,** calls. **216. outrage,** outcry. **226. purge,** clear (from suspicion).

You, to remove that siege of grief from her,
Betroth'd and would have married her perforce
To County Paris. Then comes she to me,
And, with wild looks, bid me devise some mean
To rid her from this second marriage,
Or in my cell there would she kill herself.
Then gave I her, so tutor'd by my art,
A sleeping potion; which so took effect
As I intended, for it wrought on her
The form of death. Meantime I writ to Romeo,
That he should hither come as this dire night,
To help to take her from her borrowed grave,
Being the time the potion's force should cease.
But he which bore my letter, Friar John,
Was stay'd by accident, and yesternight
Return'd my letter back. Then all alone
At the prefixed hour of her waking,
Came I to take her from her kindred's vault;
Meaning to keep her closely at my cell,
Till I conveniently could send to Romeo.
But when I came, some minute ere the time
Of her awakening, here untimely lay
The noble Paris and true Romeo dead.
She wakes; and I entreated her come forth,
And bear this work of heaven with patience.
But then a noise did scare me from the tomb;
And she, too desperate, would not go with me,
But, as it seems, did violence on herself.
All this I know; and to the marriage
Her nurse is privy; and, if aught in this
Miscarried by my fault, let my old life
Be sacrific'd, some hour before his time,
Unto the rigour of severest law.

Prince. We still have known thee for a holy man.
Where 's Romeo's man? What can he say to this?

Bal. I brought my master news of Juliet's death;
And then in post he came from Mantua
To this same place, to this same monument.
This letter he early bid me give his father,
And threaten'd me with death, going in the vault,
If I departed not and left him there.

Prince. Give me the letter; I will look on it.
Where is the County's page, that rais'd the watch?
Sirrah, what made your master in this place?

Page. He came with flowers to strew his lady's grave;
And bid me stand aloof, and so I did:
Anon comes one with light to ope the tomb,
And by and by my master drew on him;
And then I ran away to call the watch.

Prince. This letter doth make good the friar's words,
Their course of love, the tidings of her death.
And here he writes that he did buy a poison
Of a poor 'pothecary, and therewithal
Came to this vault to die, and lie with Juliet.
Where be these enemies? Capulet! Montague!
See, what a scourge is laid upon your hate,
That Heaven finds means to kill your joys with love.
And I for winking at your discords too
Have lost a brace of kinsmen. All are punish'd.

Cap. O brother Montague, give me thy hand.
This is my daughter's jointure, for no more
Can I demand.

Mon. But I can give thee more;
For I will raise her statue in pure gold;
That whiles Verona by that name is known,
There shall no figure at such rate be set
As that of true and faithful Juliet.

Cap. As rich shall Romeo's by his lady's lie,
Poor sacrifices of our enmity!

Prince. A glooming peace this morning with it brings;
The sun, for sorrow, will not show his head.
Go hence, to have more talk of these sad things;
Some shall be pardon'd, and some punished:
For never was a story of more woe
Than this of Juliet and her Romeo. *Exeunt.*

247. as this, this. **255. closely**, secretly. **273. post**, post-haste.

297. jointure, marriage-portion. **301. rate**, value.

The Merchant of Venice

The Merchant of Venice, one of the most popular of Shakespeare's plays, marks a decided advance in the poet's development not only as a practising playwright, but as an observer and interpreter of human life. Successful on the stage from the very start, it carries with it also a lesson for the thoughtful reader of to-day.

Text.—The text has come down to us in three forms of which only the first has any independent authority. This is the First Quarto entered in the Stationers' Register on July 22, 1598, by James Roberts. In October, 1600, Roberts transferred his right to Hayes, who published it late in that year. The "copy" was probably the official prompt-book.

The Second Quarto, on the other hand, also bearing the name of Roberts and the date of 1600, is now known to be one of the Pavier issues of 1619—see Introduction, pp. 78-9.

The Folio text likewise is a reprint of the First Quarto with a few more changes, some of which show alterations in the text made after the accession of James I. The First Quarto, the authentic text, is here reprinted with only the necessary modernization and corrections.

Date.—It is impossible to fix the date of the *Merchant* very precisely, but certain limits can be determined. It was, of course, on the stage in 1598 when Roberts entered it in the Stationers' Register, and it is mentioned in the same year by Meres in his well-known list. Yet there is good reason to believe that it was written several years earlier, and that the ultimate cause of its composition was a sensational trial which thrilled Shakespeare's London in 1594.

At that time Roderigo Lopez, a converted Portuguese Jew, the most distinguished member of his race in England, was physician in chief to Queen Elizabeth. He was unwary enough to entangle himself in a Spanish plot to poison his mistress, was tried, convicted in spite of his protestations of innocence, and on June 7, 1594, was hanged, drawn and quartered at Tyburn. The chief advocate of his guilt was Elizabeth's favorite, the Earl of Essex, and through Essex and his friend Southampton Shakespeare must have known all about the Lopez case. Yet the *Merchant* is not a piece of anti-Semitic propaganda. The immediate cause, so far as we can see, of Shakespeare's composition of this play was an event in the contemporary theatrical world.

Some years earlier, probably in 1589-90, Marlowe had written *The Jew of Malta,* a thrilling melodrama which told the story of a wicked Jew, who plotted, poisoned, and murdered right and left, and finally came to a horrible end shrieking out curses in a boiling cauldron. After a very successful run it had been withdrawn for about a year, but shortly after the arrest of Lopez it was revived and played to crowded houses for the rest of 1594. Most of these performances were given by the Admiral's company, the only one of the time that rivalled Shakespeare's fellows, and it is a highly reasonable conjecture that Shakespeare was urged by his company to write them a wicked Jew play which might compete in popularity with Marlowe's tragedy.

The ultimate source of the main plot of *The Merchant of Venice,* the bond story and the incident of the rings, is derived from a fourteenth century Italian collection of *novelle, Il Pecorone,* first published in 1558. Briefly the story runs as follows:

Giannetto, a young gentleman of Venice, is fitted out by his godfather, Ansaldo, for a trading voyage. On his way he puts in at the harbor of Belmont where he learns that the lady of the land has made a law that whoever enters the port must woo her. If he can obtain possession of her person, she will marry him and make him lord of the country, but if he fails, he must forfeit all his goods. Giannetto makes the trial, but fails because the lady has given him a sleeping-potion in a cup of wine. He returns to Venice, where Ansaldo equips him for a second trial in which he fails again. For a third attempt Ansaldo borrows ten thousand ducats from a Jew, pledging a pound of his flesh to be cut off by his creditor if the money were not repaid by a certain date. Thus equipped Giannetto makes a third attempt and this time wins the lady, for a friendly serving maid reveals to him the secret of the drugged cup. They are married and live happily till suddenly the youth recalls that on this very day the bond has fallen due. His wife sends him to Venice with money enough to pay the debt ten times over. Unfortunately the Jew has already arrested Ansaldo and announces that he intends to claim the pound of flesh since he would sooner kill the greatest Christian merchant than get all the gold in Venice. In the meantime the lady, disguised as a lawyer, came to Venice where she gave out that she was prepared to settle all disputed cases. Giannetto induced the Jew to refer the case to her as judge. The disguised lady first urged the Jew to take the money offered and when he refused bade him prepare to take the pound of flesh. However when the Jew, knife in hand, approached Ansaldo, she warned him not to take more or less than a pound and not to shed one drop of blood on pain of death. Thereupon the Jew declared his willingness to take the money, but was told that it was too late; he must take his bond or nothing. So he tore up the bond and left the court, having lost even the sum he had lent Ansaldo. Giannetto thanked the judge and offered him the money he had brought to free his friend, but the disguised lady would accept nothing but a ring from his finger. This the youth was loath to give because it had been presented to him by his wife who bade him always keep it as a pledge of her love. However he finally parted with the ring and returned to Belmont along with his friend Ansaldo. The lady, who had already returned there, received him coldly, asked what had become of the ring, and when Giannetto said he had given it to the judge, swore that he had given it to a woman. At last when her husband was reduced to tears, the lady burst out laughing and told him the whole story. She gave the waiting maid in marriage to Ansaldo and they all lived happily ever after.

Here, it is plain, is the main plot of *The Merchant of Venice,* but there are two minor plots in the play which do not appear in the story: the winning of the lady by the choice of the right casket and the flight of the Jew's daughter with a Christian lover. The source of the first of these is probably to be found in the *Gesta Romanorum,* a Latin collection of anecdotes, legends and moral tales compiled toward the end of the Middle Ages. An English translation published in 1577 was very popular in Shakespeare's day and he may well have read the story there. In substance it is as follows:

A certain princess was sent to Rome to become the bride of the Emperor's son. To test her fitness for the marriage, the Emperor bade her make a choice of three caskets, saying that only if she chose the right one should she wed his son. The first was made of gold, full of dead men's bones, with the inscription: "who chooseth me shall find what he deserveth." The second was of silver filled with earth and worms with the inscription: "who chooseth me shall find what his nature desireth." The third was of lead full of precious stones with the inscription: "who chooseth me shall find what God hath disposed to him." The princess rejected the first and the second casket since she said she knew not what she deserved, and she did know that what her nature desired was evil. So she chose the leaden casket because she knew that what God disposed was always for good. And so she won her husband.

The likeness between this tale, especially as regards the substance of the caskets and their inscriptions, and the story of the winning of Portia is too close to be a mere coincidence.

Neither in the Italian *novella* nor in the Latin tale is there any mention of a Jew's daughter. It seems likely that Shakespeare lifted this lady from Marlowe's popular play where the Jew's daughter, Abigail, has a Christian lover.

Construction.—Of these three sources Marlowe's play and the casket story in the English version were of course accessible to Shakespeare. There was no English translation of *Il Pecorone* in Shakespeare's time, and it is doubtful whether he could have read it in the original Italian. This is, perhaps, one of the reasons that has led scholars to look for a source of the main plot of the *Merchant* in an older dramatic version of the story. As early as 1579, Stephen Gosson, attacking the contemporary drama in his *School of Abuse,* excepted from his sweeping denunciation a play called *The Jew* "representing the greediness of worldly choosers and the bloody minds of usurers." This is a very brief description of a lost play, but we learn from it that the chief character was a Jew and a bloody-minded usurer, which would nicely fit a dramatization of the Italian tale. It is often taken for granted that Gosson's phrase "the greediness of worldly choosers" implies the existence in *The Jew* of a parallel to the casket scenes in *The Merchant of Venice.* This seems to be stretching the phrase beyond what it can reasonably bear, and we may well give Shakespeare the credit of introducing the casket device into the play. Portia is won not by a lover who evades the sleeping-potion, but by one wise enough to solve the riddle of the inscriptions, a test devised by her virtuous father to protect her against unworthy suitors. This rationalizing and moralizing of the winning of the lady is in exact accord with Shakespeare's treatment of other elements in the tale.

Consider for a moment Shakespeare's treatment of the bond. In the Italian tale no reason is given for Ansaldo's entering into such a hazardous engagement. In a very carefully planned scene of the play (I, iii) Shakespeare shows us the Jew entrapping Antonio into the bond by offering to lend the money without interest and by treating the forfeiture as a mere jest. The Jew of the story has no special reason to hate Ansaldo; Shylock bears an ancient grudge against Antonio, and as the action progresses the flight of his daughter with his gold and jewels fires his passion for revenge to fever heat. The Shylock of the Court scene is a far more realistic and credible character than the Jew of the tale. In the Court scene, too, there is another evidence of Shakespeare's transforming genius. In the tale, as in all other versions of the pound of flesh bond, the creditor is defeated by a pair of legal quibbles: he must not cut more or less than a pound; he must not shed a drop of blood. These Shakespeare retains; they are essentials of the tale, but he adds something which is not a legal quibble, but a fundamental principle of justice, the old law that condemns to death and confiscation of goods the alien who plots against the life of a Venetian citizen. It is in this predicament that Shylock stands and it is this law, the expression of the State's inalienable right to defend its citizen against alien plots, that Shakespeare makes Portia invoke against him.

Characterization.—Even more than in his handling of the plot Shakespeare's advance in his art as a dramatist is shown in the mastery of characterization which distinguishes *The Merchant of Venice* from his earlier plays. A certain number of the characters, to be sure, are mere *dramatis personæ,* or stock types; yet there are at least four fully realized characters, life-like enough for actors to differ in their impersonations and critics in their comments from Shakespeare's day to ours. First of all there is Antonio, the royal merchant, an idealist, overshadowed, like most of Shakespeare's men of thought, with a cloud of melancholy, due perhaps to his realization that he is about to lose his friend by the latter's marriage. For Antonio embodies the Renaissance conception of the high worth of friendship, a conception to which Shakespeare gave supreme expression in his sonnets. And this friend is Bassanio, a character strangely misunderstood by some modern critics; a recent commentator goes so far as to call him a fortune-hunter and a hypocrite. This is a strange piece of belated Victorianism. It certainly does not fit Shakespeare's Bassanio, "a scholar and a soldier," the companion of the Marquis of Montferrat, and "best deserving of a fair lady." These are phrases that Shakespeare uses to characterize him, and it is difficult to believe that a mere fortune-hunter would ever have won the friendship of Antonio and the love of Portia. His speech before he chooses the casket would be more fully understood by an Elizabethan auditor than by a modern reader. The little song that preludes Bassanio's choice warns him against "fancy," *i.e.* against mere sensual love, and it starts a train of thought that develops in his long soliloquy. In contrast to Morocco, who chose by appearances, and to Arragon, whose choice sprang from self-love, Bassanio chooses by the understanding which pierces below the surface and fastens upon reality.

Portia herself is, of course, the most delightful character of the play. She is one of Shakespeare's ideal women, a lady of the Renaissance, beautiful, prudent, cultured, and courteous, yet withal a simple, loving girl. She is rich, but wealth means nothing to her except as a means to the good life: the money due to Shylock is a "petty debt" which she would pay twenty times over to free her lover's friend. The famous quality of mercy speech sums up the Christian ethic of forgiveness, even as her trapping of Shylock exposes the danger of the letter-worship of the law that kills. And all these qualities are set off and enriched in her by a sly, gently mocking humor that shows in her talk with Nerissa and in the jest of the rings.

It is in the character of Shylock, however, that Shakespeare reaches a height he had never before attained. The figure of the despised and hated Jew comes to life in Shakespeare's hands; no longer the mere monster of Marlowe, Shylock is as human as any of his Christian adversaries. His racial characteristics, both for good and evil, are strongly marked: his reverence of "our sacred nation," his strong family affection, his greed of gain, his deep-rooted hatred of his persecutors, his reliance on the letter of the law, all mark him as a Jew. But he is *a* Jew, Shylock of Venice, not *the* Jew, least of all the tragic representative of his race as modern romantic actors and critics have represented him. In fact he is not a tragic hero at all. A true tragic hero would readily have laid down his life in the court to win full revenge upon his enemy; Shylock, after a vain attempt to get back at least his principal, cringes before the Duke, accepts the sentence, and slinks off muttering: "I am not well." He is the dark figure in a romantic comedy who threatens the life of the merchant and the happiness of the lovers, and is finally punished as he deserves.

Final Appreciation.—How much of the anti-Semitism of Shakespeare's day is still apparent in the play? Something, of course, remains. All the boys of Venice follow Shylock through the streets mocking his lamentations. To the clown Launcelot, the Jew is "the very devil incarnation"; Solanio calls him "the dog Jew", and the loud-mouthed Gratiano exhausts a rich vocabulary of abuse upon him. One thing, especially, sticks fast in the modern throat, the obligation laid upon the Jew to renounce his faith. We may do well, however, to remember that religious toleration was unknown in Shakespeare's day, and that to Shakespeare's audience this sentence was an act of charity since the sacrament of baptism would undoubtedly avail to save the soul of Shylock from Hell. Whether Shakespeare himself was quite sure of this may perhaps be doubted; but we may be very sure that there was no tinge of race-hatred in the poet who put into Shylock's mouth the famous vindication of the Jew's humanity. This great speech, taken in conjunction with Portia's eulogy of mercy, might, in fact, be considered as Shakespeare's plea for tolerance as opposed to the yells of the crowd that drowned the last words of the wretched Dr. Lopez.

Few plays of Shakespeare's have provoked so much theoretical discussion as *The Merchant of Venice*. It has been treated as though it were a dramatic discussion of the proper use of wealth, of the legality of usury, of the relative values of law and equity, of the supreme importance of friendship, and so on, and so on. It is none of these, but rather a romantic comedy, almost a fairy tale, rendered credible by the poet's art. And his art had now reached the stage where simply and without protestation something of his own philosophy of life might be allowed to shine through the dramatic action. We may learn from *The Merchant of Venice* something at least of the deceitfulness of appearances, of the folly of revenge, of the high quality of mercy, and of the beauty of friendship and of wedded love. And all this in a play the most vivid, realistic, and actable that Shakespeare had yet written.

The stage history of *The Merchant of Venice* presents an interesting record of varying interpretations of the play. It was acted, the title-page of the Quarto tells us, "divers times" by Shakespeare's company, and there are records of two performances at Court in 1605. After the restoration little was heard of the *Merchant* until the beginning of the eighteenth century when it was rewritten by Granville and the part of Shylock transformed into a broad comic role played by the popular clown, Doggett. Forty years later the great tragedian, Macklin, restored Shakespeare's play to the stage and reinterpreted the character of Shylock as a cold, remorseless villain. His successful performance established a tradition which persisted until the height of the Romantic era. In 1814 Edmund Kean presented Shylock as a passionate and tragic figure, rather sympathetic than repulsive. This interpretation culminated in Irving's famous presentation of Shylock as a superb representative of a martyred race, a characteristic expression of Victorian humanitarianism. Later representations have tended to restore a Shylock more in accord with what seems to have been Shakespeare's own conception.

The part of Portia has always been a favorite with actresses. From Mrs. Bracegirdle in Granville's travesty down to the present time, one great actress after another has starred in this role. Perhaps the greatest of them all was Ellen Terry, whose grave, sweet, and humorous Portia was a splendid counterpart to Irving's tragic Shylock.

THE MERCHANT OF VENICE

Dramatis Personæ

The *Duke of Venice.*
The *Prince of Morocco,* } suitors to *Portia.*
The *Prince of Arragon,* }
Antonio, a merchant of Venice.
Bassanio, his friend, suitor to *Portia.*
Solanio, } friends to *Antonio* and *Bassanio.*
Salerio, }
Gratiano, }
Lorenzo, in love with *Jessica.*
Shylock, a rich Jew.
Tubal, a Jew, friend of *Shylock.*
Launcelot Gobbo, a clown, servant to *Shylock.*
Old Gobbo, fathei to *Launcelot.*
Leonardo, servant to *Bassanio.*
Balthasar, } servants to *Portia.*
Stephano, }
Portia, a rich heiress.
Nerissa, her waiting-gentlewoman.
Jessica, daughter to *Shylock.*

Magnificoes of Venice, Officers of the Court of Justice, Jailer, Servants to Portia, and other attendants.

SCENE: *Partly at Venice and partly at Belmont, the seat of Portia.*

ACT I. Scene I. *Venice. A street.*

Enter *Antonio, Salerio,* and *Solanio.*

Ant. In sooth, I know not why I am so sad:
It wearies me; you say it wearies you;
But how I caught it, found it, or came by it,
What stuff 't is made of, whereof it is born,
I am to learn;
And such a want-wit sadness makes of me
That I have much ado to know myself.
Sal. Your mind is tossing on the ocean,
There, where your argosies with portly sail—
Like signiors and rich burghers on the flood,
Or, as it were, the pageants of the sea—
Do overpeer the petty traffickers,
That curtsy to them, do them reverence,
As they fly by them with their woven wings.
Solan. Believe me, sir, had I such venture forth,
The better part of my affections would
Be with my hopes abroad. I should be still
Plucking the grass to know where sits the wind,
Peering in maps for ports and piers and roads;
And every object that might make me fear
Misfortune to my ventures, out of doubt
Would make me sad.
Sal. My wind cooling my broth
Would blow me to an ague when I thought
What harm a wind too great at sea might do.
I should not see the sandy hour-glass run
But I should think of shallows and of flats,
And see my wealthy Andrew dock'd in sand,
Vailing her high-top lower than her ribs
To kiss her burial. Should I go to church
And see the holy edifice of stone,
And not bethink me straight of dangerous rocks,
Which, touching but my gentle vessel's side,
Would scatter all her spices on the stream,
Enrobe the roaring waters with my silks,
And, in a word, but even now worth this,
And now worth nothing? Shall I have the thought
To think on this, and shall I lack the thought
That such a thing bechanc'd would make me sad?
But tell not me; I know Antonio
Is sad to think upon his merchandise.
Ant. Believe me, no. I thank my fortune for it,
My ventures are not in one bottom trusted,
Nor to one place; nor is my whole estate
Upon the fortune of this present year:
Therefore my merchandise makes me not sad.
Solan. Why, then you are in love.
Ant. Fie, fie!
Solan. Not in love neither? Then let us say you are sad,
Because you are not merry; and 't were as easy
For you to laugh and leap and say you are merry,
Because you are not sad. Now, by two-headed Janus,

9. **argosies,** large merchant ships. 11. **pageants,** wheeled floats on which early plays were presented. 17. **still,** always. 27. **Andrew,** name of ship.

28. **Vailing,** lowering. **high-top,** topmast. 50. **Janus,** a Roman deity, had two faces looking in pposite directions, one merry, the other sad.

Nature hath fram'd strange fellows in her time;
Some that will evermore peep through their eyes
And laugh like parrots at a bag-piper,
And other of such vinegar aspect
That they 'll not show their teeth in way of smile,
Though Nestor swear the jest be laughable.

Enter *Bassanio, Lorenzo,* and *Gratiano.*

Here comes Bassanio, your most noble kinsman,
Gratiano, and Lorenzo. Fare ye well;
We leave you now with better company.
Sal. I would have stay'd till I had made you merry,
If worthier friends had not prevented me.
Ant. Your worth is very dear in my regard.
I take it, your own business calls on you
And you embrace th' occasion to depart.
Sal. Good morrow, my good lords.
Bass. Good signiors both, when shall we laugh? Say, when?
You grow exceeding strange. Must it be so?
Sal. We 'll make our leisures to attend on yours. *Exeunt Salerio and Solanio.*
Lor. My lord Bassanio, since you have found Antonio,
We two will leave you; but at dinner-time,
I pray you, have in mind where we must meet.
Bass. I will not fail you.
Gra. You look not well, Signior Antonio;
You have too much respect upon the world:
They lose it that do buy it with much care.
Believe me, you are marvellously chang'd.
Ant. I hold the world but as the world, Gratiano,
A stage where every man must play a part,
And mine a sad one.
Gra. Let me play the fool!
With mirth and laughter let old wrinkles come,
And let my liver rather heat with wine
Than my heart cool with mortifying groans.
Why should a man, whose blood is warm within,
Sit like his grandsire cut in alabaster,
Sleep when he wakes, and creep into the jaundice
By being peevish? I tell thee what, Antonio—
I love thee, and it is my love that speaks—
There are a sort of men whose visages
Do cream and mantle like a standing pond,
And do a wilful stillness entertain,
With purpose to be dress'd in an opinion
Of wisdom, gravity, profound conceit,
As who should say, "I am Sir Oracle,
And when I ope my lips let no dog bark!"
O my Antonio, I do know of those
That therefore only are reputed wise
For saying nothing; when, I am very sure,
If they should speak, would almost damn those ears
Which, hearing them, would call their brothers fools.
I 'll tell thee more of this another time;
But fish not with this melancholy bait
For this fool gudgeon, this opinion.
Come, good Lorenzo. Fare ye well awhile;
I 'll end my exhortation after dinner.
Lor. Well, we will leave you then till dinner-time.
I must be one of these same dumb wise men,
For Gratiano never lets me speak.
Gra. Well, keep me company but two years moe,
Thou shalt not know the sound of thine own tongue.
Ant. Farewell! I 'll grow a talker for this gear.
Gra. Thanks, i' faith, for silence is only commendable
In a neat's tongue dried and a maid not vendible.
Exeunt Gratiano and Lorenzo.
Ant. Is that any thing now?
Bass. Gratiano speaks an infinite deal of nothing, more than any man in all Venice. His reasons are as two grains of wheat hid in two bushels of chaff; you shall seek all day ere you find them, and when you have them, they are not worth the search.
Ant. Well, tell me now what lady is the same
To whom you swore a secret pilgrimage
That you to-day promis'd to tell me of?
Bass. 'T is not unknown to you, Antonio,
How much I have disabled mine estate
By something showing a more swelling port
Than my faint means would grant continuance:
Nor do I now make moan to be abridg'd
From such a noble rate; but my chief care
Is to come fairly off from the great debts
Wherein my time, something too prodigal,

56. Nestor, wisest and gravest of Homeric heroes. **61. prevented**, anticipated. **67. strange**, reserved. **74. respect**, consideration. **81. liver**, seat of the passions. **82. mortifying**, deadly.

89. cream and mantle, become covered with scum. **91. opinion**, reputation. **92. conceit**, thought. **98-9. damn . . . fools**, "Whosoever shall say to his brother . . . 'Thou fool,' shall be in danger of hell fire." **102. gudgeon**, a small fish. **108. moe**, more. **110. gear**, stuff, i.e., what has been said about silent people. **112. neat's**, ox's. **vendible**, marketable. **127. rate**, style of living. **129. time**, life.

Hath left me gag'd. To you, Antonio,
I owe the most, in money and in love,
And from your love I have a warranty
To unburden all my plots and purposes
How to get clear of all the debts I owe.

Ant. I pray you, good Bassanio, let me know it;
And if it stand, as you yourself still do,
Within the eye of honour, be assur'd,
My purse, my person, my extremest means,
Lie all unlock'd to your occasions.

Bass. In my school-days, when I had lost one shaft,
I shot his fellow of the self-same flight
The self-same way with more advised watch
To find the other forth, and by adventuring both
I oft found both. I urge this childhood proof,
Because what follows is pure innocence.
I owe you much, and, like a wilful youth,
That which I owe is lost; but if you please
To shoot another arrow that self way
Which you did shoot the first, I do not doubt,
As I will watch the aim, or to find both,
Or bring your latter hazard back again
And thankfully rest debtor for the first.

Ant. You know me well, and herein spend but time
To wind about my love with circumstance;
And out of doubt you do me now more wrong
In making question of my uttermost
Than if you had made waste of all I have:
Then do but say to me what I should do
That in your knowledge may by me be done,
And I am prest unto it; therefore, speak.

Bass. In Belmont is a lady richly left;
And she is fair and, fairer than that word,
Of wondrous virtues: sometimes from her eyes
I did receive fair speechless messages:
Her name is Portia, nothing undervalu'd
To Cato's daughter, Brutus' Portia.
Nor is the wide world ignorant of her worth,
For the four winds blow in from every coast
Renowned suitors; and her sunny locks
Hang on her temples like a golden fleece,
Which makes her seat of Belmont Colchos' strand,
And many Jasons come in quest of her.
O my Antonio, had I but the means
To hold a rival place with one of them,
I have a mind presages me such thrift
That I should questionless be fortunate!

Ant. Thou know'st that all my fortunes are at sea;
Neither have I money nor commodity
To raise a present sum: therefore go forth;
Try what my credit can in Venice do:
That shall be rack'd, even to the uttermost,
To furnish thee to Belmont, to fair Portia.
Go, presently inquire, and so will I,
Where money is; and I no question make
To have it of my trust or for my sake.
Exeunt.

Scene II. *Belmont. A room in Portia's house.*

Enter *Portia* with her waiting-woman, *Nerissa.*

Por. By my troth, Nerissa, my little body is aweary of this great world.

Ner. You would be, sweet madam, if your miseries were in the same abundance as your good fortunes are; and yet, for aught I see, they are as sick that surfeit with too much as they that starve with nothing. It is no mean happiness, therefore, to be seated in the mean: superfluity comes sooner by white hairs, but competency lives longer.

Por. Good sentences and well pronounced.

Ner. They would be better, if well followed.

Por. If to do were as easy as to know what were good to do, chapels had been churches and poor men's cottages princes' palaces. It is a good divine that follows his own instructions; I can easier teach twenty what were good to be done, than be one of the twenty to follow mine own teaching. The brain may devise laws for the blood, but a hot temper leaps o'er a cold decree; such a hare is madness the youth, to skip o'er the meshes of good counsel the cripple. But this reasoning is not in the fashion to choose me a husband. O me, the word choose! I may neither choose who I would nor refuse who I dislike, so is the will of a living daughter curbed by the will of a dead father. Is it not hard, Nerissa, that I cannot choose one nor refuse none?

Ner. Your father was ever virtuous, and holy men at their death have good inspirations; therefore the lottery that he hath devised in these three chests of gold, silver, and lead, whereof who chooses his meaning chooses you, will, no doubt, never be chosen by any rightly but one who you shall

143. forth, out. **144. proof,** experiment. **145. innocence,** ingenuousness. **154. wind about,** approach indirectly. **160. prest,** ready. **163. sometimes,** once. **166. Brutus' Portia,** cf. *Julius Cæsar,* a model of virtue and courage. **172. Jasons,** a reference to Jason and his expedition to Colchis in search of the golden fleece. **175. thrift,** success.

181. rack'd, stretched. **183. presently,** immediately. **185. trust,** credit. **Scene ii: 11. sentences,** maxims. **21. meshes,** snares. **22. reasoning,** talk.

rightly love. But what warmth is there in your affection towards any of these princely suitors that are already come?

Por. I pray thee, over-name them; and as thou namest them, I will describe them; and, according to my description, level at my affection.

Ner. First, there is the Neapolitan prince.

Por. Ay, that 's a colt indeed, for he doth nothing but talk of his horse; and he makes it a great appropriation to his own good parts, that he can shoe him himself. I am much afeard my lady his mother played false with a smith.

Ner. Then there is the County Palatine.

Por. He doth nothing but frown, as who should say, "If you will not have me, choose." He hears merry tales and smiles not: I fear he will prove the weeping philosopher when he grows old, being so full of unmannerly sadness in his youth. I had rather be married to a death's-head with a bone in his mouth than to either of these. God defend me from these two!

Ner. How say you by the French lord, Monsieur Le Bon?

Por. God made him, and therefore let him pass for a man. In truth, I know it is a sin to be a mocker; but, he! why, he hath a horse better than the Neapolitan's, a better bad habit of frowning than the Count Palatine. He is every man in no man: if a throstle sing, he falls straight a capering: he will fence with his own shadow: if I should marry him, I should marry twenty husbands. If he would despise me, I would forgive him, for if he love me to madness, I shall never requite him.

Ner. What say you, then, to Falconbridge, the young baron of England?

Por. You know I say nothing to him, for he understands not me, nor I him: he hath neither Latin, French, nor Italian, and you will come into the court and swear that I have a poor pennyworth in the English. He is a proper man's picture, but, alas, who can converse with a dumb-show? How oddly he is suited! I think he bought his doublet in Italy, his round hose in France, his bonnet in Germany, and his behaviour everywhere.

Ner. What think you of the Scottish lord, his neighbour?

Por. That he hath a neighbourly charity in him, for he borrowed a box of the ear of the Englishman and swore he would pay him again when he was able: I think the Frenchman became his surety and sealed under for another.

Ner. How like you the young German, the Duke of Saxony's nephew?

Por. Very vilely in the morning, when he is sober, and most vilely in the afternoon, when he is drunk: when he is best, he is a little worse than a man, and when he is worst, he is little better than a beast. An the worst fall that ever fell, I hope I shall make shift to go without him.

Ner. If he should offer to choose, and choose the right casket, you should refuse to perform your father's will, if you should refuse to accept him.

Por. Therefore, for fear of the worst, I pray thee, set a deep glass of Rhenish wine on the contrary casket, for if the devil be within and that temptation without, I know he will choose it. I will do anything, Nerissa, ere I 'll be married to a sponge.

Ner. You need not fear, lady, the having any of these lords: they have acquainted me with their determinations; which is, indeed, to return to their home and to trouble you with no more suit, unless you may be won by some other sort than your father's imposition depending on the caskets.

Por. If I live to be as old as Sibylla, I will die as chaste as Diana, unless I be obtained by the manner of my father's will. I am glad this parcel of wooers are so reasonable, for there is not one among them but I dote on his very absence, and I pray God grant them a fair departure.

Ner. Do you not remember, lady, in your father's time, a Venetian, a scholar, and a soldier, that came hither in company of the Marquis of Montferrat?

Por. Yes, yes, it was Bassanio; as I think, he was so called.

Ner. True, madam. He, of all the men that ever my foolish eyes looked upon, was the best deserving a fair lady.

Por. I remember him well, and I remember him worthy of thy praise.

Enter a *Serving-man.*

How now! what news?

Serv. The four strangers seek for you, madam, to take their leave; and there is a forerunner come from a fifth, the Prince of

41. level, aim. **43. colt,** foolish youth: the Neapolitans were famous horsemen. **45. appropriation,** addition. **52. choose,** take your choice. **53. weeping philosopher,** Heraclitus, a pessimistic thinker. **77. proper,** handsome. **79. suited,** dressed. **doublet,** close-fitting coat. **80. round hose,** breeches.

88. I think, ff., refers to constant alliance of France with Scotland against England. **sealed under for,** went surety for. **113. sort,** way. **115. imposition,** injunction. **116. Sibylla,** the Cumæan Sibyl offered by Apollo as many birthdays as there were grains in a handful of sand. **134. four strangers,** Nerissa mentions six; the English and the Scotch suitor were probably added in a revision of the play.

Morocco, who brings word the Prince his master will be here to-night.

Por. If I could bid the fifth welcome with so good a heart as I can bid the other four farewell, I should be glad of his approach: if he had the condition of a saint and the complexion of a devil, I had rather he should shrive me than wive me.
Come, Nerissa. Sirrah, go before.
While we shut the gates upon one wooer, another knocks at the door. *Exeunt.*

Scene III. *Venice. A public place.*

Enter *Bassanio* with *Shylock* the Jew.

Shy. Three thousand ducats; well.

Bass. Ay, sir, for three months.

Shy. For three months; well.

Bass. For the which, as I told you, Antonio shall be bound.

Shy. Antonio shall become bound; well.

Bass. May you stead me? Will you pleasure me? Shall I know your answer?

Shy. Three thousand ducats for three months, and Antonio bound.

Bass. Your answer to that.

Shy. Antonio is a good man.

Bass. Have you heard any imputation to the contrary?

Shy. Ho, no, no, no, no! My meaning in saying he is a good man is to have you understand me that he is sufficient. Yet his means are in supposition: he hath an argosy bound to Tripolis, another to the Indies; I understand, moreover, upon the Rialto, he hath a third at Mexico, a fourth for England, and other ventures he hath, squandered abroad. But ships are but boards, sailors but men; there be land-rats and water-rats, land-thieves and water-thieves, I mean pirates, and then there is the peril of waters, winds, and rocks. The man is, notwithstanding, sufficient. Three thousand ducats: I think I may take his bond.

Bass. Be assured you may.

Shy. I will be assured I may; and, that I may be assured, I will bethink me. May I speak with Antonio?

Bass. If it please you to dine with us.

Shy. Yes, to smell pork; to eat of the habitation which your prophet the Nazarite conjured the devil into. I will buy with you, sell with you, talk with you, walk with you, and so following; but I will not eat with you, drink with you, nor pray with you. What news on the Rialto? Who is he comes here?

Enter *Antonio.*

Bass. This is Signior Antonio.

Shy. [*Aside.*] How like a fawning publican he looks!
I hate him for he is a Christian;
But more for that in low simplicity
He lends out money gratis, and brings down
The rate of usance here with us in Venice.
If I can catch him once upon the hip,
I will feed fat the ancient grudge I bear him.
He hates our sacred nation, and he rails,
Even there where merchants most do congregate,
On me, my bargains, and my well-won thrift,
Which he calls interest. Cursed be my tribe,
If I forgive him!

Bass. Shylock, do you hear?

Shy. I am debating of my present store,
And, by the near guess of my memory,
I cannot instantly raise up the gross
Of full three thousand ducats. What of that?
Tubal, a wealthy Hebrew of my tribe,
Will furnish me: but soft! how many months
Do you desire? [*To Ant.*] Rest you fair, good signior;
Your worship was the last man in our mouths.

Ant. Shylock, although I neither lend nor borrow
By taking nor by giving of excess,
Yet, to supply the ripe wants of my friend,
I 'll break a custom. Is he yet possess'd
How much ye would?

Shy. Ay, ay, three thousand ducats.

Ant. And for three months.

Shy. I had forgot; three months; you told me so.
Well then, your bond; and let me see;—but hear you;
Methoughts you said you neither lend nor borrow
Upon advantage.

Ant. I do never use it.

Shy. When Jacob graz'd his uncle Laban's sheep—
This Jacob from our holy Abram was,
(As his wise mother wrought in his behalf)
The third possessor; ay, he was the third—

Ant. And what of him? Did he take interest?

Shy. No, not take interest, not, as you would say,
Directly int'rest. Mark what Jacob did.

143. **condition,** disposition. **Scene iii: 7. stead,** assist. **19. Rialto,** market place of Venice. **34. Nazarite,** Nazarene. The passage refers to Christ's driving the devils from the men into a herd of swine.

42. **publican,** term of abuse; cf. the biblical phrase "publicans and sinners." **46. usance,** interest. **47. catch . . . hip,** wrestling term. **63. excess,** interest. **65. possess'd,** informed. **71. advantage,** interest. **72 ff., Jacob,** cf. Genesis xxx. **75. possessor,** of God's promise to Abraham.

When Laban and himself were compromis'd
That all the eanlings which were streak'd and pied
Should fall as Jacob's hire, the ewes, being rank,
In the end of autumn turned to the rams,
And, when the work of generation was
Between these woolly breeders in the act,
The skilful shepherd pill'd me certain wands
And, in the doing of the deed of kind,
He stuck them up before the fulsome ewes,
Who then conceiving did in eaning time
Fall parti-colour'd lambs, and those were Jacob's.
This was a way to thrive, and he was blest;
And thrift is blessing, if men steal it not.

Ant. This was a venture, sir, that Jacob serv'd for;
A thing not in his power to bring to pass,
But sway'd and fashion'd by the hand of Heaven.
Was this inserted to make interest good?
Or is your gold and silver ewes and rams?

Shy. I cannot tell; I make it breed as fast.
But note me, signior.

Ant. Mark you this, Bassanio,
The devil can cite Scripture for his purpose.
An evil soul producing holy witness
Is like a villain with a smiling cheek,
A goodly apple rotten at the heart.
O, what a goodly outside falsehood hath!

Shy. Three thousand ducats; 't is a good round sum.
Three months from twelve; then, let me see; the rate—

Ant. Well, Shylock, shall we be beholding to you?

Shy. Signior Antonio, many a time and oft
In the Rialto you have rated me
About my moneys and my usances.
Still have I borne it with a patient shrug,
For suff'rance is the badge of all our tribe.
You call me misbeliever, cut-throat dog,
And spet upon my Jewish gaberdine,
And all for use of that which is mine own.
Well then, it now appears you need my help.
Go to, then! You come to me, and you say,
"Shylock, we would have moneys;" you say so—
You, that did void your rheum upon my beard
And foot me as you spurn a stranger cur
Over your threshold; moneys is your suit.
What should I say to you? Should I not say,
"Hath a dog money? Is it possible
A cur can lend three thousand ducats?" Or
Shall I bend low and in a bondman's key,
With bated breath and whisp'ring humbleness,
Say this:
"Fair sir, you spet on me on Wednesday last;
You spurn'd me such a day; another time
You call'd me dog; and for these courtesies
I 'll lend you thus much moneys"?

Ant. I am as like to call thee so again,
To spet on thee again, to spurn thee too.
If thou wilt lend this money, lend it not
As to thy friends; for when did friendship take
A breed for barren metal of his friend?
But lend it rather to thine enemy,
Who, if he break, thou mayst with better face
Exact the penalty.

Shy. Why, look you, how you storm!
I would be friends with you and have your love,
Forget the shames that you have stain'd me with,
Supply your present wants, and take no doit
Of usance for my moneys, and you 'll not hear me.
This is kind I offer.

Bass. This were kindness.

Shy. This kindness will I show.
Go with me to a notary, seal me there
Your single bond; and, in a merry sport,
If you repay me not on such a day,
In such a place, such sum or sums as are
Express'd in the condition, let the forfeit
Be nominated for an equal pound
Of your fair flesh, to be cut off and taken
In what part of your body pleaseth me.

Ant. Content, i' faith, I 'll seal to such a bond,
And say there is much kindness in the Jew.

Bass. You shall not seal to such a bond for me;
I 'll rather dwell in my necessity.

Ant. Why, fear not, man; I will not forfeit it.
Within these two months, that 's a month before
This bond expires, I do expect return
Of thrice three times the value of this bond.

Shy. O father Abram, what these Christians are,
Whose own hard dealings teaches them suspect
The thoughts of others! Pray you, tell me this:
If he should break his day, what should I gain
By the exaction of the forfeiture?
A pound of man's flesh taken from a man
Is not so estimable, profitable neither,

79. **compromis'd**, agreed. 80. **eanlings**, new-born lambs. 85. **pill'd**, peeled. 86. **kind**, nature. 89. **Fall**, give birth to. 106. **beholding**, under obligation. 113. **gaberdine**, cloak. 118. **rheum**, spittle.

135. **breed**, interest. 137. **Who**, from whom. 141. **doit**, a small coin. 146. **single**, without endorsers. 150. **equal**, exact.

As flesh of muttons, beefs, or goats. I say,
To buy his favour I extend this friendship.
If he will take it, so; if not, adieu.
And, for my love, I pray you wrong me not.
Ant. Yes, Shylock, I will seal unto this bond.
Shy. Then meet me forthwith at the notary's;
Give him direction for this merry bond,
And I will go and purse the ducats straight,
See to my house, left in the fearful guard
Of an unthrifty knave, and presently
I 'll be with you. *Exit Shylock.*
Ant. Hie thee, gentle Jew.
The Hebrew will turn Christian; he grows kind.
Bass. I like not fair terms and a villain's mind.
Ant. Come on; in this there can be no dismay;
My ships come home a month before the day.
Exeunt.

ACT II. Scene I. *Belmont. A room in Portia's house.*

Enter the *Prince of Morocco,* a tawny Moor, all in white, and three or four followers accordingly, with *Portia, Nerissa,* and their train. Flourish of cornets.

Mor. Mislike me not for my complexion,
The shadow'd livery of the burnish'd sun,
To whom I am a neighbour and near bred.
Bring me the fairest creature northward born,
Where Phœbus' fire scarce thaws the icicles,
And let us make incision for your love,
To prove whose blood is reddest, his or mine.
I tell thee, lady, this aspect of mine
Hath fear'd the valiant: by my love, I swear
The best-regarded virgins of our clime
Have lov'd it too: I would not change this hue,
Except to steal your thoughts, my gentle queen.
Por. In terms of choice I am not solely led
By nice direction of a maiden's eyes;
Besides, the lottery of my destiny
Bars me the right of voluntary choosing:
But if my father had not scanted me
And hedg'd me by his wit to yield myself
His wife who wins me by that means I told you,
Yourself, renowned Prince, then stood as fair
As any comer I have look'd on yet
For my affection.
Mor. Even for that I thank you;
Therefore, I pray you, lead me to the caskets
To try my fortune. By this scimitar
That slew the Sophy and a Persian prince
That won three fields of Sultan Solyman,
I would outstare the sternest eyes that look,
Outbrave the heart most daring on the earth,
Pluck the young sucking cubs from the she-bear,
Yea, mock the lion when 'a roars for prey,
To win thee, lady. But, alas the while!
If Hercules and Lichas play at dice
Which is the better man, the greater throw
May turn by fortunes from the weaker hand.
So is Alcides beaten by his page;
And so may I, blind fortune leading me,
Miss that which one unworthier may attain,
And die with grieving.
Por. You must take your chance,
And either not attempt to choose at all,
Or swear before you choose, if you choose wrong
Never to speak to lady afterward
In way of marriage; therefore be advis'd.
Mor. Nor will not. Come, bring me unto my chance.
Por. First, forward to the temple; after dinner
Your hazard shall be made.
Mor. Good fortune then!
To make me blest or cursed'st among men.
Cornets, and exeunt.

Scene II. *Venice. Before Shylock's house.*

Enter the Clown *Launcelot* alone.

Laun. Certainly my conscience will serve me to run from this Jew my master. The fiend is at mine elbow and tempts me, saying to me, "Gobbo, Launcelot Gobbo, good Launcelot," or "good Gobbo," or "good Launcelot Gobbo, use your legs, take the start, run away." My conscience says, "No; take heed, honest Laun-

176. fearful, untrustworthy. **Act II, Scene i: 1. shadow'd livery,** black badge. **7. reddest,** then, as now, a symbol of courage. **9. fear'd,** frightened. **14. nice,** fastidious. **17. scanted,** limited. **18. wit,** wisdom. **25. Sophy,** Shah of Persia. **26. Solyman,** Turkish sultan, 1496-1566.

30. 'a, he. **32. Lichas,** servant of Hercules, **(Alcides).**

celot; take heed, honest Gobbo," or, as aforesaid, "honest Launcelot Gobbo; do not run; scorn running with thy heels." Well, the most courageous fiend bids me pack. "Via!" says the fiend; "away!" says the fiend; "for the heavens, rouse up a brave mind," says the fiend, "and run." Well, my conscience, hanging about the neck of my heart, says very wisely to me, "My honest friend Launcelot, being an honest man's son," or rather an honest woman's son; for, indeed, my father did something smack, something grow to, he had a kind of taste,—well, my conscience says, "Launcelot, budge not." "Budge," says the fiend. "Budge not," says my conscience. "Conscience," say I, "you counsel well;" "Fiend," say I, "you counsel well." To be ruled by my conscience, I should stay with the Jew my master, who (God bless the mark) is a kind of devil; and, to run away from the Jew, I should be ruled by the fiend, who, saving your reverence, is the devil himself. Certainly the Jew is the very devil incarnation; and, in my conscience, my conscience is but a kind of hard conscience, to offer to counsel me to stay with the Jew. The fiend gives the more friendly counsel. I will run, fiend; my heels are at your commandment; I will run.

Enter *Old Gobbo,* with a basket.

Gob. Master young man, you, I pray you, which is the way to master Jew's?

Laun. [*Aside.*] O heavens! this is my true-begotten father, who, being more than sand-blind, high-gravel blind, knows me not; I will try confusions with him.

Gob. Master young gentleman, I pray you, which is the way to master Jew's?

Laun. Turn up on your right hand at the next turning, but at the next turning of all, on your left; marry at the very next turning, turn of no hand, but turn down indirectly to the Jew's house.

Gob. Be God's sonties, 't will be a hard way to hit. Can you tell me whether one Launcelot, that dwells with him, dwell with him or no?

Laun. Talk you of young Master Launcelot? [*Aside.*] Mark me now; now will I raise the waters. Talk you of young Master Launcelot?

Gob. No master, sir, but a poor man's son. His father, though I say 't, is an honest exceeding poor man and, God be thanked, well to live.

Laun. Well, let his father be what 'a will, we talk of young Master Launcelot.

Gob. Your worship's friend and Launcelot, sir.

Laun. But I pray you, ergo, old man, ergo, I beseech you, talk you of young Master Launcelot.

Gob. Of Launcelot, an 't please your mastership.

Laun. Ergo, Master Launcelot. Talk not of Master Launcelot, father; for the young gentleman, according to Fates and Destinies and such odd sayings, the Sisters Three and such branches of learning, is indeed deceased, or, as you would say in plain terms, gone to heaven.

Gob. Marry, God forbid! The boy was the very staff of my age, my very prop.

Laun. [*Aside.*] Do I look like a cudgel or a hovel-post, a staff or a prop? Do you know me, father?

Gob. Alack the day, I know you not, young gentleman; but I pray you, tell me, is my boy, God rest his soul, alive or dead?

Laun. Do you not know me, father?

Gob. Alack, sir, I am sand-blind; I know you not.

Laun. Nay, indeed, if you had your eyes, you might fail of the knowing me; it is a wise father that knows his own child. Well, old man, I will tell you news of your son; give me your blessing; truth will come to light; murder cannot be hid long; a man's son may, but in the end truth will out.

Gob. Pray you, sir, stand up. I am sure you are not Launcelot, my boy.

Laun. Pray you, let 's have no more fooling about it, but give me your blessing: I am Launcelot, your boy that was, your son that is, your child that shall be.

Gob. I cannot think you are my son.

Laun. I know not what I shall think of that; but I am Launcelot, the Jew's man, and I am sure Margery your wife is my mother.

Gob. Her name is Margery, indeed. I 'll be sworn, if thou be Launcelot, thou art mine own flesh and blood. Lord worshipped might he be! what a beard hast thou got! thou hast got more hair on thy chin than Dobbin my fill-horse has on his tail.

Laun. It should seem, then, that Dobbin's tail grows backward. I am sure he had more hair of his tail than I have of my face when I last saw him.

Gob. Lord, how art thou changed! How

10. **"Via!"**, away! 18-9. **smack, . . . grow to . . . taste,** the three phrases imply the same thing, viz., that Old Gobbo was not very honest; **grow to** may mean stick to the pot, scorch. 24. **God . . . mark,** deprecatory exclamation. 38. **high-gravel,** Launcelot's invention, a degree of blindness between sand- and stone-blind. 47. **sonties,** diminutive of sonts, i.e., saints. 51. **waters,** tears.

55. **well to live,** well to do. 99. **beard,** Launcelot kneels with his back to the old man. 100. **fill-horse,** shaft-horse.

dost thou and thy master agree? I have brought him a present. How 'gree you now?

Laun. Well, well; but, for mine own part, as I have set up my rest to run away, so I will not rest till I have run some ground. My master 's a very Jew: give him a present! give him a halter: I am famished in his service; you may tell every finger I have with my ribs. Father, I am glad you are come; give me your present to one Master Bassanio, who, indeed, gives rare new liveries: if I serve not him, I will run as far as God has any ground. O rare fortune! here comes the man. To him, father; for I am a Jew, if I serve the Jew any longer.

Enter *Bassanio,* with *Leonardo* and a follower or two.

Bass. You may do so; but let it be so hasted that supper be ready at the farthest by five of the clock. See these letters delivered; put the liveries to making, and desire Gratiano to come anon to my lodging.

Exit one of his men.

Laun. To him, father.

Gob. God bless your worship!

Bass. Gramercy! wouldst thou aught with me?

Gob. Here 's my son, sir, a poor boy,—

Laun. Not a poor boy, sir, but the rich Jew's man; that would, sir, as my father shall specify—

Gob. He hath a great infection, sir, as one would say, to serve—

Laun. Indeed, the short and the long is, I serve the Jew, and have a desire, as my father shall specify—

Gob. His master and he, saving your worship's reverence, are scarce cater-cousins—

Laun. To be brief, the very truth is that the Jew, having done me wrong, doth cause me, as my father, being, I hope, an old man, shall frutify unto you—

Gob. I have here a dish of doves that I would bestow upon your worship, and my suit is—

Laun. In very brief, the suit is impertinent to myself, as your worship shall know by this honest old man; and, though I say it, though old man, yet poor man, my father.

Bass. One speak for both. What would you?

Laun. Serve you, sir.

Gob. That is the very defect of the matter, sir.

Bass. I know thee well; thou hast obtain'd
thy suit.
Shylock thy master spoke with me this day,
And hath preferr'd thee, if it be preferment
To leave a rich Jew's service, to become
The follower of so poor a gentleman.

Laun. The old proverb is very well parted between my master Shylock and you, sir: you have the grace of God, sir, and he hath enough.

Bass. Thou speak'st it well. Go, father,
with thy son.
Take leave of thy old master, and inquire
My lodging out. Give him a livery
More guarded than his fellows'; see it done.

Laun. Father, in. I cannot get a service, no; I have ne'er a tongue in my head. Well, if any man in Italy have a fairer table, which doth offer to swear upon a book, I shall have good fortune. Go to, here 's a simple line of life! Here 's a small trifle of wives! Alas, fifteen wives is nothing! Eleven widows and nine maids is a simple coming-in for one man. And then to escape drowning thrice, and to be in peril of my life with the edge of a feather-bed; here are simple scapes. Well, if Fortune be a woman, she's a good wench for this gear. Father, come; I 'll take my leave of the Jew in the twinkling of an eye.

Exeunt Launcelot and old Gobbo.

Bass. I pray thee, good Leonardo, think on
this:
These things being bought and orderly be-
stow'd,
Return in haste, for I do feast to-night
My best esteem'd acquaintance: hie thee, go.

Leon. My best endeavours shall be done
herein.

Enter *Gratiano.*

Gra. Where 's your master?

Leon. Yonder, sir, he walks.

Exit Leonardo.

Gra. Signior Bassanio!

Bass. Gratiano!

Gra. I have a suit to you.

Bass. You have obtain'd it.

Gra. You must not deny me; I must go with you to Belmont.

Bass. Why, then you must. But hear thee,
Gratiano;
Thou art too wild, too rude and bold of voice;
Parts that become thee happily enough
And in such eyes as ours appear not faults;
But where thou art not known, why, there they
show
Something too liberal. Pray thee, take pain

110. set up my rest, resolved, bet my pile. **114. tell,** count. **128. Gramercy,** *grand merci,* many thanks. **133. infection,** affection. **139. scarce cater-cousins,** hardly good friends. **143. frutify,** certify (probably intended fructify, i.e., make fruitful). **152. defect,** for effect (purport).

158. proverb, "He that hath the grace of God hath enough." **164. guarded,** braided. **167. table,** palm; Launcelot is reading his fortune in his hand. **171. simple,** in its use throughout this speech the term means small, trifling. **coming-in,** income.

To allay with some cold drops of modesty
Thy skipping spirit, lest through thy wild behaviour
I be misconster'd in the place I go to,
And lose my hopes.
Gra. Signior Bassanio, hear me:
If I do not put on a sober habit,
Talk with respect and swear but now and then,
Wear prayer-books in my pocket, look demurely,
Nay more, while grace is saying, hood mine eyes
Thus with my hat, and sigh and say Amen,
Use all the observance of civility,
Like one well studied in a sad ostent
To please his grandam, never trust me more.
Bass. Well, we shall see your bearing.
Gra. Nay, but I bar to-night; you shall not gauge me
By what we do to-night.
Bass. No, that were pity.
I would entreat you rather to put on
Your boldest suit of mirth, for we have friends
That purpose merriment. But fare you well!
I have some business.
Gra. And I must to Lorenzo and the rest;
But we will visit you at supper-time. *Exeunt.*

Scene III. *A room in Shylock's house.*

Enter *Jessica* and the Clown *Launcelot.*

Jes. I am sorry thou wilt leave my father so:
Our house is hell, and thou, a merry devil,
Didst rob it of some taste of tediousness.
But fare thee well, there is a ducat for thee;
And, Launcelot, soon at supper shalt thou see
Lorenzo, who is thy new master's guest.
Give him this letter; do it secretly;
And so farewell: I would not have my father
See me in talk with thee.

Laun. Adieu! tears exhibit my tongue. Most beautiful pagan, most sweet Jew! if a Christian do not play the knave and get thee, I am much deceived. But, adieu! these foolish drops do something drown my manly spirit. Adieu! *Exit.*

Jes. Farewell, good Launcelot.
Alack, what heinous sin is it in me
To be asham'd to be my father's child!
But though I am a daughter to his blood,
I am not to his manners. O Lorenzo,
If thou keep promise, I shall end this strife,
Become a Christian and thy loving wife. *Exit.*

Scene IV. *A street in Venice.*

Enter *Gratiano, Lorenzo, Salerio,* and *Solanio.*

Lor. Nay, we will slink away in supper-time,
Disguise us at my lodging and return,
All in an hour.
Gra. We have not made good preparation.
Sal. We have not spoke us yet of torch-bearers.
Solan. 'T is vile unless it may be quaintly ordered,
And better in my mind not undertook.
Lor. 'T is now but four o'clock; we have two hours
To furnish us.

Enter *Launcelot,* with a letter.

Friend Launcelot, what 's the news?

Laun. An it shall please you to break up this, it shall seem to signify.

Lor. I know the hand; in faith, 't is a fair hand,
And whiter than the paper it writ on
Is the fair hand that writ.
Gra. Love-news, in faith.
Laun. By your leave, sir.
Lor. Whither goest thou?

Laun. Marry, sir, to bid my old master the Jew to sup to-night with my new master the Christian.

Lor. Hold, here, take this: tell gentle Jessica
I will not fail her; speak it privately; go.
Exit Launcelot.
Gentlemen,
Will you prepare you for this masque to-night?
I am provided of a torch-bearer.
Sal. Ay, marry, I 'll be gone about it straight.
Solan. And so will I.
Lor. Meet me and Gratiano
At Gratiano's lodging some hour hence.
Sal. 'T is good we do so.
Exeunt Salerio and Solanio.
Gra. Was not that letter from fair Jessica?
Lor. I must needs tell thee all. She hath directed
How I shall take her from her father's house,
What gold and jewels she is furnish'd with,
What page's suit she hath in readiness.

199. habit, deportment. **205. sad ostent,** grave bearing. **Scene iii: 10. exhibit,** probably for inhibit (hinder).

Scene iv: 5. spoke us of, bespoken. **6. quaintly,** elegantly. **10. break up,** open.

If e'er the Jew her father come to heaven,
It will be for his gentle daughter's sake;
And never dare misfortune cross her foot,
Unless she do it under this excuse,
That she is issue to a faithless Jew.
Come, go with me; peruse this as thou goest.
Fair Jessica shall be my torch-bearer.
Exeunt.

Scene V. *Before Shylock's house.*

Enter the Jew *Shylock* and *Launcelot* his man that was the Clown.

Shy. Well, thou shalt see, thy eyes shall be thy judge,
The difference of old Shylock and Bassanio.—
What, Jessica!—Thou shalt not gormandise,
As thou hast done with me,—What, Jessica!—
And sleep and snore, and rend apparel out;—
Why, Jessica, I say!

Laun. Why, Jessica!

Shy. Who bids thee call? I do not bid thee call.

Laun. Your worship was wont to tell me that I could do nothing without bidding.

Enter *Jessica.*

Jes. Call you? What is your will?

Shy. I am bid forth to supper, Jessica.
There are my keys. But wherefore should I go?
I am not bid for love; they flatter me;
But yet I 'll go in hate, to feed upon
The prodigal Christian. Jessica, my girl,
Look to my house. I am right loath to go:
There is some ill a-brewing towards my rest,
For I did dream of money-bags to-night.

Laun. I beseech you, sir, go. My young master doth expect your reproach.

Shy. So do I his.

Laun. And they have conspired together. I will not say you shall see a masque; but if you do, then it was not for nothing that my nose fell a-bleeding on Black Monday last at six o'clock i' th' morning, falling out that year on Ash Wednesday was four year, in th' afternoon.

Shy. What, are there masques? Hear you me, Jessica.
Lock up my doors; and when you hear the drum
And the vile squealing of the wry-neck'd fife,
Clamber not you up to the casements then,
Nor thrust your head into the public street
To gaze on Christian fools with varnish'd faces,
But stop my house's ears, I mean my casements:
Let not the sound of shallow fopp'ry enter
My sober house. By Jacob's staff I swear
I have no mind of feasting forth to-night;
But I will go. Go you before me, sirrah;
Say I will come.

Laun. I will go before, sir. Mistress, look out at a window, for all this;

There will come a Christian by,
Will be worth a Jewess' eye. *Exit.*

Shy. What says that fool of Hagar's offspring, ha?

Jes. His words were "Farewell, mistress!" nothing else.

Shy. The patch is kind enough, but a huge feeder;
Snail-slow in profit, and he sleeps by day
More than the wild-cat: drones hive not with me;
Therefore I part with him, and part with him
To one that I would have him help to waste
His borrowed purse. Well, Jessica, go in.
Perhaps I will return immediately.
Do as I bid you, shut doors after you;
Fast bind, fast find;
A proverb never stale in thrifty mind. *Exit.*

Jes. Farewell; and if my fortune be not cross'd,
I have a father, you a daughter, lost. *Exit.*

Scene VI. *Before Shylock's house.*

Enter the Maskers, *Gratiano* and *Salerio.*

Gra. This is the pent-house under which Lorenzo
Desired us to make stand.

Sal. His hour is almost past.

Gra. And it is marvel he out-dwells his hour,
For lovers ever run before the clock.

Sal. O, ten times faster Venus' pigeons fly
To seal love's bonds new-made than they are wont
To keep obliged faith unforfeited!

Gra. That ever holds: who riseth from a feast
With that keen appetite that he sits down?
Where is the horse that doth untread again

38. **faithless**, infidel. **Scene v: 5. rend**, wear. **18. to-night**, last night. **20. reproach**, for approach. **25. Black Monday**, Easter Monday. **30. wry-neck'd fife**, crooked-necked fifer.

33. **varnish'd faces**, masks, or painted faces. **44. Hagar's**, she was both a Gentile and a servant. **46. patch**, fool. **Scene vi: 1. pent-house**, projecting roof. The maskers stand under the projecting balcony of the stage. **5. Venus' pigeons**, the doves that drew Venus' chariot. **7. obliged**, already contracted. **10. untread**, retrace.

His tedious measures with the unbated fire
That he did pace them first? All things that are,
Are with more spirit chased than enjoy'd.
How like a younker or a prodigal
The scarfed bark puts from her native bay,
Hugg'd and embraced by the strumpet wind!
How like the prodigal doth she return,
With over-weather'd ribs and ragged sails,
Lean, rent and beggar'd by the strumpet wind!

Sal. Here comes Lorenzo; more of this hereafter.

Enter *Lorenzo.*

Lor. Sweet friends, your patience for my long abode;
Not I, but my affairs, have made you wait:
When you shall please to play the thieves for wives,
I 'll watch as long for you then. Approach;
Here dwells my father Jew. Ho! who 's within?

Enter *Jessica,* above.

Jes. Who are you? Tell me, for more certainty,
Albeit I 'll swear that I do know your tongue.

Lor. Lorenzo, and thy love.

Jes. Lorenzo, certain, and my love indeed,
For who love I so much? And now who knows
But you, Lorenzo, whether I am yours?

Lor. Heaven and thy thoughts are witness that thou art.

Jes. Here, catch this casket; it is worth the pains.
I am glad 't is night, you do not look on me,
For I am much asham'd of my exchange.
But love is blind and lovers cannot see
The pretty follies that themselves commit;
For if they could, Cupid himself would blush
To see me thus transformed to a boy.

Lor. Descend, for you must be my torch-bearer.

Jes. What, must I hold a candle to my shames?
They in themselves, good sooth, are too too light.
Why, 't is an office of discovery, love;
And I should be obscur'd.

Lor. So are you, sweet.
Even in the lovely garnish of a boy.
But come at once;
For the close night doth play the runaway,
And we are stay'd for at Bassanio's feast.

Jes. I will make fast the doors, and gild myself
With some moe ducats, and be with you straight. *Exit above.*

Gra. Now, by my hood, a gentle and no Jew.

Lor. Beshrew me but I love her heartily;
For she is wise, if I can judge of her,
And fair she is, if that mine eyes be true,
And true she is, as she hath prov'd herself,
And therefore, like herself, wise, fair, and true,
Shall she be placed in my constant soul.

Enter *Jessica* below.

What, art thou come? On, gentlemen; away!
Our masquing mates by this time for us stay.
Exit with Jessica and Salerio.

Enter *Antonio.*

Ant. Who 's there?

Gra. Signior Antonio!

Ant. Fie, fie, Gratiano! where are all the rest?
'T is nine o'clock; our friends all stay for you.
No masque to-night; the wind is come about,
Bassanio presently will go aboard.
I have sent twenty out to seek for you.

Gra. I am glad on 't. I desire no more delight
Than to be under sail and gone to-night.
Exeunt.

Scene VII. *Belmont. A room in Portia's house.*

Enter *Portia* with the *Prince of Morocco,* and both their trains.

Por. Go draw aside the curtains and discover
The several caskets to this noble prince.
Now make your choice.

Mor. The first, of gold, who this inscription bears,
"Who chooseth me shall gain what many men desire;"
The second, silver, which this promise carries,
"Who chooseth me shall get as much as he deserves;"
This third, dull lead, with warning all as blunt,
"Who chooseth me must give and hazard all he hath."
How shall I know if I do choose the right?

Por. The one of them contains my picture, Prince:
If you choose that, then I am yours withal.

11. measures, paces. **14. younker,** stripling. **15. scarfed,** bedecked with flags. **42. light,** (1) patent, (2) frivolous. **43. office of discovery,** the very function of torch-bearing is to reveal, not conceal. **47. close,** secret.

51. gentle, a pun on Gentile. **Scene vii: 1. discover,** disclose. **12. withal,** with it.

Mor. Some god direct my judgment! Let me see;
I will survey th' inscriptions back again.
What says this leaden casket?
"Who chooseth me must give and hazard all he hath."
Must give: for what? For lead? Hazard for lead?
This casket threatens. Men that hazard all
Do it in hope of fair advantages;
A golden mind stoops not to shows of dross.
I 'll then nor give nor hazard aught for lead.
What says the silver with her virgin hue?
"Who chooseth me shall get as much as he deserves."
As much as he deserves! Pause there, Morocco,
And weigh thy value with an even hand.
If thou be'st rated by thy estimation,
Thou dost deserve enough; and yet enough
May not extend so far as to the lady;
And yet to be afeard of my deserving
Were but a weak disabling of myself.
As much as I deserve! Why, that 's the lady.
I do in birth deserve her, and in fortunes,
In graces, and in qualities of breeding;
But more than these, in love I do deserve.
What if I stray'd no farther, but chose here?
Let 's see once more this saying grav'd in gold:
"Who chooseth me shall gain what many men desire."
Why, that 's the lady; all the world desires her.
From the four corners of the earth they come
To kiss this shrine, this mortal-breathing saint.
The Hyrcanian deserts and the vasty wilds
Of wide Arabia are as throughfares now
For princes to come view fair Portia.
The watery kingdom, whose ambitious head
Spets in the face of heaven, is no bar
To stop the foreign spirits, but they come
As o'er a brook to see fair Portia.
One of these three contains her heavenly picture.
Is 't like that lead contains her? 'T were damnation
To think so base a thought: it were too gross
To rib her cerecloth in the obscure grave.
Or shall I think in silver she 's immur'd,
Being ten times undervalued to tried gold?
O sinful thought! Never so rich a gem
Was set in worse than gold. They have in England
A coin that bears the figure of an angel
Stamp'd in gold, but that 's insculp'd upon;
But here an angel in a golden bed
Lies all within. Deliver me the key:
Here do I choose, and thrive I as I may!

Por. There, take it, Prince; and if my form lie there,
Then I am yours.

He unlocks the golden casket.

Mor. O hell! what have we here?
A carrion Death within whose empty eye
There is a written scroll! I 'll read the writing.

"All that glisters is not gold;
Often have you heard that told.
Many a man his life hath sold
But my outside to behold.
Gilded tombs do worms infold.
Had you been as wise as bold,
Young in limbs, in judgement old,
Your answer had not been inscroll'd.
Fare you well; your suit is cold."

Cold, indeed; and labour lost:
Then, farewell, heat, and welcome, frost!
Portia, adieu. I have too griev'd a heart
To take a tedious leave; thus losers part.

Exit with his train.

Por. A gentle riddance. Draw the curtains, go.
Let all of his complexion choose me so.

Exeunt.

Scene VIII. *A street in Venice.*

Enter *Salerio* and *Solanio.*

Sal. Why, man, I saw Bassanio under sail.
With him is Gratiano gone along,
And in their ship I 'm sure Lorenzo is not.

Solan. The villain Jew with outcries rais'd the Duke,
Who went with him to search Bassanio's ship.

Sal. He came too late, the ship was under sail;
But there the Duke was given to understand
That in a gondola were seen together
Lorenzo and his amorous Jessica.
Besides, Antonio certified the Duke
They were not with Bassanio in his ship.

Solan. I never heard a passion so confus'd,
So strange, outrageous, and so variable,
As the dog Jew did utter in the streets.
"My daughter! O my ducats! O my daughter!
Fled with a Christian! O my Christian ducats!
Justice! the law! my ducats, and my daughter!
A sealed bag, two sealed bags of ducats,

26. estimation, reputation. **30. disabling,** undervaluing. **41. Hyrcanian,** Hyrcania, a province in distant Asia. **51. rib,** enclose. **cerecloth,** shroud.

63. a carrion Death, a death's head.

Of double ducats, stol'n from me by my daughter!
And jewels, two stones, two rich and precious stones,
Stol'n by my daughter! Justice! find the girl;
She hath the stones upon her, and the ducats."

Sal. Why, all the boys in Venice follow him,
Crying his stones, his daughter, and his ducats.

Solan. Let good Antonio look he keep his day,
Or he shall pay for this.

Sal. Marry, well remember'd.
I reason'd with a Frenchman yesterday,
Who told me, in the narrow seas that part
The French and English, there miscarried
A vessel of our country richly fraught.
I thought upon Antonio when he told me;
And wish'd in silence that it were not his.

Solan. You were best to tell Antonio what you hear;
Yet do not suddenly, for it may grieve him.

Sal. A kinder gentleman treads not the earth.
I saw Bassanio and Antonio part;
Bassanio told him he would make some speed
Of his return; he answer'd, "Do not so;
Slubber not business for my sake, Bassanio,
But stay the very riping of the time;
And for the Jew's bond which he hath of me,
Let it not enter in your mind of love.
Be merry, and employ your chiefest thoughts
To courtship and such fair ostents of love
As shall conveniently become you there."
And even there, his eye being big with tears,
Turning his face, he put his hand behind him,
And with affection wondrous sensible
He wrung Bassanio's hand; and so they parted.

Solan. I thing he only loves the world for him.
I pray thee, let us go and find him out
And quicken his embraced heaviness
With some delight or other.

Sal. Do we so. *Exeunt.*

Scene IX. *Belmont. A room in Portia's house.*

Enter *Nerissa* and a *Servitor*

Ner. Quick, quick, I pray thee; draw the curtain straight.
The Prince of Arragon hath ta'en his oath,
And comes to his election presently.

Enter *Arragon,* his train, and *Portia* with her train.

Por. Behold, there stand the caskets, noble Prince.
If you choose that wherein I am contain'd,
Straight shall our nuptial rites be solemniz'd;
But if you fail, without more speech, my lord,
You must be gone from hence immediately.

Ar. I am enjoin'd by oath to observe three things:
First, never to unfold to any one
Which casket 't was I chose; next, if I fail
Of the right casket, never in my life
To woo a maid in way of marriage;
Lastly,
If I do fail in fortune of my choice,
Immediately to leave you and be gone.

Por. To these injunctions every one doth swear
That comes to hazard for my worthless self.

Ar. And so have I address'd me. Fortune now
To my heart's hope! Gold; silver; and base lead.
"Who chooseth me must give and hazard all he hath."
You shall look fairer, ere I give or hazard.
What says the golden chest? Ha! let me see:
"Who chooseth me shall gain what many men desire."
What many men desire! That many may be meant
By the fool multitude, that choose by show,
Not learning more than the fond eye doth teach;
Which pries not to th' interior, but, like the martlet,
Builds in the weather on the outward wall,
Even in the force and road of casualty.
I will not choose what many men desire,
Because I will not jump with common spirits
And rank me with the barbarous multitudes.
Why, then to thee, thou silver treasure-house;
Tell me once more what title thou dost bear:
"Who chooseth me shall get as much as he deserves:"
And well said too; for who shall go about
To cozen fortune and be honourable
Without the stamp of merit? Let none presume
To wear an undeserved dignity.
O, that estates, degrees, and offices
Were not deriv'd corruptly, and that clear honour

27. reason'd, talked. **30. fraught,** freighted. **39. Slubber,** slur over, do carelessly. **48. sensible,** keenly felt. **Scene ix: 3. election,** choice.

15. fortune, here as in 1. **19. Fortune,** success. **19. address'd,** prepared. **26. by,** for. **27. fond,** foolish. **28. martlet,** martin. **29. weather,** storm. **30. casualty,** mischance. **32. jump,** agree. **38. cozen,** cheat. **41. estates,** positions. **degrees,** ranks.

Were purchas'd by the merit of the wearer!
How many then should cover that stand bare!
How many be commanded that command!
How much low peasantry would then be gleaned
From the true seed of honour! and how much honour
Pick'd from the chaff and ruin of the times
To be new-varnish'd! Well, but to my choice:
"Who chooseth me shall get as much as he deserves."
I will assume desert. Give me a key for this,
And instantly unlock my fortunes here.

He opens the silver casket.

Por. Too long a pause for that which you find there.

Ar. What 's here? The portrait of a blinking idiot,
Presenting me a schedule! I will read it.
How much unlike art thou to Portia!
How much unlike my hopes and my deservings!
"Who chooseth me shall have as much as he deserves."
Did I deserve no more than a fool's head?
Is that my prize? Are my deserts no better?

Por. To offend and judge are distinct offices
And of opposed natures.

Ar. What is here?

"The fire seven times tried this;
Seven times tried that judgement is
That did never choose amiss.
Some there be that shadows kiss,
Such have but a shadow's bliss.
There be fools alive, iwis,
Silver'd o'er; and so was this.
Take what wife you will to bed,
I will ever be your head.
So be gone; you are sped."
Still more fool I shall appear
By the time I linger here.
With one fool's head I came to woo,
But I go away with two.
Sweet, adieu. I 'll keep my oath,
Patiently to bear my wroth.

Exeunt Arragon and train.

Por. Thus hath the candle sing'd the moth.
O, these deliberate fools! When they do choose,
They have the wisdom by their wit to lose.

Ner. The ancient saying is no heresy,
Hanging and wiving goes by destiny.

Por. Come, draw the curtain, Nerissa.

Enter *Messenger.*

Mess. Where is my lady?

Por. Here; what would my lord?

Mess. Madam, there is alighted at your gate
A young Venetian, one that comes before
To signify th' approaching of his lord;
From whom he bringeth sensible regreets,
To wit, besides commends and courteous breath,
Gifts of rich value. Yet I have not seen
So likely an ambassador of love.
A day in April never came so sweet,
To show how costly summer was at hand,
As this fore-spurrer comes before his lord.

Por. No more, I pray thee: I am half afeard
Thou wilt say anon he is some kin to thee,
Thou spend'st such high-day wit in praising him.
Come, come, Nerissa, for I long to see
Quick Cupid's post that comes so mannerly.

Ner. Bassanio, Lord Love, if thy will it be!

Exeunt.

ACT III. SCENE I. *A street in Venice.*

Enter *Solanio* and *Salerio.*

Solan. Now, what news on the Rialto?

Sal. Why, yet it lives there unchecked that Antonio hath a ship of rich lading wrecked on the narrow seas; the Goodwins, I think they call the place; a very dangerous flat, and fatal, where the carcases of many a tall ship lie buried, as they say, if my gossip Report be an honest woman of her word.

Solan. I would she were as lying a gossip in that as ever knapped ginger or made her neighbours believe she wept for the death of a third husband. But it is true, without any slips of prolixity or crossing the plain highway of talk, that the good Antonio, the honest Antonio,—O that I had a title good enough to keep his name company!—

Sal. Come, the full stop.

47. seed of honour, offspring of the noble. **68. iwis,** certainly. **Act III, scene i: 4. Goodwins,** Goodwin Sands off the mouth of the Thames.

78. wroth, ruth, sorrow. **85. my lord,** said mockingly. **89. sensible regreets,** tangible greetings (gifts). **94. costly,** lavish. **98. high-day,** holiday, dressed-up. **Act III, scene i: 10. knapped,** chewed.

Solan. Ha! what sayest thou? Why, the end is, he hath lost a ship.

Sal. I would it might prove the end of his losses.

Solan. Let me say Amen betimes, lest the devil cross my prayer, for here he comes in the likeness of a Jew.

Enter *Shylock.*

How now, Shylock! what news among the merchants?

Shy. You knew, none so well, none so well as you, of my daughter's flight.

Sal. That's certain; I, for my part, knew the tailor that made the wings she flew withal.

Solan. And Shylock, for his own part, knew the bird was fledged; and then it is the complexion of them all to leave the dam.

Shy. She is damned for it.

Sal. That 's certain, if the devil may be her judge.

Shy. My own flesh and blood to rebel!

Solan. Out upon it, old carrion! Rebels it at these years?

Shy. I say, my daughter is my flesh and blood.

Sal. There is more difference between thy flesh and hers than between jet and ivory; more between your bloods than there is between red wine and Rhenish. But tell us, do you hear whether Antonio have had any loss at sea or no?

Shy. There I have another bad match. A bankrupt, a prodigal, who dare scarce show his head on the Rialto; a beggar, that was used to come so smug upon the mart; let him look to his bond: he was wont to call me usurer; let him look to his bond: he was wont to lend money for a Christian curtsy; let him look to his bond.

Sal. Why, I am sure, if he forfeit, thou wilt not take his flesh. What 's that good for?

Shy. To bait fish withal. If it will feed nothing else, it will feed my revenge. He hath disgraced me, and hindered me half a million; laughed at my losses, mocked at my gains, scorned my nation, thwarted my bargains, cooled my friends, heated mine enemies; and what 's his reason? I am a Jew. Hath not a Jew eyes? Hath not a Jew hands, organs, dimensions, senses, affections, passions; fed with the same food, hurt with the same weapons, subject to the same diseases, healed by the same means, warmed and cooled by the same winter and summer, as a Christian is? If you prick us, do we not bleed? If you tickle us, do we not laugh? If you poison us, do we not die? And if you wrong us, shall we not revenge? If we are like you in the rest, we will resemble you in that. If a Jew wrong a Christian, what is his humility? Revenge. If a Christian wrong a Jew, what should his sufferance be by Christian example? Why, revenge. The villainy you teach me, I will execute, and it shall go hard but I will better the instruction.

Enter a *Man from Antonio.*

Serv. Gentlemen, my master Antonio is at his house and desires to speak with you both.

Sal. We have been up and down to seek him.

Enter *Tubal.*

Solan. Here comes another of the tribe; a third cannot be matched, unless the devil himself turn Jew.

Exeunt Solanio, Salerio, and Man.

Shy. How now, Tubal! what news from Genoa? Hast thou found my daughter?

Tub. I often came where I did hear of her, but cannot find her.

Shy. Why, there, there, there, there! A diamond gone, cost me two thousand ducats in Frankfort! The curse never fell upon our nation till now: I never felt it till now. Two thousand ducats in that; and other precious, precious jewels. I would my daughter were dead at my foot, and the jewels in her ear! would she were hearsed at my foot, and the ducats in her coffin! No news of them? Why so—and I know not what 's spent in the search: why, thou loss upon loss! the thief gone with so much, and so much to find the thief; and no satisfaction, no revenge, nor no ill luck stirring but what lights o' my shoulders, no sighs but o' my breathing, no tears but o' my shedding.

Tub. Yes, other men have ill luck too. Antonio, as I heard in Genoa,—

Shy. What, what, what? Ill luck, ill luck?

Tub. Hath an argosy cast away, coming from Tripolis.

Shy. I thank God, I thank God. Is 't true, is 't true?

Tub. I spoke with some of the sailors that escaped the wreck.

Shy. I thank thee, good Tubal; good news, good news! Ha, ha! Here? in Genoa?

Tub. Your daughter spent in Genoa, as I heard, in one night fourscore ducats.

23. **cross,** thwart. 33. **complexion,** natural disposition. 46. **match,** bargain.

72. **humility,** humiliation (as punishment). 73. **sufferance,** patient endurance; cf. 1. 3. 110. 88. **Frankfort,** famous for the jewels sold at its fair. 93. **hearsed,** on a bier.

Shy. Thou stick'st a dagger in me. I shall never see my gold again. Fourscore ducats at a sitting! Fourscore ducats!

Tub. There came divers of Antonio's creditors in my company to Venice, that swear he cannot choose but break.

Shy. I am very glad of it: I 'll plague him; I 'll torture him; I am glad of it.

Tub. One of them showed me a ring that he had of your daughter for a monkey.

Shy. Out upon her! Thou torturest me, Tubal. It was my turquoise; I had it of Leah when I was a bachelor: I would not have given it for a wilderness of monkeys.

Tub. But Antonio is certainly undone.

Shy. Nay, that 's true, that 's very true. Go, Tubal, fee me an officer; bespeak him a fortnight before. I will have the heart of him, if he forfeit; for, were he out of Venice, I can make what merchandise I will. Go, go, Tubal, and meet me at our synagogue; go, good Tubal; at our synagogue, Tubal.

Exeunt.

Scene II. *Belmont. A room in Portia's house.*

Enter *Bassanio, Portia, Gratiano, Nerissa,* and all their trains.

Por. I pray you, tarry: pause a day or two
Before you hazard; for, in choosing wrong,
I lose your company; therefore forbear awhile.
There 's something tells me (but it is not love)
I would not lose you; and you know yourself
Hate counsels not in such a quality.
But lest you should not understand me well,—
And yet a maiden hath no tongue but thought,—
I would detain you here some month or two
Before you venture for me. I could teach you
How to choose right, but then I am forsworn;
So will I never be; so may you miss me;
But if you do, you 'll make me wish a sin,
That I had been forsworn. Beshrew your eyes,
They have o'erlook'd me and divided me;
One half of me is yours, the other half yours—
Mine own, I would say; but if mine, then yours,
And so all yours. O, these naughty times
Puts bars between the owners and their rights!
And so, though yours, not yours. Prove it so,
Let fortune go to hell for it, not I.
I speak too long; but 't is to peize the time,
To eke it and to draw it out in length,
To stay you from election.

Bass. Let me choose;
For as I am, I live upon the rack.

Por. Upon the rack, Bassanio! Then confess
What treason there is mingled with your love.

Bass. None but that ugly treason of mistrust,
Which makes me fear th' enjoying of my love.
There may as well be amity and life
'Tween snow and fire, as treason and my love.

Por. Ay, but I fear you speak upon the rack,
Where men enforced do speak anything.

Bass. Promise me life, and I 'll confess the truth.

Por. Well then, confess and live.

Bass. "Confess" and "love"
Had been the very sum of my confession.
O happy torment, when my torturer
Doth teach me answer for deliverance!
But let me to my fortune and the caskets.

Por. Away, then! I am lock'd in one of them;
If you do love me, you will find me out.
Nerissa and the rest, stand all aloof.
Let music sound while he doth make his choice;
Then, if he lose, he makes a swan-like end,
Fading in music. That the comparison
May stand more proper, my eye shall be the stream
And wat'ry death-bed for him. He may win;
And what is music then? Then music is
Even as the flourish when true subjects bow
To a new-crowned monarch; such it is
As are those dulcet sounds in break of day
That creep into the dreaming bridegroom's ear
And summon him to marriage. Now he goes,
With no less presence, but with much more love,
Than young Alcides, when he did redeem
The virgin tribute paid by howling Troy
To the sea-monster: I stand for sacrifice;
The rest aloof are the Dardanian wives,
With bleared visages, come forth to view
The issue of th' exploit. Go, Hercules!
Live thou, I live: with much, much more dismay
I view the fight than thou that mak'st the fray.

A song, the whilst Bassanio comments on the caskets to himself.

Tell me where is fancy bred,
Or in the heart or in the head?

Scene ii: 6. quality, manner. **15. o'erlook'd,** bewitched. **21. Let . . . it,** Let fortune be punished for it. **22. peize,** retard by weighting.

44. swan-like, swans were supposed to sing only at their death. **49. flourish,** fanfare of trumpets. **55. Alcides,** Hercules rescued Hesione, daughter of Laomedon, King of Troy, from a sea-monster—not for love, but for a pair of horses. **58. Dardanian,** Trojan **63. fancy,** light love.

How begot, how nourished?
Reply, reply.
It is engender'd in the eyes,
With gazing fed; and fancy dies
In the cradle where it lies.
Let us all ring fancy's knell;
I'll begin it,—Ding, dong, bell.
All. Ding, dong, bell.

Bass. So may the outward shows be least themselves;
The world is still deceiv'd with ornament.
In law, what plea so tainted and corrupt
But, being season'd with a gracious voice,
Obscures the show of evil? In religion,
What damned error but some sober brow
Will bless it and approve it with a text,
Hiding the grossness with fair ornament?
There is no vice so simple but assumes
Some mark of virtue on his outward parts:
How many cowards, whose hearts are all as false
As stairs of sand, wear yet upon their chins
The beards of Hercules and frowning Mars,
Who, inward search'd, have livers white as milk;
And these assume but valour's excrement
To render them redoubted! Look on beauty,
And you shall see 't is purchas'd by the weight;
Which therein works a miracle in nature,
Making them lightest that wear most of it:
So are those crisped snaky golden locks,
Which makes such wanton gambols with the wind
Upon supposed fairness, often known
To be the dowry of a second head,
The skull that bred them in the sepulchre.
Thus ornament is but the guiled shore
To a most dangerous sea; the beauteous scarf
Veiling an Indian beauty; in a word,
The seeming truth which cunning times put on
To entrap the wisest. Therefore, thou gaudy gold,
Hard food for Midas, I will none of thee;
Nor none of thee, thou pale and common drudge
'Tween man and man; but thou, thou meagre lead,
Which rather threat'nest than dost promise aught,
Thy plainness moves me more than eloquence;
And here choose I. Joy be the consequence!
Por. [*Aside.*] How all the other passions fleet to air,
As doubtful thoughts, and rash-embrac'd despair,
And shuddering fear, and green-ey'd jealousy!
O love, be moderate; allay thy ecstasy;
In measure rain thy joy; scant this excess!
I feel too much thy blessing; make it less,
For fear I surfeit.
Bass. What find I here?
Opening the leaden casket.
Fair Portia's counterfeit! What demi-god
Hath come so near creation? Move these eyes?
Or whether, riding on the balls of mine,
Seem they in motion? Here are sever'd lips,
Parted with sugar breath; so sweet a bar
Should sunder such sweet friends. Here in her hairs
The painter plays the spider, and hath woven
A golden mesh t' entrap the hearts of men
Faster than gnats in cobwebs: but her eyes,—
How could he see to do them? Having made one,
Methinks it should have power to steal both his
And leave itself unfurnish'd. Yet look, how far
The substance of my praise doth wrong this shadow
In underprizing it, so far this shadow
Doth limp behind the substance. Here 's the scroll,
The continent and summary of my fortune.

You that choose not by the view,
Chance as fair and choose as true!
Since this fortune falls to you,
Be content and seek no new.
If you be well pleas'd with this
And hold your fortune for your bliss,
Turn you where your lady is
And claim her with a loving kiss.

A gentle scroll. Fair lady, by your leave;
I come by note, to give and to receive.
Like one of two contending in a prize,
That thinks he hath done well in people's eyes,
Hearing applause and universal shout,
Giddy in spirit, still gazing in a doubt
Whether those peals of praise be his or no;
So, thrice-fair lady, stand I, even so,
As doubtful whether what I see be true,
Until confirm'd, sign'd, ratified by you.
Por. You see me, Lord Bassanio, where I stand,
Such as I am: though for myself alone
I would not be ambitious in my wish,
To wish myself much better; yet, for you
I would be trebled twenty times myself,
A thousand times more fair, ten thousand times more rich;
That only to stand high in your account,
I might in virtues, beauties, livings, friends,

79. **approve**, justify. 81. **simple**, pure, unmixed. 86. **livers white**, sign of cowardice; cf. 2. *Hen. IV.* 4. 3. 113. 87. **excrement**, excrescence, the beard. 88. **redoubted**, feared. 92. **crisped**, curled. 97. **guiled**, treacherous.

116. **counterfeit**, portrait. 127. **unfurnish'd**, unaccompanied by its mate. 131. **continent**, inventory. 141. **by note**, by direction.

Exceed account: but the full sum of me
Is sum of—something, which, to term in gross,
Is an unlesson'd girl, unschool'd, unpractised;
Happy in this, she is not yet so old
But she may learn; happier than this,
She is not bred so dull but she can learn;
Happiest of all is that her gentle spirit
Commits itself to yours to be directed,
As from her lord, her governor, her king.
Myself and what is mine to you and yours
Is now converted. But now I was the lord
Of this fair mansion, master of my servants,
Queen o'er myself; and even now, but now,
This house, these servants, and this same myself
Are yours, my lord's; I give them with this ring;
Which when you part from, lose, or give away,
Let it presage the ruin of your love
And be my vantage to exclaim on you.

Bass. Madam, you have bereft me of all words,
Only my blood speaks to you in my veins;
And there in such confusion in my powers,
As, after some oration fairly spoke
By a beloved prince, there doth appear
Among the buzzing pleased multitude;
Where every something, being blent together,
Turns to a wild of nothing, save of joy
Express'd and not express'd. But when this ring
Parts from this finger, then parts life from hence;
O, then be bold to say Bassanio 's dead!

Ner. My lord and lady, it is now our time,
That have stood by and seen our wishes prosper,
To cry good joy. Good joy, my lord and lady!

Gra. My Lord Bassanio and my gentle lady,
I wish you all the joy that you can wish,
For I am sure you can wish none from me;
And when your honours mean to solemnize
The bargain of your faith, I do beseech you,
Even at that time I may be married too.

Bass. With all my heart, so thou canst get a wife.

Gra. I thank your lordship, you have got me one.
My eyes, my lord, can look as swift as yours.
You saw the mistress, I beheld the maid;
You lov'd, I lov'd; for intermission
No more pertains to me, my lord, than you.
Your fortune stood upon the casket there,
And so did mine too, as the matter falls;
For, wooing here until I sweat again,
And swearing till my very roof was dry
With oaths of love, at last, if promise last,
I got a promise of this fair one here
To have her love, provided that your fortune
Achiev'd her mistress.

Por. Is this true, Nerissa?

Ner. Madam, it is, so you stand pleas'd withal.

Bass. And do you, Gratiano, mean good faith?

Gra. Yes, faith, my lord.

Bass. Our feast shall be much honoured in your marriage.

Gra. We 'll play with them the first boy for a thousand ducats.

Ner. What, and stake down?

Gra. No; we shall ne'er win at that sport and stake down.
But who comes here? Lorenzo and his infidel?
What, and my old Venetian friend Salerio?

Enter *Lorenzo, Jessica,* and *Salerio,* a messenger from Venice.

Bass. Lorenzo and Salerio, welcome hither,
If that the youth of my new interest here
Have power to bid you welcome. By your leave,
I bid my very friends and countrymen,
Sweet Portia, welcome.

Por. So do I, my lord:
They are entirely welcome.

Lor. I thank your honour. For my part, my lord,
My purpose was not to have seen you here;
But meeting with Salerio by the way,
He did intreat me, past all saying nay,
To come with him along.

Sal. I did, my lord;
And I have reason for it. Signior Antonio
Commends him to you.

Gives Bassanio a letter.

Bass. Ere I ope his letter,
I pray you, tell me how my good friend doth.

Sal. Not sick, my lord, unless it be in mind,
Nor well, unless in mind: his letter there
Will show you his estate.

Bassanio opens the letter.

Gra. Nerissa, cheer yon stranger; bid her welcome.
Your hand, Salerio. What 's the news from Venice?
How doth that royal merchant, good Antonio?
I know he will be glad of our success;
We are the Jasons, we have won the fleece.

159. account, computation. **176. vantage,** opportunity. **exclaim on,** reproach. **201. intermission,** delay.

226. very, true. **235. Commends him,** sends his respects. **239. estate,** condition.

Sal. I would you had won the fleece that he hath lost.
Por. There are some shrewd contents in yon same paper,
That steals the colour from Bassanio's cheek.
Some dear friend dead; else nothing in the world
Could turn so much the constitution
Of any constant man. What, worse and worse!
With leave, Bassanio; I am half yourself,
And I must freely have the half of anything
That this same paper brings you.
Bass. O sweet Portia,
Here are a few of the unpleasant'st words
That ever blotted paper! Gentle lady,
When I did first impart my love to you,
I freely told you, all the wealth I had
Ran in my veins; I was a gentleman.
And then I told you true; and yet, dear lady,
Rating myself at nothing, you shall see
How much I was a braggart. When I told you
My state was nothing, I should then have told you
That I was worse than nothing; for, indeed,
I have engag'd myself to a dear friend,
Engag'd my friend to his mere enemy,
To feed my means. Here is a letter, lady;
The paper as the body of my friend,
And every word in it a gaping wound,
Issuing life-blood. But is it true, Salerio?
Hath all his ventures fail'd? What, not one hit?
From Tripolis, from Mexico, and England,
From Lisbon, Barbary, and India?
And not one vessel scape the dreadful touch
Of merchant-marring rocks?
Sal. Not one, my lord.
Besides, it should appear, that if he had
The present money to discharge the Jew,
He would not take it. Never did I know
A creature, that did bear the shape of man,
So keen and greedy to confound a man.
He plies the Duke at morning and at night,
And doth impeach the freedom of the state,
If they deny him justice. Twenty merchants,
The Duke himself, and the magnificoes
Of greatest port, have all persuaded with him;
But none can drive him from the envious plea
Of forfeiture, of justice, and his bond.
Jes. When I was with him I have heard him swear
To Tubal and to Chus, his countrymen,
That he would rather have Antonio's flesh
Than twenty times the value of the sum
That he did owe him; and I know, my lord,
If law, authority, and power deny not,
It will go hard with poor Antonio.
Por. Is it your dear friend that is thus in trouble?
Bass. The dearest friend to me, the kindest man,
The best-condition'd and unwearied spirit
In doing courtesies, and one in whom
The ancient Roman honour more appears
Than any that draws breath in Italy.
Por. What sum owes he the Jew?
Bass. For me, three thousand ducats.
Por. What, no more?
Pay him six thousand, and deface the bond;
Double six thousand, and then treble that,
Before a friend of this description
Shall lose a hair through Bassanio's fault.
First go with me to church and call me wife,
And then away to Venice to your friend;
For never shall you lie by Portia's side
With an unquiet soul. You shall have gold
To pay the petty debt twenty times over.
When it is paid, bring your true friend along.
My maid Nerissa and myself meantime
Will live as maids and widows. Come, away!
For you shall hence upon your wedding-day:
Bid your friends welcome, show a merry cheer;
Since you are dear bought, I will love you dear.
But let me hear the letter of your friend.
Bass. [*Reads.*]

"Sweet Bassanio, my ships have all miscarried, my creditors grow cruel, my estate is very low, my bond to the Jew is forfeit, and since in paying it, it is impossible I should live, all debts are cleared between you and I, if I might but see you at my death. Notwithstanding, use your pleasure; if your love do not persuade you to come, let not my letter."

Por. O love, dispatch all business, and be gone!
Bass. Since I have your good leave to go away,
I will make haste; but, till I come again,
No bed shall e'er be guilty of my stay,
No rest be interposer 'twixt us twain.
Exeunt.

Scene III. *Venice. A street.*

Enter *Shylock* the Jew, *Solanio, Antonio,* and the *Jailer.*

Shy. Jailer, look to him; tell not me of mercy.
This is the fool that lent out money gratis!
Jailer, look to him.
Ant. Hear me yet, good Shylock.

246. shrewd, evil. **249. constitution,** state of mind. **250. constant,** steadfast. **265. mere,** absolute, unqualified. **276. present,** in hand. **281. impeach,** call in question. **283. magnificoes,** grandees. **285. envious,** spiteful.

315. cheer, face.

Shy. I 'll have my bond; speak not against my bond.
I have sworn an oath that I will have my bond.
Thou call'dst me dog before thou hadst a cause;
But, since I am a dog, beware my fangs.
The Duke shall grant me justice. I do wonder,
Thou naughty jailer, that thou art so fond
To come abroad with him at his request.
Ant. I pray thee, hear me speak.
Shy. I 'll have my bond. I will not hear thee speak;
I 'll have my bond; and therefore speak no more.
I 'll not be made a soft and dull-ey'd fool,
To shake the head, relent, and sigh, and yield
To Christian intercessors. Follow not;
I 'll have no speaking; I will have my bond.
Exit.
Solan. It is the most impenetrable cur
That ever kept with men.
Ant. Let him alone;
I 'll follow him no more with bootless prayers.
He seeks my life; his reason well I know:
I oft deliver'd from his forfeitures
Many that have at times made moan to me;
Therefore he hates me.
Solan. I am sure the Duke
Will never grant this forfeiture to hold.
Ant. The Duke cannot deny the course of law;
For the commodity that strangers have
With us in Venice, if it be denied,
Will much impeach the justice of the state,
Since that the trade and profit of the city
Consisteth of all nations. Therefore, go.
These griefs and losses have so bated me,
That I shall hardly spare a pound of flesh
To-morrow to my bloody creditor.
Well, jailer, on. Pray God, Bassanio come
To see me pay his debt, and then I care not!
Exeunt.

Scene IV. *Belmont. A room in Portia's house.*

Enter *Portia, Nerissa, Lorenzo, Jessica,* and *Balthasar,* a man of Portia's.

Lor. Madam, although I speak it in your presence,
You have a noble and a true conceit
Of god-like amity, which appears most strongly
In bearing thus the absence of your lord.
But if you knew to whom you show this honour,
How true a gentleman you send relief,
How dear a lover of my lord your husband,
I know you would be prouder of the work
Than customary bounty can enforce you.
Por. I never did repent for doing good,
Nor shall not now: for in companions
That do converse and waste the time together,
Whose souls do bear an equal yoke of love,
There must be needs a like proportion
Of lineaments, of manners, and of spirit;
Which makes me think that this Antonio,
Being the bosom lover of my lord,
Must needs be like my lord. If it be so,
How little is the cost I have bestowed
In purchasing the semblance of my soul
From out the state of hellish misery!
This comes too near the praising of myself,
Therefore no more of it: hear other things.
Lorenzo, I commit into your hands
The husbandry and manage of my house
Until my lord's return: for mine own part,
I have toward heaven breath'd a secret vow
To live in prayer and contemplation,
Only attended by Nerissa here,
Until her husband and my lord's return.
There is a monastery two miles off;
And there will we abide. I do desire you
Not to deny this imposition,
The which my love and some necessity
Now lays upon you.
Lor. Madam, with all my heart
I shall obey you in all fair commands.
Por. My people do already know my mind,
And will acknowledge you and Jessica
In place of Lord Bassanio and myself.
And so farewell till we shall meet again.
Lor. Fair thoughts and happy hours attend on you!
Jes. I wish your ladyship all heart's content.
Por. I thank you for your wish, and am well pleas'd
To wish it back on you. Fare you well, Jessica.
Exeunt Jessica and Lorenzo.
Now, Balthasar,
As I have ever found thee honest-true,
So let me find thee still. Take this same letter,
And use thou all th' endeavour of a man
In speed to Padua: see thou render this
Into my cousin's hand, Doctor Bellario;
And, look, what notes and garments he doth give thee,
Bring them, I pray thee, with imagin'd speed

19. **kept,** dwelt. 27. **commodity,** trading facilities. 32. **bated,** reduced. **Scene iv: 2. conceit,** conception.

9. **enforce you,** cause you to be. 20. **semblance of my soul,** i.e., Bassanio, Portia's other self (cf. l. 22). 33. **imposition,** charge. 49. **Padua,** famous for its law school. 52. **imagin'd speed,** speed of thought.

Unto the traject, to the common ferry
Which trades to Venice. Waste no time in words,
But get thee gone: I shall be there before thee.

Balth. Madam, I go with all convenient speed. *Exit.*

Por. Come on, Nerissa; I have work in hand
That you yet know not of; we 'll see our husbands
Before they think of us.

Ner. Shall they see us?

Por. They shall, Nerissa; but in such a habit,
That they shall think we are accomplished
With that we lack. I 'll hold thee any wager,
When we are both accoutred like young men,
I 'll prove the prettier fellow of the two,
And wear my dagger with the braver grace,
And speak between the change of man and boy
With a reed voice, and turn two mincing steps
Into a manly stride, and speak of frays
Like a fine bragging youth, and tell quaint lies,
How honourable ladies sought my love,
Which I denying, they fell sick and died.
I could not do withal: then I 'll repent,
And wish, for all that, that I had not kill'd them;
And twenty of these puny lies I 'll tell,
That men shall swear I have discontinued school
Above a twelvemonth. I have within my mind
A thousand raw tricks of these bragging Jacks,
Which I will practise.

Ner. Why, shall we turn to men?

Por. Fie, what a question 's that,
If thou wert near a lewd interpreter!
But come, I 'll tell thee all my whole device
When I am in my coach, which stays for us
At the park gate; and therefore haste away,
For we must measure twenty miles to-day.
Exeunt.

Scene V. *At Belmont.*

Enter *Launcelot* the Clown and *Jessica.*

Laun. Yes, truly; for, look you, the sins of the father are to be laid upon the children; therefore, I promise ye, I fear you. I was always plain with you, and so now I speak my agitation of the matter; therefore be o' good cheer, for truly I think you are damned. There is but one hope in it that can do you any good; and that is but a kind of bastard hope neither.

Jes. And what hope is that, I pray thee?

Laun. Marry, you may partly hope that your father got you not, that you are not the Jew's daughter.

Jes. That were a kind of bastard hope, indeed: so the sins of my mother should be visited upon me.

Laun. Truly then I fear you are damned both by father and mother; thus when I shun Scylla, your father, I fall into Charybdis, your mother: well, you are gone both ways.

Jes. I shall be saved by my husband. He hath made me a Christian.

Laun. Truly, the more to blame he; we were Christians enow before; e'en as many as could well live, one by another. This making of Christians will raise the price of hogs: if we grow all to be pork-eaters, we shall not shortly have a rasher on the coals for money.

Enter *Lorenzo.*

Jes. I 'll tell my husband, Launcelot, what you say. Here he comes.

Lor. I shall grow jealous of you shortly, Launcelot, if you thus get my wife into corners.

Jes. Nay, you need not fear us, Lorenzo; Launcelot and I are out. He tells me flatly there is no mercy for me in heaven because I am a Jew's daughter; and he says you are no good member of the commonwealth, for in converting Jews to Christians, you raise the price of pork.

Lor. I shall answer that better to the commonwealth than you can the getting up of the negro's belly: the Moor is with child by you, Launcelot.

Laun. It is much that the Moor should be more than reason; but if she be less than an honest woman, she is indeed more than I took her for.

Lor. How every fool can play upon the word! I think the best grace of wit will shortly turn into silence, and discourse grow commendable in none only but parrots. Go in, sirrah; bid them prepare for dinner.

Laun. That is done, sir; they have all stomachs.

Lor. Goodly Lord, what a wit-snapper are you! Then bid them prepare dinner.

Laun. That is done too, sir; only cover is the word.

Lor. Will you cover then, sir?

Laun. Not so, sir, neither; I know my duty.

53. traject, ferry (Italian *traghetto*). **61. accomplished,** equipped. **72. do withal,** help it. **Scene v: 3. fear you,** fear for you. **5. agitation,** cogitation.

18. Scylla . . . Charybdis, a dangerous rock and whirlpool on either side of the narrow strait between Italy and Sicily. **54. stomachs,** appetites. **57. cover,** (1) prepare dinner, (2) put on one's hat (cf. l. 59).

Lor. Yet more quarrelling with occasion! Wilt thou show the whole wealth of thy wit in an instant? I pray thee, understand a plain man in his plain meaning: go to thy fellows; bid them cover the table, serve in the meat, and we will come in to dinner.

Laun. For the table, sir, it shall be served in; for the meat, sir, it shall be covered; for your coming in to dinner, sir, why, let it be as humours and conceits shall govern. *Exit.*

Lor. O dear discretion, how his words are suited!
The fool hath planted in his memory
An army of good words; and I do know
A many fools, that stand in better place,
Garnish'd like him, that for a tricksy word
Defy the matter. How cheer'st thou, Jessica?
And now, good sweet, say thy opinion,
How dost thou like the Lord Bassanio's wife?

Jes. Past all expressing. It is very meet
The Lord Bassanio live an upright life;
For, having such a blessing in his lady,
He finds the joys of heaven here on earth;
And if on earth he do not merit it,
In reason he should never come to heaven.
Why, if two gods should play some heavenly match
And on the wager lay two earthly women,
And Portia one, there must be something else
Pawn'd with the other, for the poor rude world
Hath not her fellow.

Lor. Even such a husband
Hast thou of me as she is for a wife.

Jes. Nay, but ask my opinion too of that.

Lor. I will anon; first, let us go to dinner.

Jes. Nay, let me praise you while I have a stomach.

Lor. No, pray thee, let it serve for table-talk;
Then, howsome'er thou speak'st, 'mong other things
I shall digest it.

Jes. Well, I'll set you forth.

Exeunt.

ACT IV. SCENE I. *Venice. A court of justice.*

Enter the *Duke,* the *Magnificoes, Antonio, Bassanio, Gratiano, Salerio,* and others.

Duke. What, is Antonio here?

Ant. Ready, so please your Grace.

Duke. I am sorry for thee: thou art come to answer
A stony adversary, an inhuman wretch,
Uncapable of pity, void and empty
From any dram of mercy.

Ant. I have heard
Your Grace hath ta'en great pains to qualify
His rigorous course; but since he stands obdurate
And that no lawful means can carry me
Out of his envy's reach, I do oppose
My patience to his fury, and am arm'd
To suffer, with a quietness of spirit,
The very tyranny and rage of his.

Duke. Go one, and call the Jew into the court.

Sal. He is ready at the door: he comes, my lord.

Enter *Shylock.*

Duke. Make room, and let him stand before our face.
Shylock, the world thinks, and I think so too,
That thou but lead'st this fashion of thy malice
To the last hour of act; and then 't is thought
Thou 'lt show thy mercy and remorse more strange
Than is thy strange apparent cruelty;
And where thou now exacts the penalty,
Which is a pound of this poor merchant's flesh,
Thou wilt not only loose the forfeiture,
But, touch'd with humane gentleness and love,
Forgive a moiety of the principal;
Glancing an eye of pity on his losses,
That have of late so huddled on his back,
Enow to press a royal merchant down
And pluck commiseration of his state
From brassy bosoms and rough hearts of flint,
From stubborn Turks and Tartars, never train'd
To offices of tender courtesy.
We all expect a gentle answer, Jew.

Shy. I have possess'd your Grace of what I purpose;
And by our holy Sabbath have I sworn
To have the due and forfeit of my bond.
If you deny it, let the danger light

60. quarrelling with occasion, cavilling, at odds with the matter in question. **70. suited,** dressed up. **74. Garnish'd,** equipped, i.e., with words. **75. Defy,** disregard. **How cheer'st thou,** what cheer. **Act IV, Scene i: 7. qualify,** moderate.

87. Pawn'd, staked. **Act IV. Scene i: 18. fashion,** pretence, mere form. **20. remorse,** pity. **strange,** extraordinary. **26. moiety,** part.

Upon your charter and your city's freedom!
You 'll ask me why I rather choose to have
A weight of carrion flesh than to receive
Three thousand ducats: I 'll not answer that!
But say it is my humour, is it answer'd?
What if my house be troubled with a rat
And I be pleas'd to give ten thousand ducats
To have it ban'd? What, are you answer'd yet?
Some men there are love not a gaping pig;
Some that are mad if they behold a cat;
And others, when the bagpipe sings i' th' nose,
Cannot contain their urine: for affection,
Master of passion, sways it to the mood
Of what it likes or loathes. Now, for your answer:
As there is no firm reason to be render'd
Why he cannot abide a gaping pig;
Why he a harmless necessary cat;
Why he a woollen bagpipe; but of force
Must yield to such inevitable shame
As to offend, himself being offended;
So can I give no reason, nor I will not,
More than a lodg'd hate and a certain loathing
I bear Antonio, that I follow thus
A losing suit against him. Are you answer'd?

Bass. This is no answer, thou unfeeling man,
To excuse the current of thy cruelty.

Shy. I am not bound to please thee with my answers.

Bass. Do all men kill the things they do not love?

Shy. Hates any man the thing he would not kill?

Bass. Every offence is not a hate at first.

Shy. What, wouldst thou have a serpent sting thee twice?

Ant. I pray you, think you question with the Jew.
You may as well go stand upon the beach
And bid the main flood bate his usual height;
You may as well use question with the wolf
Why he hath made the ewe bleat for the lamb;
You may as well forbid the mountain pines
To wag their high tops and to make no noise
When they are fretten with the gusts of heaven;
You may as well do any thing most hard,
As seek to soften that—than which what 's harder?—
His Jewish heart. Therefore, I do beseech you,
Make no moe offers, use no farther means,
But with all brief and plain conveniency
Let me have judgement and the Jew his will.

Bass. For thy three thousand ducats here is six.

Shy. If every ducat in six thousand ducats
Were in six parts, and every part a ducat,
I would not draw them; I would have my bond.

Duke. How shalt thou hope for mercy, rend'ring none?

Shy. What judgement shall I dread, doing no wrong?
You have among you many a purchas'd slave,
Which, like your asses and your dogs and mules,
You use in abject and in slavish parts,
Because you bought them: shall I say to you,
"Let them be free! Marry them to your heirs!
Why sweat they under burdens? Let their beds
Be made as soft as yours and let their palates
Be season'd with such viands"? You will answer,
"The slaves are ours." So do I answer you:
The pound of flesh, which I demand of him,
Is dearly bought; 't is mine and I will have it:
If you deny me, fie upon your law!
There is no force in the decrees of Venice.
I stand for judgement. Answer: shall I have it?

Duke. Upon my power I may dismiss this court,
Unless Bellario, a learned doctor,
Whom I have sent for to determine this,
Come here to-day.

Sal. My lord, here stays without
A messenger with letters from the doctor,
New come from Padua.

Duke. Bring us the letters; call the messenger.

Bass. Good cheer, Antonio! What, man, courage yet!
The Jew shall have my flesh, blood, bones, and all,
Ere thou shalt lose for me one drop of blood.

Ant. I am a tainted wether of the flock,
Meetest for death: the weakest kind of fruit
Drops earliest to the ground, and so let me.
You cannot better be employ'd, Bassanio,
Than to live still and write mine epitaph.

Enter *Nerissa* dressed like a lawyer's clerk.

Duke. Came you from Padua, from Bellario?

Ner. From both, my lord. Bellario greets your Grace. *Presenting a letter.*

43. humour, whim. **46. ban'd,** poisoned. **47. gaping,** roasted with mouth open. **50. affection,** natural instinct. **56. woollen,** covered with woolen cloth. **70. question,** talk. **77. fretten,** fretted.

92. parts, tasks.

Bass. Why dost thou whet thy knife so earnestly?
Shy. To cut the forfeiture from that bankrupt there.
Gra. Not on thy sole, but on thy soul, harsh Jew,
Thou mak'st thy knife keen; but no metal can—
No, not the hangman's axe—bear half the keenness
Of thy sharp envy. Can no prayers pierce thee?
Shy. No, none that thou hast wit enough to make.
Gra. O, be thou damn'd, inexorable dog!
And for thy life let justice be accus'd!
Thou almost mak'st me waver in my faith
To hold opinion with Pythagoras,
That souls of animals infuse themselves
Into the trunks of men: thy currish spirit
Govern'd a wolf, who, hang'd for human slaughter,
Even from the gallows did his fell soul fleet,
And, whilst thou layest in thy unhallowed dam,
Infus'd itself in thee; for thy desires
Are wolvish, bloody, starv'd, and ravenous.
Shy. Till thou canst rail the seal from off my bond,
Thou but offend'st thy lungs to speak so loud:
Repair thy wit, good youth, or it will fall
To cureless ruin. I stand here for law.
Duke. This letter from Bellario doth commend
A young and learned doctor to our court.
Where is he?
Ner. He attendeth here hard by,
To know your answer, whether you 'll admit him.
Duke. With all my heart. Some three or four of you
Go give him courteous conduct to this place.
Meantime the court shall hear Bellario's letter.
Clerk. [*Reads.*]

"Your Grace shall understand that at the receipt of your letter I am very sick; but in the instant that your messenger came, in loving visitation was with me a young doctor of Rome. His name is Balthazar. I acquainted him with the cause in controversy between the Jew and Antonio the merchant. We turned o'er many books together. He is furnished with my opinion; which, bettered with his own learning (the greatness whereof I cannot enough commend), comes with him, at my importunity, to fill up your Grace's request in my stead. I beseech you, let his lack of years be no impediment to let him lack a reverend estimation; for I never knew so young a body with so old a head. I leave him to your gracious acceptance, whose trial shall better publish his commendation."

162. impediment to let, impediment that will let.

Enter *Portia* for *Balthazar*, dressed like a Doctor of Laws.

Duke. You hear the learn'd Bellario, what he writes;
And here, I take it, is the doctor come.
Give me your hand. Come you from old Bellario?
Por. I did, my lord.
Duke. You are welcome; take your place.
Are you acquainted with the difference
That holds this present question in the court?
Por. I am informed throughly of the cause.
Which is the merchant here, and which the Jew?
Duke. Antonio and old Shylock, both stand forth.
Por. Is your name Shylock?
Shy. Shylock is my name.
Por. Of a strange nature is the suit you follow;
Yet in such rule that the Venetian law
Cannot impugn you as you do proceed.
You stand within his danger, do you not?
Ant. Ay, so he says.
Por. Do you confess the bond?
Ant. I do.
Por. Then must the Jew be merciful.
Shy. On what compulsion must I? Tell me that.
Por. The quality of mercy is not strain'd.
It droppeth as the gentle rain from heaven
Upon the place beneath: it is twice blest:
It blesseth him that gives and him that takes.
'T is mightiest in the mightiest; it becomes
The throned monarch better than his crown.
His sceptre shows the force of temporal power,
The attribute to awe and majesty,
Wherein doth sit the dread and fear of kings;
But mercy is above this sceptred sway;
It is enthroned in the hearts of kings;
It is an attribute to God himself;
And earthly power doth then show likest God's
When mercy seasons justice. Therefore, Jew,
Though justice be thy plea, consider this,
That, in the course of justice, none of us
Should see salvation: we do pray for mercy,
And that same prayer doth teach us all to render
The deeds of mercy. I have spoke thus much
To mitigate the justice of thy plea,

171. difference, dispute. **172. question,** discussion. **178. rule,** regular mode of procedure. **179. impugn,** oppose. **184. strain'd,** forced.

Which if thou follow, this strict court of Venice
Must needs give sentence 'gainst the merchant there.

Shy. My deeds upon my head! I crave the law,
The penalty and forfeit of my bond.

Por. Is he not able to discharge the money?

Bass. Yes, here I tender it for him in the court;
Yea, twice the sum. If that will not suffice,
I will be bound to pay it ten times o'er,
On forfeit of my hands, my head, my heart.
If this will not suffice, it must appear
That malice bears down truth. And I beseech you,
Wrest once the law to your authority;
To do a great right, do a little wrong,
And curb this cruel devil of his will.

Por. It must not be; there is no power in Venice
Can alter a decree established:
'T will be recorded for a precedent,
And many an error by the same example
Will rush into the state. It cannot be.

Shy. A Daniel come to judgement! yea, a Daniel!
O wise young judge, how I do honour thee!

Por. I pray you, let me look upon the bond.

Shy. Here 't is, most reverend doctor, here it is.

Por. Shylock, there 's thrice thy money offer'd thee.

Shy. An oath, an oath, I have an oath in heaven!
Shall I lay perjury upon my soul?
No, not for Venice.

Por. Why, this bond is forfeit;
And lawfully by this the Jew may claim
A pound of flesh, to be by him cut off
Nearest the merchant's heart. Be merciful;
Take thrice thy money; bid me tear the bond.

Shy. When it is paid according to the tenour.
It doth appear you are a worthy judge;
You know the law, your exposition
Hath been most sound: I charge you by the law,
Whereof you are a well-deserving pillar,
Proceed to judgement: by my soul I swear
There is no power in the tongue of man
To alter me. I stay here on my bond.

Ant. Most heartily I do beseech the court
To give the judgement.

Por. Why, then, thus it is;
You must prepare your bosom for his knife.

Shy. O noble judge! O excellent young man!

Por. For the intent and purpose of the law
Hath full relation to the penalty,
Which here appeareth due upon the bond.

Shy. 'T is very true. O wise and upright judge!
How much more elder art thou than thy looks!

Por. Therefore lay bare your bosom.

Shy. Ay, his breast;
So says the bond; doth it not, noble judge?
"Nearest his heart"; those are the very words.

Por. It is so. Are there balance here to weigh
The flesh?

Shy. I have them ready.

Por. Have by some surgeon, Shylock, on your charge,
To stop his wounds, lest he do bleed to death.

Shy. Is it so nominated in the bond?

Por. It is not so express'd; but what of that?
'T were good you do so much for charity.

Shy. I cannot find it; 't is not in the bond.

Por. You, merchant, have you anything to say?

Ant. But little; I am arm'd and well prepar'd.
Give me your hand, Bassanio; fare you well!
Grieve not that I am fall'n to this for you;
For herein Fortune shows herself more kind
Than is her custom: it is still her use
To let the wretched man outlive his wealth,
To view with hollow eye and wrinkled brow
An age of poverty; from which ling'ring penance
Of such misery doth she cut me off.
Commend me to your honourable wife:
Tell her the process of Antonio's end;
Say how I lov'd you, speak me fair in death,
And, when the tale is told, bid her be judge
Whether Bassanio had not once a love.
Repent but you that you shall lose your friend,
And he repents not that he pays your debt;
For if the Jew do cut but deep enough,
I 'll pay it instantly with all my heart.

Bass. Antonio, I am married to a wife
Which is as dear to me as life itself;
But life itself, my wife, and all the world,
Are not with me esteem'd above thy life.
I would lose all, ay, sacrifice them all
Here to this devil, to deliver you.

Por. Your wife would give you little thanks for that,
If she were by, to hear you make the offer.

214. truth, honesty. **223. Daniel,** the wise young judge in the apocryphal *History of Susanna.*

248. Hath full relation to, has full bearing on.

Gra. I have a wife, who, I protest, I love;
I would she were in heaven, so she could
Entreat some power to change this currish Jew.
Ner. 'T is well you offer it behind her back.
The wish would make else an unquiet house.
Shy. [*Aside.*] These be the Christian husbands. I have a daughter;
Would any of the stock of Barrabas
Had been her husband rather than a Christian!
We trifle time. I pray thee, pursue sentence.
Por. A pound of that same merchant's flesh is thine.
The court awards it, and the law doth give it.
Shy. Most rightful judge!
Por. And you must cut this flesh from off his breast.
The law allows it, and the court awards it.
Shy. Most learned judge! A sentence! Come, prepare!
Por. Tarry a little; there is something else.
This bond doth give thee here no jot of blood;
The words expressly are "a pound of flesh":
Take then thy bond, take thou thy pound of flesh;
But, in the cutting it, if thou dost shed
One drop of Christian blood, thy lands and goods
Are, by the laws of Venice, confiscate
Unto the state of Venice.
Gra. O upright judge! Mark, Jew: O learned judge!
Shy. Is that the law?
Por. Thyself shall see the act;
For, as thou urgest justice, be assur'd
Thou shalt have justice, more than thou desir'st.
Gra. O learned judge! Mark, Jew: a learned judge!
Shy. I take this offer then; pay the bond thrice
And let the Christian go.
Bass. Here is the money.
Por. Soft!
The Jew shall have all justice. Soft! no haste.
He shall have nothing but the penalty.
Gra. O Jew! an upright judge, a learned judge!
Por. Therefore prepare thee to cut off the flesh.
Shed thou no blood, nor cut thou less nor more
But just a pound of flesh: if thou cut'st more
Or less than a just pound, be it but so much
As makes it light or heavy in the substance

296. Barrabas, the thief freed by Pilate. **327. just,** exact. **328-9. substance Or the division,** whole or the fraction.

Or the division of the twentieth part
Of one poor scruple, nay, if the scale do turn
But in the estimation of a hair,
Thou diest and all thy goods are confiscate.
Gra. A second Daniel! A Daniel, Jew!
Now, infidel, I have you on the hip.
Por. Why doth the Jew pause? Take thy forfeiture.
Shy. Give me my principal, and let me go.
Bass. I have it ready for thee; here it is.
Por. He hath refus'd it in the open court.
He shall have merely justice and his bond.
Gra. A Daniel, still say I, a second Daniel!
I thank thee, Jew, for teaching me that word.
Shy. Shall I not have barely my principal?
Por. Thou shalt have nothing but the forfeiture,
To be so taken at thy peril, Jew.
Shy. Why, then the devil give him good of it!
I 'll stay no longer question.
Por. Tarry, Jew!
The law hath yet another hold on you.
It is enacted in the laws of Venice,
If it be proved against an alien
That by direct or indirect attempts
He seek the life of any citizen,
The party 'gainst the which he doth contrive
Shall seize one half his goods; the other half
Comes to the privy coffer of the state;
And the offender's life lies in the mercy
Of the Duke only, 'gainst all other voice.
In which predicament I say thou stand'st;
For it appears, by manifest proceeding,
That indirectly, and directly too,
Thou hast contriv'd against the very life
Of the defendant; and thou hast incurr'd
The danger formerly by me rehears'd.
Down therefore and beg mercy of the Duke.
Gra. Beg that thou mayst have leave to hang thyself;
And yet, thy wealth being forfeit to the state,
Thou hast not left the value of a cord;
Therefore thou must be hang'd at the state's charge.
Duke. That thou shalt see the difference of our spirits,
I pardon thee thy life before thou ask it:
For half thy wealth, it is Antonio's;
The other half comes to the general state,
Which humbleness may drive unto a fine.
Por. Ay, for the state, not for Antonio.
Shy. Nay, take my life and all; pardon not that.

330. scruple, 20 grains. **372. drive,** reduce.

You take my house when you do take the prop
That doth sustain my house; you take my life
When you do take the means whereby I live.

Por. What mercy can you render him, Antonio?

Gra. A halter gratis; nothing else, for God's sake.

Ant. So please my lord the Duke and all the court
To quit the fine for one half of his goods,
I am content; so he will let me have
The other half in use, to render it,
Upon his death, unto the gentleman
That lately stole his daughter:
Two things provided more, that, for this favour,
He presently become a Christian;
The other, that he do record a gift,
Here in the court, of all he dies possess'd,
Unto his son Lorenzo and his daughter.

Duke. He shall do this, or else I do recant
The pardon that I late pronounced here.

Por. Art thou contented, Jew? What dost thou say?

Shy. I am content.

Por. Clerk, draw a deed of gift.

Shy. I pray you give me leave to go from hence;
I am not well. Send the deed after me,
And I will sign it.

Duke. Get thee gone, but do it.

Gra. In christ'ning shalt thou have two god-fathers:
Had I been judge, thou shouldst have had ten more,
To bring thee to the gallows, not the font.

Exit Shylock.

Duke. Sir, I entreat you home with me to dinner.

Por. I humbly do desire your Grace of pardon.
I must away this night toward Padua,
And it is meet I presently set forth.

Duke. I am sorry that your leisure serves you not.
Antonio, gratify this gentleman;
For, in my mind, you are much bound to him.

Exeunt Duke and his train.

Bass. Most worthy gentleman, I and my friend
Have by your wisdom been this day acquitted
Of grievous penalties; in lieu whereof
Three thousand ducats, due unto the Jew,
We freely cope your courteous pains withal.

Ant. And stand indebted, over and above,
In love and service to you evermore.

Por. He is well paid that is well satisfied;
And I, delivering you, am satisfied
And therein do account myself well paid.
My mind was never yet more mercenary.
I pray you know me when we meet again:
I wish you well, and so I take my leave.

Bass. Dear sir, of force I must attempt you further.
Take some remembrance of us, as a tribute,
Not as a fee: grant me two things, I pray you,
Not to deny me, and to pardon me.

Por. You press me far, and therefore I will yield.
Give me your gloves, I 'll wear them for your sake;
And, for your love, I 'll take this ring from you.
Do not draw back your hand; I 'll take no more;
And you in love shall not deny me this.

Bass. This ring, good sir, alas, it is a trifle!
I will not shame myself to give you this.

Por. I will have nothing else but only this;
And now methinks I have a mind to it.

Bass. There 's more depends on this than on the value.
The dearest ring in Venice will I give you,
And find it out by proclamation;
Only for this, I pray you, pardon me.

Por. I see, sir, you are liberal in offers.
You taught me first to beg; and now methinks
You teach me how a beggar should be answer'd.

Bass. Good sir, this ring was given me by my wife;
And when she put it on, she made me vow
That I should neither sell nor give nor lose it.

Por. That 'scuse serves many men to save their gifts.
An if your wife be not a mad-woman,
And know how well I have deserv'd the ring,
She would not hold out enemy for ever,
For giving it to me. Well, peace be with you!

Exeunt Portia and Nerissa.

Ant. My Lord Bassanio, let him have the ring:
Let his deservings and my love withal
Be valued against your wife's commandment.

Bass. Go, Gratiano, run and overtake him;
Give him the ring, and bring him, if thou canst,
Unto Antonio's house. Away! make haste.

Exit Gratiano.

Come, you and I will thither presently;

381. quit, remit. **383. use,** trust. **399. ten more,** i.e., a jury of twelve. **406. gratify,** reward. **412. cope,** requite.

426. She asks for Bassanio's gloves, handsome and valuable things in those days, in order that he may draw them off and show the ring.

And in the morning early will we both
Fly toward Belmont. Come, Antonio.
Exeunt.

Scene II. *A street in Venice.*

Enter *Portia* and *Nerissa.*

Por. Inquire the Jew's house out, give him this deed
And let him sign it. We 'll away to-night,
And be a day before our husbands home.
This deed will be well welcome to Lorenzo.

Enter *Gratiano.*

Gra. Fair sir, you are well o'erta'en.
My Lord Bassanio upon more advice
Hath sent you here this ring, and doth entreat
Your company at dinner.

Por. That cannot be;
His ring I do accept most thankfully,
And so, I pray you, tell him; furthermore,
I pray you show my youth old Shylock's house.

Gra. That will I do.

Ner. Sir, I would speak with you
[*Aside to Por.*] I 'll see if I can get my husband's ring,
Which I did make him swear to keep for ever.

Por. [*Aside to Ner.*] Thou mayst, I warrant. We shall have old swearing
That they did give the rings away to men;
But we 'll outface them, and outswear them too.
[*Aloud.*] Away! make haste. Thou know'st where I will tarry.

Ner. Come, good sir, will you show me to this house? *Exeunt.*

Act V. Scene I. *Belmont. Avenue to Portia's house.*

Enter *Lorenzo* and *Jessica.*

Lor. The moon shines bright. In such a night as this,
When the sweet wind did gently kiss the trees
And they did make no noise, in such a night
Troilus methinks mounted the Troyan walls,
And sigh'd his soul toward the Grecian tents,
Where Cressid lay that night.

Jes. In such a night
Did Thisbe fearfully o'ertrip the dew,
And saw the lion's shadow ere himself
And ran dismay'd away.

Lor. In such a night
Stood Dido with a willow in her hand
Upon the wild sea banks, and waft her love
To come again to Carthage.

Jes. In such a night
Medea gathered the enchanted herbs
That did renew old Æson.

Lor. In such a night
Did Jessica steal from the wealthy Jew,
And with an unthrift love did run from Venice
As far as Belmont.

Jes. In such a night
Did young Lorenzo swear he lov'd her well,
Stealing her soul with many vows of faith
And ne'er a true one.

Lor. In such a night
Did pretty Jessica, like a little shrew,
Slander her love, and he forgave it her.

Jes. I would out-night you, did no body come;
But, hark, I hear the footing of a man.

Enter *Stephano* a Messenger.

Lor. Who comes so fast in silence of the night?

Mess. A friend.

Lor. A friend! what friend? Your name I pray you, friend?

Mess. Stephano is my name; and I bring word
My mistress will before the break of day
Be here at Belmont: she doth stray about
By holy crosses, where she kneels and prays
For happy wedlock hours.

Lor. Who comes with her?

Mess. None but a holy hermit and her maid.
I pray you, is my master yet return'd?

Lor. He is not, nor we have not heard from him.
But go we in, I pray thee, Jessica,
And ceremoniously let us prepare
Some welcome for the mistress of the house.

Scene ii: 6. advice, consideration. **Act V, Scene i: 4. Troilus.** There follow references to famous love stories of antiquity: Troilus and Cressida, Pyramus and Thisbe, Dido and Æneas. Medea for love of Jason restored his father, Æson, to youth (Ovid). **10. willow,** symbol of unrequited love. **11. waft,** beckoned.

Scene ii: 15. old, much.

Enter *Launcelot* the Clown.

Laun. Sola, sola! wo ha, ho! sola, sola!
Lor. Who calls?
Laun. Sola! did you see Master Lorenzo? Master Lorenzo, sola, sola!
Lor. Leave hollaing, man; here.
Laun. Sola where? where?
Lor. Here.
Laun. Tell him there 's a post come from my master, with his horn full of good news. My master will be here ere morning. *Exit.*
Lor. Sweet soul, let 's in, and there expect their coming.
And yet no matter; why should we go in?
My friend Stephano, signify, I pray you,
Within the house, your mistress is at hand;
And bring our music forth into the air.
Exit Messenger.
How sweet the moonlight sleeps upon this bank!
Here will we sit and let the sounds of music
Creep in our ears: soft stillness and the night
Become the touches of sweet harmony.
Sit, Jessica. Look how the floor of heaven
Is thick inlaid with patens of bright gold.
There 's not the smallest orb which thou behold'st
But in his motion like an angel sings,
Still quiring to the young-ey'd cherubins;
Such harmony is in immortal souls;
But whilst this muddy vesture of decay
Doth grossly close it in, we cannot hear it.
Come, ho! and wake Diana with a hymn;
With sweetest touches pierce your mistress' ear
And draw her home with music.
Play music.
Jes. I am never merry when I hear sweet music.
Lor. The reason is, your spirits are attentive;
For do but note a wild and wanton herd,
Or race of youthful and unhandled colts,
Fetching mad bounds, bellowing and neighing loud,
Which is the hot condition of their blood,
If they but hear perchance a trumpet sound,
Or any air of music touch their ears,
You shall perceive them make a mutual stand,
Their savage eyes turn'd to a modest gaze
By the sweet power of music; therefore the poet
Did feign that Orpheus drew trees, stones, and floods;
Since nought so stockish, hard, and full of rage,
But music for the time doth change his nature.
The man that hath no music in himself,
Nor is not mov'd with concord of sweet sounds,
Is fit for treasons, stratagems, and spoils.
The motions of his spirit are dull as night
And his affections dark as Erebus:
Let no such man be trusted. Mark the music.

Enter *Portia* and *Nerissa*.

Por. That light we see is burning in my hall.
How far that little candle throws his beams!
So shines a good deed in a naughty world.
Ner. When the moon shone, we did not see the candle.
Por. So doth the greater glory dim the less.
A substitute shines brightly as a king
Until a king be by; and then his state
Empties itself, as doth an inland brook
Into the main of waters. Music! Hark!
Ner. It is your music, madam, of the house.
Por. Nothing is good, I see, without respect;
Methinks it sounds much sweeter than by day.
Ner. Silence bestows that virtue on it, madam.
Por. The crow doth sing as sweetly as the lark
When neither is attended, and I think
The nightingale, if she should sing by day,
When every goose is cackling, would be thought
No better a musician than the wren.
How many things by season season'd are
To their right praise and true perfection!
Peace, ho! the moon sleeps with Endymion
And would not be awak'd. *Music ceases.*
Lor. That is the voice,
Or I am much deceiv'd, of Portia.
Por. He knows me as the blind man knows the cuckoo,
By the bad voice.
Lor. Dear lady, welcome home!
Por. We have been praying for our husbands' welfare,
Which speed, we hope, the better for our words.
Are they return'd?

39. Sola, imitating post horn. **59. patens,** thin metal disks. **61. sings,** the music of the spheres, inaudible to mortals (cf. l. 64ff.), was made by the revolution of the concentric spheres composing the universe. **62. quiring,** singing in harmony. **young-ey'd,** with sight ever young and keen. **66. wake,** keep awake. **79. the poet,** Ovid, Shakespeare's favorite poet.

87. affections, passions. **Erebus,** the dark hell of classical mythology. **99. respect,** i.e., to circumstances. **103. attended,** listened to. **109. Endymion,** a mortal beloved of Diana, the Moon goddess.

Lor. Madam, they are not yet;
But there is come a messenger before,
To signify their coming.
Por. Go in, Nerissa;
Give order to my servants that they take
No note at all of our being absent hence;
Nor you, Lorenzo; Jessica, nor you.
A tucket sounds.
Lor. Your husband is at hand; I hear his trumpet.
We are no tell-tales, madam; fear you not.
Por. This night methinks is but the daylight sick;
It looks a little paler: 't is a day,
Such as the day is when the sun is hid.

Enter *Bassanio, Antonio, Gratiano,* and their followers.

Bass. We should hold day with the Antipodes,
If you would walk in absence of the sun,
Por. Let me give light, but let me not be light;
For a light wife doth make a heavy husband,
And never be Bassanio so for me.
But God sort all! You 're welcome home, my lord.
Bass. I thank you, madam. Give welcome to my friend.
This is the man, this is Antonio,
To whom I am so infinitely bound.
Por. You should in all sense be much bound to him,
For, as I hear, he was much bound for you.
Ant. No more than I am well acquitted of.
Por. Sir, you are very welcome to our house:
It must appear in other ways than words,
Therefore I scant this breathing courtesy.
Gra. [*To Ner.*] By yonder moon I swear you do me wrong;
In faith, I gave it to the judge's clerk.
Would he were gelt that had it, for my part,
Since you do take it, love, so much at heart.
Por. A quarrel, ho, already! What 's the matter?
Gra. About a hoop of gold, a paltry ring
That she did give me, whose posy was
For all the world like cutler's poetry
Upon a knife, "Love me, and leave me not."
Ner. What talk you of the posy or the value?
You swore to me, when I did give it you,
That you would wear it till your hour of death,
And that it should lie with you in your grave.
Though not for me, yet for your vehement oaths,
You should have been respective and have kept it.
Gave it a judge's clerk! No, God's my judge,
The clerk will ne'er wear hair on 's face that had it.
Gra. He will, an if he live to be a man.
Ner. Ay, if a woman live to be a man.
Gra. Now, by this hand, I gave it to a youth,
A kind of boy, a little scrubbed boy,
No higher than thyself, the judge's clerk,
A prating boy, that begg'd it as a fee.
I could not for my heart deny it him.
Por. You were to blame, I must be plain with you,
To part so slightly with your wife's first gift;
A thing stuck on with oaths upon your finger
And so riveted with faith unto your flesh.
I gave my love a ring, and made him swear
Never to part with it; and here he stands.
I dare be sworn for him he would not leave it
Nor pluck it from his finger for the wealth
That the world masters. Now, in faith, Gratiano,
You give your wife too unkind a cause of grief.
An 't were to me, I should be mad at it.
Bass. [*Aside.*] Why, I were best to cut my left hand off
And swear I lost the ring defending it.
Gra. My Lord Bassanio gave his ring away
Unto the judge that begg'd it, and indeed
Deserv'd it too; and then the boy, his clerk,
That took some pains in writing, he begg'd mine;
And neither man nor master would take aught
But the two rings.
Por. What ring gave you, my lord?
Not that, I hope, which you receiv'd of me.
Bass. If I could add a lie unto a fault,
I would deny it; but you see my finger
Hath not the ring upon it; it is gone.
Por. Even so void is your false heart of truth.
By heaven, I will ne'er come in your bed
Until I see the ring.
Ner. Nor I in yours
Till I again see mine.
Bass. Sweet Portia,
If you did know to whom I gave the ring,
If you did know for whom I gave the ring,
And would conceive for what I gave the ring,

121. S. d. **tucket**, flourish of trumpets. **127. Antipodes**, the opposite side of the globe. Bassanio likens Portia to the sun. **132. sort,** dispose. **141. scant,** cut short. **breathing courtesy,** courteous words. **148. posy,** motto.

156. respective, regardful. **162. scrubbed,** scrubby **172. leave,** give up (cf. l. 196).

And how unwillingly I left the ring,
When nought would be accepted but the ring,
You would abate the strength of your displeasure.

Por. If you had known the virtue of the ring,
Or half her worthiness that gave the ring,
Or your own honour to contain the ring,
You would not then have parted with the ring.
What man is there so much unreasonable,
If you had pleas'd to have defended it
With any terms of zeal, wanted the modesty
To urge the thing held as a ceremony?
Nerissa teaches me what to believe:
I 'll die for 't but some woman had the ring.

Bass. No, by my honour, madam, by my soul,
No woman had it, but a civil doctor,
Which did refuse three thousand ducats of me
And begg'd the ring; the which I did deny him
And suffer'd him to go displeas'd away;
Even he that did uphold the very life
Of my dear friend. What should I say, sweet lady?
I was enforc'd to send it after him;
I was beset with shame and courtesy;
My honour would not let ingratitude
So much besmear it. Pardon me, good lady;
For, by these blessed candles of the night,
Had you been there, I think you would have begg'd
The ring of me to give the worthy doctor.

Por. Let not that doctor e'er come near my house.
Since he hath got the jewel that I lov'd,
And that which you did swear to keep for me,
I will become as liberal as you.
I 'll not deny him any thing I have,
No, not my body nor my husband's bed.
Know him I shall, I am well sure of it.
Lie not a night from home. Watch me like Argus.
If you do not, if I be left alone,
Now, by mine honour, which is yet mine own,
I 'll have that doctor for my bedfellow.

Ner. And I his clerk; therefore be well advis'd
How you do leave me to mine own protection.

Gra. Well, do you so; let not me take him then;
For if I do, I 'll mar the young clerk's pen.

Ant. I am th' unhappy subject of these quarrels.

Por. Sir, grieve not you; you are welcome notwithstanding.

Bass. Portia, forgive me this enforced wrong;
And in the hearing of these many friends
I swear to thee, even by thine own fair eyes,
Wherein I see myself—

Por. Mark you but that!
In both my eyes he doubly sees himself,
In each eye, one: swear by your double self,
And there 's an oath of credit.

Bass. Nay, but hear me.
Pardon this fault, and by my soul I swear
I never more will break an oath with thee.

Ant. I once did lend my body for his wealth,
Which, but for him that had your husband's ring,
Had quite miscarried. I dare be bound again,
My soul upon the forfeit, that your lord
Will never more break faith advisedly.

Por. Then you shall be his surety. Give him this
And bid him keep it better than the other.

Ant. Here, Lord Bassanio; swear to keep this ring.

Bass. By heaven, it is the same I gave the doctor!

Por. I had it of him: pardon me, Bassanio;
For, by this ring, the doctor lay with me.

Ner. And pardon me, my gentle Gratiano;
For that same scrubbed boy, the doctor's clerk,
In lieu of this last night did lie with me.

Gra. Why, this is like the mending of highways
In summer, where the ways are fair enough.
What, are we cuckolds ere we have deserv'd it?

Por. Speak not so grossly. You are all amaz'd:
Here is a letter; read it at your leisure;
It comes from Padua, from Bellario:
There you shall find that Portia was the doctor,
Nerissa there her clerk. Lorenzo here
Shall witness I set forth as soon as you
And even but now return'd; I have not yet
Enter'd my house. Antonio, you are welcome;
And I have better news in store for you
Than you expect: unseal this letter soon;
There you shall find three of your argosies
Are richly come to harbour suddenly.
You shall not know by what strange accident
I chanced on this letter.

Ant. I am dumb!

Bass. Were you the doctor and I knew you not?

Gra. Were you the clerk that is to make me cuckold?

201. **contain**, retain. 206. **ceremony**, anything held sacred. 210. **civil doctor**, doctor of civil law. 230. **Argus** had a hundred eyes.

245. **double**, two-fold and so deceitful. 249. **wealth**, welfare.

Ner. Ay, but the clerk that never means to do it,
Unless he live until he be a man.
Bass. Sweet doctor, you shall be my bed-fellow.
When I am absent, then lie with my wife.
Ant. Sweet lady, you have given me life and living;
For here I read for certain that my ships
Are safely come to road.
Por. How now, Lorenzo!
My clerk hath some good comforts too for you.
Ner. Ay, and I 'll give them him without a fee.
There do I give to you and Jessica,
From the rich Jew, a special deed of gift,
After his death, of all he dies possess'd of.

288. road, harbor.

Lor. Fair ladies, you drop manna in the way
Of starved people.
Por. It is almost morning,
And yet I am sure you are not satisfied
Of these events at full. Let us go in;
And charge us there upon inter'gatories,
And we will answer all things faithfully.
Gra. Let it be so. The first inter'gatory
That my Nerissa shall be sworn on is,
Whether till the next night she had rather stay,
Or go to bed now, being two hours to day.
But were the day come, I should wish it dark,
That I were couching with the doctor's clerk.
Well, while I live I 'll fear no other thing
So sore as keeping safe Nerissa's ring.
Exeunt.

298. charge . . . inter'gatories, question under oath.
306. fear, be concerned about.

The Tragedy of Richard the Third

Text.—Richard III was entered for publication 20 October, 1597, by Andrew Wise and late in the same year published by him as a quarto with the following title-page:

> The Tragedy of King Richard the third. Containing, His treacherous Plots against his brother Clarence: the pittiefull murther of his innocent nephewes: his tyrannical vsurpation: with the whole course of his detested life, and most deserued death. As it hath beene lately Acted by the Right honourable the Lord Chamberlaine his servants. At London Printed by Valentine Sims, for Andrew Wise, dwelling in Paules Churchyard, at the sign of the Angell, 1597.

The play was immediately popular, and a new edition was required the next year. This reprinting, known as the Second Quarto, added the name of the author to the title-page. Further editions in quarto form followed in 1602, 1605, 1612, 1622, 1629, and 1634. As each of these appears to have been printed from the edition immediately preceding without reference to any other authority, the text grew progressively worse.

In 1623 the Folio printed a text of the play differing so widely from the quartos that the problem of the source of the two versions has interested scholars ever since. It contained about two hundred and thirty lines not to be found in the quartos and in turn omitted forty lines of their text. Here was quite plainly an independent text, based apparently upon Shakespeare's own manuscript, or a transcript of it, still in the hands of his company. And it is probable that the editors in preparing the Folio for the press used this manuscript to correct and enlarge the latest quarto, 1622, which they then sent to Jaggard to put into type.

This Folio text is by no means perfect. It omits a few authentic lines, reproduces some of the misprints of Q_6, and somewhat imperfectly expunges oaths in accordance with the law of 1606. In one place, III, vii, 219-220, the excision of the oath with the line that follows and depends on it has destroyed one of the neatest and most characteristic bits of Richard's hypocrisy. But the Folio must serve as the basis of any modern edition; and the final conclusion seems to be that the quartos represent a stage version cut down for acting purposes, a copy of which, rather carelessly transcribed, was acquired by Wise in 1597; while the Folio in the main reproduces the play as Shakespeare wrote it.

Date.—There is general agreement, though no positive proof, that the play was written in the years 1593-4, near the end of the so-called "first period" of his career as a dramatist. The date of publication, 1597, is the only bit of positive external evidence unless indeed the reference on the title-page to its being acted by the Lord Chamberlain's Servants places it before July 1596, when for a period they were known as Lord Hunsdon's servants. But evidence for the early dating is drawn chiefly from the play itself: the historical accuracy and skill in handling historical material which places the play between *Henry VI,* Part III, and *Richard II,* the poetic style, the absence of prose and of comic relief, the manifest influence of Marlowe, which would have been impossible in any such like degree at a later date, say, after he had written such a play as *Richard II.*

Source.—The story of Richard's life as Shakespeare knew it derives ultimately from the accounts given in Sir Thomas More's *Life of Richard the Third* (1513) and Polydore Vergil's *Historia Angliæ* (1534), as they were the sources on which the chroniclers Hall and Holinshed drew for their facts. It would be hard indeed to imagine historians more liable to prejudice than these. They wrote in a day when the feeling against Richard was still intense and among people ready to believe any villainy of the man who was regarded as the evil genius of his own family and the nation alike. They served monarchs who believed themselves the inheritors of the Lancastrian party. More, himself Lord Chancellor under Henry VIII, got most of his account from conversations in the household of John Morton, the Bishop of Ely of our play, one of Richard's bitterest enemies; while Vergil was historiographer under Henry VII, the conqueror of Richard. It is small wonder then that while giving most of the known facts of Richard's life, they have gone beyond these to depict a perfection of villainy difficult to credit. This involves a heightening of every defect of body and character to the point of caricature: he was born, they tell us, with a full set of teeth; he was short to dwarfishness, crook-backed, with a hunchback that made one shoulder higher than the other, thin, and with a fierce face. Curiously enough while making him virtually a cripple, they credit him with really prodigious feats in battle. Circumstantial accounts are given of his participation in crimes, notably the murder of Clarence, of Anne, and of the princes in the Tower, about which less prejudiced historians are still in doubt.

On these accounts were based Hall's chronicles of the reigns of Edward IV and Richard III and the portion of Holinshed's *Chronicles of England, Scotland, and Ireland* that deals with this period, and they are Shakespeare's immediate source for most of the historical facts in the play. Remarkably little indeed in the play is not suggested at least by these histories, the principal examples of Shakespeare's pure invention being the famous wooing of Anne and the various appearances of Queen Margaret.

It seems almost certain that Shakespeare knew and made some use of an earlier play on the same subject, *The True Tragedy of Richard III* (printed 1594), a crude play at best, and preserved in such imperfect form as to make a competent judgment of it almost impossible. The famous line, "A horse! a horse! my kingdom for a horse!" has many times been noted as a possible echo of, "A horse, a horse, a fresh horse!" of that play, but that is not all. In spite of its crudities this play has anticipated Shakespeare in shifting the interest from events to the single, dominating figure of Richard himself; and in it Richard tells of a dream in which "ghoasts" came "gaping for revenge," suggesting in the first place the ghost scene of our play and in the second place the tragic motive of revenge which is common to both plays.

Eight history plays from Shakespeare's hand cover the period from approximately the year 1396 in the reign of Richard II to the accession of the house of Tudor with Henry VII in 1485: *Richard II, Henry IV,* Parts I and II, *Henry V, Henry VI,* Parts I, II, and III, and *Richard III.* Though remote in time from Shakespeare's day, these events lived in the popular mind through the currency of such accounts as Hall's, Grafton's, and Holinshed's. These were stirring, bustling times filled with wars and rumors of wars, sudden reversals of fortune for nations and individuals, usurpation, murder, civil war, all the excitement of the adventurous life. But of special interest to the patriotic Englishman were the great days of Henry V, when much of France was vassal to the English crown, and the moral of what followed during the Wars of the Roses. For the successes of Henry IV and Henry V, what may be considered the rising or successful action of a great national drama, were based after all upon the insecure foundation of Henry IV's usurpation of the throne, and there were released at his son's death the forces that brought about the inevitable reaction: punishment by a long and bitter civil war disturbing the peace and security of the nation for nearly half a century.

But with the death of Richard III all comes right once more. Henry VII was to the minds of all Elizabethans the true heir. He was himself a Lancastrian, and his marriage with the Yorkish Princess Elizabeth, daughter of Edward IV, went far to cement in friendship the jarring factions. Although to us his historic claim seems shaky, as he derived from John of Gaunt through the illegitimate Beaufort line, and although his character was somewhat less virtuous than Shakespeare and other of his apologists assert, there is no question that the popular estimate was sound: the Tudors re-established in their persons the authority and even the sanctity of the English crown, and England was once again united against the world.

As the three parts of *Henry VI* are the only plays of the eight not included in this volume, some word of them is necessary to show the connection between the events of *Henry V* and *Richard III.* The authorship of all three has been in dispute at one time or another, and there are still scholars who deny Shakespeare any considerable part in the first of the three; but while allowing for collaboration in Part I and for both collaboration and revision of material from old plays in Parts II and III, it is proper to consider them here as Shakespeare's plays, and to treat them as a stage in his development as a dramatist and as a poet.

The First Part covers the period from the death of Henry V to the marriage of Henry VI to Margaret of Anjou. It is in a sense the exposition for the whole and sets the stage for the entire action that follows. More important as a cause of conflict than the weakness of King Henry was the fact that there was one man alive at the time who had, in a strict legal sense, a better right to the throne than did the king himself: Richard Plantagenet, Duke of York, descended on his mother's side from Lionel, second son of Edward III. Ready at the slightest excuse to bid for power, great families like the Nevilles and the Howards rallied to Richard; and the resulting confusion led to the loss of a great part of the French possessions and the clear alignment of the English factions into Yorkists and Lancastrians.

The Second Part tells of the downfall of the "good duke" Humphrey of Gloucester, the last of Henry V's brothers and the last bulwark against open civil war. With him gone and Suffolk, the queen's lover and chief ally, exiled and then murdered, the way is open for York to make his attempt on the throne, and he defeats the king at the first battle of St. Albans.

The Third Part shows the swift alternation of fortune between the contending parties. It opens with the defeat and death of Richard, Duke of York, at Wakefield, and ends with the complete triumph of the House of York at the battle of Tewkesbury. Of chief interest to us is the increasing importance of Richard to the action and the clear drawing of his character. Although externally a loyal friend of Edward's and a very "packhorse in his great affairs," we soon learn from his asides and from his great speech in the second scene of the third act, where he says, "I'll make my heaven to dream upon the crown," that he is to become the scourge of his own family. And when he strikes down Prince Edward at Tewkesbury and King Henry in the Tower, we know those blows are struck to clear his own way to the crown.

The action of *Richard III* follows immediately with sufficient connectives to indicate the serial nature of the plays and the identity of authorship.

Construction.—Structurally the play of *Richard III* is Marlovian. And a play written as this was in the early nineties can be paid no higher compliment. For this means primarily the strictest compression of events and the exclusion of all material of comedy or extraneous incident that has no bearing on the character of the central figure as conceived by the author. It is true that this tends toward an over-simplification of incident and character and that Shakespeare in his maturity was able to enrich the interest by subplots and comedy without destroying the clear bearing of his main plot; but it is also true that the unity given to plays by the shift in attention from incident to character represents the most important single contribution to English drama up to 1590.

What this method did to the chronicle history play can be seen in a comparison of the *Henry VI* plays even as briefly outlined here and *Richard III.* For with all their compression of history the *Henry VI* plays are a confusion of events and characters and motives in sharp contrast to the simplicity given by the concentration of attention on the character of Richard. Where in them we have the history of a reign and a succession of important individuals, the personality of Richard so dominates his play that even after the action is taken out of his hands by the forces that accumulate to destroy him, he is still the center and focal point of attention. This structural unity in the Marlowe play is attained by means so simple as to appear to us overobvious and crude: the character of the hero is described at the outset and the action is foreshadowed if not definitely described; the motives are usually single and unmixed, such as, ambition, greed, revenge; the action deals solely with the initial success and final downfall of the hero in terms of this single motivating force.

Marlovian also, and still in a good sense, is the poetry. There is perhaps no clearer indication of Shakespeare's genius than the versification of *Richard III,* as it represents the mastery of Marlowe's technic and an improvement on it during an extremely short apprenticeship. Without losing the gusto and declamatory effect of the "mighty line," he has already toned down its artificiality and increased its flexibility by varying the pause within the line and adding syllables after the final accent; he made it in effect more musical and more compact of ideas. And this advance is not to be measured in comparison with

Marlowe's early work in *Tamburlaine* but with his latest and best work in *Edward II*.

Nowhere is the fact more evident that Shakespeare surpassed his master than in the character of Richard himself. The limitations imposed by the Marlovian type of hero-villain are evident throughout: the plain announcement of intent at the beginning, the over-simplification of motive and the over-consistency of action that tend to destroy all sense of naturalness. Then too there are the survivals of earlier drama; the Senecan chorus in the speeches of Queen Margaret and what is in a sense her personification of Nemesis; from Kyd the ghosts, the motive of revenge, the monumental curses. All of these things as they affect the story of Richard's rise and fall can be viewed as limitations on what we have come to think of as Shakespeare's peculiar genius in handling character. And yet there are by implication at least most of the elements that make his great tragic figures interesting to us. There is not in Richard the simplicity characteristic of Marlowe's heroes. His motives are mixed, and his character undergoes an unmistakable if subtle change as the action develops. It is perhaps going too far to claim for this man, who is at the opening of the play already stained with murder, a steady deterioration of moral character as the play progresses, like Macbeth for instance; but the fact remains that there is political necessity and a kind of justice in the murder of "false, fleeting, perjur'd" Clarence at the beginning, and mere blood-lust in the murder of the Princes in the Tower. Nor are we prepared by the Marlowe model for the treatment of remorse that sets in at the final curse of the Duchess of York and becomes vocal in his soliloquy on waking from his ghost-haunted sleep. These things tend to humanize the character of Richard and are but one step removed from the great tragedies in which the hero, come at last to a realization of guilt, accepts his punishment as just and makes of the catastrophe a kind of triumph.

Stage history.—The best proof of the interest in the character of Richard is the stage history of the play. Until quite recent times the part of Richard was in the repertory of every great Shakespearean actor, and in this popularity it probably ranked next to Hamlet. Much of this interest was due to its being a "big" part for the leading actor; but some was due to the fact that three centuries of acting were required to exhaust the possible interpretations of the character of Richard. These interpretations have ranged from a gloomy, savage Richard seeking vengeance on an unsympathetic world, through the type of daring sinner, matching out of pure bravado his strength and wit against the world, to the intellectual superman, outwitting with contemptuous good nature the lesser men about him. But in speaking of the stage history of *Richard III* one really refers to Colley Cibber's adaptation, for the play in the form that we read it has little recorded stage history. We assume its great popularity in Shakespeare's day from the unprecedented number of quarto editions and from the tradition that it was Burbadge's favorite part; but there are meager records of performances before the closing of the theatres in 1642, none for revivals during the Restoration, and few since the middle of the 19th century. So its great popularity during the century and a half after 1700 was in the form that Cibber gave it in that year for the stage. His adding at the beginning the scene of Richard's murder of Henry VI taken bodily from the Third Part of *Henry VI*, his omitting entirely the characters of Queen Margaret and Clarence, his adding of speeches from other plays of Shakespeare and considerable amounts of his own composition seem in the telling to mar completely Shakespeare's play and have enraged purists for a century and a half; but it must be admitted that this shortened form of the play was extremely effective on the stage and changed in no important respect the total effect aimed at by the author. Macready attempted in 1821 at Covent Garden to restore Shakespeare's play but with only partial success, as did Phelps at Sadler Wells in 1845; but it was not until Booth in 1877 and Irving in 1878 produced condensed versions of Shakespeare's text that it can be said to have re-established itself on the stage.

THE TRAGEDY OF RICHARD THE THIRD

Edward IV (1442–1483) (Reigned 1461–1483)—First of the three Yorkist kings (Edward V–Richard III). Deposed Henry VI, the last of the Lancastrian line established by Henry IV.

Edward V (1471–1483)—Reigned only a few months in 1483 before he was deposed by Richard III and confined with his brother, Richard, Duke of York (1473–1483), in the Tower. They were murdered there sometime in the summer of 1483.

George, Duke of Clarence (1449–1478)—His reputation as "false, fleeting, perjured Clarence" (I, iv, 55) is chiefly based on his desertion of Warwick, his father-in-law, for his brother Edward IV. There is no historical basis for Richard's part in his death, although they had quarrelled over their wives' inheritance (they had married daughters of Warwick, "the kingmaker").

Richard III (1452–1485) (Reigned 1483–1485)—His considered villainy is largely literary tradition built up during the reigns of the Tudors, who thought of themselves as inheritors of the Lancastrians and were glad to have the Yorkists villified. He was an able soldier and politician, but once in the way of power stopped at no savage cruelty to further his ends.

Henry, Earl of Richmond, afterwards Henry VII (1456–1509)—Through his mother, Margaret Beaufort, he was descended from John of Gaunt and Catherine Swynford. It was on this descent that he based his claim to the throne.

Thomas Cardinal Bourchier (1404–1486)—Archbishop of Canterbury, Lord Chancellor, Cardinal. Crowned Edward IV, Richard III, and Henry VII.

Thomas Rotherham, Archbishop of York (1423–1500)—Rose to prominence through the patronage of Elizabeth Woodville, Edward IV's queen.

John Morton, Bishop of Ely (1420?–1500)—Supporter of Richmond. He wrote a life of Richard III which Sir Thomas More translated into English.

Henry Stafford, second Duke of Buckingham (1454–1483). Descended on father's side from Thomas of Woodstock, Duke of Gloucester, and on his mother's from John of Gaunt. Married to Catharine Woodville, the queen's sister.

John Howard, Duke of Norfolk (1430–1485)—Killed at Bosworth, 1485.

Thomas Howard, Earl of Surrey (1443–1524)—Eldest son of Norfolk.

Anthony Woodville, Earl Rivers (1442–1463)—Brother of Queen Elizabeth; executed by Richard III at Pontefract.

Thomas Grey, Marquess of Dorset (1451–1501)—Elder son of Queen Elizabeth. Joined Richmond in Brittany and escaped Richard's wrath.

Richard, Lord Grey—Beheaded 1483 at Pontefract.

John de Vere, Earl of Oxford (1443–1513)—Followed losing cause of Warwick, the Kingmaker. Joined Richmond and held high office in his reign.

William, Baron Hastings (1430–1483)—Lord Chamberlain. Executed by Richard III.

Thomas, Lord Stanley (1435–1504)—Created Earl of Derby, 1485. Married Margaret Beaufort, mother of Richmond.

Francis Lovell, Viscount Lovell (1454–1487)—Supporter of Richard III and leader of the Yorkists after his death.

Sir Thomas Vaughan—Chamberlain to Edward, Prince of Wales (Edward V); executed by Richard, 1483.

Sir Richard Ratcliffe (d. 1485)—Executed Rivers at Pontefract and brought Edward V to London. Killed at Bosworth.

Sir William Catesby (d. 1485)—Councillor of Richard III. Connived at overthrow of Hastings. Executed after Bosworth. He, Ratcliffe, and Lovell were celebrated as "The catte, the ratte, and Lovell our dogge."

Sir James Tyrrel (d. 1502)—Supposed murderer of the princes in the Tower.

Sir James Blount.—Son of Sir Walter, Baron Mountjoy. He was Lieutenant of Hammes Castle (1476), where he was custodian of the Earl of Oxford.

Sir Walter Herbert—influential Welshman.

Sir Robert Brackenbury (d. 1483)—Constable of the Tower. Refused to murder the princes. Killed at Bosworth.

Christopher Urswick (1448–1522)—Confessor of Margaret Beaufort.

Queen Elizabeth (1437–1492)—Elizabeth Woodville. Daughter of Lord Rivers. Widow of Sir John Grey, a Lancastrian. Crowned 1464.

Margaret of Anjou (1430–1482)—Widow of Henry VI. Crowned 1445.

Duchess of York—Cicely, daughter of Ralph Neville, first Earl of Westmoreland. Married Richard, Duke of York, 1438.

Lady Anne (1456–1485)—Daughter of Richard Neville, Earl of Warwick, "the kingmaker." Betrothed to Edward, Prince of Wales, son of Henry VI.

THE TRAGEDY OF RICHARD THE THIRD

Dramatis Personæ

King Edward IV.
Edward, Prince of Wales, afterwards *King Edward V,* } sons to the King.
Richard, duke of York, }
George, duke of Clarence, } brothers to the King.
Richard, duke of Gloucester, afterwards *King Richard III,* }
A young son of Clarence.
Henry, earl of Richmond, afterwards *King Henry VII.*
Cardinal Bourchier, archbishop of Canterbury.
Thomas Rotherham, archbishop of York.
John Morton, bishop of Ely.
Duke of Buckingham.
Duke of Norfolk.
Earl of Surrey, his son.
Earl Rivers brother to *Queen Elizabeth.*
Marquis of Dorset, } her sons.
Lord Grey, }
Earl of Oxford.
Lord Hastings.
Lord Stanley, called also *Earl of Derby.*
Lord Lovel.
Sir Thomas Vaughan.
Sir Richard Ratcliff.
Sir William Catesby.
Sir James Tyrrel.
Sir James Blunt.
Sir Walter Herbert.
Sir Robert Brakenbury, lieutenant of the Tower.
Sir William Brandon.
Christopher Urswick, a priest.
Another Priest.
Tressel and *Berkeley,* gentlemen attending on the *Lady Anne.*
Lord Mayor of London.
Sheriff of Wiltshire.

Elizabeth, queen to *King Edward IV.*
Margaret, widow of *King Henry VI.*
Duchess of York, mother to *King Edward IV.*
Lady Anne, widow of *Edward Prince of Wales,* son to *King Henry VI;* afterwards married to *Richard.*
A young Daughter of Clarence (*Lady Margaret Plantagenet*).

Ghosts of those murdered by Richard III; Lords and other Attendants; a Pursuivant, a Page, Scrivener, Citizens, Murderers, Messengers, Soldiers, etc.

SCENE: *England.*

ACT I. SCENE I. *London. A street.*

Enter *Richard, Duke of Gloucester,* solus.

Glou. Now is the winter of our discontent
Made glorious summer by this sun of York;
And all the clouds that lour'd upon our house
In the deep bosom of the ocean buried.
Now are our brows bound with victorious wreaths;
Our bruised arms hung up for monuments;
Our stern alarums chang'd to merry meetings,
Our dreadful marches to delightful measures.
Grim-visag'd War hath smooth'd his wrinkled front;
And now, instead of mounting barbed steeds
To fright the souls of fearful adversaries,
He capers nimbly in a lady's chamber
To the lascivious pleasing of a lute.
But I, that am not shap'd for sportive tricks,
Nor made to court an amorous looking-glass;
I, that am rudely stamp'd, and want love's majesty
To strut before a wanton ambling nymph;
I, that am curtail'd of this fair proportion,
Cheated of feature by dissembling nature,
Deform'd, unfinish'd, sent before my time
Into this breathing world, scarce half made up,
And that so lamely and unfashionable
That dogs bark at me as I halt by them;
Why, I, in this weak piping time of peace,
Have no delight to pass away the time,
Unless to see my shadow in the sun
And descant on mine own deformity.
And therefore, since I cannot prove a lover
To entertain these fair well-spoken days,
I am determined to prove a villain
And hate the idle pleasures of these days.
Plots have I laid, inductions dangerous,
By drunken prophecies, libels, and dreams,
To set my brother Clarence and the King
In deadly hate the one against the other;

2. sun, (1) son, (2) sun. King Edward had taken a sun as his badge because of the three suns that appeared to him at the battle of Mortimer's Cross. **10. barbed,** armored. **14. sportive,** amorous.

17. ambling, affected in walking or dancing. **19. feature,** form. **22. unfashionable,** deformed. **23. halt,** limp. **27. descant,** comment on, lit., run variations on. **32. inductions,** beginnings.

And if King Edward be as true and just
As I am subtle, false, and treacherous,
This day should Clarence closely be mew'd up
About a prophecy, which says that G
Of Edward's heirs the murderer shall be.
Dive, thoughts, down to my soul; here Clarence comes.

Enter *Clarence,* guarded, and *Brakenbury.*

Brother, good day. What means this armed guard
That waits upon your Grace?
Clar. His Majesty,
Tend'ring my person's safety, hath appointed
This conduct to convey me to the Tower.
Glou. Upon what cause?
Clar. Because my name is George.
Glou. Alack, my lord, that fault is none of yours;
He should, for that, commit your godfathers.
O, belike his Majesty hath some intent
That you should be new christen'd in the Tower.
But what 's the matter, Clarence? May I know?
Clar. Yea, Richard, when I know, but I protest
As yet I do not; but, as I can learn,
He hearkens after prophecies and dreams,
And from the cross-row plucks the letter G,
And says a wizard told him that by G
His issue disinherited should be;
And, for my name of George begins with G,
It follows in his thought that I am he.
These, as I learn, and such like toys as these
Have mov'd his Highness to commit me now.
Glou. Why, this it is, when men are rul'd by women:
'T is not the King that sends you to the Tower;
My Lady Grey his wife, Clarence, 't is she
That tempts him to this harsh extremity.
Was it not she and that good man of worship,
Anthony Woodville, her brother there,
That made him send Lord Hastings to the Tower,
From whence this present day he is delivered?
We are not safe, Clarence; we are not safe.
Clar. By heaven, I think there is no man secure
But the Queen's kindred, and night-walking heralds
That trudge betwixt the King and Mistress Shore.
Heard you not what an humble suppliant
Lord Hastings was for her delivery?

38. **mew'd,** shut up, like a hawk in its cage. 55. **cross-row,** alphabet. 60. **toys,** trifles. 65. **tempts,** moulds, controls. 73. **Mistress Shore,** mistress of the king, wife of a London goldsmith. 75. **her delivery,** deliverance by her means.

Glou. Humbly complaining to her deity
Got my Lord Chamberlain his liberty.
I 'll tell you what; I think it is our way,
If we will keep in favour with the King,
To be her men and wear her livery.
The jealous o'erworn widow and herself,
Since that our brother dubb'd them gentlewomen,
Are mighty gossips in our monarchy.
Brak. I beseech your Graces both to pardon me;
His Majesty hath straitly given in charge
That no man shall have private conference,
Of what degree soever, with your brother.
Glou. Even so; an 't please your worship, Brakenbury,
You may partake of anything we say:
We speak no treason, man: we say the King
Is wise and virtuous, and his noble queen
Well struck in years, fair, and not jealous;
We say that Shore's wife hath a pretty foot,
A cherry lip, a bonny eye, a passing pleasing tongue;
And that the Queen's kindred are made gentlefolks.
How say you, sir? Can you deny all this?
Brak. With this, my lord, myself have nought to do.
Glou. Naught to do with Mistress Shore? I tell thee, fellow,
He that doth naught with her, excepting one,
Were best to do it secretly, alone.
Brak. What one, my lord?
Glou. Her husband, knave. Wouldst thou betray me?
Brak. I do beseech your Grace to pardon me, and withal
Forbear your conference with the noble Duke.
Clar. We know thy charge, Brakenbury, and will obey.
Glou. We are the Queen's abjects, and must obey.
Brother, farewell! I will unto the King;
And whatsoe'er you will employ me in,
Were it to call King Edward's widow sister,
I will perform it to enfranchise you.
Meantime, this deep disgrace in brotherhood
Touches me deeper than you can imagine.
Clar. I know it pleaseth neither of us well.
Glou. Well, your imprisonment shall not be long;
I will deliver you, or else lie for you.
Meantime, have patience.
Clar. I must perforce. Farewell.
Exeunt Clarence, Brakenbury, and Guard.
Glou. Go, tread the path that thou shalt ne'er return,

77. **Lord Chamberlain,** Hastings. 81. **widow,** i.e., the queen. 83. **gossips,** cronies. 106. **abjects,** i.e., slaves. 115. **lie,** (1) prevaricate, (2) lie in prison.

Simple, plain Clarence! I do love thee so,
That I will shortly send thy soul to heaven,
If heaven will take the present at our hands.
But who comes here? The new-delivered Hastings?

Enter *Lord Hastings.*

Hast. Good time of day unto my gracious lord!
Glou. As much unto my good Lord Chamberlain!
Well are you welcome to this open air:
How hath your lordship brook'd imprisonment?
Hast. With patience, noble lord, as prisoners must;
But I shall live, my lord, to give them thanks
That were the cause of my imprisonment.
Glou. No doubt, no doubt; and so shall Clarence too;
For they that were your enemies are his,
And have prevail'd as much on him as you.
Hast. More pity that the eagles should be mew'd,
Whiles kites and buzzards play at liberty.
Glou. What news abroad?
Hast. No news so bad abroad as this at home:
The King is sickly, weak, and melancholy,
And his physicians fear him mightily.
Glou. Now, by Saint Paul, that news is bad indeed.
O, he hath kept an evil diet long,
And overmuch consum'd his royal person:
'T is very grievous to be thought upon.
Where is he? In his bed?
Hast. He is.
Glou. Go you before, and I will follow you. *Exit Hastings.*
He cannot live, I hope; and must not die
Till George be pack'd with post-horse up to heaven.
I 'll in, to urge his hatred more to Clarence
With lies well steel'd with weighty arguments;
And, if I fail not in my deep intent,
Clarence hath not another day to live;
Which done, God take King Edward to his mercy,
And leave the world for me to bustle in!
For then I 'll marry Warwick's youngest daughter.
What though I kill'd her husband and her father?
The readiest way to make the wench amends
Is to become her husband and her father;
The which will I; not all so much for love
As for another secret close intent,
By marrying her which I must reach unto.
But yet I run before my horse to market.
Clarence still breathes; Edward still lives and reigns;
When they are gone, then must I count my gains. *Exit.*

146. **with post-horse,** i.e., speedily. 148. **steel'd,** reenforced. 154. Warwick at the battle of Barnet, Edward, Prince of Wales at Tewkesbury.

Scene II. *Another street.*

Enter the corpse of *King Henry VI, Gentlemen* with halberds to guard it, among them *Tressel* and *Berkeley; Lady Anne* being the mourner.

Anne. Set down, set down your honourable load,
If honour may be shrouded in a hearse,
Whilst I awhile obsequiously lament
Th' untimely fall of virtuous Lancaster.
The coffin is set down.
Poor key-cold figure of a holy king!
Pale ashes of the house of Lancaster!
Thou bloodless remnant of that royal blood!
Be it lawful that I invocate thy ghost
To hear the lamentations of poor Anne,
Wife to thy Edward, to thy slaughter'd son,
Stabb'd by the self-same hand that made these wounds!
Lo, in these windows that let forth thy life,
I pour the helpless balm of my poor eyes.
O cursed be the hand that made these holes!
Cursed the heart that had the heart to do it!
Cursed the blood that let this blood from hence!
More direful hap betide that hated wretch
That makes us wretched by the death of thee,
Than I can wish to wolves, to spiders, toads,
Or any creeping venom'd thing that lives!
If ever he have child, abortive be it,
Prodigious, and untimely brought to light,
Whose ugly and unnatural aspect
May fright the hopeful mother at the view;
And that be heir to his unhappiness!
If ever he have wife, let her be made
More miserable by the death of him
Than I am made by my young lord and thee!
Come, now towards Chertsey with your holy load,
Taken from Paul's to be interred there;
And still, as you are weary of this weight,
Rest you, whiles I lament King Henry's corse.
The bearers take up the coffin.

Enter *Gloucester.*

Glou. Stay, you that bear the corse, and set it down.

Scene ii: 3. obsequiously, as befits a funeral (obsequies), mournfully. 6. **Lancaster,** Henry VI murdered in the Tower 1471 by command of Edward IV, supposedly by the hand of Richard. 25. **that,** the child. **unhappiness,** evil nature. 29. **Chertsey,** town in Surrey. 30. **Paul's,** St. Paul's in London.

Anne. What black magician conjures up this fiend
To stop devoted charitable deeds?
Glou. Villains, set down the corse; or, by Saint Paul,
I 'll make a corse of him that disobeys.
Gent. My lord, stand back, and let the coffin pass.
Glou. Unmanner'd dog! stand thou, when I command.
Advance thy halberd higher than my breast,
Or, by Saint Paul, I 'll strike thee to my foot,
And spurn upon thee, beggar, for thy boldness. *The coffin is set down again.*
Anne. What, do you tremble? Are you all afraid?
Alas, I blame you not, for you are mortal,
And mortal eyes cannot endure the devil.
Avaunt, thou dreadful minister of hell!
Thou hadst but power over his mortal body,
His soul thou canst not have; therefore, be gone.
Glou. Sweet saint, for charity, be not so curst.
Anne. Foul devil, for God's sake, hence, and trouble us not;
For thou hast made the happy earth thy hell,
Fill'd it with cursing cries and deep exclaims.
If thou delight to view thy heinous deeds,
Behold this pattern of thy butcheries.
O, gentlemen, see, see! dead Henry's wounds
Open their congeal'd mouths and bleed afresh!
Blush, blush, thou lump of foul deformity;
For 't is thy presence that exhales this blood
From cold and empty veins, where no blood dwells.
Thy deed, inhuman and unnatural,
Provokes this deluge most unnatural.
O God, which this blood mad'st, revenge his death!
O earth, which this blood drink'st, revenge his death!
Either heaven with lightning strike the murd'rer dead,
Or earth gape open wide and eat him quick,
As thou dost swallow up this good king's blood,
Which his hell-govern'd arm hath butchered!
Glou. Lady, you know no rules of charity,
Which renders good for bad, blessings for curses.
Anne. Villain, thou know'st nor law of God nor man.
No beast so fierce but knows some touch of pity.
Glou. But I know none, and therefore am no beast.

54. pattern, example. **56. bleed afresh**, corpses were supposed to bleed in the presence of the murderer.

Anne. O wonderful, when devils tell the truth!
Glou. More wonderful, when angels are so angry.
Vouchsafe, divine perfection of a woman,
Of these supposed crimes, to give me leave
By circumstance but to acquit myself.
Anne. Vouchsafe, defus'd infection of a man,
For these known evils, but to give me leave,
By circumstance, to curse thy cursed self.
Glou. Fairer than tongue can name thee, let me have
Some patient leisure to excuse myself.
Anne. Fouler than heart can think thee, thou canst make
No excuse current but to hang thyself.
Glou. By such despair I should accuse myself.
Anne. And by despairing shalt thou stand excus'd
For doing worthy vengeance on thyself,
That didst unworthy slaughter upon others.
Glou. Say that I slew them not?
Anne. Then say they were not slain.
But dead they are, and, devilish slave, by thee.
Glou. I did not kill your husband.
Anne. Why, then he is alive.
Glou. Nay, he is dead; and slain by Edward's hands.
Anne. In thy foul throat thou liest! Queen Margaret saw
Thy murderous falchion smoking in his blood;
The which thou once didst bend against her breast,
But that thy brothers beat aside the point.
Glou. I was provoked by her sland'rous tongue,
That laid their guilt upon my guiltless shoulders.
Anne. Thou wast provoked by thy bloody mind,
That never dreamst on aught but butcheries.
Didst thou not kill this king?
Glou. I grant ye.
Anne. Dost grant me, hedgehog? Then, God grant me too
Thou mayst be damned for that wicked deed!
O, he was gentle, mild, and virtuous!
Glou. The better for the King of heaven, that hath him.
Anne. He is in heaven, where thou shalt never come.
Glou. Let him thank me, that holp to send him thither;
For he was fitter for that place than earth.

77. circumstance, detailed proof. **78. defus'd**, shapeless. **82. patient**, calm, quiet. **84. current**, good (of money). **94. falchion**, sword. **102. hedgehog**, a boar was in Richard's heraldic device.

Anne. And thou unfit for any place but hell.
Glou. Yes, one place else, if you will hear me name it.
Anne. Some dungeon.
Glou. Your bed-chamber.
Anne. Ill rest betide the chamber where thou liest!
Glou. So will it, madam, till I lie with you.
Anne. I hope so.
Glou. I know so. But, gentle Lady Anne,
To leave this keen encounter of our wits
And fall something into a slower method,
Is not the causer of the timeless deaths
Of these Plantagenets, Henry and Edward,
As blameful as the executioner?
Anne. Thou wast the cause, and most accurs'd effect.
Glou. Your beauty was the cause of that effect;
Your beauty, that did haunt me in my sleep
To undertake the death of all the world,
So I might live one hour in your sweet bosom.
Anne. If I thought that, I tell thee, homicide,
These nails should rend that beauty from my cheeks.
Glou. These eyes could not endure that beauty's wreck;
You should not blemish it, if I stood by.
As all the world is cheered by the sun,
So I by that; it is my day, my life.
Anne. Black night o'ershade thy day, and death thy life!
Glou. Curse not thyself, fair creature; thou art both.
Anne. I would I were, to be reveng'd on thee.
Glou. It is a quarrel most unnatural,
To be reveng'd on him that loveth thee.
Anne. It is a quarrel just and reasonable,
To be reveng'd on him that kill'd my husband.
Glou. He that bereft thee, lady, of thy husband,
Did it to help thee to a better husband.
Anne. His better doth not breathe upon the earth.
Glou. He lives that loves thee better than he could.
Anne. Name him.
Glou. Plantagenet.
Anne. Why, that was he.
Glou. The self-same name, but one of better nature.
Anne. Where is he?
Glou. Here. [*She spits at him.*] Why dost thou spit at me?
Anne. Would it were mortal poison for thy sake!
Glou. Never came poison from so sweet a place.
Anne. Never hung poison on a fouler toad.
Out of my sight! Thou dost infect mine eyes.
Glou. Thine eyes, sweet lady, have infected mine.
Anne. Would they were basilisks, to strike thee dead!
Glou. I would they were, that I might die at once;
For now they kill me with a living death.
Those eyes of thine from mine have drawn salt tears,
Sham'd their aspects with store of childish drops—
These eyes, which never shed remorseful tear,
No, when my father York and Edward wept
To hear the piteous moan that Rutland made
When black-fac'd Clifford shook his sword at him;
Nor when thy warlike father, like a child,
Told the sad story of my father's death,
And twenty times made pause to sob and weep,
That all the standers-by had wet their cheeks,
Like trees bedash'd with rain,—in that sad time
My manly eyes did scorn an humble tear;
And what these sorrows could not thence exhale,
Thy beauty hath, and made them blind with weeping.
I never sued to friend nor enemy;
My tongue could never learn sweet smoothing word;
But, now thy beauty is propos'd my fee,
My proud heart sues, and prompts my tongue to speak. *She looks scornfully at him.*
Teach not thy lip such scorn, for it was made
For kissing, lady, not for such contempt.
If thy revengeful heart cannot forgive,
Lo, here I lend thee this sharp-pointed sword;
Which if thou please to hide in this true breast,
And let the soul forth that adoreth thee,
I lay it naked to the deadly stroke,
And humbly beg the death upon my knee.
He lays his breast open: she offers at it with his sword.
Nay, do not pause; for I did kill King Henry,
But 't was thy beauty that provoked me.
Nay, now dispatch; 't was I that stabb'd young Edward,
But 't was thy heavenly face that set me on.
Here she lets fall the sword.
Take up the sword again, or take up me.

117. timeless, untimely.

151. basilisks, mythical serpents whose glance was fatal. **158. Rutland,** brother of Richard murdered by Lord Clifford (1460). **169. smoothing,** flattering. **word,** speech.

Anne. Arise, dissembler! Though I wish thy death,
I will not be thy executioner.
Glou. Then bid me kill myself, and I will do it.
Anne. I have already.
Glou. That was in thy rage:
Speak it again, and, even with the word,
This hand, which for thy love did kill thy love,
Shall for thy love kill a far truer love;
To both their deaths shalt thou be accessary.
Anne. I would I knew thy heart.
Glou. 'T is figur'd in my tongue.
Anne. I fear me both are false.
Glou. Then never man was true.
Anne. Well, well, put up your sword.
Glou. Say, then, my peace is made.
Anne. That shalt thou know hereafter.
Glou. But shall I live in hope?
Anne. All men, I hope, live so.
Glou. Vouchsafe to wear this ring.
Anne. To take is not to give.
Puts on the ring.
Glou. Look, how my ring encompasseth thy finger,
Even so thy breast encloseth my poor heart:
Wear both of them, for both of them are thine.
And if thy poor devoted servant may
But beg one favour at thy gracious hand,
Thou dost confirm his happiness for ever.
Anne. What is it?
Glou. That it may please you leave these sad designs
To him that hath most cause to be a mourner,
And presently repair to Crosby House;
Where, after I have solemnly interr'd
At Chertsey monast'ry this noble king,
And wet his grave with my repentant tears,
I will with all expedient duty see you.
For divers unknown reasons, I beseech you,
Grant me this boon.
Anne. With all my heart; and much it joys me too,
To see you are become so penitent.
Tressel and Berkeley, go along with me.
Glou. Bid me farewell.
Anne. 'T is more than you deserve;
But since you teach me how to flatter you,
Imagine I have said farewell already.
Exeunt Lady Anne, Tressel, and Berkeley.
Glou. Sirs, take up the corse.
Gent. Towards Chertsey, noble lord?
Glou. No, to White-Friars; there attend my coming. *Exeunt all but Gloucester.*
Was ever woman in this humour woo'd?
Was ever woman in this humour won?
I 'll have her; but I will not keep her long.
What! I, that kill'd her husband and his father,
To take her in her heart's extremest hate,
With curses in her mouth, tears in her eyes,
The bleeding witness of my hatred by;
Having God, her conscience, and these bars against me,
And I no friends to back my suit withal
But the plain devil and dissembling looks,
And yet to win her, all the world to nothing!
Ha!
Hath she forgot already that brave prince,
Edward, her lord, whom I, some three months since,
Stabb'd in my angry mood at Tewksbury?
A sweeter and a lovelier gentleman,
Fram'd in the prodigality of nature,
Young, valiant, wise, and, no doubt, right royal,
The spacious world cannot again afford:
And will she yet abase her eyes on me,
That cropp'd the golden prime of this sweet prince,
And made her widow to a woeful bed?
On me, whose all not equals Edward's moiety?
On me, that halts and am misshapen thus?
My dukedom to a beggarly denier,
I do mistake my person all this while.
Upon my life, she finds, although I cannot,
Myself to be a marv'llous proper man.
I 'll be at charges for a looking-glass,
And entertain a score or two of tailors,
To study fashions to adorn my body:
Since I am crept in favour with myself,
I will maintain it with some little cost.
But first I 'll turn yon fellow in his grave;
And then return lamenting to my love.
Shine out, fair sun, till I have bought a glass,
That I may see my shadow as I pass. *Exit.*

Scene III. *The palace.*

Enter *Queen Elizabeth, Lord Rivers,* and *Lord Grey.*

Riv. Have patience, madam; there 's no doubt his Majesty
Will soon recover his accustom'd health.
Grey. In that you brook it ill, it makes him worse;
Therefore, for God's sake, entertain good comfort,
And cheer his Grace with quick and merry eyes.

213. Crosby House, Richard's residence. **217. expedient,** expeditious. **218. unknown,** secret. **227. White-Friars,** the Carmelite priory in London.

237. plain, undisguised. **dissembling,** disguised. **250. moiety,** half. **252. denier,** a small coin; the twelfth part of a sou.

Q. Eliz. If he were dead, what would betide on me?
Grey. No other harm but loss of such a lord.
Q. Eliz. The loss of such a lord includes all harms.
Grey. The heavens have bless'd you with a goodly son
To be your comforter when he is gone.
Q. Eliz. Ah, he is young, and his minority
Is put unto the trust of Richard Gloucester,
A man that loves not me, nor none of you.
Riv. Is it concluded he shall be Protector?
Q. Eliz. It is determin'd, not concluded yet;
But so it must be, if the King miscarry.

Enter *Buckingham* and *Derby*.

Grey. Here comes the lords of Buckingham and Derby.
Buck. Good time of day unto your royal Grace!
Der. God make your Majesty joyful as you have been!
Q. Eliz. The Countess Richmond, good my Lord of Derby,
To your good prayer will scarcely say amen.
Yet, Derby, notwithstanding she 's your wife,
And loves not me, be you, good lord, assur'd
I hate not you for her proud arrogance.
Der. I do beseech you, either not believe
The envious slanders of her false accusers;
Or, if she be accus'd on true report,
Bear with her weakness, which, I think, proceeds
From wayward sickness, and no grounded malice.
Q. Eliz. Saw you the King to-day, my Lord of Derby?
Der. But now the Duke of Buckingham and I
Are come from visiting his Majesty.
Q. Eliz. What likelihood of his amendment, lords?
Buck. Madam, good hope; his Grace speaks cheerfully.
Q. Eliz. God grant him health! Did you confer with him?
Buck. Ay, madam. He desires to make atonement
Between the Duke of Gloucester and your brothers,
And between them and my Lord Chamberlain;
And sent to warn them to his royal presence.
Q. Eliz. Would all were well! but that will never be.
I fear our happiness is at the height.

Enter *Gloucester, Hastings,* and *Dorset.*

Glou. They do me wrong, and I will not endure it.
Who is it that complains unto the King
That I, forsooth, am stern and love them not?
By holy Paul, they love his Grace but lightly
That fill his ears with such dissentious rumours.
Because I cannot flatter and look fair,
Smile in men's faces, smooth, deceive, and cog,
Duck with French nods and apish courtesy,
I must be held a rancorous enemy.
Cannot a plain man live and think no harm,
But thus his simple truth must be abus'd
With silken, sly, insinuating Jacks?
Grey. To who in all this presence speaks your Grace?
Glou. To thee, that hast nor honesty nor grace:
When have I injur'd thee? When done thee wrong?
Or thee? or thee? or any of your faction?
A plague upon you all! His royal Grace,—
Whom God preserve better than you would wish!—
Cannot be quiet scarce a breathing-while,
But you must trouble him with lewd complaints.
Q. Eliz. Brother of Gloucester, you mistake the matter:
The King, on his own royal disposition,
And not provok'd by any suitor else,
Aiming, belike, at your interior hatred,
That in your outward action shows itself
Against my children, brothers, and myself,
Makes him to send that he may learn the ground.
Glou. I cannot tell: the world is grown so bad
That wrens make prey where eagles dare not perch.
Since every Jack became a gentleman,
There 's many a gentle person made a Jack.
Q. Eliz. Come, come, we know your meaning, brother Gloucester;
You envy my advancement and my friends'.
God grant we never may have need of you!
Glou. Meantime, God grants that I have need of you.
Our brother is imprison'd by your means,
Myself disgrac'd, and the nobility
Held in contempt; while great promotions
Are daily given to ennoble those

Scene iii: 6. betide on, become of. **15. determin'd, not concluded,** decided on but not yet executed. **16. miscarry,** die. **20. Countess Richmond,** Margaret Beaufort, formerly wife of Earl of Richmond and by him mother of Henry VII. **39. warn,** summon.

48. smooth, flatter. **cog,** cheat. **53. Jacks,** upstarts. **61. lewd,** mean, base. **77. of you,** because of you.

That scarce, some two days since, were worth a noble.
Q. Eliz. By Him that rais'd me to this careful height
From that contented hap which I enjoy'd,
I never did incense his Majesty
Against the Duke of Clarence, but have been
An earnest advocate to plead for him.
My lord, you do me shameful injury,
Falsely to draw me in these vile suspects.
Glou. You may deny that you were not the mean
Of my Lord Hastings' late imprisonment.
Riv. She may, my lord, for—
Glou. She may, Lord Rivers! Why, who knows not so?
She may do more, sir, than denying that.
She may help you to many fair preferments,
And then deny her aiding hand therein,
And lay those honours on your high desert.
What may she not? She may, ay, marry, may she,—
Riv. What, marry, may she?
Glou. What, marry, may she? Marry with a king,
A bachelor, and a handsome stripling too:
I wis your grandam had a worser match.
Q. Eliz. My Lord of Gloucester, I have too long borne
Your blunt upbraidings and your bitter scoffs:
By heaven, I will acquaint his Majesty
Of those gross taunts that oft I have endur'd.
I had rather be a country servant-maid
Than a great queen, with this condition,
To be thus baited, scorn'd, and stormed at.
Small joy have I in being England's Queen.

Enter old *Queen Margaret* behind.

Q. Mar. And lessen'd be that small, God I beseech Him!
Thy honour, state, and seat is due to me.
Glou. What! threat you me with telling of the King?
Tell him, and spare not. Look, what I have said
I will avouch 't in presence of the King.
I dare adventure to be sent to th' Tower.
'T is time to speak; my pains are quite forgot.
Q. Mar. Out, devil! I do remember them too well:
Thou kill'dst my husband Henry in the Tower,
And Edward, my poor son, at Tewksbury.
Glou. Ere you were queen, ay, or your husband king,
I was a pack-horse in his great affairs;
A weeder-out of his proud adversaries,
A liberal rewarder of his friends.
To royalize his blood I spent mine own.
Q. Mar. Ay, and much better blood than his or thine.
Glou. In all which time you and your husband Grey
Were factious for the house of Lancaster;
And, Rivers, so were you. Was not your husband
In Margaret's battle at Saint Alban's slain?
Let me put in your minds, if you forget,
What you have been ere this, and what you are;
Withal, what I have been, and what I am.
Q. Mar. A murd'rous villain, and so still thou art.
Glou. Poor Clarence did forsake his father, Warwick;
Ay, and forswore himself,—which Jesu pardon!—
Q. Mar. Which God revenge!
Glou. To fight on Edward's party for the crown;
And for his meed, poor lord, he is mewed up.
I would to God my heart were flint, like Edward's;
Or Edward's soft and pitiful, like mine.
I am too childish-foolish for this world.
Q. Mar. Hie thee to hell for shame, and leave this world,
Thou cacodemon! there thy kingdom is.
Riv. My Lord of Gloucester, in those busy days
Which here you urge to prove us enemies,
We follow'd then our lord, our sovereign king.
So should we you, if you should be our king.
Glou. If I should be! I had rather be a pedlar:
Far be it from my heart, the thought thereof!
Q. Eliz. As little joy, my lord, as you suppose
You should enjoy, were you this country's king,
As little joy you may suppose in me,
That I enjoy, being the queen thereof.
Q. Mar. A little joy enjoys the queen thereof;
For I am she, and altogether joyless.
I can no longer hold me patient. *Advancing.*
Hear me, you wrangling pirates, that fall out
In sharing that which you have pill'd from me!
Which of you trembles not that looks on me?
If not that I am queen, you bow like subjects,
Yet that by you depos'd, you quake like rebels?

82. **noble,** a coin worth 6 shillings and eight pence. 83. **careful,** full of care. 84. **hap,** fortune. 89. **suspects,** suspicions. 98. **marry,** by the Virgin Mary.

130. **battle,** army, at the battle of St. Alban's, Feb. 17, 1461. 144. **cacodemon,** evil spirit. 159. **pill'd,** pillaged. 161-2. If you bow not as subjects because I am queen, at least you quake because you have deposed me.

Ah, gentle villain, do not turn away!
Glou. Foul wrinkled witch, what mak'st thou in my sight?
Q. Mar. But repetition of what thou hast marr'd;
That will I make before I let thee go.
Glou. Wert thou not banished on pain of death?
Q. Mar. I was; but I do find more pain in banishment
Than death can yield me here by my abode.
A husband and a son thou ow'st to me;
And thou a kingdom; all of you allegiance.
This sorrow that I have, by right is yours,
And all the pleasures you usurp are mine.
Glou. The curse my noble father laid on thee,
When thou didst crown his warlike brows with paper,
And with thy scorns drew'st rivers from his eyes,
And then, to dry them, gav'st the Duke a clout
Steep'd in the faultless blood of pretty Rutland,—
His curses, then from bitterness of soul
Denounc'd against thee, are all fall'n upon thee;
And God, not we, hath plagued thy bloody deed.
Q. Eliz. So just is God, to right the innocent.
Hast. O, 't was the foulest deed to slay that babe,
And the most merciless that e'er was heard of!
Riv. Tyrants themselves wept when it was reported.
Dor. No man but prophesied revenge for it.
Buck. Northumberland, then present, wept to see it.
Q. Mar. What! were you snarling all before I came,
Ready to catch each other by the throat,
And turn you all your hatred now on me?
Did York's dread curse prevail so much with heaven
That Henry's death, my lovely Edward's death,
Their kingdom's loss, my woeful banishment,
Should all but answer for that peevish brat?
Can curses pierce the clouds and enter heaven?
Why, then, give way, dull clouds, to my quick curses!
Though not by war, by surfeit die your king,
As ours by murder to make him a king!
Edward thy son, that now is Prince of Wales,
For Edward our son, that was Prince of Wales,
Die in his youth by like untimely violence!
Thyself a queen, for me that was a queen,
Outlive thy glory, like my wretched self!
Long mayst thou live to wail thy children's death,
And see another, as I see thee now,
Deck'd in thy rights, as thou art stall'd in mine!
Long die thy happy days before thy death,
And, after many lengthen'd hours of grief,
Die neither mother, wife, nor England's Queen!
Rivers and Dorset, you were standers by,
And so wast thou, Lord Hastings, when my son
Was stabb'd with bloody daggers: God I pray him,
That none of you may live his natural age,
But by some unlook'd accident cut off!
Glou. Have done thy charm, thou hateful wither'd hag!
Q. Mar. And leave out thee? Stay, dog, for thou shalt hear me.
If heaven have any grievous plague in store
Exceeding those that I can wish upon thee,
O, let them keep it till thy sins be ripe,
And then hurl down their indignation
On thee, the troubler of the poor world's peace!
The worm of conscience still begnaw thy soul!
Thy friends suspect for traitors while thou liv'st,
And take deep traitors for thy dearest friends!
No sleep close up that deadly eye of thine,
Unless it be while some tormenting dream
Affrights thee with a hell of ugly devils!
Thou elvish-mark'd, abortive, rooting hog!
Thou that wast seal'd in thy nativity
The slave of nature and the son of hell!
Thou slander of thy heavy mother's womb!
Thou loathed issue of thy father's loins!
Thou rag of honour! thou detested—
Glou. Margaret.
Q. Mar. Richard!
Glou. Ha!
Q. Mar. I call thee not.
Glou. I cry thee mercy then, for I did think
That thou hadst call'd me all these bitter names.
Q. Mar. Why, so I did; but look'd for no reply.
O, let me make the period to my curse!

165. Only repetition of thy destruction. **171. thou,** i.e., the queen. **174ff.** At the battle of Wakefield (1460) York, father of Richard, and his brother Rutland were slain. York's head, with a paper crown, was displayed above one of the gates at York. **177. clout,** cloth. **187. Northumberland,** a grandson of Hotspur, a partisan of the Lancastrian cause. **196. quick,** active, piercing.

206. stall'd, installed. **228. elvish-mark'd,** birth-marked by elves or fairies. **230. slave of nature,** mean, contemptible by nature.

Glou. 'T is done by me, and ends in "Margaret."
Q. Eliz. Thus have you breath'd your curse against yourself.
Q. Mar. Poor painted queen, vain flourish of my fortune!
Why strew'st thou sugar on that bottled spider,
Whose deadly web ensnareth thee about?
Fool, fool! thou whet'st a knife to kill thyself:
The day will come that thou shalt wish for me
To help thee curse this poisonous bunch-back'd toad.
Hast. False-boding woman, end thy frantic curse,
Lest to thy harm thou move our patience.
Q. Mar. Foul shame upon you! you have all mov'd mine.
Riv. Were you well serv'd, you would be taught your duty.
Q. Mar. To serve me well, you all should do me duty,
Teach me to be your queen, and you my subjects.
O, serve me well, and teach yourselves that duty!
Dor. Dispute not with her; she is lunatic.
Q. Mar. Peace, master marquess, you are malapert;
Your fire-new stamp of honour is scarce current.
O, that your young nobility could judge
What 't were to lose it, and be miserable!
They that stand high have many blasts to shake them;
And if they fall, they dash themselves to pieces.
Glou. Good counsel, marry; learn it, learn it, marquess.
Dor. It touches you, my lord, as much as me.
Glou. Ay, and much more; but I was born so high,
Our aery buildeth in the cedar's top,
And dallies with the wind and scorns the sun.
Q. Mar. And turns the sun to shade; alas! alas!
Witness my son, now in the shade of death,
Whose bright out-shining beams thy cloudy wrath
Hath in eternal darkness folded up.
Your aery buildeth in our aery's nest.
O God, that seest it, do not suffer it!
As it is won with blood, lost be it so!
Buck. Peace, peace! for shame, if not for charity.
Q. Mar. Urge neither charity nor shame to me:
Uncharitably with me have you dealt,
And shamefully my hopes by you are butcher'd.
My charity is outrage, life my shame;
And in that shame still live my sorrow's rage!
Buck. Have done, have done.
Q. Mar. O princely Buckingham, I 'll kiss thy hand,
In sign of league and amity with thee:
Now fair befall thee and thy noble house!
Thy garments are not spotted with our blood,
Nor thou within the compass of my curse.
Buck. Nor no one here; for curses never pass
The lips of those that breathe them in the air.
Q. Mar. I will not think but they ascend the sky,
And there awake God's gentle-sleeping peace.
O Buckingham, take heed of yonder dog!
Look, when he fawns, he bites; and when he bites,
His venom tooth will rankle to the death.
Have not to do with him, beware of him;
Sin, death, and hell have set their marks on him,
And all their ministers attend on him.
Glou. What doth she say, my Lord of Buckingham?
Buck. Nothing that I respect, my gracious lord.
Q. Mar. What, dost thou scorn me for my gentle counsel,
And soothe the devil that I warn thee from?
O, but remember this another day,
When he shall split thy very heart with sorrow,
And say poor Margaret was a prophetess!
Live each of you the subjects to his hate,
And he to yours, and all of you to God's! *Exit.*
Buck. My hair doth stand on end to hear her curses.
Riv. And so doth mine: I muse why she 's at liberty.
Glou. I cannot blame her. By God's holy mother,
She hath had too much wrong; and I repent
My part thereof that I have done to her.
Q. Eliz. I never did her any, to my knowledge.
Glou. Yet you have all the vantage of her wrong.
I was too hot to do somebody good,
That is too cold in thinking of it now.

241. vain . . . fortune, light veneer, mere pretense of what I was in truth. **242. bottled,** big-bellied, swollen. **256. fire-new,** newly minted. **current,** in circulation (of coins). **264. aery,** brood of an eagle.

277. charity . . . outrage, instead of charity I get outrage. **291. rankle,** poison. **298. soothe,** humor. **305. muse,** wonder. **312. cold,** ungrateful.

Marry, as for Clarence, he is well repaid;
He is frank'd up to fatting for his pains.
God pardon them that are the cause thereof!
Riv. A virtuous and a Christian-like conclusion,
To pray for them that have done scath to us.
Glou. So do I ever, being well advis'd.
Speaks to himself.
For had I curs'd now, I had curs'd myself.

Enter *Catesby.*

Cates. Madam, his Majesty doth call for you;
And for your Grace; and yours, my noble lord.
Q. Eliz. Catesby, I come. Lords, will you go with me?
Riv. We wait upon your Grace.
Exeunt all but Gloucester.
Glou. I do the wrong, and first begin to brawl.
The secret mischiefs that I set abroach
I lay unto the grievous charge of others.
Clarence, who I, indeed, have cast in darkness,
I do beweep to many simple gulls,
Namely, to Derby, Hastings, Buckingham;
And tell them 't is the Queen and her allies
That stir the King against the Duke my brother.
Now, they believe it; and withal whet me
To be reveng'd on Rivers, Dorset, Grey.
But then I sigh; and, with a piece of scripture,
Tell them that God bids us do good for evil;
And thus I clothe my naked villainy
With odd old ends stol'n forth of holy writ,
And seem a saint, when most I play the devil.

Enter two *Murderers.*

But, soft! here come my executioners.
How now, my hardy, stout, resolved mates!
Are you now going to dispatch this thing?
First Murd. We are, my lord; and come to have the warrant,
That we may be admitted where he is.
Glou. Well thought upon; I have it here about me. *Gives the warrant.*
When you have done, repair to Crosby Place.
But, sirs, be sudden in the execution,
Withal obdurate, do not hear him plead;
For Clarence is well-spoken, and perhaps
May move your hearts to pity, if you mark him.
First Murd. Tut, tut, my lord, we will not stand to prate.
Talkers are no good doers; be assur'd
We go to use our hands and not our tongues.
Glou. Your eyes drop millstones, when fools' eyes fall tears.
I like you, lads; about your business straight.
Go, go, dispatch.
First Murd. We will, my noble lord.
Exeunt.

Scene IV. *London. The Tower.*

Enter *Clarence* and *Keeper.*

Keep. Why looks your Grace so heavily to-day?
Clar. O, I have pass'd a miserable night,
So full of fearful dreams, of ugly sights,
That, as I am a Christian faithful man,
I would not spend another such a night,
Though 't were to buy a world of happy days,
So full of dismal terror was the time.
Keep. What was your dream, my lord? I pray you, tell me.
Clar. Methoughts that I had broken from the Tower,
And was embark'd to cross to Burgundy;
And, in my company, my brother Gloucester,
Who from my cabin tempted me to walk
Upon the hatches: there we look'd toward England,
And cited up a thousand heavy times,
During the wars of York and Lancaster
That had befall'n us. As we pac'd along
Upon the giddy footing of the hatches,
Methought that Gloucester stumbled, and, in falling,
Struck me, that thought to stay him, overboard,
Into the tumbling billows of the main.
O Lord! methought, what pain it was to drown!
What dreadful noise of water in mine ears!
What sights of ugly death within mine eyes!
Methoughts I saw a thousand fearful wrecks;
A thousand men that fishes gnaw'd upon;
Wedges of gold, great anchors, heaps of pearl,
Inestimable stones, unvalued jewels,
All scatter'd in the bottom of the sea.
Some lay in dead men's skulls; and, in the holes
Where eyes did once inhabit, there were crept,
As 't were in scorn of eyes, reflecting gems,
That woo'd the slimy bottom of the deep,
And mock'd the dead bones that lay scatter'd by.
Keep. Had you such leisure in the time of death
To gaze upon these secrets of the deep?

314. frank'd up, shut up in a frank or sty. **317. scath,** injury. **325. set abroach,** begin. **326.** I attribute to others, lit., I place by an accusation of crime upon others.

Scene iv: 10. Burgundy, the Netherlands, where Clarence had lived as a child. **27. unvalued,** invaluable.

Clar. Methought I had. And often did I strive
To yield the ghost; but still the envious flood
Stopp'd in my soul, and would not let it forth
To find the empty, vast, and wand'ring air;
But smother'd it within my panting bulk,
Who almost burst to belch it in the sea.

Keep. Awak'd you not in this sore agony?

Clar. No, no, my dream was lengthen'd after life.
O, then began the tempest to my soul.
I pass'd, methought, the melancholy flood,
With that sour ferryman which poets write of,
Unto the kingdom of perpetual night.
The first that there did greet my stranger soul
Was my great father-in-law, renowned Warwick;
Who spake aloud, "What scourge for perjury
Can this dark monarchy afford false Clarence?"
And so he vanish'd. Then came wand'ring by
A shadow like an angel, with bright hair
Dabbled in blood; and he shriek'd out aloud,
"Clarence is come; false, fleeting, perjur'd Clarence,
That stabb'd me in the field by Tewksbury:
Seize on him, Furies, take him unto torment!"
With that, methought, a legion of foul fiends
Environ'd me, and howled in mine ears
Such hideous cries, that with the very noise
I trembling wak'd, and for a season after
Could not believe but that I was in hell,
Such terrible impression made my dream.

Keep. No marvel, lord, though it affrighted you;
I am afraid, methinks, to hear you tell it.

Clar. Ah! Keeper, Keeper, I have done these things
That now give evidence against my soul
For Edward's sake; and see how he requites me!
O God! if my deep prayers cannot appease thee,
But thou wilt be aveng'd on my misdeeds,
Yet execute thy wrath in me alone!
O, spare my guiltless wife and my poor children!
Keeper, I prithee, sit by me a while.
My soul is heavy, and I fain would sleep.

Keep. I will, my lord: God give your Grace good rest! *Clarence sleeps.*

Enter *Brakenbury*, the Lieutenant.

Brak. Sorrow breaks seasons and reposing hours,
Makes the night morning, and the noon-tide night.
Princes have but their titles for their glories,
An outward honour for an inward toil;
And, for unfelt imaginations,
They often feel a world of restless cares,
So that, between their titles and low name,
There 's nothing differs but the outward fame.

Enter the two *Murderers.*

First Murd. Ho! who 's here?

Brak. What wouldst thou, fellow, and how cam'st thou hither?

Second Murd. I would speak with Clarence, and I came hither on my legs.

Brak. What, so brief?

First Murd. 'T is better, sir, than to be tedious. Let him see our commission, and talk no more. *Brakenbury reads it.*

Brak. I am, in this, commanded to deliver
The noble Duke of Clarence to your hands.
I will not reason what is meant hereby,
Because I will be guiltless from the meaning.
There lies the Duke asleep, and there the keys.
I 'll to the King, and signify to him
That thus I have resign'd to you my charge.
Exit with Keeper.

First Murd. You may, sir, 't is a point of wisdom: fare you well.

Second Murd. What, shall we stab him as he sleeps?

First Murd. No; he 'll say 't was done cowardly, when he wakes.

Second Murd. Why, he shall never wake until the great judgement-day.

First Murd. Why, then he 'll say we stabb'd him sleeping.

Second Murd. The urging of that word "judgement" hath bred a kind of remorse in me.

First Murd. What, art thou afraid?

Second Murd. Not to kill him, having a warrant; but to be damned for killing him, from the which no warrant can defend me.

First Murd. I thought thou hadst been resolute.

Second Murd. So I am, to let him live.

First Murd. I 'll back to the Duke of Gloucester and tell him so.

Second Murd. Nay, I prithee, stay a little: I hope this passionate humour of mine will change: it was wont to hold me but while one tells twenty.

First Murd. How dost thou feel thyself now?

Second Murd. Some certain dregs of conscience are yet within me.

37. **envious**, malicious. 40. **bulk**, body. 45. **melancholy flood**, i.e., the river Styx. 46. **ferryman**, Charon. 50. **perjury**, see Clarence, *Dram. Personæ*. 53. **shadow**, Edward, Prince of Wales. 55. **fleeting**, changeable, inconstant.

80. **for unfelt imaginations**, in place of unrealized dreams of power.

First Murd. Remember our reward, when the deed 's done.

Second Murd. 'Zounds, he dies! I had forgot the reward.

First Murd. Where 's thy conscience now?

Second Murd. O, in the Duke of Gloucester's purse.

First Murd. When he opens his purse to give us our reward, thy conscience flies out.

Second Murd. 'T is no matter; let it go: there 's few or none will entertain it.

First Murd. What if it come to thee again?

Second Murd. I 'll not meddle with it; it is a dangerous thing; it makes a man a coward: a man cannot steal, but it accuseth him; a man cannot swear, but it checks him; a man cannot lie with his neighbour's wife, but it detects him. 'T is a blushing shamefaced spirit that mutinies in a man's bosom: it fills a man full of obstacles. It made me once restore a purse of gold that by chance I found: it beggars any man that keeps it: it is turn'd out of towns and cities for a dangerous thing; and every man that means to live well endeavours to trust to himself and live without it.

First Murd. 'Zounds, 't is even now at my elbow, persuading me not to kill the Duke.

Second Murd. Take the devil in thy mind, and believe him not; he would insinuate with thee but to make thee sigh.

First Murd. I am strong-framed, he cannot prevail with me.

Second Murd. Spoke like a tall man that respects thy reputation. Come, shall we fall to work?

First Murd. Take him on the costard with the hilts of thy sword, and then throw him into the malmsey-butt in the next room.

Second Murd. O excellent device! and make a sop of him.

First Murd. Soft! He wakes.

Second Murd. Strike!

First Murd. No, we 'll reason with him.

Clar. Where art thou, Keeper? Give me a cup of wine.

Second Murd. You shall have wine enough, my lord, anon.

Clar. In God's name, what art thou?

First Murd. A man, as you are.

Clar. But not, as I am, royal.

First Murd. Nor you, as we are, loyal.

Clar. Thy voice is thunder, but thy looks are humble.

First Murd. My voice is now the King's, my looks mine own.

Clar. How darkly and how deadly dost thou speak!
Your eyes do menace me: why look you pale?
Who sent you hither? Wherefore do you come?

Second Murd. To, to, to—

Clar. To murder me?

Both. Ay, ay.

Clar. You scarcely have the hearts to tell me so,
And therefore cannot have the hearts to do it.
Wherein, my friends, have I offended you?

First Murd. Offended us you have not, but the King.

Clar. I shall be reconcil'd to him again.

Second Murd. Never, my lord; therefore prepare to die.

Clar. Are you drawn forth among a world of men
To slay the innocent? What is my offence?
Where is the evidence that doth accuse me?
What lawful quest have given their verdict up
Unto the frowning judge? or who pronounc'd
The bitter sentence of poor Clarence' death?
Before I be convict by course of law,
To threaten me with death is most unlawful.
I charge you, as you hope to have redemption
By Christ's dear blood shed for our grievous sins,
That you depart and lay no hands on me:
The deed you undertake is damnable.

First Murd. What we will do, we do upon command.

Second Murd. And he that hath commanded is our King.

Clar. Erroneous vassals! the great King of kings
Hath in the table of his law commanded
That thou shalt do no murder. Will you, then,
Spurn at His edict and fulfil a man's?
Take heed; for He holds vengeance in His hand,
To hurl upon their heads that break His law.

Second Murd. And that same vengeance doth He hurl on thee
For false forswearing and for murder too:
Thou didst receive the sacrament to fight
In quarrel of the house of Lancaster.

First Murd. And, like a traitor to the name of God,
Didst break that vow; and with thy treacherous blade
Unripp'd'st the bowels of thy sov'reign's son.

Second Murd. Whom thou wast sworn to cherish and defend.

First Murd. How canst thou urge God's dreadful law to us,

151-2. **Take,** seize him, i.e., conscience, which he calls the devil. 152. **insinuate,** curry favor. 159. **costard,** head. 161. **malmsey-butt,** wine cask. 162. **sop,** bread or cake dipped in wine.

189. **quest,** inquest, jury. 192. **convict,** convicted. 200. **Erroneous,** mistaken, misled.

When thou hast broke it in such dear degree?
Clar. Alas! for whose sake did I that ill deed?
For Edward, for my brother, for his sake.
He sends you not to murder me for this,
For in that sin he is as deep as I.
If God will be avenged for the deed,
O, know you yet, He doth it publicly.
Take not the quarrel from His powerful arm;
He needs no indirect or lawless course
To cut off those that have offended Him.
First Murd. Who made thee, then, a bloody minister,
When gallant-springing brave Plantagenet,
That princely novice, was struck dead by thee?
Clar. My brother's love, the devil, and my rage.
First Murd. Thy brother's love, our duty, and thy faults
Provoke us hither now to slaughter thee.
Clar. If you do love my brother, hate not me!
I am his brother, and I love him well.
If you are hir'd for meed, go back again,
And I will send you to my brother Gloucester,
Who shall reward you better for my life
Than Edward will for tidings of my death.
Second Murd. You are deceiv'd. Your brother Gloucester hates you.
Clar. O, no, he loves me, and he holds me dear.
Go you to him from me.
First Murd. Ay, so we will.
Clar. Tell him, when that our princely father York
Bless'd his three sons with his victorious arm,
And charg'd us from his soul to love each other,
He little thought of this divided friendship:
Bid Gloucester think on this, and he will weep.
First Murd. Ay, millstones; as he lesson'd us to weep.
Clar. O, do not slander him, for he is kind.
First Murd. Right; as snow in harvest.
Come, you deceive yourself;
'T is he that sends us to destroy you here.
Clar. It cannot be; for he bewept my fortune
And hugg'd me in his arms, and swore with sobs
That he would labour my delivery.

215. dear, grievous. **227. gallant-springing,** burgeoning. **228. novice,** youth. **234. meed,** i.e., money. **248. as snow in harvest,** "As snow in summer and as rain in harvest, so honor is not seemly for a fool." (*Proverbs*, xxvi, 1). **253. labour my delivery,** work for my deliverance.

First Murd. Why, so he doth, when he delivers you
From this earth's thraldom to the joys of heaven.
Second Murd. Make peace with God, for you must die, my lord.
Clar. Have you that holy feeling in your souls,
To counsel me to make my peace with God,
And are you yet to your own souls so blind,
That you will war with God by murd'ring me?
O, sirs, consider, they that set you on
To do this deed will hate you for the deed.
Second Murd. What shall we do?
Clar. Relent, and save your souls.
First Murd. Relent! No! 't is cowardly and womanish.
Clar. Not to relent is beastly, savage, devilish.
Which of you, if you were a prince's son,
Being pent from liberty, as I am now,
If two such murderers as yourselves came to you,
Would not entreat for life?
My friend, I spy some pity in thy looks.
O, if thine eye be not a flatterer,
Come thou on my side, and entreat for me,
As you would beg, were you in my distress.
A begging prince what beggar pities not?
Second Murd. Look behind you, my lord.
First Murd. Take that, and that. If all this will not do, *Stabs him.*
I 'll drown you in the malmsey-butt within.
Exit with the body.
Second Murd. A bloody deed, and desperately dispatch'd!
How fain, like Pilate, would I wash my hands
Of this most grievous murder!

Re-enter *First Murderer.*

First Murd. How now! what mean'st thou, that thou help'st me not?
By heaven, the Duke shall know how slack you have been!
Second Murd. I would he knew that I had sav'd his brother!
Take thou the fee, and tell him what I say;
For I repent me that the Duke is slain.
Exit.
First Murd. So do not I. Go, coward as thou art.
Well, I 'll go hide the body in some hole
Till that the Duke give order for his burial;
And when I have my meed, I will away;
For this will out, and then I must not stay.
Exit.

267. pent, penned, shut off.

ACT II. Scene I. *London. The palace.*

Flourish. Enter *King Edward* sick, *Queen Elizabeth, Lord Marquess Dorset, Rivers, Hastings, Catesby, Buckingham, Woodville, Scales, Grey,* and others.

K. Edw. Why, so: now have I done a good day's work.
You peers, continue this united league:
I every day expect an embassage
From my Redeemer to redeem me hence;
And more in peace my soul shall part to heaven,
Since I have made my friends at peace on earth.
Hastings and Rivers, take each other's hand;
Dissemble not your hatred, swear your love.
Riv. By heaven, my soul is purg'd from grudging hate;
And with my hand I seal my true heart's love.
Hast. So thrive I, as I truly swear the like!
K. Edw. Take heed you dally not before your king,
Lest He that is the supreme King of kings
Confound your hidden falsehood, and award
Either of you to be the other's end.
Hast. So prosper I, as I swear perfect love!
Riv. And I, as I love Hastings with my heart!
K. Edw. Madam, your self is not exempt from this,
Nor you, son Dorset, Buckingham, nor you;
You have been factious one against the other.
Wife, love Lord Hastings, let him kiss your hand;
And what you do, do it unfeignedly.
Q. Eliz. There, Hastings; I will never more remember
Our former hatred, so thrive I and mine!
K. Edw. Dorset, embrace him; Hastings, love lord marquess.
Dor. This interchange of love, I here protest,
Upon my part shall be inviolable.
Hast. And so swear I. *They embrace.*
K. Edw. Now, princely Buckingham, seal thou this league
With thy embracements to my wife's allies,
And make me happy in your unity.
Buck. Whenever Buckingham doth turn his hate
Upon your Grace [*to the Queen*], but with all duteous love
Doth cherish you and yours, God punish me
With hate in those where I expect most love!
When I have most need to employ a friend,
And most assured that he is a friend,
Deep, hollow, treacherous, and full of guile
Be he unto me! This do I beg of Heaven,
When I am cold in love to you or yours.
They embrace.
K. Edw. A pleasing cordial, princely Buckingham,
Is this thy vow unto my sickly heart.
There wanteth now our brother Gloucester here,
To make the blessed period of this peace.
Buck. And, in good time,
Here comes Sir Richard Ratcliff and the Duke.

Enter *Gloucester* and *Ratcliff.*

Glou. Good morrow to my sovereign king and queen;
And, princely peers, a happy time of day!
K. Edw. Happy, indeed, as we have spent the day.
Gloucester, we have done deeds of charity;
Made peace of enmity, fair love of hate,
Between these swelling wrong-incensed peers.
Glou. A blessed labour, my most sovereign lord.
Among this princely heap, if any here,
By false intelligence, or wrong surmise,
Hold me a foe;
If I unwittingly, or in my rage,
Have aught committed that is hardly borne
By any in this presence, I desire
To reconcile me to his friendly peace:
'T is death to me to be at enmity;
I hate it, and desire all good men's love.
First, madam, I entreat true peace of you,
Which I will purchase with my duteous service;
Of you, my noble cousin Buckingham,
If ever any grudge were lodg'd between us;
Of you and you, Lord Rivers and of Dorset;
That all without desert have frown'd on me;
Of you, Lord Woodville, and, Lord Scales, of you;
Dukes, earls, lords, gentlemen; indeed of all:
I do not know that Englishman alive
With whom my soul is any jot at odds
More than the infant that is born to-night:
I thank my God for my humility.
Q. Eliz. A holy day shall this be kept hereafter.
I would to God all strifes were well compounded.

8. Do not merely conceal your hatred (to please me) but openly avow your love. 12. **dally**, trifle. 15. **Either**, each. 20. **been factious**, taken sides.

51. **swelling**, i.e., with anger. 53. **heap**, group. 54. **false intelligence**, wrong report. 57. **hardly borne**, resented. 67. **without desert**, without cause.

My sovereign lord, I do beseech your Highness
To take our brother Clarence to your grace.

Glou. Why, madam, have I offer'd love for this,
To be so flouted in this royal presence?
Who knows not that the gentle Duke is dead?
They all start.
You do him injury to scorn his corse.

K. Edw. Who knows not he is dead? Who knows he is?

Q. Eliz. All-seeing Heaven, what a world is this!

Buck. Look I so pale, Lord Dorset, as the rest?

Dor. Ay, my good lord; and no man in the presence
But his red colour hath forsook his cheeks.

K. Edw. Is Clarence dead? The order was revers'd.

Glou. But he, poor man, by your first order died,
And that a winged Mercury did bear;
Some tardy cripple bare the countermand,
That came too lag to see him buried.
God grant that some, less noble and less loyal,
Nearer in bloody thoughts, but not in blood,
Deserve not worse than wretched Clarence did,
And yet go current from suspicion!

Enter *Derby.*

Der. A boon, my sovereign, for my service done! *Kneels.*

K. Edw. I prithee, peace; my soul is full of sorrow.

Der. I will not rise, unless your Highness hear me.

K. Edw. Then say at once what is it thou requests.

Der. The forfeit, sovereign, of my servant's life,
Who slew to-day a riotous gentleman
Lately attendant on the Duke of Norfolk.

K. Edw. Have I a tongue to doom my brother's death,
And shall that tongue give pardon to a slave?
My brother kill'd no man; his fault was thought,
And yet his punishment was bitter death.
Who sued to me for him? Who, in my wrath,
Kneel'd at my feet, and bid me be advis'd?
Who spoke of brotherhood? Who spoke of love?
Who told me how the poor soul did forsake
The mighty Warwick, and did fight for me?
Who told me, in the field at Tewksbury,
When Oxford had me down, he rescued me,
And said, "Dear brother, live, and be a king"?
Who told me, when we both lay in the field
Frozen almost to death, how he did lap me
Even in his garments, and did give himself,
All thin and naked, to the numb cold night?
All this from my remembrance brutish wrath
Sinfully pluck'd, and not a man of you
Had so much grace to put it in my mind.
But when your carters or your waiting-vassals
Have done a drunken slaughter, and defac'd
The precious image of our dear Redeemer,
You straight are on your knees for pardon, pardon;
And I, unjustly too, must grant it you.
But for my brother not a man would speak,
Nor I, ungracious, speak unto myself
For him, poor soul. The proudest of you all
Have been beholding to him in his life;
Yet none of you would once beg for his life.
O God, I fear thy justice will take hold
On me, and you, and mine, and yours for this!
Come, Hastings, help me to my closet. Ah, poor Clarence!
Exeunt some with King and Queen.

Glou. This is the fruit of rashness! Mark'd you not
How that the guilty kindred of the Queen
Look'd pale when they did hear of Clarence' death?
O, they did urge it still unto the King!
God will revenge it. Come, lords, will you go
To comfort Edward with our company.

Buck. We wait upon your Grace.
Exeunt.

Scene II. *The palace.*

Enter the old *Duchess of York,* with the two *Children* of Clarence.

Boy. Good grandam, tell us, is our father dead?

Duch. No, boy.

Girl. Why do you weep so oft, and beat your breast,
And cry, "O Clarence, my unhappy son"?

Boy. Why do you look on us, and shake your head,
And call us orphans, wretches, castaways,
If that our noble father were alive?

Duch. My pretty cousins, you mistake me both.
I do lament the sickness of the King,
As loath to lose him, not your father's death;
It were lost sorrow to wail one that 's lost.

Boy. Then you conclude, my grandam, he is dead.

90. lag, late. **94. current from,** free from. **99.** The forfeited life of my servant, O king. **107. advis'd,** cautious.

129. beholding, beholden, under obligation. **Scene ii: 8. cousins,** relations.

The King mine uncle is to blame for it.
God will revenge it, whom I will importune
With earnest prayers all to that effect.

Girl. And so will I.

Duch. Peace, children, peace! the King doth love you well.
Incapable and shallow innocents,
You cannot guess who caus'd your father's death.

Boy. Grandam, we can; for my good uncle Gloucester
Told me the King, provok'd to it by the Queen,
Devis'd impeachments to imprison him;
And when my uncle told me so, he wept,
And pitied me, and kindly kiss'd my cheek;
Bade me rely on him as on my father,
And he would love me dearly as a child.

Duch. Ah, that deceit should steal such gentle shape,
And with a virtuous vizor hide deep vice!
He is my son, ay, and therein my shame;
Yet from my dugs he drew not this deceit.

Boy. Think you my uncle did dissemble, grandam?

Duch. Ay, boy.

Boy. I cannot think it. Hark! what noise is this?

Enter *Queen Elizabeth,* with her hair about her ears; *Rivers* and *Dorset* after her.

Q. Eliz. Ah, who shall hinder me to wail and weep,
To chide my fortune, and torment myself?
I 'll join with black despair against my soul,
And to myself become an enemy.

Duch. What means this scene of rude impatience?

Q. Eliz. To make an act of tragic violence.
Edward, my lord, thy son, our king, is dead.
Why grow the branches when the root is gone?
Why wither not the leaves that want their sap?
If you will live. lament; if die, be brief,
That our swift-winged souls may catch the King's;
Or, like obedient subjects, follow him
To his new kingdom of ne'er-changing night.

Duch. Ah, so much interest have I in thy sorrow
As I had title in thy noble husband!
I have bewept a worthy husband's death,
And liv'd with looking on his images;
But now two mirrors of his princely semblance
Are crack'd in pieces by malignant death,
And I for comfort have but one false glass,
That grieves me when I see my shame in him.
Thou art a widow; yet thou art a mother,
And hast the comfort of thy children left:
But death hath snatch'd my husband from mine arms,
And pluck'd two crutches from my feeble hands,
Clarence and Edward. O, what cause have I,
Thine being but a moiety of my moan,
To overgo thy woes and drown thy cries!

Boy. Ah! aunt, you wept not for our father's death;
How can we aid you with our kindred tears?

Girl. Our fatherless distress was left unmoan'd;
Your widow-dolour likewise be unwept!

Q. Eliz. Give me no help in lamentation,
I am not barren to bring forth complaints:
All springs reduce their currents to mine eyes,
That I, being govern'd by the watery moon,
May send forth plenteous tears to drown the world!
Ah for my husband, for my dear lord Edward!

Chil. Ah for our father, for our dear lord Clarence!

Duch. Alas for both, both mine, Edward and Clarence!

Q. Eliz. What stay had I but Edward? and he 's gone.

Chil. What stay had we but Clarence? and he 's gone.

Duch. What stays had I but they? and they are gone.

Q. Eliz. Was never widow had so dear a loss!

Chil. Were never orphans had so dear a loss!

Duch. Was never mother had so dear a loss!
Alas, I am the mother of these griefs!
Their woes are parcell'd, mine is general.
She for an Edward weeps, and so do I;
I for a Clarence weep, so doth not she;
These babes for Clarence weep, and so do I;
I for an Edward weep, so do not they.
Alas, you three, on me, threefold distress'd,
Pour all your tears! I am your sorrow's nurse,
And I will pamper it with lamentation.

Dor. Comfort, dear mother: God is much displeas'd
That you take with unthankfulness His doing.
In common worldly things, 't is call'd ungrateful,
With dull unwillingness to repay a debt
Which with a bounteous hand was kindly lent;
Much more to be thus opposite with heaven,
For it requires the royal debt it lent you.

Riv. Madam, bethink you, like a careful mother,

18. Incapable, i.e., of understanding. **shallow,** thoughtless. **28. vizor,** mask. **50. images,** i.e., children. **53. false glass,** i.e., Richard.

67. barren to, unable to. **68. reduce,** bring back. **94. opposite with,** opposed to.

Of the young prince your son: send straight for him;
Let him be crown'd; in him your comfort lives.
Drown desperate sorrow in dead Edward's grave,
And plant your joys in living Edward's throne.

Enter *Gloucester, Buckingham, Derby, Hastings,* and *Ratcliff.*

Glou. Sister, have comfort: all of us have cause
To wail the dimming of our shining star;
But none can help our harms by wailing them.
Madam, my mother, I do cry you mercy;
I did not see your Grace. Humbly on my knee
I crave your blessing.
Duch. God bless thee; and put meekness in thy breast,
Love, charity, obedience, and true duty!
Glou. Amen; [*Aside.*] and make me die a good old man!
That is the butt-end of a mother's blessing;
I marvel that her Grace did leave it out.
Buck. You cloudy princes and heart-sorrowing peers,
That bear this heavy mutual load of moan,
Now cheer each other in each other's love.
Though we have spent our harvest of this king,
We are to reap the harvest of his son.
The broken rancour of your high-swoln hates,
But lately splinter'd, knit, and join'd together,
Must gently be preserv'd, cherish'd, and kept.
Me seemeth good, that, with some little train,
Forthwith from Ludlow the young prince be fet
Hither to London, to be crown'd our king.
Riv. Why with some little train, my Lord of Buckingham?
Buck. Marry, my lord, lest, by a multitude,
The new-heal'd wound of malice should break out;
Which would be so much the more dangerous,
By how much the estate is green and yet ungovern'd.
Where every horse bears his commanding rein
And may direct his course as please himself,
As well the fear of harm, as harm apparent,
In my opinion, ought to be prevented.
Glou. I hope the King made peace with all of us;
And the compact is firm and true in me.
Riv. And so in me; and so, I think, in all.
Yet, since it is but green, it should be put
To no apparent likelihood of breach,
Which haply by much company might be urg'd;
Therefore I say with noble Buckingham,
That it is meet so few should fetch the Prince.
Hast. And so say I.
Glou. Then be it so; and go we to determine
Who they shall be that straight shall post to Ludlow.
Madam, and you, my sister, will you go
To give your censures in this business?
Q. Eliz. / *Duch.* } With all our hearts.

Exeunt all but Buckingham and Gloucester.

Buck. My lord, whoever journeys to the Prince,
For God's sake, let not us two stay at home;
For, by the way, I 'll sort occasion,
As index to the story we late talk'd of,
To part the Queen's proud kindred from the Prince.
Glou. My other self, my counsel's consistory,
My oracle, my prophet, my dear cousin,
I, as a child, will go by thy direction.
Toward Ludlow then, for we 'll not stay behind. *Exeunt.*

Scene III. *London. A street.*

Enter one *Citizen* at one door and another at the other.

First Cit. Good morrow, neighbour; whither away so fast?
Second Cit. I promise you, I scarcely know myself.
Hear you the news abroad?
First Cit. Yes, that the King is dead.
Second Cit. Ill news, by 'r lady; seldom comes the better:
I fear, I fear 't will prove a giddy world.

Enter another *Citizen.*

Third Cit. Neighbours, God speed!
First Cit. Give you good morrow, sir.
Third Cit. Doth the news hold of good King Edward's death?
Second Cit. Ay, sir, it is too true; God help the while!
Third Cit. Then, masters, look to see a troublous world.

112. **cloudy,** i.e., with sorrows. 117. The figure is that of a sore coming to a head and breaking. 118. **splinter'd,** put in splints. 121. **Ludlow,** a royal town and castle in Shropshire. **fet,** fetched. 127. **estate is green,** government, i.e., of Edward V is newly established. 128. **bears,** controls.

144. **censures,** opinions. 148. **sort,** find. 149. **index,** preface, i.e., beginning. 151. **consistory,** highest court, literally, council-chamber.

First Cit. No, no; by God's good grace his son shall reign.
Third Cit. Woe to that land that's govern'd by a child!
Second Cit. In him there is a hope of government,
That in his nonage, council under him,
And in his full and ripened years himself,
No doubt, shall then and till then govern well.
First Cit. So stood the state when Henry the Sixth
Was crown'd in Paris but at nine months old.
Third Cit. Stood the state so? No, no, good friends, God wot;
For then this land was famously enrich'd
With politic grave counsel; then the King
Had virtuous uncles to protect his Grace.
First Cit. Why, so hath this, both by his father and mother.
Second Cit. Better it were they all came by his father,
Or by his father there were none at all;
For emulation, who shall now be nearest,
Will touch us all too near, if God prevent not.
O, full of danger is the Duke of Gloucester,
And the Queen's sons and brothers haught and proud!
And were they to be rul'd, and not to rule,
This sickly land might solace as before.
First Cit. Come, come, we fear the worst; all will be well.
Third Cit. When clouds are seen, wise men put on their cloaks;
When great leaves fall, then winter is at hand;
When the sun sets, who doth not look for night?
Untimely storms makes men expect a dearth.
All may be well; but, if God sort it so,
'T is more than we deserve, or I expect.
Second Cit. Truly, the hearts of men are full of fear:
You cannot reason almost with a man
That looks not heavily and full of dread.
Third Cit. Before the days of change, still is it so.
By a divine instinct men's minds mistrust
Ensuing danger; as, by proof, we see
The water swell before a boisterous storm.
But leave it all to God. Whither away?
Second Cit. Marry, we were sent for to the justices.
Third Cit. And so was I. I 'll bear you company. *Exeunt.*

Scene iii: 11. "Woe to thee, O land, when thy king is a child." (*Ecclesiastes*, x, 16). **13. nonage,** minority. **30. solace,** be happy. **35. dearth,** famine. **36. sort,** ordain. **40. heavily,** sorrowful.

Scene IV. *London. The palace.*

Enter the *Archbishop of York,* the young *Duke of York, Queen Elizabeth,* and the *Duchess of York.*

Arch. Last night, I heard, they lay at Northampton;
At Stony-Stratford they do rest to-night.
To-morrow, or next day, they will be here.
Duch. I long with all my heart to see the Prince:
I hope he is much grown since last I saw him.
Q. Eliz. But I hear, no; they say my son of York
Has almost overta'en him in his growth.
York. Ay, mother; but I would not have it so.
Duch. Why, my good cousin, it is good to grow.
York. Grandam, one night, as we did sit at supper,
My uncle Rivers talk'd how I did grow
More than my brother. "Ay," quoth my uncle Gloucester,
"Small herbs have grace, great weeds do grow apace;"
And since, methinks I would not grow so fast,
Because sweet flowers are slow and weeds make haste.
Duch. Good faith, good faith, the saying did not hold
In him that did object the same to thee.
He was the wretched'st thing when he was young,
So long a-growing and so leisurely,
That, if his rule were true, he should be gracious.
Arch. And so, no doubt, he is, my gracious madam.
Duch. I hope he is; but yet let mothers doubt.
York. Now, by my troth, if I had been remember'd,
I could have given my uncle's Grace a flout,
To touch his growth nearer than he touch'd mine.
Duch. How, my young York? I prithee, let me hear it.
York. Marry, they say my uncle grew so fast
That he could gnaw a crust at two hours old;
'T was full two years ere I could get a tooth.
Grandam, this would have been a biting jest.
Duch. I prithee, pretty York, who told thee this?

Scene iv: 23. remember'd, reminded. **24. flout,** gibe, dig.

York. Grandam, his nurse.
Duch. His nurse! why, she was dead ere thou wast born.
York. If 't were not she, I cannot tell who told me.
Q. Eliz. A parlous boy! Go to, you are too shrewd.
Duch. Good madam, be not angry with the child.
Q. Eliz. Pitchers have ears.

Enter a *Messenger.*

Arch. Here comes a messenger. What news?
Mess. Such news, my lord, as grieves me to report.
Q. Eliz. How doth the Prince?
Mess. Well, madam, and in health.
Duch. What is thy news?
Mess. Lord Rivers and Lord Grey are sent to Pomfret,
With them Sir Thomas Vaughan, prisoners.
Duch. Who hath committed them?
Mess. The mighty dukes
Gloucester and Buckingham.
Arch. For what offence?
Mess. The sum of all I can, I have disclos'd.
Why or for what the nobles were committed
Is all unknown to me, my gracious lord.
Q. Eliz. Ay me, I see the ruin of my house!
The tiger now hath seiz'd the gentle hind;
Insulting tyranny begins to jut
Upon the innocent and aweless throne.
Welcome, destruction, blood, and massacre!
I see, as in a map, the end of all.
Duch. Accursed and unquiet wrangling days,
How many of you have mine eyes beheld!
My husband lost his life to get the crown,
And often up and down my sons were toss'd
For me to joy and weep their gain and loss;
And being seated, and domestic broils
Clean over-blown, themselves, the conquerors,
Make war upon themselves, brother to brother,
Blood to blood, self against self. O, preposterous
And frantic outrage, end thy damned spleen;
Or let me die, to look on earth no more!
Q. Eliz. Come, come, my boy; we will to sanctuary.
Madam, farewell.
Duch. Stay, I will go with you.
Q. Eliz. You have no cause.
Arch. [*To the Queen.*] My gracious lady, go;
And thither bear your treasure and your goods.
For my part, I 'll resign unto your Grace
The seal I keep; and so betide to me
As well I tender you and all of yours!
Go, I 'll conduct you to the sanctuary.
Exeunt.

ACT III. SCENE I. *London. A street.*

The trumpets sound. Enter the young *Prince,* the *Dukes of Gloucester* and *Buckingham, Cardinal Bourchier, Catesby,* and others.

Buck. Welcome, sweet prince, to London, to your chamber.
Glou. Welcome, dear cousin, my thoughts' sovereign.
The weary way hath made you melancholy.
Prince. No, uncle; but our crosses on the way
Have made it tedious, wearisome, and heavy.
I want more uncles here to welcome me.
Glou. Sweet prince, the untainted virtue of your years
Hath not yet div'd into the world's deceit.
No more can you distinguish of a man
Than of his outward show; which, God he knows,
Seldom or never jumpeth with the heart.
Those uncles which you want were dangerous;
Your Grace attended to their sugar'd words,
But look'd not on the poison of their hearts:
God keep you from them, and from such false friends!
Prince. God keep me from false friends! but they were none.
Glou. My lord, the Mayor of London comes to greet you.

Enter the *Lord Mayor* and his train.

May. God bless your Grace with health and happy days!

35. parlous, mischievous. **37.** "Little pitchers have long ears." **46. can,** know. **50. hind,** doe. **Act III, Scene i: 1. chamber,** i.e., London, the so-called *camera regis,* king's chamber. **4. crosses,** mischances, i.e., the arrest of his uncles.

51. jut Upon, overhang, threaten. **64. spleen,** anger. **66. sanctuary,** in Westminster, where protected by the church from arrest. **71. seal,** i.e., the Great Seal. **71-2. and . . . yours,** may I thrive in proportion as I take care of you and yours. **Act III, Scene i: 11. jumpeth,** agreeth.

Prince. I thank you, good my lord; and thank you all. *Mayor and train retire.*
I thought my mother and my brother York
Would long ere this have met us on the way.
Fie, what a slug is Hastings, that he comes not
To tell us whether they will come or no!

Enter *Lord Hastings.*

Buck. And, in good time, here comes the sweating lord.
Prince. Welcome, my lord! What, will our mother come?
Hast. On what occasion, God he knows, not I,
The Queen your mother, and your brother York,
Have taken sanctuary: the tender prince
Would fain have come with me to meet your Grace,
But by his mother was perforce withheld.
Buck. Fie, what an indirect and peevish course
Is this of hers! Lord Cardinal, will your Grace
Persuade the Queen to send the Duke of York
Unto his princely brother presently?
If she deny, Lord Hastings, go with him,
And from her jealous arms pluck him perforce.
Card. My Lord of Buckingham, if my weak oratory
Can from his mother win the Duke of York,
Anon expect him here; but if she be obdurate
To mild entreaties, God in heaven forbid
We should infringe the holy privilege
Of blessed sanctuary! Not for all this land
Would I be guilty of so great a sin.
Buck. You are too senseless-obstinate, my lord,
Too ceremonious and traditional.
Weigh it but with the grossness of this age,
You break not sanctuary in seizing him.
The benefit thereof is always granted
To those whose dealings have deserv'd the place,
And those who have the wit to claim the place:
This prince hath neither claim'd it nor deserv'd it,
And therefore, in mine opinion, cannot have it.
Then, taking him from thence that is not there,
You break no privilege nor charter there.
Oft have I heard of sanctuary men,
But sanctuary children ne'er till now.
Card. My lord, you shall o'er-rule my mind for once.
Come on, Lord Hastings, will you go with me?
Hast. I go, my lord.
Prince. Good lords, make all the speedy haste you may.
Exeunt Cardinal and Hastings.
Say, uncle Gloucester, if our brother come,
Where shall we sojourn till our coronation?
Glou. Where think'st best unto your royal self.
If I may counsel you, some day or two
Your Highness shall repose you at the Tower;
Then where you please, and shall be thought most fit
For your best health and recreation.
Prince. I do not like the Tower, of any place.
Did Julius Cæsar build that place, my lord?
Buck. He did, my gracious lord, begin that place;
Which, since, succeeding ages have re-edifi'd.
Prince. Is it upon record, or else reported
Successively from age to age, he built it?
Buck. Upon record, my gracious lord.
Prince. But say, my lord, it were not register'd,
Methinks the truth should live from age to age,
As 't were retail'd to all posterity,
Even to the general all-ending day.
Glou. [*Aside.*] So wise so young, they say, do never live long.
Prince. What say you, uncle?
Glou. I say, without characters, fame lives long.
[*Aside.*] Thus, like the formal vice, Iniquity,
I moralize two meanings in one word.
Prince. That Julius Cæsar was a famous man;
With what his valour did enrich his wit,
His wit set down to make his valour live:
Death makes no conquest of this conqueror;
For now he lives in fame, though not in life.
I 'll tell you what, my cousin Buckingham,—
Buck. What, my gracious lord?
Prince. An if I live until I be a man,
I 'll win our ancient right in France again,
Or die a soldier, as I liv'd a king.
Glou. [*Aside.*] Short summers lightly have a forward spring.

Enter young *York, Hastings,* and the *Cardinal.*

Buck. Now, in good time, here comes the Duke of York.
Prince. Richard of York! how fares our noble brother?

22. slug, snail. **31. indirect,** irregular. **44. senseless,** senselessly. **46. grossness,** laxness (in religious matters).

65. Tower, then a palace as well as a prison. **68. of any place,** of all places. **71. re-edifi'd,** completed. **81. characters,** (1) letters, i.e., being recorded; (2) moral character. **82. vice,** a character in the old morality plays. **94. lightly,** usually.

York. Well, my dread lord; so must I call you now.
Prince. Ay, brother, to our grief, as it is yours:
Too late he died that might have kept that title,
Which by his death hath lost much majesty.
Glou. How fares our cousin, noble Lord of York?
York. I thank you, gentle uncle. O, my lord,
You said that idle weeds are fast in growth:
The Prince my brother hath outgrown me far.
Glou. He hath, my lord.
York. And therefore is he idle?
Glou. O, my fair cousin, I must not say so.
York. Then is he more beholding to you than I.
Glou. He may command me as my sovereign;
But you have power in me as in a kinsman.
York. I pray you, uncle, give me this dagger.
Glou. My dagger, little cousin? With all my heart.
Prince. A beggar, brother?
York. Of my kind uncle, that I know will give;
And being but a toy, which is no grief to give.
Glou. A greater gift than that I 'll give my cousin.
York. A greater gift! O, that 's the sword to it.
Glou. Ay, gentle cousin, were it light enough.
York. O, then, I see, you will part but with light gifts;
In weightier things you 'll say a beggar nay.
Glou. It is too weighty for your Grace to wear.
York. I weigh it lightly, were it heavier.
Glou. What, would you have my weapon, little lord?
York. I would, that I might thank you as you call me.
Glou. How?
York. Little.
Prince. My Lord of York will still be cross in talk:
Uncle, your Grace knows how to bear with him.
York. You mean, to bear me, not to bear with me.
Uncle, my brother mocks both you and me.
Because that I am little, like an ape,
He thinks that you should bear me on your shoulders.
Buck. [*Aside to Hastings.*] With what a sharp-provided wit he reasons!
To mitigate the scorn he gives his uncle,
He prettily and aptly taunts himself.
So cunning and so young is wonderful.
Glou. My lord, will 't please you pass along?
Myself and my good cousin Buckingham
Will to your mother, to entreat of her
To meet you at the Tower and welcome you.
York. What, will you go unto the Tower, my lord?
Prince. My Lord Protector needs will have it so.
York. I shall not sleep in quiet at the Tower.
Glou. Why, what should you fear?
York. Marry, my uncle Clarence' angry ghost:
My grandam told me he was murder'd there.
Prince. I fear no uncles dead.
Glou. Nor none that live, I hope.
Prince. An if they live, I hope I need not fear.
But come, my lord; and with a heavy heart,
Thinking on them, go I unto the Tower.
A Sennet. Exeunt all but Gloucester, Buckingham, and Catesby.
Buck. Think you, my lord, this little prating York
Was not incensed by his subtle mother
To taunt and scorn you thus opprobriously?
Glou. No doubt, no doubt. O, 't is a perilous boy;
Bold, quick, ingenious, forward, capable.
He is all the mother's, from the top to toe.
Buck. Well, let them rest. Come hither, Catesby.
Thou art sworn as deeply to effect what we intend
As closely to conceal what we impart:
Thou know'st our reasons urg'd upon the way;
What think'st thou? Is it not an easy matter
To make William Lord Hastings of our mind,
For the instalment of this noble duke
In the seat royal of this famous isle?
Cate. He for his father's sake so loves the Prince,
That he will not be won to aught against him.
Buck. What think'st thou, then, of Stanley? Will not he?
Cate. He will do all in all as Hastings doth.
Buck. Well, then, no more but this: go, gentle Catesby,
And, as it were far off, sound thou Lord Hastings,
How he doth stand affected to our purpose;

99. late, lately. **121.** I should consider it a trifling gift even if it were heavier. **126. cross,** impudent. **130-1. ape . . . bear,** alluding to the custom of making a tame bear carry an ape on his back.

147. Nor . . . hope, i.e., fear for the life of the uncle imprisoned at Pomfret. **152. incensed,** set on. **170. far off,** i.e., not bluntly or directly.

And summon him to-morrow to the Tower,
To sit about the coronation.
If thou dost find him tractable to us,
Encourage him, and tell him all our reasons:
If he be leaden, icy-cold, unwilling,
Be thou so too; and so break off the talk,
And give us notice of his inclination;
For we to-morrow hold divided councils,
Wherein thyself shalt highly be employ'd.

Glou. Commend me to Lord William. Tell him, Catesby,
His ancient knot of dangerous adversaries
To-morrow are let blood at Pomfret Castle;
And bid my lord, for joy of this good news,
Give Mistress Shore one gentle kiss the more.

Buck. Good Catesby, go, effect this business soundly.

Cate. My good lords both, with all the heed I can.

Glou. Shall we hear from you, Catesby, ere we sleep?

Cate. You shall, my lord.

Glou. At Crosby House, there shall you find us both. *Exit Catesby.*

Buck. Now, my lord, what shall we do, if we perceive
Lord Hastings will not yield to our complots?

Glou. Chop off his head; something we will determine.
And, look, when I am king, claim thou of me
The earldom of Hereford, and all the movables
Whereof the King my brother was possess'd.

Buck. I 'll claim that promise at your Grace's hand.

Glou. And look to have it yielded with all kindness.
Come, let us sup betimes, that afterwards
We may digest our complots in some form.

Exeunt.

Scene II. *Before Lord Hastings' house.*

Enter a *Messenger.*

Mess. My lord! my lord!

Hast. [*Within.*] Who knocks?

Mess. One from the Lord Stanley.

Hast. [*Within.*] What is 't o'clock?

Mess. Upon the stroke of four.

Enter *Lord Hastings.*

Hast. Cannot my lord Stanley sleep these tedious nights?

Mess. So it appears by that I have to say.
First, he commends him to your noble self.

Hast. What then?

Mess. Then certifies your lordship that this night
He dreamt the boar had razed off his helm.
Besides, he says there are two councils kept;
And that may be determin'd at the one
Which may make you and him to rue at th' other.
Therefore he sends to know your lordship's pleasure,
If you will presently take horse with him,
And with all speed post with him toward the north,
To shun the danger that his soul divines.

Hast. Go, fellow, go, return unto thy lord;
Bid him not fear the separated councils:
His honour and myself are at the one,
And at the other is my good friend Catesby;
Where nothing can proceed that toucheth us
Whereof I shall not have intelligence.
Tell him his fears are shallow, without instance;
And for his dreams, I wonder he 's so simple
To trust the mock'ry of unquiet slumbers.
To fly the boar before the boar pursues,
Were to incense the boar to follow us
And make pursuit where he did mean no chase.
Go, bid thy master rise and come to me;
And we will both together to the Tower,
Where, he shall see, the boar will use us kindly.

Mess. I 'll go, my lord, and tell him what you say. *Exit.*

Enter *Catesby.*

Cate. Many good morrows to my noble lord!

Hast. Good morrow, Catesby; you are early stirring.
What news, what news, in this our tott'ring state?

Cate. It is a reeling world, indeed, my lord,
And, I believe, will never stand upright
Till Richard wear the garland of the realm.

Hast. How! wear the garland! Dost thou mean the crown?

Cate. Ay, my good lord.

Hast. I 'll have this crown of mine cut from my shoulders
Before I 'll see the crown so foul misplac'd:
But canst thou guess that he doth aim at it?

Cate. Ay, on my life; and hopes to find you forward
Upon his party for the gain thereof;
And thereupon he sends you this good news,
That this same very day your enemies,
The kindred of the Queen, must die at Pomfret.

173. **about**, concerning. 179. **divided councils**, i.e., Richard and he apart from the council planning the coronation. 183. **are let blood**, i.e., are executed. 192. **complots**, conspiracies. 200. **digest**, arrange, plan.

Scene ii: 11. **boar**, i.e., Richard. **razed off**, struck off. 47. **Upon his party**, on his side.

Hast. Indeed, I am no mourner for that news,
Because they have been still my adversaries;
But, that I 'll give my voice on Richard's side,
To bar my master's heirs in true descent,
God knows I will not do it, to the death.
Cate. God keep your lordship in that gracious mind!
Hast. But I shall laugh at this a twelvemonth hence,
That they which brought me in my master's hate,
I live to look upon their tragedy.
Well, Catesby, ere a fortnight make me older,
I 'll send some packing that yet think not on 't.
Cate. 'T is a vile thing to die, my gracious lord,
When men are unprepar'd and look not for it.
Hast. O monstrous, monstrous! and so falls it out
With Rivers, Vaughan, Grey; and so 't will do
With some men else, that think themselves as safe
As thou and I; who, as thou know'st, are dear
To princely Richard and to Buckingham.
Cate. The Princes both make high account of you,
[*Aside.*] For they account his head upon the bridge.
Hast. I know they do; and I have well deserv'd it.

Enter *Lord Stanley.*

—Come on, come on [*to Stanley*]; where is your boar-spear, man?
Fear you the boar, and go so unprovided?
Stan. My lord, good morrow; good morrow, Catesby.
You may jest on, but, by the holy rood,
I do not like these several councils, I.
Hast. My lord, I hold my life as dear as yours;
And never in my days, I do protest,
Was it so precious to me as 't is now:
Think you, but that I know our state secure,
I would be so triumphant as I am?
Stan. The lords at Pomfret, when they rode from London,
Were jocund, and suppos'd their states were sure,
And they indeed had no cause to mistrust;
But yet, you see, how soon the day o'ercast.
This sudden stab of rancour I misdoubt:
Pray God, I say, I prove a needless coward!
What, shall we toward the Tower? The day is spent.

72. bridge, London Bridge, where traitors' heads were displayed. **78. rood,** cross.

Hast. Come, come, have with you. Wot you what, my lord?
To-day the lords you talk of are beheaded.
Stan. They, for their truth, might better wear their heads
Than some that have accus'd them wear their hats.
But come, my lord, let us away.

Enter a *Pursuivant.*

Hast. Go on before; I 'll talk with this good fellow. *Exeunt Stanley and Catesby.*
How now, sirrah! how goes the world with thee?
Purs. The better that your lordship please to ask.
Hast. I tell thee, man, 't is better with me now
Than when thou met'st me last where now we meet.
Then was I going prisoner to the Tower
By the suggestion of the Queen's allies;
But now, I tell thee—keep it to thyself—
This day those enemies are put to death,
And I in better state than e'er I was.
Purs. God hold it, to your honour's good content!
Hast. Gramercy, fellow. There, drink that for me. *Throws him his purse.*
Purs. I thank your honour. *Exit.*

Enter a *Priest.*

Priest. Well met, my lord; I am glad to see your honour.
Hast. I thank thee, good Sir John, with all my heart.
I am in your debt for your last exercise;
Come the next Sabbath, and I will content you.
Priest. I 'll wait upon your lordship.

Enter *Buckingham.*

Buck. What, talking with a priest, Lord Chamberlain?
Your friends at Pomfret, they do need the priest;
Your honour hath no shriving work in hand.
Hast. Good faith, and when I met this holy man,
The men you talk of came into my mind.
What, go you toward the Tower?
Buck. I do, my lord; but long I cannot stay there:
I shall return before your lordship thence.
Hast. Nay, like enough, for I stay dinner there.

95. wear their hats, keep their offices. **S. d. Pursuivant,** an attendant or a herald. **103. suggestion,** instigation. **107. hold,** preserve. **116. shriving work,** i.e., confessing and being absolved.

Buck. [*Aside.*] And supper too, although thou know'st it not.
Come, will you go?
Hast. I 'll wait upon your lordship.
Exeunt.

Scene III. *Pomfret Castle.*

Enter *Sir Richard Ratcliff,* with halberds, carrying *Rivers, Grey,* and *Vaughan* to death.

Riv. Sir Richard Ratcliff, let me tell thee this:
To-day shalt thou behold a subject die
For truth, for duty, and for loyalty.
Grey. God bless the Prince from all the pack of you!
A knot you are of damned blood-suckers.
Vaug. You live that shall cry woe for this hereafter.
Rat. Dispatch; the limit of your lives is out.
Riv. O Pomfret, Pomfret! O thou bloody prison,
Fatal and ominous to noble peers!
Within the guilty closure of thy walls
Richard the Second here was hack'd to death;
And, for more slander to thy dismal seat,
We give to thee our guiltless blood to drink.
Grey. Now Margaret's curse is fall'n upon our heads,
When she exclaim'd on Hastings, you, and I
For standing by when Richard stabb'd her son.
Riv. Then curs'd she Richard, then curs'd she Buckingham,
Then curs'd she Hastings. O, remember, God,
To hear her prayer for them, as now for us!
And for my sister and her princely sons,
Be satisfi'd, dear God, with our true blood,
Which, as thou know'st, unjustly must be spilt.
Rat. Make haste; the hour of death is expiate.
Riv. Come, Grey, come, Vaughan, let us here embrace.
Farewell, until we meet again in heaven.
Exeunt.

Scene IV. *The Tower of London.*

Enter *Buckingham, Derby, Hastings,* the *Bishop of Ely, Ratcliff, Lovel,* with others, and take their seats at a table.

Hast. Now noble peers, the cause why we are met
Is, to determine of the coronation.
In God's name speak, when is the royal day?
Buck. Is all things ready for the royal time?
Der. It is, and wants but nomination.
Ely. To-morrow, then, I judge a happy day.
Buck. Who knows the Lord Protector's mind herein?
Who is most inward with the royal Duke?
Ely. Your Grace, we think, should soonest know his mind.
Buck. Who, I, my lord?
We know each other's faces; for our hearts,
He knows no more of mine than I of yours,
Or I of his, my lord, than you of mine.
Lord Hastings, you and he are near in love.
Hast. I thank his Grace, I know he loves me well;
But, for his purpose in the coronation,
I have not sounded him, nor he deliver'd
His gracious pleasure any way therein:
But you, my honourable lords, may name the time;
And in the Duke's behalf I 'll give my voice,
Which, I presume, he 'll take in gentle part.

Enter *Gloucester.*

Ely. In happy time, here comes the Duke himself.
Glou. My noble lords and cousins all, good morrow.
I have been long a sleeper; but, I trust,
My absence doth neglect no great design
Which by my presence might have been concluded.
Buck. Had not you come upon your cue, my lord,
William Lord Hastings had pronounc'd your part,—
I mean, your voice,—for crowning of the King.
Glou. Than my Lord Hastings no man might be bolder;
His lordship knows me well, and loves me well.
Hast. I thank your Grace.
Glou. My Lord of Ely, when I was last in Holborn,
I saw good strawberries in your garden there.
I do beseech you send for some of them.
Ely. Marry, and will, my lord, with all my heart. *Exit.*
Glou. Cousin of Buckingham, a word with you. *Drawing him aside.*
Catesby hath sounded Hastings in our business,
And finds the testy gentleman so hot
That he will lose his head ere give consent
His master's child, as worshipfully he terms it,
Shall lose the royalty of England's throne.

Scene iii: 23. expiate, ended.

Scene iv: 5. nomination, appointing, i.e., the day. 8. inward, intimate.

Buck. Withdraw yourself a while; I 'll go with you.

Exeunt Gloucester and Buckingham.

Der. We have not yet set down this day of triumph.
To-morrow, in my judgement, is too sudden;
For I myself am not so well provided
As else I would be, were the day prolong'd.

Re-enter *Bishop of Ely.*

Ely. Where is my Lord, the Duke of Gloucester? I have sent for these strawberries.

Hast. His Grace looks cheerfully and smooth this morning;
There 's some conceit or other likes him well
When that he bids good morrow with such spirit.
I think there 's never a man in Christendom
Can lesser hide his love or hate than he;
For by his face straight shall you know his heart.

Der. What of his heart perceive you in his face
By any likelihood he show'd to-day?

Hast. Marry, that with no man here he is offended;
For, were he, he had shown it in his looks.

Re-enter *Gloucester* and *Buckingham.*

Glou. I pray you all, tell me what they deserve
That do conspire my death with devilish plots
Of damned witchcraft, and that have prevail'd
Upon my body with their hellish charms?

Hast. The tender love I bear your Grace, my lord,
Makes me most forward in this princely presence
To doom th' offenders, whosoe'er they be:
I say, my lord, they have deserved death.

Glou. Then be your eyes the witness of their evil.
Look how I am bewitch'd; behold mine arm
Is, like a blasted sapling, wither'd up:
And this is Edward's wife, that monstrous witch,
Consorted with that harlot strumpet Shore,
That by their witchcraft thus have marked me.

Hast. If they have done this deed, my noble lord,—

Glou. If! Thou protector of this damned strumpet,
Talk'st thou to me of "ifs"? Thou art a traitor!
Off with his head! Now, by Saint Paul I swear,
I will not dine until I see the same.
Lovel and Ratcliff, look that it be done.
The rest, that love me, rise and follow me.

Exeunt all but Hastings, Ratcliff, and Lovel.

Hast. Woe, woe for England! not a whit for me;
For I, too fond, might have prevented this.
Stanley did dream the boar did raze our helms,
And I did scorn it and disdain to fly:
Three times to-day my foot-cloth horse did stumble,
And started, when he look'd upon the Tower,
As loath to bear me to the slaughter-house.
O, now I need the priest that spake to me;
I now repent I told the pursuivant,
As too triumphing, how mine enemies
To-day at Pomfret bloodily were butcher'd,
And I myself secure in grace and favour.
O Margaret, Margaret, now thy heavy curse
Is lighted on poor Hastings' wretched head!

Rat. Come, come, dispatch; the Duke would be at dinner.
Make a short shrift; he longs to see your head.

Hast. O momentary grace of mortal men,
Which we more hunt for than the grace of God!
Who builds his hope in air of your good looks,
Lives like a drunken sailor on a mast,
Ready, with every nod, to tumble down
Into the fatal bowels of the deep.

Lov. Come, come, dispatch; 't is bootless to exclaim.

Hast. O bloody Richard! miserable England!
I prophesy the fearfull'st time to thee
That ever wretched age hath look'd upon.
Come, lead me to the block; bear him my head.
They smile at me who shortly shall be dead.

Exeunt.

Scene V. *The Tower-walls.*

Enter *Gloucester* and *Buckingham,* in rotten armour, marvellous ill-favoured.

Glou. Come, cousin, canst thou quake, and change thy colour,
Murder thy breath in middle of a word,
And then again begin, and stop again,
As if thou were distraught and mad with terror?

Buck. Tut, I can counterfeit the deep tragedian;

47. prolong'd, put off. **50. smooth,** serene. **51. conceit,** idea. **likes,** pleases.

82. Pity England, but not me. **83. fond,** foolish. **86. foot-cloth,** cloth hanging to the ground on either side of a nobleman's horse. **stumble,** an ill-omen. **97. shrift,** confession and absolution. **100. in air,** i.e., insubstantially. **Scene v: S. d. rotten,** rusty.

Speak and look back, and pry on every side,
Tremble and start at wagging of a straw,
Intending deep suspicion: ghastly looks
Are at my service, like enforced smiles;
And both are ready in their offices,
At any time, to grace my stratagems.
But what, is Catesby gone?

Glou. He is; and, see, he brings the Mayor along.

Enter the *Mayor* and *Catesby*.

Buck. Lord Mayor,—

Glou. Look to the drawbridge there!

Buck. Hark! a drum.

Glou. Catesby, o'erlook the walls.

Buck. Lord Mayor, the reason we have sent—

Glou. Look back, defend thee, here are enemies.

Buck. God and our innocency defend and guard us!

Enter *Lovel* and *Ratcliff*, with Hastings' head.

Glou. Be patient, they are friends, Ratcliff and Lovel.

Lov. Here is the head of that ignoble traitor,
The dangerous and unsuspected Hastings.

Glou. So dear I lov'd the man, that I must weep.
I took him for the plainest harmless creature
That breath'd upon the earth a Christian;
Made him my book, wherein my soul recorded
The history of all her secret thoughts.
So smooth he daub'd his vice with show of virtue
That, his apparent open guilt omitted,
I mean his conversation with Shore's wife,
He liv'd from all attainder of suspects.

Buck. Well, well, he was the covert'st shelter'd traitor
That ever liv'd.
Would you imagine, or almost believe,
Were 't not that, by great preservation,
We live to tell it, that the subtle traitor
This day had plotted, in the council-house
To murder me and my good lord of Gloucester?

May. Had he done so?

Glou. What, think you we are Turks or infidels?
Or that we would, against the form of law,
Proceed thus rashly in the villain's death,
But that the extreme peril of the case,
The peace of England, and our persons' safety
Enforc'd us to this execution?

May. Now, fair befall you! he deserv'd his death;
And your good Graces both have well proceeded
To warn false traitors from the like attempts.
I never look'd for better at his hands,
After he once fell in with Mistress Shore.

Buck. Yet had we not determin'd he should die,
Until your lordship came to see his end;
Which now the loving haste of these our friends,
Something against our meanings, have prevented;
Because, my lord, I would have had you heard
The traitor speak, and timorously confess
The manner and the purpose of his treasons;
That you might well have signified the same
Unto the citizens, who haply may
Misconster us in him and wail his death.

May. But, my good lord, your Grace's words shall serve
As well as I had seen and heard him speak;
And do not doubt, right noble princes both,
That I'll acquaint our duteous citizens
With all your just proceedings in this case.

Glou. And to that end we wish'd your lordship here,
T' avoid the censures of the carping world.

Buck. But since you come too late of our intent,
Yet witness what you hear we did intend:
And so, my good Lord Mayor, we bid farewell.
Exit Mayor.

Glou. Go, after, after, cousin Buckingham.
The mayor towards Guildhall hies him in all post.
There, at your meetest vantage of the time,
Infer the bastardy of Edward's children:
Tell them how Edward put to death a citizen,
Only for saying he would make his son
Heir to the crown; meaning indeed his house,
Which, by the sign thereof, was termed so.
Moreover, urge his hateful luxury,
And bestial appetite in change of lust;
Which stretch'd unto their servants, daughters, wives,
Even where his raging eye or savage heart,
Without control, lusted to make a prey.
Nay, for a need, thus far come near my person:
Tell them, when that my mother went with child
Of that insatiate Edward, noble York
My princely father then had wars in France;

8. intending, pretending. **10. offices**, uses. **32. attainder of suspects**, taint of suspicion. **35. almost**, even.

73. post, haste. **74. vantage of the time**, opportunity. **75. Infer**, assert. **79.** The citizen's house was known by its sign-board, the Crown. **80. luxury**, lust **81. in change of lust**, in inconstant lust.

And, by true computation of the time,
Found that the issue was not his begot;
Which well appeared in his lineaments,
Being nothing like the noble Duke my father.
Yet touch this sparingly, as 't were far off;
Because, my lord, you know my mother lives.

Buck. Doubt not, my lord, I 'll play the orator
As if the golden fee for which I plead
Were for myself; and so, my lord, adieu.

Glou. If you thrive well, bring them to Baynard's Castle,
Where you shall find me well accompanied
With reverend fathers and well-learned bishops.

Buck. I go; and towards three or four o'clock
Look for the news that the Guildhall affords.
Exit.

Glou. Go, Lovel, with all speed to Doctor Shaw;
[*To Cate.*] Go thou to Friar Penker; bid them both
Meet me within this hour at Baynard's Castle.
Exeunt all but Gloucester.
Now will I go to take some privy order,
To draw the brats of Clarence out of sight;
And to give notice, that no manner person
Have any time recourse unto the princes.
Exit.

Scene VI. *London. A street.*

Enter a *Scrivener* with a paper in his hand.

Scriv. Here is the indictment of the good Lord Hastings,
Which in a set hand fairly is engross'd,
That it may be to-day read o'er in Paul's.
And mark how well the sequel hangs together:
Eleven hours I 've spent to write it over,
For yesternight by Catesby was it sent me;
The precedent was full as long a-doing;
And yet within these five hours Hastings liv'd,
Untainted, unexamin'd, free, at liberty.
Here 's a good world the while! Who is so gross
That cannot see this palpable device?
Yet who so bold, but says he sees it not?
Bad is the world; and all will come to nought,
When such ill dealing must be seen in thought.
Exit.

98. Baynard's Castle, on the embankment near Blackfriars, had been owned by Richard's father. **103-4. Doctor Shaw . . . Friar Penker,** popular preachers favorable to Richard. **Scene vi: 4. sequel,** order of events. **7. precedent,** original copy, i.e., the one brought by Catesby. **10. gross,** stupid.

Scene VII. *Baynard's Castle.*

Enter *Gloucester* and *Buckingham,* at several doors.

Glou. How now, how now, what say the citizens?

Buck. Now, by the holy mother of our Lord,
The citizens are mum, say not a word.

Glou. Touch'd you the bastardy of Edward's children?

Buck. I did; with his contract with Lady Lucy,
And his contract by deputy in France;
Th' unsatiate greediness of his desire,
And his enforcement of the city wives;
His tyranny for trifles; his own bastardy,
As being got, your father then in France,
And his resemblance, being not like the Duke.
Withal I did infer your lineaments,
Being the right idea of your father,
Both in your form and nobleness of mind;
Laid open all your victories in Scotland,
Your discipline in war, wisdom in peace,
Your bounty, virtue, fair humility;
Indeed, left nothing fitting for your purpose
Untouch'd or slightly handled in discourse.
And when my oratory drew toward end,
I bid them that did love their country's good
Cry, "God save Richard, England's royal king!"

Glou. And did they so?

Buck. No, so God help me, they spake not a word;
But, like dumb statuës or breathing stones,
Star'd each on other, and look'd deadly pale;
Which when I saw, I reprehended them,
And ask'd the Mayor what meant this wilful silence.
His answer was, the people were not used
To be spoke to but by the Recorder.
Then he was urg'd to tell my tale again,
"Thus saith the Duke, thus hath the Duke inferr'd;"
But nothing spoke in warrant from himself.
When he had done, some followers of mine own,
At lower end of the hall, hurl'd up their caps,
And some ten voices cried, "God save King Richard!"
And thus I took the vantage of those few,

Scene vii: 5. contract, formal betrothal constituted a legal marriage in Shakespeare's day and could invalidate subsequent marriages. The reference is to Edward's alleged betrothal to Elizabeth Lucy in England and by deputy (Warwick) to the sister of Louis XI of France, both precedent to his marriage to Elizabeth Woodville. **13. right idea,** exact likeness. **15. Scotland,** i.e., in the campaign of 1482. **30. Recorder,** keeper of the city's rolls. **33. in warrant . . . self,** on his own responsibility.

"Thanks, gentle citizens and friends," quoth I;
"This general applause and cheerful shout
Argues your wisdom and your love to Richard:"
And even here brake off, and came away.

Glou. What tongueless blocks were they! Would they not speak?

Buck. No, by my troth, my lord.

Glou. Will not the Mayor then and his brethren come?

Buck. The Mayor is here at hand: intend some fear;
Be not you spoke with, but by mighty suit;
And look you get a prayer-book in your hand,
And stand between two churchmen, good my lord,—
For on that ground I 'll make a holy descant—
And be not easily won to our requests.
Play the maid's part, still answer nay, and take it.

Glou. I go; and if you plead as well for them
As I can say nay to thee for myself,
No doubt we 'll bring it to a happy issue.

Buck. Go, go up to the leads; the Lord Mayor knocks. *Exit Gloucester.*

Enter the *Mayor* and *Citizens.*

Welcome, my lord! I dance attendance here;
I think the Duke will not be spoke withal.

Enter *Catesby.*

Now, Catesby, what says your lord to my request?

Cate. He doth entreat your Grace, my noble lord,
To visit him to-morrow or next day.
He is within, with two right reverend fathers,
Divinely bent to meditation;
And in no worldly suits would he be mov'd,
To draw him from his holy exercise.

Buck. Return, good Catesby, to the gracious Duke;
Tell him, myself, the Mayor and Aldermen,
In deep designs, in matter of great moment,
No less importing than our general good,
Are come to have some conference with his Grace.

Cate. I 'll signify so much unto him straight. *Exit.*

Buck. Ah, ha, my lord, this prince is not an Edward!
He is not lolling on a lewd love-bed,
But on his knees at meditation;
Not dallying with a brace of courtezans,
But meditating with two deep divines;
Not sleeping, to engross his idle body,
But praying, to enrich his watchful soul.
Happy were England, would this virtuous prince
Take on his Grace the sovereignty thereof;
But, sure, I fear, we shall not win him to it.

May. Marry, God defend his Grace should say us nay!

Buck. I fear he will. Here Catesby comes again.

Re-enter *Catesby.*

Now, Catesby, what says his Grace?

Cate. He wonders to what end you have assembled
Such troops of citizens to come to him,
His Grace not being warn'd thereof before.
He fears, my lord, you mean no good to him.

Buck. Sorry I am my noble cousin should
Suspect me, that I mean no good to him:
By heaven, we come to him in perfect love;
And so once more return and tell his Grace. *Exit Catesby.*
When holy and devout religious men
Are at their beads, 't is much to draw them thence,
So sweet is zealous contemplation.

Enter *Gloucester* aloft, between two Bishops. *Catesby* returns.

May. See, where his Grace stands 'tween two clergymen!

Buck. Two props of virtue for a Christian prince,
To stay him from the fall of vanity;
And, see, a book of prayer in his hand,
True ornaments to know a holy man.
Famous Plantagenet, most gracious prince,
Lend favourable ear to our requests;
And pardon us the interruption
Of thy devotion and right Christian zeal.

Glou. My lord, there needs no such apology:
I do beseech your Grace to pardon me,
Who, earnest in the service of my God,
Deferr'd the visitation of my friends.
But, leaving this, what is your Grace's pleasure?

Buck. Even that, I hope, which pleaseth God above,
And all good men of this ungovern'd isle.

Glou. I do suspect I have done some offence
That seems disgracious in the city's eye,
And that you come to reprehend my ignorance.

44. intend, pretend. **49. descant,** literally a musical variation, here a theme with comments. **55. leads,** roof.

76. engross, fatten. **94. s. d. aloft,** on the stage balcony. **97. from the fall of,** from falling into.

Buck. You have, my lord: would it might please your Grace,
On our entreaties, to amend your fault!
Glou. Else wherefore breathe I in a Christian land?
Buck. Know then, it is your fault that you resign
The supreme seat, the throne majestical,
The scepter'd office of your ancestors,
Your state of fortune, and your due of birth,
The lineal glory of your royal house,
To the corruption of a blemish'd stock;
Whiles, in the mildness of your sleepy thoughts,
Which here we waken to our country's good,
The noble isle doth want his proper limbs;
His face defac'd with scars of infamy,
His royal stock graft with ignoble plants,
And almost shoulder'd in the swallowing gulf
Of dark forgetfulness and deep oblivion.
Which to recure, we heartily solicit
Your gracious self to take on you the charge
And kingly government of this your land,
Not as protector, steward, substitute,
Or lowly factor for another's gain;
But as successively from blood to blood,
Your right of birth, your empery, your own.
For this, consorted with the citizens,
Your very worshipful and loving friends,
And by their vehement instigation,
In this just cause come I to move your Grace.
Glou. I cannot tell if to depart in silence,
Or bitterly to speak in your reproof,
Best fitteth my degree or your condition.
If not to answer, you might haply think
Tongue-tied ambition, not replying, yielded
To bear the golden yoke of sovereignty,
Which fondly you would here impose on me.
If to reprove you for this suit of yours,
So season'd with your faithful love to me,
Then, on the other side, I check'd my friends.
Therefore, to speak, and to avoid the first,
And then, in speaking, not to incur the last,
Definitively thus I answer you:
Your love deserves my thanks; but my desert
Unmeritable shuns your high request.
First, if all obstacles were cut away,
And that my path were even to the crown,
As my right revenue and due of birth;
Yet so much is my poverty of spirit,
So mighty and so many my defects,
That I would rather hide me from my greatness,
Being a bark to brook no mighty sea,
Than in my greatness covet to be hid,
And in the vapour of my glory smother'd.
But, God be thank'd, there is no need of me,
And much I need to help you, were there need:
The royal tree hath left us royal fruit,
Which, mellow'd by the stealing hours of time,
Will well become the seat of majesty,
And make, no doubt, us happy by his reign.
On him I lay that you would lay on me,
The right and fortune of his happy stars,
Which God defend that I should wring from him!
Buck. My lord, this argues conscience in your Grace;
But the respects thereof are nice and trivial,
All circumstances well considered.
You say that Edward is your brother's son:
So say we too, but not by Edward's wife;
For first was he contract to Lady Lucy—
Your mother lives a witness to his vow—
And afterward by substitute betroth'd
To Bona, sister to the King of France.
These both put off, a poor petitioner,
A care-craz'd mother to a many sons,
A beauty-waning and distressed widow,
Even in the afternoon of her best days,
Made prize and purchase of his wanton eye,
Seduc'd the pitch and height of his degree
To base declension and loath'd bigamy.
By her, in his unlawful bed, he got
This Edward, whom our manners call the Prince.
More bitterly could I expostulate,
Save that, for reverence to some alive,
I give a sparing limit to my tongue.
Then, good my lord, take to your royal self
This proffer'd benefit of dignity;
If not to bless us and the land withal,
Yet to draw forth your noble ancestry
From the corruption of abusing times,
Unto a lineal true-derived course.
May. Do, good my lord, your citizens entreat you.
Buck. Refuse not, mighty lord, this proffer'd love.
Cate. O, make them joyful, grant their lawful suit!
Glou. Alas, why would you heap this care on me?
I am unfit for state and majesty.
I do beseech you, take it not amiss;
I cannot nor I will not yield to you.
Buck. If you refuse it,—as, in love and zeal,
Loath to depose the child, your brother's son;

128. **shoulder'd**, immersed. **gulf**, whirlpool. 130. **recure**, cure, restore. 134. **factor**, agent. 136. **empery**, empire. 143. **degree**, rank. 155. **Unmeritable**, without merit. 157. **even**, smooth. 162. **to brook**, capable of enduring. 163. **covet**, wish.

166. **need**, i.e., lack ability. 175. **respects**, reasons. **nice**, over-scrupulous. 187. **purchase**, booty. 188. **pitch**, peak of elevation. 189. **declension**, deterioration. 192. **expostulate**, discuss the matter. 193. **reverence . . . some alive**, alluding to the scandalous rumor that Edward IV was the son of an adulterous amour of his mother; she is the "some alive."

As well we know your tenderness of heart
And gentle, kind, effeminate remorse,
Which we have noted in you to your kindred,
And equally indeed to all estates,—
Yet know, whe'er you accept our suit or no,
Your brother's son shall never reign our king;
But we will plant some other in the throne,
To the disgrace and downfall of your house;
And in this resolution here we leave you.—
Come, citizens! 'Zounds! I 'll entreat no more.

Glou. O, do not swear, my Lord of Buckingham.

Exit Buckingham with the Citizens.

Cate. Call them again, sweet prince, accept their suit.
If you deny them all the land will rue it.

Glou. Will you enforce me to a world of cares?
Call them again. [*Catesby goes to the Mayor, and exit.*] I am not made of stones,
But penetrable to your kind entreaties,
Albeit against my conscience and my soul.

Re-enter *Buckingham, Catesby* and the rest.

Cousin of Buckingham, and sage, grave men,
Since you will buckle Fortune on my back,
To bear her burden, whe'er I will or no,
I must have patience to endure the load:
But if black scandal or foul-fac'd reproach
Attend the sequel of your imposition,
Your mere enforcement shall acquittance me
From all the impure blots and stains thereof;
For God doth know, and you may partly see,
How far I am from the desire of this.

May. God bless your Grace! we see it, and will say it.

Glou. In saying so, you shall but say the truth.

Buck. Then I salute you with this royal title:
Long live King Richard, England's worthy king!

All. Amen.

Buck. To-morrow may it please you to be crown'd?

Glou. Even when you please, for you will have it so.

Buck. To-morrow, then, we will attend your Grace;
And so most joyfully we take our leave.

Glou. [*To the Bishops.*] Come, let us to our holy work again.
Farewell, my cousins; farewell, gentle friends.

Exeunt.

ACT IV. SCENE I. *Before the Tower.*

Enter *Queen Elizabeth*, the *Duchess of York*, and *Marquess of Dorset* at one door; *Anne, Duchess of Gloucester*, leading *Lady Margaret Plantagenet*, Clarence's Daughter at another door.

Duch. Who meets us here? My niece Plantagenet
Led in the hand of her kind aunt of Gloucester?
Now, for my life, she 's wandering to the Tower,
On pure heart's love to greet the tender prince.
Daughter, well met.

Anne. God give your Graces both
A happy and a joyful time of day!

Q. Eliz. As much to you, good sister! Whither away?

Anne. No farther than the Tower; and, as I guess,
Upon the like devotion as yourselves,
To gratulate the gentle princes there.

Q. Eliz. Kind sister, thanks; we 'll enter all together.

Enter the lieutenant *Brakenbury.*

And, in good time, here the lieutenant comes.
Master lieutenant, pray you, by your leave,
How doth the Prince, and my young son of York?

Brak. Right well, dear madam. By your patience,
I may not suffer you to visit them;
The King hath strictly charg'd the contrary.

Q. Eliz. The King! Why, who is that?

Brak. I cry you mercy! I mean the Lord Protector.

Q. Eliz. The Lord protect him from that kingly title!
Hath he set bounds between their love and me?
I am their mother; who shall bar me from them?

Duch. I am their father's mother; I will see them.

Anne. Their aunt I am in law, in love their mother;
Then bring me to their sights: I 'll bear thy blame
And take thy office from thee, on my peril.

Act IV, Scene i: 1. niece, i.e., granddaughter. **10. gratulate,** greet.

Brak. No, madam, no; I may not leave it so:
I am bound by oath, and therefore pardon me.
Exit.

Enter *Lord Stanley.*

Stan. Let me but meet you, ladies, one hour hence,
And I 'll salute your Grace of York as mother
And reverend looker on of two fair queens.
[*To Anne.*] Come, madam, you must straight to Westminster,
There to be crowned Richard's royal queen.
Q. Eliz. O, cut my lace asunder, that my pent heart
May have some scope to beat, or else I swoon
With this dead-killing news!
Anne. Despiteful tidings! O unpleasing news!
Dor. Be of good cheer. Mother, how fares your Grace?
Q. Eliz. O Dorset, speak not to me, get thee gone!
Death and destruction dogs thee at thy heels;
Thy mother's name is ominous to children.
If thou wilt outstrip death, go cross the seas,
And live with Richmond, from the reach of hell.
Go, hie thee, hie thee from this slaughter-house,
Lest thou increase the number of the dead;
And make me die the thrall of Margaret's curse,
Nor mother, wife, nor England's counted queen.
Stan. Full of wise care is this your counsel, madam.
Take all the swift advantage of the hours;
You shall have letters from me to my son
In your behalf, to meet you on the way:
Be not ta'en tardy by unwise delay.
Duch. O ill-dispersing wind of misery!
O my accursed womb, the bed of death!
A cockatrice hast thou hatch'd to the world,
Whose unavoided eye is murderous.
Stan. Come, madam, come; I in all haste was sent.
Anne. And I with all unwillingness will go.
O, would to God that the inclusive verge
Of golden metal that must round my brow
Were red-hot steel, to sear me to the brains!
Anointed let me be with deadly venom,
And die, ere men can say, "God save the Queen!"
Q. Eliz. Go, go, poor soul, I envy not thy glory;
To feed my humour, wish thyself no harm.
Anne. No! why? When he that is my husband now
Came to me, as I follow'd Henry's corse,
When scarce the blood was well wash'd from his hands
Which issued from my other angel husband
And that dear saint which then I weeping follow'd;
O, when, I say, I look'd on Richard's face,
This was my wish: "Be thou," quoth I, "accurs'd,
For making me, so young, so old a widow!
And, when thou wed'st, let sorrow haunt thy bed;
And be thy wife—if any be so mad—
More miserable by the life of thee
Than thou hast made me by my dear lord's death!"
Lo, ere I can repeat this curse again,
Within so small a time, my woman's heart
Grossly grew captive to his honey words
And prov'd the subject of mine own soul's curse,
Which hitherto hath held mine eyes from rest;
For never yet one hour in his bed
Did I enjoy the golden dew of sleep,
But with his timorous dreams was still awak'd.
Besides, he hates me for my father Warwick;
And will, no doubt, shortly be rid of me.
Q. Eliz. Poor heart, adieu! I pity thy complaining.
Anne. No more than with my soul I mourn for yours.
Dor. Farewell, thou woeful welcomer of glory!
Anne. Adieu, poor soul, that tak'st thy leave of it!
Duch. [*To Dorset.*] Go thou to Richmond, and good fortune guide thee!
[*To Anne.*] Go thou to Richard, and good angels tend thee!
[*To Queen Eliz.*] Go thou to sanctuary, and good thoughts possess thee!
I to my grave, where peace and rest lie with me!
Eighty odd years of sorrow have I seen,
And each hour's joy wreck'd with a week of teen.
Q. Eliz. Stay, yet look back with me unto the Tower.
Pity, you ancient stones, those tender babes
Whom envy hath immur'd within your walls!
Rough cradle for such little pretty ones!
Rude ragged nurse, old sullen playfellow
For tender princes, use my babies well!
So foolish sorrows bids your stones farewell.
Exeunt.

31. two fair queens, Elizabeth and Anne. **43. Richmond,** Henry Tudor, later King Henry VII. **47. counted,** accepted. **50. son,** Stanley was Richmond's step-father. **59. verge,** circlet.

65. To . . . humour, to please me. **80. grossly,** stupidly. **97. teen,** grief.

Scene II. *London. The palace.*

Sound a Sennet. Enter *Richard,* in pomp, crowned; *Buckingham, Catesby* with other nobles and a *Page.*

Rich. Stand all apart. Cousin of Buckingham!
Buck. My gracious sovereign?
Rich. Give me thy hand. [*Here he ascendeth the throne. Sound.*] Thus high, by thy advice
And thy assistance, is King Richard seated;
But shall we wear these glories for a day?
Or shall they last, and we rejoice in them?
Buck. Still live they, and for ever let them last!
Rich. Ah, Buckingham, now do I play the touch,
To try if thou be current gold indeed.
Young Edward lives: think now what I would speak.
Buck. Say on, my loving lord.
Rich. Why, Buckingham, I say, I would be king.
Buck. Why, so you are, my thrice renowned lord.
Rich. Ha! am I king? 'T is so: but Edward lives.
Buck. True, noble prince.
Rich. O bitter consequence,
That Edward still should live! "True, noble prince!"
Cousin, thou wast not wont to be so dull.
Shall I be plain? I wish the bastards dead;
And I would have it suddenly perform'd.
What say'st thou now? Speak suddenly; be brief.
Buck. Your Grace may do your pleasure.
Rich. Tut, tut, thou art all ice, thy kindness freezes.
Say, have I thy consent that they shall die?
Buck. Give me some little breath, some pause, dear lord,
Before I positively speak in this.
I will resolve you herein presently. *Exit.*
Cate. [*Aside to a stander by.*] The King is angry; see, he gnaws his lip.
Rich. I will converse with iron-witted fools
And unrespective boys; none are for me
That look into me with considerate eyes.
High-reaching Buckingham grows circumspect.
Boy!
Page. My lord?
Rich. Know'st thou not any whom corrupting gold
Will tempt unto a close exploit of death?
Page. I know a discontented gentleman,
Whose humble means match not his haughty spirit.
Gold were as good as twenty orators,
And will, no doubt, tempt him to anything.
Rich. What is his name?
Page. His name, my lord, is Tyrrel.
Rich. I partly know the man; go, call him hither. *Exit Page.*
The deep-revolving witty Buckingham
No more shall be the neighbour to my counsels.
Hath he so long held out with me untir'd,
And stops he now for breath? Well, be it so.

Enter *Stanley.*

How now, Lord Stanley, what 's the news?
Stan. Know, my loving lord,
The Marquis Dorset, as I hear, is fled
To Richmond, in the parts where he abides.
Stands apart.
Rich. Come hither, Catesby. Rumour it abroad
That Anne, my wife, is very grievous sick;
I will take order for her keeping close.
Inquire me out some mean poor gentleman,
Whom I will marry straight to Clarence' daughter;
The boy is foolish, and I fear not him.
Look, how thou dream'st! I say again, give out
That Anne my queen is sick and like to die.
About it; for it stands me much upon
To stop all hopes whose growth may damage me. *Exit Catesby.*
I must be married to my brother's daughter,
Or else my kingdom stands on brittle glass.
Murder her brothers, and then marry her!
Uncertain way of gain! But I am in
So far in blood that sin will pluck on sin!
Tear-falling pity dwells not in this eye.

Enter *Tyrrel.*

Is thy name Tyrrel?
Tyr. James Tyrrel, and your most obedient subject.
Rich. Art thou, indeed?
Tyr. Prove me, my gracious lord.
Rich. Dar'st thou resolve to kill a friend of mine?
Tyr. Please you;
But I had rather kill two enemies.

Scene ii: 8. **touch**, touchstone. The mark left by rubbing gold or silver against it indicated the purity of the metal. 28. **iron-witted**, i.e., unfeeling. 29. **unrespective**, heedless. 30. **considerate**, thoughtful.

35. **close exploit**, secret deed. 42. **deep-revolving**, thoughtful, here, scheming. **witty**, clever. 53. **close**, confined. 54. **mean**, humble. 59. **stands . . . upon**, is of the greatest importance to me. 61. **daughter**, Elizabeth of York, daughter of Edward IV. 65. **pluck**, draw.

Rich. Why, there thou hast it; two deep enemies,
Foes to my rest and my sweet sleep's disturbers
Are they that I would have thee deal upon:
Tyrrel, I mean those bastards in the Tower.
Tyr. Let me have open means to come to them,
And soon I 'll rid you from the fear of them.
Rich. Thou sing'st sweet music. Hark, come hither, Tyrrel.
Go, by this token. Rise, and lend thine ear.
Whispers.
There is no more but so; say it is done,
And I will love thee and prefer thee for it.
Tyr. I will despatch it straight.
Rich. Shall we hear from thee, Tyrrel, ere we sleep?
Tyr. Ye shall, my lord. *Exit.*

Re-enter *Buckingham.*

Buck. My lord, I have consider'd in my mind
The late request that you did sound me in.
Rich. Well, let that rest. Dorset is fled to Richmond.
Buck. I hear the news, my lord.
Rich. Stanley, he is your wife's son: well, look unto it.
Buck. My lord, I claim the gift, my due by promise,
For which your honour and your faith is pawn'd;
Th' earldom of Hereford and the movables
Which you have promised I shall possess.
Rich. Stanley, look to your wife. If she convey
Letters to Richmond, you shall answer it.
Buck. What says your Highness to my just request?
Rich. I do remember me, Henry the Sixth
Did prophesy that Richmond should be king,
When Richmond was a little peevish boy.
A king, perhaps, perhaps,—
Buck. My lord!
Rich. How chance the prophet could not at that time
Have told me, I being by, that I should kill him?
Buck. My lord, your promise for the earldom,—
Rich. Richmond! When last I was at Exeter,
The mayor in courtesy show'd me the castle,
And call'd it Rougemont; at which name I started,
Because a bard of Ireland told me once,
I should not live long after I saw Richmond.

90. he, i.e., Richmond.

Buck. My lord!
Rich. Ay, what 's o'clock?
Buck. I am thus bold to put your Grace in mind
Of what you promis'd me.
Rich. Well, but what 's o'clock?
Buck. Upon the stroke of ten.
Rich. Well, let it strike.
Buck. Why let it strike?
Rich. Because that, like a Jack, thou keep'st the stroke
Betwixt thy begging and my meditation.
I am not in the giving vein to-day.
Buck. Why, then resolve me whether you will or no.
Rich. Tut, tut,
Thou troublest me; I am not in the vein.
Exeunt all but Buckingham.
Buck. And is it thus? Repays he my deep service
With such contempt? Made I him king for this?
O, let me think on Hastings, and be gone
To Brecknock, while my fearful head is on!
Exit.

Scene III. *The palace.*

Enter *Tyrrel.*

Tyr. The tyrannous and bloody act is done,
The most arch deed of piteous massacre
That ever yet this land was guilty of.
Dighton and Forrest, who I did suborn
To do this piece of ruthless butchery,
Albeit they were flesh'd villains, bloody dogs,
Melted with tenderness and mild compassion,
Wept like two children in their death's sad story.
"O, thus," quoth Dighton, "lay the gentle babes;"
"Thus, thus," quoth Forrest, "girdling one another
Within their alabaster innocent arms.
Their lips were four red roses on a stalk,
Which in their summer beauty kiss'd each other.
A book of prayers on their pillow lay;
Which once," quoth Forrest, "almost chang'd my mind;
But O! the devil"—there the villain stopp'd;
When Dighton thus told on: "We smothered
The most replenished sweet work of Nature,
That from the prime creation e'er she framed."

117. Jack, the figure on old clocks that struck the hours. **keep'st,** maintainest. **126. Brecknock,** his castle in Wales. **Scene iii: 2. arch,** chief. **6. flesh'd,** hardened, with allusion to the practice of feeding dogs on the flesh of the game they killed. **18. replenished,** perfect. **19. prime,** first.

Hence both are gone with conscience and remorse;
They could not speak; and so I left them both,
To bear this tidings to the bloody King.

Enter *King Richard.*

And here he comes. All health, my sovereign lord!
Rich. Kind Tyrrel, am I happy in thy news?
Tyr. If to have done the thing you gave in charge
Beget your happiness, be happy then,
For it is done.
Rich. But didst thou see them dead?
Tyr. I did, my lord.
Rich. And buried, gentle Tyrrel?
Tyr. The chaplain of the Tower hath buried them;
But where, to say the truth, I do not know.
Rich. Come to me, Tyrrel, soon at after-supper,
When thou shalt tell the process of their death.
Meantime, but think how I may do thee good,
And be inheritor of thy desire.
Farewell till then.
Tyr. I humbly take my leave. *Exit.*
Rich. The son of Clarence have I pent up close;
His daughter meanly have I match'd in marriage;
The sons of Edward sleep in Abraham's bosom,
And Anne my wife hath bid this world good-night.
Now, for I know the Breton Richmond aims
At young Elizabeth, my brother's daughter,
And, by that knot, looks proudly on the crown,
To her go I, a jolly thriving wooer.

Enter *Ratcliff.*

Rat. My lord!
Rich. Good or bad news, that thou com'st in so bluntly?
Rat. Bad news, my lord. Morton is fled to Richmond;
And Buckingham, back'd with the hardy Welshmen,
Is in the field, and still his power increaseth.
Rich. Ely with Richmond troubles me more near
Than Buckingham and his rash-levied strength.
Come, I have learn'd that fearful commenting
Is leaden servitor to dull delay;
Delay leads impotent and snail-pac'd beggary:
Then fiery expedition be my wing,
Jove's Mercury, and herald for a king!
Go, muster men! My counsel is my shield;
We must be brief when traitors brave the field.
Exeunt.

Scene IV. *Before the palace.*

Enter old *Queen Margaret.*

Q. Mar. So, now prosperity begins to mellow
And drop into the rotten mouth of death.
Here in these confines slily have I lurk'd,
To watch the waning of mine enemies.
A dire induction am I witness to,
And will to France, hoping the consequence
Will prove as bitter, black, and tragical.
Withdraw thee, wretched Margaret; who comes here? *Retires.*

Enter *Queen Elizabeth* and the *Duchess of York.*

Q. Eliz. Ah, my poor princes! ah, my tender babes!
My unblown flowers, new-appearing sweets!
If yet your gentle souls fly in the air
And be not fix'd in doom perpetual,
Hover about me with your airy wings
And hear your mother's lamentation!
Q. Mar. Hover about her; say, that right for right
Hath dimm'd your infant morn to aged night.
Duch. So many miseries have craz'd my voice,
That my woe-wearied tongue is still and mute.
Edward Plantagenet, why art thou dead?
Q. Mar. Plantagenet doth quit Plantagenet.
Edward for Edward pays a dying debt.
Q. Eliz. Wilt thou, O God, fly from such gentle lambs,
And throw them in the entrails of the wolf?
When didst thou sleep when such a deed was done?
Q. Mar. When holy Harry died, and my sweet son.
Duch. Dead life, blind sight, poor mortal living ghost,

20. gone, overcome. **31. at after-supper,** at dessert. **40. Breton,** Richmond was in Brittany at this time. **42. by that knot,** by virtue of that proposed marriage. **46. Morton,** John Morton, Bishop of Ely.

51-2. fearful . . . delay, frightened speculation is the slow servant of delay. **53. leads,** is attended by. **Scene iv: 5. induction,** beginning of a play. **6. consequence,** sequel. **15. right for right,** justice. **20. Plantagenet . . . Plantagenet,** Edward V doth requite Edward, Prince of Wales, murdered at Tewkesbury. **24. When,** i.e., why. **25. holy Harry,** Henry VI.

Woe's scene, world's shame, grave's due by life usurp'd,
Brief abstract and record of tedious days,
Rest thy unrest on England's lawful earth,
Sitting down.
Unlawfully made drunk with innocent blood!
Q. Eliz. Ah, that thou wouldst as soon afford a grave
As thou canst yield a melancholy seat!
Then would I hide my bones, not rest them here.
Ah, who hath any cause to mourn but we?
Sitting down by her.
Q. Mar. [*Coming forward.*] If ancient sorrow be most reverent,
Give mine the benefit of seniory,
And let my griefs frown on the upper hand.
If sorrow can admit society,
Sitting down with them.
Tell o'er your woes again by viewing mine.
I had an Edward, till a Richard kill'd him;
I had a Harry, till a Richard kill'd him:
Thou hadst an Edward, till a Richard kill'd him;
Thou hadst a Richard, till a Richard kill'd him.
Duch. I had a Richard too, and thou didst kill him;
I had a Rutland too, thou holp'st to kill him.
Q. Mar. Thou hadst a Clarence too, and Richard kill'd him.
From forth the kennel of thy womb hath crept
A hell-hound that doth hunt us all to death:
That dog, that had his teeth before his eyes
To worry lambs and lap their gentle blood,
That foul defacer of God's handiwork,
That excellent grand tyrant of the earth
That reigns in galled eyes of weeping souls,
Thy womb let loose, to chase us to our graves.
O upright, just, and true-disposing God,
How do I thank thee, that this carnal cur
Preys on the issue of his mother's body,
And makes her pew-fellow with others' moan!
Duch. O Harry's wife, triumph not in my woes!
God witness with me, I have wept for thine.
Q. Mar. Bear with me; I am hungry for revenge,
And now I cloy me with beholding it.
Thy Edward he is dead, that kill'd my Edward;
The other Edward dead, to quit my Edward;
Young York he is but boot, because both they
Match not the high perfection of my loss:
Thy Clarence he is dead that stabb'd my Edward;
And the beholders of this frantic play,
Th' adulterate Hastings, Rivers, Vaughan, Grey,
Untimely smother'd in their dusky graves.
Richard yet lives, hell's black intelligencer,
Only reserv'd their factor, to buy souls
And send them thither; but at hand, at hand,
Ensues his piteous and unpitied end.
Earth gapes, hell burns, fiends roar, saints pray,
To have him suddenly convey'd from hence.
Cancel his bond of life, dear God, I pray,
That I may live to say, The dog is dead!
Q. Eliz. O, thou didst prophesy the time would come
That I should wish for thee to help me curse
That bottled spider, that foul bunch-back'd toad!
Q. Mar. I call'd thee then vain flourish of my fortune;
I call'd thee then poor shadow, painted queen;
The presentation of but what I was;
The flattering index of a direful pageant;
One heav'd a-high, to be hurl'd down below;
A mother only mock'd with two fair babes;
A dream of what thou wast; a garish flag
To be the aim of every dangerous shot;
A sign of dignity, a breath, a bubble;
A queen in jest, only to fill the scene.
Where is thy husband now? Where be thy brothers?
Where be thy two sons? Wherein dost thou joy?
Who sues, and kneels, and says, "God save the Queen"?
Where be the bending peers that flattered thee?
Where be the thronging troops that followed thee?
Decline all this, and see what now thou art:
For happy wife, a most distressed widow;
For joyful mother, one that wails the name;
For queen, a very caitiff crown'd with care;
For one being sued to, one that humbly sues;
For one that scorn'd at me, now scorn'd of me;
For one being fear'd of all, now fearing one;
For one commanding all, obey'd of none.
Thus hath the course of justice whirl'd about,
And left thee but a very prey to time;
Having no more but thought of what thou wast,
To torture thee the more, being what thou art.
Thou didst usurp my place, and dost thou not
Usurp the just proportion of my sorrow?

36. seniory, seniority. **37. on the upper hand,** in the superior place. **40. Edward,** i.e., her son. **42. Edward,** Edward V, killed in the Tower. **43. Richard,** Duke of York, Elizabeth's son. **44-5. Richard . . . Rutland,** her husband and son killed in the battle of Wakefield by Margaret's forces. **49. teeth,** Richard III was supposed to have had his teeth at birth. **56. carnal,** flesh-eating. **64. other Edward,** Edward V.

69. adulterate, adulterous. **71. intelligencer,** go-between. **90. sign,** mere sign. **97. Decline,** repeat. **100. caitiff,** wretch.

Now thy proud neck bears half my burden'd yoke,
From which even here I slip my wearied head,
And leave the burden of it all on thee.
Farewell, York's wife, and queen of sad mischance;
These English woes shall make me smile in France.

Q. Eliz. O thou well skill'd in curses, stay a while,
And teach me how to curse mine enemies!

Q. Mar. Forbear to sleep the night, and fast the day;
Compare dead happiness with living woe;
Think that thy babes were sweeter than they were,
And he that slew them fouler than he is.
Bett'ring thy loss makes the bad causer worse;
Revolving this will teach thee how to curse.

Q. Eliz. My words are dull; O, quicken them with thine!

Q. Mar. Thy woes will make them sharp, and pierce like mine. *Exit.*

Duch. Why should calamity be full of words?

Q. Eliz. Windy attorneys to their client woes,
Airy succeeders of intestate joys,
Poor breathing orators of miseries,
Let them have scope! though what they will impart
Help nothing else, yet do they ease the heart.

Duch. If so, then be not tongue-tied; go with me,
And in the breath of bitter words let 's smother
My damned son, that thy two sweet sons smother'd.
The trumpet sounds; be copious in exclaims.

Enter *King Richard* and his train, marching, with drums and trumpets.

Rich. Who intercepts me in my expedition?

Duch. O, she that might have intercepted thee,
By strangling thee in her accursed womb,
From all the slaughters, wretch, that thou hast done!

Q. Eliz. Hid'st thou that forehead with a golden crown,
Where should be branded, if that right were right,
The slaughter of the prince that ow'd that crown,
And the dire death of my poor sons and brothers?
Tell me, thou villain slave, where are my children?

Duch. Thou toad, thou toad, where is thy brother Clarence?
And little Ned Plantagenet, his son?

Q. Eliz. Where is the gentle Rivers, Vaughan, Grey?

Duch. Where is kind Hastings?

Rich. A flourish, trumpets! strike alarum, drums!
Let not the heavens hear these tell-tale women
Rail on the Lord's anointed. Strike, I say!
Flourish. Alarums.
Either be patient, and entreat me fair,
Or with the clamorous report of war
Thus will I drown your exclamations.

Duch. Art thou my son?

Rich. Ay, I thank God, my father, and yourself.

Duch. Then patiently hear my impatience.

Rich. Madam, I have a touch of your condition,
That cannot brook the accent of reproof.

Duch. O, let me speak!

Rich. Do then; but I 'll not hear.

Duch. I will be mild and gentle in my words.

Rich. And brief, good mother; for I am in haste.

Duch. Art thou so hasty? I have stay'd for thee,
God knows, in torment and in agony.

Rich. And came I not at last to comfort you?

Duch. No, by the holy rood, thou know'st it well,
Thou cam'st on earth to make the earth my hell.
A grievous burden was thy birth to me;
Tetchy and wayward was thy infancy;
Thy school-days frightful, desp'rate, wild, and furious,
Thy prime of manhood daring, bold, and venturous,
Thy age confirm'd, proud, subtle, sly, and bloody,
More mild, but yet more harmful, kind in hatred.
What comfortable hour canst thou name
That ever grac'd me with thy company?

Rich. Faith, none, but Humphrey Hour, that call'd your Grace
To breakfast once forth of my company.
If I be so disgracious in your eye,

122. Bett'ring, magnifying. **128. intestate**, i.e., dead, lit., dead without leaving a will. **135. exclaims**, exclamations. **136. expedition**, haste. **142. ow'd**, owned.

149. tell-tale, tattling. **157. condition**, disposition. **168. Tetchy**, peevish, fretful. **171. Thy age confirm'd**, i.e., in riper years. **175. Humphrey Hour**, men looking for invitations to supper often loitered in Duke Humphrey's (of Gloucester) walk in St. Paul's. This may mean that she was happiest when called away from Richard.

Let me march on, and not offend you, madam.
Strike up the drum.
Duch. I prithee, hear me speak.
Rich. You speak too bitterly.
Duch. Hear me a word,
For I shall never speak to thee again.
Rich. So.
Duch. Either thou wilt die by God's just ordinance,
Ere from this war thou turn a conqueror,
Or I with grief and extreme age shall perish
And never more behold thy face again.
Therefore take with thee my most grievous curse,
Which, in the day of battle, tire thee more
Than all the complete armour that thou wear'st!
My prayers on the adverse party fight;
And there the little souls of Edward's children
Whisper the spirits of thine enemies
And promise them success and victory.
Bloody thou art, bloody will be thy end;
Shame serves thy life and doth thy death attend. *Exit.*
Q. Eliz. Though far more cause, yet much less spirit to curse
Abides in me; I say amen to her.
Rich. Stay, madam; I must talk a word with you.
Q. Eliz. I have no more sons of the royal blood
For thee to slaughter; for my daughters, Richard,
They shall be praying nuns, not weeping queens;
And therefore level not to hit their lives.
Rich. You have a daughter call'd Elizabeth,
Virtuous and fair, royal and gracious.
Q. Eliz. And must she die for this? O, let her live,
And I 'll corrupt her manners, stain her beauty,
Slander myself as false to Edward's bed,
Throw over her the veil of infamy:
So she may live unscarr'd of bleeding slaughter,
I will confess she was not Edward's daughter.
Rich. Wrong not her birth, she is a royal princess.
Q. Eliz. To save her life, I 'll say she is not so.
Rich. Her life is safest only in her birth.
Q. Eliz. And only in that safety died her brothers.
Rich. Lo, at their birth good stars were opposite.
Q. Eliz. No, to their lives ill friends were contrary.
Rich. All unavoided is the doom of destiny.
Q. Eliz. True, when avoided grace makes destiny.
My babes were destin'd to a fairer death,
If grace had bless'd thee with a fairer life.
Rich. You speak as if that I had slain my cousins.
Q. Eliz. Cousins, indeed; and by their uncle cozen'd
Of comfort, kingdom, kindred, freedom, life.
Whose hand soever lanc'd their tender hearts,
Thy head, all indirectly, gave direction.
No doubt the murd'rous knife was dull and blunt
Till it was whetted on thy stone-hard heart
To revel in the entrails of my lambs.
But that still use of grief makes wild grief tame,
My tongue should to thy ears not name my boys
Till that my nails were anchor'd in thine eyes;
And I, in such a desperate bay of death,
Like a poor bark, of sails and tackling reft,
Rush all to pieces on thy rocky bosom.
Rich. Madam, so thrive I in my enterprise
And dangerous success of bloody wars,
As I intend more good to you and yours
Than ever you or yours by me were harm'd!
Q. Eliz. What good is cover'd with the face of heaven,
To be discover'd, that can do me good?
Rich. Th' advancement of your children, gentle lady.
Q. Eliz. Up to some scaffold, there to lose their heads?
Rich. Unto the dignity and height of fortune,
The high imperial type of this earth's glory.
Q. Eliz. Flatter my sorrow with report of it;
Tell me what state, what dignity, what honour,
Canst thou demise to any child of mine?
Rich. Even all I have; ay, and myself and all
Will I withal endow a child of thine;
So in the Lethe of thy angry soul
Thou drown the sad remembrance of those wrongs
Which thou supposest I have done to thee.
Q. Eliz. Be brief, lest that the process of thy kindness
Last longer telling than thy kindness' date.

195. serves, attends. **202. level,** aim. **206. manners,** morals. **213. only in,** because of. **215. opposite,** adverse.

217. unavoided, unavoidable. **218. avoided grace,** our lacking grace or kindness, i.e., Richard. **222. cozen'd,** cheated. **229. still,** constant. **236. success,** issue, result. **244. type,** sign, badge. **247. demise,** convey, transfer. **250. Lethe,** river of forgetfulness. **253. process,** story.

Rich. Then know, that from my soul I love thy daughter.
Q. Eliz. My daughter's mother thinks it with her soul.
Rich. What do you think?
Q. Eliz. That thou dost love my daughter from thy soul.
So from thy soul's love didst thou love her brothers,
And from my heart's love I do thank thee for it.
Rich. Be not so hasty to confound my meaning:
I mean, that with my soul I love thy daughter,
And do intend to make her Queen of England.
Q. Eliz. Well then, who dost thou mean shall be her king?
Rich. Even he that makes her queen. Who else should be?
Q. Eliz. What, thou?
Rich. Even so. How think you of it?
Q. Eliz. How canst thou woo her?
Rich. That I would learn of you,
As one being best acquainted with her humour.
Q. Eliz. And wilt thou learn of me?
Rich. Madam, with all my heart.
Q. Eliz. Send to her, by the man that slew her brothers,
A pair of bleeding hearts; thereon engrave
Edward and York; then haply will she weep.
Therefore present to her,—as sometime Margaret
Did to thy father, steep'd in Rutland's blood,—
A handkerchief; which, say to her, did drain
The purple sap from her sweet brother's body;
And bid her wipe her weeping eyes withal.
If this inducement move her not to love,
Send her a letter of thy noble deeds.
Tell her thou mad'st away her uncle Clarence,
Her uncle Rivers; ay, and, for her sake,
Mad'st quick conveyance with her good aunt Anne.
Rich. You mock me, madam; this is not the way
To win your daughter.
Q. Eliz. There is no other way;
Unless thou couldst put on some other shape,
And not be Richard that hath done all this.
Rich. Say that I did all this for love of her.
Q. Eliz. Nay, then indeed she cannot choose but hate thee,
Having bought love with such a bloody spoil.
Rich. Look, what is done cannot be now amended:
Men shall deal unadvisedly sometimes,
Which after hours gives leisure to repent.
If I did take the kingdom from your sons,
To make amends, I 'll give it to your daughter:
If I have kill'd the issue of your womb,
To quicken your increase, I will beget
Mine issue of your blood upon your daughter:
A grandam's name is little less in love
Than is the doting title of a mother;
They are as children but one step below,
Even of your mettle, of your very blood;
Of all one pain, save for a night of groans
Endur'd of her, for whom you bid like sorrow.
Your children were vexation to your youth,
But mine shall be a comfort to your age.
The loss you have is but a son being king,
And by that loss your daughter is made queen.
I cannot make you what amends I would,
Therefore accept such kindness as I can.
Dorset your son, that with a fearful soul
Leads discontented steps in foreign soil,
This fair alliance quickly shall call home
To high promotions and great dignity.
The King, that calls your beauteous daughter wife,
Familiarly shall call thy Dorset brother;
Again shall you be mother to a king,
And all the ruins of distressful times
Repair'd with double riches of content.
What! we have many goodly days to see.
The liquid drops of tears that you have shed
Shall come again, transform'd to orient pearl,
Advantaging their loan with interest
Of ten times double gain of happiness.
Go, then, my mother, to thy daughter go;
Make bold her bashful years with your experience;
Prepare her ears to hear a wooer's tale;
Put in her tender heart th' aspiring flame
Of golden sovereignty; acquaint the princess
With the sweet silent hours of marriage joys;
And when this arm of mine hath chastised
The petty rebel, dull-brain'd Buckingham,
Bound with triumphant garlands will I come
And lead thy daughter to a conqueror's bed;
To whom I will retail my conquest won.
And she shall be sole victress, Cæsar's Cæsar.
Q. Eliz. What were I best to say? Her father's brother
Would be her lord? Or shall I say, her uncle?
Or, he that slew her brothers and her uncles?
Under what title shall I woo for thee,
That God, the law, my honour, and her love,
Can make seem pleasing to her tender years?
Rich. Infer fair England's peace by this alliance.
Q. Eliz. Which she shall purchase with still lasting war.

258. from, the queen repeats the word in the sense of *apart from.* **274. Therefore,** i.e., for her weeping. **283. conveyance,** removal.

302. mettle, substance. **304. bid,** endured (pret. of *bide*). **307. son being king,** i.e., Edward V. **323. Advantaging,** increasing. **343. Infer,** offer, allege.

Rich. Tell her the King, that may command, entreats.
Q. Eliz. That at her hands which the King's King forbids.
Rich. Say she shall be a high and mighty queen.
Q. Eliz. To wail the title, as her mother doth.
Rich. Say, I will love her everlastingly.
Q. Eliz. But how long shall that title "ever" last?
Rich. Sweetly in force unto her fair life's end.
Q. Eliz. But how long fairly shall her sweet life last?
Rich. As long as heaven and nature lengthens it.
Q. Eliz. As long as hell and Richard likes of it.
Rich. Say, I, her sovereign, am her subject low.
Q. Eliz. But she, your subject, loathes such sovereignty.
Rich. Be eloquent in my behalf to her.
Q. Eliz. An honest tale speeds best being plainly told.
Rich. Then plainly to her tell my loving tale.
Q. Eliz. Plain and not honest is too harsh a style.
Rich. Your reasons are too shallow and too quick.
Q. Eliz. O no, my reasons are too deep and dead;
Too deep and dead, poor infants, in their graves.
Rich. Harp not on that string, madam; that is past.
Q. Eliz. Harp on it still shall I till heart-strings break.
Rich. Now, by my George, my Garter, and my crown,—
Q. Eliz. Profan'd, dishonour'd, and the third usurp'd.
Rich. I swear—
Q. Eliz. By nothing; for this is no oath.
Thy George, profan'd, hath lost his lordly honour;
Thy Garter, blemish'd, pawn'd his knightly virtue;
Thy crown, usurp'd, disgrac'd his kingly glory.
If something thou wouldst swear to be believ'd
Swear then by something that thou hast not wrong'd.
Rich. Now, by the world—
Q. Eliz. 'T is full of thy foul wrongs.
Rich. My father's death—
Q. Eliz. Thy life hath it dishonour'd.
Rich. Then, by myself—
Q. Eliz. Thyself thyself misusest.
Rich. Why then, by God—
Q. Eliz. God's wrong is most of all.
If thou did'st fear to break an oath with Him,
The unity the King my husband made
Thou hadst not broken, nor my brothers died.
If thou hadst fear'd to break an oath by Him,
Th' imperial metal, circling now thy head,
Had grac'd the tender temples of my child,
And both the Princes had been breathing here,
Which now, two tender bedfellows for dust,
Thy broken faith hath made the prey for worms.
What canst thou swear by now?
Rich. The time to come.
Q. Eliz. That thou hast wronged in the time o'erpast;
For I myself have many tears to wash
Hereafter time, for time past wrong'd by thee.
The children live, whose fathers thou hast slaughter'd,
Ungovern'd youth, to wail it with their age;
The parents live, whose children thou hast butcher'd,
Old barren plants, to wail it with their age.
Swear not by time to come; for that thou hast
Misus'd ere us'd, by times ill-us'd o'erpast.
Rich. As I intend to prosper and repent,
So thrive I in my dangerous affairs
Of hostile arms; myself myself confound;
Heaven and fortune bar me happy hours;
Day, yield me not thy light, nor, night, thy rest;
Be opposite all planets of good luck
To my proceeding, if, with dear heart's love,
Immaculate devotion, holy thoughts,
I tender not thy beauteous princely daughter!
In her consists my happiness and thine;
Without her, follows to myself and thee,
Herself, the land, and many a Christian soul,
Death, desolation, ruin, and decay.
It cannot be avoided but by this;
It will not be avoided but by this.
Therefore, dear mother,—I must call you so—
Be the attorney of my love to her.
Plead what I will be, not what I have been;
Not my deserts, but what I will deserve.
Urge the necessity and state of times,
And be not peevish-fond in great designs.
Q. Eliz. Shall I be tempted of the devil thus?
Rich. Ay, if the devil tempt you to do good.

361. **quick,** hasty (in contrast with *dead* of the following line). 366. **my George,** a pendant figure of St. George and the dragon attached to the collar of the Garter insignia.

379. **unity,** the peace made before Edward's death. See II, i. 390. **Hereafter time,** in the future. 399. **confound,** destroy. 405. **tender,** regard with tenderness.

Q. Eliz. Shall I forget myself to be myself?
Rich. Ay, if yourself's remembrance wrong yourself.
Q. Eliz. Yet thou didst kill my children.
Rich. But in your daughter's womb I bury them;
Where in that nest of spicery they will breed
Selves of themselves, to your recomforture.
Q. Eliz. Shall I go win my daughter to thy will?
Rich. And be a happy mother by the deed.
Q. Eliz. I go. Write to me very shortly,
And you shall understand from me her mind.
Rich. Bear her my true love's kiss; and so, farewell. *Exit Queen Elizabeth.*
Relenting fool, and shallow changing woman!

Enter *Ratcliff, Catesby* following.

How now! what news?
Rat. Most mighty sovereign, on the western coast
Rideth a puissant navy; to our shores
Throng many doubtful hollow-hearted friends,
Unarm'd, and unresolv'd to beat them back.
'T is thought that Richmond is their admiral;
And there they hull, expecting but the aid
Of Buckingham to welcome them ashore.
Rich. Some light-foot friend post to the Duke of Norfolk;
Ratcliff, thyself, or Catesby; where is he?
Cate. Here, my good lord.
Rich. Catesby, fly to the Duke.
Cate. I will, my lord, with all convenient haste.
Rich. Ratcliff, come hither. Post to Salisbury.
When thou com'st thither,—[*To Catesby.*] Dull unmindful villain,
Why stay'st thou here, and go'st not to the Duke?
Cate. First, mighty liege, tell me your Highness' pleasure,
What from your Grace I shall deliver to him.
Rich. O, true, good Catesby. Bid him levy straight
The greatest strength and power that he can make,
And meet me suddenly at Salisbury.
Cate. I go. *Exit.*
Rat. What, may it please you, shall I do at Salisbury?
Rich. Why, what wouldst thou do there before I go?
Rat. Your Highness told me I should post before.
Rich. My mind is chang'd.

Enter *Lord Stanley.*

Stanley, what news with you?
Stan. None good, my liege, to please you with the hearing;
Nor none so bad, but may well be reported.
Rich. Hoyday, a riddle! neither good nor bad!
What need'st thou run so many miles about
When thou mayst tell thy tale the nearest way?
Once more, what news?
Stan. Richmond is on the seas.
Rich. There let him sink, and be the seas on him!
White-liver'd runagate, what doth he there?
Stan. I know not, mighty sovereign, but by guess.
Rich. Well, as you guess?
Stan. Stirr'd up by Dorset, Buckingham, and Morton,
He makes for England, here to claim the crown.
Rich. Is the chair empty? Is the sword unsway'd?
Is the King dead? the empire unpossess'd?
What heir of York is there alive but we?
And who is England's king but great York's heir?
Then, tell me, what makes he upon the seas?
Stan. Unless for that, my liege, I cannot guess.
Rich. Unless for that he comes to be your liege,
You cannot guess wherefore the Welshman comes.
Thou wilt revolt, and fly to him, I fear.
Stan. No, my good lord, therefore mistrust me not.
Rich. Where is thy power, then, to beat him back?
Where be thy tenants and thy followers?
Are they not now upon the western shore,
Safe-conducting the rebels from their ships?
Stan. No, my good lord, my friends are in the north.
Rich. Cold friends to me! What do they in the north,
When they should serve their sovereign in the west?
Stan. They have not been commanded, mighty King.
Pleaseth your Majesty to give me leave,
I 'll muster up my friends, and meet your Grace
Where and what time your Majesty shall please.

420. Shall I forget myself as being what I am, i.e., a deeply wronged woman. **424. nest of spicery,** the phoenix was consumed in its nest of spices and arose rejuvenated. **438. hull,** float.

465. runagate, renegade. **472. York,** Richard, Duke of York. **477. Welshman,** Richmond was grandson of Owen Tudor, a Welshman who had married the widow of Henry V.

Rich. Ay, ay, thou wouldst be gone to join with Richmond;
But I 'll not trust thee.
Stan. Most mighty sovereign,
You have no cause to hold my friendship doubtful.
I never was nor never will be false.
Rich. Go, then, and muster men; but leave behind
Your son, George Stanley: look your heart be firm,
Or else his head's assurance is but frail.
Stan. So deal with him as I prove true to you. *Exit.*

Enter a *Messenger.*

First Mess. My gracious sovereign, now in Devonshire,
As I by friends am well advertised,
Sir Edward Courtney, and the haughty prelate
Bishop of Exeter, his elder brother,
With many moe confederates, are in arms.

Enter another *Messenger.*

Second Mess. In Kent, my liege, the Guildfords are in arms;
And every hour more competitors
Flock to the rebels, and their power grows strong.

Enter another *Messenger.*

Third Mess. My lord, the army of great Buckingham—
Rich. Out on ye, owls! nothing but songs of death? *He striketh him.*
There, take thou that, till thou bring better news.
Third Mess. The news I have to tell your Majesty
Is that by sudden floods and fall of waters,
Buckingham's army is dispers'd and scatter'd;
And he himself wander'd away alone,
No man knows whither.
Rich. I cry thee mercy;
There is my purse to cure that blow of thine.
Hath any well-advised friend proclaim'd
Reward to him that brings the traitor in?
Third Mess. Such proclamation hath been made, my lord.

Enter another *Messenger.*

Fourth Mess. Sir Thomas Lovel and Lord Marquis Dorset,
'T is said, my liege, in Yorkshire are in arms.
But this good comfort bring I to your Highness,
The Breton navy is dispers'd by tempest.
Richmond, in Dorsetshire, sent out a boat
Unto the shore, to ask those on the banks
If they were his assistants, yea or no;
Who answer'd him, they came from Buckingham
Upon his party: he, mistrusting them,
Hois'd sail and made his course again for Brittany.
Rich. March on, march on, since we are up in arms;
If not to fight with foreign enemies,
Yet to beat down these rebels here at home.

Re-enter *Catesby.*

Cate. My liege, the Duke of Buckingham is taken;
That is the best news: that the Earl of Richmond
Is with a mighty power landed at Milford,
Is colder news, but yet they must be told.
Rich. Away towards Salisbury! While we reason here,
A royal battle might be won and lost.
Some one take order Buckingham be brought
To Salisbury; the rest march on with me.
Flourish. Exeunt.

Scene V. *Lord Derby's house.*

Enter *Derby* and *Sir Christopher Urswick.*

Der. Sir Christopher, tell Richmond this from me,
That in the sty of the most deadly boar
My son George Stanley is frank'd up in hold;
If I revolt, off goes young George's head.
The fear of that holds off my present aid.
So get thee gone; commend me to thy lord.
Withal say that the Queen hath heartily consented
He should espouse Elizabeth her daughter.
But, tell me, where is princely Richmond now?
Chris. At Pembroke, or at Ha'rford-west, in Wales.
Der. What men of name resort to him?

501. advertised, informed. **503. elder brother,** Peter Courtenay, Bishop of Exeter, was only distantly related to Sir Edward Courtenay. **505. Guildfords,** a Kentish family. **506. competitors,** associates. **509. owls,** considered a portent of death.

528. Upon his party, on his side. **529. Hois'd,** hoisted. **535. Milford,** Milford Haven in Wales. This successful landing really followed by two years the abortive attempt described in l. 522ff. and the capture of Buckingham. **Scene v: 3. frank'd up,** penned up. **10. Ha'rford-west,** Haverfordwest, near Milford Haven. **11. name,** rank.

Christ. Sir Walter Herbert, a renowned soldier;
Sir Gilbert Talbot, Sir William Stanley,
Oxford, redoubted Pembroke, Sir James Blunt,
And Rice ap Thomas, with a valiant crew,
And many other of great name and worth;
And towards London do they bend their power,
If by the way they be not fought withal.

Der. Well, hie thee to thy lord; I kiss his hand:
My letter will resolve him of my mind.
Farewell. *Exeunt.*

ACT V. Scene I. *Salisbury. An open place.*

Enter the *Sheriff,* and *Buckingham,* with halberds, led to execution.

Buck. Will not King Richard let me speak with him?

Sher. No, my good lord; therefore be patient.

Buck. Hastings, and Edward's children, Grey and Rivers,
Holy King Henry and thy fair son Edward,
Vaughan, and all that have miscarried
By underhand corrupted foul injustice,
If that your moody discontented souls
Do through the clouds behold this present hour,
Even for revenge mock my destruction!
This is All-Souls' day, fellow, is it not?

Sher. It is, my lord.

Buck. Why, then All-Souls' day is my body's doomsday:
This is the day which, in King Edward's time,
I wish'd might fall on me, when I was found
False to his children and his wife's allies;
This is the day wherein I wish'd to fall
By the false faith of him whom most I trusted;
This, this All-Souls' day to my fearful soul
Is the determin'd respite of my wrongs.
That high All-Seer, which I dallied with,
Hath turn'd my feigned prayer on my head
And given in earnest what I begg'd in jest;
Thus doth He force the swords of wicked men
To turn their own points in their masters' bosoms.
Now Margaret's curse falls heavy on my neck:
"When he," quoth she, "shall split thy heart with sorrow,
Remember Margaret was a prophetess."
Come, lead me, officers, to the block of shame;
Wrong hath but wrong, and blame the due of blame.

Exeunt Buckingham with Officers.

Scene II. *The camp near Tamworth.*

Enter *Richmond, Oxford, Blunt, Herbert,* and others, with drum and colours.

Richm. Fellows in arms, and my most loving friends,
Bruis'd underneath the yoke of tyranny,
Thus far into the bowels of the land
Have we march'd on without impediment;
And here receive we from our father Stanley
Lines of fair comfort and encouragement.
The wretched, bloody, and usurping boar,
That spoil'd your summer fields and fruitful vines,
Swills your warm blood like wash, and makes his trough
In your embowell'd bosoms, this foul swine
Is now even in the centre of this isle,
Near to the town of Leicester, as we learn.
From Tamworth thither is but one day's march.
In God's name, cheerly on, courageous friends,
To reap the harvest of perpetual peace
By this one bloody trial of sharp war.

Oxf. Every man's conscience is a thousand men,
To fight against this guilty homicide.

Herb. I doubt not but his friends will turn to us.

Blunt. He hath no friends but what are friends for fear,
Which in his dearest need will fly from him.

Richm. All for our vantage. Then, in God's name, march!

13. **Talbot,** uncle to the Earl of Shrewsbury. **Sir William Stanley,** brother of Thomas, Lord Stanley. 14. **Pembroke,** Jasper Tudor, Earl of Pembroke, Richmond's uncle. 15. **Rice ap Thomas,** a Welsh knight. **Act V, Scene i:** 5. **miscarried,** perished. 10. **All-Souls' day,** Nov. 2. Significant here because of its being a special occasion for communicating with the dead. 19. **respite,** term, limit. **wrongs,** sinning. 26f. cf. I, iii, 300-1.

20. **resolve,** inform. **Act V, Scene ii:** 9. **wash,** swill. 10. **embowell'd,** disembowelled. 17. **conscience,** consciousness of right.

True hope is swift, and flies with swallow's wings;
Kings it makes gods, and meaner creatures kings. *Exeunt.*

Scene III. *Bosworth Field.*

Enter *King Richard,* in arms, with *Norfolk,* the *Earl of Surrey, Ratcliff* and others.

Rich. Here pitch our tent, even here in Bosworth field.
My Lord of Surrey, why look you so sad?

Sur. My heart is ten times lighter than my looks.

Rich. My Lord of Norfolk,—

Nor. Here, most gracious liege.

Rich. Norfolk, we must have knocks; ha! must we not?

Nor. We must both give and take, my loving lord.

Rich. Up with my tent! Here will I lie to-night;
But where to-morrow? Well, all 's one for that.
Who hath descried the number of the traitors?

Nor. Six or seven thousand is their utmost power.

Rich. Why, our battalia trebles that account;
Besides, the King's name is a tower of strength,
Which they upon the adverse faction want.
Up with the tent! Come, noble gentlemen,
Let us survey the vantage of the ground.
Call for some men of sound direction;
Let 's lack no discipline, make no delay;
For, lords, to-morrow is a busy day. *Exeunt.*

Enter *Richmond, Sir William Brandon, Oxford, Dorset, Blunt,* and others. Some of the Soldiers pitch Richmond's tent.

Richm. The weary sun hath made a golden set,
And, by the bright track of his fiery car,
Gives token of a goodly day to-morrow.
Sir William Brandon, you shall bear my standard.
Give me some ink and paper in my tent;
I 'll draw the form and model of our battle,
Limit each leader to his several charge,
And part in just proportion our small power.
My Lord of Oxford, you, Sir William Brandon,
And you, Sir Walter Herbert, stay with me.
The Earl of Pembroke keeps his regiment;
Good Captain Blunt, bear my good-night to him,
And by the second hour in the morning
Desire the Earl to see me in my tent:
Yet one thing more, good captain, do for me:
Where is Lord Stanley quarter'd, do you know?

Blunt. Unless I have mista'en his colours much,
Which well I am assur'd I have not done,
His regiment lies half a mile at least
South from the mighty power of the King.

Richm. If without peril it be possible,
Sweet Blunt, make some good means to speak with him,
And give him from me this most needful note.

Blunt. Upon my life, my lord, I 'll undertake it;
And so, God give you quiet rest to-night!

Richm. Good-night, good Captain Blunt.
Come, gentlemen, *Exit Blunt.*
Let us consult upon to-morrow's business:
Into my tent; the dew is raw and cold.
They withdraw into the tent.

Enter to his tent *King Richard, Norfolk, Ratcliff, Catesby* and others.

Rich. What is 't o'clock?

Cate. It 's supper-time, my lord;
It 's nine o'clock.

Rich. I will not sup to-night.
Give me some ink and paper.
What, is my beaver easier than it was,
And all my armour laid into my tent?

Cate. It is, my liege; and all things are in readiness.

Rich. Good Norfolk, hie thee to thy charge;
Use careful watch, choose trusty sentinels.

Nor. I go, my lord.

Rich. Stir with the lark to-morrow, gentle Norfolk.

Nor. I warrant you, my lord. *Exit.*

Rich. Catesby!

Cate. My lord?

Rich. Send out a pursuivant at arms
To Stanley's regiment; bid him bring his power
Before sunrising, lest his son George fall
Into the blind cave of eternal night.
Exit Catesby.
Fill me a bowl of wine. Give me a watch.
Saddle white Surrey for the field to-morrow.
Look that my staves be sound, and not too heavy.
Ratcliff!

Scene iii: 11. battalia, army. **16. direction,** judgment in military matters. **29. keeps,** remains with.

50. beaver, helmet. **59. pursuivant at arms,** assistant to a herald. **63. watch,** watch-light. **65. staves,** shafts of lances.

Rat. My lord?
Rich. Saw'st the melancholy Lord Northumberland?
Rat. Thomas the Earl of Surrey, and himself,
Much about cock-shut time, from troop to troop
Went through the army, cheering up the soldiers.
Rich. So, I am satisfied. Give me a bowl of wine:
I have not that alacrity of spirit,
Nor cheer of mind, that I was wont to have.
Set it down. Is ink and paper ready?
Rat. It is, my lord.
Rich. Bid my guard watch; leave me.
Ratcliff, about the mid of night come to my tent
And help to arm me. Leave me, I say.
Exeunt Ratcliff and the other Attendants. Richard sleeps.

Enter *Derby* to *Richmond* in his tent. Lords and others attending.

Der. Fortune and victory sit on thy helm!
Richm. All comfort that the dark night can afford
Be to thy person, noble father-in-law!
Tell me, how fares our loving mother?
Der. I, by attorney, bless thee from thy mother,
Who prays continually for Richmond's good:
So much for that. The silent hours steal on,
And flaky darkness breaks within the east.
In brief,—for so the season bids us be,—
Prepare thy battle early in the morning,
And put thy fortune to the arbitrement
Of bloody strokes and mortal-staring war.
I, as I may—that which I would I cannot,—
With best advantage will deceive the time,
And aid thee in this doubtful shock of arms;
But on thy side I may not be too forward,
Lest, being seen, thy brother, tender George,
Be executed in his father's sight.
Farewell! The leisure and the fearful time
Cuts off the ceremonious vows of love
And ample interchange of sweet discourse,
Which so long sunder'd friends should dwell upon.
God give us leisure for these rites of love!
Once more, adieu! Be valiant, and speed well!
Richm. Good lords, conduct him to his regiment:
I 'll strive with troubled thoughts, to take a nap,
Lest leaden slumber peise me down to-morrow,
When I should mount with wings of victory.
Once more, good night, kind lords and gentlemen. *Exeunt all but Richmond.*
O Thou, whose captain I account myself,
Look on my forces with a gracious eye!
Put in their hands thy bruising irons of wrath,
That they may crush down with a heavy fall
Th' usurping helmets of our adversaries!
Make us thy ministers of chastisement
That we may praise Thee in the victory!
To Thee I do commend my watchful soul
Ere I let fall the windows of mine eyes.
Sleeping and waking, O, defend me still!
Sleeps.

Enter the *Ghost of Prince Edward,* son to Henry the Sixth.

Ghost. [*To Richard.*] Let me sit heavy on thy soul to-morrow!
Think, how thou stabb'dst me in my prime of youth
At Tewksbury: despair, therefore, and die!
[*To Richmond.*] Be cheerful, Richmond; for the wronged souls
Of butcher'd princes fight in thy behalf:
King Henry's issue, Richmond, comforts thee.

Enter the *Ghost of Henry the Sixth.*

Ghost. [*To Richard.*] When I was mortal, my anointed body
By thee was punched full of deadly holes.
Think on the Tower and me: despair, and die!
Harry the Sixth bids thee despair and die.
[*To Richmond.*] Virtuous and holy, be thou conqueror!
Harry, that prophesied thou shouldst be king,
Doth comfort thee in sleep: live, and flourish!

Enter the *Ghost of Clarence.*

Ghost. [*To Richard.*] Let me sit heavy in thy soul to-morrow!
I, that was wash'd to death with fulsome wine,
Poor Clarence, by thy guile betray'd to death!
To-morrow in the battle think on me,
And fall thy edgeless sword: despair, and die!
[*To Richmond.*] Thou offspring of the house of Lancaster,
The wronged heirs of York do pray for thee:
Good angels guard thy battle! Live, and flourish!

Enter the *Ghosts of Rivers, Grey,* and *Vaughan.*

Ghost of R. [*To Richard.*] Let me sit heavy in thy soul to-morrow,

70. cock-shut time, sun-down—when poultry go to roost. **81. father-in-law,** i.e., step-father. **86. flaky,** streaked with light. **88. battle,** army in battle array. **89. arbitrement,** decision. **90. mortal-staring,** dealing death with a glance. **97. leisure,** i.e., lack of leisure.

105. peise, weigh. **132. wash'd to death,** drowned (in a butt of malmsey). **fulsome,** cloying. **135. fall,** let fall.

Rivers, that died at Pomfret! Despair, and die!
Ghost of G. [*To Richard.*] Think upon Grey, and let thy soul despair!
Ghost of V. [*To Richard.*] Think upon Vaughan, and with guilty fear
Let fall thy lance: despair, and die!
All. [*To Richmond.*] Awake, and think our wrongs in Richard's bosom
Will conquer him! Awake, and win the day!

Enter the *Ghost of Hastings.*

Ghost. [*To Richard.*] Bloody and guilty, guiltily awake,
And in a bloody battle end thy days!
Think on Lord Hastings: despair, and die!
[*To Richmond.*] Quiet untroubled soul, awake, awake!
Arm, fight, and conquer, for fair England's sake!

Enter the *Ghosts of the two young Princes.*

Ghosts. [*To Richard.*] Dream on thy cousins smothered in the Tower:
Let us be lead within thy bosom, Richard,
And weigh thee down to ruin, shame, and death!
Thy nephews' souls bid thee despair and die!
[*To Richmond.*] Sleep, Richmond, sleep in peace, and wake in joy;
Good angels guard thee from the boar's annoy!
Live, and beget a happy race of kings!
Edward's unhappy sons do bid thee flourish.

Enter the *Ghost of Anne,* his wife.

Ghost. [*To Richard.*] Richard, thy wife, that wretched Anne thy wife,
That never slept a quiet hour with thee,
Now fills thy sleep with perturbations:
To-morrow in the battle think on me,
And fall thy edgeless sword: despair, and die!
[*To Richmond.*] Thou quiet soul, sleep thou a quiet sleep;
Dream of success and happy victory!
Thy adversary's wife doth pray for thee.

Enter the *Ghost of Buckingham.*

Ghost. [*To Richard.*] The first was I that help'd thee to the crown;
The last was I that felt thy tyranny.
O, in the battle think on Buckingham,
And die in terror of thy guiltiness!
Dream on, dream on, of bloody deeds and death;
Fainting, despair; despairing, yield thy breath!
[*To Richmond.*] I died for hope ere I could lend thee aid;
But cheer thy heart, and be thou not dismay'd.
God and good angels fight on Richmond's side,
And Richard fall in height of all his pride!

The Ghosts vanish. Richard starts out of his dream.

Rich. Give me another horse! Bind up my wounds!
Have mercy, Jesu!—Soft! I did but dream.
O coward conscience, how dost thou afflict me!
The lights burn blue. It is now dead midnight.
Cold fearful drops stand on my trembling flesh.
What! do I fear myself? There 's none else by.
Richard loves Richard; that is, I am I.
Is there a murderer here? No. Yes, I am.
Then fly. What, from myself? Great reason why,
Lest I revenge. What, myself upon myself?
Alack, I love myself. Wherefore? For any good
That I myself have done unto myself?
O, no! alas, I rather hate myself
For hateful deeds committed by myself!
I am a villain: yet I lie, I am not.
Fool, of thyself speak well; fool, do not flatter.
My conscience hath a thousand several tongues,
And every tongue brings in a several tale,
And every tale condemns me for a villain.
Perjury, perjury, in the high'st degree;
Murder, stern murder, in the dir'st degree;
All several sins, all us'd in each degree,
Throng to the bar, crying all, Guilty! guilty!
I shall despair. There is no creature loves me;
And if I die, no soul shall pity me.
Nay, wherefore should they, since that I myself
Find in myself no pity to myself?
Methought the souls of all that I had murder'd
Came to my tent; and every one did threat
To-morrow's vengeance on the head of Richard.

Enter *Ratcliff.*

Rat. My lord!
Rich. 'Zounds! who is there?
Rat. Ratcliff, my lord; 't is I. The early village-cock
Hath twice done salutation to the morn;
Your friends are up, and buckle on their armour.
Rich. O Ratcliff, I have dream'd a fearful dream!

156. **boar's annoy,** i.e., Richard's assault.

173. **for hope,** in hope (of aiding you). 180. **blue,** betokened the presence of ghosts or devils. 193. **several,** separate, different. 198. **us'd,** committed.

What thinkest thou, will our friends prove all true?
Rat. No doubt, my lord.
Rich. O Ratcliff, I fear, I fear,—
Rat. Nay, good my lord, be not afraid of shadows.
Rich. By the apostle Paul, shadows to-night
Have struck more terror to the soul of Richard
Than can the substance of ten thousand soldiers
Armed in proof, and led by shallow Richmond.
It is not yet near day. Come, go with me;
Under our tents I 'll play the eaves-dropper,
To hear if any mean to shrink from me.
Exeunt.

Enter the *Lords* to *Richmond*, sitting in his tent.

Lords. Good morrow, Richmond!
Richm. Cry mercy, lords and watchful gentlemen,
That you have ta'en a tardy sluggard here.
Lords. How have you slept, my lord?
Richm. The sweetest sleep and fairest-boding dreams
That ever enter'd in a drowsy head
Have I since your departure had, my lords.
Methought their souls, whose bodies Richard murder'd,
Came to my tent, and cried on victory:
I promise you, my heart is very jocund
In the remembrance of so fair a dream.
How far into the morning is it, lords?
Lords. Upon the stroke of four.
Richm. Why, then 't is time to arm and give direction.
His oration to his soldiers.
More than I have said, loving countrymen,
The leisure and enforcement of the time
Forbids to dwell upon; yet remember this,
God and our good cause fight upon our side;
The prayers of holy saints and wronged souls,
Like high-rear'd bulwarks, stand before our faces.
Richard except, those whom we fight against
Had rather have us win than him they follow.
For what is he they follow? Truly, gentlemen,
A bloody tyrant and a homicide;
One rais'd in blood, and one in blood establish'd;
One that made means to come by what he hath,
And slaughter'd those that were the means to help him;
A base foul stone, made precious by the foil
Of England's chair, where he is falsely set;
One that hath ever been God's enemy.
Then, if you fight against God's enemy,
God will in justice ward you as his soldiers;
If you do sweat to put a tyrant down,
You sleep in peace, the tyrant being slain;
If you do fight against your country's foes,
Your country's fat shall pay your pains the hire;
If you do fight in safeguard of your wives,
Your wives shall welcome home the conquerors;
If you do free your children from the sword,
Your children's children quits it in your age.
Then, in the name of God and all these rights,
Advance your standards, draw your willing swords.
For me, the ransom of my bold attempt
Shall be this cold corpse on the earth's cold face;
But if I thrive, the gain of my attempt
The least of you shall share his part thereof.
Sound drums and trumpets boldly and cheerfully;
God and Saint George! Richmond and victory! *Exeunt.*

Re-enter *King Richard, Ratcliff, Catesby,* Attendants and Forces.

Rich. What said Northumberland as touching Richmond?
Rat. That he was never trained up in arms.
Rich. He said the truth; and what said Surrey then?
Rat. He smil'd and said, "The better for our purpose."
Rich. He was in the right; and so indeed it is. *Clock strikes.*
Tell the clock there. Give me a calendar.
Who saw the sun to-day?
Rat. Not I, my lord.
Rich. Then he disdains to shine, for by the book
He should have brav'd the east an hour ago.
A black day will it be to somebody.
Ratcliff!
Rat. My lord?
Rich. The sun will not be seen to-day;
The sky doth frown and lour upon our army.
I would these dewy tears were from the ground.
Not shine to-day! Why, what is that to me
More than to Richmond? for the self-same heaven
That frowns on me looks sadly upon him.

219. proof, tested armor. **231. cried on,** cried, named. **250. foil,** a metal setting for a jewel.

254. ward, protect. **258. fat,** wealth. **262. quits,** requite, repay. **265. ransom,** the price of failure. **276. Tell,** count. **278. book,** i.e., calendar. **279. brav'd,** made brave or glorious.

Enter *Norfolk*.

Nor. Arm, arm, my lord; the foe vaunts in the field.
Rich. Come, bustle, bustle; caparison my horse.
Call up Lord Stanley, bid him bring his power.
I will lead forth my soldiers to the plain,
And thus my battle shall be ordered:
My foreward shall be drawn out all in length,
Consisting equally of horse and foot;
Our archers shall be placed in the midst;
John Duke of Norfolk, Thomas Earl of Surrey,
Shall have the leading of this foot and horse.
They thus directed, we will follow
In the main battle, whose puissance on either side
Shall be well winged with our chiefest horse.
This, and Saint George to boot! What think'st thou, Norfolk?
Nor. A good direction, warlike sovereign.
This found I on my tent this morning.
He sheweth him a paper.
Rich. [*Reads*.]

"Jockey of Norfolk, be not so bold,
For Dickon thy master is bought and sold."

A thing devised by the enemy.
Go, gentlemen, every man to his charge.
Let not our babbling dreams affright our souls,
For conscience is a word that cowards use,
Devis'd at first to keep the strong in awe;
Our strong arms be our conscience, swords our law:
March on, join bravely, let us to 't pell-mell;
If not to heaven, then hand in hand to hell.

His oration to his Army.

What shall I say more than I have inferr'd?
Remember whom you are to cope withal;
A sort of vagabonds, rascals, and runaways,
A scum of Bretons, and base lackey peasants,
Whom their o'er-cloyed country vomits forth
To desperate ventures and assur'd destruction.
You sleeping safe, they bring you to unrest;
You having lands, and blest with beauteous wives,
They would restrain the one, distain the other.
And who doth lead them but a paltry fellow,
Long kept in Bretagne at our mother's cost?
A milk-sop, one that never in his life
Felt so much cold as over shoes in snow?
Let 's whip these stragglers o'er the seas again;
Lash hence these overweening rags of France,
These famish'd beggars, weary of their lives;
Who, but for dreaming on this fond exploit,
For want of means, poor rats, had hang'd themselves.
If we be conquered, let men conquer us,
And not these bastard Bretons; whom our fathers
Have in their own land beaten, bobb'd, and thump'd,
And on record, left them the heirs of shame.
Shall these enjoy our lands? lie with our wives?
Ravish our daughters? [*Drum afar off.*]
Hark! I hear their drum.
Fight, gentlemen of England! fight, bold yeomen!
Draw, archers, draw your arrows to the head!
Spur your proud horses hard, and ride in blood;
Amaze the welkin with your broken staves!

Enter a *Messenger*.

What says Lord Stanley? Will he bring his power?
Mess. My lord, he doth deny to come.
Rich. Off with his son George's head!
Nor. My lord, the enemy is past the marsh;
After the battle let George Stanley die.
Rich. A thousand hearts are great within my bosom.
Advance our standards, set upon our foes;
Our ancient word of courage, fair Saint George,
Inspire us with the spleen of fiery dragons!
Upon them! Victory sits on our helms.
Exeunt.

Scene IV. *Another part of the field.*

Alarum. Excursions. Enter *Norfolk* and forces; to him *Catesby*.

Cate. Rescue, my Lord of Norfolk, rescue, rescue!
The King enacts more wonders than a man,
Daring an opposite to every danger:
His horse is slain, and all on foot he fights,
Seeking for Richmond in the throat of death.
Rescue, fair lord, or else the day is lost!

Alarums. Enter *King Richard*.

Rich. A horse! a horse! my kingdom for a horse!

288. vaunts, exults. **293. foreward,** vanguard. **300. winged,** flanked. **304. Jockey,** Jack. **305. Dickon,** i.e., Richard. **312. join,** encounter the enemy. **314. inferr'd,** said, stated. **322. distain,** stain. **324. our mother's,** following his source Shakespeare falls into an error. Richmond was "kept" (supported) not by Richard's mother, but by his brother-in-law, Charles of Burgundy.

334. bobb'd, pommelled. **335. record,** history. **341. with . . . staves,** i.e., with the lances broken in the fight. **350. spleen,** wrath. **Scene iv: 3. opposite,** adversary.

Cate. Withdraw, my lord; I 'll help you to a horse.

Rich. Slave, I have set my life upon a cast,
And I will stand the hazard of the die.
I think there be six Richmonds in the field;
Five have I slain to-day instead of him.
A horse! a horse! my kingdom for a horse!

Exeunt.

Scene V. *Another part of the field.*

Alarum. Enter *Richard* and *Richmond;* they fight; *Richard* is slain. Retreat and flourish. Re-enter *Richmond, Derby,* bearing the crown, with divers other Lords.

Richm. God and your arms be prais'd, victorious friends;
The day is ours, the bloody dog is dead.

Der. Courageous Richmond, well hast thou acquit thee.
Lo, here this long-usurped royalty
From the dead temples of this bloody wretch
Have I pluck'd off, to grace thy brows withal.
Wear it, enjoy it, and make much of it.

Richm. Great God of heaven, say amen to all!
But, tell me, is young George Stanley living?

Der. He is, my lord, and safe in Leicester town;
Whither, if it please you, we may now withdraw us.

Richm. What men of name are slain on either side?

Der. John Duke of Norfolk, Walter Lord Ferrers,
Sir Robert Brakenbury, and Sir William Brandon.

Richm. Inter their bodies as become their births:
Proclaim a pardon to the soldiers fled
That in submission will return to us;
And then, as we have ta'en the sacrament,
We will unite the white rose and the red.
Smile heaven upon this fair conjunction,
That long have frown'd upon their enmity!
What traitor hears me, and says not amen?
England hath long been mad, and scarr'd herself;
The brother blindly shed the brother's blood,
The father rashly slaughtered his own son,
The son, compell'd, been butcher to the sire:
All this divided York and Lancaster,
Divided in their dire division,
O, now, let Richmond and Elizabeth,
The true succeeders of each royal house,
By God's fair ordinance conjoin together!
And let their heirs, God, if thy will be so,
Enrich the time to come with smooth-fac'd Peace,
With smiling Plenty and fair prosperous days!
Abate the edge of traitors, gracious Lord,
That would reduce these bloody days again,
And make poor England weep in streams of blood!
Let them not live to taste this land's increase
That would with treason wound this fair land's peace!
Now civil wounds are stopp'd, Peace lives again;
That she may long live here, God say amen!

Exeunt.

10. hazard of the die, turn of the die.

Scene v: 18. as . . . sacrament, as we have sworn upon the sacrament to do. 35. Abate the edge, blunt the swords. 36. reduce, bring back.

The Tragedy of Richard the Second

The play of *Richard II* possesses a special interest for the student of Shakespeare's development as a poet and dramatist, since it represents his first really independent effort in the field of historic tragedy. It cannot be said that the result is altogether satisfactory. Yet the very faults of *Richard II* reveal more to us of Shakespeare's personality and genius than the successful accomplishment of a school-piece like *Richard III*; and a study of the play shows even more clearly the drift of Shakespeare's genius toward the creation of a new tragedy, the tragedy of character foredoomed to ruin which was to reach its climax in *Hamlet, Othello, Lear,* and *Macbeth.*

Text.—Richard II was entered in the Stationers' Register by Andrew Wise on August 29, 1597, and published in the same year with the following title-page:

> The Tragedie of King Richard the second. As it hath been publikely acted by the right Honourable the Lord Chamberlain his Servants. London Printed by Valentine Simmes for Andrew Wise, and are to be sold in his shop in Paules Churchyard at the signe of the Angell. 1597.

The play was so successful that two more editions were called for at once. The Second Quarto appeared in 1598. It was set up from the First Quarto and was so full of errors that a fresh printing was needed; a Third Quarto correcting many of these also came out in 1598. This edition, like its predecessor, put the name of the author, William Shake-speare, on the title-page. All three are deficient in one rather remarkable respect; they lack the famous deposition scene. That this omission was due to state censorship there can be no doubt whatever. For some reason or other there was a tendency in the last decade of the sixteenth century to draw an analogy between the reign of Richard II and that of Elizabeth, and it was not till after the death of Elizabeth that it was allowed to appear in print. This was in the Fourth Quarto, 1608, where a special title-page called attention to this "new addition." A Fifth Quarto appeared in 1615 and the Sixth and last in 1634. The First Quarto is a good text and may well have been printed from Shakespeare's manuscript. The Folio gives a better version of the deposition scene that any preceding edition, but shows the hand of an editor in its general substitution of "heaven" for the name of "God" in accordance with the law of 1606, and in a number of minor alterations including the omission of some fifty lines. In the main the text of the present edition follows that of the First Quarto.

Date.—There is a consensus of opinion in placing the composition of *Richard II* in or about the year 1595. It is certainly later than *Richard III*—ca. 1594, and as certainly earlier than the two *Henry IV* plays, usually dated ca. 1597. It belongs in fact to a group of plays, *Midsummer Night's Dream* and *Romeo and Juliet,* which follow immediately upon Shakespeare's composition of *Venus and Adonis* and *Lucrece.* This group, like the poems, is marked by an unrestrained flow of lyric verse, as different from the rather stiff rhetorical declamation of his first plays as from the more strictly dramatic poetry of his later work.

Source.—The main source for *Richard II* is, of course, Shakespeare's favorite book, Holinshed's *Chronicles.* A few details in which he departs from his source may have been picked up from other books or invented for dramatic purposes. Among these are the age of the Queen and her devotion to Richard. Hotspur, who is introduced as a boy, was actually older than Bolingbroke, and Prince Hal, described as a dissolute youth, was only about twelve years old. Shakespeare seems already to have had in mind the conflict between these two which he was to work out in *I King Henry IV*. With the time relation of events Shakespeare takes very considerable liberty. Bolingbroke's return to England follows impossibly close upon the death of his father; and the deposition scene combines in one sequence Holinshed's account of three separate sessions of Parliament. It is plain that Shakespeare allowed himself this license in order to secure dramatic effect; after all, he was writing a play, not history.

Characterization.—Certainly Shakespeare's treatment of his theme represents a distinct departure from the technique of the popular chronicle play. Instead of beginning at the beginning of a reign and carrying on till the close, Shakespeare begins with events that immediately precede and in fact bring about the downfall of the King, and he employs all his art as a dramatist to show that this downfall was due not to external causes, but solely and directly to the character of the King himself. In other words, Shakespeare is writing an historical tragedy rather than the conventional chronicle play.

Of the various monarchs whose reigns Shakespeare had up to this time dramatized, Richard II alone was a true-born king with undisputed title to the throne. It is not flattering courtiers only who proclaim the odor of sanctity about his throne; the patriot John of Gaunt calls Richard "God's substitute," "his deputy anointed in his sight"; and the pious bishop of Carlisle styles Richard "the figure of God's majesty." It is little wonder that in such an atmosphere a youthful monarch should entertain the most exalted conception of Divine Right; and in fact it is Richard who utters the lines that embody the most complete statement of the creed of Legitimists of all ages:

Not all the water in the rough rude sea
Can wash the balm off from an anointed King;
The breath of worldly men cannot depose
The deputy elected by the Lord.

From such a conception the step to absolutism in action is short enough. There is nothing cruel or essentially tyrannical in his nature, but he does not dream of any check or limit to his will, and in every emergency he follows the easiest way to put this will in action. Thus it is plain that before the play opens he has had his turbulent uncle Gloucester quietly murdered in prison instead of bringing him to open trial. This impatient overstepping of the limits was in the end to cost Richard his throne and his life, and it is characteristic of his inability to grasp realities that he never shows consciousness of any connection between this deed and his own downfall.

Richard's action in another important matter was no less likely—one cannot say calculated—to alienate the affection of his subjects. Having squandered the ordinary revenues of the realm with "too great a court and liberal largess," he confronts an empty treasury when ready money is urgently required for his Irish war. The first expedient that comes to his mind is to "farm the royal realm," that is, to pledge the future revenues for an immediate cash payment; the second is to issue blank charters by which forced loans could be levied on his subjects. Both devices were utterly repugnant to English law and custom, and though Shakespeare, one might fancy, was not greatly interested in the collection of taxes, what he thought of these devices is plain by the words he puts into the mouth of John of Gaunt:

This dear, dear land
Is now leas'd out, I die pronouncing it,
Like to a tenement or pelting farm.

One more fatal step Richard takes before he sails for Ireland. On Gaunt's death he calmly confiscates his entire property. Even the loyal-hearted York stands aghast at such an arbitrary act and protests with unaccustomed vigor.

Richard, however, is deaf to the well-meant warning: he actually appoints the ill-boding York regent of England and turning to his queen bids her be merry before they separate.

Here is enough, one would think, of selfishness, recklessness, and arbitrary action to forfeit a claim to anything but contempt from all spectators or readers of the play. Yet it is as impossible to hate Richard as to hate a beautiful spoiled child. He is a wilful, high-spirited, and thoughtless boy, too blinded by years of adulation to see in his high office anything but the unchecked opportunity of executing his own royal will.

For one thing there is not a grain of malice in Richard's disposition. He seems to entertain a not unnatural dislike for his ambitious and popular cousin Bolingbroke, but he treats him with scrupulous courtesy. He bursts, it is true, into a rage at the stern rebuke of the dying Gaunt and talks of the scaffold and the axe, but it is the short-lived passion of a child, suddenly and for the first time scolded by an old servant. And in addition to this absence of malice there is a positive personal charm about Richard that cannot but evoke a certain sympathy. To his adoring queen he is her "fair rose," a phrase echoed in a later play by one of the very men who had pushed him from his throne; Hotspur (*I King Henry IV*, I, iii, 75) calls him "that sweet lovely rose." The poor groom of the stable who appears in the last act is devoted to his royal master. The memory of his noble father clings to him like a mantle; and in his last desperate fight he shows his father's courage. In his private life the greatest vices that he is charged with are a readiness to listen to flattery, a taste for poetry, and a love of new fashions in dress (II, i, 17ff.)—certainly no very damnable catalogue of sins.

There is a possibility, incapable, of course, of demonstration, that in writing the role of Richard, Shakespeare was preparing a part for his own interpretation as an actor. There is contemporary evidence that Shakespeare played kingly roles and the part of Richard would have fitted him like a glove. Richard, as Shakespeare has drawn him, is at heart an actor with an actor's instinctive appreciation of a telling situation and an actor's ability to play his part in it. This ability is so marked in Richard that it has been noted by almost every critic of this play; but no critic seems to have noted the bearing of this fact upon the mutual relation of the character of Richard and that of the poet-actor who wrote this part. Shakespeare must have felt, like every true actor, the peculiar joy that comes from seizing and transmitting the emotional thrill of a dramatic crisis.

Of all Shakespeare's characters none shows this delight so visibly as Richard II. We see him in the first scene playing with real gusto the role of benevolent pacificator. When this role is exhausted he takes up at Coventry that of the stern executor of justice upon stiff-necked and rebellious barons. There is not a word in either scene that shows Richard's awareness of the realities of the situation, and there is not a line that does not reveal his satisfaction in the part he is playing therein. Yet Richard's early efforts pale compared with his performance as the story develops and the emotional crises thicken. It is in the deposition scene that Richard rises to the height of his powers as an actor. He has a great situation and a splendid audience and he improves both to the uttermost. He compares himself to the betrayed Savior—a curious anticipation of the cult of King Charles the Martyr; with a fine gesture he puts the crown into his cousin's hands, and with an appeal for a sympathetic hearing—"Now mark me"—proceeds to strip himself of all the attributes of kingship:

> I give this heavy weight from off my head,
> And this unwieldy sceptre from my hand,
> The pride of kingly sway from out my heart.
> With mine own tears I wash away my balm,
> With mine own hands I give away my crown,
> With mine own tongue deny my sacred state.

The speech seems to have been carefully prepared; it is plain that Richard thoroughly enjoys his superb delivery, and he closes the scene with a bit of "business," the breaking of a mirror, as theatrically effective as it is unreal and unkingly.

Shakespeare's Richard, however, is something more than an actor; he is a poet of exquisite sensibility, lively fancy, and an almost too fluent facility of expression. This play is distinguished above all Shakespeare's historical tragedies by the rich abundance of poetic utterance, and the source and well-spring of this abundance is the character of Richard. This is especially true from Act III on, when almost every speech of Richard's is an outburst of pure poetry. In III, iii, touched by the thought of his approaching deposition, he utters a speech—"What must the King do now?"—which is a little elegiac poem. Richard is not always endowed with such sweet and simple speech. He is at times highly fantastic, abounding in conceits and over-strained analogies but these defects are exactly those of his creator, the young poet, William Shakespeare.

Whether or not Shakespeare designed the role of Richard for his own performance, it seems quite certain that he felt for this gifted and ruined character a very special sympathy. He makes Richard more than once the mouthpiece of his own emotions, his hatred of ingratitude, his brooding melancholy, his vein of pessimism. It would be absurd to say that Shakespeare has drawn himself as Richard, but it is the simple truth to say that he often puts himself in Richard's place; "Thus would I have felt," he seems to say, "thus would I have spoken, had I been Richard in this scene or in that." And so the character of Richard becomes a mirror of Shakespeare's self such as hardly another of his early plays affords us.

Bolingbroke.—There was, of course, far more in Shakespeare than that part of himself which he put into Richard, the play-acting, poetizing, sentimental part. There was, for one thing, a very definite appreciation of reality, of the power of fact, and this side he has revealed in the character of Bolingbroke. There is little need to analyze this character; it is simple enough and drawn with few strokes, but it is a life-like portrait of the realist who sees the world about him with wide-open eyes, selects his task, performs it, and moves on to something else. One speech of his (III, i. 44) seems to characterize him perfectly; he has just sent the King's favorites to the block and calls on his followers to help him chase Glendower from the English borders with the word "awhile to work and after holiday"—the true man of affairs. There is a tragic irony in the words for we know, as Shakespeare's audience knew, that the "after holiday" never came to Bolingbroke; he lived a busy and distracted life and died a weary broken man. Yet while he lived he was an efficient manager of the great business of ruling England. One cannot believe that Shakespeare loved Bolingbroke or the Bolingbroke type, but he understood it well enough to know its value in this world. His heart is with Richard but his head casts a vote unhesitatingly for his competitor.

Political Significance.—In *Richard II,* as in all Shakespeare's English history plays, the fire of patriotism burns with a clear white flame; Shakespeare places his country's welfare before all else. It is clear from many passages in this play that it is to Richard's careless neglect of this welfare and not to any personal guilt that Shakespeare attributes Richard's tragic fall. Through the mouth of old Gaunt, Shakespeare sings a hymn of praise of his native land that still remains, after so many years and so many poets, the noblest ever uttered by an Englishman. Nothing in the career of Gaunt in history or his action in the play has prepared us for such an outburst; Shakespeare is simply using him as the mouthpiece of his own passionate patriotism.

There is, however, one aspect of Shakespeare's patriotism that is, perhaps, peculiar to this play. It is, of course, a commonplace that love of country in Elizabethan days tended to identify itself with loyalty to the monarch who was, in a sense, the country. This identification of patriotism and loyalty naturally tended to lend strength to the doctrine of the Divine Right, a conception which in Shakespeare's day was gaining wide acceptance in England. That Shakespeare was familiar with this doctrine is clear from the repeated reference he makes to its chief tenet, the irresponsibility of the King to any earthly power; but that Shakespeare considered this tenet an unreal delusion is plain from the whole course of the play. The angels of God whom Richard saw ready to fight in defense of God's anointed are a poet's dream; the Percies of the North and the mob of London are stern realities.

It is small wonder that such a play as *Richard II* gave offense at the Court of Elizabeth; it is indeed a matter for wonder that the young poet-player, whose instinct, one supposes, would have been to accept implicitly courtly ideals in the body politic, should have shown himself so independent in thought and so frank in speech as Shakespeare assuredly did in this play.

Stage History.—Richard II has never been a popular stage play; yet it is a mistake to suppose as some critics have done that it was, and is, a failure theatrically. Apart from the performance in 1601 before the friends of Essex there is a curious record of its performance in 1607 on an English ship bound for the East Indies. A performance by Shakespeare's company about the same time probably led to the publication of Q_4 with the restored deposition scene. Sir Henry Herbert records another performance at the Globe in 1631. There is apparently no record of a production in the early years of the Restoration. Tate rewrote *Richard II* as *The Sicilian Usurper* in 1681, but it was suppressed as dangerous politically after a brief run of three days. A version by Theobald, 1719, was more successful, but it can hardly be recognized as Shakespeare's play. Not until the nineteenth century did the play in anything like its original form return to the stage; even then the version acted by Kean, 1815, completely alters the last act. Macready played it repeatedly, unaltered except for omissions. Charles Kean produced it as a dramatic spectacle in 1857 and Tree's magnificent production in 1903 ran for over a hundred nights. It has not often been played in America, but recent performances, 1937, by Maurice Evans in New York and elsewhere have demonstrated its appeal not merely as a theatrical pageant, but as a pathetic dramatic interpretation of character.

THE TRAGEDY OF RICHARD THE SECOND

Richard II (1367–1400)—Known as Richard of Bordeaux, at which place he was born in 1367. Son of the Black Prince. Succeeded his grandfather, Edward III, to the throne when he was ten. His connivance at the murder of his uncle, Thomas of Woodstock, Duke of Gloucester, at Calais in 1397 is used by Shakespeare, and very properly, as a motivation of the tragedy. The references to it in the play are, however, obscure. In brief, the facts are these. During Richard's nonage he was ruled by a commission of regency dominated by his uncles, Gaunt, York, and Gloucester. At the age of twenty-two he threw over this authority and for a period of nine years ruled with moderation and considerable skill. But when opportunity offered, the spirit of revenge he had nursed all along, fostered by the continued opposition of Gloucester, broke out finally in the murder of Gloucester and the ruthless assertion of absolutism that brought about his downfall.

John of Gaunt, Duke of Lancaster (1340–1399)—Born in Ghent. Fourth son of Edward III. From him the Lancastrian line of English kings takes its name.

Edmund of Langley, Duke of York (1341–1402)—Fifth son of Edward III. Progenitor of the Yorkist kings of England.

Henry Bolingbroke (1367–1413)—(See note **dramatis personæ**, *Henry IV, Part I.*)

Duke of Aumerle—(See note on **Edward, Duke of York,** *Henry V.*)

Thomas Mowbray, Duke of Norfolk (d. 1399)—As Captain of Calais where Gloucester was imprisoned, he was probably directly responsible for the murder of Gloucester. Died in banishment.

Thomas Holland, Duke of Surrey (1374–1400)—Half-brother of Richard II. Lieutenant of Ireland. Deprived of dukedom and executed by Henry IV.

John de Montacute, Earl of Salisbury (1350–1400)—With Richard in Ireland. Accused of complicity in murder of Gloucester. Killed in rebellion against Henry IV.

Sir John Bussy (Bushy) (d. 1399)—Speaker of House of Commons. Subservient to Richard. Executed at Bristol by Henry IV.

Sir William Bagot—One of "souuerain's conseillers" left in England when Richard went to Ireland. Committed to the Tower after Richard's resignation.

Earl of Northumberland—(See note *Henry IV, Part I.*)

Henry Percy (Hotspur)—(See note *Henry IV, Part I.*)

Queen Isabella (1389–1409)—Daughter of Charles VI of France. Married to Richard as his second wife at the age of seven in 1396. She was only ten years old when he was deposed.

Duchess of York—Isabel of Castile, daughter of Pedro the Cruel.

Duchess of Gloucester—Eleanor, daughter of Humphrey Bohun, Earl of Northampton.

THE TRAGEDY OF RICHARD THE SECOND

Dramatis Personæ

King Richard II.
John of Gaunt, duke of Lancaster, } uncles to
Edmund of Langley, duke of York, } the King.
Henry, surnamed *Bolingbroke,* duke of Hereford, son to *John of Gaunt;* afterwards *King Henry IV.*
Duke of Aumerle, son to the duke of York.
Thomas Mowbray, duke of Norfolk.
Duke of Surrey.
Earl of Salisbury.
Lord Berkeley.
Bushy, }
Bagot, } servants to *King Richard.*
Green, }
Earl of Northumberland.
Henry Percy, surnamed *Hotspur,* his son.
Lord Ross.
Lord Willoughby.
Lord Fitzwater.
Bishop of Carlisle.
Abbot of Westminster.
Lord Marshal.
Sir Stephen Scroop.
Sir Pierce of Exton.
Captain of a band of Welshmen.
Two Gardeners.

Queen to *King Richard.*
Duchess of York.
Duchess of Gloucester.
Lady attending on the *Queen.*

Lords, Heralds, Officers, Soldiers, Keeper, Messenger, Groom, and other Attendants.

SCENE: *England and Wales.*

ACT I. SCENE I. *London. King Richard's palace.*

Enter *King Richard, John of Gaunt,* with other Nobles and Attendants.

K. Rich. Old John of Gaunt, time-honoured Lancaster,
Hast thou, according to thy oath and band,
Brought hither Henry Hereford thy bold son,
Here to make good the boist'rous late appeal,
Which then our leisure would not let us hear,
Against the Duke of Norfolk, Thomas Mowbray?
Gaunt. I have, my liege.
K. Rich. Tell me, moreover, hast thou sounded him
If he appeal the Duke on ancient malice,
Or worthily, as a good subject should,
On some known ground of treachery in him?
Gaunt. As near as I could sift him on that argument,
On some apparent danger seen in him
Aim'd at your Highness, no inveterate malice.
K. Rich. Then call them to our presence.
Exeunt some Attendants. Face to face,
And frowning brow to brow, ourselves will hear
Th' accuser and the accused freely speak.
High-stomach'd are they both, and full of ire,
In rage deaf as the sea, hasty as fire.

2. band, bond. **9. appeal,** challenge. **18. High-stomach'd,** haughty.

Enter *Bolingbroke* and *Mowbray* with Attendants.

Boling. Many years of happy days befall
My gracious sovereign, my most loving liege!
Mow. Each day still better other's happiness,
Until the heavens, envying earth's good hap,
Add an immortal title to your crown!
K. Rich. We thank you both; yet one but flatters us,
As well appeareth by the cause you come,
Namely, to appeal each other of high treason.
Cousin of Hereford, what dost thou object
Against the Duke of Norfolk, Thomas Mowbray?
Boling. First, heaven be the record to my speech!
In the devotion of a subject's love,
Tend'ring the precious safety of my prince,
And free from other misbegotten hate,
Come I appellant to this princely presence.
Now, Thomas Mowbray, do I turn to thee,
And mark my greeting well; for what I speak
My body shall make good upon this earth,
Or my divine soul answer it in heaven.
Thou art a traitor and a miscreant,
Too good to be so, and too bad to live,
Since the more fair and crystal is the sky,
The uglier seem the clouds that in it fly.

32. Tend'ring, holding dear.

Once more, the more to aggravate the note,
With a foul traitor's name stuff I thy throat;
And wish, so please my sovereign, ere I move,
What my tongue speaks my right drawn sword may prove.

Mow. Let not my cold words here accuse my zeal.
'T is not the trial of a woman's war,
The bitter clamour of two eager tongues,
Can arbitrate this cause betwixt us twain;
The blood is hot that must be cool'd for this.
Yet can I not of such tame patience boast
As to be hush'd and nought at all to say.
First, the fair reverence of your Highness curbs me
From giving reins and spurs to my free speech,
Which else would post until it had return'd
These terms of treason doubled down his throat.
Setting aside his high blood's royalty,
And let him be no kinsman to my liege,
I do defy him, and I spit at him;
Call him a slanderous coward and a villain;
Which to maintain I would allow him odds,
And meet him, were I tied to run afoot
Even to the frozen ridges of the Alps,
Or any other ground inhabitable
Where ever Englishman durst set his foot.
Meantime let this defend my loyalty:
By all my hopes, most falsely doth he lie.

Boling. Pale trembling coward, there I throw my gage,
Disclaiming here the kindred of the King,
And lay aside my high blood's royalty,
Which fear, not reverence, makes thee to except.
If guilty dread have left thee so much strength
As to take up mine honour's pawn, then stoop.
By that and all the rites of knighthood else,
Will I make good against thee, arm to arm,
What I have spoke, or thou canst worse devise.

Mow. I take it up; and by that sword I swear,
Which gently laid my knighthood on my shoulder,
I 'll answer thee in any fair degree,
Or chivalrous design of knightly trial;
And when I mount, alive may I not light,
If I be traitor or unjustly fight!

K. Rich. What doth our cousin lay to Mowbray's charge?
It must be great that can inherit us
So much as of a thought of ill in him.

Boling. Look, what I speak, my life shall prove it true:
That Mowbray hath receiv'd eight thousand nobles
In name of lendings for your Highness' soldiers,
The which he hath detain'd for lewd employments,
Like a false traitor and injurious villain.
Besides I say, and will in battle prove,
Or here or elsewhere to the furthest verge
That ever was survey'd by English eye,
That all the treasons for these eighteen years
Complotted and contrived in this land
Fetch from false Mowbray their first head and spring.
Further I say, and further will maintain
Upon his bad life to make all this good,
That he did plot the Duke of Gloucester's death,
Suggest his soon-believing adversaries,
And consequently, like a traitor coward,
Sluic'd out his innocent soul through streams of blood;
Which blood, like sacrificing Abel's, cries,
Even from the tongueless caverns of the earth,
To me for justice and rough chastisement;
And, by the glorious worth of my descent,
This arm shall do it, or this life be spent.

K. Rich. How high a pitch his resolution soars!
Thomas of Norfolk, what say'st thou to this?

Mow. O, let my sovereign turn away his face
And bid his ears a little while be deaf,
Till I have told this slander of his blood
How God and good men hate so foul a liar.

K. Rich. Mowbray, impartial are our eyes and ears.
Were he my brother, nay, my kingdom's heir,
As he is but my father's brother's son,
Now, by my sceptre's awe, I make a vow,
Such neighbour nearness to our sacred blood
Should nothing privilege him, nor partialize
The unstooping firmness of my upright soul.
He is our subject, Mowbray; so art thou:
Free speech and fearless I to thee allow.

Mow. Then, Bolingbroke, as low as to thy heart,
Through the false passage of thy throat, thou liest.
Three parts of that receipt I had for Calais
Disburs'd I duly to his Highness' soldiers;
The other part reserv'd I by consent,
For that my sovereign liege was in my debt
Upon remainder of a dear account,

43. aggravate, intensify. **note,** stigma. **46. right,** in defense of right. **49. eager,** sharp. **63. tied,** obliged. **65. inhabitable,** uninhabitable. **74. pawn,** pledge. **80-1. fair . . . trial,** way deemed fair or in any form of combat approved by the code of chivalry. **85. inherit us,** put us in possession of.

88. nobles, 6s. 8d. **89. lendings,** probably advances. **96. Complotted,** plotted. **100. Gloucester's death,** Rich.'s uncle, Thomas of Woodstock, put to death 1397, at Calais while in Mowbray's custody. **101. suggest,** prompt criminally. **104.** "The voice of thy brother's blood crieth unto me from the ground." *Gen.*, iv, 10. **109. pitch,** the top of a falcon's flight. **130.** For the balance of a large amount.

Since last I went to France to fetch his queen:
Now swallow down that lie. For Gloucester's death
I slew him not; but to my own disgrace
Neglected my sworn duty in that case.
For you, my noble Lord of Lancaster,
The honourable father to my foe,
Once did I lay an ambush for your life,
A trespass that doth vex my grieved soul;
But ere I last receiv'd the sacrament
I did confess it, and exactly begg'd
Your Grace's pardon; and I hope I had it.
This is my fault: as for the rest appeal'd,
It issues from the rancour of a villain,
A recreant and most degenerate traitor;
Which in myself I boldly will defend,
And interchangeably hurl down my gage
Upon this overweening traitor's foot,
To prove myself a loyal gentleman
Even in the best blood chamber'd in his bosom.
In haste whereof, most heartily I pray
Your Highness to assign our trial day.

K. Rich. Wrath-kindled gentlemen, be rul'd by me;
Let 's purge this choler without letting blood:
This we prescribe, though no physician;
Deep malice makes too deep incision.
Forget, forgive; conclude and be agreed;
Our doctors say this is no month to bleed.
Good uncle, let this end where it begun;
We 'll calm the Duke of Norfolk, you your son.

Gaunt. To be a make-peace shall become my age.
Throw down, my son, the Duke of Norfolk's gage.

K. Rich. And, Norfolk, throw down his.

Gaunt. When, Harry, when!
Obedience bids I should not bid again.

K. Rich. Norfolk, throw down, we bid; there is no boot.

Mow. Myself I throw, dread sovereign, at thy foot;
My life thou shalt command, but not my shame:
The one my duty owes; but my fair name,
Despite of death that lives upon my grave,
To dark dishonour's use thou shalt not have.
I am disgrac'd, impeach'd, and baffled here,
Pierc'd to the soul with slander's venom'd spear,
The which no balm can cure but his heart-blood
Which breath'd this poison.

K. Rich. Rage must be withstood;
Give me his gage: lions make leopards tame.

Mow. Yea, but not change his spots: take but my shame,
And I resign my gage. My dear dear lord,
The purest treasure mortal times afford
Is spotless reputation; that away,
Men are but gilded loam or painted clay.
A jewel in a ten-times-barr'd-up chest
Is a bold spirit in a loyal breast.
Mine honour is my life; both grow in one;
Take honour from me, and my life is done.
Then, dear my liege, mine honour let me try;
In that I live, and for that will I die.

K. Rich. Cousin, throw up your gage. Do you begin.

Boling. O, God defend my soul from such deep sin!
Shall I seem crest-fall'n in my father's sight,
Or with pale beggar-fear impeach my height
Before this out-dar'd dastard? Ere my tongue
Shall wound my honour with such feeble wrong,
Or sound so base a parle, my teeth shall tear
The slavish motive of recanting fear,
And spit it bleeding in his high disgrace,
Where shame doth harbour, even in Mowbray's face. *Exit Gaunt.*

K. Rich. We were not born to sue, but to command;
Which since we cannot do to make you friends,
Be ready, as your lives shall answer it,
At Coventry, upon Saint Lambert's day;
There shall your swords and lances arbitrate
The swelling difference of your settled hate:
Since we cannot atone you, we shall see
Justice design the victor's chivalry.
Lord Marshal, command our officers at arms
Be ready to direct these home alarms.
Exeunt.

Scene II. *The Duke of Lancaster's palace.*

Enter *John of Gaunt* with the *Duchess of Gloucester*.

Gaunt. Alas, the part I had in Gloucester's blood
Doth more solicit me than your exclaims,
To stir against the butchers of his life!
But since correction lieth in those hands

131. queen, Isabel, daughter of Charles VI of France, Richard's second wife, who was married to him in 1396 at the age of nine. **140. exactly,** explicitly. **142. appeal'd,** charged. **144. recreant,** false. **146. interchangeably,** in return. **150. In haste whereof,** to expedite which, i.e., the proof. **156. conclude,** come to terms. **164. boot,** help. **170. baffled,** disgraced.

177. mortal times, a man's life-time. **190. out-dar'd,** dared down, cowed. **192. sound,** a trumpet note always signalled a parley. **193. motive,** i.e., tongue. **199. Lambert's day,** Sept. 17. **202. atone,** reconcile. **203. design,** designate. **victor's chivalry,** the victor, i.e., the knightly deeds that make him worthy of victory.

Which made the fault that we cannot correct,
Put we our quarrel to the will of Heaven;
Who, when they see the hours ripe on earth,
Will rain hot vengeance on offenders' heads.

Duch. Finds brotherhood in thee no sharper spur?
Hath love in thy old blood no living fire?
Edward's seven sons, whereof thyself art one,
Were as seven vials of his sacred blood,
Or seven fair branches springing from one root:
Some of those seven are dried by nature's course,
Some of those branches by the Destinies cut;
But Thomas, my dear lord, my life, my Gloucester,
One vial full of Edward's sacred blood,
One flourishing branch of his most royal root,
Is crack'd, and all the precious liquor spilt,
Is hack'd down, and his summer leaves all faded,
By Envy's hand and Murder's bloody axe.
Ah, Gaunt, his blood was thine! That bed, that womb,
That mettle, that self-mould, that fashion'd thee
Made him a man; and though thou liv'st and breath'st,
Yet art thou slain in him: thou dost consent
In some large measure to thy father's death,
In that thou seest thy wretched brother die,
Who was the model of thy father's life.
Call it not patience, Gaunt; it is despair:
In suff'ring thus thy brother to be slaughter'd,
Thou show'st the naked pathway to thy life,
Teaching stern Murder how to butcher thee:
That which in mean men we intitle patience
Is pale cold cowardice in noble breasts.
What shall I say? To safeguard thine own life,
The best way is to venge my Gloucester's death.

Gaunt. God's is the quarrel; for God's substitute,
His deputy anointed in His sight,
Hath caus'd his death; the which if wrongfully,
Let Heaven revenge; for I may never lift
An angry arm against His minister.

Duch. Where then, alas, may I complain myself?

Gaunt. To God, the widow's champion and defence.

Duch. Why, then, I will. Farewell, old Gaunt!
Thou go'st to Coventry, there to behold
Our cousin Hereford and fell Mowbray fight.
O, sit my husband's wrongs on Hereford's spear,
That it may enter butcher Mowbray's breast!
Or, if misfortune miss the first career,
Be Mowbray's sins so heavy in his bosom,
That they may break his foaming courser's back,
And throw the rider headlong in the lists,
A caitiff recreant to my cousin Hereford!
Farewell, old Gaunt! Thy sometimes brother's wife
With her companion grief must end her life.

Gaunt. Sister, farewell; I must to Coventry.
As much good stay with thee as go with me!

Duch. Yet one word more; grief boundeth where it falls,
Not with the empty hollowness, but weight:
I take my leave before I have begun,
For sorrow ends not when it seemeth done.
Commend me to thy brother, Edmund York.
Lo, this is all:—nay, yet depart not so;
Though this be all, do not so quickly go;
I shall remember more. Bid him—ah, what?—
With all good speed at Plashy visit me.
Alack, and what shall good old York there see
But empty lodgings and unfurnish'd walls,
Unpeopled offices, untrodden stones?
And what hear there for welcome but my groans?
Therefore commend me; let him not come there,
To seek out sorrow that dwells everywhere.
Desolate, desolate, will I hence and die.
The last leave of thee takes my weeping eye.

Exeunt.

Scene III. *The lists at Coventry.*

Enter the *Lord Marshal* and the *Duke of Aumerle.*

Mar. My Lord Aumerle, is Harry Hereford arm'd?

Aum. Yea, at all points; and longs to enter in.

Mar. The Duke of Norfolk, sprightfully and bold,
Stays but the summons of the appellant's trumpet.

Aum. Why, then, the champions are prepar'd, and stay
For nothing but his Majesty's approach.

The trumpets sound, and the *King* enters with his nobles, *Gaunt, Bushy, Bagot, Green,* and others. When they are set, enter *Mowbray* in arms, defendant, with a Herald.

Scene ii: 15. Destinies, the Three Fates. **21. Envy's,** malice's. **23. self-,** self-same. **28. model,** copy. **46. cousin,** here, nephew.

49. career, charge. **53. caitiff recreant,** cowardly captive.

K. Rich. Marshal, demand of yonder champion
The cause of his arrival here in arms.
Ask him his name, and orderly proceed
To swear him in the justice of his cause.
Mar. In God's name and the King's, say who thou art
And why thou com'st thus knightly clad in arms,
Against what man thou com'st, and what thy quarrel.
Speak truly, on thy knighthood and thy oath;
And so defend thee Heaven and thy valour!
Mow. My name is Thomas Mowbray, Duke of Norfolk;
Who hither come engaged by my oath—
Which God defend a knight should violate!—
Both to defend my loyalty and truth
To God, my King, and his succeeding issue,
Against the Duke of Hereford that appeals me;
And, by the grace of God and this mine arm,
To prove him, in defending of myself,
A traitor to my God, my King, and me:
And as I truly fight, defend me Heaven!

The trumpets sound. Enter *Bolingbroke,* appellant, in armour, with a Herald.

K. Rich. Marshal, ask yonder knight in arms,
Both who he is and why he cometh hither
Thus plated in habiliments of war,
And formally, according to our law,
Depose him in the justice of his cause.
Mar. What is thy name? and wherefore com'st thou hither,
Before King Richard in his royal lists?
Against whom comest thou? and what 's thy quarrel?
Speak like a true knight, so defend thee Heaven!
Boling. Harry of Hereford, Lancaster, and Derby
Am I; who ready here do stand in arms,
To prove, by God's grace and my body's valour,
In lists, on Thomas Mowbray, Duke of Norfolk,
That he 's a traitor, foul and dangerous,
To God of heaven, King Richard, and to me;
And as I truly fight, defend me Heaven!
Mar. On pain of death, no person be so bold
Or daring-hardy as to touch the lists,
Except the Marshal and such officers
Appointed to direct these fair designs.
Boling. Lord Marshal, let me kiss my sovereign's hand,
And bow my knee before his Majesty;
For Mowbray and myself are like two men
That vow a long and weary pilgrimage.
Then let us take a ceremonious leave
And loving farewell of our several friends.
Mar. The appellant in all duty greets your Highness,
And craves to kiss your hand and take his leave.
K. Rich. We will descend and fold him in our arms.
Cousin of Hereford, as thy cause is right,
So be thy fortune in this royal fight!
Farewell, my blood; which if to-day thou shed,
Lament we may, but not revenge thee dead.
Boling. O, let no noble eye profane a tear
For me, if I be gor'd with Mowbray's spear:
As confident as is the falcon's flight
Against a bird, do I with Mowbray fight.
My loving lord, I take my leave of you;
Of you, my noble cousin, Lord Aumerle;
Not sick, although I have to do with death,
But lusty, young, and cheerly drawing breath.
Lo, as at English feasts, so I regreet
The daintiest last, to make the end most sweet:
O thou, the earthly author of my blood,
Whose youthful spirit, in me regenerate,
Doth with a twofold vigour lift me up
To reach at victory above my head,
Add proof unto mine armour with thy prayers;
And with thy blessings steel my lance's point,
That it may enter Mowbray's waxen coat,
And furbish new the name of John o' Gaunt,
Even in the lusty haviour of his son.
Gaunt. God in thy good cause make thee prosperous!
Be swift like lightning in the execution;
And let thy blows, doubly redoubled,
Fall like amazing thunder on the casque
Of thy adverse pernicious enemy:
Rouse up thy youthful blood, be valiant, and live.
Boling. Mine innocency and Saint George to thrive!
Mow. However God or Fortune cast my lot,
There lives or dies, true to King Richard's throne,
A loyal, just, and upright gentleman.

Scene iii: **18. defend,** forbid. **S. d. appellant,** accuser. **28. plated,** in plate-armor. **30. Depose,** take his evidence under oath.

59-60. If I am wounded by Mowbray, it will be a profanation to shed tears for me. **66. cheerly,** cheerily. **67. regreet,** salute. **73. proof,** resistance. **75. waxen,** penetrable, as opposed to *proof* (l. 73). **81. amazing,** bewildering. **casque,** helmet.

Never did captive with a freer heart
Cast off his chains of bondage and embrace
His golden uncontroll'd enfranchisement,
More than my dancing soul doth celebrate
This feast of battle with mine adversary.
Most mighty liege, and my companion peers,
Take from my mouth the wish of happy years:
As gentle and as jocund as to jest
Go I to fight; truth hath a quiet breast.
K. Rich. Farewell, my lord; securely I espy
Virtue with valour couched in thine eye.
Order the trial, Marshal, and begin.
Mar. Harry of Hereford, Lancaster, and Derby,
Receive thy lance; and God defend the right!
Boling. Strong as a tower in hope, I cry amen.
Mar. Go bear this lance to Thomas, Duke of Norfolk.
1. Her. Harry of Hereford, Lancaster, and Derby
Stands here for God, his sovereign, and himself,
On pain to be found false and recreant,
To prove the Duke of Norfolk, Thomas Mowbray,
A traitor to his God, his king, and him;
And dares him to set forward to the fight.
2. Her. Here standeth Thomas Mowbray, Duke of Norfolk,
On pain to be found false and recreant,
Both to defend himself and to approve
Henry of Hereford, Lancaster, and Derby,
To God, his sovereign, and to him disloyal;
Courageously and with a free desire
Attending but the signal to begin.
Mar. Sound, trumpets; and set forward, combatants. *A charge sounded.*
Stay! The King hath thrown his warder down.
K. Rich. Let them lay by their helmets and their spears,
And both return back to their chairs again.
Withdraw with us; and let the trumpets sound
While we return these dukes what we decree.
A long flourish.
Draw near
And list what with our council we have done.
For that our kingdom's earth should not be soil'd
With that dear blood which it hath fostered;
And for our eyes do hate the dire aspect
Of civil wounds plough'd up with neighbours' sword;
And for we think the eagle-winged pride
Of sky-aspiring and ambitious thoughts,
With rival-hating envy, set on you
To wake our peace, which in our country's cradle
Draws the sweet infant breath of gentle sleep;
Which, so rous'd up with boist'rous untun'd drums,
With harsh-resounding trumpets' dreadful bray,
And grating shock of wrathful iron arms,
Might from our quiet confines fright fair peace
And make us wade even in our kindred's blood;
Therefore, we banish you our territories.
You, cousin Hereford, upon pain of life,
Till twice five summers have enrich'd our fields
Shall not regreet our fair dominions,
But tread the stranger paths of banishment.
Boling. Your will be done: this must my comfort be,
That sun that warms you here shall shine on me;
And those his golden beams to you here lent
Shall point on me and gild my banishment.
K. Rich. Norfolk, for thee remains a heavier doom,
Which I with some unwillingness pronounce.
The sly, slow hours shall not determinate
The dateless limit of thy dear exile;
The hopeless word of "never to return"
Breathe I against thee, upon pain of life.
Mow. A heavy sentence, my most sovereign liege,
And all unlook'd for from your Highness' mouth.
A dearer merit, not so deep a maim
As to be cast forth in the common air,
Have I deserved at your Highness' hands.
The language I have learn'd these forty years,
My native English, now I must forgo;
And now my tongue's use is to me no more
Than an unstringed viol or a harp,
Or like a cunning instrument cas'd up,
Or, being open, put into his hands
That knows no touch to tune the harmony.
Within my mouth you have enjail'd my tongue,
Doubly portcullis'd with my teeth and lips;
And dull unfeeling barren ignorance
Is made my jailer to attend on me.
I am too old to fawn upon a nurse,
Too far in years to be a pupil now.
What is thy sentence then but speechless death,
Which robs my tongue from breathing native breath?

95. jest, play a game. **97. securely,** certainly. **112. approve,** prove. **118. warder,** staff borne by the king as presiding officer of the combat. **122. return,** announce to.

150. determinate, set a limit to. **156. merit,** reward. **163. cunning,** requiring cunning in the player.

K. Rich. It boots thee not to be compassionate:
After our sentence plaining comes too late.
Mow. Then thus I turn me from my country's light,
To dwell in solemn shades of endless night.
K. Rich. Return again, and take an oath with thee.
Lay on our royal sword your banish'd hands;
Swear by the duty that you owe to God—
Our part therein we banish with yourselves—
To keep the oath that we administer:
You never shall, so help you truth and God!
Embrace each other's love in banishment;
Nor never look upon each other's face;
Nor never write, regreet, nor reconcile
This louring tempest of your home-bred hate;
Nor never by advised purpose meet
To plot, contrive, or complot any ill
'Gainst us, our state, our subjects, or our land.
Boling. I swear.
Mow. And I, to keep all this.
Boling. Norfolk, so far as to mine enemy:—
By this time, had the King permitted us,
One of our souls had wander'd in the air,
Banish'd this frail sepulchre of our flesh,
As now our flesh is banish'd from this land;
Confess thy treasons ere thou fly the realm;
Since thou hast far to go, bear not along
The clogging burden of a guilty soul.
Mow. No, Bolingbroke; if ever I were traitor,
My name be blotted from the book of life,
And I from heaven banish'd as from hence!
But what thou art, God, thou, and I do know;
And all too soon, I fear, the King shall rue.
Farewell, my liege. Now no way can I stray;
Save back to England, all the world 's my way.
Exit.
K. Rich. Uncle, even in the glasses of thine eyes
I see thy grieved heart: thy sad aspect
Hath from the number of his banish'd years
Pluck'd four away. Six frozen winters spent,
Return with welcome home from banishment.
Boling. How long a time lies in one little word!
Four lagging winters and four wanton springs
End in a word: such is the breath of kings.
Gaunt. I thank my liege, that in regard of me
He shortens four years of my son's exile;
But little vantage shall I reap thereby,
For, ere the six years that he hath to spend
Can change their moons and bring their times about,
My oil-dri'd lamp and time-bewasted light
Shall be extinct with age and endless night;
My inch of taper will be burnt and done,
And blindfold death not let me see my son.
K. Rich. Why, uncle, thou hast many years to live.
Gaunt. But not a minute, King, that thou canst give:
Shorten my days thou canst with sullen sorrow,
And pluck nights from me, but not lend a morrow.
Thou canst help Time to furrow me with age,
But stop no wrinkle in his pilgrimage.
Thy word is current with him for my death,
But dead, thy kingdom cannot buy my breath.
K. Rich. Thy son is banish'd upon good advice,
Whereto thy tongue a party-verdict gave.
Why at our justice seem'st thou then to lour?
Gaunt. Things sweet to taste prove in digestion sour.
You urg'd me as a judge; but I had rather
You would have bid me argue like a father.
O, had it been a stranger, not my child,
To smooth his fault I should have been more mild:
A partial slander sought I to avoid,
And in the sentence my own life destroy'd.
Alas, I look'd when some of you should say
I was too strict to make mine own away;
But you gave leave to my unwilling tongue
Against my will to do myself this wrong.
K. Rich. Cousin, farewell; and, uncle, bid him so.
Six years we banish him, and he shall go.
Flourish. Exeunt King Richard and train.
Aum. Cousin, farewell! What presence must not know,
From where you do remain let paper show.
Mar. My lord, no leave take I; for I will ride,
As far as land will let me, by your side.
Gaunt. O, to what purpose dost thou hoard thy words,
That thou return'st no greeting to thy friends?
Boling. I have too few to take my leave of you,
When the tongue's office should be prodigal
To breathe the abundant dolour of the heart.
Gaunt. Thy grief is but thy absence for a time.
Boling. Joy absent, grief is present for that time.

174. compassionate, sorry for thyself. **175. plaining,** complaining. **190. state,** royal condition. **208. glasses,** mirrors. **220. times about,** seasons around. **231. current,** good (as legal tender). **234. party-verdict,** vote in council. **241. partial slander,** charge of partiality. **249. presence,** royal presence-chamber. **257. dolour,** grief.

Gaunt. What is six winters? They are quickly gone.
Boling. To men in joy; but grief makes one hour ten.
Gaunt. Call it a travel that thou tak'st for pleasure.
Boling. My heart will sigh when I miscall it so,
Which finds it an inforced pilgrimage.
Gaunt. The sullen passage of thy weary steps
Esteem as foil wherein thou art to set
The precious jewel of thy home return.
Boling. Nay, rather, every tedious stride I make
Will but remember me what a deal of world
I wander from the jewels that I love.
Must I not serve a long apprenticehood
To foreign passages, and in the end,
Having my freedom, boast of nothing else
But that I was a journeyman to grief?
Gaunt. All places that the eye of heaven visits
Are to a wise man ports and happy havens.
Teach thy necessity to reason thus;
There is no virtue like necessity.
Think not the King did banish thee,
But thou the King. Woe doth the heavier sit
Where it perceives it is but faintly borne.
Go, say I sent thee forth to purchase honour
And not the King exil'd thee; or suppose
Devouring pestilence hangs in our air
And thou art flying to a fresher clime:
Look, what thy soul holds dear, imagine it
To lie that way thou goest, not whence thou com'st:
Suppose the singing birds musicians,
The grass whereon thou tread'st the presence strew'd,
The flowers fair ladies, and thy steps no more
Than a delightful measure or a dance;
For gnarling sorrow hath less power to bite
The man that mocks at it and sets it light.
Boling. O, who can hold a fire in his hand
By thinking on the frosty Caucasus?
Or cloy the hungry edge of appetite
By bare imagination of a feast?
Or wallow naked in December snow
By thinking on fantastic summer's heat?
O, no! the apprehension of the good
Gives but the greater feeling to the worse:
Fell Sorrow's tooth doth never rankle more
Than when he bites, but lanceth not the sore.
Gaunt. Come, come, my son, I 'll bring thee on thy way;
Had I thy youth and cause, I would not stay.
Boling. Then, England's ground, farewell; sweet soil, adieu;
My mother, and my nurse, that bears me yet!
Where'er I wander, boast of this I can,
Though banish'd, yet a trueborn Englishman.
Exeunt.

Scene IV. *The Court.*

Enter the *King,* with *Bagot* and *Green* at one door; and the *Lord Aumerle* at another.

K. Rich. We did observe. Cousin Aumerle,
How far brought you high Hereford on his way?
Aum. I brought high Hereford, if you call him so,
But to the next highway, and there I left him.
K. Rich. And say, what store of parting tears were shed?
Aum. Faith, none for me; except the northeast wind,
Which then blew bitterly against our faces,
Awak'd the sleeping rheum, and so by chance
Did grace our hollow parting with a tear.
K. Rich. What said our cousin when you parted with him?
Aum. "Farewell!"
And, for my heart disdained that my tongue
Should so profane the word, that taught me craft
To counterfeit oppression of such grief
That words seem'd buried in my sorrow's grave.
Marry, would the word "farewell" have lengthen'd hours
And added years to his short banishment,
He should have had a volume of farewells;
But since it would not, he had none of me.
K. Rich. He is our cousin, cousin; but 't is doubt,
When time shall call him home from banishment,
Whether our kinsman come to see his friends.
Ourself and Bushy, Bagot here and Green
Observ'd his courtship to the common people;
How he did seem to dive into their hearts
With humble and familiar courtesy,
What reverence he did throw away on slaves,
Wooing poor craftsmen with the craft of smiles
And patient underbearing of his fortune,
As 't were to banish their affects with him.

266. **foil,** metal background to set off a jewel. 272. **foreign passages,** wanderings abroad. 274. **journeyman,** worker by the day—next step above apprentice. 289. **presence strew'd,** reception room strewed with rushes. 291. **measure,** stately dance. 292. **gnarling,** snarling. 299. **fantastic,** imaginary. 300. **apprehension,** imagination.

304. **bring,** accompany. **Scene iv: 6. for me,** for my part. 13. **that,** its antecedant is the entire clause preceding. 29. **underbearing,** enduring. 30. **affects,** affections.

Off goes his bonnet to an oyster-wench;
A brace of draymen bid God speed him well
And had the tribute of his supple knee,
With "Thanks, my countrymen, my loving friends,"
As were our England in reversion his,
And he our subjects' next degree in hope.
Green. Well, he is gone; and with him go these thoughts.
Now for the rebels which stand out in Ireland,
Expedient manage must be made, my liege,
Ere further leisure yield them further means
For their advantage and your Highness' loss.
K. Rich. We will ourself in person to this war;
And, for our coffers, with too great a court
And liberal largess, are grown somewhat light,
We are inforc'd to farm our royal realm;
The revenue whereof shall furnish us
For our affairs in hand: if that come short,
Our substitutes at home shall have blank charters;
Whereto, when they shall know what men are rich,
They shall subscribe them for large sums of gold
And send them after to supply our wants;
For we will make for Ireland presently.

Enter *Bushy.*

Bushy, what news?
Bushy. Old John of Gaunt is grievous sick, my lord,
Suddenly taken; and hath sent post haste
To entreat your Majesty to visit him.
K. Rich. Where lies he?
Bushy. At Ely House.
K. Rich. Now put it, God, in the physician's mind
To help him to his grave immediately!
The lining of his coffers shall make coats
To deck our soldiers for these Irish wars.
Come, gentlemen, let 's all go visit him.
Pray God we may make haste, and come too late!
All. Amen.

Exeunt.

ACT II. Scene I. *Ely House.*

Enter *John of Gaunt,* sick, with the *Duke of York,* etc.

Gaunt. Will the King come, that I may breathe my last
In wholesome counsel to his unstaid youth?
York. Vex not yourself, nor strive not with your breath;
For all in vain comes counsel to his ear.
Gaunt. O, but they say the tongues of dying men
Enforce attention like deep harmony:
Where words are scarce, they are seldom spent in vain,
For they breathe truth that breathe their words in pain.
He that no more must say is listen'd more
Than they whom youth and ease have taught to glose.
More are men's ends mark'd than their lives before.
The setting sun, and music at the close,
As the last taste of sweets, is sweetest last,
Writ in remembrance more than things long past:
Though Richard my life's counsel would not hear,
My death's sad tale may yet undeaf his ear.
York. No; it is stopp'd with other flattering sounds,
As praises, of whose taste the wise are fond,
Lascivious metres, to whose venom sound
The open ear of youth doth always listen;
Report of fashions in proud Italy,
Whose manners still our tardy, apish nation
Limps after in base imitation.
Where doth the world thrust forth a vanity—
So it be new, there 's no respect how vile—
That is not quickly buzz'd into his ears?
Then all too late comes counsel to be heard
Where will doth mutiny with wit's regard.
Direct not him whose way himself will choose;
'T is breath thou lack'st, and that breath wilt thou lose.
Gaunt. Methinks I am a prophet new inspir'd
And thus expiring do foretell of him:
His rash fierce blaze of riot cannot last,

38. **stand out**, are in rebellion. 39. **Expedient manage**, speedy measures. 45. **farm . . . realm**, to sell for cash the right to collect all revenues. **Act II Scene i: 10. glose**, flatter. 12. **close**, cadence.

50. **subscribe them**, sign. 52. **presently**, immediately. 58. **Ely House**, the bishop of Ely's palace. **Act II, Scene i: 16. death's sad tale**, solemn dying speech. 18. **the wise**, even the wise. 25. **no respect**, no caring. 26. **buzz'd**, whispered. 28. **Where . . . regard**, where the will rebels against what the understanding esteems.

For violent fires soon burn out themselves;
Small showers last long, but sudden storms are short;
He tires betimes that spurs too fast betimes;
With eager feeding food doth choke the feeder;
Light vanity, insatiate cormorant,
Consuming means, soon preys upon itself.
This royal throne of kings, this scepter'd isle,
This earth of majesty, this seat of Mars,
This other Eden, demi-paradise,
This fortress built by Nature for herself
Against infection and the hand of war,
This happy breed of men, this little world,
This precious stone set in the silver sea,
Which serves it in the office of a wall
Or as a moat defensive to a house
Against the envy of less happier lands,
This blessed plot, this earth, this realm, this England,
This nurse, this teeming womb of royal kings,
Fear'd by their breed and famous by their birth,
Renowned for their deeds as far from home,
For Christian service and true chivalry,
As is the sepulchre in stubborn Jewry,
Of the world's ransom, blessed Mary's Son;
This land of such dear souls, this dear dear land,
Dear for her reputation through the world,
Is now leas'd out, I die pronouncing it,
Like to a tenement or pelting farm.
England, bound in with the triumphant sea,
Whose rocky shore beats back the envious siege
Of wat'ry Neptune, is now bound in with shame,
With inky blots and rotten parchment bonds:
That England, that was wont to conquer others,
Hath made a shameful conquest of itself.
Ah, would the scandal vanish with my life,
How happy then were my ensuing death!

Enter *King Richard* and *Queen, Aumerle, Bushy, Green, Bagot, Ross,* and *Willoughby.*

York. The King is come: deal mildly with his youth;
For young hot colts being rag'd do rage the more.

Queen. How fares our noble uncle Lancaster?

K. Rich. What comfort, man? How is 't with aged Gaunt?

Gaunt. O, how that name befits my composition!
Old Gaunt indeed, and gaunt in being old.
Within me Grief hath kept a tedious fast;
And who abstains from meat that is not gaunt?
For sleeping England long time have I watch'd;
Watching breeds leanness, leanness is all gaunt:
The pleasure that some fathers feed upon,
Is my strict fast; I mean, my children's looks;
And therein fasting, hast thou made me gaunt:
Gaunt am I for the grave, gaunt as a grave,
Whose hollow womb inherits nought but bones.

K. Rich. Can sick men play so nicely with their names?

Gaunt. No, misery makes sport to mock itself.
Since thou dost seek to kill my name in me,
I mock my name, great King, to flatter thee.

K. Rich. Should dying men flatter with those that live?

Gaunt. No, no, men living flatter those that die.

K. Rich. Thou, now a-dying, say'st thou flatterest me.

Gaunt. O, no! thou diest, though I the sicker be.

K. Rich. I am in health, I breathe, and see thee ill.

Gaunt. Now He that made me knows I see thee ill;
Ill in myself to see, and in thee seeing ill.
Thy death-bed is no lesser than thy land
Wherein thou liest in reputation sick;
And thou, too careless patient as thou art,
Commit'st thy anointed body to the cure
Of those physicians that first wounded thee:
A thousand flatterers sit within thy crown,
Whose compass is no bigger than thy head;
And yet, incaged in so small a verge,
The waste is no whit lesser than thy land.
O, had thy grandsire with a prophet's eye
Seen how his son's son should destroy his sons,
From forth thy reach he would have laid thy shame,
Deposing thee before thou wert possess'd,
Which art possess'd now to depose thyself.
Why, cousin, wert thou regent of the world,
It were a shame to let this land by lease;
But for thy world enjoying but this land,
Is it not more than shame to shame it so?
Landlord of England art thou now, not king.
Thy state of law is bondslave to the law,
And thou—

K. Rich. A lunatic lean-witted fool,

44. infection, pollution, contagion. **49. envy,** malice. **60. pelting,** paltry. **70. rag'd,** enraged. **73. composition,** bodily condition.

83. inherits, possesses. **84. nicely,** fantastically, idly. **102. verge,** region around a king's court. **103. waste,** destruction of property by a tenant. **114. state of law,** legal status.

Presuming on an ague's privilege,
Dar'st with thy frozen admonition
Make pale our cheek, chasing the royal blood
With fury from his native residence.
Now, by my seat's right royal majesty,
Wert thou not brother to great Edward's son,
This tongue that runs so roundly in thy head
Should run thy head from thy unreverent shoulders.

Gaunt. O, spare me not, my brother Edward's son,
For that I was his father Edward's son;
That blood already, like the pelican,
Hast thou tapp'd out and drunkenly carous'd.
My brother Gloucester, plain well-meaning soul,
Whom fair befall in heaven 'mongst happy souls!
May be a precedent and witness good
That thou respect'st not spilling Edward's blood.
Join with the present sickness that I have,
And thy unkindness be like crooked age,
To crop at once a too long wither'd flower.
Live in thy shame, but die not shame with thee!
These words hereafter thy tormentors be!
Convey me to my bed, then to my grave;
Love they to live that love and honour have.
Exit borne off by his Attendants.

K. Rich. And let them die that age and sullens have;
For both hast thou, and both become the grave.

York. I do beseech your Majesty, impute his words
To wayward sickliness and age in him:
He loves you, on my life, and holds you dear
As Harry Duke of Hereford, were he here.

K. Rich. Right, you say true: as Hereford's love, so his;
As theirs, so mine; and all be as it is.

Enter *Northumberland.*

North. My liege, old Gaunt commends him to your Majesty.

K. Rich. What says he?

North. Nay, nothing; all is said.
His tongue is now a stringless instrument;
Words, life, and all, old Lancaster hath spent.

York. Be York the next that must be bankrupt so!
Though death be poor, it ends a mortal woe.

K. Rich. The ripest fruit first falls, and so doth he;
His time is spent, our pilgrimage must be.
So much for that. Now for our Irish wars:
We must supplant those rough rug-headed kerns,
Which live like venom where no venom else
But only they have privilege to live.
And for these great affairs do ask some charge,
Towards our assistance we do seize to us
The plate, coin, revenues, and moveables,
Whereof our uncle Gaunt did stand possess'd.

York. How long shall I be patient? Ah, how long
Shall tender duty make me suffer wrong?
Not Gloucester's death, nor Hereford's banishment,
Not Gaunt's rebukes, nor England's private wrongs,
Nor the prevention of poor Bolingbroke
About his marriage, nor my own disgrace,
Have ever made me sour my patient cheek,
Or bend one wrinkle on my sovereign's face.
I am the last of noble Edward's sons,
Of whom thy father, Prince of Wales, was first.
In war was never lion rag'd more fierce,
In peace was never gentle lamb more mild,
Than was that young and princely gentleman.
His face thou hast, for even so look'd he,
Accomplish'd with the number of thy hours;
But when he frown'd, it was against the French
And not against his friends. His noble hand
Did win what he did spend and spent not that
Which his triumphant father's hand had won.
His hands were guilty of no kindred blood,
But bloody with the enemies of his kin.
O Richard! York is too far gone with grief,
Or else he never would compare between—

K. Rich. Why, uncle, what 's the matter?

York. O my liege,
Pardon me, if you please; if not, I, pleas'd
Not to be pardon'd, am content withal.
Seek you to seize and gripe into your hands
The royalties and rights of banish'd Hereford?
Is not Gaunt dead, and doth not Hereford live?
Was not Gaunt just, and is not Harry true?
Did not the one deserve to have an heir?
Is not his heir a well-deserving son?
Take Hereford's rights away, and take from Time
His charters and his customary rights;
Let not to-morrow then ensue to-day;
Be not thyself; for how art thou a king
But by fair sequence and succession?
Now, afore God—God forbid I say true!—

122. roundly, unchecked.

156. rug-, rough like coarse cloth. **kerns,** Gælic name for soldiers. **157. no venom,** i.e., snakes, cleared out by St. Patrick. **159. charge,** expense. **177. Accomplish'd,** furnished. Richard was 32 years old. **190. royalties,** privileges. **197. ensue,** follow.

If you do wrongfully seize Hereford's rights,
Call in the letters patents that he hath
By his attorneys general to sue
His livery, and deny his offer'd homage,
You pluck a thousand dangers on your head,
You lose a thousand well-disposed hearts
And prick my tender patience to those thoughts
Which honour and allegiance cannot think.

K. Rich. Think what you will, we seize into our hands
His plate, his goods, his money, and his lands.

York. I 'll not be by the while: my liege, farewell!
What will ensue hereof, there 's none can tell;
But by bad courses may be understood
That their events can never fall out good. *Exit.*

K. Rich. Go, Bushy, to the Earl of Wiltshire straight:
Bid him repair to us to Ely House
To see this business. To-morrow next
We will for Ireland; and 't is time, I trow:
And we create, in absence of ourself,
Our uncle York lord governor of England;
For he is just and always lov'd us well.
Come on, our queen; to-morrow must we part.
Be merry, for our time of stay is short.

Flourish. Exeunt King, Queen, Aumerle, Bushy, Green and *Bagot.*

North. Well lords, the Duke of Lancaster is dead.

Ross. And living too; for now his son is duke.

Willo. Barely in title, not in revenues.

North. Richly in both, if Justice had her right.

Ross. My heart is great; but it must break with silence,
Ere 't be disburden'd with a liberal tongue.

North. Nay, speak thy mind; and let him ne'er speak more
That speaks thy words again to do thee harm!

Willo. Tends that thou wouldst speak to the Duke of Hereford?
If it be so, out with it boldly, man;
Quick is mine ear to hear of good towards him.

Ross. No good at all that I can do for him;
Unless you call it good to pity him,
Bereft and gelded of his patrimony.

North. Now, afore God, 't is shame such wrongs are borne
In him, a royal prince, and many moe
Of noble blood in this declining land.
The King is not himself, but basely led
By flatterers; and what they will inform,
Merely in hate, 'gainst any of us all,
That will the King severely prosecute
'Gainst us, our lives, our children, and our heirs.

Ross. The commons hath he pill'd with grievous taxes,
And quite lost their hearts; the nobles hath he fin'd
For ancient quarrels, and quite lost their hearts.

Willo. And daily new exactions are devis'd,
As blanks, benevolences, and I wot not what:
But what, o' God's name, doth become of this?

North. Wars hath not wasted it, for warr'd he hath not,
But basely yielded upon compromise
That which his noble ancestors achiev'd with blows.
More hath he spent in peace than they in wars.

Ross. The Earl of Wiltshire hath the realm in farm.

Willo. The King 's grown bankrupt, like a broken man.

North. Reproach and dissolution hangeth over him.

Ross. He hath not money for these Irish wars,
His burdenous taxations notwithstanding,
But by the robbing of the banish'd Duke.

North. His noble kinsman: most degenerate king!
But, lords, we hear this fearful tempest sing,
Yet seek no shelter to avoid the storm;
We see the wind sit sore upon our sails,
And yet we strike not, but securely perish.

Ross. We see the very wreck that we must suffer;
And unavoided is the danger now,
For suffering so the causes of our wreck.

North. Not so; even through the hollow eyes of death
I spy life peering; but I dare not say
How near the tidings of our comfort is.

Willo. Nay, let us share thy thoughts, as thou dost ours.

Ross. Be confident to speak, Northumberland.
We three are but thyself; and, speaking so,
Thy words are but as thoughts; therefore, be bold.

North. Then thus: I have from Le Port Blanc, a bay
In Brittany, received intelligence

203-4. sue His livery, claim his inheritance. Bolingbroke had appointed attorneys to make his claim. **217. see,** see to. **228. great,** swollen (with anger). **229. liberal,** unrestrained.

243. Merely, purely. **246. pill'd,** plundered. **250. blanks,** blank charters. **benevolences,** forced loans. **265. sit sore,** press grievously. **266. securely,** heedlessly. **268. unavoided,** unavoidable.

That Harry Duke of Hereford, Rainold Lord Cobham,
The son and heir of the late Earl of Arundel,
That late broke from the Duke of Exeter,
His brother, Archbishop late of Canterbury,
Sir Thomas Erpingham, Sir John Ramston,
Sir John Norbery, Sir Robert Waterton, and Francis Coines,
All these well furnish'd by the Duke of Bretagne
With eight tall ships, three thousand men of war,
Are making hither with all due expedience
And shortly mean to touch our northern shore:
Perhaps they had ere this, but that they stay
The first departing of the King for Ireland.
If then we shall shake off our slavish yoke,
Imp out our drooping country's broken wing,
Redeem from broking pawn the blemish'd crown,
Wipe off the dust that hides our sceptre's gilt,
And make high majesty look like itself,
Away with me in post to Ravenspurgh;
But if you faint, as fearing to do so,
Stay and be secret, and myself will go.

Ross. To horse, to horse! urge doubts to them that fear.

Willo. Hold out my horse, and I will first be there. *Exeunt.*

Scene II. *Windsor Castle.*

Enter *Queen, Bushy,* and *Bagot.*

Bushy. Madam, your Majesty is too much sad.
You promis'd, when you parted with the King,
To lay aside life-harming heaviness
And entertain a cheerful disposition.

Queen. To please the King I did; to please myself
I cannot do it; yet I know no cause
Why I should welcome such a guest as Grief,
Save bidding farewell to so sweet a guest
As my sweet Richard: yet again, methinks,
Some unborn sorrow, ripe in fortune's womb,
Is coming towards me, and my inward soul
With nothing trembles: at something it grieves,
More than with parting from my lord the King.

Bushy. Each substance of a grief hath twenty shadows,
Which shows like grief itself, but is not so;
For sorrow's eyes, glazed with blinding tears,
Divides one thing entire to many objects,
Like perspectives, which rightly gaz'd upon
Show nothing but confusion—ey'd awry
Distinguish form; so your sweet Majesty,
Looking awry upon your lord's departure,
Find shapes of grief, more than himself, to wail;
Which, look'd on as it is, is nought but shadows
Of what it is not. Then, thrice-gracious Queen,
More than your lord's departure weep not: more 's not seen;
Or if it be, 't is with false sorrow's eye,
Which for things true weeps things imaginary.

Queen. It may be so; but yet my inward soul
Persuades me it is otherwise: howe'er it be,
I cannot but be sad; so heavy sad
As, though on thinking on no thought I think,
Makes me with heavy nothing faint and shrink.

Bushy. 'T is nothing but conceit, my gracious lady.

Queen. 'T is nothing less: conceit is still deriv'd
From some forefather grief; mine is not so,
For nothing hath begot my something grief,
Or something hath the nothing that I grieve:
'T is in reversion that I do possess;
But what it is, that is not yet known; what,
I cannot name; 't is nameless woe, I wot.

Enter *Green.*

Green. God save your Majesty! and well met, gentlemen:
I hope the King is not yet shipp'd for Ireland.

Queen. Why hop'st thou so? 'T is better hope he is;
For his designs crave haste, his haste good hope.
Then wherefore dost thou hope he is not shipp'd?

Green. That he, our hope, might have retir'd his power,
And driven into despair an enemy's hope,
Who strongly hath set footing in this land.
The banish'd Bolingbroke repeals himself,
And with uplifted arms is safe arriv'd
At Ravenspurgh.

Queen. Now God in heaven forbid!

Green. Ah, madam, 't is too true; and, that is worse,

280. This line, wanting in all old editions, must have been dropped from the manuscript, since it was the son and heir of Arundel who "broke from the Duke of Exeter." The line is supplied from Holinshed. **286. tall,** excellent. **292. Imp out,** graft upon. **293. broking pawn,** security in the hands of a broker. **Scene ii: 14. shadows,** false images.

18. perspectives, glasses or figures showing distorted images except when looked at from a certain angle. **rightly,** directly. **20. Distinguish form,** show distinct form. **33. conceit,** imagination. **34. less,** i.e., than conceit. **still,** always. **46. retir'd,** withdrawn. **49. repeals,** recalls. **50. uplifted,** raised in his defense. **51. Ravenspurgh,** in Yorkshire on the Humber. **52. that,** what.

The Lord Northumberland, his son young Henry Percy,
The Lords of Ross, Beaumond, and Willoughby,
With all their powerful friends, are fled to him.
Bushy. Why have you not proclaim'd Northumberland
And all the rest revolted faction traitors?
Green. We have; whereupon the Earl of Worcester
Hath broken his staff, resign'd his stewardship,
And all the household servants fled with him
To Bolingbroke.
Queen. So, Green, thou art the midwife to my woe,
And Bolingbroke my sorrow's dismal heir.
Now hath my soul brought forth her prodigy,
And I, a gasping new-deliver'd mother,
Have woe to woe, sorrow to sorrow join'd.
Bushy. Despair not, madam.
Queen. Who shall hinder me?
I will despair, and be at enmity
With cozening hope: he is a flatterer,
A parasite, a keeper back of death,
Who gently would dissolve the bands of life,
Which false hope lingers in extremity.

Enter *York.*

Green. Here comes the Duke of York.
Queen. With signs of war about his aged neck;
O, full of careful business are his looks!
Uncle, for God's sake, speak comfortable words.
York. Should I do so, I should belie my thoughts:
Comfort 's in heaven; and we are on the earth,
Where nothing lives but crosses, cares, and grief.
Your husband, he is gone to save far off,
Whilst others come to make him lose at home.
Here am I left to underprop his land,
Who, weak with age, cannot support myself:
Now comes the sick hour that his surfeit made;
Now shall he try his friends that flatter'd him.

Enter a *Servant.*

Serv. My lord, your son was gone before I came.
York. He was? Why, so! go all which way it will!
The nobles they are fled; the commons they are cold,
And will, I fear, revolt on Hereford's side.
Sirrah, get thee to Plashy, to my sister Gloucester;
Bid her send me presently a thousand pound.
Hold, take my ring.
Serv. My lord, I had forgot to tell your lordship,
To-day, as I came by, I called there,—
But I shall grieve you to report the rest.
York. What is 't, knave?
Serv. An hour before I came, the Duchess died.
York. God for his mercy! what a tide of woes
Comes rushing on this woeful land at once!
I know not what to do: I would to God,
So my untruth had not provok'd him to it,
The King had cut off my head with my brother's.
What, are there no posts dispatch'd for Ireland?
How shall we do for money for these wars?
Come, sister,—cousin, I would say,—pray, pardon me.
Go, fellow get thee home, provide some carts
And bring away the armour that is there.
Exit Servant.
Gentlemen, will you go muster men?
If I know how or which way to order these affairs
Thus disorderly thrust into my hands,
Never believe me. Both are my kinsmen:
T' one is my sovereign, whom both my oath
And duty bids defend; t' other again
Is my kinsman, whom the King hath wrong'd,
Whom conscience and my kindred bids to right.
Well, somewhat we must do. Come, cousin, I 'll
Dispose of you.
Gentlemen, go, muster up your men,
And meet me presently at Berkeley.
I should to Plashy too,
But time will not permit: all is uneven,
And everything is left at six and seven.
Exeunt York and Queen.
Bushy. The wind sits fair for news to go for Ireland,
But none returns. For us to levy power
Proportionable to the enemy
Is all unpossible.
Green. Besides, our nearness to the King in love
Is near the hate of those love not the King.
Bagot. And that 's the wavering commons, for their love
Lies in their purses; and whoso empties them

63. heir, child, not inheritor. **64. prodigy,** monstrous birth. **69. cozening,** deceiving. **72. lingers,** causes to linger. **75. careful,** anxious.

112. T' one, the one. **122. at six and seven,** in confusion. **128. those,** those who.

By so much fills their hearts with deadly hate.
Bushy. Wherein the King stands generally condemn'd.
Bagot. If judgement lie in them, then so do we,
Because we ever have been near the King.
Green. Well, I will for refuge straight to Bristol castle:
The Earl of Wiltshire is already there.
Bushy. Thither will I with you; for little office
The hateful commons will perform for us,
Except like curs to tear us all to pieces.
Will you go along with us?
Bagot. No; I will to Ireland to his Majesty.
Farewell! If heart's presages be not vain,
We three here part that ne'er shall meet again.
Bushy. That 's as York thrives to beat back Bolingbroke.
Green. Alas, poor duke! the task he undertakes
Is numb'ring sands and drinking oceans dry,
Where one on his side fights, thousands will fly.
Farewell at once, for once, for all, and ever.
Bushy. Well, we may meet again.
Bagot. I fear me, never.
Exeunt.

Scene III. *Wilds in Gloucestershire.*

Enter *Bolingbroke* and *Northumberland.*

Boling. How far is it, my lord, to Berkeley now?
North. Believe me, noble lord,
I am a stranger here in Gloucestershire:
These high wild hills and rough uneven ways
Draws out our miles, and makes them wearisome;
And yet your fair discourse hath been as sugar,
Making the hard way sweet and delectable.
But I bethink me what a weary way
From Ravenspurgh to Cotswold will be found
In Ross and Willoughby, wanting your company,
Which, I protest, hath very much beguil'd
The tediousness and process of my travel.
But theirs is sweeten'd with the hope to have
The present benefit which I possess;
And hope to joy is little less in joy
Than hope enjoy'd: by this the weary lords
Shall make their way seem short, as mine hath done
By sight of what I have, your noble company.

133. so do we, i.e., stand condemned. **138. hateful,** full of hate. **Scene iii: 12. tediousness and process,** tedious course.

Boling. Of much less value is my company
Than your good words. But who comes here?

Enter *Henry Percy.*

North. It is my son, young Harry Percy,
Sent from my brother Worcester, whencesoever.
Harry, how fares your uncle?
Percy. I had thought, my lord, to have learn'd his health of you.
North. Why, is he not with the Queen?
Percy. No, my good lord; he hath forsook the court,
Broken his staff of office, and dispers'd
The household of the King.
North. What was his reason?
He was not so resolv'd when last we spake together.
Percy. Because your lordship was proclaimed traitor.
But he, my lord, is gone to Ravenspurgh
To offer service to the Duke of Hereford,
And sent me over by Berkeley, to discover
What power the Duke of York had levied there;
Then with directions to repair to Ravenspurgh.
North. Have you forgot the Duke of Hereford, boy?
Percy. No, my good lord, for that is not forgot
Which ne'er I did remember: to my knowledge,
I never in my life did look on him.
North. Then learn to know him now; this is the Duke.
Percy. My gracious lord, I tender you my service,
Such as it is, being tender, raw, and young;
Which elder days shall ripen and confirm
To more approved service and desert.
Boling. I thank thee, gentle Percy; and be sure
I count myself in nothing else so happy
As in a soul remembering my good friends;
And, as my fortune ripens with thy love,
It shall be still thy true love's recompense:
My heart this covenant makes, my hand thus seals it.
North. How far is it to Berkeley? and what stir
Keeps good old York there with his men of war?
Percy. There stands the castle, by yon tuft of trees,
Mann'd with three hundred men, as I have heard;
And in it are the Lords of York, Berkeley, and Seymour;
None else of name and noble estimate.

Enter *Ross* and *Willoughby*.

North. Here come the Lords of Ross and Willoughby,
Bloody with spurring, fiery-red with haste.
Boling. Welcome, my lords. I wot your love pursues
A banish'd traitor. All my treasury
Is yet but unfelt thanks, which more enrich'd
Shall be your love and labour's recompense.
Ross. Your presence makes us rich, most noble lord.
Willo. And far surmounts our labour to attain it.
Boling. Evermore thanks, th' exchequer of the poor,
Which, till my infant fortune comes to years,
Stands for my bounty. But who comes here?

Enter *Berkeley*.

North. It is my Lord of Berkeley, as I guess.
Berk. My Lord of Hereford, my message is to you.
Boling. My lord, my answer is—to Lancaster;
And I am come to seek that name in England;
And I must find that title in your tongue,
Before I make reply to aught you say.
Berk. Mistake me not, my lord; 't is not my meaning
To raze one title of your honour out.
To you, my lord, I come, what lord you will,
From the most gracious regent of this land,
The Duke of York, to know what pricks you on
To take advantage of the absent time
And fright our native peace with self-borne arms.

Enter *York* attended.

Boling. I shall not need transport my words by you;
Here comes his Grace in person. My noble uncle! *Kneels.*
York. Show me thy humble heart, and not thy knee,
Whose duty is deceiveable and false.
Boling. My gracious uncle—
York. Tut, tut!
Grace me no grace, nor uncle me no uncle.
I am no traitor's uncle; and that word "grace"
In an ungracious mouth is but profane.
Why have those banish'd and forbidden legs
Dar'd once to touch a dust of England's ground?
But then more "why?" Why have they dar'd to march
So many miles upon her peaceful bosom,
Frighting her pale-fac'd villages with war
And ostentation of despised arms?
Com'st thou because the anointed King is hence?
Why, foolish boy, the King is left behind,
And in my loyal bosom lies his power.
Were I but now the lord of such hot youth
As when brave Gaunt, thy father, and myself
Rescued the Black Prince, that young Mars of men,
From forth the ranks of many thousand French,
O, then how quickly should this arm of mine,
Now prisoner to the palsy, chastise thee
And minister correction to thy fault!
Boling. My gracious uncle, let me know my fault.
On what condition stands it and wherein?
York. Even in condition of the worst degree,
In gross rebellion and detested treason:
Thou art a banish'd man, and here art come
Before the expiration of thy time,
In braving arms against thy sovereign.
Boling. As I was banish'd, I was banish'd Hereford;
But as I come, I come for Lancaster.
And, noble uncle, I beseech your Grace
Look on my wrongs with an indifferent eye.
You are my father, for methinks in you
I see old Gaunt alive. O, then, my father,
Will you permit that I shall stand condemn'd
A wandering vagabond; my rights and royalties
Pluck'd from my arms perforce, and given away
To upstart unthrifts? Wherefore was I born?
If that my cousin king be King of England,
It must be granted I am Duke of Lancaster.
You have a son, Aumerle, my noble cousin;
Had you first died, and he been thus trod down,
He should have found his uncle Gaunt a father
To rouse his wrongs and chase them to the bay.
I am denied to sue my livery here,
And yet my letters patents give me leave:
My father's goods are all distrain'd and sold,
And these and all are all amiss employ'd.
What would you have me do? I am a subject,
And I challenge law: attorneys are denied me;
And therefore personally I lay my claim
To my inheritance of free descent.
North. The noble Duke hath been too much abus'd.

61. unfelt, intangible. **79. absent time,** time of absence. **84. deceiveable,** deceptive. **91. dust,** particle.

95. despised, despicable, because shown in a bad cause. **107. condition,** quality. **112. braving,** defiant. **116. indifferent,** impartial. **131. distrain'd,** seized to meet an obligation. **136. free,** direct.

Ross. It stands your Grace upon to do him right.
Willo. Base men by his endowments are made great.
York. My lords of England, let me tell you this:
I have had feeling of my cousin's wrongs
And labour'd all I could to do him right;
But in this kind to come, in braving arms,
Be his own carver and cut out his way,
To find out right with wrong, it may not be;
And you that do abet him in this kind
Cherish rebellion and are rebels all.
North. The noble Duke hath sworn his coming is
But for his own; and for the right of that
We all have strongly sworn to give him aid;
And let him ne'er see joy that breaks that oath!
York. Well, well, I see the issue of these arms:
I cannot mend it, I must needs confess,
Because my power is weak and all ill left;
But if I could, by Him that gave me life,
I would attach you all and make you stoop
Unto the sovereign mercy of the King;
But since I cannot, be it known to you
I do remain as neuter. So, fare you well;
Unless you please to enter in the castle
And there repose you for this night.
Boling. An offer, uncle, that we will accept.
But we must win your Grace to go with us
To Bristol castle, which they say is held
By Bushy, Bagot, and their complices,
The caterpillars of the commonwealth,
Which I have sworn to weed and pluck away.
York. It may be I will go with you; but yet I 'll pause,
For I am loath to break our country's laws.
Nor friends nor foes, to me welcome you are.
Things past redress are now with me past care.
Exeunt.

Scene IV. *A camp in Wales.*

Enter *Salisbury* and a Welsh *Captain.*

Cap. My Lord of Salisbury, we have stay'd ten days,
And hardly kept our countrymen together,
And yet we hear no tidings from the King;
Therefore we will disperse ourselves: farewell!
Sal. Stay yet another day, thou trusty Welshman.
The King reposeth all his confidence in thee.
Cap. 'T is thought the King is dead; we will not stay.
The bay-trees in our country are all wither'd
And meteors fright the fixed stars of heaven;
The pale-fac'd moon looks bloody on the earth,
And lean-look'd prophets whisper fearful change;
Rich men look sad and ruffians dance and leap,
The one in fear to lose what they enjoy,
The other to enjoy by rage and war:
These signs forerun the death or fall of kings.
Farewell! Our countrymen are gone and fled,
As well assur'd Richard their king is dead.
Exit.
Sal. Ah, Richard, with the eyes of heavy mind
I see thy glory like a shooting star
Fall to the base earth from the firmament.
Thy sun sets weeping in the lowly west,
Witnessing storms to come, woe, and unrest.
Thy friends are fled to wait upon thy foes,
And crossly to thy good all fortune goes.
Exit.

ACT III. Scene I. *Bristol. Before the castle.*

Enter *Bolingbroke, York, Northumberland, Ross, Percy, Willoughby,* with *Bushy* and *Green,* prisoners.

Boling. Bring forth these men.
Bushy and Green, I will not vex your souls—
Since presently your souls must part your bodies—
With too much urging your pernicious lives,
For 't were no charity; yet, to wash your blood
From off my hands, here in the view of men
I will unfold some causes of your deaths.
You have misled a prince, a royal king,
A happy gentleman in blood and lineaments,
By you unhappied and disfigur'd clean.
You have in manner with your sinful hours
Made a divorce betwixt his queen and him,
Broke the possession of a royal bed

138. stands . . . upon, is incumbent upon. **146. in this kind,** in this way of acting. **154. ill left,** poorly provided. **156. attach,** arrest. **165. complices,** accomplices. **Act III, Scene i: 3. part,** part from. **4. urging,** emphasizing.

Scene iv: 14. to enjoy, in hope of enjoyment. **24. crossly,** adversely. **Act III, Scene i: 13. Broke,** interrupted.

And stain'd the beauty of a fair queen's cheeks
With tears drawn from her eyes by your foul wrongs.
Myself, a prince by fortune of my birth,
Near to the King in blood, and near in love
Till you did make him misinterpret me,
Have stoop'd my neck under your injuries,
And sigh'd my English breath in foreign clouds,
Eating the bitter bread of banishment;
Whilst you have fed upon my signories,
Dispark'd my parks and fell'd my forest woods,
From my own windows torn my household coat,
Raz'd out my imprese, leaving me no sign,
Save men's opinions and my living blood,
To show the world I am a gentleman.
This and much more, much more than twice all this,
Condemns you to the death. See them delivered over
To execution and the hand of death.

Bushy. More welcome is the stroke of death to me
Than Bolingbroke to England. Lords, farewell!

Green. My comfort is that heaven will take our souls
And plague injustice with the pains of hell.

Boling. My Lord Northumberland, see them dispatch'd.

Exeunt Northumberland and others, with the prisoners.

Uncle, you say the Queen is at your house;
For God's sake, fairly let her be entreated;
Tell her I send to her my kind commends.
Take special care my greetings be deliver'd.

York. A gentleman of mine I have dispatch'd
With letters of your love to her at large.

Boling. Thanks, gentle uncle. Come, lords, away,
To fight with Glendower and his complices:
Awhile to work, and after holiday. *Exeunt.*

Scene II. *The coast of Wales. A castle in view.*

Drums: flourish and colours. Enter *King Richard*, the *Bishop of Carlisle, Aumerle,* and Soldiers.

K. Rich. Barkloughly castle call they this at hand?

Aum. Yea, my lord. How brooks your Grace the air,
After your late tossing on the breaking seas?

K. Rich. Needs must I like it well; I weep for joy
To stand upon my kingdom once again.
Dear earth, I do salute thee with my hand,
Though rebels wound thee with their horses' hoofs:
As a long-parted mother with her child
Plays fondly with her tears and smiles in meeting,
So, weeping, smiling, greet I thee, my earth,
And do thee favours with my royal hands.
Feed not thy sovereign's foe, my gentle earth,
Nor with thy sweets comfort his ravenous sense;
But let thy spiders, that suck up thy venom,
And heavy-gaited toads lie in their way,
Doing annoyance to the treacherous feet
Which with usurping steps do trample thee.
Yield stinging nettles to mine enemies;
And when they from thy bosom pluck a flower,
Guard it, I pray thee, with a lurking adder
Whose double tongue may with a mortal touch
Throw death upon thy sovereign's enemies.
Mock not my senseless conjuration, lords.
This earth shall have a feeling, and these stones
Prove armed soldiers, ere her native king
Shall falter under foul rebellion's arms.

Car. Fear not, my lord; that Power that made you king
Hath power to keep you king in spite of all.
The means that heavens yield must be embrac'd,
And not neglected; else, if heaven would
And we will not, heaven's offer we refuse,
The proffer'd means of succour and redress.

Aum. He means, my lord, that we are too remiss;
Whilst Bolingbroke, through our security,
Grows strong and great in substance and in power.

K. Rich. Discomfortable cousin! know'st thou not
That when the searching eye of heaven is hid
Behind the globe, that lights the lower world,
Then thieves and robbers range abroad unseen
In murders and in outrage, boldly here;
But when from under this terrestrial ball
He fires the proud tops of the eastern pines
And darts his light through every guilty hole,
Then murders, treasons, and detested sins,
The cloak of night being pluck'd from off their backs,
Stand bare and naked, trembling at themselves?
So when this thief, this traitor, Bolingbroke,
Who all this while hath revell'd in the night,

22. **signories,** lordships. 23. **Dispark'd,** pulled down the inclosures of. 24. **coat,** coat of arms blazoned in the stained glass. 25. **imprese,** device on a scutcheon. 38. **commends,** compliments. 41. **love,** kindly feeling. Scene ii: 2. **brooks,** enjoys.

21. **double,** forked. 23. **conjuration,** adjuration. 25. **native,** by natural right. 34. **security,** carelessness.

Whilst we were wand'ring with the antipodes,
Shall see us rising in our throne, the east,
His treasons will sit blushing in his face,
Not able to endure the sight of day,
But, self-affrighted, tremble at his sin.
Not all the water in the rough rude sea
Can wash the balm off from an anointed king;
The breath of worldly men cannot depose
The deputy elected by the Lord:
For every man that Bolingbroke hath press'd
To lift shrewd steel against our golden crown,
God for his Richard hath in heavenly pay
A glorious angel; then, if angels fight,
Weak men must fall, for Heaven still guards the right.

Enter *Salisbury*.

Welcome, my lord. How far off lies your power?

Sal. Nor near nor farther off, my gracious lord,
Than this weak arm: discomfort guides my tongue
And bids me speak of nothing but despair.
One day too late, I fear me, noble lord,
Hath clouded all thy happy days on earth:
O, call back yesterday, bid time return,
And thou shalt have twelve thousand fighting men!
To-day, to-day, unhappy day, too late,
O'erthrows thy joys, friends, fortune, and thy state;
For all the Welshmen, hearing thou wert dead,
Are gone to Bolingbroke, dispers'd, and fled.

Aum. Comfort, my liege; why looks your Grace so pale?

K. Rich. But now the blood of twenty thousand men
Did triumph in my face, and they are fled;
And, till so much blood thither come again,
Have I not reason to look pale and dead?
All souls that will be safe fly from my side,
For time hath set a blot upon my pride.

Aum. Comfort, my liege; remember who you are.

K. Rich. I had forgot myself; am I not King?
Awake, thou coward majesty! thou sleepest.
Is not the King's name twenty thousand names?
Arm, arm, my name! a puny subject strikes
At thy great glory. Look not to the ground,
Ye favourites of a king; are we not high?
High be our thoughts: I know my uncle York
Hath power enough to serve our turn. But who comes here?

55. balm, consecrated oil used to anoint a king. **58. press'd,** impressed, conscripted. **64. near,** nearer.

Enter *Scroop*.

Scroop. More health and happiness betide my liege
Than can my care-tun'd tongue deliver him!

K. Rich. Mine ear is open and my heart prepar'd.
The worst is worldly loss thou canst unfold.
Say, is my kingdom lost? Why, 't was my care;
And what loss is it to be rid of care?
Strives Bolingbroke to be as great as we?
Greater he shall not be; if he serve God,
We 'll serve Him too and be his fellow so.
Revolt our subjects? That we cannot mend;
They break their faith to God as well as us.
Cry woe, destruction, ruin, and decay;
The worst is death, and death will have his day.

Scroop. Glad am I that your Highness is so arm'd
To bear the tidings of calamity.
Like an unseasonable stormy day,
Which makes the silver rivers drown their shores,
As if the world were all dissolv'd to tears,
So high above his limits swells the rage
Of Bolingbroke, covering your fearful land
With hard bright steel and hearts harder than steel.
White-beards have arm'd their thin and hairless scalps
Against thy majesty; boys, with women's voices,
Strive to speak big, and clap their female joints
In stiff unwieldy arms against thy crown;
Thy very beadsmen learn to bend their bows
Of double-fatal yew against thy state;
Yea, distaff-women manage rusty bills
Against thy seat: both young and old rebel,
And all goes worse than I have power to tell.

K. Rich. Too well, too well thou tell'st a tale so ill.
Where is the Earl of Wiltshire? Where is Bagot?
What is become of Bushy? Where is Green?
That they have let the dangerous enemy
Measure our confines with such peaceful steps?
If we prevail, their heads shall pay for it.
I warrant they have made peace with Bolingbroke.

Scroop Peace have they made with him indeed, my lord.

K. Rich. O villains, vipers, damn'd without redemption!
Dogs, easily won to fawn on any man!

102. Cry, proclaim. **114. female,** weak. **116. beadsmen,** almsmen. **117. double-fatal,** used for bows and for poison. **118. bills,** long-handled axes.

Snakes, in my heart-blood warm'd, that sting my heart!
Three Judases, each one thrice worse than Judas!
Would they make peace? Terrible hell
Make war upon their spotted souls for this!

Scroop. Sweet love, I see, changing his property,
Turns to the sourest and most deadly hate:
Again uncurse their souls; their peace is made
With heads, and not with hands: those whom you curse
Have felt the worst of death's destroying wound
And lie full low, grav'd in the hollow ground.

Aum. Is Bushy, Green, and the Earl of Wiltshire dead?

Scroop. Ay, all of them at Bristol lost their heads.

Aum. Where is the Duke my father with his power?

K. Rich. No matter where; of comfort no man speak:
Let 's talk of graves, of worms, and epitaphs;
Make dust our paper and with rainy eyes
Write sorrow on the bosom of the earth.
Let 's choose executors and talk of wills;
And yet not so; for what can we bequeath
Save our deposed bodies to the ground?
Our lands, our lives, and all are Bolingbroke's,
And nothing can we call our own but death,
And that small model of the barren earth
Which serves as paste and cover to our bones.
For God's sake, let us sit upon the ground
And tell sad stories of the death of kings:
How some have been depos'd; some slain in war;
Some haunted by the ghosts they have depos'd;
Some poison'd by their wives; some sleeping kill'd;
All murder'd: for within the hollow crown
That rounds the mortal temples of a king
Keeps Death his court, and there the antic sits,
Scoffing his state and grinning at his pomp,
Allowing him a breath, a little scene,
To monarchize, be fear'd, and kill with looks,
Infusing him with self and vain conceit,
As if this flesh which walls about our life
Were brass impregnable; and humour'd thus
Comes at the last and with a little pin
Bores through his castle wall, and—farewell king!
Cover your heads, and mock not flesh and blood
With solemn reverence: throw away respect,
Tradition, form, and ceremonious duty;
For you have but mistook me all this while:
I live with bread like you, feel want, taste grief,
Need friends: subjected thus,
How can you say to me I am a king?

Car. My lord, wise men ne'er sit and wail their woes,
But presently prevent the ways to wail.
To fear the foe, since fear oppresseth strength,
Gives in your weakness strength unto your foe,
And so your follies fight against yourself.
Fear, and be slain; no worse can come to fight;
And fight and die is death destroying death,
Where fearing dying pays death servile breath.

Aum. My father hath a power; inquire of him,
And learn to make a body of a limb.

K. Rich. Thou chid'st me well. Proud Bolingbroke, I come
To change blows with thee for our day of doom.
This ague fit of fear is over-blown;
An easy task it is to win our own.
Say, Scroop, where lies our uncle with his power?
Speak sweetly, man, although thy looks be sour.

Scroop. Men judge by the complexion of the sky
The state and inclination of the day;
So may you by my dull and heavy eye,
My tongue hath but a heavier tale to say.
I play the torturer by small and small
To lengthen out the worst that must be spoken.
Your uncle York is join'd with Bolingbroke,
And all your northern castles yielded up,
And all your southern gentlemen in arms
Upon his party.

K. Rich. Thou hast said enough.
To Aumerle. Beshrew thee, cousin, which didst lead me forth
Of that sweet way I was in to despair!
What say you now? What comfort have we now?
By heaven, I 'll hate him everlastingly
That bids me be of comfort any more.
Go to Flint castle; there I 'll pine away;
A king, woe's slave, shall kingly woe obey.
That power I have, discharge; and let them go
To ear the land that hath some hope to grow,
For I have none. Let no man speak again
To alter this, for counsel is but vain.

Aum. My liege, one word.

135. property, nature. **153. model,** image. **162. antic,** grotesque figure. **163. Scoffing his state,** scoffing at his majesty. **166. self,** selfish. **168. humour'd thus,** possessed of this humor (conceit).

184-5. And fight . . . breath, one who dies in fighting, triumphs over Death; but one who dies in fear, dies in subjection to Death. **212. ear,** plow.

K. Rich. He does me double wrong
That wounds me with the flatteries of his tongue.
Discharge my followers; let them hence away,
From Richard's night to Bolingbroke's fair day. *Exeunt.*

Scene III. *Wales. Before Flint Castle.*

Enter, with drum and colours, *Bolingbroke, York, Northumberland,* Attendants and forces.

Boling. So that by this intelligence we learn
The Welshmen are dispers'd and Salisbury
Is gone to meet the King, who lately landed
With some few private friends upon this coast.
North. The news is very fair and good, my lord.
Richard not far from hence hath hid his head.
York. It would beseem the Lord Northumberland
To say King Richard. Alack the heavy day
When such a sacred king should hide his head!
North. Your Grace mistakes; only to be brief
Left I his title out.
York. The time hath been,
Would you have been so brief with him, he would
Have been so brief with you, to shorten you,
For taking so the head, your whole head's length.
Boling. Mistake not, uncle, further than you should.
York. Take not, good cousin, further than you should,
Lest you mistake: the heavens are o'er our heads.
Boling. I know it, uncle, and oppose not myself
Against their will. But who comes here?

Enter *Percy.*

Welcome, Harry. What, will not this castle yield?
Percy. The castle royally is mann'd, my lord,
Against thy entrance.
Boling. Royally!
Why, it contains no king?
Percy. Yes, my good lord,
It doth contain a king. King Richard lies
Within the limits of yon lime and stone;
And with him are the Lord Aumerle, Lord Salisbury,
Sir Stephen Scroop, besides a clergyman
Of holy reverence; who, I cannot learn.
North. O, belike it is the Bishop of Carlisle.
Boling. Noble lords,
Go to the rude ribs of that ancient castle;
Through brazen trumpet send the breath of parley
Into his ruin'd ears, and thus deliver:
Henry Bolingbroke
On both his knees doth kiss King Richard's hand
And sends allegiance and true faith of heart
To his most royal person, hither come
Even at his feet to lay my arms and power,
Provided that my banishment repeal'd
And lands restor'd again be freely granted.
If not, I 'll use th' advantage of my power
And lay the summer's dust with showers of blood
Rain'd from the wounds of slaughter'd Englishmen;
The which, how far off from the mind of Bolingbroke
It is, such crimson tempest should bedrench
The fresh green lap of fair King Richard's land,
My stooping duty tenderly shall show.
Go, signify as much, while here we march
Upon the grassy carpet of this plain.
Let 's march without the noise of threat'ning drum,
That from this castle's tatter'd battlements
Our fair appointments may be well perus'd.
Methinks King Richard and myself should meet
With no less terror than the elements
Of fire and water, when their thund'ring shock
At meeting tears the cloudy cheeks of heaven.
Be he the fire, I 'll be the yielding water;
The rage be his, whilst on the earth I rain
My waters; on the earth, and not on him.
March on, and mark King Richard how he looks.

Parle without and answer within: then a flourish. Enter on the walls, *King Richard,* the *Bishop of Carlisle, Aumerle, Scroop,* and *Salisbury.*

See, see, King Richard doth himself appear,
As doth the blushing discontented sun
From out the fiery portal of the east,
When he perceives the envious clouds are bent
To dim his glory and to stain the track
Of his bright passage to the occident.
York. Yet looks he like a king! Behold, his eye,
As bright as is the eagle's, lightens forth

Scene iii: 13. to, as to. **14. head,** title.

32. rude ribs, the walls. **34. deliver,** announce.

Controlling majesty. Alack, alack, for woe,
That any harm should stain so fair a show!

K. Rich. We are amaz'd; and thus long have we stood *To Northumberland.*
To watch the fearful bending of thy knee,
Because we thought ourself thy lawful king;
And if we be, how dare thy joints forget
To pay their awful duty to our presence?
If we be not, show us the hand of God
That hath dismiss'd us from our stewardship;
For well we know, no hand of blood and bone
Can gripe the sacred handle of our sceptre,
Unless he do profane, steal, or usurp.
And though you think that all, as you have done,
Have torn their souls by turning them from us,
And we are barren and bereft of friends,
Yet know, my master, God omnipotent,
Is mustering in his clouds on our behalf
Armies of pestilence; and they shall strike
Your children yet unborn and unbegot,
That lift your vassal hands against my head
And threat the glory of my precious crown.
Tell Bolingbroke—for yon methinks he stands—
That every stride he makes upon my land
Is dangerous treason. He is come to open
The purple testament of bleeding war;
But ere the crown he looks for live in peace,
Ten thousand bloody crowns of mothers' sons
Shall ill become the flower of England's face,
Change the complexion of her maid-pale peace
To scarlet indignation, and bedew
Her pastures' grass with faithful English blood.

North. The King of heaven forbid our lord the King
Should so with civil and uncivil arms
Be rush'd upon! Thy thrice noble cousin
Harry Bolingbroke doth humbly kiss thy hand;
And by the honourable tomb he swears,
That stands upon your royal grandsire's bones,
And by the royalties of both your bloods,
Currents that spring from one most gracious head,
And by the buried hand of warlike Gaunt,
And by the worth and honour of himself,
Comprising all that may be sworn or said,
His coming hither hath no further scope
Than for his lineal royalties, and to beg
Enfranchisement immediate on his knees;
Which on thy royal party granted once,
His glittering arms he will commend to rust,
His barbed steeds to stables, and his heart
To faithful service of your Majesty.
This swears he, as he is a prince, is just;
And, as I am a gentleman, I credit him.

K. Rich. Northumberland, say thus the King returns:
His noble cousin is right welcome hither;
And all the number of his fair demands
Shall be accomplish'd without contradiction.
With all the gracious utterance thou hast
Speak to his gentle hearing kind commends.

Northumberland withdraws to Bolingbroke.

[*To Aumerle.*] We do debase ourselves, cousin, do we not,
To look so poorly and to speak so fair?
Shall we call back Northumberland, and send
Defiance to the traitor, and so die?

Aum. No, good my lord; let 's fight with gentle words
Till time lend friends, and friends their helpful swords.

K. Rich. O God, O God! that e'er this tongue of mine,
That laid the sentence of dread banishment
On yon proud man, should take it off again
With words of sooth! O that I were as great
As is my grief, or lesser than my name!
Or that I could forget what I have been,
Or not remember what I must be now!
Swell'st thou, proud heart? I 'll give thee scope to beat,
Since foes have scope to beat both thee and me.

Aum. Northumberland comes back from Bolingbroke.

K. Rich. What must the King do now? Must he submit?
The King shall do it. Must he be depos'd?
The King shall be contented. Must he lose
The name of king? O' God's name, let it go.
I 'll give my jewels for a set of beads,
My gorgeous palace for a hermitage,
My gay apparel for an almsman's gown,
My figur'd goblets for a dish of wood,
My sceptre for a palmer's walking-staff,
My subjects for a pair of carved saints,
And my large kingdom for a little grave,
A little little grave, an obscure grave;
Or I 'll be buried in the King's highway,
Some way of common trade, where subjects' feet
May hourly trample on their sovereign's head;
For on my heart they tread now whilst I live,
And buried once, why not upon my head?

81. **profane**, commit sacrilege. 83. **torn**, perjured. 94. **purple testament**, blood-stained will. 97-100. **Shall . . . blood**, a bold and involved figure. At first Richard thinks of the blooming surface of England; but in the next line, the land has become the flower-like human face of England. 102. **civil**, as in civil war. **uncivil**, violent. 112. **scope**, aim. 114. **enfranchisement**, restoration of rights as citizen.

115. **party**, side. 121. **returns**, i.e., an answer. 136. **sooth**, flattery. 147. **set of beads**, a rosary. 156. **trade**, traffic.

Aumerle, thou weep'st, my tender-hearted cousin!
We 'll make foul weather with despised tears.
Our sighs and they shall lodge the summer corn,
And make a dearth in this revolting land.
Or shall we play the wantons with our woes,
And make some pretty match with shedding tears?
As thus, to drop them still upon one place,
Till they have fretted us a pair of graves
Within the earth; and, therein laid,—there lies
Two kinsmen digg'd their graves with weeping eyes.
Would not this ill do well? Well, well, I see
I talk but idly, and you laugh at me.
Most mighty prince, my lord Northumberland,
What says King Bolingbroke? Will his Majesty
Give Richard leave to live till Richard die?
You make a leg, and Bolingbroke says ay.

North. My lord, in the base court he doth attend
To speak with you, may it please you to come down.

K. Rich. Down, down I come; like glist'ring Phaethon,
Wanting the manage of unruly jades.
In the base court? Base court, where kings grow base,
To come at traitors' calls and do them grace.
In the base court? Come down? Down, court! down, king!
For night-owls shriek where mounting larks should sing. *Exeunt from above.*

Boling. What says his Majesty?

North. Sorrow and grief of heart
Makes him speak fondly, like a frantic man;
Yet he is come.

Enter *King Richard* and his Attendants below.

Boling. Stand all apart,
And show fair duty to his Majesty.
He kneels down.
My gracious lord,—

K. Rich. Fair cousin, you debase your princely knee
To make the base earth proud with kissing it.
Me rather had my heart might feel your love
Than my unpleas'd eye see your courtesy.
Up, cousin, up; your heart is up, I know,
Thus high at least [*touching his own head*], although your knee be low.

Boling. My gracious lord, I come but for mine own.

K. Rich. Your own is yours, and I am yours, and all.

Boling. So far be mine, my most redoubted lord,
As my true service shall deserve your love.

K. Rich. Well you deserve; they well deserve to have,
That know the strong'st and surest way to get.
Uncle, give me your hands: nay, dry your eyes;
Tears show their love, but want their remedies.
Cousin, I am too young to be your father,
Though you are old enough to be my heir.
What you will have, I 'll give, and willing too;
For do we must what force will have us do.
Set on towards London, cousin, is it so?

Boling. Yea, my good lord.

K. Rich. Then I must not say no.
Flourish. Exeunt.

Scene IV. *Langley. The Duke of York's garden.*

Enter the *Queen* and two *Ladies.*

Queen. What sport shall we devise here in this garden
To drive away the heavy thought of care?

Lady. Madam, we'll play at bowls.

Queen. 'T will make me think the world is full of rubs,
And that my fortune runs against the bias.

Lady. Madam, we 'll dance.

Queen. My legs can keep no measure in delight,
When my poor heart no measure keeps in grief;
Therefore, no dancing, girl; some other sport.

Lady. Madam, we'll tell tales.

Queen. Of sorrow or of joy?

Lady. Of either, madam.

Queen. Of neither, girl;
For if of joy, being altogether wanting,
It doth remember me the more of sorrow;
Or if of grief, being altogether had,
It adds more sorrow to my want of joy;
For what I have I need not to repeat,
And what I want it boots not to complain.

Lady. Madam, I'll sing.

Queen. 'T is well that thou hast cause;
But thou shouldst please me better, wouldst thou weep.

Lady. I could weep, madam, would it do you good.

162. lodge, lay low. **167. fretted,** worn. **175. make a leg,** make an obeisance. **176. base court,** the outer courtyard was usually on a lower level than the inner one. **179. manage of,** control of. **jades,** broken-down horses.

203. want, are devoid of. **204. young,** Richard and Bolingbroke were both born in 1367. **Scene iv: 4. rubs,** diversion of a bowl from its course by anything but the **bias** (l. 5), the weighted side of the ball that causes it to swerve. **14. remember,** remind. **15. being altogether had,** possessing me completely.

Queen. And I could sing, would weeping do me good,
And never borrow any tear of thee.

Enter a *Gardener* and two *Servants.*

But stay, here come the gardeners:
Let 's step into the shadow of these trees.
My wretchedness unto a row of pins,
They 'll talk of state; for every one doth so
Against a change; woe is forerun with woe.
Queen and Ladies retire.

Gard. Go, bind thou up yond dangling apricocks,
Which, like unruly children, make their sire
Stoop with oppression of their prodigal weight;
Give some supportance to the bending twigs.
Go thou, and like an executioner,
Cut off the heads of too fast growing sprays,
That look too lofty in our commonwealth;
All must be even in our government.
You thus employ'd, I will go root away
The noisome weeds, which without profit suck
The soil's fertility from wholesome flowers.

Serv. Why should we in the compass of a pale
Keep law and form and due proportion,
Showing, as in a model, our firm estate,
When our sea-walled garden, the whole land,
Is full of weeds, her fairest flowers chok'd up,
Her fruit-trees all unprun'd, her hedges ruin'd,
Her knots disorder'd and her wholesome herbs
Swarming with caterpillars?

Gard. Hold thy peace.
He that hath suffer'd this disorder'd spring
Hath now himself met with the fall of leaf.
The weeds which his broad-spreading leaves did shelter,
That seem'd in eating him to hold him up,
Are pluck'd up root and all by Bolingbroke,
I mean the Earl of Wiltshire, Bushy, Green.

Serv. What, are they dead?

Gard. They are; and Bolingbroke
Hath seiz'd the wasteful King. O, what pity is it
That he had not so trimm'd and dress'd his land
As we this garden! We at time of year
Do wound the bark, the skin of our fruit-trees,
Lest, being over-proud in sap and blood,
With too much riches it confound itself;
Had he done so to great and growing men,
They might have liv'd to bear and he to taste
Their fruits of duty. Superfluous branches
We lop away, that bearing boughs may live;
Had he done so, himself had borne the crown,
Which waste of idle hours hath quite thrown down.

Serv. What, think you the King shall be depos'd?

Gard. Depress'd he is already, and depos'd
'T is doubt he will be. Letters came last night
To a dear friend of the good Duke of York's,
That tell black tidings.

Queen. O, I am press'd to death through want of speaking! *Coming forward.*
Thou, old Adam's likeness, set to dress this garden,
How dares thy harsh rude tongue sound this unpleasing news?
What Eve, what serpent, hath suggested thee
To make a second fall of cursed man?
Why dost thou say King Richard is depos'd?
Dar'st thou, thou little better thing than earth,
Divine his downfall? Say, where, when, and how,
Cam'st thou by this ill tidings? Speak, thou wretch.

Gard. Pardon me, madam; little joy have I
To breathe this news; yet what I say is true.
King Richard, he is in the mighty hold
Of Bolingbroke: their fortunes both are weigh'd.
In your lord's scale is nothing but himself,
And some few vanities that make him light;
But in the balance of great Bolingbroke,
Besides himself, are all the English peers,
And with that odds he weighs King Richard down.
Post you to London, and you 'll find it so;
I speak no more than every one doth know.

Queen. Nimble Mischance, that art so light of foot,
Doth not thy embassage belong to me,
And am I last that knows it? O, thou think'st
To serve me last, that I may longest keep
Thy sorrow in my breast. Come, ladies, go,
To meet at London London's king in woe.
What, was I born to this, that my sad look
Should grace the triumph of great Bolingbroke?
Gardener, for telling me these news of woe,
Pray God the plants thou graft'st may never grow. *Exeunt Queen and Ladies.*

Gard. Poor queen! so that thy state might be no worse,
I would my skill were subject to thy curse.
Here did she fall a tear; here in this place
I 'll set a bank of rue, sour herb of grace.
Rue, even for ruth, here shortly shall be seen,
In the remembrance of a weeping queen.
Exeunt.

22. And . . . good, if my troubles were of the sort to be relieved by tears, I could sing for joy. **28. Against a change,** when a change is about to occur. **woe . . . woe,** grief is a herald of disaster. **29. apricocks,** apricots. **35. look too lofty,** aspire too high. **40. pale,** enclosure. **42. firm estate,** settled condition. **46. knots,** flower beds arranged in strange shapes. **57. time,** proper time. **60. confound,** destroy.

69. doubt, fear. **83. hold,** grasp. **104. fall,** let fall.

ACT IV. Scene I. *Westminster Hall.*

Enter as to the Parliament *Bolingbroke, Aumerle, Northumberland, Percy, Fitzwater, Surrey,* the *Bishop of Carlisle,* the *Abbot of Westminster* and another *Lord,* Herald, and Officers.

Boling. Call forth Bagot.

Enter *Bagot.*

Now, Bagot, freely speak thy mind;
What thou dost know of noble Gloucester's death,
Who wrought it with the King, and who perform'd
The bloody office of his timeless end.

Bagot. Then set before my face the Lord Aumerle.

Boling. Cousin, stand forth, and look upon that man.

Bagot. My Lord Aumerle, I know your daring tongue
Scorns to unsay what once it hath deliver'd.
In that dead time when Gloucester's death was plotted,
I heard you say, "Is not my arm of length,
That reacheth from the restful English court
As far as Calais, to mine uncle's head?"
Amongst much other talk, that very time,
I heard you say that you had rather refuse
The offer of an hundred thousand crowns
Than Bolingbroke's return to England;
Adding withal, how blest this land would be
In this your cousin's death.

Aum. Princes and noble lords,
What answer shall I make to this base man?
Shall I so much dishonour my fair stars,
On equal terms to give him chastisement?
Either I must, or have mine honour soil'd
With the attainder of his sland'rous lips.
There is my gage, the manual seal of death,
That marks thee out for hell: I say, thou liest,
And will maintain what thou hast said is false
In thy heart-blood, though being all too base
To stain the temper of my knightly sword.

Boling. Bagot, forbear; thou shalt not take it up.

Aum. Excepting one, I would he were the best
In all this presence that hath mov'd me so.

Fitz. If that thy valour stand on sympathy,
There is my gage, Aumerle, in gage to thine:
By that fair sun which shows me where thou stand'st,
I heard thee say, and vauntingly thou spak'st it,
That thou wert cause of noble Gloucester's death.
If thou deny'st it twenty times, thou liest;
And I will turn thy falsehood to thy heart,
Where it was forged, with my rapier's point.

Aum. Thou dar'st not, coward, live to see that day.

Fitz. Now, by my soul, I would it were this hour.

Aum. Fitzwater, thou art damn'd to hell for this.

Percy. Aumerle, thou liest; his honour is as true
In this appeal as thou art all unjust;
And that thou art so, there I throw my gage,
To prove it on thee to the extremest point
Of mortal breathing. Seize it, if thou dar'st.

Aum. An if I do not, may my hands rot off
And never brandish more revengeful steel
Over the glittering helmet of my foe!

Another Lord. I task the earth to the like, forsworn Aumerle;
And spur thee on with full as many lies
As may be halloaed in thy treacherous ear
From sun to sun: there is my honour's pawn;
Engage it to the trial, if thou darest.

Aum. Who sets me else? By heaven, I 'll throw at all!
I have a thousand spirits in one breast,
To answer twenty thousand such as you.

Surrey. My Lord Fitzwater, I do remember well
The very time Aumerle and you did talk.

Fitz. 'T is very true; you were in presence then,
And you can witness with me this is true.

Surrey. As false, by heaven, as heaven itself is true.

Fitz. Surrey, thou liest.

Surrey. Dishonourable boy!
That lie shall lie so heavy on my sword,
That it shall render vengeance and revenge
Till thou the lie-giver and that lie do lie
In earth as quiet as thy father's skull;
In proof whereof, there is my honour's pawn;
Engage it to the trial, if thou dar'st.

Fitz. How fondly dost thou spur a forward horse!
If I dare eat, or drink, or breathe, or live,

Act IV, Scene i: 4. wrought it, influenced the king to do it. **5. timeless,** untimely. **10. dead,** death-like, i.e., utterly dark. **21. stars,** i.e., destiny. **33. sympathy,** external equality.

52. I . . . like, I lay on the earth the task of bearing my like gage. **55. pawn,** pledge. **57. Who sets me else,** who else challenges me?

I dare meet Surrey in a wilderness,
And spit upon him, whilst I say he lies,
And lies, and lies. There is my bond of faith,
To tie thee to my strong correction.
As I intend to thrive in this new world,
Aumerle is guilty of my true appeal;
Besides, I heard the banish'd Norfolk say
That thou, Aumerle, didst send two of thy men
To execute the noble Duke at Calais.

Aum. Some honest Christian trust me with a gage,
That Norfolk lies. Here do I throw down this,
If he may be repeal'd, to try his honour.

Boling. These differences shall all rest under gage
Till Norfolk be repeal'd: repeal'd he shall be,
And, though mine enemy, restor'd again
To all his lands and signories. When he 's return'd,
Against Aumerle we will enforce his trial.

Car. That honourable day shall ne'er be seen.
Many a time hath banish'd Norfolk fought
For Jesu Christ in glorious Christian field,
Streaming the ensign of the Christian cross
Against black pagans, Turks, and Saracens;
And, toil'd with works of war, retir'd himself
To Italy; and there at Venice gave
His body to that pleasant country's earth,
And his pure soul unto his captain Christ,
Under whose colours he had fought so long.

Boling. Why, Bishop, is Norfolk dead?

Car. As surely as I live, my lord.

Boling. Sweet Peace conduct his sweet soul to the bosom
Of good old Abraham! Lords appellants,
Your differences shall all rest under gage
Till we assign you to your days of trial.

Enter *York* attended.

York. Great Duke of Lancaster, I come to thee
From plume-pluck'd Richard; who with willing soul
Adopts thee heir, and his high sceptre yields
To the possession of thy royal hand.
Ascend his throne, descending now from him;
And long live Henry, fourth of that name!

Boling. In God's name, I 'll ascend the regal throne.

Car. Marry, God forbid!
Worst in this royal presence may I speak,
Yet best beseeming me to speak the truth.
Would God that any in this noble presence
Were enough noble to be upright judge
Of noblè Richard! Then true noblesse would
Learn him forbearance from so foul a wrong.
What subject can give sentence on his king?
And who sits here that is not Richard's subject?
Thieves are not judg'd but they are by to hear,
Although apparent guilt be seen in them;
And shall the figure of God's majesty,
His captain, steward, deputy elect,
Anointed, crowned, planted many years,
Be judg'd by subject and inferior breath,
And he himself not present? O, forfend it, God,
That in a Christian climate souls refin'd
Should show so heinous, black, obscene a deed!
I speak to subjects, and a subject speaks,
Stirr'd up by God, thus boldly for his king.
My Lord of Hereford here, whom you call king,
Is a foul traitor to proud Hereford's king;
And if you crown him, let me prophesy,
The blood of English shall manure the ground,
And future ages groan for this foul act.
Peace shall go sleep with Turks and infidels,
And in this seat of peace tumultuous wars
Shall kin with kin and kind with kind confound.
Disorder, horror, fear, and mutiny
Shall here inhabit, and this land be call'd
The field of Golgotha and dead men's skulls.
O, if you raise this house against this house,
It will the woefullest division prove
That ever fell upon this cursed earth.
Prevent it, resist it, let it not be so,
Lest child, child's children, cry against you "woe!"

North. Well have you argu'd, sir; and, for your pains,
Of capital treason we arrest you here.
My Lord of Westminster, be it your charge
To keep him safely till his day of trial.
May it please you, lords, to grant the commons' suit?

Boling. Fetch hither Richard, that in common view
He may surrender; so we shall proceed
Without suspicion.

York. I will be his conduct. *Exit.*

Boling. Lords, you that here are under our arrest,
Procure your sureties for your days of answer:
Little are we beholding to your love,
And little look'd for at your helping hands.

78. **world**, era. 79. **appeal**, accusation involving a challenge. 85. **repeal'd**, recalled from banishment. 96. **toil'd**, worn out. 115. **Worst**, of least importance.

120. **Learn**, teach. 123. **judg'd**, condemned. 124. **apparent**, evident. 130. **climate**, region. 131. **obscene**, foul. 145. **raise**, rouse. 157. **conduct**, guide.

Re-enter York, with Richard and Officers bearing the crown and sceptre.

K. Rich. Alack, why am I sent for to a king,
Before I have shook off the regal thoughts
Wherewith I reign'd? I hardly yet have learn'd
To insinuate, flatter, bow, and bend my knee.
Give sorrow leave a while to tutor me
To this submission. Yet I well remember
The favours of these men: were they not mine?
Did they not sometime cry, "All hail!" to me?
So Judas did to Christ; but He, in twelve,
Found truth in all but one; I, in twelve thousand, none.
God save the King!—Will no man say amen?
Am I both priest and clerk? Well then, amen.
God save the King! although I be not he;
And yet, amen, if heaven do think him me.—
To do what service am I sent for hither?

York. To do that office of thine own good will
Which tired majesty did make thee offer,
The resignation of thy state and crown
To Henry Bolingbroke.

K. Rich. Give me the crown.—Here, cousin, seize the crown;
Here, cousin,
On this side my hand, and on that side thine.
Now is this golden crown like a deep well
That owes two buckets, filling one another,
The emptier ever dancing in the air,
The other down, unseen, and full of water.
That bucket down and full of tears am I,
Drinking my griefs, whilst you mount up on high.

Boling. I thought you had been willing to resign.

K. Rich. My crown I am; but still my griefs are mine.
You may my glories and my state depose,
But not my griefs; still am I king of those.

Boling. Part of your cares you give me with your crown.

K. Rich. Your cares set up do not pluck my cares down.
My care is loss of care, by old care done;
Your care is gain of care, by new care won.
The cares I give I have, though given away;
They 'tend the crown, yet still with me they stay.

Boling. Are you contented to resign the crown?

K. Rich. Ay, no; no, ay; for I must nothing be;
Therefore no no, for I resign to thee.
Now mark me, how I will undo myself.
I give this heavy weight from off my head,
And this unwieldy sceptre from my hand,
The pride of kingly sway from out my heart.
With mine own tears I wash away my balm,
With mine own hands I give away my crown,
With mine own tongue deny my sacred state,
With mine own breath release all duteous oaths;
All pomp and majesty I do forswear;
My manors, rents, revenues I forgo;
My acts, decrees, and statutes I deny:
God pardon all oaths that are broke to me!
God keep all vows unbroke are made to thee!
Make me, that nothing have, with nothing griev'd,
And thou with all pleas'd, that hast all achiev'd!
Long mayst thou live in Richard's seat to sit,
And soon lie Richard in an earthy pit!
God save King Henry, unking'd Richard says,
And send him many years of sunshine days!
—What more remains?

North. No more, but that you read *Presenting a paper.*
These accusations and these grievous crimes
Committed by your person and your followers
Against the state and profit of this land;
That, by confessing them, the souls of men
May deem that you are worthily depos'd.

K. Rich. Must I do so? and must I ravel out
My weav'd-up follies? Gentle Northumberland,
If thy offences were upon record,
Would it not shame thee in so fair a troop
To read a lecture of them? If thou wouldst,
There shouldst thou find one heinous article,
Containing the deposing of a king
And cracking the strong warrant of an oath,
Mark'd with a blot, damn'd in the book of heaven.
Nay, all of you that stand and look upon me
Whilst that my wretchedness doth bait myself,
Though some of you with Pilate wash your hands
Showing an outward pity; yet you Pilates
Have here deliver'd me to my sour cross,
And water cannot wash away your sin.

North. My lord, dispatch; read o'er these articles.

K. Rich. Mine eyes are full of tears, I cannot see;
And yet salt water blinds them not so much
But they can see a sort of traitors here.
Nay, if I turn mine eyes upon myself,
I find myself a traitor with the rest;

168. favours, faces. **185. owes,** owns. **199. 'tend,** attend. **201. Ay, no,** this is over-ingenious punning. *Ay* equals *I*, which in turn is equal to nothing or *no*.

225. state and profit, existing order and material interests. **238. bait,** worry.

For I have given here my soul's consent
T' undeck the pompous body of a king;
Made glory base, a sovereignty a slave,
Proud majesty a subject, state a peasant.
North. My lord,—
K. Rich. No lord of thine, thou haught insulting man.
Nor no man's lord. I have no name, no title;
No, not that name was given me at the font,
But 't is usurp'd. Alack the heavy day,
That I have worn so many winters out,
And know not now what name to call myself!
O that I were a mockery king of snow,
Standing before the sun of Bolingbroke,
To melt myself away in water-drops!
Good king, great king, and yet not greatly good,
An if my word be sterling yet in England,
Let it command a mirror hither straight,
That it may show me what a face I have,
Since it is bankrupt of his majesty.
Boling. Go some of you and fetch a looking-glass. *Exit an attendant.*
North. Read o'er this paper while the glass doth come.
K. Rich. Fiend, thou torments me e'er I come to hell!
Boling. Urge it no more, my Lord Northumberland.
North. The commons will not then be satisfi'd.
K. Rich. They shall be satisfied: I 'll read enough,
When I do see the very book indeed
Where all my sins are writ, and that 's myself.

Re-enter Attendant, with a glass.

Give me that glass, and therein will I read.
No deeper wrinkles yet? Hath sorrow struck
So many blows upon this face of mine,
And made no deeper wounds? O flatt'ring glass,
Like to my followers in prosperity,
Thou dost beguile me! Was this face the face
That every day under his household roof
Did keep ten thousand men? Was this the face
That, like the sun, did make beholders wink?
Is this the face which fac'd so many follies,
That was at last out-fac'd by Bolingbroke?
A brittle glory shineth in this face;
As brittle as the glory is the face,
Dashes the glass against the ground.
For there it is, crack'd in an hundred shivers.
Mark, silent king, the moral of this sport,
How soon my sorrow hath destroy'd my face.

250. pompous, magnificent. **254. haught,** haughty. **281. beguile,** deceive. **284. wink,** close the eye. **285. fac'd,** braved.

Boling. The shadow of your sorrow hath destroy'd
The shadow of your face.
K. Rich. Say that again.
The shadow of my sorrow! Ha! let 's see.
'T is very true, my grief lies all within;
And these external manners of laments
Are merely shadows to the unseen grief
That swells with silence in the tortur'd soul.
There lies the substance; and I thank thee, King,
For thy great bounty, that not only giv'st
Me cause to wail but teachest me the way
How to lament the cause. I 'll beg one boon,
And then be gone and trouble you no more.
Shall I obtain it?
Boling. Name it, fair cousin.
K. Rich. "Fair cousin"? I am greater than a king;
For when I was a king, my flatterers
Were then but subjects; being now a subject,
I have a king here to my flatterer.
Being so great, I have no need to beg.
Boling. Yet ask.
K. Rich. And shall I have?
Boling. You shall.
K. Rich. Then give me leave to go.
Boling. Whither?
K. Rich. Whither you will, so I were from your sights.
Boling. Go, some of you convey him to the Tower.
K. Rich. O, good! convey! Conveyers are you all,
That rise thus nimbly by a true king's fall.
Exeunt King Richard, some Lords, and a Guard.
Boling. On Wednesday next we solemnly set down
Our coronation. Lords, prepare yourselves.
Exeunt all but the Bishop of Carlisle, the Abbot of Westminster, and Aumerle.
Abbot. A woeful pageant have we here beheld.
Car. The woe 's to come; the children yet unborn
Shall feel this day as sharp to them as thorn.
Aum. You holy clergymen, is there no plot
To rid the realm of this pernicious blot?
Abbot. My lord,
Before I freely speak my mind herein,
You shall not only take the sacrament
To bury mine intents, but also to effect
Whatever I shall happen to devise.
I see your brows are full of discontent,
Your hearts of sorrow and your eyes of tears.
Come home with me to supper; and I 'll lay
A plot shall show us all a merry day. *Exeunt.*

308. to, as. **317. conveyers,** cant term for thieves.

ACT V. SCENE I. *London. A street leading to the Tower.*

Enter *Queen* and Ladies.

Queen. This way the King will come; this is the way
To Julius Cæsar's ill-erected tower,
To whose flint bosom my condemned lord
Is doom'd a prisoner by proud Bolingbroke.
Here let us rest, if this rebellious earth
Have any resting for her true king's queen.

Enter *Richard* and Guard.

But soft, but see, or rather do not see,
My fair rose wither; yet look up, behold,
That you in pity may dissolve to dew,
And wash him fresh again with true-love tears.
Ah, thou, the model where old Troy did stand,
Thou map of honour, thou King Richard's tomb,
And not King Richard; thou most beauteous inn,
Why should hard-favour'd Grief be lodg'd in thee,
When Triumph is become an alehouse guest?

K. Rich. Join not with grief, fair woman, do not so,
To make my end too sudden: learn, good soul,
To think our former state a happy dream;
From which awak'd, the truth of what we are
Shows us but this. I am sworn brother, sweet,
To grim Necessity; and he and I
Will keep a league till death. Hie thee to France
And cloister thee in some religious house.
Our holy lives must win a new world's crown,
Which our profane hours here have thrown down.

Queen. What, is my Richard both in shape and mind
Transform'd and weaken'd? Hath Bolingbroke depos'd
Thine intellect? Hath he been in thy heart?
The lion dying thrusteth forth his paw,
And wounds the earth, if nothing else, with rage
To be o'erpower'd; and wilt thou, pupil-like,
Take the correction, mildly kiss the rod,
And fawn on rage with base humility,
Which art a lion and the king of beasts?

K. Rich. A king of beasts, indeed; if aught but beasts,
I had been still a happy king of men.
Good sometimes queen, prepare thee hence for France.
Think I am dead, and that even here thou tak'st,
As from my death-bed, thy last living leave.
In winter's tedious nights sit by the fire
With good old folks and let them tell thee tales
Of woeful ages long ago betid;
And ere thou bid good night, to quite their griefs
Tell thou the lamentable tale of me
And send the hearers weeping to their beds:
For why, the senseless brands will sympathize
The heavy accent of thy moving tongue,
And in compassion weep the fire out;
And some will mourn in ashes, some coal-black,
For the deposing of a rightful king.

Enter *Northumberland* and others.

North. My lord, the mind of Bolingbroke is chang'd;
You must to Pomfret, not unto the Tower.
And, madam, there is order ta'en for you;
With all swift speed you must away to France.

K. Rich. Northumberland, thou ladder wherewithal
The mounting Bolingbroke ascends my throne,
The time shall not be many hours of age
More than it is, ere foul sin gathering head
Shall break into corruption: thou shalt think,
Though he divide the realm and give thee half,
It is too little, helping him to all;
He shall think that thou, which knowest the way
To plant unrightful kings, wilt know again,
Being ne'er so little urg'd, another way
To pluck him headlong from the usurped throne.
The love of wicked men converts to fear;
That fear to hate, and hate turns one or both
To worthy danger and deserved death.

North. My guilt be on my head, and there an end.
Take leave and part; for you must part forthwith.

K. Rich. Doubly divorc'd! Bad men, you violate
A twofold marriage, 'twixt my crown and me,
And then betwixt me and my married wife.
Let me unkiss the oath 'twixt thee and me;
And yet not so, for with a kiss 't was made.

Act V, Scene i: 2. ill-erected, erected for evil purposes. **11-13. Ah . . . inn**, the figures of speech indicate Richard as but the ruin of his former self. A "model" is a ground plan, here of a ruined city; a map is a mere outline; an inn, too, is but a temporary lodging for grief. **24. new world's**, heaven's. **28-29. Hath . . . heart**, i.e., stolen your courage also. **31. to be** at being.

42. betid, past. **43. quite**, requite. **griefs**, sad tales. **46. For why**, because. **68. worthy**, merited. **74.** Annul the oath sealed with a kiss.

Part us, Northumberland; I towards the north,
Where shivering cold and sickness pines the clime;
My wife to France; from whence, set forth in pomp,
She came adorned hither like sweet May,
Sent back like Hallowmas or short'st of day.

Queen. And must we be divided? Must we part?

K. Rich. Ay, hand from hand, my love, and heart from heart.

Queen. Banish us both, and send the King with me.

North. That were some love but little policy.

Queen. Then whither he goes, thither let me go.

K. Rich. So two, together weeping, make one woe.
Weep thou for me in France, I for thee here;
Better far off than near, be ne'er the near.
Go, count thy way with sighs; I mine with groans.

Queen. So longest way shall have the longest moans.

K. Rich. Twice for one step I 'll groan, the way being short,
And piece the way out with a heavy heart.
Come, come, in wooing sorrow let 's be brief,
Since, wedding it, there is such length in grief.
One kiss shall stop our mouths, and dumbly part;
Thus give I mine, and thus take I thy heart.

Queen. Give me mine own again; 't were no good part
To take on me to keep and kill thy heart.—
So, now I have mine own again, be gone,
That I may strive to kill it with a groan.

K. Rich. We make woe wanton with this fond delay.
Once more, adieu; the rest let sorrow say.
Exeunt.

Scene II. *The Duke of York's palace.*

Enter *York* and his *Duchess.*

Duch. My lord, you told me you would tell the rest,
When weeping made you break the story off,
Of our two cousins coming into London.

York. Where did I leave?

Duch. At that sad stop, my lord,
Where rude misgovern'd hands from windows' tops
Threw dust and rubbish on King Richard's head.

York. Then, as I said, the Duke, great Bolingbroke,
Mounted upon a hot and fiery steed
Which his aspiring rider seem'd to know,
With slow but stately pace kept on his course,
Whilst all tongues cried, "God save thee, Bolingbroke!"
You would have thought the very windows spake,
So many greedy looks of young and old
Through casements darted their desiring eyes
Upon his visage, and that all the walls
With painted imagery had said at once,
"Jesu preserve thee! Welcome, Bolingbroke!"
Whilst he, from the one side to the other turning,
Bareheaded, lower than his proud steed's neck,
Bespake them thus: "I thank you, countrymen."
And thus still doing, thus he pass'd along.

Duch. Alack, poor Richard! where rode he the whilst?

York. As in a theatre, the eyes of men,
After a well-grac'd actor leaves the stage,
Are idly bent on him that enters next,
Thinking his prattle to be tedious;
Even so, or with much more contempt, men's eyes
Did scowl on gentle Richard. No man cried, "God save him!"
No joyful tongue gave him his welcome home;
But dust was thrown upon his sacred head,
Which with such gentle sorrow he shook off,
His face still combating with tears and smiles,
The badges of his grief and patience,
That had not God, for some strong purpose, steel'd
The hearts of men, they must perforce have melted,
And barbarism itself have pitied him.
But Heaven hath a hand in these events,
To whose high will we bow our calm contents.
To Bolingbroke are we sworn subjects now,
Whose state and honour I for aye allow.

Enter *Aumerle.*

Duch. Here comes my son Aumerle.

York. Aumerle that was;
But that is lost for being Richard's friend,
And, madam, you must call him Rutland now:
I am in parliament pledge for his truth
And lasting fealty to the new made king.

77. pines, distresses, causes to suffer. **80. Hallowmas,** Nov. 1. **88. Better . . . near,** better to be far off than near without hope of meeting. **Scene ii: 4. Leave,** leave off.

16. painted imagery, figured tapestry. **25. idly,** casually. **38. To . . . contents,** in deference to whose will we acquiesce in limiting our desires. **40. allow,** accept. **41. Aumerle that was,** he had been deprived of that title by Henry's first Parliament, so that he was merely the Earl of Rutland.

Duch. Welcome, my son! Who are the violets now
That strew the green lap of the new come spring?
Aum. Madam, I know not, nor I greatly care not.
God knows I had as lief be none as one.
York. Well, bear you well in this new spring of time,
Lest you be cropp'd before you come to prime.
What news from Oxford? Do these jousts and triumphs hold?
Aum. For aught I know, my lord, they do.
York. You will be there, I know.
Aum. If God prevent not, I purpose so.
York. What seal is that, that hangs without thy bosom?
Yea, look'st thou pale? Let me see the writing.
Aum. My lord, 't is nothing.
York. No matter, then, who see it.
I will be satisfied; let me see the writing.
Aum. I do beseech your Grace to pardon me.
It is a matter of small consequence,
Which for some reasons I would not have seen.
York. Which for some reasons, sir, I mean to see.
I fear, I fear,—
Duch. What should you fear?
'T is nothing but some band, that he is enter'd into
For gay apparel 'gainst the triumph day.
York. Bound to himself! What doth he with a bond
That he is bound to? Wife, thou art a fool.
Boy, let me see the writing.
Aum. I do beseech you, pardon me. I may not show it.
York. I will be satisfied; let me see it, I say.

He plucks it out of his bosom and reads it.

Treason! foul treason! Villain! traitor! slave!
Duch. What is the matter, my lord?
York. Ho! who is within there?

Enter a Servant.

Saddle my horse.
God for his mercy, what treachery is here!
Duch. Why, what is it, my lord?
York. Give me my boots, I say; saddle my horse. *Exit Servant.*
Now, by mine honour, by my life, by my troth,
I will appeach the villain.
Duch. What is the matter?
York. Peace, foolish woman.
Duch. I will not peace. What is the matter, Aumerle?
Aum. Good mother, be content; it is no more
Than my poor life must answer.
Duch. Thy life answer!
York. Bring me my boots; I will unto the King.

Re-enter Servant with boots.

Duch. Strike him, Aumerle. Poor boy, thou art amaz'd.
—Hence, villain! never more come in my sight.
York. Give me my boots, I say.
Duch. Why, York, what wilt thou do?
Wilt thou not hide the trespass of thine own?
Have we more sons? or are we like to have?
Is not my teeming date drunk up with time?
And wilt thou pluck my fair son from mine age,
And rob me of a happy mother's name?
Is he not like thee? Is he not thine own?
York. Thou fond mad woman,
Wilt thou conceal this dark conspiracy?
A dozen of them here have ta'en the sacrament,
And interchangeably set down their hands,
To kill the King at Oxford.
Duch. He shall be none;
We 'll keep him here; then what is that to him?
York. Away, fond woman! were he twenty times my son,
I would appeach him.
Duch. Hadst thou groan'd for him
As I have done, thou wouldst be more pitiful.
But now I know thy mind; thou dost suspect
That I have been disloyal to thy bed,
And that he is a bastard, not thy son.
Sweet York, sweet husband, be not of that mind.
He is as like thee as a man may be,
Not like to me, or any of my kin,
And yet I love him.
York. Make way, unruly woman! *Exit.*
Duch. After, Aumerle! mount thee upon his horse;
Spur post, and get before him to the King,
And beg thy pardon ere he do accuse thee.
I 'll not be long behind; though I be old,
I doubt not but to ride as fast as York.

52. **triumphs,** public festivities or shows. 65. **band,** bond. 79. **appeach,** accuse.

85. **him,** i.e., the servant. **amaz'd,** bewildered. 91. **teeming date,** period of childbearing. 98. **And . . . hands,** the conspirators had signed each of the articles of the agreement.

And never will I rise up from the ground
Till Bolingbroke have pardon'd thee. Away, be gone! *Exeunt.*

Scene III. *Windsor Castle.*

Enter *Bolingbroke, Percy,* and other Lords.

Boling. Can no man tell me of my unthrifty son?
'T is full three months since I did see him last.
If any plague hang over us, 't is he:
I would to God, my lords, he might be found:
Inquire at London, 'mongst the taverns there,
For there, they say, he daily doth frequent
With unrestrained loose companions,
Even such, they say, as stand in narrow lanes,
And beat our watch, and rob our passengers;
Which he, young wanton and effeminate boy,
Takes on the point of honour to support
So dissolute a crew.

Percy. My lord, some two days since I saw the Prince,
And told him of those triumphs held at Oxford.

Boling. And what said the gallant?

Percy. His answer was, he would unto the stews,
And from the common'st creature pluck a glove,
And wear it as a favour; and with that
He would unhorse the lustiest challenger.

Boling. As dissolute as desperate; yet through both
I see some sparks of better hope, which elder years
May happily bring forth. But who comes here?

Enter *Aumerle,* amazed.

Aum. Where is the King?

Boling. What means our cousin, that he stares and looks
So wildly?

Aum. God save your Grace! I do beseech your Majesty,
To have some conference with your Grace alone.

Boling. Withdraw yourselves, and leave us here alone. *Exeunt Percy and Lords.*
What is the matter with our cousin now?

Aum. For ever may my knees grow to the earth, *Kneeling.*
My tongue cleave to my roof within my mouth,
Unless a pardon ere I rise or speak.

Boling. Intended or committed was this fault?
If on the first, how heinous e'er it be,
To win thy after-love I pardon thee.

Aum. Then give me leave that I may turn the key,
That no man enter till my tale be done.

Boling. Have thy desire.

York knocks at the door and crieth.

York. My liege, beware! Look to thyself;
Thou hast a traitor in thy presence there.

Boling. Villain, I 'll make thee safe. *Drawing.*

Aum. Stay thy revengeful hand; thou hast no cause to fear.

York. [*Within.*] Open the door, secure, foolhardy King!
Shall I for love speak treason to thy face?
Open the door, or I will break it open.

Enter *York.*

Boling. What is the matter, uncle? Speak;
Recover breath; tell us how near is danger,
That we may arm us to encounter it.

York. Peruse this writing here, and thou shalt know
The treason that my haste forbids me show.

Aum. Remember, as thou read'st, thy promise pass'd.
I do repent me; read not my name there.
My heart is not confederate with my hand.

York. It was, villain, ere thy hand did set it down.
I tore it from the traitor's bosom, King;
Fear, and not love, begets his penitence.
Forget to pity him, lest thy pity prove
A serpent that will sting thee to the heart.

Boling. O heinous, strong, and bold conspiracy!
O loyal father of a treacherous son!
Thou sheer, immaculate, and silver fountain,
From whence this stream through muddy passages
Hath held his current and defil'd himself!
Thy overflow of good converts to bad,
And thy abundant goodness shall excuse
This deadly blot in thy digressing son.

York. So shall my virtue be his vice's bawd;
And he shall spend mine honour with his shame,
As thriftless sons their scraping fathers' gold.
Mine honour lives when his dishonour dies,

Scene iii: 1. unthrifty, worthless. **9. passengers,** passers-by. **10. effeminate,** capricious. **20. desperate,** reckless. **23. s. d. amazed,** in confusion.

43. secure, without suspicion of danger. **44. treason,** i.e., by calling him "foolhardy." **61. sheer,** pure. **66. digressing,** transgressing.

Or my sham'd life in his dishonour lies:
Thou kill'st me in his life; giving him breath,
The traitor lives, the true man 's put to death.

Duch. [*Within.*] What ho, my liege! for God's sake, let me in.

Boling. What shrill-voiced suppliant makes this eager cry?

Duch. A woman, and thy aunt, great King; 't is I.
Speak with me, pity me, open the door!
A beggar begs that never begg'd before.

Boling. Our scene is alter'd from a serious thing,
And now chang'd to "The Beggar and the King."
My dangerous cousin, let your mother in:
I know she 's come to pray for your foul sin.

York. If thou do pardon, whosoever pray,
More sins for this forgiveness prosper may.
This fester'd joint cut off, the rest rest sound;
This let alone will all the rest confound.

Enter *Duchess.*

Duch. O King, believe not this hard-hearted man!
Love loving not itself none other can.

York. Thou frantic woman, what dost thou make here?
Shall thy old dugs once more a traitor rear?

Duch. Sweet York, be patient. Hear me, gentle liege. *She kneels.*

Boling. Rise up, good aunt.

Duch. Not yet, I thee beseech.
For ever will I walk upon my knees,
And never see day that the happy sees,
Till thou give joy; until thou bid me joy,
By pardoning Rutland, my transgressing boy.

Aum. Unto my mother's prayers I bend my knee. *Kneels.*

York. Against them both my true joints bended be. *Kneels.*
Ill mayst thou thrive, if thou grant any grace!

Duch. Pleads he in earnest? Look upon his face;
His eyes do drop no tears, his prayers are in jest;
His words come from his mouth, ours from our breast.
He prays but faintly and would be deni'd;
We pray with heart and soul and all beside.
His weary joints would gladly rise, I know;
Our knees shall kneel till to the ground they grow.
His prayers are full of false hypocrisy;
Ours of true zeal and deep integrity:
Our prayers do out-pray his; then let them have
That mercy which true prayer ought to have.

Boling. Good aunt, stand up.

Duch. Nay, do not say, "Stand up";
Say "Pardon" first, and afterwards "Stand up."
An if I were thy nurse, thy tongue to teach,
"Pardon" should be the first word of thy speech.
I never long'd to hear a word till now.
Say "pardon," King; let pity teach thee how.
The word is short, but not so short as sweet;
No word like "pardon" for kings' mouths so meet.

York. Speak it in French, King; say, "*Pardonne moi.*"

Duch. Dost thou teach pardon pardon to destroy?
Ah, my sour husband, my hard-hearted lord,
That set'st the word itself against the word!
Speak "pardon" as 't is current in our land;
The chopping French we do not understand.
Thine eye begins to speak; set thy tongue there;
Or in thy piteous heart plant thou thine ear;
That hearing how our plaints and prayers do pierce,
Pity may move thee "pardon" to rehearse.

Boling. Good aunt, stand up.

Duch. I do not sue to stand;
Pardon is all the suit I have in hand.

Boling. I pardon him, as God shall pardon me.

Duch. O happy vantage of a kneeling knee!
Yet am I sick for fear: speak it again,
Twice saying "pardon" doth not pardon twain,
But makes one pardon strong.

Boling. I pardon him with all my heart.

Duch. A god on earth thou art.

Boling. But for our trusty brother-in-law and the abbot,
With all the rest of that consorted crew,
Destruction straight shall dog them at the heels.
Good uncle, help to order several powers
To Oxford, or where'er these traitors are.
They shall not live within this world, I swear,
But I will have them, if I once know where.
Uncle, farewell; and, cousin, adieu!
Your mother well hath pray'd, and prove you true.

Duch. Come, my old son; I pray God make thee new. *Exeunt.*

80. **"The . . . King,"** a reference to the ballad *King Cophetua and the Beggar-maid.* 86. **confound,** destroy. 88. **none other can,** can love no one else (not even you). 89. **make,** do.

124. **chopping,** mincing, affected. 128. **rehearse,** pronounce aloud. 137. **brother-in-law,** the Earl of Huntingdon had married Bolingbroke's sister Elizabeth. He was half-brother of Richard and is the Exeter of II, i, 281. 138. **consorted,** confederate. 140. **several powers,** separate bodies of troops. 146. **old,** unreformed.

Scene IV. *Another room in the same.*

Enter *Exton* and *Servant.*

Exton. Didst thou not mark the King, what words he spake,
"Have I no friend will rid me of this living fear?"
Was it not so?
Serv. These were his very words.
Exton. "Have I no friend?" quoth he. He spake it twice,
And urg'd it twice together, did he not?
Serv. He did.
Exton. And speaking it, he wistly look'd on me,
As who should say, "I would thou wert the man
That would divorce this terror from my heart;"
Meaning the King at Pomfret. Come, let 's go.
I am the King's friend, and will rid his foe.
Exeunt.

Scene V. *Pomfret Castle.*

Enter *King Richard.*

K. Rich. I have been studying how I may compare
This prison where I live unto the world;
And for because the world is populous
And here is not a creature but myself,
I cannot do it; yet I 'll hammer it out.
My brain I 'll prove the female to my soul,
My soul the father; and these two beget
A generation of still-breeding thoughts,
And these same thoughts people this little world,
In humours like the people of this world,
For no thought is contented. The better sort,
As thoughts of things divine, are intermix'd
With scruples and do set the word itself
Against the word:
As thus, "Come, little ones," and then again,
"It is as hard to come as for a camel
To thread the postern of a small needle's eye."
Thoughts tending to ambition, they do plot
Unlikely wonders: how these vain weak nails
May tear a passage through the flinty ribs
Of this hard world, my ragged prison walls,
And, for they cannot, die in their own pride.
Thoughts tending to content flatter themselves
That they are not the first of fortune's slaves,
Nor shall not be the last; like silly beggars
Who sitting in the stocks refuge their shame,
That many have and others must sit there;
And in this thought they find a kind of ease,
Bearing their own misfortunes on the back
Of such as have before endur'd the like.
Thus play I in one person many people,
And none contented. Sometimes am I king;
Then treasons make me wish myself a beggar;
And so I am. Then crushing penury
Persuades me I was better when a king;
Then am I king'd again: and by and by
Think that I am unking'd by Bolingbroke,
And straight am nothing. But whate'er I be,
Nor I nor any man that but man is
With nothing shall be pleas'd, till he be eas'd
With being nothing. Music do I hear?
The music plays.
Ha, ha! keep time! How sour sweet music is,
When time is broke and no proportion kept!
So is it in the music of men's lives.
And here have I the daintiness of ear
To check time broke in a disorder'd string;
But for the concord of my state and time
Had not an ear to hear my true time broke.
I wasted time, and now doth Time waste me;
For now hath Time made me his numb'ring clock.
My thoughts are minutes; and with sighs they jar
Their watches on unto mine eyes, the outward watch,
Whereto my finger, like a dial's point,
Is pointing still, in cleansing them from tears.
Now sir, the sound that tells what hour it is
Are clamorous groans, which strike upon my heart,
Which is the bell: so sighs and tears and groans
Show minutes, times, and hours; but my time
Runs posting on in Bolingbroke's proud joy,
While I stand fooling here, his Jack o' the clock.
This music mads me; let it sound no more;
For though it have holp madmen to their wits,
In me it seems it will make wise men mad.
Yet blessing on his heart that gives it me!
For 't is a sign of love; and love to Richard
Is a strange brooch in this all-hating world.

Scene iv: 5. urg'd, emphasized. **7. wistly,** fixedly. **11. rid,** take off. **Scene v: 8. still-breeding,** constantly breeding. **10. humours,** peculiarities of disposition. **13-14. do . . . word,** set one passage of Scripture off against another. **17. postern,** narrow gate. **21. ragged,** rugged.

25. silly, simple. **26. refuge,** find a refuge for. **46. check,** reprove. **50. numb'ring clock,** a clock by which he can count seconds and minutes as well as hours. Richard compares three manifestations of grief to a clock's three-fold measure of time. His sighs are like the ticking of the pendulum, which watches (numbers) the seconds. His tears, wiped away by the finger which is like the dial's point, are like the measurement of time upon the outward watch or dial by the minute hand. Finally his groans are like the bell which strikes the hours. **60. Jack,** figure which strikes the hours. **66. brooch,** ornament.

Enter a *Groom* of the Stable.

Groom. Hail, royal prince!
K. Rich. Thanks, noble peer!
The cheapest of us is ten groats too dear.
What art thou? and how com'st thou hither,
Where no man never comes but that sad dog
That brings me food to make misfortune live?
Groom. I was a poor groom of thy stable, King,
When thou wert king; who, travelling towards York,
With much ado at length have gotten leave
To look upon my sometimes royal master's face.
O, how it yearn'd my heart when I beheld
In London streets, that coronation-day,
When Bolingbroke rode on roan Barbary,
That horse that thou so often hast bestrid,
That horse that I so carefully have dress'd!
K. Rich. Rode he on Barbary? Tell me, gentle friend,
How went he under him?
Groom. So proudly as if he disdain'd the ground.
K. Rich. So proud that Bolingbroke was on his back!
That jade hath eat bread from my royal hand;
This hand hath made him proud with clapping him.
Would he not stumble? Would he not fall down,
Since pride must have a fall, and break the neck
Of that proud man that did usurp his back?
Forgiveness, horse! why do I rail on thee,
Since thou, created to be aw'd by man,
Wast born to bear? I was not made a horse;
And yet I bear a burden like an ass,
Spurr'd, gall'd, and tir'd by jauncing Bolingbroke.

Enter *Keeper,* with a dish.

Keep. Fellow, give place; here is no longer stay.
K. Rich. If thou love me, 't is time thou wert away.
Groom. What my tongue dares not, that my heart shall say. *Exit.*
Keep. My lord, will 't please you to fall to?
K. Rich. Taste of it first, as thou art wont to do.
Keep. My lord, I dare not. Sir Pierce of Exton,
Who lately came from th' King, commands the contrary.
K. Rich. The devil take Henry of Lancaster and thee!
Patience is stale, and I am weary of it.
Keep. Help, help, help! *Beats the Keeper.*

Enter *Exton* and Servants, the murderers rush in.

K. Rich. How now! what means death in this rude assault?
Villain, thy own hand yields thy death's instrument.
Snatching an axe from a Servant and killing him.
Go thou, and fill another room in hell.
He kills another. Here Exton strikes him down.
That hand shall burn in never-quenching fire
That staggers thus my person. Exton, thy fierce hand
Hath with the King's blood stained the King's own land.
Mount, mount, my soul! thy seat is up on high;
Whilst my gross flesh sinks downward, here to die. *Dies.*
Exton. As full of valour as of royal blood!
Both have I spill'd; O would the deed were good!
For now the devil, that told me I did well,
Says that this deed is chronicled in hell.
This dead king to the living king I 'll bear:
Take hence the rest, and give them burial here. *Exeunt.*

Scene VI. *Windsor Castle.*

Flourish. Enter *Bolingbroke, York,* with other Lords, and Attendants.

Boling. Kind uncle York, the latest news we hear
Is that the rebels have consum'd with fire
Our town of Cicester in Gloucestershire;
But whether they be ta'en or slain we hear not.

Enter *Northumberland.*

Welcome, my lord, what is the news?
North. First, to thy sacred state wish I all happiness.
The next news is, I have to London sent
The heads of Oxford, Salisbury, Blunt, and Kent.
The manner of their taking may appear
At large discoursed in this paper here.
Boling. We thank thee, gentle Percy, for thy pains;
And to thy worth will add right worthy gains.

68. ten groats, the difference between a *noble* (6s. 8d.) and a *royal* (10s.) was 10 groats. A groat was 4d. **76. yearn'd,** made miserable. **94. jauncing,** fretting a horse to make it prance.

Enter *Fitzwater*.

Fitz. My lord, I have from Oxford sent to London
The heads of Brocas and Sir Bennet Seely,
Two of the dangerous consorted traitors
That sought at Oxford thy dire overthrow.
Boling. Thy pains, Fitzwater, shall not be forgot;
Right noble is thy merit, well I wot.

Enter *Percy*, and the *Bishop of Carlisle*.

Percy. The grand conspirator, Abbot of Westminster,
With clog of conscience and sour melancholy
Hath yielded up his body to the grave;
But here is Carlisle living, to abide
Thy kingly doom and sentence of his pride.
Boling. Carlisle, this is your doom:
Choose out some secret place, some reverend room,
More than thou hast, and with it joy thy life.
So as thou liv'st in peace, die free from strife;
For though mine enemy thou hast ever been,
High sparks of honour in thee have I seen.

Enter *Exton*, with Attendants bearing a coffin.

Exton. Great King, within this coffin I present
Thy buried fear. Herein all breathless lies
The mightiest of thy greatest enemies,
Richard of Bordeaux, by me hither brought.
Boling. Exton, I thank thee not; for thou hast wrought
A deed of slander with thy fatal hand
Upon my head and all this famous land.
Exton. From your own mouth, my lord, did I this deed.
Boling. They love not poison that do poison need,
Nor do I thee: though I did wish him dead,
I hate the murderer, love him murdered.
The guilt of conscience take thou for thy labour,
But neither my good word nor princely favour.
With Cain go wander through the shades of night,
And never show thy head by day nor light.
Lords, I protest, my soul is full of woe
That blood should sprinkle me to make me grow:
Come, mourn with me for what I do lament,
And put on sullen black incontinent:
I 'll make a voyage to the Holy Land,
To wash this blood off from my guilty hand.
March sadly after; grace my mournings here
In weeping after this untimely bier. *Exeunt*.

22. abide, suffer, endure. **26. joy,** enjoy.

35. deed of slander, deed stimulating slanderous talk. **48. incontinent,** immediately.

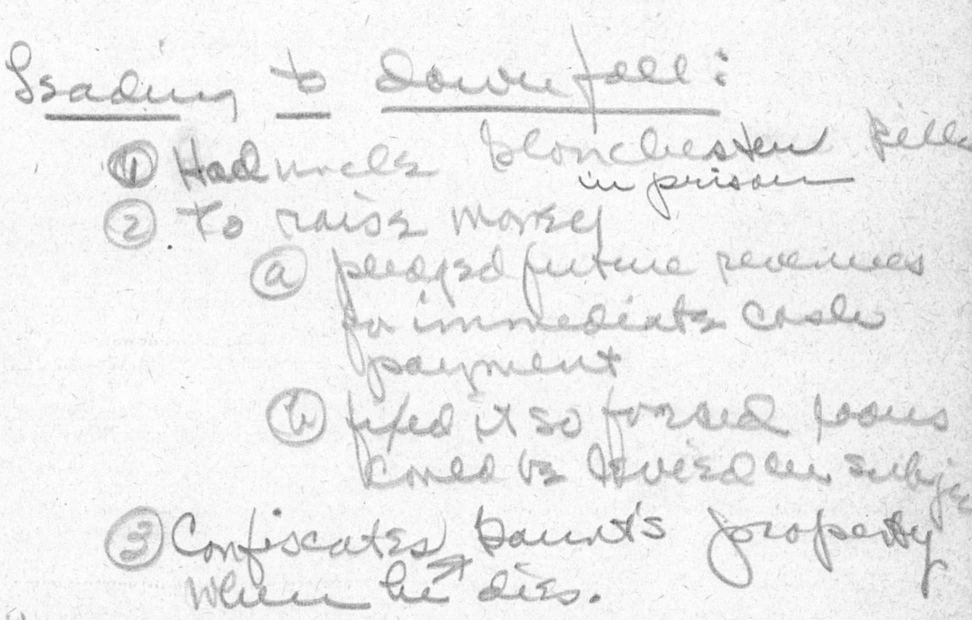

Leading to Downfall:
(1) Had uncle Gloucester killed in prison
(2) To raise money
(a) pledged future revenues for immediate cash payment
(b) fixed it so forced loans
(3) Confiscates Gaunt's property when he dies.
341
306
35 pp.

THE FIRST PART OF HENRY THE FOURTH

Of all Shakespeare's Histories there is none that was so successful in his own day and has been the source of such delight ever since as the First Part of *King Henry the Fourth,* or, as the first publisher called it on a title-page which served the purpose of an advertisement, *The History of Henrie the Fourth; With the battell at Shrewsburie, between the King and Lord Henry Percy, surnamed Henrie Hotspur of the North. With the humorous conceits of Sir John Falstalffe. Printed by P. S. for Andrew Wise.*

Text.—This edition, the First Quarto, appeared in 1598, probably soon after the entry, for copyright purposes, of the play in the Stationers' Register on February 25, 1598. A whole flock of quartos followed in 1599, 1604, 1608, 1613, 1622, 1632, and 1639. One of these, the Quarto of 1613, seems to have been used as the copy from which the Folio text was printed with some corrections derived from the earlier editions. The First Quarto, however, remains the authoritative text.

Date.—It has usually been held that Shakespeare wrote this play shortly before its publication, that is, in 1597. But there is some reason to believe that in its first form, at least, it must be dated some years earlier. It forms part of a tetralogy of which *Richard II* is the first member and probably was composed immediately after that play, for which the generally accepted date is 1595. Some rather amusing evidence exists to show that *Henry IV* was carefully revised by Shakespeare and that the revision was completed some time, perhaps immediately, before the publication. In a quaint old play, *The Famous Victories of Henry the Fifth,* of which we shall have more to say hereafter, Prince Hal's riotous companions included a certain Sir John Oldcastle. Now the historic Sir John Oldcastle, Lord Cobham, had indeed been a friend of Henry's youth, but he was anything but a riotous companion. On the contrary he was a brave soldier, a deeply religious man, and in the end a martyr, for he was condemned as a heretic, hanged on a gallows and burnt, "gallows and all." Shakespeare with his usual indifference to historical fact took over the name of Oldcastle from the old play and promoted its bearer to be the chief of Prince Henry's boon companions, a haunter of taverns, a highway robber, and a witty, but at times a rather foul-mouthed, jester. That he did so is shown by Prince Henry's calling this friend "my old lad of the castle" (I, ii, 7–8). A still stronger piece of evidence is found in a play dating 1618 which speaks of

"The play where the fat knight, hight Oldcastle,
Did tell you plainly what this honour was."

There was instant protest against such a caricature of the good knight, especially by one of his indirect descendants, a Lord Cobham who held high office at the court of Elizabeth. Shakespeare was forced to apologize—see his words in the *Epilogue* to the *Second Part,* "Oldcastle died a martyr and this (*i.e.* Falstaff) is not the man"—and to revise his play, substituting another name for that of Oldcastle. Looking about in history, or rather perhaps in dramatic tradition, he came upon the name of another Sir John, a Fastolfe this time, who had once owned the Boar's Head Tavern where Prince Hal was supposed to have gloried and drunk deep, and who was charged with having run away from battle in France. A slight alteration changed Fastolfe into Falstaff (or Falstalffe as it was first spelled) and so we get the name of Shakespeare's immortal hero.

It seems more than likely that when Shakespeare was forced to revise his play he gave it a thorough overhauling, cut down the historical scenes written in a somewhat stiff blank verse, and expanded the prose scenes into those masterpieces of comic humor which have been the delight of generations since. There was no descendant of Sir John Fastolfe to protest against such a portrayal of his ancestor as Shakespeare gave in the tavern scenes, on the highway near Gadshill, or on the battlefield of Shrewsbury.

Source.—Shakespeare drew the historical basis of his play from the standard English history of his day, Holinshed's *Chronicles,* which he had already used for his former plays on English history. In the main he followed his authority fairly closely. Certain changes he seems to have made for dramatic purposes.

He represents the King as an old man (V, i, 13), evidently to contrast him with the exuberant youth of the Prince, whereas Henry IV was in the very prime of life at the battle of Shrewsbury where he is reported to have slain with his own hand thirty-six of his enemies. For a similar reason he has changed the age of Hotspur. As a matter of fact Henry Percy was older than the King, but Shakespeare planned to make him at once a rival and a foil to the Prince and therefore represents him as of the same age as Hal (III, ii, 103). There is no warrant in history for the Prince's challenge to Hotspur nor for his slaying him in single combat; Henry Percy fell by an unknown hand in the rout of the rebel army. Hal's rescue of his father from the sword of Douglas seems to be taken from a poet's story of the war (Daniel—*Civil Wars*) rather than from history. And finally the interview between Hal and the King, in which the Prince regains his father's favor, took place not before the battle of Shrewsbury, but nearly ten years later. It is easy to see how much these changes add to the interest and heighten the dramatic value of the play.

Another quite different source supplied Shakespeare with some of the comic material of the play. This was the old play, *The Famous Victories of Henry the Fifth.* Author and date of composition are unknown, but it was certainly on the stage before 1588, since the famous clown Tarleton, who is known to have acted in it, died in that year. We may well believe that it was one of the first plays that Shakespeare saw after he came to London, and naturally enough it left its mark upon him. But it would be a mistake to think that Shakespeare borrowed largely from this crude and early work; what he derived from it were certain hints and suggestions for scenes which he elaborated and developed with extraordinary comic power. Chief among these are the highway robbery, although the trick played by the Prince and Poins on Falstaff seems to be Shakespeare's own invention, and a scene of a mock rehearsal of Hal's striking the Chief Justice, which gave him the suggestion for the inimitable scene in which Falstaff and the Prince in turn rehearse his approaching interview with the King. In general it may be said that Shakespeare used all his art to tone down the picture of the riotous Prince presented in the old play. He does not let his hero actually rob the King's servants on the highway; he omits the scene of Hal's abuse of the Chief Justice, and he transforms the vulgar ruffian of the *Famous Victories* into a madcap prince whose escapades are easily pardoned on the ground of youth and wild blood.

Type of Play.—Widely as Shakespeare departed from the conception of Prince Hal in the *Famous Victories,* it still seems clear that his use of that early work drew him back into the old, native tradition of the chronicle play and as he reverted to that type his strength was renewed like that of the fabled giant. For the rough farce of the older chronicle he substituted the gayest scenes of broad comedy in English and grouped them about the most superb comic figure in all literature, Sir John Falstaff.

Falstaff.—Volumes have been written to analyze the character of Falstaff. It seems love's labors lost, for no reader so strait-laced as not to love old Jack will ever be moved to open his heart to him by the appeal of critical analysis. By universal consent the character of Falstaff is one of the supreme achievements of Shakespeare's genius. He derives ultimately from the stock character of Latin comedy, the Miles Gloriosus, the soldier who is at once a braggart and a coward. There are many presentations of the Miles; there is but one Falstaff. In the first place he is not a coward, at least not in the ordinary sense of that word; he will fight, but no "longer than he sees reason" (I, ii, 206–7). In his own words "the better part of valour is discretion." But he never exhibits such base and panic fear as characterizes the stock figure of the Miles.

Perhaps the most striking feature of Falstaff's character and one which adds immensely to its comic force is the extraordinary bundle of incongruities of which he is composed. Old, fat, and bibulous, he is yet an active highway robber; a gentleman by birth and breeding and an intimate of the Prince, he is a haunter of taverns and an associate with footpads; a soldier of some reputation and an officer in the King's army, he is not ashamed to abuse "the King's press," to feign death rather than fight it out, and to claim a victory that he has never won. A fluent and outrageous liar, his lies are never told with intent to deceive; no sensible man can think that Falstaff expected the Prince to believe his fantastic tale of the fifty or more men he fought with in the dark at Gadshill. A knight trained up in the court of a famous Duke of Norfolk (Pt. II, III, ii, 28-9) he scoffs at honor as a mere word of no substantial value. Could contradictions further go?

What endears Falstaff, however, to all right-minded readers is not his bundle of incongruities, but his quenchless and inexhaustible good humor. No matter into what scrapes he falls or what dangers confront him, he never loses his cheery self-assurance. His world of thieves, politicians, and fighting men seems to him little more than a game, and he is always ready to play a part, any part in fact, in the spectacle. He will be a young robber stripping "fat chuffs" of their gold on the highway, or an indignant protester against having his own pockets picked while he took his ease in his inn. He can play the part of an offended king or a prodigal prince with equal ease, and his apologia spoken in the Prince's role for the character of the abused Falstaff is a masterpiece of specious and witty pleading. And Falstaff's wit is contagious; he is not only witty himself but the source of wit in others. Like Yorick his flashes of merriment set the table in a roar, and it is not surprising that Prince Hal fled the gloom and formality of his father's court to seek the society of this all-licensed jester at an Eastcheap tavern.

Prince Hal.—To the reader of to-day *King Henry IV* is the play of Falstaff. It is more than doubtful whether this was Shakespeare's purpose. The character of the fat knight, Oldcastle-Falstaff, seems to have grown on his hands until it tended to dominate the play. What Shakespeare planned, it seems plain, was to write a play centering about the youth of Henry V, the last great hero-king of England, the "mirror of all Christian kings." A tradition had firmly established itself in the folk-mind of Shakespeare's day that this hero had sown his wild oats with a liberal and reckless hand in the days of his youth, and on coming to the throne had experienced a sudden and almost miraculous conversion. Shakespeare, we may believe, had little faith in such miracles, but he would be profoundly interested in the transformation of the wild prince into the hero-king; a character study of this kind always interested him, and there was in this case the additional reason that a play on this idol of folk tradition would pack the theatre. It would, perhaps, be better to say a set of plays, for it is clear that from the beginning Shakespeare meant to carry on his hero from his first gay pranks to his crowning victory at Agincourt, to expand the short, crude *Famous Victories* into a trilogy like that on Henry VI, probably on the boards of Shakespeare's theatre at this very time. For *King Henry IV, Part I,* does not stand alone; it is the first of a three-part play of which *King Henry V* is the final member, and Hal as Prince and King is the protagonist of all three.

Regarded from this point of view all the characters of the play—and there is no play of Shakespeare's youth so crowded with clearly drawn and interesting characters—seem to fall into place about the central figure for whom they serve as foils and contrasts. There is first the old King, the politician and usurper, fighting hard to keep the crown he had won by crooked ways, suspicious of former friends, jealous of the power and reputation of Hotspur, and bitterly disappointed in his hopes for his son in whom with his embittered disposition he can see nothing but at best a wanton reveller, at worst an enemy of his throne and life. There is the group of rebels, among them the crafty and deceitful Worcester, a debased copy of the King, the weak and cowardly Northumberland, the headstrong and impetuous Percy, "the Hotspur of the North," covetous only of the honor to be won in fight. And there is the company of the Prince's friends among whom Falstaff shines pre-eminent, and Falstaff's utter irresponsibility, his cheerful contempt of honor and of duty, all contrast, and are meant to contrast, with the behavior of the Prince when the call to action comes. Henry has been called Shakespeare's "ideal man of action" and the phrase is, perhaps, the best key to Shakespeare's treatment of his character development, his gradual, rather than sudden, transformation. At the beginning of the play in a time of peace Henry turns from the formal councils and intrigues of his father's court to find vent for his energies in practical jokes and high revelry with Falstaff and his gang. His much debated soliloquy (I, ii) may be taken in part as Shakespeare's explanation to the audience that *his* prince was not quite the thoughtless scamp of popular tradition, but it is something more; it is Henry's avowal that he is content to play the madcap for a time, but that when the call comes he will rise and shine. In his interview with his father he makes little attempt to apologize for his way of life, suggests that he has been slandered by pickthanks and newsmongers, and only breaks out in passion when the blinded King insults him with the suggestion that he is likely to enlist under the rebel Percy. This unbearable accusation is the call to action, and the Prince vows to "make this northern youth exchange his glorious deeds for my indignities." The rest of the play is devoted in the main to showing how he kept this vow.

The evolution of Hal's character does not end with this play. Every reader should follow it through the Second Part and note the widening breach between Falstaff and the Prince and the final renunciation of Sir John by the new-crowned King: To every careful reader of the play it should be clear that Henry as King must break sharply and at once all the ties that bound him to such a rogue as Falstaff, and the touch of bitterness in his final speech may be explained perhaps by a lingering sense of shame that he had once stooped to make merry in the fat knight's company. He has other things to think of now; civil dissension to be composed, the conquest of France to be achieved. He is no longer the wild prince, nor even the soldier of Shrewsbury, but a king with all a king's opportunities, cares, and duties. And in the last play of the series, *Henry V,* Shakespeare shows us his hero in the role of king and conqueror.

Political Significance.—One other phase of this play deserves at least passing mention, its political significance. This may not be at once apparent to the reader of today; it can hardly have failed to appeal to the audience of Shakespeare's time. It is a well-worn commonplace that the age of Elizabeth was marked by an outburst of patriotism. It is, perhaps, less generally recognized that this patriotism centered around the figure of the sovereign; Elizabeth was England. The age of feudalism was passing into history; the age of monarchy, more or less absolute, was approaching. The Tudor dynasty in England achieved the final overthrow of the great feudal barons who were mainly responsible for the devastating Wars of the Roses; but this was not accomplished without a struggle. The success of Tudor monarchs in dealing with the last struggles of feudalism is to be attributed in the main to popular support. The nation had come to realize that only through the monarch could unity and civil peace be obtained and preserved, and the Tudors were, in the best sense of the word, popular monarchs.

Here as elsewhere Shakespeare is a true representative of his age, and the picture that he gives us in this play is of a struggle between the two opposing principles of feudalism and monarchy. He is not unfair to the past; in fact the character of Hotspur, the incarnation of the feudal age, is so nobly presented that a modern reader might be tempted to prefer him to the Prince. But Shakespeare has labelled him once for all in the phrase "a very valiant rebel." It is quite wrong to think of Hotspur as a type of medieval chivalry; he is no "very perfect gentle knight," but one of the turbulent barons of the late middle ages who made and deposed kings, and who cherished personal ambition and family pride above loyalty or patriotism. The great scene of Act III when the conspirators parcel out the kingdom between them may delight a reader of today by its brilliant wit and vivid characterization; it had a deeper significance in Shakespeare's time. Here, he seems to say, is what a feudal baron would do if he had the power, turn over all the West to a Welshman, seize the North for himself, and confine the titular king of England to the narrow limits of the South.

Over against this splendid representation of a dying age Shakespeare places the figure of the Prince, the embodiment of all that Elizabethans desired in a sovereign; bravery, affability, generosity and above all loyalty to the throne and the idea of national unity. Hal has no personal grudge against Hotspur, but he is very sure that "one England cannot brook a double reign." And so Hotspur falls and deserves to fall, all good Elizabethans would think; the sword of the Prince is the symbol of the power of the sovereign.

Final appreciation.—Such then is this play, a chronicle history of the old native type, a genial blend of historic fact and comedy, written by the greatest of English dramatists at the very height of his power, crowded with brilliant characters, presenting the supreme figure of irresponsible mirth, and containing, for its day, at least, a deep and true lesson of loyalty and patriotism.

Stage history.—Many contemporary references indicate the popularity of this play in Shakespeare's lifetime. Curiously, however, there is no record of a performance under its published name. The first clear reference to a performance, 1600, speaks of it as *Sir John Oldcastle,* an interesting testimony to the fact that the memory of this name lingered after Shakespeare had altered it to Falstaff. In fact the last record of a performance, 1638–9, before the closing of the theaters calls it simply "ould Castel." Payments made for performances at Court in honor of the Princess Elizabeth's marriage, 1613, show that it was played there under the title of *The Hotspur;* another entry in the same record speaks of a play *Sir John Falstaff,* possibly the second part of *King Henry IV.* In 1625 Sir Henry Herbert records a performance of the *"First part of Sir John Falstaff"* at Court.

The play was promptly revived after the Restoration. Pepys saw a performance as early as December 31, 1660, and was rather disappointed, but later in 1661 he pronounced it a good play. In 1667 he was specially pleased with Cartwright in the role of Falstaff. Hart, a famous actor of the day, played Hotspur. This role was taken over by Betterton in 1682, who played it with great success for years, until about 1700, when he exchanged it for that of Falstaff, in which he was said to have "hit the humor" of that character better than any before him. Betterton's acting version of the play is remarkable among Restoration versions of Shakespeare for its adherence to the original text.

In the early eighteenth century Booth played Hotspur and Quin Falstaff. The young Garrick in 1746 played Hotspur to old Quin's Falstaff but without marked success, and he soon abandoned the role. A succession of famous actors took these parts throughout the later eighteenth century, but in the romantic age the enjoyment of Falstaff's humor began to wane. John Philip Kemble preferred the part of Hotspur, 1802, and later played the King in Part II to the Prince Hal of his brother Charles. When Charles played Falstaff, 1824, he invested it, we are told, "with a certain gentility." This seems to foreshadow a Victorian aversion to Falstaff, and it is interesting to note that the Victorian age produced no great interpreter of Shakespeare's greatest comic character—at least in the *Henry IV* plays; the role in *The Merry Wives* has always been a favorite. In comparatively recent times the play has been in the repertoires of Tree and Benson, and it has been repeatedly performed in American colleges, at Harvard in 1886, Yale 1906, Princeton 1910, Northwestern 1936, and no doubt elsewhere.

THE FIRST PART OF HENRY THE FOURTH

Henry IV (1367–1413)—Henry, son of John of Gaunt, Duke of Lancaster (called Bolingbroke from his birthplace), was exiled by Richard II. The following year at the death of John of Gaunt, Richard seized upon the vast Lancastrian estates. This gave Henry an excuse to return; and he landed at Ravenspurgh, 4 July, 1399, declaring that his sole motive was the recovery of his properties. But the country, tired of Richard's misgovernment, rallied to him. Richard, who was just returning from an expedition to Ireland, was seized and deposed by Parliament, and Henry was proclaimed Henry IV. Richard died or was killed in prison within the year.

But the Percies, a powerful family in the north that had been instrumental in putting Henry on the throne, soon grew restive under his restraint; and in 1403 a confederation under Henry Percy (Hotspur) broke into open rebellion. The quelling of this revolt involved the country in civil war for the greater part of Henry's reign; but the end was success for the king, and at his death in 1413 his successor, Prince Hal, succeeded to an undisputed throne.

Prince Hal (1387–1422)—Henry, Prince of Wales, was only sixteen at the battle of Shrewsbury. Even before that he had seen military service in the Welsh campaigns with his father. After his father's death he carried on a series of brilliant campaigns in France, culminating in the victory of Agincourt. This battle, followed by his marriage to a French princess, marks the high tide of the Lancastrian rule in England. He was succeeded at his death in 1422 by his son, Henry VI, the last of the Lancastrian kings.

John of Lancaster (d. 1435)—John was the third son of Henry IV. There is no historical evidence of his presence at the battle of Shrewsbury. Shakespeare introduces him for the purpose of contrast with Hal.

Ralph Neville, first Earl of Westmoreland (1364–1425), was one of the most powerful of the northern barons. He was created earl by Richard II, but joined Henry at Ravenspurgh and was made by him Marshal of England.

Sir Walter Blount (d. 1403) was a loyal supporter of Henry IV. He carried the king's standard at Shrewsbury and was killed in that battle.

Thomas Percy, Earl of Worcester (c. 1344–1403), was a younger brother of Northumberland. He had had an active military career before Henry came to the throne, serving in France under Edward III and in Spain under John of Gaunt. Upon Henry's accession he was made admiral of the fleet and tutor to Prince Hal.

Henry Percy, first Earl of Northumberland (1342–1408), was created earl by Richard II but quarrelled with him and refused to join him in Ireland in 1398. He joined Henry on his landing at Ravenspurgh and was a chief factor in his elevation to the throne. In return he was made high constable of England and intrusted with the defense of the northern border. The story of his part in the rebellion after the death of his son at Shrewsbury is told in the second part of Henry IV.

Henry Percy (Hotspur) (1364–1403) was the eldest son of Northumberland. He had a brilliant career as a soldier, he was knighted by Edward III, and served under Richard II and Henry IV. Partly because he felt that he was not sufficiently rewarded for his service against the Welsh and Scots and particularly because of Henry's demands after the battle of Holmedon Hill, in which he defeated Douglas, Hotspur headed the revolt against the king.

Edmund de Mortimer (1376–1409?) was the second son of Edmund de Mortimer, third Earl of March. When he was captured by Glendower, Henry suspected his good faith and refused to allow his cousins, the Percies, to ransom him. As a consequence he allied himself with Glendower, married his daughter, and proclaimed himself as favoring the claim of his nephew, Edmund Mortimer, to the throne.

This **Edmund Mortimer, Earl of March (1391–1425)** was the son of Roger Mortimer, fourth Earl of March, who had claimed the throne by descent through his mother Philippa, the daughter of Lionel, second son of Edward III, and who had been declared heir to the throne by Richard II in 1385.

It will be seen at once that Shakespeare has confused these two and has combined them into one.

Archibald Douglas, fourth Earl of Douglas (1372–1424), was a grandson of the famous James, the second Earl, who was killed at the battle of Otterburn. He succeeded to the headship of the great Border family in 1400. His defeat at the hands of Hotspur at Holmedon Hill in 1402 is one of the incidents with which the play opens. He was drawn to the Percy side by the offer of Berwick and a part of Northumberland.

Richard Scroop (1350?–1405) was made Archbishop of York by Richard II. He joined the rebels because his brother, Lord Scroop, had been beheaded by Henry at Bristow. He was not at the battle of Shrewsbury but was captured and executed in 1405.

Owen Glendower (1359?–1415) was a Welsh squire who had been educated in law at Westminster in London. Failing to obtain redress from the English government for incroachments made on his lands by the English, he threw over his allegiance to the king and made a series of raids over the English border. Gradually he put himself at the head of a national Welsh movement to set up an independent kingdom. Throughout the first decade of the fifteenth century he was the terror of the English counties along the Welsh border, and it was not until after the Percy rebellion that Henry was able to break his power.

He allied himself with Mortimer and the Percies, but was either unable or unwilling to join them at Shrewsbury. The exact date and circumstances of his death are unknown.

THE FIRST PART OF HENRY THE FOURTH

Dramatis Personæ

King Henry IV.
Henry, Prince of Wales, } sons to the King.
John of Lancaster, }
Earl of Westmoreland.
Sir Walter Blunt.
Thomas Percy, earl of Worcester.
Henry Percy, earl of Northumberland.
Henry Percy, surnamed *Hotspur,* his son.
Edmund Mortimer, earl of March.
Richard Scroop, archbishop of York.
Archibald, earl of Douglas.
Owen Glendower.
Sir Richard Vernon.
Sir John Falstaff.
Sir Michael, a friend to the archbishop of York.
Poins.
Gadshill.
Peto.
Bardolph.

Lady Percy, wife to *Hotspur,* and sister to *Mortimer.*
Lady Mortimer, daughter to *Glendower,* and wife to *Mortimer.*
Mistress Quickly, hostess of a tavern in Eastcheap.

Lords, Officers, Sheriff, Vintner, Chamberlain, Drawers, two Carriers, Travellers, and Attendants.

SCENE: *England and Wales.*

ACT I. Scene I. *London. The palace.*

Enter *King Henry, Lord John of Lancaster,* the *Earl of Westmoreland, Sir Walter Blunt* with others.

King. So shaken as we are, so wan with care,
Find we a time for frighted Peace to pant,
And breathe short-winded accents of new broils
To be commenc'd in strands afar remote.
No more the thirsty entrance of this soil
Shall daub her lips with her own children's blood;
No more shall trenching war channel her fields,
Nor bruise her flowerets with the armed hoofs
Of hostile paces. Those opposed eyes,
Which, like the meteors of a troubled heaven,
All of one nature, of one substance bred,
Did lately meet in the intestine shock
And furious close of civil butchery,
Shall now, in mutual well-beseeming ranks,
March all one way and be no more oppos'd
Against acquaintance, kindred, and allies.
The edge of war, like an ill-sheathed knife,
No more shall cut his master. Therefore, friends,
As far as to the sepulchre of Christ,
Whose soldier now under whose blessed cross
We are impressed and engag'd to fight,
Forthwith a power of English shall we levy;
Whose arms were moulded in their mothers' womb
To chase these pagans in those holy fields
Over whose acres walk'd those blessed feet
Which fourteen hundred years ago were nail'd
For our advantage on the bitter cross.
But this our purpose now is twelve months old,
And bootless 'tis to tell you we will go;
Therefore we meet not now. Then let me hear
Of you, my gentle cousin Westmoreland,
What yesternight our council did decree
In forwarding this dear expedience.
West. My liege, this haste was hot in question,
And many limits of the charge set down
But yesternight; when all athwart there came
A post from Wales loaden with heavy news;
Whose worst was that the noble Mortimer,
Leading the men of Herefordshire to fight
Against the irregular and wild Glendower,
Was by the rude hands of that Welshman taken,
A thousand of his people butchered;
Upon whose dead corpses there was such misuse,
Such beastly shameless transformation,

12. intestine, internal. **21. impressed,** enlisted.

30. Therefore, for this. **33. dear expedience,** important expedition. **34. hot in question,** being warmly debated. **35. charge,** expense. **40. irregular,** lawless. **44. transformation,** mutilation.

Civil war has been going on now over.

By those Welshwomen done as may not be
Without much shame retold or spoken of.
King. It seems then that the tidings of this broil
Brake off our business for the Holy Land.
West. This match'd with other did, my gracious lord;
For more uneven and unwelcome news
Came from the north, and thus it did import:
On Holy-rood day, the gallant Hotspur there,
Young Harry Percy, and brave Archibald,
That ever-valiant and approved Scot,
At Holmedon met,
Where they did spend a sad and bloody hour,
As by discharge of their artillery,
And shape of likelihood, the news was told;
For he that brought them, in the very heat
And pride of their contention did take horse,
Uncertain of the issue any way.
King. Here is a dear, a true industrious friend,
Sir Walter Blunt, new lighted from his horse,
Stain'd with the variation of each soil
Betwixt that Holmedon and this seat of ours;
And he hath brought us smooth and welcome news.
The Earl of Douglas is discomfited.
Ten thousand bold Scots, two and twenty knights,
Balk'd in their own blood did Sir Walter see
On Holmedon's plains. Of prisoners, Hotspur took
Mordake Earl of Fife, and eldest son
To beaten Douglas; and the Earl of Athole,
Of Murray, Angus, and Menteith:
And is not this an honourable spoil?
A gallant prize, ha, cousin, is it not?
West. In faith,
It is a conquest for a prince to boast of.
King. Yea, there thou mak'st me sad, and mak'st me sin
In envy that my Lord Northumberland
Should be the father to so blest a son,
A son who is the theme of Honour's tongue,
Amongst a grove the very straightest plant,
Who is sweet Fortune's minion and her pride;
Whilst I, by looking on the praise of him,
See riot and dishonour stain the brow
Of my young Harry. O that it could be prov'd
That some night-tripping fairy had exchang'd
In cradle-clothes our children where they lay,
And call'd mine Percy, his Plantagenet!
Then would I have his Harry, and he mine.
But let him from my thoughts. What think you, coz,
Of this young Percy's pride? The prisoners,
Which he in this adventure hath surpris'd,
To his own use he keeps; and sends me word,
I shall have none but Mordake Earl of Fife.
West. This is his uncle's teaching. This is Worcester,
Malevolent to you in all aspects;
Which makes him prune himself, and bristle up
The crest of youth against your dignity.
King. But I have sent for him to answer this;
And for this cause awhile we must neglect
Our holy purpose to Jerusalem.
Cousin, on Wednesday next our council we
Will hold at Windsor; so inform the lords;
But come yourself with speed to us again,
For more is to be said and to be done
Than out of anger can be uttered.
West. I will, my liege. *Exeunt.*

52. Holy-rood day, Sept. 14. **55. Holmedon,** a town in Northumberland. **58. shape of likelihood,** probable evidence. **60. pride,** height, a term in falconry; cf. *Macb.* II, iv, 12. **69. Balk'd,** heaped up. **71-2. Mordake . . . eldest son to beaten Douglas,** Mordake Stewart was really the son of Robert, Duke of Albany. The omission of a comma after **governour** in Holinshed—"And of prisoners, Mordacke earl of Fife, son to the governour Archembald earle of Douglas, etc." misled Shakespeare. **83. minion,** darling.

95. I shall have none but . . ., by the law of arms Percy had a right to keep all prisoners except those of blood royal. Mordake was a grandson of King Robert II of Scotland. **98. prune,** preen, ruffle up, a term in falconry.

Scene II. *London. An apartment of the Prince's.*

Enter the *Prince of Wales* and *Falstaff.*

Fal. Now, Hal, what time of day is it, lad?

Prince. Thou art so fat-witted, with drinking of old sack and unbuttoning thee after supper and sleeping upon benches after noon, that thou hast forgotten to demand that truly which thou wouldest truly know. What a devil hast thou to do with the time of the day? Unless hours were cups of sack, and minutes capons, and clocks the tongues of bawds, and dials the signs of leaping-houses, and the blessed sun himself a fair hot wench in flame-coloured taffeta, I see no reason why thou shouldst be so superfluous to demand the time of the day.

Fal. Indeed, you come near me now, Hal; for we that take purses go by the moon and the seven stars, and not by Phœbus, he, "that wand'ring knight so fair." And, I prithee, sweet wag, when thou art king, as, God save thy Grace,—Majesty I should say, for grace thou wilt have none,—

Prince. What, none?

Fal. No, by my troth, not so much as will serve to be prologue to an egg and butter.

Scene ii: 3. sack, a white wine. **4. benches,** privies; cf. *A. and C.* IV, vii, 9. **9. leaping-houses,** brothels. **16. seven stars,** the Pleiades.

Prince. Well, how then? Come, roundly, roundly.

Fal. Marry, then, sweet wag, when thou art king, let not us that are squires of the night's body be called thieves of the day's beauty. Let us be Diana's foresters, gentlemen of the shade, minions of the moon; and let men say we be men of good government, being governed, as the sea is, by our noble and chaste mistress the moon, under whose countenance we steal.

Prince. Thou say'st well, and it holds well too; for the fortune of us that are the moon's men doth ebb and flow like the sea, being governed, as the sea is, by the moon. As, for proof, now: a purse of gold most resolutely snatched on Monday night and most dissolutely spent on Tuesday morning; got with swearing "Lay by" and spent with crying "Bring in"; now in as low an ebb as the foot of the ladder, and by and by in as high a flow as the ridge of the gallows.

Fal. By the Lord, thou say'st true, lad. And is not my hostess of the tavern a most sweet wench?

Prince. As the honey of Hybla, my old lad of the castle. And is not a buff jerkin a most sweet robe of durance?

Fal. How now, how now, mad wag! What, in thy quips and thy quiddities, what a plague have I to do with a buff jerkin?

Prince. Why, what a pox have I to do with my hostess of the tavern?

Fal. Well, thou hast called her to a reckoning many a time and oft.

Prince. Did I ever call for thee to pay thy part?

Fal. No; I 'll give thee thy due, thou hast paid all there.

Prince. Yea, and elsewhere, so far as my coin would stretch; and where it would not, I have used my credit.

Fal. Yea, and so used it that, were it not here apparent that thou art heir apparent— But, I prithee, sweet wag, shall there be gallows standing in England when thou art king? and resolution thus fobbed as it is with the rusty curb of old father antic the law? Do not thou, when thou art king, hang a thief.

Prince. No; thou shalt.

Fal. Shall I? O rare! By the Lord, I 'll be a brave judge.

Prince. Thou judgest false already. I mean, thou shalt have the hanging of the thieves and so become a rare hangman.

Fal. Well, Hal, well; and in some sort it jumps with my humour as well as waiting in the court, I can tell you.

Prince. For obtaining of suits?

Fal. Yea, for obtaining of suits, whereof the hangman hath no lean wardrobe. 'Sblood, I am as melancholy as a gib cat or a lugged bear.

Prince. Or an old lion, or a lover's lute.

Fal. Yea, or the drone of a Lincolnshire bagpipe.

Prince. What sayest thou to a hare, or the melancholy of Moor-ditch?

Fal. Thou hast the most unsavoury similes and art indeed the most comparative, rascalliest, sweet young prince. But, Hal, I prithee, trouble me no more with vanity. I would to God thou and I knew where a commodity of good names were to be bought. An old lord of the council rated me the other day in the street about you, sir, but I marked him not; and yet he talked very wisely, but I regarded him not; and yet he talked wisely, and in the street too.

Prince. Thou didst well; for wisdom cries out in the streets, and no man regards it.

Fal. O, thou hast damnable iteration and art indeed able to corrupt a saint. Thou hast done much harm upon me, Hal; God forgive thee for it! Before I knew thee, Hal, I knew nothing; and now am I, if a man should speak truly, little better than one of the wicked. I must give over this life, and I will give it over. By the Lord, an I do not, I am a villain. I 'll be damned for never a king's son in Christendom.

Prince. Where shall we take a purse tomorrow, Jack?

Fal. 'Zounds, where thou wilt, lad; I 'll make one. An I do not, call me villain and baffle me.

Prince. I see a good amendment of life in thee; from praying to purse-taking.

Fal. Why, Hal, 't is my vocation, Hal: 't is no sin for a man to labour in his vocation.

Enter *Poins.*

Poins! Now shall we know if Gadshill have set a match. O, if men were to be saved by merit,

24. roundly, plainly. **33. countenance,** favor. **41. Lay by,** robbers' cry, like "Hands up." **47. Hybla,** town in Sicily, famous for its honey. **47-8. my old lad of the castle,** see Introduction. **48. buff jerkin,** leather jacket worn by sheriff's men. **49. durance,** (1) stout cloth, (2) imprisonment. **51. quips,** sharp jests. **quiddities,** subtilities. **68. fobbed,** cheated. **69. antic,** mountebank. **73. brave,** fine.

78. jumps with, suits. **83. gib cat,** tom cat, **lugged bear,** led bear. **85. drone,** large pipe, with deep sustained note. **88. Moor-ditch,** stagnant ditch in Moorfields near London. **90. comparative,** witty, fertile in comparisons. **93. commodity,** store. **99-100.** Proverbs 1:20-24. "Wisdom crieth in the streets, and no man regardeth." Falstaff's **damnable iteration** accuses the prince of citing Scripture profanely. **101. iteration,** habit of quoting. **113. baffle,** disgrace. **118-9. set a match,** planned a meeting.

what hole in hell were hot enough for him? This is the most omnipotent villain that ever cried "Stand!" to a true man.

Prince. Good morrow, Ned.

Poins. Good morrow, sweet Hal. What says Monsieur Remorse? What says Sir John Sack and Sugar? Jack! how agrees the devil and thee about thy soul, that thou soldest him on Good Friday last for a cup of Madeira and a cold capon's leg?

Prince. Sir John stands to his word, the devil shall have his bargain; for he was never yet a breaker of proverbs. He will give the devil his due.

Poins. Then art thou damned for keeping thy word with the devil.

Prince. Else he had been damned for cozening the devil.

Poins. But, my lads, my lads, to-morrow morning, by four o'clock, early at Gadshill! There are pilgrims going to Canterbury with rich offerings, and traders riding to London with fat purses. I have vizards for you all; you have horses for yourselves: Gadshill lies to-night in Rochester: I have bespoke supper to-morrow night in Eastcheap: we may do it as secure as sleep. If you will go, I will stuff your purses full of crowns; if you will not, tarry at home and be hanged.

Fal. Hear ye, Yedward; if I tarry at home and go not, I 'll hang you for going.

Poins. You will, chops?

Fal. Hal, wilt thou make one?

Prince. Who, I rob? I a thief? Not I, by my faith.

Fal. There 's neither honesty, manhood, nor good fellowship in thee, nor thou cam'st not of the blood royal, if thou dar'st not stand for ten shillings.

Prince. Well, then, once in my days I 'll be a madcap.

Fal. Why, that 's well said.

Prince. Well, come what will, I 'll tarry at home.

Fal. By the lord, I 'll be a traitor then, when thou art king.

Prince. I care not.

Poins. Sir John, I prithee, leave the Prince and me alone. I will lay him down such reasons for this adventure that he shall go.

Fal. Well, God give thee the spirit of persuasion and him the ears of profiting, that what thou speakest may move and what he hears may be believed, that the true prince may, for recreation sake, prove a false thief; for the poor abuses of the time want countenance. Farewell; you shall find me in Eastcheap.

Prince. Farewell, the latter spring! Farewell, All-hallown summer! *Exit Falstaff.*

Poins. Now, my good sweet honey lord, ride with us to-morrow; I have a jest to execute that I cannot manage alone. Falstaff, Bardolph, Peto, and Gadshill shall rob those men that we have already waylaid; yourself and I will not be there; and when they have the booty, if you and I do not rob them, cut this head off from my shoulders.

Prince. How shall we part with them in setting forth?

Poins. Why, we will set forth before or after them, and appoint them a place of meeting, wherein it is at our pleasure to fail, and then will they adventure upon the exploit themselves; which they shall have no sooner achieved, but we 'll set upon them.

Prince. Yea, but 't is like that they will know us by our horses, by our habits, and by every other appointment, to be ourselves.

Poins. Tut! our horses they shall not see; I 'll tie them in the wood; our vizards we will change after we leave them; and, sirrah, I have cases of buckram for the nonce, to immask our noted outward garments.

Prince. Yea, but I doubt they will be too hard for us.

Poins. Well, for two of them, I know them to be as true-bred cowards as ever turned back; and for the third, if he fight longer than he sees reason, I 'll forswear arms. The virtue of this jest will be the incomprehensible lies that this same fat rogue will tell us when we meet at supper; how thirty, at least, he fought with; what wards, what blows, what extremities he endured; and in the reproof of this lies the jest.

Prince. Well, I 'll go with thee: provide us all things necessary and meet me to-morrow night in Eastcheap; there I 'll sup. Farewell.

Poins. Farewell, my lord. *Exit.*

Prince. I know you all, and will a while
uphold
The unyok'd humour of your idleness;
Yet herein will I imitate the sun,
Who doth permit the base contagious clouds
To smother up his beauty from the world,
That when he please again to be himself,

138. **Gadshill,** the character in the play takes his name from a hill near Rochester, famous for its robberies. 139. **Canterbury,** to Thomas à Becket's shrine. 141. **vizards,** masks. 143. **Rochester,** in Kent on the road to Canterbury. 144. **Eastcheap,** a quarter in the eastern part of London. 157. **royal,** a pun—the royal was a coin worth 10s.

178. **All-hallown summer,** All-hallows or All Saint's Day is November first. The sense is that Falstaff has kept his youth (summer) long past its time. 196. **habits,** clothes. 201. **cases of buckram,** suits of stiffened linen. **nonce,** occasion. 202. **noted,** known. 203. **doubt,** fear. 211. **wards,** fencing guards. 212. **reproof,** refutation. 221. **contagious,** pestilence-breeding.

Being wanted, he may be more wonder'd at
By breaking through the foul and ugly mists
Of vapours that did seem to strangle him.
If all the year were playing holidays,
To sport would be as tedious as to work;
But when they seldom come, they wish'd for come,
And nothing pleaseth but rare accidents.
So, when this loose behaviour I throw off
And pay the debt I never promised,
By how much better than my word I am,
By so much shall I falsify men's hopes;
And like bright metal on a sullen ground,
My reformation, glitt'ring o'er my fault,
Shall show more goodly and attract more eyes
Than that which hath no foil to set it off.
I 'll so offend, to make offence a skill,
Redeeming time when men think least I will.
Exit.

Scene III. *London. The palace.*

Enter the *King, Northumberland, Worcester, Hotspur, Sir Walter Blunt,* with others.

King. My blood hath been too cold and temperate,
Unapt to stir at these indignities,
And you have found me; for accordingly
You tread upon my patience. But be sure
I will from henceforth rather be myself,
Mighty and to be fear'd, than my condition;
Which hath been smooth as oil, soft as young down,
And therefore lost that title of respect
Which the proud soul ne'er pays but to the proud.

Wor. Our house, my sovereign liege, little deserves
The scourge of greatness to be us'd on it;
And that same greatness too which our own hands
Have holp to make so portly.

North. My lord,—

King. Worcester, get thee gone; for I do see
Danger and disobedience in thine eye.
O, sir, your presence is too bold and peremptory,
And majesty might never yet endure
The moody frontier of a servant brow.
You have good leave to leave us. When we need
Your use and counsel, we shall send for you.
Exit Worcester.
You were about to speak.

North. Yea, my good lord.
Those prisoners in your Highness' name demanded,
Which Harry Percy here at Holmedon took,
Were, as he says, not with such strength denied
As is delivered to your Majesty.
Either envy, therefore, or misprision
Is guilty of this fault, and not my son.

Hot. My liege, I did deny no prisoners.
But I remember, when the fight was done,
When I was dry with rage and extreme toil,
Breathless and faint, leaning upon my sword,
Came there a certain lord, neat, and trimly dress'd,
Fresh as a bridegroom; and his chin new reap'd
Show'd like a stubble-land at harvest-home.
He was perfumed like a milliner;
And 'twixt his finger and his thumb he held
A pouncet-box, which ever and anon
He gave his nose and took 't away again;
Who therewith angry, when it next came there,
Took it in snuff· and still he smil'd and talk'd,
And as the soldiers bore dead bodies by,
He call'd them untaught knaves, unmannerly,
To bring a slovenly unhandsome corse
Betwixt the wind and his nobility.
With many holiday and lady terms
He question'd me; amongst the rest, demanded
My prisoners in your Majesty's behalf.
I then, all smarting with my wounds being cold,
To be so pester'd with a popinjay,
Out of my grief, and my impatience
Answer'd neglectingly—I know not what,
He should, or he should not; for he made me mad
To see him shine so brisk and smell so sweet
And talk so like a waiting-gentlewoman
Of guns and drums and wounds,—God save the mark!—
And telling me the sovereign'st thing on earth
Was parmaceti for an inward bruise;
And that it was great pity, so it was,
This villanous salt-petre should be digg'd
Out of the bowels of the harmless earth,
Which many a good tall fellow had destroy'd
So cowardly; and but for these vile guns,
He would himself have been a soldier.
This bald unjointed chat of his, my lord,
I answered indirectly, as I said;
And I beseech you, let not his report
Come current for an accusation
Betwixt my love and your high Majesty.

224. wanted, needed. **230. accidents,** occurrences. **235. sullen ground,** dark background. **238. foil,** contrast, literally, setting. **Scene iii: 3. found me,** discovered my nature. **6. condition,** natural disposition. **13. portly,** imposing. **19. frontier,** military outworks.

27. misprision, misunderstanding. **38. pouncet-box,** perfume box. **46. holiday,** elegant. **50. popinjay,** parrot. **51. grief,** pain. **52. neglectingly,** absentmindedly. **58. parmaceti,** spermaceti. **62. tall,** brave. **66. indirectly,** vaguely. **68. Come current,** be accepted (as good coin).

Blunt. The circumstance considered, good my lord,
Whate'er Lord Harry Percy then had said
To such a person and in such a place,
At such a time, with all the rest retold,
May reasonably die and never rise
To do him wrong or any way impeach
What then he said, so he unsay it now.

King. Why, yet he doth deny his prisoners
But with proviso and exception
That we at our own charge shall ransom straight
His brother-in-law, the foolish Mortimer;
Who, on my soul, hath wilfully betray'd
The lives of those that he did lead to fight
Against that great magician, damn'd Glendower,
Whose daughter, as we hear, that Earl of March
Hath lately married. Shall our coffers, then,
Be emptied to redeem a traitor home?
Shall we buy treason, and indent with fears,
When they have lost and forfeited themselves?
No, on the barren mountains let him starve;
For I shall never hold that man my friend
Whose tongue shall ask me for one penny cost
To ransom home revolted Mortimer.

Hot. Revolted Mortimer!
He never did fall off, my sovereign liege,
But by the chance of war: to prove that true
Needs no more but one tongue for all those wounds,
Those mouthed wounds, which valiantly he took,
When on the gentle Severn's sedgy bank,
In single opposition, hand to hand,
He did confound the best part of an hour
In changing hardiment with great Glendower.
Three times they breath'd and three times did they drink,
Upon agreement, of swift Severn's flood;
Who then, affrighted with their bloody looks,
Ran fearfully among the trembling reeds,
And hid his crisp head in the hollow bank
Bloodstained with these valiant combatants.
Never did base and rotten policy
Colour her working with such deadly wounds;
Nor never could the noble Mortimer
Receive so many, and all willingly.
Then let not him be slander'd with revolt.

King. Thou dost belie him, Percy, thou dost belie him;
He never did encounter with Glendower.
I tell thee,
He durst as well have met the devil alone
As Owen Glendower for an enemy.
Art thou not asham'd? But, sirrah, henceforth
Let me not hear you speak of Mortimer.
Send me your prisoners with the speediest means,
Or you shall hear in such a kind from me
As will displease you. My Lord Northumberland,
We license your departure with your son.
Send us your prisoners, or you 'll hear of it.

Exeunt King Henry, Blunt, and train.

Hot. An if the devil come and roar for them,
I will not send them. I will after straight
And tell him so; for I will ease my heart,
Albeit I make a hazard of my head.

North. What, drunk with choler? Stay and pause a while.
Here comes your uncle.

Re-enter *Worcester.*

Hot. Speak of Mortimer!
'Zounds, I will speak of him; and let my soul
Want mercy, if I do not join with him.
Yea, on his part I 'll empty all these veins,
And shed my dear blood drop by drop in the dust,
But I will lift the down-trod Mortimer
As high in the air as this unthankful king,
As this ingrate and canker'd Bolingbroke.

North. Brother, the King hath made your nephew mad.

Wor. Who struck this heat up after I was gone?

Hot. He will, forsooth, have all my prisoners;
And when I urg'd the ransom once again
Of my wife's brother, then his cheek look'd pale,
And on my face he turn'd an eye of death,
Trembling even at the name of Mortimer.

Wor. I cannot blame him. Was not he proclaim'd
By Richard, that dead is, the next of blood?

North. He was; I heard the proclamation.
And then it was when the unhappy king,—
Whose wrongs in us God pardon!—did set forth
Upon his Irish expedition;
From whence he intercepted did return
To be depos'd and shortly murdered.

Wor. And for whose death we in the world's wide mouth
Live scandaliz'd and foully spoken of.

75. impeach, call in question. **80.** Percy's brother-in-law was Sir Edmund Mortimer, the uncle of Mortimer, Earl of March. Cf. Explanation of *dramatis personæ*, p. 348. Cf. also I, iii, 145-6. **87. indent,** bargain. **94. fall off,** desert. **100. confound,** spend. **101. changing hardiment,** exchanging valiant blows. **103. Severn,** river between England and Wales. **106. crisp,** wavy, rippled. **109. Colour,** disguise.

121. kind, manner. **137. canker'd,** corrupted.

Hot. But, soft, I pray you; did King Richard then
Proclaim my brother Edmund Mortimer
Heir to the crown?
North. He did; myself did hear it.
Hot. Nay, then I cannot blame his cousin king,
That wish'd him on the barren mountains starve.
But shall it be, that you, that set the crown
Upon the head of this forgetful man
And for his sake wear the detested blot
Of murderous subornation, shall it be,
That you a world of curses undergo,
Being the agents, or base second means,
The cords, the ladder, or the hangman rather?
O, pardon me that I descend so low,
To show the line and the predicament
Wherein you range under this subtle king!
Shall it for shame be spoken in these days,
Or fill up chronicles in time to come,
That men of your nobility and power
Did gage them both in an unjust behalf,
As both of you—God pardon it!—have done,
To put down Richard, that sweet lovely rose,
And plant this thorn, this canker, Bolingbroke?
And shall it in more shame be further spoken,
That you are fool'd, discarded, and shook off
By him for whom these shames ye underwent?
No; yet time serves wherein you may redeem
Your banish'd honours and restore yourselves
Into the good thoughts of the world again,
Revenge the jeering and disdain'd contempt
Of this proud king, who studies day and night
To answer all the debt he owes to you
Even with the bloody payment of your deaths.
Therefore, I say,—
Wor. Peace, cousin, say no more;
And now I will unclasp a secret book,
And to your quick-conceiving discontents
I 'll read you matter deep and dangerous,
As full of peril and adventurous spirit
As to o'er-walk a current roaring loud
On the unsteadfast footing of a spear.
Hot. If he fall in, good night! or sink or swim.
Send Danger from the east unto the west,
So Honour cross it from the north to south,
And let them grapple: O, the blood more stirs
To rouse a lion than to start a hare!
North. Imagination of some great exploit
Drives him beyond the bounds of patience.
Hot. By heaven, methinks it were an easy leap,
To pluck bright Honour from the pale-fac'd moon,
Or dive into the bottom of the deep,
Where fathom-line could never touch the ground,
And pluck up drowned Honour by the locks;
So he that doth redeem her thence might wear
Without corrival all her dignities.
But out upon this half-fac'd fellowship!
Wor. He apprehends a world of figures here,
But not the form of what he should attend.
Good cousin, give me audience for a while
Hot. I cry you mercy.
Wor. Those same noble Scots
That are your prisoners,—
Hot. I 'll keep them all!
By God, he shall not have a Scot of them;
No, if a Scot would save his soul, he shall not!
I 'll keep them, by this hand.
Wor. You start away
And lend no ear unto my purposes.
Those prisoners you shall keep.
Hot. Nay, I will; that 's flat.
He said he would not ransom Mortimer;
Forbad my tongue to speak of Mortimer;
But I will find him when he lies asleep,
And in his ear I 'll holla "Mortimer!"
Nay,
I 'll have a starling shall be taught to speak
Nothing but "Mortimer," and give it him,
To keep his anger still in motion.
Wor. Hear you, cousin; a word.
Hot. All studies here I solemnly defy,
Save how to gall and pinch this Bolingbroke;
And that same sword-and-buckler Prince of Wales,
But that I think his father loves him not
And would be glad he met with some mischance,
I would have him poison'd with a pot of ale.
Wor. Farewell, kinsman! I 'll talk to you
When you are better temper'd to attend.
North. Why, what a wasp-stung and impatient fool
Art thou to break into this woman's mood,
Tying thine ear to no tongue but thine own!
Hot. Why, look you, I am whipp'd and scourg'd with rods,
Nettled and stung with pismires, when I hear
Of this vile politician, Bolingbroke.
In Richard's time,—what do you call the place?—
A plague upon it, it is in Gloucestershire;
'T was where the madcap duke his uncle kept,

163. subornation, perjury, here "collusion." **168. line**, rank. **predicament**, class. **173. gage**, engage. **176. canker**, dog-rose. **183. disdain'd**, disdainful. **206. So**, provided that. **207. corrival**, competitor. **226. still**, always. **228. defy**, renounce. **240. pismires**, ants. **244. kept**, resided.

His uncle York; where I first bow'd my knee
Unto this king of smiles, this Bolingbroke,—
'Sblood!—
When you and he came back from Ravenspurgh.

North. At Berkley castle.

Hot. You say true.
Why, what a candy deal of courtesy
This fawning greyhound then did proffer me!
Look, "when his infant fortune came to age,"
And "gentle Harry Percy," and "kind cousin;"
O, the devil take such cozeners!—God forgive me!
Good uncle, tell your tale; for I have done.

Wor. Nay, if you have not, to 't again;
We 'll stay your leisure.

Hot. I have done, i' faith.

Wor. Then once more to your Scottish prisoners.
Deliver them up without their ransom straight,
And make the Douglas' son your only mean
For powers in Scotland; which, for divers reasons
Which I shall send you written, be assur'd,
Will easily be granted. You, my lord,
To Northumberland.
Your son in Scotland being thus employ'd,
Shall secretly into the bosom creep
Of that same noble prelate, well belov'd,
The Archbishop.

Hot. Of York, is it not?

Wor. True; who bears hard
His brother's death at Bristow, the Lord Scroop.
I speak not this in estimation,
As what I think might be, but what I know
Is ruminated, plotted, and set down,
And only stays but to behold the face
Of that occasion that shall bring it on.

Hot. I smell it. Upon my life, it will do well.

North. Before the game 's afoot, thou still let'st slip.

Hot. Why, it cannot choose but be a noble plot:
And then the power of Scotland and of York,
To join with Mortimer, ha?

Wor. And so they shall.

Hot. In faith, it is exceedingly well aim'd.

Wor. And 't is no little reason bids us speed,
To save our heads by raising of a head;
For, bear ourselves as even as we can,
The King will always think him in our debt,
And think we think ourselves unsatisfied,
Till he hath found a time to pay us home.
And see already how he doth begin
To make us strangers to his looks of love.

Hot. He does, he does. We 'll be reveng'd on him.

Wor. Cousin, farewell! No further go in this
Than I by letters shall direct your course.
When time is ripe, which will be suddenly,
I 'll steal to Glendower and Lord Mortimer;
Where you and Douglas and our powers at once,
As I will fashion it, shall happily meet,
To bear our fortunes in our own strong arms,
Which now we hold at much uncertainty.

North. Farewell, good brother! We shall thrive, I trust.

Hot. Uncle, adieu! O, let the hours be short
Till fields and blows and groans applaud our sport!
Exeunt.

ACT II. SCENE I. *Rochester. An inn yard.*

Enter a *Carrier* with a lantern in his hand.

First Car. Heigh-ho! an it be not four by the day, I 'll be hanged. Charles' wain is over the new chimney, and yet our horse not packed. What, ostler!

Ost. [*Within.*] Anon, anon.

First Car. I prithee, Tom, beat Cut's saddle, put a few flocks in the point: the poor jade is wrung in the withers out of all cess.

Enter another *Carrier.*

Second Car. Peas and beans are as dank here as a dog, and that is the next way to give poor jades the bots: this house is turned upside down since Robin Ostler died.

First Car. Poor fellow, never joyed since the price of oats rose; it was the death of him.

Second Car. I think this be the most villanous house in all London road for fleas: I am stung like a tench.

251. candy, sugared. **255. cozeners**, cheaters. **261. only mean**, sole agent. **271. Bristow**, Bristol. **Scroop**, see note, page 348. **272. estimation**, conjecture. **Act II, Scene i: 2. Charles' wain**, the Great Bear. **4. anon**, coming at once. **7. flocks**, tufts of wool. **point**, pummel. **8. cess**, measure.

278. let'st slip, lettest loose the hounds. **284. head**, force. **285. even**, temperately. **Act II, Scene i: 11. bots**, worms. **17. stung like a tench**, there was a belief that the spots on the tench, a fish, were caused by fleabites.

First Car. Like a tench! by the mass, there is ne'er a king christen could be better bit than I have been since the first cock.

Second Car. Why, they will allow us ne'er a jordan, and then we leak in your chimney; and your chamber-lye breeds fleas like a loach.

First Car. What, ostler! come away and be hanged! Come away.

Second Car. I have a gammon of bacon and two razes of ginger, to be delivered as far as Charing-cross.

First Car. God's body! the turkeys in my pannier are quite starved. What, ostler! A plague on thee! hast thou never an eye in thy head? Canst not hear? An 't were not as good deed as drink, to break the pate on thee, I am a very villain. Come, and be hanged! Hast no faith in thee?

Enter *Gadshill.*

Gads. Good morrow, carriers. What 's o'clock?

First Car. I think it be two o'clock.

Gads. I prithee, lend me thy lantern, to see my gelding in the stable.

First Car. Nay, by God, soft; I know a trick worth two of that, i' faith.

Gads. I pray thee, lend me thine.

Second Car. Ay, when? canst tell? Lend me thy lantern, quoth he? Marry, I 'll see thee hanged first.

Gads. Sirrah carrier, what time do you mean to come to London?

Second Car. Time enough to go to bed with a candle, I warrant thee. Come, neighbour Mugs, we 'll call up the gentlemen: they will along with company, for they have great charge. *Exeunt Carriers.*

Enter *Chamberlain.*

Gads. What, ho! chamberlain!

Cham. At hand, quoth pick-purse.

Gads. That 's even as fair as—at hand, quoth the chamberlain; for thou variest no more from picking of purses than giving direction doth from labouring; thou lay'st the plot how.

Cham. Good morrow, Master Gadshill. It holds current that I told you yesternight: there 's a franklin in the wild of Kent hath brought three hundred marks with him in gold. I heard him tell it to one of his company last night at supper; a kind of auditor; one that hath abundance of charge too, God knows what. They are up already, and call for eggs and butter: they will away presently.

Gads. Sirrah, if they meet not with Saint Nicholas' clerks, I 'll give thee this neck.

Cham. No, I 'll none of it. I pray thee, keep that for the hangman; for I know thou worshippest Saint Nicholas as truly as a man of falsehood may.

Gads. What talkest thou to me of the hangman? If I hang, I 'll make a fat pair of gallows; for if I hang, old Sir John hangs with me, and thou knowest he is no starveling. Tut! there are other Troians that thou dream'st not of, the which for sport sake are content to do the profession some grace, that would, if matters should be looked into, for their own credit sake, make all whole. I am joined with no foot land-rakers, no long-staff sixpenny strikers, none of these mad mustachio purple-hued malt-worms; but with nobility and tranquillity, burgomasters and great oneyers; such as can hold in, such as will strike sooner than speak, and speak sooner than drink, and drink sooner than pray; and yet, 'zounds, I lie; for they pray continually to their saint, the commonwealth; or rather, not pray to her, but prey on her, for they ride up and down on her and make her their boots.

Cham. What, the commonwealth their boots? Will she hold out water in foul way?

Gads. She will, she will; justice hath liquored her. We steal as in a castle, cock-sure; we have the receipt of fern-seed, we walk invisible.

Cham. Nay, by my faith, I think you are more beholding to the night than to fern-seed for your walking invisible.

Gads. Give me thy hand: thou shalt have a share in our purchase, as I am a true man.

Cham. Nay, rather let me have it as you are a false thief.

Gads. Go to; *homo* is a common name to all men. Bid the ostler bring my gelding out of the stable. Farewell, you muddy knave. *Exeunt.*

Scene II. *The highway, near Gadshill.*

Enter *Prince Henry* and *Poins.*

Poins. Come, shelter, shelter! I have removed Falstaff's horse, and he frets like a gummed velvet. *They step back.*

23. chamber-lye, urine. **loach,** a prolific fish. **27. razes,** bundles of root. **52. chamberlain,** servant in charge of rooms. **60. franklin,** freeholder. **wild,** weald, forest. **61. mark,** 13s. 4d.

67-8. Saint Nicholas' clerks, thieves. **77. Troians,** a cant name for dissolute fellows or boon companions. Gadshill may well be thinking of the prince. **81. foot land-rakers,** footpads. **82. strikers,** robbers. **83. malt-worms,** tipplers. **84. oneyers,** probably ones. **93. foul,** muddy. **95. liquored,** (1) waterproofed, (2) intoxicated. **96. we have the receipt of fern-seed,** the recipe for gathering fern-seed, which was popularly supposed to make the possessor invisible. **101. purchase,** plunder. **Scene ii: 3. gummed,** cheap velvets were often stiffened with gum, which would fret or rub when worn.

Prince. Stand close.

Enter *Falstaff.*

Fal. Poins! Poins, and be hanged! Poins!

Prince. [*Coming forward.*] Peace, ye fat-kidneyed rascal! what a brawling dost thou keep!

Fal. Where 's Poins, Hal?

Prince. He is walked up to the top of the hill; I 'll go seek him. *Withdraws.*

Fal. I am accursed to rob in that thief's company: the rascal hath removed my horse, and tied him I know not where. If I travel but four foot by the squire further afoot, I shall break my wind. Well, I doubt not but to die a fair death for all this, if I scape hanging for killing that rogue. I have forsworn his company hourly any time this two and twenty years, and yet I am bewitched with the rogue's company. If the rascal have not given me medicines to make me love him, I 'll be hanged. It could not be else; I have drunk medicines. Poins! Hal! a plague upon you both! Bardolph! Peto! I 'll starve ere I 'll rob a foot further. An 't were not as good a deed as drink, to turn true man and to leave these rogues, I am the veriest varlet that ever chewed with a tooth. Eight yards of uneven ground is three score and ten miles afoot with me; and the stony-hearted villains know it well enough. A plague upon it when thieves cannot be true one to another! [*They whistle.*] Whew! A plague upon you all! Give me my horse, you rogues; give me my horse, and be hanged!

Prince. [*Coming forward.*] Peace ye fat-guts! lie down: lay thine ear close to the ground and list if thou canst hear the tread of travellers.

Fal. Have you any levers to lift me up again, being down? 'Sblood, I 'll not bear mine own flesh so far afoot again for all the coin in thy father's exchequer. What a plague mean ye to colt me thus?

Prince. Thou liest; thou art not colted, thou art uncolted.

Fal. I prithee, good Prince Hal, help me to my horse, good king's son.

Prince. Out, ye rogue! shall I be your ostler?

Fal. Hang thyself in thine own heir-apparent garters! If I be ta'en, I 'll peach for this. An I have not ballads made on you all and sung to filthy tunes, let a cup of sack be my poison. When a jest is so forward, and afoot too! I hate it.

Enter *Gadshill, Bardolph,* and *Peto* with him.

Gads. Stand.

Fal. So I do, against my will.

Poins. [*Coming forward.*] O, 't is our setter; I know his voice. Bardolph, what news?

Bard. Case ye, case ye; on with your vizards: there 's money of the King's coming down the hill; 't is going to the King's exchequer.

Fal. You lie, ye rogue; 't is going to the King's tavern.

Gads. There 's enough to make us all.

Fal. To be hanged.

Prince. Sirs, you four shall front them in the narrow lane; Ned Poins and I will walk lower: if they scape from your encounter, then they light on us.

Peto. How many be there of them?

Gads. Some eight or ten.

Fal. 'Zounds, will they not rob us?

Prince. What, a coward, Sir John Paunch?

Fal. Indeed, I am not John of Gaunt, your grandfather; but yet no coward, Hal.

Prince. Well, we leave that to the proof.

Poins. Sirrah Jack, thy horse stands behind the hedge; when thou need'st him, there thou shalt find him. Farewell, and stand fast.

Fal. Now cannot I strike him, if I should be hanged.

Prince. [*Aside.*] Ned, where are our disguises.

Poins. [*Aside.*] Here, hard by: stand close.
Exeunt Prince and Poins.

Fal. Now, my masters, happy man be his dole, say I: every man to his business.

Enter the *Travellers.*

First Trav. Come, neighbour; the boy shall lead our horses down the hill: we 'll walk afoot a while, and ease our legs.

Thieves. Stand!

Travellers. Jesus bless us!

Fal. Strike; down with them! Cut the villains' throats! Ah! whoreson caterpillars! bacon-fed knaves! they hate us youth. Down with them! Fleece them!

Travellers. O, we are undone, both we and ours for ever!

Fal. Hang ye, gorbellied knaves, are ye undone? No, ye fat chuffs; I would your store were here! On, bacons, on! What, ye knaves! young men must live. You are grandjurors, are ye? We 'll jure ye, faith.

Here they rob them and bind them.
Exeunt.

13. squire, square, foot-rule. **14. for,** in spite of. **40. colt,** fool.

53. setter, Gadshill, the arranger of the robbery. **93. gorbellied,** fat-bellied. **94. chuffs,** miserly churls. **your store,** all you have.

Re-enter *Prince Henry* and *Poins* in buckram.

Prince. The thieves have bound the true men. Now, could thou and I rob the thieves and go merrily to London, it would be argument for a week, laughter for a month, and a good jest for ever.

Poins. Stand close; I hear them coming.

Enter the *Thieves* again.

Fal. Come, my masters, let us share, and then to horse before day. An the Prince and Poins be not two arrant cowards, there 's no equity stirring. There 's no more valour in that Poins than in a wild-duck.

Prince. Your money!

Poins. Villains!

As they are sharing, the Prince and Poins set upon them; they all run away; and Falstaff, after a blow or two, runs away too, leaving the booty behind them.

Prince. Got with much ease. Now merrily to horse.
The thieves are all scatter'd and possess'd with fear
So strongly that they dare not meet each other;
Each takes his fellow for an officer.
Away, good Ned. Falstaff sweats to death,
And lards the lean earth as he walks along.
Were 't not for laughing, I should pity him.

Poins. How the rogue roar'd! *Exeunt.*

Scene III. *Warkworth Castle.*

Enter *Hotspur,* solus, reading a letter.

Hot. "But, for mine own part, my lord, I could be well contented to be there, in respect of the love I bear your house." He could be contented: why is he not, then? In respect of the love he bears our house: he shows in this, he loves his own barn better than he loves our house. Let me see some more. "The purpose you undertake is dangerous;"—why, that 's certain. 'T is dangerous to take a cold, to sleep, to drink; but I tell you, my lord fool, out of this nettle, danger, we pluck this flower, safety. "The purpose you undertake is dangerous; the friends you have named uncertain; the time itself unsorted; and your whole plot too light for the counterpoise of so great an opposition." Say you so, say you so? I say unto you again, you are a shallow, cowardly hind, and you lie. What a lack-brain is this! By the Lord, our plot is a good plot as ever was laid; our friends true and constant: a good plot, good friends, and full of expectation; an excellent plot, very good friends. What a frosty-spirited rogue is this! Why, my Lord of York commends the plot and the general course of the action. 'Zounds, an I were now by this rascal, I could brain him with his lady's fan. Is there not my father, my uncle, and myself? Lord Edmund Mortimer, my Lord of York, and Owen Glendower? Is there not besides the Douglas? Have I not all their letters to meet me in arms by the ninth of the next month? and are they not some of them set forward already? What a pagan rascal is this! an infidel! Ha! you shall see now in very sincerity of fear and cold heart, will he to the King and lay open all our proceedings. O, I could divide myself and go to buffets, for moving such a dish of skim-milk with so honourable an action! Hang him! let him tell the King; we are prepared. I will set forward to-night.

Enter his *Lady.*

How now, Kate! I must leave you within these two hours.

Lady. O, my good lord, why are you thus alone?
For what offence have I this fortnight been
A banish'd woman from my Harry's bed?
Tell me, sweet lord, what is 't that takes from thee
Thy stomach, pleasure, and thy golden sleep?
Why dost thou bend thine eyes upon the earth,
And start so often when thou sit'st alone?
Why hast thou lost the fresh blood in thy cheeks,
And given my treasures and my rights of thee
To thick-ey'd musing and curst melancholy?
In thy faint slumbers I by thee have watch'd,
And heard thee murmur tales of iron wars;
Speak terms of manage to thy bounding steed;
Cry "Courage! to the field!" And thou hast talk'd
Of sallies and retires, of trenches, tents,
Of palisadoes, frontiers, parapets,
Of basilisks, of cannon, culverin,
Of prisoners' ransom, and of soldiers slain,
And all the currents of a heady fight.
Thy spirit within thee hath been so at war
And thus hath so bestirr'd thee in thy sleep,
That beads of sweat have stood upon thy brow,
Like bubbles in a late-disturbed stream;

107. equity, justice. **Scene iii: 13. unsorted,** ill-chosen.

20. expectation, promise. **44. stomach,** appetite. **52. terms of manage,** words used in training a horse. **56. basilisks,** large brass cannon. **culverin,** long cannon. **58. currents,** occurrences. **heady,** impetuous.

Hotspur rejects wife — his life — fighting.

And in thy face strange motions have appear'd,
Such as we see when men restrain their breath
On some great sudden hest. O, what portents are these?
Some heavy business hath my lord in hand,
And I must know it, else he loves me not.

Hot. What, ho!

Enter *Servant.*

Is Gilliams with the packet gone?

Serv. He is, my lord, an hour ago.

Hot. Hath Butler brought those horses from the sheriff?

Serv. One horse, my lord, he brought even now.

Hot. What horse? A roan, a crop-ear, is it not?

Serv. It is, my lord.

Hot. That roan shall be my throne.
Well, I will back him straight. O *Esperance!*
Bid Butler lead him forth into the park.

Exit Servant.

Lady. But hear you, my lord.

Hot. What say'st thou, my lady?

Lady. What is it carries you away?

Hot. Why, my horse, my love, my horse.

Lady. Out, you mad-headed ape!
A weasel hath not such a deal of spleen
As you are toss'd with. In faith,
I 'll know your business, Harry, that I will.
I fear my brother Mortimer doth stir
About his title, and hath sent for you
To line his enterprise; but if you go,—

Hot. So far afoot, I shall be weary, love.

Lady. Come, come, you paraquito, answer me
Directly unto this question that I ask.
In faith, I 'll break thy little finger, Harry,
An if thou wilt not tell me all things true.

Hot. Away,
Away, you trifler! Love! I love thee not,
I care not for thee, Kate: this is no world
To play with mammets and to tilt with lips:
We must have bloody noses and crack'd crowns,
And pass them current too. God 's me, my horse!
What say'st thou, Kate? What would'st thou have with me?

Lady. Do you not love me? Do you not, indeed?
Well, do not then; for since you love me not,
I will not love myself. Do you not love me?
Nay, tell me if you speak in jest or no.

Hot. Come, wilt thou see me ride?
And when I am a-horseback, I will swear
I love thee infinitely. But hark you, Kate;
I must not have you henceforth question me
Whither I go, nor reason whereabout.
Whither I must, I must; and, to conclude,
This evening must I leave you, gentle Kate.
I know you wise; but yet no farther wise
Than Harry Percy's wife. Constant you are,
But yet a woman; and for secrecy,
No lady closer; for I well believe
Thou wilt not utter what thou dost not know;
And so far will I trust thee, gentle Kate.

Lady. How! so far?

Hot. Not an inch further. But hark you, Kate:
Whither I go, thither shall you go too;
To-day will I set forth, to-morrow you.
Will this content you, Kate?

Lady. It must of force. *Exeunt.*

Scene IV. *The Boar's-Head Tavern, Eastcheap.*

Enter the *Prince* and *Poins.*

Prince. Ned, prithee, come out of that fat room, and lend me thy hand to laugh a little.

Poins. Where hast been, Hal?

Prince. With three or four loggerheads amongst three or four score hogsheads. I have sounded the very base-string of humility. Sirrah, I am sworn brother to a leash of drawers; and can call them all by their christen names, as Tom, Dick, and Francis. They take it already upon their salvation, that though I be but Prince of Wales, yet I am the king of courtesy; and tell me flatly I am no proud Jack, like Falstaff, but a Corinthian, a lad of mettle, a good boy, (by the Lord, so they call me,) and when I am King of England, I shall command all the good lads in Eastcheap. They call drinking deep, dyeing scarlet; and when you breathe in your watering, they cry "hem!" and bid you play it off. To conclude, I am so good a proficient in one quarter of an hour, that I can drink with any tinker in his own language during my life. I tell thee, Ned, thou hast lost much honour, that thou wert not with me in this action. But, sweet Ned,—to sweeten which name of Ned, I give thee this pennyworth of sugar, clapped even now into my hand by an under-skinker, one that never spake other English in his life than "Eight shillings and sixpence," and "You are welcome," with this shrill addition, "Anon, anon, sir! Score a pint of bastard in the Half-moon," or so. But, Ned, to drive away the time till Falstaff come, I prithee, do thou stand

65. **hest**, command. 74. *Esperance*, motto of the Percies. 86. **line**, support. 95. **mammets**, dolls, puppets.

107. **whereabout**, on what errand. **Scene iv: 1-2. fat room**, probably vat room. 12. **Corinthian**, a gay fellow. 17. **watering**, drinking. 18. **play it off**, drink it down. 25. **under-skinker**, tapster's boy. 29. **bastard**, a sweet Spanish wine. **Half-moon**, a room in the tavern.

in some by-room, while I question my puny drawer to what end he gave me the sugar; and do thou never leave calling "Francis," that his tale to me may be nothing but "Anon." Step aside, and I 'll show thee a precedent.

Poins. Francis!

Prince. Thou art perfect.

Poins. Francis! *Exit Poins.*

Enter *Francis,* a drawer.

Fran. Anon, anon, sir. Look down into the Pomgarnet, Ralph.

Prince. Come hither, Francis.

Fran. My lord?

Prince. How long hast thou to serve, Francis?

Fran. Forsooth, five years, and as much as to—

Poins. [*Within.*] Francis!

Fran. Anon, anon, sir.

Prince. Five year! by 'r lady, a long lease for the clinking of pewter. But, Francis, darest thou be so valiant as to play the coward with thy indenture and show it a fair pair of heels and run from it?

Fran. O Lord, sir, I 'll be sworn upon all the books in England, I could find in my heart—

Poins. [*Within.*] Francis!

Fran. Anon, sir.

Prince. How old art thou, Francis?

Fran. Let me see—about Michaelmas next I shall be—

Poins. [*Within.*] Francis!

Fran. Anon, sir. Pray, stay a little, my lord.

Prince. Nay, but hark you, Francis: for the sugar thou gavest me, 't was a pennyworth, was 't not?

Fran. O Lord, I would it had been two!

Prince. I will give thee for it a thousand pound. Ask me when thou wilt, and thou shalt have it.

Poins. [*Within.*] Francis!

Fran. Anon, anon.

Prince. Anon, Francis? No, Francis; but to-morrow, Francis; or Francis, o' Thursday; or indeed, Francis, when thou wilt. But, Francis!

Fran. My lord?

Prince. Wilt thou rob this leathern jerkin, crystal-button, not-pated, agate-ring, puke-stocking, caddis-garter, smooth-tongue, Spanish-pouch,—

Fran. O Lord, sir, who do you mean?

Prince. Why, then, your brown bastard is your only drink; for look you, Francis, your white canvas doublet will sully. In Barbary, sir, it cannot come to so much.

Fran. What, sir?

Poins. [*Within.*] Francis!

Prince. Away, you rogue! dost thou not hear them call?

Here they both call him; the drawer stands amazed, not knowing which way to go.

Enter *Vintner.*

Vint. What, stand'st thou still, and hear'st such a calling? Look to the guests within. [*Exit Francis.*] My lord, old Sir John with half-a-dozen more are at the door; shall I let them in?

Prince. Let them alone a while, and then open the door. [*Exit Vintner.*] Poins!

Poins. [*Within.*] Anon, anon, sir.

Re-enter *Poins.*

Prince. Sirrah, Falstaff and the rest of the thieves are at the door; shall we be merry?

Poins. As merry as crickets, my lad. But hark ye; what cunning match have you made with this jest of the drawer? Come, what 's the issue?

Prince. I am now of all humours that have showed themselves humours since the old days of goodman Adam to the pupil age of this present twelve o'clock at midnight.

Re-enter *Francis.*

What 's o'clock, Francis?

Fran. Anon, anon, sir. *Exit.*

Prince. That ever this fellow should have fewer words than a parrot, and yet the son of a woman! His industry is upstairs and downstairs; his eloquence the parcel of a reckoning. I am not yet of Percy's mind, the Hotspur of the north; he that kills me some six or seven dozen of Scots at a breakfast, washes his hands, and says to his wife, "Fie upon this quiet life! I want work." "O my sweet Harry," says she, "how many hast thou killed to-day?" "Give my roan horse a drench," says he; and answers, "Some fourteen," an hour after; "a trifle, a trifle." I prithee, call in Falstaff. I 'll play Percy, and that damned brawn shall play Dame Mortimer his wife. "Rivo!" says the drunkard. Call in ribs, call in tallow.

36. **precedent,** example. 42. **Pomgarnet,** Pomegranate, another room in the tavern. 53. **indenture,** apprentice agreement. 56. **books,** Bibles. 60. **Michaelmas,** Sept. 29. 77-80. This is a jesting description of the vintner, who appears at line 90. The costume was typical of that worn by landlords: **not-pated,** hair close-cropped; **puke-stocking,** stockings of a dull gray color; **caddis-garter,** garter of worsted lace; **Spanish-pouch,** a reference to the purse of Spanish leather he carried. The next speech of the Prince is mere nonsense to bewilder the waiter.

101. **match,** game. 106. **pupil age,** youth. 113. **parcel,** item. 119. **drench,** bran and water. 124. **Rivo,** drunkard's exclamation.

Enter *Falstaff, Gadshill, Bardolph,* and *Peto; Francis* following with wine.

Poins. Welcome, Jack! Where hast thou been?

Fal. A plague of all cowards, I say, and a vengeance too! marry, and amen! Give me a cup of sack, boy. Ere I lead this life long, I 'll sew nether stocks, and mend them and foot them too. A plague of all cowards! Give me a cup of sack, rogue. Is there no virtue extant? *He drinketh.*

Prince. Didst thou never see Titan kiss a dish of butter, pitiful-hearted Titan, that melted at the sweet tale of the sun? If thou didst, then behold that compound.

Fal. You rogue, here 's lime in this sack too: there is nothing but roguery to be found in villanous man; yet a coward is worse than a cup of sack with lime in it. A villanous coward! Go thy ways, old Jack; die when thou wilt, if manhood, good manhood, be not forgot upon the face of the earth, then am I a shotten herring. There lives not three good men unhanged in England; and one of them is fat and grows old. God help the while! a bad world, I say. I would I were a weaver; I could sing psalms or anything. A plague of all cowards, I say still.

Prince. How now, wool-sack! what mutter you?

Fal. A king's son! If I do not beat thee out of thy kingdom with a dagger of lath, and drive all thy subjects afore thee like a flock of wild-geese, I 'll never wear hair on my face more. You Prince of Wales!

Prince. Why, you whoreson round man, what 's the matter?

Fal. Are not you a coward? Answer me to that; and Poins there?

Poins. 'Zounds, ye fat paunch, an ye call me coward, by the Lord, I 'll stab thee.

Fal. I call thee coward! I 'll see thee damned ere I call thee coward; but I would give a thousand pound I could run as fast as thou canst. You are straight enough in the shoulders; you care not who sees your back: call you that backing of your friends? A plague upon such backing! give me them that will face me. Give me a cup of sack. I am a rogue, if I drunk to-day.

Prince. O villain! thy lips are scarce wiped since thou drunk'st last.

Fal. All 's one for that. [*He drinketh.*] A plague of all cowards, still say I.

Prince. What 's the matter?

Fal. What 's the matter? There be four of us here have ta'en a thousand pound this day morning.

Prince. Where is it, Jack? where is it?

Fal. Where is it? Taken from us it is; a hundred upon poor four of us.

Prince. What, a hundred, man?

Fal. I am a rogue, if I were not at half-sword with a dozen of them two hours together. I have scaped by miracle. I am eight times thrust through the doublet, four through the hose; my buckler cut through and through; my sword hack'd like a hand-saw—*ecce signum!* I never dealt better since I was a man; all would not do. A plague of all cowards! Let them speak; if they speak more or less than truth, they are villains and the sons of darkness.

Prince. Speak, sirs; how was it?

Gads. We four set upon some dozen—

Fal. Sixteen at least, my lord.

Gads. And bound them.

Peto. No, no, they were not bound.

Fal. You rogue, they were bound, every man of them, or I am a Jew else, an Ebrew Jew.

Gads. As we were sharing, some six or seven fresh men set upon us—

Fal. And unbound the rest, and then come in the other.

Prince. What, fought you with them all?

Fal. All! I know not what you call all; but if I fought not with fifty of them, I am a bunch of radish. If there were not two or three and fifty upon poor old Jack, then am I no two-legg'd creature.

Prince. Pray God you have not murdered some of them.

Fal. Nay, that 's past praying for; I have peppered two of them. Two I am sure I have paid, two rogues in buckram suits. I tell thee what, Hal, if I tell thee a lie, spit in my face, call me horse. Thou knowest my old ward: here I lay, and thus I bore my point. Four rogues in buckram let drive at me—

Prince. What, four? Thou saidst but two even now.

Fal. Four, Hal; I told thee four.

Poins. Ay, ay, he said four.

Fal. These four came all a-front, and mainly thrust at me. I made me no more ado but took all their seven points in my target, thus.

Prince. Seven? why, there were but four even now.

130. nether stocks, stockings. **132. virtue,** courage. **134. pitiful-hearted Titan,** Hyperion, the sun. The relative clause beginning "that melted" refers back to **butter** and not to **Titan. 137. lime,** a preservative. **143. shotten herring,** a herring that has spawned. **145. while,** present age.

182-3. at half-sword, at close quarters. **187.** *ecce signum* behold the proof. **213. paid,** killed. **215. ward,** posture of defense. **223. mainly,** mightily. **224. target,** shield.

Fal. In buckram?

Poins. Ay, four, in buckram suits.

Fal. Seven, by these hilts, or I am a villain else.

Prince. Prithee, let him alone; we shall have more anon.

Fal. Dost thou hear me, Hal?

Prince. Ay, and mark thee too, Jack.

Fal. Do so, for it is worth the listening to. These nine in buckram that I told thee of—

Prince. So, two more already.

Fal. Their points being broken,—

Poins. Down fell their hose.

Fal. Began to give me ground; but I followed me close, came in foot and hand, and with a thought seven of the eleven I paid.

Prince. O monstrous! eleven buckram men grown out of two!

Fal. But, as the devil would have it, three misbegotten knaves in Kendal green came at my back and let drive at me; for it was so dark, Hal, that thou couldst not see thy hand.

Prince. These lies are like their father that begets them; gross as a mountain, open, palpable. Why thou clay-brained guts, thou knotty-pated fool, thou whoreson, obscene, greasy tallow-catch,—

Fal. What, art thou mad? art thou mad? Is not the truth the truth?

Prince. Why, how couldst thou know these men in Kendal green, when it was so dark thou couldst not see thy hand? Come, tell us your reason; what say'st thou to this?

Poins. Come, your reason, Jack, your reason.

Fal. What, upon compulsion? 'Zounds, an I were at the strappado, or all the racks in the world, I would not tell you on compulsion. Give you a reason on compulsion! If reasons were as plenty as blackberries, I would give no man a reason upon compulsion, I.

Prince. I 'll be no longer guilty of this sin. This sanguine coward, this bed-presser, this horseback-breaker, this huge hill of flesh,—

Fal. 'Sblood, you starveling, you elf-skin, you dried neat's tongue, you bull's pizzle, you stockfish! O for breath to utter what is like thee! you tailor's-yard, you sheath, you bow-case, you vile standing-tuck,—

Prince. Well, breathe a while, and then to it again; and when thou hast tired thyself in base comparisons, hear me speak but this:—

Poins. Mark, Jack.

Prince. We two saw you four set on four and bound them, and were masters of their wealth. Mark now, how a plain tale shall put you down. Then did we two set on you four; and, with a word, out-faced you from your prize, and have it, yea, and can show it you here in the house; and, Falstaff, you carried your guts away as nimbly, with as quick dexterity, and roared for mercy, and still run and roared, as ever I heard bull-calf. What a slave art thou, to hack thy sword as thou hast done, and then say it was in fight! What trick, what device, what starting-hole, canst thou now find out to hide thee from this open and apparent shame?

Poins. Come, let 's hear, Jack; what trick hast thou now?

Fal. By the Lord, I knew ye as well as he that made ye. Why, hear you, my masters: was it for me to kill the heir-apparent? Should I turn upon the true prince? Why, thou knowest I am as valiant as Hercules; but beware instinct; the lion will not touch the true prince. Instinct is a great matter; I was now a coward on instinct. I shall think the better of myself and thee during my life; I for a valiant lion, and thou for a true prince. But, by the Lord, lads, I am glad you have the money. Hostess, clap to the doors! Watch to-night, pray to-morrow. Gallants, lads, boys, hearts of gold, all the titles of good fellowship come to you! What, shall we be merry? Shall we have a play extempore?

Prince. Content; and the argument shall be thy running away.

Fal. Ah, no more of that, Hal, an thou lovest me!

Enter *Hostess.*

Host. O Jesu, my lord the Prince!

Prince. How now, my lady the hostess! what say'st thou to me?

Host. Marry, my lord, there is a nobleman of the court at door would speak with you. He says he comes from your father.

Prince. Give him as much as will make him a royal man, and send him back again to my mother.

Fal. What manner of man is he?

Host. An old man.

Fal. What doth Gravity out of his bed at midnight? Shall I give him his answer?

Prince. Prithee, do, Jack.

Fal. Faith, and I 'll send him packing. *Exit.*

Prince. Now, sirs, by 'r lady, you fought fair; so did you, Peto; so did you, Bardolph.

238. points, (1) points of swords, (2) laces of doublet. **253. catch,** ketch or tub. **262. strappado,** a species of torture. **268. sanguine.** red-faced. **271. neat's,** ox's. **272. stockfish.** dried cod. **274. standing-tuck,** rapier standing upright.

290. starting-hole, loop-hole. **317-21. nobleman . . . royal man,** pun on names of coins—noble 6s. 8d.; royal 10s.

You are lions too, you ran away upon instinct, you will not touch the true prince; no, fie!

Bard. Faith, I ran when I saw others run.

Prince. Tell me now in earnest, how came Falstaff's sword so hacked?

Peto. Why, he hacked it with his dagger, and said he would swear truth out of England but he would make you believe it was done in fight, and persuaded us to do the like.

Bard. Yea, and to tickle our noses with spear-grass to make them bleed, and then to beslubber our garments with it and swear it was the blood of true men. I did that I did not this seven year before, I blushed to hear his monstrous devices.

Prince. O villain, thou stolest a cup of sack eighteen years ago, and wert taken with the manner, and ever since thou hast blushed extempore. Thou hadst fire and sword on thy side, and yet thou ran'st away; what instinct hadst thou for it?

Bard. My lord, do you see these meteors? Do you behold these exhalations?

Pointing to his own face.

Prince. I do.

Bard. What think you they portend?

Prince. Hot livers and cold purses.

Bard. Choler, my lord, if rightly taken.

Re-enter *Falstaff.*

Prince. No, if rightly taken, halter. Here comes lean Jack, here comes bare-bone. How now, my sweet creature of bombast! How long is 't ago, Jack, since thou sawest thine own knee?

Fal. My own knee? When I was about thy years, Hal, I was not an eagle's talon in the waist; I could have crept into any alderman's thumb-ring: a plague of sighing and grief! it blows a man up like a bladder. There 's villanous news abroad: here was Sir John Bracy from your father; you must to the court in the morning. That same mad fellow of the north, Percy, and he of Wales that gave Amamon the bastinado and made Lucifer cuckold and swore the devil his true liegeman upon the cross of a Welsh hook—what a plague call you him?

Poins. O, Glendower.

Fal. Owen, Owen, the same; and his son-in-law Mortimer, and old Northumberland, and that sprightly Scot of Scots, Douglas, that runs a-horseback up a hill perpendicular,—

Prince. He that rides at high speed and with his pistol kills a sparrow flying.

Fal. You have hit it.

Prince. So did he never the sparrow.

Fal. Well, that rascal hath good mettle in him; he will not run.

Prince. Why, what a rascal art thou then, to praise him so for running!

Fal. A-horseback, ye cuckoo; but afoot he will not budge a foot.

Prince. Yes, Jack, upon instinct.

Fal. I grant ye, upon instinct. Well, he is there too, and one Mordake, and a thousand blue-caps more: Worcester is stolen away tonight: thy father's beard is turn'd white with the news: you may buy land now as cheap as stinking mackerel.

Prince. Why, then, it is like, if there come a hot June and this civil buffeting hold, we shall buy maidenheads as they buy hob-nails, by the hundreds.

Fal. By the mass, lad, thou say'st true; it is like we shall have good trading that way. But tell me, Hal, art not thou horrible afeard? Thou being heir-apparent, could the world pick thee out three such enemies again as that fiend Douglas, that spirit Percy, and that devil Glendower? Art thou not horribly afraid? Doth not thy blood thrill at it?

Prince. Not a whit, i' faith; I lack some of thy instinct.

Fal. Well, thou wilt be horribly chid tomorrow when thou comest to thy father: if thou love me, practise an answer.

Prince. Do thou stand for my father, and examine me upon the particulars of my life.

Fal. Shall I? Content. This chair shall be my state, this dagger my sceptre, and this cushion my crown.

Prince. Thy state is taken for a joined-stool, thy golden sceptre for a leaden dagger, and thy precious rich crown for a pitiful bald crown!

Fal. Well, an the fire of grace be not quite out of thee, now shalt thou be moved. Give me a cup of sack to make my eyes look red, that it may be thought I have wept; for I must speak in passion, and I will do it in King Cambyses' vein.

Prince. Well, here is my leg.

Fal. And here is my speech. Stand aside, nobility.

Host. O Jesu, this is excellent sport, i' faith!

Fal. Weep not, sweet queen; for trickling tears are vain.

Host. O, the father, how he holds his countenance!

346-7. **taken with the manner**, taken in the act. 355. **Hot livers**, drunkenness. **cold purses**, poverty. 357. **halter**, punning reference to choler, or collar. 359. **bombast**, raw cotton, padding. 369-70. **Amamon**, a devil. 370. **bastinado**, a beating. 372. **Welsh hook**, a pike with a hook below the spearhead.

392. **blue-caps**, blue-bonneted Scotchmen. 416. **state**, throne. 425-6. **King Cambyses' vein**, reference to Thomas Preston's *A Lamentable Tragedie*—containing the life of Cambises, King of Persia, 1570. The bombastic, high flown style of this play became proverbial. 427. **leg**, bow.

Fal. For God's sake, lords, convey my tristful queen;
For tears do stop the flood-gates of her eyes.

Host. O Jesu, he doth it as like one of these harlotry players as ever I see!

Fal. Peace, good pint-pot; peace, good tickle-brain. Harry, I do not only marvel where thou spendest thy time, but also how thou art accompanied; for though the camomile, the more it is trodden on the faster it grows, so youth, the more it is wasted the sooner it wears. That thou art my son, I have partly thy mother's word, partly my own opinion, but chiefly a villanous trick of thine eye and a foolish hanging of thy nether lip, that doth warrant me. If then thou be son to me, here lies the point; why, being son to me, art thou so pointed at? Shall the blessed sun of heaven prove a micher and eat blackberries? a question not to be asked. Shall the son of England prove a thief and take purses? a question to be asked. There is a thing, Harry, which thou hast often heard of and it is known to many in our land by the name of pitch. This pitch, as ancient writers do report, doth defile; so doth the company thou keepest: for, Harry, now I do not speak to thee in drink but in tears; not in pleasure but in passion, not in words only, but in woes also; and yet there is a virtuous man whom I have often noted in thy company, but I know not his name.

Prince. What manner of man, an it like your Majesty?

Fal. A goodly portly man, i' faith, and a corpulent; of a cheerful look, a pleasing eye, and a most noble carriage; and, as I think, his age some fifty, or, by 'r lady, inclining to threescore; and now I remember me, his name is Falstaff. If that man should be lewdly given, he deceiveth me; for, Harry, I see virtue in his looks. If then the tree may be known by the fruit, as the fruit by the tree, then, peremptorily I speak it, there is virtue in that Falstaff; him keep with, the rest banish. And tell me now, thou naughty varlet, tell me, where hast thou been this month?

Prince. Dost thou speak like a king? Do thou stand for me, and I 'll play my father.

Fal. Depose me? If thou dost it half so gravely, so majestically, both in word and matter, hang me up by the heels for a rabbit-sucker or a poulter's hare.

Prince. Well, here I am set.

Fal. And here I stand: judge, my masters.

Prince. Now, Harry, whence come you?

Fal. My noble lord, from Eastcheap.

Prince. The complaints I hear of thee are grievous.

Fal. 'Sblood, my lord, they are false.—Nay, I 'll tickle ye for a young prince, i' faith.

Prince. Swearest thou, ungracious boy? Henceforth ne'er look on me. Thou art violently carried away from grace: there is a devil haunts thee in the likeness of an old fat man; a tun of man is thy companion. Why dost thou converse with that trunk of humours, that bolting-hutch of beastliness, that swollen parcel of dropsies, that huge bombard of sack, that stuffed cloak-bag of guts, that roasted Manningtree ox with the pudding in his belly, that reverend vice, that grey iniquity, that father ruffian, that vanity in years? Wherein is he good, but to taste sack and drink it? wherein neat and cleanly, but to carve a capon and eat it? wherein cunning, but in craft? wherein crafty, but in villainy? wherein villanous, but in all things? wherein worthy, but in nothing?

Fal. I would your Grace would take me with you: whom means your Grace?

Prince. That villanous abominable misleader of youth, Falstaff, that old white-bearded Satan.

Fal. My lord, the man I know.

Prince. I know thou dost.

Fal. But to say I know more harm in him than in myself, were to say more than I know. That he is old, the more the pity, his white hairs do witness it; but that he is, saving your reverence, a whoremaster, that I utterly deny. If sack and sugar be a fault, God help the wicked! If to be old and merry be a sin, than many an old host that I know is damned. If to be fat be to be hated, then Pharaoh's lean kine are to be loved. No, my good lord; banish Peto, banish Bardolph, banish Poins; but for sweet Jack Falstaff, kind Jack Falstaff, true Jack Falstaff, valiant Jack Falstaff, and therefore more valiant, being, as he is, old Jack Falstaff, banish not him thy Harry's company, banish not him thy Harry's company. Banish plump Jack, and banish all the world.

Prince. I do, I will.

A knocking heard. Exeunt Hostess, Francis, and Bardolph.

439. tickle-brain, strong liquor. **441. though the camomile,** the two long speeches of Falstaff in the rôle of the King are an elaborate parody of the style made popular by Lyly's *Euphues* in 1578. It was a highly artificial prose style which had as distinguishing traits the use of antithesis—the setting off of one clause or phrase against another—the marking of this antithesis by alliteration, the use of rhetorical questions, and the use of illustrations drawn from false natural history. The reference to the camomile, a creeping herb, is an example of the last. **446. nether,** lower. **450. micher,** truant.

480-1. rabbit-sucker, a sucking rabbit. **481. poulter's,** poulterer's. **494. humours,** caprices. **495. bolting-hutch,** miller's bin. **496. bombard,** leather vessel for holding liquor.

Re-enter *Bardolph,* running.

Bard. O, my lord, my lord! the sheriff with a most monstrous watch is at the door.

Fal. Out, ye rogue! Play out the play; I have much to say in the behalf of that Falstaff.

Re-enter the *Hostess.*

Host. O Jesu, my lord, my lord!

Prince. Heigh, heigh! the devil rides upon a fiddlestick: what 's the matter?

Host. The sheriff and all the watch are at the door; they are come to search the house. Shall I let them in?

Fal. Dost thou hear, Hal? Never call a true piece of gold a counterfeit: thou art essentially mad, without seeming so.

Prince. And thou a natural coward, without instinct.

Fal. I deny your major: if you will deny the sheriff, so; if not, let him enter. If I become not a cart as well as another man, a plague on my bringing up! I hope I shall as soon be strangled with a halter as another.

Prince. Go, hide thee behind the arras; the rest walk up above. Now, my masters, for a true face and good conscience.

Fal. Both which I have had; but their date is out, and therefore I 'll hide me. *Exit.*

Prince. Call in the sheriff.

Exeunt all except the Prince and Peto.

Enter *Sheriff* and the *Carrier.*

Now, master sheriff, what is your will with me?

Sher. First, pardon me, my lord. A hue and cry
Hath followed certain men unto this house.

Prince. What men?

Sher. One of them is well known, my gracious lord,
A gross fat man.

Car. As fat as butter.

Prince. The man, I do assure you, is not here,
For I myself at this time have employ'd him.
And, sheriff, I will engage my word to thee
That I will, by to-morrow dinner-time,
Send him to answer thee or any man
For anything he shall be charg'd withal.
And so let me entreat you leave the house.

Sher. I will, my lord. There are two gentlemen
Have in this robbery lost three hundred marks.

Prince. It may be so: if he have robb'd these men,
He shall be answerable; and so farewell.

Sher. Good night, my noble lord.

Prince. I think it is good morrow, is it not?

Sher. Indeed, my lord, I think it be two o'clock. *Exeunt Sheriff and Carrier.*

Prince. This oily rascal is known as well as Paul's. Go, call him forth.

Peto. Falstaff!—Fast asleep behind the arras, and snorting like a horse.

Prince. Hark, how hard he fetches breath. Search his pockets. [*He searcheth his pockets, and findeth certain papers.*] What hast thou found?

Peto. Nothing but papers, my lord.

Prince. Let 's see what they be. Read them.

Peto. [*Reads.*]

Item, A capon....................2s. 2d.
Item, Sauce ....4d.
Item, Sack, two gallons...........5s. 8d.
Item, Anchovies and sack after supper. 2s. 6d.
Item, Bread ....ob.

Prince. O monstrous! but one half-pennyworth of bread to this intolerable deal of sack! What there is else, keep close; we 'll read it at more advantage: there let him sleep till day. I 'll to the court in the morning. We must all to the wars, and thy place shall be honourable. I 'll procure this fat rogue a charge of foot; and I know his death will be a march of twelve-score. The money shall be paid back again with advantage. Be with me betimes in the morning; and so, good morrow, Peto.

Peto. Good morrow, good my lord.

Exeunt.

539-41. This speech may refer not to playing out the play but to the coming of the sheriff. Falstaff is anxious for Hal to take the matter seriously. To paraphrase: This alarm is no counterfeit. To make light of it will show that you are demented. And your fear about it, retorts the prince, shows that you are a coward. **544. major,** major premise. **545. so,** very well. **546. cart,** hangman's cart. **549. arras,** tapestry curtain. **552-3. their date is out,** they're out of date with me; cf. *R. and J.* I, iv, 3.

569. mark, 13s. 4d. **576. Paul's,** St. Paul's Cathedral. **590. ob,** obolus, a half-penny. **598-9. death . . . twelve-score,** a march of twelve-score yards will kill him. **600. advantage,** interest.

ACT III. Scene I. *Bangor. The Archdeacon's house.*

Enter *Hotspur, Worcester, Lord Mortimer,* and *Owen Glendower.*

Mort. These promises are fair, the parties sure,
And our induction full of prosperous hope.
Hot. Lord Mortimer, and cousin Glendower,
Will you sit down?
And uncle Worcester,—a plague upon it!
I have forgot the map.
Glend. No, here it is.
Sit, cousin Percy; sit, good cousin Hotspur,
For by that name as oft as Lancaster
Doth speak of you, his cheek looks pale and with
A rising sigh he wisheth you in heaven.
Hot. And you in hell, as oft as he hears
Owen Glendower spoke of.
Glend. I cannot blame him: at my nativity
The front of heaven was full of fiery shapes,
Of burning cressets; and at my birth
The frame and huge foundation of the earth
Shak'd like a coward.
Hot. Why, so it would have done at the same season, if your mother's cat had but kittened, though yourself had never been born.
Glend. I say the earth did shake when I was born.
Hot. And I say the earth was not of my mind,
If you suppose as fearing you it shook.
Glend. The heavens were all on fire, the earth did tremble.
Hot. O, then the earth shook to see the heavens on fire,
And not in fear of your nativity.
Diseased nature oftentimes breaks forth
In strange eruptions; oft the teeming earth
Is with a kind of colic pinch'd and vex'd
By the imprisoning of unruly wind
Within her womb; which, for enlargement striving,
Shakes the old beldam earth, and topples down
Steeples and moss-grown towers. At your birth
Our grandam earth, having this distemperature,
In passion shook.
Glend. Cousin, of many men
I do not bear these crossings. Give me leave
To tell you once again that at my birth
The front of heaven was full of fiery shapes,
The goats ran from the mountains, and the herds
Were strangely clamorous to the frighted fields.
These signs have mark'd me extraordinary;
And all the courses of my life do show
I am not in the roll of common men.
Where is he living, clipp'd in with the sea
That chides the banks of England, Scotland, Wales,
Which calls me pupil, or hath read to me?
And bring him out that is but woman's son
Can trace me in the tedious ways of art
And hold me pace in deep experiments.
Hot. I think there 's no man speaks better
Welsh. I 'll to dinner.
Mort. Peace, cousin Percy; you will make him mad.
Glend. I can call spirits from the vasty deep.
Hot. Why, so can I, or so can any man;
But will they come when you do call for them?
Glend. Why, I can teach you, cousin, to command
The devil.
Hot. And I can teach thee, coz, to shame the devil
By telling truth. "Tell truth and shame the devil."
If thou have power to raise him, bring him hither,
And I 'll be sworn I have power to shame him hence.
O, while you live, tell truth and shame the devil!
Mort. Come, come, no more of this unprofitable chat.
Glend. Three times hath Henry Bolingbroke made head
Against my power; thrice from the banks of Wye
And sandy-bottom'd Severn have I sent him
Bootless home and weather-beaten back.
Hot. Home without boots, and in foul weather too!
How scapes he agues, in the devil's name?
Glend. Come, here 's the map: shall we divide our right
According to our threefold order ta'en?
Mort. The Archdeacon hath divided it
Into three limits very equally.
England, from Trent and Severn hitherto,
By south and east is to my part assign'd;
All westward, Wales beyond the Severn shore,
And all the fertile land within that bound,

Act III, Scene i: 2. induction, beginning. **15. cressets,** vessels containing fire. **32. beldam,** grandmother. **34. distemperature,** disorder. **46. read to me,** instructed me. **48. trace,** follow. **art,** magic. **67. bootless,** without advantage. **74. hitherto,** to this point.

To Owen Glendower; and, dear coz, to you
The remnant northward, lying off from Trent.
And our indentures tripartite are drawn;
Which being sealed interchangeably,
A business that this night may execute,
To-morrow, cousin Percy, you and I
And my good Lord of Worcester will set forth
To meet your father and the Scottish power,
As is appointed us, at Shrewsbury.
My father Glendower is not ready yet,
Nor shall we need his help these fourteen days.
Within that space you may have drawn together
Your tenants, friends, and neighbouring gentlemen.
Glend. A shorter time shall send me to you, lords;
And in my conduct shall your ladies come,
From whom you now must steal and take no leave,
For there will be a world of water shed
Upon the parting of your wives and you.
Hot. Methinks my moiety, north from Burton here,
In quantity equals not one of yours.
See how this river comes me cranking in,
And cuts me from the best of all my land
A huge half-moon, a monstrous cantle out.
I 'll have the current in this place damm'd up;
And here the smug and silver Trent shall run
In a new channel, fair and evenly.
It shall not wind with such a deep indent,
To rob me of so rich a bottom here.
Glend. Not wind? It shall, it must; you see it doth.
Mort. Yea, but
Mark how he bears his course, and runs me up
With like advantage on the other side;
Gelding the opposed continent as much
As on the other side it takes from you.
Wor. Yea, but a little charge will trench him here
And on this north side win this cape of land;
And then he runs straight and even.
Hot. I 'll have it so; a little charge will do it.
Glend. I 'll not have it alter'd.
Hot. Will not you?
Glend. No, nor you shall not.
Hot. Who shall say me nay?
Glend. Why, that will I.
Hot. Let me not understand you, then; speak it in Welsh.
Glend. I can speak English, lord, as well as you;
For I was train'd up in the English court;
Where, being but young, I framed to the harp
Many an English ditty lovely well
And gave the tongue a helpful ornament,
A virtue that was never seen in you.
Hot. Marry,
And I am glad of it with all my heart.
I had rather be a kitten and cry mew
Than one of these same metre ballad-mongers;
I had rather hear a brazen canstick turn'd,
Or a dry wheel grate on the axle-tree;
And that would set my teeth nothing on edge,
Nothing so much as mincing poetry.
'T is like the forc'd gait of a shuffling nag.
Glend. Come, you shall have Trent turn'd.
Hot. I do not care. I 'll give thrice so much land
To any well-deserving friend;
But in the way of bargain, mark ye me,
I 'll cavil on the ninth part of a hair.
Are the indentures drawn? Shall we be gone?
Glend. The moon shines fair; you may away by night.
I 'll haste the writer, and withal
Break with your wives of your departure hence.
I am afraid my daughter will run mad,
So much she doteth on her Mortimer. *Exit.*
Mort. Fie, cousin Percy! how you cross my father!
Hot. I cannot choose. Sometime he angers me
With telling me of the moldwarp and the ant,
Of the dreamer Merlin and his prophecies,
And of a dragon and a finless fish,
A clip-wing'd griffin and a moulten raven,
A couching lion and a ramping cat,
And such a deal of skimble-skamble stuff
As puts me from my faith. I tell you what:
He held me last night at least nine hours
In reckoning up the several devils' names
That were his lackeys. I cried "hum," and "well, go to,"
But mark'd him not a word. O, he is as tedious
As a tired horse, a railing wife;
Worse than a smoky house. I had rather live
With cheese and garlic in a windmill, far,
Than feed on cates and have him talk to me
In any summer-house in Christendom.
Mort. In faith, he is a worthy gentleman,

80. indentures tripartite, signed papers in three copies. **96. moiety,** portion. **98. cranking,** bending. **100. cantle,** piece. **104. indent,** indentation. **110. Gelding,** cutting from. **continent,** land. **112. charge,** expense.

130. canstick, candlestick. **144. Break with,** inform. **149. moldwarp,** mole. **149-55. the moldwarp and the ant,** Holinshed says: "This (the dividing of the kingdom) was done (as some have said) through a foolish credit given to a vaine prophesie, as though King Henrie was the moldwarp, cursssed of God's owne mouth, and they three were the dragon, the lion, and the woolfe, which should divide the realme betweene them." The **skimble-skamble stuff** is made up of garbled fragments of Glendower's talk: **Merlin** (Arthurian Magician); **moulten** (probably moulting); **couching** (heraldic term "couchant"); **ramping** (heraldic term, 'rampant'). **163. cates,** delicacies.

Exceedingly well read, and profited
In strange concealments, valiant as a lion
And wondrous affable, and as bountiful
As mines of India. Shall I tell you, cousin?
He holds your temper in a high respect
And curbs himself even of his natural scope
When you come 'cross his humour; faith, he does.
I warrant you, that man is not alive
Might so have tempted him as you have done,
Without the taste of danger and reproof:
But do not use it oft, let me entreat you.

Wor. In faith, my lord, you are too wilful-blame;
And since your coming hither have done enough
To put him quite besides his patience.
You must needs learn, lord, to amend this fault.
Though sometimes it show greatness, courage, blood,—
And that 's the dearest grace it renders you,—
Yet oftentimes it doth present harsh rage,
Defect of manners, want of government,
Pride, haughtiness, opinion, and disdain;
The least of which haunting a nobleman
Loseth men's hearts and leaves behind a stain
Upon the beauty of all parts besides,
Beguiling them of commendation.

Hot. Well, I am school'd: good manners be your speed!
Here come our wives, and let us take our leave.

Re-enter *Glendower* with the Ladies.

Mort. This is the deadly spite that angers me;
My wife can speak no English, I no Welsh.

Glend. My daughter weeps; she 'll not part with you;
She 'll be a soldier too, she 'll to the wars.

Mort. Good father, tell her that she and my aunt Percy
Shall follow in your conduct speedily.

Glendower speaks to her in Welsh, and she answers him in the same.

Glend. She is desperate here; a peevish self-willed harlotry, one that no persuasion can do good upon. *The lady speaks in Welsh.*

Mort. I understand thy looks: that pretty Welsh
Which thou pourest down from these swelling heavens
I am too perfect in; and, but for shame,
In such a parley should I answer thee.

The lady speaks again in Welsh.

I understand thy kisses and thou mine,
And that 's a feeling disputation:
But I will never be a truant, love,
Till I have learn'd thy language; for thy tongue
Makes Welsh as sweet as ditties highly penn'd,
Sung by a fair queen in a summer's bower,
With ravishing division, to her lute.

Glend. Nay, if you melt, then will she run mad. *The lady speaks again in Welsh.*

Mort. O, I am ignorance itself in this!

Glend. She bids you on the wanton rushes lay you down
And rest your gentle head upon her lap,
And she will sing the song that pleaseth you
And on your eyelids crown the god of sleep,
Charming your blood with pleasing heaviness,
Making such difference 'twixt wake and sleep
As is the difference betwixt day and night
The hour before the heavenly-harness'd team
Begins his golden progress in the east.

Mort. With all my heart I 'll sit and hear her sing:
By that time will our book, I think, be drawn.

Glend. Do so;
And those musicians that shall play to you
Hang in the air a thousand leagues from hence,
And straight they shall be here: sit, and attend.

Hot. Come, Kate, thou art perfect in lying down: come, quick, quick, that I may lay my head in thy lap.

Lady P. Go, ye giddy goose.

The music plays.

Hot. Now I perceive the devil understands Welsh;
And 't is no marvel he is so humorous.
By 'r lady, he is a good musician.

Lady P. Then should you be nothing but musical, for you are altogether governed by humours. Lie still, ye thief, and hear the lady sing in Welsh.

Hot. I had rather hear Lady, my brach, howl in Irish.

Lady P. Wouldst thou have thy head broken?

Hot. No.

Lady P. Then be still.

Hot. Neither; 't is a woman's fault.

Lady P. Now God help thee!

Hot. To the Welsh lady's bed.

Lady P. What 's that?

Hot. Peace! she sings.

Here the lady sings a Welsh song.

Hot. Come, Kate, I 'll have your song too.

Lady P. Not mine, in good sooth.

Hot. Not yours, in good sooth! Heart, you swear like a comfit-maker's wife. "Not

166. **profited,** skilled. 167. **concealments,** mysteries. 177. **wilful-blame,** wilfully blameworthy. 181. **blood,** spirit. 182. **dearest,** best. 183. **present,** represent. 199. **harlotry,** hussy.

206. **disputation,** conversation. 211. **division,** melody. 214. **wanton,** luxuriant. 224. **book,** indentures. 240. **brach,** bitch. 253. **comfit-maker,** confectioner.

you, in good sooth," and "as true as I live," and "as God shall mend me," and "as sure as day;"
And givest such sarcenet surety for thy oaths
As if thou never walk'st further than Finsbury.
Swear me, Kate, like a lady as thou art,
A good mouth-filling oath, and leave "in sooth,"
And such protest of pepper-gingerbread,
To velvet-guards and Sunday-citizens.
Come, sing.

Lady P. I will not sing.

Hot. 'T is the next way to turn tailor, or be red-breast teacher. An the indentures be drawn, I 'll away within these two hours; and so, come in when ye will. *Exit.*

Glend. Come, come, Lord Mortimer; you are as slow
As hot Lord Percy is on fire to go.
By this our book is drawn; we 'll but seal,
And then to horse immediately.

Mort. With all my heart. *Exeunt.*

Scene II. *London. The palace.*

Enter the *King, Prince of Wales,* and others.

King. Lords, give us leave; the Prince of Wales and I
Must have some private conference; but be near at hand,
For we shall presently have need of you.
Exeunt Lords.
I know not whether God will have it so,
For some displeasing service I have done,
That, in his secret doom, out of my blood
He 'll breed revengement and a scourge for me;
But thou dost in thy passages of life
Make me believe that thou art only mark'd
For the hot vengeance and the rod of heaven
To punish my mistreadings. Tell me else,
Could such inordinate and low desires,
Such poor, such bare, such lewd, such mean attempts,
Such barren pleasures, rude society,
As thou art match'd withal and grafted to,
Accompany the greatness of thy blood
And hold their level with thy princely heart?

Prince. So please your Majesty, I would I could
Quit all offences with as clear excuse
As well as I am doubtless I can purge
Myself of many I am charg'd withal:
Yet such extenuation let me beg,
As, in reproof of many tales devis'd,
Which oft the ear of greatness needs must hear,
By smiling pick-thanks and base newsmongers,
I may, for some things true, wherein my youth
Hath faulty wander'd and irregular,
Find pardon on my true submission.

King. God pardon thee! yet let me wonder, Harry,
At thy affections, which do hold a wing
Quite from the flight of all thy ancestors.
Thy place in council thou hast rudely lost,
Which by thy younger brother is supplied,
And art almost an alien to the hearts
Of all the court and princes of my blood:
The hope and expectation of thy time
Is ruin'd, and the soul of every man
Prophetically do forethink thy fall.
Had I so lavish of my presence been,
So common-hackney'd in the eyes of men,
So stale and cheap to vulgar company,
Opinion, that did help me to the crown,
Had still kept loyal to possession
And left me in reputeless banishment,
A fellow of no mark nor likelihood.
By being seldom seen, I could not stir
But like a comet I was wonder'd at;
That men would tell their children, "This is he;"
Others would say, "Where, which is Bolingbroke?"
And then I stole all courtesy from heaven,
And dress'd myself in such humility
That I did pluck allegiance from men's hearts,
Loud shouts and salutations from their mouths,
Even in the presence of the crowned King.
Thus did I keep my person fresh and new,
My presence, like a robe pontifical,
Ne'er seen but wonder'd at; and so my state,
Seldom but sumptuous, show'd like a feast
And won by rareness such solemnity.
The skipping King, he ambled up and down
With shallow jesters and rash bavin wits,
Soon kindled and soon burnt; carded his state,
Mingled his royalty with cap'ring fools,
Had his great name profaned with their scorns,
And gave his countenance, against his name,
To laugh at gibing boys and stand the push
Of every beardless vain comparative;
Grew a companion to the common streets,
Enfeoff'd himself to popularity;

256. **sarcenet,** silken, flimsy. 257. **Finsbury,** pleasure ground of London citizens. 261. **velvet-guards,** citizens' wives. 265. **red-breast teacher,** trainer of songbirds. **Scene ii:** 6. **doom,** judgment. 8. **passages,** actions. 19. **quit,** clear myself of.

23. **reproof,** refutation. 25. **pick-thanks,** flatterers. 36. **time,** reign. 42. **Opinion,** public opinion. 43. **possession,** the possessor, i.e., Richard II. 61. **bavin,** brushwood. 62. **carded,** debased by mixing. 66. **stand the push,** engage in battle. 67. **comparative,** one who affects wit. 69. **Enfeoff'd,** gave in vassalage. **popularity,** vulgarity.

That, being daily swallowed by men's eyes,
They surfeited with honey and began
To loathe the taste of sweetness, whereof a little
More than a little is by much too much.
So when he had occasion to be seen,
He was but as the cuckoo is in June,
Heard, not regarded; seen, but with such eyes
As, sick and blunted with community,
Afford no extraordinary gaze,
Such as is bent on sun-like majesty
When it shines seldom in admiring eyes;
But rather drows'd and hung their eyelids down,
Slept in his face and render'd such aspect
As cloudy men use to their adversaries,
Being with his presence glutted, gorg'd and full.
And in that very line, Harry, standest thou;
For thou hast lost thy princely privilege
With vile participation. Not an eye
But is a-weary of thy common sight,
Save mine, which hath desir'd to see thee more;
Which now doth that I would not have it do,
Make blind itself with foolish tenderness.

Prince. I shall hereafter, my thrice gracious lord,
Be more myself.

King. For all the world
As thou art to this hour was Richard then
When I from France set foot at Ravenspurgh,
And even as I was then is Percy now.
Now, by my sceptre and my soul to boot,
He hath more worthy interest to the state
Than thou, the shadow of succession.
For of no right, nor colour like to right,
He doth fill fields with harness in the realm,
Turns head against the lion's armed jaws,
And, being no more in debt to years than thou,
Leads ancient lords and reverend bishops on
To bloody battles and to bruising arms.
What never-dying honour hath he got
Against renowned Douglas! whose high deeds,
Whose hot incursions and great name in arms
Holds from all soldiers chief majority
And military title capital
Through all the kingdoms that acknowledge Christ.
Thrice hath this Hotspur, Mars in swathling clothes,
This infant warrior, in his enterprises
Discomfited great Douglas, ta'en him once,
Enlarged him and made a friend of him,
To fill the mouth of deep defiance up
And shake the peace and safety of our throne.
And what say you to this? Percy, Northumberland,
The Archbishop's grace of York, Douglas, Mortimer,
Capitulate against us and are up.
But wherefore do I tell these news to thee?
Why, Harry, do I tell thee of my foes,
Which art my near'st and dearest enemy?
Thou that art like enough, through vassal fear,
Base inclination, and the start of spleen,
To fight against me under Percy's pay,
To dog his heels and curtsy at his frowns,
To show how much thou art degenerate.

Prince. Do not think so; you shall not find it so:
And God forgive them that so much have sway'd
Your Majesty's good thoughts away from me!
I will redeem all this on Percy's head,
And in the closing of some glorious day
Be bold to tell you that I am your son;
When I will wear a garment all of blood
And stain my favours in a bloody mask,
Which, wash'd away, shall scour my shame with it:
And that shall be the day, whene'er it lights,
That this same child of honour and renown,
This gallant Hotspur, this all-praised knight,
And your unthought-of Harry chance to meet.
For every honour sitting on his helm,
Would they were multitudes, and on my head
My shames redoubled! For the time will come,
That I shall make this northern youth exchange
His glorious deeds for my indignities.
Percy is but my factor, good my lord,
To engross up glorious deeds on my behalf;
And I will call him to so strict account
That he shall render every glory up,
Yea, even the slightest worship of his time,
Or I will tear the reckoning from his heart.
This, in the name of God, I promise here;
The which if He be pleas'd I shall perform,
I do beseech your Majesty may salve
The long-grown wounds of my intemperance:
If not, the end of life cancels all bands;
And I will die a hundred thousand deaths
Ere break the smallest parcel of this vow.

King. A hundred thousand rebels die in this.
Thou shalt have charge and sovereign trust herein.

Enter *Blunt*.

How now, good Blunt? Thy looks are full of speed.

77. **community,** familiarity. 83. **cloudy,** sullen. 87. **vile participation,** low companionship. 98. **interest,** claim. 101. **harness,** armor. 109. **majority,** pre-eminence. 110. **capital,** supreme.

120. **Capitulate,** agree together. 125. **start of spleen,** angry impulse. 136. **favours,** features. 147. **factor,** agent. 148. **engross up,** collect. 157. **bands,** bonds.

Blunt. So hath the business that I come to speak of.
Lord Mortimer of Scotland hath sent word
That Douglas and the English rebels met
The eleventh of this month at Shrewsbury.
A mighty and a fearful head they are,
If promises be kept on every hand,
As ever offer'd foul play in a state.

King. The Earl of Westmoreland set forth to-day,
With him my son, Lord John of Lancaster,
For this advertisement is five days old.
On Wednesday next, Harry, you shall set forward;
On Thursday we ourselves will march. Our meeting
Is Bridgenorth: and, Harry, you shall march
Through Gloucestershire; by which account,
Our business valued, some twelve days hence
Our general forces at Bridgenorth shall meet.
Our hands are full of business; let 's away.
Advantage feeds him fat, while men delay.
Exeunt.

Scene III. *Eastcheap. The Boar's-Head Tavern.*

Enter *Falstaff* and *Bardolph.*

Fal. Bardolph, am I not fallen away vilely since this last action? Do I not bate? Do I not dwindle? Why, my skin hangs about me like an old lady's loose gown; I am withered like an old apple-john. Well, I 'll repent, and that suddenly, while I am in some liking: I shall be out of heart shortly, and then I shall have no strength to repent. An I have not forgotten what the inside of a church is made of, I am a peppercorn, a brewer's horse. The inside of a church! Company, villanous company, hath been the spoil of me.

Bard. Sir John, you are so fretful, you cannot live long.

Fal. Why, there is it: come sing me a bawdy song; make me merry. I was as virtuously given as a gentleman need to be; virtuous enough, swore little, diced not above seven times a week, went to a bawdy-house not above once in a quarter—of an hour, paid money that I borrowed three or four times, lived well and in good compass; and now I live out of all order, out of all compass.

Bard. Why, you are so fat, Sir John, that you must needs be out of all compass, out of all reasonable compass, Sir John.

Fal. Do thou amend thy face, and I 'll amend my life: thou art our admiral; thou bearest the lantern in the poop, but 't is in the nose of thee: thou art the Knight of the Burning Lamp.

Bard. Why, Sir John, my face does you no harm.

Fal. No, I 'll be sworn; I make as good use of it as many a man doth of a Death's-head or a *memento mori;* I never see thy face but I think upon hell-fire and Dives that lived in purple; for there he is in his robes, burning, burning. If thou wert any way given to virtue, I would swear by thy face; my oath should be, "By this fire, that 's God's angel;" but thou art altogether given over, and wert indeed, but for the light in thy face, the son of utter darkness. When thou ran'st up Gadshill in the night to catch my horse, if I did not think thou hadst been an *ignis fatuus* or a ball of wildfire, there 's no purchase in money. O, thou art a perpetual triumph, an everlasting bonfire-light! Thou hast saved me a thousand marks in links and torches, walking with thee in the night betwixt tavern and tavern; but the sack that thou hast drunk me would have bought me lights as good cheap at the dearest chandler's in Europe. I have maintain'd that salamander of yours with fire any time this two and thirty years; God reward me for it.

Bard. 'Sblood, I would my face were in your belly!

Fal. God-a-mercy! so should I be sure to be heart-burn'd.

Enter *Hostess.*

How now, Dame Partlet the hen! have you inquired yet who picked my pocket?

Host. Why, Sir John, what do you think, Sir John? Do you think I keep thieves in my house? I have searched, I have inquired, so has my husband, man by man, boy by boy, servant by servant: the tithe of a hair was never lost in my house before.

Fal. Ye lie, hostess: Bardolph was shaved and lost many a hair; and I 'll be sworn my pocket was picked. Go to, you are a woman, go.

Host. Who? I? No; I defy thee. God's light, I was never called so in mine own house before.

Fal. Go to, I know you well enough.

Host. No, Sir John; you do not know me.

164. Lord Mortimer of Scotland, this is George Dunbar, Lord March of Scotland. Shakespeare gives him the name **Mortimer**, evidently confusing him with the English Earl of March. **167. head,** armed force. **172. advertisement,** news. **177. valued,** estimated. **Scene iii: 5. apple-john,** a kind of apple that keeps a long time. **6. liking,** good condition. **10. peppercorn,** berry of the pepper-plant.

28. admiral, flag-ship. **35. Dives,** *Luke,* 16:19-31. **39. God's angel,** *Psalms,* 104.4. **48. links,** torches of tow and pitch. **53. salamander,** lizard supposed to live in fire. **60. Partlet,** a common name for hen.

Sir John. I know you, Sir John; you owe me money, Sir John; and now you pick a quarrel to beguile me of it: I bought you a dozen of shirts to your back.

Fal. Dowlas, filthy dowlas. I have given them away to bakers' wives; they have made bolters of them.

Host. Now, as I am a true woman, holland of eight shillings an ell. You owe money here besides, Sir John, for your diet, and by-drinkings, and money lent you, four and twenty pound.

Fal. He had his part of it; let him pay.

Host. He? Alas, he is poor; he hath nothing.

Fal. How! poor? Look upon his face; what call you rich? Let them coin his nose, let them coin his cheeks: I 'll not pay a denier. What, will you make a younker of me? Shall I not take mine ease in mine inn but I shall have my pocket picked? I have lost a seal-ring of my grandfather's worth forty mark.

Host. O Jesu, I have heard the Prince tell him, I know not how oft, that that ring was copper!

Fal. How! the Prince is a Jack, a sneak-cup: 'sblood, an he were here, I would cudgel him like a dog, if he would say so.

Enter the *Prince* and *Poins,* marching, and *Falstaff* meets them playing on his truncheon like a fife.

How now, lad! is the wind in that door, i' faith? Must we all march?

Bard. Yea, two and two, Newgate fashion.

Host. My lord, I pray you, hear me.

Prince. What say'st thou, Mistress Quickly? How doth thy husband? I love him well; he is an honest man.

Host. Good my lord, hear me.

Fal. Prithee, let her alone, and list to me.

Prince. What say'st thou, Jack?

Fal. The other night I fell asleep here behind the arras and had my pocket picked. This house is turned bawdy-house; they pick pockets.

Prince. What didst thou lose, Jack?

Fal. Wilt thou believe me, Hal? Three or four bonds of forty pound a-piece, and a seal-ring of my grandfather's.

Prince. A trifle, some eight-penny matter.

Host. So I told him, my lord, and I said I heard your Grace say so; and, my lord, he speaks most vilely of you, like a foul-mouthed man as he is, and said he would cudgel you.

Prince. What! he did not?

Host. There 's neither faith, truth, nor womanhood in me else.

Fal. There 's no more faith in thee than in a stewed prune; nor no more truth in thee than in a drawn fox; and for womanhood, Maid Marian may be the deputy's wife of the ward to thee. Go, you thing, go.

Host. Say, what thing? what thing?

Fal. What thing? Why, a thing to thank God on.

Host. I am no thing to thank God on, I would thou shouldst know it: I am an honest man's wife; and, setting thy knighthood aside, thou art a knave to call me so.

Fal. Setting thy womanhood aside, thou art a beast to say otherwise.

Host. Say, what beast, thou knave, thou?

Fal. What beast? Why, an otter.

Prince. An otter, Sir John! Why an otter?

Fal. Why, she 's neither fish nor flesh; a man knows not where to have her.

Host. Thou art an unjust man in saying so: thou or any man knows where to have me, thou knave, thou!

Prince. Thou say'st true, hostess; and he slanders thee most grossly.

Host. So he doth you, my lord; and said this other day you ought him a thousand pound.

Prince. Sirrah, do I owe you a thousand pound?

Fal. A thousand pound, Hal! A million. Thy love is worth a million; thou owest me thy love.

Host. Nay, my lord, he called you Jack, and said he would cudgel you.

Fal. Did I, Bardolph?

Bard. Indeed, Sir John, you said so.

Fal. Yea, if he said my ring was copper.

Prince. I say 't is copper: dar'st thou be as good as thy word now?

Fal. Why, Hal, thou knowest, as thou art but man, I dare; but as thou art Prince, I fear thee as I fear the roaring of the lion's whelp.

Prince. And why not as the lion?

Fal. The King himself is to be feared as the lion: dost thou think I 'll fear thee as I fear thy father? Nay, an I do, I pray God my girdle break.

Prince. O, if it should, how would thy guts fall about thy knees! But, sirrah, there 's no room for faith, truth, nor honesty in this bosom of thine; it is all filled up with guts and

79. Dowlas, coarse linen. **81. bolters,** cloth sieves. **82. holland,** fine linen. **83. ell.** 45 inches. **92. denier,** one-tenth of a penny. **younker,** greenhorn. **104. Newgate.** a London prison.

129. drawn, separated from his hole and so full of tricks. **129-30. Maid Marian,** character of questionable reputation in May-games. **145. have,** place, classify. **152. ought,** owed.

midriff. Charge an honest woman with picking thy pocket! Why, thou whoreson, impudent, embossed rascal, if there were anything in thy pocket but tavern-reckonings, memorandums of bawdy-houses, and one poor penny-worth of sugar-candy to make thee long-winded, if thy pocket were enriched with any other injuries but these, I am a villain: and yet you will stand to it; you will not pocket up wrong: art thou not ashamed?

Fal. Dost thou hear, Hal? Thou knowest in the state of innocency Adam fell; and what should poor Jack Falstaff do in the days of villainy? Thou seest I have more flesh than another man, and therefore more frailty. You confess then, you picked my pocket?

Prince. It appears so by the story.

Fal. Hostess, I forgive thee: go, make ready breakfast; love thy husband, look to thy servants, cherish thy guests: thou shalt find me tractable to any honest reason; thou seest I am pacified still. Nay, prithee, be gone. *Exit Hostess.*

Now, Hal, to the news at court: for the robbery, lad, how is that answered?

Prince. O, my sweet beef, I must still be good angel to thee: the money is paid back again.

Fal. O, I do not like that paying back; 't is a double labour.

Prince. I am good friends with my father and may do anything.

Fal. Rob me the exchequer the first thing thou doest, and do it with unwashed hands too.

Bard. Do, my lord.

Prince. I have procured thee, Jack, a charge of foot.

Fal. I would it had been of horse. Where shall I find one that can steal well? O for a fine thief, of the age of two and twenty or thereabouts! I am heinously unprovided. Well, God be thanked for these rebels, they offend none but the virtuous. I laud them, I praise them.

Prince. Bardolph!

Bard. My lord?

Prince. Go bear this letter to Lord John of Lancaster, to my brother John; this to my Lord of Westmoreland. [*Exit Bardolph.*] Go, Poins, to horse, to horse; for thou and I have thirty miles to ride yet ere dinner time. [*Exit Poins.*] Jack, meet me to-morrow in the Temple hall at two o'clock in the afternoon.
There shalt thou know thy charge, and there receive
Money and order for their furniture.
The land is burning; Percy stands on high;
And either we or they must lower lie. *Exit.*

Fal. Rare words! brave world! Hostess, my breakfast, come!
O, I could wish this tavern were my drum! *Exit.*

ACT IV. SCENE I. *The rebel camp near Shrewsbury.*

Enter *Harry Hotspur, Worcester,* and *Douglas.*

Hot. Well said, my noble Scot! If speaking truth
In this fine age were not thought flattery,
Such attribution should the Douglas have
As not a soldier of this season's stamp
Should go so general current through the world.
By God, I cannot flatter; I do defy
The tongues of soothers; but a braver place
In my heart's love hath no man than yourself.
Nay, task me to my word; approve me, lord.

Doug. Thou art the king of honour.
No man so potent breathes upon the ground
But I will beard him.

Enter a *Messenger* with letters.

Hot. Do so, and 't is well.—
What letters hast thou there?—I can but thank you.

Mess. These letters come from your father.

Hot. Letters from him! Why comes he not himself?

Mess. He cannot come, my lord; he is grievous sick.

Hot. 'Zounds! how has he the leisure to be sick
In such a justling time? Who leads his power?
Under whose government come they along?

Mess. His letters bears his mind, not I, my lord.

Wor. I prithee, tell me, doth he keep his bed?

177. embossed, swollen. **Act IV, Scene i: 3. attribution,** praise, character ascribed to one. **7. soothers,** flatterers. **9. approve,** test.

206. with unwashed hands, in haste. **226. furniture,** equipment.

Mess. He did, my lord, four days ere I set forth;
And at the time of my departure thence
He was much fear'd by his physicians.
Wor. I would the state of time had first been whole
Ere he by sickness had been visited.
His health was never better worth than now.
Hot. Sick now! droop now! This sickness doth infect
The very life-blood of our enterprise;
'T is catching hither, even to our camp.
He writes me here, that inward sickness—
And that his friends by deputation could not
So soon be drawn, nor did he think it meet
To lay so dangerous and dear a trust
On any soul remov'd but on his own.
Yet doth he give us bold advertisement
That with our small conjunction we should on
To see how fortune is dispos'd to us;
For, as he writes, there is no quailing now,
Because the King is certainly possess'd
Of all our purposes. What say you to it?
Wor. Your father's sickness is a maim to us.
Hot. A perilous gash, a very limb lopp'd off.
And yet, in faith, 't is not; his present want
Seems more than we shall find it: were it good
To set the exact wealth of all our states
All at one cast? to set so rich a main
On the nice hazard of one doubtful hour?
It were not good; for therein should we read
The very bottom and the soul of hope,
The very list, the very utmost bound
Of all our fortunes.
Doug. Faith, and so we should;
Where now remains a sweet reversion,
We may boldly spend upon the hope
Of what is to come in.
A comfort of retirement lives in this.
Hot. A rendezvous, a home to fly unto,
If that the devil and mischance look big
Upon the maidenhead of our affairs.
Wor. But yet I would your father had been here.
The quality and hair of our attempt
Brooks no division: it will be thought
By some that know not why he is away,
That wisdom, loyalty, and mere dislike
Of our proceedings kept the earl from hence;
And think how such an apprehension
May turn the tide of fearful faction
And breed a kind of question in our cause;
For well you know we of the off'ring side
Must keep aloof from strict arbitrement,
And stop all sight-holes, every loop from whence
The eye of reason may pry in upon us:
This absence of your father's draws a curtain,
That shows the ignorant a kind of fear
Before not dreamt of.
Hot. You strain too far.
I rather of his absence make this use:
It lends a lustre and more great opinion,
A larger dare to our great enterprise,
Than if the earl were here; for men must think,
If we without his help can make a head
To push against a kingdom, with his help
We shall o'erturn it topsy-turvy down.
Yet all goes well, yet all our joints are whole.
Doug. As heart can think: there is not such a word
Spoke of in Scotland as this term of fear.

Enter *Sir Richard Vernon.*

Hot. My cousin Vernon! welcome, by my soul.
Ver. Pray God my news be worth a welcome, lord.
The Earl of Westmoreland, seven thousand strong,
Is marching hitherwards; with him Prince John.
Hot. No harm. What more?
Ver. And further, I have learn'd,
The King himself in person is set forth,
Or hitherwards intended speedily,
With strong and mighty preparation.
Hot. He shall be welcome too. Where is his son,
The nimble-footed madcap Prince of Wales,
And his comrades, that daff'd the world aside,
And bid it pass?
Ver. All furnish'd, all in arms;
All plum'd like estridges that with the wind
Bated, like eagles having lately bath'd;
Glittering in golden coats, like images;
As full of spirit as the month of May,
And gorgeous as the sun at midsummer;
Wanton as youthful goats, wild as young bulls.
I saw young Harry, with his beaver on,
His cuisses on his thighs, gallantly arm'd,
Rise from the ground like feathered Mercury,
And vaulted with such ease into his seat,
As if an angel dropp'd down from the clouds
To turn and wind a fiery Pegasus
And witch the world with noble horsemanship.
Hot. No more, no more! Worse than the sun in March,

32. by deputation, by means of agents. **36. advertisement**, advice. **37. conjunction**, allied forces. **44. want**, absence. **47. main**, stake. **51. list**, limit. **53. Where**, whereas. **reversion**, future hope. **61. hair**, character. **69. off'ring**, attacking. **70. arbitrement**, arbitration.

77. opinion, reputation. **96. daff'd**, thrust. **98. estridges**, goshawks. **99. Bated**, beat their wings. **104. beaver**, visor, part of the helmet, used here in the sense of the whole helm. **105. cuisses**, thigh-armor. **109. wind**, to move in a circle.

This praise doth nourish agues. Let them come!
They come like sacrifices in their trim,
And to the fire-ey'd maid of smoky war
All hot and bleeding will we offer them:
The mailed Mars shall on his altar sit
Up to the ears in blood. I am on fire
To hear this rich reprisal is so nigh
And yet not ours. Come, let me taste my horse,
Who is to bear me like a thunderbolt
Against the bosom of the Prince of Wales:
Harry to Harry shall, hot horse to horse,
Meet and ne'er part till one drop down a corse.
O that Glendower were come!

Ver. There is more news.
I learn'd in Worcester, as I rode along,
He cannot draw his power this fourteen days.

Doug. That 's the worst tidings that I hear of yet.

Wor. Ay, by my faith, that bears a frosty sound.

Hot. What may the King's whole battle reach unto?

Ver. To thirty thousand.

Hot. Forty let it be!
My father and Glendower being both away,
The powers of us may serve so great a day.
Come, let us take a muster speedily.
Doomsday is near; die all, die merrily.

Doug. Talk not of dying; I am out of fear
Of death or death's hand for this one-half year. *Exeunt.*

Scene II. *A public road near Coventry.*

Enter *Falstaff* and *Bardolph*.

Fal. Bardolph, get thee before to Coventry; fill me a bottle of sack: our soldiers shall march through; we 'll to Sutton Cop-hill to-night.

Bard. Will you give me money, captain?

Fal. Lay out, lay out.

Bard. This bottle makes an angel.

Fal. An if it do, take it for thy labour; and if it make twenty, take them all; I 'll answer the coinage. Bid my lieutenant Peto meet me at town's end.

Bard. I will, captain; farewell. *Exit.*

Fal. If I be not ashamed of my soldiers, I am a soused gurnet. I have misused the King's press damnably. I have got, in exchange of a hundred and fifty soldiers, three hundred and odd pounds. I press me none but good householders, yeoman's sons; inquire me out contracted bachelors, such as had been asked twice on the banns; such a commodity of warm slaves, as had as lieve hear the devil as a drum; such as fear the report of a caliver worse than a struck fowl or a hurt wild-duck. I pressed me none but such toasts-and-butter, with hearts in their bellies no bigger than pins' heads; and they have bought out their services; and now my whole charge consists of ancients, corporals, lieutenants, gentlemen of companies, slaves as ragged as Lazarus in the painted cloth, where the glutton's dogs licked his sores; and such as, indeed, were never soldiers, but discarded unjust serving-men, younger sons to younger brothers, revolted tapsters and ostlers trade-fallen, the cankers of a calm world and a long peace, ten times more dishonourable ragged than an old feazed ancient: and such have I, to fill up the rooms of them as have bought out their services, that you would think that I had a hundred and fifty tattered prodigals lately come from swine-keeping, from eating draff and husks. A mad fellow met me on the way and told me I had unloaded all the gibbets and pressed the dead bodies. No eye hath seen such scarecrows. I 'll not march through Coventry with them, that 's flat: nay, and the villains march wide betwixt the legs, as if they had gyves on; for indeed I had the most of them out of prison. There 's not a shirt and a half in all my company; and the half shirt is two napkins tacked together and thrown over the shoulders like an herald's coat without sleeves; and the shirt, to say the truth, stolen from my host at Saint Alban's, or the red-nose inn-keeper of Daventry. But that 's all one; they 'll find linen enough on every hedge.

Enter the *Prince* and the *Lord of Westmoreland.*

Prince. How now, blown Jack! how now, quilt!

Fal. What, Hal! how now, mad wag! what a devil dost thou in Warwickshire? My good Lord of Westmoreland, I cry you mercy! I thought your honour had already been at Shrewsbury.

West. Faith, Sir John, 't is more than time that I were there, and you too; but my powers are there already. The King, I can tell you, looks for us all: we must away all night.

Fal. Tut, never fear me: I am as vigilant as a cat to steal cream.

Prince. I think, to steal cream indeed, for

118. reprisal, prize. **129. battle,** army. **Scene ii: 5. Lay out,** spend freely. **6. angel,** 10s. **13. soused gurnet,** pickled fish. **15. press,** warrant for conscripting troops.

18. commodity, lot, assortment. **20. caliver,** musket. **26. ancients,** ensigns. **28. painted cloth,** cloth with designs or pictures painted on it was often used as a substitute for tapestry. **34. feazed ancient,** frayed flag. **38. draff,** refuse. **45. gyves,** fetters.

thy theft hath already made thee butter. But tell me, Jack, whose fellows are these that come after?

Fal. Mine, Hal, mine.

Prince. I did never see such pitiful rascals.

Fal. Tut, tut; good enough to toss; food for powder, food for powder; they 'll fill a pit as well as better: tush, man, mortal men, mortal men.

West. Ay, but, Sir John, methinks they are exceeding poor and bare, too beggarly.

Fal. Faith, for their poverty, I know not where they had that; and for their bareness, I am sure they never learned that of me.

Prince. No, I 'll be sworn; unless you call three fingers on the ribs bare. But, sirrah, make haste. Percy is already in the field.

Fal. What, is the King encamp'd?

West. He is, Sir John: I fear we shall stay too long.

Fal. Well,
To the latter end of a fray and the beginning of a feast
Fits a dull fighter and a keen guest. *Exeunt.*

Scene III. *The rebel camp near Shrewsbury.*

Enter *Hotspur, Worcester, Douglas,* and *Vernon.*

Hot. We 'll fight with him to-night.
Wor. It may not be.
Doug. You give him then advantage.
Ver. Not a whit.
Hot. Why say you so? Looks he not for supply?
Ver. So do we.
Hot. His is certain, ours is doubtful.
Wor. Good cousin, be advis'd; stir not to-night.
Ver. Do not, my lord.
Doug. You do not counsel well.
You speak it out of fear and cold heart.
Ver. Do me no slander, Douglas. By my life,
And I dare well maintain it with my life,
If well-respected honour bid me on,
I hold as little counsel with weak fear
As you, my lord, or any Scot that this day lives.
Let it be seen to-morrow in the battle
Which of us fears.
Doug. Yea, or to-night.
Ver. Content.
Hot. To-night, say I.
Ver. Come, come, it may not be. I wonder much,
Being men of such great leading as you are,

Scene iii: 17. leading, generalship.

That you foresee not what impediments
Drag back our expedition: certain horse
Of my cousin Vernon's are not yet come up;
Your uncle Worcester's horse came but to-day;
And now their pride and mettle is asleep,
Their courage with hard labour tame and dull,
That not a horse is half the half of himself.
Hot. So are the horses of the enemy
In general, journey-bated and brought low.
The better part of ours are full of rest.
Wor. The number of the King exceedeth ours.
For God's sake, cousin, stay till all come in.
The trumpet sounds a parley.

Enter *Sir Walter Blunt.*

Blunt. I come with gracious offers from the King,
If you vouchsafe me hearing and respect.
Hot. Welcome, Sir Walter Blunt; and would to God
You were of our determination!
Some of us love you well; and even those some
Envy your great deservings and good name,
Because you are not of our quality,
But stand against us like an enemy.
Blunt. And God defend but still I should stand so,
So long as out of limit and true rule
You stand against anointed majesty.
But to my charge. The King hath sent to know
The nature of your griefs, and whereupon
You conjure from the breast of civil peace
Such bold hostility, teaching his duteous land
Audacious cruelty. If that the King
Have any way your good deserts forgot,
Which he confesseth to be manifold,
He bids you name your griefs; and with all speed
You shall have your desires with interest
And pardon absolute for yourself and these
Herein misled by your suggestion.
Hot. The King is kind; and well we know the King
Knows at what time to promise, when to pay.
My father and my uncle and myself
Did give him that same royalty he wears;
And when he was not six and twenty strong,
Sick in the world's regard, wretched and low,
A poor unminded outlaw sneaking home,
My father gave him welcome to the shore;
And when he heard him swear and vow to God
He came but to be Duke of Lancaster,
To sue his livery and beg his peace,

19. expedition, haste. **36. quality,** party. **42. whereupon,** for what reason. **51. suggestion,** instigation. **62. sue his livery,** claim his estate.

With tears of innocence and terms of zeal,
My father, in kind heart and pity mov'd,
Swore him assistance and perform'd it too.
Now when the lords and barons of the realm
Perceiv'd Northumberland did lean to him,
The more and less came in with cap and knee;
Met him in boroughs, cities, villages,
Attended him on bridges, stood in lanes,
Laid gifts before him, proffer'd him their oaths,
Gave him their heirs as pages, followed him
Even at the heels in golden multitudes.
He presently, as greatness knows itself,
Steps me a little higher than his vow
Made to my father, while his blood was poor,
Upon the naked shore at Ravenspurgh;
And now, forsooth, takes on him to reform
Some certain edicts and some strait decrees
That lie too heavy on the commonwealth,
Cries out upon abuses, seems to weep
Over his country's wrongs; and by this face,
This seeming brow of justice, did he win
The hearts of all that he did angle for;
Proceeded further; cut me off the heads
Of all the favourites that the absent king
In deputation left behind him here,
When he was personal in the Irish war.

Blunt. Tut, I came not to hear this.

Hot. Then to the point.
In short time after, he depos'd the King;
Soon after that, depriv'd him of his life;
And in the neck of that, task'd the whole state.
To make that worse, suffer'd his kinsman March,
(Who is, if every owner were well plac'd,
Indeed his king) to be engag'd in Wales,
There without ransom to lie forfeited;
Disgrac'd me in my happy victories,
Sought to entrap me by intelligence;
Rated mine uncle from the council-board;
In rage dismiss'd my father from the court;
Broke oath on oath, committed wrong on wrong,
And in conclusion drove us to seek out
This head of safety; and withal to pry
Into his title, the which we find
Too indirect for long continuance.

Blunt. Shall I return this answer to the King?

Hot. Not so, Sir Walter; we 'll withdraw a while.
Go to the King; and let there be impawn'd
Some surety for a safe return again,
And in the morning early shall mine uncle
Bring him our purposes: and so farewell.

Blunt. I would you would accept of grace and love.

Hot. And may be so we shall.

Blunt. Pray God you do.

Exeunt.

Scene IV. *York. The Archbishop's palace.*

Enter the *Archbishop of York* and *Sir Michael.*

Arch. Hie, good Sir Michael; bear this sealed brief
With winged haste to the Lord Marshal,
This to my cousin Scroop, and all the rest
To whom they are directed. If you knew
How much they do import, you would make haste.

Sir M. My good lord,
I guess their tenour.

Arch. Like enough you do.
To-morrow, good Sir Michael, is a day
Wherein the fortune of ten thousand men
Must bide the touch; for, sir, at Shrewsbury,
As I am truly given to understand,
The King with mighty and quick-raised power
Meets with Lord Harry; and, I fear, Sir Michael,
What with the sickness of Northumberland,
Whose power was in the first proportion,
And what with Owen Glendower's absence thence,
Who with them was a rated sinew too
And comes not in, over-rul'd by prophecies,
I fear the power of Percy is too weak
To wage an instant trial with the King.

Sir M. Why, my good lord, you need not fear;
There is Douglas and Lord Mortimer.

Arch. No, Mortimer is not there.

Sir M. But there is Mordake, Vernon, Lord Harry Percy,
And there is my Lord of Worcester, and a head
Of gallant warriors, noble gentlemen.

Arch. And so there is; but yet the King hath drawn
The special head of all the land together:
The Prince of Wales, Lord John of Lancaster,
The noble Westmoreland, and warlike Blunt;
And many moe corrivals and dear men
Of estimation and command in arms.

Sir M. Doubt not, my lord, they shall be well oppos'd.

68. more and less, all classes. **79. strait,** strict. **88. personal,** in person. **92. task'd,** taxed. **98. intelligence,** spies. **99. Rated,** berated. **103. head of safety,** army to insure safety. **105. indirect,** unjust.

Scene iv: 15. proportion, magnitude. **17. rated sinew,** force counted upon. **31. moe,** more. **dear,** worthy.

Arch. I hope no less, yet needful 't is to fear;
And, to prevent the worst, Sir Michael, speed;
For if Lord Percy thrive not, ere the King
Dismiss his power he means to visit us,
For he hath heard of our confederacy,
And 't is but wisdom to make strong against him:
Therefore make haste. I must go write again
To other friends; and so farewell, Sir Michael.
Exeunt.

ACT V. Scene I. *The King's camp near Shrewsbury.*

Enter the *King, Prince of Wales, Lord John of Lancaster, Sir Walter Blunt,* and *Falstaff.*

King. How bloodily the sun begins to peer
Above yon busky hill! The day looks pale
At his distemperature.
Prince. The southern wind
Doth play the trumpet to his purposes,
And by his hollow whistling in the leaves
Foretells a tempest and a blust'ring day.
King. Then with the losers let it sympathize,
For nothing can seem foul to those that win.
The trumpet sounds.

Enter *Worcester* and *Vernon.*

How now, my Lord of Worcester! 't is not well
That you and I should meet upon such terms
As now we meet. You have deceiv'd our trust,
And made us doff our easy robes of peace,
To crush our old limbs in ungentle steel:
This is not well, my lord, this is not well.
What say you to it? Will you again unknit
This churlish knot of all-abhorred war?
And move in that obedient orb again
Where you did give a fair and natural light,
And be no more an exhal'd meteor,
A prodigy of fear and a portent
Of broached mischief to the unborn times?
Wor. Hear me, my liege.
For mine own part, I could be well content
To entertain the lag-end of my life
With quiet hours; for I do protest,
I have not sought the day of this dislike.
King. You have not sought it! How comes it, then?
Fal. Rebellion lay in his way, and he found it.
Prince. Peace, chewet, peace!
Wor. It pleas'd your Majesty to turn your looks
Of favour from myself and all our house;
And yet I must remember you, my lord,
We were the first and dearest of your friends.
For you my staff of office did I break
In Richard's time; and posted day and night
To meet you on the way, and kiss your hand,
When yet you were in place and in account
Nothing so strong and fortunate as I.
It was myself, my brother, and his son,
That brought you home and boldly did outdare
The dangers of the time. You swore to us,
And you did swear that oath at Doncaster,
That you did nothing purpose 'gainst the state;
Nor claim no further than your new-fall'n right,
The seat of Gaunt, dukedom of Lancaster.
To this we swore our aid. But in short space
It rain'd down fortune show'ring on your head;
And such a flood of greatness fell on you,
What with our help, what with the absent King,
What with the injuries of a wanton time,
The seeming sufferances that you had borne,
And the contrarious winds that held the King
So long in his unlucky Irish wars
That all in England did repute him dead;
And from this swarm of fair advantages
You took occasion to be quickly woo'd
To gripe the general sway into your hand;
Forgot your oath to us at Doncaster;
And being fed by us you us'd us so
As that ungentle gull, the cuckoo's bird,
Useth the sparrow; did oppress our nest;
Grew by our feeding to so great a bulk
That even our love durst not come near your sight
For fear of swallowing; but with nimble wing
We were enforc'd, for safety sake, to fly
Out of your sight and raise this present head;

Act V, Scene i: 2. busky, wooded. **3. distemperature,** unusual appearance. **21. broached,** already begun. **29. chewet,** chatterer (lit. jackdaw).

32. remember, remind. **51. sufferances,** sufferings. **60. gull,** nestling bird. The cuckoo lays its eggs in the nests of smaller birds, which hatch and rear its young. Because of their size, these cuckoo nestlings often crowd the rightful owners out of the nest. Cf. *Lear,* I, iv, 235-6.

Whereby we stand opposed by such means
As you yourself have forg'd against yourself
By unkind usage, dangerous countenance,
And violation of all faith and troth
Sworn to us in your younger enterprise.

King. These things indeed you have articulate,
Proclaim'd at market-crosses, read in churches,
To face the garment of rebellion
With some fine colour that may please the eye
Of fickle changelings and poor discontents,
Which gape and rub the elbow at the news
Of hurly-burly innovation.
And never yet did insurrection want
Such water-colours to impaint his cause;
Nor moody beggars, starving for a time
Of pell-mell havoc and confusion.

Prince. In both your armies there is many a soul
Shall pay full dearly for this encounter,
If once they join in trial. Tell your nephew,
The Prince of Wales doth join with all the world
In praise of Henry Percy: by my hopes,
This present enterprise set off his head,
I do not think a braver gentleman,
More active-valiant or more valiant-young,
More daring or more bold, is now alive
To grace this latter age with noble deeds.
For my part, I may speak it to my shame,
I have a truant been to chivalry;
And so I hear he doth account me too;
Yet this before my father's majesty:
I am content that he shall take the odds
Of his great name and estimation,
And will, to save the blood on either side,
Try fortune with him in a single fight.

King. And, Prince of Wales, so dare we venture thee,
Albeit considerations infinite
Do make against it. No, good Worcester, no,
We love our people well; even those we love
That are misled upon your cousin's part;
And, will they take the offer of our grace,
Both he and they and you, yea, every man
Shall be my friend again and I 'll be his:
So tell your cousin, and bring me word
What he will do. But if he will not yield,
Rebuke and dread correction wait on us
And they shall do their office. So, be gone;
We will not now be troubled with reply.
We offer fair; take it advisedly.

Exeunt Worcester and Vernon.

Prince. It will not be accepted, on my life.
The Douglas and the Hotspur both together
Are confident against the world in arms.

King. Hence, therefore, every leader to his charge,
For, on their answer, will we set on them;
And God befriend us, as our cause is just!

Exeunt all but the Prince of Wales and Falstaff.

Fal. Hal, if thou see me down in the battle and bestride me, so; 't is a point of friendship.

Prince. Nothing but a colossus can do thee that friendship. Say thy prayers, and farewell.

Fal. I would 't were bed-time, Hal, and all well.

Prince. Why, thou owest God a death. *Exit.*

Fal. 'T is not due yet; I would be loath to pay him before his day. What need I be so forward with him that calls not on me? Well, 't is no matter; honour pricks me on. Yea, but how if honour prick me off when I come on? How then? Can honour set to a leg? No. Or an arm? No. Or take away the grief of a wound? No. Honour hath no skill in surgery, then? No. What is honour? A word. What is in that word honour? What is that honour? Air; a trim reckoning! Who hath it? He that died o' Wednesday. Doth he feel it? No. Doth he hear it? No. 'T is insensible, then? Yea, to the dead. But will it not live with the living? No. Why? Detraction will not suffer it. Therefore I 'll none of it. Honour is a mere scutcheon; and so ends my catechism. *Exit.*

Scene II. *The rebel camp.*

Enter *Worcester* and *Vernon.*

Wor. O, no, my nephew must not know, Sir Richard,
The liberal and kind offer of the King.

Ver. 'T were best he did.

Wor. Then are we all undone.
It is not possible, it cannot be,
The King should keep his word in loving us.
He will suspect us still, and find a time
To punish this offence in other faults:
Supposition all our lives shall be stuck full of eyes;
For treason is but trusted like the fox,
Who, ne'er so tame, so cherish'd and lock'd up,
Will have a wild trick of his ancestors.
Look how we can, or sad or merrily,
Interpretation will misquote our looks,

69. **dangerous,** threatening. 72. **articulate,** expressed in articles. 74. **face,** ornament. 78. **innovation,** insurrection. 79. **want,** lack. 88. **set off his head,** not put to his account.

143. **scutcheon,** coat-of-arms borne in funeral processions or hung in churches. **Scene ii:** 8. **Supposition,** suspicion.

And we shall feed like oxen at a stall,
The better cherish'd, still the nearer death.
My nephew's trespass may be well forgot;
It hath the excuse of youth and heat of blood,
And an adopted name of privilege,
A hare-brain'd Hotspur, govern'd by a spleen.
All his offences live upon my head
And on his father's. We did train him on,
And, his corruption being ta'en from us,
We, as the spring of all, shall pay for all.
Therefore, good cousin, let not Harry know,
In any case, the offer of the King.
Ver. Deliver what you will; I 'll say 't is so.
Here comes your cousin.

Enter *Hotspur* and *Douglas.*

Hot. My uncle is return'd;
Deliver up my Lord of Westmoreland.
Uncle, what news?
Wor. The King will bid you battle presently.
Doug. Defy him by the Lord of Westmoreland.
Hot. Lord Douglas, go you and tell him so.
Doug. Marry, and shall, and very willingly. *Exit.*
Wor. There is no seeming mercy in the King.
Hot. Did you beg any? God forbid!
Wor. I told him gently of our grievances,
Of his oath-breaking; which he mended thus,
By now forswearing that he is forsworn.
He calls us rebels, traitors; and will scourge
With haughty arms this hateful name in us.

Re-enter *Douglas.*

Doug. Arm, gentlemen; to arms! for I have thrown
A brave defiance in King Henry's teeth,
And Westmoreland, that was engag'd, did bear it;
Which cannot choose but bring him quickly on.
Wor. The Prince of Wales stepp'd forth before the King,
And, nephew, challeng'd you to single fight.
Hot. O, would the quarrel lay upon our heads,
And that no man might draw short breath to-day
But I and Harry Monmouth! Tell me, tell me,
How show'd his tasking? Seem'd it in contempt?
Ver. No, by my soul; I never in my life
Did hear a challenge urg'd more modestly,
Unless a brother should a brother dare
To gentle exercise and proof of arms.
He gave you all the duties of a man,
Trimm'd up your praises with a princely tongue,
Spoke your deservings like a chronicle,
Making you ever better than his praise
By still dispraising praise valued with you;
And, which became him like a prince indeed,
He made a blushing cital of himself,
And chid his truant youth with such a grace
As if he master'd there a double spirit
Of teaching and of learning instantly.
There did he pause; but let me tell the world,
If he outlive the envy of this day,
England did never owe so sweet a hope,
So much misconstrued in his wantonness.
Hot. Cousin, I think thou art enamoured
On his follies: never did I hear
Of any prince so wild a liberty.
But be he as he will, yet once ere night
I will embrace him with a soldier's arm,
That he shall shrink under my courtesy.
Arm, arm with speed! and, fellows, soldiers, friends,
Better consider what you have to do
Than I, that have not well the gift of tongue,
Can lift your blood up with persuasion.

Enter a *Messenger.*

Mess. My lord, here are letters for you.
Hot. I cannot read them now.
O gentlemen, the time of life is short!
To spend that shortness basely were too long,
If life did ride upon a dial's point,
Still ending at the arrival of an hour.
An if we live, we live to tread on kings;
If die, brave death, when princes die with us!
Now, for our consciences, the arms are fair,
When the intent of bearing them is just.

Enter another *Messenger.*

Second Mess. My lord, prepare; the King comes on apace.
Hot. I thank him that he cuts me from my tale,
For I profess not talking; only this—
Let each man do his best; and here draw I
A sword, whose temper I intend to stain
With the best blood that I can meet withal
In the adventure of this perilous day.
Now *Esperance!* Percy! and set on.
Sound all the lofty instruments of war,
And by that music let us all embrace;
For, heaven to earth, some of us never shall
A second time do such a courtesy.
They embrace and exeunt.

18. The name of Hotspur will privilege him from censure. **51. tasking,** challenge.

56. duties, due merits. **62. cital,** mention. **68. owe,** own. **84. dial's point,** hand of clock.

Douglas kills Blunt mistaking him for the King. Blunt allows it for the king.

Scene III. *Plain between the camps.*

The trumpets sound. The *King* enters with his power and passes over. Alarum to the battle. Then enter *Douglas* and *Sir Walter Blunt*.

Blunt. What is thy name, that in the battle thus
Thou crossest me? What honour dost thou seek
Upon my head?

Doug. Know then, my name is Douglas;
And I do haunt thee in the battle thus
Because some tell me that thou art a king.

Blunt. They tell thee true.

Doug. The Lord of Stafford dear to-day hath bought
Thy likeness, for instead of thee, King Harry,
This sword hath ended him. So shall it thee,
Unless thou yield thee as my prisoner.

Blunt. I was not born a yielder, thou proud Scot;
And thou shalt find a king that will revenge
Lord Stafford's death.

They fight. Douglas kills Blunt.

Enter *Hotspur.*

Hot. O Douglas, hadst thou fought at Holmedon thus,
I never had triumph'd upon a Scot.

Doug. All 's done, all 's won; here breathless lies the King.

Hot. Where?

Doug. Here.

Hot. This, Douglas? No. I know this face full well.
A gallant knight he was, his name was Blunt;
Semblably furnish'd like the King himself.

Doug. A fool go with thy soul, whither it goes!
A borrowed title hast thou bought too dear:
Why didst thou tell me that thou wert a king?

Hot. The King hath many marching in his coats.

Doug. Now, by my sword, I will kill all his coats;
I 'll murder all his wardrobe, piece by piece,
Until I meet the King.

Hot. Up, and away!
Our soldiers stand full fairly for the day.

Exeunt.

Alarum. Enter *Falstaff,* solus.

Fal. Though I could scape shot-free at London, I fear the shot here; here 's no scoring but upon the pate. Soft! who are you? Sir Walter Blunt: there 's honour for you! Here 's no vanity! I am as hot as molten lead, and as heavy too: God keep lead out of me! I need no more weight than mine own bowels. I have led my ragamuffins where they are peppered. There 's not three of my hundred and fifty left alive; and they are for the town's end, to beg during life. But who comes here?

Enter the *Prince.*

Prince. What, stands thou idle here? Lend me thy sword.
Many a nobleman lies stark and stiff
Under the hoofs of vaunting enemies,
Whose deaths are yet unreveng'd. I prithee, lend me thy sword.

Fal. O Hal, I prithee, give me leave to breathe a while. Turk Gregory never did such deeds in arms as I have done this day. I have paid Percy, I have made him sure.

Prince. He is, indeed; and living to kill thee. I prithee, lend me thy sword.

Fal. Nay, before God, Hal, if Percy be alive, thou gets not my sword; but take my pistol, if thou wilt.

Prince. Give it me. What, is it in the case?

Fal. Ay, Hal; 't is hot, 't is hot: there 's that will sack a city.

The Prince draws it out, and finds it to be a bottle of sack.

Prince. What, is it a time to jest and dally now? *He throws the bottle at him. Exit.*

Fal. Well, if Percy be alive, I 'll pierce him. If he do come in my way, so; if he do not, if I come in his willingly, let him make a carbonado of me. I like not such grinning honour as Sir Walter hath: give me life, which if I can save, so; if not, honour comes unlooked for, and there 's an end. *Exit.*

Scene IV. *Another part of the field.*

Alarum. Excursions. Enter the *King,* the *Prince, Lord John of Lancaster,* and *Earl of Westmoreland.*

King. I prithee,
Harry, withdraw thyself; thou bleedest too much.
Lord John of Lancaster, go you with him.

Lan. Not I, my lord, unless I did bleed too.

Prince. I beseech your Majesty, make up,
Lest your retirement do amaze your friends.

Scene iii: 21. Semblably, similarly. **22. A fool go with,** a semi-proverbial expression of contempt. **30. shot-free,** without paying the bill.

46. Turk Gregory, Pope Gregory VII, also known as Hildebrand, was so fierce an opponent of the Emperor that he was as dreaded as the Turk. **62. carbonado,** meat scored across for broiling. **Scene iv: 5. make up,** advance. **6. amaze,** alarm, confuse.

King. I will do so.
My Lord of Westmoreland, lead him to his tent.

West. Come, my lord, I 'll lead you to your tent.

Prince. Lead me, my lord? I do not need your help:
And God forbid a shallow scratch should drive
The Prince of Wales from such a field as this,
Where stain'd nobility lies trodden on,
And rebels' arms triumph in massacres!

Lan. We breathe too long. Come, cousin Westmoreland,
Our duty this way lies; for God's sake, come.

Exeunt Prince John and Westmoreland.

Prince. By God, thou hast deceiv'd me, Lancaster;
I did not think thee lord of such a spirit.
Before, I lov'd thee as a brother, John;
But now, I do respect thee as my soul.

King. I saw him hold Lord Percy at the point
With lustier maintenance than I did look for
Of such an ungrown warrior.

Prince. O, this boy
Lends mettle to us all! *Exit.*

Enter *Douglas.*

Doug. Another king! they grow like Hydra's heads.
I am the Douglas, fatal to all those
That wear those colours on them. What art thou,
That counterfeit'st the person of a king?

King. The King himself; who, Douglas, grieves at heart
So many of his shadows thou hast met
And not the very King. I have two boys
Seek Percy and thyself about the field;
But, seeing thou fall'st on me so luckily,
I will assay thee; so, defend thyself.

Doug. I fear thou art another counterfeit;
And yet, in faith, thou bear'st thee like a king.
But mine I am sure thou art, whoe'er thou be,
And thus I win thee.

They fight; the *King* being in danger, re-enter *Prince of Wales.*

Prince. Hold up thy head, vile Scot, or thou art like
Never to hold it up again! The spirits
Of valiant Shirley, Stafford, Blunt, are in my arms.
It is the Prince of Wales that threatens thee,
Who never promiseth but he means to pay.

They fight: Douglas flies.

Cheerly, my lord, how fares your Grace?
Sir Nicholas Gawsey hath for succour sent,
And so hath Clifton: I 'll to Clifton straight.

King. Stay, and breathe a while.
Thou hast redeem'd thy lost opinion,
And show'd thou mak'st some tender of my life,
In this fair rescue thou hast brought to me.

Prince. O God! they did me too much injury
That ever said I hearken'd for your death.
If it were so, I might have let alone
The insulting hand of Douglas over you,
Which would have been as speedy in your end
As all the poisonous potions in the world,
And sav'd the treacherous labour of your son.

King. Make up to Clifton: I 'll to Sir Nicholas Gawsey. *Exit.*

Enter *Hotspur.*

Hot. If I mistake not, thou are Harry Monmouth.

Prince. Thou speak'st as if I would deny my name.

Hot. My name is Harry Percy.

Prince. Why, then I see
A very valiant rebel of the name.
I am the Prince of Wales; and think not, Percy,
To share with me in glory any more:
Two stars keep not their motion in one sphere;
Nor can one England brook a double reign
Of Harry Percy and the Prince of Wales.

Hot. Nor shall it, Harry; for the hour is come
To end the one of us; and would to God
Thy name in arms were now as great as mine!

Prince. I 'll make a greater ere I part from thee;
And all the budding honours on thy crest
I 'll crop, to make a garland for my head.

Hot. I can no longer brook thy vanities. *They fight.*

Enter *Falstaff.*

Fal. Well said, Hal! to it, Hal! Nay, you shall find no boy's play here, I can tell you.

Re-enter *Douglas;* he fights with *Falstaff,* who falls down as if he were dead and exit *Douglas.* The *Prince* killeth *Percy.*

Hot. O, Harry, thou hast robb'd me of my youth!
I better brook the loss of brittle life

22. maintenance, bearing, behavior.

49. mak'st some tender of, hast some regard for. **52. hearken'd,** waited eagerly for news of. **65. Two stars keep not their motion in one sphere,** according to the Ptolemaic system of astronomy, each sphere that revolved about the earth had only one planet in it.

Falstaff pretending to be dead — being discreet — dissertation on counterfeit

Than those proud titles thou hast won of me:
They wound my thoughts worse than thy sword my flesh:
But thought 's the slave of life, and life time 's fool;
And time, that takes survey of all the world,
Must have a stop. O, I could prophesy,
But that the earthy and cold hand of death
Lies on my tongue: no, Percy, thou art dust,
And food for— *Dies.*

Prince. For worms, brave Percy: fare thee well, great heart!
Ill-weav'd ambition, how much art thou shrunk!
When that this body did contain a spirit,
A kingdom for it was too small a bound;
But now two paces of the vilest earth
Is room enough: this earth that bears thee dead
Bears not alive so stout a gentleman.
If thou wert sensible of courtesy,
I should not make so dear a show of zeal;
But let my favours hide thy mangled face;
And, even in thy behalf, I 'll thank myself
For doing these fair rites of tenderness.
Adieu, and take thy praise with thee to heaven!
Thy ignomy sleep with thee in the grave,
But not remember'd in thy epitaph!

He spieth Falstaff on the ground.

What, old acquaintance! could not all this flesh
Keep in a little life? Poor Jack, farewell!
I could have better spar'd a better man:
O, I should have a heavy miss of thee,
If I were much in love with vanity!
Death hath not struck so fat a deer to-day,
Though many dearer, in this bloody fray.
Embowell'd will I see thee by and by;
Till then in blood by noble Percy lie. *Exit.*

Fal. [*Rising up.*] Embowelled! if thou embowel me to-day, I 'll give you leave to powder me and eat me too to-morrow. 'Sblood, 't was time to counterfeit, or that hot termagant Scot had paid me scot and lot too. Counterfeit? I lie, I am no counterfeit: to die is to be a counterfeit, for he is but the counterfeit of a man who hath not the life of a man; but to counterfeit dying, when a man thereby liveth, is to be no counterfeit, but the true and perfect image of life indeed. The better part of valour is discretion; in the which better part I have saved my life. 'Zounds, I am afraid of this gunpowder Percy, though he be dead: how, if he should counterfeit too and rise? By my faith, I am afraid he would prove the better counterfeit. Therefore I 'll make him sure; yea, and I 'll swear I killed him. Why may not he rise as well as I? Nothing confutes me but eyes, and nobody sees me. Therefore, sirrah [*stabbing him*], with a new wound in your thigh, come you along with me.

He takes up Hotspur on his back.

Re-enter *Prince* and *John of Lancaster.*

Prince. Come, brother John; full bravely hast thou flesh'd
Thy maiden sword.

Lan. But, soft! whom have we here?
Did you not tell me this fat man was dead?

Prince. I did; I saw him dead,
Breathless and bleeding on the ground. Art thou alive?
Or is it fantasy that plays upon our eyesight?
I prithee, speak; we will not trust our eyes
Without our ears: thou art not what thou seem'st.

Fal. No, that 's certain; I am not a double man; but if I be not Jack Falstaff, then am I a Jack. There is Percy [*throwing the body down*]. If your father will do me any honour, so; if not, let him kill the next Percy himself. I look to be either earl or duke, I can assure you.

Prince. Why, Percy I killed myself, and saw thee dead.

Fal. Didst thou? Lord, Lord, how this world is given to lying! I grant you I was down and out of breath, and so was he; but we rose both at an instant and fought a long hour by Shrewsbury clock. If I may be believed, so; if not, let them that should reward valour bear the sin upon their own heads. I 'll take it upon my death, I gave him this wound in the thigh: if the man were alive and would deny it, 'zounds, I would make him eat a piece of my sword.

Lan. This is the strangest tale that ever I heard.

Prince. This is the strangest fellow, brother John.
Come, bring your luggage nobly on your back.
For my part, if a lie may do thee grace,
I 'll gild it with the happiest terms I have.

A retreat is sounded.

The trumpet sounds retreat; the day is ours.
Come, brother, let us to the highest of the field,
To see what friends are living, who are dead.

Exeunt Prince and Lancaster.

Fal. I 'll follow, as they say, for reward. He that rewards me, God reward him! If I do grow great, I 'll grow less; for I 'll purge, and

90. bound, enclosure. **95. dear,** heartfelt. **96. favours,** scarf. **109. Embowell'd,** disembowelled for embalming. **112. powder,** salt. **113. termagant,** violent, quarrelsome. **114. scot and lot,** utterly.

141-2. I am not a double man, refers to his carrying Percy on his back.

Falstaff pretends to have killed Hotspur — he then resolves to stop drinking + to live decently

leave sack, and live cleanly as a nobleman should do. *Exit.*

Scene V. *Another part of the field.*

The trumpets sound. Enter the *King, Prince of Wales, Lord John of Lancaster, Earl of Westmoreland,* with *Worcester* and *Vernon* prisoners.

King. Thus ever did rebellion find rebuke.
Ill-spirited Worcester! did not we send grace,
Pardon, and terms of love to all of you?
And wouldst thou turn our offers contrary?
Misuse the tenour of thy kinsman's trust?
Three knights upon our party slain to-day,
A noble earl, and many a creature else
Had been alive this hour,
If like a Christian thou hadst truly borne
Betwixt our armies true intelligence.
Wor. What I have done my safety urg'd me to;
And I embrace this fortune patiently,
Since not to be avoided it falls on me.
King. Bear Worcester to the death and Vernon too.
Other offenders we will pause upon.
Exeunt Worcester and Vernon guarded.
How goes the field?
Prince. The noble Scot, Lord Douglas, when he saw
The fortune of the day quite turn'd from him,
The noble Percy slain, and all his men
Upon the foot of fear, fled with the rest;
And falling from a hill, he was so bruis'd
That the pursuers took him. At my tent
The Douglas is; and I beseech your Grace
I may dispose of him.
King. With all my heart.
Prince. Then, brother John of Lancaster, to you
This honourable bounty shall belong.
Go to the Douglas, and deliver him
Up to his pleasure, ransomless and free:
His valours shown upon our crests to-day
Have taught us how to cherish such high deeds
Even in the bosom of our adversaries.
Lan. I thank your Grace for this high courtesy,
Which I shall give away immediately.
King. Then this remains, that we divide our power.
You, son John, and my cousin Westmoreland
Towards York shall bend you with your dearest speed.
To meet Northumberland and the prelate Scroop,
Who, as we hear, are busily in arms:
Myself and you, son Harry, will towards Wales,
To fight with Glendower and the Earl of March.
Rebellion in this land shall lose his sway,
Meeting the check of such another day;
And since this business so fair is done,
Let us not leave till all our own be won.
Exeunt.

Scene v: 4. turn . . . contrary, misrepresent. **5. tenour,** purport.

THE SECOND PART OF HENRY THE FOURTH

The Second Part of *King Henry IV* is one of the least familiar of Shakespeare's historical plays to the general reader. Like most continuations it falls below its predecessor. Many a reader who has learned to know and enjoy Falstaff in the First Part fails to continue the fascinating acquaintance in the sequel and has only a general knowledge of the fact that in the end the fat knight was rejected by his former crony Prince Hal, now become King. This is, however, a real misfortune. Even though the Second Part lacks the brilliant dramatic qualities of the First, it is a capital reading play. Falstaff is at his very best in a number of scenes, and Shakespeare has added to his entourage a group of "irregular humorists": Dame Quickly, Pistol, and Justice Shallow, whose talk and action add life and luster to the fascinating comic scenes.

The Second Part was entered in the Stationers' Register on August 23, 1600, and appeared in the same year with the following title-page:

The Second part of Henrie the fourth, continuing to his death, and coronation of Henrie the fift. With the humours of Sir John Falstaffe and swaggering Pistoll. As it hath been sundrie times publikely acted by the right honourable, the Lord Chamberlaine his servants. Written by William Shakespeare. London. Printed by V. S. [*Valentine Simmes*] *for Andrew Wise and William Aspley. 1600.*

Text.—The "copy" from which this edition, the first and only quarto, was printed was probably the prompt-book, or a transcript thereof, sold by Shakespeare's company to the publishers. It had evidently been cut for representation since it lacks about 170 lines which appear in the Folio text. It contains, however, some 40 lines wanting in the Folio, an absence due in part to careless printing, in part to emendation and censorship. No other edition of the play appeared before the Folio of 1623, a strange contrast to the six quartos of the first part; it is possible, but not very likely, that other published editions have been lost.

The Folio text may have been printed from the Quarto, but if so the early text was collated with a better manuscript—possibly Shakespeare's original autograph—in the possession of the company. Like most Folio texts, however, it shows plain signs of editorial revision, and the present edition follows in the main the Quarto version.

Date.—The composition of the Second Part must have followed close upon that of the First. In fact the last lines of the First Part clearly indicate the author's purpose of continuing the story. It is an interesting fact that the Second Part must have been written while the fat knight was still called Oldcastle, as is shown by the appearance of the speech-heading *Old.* instead of *Fal.* in the Quarto at I, ii, 137; evidently this name was still in the author's mind and slipped unconsciously off his pen. Since the accepted date for *I King Henry IV* is 1597 the Second Part must have been written in the same year or at least not later than 1598. Jonson's *Every Man Out* (V, ii), played by Shakespeare's company in 1599, alludes to Justice Silence, a character in Shakespeare's play, and so presupposes the existence of that play on the boards in 1599 or the preceding year.

Source.—For the historical scenes of this play Shakespeare's source is Holinshed's *Chronicles.* As usual he takes a playwright's liberties with history, condensing and arranging the sequence of events to secure unity and dramatic effect. The scene in which the Prince takes the crown from the bedside of his sleeping father and that in which as King he banishes his former companions are drawn from the old play of the *Famous Victories.* Most of the scenes, however, in which Falstaff figures are Shakespeare's own invention, even that in which he takes prisoner the "famous rebel," Colville of the Dale.

Characters.—As in the First Part, Shakespeare alternates scenes from history with purely comic scenes, but the historical section of this play is far inferior to that of its predecessor. The reason is evident: there are no such imposing and exciting figures to stand in opposition to the King and Prince Hal as "that fiend Douglas, that spirit Percy, and that devil Glendower." The craven Northumberland and the long-winded Archbishop are poor substitutes for such enemies. In particular one misses the dramatic conflict implied in the opposition of the two Harries, Hotspur and the Prince. It is remarkable, indeed, that in this play Shakespeare seems purposely to keep the Prince out of the scenes that deal with the rebellion and entrusts the inglorious victory, gained by scandalous breach of faith rather than by valor, to his brother, Prince John. One hears, to be sure, of Hal's expedition against the Welsh but one never sees him in action. It is as though Shakespeare thought it unfitting to show him fighting against such feeble adversaries. It is not till the close of the play in the scenes with his dying father and later as King that he shows us the true Prince, and it is only in these scenes that we catch the voice of the poet-dramatist. Much of the earlier verse reads as if it had been written in hours when the tide of inspiration was at a very low ebb.

With the comic scenes centering as they do about the great figure of Falstaff it is far otherwise. Shakespeare's prose is here at its highest, wittiest, and most fluent, and Shakespeare's power of characterization nowhere more apparent. He has enlarged and elaborated the slightly sketched Hostess of Part I into the inimitable Dame Quickly of this play. He has introduced a new "humorist," somewhat in the fashion of Jonson, but with more fire and life than Jonson ever dreamed of, in the person of swaggering Pistol. Much of the fun of Pistol's speech with its incessant parody of old plays has lost its pristine freshness, but the character itself, the cowardly, drunken, grandiloquent braggart is a masterpiece. The part must have seemed like God's gift to the actor whose happy lot it was to play Pistol on the stage. Indeed Shakespeare himself seems to have enjoyed him so well that he carries him over into both *Henry V* and *The Merry Wives*. Justice Shallow, too, is a most happy and original creation: the loquacious, self-satisfied, self-important country magnate with his reminiscences of wild old days in London is a living, breathing figure. Shakespeare must have known such a one in Warwick or Gloucestershire, and indeed the scenes in which Shallow figures are full of little touches that reveal Shakespeare's intimate knowledge of local conditions in the Cotswold hills. Like Pistol, Shallow carries over into the comedy of *The Merry Wives*.

Falstaff is, of course, the dominant figure of all the comic scenes. His character has been discussed in the introduction to the First Part, but it is worth while to consider here Shakespeare's treatment of the role in the Second Part. It is evident, notwithstanding Shakespeare's own delight in his creation of this supreme comic character, that he has deliberately planned to degrade Falstaff, morally, if not dramatically, throughout the play, and so prepare the audience for the shock of the rejection in the last scene. Falstaff in Part I is a most delightful and quite harmless rogue; even the highway robbery in which he takes part is little more than a practical joke; no one is hurt and the money is paid back. We hear indeed of his abuse of the King's press, but in the second part we see it practised at the home of Shallow when his hanger-on, Bardolph, takes bribes to release the able-bodied conscripts and impresses such miserable substitutes as Feeble, Shallow, and the ragged Wart—bribes which of course go into Falstaff's pocket. We hear in the First Part of his excessive drinking and his intimate acquaintance with *bona robas;* in the second we see him half-drunk and embracing Doll Tearsheet, a wench "as common as the way between St. Alban's and London." In the First Part he evades the sheriff and the watch by the kindly aid of Prince Hal; in the Second he resists arrest by force of arms, and confronts the Chief Justice in a manner as insolent as it is entertaining. He rises to the final and fatal pitch of arrogant assumption when he hears that his old crony, Prince Hal, is now the King. The news comes to him in the country and he sets out forthwith to ride all night to town; "take any man's horses"; he cries, "the laws of England are at my commandment. Blessed are they that have been my friends; and woe to my Lord Chief Justice." Shakespeare has already warned us in the scene which immediately precedes this that the new King, far from sharing Falstaff's views, has confirmed the Chief Justice in his office and has declared his wish to respect him as a father. It need be no surprise then that in the rejection scene Henry resents and rebuffs the outrageous attempt of Falstaff to fasten a claim of former intimacy upon him. Shakespeare has in fact taken some pains to show that this intimacy was already a thing of the past. In the First Part Hal and Falstaff are almost inseparable; they are together on the field of battle as well as in the tavern; in the Second they are together only once and that in a scene where Hal, returning weary from a hard campaign, seeks a little recreation by playing one of his old jokes on Falstaff. The joke is interrupted by an imperative call to duty; the Prince is needed at the sick King's side and a dozen captains are asking for Sir John, who should long since have been on his way to the war instead of boozing and kissing Doll in the Boar's Head Tavern. It is in a mood of sharp impatience, if not of anger, that Hal takes leave of his old friend: "give me my sword and cloak. Falstaff, goodnight"; and the two never meet again until Falstaff attempts to force himself upon the new-crowned King with the cry "God save thee, my sweet boy."

It has been well said that the main source of our delight in Falstaff is his humorous superiority to everything serious and the freedom of soul which he enjoys in this. Yet this freedom is an illusion; it cannot endure for long the shock of reality. There is no place for Falstaff in a realm ruled by Henry, son and heir of the hard realist, Bolingbroke. Shakespeare seems at one time to have entertained the idea, as the Epilogue tells us, of continuing the role and taking Sir John along with Henry to France, but he soon became aware of the impropriety of such a plan. Accordingly all we hear of Sir John in the play that follows this is the report of his sickness and death. We may well believe that it cost Shakespeare a pang to part with so delightful a character, and the few words in *Henry V* that tell us how the old knight's heart is "fracted and corroborate," and how he "went away an it had been any christom child," breathe Shakespeare's sigh of regret over the passing of Sir John. A Falstaff does indeed appear in *The Merry Wives* [1] but he resembles the true Sir John in little but his name: "Falstaff he is dead and we must yearn therefore."

Stage History.—There is no trace of the Second Part upon the public stage in Shakespeare's lifetime. A scrap of paper, apparently from the records of the Master of the Revels, tells of a performance at Court in 1619. It is said that Betterton's success as Falstaff in Part I induced him to revive the Second Part, but there is no certainty as to this, and the so-called Betterton adaptation in 1719–20 not only lacks his name—Mills appears as Falstaff in the cast of characters—but shows a license in altering Shakespeare's diction which is unlike Betterton's restraint in his acting version of Part I. This adaptation cuts the historic scenes very heavily, omitting the character of Northumberland altogether, and tries to make amends for this by closing with a brief version of the first scene of *Henry V*. Colley Cibber played the part of Shallow in this version, 1720, as he did later, 1736, with Quin in his favorite role of Falstaff. Garrick in 1758 acted the King, as Kemble and Macready did after him. In 1761 an adaptation with a magnificent coronation pageant in honor of the accession of George II ran for twenty-two days. Macready revived this spectacle in 1821 at the coronation of William IV, using the adaptation prepared by Kemble about 1804. This version follows the lines of that of 1720, except that it omits the fragment of *Henry V* with which the former closes, and ends the play with the wise and friendly words of the new King to the Chief Justice. In his series of performances at Sadler's Wells Phelps performed the seemingly impossible feat of doubling as the King and Justice Shallow. Little is heard of this play on the boards after a Phelps performance in 1874. In America Julia Marlowe played Prince Hal in a condensed version of both parts; otherwise it would seem to be unknown to the stage of this country.

[1] For the whole probable reason of this transformation see General Introduction, p. 56.

THE SECOND PART OF HENRY THE FOURTH

Henry IV—(See note *Henry IV, Part I.*)

Henry V—(See note *Henry IV, Part I.*)

Prince John of Lancaster—(See note *Henry IV, Part I.*)

Prince Humphrey of Gloucester—(See note *Henry V.*)

Prince Thomas of Clarence (1388–1421)—Second son of Henry IV. King Henry's reference to him as the favorite brother of Prince Hal is not borne out by history, as they were often in opposition. Later, however, they campaigned together in France, where Clarence was killed at the battle of Beaugé in 1421.

Northumberland—(See note *Henry IV, Part I.*)

Scroop, Archbi hop of York—(See note *Henry IV, Part I.*)

Lord Thomas Mowbray (1385–1405)—Son of Thomas, first Duke of Norfolk, banished by Richard II. At Henry IV's accession he was restored to his hereditary office of earl-marshal; but he was taken in Scroop's rebellion and beheaded in 1405.

Lord Hastings (d. 1405)—One of Scroop's associates, beheaded by Henry at Durham.

Lord Thomas Bardolph (1368–1408)—Mentioned in Holinshed along with others as associated with Scroop. Later he joined the rebellious Northumberland and fell in 1408 at the battle of Branham Moor.

Sir John Colville (d. 1405)—Mentioned in Holinshed as "convicted of the conspiracy" and beheaded at Durham.

Earl of Warwick—(See note *Henry V.*)

Earl of Westmoreland—(See note *Henry IV, Part I.*)

Thomas Fitzalan, Earl of Arundel and Surrey (1381–1415)—Son of Richard, Earl of Arundel, one of the "lords appellant" beheaded by Richard II in 1397. Thomas escaped from the Duke of Exeter (see *Richard II*, II, i, 280), who held him in captivity, and returned to England with Bolingbroke, who restored him to his father's titles and estates. He was a faithful servant of Henry IV and Henry V.

Sir John Blunt—Son of Sir Walter Blunt (*Henry IV, Part I.*)

THE SECOND PART OF HENRY THE FOURTH

Names of the Actors

Rumour, the Presenter.
King Henry IV.
Prince Henry, afterwards crowned King Henry V.
Prince John of Lancaster, *Prince Humphrey of Gloucester*, *Prince Thomas of Clarence*, — sons to *Henry IV* and brethren to *Henry V*.
Earl of Northumberland, *Scroop*, The Archbishop of York, *Mowbray*, *Hastings*, *Lord Bardolph*, *Travers*, *Morton*, *Colville*, — opposites against *King Henry IV*.
Warwick, *Westmoreland*, *Surrey*, *Gower*, *Harcourt*, *Lord Chief Justice*, — of the King's Party.
Falstaff, His *Page*, *Poins*, *Bardolph*, *Pistol*, *Peto*, — irregular Humourists.
Shallow, *Silence*, — both country Justices.
Davy, servant to *Shallow*.
Fang and *Snare*, two Sergeants.
Mouldy, *Shadow*, *Wart*, *Feeble*, *Bullcalf*, — country soldiers.
Northumberland's Wife.
Percy's Widow.
Hostess Quickly.
Doll Tearsheet.

Lords and attendants; Porter, Drawers, Beadles, Grooms, Servants, etc.

A Dancer as Epilogue.

[This list appears at the end of the play in the Folio.]

SCENE: *England*.

Induction

Warkworth. Before the castle.

Enter *Rumour*, painted full of tongues.

Rum. Open your ears; for which of you will stop
The vent of hearing when loud Rumour speaks?
I, from the orient to the drooping west,
Making the wind my post-horse, still unfold
The acts commenced on this ball of earth.
Upon my tongues continual slanders ride,
The which in every language I pronounce,
Stuffing the ears of men with false reports.
I speak of peace, while covert enmity
Under the smile of safety wounds the world;
And who but Rumour, who but only I,
Make fearful musters and prepar'd defence,
Whiles the big year, swoln with some other grief,
Is thought with child by the stern tyrant war,
And no such matter? Rumour is a pipe
Blown by surmises, jealousies, conjectures,
And of so easy and so plain a stop
That the blunt monster with uncounted heads,
The still-discordant wav'ring multitude,
Can play upon it. But what need I thus
My well-known body to anatomize
Among my household? Why is Rumour here?
I run before King Harry's victory,
Who in a bloody field by Shrewsbury
Hath beaten down young Hotspur and his troops,
Quenching the flame of bold rebellion
Even with the rebel's blood. But what mean I
To speak so true at first? My office is
To noise abroad that Harry Monmouth fell
Under the wrath of noble Hotspur's sword,
And that the King before the Douglas' rage

S. d. tongues, rumor is described by Virgil (*Aeneid*, iv, 174) as covered with ears, eyes, and tongues. **4. still**, always.

15. pipe, wind instrument. **17. stop**, hole for regulating sound. **18. blunt**, stupid. **23. King Harry's**, Henry IV.

Stoop'd his anointed head as low as death.
This have I rumour'd through the peasant towns
Between that royal field of Shrewsbury
And this worm-eaten hold of ragged stone,
Where Hotspur's father, old Northumberland,
Lies crafty-sick. The posts come tiring on,
And not a man of them brings other news
Than they have learn'd of me: from Rumour's tongues
They bring smooth comforts false, worse than true wrongs. *Exit.*

ACT I. SCENE I. *The same.*

Enter *Lord Bardolph* at one door.

L. Bard. Who keeps the gate here, ho?

Enter the *Porter.*

Where is the Earl?
Port. What shall I say you are?
L. Bard. Tell thou the Earl
That the Lord Bardolph doth attend him here.
Port. His lordship is walk'd forth into the orchard.
Please it your honour, knock but at the gate,
And he himself will answer.

Enter the *Earl of Northumberland.*

L. Bard. Here comes the Earl.
North. What news, Lord Bardolph? Every minute now
Should be the father of some stratagem.
The times are wild; contention, like a horse
Full of high feeding, madly hath broke loose
And bears down all before him.
L. Bard. Noble Earl,
I bring you certain news from Shrewsbury.
North. Good, an God will!
L. Bard. As good as heart can wish.
The King is almost wounded to the death;
And, in the fortune of my lord your son,
Prince Harry slain outright; and both the Blunts
Kill'd by the hand of Douglas; young Prince John
And Westmoreland and Stafford fled the field;
And Harry Monmouth's brawn, the hulk Sir John,
Is prisoner to your son: O, such a day,
So fought, so follow'd, and so fairly won,
Came not till now to dignify the times,
Since Cæsar's fortunes!
North. How is this deriv'd?
Saw you the field? Came you from Shrewsbury?
L. Bard. I spake with one, my lord, that came from thence,
A gentleman well bred and of good name,
That freely render'd me these news for true.
North. Here comes my servant Travers, who I sent
On Tuesday last to listen after news.

Enter *Travers.*

L. Bard. My lord, I over-rode him on the way;
And he is furnish'd with no certainties
More than he haply may retail from me.
North. Now, Travers, what good tidings comes with you?
Tra. My lord, Sir John Umfrevile turn'd me back
With joyful tidings; and, being better hors'd,
Out-rode me. After him came spurring hard
A gentleman, almost forspent with speed,
That stopp'd by me to breath his bloodied horse.
He ask'd the way to Chester; and of him
I did demand what news from Shrewsbury.
He told me that rebellion had bad luck,
And that young Harry Percy's spur was cold.
With that he gave his able horse the head,
And bending forward struck his armed heels
Against the panting side of his poor jade
Up to the rowel-head, and starting so
He seem'd in running to devour the way,
Staying no longer question.
North. Ha! Again:
Said he young Harry Percy's spur was cold?
Of Hotspur Coldspur? That rebellion
Had met ill luck?
L. Bard. My lord, I 'll tell you what:
If my young lord your son have not the day,
Upon mine honour, for a silken point
I 'll give my barony. Never talk of it.
North. Why should that gentleman that rode by Travers
Give then such instances of loss?
L. Bard. Who, he?
He was some hilding fellow that had stol'n

33. **peasant**, provincial. 35. **hold**, stronghold. **Act I, Scene i:** 2. **What**, who. 19. **brawn**, fat friend. 37. **crafty-sick**, feigning illness. **tiring**, riding until tired. **Act I, Scene i:** 48. **Staying**, awaiting. 53. **point**, lace to tie breeches to doublet. 57. **hilding**, worthless.

The horse he rode on, and, upon my life,
Spoke at a venture. Look, here comes more news.

Enter *Morton*.

North. Yea, this man's brow, like to a title-leaf,
Foretells the nature of a tragic volume.
So looks the strand whereon the imperious flood
Hath left a witness'd usurpation.
Say, Morton, didst thou come from Shrewsbury?

Mor. I ran from Shrewsbury, my noble lord,
Where hateful Death put on his ugliest mask
To fright our party.

North. How doth my son and brother?
Thou tremblest; and the whiteness in thy cheek
Is apter than thy tongue to tell thy errand.
Even such a man, so faint, so spiritless,
So dull, so dead in look, so woe-begone,
Drew Priam's curtain in the dead of night,
And would have told him half his Troy was burnt;
But Priam found the fire ere he his tongue,
And I my Percy's death ere thou report'st it.
This thou wouldst say, "Your son did thus and thus;
Your brother thus; so fought the noble Douglas;"
Stopping my greedy ear with their bold deeds;
But in the end, to stop my ear indeed,
Thou hast a sigh, to blow away this praise,
Ending with "Brother, son, and all are dead."

Mor. Douglas is living, and your brother yet;
But, for my lord your son,—

North. Why, he is dead.
See what a ready tongue suspicion hath!
He that but fears the thing he would not know
Hath by instinct knowledge from others' eyes
That what he fear'd is chanced. Yet speak, Morton;
Tell thou an earl his divination lies,
And I will take it as a sweet disgrace
And make thee rich for doing me such wrong.

Mor. You are too great to be by me gainsaid;
Your spirit is too true, your fears too certain.

North. Yet, for all this, say not that Percy 's dead.
I see a strange confession in thine eye.
Thou shak'st thy head and hold'st it fear or sin
To speak a truth. If he be slain, say so;
The tongue offends not that reports his death;
And he doth sin that doth belie the dead,
Not he which says the dead is not alive.
Yet the first bringer of unwelcome news
Hath but a losing office, and his tongue
Sounds ever after as a sullen bell,
Remember'd tolling a departing friend.

L. Bard. I cannot think, my lord, your son is dead.

Mor. I am sorry I should force you to believe
That which I would to God I had not seen;
But these mine eyes saw him in bloody state,
Rendering faint quittance, wearied and outbreath'd,
To Harry Monmouth; whose swift wrath beat down
The never-daunted Percy to the earth,
From whence with life he never more sprung up.
In few, his death, whose spirit lent a fire
Even to the dullest peasant in his camp,
Being bruited once, took fire and heat away
From the best-temper'd courage in his troops;
For from his mettle was his party steel'd;
Which once in him abated, all the rest
Turn'd on themselves, like dull and heavy lead.
And as the thing that 's heavy in itself,
Upon enforcement flies with greatest speed,
So did our men, heavy in Hotspur's loss,
Lend to this weight such lightness with their fear
That arrows fled not swifter toward their aim
Than did our soldiers, aiming at their safety,
Fly from the field. Then was that noble Worcester
Too soon ta'en prisoner; and that furious Scot,
The bloody Douglas, whose well-labouring sword
Had three times slain th' appearance of the King,
Gan vail his stomach and did grace the shame
Of those that turn'd their backs, and in his flight,
Stumbling in fear, was took. The sum of all
Is that the King hath won, and hath sent out
A speedy power to encounter you, my lord,
Under the conduct of young Lancaster
And Westmoreland. This is the news at full.

North. For this I shall have time enough to mourn.

63. **witness'd usurpation,** a witness, i.e., traces of its destruction. 72. **Priam,** King of Troy. 87. **chanced,** come to pass.

101. **a losing office,** unfortunate employment. 108. **quittance,** return of blows. 112. **In few,** in brief. 114. **bruited,** reported. 120. **enforcement,** compulsion. 128. **appearance,** i.e., noblemen dressed to look like the king. 129. **Gan vail his stomach,** began to lower (let fall) his courage.

In poison there is physic; and these news,
Having been well, that would have made me sick,
Being sick, have in some measure made me well:
And as the wretch, whose fever-weaken'd joints,
Like strengthless hinges, buckle under life,
Impatient of his fit, breaks like a fire
Out of his keeper's arms, even so my limbs,
Weaken'd with grief, being now enrag'd with grief,
Are thrice themselves. Hence, therefore, thou nice crutch!
A scaly gauntlet now with joints of steel
Must glove this hand; and hence, thou sickly quoif!
Thou art a guard too wanton for the head
Which princes, flesh'd with conquest, aim to hit.
Now bind my brows with iron; and approach
The ragged'st hour that time and spite dare bring
To frown upon th' enrag'd Northumberland!
Let heaven kiss earth! Now let not Nature's hand
Keep the wild flood confin'd! Let order die!
And let this world no longer be a stage
To feed contention in a ling'ring act;
But let one spirit of the first-born Cain
Reign in all bosoms, that, each heart being set
On bloody courses, the rude scene may end,
And darkness be the burier of the dead!

Tra. This strained passion doth you wrong, my lord.

L. Bard. Sweet Earl, divorce not wisdom from your honour.

Mor. The lives of all your loving complices
Lean on your health; the which, if you give o'er
To stormy passion, must perforce decay.
You cast th' event of war, my noble lord,
And summ'd the account of chance, before you said,
"Let us make head." It was your presurmise,
That, in the dole of blows, your son might drop.
You knew he walk'd o'er perils, on an edge,
More likely to fall in than to get o'er;
You were advis'd his flesh was capable
Of wounds and scars, and that his forward spirit
Would lift him where most trade of danger rang'd;
Yet did you say, "Go forth!" and none of this,
Though strongly apprehended, could restrain
The stiff-borne action. What hath then befall'n,
Or what hath this bold enterprise brought forth,
More than that being which was like to be?

L. Bard. We all that are engaged to this loss
Knew that we ventur'd on such dangerous seas
That if we wrought out life 't was ten to one;
And yet we ventur'd, for the gain propos'd
Chok'd the respect of likely peril fear'd;
And since we are o'erset, venture again,
Come, we will all put forth, body and goods.

Mor. 'T is more than time; and, my most noble lord,
I hear for certain, and do speak the truth,
The gentle Archbishop of York is up
With well-appointed powers: he is a man
Who with a double surety binds his followers.
My lord your son had only but the corpse,
But shadows and the shows of men, to fight;
For that same word, rebellion, did divide
The action of their bodies from their souls;
And they did fight with queasiness, constrain'd,
As men drink potions, that their weapons only
Seem'd on our side; but, for their spirits and souls,
This word, rebellion, it had froze them up,
As fish are in a pond. But now the Bishop
Turns insurrection to religion.
Suppos'd sincere and holy in his thoughts,
He 's follow'd both with body and with mind;
And doth enlarge his rising with the blood
Of fair King Richard, scrap'd from Pomfret stones;
Derives from heaven his quarrel and his cause;
Tells them he doth bestride a bleeding land,
Gasping for life under great Bolingbroke;
And more and less do flock to follow him.

North. I knew of this before; but, to speak truth,
This present grief had wip'd it from my mind.
Go in with me; and counsel every man
The aptest way for safety and revenge.
Get posts and letters, and make friends with speed;
Never so few, and never yet more need.

Exeunt.

144. **grief**, pain. **grief**, sorrow. 145. **nice**, dainty. 147. **sickly quoif**, invalid's cap. 148. **wanton**, light. 149. **flesh'd**, aroused, lit. like a dog fed on raw meat. 151. **ragged'st**, roughest. 166. **cast the event**, considered the outcome. 168. **make head**, muster troops. 169. **dole**, dealing. 172. **advis'd**, aware.

177. **stiff-borne**, obstinately carried out. 179. More than that happening which was likely to happen. 180. **engaged to**, involved in. 184. **Chok'd the respect of**, stopped consideration of. 192. **corpse**, body. 196. **queasiness**, nausea. 205. **Pomfret**, Richard II was murdered at Pomfret Castle. 209. **more and less**, high and low. 214. **make**, collect.

Scene II. *London. A street.*

Enter *Falstaff*, with his *Page* bearing his sword and buckler.

Fal. Sirrah, you giant, what says the doctor to my water?

Page. He said, sir, the water itself was a good healthy water; but, for the party that owed it, he might have moe diseases than he knew for.

Fal. Men of all sorts take a pride to gird at me: the brain of this foolish-compounded clay, man, is not able to invent anything that intends to laughter, more than I invent or is invented on me: I am not only witty in myself, but the cause that wit is in other men. I do here walk before thee like a sow that hath overwhelmed all her litter but one. If the Prince put thee into my service for any other reason than to set me off, why then I have no judgement. Thou whoreson mandrake, thou art fitter to be worn in my cap than to wait at my heels. I was never manned with an agate till now; but I will inset you neither in gold nor silver, but in vile apparel, and send you back again to your master, for a jewel,—the juvenal, the Prince your master, whose chin is not yet fledge. I will sooner have a beard grow in the palm of my hand than he shall get one off his cheek; and yet he will not stick to say his face is a face royal: God may finish it when he will, 't is not a hair amiss yet: he may keep it still at a face royal, for a barber shall never earn sixpence out of it; and yet he 'll be crowing as if he had writ man ever since his father was a bachelor. He may keep his own grace, but he 's almost out of mine, I can assure him. What said Master Dommelton about the satin for my short cloak and my slops?

Page. He said, sir, you should procure him better assurance than Bardolph. He would not take his band and yours. He liked not the security.

Fal. Let him be damned like the glutton! Pray God his tongue be hotter! A whoreson Achitophel! a rascally yea-for-sooth knave! to bear a gentleman in hand, and then stand upon security! The whoreson smooth-pates do now wear nothing but high shoes and bunches of keys at their girdles; and if a man is through with them in honest taking up, then they must stand upon security: I had as lief they would put ratsbane in my mouth as offer to stop it with security. I looked 'a should have sent me two and twenty yards of satin, as I am a true knight, and he sends me security. Well, he may sleep in security; for he hath the horn of abundance, and yet the lightness of his wife shines through it; and yet cannot he see, though he have his own lanthorn to light him. Where 's Bardolph?

Page. He 's gone into Smithfield to buy your worship a horse.

Fal. I bought him in Paul's, and he 'll buy me a horse in Smithfield: an I could get me but a wife in the stews, I were manned, horsed, and wived.

Enter the *Lord Chief Justice* and *Servant.*

Page. Sir, here comes the nobleman that committed the Prince for striking him about Bardolph.

Fal. Wait close; I will not see him.

Ch. Just. What 's he that goes there?

Serv. Falstaff, an 't please your lordship.

Ch. Just. He that was in question for the robbery?

Serv. He, my lord; but he hath since done good service at Shrewsbury, and, as I hear, is now going with some charge to the Lord John of Lancaster.

Ch. Just. What, to York? Call him back again.

Serv. Sir John Falstaff!

Fal. Boy, tell him I am deaf.

Page. You must speak louder; my master is deaf.

Ch. Just. I am sure he is, to the hearing of anything good. Go, pluck him by the elbow; I must speak with him.

Serv. Sir John!

Fal. What! a young knave, and begging! Is there not wars? Is there not employment? Doth not the King lack subjects? Do not the rebels need soldiers? Though it be a shame to be on any side but one, it is worse shame to beg than to be on the worst side, were it worse than the name of rebellion can tell how to make it.

Serv. You mistake me, sir.

Fal. Why, sir, did I say you were an honest man? Setting my knighthood and my soldiership aside, I had lied in my throat, if I had said so.

Serv. I pray you, sir, then set your knighthood and your soldiership aside; and give me

Scene ii: 5. owed, owned. **7. gird,** mock. **18. mandrake,** a poisonous plant with a forked root often likened to the human figure. **18. agate,** stone often cut into tiny figures. **28. face royal,** (1) coin, 10 s, (2) royal face. **35. slops,** loose breeches. **37. band,** bond. **39. glutton,** Dives (*Luke,* xvi, 19-31). **41. Achitophel,** Counsellor of Absalom (*II Samuel,* xv-xvii). **yea-for-sooth,** a lady-like oath. **42. bear . . . in hand,** delude with false hopes. **45. through,** serious. **taking up,** buying on credit.

52ff. horn . . . lightness . . . lanthorn, complicated punning on the invisible horns of cuckolds and the "lightness" of their unfaithful wives. **58. Paul's,** St. Paul's Cathedral. **60. stews,** houses of ill fame. **63. committed,** etc. reference to episode in *The Famous Victories of Henry V.*

leave to tell you you lie in your throat if you say I am any other than an honest man.

Fal. I give thee leave to tell me so? I lay aside that which grows to me? If thou get'st any leave of me, hang me; if thou tak'st leave, thou wert better be hanged. You hunt counter; hence! avaunt!

Serv. Sir, my lord would speak with you.

Ch. Just. Sir John Falstaff, a word with you.

Fal. My good lord! God give your lordship good time of day. I am glad to see your lordship abroad: I heard say your lordship was sick; I hope your lordship goes abroad by advice. Your lordship, though not clean past your youth, hath yet some smack of age in you, some relish of the saltness of time in you; and I most humbly beseech your lordship to have a reverend care of your health.

Ch. Just. Sir John, I sent for you before your expedition to Shrewsbury.

Fal. An 't please your lordship, I hear his Majesty is return'd with some discomfort from Wales.

Ch. Just. I talk not of his Majesty. You would not come when I sent for you.

Fal. And I hear, moreover, his Highness is fallen into the same whoreson apoplexy.

Ch. Just. Well, God mend him! I pray you, let me speak with you.

Fal. This apoplexy, as I take it, is a kind of lethargy, an 't please your lordship, a kind of sleeping in the blood, a whoreson tingling.

Ch. Just. What tell you me of it? Be it as it is.

Fal. It hath it original from much grief, from study, and perturbation of the brain. I have read the cause of his effects in Galen: it is a kind of deafness.

Ch. Just. I think you are fallen into the disease; for you hear not what I say to you.

Fal. Very well, my lord, very well: rather, an 't please you, it is the disease of not list'ning, the malady of not marking, that I am troubled withal.

Ch. Just. To punish you by the heels would amend the attention of your ears; and I care not if I do become your physician.

Fal. I am as poor as Job, my lord, but not so patient: your lordship may minister the potion of imprisonment to me in respect of poverty; but how I should be your patient to follow your prescriptions, the wise may make some dram of a scruple, or indeed a scruple itself.

Ch. Just. I sent for you, when there were matters against you for your life, to come speak with me.

Fal. As I was then advised by my learned counsel in the laws of this land-service, I did not come.

Ch. Just. Well, the truth is, Sir John, you live in great infamy.

Fal. He that buckles himself in my belt cannot live in less.

Ch. Just. Your means are very slender, and your waste is great.

Fal. I would it were otherwise; I would my means were greater, and my waist slenderer.

Ch. Just. You have misled the youthful prince.

Fal. The young prince hath misled me. I am the fellow with the great belly, and he my dog.

Ch. Just. Well, I am loath to gall a new-healed wound. Your day's service at Shrewsbury hath a little gilded over your night's exploit on Gadshill. You may thank the unquiet time for your quiet o'er-posting that action.

Fal. My lord?

Ch. Just. But since all is well, keep it so: wake not a sleeping wolf.

Fal. To wake a wolf is as bad as smell a fox.

Ch. Just. What! you are as a candle, the better part burnt out.

Fal. A wassail candle, my lord, all tallow. If I did say of wax, my growth would approve the truth.

Ch. Just. There is not a white hair in your face but should have his effect of gravity.

Fal. His effect of gravy, gravy, gravy.

Ch. Just. You follow the young prince up and down, like his ill angel.

Fal. Not so, my lord. Your ill angel is light; but I hope he that looks upon me will take me without weighing; and yet, in some respects, I grant, I cannot go; I cannot tell. Virtue is of so little regard in these costermongers' times that true Valour is turned bearherd; Pregnancy is made a tapster, and his quick wit wasted in giving reckonings; all the other gifts appertinent to man, as the malice of this age shapes them, are not worth a gooseberry. You that are old consider not the capacities of us that are young; you do measure the heat of our livers with the bitterness

102. hunt counter, hunting term, at fault or going the wrong direction on the trail. **129. What,** why. **131. it original,** its origin. **133. Galen,** famous ancient physician. **141. by the heels,** imprisonment. **146. in respect of,** on account of. **148. dram of a scruple,** trifle of doubt, with pun on "dram" and "scruple" as small weights.

154. land-service, military service. **171. o'er-posting,** avoiding the consequences of. **175. smell a fox,** be suspicious. **179. wassail candle,** large candle used at feasts. **183. have his effect,** be the outward sign. **187. ill angel,** the edges of gold or silver coins were often clipped for the metal. Such coins were "light" and not current (cf. cannot go, l. 189). **189. tell,** count, like a good coin. **190. costermongers',** commercial. **192. Pregnancy,** quickness of wit.

of your galls; and we that are in the vaward of our youth, I must confess, are wags too.

Ch. Just. Do you set down your name in the scroll of youth, that are written down old with all the characters of age? Have you not a moist eye, a dry hand, a yellow cheek, a white beard, a decreasing leg, an increasing belly? Is not your voice broken, your wind short, your chin double, your wit single, and every part about you blasted with antiquity? And will you yet call yourself young? Fie, fie, fie, Sir John!

Fal. My lord, I was born about three of the clock in the afternoon, with a white head and something a round belly. For my voice, I have lost it with hallooing and singing of anthems. To approve my youth further, I will not: the truth is, I am only old in judgement and understanding; and he that will caper with me for a thousand marks, let him lend me the money, and have at him! For the box of the ear that the Prince gave you, he gave it like a rude prince, and you took it like a sensible lord. I have checked him for it, and the young lion repents; marry, not in ashes and sackcloth, but in new silk and old sack.

Ch. Just. Well, God send the Prince a better companion!

Fal. God send the companion a better prince! I cannot rid my hands of him.

Ch. Just. Well, the King hath severed you and Prince Harry: I hear you are going with Lord John of Lancaster against the Archbishop and the Earl of Northumberland.

Fal. Yea, I thank your pretty sweet wit for it. But look you pray, all you that kiss my lady Peace at home, that our armies join not in a hot day; for, by the Lord, I take but two shirts out with me, and I mean not to sweat extraordinarily: if it be a hot day, and I brandish anything but a bottle, I would I might never spit white again. There is not a dangerous action can peep out his head but I am thrust upon it: well, I cannot last ever; but it was alway yet the trick of our English nation, if they have a good thing, to make it too common. If ye will needs say I am an old man, you should give me rest. I would to God my name were not so terrible to the enemy as it is. I were better to be eaten to death with a rust than to be scoured to nothing with perpetual motion.

Ch. Just. Well, be honest, be honest; and God bless your expedition!

Fal. Will your lordship lend me a thousand pound to furnish me forth?

Ch. Just. Not a penny, not a penny; you are too impatient to bear crosses. Fare you well! Commend me to my cousin Westmoreland.

Exeunt Chief Justice and Servant.

Fal. If I do, fillip me with a three-man beetle. A man can no more separate age and covetousness than 'a can part young limbs and lechery; but the gout galls the one, and the pox pinches the other, and so both the degrees prevent my curses. Boy!

Page. Sir?

Fal. What money is in my purse?

Page. Seven groats and two pence.

Fal. I can get no remedy against this consumption of the purse: borrowing only lingers and lingers it out, but the disease is incurable. Go bear this letter to my Lord of Lancaster; this to the Prince; this to the Earl of Westmoreland; and this to old Mistress Ursula, whom I have weekly sworn to marry since I perceived the first white hair of my chin. About it. You know where to find me. [*Exit Page.*] A pox of this gout! or, a gout of this pox! for the one or the other plays the rogue with my great toe. 'T is no matter if I do halt; I have the wars for my colour, and my pension shall seem the more reasonable. A good wit will make use of anything: I will turn diseases to commodity. *Exit.*

Scene III. *York. The Archbishop's palace.*

Enter the *Archbishop, Thomas Mowbray,* (*Earl Marshal*) the *Lords Hastings* and *Bardolph.*

Arch. Thus have you heard our cause and known our means;
And, my most noble friends, I pray you all,
Speak plainly your opinions of our hopes.
And first, Lord Marshal, what say you to it?
Mowb. I well allow the occasion of our arms;
But gladly would be better satisfied
How in our means we should advance ourselves
To look with forehead bold and big enough
Upon the power and puissance of the King.
Hast. Our present musters grow upon the file
To five and twenty thousand men of choice;

199. vaward, vanguard. **217. marks,** coins worth 13s. 4d. **218. box of the ear,** another reference to the old play *The Famous Victories of Henry V.* **222. sack,** Spanish wine. **238. spit white,** be thirsty.

253. crosses, (1) affliction, (2) coins, often marked with crosses. **255. fillip . . . beetle,** it would take a mallet (beetle) wielded by three men to fillip Falstaff into the air. From the game, *Filliping the Toad,* in which a weight was thrown into the air from one end of a board set across a log and struck on the other end. **260. prevent,** anticipate. **263. groats,** 4d. **274. halt,** limp. **275. colour,** excuse. **278. commodity,** profit. **Scene iii: 7. in,** with. **10. file,** roster.

And our supplies live largely in the hope
Of great Northumberland, whose bosom burns
With an incensed fire of injuries.

L. Bard. The question then, Lord Hastings, standeth thus:
Whether our present five and twenty thousand
May hold up head without Northumberland?

Hast. With him, we may.

L. Bard. Yea, marry, there 's the point!
But if without him we be thought too feeble,
My judgement is, we should not step too far
Till we had his assistance by the hand;
For, in a theme so bloody-fac'd as this,
Conjecture, expectation, and surmise
Of aids incertain should not be admitted.

Arch. 'T is very true, Lord Bardolph; for indeed
It was young Hotspur's case at Shrewsbury.

L. Bard. It was, my lord; who lin'd himself with hope,
Eating the air, on promise of supply,
Flatt'ring himself in project of a power
Much smaller than the smallest of his thoughts;
And so, with great imagination
Proper to madmen, led his powers to death,
And winking leap'd into destruction.

Hast. But, by your leave, it never yet did hurt
To lay down likelihoods and forms of hope.

L. Bard. Yes, if this present quality of war—
Indeed the instant action—a cause on foot,
Lives so in hope as in an early spring
We see th' appearing buds, which to prove fruit
Hope gives not so much warrant, as despair
That frosts will bite them. When we mean to build,
We first survey the plot, then draw the model;
And when we see the figure of the house,
Then must we rate the cost of the erection;
Which if we find outweighs ability,
What do we then but draw anew the model
In fewer offices, or at least desist
To build at all? Much more, in this great work,
Which is almost to pluck a kingdom down
And set another up, should we survey
The plot of situation and the model,
Consent upon a sure foundation,
Question surveyors, know our own estate,
How able such a work to undergo,
To weigh against his opposite; or else
We fortify in paper and in figures,
Using the names of men instead of men;
Like one that draws the model of a house
Beyond his power to build it; who, half through,
Gives o'er and leaves his part-created cost
A naked subject to the weeping clouds
And waste for churlish winter's tyranny.

Hast. Grant that our hopes, yet likely of fair birth,
Should be still-born, and that we now possess'd
The utmost man of expectation,
I think we are a body strong enough,
Even as we are, to equal with the King.

L. Bard. What, is the King but five and twenty thousand?

Hast. To us no more; nay, not so much, Lord Bardolph.
For his divisions, as the times do brawl,
Are in three heads: one power against the French,
And one against Glendower; perforce a third
Must take up us. So is the unfirm King
In three divided; and his coffers sound
With hollow poverty and emptiness.

Arch. That he should draw his several strengths together
And come against us in full puissance,
Need not to be dreaded.

Hast. If he should do so,
To French and Welsh he leaves his back unarm'd,
They baying him at the heels. Never fear that.

L. Bard. Who is it like should lead his forces hither?

Hast. The Duke of Lancaster and Westmoreland;
Against the Welsh, himself and Harry Monmouth;
But who is substituted 'gainst the French,
I have no certain notice.

Arch. Let us on,
And publish the occasion of our arms.
The commonwealth is sick of their own choice;
Their over-greedy love hath surfeited:
An habitation giddy and unsure
Hath he that buildeth on the vulgar heart.
O thou fond many, with what loud applause
Didst thou beat heaven with blessing Bolingbroke,
Before he was what thou wouldst have him be!
And being now trimm'd in thine own desires,
Thou, beastly feeder, art so full of him,
That thou provok'st thyself to cast him up.
So, so, thou common dog, didst thou disgorge

12. supplies, reinforcements. **27. lin'd,** strengthened. **29. project,** anticipation. **33. winking,** with eyes shut. 36-9. A possibly corrupt passage, but it may be interpreted: Yes, it does do harm if a cause like the present, an action on foot, lives only in hope like buds in early spring. **47. offices,** rooms. **52. Consent,** agree. **55. opposite,** opponent.

60. part-created cost, costly fragment. **70. do brawl,** are turbulent. **91. fond many,** foolish multitude.

Thy glutton bosom of the royal Richard;
And now thou wouldst eat thy dead vomit up,
And howl'st to find it. What trust is in these times?
They that, when Richard liv'd, would have him die,
Are now become enamour'd on his grave.
Thou, that threw'st dust upon his goodly head
When through proud London he came sighing on
After th' admired heels of Bolingbroke,
Cri'st now, "O earth, yield us that king again,
And take thou this!" O thoughts of men accurs'd!
Past and to come seem best; things present worst.

Mowb. Shall we go draw our numbers and set on?

Hast. We are Time's subjects, and Time bids be gone. *Exeunt.*

Act II. Scene I. *London. A street.*

Enter *Hostess* of the Tavern with two officers, *Fang* and his boy; *Snare.*

Host. Master Fang, have you entered the action?

Fang. It is entered.

Host. Where 's your yeoman? Is 't a lusty yeoman? Will 'a stand to 't?

Fang. Sirrah, where 's Snare?

Host. O Lord, ay! good Master Snare.

Snare. Here, here.

Fang. Snare, we must arrest Sir John Falstaff.

Host. Yea, good Master Snare; I have entered him and all.

Snare. It may chance cost some of us our lives, for he will stab.

Host. Alas the day! take heed of him. He stabbed me in mine own house, most beastly: in good faith: 'a cares not what mischief he does, if his weapon be out: he will foin like any devil; he will spare neither man, woman, nor child.

Fang. If I can close with him, I care not for his thrust.

Host. No, nor I neither. I 'll be at your elbow.

Fang. An I but fist him once; an 'a come but within my vice,—

Host. I am undone by his going; I warrant you, he 's an infinitive thing upon my score. Good Master Fang, hold him sure: good Master Snare, let him not scape. 'A comes continuantly to Pie-corner—saving your manhoods—to buy a saddle; and he is indited to dinner to the Lubber's-head in Lumbert street, to Master Smooth's the silk-man. I pray you, since my exion is entered and my case so openly known to the world, let him be brought in to his answer. A hundred mark is a long one for a poor lone woman to bear; and I have borne, and borne, and borne, and have been fubbed off, and fubbed off, and fubbed off, from this day to that day, that it is a shame to be thought on. There is no honesty in such dealing; unless a woman should be made an ass and a beast, to bear every knave's wrong. Yonder he comes; and that arrant malmsey-nose knave, Bardolph, with him. Do your offices, do your offices, Master Fang and Master Snare; do me, do me, do me your offices.

Enter *Falstaff, Bardolph,* and *Page.*

Fal. How now! whose mare 's dead? What 's the matter?

Fang. Sir John, I arrest you at the suit of Mistress Quickly.

Fal. Away, varlets! Draw, Bardolph; cut me off the villain's head: throw the quean in the channel.

Host. Throw me in the channel? I 'll throw thee in the channel. Wilt thou? wilt thou? thou bastardly rogue! Murder, murder! Ah, thou honey-suckle villain! wilt thou kill God's officers and the King's? Ah, thou honey-seed rogue! thou art a honey-seed, a man-queller, and a woman-queller.

Fal. Keep them off, Bardolph.

Fang. A rescue! a rescue!

Host. Good people, bring a rescue or two. Thou wo 't, wo 't thou? thou wo 't, wo 't ta? Do, do, thou rogue! do, thou hempseed!

Page. Away, you scullion! you rampallian! you fustilarian! I 'll tickle your catastrophe.

109. draw, assemble. **Act II, Scene i: 38. fubb'd off,** for fobbed of, i.e., put off. **43. malmsey-nose,** red nosed from drinking wine. **51. quean,** wench. **52. channel,** gutter. **56. honey-suckle,** for homicidal. **57. honey-seed,** for homicide. **58. man-queller,** man killer. **63. ta,** thou. **65. rampallian,** rapscallion. **66. fustilarian,** from fustilugs, a fat, frowsy woman. **catastrophe,** end, backside.

Act II, Scene i: 4. yeoman, sheriff's officer. **10. entered,** brought suit against. **17. foin,** thrust in fencing. **23. fist,** grasp. **24. vice,** grip. **30.** The Leopard's Head in Lombard Street. **33. exion,** for action.

Enter the *Lord Chief Justice*, and his men.

Ch. Just. What is the matter? Keep the peace here, ho!

Host. Good my lord, be good to me. I beseech you, stand to me.

Ch. Just. How now, Sir John! what, are you brawling here?
Doth this become your place, your time and business?
You should have been well on your way to York.
Stand from him, fellow; wherefore hang'st thou upon him?

Host. O my most worshipful lord, an 't please your Grace, I am a poor widow of Eastcheap, and he is arrested at my suit.

Ch. Just. For what sum?

Host. It is more than for some, my lord; it is for all I have. He hath eaten me out of house and home; he hath put all my substance into that fat belly of his: but I will have some of it out again, or I will ride thee o' nights like the mare.

Fal. I think I am as like to ride the mare, if I have any vantage of ground to get up.

Ch. Just. How comes this, Sir John? Fie! what man of good temper would endure this tempest of exclamation? Are you not ashamed to enforce a poor widow to so rough a course to come by her own?

Fal. What is the gross sum that I owe thee?

Host. Marry, if thou wert an honest man, thyself and the money too. Thou didst swear to me upon a parcel-gilt goblet, sitting in my Dolphin chamber, at the round table, by a sea-coal fire, upon Wednesday in Wheeson week, when the Prince broke thy head for liking his father to a singing-man of Windsor, thou didst swear to me then, as I was washing thy wound, to marry me and make me my lady thy wife. Canst thou deny it? Did not good wife Keech, the butcher's wife, come in then and call me gossip Quickly? coming in to borrow a mess of vinegar, telling us she had a good dish of prawns; whereby thou didst desire to eat some; whereby I told thee they were ill for a green wound? And didst thou not, when she was gone downstairs, desire me to be no more so familiarity with such poor people, saying that ere long they should call me madam? And didst thou not kiss me and bid me fetch thee thirty shillings? I put thee now to thy book-oath: deny it, if thou canst.

Fal. My lord, this is a poor mad soul; and she says up and down the town that her eldest son is like you: she hath been in good case, and the truth is, poverty hath distracted her. But for these foolish officers, I beseech you I may have redress against them.

Ch. Just. Sir John, Sir John, I am well acquainted with your manner of wrenching the true cause the false way. It is not a confident brow, nor the throng of words that come with such more than impudent sauciness from you, can thrust me from a level consideration. You have, as it appears to me, practised upon the easy-yielding spirit of this woman, and made her serve your uses both in purse and in person.

Host. Yea, in truth, my lord.

Ch. Just. Pray thee, peace. Pay her the debt you owe her, and unpay the villainy you have done with her: the one you may do with sterling money, and the other with current repentance.

Fal. My lord, I will not undergo this sneap without reply. You call honourable boldness impudent sauciness; if a man will make curtsy and say nothing, he is virtuous. No, my lord, my humble duty remembered, I will not be your suitor. I say to you, I do desire deliverance from these officers, being upon hasty employment in the King's affairs.

Ch. Just. You speak as having power to do wrong; but answer in th' effect of your reputation, and satisfy the poor woman.

Fal. Come hither, hostess.

Enter *Gower*.

Ch. Just. Now, Master Gower, what news?

Gow. The King, my lord, and Harry Prince of Wales
Are near at hand: the rest the paper tells.

Fal. As I am a gentleman.

Host. Faith, you said so before.

Fal. As I am a gentleman. Come, no more words of it.

Host. By this heavenly ground I tread on, I must be fain to pawn both my plate and the tapestry of my dining-chambers.

Fal. Glasses, glasses, is the only drinking; and for thy walls, a pretty slight drollery, or the story of the Prodigal, or the German hunting in water-work, is worth a thousand of these bed-hangers and these fly-bitten tapestries. Let it be ten pound, if thou canst. Come, an 't were not for thy humours, there 's not a better

83. mare, nightmare. **94. parcel-gilt,** partly gilt. **96. Wheeson,** Whitsun. **103. gossip,** familiar term of address. **105. prawns,** shrimps. **107. green,** fresh.

115. in good case, well to do. **124. level,** balanced. **132. current,** genuine. **133. sneap,** reprimand. **142. in th' effect of,** as befits. **155. Glasses,** to replace her silver goblets. **156. drollery,** comic scene. **158. water-work,** water color. **161. humours,** caprices.

wench in England. Go, wash thy face, and draw the action. Come, thou must not be in this humour with me; dost not know me? Come, come, I know thou wast set on to this.

Host. Pray thee, Sir John, let it be but twenty nobles: i' faith, I am loath to pawn my plate, so God save me, la!

Fal. Let it alone; I 'll make other shift: you 'll be a fool still.

Host. Well, you shall have it, though I pawn my gown. I hope you 'll come to supper. You 'll pay me altogether?

Fal. Will I live? [*To Bardolph.*] Go, with her, with her; hook on, hook on.

Host. Will you have Doll Tearsheet meet you at supper?

Fal. No more words; let 's have her.

Exeunt Hostess, Bardolph, Officers, and Boy.

Ch. Just. I have heard better news.

Fal. What 's the news, my lord?

Ch. Just. Where lay the King to-night?

Gow. At Basingstoke, my lord.

Fal. I hope, my lord, all 's well. What is the news, my lord?

Ch. Just. Come all his forces back?

Gow. No; fifteen hundred foot, five hundred horse,
Are march'd up to my Lord of Lancaster.
Against Northumberland and the Archbishop.

Fal. Comes the King back from Wales, my noble lord?

Ch. Just. You shall have letters of me presently.
Come, go along with me, good Master Gower.

Fal. My lord!

Ch. Just. What 's the matter?

Fal. Master Gower, shall I entreat you with me to dinner?

Gow. I must wait upon my good lord here; I thank you, good Sir John.

Ch. Just. Sir John, you loiter here too long, being you are to take soldiers up in counties as you go.

Fal. Will you sup with me, Master Gower?

Ch. Just. What foolish master taught you these manners, Sir John?

Fal. Master Gower, if they become me not, he was a fool that taught them me. This is the right fencing grace, my lord; tap for tap, and so part fair.

Ch. Just. Now the Lord lighten thee! thou art a great fool. *Exeunt.*

163. draw, withdraw. **199. take . . . up,** levy. **208. lighten,** enlighten.

Scene II. *London. Another street.*

Enter *Prince Henry* and *Poins.*

Prince. Before God, I am exceeding weary.

Poins. Is 't come to that? I had thought weariness durst not have attached one of so high blood.

Prince. Faith, it does me, though it discolours the complexion of my greatness to acknowledge it. Doth it not show vilely in me to desire small beer?

Poins. Why, a prince should not be so loosely studied as to remember so weak a composition.

Prince. Belike then my appetite was not princely got, for, by my troth, I do now remember the poor creature, small beer. But, indeed, these humble considerations make me out of love with my greatness. What a disgrace is it to me to remember thy name! or to know thy face to-morrow! or to take note how many pair of silk stockings thou hast, viz., these, and those that were thy peach-coloured ones! or to bear the inventory of thy shirts, as, one for superfluity, and another for use! But that the tennis-court-keeper knows better than I; for it is a low ebb of linen with thee when thou keepest not racket there; as thou hast not done a great while, because the rest of the low countries have made a shift to eat up thy holland: and God knows, whether those that bawl out the ruins of thy linen shall inherit his kingdom: but the midwives say the children are not in the fault; whereupon the world increases, and kindreds are mightily strengthened.

Poins. How ill it follows, after you have laboured so hard, you should talk so idlely! Tell me, how many good young princes would do so, their fathers being so sick as yours at this time is?

Prince. Shall I tell thee one thing, Poins?

Poins. Yes, faith; and let it be an excellent good thing.

Prince. It shall serve among wits of no higher breeding than thine.

Poins. Go to; I stand the push of your one thing that you will tell.

Prince. Marry, I tell thee, it is not meet that I should be sad, now my father is sick; albeit I could tell to thee, as to one it pleases

Scene ii: 5. discolours the complexion, causes to blush. **9. studied,** inclined. **weak a composition,** i.e., small beer (l. 7). **27. holland,** linen. Puns on Holland, where linen was made and Low Country. **27ff.** Reference to Poins' illegitimate children, who wear his cast-off shirts. **40. push,** thrust.

me, for fault of a better, to call my friend, I could be sad, and sad indeed too.

Poins. Very hardly upon such a subject.

Prince. By this hand, thou think'st me as far in the devil's book as thou and Falstaff for obduracy and persistency. Let the end try the man. But I tell thee, my heart bleeds inwardly that my father is so sick; and keeping such vile company as thou art hath in reason taken from me all ostentation of sorrow.

Poins. The reason?

Prince. What wouldst thou think of me, if I should weep?

Poins. I would think thee a most princely hypocrite.

Prince. It would be every man's thought; and thou art a blessed fellow to think as every man thinks: never a man's thought in the world keeps the road-way better than thine: every man would think me an hypocrite indeed. And what accites your most worshipful thought to think so?

Poins. Why, because you have been so lewd and so much engraffed to Falstaff.

Prince. And to thee.

Poins. By this light, I am well spoke on; I can hear it with mine own ears: the worst that they can say of me is that I am a second brother and that I am a proper fellow of my hands; and those two things, I confess, I cannot help. By the mass, here comes Bardolph.

Enter *Bardolph* and *Page.*

Prince. And the boy that I gave Falstaff. 'A had him from me Christian; and look, if the fat villain have not transformed him ape.

Bard. God save your Grace!

Prince. And yours, most noble Bardolph!

Poins. Come, you virtuous ass, you bashful fool, must you be blushing? Wherefore blush you now? What a maidenly man-at-arms are you become! Is 't such a matter to get a pottle-pot's maidenhead?

Page. 'A calls me e'en now, my lord, through a red lattice, and I could discern no part of his face from the window: at last I spied his eyes, and methought he had made two holes in the ale-wife's new petticoat and so peeped through.

Prince. Has not the boy profited?

Bard. Away, you whoreson upright rabbit, away!

Page. Away, you rascally Althæa's dream, away!

Prince. Instruct us, boy; what dream, boy?

Page. Marry, my lord, Althæa dreamed she was delivered of a fire-brand; and therefore I call him her dream.

Prince. A crown's worth of good interpretation: there 't is, boy.

Poins. O, that this good blossom could be kept from cankers! Well, there is sixpence to preserve thee.

Bard. An you do not make him hanged among you, the gallows shall have wrong.

Prince. And how doth thy master, Bardolph?

Bard. Well, my lord. He heard of your Grace's coming to town. There 's a letter for you.

Poins. Delivered with good respect. And how doth the Martlemas, your master?

Bard. In bodily health, sir.

Poins. Marry, the immortal part needs a physician; but that moves not him: though that be sick, it dies not.

Prince. I do allow this wen to be as familiar with me as my dog, and he holds his place, for look you how he writes.

Poins. [*Reads.*] "John Falstaff, knight,"— Every man must know that, as oft as he has occasion to name himself; even like those that are kin to the King, for they never prick their finger but they say, "There 's some of the King's blood spilt." "How comes that?" says he, that takes upon him not to conceive. The answer is as ready as a borrower's cap, "I am the King's poor cousin, sir."

Prince. Nay, they will be kin to us, or they will fetch it from Japhet. But the letter: [*Reads.*] "Sir John Falstaff, knight, to the son of the King nearest his father, Harry Prince of Wales, greeting."

Poins. Why, this is a certificate.

Prince. Peace! [*Reads.*] "I will imitate the honourable Romans in brevity."

Poins. He sure means brevity in breath, short-winded.

Prince. [*Reads.*] "I commend me to thee, I commend thee, and I leave thee. Be not too familiar with Poins; for he misuses thy favours so much, that he swears thou art to marry his sister Nell. Repent at idle times as thou mayest; and so, farewell.

64. accites, excites. **72. proper . . . hands,** i.e., for fighting, perhaps, stealing. **84. pottle-pot's,** two-quart tankard's. **93. Althæa's,** she dreamed that her son would live only so long as the brand burned in the fire.

96ff. Hecuba's dream, not Althæa's. 102. cankers, canker-worms. **110. Martlemas,** Martinmas (St. Martin's Day, Nov. 11) was season for killing and salting beef for the winter. Reference to Falstaff as beef or ox. **115. wen,** swelling tumor. **118. s. d. Reads,** apparently the Prince hands the letter to Poins who reads the opening phrase, comments on it, and hands the letter back to Hal, who proceeds to read it aloud. **124. conceive,** understand. **128. fetch it from Japhet,** trace kinship through this son of Noah.

"Thine, by yea and no, which is as much as to say, as thou usest him, *Jack Falstaff* with my familiars, *John* with my brothers and sisters, and *Sir John* with all Europe."

Poins. My lord, I 'll steep this letter in sack and make him eat it.

Prince. That 's to make him eat twenty of his words. But do you use me thus, Ned? Must I marry your sister?

Poins. God send the wench no worse fortune! But I never said so.

Prince. Well, thus we play the fools with the time, and the spirits of the wise sit in the clouds and mock us. Is your master here in London?

Bard. Yea, my lord.

Prince. Where sups he? Doth the old boar feed in the old frank?

Bard. At the old place, my lord, in Eastcheap.

Prince. What company?

Page. Ephesians, my lord, of the old church.

Prince. Sup any women with him?

Page. None, my lord, but old Mistress Quickly and Mistress Doll Tearsheet.

Prince. What pagan may that be?

Page. A proper gentlewoman, sir, and a kinswoman of my master's.

Prince. Even such kin as the parish heifers are to the town bull. Shall we steal upon them, Ned, at supper?

Poins. I am your shadow, my lord; I 'll follow you.

Prince. Sirrah, you boy, and Bardolph, no word to your master that I am yet come to town. There 's for your silence.

Bard. I have no tongue, sir.

Page. And for mine, sir, I will govern it.

Prince. Fare you well; go. [*Exeunt Bardolph and Page.*] This Doll Tearsheet should be some road.

Poins. I warrant you, as common as the way between Saint Alban's and London.

Prince. How might we see Falstaff bestow himself to-night in his true colours, and not ourselves be seen?

Poins. Put on two leathern jerkins and aprons, and wait upon him at his table as drawers.

Prince. From a God to a bull? a heavy descension! It was Jove's case. From a prince to a prentice? a low transformation! That shall be mine; for in everything the purpose must weigh with the folly. Follow me, Ned.

Exeunt.

160. **frank**, sty. 164. **Ephesians**, boon companions. 168. **pagan**, strumpet. 186. **bestow**, behave. 192. **God to a bull**, story of Jupiter and Europa. 196. **weigh with**, equal.

Scene III. *Warkworth. Before the castle.*

Enter *Northumberland*, his *Lady* and *Harry Percy's Lady*.

North. I pray thee, loving wife and gentle daughter,
Give even way unto my rough affairs;
Put not you on the visage of the times
And be like them to Percy troublesome.

Lady N. I have given over, I will speak no more.
Do what you will; your wisdom be your guide.

North. Alas, sweet wife, my honour is at pawn;
And, but my going, nothing can redeem it.

Lady P. O yet, for God's sake, go not to these wars!
The time was, father, that you broke your word,
When you were more endear'd to it than now;
When your own Percy, when my heart's dear Harry,
Threw many a northward look to see his father
Bring up his powers; but he did long in vain.
Who then persuaded you to stay at home?
There were two honours lost, yours and your son's.
For yours, the God of heaven brighten it!
For his, it stuck upon him as the sun
In the grey vault of heaven, and by his light
Did all the chivalry of England move
To do brave acts: he was indeed the glass
Wherein the noble youth did dress themselves.
He had no legs, that practis'd not his gait;
And speaking thick, which nature made his blemish,
Became the accents of the valiant;
For those that could speak low and tardily
Would turn their own perfection to abuse,
To seem like him; so that in speech, in gait,
In diet, in affections of delight,
In military rules, humours of blood,
He was the mark and glass, copy and book,
That fashion'd others. And him, O wondrous him!
O miracle of men! him did you leave,
Second to none, unseconded by you,
To look upon the hideous god of war
In disadvantage; to abide a field
Where nothing but the sound of Hotspur's name
Did seem defensible: so you left him.
Never, O never, do his ghost the wrong
To hold your honour more precise and nice
With others than with him! Let them alone.

Scene iii: 11. endear'd, bound. **24. thick**, fast. **29. affections of delight**, pastimes. **30. humours of blood**, disposition. **38. defensible**, capable of making defense.

The Marshal and the Archbishop are strong.
Had my sweet Harry had but half their numbers,
To-day might I, hanging on Hotspur's neck,
Have talk'd of Monmouth's grave.

North. Beshrew your heart,
Fair daughter, you do draw my spirits from me
With new lamenting ancient oversights.
But I must go and meet with danger there,
Or it will seek me in another place
And find me worse provided.

Lady N. O, fly to Scotland,
Till that the nobles and the armed commons
Have of their puissance made a little taste.

Lady P. If they get ground and vantage of the King,
Then join you with them, like a rib of steel,
To make strength stronger; but, for all our loves,
First let them try themselves. So did your son;
He was so suff'red; so came I a widow;
And never shall have length of life enough
To rain upon remembrance with mine eyes,
That it may grow and sprout as high as heaven,
For recordation to my noble husband.

North. Come, come, go in with me. 'T is with my mind
As with the tide swell'd up unto his height,
That makes a still stand, running neither way.
Fain would I go to meet the Archbishop,
But many thousand reasons hold me back.
I will resolve for Scotland: there am I,
Till time and vantage crave my company.
Exeunt.

Scene IV. *London. The Boar's-Head Tavern in Eastcheap.*

Enter two *Drawers.*

1. Draw. What the devil hast thou brought there? Apple-johns? Thou know'st Sir John cannot endure an apple-john.

2. Draw. Mass, thou say'st true. The Prince once set a dish of apple-johns before him, and told him there were five more Sir Johns, and, putting off his hat, said, "I will now take my leave of these six dry, round, old, withered knights." It angered him to the heart; but he hath forgot that.

1. Draw. Why, then, cover, and set them down; and see if thou canst find out Sneak's noise: Mistress Tearsheet would fain hear some music. Dispatch! The room where they supped is too hot; they 'll come in straight.

2. Draw. Sirrah, here will be the Prince and Master Poins anon; and they will put on two of our jerkins and aprons; and Sir John must not know of it. Bardolph hath brought word.

1. Draw. By the mass, here will be old utis; it will be an excellent stratagem.

2. Draw. I 'll see if I can find out Sneak.
Exit.

Enter *Hostess* and *Doll Tearsheet.*

Host. I' faith, sweetheart, methinks now you are in an excellent good temperality. Your pulsidge beats as extraordinarily as heart would desire; and your colour, I warrant you, is as red as any rose, in good truth, la! But, i' faith, you have drunk too much canaries; and that 's a marvellous searching wine, and it perfumes the blood ere one can say, "What 's this?" How do you now?

Dol. Better than I was. Hem!

Host. Why, that 's well said; a good heart 's worth gold. Lo, here comes Sir John.

Enter *Falstaff.*

Fal. [*Singing.*] "When Arthur first in court"—Empty the jordan. [*Exit 1. Drawer.*]—[*Singing.*] "And was a worthy king." How now, Mistress Doll!

Host. Sick of a calm; yea, good faith.

Fal. So is all her sect; an they be once in a calm, they are sick.

Dol. A pox damn you, you muddy rascal, is that all the comfort you give me?

Fal. You make fat rascals, Mistress Doll.

Dol. I make them? Gluttony and diseases make them; I make them not.

Fal. If the cook help to make the gluttony, you help to make the diseases, Doll: we catch of you, Doll, we catch of you: grant that, my poor virtue, grant that.

Dol. Yea, joy, our chains and our jewels.

Fal. "Your brooches, pearls, and ouches." For to serve bravely is to come halting off, you know; to come off the breach with his pike bent bravely, and to surgery bravely; to venture upon the charged chambers bravely,—

Dol. Hang yourself, you muddy conger, hang yourself!

Host. By my troth, this is the old fashion;

46. spirits, courage. **61. recordation,** remembrance. **Scene iv: 2. Apple-johns,** a variety of apple that shrivelled without decaying. **13. noise,** band of musicians.

21. old utis, rare sport. **25. temperality,** for temper. **26. extraordinarily,** for ordinarily. **36. "When Arthur," etc.,** from ballad *Sir Lancelot du Lake.* **40. calm,** for qualm. **53.** From another old ballad. **ouches,** jewels. **57. chambers,** small cannon. **58. conger,** eel.

you two never meet but you fall to some discord. You are both, i' good truth, as rheumatic as two dry toasts; you cannot one bear with another's confirmities. What the good-year! one must bear, and that must be you; you are the weaker vessel, as they say, the emptier vessel.

Dol. Can a weak empty vessel bear such a huge full hogshead? There 's a whole merchant's venture of Bourdeaux stuff in him; you have not seen a hulk better stuffed in the hold. Come, I 'll be friends with thee, Jack: thou art going to the wars; and whether I shall ever see thee again or no, there is nobody cares.

Re-enter *First Drawer.*

1. Draw. Sir, Ancient Pistol's below, and would speak with you.

Dol. Hang him, swaggering rascal! let him not come hither: it is the foul-mouth'd'st rogue in England.

Host. If he swagger, let him not come here; no, by my faith: I must live among my neighbours; I 'll no swaggerers: I am in good name and fame with the very best. Shut the door; there comes no swaggerers here: I have not lived all this while, to have swaggering now. Shut the door, I pray you.

Fal. Dost thou hear, hostess?

Host. Pray ye, pacify yourself, Sir John. There comes no swaggerers here.

Fal. Dost thou hear? It is mine ancient.

Host. Tilly-fally, Sir John, ne'er tell me; your ancient swaggerer comes not in my doors. I was before Master Tisick, the debuty, t' other day; and, as he said to me, 't was no longer ago than Wednesday last, "I' good faith, neighbour Quickly," says he; Master Dumbe, our minister, was by then; "neighbour Quickly," says he, "receive those that are civil; for," said he, "you are in an ill name." Now 'a said so, I can tell whereupon; "for," says he, "you are an honest woman, and well thought on; therefore take heed what guests you receive. Receive," says he, "no swaggering companions." There comes none here: you would bless you to hear what he said. No, I 'll no swaggerers.

Fal. He 's no swaggerer, hostess; a tame cheater, i' faith; you may stroke him as gently as a puppy greyhound: he 'll not swagger with a Barbary hen, if her feathers turn back in any show of resistance. Call him up, drawer.

Exit 1. Drawer.

Host. Cheater, call you him? I will bar no honest man my house, nor no cheater; but I do not love swaggering, by my troth. I am the worse, when one says swagger. Feel, masters, how I shake; look you, I warrant you.

Dol. So you do, hostess.

Host. Do I? yea, in very truth, do I, an 't were an aspen leaf. I cannot abide swaggerers.

Enter *Pistol, Bardolph,* and *Page.*

Pist. God save you, Sir John!

Fal. Welcome, Ancient Pistol. Here, Pistol, I charge you with a cup of sack; do you discharge upon mine hostess.

Pist. I will discharge upon her, Sir John, with two bullets.

Fal. She is pistol-proof, sir; you shall hardly offend her.

Host. Come, I 'll drink no proofs nor no bullets: I 'll drink no more than will do me good, for no man's pleasure, I.

Pist. Then to you, Mistress Dorothy; I will charge you.

Dol. Charge me! I scorn you, scurvy companion. What! you poor, base, rascally, cheating, lack-linen mate! Away, you mouldy rogue, away! I am meat for your master.

Pist. I know you, Mistress Dorothy.

Dol. Away, you cut-purse rascal! you filthy bung, away! By this wine, I 'll thrust my knife in your mouldy chaps, an you play the saucy cuttle with me. Away, you bottle-ale rascal! you basket-hilt stale juggler, you! Since when, I pray you, sir? God's light, with two points on your shoulder? Much!

Pist. God let me not live, but I will murder your ruff for this.

Fal. No more, Pistol; I would not have you go off here: discharge yourself of our company, Pistol.

Host. No, good Captain Pistol; not here, sweet captain.

Dol. Captain thou abominable damned cheater, art thou not ashamed to be called captain? An captains were of my mind, they would truncheon you out, for taking their names upon you before you have earned them. You a captain! you slave, for what? For tearing a poor whore's ruff in a bawdy-house? He a captain! Hang him, rogue! he lives upon mouldy stewed prunes and dried cakes. A cap-

61. **rheumatic,** may be for choleric. 63. **confirmities,** for infirmities. 64. **good-year,** an expletive of uncertain meaning, sometimes interpreted as equivalent to "pox," sometimes to "devil." 74. **Ancient,** ensign. 92. **debuty,** deputy. 105. **tame cheater,** gamester's decoy, with perhaps a pun on **chetah,** the hunting leopard. Quickly mistakes it for **escheator,** an officer of the exchequer.

108. **Barbary hen,** collared dove. 138. **bung,** pickpocket. 139. **chaps,** jaws. 140. **cuttle,** cut-purse. 141. **basket-hilt stale juggler,** worn-out sword trickster. 143. **point,** perhaps a sign of rank. 154. **truncheon,** beat with their staffs of office.

tain! God's light, these villains will make the word as odious as the word "occupy"; [161 which was an excellent good word before it was ill sorted; therefore captains had need look to 't.

Bard. Pray thee, go down, good ancient.

Fal. Hark thee hither, Mistress Doll. 165

Pist. Not I: I tell thee what, Corporal Bardolph, I could tear her: I 'll be reveng'd of her.

Page. Pray thee, go down.

Pist. I 'll see her damned first; to Pluto's damned lake, by this hand, to th' infernal deep, with Erebus and tortures vile also. Hold hook and line, say I. Down, down, dogs! down, faitors! Have we not Hiren here? 173

Host. Good Captain Peesel, be quiet; 't is very late, i' faith: I beseek you now, aggravate your choler.

Pist. These be good humours, indeed! Shall pack-horses
And hollow pamper'd jades of Asia,
Which cannot go but thirty mile a-day, 179
Compare with Cæsars and with Cannibals
And Troian Greeks? Nay, rather damn them with
King Cerberus, and let the welkin roar.
Shall we fall foul for toys?

Host. By my troth, captain, these are very bitter words. 185

Bard. Be gone, good ancient. This will grow to a brawl anon.

Pist. Die men like dogs! Give crowns like pins! Have we not Hiren here? 189

Host. O' my word, captain, there 's none such here. What the good-year! do you think I would deny her? For God's sake, be quiet.

Pist. Then feed, and be fat, my fair Calipolis.
Come, give 's some sack. 194
"Si fortune me tormente, sperato me contento."
Fear we broadsides? No, let the fiend give fire.
Give me some sack; and, sweetheart, lie thou there. *Laying down his sword.*
Come we to full points here; and are etceteras nothing?

Fal. Pistol, I would be quiet. 199

Pist. Sweet knight, I kiss thy neaf. What! we have seen the seven stars.

Dol. For God's sake, thrust him downstairs. I cannot endure such a fustian rascal.

Pist. Thrust him downstairs! Know we not Galloway nags? 205

Fal. Quoit him down, Bardolph, like a shove-groat shilling: nay, an 'a do nothing but speak nothing, 'a shall be nothing here.

Bard. Come, get you downstairs.

Pist. What! shall we have incision? Shall we imbrue? [*Snatching up his sword.*] 210
Then death rock me asleep, abridge my doleful days!
Why, then, let grievous, ghastly, gaping wounds
Untwine the Sisters Three! Come, Atropos, I say!

Host. Here 's goodly stuff toward! 214

Fal. Give me my rapier, boy.

Dol. I pray thee, Jack, I pray thee, do not draw.

Fal. Get you downstairs. 218

Drawing, and driving Pistol out.

Host. Here 's a goodly tumult! I 'll forswear keeping house, afore I 'll be in these tirrits and frights. So; murder, I warrant now. Alas, alas! put up your naked weapons, put up your naked weapons. 223

Exeunt Pistol and Bardolph.

Dol. I pray thee, Jack, be quiet; the rascal 's gone. Ah, you whoreson little valiant villain, you!

Host. Are you not hurt i' th' groin? Methought 'a made a shrewd thrust at your belly. 228

Re-enter *Bardolph.*

Fal. Have you turned him out o' doors?

Bard. Yea, sir; the rascal 's drunk. You have hurt him, sir, i' th' shoulder.

Fal. A rascal! to brave me! 232

Dol. Ah, you sweet little rogue, you! Alas, poor ape, how thou sweat'st! Come, let me wipe thy face. Come on, you whoreson chops. Ah, rogue! i' faith, I love thee: thou art as valorous as Hector of Troy, worth five of Agamemnon, and ten times better than the Nine Worthies. Ah, villain! 239

Fal. A rascally slave! I will toss the rogue in a blanket.

Dol. Do, an thou dar'st for thy heart. An thou dost, I 'll canvass thee between a pair of sheets. 244

161. **occupy**, because of its obscene meaning the word was out of polite usage for three centuries. 173. **faitors**, impostors. 173. **Hiren**, Irene in Peale's lost play, *Turkish Mahomet and the Fair Greek*. 175. **beseek**, for beseech. **aggravate**, for moderate. 178f. Misquoted from Marlowe's *Tamburlaine*, Pt. II, iv, 4, 1-2. 183. **toys**, trifles. 193. **Calipolis**, character in Peale's *Battle of Alcazar*. 195. **If fortune torments me, hope contents me**, a widely current motto. 198. **full points**, full stop. 200. **neaf**, fist. 201. **seven stars**, Pleiades.

203. **fustian**, nonsensical. 205. **Galloway nags**, scrubby breed of horses. 206. **Quoit**, pitch. 207. **shove-groat**, a game in which coins were shoved or thrown at marks. 210. **imbrue**, draw blood. 213. **Sisters Three**, the fates. 214. **toward**, at hand. 221. **tirrits**, for terrors. 235. **chops**, fat jaws. 238. **Nine Worthies**, Hector, Alexander, Julius Cæsar, Joshua, David, Judas Maccabeus, Arthur, Charlemagne, Godfrey of Bouillon.

Enter Music.

Page. The music is come, sir.

Fal. Let them play. Play, sirs. Sit on my knee, Doll. A rascal bragging slave! The rogue fled from me like quicksilver.

Dol. I' faith, and thou follow'dst him like a church. Thou whoreson little tidy Bartholomew boar-pig, when wilt thou leave fighting o' days and foining o' nights, and begin to patch up thine old body for heaven?

Enter behind, *Prince Henry* and *Poins,* disguised.

Fal. Peace, good Doll! do not speak like a death's-head: do not bid me remember mine end.

Dol. Sirrah, what humour 's the Prince of?

Fal. A good shallow young fellow: 'a would have made a good pantler; 'a would ha' chipped bread well.

Dol. They say Poins has a good wit.

Fal. He a good wit? Hang him, baboon! His wit 's as thick as Tewksbury mustard; there 's no more conceit in him than is in a mallet.

Dol. Why does the Prince love him so, then?

Fal. Because their legs are both of a bigness, and 'a plays at quoits well, and eats conger and fennel, and drinks off candles' ends for flap-dragons, and rides the wild-mare with the boys, and jumps upon joined stools, and swears with a good grace, and wears his boots very smooth, like unto the sign of The Leg, and breeds no bate with telling of discreet stories; and such other gambol faculties 'a has, that show a weak mind and an able body, for the which the Prince admits him: for the Prince himself is such another; the weight of a hair will turn the scales between their avoirdupois.

Prince. Would not this nave of a wheel have his ears cut off?

Poins. Let 's beat him before his whore.

Prince. Look, whe'er the withered elder hath not his poll clawed like a parrot.

Poins. Is it not strange that desire should so many years outlive performance?

Fal. Kiss me, Doll.

Prince. Saturn and Venus this year in conjunction! What says th' almanac to that?

Poins. And, look, whether the fiery Trigon, his man, be not lisping to his master's old tables, his note-book, his counsel-keeper.

Fal. Thou dost give me flattering busses.

Dol. By my troth, I kiss thee with a most constant heart.

Fal. I am old, I am old.

Dol. I love thee better than I love e'er a scurvy young boy of them all.

Fal. What stuff wilt have a kirtle of? I shall receive money o' Thursday: shalt have a cap to-morrow. A merry song, come! It grows late; we 'll to bed. Thou 't forget me when I am gone.

Dol. By my troth, thou 't set me a-weeping, an thou say'st so: prove that ever I dress myself handsome till thy return. Well, hearken at the end.

Fal. Some sack, Francis.

Prince. } *Poins.* } Anon, anon, sir.

Coming forward.

Fal. Ha! a bastard son of the King's? And art not thou Poins his brother?

Prince. Why, thou globe of sinful continents, what a life dost thou lead!

Fal. A better than thou: I am a gentleman; thou art a drawer.

Prince. Very true, sir; and I come to draw you out by the ears.

Host. O, the Lord preserve thy Grace! By my troth, welcome to London. Now, the Lord bless that sweet face of thine! O Jesu, are you come from Wales?

Fal. Thou whoreson mad compound of majesty, by this light flesh and corrupt blood, thou art welcome.

Dol. How, you fat fool! I scorn you.

Poins. My lord, he will drive you out of your revenge and turn all to a merriment, if you take not the heat.

Prince. You whoreson candle-mine, you, how vilely did you speak of me even now before this honest, virtuous, civil gentlewoman!

Host. God's blessing of your good heart! and so she is, by my troth.

Fal. Didst thou hear me?

Prince. Yea, and you knew me, as you did when you ran away by Gadshill: you knew I was at your back, and spoke it on purpose to try my patience.

Fal. No, no, no; not so; I did not think thou wast within hearing.

Prince. I shall drive you then to confess the wilful abuse, and then I know how to handle you.

250. Bartholomew boar-pig, roast pig was served on St. Bartholomew's Day. **258. pantler,** servant in the pantry. **262. conceit,** wit. **268. flap-dragons,** raisins snapped out of burning brandy in the game of snapdragon. **wild-mare,** see-saw. **269. join'd stools,** made by joiner. **272. bate,** quarrel. **273. gambol,** sportive. **278. nave,** (1) hub (round). (2) knave. **288. fiery Trigon,** Bardolph, the fiery division (trigon) of the zodiac included: Aries, Leo, Sagittarius.

289. lisping, i.e., making love. **290. tables,** account book, i.e., the hostess. **291. busses,** kisses. **297. kirtle,** skirt. **304. hearken at,** judge. **325. take . . . the heat,** strike not while the iron is hot. **326. candle-mine,** mine of tallow.

Fal. No abuse, Hal, o' mine honour; no abuse.

Prince. Not to dispraise me, and call me pantler and bread-chipper and I know not what?

Fal. No abuse, Hal.

Poins. No abuse?

Fal. No abuse, Ned, i' th' world; honest Ned, none. I dispraised him before the wicked, that the wicked might not fall in love with him; in which doing, I have done the part of a careful friend and a true subject, and thy father is to give me thanks for it. No abuse, Hal; none, Ned, none; no, faith, boys, none.

Prince. See now, whether pure fear and entire cowardice doth not make thee wrong this virtuous gentlewoman to close with us? Is she of the wicked? Is thine hostess here of the wicked? Or is thy boy of the wicked? Or honest Bardolph, whose zeal burns in his nose, of the wicked?

Poins. Answer, thou dead elm, answer.

Fal. The fiend hath pricked down Bardolph irrecoverable; and his face is Lucifer's privy-kitchen, where he doth nothing but roast malt-worms. For the boy, there is a good angel about him; but the devil blinds him too.

Prince. For the women?

Fal. For one of them, she is in hell already, and burns poor souls. For th' other, I owe her money; and whether she be damned for that, I know not.

Host. No, I warrant you.

Fal. No, I think thou art not; I think thou art quit for that. Marry, there is another indictment upon thee, for suffering flesh to be eaten in thy house, contrary to the law; for the which I think thou wilt howl.

Host. All victuallers do so: what 's a joint of mutton or two in a whole Lent?

Prince. You, gentlewoman,—

Dol. What says your Grace?

Fal. His grace says that which his flesh rebels against. *Peto knocks at door.*

Host. Who knocks so loud at door? Look to the door there, Francis.

Enter *Peto.*

Prince. Peto, how now! what news?

Peto. The King your father is at Westminster;
And there are twenty weak and wearied posts
Come from the north; and, as I came along,
I met and overtook a dozen captains,
Bare-headed, sweating, knocking at the taverns,
And asking every one for Sir John Falstaff.

Prince. By heaven, Poins, I feel me much to blame,
So idly to profane the precious time,
When tempest of commotion, like the south
Borne with black vapour, doth begin to melt
And drop upon our bare unarmed heads.
Give me my sword and cloak. Falstaff, good night.

Exeunt Prince Henry, Poins, and Peto.

Fal. Now comes in the sweetest morsel of the night, and we must hence and leave it unpicked. [*Knocking within.*] More knocking at the door! How now! what 's the matter?

Bard. You must away to court, sir, presently;
A dozen captains stay at door for you.

Fal. Pay the musicians, sirrah. Farewell, hostess; farewell, Doll. You see, my good wenches, how men of merit are sought after: the undeserver may sleep, when the man of action is called on. Farewell, good wenches; if I be not sent away post, I will see you again ere I go.

Dol. I cannot speak: if my heart be not ready to burst,—well, sweet Jack, have a care of thyself.

Fal. Farewell, farewell.

Exeunt Falstaff and Bardolph.

Host. Well, fare thee well: I have known thee these twenty-nine years, come peascod-time; but an honester and truer-hearted man,—well, fare thee well.

Bard. [*Within.*] Mistress Tearsheet!

Host. What 's the matter?

Bard. [*Within.*] Bid Mistress Tearsheet come to my master.

Host. O, run, Doll, run; run, good Doll. Come. She comes blubbered. Yea, will you come, Doll? *Exeunt.*

354. **close,** make peace. 359. **pricked,** marked. 362. **malt-worms,** topers. 363. **blinds,** i.e., in spite of the boy's good angel the devil blinds and misleads him.

392. **south,** south wind. 393. **Borne,** laden. 400. Bardolph has got the message from the knocker at the door. In l. 403 Falstaff bids him pay the musicians, cf. *I K. H. IV.* IV, ii, 5. 408. **post,** in haste. 420. The words "She comes blubbered" (i.e., in tears) have been restored to the text where they appear in the first edition; modern editors treat them as a stage direction. It seems clear that the Hostess calls to Bardolph to say that Doll is coming in tears.

ACT III. Scene I. *Westminster. The palace.*

Enter the *King* in his nightgown, with a *Page.*

King. Go call the Earls of Surrey and of Warwick;
But, ere they come, bid them o'er-read these letters,
And well consider of them: make good speed.
Exit Page.
How many thousand of my poorest subjects
Are at this hour asleep! O Sleep, O gentle Sleep,
Nature's soft nurse, how have I frighted thee,
That thou no more wilt weigh my eyelids down
And steep my senses in forgetfulness?
Why rather, Sleep, liest thou in smoky cribs,
Upon uneasy pallets stretching thee,
And hush'd with buzzing night-flies to thy slumber,
Than in the perfum'd chambers of the great,
Under the canopies of costly state,
And lull'd with sound of sweetest melody?
O thou dull god, why liest thou with the vile
In loathsome beds, and leav'st the kingly couch
A watch-case or a common 'larum-bell?
Wilt thou upon the high and giddy mast
Seal up the ship-boy's eyes, and rock his brains
In cradle of the rude imperious surge
And in the visitation of the winds,
Who take the ruffian billows by the top,
Curling their monstrous heads and hanging them
With deafening clamour in the slippery clouds,
That, with the hurly, death itself awakes?
Canst thou, O partial Sleep, give thy repose
To the wet sea-boy in an hour so rude,
And in the calmest and most stillest night,
With all appliances and means to boot,
Deny it to a king? Then happy low, lie down!
Uneasy lies the head that wears a crown.

Enter *Warwick* and *Surrey.*

War. Many good morrows to your Majesty!
King. Is it good morrow, lords?
War. 'T is one o'clock, and past.
King. Why, then, good morrow to you all, my lords.
Have you read o'er the letters that I sent you?
War. We have, my liege.
King. Then you perceive the body of our kingdom
How foul it is; what rank diseases grow,
And with what danger, near the heart of it.
War. It is but as a body yet distemper'd;
Which to his former strength may be restor'd
With good advice and little medicine.
My Lord Northumberland will soon be cool'd.
King. O God! that one might read the book of fate,
And see the revolution of the times
Make mountains level, and the continent,
Weary of solid firmness, melt itself
Into the sea! and, other times, to see
The beachy girdle of the ocean
Too wide for Neptune's hips; how chances mock,
And changes fill the cup of alteration
With divers liquors! O, if this were seen,
The happiest youth, viewing his progress through,
What perils past, what crosses to ensue,
Would shut the book, and sit him down and die.
'T is not ten years gone
Since Richard and Northumberland, great friends,
Did feast together, and in two years after
Were they at wars. It is but eight years since
This Percy was the man nearest my soul,
Who like a brother toil'd in my affairs
And laid his love and life under my foot;
Yea, for my sake, even to the eyes of Richard
Gave him defiance. But which of you was by—
You, cousin Nevil, as I may remember—
To Warwick.
When Richard, with his eye brimful of tears,
Then check'd and rated by Northumberland,
Did speak these words, now prov'd a prophecy?
"Northumberland, thou ladder by the which
My cousin Bolingbroke ascends my throne,—"
Though then, God knows, I had no such intent,
But that necessity so bow'd the state
That I and greatness were compell'd to kiss;—
"The time shall come," thus did he follow it,
"The time will come, that foul sin, gathering head,
Shall break into corruption:" so went on,
Foretelling this same time's condition
And the division of our amity.
War. There is a history in all men's lives,
Figuring the nature of the times deceas'd;
The which observ'd, a man may prophesy,

Act III, Scene i: S. d. nightgown, dressing gown. **9. cribs,** hovels. **17. watch-case,** sentry-box.

70. *Rich. II*, **V, i, 55ff. 81. Figuring,** symbolizing.

With a near aim, of the main chance of things
As yet not come to life, who in their seeds
And weak beginnings lie intreasured.
Such things become the hatch and brood of time;
And by the necessary form of this
King Richard might create a perfect guess
That great Northumberland, then false to him,
Would of that seed grow to a greater falseness;
Which should not find a ground to root upon,
Unless on you.

King. Are these things then necessities?
Then let us meet them like necessities.
And that same word even now cries out on us.
They say the Bishop and Northumberland
Are fifty thousand strong.

War. It cannot be, my lord.
Rumour doth double, like the voice and echo,
The numbers of the feared. Please it your Grace
To go to bed. Upon my soul, my lord,
The powers that you already have sent forth
Shall bring this prize in very easily.
To comfort you the more, I have receiv'd
A certain instance that Glendower is dead.
Your Majesty hath been this fortnight ill,
And these unseason'd hours perforce must add
Unto your sickness.

King. I will take your counsel:
And were these inward wars once out of hand,
We would, dear lords, unto the Holy Land.
Exeunt.

Scene II. *Gloucestershire. Before Justice Shallow's house.*

Enter *Shallow* and *Silence* meeting; *Mouldy, Shadow, Wart, Feeble, Bullcalf,* a Servant or two with them.

Shal. Come on, come on, come on, sir; give me your hand, sir, give me your hand, sir: an early stirrer, by the rood! And how doth my good cousin Silence?

Sil. Good morrow, good cousin Shallow.

Shal. And how doth my cousin, your bedfellow? and your fairest daughter and mine, my god-daughter Ellen?

Sil. Alas, a black ousel, cousin Shallow!

Shal. By yea and no, sir, I dare say my cousin William is become a good scholar: he is at Oxford still, is he not?

Sil. Indeed, sir, to my cost.

Shal. 'A must, then, to the Inns o' Court shortly. I was once of Clement's Inn, where I think they will talk of mad Shallow yet.

Sil. You were called lusty Shallow then, cousin.

Shal. By the mass, I was called anything; and I would have done anything indeed too, and roundly too. There was I, and little John Doit of Staffordshire, and black George Barnes, and Francis Pickbone, and Will Squele, a Cotsol man: you had not four such swinge-bucklers in all the Inns o' Court again; and I may say to you, we knew where the bona-robas were and had the best of them all at commandment. Then was Jack Falstaff, now Sir John, a boy, and page to Thomas Mowbray, Duke of Norfolk.

Sil. Cousin, this Sir John that comes hither anon about soldiers?

Shal. The same Sir John, the very same. I see him break Skogan's head at the court-gate, when 'a was a crack not thus high; and the very same day did I fight with one Sampson Stockfish, a fruiterer, behind Gray's Inn. Jesu, Jesu, the mad days that I have spent! And to see how many of my old acquaintance are dead!

Sil. We shall all follow, cousin.

Shal. Certain, 't is certain; very sure, very sure: death, as the Psalmist saith, is certain to all; all shall die. How a good yoke of bullocks at Stamford fair?

Sil. By my troth, I was not there.

Shal. Death is certain. Is old Double of your town living yet?

Sil Dead, sir.

Shal. Jesu, Jesu, dead! 'A drew a good bow; and dead! 'A shot a fine shoot. John o' Gaunt loved him well, and betted much money on his head. Dead! 'a would have clapped i' th' clout at twelve score; and carried you a forehand shaft at fourteen and fourteen and a half, that it would have done a man's heart good to see. How a score of ewes now?

Sil. Thereafter as they be; a score of good ewes may be worth ten pounds.

Shal. And is old Double dead?

Sil. Here come two of Sir John Falstaff's men, as I think.

85. **intreasured,** stored up. 87. **necessary form,** logical necessity. 103. **instance,** proof. 105. **unseason'd,** unseasonable. **Scene ii: 3. rood,** cross. 9. **ousel,** blackbird.

15. **Clement's Inn,** one of the inns of court (colleges of law) at London. 25. **swinge-bucklers,** roisterers. 27. **bona-robas,** showily dressed harlots. 33. **Skogan's,** possibly the John Skogan who was court jester to Ed. IV. 34. **crack,** pert young boy. 42. **How,** how much. 51-2. **clapped, . . . score,** hit the bull's eye at twelve score yards. 53. **forehand shaft,** arrow for shooting straight ahead.

Enter *Bardolph* and one with him.

Good morrow, honest gentlemen.

Bard. I beseech you, which is Justice Shallow?

Shal. I am Robert Shallow, sir; a poor esquire of this county, and one of the King's justices of the peace. What is your good pleasure with me?

Bard. My captain, sir, commends him to you; my captain, Sir John Falstaff, a tall gentleman, by heaven, and a most gallant leader.

Shal. He greets me well, sir, I knew him a good backsword man. How doth the good knight? May I ask how my lady his wife doth?

Bard. Sir, pardon; a soldier is better accommodated than with a wife.

Shal. It is well said, in faith, sir; and it is well said indeed too. Better accommodated! it is good; yea, indeed, is it: good phrases are surely, and ever were, very commendable. Accommodated! it comes of *accommodo:* very good; a good phrase.

Bard. Pardon me, sir; I have heard the word. Phrase call you it? By this good day, I know not the phrase; but I will maintain the word with my sword to be a soldier-like word, and a word of exceeding good command, by heaven. Accommodated; that is, when a man is, as they say, accommodated; or when a man is, being, whereby 'a may be thought to be accommodated; which is an excellent thing.

Enter *Sir John Falstaff.*

Shal. It is very just. Look, here comes good Sir John. Give me your good hand, give me your worship's good hand. By my troth, you like well and bear your years very well: welcome, good Sir John.

Fal. I am glad to see you well, good Master Robert Shallow. Master Surecard, as I think?

Shal. No, Sir John; it is my cousin Silence in commission with me.

Fal. Good Master Silence, it well befits you should be of the peace.

Sil. Your good worship is welcome.

Fal. Fie! this is hot weather, gentlemen. Have you provided me here half a dozen sufficient men?

Shal. Marry, have we, sir. Will you sit?

Fal. Let me see them, I beseech you.

Shal. Where 's the roll? where 's the roll? where 's the roll? Let me see, let me see, let me see. So, so, so, so, so, so, so; yea, marry, sir. Ralph Mouldy! Let them appear as I call; let them do so, let them do so. Let me see; where is Mouldy?

Moul. Here, an it please you.

Shal. What think you, Sir John? A good-limbed fellow; young, strong, and of good friends.

Fal. Is thy name Mouldy?

Moul. Yea, an 't please you.

Fal. 'T is the more time thou wert used.

Shal. Ha, ha, ha! most excellent, i' faith! Things that are mouldy lack use. Very singular good! In faith, well said, Sir John, very well said.

Fal. Prick him.

Moul. I was pricked well enough before, an you could have let me alone: my old dame will be undone now for one to do her husbandry and her drudgery: you need not to have pricked me; there are other men fitter to go out than I.

Fal. Go to; peace, Mouldy; you shall go. Mouldy, it is time you were spent.

Moul. Spent!

Shal. Peace, fellow, peace; stand aside; know you where you are? For th' other, Sir John, let me see. Simon Shadow!

Fal. Yea, marry, let me have him to sit under; he 's like to be a cold soldier.

Shal. Where 's Shadow?

Shad. Here, sir.

Fal. Shadow, whose son art thou?

Shad. My mother's son, sir.

Fal. Thy mother's son; like enough, and thy father's shadow. So the son of the female is the shadow of the male: it is often so, indeed; but much of the father's substance!

Shal. Do you like him, Sir John?

Fal. Shadow will serve for summer: prick him, for we have a number of shadows to fill up the muster-book.

Shal. Thomas Wart!

Fal. Where 's he?

Wart. Here, sir.

Fal. Is thy name Wart?

Wart. Yea, sir.

Fal. Thou art a very ragged wart.

Shal. Shall I prick him, Sir John?

Fal. It were superfluous; for his apparel is built upon his back and the whole frame stands upon pins: prick him no more.

Shal. Ha, ha, ha! you can do it, sir; you can do it; I commend you well. Francis Feeble!

Fee. Here, sir.

Fal. What trade art thou, Feeble?

Fee. A woman's tailor, sir.

Shal. Shall I prick him, sir?

Fal. You may; but if he had been a man's

67. tall, brave. **70. backsword man,** single-stick fencer. **72. accommodated,** furnished, an affected, "holiday" term. **92. like,** thrive. **97. commission,** office. **102. sufficient,** fit.

145. shadows, false entries on the muster roll.

tailor, he 'd 'a' pricked you. Wilt thou make as many holes in an enemy's battle as thou hast done in a woman's petticoat?

Fee. I will do my good will, sir; you can have no more.

Fal. Well said, good woman's tailor! well said, courageous Feeble! Thou wilt be as valiant as the wrathful dove or most magnanimous mouse. Prick the woman's tailor well, Master Shallow; deep, Master Shallow.

Fee. I would Wart might have gone, sir.

Fal. I would thou wert a man's tailor, that thou mightst mend him and make him fit to go. I cannot put him to a private soldier that is the leader of so many thousands: let that suffice, most forcible Feeble.

Fee. It shall suffice, sir.

Fal. I am bound to thee, reverend Feeble. Who is next?

Shal. Peter Bullcalf o' th' green!

Fal. Yea, marry, let 's see Bullcalf.

Bull. Here, sir.

Fal. 'Fore God, a likely fellow! Come, prick me Bullcalf till he roar again.

Bull. O Lord! good my lord captain,—

Fal. What, dost thou roar before thou art pricked?

Bull. O Lord, sir! I am a diseased man.

Fal. What disease hast thou?

Bull. A whoreson cold, sir, a cough, sir, which I caught with ringing in the King's affairs upon his coronation-day, sir.

Fal. Come, thou shalt go to the wars in a gown. We will have away thy cold; and I will take such order that thy friends shall ring for thee. Is here all?

Shal. Here is two more called than your number; you must have but four here, sir: and so, I pray you, go in with me to dinner.

Fal. Come, I will go drink with you, but I cannot tarry dinner. I am glad to see you, by my troth, Master Shallow.

Shal. O, Sir John, do you remember since we lay all night in the windmill in Saint George's field?

Fal. No more of that, good Master Shallow, no more of that.

Shal. Ha! 't was a merry night. And is Jane Nightwork alive?

Fal. She lives, Master Shallow.

Shal. She never could away with me.

Fal. Never, never; she would always say she could not abide Master Shallow.

Shal. By the mass, I could anger her to th' heart. She was then a bona-roba. Doth she hold her own well?

Fal. Old, old, Master Shallow.

Shal. Nay, she must be old; she cannot choose but be old; certain she 's old; and had Robin Nightwork by old Nightwork before I came to Clement's Inn.

Sil. That 's fifty-five year ago.

Shal. Ha, cousin Silence, that thou hadst seen that that this knight and I have seen! Ha, Sir John, said I well?

Fal. We have heard the chimes at midnight, Master Shallow.

Shal. That we have, that we have, that we have; in faith, Sir John, we have. Our watchword was "Hem, boys!" Come, let 's to dinner; come, let 's to dinner. Jesu, the days that we have seen! Come, come.

Exeunt Falstaff and the Justices.

Bull. Good Master Corporate Bardolph, stand my friend; and here 's four Harry ten shillings in French crowns for you. In very truth, sir, I had as lief be hanged sir, as go; and yet for mine own part, sir, I do not care; but rather, because I am unwilling, and, for mine own part, have a desire to stay with my friends; else, sir, I did not care, for mine own part, so much.

Bard. Go to; stand aside.

Moul. And, good master corporal captain, for my old dame's sake, stand my friend: she has nobody to do anything about her when I am gone; and she is old, and cannot help herself. You shall have forty, sir.

Bard. Go to; stand aside.

Fee. By my troth, I care not; a man can die but once; we owe God a death. I 'll ne'er bear a base mind: an 't be my destiny, so; an 't be not, so: no man 's too good to serve 's prince; and let it go which way it will, he that dies this year is quit for the next.

Bard. Well said; th' art a good fellow.

Fee. Faith, I 'll bear no base mind.

Re-enter *Falstaff* and the *Justices.*

Fal. Come, sir, which men shall I have?

Shal. Four of which you please.

Bard. [*Aside to Fal.*] Sir, a word with you. I have three pound to free Mouldy and Bullcalf.

Fal. Go to; well.

Shal. Come, Sir John, which four will you have?

Fal. Do you choose for me.

Shal. Marry, then, Mouldy, Bullcalf, Feeble, and Shadow.

Fal. Mouldy and Bullcalf! for you, Mouldy, stay at home till you are past service; and for your part, Bullcalf, grow till you come unto it. I will none of you.

165. battle, army. **178. thousands**, i.e., of vermin.

236. four . . . crowns, the equivalent in French crowns of four King Henry's 10-shilling pieces. As a matter of fact the first coinage of such pieces was in Henry VII's reign. **255. quit for**, exempt.

Shal. Sir John, Sir John, do not yourself wrong: they are your likeliest men, and I would have you served with the best.

Fal. Will you tell me, Master Shallow, how to choose a man? Care I for the limb, the thews, the stature, bulk, and big assemblance of a man! Give me the spirit, Master Shallow. Here 's Wart; you see what a ragged appearance it is: 'a shall charge you and discharge you with the motion of a pewterer's hammer, come off and on swifter than he that gibbets on the brewer's bucket. And this same half-faced fellow, Shadow; give me this man: he presents no mark to the enemy; the foeman may with as great aim level at the edge of a penknife. And for a retreat; how swiftly will this Feeble the woman's tailor run off! O, give me the spare men, and spare me the great ones. Put me a caliver into Wart's hand, Bardolph.

Bard. Hold, Wart, traverse; thus, thus, thus.

Fal. Come, manage me your caliver. So: very well; go to; very good, exceeding good. O, give me always a little, lean, old chapt, bald shot. Well said, i' faith, Wart; thou 'rt a good scab. Hold, there 's a tester for thee.

Shal. He is not his craft's master; he doth not do it right. I remember at Mile-end Green, when I lay at Clement's Inn,—I was then Sir Dagonet in Arthur's show,—there was a little quiver fellow, and 'a would manage you his piece thus; and 'a would about and about, and come you in and come you in. "Rah, tah, tah," would 'a say; "bounce" would 'a say; and away again would 'a go, and again would 'a come: I shall ne'er see such a fellow.

Fal. These fellows will do well, Master Shallow. God keep you, Master Silence; I will not use many words with you. Fare you well, gentlemen both; I thank you: I must a dozen mile to-night. Bardolph, give the soldiers coats.

Shal. Sir John, the Lord bless you! God prosper your affairs! God send us peace! At your return visit our house; let our old acquaintance be renewed: peradventure I will with ye to the court.

Fal. 'Fore God, would you would, Master Shallow.

Shal. Go to; I have spoke at a word. God keep you!

Fal. Fare you well, gentle gentlemen. [*Exeunt Justices.*] On, Bardolph; lead the men away. [*Exeunt Bardolph, recruits, etc.*] As I return, I will fetch off these justices. I do see the bottom of Justice Shallow. Lord, Lord, how subject we old men are to this vice of lying! This same starved justice hath done nothing but prate to me of the wildness of his youth, and the feats he hath done about Turnbull Street; and every third word a lie, duer paid to the hearer than the Turk's tribute. I do remember him at Clement's Inn like a man made after supper of a cheese-paring: when 'a was naked, he was, for all the world, like a forked radish, with a head fantastically carv'd upon it with a knife: 'a was so forlorn, that his dimensions to any thick sight were invincible: 'a was the very genius of famine, yet lecherous as a monkey, and the whores called him mandrake: 'a came ever in the rearward of the fashion, and sung those tunes to the overscutched huswives that he heard the carmen whistle, and sware they were his fancies or his good-nights. And now is this Vice's dagger become a squire, and talks as familiarly of John o' Gaunt as if he had been sworn brother to him; and I 'll be sworn 'a ne'er saw him but once in the Tilt-yard; and then he burst his head for crowding among the marshal's men. I saw it, and told John o' Gaunt he beat his own name; for you might have thrust him and all his apparel into an eel-skin: the case of a treble hautboy was a mansion for him, a court; and now has he land and beeves. Well, I 'll be acquainted with him, if I return; and it shall go hard but I will make him a philosopher's two stones to me. If the young dace be a bait for the old pike, I see no reason in the law of nature but I may snap at him. Let time shape, and there an end. *Exit.*

277. **assemblance**, appearance. 282. **gibbets on**, swing onto the gibbet or yoke for carrying buckets. 289. **caliver**, light musket. 291. **traverse**, march. 295. **shot**, marksman. 296. **scab**, term of contempt. **tester**, sixpence. 300. **Arthur's show**, annual archery exhibiton at Mile-end Green. Each of the 58 members of the club took names of Arthurian characters. Shallow was the fool, Sir Dagonet. 301. **quiver**, nimble.

319. **at a word**, briefly. 324. **fetch off**, fleece. 330. **duer**, more duly. 338. **invincible**, not to be made out. 341. **overscutched huswives**, worn-out prostitutes. 342. **carmen**, teamsters. 343. **fancies . . . goodnights**, common names for light lyrics. 344. **Vice's dagger**, The Vice, comic character in the morality plays, carried a thin wooden dagger. 352. **hautboy**, oboe. 356. **philosopher's two stones**, twice the power of the one stone that was supposed to transmute base metals into gold.

ACT IV. Scene I. *Yorkshire. The Forest of Gaultree.*

Enter the *Archbishop of York, Mowbray, Hastings* and others.

Arch. What is this forest call'd?
Hast. 'T is Gaultree Forest, an 't shall please your Grace.
Arch. Here stand, my lords; and send discoverers forth
To know the numbers of our enemies.
Hast. We have sent forth already.
Arch. 'T is well done.
My friends and brethren in these great affairs,
I must acquaint you that I have receiv'd
New-dated letters from Northumberland;
Their cold intent, tenour, and substance, thus:
Here doth he wish his person, with such powers
As might hold sortance with his quality.
The which he could not levy; whereupon
He is retir'd, to ripe his growing fortunes,
To Scotland; and concludes in hearty prayers
That your attempts may overlive the hazard
And fearful meeting of their opposite.
Mowb. Thus do the hopes we have in him touch ground
And dash themselves to pieces.

Enter a *Messenger.*

Hast. Now, what news?
Mess. West of this forest, scarcely off a mile,
In goodly form comes on the enemy;
And, by the ground they hide, I judge their number
Upon or near the rate of thirty thousand.
Mowb. The just proportion that we gave them out.
Let us sway on and face them in the field.
Arch. What well-appointed leader fronts us here?

Enter *Westmoreland.*

Mowb. I think it is my Lord of Westmoreland.
West. Health and fair greeting from our general,
The Prince, Lord John and Duke of Lancaster.
Arch. Say on, my Lord of Westmoreland, in peace,
What doth concern your coming.
West. Then, my lord,
Unto your Grace do I in chief address
The substance of my speech. If that rebellion
Came like itself, in base and abject routs,
Led on by bloody youth, guarded with rags,
And countenanc'd by boys and beggary,—
I say, if damn'd commotion so appear'd,
In his true, native, and most proper shape,
You, reverend father, and these noble lords
Had not been here, to dress the ugly form
Of base and bloody insurrection
With your fair honours. You, Lord Archbishop,
Whose see is by a civil peace maintain'd,
Whose beard the silver hand of peace hath touch'd,
Whose learning and good letters peace hath tutor'd,
Whose white investments figure innocence,
The dove, and very blessed spirit of peace,
Wherefore do you so ill translate yourself
Out of the speech of peace that bears such grace,
Into the harsh and boist'rous tongue of war;
Turning your books to graves, your ink to blood,
Your pens to lances and your tongue divine
To a loud trumpet and a point of war?
Arch. Wherefore do I this? so the question stands.
Briefly to this end: we are all diseas'd,
And with our surfeiting and wanton hours
Have brought ourselves into a burning fever,
And we must bleed for it; of which disease
Our late king, Richard, being infected, died.
But, my most noble Lord of Westmoreland,
I take not on me here as a physician,
Nor do I as an enemy to peace
Troop in the throngs of military men;
But rather show awhile like fearful war
To diet rank minds sick of happiness,
And purge th' obstructions which begin to stop
Our very veins of life. Hear me more plainly.
I have in equal balance justly weigh'd
What wrongs our arms may do, what wrongs we suffer,
And find our griefs heavier than our offences.
We see which way the stream of time doth run,
And are enforc'd from our most quiet there
By the rough torrent of occasion;
And have the summary of all our griefs,
When time shall serve, to show in articles;
Which long ere this we offer'd to the King,
And might by no suit gain our audience:

Act IV, Scene i: 11. hold sortance, accord. **15. overlive,** outlive. **23. just proportion,** exact size.

33. routs, mobs. **34. bloody,** passionate. **guarded,** decked. **52. point,** trumpet signal. **69. griefs,** grievances.

When we are wrong'd and would unfold our griefs,
We are denied access unto his person
Even by those men that most have done us wrong.
The dangers of the days but newly gone,
Whose memory is written on the earth
With yet appearing blood, and the examples
Of every minute's instance, present now,
Hath put us in these ill-beseeming arms,
Not to break peace or any branch of it,
But to establish here a peace indeed,
Concurring both in name and quality.

West. When ever yet was your appeal denied?
Wherein have you been galled by the King?
What peer hath been suborn'd to grate on you,
That you should seal this lawless bloody book
Of forg'd rebellion with a seal divine
And consecrate commotion's bitter edge?

Arch. My brother general, the commonwealth,
To brother born an household cruelty.
I make my quarrel in particular.

West. There is no need of any such redress;
Or if there were, it not belongs to you.

Mowb. Why not to him in part, and to us all
That feel the bruises of the days before,
And suffer the condition of these times
To lay a heavy and unequal hand
Upon our honours?

West. O, my good Lord Mowbray,
Construe the times to their necessities,
And you shall say indeed, it is the time,
And not the King, that doth you injuries.
Yet for your part, it not appears to me
Either from the King or in the present time
That you should have an inch of any ground
To build a grief on: were you not restor'd
To all the Duke of Norfolk's signories,
Your noble and right well-remember'd father's?

Mowb. What thing, in honour, had my father lost,
That need to be reviv'd and breath'd in me?
The King that lov'd him, as the state stood then,
Was, force perforce, compell'd to banish him;
And then that Henry Bolingbroke and he,
Being mounted and both roused in their seats,
Their neighing coursers daring of the spur,
Their armed staves in charge, their beavers down,
Their eyes of fire sparkling through sights of steel,
And the loud trumpet blowing them together,
Then, then, when there was nothing could have stay'd
My father from the breast of Bolingbroke,
O, when the King did throw his warder down—
His own life hung upon the staff he threw,—
Then threw he down himself and all their lives
That by indictment and by dint of sword
Have since miscarried under Bolingbroke.

West. You speak, Lord Mowbray, now you know not what.
The Earl of Hereford was reputed then
In England the most valiant gentleman.
Who knows on whom Fortune would then have smil'd?
But if your father had been victor there,
He ne'er had borne it out of Coventry;
For all the country in a general voice
Cried hate upon him; and all their prayers and love
Were set on Hereford, whom they doted on
And bless'd and grac'd, indeed, more than the King,—
But this is mere digression from my purpose.
Here come I from our princely general
To know our griefs; to tell you from his Grace
That he will give you audience; and wherein
It shall appear that your demands are just,
You shall enjoy them, everything set off
That might so much as think you enemies.

Mowb. But he hath forc'd us to compel this offer;
And it proceeds from policy, not love.

West. Mowbray, you overween to take it so;
This offer comes from mercy, not from fear.
For, lo! within a ken our army lies,
Upon mine honour, all too confident
To give admittance to a thought of fear.
Our battle is more full of names than yours,
Our men more perfect in the use of arms,
Our armour all as strong, our cause the best;
Then reason will our hearts should be as good.
Say you not then our offer is compell'd.

Mowb. Well, by my will we shall admit no parley.

West. That argues but the shame of your offence.
A rotten case abides no handling.

Hast. Hath the Prince John a full commission,
In very ample virtue of his father,
To hear and absolutely to determine

94-6. Passage obviously corrupt. It is possible, however, that he refers both to his private quarrel with the king (his brother, Lord Scroop, was beheaded by Henry) and to his quarrel on behalf of the commonwealth. **104. to,** according to. **114. breath'd,** endowed with breath. **115ff.** Cf. *R. II*, I, iii. **120. armed . . . charge,** lances in rest. **beavers,** visors.

125. warder, staff. **129. miscarried,** perished. **131. Hereford,** i.e. Bolingbroke. **145. set off,** ignored. **149. overween,** are presumptuous. **151. within a ken,** within sight. **163. virtue,** authority.

Of what conditions we shall stand upon?
West. That is intended in the general's name.
I muse you make so slight a question.
Arch. Then take, my Lord of Westmoreland, this schedule,
For this contains our general grievances:
Each several article herein redress'd,
All members of our cause, both here and hence,
That are insinewed to this action,
Acquitted by a true substantial form
And present execution of our wills
To us and to our purposes confin'd,
We come within our awful banks again
And knit our powers to the arm of peace.
West. This will I show the general. Please you, lords,
In sight of both our battles we may meet;
And either end in peace, which God so frame!
Or to the place of difference call the swords
Which must decide it. *Exit Westmoreland.*
Arch. My lord, we will do so.
Mowb. There is a thing within my bosom tells me
That no conditions of our peace can stand.
Hast. Fear you not that: if we can make our peace
Upon such large terms and so absolute
As our conditions shall consist upon,
Our peace shall stand as firm as rocky mountains.
Mowb. Yea, but our valuation shall be such
That every slight and false-derived cause,
Yea, every idle, nice, and wanton reason
Shall to the King taste of this action;
That, were our royal faiths martyrs in love,
We shall be winnow'd with so rough a wind
That even our corn shall seem as light as chaff
And good from bad find no partition.
Arch. No, no, my lord. Note this: the King is weary
Of dainty and such picking grievances;
For he hath found to end one doubt by death
Revives two greater in the heirs of life,
And therefore will he wipe his tables clean
And keep no tell-tale to his memory
That may repeat and history his loss
To new remembrance; for full well he knows
He cannot so precisely weed this land
As his misdoubts present occasion.
His foes are so enrooted with his friends
That, plucking to unfix an enemy,
He doth unfasten so and shake a friend;
So that this land, like an offensive wife
That hath enrag'd him on to offer strokes,
As he is striking, holds his infant up
And hangs resolv'd correction in the arm
That was uprear'd to execution.
Hast. Besides, the King hath wasted all his rods
On late offenders, that he now doth lack
The very instruments of chastisement;
So that his power, like to a fangless lion,
May offer, but not hold.
Arch. 'T is very true;
And therefore be assur'd, my good Lord Marshal,
If we do now make our atonement well,
Our peace will, like a broken limb united,
Grow stronger for the breaking.
Mowb. Be it so.
Here is return'd my Lord of Westmoreland.

Re-enter *Westmoreland.*

West. The Prince is here at hand. Pleaseth your lordship
To meet his Grace just distance 'tween our armies.
Mowb. Your Grace of York, in God's name, then, set forward.
Arch. Before, and greet his Grace, my lord. We come. *Exeunt.*

Scene II. *Another part of the forest.*

Enter *Prince John of Lancaster* and *Westmoreland,* meeting the *Archbishop, Mowbray, Hastings,* and Officers.

Lan. You are well encounter'd here, my cousin Mowbray.
Good day to you, gentle Lord Archbishop;
And so to you, Lord Hastings, and to all.
My Lord of York, it better show'd with you
When that your flock, assembled by the bell,
Encircled you to hear with reverence
Your exposition on the holy text
Than now to see you here an iron man,
Cheering a rout of rebels with your drum,
Turning the word to sword and life to death.
That man that sits within a monarch's heart,
And ripens in the sunshine of his favour,
Would he abuse the countenance of the King,
Alack, what mischiefs might he set abroach
In shadow of such greatness! With you, Lord Bishop,
It is even so. Who hath not heard it spoken
How deep you were within the books of God?
To us the speaker in His parliament;

166. intended, implied. **172. insinewed**, bound as by sinews. **176. awful banks**, bounds of respect or awe. **189. our valuation**, the king's estimation of us. **193. royal faiths**, loyalty to the king. **198. picking**, picked-over. **203. history**, record.

213. hangs resolv'd correction, stops punishment resolved upon. **219. offer**, threaten. **226. just**, exact. **Scene ii: 14. set abroach**, cause.

To us th' imagin'd voice of God himself;
The very opener and intelligencer
Between the grace, the sanctities, of Heaven
And our dull workings. O, who shall believe
But you misuse the reverence of your place,
Employ the countenance and grace of Heaven,
As a false favourite doth his prince's name,
In deeds dishonourable? You have ta'en up,
Under the counterfeited zeal of God,
The subjects of His substitute, my father,
And both against the peace of Heaven and him
Have here upswarm'd them.
Arch. Good my Lord of Lancaster,
I am not here against your father's peace;
But, as I told my Lord of Westmoreland,
The time misorder'd doth, in common sense,
Crowd us and crush us to this monstrous form,
To hold our safety up. I sent your Grace
The parcels and particulars of our grief,
The which hath been with scorn shov'd from the court,
Whereon this Hydra son of war is born;
Whose dangerous eyes may well be charm'd asleep
With grant of our most just and right desires;
And true obedience, of this madness cur'd,
Stoop tamely to the foot of majesty.
Mowb. If not, we ready are to try our fortunes
To the last man.
Hast. And though we here fall down,
We have supplies to second our attempt.
If they miscarry, theirs shall second them;
And so success of mischief shall be born,
And heir from heir shall hold this quarrel up
While England shall have generation.
Lan. You are too shallow, Hastings, much too shallow,
To sound the bottom of the after-times.
West. Pleaseth your Grace to answer them directly
How far forth you do like their articles.
Lan. I like them all, and do allow them well,
And swear here, by the honour of my blood,
My father's purposes have been mistook,
And some about him have too lavishly
Wrested his meaning and authority.
My lord, these griefs shall be with speed redress'd;
Upon my soul, they shall. If this may please you,
Discharge your powers unto their several counties,
As we will ours; and here between the armies
Let 's drink together friendly and embrace,
That all their eyes may bear those tokens home
Of our restored love and amity.
Arch. I take your princely word for these redresses.
Lan. I give it you, and will maintain my word;
And thereupon I drink unto your Grace.
Hast. Go, captain, and deliver to the army
This news of peace. Let them have pay, and part.
I know it will well please them. Hie thee, captain. *Exit Officer.*
Arch. To you, my noble Lord of Westmoreland.
West. I pledge your Grace; and, if you knew what pains
I have bestow'd to breed this present peace,
You would drink freely: but my love to ye
Shall show itself more openly hereafter.
Arch. I do not doubt you.
West. I am glad of it.
Health to my lord and gentle cousin, Mowbray.
Mowb. You wish me health in very happy season;
For I am, on the sudden, something ill.
Arch. Against ill chances men are ever merry;
But heaviness foreruns the good event.
West. Therefore be merry, coz; since sudden sorrow
Serves to say thus, some good thing comes tomorrow.
Arch. Believe me, I am passing light in spirit.
Mowb. So much the worse, if your own rule be true. *Shouts within.*
Lan. The word of peace is render'd. Hark, how they shout!
Mowb. This had been cheerful after victory.
Arch. A peace is of the nature of a conquest;
For then both parties nobly are subdued,
And neither party loser.
Lan. Go, my lord,
And let our army be discharged too.
Exit Westmoreland.
And, good my lord, so please you, let your trains
March by us, that we may peruse the men
We should have cop'd withal.
Arch. Go, good Lord Hastings,

20. opener, interpreter. **intelligencer,** mediator. **22. dull workings,** stupid actions. **26. ta'en up,** levied. **38. Hydra,** many-headed. **42. Stoop tamely,** submit. **47. success,** succession. **49. generation,** offspring.

81. Against, before. **85. passing,** exceedingly. **87. render'd,** reported. **95. cop'd withal,** encountered.

And, ere they be dismiss'd, let them march by. *Exit Hastings.*

Re-enter *Westmoreland.*

Lan. I trust, lords, we shall lie to-night together.
Now cousin, wherefore stands our army still?
West. The leaders, having charge from you to stand,
Will not go off until they hear you speak.
Lan. They know their duties.

Re-enter *Hastings.*

Has. My lord, our army is dispers'd already.
Like youthful steers unyok'd, they take their courses
East, west, north, south; or, like a school broke up,
Each hurries toward his home and sporting-place.
West. Good tidings, my Lord Hastings; for the which
I do arrest thee, traitor, of high treason;
And you, Lord Archbishop, and you, Lord Mowbray,
Of capital treason I attach you both.
Mowb. Is this proceeding just and honourable?
West. Is your assembly so?
Arch. Will you thus break your faith?
Lan. I pawn'd thee none.
I promis'd you redress of these same grievances
Whereof you did complain; which, by mine honour,
I will perform with a most Christian care.
But for you, rebels, look to taste the due
Meet for rebellion and such acts as yours.
Most shallowly did you these arms commence,
Fondly brought here and foolishly sent hence.
Strike up our drums, pursue the scatter'd stray.
God, and not we, hath safely fought to-day.
Some guard these traitors to the block of death,
Treason's true bed and yielder up of breath.
Exeunt.

Scene III. *Another part of the forest.*

Alarums. Excursion. Enter *Falstaff* and *Colville* meeting.

Fal. What 's your name, sir? Of what condition are you, and of what place, I pray?

Col. I am a knight, sir; and my name is Colville of the Dale.

Fal. Well, then, Colville is your name, a knight is your degree, and your place the Dale. Colville shall be still your name, a traitor your degree, and the dungeon your place, a place deep enough; so shall you be still Colville of the Dale.

Col. Are not you Sir John Falstaff?

Fal. As good a man as he, sir, whoe'er I am. Do ye yield, sir, or shall I sweat for you? If I do sweat, they are the drops of thy lovers, and they weep for thy death; therefore rouse up fear and trembling, and do observance to my mercy.

Col. I think you are Sir John Falstaff, and in that thought yield me.

Fal. I have a whole school of tongues in this belly of mine, and not a tongue of them all speaks any other word but my name. An I had but a belly of any indifferency, I were simply the most active fellow in Europe: my womb, my womb, my womb, undoes me. Here comes our general.

Enter *Prince John of Lancaster, Westmoreland, Blunt* and others.

Lan. The heat is past; follow no further now.
Call in the powers, good cousin Westmoreland. *Exit Westmoreland.*
Now, Falstaff, where have you been all this while?
When everything is ended, then you come.
These tardy tricks of yours will, on my life,
One time or other break some gallows' back.

Fal. I would be sorry, my lord, but it should be thus: I never knew yet but rebuke and check was the reward of valour. Do you think me a swallow, an arrow, or a bullet? Have I, in my poor and old motion, the expedition of thought? I have speeded hither with the very extremest inch of possibility; I have foundered ninescore and odd posts; and here, travel-tainted as I am, have, in my pure and immaculate valour, taken Sir John Colville of the Dale, a most furious knight and valorous enemy. But what of that? He saw me, and yielded; that I may justly say, with the hook-nosed fellow of Rome, "I came, saw, and overcame."

Lan. It was more of his courtesy than your deserving.

Fal. I know not: here he is, and here I yield him; and I beseech your Grace, let it be booked with the rest of this day's deeds; or,

118. shallowly, thoughtlessly. **120. stray,** stragglers. **Scene iii: 1. condition,** rank.

23. indifferency, moderate size. **37. expedition,** speed. **41 posts,** post-horses.

by the Lord, I will have it in a particular ballad else, with mine own picture on the top on 't, Colville kissing my foot; to the which course if I be enforced, if you do not all show like gilt twopences to me, and I in the clear sky of fame o'ershine you as much as the full moon doth the cinders of the element, which show like pins' heads to her, believe not the word of the noble: therefore let me have right, and let desert mount.

Lan. Thine 's too heavy to mount.

Fal. Let it shine, then.

Lan. Thine 's too thick to shine.

Fal. Let it do something, my good lord, that may do me good, and call it what you will.

Lan. Is thy name Colville?

Col. It is, my lord.

Lan. A famous rebel art thou, Colville.

Fal. And a famous true subject took him.

Col. I am, my lord, but as my betters are
That led me hither: had they been rul'd by me,
You should have won them dearer than you have.

Fal. I know not how they sold themselves; but thou, like a kind fellow, gav'st thyself away gratis; and I thank thee for thee.

Re-enter *Westmoreland.*

Lan. Now, have you left pursuit?

West. Retreat is made and execution stay'd.

Lan. Send Colville with his confederates
To York, to present execution.
Blunt, lead him hence; and see you guard him sure. *Exeunt Blunt with Colville.*
And now dispatch we toward the court, my lords;
I hear the King my father is sore sick.
Our news shall go before us to his Majesty,
Which, cousin, you shall bear to comfort him.
And we with sober speed will follow you.

Fal. My lord, I beseech you, give me leave to go
Through Gloucestershire; and, when you come to court,
Stand my good lord, pray, in your good report.

Lan. Fare you well, Falstaff: I, in my condition,
Shall better speak of you than you deserve.
Exeunt all but Falstaff.

Fal. I would you had but the wit; 't were better than your dukedom. Good faith, this same young sober-blooded boy doth not love me, nor a man cannot make him laugh; but that 's no marvel, he drinks no wine. There 's never none of these demure boys come to any proof; for thin drink doth so over-cool their blood, and making many fish-meals, that they fall into a kind of male green-sickness; and then, when they marry, they get wenches. They are generally fools and cowards; which some of us should be too, but for inflammation. A good sherris-sack hath a two-fold operation in it: it ascends me into the brain; dries me there all the foolish and dull and crudy vapours which environ it; makes it apprehensive, quick, forgetive, full of nimble, fiery, and delectable shapes; which, delivered o'er to the voice, the tongue, which is the birth, becomes excellent wit. The second property of your excellent sherris is, the warming of the blood; which, before cold and settled, left the liver white and pale, which is the badge of pusillanimity and cowardice; but the sherris warms it and makes it course from the inwards to the parts extremes: it illumineth the face, which as a beacon gives warning to all the rest of this little kingdom, man, to arm; and then the vital commoners and inland petty spirits muster me all to their captain, the heart, who, great and puffed up with this retinue, doth any deed of courage; and this valour comes of sherris. So that skill in the weapon is nothing without sack, for that sets it a-work; and learning a mere hoard of gold kept by a devil, till sack commences it and sets it in act and use. Hereof comes it that Prince Harry is valiant; for the cold blood he did naturally inherit of his father, he hath, like lean, sterile, and bare land, manured, husbanded, and tilled with excellent endeavour of drinking good and good store of fertile sherris, that he is become very hot and valiant. If I had a thousand sons, the first humane principle I would teach them should be, to forswear thin potations and to addict themselves to sack.

Enter *Bardolph.*

How now, Bardolph?

Bard. The army is discharged all and gone.

Fal. Let them go. I 'll through Gloucestershire; and there will I visit Master Robert Shallow, Esquire: I have him already tempering between my finger and my thumb, and shortly will I seal with him. Come away.

Exeunt.

58. cinders of the element, stars. **80. present,** immediate. **89. Stand my good lord,** be my sponsor. **90. condition,** official capacity.

97-8. come to any proof, turn out well. **104. sherris-sack,** sherry. **107. crudy,** raw, crude. **108. apprehensive,** quick of apprehension. **forgetive,** inventive. **140. tempering,** warming (like sealing wax).

Scene IV. *Westminster. The Jerusalem Chamber.*

Enter the *King, Thomas of Clarence* and *Humphrey of Gloucester, Warwick* and others.

King. Now, lords, if God doth give successful end
To this debate that bleedeth at our doors,
We will our youth lead on to higher fields,
And draw no swords but what are sanctified.
Our navy is address'd, our power collected,
Our substitutes in absence well invested,
And everything lies level to our wish.
Only, we want a little personal strength;
And pause us, till these rebels, now afoot,
Come underneath the yoke of government.

War. Both which we doubt not but your Majesty
Shall soon enjoy.

King. Humphrey, my son of Gloucester,
Where is the Prince your brother?

Glou. I think he 's gone to hunt, my lord, at Windsor.

King. And how accompanied?

Glou. I do not know, my lord.

King. Is not his brother, Thomas of Clarence, with him?

Glou. No, my good lord; he is in presence here.

Clar. What would my lord and father?

King. Nothing but well to thee, Thomas of Clarence.
How chance thou art not with the Prince thy brother?
He loves thee, and thou dost neglect him, Thomas.
Thou hast a better place in his affection
Than all thy brothers: cherish it, my boy,
And noble offices thou mayst effect
Of mediation, after I am dead,
Between his greatness and thy other brethren.
Therefore omit him not; blunt not his love,
Nor lose the good advantage of his grace
By seeming cold or careless of his will.
For he is gracious, if he be observ'd;
He hath a tear for pity, and a hand
Open as day for melting charity;
Yet notwithstanding, being incens'd, he 's flint,
As humorous as winter, and as sudden
As flaws congealed in the spring of day.
His temper, therefore, must be well observ'd.
Chide him for faults, and do it reverently,
When you perceive his blood inclin'd to mirth;
But, being moody, give him time and scope,
Till that his passions, like a whale on ground,
Confound themselves with working. Learn this, Thomas,
And thou shalt prove a shelter to thy friends,
A hoop of gold to bind thy brothers in,
That the united vessel of their blood,
Mingled with venom of suggestion,
As, force perforce, the age will pour it in,
Shall never leak, though it do work as strong
As aconitum or rash gunpowder.

Clar. I shall observe him with all care and love.

King. Why art thou not at Windsor with him, Thomas?

Clar. He is not there to-day; he dines in London.

King. And how accompanied? Canst thou tell that?

Clar. With Poins, and other his continual followers.

King. Most subject is the fattest soil to weeds,
And he, the noble image of my youth,
Is overspread with them; therefore my grief
Stretches itself beyond the hour of death.
The blood weeps from my heart when I do shape
In forms imaginary th' unguided days
And rotten times that you shall look upon
When I am sleeping with my ancestors.
For when his headstrong riot hath no curb,
When rage and hot blood are his counsellors,
When means and lavish manners meet together,
O, with what wings shall his affections fly
Towards fronting peril and oppos'd decay!

War. My gracious lord, you look beyond him quite.
The Prince but studies his companions
Like a strange tongue, wherein, to gain the language,
'T is needful that the most immodest word
Be look'd upon and learn'd; which once attain'd,
Your Highness knows, comes to no further use
But to be known and hated. So, like gross terms,
The Prince will in the perfectness of time
Cast off his followers; and their memory
Shall as a pattern or a measure live,
By which his Grace must mete the lives of others,
Turning past evils to advantages.

Scene iv: 3. higher fields, i.e., the Holy Land. **5. address'd,** prepared. **27. omit,** neglect. **30. observ'd,** paid respect to. **33. flint,** either (1) **hard** as opposed to **charitable,** or, (2) capable of emitting sparks. **34. humorous,** capricious. **35. flaws,** hailstorms.

44. united . . . blood, i.e., the royal family. **45. suggestion,** malicious gossip. **48. aconitum,** the poison, wolf's bane. **65. affections,** inclinations. **66. fronting . . . decay,** the peril and decay that confront him. **67. look beyond,** misjudge. **77. mete,** measure.

King. 'T is seldom when the bee doth leave her comb
In the dead carrion.

Enter *Westmoreland.*

Who 's here? Westmoreland?
West. Health to my sovereign, and new happiness
Added to that that I am to deliver!
Prince John, your son, doth kiss your Grace's hand.
Mowbray, the Bishop Scroop, Hastings and all
Are brought to the correction of your law.
There is not now a rebel's sword unsheath'd,
But Peace puts forth her olive everywhere.
The manner how this action hath been borne
Here at more leisure may your Highness read,
With every course in his particular.
King. O Westmoreland, thou art a summer bird,
Which ever in the haunch of winter sings
The lifting up of day.

Enter *Harcourt.*

Look, here 's more news.
Har. From enemies heaven keep your Majesty;
And, when they stand against you, may they fall
As those that I am come to tell you of!
The Earl Northumberland and the Lord Bardolph,
With a great power of English and of Scots,
Are by the shrieve of Yorkshire overthrown.
The manner and true order of the fight
This packet, please it you, contains at large.
King. And wherefore should these good news make me sick?
Will Fortune never come with both hands full,
But write her fair words still in foulest letters?
She either gives a stomach and no food;
(Such are the poor, in health), or else a feast
And takes away the stomach—such are the rich,
That have abundance and enjoy it not.
I should rejoice now at this happy news;
And now my sight fails, and my brain is giddy.
O me! come near me; now I am much ill.
Glou. Comfort, your Majesty!
Clar. O my royal father!
West. My sovereign lord, cheer up yourself, look up.
War. Be patient, Princes; you do know, these fits
Are with his Highness very ordinary.
Stand from him, give him air: he 'll straight be well.
Clar. No, no, he cannot long hold out these pangs.
Th' incessant care and labour of his mind
Hath wrought the mure that should confine it in
So thin that life looks through and will break out.
Glou. The people fear me; for they do observe
Unfather'd heirs and loathly births of nature:
The seasons change their manners, as the year
Had found some months asleep and leap'd them over.
Clar. The river hath thrice flow'd, no ebb between;
And the old folk, time's doting chronicles,
Say it did so a little time before
That our great-grandsire, Edward, sick'd and died.
War. Speak lower, Princes, for the King recovers.
Glou. This apoplexy will certain be his end.
King. I pray you, take me up, and bear me hence
Into some other chamber. Softly, pray.
Exeunt.

Scene V. *Another chamber.*

The *King* on a bed: *Clarence, Gloucester, Warwick,* and others in attendance.

King. Let there be no noise made, my gentle friends;
Unless some dull and favourable hand
Will whisper music to my weary spirit.
War. Call for the music in the other room.
King. Set me the crown upon my pillow here.
Clar. His eye is hollow, and he changes much.
War. Less noise, less noise!

Enter *Prince Henry.*

Prince. Who saw the Duke of Clarence?
Clar. I am here, brother, full of heaviness.
Prince. How now! rain within doors, and none abroad!
How doth the King?
Glou. Exceeding ill.
Prince. Heard he the good news yet?
Tell it him.

90. **particular,** detail. 92. **haunch,** end. 99. **shrieve,** sheriff. 105. **stomach,** appetite.

119. **wrought the mure,** worn the wall (of flesh). 121. **fear,** frighten. 123. **as,** as if. 125. **flow'd,** been at flood tide (the Thames at London is affected by the tides). **Scene v:** 2. **dull,** soothing, drowsy. 6. **changes much,** grows pale.

Glou. He alter'd much upon the hearing it.
Prince. If he be sick with joy, he 'll recover without physic.
War. Not so much noise, my lords: sweet Prince, speak low;
The King, your father, is dispos'd to sleep.
Clar. Let us withdraw into the other room.
War. Will 't please your Grace to go along with us?
Prince. No; I will sit and watch here by the King. *Exeunt all but the Prince.*
Why doth the crown lie there upon his pillow,
Being so troublesome a bedfellow?
O polish'd perturbation! golden care!
That keep'st the ports of slumber open wide
To many a watchful night! Sleep with it now!
Yet not so sound and half so deeply sweet
As he whose brow with homely biggen bound
Snores out the watch of night. O majesty!
When thou dost pinch thy bearer, thou dost sit
Like a rich armour worn in heat of day,
That scald'st with safety. By his gates of breath
There lies a dowlny feather which stirs not.
Did he suspire, that light and weightless dowle
Perforce must move. My gracious lord! my father!
This sleep is sound indeed; this is a sleep
That from this golden rigol hath divorc'd
So many English kings. Thy due from me
Is tears and heavy sorrows of the blood,
Which nature, love, and filial tenderness
Shall, O dear father, pay thee plenteously:
My due from thee is this imperial crown,
Which, as immediate from thy place and blood,
Derives itself to me. [*Puts on the crown.*]
Lo, where it sits,
Which God shall guard; and put the world's whole strength
Into one giant arm, it shall not force
This lineal honour from me. This from thee
Will I to mine leave, as 't is left to me. *Exit.*
King. Warwick! Gloucester! Clarence!

Re-enter *Warwick, Gloucester, Clarence.*

Clar. Doth the King call?
War. What would your Majesty? How fares your Grace?
King. Why did you leave me here alone, my lords?
Clar. We left the Prince my brother here, my liege,
Who undertook to sit and watch by you.

27. **biggen,** nightcap. 31. **scald'st with safety,** burns while it gives safety. 32. **dowlny,** downy. 33. **suspire,** breathe. **dowle,** feather. 36. **rigol,** circle, crown. 42. **immediate,** next in line.

King. The Prince of Wales! Where is he? Let me see him.
He is not here.
War. This door is open; he is gone this way.
Glou. He came not through the chamber where we stay'd.
King. Where is the crown? Who took it from my pillow?
War. When we withdrew, my liege, we left it here.
King. The Prince hath ta'en it hence. Go, seek him out.
Is he so hasty that he doth suppose
My sleep my death?
Find him, my Lord of Warwick; chide him hither. *Exit Warwick.*
This part of his conjoins with my disease,
And helps to end me. See, sons, what things you are!
How quickly nature falls into revolt
When gold becomes her object!
For this the foolish over-careful fathers
Have broke their sleep with thoughts, their brains with care,
Their bones with industry;
For this they have engrossed and pil'd up
The canker'd heaps of strange-achieved gold;
For this they have been thoughtful to invest
Their sons with arts and martial exercises;
When, like the bee, tolling from every flower
The virtuous sweets,
Our thighs pack'd with wax, our mouths with honey,
We bring it to the hive, and, like the bees,
Are murder'd for our pains. This bitter taste
Yields his engrossments to the ending father.

Re-enter *Warwick.*

Now, where is he that will not stay so long
Till his friend sickness hath determin'd me?
War. My lord, I found the Prince in the next room,
Washing with kindly tears his gentle cheeks,
With such a deep demeanour in great sorrow
That Tyranny, which never quaff'd but blood,
Would, by beholding him, have wash'd his knife
With gentle eye-drops. He is coming hither.
King. But wherefore did he take away the crown?

Re-enter *Prince Henry.*

Lo, where he comes. Come hither to me, Harry.
Depart the chamber, leave us here alone.
Exeunt Warwick and the rest.

64. **part,** act. 71. **engrossed,** amassed. 72. **canker'd,** tarnished. **strange-achieved,** got in strange ways. 82. **determin'd,** ended. 84. **kindly,** natural.

Prince. I never thought to hear you speak again.
King. Thy wish was father, Harry, to that thought:
I stay too long by thee, I weary thee.
Dost thou so hunger for mine empty chair
That thou wilt needs invest thee with mine honours
Before thy hour be ripe? O foolish youth!
Thou seek'st the greatness that will overwhelm thee.
Stay but a little; for my cloud of dignity
Is held from falling with so weak a wind
That it will quickly drop: my day is dim.
Thou hast stol'n that which after some few hours
Were thine without offence; and at my death
Thou hast seal'd up my expectation.
Thy life did manifest thou lov'dst me not,
And thou wilt have me die assur'd of it.
Thou hid'st a thousand daggers in thy thoughts,
Which thou hast whetted on thy stony heart,
To stab at half an hour of my life.
What! canst thou not forbear me half an hour?
Then get thee gone and dig my grave thyself,
And bid the merry bells ring to thine ear
That thou art crowned, not that I am dead.
Let all the tears that should bedew my hearse
Be drops of balm to sanctify thy head;
Only compound me with forgotten dust;
Give that which gave thee life unto the worms.
Pluck down my officers, break my decrees;
For now a time is come to mock at form.
Harry the Fifth is crown'd! Up, vanity!
Down, royal state! All you sage counsellors, hence!
And to the English court assemble now,
From every region, apes of idleness!
Now, neighbour confines, purge you of your scum!
Have you a ruffian that will swear, drink, dance,
Revel the night, rob, murder, and commit
The oldest sins the newest kind of ways?
Be happy, he will trouble you no more.
England shall double gild his treble guilt,
England shall give him office, honour, might;
For the fifth Harry from curb'd license plucks
The muzzle of restraint, and the wild dog
Shall flesh his tooth on every innocent.
O my poor kingdom, sick with civil blows!
When that my care could not withhold thy riots,
What wilt thou do when riot is thy care?
O, thou wilt be a wilderness again,
Peopled with wolves, thy old inhabitants!
Prince. O, pardon me, my liege! but for my tears,
The moist impediments unto my speech,
I had forestall'd this dear and deep rebuke
Ere you with grief had spoke and I had heard
The course of it so far. There is your crown;
And He that wears the crown immortally
Long guard it yours! If I affect it more
Than as your honour and as your renown,
Let me no more from this obedience rise.
Kneels.
Which my most inward, true, and duteous spirit
Teacheth, this prostrate and exterior bending.
God witness with me, when I here came in,
And found no course of breath within your Majesty,
How cold it struck my heart! If I do feign,
O, let me in my present wildness die
And never live to show th' incredulous world
The noble change that I have purposed!
Coming to look on you, thinking you dead,
And dead almost, my liege, to think you were,
I spake unto this crown as having sense,
And thus upbraided it: "The care on thee depending
Hath fed upon the body of my father;
Therefore thou best of gold art worst of gold.
Other, less fine in carat, is more precious,
Preserving life in med'cine potable;
But thou, most fine, most honour'd, most renown'd,
Hast eat thy bearer up." Thus, my most royal liege,
Accusing it, I put it on my head,
To try with it, as with an enemy
That had before my face murder'd my father,
The quarrel of a true inheritor.
But if it did infect my blood with joy,
Or swell my thoughts to any strain of pride;
If any rebel or vain spirit of mine
Did with the least affection of a welcome
Give entertainment to the might of it,
Let God for ever keep it from my head
And make me as the poorest vassal is
That doth with awe and terror kneel to it!
King. O my son,
God put it in thy mind to take it hence,
That thou mightst win the more thy father's love,
Pleading so wisely in excuse of it!
Come hither, Harry, sit thou by my bed;
And hear, I think, the very latest counsel

104. seal'd up, confirmed fully. **119. form,** order. **120. vanity,** folly. **135. care,** special study.

141. dear and deep, earnest and severe. **145. affect,** love. **163. med'cine potable,** cf. Chaucer's *Prologue*, "For gold in physic is a cordial." **171. strain,** impulse.

That ever I shall breathe. God knows, my son,
By what by-paths and indirect crook'd ways
I met this crown; and I myself know well
How troublesome it sat upon my head.
To thee it shall descend with better quiet,
Better opinion, better confirmation;
For all the soil of the achievement goes
With me into the earth. It seem'd in me
But as an honour snatch'd with boist'rous hand,
And I had many living to upbraid
My gain of it by their assistances;
Which daily grew to quarrel and to bloodshed,
Wounding supposed peace. All these bold fears
Thou see'st with peril I have answered;
For all my reign hath been but as a scene
Acting that argument; and now my death
Changes the mode; for what in me was purchas'd,
Falls upon thee in a more fairer sort;
So thou the garland wear'st successively.
Yet, though thou stand'st more sure than I could do,
Thou art not firm enough, since griefs are green;
And all my friends, which thou must make thy friends,
Have but their stings and teeth newly ta'en out;
By whose fell working I was first advanc'd
And by whose power I well might lodge a fear
To be again displac'd; which to avoid,
I cut them off; and had a purpose now
To lead out many to the Holy Land,
Lest rest and lying still might make them look
Too near unto my state. Therefore, my Harry,
Be it thy course to busy giddy minds
With foreign quarrels, that action, hence borne out,
May waste the memory of the former days.
More would I, but my lungs are wasted so
That strength of speech is utterly denied me.
How I came by the crown, O God forgive;
And grant it may with thee in true peace live!

Prince. My gracious liege,
You won it, wore it, kept it, gave it me;
Then plain and right must my possession be,
Which I with more than with a common pain
'Gainst all the world will rightfully maintain.

Enter *Lord John of Lancaster* and *Warwick.*

King. Look, look, here comes my John of Lancaster.

Lan. Health, peace, and happiness to my royal father!

King. Thou bring'st me happiness and peace, son John;
But health, alack, with youthful wings is flown
From this bare wither'd trunk. Upon thy sight
My worldly business makes a period.
Where is my Lord of Warwick?

Prince. My Lord of Warwick!

King. Doth any name particular belong
Unto the lodging where I first did swound?

War. 'T is call'd Jerusalem, my noble lord.

King. Laud be to God! even there my life must end.
It hath been prophesied to me many years,
I should not die but in Jerusalem;
Which vainly I suppos'd the Holy Land.
But bear me to that chamber; there I 'll lie;
In that Jerusalem shall Harry die. *Exeunt.*

ACT V. SCENE I. *Gloucestershire. Shallow's house.*

Enter *Shallow, Falstaff, Bardolph,* and *Page.*

Shal. By cock and pie, sir, you shall not away to-night. What, Davy, I say!

Fal. You must excuse me, Master Robert Shallow.

Shal. I will not excuse you; you shall not be excused; excuses shall not be admitted; there is no excuse shall serve; you shall not be excused. Why, Davy!

Enter *Davy.*

Davy. Here, sir.

Shal. Davy, Davy, Davy, Davy, let me see, Davy; let me see, Davy; let me see. Yea, marry, William cook, bid him come hither. Sir John, you shall not be excused.

Davy. Marry, sir, thus; those precepts

189. **opinion,** public opinion. 190. **soil,** pollution. 199. **argument,** story. 200. **mode,** mood, musical key. 202. **successively,** by right of succession. 207. **fell,** evil. **Act V, Scene i: 1. cock and pie,** an oath.

215. **hence,** in foreign lands. 216. **waste,** efface. 235. **Jerusalem,** a chamber in Westminster Abbey. **Act V, Scene i: 14. precepts,** summonses.

cannot be served; and, again, sir, shall we sow the headland with wheat?

Shal. With red wheat, Davy. But for William cook: are there no young pigeons?

Davy. Yes, sir. Here is now the smith's note for shoeing and plough-irons.

Shal. Let it be cast and paid. Sir John, you shall not be excused.

Davy. Now, sir, a new link to the bucket must needs be had; and, sir, do you mean to stop any of William's wages, about the sack he lost the other day at Hinckley fair?

Shal. 'A shall answer it. Some pigeons, Davy, a couple of short-legged hens, a joint of mutton, and any pretty little tiny kickshaws, tell William cook.

Davy. Doth the man of war stay all night, sir?

Shal. Yea, Davy; I will use him well: a friend i' th' court is better than a penny in purse. Use his men well, Davy; for they are arrant knaves, and will backbite.

Davy. No worse than they are backbitten, sir; for they have marvellous foul linen.

Shal. Well conceited, Davy: about thy business, Davy.

Davy. I beseech you, sir, to countenance William Visor of Woncot against Clement Perkes o' th' hill.

Shal. There is many complaints, Davy, against that Visor: that Visor is an arrant knave, on my knowledge.

Davy. I grant your worship that he is a knave, sir; but yet, God forbid, sir, but a knave should have some countenance at his friend's request. An honest man, sir, is able to speak for himself, when a knave is not. I have served your worship truly, sir, this eight years; and if I cannot once or twice in a quarter bear out a knave against an honest man, I have but a very little credit with your worship. The knave is mine honest friend, sir; therefore, I beseech you, let him be countenanced.

Shal. Go to; I say he shall have no wrong. Look about, Davy. [*Exit Davy.*] Where are you, Sir John? Come, come, come, off with your boots. Give me your hand, Master Bardolph.

Bard. I am glad to see your worship.

Shal. I thank thee with all my heart, kind Master Bardolph: and welcome, my tall fellow [*to the Page*]. Come, Sir John.

Fal. I 'll follow you, good Master Robert Shallow. [*Exit Shallow.*] Bardolph, look to our horses. [*Exeunt Bardolph and Page.*] If I were sawed into quantities, I should make four dozen of such bearded hermits' staves as Master Shallow. It is a wonderful thing to see the semblable coherence of his men's spirits and his. They, by observing of him, do bear themselves like foolish justices; he, by conversing with them, is turned into a justice-like serving-man: their spirits are so married in conjunction with the participation of society that they flock together in consent, like so many wild-geese. If I had a suit to Master Shallow, I would humour his men with the imputation of being near their master; if to his men, I would curry with Master Shallow that no man could better command his servants. It is certain that either wise bearing or ignorant carriage is caught, as men take diseases, one of another; therefore let men take heed of their company. I will devise matter enough out of this Shallow to keep Prince Harry in continual laughter the wearing out of six fashions, which is four terms, or two actions, and 'a shall laugh without intervallums. O, it is much that a lie with a slight oath and a jest with a sad brow will do with a fellow that never had the ache in his shoulders! O, you shall see him laugh till his face be like a wet cloak ill laid up.

Shal. [*Within.*] Sir John!

Fal. I come, Master Shallow; I come, Master Shallow. *Exit.*

20. **note,** bill. 21. **cast,** reckoned. 29. **kickshaws,** fancy dishes. 39. **Well conceited,** well punned. 41. **countenance,** favor. 42. **Visor . . . Perkes,** these Gloucestershire names are supposed to show some connection between Shakespeare and that county. Cf. Introduction, p. 388.

69. **quantities,** small pieces. 72. **semblable coherence,** resemblance. 78. **consent,** agreement. 89. **terms,** i.e., of court. 90. **actions,** law-suits. 91. **intervallums,** intervals. 92. **sad,** sober.

Scene II. *Westminster. The palace.*

Enter *Warwick* meeting the *Lord Chief Justice.*

War. How now, my Lord Chief Justice: whither away?
Ch. Just. How doth the King?
War. Exceeding well; his cares are now all ended.
Ch. Just. I hope, not dead.
War. He 's walk'd the way of nature;
And to our purposes he lives no more.
Ch. Just. I would his Majesty had call'd me with him.
The service that I truly did his life
Hath left me open to all injuries.
War. Indeed I think the young King loves you not.
Ch. Just. I know he doth not, and do arm myself
To welcome the condition of the time,
Which cannot look more hideously upon me
Than I have drawn it in my fantasy.

Enter *Lancaster, Clarence, Gloucester, Westmoreland,* and others.

War. Here come the heavy issue of dead Harry:
O that the living Harry had the temper
Of him, the worst of these three gentlemen!
How many nobles then should hold their places,
That must strike sail to spirits of vile sort!
Ch. Just. O God, I fear all will be overturn'd!
Lan. Good morrow, cousin Warwick, good morrow.
Glou. } *Clar.* } Good morrow, cousin.
Lan. We meet like men that had forgot to speak.
War. We do remember; but our argument
Is all too heavy to admit much talk.
Lan. Well, peace be with him that hath made us heavy!
Ch. Just. Peace we with us, lest we be heavier!
Glou. O, good my lord, you have lost a friend indeed;
And I dare swear you borrow not that face
Of seeming sorrow; it is sure your own.
Lan. Though no man be assur'd what grace to find,
You stand in coldest expectation.
I am the sorrier; would 't were otherwise!
Clar. Well, you must now speak Sir John Falstaff fair;
Which swims against your stream of quality.
Ch. Just. Sweet princes, what I did, I did in honour,
Led by the impartial conduct of my soul;
And never shall you see that I will beg
A ragged and forestall'd remission.
If truth and upright innocency fail me,
I 'll to the King my master that is dead,
And tell him who hath sent me after him.
War. Here comes the Prince.

Enter *King Henry the Fifth* attended.

Ch. Just. Good morrow; and God save your Majesty!
King. This new and gorgeous garment, majesty,
Sits not so easy on me as you think.
Brothers, you mix your sadness with some fear.
This is the English, not the Turkish court;
Not Amurath an Amurath succeeds,
But Harry Harry. Yet be sad, good brothers,
For, by my faith, it very well becomes you.
Sorrow so royally in you appears
That I will deeply put the fashion on
And wear it in my heart. Why then, be sad;
But entertain no more of it, good brothers,
Than a joint burden laid upon us all.
For me, by heaven, I bid you be assur'd,
I 'll be your father and your brother too.
Let me but bear your love, I 'll bear your cares:
Yet weep that Harry 's dead, and so will I;
But Harry lives, that shall convert those tears
By number into hours of happiness.
Princes. We hope no other from your Majesty.
King. You all look strangely on me, and you most.
You are, I think, assur'd I love you not.
Ch. Just. I am assur'd, if I be measur'd rightly,
Your Majesty hath no just cause to hate me.
King. No?
How might a prince of my great hopes forget
So great indignities you laid upon me?
What! rate, rebuke, and roughly send to prison
The immediate heir of England! Was this easy?
May this be wash'd in Lethe, and forgotten?
Ch. Just. I then did use the person of your father;
The image of his power lay then in me;
And, in th' administration of his law,
Whiles I was busy for the commonwealth,
Your Highness pleased to forget my place,
The majesty and power of law and justice,
The image of the King whom I presented,
And struck me in my very seat of judgement;
Whereon, as an offender to your father,
I gave bold way to my authority
And did commit you. If the deed were ill,
Be you contented, wearing now the garland,
To have a son set your decrees at nought,
To pluck down justice from your awful bench,
To trip the course of law and blunt the sword
That guards the peace and safety of your person;
Nay, more, to spurn at your most royal image
And mock your workings in a second body.
Question your royal thoughts, make the case yours:
Be now the father and propose a son,
Hear your own dignity so much profan'd,
See your most dreadful laws so loosely slighted,

14. heavy, sorrowful. **23. argument,** subject-matter. **31. coldest expectation,** least hopeful position. **34.** goes against the grain of your character. **38. ragged,** beggarly. **forestall'd remission,** a pardon sure to be refused. **48.** Amurath IV on his succession strangled his brothers.

71. easy, trivial. **72. Lethe,** river of oblivion. **73. use the person,** stand as the representative. **79. presented,** represented. **86. awful,** awe-inspiring. **90. second body,** deputy. **92. propose,** imagine.

Behold yourself so by a son disdained;
And then imagine me taking your part
And in your power soft silencing your son.
After this cold considerance, sentence me;
And, as you are a king, speak in your state
What I have done that misbecame my place,
My person, or my liege's sovereignty.

King. You are right, Justice, and you weigh this well,
Therefore still bear the balance and the sword,
And I do wish your honours may increase,
Till you do live to see a son of mine
Offend you and obey you, as I did.
So shall I live to speak my father's words:
"Happy am I, that have a man so bold,
That dares do justice on my proper son;
And not less happy, having such a son
That would deliver up his greatness so
Into the hands of justice." You did commit me;
For which, I do commit into your hand
Th' unstained sword that you have us'd to bear;
With this remembrance, that you use the same
With the like bold, just, and impartial spirit
As you have done 'gainst me. There is my hand;
You shall be as a father to my youth,
My voice shall sound as you do prompt mine ear,
And I will stoop and humble my intents
To your well-practis'd wise directions.
And, princes all, believe me, I beseech you,
My father is gone wild into his grave,
For in his tomb lie my affections;
And with his spirit sadly I survive,
To mock the expectation of the world,
To frustrate prophecies, and to raze out
Rotten opinion, who hath writ me down
After my seeming. The tide of blood in me
Hath proudly flow'd in vanity till now:
Now doth it turn and ebb back to the sea,
Where it shall mingle with the state of floods
And flow henceforth in formal majesty.
Now call we our high court of parliament;
And let us choose such limbs of noble counsel,
That the great body of our state may go
In equal rank with the best govern'd nation;
That war, or peace, or both at once, may be
As things acquainted and familiar to us;
In which you, father, shall have foremost hand.
Our coronation done, we will accite,
As I before remember'd, all our state;
And, God consigning to my good intents,
No prince nor peer shall have just cause to say,
God shorten Harry's happy life one day!

Exeunt.

Scene III. *Gloucestershire. Shallow's orchard.*

Enter *Falstaff, Shallow, Silence, Davy, Bardolph,* and *Page.*

Shal. Nay, you shall see my orchard, where, in an arbour, we will eat a last year's pippin of mine own graffing, with a dish of caraways, and so forth,—come, cousin Silence,—and then to bed.

Fal. 'Fore God, you have here a goodly dwelling and a rich.

Shal. Barren, barren, barren; beggars all, beggars all, Sir John: marry, good air. Spread, Davy; spread, Davy. Well said, Davy.

Fal. This Davy serves you for good uses; he is your serving-man and your husband.

Shal. A good varlet, a good varlet, a very good varlet, Sir John. By the mass, I have drunk too much sack at supper. A good varlet. Now sit down, now sit down. Come, cousin.

Sil. Ah, sirrah! quoth-a, we shall [*Singing.*]

"Do nothing but eat, and make good cheer,
And praise God for the merry year,
When flesh is cheap and females dear,
And lusty lads roam here and there
So merrily,
And ever among so merrily."

Fal. There 's a merry heart! Good Master Silence, I 'll give you a health for that anon.

Shal. Give Master Bardolph some wine, Davy.

Davy. Sweet sir, sit; I 'll be with you anon; most sweet sir, sit. Master page, good master page, sit. Proface! What you want in meat, we 'll have in drink; but you must bear: the heart 's all. *Exit.*

Shal. Be merry, Master Bardolph; and, my little soldier there, be merry.

Sil. [*Singing.*]

"Be merry, be merry, my wife has all;
For women are shrews, both short and tall.
'T is merry in hall when beards wag all,
And welcome merry Shrove-tide.
Be merry, be merry."

97. **soft,** softly. 98. **cold considerance,** calm consideration. 99. **state,** official capacity. 109. **proper,** own. 115. **remembrance,** admonition. 123-4. His waywardness lies buried with his father. 132. **state of floods,** majesty of the ocean. 137. **In equal rank,** step by step. 141. **accite,** summon.

142. **remember'd,** mentioned. 143. **consigning to,** sanctioning. **Scene iii:** 3. **graffing,** grafting. 4. **caraways,** confection containing caraway seeds. 10. **said,** done. 12. **husband,** husbandman, manager. 23. **ever among,** all the while. 30. **Proface,** may it do you good. 38. **Shrove-tide,** period of merry-making before Ash-Wednesday.

Fal. I did not think Master Silence had been a man of this mettle.

Sil. Who? I? I have been merry twice and once ere now.

Re-enter *Davy*.

Davy. There 's a dish of leather-coats for you. *To Bardolph.*

Shal. Davy!

Davy. Your worship! I 'll be with you straight. A cup of wine, sir?

Sil. [*Singing.*]

"A cup of wine that's brisk and fine,
And drink unto the leman mine;
And a merry heart lives long-a."

Fal. Well said, Master Silence.

Sil. An we shall be merry, now comes in the sweet o' the night.

Fal. Health and long life to you, Master Silence.

Sil. [*Singing.*]

"Fill the cup, and let it come;
I'll pledge you a mile to the bottom."

Shal. Honest Bardolph, welcome: if thou want'st anything, and wilt not call, beshrew thy heart. Welcome, my little tiny thief [*to the Page*], and welcome indeed too. I 'll drink to Master Bardolph, and to all the cavaleros about London.

Davy. I hope to see London once ere I die.

Bard. An I might see you there, Davy,—

Shal. By the mass, you 'll crack a quart together, ha! will you not, Master Bardolph?

Bard. Yea, sir, in a pottle-pot.

Shal. By God's liggens, I thank thee: the knave will stick by thee, I can assure thee that. 'A will not out; 'a is true bred.

Bard. And I 'll stick by him, sir.

One knocks at door.

Shal. Why, there spoke a king. Lack nothing; be merry! Look who 's at door there. Ho! who knocks? *Exit Davy.*

Fal. Why, now you have done me right.

To Silence, seeing him take off a bumper.

Sil. [*Singing.*]

"Do me right,
And dub me knight:
Samingo."

Is 't not so?

Fal. 'T is so.

Sil. Is 't so? Why then, say an old man can do somewhat.

Re-enter *Davy*.

Davy. An 't please your worship, there 's one Pistol come from the court with news.

Fal. From the court! Let him come in.

Enter *Pistol*.

How now, Pistol!

Pist. Sir John, God save you!

Fal. What wind blew you hither, Pistol?

Pist. Not the ill wind which blows no man to good. Sweet knight, thou art now one of the greatest men in this realm.

Sil. By 'r lady, I think 'a be, but goodman Puff of Barson.

Pist. Puff!
Puff i' thy teeth, most recreant coward base!
Sir John, I am thy Pistol and thy friend,
And helter-skelter have I rode to thee,
And tidings do I bring, and lucky joys
And golden times and happy news of price.

Fal. I pray thee now, deliver them like a man of this world.

Pist. A foutra for the world and worldlings base!
I speak of Africa and golden joys.

Fal. O base Assyrian knight, what is thy news?
Let King Cophetua know the truth thereof.

Sil. [*Singing.*] "And Robin Hood, Scarlet, and John."

Pist. Shall dunghill curs confront the Helicons?
And shall good news be baffled?
Then, Pistol, lay thy head in Furies' lap.

Sil. Honest gentleman, I know not your breeding.

Pist. Why then, lament therefore.

Shal. Give me pardon, sir. If, sir, you come with news from the court, I take it there 's but two ways, either to utter them, or to conceal them. I am, sir, under the King, in some authority.

Pist. Under which King, Besonian? Speak, or die.

Shal. Under King Harry.

Pist. Harry the Fourth or Fifth?

Shal. Harry the Fourth.

Pist. A foutra for thine office!
Sir John, thy tender lambkin now is king;
Harry the Fifth 's the man. I speak the truth.
When Pistol lies, do this, and fig me like
The bragging Spaniard.

44. leather-coats, russet apples. **49. leman**, sweetheart. **62. cavaleros**, cavaliers. **68. pottle-pot**, two-quart tankard. **69. liggens**, an oath original with Shallow. **71. will not out**, will not fail you. **76. have done me right**, have drunk with me. **79. Samingo**, San Domingo.

93. but, except. **103. foutra**, term of contempt. **106-7.** References to ballads *King Cophetua and the Beggar-Maid* and *Robin Hood*. Pistol (l. 108) resents such low company being admitted to Helicon, the abode of the muses. **119. Besonian**, beggar. **124. fig**, to insult by thrusting the thumb between first two fingers.

Fal. What, is the old king dead?

Pist. As nail in door. The things I speak are just.

Fal. Away, Bardolph! saddle my horse. Master Robert Shallow, choose what office thou wilt in the land, 't is thine. Pistol, I will double-charge thee with dignities.

Bard. O joyful day!
I would not take a knighthood for my fortune.

Pist. What! I do bring good news.

Fal. Carry Master Silence to bed. Master Shallow, my Lord Shallow,—be what thou wilt; I am Fortune's steward—get on thy boots. We 'll ride all night. O sweet Pistol! Away, Bardolph. [*Exit Bardolph.*] Come, Pistol, utter more to me; and withal devise something to do thyself good. Boot, boot, Master Shallow! I know the young king is sick for me. Let us take any man's horses; the laws of England are at my commandment. Blessed are they that have been my friends; and woe to my Lord Chief Justice!

Pist. Let vultures vile seize on his lungs also!
"Where is the life that late I led?" say they.
Why here it is; welcome these pleasant days!
Exeunt.

Scene IV. *London. A street.*

Enter *Beadles,* dragging in *Hostess Quickly* and *Doll Tearsheet.*

Host. No, thou arrant knave; I would to God that I might die, that I might have thee hanged. Thou hast drawn my shoulder out of joint.

1. Bead. The constables have delivered her over to me; and she shall have whipping-cheer enough, I warrant her. There hath been a man or two lately killed about her.

Dol. Nut-hook, nut-hook, you lie. Come on! I 'll tell thee what, thou damned tripe-visaged rascal, an the child I now go with do miscarry, thou wert better thou hadst struck thy mother, thou paper-faced villain!

Host. O the Lord, that Sir John were come! He would make this a bloody day to somebody. But I pray God the fruit of her womb miscarry.

1. Bead. If it do, you shall have a dozen of cushions again; you have but eleven now. Come, I charge you both go with me; for the man is dead that you and Pistol beat amongst you.

Dol. I 'll tell you what, you thin man in a censer, I will have you as soundly swinged for this,—you blue-bottle rogue, you filthy famished correctioner, if you be not swinged, I 'll forswear half-kirtles.

1. Bead. Come, come, you she knight-errant, come.

Host. O God, that right should thus overcome might! Well, of sufferance comes ease.

Dol. Come, you rogue, come; bring me to a justice.

Host. Ay, come, you starved blood-hound.

Dol. Goodman death, goodman bones!

Host. Thou atomy, thou!

Dol. Come, you thin thing; come, you rascal.

1. Bead. Very well. *Exeunt.*

Scene V. *A public place near Westminster Abbey*

Enter two *Grooms,* strewing rushes.

1. Groom. More rushes, more rushes.

2. Groom. The trumpets have sounded twice.

1. Groom. 'T will be two o'clock ere they come from the coronation: dispatch, dispatch. *Exeunt.*

Trumpets sound, and the *King* and his train pass over the stage. After them enter *Falstaff, Shallow, Pistol, Bardolph,* and *Page.*

Fal. Stand here by me, Master Robert Shallow; I will make the King do you grace. I will leer upon him as he comes by; and do but mark the countenance that he will give me.

Pist. God bless thy lungs, good knight.

Fal. Come here, Pistol; stand behind me. O, if I had had time to have made new liveries, I would have bestowed the thousand pound I borrowed of you. But 't is no matter; this poor show doth better; this doth infer the zeal I had to see him.

Shal. It doth so.

Fal. It shows my earnestness of affection,—

Shal. It doth so.

Fal. My devotion,—

Shal. It doth, it doth, it doth.

Fal. As it were, to ride day and night; and not to deliberate, not to remember, not to have patience to shift me,—

Shal. It is best, certain.

Fal. But to stand stained with travel, and sweating with desire to see him; thinking of nothing else, putting all affairs else in oblivion,

Scene iv: 8. Nut-hook, hook for pulling branches of nuts within reach. **9. tripe-visaged,** pale. **20. thin . . . censer,** i.e., figure embossed on a censer. **21. swinged,** whipped. **22. blue-bottle,** beadles wore blue coats. **24. half-kirtles,** short kirtle or skirt. **28. sufferance,** suffering. **33. atomy,** anatomy, skeleton.

as if there were nothing else to be done but to see him.

Pist. 'T is "*semper idem*," for "*absque hoc nihil est.*" 'T is all in every part.

Shal. 'T is so, indeed.

Pist. My knight, I will inflame thy noble liver,
And make thee rage.
Thy Doll, and Helen of thy noble thoughts,
Is in base durance and contagious prison;
Hal'd thither
By most mechanical and dirty hand.
Rouse up revenge from ebon den with fell Alecto's snake,
For Doll is in. Pistol speaks nought but truth.

Fal. I will deliver her.

Pist. There roar'd the sea, and trumpet-clangor sounds.

The trumpets sound. Enter the *King* and his train, the *Lord Chief Justice* among them.

Fal. God save thy Grace, King Hal! my royal Hal!

Pist. The heavens thee guard and keep, most royal imp of fame!

Fal. God save thee, my sweet boy!

King. My Lord Chief Justice, speak to that vain man.

Ch. Just. Have you your wits? Know you what 't is you speak?

Fal. My king! my Jove! I speak to thee, my heart!

King. I know thee not, old man; fall to thy prayers:
How ill white hairs become a fool and jester!
I have long dream'd of such a kind of man,
So surfeit-swell'd, so old, and so profane;
But, being awak'd, I do despise my dream.
Make less thy body hence, and more thy grace;
Leave gormandizing; know the grave doth gape
For thee thrice wider than for other men.
Reply not to me with a fool-born jest.
Presume not that I am the thing I was;
For God doth know, so shall the world perceive,
That I have turn'd away my former self;
So will I those that kept me company.
When thou dost hear I am as I have been,
Approach me, and thou shalt be as thou wast,
The tutor and the feeder of my riots;
Till then, I banish thee, on pain of death,
As I have done the rest of my misleaders,
Not to come near our person by ten mile.
For competence of life I will allow you,
That lack of means enforce you not to evils;
And, as we hear you do reform yourselves,
We will, according to your strengths and qualities,
Give you advancement. Be it your charge, my lord,
To see perform'd the tenour of my word.
Set on. *Exeunt King with his train.*

Fal. Master Shallow, I owe you a thousand pound.

Shal. Yea, marry, Sir John; which I beseech you to let me have home with me.

Fal. That can hardly be, Master Shallow. Do not you grieve at this; I shall be sent for in private to him. Look you, he must seem thus to the world. Fear not your advancements; I will be the man yet that shall make you great.

Shal. I cannot well perceive how, unless you should give me your doublet and stuff me out with straw. I beseech you, good Sir John, let me have five hundred of my thousand.

Fal. Sir, I will be as good as my word. This that you heard was but a colour.

Shal. A colour that I fear you will die in, Sir John.

Fal. Fear no colours; go with me to dinner. Come, Lieutenant Pistol; come, Bardolph. I shall be sent for soon at night.

Re-enter *Prince John*, the *Lord Chief Justice*, Officers with them.

Ch. Just. Go, carry Sir John Falstaff to the Fleet.
Take all his company along with him.

Fal. My lord, my lord,—

Ch. Just. I cannot now speak; I will hear you soon.
Take them away.

Pist. *Si fortuna me tormenta, spero contenta.*

Exeunt all but Prince John and the Chief Justice.

Lan. I like this fair proceeding of the King's.
He hath intent his wonted followers
Shall all be very well provided for;
But all are banish'd till their conversations
Appear more wise and modest to the world.

Ch. Just. And so they are.

Lan. The King hath call'd his parliament, my lord.

Ch. Just. He hath.

Lan. I will lay odds that, ere this year expire,
We bear our civil swords and native fire
As far as France. I heard a bird so sing,

Scene v: 30-1. "*semper . . . est,*" it is aways the same, for without this there is nothing. **38. mechanical,** base. **39. Alecto,** one of the furies.

91. colour, pretext, with punning reference to: (1) choler; (2) collar, halter, l. 92; (3) flags, l. 94. **97 Fleet,** a prison. **102.** *Si . . . contenta,* cf. II, iv, 195.

Whose music, to my thinking, pleas'd the King.
Come, will you hence? *Exeunt.*

Epilogue

Spoken by a *Dancer.*

First my fear; then my curtsy; last my speech. My fear is, your displeasure; my curtsy, my duty; and my speech, to beg your pardons. If you look for a good speech now, you undo me; for what I have to say is of mine own making; and what indeed I should say will, I doubt, prove mine own marring. But to the purpose, and so to the venture. Be it known to you, as it is very well, I was lately here in the end of a displeasing play, to pray your patience for it and to promise you a better. I meant indeed to pay you with this; which, if like an ill venture it come unluckily home, I break, and you, my gentle creditors, lose. Here I promised you I would be, and here I commit my body to your mercies. Bate me some and I will pay you some and, as most debtors do, promise you infinitely.

If my tongue cannot entreat you to acquit me, will you command me to use my legs? And yet that were but light payment, to dance out of your debt. But a good conscience will make any possible satisfaction, and so would I. All the gentlewomen here have forgiven me; if the gentlemen will not, then the gentlemen do not agree with the gentlewomen, which was never seen before in such an assembly.

One word more, I beseech you. If you be not too much cloyed with fat meat, our humble author will continue the story, with Sir John in it, and make you merry with fair Katharine of France; where, for anything I know, Falstaff shall die of a sweat, unless already 'a be killed with your hard opinions; for Oldcastle died a martyr, and this is not the man. My tongue is weary; when my legs are too, I will bid you good night; and so kneel down before you; but, indeed, to pray for the Queen.

Epi.: 16. Bate, remit. **27ff.** This last paragraph is obviously an addition to explain the change of Oldcastle to Falstaff. It must have been added between the date of composition of this play and February 25, 1598, when Part One was entered for publication as containing "the conceipted mirth of Sir John Falstaff." For a discussion of this change see Introduction, p. 55. It is interesting to note that Falstaff is promised but does not appear in the new play of *Henry V.*

The Life of Henry the Fifth

King Henry V is the last of Shakespeare's long series of chronicle plays. He had attained complete mastery of this form in his two-part drama, *King Henry IV*. The two plays show the evolution of the Prince from the rake of Eastcheap to the sober, righteous, and godly King. It seems to have been Shakespeare's purpose from the beginning to complete the story of his hero and to show him as the "mirror of all Christian Kings," the conqueror of Agincourt, and the embodiment of the national spirit of England. He promised his audience as much in the Epilogue to *II King Henry IV* and fulfilled it in a play which set the capstone on all his earlier work of this type, and having done this he turned to other fields. After *Henry V* Shakespeare wrote no more histories.

Text.—The text of *Henry V* has come down to us in two forms, the Quarto of 1600, and the Folio of 1623. The first of these is one of the "bad quartos" of recent Shakespearean criticism. The original and only true text is that of the Folio.

Date.—It is possible to date the composition of *Henry V* with some degree of accuracy. The well-known reference to Essex (chorus to Act V) enables us to fix the summer of 1599 as the time when the play was finished. The lines speak of Essex as engaged in suppressing rebellion in Ireland and express the confident hope that he will return victorious. Now Essex went to Ireland in March, 1599, and returned—anything but a victor—in September of the same year. The passage must, then, have been written in this interval, and, unless it is an interpolation, this means that Shakespeare was finishing the play between March and September, 1599.

Source.—As in his other histories Shakespeare's main source for *Henry V* is Holinshed's *Chronicles*. With a single exception all the scenes that present the figure of the King are drawn from Holinshed. At times, indeed, Shakespeare borrows the very words of Holinshed and merely transforms them into verse, as when he makes Henry say, "We shall your tawny ground with your red blood discolor"; Holinshed: "I wish not any of you so unadvised, as to be the occasion that I die your tawny ground with your red blood." Shakespeare knew a good phrase when he saw it.

It goes without saying that Shakespeare does not follow his source slavishly. He omits, compresses, and even allows himself certain violations of historic truth. The Dauphin, for example, was not present at Agincourt; Shakespeare brings him there to shame by disgraceful defeat the boaster who had mocked Henry with the gift of tennis balls. He omits all mention of the insurrection of the Lollards at the very beginning of the reign, for the good reason that he wishes to show Henry as King of a united England. And to obtain dramatic speed he closes the play with a treaty of peace and a marriage directly after Agincourt, omitting all mention of the tedious series of sieges and negotiations which followed that battle. After all, Shakespeare was writing not a chronicle but a play for the stage. And in composing his play he was guided to an extent not always realized by the popular old play, the *Famous Victories*. Only about a third of this play deals with the actual reign of Henry, but from this third Shakespeare has caught more than one hint. The Dauphin's scorn of Henry in the French councils, the scene between Pistol and his captive, and more especially the wooing of Katharine are all taken over, enlarged, and vastly improved from the old play.

Henry V, then, is a chronicle play founded upon what was to Shakespeare authoritative history; but it differs in a marked degree from the earlier histories of Shakespeare. There is none of the headlong rush of action that marks *Richard III,* of the lyrical outbursts of *Richard II,* or of the character contrast and character development so brilliantly achieved in the two parts of *Henry IV*. It has often been remarked that the interest of *Henry V* is epic rather than dramatic and indeed it possesses certain characteristics of the epic. Shakespeare himself seems to have been conscious of the impossibility of representing on the stage the national combat of England with her ancient enemy, and in the choruses he expends all his magnificent strength in an appeal to his audience to lift their imagination to the level of his great theme: "Think," he cries, "when we talk of horses that you see them." "This cockpit"—the narrow confine of the Elizabethan theater—cannot hold "the vasty fields of France" nor show "the very casques that did affright the air at Agincourt." Shakespeare had shown no such distrust of the resources of his theater in his earlier historical plays. It is singular that there is not a battle, not even a single broad-sword contest, represented on the stage in a play which purports to tell the tale of England's last great victory upon the Continent. It is interesting to note that in the plays which immediately follow *Henry V*, *Julius Cæsar*, and *Hamlet*, Shakespeare shifts from the external to the internal, from historic to psychologic tragedy. In more ways than one *Henry V* marks a turning point in the evolution of Shakespeare's art.

Character of Henry.—Like many of Shakespeare's dramas *Henry V* is a one-star play. The whole interest and action centers about the person of the royal protagonist. There is a reason for this. Shakespeare was crowning his series of chronicle plays by one which dealt with the last great hero-king of England. Whatever modern historians or moralists may think of Henry, there is no doubt that to his contemporaries and to all succeeding chroniclers down to Shakespeare's time he was the ideal monarch. Holinshed, in particular, overflows with eulogy: "This Henry," he says, "was a king, of life without spot; a prince of all men loved . . . that both lived and died a pattern in princehood, a lodestar in honor, and mirror of magnificence." And Shakespeare, accepting without question this portrait of the great King, set himself to the task of exhibiting him dramatically in action. No other character could be allowed to rival Henry or even for a moment distract our interest from him as Hotspur does to some extent in *I King Henry IV*. The King stands supreme and alone.

On the other hand this play differs from most of Shakespeare's in that there is little if any character development in the person of the hero. The reason is plain enough; *Henry V* does not stand alone; it is the third member of a trilogy, in the earlier parts of which the development of the hero's character had been treated at full length. It remained for Shakespeare to show him in his final phase and this he does in a series of scenes which present the King in one situation after another dealing with each as it arises with perfect wisdom, courage, and good humor. A brief analysis of the play will make this plain.

In the opening scene the Archbishop dwells on the sudden and complete transformation of Henry's character after his father's death. This was part of the legend that had grown up around the historic figure, but Shakespeare had already shown in the earlier plays the gradual rather than the sudden change in the Prince. Then comes the long scene in which Henry demands from the Archbishop a justification of his claim to the throne of France. To us moderns the scene is not only tedious, but carries a suspicion of insincerity, as if Henry were only seeking for a pretext to make war upon his neighbor; but we should remember that Shakespeare and his age had no such horror of war as is felt today, and that hereditary rights to territorial possessions, kingdoms as well as private lands, were universally acknowledged. Henry's claim was no new one; and the only legal bar to it was the so-called Salic law which the French discovered, or invented, to oppose it. We may assume without hesitation that Shakespeare means to show us his hero determined to get an authoritative exposition of his rights before drawing the sword to maintain them. It is worth noting, too, that in this scene Henry is working in perfect harmony with his peers and that he does not plunge into war abroad without making preparations for defense at home. Lastly we may note his proud but dignified reply to the Dauphin's mockery and his appeal to God to justify his cause. The note of piety struck here is re-echoed through the play and is as characteristic of the dramatic as it seems to have been of the historic Henry.

The scene with the conspirators (II, ii) shows Henry at once as a merciful, a just, and an able ruler. He frees a poor wretch who has abused him, makes this incident a means to bar a plea for pardon from the traitors, exposes their treason and sentences them to death, not out of revenge, but because a conspiracy against the King is a betrayal of the kingdom, a maxim very close to the heart of every loyal Elizabethan. It might be noted in passing that Henry's outburst against the familiar friend who had betrayed him shows none of the grieved and disillusioned idealism of a Hamlet, but only the honest anger of an honest man at sudden and surprising villainy.

The famous speech of Henry to his soldiers before the walls of Harfleur has lost with the passing years something of its first appeal. It is magnificent rhetoric, but one wonders whether so good a soldier as Henry would waste so many words in exhorting his men to make faces at the enemy. A set speech before battle was, however, a convention of the Elizabethan stage and Shakespeare follows the rule. Only in the last lines with Henry's call on the good yeomen to show the mettle of their pasture do we get something of that touch of sympathy with the common man that distinguishes this character from all the rest of Shakespeare's kings. His speech to the Governor has been sharply condemned as more befitting a Tamburlaine than a Christian King, but the moralist might remember that by the medieval law of war a city that refused to surrender was given over to sack when stormed. Henry spoke only the truth when he warned the Governor of the terrors that awaited the town, and his warning brought about, as no doubt he expected, a prompt surrender.

It is in the scenes that center around Agincourt that Henry's character is most fully and most favorably portrayed. At this crisis of his fortune, confronted by an overwhelming hostile force, his own dwindling army enfeebled by sickness and starvation, he rises to the height of noble manhood. There is even a certain genial note of fellowship in his behavior alike to nobles and commons that has not appeared since his old tavern days. All his men are "brothers, friends and countrymen." He borrows a cloak of old Sir Thomas to pass disguised among his soldiers and talks with the privates as man to man. He sees through the veil of ceremony that surrounds the office of a King to the hard realities that underlie it, and in the fierce trial that awaits him he is sustained by an unfaltering trust in God and in his own good cause. And when the strain is over and the impossible achieved, Henry shows no trace of boasting or satisfaction in his own achievement, but attributes the almost miraculous victory to God alone, and relaxes into a jesting mood with the soldier Williams and the comic Welshman, Gower.

Finally we have the scene in which Henry, statesman, soldier, and King, is shown as a wooer. Shakespeare had promised his audience at the close of *II King Henry IV* to make them merry in a new play with fair Katharine of France. He kept his promise, and it can hardly be denied that the scene adds a touch of comedy to what has been in the main a drum-and-trumpet sort of play. But what shall we say of Henry's behavior in the scene, what light does it throw upon his character? A fair answer, perhaps, is that his behavior is the only one possible and that it shows him in the same human light as Shakespeare has thrown upon him from the first. How is the conqueror to behave toward the timid girl who is handed over to him by her parents as part of the price of peace? To affect the lover *à la mode,* to play the Romeo, would be a piece of gross hypocrisy of which Henry is incapable. To treat her as the captive of his bow and spear would be inhuman. What he actually does is to laugh with her and at her, to "jolly her along" in the slang phrase, till he has persuaded her that the terrible enemy of France is after all a good heart and "the best king of good fellows." The friendly violence with which he finally breaks down her demure observance of her country's fashion and kisses first her hand and then her lips is hardly likely to frighten or repel her. In short since the scene had to be written and presented, it would seem the Shakespeare has here shown his Henry master of this situation as of others, as successful a wooer as he had been a warrior.

What is the final impression left upon the reader's mind of the character of Henry? It differs, no doubt, from the impression derived by the first spectators in the Elizabethan theater. To them, Henry was the ideal king, a miracle of wisdom, valor, and triumphant success. The modern reader is less enthusiastic, but even the modern reader must grant that Shakespeare has here drawn the perfect picture of the man of action placed in a sphere where his abilities have full scope. Compared with all the rest of Shakespeare's kings, Henry towers above them head and shoulders. But this is by no means to say that he is Shakespeare's ideal man; we may well believe that Shakespeare's heart went out more fully to some of his failures in the world of affairs, to Brutus, to Hamlet, even to the unhappy Richard II. To Shakespeare, we may well believe, the highest human faculty was that of love; the noblest man was he who loved and was beloved by his fellows; and there is little in this play, or in its predecessors, to show either that Henry loved or was beloved by any, except perhaps by the reprobate Falstaff whose heart was "fracted and corroborate" by Henry's cold rejection of his claim. It may perhaps be taken as an axiom of criticism that when Shakespeare profoundly sympathizes with one of his characters he fills that character's mouth with the noblest poetry; and there is little poetry—though much of resounding rhetoric—to be found in the mouth of Henry V. Only at certain moments, as in his judgment on the traitors, or in his soliloquy before the battle, when his soul is touched to higher issues, does Henry' speech rise to the level of Shakespeare's finest verse. And why should we ask for more? Henry is no poet; he expresses his dislike for poetry plainly enough in his speech to Katharine. He is simply the successful man of action in a world where action means strife, and success the ability to use the weapons of war.

Patriotism.—Finally we may remark that Shakespeare's love of country finds its full expression in this play. Not only in the action but in the splendid poetry of the choruses we find Shakespeare hymning the virtues and the glories of his beloved England. The play is in one sense at least an appeal to the poet's contemporaries to forget their private quarrels and to unite like Henry's band of brothers against the foreign foe. To Shakespeare as to his contemporaries the sovereign was God's anointed, and loyalty was the first duty of the subject. But in *Henry V* Shakespeare has shown the other side of the shield. If the subject must be loyal, the monarch must be just, wise, brave, and merciful. The King does not stand apart and alone above a crowd of slaves; he is, or should be, like Henry, the very incarnation of his country, the embodiment of her spirit, the achiever of her destined purposes. His subjects are his brothers, friends, and countrymen. Toward such a king the spirit of patriotism may flow in full measure and perhaps the final lesson of this last of Shakespeare's histories is the dear worth of love of country and of the reciprocal tie which unites the leader and the led.

Stage History.—Henry V was at once successful on the stage with Richard Burbage in the part of King Henry. There is a record of a performance at Court, January 7, 1605, but after that we lose sight of the play for many years.

Its place in Restoration days was taken apparently by Orrery's *History of Henry V*, one of the earliest rhymed "heroic plays." Pepys saw a performance of this drama, August 13, 1664, and pronounced it "a most noble play—full of height and raptures of sense"—whatever that may mean.

With the dawning revival of interest in Shakespeare in the eighteenth century, Aaron Hill brought out a *Henry V or the Conquest of France.* He helped himself liberally to lines from Shakespeare but struck a note that Shakespeare would have been ashamed of, Henry's desertion of a maid he had seduced, a characteristic touch of sentimental tragedy. Shakespeare's play returned to the stage in 1738 and was revived in 1745, perhaps to rouse the fire of patriotism in London when Prince Charlie was threatening the throne. Two years later Garrick produced the play, but contented himself with speaking the lines of the chorus.

Since Garrick's day the play has been revived from time to time, usually as a grand spectacle. Kemble produced it, 1789, with careful attention to costumes and scenery. Macready's production, 1839, was distinguished by pictorial illustrations, a moving diorama of the English fleet, of the armies on the eve of Agincourt, and so on. Charles Kean's production presenting Henry's triumphal entry into London was called a "stupendous show"; it ran eighty-four nights.

It is interesting to note that later revivals in England coincide with periods when an appeal to patriotism on the stage was well-timed. Thus Waller produced it in London during the Boer War, and a revival in 1916 during the World War played to crowded houses. The one famous American production was that of Richard Mansfield in 1900.

THE LIFE OF HENRY THE FIFTH

Henry V (1387–1422)—The *Prince Hal* of the First and Second parts of *Henry IV*. He was born at Monmouth, 9 August 1387, succeeded his father, Henry IV, as king, 20 March 1413, and died at Vincennes in France, 1 September 1422.

Humphrey, Duke of Gloucester (1391–1447), was the youngest son of Henry IV. He was a member of Henry V's council and was with him at Harfleur and Agincourt. After Henry's death he was deputy-protector of England under Bedford.

John, Duke of Bedford (1389–1435)—The *John of Lancaster* of the *Henry IV* plays. He was the third son of Henry IV. During Henry V's campaigns in France he remained in England as "lieutenant of the kingdom" and at Henry's death was appointed regent of France and protector of England.

Thomas Beaufort, Duke of Exeter (d. 1427), was the youngest illegitimate son of John of Gaunt by Catherine Swynford and half-brother of Henry IV. He was at Harfleur and Agincourt.

Edward, Duke of York (1373–1415), the *Aumerle* of *Richard II,* was the son of Edmund de Langley, Duke of Cambridge and York, the fifth son of Edward III. His younger brother was the Earl of Cambridge (q. v.). He was killed at Agincourt.

Thomas de Montacute, Earl of Salisbury (1388–1428), was with Henry at Harfleur and Agincourt. His daughter Alice married Richard Neville, third son of Westmoreland. This accounts for his addressing Westmoreland as "my kind kinsman" in IV, iii, 10.

Ralph Neville, Earl of Westmoreland (1364–1425), appears in both parts of *Henry IV*. He was "cousin" or kinsman of Henry V (IV, iii, 19) by virtue of his taking as his second wife Joan Beaufort, natural daughter of John of Gaunt. He was not at Agincourt.

Richard de Beauchamp, Earl of Warwick (1382–1439), was a great soldier and traveler of his time and one of Henry's trusted lieutenants. He was present at the siege of Harfleur but was sent back to England on a mission and was not at Agincourt.

Henry Chicheley, Archbishop of Canterbury (1364–1443), succeeded Arundel to the see of Canterbury in 1414.

John Fordham, Bishop of Ely, was transferred from Durham to Ely in 1388.

Richard de Langley, Earl of Cambridge (d. 1415), was the second son of Edmund, first Duke of York, and brother to Edward, second Duke of York, who was killed at Agincourt. He was convicted of plotting with Scrope and Sir Thomas Grey to kill Henry and put Edmund Mortimer, Earl of March, on the throne, and was executed in 1415.

Henry de Scrope, Baron Scrope of Masham (1376–1415), was a nephew of Archbishop Scrope of the *Henry IV* plays. Beheaded for high treason in 1415.

Sir Thomas Grey, of Heaton, Northumberland (d. 1415), was a son-in-law of Westmoreland. Executed for high treason in 1415.

Sir Thomas Erpingham is cited in the Agincourt Roll as "steward of the King's house." He is mentioned by Drayton (*Ballad of Agincourt*) as commander of the English archers.

Charles VI of France (1368–1422) was insane during a great part of his life. His queen, Isabel of Bavaria, was unable to cope with the two parties that fought for control and opened the way for English conquest. One of these was headed by the Duke of Burgundy, cousin of the King, and the other (the Armagnacs) by the Duke of Orleans, his brother.

Lewis the Dauphin (d. 1415) was a weakling. He was not present at the battle of Agincourt.

Philip the Good, Duke of Burgundy (1396–1467)—He succeeded to the dukedom in 1419, when his father, *"Jean sans peur,"* was murdered by the Dauphin Charles. As a result he sided immediately with the English and forced Charles VI to accept the Treaty of Troyes, excluding the Dauphin from the succession. As regent of France he signed the treaty.

Charles, Duke of Orleans (1391–1465), was the son of Lewis, Duke of Orleans, who was murdered by order of Jean, Duke of Burgundy, in 1407. He was taken prisoner at Agincourt and not released until 1440.

Jean, Duke of Bourbon (1381–1434), was taken prisoner at Agincourt and confined in England until his death.

Charles d'Albert (d. 1415), (Holinshed and Shakespeare "Delabreth")—Constable of France, commanded the French army at Agincourt and was killed there.

"Montjoy" was not a proper name but the title of the "king at arms" or chief herald of France.

Isabel of Bavaria, Queen of France (1371–1435), was the wife of Charles VI. She consented to the Treaty of Troyes in which Henry V supplanted her son, the Dauphin Charles, as heir to the French throne.

Katharine, Queen of England (1401–1438), was the third daughter of Charles VI and Isabel. She married Henry V, 2 June, 1420, and became the mother of Henry VI. After Henry's death she married Owen Tudor. From this union came the Tudor dynasty.

THE LIFE OF HENRY THE FIFTH

Dramatis Personæ

King Henry the Fifth.
Duke of Gloucester, } brothers to the King.
Duke of Bedford, }
Duke of Exeter, uncle to the King.
Duke of York, cousin to the King.
Earls of Salisbury, Westmoreland, and *Warwick.*
Archbishop of Canterbury.
Bishop of Ely.
Earl of Cambridge.
Lord Scroop.
Sir Thomas Grey.
Sir Thomas Erpingham, }
Gower, }
Fluellen, } officers in *King Henry's* army.
Macmorris, }
Jamy, }
Bates, }
Court, } soldiers in the same.
Williams, }
Pistol.
Nym.
Bardolph.
Boy.
A Herald.

Charles the Sixth, king of France.
Lewis, the Dauphin.
Dukes of Burgundy, Orleans, and *Bourbon.*
The Constable of France.
Rambures, } French Lords.
Grandpré, }
Governor of Harfleur.
Montjoy, a French Herald.
Ambassadors to the King of England.

Isabel, queen of France.
Katharine, daughter to *Charles* and *Isabel.*
Alice, a lady attending on her.
Hostess of a tavern in Eastcheap, formerly Mistress Quickly, now married to *Pistol.*

Chorus.

Lords, Ladies, Officers, Soldiers, Citizens, Messengers, and Attendants.

SCENE: *England; afterwards France.*

Prologue

Enter *Chorus.*

Chor. O for a Muse of fire, that would ascend
The brightest heaven of invention,
A kingdom for a stage, princes to act,
And monarchs to behold the swelling scene!
Then should the warlike Harry, like himself,
Assume the port of Mars; and at his heels,
Leash'd in like hounds, should famine, sword, and fire
Crouch for employment. But pardon, gentles all,
The flat unraised spirits that hath dar'd
On this unworthy scaffold to bring forth
So great an object: can this cockpit hold
The vasty fields of France? Or may we cram
Within this wooden O the very casques
That did affright the air at Agincourt?
O, pardon! since a crooked figure may
Attest in little place a million;
And let us, ciphers to this great accompt,
On your imaginary forces work.
Suppose within the girdle of these walls
Are now confin'd two mighty monarchies,
Whose high upreared and abutting fronts
The perilous narrow ocean parts asunder:
Piece out our imperfections with your thoughts;
Into a thousand parts divide one man,
And make imaginary puissance;
Think, when we talk of horses, that you see them
Printing their proud hoofs i' th' receiving earth;
For 't is your thoughts that now must deck our kings,
Carry them here and there, jumping o'er times,
Turning the accomplishment of many years
Into an hour-glass: for the which supply,
Admit me Chorus to this history;
Who, prologue-like, your humble patience pray,
Gently to hear, kindly to judge, our play.
Exit.

6. port, bearing. **9. unraised,** unaspiring. **10ff.** The **scaffold** (l. 10) is the stage. **Cockpit** (l. 11) means literally the place where cockfights were held, but here the theatre as a whole. **This wooden O** (l. 13) probably refers to the Globe Theatre. **13. casques,** helmets. **15. crooked figure,** either a **cipher** (referred to l. 17) or small figure used to stand for a million, such as 10^7.

18. imaginary forces, forces of imagination. **29. jumping o'er times,** events in the play cover the period 1414-20. **31. for . . . supply,** for supplying gaps in the action.

ACT I. Scene I. *London. An ante-chamber in the King's palace.*

Enter the *Archbishop of Canterbury* and the *Bishop of Ely.*

Cant. My lord, I 'll tell you: that self bill is urg'd,
Which in th' eleventh year of the last king's reign
Was like, and had indeed against us pass'd,
But that the scambling and unquiet time
Did push it out of farther question.
Ely. But how, my lord, shall we resist it now?
Cant. It must be thought on. If it pass against us,
We lose the better half of our possession;
For all the temporal lands, which men devout
By testament have given to the Church,
Would they strip from us; being valued thus:
As much as would maintain, to the King's honour,
Full fifteen earls and fifteen hundred knights,
Six thousand and two hundred good esquires;
And, to relief of lazars and weak age,
Of indigent faint souls past corporal toil,
A hundred almshouses right well supplied;
And to the coffers of the King beside,
A thousand pounds by the year. Thus runs the bill.
Ely. This would drink deep.
Cant. 'T would drink the cup and all.
Ely. But what prevention?
Cant. The King is full of grace and fair regard.
Ely. And a true lover of the holy Church.
Cant. The courses of his youth promis'd it not.
The breath no sooner left his father's body,
But that his wildness, mortified in him,
Seem'd to die too; yea, at that very moment
Consideration like an angel came
And whipp'd the offending Adam out of him,
Leaving his body as a paradise
To envelope and contain celestial spirits.
Never was such a sudden scholar made;
Never came reformation in a flood
With such a heady currance, scouring faults;
Nor never Hydra-headed wilfulness
So soon did lose his seat, and all at once,
As in this king.
Ely. We are blessed in the change.
Cant. Hear him but reason in divinity,
And, all-admiring, with an inward wish
You would desire the King were made a prelate;
Hear him debate of commonwealth affairs,
You would say it hath been all in all his study;
List his discourse of war, and you shall hear
A fearful battle render'd you in music;
Turn him to any cause of policy,
The Gordian knot of it he will unloose,
Familiar as his garter; that, when he speaks,
The air, a charter'd libertine, is still,
And the mute wonder lurketh in men's ears,
To steal his sweet and honey'd sentences;
So that the art and practic part of life
Must be the mistress to this theoric:
Which is a wonder how his Grace should glean it,
Since his addiction was to courses vain,
His companies unletter'd, rude, and shallow,
His hours fill'd up with riots, banquets, sports,
And never noted in him any study,
Any retirement, any sequestration
From open haunts and popularity.
Ely. The strawberry grows underneath the nettle,
And wholesome berries thrive and ripen best
Neighbour'd by fruit of baser quality;
And so the Prince obscur'd his contemplation
Under the veil of wildness; which, no doubt,
Grew like the summer grass, fastest by night,
Unseen, yet crescive in his faculty.
Cant. It must be so; for miracles are ceas'd,
And therefore we must needs admit the means
How things are perfected.
Ely. But, my good lord,
How now for mitigation of this bill
Urg'd by the commons? Doth his Majesty
Incline to it, or no?
Cant. He seems indifferent,
Or rather swaying more upon our part
Than cherishing the exhibiters against us;
For I have made an offer to his Majesty,
Upon our spiritual convocation
And in regard of causes now in hand,
Which I have open'd to his Grace at large,
As touching France, to give a greater sum
Than ever at one time the clergy yet
Did to his predecessors part withal.
Ely. How did this offer seem receiv'd, my lord?

Act I, Scene i: 1. self, same. **3. like,** likely (to pass). **4. scambling,** disordered. **5. question,** consideration. **15. lazars,** lepers. **28. Consideration,** reflection. **34. heady currance,** impetuous current. **35. Hydra-headed,** many-headed.

45. cause of policy, affair of state. **48. charter'd libertine,** free as by charter. **51. art,** here synonymous with practical (**practic** l. 51) part of life. Henry has reversed the usual process and learned the theory (**theoric** l. 52) from the art and practice of life. This is all the more strange because his frivolous young days have seemed to give him no experience of statecraft. **55. companies,** companions. **57. never noted,** there was never noted. **59. popularity,** vulgar company. **66. crescive in his faculty,** growing by its own strength. **74. exhibiters,** sponsors of a bill. **76. Upon our spiritual convocation,** by the authority of or on behalf of the assembly of bishops and clergy.

Cant. With good acceptance of his Majesty;
Save that there was not time enough to hear,
As I perceiv'd his Grace would fain have done,
The severals and unhidden passages
Of his true titles to some certain dukedoms,
And generally to the crown and seat of France
Deriv'd from Edward, his great-grandfather.
Ely. What was the impediment that broke this off?
Cant. The French ambassador upon that instant
Crav'd audience; and the hour, I think, is come
To give him hearing. Is it four o'clock?
Ely. It is.
Cant. Then go we in, to know his embassy;
Which I could with a ready guess declare,
Before the Frenchman speak a word of it.
Ely. I 'll wait upon you, and I long to hear it. *Exeunt.*

Scene II. *The same. The presence chamber.*

Enter *King Henry, Gloucester, Bedford, Exeter, Warwick, Westmoreland* and Attendants.

K. Hen. Where is my gracious Lord of Canterbury?
Exe. Not here in presence.
K. Hen. Send for him, good uncle.
West. Shall we call in the ambassador, my liege?
K. Hen. Not yet, my cousin: we would be resolv'd,
Before we hear him, of some things of weight
That task our thoughts, concerning us and France.

Enter the *Archbishop of Canterbury* and the *Bishop of Ely.*

Cant. God and his angels guard your sacred throne
And make you long become it!
K. Hen. Sure, we thank you.
My learned lord, we pray you to proceed
And justly and religiously unfold
Why the law Salique that they have in France
Or should, or should not, bar us in our claim;
And God forbid, my dear and faithful lord,
That you should fashion, wrest, or bow your reading,
Or nicely charge your understanding soul
With opening titles miscreate, whose right
Suits not in native colours with the truth;
For God doth know how many now in health
Shall drop their blood in approbation
Of what your reverence shall incite us to.
Therefore take heed how you impawn our person,
How you awake our sleeping sword of war:
We charge you, in the name of God, take heed;
For never two such kingdoms did contend
Without much fall of blood, whose guiltless drops
Are every one a woe, a sore complaint
'Gainst him whose wrong gives edge unto the swords
That makes such waste in brief mortality.
Under this conjuration speak, my lord;
For we will hear, note, and believe in heart
That what you speak is in your conscience wash'd
As pure as sin with baptism.
Cant. Then hear me, gracious sovereign, and you peers,
That owe yourselves, your lives, and services
To this imperial throne. There is no bar
To make against your Highness' claim to France
But this, which they produce from Pharamond:
"In terram Salicam mulieres ne succedant,"
"No woman shall succeed in Salique land";
Which Salique land the French unjustly gloze
To be the realm of France, and Pharamond
The founder of this law and female bar.
Yet their own authors faithfully affirm
That the land Salique is in Germany,
Between the floods of Sala and of Elbe;
Where Charles the Great, having subdued the Saxons,
There left behind and settled certain French;
Who, holding in disdain the German women
For some dishonest manners of their life,
Establish'd then this law; to wit, no female
Should be inheritrix in Salique land;
Which Salique, as I said, 'twixt Elbe and Sala,
Is at this day in Germany called Meisen.
Then doth it well appear the Salique law
Was not devised for the realm of France;
Nor did the French possess the Salique land
Until four hundred one and twenty years
After defunction of King Pharamond,
Idly suppos'd the founder of this law,

86. severals, particulars. **unhidden passages,** clear lines of succession. **Scene ii: 4-5. resolv'd . . . of,** satisfied about. **11. law Salique,** Henry's claim to the French throne was through his great-great-grandmother, Isabelle, daughter of Philip IV. The bearings of this law are clearly enough indicated in the speeches that follow. In them Shakespeare follows closely his chief source: Holinshed's "Chronicles of England, Scotland and Ireland."

15. nicely, subtly. **16. opening,** disclosing. **miscreate,** illegitimate. **19. approbation,** proving, establishing. **21. impawn,** pledge. **28. mortality,** human life. **37. Pharamond,** early Frankish king. **40. gloze,** interpret. **49. dishonest,** unchaste. **58. defunction,** death.

Who died within the year of our redemption
Four hundred twenty-six; and Charles the Great
Subdued the Saxons, and did seat the French
Beyond the river Sala, in the year
Eight hundred five. Besides, their writers say,
King Pepin, which deposed Childeric,
Did, as heir general, being descended
Of Blithild, which was daughter to King Clothair,
Make claim and title to the crown of France.
Hugh Capet also, who usurp'd the crown
Of Charles the Duke of Lorraine, sole heir male
Of the true line and stock of Charles the Great,
To find his title with some shows of truth,
Though, in pure truth, it was corrupt and naught,
Convey'd himself as the heir to th' Lady Lingare,
Daughter to Charlemain, who was the son
To Lewis the Emperor, and Lewis the son
Of Charles the Great. Also, King Lewis the Tenth,
Who was sole heir to the usurper Capet,
Could not keep quiet in his conscience,
Wearing the crown of France, till satisfied
That fair Queen Isabel, his grandmother,
Was lineal of the Lady Ermengare,
Daughter to Charles, the foresaid Duke of Lorraine;
By the which marriage the line of Charles the Great
Was re-united to the crown of France.
So that, as clear as is the summer's sun,
King Pepin's title and Hugh Capet's claim,
King Lewis his satisfaction, all appear
To hold in right and title of the female.
So do the kings of France unto this day,
Howbeit they would hold up this Salique law
To bar your Highness claiming from the female,
And rather choose to hide them in a net
Than amply to imbar their crooked titles
Usurp'd from you and your progenitors.

K. Hen. May I with right and conscience make this claim?

Cant. The sin upon my head, dread sovereign!
For in the book of Numbers is it writ,
When the man dies, let the inheritance
Descend unto the daughter. Gracious lord,
Stand for your own! Unwind your bloody flag!
Look back into your mighty ancestors!
Go, my dread lord, to your great-grandsire's tomb,
From whom you claim; invoke his warlike spirit,
And your great-uncle's, Edward the Black Prince,
Who on the French ground play'd a tragedy,
Making defeat on the full power of France,
Whiles his most mighty father on a hill
Stood smiling to behold his lion's whelp
Forage in blood of French nobility.
O noble English, that could entertain
With half their forces the full pride of France
And let another half stand laughing by,
All out of work and cold for action!

Ely. Awake remembrance of these valiant dead,
And with your puissant arm renew their feats:
You are their heir; you sit upon their throne;
The blood and courage that renowned them
Runs in your veins; and my thrice-puissant liege
Is in the very May-morn of his youth,
Ripe for exploits and mighty enterprises.

Exe. Your brother kings and monarchs of the earth
Do all expect that you should rouse yourself,
As did the former lions of your blood.

West. They know your Grace hath cause and means and might;
So hath your Highness: never King of England
Had nobles richer, and more loyal subjects,
Whose hearts have left their bodies here in England
And lie pavilion'd in the fields of France.

Cant. O, let their bodies follow, my dear liege,
With blood and sword and fire to win your right;
In aid whereof we of the spiritualty
Will raise your Highness such a mighty sum
As never did the clergy at one time
Bring in to any of your ancestors.

K. Hen. We must not only arm to invade the French,
But lay down our proportions to defend
Against the Scot, who will make road upon us
With all advantages.

72. **find,** provide. 74. **Convey'd himself,** passed himself off. 75. **Charlemain,** not Charlemagne, i.e., Charles the Great (l. 77), but Charles the Bald, son of Lewis the Pious. 77. **Lewis the Tenth,** mistake for Lewis the Ninth (St. Louis). Shakespeare here, as in the greater part of this passage, has followed Holinshed. 93-5. **And . . . progenitors,** the reading of this passage turns upon the meaning of **imbar,** which has been variously interpreted. If it means **bar in, secure, defend,** the passage would read: "They prefer to involve themselves in contradictions rather than fully to defend their own false titles." Their defense, of course, would be that their line of descent, even though it was through the female, was better than the English.

98. **Numbers,** 27:1-11. 103-14. Battle of Crécy, 26 August, 1346. 114. **for,** for want of. 132. **spiritualty,** clergy. 137. **proportions,** number of troops. 138. **road,** inroad.

Cant. They of those marches, gracious sovereign,
Shall be a wall sufficient to defend
Our inland from the pilfering borderers.
K. Hen. We do not mean the coursing snatchers only,
But fear the main intendment of the Scot,
Who hath been still a giddy neighbour to us;
For you shall read that my great-grandfather
Never went with his forces into France
But that the Scot on his unfurnish'd kingdom
Came pouring, like the tide into a breach,
With ample and brim fullness of his force,
Galling the gleaned land with hot assays,
Girding with grievous siege castles and towns;
That England, being empty of defence,
Hath shook and trembled at th' ill neighbourhood.
Cant. She hath been then more fear'd than harm'd, my liege;
For hear her but exampled by herself:
When all her chivalry hath been in France,
And she a mourning widow of her nobles,
She hath herself not only well defended
But taken and impounded as a stray
The King of Scots; whom she did send to France
To fill King Edward's fame with prisoner kings,
And make her chronicle as rich with praise
As is the ooze and bottom of the sea
With sunken wrack and sumless treasuries.
West. But there 's a saying very old and true:
"If that you will France win,
Then with Scotland first begin."
For once the eagle England being in prey,
To her unguarded nest the weasel Scot
Comes sneaking and so sucks her princely eggs,
Playing the mouse in absence of the cat,
To tear and havoc more than she can eat.
Exe. It follows then the cat must stay at home;
Yet that is but a crush'd necessity,
Since we have locks to safeguard necessaries,
And pretty traps to catch the petty thieves.
While that the armed hand doth fight abroad,
Th' advised head defends itself at home;
For government, though high and low and lower,
Put into parts, doth keep in one consent,
Congreeing in a full and natural close,
Like music.

140. marches, borders. **143. coursing snatchers,** swift-riding marauders. **144. intendment,** intention. **145. still,** always. **giddy,** unstable. **148. unfurnish'd,** unprotected. **151. assays,** attacks. **155. fear'd,** frightened. **161. King of Scots,** David Bruce, 1346. **169. in prey,** in search of prey. **175. crush'd,** forced, strained. **181. parts,** as in music. **consent,** harmony. **182. congreeing,** agreeing. **close,** cadence.

Cant. Therefore doth heaven divide
The state of man in divers functions,
Setting endeavour in continual motion,
To which is fixed, as an aim or butt,
Obedience; for so work the honey-bees,
Creatures that by a rule in nature teach
The act of order to a peopled kingdom.
They have a king and officers of sorts,
Where some, like magistrates, correct at home,
Others, like merchants, venture trade abroad,
Others, like soldiers, armed in their stings,
Make boot upon the summer's velvet buds,
Which pillage they with merry march bring home
To the tent-royal of their emperor;
Who busied in his majesty, surveys
The singing masons building roofs of gold,
The civil citizens kneading up the honey,
The poor mechanic porters crowding in
Their heavy burdens at his narrow gate,
The sad-eyed justice, with his surly hum,
Delivering o'er to executors pale
The lazy yawning drone. I this infer,
That many things, having full reference
To one consent, may work contrariously.
As many arrows, loosed several ways,
Come to one mark; as many ways meet in one town;
As many fresh streams meet in one salt sea;
As many lines close in the dial's centre;
So may a thousand actions, once afoot,
End in one purpose, and be all well borne
Without defeat. Therefore to France, my liege!
Divide your happy England into four,
Whereof take you one quarter into France,
And you withal shall make all Gallia shake.
If we, with thrice such powers left at home,
Cannot defend our own doors from the dog,
Let us be worried and our nation lose
The name of hardiness and policy.
K. Hen. Call in the messengers sent from the Dauphin. *Exeunt some Attendants.*
Now are we well resolv'd; and, by God's help,
And yours, the noble sinews of our power,
France being ours, we 'll bend it to our awe,
Or break it all to pieces. Or there we 'll sit,
Ruling in large and ample empery
O'er France and all her almost kingly dukedoms,
Or lay these bones in an unworthy urn,
Tombless, with no remembrance over them:
Either our history shall with full mouth
Speak freely of our acts, or else our grave,
Like Turkish mute, shall have a tongueless mouth,
Not worshipp'd with a waxen epitaph.

190. sorts, different ranks. **194. make boot,** plunder. **220. policy,** wisdom. **226. empery,** power. **233. worshipp'd,** honored. **waxen,** perishable.

Enter *Ambassadors* of France.

Now are we well prepar'd to know the pleasure
Of our fair cousin Dauphin; for we hear
Your greeting is from him, not from the King.

1. Amb. May 't please your Majesty to give us leave
Freely to render what we have in charge;
Or shall we sparingly show you far off
The Dauphin's meaning and our embassy?

K. Hen. We are no tyrant, but a Christian king,
Unto whose grace our passion is as subject
As is our wretches fetter'd in our prisons;
Therefore with frank and with uncurbed plainness
Tell us the Dauphin's mind.

1. Amb. Thus, then, in few.
Your Highness, lately sending into France,
Did claim some certain dukedoms, in the right
Of your great predecessor, King Edward the Third.
In answer of which claim, the Prince our master
Says that you savour too much of your youth,
And bids you be advis'd. There 's nought in France
That can be with a nimble galliard won;
You cannot revel into dukedoms there.
He therefore sends you, meeter for your spirit,
This tun of treasure; and, in lieu of this,
Desires you let the dukedoms that you claim
Hear no more of you. This the Dauphin speaks.

K. Hen. What treasure, uncle?

Exe. Tennis-balls, my liege.

K. Hen. We are glad the Dauphin is so pleasant with us;
His present and your pains we thank you for:
When we have match'd our rackets to these balls,
We will, in France, by God's grace, play a set
Shall strike his father's crown into the hazard.
Tell him he hath made a match with such a wrangler
That all the courts of France will be disturb'd
With chaces. And we understand him well,
How he comes o'er us with our wilder days,
Not measuring what use we made of them.
We never valued this poor seat of England;
And therefore, living hence, did give ourself
To barbarous license; as 't is ever common
That men are merriest when they are from home.
But tell the Dauphin I will keep my state,
Be like a king, and show my sail of greatness
When I do rouse me in my throne of France:
For that I have laid by my majesty
And plodded like a man for working-days,
But I will rise there with so full a glory
That I will dazzle all the eyes of France,
Yea, strike the Dauphin blind to look on us.
And tell the pleasant prince this mock of his
Hath turn'd his balls to gun-stones, and his soul
Shall stand sore charged for the wasteful vengeance
That shall fly with them; for many a thousand widows
Shall this his mock mock out of their dear husbands,
Mock mothers from their sons, mock castles down;
And some are yet ungotten and unborn
That shall have cause to curse the Dauphin's scorn.
But this lies all within the will of God,
To whom I do appeal; and in whose name
Tell you the Dauphin I am coming on
To venge me as I may, and to put forth
My rightful hand in a well-hallow'd cause.
So get you hence in peace; and tell the Dauphin
His jest will savour but of shallow wit,
When thousands weep more than did laugh at it.
Convey them with safe conduct. Fare you well. *Exeunt Ambassadors.*

Exe. This was a merry message.

K. Hen. We hope to make the sender blush at it.
Therefore, my lords, omit no happy hour
That may give furtherance to our expedition;
For we have now no thought in us but France,
Save those to God, that run before our business.
Therefore, let our proportions for these wars
Be soon collected, and all things thought upon
That may with reasonable swiftness add
More feathers to our wings; for, God before,
We 'll chide this Dauphin at his father's door.
Therefore let every man now task his thought,
That this fair action may on foot be brought.

Exeunt.

245. in few, in few words. **252. galliard,** a lively dance. **255. tun,** a cask. **262-6. Hazard** (l. 263), part of court, **wrangler** (l. 264), an opponent, **chaces** (l. 266), a particular stroke or play, were all terms used in the old game of court tennis. **Hazard, court,** and **chaces** are puns. **267. comes o'er,** taunts. **269. seat,** throne.

270. hence, away from court. **282. gun-stones,** stone cannon-balls. **307. God before,** God helping us.

ACT II

Flourish. Enter *Chorus.*

Chor. Now all the youth of England are on fire,
And silken dalliance in the wardrobe lies.
Now thrive the armourers, and honour's thought
Reigns solely in the breast of every man:
They sell the pasture now to buy the horse,
Following the mirror of all Christian kings,
With winged heels, as English Mercuries.
For now sits Expectation in the air,
And hides a sword from hilts unto the point
With crowns imperial, crowns, and coronets,
Promis'd to Harry and his followers.
The French, advis'd by good intelligence
Of this most dreadful preparation,
Shake in their fear, and with pale policy
Seek to divert the English purposes.
O England! model to thy inward greatness,
Like little body with a mighty heart,
What mightst thou do, that honour would thee do,
Were all thy children kind and natural!
But see, thy fault France hath in thee found out,
A nest of hollow bosoms, which he fills
With treacherous crowns; and three corrupted men,
One, Richard Earl of Cambridge, and the second,
Henry Lord Scroop of Masham, and the third,
Sir Thomas Grey, knight, of Northumberland,
Have, for the gilt of France,—O guilt indeed!—
Confirm'd conspiracy with fearful France;
And by their hands this grace of kings must die,
If hell and treason hold their promises,
Ere he take ship for France, and in Southampton.
Linger your patience on, and we 'll digest
The abuse of distance, force a play.
The sum is paid; the traitors are agreed;
The King is set from London; and the scene
Is now transported, gentles, to Southampton.
There is the playhouse now, there must you sit;
And thence to France shall we convey you safe,
And bring you back, charming the narrow seas
To give you gentle pass; for, if we may,
We 'll not offend one stomach with our play.
But, till the King come forth, and not till then,
Unto Southampton do we shift our scene.
Exit.

Scene I. *London. A street.*

Enter *Corporal Nym* and *Lieutenant Bardolph.*

Bard. Well met, Corporal Nym.

Nym. Good morrow, Lieutenant Bardolph.

Bard. What, are Ancient Pistol and you friends yet?

Nym. For my part, I care not: I say little; but when time shall serve, there shall be smiles; but that shall be as it may. I dare not fight, but I will wink and hold out mine iron. It is a simple one, but what though? It will toast cheese, and it will endure cold as another man's sword will; and there 's an end.

Bard. I will bestow a breakfast to make you friends; and we 'll be all three sworn brothers to France: let it be so, good Corporal Nym.

Nym. Faith, I will live so long as I may, that 's the certain of it; and when I cannot live any longer, I will do as I may: that is my rest, that is the rendezvous of it.

Bard. It is certain, corporal, that he is married to Nell Quickly; and certainly she did you wrong, for you were troth-plight to her.

Nym. I cannot tell: things must be as they may: men may sleep, and they may have their throats about them at that time; and some say knives have edges. It must be as it may: though patience be a tired mare, yet she will plod. There must be conclusions. Well, I cannot tell.

Enter *Pistol* and *Hostess.*

Bard. Here come Ancient Pistol and his wife. Good corporal, be patient here. How now, mine host Pistol!

Pist. Base tike, call'st thou me host?
Now, by this hand, I swear, I scorn the term;
Nor shall my Nell keep lodgers.

Host. No, by my troth, not long; for we cannot lodge and board a dozen or fourteen gentlewomen that live honestly by the prick of

Act II, Chorus: 12. intelligence, information. **14. policy,** cunning. **18. would,** would have. **22. crowns,** pieces of money. **26. gilt,** gold. **31-2.** Paraphrase: Continue, extend **(linger l. 31)** your patience and we 'll reduce to nothing **(digest l. 31)** the limitations imposed by distance and force into a play events widely separated in time and place. **39. pass,** passage.

Act II, Scene i: 3. Ancient, ensign. **18. rest,** a term in the game of Primero, meaning the hand of cards on which one staked one's chance of winning or the stake itself. Most of Nym's phrases were current in his day but are meaningless in his context. **Rendezvous** (l. 18) is typical. **31. tike,** cur.

their needles, but it will be thought we keep a bawdy house straight. [*Nym and Pistol draw.*] O well a day, Lady, if he be not drawn now! We shall see wilful adultery and murder committed.

Bard. Good lieutenant! good corporal! offer nothing here.

Nym. Pish!

Pist. Pish for thee, Iceland dog! thou prick-ear'd cur of Iceland!

Host. Good Corporal Nym, show thy valour, and put up your sword.

Nym. Will you shog off? I would have you solus.

Pist. "Solus," egregious dog! O viper vile!
The "solus" in thy most mervailous face;
The "solus" in thy teeth, and in thy throat,
And in thy hateful lungs, yea, in thy maw, perdy,
And, which is worse, within thy nasty mouth!
I do retort the "solus" in thy bowels;
For I can take, and Pistol's cock is up,
And flashing fire will follow.

Nym. I am not Barbason; you cannot conjure me. I have an humour to knock you indifferently well. If you grow foul with me, Pistol, I will scour you with my rapier, as I may, in fair terms: if you would walk off, I would prick your guts a little, in good terms, as I may; and that 's the humour of it.

Pist. O braggart vile and damned furious wight!
The grave doth gape, and doting death is near,
Therefore exhale.

Bard. Hear me, hear me what I say: he that strikes the first stroke, I 'll run him up to the hilts, as I am a soldier. *Draws.*

Pist. An oath of mickle might; and fury shall abate.
Give me thy fist, thy fore-foot to me give;
Thy spirits are most tall.

Nym. I will cut thy throat, one time or other, in fair terms: that is the humour of it.

Pist. *"Couple a gorge!"*
That is the word. I thee defy again.
O hound of Crete, think'st thou my spouse to get?
No! to the spital go,
And from the powdering-tub of infamy
Fetch forth the lazar kite of Cressid's kind,
Doll Tearsheet she by name, and her espouse:
I have, and I will hold, the quondam Quickly
For the only she; and—*pauca,* there 's enough.
Go to.

Enter the *Boy.*

Boy. Mine host Pistol, you must come to my master, and you, hostess: he is very sick, and would to bed. Good Bardolph, put thy face between his sheets, and do the office of a warming-pan. Faith, he 's very ill.

Bard. Away, you rogue!

Host. By my troth, he 'll yield the crow a pudding one of these days. The King has killed his heart. Good husband, come home presently.

Exeunt Hostess and Boy.

Bard. Come, shall I make you two friends? We must to France together; why the devil should we keep knives to cut one another's throats?

Pist. Let floods o'erswell, and fiends for food howl on!

Nym. You 'll pay me the eight shillings I won of you at betting?

Pist. Base is the slave that pays.

Nym. That now I will have: that 's the humour of it.

Pist. As manhood shall compound. Push home. *They draw.*

Bard. By this sword, he that makes the first thrust, I 'll kill him; by this sword, I will.

Pist. Sword is an oath, and oaths must have their course.

Bard. Corporal Nym, an thou wilt be friends, be friends; an thou wilt not, why, then, be enemies with me too. Prithee, put up.

Nym. I shall have my eight shillings I won from you at betting?

Pist. A noble shalt thou have, and present pay;
And liquor likewise will I give to thee,
And friendship shall combine, and brotherhood:
I 'll live by Nym, and Nym shall live by me.
Is not this just? For I shall sutler be
Unto the camp, and profits will accrue.
Give me thy hand.

Nym. I shall have my noble?

Pist. In cash most justly paid.

Nym. Well, then that 's the humour of 't.

Re-enter *Hostess.*

Host. As ever you come of women, come in quickly to Sir John. Ah, poor heart! he is so shaked of a burning quotidian tertian, that

39. Lady, by the Virgin Mary. **43. Iceland dog,** imported into Elizabethan England as pet dogs. They were of shaggy appearance and evil temper. **47. shog,** move. **55. take,** harm. **57. Barbason,** name of a fiend. **72. tall,** courageous. **75. Couple a gorge,** couper la gorge. **78. spital,** hospital. **79. powdering tub,** tub used for salting meat. Here it refers to the hot bath used in the treatment of venereal diseases. **80. lazar kite of Cressid's kind,** in Henryson's "Testament of Cresseid" Cressida becomes a leprous beggar.

83. *pauca,* briefly. **93. presently,** immediately. **102. compound,** determine. **112. noble,** 6s. 8d. **116. sutler,** provisioner. **124. quotidian tertian,** fever (ridiculous confusion of medical terms).

it is most lamentable to behold. Sweet men, come to him.

Nym. The King hath run bad humours on the knight; that 's the even of it.

Pist. Nym, thou hast spoke the right.
His heart is fracted and corroborate.

Nym. The king is a good King; but it must be as it may; he passes some humours and careers.

Pist. Let us condole the knight; for, lambkins, we will live. *Exeunt.*

Scene II. *Southampton. A council-chamber.*

Enter *Exeter, Bedford,* and *Westmoreland.*

Bed. 'Fore God, his Grace is bold, to trust these traitors.

Exe. They shall be apprehended by and by.

West. How smooth and even they do bear themselves!
As if allegiance in their bosoms sat,
Crowned with faith and constant loyalty.

Bed. The King hath note of all that they intend,
By interception which they dream not of.

Exe. Nay, but the man that was his bed-fellow,
Whom he hath dull'd and cloy'd with gracious favours,
That he should, for a foreign purse, so sell
His sovereign's life to death and treachery.

Trumpets sound. Enter *King Henry, Scroop, Cambridge,* and *Grey.*

K. Hen. Now sits the wind fair, and we will aboard.
My Lord of Cambridge, and my kind Lord of Masham,
And you, my gentle knight, give me your thoughts:
Think you not that the powers we bear with us
Will cut their passage through the force of France,
Doing the execution and the act
For which we have in head assembled them?

Scroop. No doubt, my liege, if each man do his best.

K. Hen. I doubt not that, since we are well persuaded
We carry not a heart with us from hence
That grows not in a fair consent with ours,
Nor leave not one behind that doth not wish
Success and conquest to attend on us.

Cam. Never was monarch better fear'd and lov'd
Than is your Majesty: there 's not, I think, a subject
That sits in heart-grief and uneasiness
Under the sweet shade of your government.

Grey. True; those that were your father's enemies
Have steep'd their galls in honey, and do serve you
With hearts create of duty and of zeal.

K. Hen. We therefore have great cause of thankfulness,
And shall forget the office of our hand
Sooner than quittance of desert and merit
According to the weight and worthiness.

Scroop. So service shall with steeled sinews toil,
And labour shall refresh itself with hope,
To do your Grace incessant services.

K. Hen. We judge no less. Uncle of Exeter,
Enlarge the man committed yesterday,
That rail'd against our person: we consider
It was excess of wine that set him on,
And on his more advice we pardon him.

Scroop. That 's mercy, but too much security:
Let him be punish'd, sovereign, lest example
Breed, by his sufferance, more of such a kind.

K. Hen. O, let us yet be merciful.

Cam. So may your Highness, and yet punish too.

Grey. Sir,
You show great mercy if you give him life
After the taste of much correction.

K. Hen. Alas, your too much love and care of me
Are heavy orisons 'gainst this poor wretch!
If little faults, proceeding on distemper,
Shall not be wink'd at, how shall we stretch our eye
When capital crimes, chew'd, swallow'd and digested,
Appear before us? We 'll yet enlarge that man,
Though Cambridge, Scroop, and Grey, in their dear care
And tender preservation of our person,
Would have him punish'd. And now to our French causes.
Who are the late commissioners?

Cam. I one, my lord.
Your Highness bade me ask for it to-day.

Scroop. So did you me, my liege.

130. **fracted,** broken. **corroborate,** made strong (misuse). 132. **passes,** gives vent to. **careers,** wild courses. 133. **condole,** lament. **Scene ii: 2. by and by,** immediately. 18. **head,** organized force.

33. **office of our hand,** royal power. 34. **quittance,** reward. 43. **advice,** reflection, consideration. 44. **security,** want of caution. 46. **by his sufferance,** by his being pardoned. 53. **orisons,** prayers. 54. **distemper,** drunkenness. 55. **stretch our eye,** open the eye wide to view great crimes. 61. **late,** lately appointed. 63. **it,** the commission.

Grey. And I, my royal sovereign.
K. Hen. Then, Richard Earl of Cambridge, there is yours;
There yours, Lord Scroop of Masham; and, sir knight,
Grey of Northumberland, this same is yours.
Read them, and know I know your worthiness.
My Lord of Westmoreland, and uncle Exeter,
We will aboard to-night.—Why, how now, gentlemen!
What see you in those papers that you lose
So much complexion?—Look ye, how they change!
Their cheeks are paper.—Why, what read you there,
That have so cowarded and chas'd your blood
Out of appearance?
Cam. I do confess my fault,
And do submit me to your Highness' mercy.
Grey. } *Scroop.* } To which we all appeal.
K. Hen. The mercy that was quick in us but late,
By your own counsel is suppress'd and kill'd:
You must not dare, for shame, to talk of mercy,
For your own reasons turn into your bosoms,
As dogs upon their masters, worrying you.
See you, my princes and my noble peers,
These English monsters! My Lord of Cambridge here,
You know how apt our love was to accord
To furnish him with all appertinents
Belonging to his honour; and this man
Hath, for a few light crowns, lightly conspir'd
And sworn unto the practices of France
To kill us here in Hampton; to the which
This knight, no less for bounty bound to us
Than Cambridge is, hath likewise sworn. But, O
What shall I say to thee, Lord Scroop? thou cruel,
Ingrateful, savage, and inhuman creature!
Thou that didst bear the key of all my counsels,
That knew'st the very bottom of my soul,
That almost mightst have coin'd me into gold,
Wouldst thou have practis'd on me for thy use,—
May it be possible that foreign hire
Could out of thee extract one spark of evil
That might annoy my finger? 'T is so strange,
That, though the truth of it stands off as gross
As black and white, my eye will scarcely see it.
Treason and murder ever kept together,
As two yoke-devils sworn to either's purpose,
Working so grossly in a natural cause
That admiration did not whoop at them;
But thou, 'gainst all proportion, didst bring in
Wonder to wait on treason and on murder;
And whatsoever cunning fiend it was
That wrought upon thee so preposterously
Hath got the voice in hell for excellence;
And other devils that suggest by treasons
Do botch and bungle up damnation
With patches, colours, and with forms being fetch'd
From glist'ring semblances of piety;
But he that temper'd thee bade thee stand up,
Gave thee no instance why thou shouldst do treason,
Unless to dub thee with the name of traitor.
If that same demon that hath gull'd thee thus
Should with his lion gait walk the whole world,
He might return to vasty Tartar back,
And tell the legions, "I can never win
A soul so easy as that Englishman's."
O, how hast thou with jealousy infected
The sweetness of affiance! Show men dutiful?
Why, so didst thou. Seem they grave and learned?
Why, so didst thou. Come they of noble family?
Why, so didst thou. Seem they religious?
Why, so didst thou. Or are they spare in diet,
Free from gross passion or of mirth or anger,
Constant in spirit, not swerving with the blood,
Garnish'd and deck'd in modest complement,
Not working with the eye without the ear,
And but in purged judgement trusting neither?
Such and so finely bolted didst thou seem:
And thus thy fall hath left a kind of blot
To mark the full-fraught man and best indued
With some suspicion. I will weep for thee;
For this revolt of thine, methinks, is like
Another fall of man. Their faults are open.
Arrest them to the answer of the law;
And God acquit them of their practices!

Exe. I arrest thee of high treason, by the name of Richard Earl of Cambridge.

I arrest thee of high treason, by the name of Henry Lord Scroop of Masham.

I arrest thee of high treason, by the name of Thomas Grey, knight, of Northumberland.

Scroop. Our purposes God justly hath discover'd,

79. quick, alive. **86. accord,** agree. **90. practices,** plots. **103. gross,** palpable. **107. natural,** human.

108. admiration, wonder. **112. preposterously,** contrary to the natural order of things. **114-20.** "Other devils who tempt one to treason cover up the damnable sin by some semblance of piety. But he who fashioned you commanded you to stand up as his man and gave no reason for your treason except that you might be called traitor." **114. suggest,** seduce. **115. botch,** patch clumsily. **118. temper'd,** fashioned. **121. gull'd,** fooled. **123. Tartar,** Tartarus. **127. affiance,** trust. **Show,** appear. **133. blood,** passion. **134. complement,** outward appearance. **137. bolted,** sifted (like flour). **139. full-fraught,** freighted (with virtue). **151. discover'd,** disclosed.

And I repent my fault more than my death,
Which I beseech your Highness to forgive,
Although my body pay the price of it.
Cam. For me, the gold of France did not seduce,
Although I did admit it as a motive
The sooner to effect what I intended:
But God be thanked for prevention,
Which I in sufferance heartily will rejoice,
Beseeching God and you to pardon me.
Grey. Never did faithful subject more rejoice
At the discovery of most dangerous treason
Than I do at this hour joy o'er myself,
Prevented from a damned enterprise.
My fault, but not my body, pardon, sovereign.
K. Hen. God quit you in his mercy! Hear your sentence.
You have conspir'd against our royal person,
Join'd with an enemy proclaim'd, and from his coffers
Received the golden earnest of our death;
Wherein you would have sold your king to slaughter,
His princes and his peers to servitude,
His subjects to oppression and contempt,
And his whole kingdom into desolation.
Touching our person seek we no revenge;
But we our kingdom's safety must so tender,
Whose ruin you have sought, that to her laws
We do deliver you. Get you therefore hence,
Poor miserable wretches, to your death,
The taste whereof God of his mercy give
You patience to endure, and true repentance
Of all your dear offences! Bear them hence.
Exeunt Cambridge, Scroop, and Grey, guarded.
Now, lords, for France; the enterprise whereof
Shall be to you, as us, like glorious.
We doubt not of a fair and lucky war,
Since God so graciously hath brought to light
This dangerous treason lurking in our way
To hinder our beginnings. We doubt not now
But every rub is smoothed on our way.
Then forth, dear countrymen! Let us deliver
Our puissance into the hand of God,
Putting it straight in expedition.
Cheerly to sea; the signs of war advance!
No king of England, if not king of France!
Flourish. Exeunt.

159. **in sufferance,** in suffering my punishment. 169. **golden earnest,** pledge money. 175. **tender,** cherish. 181. **dear,** grievous. 183. **like,** alike. 188. **rub,** obstacle. 191. **expedition,** motion. 192. **signs,** standards

Scene III. *London. Before a tavern.*

Enter *Pistol, Nym, Bardolph, Boy,* and *Hostess.*

Host. Prithee honey, sweet husband, let me bring thee to Staines.

Pist. No; for my manly heart doth yearn.
Bardolph, be blithe; Nym, rouse thy vaunting veins;
Boy, bristle thy courage up; for Falstaff he is dead,
And we must yearn therefore.

Bard. Would I were with him, wheresome'er he is, either in heaven or in hell!

Host. Nay, sure, he 's not in hell: he 's in Arthur's bosom, if ever man went to Arthur's bosom. 'A made a finer end and went away an it had been any christom child: 'a parted even just between twelve and one, even at the turning o' th' tide: for after I saw him fumble with the sheets, and play with flowers, and smile upon his fingers' ends, I knew there was but one way; for his nose was as sharp as a pen, and 'a babbled of green fields. "How now, Sir John!" quoth I; "what, man! be o' good cheer." So 'a cried out, "God, God, God!" three or four times: now I, to comfort him, bid him 'a should not think of God; I hoped there was no need to trouble himself with any such thoughts yet. So 'a bade me lay more clothes on his feet: I put my hand into the bed and felt them, and they were as cold as any stone; then I felt to his knees, and so upward and upward, and all was as cold as any stone.

Nym. They say he cried out of sack.

Host. Ay, that 'a did.

Bard. And of women.

Host. Nay, that 'a did not.

Boy. Yes, that 'a did; and said they were devils incarnate.

Host. 'A could never abide carnation; 't was a colour he never liked.

Boy. 'A said once, the devil would have him about women.

Host. 'A did in some sort, indeed, handle women; but then he was rheumatic, and talked of the whore of Babylon.

Boy. Do you not remember, 'a saw a flea stick upon Bardolph's nose, and 'a said it was a black soul burning in hell-fire?

Scene iii: 12. christom, chrisom, newly christened babe less than a month old. **18. and 'a babbled of green fields,** this is one of the most famous emendations in the text of Shakespeare. The Folio reading "and a Table of greene fields" was never satisfactorily explained until Theobald in the 18th century suggested this possible reading. **29. of,** against. **sack,** a white wine. **39. handle,** talk of. **40. rheumatic,** she means "lunatic."

Bard. Well, the fuel is gone that maintained that fire: that 's all the riches I got in his service.

Nym. Shall we shog? The King will be gone from Southampton.

Pist. Come, let 's away. My love, give me thy lips.
Look to my chattels and my movables:
Let senses rule; the word is "Pitch and Pay."
Trust none;
For oaths are straws, men's faiths are wafer-cakes,
And hold-fast is the only dog, my duck;
Therefore, *Caveto* be thy counsellor.
Go, clear thy crystals. Yoke-fellows in arms,
Let us to France; like horse-leeches, my boys,
To suck, to suck, the very blood to suck!

Boy. And that 's but unwholesome food, they say.

Pist. Touch her soft mouth, and march.

Bard. Farewell, hostess. *Kissing her.*

Nym. I cannot kiss; that is the humour of it; but, adieu.

Pist. Let housewifery appear. Keep close, I thee command.

Host. Farewell; adieu. *Exeunt.*

Scene IV. *France. The King's palace.*

Flourish. Enter the *French King,* the *Dauphin,* the *Dukes of Berri* and *Bretagne,* the *Constable,* and others.

Fr. King. Thus comes the English with full power upon us,
And more than carefully it us concerns
To answer royally in our defences.
Therefore the Dukes of Berri and of Bretagne,
Or Brabant and of Orleans, shall make forth,
And you, Prince Dauphin, with all swift dispatch,
To line and new repair our towns of war
With men of courage and with means defendant;
For England his approaches makes as fierce
As waters to the sucking of a gulf.
It fits us then to be as provident
As fears may teach us out of late examples
Left by the fatal and neglected English
Upon our fields.

Dau. My most redoubted father,
It is most meet we arm us 'gainst the foe;
For peace itself should not so dull a kingdom,
Though war nor no known quarrel were in question,
But that defences, musters, preparations,
Should be maintain'd, assembled, and collected,
As were a war in expectation.
Therefore, I say, 't is meet we all go forth
To view the sick and feeble parts of France.
And let us do it with no show of fear;
No, with no more than if we heard that England
Were busied with a Whitsun morris-dance;
For, my good liege, she is so idly king'd,
Her sceptre so fantastically borne
By a vain, giddy, shallow, humorous youth,
That fear attends her not.

Con. O peace, Prince Dauphin!
You are too much mistaken in this king.
Question your Grace the late ambassadors
With what great state he heard their embassy,
How well supplied with noble counsellors,
How modest in exception, and withal
How terrible in constant resolution,
And you shall find his vanities forespent
Were but the outside of the Roman Brutus,
Covering discretion with a coat of folly,
As gardeners do with ordure hide those roots
That shall first spring and be most delicate.

Dau. Well, 't is not so, my Lord High Constable;
But though we think it so, it is no matter:
In cases of defence 't is best to weigh
The enemy more mighty than he seems,
So the proportions of defence are fill'd;
Which, of a weak and niggardly projection,
Doth, like a miser, spoil his coat with scanting
A little cloth.

Fr. King. Think we King Harry strong;
And, Princes, look you strongly arm to meet him.
The kindred of him hath been flesh'd upon us;
And he is bred out of that bloody strain
That haunted us in our familiar paths:
Witness our too much memorable shame
When Cressy battle fatally was struck,
And all our princes captiv'd by the hand
Of that black name, Edward, Black Prince of Wales;
Whiles that his mountain sire, on mountain standing,
Up in the air, crown'd with the golden sun,
Saw his heroical seed, and smil'd to see him,
Mangle the work of nature and deface

51. **"Pitch and Pay,"** pay cash. 55. *Caveto,* be cautious. 64. **housewifery,** thrift. **Scene iv: 7. line,** strengthen. 10. **gulf,** whirlpool. 13. **fatal and neglected**, deadly and underrated.

25. **Whitsun,** Whitsuntide, the week following Whitsunday (7th Sunday after Easter); **morris-dance,** morisco-dance, was introduced by the Moors into Spain. The dance was formerly associated with the May games and had as its characters Robin Hood, Maid Marian, etc. 26. **idly,** foolishly. 28. **humorous,** full of whims. 34. **in exception,** in offering objections. 36. **forespent,** past. 37. **Roman Brutus,** Lucius Junius Brutus, who pretended madness in order to conceal his plots against the tyrant Tarquinius Superbus. 46. **projection,** calculation. 50. **flesh'd,** fed with flesh. 57. **mountain sire,** great father.

The patterns that by God and by French fathers
Had twenty years been made. This is a stem
Of that victorious stock; and let us fear
The native mightiness and fate of him.

Enter a *Messenger.*

Mess. Ambassadors from Harry King of England
Do crave admittance to your Majesty.

Fr. King. We 'll give them present audience. Go, and bring them.

Exeunt Messenger and certain Lords.

You see this chase is hotly follow'd, friends.

Dau. Turn head, and stop pursuit; for coward dogs
Most spend their mouths when what they seem to threaten
Runs far before them. Good my sovereign,
Take up the English short, and let them know
Of what a monarchy you are the head:
Self-love, my liege, is not so vile a sin
As self-neglecting.

Enter *Exeter.*

Fr. King. From our brother of England?

Exe. From him; and thus he greets your Majesty:
He wills you, in the name of God Almighty,
That you divest yourself, and lay apart
The borrowed glories that by gift of heaven,
By law of nature and of nations, longs
To him and to his heirs; namely, the crown
And all wide-stretched honours that pertain
By custom and the ordinance of times
Unto the crown of France. That you may know
'T is no sinister nor no awkward claim
Pick'd from the worm-holes of long-vanish'd days,
Nor from the dust of old oblivion rak'd,
He sends you this most memorable line,
In every branch truly demonstrative;
Willing you overlook this pedigree;
And when you find him evenly deriv'd
From his most fam'd of famous ancestors,
Edward the Third, he bids you then resign
Your crown and kingdom, indirectly held
From him, the native and true challenger.

Fr. King. Or else what follows?

Exe. Bloody constraint; for if you hide the crown
Even in your hearts, there will he rake for it:
Therefore in fierce tempest he is coming,
In thunder and in earthquake, like a Jove,
That, if requiring fail, he will compel;
And bids you, in the bowels of the Lord,
Deliver up the crown, and to take mercy
On the poor souls for whom this hungry war
Opens his vasty jaws; and on your head
Turning the widow's tears, the orphans' cries,
The dead men's blood, and the pining maidens' groans,
For husbands, fathers, and betrothed lovers,
That shall be swallowed in this controversy.
This is his claim, his threat'ning, and my message;
Unless the Dauphin be in presence here,
To whom expressly I bring greeting too.

Fr. King. For us, we will consider of this further:
To-morrow shall you bear our full intent
Back to our brother of England.

Dau. For the Dauphin,
I stand here for him: what to him from England?

Exe. Scorn and defiance; slight regard, contempt,
And anything that may not misbecome
The mighty sender, doth he prize you at.
Thus says my king: an if your father's Highness
Do not, in grant of all demands at large,
Sweeten the bitter mock you sent his Majesty,
He 'll call you to so hot an answer of it,
That caves and womby vaultages of France
Shall chide your trespass and return your mock
In second accent of his ordinance.

Dau. Say, if my father render fair return,
It is against my will; for I desire
Nothing but odds with England: to that end,
As matching to his youth and vanity,
I did present him with the Paris balls.

Exe. He 'll make your Paris Louvre shake for it,
Were it the mistress-court of mighty Europe;
And, be assur'd, you 'll find a difference,
As we his subjects have in wonder found,
Between the promise of his greener days
And these he masters now. Now he weighs time
Even to the utmost grain: that you shall read
In your own losses, if he stay in France.

Fr. King. To-morrow shall you know our mind at full.

Exe. Dispatch us with all speed, lest that our king
Come here himself to question our delay;
For he is footed in this land already.

Fr. King. You shall be soon dispatch'd with fair conditions.
A night is but small breath and little pause
To answer matters of this consequence.

Flourish. Exeunt.

64. fate, what he is destined to do. **80. longs,** belong. **83. ordinance,** established rule. **85. sinister,** illegitimate. **91. evenly,** directly. **94. indirectly,** wrongfully. **101. requiring,** demanding.

124. womby vaultages, deep caverns. **126. second . . . ordinance,** echo of his artillery. **137. masters,** possesses. **143. footed,** landed in force. **145. breath,** breathing-space.

Act III

Flourish. Enter *Chorus.*

Chor. Thus with imagin'd wing our swift scene flies
In motion of no less celerity
Than that of thought. Suppose that you have seen
The well-appointed king at Hampton pier
Embark his royalty, and his brave fleet
With silken streamers the young Phœbus fanning:
Play with your fancies, and in them behold
Upon the hempen tackle ship-boys climbing;
Hear the shrill whistle which doth order give
To sounds confus'd; behold the threaden sails,
Borne with the invisible and creeping wind,
Draw the huge bottoms through the furrowed sea,
Breasting the lofty surge. O, do but think
You stand upon the rivage and behold
A city on the inconstant billows dancing;
For so appears this fleet majestical,
Holding due course to Harfleur. Follow, follow!
Grapple your minds to sternage of this navy,
And leave your England, as dead midnight still,
Guarded with grandsires, babies, and old women,
Either past or not arriv'd to pith and puissance:
For who is he, whose chin is but enrich'd
With one appearing hair, that will not follow
These cull'd and choice-drawn cavaliers to France?
Work, work your thoughts, and therein see a siege;
Behold the ordinance on their carriages,
With fatal mouths gaping on girded Harfleur.
Suppose th' ambassador from the French comes back,
Tells Harry that the King doth offer him
Katharine his daughter, and with her, to dowry,
Some petty and unprofitable dukedoms.
The offer likes not; and the nimble gunner
With linstock now the devilish cannon touches,
Alarum, and chambers go off.
And down goes all before them. Still be kind,
And eke out our performance with your mind. *Exit.*

Act III, Chorus: 1. imagin'd wing, wing of imagination. **14. rivage,** shore. **18. sternage,** the sterns. **32. likes,** pleases. **33. linstock,** stick that held the gunner's match. **S. d. chambers,** small cannon used in the theatre.

Scene I. *France. Before Harfleur.*

Alarum. Enter *King Henry, Exeter, Bedford, Gloucester,* and Soldiers, with scaling-ladders.

K. Hen. Once more unto the breach, dear friends, once more,
Or close the wall up with our English dead.
In peace there 's nothing so becomes a man
As modest stillness and humility;
But when the blast of war blows in our ears,
Then imitate the action of the tiger;
Stiffen the sinews, summon up the blood,
Disguise fair nature with hard-favour'd rage;
Then lend the eye a terrible aspect;
Let it pry through the portage of the head
Like the brass cannon; let the brow o'erwhelm it
As fearfully as doth a galled rock
O'erhang and jutty his confounded base,
Swill'd with the wild and wasteful ocean.
Now set the teeth and stretch the nostril wide,
Hold hard the breath, and bend up every spirit
To his full height. On, on, you noblest English,
Whose blood is fet from fathers of war-proof!
Fathers that, like so many Alexanders,
Have in these parts from morn till even fought,
And sheath'd their swords for lack of argument.
Dishonour not your mothers; now attest
That those whom you call'd fathers did beget you.
Be copy now to men of grosser blood,
And teach them how to war. And you, good yeomen,
Whose limbs were made in England, show us here
The mettle of your pasture; let us swear
That you are worth your breeding, which I doubt not;
For there is none of you so mean and base,
That hath not noble lustre in your eyes.
I see you stand like greyhounds in the slips,
Straining upon the start. The game 's afoot!
Follow your spirit, and upon this charge
Cry, "God for Harry! England and Saint George!"
Exeunt. Alarum, and chambers go off.

Act III, Scene i: 8. hard-favour'd, ugly. **10. portage,** porthole. **11. o'erwhelm,** overhang. **12. galled,** chafed. **13. jutty,** project beyond. **confounded,** worn away. **14. Swill'd,** gulped down. **18. fet,** fetched. **21. argument,** reason for fighting. **27. pasture,** rearing. **31. in the slips,** in leash.

Scene II. *The same.*

Enter *Nym, Bardolph, Pistol,* and *Boy.*

Bard. On, on, on, on, on! To the breach, to the breach!

Nym. Pray thee, corporal, stay: the knocks are too hot; and, for mine own part, I have not a case of lives: the humour of it is too hot; that is the very plain-song of it.

Pist. The plain-song is most just, for humours do abound.

"Knocks go and come; God's vassals
drop and die;
And sword and shield,
In bloody field,
Doth win immortal fame."

Boy. Would I were in an alehouse in London! I would give all my fame for a pot of ale and safety.

Pist. And I.

"If wishes would prevail with me,
My purpose should not fail with me,
But thither would I hie."

Boy.

"As duly, but not as truly,
As bird doth sing on bough."

Enter *Fluellen.*

Flu. Up to the breach, you dogs! Avaunt, you cullions! *Driving them forward.*

Pist. Be merciful, great Duke, to men of mould.
Abate thy rage, abate thy manly rage,
Abate thy rage, great Duke!
Good bawcock, bate thy rage; use lenity, sweet chuck!

Nym. These be good humours! Your honour wins bad humours. *Exeunt all but Boy.*

Boy. As young as I am, I have observed these three swashers. I am boy to them all three; but all they three, though they would serve me, could not be man to me; for indeed three such antics do not amount to a man. For Bardolph, he is white-livered and red-faced; by the means whereof 'a faces it out, but fights not. For Pistol, he hath a killing tongue and a quiet sword; by the means whereof 'a breaks words, and keeps whole weapons. For Nym, he hath heard that men of few words are the best men; and therefore he scorns to say his prayers, lest 'a should be thought a coward: but his few bad words are matched with as few good deeds; for 'a never broke any man's head but his own, and that was against a post when he was drunk. They will steal anything, and call it purchase. Bardolph stole a lute-case, bore it twelve leagues, and sold it for three half-pence. Nym and Bardolph are sworn brothers in filching, and in Calais they stole a fire-shovel: I knew by that piece of service the men would carry coals. They would have me as familiar with men's pockets as their gloves or their handkerchers; which makes much against my manhood, if I should take from another's pocket to put into mine; for it is plain pocketing up of wrongs. I must leave them, and seek some better service. Their villainy goes against my weak stomach, and therefore I must cast it up. *Exit.*

Enter *Gower* and *Fluellen.*

Gow. Captain Fluellen, you must come presently to the mines: the Duke of Gloucester would speak with you.

Flu. To the mines! Tell you the Duke, it is not so good to come to the mines; for, look you, the mines is not according to the disciplines of the war: the concavities of it is not sufficient; for, look you, th' athversary, you may discuss unto the Duke, look you, is digt himself four yard under the countermines: by Cheshu, I thing 'a will plow up all, if there is not better directions.

Gow. The Duke of Gloucester, to whom the order of the siege is given, is altogether directed by an Irishman, a very valiant gentleman, i' faith.

Flu. It is Captain Macmorris, is it not?

Gow. I think it be.

Flu. By Cheshu, he is an ass, as in the world: I will verify as much in his beard: he has no more directions in the true disciplines of the wars, look you, of the Roman disciplines, than is a puppy-dog.

Enter *Macmorris* and *Captain Jamy.*

Gow. Here 'a comes; and the Scots captain, Captain Jamy with him.

Flu. Captain Jamy is a marvellous falorous gentleman, that is certain; and of great expedition and knowledge in th' aunchient wars, upon my particular knowledge of his directions: by Cheshu, he will maintain his argument as well as any military man in the world, in the disciplines of the pristine wars of the Romans.

Jamy. I say gud-day, Captain Fluellen.

Flu. God-den to your worship, good Captain James.

Gow. How now, Captain Macmorris! have

Scene ii: 5. case, set. **6. plain-song,** lit., simple melody. **22. cullions,** vile creatures. **23. mould,** earth. **26. bawcock,** *beau coq,* fine fellow. **30. swashers,** swaggerers. **32. antics,** buffoons.

49-50. carry coals, endure insults. **66. discuss,** explain. **68. Cheshu,** Jesu. **89. God-den,** Good evening.

you quit the mines? Have the pioners given o'er?

Mac. By Chrish, la! 'tish ill done: the work ish give over, the trompet sound the retreat. By my hand I swear, and my father's soul, the work ish ill done; it ish give over: I would have blowed up the town, so Chrish save me, la! in an hour. O, 'tish ill done, 'tish ill done; by my hand, 'tish ill done!

Flu. Captain Macmorris, I beseech you now, will you voutsafe me, look you, a few disputations with you, as partly touching or concerning the disciplines of the war, the Roman wars, in the way of argument, look you, and friendly communication; partly to satisfy my opinion, and partly for the satisfaction, look you, of my mind, as touching the direction of the military discipline; that is the point.

Jamy. It sall be very gud, gud feith, gud captains bath: and I sall quit you with gud leve, as I may pick occasion; that sall I, marry.

Mac. It is no time to discourse, so Chrish save me: the day is hot, and the weather, and the wars, and the King, and the Dukes: it is no time to discourse. The town is beseeched, and the trumpet call us to the breach, and we talk, and, be Chrish, do nothing: 't is shame for us all: so God sa' me, 't is shame to stand still; it is shame, by my hand; and there is throats to be cut, and works to be done; and there ish nothing done, so Chrish sa' me, la!

Jamy. By the mess, ere theise eyes of mine take themselves to slomber, ay 'll de gud service, or ay 'll lig i' th' grund for it; ay, or go to death; and I 'll pay 't as valourously as I may, that sall I suerly do, that is the breff and the long. Marry, I wad full fain heard some question 'tween you tway.

Flu. Captain Macmorris, I think, look you, under your correction, there is not many of your nation—

Mac. Of my nation! What ish my nation? Ish a villain, and a bastard, and a knave, and a rascal. What ish my nation? Who talks of my nation?

Flu. Look you, if you take the matter otherwise than is meant, Captain Macmorris, peradventure I shall think you do not use me with that affability as in discretion you ought to use me, look you, being as good a man as yourself, both in the disciplines of war, and in the derivation of my birth, and in other particularities.

Mac. I do not know you so good a man as myself: so Chrish save me, I will cut off your head.

Gow. Gentlemen both, you will mistake each other.

Jamy. Ah! that 's a foul fault.

A parley sounded.

Gow. The town sounds a parley.

Flu. Captain Macmorris, when there is more better opportunity to be required, look you, I will be so bold as to tell you I know the disciplines of war; and there is an end.

Exeunt.

Scene III. *Before the gates of Harfleur.*

The *Governor* and some *Citizens* on the walls; Enter *King Henry* and all his train.

K. Hen. How yet resolves the governor of the town?
This is the latest parle we will admit;
Therefore to our best mercy give yourselves,
Or like to men proud of destruction
Defy us to our worst; for, as I am a soldier,
A name that in my thoughts becomes me best,
If I begin the battery once again,
I will not leave the half-achieved Harfleur
Till in her ashes she lies buried.
The gates of mercy shall be all shut up,
And the flesh'd soldier, rough and hard of heart,
In liberty of bloody hand shall range
With conscience wide as hell, mowing like grass
Your fresh fair virgins and your flow'ring infants.
What is it then to me, if impious War,
Array'd in flames like to the prince of fiends,
Do with his smirch'd complexion all fell feats
Enlink'd to waste and desolation?
What is 't to me, when you yourselves are cause,
If your pure maidens fall into the hand
Of hot and forcing violation?
What rein can hold licentious wickedness
When down the hill he holds his fierce career?
We may as bootless spend our vain command
Upon th' enraged soldiers in their spoil
As send precepts to the leviathan
To come ashore. Therefore, you men of Harfleur,
Take pity of your town and of your people,
Whiles yet my soldiers are in my command,
Whiles yet the cool and temperate wind of grace
O'erblows the filthy and contagious clouds
Of heady murder, spoil, and villainy.

92. **pioners**, pioneers, workers on fortifications. 109. **quit**, requite. 114. **beseeched**, besieged. 122. **mess**, mass. 124. **lig**, lie. 128. **tway**, two.

Scene iii: 2. **parle**, parley. 11. **flesh'd**, having tasted blood. 31. **O'erblows**, blows away. 32. **heady**, headstrong.

If not, why, in a moment look to see
The blind and bloody soldier with foul hand
Defile the locks of your shrill-shrieking daughters;
Your fathers taken by the silver beards,
And their most reverend heads dash'd to the walls;
Your naked infants spitted upon pikes,
Whiles the mad mothers with their howls confus'd
Do break the clouds, as did the wives of Jewry
At Herod's bloody-hunting slaughtermen.
What say you? Will you yield, and this avoid,
Or, guilty in defence, be thus destroy'd?

Gov. Our expectation hath this day an end.
The Dauphin, whom of succours we entreated,
Returns us that his powers are yet not ready
To raise so great a siege. Therefore, great King,
We yield our town and lives to thy soft mercy.
Enter our gates; dispose of us and ours;
For we no longer are defensible.

K. Hen. Open your gates. Come, uncle Exeter,
Go you and enter Harfleur; there remain,
And fortify it strongly 'gainst the French.
Use mercy to them all. For us, dear uncle,
The winter coming on, and sickness growing
Upon our soldiers, we will retire to Calais.
To-night in Harfleur will we be your guest;
To-morrow for the march are we addrest.

Flourish. The King and his train enter the town.

Scene IV. *The French King's palace.*

Enter *Katharine* and *Alice* an old Gentlewoman.

Kath. Alice, tu as été en Angleterre, et tu parles bien le langage.

Alice. Un peu, madame.

Kath. Je te prie, m'enseignez; il faut que j'apprenne à parler. Comment appelez-vous la main en Anglois?

Alice. La main? Elle est appelée de hand.

Kath. De hand. Et les doigts?

Alice. Les doigts? Ma foi, j'oublie les doigts; mais je me souviendrai. Les doigts? Je pense qu'ils sont appelés de fingres; oui, de fingres.

Kath. La main, de hand; les doigts, de fingres. Je pense que je suis le bon écolier; j'ai gagné deux mots d'Anglois vîtement. Comment appelez-vous les ongles?

Alice. Les ongles? Nous les appelons de nails.

Kath. De nails. Écoutez; dites-moi, si je parle bien: de hand, de fingres, et de nails.

Alice. C'est bien dit, madame; il est fort bon Anglois.

Kath. Dites-moi l'Anglois pour le bras.

Alice. De arm, madame.

Kath. Et le coude?

Alice. D' elbow.

Kath. D' elbow. Je m'en fais la répétition de tous les mots que vous m'avez appris dès à présent.

Alice. Il est trop difficile, madame, comme je pense.

Kath. Excusez-moi, Alice; écoutez: D' hand, de fingres, de nails, d' arma, de bilbow.

Alice. D' elbow, madame.

Kath. O Seigneur Dieu, je me'en oublie! D' elbow. Comment appelez-vous le col?

Alice. De nick, madame.

Kath. De nick. Et le menton?

Alice. De chin.

Kath. De sin. Le col, de nick; le menton, de sin.

Alice. Oui. Sauf votre honneur, en vérité, vous prononcez les mots aussi droit que les natifs d'Angleterre.

Kath. Je ne doute point d'apprendre, par la grace de Dieu, et en peu de temps.

Alice. N'avez vous pas déjà oublié ce que je vous ai enseigné?

Kath. Non, je reciterai à vous promptement: d' hand, de fingres, de mails,—

Alice. De nails, madame.

Kath. De nails, de arm, de ilbow.

Alice. Sauf votre honneur, de elbow.

Kath. Ainsi dis-je; d' elbow, de nick, et de sin. Comment appelez-vous le pied et la robe?

Alice. De foot, madame; et de coun.

Kath. De foot et de coun! O Seigneur Dieu! ce sont mots de son mauvais, corruptible, gros, et impudique, et non pour les dames d'honneur d'user. Je ne voudrais prononcer ces mots devant les seigneurs de France pour tout le monde. Foh! le foot et le coun! Néanmoins, je réciterai une autre fois ma leçon ensemble: d' hand, de fingres, de nails, d' arm, d' elbow, de nick, de sin, de foot, de coun.

Alice. Excellent, madame!

Kath. C'est assez pour une fois: allons-nous à dîner. *Exeunt.*

Scene V. *The same.*

Enter the *King of France,* the *Dauphin,* the *Duke of Bourbon,* the *Constable of France,* and others.

Fr. King. 'T is certain he hath pass'd the river Somme.

Con. An if he be not fought withal, my lord,

40-1. wives . . . slaughtermen, The Massacre of the Innocents, *Matt.* ii. 16-8. **58. addrest,** in readiness.

Let us not live in France; let us quit all
And give our vineyards to a barbarous people.
Dau. *O Dieu vivant!* shall a few sprays of us,
The emptying of our fathers' luxury,
Our scions put in wild and savage stock,
Spirt up so suddenly into the clouds,
And overlook their grafters?
Bour. Normans, but bastard Normans, Norman bastards!
Mort de ma vie! if they march along
Unfought withal, but I will sell my dukedom,
To buy a slobbery and a dirty farm
In that nook-shotten isle of Albion.
Con. *Dieu de batailles!* where have they this mettle?
Is not their climate foggy, raw, and dull,
On whom, as in despite, the sun looks pale,
Killing their fruit with frowns? Can sodden water,
A drench for sur-rein'd jades, their barley-broth,
Decoct their cold blood to such valiant heat?
And shall our quick blood, spirited with wine,
Seem frosty? O, for honour of our land,
Let us not hang like roping icicles
Upon our houses' thatch, whiles a more frosty people
Sweat drops of gallant youth in our rich fields!—
Poor we may call them in their native lords.
Dau. By faith and honour,
Our madams mock at us, and plainly say
Our mettle is bred out, and they will give
Their bodies to the lust of English youth
To new-store France with bastard warriors.
Bour. They bid us to the English dancing-schools,
And teach lavoltas high, and swift corantos;
Saying our grace is only in our heels,
And that we are most lofty runaways.
Fr. King. Where is Montjoy the herald? Speed him hence.
Let him greet England with our sharp defiance.
Up, princes! and, with spirit of honour edged
More sharper than your swords, hie to the field!
Charles Delabreth, High Constable of France;
You Dukes of Orleans, Bourbon, and of Berri,
Alençon, Brabant, Bar, and Burgundy;
Jacques Chatillon, Rambures, Vaudemont,
Beaumont, Grandpré, Roussi, and Fauconberg,
Foix, Lestrale, Bouciqualt, and Charolois;
High dukes, great princes, barons, lords, and knights,
For your great seats now quit you of great shames.
Bar Harry England, that sweeps through our land
With pennons painted in the blood of Harfleur:
Rush on his host, as doth the melted snow
Upon the valleys, whose low vassal seat
The Alps doth spit and void his rheum upon:
Go down upon him, you have power enough,
And in a captive chariot into Rouen
Bring him our prisoner.
Con. This becomes the great.
Sorry am I his numbers are so few,
His soldiers sick and famish'd in their march;
For I am sure, when he shall see our army,
He 'll drop his heart into the sink of fear
And for achievement offer us his ransom.
Fr. King. Therefore, Lord Constable, haste on Montjoy,
And let him say to England that we send
To know what willing ransom he will give.
Prince Dauphin, you shall stay with us in Rouen.
Dau. Not so, I do beseech your Majesty.
Fr. King. Be patient, for you shall remain with us.
Now forth, Lord Constable and princes all,
And quickly bring us word of England's fall.
Exeunt.

Scene VI. *The English camp in Picardy.*

Enter *Gower* and *Fluellen* meeting.

Gow. How now, Captain Fluellen! come you from the bridge?

Flu. I assure you, there is very excellent services committed at the bridge.

Gow. Is the Duke of Exeter safe?

Flu. The Duke of Exeter is as magnanimous as Agamemnon; and a man that I love and honour with my soul, and my heart, and my duty, and my live, and my living, and my uttermost power: he is not—God be praised and blessed!—any hurt in the world; but keeps the bridge most valiantly, with excellent discipline. There is an aunchient lieutenant there at the pridge, I think in my very conscience he is as valiant a man as Mark An-

Scene v: 5-9. This figurative passage—the figure is that of grafting trees—refers to the Norman-French blood in the English: "Shall a few branches (**sprays** l. 5) of us, the issue (**emptying** l. 6) of our fathers' lust (**luxury** l. 6), our cutting (**scions** l. 7) grafted on wild and savage stock, sprout (**spirt** l. 8) up so suddenly into the clouds and overtop (**overlook** l. 9) their grafters. **11-12.** The but-clause depends grammatically on the imprecation **"Mort de ma vie"**: "If they march along unfought with, may death take me if I do not sell my dukedom." **13. slobbery**, wet. **14. nook-shotten**, full of nooks and promontories. **18. sodden**, boiled. **19. drench**, bran mash. **sur-rein'd jades**, overworked horses. **20. Decoct**, warm up. **23. roping**, dripping. **33. lavoltas, corantos**, lively dances.

47. quit you, absolve yourselves. **60. for achievement**, instead of letting us conquer him.

tony; and he is a man of no estimation in the world, but I did see him do as gallant service.

Gow. What do you call him?

Flu. He is called Aunchient Pistol.

Gow. I know him not.

Enter *Pistol.*

Flu. Here is the man.

Pist. Captain, I thee beseech to do me favours.
The Duke of Exeter doth love thee well.

Flu. Ay, I praise God; and I have merited some love at his hands.

Pist. Bardolph, a soldier, firm and sound of heart,
And of buxom valour, hath, by cruel fate,
And giddy Fortune's furious fickle wheel,
That goddess blind,
That stands upon the rolling restless stone—

Flu. By your patience, Aunchient Pistol. Fortune is painted blind, with a muffler afore his eyes, to signify to you that Fortune is blind; and she is painted also with a wheel, to signify to you, which is the moral of it, that she is turning, and inconstant, and mutability, and variation; and her foot, look you, is fixed upon a spherical stone, which rolls, and rolls, and rolls: in good truth, the poet makes a most excellent description of it: fortune is an excellent moral.

Pist. Fortune is Bardolph's foe, and frowns on him;
For he hath stolen a pax, and hanged must 'a be,—
A damned death!
Let gallows gape for dog; let man go free,
And let not hemp his windpipe suffocate.
But Exeter hath given the doom of death
For pax of little price.
Therefore, go speak; the Duke will hear thy voice;
And let not Bardolph's vital thread be cut
With edge of penny cord and vile reproach.
Speak, captain, for his life, and I will thee requite.

Flu. Aunchient Pistol, I do partly understand your meaning.

Pist. Why then, rejoice therefore.

Flu. Certainly, aunchient, it is not a thing to rejoice at; for if, look you, he were my brother, I would desire the Duke to use his good pleasure, and put him to execution; for discipline ought to be used.

Pist. Die and be damned! and *figo* for thy friendship!

Flu. It is well.

Pist. The fig of Spain. *Exit.*

Flu. Very good.

Gow. Why, this is an arrant counterfeit rascal. I remember him now; a bawd, a cutpurse.

Flu. I 'll assure you, 'a uttered as prave words at the pridge as you shall see in a summer's day. But it is very well; what he has spoke to me, that is well, I warrant you, when time is serve.

Gow. Why, 't is a gull, a fool, a rogue, that now and then goes to the wars, to grace himself at his return into London under the form of a soldier. And such fellows are perfect in the great commanders' names; and they will learn you by rote where services were done; at such and such a sconce, at such a breach, at such a convoy; who came off bravely, who was shot, who disgraced, what terms the enemy stood on; and this they con perfectly in the phrase of war, which they trick up with new-tuned oaths: and what a beard of the general's cut and a horrid suit of the camp will do among foaming bottles and ale-washed wits, is wonderful to be thought on. But you must learn to know such slanders of the age, or else you may be marvellously mistook.

Flu. I tell you what, Captain Gower; I do perceive he is not the man that he would gladly make show to the world he is: if I find a hole in his coat, I will tell him my mind. [*Drum heard.*] Hark you, the King is coming, and I must speak with him from the pridge.

Drum and colours. Enter *King Henry, Gloucester,* and his poor Soldiers.

God bless your Majesty!

K. Hen. How now, Fluellen! cam'st thou from the bridge?

Flu. Ay, so please your Majesty. The Duke of Exeter has very gallantly maintained the pridge. The French is gone off, look you; and there is gallant and most prave passages. Marry th' athversary was have possession of the pridge; but he is enforced to retire, and the Duke of Exeter is master of the pridge: I can tell your Majesty, the Duke is a prave man.

K. Hen. What men have you lost, Fluellen?

Flu. The perdition of th' athversary hath been very great, reasonable great: marry, for my part, I think the Duke hath lost never a man, but one that is like to be executed for robbing a church, one Bardolph, if your Majesty know the man: his face is all bubukles, and whelks, and knobs, and flames o'

Scene vi: 42. pax, a piece of wood or metal with Christ's picture on it offered, as a symbol of peace, to be kissed by the people during Mass. Shakespeare has probably confused this with the pix, a much more sacred object, a box containing the Host or consecrated wafer. There is record of Henry's having executed a soldier for stealing a pix.

70. gull, simpleton. **75. sconce,** a small fort. **77. stood on,** insisted on. **107. bubukles,** carbuncles. **108. whelks,** pimples.

fire; and his lips blows at his nose, and it is like a coal of fire, sometimes plue and sometimes red; but his nose is executed, and his fire 's out.

K. Hen. We would have all such offenders so cut off; and we give express charge, that in our marches through the country, there be nothing compelled from the villages, nothing taken but paid for, none of the French upbraided or abused in disdainful language; for when lenity and cruelty play for a kingdom, the gentler gamester is the soonest winner.

Tucket. Enter *Montjoy.*

Mont. You know me by my habit.
K. Hen. Well then I know thee. What shall I know of thee?
Mont. My master's mind.
K. Hen. Unfold it.

Mont. Thus says my King: Say thou to Harry of England: Though we seem'd dead, we did but sleep; advantage is a better soldier than rashness. Tell him we could have rebuked him at Harfleur, but that we thought not good to bruise an injury till it were full ripe. Now we speak upon our cue, and our voice is imperial: England shall repent his folly, see his weakness, and admire our sufferance. Bid him therefore consider of his ransom; which must proportion the losses we have borne, the subjects we have lost, the disgrace we have digested; which in weight to re-answer, his pettiness would bow under. For our losses, his exchequer is too poor; for the effusion of our blood, the muster of his kingdom too faint a number; and for our disgrace, his own person, kneeling at our feet, but a weak and worthless satisfaction. To this add defiance; and tell him, for conclusion, he hath betrayed his followers, whose condemnation is pronounced. So far my King and master; so much my office.

K. Hen. What is thy name? I know thy quality.
Mont. Montjoy.
K. Hen. Thou dost thy office fairly. Turn thee back,
And tell thy King I do not seek him now,
But could be willing to march on to Calais
Without impeachment; for, to say the sooth,
Though 't is no wisdom to confess so much
Unto an enemy of craft and vantage,
My people are with sickness much enfeebled,
My numbers lessen'd, and those few I have
Almost no better than so many French;
Who when they were in health, I tell thee, herald,
I thought upon one pair of English legs
Did march three Frenchmen. Yet, forgive me, God,
That I do brag thus! This your air of France
Hath blown that vice in me. I must repent.
Go therefore, tell thy master here I am;
My ransom is this frail and worthless trunk,
My army but a weak and sickly guard;
Yet, God before, tell him we will come on,
Though France himself and such another neighbour
Stand in our way. There 's for thy labour, Montjoy.
Go, bid thy master well advise himself.
If we may pass, we will; if we be hinder'd,
We shall your tawny ground with your red blood
Discolour; and so, Montjoy, fare you well.
The sum of all our answer is but this:
We would not seek a battle, as we are;
Nor, as we are, we say we will not shun it.
So tell your master.
Mont. I shall deliver so. Thanks to your Highness. *Exit.*
Glou. I hope they will not come upon us now.
K. Hen. We are in God's hands, brother, not in theirs.
March to the bridge; it now draws toward night:
Beyond the river we 'll encamp ourselves,
And on to-morrow bid them march away.
Exeunt.

Scene VII. *The French camp, near Agincourt.*

Enter the *Constable of France,* the *Lord Rambures, Orleans, Dauphin,* with others.

Con. Tut! I have the best armour of the world. Would it were day!

Orl. You have an excellent armour; but let my horse have his due.

Con. It is the best horse of Europe.

Orl. Will it never be morning?

Dau. My Lord of Orleans, and my Lord High Constable, you talk of horse and armour?

Orl. You are as well provided of both as any prince in the world.

Dau. What a long night is this! I will not change my horse with any that treads but on four pasterns. *Ca, ha!* he bounds from the earth, as if his entrails were hairs; *le cheval*

S. d. **Tucket,** trumpet call. **121. habit,** dress. **127. advantage,** favorable opportunity. **130. upon our cue,** in our turn. **136. re-answer,** compensate, make amends for. **146. quality,** profession. **151. impeachment,** hindrance.

Scene vii: 14. as . . . hairs, stuffed with hair like a tennis ball.

volant, the Pegasus, *chez les narines de feu!* When I bestride him, I soar, I am a hawk; he trots the air; the earth sings when he touches it; the basest horn of his hoof is more musical than the pipe of Hermes.

Orl. He 's of the colour of the nutmeg.

Dau. And of the heat of the ginger. It is a beast for Perseus: he is pure air and fire; and the dull elements of earth and water never appear in him, but only in patient stillness while his rider mounts him: he is indeed a horse, and all other jades you may call beasts.

Con. Indeed, my lord, it is a most absolute and excellent horse.

Dau. It is the prince of palfreys; his neigh is like the bidding of a monarch, and his countenance enforces homage.

Orl. No more, cousin.

Dau. Nay, the man hath no wit that cannot, from the rising of the lark to the lodging of the lamb, vary deserved praise on my palfrey: it is a theme as fluent as the sea; turn the sands into eloquent tongues, and my horse is argument for them all: 't is a subject for a sovereign to reason on, and for a sovereign's sovereign to ride on; and for the world, familiar to us and unknown, to lay apart their particular functions and wonder at him. I once writ a sonnet in his praise and began thus: "Wonder of nature,"—

Orl. I have heard a sonnet begin so to one's mistress.

Dau. Then did they imitate that which I composed to my courser, for my horse is my mistress.

Orl. Your mistress bears well.

Dau. Me well; which is the prescript praise and perfection of a good and particular mistress.

Con. Nay, for methought yesterday your mistress shrewdly shook your back.

Dau. So perhaps did yours.

Con. Mine was not bridled.

Dau. O then belike she was old and gentle; and you rode, like a kern of Ireland, your French hose off, and in your strait strossers.

Con. You have good judgement in horsemanship.

Dau. Be warned by me, then; they that ride so and ride not warily, fall into foul bogs. I had rather have my horse to my mistress.

Con. I had as lief have my mistress a jade.

Dau. I tell thee, Constable, my mistress wears his own hair.

Con. I could make as true a boast as that, if I had a sow to my mistress.

Dau. *"Le chien est retourné à son propre vomissement, et la truie lavée au bourbier:"* thou mak'st use of anything.

Con. Yet do I not use my horse for my mistress, or any such proverb so little kin to the purpose.

Ram. My Lord Constable, the armour that I saw in your tent to-night, are those stars or suns upon it?

Con. Stars, my lord.

Dau. Some of them will fall to-morrow, I hope.

Con. And yet my sky shall not want.

Dau. That may be, for you bear a many superfluously, and 't were more honour some were away.

Con. Even as your horse bears your praises; who would trot as well, were some of your brags dismounted.

Dau. Would I were able to load him with his desert! Will it never be day? I will trot to-morrow a mile, and my way shall be paved with English faces.

Con. I will not say so, for fear I should be faced out of my way: but I would it were morning; for I would fain be about the ears of the English.

Ram. Who will go to hazard with me for twenty prisoners?

Con. You must first go yourself to hazard, ere you have them.

Dau. 'T is midnight; I 'll go arm myself. *Exit.*

Orl. The Dauphin longs for morning.

Ram. He longs to eat the English.

Con. I think he will eat all he kills.

Orl. By the white hand of my lady, he 's a gallant prince.

Con. Swear by her foot that she may tread out the oath.

Orl. He is simply the most active gentleman of France.

Con. Doing is activity; and he will still be doing.

Orl. He never did harm, that I heard of.

Con. Nor will do none to-morrow. He will keep that good name still.

Orl. I know him to be valiant.

Con. I was told that by one that knows him better than you.

Orl. What 's he?

Con. Marry, he told me so himself; and he said he cared not who knew it.

Orl. He needs not; it is no hidden virtue in him.

22. **beast for Perseus,** the winged horse Pegasus, first ridden by Perseus. 27. **absolute,** perfect. 37. **argument,** theme. 49. **prescript,** prescribed. 52. **shrewdly,** cursedly. 56. **kern,** light-armed Irish soldier. 57. **French hose,** loose breeches. **strait strossers,** tight trousers.

68-9. "The dog is turned to his own vomit again; and the sow that was washed to her wallowing in the mire"—II Peter 2:22. 93. **go to hazard,** gamble.

Con. By my faith, sir, but it is; never anybody saw it but his lackey: 't is a hooded valour; and when it appears, it will bate.

Orl. "Ill will never said well."

Con. I will cap that proverb with "There is flattery in friendship."

Orl. And I will take up that with "Give the devil his due."

Con. Well placed: there stands your friend for the devil; have at the very eye of that proverb with "A pox of the devil."

Orl. You are the better at proverbs, by how much "A fool's bolt is soon shot."

Con. You have shot over.

Orl. 'T is not the first time you were overshot.

Enter a *Messenger*.

Mess. My Lord High Constable, the English lie within fifteen hundred paces of your tents.

Con. Who hath measured the ground?

Mess. The Lord Grandpré.

Con. A valiant and most expert gentleman. Would it were day! Alas, poor Harry of England, he longs not for the dawning as we do.

Orl. What a wretched and peevish fellow is this King of England, to mope with his fat-brained followers so far out of his knowledge!

Con. If the English had any apprehension, they would run away.

Orl. That they lack; for if their heads had any intellectual armour, they could never wear such heavy head-pieces.

Ram. That island of England breeds very valiant creatures: their mastiffs are of unmatchable courage.

Orl. Foolish curs, that run winking into the mouth of a Russian bear and have their heads crushed like rotten apples! You may as well say, that 's a valiant flea that dare eat his breakfast on the lip of a lion.

Con. Just, just; and the men do sympathize with the mastiffs in robustious and rough coming on, leaving their wits with their wives; and then, give them great meals of beef and iron and steel, they will eat like wolves and fight like devils.

Orl. Ay, but these English are shrewdly out of beef.

Con. Then shall we find to-morrow they have only stomachs to eat and none to fight. Now is the time to arm. Come, shall we about it?

Orl. It is now two o'clock; but, let me see, by ten
We shall have each a hundred Englishmen.

Exeunt.

ACT IV

Enter *Chorus*.

Chor. Now entertain conjecture of a time
When creeping murmur and the poring dark
Fills the wide vessel of the universe.
From camp to camp through the foul womb of night
The hum of either army stilly sounds,
That the fix'd sentinels almost receive
The secret whispers of each other's watch;
Fire answers fire, and through their paly flames
Each battle sees the other's umber'd face;
Steed threatens steed, in high and boastful neighs
Piercing the night's dull ear; and from the tents
The armourers, accomplishing the knights,
With busy hammers closing rivets up,
Give dreadful note of preparation.
The country cocks do crow, the clocks do toll,
And the third hour of drowsy morning name.
Proud of their numbers and secure in soul,
The confident and over-lusty French
Do the low-rated English play at dice;
And chide the cripple tardy-gaited Night
Who, like a foul and ugly witch, doth limp
So tediously away. The poor condemned English,
Like sacrifices, by their watchful fires
Sit patiently and inly ruminate
The morning's danger; and their gesture sad,
Investing lank-lean cheeks and war-worn coats,
Presented them unto the gazing moon
So many horrid ghosts. O now, who will behold
The royal captain of this ruin'd band

121-2. 't is a hooded valour; and when it appears it will bate, the falcon was hooded (its head covered) until the game was sighted. When the hood was removed, it immediately flapped its wings (bated) preparatory to flight. Bate may also mean here abate, diminish. **134. overshot,** beaten, outshot. **142. peevish,** foolish. **143. mope,** be in a daze. **144. out . . . knowledge,** without reason or reflection. **Act IV, Chorus: 2. poring,** dull-eyed. **9. battle,** army. **umber'd,** darkened. **12. accomplishing,** equipping.

153. winking, with eyes shut. **158. sympathize with,** resemble. **Act IV, Chorus: 19. low-rated,** despised. **25. gesture sad,** grave bearing. **26. Investing,** accompanying.

Walking from watch to watch, from tent to tent,
Let him cry, "Praise and glory on his head!"
For forth he goes and visits all his host,
Bids them good morrow with a modest smile,
And calls them brothers, friends, and countrymen.
Upon his royal face there is no note
How dread an army hath enrounded him;
Nor doth he dedicate one jot of colour
Unto the weary and all-watched night,
But freshly looks, and over-bears attaint
With cheerful semblance and sweet majesty;
That every wretch, pining and pale before,
Beholding him, plucks comfort from his looks.
A largess universal like the sun
His liberal eye doth give to every one,
Thawing cold fear, that mean and gentle all
Behold, as may unworthiness define,
A little touch of Harry in the night.
And so our scene must to the battle fly,
Where—O for pity!—we shall much disgrace
With four or five most vile and ragged foils,
Right ill-dispos'd in brawl ridiculous,
The name of Agincourt. Yet sit and see,
Minding true things by what their mockeries be. *Exit.*

Scene I. *The English camp at Agincourt.*

Enter *King Henry, Bedford,* and *Gloucester.*

K. Hen. Gloucester, 't is true that we are in great danger;
The greater therefore should our courage be.
Good morrow, brother Bedford. God Almighty!
There is some soul of goodness in things evil,
Would men observingly distil it out;
For our bad neighbour makes us early stirrers,
Which is both healthful and good husbandry.
Besides, they are our outward consciences,
And preachers to us all, admonishing
That we should dress us fairly for our end.
Thus may we gather honey from the weed,
And make a moral of the devil himself.

Enter *Erpingham.*

Good morrow, old Sir Thomas Erpingham.
A good soft pillow for that good white head
Were better than a churlish turf of France.

Erp. Not so, my liege; this lodging likes me better,
Since I may say, "Now lie I like a king."

K. Hen. 'T is good for men to love their present pains
Upon example; so the spirit is eased;
And when the mind is quicken'd, out of doubt,
The organs, though defunct and dead before,
Break up their drowsy grave and newly move,
With casted slough and fresh legerity.
Lend me thy cloak, Sir Thomas. Brothers both,
Commend me to the princes in our camp;
Do my good morrow to them, and anon
Desire them all to my pavilion.

Glou. We shall, my liege.

Erp. Shall I attend your Grace?

K. Hen. No, my good knight;
Go with my brothers to my lords of England:
I and my bosom must debate a while,
And then I would no other company.

Erp. The Lord in heaven bless thee, noble Harry! *Exeunt all but King.*

K. Hen. God-a-mercy, old heart! thou speak'st cheerfully.

Enter *Pistol.*

Pist. *Qui va là?*

K. Hen. A friend.

Pist. Discuss unto me; art thou officer?
Or art thou base, common, and popular?

K. Hen. I am a gentleman of a company.

Pist. Trail'st thou the puissant pike?

K. Hen. Even so. What are you?

Pist. As good a gentleman as the Emperor.

K. Hen. Then you are a better than the King.

Pist. The King 's a bawcock, and a heart of gold,
A lad of life, an imp of fame;
Of parents good, of fist most valiant.
I kiss his dirty shoe, and from heart-string
I love the lovely bully. What is thy name?

K. Hen. Harry le Roy.

Pist. Le Roy! a Cornish name. Art thou of Cornish crew?

K. Hen. No, I am a Welshman.

Pist. Know'st thou Fluellen?

K. Hen. Yes.

Pist. Tell him, I 'll knock his leek about his pate
Upon Saint Davy's day.

K. Hen. Do not you wear your dagger in your cap that day, lest he knock that about yours.

Pist. Art thou his friend?

K. Hen. And his kinsman too.

Pist. The *figo* for thee, then!

39. over-bears attaint, subdues dejection. **53. Minding,** conceiving. **Scene i: 19. Upon example,** by comparison with another's suffering.

23. casted slough, cast-off skin. **legerity,** activity, nimbleness. **27. Desire,** summon. **38. popular,** plebeian. **45. imp,** youngling. **48. bully,** fine fellow. **55. Saint Davy's day,** March 1. The Welsh wore leeks in their hats to commemorate the victory of King Arthur over the Saxons in 540 A.D. Saint David is supposed to have ordered them to pluck leeks from the garden where they had fought and to wear them in their caps. **Cf. IV, vii, 104. 59. kinsman,** fellow-countryman.

K. Hen. I thank you: God be with you!
Pist. My name is Pistol call'd. *Exit.*
K. Hen. It sorts well with your fierceness.

Enter *Fluellen* and *Gower.*

Gow. Captain Fluellen!

Flu. So! in the name of Jesu Christ, speak lower. It is the greatest admiration in the universal world, when the true and aunchient prerogatifes and laws of the wars is not kept. If you would take the pains but to examine the wars of Pompey the Great, you shall find, I warrant you, that there is no tiddle taddle nor pibble pabble in Pompey's camp: I warrant you, you shall find the ceremonies of the wars, and the cares of it, and the forms of it, and the sobriety of it, and the modesty of it, to be otherwise.

Gow. Why, the enemy is loud; you hear him all night.

Flu. If the enemy is an ass and a fool and a prating coxcomb, is it meet, think you, that we should also, look you, be an ass and a fool and a prating coxcomb? In your own conscience, now?

Gow. I will speak lower.

Flu. I pray you and beseech you that you will. *Exeunt Gower and Fluellen.*

K. Hen. Though it appear a little out of fashion,
There is much care and valour in this Welshman.

Enter three soldiers, *John Bates, Alexander Court,* and *Michael Williams.*

Court. Brother John Bates, is not that the morning which breaks yonder?

Bates. I think it be; but we have no great cause to desire the approach of day.

Will. We see yonder the beginning of the day, but I think we shall never see the end of it. Who goes there?

K. Hen. A friend.

Will. Under what captain serve you?

K. Hen. Under Sir Thomas Erpingham.

Will. A good old commander and a most kind gentleman: I pray you, what thinks he of our estate?

K. Hen. Even as men wrecked upon a sand, that look to be washed off the next tide.

Bates. He hath not told his thought to the King?

K. Hen. No; nor it is not meet he should. For, though I speak it to you, I think the King is but a man, as I am: the violet smells to him as it does to me; the element shows to him as it doth to me; all his senses have but human conditions: his ceremonies laid by, in his nakedness he appears but a man; and though his affections are higher mounted than ours, yet, when they stoop, they stoop with the like wing. Therefore, when he sees reason of fears as we do, his fears, out of doubt, be of the same relish as ours are; yet, in reason, no man should possess him with any appearance of fear, lest he, by showing it, should dishearten his army.

Bates. He may show what outward courage he will; but I believe, as cold a night as 't is, he could wish himself in Thames up to the neck; and so I would he were, and I by him, at all adventures, so we were quit here.

K. Hen. By my troth, I will speak my conscience of the King: I think he would not wish himself anywhere but where he is.

Bates. Then I would he were here alone; so should he be sure to be ransomed, and a many poor men's lives saved.

K. Hen. I dare say you love him not so ill to wish him here alone, howsoever you speak this to feel other men's minds: methinks I could not die anywhere so contented as in the King's company, his cause being just and his quarrel honourable.

Will. That 's more than we know.

Bates. Ay, or more than we should seek after; for we know enough, if we know we are the King's subjects. If his cause be wrong, our obedience to the King wipes the crime of it out of us.

Will. But if the cause be not good, the King himself hath a heavy reckoning to make, when all those legs and arms and heads, chopped off in a battle, shall join together at the latter day and cry all, "We died at such a place"; some swearing, some crying for a surgeon, some upon their wives left poor behind them, some upon the debts they owe, some upon their children rawly left. I am afeard there are few die well that die in a battle; for how can they charitably dispose of anything, when blood is their argument? Now, if these men do not die well, it will be a black matter for the King that led them to it; who to disobey were against all proportion of subjection.

K. Hen. So, if a son that is by his father sent about merchandise do sinfully miscarry upon the sea, the imputation of his wickedness, by your rule, should be imposed upon his father that sent him; or if a servant, under his master's command transporting a sum of money, be assailed by robbers and die in many irreconciled iniquities, you may call the busi-

106. **element,** sky. 108. **ceremonies,** insignia of office.

111. **stoop,** used of a hawk descending on its prey. 114. **relish,** quality. 123-4. **conscience,** innermost thought. 147. **rawly,** without due provision. 153. **proportion of subjection,** proper relation of subject to king. 155. **sinfully miscarry,** perish in sin.

ness of the master the author of the servant's damnation. But this is not so: the King is not bound to answer the particular endings of his soldiers, the father of his son, nor the master of his servant; for they purpose not their death, when they purpose their services. Besides, there is no king, be his cause never so spotless, if it come to the arbitrement of swords, can try it out with all unspotted soldiers. Some, peradventure, have on them the guilt of premeditated and contrived murder; some, of beguiling virgins with the broken seals of perjury; some, making the wars their bulwark, that have before gored the gentle bosom of Peace with pillage and robbery. Now, if these men have defeated the law and outrun native punishment, though they can outstrip men, they have no wings to fly from God. War is his beadle, war is his vengeance; so that here men are punished for before-breach of the King's laws in now the King's quarrel: where they feared the death, they have borne life away; and where they would be safe, they perish. Then if they die unprovided, no more is the King guilty of their damnation than he was before guilty of those impieties for the which they are now visited. Every subject's duty is the King's; but every subject's soul is his own. Therefore should every soldier in the wars do as every sick man in his bed, wash every mote out of his conscience; and dying so, death is to him advantage; or not dying, the time was blessedly lost wherein such preparation was gained; and in him that escapes, it were not sin to think that, making God so free an offer, He let him outlive that day to see His greatness and to teach others how they should prepare.

Will. 'T is certain, every man that dies ill, the ill upon his own head, the King is not to answer it.

Bates. I do not desire he should answer for me; and yet I determine to fight lustily for him.

K. Hen. I myself heard the King say he would not be ransomed.

Will. Ay, he said so, to make us fight cheerfully; but when our throats are cut, he may be ransomed, and we ne'er the wiser.

K. Hen. If I live to see it, I will never trust his word after.

Will. You pay him then. That 's a perilous shot out of an elder-gun, that a poor and a private displeasure can do against a monarch! You may as well go about to turn the sun to ice with fanning in his face with a peacock's feather. You 'll never trust his word after! Come, 't is a foolish saying.

K. Hen. Your reproof is something too round: I should be angry with you, if the time were convenient.

Will. Let it be a quarrel between us, if you live.

K. Hen. I embrace it.

Will. How shall I know thee again?

K. Hen. Give me any gage of thine, and I will wear it in my bonnet; then, if ever thou dar'st acknowledge it, I will make it my quarrel.

Will. Here 's my glove; give me another of thine.

K. Hen. There.

Will. This will I also wear in my cap: if ever thou come to me and say, after to-morrow, "This is my glove," by this hand, I will take thee a box on the ear.

K. Hen. If ever I live to see it, I will challenge it.

Will. Thou dar'st as well be hanged.

K. Hen. Well, I will do it, though I take thee in the King's company.

Will. Keep thy word; fare thee well.

Bates. Be friends, you English fools, be friends. We have French quarrels enow, if you could tell how to reckon. *Exeunt soldiers.*

K. Hen. Indeed, the French may lay twenty French crowns to one they will beat us, for they bear them on their shoulders; but it is no English treason to cut French crowns, and to-morrow the King himself will be a clipper.
Upon the King! let us our lives, our souls,
Our debts, our careful wives,
Our children, and our sins lay on the King!
We must bear all. O hard condition,
Twin-born with greatness, subject to the breath
Of every fool, whose sense no more can feel
But his own wringing! What infinite heart's-ease
Must kings neglect, that private men enjoy!
And what have kings, that privates have not too,
Save ceremony, save general ceremony?
And what art thou, thou idol Ceremony?
What kind of god art thou, that suffer'st more
Of mortal griefs than do thy worshippers?
What are thy rents? What are thy comings in?
O Ceremony, show me but thy worth!
What is thy soul of adoration?

176. **native,** in their native country. 183. **unprovided,** unprepared. 209. **pay,** punish. 210. **elder-gun,** popgun.

217. **round,** downright. 223. **gage,** pledge. 243. **French crowns,** this reference through line 246 is an elaborate pun on crowns = French coins; crowns = heads (l. 244); **clipper** (l. 246) alludes to the criminal practice of clipping the edges of coins for the gold and silver in them. 248. **careful,** full of care. 253. **wringing,** suffering. 262. **What is thy soul of adoration?** What is the essence, the real reason, men adore thee?

Art thou aught else but place, degree, and form,
Creating awe and fear in other men?
Wherein thou art less happy being fear'd
Than they in fearing.
What drink'st thou oft, instead of homage sweet,
But poison'd flattery? O, be sick, great greatness,
And bid thy Ceremony give thee cure!
Think'st thou the fiery fever will go out
With titles blown from adulation?
Will it give place to flexure and low bending?
Canst thou, when thou command'st the beggar's knee,
Command the health of it? No, thou proud dream,
That play'st so subtly with a king's repose;
I am a king that find thee, and I know
'T is not the balm, the sceptre, and the ball,
The sword, the mace, the crown imperial,
The intertissued robe of gold and pearl,
The farced title running 'fore the King,
The throne he sits on, nor the tide of pomp
That beats upon the high shore of this world,
No, not all these, thrice-gorgeous Ceremony,
Not all these, laid in bed majestical,
Can sleep so soundly as the wretched slave,
Who with a body fill'd and vacant mind
Gets him to rest, cramm'd with distressful bread,
Never sees horrid night, the child of hell,
But, like a lackey, from the rise to set
Sweats in the eye of Phœbus, and all night
Sleeps in Elysium; next day after dawn,
Doth rise and help Hyperion to his horse,
And follows so the ever-running year,
With profitable labour, to his grave:
And, but for ceremony, such a wretch,
Winding up days with toil and nights with sleep,
Had the fore-hand and vantage of a king.
The slave, a member of the country's peace,
Enjoys it, but in gross brain little wots
What watch the King keeps to maintain the peace,
Whose hours the peasant best advantages.

Enter *Erpingham.*

Erp. My lord, your nobles, jealous of your absence,
Seek through your camp to find you.
K. Hen. Good old knight,
Collect them all together at my tent.
I 'll be before thee.
Erp. I shall do 't, my lord.
Exit.
K. Hen. O God of battles! steel my soldiers' hearts.
Possess them not with fear: take from them now
The sense of reckoning, if th' opposed numbers
Pluck their hearts from them. Not to-day, O Lord,
O, not to-day, think not upon the fault
My father made in compassing the crown!
I Richard's body have interred new,
And on it have bestowed more contrite tears
Than from it issued forced drops of blood.
Five hundred poor I have in yearly pay,
Who twice a day their wither'd hands hold up
Toward heaven, to pardon blood; and I have built
Two chantries, where the sad and solemn priests
Sing still for Richard's soul. More will I do;
Though all that I can do is nothing worth,
Since that my penitence comes after all,
Imploring pardon.

Enter *Gloucester.*

Glou. My liege!
K. Hen. My brother Gloucester's voice? Ay;
I know thy errand, I will go with thee.
The day, my friends, and all things stay for me. *Exeunt.*

Scene II. *The French camp.*

Enter the *Dauphin, Orleans, Rambures,* and *Beaumont.*

Orl. The sun doth gild our armour; up, my lords!
Dau. *Montez à cheval!* My horse, varlet! lackey! ha!
Orl. O brave spirit!
Dau. *Via! les eaux et la terre.*
Orl. *Rien puis? L'air et le feu.*
Dau. *Ciel,* cousin Orleans.

Enter *Constable.*

Now, my Lord Constable!
Con. Hark, how our steeds for present service neigh!
Dau. Mount them, and make incision in their hides,

271. adulation, flattery. **272. flexure,** bowing. **277. balm,** anointing oil. **ball,** emblem of sovereignty. **279. intertissued,** interwoven. **280. farced,** stuffed, bombastic. **287. distressful,** hard earned. **297. Had,** would have. **298. member,** sharer. **301. advantages,** advantages is best taken as a verb whose subject is **hours** and object **peasant.**

311. compassing, securing.

That their hot blood may spin in English eyes,
And dout them with superfluous courage, ha!
Ram. What, will you have them weep our horses' blood?
How shall we, then, behold their natural tears?

Enter *Messenger.*

Mess. The English are embattl'd, you French peers.
Con. To horse, you gallant princes! straight to horse!
Do but behold yond poor and starved band,
And your fair show shall suck away their souls,
Leaving them but the shales and husks of men.
There is not work enough for all our hands;
Scarce blood enough in all their sickly veins
To give each naked curtle-axe a stain,
That our French gallants shall to-day draw out,
And sheathe for lack of sport. Let us but blow on them,
The vapour of our valour will o'erturn them.
'T is positive 'gainst all exceptions, lords,
That our superfluous lackeys and our peasants,
Who in unnecessary action swarm
About our squares of battle, were enow
To purge this field of such a hilding foe,
Though we upon this mountain's basis by
Took stand for idle speculation:
But that our honours must not. What 's to say?
A very little little let us do,
And all is done. Then let the trumpets sound
The tucket sonance and the note to mount;
For our approach shall so much dare the field
That England shall crouch down in fear and yield.

Enter *Grandpré.*

Grand. Why do you stay so long, my lords of France?
Yond island carrions, desperate of their bones,
Ill-favouredly become the morning field.
Their ragged curtains poorly are let loose,
And our air shakes them passing scornfully.
Big Mars seems bankrupt in their beggar'd host
And faintly through a rusty beaver peeps;
The horsemen sit like fixed candlesticks
With torch-staves in their hand; and their poor jades
Lob down their heads, drooping the hides and hips,
The gum down-roping from their pale-dead eyes,
And in their pale dull mouths the gimmal bit
Lies foul with chew'd grass, still, and motionless;
And their executors, the knavish crows,
Fly o'er them, all impatient for their hour.
Description cannot suit itself in words
To demonstrate the life of such a battle,
In life so lifeless as it shows itself.
Con. They have said their prayers, and they stay for death.
Dau. Shall we go send them dinners and fresh suits
And give their fasting horses provender,
And after fight with them?
Con. I stay but for my guard; on to the field!
I will the banner from a trumpet take,
And use it for my haste. Come, come, away!
The sun is high, and we outwear the day.
Exeunt.

Scene III. *The English camp.*

Enter *Gloucester, Bedford, Exeter, Erpingham,* with all his host: *Salisbury* and *Westmoreland.*

Glou. Where is the King?
Bed. The King himself is rode to view their battle.
West. Of fighting men they have full threescore thousand.
Exe. There 's five to one; besides, they all are fresh.
Sal. God's arm strike with us! 't is a fearful odds.
God be wi' you, princes all; I 'll to my charge.
If we no more meet till we meet in heaven,
Then, joyfully, my noble Lord of Bedford,
My dear Lord Gloucester, and my good Lord Exeter,
And my kind kinsman, warriors all, adieu!
Bed. Farewell, good Salisbury, and good luck go with thee!
Exe. Farewell, kind lord; fight valiantly today!
And yet I do thee wrong to mind thee of it,
For thou art fram'd of the firm truth of valour.
Exit Salisbury.
Bed. He is as full of valour as of kindness,
Princely in both.

Scene ii: 11. dout, extinguish. **courage,** figuratively, blood. **18. shales,** shells. **21. curtle-axe,** cutlass. **25. exceptions,** objections. **29. hilding,** contemptible. **31. speculation,** onlooking. **35. sonance,** note. **36. dare the field,** put fear into the enemy. The term **dare** is taken from falconry, and is used when the object of the hunt, frightened by the hawk, stays close to the ground. **41. curtains,** banners. **47. Lob down,** droop. **49. gimmal,** double-hinged.
Scene iii: 10. kinsman, i.e., Westmoreland.

Enter the *King*.

West. O that we now had here
But one ten thousand of those men in England
That do no work to-day!
K. Hen. What 's he that wishes so?
My cousin Westmoreland? No, my fair cousin.
If we are mark'd to die, we are enow
To do our country loss; and if to live,
The fewer men, the greater share of honour.
God's will! I pray thee, wish not one man more.
By Jove, I am not covetous for gold,
Nor care I who doth feed upon my cost;
It yearns me not if men my garments wear;
Such outward things dwell not in my desires;
But if it be a sin to covet honour,
I am the most offending soul alive.
No, faith, my coz, wish not a man from England.
God's peace! I would not lose so great an honour
As one man more, methinks, would share from me
For the best hope I have. O, do not wish one more!
Rather proclaim it, Westmoreland, through my host,
That he which hath no stomach to this fight,
Let him depart: his passport shall be made,
And crowns for convoy put into his purse:
We would not die in that man's company
That fears his fellowship to die with us.
This day is call'd the feast of Crispian.
He that outlives this day, and comes safe home,
Will stand a tip-toe when this day is named,
And rouse him at the name of Crispian.
He that shall live this day, and see old age,
Will yearly on the vigil feast his neighbours,
And say, "To-morrow is Saint Crispian."
Then will he strip his sleeve and show his scars,
And say, "These wounds I had on Crispian's day."
Old men forget; yet all shall be forgot,
But he 'll remember with advantages
What feats he did that day. Then shall our names,
Familiar in his mouth as household words,
Harry the King, Bedford, and Exeter,
Warwick and Talbot, Salisbury and Gloucester,
Be in their flowing cups freshly remember'd.
This story shall the good man teach his son;
And Crispin Crispian shall ne'er go by,
From this day to the ending of the world,
But we in it shall be remember'd,
We few, we happy few, we band of brothers;
For he to-day that sheds his blood with me
Shall be my brother; be he ne'er so vile,
This day shall gentle his condition;
And gentlemen in England now a-bed
Shall think themselves accurs'd they were not here,
And hold their manhoods cheap whiles any speaks
That fought with us upon Saint Crispin's day.

Re-enter *Salisbury*.

Sal. My sovereign lord, bestow yourself with speed:
The French are bravely in their battles set,
And will with all expedience charge on us.
K. Hen. All things are ready, if our minds be so.
West. Perish the man whose mind is backward now!
K. Hen. Thou dost not wish more help from England, coz?
West. God's will! my liege, would you and I alone,
Without more help, could fight this royal battle!
K. Hen. Why, now thou hast unwish'd five thousand men,
Which likes me better than to wish us one.
You know your places: God be with you all!

Tucket. Enter *Montjoy*.

Mont. Once more I come to know of thee, King Harry,
If for thy ransom thou wilt now compound,
Before thy most assured overthrow;
For certainly thou art so near the gulf,
Thou needs must be englutted. Besides, in mercy,
The Constable desires thee thou wilt mind
Thy followers of repentance; that their souls
May make a peaceful and a sweet retire
From off these fields, where, wretches, their poor bodies
Must lie and fester.
K. Hen. Who hath sent thee now?
Mont. The Constable of France.
K. Hen. I pray thee, bear my former answer back:
Bid them achieve me and then sell my bones.
Good God! why should they mock poor fellows thus?
The man that once did sell the lion's skin

26. yearns, grieves. **40. Crispian,** October 25th. **45. vigil,** eve of a saint's day. **50. advantages,** additions, lit., interest. **57.** The brothers, Crispinus and Crispianus, patron saints of shoemakers, were martyred at Soissons in France in the late third or early fourth century.

62. vile, low born. **63. gentle his condition,** make him a gentleman. **68. bestow,** place. **69. bravely,** with great display. **70. expedience,** speed. **80. compound,** make terms. **83. englutted,** swallowed up. **91. achieve,** win.

While the beast liv'd, was kill'd with hunting him.
A many of our bodies shall no doubt
Find native graves, upon the which, I trust,
Shall witness live in brass of this day's work;
And those that leave their valiant bones in France,
Dying like men, though buried in your dunghills,
They shall be fam'd; for there the sun shall greet them,
And draw their honours reeking up to heaven;
Leaving their earthly parts to choke your clime,
The smell whereof shall breed a plague in France.
Mark then abounding valour in our English,
That being dead, like to the bullet's grazing,
Break out into a second course of mischief,
Killing in relapse of mortality.
Let me speak proudly: tell the Constable
We are but warriors for the working-day.
Our gayness and our gilt are all besmirch'd
With rainy marching in the painful field;
There 's not a piece of feather in our host—
Good argument, I hope, we will not fly—
And time hath worn us into slovenry;
But, by the mass, our hearts are in the trim;
And my poor soldiers tell me, yet ere night
They 'll be in fresher robes, or they will pluck
The gay new coats o'er the French soldiers' heads
And turn them out of service. If they do this—
As, if God please, they shall,—my ransom then
Will soon be levied. Herald, save thou thy labour.
Come thou no more for ransom, gentle herald.
They shall have none, I swear, but these my joints;
Which if they have as I will leave 'em them,
Shall yield them little, tell the Constable.

Mont. I shall, King Harry. And so fare thee well;
Thou never shalt hear herald any more. *Exit.*

K. Hen. I fear thou 'lt once more come again for ransom.

Enter *York.*

York. My lord, most humbly on my knee I beg
The leading of the vaward.

K. Hen. Take it, brave York. Now, soldiers, march away;
And how thou pleasest, God, dispose the day!
Exeunt.

107. in . . . mortality, in a deadly rebound. **130. vaward,** vanguard.

Scene IV. *The field of battle.*

Alarum. Excursions. Enter *Pistol, French Soldier,* and *Boy.*

Pist. Yield, cur!

Fr. Sol. *Je pense que vous êtes le gentilhomme de bonne qualité.*

Pist. *Qualtitie calmie custure me!* Art thou a gentleman? What is thy name? Discuss.

Fr. Sol. *O Seigneur Dieu!*

Pist. O, signieur Dew should be a gentleman.
Perpend my words, O Signieur Dew, and mark:
O Signieur Dew, thou diest on point of fox,
Except, O signieur, thou do give to me
Egregious ransom.

Fr. Sol. *O, prenez miséricorde! ayez pitié de moi!*

Pist. Moy shall not serve; I will have forty moys,
Or I will fetch thy rim out at thy throat
In drops of crimson blood.

Fr. Sol. *Est-il impossible d'échapper la force de ton bras?*

Pist. Brass, cur!
Thou damned and luxurious mountain goat,
Offer'st me brass?

Fr. Sol. *O pardonnez moi!*

Pist. Say'st thou me so? Is that a ton of moys?
Come hither, boy; ask me this slave in French
What is his name.

Boy. *Écoutez: comment êtes-vous appelé?*

Fr. Sol. *Monsieur le Fer.*

Boy. He says his name is Master Fer.

Pist. Master Fer! I 'll fer him, and firk him, and ferret him: discuss the same in French unto him.

Boy. I do not know the French for fer, and ferret, and firk.

Pist. Bid him prepare; for I will cut his throat.

Fr. Sol. *Que dit-il, monsieur?*

Boy. *Il me commande à vous dire que vous faites vous prêt; car ce soldat ici est disposé tout à cette heure de couper votre gorge.*

Pist. *Owy, cuppele gorge, permafoy,*

4. Qualtitie calmie custure me, Qualtitie is obviously Pistol's attempt at **"Qualité,"** the last word spoken by the French soldier. The remainder may have been suggested by the refrain of a contemporary Irish song: "Calen, O custure me!" This in turn is a corruption of the phrase, "Colleen, oge asture," which means, "Young girl, my treasure." **9. fox,** sword. **14. moys,** the Portuguese coin, a **moi,** worth about seven dollars. **15. rim,** midriff. **20. luxurious,** lustful. **29. firk,** beat. **30. ferret,** worry, as a ferret does it prey.

Peasant, unless thou give me crowns, brave crowns,
Or mangled shalt thou be by this my sword.

Fr. Sol. *O, je vous supplie, pour l'amour le Dieu, me pardonner! Je suis le gentilhomme de bonne maison; gardez ma vie, et je vous donnerai deux cents écus.*

Pist. What are his words?

Boy. He prays you to save his life: he is a gentleman of a good house; and for his ransom he will give you two hundred crowns.

Pist. Tell him my fury shall abate, and I
The crowns will take.

Fr. Sol. *Petit monsieur, que dit-il?*

Boy. *Encore qu'il est contre son jurement de pardonner aucun prisonnier; néanmoins, pour les écus que vous l'avez promis, il est content de vous donner la liberté, le franchisement.*

Fr. Sol. *Sur mes genoux je vous donne mille remercîmens; et je m'estime heureux que je suis tombé entre les mains d'un chevalier, je pense, le plus brave, vaillant, et très distingué seigneur d'Angleterre.*

Pist. Expound unto me, boy.

Boy. He gives you upon his knee, a thousand thanks; and he esteems himself happy that he hath fall'n into the hands of one, as he thinks, the most brave, valorous, and thrice-worthy seigneur of England.

Pist. As I suck blood, I will some mercy show. Follow me!

Boy. *Suivez-vous le grande capitaine.* [*Exeunt Pistol, and French Soldier.*] I did never know so full a voice issue from so empty a heart; but the saying is true, "The empty vessel makes the greatest sound." Bardolph and Nym had ten times more valour than this roaring devil i' th' old play, that every one may pare his nails with a wooden dagger; and they are both hanged; and so would this be, if he durst steal anything adventurously. I must stay with the lackeys with the luggage of our camp: the French might have a good prey of us, if he knew of it; for there is none to guard it but boys. *Exit.*

Scene V. *Another part of the field.*

Enter *Constable, Orleans, Bourbon, Dauphin,* and *Rambures.*

Con. *O diable!*

Orl. *O seigneur! le jour est perdu, tout est perdu!*

Dau. *Mort de ma vie!* all is confounded, all!
Reproach and everlasting shame
Sits mocking in our plumes. *O méchante fortune!*
Do not run away. *A short alarum.*

Con. Why, all our ranks are broke.

Dau. O perdurable shame! let 's stab ourselves.
Be these the wretches that we play'd at dice for?

Orl. Is this the king we sent to for his ransom?

Bour. Shame and eternal shame, nothing but shame!
Let 's die in honour! Once more back again!
And he that will not follow Bourbon now,
Let him go hence, and with his cap in hand,
Like a base pandar, hold the chamber door
Whilst by a slave, no gentler than my dog,
His fairest daughter is contaminated.

Con. Disorder, that hath spoil'd us, friend us now!
Let us on heaps go offer up our lives.

Orl. We are enow yet living in the field
To smother up the English in our throngs,
If any order might be thought upon.

Bour. The devil take order now! I 'll to the throng.
Let life be short, else shame will be too long.
Exeunt.

Scene VI. *Another part of the field.*

Alarum. Enter *King Henry* and his train, with prisoners.

K. Hen. Well have we done, thrice valiant countrymen:
But all 's not done; yet keep the French the field.

Exe. The Duke of York commends him to your Majesty.

K. Hen. Lives he, good uncle? Thrice within this hour
I saw him down; thrice up again, and fighting;
From helmet to the spur all blood he was.

Exe. In which array, brave soldier, doth he lie,
Larding the plain; and by his bloody side,
Yoke-fellow to his honour-owing wounds,
The noble Earl of Suffolk also lies.
Suffolk first died; and York, all haggled over,
Comes to him, where in gore he lay insteeped,
And takes him by the beard; kisses the gashes
That bloodily did yawn upon his face.

75. **roaring devil i' th' old play,** the devil of the Morality plays was a stock comic character, a braggart and coward like Pistol, and was put to flight by the Vice, or buffoon, armed with a wooden dagger. It was evidently common for Vice to pare the devil's claws or nails with his dagger.

Scene v: 7. perdurable, lasting. **Scene vi: 8. Larding,** enriching (with his blood). **9. owing,** owning, possessing. **11. haggled,** hacked.

He cries aloud, "Tarry, my cousin Suffolk!
My soul shall thine keep company to heaven;
Tarry, sweet soul, for mine, then fly abreast,
As in this glorious and well-foughten field
We kept together in our chivalry!"
Upon these words I came and cheer'd him up.
He smil'd me in the face, raught me his hand,
And, with a feeble gripe, says, "Dear my lord,
Commend my service to my sovereign."
So did he turn and over Suffolk's neck
He threw his wounded arm and kiss'd his lips;
And so espous'd to death, with blood he seal'd
A testament of noble-ending love.
The pretty and sweet manner of it forc'd
Those waters from me which I would have stopp'd;
But I had not so much of man in me,
And all my mother came into mine eyes
And gave me up to tears.

K. Hen. I blame you not;
For, hearing this, I must perforce compound
With mistful eyes, or they will issue too.
Alarum.
But, hark! what new alarum is this same?
The French have reinforc'd their scatter'd men:
Then every soldier kill his prisoners;
Give the word through. *Exeunt.*

Scene VII. *Another part of the field.*

Enter *Fluellen* and *Gower.*

Flu. Kill the poys and the luggage! 'T is expressly against the law of arms: 't is as arrant a piece of knavery, mark you now, as can be offer't; in your conscience, now, is it not?

Gow. 'T is certain there 's not a boy left alive; and the cowardly rascals that ran from the battle ha' done this slaughter: besides, they have burned and carried away all that was in the King's tent; wherefore the King, most worthily, hath caused every soldier to cut his prisoner's throat. O, 't is a gallant king!

Flu. Ay, he was porn at Monmouth, Captain Gower. What call you the town's name where Alexander the Pig was born!

Gow. Alexander the Great.

Flu. Why, I pray you, is not pig great? The pig, or the great, or the mighty, or the huge, or the magnanimous, are all oné reckonings, save the phrase is a little variations.

Gow. I think Alexander the Great was born in Macedon: his father was called Philip of Macedon, as I take it.

Flu. I think it is in Macedon where Alexander is porn. I tell you, captain, if you look in the maps of the 'orld, I warrant you sall find, in the comparisons between Macedon and Monmouth, that the situations, look you, is both alike. There is a river in Macedon; and there is also moreover a river at Monmouth: it is call'd Wye at Monmouth; but it is out of my prains what is the name of the other river; but 't is all one, 't is alike as my fingers is to my fingers, and there is salmons in both. If you mark Alexander's life well, Harry of Monmouth's life is come after it indifferent well; for there is figures in all things. Alexander, God knows, and you know, in his rages, and his furies, and his wraths, and his cholers, and his moods, and his displeasures, and his indignations, and also being a little intoxicates in his prains, did, in his ales and his angers, look you, kill his best friend, Cleitus.

Gow. Our King is not like him in that. He never killed any of his friends.

Flu. It is not well done, mark you now, to take the tales out of my mouth, ere it is made and finished. I speak but in the figures and comparisons of it. As Alexander killed his friend Cleitus, being in his ales and his cups; so also Harry Monmouth, being in his right wits and his good judgements, turned away the fat knight with the great belly doublet: he was full of jests, and gipes, and knaveries, and mocks; I have forgot his name.

Gow. Sir John Falstaff.

Flu. That is he. I 'll tell you there is good men porn at Monmouth.

Gow. Here comes his Majesty.

Alarum. Enter *King Henry* and forces; *Warwick, Gloucester, Exeter,* with prisoners. Flourish.

K. Hen. I was not angry since I came to France
Until this instant. Take a trumpet, herald;
Ride thou unto the horsemen on yond hill:
If they will fight with us, bid them come down,
Or void the field; they do offend our sight.
If they 'll do neither, we will come to them,
And make them skirr away, as swift as stones
Enforced from the old Assyrian slings.
Besides, we 'll cut the throats of those we have,
And not a man of them that we shall take
Shall taste our mercy. Go and tell them so.

Enter *Montjoy.*

Exe. Here comes the herald of the French, my liege.

21. raught, reached. **33. compound,** come to terms. **34. issue,** shed tears.

Scene vii: 35. figures, comparisons. **51. gipes,** gibes **64. skirr,** scurry. **65. Enforced,** hurled.

Glou. His eyes are humbler than they us'd to be.
K. Hen. How now! what means this, herald? Know'st thou not
That I have fin'd these bones of mine for ransom?
Com'st thou again for ransom?
Mont. No, great King;
I come to thee for charitable license,
That we may wander o'er this bloody field
To book our dead, and then to bury them;
To sort our nobles from our common men.
For many of our princes—woe the while!—
Lie drown'd and soak'd in mercenary blood;
So do our vulgar drench their peasant limbs
In blood of princes; and the wounded steeds
Fret fetlock deep in gore, and with wild rage
Yerk out their armed heels at their dead masters,
Killing them twice. O, give us leave, great King,
To view the field in safety, and dispose
Of their dead bodies!
K. Hen. I tell thee truly, herald,
I know not if the day be ours or no;
For yet a many of your horsemen peer
And gallop o'er the field.
Mont. The day is yours.
K. Hen. Praised be God, and not our strength, for it!
What is this castle call'd that stands hard by?
Mont. They call it Agincourt.
K. Hen. Then call we this the field of Agincourt,
Fought on the day of Crispin Crispianus.

Flu. Your grandfather of famous memory, an 't please your Majesty, and your great-uncle Edward the Plack Prince of Wales, as I have read in the chronicles, fought a most prave pattle here in France.

K. Hen. They did, Fluellen.

Flu. Your Majesty says very true. If your Majesties is remember'd of it, the Welshmen did good service in a garden where leeks did grow, wearing leeks in their Monmouth caps; which, your Majesty know, to this hour is an honourable badge of the service; and I do believe your Majesty takes no scorn to wear the leek upon Saint Tavy's day.

K. Hen. I wear it for a memorable honour;
For I am Welsh, you know, good countryman.

Flu. All the water in Wye cannot wash your Majesty's Welsh plood out of your pody, I can tell you that. God pless it and preserve it, as long as it pleases His grace, and His majesty too!

K. Hen. Thanks, good my countryman.

Flu. By Jeshu, I am your Majesty's countryman, I care not who know it: I will confess it to all the 'orld: I need not to be ashamed of your Majesty, praised be God, so long as your Majesty is an honest man.

K. Hen. God keep me so!

Enter *Williams.*

Our heralds go with him;
Bring me just notice of the numbers dead
On both our parts. Call yonder fellow hither.
Exeunt Heralds with Montjoy.

Exe. Soldier, you must come to the King.

K. Hen. Soldier, why wear'st thou that glove in thy cap?

Will. An 't please your Majesty, 't is the gage of one that I should fight withal, if he be alive.

K. Hen. An Englishman?

Will. An 't please your Majesty, a rascal that swaggered with me last night; who, if alive and ever dare to challenge this glove, I have sworn to take him a box o' th' ear; or if I can see my glove in his cap, which he swore, as he was a soldier, he would wear if alive, I will strike it out soundly.

K. Hen. What think you, Captain Fluellen? Is it fit this soldier keep his oath?

Flu. He is a craven and a villain else, an 't please your Majesty, in my conscience.

K. Hen. It may be his enemy is a gentleman of great sort, quite from the answer of his degree.

Flu. Though he be as good a gentleman as the devil is, as Lucifer and Belzebub himself, it is necessary, look your Grace, that he keep his vow and his oath. If he be perjured, see you now, his reputation is as arrant a villain and a Jack-sauce, as ever his black shoe trod upon God's ground and His earth, in my conscience, la!

K. Hen. Then keep thy vow, sirrah, when thou meet'st the fellow.

Will. So I will, my liege, as I live.

K. Hen. Who serv'st thou under?

Will. Under Captain Gower, my liege.

Flu. Gower is a good captain, and is good knowledge and literatured in the wars.

K. Hen. Call him hither to me, soldier.

Will. I will, my liege. *Exit.*

K. Hen. Here, Fluellen; wear thou this favour for me and stick it in thy cap. When Alençon and myself were down together, I plucked this glove from his helm: if any man challenge this, he is a friend to Alençon, and an enemy to our person: if thou encounter

72. **fin'd,** agreed to pay as a fine. 83. **Yerk,** kick. 88. **peer,** appear. 95. **Your grandfather,** Henry's grandfather, John of Gaunt, was only six at the battle of Crecy. Fluellen means his great-grandfather, Edward III. 103. **garden,** see n. IV. i. 55.

142. **sort,** rank. 142-3. **quite from the answer of his degree,** quite above answering the challenge of a man of his rank. 149. **Jack-sauce,** impudent fellow.

any such, apprehend him, an thou dost me love.

Flu. Your Grace doo's me as great honours as can be desired in the hearts of his subjects: I would fain see the man, that has but two legs, that shall find himself aggriefed at this glove; that is all: but I would fain see it once, an please God of His grace that I might see.

K. Hen. Know'st thou Gower?

Flu. He is my dear friend, an please you.

K. Hen. Pray thee, go seek him, and bring him to my tent.

Flu. I will fetch him. *Exit.*

K. Hen. My Lord of Warwick, and my brother Gloucester,
Follow Fluellen closely at the heels.
The glove which I have given him for a favour
May haply purchase him a box o' th' ear.
It is the soldier's; I by bargain should
Wear it myself. Follow, good cousin Warwick.
If that the soldier strike him, as I judge
By his blunt bearing he will keep his word,
Some sudden mischief may arise of it;
For I do know Fluellen valiant
And, touch'd with choler, hot as gunpowder,
And quickly will return an injury.
Follow, and see there be no harm between them.
Go you with me, uncle of Exeter. *Exeunt.*

Scene VIII. *Before King Henry's pavilion.*

Enter *Gower* and *Williams.*

Will. I warrant it is to knight you, captain.

Enter *Fluellen.*

Flu. God's will and his pleasure, captain, I beseech you now, come apace to the King: there is more good toward you peradventure than is in your knowledge to dream of.

Will. Sir, know you this glove?

Flu. Know the glove! I know the glove is a glove.

Will. I know this; and thus I challenge it. *Strikes him.*

Flu. 'Sblood! an arrant traitor as any is in the universal world, or in France, or in England!

Gow. How now, sir! you villain!

Will. Do you think I 'll be forsworn?

Flu. Stand away, Captain Gower: I will give treason his payment into plows, I warrant you.

Will. I am no traitor.

Flu. That 's a lie in thy throat. I charge you in his Majesty's name, apprehend him; he 's a friend of the Duke Alençon's.

Enter *Warwick* and *Gloucester.*

War. How now, how now! what 's the matter?

Flu. My Lord of Warwick, here is—praised be God for it!—a most contagious treason come to light, look you, as you shall desire in a summer's day. Here is his Majesty

Enter *King Henry* and *Exeter.*

K. Hen. How now! what 's the matter?

Flu. My liege, here is a villain and a traitor, that, look your Grace, has struck the glove which your Majesty is take out of the helmet of Alençon.

Will. My liege, this was my glove; here is the fellow of it; and he that I gave it to in change promised to wear it in his cap: I promis'd to strike him, if he did: I met this man with my glove in his cap, and I have been as good as my word.

Flu. Your Majesty hear now, saving your Majesty's manhood, what an arrant, rascally, beggarly, lousy knave it is. I hope your Majest is pear me testimony and witness, and will avouchment, that this is the glove of Alençon that your Majesty is give me; in your conscience, now?

K. Hen. Give me thy glove, soldier. Look, here is the fellow of it.
'T was I, indeed, thou promisedst to strike;
And thou hast given me most bitter terms.

Flu. An it please your Majesty, let his neck answer for it, if there is any martial law in the world.

K. Hen. How canst thou make me satisfaction?

Will. All offences, my lord, come from the heart: never came any from mine that might offend your Majesty.

K. Hen. It was ourself thou didst abuse.

Will. Your Majesty came not like yourself: you appeared to me but as a common man; witness the night, your garments, your lowliness; and what your Highness suffered under that shape, I beseech you take it for your own fault and not mine; for had you been as I took you for, I made no offence; therefore, I beseech your Highness, pardon me.

K. Hen. Here, uncle Exeter, fill this glove with crowns,
And give it to this fellow. Keep it, fellow;
And wear it for an honour in thy cap
Till I do challenge it. Give him his crowns;
And, captain, you must needs be friends with him.

Flu. By this day and this light, the fellow

38. is pear, will bear. **39. avouchment,** acknowledge.

has mettle enough in his belly. Hold, there is twelve pence for you; and I pray you to serve God, and keep you out of prawls, and prabbles, and quarrels, and dissensions, and, I warrant you, it is the better for you.

Will. I will none of your money.

Flu. It is with a good will; I can tell you, it will serve you to mend your shoes: come, wherefore should you be so pashful? Your shoes is not so good: 't is a good silling, I warrant you, or I will change it.

Enter an English *Herald*.

K. Hen. Now, herald, are the dead number'd?

Her. Here is the number of the slaughter'd French.

K. Hen. What prisoners of good sort are taken, uncle?

Exe. Charles Duke of Orleans, nephew to the King;
John Duke of Bourbon, and Lord Bouciqualt;
Of other lords and barons, knights and squires,
Full fifteen hundred, besides common men.

K. Hen. This note doth tell me of ten thousand French
That in the field lie slain; of princes, in this number,
And nobles bearing banners, there lie dead
One hundred twenty-six; added to these,
Of knights, esquires, and gallant gentlemen,
Eight thousand and four hundred; of the which,
Five hundred were but yesterday dubb'd knights;
So that, in these ten thousand they have lost,
There are but sixteen hundred mercenaries;
The rest are princes, barons, lords, knights, squires,
And gentlemen of blood and quality.
The names of those their nobles that lie dead:
Charles Delabreth, High Constable of France;
Jacques of Chatillon, Admiral of France;
The master of the cross-bows, Lord Rambures;
Great Master of France, the brave Sir Guichard Dauphin,
John Duke of Alençon, Anthony Duke of Brabant,
The brother to the Duke of Burgundy,
And Edward Duke of Bar; of lusty earls,
Grandpré and Roussi, Fauconberg and Foix,
Beaumont and Marle, Vaudemont and Lestrale.
Here was a royal fellowship of death!
Where is the number of our English dead?

Herald shows him another paper.

Edward the Duke of York, the Earl of Suffolk,
Sir Richard Ketly, Davy Gam, esquire;
None else of name; and of all other men
But five and twenty.—O God, thy arm was here;
And not to us, but to thy arm alone,
Ascribe we all! When, without stratagem,
But in plain shock and even play of battle,
Was ever known so great and little loss
On one part and on the other? Take it, God,
For it is none but thine!

Exe. 'T is wonderful!

K. Hen. Come, go we in procession to the village;
And be it death proclaimed through our host
To boast of this or take that praise from God
Which is His only.

Flu. Is it not lawful, an please your Majesty, to tell how many is killed?

K. Hen. Yes, captain, but with this acknowledgement,
That God fought for us.

Flu. Yes, my conscience, He did us great good.

K. Hen. Do we all holy rites.
Let there be sung *Non nobis* and *Te Deum*,
The dead with charity enclos'd in clay,
And then to Calais; and to England then,
Where ne'er from France arriv'd more happy men. *Exeunt.*

ACT V

Enter *Chorus*.

Chor. Vouchsafe to those that have not read the story,
That I may prompt them; and of such as have,
I humbly pray them to admit th' excuse
Of time, of numbers, and due course of things,
Which cannot in their huge and proper life
Be here presented. Now we bear the King
Toward Calais; grant him there; there seen,
Heave him away upon your winged thoughts
Athwart the sea. Behold, the English beach
Pales in the flood with men, with wives and boys,
Whose shouts and claps out-voice the deep-mouth'd sea,

69. prabbles, squabbles. 76. silling. shilling.

Act V, Chorus: 10. Pales in, fences in.

Which like a mighty whiffler 'fore the King
Seems to prepare his way: so let him land,
And solemnly see him set on to London.
So swift a pace hath thought that even now
You may imagine him upon Blackheath,
Where that his lords desire him to have borne
His bruised helmet and his bended sword
Before him through the city: he forbids it,
Being free from vainness and self-glorious pride;
Giving full trophy, signal, and ostent
Quite from himself to God. But now behold,
In the quick forge and working-house of thought,
How London doth pour out her citizens!
The mayor and all his brethren in best sort,
Like to the senators of th' antique Rome,
With the plebeians swarming at their heels,
Go forth and fetch their conqu'ring Cæsar in;
As, by a lower but loving likelihood,
Were now the general of our gracious Empress,
As in good time he may, from Ireland coming,
Bringing rebellion broached on his sword,
How many would the peaceful city quit,
To welcome him! Much more, and much more cause,
Did they this Harry. Now in London place him;
As yet the lamentation of the French
Invites the King of England's stay at home,—
The Emperor's coming in behalf of France,
To order peace between them;—and omit
All the occurrences, whatever chanc'd,
Till Harry's back-return again to France.
There must we bring him; and myself have play'd
The interim, by rememb'ring you 't is past.
Then brook abridgement, and your eyes advance
After your thoughts, straight back again to France. *Exit.*

Scene I. *France. The English camp.*

Enter *Fluellen* and *Gower*.

Gow. Nay, that 's right; but why wear you your leek to-day? Saint Davy's day is past.

Flu. There is occasions and causes why and wherefore in all things: I will tell you asse my friend, Captain Gower. The rascally, scald, beggarly, lousy, pragging knave, Pistol, which you and yourself and all the world know to be no petter than a fellow, look you now, of no merits, he is come to me and prings me pread and salt yesterday, look you, and bid me eat my leek. It was in a place where I could not breed no contention with him; but I will be so bold as to wear it in my cap till I see him once again, and then I will tell him a little piece of my desires.

Enter *Pistol.*

Gow. Why, here he comes, swelling like a turkey-cock.

Flu. 'T is no matter for his swellings nor his turkey-cocks. God pless you, Aunchient Pistol! you scurfy, lousy knave, God pless you!

Pist. Ha! art thou bedlam? Dost thou thirst, base Trojan,
To have me fold up Pasca's fatal web?
Hence! I am qualmish at the smell of leek.

Flu. I peseech you heartily, scurfy, lousy knave, at my desires, and my requests, and my petitions, to eat, look you, this leek: because, look you, you do not love it, nor your affections and your appetites and your disgestions doo's not agree with it, I would desire you to eat it.

Pist. Not for Cadwallader and all his goats.

Flu. There is one goat for you. [*Strikes him.*] Will you be so good, scald knave, as eat it?

Pist. Base Trojan, thou shalt die.

Flu. You say very true, scald knave, when God's will is. I will desire you to live in the mean time, and eat your victuals: come, there is sauce for it. [*Strikes him.*] You called me yesterday mountain-squire; but I will make you to-day a squire of low degree. I pray you, fall to; if you can mock a leek, you can eat a leek.

Gow. Enough, captain; you have astonished him.

Flu. I say, I will make him eat some part of my leek, or I will peat his pate four days. Bite, I pray you; it is good for your green wound and your ploody coxcomb.

Pist. Must I bite?

12. whiffler, one who clears the way for a procession. **21. signal,** token of victory. **ostent,** external signs of honor. **30. the general of our gracious Empress,** Robert Devereux, Earl of Essex, went to Ireland March 27, 1599, to suppress Tyrone's rebellion. He was unsuccessful and returned the same year, Sept. 28th. **32. broached,** spitted. **38. The Emperor's coming,** the Emperor of Germany, Sigismund, arrived May 1, 1416, to make peace between England and France. The peace treaty was not signed, however, until May 1, 1420. **44. brook abridgement,** accept this cutting short of history.

Scene i: 5. scald, scurvy. **20. bedlam,** mad. **21. Parca's,** Fate's. **29. Cadwallader,** a famous British king. He defended Wales against the Saxons in the 7th century. Goats were associated with Wales. **40. astonished,** stunned.

Flu. Yes, certainly, and out of doubt and out of question too, and ambiguities.

Pist. By this leek, I will most horribly revenge. I eat and eat, I swear—

Flu. Eat, I pray you. Will you have some more sauce to your leek? There is not enough leek to swear by.

Pist. Quiet thy cudgel; thou dost see I eat.

Flu. Much good do you, scald knave, heartily. Nay, pray you, throw none away; the skin is good for your broken coxcomb. When you take occasions to see leeks hereafter, I pray you, mock at 'em; that is all.

Pist. Good.

Flu. Ay, leeks is good. Hold you, there is a groat to heal your pate.

Pist. Me a groat!

Flu. Yes, verily and in truth you shall take it; or I have another leek in my pocket, which you shall eat.

Pist. I take thy groat in earnest of revenge.

Flu. If I owe you anything, I will pay you in cudgels: you shall be a woodmonger, and buy nothing of me but cudgels. God be wi' you, and keep you, and heal your pate. *Exit.*

Pist. All hell shall stir for this.

Gow. Go, go; you are a counterfeit cowardly knave. Will you mock at an ancient tradition, begun upon an honourable respect, and worn as a memorable trophy of predeceased valour, and dare not avouch in your deeds any of your words? I have seen you gleeking and galling at this gentleman twice or thrice. You thought, because he could not speak English in the native garb, he could not therefore handle an English cudgel: you find it otherwise; and henceforth let a Welsh correction teach you a good English condition. Fare ye well. *Exit.*

Pist. Doth Fortune play the huswife with me now?
News have I, that my Doll is dead i' th' spital
Of malady of France;
And there my rendezvous is quite cut off.
Old I do wax; and from my weary limbs
Honour is cudgell'd. Well, bawd I 'll turn,
And something lean to cutpurse of quick hand,
To England will I steal, and there I 'll steal;
And patches will I get unto these cudgell'd scars,
And swear I got them in the Gallia wars.
Exit.

62. **groat**, 4d. 75. **respect**, reason. 78. **gleeking**, jeering. 79. **galling**, scoffing. 83. **condition**, disposition. 85. **huswife**, hussy, jilt. 86. **Doll**, Pistol's wife was Nell (Quickly) not Doll (Tearsheet). There are other examples of mistaken names in this play.

Scene II. *France. A royal palace.*

Enter, at one door, *King Henry, Exeter, Bedford, Gloucester, Warwick, Westmoreland,* and other Lords; at another, the *French King, Queen Isabel,* the *Princess Katharine, Alice,* and other Ladies; the *Duke of Burgundy,* and other French.

K. Hen. Peace to this meeting, wherefore we are met!
Unto our brother France, and to our sister,
Health and fair time of day; joy and good wishes
To our most fair and princely cousin Katharine;
And, as a branch and member of this royalty,
By whom this great assembly is contriv'd,
We do salute you, Duke of Burgundy;
And, princes French, and peers, health to you all!

Fr. King. Right joyous are we to behold your face.
Most worthy brother England; fairly met!
So are you, princes English, every one.

Q. Isa. So happy be the issue, brother England,
Of this good day and of this gracious meeting,
As we are now glad to behold your eyes;
Your eyes, which hitherto have borne in them
Against the French that met them in their bent
The fatal balls of murdering basilisks:
The venom of such looks, we fairly hope,
Have lost their quality, and that this day
Shall change all griefs and quarrels into love.

K. Hen. To cry amen to that, thus we appear.

Q. Isa. You English princes all, I do salute you.

Bur. My duty to you both, on equal love,
Great Kings of France and England! That I have labour'd,
With all my wits, my pains, and strong endeavours,
To bring your most imperial Majesties
Unto this bar and royal interview,
Your mightiness on both parts best can witness.
Since then my office hath so far prevail'd
That, face to face and royal eye to eye,
You have congreeted, let it not disgrace me,
If I demand, before this royal view,
What rub or what impediment there is,
Why that the naked, poor, and mangled Peace,
Dear nurse of arts, plenties, and joyful births,

16. **bent**, direction, glance. 17. **basilisks**, large cannon, named after the fabulous serpent whose glance was supposed to kill. 27. **bar**, meeting-place. 31. **congreeted**, greeted each other.

Should not in this best garden of the world,
Our fertile France, put up her lovely visage?
Alas, she hath from France too long been chas'd,
And all her husbandry doth lie on heaps,
Corrupting in it own fertility.
Her vine, the merry cheerer of the heart,
Unpruned dies; her hedges even-pleach'd,
Like prisoners wildly overgrown with hair,
Put forth disorder'd twigs; her fallow leas
The darnel, hemlock, and rank fumitory
Doth root upon, while that the coulter rusts
That should deracinate such savagery;
The even mead, that erst brought sweetly forth
The freckled cowslip, burnet, and green clover,
Wanting the scythe, all uncorrected, rank,
Conceives by idleness, and nothing teems
But hateful docks, rough thistles, kexes, burs,
Losing both beauty and utility;
And all our vineyards, fallows, meads, and hedges,
Defective in their natures, grow to wildness.
Even so our houses and ourselves and children
Have lost, or do not learn for want of time,
The sciences that should become our country;
But grow like savages,—as soldiers will
That nothing do but meditate on blood,—
To swearing and stern looks, diffus'd attire,
And everything that seems unnatural.
Which to reduce into our former favour
You are assembled; and my speech entreats
That I may know the let, why gentle Peace
Should not expel these inconveniences
And bless us with her former qualities.

K. Hen. If, Duke of Burgundy, you would the peace,
Whose want gives growth to th' imperfections
Which you have cited, you must buy that peace
With full accord to all our just demands;
Whose tenours and particular effects
You have enschedul'd briefly in your hands.

Bur. The King hath heard them; to the which as yet
There is no answer made.

K. Hen. Well, then, the peace,
Which you before so urg'd, lies in his answer.

Fr. King. I have but with a cursorary eye
O'erglanc'd the articles: pleaseth your Grace
To appoint some of your council presently
To sit with us once more, with better heed
To re-survey them, we will suddenly
Pass our accept and peremptory answer.

40. it, its. **42. even-pleach'd,** evenly interwoven. **44. leas,** arable land. **46. coulter,** ploughshare. **47. deracinate,** uproot. **52. kexes,** dry stocks of weeds. **61. diffus'd,** disordered. **63. favour,** appearance. **65. let,** hindrance. **72. tenours,** purport. **73. enschedul'd,** written down. **77. cursorary,** cursory. **82. accept,** decisive. **peremptory,** final.

K. Hen. Brother, we shall. Go, uncle Exeter,
And brother Clarence, and you, brother Gloucester,
Warwick, and Huntingdon, go with the King;
And take with you free power to ratify,
Augment, or alter, as your wisdoms best
Shall see advantageable for our dignity,
Anything in or out of our demands,
And we 'll consign thereto. Will you, fair sister,
Go with the princes, or stay here with us?

Q. Isa. Our gracious brother, I will go with them:
Haply a woman's voice may do some good,
When articles too nicely urg'd be stood on.

K. Hen. Yet leave our cousin Katharine here with us:
She is our capital demand, compris'd
Within the fore-rank of our articles.

Q. Isa. She hath good leave.

Exeunt all except Henry, Katharine and Alice.

K. Hen. Fair Katharine, and most fair,
Will you vouchsafe to teach a soldier terms
Such as will enter at a lady's ear
And plead his love-suit to her gentle heart?

Kath. Your Majesty shall mock at me; I cannot speak your England.

K. Hen. O fair Katharine, if you will love me soundly with your French heart, I will be glad to hear you confess it brokenly with your English tongue. Do you like me, Kate?

Kath. Pardonnez-moi, I cannot tell wat is "like me."

K. Hen. An angel is like you, Kate, and you are like an angel.

Kath. Que dit-il? Que je suis semblable à les anges?

Alice. Oui, vraiment, sauf votre grace, ainsi dit-il.

K. Hen. I said so, dear Katharine; and I must not blush to affirm it.

Kath. O bon Dieu! les langues des hommes sont pleines de tromperies.

K. Hen. What says she, fair one? That the tongues of men are full of deceits?

Alice. Oui, dat de tongues of de mans is be full of deceits: dat is de Princess.

K. Hen. The Princess is the better Englishwoman. I' faith, Kate, my wooing is fit for thy understanding: I am glad thou canst speak no better English; for, if thou couldst, thou wouldst find me such a plain king that thou wouldst think I had sold my farm to buy my crown. I know no ways to mince it in love, but directly to say, "I love you"; then if you urge me farther than to say, "Do you in

90. consign, agree.

faith?" I wear out my suit. Give me your answer; i' faith, do; and so clap hands and a bargain. How say you, lady?

Kath. *Sauf votre honneur,* me understand well.

K. Hen. Marry, if you would put me to verses, or to dance for your sake, Kate, why you undid me; for the one, I have neither words nor measure, and for the other I have no strength in measure, yet a reasonable measure in strength. If I could win a lady at leap-frog, or by vaulting into my saddle with my armour on my back, under the correction of bragging be it spoken, I should quickly leap into a wife. Or if I might buffet for my love, or bound my horse for her favours, I could lay on like a butcher and sit like a jack-an-apes, never off. But, before God, Kate, I cannot look greenly, nor gasp out my eloquence, nor I have no cunning in protestation; only downright oaths, which I never use till urged, nor never break for urging. If thou canst love a fellow of this temper, Kate, whose face is not worth sunburning, that never looks in his glass for love of anything he sees there, let thine eye be thy cook. I speak to thee plain soldier: if thou canst love me for this, take me; if not, to say to thee that I shall die, is true; but for thy love, by the Lord, no; yet I love thee too. And while thou liv'st, dear Kate, take a fellow of plain and uncoined constancy; for he perforce must do thee right, because he hath not the gift to woo in other places; for these fellows of infinite tongue, that can rhyme themselves into ladies' favours, they do always reason themselves out again. What! a speaker is but a prater; a rhyme is but a ballad. A good leg will fall; a straight back will stoop; a black beard will turn white; a curled pate will grow bald; a fair face will wither; a full eye will wax hollow; but a good heart, Kate, is the sun and the moon; or rather the sun and not the moon; for it shines bright and never changes, but keeps his course truly. If thou would have such a one, take me; and take me, take a soldier; take a soldier, take a king. And what say'st thou then to my love? Speak, my fair, and fairly, I pray thee.

Kath. Is it possible dat I should love de enemy of France?

K. Hen. No; it is not possible you should love the enemy of France, Kate; but, in loving me, you should love the friend of France; for I love France so well that I will not part with a village of it; I will have it all mine; and, Kate, when France is mine and I am yours, then yours is France and you are mine.

Kath. I cannot tell wat is dat.

K. Hen. No, Kate? I will tell thee in French; which I am sure will hang upon my tongue like a new-married wife about her husband's neck, hardly to be shook off. *Je quand sur le possession de France, et quand vous avez le possession de moi,*—let me see, what then? Saint Denis be my speed!—*donc votre est France et vous êtes mienne.* It is as easy for me, Kate, to conquer the kingdom as to speak so much more French: I shall never move thee in French, unless it be to laugh at me.

Kath. *Sauf votre honneur, le François que vous parlez, il est meilleur que l'Anglois lequel je parle.*

K. Hen. No, faith, is 't not, Kate; but thy speaking of my tongue, and I thine, most truly-falsely, must needs be granted to be much at one. But, Kate, dost thou understand thus much English: canst thou love me?

Kath. I cannot tell.

K. Hen. Can any of your neighbours tell, Kate? I 'll ask them. Come, I know thou lovest me; and at night, when you come into your closet, you 'll question this gentlewoman about me; and I know, Kate, you will to her dispraise those parts in me that you love with your heart: but, good Kate, mock me mercifully; the rather, gentle princess, because I love thee cruelly. If ever thou beest mine, Kate, as I have a saving faith within me tells me thou shalt, I get thee with scambling, and thou must therefore needs prove a good soldier-breeder. Shalt not thou and I, between Saint Denis and Saint George, compound a boy, half French, half English, that shall go to Constantinople and take the Turk by the beard? Shall we not? What say'st thou, my fair flower-de-luce?

Kath. I do not know dat.

K. Hen. No; 't is hereafter to know, but now to promise: do but now promise, Kate, you will endeavour for your French part of such a boy; and for my English moiety, take the word of a king and a bachelor. How answer you, *la plus belle Katharine du monde, mon très cher et devin déesse?*

Kath. Your Majestee ave fausse French enough to deceive de most sage demoiselle dat is en France.

K. Hen. Now, fie upon my false French! By mine honour, in true English, I love thee, Kate; by which honour I dare not swear thou

139. **measure,** metre; dancing (l. 140); amount (l. 141). 146. **bound my horse,** make my horse bound. 148. **jack-an-apes,** ape. 148. **greenly,** sheepishly. 156. **let thine eye be thy cook,** let thine eye garnish me with attractions to suit its taste. 160. **uncoined constancy,** constancy that has not been coined so as to pass current. Henry's constancy would remain Kate's private possession. 166. **fall,** shrink.

211. **closet,** chamber. 217. **scambling,** fighting. 229. **moiety,** half.

lovest me; yet my blood begins to flatter me that thou dost, notwithstanding the poor and untempering effect of my visage. Now, beshrew my father's ambition! he was thinking of civil wars when he got me; therefore was I created with a stubborn outside, with an aspect of iron, that, when I come to woo ladies, I fright them. But, in faith, Kate, the elder I wax, the better I shall appear. My comfort is, that old age, that ill layer up of beauty, can do no more spoil upon my face. Thou hast me, if thou hast me, at the worst; and thou shalt wear me, if thou wear me, better and better; and therefore tell me, most fair Katharine, will you have me? Put off your maiden blushes; avouch the thoughts of your heart with the looks of an empress; take me by the hand, and say, Harry of England, I am thine; which word thou shalt no sooner bless mine ear withal, but I will tell thee aloud, England is thine, Ireland is thine, France is thine, and Henry Plantagenet is thine; who, though I speak it before his face, if he be not fellow with the best king, thou shalt find the best king of good fellows. Come, your answer in broken music; for thy voice is music and thy English broken; therefore, queen of all, Katharine, break thy mind to me in broken English. Wilt thou have me?

Kath. Dat is as it shall please de *roi mon père.*

K. Hen. Nay, it will please him well, Kate; it shall please him, Kate.

Kath. Den it sall also content me.

K. Hen. Upon that I kiss your hand, and call you my queen.

Kath. Laissez, mon seigneur, laissez, laissez! Ma foi, je ne veux point que vous abaissez votre grandeur en baisant la main d'une de votre Seigneurie indigne serviteur. Excusez-moi, je vous supplie, mon très-puissant seigneur.

K. Hen. Then I will kiss your lips, Kate.

Kath. Les dames et demoiselles pour être baisées devant leur noces, il n'est pas la coutume de France.

K. Hen. Madam my interpreter, what says she?

Alice. Dat it is not be de fashion pour les ladies of France,—I cannot tell what is *baiser* en Anglish.

K. Hen. To kiss.

Alice. Your Majesty *entendre* bettre *que moi.*

K. Hen. It is not the fashion for the maids in France to kiss before they are married, would she say?

Alice. Oui, vraiment.

K. Hen. O Kate, nice customs curtsy to great kings. Dear Kate, you and I cannot be confined within the weak list of a country's fashion: we are the makers of manners, Kate; and the liberty that follows our places stops the mouth of all find-faults, as I will do yours, for upholding the nice fashion of your country in denying me a kiss; therefore, patiently and yielding. [*Kissing her.*] You have witchcraft in your lips, Kate; there is more eloquence in a sugar touch of them than in the tongues of the French council; and they should sooner persuade Harry of England than a general petition of monarchs. Here comes your father.

Re-enter the *French Power* and the *English Lords.*

Bur. God save your Majesty! My royal cousin, teach you our princess English?

K. Hen. I would have her learn, my fair cousin, how perfectly I love her; and that is good English.

Bur. Is she not apt?

K. Hen. Our tongue is rough, coz, and my condition is not smooth; so that, having neither the voice nor the heart of flattery about me, I cannot so conjure up the spirit of love in her, that he will appear in his true likeness.

Bur. Pardon the frankness of my mirth, if I answer you for that. If you would conjure in her, you must make a circle; if conjure up Love in her in his true likeness, he must appear naked and blind. Can you blame her then, being a maid yet rosed over with the virgin crimson of modesty, if she deny the appearance of a naked blind boy in her naked seeing self? It were, my lord, a hard condition for a maid to consign to.

K. Hen. Yet they do wink and yield, as love is blind and enforces.

Bur. They are then excused, my lord, when they see not what they do.

K. Hen. Then, good my lord, teach your cousin to consent winking.

Bur. I will wink on her to consent, my lord, if you will teach her to know my meaning; for maids, well summered and warm kept, are like flies at Bartholomew-tide, blind, though they have their eyes; and then they will endure handling, which before would not abide looking on.

K. Hen. This moral ties me over to time and a hot summer; and so I shall catch the fly,

241. untempering, incapable of softening. **263. broken music,** broken music is so called when a different instrument is introduced into a "consort" or set of like instruments. This is essentially the "part music" of today. **265. break,** disclose.

295. list, limit, bound. **327. wink,** shut their eyes. **336. Bartholomew-tide,** August 24th.

your cousin, in the latter end, and she must be blind too.

Bur. As love is, my lord, before it loves.

K. Hen. It is so; and you may, some of you, thank love for my blindness, who cannot see many a fair French city for one fair French maid that stands in my way.

Fr. King. Yes, my lord, you see them perspectively, the cities turn'd into a maid; for they are all girdled with maiden walls that war hath never enter'd.

K. Hen. Shall Kate be my wife?

Fr. King. So please you.

K. Hen. I am content, so the maiden cities you talk of may wait on her; so the maid that stood in the way for my wish shall show me the way to my will.

Fr. King. We have consented to all terms of reason.

K. Hen. Is 't so, my lords of England?

West. The King hath granted every article;
His daughter first, and then in sequel all,
According to their firm proposed natures.

Exe. Only he hath not yet subscribed this: where your Majesty demands, that the King of France, having any occasion to write for matter of grant, shall name your Highness in this form and with this addition, in French, *Notre très-cher fils Henri, Roi d'Angleterre, Héritier de France;* and thus in Latin, *Præclarissimus filius noster Henricus, Rex Angliæ, et Hæres Franciæ.*

Fr. King. Nor this I have not, brother, so denied,
But your request shall make me let it pass.

K. Hen. I pray you then, in love and dear alliance,
Let that one article rank with the rest;
And thereupon give me your daughter.

Fr. King. Take her, fair son, and from her blood raise up
Issue to me; that the contending kingdoms
Of France and England, whose very shores look pale
With envy of each other's happiness,
May cease their hatred, and this dear conjunction
Plant neighbourhood and Christian-like accord
In their sweet bosoms, that never war advance
His bleeding sword 'twixt England and fair France.

Lords. Amen!

K. Hen. Now, welcome, Kate; and bear me witness all,
That here I kiss her as my sovereign queen.

Flourish.

Q. Isa. God, the best maker of all marriages,
Combine your hearts in one, your realms in one!
As man and wife, being two, are one in love,
So be there 'twixt your kingdoms such a spousal,
That never may ill office, or fell jealousy,
Which troubles oft the bed of blessed marriage,
Thrust in between the paction of these kingdoms,
To make divorce of their incorporate league;
That English may as French, French Englishmen,
Receive each other. God speak this Amen!

All. Amen!

K. Hen. Prepare we for our marriage; on which day,
My Lord of Burgundy, we 'll take your oath,
And all the peers', for surety of our leagues.
Then shall I swear to Kate, and you to me;
And may our oaths well kept and prosp'rous be!

Sennet. Exeunt.

Epilogue

Enter *Chorus.*

Chor. Thus far, with rough and all-unable pen,
Our bending author hath pursu'd the story,
In little room confining mighty men,
Mangling by starts the full course of their glory.
Small time, but in that small most greatly lived
This star of England. Fortune made his sword,
By which the world's best garden he achieved,
And of it left his son imperial lord.
Henry the Sixth, in infant bands crown'd King
Of France and England, did this king succeed;
Whose state so many had the managing,
That they lost France and made his England bleed;
Which oft our stage hath shown; and, for their sake,
In your fair minds let this acceptance take.

Exit.

347-8. perspectively, a "perspective" was an optical instrument or glass showing, if viewed at different angles, different images. **367. addition,** title. **Epilogue: 2. bending,** i.e., under the burden. **4. starts,** desultory treatment.

381. neighbourhood, neighborliness. **393. paction,** compact. **403. S. d. Sennet,** a trumpet call. **Epilogue: 13. oft our stage,** a reference to the three plays on the reign of Henry VI performed by Shakespeare's company. **14. this,** this work.

Much Ado About Nothing

Much Ado About Nothing is the first in time of the three "joyous comedies" of Shakespeare's middle period and it is in some ways the most brilliant of the three. It has little of Shakespeare's loveliest verse; his "native wood notes wild" are heard to better advantage in the Forest of Arden than in the Court of Messina, but no other comedy of Shakespeare's sparkles with such a coruscating fire of wit.

Text.—*Much Ado* was first published in quarto form in 1600 with the following title-page:

Much adoe about Nothing. As it hath been sundrie times publickely acted by the right honourable, the Lord Chamberlaine his servants. Written by William Shakespeare.

There is every reason to believe that the publishers, Wise and Aspley, obtained their copy direct from the company. When material was being collected for the publication of the Folio, a copy of this quarto, the only printed edition up to that time, corrected here and there on the margin, was used to print the Folio text. So far as the two texts differ the quarto appears generally to be correct; a few lines omitted in the Folio are probably due to careless printing.

Date.—The date of *Much Ado* can be fixed within rather narrow limits. As it is not mentioned by Meres in 1598, we may conclude that it was not on the boards when he compiled his list of Shakespeare's plays, and since Kemp, who certainly acted in it, left the company about the middle of 1599, the play must have been produced between those dates, *i.e.* late in 1598 or early in 1599.

Source.—The source of the main plot, the Claudio-Hero story, goes back in the end to an Italian novel by Bandello. Briefly the old tale runs as follows:

A young noble, Don Timbreo, who had distinguished himself in the wars of King Pedro of Aragon, came with that king and his court to Messina. There he beheld a lovely lady, Fenicia by name, daughter of Lionato, a poor but noble gentleman. He asked a friend to require her in marriage from her father and a match was arranged to the joy of Fenicia, Lionato, and the whole city over so brilliant a marriage for so good and beautiful a girl. But another gentleman of the city, Girondo, had long loved her in secret, and mad with jealousy determined to break the match, hoping thereafter to win Fenicia himself. He sent an acquaintance of his to tell Timbreo that Fenicia was unchaste and often received a lover at a window in her father's house, and further promised to give Timbreo ocular proof of her guilt if he would go that evening and watch the house. The credulous Timbreo consented and actually saw a ladder set to the window and a man enter the room. Convinced of his lady's guilt he sent word to her father that he would not marry her and that she had better wed the lover whom she had chosen for herself. Overcome by this sudden and dreadful charge, Fenicia swooned and lay like dead. In fact she was believed dead by her family, the doctors, and all the town. Only when she was being actually prepared for the grave did she return to life; whereupon her father sent her secretly to his brother's house in the country, buried an empty coffin in the church, and inscribed an epitaph on her tombstone telling how she had been killed by a slanderous report. Don Timbreo began to wonder whether he had not been too credulous, but Girondo was completely overcome by remorse, and asking Timbreo to meet him at the grave confessed to his villainy and begged the injured man to kill him. Timbreo, however, forgave him and went with him to the house of Lionato where Girondo repeated his tale and Timbreo declared himself ready to do whatever the old man should require by way of atonement. Lionato answered that he would ask but one thing, namely that, when Timbreo desired again to marry, he would take a wife of Lionato's choosing. To this the remorseful lover at once consented. Meanwhile at her uncle's house Fenicia recovered her health and grew so much more beautiful than before that no one would have recognized her. When a year or so had passed Lionato claimed his promise of Timbreo, took him into the country and introduced him to a beautiful girl called Lucilla, whom he desired Timbreo to marry. At the wedding feast Lucilla revealed herself as the supposedly dead Fenicia and the lovers, parted by slander, were now happily united. To make the joy complete her sister Belfiore was given in marriage to Girondo.

This tale was translated into French by Belleforest, *Histoires Tragiques,* in 1582. Shakespeare may have read it in either the French or Italian version. But it is not his sole source. A somewhat similar story occurs in Ariosto's *Orlando* where the lover is deceived by seeing at his lady's window her maid, dressed in the lady's clothes, receiving a lover. Spenser translated this episode (*Faerie Queene* II, v.) and Shakespeare, who had certainly read *The Faerie Queene* if not the Italian poem, recognized the dramatic value of this substitution.

As usual Shakespeare handled his source with complete freedom. Not only did he bring in the maid at the window from Ariosto's tale, but he altered completely the renunciation scene. Shakespeare's alteration, in which Claudio denounces his lady at the very altar and before all the world, has long been considered the chief blot in this brilliant comedy: "What, bear her in hand until they come to take hands; and then, with public accusation, uncovered slander, unmitigated rancour"—it more than justifies the indignant cry of Beatrice, "O God that I were a man! I would eat his heart in the market-place." As usual, however, there is a reason and a good reason for Shakespeare's change. Little could be made dramatically of the quiet household scene of the story; the scene of denunciation in the church is the most theatrically effective of the whole play. It is true that this change distinctly degrades the lover of the play below the hero of the story, but it may be suggested that Shakespeare did not find the credulous and sentimental Timbreo a very sympathetic character and was little concerned to support or to ennoble him. Shakespeare's Claudio is at any rate a perfectly consistent and comprehensible character: young, vain, easily moved to love or to suspicion, his match with Hero is one that has been promoted by his master, Don Pedro, and since that master shares his belief in Hero's guilt, he feels it incumbent on him by a striking demonstration to wash off the stain upon his honor.

There was, moreover, another reason which impelled Shakespeare to this alteration. If he had little sympathy for the nominal hero, Timbreo-Claudio, he was profoundly interested in two other characters, Benedick and Beatrice, the champions of their respective sexes in the eternal duel of male and female.

Earlier in the play he had devised a comic trick by which each was led to believe in the other's love, but this he must have felt was unsatisfactory. Something more was needed to bring them together, some crisis in which their two hearts would beat alike and their common sympathy for an injured lady would reveal them to each other as they really are, not flippant scoffers, but generous champions of the truth. It is to be noted that when her lover, her prince, her very father, all believe in Hero's guilt, Beatrice and Benedick remain incredulous. "Surely I do believe your fair cousin is wrong'd," says he, and his clear vision puts him at once on the trail of the truth, "the practice of this lives in John the Bastard"; while from first to last Beatrice is strong in affirmation of her cousin's innocence. There is no finer scene, no more vivid and telling dialogue, in all the comedies of Shakespeare than this in which Benedick and Beatrice join hands over the corpse of Hero's slandered honor. To Shakespeare as to us the chief interest of the play centers about Benedick and Beatrice, and this scene was written primarily for them. They are Shakespeare's creations added by him to put the salt of life into the borrowed unreal and sentimental plot.

There remains a third strand in the texture of the play, the Dogberry-Verges action. Here certainly there is no need to look for a source. We have here a cross-section of English life in the tradition of the native realism. Shakespeare was never happier than when he brought the delightful absurdities of his own countrymen, especially those of the middle or lower classes, upon the stage, and he was never weary of so doing. But he never touched off the manners of his own people with happier humor than when he drew the pompous ass and Jack-in-office, Dogberry, and his running-mate, Goodman Verges, "an old man, sir, and his wits are not so blunt as, God help, I would desire they were; but, in faith, honest as the skin between his brows."

Structure.—These three strands, the Italianate tragi-comic, the native English realistic, and the genuine Shakespearean comedy of character, are woven together with the utmost skill. A brief survey of the structure will throw some light upon the master's art.

The play opens with a brief exposition, the return from the wars of the victorious Prince and his brave young favorite, Claudio. The mocking queries of Beatrice as to the welfare of Benedick serve to introduce the strain of character comedy immediately carried to a high pitch by the war of words which takes place between them on his entrance. No sooner is this ended than the theme of Claudio's love for Hero is introduced in not too passionate a strain; Claudio is no Romeo, but a young gentleman well content to marry Leonato's only heir. The second and third scenes prepare us for the first misunderstanding in this play of cross-purposes, and introduce the malcontent Don John, who sees in the suit of Claudio a chance to revenge himself on "that young up-start."

The second act promptly brings matters to a head. At the masked ball the Prince woos Hero for Claudio, and the sensitive and credulous nature of the young lover is revealed when at a whispered word from Don John and a jest from Benedick he at once believes that his patron has played him false, thus preparing the way for his later hasty belief in his lady's guilt. His suspicions are as easily removed, however, as they have been aroused, and the scene closes with his formal betrothal to Hero.

To pass the time before the marriage the company now plan to bring Benedick and Beatrice "into a mountain of affection, the one for the other." The next scene gives us the plot of John against the betrothed pair, a plot framed by his servant Borachio, whose very name, meaning Drunkard, prepares us for the way in which he will later babble out his guilty secret. The last scene of this act and the first of the next are filled up with the device by which Benedick and Beatrice in turn are led each to believe that the other is dying of love, but is too proud to speak out. In the second scene of Act III Don John utters his slander against Hero and offers to give her lover and the Prince ocular proof. And now by a skilful turn of the hand Shakespeare introduces the night watch of Messina. He has kept them off-stage till now to introduce them when they are most needed. After a charge from Dogberry, the master constable, which prepares us for his verbose stupidity—of prime importance in a later scene—they retire to sit upon the church bench till two and then to bed. Here they overhear Borachio, very evidently flustered with new wine, gleefully relate to his fellow Conrade the success of the trick he has played and Claudio's rash vow to denounce Hero at the altar. The watch is too dull to understand the story, but not too stupid to miss the fact that some villainy is on foot, and they promptly arrest the pair. This is, or at least should be, enough to let the audience know that the plot is already foiled. Had Shakespeare staged the window scene and shown us Claudio's rage we might have taken the whole affair too seriously and not understood that it was much ado about nothing. With the arrest of the plotters who will be taken before Hero's father for examination one might suppose that the plot would be revealed; but Shakespeare has another trick in reserve. Dogberry and Verges come on the morning of the wedding to tell Leonato of the arrest of "a couple of arrant knaves," but the prolixity of the one and the dullness of the other so weary the old gentleman that he bids them take the examination themselves. A little less of Dogberry's tediousness, a little more patience on the part of Leonato, and the church scene toward which Shakespeare has been heading would be frustrated.

This scene, the first of the fourth, is the high-water mark of the play. Had we not been prepared for it we might have taken it too seriously. Benedick and Beatrice, however, have not been so prepared, they do as a matter of fact take it most seriously, and it is their common sympathy with the slandered Hero that leads to the frank avowal of their mutual love. But the price of Beatrice's love is that Benedick shall kill the slanderer. Once more we are on serious ground, and once more by a deft turn Shakespeare averts the threatened disaster. For upon the tense strain of the church scene follows the examination of the prisoners. Dogberry's stupidity and self-conceit might even now have hindered a disclosure and indeed he does all that a fool in office can do to block the revelation; but one sensible man and one accurate witness manage to elicit the truth in spite of him, and we know that the good ship of Shakespeare's comedy is in sight of the haven.

The last act sees her safe at anchor; a bit of a ruffle between Hero's father and his brother on one side with Claudio and Don Pedro on the other, the whispered challenge of Benedick to Claudio, and then the treason is disclosed. Following his source Shakespeare makes the father insist that Claudio shall make reparation by marrying into his family, the new bride being a supposed niece. Only two short scenes intervene before the close in which Claudio gives his hand in marriage to a masked lady, who, of course, is none other than Hero.

And this leads, naturally, to the open avowal of the secret love of the two best people in the play. The news that Don John has been arrested adds a final touch, but the "brave punishments" that Benedick promises to devise for him will probably be little more than a scoff or two. The pipers strike up and the company dances off the stage—All's Well That Ends Well, or Much Ado About Nothing, either title would fit the play.

The technical skill of the playwright is a source of delight to the student of the drama, but it is not this which wins the favor of the theatre-going public. To win this favor the playwright must first tell them an entertaining story and then excite their interest in real human beings caught in the meshes of the plot. Shakespeare did not find such characters in the old tale which served as his source and accordingly he created them, to the immense advantage of the play. For after all, *Much Ado* lives, on the stage and in the study, by the characters of Benedick and Beatrice. That they are real and recognizable characters is plain enough. We all know the young gentleman who scoffs at love and lovers, only to fall victim to a pretty face, and the young lady who rails at mankind and swearing she will never consent consents at last with only feigned reluctance. But Benedick and Beatrice are something more than mere type figures. There is in each case a genuine fear of that loss of independence and individuality implied in the bond of marriage, and the first stirrings of the attraction which each feels for the other quicken that fear and give rise to the railleries by which each strives to drive away the other, a mate at once desired and feared. How much more of human interest is there in such a complex relation than in the simple desire and quick aversion of Claudio for his lady. It is a genuine relief to find in a romantic comedy a pair of lovers drawn together by the mutual attraction of man for maid without the least trace of the sentimentality which so often mars that relation.

In fact there is so little sentimentality in the relation of Benedick and Beatrice that the greater part of their time is spent in railing at each other. The fashion of wit passes, but humor remains and both characters are instinct with humor. Who can forget Benedick's "when I said I would die a bachelor I did not think I should live till I were married" or Beatrice's advice to her cousin on marriage: "For all that, cousin, let him be a handsome fellow, or else make another curtsy and say 'Father, as it please me.' " That two such characters, so witty, so humorous, so defiant of the claims of love, should so long resist his claims and at last fall happy victims to them is a sheer triumph of the comic spirit. And it is this comic spirit which gives immortal life to *Much Ado About Nothing.*

Stage history.—We know from the title-page of the First Quarto that *Much Ado* had been performed by Shakespeare's Company before its publication in 1600. It was twice acted during the festivities celebrating the marriage of the Princess Elizabeth, 1613, once under the title, *Benedicte and Betteris.*

After the Restoration Davenant lifted the Benedick-Beatrice action from it for insertion in his adaptation of *Measure for Measure,* called *The Law Against Lovers.* Pepys saw this on the 18th of February, 1662, and called it a "good play and well performed." There is no sign that this audacious attempt to improve Shakespeare held the stage for any length of time. In fact *Much Ado,* even in this partial form, disappears altogether till well on into the next century. It did not really attract public attention until it came into the hands of Garrick in 1748. Benedick was one of his favorite parts in comedy and he played it repeatedly to the Beatrice of Mrs. Pritchard.

From Garrick's time to the present it has, with certain intermissions, held the stage and, as a rule, in its true form. Kemble and Macready both played the part of Benedick. The most famous production, however, was that of Irving in 1882, which ran for two hundred and twelve nights, a performance pronounced by contemporaries as near perfect as possible. Ellen Terry was the Beatrice of this production and was never more charming than in her scenes with Benedick.

MUCH ADO ABOUT NOTHING

Dramatis Personæ

Don Pedro, prince of Arragon.
Don John, his bastard brother.
Claudio, a young lord of Florence.
Benedick, a young lord of Padua.
Leonato, governor of Messina.
Antonio, his brother.
Balthasar, esquire to *Don Pedro.*
Conrade, } followers of *Don John.*
Borachio, }
Friar Francis.

Dogberry, a constable.
Verges, a headborough.
A Sexton.
A Boy.

Hero, daughter to *Leonato.*
Beatrice, niece to *Leonato.*
Margaret, } gentlewomen attending on *Hero.*
Ursula, }

Messengers, Watch, Attendants, etc.

Scene: *Messina.*

Act I. Scene I. *Before Leonato's house.*

Enter *Leonato,* Governor of Messina, *Hero,* his daughter, and *Beatrice,* his niece, with a *Messenger.*

Leon. I learn in this letter that Don Pedro of Arragon comes this night to Messina.

Mess. He is very near by this: he was not three leagues off when I left him.

Leon. How many gentlemen have you lost in this action?

Mess. But few of any sort, and none of name.

Leon. A victory is twice itself when the achiever brings home full numbers. I find here that Don Pedro hath bestowed much honour on a young Florentine called Claudio.

Mess. Much deserved on his part and equally remembered by Don Pedro: he hath borne himself beyond the promise of his age, doing, in the figure of a lamb, the feats of a lion: he hath indeed better bettered expectation than you must expect of me to tell you how.

Leon. He hath an uncle here in Messina will be very much glad of it.

Mess. I have already delivered him letters, and there appears much joy in him; even so much that joy could not show itself modest enough without a badge of bitterness.

Leon. Did he break out into tears?

Mess. In great measure.

Leon. A kind overflow of kindness: there are no faces truer than those that are so washed. How much better is it to weep at joy than to joy at weeping!

Beat. I pray you, is Signior Mountanto returned from the wars or no?

Mess. I know none of that name, lady: there was none such in the army of any sort.

Leon. What is he that you ask for, niece?

Hero. My cousin means Signior Benedick of Padua.

Mess. O, he 's returned; and as pleasant as ever he was.

Beat. He set up his bills here in Messina and challenged Cupid at the flight; and my uncle's fool, reading the challenge, subscribed for Cupid, and challenged him at the bird-bolt. I pray you, how many hath he killed and eaten in these wars? But how many hath he killed? for indeed I promised to eat all of his killing.

Leon. Faith, niece, you tax Signior Benedick too much; but he 'll be meet with you, I doubt it not.

Mess. He hath done good service, lady, in these wars.

Beat. You had musty victual, and he hath holp to eat it: he is a very valiant trencherman; he hath an excellent stomach.

Mess. And a good soldier too, lady.

Beat. And a good soldier to a lady: but what is he to a lord?

Mess. A lord to a lord, a man to a man; stuffed with all honourable virtues.

Beat. It is so, indeed; he is no less than a stuffed man: but for the stuffing,—well, we are all mortal.

7. name, distinction. **26. kind,** natural.

30. Mountanto, an upward thrust in fencing. **37. pleasant,** facetious. **39. bills,** notices of a challenge. **40. flight,** light arrow for long ranges. **42. bird-bolt,** blunt arrow for shooting birds. **47. meet,** even. **59. stuffed man,** puppet, man of straw.

Leon. You must not, sir, mistake my niece. There is a kind of merry war betwixt Signior Benedick and her: they never meet but there 's a skirmish of wit between them.

Beat. Alas! he gets nothing by that. In our last conflict four of his five wits went halting off, and now is the whole man governed with one; so that if he have wit enough to keep himself warm, let him bear it for a difference between himself and his horse; for it is all the wealth that he hath left, to be known a reasonable creature. Who is his companion now? He hath every month a new sworn brother.

Mess. Is 't possible?

Beat. Very easily possible: he wears his faith but as the fashion of his hat; it ever changes with the next block.

Mess. I see, lady, the gentleman is not in your books.

Beat. No; an he were, I would burn my study. But, I pray you, who is his companion? Is there no young squarer now that will make a voyage with him to the devil?

Mess. He is most in the company of the right noble Claudio.

Beat. O Lord, he will hang upon him like a disease: he is sooner caught than the pestilence, and the taker runs presently mad. God help the noble Claudio! If he have caught the Benedick, it will cost him a thousand pounds ere 'a be cured.

Mess. I will hold friends with you, lady.

Beat. Do, good friend.

Leon. You will never run mad, niece.

Beat. No, not till a hot January.

Mess. Don Pedro is approached.

Enter *Don Pedro, Claudio, Benedick, Balthasar,* and *John* the Bastard.

D. Pedro. Good Signior Leonato, are you come to meet your trouble? The fashion of the world is to avoid cost, and you encounter it.

Leon. Never came trouble to my house in the likeness of your Grace, for trouble being gone, comfort should remain; but when you depart from me, sorrow abides and happiness takes his leave.

D. Pedro. You embrace your charge too willingly. I think this is your daughter.

Leon. Her mother hath many times told me so.

Bene. Were you in doubt, sir, that you asked her?

Leon. Signior Benedick, no; for then were you a child.

D. Pedro. You have it full, Benedick: we may guess by this what you are, being a man. Truly, the lady fathers herself. Be happy, lady; for you are like an honourable father.

Bene. If Signior Leonato be her father, she would not have his head on her shoulders for all Messina, as like him as she is.

Beat. I wonder that you will still be talking, Signior Benedick: nobody marks you.

Bene. What, my dear Lady Disdain! are you yet living?

Beat. Is it possible Disdain should die while she hath such meet food to feed it as Signior Benedick? Courtesy itself must convert to disdain, if you come in her presence.

Bene. Then is courtesy a turncoat. But it is certain I am loved of all ladies, only you excepted; and I would I could find in my heart that I had not a hard heart, for truly I love none.

Beat. A dear happiness to women; they would else have been troubled with a pernicious suitor. I thank God and my cold blood, I am of your humour for that. I had rather hear my dog bark at a crow than a man swear he loves me.

Bene. God keep your ladyship still in that mind! So some gentleman or other shall scape a predestinate scratched face.

Beat. Scratching could not make it worse, an 't were such a face as yours were.

Bene. Well, you are a rare parrot-teacher.

Beat. A bird of my tongue is better than a beast of yours.

Bene. I would my horse had the speed of your tongue, and so good a continuer. But keep your way, a God's name; I have done.

Beat. You always end with a jade's trick; I know you of old.

D. Pedro. That is the sum of all, Leonato. Signior Claudio and Signior Benedick, my dear friend Leonato hath invited you all. I tell him we shall stay here at the least a month; and he heartily prays some occasion may detain us longer. I dare swear he is no hypocrite, but prays from his heart.

Leon. If you swear, my lord, you shall not be forsworn. [*To Don John.*] Let me bid you welcome, my lord: being reconciled to the Prince, your brother, I owe you all duty.

D. John. I thank you: I am not of many words, but I thank you.

Leon. Please it your Grace lead on?

66-7. **halting**, limping. 68. **difference**, distinguishing mark in heraldry. 77. **block**, hat-mould. 78-9. **in your books**, in your good graces. 82. **squarer**, brawler. 103. **charge**, burden.

112. **fathers herself**, shows who her father is. 117. **still**, always. 123. **convert**, change. 128. **dear happiness**, rare good fortune. 145. **jade's trick**, a jade was a nag. Here perhaps a reference to a horse's slipping its head out of the collar and escaping.

D. Pedro. Your hand, Leonato; we will go together. *Exeunt all except Benedick and Claudio.*

Claud. Benedick, didst thou note the daughter of Signior Leonato?

Bene. I noted her not; but I looked on her.

Claud. Is she not a modest young lady?

Bene. Do you question me, as an honest man should do, for my simple true judgement; or would you have me speak after my custom, as being a professed tyrant to their sex?

Claud. No; I pray thee speak in sober judgement.

Bene. Why, i' faith, methinks she 's too low for a high praise, too brown for a fair praise and too little for a great praise; only this commendation I can afford her, that were she other than she is, she were unhandsome; and being no other but as she is, I do not like her.

Claud. Thou thinkest I am in sport: I pray thee tell me truly how thou lik'st her.

Bene. Would you buy her, that you inquire after her?

Claud. Can the world buy such a jewel?

Bene. Yea, and a case to put it into. But speak you this with a sad brow, or do you play the flouting Jack, to tell us Cupid is a good hare-finder and Vulcan a rare carpenter? Come, in what key shall a man take you, to go in the song?

Claud. In mine eye she is the sweetest lady that ever I looked on.

Bene. I can see yet without spectacles and I see no such matter: there 's her cousin, an she were not possessed with a fury, exceeds her as much in beauty as the first of May doth the last of December. But I hope you have no intent to turn husband, have you?

Claud. I would scarce trust myself, though I had sworn the contrary, if Hero would be my wife.

Bene. Is 't come to this? In faith, hath not the world one man but he will wear his cap with suspicion? Shall I never see a bachelor of threescore again? Go to, i' faith, an thou wilt needs thrust thy neck into a yoke, wear the print of it, and sigh away Sundays. Look! Don Pedro is returned to seek you.

Re-enter *Don Pedro.*

D. Pedro. What secret hath held you here, that you followed not to Leonato's?

Bene. I would your Grace would constrain me to tell.

D. Pedro. I charge thee on thy allegiance.

Bene. You hear, Count Claudio: I can be secret as a dumb man; I would have you think so; but, on my allegiance, mark you this, on my allegiance. He is in love. With who? Now that is your Grace's part. Mark how short his answer is:—With Hero, Leonato's short daughter.

Claud. If this were so, so were it uttered.

Bene. Like the old tale, my lord: "It is not so, nor 't was not so, but, indeed, God forbid it should be so."

Claud. If my passion change not shortly, God forbid it should be otherwise.

D. Pedro. Amen, if you love her; for the lady is very well worthy.

Claud. You speak this to fetch me in, my lord.

D. Pedro. By my troth, I speak my thought.

Claud. And, in faith, my lord, I spoke mine.

Bene. And, by my two faiths and troths, my lord, I spoke mine.

Claud. That I love her, I feel.

D. Pedro. That she is worthy, I know.

Bene. That I neither feel how she should be loved nor know how she should be worthy, is the opinion that fire cannot melt out of me: I will die in it at the stake.

D. Pedro. Thou wast ever an obstinate heretic in the despite of beauty.

Claud. And never could maintain his part but in the force of his will.

Bene. That a woman conceived me, I thank her; that she brought me up, I likewise give her most humble thanks; but that I will have a recheat winded in my forehead, or hang my bugle in an invisible baldrick, all women shall pardon me. Because I will not do them the wrong to mistrust any, I will do myself the right to trust none; and the fine is, for the which I may go the finer, I will live a bachelor.

D. Pedro. I shall see thee, ere I die, look pale with love.

Bene. With anger, with sickness, or with hunger, my lord, not with love: prove that ever I lose more blood with love than I will get again with drinking, pick out mine eyes with a ballad-maker's pen and hang me up at the

170. tyrant, merciless critic. **184. sad,** serious. **185. flouting Jack,** mocking knave. **185-6. Cupid, etc.,** the absurdity of making the blind Cupid a keen-eyed hunter or the blacksmith Vulcan a carpenter is evident. **201. with suspicion,** a reference to the invisible horns supposed to grow in the foreheads of men whose wives were unfaithful. Such a man was called a "cuckold." **204. Sundays,** the day he had to stay with his wife.

224. fetch me in, entrap me. **243. A recheat** was a series of notes blown or "winded" on a hunting horn to recall the hounds. **A baldrick** was the belt by which the horn was suspended. The whole passage is another play of words upon the horns of the cuckold. **246. fine,** end. **247. go the finer,** wear finer clothes.

door of a brothel-house for the sign of blind Cupid.

D. Pedro. Well, if ever thou dost fall from this faith, thou wilt prove a notable argument.

Bene. If I do, hang me in a bottle like a cat and shoot at me; and he that hits me, let him be clapped on the shoulder and called Adam.

D. Pedro. Well, as time shall try.
"In time the savage bull doth bear the yoke."

Bene. The savage bull may; but if ever the sensible Benedick bear it, pluck off the bull's horns and set them in my forehead; and let me be vilely painted, and in such great letters as they write "Here is good horse to hire," let them signify under my sign, "Here you may see Benedick the married man."

Claud. If this should ever happen, thou wouldst be horn-mad.

D. Pedro. Nay, if Cupid have not spent all his quiver in Venice, thou wilt quake for this shortly.

Bene. I look for an earthquake too, then.

D. Pedro. Well, you will temporize with the hours. In the meantime, good Signior Benedick, repair to Leonato's; commend me to him, and tell him I will not fail him at supper; for indeed he hath made great preparation.

Bene. I have almost matter enough in me for such an embassage; and so I commit you—

Claud. To the tuition of God. From my house,—if I had it,—

D. Pedro. The sixth of July. Your loving friend, Benedick.

Bene. Nay, mock not, mock not. The body of your discourse is sometime guarded with fragments, and the guards are but slightly basted on neither. Ere you flout old ends any further, examine your conscience; and so I leave you. *Exit.*

Claud. My liege, your Highness now may do me good.
D. Pedro. My love is thine to teach; teach it but how,
And thou shalt see how apt it is to learn
Any hard lesson that may do thee good.
Claud. Hath Leonato any son, my lord?
D. Pedro. No child but Hero; she 's his only heir.
Dost thou affect her, Claudio?
Claud. O, my lord,
When you went onward on this ended action,
I look'd upon her with a soldier's eye,
That lik'd, but had a rougher task in hand
Than to drive liking to the name of love.
But now I am return'd and that war-thoughts
Have left their places vacant, in their rooms
Come thronging soft and delicate desires,
All prompting me how fair young Hero is,
Saying, I lik'd her ere I went to wars.
D. Pedro. Thou wilt be like a lover presently
And tire the hearer with a book of words.
If thou dost love fair Hero, cherish it,
And I will break with her and with her father,
And thou shalt have her. Was 't not to this end
That thou began'st to twist so fine a story?
Claud. How sweetly you do minister to love,
That know love's grief by his complexion!
But lest my liking might too sudden seem,
I would have salv'd it with a longer treatise.
D. Pedro. What need the bridge much broader than the flood?
The fairest grant is the necessity.
Look, what will serve is fit: 't is once, thou lovest,
And I will fit thee with the remedy.
I know we shall have revelling to-night.
I will assume thy part in some disguise
And tell fair Hero I am Claudio,
And in her bosom I 'll unclasp my heart
And take her hearing prisoner with the force
And strong encounter of my amorous tale;
Then after to her father will I break;
And the conclusion is, she shall be thine.
In practice let us put it presently. *Exeunt.*

Scene II. *A room in Leonato's house.*

Enter *Leonato* and an old man, *Antonio* his brother, meeting.

Leon. How now, brother! Where is my cousin, your son? Hath he provided this music?

Ant. He is very busy about it. But, brother, I can tell you strange news that you yet dreamt not of.

Leon. Are they good?

Ant. As the events stamps them; but they have a good cover, they show well outward. The Prince and Count Claudio, walking in a thick-pleached alley in mine orchard, were thus much overheard by a man of mine. The Prince discovered to Claudio that he loved my niece your daughter and meant to acknowledge it this night in a dance; and if he found her

258. argument, topic for discussion. **259. bottle,** wicker basket. **261. Adam,** Adam Bell, famous archer of the ballads. **274. Venice,** famous then for its dissoluteness. **276. temporize,** come to terms. **283. tuition,** protection. **288. guarded,** trimmed. **298. affect,** love.

311. break with, broach the subject. **315. complexion,** appearance. **319.** The best help is that which is suited to the need. **320. once,** once for all. **Scene ii: 2. cousin,** in general sense of "relative." **7. events,** outcome. **10. pleached,** interwoven.

accordant, he meant to take the present time by the top and instantly break with you of it.

Leon. Hath the fellow any wit that told you this?

Ant. A good sharp fellow: I will send for him; and question him yourself.

Leon. No, no; we will hold it as a dream till it appear itself; but I will acquaint my daughter withal, that she may be the better prepared for an answer, if peradventure this be true. Go you and tell her of it.

Exit Antonio. Enter his son and a musician.

Cousin, you know what you have to do. O, I cry you mercy, friend; go you with me, and I will use your skill. Good cousin, have a care this busy time. *Exeunt.*

Scene III. *The same.*

Enter *Sir John* the Bastard and *Conrade*, his Companion.

Con. What the good-year, my lord! Why are you thus out of measure sad?

D. John. There is no measure in the occasion that breeds; therefore the sadness is without limit.

Con. You should hear reason.

D. John. And when I have heard it, what blessing brings it?

Con. If not a present remedy, at least a patient sufferance.

D. John. I wonder that thou (being, as thou say'st thou art, born under Saturn) goest about to apply a moral medicine to a mortifying mischief. I cannot hide what I am. I must be sad when I have cause, and smile at no man's jests; eat when I have stomach, and wait for no man's leisure; sleep when I am drowsy, and tend on no man's business; laugh when I am merry, and claw no man in his humour.

Con. Yea, but you must not make the full show of this till you may do it without controlment. You have of late stood out against your brother, and he hath ta'en you newly into his grace; where it is impossible you should take true root but by the fair weather that you make yourself: it is needful that you frame the season for your own harvest.

D. John. I had rather be a canker in a hedge than a rose in his grace, and it better fits my blood to be disdained of all than to fashion a carriage to rob love from any: in this, though I cannot be said to be a flattering honest man, it must not be denied but I am a plain-dealing villain. I am trusted with a muzzle and enfranchised with a clog; therefore I have decreed not to sing in my cage. If I had my mouth, I would bite; if I had my liberty, I would do my liking: in the meantime let me be that I am and seek not to alter me.

Con. Can you make no use of your discontent?

D. John. I make all use of it, for I use it only. Who comes here?

Enter *Borachio.*

What news, Borachio?

Bora. I came yonder from a great supper. The Prince your brother is royally entertained by Leonato; and I can give you intelligence of an intended marriage.

D. John. Will it serve for any model to build mischief on? What is he for a fool that betroths himself to unquietness?

Bora. Marry, it is your brother's right hand.

D. John. Who? The most exquisite Claudio?

Bora. Even he.

D. John. A proper squire! And who? and who? Which way looks he?

Bora. Marry, on Hero, the daughter and heir of Leonato.

D. John. A very forward March-chick! How came you to this?

Bora. Being entertained for a perfumer, as I was smoking a musty room, comes me the Prince and Claudio, hand in hand, in sad conference: I whipt me behind the arras, and there heard it agreed upon that the Prince should woo Hero for himself, and having obtained her, give her to Count Claudio.

D. John. Come, come, let us thither; this may prove food to my displeasure. That young start-up hath all the glory of my overthrow: if I can cross him any way, I bless myself every way. You are both sure, and will assist me?

Con. To the death, my lord.

D. John. Let us to the great supper; their cheer is the greater than I am subdued. Would the cook were o' my mind! Shall we go prove what 's to be done?

Bora. We 'll wait upon your lordship.

Exeunt.

15. **accordant**, consenting. 16. **top**, forelock. **Scene iii: 1. good-year**, an expletive. 12. **born under Saturn**, people born under the domination of the planet Saturn were supposed to be of a morose and melancholy disposition. 13-14. **mortifying mischief**, deadly disease. 18. **claw**, flatter. 21-2. **controlment**, restraint. 28. **canker**, dog-rose.

31. **carriage**, behavior. 35. **enfranchised**, freed. **clog**, encumbrance. 54. **proper**, fine. 58. **March-chick**, prematurely hatched chicken. 61. **smoking a musty room**, Juniper or some other plant giving off a pungent smoke was often used to fumigate rooms that had not been used for some time. 71. **sure**, trustworthy.

ACT II. SCENE I. *A hall in Leonato's house.*

Enter *Leonato, Antonio, Hero, Beatrice, Margaret* and *Ursula,* and a kinsman.

Leon. Was not Count John here at supper?

Ant. I saw him not.

Beat. How tartly that gentleman looks! I never can see him but I am heart-burned an hour after.

Hero. He is of a very melancholy disposition.

Beat. He were an excellent man that were made just in the midway between him and Benedick: the one is too like an image and says nothing, and the other too like my lady's eldest son, evermore tattling.

Leon. Then half Signior Benedick's tongue in Count John's mouth, and half Count John's melancholy in Signior Benedick's face,—

Beat. With a good leg and a good foot, uncle, and money enough in his purse, such a man would win any woman in the world, if 'a could get her good-will.

Leon. By my troth, niece, thou wilt never get thee a husband, if thou be so shrewd of thy tongue.

Ant. In faith, she 's too curst.

Beat. Too curst is more than curst: I shall lessen God's sending that way; for it is said, "God sends a curst cow short horns;" but to a cow too curst he sends none.

Leon. So, by being too curst, God will send you no horns.

Beat. Just, if he send me no husband; for the which blessing I am at him upon my knees every morning and evening. Lord, I could not endure a husband with a beard on his face! I had rather lie in the woollen.

Leon. You may light on a husband that hath no beard.

Beat. What should I do with him? Dress him in my apparel and make him my waiting-gentlewoman? He that hath a beard is more than a youth, and he that hath no beard is less than a man; and he that is more than a youth is not for me, and he that is less than a man, I am not for him; therefore I will even take sixpence in earnest of the bear-ward, and lead his apes into hell.

Leon. Well, then, go you into hell?

Beat. No, but to the gate; and there will the devil meet me, like an old cuckold, with horns on his head, and say, "Get you to heaven, Beatrice, get you to heaven; here 's no place for you maids:" so deliver I up my apes, and away to Saint Peter for the heavens: he shows me where the bachelors sit, and there live we as merry as the day is long.

Ant. [*To Hero.*] Well, niece, I trust you will be ruled by your father.

Beat. Yes, faith; it is my cousin's duty to make curtsy and say, "Father, as it please you:" but yet for all that, cousin, let him be a handsome fellow, or else make another curtsy and say, "Father, as it please me."

Leon. Well, niece, I hope to see you one day fitted with a husband.

Beat. Not till God make men of some other mettle than earth. Would it not grieve a woman to be overmastered with a piece of valiant dust? to make an account of her life to a clod of wayward marl? No uncle, I 'll none: Adam's sons are my brethren; and truly I hold it a sin to match in my kindred.

Leon. Daughter, remember what I told you: if the Prince do solicit you in that kind, you know your answer.

Beat. The fault will be in the music, cousin, if you be not wooed in good time: if the Prince be too important, tell him there is measure in every thing and so dance out the answer. For, hear me, Hero: wooing, wedding, and repenting, is as a Scotch jig, a measure, and a cinque-pace; the first suit is hot and hasty, like a Scotch jig, and full as fantastical; the wedding mannerly-modest, as a measure, full of state and ancientry; and then comes repentance and, with his bad legs, falls into the cinque-pace faster and faster, till he sink into his grave.

Leon. Cousin, you apprehend passing shrewdly.

Beat. I have a good eye, uncle; I can see a church by daylight.

Leon. The revellers are entering, brother; make good room.

Antonio dons a mask.

Enter *Don Pedro, Claudio, Benedick, Balthasar, Don John, Borachio,* and others, masked, with a drum.

D. Pedro. Lady, will you walk a bout with your friend?

Hero. So you walk softly and look sweetly

Act II, Scene i: 11. eldest son, a spoiled child. **20. shrewd,** shrewish. **22. curst,** bitter. **33. woollen,** between blankets. **43-4. earnest of the bear-ward, and lead his apes into hell,** advance payment from the bear-ward (trainer of bears and sometimes apes) and lead his (the bear-ward's) apes into hell. Old maids were supposed to lead apes in hell, perhaps as punishment for not undergoing the trouble of children while they were on earth.

63. mettle, stuff of life. **66. marl,** clay. **74. important,** importunate. **75. measure,** (1) moderation, (2) a slow dance. **78. cinque-pace,** lively five-step dance. **81. ancientry,** antique fashion. S. d., **drum,** drummer. **90. walk a bout,** tread a measure. **friend,** lover.

and say nothing, I am yours for the walk; and especially when I walk away.

D. Pedro. With me in your company?

Hero. I may say so when I please.

D. Pedro. And when please you to say so?

Hero. When I like your favour; for God defend the lute should be like the case!

D. Pedro. My visar is Philemon's roof; within the house is Jove.

Hero. Why, then, your visor should be thatched.

D. Pedro. Speak low, if you speak love.

Drawing her aside.

Balth. Well, I would you did like me.

Marg. So would not I, for your own sake; for I have many ill qualities.

Balth. Which is one?

Marg. I say my prayers aloud.

Balth. I love you the better; the hearers may cry, Amen.

Marg. God match me with a good dancer!

Balth. Amen.

Marg. And God keep you out of my sight when the dance is done! Answer, clerk.

Balth. No more words; the clerk is answered.

Urs. I know you well enough; you are Signior Antonio.

Ant. At a word, I am not.

Urs. I know you by the waggling of your head.

Ant. To tell you true, I counterfeit him.

Urs. You could never do him so ill-well, unless you were the very man. Here 's his dry hand up and down: you are he, you are he.

Ant. At a word, I am not.

Urs. Come, come, do you think I do not know you by your excellent wit? Can virtue hide itself? Go to, mum, you are he: graces will appear, and there 's an end.

Beat. Will you not tell me who told you so?

Bene. No, you shall pardon me.

Beat. Nor will you not tell me who you are?

Bene. Not now.

Beat. That I was disdainful, and that I had my good wit out of the "Hundred Merry Tales":—well, this was Signior Benedick that said so.

Bene. What 's he?

Beat. I am sure you know him well enough.

Bene. Not I, believe me.

Beat. Did he never make you laugh?

Bene. I pray you, what is he?

Beat. Why, he is the Prince's jester, a very dull fool; only his gift is in devising impossible slanders: none but libertines delight in him, and the commendation is not in his wit but in his villainy; for he both pleases men and angers them, and then they laugh at him and beat him. I am sure he is in the fleet; I would he had boarded me.

Bene. When I know the gentleman, I 'll tell him what you say.

Beat. Do, do: he 'll but break a comparison or two on me; which, peradventure not marked or not laughed at, strikes him into melancholy; and then there 's a partridge wing saved, for the fool will eat no supper that night. [*Music.*] We must follow the leaders.

Bene. In every good thing.

Beat. Nay, if they lead to any ill, I will leave them at the next turning.

Dance. Then exeunt all except Don John, Borachio, and Claudio.

D. John. Sure my brother is amorous on Hero and hath withdrawn her father to break with him about it. The ladies follow her and but one visor remains.

Bora. And that is Claudio: I know him by his bearing.

D. John. Are not you Signior Benedick?

Claud. You know me well; I am he.

D. John. Signior, you are very near my brother in his love: he is enamoured on Hero. I pray you, dissuade him from her; she is no equal for his birth. You may do the part of an honest man in it.

Claud. How know you he loves her?

D. John. I heard him swear his affection.

Bora. So did I too; and he swore he would marry her to-night.

D. John. Come, let us to the banquet.

Exeunt Don John and Borachio.

Claud. Thus answer I in name of Benedick,
But hear these ill news with the ears of Claudio.
'T is certain so; the Prince wooes for himself.
Friendship is constant in all other things
Save in the office and affairs of love;
Therefore all hearts in love use their own tongues.
Let every eye negotiate for itself
And trust no agent; for beauty is a witch

97. **favour,** face. 99. **Philemon's roof,** the reference is to Ovid's version of the story of Baucis and Philemon, who entertained Jove in their small thatched cottage. 113. **clerk,** this is suggested by the "**Amen**" of l. 112. The parish clerk read the responses in the church service. 122. **do . . . ill-well,** so successfully imitate a defect. 123-4. **dry hand,** sign of old age. 134-5. **"Hundred Merry Tales,"** a collection of coarse anecdotes.

143. **only his gift,** his only gift. 147. **fleet,** i.e., company. 152. **break a comparison,** crack a joke.

Against whose charms faith melteth into blood.
This is an accident of hourly proof,
Which I mistrusted not. Farewell, therefore, Hero!

Re-enter *Benedick*.

Bene. Count Claudio?

Claud. Yea, the same.

Bene. Come, will you go with me?

Claud. Whither?

Bene. Even to the next willow, about your own business, County. What fashion will you wear the garland of? About your neck, like an usurer's chain, or under your arm, like a lieutenant's scarf? You must wear it one way, for the Prince hath got your Hero.

Claud. I wish him joy of her.

Bene. Why, that 's spoken like an honest drover; so they sell bullocks. But did you think the Prince would have served you thus?

Claud. I pray you, leave me.

Bene. Ho! now you strike like the blind man. 'T was the boy that stole your meat, and you 'll beat the post.

Claud. If it will not be, I 'll leave you. *Exit.*

Bene. Alas, poor hurt fowl! now will he creep into sedges. But that my Lady Beatrice should know me, and not know me! The Prince's fool! Ha? It may be I go under that title because I am merry. Yea, but so I am apt to do myself wrong: I am not so reputed: it is the base, though bitter, disposition of Beatrice that puts the world into her person, and so gives me out. Well, I 'll be revenged as I may.

Re-enter *Don Pedro, Hero* and *Leonato*.

D. Pedro. Now, signior, where 's the Count? Did you see him?

Bene. Troth, my lord, I have played the part of Lady Fame. I found him here as melancholy as a lodge in a warren. I told him, and I think I told him true, that your Grace had got the good will of this young lady; and I offered him my company to a willow-tree, either to make him a garland, as being forsaken, or to bind him up a rod, as being worthy to be whipped.

D. Pedro. To be whipped! What 's his fault?

Bene. The flat transgression of a schoolboy, who, being overjoyed with finding a birds' nest, shows it his companion, and he steals it.

D. Pedro. Wilt thou make a trust a transgression? The transgression is in the stealer.

Bene. Yet it had not been amiss the rod had been made, and the garland too; for the garland he might have worn himself, and the rod he might have bestowed on you, who, as I take it, have stolen his birds' nest.

D. Pedro. I will but teach them to sing, and restore them to the owner.

Bene. If their singing answer your saying, by my faith, you say honestly.

D. Pedro. The Lady Beatrice hath a quarrel to you: the gentleman that danced with her told her she is much wronged by you.

Bene. O, she misused me past the endurance of a block! An oak but with one green leaf on it would have answered her: my very visor began to assume life and scold with her. She told me, not thinking I had been myself, that I was the Prince's jester, that I was duller than a great thaw; huddling jest upon jest with such impossible conveyance upon me that I stood like a man at a mark, with a whole army shooting at me. She speaks poniards, and every word stabs: if her breath were as terrible as her terminations, there were no living near her; she would infect to the north star. I would not marry her, though she were endowed with all that Adam had left him before he transgressed. She would have made Hercules have turned spit, yea, and have cleft his club to make the fire too. Come, talk not of her; you shall find her the infernal Ate in good apparel. I would to God some scholar would conjure her; for certainly while she is here, a man may live as quiet in hell as in a sanctuary; and people sin upon purpose, because they would go thither; so, indeed, all disquiet, horror, and perturbation follows her.

Enter *Claudio* and *Beatrice*.

D. Pedro. Look, here she comes.

Bene. Will your Grace command me any service to the world's end? I will go on the slightest errand now to the Antipodes that you can devise to send me on; I will fetch you a toothpicker now from the furthest inch of Asia, bring you the length of Prester

187. **blood,** passion. 193. **willow,** emblem of unhappy love. 209. Wounded water-fowl often hide in the sedges along the edge of the water. 214. **base, though bitter,** the mean, although ironical, nature of Beatrice makes her misreport what the world says of me. 215. **puts . . . person,** speaks for the world. 222. **lodge in a warren,** isolated gamekeeper's house.

241. **If . . . saying,** i.e., if Hero consents to marry Claudio. 252. **impossible conveyance,** incredible dexterity. 256. **terminations,** epithets. 257. Her breath would taint everything to the farthest reaches of space. 261. **Hercules . . . spit,** i.e., do domestic service. 263. **Ate,** goddess of discord. 263-4. **I would to God some scholar would conjure her,** scholars were supposed to be able to control evil spirits by appropriate conjuration. 275-6. **Prester John's,** fabled eastern king's.

John's foot, fetch you a hair off the great Cham's beard, do you any embassage to the Pigmies, rather than hold three words' conference with this harpy. You have no employment for me?

D. Pedro. None, but to desire your good company.

Bene. O God, sir, here 's a dish I love not: I cannot endure my Lady Tongue. *Exit.*

D. Pedro. Come, lady, come; you have lost the heart of Signior Benedick.

Beat. Indeed, my lord, he lent it me awhile; and I gave him use for it, a double heart for his single one: marry, once before he won it of me with false dice, therefore your Grace may well say I have lost it.

D. Pedro. You have put him down, lady, you have put him down.

Beat. So I would not he should do me, my lord, lest I should prove the mother of fools. I have brought Count Claudio, whom you sent me to seek.

D. Pedro. Why, how now, Count! wherefore are you sad?

Claud. Not sad, my lord.

D. Pedro. How, then? Sick?

Claud. Neither, my lord.

Beat. The count is neither sad, nor sick, nor merry, nor well; but civil count, civil as an orange, and something of that jealous complexion.

D. Pedro. I' faith, lady, I think your blazon to be true; though, I 'll be sworn, if he be so, his conceit is false. Here, Claudio, I have wooed in thy name, and fair Hero is won: I have broke with her father, and his good will obtained: name the day of marriage, and God give thee joy!

Leon. Count, take of me my daughter, and with her my fortunes: his Grace hath made the match, and all grace say Amen to it.

Beat. Speak, Count, 't is your cue.

Claud. Silence is the perfectest herald of joy; I were but little happy, if I could say how much. Lady, as you are mine, I am yours: I give away myself for you and dote upon the exchange.

Beat. Speak, cousin; or, if you cannot, stop his mouth with a kiss, and let not him speak neither.

D. Pedro. In faith, lady, you have a merry heart.

Beat. Yea, my lord; I thank it, poor fool, it keeps on the windy side of care. My cousin tells him in his ear that he is in her heart.

Claud. And so she doth, cousin.

Beat. Good Lord, for alliance! Thus goes every one to the world but I, and I am sunburnt: I may sit in a corner and cry "Heigh-ho for a husband!"

D. Pedro. Lady Beatrice, I will get you one.

Beat. I would rather have one of your father's getting. Hath your Grace ne'er a brother like you? Your father got excellent husbands, if a maid could come by them.

D. Pedro. Will you have me, lady?

Beat. No, my lord, unless I might have another for working-days: your Grace is too costly to wear every day. But, I beseech your Grace, pardon me; I was born to speak all mirth and no matter.

D. Pedro. Your silence most offends me, and to be merry best becomes you; for, out o' question, you were born in a merry hour.

Beat. No, sure, my lord, my mother cried; but then there was a star danced, and under that was I born. Cousins, God give you joy!

Leon. Niece, will you look to those things I told you of?

Beat. I cry you mercy, uncle. By your Grace's pardon. *Exit.*

D. Pedro. By my troth, a pleasant-spirited lady.

Leon. There 's little of the melancholy element in her, my lord: she is never sad but when she sleeps, and not ever sad then; for I have heard my daughter say, she hath often dreamt of unhappiness and waked herself with laughing.

D. Pedro. She cannot endure to hear tell of a husband.

Leon. O, by no means; she mocks all her wooers out of suit.

D. Pedro. She were an excellent wife for Benedick.

Leon. O Lord, my lord, if they were but a week married, they would talk themselves mad.

D. Pedro. County Claudio, when mean you to go to church?

Claud. To-morrow, my lord: time goes on crutches till love have all his rites.

Leon. Not till Monday, my dear son, which is hence a just seven-night; and a time too brief, too, to have all things answer my mind.

D. Pedro. Come, you shake the head at so long a breathing; but, I warrant thee,

276-7. great Cham's, Grand Khan of the Mongols. **288. use,** interest. **304-5. civil as an orange,** the pun on **civil** is twofold: (1) civil and Seville were spelled and pronounced alike; (2) Seville oranges were "civil" in that they were neither sweet nor sour The yellow color of the orange suggests jealousy. (Cf. l. 305). **308. blazon,** description. **309. conceit,** conception, idea.

327. windy, windward (in combat, the side of advantage). **330. alliance,** i.e., by marriage. **goes . . . to the world,** marries. **331-2. sunburnt,** ill-favored, unattractive. **359. ever,** always. **365. suit,** courtship. **378. breathing,** delay.

Claudio, the time shall not go dully by us. I will in the interim undertake one of Hercules' labours; which is, to bring Signior Benedick and the Lady Beatrice into a mountain of affection th' one with th' other. I would fain have it a match, and I doubt not but to fashion it, if you three will but minister such assistance as I shall give you direction.

Leon. My lord, I am for you, though it cost me ten nights' watchings.

Claud. And I, my lord.

D. Pedro. And you too, gentle Hero?

Hero. I will do any modest office, my lord, to help my cousin to a good husband.

D. Pedro. And Benedick is not the unhopefullest husband that I know. Thus far can I praise him: he is of a noble strain, of approved valour, and confirmed honesty. I will teach you how to humour your cousin, that she shall fall in love with Benedick; and I, with your two helps, will so practise on Benedick that, in despite of his quick wit and his queasy stomach, he shall fall in love with Beatrice. If we can do this, Cupid is no longer an archer. His glory shall be ours, for we are the only love-gods. Go in with me, and I will tell you my drift. *Exeunt.*

Scene II. *The same.*

Enter *Don John* and *Borachio.*

D. John. It is so; the Count Claudio shall marry the daughter of Leonato.

Bora. Yea, my lord; but I can cross it.

D. John. Any bar, any cross, any impediment will be med'cinable to me: I am sick in displeasure to him, and whatsoever comes athwart his affection ranges evenly with mine. How canst thou cross this marriage?

Bora. Not honestly, my lord; but so covertly that no dishonesty shall appear in me.

D. John. Show me briefly how.

Bora. I think I told your lordship a year since how much I am in the favour of Margaret, the waiting gentlewoman to Hero.

D. John. I remember.

Bora. I can, at any unseasonable instant of the night, appoint her to look out at her lady's chamber-window.

D. John. What life is in that, to be the death of this marriage?

Bora. The poison of that lies in you to temper. Go you to the Prince your brother; spare not to tell him that he hath wronged his honour in marrying the renowned Claudio—whose estimation do you mightily hold up—to a contaminated stale, such a one as Hero.

D. John. What proof shall I make of that?

Bora. Proof enough to misuse the Prince, to vex Claudio, to undo Hero, and kill Leonato. Look you for any other issue?

D. John. Only to despite them, I will endeavour anything.

Bora. Go, then; find me a meet hour to draw Don Pedro and the Count Claudio alone; tell them that you know that Hero loves me; intend a kind of zeal both to the Prince and Claudio, as,—in love of your brother's honour, who hath made this match, and his friend's reputation, who is thus like to be cozened with the semblance of a maid,—that you have discovered thus. They will scarcely believe this without trial. Offer them instances; which shall bear no less likelihood than to see me at her chamber-window, hear me call Margaret Hero, hear Margaret term me Claudio; and bring them to see this the very night before the intended wedding,—for in the meantime I will so fashion the matter that Hero shall be absent,—and there shall appear such seeming truth of Hero's disloyalty, that jealousy shall be called assurance and all the preparation overthrown.

D. John. Grow this to what adverse issue it can, I will put it in practice. Be cunning in the working this, and thy fee is a thousand ducats.

Bora. Be you constant in the accusation, and my cunning shall not shame me.

D. John. I will presently go learn their day of marriage. *Exeunt.*

Scene III. *Leonato's orchard.*

Enter *Benedick* alone.

Bene. Boy!

Enter *Boy.*

Boy. Signior?

Bene. In my chamber-window lies a book; bring it hither to me in the orchard.

Boy. I am here already, sir.

Bene. I know that; but I would have thee hence, and here again. [*Exit Boy.*] I do much wonder that one man, seeing how much an-

394. **strain,** lineage. 395. **approved,** proved. 399. **queasy,** squeamish. 403. **drift,** scheme. **Scene ii: 7. affection,** desire. **ranges evenly,** runs parallel. 22. **temper,** mix.

25. **estimation,** worth. 26. **stale,** loose woman. 28. **misuse,** mislead. 35. **intend,** pretend. 39. **cozened,** cheated. 41. **instances,** proofs. 44-5. **hear Margaret term me Claudio,** this has seemed confusing to many editors, and some have substituted "Borachio" for "Claudio." But if we want to think Margaret guiltless of conspiring against her mistress, we must suppose that she was induced by the romance of the thing to act out a love scene from high life, she taking the part of Hero and Borachio the part of Claudio. 50. **assurance, certainty.**

Don Pedro + Claudio knowing Benedict is hiding tell of how much Beatrice loves him – he hears of

other man is a fool when he dedicates his behaviours to love, will, after he hath laughed at such shallow follies in others, become the argument of his own scorn by falling in love, and such a man is Claudio. I have known when there was no music with him but the drum and the fife; and now had he rather hear the tabor and the pipe. I have known when he would have walked ten miles a-foot to see a good armour; and now will he lie ten nights awake, carving the fashion of a new doublet. He was wont to speak plain and to the purpose, like an honest man and a soldier; and now is he turned orthography; his words are a very fantastical banquet, just so many strange dishes. May I be so converted and see with these eyes? I cannot tell; I think not. I will not be sworn but love may transform me to an oyster; but I 'll take my oath on it, till he have made an oyster of me, he shall never make me such a fool. One woman is fair, yet I am well; another is wise, yet I am well; another virtuous, yet I am well; but till all graces be in one woman, one woman shall not come in my grace. Rich she shall be, that 's certain; wise, or I 'll none; virtuous, or I 'll never cheapen her; fair, or I 'll never look on her; mild, or come not near me; noble, or not I for an angel; of good discourse, an excellent musician, and her hair shall be of what colour it please God. Ha! the Prince and Monsieur Love! I will hide me in the arbour. *Withdraws.*

Enter *Don Pedro, Claudio,* and *Leonato.* Music within.

D. Pedro. Come, shall we hear this music?

Claud. Yea, my good lord. How still the evening is,
As hush'd on purpose to grace harmony!

D. Pedro. See you where Benedick hath hid himself?

Claud. O, very well, my lord. The music ended,
We 'll fit the hid-fox with a pennyworth.

Enter *Balthasar* with music.

D. Pedro. Come, Balthasar, we 'll hear that song again.

Balth. O, good my lord, tax not so bad a voice
To slander music any more than once.

D. Pedro. It is the witness still of excellency
To put a strange face on his own perfection.
I pray thee, sing, and let me woo no more.

Balth. Because you talk of wooing, I will sing;
Since many a wooer doth commence his suit
To her he thinks not worthy, yet he wooes,
Yet will he swear he loves.

D. Pedro. Now, pray thee, come;
Or, if thou wilt hold longer argument,
Do it in notes.

Balth. Note this before my notes;
There 's not a note of mine that 's worth the noting.

D. Pedro. Why, these are very crotchets that he speaks;
Note, notes, forsooth, and nothing. *Music.*

Bene. Now, divine air! now is his soul ravished! Is it not strange that sheeps' guts should hale souls out of men's bodies? Well, a horn for my money, when all 's done.

The Song

Balth.

Sigh no more, ladies, sigh no more,
  Men were deceivers ever,
One foot in sea and one on shore,
  To one thing constant never.
Then sigh not so, but let them go,
  And be you blithe and bonny,
Converting all your sounds of woe
  Into Hey nonny nonny.

Sing no more ditties, sing no moe,
  Of dumps so dull and heavy;
The fraud of men was ever so,
  Since summer first was leavy.
    Then sigh not so, etc.

D. Pedro. By my troth, a good song.

Balth. And an ill singer, my lord.

D. Pedro. Ha, no, no, faith; thou sing'st well enough for a shift.

Bene. An he had been a dog that should have howled thus, they would have hanged him; and I pray God his bad voice bode no mischief. I had as lief have heard the night-raven, come what plague could have come after it.

D. Pedro. Yea, marry. Dost thou hear, Balthasar? I pray thee, get us some excellent music; for to-morrow night we would have it at the Lady Hero's chamber-window.

Balth. The best I can, my lord.

Exit Balthasar.

D. Pedro. Do so; farewell. Come hither,

15. **tabor**, small drum. 18. **carving**, planning. 21. **orthography**, correct speaking and spelling. 34. **cheapen**, ask the price of. 36. **noble . . . angel**, this is one of the many punning references to coins of these names. The noble was worth 6s. 8d., and the angel 10s. 44. We'll give this hidden fox (cf. *Ham.* iv. ii, 33) his money's worth. 46. **tax**, impose as a task.

48-9. It is always (still) a proof of excellency for one to fail to recognize (to put a strange face on) one's own perfection. 58. **crotchets**, (1) whims, (2) quarter-notes. 59. **nothing**, pronounced like "noting" (l. 57). 72. **moe**, more. 73. **dumps**, doleful tunes. 80. **shift**, makeshift.

Leonato. What was it you told me of to-day, that your niece Beatrice was in love with Signior Benedick.

Claud. [*Aside.*] O, ay, stalk on, stalk on; the fowl sits.—I did never think that lady would have loved any man.

Leon. No, nor I neither; but most wonderful that she should so dote on Signior Benedick, whom she hath in all outward behaviours seemed ever to abhor.

Bene. Is 't possible? Sits the wind in that corner?

Leon. By my troth, my lord, I cannot tell what to think of it but that she loves him with an enraged affection: it is past the infinite of thought.

D. Pedro. May be she doth but counterfeit.

Claud. Faith, like enough.

Leon. O God, counterfeit! There was never counterfeit of passion came so near the life of passion as she discovers it.

D. Pedro. Why, what effects of passion shows she?

Claud. [*Aside.*] Bait the hook well; this fish will bite.

Leon. What effects, my lord? She will sit you,—you heard my daughter tell you how.

Claud. She did, indeed.

D. Pedro. How, how, I pray you? You amaze me; I would have thought her spirit had been invincible against all assaults of affection.

Leon. I would have sworn it had, my lord; especially against Benedick.

Bene. I should think this a gull, but that the white-bearded fellow speaks it. Knavery cannot, sure, hide himself in such reverence.

Claud. [*Aside.*] He hath ta'en the infection. Hold it up.

D. Pedro Hath she made her affection known to Benedick?

Leon. No; and swears she never will: that 's her torment.

Claud. 'T is true, indeed; so your daughter says. "Shall I," says she, "that have so oft encountered him with scorn, write to him that I love him?"

Leon. This says she now when she is beginning to write to him; for she 'll be up twenty times a night, and there will she sit in her smock till she have writ a sheet of paper. My daughter tells us all.

Claud. Now you talk of a sheet of paper, I remember a pretty jest your daughter told us of.

Leon. O, when she had writ it and was reading it over, she found Benedick and Beatrice between the sheet?

Claud. That.

Leon. O, she tore the letter into a thousand halfpence; railed at herself, that she should be so immodest to write to one that she knew would flout her. "I measure him," says she, "by my own spirit; for I should flout him, if he writ to me; yea, though I love him, I should."

Claud. Then down upon her knees she falls, weeps, sobs, beats her heart, tears her hair, prays, curses: "O sweet Benedick! God give me patience!"

Leon. She doth indeed, my daughter says so; and the ecstasy hath so much overborne her that my daughter is sometime afeard she will do a desperate outrage to herself: it is very true.

D. Pedro. It were good that Benedick knew of it by some other, if she will not discover it.

Claud. To what end? He would make but a sport of it and torment the poor lady worse.

D. Pedro. An he should, it were an alms to hang him. She 's an excellent sweet lady and, out of all suspicion, she is virtuous.

Claud. And she is exceeding wise.

D. Pedro. In every thing but in loving Benedick.

Leon. O, my lord, wisdom and blood combating in so tender a body, we have ten proofs to one that blood hath the victory. I am sorry for her, as I have just cause, being her uncle and her guardian.

D. Pedro. I would she had bestowed this dotage on me; I would have daffed all other respects and made her half myself. I pray you, tell Benedick of it, and hear what 'a will say.

Leon. Were it good, think you?

Claud. Hero thinks surely she will die; for she says she will die, if he love her not, and she will die, ere she make her love known, and she will die, if he woo her, rather than she will bate one breath of her accustomed crossness.

D. Pedro. She doth well: if she should make tender of her love, 't is very possible he 'll scorn it; for the man, as you know all, hath a contemptible spirit.

Claud. He is a very proper man.

D. Pedro. He hath indeed a good outward happiness.

Claud. Before God! and, in my mind, very wise.

104. enraged, frenzied. **111. discovers,** reveals. **123. gull,** trick. **127. Hold it up,** Keep it up.

157. ecstasy, frenzy. **164. an alms,** a good deed. **176-7. daffed . . . respects,** put aside all other considerations. **186. tender,** offer. **188. contemptible,** contemptuous. **189. proper,** handsome. **190-1. outward happiness,** happy or goodly exterior.

Benedict decides he must return his great love of Beatrice's

D. Pedro. He doth indeed show some sparks that are like wit.

Claud. And I take him to be valiant.

D. Pedro. As Hector, I assure you; and in the managing of quarrels you may say he is wise, for either he avoids them with great discretion, or undertakes them with a most Christian-like fear.

Leon. If he do fear God, 'a must necessarily keep peace: if he break the peace, he ought to enter into a quarrel with fear and trembling.

D. Pedro. And so will he do; for the man doth fear God, howsoever it seems not in him by some large jests he will make. Well, I am sorry for your niece. Shall we go seek Benedick and tell him of her love?

Claud. Never tell him, my lord: let her wear it out with good counsel.

Leon. Nay, that 's impossible; she may wear her heart out first.

D. Pedro. Well, we will hear further of it by your daughter: let it cool the while. I love Benedick well; and I could wish he would modestly examine himself, to see how much he is unworthy so good a lady.

Leon. My lord, will you walk? Dinner is ready.

Claud. [*Aside.*] If he do not dote on her upon this, I will never trust my expectation.

D. Pedro. [*Aside.*] Let there be the same net spread for her; and that must your daughter and her gentlewomen carry. The sport will be, when they hold one an opinion of another's dotage, and no such matter; that 's the scene that I would see, which will be merely a dumb-show. Let us send her to call him in to dinner.

Exeunt Don Pedro, Claudio, and Leonato.

Bene. [*Coming forward.*] This can be no trick; the conference was sadly borne. They have the truth of this from Hero. They seem to pity the lady; it seems her affections have their full bent. Love me! why, it must be requited. I hear how I am censured: they say I will bear myself proudly if I perceive the love come from her; they say too that she will rather die than give any sign of affection. I did never think to marry: I must not seem proud: happy are they that hear their detractions and can put them to mending. They say the lady is fair; 't is a truth, I can bear them witness; and virtuous; 't is so, I cannot reprove it; and wise, but for loving me; by my troth, it is no addition to her wit, nor no great argument of her folly, for I will be horribly in love with her. I may chance have some odd quirks and remnants of wit broken on me, because I have railed so long against marriage; but doth not the appetite alter? A man loves the meat in his youth that he cannot endure in his age. Shall quips and sentences and these paper bullets of the brain awe a man from the career of his humour? No, the world must be peopled. When I said I would die a bachelor, I did not think I should live till I were married. Here comes Beatrice. By this day! she 's a fair lady. I do spy some marks of love in her.

Enter *Beatrice.*

Beat. Against my will I am sent to bid you come in to dinner.

Bene. Fair Beatrice, I thank you for your pains.

Beat. I took no more pains for those thanks than you take pains to thank me: if it had been painful, I would not have come.

Bene. You take pleasure then in the message?

Beat. Yea, just so much as you may take upon a knife's point and choke a daw withal. You have no stomach, signior: fare you well. *Exit.*

Bene. Ha! "Against my will I am sent to bid you come in to dinner"; there 's a double meaning in that. "I took no more pains for those thanks than you took pains to thank me"; that 's as much as to say, "Any pains that I take for you is as easy as thanks." If I do not take pity of her, I am a villain; if I do not love her, I am a Jew. I will go get her picture. *Exit.*

ACT III. Scene I. *Leonato's orchard.*

Enter *Hero* and two Gentlewomen, *Margaret* and *Ursula.*

Hero. Good Margaret, run thee to the parlour;
There shalt thou find my cousin Beatrice
Proposing with the Prince and Claudio.
Whisper her ear and tell her, I and Ursley
Walk in the orchard and our whole discourse
Is all of her; say that thou overheard'st us,

205. large, broad. **224. no such matter,** no such thing exists. **228. sadly borne,** gravely conducted. **231. full bent,** extreme extent.

241. reprove, disprove. **249. sentences,** wise sayings. **250. career,** ground on which race is run. **Act III, Scene i: 3. Proposing,** conversing.

Hero + Ursula, knowing Beatrice can hear, talk of how much Benedict loves her.

And bid her steal into the pleached bower,
Where honeysuckles, ripened by the sun,
Forbid the sun to enter, like favourites
Made proud by princes, that advance their pride
Against that power that bred it: there will she hide her,
To listen our propose. This is thy office;
Bear thee well in it and leave us alone.

Marg. I 'll make her come, I warrant you, presently. *Exit.*

Hero. Now, Ursula, when Beatrice doth come,
As we do trace this alley up and down,
Our talk must only be of Benedick.
When I do name him, let it be thy part
To praise him more than ever man did merit:
My talk to thee must be how Benedick
Is sick in love with Beatrice. Of this matter
Is little Cupid's crafty arrow made,
That only wounds by hearsay. Now begin;

Enter *Beatrice* behind.

For look where Beatrice, like a lapwing, runs
Close by the ground, to hear our conference.

Urs. The pleasant'st angling is to see the fish
Cut with her golden oars the silver stream,
And greedily devour the treacherous bait:
So angle we for Beatrice, who even now
Is couched in the woodbine coverture.
Fear you not my part of the dialogue.

Hero. Then go we near her, that her ear lose nothing
Of the false sweet bait that we lay for it.
Approaching the bower.
No, truly. Ursula, she is too disdainful.
I know her spirits are as coy and wild
As haggards of the rock.

Urs. But are you sure
That Benedick loves Beatrice so entirely?

Hero. So says the Prince and my new-trothed lord.

Urs. And did they bid you tell her of it, madam?

Hero. They did entreat me to acquaint her of it;
But I persuaded them, if they lov'd Benedick,
To wish him wrestle with affection,
And never to let Beatrice know of it.

Urs. Why did you so? Doth not the gentleman
Deserve as full as fortunate a bed
As ever Beatrice shall couch upon?

Hero. O god of love! I know he doth deserve
As much as may be yielded to a man;
But Nature never fram'd a woman's heart
Of prouder stuff than that of Beatrice.
Disdain and scorn ride sparkling in her eyes,
Misprising what they look on, and her wit
Values itself so highly that to her
All matter else seems weak: she cannot love,
Nor take no shape nor project of affection,
She is so self-endeared.

Urs. Sure, I think so;
And therefore certainly it were not good
She knew his love, lest she 'll make sport at it.

Hero. Why, you speak truth. I never yet saw man,
How wise, how noble, young, how rarely featur'd,
But she would spell him backward. If fair-fac'd,
She would swear the gentleman should be her sister;
If black, why, Nature, drawing of an antic,
Made a foul blot: if tall, a lance ill-headed;
If low, an agate very vilely cut;
If speaking, why, a vane blown with all winds;
If silent, why, a block moved with none.
So turns she every man the wrong side out,
And never gives to truth and virtue that
Which simpleness and merit purchaseth.

Urs. Sure, sure, such carping is not commendable.

Hero. No; not to be so odd and from all fashions
As Beatrice is, cannot be commendable.
But who dare tell her so? If I should speak,
She would mock me into air; O, she would laugh me
Out of myself, press me to death with wit.
Therefore let Benedick, like cover'd fire,
Consume away in sighs, waste inwardly.
It were a better death than die with mocks,
Which is as bad as die with tickling.

Urs. Yet tell her of it; hear what she will say.

Hero. No; rather I will go to Benedick
And counsel him to fight against his passion;
And, truly, I 'll devise some honest slanders
To stain my cousin with: one doth not know
How much an ill word may empoison liking.

Urs. O, do not do your cousin such a wrong.
She cannot be so much without true judgement—
Having so swift and excellent a wit
As she is priz'd to have—as to refuse
So rare a gentleman as Signior Benedick.

12. **propose**, conversation. 16. **trace**, pace. 36. **haggards**, untamed hawks.

52. **Misprising**, undervaluing. 55. **project**, idea. 61. **spell him backward**, that is, make his virtues look like faults. Witches were supposed to say their prayers backwards. 63. **antic**, a grotesque figure. 65. **agate**, a tiny figure cut in an agate stone. 84. **honest**, not injurious to her honor.

Hero. He is the only man of Italy,
Always excepted my dear Claudio.
Urs. I pray you, be not angry with me, madam,
Speaking my fancy; Signior Benedick,
For shape, for bearing, argument, and valour,
Goes foremost in report through Italy.
Hero. Indeed, he hath an excellent good name.
Urs. His excellence did earn it, ere he had it.
When are you married, madam?
Hero. Why, every day, to-morrow. Come, go in;
I 'll show thee some attires, and have thy counsel
Which is the best to furnish me to-morrow.
Urs. [*Aside.*] She 's limed, I warrant you. We have caught her, madam.
Hero. [*Aside*] If it proves so, then loving goes by haps:
Some Cupid kills with arrows, some with traps. *Exeunt Hero and Ursula.*
Beat. [*Coming forward.*] What fire is in mine ears? Can this be true?
Stand I condemn'd for pride and scorn so much?
Contempt, farewell! and maiden pride, adieu!
No glory lives behind the back of such.
And, Benedick, love on; I will requite thee,
Taming my wild heart to thy loving hand.
If thou dost love, my kindness shall incite thee
To bind our loves up in a holy band;
For others say thou dost deserve, and I
Believe it better than reportingly. *Exit.*

Scene II. *A room in Leonato's house.*

Enter *Don Pedro, Claudio, Benedick,* and *Leonato.*

D. Pedro. I do but stay till your marriage be consummate, and then go I toward Arragon.

Claud. I 'll bring you thither, my lord, if you 'll vouchsafe me.

D. Pedro. Nay, that would be as great a soil in the new gloss of your marriage as to show a child his new coat and forbid him to wear it. I will only be bold with Benedick for his company; for, from the crown of his head to the sole of his foot, he is all mirth: he hath twice or thrice cut Cupid's bowstring, and the little hangman dare not shoot at him. He hath a heart as sound as a bell and his tongue is the clapper, for what his heart thinks his tongue speaks.

Bene. Gallants, I am not as I have been.

Leon. So say I; methinks you are sadder.

Claud. I hope he be in love.

D. Pedro. Hang him, truant! There 's no true drop of blood in him, to be truly touched with love. If he be sad, he wants money.

Bene. I have the toothache.

D. Pedro. Draw it.

Bene. Hang it!

Claud. You must hang it first, and draw it afterwards.

D. Pedro. What! sigh for the toothache?

Leon. Where is but a humour or a worm.

Bene. Well, every one can master a grief but he that has it.

Claud. Yet say I, he is in love.

D. Pedro. There is no appearance of fancy in him, unless it be a fancy that he hath to strange disguises; as, to be a Dutchman to-day, a Frenchman to-morrow, or in the shape of two countries at once, as, a German from the waist downward, all slops, and a Spaniard from the hip upward, no doublet. Unless he have a fancy to this foolery, as it appears he hath, he is no fool for fancy, as you would have it appear he is.

Claud. If he be not in love with some woman, there is no believing old signs: 'a brushes his hat a mornings; what should that bode?

D. Pedro. Hath any man seen him at the barber's?

Claud. No, but the barber's man hath been seen with him, and the old ornament of his cheek hath already stuffed tennis-balls.

Leon. Indeed, he looks younger than he did, by the loss of a beard.

D. Pedro. Nay, 'a rubs himself with civet: can you smell him out by that?

Claud. That 's as much as to say, the sweet youth 's in love.

D. Pedro. The greatest note of it is his melancholy.

Claud. And when was he wont to wash his face?

D. Pedro. Yea, or to paint himself? For the which, I hear what they say of him.

Claud. Nay, but his jesting spirit; which is now crept into a lute-string and now governed by stops.

101. every day, this may mean for all time; it may refer to the day by day postponement; or it may indicate that the marriage is always in her thoughts. **104. limed,** snared, as with birdlime. **105. haps,** chances. **110. No glory lives behind the back of such,** contemptuous and scornful people are not spoken well of behind their backs.

Scene ii: 24. A reference to the hanging and drawing (disembowelling) of traitors and also to the practice of hanging up extracted teeth in a barber's shop. **27. humour or a worm,** toothache was supposed to be caused either by unhealthful bodily fluids (humors) or by worms. **31. fancy,** love. **35. slops,** loose breeches. **50. civet,** a perfume. **56. wash,** i.e., at the barber's. **62. stops,** frets of a stringed instrument.

D. Pedro. Indeed, that tells a heavy tale for him: conclude, conclude, he is in love.

Claud. Nay, but I know who loves him.

D. Pedro. That would I know too: I warrant, one that knows him not.

Claud. Yes, and his ill conditions; and, in despite of all, dies for him.

D. Pedro. She shall be buried with her face upwards.

Bene. Yet is this no charm for the toothache. Old signior, walk aside with me; I have studied eight or nine wise words to speak to you, which these hobby-horses must not hear.

Exeunt Benedick and Leonato.

D. Pedro. For my life, to break with him about Beatrice.

Claud. 'T is even so. Hero and Margaret have by this played their parts with Beatrice; and then the two bears will not bite one another when they meet.

Enter *John* the Bastard.

D. John. My lord and brother, God save you!

D. Pedro. Good den, brother.

D. John. If your leisure served, I would speak with you.

D. Pedro. In private?

D. John. If it please you; yet Count Claudio may hear, for what I would speak of concerns him.

Claud. What 's the matter?

D. John. [*To Claudio.*] Means your lordship to be married to-morrow?

D. Pedro. You know he does.

D. John. I know not that, when he knows what I know.

Claud. If there be any impediment, I pray you discover it.

D. John. You may think I love you not; let that appear hereafter, and aim better at me by that I now will manifest. For my brother, I think he holds you well, and in dearness of heart hath holp to effect your ensuing marriage;—surely suit ill spent and labour ill bestowed.

D. Pedro. Why, what 's the matter?

D. John. I came hither to tell you; and, circumstances shortened, for she has been too long a talking of, the lady is disloyal.

Claud. Who? Hero?

D. John. Even she; Leonato's Hero, your Hero, every man's Hero.

Claud. Disloyal?

D. John. The word is too good to paint out her wickedness; I could say she were worse; think you of a worse title, and I will fit her to it. Wonder not till further warrant: go but with me to-night; you shall see her chamber-window entered, even the night before her wedding-day: if you love her then, to-morrow wed her; but it would better fit your honour to change your mind.

Claud. May this be so?

D. Pedro. I will not think it.

D. John. If you dare not trust that you see, confess not that you know: if you will follow me, I will show you enough; and when you have seen more and heard more, proceed accordingly

Claud. If I see any thing to-night why I should not marry her to-morrow, in the congregation, where I should wed, there will I shame her.

D. Pedro. And, as I wooed for thee to obtain her, I will join with thee to disgrace her.

D. John. I will disparage her no farther till you are my witnesses: bear it coldly but till midnight, and let the issue show itself.

D. Pedro. O day untowardly turned!

Claud. O mischief strangely thwarting!

D. John. O plague right well prevented! So will you say when you have seen the sequel.

Exeunt.

Scene III. *A street.*

Enter *Dogberry* and his compartner *Verges* with the *Watch.*

Dog. Are you good men and true?

Verg. Yea, or else it were pity but they should suffer salvation, body and soul.

Dog. Nay, that were a punishment too good for them, if they should have any allegiance in them, being chosen for the Prince's watch.

Verg. Well, give them their charge, neighbour Dogberry.

Dog. First, who think you the most desartless man to be constable?

1. Watch. Hugh Oatcake, sir, or George Seacole; for they can write and read.

Dog. Come hither, neighbour Seacole. God hath blessed you with a good name. To be a well-favoured man is the gift of fortune, but to write and read comes by nature.

2. Watch. Both which, master constable,—

Dog. You have: I knew it would be your

70-1. buried with her face upwards, suicides were buried face downwards. Beatrice will not die by her own hand, Benedick will be the cause of her death. **75. hobby-horses,** jack-asses, lit. fantastic characters in the morris-dance. **99-100. aim . . . me,** form a better opinion of me. **106. circumstances shortened,** without beating about the bush.

112. paint out, depict. **114. warrant,** proof. **134. untowardly turned,** unfortunately altered. **Scene iii: 15. well-favoured,** handsome.

answer. Well, for your favour, sir, why, give God thanks, and make no boast of it; and for your writing and reading, let that appear when there is no need of such vanity. You are thought here to be the most senseless and fit man for the constable of the watch; therefore bear you the lantern. This is your charge: you shall comprehend all vagrom men; you are to bid any man stand, in the Prince's name.

2. Watch. How if 'a will not stand?

Dog. Why, then, take no note of him, but let him go; and presently call the rest of the watch together, and thank God you are rid of a knave.

Verg. If he will not stand when he is bidden, he is none of the Prince's subjects.

Dog. True, and they are to meddle with none but the Prince's subjects. You shall also make no noise in the streets; for for the watch to babble and to talk is most tolerable and not to be endured.

2. Watch. We will rather sleep than talk; we know what belongs to a watch.

Dog. Why, you speak like an ancient and most quiet watchman, for I cannot see how sleeping should offend; only, have a care that your bills be not stolen. Well, you are to call at all the ale-houses, and bid those that are drunk get them to bed.

2. Watch. How if they will not?

Dog. Why, then, let them alone till they are sober: if they make you not then the better answer, you may say they are not the men you took them for.

2. Watch. Well, sir.

Dog. If you meet a thief, you may suspect him, by virtue of your office, to be no true man; and, for such kind of men, the less you meddle or make with them, why, the more is for your honesty.

2. Watch. If we know him to be a thief, shall we not lay hands on him?

Dog. Truly, by your office, you may; but I think they that touch pitch will be defiled. The most peaceable way for you, if you do take a thief, is to let him show himself what he is and steal out of your company.

Verg. You have been always called a merciful man, partner.

Dog. Truly, I would not hang a dog by my will, much more a man who hath any honesty in him.

Verg. If you hear a child cry in the night, you must call to the nurse and bid her still it.

2. Watch. How if the nurse be asleep and will not hear us?

Dog. Why, then, depart in peace, and let the child wake her with crying; for the ewe that will not hear her lamb when it baes will never answer a calf when he bleats.

Verg. 'T is very true.

Dog. This is the end of the charge: you, constable, are to present the Prince's own person: if you meet the Prince in the night, you may stay him.

Verg. Nay, by 'r lady, that I think 'a cannot.

Dog. Five shillings to one on 't, with any man that knows the statues, he may stay him; marry, not without the Prince be willing; for, indeed, the watch ought to offend no man, and it is an offence to stay a man against his will.

Verg. By 'r lady, I think it be so.

Dog. Ha, ah ha! Well, masters, good night. And there be any matter of weight chances, call up me: keep your fellows' counsels and your own, and good night. Come, neighbour.

2. Watch. Well, masters, we hear our charge: let us go sit here upon the church-bench till two, and then all to bed.

Dog. One word more, honest neighbours. I pray you, watch about Signior Leonato's door; for the wedding being there to-morrow, there is a great coil to-night. Adieu! Be vigitant, I beseech you.

Exeunt Dogberry and Verges.

Enter *Borachio* and *Conrade*.

Bora. What, Conrade!

2. Watch. [*Aside.*] Peace! stir not.

Bora. Conrade, I say!

Con. Here, man; I am at thy elbow.

Bora. Mass, and my elbow itched; I thought there would a scab follow.

Con. I will owe thee an answer for that; and now forward with thy tale.

Bora. Stand thee close, then, under this pent-house, for it drizzles rain; and I will, like a true drunkard, utter all to thee.

2. Watch. [*Aside.*] Some treason, masters; yet stand close.

Bora. Therefore know I have earned of Don John a thousand ducats.

Con. Is it possible that any villainy should be so dear?

Bora. Thou shouldst rather ask if it were possible any villainy should be so rich; for when rich villains have need of poor ones, poor ones may make what price they will.

Con. I wonder at it.

Bora. That shows thou art unconfirmed.

25. **comprehend**, apprehend. **vagrom**, vagrant. 44. **bills**, halberds. 55. **make**, have to do with.

79. **present**, represent. 84. **statues**, statutes. 100. **coil**, bustle. 111. **pent-house**, projecting roof. 124. **unconfirmed**, inexperienced.

Thou knowest that the fashion of a doublet, or a hat, or a cloak, is nothing to a man.

Con. Yes, it is apparel.

Bora. I mean, the fashion.

Con. Yes, the fashion is the fashion.

Bora. Tush! I may as well say the fool 's the fool. But seest thou not what a deformed thief this fashion is?

2. Watch [*Aside.*] I know that Deformed; 'a has been a vile thief this seven year: 'a goes up and down like a gentleman: I remember his name.

Bora. Didst thou not hear somebody?

Con. No; 't was the vane on the house.

Bora. Seest thou not, I say, what a deformed thief this fashion is, how giddily 'a turns about all the hot bloods between fourteen and five-and-thirty, sometimes fashioning them like Pharaoh's soldiers in the reechy painting, sometime like god Bel's priests in the old church-window, sometime like the shaven Hercules in the smirched worm-eaten tapestry, where his codpiece seems as massy as his club?

Con. All this I see; and I see that the fashion wears out more apparel than the man. But art not thou thyself giddy with the fashion too, that thou hast shifted out of thy tale into telling me of the fashion?

Bora. Not so, neither; but know that I have to-night wooed Margaret, the Lady Hero's gentlewoman, by the name of Hero: she leans me out at her mistress' chamber-window, bids me a thousand times good night,—I tell this tale vilely:—I should first tell thee how the Prince, Claudio, and my master, planted and placed and possessed by my master Don John, saw afar off in the orchard this amiable encounter.

Con. And thought they Margaret was Hero?

Bora. Two of them did, the Prince and Claudio; but the devil my master knew she was Margaret; and partly by his oaths, which first possessed them, partly by the dark night, which did deceive them, but chiefly by my villainy, which did confirm any slander that Don John had made, away went Claudio enraged; swore he would meet her, as he was appointed, next morning at the temple, and there, before the whole congregation, shame her with what he saw o'er night, and send her home again without a husband.

2. Watch. We charge you, in the Prince's name, stand!

1. Watch. Call up the right master constable. We have here recovered the most dangerous piece of lechery that ever was known in the commonwealth.

2. Watch. And one Deformed is one of them. I know him; 'a wears a lock.

Con. Masters, masters,—

2. Watch. You 'll be made bring Deformed forth, I warrant you.

Con. Masters,—

1. Watch. Never speak. We charge you let us obey you to go with us.

Bora. We are like to prove a goodly commodity, being taken up of these men's bills.

Con. A commodity in question, I warrant you. Come, we 'll obey you. *Exeunt.*

Scene IV. *Hero's apartment.*

Enter *Hero, Margaret,* and *Ursula.*

Hero. Good Ursula, wake my cousin Beatrice, and desire her to rise.

Urs. I will, lady.

Hero. And bid her come hither.

Urs. Well. *Exit.*

Marg. Troth, I think your other rebato were better.

Hero. No, pray thee, good Meg, I 'll wear this.

Marg. By my troth, 's not so good; and I warrant your cousin will say so.

Hero. My cousin 's a fool, and thou art another: I 'll wear none but this.

Marg. I like the new tire within excellently, if the hair were a thought browner; and your gown 's a most rare fashion, i' faith. I saw the Duchess of Milan's gown that they praise so.

Hero. O, that exceeds, they say.

Marg. By my troth, 's but a night-gown in respect of yours: cloth o' gold, and cuts, and laced with silver, set with pearls, down sleeves, side sleeves, and skirts, round underborne with a bluish tinsel; but for a fine, quaint, graceful, and excellent fashion, yours is worth ten on 't.

Hero. God give me joy to wear it! for my heart is exceeding heavy.

Marg. 'T will be heavier soon by the weight of a man.

Hero. Fie upon thee! art not ashamed?

Marg. Of what, lady? Of speaking honour-

144. reechy, smoke-stained. **god Bel's priests,** alluding to the story of Bel and the Dragon told in the apocryphal addition to *Daniel.* **146. codpiece,** part of man's breeches. **159. possessed,** i.e., as by a devil.

183. lock, love-lock. **190-1. commodity . . . bills, commodity,** (1) goods, (2) a bargain; **taken up,** (1) got on credit, (2) arrested; **bills,** (1) bonds, (2) weapons, halberds. **192. in question,** subject to examination and trial. **Scene iv: 6. rebato,** ruff for the neck. **13. tire,** head-dress. **14. the hair,** false hair inside tire. **18. night-gown,** dressing-gown. **19. cuts,** slashes to show fabric beneath. **19-20. down sleeves,** sleeves fitted to the arm. **20. side sleeves,** ornamental sleeves hanging from shoulder. **20-1. underborne,** lined.

(Beatrice says she is ill, too - Margaret says it's love.

ably? Is not marriage honourable in a beggar? Is not your lord honourable without marriage? I think you would have me say, "saving your reverence, a husband:" an bad thinking do not wrest true speaking, I 'll offend nobody: is there any harm in "the heavier for a husband"? None, I think, an it be the right husband and the right wife; otherwise 't is light, and not heavy: ask my Lady Beatrice else; here she comes.

Enter *Beatrice.*

Hero. Good morrow, coz.

Beat. Good morrow, sweet Hero.

Hero. Why, how now? Do you speak in the sick tune?

Beat. I am out of all other tune, methinks.

Marg. Clap 's into "Light o' love"; that goes without a burden: do you sing it, and I 'll dance it.

Beat. Ye light o' love with your heels! then, if your husband have stables enough, you 'll see he shall lack no barns.

Marg. O illegitimate construction! I scorn that with my heels.

Beat. 'T is almost five o'clock, cousin; 't is time you were ready. By my troth, I am exceeding ill: heigh-ho!

Marg. For a hawk, a horse, or a husband?

Beat. For the letter that begins them all, H.

Marg. Well, an you be not turned Turk, there 's no more sailing by the star.

Beat. What means the fool, trow?

Marg. Nothing I; but God send every one their heart's desire!

Hero. These gloves the count sent me; they are an excellent perfume.

Beat. I am stuffed, cousin; I cannot smell.

Marg. A maid, and stuffed! There 's goodly catching of cold.

Beat. O God help me! God help me! How long have you professed apprehension?

Marg. Ever since you left it. Doth not my wit become me rarely?

Beat. It is not seen enough, you should wear it in your cap. By my troth, I am sick.

Marg. Get you some of this distilled Carduus Benedictus, and lay it to your heart: it is the only thing for a qualm.

Hero. There thou prick'st her with a thistle.

Beat. Benedictus! why Benedictus? You have some moral in this Benedictus.

Marg. Moral! no, by my troth, I have no moral meaning; I meant, plain holy-thistle. You may think perchance that I think you are in love: nay, by 'r lady, I am not such a fool to think what I list, nor I list not to think what I can, nor indeed I cannot think, if I would think my heart out of thinking, that you are in love or that you will be in love or that you can be in love. Yet Benedick was such another, and now is he become a man: he swore he would never marry, and yet now, in despite of his heart, he eats his meat without grudging; and how you may be converted I know not, but methinks you look with your eyes as other women do.

Beat. What pace is this that thy tongue keeps?

Marg. Not a false gallop.

Re-enter *Ursula.*

Urs. Madam, withdraw; the Prince, the Count, Signior Benedick, Don John, and all the gallants of the town, are come to fetch you to church.

Hero. Help to dress me, good coz, good Meg, good Ursula. *Exeunt.*

Scene V. *The Hall in Leonato's house.*

Enter *Leonato,* with the Constable *Dogberry* and the Headborough *Verges.*

Leon. What would you with me, honest neighbour?

Dog. Marry, sir, I would have some confidence with you that decerns you nearly.

Leon. Brief, I pray you; for you see it is a busy time with me.

Dog. Marry, this it is, sir.

Verg. Yes, in truth it is, sir.

Leon. What is it, my good friends?

Dog. Goodman Verges, sir, speaks a little off the matter; an old man, sir, and his wits are not so blunt as, God help, I would desire they were; but, in faith, honest as the skin between his brows.

Verg. Yes, I thank God I am as honest as any man living that is an old man and no honester than I.

Dog. Comparisons are odorous: palabras, neighbour Verges.

Leon. Neighbours, you are tedious.

Dog. It pleases your worship to say so, but we are the poor Duke's officers; but truly,

37. **light,** wanton. 45. **burden,** bass accompaniment, i.e., no men needed for this song. 49. **barns,** bairns (children). 56. **H,** in Shakespeare's time the word ache was pronounced exactly like this letter, a similarity of sound that gave rise to endless puns. 57. **turned Turk,** become renegade, i.e., fallen in love. 68. **professed apprehension,** set up as a wit. 74. **Carduus Benedictus,** "blessed thistle," a medicinal herb.

78. **moral,** secret meaning. **Scene v: S. d. Headborough,** tithing-man. 18. **palabras,** a scrap of Spanish from the phrase *pocas palabras,* few words.

for mine own part, if I were as tedious as a king, I could find in my heart to bestow it all of your worship.

Leon. All thy tediousness on me, ah?

Dog. Yea, an 't were a thousand pound more than 't is; for I hear as good exclamation on your worship as of any man in the city; and though I be but a poor man, I am glad to hear it.

Verg. And so am I.

Leon. I would fain know what you have to say.

Verg. Marry, sir, our watch to-night, excepting your worship's presence, ha' ta'en a couple of as arrant knaves as any in Messina.

Dog. A good old man, sir; he will be talking: as they say, When the age is in, the wit is out. God help us! It is a world to see. Well said, i' faith, neighbour Verges! Well, God 's a good man; an two men ride of a horse, one must ride behind. An honest soul, i' faith, sir; by my troth he is, as ever broke bread; but God is to be worshipped; all men are not alike; alas, good neighbour!

Leon. Indeed, neighbour, he comes too short of you.

Dog. Gifts that God gives.

Leon I must leave you.

Dog. One word, sir: our watch, sir, have indeed comprehended two aspicious persons, and we would have them this morning examined before your worship.

Leon. Take their examination yourself and bring it me: I am now in great haste, as it may appear unto you.

Dog. It shall be suffigance.

Leon. Drink some wine ere you go: fare you well.

Enter a *Messenger.*

Mess. My lord, they stay for you to give your daughter to her husband.

Leon. I 'll wait upon them; I am ready.

Exeunt Leonato and Messenger.

Dog. Go, good partner, go, get you to Francis Seacole; bid him bring his pen and inkhorn to the jail: we are now to examination these men.

Verg. And we must do it wisely.

Dog. We will spare for no wit, I warrant you: here 's that shall drive some of them to a non-come; only get the learned writer to set down our excommunication, and meet me at the jail. *Exeunt.*

ACT IV. Scene I. *A church.*

Enter *Don Pedro, John* the Bastard, *Leonato, Friar Francis, Claudio, Benedick, Hero, Beatrice* and attendants.

Leon. Come, Friar Francis, be brief; only to the plain form of marriage, and you shall recount their particular duties afterwards.

Friar. You come hither, my lord, to marry this lady?

Claud. No.

Leon. To be married to her: friar, you come to marry her.

Friar. Lady, you come hither to be married to this count?

Hero. I do.

Friar. If either of you know any inward impediment why you should not be conjoined, I charge you, on your souls, to utter it.

Claud. Know you any, Hero?

Hero. None, my lord.

Friar. Know you any, Count?

Leon. I dare make his answer—none.

Claud. O, what men dare do! What men may do! What men daily do, not knowing what they do!

Bene. How now! interjections? Why, then, some be of laughing, as, ah, ha, he!

Claud. Stand thee by, friar. Father, by your leave.
Will you with free and unconstrained soul
Give me this maid, your daughter?

Leon. As freely, son, as God did give her me.

Claud. And what have I to give you back, whose worth
May counterpoise this rich and precious gift?

D. Pedro. Nothing, unless you render her again.

Claud. Sweet Prince, you learn me noble thankfulness.
There, Leonato, take her back again:
Give not this rotten orange to your friend;
She 's but the sign and semblance of her honour.
Behold how like a maid she blushes here!
O, what authority and show of truth

63. non-come, *non compos mentis.* He means *non plus.* **Act IV, Scene i: 22-3.** Benedick is quoting from the school grammar. **Cf.** Lyly's **Endymion,** iii, 3: "An interjection, whereof some are of mourning; as eho, vah."

Can cunning sin cover itself withal!
Comes not that blood as modest evidence
To witness simple virtue? Would you not swear,
All you that see her, that she were a maid,
By these exterior shows? But she is none:
She knows the heat of a luxurious bed;
Her blush is guiltiness, not modesty.

Leon. What do you mean, my lord?

Claud. Not to be married;
Not to knit my soul to an approved wanton.

Leon. Dear my lord, if you, in your own proof,
Have vanquish'd the resistance of her youth,
And made defeat of her virginity,—

Claud. I know what you would say: if I have known her,
You will say she did embrace me as a husband,
And so extenuate the 'forehand sin.
No, Leonato.
I never tempted her with word too large;
But, as a brother to his sister, show'd
Bashful sincerity and comely love.

Hero. And seem'd I ever otherwise to you?

Claud. Out on the seeming! I will write against it:
You seem to me as Dian in her orb,
As chaste as is the bud ere it be blown;
But you are more intemperate in your blood
Than Venus, or those pamper'd animals
That rage in savage sensuality.

Hero. Is my lord well, that he doth speak so wide?

Leon. Sweet Prince, why speak not you?

D. Pedro. What should I speak?
I stand dishonour'd, that have gone about
To link my dear friend to a common stale.

Leon. Are these things spoken, or do I but dream?

D. John. Sir, they are spoken, and these things are true.

Bene. This looks not like a nuptial.

Hero. True! O God!

Claud. Leonato, stand I here?
Is this the Prince? Is this the Prince's brother?
Is this face Hero's? Are our eyes our own?

Leon. All this is so; but what of this, my lord?

Claud. Let me but move one question to your daughter;
And, by that fatherly and kindly power
That you have in her, bid her answer truly.

Leon. I charge thee do so, as thou art my child.

Hero. O, God defend me! how am I beset!
What kind of catechising call you this?

Claud. To make you answer truly to your name.

Hero. Is it not Hero? Who can blot that name
With any just reproach?

Claud. Marry, that can Hero;
Hero itself can blot out Hero's virtue.
What man was he talk'd with you yester-night
Out at your window betwixt twelve and one?
Now, if you are a maid, answer to this.

Hero. I talk'd with no man at that hour, my lord.

D. Pedro. Why, then are you no maiden. Leonato,
I am sorry you must hear: upon mine honour,
Myself, my brother, and this grieved count
Did see her, hear her, at that hour last night
Talk with a ruffian at her chamber-window;
Who hath indeed, most like a liberal villain,
Confess'd the vile encounters they have had
A thousand times in secret.

D. John. Fie, fie! they are not to be named, my lord,
Not to be spoke of;
There is not chastity enough in language
Without offence to utter them. Thus, pretty lady,
I am sorry for thy much misgovernment.

Claud. O Hero, what a Hero hadst thou been,
If half thy outward graces had been plac'd
About the thoughts and counsels of thy heart!
But fare thee well, most foul, most fair! Farewell,
Thou pure impiety and impious purity!
For thee I 'll lock up all the gates of love,
And on my eyelids shall conjecture hang,
To turn all beauty into thoughts of harm,
And never shall it more be gracious.

Leon. Hath no man's dagger here a point for me? *Hero swoons.*

Beat. Why, how now, cousin! wherefore sink you down?

D. John. Come, let us go. These things, come thus to light,
Smother her spirits up.

Exeunt Don Pedro, Don John, and Claudio.

Bene. How doth the lady?

Beat. Dead, I think. Help, uncle!
Hero! why, Hero! Uncle! Signior Benedick! Friar!

Leon. O Fate take not away thy heavy hand.
Death is the fairest cover for her shame

42. luxurious, lustful. **45. approved,** proved. **46. in . . . proof,** in tempting her yourself. **53. large,** immodest. **63. so wide,** so far from the truth. **74. move,** propose. **75. kindly,** natural.

93. liberal, licentious. **107. conjecture,** suspicion.

That may be wish'd for.
Beat. How now, cousin Hero!
Friar. Have comfort, lady.
Leon. Dost thou look up?
Friar. Yea, wherefore should she not?
Leon. Wherefore! Why, doth not every earthly thing
Cry shame upon her? Could she here deny
The story that is printed in her blood?
Do not live, Hero; do not ope thine eyes;
For, did I think thou wouldst not quickly die,
Thought I thy spirits were stronger than thy shames,
Myself would, on the rearward of reproaches,
Strike at thy life. Grieved I, I had but one?
Chid I for that a frugal nature's frame?
O, one too much by thee! Why had I one?
Why ever wast thou lovely in my eyes?
Why had I not with charitable hand
Took up a beggar's issue at my gates,
Who smirched thus and mir'd with infamy,
I might have said "No part of it is mine.
This shame derives itself from unknown loins"?
But mine, and mine I lov'd, and mine I prais'd,
And mine that I was proud on, mine so much
That I myself was to myself not mine,
Valuing of her,—why, she, O, she is fallen
Into a pit of ink, that the wide sea
Hath drops too few to wash her clean again,
And salt too little which may season give
To her foul-tainted flesh!
Bene. Sir, sir, be patient.
For my part, I am so attir'd in wonder,
I know not what to say.
Beat. O, on my soul, my cousin is belied!
Bene. Lady, were you her bedfellow last night?
Beat. No, truly not; although, until last night,
I have this twelvemonth been her bedfellow.
Leon. Confirm'd, confirm'd! O, that is stronger made
Which was before barr'd up with ribs of iron!
Would the two princes lie, and Claudio lie,
Who lov'd her so, that, speaking of her foulness,
Wash'd it with tears? Hence from her! Let her die.
Friar. Hear me a little;
For I have only been silent so long
And given way unto this course of fortune,
By noting of the lady. I have mark'd
A thousand blushing apparitions
To start into her face, a thousand innocent shames
In angel whiteness beat away those blushes;
And in her eye there hath appear'd a fire
To burn the errors that these princes hold
Against her maiden truth. Call me a fool;
Trust not my reading nor my observations,
Which with experimental seal doth warrant
The tenour of my book; trust not my age,
My reverence, calling, nor divinity,
If this sweet lady lie not guiltless here
Under some biting error.
Leon. Friar, it cannot be.
Thou seest that all the grace that she hath left
Is that she will not add to her damnation
A sin of perjury; she not denies it.
Why seek'st thou then to cover with excuse
That which appears in proper nakedness?
Friar. Lady, what man is he you are accus'd of?
Hero. They know that do accuse me; I know none.
If I know more of any man alive
Than that which maiden modesty doth warrant,
Let all my sins lack mercy! O my father,
Prove you that any man with me convers'd
At hours unmeet, or that I yesternight
Maintain'd the change of words with any creature,
Refuse me, hate me, torture me to death!
Friar. There is some strange misprision in the princes.
Bene. Two of them have the very bent of honour;
And if their wisdoms be misled in this,
The practice of it lives in John the Bastard,
Whose spirits toil in frame of villainies.
Leon. I know not. If they speak but truth of her,
These hands shall tear her; if they wrong her honour,
The proudest of them shall well hear of it.
Time hath not yet so dried this blood of mine,
Nor age so eat up my invention,
Nor fortune made such havoc of my means,
Nor my bad life reft me so much of friends,
But they shall find, awak'd in such a kind,
Both strength of limb and policy of mind,
Ability in means and choice of friends,
To quit me of them throughly.
Friar. Pause awhile,
And let my counsel sway you in this case.
Your daughter here the princes left for dead:
Let her awhile be secretly kept in,
And publish it that she is dead indeed:

124. printed in her blood, revealed by her blushes. **128. on . . . reproaches,** after I had reproached thee. **130. frame,** plan, scheme. **140-1.** i.e., that I set no value on myself compared to her.

168-9. which . . . book, which with the test of experience (experimental seal) doth confirm (warrant) the general bearing (tenour) of my reading (book). **187. misprision,** mistake. **188. bent,** disposition. **190. practice,** contrivance. **191. frame,** framing. **202. quit . . . of,** repay.

Friar suggests pretending Hero is dead + then Claudio would be sorry for what he said about her.

Maintain a mourning ostentation
And on your family's old monument
Hang mournful epitaphs, and do all rites
That appertain unto a burial.

Leon. What shall become of this? What will this do?

Friar. Marry, this well carried shall on her behalf
Change slander to remorse; that is some good:
But not for that dream I on this strange course,
But on this travail look for greater birth.
She dying, as it must be so maintain'd,
Upon the instant that she was accus'd,
Shall be lamented, pitied, and excus'd
Of every hearer; for it so falls out
That what we have we prize not to the worth
Whiles we enjoy it, but being lack'd and lost,
Why, then we rack the value; then we find
The virtue that possession would not show us
Whiles it was ours. So will it fare with Claudio.
When he shall hear she died upon his words,
Th' idea of her life shall sweetly creep
Into his study of imagination,
And every lovely organ of her life
Shall come apparell'd in more precious habit,
More moving-delicate and full of life,
Into the eye and prospect of his soul,
Than when she liv'd indeed: then shall he mourn,
If ever love had interest in his liver,
And wish he had not so accused her,
No, though he thought his accusation true.
Let this be so, and doubt not but success
Will fashion the event in better shape
Than I can lay it down in likelihood.
But if all aim but this be levell'd false,
The supposition of the lady's death
Will quench the wonder of her infamy.
And if it sort not well, you may conceal her,
As best befits her wounded reputation,
In some reclusive and religious life,
Out of all eyes, tongues, minds, and injuries.

Bene. Signior Leonato, let the friar advise you;
And though you know my inwardness and love
Is very much unto the Prince and Claudio,
Yet, by mine honour, I will deal in this
As secretly and justly as your soul
Should with your body.

Leon. Being that I flow in grief,
The smallest twine may lead me.

207. mourning ostentation, show of mourning. **208. monument,** tomb. **222. rack,** exaggerate. **227. study of imagination,** imaginative reflection. **228. organ,** feature. **231. prospect,** view. **233. liver,** supposed seat of affections, like our "heart." **239. levell'd false,** miss the mark. **240. supposition . . . death,** the supposed death. **242. sort,** turn out.

Friar. 'T is well consented; presently away,
For to strange sores strangely they strain the cure.
Come, lady, die to live: this wedding-day
Perhaps is but prolong'd; have patience and endure.

Exeunt all but Benedick and Beatrice.

Bene. Lady Beatrice, have you wept all this while?

Beat. Yea, and I will weep a while longer.

Bene. I will not desire that.

Beat. You have no reason; I do it freely.

Bene. Surely I do believe your fair cousin is wronged.

Beat. Ah, how much might the man deserve of me that would right her!

Bene. Is there any way to show such friendship?

Beat. A very even way, but no such friend.

Bene. May a man do it?

Beat. It is a man's office, but not yours.

Bene. I do love nothing in the world so well as you—is not that strange?

Beat. As strange as the thing I know not. It were as possible for me to say I loved nothing so well as you: but believe me not; and yet I lie not: I confess nothing, nor I deny nothing. I am sorry for my cousin.

Bene. By my sword, Beatrice, thou lovest me.

Beat. Do not swear, and eat it.

Bene. I will swear by it that you love me; and I will make him eat it that says I love not you.

Beat. Will you not eat your word?

Bene. With no sauce that can be devised to it. I protest I love thee.

Beat. Why, then, God forgive me!

Bene. What offence, sweet Beatrice?

Beat. You have stayed me in a happy hour. I was about to protest I loved you.

Bene. And do it with all thy heart.

Beat. I love you with so much of my heart that none is left to protest.

Bene. Come, bid me do any thing for thee.

Beat. Kill Claudio.

Bene. Ha! not for the wide world.

Beat. You kill me to deny it. Farewell.

Bene. Tarry, sweet Beatrice.

Beat. I am gone, though I am here: there is no love in you: nay, I pray you, let me go.

Bene. Beatrice,—

Beat. In faith, I will go.

Bene. We 'll be friends first.

Beat. You dare easier be friends with me than fight with mine enemy.

Bene. Is Claudio thine enemy?

256. prolong'd, postponed. **264. even,** plain.

Beatrice + Benedick brought together as they feel the same way - revealed to each other.

Beat. Is 'a not approved in the height a villain, that hath slandered, scorned, dishonoured my kinswoman? O that I were a man! What, bear her in hand until they come to take hands; and then, with public accusation, uncovered slander, unmitigated rancour, —O God, that I were a man! I would eat his heart in the market-place.

Bene. Hear me, Beatrice,—

Beat. Talk with a man out at a window! A proper saying!

Bene. Nay, but, Beatrice,—

Beat. Sweet Hero! She is wronged, she is slandered, she is undone.

Bene. Beat—

Beat. Princes and Counties! Surely, a princely testimony, a goodly count, Count Comfect; a sweet gallant, surely! O that I were a man for his sake! or that I had any friend would be a man for my sake! But manhood is melted into curtsies, valour into compliment, and men are only turned into tongue, and trim ones too: he is now as valiant as Hercules that only tells a lie and swears it. I cannot be a man with wishing, therefore I will die a woman with grieving.

Bene. Tarry, good Beatrice. By this hand, I love thee.

Beat. Use it for my love some other way than swearing by it.

Bene. Think you in your soul the Count Claudio hath wronged Hero?

Beat. Yea, as sure as I have a thought or a soul.

Bene. Enough! I am engaged; I will challenge him. I will kiss your hand, and so I leave you. By this hand, Claudio shall render me a dear account. As you hear of me, so think of me. Go, comfort your cousin: I must say she is dead; and so, farewell. *Exeunt.*

Scene II. *A prison.*

Enter the Constables *Dogberry*, *Verges*, and *Sexton* in gowns, and the *Watch*, with *Conrade* and *Borachio*.

Dog. Is our whole dissembly appeared?

Verg. O, a stool and a cushion for the sexton.

Sex. Which be the malefactors?

Dog. Marry, that am I and my partner.

Verg. Nay, that 's certain; we have the exhibition to examine.

Sex. But which are the offenders that are to be examined? Let them come before master constable.

Dog. Yea, marry, let them come before me. What is your name, friend?

Bora. Borachio.

Dog. Pray, write down Borachio. Yours, sirrah?

Con. I am a gentleman, sir, and my name is Conrade.

Dog. Write down, master gentleman Conrade. Masters, do you serve God?

Con. } *Bora.* } Yea, sir, we hope.

Dog. Write down, that they hope they serve God; and write God first; for God defend but God should go before such villains! Masters, it is proved already that you are little better than false knaves; and it will go near to be thought so shortly. How answer you for yourselves?

Con. Marry, sir, we say we are none.

Dog. A marvellous witty fellow, I assure you; but I will go about with him. Come you hither, sirrah; a word in your ear, sir. I say to you, it is thought you are false knaves.

Bora. Sir, I say to you we are none.

Dog. Well, stand aside. 'Fore God, they are both in a tale. Have you writ down, that they are none?

Sex. Master constable, you go not the way to examine: you must call forth the watch that are their accusers.

Dog. Yea, marry, that 's the eftest way. Let the watch come forth. Masters, I charge you, in the Prince's name, accuse these men.

1. Watch. This man said, sir, that Don John, the Prince's brother, was a villain.

Dog. Write down Prince John a villain. Why, this is flat perjury, to call a prince's brother villain.

Bora. Master constable,—

Dog. Pray thee, fellow, peace: I do not like thy look, I promise thee.

Sex. What heard you him say else?

2. Watch. Marry, that he had received a thousand ducats of Don John for accusing the Lady Hero wrongfully.

Dog. Flat burglary as ever was committed.

Verg. Yea, by mass, that it is.

Sex. What else, fellow?

1. Watch. And that Count Claudio did mean, upon his words, to disgrace Hero before the whole assembly, and not marry her.

Dog. O villain! thou wilt be condemned into everlasting redemption for this.

Sex. What else?

Watchmen. This is all.

Sex. And this is more, masters, than you can deny. Prince John is this morning secretly stolen away: Hero was in this manner accused,

305. bear her in hand, delude her by false promises. **307. uncovered,** open. **318. Comfect,** comfit, candy. **Scene ii: 6. exhibition,** legal term "allowance," misused by Verges.

28. go about with, circumvent. **33. both in a tale,** both tell the same story. **38. eftest,** quickest.

in this very manner refused, and upon the grief of this suddenly died. Master constable, let these men be bound, and brought to Leonato's: I will go before and show him their examination. *Exit.*

Dog. Come, let them be opinioned.

Verg. Let them be in the hands—

Con. Off, coxcomb!

Dog. God 's my life, where 's the sexton? Let him write down the Prince's officer coxcomb. Come, bind them. Thou naughty varlet!

Con. Away! you are an ass, you are an ass.

Dog. Dost thou not suspect my place? Dost thou not suspect my years? O that he were here to write me down an ass! But, masters, remember that I am an ass; though it be not written down, yet forget not that I am an ass. No, thou villain, thou art full of piety, as shall be proved upon thee by good witness. I am a wise fellow, and, which is more, an officer, and, which is more, a householder, and, which is more, as pretty a piece of flesh as any is in Messina, and one that knows the law, go to; and a rich fellow enough, go to; and a fellow that hath had losses, and one that hath two gowns and every thing handsome about him. Bring him away. O that I had been writ down an ass! *Exeunt.*

ACT V. Scene I. *Before Leonato's house.*

Enter *Leonato* and his brother *Antonio.*

Ant. If you go on thus, you will kill yourself;
And 't is not wisdom thus to second grief
Against yourself.

Leon. I pray thee, cease thy counsel,
Which falls into mine ears as profitless
As water in a sieve: give not me counsel;
Nor let no comforter delight mine ear
But such a one whose wrongs do suit with mine.
Bring me a father that so lov'd his child,
Whose joy of her is overwhelm'd like mine,
And bid him speak of patience;
Measure his woe the length and breadth of mine,
And let it answer every strain for strain,
As thus for thus, and such a grief for such,
In every lineament, branch, shape, and form;
If such a one will smile and stroke his beard,
And, sorry wag, cry "hem!" when he should groan,
Patch grief with proverbs, make misfortune drunk
With candle-wasters; bring him yet to me,
And I of him will gather patience.
But there is no such man; for, brother, men
Can counsel and speak comfort to that grief
Which they themselves not feel; but, tasting it,
Their counsel turns to passion, which before
Would give preceptial medicine to rage,
Fetter strong madness in a silken thread,
Charm ache with air and agony with words.
No, no; 't is all men's office to speak patience
To those that wring under the load of sorrow,
But no man's virtue nor sufficiency
To be so moral when he shall endure
The like himself. Therefore give me no counsel;
My griefs cry louder than advertisement.

Ant. Therein do men from children nothing differ.

Leon. I pray thee, peace: I will be flesh and blood;
For there was never yet philosopher
That could endure the toothache patiently,
However they have writ the style of gods
And made a push at chance and sufferance.

Ant. Yet bend not all the harm upon yourself;
Make those that do offend you suffer too.

Leon. There thou speak'st reason: nay, I will do so.
My soul doth tell me Hero is belied;
And that shall Claudio know; so shall the Prince
And all of them that thus dishonour her.

Enter *Don Pedro* and *Claudio.*

Ant. Here comes the Prince and Claudio hastily.

D. Pedro. Good den, good den.

Claud. Good day to both of you

Leon. Hear you, my lords,—

D. Pedro. We have some haste, Leonato

Act V, scene i: 7. suit, match. **16. sorry wag,** pitiful jester. **18. candle-wasters,** students. **24. preceptial,** made of precepts. **30. moral,** moralizing. **32. advertisement,** advice. **37. writ the style of gods,** claimed superiority to mankind. **38. made a push at,** pooh-poohed.

Leon. Some haste, my lord! Well, fare you well, my lord.
Are you so hasty now? Well, all is one.

D. Pedro. Nay, do not quarrel with us, good old man.

Ant. If he could right himself with quarrelling,
Some of us would lie low.

Claud. Who wrongs him?

Leon. Marry, thou dost wrong me; thou dissembler, thou,—
Nay, never lay thy hand upon thy sword;
I fear thee not.

Claud. Marry, beshrew my hand,
If it should give your age such cause of fear.
In faith, my hand meant nothing to my sword.

Leon. Tush, tush, man; never fleer and jest at me.
I speak not like a dotard nor a fool,
As under privilege of age to brag
What I have done being young, or what would do
Were I not old. Know, Claudio, to thy head,
Thou hast so wrong'd mine innocent child and me
That I am forc'd to lay my reverence by
And, with grey hairs and bruise of many days,
Do challenge thee to trial of a man.
I say thou hast belied mine innocent child!
Thy slander hath gone through and through her heart,
And she lies buried with her ancestors,
O, in a tomb where never scandal slept,
Save this of hers, fram'd by thy villainy!

Claud. My villainy?

Leon. Thine, Claudio; thine, I say.

D. Pedro. You say not right, old man.

Leon. My lord, my lord,
I 'll prove it on his body, if he dare,
Despite his nice fence and his active practice,
His May of youth and bloom of lustihood.

Claud. Away! I will not have to do with you.

Leon. Canst thou so daff me? Thou hast kill'd my child.
If thou kill'st me, boy, thou shalt kill a man.

Ant. He shall kill two of us, and men indeed.
But that 's no matter; let him kill one first.
Win me and wear me; let him answer me.
Come, follow me, boy; come, sir boy, come, follow me:
Sir boy, I 'll whip you from your foining fence;
Nay, as I am a gentleman, I will.

Leon. Brother,—

Ant. Content yourself. God knows I lov'd my niece;
And she is dead, slander'd to death by villains,
That dare as well answer a man indeed
As I dare take a serpent by the tongue.
Boys, apes, braggarts, Jacks, milksops!

Leon. Brother Antony,—

Ant. Hold you content. What, man! I know them, yea,
And what they weigh, even to the utmost scruple,—
Scambling, out-facing, fashion-monging boys,
That lie and cog and flout, deprave and slander,
Go anticly and show outward hideousness,
And speak off half a dozen dangerous words,
How they might hurt their enemies, if they durst;
And this is all.

Leon. But, brother Antony,—

Ant. Come, 't is no matter.
Do not you meddle; let me deal in this.

D. Pedro. Gentlemen both, we will not wake your patience.
My heart is sorry for your daughter's death;
But, on my honour, she was charg'd with nothing
But what was true and very full of proof.

Leon. My lord, my lord,—

D. Pedro. I will not hear you.

Leon. No? Come, brother, away! I will be heard.

Ant. And shall, or some of us will smart for it. *Exeunt Leonato and Antonio.*

Enter *Benedick*.

D. Pedro. See, see; here comes the man we went to seek.

Claud. Now, signior, what news?

Bene. Good day, my lord.

D. Pedro. Welcome, signior: you are almost come to part almost a fray.

Claud. We had liked to have had our two noses snapped off with two old men without teeth.

D. Pedro. Leonato and his brother. What think'st thou? Had we fought, I doubt we should have been too young for them.

Bene. In a false quarrel there is no true valour. I came to seek you both.

Claud. We have been up and down to seek thee; for we are high-proof melancholy and would fain have it beaten away. Wilt thou use thy wit?

Bene. It is in my scabbard; shall I draw it?

55. beshrew, curse. **58. fleer,** sneer. **75. fence,** fencing. **78. daff,** put off. **84. foining,** thrusting.

94. Scambling, quarrelsome. **out-facing,** swaggering. **95. cog,** cheat. **96. anticly,** fantastically dressed. **102. wake,** rouse. **123. high-proof,** high test, i.e., exceedingly.

Bendick challenges Claudio + says can no longer associate c̄ D. Pedro cs they killed Hero.

D. Pedro. Dost thou wear thy wit by thy side?

Claud. Never any did so, though very many have been beside their wit. I will bid thee draw, as we do the minstrels; draw, to pleasure us.

D. Pedro. As I am an honest man, he looks pale. Art thou sick, or angry?

Claud. What, courage, man! What though care killed a cat, thou hast mettle enough in thee to kill care.

Bene. Sir, I shall meet your wit in the career, an you charge it against me. I pray you choose another subject.

Claud. Nay, then, give him another staff: this last was broke across.

D. Pedro. By this light, he changes more and more. I think he be angry indeed.

Claud. If he be, he knows how to turn his girdle.

Bene. Shall I speak a word in your ear?

Claud. God bless me from a challenge!

Bene. [*Aside to Claudio.*] You are a villain: I jest not. I will make it good how you dare, with what you dare, and when you dare. Do me right, or I will protest your cowardice. You have killed a sweet lady, and her death shall fall heavy on you. Let me hear from you.

Claud. Well, I will meet you, so I may have good cheer.

D. Pedro. What, a feast, a feast?

Claud. I' faith, I thank him. He hath bid me to a calf's head and a capon; the which if I do not carve most curiously, say my knife 's naught. Shall I not find a woodcock too?

Bene. Sir, your wit ambles well; it goes easily.

D. Pedro. I 'll tell thee how Beatrice praised thy wit the other day. I said, thou hadst a fine wit. "True," said she, "a fine little one." "No," said I, "a great wit." "Right," says she, "a great gross one." "Nay," said I, "a good wit." "Just," said she, "it hurts nobody." "Nay," said I, "the gentleman is wise." "Certain," said she, "a wise gentleman." "Nay," said I, "he hath the tongues." "That I believe," said she, "for he swore a thing to me on Monday night, which he forswore on Tuesday morning. There 's a double tongue; there 's two tongues." Thus did she, an hour together, trans-shape thy particular virtues; yet at last she concluded with a sigh, thou wast the proper'st man in Italy.

Claud. For the which she wept heartily and said she cared not.

D. Pedro. Yea, that she did; but yet, for all that, an if she did not hate him deadly, she would love him dearly. The old man's daughter told us all.

Claud. All, all; and, moreover, God saw him when he was hid in the garden.

D. Pedro. But when shall we set the savage bull's horns on the sensible Benedick's head?

Claud. Yea, and text underneath, "Here dwells Benedick the married man"?

Bene. Fare you well, boy; you know my mind. I will leave you now to your gossip-like humour: you break jests as braggarts do their blades, which, God be thanked, hurt not. My lord, for your many courtesies I thank you: I must discontinue your company. Your brother the bastard is fled from Messina: you have among you killed a sweet and innocent lady. For my Lord Lackbeard there, he and I shall meet; and, till then, peace be with him. *Exit.*

D. Pedro. He is in earnest.

Claud. In most profound earnest; and, I 'll warrant you, for the love of Beatrice.

D. Pedro. And hath challenged thee?

Claud. Most sincerely.

D. Pedro. What a pretty thing man is when he goes in his doublet and hose and leaves off his wit!

Claud. He is then a giant to an ape; but then is an ape a doctor to such a man.

D. Pedro. But, soft you, let me be: pluck up, my heart, and be sad. Did he not say, my brother was fled?

Enter Constables *Dogberry, Verges,* and the Watch, with *Conrade* and *Borachio.*

Dog. Come you, sir: if justice cannot tame you, she shall ne'er weigh more reasons in her balance: nay, an you be a cursing hypocrite once, you must be looked to.

D. Pedro. How now? Two of my brother's men bound! Borachio one!

Claud. Hearken after their offence, my lord.

D. Pedro. Officers, what offence have these men done?

Dog. Marry, sir, they have committed false report; moreover, they have spoken untruths; secondarily, they are slanders; sixth and lastly, they have belied a lady; thirdly,

135-6. in the career, in the lists. **138. staff,** lance. **139. broke across,** a skillfully handled lance in a tournament would either unseat an opponent or be shivered from end to end. Clumsy handling would result in its being broken across. **142-3. turn his girdle,** this is variously explained. It may mean the scornful "If you don't like it, you can lump it"; or it may mean the turning of the belt buckle to the rear in preparation for combat. **148. protest,** proclaim. **157. curiously,** carefully. **158. woodcock,** a stupid bird. **167. hath the tongues,** is a linguist.

171. trans-shape, distort. **205. giant,** i.e., in stature. **216. Hearken after,** ask about.

they have verified unjust things; and, to conclude, they are lying knaves.

D. Pedro. First, I ask thee what they have done; thirdly, I ask thee what 's their offence; sixth and lastly, why they are committed; and, to conclude, what you lay to their charge.

Claud. Rightly reasoned, and in his own division; and, by my troth, there 's one meaning well suited.

D. Pedro. Who have you offended, masters, that you are thus bound to your answer? This learned constable is too cunning to be understood. What 's your offence?

Bora. Sweet Prince, let me go no farther to mine answer: do you hear me, and let this Count kill me. I have deceived even your very eyes: what your wisdoms could not discover, these shallow fools have brought to light, who in the night overheard me confessing to this man how Don John your brother incensed me to slander the Lady Hero, how you were brought into the orchard and saw me court Margaret in Hero's garments, how you disgraced her, when you should marry her. My villainy they have upon record; which I had rather seal with my death than repeat over to my shame. The lady is dead upon mine and my master's false accusation; and, briefly, I desire nothing but the reward of a villain.

D. Pedro. Runs not this speech like iron through your blood?

Claud. I have drunk poison whiles he utter'd it.

D. Pedro. But did my brother set thee on to this?

Bora. Yea, and paid me richly for the practice of it.

D. Pedro. He is compos'd and fram'd of treachery,
And fled he is upon this villainy.

Claud. Sweet Hero! now thy image doth appear
In the rare semblance that I lov'd it first.

Dog. Come, bring away the plaintiffs: by this time our sexton hath reformed Signior Leonato of the matter; and, masters, do not forget to specify, when time and place shall serve, that I am an ass.

Verg. Here, here comes master Signior Leonato, and the sexton too.

Re-enter *Leonato* and *Antonio*, with the *Sexton*.

Leon. Which is the villain? Let me see his eyes,
That, when I note another man like him,
I may avoid him. Which of these is he?

Bora. If you would know your wronger, look on me.

Leon. Art thou the slave that with thy breath has kill'd
Mine innocent child?

Bora. Yea, even I alone.

Leon. No, not so, villain; thou beliest thyself.
Here stand a pair of honourable men,—
A third is fled—that had a hand in it.
I thank you, princes, for my daughter's death.
Record it with your high and worthy deeds.
'T was bravely done, if you bethink you of it.

Claud. I know not how to pray your patience;
Yet I must speak. Choose your revenge yourself;
Impose me to what penance your invention
Can lay upon my sin; yet sinn'd I not
But in mistaking.

D. Pedro. By my soul, nor I;
And yet, to satisfy this good old man,
I would bend under any heavy weight
That he 'll enjoin me to.

Leon. I cannot bid you bid my daughter live,—
That were impossible—but, I pray you both,
Possess the people in Messina here
How innocent she died; and if your love
Can labour ought in sad invention,
Hang her an epitaph upon her tomb
And sing it to her bones, sing it to-night.
To-morrow morning come you to my house,
And since you could not be my son-in-law,
Be yet my nephew: my brother hath a daughter,
Almost the copy of my child that 's dead,
And she alone is heir to both of us.
Give her the right you should have given her cousin,
And so dies my revenge.

Claud. O noble sir,
Your over-kindness doth wring tears from me!
I do embrace your offer; and dispose
For henceforth of poor Claudio.

Leon. To-morrow then I will expect your coming;
To-night I take my leave. This naughty man
Shall face to face be brought to Margaret,
Who I believe was pack'd in all this wrong,
Hir'd to it by your brother.

Bora. No, by my soul, she was not,
Nor knew not what she did when she spoke to me,

231. well suited, well clothed. In the preceding speech the same meaning is put in four different ways or "suits." **241. incensed,** instigated.

291. possess, inform. **309. pack'd,** confederate.

But always hath been just and virtuous
In any thing that I do know by her.

Dog. Moreover, sir, which indeed is not under white and black, this plaintiff here, the offender, did call me ass: I beseech you, let it be remembered in his punishment. And also, the watch heard them talk of one Deformed: they say he wears a key in his ear and a lock hanging by it, and borrows money in God's name, the which he hath used so long and never paid that now men grow hard-hearted and will lend nothing for God's sake: pray you, examine him upon that point.

Leon. I thank thee for thy care and honest pains.

Dog. Your worship speaks like a most thankful and reverend youth, and I praise God for you.

Leon. There 's for thy pains.

Dog. God save the foundation!

Leon. Go, I discharge thee of thy prisoner, and I thank thee.

Dog. I leave an arrant knave with your worship; which I beseech your worship to correct yourself, for the example of others. God keep your worship! I wish your worship well. God restore you to health! I humbly give you leave to depart; and if a merry meeting may be wished, God prohibit it! Come, neighbour. *Exeunt Dogberry and Verges.*

Leon. Until to-morrow morning, lords, farewell.

Ant. Farewell, my lords: we look for you to-morrow.

D. Pedro. We will not fail.

Claud. To-night I 'll mourn with Hero.

Leon. [*To the Watch.*] Bring you these fellows on. We 'll talk with Margaret,
How her acquaintance grew with this lewd fellow. *Exeunt.*

Scene II. *Leonato's garden.*

Enter *Benedick* and *Margaret.*

Bene. Pray thee, sweet Mistress Margaret, deserve well at my hands by helping me to the speech of Beatrice.

Marg. Will you then write me a sonnet in praise of my beauty?

Bene. In so high a style, Margaret, that no man living shall come over it; for, in most comely truth, thou deservest it.

Marg. To have no man come over me! Why, shall I always keep below stairs?

Bene. Thy wit is as quick as the greyhound's mouth; it catches.

Marg. And yours as blunt as the fencer's foils, which hit, but hurt not.

Bene. A most manly wit, Margaret; it will not hurt a woman: and so, I pray thee, call Beatrice; I give thee the bucklers.

Marg. Give us the swords; we have bucklers of our own.

Bene. If you use them, Margaret, you must put in the pikes with a vice; and they are dangerous weapons for maids.

Marg. Well, I will call Beatrice to you, who I think hath legs. *Exit Margaret.*

Bene. And therefore will come.

Sings.

The god of love,
That sits above,
And knows me, and knows me,
How pitiful I deserve,—

I mean in singing; but in loving, Leander the good swimmer, Troilus the first employer of panders, and a whole bookful of these quondam carpet-mongers, whose names yet run smoothly in the even road of a blank verse, why, they were never so truly turned over and over as my poor self in love. Marry, I cannot show it in rhyme: I have tried: I can find out no rhyme to "lady" but "baby," an innocent rhyme; for "scorn," "horn," a hard rhyme; for "school," "fool," a babbling rhyme, very ominous endings: no, I was not born under a rhyming planet, nor I cannot woo in festival terms.

Enter *Beatrice.*

Sweet Beatrice, wouldst thou come when I called thee?

Beat. Yea, signior, and depart when you bid me.

Bene. O, stay but till then!

Beat. "Then" is spoken; fare you well now: and yet, ere I go, let me go with that I came for; which is, with knowing what hath passed between you and Claudio.

Bene. Only foul words; and thereupon I will kiss thee.

Beat. Foul words is but foul wind, and foul wind is but foul breath, and foul breath is noisome; therefore I will depart unkissed.

Bene. Thou hast frighted the word out of his right sense, so forcible is thy wit. But I must tell thee plainly, Claudio undergoes my challenge; and either I must shortly hear from him, or I will subscribe him a coward. And, I

312. by, of. **328. God save the foundation,** a phrase used in thanking a charitable foundation for assistance. **Scene ii: 6. style,** with pun on "stile." **7. come over,** (1) surpass, (2) mount (the stile). **10. keep below stairs,** remain a servant.

17. I . . . bucklers, I yield. **21. pikes,** spikes in buckler. **vice,** (1) screw, (2) sin. **32-3. quondam carpet-mongers,** carpet-knights of former times. **56. undergoes,** has received. **58. subscribe,** write down.

pray thee now, tell me for which of my bad parts didst thou first fall in love with me?

Beat. For them all together, which maintained so politic a state of evil that they will not admit any good part to intermingle with them. But for which of my good parts did you first suffer love for me?

Bene. Suffer love! a good epithet! I do suffer love indeed, for I love thee against my will.

Beat. In spite of your heart, I think; alas, poor heart! If you spite it for my sake, I will spite it for yours; for I will never love that which my friend hates.

Bene. Thou and I are too wise to woo peaceably.

Beat. It appears not in this confession: there 's not one wise man among twenty that will praise himself.

Bene. An old, an old instance, Beatrice, that lived in the time of good neighbours. If a man do not erect in this age his own tomb ere he dies, he shall live no longer in monument than the bell rings and the widow weeps.

Beat. And how long is that, think you?

Bene. Question! Why, an hour in clamour and a quarter in rheum; therefore is it most expedient for the wise, if Don Worm, his conscience, find no impediment to the contrary, to be the trumpet of his own virtues, as I am to myself. So much for praising myself, who, I myself will bear witness, is praiseworthy. And now tell me, how doth your cousin?

Beat. Very ill.

Bene. And how do you?

Beat. Very ill too.

Bene. Serve God, love me, and mend. There will I leave you too, for here comes one in haste.

Enter *Ursula.*

Urs. Madam, you must come to your uncle. Yonder 's old coil at home: it is proved my Lady Hero hath been falsely accused, the Prince and Claudio mightily abused; and Don John is the author of all, who is fled and gone. Will you come presently?

Beat. Will you go hear this news, signior?

Bene. I will live in thy heart, die in thy lap, and be buried in thy eyes; and moreover I will go with thee to thy uncle's. *Exeunt.*

78-9. An old instance . . . in the time of good neighbours, an old saying (instance) that existed in the good old days when neighbours praised each other. **84. rheum,** tears. **85. Don Worm,** in old miracle plays Conscience sometimes appeared as a worm, i.e., snake or dragon. **98. old coil, a great stir. 100. abused,** deceived.

Scene III. *A church-yard.*

Enter *Don Pedro, Claudio,* and three or four with tapers.

Claud. Is this the monument of Leonato?
A Lord. It is, my lord.
Claud. [*Reading out of a scroll.*]

Epitaph

"Done to death by slanderous tongues
Was the Hero that here lies.
Death, in guerdon of her wrongs,
Gives her fame which never dies.
So the life that died with shame
Lives in death with glorious fame."

Hang thou there upon the tomb,
Hanging up the scroll.
Praising her when I am dumb.
Now, music, sound, and sing your solemn hymn.

Song

"Pardon, goddess of the night,
Those that slew thy virgin knight;
For the which, with songs of woe,
Round about her tomb they go.
Midnight, assist our moan;
Help us to sigh and groan,
Heavily, heavily.
Graves, yawn and yield your dead,
Till death be uttered,
Heavily, heavily."

Claud. Now unto thy bones good night!
Yearly will I do this rite.
D. Pedro. Good morrow, masters; put your torches out.
The wolves have prey'd; and look, the gentle day,
Before the wheels of Phœbus, round about
Dapples the drowsy east with spots of grey.
Thanks to you all, and leave us: fare you well.
Claud. Good morrow, masters: each his several way.
D. Pedro. Come, let us hence, and put on other weeds;
And then to Leonato's we will go.
Claud. And Hymen now with luckier issue speeds
Than this for whom we render'd up this woe.
Exeunt.

Scene IV. *A room in Leonato's house.*

Enter *Leonato, Antonio, Benedick, Beatrice, Margaret, Ursula, Friar Francis,* and *Hero.*

Friar. Did I not tell you she was innocent?
Leon. So are the Prince and Claudio, who accus'd her

Scene iii: 20. uttered, expelled, i.e., at the Last Judgment. **30. weeds,** clothes.

Upon the error that you heard debated:
But Margaret was in some fault for this,
Although against her will, as it appears
In the true course of all the question.

Ant. Well, I am glad that all things sorts so well.

Bene. And so am I, being else by faith enforc'd
To call young Claudio to a reckoning for it.

Leon. Well, daughter, and you gentlewomen all,
Withdraw into a chamber by yourselves,
And when I send for you, come hither mask'd.
The Prince and Claudio promis'd by this hour
To visit me. You know your office, brother:
You must be father to your brother's daughter,
And give her to young Claudio.

Exeunt Ladies.

Ant. Which I will do with confirm'd countenance.

Bene. Friar, I must entreat your pains, I think.

Friar. To do what, signior?

Bene. To bind me, or undo me; one of them.
Signior Leonato, truth it is, good signior,
Your niece regards me with an eye of favour.

Leon. That eye my daughter lent her; 't is most true.

Bene. And I do with an eye of love requite her.

Leon. The sight whereof I think you had from me,
From Claudio, and the Prince. But what 's your will?

Bene. Your answer, sir, is enigmatical;
But, for my will, my will is your good will
May stand with ours, this day to be conjoin'd
In the state of honourable marriage;
In which, good friar, I shall desire your help.

Leon. My heart is with your liking.

Friar. And my help.
Here comes the Prince and Claudio.

Enter *Don Pedro* and *Claudio,* and two or three other.

D. Pedro. Good morrow to this fair assembly.

Leon. Good morrow, Prince; good morrow Claudio;
We here attend you. Are you yet determin'd
To-day to marry with my brother's daughter?

Claud. I 'll hold my mind, were she an Ethiope.

Leon. Call her forth, brother; here 's the friar ready. *Exit Antonio.*

D. Pedro. Good morrow, Benedick. Why, what 's the matter,
That you have such a February face,
So full of frost, of storm and cloudiness?

Claud. I think he thinks upon the savage bull.
Tush, fear not, man; we 'll tip thy horns with gold
And all Europa shall rejoice at thee,
As once Europa did at lusty Jove,
When he would play the noble beast in love.

Bene. Bull Jove, sir, had an amiable low;
And some such strange bull leap'd your father's cow,
And got a calf in that same noble feat
Much like to you, for you have just his bleat.

Re-enter *Antonio,* with the *Ladies* masked.

Claud. For this I owe you: here comes other reck'nings.
Which is the lady I must seize upon?

Ant. This same is she, and I do give you her.

Claud. Why, then she 's mine. Sweet, let me see your face.

Leon. No, that you shall not, till you take her hand
Before this friar and swear to marry her.

Claud. Give me your hand: before this holy friar:
I am your husband, if you like of me.

Hero. And when I liv'd, I was your other wife; *Unmasking*
And when you lov'd, you were my other husband.

Claud. Another Hero!

Hero. Nothing certainer.
One Hero died defil'd, but I do live;
And surely as I live, I am a maid.

D. Pedro. The former Hero! Hero that is dead!

Leon. She died, my lord, but whiles her slander liv'd.

Friar. All this amazement can I qualify;
When after that the holy rites are ended,
I 'll tell you largely of fair Hero's death.
Meantime let wonder seem familiar,
And to the chapel let us presently.

Bene. Soft and fair, friar. Which is Beatrice?

Beat. [*Unmasking.*] I answer to that name. What is your will?

Bene. Do not you love me?

Beat. Why, no; no more than reason.

Bene. Why, then your uncle and the Prince and Claudio
Have been deceived. They swore you did.

7. sorts, turn out. **17. confirm'd,** unmoved.

46-7. The allusion is to Jove's transforming himself into a bull and abducting Europa. Shakespeare knew the version in Ovid's *Metamorphoses.* **67. qualify,** moderate. **69. largely,** in detail.

Beat. Do not you love me?
Bene. Troth, no; no more than reason.
Beat. Why, then my cousin, Margaret, and Ursula
Are much deceiv'd, for they did swear you did.
Bene. They swore that you were almost sick for me.
Beat. They swore that you were well-nigh dead for me.
Bene. 'T is no such matter. Then you do not love me?
Beat. No truly, but in friendly recompense.
Leon. Come, cousin, I am sure you love the gentleman.
Claud. And I 'll be sworn upon 't that he loves her;
For here 's a paper written in his hand,
A halting sonnet of his own pure brain,
Fashion'd to Beatrice.
Hero. And here 's another
Writ in my cousin's hand, stol'n from her pocket,
Containing her affection unto Benedick.

Bene. A miracle! here 's our own hands against our hearts. Come, I will have thee; but, by this light, I take thee for pity.

Beat. I would not deny you; but, by this good day, I yield upon great persuasion; and partly to save your life, for I was told you were in a consumption.

Bene. Peace! I will stop your mouth.

Kissing her.

D. Pedro. How dost thou, Benedick, the married man?

Bene. I 'll tell thee what, Prince; a college of wit-crackers cannot flout me out of my humour. Dost thou think I care for a satire or an epigram? No; if a man will be beaten with brains, 'a shall wear nothing handsome about him. In brief, since I do purpose to marry, I will think nothing to any purpose that the world can say against it; and therefore never flout at me for what I have said against it, for man is a giddy thing, and this is my conclusion. For thy part, Claudio, I did think to have beaten thee; but in that thou art like to be my kinsman, live unbruised and love my cousin.

Claud. I had well hoped thou wouldst have denied Beatrice, that I might have cudgelled thee out of thy single life, to make thee a double-dealer; which, out of question, thou wilt be, if my cousin do not look exceeding narrowly to thee.

Bene. Come, come, we are friends: let 's have a dance ere we are married, that we may lighten our own hearts and our wives' heels.

Leon. We 'll have dancing afterward.

Bene. First, of my word; therefore play, music. Prince, thou art sad; get thee a wife, get thee a wife: there is no staff more reverend than one tipped with horn.

Enter a *Messenger.*

Mess. My lord, your brother John is ta'en in flight,
And brought with armed men back to Messina.
Bene. Think not on him till to-morrow: I 'll devise thee brave punishments for him. Strike up, pipers. *Dance. Exeunt.*

116. double-dealer, (1) **a married man,** (2) **an unfaithful husband.**

As You Like It

As You Like It, one of the happiest of Shakespeare's comedies, presents few problems of interest to the critical student. It is rather a play to be enjoyed than analyzed, delightful on the stage, more fascinating still, perhaps, in the study.

Text.—It appears in print for the first time in the Folio of 1623, but there is evidence that publication was at least contemplated many years earlier. On August 4, 1600, it was entered in the Stationers' Register along with *Henry V, Much Ado,* and Jonson's *Everyman In* as plays "to be staid." Shakespeare's company probably allowed their printer Roberts to make this entry in the hope of forestalling unauthorized publication of this group of new plays. In this attempt they were only partially successful. The popular *Henry V* escaped their hands and was published in a badly reported version in that very year. *Much Ado* and *Everyman In* were later entered and published in proper form. *As You Like It,* however, was still "staid," possibly because it was so good a drawing card that the company declined to allow its publication.

The text of the Folio is in the main satisfactory. It was probably set up from a transcript of the theatrical prompt-book.

Date.—It is possible to fix the date of *As You Like It* within fairly close limits. It must be later than 1598, since it is not included in the Meres catalogue of that year, and it must precede the entry of 1600 already mentioned. Inasmuch as the clown's part of Touchstone is evidently designed for a new member of the company rather than for Kemp, who deserted his old fellows in 1599, it seems fairly certain that Shakespeare wrote the play late in 1599 and brought it out early in 1600.

Source.—Lodge's pastoral romance *Rosalynde* has long been recognized as the source of Shakespeare's play. The story, Lodge tells us, was written on shipboard to beguile the tedium of a voyage, ca. 1588, to the Canaries. Lodge's work, in turn, rests upon a late medieval poem, *Gamelyn,* falsely ascribed to Chaucer. *Gamelyn* is the tale of a younger brother, abused by his elder, who triumphs in a wrestling match, escapes the machinations of his brother, flies to the woods, becomes captain of a band of outlaws, hangs his brother, now the King's sheriff—a genuine Robin Hood touch—and ends as a loyal subject of the King. Much of this Lodge retained, but he softened the harsh ending by bringing about a reconciliation between the brothers and attaching them both to the party of an exiled King of France. He did more than this, however; the main interest of his story centers about the love affair of Rosader (Shakespeare's Orlando) and Rosalynde, daughter of the banished King. This is set in the Forest of Arden to which both the lady and her lover have fled, he from the plots of his wicked brother; she disguised as Ganymede in the company of the usurper's daughter, Alinda, later called Aliena. Lodge's tale, though rather long-drawn-out and packed with highly euphuistic speeches by the lovers, is well worth reading. It is a characteristic bit of Elizabethan prose, diversified by a group of charming lyrics and stressing in genuine Elizabethan fashion the love-interest entirely wanting in the tale of Gamelyn.

Enough has been said to show how closely in the main outlines Shakespeare follows his source: the quarrel between the brothers, the wrestling match, the flight to Arden, the wooing of the disguised heroine by her lover, even the minor love affair of Phebe and Silvius, and the marriage of the repentant elder brother to Celia, all come from Lodge. The somewhat puzzling title of Shakespeare's play was probably suggested by a phrase in Lodge's dedication of his tale: "If you like it, so." Evidently Shakespeare thought they did like it, and liked it well enough to pay to see it on the stage. What Shakespeare has left out as unsuitable to his bright pastoral play are the more violent incidents which Lodge took over from *Gamelyn.* He altered names at will: Rosader and Saladyne of the story become Orlando and Oliver—names suggested by Lodge's mention of the twelve peers of France—Alinda becomes Celia, and the two Kings, Torismond and Gerismond, appear in the play as Duke Frederick and his nameless banished brother.

Characters.—What Shakespeare added to his source, however, is of more importance than his omissions or minor alterations. A number of characters appear for the first time. Some of them are merely incidental, like the courtier Le Beau and the singing lords in the forest. Others are introduced for a very definite dramatic purpose. To add a touch of true country life to the fantastic pastoralism of Lodge's tale Shakespeare invents the old shepherd Corin whose hands are greasy with handling his ewes, the country wench Audrey who knows not the word "poetical," and her discarded suitor, the country bumpkin, William. Like the rude mechanicals of *Midsummer Night's Dream* these figures give a background of reality to the scene.

In contrast to this group of rustics Shakespeare introduces the Court Fool, Touchstone. It was Shakespeare's business, of course, to provide in every play a good part for the comedian of his company. Up to the summer of 1599 Kemp had been the clown of the company, and for Kemp, Shakespeare had written such parts as Peter in *Romeo and Juliet,* bully Bottom, and the immortal Dogberry. There is a family likeness in all these roles; they are bumptious, conceited, and withal stupid, characters to be laughed at. But Armin, who succeeded Kemp, was of a different type, in a small way an author as well as an actor, and something of a wit. It was for him that Shakespeare created the role of Touchstone, the professional jester, a role that looks forward to Feste, and to the wonderful part of the Fool in *Lear*. He has little real connection with the story; the plot develops along the lines of the source without his interference. He stands aside to laugh and mock, to parody the fantastic love-affair of Silvius and Phebe by his frankly sensual pursuit of Audrey, to dumbfound the rustics by his display of learning and logic, and to make a mockery of the shams and conventions of Court life. He is a sharp wind of realism blowing upon the pastoral convention of the play.

Jaques also is Shakespeare's addition to the *dramatis personæ*. Like Touchstone he has no prototype in the source, and like him he has no effective action in the plot. Yet the play would be the poorer without Jaques. He is a "humour" character such as Jonson in these last years had been bringing upon the boards of Shakespeare's theatre. His "humour" is that of melancholy; in the phrase of the day he is a malcontent. Where Touchstone laughs and mocks, Jaques sneers and satirizes. Yet Jaques is not a mere type character; Shakespeare has taken some pains to individualize him. He has been a traveller and, it would seem, indulged in all the vices which the Elizabethan Englishman ascribed to foreign lands; the Duke calls him "a libertine, as sensual as the brutish sting." He has come back with experience indeed, but it is an experience that saddens him. His famous speech, "All the world's a stage," is a theatrical expansion of the Preacher's *vanitas vanitatum.* We are not told how he drifted into Arden; he seems out of place there, a passing shadow on that sunny life. It is interesting to note that he does not return to the life he despises when the banished Duke is restored to his throne; on the contrary he seeks out the cell of the penitent usurper to converse with him, for there is much matter to be learned from these convertites; Jaques is for other than the dancing measures of the general marrying with which the play ends.

Of the characters who make up the main action of the play there is, with one exception, little to be said. Duke Frederick is a bad-tempered and capricious tyrant; he escapes the fate suffered by Torismond in the story only because Shakespeare does not wish to mar his happy ending by anybody's death. His banished brother is a friendly and genial soul, the mouthpiece of some lovely poetry, but otherwise a rather indistinct figure. The two brothers Oliver and Orlando are of course sharply contrasted in the play as in the story. Oliver is a designing villain, a little too bad, perhaps, to be true. His sudden repentance and reconciliation is hardly credible, but here Shakespeare is following his source and is evidently hurrying on to his conclusion. The same may be said of the sudden love which springs up between him and Celia—"they no sooner met but they looked, no sooner looked but they loved" and so on. Again Shakespeare is following his source; but while the scope of the novel allows some time for Oliver's counterpart to win the love of Aliena, Shakespeare's haste and the convention of Elizabethan comedy, which insisted on the marriage of all marriageable females in the play, forced him to dismiss the matter in the brief report by Rosalind already quoted. This particular marriage has been denounced as an ugly blot on the shining canvas of the play, but it is hardly to be taken seriously. Certainly matters were not mended when an eighteenth century adapter handed Celia over to Jaques —a device followed by George Sand in her adaptation.

Orlando, the hero of the main plot, is a fine upstanding young fellow. Less sentimental than Romeo who precedes or Orsino who follows him, he is a typical example of the athletic young Englishman. High-spirited, handsome, strong, and brave, he is just the man to win a lady's heart, and if his wit is no match for the sparkling effervescence of Rosalind, the match is none the worse for that. He and his Rosalind are less likely to wrangle than such an evenly matched pair in the war of wits as Benedick and Beatrice.

Silvius and Phebe, drawn like the other lovers from the source, are not so much real characters as stock figures of the pastoral romance, the hopeless lover and the hard-hearted lady. His somewhat lacrimose devotion and her sudden passion for the youth Ganymede, who has upbraided her so roundly, are a designed contrast to the natural human affection which springs up at first sight between Orlando and Rosalind, even as her affected scorn of Silvius contrasts with Rosalind's merry and mocking play with her true lover. They represent, it would seem, Shakespeare's sense of the unreality and absurdity of the extravagances of the pastoral romance so popular in his day.

The one exception already referred to is, of course, Rosalind. Like the other persons of the main plot this character derives from the source, but Shakespeare has wrought on her a complete transfiguration. Lodge's Rosalynd is a rather long-winded lady who decorates her speech with the choicest flowers of euphuism, is given to balancing *pros* and *cons,* and indulges at times in citations from the classic poets. She has none of Rosalind's mirth and mingled wit and tenderness. Of all the "wise girls that mock their lovers" in the gay gallery of Shakespeare's comedies, Rosalind is perhaps the most charming. Less sharp of tongue and aggressive of temper than Beatrice, less imbued with tender sentiment than Viola, the heroines nearest to her in the succession of Shakespeare's plays, she has a fascination that is all her own. This fascination indeed does not appear at first; the Rosalind of the first act is a rather timid girl living on sufferance at the usurper's court under the protection of her gentle cousin. But once she dons doublet and hose and escapes to the greenwood, she becomes another creature. It is as if her creator's spirit caught fire when he brought her out of the court into the freedom of the woods and fields. There she finds the youth whom she has already learned to love, though with none of the passion of Juliet or the hopeless longing of Viola, and her frank delight in listening, disguised as a boy, to his protestations of love for his Rosalind, and her mischievous joy in mocking his vows, give rise to the gayest and wittiest scenes of the whole play. It is an interesting example of Shakespeare's transforming power, that while Lodge's Ganymede offers to play the part of Rosalind to her lover, Shakespeare's lady does so with the professed purpose of curing him of the disease of love. Rosalind alone of Shakespeare's heroines has the happy lot of loving and finding herself beloved, without the necessity of fighting for her love against parental control or outward circumstance. And with all her audacious wit and mockery there is something essentially feminine in Rosalind, a quality that shows itself alike in her rebuke of Phebe for scorning a good man's love and in her sudden swoon at the sight of her lover's blood.

Construction.—As You Like It is anything but a well-made play. It has little or no plot interest; spectator and reader alike are sure from the beginning that Rosalind will get her lover and the banished Duke regain his throne. There is no threat of impending disaster such as heightens the interest in *Much Ado,* no such laughable entrapping of a comic figure as enlivens *Twelfth Night.* The denouement, in particular, is hasty, not to say hurried; the mythological Hymen is strangely out of place in the forest of Arden. Shakespeare did better than this when he devised the wedding-masque in *The Tempest.* There are, it would seem, two reasons for this weakness of construction. In the first place Shakespeare is simply dramatizing a popular novel; it had entertained readers for a decade or more, and he knew that it would amuse spectators in his theatre. The story that he dramatized is slow-moving and rather incoherent, but it was a good story and Shakespeare held fast to its main outline. Some of the changes that he made have already been noted. The hasty Hymeneal conclusion is evidently Shakespeare's device to cut down the long-drawn-out close of Lodge's story and to end his play with music, a masque, and dancing.

Moreover there is some reason to suppose that Shakespeare spent little time or thought on the composition of this play. The year 1599-1600 must have been one of the busiest of his life. His company had just moved into their new theatre, the Globe, and Shakespeare as shareholder, actor, and playwright had his hands extremely full. *As You Like It* falls between two of his best constructed comedies, *Much Ado* and *Twelfth Night;* it comes in the same year that saw the first of his long roll of tragedies, *Julius Cæsar,* at a time when he was probably wrestling with the problem of the reconstruction of the old *Hamlet.* Instead of blaming Shakespeare for the transparent dramatic faults of *As You Like It,* we should be grateful for what he has given us.

For *As You Like It* is a joy forever; it is something better than a well-made play. It is a romance of true love, of freedom, and of happiness, set against a background of Robin Hood's greenwood. The atmosphere, in fact, means more to the sympathetic reader than the action. As we surrender to the spell of Shakespeare's magic we, too, are free for the moment from the conventions and restraints of this work-a-day world, and linger in an enchanted wood to listen to the moralizing of Jaques, the jests of Touchstone, the laughing wit of Rosalind, and last but by no means least the lovely songs with which Shakespeare has adorned this play. If he put little intellectual labor into the construction of the plot, he lavished the treasures of his genius on the sparkling prose, the lyric verse, and above all on the creation of the ideal lady of this world of fantasy, the well-beloved Rosalind.

Stage History.—Little or nothing is known of the early history of *As You Like It* on the stage. There is a credible, if not substantiated, tradition that it was one of the first plays that James I saw in England, played before him at Wilton while the plague raged in London in December, 1603. Another tradition of even less authority, but quite possibly rooted in theatrical reminiscence, declares that Shakespeare himself played the part of Adam. We have no record of a performance in Restoration times and indeed no play of Shakespeare's was less fitted to please the sophisticated urban audience of that day than this carefree romance. In 1723 the first attempt was made to bring *As You Like It* back to the stage. This adaptation, *Love in a Forest,* was the work of a practical playwright, Charles Johnson, but his practice was one that would evoke loud cries of reprobation today. He altered the plot at will, set Orlando and Charles fighting with rapiers like Hamlet and Laertes, lifted lines from other plays to pad thin parts, and introduced the burlesque of Pyramus and Thisbe as an entertainment before the banished Duke. Colley Cibber played the part of Jaques and it was no doubt his influence as actor-manager which led to the fattening of his part and to his acquisition of Celia in marriage.

A better era begins in 1740 with a performance at Drury Lane, when Quin, the famous Falstaff of the day, played the part of Jaques and the charming actresses, Mrs. Pritchard and Kitty Clive, took the roles of Rosalind and Celia. From that time on *As You Like It* has held the stage, as a rule in comparatively unaltered form. Its popularity is in the main due to the fact that a long line of great actresses found the role of Rosalind an almost perfect vehicle for their art; Peg Woffington, Mrs. Barry, "tender, animated, and playful," and Mrs. Jordan, all were famous Rosalinds. Strange as it may seem, the queen of tragedy, Mrs. Siddons, also played this part. Macready staged a beautiful production at Covent Garden in the late 1830s, and Helen Faucit, who at one time played Rosalind under him, was called the perfect embodiment of that role.

It has always been a popular play in America, where it was first performed by an English company in 1786. Daly's adaptation of the play, 1889-90, was glorified by Ada Rehan's impersonation of a Rosalind, "all sweetness and brilliancy." The long partnership of Sothern and Marlowe carried it in their repertoire, and in Ben Greet's company the sweet-voiced Edith Wynn Matheson was a very lovely Rosalind.

AS YOU LIKE IT

Dramatis Personæ

Duke, living in banishment.
Frederick, his brother, and usurper of his dominions.
Amiens, *Jaques*, } lords attending on the banished *Duke*.
Le Beau, a courtier attending upon *Frederick*.
Charles, wrestler to *Frederick*.
Oliver, *Jaques*, *Orlando*, } sons of *Sir Roland de Boys*.
Adam, *Dennis*, } servants to *Oliver*.
Touchstone, a clown.
Sir Oliver Martext, a vicar.
Corin, *Silvius*, } shepherds.
William, a country fellow, in love with *Audrey*.
A person representing *Hymen*.

Rosalind, daughter to the banished *Duke*.
Celia, daughter to *Frederick*.
Phebe, a shepherdess.
Audrey, a country wench.

Lords, pages, attendants, etc.

SCENE: *Oliver's house; Duke Frederick's court; and the Forest of Arden.*

ACT I. SCENE I. *Orchard of Oliver's house.*

Enter *Orlando* and *Adam*.

Orl. As I remember, Adam, it was upon this fashion: bequeathed me by will but poor a thousand crowns, and, as thou sayest, charged my brother, on his blessing, to breed me well; and there begins my sadness. My brother Jaques he keeps at school, and report speaks goldenly of his profit: for my part, he keeps me rustically at home, or, to speak more properly, stays me here at home unkept; for call you that keeping for a gentleman of my birth, that differs not from the stalling of an ox? His horses are bred better; for, besides that they are fair with their feeding, they are taught their manage, and to that end riders dearly hired; but I, his brother, gain nothing under him but growth; for the which his animals on his dunghills are as much bound to him as I. Besides this nothing that he so plentifully gives me, the something that nature gave me his countenance seems to take from me: he lets me feed with his hinds, bars me the place of a brother, and, as much as in him lies, mines my gentility with my education. This is it, Adam, that grieves me; and the spirit of my father, which I think is within me, begins to mutiny against this servitude. I will no longer endure it, though yet I know no wise remedy how to avoid it.

Enter *Oliver*.

Adam. Yonder comes my master, your brother.

Orl. Go apart, Adam, and thou shalt hear how he will shake me up.

Oli. Now, sir! what make you here?

Orl. Nothing. I am not taught to make any thing.

Oli. What mar you then, sir?

Orl. Marry, sir, I am helping you to mar that which God made, a poor unworthy brother of yours, with idleness.

Oli. Marry, sir, be better employed, and be naught awhile.

Orl. Shall I keep your hogs and eat husks with them? What prodigal portion have I spent, that I should come to such penury?

Oli. Know you where you are, sir?

Orl. O, sir, very well; here in your orchard.

Oli. Know you before whom, sir?

Orl. Ay, better than him I am before knows me. I know you are my eldest brother; and, in the gentle condition of blood, you should so know me. The courtesy of nations allows you my better, in that you are the first-born; but the same tradition takes not away my blood, were there twenty brothers betwixt us: I have as much of my father in me as you; albeit, I confess, your coming before me is nearer to his reverence.

Oli. What, boy! *Strikes him.*

Orl. Come, come, elder brother, you are too young in this. *Seizes him.*

Oli. Wilt thou lay hands on me, villain?

Orl. I am no villain; I am the youngest son

4. on his blessing, on condition of obtaining his blessing. **breed,** educate. **6. school,** university. **7. profit,** proficiency. **9. stays,** detains. **14. manage,** action and paces. **20. countenance,** treatment. **21. hinds,** menials. **23. mines,** undermines.

31. make, do. **39. be naught awhile,** a proverbial petty curse. Sometimes=merely "get you gone." **49. courtesy of nations,** acknowledgment of the law of primogeniture by all nations. **53-4. your coming before . . . reverence,** your being older than I gives you a nearer claim to the respect which was due him.

of Sir Roland de Boys. He was my father, and he is thrice a villain that says such a father begot villains. Wert thou not my brother, I would not take this hand from thy throat till this other had pulled out thy tongue for saying so: thou hast railed on thyself.

Adam. Sweet masters, be patient; for your father's remembrance, be at accord.

Oli. Let me go, I say.

Orl. I will not, till I please: you shall hear me. My father charged you in his will to give me a good education: you have trained me like a peasant, obscuring and hiding from me all gentleman-like qualities. The spirit of my father grows strong in me, and I will no longer endure it; therefore allow me such exercises as may become a gentleman, or give me the poor allottery my father left me by testament: with that I will go buy my fortunes.

Oli. And what wilt thou do? Beg, when that is spent? Well, sir, get you in. I will not long be troubled with you; you shall have some part of your will: I pray you, leave me.

Orl. I will no further offend you than becomes me for my good.

Oli. Get you with him, you old dog.

Adam. Is "old dog" my reward? Most true, I have lost my teeth in your service. God be with my old master! He would not have spoke such a word.

Exeunt Orlando and Adam.

Oli. Is it even so? Begin you to grow upon me? I will physic your rankness, and yet give no thousand crowns neither. Holla, Dennis!

Enter *Dennis.*

Den. Calls your worship?

Oli. Was not Charles, the Duke's wrestler, here to speak with me?

Den. So please you, he is here at the door and importunes access to you.

Oli. Call him in. [*Exit Dennis.*] 'T will be a good way; and to-morrow the wrestling is.

Enter *Charles.*

Cha. Good morrow to your worship.

Oli. Good Monsieur Charles, what 's the new news at the new court?

Cha. There 's no news at the court, sir, but the old news: that is, the old Duke is banished by his younger brother the new Duke; and three or four loving lords have put themselves into voluntary exile with him, whose lands and revenues enrich the new Duke; therefore he gives them good leave to wander.

Oli. Can you tell if Rosalind, the Duke's daughter, be banished with her father?

Cha. O, no; for the Duke's daughter, her cousin, so loves her, being ever from their cradles bred together, that she would have followed her exile, or have died to stay behind her. She is at the court, and no less beloved of her uncle than his own daughter; and never two ladies loved as they do.

Oli. Where will the old Duke live?

Cha. They say he is already in the forest of Arden, and a many merry men with him; and there they live like the old Robin Hood of England. They say many young gentlemen flock to him every day, and fleet the time carelessly, as they did in the golden world.

Oli. What, you wrestle to-morrow before the new Duke?

Cha. Marry, do I, sir; and I came to acquaint you with a matter. I am given, sir, secretly to understand that your younger brother, Orlando, hath a disposition to come in disguised against me to try a fall. To-morrow, sir, I wrestle for my credit; and he that escapes me without some broken limb shall acquit him well. Your brother is but young and tender; and, for your love, I would be loath to foil him, as I must, for my own honour, if he come in; therefore, out of my love to you, I came hither to acquaint you withal, that either you might stay him from his intendment, or brook such disgrace well as he shall run into, in that it is a thing of his own search, and altogether against my will.

Oli. Charles, I thank thee for thy love to me, which thou shalt find I will most kindly requite. I had myself notice of my brother's purpose herein, and have by underhand means laboured to dissuade him from it, but he is resolute. I 'll tell thee, Charles, it is the stubbornest young fellow of France; full of ambition, an envious emulator of every man's good parts, a secret and villanous contriver against me his natural brother; therefore use thy discretion; I had as lief thou didst break his neck as his finger. And thou wert best look to 't; for if thou dost him any slight disgrace, or if he do not mightily grace himself on thee, he will practise against thee by poison, entrap thee by some treacherous device, and never leave thee till he hath ta'en thy life by some indirect means or other; for, I assure thee, (and almost with

61. **villain,** Orlando plays upon the other meaning of the word, i.e., "serf." 66-7. **for your father's remembrance,** in remembrance of your father. 77. **allottery,** allotment. 90. **grow upon,** take liberties with. 91. **rankness,** exuberant growth: here insolence. 109. **good leave,** easy permission.

121. **Arden,** the name is taken from Lodge's novel. There was an ancient forest of Ardennes in the north-eastern part of France near the Belgian border. 125. **golden world,** i.e., in the golden age. 134. **shall,** will be compelled to. 140. **intendment,** intention. 145. **underhand,** indirect. 151. **natural,** in the course of nature, not as now, "illegitimate." 156. **grace himself on,** gain honor in contest with. 156. **practise,** plot.

tears I speak it), there is not one so young and so villanous this day living. I speak but brotherly of him; but should I anatomize him to thee as he is, I must blush and weep, and thou must look pale and wonder.

Cha. I am heartily glad I came hither to you. If he come to-morrow, I 'll give him his payment: if ever he go alone again, I 'll never wrestle for prize more: and so, God keep your worship! *Exit.*

Oli. Farewell, good Charles.

Now will I stir this gamester: I hope I shall see an end of him; for my soul (yet I know not why) hates nothing more than he. Yet he 's gentle; never schooled, and yet learned; full of noble device; of all sorts enchantingly beloved; and indeed so much in the heart of the world, and especially of my own people, who best know him, that I am altogether misprised: but it shall not be so long; this wrestler shall clear all: nothing remains but that I kindle the boy thither, which now I 'll go about. *Exit.*

Scene II. *A lawn before the Duke's palace.*

Enter *Rosalind* and *Celia.*

Cel. I pray thee, Rosalind, sweet my coz, be merry.

Ros. Dear Celia, I show more mirth than I am mistress of; and would you yet I were merrier? Unless you could teach me to forget a banished father, you must not learn me how to remember any extraordinary pleasure.

Cel. Herein I see thou lov'st me not with the full weight that I love thee. If my uncle, thy banished father, had banished thy uncle, the Duke my father, so thou hadst been still with me, I could have taught my love to take thy father for mine: so wouldst thou, if the truth of thy love to me were so righteously tempered as mine is to thee.

Ros. Well, I will forget the condition of my estate, to rejoice in yours.

Cel. You know my father hath no child but I, nor none is like to have; and, truly, when he dies, thou shalt be his heir; for what he hath taken away from thy father perforce, I will render thee again in affection: by mine honour, I will; and when I break that oath, let me turn monster: therefore, my sweet Rose, my dear Rose, be merry.

Ros. From henceforth I will, coz, and devise sports. Let me see; what think you of falling in love?

Cel. Marry, I prithee, do, to make sport withal: but love no man in good earnest, nor no further in sport neither than with safety of a pure blush thou mayst in honour come off again.

Ros. What shall be our sport, then?

Cel. Let us sit and mock the good housewife Fortune from her wheel, that her gifts may henceforth be bestowed equally.

Ros. I would we could do so; for her benefits are mightily misplaced, and the bountiful blind woman doth most mistake in her gifts to women.

Cel. 'T is true; for those that she makes fair she scarce makes honest, and those that she makes honest she makes very ill-favouredly.

Ros. Nay, now thou goest from Fortune's office to Nature's: Fortune reigns in gifts of the world, not in the lineaments of Nature.

Enter *Touchstone* the Clown.

Cel. No? When Nature hath made a fair creature, may she not by Fortune fall into the fire? Though Nature hath given us wit to flout at Fortune, hath not Fortune sent in this fool to cut off the argument?

Ros. Indeed, there is Fortune too hard for Nature, when Fortune makes Nature's natural the cutter-off of Nature's wit.

Cel. Peradventure this is not Fortune's work neither, but Nature's; who, perceiveth our natural wits too dull to reason of such goddesses, and hath sent this natural for our whetstone; for always the dulness of the fool is the whetstone of the wits. How now, wit! whither wander you?

Touch. Mistress, you must come away to your father.

Cel. Were you made the messenger?

Touch. No, by mine honour, but I was bid to come for you.

Ros. Where learned you that oath, fool?

Touch. Of a certain knight that swore by his honour they were good pancakes, and swore by his honour the mustard was naught: now I 'll stand to it, the pancakes were naught and the mustard was good, and yet was not the knight forsworn.

Cel. How prove you that in the great heap of your knowledge?

Ros. Ay, marry, now unmuzzle your wisdom.

Touch. Stand you both forth now:

162. **anatomize,** dissect, analyze. 170. **gamester,** athlete, sport. 174. **noble device,** noble ideals. **sorts,** ranks. **enchantingly,** as if under enchantment. 177. **misprised,** despised. 180. **kindle . . . thither,** incite to the wrestling match. **Scene ii:** 7. **extraordinary,** i.e., beyond my capacity. 10. **so,** provided that. 15. **temper'd,** composed.

31. **pure,** mere. **come off,** escape. 34. **housewife,** hussy. 41. **honest,** chaste. 42. **ill-favouredly,** ugly. 49. **flout,** mock. 52. **natural,** idiot. 68. **naught,** worthless.

stroke your chins, and swear by your beards that I am a knave.

Cel. By our beards (if we had them) thou art.

Touch. By my knavery (if I had it) then I were. But if you swear by that that is not, you are not forsworn: no more was this knight, swearing by his honour, for he never had any; or if he had, he had sworn it away before ever he saw those pancakes or that mustard.

Cel. Prithee, who is 't that thou meanest?

Touch. One that old Frederick, your father, loves.

Cel. My father's love is enough to honour him. Enough! speak no more of him: you 'll be whipped for taxation one of these days.

Touch. The more pity, that fools may not speak wisely what wise men do foolishly.

Cel. By my troth, thou sayest true; for since the little wit that fools have was silenced, the little foolery that wise men have makes a great show. Here comes Monsieur the Beau.

Enter *Le Beau.*

Ros. With his mouth full of news.

Cel. Which he will put on us, as pigeons feed their young.

Ros. Then shall we be news-crammed.

Cel. All the better; we shall be the more marketable. *Bon jour,* Monsieur Le Beau. What 's the news?

Le Beau. Fair princess, you have lost much good sport.

Cel. Sport? Of what colour?

Le Beau. What colour, madam? How shall I answer you?

Ros. As wit and fortune will.

Touch. Or as the Destinies decrees.

Cel. Well said: that was laid on with a trowel.

Touch. Nay, if I keep not my rank,—

Ros. Thou losest thy old smell.

Le Beau. You amaze me, ladies: I would have told you of good wrestling, which you have lost the sight of.

Ros. Yet tell us the manner of the wrestling.

Le Beau. I will tell you the beginning; and, if it please your ladyships, you may see the end. For the best is yet to do; and here, where you are, they are coming to perform it.

Cel. Well, the beginning, that is dead and buried.

Le Beau. There comes an old man and his three sons,—

Cel. I could match this beginning with an old tale.

Le Beau. Three proper young men, of excellent growth and presence.

Ros. With bills on their necks, "Be it known unto all men by these presents."

Le Beau. The eldest of the three wrestled with Charles, the Duke's wrestler; which Charles in a moment threw him, and broke three of his ribs, that there is little hope of life in him. So he served the second, and so the third. Yonder they lie; the poor old man, their father, making such pitiful dole over them that all the beholders take his part with weeping.

Ros. Alas!

Touch. But what is the sport, monsieur, that the ladies have lost?

Le Beau. Why, this that I speak of.

Touch. Thus men may grow wiser every day. It is the first time that ever I heard breaking of ribs was sport for ladies.

Cel. Or I, I promise thee.

Ros. But is there any else longs to see this broken music in his sides? Is there yet another dotes upon rib-breaking? Shall we see this wrestling, cousin?

Le Beau. You must, if you stay here; for here is the place appointed for the wrestling, and they are ready to perform it.

Cel. Yonder, sure, they are coming. Let us now stay and see it.

Flourish. Enter *Duke Frederick, Lords, Orlando, Charles,* and *Attendants.*

Duke F. Come on: since the youth will not be entreated, his own peril on his forwardness.

Ros. Is yonder the man?

Le Beau. Even he, madam.

Cel. Alas, he is too young! Yet he looks successfully.

Duke F. How now, daughter and cousin! Are you crept hither to see the wrestling?

Ros. Ay, my liege, so please you give us leave.

Duke F. You will take little delight in it, I can tell you, there is such odds in the man. In pity of the challenger's youth I would fain dissuade him, but he will not be entreated. Speak to him, ladies; see if you can move him.

Cel. Call him hither, good Monsieur Le Beau.

Duke F. Do so; I 'll not be by.

Le Beau. Monsieur the challenger, the princess calls for you.

91. taxation, satire. **99. put on,** pass off on. **107. colour,** nature.

129. proper, handsome. **131. bills,** (1) pikes, (2) legal instruments. **139. dole,** grief. **150. broken music,** part music played by different instruments with a reference to the broken ribs of l. 147. **163. successfully,** as though he would be successful. **169. odds in the man,** superiority in Charles.

Orl. I attend them with all respect and duty.

Ros. Young man, have you challenged Charles the wrestler?

Orl. No, fair princess; he is the general challenger: I come but in, as others do, to try with him the strength of my youth.

Cel. Young gentleman, your spirits are too bold for your years. You have seen cruel proof of this man's strength: if you saw yourself with your eyes, or knew yourself with your judgement, the fear of your adventure would counsel you to a more equal enterprise. We pray you, for your own sake, to embrace your own safety, and give over this attempt.

Ros. Do, young sir; your reputation shall not therefore be misprised: we will make it our suit to the Duke that the wrestling might not go forward.

Orl. I beseech you, punish me not with your hard thoughts, wherein I confess me much guilty, to deny so fair and excellent ladies any thing. But let your fair eyes and gentle wishes go with me to my trial; wherein if I be foiled, there is but one shamed that was never gracious; if killed, but one dead that is willing to be so: I shall do my friends no wrong, for I have none to lament me; the world no injury, for in it I have nothing: only in the world I fill up a place, which may be better supplied when I have made it empty.

Ros. The little strength that I have, I would it were with you.

Cel. And mine to eke out hers.

Ros. Fare you well: pray heaven I be deceived in you!

Cel. Your heart's desires be with you!

Cha. Come, where is this young gallant that is so desirous to lie with his mother earth?

Orl. Ready, sir; but his will hath in it a more modest working.

Duke F. You shall try but one fall.

Cha. No, I warrant your Grace, you shall not entreat him to a second, that have so mightily persuaded him from a first.

Orl. You mean to mock me after; you should not have mocked me before: but come your ways.

Ros. Now Hercules be thy speed, young man!

Cel. I would I were invisible, to catch the strong fellow by the leg. *They wrestle.*

Ros. O excellent young man!

Cel. If I had a thunderbolt in mine eye I can tell who should down.

Shout. Charles is thrown.

Duke F. No more, no more.

Orl. Yes, I beseech your Grace, I am not yet well breath'd.

Duke F. How dost thou, Charles?

Le Beau. He cannot speak, my lord.

Duke F. Bear him away. What is thy name, young man?

Orl. Orlando, my liege; the youngest son of Sir Roland de Boys.

Duke F. I would thou hadst been son to some man else.
The world esteem'd thy father honourable,
But I did find him still mine enemy:
Thou shouldst have better pleas'd me with this deed,
Hadst thou descended from another house.
But fare thee well; thou art a gallant youth.
I would thou hadst told me of another father.

Exeunt Duke Frederick, train, and Le Beau.

Cel. Were I my father, coz, would I do this?

Orl. I am more proud to be Sir Roland's son,
His youngest son,—and would not change that calling,
To be adopted heir to Frederick.

Ros. My father lov'd Sir Roland as his soul,
And all the world was of my father's mind.
Had I before known this young man his son,
I should have given him tears unto entreaties,
Ere he should thus have ventur'd.

Cel. Gentle cousin,
Let us go thank him and encourage him.
My father's rough and envious disposition
Sticks me at heart. Sir, you have well deserv'd:
If you do keep your promises in love
But justly, as you have exceeded all promise,
Your mistress shall be happy.

Ros. Gentleman,
Giving him a chain from her neck.
Wear this for me, one out of suits with fortune,
That could give more, but that her hand lacks means.
Shall we go, coz?

Cel. Ay. Fare you well, fair gentleman.

Orl. Can I not say, I thank you? My better parts
Are all thrown down, and that which here stands up
Is but a quintain, a mere lifeless block.

200. gracious, favored. **215. working**, operation. **223. speed**, good fortune.

245. calling, name. **254. sticks**, pierces. **256. justly**, exactly. **258. out of suits with fortune**, stripped of fortune's livery, discharged. **263. quintain**, wooden figure to tilt at.

Ros. He calls us back: my pride fell with my fortunes;
I 'll ask him what he would. Did you call, sir?
Sir, you have wrestled well, and overthrown
More than your enemies.

Cel. Will you go, coz?

Ros. Have with you. Fare you well.

Exeunt Rosalind and Celia.

Orl. What passion hangs these weights upon my tongue?
I cannot speak to her, yet she urg'd conference.

Re-enter *Le Beau.*

O poor Orlando, thou art overthrown!
Or Charles or something weaker masters thee.

Le Beau. Good sir; I do in friendship counsel you
To leave this place. Albeit you have deserv'd
High commendation, true applause, and love,
Yet such is now the Duke's condition,
That he misconsters all that you have done.
The Duke is humorous:—what he is, indeed,
More suits you to conceive than I to speak of.

Orl. I thank you, sir; and, pray you, tell me this:
Which of the two was daughter of the Duke,
That here was at the wrestling?

Le Beau. Neither his daughter, if we judge by manners;
But yet, indeed, the smaller is his daughter.
The other is daughter to the banish'd Duke,
And here detain'd by her usurping uncle
To keep his daughter company; whose loves
Are dearer than the natural bond of sisters.
But I can tell you that of late this Duke
Hath ta'en displeasure 'gainst his gentle niece,
Grounded upon no other argument
But that the people praise her for her virtues,
And pity her for her good father's sake;
And, on my life, his malice 'gainst the lady
Will suddenly break forth. Sir, fare you well.
Hereafter, in a better world than this,
I shall desire more love and knowledge of you.

Orl. I rest much bounden to you; fare you well. *Exit Le Beau.*
Thus must I from the smoke into the smother,
From tyrant Duke unto a tyrant brother.
But heavenly Rosalind! *Exit.*

276. **condition,** state of mind. 278. **humorous,** capricious. 291. **argument,** cause. 299. **smoke into the smother,** frying-pan into the fire.

Scene III. *A room in the palace.*

Enter *Celia* and *Rosalind.*

Cel. Why, cousin! why, Rosalind! Cupid have mercy! not a word?

Ros. Not one to throw at a dog.

Cel. No, thy words are too precious to be cast away upon curs; throw some of them at me: come, lame me with reasons.

Ros. Then there were two cousins laid up, when the one should be lamed with reasons and the other mad without any.

Cel. But is all this for your father?

Ros. No, some of it is for my child's father. O, how full of briers is this working-day world!

Cel. They are but burs, cousin, thrown upon thee in holiday foolery: if we walk not in the trodden paths, our very petticoats will catch them.

Ros. I could shake them off my coat: these burs are in my heart.

Cel. Hem them away.

Ros. I would try, if I could cry hem and have him.

Cel. Come, come, wrestle with thy affections.

Ros. O, they take the part of a better wrestler than myself!

Cel. O, a good wish upon you! you will try in time, in despite of a fall. But, turning these jests out of service, let us talk in good earnest. Is it possible, on such a sudden you should fall into so strong a liking with old Sir Roland's youngest son?

Ros. The Duke my father lov'd his father dearly.

Cel. Doth it therefore ensue that you should love his son dearly? By this kind of chase, I should hate him, for my father hated his father dearly; yet I hate not Orlando.

Ros. No, faith, hate him not, for my sake.

Cel. Why should I not? Doth he not deserve well?

Ros. Let me love him for that, and do you love him because I do. Look, here comes the Duke.

Enter *Duke Frederick,* with *Lords.*

Cel. With his eyes full of anger.

Duke F. Mistress, dispatch you with your safest haste,
And get you from our court.

Ros. Me, uncle?

Duke F. You, cousin:

Scene iii: 12. **working-day world,** common life of every day. 18. **Hem,** cough. 37. **deserve well,** i.e., to be hated.

Within these ten days if that thou be'st found
So near our public court as twenty miles,
Thou diest for it.

Ros. I do beseech your Grace,
Let me the knowledge of my fault bear with me:
If with myself I hold intelligence,
Or have acquaintance with mine own desires;
If that I do not dream, or be not frantic,—
As I do trust I am not—then, dear uncle,
Never so much as in a thought unborn
Did I offend your Highness.

Duke F. Thus do all traitors:
If their purgation did consist in words,
They are as innocent as grace itself:
Let it suffice thee that I trust thee not.

Ros. Yet your mistrust cannot make me a traitor.
Tell me whereon the likelihoods depends.

Duke F. Thou art thy father's daughter; there 's enough.

Ros. So was I when your Highness took his dukedom.
So was I when your Highness banish'd him.
Treason is not inherited, my lord;
Or, if we did derive it from our friends,
What 's that to me? My father was no traitor:
Then, good my liege, mistake me not so much
To think my poverty is treacherous.

Cel. Dear sovereign, hear me speak.

Duke F. Ay, Celia; we stay'd her for your sake,
Else had she with her father rang'd along.

Cel. I did not then entreat to have her stay;
It was your pleasure and your own remorse:
I was too young that time to value her,
But now I know her: if she be a traitor,
Why so am I: we still have slept together,
Rose at an instant, learn'd, play'd, eat together;
And wheresoe'er we went, like Juno's swans,
Still we went coupled and inseparable.

Duke F. She is too subtle for thee; and her smoothness,
Her very silence, and her patience
Speak to the people, and they pity her.
Thou art a fool: she robs thee of thy name,
And thou wilt show more bright and seem more virtuous
When she is gone. Then open not thy lips.
Firm and irrevocable is my doom
Which I have pass'd upon her; she is banish'd.

Cel. Pronounce that sentence then on me, my liege;
I cannot live out of her company.

Duke F. You are a fool. You, niece, provide yourself:
If you outstay the time, upon mine honour,
And in the greatness of my word, you die.

Exeunt Duke Frederick and Lords.

Cel. O my poor Rosalind, whither wilt thou go?
Wilt thou change fathers? I will give thee mine.
I charge thee, be not thou more griev'd than I am.

Ros. I have more cause.

Cel. Thou hast not, cousin;
Prithee, be cheerful. Know'st thou not, the Duke
Hath banish'd me, his daughter?

Ros. That he hath not.

Cel. No, hath not? Rosalind lacks then the love
Which teacheth thee that thou and I am one.
Shall we be sunder'd? Shall we part, sweet girl?
No; let my father seek another heir.
Therefore devise with me how we may fly,
Whither to go and what to bear with us;
And do not seek to take your charge upon you,
To bear your griefs yourself, and leave me out;
For, by this heaven, now at our sorrows pale,
Say what thou canst, I 'll go along with thee.

Ros. Why, whither shall we go?

Cel. To seek my uncle in the forest of Arden.

Ros. Alas, what danger will it be to us,
Maids as we are, to travel forth so far!
Beauty provoketh thieves sooner than gold.

Cel. I 'll put myself in poor and mean attire,
And with a kind of umber smirch my face.
The like do you: so shall we pass along
And never stir assailants.

Ros. Were it not better,
Because that I am more than common tall,
That I did suit me all points like a man?
A gallant curtle-axe upon my thigh,
A boar-spear in my hand; and—in my heart
Lie there what hidden woman's fear there will—
We 'll have a swashing and a martial outside,
As many other mannish cowards have
That do outface it with their semblances.

Cel. What shall I call thee when thou art a man?

Ros. I 'll have no worse a name than Jove's own page,

55. **purgation**, exculpation from a charge of crime. 72. **remorse**, compassion. 77. **Juno's swans**, the swan was sacred to Venus, not to Juno.

104. **charge**, burden. 114. **umber**, brown pigment. 119. **curtle-axe**, cutlass. 122. **swashing**, swaggering.

And therefore look you call me Ganymede.
But what will you be call'd?
Cel. Something that hath a reference to my state:
No longer Celia, but Aliena.
Ros. But, cousin, what if we assay'd to steal
The clownish fool out of your father's court?
Would he not be a comfort to our travel?
Cel. He 'll go along o'er the wide world with me.
Leave me alone to woo him. Let 's away,
And get our jewels and our wealth together,
Devise the fittest time and safest way
To hide us from pursuit that will be made
After my flight. Now go we in content
To liberty and not to banishment.
Exeunt.

ACT II. SCENE I. *The Forest of Arden.*

Enter *Duke* senior, *Amiens,* and two or three *Lords,* like foresters.

Duke S. Now, my co-mates and brothers in exile,
Hath not old custom made this life more sweet
Than that of painted pomp? Are not these woods
More free from peril than the envious court?
Here feel we not the penalty of Adam,
The seasons' difference—as the icy fang
And churlish chiding of the winter's wind,
Which, when it bites and blows upon my body,
Even till I shrink with cold, I smile and say,
"This is no flattery: these are counsellors
That feelingly persuade me what I am."
Sweet are the uses of adversity,
Which, like the toad, ugly and venomous,
Wears yet a precious jewel in his head;
And this our life, exempt from public haunt,
Finds tongues in trees, books in the running brooks,
Sermons in stones, and good in every thing.
I would not change it.
Ami. Happy is your Grace,
That can translate the stubbornness of fortune
Into so quiet and so sweet a style.
Duke S. Come, shall we go and kill us venison?
And yet it irks me the poor dappled fools,
Being native burghers of this desert city,
Should in their own confines with forked heads
Have their round haunches gor'd.
1. Lord. Indeed, my lord,
The melancholy Jaques grieves at that;
And, in that kind, swears you do more usurp
Than doth your brother that hath banish'd you.
To-day my Lord of Amiens and myself
Did steal behind him as he lay along
Under an oak whose antique root peeps out
Upon the brook that brawls along this wood;
To the which place a poor sequester'd stag,
That from the hunter's aim had ta'en a hurt,
Did come to languish; and indeed, my lord,
The wretched animal heav'd forth such groans,
That their discharge did stretch his leathern coat
Almost to bursting, and the big round tears
Cours'd one another down his innocent nose
In piteous chase; and thus the hairy fool,
Much marked of the melancholy Jaques,
Stood on th' extremest verge of the swift brook,
Augmenting it with tears.
Duke S. But what said Jaques?
Did he not moralize this spectacle?
1. Lord. O, yes, into a thousand similes.
First, for his weeping into the needless stream:
"Poor deer," quoth he, "thou mak'st a testament
As worldlings do, giving thy sum of more
To that which had too much": then, being there alone,
Left and abandoned of his velvet friends,
"'T is right," quoth he; "thus misery doth part
The flux of company": anon a careless herd,
Full of the pasture, jumps along by him
And never stays to greet him; "Ay," quoth Jaques,
"Sweep on, you fat and greasy citizens.
'T is just the fashion: wherefore do you look
Upon that poor and broken bankrupt there?"
Thus most invectively he pierceth through
The body of the country, city, court,
Yea, and of this our life; swearing that we
Are mere usurpers, tyrants, and what 's worse,

Act II, Scene i: 5. penalty of Adam, "In the sweat of thy face shalt thou eat bread." *Gen.* III, 19. **13-14.** It was believed that the toad was venomous and had a jewel (the toadstone) in its head. **15. exempt,** cut off from. **24. forked heads,** i.e., arrow heads.

31. antique, ancient. **44. moralize,** draw a moral from. **46. needless,** without need. **50. velvet,** courtier-like, alluding to the velvety horns of the deer. **58. invectively,** in railing terms.

To fright the animals and to kill them up
In their assign'd and native dwelling-place.
Duke S. And did you leave him in this contemplation?
2. Lord. We did, my lord, weeping and commenting
Upon the sobbing deer.
Duke S. Show me the place.
I love to cope him in these sullen fits,
For then he 's full of matter.
1. Lord. I 'll bring you to him straight.
Exeunt.

Scene II. *A room in the palace.*

Enter *Duke Frederick,* with *Lords.*

Duke F. Can it be possible that no man saw them?
It cannot be: some villains of my court
Are of consent and sufferance in this.
1. Lord. I cannot hear of any that did see her.
The ladies, her attendants of her chamber,
Saw her a-bed, and in the morning early
They found the bed untreasur'd of their mistress.
2. Lord. My lord, the roynish clown, at whom so oft
Your Grace was wont to laugh, is also missing.
Hisperia, the princess' gentlewoman,
Confesses that she secretly o'erheard
Your daughter and her cousin much commend
The parts and graces of the wrestler
That did but lately foil the sinewy Charles;
And she believes, wherever they are gone,
That youth is surely in their company.
Duke F. Send to his brother; fetch that gallant hither.
If he be absent, bring his brother to me;
I 'll make him find him: do this suddenly,
And let not search and inquisition quail
To bring again these foolish runaways.
Exeunt.

Scene III. *Before Oliver's house.*

Enter *Orlando* and *Adam,* meeting.

Orl. Who 's there?
Adam. What, my young master? O my gentle master!
O my sweet master! O you memory
Of old Sir Roland! Why, what make you here?
Why are you virtuous? Why do people love you?
And wherefore are you gentle, strong, and valiant?
Why would you be so fond to overcome
The bonny priser of the humorous Duke?
Your praise is come too swiftly home before you.
Know you not, master, to some kind of men
Their graces serve them but as enemies?
No more do yours: your virtues, gentle master,
Are sanctified and holy traitors to you.
O, what a world is this, when what is comely
Envenoms him that bears it!
Orl. Why, what 's the matter?
Adam. O unhappy youth!
Come not within these doors: within this roof
The enemy of all your graces lives:
Your brother—no, no brother; yet the son—
(Yet not the son, I will not call him son
Of him I was about to call his father)
Hath heard your praises, and this night he means
To burn the lodging where you use to lie
And you within it: if he fail of that,
He will have other means to cut you off.
I overheard him and his practices.
This is no place; this house is but a butchery.
Abhor it, fear it, do not enter it.
Orl. Why, whither, Adam, wouldst thou have me go?
Adam. No matter whither, so you come not here.
Orl. What, wouldst thou have me go and beg my food?
Or with a base and boist'rous sword enforce
A thievish living on the common road?
This I must do, or know not what to do;
Yet this I will not do, do how I can.
I rather will subject me to the malice
Of a diverted blood and bloody brother.
Adam. But do not so. I have five hundred crowns,
The thrifty hire I saved under your father,
Which I did store to be my foster-nurse
When service should in my old limbs lie lame,
And unregarded age in corners thrown.
Take that, and He that doth the ravens feed,
Yea, providently caters for the sparrow,
Be comfort to my age! Here is the gold.
All this I give you. Let me be your servant.
Though I look old, yet I am strong and lusty;

67. cope, encounter. **68. matter,** good sense. **Scene ii: 8. roynish,** scurvy, rough. **19. suddenly,** at once. **20. inquisition quail,** inquiry slacken. **21. again,** back. **Scene iii: 3. memory,** memorial.

8. bonny priser, stalwart competitor for a prize, champion. **26. practices,** plots. **27. place,** dwelling-place. **butchery,** slaughter-house. **37. diverted blood,** unnatural kin. **39. thrifty hire,** wages saved by thrift.

For in my youth I never did apply
Hot and rebellious liquors in my blood,
Nor did not with unbashful forehead woo
The means of weakness and debility;
Therefore my age is as a lusty winter,
Frosty, but kindly: let me go with you;
I 'll do the service of a younger man
In all your business and necessities.

Orl. O good old man, how well in thee appears
The constant service of the antique world,
When service sweat for duty, not for meed!
Thou art not for the fashion of these times,
Where none will sweat but for promotion,
And having that do choke their service up
Even with the having: it is not so with thee.
But, poor old man, thou prun'st a rotten tree,
That cannot so much as a blossom yield
In lieu of all thy pains and husbandry.
But come thy ways; we 'll go along together,
And ere we have thy youthful wages spent,
We 'll light upon some settled low content.

Adam. Master, go on, and I will follow thee
To the last gasp, with truth and loyalty.
From seventeen years till now almost four-score
Here lived I, but now live here no more.
At seventeen years many their fortunes seek,
But at fourscore it is too late a week;
Yet fortune cannot recompense me better
Than to die well and not my master's debtor.
Exeunt.

Scene IV. *The Forest of Arden.*

Enter *Rosalind* for Ganymede, *Celia* for Aliena, and Clown, alias *Touchstone.*

Ros. O Jupiter, how weary are my spirits!

Touch. I care not for my spirit, if my legs were not weary.

Ros. I could find in my heart to disgrace my man's apparel and to cry like a woman; but I must comfort the weaker vessel, as doublet and hose ought to show itself courageous to petticoat; therefore, courage, good Aliena.

Cel. I pray you, bear with me; I cannot go no further.

Touch. For my part, I had rather bear with you than bear you. Yet I should bear no cross if I did bear you, for I think you have no money in your purse.

Ros. Well, this is the forest of Arden.

Touch. Ay, now am I in Arden, the more fool I: when I was at home, I was in a better place; but travellers must be content.

Enter *Corin* and *Silvius.*

Ros. Ay, be so, good Touchstone. Look you, who comes here; a young man and an old in solemn talk.

Cor. That is the way to make her scorn you still.

Sil. O Corin, that thou knew'st how I do love her!

Cor. I partly guess; for I have lov'd ere now.

Sil. No, Corin, being old, thou canst not guess,
Though in thy youth thou wast as true a lover
As ever sigh'd upon a midnight pillow.
But if thy love were ever like to mine,—
As sure I think did never man love so—
How many actions most ridiculous
Hast thou been drawn to by thy fantasy?

Cor. Into a thousand that I have forgotten.

Sil. O, thou didst then ne'er love so heartily!
If thou rememb'rest not the slightest folly
That ever love did make thee run into,
Thou hast not lov'd;
Or if thou hast not sat as I do now,
Wearing thy hearer in thy mistress' praise,
Thou hast not lov'd;
Or if thou hast not broke from company
Abruptly, as my passion now makes me,
Thou hast not lov'd.
O Phebe, Phebe, Phebe! *Exit.*

Ros. Alas, poor shepherd! searching of thy wound,
I have by hard adventure found mine own.

Touch. And I mine. I remember, when I was in love I broke my sword upon a stone, and bid him take that for coming a-night to Jane Smile; and I remember the kissing of her batlet and the cow's dugs that her pretty chopt hands had milk'd; and I remember the wooing of a peascod instead of her; from whom I took two cods and, giving her them again, said with weeping tears, "Wear these for my sake." We that are true lovers run into strange capers; but as all is mortal in nature, so is all nature in love mortal in folly.

Ros. Thou speak'st wiser than thou art ware of.

Touch. Nay, I shall ne'er be ware of mine own wit till I break my shins against it.

58. meed, reward. **61. choke . . . up,** extinguish, leave off. **65. In lieu of,** in return for. **68. content,** state of contentment. **74. too late a week,** i.e., a good deal too late. **Scene iv: 13. cross,** silver coins had crosses on them.

31. fantasy, fancy, love. **38. Wearing,** wearing out. **44. searching,** probing. **49. batlet,** small bat to beat clothes in the wash. **50. chopt,** chapped. **51. peascod,** pea pod, used by rustics as a means of divination in their love affairs. **57. mortal,** excessive.

Ros. Jove, Jove! this shepherd's passion
Is much upon my fashion.

Touch. And mine; but it grows something stale with me.

Cel. I pray you, one of you question yond man
If he for gold will give us any food.
I faint almost to death.

Touch. Holla, you clown!

Ros. Peace, fool; he 's not thy kinsman.

Cor. Who calls?

Touch. Your betters, sir.

Cor. Else are they very wretched.

Ros. Peace, I say. Good even to you, friend.

Cor. And to you, gentle sir, and to you all.

Ros. I prithee, shepherd, if that love or gold
Can in this desert place buy entertainment,
Bring us where we may rest ourselves and feed.
Here 's a young maid with travel much oppressed
And faints for succour.

Cor. Fair sir, I pity her,
And wish, for her sake more than for mine own,
My fortunes were more able to relieve her;
But I am shepherd to another man,
And do not shear the fleeces that I graze:
My master is of churlish disposition,
And little recks to find the way to heaven
By doing deeds of hospitality.
Besides, his cote, his flocks, and bounds of feed
Are now on sale, and at our sheep-cote now,
By reason of his absence, there is nothing
That you will feed on; but what is, come see,
And in my voice most welcome shall you be.

Ros. What is he that shall buy his flock and pasture?

Cor. That young swain that you saw here but erewhile,
That little cares for buying any thing.

Ros. I pray thee, if it stand with honesty,
Buy thou the cottage, pasture, and the flock,
And thou shalt have to pay for it of us.

Cel. And we will mend thy wages. I like this place,
And willingly could waste my time in it.

Cor. Assuredly the thing is to be sold.
Go with me: if you like upon report
The soil, the profit, and this kind of life,
I will your very faithful feeder be.
And buy it with your gold right suddenly.

Exeunt.

62. upon, according to. **75. for succour,** for want of help. **80. churlish,** miserly. **81. recks,** cares. **83. cote,** cottage. **bounds of feed,** pasturage. **87. voice,** vote. **91. stand,** be consistent. **99. feeder,** shepherd.

Scene V. *The forest.*

Enter *Amiens, Jaques,* and others.

Song.

Amiens.

Under the greenwood tree
Who loves to lie with me,
And turn his merry note
Unto the sweet bird's throat,
Come hither, come hither, come hither!
Here shall he see
No enemy
But winter and rough weather.

Jaq. More, more, I prithee, more.

Ami. It will make you melancholy, Monsieur Jaques.

Jaq. I thank it. More, I prithee, more. I can suck melancholy out of a song, as a weasel sucks eggs. More, I prithee, more.

Ami. My voice is ragged. I know I cannot please you.

Jaq. I do not desire you to please me; I do desire you to sing. Come, more; another stanzo. Call you 'em stanzos?

Ami. What you will, Monsieur Jaques.

Jaq. Nay, I care not for their names; they owe me nothing. Will you sing?

Ami. More at your request than to please myself.

Jaq. Well then, if ever I thank any man, I 'll thank you; but that they call compliment is like the encounter of two dog-apes; and when a man thanks me heartily, methinks I have given him a penny and he renders me the beggarly thanks. Come, sing; and you that will not, hold your tongues.

Ami. Well, I 'll end the song. Sirs, cover the while; the Duke will drink under this tree. He hath been all this day to look you.

Jaq. And I have been all this day to avoid him. He is too disputable for my company. I think of as many matters as he; but I give heaven thanks, and make no boast of them. Come, warble, come.

Song.

All together here.

Who doth ambition shun,
And loves to live i' th' sun,
Seeking the food he eats,
And pleased with what he gets,
Come hither, come hither, come hither!
Here shall he see
No enemy
But winter and rough weather.

Jaq. I 'll give you a verse to this note, that I made yesterday in despite of my invention.

Scene v: 3. turn, adapt. **15. ragged,** rough. **21. names,** with a pun on signatures. **27. dog-apes,** dog-faced apes. **32. cover the while,** set the table in the meantime. **36. disputable,** disputatious.

Ami. And I 'll sing it.
Jaq. Thus it goes:—

If it do come to pass
That any man turn ass,
Leaving his wealth and ease
A stubborn will to please,
Ducdame, ducdame, ducdame!
Here shall he see
Gross fools as he,
An if he will come to me.

Ami. What 's that "ducdame"?
Jaq. 'T is a Greek invocation, to call fools into a circle. I 'll go sleep, if I can; if I cannot, I 'll rail against all the first-born of Egypt.
Ami. And I 'll go seek the Duke; his banquet is prepared. *Exeunt.*

Scene VI. *The forest.*

Enter *Orlando* and *Adam.*

Adam. Dear master, I can go no further: O, I die for food! Here lie I down, and measure out my grave. Farewell, kind master.
Orl. Why, how now, Adam! no greater heart in thee? Live a little; comfort a little; cheer thyself a little. If this uncouth forest yield any thing savage, I will either be food for it or bring it for food to thee. Thy conceit is nearer death than thy powers. For my sake be comfortable; hold death awhile at the arm's end: I will here be with thee presently; and if I bring thee not something to eat, I will give thee leave to die; but if thou diest before I come, thou art a mocker of my labour. Well said! thou look'st cheerly, and I 'll be with thee quickly. Yet thou liest in the bleak air. Come, I will bear thee to some shelter; and thou shalt not die for lack of a dinner if there live any thing in this desert. Cheerly, good Adam! *Exeunt.*

Scene VII. *The forest.*

A table set out. Enter *Duke* senior, *Amiens* and *Lords,* like outlaws.

Duke S. I think he be transform'd into a beast,
For I can no where find him like a man.
1. Lord. My lord, he is but even now gone hence.
Here was he merry, hearing of a song.
Duke S. If he, compact of jars, grow musical,
We shall have shortly discord in the spheres.
Go, seek him; tell him I would speak with him.

Enter *Jaques.*

1. Lord. He saves my labour by his own approach.
Duke S. Why, how now, monsieur! what a life is this,
That your poor friends must woo your company?
What, you look merrily!
Jaq. A fool, a fool! I met a fool i' th' forest,
A motley fool—a miserable world—
As I do live by food, I met a fool;
Who laid him down and bask'd him in the sun,
And rail'd on Lady Fortune in good terms,
In good set terms, and yet a motley fool.
"Good morrow, fool," quoth I. "No, sir," quoth he,
"Call me not fool till heaven hath sent me fortune."
And then he drew a dial from his poke,
And, looking on it with lack-lustre eye,
Says very wisely, "It is ten o'clock.
Thus we may see," quoth he, "how the world wags.
'T is but an hour ago since it was nine;
And after one hour more 't will be eleven;
And so, from hour to hour, we ripe and ripe,
And then, from hour to hour, we rot and rot;
And thereby hangs a tale." When I did hear
The motley fool thus moral on the time,
My lungs began to crow like chanticleer,
That fools should be so deep-contemplative;
And I did laugh sans intermission
An hour by his dial. O noble fool!
A worthy fool! Motley's the only wear.
Duke S. What fool is this?
Jaq. O worthy fool! One that hath been a courtier,
And says, if ladies be but young and fair,
They have the gift to know it; and in his brain,
Which is as dry as the remainder biscuit
After a voyage, he hath strange places cramm'd
With observation, the which he vents
In mangled forms. O that I were a fool!
I am ambitious for a motley coat.
Duke S. Thou shalt have one.
Jaq. It is my only suit;—

56. **Ducdame,** meaningless jargon, perhaps a corruption of a gypsy word. 63. **first-born of Egypt,** perhaps the high-born. 64. **banquet,** wine and dessert served after dinner. **Scene vi: 5. comfort,** comfort thee. 9. **conceit,** imagination. **Scene vii: 5. compact of jars,** composed of discords.

6. **spheres,** i.e., of the Ptolemaic solar system, which in their turning made music. 13. **motley,** a parti-colored costume worn by court jesters. 20. **dial,** watch or portable sundial. **poke,** pouch. 29. **moral,** moralize. 39. **dry,** in the physiology of Shakespeare's time a dry brain was slow and retentive. 40. **places,** topics of conversation. 44. **suit,** (1) dress, (2) petition.

Provided that you weed your better judgements
Of all opinion that grows rank in them
That I am wise. I must have liberty
Withal, as large a charter as the wind,
To blow on whom I please; for so fools have;
And they that are most galled with my folly,
They most must laugh. And why, sir, must they so?
The "why" is plain as way to parish church.
He that a fool doth very wisely hit
Doth very foolishly, although he smart,
Not to seem senseless of the bob; if not,
The wise man's folly is anatomiz'd
Even by the squand'ring glances of the fool.
Invest me in my motley. Give me leave
To speak my mind, and I will through and through
Cleanse the foul body of th' infected world,
If they will patiently receive my medicine.

Duke S. Fie on thee! I can tell what thou wouldst do.

Jaq. What, for a counter, would I do but good?

Duke S. Most mischievous foul sin, in chiding sin.
For thou thyself hast been a libertine,
As sensual as the brutish sting itself;
And all th' embossed sores and headed evils,
That thou with license of free foot hast caught,
Wouldst thou disgorge into the general world.

Jaq. Why, who cries out on pride,
That can therein tax any private party?
Doth it not flow as hugely as the sea,
Till that the wearer's very means do ebb?
What woman in the city do I name,
When that I say the city-woman bears
The cost of princes on unworthy shoulders?
Who can come in and say that I mean her,
When such a one as she such is her neighbour?
Or what is he of basest function,
That says his bravery is not on my cost,
Thinking that I mean him, but therein suits
His folly to the mettle of my speech?
There then; how then? what then? Let me see wherein
My tongue hath wrong'd him. If it do him right,
Then he hath wrong'd himself. If he be free,
Why then my taxing like a wild-goose flies,
Unclaim'd of any man. But who comes here?

Enter *Orlando* with his sword drawn.

Orl. Forbear, and eat no more.

Jaq. Why, I have eat none yet.

Orl. Nor shalt not, till necessity be serv'd.

Jaq. Of what kind should this cock come of?

Duke S. Art thou thus bolden'd, man, by thy distress?
Or else a rude despiser of good manners,
That in civility thou seem'st so empty?

Orl. You touch'd my vein at first: the thorny point
Of bare distress hath ta'en from me the show
Of smooth civility: yet am I inland bred
And know some nurture. But forbear, I say:
He dies that touches any of this fruit
Till I and my affairs are answered.

Jaq. An you will not be answered with reason, I must die.

Duke S. What would you have? Your gentleness shall force,
More than your force move us to gentleness.

Orl. I almost die for food; and let me have it.

Duke S. Sit down and feed, and welcome to our table.

Orl. Speak you so gently? Pardon me, I pray you.
I thought that all things had been savage here,
And therefore put I on the countenance
Of stern commandment. But whate'er you are
That in this desert inaccessible
Under the shade of melancholy boughs
Lose and neglect the creeping hours of time;
If ever you have look'd on better days,
If ever been where bells have knoll'd to church,
If ever sat at any good man's feast,
If ever from your eyelids wip'd a tear
And know what 't is to pity and be pitied,
Let gentleness my strong enforcement be;
In the which hope I blush, and hide my sword.

Duke S. True is it that we have seen better days,
And have with holy bell been knoll'd to church,
And sat at good men's feasts, and wip'd our eyes
Of drops that sacred pity hath engender'd;
And therefore sit you down in gentleness
And take upon command what help we have
That to your wanting may be minister'd.

Orl. Then but forbear your food a little while,
Whiles, like a doe, I go to find my fawn
And give it food. There is an old poor man,

48. **as large a charter,** the wind bloweth where it listeth. 55. **bob,** jest, gibe. 57. **squand'ring glances,** random glancing blows. 63. **counter,** worthless metal disc used in counting. 66. **brutish sting,** animal passion. 67. **embossed,** bulging. **headed,** come to a head. 71. **tax,** censure. 79. **function,** office. 80. **bravery,** finery. 85. **free,** innocent.

96. **civility,** good breeding. **inland bred,** i.e., civilized. 97. **nurture,** training. 109. **commandment,** command. 118. **enforcement,** support.

Who after me hath many a weary step
Limp'd in pure love: till he first suffic'd,
Oppress'd with two weak evils, age and hunger,
I will not touch a bit.

Duke S. Go find him out,
And we will nothing waste till you return.

Orl. I thank ye; and be blest for your good comfort! *Exit.*

Duke S. Thou seest we are not all alone unhappy:
This wide and universal theatre
Presents more woeful pageant than the scene
Wherein we play in.

Jaq. All the world 's a stage,
And all the men and women merely players:
They have their exits and their entrances,
And one man in his time plays many parts,
His acts being seven ages. At first the infant,
Mewling and puking in the nurse's arms.
Then the whining school-boy, with his satchel
And shining morning face, creeping like snail
Unwillingly to school. And then the lover,
Sighing like furnace, with a woeful ballad
Made to his mistress' eyebrow. Then a soldier,
Full of strange oaths, and bearded like the pard,
Jealous in honour, sudden, and quick in quarrel,
Seeking the bubble reputation
Even in the cannon's mouth. And then the justice,
In fair round belly with good capon lin'd,
With eyes severe and beard of formal cut,
Full of wise saws and modern instances;
And so he plays his part. The sixth age shifts
Into the lean and slipper'd pantaloon,
With spectacles on nose and pouch on side,
His youthful hose, well sav'd, a world too wide
For his shrunk shank; and his big manly voice,
Turning again toward childish treble, pipes
And whistles in his sound. Last scene of all,
That ends this strange eventful history,
Is second childishness and mere oblivion,
Sans teeth, sans eyes, sans taste, sans every thing.

132. **weak evils**, evils causing weakness. 144. **Mewling**, squalling. 150. **bearded like the pard**, with long moustaches like a leopard's whiskers. 156. **saws**, sayings. **modern instances**, commonplace proverbs. 158. **pantaloon**, feeble old man.

Re-enter *Orlando*, with *Adam*.

Duke S. Welcome. Set down your venerable burden,
And let him feed.

Orl. I thank you most for him.

Adam. So had you need;
I scarce can speak to thank you for myself.

Duke S. Welcome: fall to. I will not trouble you
As yet, to question you about your fortunes.
Give us some music; and, good cousin, sing.

Song.

Amiens.

Blow, blow, thou winter wind,
Thou art not so unkind
As mans' ingratitude;
Thy tooth is not so keen,
Because thou art not seen,
Although thy breath be rude.
Heigh-ho! sing, heigh-ho! unto the green holly.
Most friendship is feigning, most loving mere folly.
Then, heigh-ho, the holly!
This life is most jolly.

Freeze, freeze, thou bitter sky,
That dost not bite so nigh
As benefits forgot;
Though thou the waters warp,
Thy sting is not so sharp
As friend rememb'red not.
Heigh-ho! sing, etc.

Duke S. If that you were the good Sir Roland's son,
As you have whisper'd faithfully you were,
And as mine eye doth his effigies witness
Most truly limn'd and living in your face,
Be truly welcome hither: I am the Duke
That lov'd your father. The residue of your fortune,
Go to my cave and tell me. Good old man,
Thou art right welcome as thy master is.
Support him by the arm: give me your hand,
And let me all your fortunes understand.

Exeunt.

175. **unkind**, unnatural. 193. **effigies**, likeness. 194. **limn'd**, painted.

ACT III. Scene I. *A room in the palace.*

Enter *Duke Frederick, Oliver,* and *Lords.*

Duke F. Not see him since? Sir, sir, that cannot be.
But were I not the better part made mercy,
I should not seek an absent argument
Of my revenge, thou present. But look to it.
Find out thy brother, wheresoe'er he is.
Seek him with candle! Bring him dead or living
Within this twelvemonth, or turn thou no more
To seek a living in our territory.
Thy lands and all things that thou dost call thine
Worth seizure do we seize into our hands,
Till thou canst quit thee by thy brother's mouth
Of what we think against thee.

Oli. O that your Highness knew my heart in this!
I never lov'd my brother in my life.

Duke F. More villain thou. Well, push him out of doors;
And let my officers of such a nature
Make an extent upon his house and lands.
Do this expediently and turn him going.
Exeunt.

Scene II. *The forest.*

Enter *Orlando* with a paper.

Orl. Hang there, my verse, in witness of my love;
And thou, thrice-crowned queen of night, survey
With thy chaste eye, from thy pale sphere above,
Thy huntress' name that my full life doth sway.
O Rosalind! these trees shall be my books,
And in their barks my thoughts I 'll character;
That every eye which in this forest looks
Shall see thy virtue witness'd every where.
Run, run Orlando; carve on every tree
The fair, the chaste, and unexpressive she.
Exit.

Enter *Corin* and Clown *Touchstone.*

Cor. And how like you this shepherd's life, Master Touchstone?

Touch. Truly, shepherd, in respect of itself, it is a good life; but in respect that it is a shepherd's life, it is naught. In respect that it is solitary, I like it very well; but in respect that it is private, it is a very vile life. Now, in respect it is in the fields, it pleaseth me well; but in respect it is not in the court, it is tedious. As it is a spare life, look you, it fits my humour well; but as there is no more plenty in it, it goes much against my stomach. Hast any philosophy in thee, shepherd?

Cor. No more but that I know the more one sickens the worse at ease he is; and that he that wants money, means, and content is without three good friends; that the property of rain is to wet and fire to burn; that good pasture makes fat sheep, and that a great cause of the night is lack of the sun; that he that hath learned no wit by nature nor art may complain of good breeding or comes of a very dull kindred.

Touch. Such a one is a natural philosopher. Wast ever in court, shepherd?

Cor. No, truly.

Touch. Then thou art damned.

Cor. Nay, I hope.

Touch. Truly, thou art damned, like an ill-roasted egg all on one side.

Cor. For not being at court? Your reason.

Touch. Why, if thou never wast at court, thou never saw'st good manners; if thou never saw'st good manners, then thy manners must be wicked; and wickedness is sin, and sin is damnation. Thou art in a parlous state, shepherd.

Cor. Not a whit, Touchstone. Those that are good manners at the court are as ridiculous in the country as the behaviour of the country is most mockable at the court. You told me you salute not at the court but you kiss your hands: that courtesy would be uncleanly if courtiers were shepherds.

Touch. Instance, briefly; come, instance.

Cor. Why, we are still handling our ewes, and their fells, you know, are greasy.

Touch. Why, do not your courtier's hands sweat? And is not the grease of a mutton as wholesome as the sweat of a man? Shallow, shallow. A better instance, I say; come.

Cor. Besides, our hands are hard.

Act III, Scene i: 3. argument, reason for. **6. candle,** "What woman having ten pieces of silver, if she lose one piece, doth not light a candle and sweep the house, and search diligently until she find it." *Luke,* xv, 8. **11. quit,** acquit. **16. of such a nature,** whose duty it is. **17. extent,** i.e., seizure, lit., a writ to recover debts. **18. expediently,** expeditiously. **Scene ii: 2. thrice-crowned,** Diana: Luna in heaven; Diana on earth; Proserpine or Hecate in the underworld. **6. character,** inscribe. **10. unexpressive,** inexpressible.

16. private, lonely. **31. of good breeding,** of lack of good breeding. **45. parlous,** perilous. **50. but you kiss,** without kissing. **55. fells,** hides with the wool on them.

Touch. Your lips will feel them the sooner. Shallow again. A more sounder instance, come.

Cor. And they are often tarred over with the surgery of our sheep; and would you have us kiss tar? The courtier's hands are perfumed with civet.

Touch. Most shallow man! thou worm's-meat, in respect of a good piece of flesh indeed! Learn of the wise, and perpend: civet is of a baser birth than tar, the very uncleanly flux of a cat. Mend the instance, shepherd.

Cor. You have too courtly a wit for me: I 'll rest.

Touch. Wilt thou rest damned? God help thee, shallow man! God make incision in thee! Thou art raw.

Cor. Sir, I am a true labourer: I earn that I eat, get that I wear, owe no man hate, envy no man's happiness, glad of other men's good, content with my harm, and the greatest of my pride is to see my ewes graze and my lambs suck.

Touch. That is another simple sin in you, to bring the ewes and the rams together, and to offer to get your living by the copulation of cattle; to be bawd to a bell-wether, and to betray a she-lamb of a twelvemonth to a crooked-pated, old, cuckoldly ram, out of all reasonable match. If thou beest not damn'd for this, the devil himself will have no shepherds. I cannot see else how thou shouldst scape.

Cor. Here comes young Master Ganymede, my new mistress's brother.

Enter *Rosalind* with a paper, reading.

Ros.

From the east to western Ind,
No jewel is like Rosalind.
Her worth, being mounted on the wind,
Through all the world bears Rosalind.
All the pictures fairest lin'd
Are but black to Rosalind.
Let no face be kept in mind
But the fair of Rosalind.

Touch. I 'll rhyme you so eight years together, dinners and suppers and sleeping-hours excepted. It is the right butter-women's rank to market.

Ros. Out, fool!

Touch. For a taste:—

If a hart do lack a hind,
Let him seek out Rosalind.
If the cat will after kind,
So be sure will Rosalind.
Winter'd garments must be lin'd,
So must slender Rosalind.
They that reap must sheaf and bind,
Then to cart with Rosalind.
Sweetest nut hath sourest rind,
Such a nut is Rosalind.
He that sweetest rose will find,
Must find love's prick and Rosalind.

This is the very false gallop of verses: why do you infect yourself with them?

Ros. Peace, you dull fool! I found them on a tree.

Touch. Truly, the tree yields bad fruit.

Ros. I 'll graff it with you, and then I shall graff it with a medlar: then it will be the earliest fruit i' th' country; for you 'll be rotten ere you be half ripe, and that 's the right virtue of the medlar.

Touch. You have said; but whether wisely or no, let the forest judge.

Enter *Celia,* with a writing.

Ros. Peace!
Here comes my sister, reading; stand aside.

Cel. [*Reads.*]

Why should this a desert be?
 For it is unpeopled? No!
Tongues I 'll hang on every tree,
 That shall civil sayings show:
Some, how brief the life of man
 Runs his erring pilgrimage,
That the stretching of a span
 Buckles in his sum of age;
Some, of violated vows
 'Twixt the souls of friend and friend;
But upon the fairest boughs,
 Or at every sentence end,
Will I Rosalinda write,
 Teaching all that read to know
The quintessence of every sprite
 Heaven would in little show.
Therefore Heaven Nature charg'd
 That one body should be fill'd
With all graces wide-enlarg'd.
 Nature presently distill'd
Helen's cheek, but not her heart,
 Cleopatra's majesty,
Atalanta's better part,
 Sad Lucretia's modesty.
Thus Rosalind of many parts
 By heavenly synod was devis'd;
Of many faces, eyes, and hearts,
 To have the touches dearest priz'd.
Heaven would that she these gifts should have,
And I to live and die her slave.

Ros. O most gentle pulpiter! what tedious homily of love have you wearied your parish-

68. in respect of, in comparison with. **69. perpend,** consider. **75. incision,** i.e., for blood-letting. **76. raw,** inexperienced. **80. content with my harm,** patient under adversity. **93. Ind,** Indies. **97. lin'd,** drawn. **100. fair,** beauty. **103. rank,** row, like a row of butter women jogging to market.

119. false gallop, canter. **124. medlar,** (1) meddler, (2) an apple-like fruit half rotten before it can be eaten. **136. civil sayings,** grave maxims. **138. erring,** wandering. **140. Buckles in,** includes. **155. better part,** grace and fleetness. **156. Sad,** serious. **160. touches,** traits.

ioners withal, and never cried "Have patience, good people!"

Cel. How now! Back, friends! Shepherd, go off a little. Go with him, sirrah.

Touch. Come, shepherd, let us make an honourable retreat; though not with bag and baggage, yet with scrip and scrippage.

Exeunt Corin and Touchstone.

Cel. Didst thou hear these verses?

Ros. O, yes, I heard them all, and more, too; for some of them had in them more feet than the verses would bear.

Cel. That 's no matter: the feet might bear the verses.

Ros. Ay, but the feet were lame and could not bear themselves without the verse, and therefore stood lamely in the verse.

Cel. But didst thou hear without wondering how thy name should be hanged and carved upon these trees?

Ros. I was seven of the nine days out of the wonder before you came; for look here what I found on a palm tree. I was never so berhymed since Pythagoras' time, that I was an Irish rat, which I can hardly remember.

Cel. Trow you who hath done this?

Ros. Is it a man?

Cel. And a chain that you once wore about his neck. Change you colour?

Ros. I prithee, who?

Cel. O Lord, Lord! it is a hard matter for friends to meet; but mountains may be removed with earthquakes and so encounter.

Ros. Nay, but who is it?

Cel. Is it possible?

Ros. Nay, I prithee now with most petitionary vehemence, tell me who it is.

Cel. O wonderful, wonderful, and most wonderful wonderful! and yet again wonderful, and after that, out of all whooping!

Ros. Good my complexion! dost thou think, though I am caparisoned like a man, I have a doublet and hose in my disposition? One inch of delay more is a South-sea of discovery. I prithee, tell me who is it quickly, and speak apace. I would thou couldst stammer, that thou might'st pour this concealed man out of thy mouth, as wine comes out of a narrow-mouth'd bottle, either too much at once, or none at all. I prithee, take the cork out of thy mouth that I may drink thy tidings.

Cel. So you may put a man in your belly.

Ros. Is he of God's making? What manner of man? Is his head worth a hat? or his chin worth a beard?

Cel. Nay, he hath but a little beard.

Ros. Why, God will send more, if the man will be thankful: let me stay the growth of his beard, if thou delay me not the knowledge of his chin.

Cel. It is young Orlando, that tripped up the wrestler's heels and your heart both in an instant.

Ros. Nay, but the devil take mocking: speak sad brow and true maid.

Cel. I' faith, coz, 't is he.

Ros. Orlando?

Cel. Orlando.

Ros. Alas the day! what shall I do with my doublet and hose? What did he when thou saw'st him? What said he? How looked he? Wherein went he? What makes he here? Did he ask for me? Where remains he? How parted he with thee? And when shalt thou see him again? Answer me in one word.

Cel. You must borrow me Gargantua's mouth first: 't is a word too great for any mouth of this age's size. To say ay and no to these particulars is more than to answer in a catechism.

Ros. But doth he know that I am in this forest and in man's apparel? Looks he as freshly as he did the day he wrestled?

Cel. It is as easy to count atomies as to resolve the propositions of a lover. But take a taste of my finding him, and relish it with good observance. I found him under a tree, like a dropped acorn.

Ros. It may well be called Jove's tree, when it drops forth such fruit.

Cel. Give me audience, good madam.

Ros. Proceed.

Cel. There lay he, stretched along, like a wounded knight.

Ros. Though it be pity to see such a sight, it well becomes the ground.

Cel. Cry "holla" to thy tongue, I prithee; it curvets unseasonably. He was furnished like a hunter.

Ros. O, ominous! he comes to kill my heart.

Cel. I would sing my song without a burden. Thou bring'st me out of tune.

Ros. Do you not know I am a woman? When I think, I must speak. Sweet, say on.

171. scrip, wallet. **188. berhymed . . . rat,** refers to the theory of the transmigration of souls credited to Pythagoras, a Greek philosopher, and to the belief that rats in Ireland were killed by rhymed spells. **189. Trow,** know. **194-6.** "Friends may meet, but mountains never greet." **199. petitionary,** entreating. **204. Good my complexion,** reference to her blushing. **206. delay . . . discovery,** the least delay in answering will mean an ocean of guessing.

221. stay, wait for. **227. sad brow,** serious expression. **234. Wherein went he,** how was he dressed. **237. Gargantua's mouth,** Rabelais' giant swallowed five pilgrims at once. **245. atomies,** motes in the sunbeams. **246. resolve,** solve. **248. observance,** observation. **249. Jove's tree,** the oak. **257. Cry "holla,"** check. **261. burden,** refrain.

Cel. You bring me out. [*Enter Orlando and Jaques.*] Soft! comes he not here?

Ros. 'T is he: slink by, and note him.

Jaq. I thank you for your company; but, good faith, I had as lief have been myself alone.

Orl. And so had I; but yet, for fashion sake, I thank you too for your society.

Jaq. God buy you; let 's meet as little as we can.

Orl. I do desire we may be better strangers.

Jaq. I pray you mar no more trees with writing love-songs in their barks.

Orl. I pray you mar no moe of my verses with reading them ill-favouredly.

Jaq. Rosalind is your love's name?

Orl. Yes, just.

Jaq. I do not like her name.

Orl. There was no thought of pleasing you when she was christened.

Jaq. What stature is she of?

Orl. Just as high as my heart.

Jaq. You are full of pretty answers. Have you not been acquainted with goldsmiths' wives, and conned them out of rings?

Orl. Not so; but I answer you right painted cloth, from whence you have studied your questions.

Jaq. You have a nimble wit. I think 't was made of Atalanta's heels. Will you sit down with me? and we two will rail against our mistress the world, and all our misery.

Orl. I will chide no breather in the world but myself, against whom I know most faults.

Jaq. The worst fault you have is to be in love.

Orl. 'T is a fault I will not change for your best virtue. I am weary of you.

Jaq. By my troth, I was seeking for a fool when I found you.

Orl. He is drowned in the brook: look but in, and you shall see him.

Jaq. There I shall see mine own figure.

Orl. Which I take to be either a fool or a cipher.

Jaq. I 'll tarry no longer with you: farewell, good Signior Love.

Orl. I am glad of your departure: adieu, good Monsieur Melancholy. *Exit Jaques.*

Ros. [*Aside to Celia.*] I will speak to him like a saucy lackey, and under that habit play the knave with him. Do you hear, forester?

Orl. Very well: what would you?

Ros. I pray you, what is 't o'clock?

Orl. You should ask me what time o' day: there 's no clock in the forest.

Ros. Then there is no true lover in the forest; else sighing every minute and groaning every hour would detect the lazy foot of Time as well as a clock.

Orl. And why not the swift foot of Time? Had not that been as proper?

Ros. By no means, sir: time travels in divers paces with divers persons. I 'll tell you who Time ambles withal, who Time trots withal, who Time gallops withal, and who he stands still withal.

Orl. I prithee, who doth he trot withal?

Ros. Marry, he trots hard with a young maid between the contract of her marriage and the day it is solemnized: if the interim be but a se'nnight, Time's pace is so hard that it seems the length of seven year.

Orl. Who ambles Time withal?

Ros. With a priest that lacks Latin, and a rich man that hath not the gout; for the one sleeps easily because he cannot study, and the other lives merrily because he feels no pain; the one lacking the burden of lean and wasteful learning, the other knowing no burden of heavy tedious penury. These Time ambles withal.

Orl. Who doth he gallop withal?

Ros. With a thief to the gallows; for though he go as softly as foot can fall, he thinks himself too soon there.

Orl. Who stays it still withal?

Ros. With lawyers in the vacation; for they sleep between term and term, and then they perceive not how Time moves.

Orl. Where dwell you, pretty youth?

Ros. With this shepherdess, my sister; here in the skirts of the forest, like fringe upon a petticoat.

Orl. Are you native of this place?

Ros. As the cony that you see dwell where she is kindled.

Orl. Your accent is something finer than you could purchase in so removed a dwelling.

Ros. I have been told so of many; but indeed an old religious uncle of mine taught me to speak, who was in his youth an inland man; one that knew courtship too well, for there he fell in love. I have heard him read many lectures against it, and I thank God I am not a woman, to be touched with so many giddy offences as he hath generally taxed their whole sex withal.

273. **buy,** be with. Cf., our "good-by." 281. **just,** just so. 289. **conn'd . . . rings,** memorized the mottoes carved in the inside of rings. 291. **painted cloth,** the painted canvas wall hangings were often decorated with Biblical scenes and moral maxims.

334. **se'nnight,** week. 357. **cony,** rabbit. 358. **kindled,** littered. 360. **purchase,** acquire. 362. **religious,** of a religious order. 364. **courtship,** (1) courtly manners, (2) wooing.

Orl. Can you remember any of the principal evils that he laid to the charge of women?

Ros. There were none principal; they were all like one another as half-pence are, every one fault seeming monstrous till his fellow-fault came to match it.

Orl. I prithee, recount some of them.

Ros. No, I will not cast away my physic but on those that are sick. There is a man haunts the forest, that abuses our young plants with carving Rosalind on their barks; hangs odes upon hawthorns and elegies on brambles; all, forsooth, deifying the name of Rosalind. If I could meet that fancy-monger, I would give him some good counsel, for he seems to have the quotidian of love upon him.

Orl. I am he that is so love-shaked. I pray you, tell me your remedy.

Ros. There is none of my uncle's marks upon you: he taught me how to know a man in love, in which cage of rushes I am sure you are not prisoner.

Orl. What were his marks?

Ros. A lean cheek, which you have not; a blue eye and sunken, which you have not; an unquestionable spirit, which you have not; a beard neglected, which you have not; but I pardon you for that, for simply your having in beard is a younger brother's revenue. Then your hose should be ungartered, your bonnet unbanded, your sleeve unbuttoned, your shoe untied, and every thing about you demonstrating a careless desolation. But you are no such man; you are rather point-device in your accoutrements, as loving yourself than seeming the lover of any other.

Orl. Fair youth, I would I could make thee believe I love.

Ros. Me believe it? You may as soon make her that you love believe it; which, I warrant, she is apter to do than to confess she does: that is one of the points in the which women still give the lie to their consciences. But, in good sooth, are you he that hangs the verses on the trees, wherein Rosalind is so admired?

Orl. I swear to thee, youth, by the white hand of Rosalind, I am that he, that unfortunate he.

Ros. But are you so much in love as your rhymes speak?

Orl. Neither rhyme nor reason can express how much.

Ros. Love is merely a madness, and, I tell you, deserves as well a dark house and a whip as madmen do; and the reason why they are not so punished and cured is, that the lunacy is so ordinary that the whippers are in love too. Yet I profess curing it by counsel.

Orl. Did you ever cure any so?

Ros. Yes, one, and in this manner. He was to imagine me his love, his mistress, and I set him every day to woo me. At which time would I, being but a moonish youth, grieve, be effeminate, changeable, longing and liking, proud, fantastical, apish, shallow, inconstant, full of tears, full of smiles; for every passion something and for no passion truly any thing, as boys and women are for the most part cattle of this colour; would now like him, now loathe him; then entertain him, then forswear him; now weep for him, then spit at him; that I drave my suitor from his mad humour of love to a living humour of madness; which was, to forswear the full stream of the world and to live in a nook, merely monastic. And thus I cured him; and this way will I take upon me to wash your liver as clean as a sound sheep's heart, that there shall not be one spot of love in 't.

Orl. I would not be cured, youth.

Ros. I would cure you, if you would but call me Rosalind and come every day to my cote and woo me.

Orl. Now, by the faith of my love, I will. Tell me where it is.

Ros. Go with me to it and I 'll show it you; and by the way you shall tell me where in the forest you live. Will you go?

Orl. With all my heart, good youth.

Ros. Nay, you must call me Rosalind. Come, sister, will you go? *Exeunt.*

Scene III. *The forest.*

Enter Clown *Touchstone* and *Audrey;* *Jaques* behind.

Touch. Come apace, good Audrey. I will fetch up your goats, Audrey: and how, Audrey, am I the man yet? Doth my simple feature content you?

Aud. Your features? Lord warrant us! what features?

Touch. I am here with thee and thy goats, as the most capricious poet, honest Ovid, was among the Goths.

Jaq. [*Aside.*] O knowledge ill-inhabited, worse than Jove in a thatch'd house!

382. fancy-monger, dealer in love. **384. quotidian,** daily fever. **393. blue eye,** blue under the eye. **394. unquestionable,** averse to conversation. **395-6. for simply . . . revenue,** i.e., for all you have of beard is like a younger brother's income. **401-2. point-device,** affectedly faultless.

430. moonish, inconstant. **442. merely,** entirely. **444. liver,** supposed to be the seat of love. **Scene iii: 4. feature,** shape. **7-9. goats, etc.,** capricious; suggests Latin *caper*, goat; Ovid, a pastoral poet, was banished to the land of Getae, or Goths; Goths, pun on goats. **10. ill-inhabited,** ill-housed.

Touch. When a man's verses cannot be understood, nor a man's good wit seconded with the forward child, understanding, it strikes a man more dead than a great reckoning in a little room. Truly, I would the gods had made thee poetical.

Aud. I do not know what "poetical" is. Is it honest in deed and word? Is it a true thing?

Touch. No, truly; for the truest poetry is the most feigning; and lovers are given to poetry, and what they swear in poetry may be said as lovers they do feign.

Aud. Do you wish then that the gods had made me poetical?

Touch. I do, truly; for thou swearest to me thou art honest. Now, if thou wert a poet, I might have some hope thou didst feign.

Aud. Would you not have me honest?

Touch. No, truly, unless thou wert hard-favour'd; for honesty coupled to beauty is to have honey a sauce to sugar.

Jaq. [*Aside.*] A material fool!

Aud. Well, I am not fair; and therefore I pray the gods make me honest.

Touch. Truly, and to cast away honesty upon a foul slut were to put good meat into an unclean dish.

Aud. I am not a slut, though I thank the gods I am foul.

Touch. Well, praised be the gods for thy foulness! Sluttishness may come hereafter. But be it as it may be, I will marry thee, and to that end I have been with Sir Oliver Martext, the vicar of the next village, who hath promised to meet me in this place of the forest and to couple us.

Jaq. [*Aside.*] I would fain see this meeting.

Aud. Well, the gods give us joy!

Touch. Amen. A man may, if he were of a fearful heart, stagger in this attempt; for here we have no temple but the wood, no assembly but horn-beasts. But what though? Courage! As horns are odious, they are necessary. It is said, "Many a man knows no end of his goods." Right; many a man has good horns, and knows no end of them. Well, that is the dowry of his wife; 't is none of his own getting. Horns?—even so. Poor men alone? No, no; the noblest deer hath them as huge as the rascal. Is the single man therefore blessed? No: as a walled town is more worthier than a village, so is the forehead of a married man more honourable than the bare brow of a bachelor; and by how much defence is better than no skill, by so much is a horn more precious than to want.

Enter *Sir Oliver Martext.*

Here comes Sir Oliver. Sir Oliver Martext, you are well met. Will you dispatch us here under this tree, or shall we go with you to your chapel?

Sir Oli. Is there none here to give the woman?

Touch. I will not take her on gift of any man.

Sir Oli. Truly, she must be given, or the marriage is not lawful.

Jaq. Proceed, proceed: I 'll give her.

Touch. Good even, good Master What-ye-call 't; how do you, sir? You are very well met. God 'ild you for your last company: I am very glad to see you: even a toy in hand here, sir. Nay, pray be covered.

Jaq. Will you be married, motley?

Touch. As the ox hath his bow, sir, the horse his curb, and the falcon her bells, so man hath his desires; and as pigeons bill, so wedlock would be nibbling.

Jaq. And will you, being a man of your breeding, be married under a bush like a beggar? Get you to church, and have a good priest that can tell you what marriage is: this fellow will but join you together as they join wainscot; then one of you will prove a shrunk panel, and like green timber warp, warp.

Touch. [*Aside.*] I am not in the mind but I were better to be married of him than of another; for he is not like to marry me well; and not being well married, it will be a good excuse for me hereafter to leave my wife.

Jaq. Go thou with me, and let me counsel thee.

Touch. Come, sweet Audrey;
We must be married, or we must live in bawdry.
Farewell, good Master Oliver: not,—

O sweet Oliver,
O brave Oliver,
Leave me not behind thee;

but,—

Wind away,
Begone, I say,
I will not to wedding with thee.

Exeunt Jaques, Touchstone, and Audrey.

Sir Oli. 'T is no matter. Ne'er a fantastical knave of them all shall flout me out of my calling. *Exit.*

14. great reckoning, big bill. **20. feigning,** (1) imaginative, (2) dissembling. **32. material,** full of ideas. **43. Sir,** title of priest. **49. stagger,** hesitate. **51. But what though,** but what of it? **52. necessary,** unavoidable. **58. rascal,** young deer out of season.

75. 'ild, reward. **78. be covered,** put on your hat. **80. bow,** yoke.

Scene IV. *The forest.*

Enter *Rosalind* and *Celia.*

Ros. Never talk to me; I will weep.

Cel. Do, I prithee; but yet have the grace to consider that tears do not become a man.

Ros. But have I not cause to weep?

Cel. As good cause as one would desire; therefore weep.

Ros. His very hair is of the dissembling colour.

Cel. Something browner than Judas's. Marry, his kisses are Judas's own children.

Ros. I' faith his hair is of a good colour.

Cel. An excellent colour: your chestnut was ever the only colour.

Ros. And his kissing is as full of sanctity as the touch of holy bread.

Cel. He hath bought a pair of cast lips of Diana: a nun of winter's sisterhood kisses not more religiously; the very ice of chastity is in them.

Ros. But why did he swear he would come this morning, and comes not?

Cel. Nay, certainly, there is no truth in him.

Ros. Do you think so?

Cel. Yes; I think he is not a pick-purse nor a horse-stealer; but for his verity in love, I do think him as concave as a covered goblet or a worm-eaten nut.

Ros. Not true in love?

Cel. Yes, when he is in; but I think he is not in.

Ros. You have heard him swear downright he was.

Cel. "Was" is not "is": besides, the oath of a lover is no stronger than the word of a tapster; they are both the confirmer of false reckonings. He attends here in the forest on the Duke your father.

Ros. I met the Duke yesterday and had much question with him: he asked me of what parentage I was. I told him, of as good as he; so he laughed and let me go. But what talk we of fathers, when there is such a man as Orlando?

Cel. O, that 's a brave man! He writes brave verses, speaks brave words, swears brave oaths and breaks them bravely, quite traverse, athwart the heart of his lover; as a puisny tilter, that spurs his horse but on one side, breaks his staff like a noble goose: but all 's brave that youth mounts and folly guides. Who comes here?

Enter *Corin.*

Cor. Mistress and master, you have oft inquired
After the shepherd that complain'd of love,
Who you saw sitting by me on the turf,
Praising the proud disdainful shepherdess
That was his mistress.

Cel. Well, and what of him?

Cor. If you will see a pageant truly play'd,
Between the pale complexion of true love
And the red glow of scorn and proud disdain,
Go hence a little and I shall conduct you,
If you will mark it.

Ros. O, come, let us remove;
The sight of lovers feedeth those in love.
Bring us to this sight, and you shall say
I 'll prove a busy actor in their play. *Exeunt.*

Scene V. *Another part of the forest.*

Enter *Silvius* and *Phebe.*

Sil. Sweet Phebe, do not scorn me; do not, Phebe;
Say that you love me not, but say not so
In bitterness. The common executioner,
Whose heart th' accustom'd sight of death makes hard,
Falls not the axe upon the humbled neck
But first begs pardon. Will you sterner be
Than he that dies and lives by bloody drops?

Enter *Rosalind, Celia,* and *Corin* behind.

Phe. I would not be thy executioner:
I fly thee, for I would not injure thee.
Thou tell'st me there is murder in mine eye:
'T is pretty, sure, and very probable,
That eyes, that are the frail'st and softest things,
Who shut their coward gates on atomies,
Should be called tyrants, butchers, murderers!
Now I do frown on thee with all my heart;
And if mine eyes can wound, now let them kill thee:
Now counterfeit to swound; why, now fall down;
Or if thou canst not, O, for shame, for shame,
Lie not, to say mine eyes are murderers!
Now show the wound mine eye hath made in thee:
Scratch thee but with a pin, and there remains
Some scar of it; lean but upon a rush,

Scene iv: 9. browner than Judas's, Judas is represented as having red hair. **15. holy bread,** the bread of the sacrament. **16. cast,** cast-off. **44. traverse,** across. It was disgraceful to break a lance athwart the body of an adversary instead of by a direct blow on his shield. **45. puisny,** unskilful.

56. pale, sighing was supposed to thin the blood.
Scene v: 7. dies and lives, makes his living.

The cicatrice and capable impressure
Thy palm some moment keeps; but now mine eyes,
Which I have darted at thee, hurt thee not,
Nor, I am sure, there is no force in eyes
That can do hurt.
Sil. O dear Phebe,
If ever—as that ever may be near—
You meet in some fresh cheek the power of fancy,
Then shall you know the wounds invisible
That love's keen arrows make.
Phe. But till that time
Come not thou near me; and when that time comes,
Afflict me with thy mocks, pity me not,
As till that time I shall not pity thee.
Ros. And why, I pray you? Who might be your mother,
That you insult, exult, and all at once,
Over the wretched? What though you have no beauty,—
As, by my faith, I see no more in you
Than without candle may go dark to bed—
Must you be therefore proud and pitiless?
Why, what means this? Why do you look on me?
I see no more in you than in the ordinary
Of nature's sale-work. 'Od's my little life,
I think she means to tangle my eyes too!
No, faith, proud mistress, hope not after it.
'T is not your inky brows, your black silk hair,
Your bugle eyeballs, nor your cheek of cream
That can entame my spirits to your worship.
You foolish shepherd, wherefore do you follow her,
Like foggy south, puffing with wind and rain?
You are a thousand times a properer man
Than she a woman. 'T is such fools as you
That makes the world full of ill-favour'd children:
'T is not her glass, but you, that flatters her;
And out of you she sees herself more proper
Than any of her lineaments can show her.
But, mistress, know yourself: down on your knees,
And thank heaven, fasting, for a good man's love;
For I must tell you friendly in your ear,
Sell when you can; you are not for all markets.
Cry the man mercy; love him; take his offer.
Foul is most foul, being foul to be a scoffer.
So take her to thee, shepherd: fare you well.
Phe. Sweet youth, I pray you, chide a year together.
I had rather hear you chide than this man woo.
Ros. He 's fallen in love with your foulness, and she 'll fall in love with my anger. If it be so, as fast as she answers thee with frowning looks, I 'll sauce her with bitter words. Why look you so upon me?
Phe. For no ill will I bear you.
Ros. I pray you, do not fall in love with me,
For I am falser than vows made in wine.
Besides, I like you not. If you will know my house,
'T is at the tuft of olives here hard by.
Will you go, sister? Shepherd, ply her hard.
Come, sister. Shepherdess, look on him better,
And be not proud: though all the world could see,
None could be so abus'd in sight as he.
Come, to our flock.
Exeunt Rosalind, Celia, and Corin
Phe. Dead shepherd, now I find thy saw of might,
"Who ever lov'd that lov'd not at first sight?"
Sil. Sweet Phebe,—
Phe. Ha, what say'st thou, Silvius?
Sil. Sweet Phebe, pity me.
Phe. Why, I am sorry for thee, gentle Silvius.
Sil. Wherever sorrow is, relief would be.
If you do sorrow at my grief in love,
By giving love, your sorrow and my grief
Were both extermin'd.
Phe. Thou hast my love: is not that neighbourly?
Sil. I would have you.
Phe. Why, that were covetousness.
Silvius, the time was that I hated thee,
And yet it is not that I bear thee love;
But since that thou canst talk of love so well,
Thy company, which erst was irksome to me,
I will endure, and I 'll employ thee too.
But do not look for further recompense
Than thine own gladness that thou art employ'd.
Sil. So holy and so perfect is my love,
And I in such a poverty of grace,
That I shall think it a most plenteous crop
To glean the broken ears after the man
That the main harvest reaps: loose now and then
A scatter'd smile, and that I 'll live upon.

23. cicatrice and capable impressure, mark and perceptible impression. **43. sale-work,** ready-made work. **47. bugle,** bead of black glass. **51. properer,** handsomer. **62. Foul,** (1) ugly, (2) morally bad. You are doubly bad in being both ugly and a scoffer.

79. abus'd, deceived. **81. Dead shepherd,** Christopher Marlowe, killed in a brawl June, 1593. The quotation is from his poem, *Hero and Leander*. **89. extermin'd,** exterminated.

Phe. Know'st thou the youth that spoke to me erewhile?
Sil. Not very well, but I have met him oft;
And he hath bought the cottage and the bounds
That the old carlot once was master of.
Phe. Think not I love him, though I ask for him;
'T is but a peevish boy; yet he talks well.
But what care I for words? Yet words do well
When he that speaks them pleases those that hear.
It is a pretty youth; not very pretty;
But, sure, he 's proud, and yet his pride becomes him.
He 'll make a proper man: the best thing in him
Is his complexion; and faster than his tongue
Did make offence his eye did heal it up.
He is not very tall; yet for his years he 's tall.
His leg is but so so; and yet 't is well.
There was a pretty redness in his lip,
A little riper and more lusty red
Than that mix'd in his cheek; 't was just the difference
Betwixt the constant red and mingled damask.
There be some women, Silvius, had they mark'd him
In parcels as I did, would have gone near
To fall in love with him; but, for my part,
I love him not nor hate him not; and yet
I have more cause to hate him than to love him,
For what had he to do to chide at me?
He said mine eyes were black and my hair black;
And, now I am remember'd, scorn'd at me:
I marvel why I answer'd not again:
But that 's all one; omittance is no quittance.
I 'll write to him a very taunting letter,
And thou shalt bear it; wilt thou, Silvius?
Sil. Phebe, with all my heart.
Phe. I 'll write it straight;
The matter 's in my head and in my heart.
I will be bitter with him and passing short.
Go with me, Silvius. *Exeunt.*

ACT IV. Scene I. *The forest.*

Enter *Rosalind, Celia,* and *Jaques.*

Jaq. I prithee, pretty youth, let me be better acquainted with thee.

Ros. They say you are a melancholy fellow.

Jaq. I am so; I do love it better than laughing.

Ros. Those that are in extremity of either are abominable fellows, and betray themselves to every modern censure worse than drunkards.

Jaq. Why, 't is good to be sad and say nothing.

Ros. Why then, 't is good to be a post.

Jaq. I have neither the scholar's melancholy, which is emulation; nor the musician's, which is fantastical; nor the courtier's, which is proud; nor the soldier's, which is ambitious; nor the lawyer's, which is politic; nor the lady's, which is nice; nor the lover's, which is all these: but it is a melancholy of mine own, compounded of many simples, extracted from many objects; and indeed the sundry contemplation of my travels, in which my often rumination wraps me in a most humorous sadness—

Ros. A traveller! By my faith, you have great reason to be sad: I fear you have sold your own lands to see other men's; then, to have seen much, and to have nothing, is to have rich eyes and poor hands.

Jaq. Yes, I have gained my experience.

Enter *Orlando.*

Ros. And your experience makes you sad: I had rather have a fool to make me merry than experience to make me sad; and to travel for it too!

Orl. Good-day and happiness, dear Rosalind!

Jaq. Nay, then, God buy you, an you talk in blank verse. *Exit.*

Ros. Farewell, Monsieur Traveller: look you lisp and wear strange suits, disable all the benefits of your own country, be out of love with your nativity, and almost chide God for making you that countenance you are, or I will scarce think you have swam in a gondola.

107. bounds, pastures. **108. carlot,** rustic, dim. of churl. **Act IV, Scene i: 7. modern censure,** ordinary judgment. **14. politic,** a matter of policy, insincere. **15. nice,** fastidious. **17. simples,** single ingredients.

123. mingled damask, red and white (pink). **125. In parcels,** piecemeal. **Act IV, Scene i: 20. humorous,** temperamental. **33. disable,** disparage. **37. swam in a gondola,** i.e., been in Venice.

Why, how now, Orlando! Where have you been all this while? You a lover! An you serve me such another trick, never come in my sight more.

Orl. My fair Rosalind, I come within an hour of my promise.

Ros. Break an hour's promise in love! He that will divide a minute into a thousand parts, and break but a part of the thousandth part of a minute in the affairs of love, it may be said of him that Cupid hath clapped him o' th' shoulder, but I'll warrant him heart-whole.

Orl. Pardon me, dear Rosalind.

Ros. Nay, an you be so tardy, come no more in my sight. I had as lief be wooed of a snail.

Orl. Of a snail?

Ros. Ay, of a snail; for though he comes slowly, he carries his house on his head; a better jointure, I think, than you make a woman: besides, he brings his destiny with him.

Orl. What 's that?

Ros. Why, horns, which such as you are fain to be beholding to your wives for: but he comes armed in his fortune and prevents the slander of his wife.

Orl. Virtue is no horn-maker; and my Rosalind is virtuous.

Ros. And I am your Rosalind.

Cel. It pleases him to call you so; but he hath a Rosalind of a better leer than you.

Ros. Come, woo me, woo me; for now I am in a holiday humour and like enough to consent. What would you say to me now, an I were your very very Rosalind?

Orl. I would kiss before I spoke.

Ros. Nay, you were better speak first; and when you were gravelled for lack of matter, you might take occasion to kiss. Very good orators, when they are out, they will spit; and for lovers lacking—God warn us!—matter, the cleanliest shift is to kiss.

Orl. How if the kiss be denied?

Ros. Then she puts you to entreaty and there begins new matter.

Orl. Who could be out, being before his beloved mistress?

Ros. Marry, that should you if I were your mistress, or I should think my honesty ranker than my wit.

Orl. What, of my suit?

Ros. Not out of your apparel, and yet out of your suit. Am not I your Rosalind?

Orl. I take some joy to say you are, because I would be talking of her.

Ros. Well, in her person, I say I will not have you.

Orl. Then in mine own person I die.

Ros. No, faith, die by attorney. The poor world is almost six thousand years old, and in all this time there was not any man died in his own person, videlicet, in a love-cause. Troilus had his brains dashed out with a Grecian club; yet he did what he could to die before, and he is one of the patterns of love. Leander, he would have lived many a fair year though Hero had turned nun, if it had not been for a hot mid-summer night; for, good youth, he went but forth to wash him in the Hellespont and being taken with the cramp was drowned; and the foolish chroniclers of that age found it was—Hero of Sestos. But these are all lies. Men have died from time to time and worms have eaten them, but not for love.

Orl. I would not have my right Rosalind of this mind; for, I protest, her frown might kill me.

Ros. By this hand, it will not kill a fly. But come, now I will be your Rosalind in a more coming-on disposition; and ask me what you will, I will grant it.

Orl. Then love me, Rosalind.

Ros. Yes, faith, will I, Fridays and Saturdays and all.

Orl. And wilt thou have me?

Ros. Ay, and twenty such.

Orl. What sayest thou?

Ros. Are you not good?

Orl. I hope so.

Ros. Why then, can one desire too much of a good thing? Come, sister, you shall be the priest and marry us. Give me your hand, Orlando. What do you say, sister?

Orl. Pray thee, marry us.

Cel. I cannot say the words.

Ros. You must begin, "Will you, Orlando,"—

Cel. Go to. Will you, Orlando, have to wife this Rosalind?

Orl. I will.

Ros. Ay, but when?

Orl. Why now; as fast as she can marry us.

Ros. Then you must say, "I take thee, Rosalind, for wife."

Orl. I take thee, Rosalind, for wife.

Ros. I might ask you for your commission; but I do take thee, Orlando, for my hus-

47-8. clapped . . . shoulder, i.e., arrested him. **56. jointure,** dowry. **60. beholding,** indebted. **61. prevents,** anticipates. **67. leer,** face, look. **74. gravelled,** at a standstill. **76. out,** at a loss. **77. warn,** defend. **85. honesty ranker,** chastity better grown, greater.

97-106. Troilus . . ., Rosalind belittles the famous loves of Troilus and Cressida, and Hero and Leander by the use of the homely terms *club* (l. 98), *wash* (l. 103) and *cramp* (l. 104).

band. There 's a girl goes before the priest; and certainly a woman's thought runs before her actions.

Orl. So do all thoughts; they are winged.

Ros. Now tell me how long you would have her after you have possessed her.

Orl. For ever and a day.

Ros. Say "a day," without the "ever." No, no, Orlando. Men are April when they woo, December when they wed; maids are May when they are maids, but the sky changes when they are wives. I will be more jealous of thee than a Barbary cock-pigeon over his hen, more clamorous than a parrot against rain, more new-fangled than an ape, more giddy in my desires than a monkey. I will weep for nothing, like Diana in the fountain, and I will do that when you are disposed to be merry. I will laugh like a hyen, and that when thou art inclined to sleep.

Orl. But will my Rosalind do so?

Ros. By my life, she will do as I do.

Orl. O, but she is wise.

Ros. Or else she could not have the wit to do this: the wiser, the waywarder: make the doors upon a woman's wit and it will out at the casement; shut that and 't will out at the key-hole; stop that, 't will fly with the smoke out at the chimney.

Orl. A man that had a wife with such a wit, he might say, "Wit, whither wilt?"

Ros. Nay, you might keep that check for it, till you met your wife's wit going to your neighbour's bed.

Orl. And what wit could wit have to excuse that?

Ros. Marry, to say she came to seek you there. You shall never take her without her answer, unless you take her without her tongue. O, that woman that cannot make her fault her husband's occasion, let her never nurse her child herself, for she will breed it like a fool!

Orl. For these two hours, Rosalind, I will leave thee.

Ros. Alas, dear love, I cannot lack thee two hours!

Orl. I must attend the Duke at dinner: by two o'clock I will be with thee again.

Ros. Ay, go your ways, go your ways; I knew what you would prove: my friends told me as much, and I thought no less: that flattering tongue of yours won me: 't is but one cast away, and so, come, death! Two o'clock is your hour?

Orl. Ay, sweet Rosalind.

Ros. By my troth, and in good earnest, and so God mend me, and by all pretty oaths that are not dangerous, if you break one jot of your promise or come one minute behind your hour, I will think you the most pathetical break-promise, and the most hollow lover, and the most unworthy of her you call Rosalind, that may be chosen out of the gross band of the unfaithful; therefore beware my censure and keep your promise.

Orl. With no less religion than if thou wert indeed my Rosalind; so adieu.

Ros. Well, Time is the old justice that examines all such offenders, and let Time try. Adieu. *Exit Orlando.*

Cel. You have simply misused our sex in your love-prate. We must have your doublet and hose plucked over your head, and show the world what the bird hath done to her own nest.

Ros. O coz, coz, coz, my pretty little coz, that thou didst know how many fathom deep I am in love! But it cannot be sounded: my affection hath an unknown bottom, like the bay of Portugal.

Cel. Or rather, bottomless; that as fast as you pour affection in, it runs out.

Ros. No, that same wicked bastard of Venus that was begot of thought, conceived of spleen, and born of madness, that blind rascally boy that abuses every one's eyes because his own are out, let him be judge how deep I am in love. I 'll tell thee, Aliena, I cannot be out of the sight of Orlando; I 'll go find a shadow and sigh till he come.

Cel. And I 'll sleep. *Exeunt.*

Scene II. *The forest.*

Enter *Jaques, Lords,* and *Foresters.*

Jaq. Which is he that killed the deer?

A Lord. Sir, it was I.

Jaq. Let 's present him to the Duke, like a Roman conqueror; and it would do well to set the deer's horns upon his head, for a branch of victory. Have you no song, forester, for this purpose?

1. For. Yes, sir.

Jaq. Sing it. 'T is no matter how it be in tune, so it make noise enough.

Song *Music.*

1. For.

What shall he have that killed the deer?
His leather skin and horns to wear.

152. **new-fangled,** eager for novelty. 156. **hyen,** hyena. 162. **make,** close. 168. **"Wit, whither wilt,"** cant expression to cut short another's talk. 178. **occasion,** i.e., occasion against, to get the better of him. 182. **lack,** be without.

195. **pathetical,** shocking. Probably a girl's cant adjective of the time, like the modern "awful." 201. **religion,** sense of obligation. 205. **simply misused,** absolutely abused. 218. **spleen,** any irrational impulse.

Then sing him home.
[*The rest shall bear this burden.*]
Take thou no scorn to wear the horn;
It was a crest ere thou wast born;
Thy father's father wore it,
And thy father bore it.
The horn, the horn, the lusty horn
Is not a thing to laugh to scorn.
Exeunt.

Scene III. *The forest.*

Enter *Rosalind* and *Celia.*

Ros. How say you now? Is it not past two o'clock? And here much Orlando!

Cel. I warrant you, with pure love and troubled brain, [*Enter Silvius*] he hath ta'en his bow and arrows and is gone forth—to sleep. Look, who comes here.

Sil. My errand is to you, fair youth;
My gentle Phebe bid me give you this.
I know not the contents; but, as I guess
By the stern brow and waspish action
Which she did use as she was writing of it,
It bears an angry tenour: pardon me,
I am but as a guiltless messenger.

Ros. Patience herself would startle at this letter
And play the swaggerer: bear this, bear all.
She says I am not fair, that I lack manners.
She calls me proud, and that she could not love me,
Were man as rare as phœnix. 'Od's my will!
Her love is not the hare that I do hunt.
Why writes she so to me? Well, shepherd, well,
This is a letter of your own device.

Sil. No, I protest, I know not the contents:
Phebe did write it.

Ros. Come, come, you are a fool,
And turn'd into the extremity of love.
I saw her hand; she has a leathern hand,
A freestone-coloured hand. I verily did think
That her old gloves were on, but 't was her hands;
She has a huswife's hand; but that 's no matter.
I say she never did invent this letter.
This is a man's invention and his hand.

Sil. Sure, it is hers.

Ros. Why, 't is a boisterous and a cruel style,
A style for challengers: why, she defies me,
Like Turk to Christian: women's gentle brain
Could not drop forth such giant-rude invention,
Such Ethiope words, blacker in their effect
Than in their countenance. Will you hear the letter?

Sil. So please you, for I never heard it yet;
Yet heard too much of Phebe's cruelty.

Ros. She Phebes me. Mark how the tyrant writes.
[*Reads.*]

"Art thou god to shepherd turn'd,
That a maiden's heart hath burn'd?"

Can a woman rail thus?

Sil. Call you this railing?

Ros. [*Reads.*]

"Why, thy godhead laid apart,
Warr'st thou with a woman's heart?"

Did you ever hear such railing?

"Whiles the eye of man did woo me,
That could do no vengeance to me."

Meaning me a beast.

"If the scorn of your bright eyne
Have power to raise such love in mine,
Alack, in me what strange effect
Would they work in mild aspect!
Whiles you chid me, I did love;
How then might your prayers move!
He that brings this love to thee
Little knows this love in me;
And by him seal up thy mind,
Whether that thy youth and kind
Will the faithful offer take
Of me and all that I can make;
Or else by him my love deny,
And then I'll study how to die."

Sil. Call you this chiding?

Cel. Alas, poor shepherd!

Ros. Do you pity him? No, he deserves no pity. Wilt thou love such a woman? What, to make thee an instrument and play false strains upon thee! Not to be endured! Well, go your way to her—for I see love hath made thee a tame snake—and say this to her: that if she love me, I charge her to love thee; if she will not, I will never have her unless thou entreat for her. If you be a true lover, hence, and not a word; for here comes more company. *Exit Silvius.*

Enter *Oliver.*

Oli. Good morrow, fair ones. Pray you, if you know,
Where in the purlieus of this forest stands

Scene iii: 17. phœnix, the fabulous bird of Arabia that renewed itself by fire every five hundred years. **23. turn'd into,** brought to. **25. freestone,** brown brick. **44. apart,** aside. **48. vengeance,** mischief. **59. youth and kind,** youthful nature. **68. instrument,** (1) tool, (2) musical instrument. **77. purlieus,** borders of a forest.

A sheep-cote fenc'd about with olive-trees?
Cel. West of this place, down in the neighbour bottom.
The rank of osiers by the murmuring stream
Left on your right hand brings you to the place.
But at this hour the house doth keep itself;
There 's none within.
Oli. If that an eye may profit by a tongue,
Then should I know you by description;
Such garments and such years. "The boy is fair,
Of female favour, and bestows himself
Like a ripe sister; the woman low,
And browner than her brother." Are not you
The owner of the house I did enquire for?
Cel. It is no boast, being ask'd, to say we are.
Oli. Orlando doth commend him to you both,
And to that youth he calls his Rosalind
He sends this bloody napkin. Are you he?
Ros. I am: what must we understand by this?
Oli. Some of my shame, if you will know of me
What man I am, and how, and why, and where
This handkercher was stain'd.
Cel. I pray you, tell it.
Oli. When last the young Orlando parted from you
He left a promise to return again
Within an hour; and pacing through the forest,
Chewing the food of sweet and bitter fancy,
Lo, what befell! He threw his eye aside,
And mark what object did present itself.
Under an old oak, whose boughs were moss'd with age
And high top bald with dry antiquity,
A wretched ragged man, o'ergrown with hair,
Lay sleeping on his back: about his neck
A green and gilded snake had wreath'd itself,
Who with her head nimble in threats approach'd
The opening of his mouth; but suddenly,
Seeing Orlando, it unlink'd itself.
And with indented glides did slip away
Into a bush; under which bush's shade
A lioness, with udders all drawn dry,
Lay couching, head on ground, with catlike watch,
When that the sleeping man should stir; for 't is
The royal disposition of that beast
To prey on nothing that doth seem as dead.
This seen, Orlando did approach the man
And found it was his brother, his elder brother.
Cel. O, I have heard him speak of that same brother;
And he did render him the most unnatural
That liv'd amongst men.
Oli. And well he might do so,
For well I know he was unnatural.
Ros. But, to Orlando. Did he leave him there,
Food to the suck'd and hungry lioness?
Oli. Twice did he turn his back and purpos'd so;
But kindness, nobler ever than revenge,
And nature, stronger than his just occasion,
Made him give battle to the lioness,
Who quickly fell before him; in which hurtling
From miserable slumber I awaked.
Cel. Are you his brother?
Ros. Was 't you he rescu'd?
Cel. Was 't you that did so oft contrive to kill him?
Oli. 'T was I; but 't is not I. I do not shame
To tell you what I was, since my conversion
So sweetly tastes, being the thing I am.
Ros. But, for the bloody napkin?
Oli. By and by.
When from the first to last betwixt us two
Tears our recountments had most kindly bath'd,
As how I came into that desert place,—
In brief, he led me to the gentle Duke,
Who gave me fresh array and entertainment,
Committing me unto my brother's love;
Who led me instantly unto his cave,
There stripp'd himself, and here upon his arm
The lioness had torn some flesh away,
Which all this while had bled; and now he fainted
And cried, in fainting, upon Rosalind.
Brief, I recover'd him, bound up his wound;
And, after some small space, being strong at heart,
He sent me hither, stranger as I am,
To tell this story, that you might excuse
His broken promise, and to give this napkin,
Dyed in his blood, unto the shepherd youth
That he in sport doth call his Rosalind.
Rosalind swoons.
Cel. Why, how now, Ganymede! sweet Ganymede!

79. **neighbour bottom**, neighboring valley. 80. **rank of osiers**, row of water-willows. 87. **favour**, aspect. **bestows himself**, acts. 88. **ripe**, mature. 94. **napkin**, handkerchief. 113. **indented**, undulating.

123. **render**, describe. 130. **just occasion**, fair opportunity. 132. **hurtling**, uproar. 135. **contrive**, plot. 141. **recountments**, tales. 151. **recover'd**, restored.

Oli. Many will swoon when they do look on blood.

Cel. There is more in it. Cousin Ganymede!

Oli. Look, he recovers.

Ros. I would I were at home.

Cel. We 'll lead you thither.
I pray you, will you take him by the arm?

Oli. Be of good cheer, youth. You a man!
You lack a man's heart.

Ros. I do so, I confess it. Ah, sirrah, a body would think this was well counterfeited! I pray you, tell your brother how well I counterfeited. Heigh-ho!

Oli. This was not counterfeit: there is too great testimony in your complexion that it was a passion of earnest.

Ros. Counterfeit, I assure you.

Oli. Well then, take a good heart and counterfeit to be a man.

Ros. So I do: but, i' faith, I should have been a woman by right.

Cel. Come, you look paler and paler: pray you, draw homewards. Good sir, go with us.

Oli. That will I, for I must bear answer back
How you excuse my brother, Rosalind.

Ros. I shall devise something; but, I pray you, commend my counterfeiting to him. Will you go? *Exeunt.*

ACT V. SCENE I. *The forest.*

Enter Clown *Touchstone* and *Audrey.*

Touch. We shall find a time, Audrey; patience, gentle Audrey.

Aud. Faith, the priest was good enough, for all the old gentleman's saying.

Touch. A most wicked Sir Oliver, Audrey, a most vile Martext. But, Audrey, there is a youth here in the forest lays claim to you.

Aud. Ay, I know who 't is; he hath no interest in me in the world: here comes the man you mean.

Enter *William.*

Touch. It is meat and drink to me to see a clown: by my troth, we that have good wits have much to answer for; we shall be flouting; we cannot hold.

Will. Good ev'n, Audrey.

Aud. God ye good ev'n, William.

Will. And good ev'n to you, sir.

Touch. Good ev'n, gentle friend. Cover thy head, cover thy head; nay, prithee, be covered. How old are you, friend?

Will. Five and twenty, sir.

Touch. A ripe age. Is thy name William?

Will. William, sir.

Touch. A fair name. Wast born i' th' forest here?

Will. Ay, sir, I thank God.

Touch. "Thank God"—a good answer. Art rich?

Will. Faith, sir, so so.

Touch. "So so" is good, very good, very excellent good; and yet it is not; it is but so so. Art thou wise?

Will. Ay, sir, I have a pretty wit.

Touch. Why, thou say'st well. I do now remember a saying: "The fool doth think he is wise, but the wise man knows himself to be a fool." The heathen philosopher, when he had a desire to eat a grape, would open his lips when he put it into his mouth; meaning thereby that grapes were made to eat and lips to open. You do love this maid?

Will. I do, sir.

Touch. Give me your hand. Art thou learned?

Will. No, sir.

Touch. Then learn this of me: to have, is to have; for it is a figure in rhetoric that drink, being poured out of a cup into a glass, by filling the one doth empty the other. For all your writers do consent that *ipse* is he: now, you are not *ipse*, for I am he.

Will. Which he, sir?

Touch. He, sir, that must marry this woman. Therefore, you clown, abandon—which is in the vulgar leave—the society—which in the boorish is company—of this female—which in the common is woman; which together is, abandon the society of this female; or, clown, thou perishest; or, to thy better understanding, diest; or, to wit, I kill thee, make thee away, translate thy life into death, thy liberty into bondage: I will deal in poison with thee, or in bastinado, or in steel: I will bandy with thee in faction, I will o'er-run thee with policy: I will kill thee a hundred and fifty ways: therefore tremble, and depart.

Act V, Scene i: 12. clown, countryman. **13. shall be flouting,** must jest.

61. bastinado, beating with a cudgel. **bandy,** contend. **62. faction,** dissensions (as opposed to physical encounters). **63. policy,** stratagems.

Aud. Do, good William.

Will. God rest you merry, sir. *Exit.*

Enter *Corin.*

Cor. Our master and mistress seeks you. Come, away, away!

Touch. Trip, Audrey! trip, Audrey! I attend, I attend. *Exeunt.*

Scene II. *The forest.*

Enter *Orlando* and *Oliver.*

Orl. Is 't possible that on so little acquaintance you should like her? That but seeing you should love her? And loving woo? And, wooing, she should grant? And will you persever to enjoy her?

Oli. Neither call the giddiness of it in question, the poverty of her, the small acquaintance, my sudden wooing, nor her sudden consenting; but say with me, I love Aliena; say with her that she loves me; consent with both that we may enjoy each other: it shall be to your good; for my father's house and all the revenue that was old Sir Roland's will I estate upon you, and here live and die a shepherd.

Enter *Rosalind.*

Orl. You have my consent. Let your wedding be to-morrow; thither will I invite the Duke and all 's contented followers. Go you and prepare Aliena; for look you, here comes my Rosalind.

Ros. God save you, brother.

Oli. And you, fair sister. *Exit.*

Ros. O, my dear Orlando, how it grieves me to see thee wear thy heart in a scarf!

Orl. It is my arm.

Ros. I thought thy heart had been wounded with the claws of a lion.

Orl. Wounded it is, but with the eyes of a lady.

Ros. Did your brother tell you how I counterfeited to swoun when he show'd me your handkercher?

Orl. Ay, and greater wonders than that.

Ros. O, I know where you are: nay, 't is true. There was never any thing so sudden but the fight of two rams, and Cæsar's thrasonical brag of "I came, saw, and overcame." For your brother and my sister no sooner met but they looked; no sooner looked but they loved; no sooner loved but they sighed; no sooner sighed but they asked one another the reason; no sooner knew the reason but they sought the remedy; and in these degrees have they made a pair of stairs to marriage which they will climb incontinent, or else be incontinent before marriage: they are in the very wrath of love and they will together. Clubs cannot part them.

Orl. They shall be married to-morrow, and I will bid the Duke to the nuptial. But, O, how bitter a thing it is to look into happiness through another man's eyes! By so much the more shall I to-morrow be at the height of heart-heaviness, by how much I shall think my brother happy in having what he wishes for.

Ros. Why then, to-morrow I cannot serve your turn for Rosalind?

Orl. I can live no longer by thinking.

Ros. I will weary you, then, no longer with idle talking. Know of me, then, (for now I speak to some purpose), that I know you are a gentleman of good conceit. I speak not this that you should bear a good opinion of my knowledge, insomuch I say I know you are; neither do I labour for a greater esteem than may in some little measure draw a belief from you, to do yourself good and not to grace me. Believe then, if you please, that I can do strange things: I have, since I was three year old, conversed with a magician, most profound in his art and yet not damnable. If you do love Rosalind so near the heart as your gesture cries it out, when your brother marries Aliena, shall you marry her. I know into what straits of fortune she is driven; and it is not impossible to me, if it appear not inconvenient to you, to set her before your eyes to-morrow, human as she is, and without any danger.

Orl. Speak'st thou in sober meanings?

Ros. By my life, I do; which I tender dearly, though I say I am a magician. Therefore, put you in your best array; bid your friends; for if you will be married to-morrow, you shall; and to Rosalind, if you will.

Enter *Silvius* and *Phebe.*

Look, here comes a lover of mine and a lover of hers.

Phe. Youth, you have done me much ungentleness,
To show the letter that I writ to you.

Scene ii: 14. estate, settle. **34. thrasonical,** like Thraso, the braggart in Terence's comedy *The Eunuch.*

42-3. incontinent . . . incontinent, immediately . . . unchaste. **45. Clubs,** the weapons of citizens, often used to part street frays; cf. *R. and J.*, I, i, 80. **58. conceit,** intellect. **66. conversed,** associated. **67. not damnable,** not worthy of legal condemnation. **69. gesture,** behavior. **77. tender dearly,** value highly.

Ros. I care not if I have. It is my study
To seem despiteful and ungentle to you.
You are there followed by a faithful shepherd;
Look upon him, love him. He worships you.

Phe. Good shepherd, tell this youth what 't is to love.

Sil. It is to be all made of sighs and tears;
And so am I for Phebe.

Phe. And I for Ganymede.

Orl. And I for Rosalind.

Ros. And I for no woman.

Sil. It is to be all made of faith and service;
And so am I for Phebe.

Phe. And I for Ganymede.

Orl. And I for Rosalind.

Ros. And I for no woman.

Sil. It is to be all made of fantasy.
All made of passion, and all made of wishes;
All adoration, duty, and obedience,
All humbleness, all patience, and impatience,
All purity, all trial, all observance;
And so am I for Phebe.

Phe. And so am I for Ganymede.

Orl. And so am I for Rosalind.

Ros. And so am I for no woman.

Phe. If this be so, why blame you me to love you?

Sil. If this be so, why blame you me to love you?

Orl. If this be so, why blame you me to love you?

Ros. Who do you speak to, "Why blame you me to love you?"

Orl. To her that is not here, nor doth not hear.

Ros. Pray you, no more of this; 't is like the howling of Irish wolves against the moon. [*To Silvius.*] I will help you, if I can. [*To Phebe.*] I would love you, if I could. To-morrow meet me all together. [*To Phebe.*] I will marry you, if ever I marry woman, and I 'll be married to-morrow. [*To Orlando.*] I will satisfy you, if ever I satisfied man, and you shall be married to-morrow. [*To Silvius.*] I will content you, if what pleases you contents you, and you shall be married to-morrow. [*To Orlando.*] As you love Rosalind, meet. [*To Silvius.*] As you love Phebe, meet. And as I love no woman, I 'll meet. So, fare you well. I have left you commands.

Sil. I 'll not fail, if I live.

Phe. Nor I.

Orl. Nor I.

Exeunt.

104. observance, homage.

Scene III. *The forest.*

Enter Clown *Touchstone* and *Audrey.*

Touch. To-morrow is the joyful day, Audrey; to-morrow will we be married.

Aud. I do desire it with all my heart; and I hope it is no dishonest desire to desire to be a woman of the world. Here come two of the banished Duke's pages.

Enter two *Pages.*

1. Page. Well met, honest gentlemen.

Touch. By my troth, well met. Come, sit, sit, and a song.

2. Page. We are for you: sit i' th' middle.

1. Page. Shall we clap into 't roundly, without hawking or spitting or saying we are hoarse, which are the only prologues to a bad voice?

2. Page. I' faith, i' faith; and both in a tune, like two gipsies on a horse.

Song.

It was a lover and his lass,
With a hey, and a ho, and a hey nonino,
That o'er the green corn-field did pass
In the spring time, the only pretty ring time,
When birds do sing, hey ding a ding, ding;
Sweet lovers love the spring.

Between the acres of the rye,
With a hey, and a ho, and hey nonino,
These pretty country folks would lie,
In spring time, &c.

This carol they began that hour,
With a hey, and a ho, and hey nonino,
How that a life was but a flower
In spring time, &c.

And therefore take the present time,
With a hey, and a ho, and hey nonino,
For love is crowned with the prime
In spring time, &c.

Touch. Truly, young gentlemen, though there was no great matter in the ditty, yet the note was very untuneable.

1. Page. You are deceived, sir: we kept time, we lost not our time.

Touch. By my troth, yes; I count it but time lost to hear such a foolish song. God buy you—and God mend your voices! Come, Audrey. *Exeunt.*

Scene IV. *The forest.*

Enter *Duke* senior, *Amiens, Jaques, Orlando, Oliver,* and *Celia.*

Duke S. Dost thou believe, Orlando, that the boy

Scene iii: 4. dishonest, immodest. **5. woman of the world,** married woman. **11. roundly,** briskly. **13. the only,** only the. **15. in a tune,** in unison. **20. ring time,** marriage time. **36. matter,** meaning.

Can do all this that he hath promised?
Orl. I sometimes do believe, and sometimes do not;
As those that fear they hope, and know they fear.

Enter *Rosalind, Silvius,* and *Phebe.*

Ros. Patience once more, whiles our compact is urg'd.
You say, if I bring in your Rosalind,
You will bestow her on Orlando here?
Duke S. That would I, had I kingdoms to give with her.
Ros. And you say, you will have her, when I bring her.
Orl. That would I, were I of all kingdoms king.
Ros. You say, you 'll marry me, if I be willing?
Phe. That will I, should I die the hour after.
Ros. But if you do refuse to marry me,
You 'll give yourself to this most faithful shepherd?
Phe. So is the bargain.
Ros. You say, that you 'll have Phebe, if she will?
Sil. Though to have her and death were both one thing.
Ros. I have promis'd to make all this matter even.
Keep you your word, O Duke, to give your daughter;
You yours, Orlando, to receive his daughter;
Keep your word, Phebe, that you 'll marry me,
Or else, refusing me, to wed this shepherd;
Keep your word, Silvius, that you 'll marry her,
If she refuse me; and from hence I go,
To make these doubts all even.
Exeunt Rosalind and Celia.
Duke S. I do remember in this shepherd boy
Some lively touches of my daughter's favour.
Orl. My lord, the first time that I ever saw him
Methought he was a brother to your daughter.
But, my good lord, this boy is forest-born,
And hath been tutor'd in the rudiments
Of many desperate studies by his uncle,
Whom he reports to be a great magician,
Obscured in the circle of this forest.

Enter *Touchstone* and *Audrey.*

Jaq. There is, sure, another flood toward, and these couples are coming to the ark. Here comes a pair of very strange beasts, which in all tongues are called fools.

Touch. Salutation and greeting to you all!

Jaq. Good my lord, bid him welcome: this is the motley-minded gentleman that I have so often met in the forest: he hath been a courtier, he swears.

Touch. If any man doubt that, let him put me to my purgation. I have trod a measure; I have flattered a lady; I have been politic with my friend, smooth with mine enemy; I have undone three tailors; I have had four quarrels, and like to have fought one.

Jaq. And how was that ta'en up?

Touch. Faith, we met, and found the quarrel was upon the seventh cause.

Jaq. How seventh cause? Good my lord, like this fellow.

Duke S. I like him very well.

Touch. God 'ild you, sir; I desire you of the like. I press in here, sir, amongst the rest of the country copulatives, to swear and to forswear, according as marriage binds and blood breaks. A poor virgin, sir, an ill-favoured thing, sir, but mine own. A poor humour of mine, sir, to take that that no man else will: rich honesty dwells like a miser, sir, in a poor house, as your pearl in your foul oyster.

Duke S. By my faith, he is very swift and sententious.

Touch. According to the fool's bolt, sir, and such dulcet diseases.

Jaq. But, for the seventh cause,—how did you find the quarrel on the seventh cause?

Touch. Upon a lie seven times removed,—bear your body more seeming, Audrey,—as thus, sir. I did dislike the cut of a certain courtier's beard: he sent me word, if I said his beard was not cut well, he was in the mind it was: this is call'd the Retort Courteous. If I sent him word again "it was not well cut," he would send me word, he cut it to please himself: this is call'd the Quip Modest. If again "it was not well cut," he disabled my judgement: this is called the Reply Churlish. If again "it was not well cut," he would answer, I spake not true: this is called the Reproof Valiant. If again "it was not well cut," he would say, I lie: this is call'd the Countercheck Quarrelsome: and so to Lie Circumstantial and the Lie Direct.

Scene iv: 4. As those who fear to trust their hope and are certain only of their fear. **5. urg'd,** examined. **19. to make . . . even,** to fulfil. **25. doubts all even,** clear up the doubts. **27. lively touches,** life-like traits. **32. desperate,** because they deal with forbidden arts.

35. toward, at hand. **45. purgation,** proof (of honesty). **measure,** dignified dance. **46. politic,** cunning. **50. ta'en up,** made up. **60. blood,** passion. **65. swift and sententious,** quick and pithy. **67. bolt,** blunt arrow. "A fool's bolt is soon shot." **72. seeming,** seemly. **73. dislike,** express dislike for. **78. Quip,** jest. **79. disabled,** disparaged.

Jaq. And how oft did you say his beard was not well cut?

Touch. I durst go no further than the Lie Circumstantial, nor he durst not give me the Lie Direct; and so we measured swords and parted.

Jaq. Can you nominate in order now the degrees of the lie?

Touch. O sir, we quarrel in print, by the book, as you have books for good manners: I will name you the degrees. The first, the Retort Courteous; the second, the Quip Modest; the third, the Reply Churlish; the fourth, the Reproof Valiant; the fifth, the Countercheck Quarrelsome; the sixth, the Lie with Circumstance; the seventh, the Lie Direct. All these you may avoid but the Lie Direct; and you may avoid that too, with an If. I knew when seven justices could not take up a quarrel, but when the parties were met themselves, one of them thought but of an If, as, "If you said so, then I said so"; and they shook hands and swore brothers. Your If is the only peace-maker; much virtue in If.

Jaq. Is not this a rare fellow, my lord? He 's as good at any thing. and yet a fool.

Duke S. He uses his folly like a stalking-horse and under the presentation of that he shoots his wit.

Enter *Hymen, Rosalind,* and *Celia.*

Still Music.

Hym. Then is there mirth in heaven,
When earthly things made even
Atone together.
Good Duke, receive thy daughter.
Hymen from heaven brought her,
Yea, brought her hither,
That thou mightst join her hand with his
Whose heart within his bosom is.

Ros. [*To the Duke.*] To you I give myself, for I am yours.
[*To Orlando.*] To you I give myself, for I am yours.

Duke S. If there be truth in sight, you are my daughter.

Orl. If there be truth in sight, you are my Rosalind.

Phe. If sight and shape be true,
Why then, my love adieu!

Ros. I 'll have no father, if you be not he;
I 'll have no husband, if you be not he;
Nor ne'er wed woman, if you be not she.

Hym. Peace, ho! I bar confusion.
'T is I must make conclusion
Of these most strange events:
Here 's eight that must take hands
To join in Hymen's bands,
If truth holds true contents.
You and you no cross shall part;
You and you are heart in heart;
You to his love must accord,
Or have a woman to your lord;
You and you are sure together,
As the winter to foul weather.
Whiles a wedlock-hymn we sing,
Feed yourselves with questioning;
That reason wonder may diminish,
How thus we met, and these things finish.

Song.

Wedding is great Juno's crown
O blessed bond of board and bed!
'T is Hymen peoples every town;
High wedlock then be honoured.
Honour, high honour, and renown,
To Hymen, god of every town!

Duke S. O my dear niece, welcome thou art to me!
Even daughter, welcome in no less degree.

Phe. I will not eat my word, now thou art mine;
Thy faith my fancy to thee doth combine.

Enter Second Brother *Jaques de Boys.*

Jaq. de Boys. Let me have audience for a word or two:
I am the second son of old Sir Roland,
That bring these tidings to this fair assembly.
Duke Frederick, hearing how that every day
Men of great worth resorted to this forest,
Address'd a mighty power, which were on foot,
In his own conduct, purposely to take
His brother here and put him to the sword;
And to the skirts of this wild wood he came,
Where meeting with an old religious man,
After some question with him, was converted
Both from his enterprise and from the world;
His crown bequeathing to his banish'd brother,
And all their lands restor'd to them again
That were with him exil'd. This to be true,
I do engage my life.

Duke S. Welcome, young man;
Thou offer'st fairly to thy brothers' wedding:
To one his lands withheld; and to the other
A land itself at large, a potent dukedom.

95. by the book, he is ridiculing the books on dueling. **111. stalking-horse,** horse real or artificial for stalking game. **112. presentation,** semblance. **S. d.** *Still music,* soft music. **116. Atone together,** become reconciled. **131. bar,** prohibit.

136. holds true contents, is true. **141. sure,** united. **150. High,** solemn. **156. combine,** bind. **162. Address'd,** equipped. **163. In his own conduct,** under his own guidance. **167. question,** conversation. **173. offer'st,** contributest.

First, in this forest let us do those ends
That here were well begun and well begot;
And after, every of this happy number,
That have endur'd shrewd days and nights with us,
Shall share the good of our returned fortune,
According to the measure of their states.
Meantime, forget this new-fallen dignity,
And fall into our rustic revelry.
Play, music! And you, brides and bridegrooms all,
With measure heap'd in joy, to the measures fall.

Jaq. Sir, by your patience. If I heard you rightly,
The Duke hath put on a religious life
And thrown into neglect the pompous court?

Jaq. de B. He hath.

Jaq. To him will I. Out of these convertites
There is much matter to be heard and learn'd.
[*To Duke S.*] You to your former honour I bequeath;
Your patience and your virtue well deserves it:
[*To Orlando.*] You to a love, that your true faith doth merit:
[*To Oliver.*] You to your land, and love, and great allies:
[*To Silvius.*] You to a long and well-deserved bed:
[*To Touchstone.*] And you to wrangling; for thy loving voyage
Is but for two months victuall'd. So, to your pleasures;
I am for other than for dancing measures.

Duke S. Stay, Jaques, stay.

176. do those ends, accomplish those purposes. **179. shrewd,** bad. **181. states,** estates. **190. convertites,** converts.

Jaq. To see no pastime I. What you would have
I 'll stay to know at your abandon'd cave.
Exit.

Duke S. Proceed, proceed: we 'll begin these rites,
As we do trust they 'll end, in true delights.
A dance. Exeunt.

Epilogue

Ros. It is not the fashion to see the lady the epilogue, but it is no more unhandsome than to see the lord the prologue. If it be true that good wine needs no bush, 't is true that a good play needs no epilogue. Yet to good wine they do use good bushes, and good plays prove the better by the help of good epilogues. What a case am I in then, that am neither a good epilogue, nor cannot insinuate with you in the behalf of a good play! I am not furnished like a beggar, therefore to beg will not become me. My way is to conjure you, and I 'll begin with the women. I charge you, O women, for the love you bear to men, to like as much of this play as please you; and I charge you, O men, for the love you bear to women,—as I perceive by your simp'ring, none of you hates them—that between you and the women the play may please. If I were a woman I would kiss as many of you as had beards that pleased me, complexions that liked me, and breaths that I defied not; and, I am sure, as many as have good beards or good faces or sweet breaths will, for my kind offer, when I make curtsy, bid me farewell. *Exit.*

Epi.: 2. unhandsome, in bad taste. **4. bush,** the ivy bush or holly garland was the sign of a vintner. The proverb means in effect that good wine needs no advertising. **9. insinuate,** bring myself into favor. **21. liked,** pleased. **defied,** disliked strongly.

Twelfth Night, or What You Will

Twelfth Night, the third in time of Shakespeare's glorious triad of romantic comedies, is in some ways the most delightful, in many ways the most perfectly finished of the three. It lacks, to be sure, the greenwood atmosphere of *As You Like It;* it has no such rapier thrusts of repartee as we find in the wit-combats of *Much Ado.* On the other hand, the smooth rhythm of its action is not broken by the manifest improbabilities of the former, nor its lovely harmony of tone marred by such discords as the baseness of Don John and the credulity of Claudio. Nowhere else, not even in Shakespeare, are romance and realism so happily blended in lovely poetry and laughing prose. From the time of its first appearance on the stage of the Globe it has been one of the few plays of Shakespeare that has held the boards with very little alteration. Lamb's delightful essay *On Some of the Old Actors* brings before our eyes a group of players who filled the parts of this comedy in his young days and is, in some ways, the best of introductions to the play itself.

Text.—There is no earlier version of *Twelfth Night* than that of the First Folio, 1623. Shakespeare's company were able, it seems, to prevent a prior publication of the play, and we are forced to rely for the text upon the Folio version. Fortunately this was printed from a good manuscript and is remarkably free from errors and corruptions.

Date.—The date of *Twelfth Night* can be fixed within certain rather narrow limits. It is not mentioned by Meres in his well-known list of Shakespeare's plays in 1598, and we have a record of its performance early in 1602 in the Middle Temple. Somewhere between these dates it must have been composed, and an accumulation of minor details points toward the later date. Certainly it was written after Armin, who played the part of Feste, succeeded Kemp, the Dogberry of *Much Ado,* early in 1600. It is fairly safe therefore to date *Twelfth Night* late in 1600 or some time in 1601. There is, indeed, a bare possibility that the title, *Twelfth Night,* points to a first production of the play on this festival day, the sixth of January, in 1601. Shakespeare seems to have been quite careless as to the titles of his plays and when pressed for a name for the new play to be presented on this date may have told his fellows: "Call it the play of *Twelfth Night* or *What You Will,*" *i.e.,* anything you wish.

Sources.—There has been much shedding of ink in the search for the sources of *Twelfth Night.* The quest began in the first record of the play. Manningham, one of the lawyers who attended the performance in the Middle Temple, noted in his diary that "Twelve Night or What you will" was "much like . . . Menechmi in Plautus, but most like and near to that in Italian called *Inganni.*" Now there are two sixteenth century Italian plays of that name, but neither bears any close relation to *Twelfth Night,* although in one of them the disguised heroine takes the name of Cesare, which certainly suggests Viola's assumed name, Cesario. But there is a third Italian play older than either of these, *Gl'Ingannati* (The Deceived), which shows a much nearer resemblance. It was first published in 1537, frequently reprinted, translated into French and Spanish, and finally into Latin by an English scholar, in which form it was acted at Queen's College, Cambridge, under the name of *Laelia* in 1590 and again in 1598. In other words it was an exceedingly popular play, so much so that its plot was retold by various novelists, Bandello in Italian prose, Belleforest in French, and Barnaby Riche in English. This last version, known as *Apolonius and Silla,* is the second of a group of tales in a volume entitled *Riche his Farewell to the Military Profession,* 1581, a work which almost certainly came into Shakespeare's hands.

What does all this amount to? Briefly the central idea of the plot, the indistinguishable likeness of twins, goes back to Plautus and behind him to Greek comedy. An unknown Italian playwright introduced a new and skillful variation by making the twins brother and sister. He went further and made the girl disguise herself as a page to follow the man she loves. As his page she is employed to carry love-letters to the lady he loves, who in turn falls in love with the page. In the meantime her brother—long absent from the scene—arrives and is mistaken by the lady for the page, his sister. When she makes love to him, he promptly responds and marries her. The page is accused by her master of betraying him, but on the revelation of her true sex is rewarded with his hand in marriage. Such with many minor variations is the story as it came to Shakespeare; he probably knew more than one of the many versions, borrowed from each what suited him, and compiled the charming plot of *Twelfth Night*.

It will be noted that there has been no word so far of the minor plot, the trick played on Malvolio and the revels of Sir Toby, Sir Andrew, and the clown. This, so far as we know, is Shakespeare's own invention, though he may well have caught a hint here and there in his reading. One of Riche's stories tells how a husband shut his scolding wife up in a dark room pretending that she was mad; the neighbors who believe his report come to visit her and reply to her wild protests by bidding her "forget these idle speeches and call upon God." This may have suggested one phase of the Malvolio story to Shakespeare, but the device of the letter, the behavior of Malvolio before his mistress, and the manner in which characters of the underplot, Sir Andrew and Sir Toby, are employed to bring about the denouement of the main story, are certainly his own.

Construction.—The main plot of *Twelfth Night* is, of course, the romantic tale of Viola and Sebastian, twin brother and sister, their separation in a shipwreck, their love affairs, and final reunion. Over against this as a foil, to preserve the play from sinking into an excess of sentiment, Shakespeare develops a group of broad comedy figures, gathered at the house of Olivia, whose pranks serve as a refreshing interlude to the romantic plot. Let us see how the two are interwoven.

A short scene at the beginning introduces us to the amorous Duke of Illyria, and his sentimental passion for the hard-hearted Lady Olivia. Then the shipwrecked heroine appears, and we learn that she means to disguise herself as a page and take service with the Duke. The third scene introduces the comic characters, Sir Toby, Sir Andrew, and Maria. So far we have had swift and clear exposition; with the fourth scene the action begins. Viola, now known as the page Cesario, has won the favor of the Duke and has fallen in love with him. Love at first sight is here, as elsewhere, of course, a convention of romantic comedy. With her dispatch to Olivia as the Duke's messenger of love the plot advances and it is at once complicated by the fact that Olivia falls in love at first sight with the page. And now to prepare us for further complications Shakespeare introduces the twin brother, like Viola rescued from the sea and bound to Orsino's court. After a brief scene in which Viola learns that Olivia has fallen in love with her we get, by way of relief, a passage of uproarious midnight revelry—perhaps the jolliest scene that Shakespeare ever penned. The resentment of the revelers at the interruption and harsh rebuke of the steward, Malvolio, leads them to plot his downfall. The plot is immediately and completely successful in the last scene of the act. In between, however, for fear we should forget Viola, Shakespeare interposes the loveliest scene of the play in which the heroine and her master talk of man's love and woman's, and the unhappy lady tells her own story under the pretense of speaking of a sister's sorrow. The third act brings matters to a head; Olivia openly avows her passion to the page; Sir Andrew, her foolish suitor, is encouraged by his friends to challenge the page and thus win Olivia's favor. And now to keep him before our eyes Sebastian is again introduced accompanied by his rescuer the old sea-captain, Antonio. They part, Sebastian bearing the captain's purse which has been thrust upon him, and we know that the time is at hand for the brother and sister to be mistaken one for the other. And this occurs almost at once. After a scene in which the gulled Malvolio's behavior leads his mistress to believe him mad and to turn him over to the tender mercies of Sir Toby, we get the delightful episode of the mock duel, if so it can be called, between the page and Sir Andrew. Here for the first time the romantic and comic plots touch, and henceforth they are closely interwoven. Antonio, mistaking the page for Sebastian, comes to his aid and is promptly arrested as an old enemy of the Duke by that lord's officers. Calling on the page for his purse, he addresses him as Sebastian, and this leads Viola to hope that her brother may still be living. The short fourth act complicates the intrigue still more closely, for now Sebastian is mistaken for his sister. Attacked by Sir Andrew and Sir Toby, he defends himself in quite another manner than she had done, and a dangerous brawl is interrupted by Olivia, who rescues, as she believes, her beloved page and carries him off with her. After a comic interlude in which Malvolio confined in darkness is mocked by Sir Toby and the Clown, we get the marriage, or perhaps, one should say the formal betrothal of Sebastian and Olivia. Some carping critics have objected to the haste with which this engagement takes place. They forget that the story tells of Elizabethans, not of prudent modern folk. Sebastian would differ widely from the usual Elizabethan gallant if, finding himself alone and unfriended in a foreign land, he did not accept the good fortune which offered him for a wife a lady wellborn, beautiful, and rich.

The long unbroken scene which constitutes the last act brings about the final solution. All the actors gather one by one before Olivia's house. The Duke comes in person attended by his page to make a last effort to win his suit. Antonio dragged before him denounces the ingratitude of Sebastian, *i.e.*, the page; Olivia appears to claim the page, *i.e.*, Sebastian, as her husband; the Duke's wrath is aroused, and things might have gone hard with the page, when a burst of comedy clears up the whole. Sir Andrew and Sir Toby have once more attacked Sebastian as the page; he has given each of them a bloody coxcomb, and they now appear, Andrew whimpering, Sir Toby hiccuping, to get their wounds dressed. They are closely followed by Sebastian, who comes to apologize to his mistress for his rough treatment of her kinsman. Now for the first time brother and sister meet on the stage. They recognize each other, the whole comedy of errors is dissolved; Olivia is satisfied with the gallant husband she has won by mistake; the Duke rewards the devotion of his page by a promise of his hand; Malvolio is freed from his confinement, and the Clown ends all with a merry song. Nowhere else in Shakespeare's comedies do we have so deft, so entertaining, and so happy a piece of plot-construction.

Characters.—High comedy such as *Twelfth Night*, is marked even more by power and subtlety of characterization than by deft and entertaining plot. And it is not too much to say that the characters of this play rank high in Shakespeare's gallery of masterpieces. It required no little skill in character portrayal to keep such a sentimentalist as the Duke from becoming a ridiculous, if not a contemptible, figure, and to make him what he is, in truth, a charming and really lovable gentleman. And this he must be to justify Viola's love. With the same art Olivia, for all her fantastical and headstrong nature, is presented as a great and honorable lady, not the mere coquette or wanton of her predecessors in the sources. It is in the character of Viola, however, that Shakespeare achieves his supreme triumph in the play. In the earlier versions the heroine deliberately leaves her home and assumes man's disguise to follow the man she loves, although he cares nothing for her. In one of them, at least, she actually attempts to gain her end by suggesting that she, in her character of page, might consent to love Olivia's prototype, if that lady will definitely dismiss the suitor who corresponds to the Duke. Such willfulness, such trickery, is altogether foreign to Shakespeare's heroine; she is the most modest, the most wistful, of all his ladies of romance. It is the misfortune of shipwreck, not her own desire, that brings her to the Duke's court; it is for protection rather than for pursuit that she dons a page's dress; and it is her fate, not her voluntary choice, that makes her love her master. In her love, moreover, there is a note of loyalty and unselfish devotion that is peculiarly her own. Even her feminine shrinking at the thought of drawn swords, her confession that she would rather "go with sir priest than sir knight," endears her to us.

The characters of the comic plot are all sharply drawn, distinctly individualized. Sir Toby, indeed, belongs to the family of Falstaff, but he lacks the fat knight's irrepressible and unfailing wit; he is a little prompter than Sir John to proceed from words to blows; something of a rudesby and a roisterer. One can hardly imagine a Prince Hal delighting in his companionship. His running mate, Sir Andrew, is surely the most perfect and complete picture of a fool that Shakespeare ever drew. If ever it is permissible to laugh at hopeless folly, it is here where the incongruity between his character, or rather want of it, and his title, between his pretensions to Olivia's hand and his behavior in her house, is so gross and palpable. The Clown, too, is the merriest of all Shakespeare's jesters: not so witty as Touchstone, not so keen-sighted as the Fool of *Lear,* he is, one feels, happier than either of them, and fits more perfectly into the atmosphere of this happy comedy.

There is but one character in the play in the least likely to be misunderstood. That is, of course, Malvolio. One misunderstanding seems to be due to the interpretation of the part by a line of actors who gave to the role a note of Quixotic dignity that threw a certain tragic interest over the steward's downfall. This, it would seem, is quite contrary to Shakespeare's intention. To his auditors, we may be sure, Malvolio was what a contemporary calls him "that cross-gartered gull." Make what allowance one may for Malvolio's rank as major-domo of a great lady's household, for his honesty, respectability, and so forth, the fact remains that he is, as his quick-witted mistress tells him, "sick of self-love," a vain and pompous prig. Utterly without a sense of humor his absurd conceit makes it a "ground of faith" with him that "all that look on him love him," and so delivers him helplessly into the trap that is laid for him. To prick a swollen bubble of vanity is a fit task for the comic spirit; it might be maintained that he who feels a tragic sympathy for Malvolio is well-nigh as devoid of humor as Malvolio himself. Another and a slighter error is due perhaps to academic critics who have declared Malvolio to be the poet's satiric portrait of the Puritan. One phrase of Maria's should be enough to dispel this illusion: "the devil of a Puritan he is." When an Elizabethan dramatist whetted his knife for the Puritan enemies of his profession he left his audience in no doubts as to his meaning. Malvolio shares with the Puritan, to be sure, a strong objection to all pleasures that do not please him. He got Fabian into trouble with his lady about a bear-baiting—one recalls that the Puritan Colonel Pride shot the bears that had long furnished this sport for London citizens. He appears to hold, with certain modern thinkers, that because he is virtuous there shall be no more cakes and ale. But the crying vice of the Puritan in all ages is hypocrisy, and there is nothing of the hypocrite about Malvolio. Let him pass with the labels his lady and Maria pin on him—"sick of self-love" and "an affectioned (*i.e.,* affected) ass."

Beauty of phrase.—There is mirth enough in *Twelfth Night,* but there is beauty too. In fact the special charm of the play lies in its happy mingling of laughter and romantic beauty. There is the clear-cut diction such as all high comedy must have, winged words and phrases that have woven themselves into the web of English speech—Sir Toby's "cakes and ale," the Clown's "ginger hot in the mouth." And the verse of the romantic scenes has its own peculiar charm, a certain wistful beauty smiling at grief. Such a lyric as "Come away death" would be out of place, one feels, in robuster realistic comedy. The play opens to music and closes with the Clown's song of the wind and the rain. "The comic Spirit," says Meredith, "is not hostile to the sweetest songfully poetic"—and no better proof of this apparent paradox could be found than this sweet and songful comedy of Shakespeare's.

Stage history.—The stage history of *Twelfth Night* begins with the record of the performance at the Middle Temple on February 2, 1602. We know that it was played at Court in 1618 and again under the title of *Malvolio* in 1623. A reference in verses prefixed to the 1640 edition of Shakespeare's *Poems,*

> The Cockpit, galleries, boxes all are full
> To hear Malvoglio that cross garter'd Gull

attests the popularity of the play up to the closing of the theatres. Like the other romantic comedies of Shakespeare, *Twelfth Night* had little charm for the Restoration. Pepys saw a production in 1661, and attended two later performances. He called it a silly play, "one of the worst that ever I saw."

It regained popularity in the eighteenth century, mainly because a succession of charming actresses—Mrs. Pritchard, Peg Woffington, and Mrs. Jordan—played the part of Viola. Lamb's Bensley and later John Philip Kemble played Malvolio with a certain stately dignity which culminated in Irving's almost tragic rendering. Ellen Terry played Viola to Irving's Malvolio in 1884.

In America, Julia Marlowe, Ada Rehan, and Maude Adams have all triumphed in the role of Viola. Except for its brief eclipse in the Restoration period it has been one of the most successful of Shakespeare's comedies upon the stage.

TWELFTH NIGHT

OR

WHAT YOU WILL

Dramatis Personæ

Orsino, Duke of Illyria.
Sebastian, brother to *Viola.*
Antonio, a sea-captain, friend to *Sebastian.*
A Sea-Captain, friend to *Viola.*
Valentine, }
Curio, } gentlemen attending on the Duke.
Sir Toby Belch, uncle to *Olivia.*
Sir Andrew Aguecheek.

Malvolio, steward to *Olivia.*
Fabian, a gentleman, }
Feste, a clown, } servants to *Olivia.*

Olivia, a rich countess.
Viola.
Maria, Olivia's woman.

Lords, Priests, Sailors, Officers, Musicians, and other Attendants.

SCENE: *A city in Illyria, and the sea-coast near it.*

ACT I. Scene I. *The Duke's palace.*

Enter *Orsino,* Duke of Illyria, *Curio,* and other Lords, Musicians attending.

Duke. If music be the food of love, play on!
Give me excess of it, that, surfeiting,
The appetite may sicken, and so die.
That strain again! It had a dying fall.
O, it came o'er my ear like the sweet sound
That breathes upon a bank of violets,
Stealing and giving odour. Enough! no more!
'T is not so sweet now as it was before.
O spirit of love, how quick and fresh art thou,
That, notwithstanding thy capacity
Receiveth as the sea, nought enters there,
Of what validity and pitch soe'er,
But falls into abatement and low price
Even in a minute! So full of shapes is fancy
That it alone is high fantastical.
Cur. Will you go hunt, my lord?
Duke. What, Curio?
Cur. The hart.
Duke. Why, so I do, the noblest that I have.
O, when mine eyes did see Olivia first,
Methought she purg'd the air of pestilence!
That instant was I turn'd into a hart;
And my desires, like fell and cruel hounds,
E'er since pursue me.

Enter *Valentine.*

How now! what news from her?
Val. So please my lord, I might not be admitted,
But from her handmaid do return this answer:
The element itself, till seven years' heat,
Shall not behold her face at ample view;
But like a cloistress she will veiled walk,
And water once a day her chamber round
With eye-offending brine: all this to season
A brother's dead love, which she would keep fresh
And lasting in her sad remembrance.
Duke. O, she that hath a heart of that fine frame
To pay this debt of love but to a brother,
How will she love when the rich golden shaft
Hath kill'd the flock of all affections else
That live in her; when liver, brain, and heart,
These sovereign thrones, are all supplied, and fill'd
Her sweet perfections with one self king!
Away before me to sweet beds of flowers;
Love-thoughts lie rich when canopied with bowers. *Exeunt.*

Scene II. *The sea-coast.*

Enter *Viola,* a *Captain,* and Sailors.

Vio. What country, friends, is this?
Cap. This is Illyria, lady.
Vio. And what should I do in Illyria?
My brother he is in Elysium.
Perchance he is not drown'd. What think you, sailors?
Cap. It is perchance that you yourself were saved.

9. quick, living. **12. validity,** value. **pitch,** height. **13. abatement,** lower estimation. **14. fancy,** love. **15. high fantastical,** highly imaginative. **21-3.** Actaeon, who saw Diana bathing, was transformed by her into a hart, pursued, and killed by his own hounds.

26. element, sky. **seven years' heat,** seven summers. **30. season,** keep fresh. **39. one self king,** one sole monarch.

Vio. O my poor brother! and so perchance may he be.
Cap. True, madam; and, to comfort you with chance,
Assure yourself, after our ship did split,
When you and those poor number saved with you
Hung on our driving boat, I saw your brother,
Most provident in peril, bind himself,
Courage and hope both teaching him the practice,
To a strong mast that liv'd upon the sea;
Where, like Arion on the dolphin's back,
I saw him hold acquaintance with the waves
So long as I could see.
Vio. For saying so, there 's gold.
Mine own escape unfoldeth to my hope,
Whereto thy speech serves for authority,
The like of him. Know'st thou this country?
Cap. Ay, madam, well; for I was bred and born
Not three hours' travel from this very place.
Vio. Who governs here?
Cap. A noble duke, in nature as in name.
Vio. What is his name?
Cap. Orsino.
Vio. Orsino! I have heard my father name him.
He was a bachelor then.
Cap. And so is now, or was so very late;
For but a month ago I went from hence,
And then 't was fresh in murmur—as, you know,
What great ones do the less will prattle of—
That he did seek the love of fair Olivia.
Vio. What 's she?
Cap. A virtuous maid, the daughter of a count
That died some twelvemonth since, then leaving her
In the protection of his son, her brother,
Who shortly also died; for whose dear love,
They say, she hath abjur'd the company
And sight of men.
Vio. O that I serv'd that lady,
And might not be delivered to the world,
Till I had made mine own occasion mellow,
What my estate is!
Cap. That were hard to compass,
Because she will admit no kind of suit,
No, not the Duke's.
Vio. There is a fair behaviour in thee, captain;
And though that nature with a beauteous wall
Doth oft close in pollution, yet of thee
I will believe thou hast a mind that suits
With this thy fair and outward character.
I prithee, and I 'll pay thee bounteously,
Conceal me what I am, and be my aid
For such disguise as haply shall become
The form of my intent. I 'll serve this duke.
Thou shalt present me as an eunuch to him.
It may be worth thy pains, for I can sing
And speak to him in many sorts of music
That will allow me very worth his service.
What else may hap, to time I will commit,
Only shape thou thy silence to my wit.
Cap. Be you his eunuch, and your mute I 'll be.
When my tongue blabs, then let mine eyes not see.
Vio. I thank thee. Lead me on. *Exeunt.*

Scene III. *Olivia's house.*

Enter *Sir Toby Belch* and *Maria.*

Sir To. What a plague means my niece, to take the death of her brother thus? I am sure care 's an enemy to life.

Mar. By my troth, Sir Toby, you must come in earlier o' nights. Your cousin, my lady, takes great exceptions to your ill hours.

Sir To. Why, let her except before excepted.

Mar. Ay, but you must confine yourself within the modest limits of order.

Sir To. Confine? I 'll confine myself no finer than I am. These clothes are good enough to drink in, and so be these boots too; an they be not, let them hang themselves in their own straps.

Mar. That quaffing and drinking will undo you. I heard my lady talk of it yesterday, and of a foolish knight that you brought in one night here to be her wooer.

Sir To. Who? Sir Andrew Aguecheek?

Mar. Ay, he.

Sir To. He 's as tall a man as any 's in Illyria.

Mar. What 's that to the purpose?

Sir To. Why, he has three thousand ducats a year.

Mar. Ay, but he 'll have but a year in all these ducats. He 's a very fool and a prodigal.

Sir To. Fie, that you 'll say so! He plays o' the viol-de-gamboys, and speaks three or four languages word for word without book, and hath all the good gifts of nature.

Mar. He hath indeed, almost natural; for

Scene ii: 15. Arion was a Greek poet, who in order to escape the murderous intent of robber sailors leapt into the sea. The music of his lyre so charmed the dolphins that they bore him to land. **42-4.** And might not have my identity disclosed until I find a suitable opportunity.

56. as an eunuch, as a singing boy. Originally it seems the boy who played Viola was meant to sing the songs in this play. Later they were given to Armin who played the part of Feste. **Scene iii: 7. except before excepted,** legal phrase meaning "with the exceptions before named." **19. tall,** valiant. **27. viol-de-gamboys,** viol da gamba. **30. natural,** idiot.

besides that he 's a fool, he 's a great quarreller; and but that he hath the gift of a coward to allay the gust he hath in quarrelling, 't is thought among the prudent he would quickly have the gift of a grave.

Sir To. By this hand, they are scoundrels and substractors that say so of him. Who are they?

Mar. They that add, moreover, he 's drunk nightly in your company.

Sir To. With drinking healths to my niece. I 'll drink to her as long as there is a passage in my throat and drink in Illyria. He 's a coward and a coystrill that will not drink to my niece till his brains turn o' the toe like a parish-top. What, wench! *Castiliano vulgo!* for here comes Sir Andrew Agueface.

Enter *Sir Andrew.*

Sir And. Sir Toby Belch! How now, Sir Toby Belch!

Sir To. Sweet Sir Andrew!

Sir And. Bless you, fair shrew.

Mar. And you too, sir.

Sir To. Accost, Sir Andrew, accost.

Sir And. What 's that?

Sir To. My niece's chambermaid.

Sir And. Good Mistress Accost, I desire better acquaintance.

Mar. My name is Mary, sir.

Sir And. Good Mistress Mary Accost,—

Sir To. You mistake, knight. "Accost" is front her, board her, woo her, assail her.

Sir And. By my troth, I would not undertake her in this company. Is that the meaning of "accost"?

Mar. Fare you well, gentlemen.

Sir To. An thou let part so, Sir Andrew, would thou mightst never draw sword again.

Sir And. An you part so, mistress, I would I might never draw sword again. Fair lady, do you think you have fools in hand?

Mar. Sir, I have not you by the hand.

Sir And. Marry, but you shall have; and here 's my hand.

Mar. Now, sir, "thought is free." I pray you, bring your hand to the buttery-bar and let it drink.

Sir And. Wherefore, sweetheart? What 's your metaphor?

Mar. It 's dry, sir.

Sir And. Why, I think so. I am not such an ass but I can keep my hand dry. But what 's your jest?

Mar. A dry jest, sir.

Sir And. Are you full of them?

Mar. Ay, sir, I have them at my fingers' ends. Marry, now I let go your hand, I am barren. *Exit.*

Sir To. O knight, thou lack'st a cup of canary. When did I see thee so put down?

Sir And. Never in your life, I think, unless you see canary put me down. Methinks sometimes I have no more wit than a Christian or an ordinary man has; but I am a great eater of beef and I believe that does harm to my wit.

Sir To. No question.

Sir And. An I thought that, I 'd forswear it. I 'll ride home to-morrow, Sir Toby.

Sir To. *Pourquoi,* my dear knight?

Sir And. What is "*pourquoi*"? Do or not do? I would I had bestowed that time in the tongues that I have in fencing, dancing, and bear-baiting. O, had I but followed the arts!

Sir To. Then hadst thou had an excellent head of hair.

Sir And. Why, would that have mended my hair?

Sir To. Past question; for thou seest it will not curl by nature.

Sir And. But it becomes me well enough, does 't not?

Sir To. Excellent; it hangs like flax on a distaff, and I hope to see a housewife take thee between her legs, and spin it off.

Sir And. Faith, I 'll home to-morrow, Sir Toby. Your niece will not be seen, or if she be, it 's four to one she 'll none of me. The Count himself here hard by wooes her.

Sir To. She 'll none o' the Count. She 'll not match above her degree, neither in estate, years, nor wit; I have heard her swear 't. Tut, there 's life in 't, man.

Sir And. I 'll stay a month longer. I am a fellow o' the strangest mind in the world; I delight in masques and revels sometimes altogether.

Sir To. Art thou good at these kickshawses, knight?

Sir And. As any man in Illyria, whatsoever he be, under the degree of my betters; and yet I will not compare with an old man.

Sir To. What is thy excellence in a galliard, knight?

Sir And. Faith, I can cut a caper.

33. gust, zest. **37. substractors,** detractors. **43. coystrill,** knave. **45.** A large top kept in each parish to amuse and exercise the villagers. It was kept in motion by constant whipping. **Castiliano vulgo,** probably nonsense. If Sir Toby uses "vulgo" for "volto" by mistake, it means "look grave like a Castilian." **78-81.** There is here a play on the various significances of "dry." In l. 77 it has the sense of "old" or the opposite of amorous; in **l. 80, "dry"** as opposed to "moist"; in **l. 81, "dull."**

86. canary, a sweet wine. **101.** Possibly a pun on **tongues** (l. 98) and **tongs** (curling tongs); or it is to be explained by Sir Toby's next speech, which implies that his hair would curl by art if not by nature. **118. there 's life in 't,** there's hope still. **122. kickshawses,** trifles. **127. galliard,** a lively dance.

Duke already likes Viola (Caesario) sends her to see Olivia & tell her of Duke's love. Viola loves Duke.

Sir To. And I can cut the mutton to 't.

Sir And. And I think I have the back-trick simply as strong as any man in Illyria.

Sir To. Wherefore are these things hid? Wherefore have these gifts a curtain before 'em? Are they like to take dust, like Mistress Mall's picture? Why dost thou not go to church in a galliard and come home in a coranto? My very walk should be a jig. I would not so much as make water but in a sink-a-pace. What dost thou mean? Is it a world to hide virtues in? I did think, by the excellent constitution of thy leg, it was formed under the star of a galliard.

Sir And. Ay, 't is strong, and it does indifferent well in a damned coloured stock. Shall we set about some revels?

Sir To. What shall we do else? Were we not born under Taurus?

Sir And. Taurus! That 's sides and heart.

Sir To. No, sir, it is legs and thighs. Let me see thee caper. Ha! Higher! Ha, ha! Excellent! *Exeunt.*

Scene IV. *The Duke's palace.*

Enter *Valentine,* and *Viola* in man's attire.

Val. If the Duke continue these favours towards you, Cesario, you are like to be much advanced. He hath known you but three days, and already you are no stranger.

Vio. You either fear his humour or my negligence, that you call in question the continuance of his love. Is he inconstant, sir, in his favours?

Val. No, believe me.

Enter *Duke, Curio,* and Attendants.

Vio. I thank you. Here comes the Count.

Duke. Who saw Cesario, ho?

Vio. On your attendance, my lord; here.

Duke. Stand you a while aloof. Cesario,
Thou know'st no less but all. I have unclasp'd
To thee the book even of my secret soul;
Therefore, good youth, address thy gait unto her.
Be not denied access, stand at her doors,
And tell them, there thy fixed foot shall grow
Till thou have audience.

Vio. Sure, my noble lord,
If she be so abandon'd to her sorrow
As it is spoke, she never will admit me.

Duke. Be clamorous and leap all civil bounds
Rather than make unprofited return.

Vio. Say I do speak with her, my lord, what then?

Duke. O, then unfold the passion of my love,
Surprise her with discourse of my dear faith.
It shall become thee well to act my woes.
She will attend it better in thy youth
Than in a nuncio's of more grave aspect.

Vio. I think not so, my lord.

Duke. Dear lad, believe it;
For they shall yet belie thy happy years,
That say thou art a man. Diana's lip
Is not more smooth and rubious; thy small pipe
Is as the maiden's organ, shrill and sound;
And all is semblative a woman's part.
I know thy constellation is right apt
For this affair. Some four or five attend him,—
All, if you will; for I myself am best
When least in company. Prosper well in this,
And thou shalt live as freely as thy lord,
To call his fortunes thine.

Vio. I 'll do my best
To woo your lady,—[*aside*] yet, a barful strife!
Whoe'er I woo, myself would be his wife.
Exeunt.

Scene V. *Olivia's house.*

Enter *Maria* and *Clown.*

Mar. Nay, either tell me where thou hast been, or I will not open my lips so wide as a bristle may enter in way of thy excuse. My lady will hang thee for thy absence.

Clo. Let her hang me! He that is well hanged in this world needs to fear no colours.

Mar. Make that good.

Clo. He shall see none to fear.

Mar. A good lenten answer. I can tell thee where that saying was born, of "I fear no colours."

Clo. Where, good Mistress Mary?

Mar. In the wars; and that may you be bold to say in your foolery.

Clo. Well, God give them wisdom that have it; and those that are fools, let them use their talents.

Mar. Yet you will be hanged for being so

130. mutton, the flower of the caper-bush was used in pickling mutton. **131. back-trick,** caper backwards in dancing. **136-7. coranto,** quick dance. **138-9. sink-a-pace,** cinque-pace, a five-step dance. **144. damned coloured,** possibly a fiery red, like the flames of hell. The text has often been changed to read "flame-colored" or "dun-colored." **stock,** stockings. **147. Taurus,** constellation supposed to govern neck, throat, and voice.

Scene iv: 32. rubious, rosy. **33. sound,** clear. **34. semblative,** seeming like. **35. constellation,** nature (determined by stars). **41. barful,** full of impediments. **Scene v: 6. fear no colours,** (1) fear no enemy, (2) hempen collar of hangman's noose. **9. lenten,** short, scanty.

long absent; or, to be turned away, is not that as good as a hanging to you?

Clo. Many a good hanging prevents a bad marriage; and, for turning away, let summer bear it out.

Mar. You are resolute, then?

Clo. Not so, neither; but I am resolved on two points.

Mar. That if one break, the other will hold; or, if both break, your gaskins fall.

Clo. Apt, in good faith; very apt. Well, go thy way. If Sir Toby would leave drinking, thou wert as witty a piece of Eve's flesh as any in Illyria.

Mar. Peace, you rogue, no more o' that. Here comes my lady. Make your excuse wisely, you were best. *Exit.*

Enter *Lady Olivia* and retinue with *Malvolio.*

Clo. Wit, an 't be thy will, put me into good fooling! Those wits, that think they have thee, do very oft prove fools; and I, that am sure I lack thee, may pass for a wise man; for what says Quinapalus? "Better a witty fool than a foolish wit."—God bless thee, lady!

Oli. Take the fool away.

Clo. Do you not hear, fellows? Take away the lady.

Oli. Go to, you 're a dry fool. I 'll no more of you; besides, you grow dishonest.

Clo. Two faults, madonna, that drink and good counsel will amend; for give the dry fool drink, then is the fool not dry: bid the dishonest man mend himself; if he mend, he is no longer dishonest; if he cannot, let the botcher mend him. Any thing that 's mended is but patched; virtue that transgresses is but patched with sin, and sin that amends is but patched with virtue. If that this simple syllogism will serve, so; if it will not, what remedy? As there is no true cuckold but calamity, so beauty 's a flower. The lady bade take away the fool; therefore, I say again, take her away.

Oli. Sir, I bade them take away you.

Clo. Misprision in the highest degree! Lady, *"cucullus non facit monachum"*; that 's as much to say as I wear not motley in my brain. Good madonna, give me leave to prove you a fool.

Oli. Can you do it?

Clo. Dexteriously, good madonna.

Oli. Make your proof.

Clo. I must catechise you for it, madonna. Good my mouse of virtue, answer me.

Oli. Well, sir, for want of other idleness, I 'll bide your proof.

Clo. Good madonna, why mourn'st thou?

Oli. Good fool, for my brother's death.

Clo. I think his soul is in hell, madonna.

Oli. I know his soul is in heaven, fool.

Clo. The more fool, madonna, to mourn for your brother's soul being in heaven. Take away the fool, gentlemen.

Oli. What think you of this fool, Malvolio? Doth he not mend?

Mal. Yes, and shall do till the pangs of death shake him. Infirmity, that decays the wise, doth ever make the better fool.

Clo. God send you, sir, a speedy infirmity, for the better increasing your folly! Sir Toby will be sworn that I am no fox, but he will not pass his word for twopence that you are no fool.

Oli. How say you to that, Malvolio?

Mal. I marvel your ladyship takes delight in such a barren rascal. I saw him put down the other day with an ordinary fool that has no more brain than a stone. Look you now, he 's out of his guard already. Unless you laugh and minister occasion to him, he is gagged. I protest, I take these wise men, that crow so at these set kind of fools, no better than the fools' zanies.

Oli. O, you are sick of self-love, Malvolio, and taste with a distempered appetite. To be generous, guiltless, and of free disposition, is to take those things for bird-bolts that you deem cannon-bullets. There is no slander in an allowed fool, though he do nothing but rail; nor no railing in a known discreet man, though he do nothing but reprove.

Clo. Now Mercury endue thee with leasing, for thou speak'st well of fools!

Re-enter *Maria.*

Mar. Madam, there is at the gate a young gentleman much desires to speak with you.

Oli. From the Count Orsino, is it?

Mar. I know not, madam. 'T is a fair young man, and well attended.

Oli. Who of my people hold him in delay?

Mar. Sir Toby, madam, your kinsman.

Oli. Fetch him off, I pray you. He speaks nothing but madman; fie on him! [*Exit Maria.*] Go you, Malvolio; if it be a suit from the Count, I am sick, or not at home,—what you will, to dismiss it. [*Exit Malvolio.*] Now

25-7. Pun on "points," the lace tags that held up the gaskins (breeches). **39. Quinapalus,** a coined name. **45. dry,** dull. **47. madonna,** my lady. **51. botcher,** mender of old clothes. **52. patched,** like a fool's motley or parti-colored dress. **56-7.** Meaningless, nonsense. **61. Misprision,** misapprehension (lit. concealment of treason). **62.** *"cucullus,"* etc., the cowl does not make the monk.

69. mouse, term of endearment. **89. barren,** stupid. **96. zanies,** foolish imitators. **99. bird-bolts,** blunt arrows. **101. allowed,** licensed. **105. leasing,** lying.

you see, sir, how your fooling grows old, and people dislike it.

Clo. Thou hast spoke for us, madonna, as if thy eldest son should be a fool; whose skull Jove cram with brains! for—here he comes—

Enter *Sir Toby.*

one of thy kin has a most weak *pia mater.*

Oli. By mine honour, half drunk. What is he at the gate, cousin?

Sir To. A gentleman.

Oli. A gentleman! What gentleman?

Sir To. 'T is a gentleman here—a plague o' these pickle-herring! How now, sot!

Clo. Good Sir Toby!

Oli. Cousin, cousin, how have you come so early by this lethargy?

Sir To. Lechery! I defy lechery. There 's one at the gate.

Oli. Ay, marry, what is he?

Sir To. Let him be the devil, an he will, I care not; give me faith, say I. Well, it 's all one. *Exit.*

Oli. What 's a drunken man like, fool?

Clo. Like a drowned man, a fool, and a madman. One draught above heat makes him a fool, the second mads him, and a third drowns him.

Oli. Go thou and seek the crowner and let him sit o' my coz, for he 's in the third degree of drink, he 's drowned. Go, look after him.

Clo. He is but mad yet, madonna; and the fool shall look to the madman. *Exit.*

Re-enter *Malvolio.*

Mal. Madam, yond young fellow swears he will speak with you. I told him you were sick: he takes on him to understand so much, and therefore comes to speak with you. I told him you were asleep: he seems to have a fore-knowledge of that too, and therefore comes to speak with you. What is to be said to him, lady? He 's fortified against any denial.

Oli. Tell him he shall not speak with me.

Mal. Has been told so; and he says, he 'll stand at your door like a sheriff's post, and be the supporter to a bench, but he 'll speak with you.

Oli. What kind o' man is he?

Mal. Why, of mankind.

Oli. What manner of man?

Mal. Of very ill manner. He 'll speak with you, will you or no.

Oli. Of what personage and years is he?

Mal. Not yet old enough for a man, nor young enough for a boy; as a squash is before 't is a peascod, or a codling when 't is almost an apple: 't is with him in standing water, between boy and man. He is very well-favoured and he speaks very shrewishly: one would think his mother's milk were scarce out of him.

Oli. Let him approach. Call in my gentlewoman.

Mal. Gentlewoman, my lady calls. *Exit.*

Re-enter *Maria.*

Oli. Give me my veil. Come, throw it o'er
my face.
We 'll once more hear Orsino's embassy.

Enter *Viola.*

Vio. The honourable lady of the house, which is she?

Oli. Speak to me; I shall answer for her. Your will?

Vio. Most radiant, exquisite, and unmatchable beauty,—I pray you, tell me if this be the lady of the house, for I never saw her. I would be loath to cast away my speech, for besides that it is excellently well penned, I have taken great pains to con it. Good beauties, let me sustain no scorn. I am very comptible, even to the least sinister usage.

Oli. Whence came you, sir?

Vio. I can say little more than I have studied, and that question 's out of my part. Good gentle one, give me modest assurance if you be the lady of the house, that I may proceed in my speech.

Oli. Are you a comedian?

Vio. No, my profound heart; and yet, by the very fangs of malice I swear, I am not that I play. Are you the lady of the house?

Oli. If I do not usurp myself, I am.

Vio. Most certain, if you are she, you do usurp yourself; for what is yours to bestow is not yours to reserve. But this is from my commission. I will on with my speech in your praise, and then show you the heart of my message.

Oli. Come to what is important in 't. I forgive you the praise.

Vio. Alas, I took great pains to study it, and 't is poetical.

Oli. It is the more like to be feigned. I pray you, keep it in. I heard you were saucy at my gates, and allowed your approach

123. *pia mater,* brain (lit. membrane covering brain). **125. cousin,** kinsman. **132. lethargy,** drunken state. **142. crowner,** coroner. **157. sheriff's post,** post for notices at sheriff's door.

166. squash, unripe peascod. **167. codling,** unripe apple. **168-9. standing water,** at the turn of the tide. **186. con,** learn by heart. **188. comptible,** sensitive. **199. usurp,** counterfeit.

rather to wonder at you than to hear you. If you be not mad, be gone: if you have reason, be brief: 't is not that time of moon with me to make one in so skipping a dialogue.

Mar. Will you hoist sail, sir? Here lies your way.

Vio. No, good swabber, I am to hull here a little longer. Some mollification for your giant, sweet lady. Tell me your mind. I am a messenger.

Oli. Sure, you have some hideous matter to deliver, when the courtesy of it is so fearful. Speak your office.

Vio. It alone concerns your ear. I bring no overture of war, no taxation of homage: I hold the olive in my hand: my words are as full of peace as matter.

Oli. Yet you began rudely. What are you? What would you?

Vio. The rudeness that hath appeared in me have I learned from my entertainment. What I am, and what I would, are as secret as maidenhead; to your ears, divinity; to any other's, profanation.

Oli. Give us the place alone; we will hear this divinity. [*Exit Maria.*] Now, sir, what is your text?

Vio. Most sweet lady,—

Oli. A comfortable doctrine, and much may be said of it. Where lies your text?

Vio. In Orsino's bosom.

Oli. In his bosom! In what chapter of his bosom?

Vio. To answer by the method, in the first of his heart.

Oli. O, I have read it; it is heresy. Have you no more to say?

Vio. Good madam, let me see your face.

Oli. Have you any commission from your lord to negotiate with my face? You are now out of your text, but we will draw the curtain and show you the picture. Look you, sir, such a one I was this present. Is 't not well done? *Unveiling.*

Vio. Excellently done, if God did all.

Oli. 'T is in grain, sir; 't will endure wind and weather.

Vio. 'T is beauty truly blent, whose red and white
Nature's own sweet and cunning hand laid on.
Lady, you are the cruell'st she alive,
If you will lead these graces to the grave
And leave the world no copy.

Oli. O, sir, I will not be so hard-hearted; I will give out divers schedules of my beauty. It shall be inventoried, and every particle and utensil labelled to my will: as, item, two lips, indifferent red; item, two grey eyes, with lids to them; item, one neck, one chin, and so forth. Were you sent hither to praise me?

Vio. I see you what you are, you are too proud;
But, if you were the devil, you are fair.
My lord and master loves you. O, such love
Could be but recompens'd, though you were crown'd
The nonpareil of beauty!

Oli. How does he love me?

Vio. With adorations, with fertile tears,
With groans that thunder love, with sighs of fire.

Oli. Your lord does know my mind; I cannot love him.
Yet I suppose him virtuous, know him noble;
Of great estate, of fresh and stainless youth,
In voices well divulg'd, free, learn'd, and valiant,
And in dimension and the shape of nature
A gracious person: but yet I cannot love him.
He might have took his answer long ago.

Vio. If I did love you in my master's flame,
With such a suff'ring, such a deadly life,
In your denial I would find no sense.
I would not understand it.

Oli. Why, what would you?

Vio. Make me a willow cabin at your gate,
And call upon my soul within the house;
Write loyal cantons of contemned love
And sing them loud even in the dead of night;
Halloo your name to the reverberate hills
And make the babbling gossip of the air
Cry out "Olivia!" O, you should not rest
Between the elements of air and earth,
But you should pity me!

Oli. You might do much.
What is your parentage?

Vio. Above my fortunes, yet my state is well.
I am a gentleman.

Oli. Get you to your lord.
I cannot love him. Let him send no more,—
Unless, perchance, you come to me again
To tell me how he takes it. Fare you well!
I thank you for your pains: spend this for me.

214. **skipping,** mad. 217. **swabber,** deck-swabber. **hull,** float. 218. **your giant,** a reference to the diminutive size of the actor playing Maria; see also "little villain," II, v, 16; "beagle," i.e., small dog, II, iii, 195; and "youngest wren of nine," III, ii, 70. 225. **taxation,** demand. 252. **this present,** this moment. 255. **in grain,** natural, a "fast" color.

264. **labelled to my will,** appended to my will (like an inventory). 267. **praise,** appraise. 279. **In voices well divulg'd,** highly spoken of. 280. **dimension,** body 284. **deadly,** deathlike. 289. **cantons,** songs. 297. **state,** condition.

Vio. I am no fee'd post, lady. Keep your purse.
My master, not myself, lacks recompense.
Love make his heart of flint that you shall love;
And let your fervour, like my master's, be
Plac'd in contempt! Farewell, fair cruelty.
Exit.

Oli. "What is your parentage?"
"Above my fortunes, yet my state is well.
I am a gentleman." I 'll be sworn thou art.
Thy tongue, thy face, thy limbs, actions, and spirit
Do give thee five-fold blazon. Not too fast! Soft, soft!
Unless the master were the man. How now!
Even so quickly may one catch the plague?
Methinks I feel this youth's perfections
With an invisible and subtle stealth
To creep in at mine eyes. Well, let it be.
What ho, Malvolio!

Re-enter *Malvolio.*

Mal. Here, madam, at your service.

Oli. Run after that same peevish messenger,
The County's man. He left this ring behind him,
Would I or not. Tell him I 'll none of it.
Desire him not to flatter with his lord,
Nor hold him up with hopes. I 'm not for him.
If that the youth will come this way to-morrow,
I 'll give him reasons for 't. Hie thee, Malvolio.

Mal. Madam, I will. *Exit.*

Oli. I do I know not what, and fear to find
Mine eye too great a flatterer for my mind.
Fate, show thy force; ourselves we do not owe;
What is decreed must be, and be this so.
Exit.

ACT II. SCENE I. *The sea-coast.*

Enter *Antonio* and *Sebastian.*

Ant. Will you stay no longer? Nor will you not that I go with you?

Seb. By your patience, no. My stars shine darkly over me. The malignancy of my fate might perhaps distemper yours, therefore I shall crave of you your leave that I may bear my evils alone. It were a bad recompense for your love, to lay any of them on you.

Ant. Let me yet know of you whither you are bound.

Seb. No, sooth, sir: my determinate voyage is mere extravagancy. But I perceive in you so excellent a touch of modesty, that you will not extort from me what I am willing to keep in; therefore it charges me in manners the rather to express myself. You must know of me then, Antonio, my name is Sebastian, which I called Roderigo. My father was that Sebastian of Messaline, whom I know you have heard of. He left behind him myself and a sister, both born in an hour. If the heavens had been pleased, would we had so ended! But you, sir, altered that; for some hour before you took me from the breach of the sea was my sister drowned.

Ant. Alas the day!

Seb. A lady, sir, though it was said she much resembled me, was yet of many accounted beautiful; but, though I could not with such estimable wonder overfar believe that, yet thus far I will boldly publish her: she bore a mind that envy could not but call fair. She is drowned already, sir, with salt water, though I seem to drown her remembrance again with more.

Ant. Pardon me, sir, your bad entertainment.

Seb. O good Antonio, forgive me your trouble.

Ant. If you will not murder me for my love, let me be your servant.

Seb. If you will not undo what you have done, that is, kill him whom you have recovered, desire it not. Fare ye well at once. My bosom is full of kindness, and I am yet so near the manners of my mother, that upon the least occasion more mine eyes will tell tales of me. I am bound to the Count Orsino's court. Farewell. *Exit.*

Ant. The gentleness of all the gods go with thee!
I have many enemies in Orsino's court,

312. blazon, coat-of-arms. **313. Unless . . . man,** unless Orsino were in Cesario's place. **Act II, scene i: 5. distemper,** disorder. **11. determinate,** fixed. **12. extravagancy,** vagrancy, aimless wandering. **13. touch,** feeling. **modesty,** moderation, decency. **16. express,** reveal. **23. breach.** breakers.

319. peevish, foolish. **322. flatter with,** deceive with hopes. **327-8.** "I fear that my eye deceived me with hopes beyond what my sober judgment will justify." **329. owe,** own. **Act II, scene i: 29. estimable wonder,** admiring judgment. **45. gentleness,** goodwill.

Viola recieves ring knows Duke ledin' + rena + to Olivia + realizes Olivia loves Page.

Else would I very shortly see thee there.
But, come what may, I do adore thee so.
That danger shall seem sport, and I will go.
Exit.

Scene II. *A street.*

Enter *Viola* and *Malvolio,* at several doors.

Mal. Were you not e'en now with the Countess Olivia?

Vio. Even now, sir. On a moderate pace I have since arrived but hither.

Mal. She returns this ring to you, sir: you might have saved me my pains, to have taken it away yourself. She adds, morever, that you should put your lord into a desperate assurance she will none of him; and one thing more, that you be never so hardy to come again in his affairs, unless it be to report your lord's taking of this. Receive it so.

Vio. She took the ring of me. I 'll none of it.

Mal. Come, sir, you peevishly threw it to her; and her will is, it should be so returned. If it be worth stooping for, there it lies in your eye; if not, be it his that finds it. *Exit.*

Vio. I left no ring with her: what means this lady?
Fortune forbid my outside have not charm'd her!
She made good view of me; indeed so much,
That sure methought her eyes had lost her tongue,
For she did speak in starts distractedly.
She loves me, sure: the cunning of her passion
Invites me in this churlish messenger.
None of my lord's ring! Why, he sent her none.
I am the man: if it be so, as 't is,
Poor lady, she were better love a dream.
Disguise, I see thou art a wickedness
Wherein the pregnant enemy does much.
How easy is it for the proper-false
In women's waxen hearts to set their forms!
Alas, our frailty is the cause, not we!
For such as we are made of, such we be.
How will this fadge? My master loves her dearly;
And I, poor monster, fond as much on him;
And she, mistaken, seems to dote on me.
What will become of this? As I am man,
My state is desperate for my master's love;
As I am woman,—now alas the day!—
What thriftless sighs shall poor Olivia breathe!
O time! thou must untangle this, not I.
It is too hard a knot for me t' untie! *Exit.*

Scene ii: 7. desperate, hopeless. **29. pregnant,** clever, quick-witted. **30. proper-false,** handsome deceivers. **34. fadge,** turn out. **35. fond,** dote.

Scene III. *Olivia's house.*

Enter *Sir Toby* and *Sir Andrew.*

Sir To. Approach, Sir Andrew. Not to be a-bed after midnight is to be up betimes; and *"diliculo surgere,"* thou know'st,—

Sir And. Nay, by my troth, I know not; but I know, to be up late is to be up late.

Sir To. A false conclusion: I hate it as an unfilled can. To be up after midnight and to go to bed then, is early; so that to go to bed after midnight is to go to bed betimes. Does not our lives consist of the four elements?

Sir And. Faith, so they say; but I think it rather consists of eating and drinking.

Sir To. Thou 'rt a scholar; let us therefore eat and drink. Marian, I say! a stoup of wine!

Enter *Clown.*

Sir And. Here comes the fool, i' faith.

Clo. How now, my hearts! Did you never see the picture of "we three"?

Sir To. Welcome, ass. Now let 's have a catch.

Sir And. By my troth, the fool has an excellent breast. I had rather than forty shillings I had such a leg, and so sweet a breath to sing, as the fool has. In sooth, thou wast in very gracious fooling last night, when thou spok'st of Pigrogromitus, of the Vapians passing the equinoctial of Queubus. 'T was very good, i' faith. I sent thee sixpence for thy leman. Hadst it?

Clo. I did impeticos thy gratillity; for Malvolio's nose is no whipstock. My lady has a white hand, and the Mermidons are no bottle-ale houses.

Sir And. Excellent! Why, this is the best fooling, when all is done. Now, a song.

Sir To. Come on; there is sixpence for you. Let 's have a song.

Sir And. There 's a testril of me too. If one knight give a—

Clo. Would you have a love-song, or a song of good life?

Sir To. A love-song, a love-song.

Sir And. Ay, ay. I care not for good life.

Clo. [*Sings.*]

O mistress mine, where are you roaming?
O, stay and hear, your true love 's coming,
That can sing both high and low.

Scene iii: 3. *"diliculo surgere saluberrimum est,"* to rise early is most healthful. **14. stoup,** cup. **17.** A picture commonly found in inns of two asses or fools, with the inscription, "We three loggerheads be." The spectator was supposed to make the third. **19. breast,** voice. **23. Pigrogromitus,** etc., learned nonsense. **26. leman,** sweetheart. **27. impeticos thy gratillity,** pocket thy gratuity. **34. testril,** sixpence.

Trip no further, pretty sweeting;
Journeys end in lovers meeting,
Every wise man's son doth know.

Sir And. Excellent good, i' faith.

Sir To. Good, good.

Clo. [*Sings.*]

What is love? 'T is not hereafter.
Present mirth hath present laughter;
What 's to come is still unsure.
In delay there lies no plenty;
Then come kiss me, sweet and twenty,
Youth 's a stuff will not endure.

Sir And. A mellifluous voice, as I am true knight.

Sir To. A contagious breath.

Sir And. Very sweet and contagious, i' faith.

Sir To. To hear by the nose, it is dulcet in contagion. But shall we make the welkin dance indeed? Shall we rouse the night-owl in a catch that will draw three souls out of one weaver? Shall we do that?

Sir And. An you love me, let 's do 't. I am dog at a catch.

Clo. By 'r lady, sir, and some dogs will catch well.

Sir And. Most certain. Let our catch be, "Thou knave."

Clo. "Hold thy peace, thou knave," knight? I shall be constrained in 't to call thee knave, knight.

Sir And. 'T is not the first time I have constrained one to call me knave. Begin, fool. It begins, "Hold thy peace."

Clo. I shall never begin if I hold my peace.

Sir And. Good, i' faith. Come, begin.

Catch sung.

Enter *Maria.*

Mar. What a caterwauling do you keep here! If my lady have not called up her steward Malvolio and bid him turn you out of doors, never trust me.

Sir To. My lady 's a Cataian, we are politicians, Malvolio 's a Peg-a-Ramsey, and "Three merry men be we." Am not I consanguineous? Am I not of her blood? Tilly-vally. Lady! [*Sings.*] "There dwelt a man in Babylon, lady, lady!"

Clo. Beshrew me, the knight's in admirable fooling.

Sir And. Ay, he does well enough if he be disposed, and so do I too. He does it with a better grace, but I do it more natural.

Sir To. [*Sings.*] "O, the twelfth day of December,"—

Mar. For the love o' God, peace!

Enter *Malvolio.*

Mal. My masters, are you mad, or what are you? Have you no wit, manners, nor honesty, but to gabble like tinkers at this time of night? Do ye make an alehouse of my lady's house, that ye squeak out your coziers' catches without any mitigation or remorse of voice? Is there no respect of place, persons, nor time in you?

Sir To. We did keep time, sir, in our catches. Sneck up!

Mal. Sir Toby, I must be round with you. My lady bade me tell you that, though she harbours you as her kinsman, she 's nothing allied to your disorders. If you can separate yourself and your misdemeanours, you are welcome to the house; if not, an it would please you to take leave of her, she is very willing to bid you farewell.

Sir To. "Farewell, dear heart, since I must needs be gone."

Mar. Nay, good Sir Toby.

Clo. "His eyes do show his days are almost done."

Mal. Is 't even so?

Sir To. "But I will never die."

Clo. Sir Toby, there you lie.

Mal. This is much credit to you.

Sir To. "Shall I bid him go?"

Clo. "What an if you do?"

Sir To. "Shall I bid him go, and spare not?"

Clo. "O no, no, no, no, you dare not."

Sir To. Out o' tune, sir! Ye lie. Art any more than a steward? Dost thou think, because thou art virtuous, there shall be no more cakes and ale?

Clo. Yes, by Saint Anne, and ginger shall be hot i' the mouth too.

Sir To. Thou 'rt i' the right. Go, sir, rub your chain with crumbs. A stoup of wine, Maria!

Mal. Mistress Mary, if you prized my lady's favour at anything more than contempt, you would not give means for this uncivil rule. She shall know of it, by this hand.

Exit.

Mar. Go shake your ears.

Sir And. 'T were as good a deed as to drink when a man 's a-hungry, to challenge him the field, and then to break promise with him and make a fool of him.

56. contagious breath, catchy tune. **61.** Weavers were mostly psalm-singing Calvinist refugees from the Netherlands. **80. Cataian,** Chinese, here means rogue. **81. Peg-a-Ramsey,** character in ballad All the quotations that follow are from songs of th' day. **83. Tilly-vally,** expression, of contempt.

95. tinkers, proverbially a drunken lot. **97. coziers',** cobblers'. **101. Sneck up,** go and be hanged. **129. chain,** steward's badge of office. **132. rule,** conduct.

Sir To. Do 't, knight. I 'll write thee a challenge, or I 'll deliver thy indignation to him by word of mouth.

Mar. Sweet Sir Toby, be patient for to-night. Since the youth of the Count's was to-day with my lady, she is much out of quiet. For Monsieur Malvolio, let me alone with him. If I do not gull him into a nayword, and make him a common recreation, do not think I have wit enough to lie straight in my bed. I know I can do it.

Sir To. Possess us, possess us. Tell us something of him.

Mar. Marry, sir, sometimes he is a kind of puritan.

Sir And. O, if I thought that, I 'd beat him like a dog!

Sir To. What, for being a puritan? Thy exquisite reason, dear knight?

Sir And. I have no exquisite reason for 't, but I have reason good enough.

Mar. The devil a puritan that he is, or anything constantly, but a time-pleaser; an affectioned ass, that cons state without book and utters it by great swarths; the best persuaded of himself, so crammed, as he thinks, with excellencies, that it is his grounds of faith that all that look on him love him; and on that vice in him will my revenge find notable cause to work.

Sir To. What wilt thou do?

Mar. I will drop in his way some obscure epistles of love; wherein, by the colour of his beard, the shape of his leg, the manner of his gait, the expressure of his eye, forehead, and complexion, he shall find himself most feelingly personated. I can write very like my lady your niece. On a forgotten matter we can hardly make distinction of our hands.

Sir To. Excellent! I smell a device.

Sir And. I have 't in my nose too.

Sir To. He shall think by the letters that thou wilt drop that they come from my niece, and that she 's in love with him.

Mar. My purpose is, indeed, a horse of that colour.

Sir And. And your horse now would make him an ass.

Mar. Ass, I doubt not.

Sir And. O, 't will be admirable!

Mar. Sport royal, I warrant you. I know my physic will work with him. I will plant you two, and let the fool make a third, where he shall find the letter: observe his construction of it. For this night, to bed, and dream on the event. Farewell. *Exit.*

Sir To. Good night, Penthesilea.

Sir And. Before me, she 's a good wench.

Sir To. She 's a beagle, true-bred, and one that adores me. What o' that?

Sir And. I was adored once too.

Sir To. Let 's to bed, knight. Thou hadst need send for more money.

Sir And. If I cannot recover your niece, I am a foul way out.

Sir To. Send for money, knight. If thou hast her not i' th' end, call me cut.

Sir And. If I do not, never trust me, take it how you will.

Sir To. Come, come, I 'll go burn some sack; 't is too late to go to bed now. Come, knight; come, knight. *Exeunt.*

Scene IV. *The Duke's palace.*

Enter *Duke, Viola, Curio,* and others.

Duke. Give me some music. Now,—good morrow, friends,—
Now, good Cesario, but that piece of song,
That old and antic song we heard last night.
Methought it did relieve my passion much,
More than light airs and recollected terms
Of these most brisk and giddy-paced times.
Come, but one verse.

Cur. He is not here, so please your lordship, that should sing it.

Duke. Who was it?

Cur. Feste, the jester, my lord; a fool that the lady Olivia's father took much delight in. He is about the house.

Duke. Seek him out, and play the tune the while. *Exit Curio. Music plays.*
Come hither, boy. If ever thou shalt love,
In the sweet pangs of it remember me;
For such as I am all true lovers are,
Unstaid and skittish and in all motions else,
Save in the constant image of the creature
That is belov'd. How dost thou like this tune?

Vio. It gives a very echo to the seat
Where Love is thron'd.

Duke. Thou dost speak masterly.
My life upon 't, young though thou art, thine eye
Hath stay'd upon some favour that it loves.
Hath it not, boy?

Vio. A little, by your favour.

Duke. What kind of woman is 't?

145. **nayword,** byword. 149. **possess,** inform. 161. **affectioned,** affected. 161-2. **cons . . . book,** learns courtly terms by heart. 162. **swarths,** swaths. 170. **expressure,** expression.

192. **Penthesilea,** Queen of the Amazons. 193. **Before me,** by my soul. 200. **recover,** win. 203. **cut,** docked horse. 206. **burn,** heat and spice. 207. **sack,** a Spanish wine. **Scene iv:** 2. **but,** only. 3. **antic,** quaint. 5. Meaning obscure. Probably means reworked, elaborated musical phrases like Sir Toby's "catches," as opposed to the simpler old airs. 18. **motions,** emotions. 25. **favour,** face.

Viola & Duke talk of love — She tells her story as if it were her sister's. He sends her to Olivia.

Vio. Of your complexion.

Duke. She is not worth thee, then. What years, i' faith?

Vio. About your years, my lord.

Duke. Too old, by heaven. Let still the woman take
An elder than herself; so wears she to him,
So sways she level in her husband's heart.
For, boy, however we do praise ourselves,
Our fancies are more giddy and unfirm,
More longing, wavering, sooner lost and worn,
Than women's are.

Vio. I think it well, my lord.

Duke. Then let thy love be younger than thyself,
Or thy affection cannot hold the bent.
For women are as roses, whose fair flower
Being once display'd, doth fall that very hour.

Vio. And so they are; alas, that they are so!
To die, even when they to perfection grow!

Re-enter *Curio* and *Clown.*

Duke. O, fellow, come, the song we had last night.
Mark it, Cesario, it is old and plain.
The spinsters and the knitters in the sun
And the free maids that weave their thread with bones
Do use to chant it. It is silly sooth,
And dallies with the innocence of love,
Like the old age.

Clo. Are you ready, sir?

Duke. Ay; prithee, sing. *Music.*

Song.

Clo.

Come away, come away, death,
And in sad cypress let me be laid.
Fly away, fly away, breath;
I am slain by a fair cruel maid.
My shroud of white, stuck all with yew,
O, prepare it!
My part of death, no one so true
Did share it.

Not a flower, not a flower sweet,
On my black coffin let there be strown.
Not a friend, not a friend greet
My poor corpse, where my bones shall be thrown.
A thousand thousand sighs to save,
Lay me, O, where
Sad true lover never find my grave,
To weep there!

Duke. There 's for thy pains.

Clo. No pains, sir; I take pleasure in singing, sir.

Duke. I 'll pay thy pleasure then.

Clo. Truly, sir, and pleasure will be paid, one time or another.

Duke. Give me now leave to leave thee.

Clo. Now, the melancholy god protect thee, and the tailor make thy doublet of changeable taffeta, for thy mind is a very opal. I would have men of such constancy put to sea, that their business might be everything and their intent everywhere; for that 's it that always makes a good voyage of nothing. Farewell. *Exit.*

Duke. Let all the rest give place.

Curio and Attendants retire.

Once more, Cesario,
Get thee to yond same sovereign cruelty.
Tell her, my love, more noble than the world,
Prizes not quantity of dirty lands.
The parts that fortune hath bestow'd upon her,
Tell her, I hold as giddily as fortune;
But 't is that miracle and queen of gems
That nature pranks her in attracts my soul.

Vio. But if she cannot love you, sir?

Duke. I cannot be so answer'd.

Vio. Sooth, but you must.
Say that some lady, as perhaps there is,
Hath for your love as great a pang of heart
As you have for Olivia. You cannot love her.
You tell her so. Must she not then be answer'd?

Duke. There is no woman's sides
Can bide the beating of so strong a passion
As love doth give my heart; no woman's heart
So big, to hold so much: they lack retention.
Alas, their love may be call'd appetite,
No motion of the liver, but the palate,
That suffer surfeit, cloyment, and revolt;
But mine is all as hungry as the sea,
And can digest as much. Make no compare
Between that love a woman can bear me
And that I owe Olivia.

Vio. Ay, but I know—

Duke. What dost thou know?

Vio. Too well what love women to men may owe.
In faith, they are as true of heart as we.
My father had a daughter lov'd a man,
As it might be, perhaps, were I a woman,
I should your lordship.

Duke. And what 's her history?

Vio. A blank, my lord. She never told her love,
But let concealment, like a worm i' the bud,
Feed on her damask cheek. She pin'd in thought,

35. worn, worn out. **38. bent,** tension (of a bow). **46. free,** carefree. **bones,** bone pins or bobbins. **47. silly sooth,** simple truth. **49. old age,** ancient time. **53. cypress,** crape shroud.

87. giddily, indifferently. **89. pranks,** adorns. **101. liver,** seat of the emotions.

Fabian, Toby & Andrew hide while Malvolio finds Maria's letter. Malvolio imagines he is married to Olivia & plays what he would do.

And with a green and yellow melancholy
She sat, like Patience on a monument,
Smiling at grief. Was not this love indeed?
We men may say more, swear more; but indeed
Our shows are more than will, for still we prove
Much in our vows, but little in our love.

Duke. But died thy sister of her love, my boy?

Vio. I am all the daughters of my father's house,
And all the brothers too;—and yet I know not.
Sir, shall I to this lady?

Duke. Ay, that 's the theme.
To her in haste. Give her this jewel: say
My love can give no place, bide no denay.

Exeunt.

Scene V. *Olivia's garden.*

Enter *Sir Toby, Sir Andrew,* and *Fabian.*

Sir To. Come thy ways, Signior Fabian.

Fab. Nay, I 'll come. If I lose a scruple of this sport, let me be boiled to death with melancholy.

Sir To. Wouldst thou not be glad to have the niggardly rascally sheep-biter come by some notable shame?

Fab. I would exult, man. You know, he brought me out o' favour with my lady about a bear-baiting here.

Sir To. To anger him we 'll have the bear again, and we will fool him black and blue. Shall we not, Sir Andrew?

Sir And. An we do not, it is pity of our lives.

Enter *Maria.*

Sir To. Here comes the little villain. How now, my metal of India!

Mar. Get ye all three into the box-tree; Malvolio 's coming down this walk. He has been yonder i' the sun practising behaviour to his own shadow this half hour. Observe him, for the love of mockery, for I know this letter will make a contemplative idiot of him. Close, in the name of jesting! Lie thou there [*throws down a letter*], for here comes the trout that must be caught with tickling.

Exit.

Enter *Malvolio.*

Mal. 'T is but fortune. All is fortune. Maria once told me she did affect me; and I have heard herself come thus near, that, should she fancy, it should be one of my complexion. Besides, she uses me with a more exalted respect than any one else that follows her. What should I think on 't?

Sir To. Here 's an overweening rogue!

Fab. O, peace! Contemplation makes a rare turkey-cock of him. How he jets under his advanced plumes!

Sir And. 'S light, I could so beat the rogue!

Fab. Peace, I say.

Mal. To be Count Malvolio!

Sir To. Ah, rogue!

Sir And. Pistol him, pistol him.

Fab. Peace, peace!

Mal. There is example for 't. The lady of the Strachy married the yeoman of the wardrobe.

Sir And. Fie on him, Jezebel!

Fab. O, peace! now he 's deeply in. Look how imagination blows him.

Mal. Having been three months married to her, sitting in my state,—

Sir To. O, for a stone-bow, to hit him in the eye!

Mal. Calling my officers about me, in my branched velvet gown, having come from a day-bed, where I have left Olivia sleeping,—

Sir To. Fire and brimstone!

Fab. O, peace, peace!

Mal. And then to have the humour of state; and after a demure travel of regard, telling them I know my place as I would they should do theirs, to ask for my kinsman Toby,—

Sir To. Bolts and shackles!

Fab. O peace, peace, peace! Now, now.

Mal. Seven of my people, with an obedient start, make out for him. I frown the while, and perchance wind up my watch, or play with my—some rich jewel. Toby approaches, curtsies there to me,—

Sir To. Shall this fellow live?

Fab. Though our silence be drawn from us with cars, yet peace.

Mal. I extend my hand to him thus, quenching my familiar smile with an austere regard of control,—

116. **green** for hope; **yellow** for jealousy, expressing Viola's melancholy passion for the Duke. 117. **monument,** tomb. 120. **Our . . . will,** our professions are stronger than our will to put them into effect. 127. **denay,** denial. **Scene v:** 6. **sheep-biter,** vicious cur. 17. **metal of India,** gold. 26. **trout . . . tickling,** trout in holes or pools where they could be reached by the hand were often taken by being rubbed under the gills until they became quiet enough to be grasped and landed.

28. **she,** Olivia. 36. **jets,** struts. 44-5. This reference to the lady of the Strachy has never been explained. It is obviously a reference to some unequal marriage. 50. **state,** canopied chair. 51. **stone-bow,** cross-bow which threw stones. 54. **branched,** flowered. 58. **humour of state,** caprice of authority. 59. **travel of regard,** glance around. 66. **play with my—,** is about to say "chain," i.e., steward's badge of office. 74. **regard of control** look of authority.

Sir To. And does not Toby take you a blow o' the lips then?

Mal. Saying, "Cousin Toby, my fortunes, having cast me on your niece, give me this prerogative of speech,"—

Sir To. What, what?

Mal. "You must amend your drunkenness."

Sir To. Out, scab!

Fab. Nay, patience, or we break the sinews of our plot.

Mal. "Besides, you waste the treasure of your time with a foolish knight,"—

Sir And. That 's me, I warrant you.

Mal. "One Sir Andrew,"—

Sir And. I knew 't was I; for many do call me fool.

Mal. What employment have we here?

Taking up the letter.

Fab. Now is the woodcock near the gin.

Sir To. O, peace, and the spirit of humours intimate reading aloud to him!

Mal. By my life, this is my lady's hand. These be her very C's, her U's, and her T's; and thus makes she her great P's. It is, in contempt of question, her hand.

Sir And. Her C's, her U's, and her T's: why that?

Mal. [*Reads.*] "To the unknown beloved, this, and my good wishes":—her very phrases! By your leave, wax. Soft! And the impressure her Lucrece, with which she uses to seal: 't is my lady. To whom should this be?

Fab. This wins him, liver and all.

Mal. [*Reads.*]

"Jove knows I love;
But who?
Lips, do not move;
No man must know."

"No man must know." What follows? The numbers altered! "No man must know!" If this should be thee, Malvolio?

Sir T. Marry, hang thee, brock!

Mal. [*Reads.*]

"I may command where I adore;
But silence, like a Lucrece knife.
With bloodless stroke my heart doth gore.
M, O, A, I, doth sway my life."

Fab. A fustian riddle!

Sir To. Excellent wench, say I.

Mal. "M, O, A, I, doth sway my life." Nay, but first, let me see, let me see, let me see.

Fab. What dish o' poison has she dressed him!

Sir To. And with what wing the staniel checks at it!

Mal. "I may command where I adore." Why, she may command me: I serve her: she is my lady. Why, this is evident to any formal capacity, there is no obstruction in this. And the end,—what should that alphabetical position portend? If I could make that resemble something in me!—Softly! M, O, A, I,—

Sir To. O, ay, make up that. He is now at a cold scent.

Fab. Sowter will cry upon 't for all this, though it be as rank as a fox.

Mal. M,—Malvolio; M,—why, that begins my name.

Fab. Did not I say he would work it out? The cur is excellent at faults.

Mal. M,—but then there is no consonancy in the sequel: that suffers under probation: A should follow, but O does.

Fab. And O shall end, I hope.

Sir To. Ay, or I 'll cudgel him, and make him cry O!

Mal. And then I comes behind.

Fab. Ay, an you had any eye behind you, you might see more detraction at your heels than fortunes before you.

Mal. M, O, A, I; this simulation is not as the former; and yet, to crush this a little, it would bow to me, for every one of these letters are in my name. Soft! here follows prose.

[*Reads.*] "If this fall into thy hand, revolve. In my stars I am above thee, but be not afraid of greatness: some are born great, some achieves greatness, and some have greatness thrust upon 'em. Thy Fates open their hands, let thy blood and spirit embrace them; and, to inure thyself to what thou art like to be, cast thy humble slough and appear fresh. Be opposite with a kinsman, surly with servants; let thy tongue tang arguments of state; put thyself into the trick of singularity: she thus advises thee that sighs for thee. Remember who commended thy yellow stockings, and wished to see thee ever cross-gartered. I say, remember. Go to, thou art made, if thou desir'st to be so; if not, let me see thee a steward still, the fellow of servants, and not worthy to touch Fortune's fingers. Farewell. She that would alter services with thee,

THE FORTUNATE—UNHAPPY."

92. woodcock, bird, emblem of stupidity. **gin,** snare. **97-8. in . . . question,** without doubt. **103. impressure,** impression. **112. numbers,** metre. **114. brock,** badger, term of contempt. **119. fustian,** nonsensical.

124-5. Terms taken from falconry. The **staniel** (untrained hawk) **checks** (turns aside) after inferior game instead of following the proper object of its hunt. **128-9. formal capacity,** ordinary intelligence. **135.** Even Sowter (contemptuous name for dog) will find this scent, though as a matter of fact it's as plain as can be. **140. faults.** breaks in the line of scent. **141. consonancy,** agreement. **142. probation,** test. **151. simulation.** disguised meaning. **152. crush,** strain (the meaning). **155. revolve.** consider. **162. slough,** snake-skin. **opposite,** antagonistic.

Daylight and champian discovers not more: this is open. I will be proud, I will read politic authors, I will baffle Sir Toby, I will wash off gross acquaintance, I will be point-device the very man. I do not now fool myself, to let imagination jade me; for every reason excites to this, that my lady loves me. She did commend my yellow stockings of late, she did praise my leg being cross-gartered; and in this she manifests herself to my love, and with a kind of injunction drives me to these habits of her liking. I thank my stars I am happy, I will be strange, stout, in yellow stockings, and cross-gartered, even with the swiftness of putting on. Jove and my stars be praised! Here is yet a postscript.

[*Reads.*] "Thou canst not choose but know who I am. If thou entertain'st my love, let it appear in thy smiling. Thy smiles become thee well; therefore in my presence still smile, dear my sweet, I prithee."

Jove, I thank thee. I will smile; I will do everything that thou wilt have me. *Exit.*

Fab. I will not give my part of this sport for a pension of thousands to be paid from the Sophy.

Sir To. I could marry this wench for this device—

Sir And. So could I too.

Sir To. And ask no other dowry with her but such another jest.

Re-enter *Maria.*

Sir And. Nor I neither.

Fab. Here comes my noble gull-catcher.

Sir To. Wilt thou set thy foot o' my neck?

Sir And. Or o' mine either?

Sir To. Shall I play my freedom at tray-trip, and become thy bond-slave?

Sir And. I' faith, or I either?

Sir To. Why, thou hast put him in such a dream, that when the image of it leaves him he must run mad.

Mar. Nay, but say true: does it work upon him?

Sir To. Like aqua-vitæ with a midwife.

Mar. If you will then see the fruits of the sport, mark his first approach before my lady. He will come to her in yellow stockings, and 't is a colour she abhors, and cross-gartered, a fashion she detests; and he will smile upon her, which will now be so unsuitable to her disposition, being addicted to a melancholy as she is, that it cannot but turn him into a notable contempt. If you will see it, follow me.

Sir To. To the gates of Tartar, thou most excellent devil of wit!

Sir And. I 'll make one too. *Exeunt.*

ACT III. SCENE I. *Olivia's garden.*

Enter *Viola* and *Clown* with a tabor.

Vio. Save thee, friend, and thy music! Dost thou live by thy tabor?

Clo. No, sir, I live by the church.

Vio. Art thou a churchman?

Clo. No such matter, sir; I do live by the church; for I do live at my house, and my house doth stand by the church.

Vio. So thou mayst say, the king lies by a beggar, if a beggar dwells near him; or, the church stands by thy tabor, if thy tabor stand by the church.

Clo. You have said, sir. To see this age! A sentence is but a cheveril glove to a good wit. How quickly the wrong side may be turned outward!

Vio. Nay, that 's certain. They that dally nicely with words may quickly make them wanton.

Clo. I would, therefore, my sister had had no name, sir.

Vio. Why, man?

Clo. Why, sir, her name 's a word, and to dally with that word might make my sister wanton. But, indeed, words are very rascals since bonds disgraced them.

Vio. Thy reason, man?

Clo. Troth, sir, I can yield you none without words; and words are grown so false, I am loath to prove reason with them.

Vio. I warrant thou art a merry fellow and car'st for nothing.

Clo. Not so, sir, I do care for something; but in my conscience, sir, I do not care for

173. champian, open country. **175. politic**, treating of statecraft. **baffle**, treat contemptuously. **177. point-device**, precisely. **178. jade**, abuse. **185. stout**, overbearing. **198. Sophy**, Shah of Persia. **Act III, Scene i: 2. tabor**, small drum. **13. cheveril**, kid.

208. tray-trip, a dice game. **226. Tartar**, Tartarus. **Act III, Scene i: 17. nicely**, subtly. **18. wanton**, light, frivolous (l. 24, lustful). **25. since bonds disgraced them**, implies that a man's word is no longer as good as his bond since a bond has become necessary.

you: if that be to care for nothing, sir, I would it would make you invisible.

Vio. Art not thou the Lady Olivia's fool?

Clo. No, indeed, sir; the Lady Olivia has no folly. She will keep no fool, sir, till she be married; and fools are as like husbands as pilchards are to herrings, the husband 's the bigger. I am indeed not her fool, but her corrupter of words.

Vio. I saw thee late at the Count Orsino's.

Clo. Foolery, sir, does walk about the orb like the sun, it shines everywhere. I would be sorry, sir, but the fool should be as oft with your master as with my mistress. I think I saw your wisdom there.

Vio. Nay, an thou pass upon me, I 'll no more with thee. Hold, there 's expenses for thee.

Clo. Now Jove, in his next commodity of hair, send thee a beard!

Vio. By my troth, I 'll tell thee, I am almost sick for one,—[*aside*] though I would not have it grow on my chin. Is thy lady within?

Clo. Would not a pair of these have bred, sir?

Vio. Yes, being kept together and put to use.

Clo. I would play Lord Pandarus of Phrygia, sir, to bring a Cressida to this Troilus.

Vio. I understand you, sir; 't is well begged.

Clo. The matter, I hope, is not great, sir, begging but a beggar. Cressida was a beggar. My lady is within, sir. I will conster to them whence you come: who you are and what you would are out of my welkin—I might say "element," but the word is overworn. *Exit.*

Vio. This fellow is wise enough to play the fool,
And to do that well craves a kind of wit.
He must observe their mood on whom he jests,
The quality of persons, and the time,
And, like the haggard, check at every feather
That comes before his eye. This is a practice
As full of labour as a wise man's art;
For folly that he wisely shows is fit;
But wise men, folly-fall'n, quite taint their wit.

Enter *Sir Toby* and *Sir Andrew*.

Sir To. Save you, gentleman.

Vio. And you, sir.

Sir And. *Dieu vous garde, monsieur.*

Vio. *Et vous aussi; votre serviteur.*

Sir And. I hope, sir, you are; and I am yours.

Sir To. Will you encounter the house? My niece is desirous you should enter, if your trade be to her.

Vio. I am bound to your niece, sir; I mean, she is the list of my voyage.

Sir To. Taste your legs, sir; put them to motion.

Vio. My legs do better understand me, sir, than I understand what you mean by bidding me taste my legs.

Sir To. I mean, to go, sir, to enter.

Vio. I will answer you with gait and entrance. But we are prevented.

Enter *Olivia* and *Maria* her Gentlewoman.

Most excellent accomplished lady, the heavens rain odours on you!

Sir And. That youth 's a rare courtier. "Rain odours;" well.

Vio. My matter hath no voice, lady, but to your own most pregnant and vouchsafed ear.

Sir And. "Odours," "pregnant," and "vouchsafed"; I 'll get 'em all three all ready.

Oli. Let the garden door be shut, and leave me to my hearing. [*Exeunt all but Olivia and Viola.*] Give me your hand, sir.

Vio. My duty, madam, and most humble service.

Oli. What is your name?

Vio. Cesario is your servant's name, fair princess.

Oli. My servant, sir! 'T was never merry world
Since lowly feigning was call'd compliment.
You 're servant to the Count Orsino, youth.

Vio. And he is yours, and his must needs be yours.
Your servant's servant is your servant, madam.

Oli. For him, I think not on him: for his thoughts,
Would they were blanks, rather than fill'd with me!

Vio. Madam, I come to whet your gentle thoughts
On his behalf.

Oli. O, by your leave, I pray you,
I bade you never speak again of him;
But, would you undertake another suit,
I had rather hear you to solicit that
Than music from the spheres.

Vio. Dear lady,—

40. **pilchards**, a fish which looks like a herring. 48. **pass upon**, thrust at. 50. **commodity**, consignment. 56. **use**, interest. 57. **Pandarus**, Cressida's uncle, arranged the meeting between her and Troilus. In one version of the story Cressida became a leper and begged for alms (l. 62). 63. **conster**, construe, explain. 71. **haggard**, untrained hawk. **check at**, turn aside. 75. **folly-fall'n**, when they speak like fools. **wit**, understanding, intelligence.

82. **encounter**, approach. 86. **list**, goal. 94. **prevented**, anticipated. 100. **pregnant**, receptive. **vouchsafed**, willing.

Oli. Give me leave, beseech you. I did send,
After the last enchantment you did here,
A ring in chase of you; so did I abuse
Myself, my servant, and, I fear me, you.
Under your hard construction must I sit,
To force that on you, in a shameful cunning,
Which you knew none of yours. What might you think?
Have you not set mine honour at the stake
And baited it with all th' unmuzzled thoughts
That tyrannous heart can think? To one of your receiving
Enough is shown. A cypress, not a bosom,
Hides my heart. So, let me hear you speak.

Vio. I pity you.

Oli. That 's a degree to love.

Vio. No, not a grize; for 't is a vulgar proof,
That very oft we pity enemies.

Oli. Why, then, methinks 't is time to smile again.
O world, how apt the poor are to be proud!
If one should be a prey, how much the better
To fall before the lion than the wolf!
Clock strikes.
The clock upbraids me with the waste of time.
Be not afraid, good youth, I will not have you;
And yet, when wit and youth is come to harvest,
Your wife is like to reap a proper man.
There lies your way, due west.

Vio. Then westward-ho!
Grace and good disposition
Attend your ladyship!
You 'll nothing, madam, to my lord by me?

Oli. Stay!
I prithee, tell me what thou think'st of me.

Vio. That you do think you are not what you are.

Oli. If I think so, I think the same of you.

Vio. Then think you right. I am not what I am.

Oli. I would you were as I would have you be!

Vio. Would it be better, madam, than I am?
I wish it might, for now I am your fool.

Oli. O, what a deal of scorn looks beautiful
In the contempt and anger of his lip!
A murd'rous guilt shows not itself more soon
Than love that would seem hid. Love's night is noon.
Cesario, by the roses of the spring,
By maidhood, honour, truth, and everything,
I love thee so, that, maugre all thy pride,
Nor wit nor reason can my passion hide.
Do not extort thy reasons from this clause,
For that I woo, thou therefore hast no cause;
But rather reason thus with reason fetter,
Love sought is good, but given unsought is better.

Vio. By innocence I swear, and by my youth,
I have one heart, one bosom, and one truth,
And that no woman has; nor never none
Shall mistress be of it, save I alone.
And so adieu, good madam; nevermore
Will I my master's tears to you deplore.

Oli. Yet come again; for thou perhaps mayst move
That heart, which now abhors, to like his love.
Exeunt.

Scene II. *Olivia's house.*

Enter *Sir Toby, Sir Andrew,* and *Fabian.*

Sir And. No, faith, I 'll not stay a jot longer.

Sir To. Thy reason, dear venom, give thy reason.

Fab. You must needs yield your reason, Sir Andrew.

Sir And. Marry, I saw your niece do more favours to the Count's serving-man than ever she bestowed upon me. I saw 't i' th' orchard.

Sir To. Did she see thee the while, old boy? Tell me that.

Sir And. As plain as I see you now.

Fab. This was a great argument of love in her toward you.

Sir And. 'S light, will you make an ass o' me?

Fab. I will prove it legitimate, sir, upon the oaths of judgement and reason.

Sir To. And they have been grand-jurymen since before Noah was a sailor.

Fab. She did show favour to the youth in your sight only to exasperate you, to awake your dormouse valour, to put fire in your heart, and brimstone in your liver. You should then have accosted her; and with some excellent jests, fire-new from the mint, you should have banged the youth into dumbness. This was looked for at your hand, and this was balked: the double gilt of this opportunity you let time wash off, and you are now sailed into the north of my lady's opinion, where you will hang like an icicle on a Dutchman's beard,

123. enchantment, charm. **124. abuse**, deceive. **130. baited it with all th' unmuzzled thoughts**, in bear-baiting the bear was tied to a stake and set upon by large dogs. **131. receiving**, understanding. **132. cypress**, transparent crape. **135. grize**, step. **vulgar proof**, common experience.

163. maugre, in spite of. **165-6.** Do not extort (wrest) from this declaration of my love excuses for not wooing me. **166. For that**, because. **Scene ii: 12. argument**, proof. **28. north**, region of cold disdain. **29. Dutchman's beard**, probably reference to William Barendz's enduring an arctic winter in Nova Zembla in 1596.

unless you do redeem it by some laudable attempt either of valour or policy.

Sir And. An 't be any way, it must be with valour; for policy I hate: I had as lief be a Brownist as a politician.

Sir To. Why, then, build me thy fortunes upon the basis of valour. Challenge me the Count's youth to fight with him; hurt him in eleven places; my niece shall take note of it; and assure thyself, there is no love-broker in the world can more prevail in man's commendation with woman than report of valour.

Fab. There is no way but this, Sir Andrew.

Sir And. Will either of you bear me a challenge to him?

Sir To. Go, write it in a martial hand. Be curst and brief. It is no matter how witty, so it be eloquent and full of invention: taunt him with the license of ink: if thou thou'st him some thrice, it shall not be amiss; and as many lies as will lie in thy sheet of paper, although the sheet were big enough for the bed of Ware in England, set 'em down: go about it. Let there be gall enough in thy ink, though thou write with a goose-pen, no matter: about it.

Sir And. Where shall I find you?

Sir To. We 'll call thee at the cubiculo. Go.

Exit Sir Andrew.

Fab. This is a dear manakin to you, Sir Toby.

Sir To. I have been dear to him, lad, some two thousand strong, or so.

Fab. We shall have a rare letter from him. But you 'll not deliver 't?

Sir To. Never trust me, then; and by all means stir on the youth to an answer. I think oxen and wainropes cannot hale them together. For Andrew, if he were opened, and you find so much blood in his liver as will clog the foot of a flea, I 'll eat the rest of th' anatomy.

Fab. And his opposite, the youth, bears in his visage no great presage of cruelty.

Enter *Maria.*

Sir To. Look, where the youngest wren of mine comes.

Mar. If you desire the spleen, and will laugh yourselves into stitches, follow me. Yond gull Malvolio is turned heathen, a very renegado; for there is no Christian, that means to be saved by believing rightly, can ever believe such impossible passages of grossness. He 's in yellow stockings.

Sir To. And cross-gartered?

Mar. Most villanously; like a pedant that keeps a school i' the church. I have dogged him like his murderer. He does obey every point of the letter that I dropped to betray him. He does smile his face into more lines than is in the new map with the augmentation of the Indies. You have not seen such a thing as 't is. I can hardly forbear hurling things at him. I know my lady will strike him: if she do, he 'll smile and take 't for a great favour.

Sir To. Come, bring us, bring us where he is.

Exeunt.

Scene III. *A street.*

Enter *Sebastian* and *Antonio.*

Seb. I would not by my will have troubled you;
But since you make your pleasure of your pains,
I will no further chide you.

Ant. I could not stay behind you: my desire,
More sharp than filed steel, did spur me forth,
And not all love to see you, though so much
As might have drawn one to a longer voyage,
But jealousy what might befall your travel,
Being skilless in these parts; which to a stranger,
Unguided and unfriended, often prove
Rough and unhospitable: my willing love,
The rather by these arguments of fear,
Set forth in your pursuit.

Seb. My kind Antonio,
I can no other answer make but thanks,
And thanks, and ever thanks; and oft good turns
Are shuffled off with such uncurrent pay;
But, were my worth as is my conscience firm,
You should find better dealing. What 's to do?
Shall we go see the reliques of this town?

Ant. To-morrow, sir: best first go see your lodging.

Seb. I am not weary, and 't is long to night.
I pray you, let us satisfy our eyes
With the memorials and the things of fame
That do renown this city.

34. Brownist, member of an unpopular Puritan sect. **46. curst,** ill-tempered. **48. thou'st,** "thou" used to intimates and inferiors, here an insult. **51.** A famous bed—10 feet 9 inches square—in an inn at Ware. Four couples could sleep in it comfortably. **56. cubiculo,** apartment. **72. spleen,** fit of laughter. **77. passages of grossness,** acts of absurdity.

80. pedant, schoolmaster. **85-6. The new map with the augmentation of the Indies,** this reference has helped to date the play, as the map referred to, probably that bound into certain copies of the 1599 edition of Hakluyt's voyages, has information that would not have been known in England before 1588-9. It contained fuller information about the East Indies than its predecessors and had more lines on it. **Scene iii: 8. jealousy,** apprehension. **17. worth,** wealth. **conscience,** recognition of the debt. **19. reliques,** see l. 23.

Ant. Would you 'd pardon me.
I do not without danger walk these streets.
Once, in a sea-fight, 'gainst the Count his galleys
I did some service; of such note indeed,
That were I ta'en here it would scarce be answer'd.

Seb. Belike you slew great number of his people.

Ant. Th' offence is not of such a bloody nature,
Albeit the quality of the time and quarrel
Might well have given us bloody argument.
It might have since been answer'd in repaying
What we took from them, which, for traffic's sake,
Most of our city did; only myself stood out,
For which, if I be lapsed in this place,
I shall pay dear.

Seb. Do not then walk too open.

Ant. It doth not fit me. Hold, sir, here 's my purse.
In the south suburbs, at the Elephant
Is best to lodge. I will bespeak our diet,
Whiles you beguile the time and feed your knowledge
With viewing of the town. There shall you have me.

Seb. Why I your purse?

Ant. Haply your eye shall light upon some toy
You have desire to purchase; and your store,
I think, is not for idle markets, sir.

Seb. I 'll be your purse-bearer and leave you for
An hour.

Ant. To th' Elephant.

Seb. I do remember.

Exeunt.

Scene IV. *Olivia's garden.*

Enter *Olivia* and *Maria.*

Oli. I have sent after him; he says he 'll come.
How shall I feast him? What bestow of him?
For youth is bought more oft than begg'd or borrow'd.
I speak too loud.
Where 's Malvolio? He is sad and civil,
And suits well for a servant with my fortunes.
Where is Malvolio?

Mar. He 's coming, madam, but in very strange manner. He is, sure, possessed, madam.

Oli. Why, what 's the matter? Does he rave?

Mar. No, madam, he does nothing but smile. Your ladyship were best to have some guard about you, if he come; for sure the man is tainted in 's wits.

Oli. Go call him hither. *Exit Maria.*
I am as mad as he,
If sad and merry madness equal be.

Enter *Malvolio,* with *Maria.*

How now, Malvolio!

Mal. Sweet lady, ho, ho.

Oli. Smil'st thou?
I sent for thee upon a sad occasion.

Mal. Sad, lady? I could be sad. This does make some obstruction in the blood, this cross-gartering; but what of that? If it please the eye of one, it is with me as the very true sonnet is "Please one, and please all."

Oli. Why, how dost thou, man? What is the matter with thee?

Mal. Not black in my mind, though yellow in my legs. It did come to his hands, and commands shall be executed. I think we do know the sweet Roman hand.

Oli. Wilt thou go to bed, Malvolio?

Mal. To bed! Ay, sweet heart, and I 'll come to thee.

Oli. God comfort thee! Why dost thou smile so and kiss thy hand so oft?

Mar. How do you, Malvolio?

Mal. At your request? Yes: nightingales answer daws.

Mar. Why appear you with this ridiculous boldness before my lady?

Mal. "Be not afraid of greatness:" 't was well writ.

Oli. What mean'st thou by that, Malvolio?

Mal. "Some are born great,"—

Oli. Ha?

Mal. "Some achieve greatness,"—

Oli. What say'st thou?

Mal. "And some have greatness thrust upon them."

Oli. Heaven restore thee!

Mal. "Remember who commended thy yellow stockings,"—

Oli. Thy yellow stockings!

Mal. "And wish'd to see thee cross-gartered."

Oli. Cross-gartered!

Mal. "Go to, thou art made, if thou desir'st to be so;"—

Oli. Am I made?

Mal. "If not, let me see thee a servant still."

Oli. Why, this is very midsummer madness.

31. quality, nature. **36. lapsed,** surprised, arrested. **Scene iv: 5. sad,** grave.

25. "Please . . . all," an old ballad. **31. Roman hand,** a style of handwriting used by educated people.

Enter *Servant.*

Ser. Madam, the young gentleman of the Count Orsino's is returned. I could hardly entreat him back. He attends your ladyship's pleasure.

Oli. I 'll come to him. [*Exit Servant.*] Good Maria, let this fellow be looked to. Where 's my cousin Toby? Let some of my people have a special care of him: I would not have him miscarry for the half of my dowry.

Exeunt Olivia and Maria.

Mal. O, ho! do you come near me now? No worse man than Sir Toby to look to me! This concurs directly with the letter: she sends him on purpose, that I may appear stubborn to him, for she incites me to that in the letter. "Cast thy humble slough," says she; "be opposite with a kinsman, surly with servants; let thy tongue tang with arguments of state; put thyself into the trick of singularity;" and consequently sets down the manner how; as, a sad face, a reverend carriage, a slow tongue, in the habit of some sir of note, and so forth. I have limed her; but it is Jove's doing, and Jove make me thankful! And when she went away now, "Let this fellow be looked to"; "fellow!" not Malvolio, nor after my degree, but "fellow." Why, everything adheres together, that no dram of a scruple, no scruple of a scruple, no obstacle, no incredulous or unsafe circumstance—What can be said? Nothing that can be can come between me and the full prospect of my hopes. Well, Jove, not I, is the doer of this, and he is to be thanked.

Re-enter *Maria,* with *Sir Toby* and *Fabian.*

Sir To. Which way is he, in the name of sanctity? If all the devils of hell be drawn in little, and Legion himself possessed him, yet I 'll speak to him.

Fab. Here he is, here he is. How is 't with you, sir? How is 't with you, man?

Mal. Go off; I discard you: let me enjoy my private: go off.

Mar. Lo, how hollow the fiend speaks within him! Did not I tell you? Sir Toby, my lady prays you to have a care of him.

Mal. Ah, ha! Does she so?

Sir To. Go to, go to; peace, peace. We must deal gently with him: let me alone. How do you Malvolio? How is 't with you? What man, defy the devil! Consider, he 's an enemy to mankind.

Mal. Do you know what you say?

Mar. La you! and you speak ill of the devil, how he takes it at heart! Pray God he be not bewitched!

Fab. Carry his water to the wise woman.

Mar. Marry, and it shall be done to-morrow morning if I live. My lady would not lose him for more than I 'll say.

Mal. How now, mistress!

Mar. O Lord!

Sir To. Prithee, hold thy peace; this is not the way: do you not see you move him? Let me alone with him.

Fab. No way but gentleness; gently, gently: the fiend is rough, and will not be roughly used.

Sir To. Why, how now, my bawcock! How dost thou, chuck?

Mal. Sir!

Sir To. Ay, "Biddy, come with me." What, man, 't is not for gravity to play at cherry-pit with Satan. Hang him, foul collier!

Mar. Get him to say his prayers, good Sir Toby, get him to pray.

Mal. My prayers, minx!

Mar. No, I warrant you, he will not hear of godliness.

Mal. Go, hang yourselves all! You are idle shallow things; I am not of your element. You shall know more hereafter. *Exit.*

Sir To. Is 't possible?

Fab. If this were played upon a stage now, I could condemn it as an improbable fiction.

Sir To. His very genius hath taken the infection of the device, man.

Mar. Nay, pursue him now, lest the device take air and taint.

Fab. Why, we shall make him mad indeed.

Mar. The house will be the quieter.

Sir To. Come, we 'll have him in a dark room and bound. My niece is already in the belief that he 's mad. We may carry it thus, for our pleasure and his penance, till our very pastime, tired out of breath, prompt us to have mercy on him; at which time we will bring the device to the bar and crown thee for a finder of madmen. But see, but see.

Enter *Sir Andrew.*

Fab. More matter for a May morning.

Sir And. Here 's the challenge, read it: I warrant there 's vinegar and pepper in 't.

Fab. Is 't so saucy?

Sir And. Ay, is 't, I warrant him: do but read.

70. **miscarry**, come to harm. 79. **consequently**, in what follows. 82. **limed**, snared as with birdline. 87. **scruple**, pun (1) unit of measurement, (2) doubt. 87. **incredulous**, incredible. 95. **Legion**, the devils cast out by Christ, cf. Mark v. 9.

125. **bawcock**, beau coq—good fellow. 126. **chuck**, chick. 129. **cherry-pit**, a child's game of pitching cherry-stones into small hole. 137. **element**, sphere (of society). 142. **genius**, guiding spirit, soul. 145. **take air and taint**, become known and be discredited.

Sir To. Give me. [*Reads.*] "Youth, whatsoever thou art, thou art but a scurvy fellow."

Fab. Good and valiant.

Sir To. [*Reads.*] "Wonder not, nor admire not in thy mind, why I do call thee so, for I will show thee no reason for 't."

Fab. A good note. That keeps you from the blow of the law.

Sir To. [*Reads.*] "Thou com'st to the lady Olivia, and in my sight she uses thee kindly. But thou liest in thy throat; that is not the matter I challenge thee for."

Fab. Very brief, and to exceeding good sense—less.

Sir To. [*Reads.*] "I will waylay thee going home; where if it be thy chance to kill me,"—

Fab. Good.

Sir To. [*Reads.*] "Thou kill'st me like a rogue and a villain."

Fab. Still you keep o' the windy side of the law; good.

Sir To. [*Reads.*] "Fare thee well, and God have mercy upon one of our souls! He may have mercy upon mine; but my hope is better, and so look to thyself. Thy friend, as thou usest him, and thy sworn enemy,

ANDREW AGUECHEEK."

If this letter move him not, his legs cannot. I 'll give 't him.

Mar. You may have very fit occasion for 't. He is now in some commerce with my lady, and will by and by depart.

Sir To. Go, Sir Andrew, scout me for him at the corner of the orchard like a bum-baily. So soon as ever thou seest him, draw; and, as thou draw'st, swear horrible; for it comes to pass oft that a terrible oath, with a swaggering accent sharply twanged off, gives manhood more approbation than ever proof itself would have earned him. Away!

Sir And. Nay, let me alone for swearing. *Exit.*

Sir To. Now will not I deliver his letter; for the behaviour of the young gentleman gives him out to be of good capacity and breeding; his employment between his lord and my niece confirms no less; therefore this letter, being so excellently ignorant, will breed no terror in the youth; he will find it comes from a clodpole. But, sir, I will deliver his challenge by word of mouth, set upon Aguecheek a notable report of valour, and drive the gentleman, as I know his youth will aptly receive it, into a most hideous opinion of his rage, skill, fury, and impetuosity. This will so fright them both that they will kill one another by the look, like cockatrices.

Re-enter *Olivia* with *Viola.*

Fab. Here he comes with your niece. Give them way till he take leave, and presently after him.

Sir To. I will meditate the while upon some horrid message for a challenge.

Exeunt Sir Toby, Fabian, and Maria.

Oli. I have said too much unto a heart of stone,
And laid mine honour too unchary on 't.
There 's something in me that reproves my fault;
But such a headstrong potent fault it is,
That it but mocks reproof.

Vio. With the same 'haviour that your passion bears
Goes on my master's grief.

Oli. Here, wear this jewel for me, 't is my picture.
Refuse it not; it hath no tongue to vex you;
And I beseech you come again to-morrow.
What shall you ask of me that I 'll deny,
That honour sav'd may upon asking give?

Vio. Nothing but this—your true love for my master.

Oli. How with mine honour may I give him that
Which I have given to you?

Vio. I will acquit you.

Oli. Well, come again to-morrow: fare thee well!
A fiend like thee might bear my soul to hell.
Exit.

Re-enter *Sir Toby* and *Fabian.*

Sir To. Gentleman, God save thee!

Vio. And you, sir.

Sir To. That defence thou hast, betake thee to 't. Of what nature the wrongs are thou hast done him, I know not; but thy intercepter, full of despite, bloody as the hunter, attends thee at the orchard-end. Dismount thy tuck, be yare in thy preparation, for thy assailant is quick, skilful, and deadly.

Vio. You mistake, sir, I am sure: no man hath any quarrel to me: my remembrance is very free and clear from any image of offence done to any man.

Sir To. You 'll find it otherwise, I assure you; therefore, if you hold your life at any price, betake you to your guard; for your opposite hath in him what youth, strength, skill, and wrath can furnish man withal.

165. **admire**, be surprised. 191. **commerce**, conversation. 194. **bum-baily**, bailiff who arrests for debt. 199. **approbation**, attestation. 208. **clodpole**, blockhead.

215. **cockatrices**, mythical animal, supposed to kill by a glance. 217. **presently**, immediately. 222. **unchary**, heedlessly. 243. **bloody**, bloodthirsty. 244-5. **Dismount thy tuck**, draw thy sword. 245. **yare**, ready, nimble.

Vio. I pray you, sir, what is he?

Sir To. He is knight, dubbed with unhatched rapier and on carpet consideration; but he is a devil in private brawl: souls and bodies hath he divorced three; and his incensement at this moment is so implacable, that satisfaction can be none but by pangs of death and sepulchre. Hob, nob, is his word; give 't or take 't.

Vio. I will return again into the house and desire some conduct of the lady. I am no fighter. I have heard of some kind of men that put quarrels purposely on others, to taste their valour: belike this is a man of that quirk.

Sir To. Sir, no; his indignation derives itself out of a very competent injury; therefore, get you on and give him his desire. Back you shall not to the house, unless you undertake that with me which with as much safety you might answer him; therefore, on, or strip your sword stark naked; for meddle you must, that 's certain, or forswear to wear iron about you.

Vio. This is as uncivil as strange. I beseech you, do me this courteous office, as to know of the knight what my offence to him is: it is something of my negligence, nothing of my purpose.

Sir To. I will do so. Signor Fabian, stay you by this gentleman till my return. *Exit.*

Vio. Pray you, sir, do you know of this matter?

Fab. I know the knight is incensed against you, even to a mortal arbitrement, but nothing of the circumstance more.

Vio. I beseech you, what manner of man is he?

Fab. Nothing of that wonderful promise, to read him by his form, as you are like to find him in the proof of his valour. He is, indeed, sir, the most skilful, bloody, and fatal opposite that you could possibly have found in any part of Illyria. Will you walk towards him? I will make your peace with him if I can.

Vio. I shall be much bound to you for 't: I am one that had rather go with sir priest than sir knight; I care not who knows so much of my mettle. *Exeunt.*

Re-enter *Sir Toby*, with *Sir Andrew.*

Sir To. Why, man, he 's a very devil; I have not seen such a firago. I had a pass with him, rapier, scabbard, and all, and he gives me the stuck in with such a mortal motion, that it is inevitable; and on the answer, he pays you as surely as your feet hits the ground they step on. They say he has been fencer to the Sophy.

Sir And. Pox on 't, I 'll not meddle with him.

Sir To. Ay, but he will not now be pacified. Fabian can scarce hold him yonder.

Sir And. Plague on 't, an I thought he had been valiant and so cunning in fence, I 'd have seen him damned ere I 'd have challenged him. Let him let the matter slip, and I 'll give him my horse, grey Capilet.

Sir To. I 'll make the motion. Stand here; make a good show on 't: this shall end without the perdition of souls. [*Aside.*] Marry, I 'll ride your horse as well as I ride you.

Re-enter *Fabian* and *Viola.*

[*To Fabian.*] I have his horse to take up the quarrel. I have persuaded him the youth 's a devil.

Fab. He is as horribly conceited of him; and pants and looks pale, as if a bear were at his heels.

Sir To. [*To Vio.*] There 's no remedy, sir; he will fight with you for 's oath sake. Marry, he hath better bethought him of his quarrel, and he finds that now scarce to be worth talking of; therefore draw, for the supportance of his vow: he protests he will not hurt you.

Vio. [*Aside.*] Pray God defend me! A little thing would make me tell them how much I lack of a man.

Fab. Give ground, if you see him furious.

Sir To. Come, Sir Andrew, there 's no remedy; the gentleman will, for his honour's sake, have one bout with you: he cannot by the duello avoid it; but he has promised me, as he is a gentleman and a soldier, he will not hurt you. Come on; to 't.

Sir And. Pray God, he keep his oath!

Enter *Antonio.*

Vio. I do assure you, 't is against my will. *They draw.*

Ant. Put up your sword. If this young gentleman
Have done offence, I take the fault on me;
If you offend him, I for him defy you.

Sir To. You, sir! Why, what are you?

Ant. One sir, that for his love dares yet do more

257. unhatched, unhacked. **258.** A carpet knight was one who was knighted not on the battle field but on a carpet in the king's hall and often for a material consideration. King James is said to have sold knighthoods for thirty pounds sterling. **262. Hob, nob,** have or have not. **265. conduct,** escort. **268. quirk,** humor. **275. meddle,** fight. **286. arbitrement,** decision. **302. firago,** virago.

303. stuck, thrust (Italian stoccata), **304. on the answer,** in the riposte, fencing term. **320. take up,** settle. **322. He is . . . conceited,** has as horrible a conception. **329. supportance,** maintaining. **338. duello,** laws of duelling.

Than you have heard him brag to you he will.

Sir To. Nay, if you be an undertaker, I am for you. *They draw.*

Enter *Officers.*

Fab. O good Sir Toby, hold! Here come the officers.

Sir To. I 'll be with you anon.

Vio. Pray, sir, put your sword up, if you please.

Sir And. Marry, will I, sir; and, for that I promised you, I 'll be as good as my word. He will bear you easily and reins well.

1. Off. This is the man; do thy office.

2. Off. Antonio, I arrest thee at the suit of Count Orsino.

Ant. You do mistake me, sir.

1. Off. No, sir, no jot. I know your favour well,
Though now you have no sea-cap on your head.
Take him away; he knows I know him well.

Ant. I must obey. [*To Viola.*] This comes with seeking you.
But there 's no remedy; I shall answer it.
What will you do, now my necessity
Makes me to ask you for my purse? It grieves me
Much more for what I cannot do for you
Than what befalls myself. You stand amaz'd,
But be of comfort.

2. Off. Come, sir, away.

Ant. I must entreat of you some of that money.

Vio. What money, sir?
For the fair kindness you have show'd me here,
And, part, being prompted by your present trouble,
Out of my lean and low ability
I 'll lend you something. My having is not much.
I 'll make division of my present with you.
Hold, there 's half my coffer.

Ant. Will you deny me now?
Is 't possible that my deserts to you
Can lack persuasion? Do not tempt my misery,
Lest that it make me so unsound a man
As to upbraid you with those kindnesses
That I have done for you.

Vio. I know of none,
Nor know I you by voice or any feature.
I hate ingratitude more in a man
Than lying, vainness, babbling drunkenness,
Or any taint of vice whose strong corruption
Inhabits our frail blood.

Ant. O heavens themselves!

2. Off. Come, sir, I pray you, go.

Ant. Let me speak a little. This youth that you see here
I snatch'd one half out of the jaws of death,
Reliev'd him with such sanctity of love,
And to his image, which methought did promise
Most venerable worth, did I devotion.

1. Off. What 's that to us? The time goes by; away!

Ant. But, O, how vile an idol proves this god!
Thou hast, Sebastian, done good feature shame.
In nature there 's no blemish but the mind;
None can be call'd deform'd but the unkind.
Virtue is beauty, but the beauteous evil
Are empty trunks o'erflourish'd by the devil.

1. Off. The man grows mad; away with him!
Come, come, sir.

Ant. Lead me on. *Exit with Officers.*

Vio. Methinks his words do from such passion fly,
That he believes himself; so do not I.
Prove true, imagination, O, prove true,
That I, dear brother, be now ta'en for you!

Sir To. Come hither, knight; come hither, Fabian; we 'll whisper o'er a couplet or two of most sage saws.

Vio. He nam'd Sebastian. I my brother know
Yet living in my glass; even such and so
In favour was my brother, and he went
Still in this fashion, colour, ornament,
For him I imitate. O, if it prove,
Tempests are kind and salt waves fresh in love. *Exit.*

Sir To. A very dishonest paltry boy, [and more a coward than a hare. His dishonesty appears in leaving his friend here in necessity and denying him; and, for his cowardship, ask Fabian.

Fab. A coward, a most devout coward, religious in it.

Sir And. 'Slid, I 'll after him again and beat him.

Sir To. Do; cuff him soundly, but never draw thy sword

Sir And. An I do not,—

Fab. Come, let 's see the event.

Sir To. I dare lay any money 't will be nothing yet. *Exeunt.*

349. undertaker, meddler. **363. favour,** face. **377. part,** partly. **379. having,** wealth. **380. present,** present money. **384. unsound,** weak.

397. venerable, worthy of veneration. **402. unkind,** unnatural. **415. yet . . . glass,** reflected exactly in my dress and person.

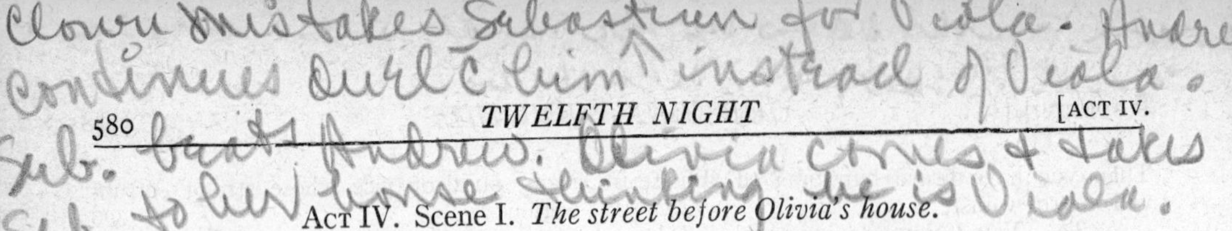

ACT IV. Scene I. *The street before Olivia's house.*

Enter *Sebastian* and *Clown.*

Clo. Will you make me believe that I am not sent for you?

Seb. Go to, go to, thou art a foolish fellow; let me be clear of thee.

Clo. Well held out, i' faith! No, I do not know you; nor I am not sent to you by my lady, to bid you come speak with her; nor your name is not Master Cesario; nor this is not my nose neither. Nothing that is so is so.

Seb. I prithee, vent thy folly somewhere else. Thou know'st not me.

Clo. Vent my folly! He has heard that word of some great man and now applies it to a fool. Vent my folly! I am afraid this great lubber, the world, will prove a cockney. I prithee now, ungird thy strangeness and tell me what I shall vent to my lady. Shall I vent to her that thou art coming?

Seb. I prithee, foolish Greek, depart from me.
There 's money for thee: if you tarry longer,
I shall give worse payment.

Clo. By my troth, thou hast an open hand. These wise men that give fools money get themselves a good report—after fourteen years' purchase.

Enter *Sir Andrew, Sir Toby,* and *Fabian.*

Sir And. Now, sir, have I met you again? There 's for you. *Striking Sebastian.*

Seb. Why, there 's for thee, and there, and there. Are all the people mad? *Beating Sir Andrew.*

Sir To. Hold, sir, or I 'll throw your dagger o'er the house.

Clo. This will I tell my lady straight. I would not be in some of your coats for two pence. *Exit.*

Sir To. Come on, sir. Hold!

Sir And. Nay, let him alone: I 'll go another way to work with him: I 'll have an action of battery against him, if there be any law in Illyria. Though I struck him first, yet it 's no matter for that.

Seb. Let go thy hand.

Sir To. Come, sir, I will not let you go. Come, my young soldier, put up your iron; you are well flesh'd. Come on.

Seb. I will be free from thee. What wouldst thou now?
If thou dar'st tempt me further, draw thy sword. *Draws.*

Sir To. What, what? Nay, then I must have an ounce or two of this malapert blood from you. *Draws.*

Enter *Olivia.*

Oli. Hold, Toby! On thy life I charge thee, hold!

Sir To. Madam—

Oli. Will it be ever thus? Ungracious wretch,
Fit for the mountains and the barbarous caves,
Where manners ne'er were preach'd! Out of my sight!
Be not offended, dear Cesario.
Rudesby, be gone!
Exeunt Sir Toby, Sir Andrew, and Fabian.
I prithee, gentle friend,
Let thy fair wisdom, not thy passion, sway
In this uncivil and unjust extent
Against thy peace. Go with me to my house,
And hear thou there how many fruitless pranks
This ruffian hath botch'd up, that thou thereby
Mayst smile at this. Thou shalt not choose but go.
Do not deny. Beshrew his soul for me,
He started one poor heart of mine in thee.

Seb. What relish is in this? How runs the stream?
Or I am mad, or else this is a dream.
Let fancy still my sense in Lethe steep.
If it be thus to dream, still let me sleep!

Oli. Nay, come, I prithee. Would thou 'dst be rul'd by me!

Seb. Madam, I will.

Oli. O, say so, and so be! *Exeunt.*

Scene II. *Olivia's house.*

Enter *Maria* and *Clown.*

Mar. Nay, I prithee, put on this gown and this beard: make him believe thou art Sir

Act iv, scene i: 14-5. I am afraid this great lubber, the world, will prove a cockney, if such words as "vent" are applied to fools the world will become a foppish cockney. **19. Greek,** jester. **24-5. after fourteen years' purchase,** at a high price. The price of land was computed by its total yearly income and stated in years. In Shakespeare's day twelve years' purchase was the normal price.

43. flesh'd, initiated in bloodshed. **47. malapert,** saucy. **55. Rudesby,** ruffian. **57. extent,** behavior. **60. botch'd up,** patched clumsily. **63. started,** roused, alarmed.

Clown pretends to be Sir Topas the curate + visits Malvolio the lunatic.

Topas the curate: do it quickly; I 'll call Sir Toby the whilst. *Exit.*

Clo. Well, I 'll put it on, and I will dissemble myself in 't; and I would I were the first that ever dissembled in such a gown. I am not tall enough to become the function well, nor lean enough to be thought a good student; but to be said an honest man and a good housekeeper goes as fairly as to say a careful man and a great scholar. The competitors enter.

Enter *Sir Toby* and *Maria.*

Sir To. Jove bless thee, master Parson.

Clo. *Bonos dies,* Sir Toby: for, as the old hermit of Prague, that never saw pen and ink, very wittily said to a niece of King Gorboduc, "That that is is"; so I, being master Parson, am master Parson; for, what is "that" but "that," and "is" but "is"?

Sir To. To him, Sir Topas.

Clo. What, ho, I say! Peace in this prison!

Sir To. The knave counterfeits well; a good knave.

Mal. [*Within.*] Who calls there?

Clo. Sir Topas the curate, who comes to visit Malvolio the lunatic.

Mal. Sir Topas, Sir Topas, good Sir Topas, go to my lady.

Clo. Out, hyperbolical fiend! How vexest thou this man! Talkest thou nothing but of ladies?

Sir To. Well said, master Parson.

Mal. Sir Topas, never was man thus wronged. Good Sir Topas, do not think I am mad. They have laid me here in hideous darkness.

Clo. Fie, thou dishonest Satan! I call thee by the most modest terms, for I am one of those gentle ones that will use the devil himself with courtesy. Say'st thou that house is dark?

Mal. As hell, Sir Topas.

Clo. Why, it hath bay windows transparent as barricadoes, and the clerestories toward the south north are as lustrous as ebony; and yet complainest thou of obstruction?

Mal. I am not mad, Sir Topas. I say to you, this house is dark.

Clo. Madman, thou errest: I say, there is no darkness but ignorance, in which thou art more puzzled than the Egyptians in their fog.

Mal. I say, this house is dark as ignorance, though ignorance were as dark as hell; and I say, there was never man thus abused. I am no more mad than you are: make the trial of it in any constant question.

Clo. What is the opinion of Pythagoras concerning wild fowl?

Mal. That the soul of our grandam might haply inhabit a bird.

Clo. What think'st thou of his opinion?

Mal. I think nobly of the soul, and no way approve his opinion.

Clo. Fare thee well! Remain thou still in darkness. Thou shalt hold the opinion of Pythagoras ere I will allow of thy wits, and fear to kill a woodcock, lest thou dispossess the soul of thy grandam. Fare thee well.

Mal. Sir Topas, Sir Topas!

Sir To. My most exquisite Sir Topas!

Clo. Nay, I am for all waters.

Mar. Thou mightst have done this without thy beard and gown. He sees thee not.

Sir To. To him in thine own voice, and bring me word how thou find'st him. I would we were well rid of this knavery. If he may be conveniently delivered, I would he were, for I am now so far in offence with my niece that I cannot pursue with any safety this sport to the upshot. Come by and by to my chamber.

Exit with Maria.

Clo. [*Singing.*]
"Hey, Robin, jolly Robin,
Tell me how thy lady does."

Mal. Fool!

Clo. "My lady is unkind, perdy."

Mal. Fool!

Clo. "Alas, why is she so?"

Mal. Fool, I say!

Clo. "She loves another"—Who calls, ha?

Mal. Good fool, as ever thou wilt deserve well at my hand, help me to a candle, and pen, ink, and paper. As I am a gentleman, I will live to be thankful to thee for 't.

Clo. Master Malvolio?

Mal. Ay, good fool.

Clo. Alas, sir, how fell you besides your five wits?

Mal. Fool, there was never man so notoriously abused. I am as well in my wits, fool, as thou art.

Clo. But as well? Then you are mad in-

Scene ii: 2-3. Sir Topas. The name is used by Chaucer. Perhaps Shakespeare chose it because the topaz was supposed to be a cure for lunacy. All bachelors of arts were called "dominus," a title usually rendered as "Sir" and given to parish priests. **5. dissemble,** disguise. **8. tall,** robust. **11. competitors,** confederates. **17. Gorboduc,** legendary British king. **29. hyperbolical,** extravagant. **41. clerestories,** upper galleries with windows in churches.

48. Egyptians . . . fog, darkness cast over Egypt by Moses. Cf. Exodus 10.21. **53. constant question,** logical debate. **68. I . . . waters,** I can turn my hand to anything. **93. five wits,** common wit, imagination, fantasy, estimation, memory. **94-5. notoriously,** outrageously.

deed, if you be no better in your wits than a fool.

Mal. They have here propertied me, keep me in darkness, send ministers to me, asses, and do all they can to face me out of my wits.

Clo. Advise you what you say; the minister is here. Malvolio, Malvolio, thy wits the heavens restore! Endeavour thyself to sleep, and leave thy vain bibble babble.

Mal. Sir Topas!

Clo. Maintain no words with him, good fellow. Who, I, sir? Not I, sir. God buy you, good Sir Topas. Marry, amen. I will, sir, I will.

Mal. Fool, fool, fool, I say!

Clo. Alas, sir, be patient. What say you, sir? I am shent for speaking to you.

Mal. Good fool, help me to some light and some paper. I tell thee, I am as well in my wits as any man in Illyria.

Clo. Well-a-day that you were, sir!

Mal. By this hand, I am. Good fool, some ink, paper, and light; and convey what I will set down to my lady. It shall advantage thee more than ever the bearing of letter did.

Clo. I will help you to 't. But tell me true, are you not mad indeed, or do you but counterfeit?

Mal. Believe me, I am not. I tell thee true.

Clo. Nay, I 'll ne'er believe a madman till I see his brains. I will fetch you light and paper and ink.

Mal. Fool, I 'll requite it in the highest degree. I prithee, be gone.

Clo. [*Singing.*]

I am gone, sir,
And anon, sir,
I 'll be with you again,
In a trice,
Like to the old Vice,
Your need to sustain;

Who, with dagger of lath,
In his rage and his wrath,
Cries, ah, ha! to the devil,
Like a mad lad.
Pare thy nails, dad.
Adieu, goodman devil.

Exit.

98. **propertied,** used as tool (perhaps, thrust backstage among the properties). 100. **face,** bluff. 102. **Advise you,** be careful. 103. From l. 103 to l. 109 we are supposed to hear a dialogue between Sir Topas and Feste speaking once more in his own voice. The parts can easily be assigned by any intelligent reader. 108. **God buy you,** God be with you. 112. **shent,** reproved. 134. **Vice,** a stock comic character in the "morality" plays.

Scene III. *Olivia's garden.*

Enter *Sebastian.*

Seb. This is the air, that is the glorious sun,
This pearl she gave me, I do feel 't and see 't;
And though 't is wonder that enwraps me thus,
Yet 't is not madness. Where 's Antonio, then?
I could not find him at the Elephant;
Yet there he was, and there I found this credit,
That he did range the town to seek me out.
His counsel now might do me golden service;
For though my soul disputes well with my sense,
That this may be some error, but no madness,
Yet doth this accident and flood of fortune
So far exceed all instance, all discourse,
That I am ready to distrust mine eyes
And wrangle with my reason that persuades me
To any other trust but that I am mad
Or else the lady 's mad; yet, if 't were so,
She could not sway her house, command her followers,
Take and give back affairs and their dispatch
With such a smooth, discreet, and stable bearing
As I perceive she does. There 's something in 't
That is deceivable. But here the lady comes.

Enter *Olivia* and *Priest.*

Oli. Blame not this haste of mine. If you mean well,
Now go with me and with this holy man
Into the chantry by; there, before him,
And underneath that consecrated roof,
Plight me the full assurance of your faith,
That my most jealous and too doubtful soul
May live at peace. He shall conceal it
Whiles you are willing it shall come to note,
What time we will our celebration keep
According to my birth. What do you say?

Seb. I 'll follow this good man, and go with you;
And, having sworn truth, ever will be true.

Oli. Then lead the way, good father; and heavens so shine
That they may fairly note this act of mine!

Exeunt.

Scene iii: 6. **was,** had been. **credit,** belief, opinion. 12. **instance,** example. **discourse,** reasoning. 21. **deceivable,** deceptive. 24. **chantry,** private chapel. 29. **Whiles,** until. 30. **What,** at which.

ACT V. Scene I. *Before Olivia's house.*

Enter *Clown* and *Fabian.*

Fab. Now, as thou lov'st me, let me see his letter.

Clo. Good Master Fabian, grant me another request.

Fab. Anything.

Clo. Do not desire to see this letter.

Fab. This is to give a dog and in recompense desire my dog again.

Enter *Duke, Viola, Curio,* and *Lords.*

Duke. Belong you to the Lady Olivia, friends?

Clo. Ay, sir! we are some of her trappings.

Duke. I know thee well; how dost thou, my good fellow?

Clo. Truly, sir, the better for my foes and the worse for my friends.

Duke. Just the contrary; the better for thy friends.

Clo. No, sir, the worse.

Duke. How can that be?

Clo. Marry, sir, they praise me and make an ass of me. Now my foes tell me plainly I am an ass; so that by my foes, sir, I profit in the knowledge of myself, and by my friends I am abused; so that, conclusions to be as kisses, if your four negatives make your two affirmatives, why then, the worse for my friends and the better for my foes.

Duke. Why, this is excellent.

Clo. By my troth, sir, no; though it please you to be one of my friends.

Duke. Thou shalt not be the worse for me. There 's gold.

Clo. But that it would be double-dealing, sir, I would you could make it another.

Duke. O, you give me ill counsel.

Clo. Put your grace in your pocket, sir, for this once, and let your flesh and blood obey it.

Duke. Well, I will be so much a sinner, to be a double-dealer. There 's another.

Clo. Primo, secundo, tertio, is a good play; and the old saying is, the third pays for all. The triplex, sir, is a good tripping measure; or the bells of Saint Bennet, sir, may put you in mind; one, two, three.

Duke. You can fool no more money out of me at this throw: if you will let your lady know I am here to speak with her, and bring her along with you, it may awake my bounty further.

Clo. Marry, sir, lullaby to your bounty till I come again. I go, sir, but I would not have you to think that my desire of having is the sin of covetousness; but, as you say, sir, let your bounty take a nap, I will awake it anon. *Exit.*

Enter *Antonio* and *Officers.*

Vio. Here comes the man, sir, that did rescue me.
Duke. That face of his I do remember well,
Yet when I saw it last, it was besmear'd
As black as Vulcan in the smoke of war.
A bawbling vessel was he captain of,
For shallow draught and bulk unprizable,
With which such scathful grapple did he make
With the most noble bottom of our fleet,
That very envy and the tongue of loss
Cried fame and honour on him. What 's the matter?
1. Off. Orsino, this is that Antonio
That took the *Phœnix* and her fraught from Candy,
And this is he that did the *Tiger* board,
When your young nephew Titus lost his leg.
Here in the streets, desperate of shame and state,
In private brabble did we apprehend him.
Vio. He did me kindness, sir, drew on my side,
But in conclusion put strange speech upon me.
I know not what 't was but distraction.
Duke. Notable pirate! Thou salt-water thief!
What foolish boldness brought thee to their mercies
Whom thou, in terms so bloody and so dear,
Hast made thine enemies?
Ant. Orsino, noble sir,
Be pleas'd that I shake off these names you give me.
Antonio never yet was thief or pirate,
Though I confess, on base and ground enough,
Orsino's enemy. A witchcraft drew me hither.
That most ingrateful boy there by your side,
From the rude sea's enrag'd and foamy mouth
Did I redeem; a wreck past hope he was:

Act V, Scene i: 7-8. Some such story as this is told of Queen Elizabeth who begged a dog of her kinsman, promising to give him whatever he wanted in return. He gave her the dog and asked for it back again. **22. conclusions to be as kisses**, as two people are necessary to a kiss, so are two premises necessary to a conclusion. **41. Saint Bennet**, St. Benedict's church in London.

57. bawbling, insignificant. **58. unprizable**, valueless. **59. scathful**, destructive. **61. tongue of loss**, voices of the losers. **64. Candy**, now Crete. **67. desperate**, reckless. **68. brabble**, brawl. **71. distraction**, madness. **74. dear**, grievous.

His life I gave him, and did thereto add
My love, without retention or restraint,
All his in dedication. For his sake
Did I expose myself, pure for his love,
Into the danger of this adverse town;
Drew to defend him when he was beset;
Where being apprehended, his false cunning,
Not meaning to partake with me in danger,
Taught him to face me out of his acquaintance,
And grew a twenty years removed thing
While one would wink; denied me mine own purse,
Which I had recommended to his use
Not half an hour before.

Vio. How can this be?

Duke. When came he to this town?

Ant. To-day, my lord; and for three months before,
No interim, not a minute's vacancy,
Both day and night did we keep company.

Enter *Olivia* and Attendants.

Duke. Here comes the countess; now heaven walks on earth.
But for thee, fellow; fellow, thy words are madness.
Three months this youth hath tended upon me;
But more of that anon. Take him aside.

Oli. What would my lord, but that he may not have,
Wherein Olivia may seem serviceable?
Cesario, you do not keep promise with me.

Vio. Madam!

Duke. Gracious Olivia,—

Oli. What do you say, Cesario? Good my lord,—

Vio. My lord would speak; my duty hushes me.

Oli. If it be aught to the old tune, my lord,
It is as fat and fulsome to mine ear
As howling after music.

Duke. Still so cruel!

Oli. Still so constant, lord.

Duke. What, to perverseness? You uncivil lady,
To whose ingrate and unauspicious altars
My soul the faithfull'st offerings have breath'd out
That e'er devotion tender'd! What shall I do?

Oli. Even what it please my lord, that shall become him.

Duke. Why should I not, had I the heart to do it,
Like to th' Egyptian thief at point of death,
Kill what I love?—a savage jealousy
That sometimes savours nobly. But hear me this:
Since you to non-regardance cast my faith,
And that I partly know the instrument
That screws me from my true place in your favour,
Live you the marble-breasted tyrant still;
But this your minion, whom I know you love,
And whom, by heaven I swear, I tender dearly,
Him will I tear out of that cruel eye,
Where he sits crowned in his master's spite.
Come, boy, with me; my thoughts are ripe in mischief.
I 'll sacrifice the lamb that I do love,
To spite a raven's heart within a dove.

Vio. And I, most jocund, apt, and willingly,
To do you rest, a thousand deaths would die.

Oli. Where goes Cesario?

Vio. After him I love
More than I love these eyes, more than my life,
More, by all mores, than e'er I shall love wife.
If I do feign, you witnesses above
Punish my life for tainting of my love!

Oli. Ay me, detested! How am I beguil'd!

Vio. Who does beguile you? Who does do you wrong?

Oli. Hast thou forgot thyself? Is it so long?
Call forth the holy father.

Duke. Come, away!

Oli. Whither, my lord? Cesario, husband, stay.

Duke. Husband?

Oli. Ay, husband! Can he that deny?

Duke. Her husband, sirrah?

Vio. No, my lord, not I.

Oli. Alas, it is the baseness of thy fear
That makes thee strangle thy propriety.
Fear not, Cesario; take thy fortunes up.
Be that thou know'st thou art, and then thou art
As great as that thou fear'st.

Enter *Priest*.

O, welcome, father!
Father, I charge thee by thy reverence,
Here to unfold, though lately we intended
To keep in darkness what occasion now
Reveals before 't is ripe, what thou dost know
Hath newly pass'd between this youth and me.

Priest. A contract of eternal bond of love,
Confirm'd by mutual joinder of your hands,
Attested by the holy close of lips,

112. **fat and fulsome**, dull and disgusting. 121. In the *Ethiopica* of Heliodorus an Egyptian pirate, Thyamis, fell in love with his captive, Chariclea, and when about to be captured and executed, tried to kill her first.

128. **minion**, favorite. 129. **tender**, cherish. 150. **strangle thy propriety**, deny your identity.

Strengthen'd by interchangement of your rings;
And all the ceremony of this compact
Seal'd in my function, by my testimony;
Since when, my watch hath told me, toward my grave
I have travell'd but two hours.

Duke. O thou dissembling cub! What wilt thou be
When time hath sow'd a grizzle on thy case?
Or will not else thy craft so quickly grow,
That thine own trip shall be thine overthrow?
Farewell, and take her; but direct thy feet
Where thou and I henceforth may never meet.

Vio. My lord, I do protest—

Oli. O, do not swear!
Hold little faith, though thou hast too much fear.

Enter *Sir Andrew*.

Sir And. For the love of God, a surgeon! Send one presently to Sir Toby.

Oli. What 's the matter?

Sir And. Has broke my head across and has given Sir Toby a bloody coxcomb too. For the love of God, your help! I had rather than forty pound I were at home.

Oli. Who has done this, Sir Andrew?

Sir And. The Count's gentleman, one Cesario: we took him for a coward, but he 's the very devil incardinate.

Duke. My gentleman, Cesario?

Sir And. 'Od's lifelings, here he is! You broke my head for nothing; and that that I did, I was set on to do 't by Sir Toby.

Vio. Why do you speak to me? I never hurt you.
You drew your sword upon me without cause;
But I bespake you fair, and hurt you not.

Enter *Sir Toby* and *Clown*.

Sir And. If a bloody coxcomb be a hurt, you have hurt me: I think you set nothing by a bloody coxcomb. Here comes Sir Toby halting: you shall hear more; but if he had not been in drink, he would have tickled you othergates than he did.

Duke. How now, gentleman! How is 't with you?

Sir To. That 's all one. Has hurt me, and there 's the end on 't. Sot, didst see Dick surgeon, sot?

Clo. O, he 's drunk, Sir Toby, an hour agone. His eyes were set at eight i' the morning.

Sir To. Then he 's a rogue, and a passy measures pavin. I hate a drunken rogue.

Oli. Away with him! Who hath made this havoc with them?

Sir And. I 'll help you, Sir Toby, because we 'll be dressed together.

Sir To. Will you help?—an ass-head and a coxcomb and a knave, a thin-faced knave, a gull!

Oli. Get him to bed, and let his hurt be look'd to.

Exeunt Clown, Fabian, Sir Toby, and Sir Andrew.

Enter *Sebastian*.

Seb. I am sorry, madam, I have hurt your kinsman;
But, had it been the brother of my blood,
I must have done no less with wit and safety.
You throw a strange regard upon me, and by that
I do perceive it hath offended you.
Pardon me, sweet one, even for the vows
We made each other but so late ago.

Duke. One face, one voice, one habit, and two persons,
A natural perspective, that is and is not!

Seb. Antonio, O my dear Antonio!
How have the hours rack'd and tortur'd me,
Since I have lost thee!

Ant. Sebastian are you?

Seb. Fear'st thou that, Antonio?

Ant. How have you made division of yourself?
An apple, cleft in two, is not more twin
Than these two creatures. Which is Sebastian?

Oli. Most wonderful!

Seb. Do I stand there? I never had a brother,
Nor can there be that deity in my nature,
Of here and everywhere. I had a sister,
Whom the blind waves and surges have devour'd.
Of charity, what kin are you to me?
What countryman? What name? What parentage?

Vio. Of Messaline; Sebastian was my father;
Such a Sebastian was my brother too;
So went he suited to his watery tomb.
If spirits can assume both form and suit
You come to fright us.

Seb. A spirit I am indeed;
But am in that dimension grossly clad

164. function, official capacity. **168. grizzle,** grey (beard). **case,** skin. **179. coxcomb,** head. **185. incardinate,** incarnate. **198. othergates,** in another manner.

206-7. passy measures pavin (Italian, Passamezzo Pavana) a stately dance with eight bars to each strain of music, suggested to Toby by "set at eight" in l. 205. **219. regard,** look. **224. natural perspective,** a deception produced by nature which is ordinarily produced only by an optical instrument or special glass. **228. Fear'st,** doubtest. **234-5. Nor . . . everywhere,** Nor can I, like a god, be everywhere at once. **241. suited,** dressed. **244. dimension,** bodily form.

Which from the womb I did participate.
Were you a woman, as the rest goes even,
I should my tears let fall upon your cheek,
And say, "Thrice welcome, drowned Viola!"
Vio. My father had a mole upon his brow.
Seb. And so had mine.
Vio. And died that day when Viola from her birth
Had number'd thirteen years.
Seb. O, that record is lively in my soul!
He finished indeed his mortal act
That day that made my sister thirteen years.
Vio. If nothing lets to make us happy both
But this my masculine usurp'd attire,
Do not embrace me till each circumstance
Of place, time, fortune, do cohere and jump
That I am Viola; which to confirm,
I 'll bring you to a captain in this town,
Where lie my maiden weeds; by whose gentle help
I was preserv'd to serve this noble count.
All the occurrence of my fortunes since
Hath been between this lady and this lord.
Seb. [*To Olivia.*] So comes it, lady, you have been mistook;
But nature to her bias drew in that.
You would have been contracted to a maid;
Nor are you therein, by my life, deceiv'd,
You are betroth'd both to a maid and man.
Duke. Be not amaz'd, right noble is his blood.
If this be so, as yet the glass seems true,
I shall have share in this most happy wreck.
[*To Viola.*] Boy, thou hast said to me a thousand times
Thou never shouldst love woman like to me.
Vio. And all those sayings will I over-swear;
And all those swearings keep as true in soul
As doth that orbed continent the fire
That severs day from night.
Duke. Give me thy hand,
And let me see thee in thy woman's weeds.
Vio. The captain that did bring me first on shore
Hath my maid's garments. He upon some action
Is now in durance, at Malvolio's suit,
A gentleman, and follower of my lady's.
Oli. He shall enlarge him; fetch Malvolio hither.
And yet, alas, now I remember me,
They say, poor gentleman, he 's much distract.

Re-enter Clown *with a letter, and* Fabian.

A most extracting frenzy of mine own
From my remembrance clearly banish'd his.
How does he, sirrah?
Clo. Truly, madam, he holds Belzebub at the stave's end as well as a man in his case may do. Has here writ a letter to you. I should have given 't you to-day morning, but as a madman's epistles are no gospels, so it skills not much when they are delivered.
Oli. Open 't, and read it.
Clo. Look then to be well edified when the fool delivers the madman. [*Reads.*] "By the Lord, madam,"—
Oli. How now, art thou mad?
Clo. No, madam, I do but read madness: an your ladyship will have it as it ought to be, you must allow Vox.
Oli. Prithee, read i' thy right wits.
Clo. So I do, madonna; but to read his right wits is to read thus; therefore perpend, my princess, and give ear.
Oli. Read it you, sirrah. [*To Fabian.*]
Fab. [*Reads.*]

"By the Lord, madam, you wrong me, and the world shall know it: though you have put me into darkness and given your drunken cousin rule over me, yet have I the benefit of my senses as well as your ladyship. I have your own letter that induced me to the semblance I put on; with the which I doubt not but to do myself much right, or you much shame. Think of me as you please. I leave my duty a little unthought of and speak out of my injury.

"THE MADLY-USED MALVOLIO."

Oli. Did he write this?
Clo. Ay, madam.
Duke. This savours not much of distraction.
Oli. See him deliver'd, Fabian; bring him hither. *Exit Fabian.*
My lord, so please you, these things further thought on,
To think me as well a sister as a wife,
One day shall crown the alliance on 't, so please you,
Here at my house and at my proper cost.
Duke. Madam, I am most apt t' embrace your offer.
[*To Viola.*] Your master quits you; and for your service done him,
So much against the mettle of your sex,
So far beneath your soft and tender breeding,
And since you call'd me master for so long,
Here is my hand. You shall from this time be
Your master's mistress.
Oli. A sister! You are she.

245. participate, possesses like other men. **246. goes even,** accords. **256. lets,** prevents. **259. jump,** agree. **264. occurrence,** course of events. **267.** The "bias" was the lead weight in one side of a bowl which made it change direction. Nature obeyed her bias in making Olivia fall in love with Sebastian's counterpart. **272. glass,** the "perspective" of l. 224. **278. orbed continent,** the firmament, which holds the sun.

288. extracting, distracting. **292. stave's end,** arm's length. **295. skills,** matters. **304. Vox,** loud voice. **307. perpend,** consider. **327. proper,** own. **328. apt,** ready. **329. quits,** releases. **330. mettle,** disposition.

Enter *Malvolio* and *Fabian*.

Duke. Is this the madman?
Oli. Ay, my lord, this same.
How now, Malvolio!
Mal. Madam, you have done me wrong,
Notorious wrong.
Oli. Have I, Malvolio? No.
Mal. Lady, you have. Pray you, peruse that letter;
You must not now deny it is your hand.
Write from it, if you can, in hand or phrase;
Or say 't is not your seal, not your invention.
You can say none of this. Well, grant it then
And tell me, in the modesty of honour,
Why you have given me such clear lights of favour,
Bade me come smiling and cross-garter'd to you,
To put on yellow stockings and to frown
Upon Sir Toby and the lighter people;
And, acting this in an obedient hope,
Why have you suffer'd me to be imprison'd,
Kept in a dark house, visited by the priest,
And made the most notorious geck and gull
That e'er invention played on? Tell me why.
Oli. Alas, Malvolio, this is not my writing,
Though, I confess, much like the character;
But out of question 't is Maria's hand.
And now I do bethink me, it was she
First told me thou wast mad. Then cam'st in smiling,
And in such forms which here were presuppos'd
Upon thee in the letter. Prithee, be content.
This practice hath most shrewdly pass'd upon thee;
But when we know the grounds and authors of it,
Thou shalt be both the plaintiff and the judge
Of thine own cause.
Fab. Good madam, hear me speak,
And let no quarrel nor no brawl to come
Taint the condition of this present hour,
Which I have wonder'd at. In hope it shall not,
Most freely I confess, myself and Toby
Set this device against Malvolio here,
Upon some stubborn and uncourteous parts
We had conceiv'd against him. Maria writ
The letter at Sir Toby's great importance,
In recompense whereof he hath married her.
How with a sportful malice it was follow'd
May rather pluck on laughter than revenge,
If that the injuries be justly weigh'd
That have on both sides pass'd.
Oli. Alas, poor fool, how have they baffl'd thee!
Clo. Why, "some are born great, some achieve greatness, and some have greatness thrown upon them." I was one, sir, in this interlude; one Sir Topas, sir; but that 's all one. "By the Lord, fool, I am not mad." But do you remember? "Madam, why laugh you at such a barren rascal? An you smile not, he 's gagged." And thus the whirligig of time brings in his revenges.
Mal. I 'll be reveng'd on the whole pack of you. *Exit.*
Oli. He hath been most notoriously abus'd.
Duke. Pursue him, and entreat him to a peace;
He hath not told us of the captain yet.
When that is known and golden time convents,
A solemn combination shall be made
Of our dear souls. Meantime, sweet sister,
We will not part from hence. Cesario, come;
For so you shall be, while you are a man;
But when in other habits you are seen,
Orsino's mistress and his fancy's queen.
Exeunt all, except Clown.
Clo. [*Sings.*]

When that I was and a little tiny boy,
With hey, ho, the wind and the rain,
A foolish thing was but a toy,
For the rain it raineth every day.

But when I came to man's estate,
With hey, ho, &c.
'Gainst knaves and thieves men shut their gate,
For the rain, &c.

But when I came, alas! to wive,
With hey, ho, &c.
By swaggering could I never thrive,
For the rain, &c.

But when I came unto my beds,
With hey, ho, &c.
With toss-pots still had drunken heads,
For the rain, &c.

A great while ago the world begun,
With hey, ho, &c.
But that 's all one, our play is done,
And we 'll strive to please you every day.
Exit.

340. from it, differently. **347. lighter,** of less importance. **351. geck,** dupe. **358. presuppos'd,** suggested. **360. practice,** plot. **371. importance,** importunity.

374. pluck on, excite. **391. convents,** suits.

Measure for Measure

Measure for Measure, the only one of the "bitter comedies" included in this collection, is a strange and puzzling play. It has been the despair of commentators. It is in a double sense a problem play; it propounds an ethical and an esthetic problem. The first of these is apparently evaded rather than answered; the second can perhaps be solved by a study of the sources and a consideration of Shakespeare's treatment of the material offered him. The theme and the setting are essentially realistic; the treatment is conventionally romantic. Ostensibly a comedy with a happy ending, it belongs to Shakespeare's tragic period and the great scenes for which it is remembered are treated with tragic force and dignity.

Text.—The text of *Measure for Measure* appears for the first time in the Folio of 1623. It is far from satisfactory; it abounds in confusions, errors, and difficulties. This is probably due to the way in which it has come down to us. The play was no doubt produced at the Globe, then revised and shortened for a Court performance, then altered again, for later public productions. The "copy" furnished the printer in 1623 seems to have been a transcript of a prompt-book badly confused by repeated alterations.

Date.—*Measure for Measure* was played at Court on December 26, 1604. The London theatres had been closed from May, 1603, to April, 1604, because of the prevalence of the plague. Presumably *Measure for Measure* was the comedy as *Othello* was the tragedy which Shakespeare's company presented in the summer of that year. Stylistic and metrical characteristics connect *Measure for Measure* closely with *Hamlet,* and it is a plausible assumption that Shakespeare composed it soon after he finished his final revision of that tragedy.

Source.—Some account of the source of *Measure for Measure* has already been given—General Introduction, p. 59. It will suffice here to note its remote origin and mark the changes that it underwent. It derives apparently from an actual occurrence in Italy. A letter written in 1547 by a Hungarian student gives the main facts substantially as follows:

> In an Italian town near Milan a citizen was condemned to death for murder. His beautiful wife begged the judge to pardon him. He offered to do so at the price of her honor. She yielded, but the judge none the less had the prisoner beheaded. The lady appealed to the Imperial Viceroy who forced the judge to marry her and straightway put him to death.

This grimly tragic tale came to the knowledge of the Italian novelist Cinthio who included a version of it in his *Hecatommithi* with various romanticizing alterations. The crime is the violation of a virgin; the intercessor is the prisoner's sister, a lady of great beauty and virtue. She at first refuses the shameful offer of the judge, but on her brother's entreaty at last yields to him. The wicked judge sends her the headless body of her brother, whereupon she appeals to the Emperor who makes him marry her to restore her honor and then condemns him to death. The virtuous lady, however, begs his life of the Emperor and it is said that they lived happily thereafter.

Some years later Cinthio dramatized the story in a play, *Epitia,* the heroine's name, first published in 1583, ten years after his death. Here at the very end of the play the lady learns that her brother still lives; a merciful jailer beheaded another criminal and sent her the body dressed in her brother's clothes. She now consents to beg the judge's life and accept him as her husband.

Whetstone's play, *Promos and Cassandra,* like Cinthio's, spares the brother's life. He appears at the last moment and joins his sister in her plea for mercy for her new-made husband. Some years later, 1582, Whetstone retold the tale in his *Heptameron* with no essential alteration.

Shakespeare may have read the story in the original Italian or in a French translation; he doubtless knew both the English versions. In the main he follows Whetstone, but he makes a final and most important change in the action. In all the earlier versions the heroine sacrifices her honor and later weds the man who has basely and cruelly betrayed her. Shakespeare felt quite rightly that such a sacrifice and such a marriage was altogether outside the field of English comedy. He evidently planned from the beginning to save his heroine and it is interesting to see how he proceeds to accomplish this.

Construction.—Technically *Measure for Measure* is a comedy of intrigue and it opens by introducing the Duke who devises and directs the whole action of the plot. In the earlier versions the supreme ruler, Emperor or King, sends his delegate to a distant city to administer justice. Here the Duke leaves his city of Vienna and appoints Angelo, a well-known and worthy citizen, to rule in his stead. No reason is assigned for this delegation of authority, but we soon learn (I, iii) that the Duke intends to remain in Vienna disguised as a Friar to watch the administration of the law and in particular to test the character of his deputy. This, of course, is an old device of comedy; the presence of the disguised ruler serves to assure us that in the end all will be well. That his presence and later interposition are necessary is quickly made apparent, for Angelo begins to enforce obsolete laws with the utmost rigor and in particular condemns to death a young gentleman, Claudio, for extra-marital relations with his betrothed bride—an offence, by the way, that would seem little more than a venial irregularity to Shakespeare's Elizabethan audience. Claudio's sister Isabella is called from the nunnery where she has entered on her novitiate to intercede for her brother, and the action is now in full swing.

In the second act the plot develops rapidly. Isabella in the first of the three great scenes of the play pleads for her brother's life with such matchless eloquence that Angelo is moved, not indeed to pardon her brother, but rather to lust after the fair intercessor. He bids her come to him again, but before their second meeting we see the disguised Duke visiting the prison and informing himself of the situation, a plain hint that he will at his own good time take a hand in the action. In his second interview with Isabella the deputy makes his shameful offer to spare her brother at the price of her honor. She refuses indignantly and departs to visit her brother in prison assured that his "mind of honor" will approve her stand.

The third act rises to the climax. In a great scene written with overpowering force Claudio breaks down and begs Isabella to save him by paying the required price. Far from yielding, as in the earlier versions, she turns on him in fury, denounces him as a shameful coward, and bids him die quickly. Here certainly in the clash of wills is a tragic situation, out of which it would seem there can be only a tragic issue. But Shakespeare has planned it otherwise. The disguised Duke has overheard the interview between brother and sister and now takes charge of the situation. He intercepts Isabella and suggests a scheme which will at once save her brother's life and her own honor; she shall *seem* to consent to the deputy's demand and he will provide a substitute, Mariana the betrothed and deserted bride of Angelo. This suggestion has shocked modern critics; but there was nothing offensive to Shakespeare's audience in the Duke's proposal or in Mariana's consent; Shakespeare had already tested popular approval of this device by using it in an earlier play, *All's Well*. That Isabella, however, at the very height of her righteous indignation should without remonstrance creep back to Angelo and seem to consent to his desire is hardly what one would expect of the character that Shakespeare has drawn so far. As a matter of fact, however, the character of Isabella seems to break up and dissolve in the remaining scenes of the play. Shakespeare wisely keeps her off the stage as much as possible: it would have taxed even his power, one imagines, to have written a scene in which she feigned consent to Angelo's desire. Her outburst of grief and rage when she hears of the false news of her brother's death is brief and perfunctory and she again accepts without demur the guidance of the Friar-Duke. It is not until the very end of the play that the true Isabella appears again when she joins Mariana in her plea for mercy.

Meantime the intrigue runs its course directed by the Duke. Once more a visitor in the prison he learns of Angelo's perfidy and provides a substitute for Claudio as he had done for his sister. He persuades Isabella to accuse Angelo before the returning Duke, not only of the death of Claudio, but of the violation of her honor. Both charges, to be sure, are false, but the Duke means to apply craft against vice; or perhaps we had better say that Shakespeare, careless for once of consistency of character, is planning the charges, counter-charges, and amazing denouement of the long scene which occupies the final act.

Act V

It would take too long to run through all the changes of this kaleidoscopic scene. It leads up, of course, to the unveiling of Angelo after he has shown himself in public the villain he has become; but the Duke's design goes further than this. Still concealing from Isabella the fact that her brother lives, he brings it about that she falls on her knees before him in a plea for the life of Angelo—a plea that goes far to redeem her character from its former inhumanity. For this scene, where the love of Mariana and the pity of Isabella implore mercy for the man who has wronged them both, we may well forgive all the wiles and subterfuges of the Duke of dark corners. In the end as at the beginning it is the Duke who dominates the action.

Enough has been said to show how completely the original tragic tale has changed in Shakespeare's hands into a comedy of intrigue. Yet it is not a happy comedy; the cruel trials of Claudio and Isabella, the sad fall of Angelo from self-complacent virtue to hateful vice, are not the stuff that comedy is made of. And if further proof is needed that when Shakespeare wrote *Measure for Measure* the old spirit of mirth had deserted him, we have only to look at the minor characters who serve to fill up the background and set the atmosphere of this strange play. The foolish constable, the bawd, her cheerful servant Pompey, the hardened Barnardine, the scandal-loving Lucio, are all vividly realized characters; Shakespeare had known such in real life; they are the work-a-day world against which the tragic figures of Angelo and Isabella stand out in high relief. *Measure for Measure* is a comedy by courtesy; a comedy written to order, we may well believe, when Shakespeare was wrestling with the problem of evil and his imagination was obsessed with the doubts of Hamlet and the agonies of Othello.

Characters.—Perhaps after all it is better to label this play, if a label is needed, a tragi-comedy, the type of play in which a tragic beginning is skillfully and surprisingly conducted to a happy close. In tragi-comedy, as has been often said, the plot makes the characters, not the characters the plot; we rather admire the skill of the dramatist's technique than praise the lifelike consistency of his characterization. And so in great part it is in *Measure for Measure.* Pages have been written, for example, about the Duke. He has been blamed as derelict in duty; he has been extolled as an earthly Providence watching over wayward children. All this is beating the wind; the Duke is not a living man at all, but a *deus ex machina* devised by Shakespeare to steer the action through storm and stress into the final haven. He is a mere bundle of inconsistencies; he does not like to stage himself in people's eyes, yet he indulges in a most spectacular bit of self-revelation; he preaches a long sermon to Claudio to prepare him for death when he is fully purposed to save the poor boy's life. If we cease to analyze his character we may overlook its inconsistency and admire the art with which Shakespeare makes him serve the end for which he was designed. And what can be said of Escalus, of the Provost, of the two Friars, Thomas and Peter, except that they are puppets who play their hour upon the stage?

Three characters, however, are exempt from this charge of unreality: the condemned man, his sister, and the deputy; and it is an interesting and important fact that they all belong to the original tragic theme. Shakespeare, it would seem, was not greatly interested in Claudio; he takes no pains to develop his character and dismisses him at the end without a word. But in the great scene with his sister he suddenly comes to life. Condemned for a fault that seems to him no crime, hoping against hope for a reprieve, he learns that a way of escape is open. It is a shameful way, and his better nature at first rejects it, but the fear of death—now first fully realized—floods him like a wave and he cries "sweet sister, let me live." It is not admirable, but it is very human, as human as his shame a little later: "Let me ask my sister pardon, I am so out of love with life that I will sue to be rid of it."

His sweet sister has been lauded to the skies as one of Shakespeare's ideal women. She hardly seems so to modern eyes; there is something almost too bright and good for human nature in her hard, defiant virtue. Yet Shakespeare must have loved her or he would not have devised so artful a plot to save her from the fate that overtook her predecessors in the story. And indeed up to the moment when she ceases to be an active figure in the plot she is a magnificently drawn and wholly consistent character. We are not required to sympathize with her fierce denunciation of her brother, but we can quite understand it. Shakespeare's Isabella is not the woman to sacrifice a virtue that is more to her than life to save a man who begs for life on shameful terms.

Of these three characters the most fully realized is Angelo, a figure better fitted for a play like *Hamlet* than for this tragi-comedy. Angelo is no hypocrite; he does not pretend a virtue which is not his own. Nor is he from the beginning a villain. He is a well-known type, virtuous because untried, overcome by irresistible temptation, and sinking ever deeper into sin. Confident in his own righteousness, he administers the letter of the law without mercy until the fatal moment when the beauty and the goodness of Isabella overcome him. He feels for the first time the sting of sensual desire; he recognizes it, struggles against it, prays against it even, but with empty words, while his thoughts anchor on Isabella. The opportunity afforded by his place and power for sweet and secret sin opens the door for his proposal; her refusal only hardens him in his determination and he sinks to threats of torturing her brother. His worst crime is his promise-breach, the treacherous order for the instant death of Claudio, and this, it is quite clear, was not planned from the beginning, but due to fear, and fear can be crueller even than hate. Angelo is no hardened villain. At the end, after fighting his accusers with the fierce instinct of self-preservation, he breaks down completely. This is not one of the sudden conversions too common in Elizabethan drama, but the natural and necessary consequence of his character in action. What should such an Angelo do but beg for "immediate sentence and sequent death". It is the women who implore his life; he makes no plea for mercy, recognizing only too well that he has shown none. The claim of justice seems indeed baffled when he is let off with a warning to love his wife, but what other conclusion could be expected in such a play as this. We should be thankful that he does not as in the sources marry Isabella.

Few of Shakespeare's plays provoke so many questions or better repay careful and unprejudiced consideration than *Measure for Measure*. The central theme is repulsive; the characters are for the most part unsympathetic, the background is of an unwonted sordidness. The apparent problem, whether a maid's chastity rates higher than a man's life, is evaded by Shakespeare's invention of Mariana. And yet the play appeals. If the ostensible problem is not solved a deeper and graver one is set and answered, the conflicting claims of justice and of mercy, and Shakespeare tips the scales for mercy. It is a bad world we live in, he seems to say; but it is peopled by human beings who are weak rather than wicked. What man dare play the part of Angelo and judge his brother? Let him remember the words of Christ: "with what measure ye mete, it shall be measured to you again." This is the implied moral of the play, summed up in its fit and warning title, *Measure for Measure*.

Stage History.—Apart from the Court performance of 1604 there is no record of *Measure for Measure* on the stage before the closing of the theatres. It was one of the first of Shakespeare's plays that Davenant adapted for the Restoration stage. His *The Law Against Lovers* is an extraordinary production, hardly recognizable as Shakespeare. It omits all the low comedy and most of the semi-tragic scenes. In the end all comes right and Angelo marries Isabella. Pepys, who saw this play, February 18, 1662, was delighted with "the little girl's singing and dancing." Needless to say "the little girl" is a Davenant invention, Viola, the sister of Beatrice, a forward minx who dances a saraband to the clatter of castanets.

Nothing more is heard of *Measure for Measure* till 1720, when it was turned into an operatic and spectacular performance, with music and an elaborate masque, *Beauty the Best Advocate,* by Charles Gildon. About 1738 Shakespeare's play came back to the stage in something like its original form and from that time on it was acted fairly steadily throughout the century. A succession of great actresses, Yates, Barry, and Siddons, took the part of Isabella. Victorian prudery may have been partly responsible for the almost unbroken absence of this play from the stage in the nineteenth century, but it is interesting to note that occasional revivals were due to the desire of actresses to play the role of the heroine. Thus Adelaide Neilson revived it in 1876 and Modjeska repeatedly played Isabella in this country.

MEASURE FOR MEASURE

The Names of all the Actors

Vincentio, the Duke.
Angelo, the Deputy.
Escalus, an ancient Lord.
Claudio, a young gentleman.
Lucio, a fantastic.
Two other like gentlemen.
Provost.
Thomas, } two friars.
Peter, }
A Justice.
Varrius.

Elbow, a simple constable.
Froth, a foolish gentleman.
Pompey, the clown, servant to *Mistress Overdone.*
Abhorson, an executioner.
Barnardine, a dissolute prisoner.

Isabella, sister to *Claudio.*
Mariana, betrothed to *Angelo.*
Juliet, beloved of *Claudio.*
Francisca, a nun.
Mistress Overdone, a bawd.

Lords, Officers, Citizens, Boy, and Attendants.

[This list appears in practically the present form at the end of the play in the Folio.]

SCENE: *Vienna.*

ACT I. Scene I. *The Duke's palace.*

Enter *Duke, Escalus,* Lords and Attendants.

Duke. Escalus.
Escal. My lord.
Duke. Of government the properties to unfold
Would seem in me t' affect speech and discourse,
Since I am put to know that your own science
Exceeds, in that, the lists of all advice
My strength can give you: then no more remains,
But that to your sufficiency as your worth is able,
And let them work. The nature of our people,
Our city's institutions, and the terms
For common justice, you 're as pregnant in
As art and practice hath enriched any
That we remember. There is our commission,
From which we would not have you warp. Call hither,
I say, bid come before us Angelo.
Exit an attendant.
What figure of us think you he will bear?
For you must know, we have with special soul
Elected him our absence to supply,
Lent him our terror, dress'd him with our love,
And given his deputation all the organs
Of our own power. What think you of it?
Escal. If any in Vienna be of worth
To undergo such ample grace and honour,
It is Lord Angelo.

Enter *Angelo.*

Duke. Look where he comes.
Ang. Always obedient to your Grace's will,
I come to know your pleasure.
Duke. Angelo,
There is a kind of character in thy life,
That to th' observer doth thy history
Fully unfold: thyself and thy belongings
Are not thine own so proper as to waste
Thyself upon thy virtues, they on thee.
Heaven doth with us as we with torches do,
Not light them for themselves; for if our virtues
Did not go forth of us, 't were all alike
As if we had them not. Spirits are not finely touch'd
But to fine issues, nor Nature never lends
The smallest scruple of her excellence
But, like a thrifty goddess, she determines
Herself the glory of a creditor,
Both thanks and use. But I do bend my speech
To one that can my part in him advertise.
Hold therefore, Angelo:

5. put, made. **6. lists,** limits. **12. pregnant,** expert. **15. warp,** deviate. **17. figure,** image. Reference to the image on a coin that gives it currency. **18. soul,** interest of love. **21. deputation,** vice-regency.

24. undergo, bear. **28. character,** writing. **31. so proper,** i.e., so exclusively. **as . . . virtues,** as to allow you to live to yourself alone. **38. scruple,** third part of a dram, i.e., small quantity. **40. glory,** just pride. The credit or glories in "both thanks and use." **41-2. But . . . advertise,** but I do direct (bend) my speech to one who can instruct (advertise) me in the duties I am delegating to him. **43. Hold,** retain (what follows).

In our remove be thou at full ourself.
Mortality and mercy in Vienna
Live in thy tongue and heart. Old Escalus,
Though first in question, is thy secondary.
Take thy commission.
Ang. Now, good my lord,
Let there be some more test made of my mettle
Before so noble and so great a figure
Be stamp'd upon it.
Duke. No more evasion.
We have with a leaven'd and prepared choice
Proceeded to you; therefore take your honours.
Our haste from hence is of so quick condition
That it prefers itself and leaves unquestion'd
Matters of needful value. We shall write to you,
As time and our concernings shall importune,
How it goes with us, and do look to know
What doth befall you here. So, fare you well:
To th' hopeful execution do I leave you
Of your commissions.
Ang. Yet give leave, my lord,
That we may bring you something on the way.
Duke. My haste may not admit it;
Nor need you, on mine honour, have to do
With any scruple: your scope is as mine own,
So to enforce or qualify the laws
As to your soul seems good. Give me your hand;
I 'll privily away: I love the people,
But do not like to stage me to their eyes:
Though it do well, I do not relish well
Their loud applause and Aves vehement;
Nor do I think the man of safe discretion
That does affect it. Once more, fare you well.
Ang. The heavens give safety to your purposes!
Escal. Lead forth and bring you back in happiness!
Duke. I thank you. Fare you well. *Exit.*
Escal. I shall desire you, sir, to give me leave
To have free speech with you; and it concerns me
To look into the bottom of my place:
A power I have, but of what strength and nature
I am not yet instructed.
Ang. 'T is so with me. Let us withdraw together,
And we may soon our satisfaction have
Touching that point.
Escal. I 'll wait upon your honour.
Exeunt.

44. **remove,** absence. 47. **first in question,** first in consideration. 52. **leaven'd,** ripened. 55. **prefers itself,** takes precedence. 57. **concernings,** affairs, concerns. 69. **stage me,** exhibit myself. 70. **do well,** is fit. 71. **Aves,** hails.

Scene II. *A street.*

Enter *Lucio* and two other *Gentlemen.*

Lucio. If the Duke with the other dukes come not to composition with the King of Hungary, why then all the dukes fall upon the King.

1. Gent. Heaven grant us its peace, but not the King of Hungary's!

2. Gent. Amen.

Lucio. Thou conclud'st like the sanctimonious pirate, that went to sea with the Ten Commandments, but scraped one out of the table.

2. Gent. "Thou shalt not steal"?

Lucio. Ay, that he razed.

1. Gent. Why, 't was a commandment to command the captain and all the rest from their functions; they put forth to steal. There 's not a soldier of us all, that, in the thanksgiving before meat, do relish the petition well that prays for peace.

2. Gent. I never heard any soldier dislike it.

Lucio. I believe thee; for I think thou never wast where grace was said.

2. Gent. No? A dozen times at least.

1. Gent. What, in metre?

Lucio. In any proportion or in any language.

1. Gent. I think, or in any religion.

Lucio. Ay, why not? Grace is grace, despite of all controversy; as, for example, thou thyself art a wicked villain, despite of all grace.

1. Gent. Well, there went but a pair of shears between us.

Lucio. I grant; as there may between the lists and the velvet. Thou art the list.

1. Gent. And thou the velvet: thou art good velvet; thou 'rt a three-piled piece, I warrant thee. I had as lief be a list of an English kersey as be piled, as thou art piled, for a French velvet. Do I speak feelingly now?

Lucio. I think thou dost; and, indeed, with most painful feeling of thy speech: I will, out of thine own confession, learn to begin thy health; but, whilst I live, forget to drink after thee.

1. Gent. I think I have done myself wrong, have I not?

Scene ii: 2. composition, agreement. **22. in metre,** metrical graces were not unknown on Shakespeare's stage. **23. proportion,** length. **28-9. there . . . us,** we were cut from the same cloth. **31. lists,** selvedge or outer edge of any cloth (here of velvet). **33. three-pil'd,** deep-napped, fine. There follows punning on **piled** as **peeled** (bald), the result of the "French disease," i.e., syphilis. **34. kersey,** coarse woollen cloth. **35-6. Do . . . now,** do I touch you now. Lucio takes **feelingly** for **in a heartfelt way** (from experience of the disease).

2. Gent. Yes, that thou hast, whether thou art tainted or free.

Enter *Mistress Overdone* the Bawd.

Lucio. Behold, behold, where Madam Mitigation comes! I have purchased as many diseases under her roof as come to—

2. Gent. To what, I pray?

Lucio. Judge.

2. Gent. To three thousand dolours a year.

1. Gent. Ay, and more.

Lucio. A French crown more.

1. Gent. Thou art always figuring diseases in me; but thou art full of error; I am sound.

Lucio. Nay, not as one would say, healthy; but so sound as things that are hollow. Thy bones are hollow; impiety has made a feast of thee.

1. Gent. How now! which of your hips has the most profound sciatica?

Over. Well, well; there 's one yonder arrested and carried to prison was worth five thousand of you all.

2. Gent. Who 's that, I pray thee?

Over. Marry, sir, that 's Claudio, Signior Claudio.

1. Gent. Claudio to prison? 'T is not so.

Over. Nay, but I know 't is so. I saw him arrested, saw him carried away; and, which is more, within these three days his head to be chopped off.

Lucio. But, after all this fooling, I would not have it so. Art thou sure of this?

Over. I am too sure of it; and it is for getting Madam Julietta with child.

Lucio. Believe me, this may be. He promised to meet me two hours since, and he was ever precise in promise-keeping.

2. Gent. Besides, you know, it draws something near to the speech we had to such a purpose.

1. Gent. But, most of all, agreeing with the proclamation.

Lucio. Away! let 's go learn the truth of it.

Exeunt Lucio and Gentlemen.

Over. Thus, what with the war, what with the sweat, what with the gallows, and what with poverty, I am custom-shrunk.

Enter *Pompey* the Clown.

How now! what 's the news with you?

Pom. Yonder man is carried to prison.

Over. Well; what has he done?

Pom. A woman.

Over. But what 's his offence?

Pom. Groping for trouts in a peculiar river.

Over. What, is there a maid with child by him?

Pom. No, but there 's a woman with maid by him. You have not heard of the proclamation, have you?

Over. What proclamation, man?

Pom. All houses in the suburbs of Vienna must be plucked down.

Over. And what shall become of those in the city?

Pom. They shall stand for seed: they had gone down too, but that a wise burgher put in for them.

Over. But shall all our houses of resort in the suburbs be pulled down?

Pom. To the ground, mistress.

Over. Why, here 's a change indeed in the commonwealth! What shall become of me?

Pom. Come, fear not you; good counsellors lack no clients: though you change your place, you need not change your trade: [I 'll be your tapster still. Courage! there will be pity taken on you: you that have worn your eyes almost out in the service, you will be considered.

Over. What 's to do here, Thomas tapster? Let 's withdraw.

Pom. Here comes Signior Claudio, led by the provost to prison; and there 's Madam Juliet. *Exeunt.*

Enter *Provost, Claudio, Juliet,* and Officers.

Claud. Fellow, why dost thou show me
thus to th' world?
Bear me to prison, where I am committed.

Prov. I do it not in evil disposition,
But from Lord Angelo by special charge.

Claud. Thus can the demigod authority
Make us pay down for our offence by weight.
The words of heaven: on whom it will, it
will;
On whom it will not, so; yet still 't is just.

Re-enter *Lucio* and two Gentlemen.

Lucio. Why, how now, Claudio! whence
comes this restraint?

Claud. From too much liberty, my Lucio,
liberty:
As surfeit is the father of much fast,
So every scope by the immoderate use
Turns to restraint. Our natures do pursue,

50. dolours, (1) sorrows, (2) dollars. **52. French crown,** (1) coin, (2) bald head. **53. figuring,** imagining. **84. sweat,** sweating sickness, plague.

119. provost, jailer. **125. by weight,** in just proportion, exactly. **126. words of heaven,** I will have mercy on whom I will have mercy, and I will have compassion on whom I will have compassion. *Romans,* ix, 15. **131. scope,** liberty.

Like rats that ravin down their proper bane,
A thirsty evil; and when we drink we die.

Lucio. If I could speak so wisely under an arrest, I would send for certain of my creditors; and yet, to say the truth, I had as lief have the foppery of freedom as the mortality of imprisonment. What 's thy offence, Claudio?

Claud. What but to speak of would offend again.

Lucio. What, is 't murder?

Claud. No.

Lucio. Lechery?

Claud. Call it so.

Prov. Away, sir! you must go.

Claud. One word, good friend. Lucio, a word with you.

Lucio. A hundred, if they 'll do you any good.
Is lechery so look'd after?

Claud. Thus stands it with me: upon a true contract
I got possession of Julietta's bed.
You know the lady; she is fast my wife,
Save that we do the denunciation lack
Of outward order. This we came not to,
Only for propagation of a dower
Remaining in the coffer of her friends,
From whom we thought it meet to hide our love
Till time had made them for us. But it chances
The stealth of our most mutual entertainment
With character too gross is writ on Juliet.

Lucio. With child, perhaps?

Claud. Unhappily, even so.
And the new deputy now for the Duke—
Whether it be the fault and glimpse of newness,
Or whether that the body public be
A horse whereon the governor doth ride,
Who, newly in the seat, that it may know
He can command, lets it straight feel the spur;
Whether the tyranny be in his place,
Or in his eminence that fills it up,
I stagger in:—but this new governor
Awakes me all the enrolled penalties
Which have, like unscour'd armour, hung by the wall
So long that nineteen zodiacs have gone round
And none of them been worn; and, for a name,
Now puts the drowsy and neglected act
Freshly on me: 't is surely for a name.

Lucio. I warrant it is; and thy head stands so tickle on thy shoulders that a milkmaid, if she be in love, may sigh it off. Send after the Duke and appeal to him.

Claud. I have done so, but he 's not to be found.
I prithee, Lucio, do me this kind service.
This day my sister should the cloister enter
And there receive her approbation.
Acquaint her with the danger of my state;
Implore her, in my voice, that she make friends
To the strict deputy; bid herself assay him.
I have great hope in that; for in her youth
There is a prone and speechless dialect,
Such as move men; beside, she hath prosperous art
When she will play with reason and discourse,
And well she can persuade.

Lucio. I pray she may; as well for the encouragement of the like, which else would stand under grievous imposition, as for the enjoying of thy life, who I would be sorry should be thus foolishly lost at a game of tick-tack. I 'll to her.

Claud. I thank you, good friend Lucio.

Lucio. Within two hours.

Claud. Come, officer, away!

Exeunt.

Scene III. *A monastery.*

Enter *Duke* and *Friar Thomas.*

Duke. No, holy father; throw away that thought.
Believe not that the dribbling dart of love
Can pierce a complete bosom: why I desire thee
To give me secret harbour, hath a purpose
More grave and wrinkled than the aims and ends
Of burning youth.

Fri. T. May your Grace speak of it?

Duke. My holy sir, none better knows than you
How I have ever lov'd the life removed,
And held in idle price to haunt assemblies
Where youth and cost a witless bravery keeps.
I have delivered to Lord Angelo,
(A man of stricture and firm abstinence)

133. ravin, gulp. **proper bane,** own peculiar poison. **138. foppery,** folly. **mortality,** death. **148. look'd after,** frowned upon. **151. fast,** securely. **152. denunciation,** formal declaration. **154. propagation,** increase, i.e., by investment. **162. fault and glimpse,** faulty glance, imperfect vision. **167. place,** office. **168. eminence,** moral loftiness. **169. I stagger in,** i.e., I hesitate to say. **172. zodiacs,** i.e., years.

174. drowsy, i.e., from long disuse. **177. tickle,** unstable. **183. receive her approbation,** begin her probation or novitiate. **186. assay,** attempt. **188. prone and speechless,** mutely eager or earnest. **193. like,** i.e., lechery. **194. imposition,** i.e., punishment. **Scene iii: 2. dribbling,** weakly shot. **3. complete,** sound, perfect. **9. in idle price,** as little worth. **10. cost,** pomp. **bravery,** splendor. **12. stricture,** strictness.

My absolute power and place here in Vienna,
And he supposes me travell'd to Poland;
For so I have strew'd it in the common ear,
And so it is receiv'd. Now, pious sir,
You will demand of me why I do this.

Fri. T. Gladly, my lord.

Duke. We have strict statutes and most biting laws,
(The needful bits and curbs to headstrong steeds)
Which for this fourteen years we have let sleep;
Even like an o'ergrown lion in a cave,
That goes not out to prey. Now, as fond fathers,
Having bound up the threat'ning twigs of birch,
Only to stick it in their children's sight
For terror, not to use, in time the rod
Becomes more mock'd than fear'd; so our decrees,
Dead to infliction, to themselves are dead,
And liberty plucks justice by the nose,
The baby beats the nurse, and quite athwart
Goes all decorum.

Fri. T. It rested in your Grace
To unloose this tied-up justice when you pleas'd:
And it in you more dreadful would have seem'd
Than in Lord Angelo.

Duke. I do fear, too dreadful.
Sith 't was my fault to give the people scope,
'T would be my tyranny to strike and gall them
For what I bid them do; for we bid this be done,
When evil deeds have their permissive pass
And not the punishment. Therefore indeed, my father,
I have on Angelo impos'd the office;
Who may, in th' ambush of my name, strike home,
And yet my nature never in the fight
To do it slander. And to behold his sway,
I will, as 't were a brother of your order,
Visit both prince and people; therefore, I prithee,
Supply me with the habit and instruct me
How I may formally in person bear me
Like a true friar. Moe reasons for this action
At our more leisure shall I render you;
Only, this one: Lord Angelo is precise,
Stands at a guard with envy, scarce confesses
That his blood flows, or that his appetite
Is more to bread than stone; hence shall we see,
If power change purpose, what our seemers be. *Exeunt.*

Scene IV. *A nunnery.*

Enter *Isabella* and *Francisca,* a Nun.

Isab. And have you nuns no farther privileges?

Fran. Are not these large enough?

Isab. Yes, truly: I speak not as desiring more,
But rather wishing a more strict restraint
Upon the sisterhood, the votaries of Saint Clare.

Lucio. [*Within.*] Ho! Peace be in this place!

Isab. Who 's that which calls?

Fran. It is a man's voice: gentle Isabella,
Turn you the key, and know his business of him.
You may, I may not; you are yet unsworn.
When you have vow'd, you must not speak with men
But in the presence of the prioress;
Then, if you speak, you must not show your face,
Or, if you show your face, you must not speak.
He calls again; I pray you, answer him. *Exit.*

Isab. Peace and prosperity! Who is 't that calls?

Enter *Lucio.*

Lucio. Hail, virgin, if you be, as those cheek-roses
Proclaim you are no less! Can you so stead me
As bring me to the sight of Isabella,
A novice of this place and the fair sister
To her unhappy brother Claudio?

Isab. Why "her unhappy brother"? let me ask,
The rather for I now must make you know
I am that Isabella and his sister.

Lucio. Gentle and fair, your brother kindly greets you.
Not to be weary with you, he 's in prison.

Isab. Woe me! for what?

Lucio. For that which, if myself might be his judge,
He should receive his punishment in thanks:
He hath got his friend with child.

Isab. Sir, make me not your story.

Lucio. 'T is true.
I would not—though 't is my familiar sin
With maids to seem the lapwing and to jest,

28. infliction, execution. **30. athwart**, wrongly, perversely. **35. Sith**, since. **41. in th' ambush**, under the cover. **42. nature**, personality. **43. it**, itself. **47. formally**, externally. **51. Stands . . . envy**, guards against malice.

Scene iv: 17. stead, help. **25. weary**, tedious. **30. make me**, make up for me. **31. familiar**, habitual. **32. lapwing**, diverts attention of hunters from its nest by pretending to be injured and similar tricks.

Tongue far from heart—play with all virgins so:
I hold you as a thing enskied and sainted,
By your renouncement an immortal spirit,
And to be talk'd with in sincerity,
As with a saint.

Isab. You do blaspheme the good in mocking me.

Lucio. Do not believe it. Fewness and truth, 't is thus:
Your brother and his lover have embrac'd:
As those that feed grow full, as blossoming time
That from the seedness the bare fallow brings
To teeming foison, even so her plenteous womb
Expresseth his full tilth and husbandry.

Isab. Some one with child by him? My cousin Juliet?

Lucio. Is she your cousin?

Isab. Adoptedly; as school-maids change their names
By vain though apt affection.

Lucio. She it is.

Isab. O, let him marry her.

Lucio. This is the point.
The Duke is very strangely gone from hence;
Bore many gentlemen, myself being one,
In hand, in hope of action; but we do learn
By those that know the very nerves of state,
His givings-out were of an infinite distance
From his true-meant design. Upon his place,
And with full line of his authority,
Governs Lord Angelo, a man whose blood
Is very snow-broth, one who never feels
The wanton stings and motions of the sense,
But doth rebate and blunt his natural edge
With profits of the mind, study, and fast.
He—to give fear to use and liberty,
Which have for long run by the hideous law,
As mice by lions—hath pick'd out an act,
Under whose heavy sense your brother's life
Falls into forfeit; he arrests him on it;
And follows close the rigour of the statute,
To make him an example. All hope is gone,
Unless you have the grace by your fair prayer
To soften Angelo: and that 's my pith
Of business 'twixt you and your poor brother.

Isab. Doth he so seek his life?

Lucio. Has censur'd him
Already; and, as I hear, the Provost hath
A warrant for his execution.

Isab. Alas! what poor ability 's in me
To do him good?

Lucio. Assay the power you have.

Isab. My power? Alas, I doubt—

Lucio. Our doubts are traitors,
And makes us lose the good we oft might win
By fearing to attempt. Go to Lord Angelo,
And let him learn to know, when maidens sue
Men give like gods; but when they weep and kneel,
All their petitions are as freely theirs
As they themselves would owe them.

Isab. I 'll see what I can do.

Lucio. But speedily.

Isab. I will about it straight,
No longer staying but to give the Mother
Notice of my affair. I humbly thank you.
Commend me to my brother: soon at night
I 'll send him certain words of my success.

Lucio. I take my leave of you.

Isab. Good sir, adieu.

Exeunt.

ACT II. Scene I. *Court of Justice.*

Enter *Angelo, Escalus,* a *Justice,* and Servants.

Ang. We must not make a scarecrow of the law,
Setting it up to fear the birds of prey,
And let it keep one shape, till custom make it
Their perch and not their terror.

Escal. Ay, but yet
Let us be keen, and rather cut a little,
Than fall, and bruise to death. Alas, this gentleman
Whom I would save had a most noble father!
Let but your honour know,
(Whom I believe to be most strait in virtue,)
That, in the working of your own affections,
Had time coher'd with place or place with wishing,
Or that the resolute acting of your blood
Could have attain'd th' effect of your own purpose,

34. enskied, in heaven. **39. Fewness and truth,** briefly and truthfully. **42. seedness,** seeding. **fallow,** plowed land. **43. foison,** rich harvest. **48. apt,** natural. **51-2. Bore . . . in hand,** deluded. **52. action,** military action. **53. nerves,** sinews. **54. givings-out,** announced plans. **56. line,** free scope. **60. rebate,** dull. **Act II, Scene i: 2. fear,** frighten.

62. use and liberty, practice of liberty. **72. censur'd,** sentenced. **83. As,** as if. **would owe,** possessed. **Act II, Scene i: 6. fall,** let fall.

Whether you had not sometime in your life
Err'd in this point which now you censure him,
And pull'd the law upon you.

Ang. 'T is one thing to be tempted, Escalus,
Another thing to fall. I not deny,
The jury, passing on the prisoner's life,
May in the sworn twelve have a thief or two
Guiltier than him they try. What 's open made to justice,
That justice seizes. What knows the laws
That thieves do pass on thieves? 'T is very pregnant,
The jewel that we find, we stoop and take 't
Because we see it; but what we do not see
We tread upon, and never think of it.
You may not so extenuate his offence
For I have had such faults; but rather tell me,
When I, that censure him, do so offend,
Let mine own judgement pattern out my death,
And nothing come in partial. Sir, he must die.

Enter Provost.

Escal. Be it as your wisdom will.

Ang. Where is the Provost?

Prov. Here, if it like your honour.

Ang. See that Claudio
Be executed by nine to-morrow morning.
Bring him his confessor, let him be prepar'd;
For that 's the utmost of his pilgrimage.

Exit Provost.

Escal. Well, Heaven forgive him! and forgive us all!
Some rise by sin, and some by virtue fall.
Some run from brakes of vice, and answer none;
And some condemned for a fault alone.

Enter *Elbow, Froth, Pompey* the Clown and Officers.

Elb. Come, bring them away: if these be good people in a commonweal that do nothing but use their abuses in common houses, I know no law: bring them away.

Ang. How now, sir, what 's your name, and what 's the matter?

Elb. If it please your honour, I am the poor Duke's constable, and my name is Elbow: I do lean upon justice, sir, and do bring in here before your good honour two notorious benefactors.

Ang. Benefactors? Well, what benefactors are they? Are they not malefactors?

Elb. If it please your honour, I know not well what they are; but precise villains they are, that I am sure of; and void of all profanation in the world that good Christians ought to have.

Escal. This comes off well. Here 's a wise officer.

Ang. Go to; what quality are they of? Elbow is your name? Why dost thou not speak, Elbow?

Pom. He cannot, sir; he 's out at elbow.

Ang. What are you, sir?

Elb. He, sir! A tapster, sir; parcel-bawd; one that serves a bad woman, whose house, sir, was, as they say, plucked down in the suburbs; and now she professes a hot-house, which, I think, is a very ill house too.

Escal. How know you that?

Elb. My wife, sir, whom I detest before Heaven and your honour,—

Escal. How? Thy wife?

Elb. Ay, sir; whom, I thank Heaven, is an honest woman,—

Escal. Dost thou detest her therefore?

Elb. I say, sir, I will detest myself also, as well as she, that this house, if it be not a bawd's house, it is pity of her life, for it is a naughty house.

Escal. How dost thou know that, constable?

Elb. Marry, sir, by my wife; who if she had been a woman cardinally given, might have been accused in fornication, adultery, and all uncleanliness there.

Escal. By the woman's means?

Elb. Ay, sir, by Mistress Overdone's means; but as she spit in his face, so she defied him.

Pom. Sir, if it please your honour, this is not so.

Elb. Prove it before these varlets, here, thou honourable man; prove it.

Escal. Do you hear how he misplaces?

Pom. Sir, she came in great with child, and longing (saving your honour's reverence) for stewed prunes: sir, we had but two in the house, which at that very distant time stood, as it were, in a fruit-dish, a dish of some threepence: your honours have seen such dishes; they are not china dishes, but very good dishes,—

Escal. Go to, go to; no matter for the dish, sir.

Pom. No, indeed, sir, not of a pin; you are therein in the right: but to the point. As I say, this Mistress Elbow, being, as I say, with

21. open, evident, plain. **23. pregnant,** evident, visible, **31. nothing . . . partial,** i.e., none be shown partiality. **39. brakes,** thickets. **43. abuses,** corrupt practices.

54. precise, puritanical. **55. profanation,** irreverence, for reverence. **63. parcel-bawd,** part bawd. **66. hot-house,** bath-house. **69. detest,** for protest. **81. cardinally,** for carnally

child, and being great-bellied, and longing, as I said, for prunes; and having but two in the dish, as I said, Master Froth here, this very man, having eaten the rest, as I said, and, as I say, paying for them very honestly; for, as you know, Master Froth, I could not give you three-pence again.

Froth. No, indeed.

Pom. Very well; you being then, if you be remembered, cracking the stones of the foresaid prunes,—

Froth. Ay, so I did indeed.

Pom. Why, very well: I telling you then, if you be remembered, that such a one and such a one were past cure of the thing you wot of, unless they kept very good diet, as I told you,—

Froth. All this is true.

Pom. Why, very well, then,—

Escal. Come, you are a tedious fool: to the purpose. What was done to Elbow's wife, that he hath cause to complain of? Come me to what was done to her.

Pom. Sir, your honour cannot come to that yet.

Escal. No, sir, nor I mean it not.

Pom. Sir, but you shall come to it, by your honour's leave. And, I beseech you, look into Master Froth here, sir; a man of fourscore pound a year; whose father died at Hallowmas. Was 't not at Hallowmas, Master Froth?

Froth. All-hallond eve.

Pom. Why, very well; I hope here be truths. He, sir, sitting, as I say, in a lower chair, sir; 't was in the Bunch of Grapes, where indeed you have a delight to sit, have you not?

Froth. I have so; because it is an open room and good for winter.

Pom. Why, very well, then; I hope here be truths.

Ang. This will last out a night in Russia,
When nights are longest there: I 'll take my leave,
And leave you to the hearing of the cause,
Hoping you 'll find good cause to whip them all.

Escal. I think no less. Good morrow to your lordship. *Exit Angelo.*
Now, sir, come on. What was done to Elbow's wife, once more?

Pom. Once, sir? There was nothing done to her once.

Elb. I beseech you, sir, ask him what this man did to my wife.

Pom. I beseech your honour, ask me.

Escal. Well, sir; what did this gentleman to her?

Pom. I beseech you, sir, look in this gentleman's face. Good Master Froth, look upon his honour; 't is for a good purpose. Doth your honour mark his face?

Escal. Ay, sir, very well.

Pom. Nay, I beseech you, mark it well.

Escal. Well, I do so.

Pom. Doth your honour see any harm in his face?

Escal. Why, no.

Pom. I 'll be supposed upon a book, his face is the worst thing about him. Good, then; if his face be the worst thing about him, how could Master Froth do the constable's wife any harm? I would know that of your honour.

Escal. He 's in the right. Constable, what say you to it?

Elb. First, an it like you, the house is a respected house; next, this is a respected fellow; and his mistress is a respected woman.

Pom. By this hand, sir, his wife is a more respected person than any of us all.

Elb. Varlet, thou liest! Thou liest, wicked varlet! The time is yet to come that she was ever respected with man, woman, or child.

Pom. Sir, she was respected with him before he married with her.

Escal. Which is the wiser here, Justice or Iniquity? Is this true?

Elb. O thou caitiff! O thou varlet! O thou wicked Hannibal! I respected with her before I was married to her! If ever I was respected with her, or she with me, let not your worship think me the poor Duke's officer. Prove this, thou wicked Hannibal, or I 'll have mine action of battery on thee.

Escal. If he took you a box o' th' ear, you might have your action of slander too.

Elb. Marry, I thank your good worship for it: what is 't your worship's pleasure I shall do with this wicked caitiff?

Escal. Truly, officer, because he hath some offences in him that thou wouldst discover if thou couldst, let him continue in his courses till thou know'st what they are.

Elb. Marry, I thank your worship for it. Thou seest, thou wicked varlet, now, what 's come upon thee. Thou art to continue now, thou varlet; thou art to continue.

Escal. Where were you born, friend?

Froth. Here in Vienna, sir.

Escal. Are you of fourscore pounds a year?

Froth. Yes, an 't please you, sir.

121. Come me, bring me. **132. lower,** easy, reclining. **133. Bunch of Grapes,** name of room in the inn. **135. open,** public.

163. supposed, for deposed or sworn. **171. respected,** misused here and in the following speeches for "suspected" or "ill-reputed." **180-1. Justice or Iniquity,** constable or clown.

Escal. So. What trade are you of, sir?

Pom. A tapster; a poor widow's tapster.

Escal. Your mistress' name?

Pom. Mistress Overdone.

Escal. Hath she had any more than one husband?

Pom. Nine, sir; Overdone by the last.

Escal. Nine! Come hither to me, Master Froth. Master Froth, I would not have you acquainted with tapsters; they will draw you, Master Froth, and you will hang them. Get you gone, and let me hear no more of you.

Froth. I thank your worship. For mine own part, I never come into any room in a taphouse, but I am drawn in.

Escal. Well, no more of it, Master Froth. Farewell. [*Exit Froth.*] Come you hither to me, Master tapster: what 's your name, Master tapster?

Pom. Pompey.

Escal. What else?

Pom. Bum, sir.

Escal. Troth, and your bum is the greatest thing about you, so that in the beastliest sense you are Pompey the Great. Pompey, you are partly a bawd, Pompey, howsoever you colour it in being a tapster, are you not? Come, tell me true; it shall be the better for you.

Pom. Truly, sir, I am a poor fellow that would live.

Escal. How would you live, Pompey? By being a bawd? What do you think of the trade, Pompey? Is it a lawful trade?

Pom. If the law would allow it, sir.

Escal. But the law will not allow it, Pompey; nor it shall not be allowed in Vienna.

Pom. Does your worship mean to geld and splay all the youth of the city?

Escal. No, Pompey.

Pom. Truly, sir, in my poor opinion, they will to 't then. If your worship will take order for the drabs and the knaves, you need not to fear the bawds.

Escal. There is pretty orders beginning, I can tell you: it is but heading and hanging.

Pom. If you head and hang all that offend that way but for ten year together, you 'll be glad to give out a commission for more heads. If this law hold in Vienna ten year, I 'll rent the fairest house in it after three-pence a bay: if you live to see this come to pass, say Pompey told you so.

Escal. Thank you, good Pompey; and, in requital of your prophecy, hark you: I advise you, let me not find you before me again upon any complaint whatsoever; no, not for dwelling where you do: if I do, Pompey, I shall beat you to your tent, and prove a shrewd Cæsar to you; in plain dealing, Pompey, I shall have you whipt: so, for this time, Pompey, fare you well.

Pom. I thank your worship for your good counsel; [*aside*] but I shall follow it as the flesh and fortune shall better determine.
Whip me? No, no; let carman whip his jade;
The valiant heart 's not whipt out of his trade. *Exit.*

Escal. Come hither to me, Master Elbow; come hither, Master constable. How long have you been in this place of constable?

Elb. Seven year and a half, sir.

Escal. I thought, by the readiness in the office, you had continued in it some time. You say, seven years together?

Elb. And a half, sir.

Escal. Alas, it hath been great pains to you: they do you wrong to put you so oft upon 't. Are there not men in your ward sufficient to serve it?

Elb. Faith, sir, few of any wit in such matters: as they are chosen, they are glad to choose me for them; I do it for some piece of money, and go through with all.

Escal. Look you bring me in the names of some six or seven, the most sufficient of your parish.

Elb. To your worship's house, sir?

Escal. To my house. Fare you well.

Exit Elbow.

What 's o'clock, think you?

Just. Eleven, sir.

Escal. I pray you home to dinner with me.

Just. I humbly thank you.

Escal. It grieves me for the death of Claudio;
But there 's no remedy.

Just. Lord Angelo is severe.

Escal. It is but needful.
Mercy is not itself, that oft looks so;
Pardon is still the nurse of second woe.
But yet,—poor Claudio! There is no remedy.
Come, sir. *Exeunt.*

Scene II. *Another room in the court.*

Enter *Provost* and a *Servant.*

Serv. He 's hearing of a cause; he will come straight.
I 'll tell him of you.

Prov. Pray you, do.

Exit Servant.

215. draw you, (1) draw you liquor, (2) get you hung, drawn, and quartered. **228. bum,** buttocks. **231. bawd,** procurer. **247. drabs,** strumpets. **250. heading,** beheading. **255. after,** at. **bay,** section.

263. beat . . . tent, Battle of Pharsalia, 48 B.C. **shrewd,** vexatious. **269. carman,** teamster. **jade,** horse. **275. readiness,** facility. **281. sufficient,** fit, able.

I 'll know
His pleasure; may be he will relent. Alas,
He hath but as offended in a dream!
All sects, all ages smack of this vice; and he
To die for 't!

Enter *Angelo*.

Ang. Now, what 's the matter, Provost?
Prov. Is it your will Claudio shall die tomorrow?
Ang. Did not I tell thee yea? Hadst thou not order?
Why dost thou ask again?
Prov. Lest I might be too rash.
Under your good correction, I have seen
When, after execution, judgement hath
Repented o'er his doom.
Ang. Go to; let that be mine.
Do you your office, or give up your place,
And you shall well be spar'd.
Prov. I crave your honour's pardon.
What shall be done, sir, with the groaning Juliet?
She 's very near her hour.
Ang. Dispose of her
To some more fitter place, and that with speed.

Re-enter *Servant*.

Serv. Here is the sister of the man condemn'd
Desires access to you.
Ang. Hath he a sister?
Prov. Ay, my good lord; a very virtuous maid,
And to be shortly of a sisterhood,
If not already.
Ang. Well, let her be admitted.
Exit Servant.
See you the fornicatress be remov'd.
Let her have needful but not lavish means;
There shall be order for 't.

Enter *Lucio* and *Isabella*.

Prov. Save your honour!
Ang. Stay a little while. [*To Isab.*]
You 're welcome; what 's your will?
Isab. I am a woeful suitor to your honour,
Please but your honour hear me.
Ang. Well; what 's your suit?
Isab. There is a vice that most I do abhor,
And most desire should meet the blow of justice;
For which I would not plead, but that I must;
For which I must not plead, but that I am
At war 'twixt will and will not.
Ang. Well; the matter?
Isab. I have a brother is condemn'd to die:
I do beseech you, let it be his fault,
And not my brother.
Prov. [*Aside.*] Heaven give thee moving graces!
Ang. Condemn the fault, and not the actor of it?
Why, every fault 's condemn'd ere it be done:
Mine were the very cipher of a function,
To fine the faults whose fine stands in record,
And let go by the actor.
Isab. O just but severe law!
I had a brother, then.—Heaven keep your honour!
Lucio. [*Aside to Isab.*] Give 't not o'er so: to him again, entreat him,
Kneel down before him, hang upon his gown.
You are too cold: if you should need a pin,
You could not with more tame a tongue desire it.
To him, I say!
Isab. Must he needs die?
Ang. Maiden, no remedy.
Isab. Yes; I do think that you might pardon him,
And neither heaven nor man grieve at the mercy.
Ang. I will not do 't.
Isab. But can you, if you would?
Ang. Look, what I will not, that I cannot do.
Isab. But might you do 't, and do the world no wrong,
If so your heart were touch'd with that remorse
As mine is to him?
Ang. He 's sentenc'd; 't is too late.
Lucio. [*Aside to Isab.*] You are too cold.
Isab. Too late? Why, no, I, that do speak a word,
May call it back again. Well, believe this,
No ceremony that to great ones longs,
Not the king's crown, nor the deputed sword,
The marshal's truncheon, nor the judge's robe,
Become them with one half so good a grace
As mercy does.
If he had been as you and you as he,
You would have slipt like him; but he, like you,
Would not have been so stern.
Ang. Pray you, be gone.
Isab. I would to heaven I had your potency,
And you were Isabel! Should it then be thus?
No; I would tell what 't were to be a judge,
And what a prisoner.
Lucio. [*Aside to Isab.*] Ay, touch him; there 's the vein.

Scene ii: 39. function, office. **40. fine**, punish. **46. tame**, spiritless. **desire**, ask. **59. longs**, belongs. **60. deputed sword**, the sword that by deputy represents the king's authority. **61. truncheon**, staff of office. **69. tell**, show.

Ang. Your brother is a forfeit of the law,
And you but waste your words.
Isab. Alas, alas!
Why, all the souls that were were forfeit once;
And He that might the vantage best have took
Found out the remedy. How would you be,
If He, which is the top of judgement, should
But judge you as you are? O, think on that;
And mercy then will breathe within your lips,
Like man new made.
Ang. Be you content, fair maid.
It is the law, not I condemn your brother.
Were he my kinsman, brother, or my son,
It should be thus with him: he must die to-morrow.
Isab. To-morrow? O, that 's sudden! Spare him, spare him!
He 's not prepar'd for death: even for our kitchens
We kill the fowl of season: shall we serve Heaven
With less respect than we do minister
To our gross selves? Good, good my lord, bethink you:
Who is it that hath died for this offence?
There 's many have committed it.
Lucio. [*Aside to Isab.*] Ay, well said.
Ang. The law hath not been dead, though it hath slept.
Those many had not dar'd to do that evil,
If the first that did th' edict infringe
Had answer'd for his deed. Now 't is awake,
Takes note of what is done, and, like a prophet,
Looks in a glass that shows what future evils,
Either new, or by remissness new-conceiv'd,
And so in progress to be hatch'd and born,
Are now to have no successive degrees,
But, ere they live, to end.
Isab. Yet show some pity.
Ang. I show it most of all when I show justice,
For then I pity those I do not know,
Which a dismiss'd offence would after gall;
And do him right that, answering one foul wrong,
Lives not to act another. Be satisfied;
Your brother dies to-morrow; be content.
Isab. So you must be the first that gives this sentence,
And he, that suffers. O, it is excellent
To have a giant's strength; but it is tyrannous
To use it like a giant.
Lucio. [*Aside to Isab.*] That 's well said.
Isab. Could great men thunder
As Jove himself does, Jove would never be quiet;
For every pelting, petty officer
Would use his heaven for thunder,
Nothing but thunder! Merciful Heaven,
Thou rather with thy sharp and sulphurous bolt
Splits the unwedgeable and gnarled oak
Than the soft myrtle; but man, proud man,
Dress'd in a little brief authority,
Most ignorant of what he 's most assur'd,—
His glassy essence—like an angry ape,
Plays such fantastic tricks before high heaven
As makes the angels weep; who, with our spleens,
Would all themselves laugh mortal.
Lucio. [*Aside to Isab.*] O, to him, to him, wench! he will relent.
He 's coming; I perceive 't.
Prov. [*Aside.*] Pray Heaven she win him!
Isab. We cannot weigh our brother with ourself.
Great men may jest with saints; 't is wit in them,
But in the less foul profanation.
Lucio. Thou 'rt i' th' right, girl. More o' that.
Isab. That in the captain 's but a choleric word,
Which in the soldier is flat blasphemy.
Lucio. [*Aside to Isab.*] Art avis'd o' that? More on 't.
Ang. Why do you put these sayings upon me?
Isab. Because authority, though it err like others,
Hath yet a kind of medicine in itself,
That skins the vice o' th' top; go to your bosom,
Knock there, and ask your heart what it doth know
That 's like my brother's fault: if it confess
A natural guiltiness such as is his,
Let it not sound a thought upon your tongue
Against my brother's life.
Ang. [*Aside.*] She speaks, and 't is
Such sense, that my sense breeds with it.—Fare you well.
Isab. Gentle my lord, turn back.
Ang. I will bethink me. Come again to-morrow.
Isab. Hark how I 'll bribe you. Good my lord, turn back.
Ang. How! bribe me?
Isab. Ay, with such gifts that Heaven shall share with you.

85. of season, i.e., matured, fattened. **95. glass,** a magic glass of beryl or crystal. **98. successive degrees,** descendants. **107. that suffers,** i.e., the first that suffers. **112. pelting,** paltry.

116. unwedgeable, not to be split with wedges. **119. assur'd,** sure of, dogmatic about. **120. His glassy essence,** his nature like glass, fragile and incapable of lasting impressions. **122. spleens,** fits of laughter. **123.** Laugh themselves to death. **132. avis'd,** advised, informed. **136. skins,** covers with skin. **142. breeds,** quickens.

Lucio. [*Aside to Isab.*] You had marr'd all else.
Isab. Not with fond shekels of the tested gold,
Or stones whose rate are either rich or poor
As fancy values them; but with true prayers
That shall be up at heaven and enter there
Ere sun-rise, prayers from preserved souls,
From fasting maids whose minds are dedicate
To nothing temporal.
Ang. Well, come to me to-morrow.
Lucio. [*Aside to Isab.*] Go to; 't is well. Away!
Isab. Heaven keep your honour safe!
Ang. [*Aside.*] Amen!
For I am that way going to temptation,
Where prayers cross.
Isab. At what hour to-morrow
Shall I attend your lordship?
Ang. At any time 'fore noon.
Isab. 'Save your honour!
Exeunt Isabella, Lucio, and Provost.
Ang. From thee: even from thy virtue.
What 's this, what 's this? Is this her fault or mine?
The tempter or the tempted, who sins most?
Ha!
Not she, nor doth she tempt; but it is I
That, lying by the violet in the sun,
Do as the carrion does, not as the flower,
Corrupt with virtuous season. Can it be
That modesty may more betray our sense
Than woman's lightness? Having waste ground enough,
Shall we desire to raze the sanctuary
And pitch our evils there? O, fie, fie, fie!
What dost thou, or what art thou, Angelo?
Dost thou desire her foully for those things
That make her good? O, let her brother live!
Thieves for their robbery have authority
When judges steal themselves. What, do I love her,
That I desire to hear her speak again
And feast upon her eyes? What is 't I dream on?
O cunning enemy, that, to catch a saint,
With saints dost bait thy hook! Most dangerous
Is that temptation that doth goad us on
To sin in loving virtue: never could the strumpet,
With all her double vigour, art and nature,
Once stir my temper; but this virtuous maid
Subdues me quite. Ever till now,
When men were fond, I smil'd and wonder'd how. *Exit.*

Scene III. *A room in a prison.*

Enter *Duke* disguised as a friar and *Provost.*

Duke. Hail to you, Provost! so I think you are.
Prov. I am the Provost. What 's your will, good friar?
Duke. Bound by my charity and my blest order,
I come to visit the afflicted spirits
Here in the prison: do me the common right
To let me see them and to make me know
The nature of their crimes, that I may minister
To them accordingly.
Prov. I would do more than that, if more were needful.

Enter *Juliet.*

Look, here comes one; a gentlewoman of mine,
Who, falling in the flames of her own youth,
Hath blister'd her report. She is with child;
And he that got it, sentenc'd; a young man
More fit to do another such offence
Than die for this.
Duke. When must he die?
Prov. As I do think, to-morrow.
I have provided for you. Stay awhile,
[*To Juliet.*]
And you shall be conducted.
Duke. Repent you, fair one, of the sin you carry?
Jul. I do; and bear the shame most patiently.
Duke. I 'll teach you how you shall arraign your conscience,
And try your penitence, if it be sound
Or hollowly put on.
Jul. I 'll gladly learn.
Duke. Love you the man that wrong'd you?
Jul. Yes, as I love the woman that wrong'd him.
Duke. So then it seems your most offenceful act
Was mutually committed?
Jul. Mutually.
Duke. Then was your sin of heavier kind than his.
Jul. I do confess it, and repent it, father.
Duke. 'T is meet so, daughter; but lest you do repent,
As that the sin hath brought you to this shame,
Which sorrow is always towards ourselves, not heaven,

150. rate, estimate, value. **168. Corrupt . . . season,** decay in summer. **169. betray,** ensnare.

Scene iii: **12. report,** reputation. **23. hollowly,** insincerely.

Showing we would not spare heaven as we love it,
But as we stand in fear,—
Jul. I do repent me, as it is an evil,
And take the shame with joy.
Duke. There rest.
Your partner, as I hear, must die to-morrow,
And I am going with instruction to him.
Grace go with you, *Benedicte!* *Exit.*
Jul. Must die to-morrow? O injurious law,
That respites me a life whose very comfort
Is still a dying horror!
Prov. 'T is pity of him.
Exeunt.

Scene IV. *A room in Angelo's house.*

Enter *Angelo.*

Ang. When I would pray and think, I think and pray
To several subjects: heaven hath my empty words,
Whilst my invention, hearing not my tongue,
Anchors on Isabel; heaven in my mouth,
As if I did but only chew his name,
And in my heart the strong and swelling evil
Of my conception. The state, whereon I studied,
Is like a good thing, being often read,
Grown sere and tedious; yea, my gravity,
Wherein—let no man hear me—I take pride,
Could I with boot change for an idle plume,
Which the air beats for vain. O place, O form,
How often dost thou with thy case, thy habit,
Wrench awe from fools and tie the wiser souls
To thy false seeming! Blood, thou art blood.
Let 's write "good angel" on the devil's horn;
'T is not the devil's crest.

Enter a *Servant.*

How now! who 's there?
Serv. One Isabel, a sister, desires access to you.
Ang. Teach her the way. [*Exit Serv.*] O heavens!
Why does my blood thus muster to my heart,
Making both it unable for itself,
And dispossessing all my other parts
Of necessary fitness?
So play the foolish throngs with one that swounds,
Come all to help him, and so stop the air
By which he should revive; and even so
The general subject to a well-wish'd king
Quit their own part, and in obsequious fondness
Crowd to his presence, where their untaught love
Must needs appear offence.

Enter *Isabella.*

How now, fair maid?
Isab. I am come to know your pleasure.
Ang. That you might know it, would much better please me
Than to demand what 't is. Your brother cannot live.
Isab. Even so. Heaven keep your honour!
Ang. Yet may he live a while; and, it may be,
As long as you or I: yet he must die.
Isab. Under your sentence?
Ang. Yea.
Isab. When, I beseech you? that in his reprieve,
Longer or shorter, he may be so fitted
That his soul sicken not.
Ang. Ha! fie, these filthy vices! It were as good
To pardon him that hath from nature stol'n
A man already made, as to remit
Their saucy sweetness that do coin Heaven's image
In stamps that are forbid: 't is all as easy
Falsely to take away a life true made
As to put metal in restrained means
To make a false one.
Isab. 'T is set down so in heaven, but not in earth.
Ang. Say you so? Then I shall pose you quickly.
Which had you rather, that the most just law
Now took your brother's life; or, to redeem him,
Give up your body to such sweet uncleanness
As she that he hath stain'd?
Isab. Sir, believe this,
I had rather give my body than my soul.
Ang. I talk not of your soul; our compell'd sins
Stand more for number than for accompt.
Isab. How say you?

33. **spare,** i.e., refrain from offending. 38. **instruction,** i.e., spiritual advice. **Scene iv: 2. several subjects,** different objects. 3. **invention,** thinking. 5. **his,** its. 12. **beats for vain,** fans to no purpose. 13. **case,** outward show. 16-17. **Let's write . . . crest,** even if we write "good angel," as a badge or cognizance on the devil's horn, it is not the true "crest," i.e., device, of Satan. 19. **Teach,** show. 20. **muster,** rush, assemble.

22. **parts,** organs. 24. **swounds,** swoons. 27. **general subject,** subjects. 28. **part,** tasks. 40. **fitted,** prepared (by a priest). 46. **stamps,** dies (for making coins). 46. **'t is all as easy,** i.e., it is no worse. 48. **restrained,** forbidden. 51. **pose,** puzzle with a question. 58. Are rather numbered than charged against us.

Ang. Nay, I 'll not warrant that; for I can speak
Against the thing I say. Answer to this:
I, now the voice of the recorded law,
Pronounce a sentence on your brother's life:
Might there not be a charity in sin
To save this brother's life?
Isab. Please you to do 't,
I 'll take it as a peril to my soul,
It is no sin at all, but charity.
Ang. Pleas'd you to do 't at peril of your soul,
Were equal poise of sin and charity.
Isab. That I do beg his life, if it be sin,
Heaven let me bear it! You granting of my suit,
If that be sin, I 'll make it my morn prayer
To have it added to the faults of mine,
And nothing of your answer.
Ang. Nay, but hear me;
Your sense pursues not mine: either you are ignorant,
Or seem so craftily; and that 's not good.
Isab. Let me be ignorant, and in nothing good,
But graciously to know I am no better.
Ang. Thus wisdom wishes to appear most bright
When it doth tax itself; as these black masks
Proclaim an enshield beauty ten times louder
Than beauty could, display'd. But mark me:
To be received plain, I 'll speak more gross:
Your brother is to die.
Isab. So.
Ang. And his offence is so, as it appears,
Accountant to the law upon that pain.
Isab. True.
Ang. Admit no other way to save his life,—
As I subscribe not that, nor any other,
But in the loss of question,—that you, his sister,
Finding yourself desir'd of such a person,
Whose credit with the judge, or own great place,
Could fetch your brother from the manacles
Of the all-binding law; and that there were
No earthly mean to save him, but that either
You must lay down the treasures of your body
To this supposed, or else to let him suffer;
What would you do?
Isab. As much for my poor brother as myself:
That is, were I under the terms of death,
Th' impression of keen whips I 'd wear as rubies,
And strip myself to death, as to a bed
That longings have been sick for, ere I 'd yield
My body up to shame.
Ang. Then must your brother die.
Isab. And 't were the cheaper way.
Better it were a brother died at once,
Than that a sister, by redeeming him,
Should die for ever.
Ang. Were not you then as cruel as the sentence
That you have slander'd so?
Isab. Ignomy in ransom and free pardon
Are of two houses: lawful mercy
Is nothing kin to foul redemption.
Ang. You seem'd of late to make the law a tyrant;
And rather prov'd the sliding of your brother
A merriment than a vice.
Isab. O, pardon me, my lord, it oft falls out,
To have what we would have, we speak not what we mean.
I something do excuse the thing I hate,
For his advantage that I dearly love.
Ang. We are all frail.
Isab. Else let my brother die,
If not a fedary, but only he
Owe and succeed thy weakness.
Ang. Nay, women are frail too.
Isab. Ay, as the glasses where they view themselves;
Which are as easy broke as they make forms.
Women! Help, Heaven! men their creation mar
In profiting by them. Nay, call us ten times frail;
For we are soft as our complexions are,
And credulous to false prints.
Ang. I think it well;
And from this testimony of your own sex,—
Since I suppose we are made to be no stronger
Than faults may shake our frames,—let me be bold:
I do arrest your words. Be that you are,
That is, a woman; if you be more, you 're none;
If you be one (as you are well express'd
By all external warrants) show it now,
By putting on the destin'd livery.

59. I'll not warrant that, I'll not be surety for that. **68. poise,** weight. **73. answer,** responsibility. **79. tax,** censure. **80. enshield,** hidden. **86. Accountant,** accountable. **pain,** punishment. **88. Admit,** suppose (there were). **89-90. As . . . question,** I grant that or any other supposition only for the sake of argument.

111. Ignomy, ignominy. **115. sliding,** backsliding, sinning. **121-3. Else . . . weakness,** otherwise (if we are not all frail) let my brother die, since in that case no confederate but he alone owns and inherits man's weakness. **127. creation,** i.e., women's natures. **134. arrest,** seize upon. **138. destin'd livery,** i.e., frailty.

Isab. I have no tongue but one; gentle my lord,
Let me entreat you speak the former language.
Ang. Plainly conceive, I love you.
Isab. My brother did love Juliet,
And you tell me that he shall die for it.
Ang. He shall not, Isabel, if you give me love.
Isab. I know your virtue hath a license in 't,
Which seems a little fouler than it is,
To pluck on others.
Ang. Believe me, on mine honour,
My words express my purpose.
Isab. Ha! little honour to be much believ'd,
And most pernicious purpose! Seeming, seeming!
I will proclaim thee, Angelo; look for 't!
Sign me a present pardon for my brother,
Or with an outstretch'd throat I 'll tell the world aloud
What man thou art.
Ang. Who will believe thee, Isabel?
My unsoil'd name, th' austereness of my life,
My vouch against you, and my place i' th' state,
Will so your accusation overweigh,
That you shall stifle in your own report
And smell of calumny. I have begun,
And now I give my sensual race the rein.
Fit thy consent to my sharp appetite;
Lay by all nicety and prolixious blushes
That banish what they sue for; redeem thy brother
By yielding up thy body to my will;
Or else he must not only die the death,
But thy unkindness shall his death draw out
To lingering sufferance. Answer me to-morrow,
Or, by the affection that now guides me most,
I 'll prove a tyrant to him. As for you,
Say what you can, my false o'erweighs your true. *Exit.*
Isab. To whom should I complain? Did I tell this,
Who would believe me? O perilous mouths,
That bear in them one and the self-same tongue,
Either of condemnation or approof;
Bidding the law make curtsy to their will;
Hooking both right and wrong to th' appetite,
To follow as it draws. I 'll to my brother.
Though he hath fall'n by prompture of the blood,
Yet hath he in him such a mind of honour
That, had he twenty heads to tender down
On twenty bloody blocks, he 'd yield them up,
Before his sister should her body stoop
To such abhorr'd pollution.
Then, Isabel, live chaste, and, brother, die;
More than our brother is our chastity.
I 'll tell him yet of Angelo's request,
And fit his mind to death, for his soul's rest.
Exit.

ACT III. Scene I. *A room in the prison.*

Enter *Duke* disguised, *Claudio*, and *Provost*.

Duke. So then you hope of pardon from Lord Angelo?
Claud. The miserable have no other medicine
But only hope.
I 've hope to live, and am prepar'd to die.
Duke. Be absolute for death; either death or life
Shall thereby be the sweeter. Reason thus with life:
If I do lose thee, I do lose a thing
That none but fools would keep: a breath thou art,
Servile to all the skyey influences,
That dost this habitation where thou keep'st
Hourly afflict. Merely, thou art Death's fool;
For him thou labour'st by thy flight to shun
And yet runn'st ward him still. Thou art not noble;
For all th' accommodations that thou bear'st
Are nurs'd by baseness: thou 'rt by no means valiant;
For thou dost fear the soft and tender fork
Of a poor worm: thy best of rest is sleep,
And that thou oft provok'st; yet grossly fear'st

140. former language, previous sentiments. **147. pluck on,** stir up, incite. **156. vouch,** testimony. **Act III. Scene i: 5. absolute,** resolved.

162. prolixious, tiresome and superfluous. **167. sufferance,** suffering. **174. approof,** approval. **178. prompture,** prompting, instigation. **180. tender,** offer. **182. stoop,** yield. **186. yet,** nevertheless. **Act III, Scene i: 9. skyey,** i.e., of the stars. **10. keep'st,** livest. **14. accommodations,** comforts. **15. nurs'd by baseness,** provided by the base-born. **16. fork,** forked tongue.

Thy death, which is no more. Thou art not thyself;
For thou exists on many a thousand grains
That issue out of dust. Happy thou art not;
For what thou hast not, still thou striv'st to get,
And what thou hast, forget'st. Thou art not certain;
For thy complexion shifts to strange effects,
After the moon. If thou art rich, thou 'rt poor;
For, like an ass whose back with ingots bows,
Thou bear'st thy heavy riches but a journey,
And Death unloads thee. Friend hast thou none;
For thine own bowels, which do call thee sire,
The mere effusion of thy proper loins,
Do curse the gout, serpigo, and the rheum,
For ending thee no sooner. Thou hast nor youth nor age,
But as it were an after-dinner's sleep,
Dreaming on both; for all thy blessed youth
Becomes as aged, and doth beg the alms
Of palsied Eld; and when thou art old and rich,
Thou hast neither heat, affection, limb, nor beauty,
To make thy riches pleasant. What 's yet in this
That bears the name of life? Yet in this life
Lie hid moe thousand deaths; yet death we fear,
That makes these odds all even.

Claud. I humbly thank you.
To sue to live, I find I seek to die;
And, seeking death, find life. Let it come on.

Isab. [*Within.*] What, ho! Peace here; grace and good company!

Prov. Who 's there? Come in; the wish deserves a welcome.

Duke. Dear sir, ere long I 'll visit you again.

Claud. Most holy sir, I thank you.

Enter *Isabella.*

Isab. My business 's a word or two with Claudio.

Prov. And very welcome. Look, signior, here 's your sister.

Duke. Provost, a word with you.

Prov. As many as you please.

Duke. Bring me to hear them speak, where I may be concealed.

Exeunt Duke and Provost.

Claud. Now, sister, what 's the comfort?

Isab. Why,
As all comforts are; most good, most good indeed.
Lord Angelo, having affairs to heaven,
Intends you for his swift ambassador,
Where you shall be an everlasting leiger;
Therefore your best appointment make with speed,
To-morrow you set on.

Claud. Is there no remedy?

Isab. None but such remedy as, to save a head,
To cleave a heart in twain.

Claud. But is there any?

Isab. Yes, brother, you may live.
There is a devilish mercy in the judge,
If you 'll implore it, that will free your life,
But fetter you till death.

Claud. Perpetual durance?

Isab. Ay, just; perpetual durance, a restraint,
Though all the world's vastidity you had,
To a determin'd scope.

Claud. But in what nature?

Isab. In such a one as, you consenting to 't,
Would bark your honour from that trunk you bear,
And leave you naked.

Claud. Let me know the point.

Isab. O, I do fear thee, Claudio; and I quake,
Lest thou a feverous life shouldst entertain,
And six or seven winters more respect
Than a perpetual honour. Dar'st thou die?
The sense of death is most in apprehension;
And the poor beetle, that we tread upon,
In corporal sufferance finds a pang as great
As when a giant dies.

Claud. Why give you me this shame?
Think you I can a resolution fetch
From flow'ry tenderness? If I must die,
I will encounter darkness as a bride,
And hug it in mine arms.

Isab. There spake my brother; there my father's grave
Did utter forth a voice. Yes, thou must die.
Thou art too noble to conserve a life
In base appliances. This outward-sainted deputy,
Whose settled visage and deliberate word
Nips youth i' th' head and follies doth enmew
As falcon doth the fowl, is yet a devil;

24. complexion, outward appearance. **25. moon,** symbol of instability. **29. bowels,** i.e., children. **31. serpigo,** skin disease. **rheum,** rheumatism. **35-6. Becomes . . . Eld,** is like age and begs alms like palsied old age. **37. limb,** bodily vigor.

59. leiger, ambassador. **60. appointment,** preparation. **69. vastidity,** vastness. **70. determin'd scope,** set limits. **75. entertain,** i.e., in your mind. **78. apprehension,** imagination. **82. fetch,** derive. **83. From . . . tenderness,** i.e., from tenderness soft as flowers. **89. In base appliances,** by base remedies or means. **90. settled,** composed, grave. **91. enmew,** keep in, coop up. Fear of the falcon makes chickens stay indoors.

His filth within being cast, he would appear
A pond as deep as hell.
Claud. The prenzie Angelo!
Isab. O, 't is the cunning livery of hell,
The damned'st body to invest and cover
In prenzie guards! Dost thou think, Claudio?
If I would yield him my virginity,
Thou mightst be freed.
Claud. O heavens! it cannot be.
Isab. Yes, he would give 't thee, from this rank offence,
So to offend him still. This night 's the time
That I should do what I abhor to name,
Or else thou diest to-morrow.
Claud. Thou shalt not do 't.
Isab. O, were it but my life,
I 'd throw it down for your deliverance
As frankly as a pin.
Claud. Thanks, dear Isabel.
Isab. Be ready, Claudio, for your death to-morrow.
Claud. Yes. Has he affections in him,
That thus can make him bite the law by th' nose,
When he would force it? Sure, it is no sin;
Or of the deadly seven it is the least.
Isab. Which is the least?
Claud. If it were damnable, he being so wise,
Why would he for the momentary trick
Be perdurably fin'd? O Isabel!
Isab. What says my brother?
Claud. Death is a fearful thing.
Isab. And shamed life a hateful.
Claud. Ay, but to die, and go we know not where;
To lie in cold obstruction and to rot;
This sensible warm motion to become
A kneaded clod, and the delighted spirit
To bathe in fiery floods, or to reside
In thrilling region of thick-ribbed ice;
To be imprison'd in the viewless winds,
And blown with restless violence round about
The pendent world; or to be worse than worst
Of those that lawless and incertain thought
Imagine howling; 't is too horrible!
The weariest and most loathed worldly life
That age, ache, penury, and imprisonment
Can lay on nature is a paradise
To what we fear of death.
Isab. Alas, alas!
Claud. Sweet sister, let me live.
What sin you do to save a brother's life,
Nature dispenses with the deed so far
That it becomes a virtue.
Isab. O you beast!
O faithless coward! O dishonest wretch!
Wilt thou be made a man out of my vice?
Is 't not a kind of incest, to take life
From thine own sister's shame? What should I think?
Heaven shield my mother play'd my father fair!
For such a warped slip of wilderness
Ne'er issu'd from his blood. Take my defiance!
Die, perish! Might but my bending down
Reprieve thee from thy fate, it should proceed.
I 'll pray a thousand prayers for thy death,
No word to save thee.
Claud. Nay, hear me, Isabel.
Isab. O, fie, fie, fie!
Thy sin 's not accidental, but a trade.
Mercy to thee would prove itself a bawd;
'T is best that thou diest quickly.
Claud. O hear me, Isabella!

Re-enter *Duke*.

Duke. Vouchsafe a word, young sister, but one word.
Isab. What is your will?
Duke. Might you dispense with your leisure, I would by and by have some speech with you: the satisfaction I would require is likewise your own benefit.

Isab. I have no superfluous leisure; my stay must be stolen out of other affairs; but I will attend you a while. *Walks apart.*

Duke. Son, I have overheard what hath passed between you and your sister. Angelo had never the purpose to corrupt her; only he hath made an assay of her virtue to practise his judgement with the disposition of natures. She, having the truth of honour in her, hath made him that gracious denial which he is most glad to receive: I am confessor to Angelo, and I know this to be true; therefore prepare yourself to death: do not satisfy your resolution with hopes that are fallible. To-morrow you must die; go to your knees and make ready.

Claud. Let me ask my sister pardon. I am so out of love with life that I will sue to be rid of it.

Duke. Hold you there! Farewell. [*Exit Claudio.*] Provost, a word with you!

Re-enter *Provost*.

Prov. What 's your will, father?
Duke. That now you are come, you will be gone: leave me a while with the maid. My

93. **cast**, cast up, vomitted. 94. **prenzie**, prim, demure. 97. **guards**, trappings. 101. **So . . . still**, so that you can sin again. 106. **frankly**, freely. 109. **bite . . . nose**, mock the law. 110. **force**, enforce. 114. **trick**, foolish act. 115. **perdurably fin'd**, everlastingly punished. 119. **obstruction**, stagnation. 121. **kneaded**, i.e., like dough. **delighted**, capable of giving delight. 123. **thrilling**, i.e., with cold.

135. **dispenses**, excuses. 141. **shield**, forbid. 169-70. **satisfy your resolution**, sustain your courage. 171. **fallible**, false.

mind promises with my habit no loss shall touch her by my company.

Prov. In good time.

Exit Provost. Isabella comes forward.

Duke. The hand that hath made you fair hath made you good; the goodness that is cheap in beauty makes beauty brief in goodness; but grace, being the soul of your complexion, shall keep the body of it ever fair. The assault that Angelo hath made to you, fortune hath conveyed to my understanding; and, but that frailty hath examples for his falling, I should wonder at Angelo. How will you do to content this substitute, and to save your brother?

Isab. I am now going to resolve him: I had rather my brother die by the law than my son should be unlawfully born. But, O, how much is the good Duke deceived in Angelo! If ever he return and I can speak to him, I will open my lips in vain, or discover his government.

Duke. That shall not be much amiss; yet, as the matter now stands, he will avoid your accusation; he made trial of you only. Therefore fasten your ear on my advisings. To the love I have in doing good a remedy presents itself. I do make myself believe that you may most uprighteously do a poor wronged lady a merited benefit, redeem your brother from the angry law, do no stain to your own gracious person, and much please the absent Duke, if peradventure he shall ever return to have hearing of this business.

Isab. Let me hear you speak farther: I have spirit to do anything that appears not foul in the truth of my spirit.

Duke. Virtue is bold, and goodness never fearful. Have you not heard speak of Mariana, the sister of Frederick, the great soldier who miscarried at sea?

Isab. I have heard of the lady, and good words went with her name.

Duke. She should this Angelo have married; was affianced to her by oath, and the nuptial appointed; between which time of the contract and limit of the solemnity, her brother Frederick was wrecked at sea, having in that perished vessel the dowry of his sister. But mark how heavily this befell to the poor gentlewoman. There she lost a noble and renowned brother, in his love toward her ever most kind and natural; with him, the portion and sinew of her fortune, her marriage-dowry; with both, her combinate husband, this well-seeming Angelo.

Isab. Can this be so? Did Angelo so leave her?

Duke. Left her in her tears, and dried not one of them with his comfort; swallowed his vows whole, pretending in her discoveries of dishonour; in few, bestowed her on her own lamentation, which she yet wears for his sake; and he, a marble to her tears, is washed with them, but relents not.

Isab. What a merit were it in death to take this poor maid from the world! What corruption in this life, that it will let this man live! But how out of this can she avail?

Duke. It is a rupture that you may easily heal; and the cure of it not only saves your brother, but keeps you from dishonour in doing it.

Isab. Show me how, good father.

Duke. This forenamed maid hath yet in her the continuance of her first affection; his unjust unkindness, that in all reason should have quenched her love, hath like an impediment in the current, made it more violent and unruly. Go you to Angelo; answer his requiring with a plausible obedience; agree with his demands to the point; only refer yourself to this advantage, first, that your stay with him may not be long; that the time may have all shadow and silence in it; and the place answer to convenience. This being granted in course,—and now follows all,—we shall advise this wronged maid to stead up your appointment, go in your place: if the encounter acknowledge itself hereafter, it may compel him to her recompense; and here, by this is your brother saved, your honour untainted, the poor Mariana advantaged, and the corrupt deputy scaled. The maid will I frame and make fit for his attempt. If you think well to carry this as you may, the doubleness of the benefit defends the deceit from reproof. What think you of it?

Isab. The image of it gives me content already; and I trust it will grow to a most prosperous perfection.

Duke. It lies much in your holding up. Haste you speedily to Angelo: if for this night he entreat you to his bed, give him promise of satisfaction. I will presently to Saint Luke's; there, at the moated grange, resides this dejected Mariana: at that place call upon me; and dispatch with Angelo, that it may be quickly.

Isab. I thank you for this comfort. Fare you well, good father.

Exeunt.

183. In good time, very well. **199. discover,** reveal. **government,** conduct. **218. miscarried,** perished. **232. combinate,** betrothed.

243. avail, profit. **254. refer,** have recourse. **255. advantage,** favorable condition. **257. shadow,** darkness. **258. answer to convenience,** agree with propriety. **260. stead up,** replace (you in). **266. scaled,** weighed. **267. frame and make fit,** instruct and prepare. **268. carry,** do, execute. **270. image,** thought. **277. moated grange,** farm house surrounded by a moat. **279. dispatch,** come to an agreement.

Scene II. *The street before the prison.*

Enter on one side, *Duke,* disguised; on the other, *Elbow* and Officers with *Pompey,* the Clown.

Elb. Nay, if there be no remedy for it but that you will needs buy and sell men and women like beasts, we shall have all the world drink brown and white bastard.

Duke. O heavens! what stuff is here?

Pom. 'T was never merry world since, of two usuries, the merriest was put down, and the worser allowed by order of law a furred gown to keep him warm; and furred with fox on lambskins too, to signify that craft, being richer than innocency, stands for the facing.

Elb. Come your way, sir. 'Bless you, good father friar.

Duke. And you, good brother father. What offence
Hath this man made you, sir?

Elb. Marry, sir, he hath offended the law; and, sir, we take him to be a thief too, sir, for we have found upon him, sir, a strange picklock, which we have sent to the deputy.

Duke. Fie, sirrah! a bawd, a wicked bawd!
The evil that thou causest to be done,
That is thy means to live. Do thou but think
What 't is to cram a maw or clothe a back
From such a filthy vice; say to thyself,
From their abominable and beastly touches
I drink, I eat, array myself, and live.
Canst thou believe thy living is a life,
So stinkingly depending? Go mend, go mend.

Pom. Indeed, it does stink in some sort, sir; but yet, sir, I would prove—

Duke. Nay, if the devil have given thee proofs for sin,
Thou wilt prove his. Take him to prison, officer:
Correction and instruction must both work
Ere this rude beast will profit.

Elb. He must before the deputy, sir; he has given him warning: the deputy cannot abide a whoremaster: if he be a whoremonger, and comes before him, he were as good go a mile on his errand.

Duke. That we were all, as some would seem to be,
Free from our faults, as faults from seeming, free!

Enter *Lucio.*

Elb. His neck will come to your waist,—a cord, sir.

Pom. I spy comfort; I cry bail. Here 's a gentleman and a friend of mine.

Lucio. How now, noble Pompey! What, at the wheels of Cæsar? Art thou led in triumph? What, is there none of Pygmalion's images, newly made woman, to be had now, for putting the hand in the pocket and extracting it clutched? What reply, ha? What say'st thou to this tune, matter, and method? Is 't not drowned i' th' last rain, ha? What say'st thou, Trot? Is the world as it was, man? Which is the way? Is it sad, and few words? or how? The trick of it?

Duke. Still thus, and thus; still worse!

Lucio. How doth my dear morsel, thy mistress? Procures she still, ha?

Pom. Troth, sir, she hath eaten up all her beef, and she is herself in the tub.

Lucio. Why, 't is good; it is the right of it; it must be so. Ever your fresh whore and your powdered bawd; an unshunned consequence; it must be so. Art going to prison, Pompey?

Pom. Yes, faith, sir.

Lucio. Why, 't is not amiss, Pompey: farewell: go, say I sent thee thither. For debt, Pompey? or how?

Elb. For being a bawd, for being a bawd.

Lucio. Well, then, imprison him: if imprisonment be the due of a bawd, why, 't is his right. Bawd is he doubtless, and of antiquity too; bawd-born. Farewell, good Pompey. Commend me to the prison, Pompey. You will turn good husband now, Pompey; you will keep the house.

Pom. I hope, sir, your good worship will be my bail.

Lucio. No, indeed, will I not, Pompey; it is not the wear. I will pray, Pompey, to increase your bondage: if you take it not patiently, why, your mettle is the more. Adieu, trusty Pompey. 'Bless you, friar.

Duke. And you.

Lucio. Does Bridget paint still, Pompey, ha?

Elb. Come your ways, sir; come.

Pom. You will not bail me, then, sir?

Lucio. Then, Pompey, nor now. What news abroad, friar? what news?

Elb. Come your ways, sir; come.

Lucio. Go to kennel, Pompey; go. [*Exeunt Elbow, Pompey, and Officers.*] What news, friar, of the Duke?

Scene ii: 4. bastard, a Spanish wine. **7. two usuries,** i.e., procuring and money-lending. **28. So stinkingly depending,** supported as it is by such a disgusting business.

47. Pygmalion's, his statue of a beautiful woman was given life by Aphrodite. **50. tune,** humor. **52. Trot,** decrepit old woman. **59. tub,** (1) sweating tub for treating disease, (2) salting tub for curing beef. **62. powdered,** salted. **unshunned,** inevitable. **78. wear,** fashion.

Lucio gossips c̄ Duke about the deputy + also about the "absent" Duke + mentions Claudio

Duke. I know none: can you tell me of any?

Lucio. Some say he is with the Emperor of Russia; other some, he is in Rome; but where is he, think you?

Duke. I know not where; but wheresoever, I wish him well.

Lucio. It was a mad fantastical trick of him to steal from the state, and usurp the beggary he was never born to. Lord Angelo dukes it well in his absence; he puts transgression to 't.

Duke. He does well in 't.

Lucio. A little more lenity to lechery would do no harm in him: something too crabbed that way, friar.

Duke. It is too general a vice, and severity must cure it.

Lucio. Yes, in good sooth, the vice is of a great kindred, it is well allied; but it is impossible to extirp it quite, friar, till eating and drinking be put down. They say this Angelo was not made by man and woman after this downright way of creation: is it true, think you?

Duke. How should he be made, then?

Lucio. Some report a sea-maid spawned him; some that he was begot between two stock-fishes. But it is certain that when he makes water his urine is congealed ice; that I know to be true: and he is a motion generative; that 's infallible.

Duke. You are pleasant, sir, and speak apace.

Lucio. Why, what a ruthless thing is this in him, for the rebellion of a codpiece to take away the life of a man! Would the Duke that is absent have done this? Ere he would have hanged a man for the getting a hundred bastards, he would have paid for the nursing a thousand. He had some feeling of the sport; he knew the service, and that instructed him to mercy.

Duke. I never heard the absent Duke much detected for women: he was not inclined that way.

Lucio. O, sir, you are deceived.

Duke. 'T is not possible.

Lucio. Who, not the Duke? Yes, your beggar of fifty; and his use was to put a ducat in her clack-dish: the Duke had crotchets in him. He would be drunk too; that let me inform you.

Duke. You do him wrong, surely.

Lucio. Sir, I was an inward of his. A shy fellow was the Duke; and I believe I know the cause of his withdrawing.

Duke. What, I prithee, might be the cause?

Lucio. No, pardon; 't is a secret must be locked within the teeth and the lips: but this I can let you understand, the greater file of the subject held the Duke to be wise.

Duke. Wise! Why, no question but he was.

Lucio. A very superficial, ignorant, unweighing fellow.

Duke. Either this is envy in you, folly, or mistaking. The very stream of his life and the business he hath helmed must upon a warranted need give him a better proclamation. Let him be but testimonied in his own bringings-forth, and he shall appear to the envious a scholar, a statesman, and a soldier. Therefore you speak unskilfully; or if your knowledge be more it is much darkened in your malice.

Lucio. Sir, I know him, and I love him.

Duke. Love talks with better knowledge, and knowledge with dearer love.

Lucio. Come, sir, I know what I know.

Duke. I can hardly believe that, since you know not what you speak. But, if ever the Duke return, as our prayers are he may, let me desire you to make your answer before him: if it be honest you have spoke, you have courage to maintain it. I am bound to call upon you; and, I pray you, your name?

Lucio. Sir, my name is Lucio; well known to the Duke.

Duke. He shall know you better, sir, if I may live to report you.

Lucio. I fear you not.

Duke. O, you hope the Duke will return no more; or you imagine me too unhurtful an opposite. But indeed I can do you little harm; you 'll forswear this again.

Lucio. I 'll be hanged first; thou art deceived in me, friar. But no more of this. Canst thou tell if Claudio die to-morrow or no?

Duke. Why should he die, sir?

Lucio. Why? For filling a bottle with a tun-dish. I would the Duke we talk of were returned again. This ungenitured agent will unpeople the province with continency. Sparrows must not build in his house-eaves, because they are lecherous. The Duke yet would have dark deeds darkly answered; he would never bring them to light: would he

103. lenity to, mildness toward. **110. extirp,** extirpate. **117. stock-fishes,** dried cod. **118. motion generative,** a puppet, capable of procreation. **130. detected for,** accused of. **135. clack-dish,** wooden dish carried by beggars. They clicked the cover to attract attention. **138. inward,** intimate friend.

144. greater file, larger number. **148. envy,** malice. **150. helmed,** steered, directed. **upon . . . need,** if surety is needed. **152. testimonied,** witnessed, attested. **155. unskilfully,** without knowledge. **176. opposite,** opponent. **183. tun-dish,** funnel. **184. ungenitured,** impotent.

were returned! Marry, this Claudio is condemned foı untrussing. Farewell, good friar; I prithee, pray for me. The Duke, I say to thee again, would eat mutton on Fridays. He 's not past it; yet, and I say 't to thee, he would mouth with a beggar, though she smelt brown bread and garlic. Say that I said so. Farewell. *Exit.*

Duke. No might nor greatness in mortality
Can censure scape; back-wounding calumny
The whitest virtue strikes. What king so strong
Can tie the gall up in the slanderous tongue?
But who comes here?

Enter *Escalus, Provost,* and Officers with *Mistress Overdone* the Bawd.

Escal. Go; away with her to prison!

Over. Good my lord, be good to me; your honour is accounted a merciful man: good my lord!

Escal. Double and treble admonition, and still forfeit in the same kind! This would make mercy swear and play the tyrant.

Prov. A bawd of eleven years' continuance, may it please your honour.

Over. My lord, this is one Lucio's information against me. Mistress Kate Keepdown was with child by him in the Duke's time: he promised her marriage: his child is a year and a quarter old, come Philip and Jacob: I have kept it myself, and see how he goes about to abuse me!

Escal. That fellow is a fellow of much license; let him be called before us. Away with her to prison! Go to; no more words. [*Exeunt Officers with Mistress Overdone.*] Provost, my brother Angelo will not be altered; Claudio must die to-morrow. Let him be furnished with divines, and have all charitable preparation. If my brother wrought by my pity, it should not be so with him.

Prov. So please you, this friar hath been with him, and advised him for the entertainment of death.

Escal. Good even, good father.

Duke. Bliss and goodness on you!

Escal. Of whence are you?

Duke. Not of this country, though my chance is now
To use it for my time: I am a brother
Of gracious order, late come from the See
In special business from his Holiness.

Escal. What news abroad i' th' world?

Duke. None, but that there is so great a fever on goodness, that the dissolution of it must cure it. Novelty is only in request; and it is as dangerous to be aged in any kind of course, as it is virtuous to be inconstant in any undertaking. There is scarce truth enough alive to make societies secure; but security enough to make fellowships accurst. Much upon this riddle runs the wisdom of the world. This news is old enough, yet it is every day's news. I pray you, sir, of what disposition was the Duke?

Escal. One that, above all other strifes, contended especially to know himself.

Duke. What pleasure was he given to?

Escal. Rather rejoicing to see another merry, than merry at anything which professed to make him rejoice; a gentleman of all temperance. But leave we him to his events, with a prayer they may prove prosperous; and let me desire to know how you find Claudio prepared. I am made to understand that you have lent him visitation.

Duke. He professes to have received no sinister measure from his judge, but most willingly humbles himself to the determination of justice; yet had he framed to himself, by the instruction of his frailty, many deceiving promises of life, which I by my good leisure have discredited to him, and now is he resolved to die.

Escal. You have paid the heavens your function, and the prisoner the very debt of your calling. I have laboured for the poor gentleman to the extremest shore of my modesty; but my brother justice have I found so severe, that he hath forced me to tell him he is indeed Justice.

Duke. If his own life answer the straitness of his proceeding, it shall become him well; wherein if he chance to fail, he hath sentenced himself.

Escal. I am going to visit the prisoner Fare you well.

Duke. Peace be with you!

Exeunt Escalus and Provost.

He who the sword of heaven will bear
Should be as holy as severe;
Pattern in himself to know
Grace to stand, and virtue go;
More nor less to others paying
Than by self-offences weighing.
Shame to him whose cruel striking
Kills for faults of his own liking!

190. **untrussing,** undressing. 192. **mutton,** (1) meat, (2) a loose woman. 206. **forfeit in the same kind,** liable to punishment for the same offense. 214. **Philip and Jacob,** St. Philip's and St. James's day—May first. 231. **time,** present time. 232. **See,** i.e., of Rome.

236. **the dissolution of it,** its death. 240. **security,** suretyship, requests for surety. 241. **fellowships,** friendships. 253. **events,** affairs. 257. **sinister measure,** unjust dealing. 260. **instruction,** prompting. 261. **by . . . leisure,** by taking fit occasion to do so. 278. **go,** to go ahead.

Twice treble shame on Angelo,
To weed my vice and let his grow!
O, what may man within him hide,
Though angel on the outward side!
How may likeness made in crimes,
Making practice on the times,
To draw with idle spiders' strings
Most ponderous and substantial things!
Craft against vice I must apply.
With Angelo to-night shall lie
His old betrothed but despised;
So disguise shall, by the disguised,
Pay with falsehood false exacting,
And perform an old contracting. *Exit.*

ACT IV. SCENE I. *The moated grange.*

Enter *Mariana,* and Boy singing.

Song

Take, O, take those lips away,
That so sweetly were forsworn;
And those eyes, the break of day,
Lights that do mislead the morn;
But my kisses bring again, bring again;
Seals of love, but seal'd in vain, seal'd in vain.

Enter *Duke* disguised.

Mari. Break off thy song, and haste thee quick away.
Here comes a man of comfort, whose advice
Hath often still'd my brawling discontent.
Exit Boy.
I cry you mercy, sir; and well could wish
You had not found me here so musical.
Let me excuse me, and believe me so,
My mirth it much displeas'd, but pleas'd my woe.

Duke. 'T is good; though music oft hath such a charm
To make bad good, and good provoke to harm.
I pray you, tell me, hath anybody inquired for me here to-day? Much upon this time have I promised here to meet.

Mari. You have not been inquired after. I have sat here all day.

Enter *Isabella.*

Duke. I do constantly believe you. The time is come even now. I shall crave your forbearance a little: may be I will call upon you anon, for some advantage to yourself.

Mari. I am always bound to you. *Exit.*

Duke. Very well met, and well come.
What is the news from this good deputy?

Isab. He hath a garden circummur'd with brick,
Whose western side is with a vineyard back'd,
And to that vineyard is a planched gate,
That makes his opening with this bigger key.
This other doth command a little door
Which from the vineyard to the garden leads;
There have I made my promise
Upon the heavy middle of the night
To call upon him.

Duke. But shall you on your knowledge find this way?

Isab. I have ta'en a due and wary note upon 't.
With whispering and most guilty diligence,
In action all of precept, he did show me
The way twice o'er.

Duke. Are there no other tokens
Between you 'greed concerning her observance?

Isab. No, none, but only a repair i' th' dark;
And that I have possess'd him my most stay
Can be but brief; for I have made him know
I have a servant comes with me along,
That stays upon me, whose persuasion is
I come about my brother.

Duke. 'T is well borne up.
I have not yet made known to Mariana
A word of this. What, ho! within! come forth!

Re-enter *Mariana.*

I pray you, be acquainted with this maid;
She comes to do you good.

Isab. I do desire the like.

Duke. Do you persuade yourself that I respect you?

Mari. Good friar, I know you do, and have found it.

287-90. An obscure passage. The sense seems to be that "likeness," false seeming, composed of guilt within, makes a practise of drawing important things by the spider webs of craft. **288. Making practice,** using stratagems. **Act IV, Scene i: 9. brawling,** scolding. **13.** It did not please me to the point of making me mirthful, but soothed my woe. **17. Much . . . time,** at almost this exact time. **21. constantly,** certainly.

295. exacting, extortion. **Act IV, Scene i: 28. circummur'd,** walled about. **30. planched,** made of planks. **40. In . . . precept,** with gestures of instruction. **42. concerning her observance,** which concerns her (Mariana) to observe (in her role). **44. possess'd,** informed. **47. persuasion,** understanding of the matter. **48. borne up,** devised, planned.

Duke. Take, then, this your companion by the hand,
Who hath a story ready for your ear:
I shall attend your leisure; but make haste;
The vaporous night approaches.

Mari. Will 't please you walk aside?

Exeunt Mariana and Isabella.

Duke. O place and greatness! millions of false eyes
Are stuck upon thee: volumes of report
Run with these false and most contrarious quests
Upon thy doings; thousand escapes of wit
Make thee the father of their idle dream
And rack thee in their fancies.

Re-enter *Mariana* and *Isabella.*

Welcome, how agreed?

Isab. She 'll take the enterprise upon her, father,
If you advise it.

Duke. It is not my consent,
But my entreaty too.

Isab. Little have you to say
When you depart from him, but, soft and low,
"Remember now my brother."

Mari. Fear me not.

Duke. Nor, gentle daughter, fear you not at all.
He is your husband on a pre-contract:
To bring you thus together, 't is no sin,
Sith that the justice of your title to him
Doth flourish the deceit. Come, let us go.
Our corn 's to reap, for yet our tilth 's to sow.

Exeunt.

Scene II. *A room in the prison.*

Enter *Provost* and *Pompey* the Clown.

Prov. Come hither, sirrah. Can you cut off a man's head?

Pom. If the man be a bachelor, sir, I can; but if he be a married man, he 's his wife's head, and I can never cut off a woman's head.

Prov. Come, sir, leave me your snatches, and yield me a direct answer. To-morrow morning are to die Claudio and Barnardine: here is in our prison a common executioner, who in his office lacks a helper. If you will take it on you to assist him, it shall redeem you from your gyves; if not, you shall have your full time of imprisonment, and your deliverance with an unpitied whipping, for you have been a notorious bawd.

Pom. Sir, I have been an unlawful bawd time out of mind; but yet I will be content to be a lawful hangman. I would be glad to receive some instruction from my fellow partner.

Prov. What, ho! Abhorson! Where 's Abhorson, there?

Enter *Abhorson.*

Abhor. Do you call, sir?

Prov. Sirrah, here 's a fellow will help you to-morrow in your execution: if you think it meet, compound with him by the year, and let him abide here with you; if not, use him for the present and dismiss him: he cannot plead his estimation with you; he hath been a bawd.

Abhor. A bawd, sir? Fie upon him! he will discredit our mystery.

Prov. Go to, sir; you weigh equally. A feather will turn the scale. *Exit.*

Pom. Pray, sir, by your good favour,—for surely, sir, a good favour you have, but that you have a hanging look,—do you call, sir, your occupation a mystery?

Abhor. Ay, sir; a mystery.

Pom. Painting, sir, I have heard say, is a mystery; and your whores, sir, being members of my occupation, using painting, do prove my occupation a mystery; but what mystery there should be in hanging, if I should be hanged, I cannot imagine.

Abhor. Sir, it is a mystery.

Pom. Proof?

Abhor. Every true man's apparel fits your thief. If it be too little for your thief, your true man thinks it big enough; if it be too big for your thief, your thief thinks it little enough; so every true man's apparel fits your thief.

Re-enter *Provost.*

Prov. Are you agreed?

Pom. Sir, I will serve him, for I do find your hangman is a more penitent trade than your bawd; he doth oftener ask forgiveness.

Prov. You, sirrah, provide your block and your axe to-morrow four o'clock.

Abhor. Come on, bawd, I will instruct thee in my trade: follow.

Pom. I do desire to learn, sir; and I hope, if you have occasion to use me for your own turn, you shall find me yare; for truly sir, for your kindness I owe you a good turn. *Exit.*

60. place and greatness, place of greatness. **false,** deceitful. **61. stuck,** fixed. **62. Run with,** are spread by. **contrarious quests,** inconsistent inquiries. **63. escapes,** sallies. **65. rack,** stretch, distort. **75. flourish,** gloss over. **76. tilth 's,** tillage (plowed land) is. **Scene ii: 6. snatches,** scraps of wit. **9. common,** public.

12. gyves, fetters. **30. mystery,** profession. **61. yare,** quick.

Prov. Call hither Barnardine and Claudio.
Exit Abhorson.
Th' one has my pity; not a jot the other,
Being a murderer, though he were my brother.

Enter *Claudio*.

Look, here 's the warrant, Claudio, for thy death.
'T is now dead midnight, and by eight to-morrow
Thou must be made immortal. Where 's Barnardine?
Claud. As fast lock'd up in sleep as guiltless labour
When it lies starkly in the traveller's bones.
He will not wake.
Prov. Who can do good on him?
Well, go, prepare yourself. *Knocking within.*
But, hark, what noise?
Heaven give your spirit comfort! [*Exit Claudio.*] By and by.
I hope it is some pardon or reprieve
For the most gentle Claudio.

Enter *Duke* disguised.

Welcome, father.
Duke. The best and wholesom'st spirits of the night
Envelop you, good Provost! Who call'd here of late?
Prov. None, since the curfew rung.
Duke. Not Isabel?
Prov. No.
Duke. They will, then, ere 't be long.
Prov. What comfort is for Claudio?
Duke. There 's some in hope.
Prov. It is a bitter deputy.
Duke. Not so, not so; his life is parallel'd
Even with the stroke and line of his great justice:
He doth with holy abstinence subdue
That in himself which he spurs on his power
To qualify in others: were he meal'd with that
Which he corrects, then were he tyrannous;
But this being so, he 's just.
Knocking within.
Now are they come.
Exit Provost.
This is a gentle Provost: seldom when
The steeled gaoler is the friend of men.
Knocking within.
How now! what noise? That spirit 's possess'd with haste
That wounds th' unsisting postern with these strokes.

Re-enter *Provost*.

Prov. There he must stay until the officer
Arise to let him in. He is call'd up.
Duke. Have you no countermand for Claudio yet,
But he must die to-morrow?
Prov. None, sir, none.
Duke. As near the dawning, Provost, as it is,
You shall hear more ere morning.
Prov. Happily
You something know, yet I believe there comes
No countermand; no such example have we:
Besides, upon the very siege of justice
Lord Angelo hath to the public ear
Profess'd the contrary.

Enter a *Messenger*.

This is his lordship's man.
Duke. And here comes Claudio's pardon.
Mes. [*Giving a paper.*] My lord hath sent you this note; and by me this further charge, that you swerve not from the smallest article of it, neither in time, matter, or other circumstance. Good morrow; for, as I take it, it is almost day.
Prov. I shall obey him. *Exit Messenger.*
Duke. [*Aside.*] This is his pardon, purchas'd by such sin
For which the pardoner himself is in:
Hence hath offence his quick celerity,
When it is borne in high authority.
When vice makes mercy, mercy 's so extended,
That for the fault's love is th' offender friended.
Now, sir, what news?
Prov. I told you. Lord Angelo, belike thinking me remiss in mine office, awakens me with this unwonted putting-on; methinks strangely, for he hath not used it before.
Duke. Pray you, let 's hear.
Prov. [*Reads the letter.*]

"Whatsoever you may hear to the contrary, let Claudio be executed by four of the clock; and in the afternoon Barnardine. For my better satisfaction, let me have Claudio's head sent me by five. Let this be duly performed, with a thought that more depends on it than we must yet deliver. Thus fail not to do your office, as you will answer it at your peril."

What say you to this, sir?
Duke. What is that Barnardine who is to be executed in th' afternoon?
Prov. A Bohemian born, but here nursed

70. **starkly**, stiffly. 83. **stroke and line**, line marked out. 86. **qualify**, check. **meal'd**, tainted. 90. **steeled**, hardened. 92. **unsisting**, unresisting.

98. **Happily**, perhaps. 101. **siege**, seat. 113. **quick celerity**, swift speed. 118. **belike**, perhaps. 120. **putting-on**, instigation, goading.

up and bred; one that is a prisoner nine years old.

Duke. How came it that the absent Duke had not either delivered him to his liberty or executed him? I have heard it was ever his manner to do so.

Prov. His friends still wrought reprieves for him; and, indeed, his fact, till now in the government of Lord Angelo, came not to an undoubtful proof.

Duke. It is now apparent?

Prov. Most manifest, and not denied by himself.

Duke. Hath he borne himself penitently in prison? How seems he to be touched?

Prov. A man that apprehends death no more dreadfully but as a drunken sleep; careless, reckless, and fearless of what 's past, present, or to come; insensible of mortality, and desperately mortal.

Duke. He wants advice.

Prov. He will hear none: he hath evermore had the liberty of the prison; give him leave to escape hence, he would not; drunk many times a day, if not many days entirely drunk. We have very oft awaked him, as if to carry him to execution, and showed him a seeming warrant for it; it hath not moved him at all.

Duke. More of him anon. There is written in your brow, Provost, honesty and constancy: if I read it not truly, my ancient skill beguiles me; but, in the boldness of my cunning, I will lay myself in hazard. Claudio, whom here you have warrant to execute, is no greater forfeit to the law than Angelo who hath sentenced him. To make you understand this in a manifested effect, I crave but four days' respite; for the which you are to do me both a present and a dangerous courtesy.

Prov. Pray, sir, in what?

Duke. In the delaying death.

Prov. Alack, how may I do it, having the hour limited, and an express command, under penalty, to deliver his head in the view of Angelo? I may make my case as Claudio's, to cross this in the smallest.

Duke. By the vow of mine order I warrant you, if my instructions may be your guide. Let this Barnardine be this morning executed, and his head borne to Angelo.

Prov. Angelo hath seen them both, and will discover the favour.

Duke. O, death 's a great disguiser, and you may add to it. Shave the head, and tie the beard; and say it was the desire of the penitent to be so bared before his death: you know the course is common. If anything fall to you upon this, more than thanks and good fortune, by the saint whom I profess, I will plead against it with my life.

Prov. Pardon me, good father; it is against my oath.

Duke. Were you sworn to the Duke, or to the deputy?

Prov. To him, and to his substitutes.

Duke. You will think you have made no offence, if the Duke avouch the justice of your dealing?

Prov. But what likelihood is in that?

Duke. Not a resemblance, but a certainty. Yet since I see you fearful, that neither my coat, integrity, nor persuasion can with ease attempt you, I will go further than I meant, to pluck all fears out of you. Look you, sir, here is the hand and seal of the Duke: you know the character, I doubt not; and the signet is not strange to you.

Prov. I know them both.

Duke. The contents of this is the return of the Duke: you shall anon over-read it at your pleasure; where you shall find within these two days he will be here. This is a thing that Angelo knows not; for he this very day receives letters of strange tenour, perchance of the Duke's death, perchance entering into some monastery, but, by chance, nothing of what is here writ. Look, th' unfolding star calls up the shepherd. Put not yourself into amazement how these things should be: all difficulties are but easy when they are known. Call your executioner, and off with Barnardine's head. I will give him a present shrift and advise him for a better place. Yet you are amazed, but this shall absolutely resolve you. Come away; it is almost clear dawn.

Exeunt.

Scene III. *Another room in the prison.*

Enter *Pompey the Clown.*

Pom. I am as well acquainted here as I was in our house of profession: one would think it were Mistress Overdone's own house, for here be many of her old customers. First, here 's young Master Rash: he 's in for a commodity of brown paper and old ginger, nine-score and seventeen pounds; of which he

141. fact, crime. **153. desperately,** i.e., without hope of salvation. **165. hazard,** danger. **169. in . . . effect,** by means of manifest proof. **175. limited,** delimited, fixed. **179. warrant,** will be surety for. **185. discover the favour,** recognize the face.

208. character, writing. **218. unfolding star,** morning star, signal for turning the sheep out. **224. shrift,** confession and absolution. **Scene iii: 5. commodity,** quantity. The usurer, to make the loan appear a legitimate purchase, gave some articles of little value along with the money.

made five marks, ready money: marry, then ginger was not much in request, for the old women were all dead. Then is there here one Master Caper, at the suit of Master Three-pile the mercer, for some four suits of peach-coloured satin, which now peaches him a beggar. Then have we here young Dizie, and young Master Deep-vow, and Master Copper-spur, and Master Starve-lackey the rapier and dagger man, and young Drop-heir that killed lusty Pudding, and Master Forthright the tilter, and brave Master Shootie the great traveller, and wild Half-can that stabbed Pots, and, I think, forty more; all great doers in our trade, and are now "for the Lord's sake."

Enter *Abhorson.*

Abhor. Sirrah, bring Barnardine hither.

Pom. Master Barnardine! You must rise and be hanged, Master Barnardine!

Abhor. What, ho, Barnardine!

Bar. [*Within.*] A pox o' your throats! Who makes that noise there? What are you?

Pom. Your friends, sir; the hangman. You must be so good, sir, to rise and be put to death.

Bar. [*Within.*] Away, you rogue, away! I am sleepy.

Abhor. Tell him he must awake, and that quickly too.

Pom. Pray, Master Barnardine, awake till you are executed, and sleep afterwards.

Abhor. Go in to him, and fetch him out.

Pom. He is coming, sir, he is coming. I hear his straw rustle.

Enter *Barnardine.*

Abhor. Is the axe upon the block, sirrah?

Pom. Very ready, sir.

Bar. How now, Abhorson? What 's the news with you?

Abhor. Truly, sir, I would desire you to clap into your prayers; for, look you, the warrant 's come.

Bar. You rogue, I have been drinking all night; I am not fitted for 't.

Pom. O, the better, sir; for he that drinks all night, and is hanged betimes in the morning, may sleep the sounder all the next day.

Enter *Duke* disguised.

Abhor. Look you, sir; here comes your ghostly father: do we jest now, think you?

Duke. Sir, induced by my charity, and hearing how hastily you are to depart, I am come to advise you, comfort you, and pray with you.

Bar. Friar, not I: I have been drinking hard all night, and I will have more time to prepare me, or they shall beat out my brains with billets. I will not consent to die this day, that 's certain.

Duke. O, sir, you must; and therefore I beseech you
Look forward on the journey you shall go.

Bar. I swear I will not die to-day for any man's persuasion.

Duke. But hear you—

Bar. Not a word: if you have anything to say to me, come to my ward; for thence will not I to-day. *Exit.*

Re-enter *Provost.*

Duke. Unfit to live or die, O gravel heart!
After him, fellows; bring him to the block.
Exeunt Abhorson and Pompey.

Prov. Now sir, how do you find the prisoner?

Duke. A creature unprepar'd, unmeet for death;
And to transport him in the mind he is
Were damnable.

Prov. Here in the prison, father,
There died this morning of a cruel fever
One Ragozine, a most notorious pirate,
A man of Claudio's years; his beard and head
Just of his colour. What if we do omit
This reprobate till he were well inclin'd,
And satisfy the deputy with the visage
Of Ragozine, more like to Claudio?

Duke. O, 't is an accident that Heaven provides!
Dispatch it presently. The hour draws on
Prefix'd by Angelo. See this be done,
And sent according to command, whiles I
Persuade this rude wretch willingly to die.

Prov. This shall be done, good father, presently.
But Barnardine must die this afternoon;
And how shall we continue Claudio,
To save me from the danger that might come
If he were known alive?

Duke. Let this be done.
Put them in secret holds, both Barnardine and Claudio.
Ere twice the sun hath made his journal greeting
To th' under generation, you shall find
Your safety manifested.

Prov. I am your free dependant.

Duke. Quick, dispatch, and send the head to Angelo. *Exit Provost.*

8. ginger, used as medicine. **11. mercer,** dry-goods merchant. **12. peaches him,** denounces him as. **18. tilter,** fencer. **21. "for the Lord's sake,"** i.e., begging alms.

59. billets, small logs. **68. gravel heart,** stony heart. **77. omit,** pass by. **88. continue,** keep. **92. journal,** daily. **93. under generation,** race down under, antipodes. **95. free dependant,** willing slave.

Now will I write letters to Varrius,
The Provost, he shall bear them,—whose contents
Shall witness to him I am near at home,
And that, by great injunctions, I am bound
To enter publicly: him I 'll desire
To meet me at the consecrated fount
A league below the city; and from thence,
By cold gradation and well-balanc'd form,
We shall proceed with Angelo.

Re-enter *Provost.*

Prov. Here is the head: I 'll carry it myself.
Duke. Convenient is it. Make a swift return;
For I would commune with you of such things
That want no ear but yours.
Prov. I 'll make all speed. *Exit.*
Isab. [*Within.*] Peace, ho, be here!
Duke. The tongue of Isabel. She 's come to know
If yet her brother's pardon be come hither.
But I will keep her ignorant of her good,
To make her heavenly comforts of despair,
When it is least expected.

Enter *Isabella.*

Isab. Ho, by your leave!
Duke. Good morning to you, fair and gracious daughter.
Isab. The better, given me by so holy a man.
Hath yet the deputy sent my brother's pardon?
Duke. He hath releas'd him, Isabel, from the world.
His head is off and sent to Angelo.
Isab. Nay, but it is not so.
Duke. It is no other. Show your wisdom, daughter,
In your close patience.
Isab. O, I will to him and pluck out his eyes!
Duke. You shall not be admitted to his sight.
Isab. Unhappy Claudio! Wretched Isabel!
Injurious world! Most damned Angelo!
Duke. This nor hurts him nor profits you a jot.
Forbear it therefore; give your cause to heaven.
Mark what I say, which you shall find
By every syllable a faithful verity.
The Duke comes home to-morrow;—nay, dry your eyes;—
One of our covent, and his confessor,
Gives me this instance. Already he hath carried
Notice to Escalus and Angelo,
Who do prepare to meet him at the gates,
There to give up their power. If you can, pace your wisdom
In that good path that I would wish it go,
And you shall have your bosom on this wretch,
Grace of the Duke, revenges to your heart,
And general honour.
Isab. I am directed by you.
Duke. This letter, then, to Friar Peter give;
'T is that he sent me of the Duke's return.
Say, by this token, I desire his company
At Mariana's house to-night. Her cause and yours
I 'll perfect him withal, and he shall bring you
Before the Duke, and to the head of Angelo
Accuse him home and home. For my poor self,
I am combined by a sacred vow
And shall be absent. Wend you with this letter.
Command these fretting waters from your eyes
With a light heart: trust not my holy order,
If I pervert your course. Who 's here?

Enter *Lucio.*

Lucio. Good even. Friar, where 's the Provost?
Duke. Not within, sir.
Lucio. O pretty Isabella, I am pale at mine heart to see thine eyes so red: thou must be patient. I am fain to dine and sup with water and bran. I dare not for my head fill my belly; one fruitful meal would set me to 't. But they say the Duke will be here to-morrow. By my troth, Isabel, I loved thy brother. If the old fantastical Duke of dark corners had been at home, he had lived. *Exit Isabella.*
Duke. Sir, the Duke is marvellous little beholding to your reports; but the best is, he lives not in them.
Lucio. Friar, thou knowest not the Duke so well as I do: he 's a better woodman than thou tak'st him for.
Duke. Well, you 'll answer this one day. Fare ye well.

100. great injunctions, urgent motives. **104-5.** With unhurried steps and duly weighed forms of law shall we proceed against Angelo. **123. close,** secretive, silent.

133. covent, convent. **134. instance,** information. **139. bosom,** desire. **146. perfect,** inform. **147. head,** face. **148. home,** sharply, energetically. **149. combined,** bound. **159. fain,** constrained. **167. beholding,** obliged. **168. lives . . . them,** is not like them. **170. woodman,** huntsman (of women).

Lucio. Nay, tarry; I 'll go along with thee:
I can tell thee pretty tales of the Duke.

Duke. You have told me too many of him already, sir, if they be true; if not true, none were enough.

Lucio. I was once before him for getting a wench with child.

Duke. Did you such a thing?

Lucio. Yes, marry, did I; but I was fain to forswear it: they would else have married me to the rotten medlar.

Duke. Sir, your company is fairer than honest: rest you well.

Lucio. By my troth, I 'll go with thee to the lane's end. If bawdy talk offend you, we 'll have very little of it. Nay, friar, I am a kind of burr; I shall stick. *Exeunt.*

Scene IV. *Angelo's house.*

Enter *Angelo* and *Escalus.*

Escal. Every letter he hath writ hath disvouched other.

Ang. In most uneven and distracted manner. His actions show much like to madness; pray Heaven his wisdom be not tainted! And why meet him at the gates, and redeliver our authorities there?

Escal. I guess not.

Ang. And why should we proclaim it in an hour before his entering, that if any crave redress of injustice, they should exhibit their petitions in the street?

Escal. He shows his reason for that: to have a dispatch of complaints, and to deliver us from devices hereafter, which shall then have no power to stand against us.

Ang. Well, I beseech you let it be proclaim'd.
Betimes, i' th' morn I 'll call you at your house;
Give notice to such men of sort and suit
As are to meet him.

Escal. I shall, sir. Fare you well.
Exit Escalus.

Ang. Good night.
This deed unshapes me quite, makes me unpregnant
And dull to all proceedings. A deflower'd maid!
And by an eminent body that enforc'd
The law against it! But that her tender shame
Will not proclaim against her maiden loss,
How might she tongue me! Yet reason dares her no;
For my authority bears of a credent bulk,
That no particular scandal once can touch
But it confounds the breather. He should have liv'd,
Save that his riotous youth, with dangerous sense,
Might in the times to come have ta'en revenge,
By so receiving a dishonour'd life
With ransom of such shame. Would yet he had lived!
Alack, when once our grace we have forgot,
Nothing goes right; we would, and we would not. *Exit.*

Scene V. *Fields without the town.*

Enter *Duke* in his own habit and *Friar Peter.*

Duke. These letters at fit time deliver me.
Giving letters.
The Provost knows our purpose and our plot.
The matter being afoot, keep your instruction,
And hold you ever to our special drift,
Though sometimes you do blench from this to that,
As cause doth minister. Go call at Flavius' house,
And tell him where I stay: give the like notice
To Valentius, Rowland, and to Crassus,
And bid them bring the trumpets to the gate:
But send me Flavius first.

Fri. P. It shall be speeded well.
Exit.

Enter *Varrius.*

Duke. I thank thee, Varrius; thou hast made good haste:
Come, we will walk. There 's other of our friends
Will greet us here anon, my gentle Varrius.
Exeunt.

Scene VI. *Street near the city gate.*

Enter *Isabella* and *Mariana.*

Isab. To speak so indirectly I am loath.
I would say the truth; but to accuse him so,
That is your part: yet I am advis'd to do it,
He says, to veil full purpose.

Mari. Be rul'd by him.

Isab. Besides, he tells me that, if peradventure

184. medlar, a kind of apple edible only when partially decayed. **Scene iv: 1. disvouched other**, contradicted the other. **15. devices**, plots. **18. Betimes**, early. **19. sort**, rank. **suit**, with petitions. **23. unshapes**, confounds. **unpregnant**, indisposed. **28. tongue**, i.e., accuse. **dares her no**, frightens her into saying no.

29. credent bulk, weight of credit or credibility. **Scene v: 1. me**, for me. **5. blench**, shift. **9. trumpets**, trumpeters.

He speak against me on the adverse side,
I should not think it strange; for 't is a physic
That 's bitter to sweet end.

Enter *Friar Peter*.

Mari. I would Friar Peter—
Isab. O, peace! the friar is come.
Fri. P. Come, I have found you out a stand most fit,
Where you may have such vantage on the Duke,
He shall not pass you. Twice have the trumpets sounded,
The generous and gravest citizens
Have hent the gates, and very near upon
The Duke is ent'ring; therefore, hence, away!

Exeunt.

Act V. Scene I. *The city gate.*

Enter *Duke, Varrius*, Lords, *Angelo, Escalus, Lucio*, Provost, Officers, and Citizens, at several doors.

Duke. My very worthy cousin, fairly met!
Our old and faithful friend, we are glad to see you.
Ang. } Happy return be to your
Escal. } royal Grace!
Duke. Many and hearty thankings to you both!
We have made inquiry of you, and we hear
Such goodness of your justice, that our soul
Cannot but yield you forth to public thanks,
Forerunning more requital.
Ang. You make my bonds still greater.
Duke. O, your desert speaks loud; and I should wrong it,
To lock it in the wards of covert bosom,
When it deserves, with characters of brass,
A forted residence 'gainst the tooth of time
And razure of oblivion. Give me your hand,
And let the subject see, to make them know
That outward courtesies would fain proclaim
Favours that keep within. Come, Escalus,
You must walk by us on our other hand;
And good supporters are you.

Enter *Friar Peter* and *Isabella*.

Fri. P. Now is your time. Speak loud and kneel before him.
Isab. Justice, O royal Duke! Vail your regard
Upon a wrong'd—I would fain have said, a maid!
O worthy Prince, dishonour not your eye
By throwing it on any other object
Till you have heard me in my true complaint
And given me justice, justice, justice, justice!
Duke. Relate your wrongs. In what? By whom? Be brief.
Here is Lord Angelo shall give you justice:
Reveal yourself to him.
Isab. O worthy Duke,
You bid me seek redemption of the devil!
Hear me yourself; for that which I must speak
Must either punish me, not being believ'd,
Or wring redress from you. Hear me, O hear me, here!
Ang. My lord, her wits, I fear me, are not firm:
She hath been a suitor to me for her brother,
Cut off by course of justice,—
Isab. By course of justice!
Ang. And she will speak most bitterly and strange.
Isab. Most strange: but yet most truly, will I speak.
That Angelo 's forsworn, is it not strange?
That Angelo 's a murderer, is 't not strange?
That Angelo is an adulterous thief,
An hypocrite, a virgin-violator,
Is it not strange and strange?
Duke. Nay, it is ten times strange.
Isab. It is not truer he is Angelo
Than this is all as true as it is strange.
Nay, it is ten times true; for truth is truth
To the end of reckoning.
Duke. Away with her! Poor soul,
She speaks this in th' infirmity of sense.
Isab. O Prince, I conjure thee, as thou believ'st
There is another comfort than this world,
That thou neglect me not, with that opinion
That I am touch'd with madness! Make not impossible
That which but seems unlike. 'T is not impossible
But one, the wicked'st caitiff on the ground,
May seem as shy, as grave, as just, as absolute
As Angelo: even so may Angelo,

13. generous, of noble birth. **14. hent,** passed. **very near upon,** soon. **Act V, Scene i: 7. yield you forth,** give you. **10. wards,** prison-cells. **covert,** secret. **11. characters,** letters. **12. forted,** fortified. **13. razure,** erasure. **20. Vail,** let fall. **51. Make,** consider. **52. unlike,** unlikely.

In all his dressings, caracts, titles, forms,
Be an arch-villain. Believe it, royal Prince!
If he be less, he 's nothing; but he 's more,
Had I more name for badness.

Duke. By mine honesty,
If she be mad,—as I believe no other,—
Her madness hath the oddest frame of sense,
Such a dependency of thing on thing,
As e'er I heard in madness.

Isab. O gracious Duke,
Harp not on that, nor do not banish reason
For inequality; but let your reason serve
To make the truth appear where it seems hid,
And hide the false seems true.

Duke. Many that are not mad
Have, sure, more lack of reason. What would you say?

Isab. I am the sister of one Claudio
Condemn'd upon the act of fornication
To lose his head; condemn'd by Angelo.
I, in probation of a sisterhood,
Was sent to by my brother; one Lucio
As then the messenger,—

Lucio. That 's I, an 't like your Grace:
I came to her from Claudio, and desir'd her
To try her gracious fortune with Lord Angelo
For her poor brother's pardon.

Isab. That 's he indeed.

Duke. You were not bid to speak.

Lucio. No, my good lord;
Nor wish'd to hold my peace.

Duke. I wish you now, then.
Pray you, take note of it; and when you have
A business for yourself, pray Heaven you then
Be perfect.

Lucio. I warrant your honour.

Duke. The warrant 's for yourself; take heed to 't.

Isab. This gentleman told somewhat of my tale,—

Lucio. Right.

Duke. It may be right, but you are i' the wrong
To speak before your time. Proceed.

Isab. I went
To this pernicious caitiff deputy,—

Duke. That 's somewhat madly spoken.

Isab. Pardon it;
The phrase is to the matter.

Duke. Mended again. The matter; proceed.

Isab. In brief, to set the needless process by,
How I persuaded, how I pray'd, and kneel'd,
How he refell'd me, and how I replied,—
For this was of much length,—the vile conclusion
I now begin with grief and shame to utter.
He would not, but by gift of my chaste body
To his concupiscible intemperate lust,
Release my brother; and, after much debatement,
My sisterly remorse confutes mine honour,
And I did yield to him; but the next morn betimes,
His purpose surfeiting, he sends a warrant
For my poor brother's head.

Duke. This is most likely!

Isab. O, that it were as like as it is true!

Duke. By heaven, fond wretch, thou know'st not what thou speak'st,
Or else thou art suborn'd against his honour
In hateful practice. First, his integrity
Stands without blemish: next, it imports no reason
That with such vehemency he should pursue
Faults proper to himself: if he had so offended,
He would have weigh'd thy brother by himself,
And not have cut him off. Some one hath set you on.
Confess the truth, and say by whose advice
Thou cam'st here to complain.

Isab. And is this all?
Then, O you blessed ministers above,
Keep me in patience, and with ripened time
Unfold the evil which is here wrapt up
In countenance! Heaven shield your Grace from woe,
As I, thus wrong'd, hence unbelieved go!

Duke. I know you 'd fain be gone. An officer!
To prison with her! Shall we thus permit
A blasting and a scandalous breath to fall
On him so near us? This needs must be a practice.
Who knew of your intent and coming hither?

Isab. One that I would were here, Friar Lodowick.

Duke. A ghostly father, belike. Who knows that Lodowick?

Lucio. My lord, I know him; 't is a meddling friar.
I do not like the man: had he been lay, my lord,
For certain words he spake against your Grace
In your retirement, I had swing'd him soundly.

Duke. Words against me! This a good friar, belike!

56. **caracts**, distinctive marks. 67. **seems**, i.e., where it seems. 90. **matter**, point in question. 94. **refell'd**, refuted.

98. **concupiscible**, lewd. 106. **suborn'd**, bribed to witness falsely. 107. **practice**, plot. 110. **proper**, peculiar. 118. **countenance**, authority. 126. **ghostly**, spiritual. 128. **lay**, a layman.

And to set on this wretched woman here
Against our substitute! Let this friar be found.
Lucio. But yesternight, my lord, she and that friar,
I saw them at the prison: a saucy friar,
A very scurvy fellow.
Fri. P. Blessed be your royal Grace!
I have stood by, my lord, and I have heard
Your royal ear abus'd. First, hath this woman
Most wrongfully accus'd your substitute,
Who is as free from touch or soil with her
As she from one ungot.
Duke. We did believe no less.
Know you that Friar Lodowick that she speaks of?
Fri. P. I know him for a man divine and holy;
Not scurvy, nor a temporary meddler,
As he 's reported by this gentleman;
And, on my trust, a man that never yet
Did, as he vouches, misreport your Grace.
Lucio. My lord, most villanously; believe it.
Fri. P. Well, he in time may come to clear himself;
But at this instant he is sick, my lord,
Of a strange fever. Upon his mere request,
Being come to knowledge that there was complaint
Intended 'gainst Lord Angelo, came I hither,
To speak, as from his mouth, what he doth know
Is true and false; and what he with his oath
And all probation will make up full clear,
Whensoever he 's convented. First, for this woman,
To justify this worth nobleman,
So vulgarly and personally accus'd,
Her shall you hear disproved to her eyes,
Till she herself confess it.
Duke. Good friar, let 's hear it.
Isabella is carried off guarded.
Do you not smile at this, Lord Angelo?
O heaven, the vanity of wretched fools!
Give us some seats. Come, cousin Angelo;
In this I 'll be impartial: be you judge
Of your own cause. Is this the witness, friar?

Enter *Mariana* veiled.

First, let her show her face, and after speak.
Mari. Pardon, my lord; I will not show my face
Until my husband bid me.
Duke. What, are you married?
Mari. No, my lord.
Duke. Are you a maid?
Mari. No, my lord.
Duke. A widow, then?
Mari. Neither, my lord.
Duke. Why, you are nothing then: neither maid, widow, nor wife?
Lucio. My lord, she may be a punk; for many of them are neither maid, widow, nor wife.
Duke. Silence that fellow. I would he had some cause
To prattle for himself.
Lucio. Well, my lord.
Mari. My lord, I do confess I ne'er was married;
And I confess besides I am no maid.
I have known my husband; yet my husband
Knows not that ever he knew me.
Lucio. He was drunk then, my lord; it can be no better.
Duke. For the benefit of silence, would thou wert so too!
Lucio. Well, my lord.
Duke. This is no witness for Lord Angelo.
Mari. Now I come to 't, my lord.
She that accuses him of fornication,
In self-same manner doth accuse my husband,
And charges him, my lord, with such a time
When I 'll depose I had him in mine arms
With all th' effect of love.
Ang. Charges she moe than me?
Mari. Not that I know.
Duke. No? You say your husband.
Mari. Why, just, my lord, and that is Angelo,
Who thinks he knows that he ne'er knew my body,
But knows he thinks that he knows Isabel's.
Ang. This is a strange abuse. Let 's see thy face.
Mari. My husband bids me; now I will unmask. *Unveiling.*
This is that face, thou cruel Angelo,
Which once thou swor'st was worth the looking on;
This is the hand which, with a vow'd contract,
Was fast belock'd in thine; this is the body
That took away the match from Isabel,
And did supply thee at thy garden-house
In her imagin'd person.
Duke. Know you this woman?
Lucio. Carnally, she says.
Duke. Sirrah, no more!
Lucio. Enough, my lord.
Ang. My lord, I must confess I know this woman;
And five years since there was some speech of marriage
Betwixt myself and her; which was broke off,

141. soil, taint. **142. ungot,** unbegotten, i.e., unborn. **145. temporary meddler,** meddler in temporal matters. **152. Upon . . . request,** only at his request. **157. probation,** proof. **158. convented,** summoned.

179. punk, strumpet. **198. depose,** swear. **200. moe than,** other than. **211. match,** meeting, appointment.

Partly for that her promis'd proportions
Came short of composition, but in chief
For that her reputation was disvalued
In levity: since which time of five years
I never spake with her, saw her, nor heard from her,
Upon my faith and honour.

Mari. Noble Prince,
As there comes light from heaven and words from breath,
As there is sense in truth and truth in virtue,
I am affianced this man's wife as strongly
As words could make up vows; and, my good lord,
But Tuesday night last gone in 's garden-house
He knew me as a wife. As this is true,
Let me in safety raise me from my knees;
Or else for ever be confixed here,
A marble monument!

Ang. I did but smile till now.
Now, good my lord, give me the scope of justice.
My patience here is touch'd: I do perceive
These poor informal women are no more
But instruments of some more mightier member
That sets them on. Let me have way, my lord,
To find this practice out.

Duke. Ay, with my heart;
And punish them unto your height of pleasure.
Thou foolish friar, and thou pernicious woman,
Compact with her that 's gone, think'st thou thy oaths,
Though they would swear down each particular saint,
Were testimonies against his worth and credit
That 's seal'd in approbation? You, Lord Escalus,
Sit with my cousin: lend him your kind pains
To find out this abuse, whence 't is deriv'd.
There is another friar that set them on;
Let him be sent for.

Fri. P. Would he were here, my lord, for he indeed
Hath set the woman on to this complaint.
Your provost knows the place where he abides,
And he may fetch him.

Duke. Go, do it instantly.
Exit Provost.
And you, my noble and well-warranted cousin,
Whom it concerns to hear this matter forth,
Do with your injuries as seems you best,
In any chastisement; I for a while will leave you;
But stir not you till you have well determin'd
Upon these slanderers.

Escal. My lord, we 'll do it throughly.
Exit Duke.
Signior Lucio, did not you say you knew that Friar Lodowick to be a dishonest person?

Lucio. *Cucullus non facit monachum:* honest in nothing but in his clothes; and one that hath spoke most villanous speeches of the Duke.

Escal. We shall entreat you to abide here till he come and enforce them against him: we shall find this friar a notable fellow.

Lucio. As any in Vienna, on my word.

Escal. Call that same Isabel here once again; I would speak with her. [*Exit an attendant.*] Pray you, my lord, give me leave to question; you shall see how I 'll handle her.

Lucio. Not better than he, by her own report.

Escal. Say you?

Lucio. Marry, sir, I think, if you handled her privately, she would sooner confess: perchance, publicly, she 'll be ashamed.

Re-enter Officers with *Isabella;* and *Provost* with the *Duke* in his friar's habit.

Escal. I will go darkly to work with her.

Lucio. That 's the way, for woman are light at midnight.

Escal. Come on, mistress. Here 's a gentlewoman denies all that you have said.

Lucio. My lord, here comes the rascal I spoke of; here with the Provost.

Escal. In very good time: speak not you to him till we call upon you.

Lucio. Mum.

Escal. Come, sir, did you set these women on to slander Lord Angelo? They have confessed you did.

Duke. 'T is false.

Escal. How! know you where you are?

Duke. Respect to your great place! and let the devil
Be sometime honour'd for his burning throne!
Where is the Duke? 'T is he should hear me speak.

Escal. The Duke 's in us; and we will hear you speak.
Look you speak justly.

Duke. Boldly, at least. But, O, poor souls,
Come you to seek the lamb here of the fox?
Good night to your redress! Is the Duke gone?
Then is your cause gone too. The Duke 's unjust

219. proportions, marriage-portion. **220. composition,** the agreement. **221-2. was . . . levity,** became light, lit. depreciated into levity. **232. confixed,** fastened, fixed. **236. informal,** foolish. **242. Compact,** confederated. **246. pains,** effort.

258. determin'd, decided, judged. **263.** *Cucullus . . . monachum,* a cowl does not make a monk. **268. notable,** worth watching. **279. darkly,** obscurely, indirectly.

Thus to retort your manifest appeal,
And put your trial in the villain's mouth
Which here you come to accuse.

Lucio. This is the rascal; this is he I spoke of.

Escal. Why, thou unreverend and unhallowed friar,
Is 't not enough thou hast suborn'd these women
To accuse this worthy man, but, in foul mouth
And in the witness of his proper ear,
To call him villain, and then to glance from him
To th' Duke himself, to tax him with injustice?
Take him hence; to th' rack with him! We 'll touse you
Joint by joint, but we will know his purpose.
What, "unjust"!

Duke. Be not so hot: the Duke
Dare no more stretch this finger of mine than he
Dare rack his own: his subject am I not,
Nor here provincial. My business in this state
Made me a looker on here in Vienna,
Where I have seen corruption boil and bubble
Till it o'er-run the stew; laws for all faults,
But faults so countenanc'd, that the strong statutes
Stand like the forfeits in a barber's shop,
As much in mock as mark.

Escal. Slander to the state! Away with him to prison!

Ang. What can you vouch against him, Signior Lucio?
Is this the man that you did tell us of?

Lucio. 'T is he, my lord. Come hither, good-man bald-pate: do you know me?

Duke. I remember you, sir, by the sound of your voice: I met you at the prison, in the absence of the Duke.

Lucio. O, did you so? And do you remember what you said of the Duke?

Duke. Most notedly, sir.

Lucio. Do you so, sir? And was the Duke a fleshmonger, a fool, and a coward, as you then reported him to be?

Duke. You must, sir, change persons with me, ere you make that my report: you, indeed, spoke so of him, and much more, much worse.

Lucio. O thou damnable fellow! Did not I pluck thee by the nose for thy speeches?

Duke. I protest I love the Duke as I love myself.

Ang. Hark, how the villain would close now, after his treasonable abuses!

Escal. Such a fellow is not to be talked withal. Away with him to prison! Where is the Provost? Away with him to prison! Lay bolts enough upon him: let him speak no more. Away with those giglots too, and with the other confederate companion!

The Provost lays hands on the Duke.

Duke. Stay, sir; stay awhile.

Ang. What, resists he? Help him, Lucio.

Lucio. Come, sir; come, sir; come, sir; foh, sir! Why, you bald-pated, lying rascal, you must be hooded, must you? Show your knave's visage, with a pox to you! Show your sheep-biting face, and be hanged an hour! Will 't not off?

Pulls off the friar's hood and discovers the Duke.

Duke. Thou art the first knave that e'er mad'st a duke.
First, Provost, let me bail these gentle three.
[*To Lucio.*] Sneak not away, sir; for the friar and you
Must have a word anon. Lay hold on him.

Lucio. This may prove worse than hanging.

Duke. [*To Escalus.*] What you have spoke I pardon. Sit you down;
We 'll borrow place of him. Sir, [*taking Angelo's seat*] by your leave.
Hast thou or word, or wit, or impudence,
That yet can do thee office? If thou hast,
Rely upon it till my tale be heard,
And hold no longer out.

Ang. O my dread lord,
I should be guiltier than my guiltiness,
To think I can be undiscernible,
When I perceive your Grace, like power divine,
Hath look'd upon my passes. Then, good Prince,
No longer session hold upon my shame,
But let my trial be mine own confession.
Immediate sentence, then, and sequent death
Is all the grace I beg.

Duke. Come hither, Mariana.
Say, wast thou e'er contracted to this woman?

Ang. I was, my lord.

Duke. Go take her hence, and marry her instantly.
Do you the office, friar; which consummate,
Return him here again. Go with him, Provost.

Exeunt Angelo, Mariana, Friar Peter, and Provost.

303. retort, throw back, reject. **310. proper,** own. **313. touse,** tear. **318. provincial,** under the jurisdiction of an ecclesiastical province. **323. forfeits,** barbers were the dentists of the time, and extracted teeth were hung up in their shops. **324. in mock as mark,** laughed at as obeyed. **335. notedly,** exactly.

346. close, make reparation. **352. giglots,** lewd women. **353. other,** i.e., Friar Peter. **369. do thee office,** help thee out. **371. hold . . . out,** play your part no longer. **375. passes,** acts. **378. sequent,** consequent. **383. consummate,** performed.

Duke condemns Angelo to death for killing Claudio, still pretends C. is dead.

Escal. My lord, I am more amaz'd at his dishonour
Than at the strangeness of it.
Duke. Come hither, Isabel.
Your friar is now your prince. As I was then
Advertising and holy to your business,
Not changing heart with habit, I am still
Attorney'd at your service.
Isab. O, give me pardon,
That I, your vassal, have employ'd and pain'd
Your unknown sovereignty!
Duke. You are pardon'd, Isabel;
And now, dear maid, be you as free to us.
Your brother's death, I know, sits at your heart;
And you may marvel why I obscur'd myself,
Labouring to save his life, and would not rather
Make rash remonstrance of my hidden power
Than let him so be lost. O most kind maid,
It was the swift celerity of his death,
Which I did think with slower foot came on,
That brain'd my purpose: but, peace be with him!
That life is better life, past fearing death,
Than that which lives to fear: make it your comfort,
So happy is your brother.

Re-enter *Angelo, Mariana, Friar Peter,* and *Provost.*

Isab. I do, my lord.
Duke. For this new-married man approaching here,
Whose salt imagination yet hath wrong'd
Your well defended honour, you must pardon
For Mariana's sake; but as he adjudg'd your brother,—
Being criminal, in double violation
Of sacred chastity and of promise-breach
Thereon dependent, for your brother's life,—
The very mercy of the law cries out
Most audible, even from his proper tongue,
"An Angelo for Claudio, death for death!"
Haste still pays haste, and leisure answers leisure;
Like doth quit like, and *Measure* still *for Measure.*
Then, Angelo, thy fault 's thus manifested;
Which, though thou wouldst deny, denies thee vantage.
We do condemn thee to the very block
Where Claudio stoop'd to death, and with like haste.
Away with him!
Mari. O my most gracious lord,
I hope you will not mock me with a husband.
Duke. It is your husband mock'd you with a husband.
Consenting to the safeguard of your honour,
I thought your marriage fit; else imputation,
For that he knew you, might reproach your life
And choke your good to come. For his possessions,
Although by confiscation they are ours,
We do instate and widow you withal,
To buy you a better husband.
Mari. O my dear lord,
I crave no other, nor no better man.
Duke. Never crave him; we are definitive.
Mari. Gentle my liege,— *Kneeling.*
Duke. You do but lose your labour.
Away with him to death! [*To Lucio.*] Now, sir, to you.
Mari. O my good lord! Sweet Isabel, take my part!
Lend me your knees, and all my life to come
I 'll lend you all my life to do you service.
Duke. Against all sense you do importune her.
Should she kneel down in mercy of this fact,
Her brother's ghost his paved bed would break,
And take her hence in horror.
Mari. Isabel,
Sweet Isabel, do yet but kneel by me.
Hold up your hands, say nothing; I 'll speak all.
They say, best men are moulded out of faults,
And, for the most, become much more the better
For being a little bad; so may my husband.
O Isabel, will you not lend a knee?
Duke. He dies for Claudio's death.
Isab. [*Kneeling.*] Most bounteous sir,
Look, if it please you, on this man condemn'd,
As if my brother liv'd. I partly think
A due sincerity governed his deeds,
Till he did look on me: since it is so,
Let him not die. My brother had but justice,
In that he did the thing for which he died;
For Angelo,

388. **Advertising,** attentive. **holy,** consecrated (like a priest). 390. **Attorney'd,** employed as an attorney. 391. **pain'd,** caused to work or take pains. 393. **free,** bountiful, i.e., to forgive my part in your brother's death. 397. **rash remonstrance,** hasty demonstration. 401. **brain'd,** defeated, killed. [illegible] **yet,** hitherto. 409. **criminal,** guilty. 418. **vantage,** advantage.

425. **imputation,** censure. 429. **instate . . . withal,** invest you with it (possessions) and widow you. 432. **definitive,** resolved. 439. **fact,** crime. 440. **paved,** lined with stone. 442. **yet,** at least. 445. **for the most,** the most part.

Duke shows Claudio to be alive so pardons Angelo
He makes Lucio marry a whore he impregnated for slandering the Duke.

His act did not o'ertake his bad intent,
And must be buried but as an intent
That perish'd by the way. Thoughts are no subjects;
Intents, but merely thoughts.

Mari. Merely, my lord.

Duke. Your suit 's unprofitable; stand up, I say.
I have bethought me of another fault.
Provost, how came it Claudio was beheaded
At an unusual hour?

Prov. It was commanded so.

Duke. Had you a special warrant for the deed?

Prov. No, my good lord; it was by private message.

Duke. For which I do discharge you of your office:
Give up your keys.

Prov. Pardon me, noble lord.
I thought it was a fault, but knew it not;
Yet did repent me, after more advice.
For testimony whereof, one in the prison,
That should by private order else have died,
I have reserv'd alive.

Duke. What 's he?

Prov. His name is Barnardine.

Duke. I would thou hadst done so by Claudio.
Go fetch him hither; let me look upon him.

Exit Provost.

Escal. I am sorry, one so learned and so wise
As you, Lord Angelo, have still appear'd,
Should slip so grossly, both in the heat of blood,
And lack of temper'd judgement afterward.

Ang. I am sorry that such sorrow I procure;
And so deep sticks it in my penitent heart
That I crave death more willingly than mercy.
'T is my deserving, and I do entreat it.

Re-enter *Provost*, with *Barnardine, Claudio* muffled, and *Juliet*.

Duke. Which is that Barnardine?

Prov. This, my lord.

Duke. There was a friar told me of this man.
Sirrah, thou art said to have a stubborn soul,
That apprehends no further than this world,
And squar'st thy life according. Thou 'rt condemn'd;
But, for those earthly faults, I quit them all;
And pray thee take this mercy to provide
For better times to come. Friar, advise him;
I leave him to your hand. What muffled fellow 's that?

Prov. This is another prisoner that I sav'd,
Who should have died when Claudio lost his head;
As like almost to Claudio as himself.

Unmuffles Claudio.

Duke. [*To Isabella.*] If he be like your brother, for his sake
Is he pardon'd; and, for your lovely sake—
Give me your hand and say you will be mine—
He is my brother too. But fitter time for that.
By this Lord Angelo perceives he 's safe;
Methinks I see a quick'ning in his eye.
Well, Angelo, your evil quits you well.
Look that you love your wife; her worth worth yours.
I find an apt remission in myself;
And yet here 's one in place I cannot pardon.
[*To Lucio.*] You, sirrah, that knew me for a fool, a coward,
One all of luxury, an ass, a madman,
Wherein have I so deserv'd of you,
That you extol me thus?

Lucio. Faith, my lord, I spoke it but according to the trick: if you will hang me for it, you may; but I had rather it would please you I might be whipped.

Duke. Whipp'd first, sir, and hang'd after.
Proclaim it, Provost, round about the city,
If any woman wrong'd by this lewd fellow,
As I have heard him swear himself there 's one
Whom he begot with child, let her appear,
And he shall marry her. The nuptial finish'd,
Let him be whipp'd and hang'd.

Lucio. I beseech your Highness do not marry me to a whore. Your Highness said even now, I made you a duke; good my lord, do not recompense me in making me a cuckold.

Duke. Upon mine honour, thou shalt marry her.
Thy slanders I forgive; and therewithal
Remit thy other forfeits. Take him to prison;
And see our pleasure herein executed.

Lucio. Marrying a punk, my lord, is pressing to death, whipping, and hanging.

Duke. Slandering a prince deserves it.

Exeunt Officers with Lucio.

She, Claudio, that you wrong'd, look you restore.
Joy to you, Mariana! Love her, Angelo!
I have confess'd her and I know her virtue.
Thanks, good friend Escalus, for thy much goodness;

458. **subjects,** real, existing things. 479. **procure,** cause. 488. **quit,** remit, pardon.

501. **quits,** requites, repays. 502. **yours,** i.e., your worth. 503. **apt remission,** inclination to pardon. 504. **in place,** present. 506. **luxury,** lust. 510. **according to the trick,** in character (as a jest). 526. **forfeits,** i.e., whipping and hanging.

There 's more behind that is more gratulate.
Thanks, Provost, for thy care and secrecy;
We shall employ thee in a worthier place.
Forgive him, Angelo, that brought you home
The head of Ragozine for Claudio's;
The offence pardons itself. Dear Isabel,
I have a motion much imports your good;
Whereto if you 'll a willing ear incline,
What 's mine is yours, and what is yours is mine.
So, bring us to our palace, where we 'll show
What 's yet behind, that 's meet you all should know. *Exeunt.*

535. behind, to come. **gratulate,** gratifying.

The Tragedy of Julius Cæsar

Julius Cæsar marks the beginning of another stage in the development of Shakespeare's genius. It is a link-play bridging the transition from the histories of his second to the tragedies of his third period. Outwardly a history rather than a tragedy, it abandons the type of chronicle play which had reached its climax in *Henry V,* discards the comic scenes and characters that gave life and color to the Lancastrian trilogy, and concentrates on the tragic fate of the central character of the story. Something like this Shakespeare had already done in *Richard II,* but there is a vast difference between the exuberant lyricism of that play and the classic restraint of *Julius Cæsar*. Over *Julius Cæsar* the clouds are gathering that are to darken into the night of the great tragedies.

Text.—*Julius Cæsar* was published for the first time in the Folio of 1623. It is a clean, well-printed text, probably based upon the acting version in the hands of the company at that time. It is one of the shortest of Shakespeare's plays, a fact which points to the possibility of drastic cutting in the theatre, but it would take more than human intelligence or insight to indicate the gaps or supply the scenes omitted by the actors. The present edition follows the Folio text, accepting only such emendations as seem absolutely necessary.

Date.—Meres does not mention *Julius Cæsar* in his list of Shakespeare's plays in 1598, but it must have been on the stage in the following year, for Plattner, a Swiss physician travelling in England, saw a play on the 21st of September, 1599, which can hardly have been other than Shakespeare's tragedy. Jonson parodies the line "judgement, thou art fled to brutish beasts" and repeats *Et tu Brute* in his *Every Man Out of His Humour,* a play acted by Shakespeare's company in that same year. A reference in Weever's *Mirror of Martyrs,* published in 1601 but written two years earlier, contains an unmistakable reference to the orations of Brutus and Mark Antony. It is probable that Shakespeare turned to the composition of *Julius Cæsar* immediately after finishing the last of his English history plays.

Source.—The one main source of *Julius Cæsar* is Plutarch in the noble translation of Sir Thomas North. It is possible that Shakespeare caught a hint or two from other histories or earlier plays, but all the essential matter of the drama comes direct from the three *Lives* of Cæsar, Brutus, and Mark Antony in Plutarch. Shakespeare follows his source here, as he was later to do in *Antony and Cleopatra* and in *Coriolanus,* with scrupulous fidelity. There is hardly an incident in the play important or trivial which is not also found in Plutarch. At times he even rewrites in sonorous verse the splendid prose of North, perhaps the greatest master of prose rhythms of all Elizabethan translators. The characters, too, all come from the source—only the boy, Lucius, introduced mainly to show the gentler side of Brutus, is a creation of Shakespeare's.

There were special reasons for Shakespeare's scrupulous fidelity in *Julius Cæsar* to his source. Plutarch's *Lives,* long lost in the Middle Ages and rediscovered in the early Renaissance, had become a sort of gospel to the intellectual aristocracy of that age. Widely read in Latin versions, translated into French by Amyot, 1559, and from Amyot into English by North, 1579, the *Lives* opened to the sixteenth century a treasury of history, biography, and political-moral maxims such as Western Europe had not known for centuries. "Plutarch," says Montaigne, "became our breviary." Henry of Navarre writing to his young wife congratulates her on having discovered and fallen in love with Plutarch. "To love him is to love me," he writes. "He was the instructor of my early years; my good mother put the book into my hands when I was little more than an infant. It has been as my conscience and has whispered to me many maxims for my conduct and the government of my affairs." "Among all profane books," says North in the preface of his translation, "that are in reputation at this day there is none that teaches so much honor, love, obedience, reverence, zeal, and devotion to princes as these *Lives* of Plutarch do." Shakespeare would have been other than the child of the Renaissance he was had he not shared this reverence for the great classic.

There was, moreover, another and special reason for Shakespeare's close adherence to his source in this play. He found in Plutarch what no other of his varied sources gave him, a lively interest in man's life in the world of affairs, a vigorous power of characterization, and above all a keen sense of the dramatic in history, which must have had for him a very peculiar appeal. Plutarch is not a historian in the true sense of the word; he presents no such masterpieces of historical narrative as Thucydides or Livy; much less does he attempt to interpret the course of events and unfold their social and economic causes like a modern historian. He was primarily a biographer, a psychological biographer even, since his interest lay not so much in narrating the events of heroes' lives as in interpreting their characters. And of all the *Lives* none is so vivid, so rich in character contrasts, so dramatic in spirit and in presentation as the two, *Cæsar* and *Brutus,* that center round the death of the great dictator. Here was the richest of mines for the dramatist to explore. Rich as was the material, however, it was fragmentary and scattered through many pages of North's translation. It fell to Shakespeare to assemble and mold it into a perfect whole, and this task he performed with a skill acquired by his long practice in dramatizing tales from English history. Yet *Julius Cæsar* is something more than a chronicle history, the "Life and Death of Julius Cæsar," as his first editors called it in the Folio table of contents. It has one central and unifying theme, the death of Cæsar, and it presents the causes and consequences of this great tragic act.

Construction.—The play opens with swift and masterly exposition in which the opposing forces, aristocratic republicanism and Cæsarism, dictatorship based on popular favor, are brought face to face. In Cassius and Brutus we find incarnate the two eternal enemies of Cæsarism, personal jealousy and unselfish devotion to republican ideals. Cassius takes the initiative in plotting to overthrow Cæsar, already monarch in all but name. The night of omens with which the first act closes sets the tragic atmosphere befitting the theme:

> The heavens themselves blaze forth the death of princes.

The second act quickens the movement toward the climax. Brutus persuades himself of the necessity of Cæsar's death, joins Cassius and his fellows, and throws around the project of privy conspiracy and murder the mantle of ideal republicanism. His moral authority makes him the gladly accepted leader of the plot; his inability to recognize the realities of life sows in it at the very outset the seeds of failure. The second scene shows Cæsar's fatal decision to attend the Senate on the morning set for his murder. Two brief scenes indicating the possibility of the conspiracy's failure lead up to the third act.

This act, one of Shakespeare's supreme masterpieces, rises to the climax with the murder of Cæsar and at once introduces the counteraction. Antony, the champion of Cæsarism, feigns adherence to the conspirators, secures from Brutus permission to deliver the funeral oration for the dead dictator, and by his powerful appeal to the emotions of the mob rouses them to fury against the murderers. They flee from the Rome they had sought to save and Antony joins hands with Cæsar's heir, Octavius. The great central action of the play has occurred; the blow for the ancient liberty of Rome has been struck in vain, and the rest of the play develops the consequences of the failure.

The fourth act continues the downward movement. We see first the power that has succeeded to the gentle rule of Julius, a military autocracy, greedy, cruel, and treacherous. The scene shifts to the camp of Brutus to reveal his growing disillusion and the impending downfall of his cause. The famous quarrel scene, sometimes attacked as not contributing to the action, in fact leads up to and explains the catastrophe. The conflict between the unworldly idealism of Brutus and the harsh necessities of war accepted and practised by his brother-in-arms betrays a weakness quite incapable of opposing the ruthless efficiency of Cæsar's revengers. The moral ascendency of Brutus over the older and better soldier leads to the last fatal error of the republicans, the decision to abandon their post of vantage, and the ghost of Cæsar warns of their now inevitable ruin.

The last act, a series of battle scenes, as in an old chronicle play, rounds off the tragic history. Cæsar's assassins and his avengers join conflict, but the end is certain, foretold by omens that shock the skeptic Cassius and by the foreboding of Brutus that the self-inflicted death he had held unlawful might yet be necessary. The spirit of Cæsar hovers over the field like an angry Nemesis, and one by one his murderers fall on their own swords. The victors pronounce the funeral elegy of Brutus and give orders for his honorable burial.

Here if anywhere in Shakespeare we find unity of design and harmony of details. There are no digressions, under-plots, or episodes; the theme announced at the beginning is held singly and strictly to the very end. It is more than a coincidence that Shakespeare's dramatic version of the greatest event in classical history should be the most classically perfect of all his plays in structure.

Characters.—Shakespeare's purpose in *Julius Cæsar,* as in his English history plays, was to present upon the stage a living picture of the past. He is not concerned like his contemporary Jonson about accuracy of details; he is careless of anachronism, as when he sets a clock to strike the hour in ancient Rome; he omits important actions that do not bear upon his theme, and compresses the sequence of events to secure swiftness and unity. Following the tradition of the miracle plays and the earlier chronicles, Shakespeare devotes himself to the re-creation of historic characters in such form that they might seem to his hearers men like themselves, that the dead past might become for an hour the living present, and the very groundlings of his theatre behold the grandeur that was Rome at the hour of her supreme tragedy. Of his success it seems hardly necessary to speak. From the day that *Julius Cæsar* was first acted until the present the characters of the play have, with one exception, established themselves in the literary and historical consciousness of the English world. To speak of Antony, of Brutus, or of Cassius is to recall at once the characters of Shakespeare's play rather than those of history. And these main characters are surrounded by a group of others into whom Shakespeare has breathed the breath of life, the blunt Casca, the devoted Portia, the cool and calculating Octavius, to say nothing of the fickle and unruly mob. No other of Shakespeare's historical plays, it would seem, conveys so strongly to reader or spectator such a sense of the reality of the characters who play their part in it.

There is, no doubt, one exception to be made to such praise of Shakespeare's characterization in this play. His treatment of Cæsar has been challenged, and rightly so, if it were his purpose to present a full-length portrait of "the mightiest Julius." But this is not his purpose here. Shakespeare is not dramatizing the life of Julius Cæsar. He leaves untouched, save for the brief reference in the speech of Antony, the earlier events of Cæsar's life and shows him as he appeared to the world of his day in the brief interval between his latest triumph and his death. For this he borrows and even stresses all that he can gather from Plutarch: Cæsar's physical weakness, the "falling sickness," his superstition, his reckless defiance of danger, his arbitrary treatment of the Senate, and his ill-disguised desire for the title as well as the power of a King. Shakespeare of course, relied upon Plutarch; to have drawn a Cæsar such as later Cæsarians —Mommsen and Froude, for example—have presented, would have been to falsify history as he knew it; in particular it would have annihilated all sympathy for his opponent, Brutus, to Shakespeare as to Plutarch the hero of the action and the incarnation of the Renaissance idea of civic liberty.

To a modern reader the most offensive trait in Shakespeare's Cæsar is his pompous and arrogant manner of speech: "Always I am Cæsar"; "Danger knows full well that Cæsar is more terrible than he"; "Cæsar doth not wrong"—a line, by the way, which originally ended "but with just cause." Of such arrogance there is little trace in Plutarch; it is a device of Shakespeare's for dramatic reasons. There was in the first place an old dramatic convention presenting Cæsar as a boastful conqueror whose pride—*hybris*—brought down on him the vengeance of the gods. Shakespeare accepted this convention but he had another and a better reason. He wished to show Cæsar as the embodiment of Cæsarism, of absolute and autocratic power, a man bestriding the narrow world like a Colossus. Limits of time and necessity of action forbade him to write long scenes developing this phase of Cæsar's character; he did it in the simplest way by putting into Cæsar's mouth language unfit for mortal man, much less for the citizen of a free Republic. For Shakespeare's Cæsar, indeed, the Republic has already vanished; the Senate he calls "my Senate," "graybeards" obedient to his will; "tell them," he says when asked to give a reason for his refusal to appear before them:

> The cause is in my will; I will not come;
> That is enough to satisfy the Senate.

Regis voluntas suprema lex, the maxim of autocrats, could not be more succinctly stated. To Shakespeare's eyes the tragedy of Cæsar's fall lay in the ironic contrast between such extravagant claims and the realities of life. So long as Romans lived still mindful of the past, Romans who would brook

> The eternal devil to keep his state in Rome
> As easily as a King,

so long was Cæsar's tyranny and Cæsar's life in danger. In his calmer moments Cæsar himself knows this; he feels instinctively that men like Cassius, "never at heart's ease while they behold a greater than themselves," are very dangerous; but he is blinded by his belief in himself and falls at last a victim alone and undefended under the swords of a group of nobles who represent old Rome.

The two leaders of this group are sharply contrasted characters. Cassius, the leader, is a malcontent. In spite of his fine words it is no abstract love of liberty that inspires him but a personal grudge against the tyrant. He stresses Cæsar's physical weakness as if strength of body alone gave title to supreme power, and he knows himself a stronger man than Cæsar. There is something mordant, bitter, almost misanthropic in his nature; "he loves no plays; he hears no music"; and such a man, Shakespeare knew, was "fit for treasons." He is suspicious by nature and his suspicions are often justified. Yet he has a weakness which shows him the more human, his reverence for the moral nobleness of Brutus and his deep affection for this friend. He is shrewd enough to see that the adherence of Brutus is necessary to the success of his conspiracy, but it is not shrewdness that compels him more than once to renounce his own wise plans of action at the bidding of his moral superior. Hard practical man of the world he yet worships virtue, and virtue embodied in the character of Brutus commands his obedience.

Brutus is, of course, the most important figure, if not the hero of the play. It is hardly too much to say that Shakespeare dramatizes the story from the point of view of Brutus. He takes over the character as he found it in Plutarch and idealizes the already idealized portrait of a Roman patrician. He is a student, a stoic, a patriot devoid of self-seeking, constant of purpose, beloved by his friends, reverenced even by his enemies. Shakespeare lays emphasis on the human side of this ideal figure, on his courtesy, his gentleness even to inferiors, his love of Portia, his abhorrence of bloodshed. Yet he is no model of superhuman perfection. He is overshadowed by melancholy, ignorant of the world about him, blinded to realities by a self-satisfaction that at times approaches self-complacency. Doggedly obstinate in his plans, deaf to all advice that conflicts with them, he is yet susceptible to subtle flattery. His decision to murder Cæsar rests upon a sense of duty, but this sense has been awakened by the artful appeal of Cassius and by the forged letters which he mistakes for the voice of Rome. This sense of duty, moreover, is inextricably intertwined with personal and family pride. It is because he is a Brutus, descendant of the Brutus who drove out kings from Rome, that he feels himself called upon to save his country, and it is with an air of high self-sufficiency that he promises to grant his imagined supplicating Rome her "full petition." Too much has been made at times of his love for Cæsar and of his sacrifice of this love at the call of duty. There are, it is true, repeated references in the play to the affection supposed to exist between them, but we never see them togther on terms of intimacy, nor is there any allusion in the soliloquy of Brutus, which justifies the murder, to his affection for the man he has resolved to kill. This speech is an extraordinary example of Shakespeare's insight into human nature, particularly into its tendency to seek a moral justification for ignoble deeds. Brutus shrinks from the murder, not because it involves the death of a friend, but because of his instinctive detestation of the "monstrous visage of Conspiracy." Before he has been able to persuade himself of its righteousness his mind has been distracted as by civil war and the tumult in his soul has been reflected in his outward behavior until he has grown ungentle even toward his beloved wife. But once the deed is justified to his conscience there is neither hesitation before it is performed nor remorse thereafter. Even when Brutus is completely disillusioned as to the consequences of his action he preserves in perfect calm the illusion of his own righteousness. Weary of life and about to fall on his sword, he is yet assured that he shall have more glory in defeat than Octavius and Antony by their "vile conquest." Accepting but modifying for his own ends the material which he drew from Plutarch, Shakespeare has drawn in Brutus an immortal portrait of the idealist in conflict with unknown or ignored realities. The contrast with his recent portrayal of the heroic man of action, Henry V, is perfect; the transition from Brutus to Hamlet is the next step.

Little need be said of the character of Antony as he appears in the play. In strong contrast to Brutus he lives by his emotions. Devoted to Cæsar in his life, he becomes his avenger after the murder, but not without a firm determination to profit by his revenge. A past master in dissimulation, he finds it as easy to deceive the single-minded Brutus as to sway the fickle mob. His famous oration is a superb example of the art of the demagogue, but it would have been impossible for Antony so to have stirred the mob had he not himself been moved to the depth of his being by the murder of his friend and master.

Political Significance.—The question of the political significance of *Julius Cæsar* has often been discussed, but it is an idle question. There was the least resemblance possible between the decadent Roman republic and the popular monarchy of Elizabeth. A true English conservative, Shakespeare was not likely to approve the classical virtue of tyrannicide, and equally unlikely to favor the rule of the mob. What Antony and Octavius made of their victory he was to show in a later play; the issue between patrician and plebeian rule is fought out in *Coriolanus*. Shakespeare wrote *Julius Cæsar* not to teach any political lesson, but to exhibit on the stage a great action and to give immortal life to the actors in that deed. It is not to *Julius Cæsar* but to *Henry V* that we must turn for Shakespeare's conception of the ideal government and governor.

Stage History.—From the beginning *Julius Cæsar* has been a successful play upon the stage. Apart from the Plattner performance already noticed we have records of performances at Court in 1613 and before Charles I in 1636 and 1639. Digges in the verses prefixed to the *Poems*, 1640, calls attention to the popularity of Shakespeare's play as compared with Jonson's.

When Cæsar would appear,
And on the stage at half-sword parley were
Brutus and Cassius: oh how the audience
Were ravish'd, with what wonder they went thence,
When some new day they would not brook a line
Of tedious (though well laboured) *Cataline*.

The classical theme and sobriety of language commended *Julius Cæsar* to the Restoration audience and it was fortunate in escaping the transformation wrought upon other of Shakespeare's tragedies. Betterton was a famous Brutus and his acting in the quarrel scene is praised by Cibber for its fine restraint: "with a settled dignity of contempt like an unheeding rock he repelled upon himself the foam of Cassius."

Some alterations, cutting, patching, and doubling of parts appear in eighteenth century versions, but on the whole the play runs an unbroken course. It is a play for male actors; with the exception of Garrick every great actor from Barton Booth to Kemble played the part of Brutus. Kemble's revival in 1811-12 is said to have been staged with "scenic splendor" and even this was surpassed by Tree's magnificent production, designed by the painter Alma Tadema, which ran for a hundred nights in 1898.

It was produced in America even before the Revolution in 1774 at Charleston. For three decades from the 60s to the 80s Edwin Booth's Brutus and Barrett's Cassius were twin stars in the American theatre. As recently as 1937 a performance in modern dress with a decided anti-fascist slant evoked considerable comment and high praise in New York.

THE TRAGEDY OF JULIUS CÆSAR

Dramatis Personæ

Julius Cæsar.
Octavius Cæsar, *Marcus Antonius,* *M. Æmilius Lepidus,* — triumvirs after the death of *Julius Cæsar.*
Cicero, *Publius,* *Popilius Lena,* — senators.
Marcus Brutus, *Cassius,* *Casca,* *Trebonius,* *Ligarius,* *Decius Brutus,* *Metellus Cimber,* *Cinna,* — conspirators against *Julius Cæsar.*
Flavius and *Marullus,* tribunes.
Artemidorus, a teacher of Rhetoric.
A Soothsayer.
Cinna, a poet.
Another Poet.
Lucilius, *Titinius,* *Messala,* Young *Cato,* *Volumnius,* — friends to ***Brutus*** and ***Cassius.***
Varro, *Clitus,* *Claudius,* *Strato,* *Lucius,* *Dardanius,* — servants to ***Brutus.***
Pindarus, servant to *Cassius.*
Calpurnia, wife to *Cæsar.*
Portia, wife to *Brutus.*
The Ghost of *Cæsar.*

Senators, Citizens, Guards, Attendants, etc.

SCENE: *Rome; the neighbourhood near Sardis; near Philippi.*

ACT I. Scene I. *Rome. A street.*

Enter *Flavius, Marullus,* and certain *Commoners* over the stage.

Flav. Hence! home, you idle creatures, get you home!
Is this a holiday? What! know you not,
Being mechanical, you ought not walk
Upon a labouring day without the sign
Of your profession? Speak, what trade art thou?

Car. Why, sir, a carpenter.

Mar. Where is thy leather apron and thy rule?
What dost thou with thy best apparel on?
You, sir, what trade are you?

Cob. Truly, sir, in respect of a fine workman, I am but, as you would say, a cobbler.

Mar. But what trade art thou? Answer me directly.

Cob. A trade, sir, that I hope I may use with a safe conscience; which is, indeed, sir, a mender of bad soles.

Flav. What trade, thou knave? thou naughty knave, what trade?

Cob. Nay, I beseech you, sir, be not out with me; yet, if you be out, sir, I can mend you.

Mar. What mean'st thou by that? Mend me, thou saucy fellow!

Cob. Why, sir, cobble you.

Flav. Thou art a cobbler, art thou?

Cob. Truly, sir, all that I live by is with the awl. I meddle with no tradesman's matters, nor women's matters, but with all. I am, indeed, sir, a surgeon to old shoes; when they are in great danger, I re-cover them. As proper men as ever trod upon neat's leather have gone upon my handiwork.

Flav. But wherefore art not in thy shop today?
Why dost thou lead these men about the streets?

Cob. Truly, sir, to wear out their shoes, to get myself into more work. But, indeed, sir, we make holiday, to see Cæsar and to rejoice in his triumph.

Mar. Wherefore rejoice? What conquest brings he home?
What tributaries follow him to Rome

3. mechanical, of the working class. **4. sign,** dress, tools. **10. respect of,** comparison with. **11. cobbler,** (1) mender of shoes, (2) bungler. **17. naughty,** worthless. **18. out,** out of temper.

19. out, have shoe worn out. **26. with all,** a play on "with all" and 'with awl," the cobbler's tool. **29. proper,** handsome, fine. **neat's leather,** cowhide. **36. triumph,** the triumphal entry into Rome, the highest honor accorded to victorious generals. Cæsar had defeated Pompey's sons in Spain, at the battle of Munda.

To grace in captive bonds his chariot-wheels?
You blocks, you stones, you worse than senseless things!
O you hard hearts, you cruel men of Rome,
Knew you not Pompey? Many a time and oft
Have you climb'd up to walls and battlements,
To towers and windows, yea, to chimney-tops,
Your infants in your arms, and there have sat
The live-long day, with patient expectation,
To see great Pompey pass the streets of Rome,
And when you saw his chariot but appear
Have you not made an universal shout,
That Tiber trembled underneath her banks
To hear the replication of your sounds
Made in her concave shores?
And do you now put on your best attire?
And do you now cull out a holiday?
And do you now strew flowers in his way
That comes in triumph over Pompey's blood?
Be gone!
Run to your houses, fall upon your knees,
Pray to the gods to intermit the plague
That needs must light on this ingratitude.

Flav. Go, go, good countrymen, and, for this fault,
Assemble all the poor men of your sort;
Draw them to Tiber banks, and weep your tears
Into the channel, till the lowest stream
Do kiss the most exalted shores of all.

Exeunt all the Commoners.

See, whe'er their basest metal be not mov'd;
They vanish tongue-tied in their guiltiness.
Go you down that way towards the Capitol;
This way will I. Disrobe the images
If you do find them deck'd with ceremonies.

Mar. May we do so?
You know it is the feast of Lupercal.

Flav. It is no matter; let no images
Be hung with Cæsar's trophies. I'll about
And drive away the vulgar from the streets;
So do you too, where you perceive them thick.
These growing feathers pluck'd from Cæsar's wing
Will make him fly an ordinary pitch,
Who else would soar above the view of men
And keep us all in servile fearfulness.

Exeunt.

42. **Pompey,** Gnæus Pompeius Magnus, the conqueror of the East. Civil war between him and Cæsar ended in his defeat at Pharsalia, and he was shortly after assassinated. 51. **replication,** echo. 54. **cull out,** choose this as. 56. **Pompey's blood,** see note on l. 36. 59. **intermit,** withhold. 66. **whe'er,** whether. 69. **images,** statues. 70. **ceremonies,** ceremonial decorations. 72. **feast of Lupercal,** the Lupercalia, an ancient festival of purification and fertility. The priests, *Luperci* (of whom Antony was one on this occasion), ran through the streets striking women with goatskin thongs. The blows were thought to cure barrenness. 78. **pitch,** height.

Scene II. *A public place.*

Enter *Cæsar; Antony,* for the course; *Calpurnia, Portia, Decius, Cicero, Brutus, Cassius,* and *Casca,* a *Soothsayer:* after them *Marullus* and *Flavius.*

Cæs. Calpurnia!
Casca. Peace ho! Cæsar speaks.
Cæs. Calpurnia!
Cal. Here, my lord.
Cæs. Stand you directly in Antonius' way
When he doth run his course. Antonius!
Ant. Cæsar, my lord?
Cæs. Forget not, in your speed, Antonius,
To touch Calpurnia; for our elders say,
The barren, touched in this holy chase,
Shake off their sterile curse.
Ant. I shall remember:
When Cæsar says, "Do this," it is perform'd.
Cæs. Set on; and leave no ceremony out.
Sooth. Cæsar!
Cæs. Ha! who calls?
Casca. Bid every noise be still; peace yet again!
Cæs. Who is it in the press that calls on me?
I hear a tongue, shriller than all the music,
Cry "Cæsar!" Speak; Cæsar is turn'd to hear.
Sooth. Beware the ides of March.
Cæs. What man is that?
Bru. A soothsayer bids you beware the ides of March.
Cæs. Set him before me; let me see his face.
Cas. Fellow, come from the throng; look upon Cæsar.
Cæs. What say'st thou to me now? Speak once again.
Sooth. Beware the ides of March.
Cæs. He is a dreamer; let us leave him. Pass.

Sennet. Exeunt all but Brutus and Cassius.

Cas. Will you go see the order of the course?
Bru. Not I.
Cas. I pray you, do.
Bru. I am not gamesome; I do lack some part
Of that quick spirit that is in Antony.
Let me not hinder, Cassius, your desires;
I'll leave you.
Cas. Brutus, I do observe you now of late;
I have not from your eyes that gentleness
And show of love as I was wont to have:

Scene ii: s. d., for the course, to run the sacred race. 9. **sterile curse,** curse of childlessness. 15. **press,** crowd. 18. **ides of March,** fifteenth of March. 24. **Pass,** let us move on. **S. d., Sennet,** a trumpet call. 25. **see . . . course,** watch the running.

You bear too stubborn and too strange a hand
Over your friend that loves you.

Bru. Cassius,
Be not deceiv'd. If I have veil'd my look,
I turn the trouble of my countenance
Merely upon myself. Vexed I am
Of late with passions of some difference,
Conceptions only proper to myself,
Which give some soil perhaps to my behaviours;
But let not therefore my good friends be griev'd—
Among which number, Cassius, be you one—
Nor construe any further my neglect,
Than that poor Brutus, with himself at war,
Forgets the shows of love to other men.

Cas. Then, Brutus, I have much mistook your passion;
By means whereof this breast of mine hath buried
Thoughts of great value, worthy cogitations.
Tell me, good Brutus, can you see your face?

Bru. No, Cassius; for the eye sees not itself
But by reflection, by some other things.

Cas. 'T is just;
And it is very much lamented, Brutus,
That you have no such mirrors as will turn
Your hidden worthiness into your eye,
That you might see your shadow. I have heard,
Where many of the best respect in Rome,
(Except immortal Cæsar), speaking of Brutus
And groaning underneath this age's yoke,
Have wish'd that noble Brutus had his eyes.

Bru. Into what dangers would you lead me, Cassius,
That you would have me seek into myself
For that which is not in me?

Cas. Therefore, good Brutus, be prepar'd to hear;
And since you know you cannot see yourself
So well as by reflection, I, your glass,
Will modestly discover to yourself
That of yourself which you yet know not of.
And be not jealous on me, gentle Brutus.
Were I a common laugher, or did use
To stale with ordinary oaths my love
To every new protester; if you know
That I do fawn on men and hug them hard
And after scandal them, or if you know
That I profess myself in banqueting
To all the rout, then hold me dangerous.
Flourish and shout.

Bru. What means this shouting? I do fear, the people
Choose Cæsar for their king.

Cas. Ay, do you fear it?
Then must I think you would not have it so.

Bru. I would not, Cassius; yet I love him well.
But wherefore do you hold me here so long?
What is it that you would impart to me?
If it be aught toward the general good,
Set honour in one eye and death i' th' other,
And I will look on both indifferently;
For let the gods so speed me as I love
The name of honour more than I fear death.

Cas. I know that virtue to be in you, Brutus,
As well as I do know your outward favour.
Well, honour is the subject of my story.
I cannot tell what you and other men
Think of this life; but, for my single self,
I had as lief not be as live to be
In awe of such a thing as I myself.
I was born free as Cæsar, so were you;
We both have fed as well, and we can both
Endure the winter's cold as well as he;
For once, upon a raw and gusty day,
The troubled Tiber chafing with her shores,
Cæsar said to me, "Dar'st thou, Cassius, now
Leap with me into this angry flood,
And swim to yonder point?" Upon the word,
Accoutred as I was, I plunged in
And bade him follow; so indeed he did.
The torrent roar'd, and we did buffet it
With lusty sinews, throwing it aside
And stemming it with hearts of controversy;
But ere we could arrive the point propos'd,
Cæsar cried, "Help me, Cassius, or I sink!"
I, as Æneas, our great ancestor,
Did from the flames of Troy upon his shoulder
The old Anchises bear, so from the waves of Tiber
Did I the tired Cæsar. And this man
Is now become a god, and Cassius is
A wretched creature, and must bend his body
If Cæsar carelessly but nod on him.
He had a fever when he was in Spain,
And when the fit was on him, I did mark
How he did shake—'t is true, this god did shake—
His coward lips did from their colour fly,

35. **stubborn,** rough. 39. **Merely,** wholly. 40. **of some difference,** conflicting. 41. **only proper to,** concerning. 42. **give . . . to,** sully, alter. 49. **By means whereof,** on which account. 54. **just,** true. 58. **shadow,** reflection. 69. **modestly,** in a moderate way. 73. **stale,** make stale, cheap. **ordinary,** customary, frequent. 74. **protester,** person who professes friendship. 76. **scandal,** slander.

77. **profess myself,** make profession of friendship. 87. **indifferently,** impartially. 91. **favour,** appearance. 109. **of controversy,** stirred by rivalry. 112ff. **Æneas,** the founder of Rome, carried his father Anchises from the sack of Troy. 122. **His . . . fly,** his lips lost their redness as cowardly soldiers desert the colors.

And that same eye whose bend doth awe the world
Did lose his lustre; I did hear him groan.
Ay, and that tongue of his that bade the Romans
Mark him and write his speeches in their books,
Alas, it cried, "Give me some drink, Titinius,"
As a sick girl. Ye gods, it doth amaze me
A man of such a feeble temper should
So get the start of the majestic world
And bear the palm alone. *Shout. Flourish.*

Bru. Another general shout!
I do believe that these applauses are
For some new honours that are heap'd on Cæsar.

Cas. Why, man, he doth bestride the narrow world
Like a Colossus, and we petty men
Walk under his huge legs, and peep about
To find ourselves dishonourable graves.
Men at some time are masters of their fates;
The fault, dear Brutus, is not in our stars,
But in ourselves, that we are underlings.
Brutus and Cæsar: what should be in that "Cæsar"?
Why should that name be sounded more than yours?
Write them together, yours is as fair a name;
Sound them, it doth become the mouth as well;
Weigh them, it is as heavy; conjure with 'em,
"Brutus" will start a spirit as soon as "Cæsar."
Now, in the names of all the gods at once,
Upon what meat doth this our Cæsar feed
That he is grown so great? Age, thou art sham'd!
Rome, thou hast lost the breed of noble bloods!
When went there by an age, since the great flood,
But it was fam'd with more than with one man?
When could they say, till now, that talk'd of Rome,
That her wide walks encompass'd but one man?
Now is it Rome indeed and room enough,
When there is in it but one only man.
O, you and I have heard our fathers say
There was a Brutus once that would have brook'd
Th' eternal devil to keep his state in Rome
As easily as a king.

Bru. That you do love me, I am nothing jealous;
What you would work me to, I have some aim.
How I have thought of this and of these times,
I shall recount hereafter; for this present,
I would not—so with love I might entreat you—
Be any further mov'd. What you have said
I will consider: what you have to say
I will with patience hear, and find a time
Both meet to hear and answer such high things.
Till then, my noble friend, chew upon this:
Brutus had rather be a villager
Than to repute himself a son of Rome
Under these hard conditions as this time
Is like to lay upon us.

Cas. I am glad that my weak words
Have struck but thus much show of fire from Brutus.

Re-enter *Cæsar* and his train.

Bru. The games are done and Cæsar is returning.

Cas. As they pass by, pluck Casca by the sleeve;
And he will, after his sour fashion, tell you
What hath proceeded worthy note to-day.

Bru. I will do so. But, look you, Cassius,
The angry spot doth glow on Cæsar's brow,
And all the rest look like a chidden train.
Calpurnia's cheek is pale and Cicero
Looks with such ferret and such fiery eyes
As we have seen him in the Capitol,
Being cross'd in conference by some senators.

Cas. Casca will tell us what the matter is.

Cæs. Antonius!

Ant. Cæsar?

Cæs. Let me have men about me that are fat,
Sleek-headed men and such as sleep a-nights.
Yond Cassius has a lean and hungry look,
He thinks too much; such men are dangerous.

Ant. Fear him not, Cæsar; he's not dangerous;
He is a noble Roman and well given.

Cæs. Would he were fatter! but I fear him not.

123. bend, glance. **129. temper,** constitution. **136. Colossus,** a huge statue which was said to bestride the entrance to the harbor of Rhodes, so that ships sailed under its legs. **147. start,** raise. **152. the great flood,** the legendary flood of which Deucalion and Pyrrha were the only survivors. **155. wide walks,** the belt of parks and gardens around ancient Rome. **156.** "room" was pronounced like "Rome."

159. a Brutus once, the Lucius Junius Brutus who took a leading part in expelling the Tarquins and founding the Roman state. **brook'd,** allowed. **160. keep his state,** rule. **162. nothing jealous,** not at all doubtful. **163. work,** urge. **aim,** inkling. **166. so,** if. **186. ferret,** like a ferret's, i.e., sharp and red. **188. conference,** debate. **197. given,** disposed.

Yet if my name were liable to fear,
I do not know the man I should avoid
So soon as that spare Cassius. He reads much;
He is a great observer, and he looks
Quite through the deeds of men. He loves no plays
As thou dost, Antony; he hears no music;
Seldom he smiles, and smiles in such a sort
As if he mock'd himself and scorn'd his spirit
That could be mov'd to smile at anything.
Such men as he be never at heart's ease
Whiles they behold a greater than themselves,
And therefore are they very dangerous.
I rather tell thee what is to be fear'd
Than what I fear; for always I am Cæsar.
Come on my right hand, for this ear is deaf,
And tell me truly what thou think'st of him.

Sennet. Exeunt Cæsar and all his train but Casca.

Casca. You pull'd me by the cloak; would you speak with me?

Bru. Ay, Casca; tell us what hath chanc'd to-day
That Cæsar looks so sad.

Casca. Why, you were with him, were you not?

Bru. I should not then ask Casca what had chanc'd.

Casca. Why, there was a crown offered him; and being offered him, he put it by with the back of his hand, thus; and then the people fell a-shouting.

Bru. What was the second noise for?

Casca. Why, for that too.

Cas. They shouted thrice; what was the last cry for?

Casca. Why, for that too.

Bru. Was the crown offered him thrice?

Casca. Ay, marry, was 't, and he put it by thrice, every time gentler than other; and at every putting-by mine honest neighbours shouted.

Cas. Who offer'd him the crown?

Casca. Why, Antony.

Bru. Tell us the manner of it, gentle Casca.

Casca. I can as well be hanged as tell the manner of it: it was mere foolery; I did not mark it. I saw Mark Antony offer him a crown—yet 't was not a crown neither, 't was one of these coronets—and, as I told you, he put it by once; but, for all that, to my thinking, he would fain have had it. Then he offered it to him again; then he put it by again; but, to my thinking, he was very loath to lay his fingers off it. And then he offered it the third time; he put it the third time by; and still as he refused it, the rabblement hooted and clapped their chopped hands and threw up their sweaty night-caps and uttered such a deal of stinking breath because Cæsar refused the crown, that it had almost choked Cæsar, for he swounded and fell down at it; and for mine own part, I durst not laugh, for fear of opening my lips and receiving the bad air.

Cas. But, soft, I pray you; what, did Cæsar swound?

Casca. He fell down in the market-place, and foamed at mouth, and was speechless.

Bru. 'T is very like; he hath the falling sickness.

Cas. No, Cæsar hath it not; but you and I
And honest Casca, we have the falling sickness.

Casca. I know not what you mean by that, but I am sure Cæsar fell down. If the tag-rag people did not clap him and hiss him, according as he pleased and displeased them, as they use to do the players in the theatre, I am no true man.

Bru. What said he when he came unto himself?

Casca. Marry, before he fell down, when he perceived the common herd was glad he refused the crown, he plucked me ope his doublet and offered them his throat to cut. An I had been a man of any occupation, if I would not have taken him at a word, I would I might go to hell among the rogues. And so he fell. When he came to himself again, he said, if he had done or said anything amiss, he desired their worships to think it was his infirmity. Three or four wenches, where I stood, cried, "Alas, good soul!" and forgave him with all their hearts: but there's no heed to be taken of them; if Cæsar had stabbed their mothers, they would have done no less.

Bru. And after that, he came thus sad away?

Casca. Ay.

Cas. Did Cicero say anything?

Casca. Ay, he spoke Greek.

Cas. To what effect?

Casca. Nay, an I tell you that, I'll ne'er look you i' th' face again. But those that understood him smiled at one another and shook their heads; but, for mine own part, it was Greek to me. I could tell you more news too: Marullus and Flavius, for pulling scarfs off Cæsar's images, are put to silence. Fare

199. **my name**, I, Cæsar. 204. **hears no music**, cf. *Merchant of Venice*, V. i, 83ff. 217. **sad**, serious. 238. **coronets**, chaplets, garlands.

244. **still**, always. 245. **chopped**, chapped. 250. **swounded**, swooned. 256. **like**, likely. **falling sickness**, epilepsy. 267. **ope**, open. **doublet**, Elizabethan jacket. 269. **man . . . occupation**, workman. 269. **at a**, at this. 289. **scarfs**, wreaths, fillets. 290. **put to silence**, removed from office.

you well. There was more foolery yet, if I could remember it.

Cas. Will you sup with me to-night, Casca?

Casca. No, I am promised forth.

Cas. Will you dine with me to-morrow?

Casca. Ay, if I be alive and your mind hold and your dinner worth the eating.

Cas. Good; I will expect you.

Casca. Do so. Farewell, both; *Exit*

Bru. What a blunt fellow is this grown to be!
He was quick mettle when he went to school.

Cas. So is he now in execution
Of any bold or noble enterprise,
However he puts on this tardy form.
This rudeness is a sauce to his good wit,
Which gives men stomach to digest his words
With better appetite.

Bru. And so it is. For this time I will leave you;
To-morrow, if you please to speak with me,
I will come home to you; or, if you will,
Come home to me, and I will wait for you.

Cas. I will do so; till then, think of the world. *Exit Brutus.*
Well, Brutus, thou art noble; yet, I see,
Thy honourable metal may be wrought
From that it is dispos'd; therefore it is meet
That noble minds keep ever with their likes;
For who so firm that cannot be seduc'd?
Cæsar doth bear me hard, but he loves Brutus.
If I were Brutus now and he were Cassius,
He should not humour me. I will this night,
In several hands, in at his windows throw,
As if they came from several citizens,
Writings all tending to the great opinion
That Rome holds of his name; wherein obscurely
Cæsar's ambition shall be glanced at;
And after this let Cæsar seat him sure,
For we will shake him, or worse days endure.
Exit.

Scene III. *A street in Rome.*

Thunder and lightning. Enter *Casca* with his sword drawn and *Cicero.*

Cic. Good even, Casca; brought you Cæsar home?
Why are you breathless, and why stare you so?

Casca. Are not you mov'd, when all the sway of earth
Shakes like a thing unfirm? O Cicero,
I have seen tempests when the scolding winds
Have riv'd the knotty oaks, and I have seen
Th' ambitious ocean swell and rage and foam
To be exalted with the threat'ning clouds;
But never till to-night, never till now,
Did I go through a tempest dropping fire.
Either there is a civil strife in heaven,
Or else the world, too saucy with the gods,
Incenses them to send destruction.

Cic. Why, saw you anything more wonderful?

Casca. A common slave—you know him well by sight—
Held up his left hand, which did flame and burn
Like twenty torches join'd, and yet his hand,
Not sensible of fire, remain'd unscorch'd.
Besides—I ha' not since put up my sword—
Against the Capitol I met a lion,
Who glaz'd upon me, and went surly by
Without annoying me. And there were drawn
Upon a heap a hundred ghastly women,
Transformed with their fear, who swore they saw
Men all in fire walk up and down the streets.
And yesterday the bird of night did sit
Even at noon-day upon the market-place,
Hooting and shrieking. When these prodigies
Do so conjointly meet, let not men say,
"These are their reasons; they are natural";
For, I believe, they are portentous things
Unto the climate that they point upon.

Cic. Indeed, it is a strange-disposed time;
But men may construe things after their fashion
Clean from the purpose of the things themselves.
Comes Cæsar to the Capitol to-morrow?

Casca. He doth; for he did bid Antonius
Send word to you he would be there to-morrow.

Cic. Good-night then, Casca; this disturbed sky
Is not to walk in.

Casca. Farewell, Cicero.
Exit Cicero.

Enter *Cassius.*

Cas. Who's there?

Casca. A Roman.

Cas. Casca, by your voice.

Casca. Your ear is good. Cassius, what night is this!

Cas. A very pleasing night to honest men.

293. **promis'd forth,** engaged for dinner. 300. **quick mettle,** high-spirited. 303. **tardy form,** sluggish manner. 313-4. **Thy . . . dispos'd,** your noble nature, through association with persons less noble, may be made to swerve from its true course. 317. **doth bear me hard,** is hostile to me. 320. **several hands,** different handwritings. **Scene iii:** 3. **sway,** settled order, or, weight.

18. **sensible of,** sensitive to. 21. **glaz'd,** glared. 22-3. **drawn . . . heap,** crowded together. 26. **bird of night,** owl. 32. **climate,** region. **point upon,** concern. 35. **Clean . . . themselves,** quite contrary to their true meaning. 42. **what night,** what a night.

Casca. Who ever knew the heavens menace so?
Cas. Those that have known the earth so full of faults.
For my part, I have walk'd about the streets,
Submitting me unto the perilous night,
And, thus unbraced, Casca, as you see,
Have bar'd my bosom to the thunder-stone;
And when the cross blue lightning seem'd to open
The breast of heaven, I did present myself
Even in the aim and very flash of it.
Casca. But wherefore did you so much tempt the heavens?
It is the part of men to fear and tremble
When the most mighty gods by tokens send
Such dreadful heralds to astonish us.
Cas. You are dull, Casca, and those sparks of life
That should be in a Roman you do want,
Or else you use not. You look pale and gaze
And put on fear and cast yourself in wonder,
To see the strange impatience of the heavens;
But if you would consider the true cause
Why all these fires, why all these gliding ghosts,
Why birds and beasts from quality and kind,
Why old men, fools, and children calculate,
Why all these things change from their ordinance
Their natures and preformed faculties
To monstrous quality, why, you shall find
That Heaven hath infus'd them with these spirits,
To make them instruments of fear and warning
Unto some monstrous state.
Now could I, Casca, name to thee a man
Most like this dreadful night,
That thunders, lightens, opens graves, and roars
As doth the lion in the Capitol,
A man no mightier than thyself or me
In personal action, yet prodigious grown
And fearful, as these strange eruptions are.
Casca. 'T is Cæsar that you mean; is it not, Cassius?
Cas. Let it be who it is; for Romans now
Have thews and limbs like to their ancestors,
But, woe the while! our fathers' minds are dead,
And we are govern'd with our mothers' spirits;
Our yoke and sufferance show us womanish.
Casca. Indeed, they say the senators to-morrow
Mean to establish Cæsar as a king;
And he shall wear his crown by sea and land,
In every place, save here in Italy.
Cas. I know where I will wear this dagger then;
Cassius from bondage will deliver Cassius.
Therein, ye gods, you make the weak most strong;
Therein, ye gods, you tyrants do defeat;
Nor stony tower, nor walls of beaten brass,
Nor airless dungeon, nor strong links of iron,
Can be retentive to the strength of spirit;
But life, being weary of these worldly bars,
Never lacks power to dismiss itself.
If I know this, know all the world besides,
That part of tyranny that I do bear
I can shake off at pleasure. *Thunder still.*
Casca. So can I;
So every bondman in his own hand bears
The power to cancel his captivity.
Cas. And why should Cæsar be a tyrant then?
Poor man! I know he would not be a wolf,
But that he sees the Romans are but sheep;
He were no lion, were not Romans hinds.
Those that with haste will make a mighty fire
Begin it with weak straws. What trash is Rome,
What rubbish and what offal, when it serves
For the base matter to illuminate
So vile a thing as Cæsar! But, O grief,
Where hast thou led me? I, perhaps, speak this
Before a willing bondman; then I know
My answer must be made. But I am arm'd,
And dangers are to me indifferent.
Casca. You speak to Casca, and to such a man
That is no fleering tell-tale. Hold, my hand:
Be factious for redress of all these griefs,
And I will set this foot of mine as far
As who goes farthest.
Cas. There's a bargain made.
Now know you, Casca, I have mov'd already
Some certain of the noblest-minded Romans
To undergo with me an enterprise
Of honourable-dangerous consequence;
And I do know, by this they stay for me
In Pompey's porch; for now, this fearful night,
There is no stir or walking in the streets;

48. unbraced, with doublet open. **49. thunder-stone,** thunder-bolt. **50. cross,** forked. **60. put on,** show. **cast . . . in,** give way to. **64. from . . . kind,** contrary to their nature. **66. ordinance,** normal character. **67. preformed,** original. **71. Unto . . . state,** of an unnatural state of affairs. **78. fearful,** fear-inspiring. **eruptions,** portents. **82. woe the while,** woe for the times.

84. yoke and sufferance, submission to the yoke. **106. hinds,** female deer; also, rustics, serfs. **117. fleering,** mocking. **118. Be factious,** be zealous, or, form a party. **123. undergo,** undertake. **126. Pompey's porch,** a colonnade attached to the theatre built by Pompey.

And the complexion of the element
In favour 's like the work we have in hand,
Most bloody, fiery, and most terrible.

Enter *Cinna*.

Casca. Stand close a while, for here comes one in haste.
Cas. 'T is Cinna, I do know him by his gait;
He is a friend. Cinna, where haste you so?
Cin. To find out you. Who's that? Metellus Cimber?
Cas. No, it is Casca, one incorporate
To our attempts. Am I not stay'd for, Cinna?
Cin. I am glad on't. What a fearful night is this!
There 's two or three of us have seen strange sights.
Cas. Am I not stay'd for? tell me.
Cin. Yes, you are.
O Cassius, if you could
But win the noble Brutus to our party—
Cas. Be you content. Good Cinna, take this paper,
And look you lay it in the prætor's chair,
Where Brutus may but find it; and throw this
In at his window; set this up with wax
Upon old Brutus' statue: all this done,
Repair to Pompey's porch, where you shall find us.
Is Decius Brutus and Trebonius there?
Cin. All but Metullus Cimber; and he's gone
To seek you at your house. Well, I will hie
And so bestow these papers as you bade me.
Cas. That done, repair to Pompey's theatre.

Exit Cinna.

Come, Casca, you and I will yet ere day
See Brutus at his house: three parts of him
Is ours already, and the man entire
Upon the next encounter yields him ours,
Casca. O, he sits high in all the people's hearts;
And that which would appear offence in us,
His countenance, like richest alchemy,
Will change to virtue and to worthiness.
Cas. Him and his worth and our great need of him
You have right well conceited. Let us go,
For it is after midnight; and ere day
We will awake him and be sure of him.

Exeunt.

ACT II. Scene I. *Rome.*

Enter *Brutus* in his orchard.

Bru. What, Lucius, ho!
I cannot by the progress of the stars
Give guess how near to day. Lucius, I say!
I would it were my fault to sleep so soundly.
When, Lucius, when! Awake, I say! What, Lucius!

Enter *Lucius*.

Luc. Call'd you, my lord?
Bru. Get me a taper in my study, Lucius.
When it is lighted, come and call me here.
Luc. I will, my lord. *Exit*
Bru. It must be by his death; and for my part,
I know no personal cause to spurn at him
But for the general. He would be crown'd:
How that might change his nature, there's the question.
It is the bright day that brings forth the adder,
And that craves wary walking. Crown him?—that!—
And then, I grant, we put a sting in him
That at his will he may do danger with.
Th' abuse of greatness is, when it disjoins
Remorse from power; and, to speak truth of Cæsar,
I have not known when his affections sway'd
More than his reason. But 't is a common proof
That lowliness is young Ambition's ladder,
Whereto the climber-upward turns his face;
But when he once attains the upmost round,
He then unto the ladder turns his back,
Looks in the clouds, scorning the base degrees
By which he did ascend. So Cæsar may;

128. complexion of the element, look of the sky. **129. favour 's,** appearance is. **135-6. incorporate to,** confederate in. **143. prætor's chair,** Brutus was one of the prætors, magistrates ranking next to the consuls. **Act II, Scene i: 11. spurn at,** attack. **12. the general,** the public good.

146. old Brutus' statue, see above, note on I, ii, 159. **159. countenance,** support. **alchemy,** the supposed science of transmuting inferior metals into gold. **162. conceited,** understood, described. **Act II, Scene i: 15. craves,** necessitates. **Crown him?—that!,** give him the crown? do that! **19. Remorse,** pity. **20. affections,** passions. **21. proof,** experience. **26. degrees,** rungs.

Then, lest he may, prevent. And, since the quarrel
Will bear no colour for the thing he is,
Fashion it thus: that what he is, augmented,
Would run to these and these extremities;
And therefore think him as a serpent's egg
Which, hatch'd, would, as his kind, grow mischievous,
And kill him in the shell.

Re-enter *Lucius.*

Luc. The taper burneth in your closet, sir.
Searching the window for a flint, I found
This paper, thus seal'd up; and I am sure
It did not lie there when I went to bed.
Gives him the letter.

Bru. Get you to bed again; it is not day.
Is not to-morrow, boy, the ides of March?

Luc. I know not, sir.

Bru. Look in the calendar, and bring me word.

Luc. I will, sir. *Exit*

Bru. The exhalations whizzing in the air
Give so much light that I may read by them.
Opens the letter and reads.

"Brutus, thou sleep'st; awake, and see thyself!
Shall Rome, etc. Speak, strike, redress!"
"Brutus, thou sleep'st; awake!"

Such instigations have been often dropp'd
Where I have took them up.
"Shall Rome, etc." Thus must I piece it out:
Shall Rome stand under one man's awe? What, Rome?
My ancestors did from the streets of Rome
The Tarquin drive, when he was call'd a king.
"Speak, strike, redress!" Am I entreated
To speak and strike? O Rome, I make thee promise,
If the redress will follow, thou receivest
Thy full petition at the hand of Brutus!

Re-enter *Lucius.*

Luc. Sir, March is wasted fifteen days.
Knocking within.

Bru. 'T is good. Go to the gate; somebody knocks. *Exit Lucius.*
Since Cassius first did whet me against Cæsar,
I have not slept.
Between the acting of a dreadful thing
And the first motion, all the interim is
Like a phantasma or a hideous dream.
The Genius and the mortal instruments
Are then in council; and the state of man,
Like to a little kingdom, suffers then
The nature of an insurrection.

Re-enter *Lucius.*

Luc. Sir, 't is your brother Cassius at the door,
Who doth desire to see you.

Bru. Is he alone?

Luc. No, sir, there are moe with him.

Bru. Do you know them?

Luc. No, sir; their hats are pluck'd about their ears
And half their faces buried in their cloaks,
That by no means I may discover them
By any mark of favour.

Bru. Let 'em enter.
Exit Lucius.
They are the faction. O Conspiracy,
Sham'st thou to show thy dang'rous brow by night,
When evils are most free? O, then by day
Where wilt thou find a cavern dark enough
To mask thy monstrous visage? Seek none, Conspiracy!
Hide it in smiles and affability;
For if thou path, thy native semblance on,
Not Erebus itself were dim enough
To hide thee from prevention.

Enter the conspirators, *Cassius, Casca, Decius, Cinna, Metellus Cimber,* and *Trebonius.*

Cas. I think we are too bold upon your rest:
Good morrow, Brutus; do we trouble you?

Bru. I have been up this hour, awake all night.
Know I these men that come along with you?

Cas. Yes, every man of them; and no man here
But honours you; and every one doth wish
You had but that opinion of yourself
Which every noble Roman bears of you.
This is Trebonius.

Bru. He is welcome hither.

Cas. This, Decius Brutus.

Bru. He is welcome too.

Cas. This, Casca; this, Cinna; and this, Metellus Cimber.

Bru. They are all welcome.
What watchful cares do interpose themselves
Betwixt your eyes and night?

28-30. And . . . thus, since Cæsar's present conduct will not be thought to justify his removal, look at the case in this way. **33. as his kind,** according to his nature. **35. closet,** study. **44. exhalations,** meteors. **52. under one man's awe,** in awe of one man. **58. full petition,** everything asked for. **65. phantasma,** vision. **66-9. The Genius . . . insurrection,** the mind and the bodily agents are debating with each other. See note on *Macbeth,* I, iii, 140. **70. brother,** Cassius had married Brutus' sister. **76. favour,** appearance. **77. faction,** party of conspirators. **83. path,** proceed. **thy . . . on,** without disguise. **84. Erebus,** the space of darkness between earth and Hades. **85. prevention,** discovery.

Cas. Shall I entreat a word?
They whisper.
Dec. Here lies the east; doth not the day break here?
Casca. No.
Cin. O, pardon, sir, it doth; and yon grey lines
That fret the clouds are messengers of day.
Casca. You shall confess that you are both deceiv'd.
Here, as I point my sword, the sun arises,
Which is a great way growing on the south,
Weighing the youthful season of the year.
Some two months hence up higher toward the north
He first presents his fire; and the high east
Stands, as the Capitol, directly here.
Bru. Give me your hands all over, one by one.
Cas. And let us swear our resolution.
Bru. No, not an oath! If not the face of men,
The sufferance of our souls, the time's abuse,—
If these be motives weak, break off betimes,
And every man hence to his idle bed;
So let high-sighted tyranny range on,
Till each man drop by lottery. But if these
(As I am sure they do) bear fire enough
To kindle cowards and to steel with valour
The melting spirits of women, then, countrymen,
What need we any spur but our own cause,
To prick us to redress? what other bond
Than secret Romans, that have spoke the word,
And will not palter? and what other oath
Than honesty to honesty engag'd,
That this shall be, or we will fall for it?
Swear priests and cowards and men cautelous,
Old feeble carrions and such suffering souls
That welcome wrongs; unto bad causes swear
Such creatures as men doubt; but do not stain
The even virtue of our enterprise,
Nor th' insuppressive mettle of our spirits,
To think that or our cause or our performance
Did need an oath; when every drop of blood
That every Roman bears, and nobly bears,
Is guilty of a several bastardy,
If he do break the smallest particle
Of any promise that hath pass'd from him.

104. fret, interlace. **107. growing on,** toward. **108. weighing,** allowing for. **112. all over,** in turn. **114. face of men,** evidence of suffering in people's looks. **115. the time's abuse,** abuses of the times. **118. high-sighted,** arrogant. **119. by lottery,** in turn (i.e., by proscription). **125. secret,** conspiring. **126. palter,** use trickery. **129. cautelous,** deceitful. **130. suffering,** tamely submissive. **135. to think,** by thinking. **or . . . or,** either . . . or.

Cas. But what of Cicero? Shall we sound him?
I think he will stand very strong with us.
Casca. Let us not leave him out.
Cin. No, by no means.
Met. O, let us have him, for his silver hairs
Will purchase us a good opinion
And buy men's voices to commend our deeds.
It shall be said, his judgment rul'd our hands;
Our youths and wildness shall no whit appear,
But all be buried in his gravity.
Bru. O, name him not; let us not break with him,
For he will never follow anything
That other men begin.
Cas. Then leave him out.
Casca. Indeed he is not fit.
Dec. Shall no man else be touch'd but only Cæsar?
Cas. Decius, well urg'd. I think it is not meet,
Mark Antony, so well belov'd of Cæsar,
Should outlive Cæsar: we shall find of him
A shrewd contriver; and, you know, his means,
If he improve them, may well stretch so far
As to annoy us all; which to prevent,
Let Antony and Cæsar fall together.
Bru. Our course will seem too bloody, Caius Cassius,
To cut the head off and then hack the limbs,
Like wrath in death and envy afterwards;
For Antony is but a limb of Cæsar.
Let 's be sacrificers, but not butchers, Caius.
We all stand up against the spirit of Cæsar,
And in the spirit of men there is no blood;
O, that we then could come by Cæsar's spirit,
And not dismember Cæsar! But, alas,
Cæsar must bleed for it! And, gentle friends,
Let 's kill him boldly, but not wrathfully;
Let 's carve him as a dish fit for the gods,
Not hew him as a carcass fit for hounds;
And let our hearts, as subtle masters do,
Stir up their servants to an act of rage,
And after seem to chide 'em. This shall make
Our purpose necessary and not envious;
Which so appearing to the common eyes,
We shall be call'd purgers, not murderers.
And for Mark Antony, think not of him;
For he can do no more than Cæsar's arm
When Cæsar's head is off.
Cas. Yet I fear him;
For in the ingrafted love he bears to Cæsar—
Bru. Alas, good Cassius, do not think of him.

150. break with, confide in. **157. of,** in. **158. shrewd contriver,** dangerous schemer. **160. annoy,** injure. **164. envy,** vindictiveness. **176. servants,** i.e., our arms. **184. ingrafted,** deep-rooted.

If he love Cæsar, all that he can do
Is to himself, take thought and die for Cæsar;
And that were much he should, for he is given
To sports, to wildness, and much company.
Treb. There is no fear in him; let him not die;
For he will live, and laugh at this hereafter.
Clock strikes.
Bru. Peace! count the clock.
Cas. The clock hath stricken three.
Treb. 'T is time to part.
Cas. But it is doubtful yet
Whether Cæsar will come forth to-day, or no;
For he is superstitious grown of late,
Quite from the main opinion he held once
Of fantasy, of dreams, and ceremonies.
It may be these apparent prodigies,
The unaccustom'd terror of this night,
And the persuasion of his augurers,
May hold him from the Capitol to-day.
Dec. Never fear that. If he be so resolv'd,
I can o'ersway him; for he loves to hear
That unicorns may be betray'd with trees,
And bears with glasses, elephants with holes,
Lions with toils, and men with flatterers;
But when I tell him he hates flatterers
He says he does, being then most flattered.
Let me work;
For I can give his humour the true bent,
And I will bring him to the Capitol.
Cas. Nay, we will all of us be there to fetch him.
Bru. By the eighth hour; is that the uttermost?
Cin. Be that the uttermost, and fail not then.
Met. Caius Ligarius doth bear Cæsar hard,
Who rated him for speaking well of Pompey.
I wonder none of you have thought of him.
Bru. Now, good Metellus, go along by him.
He loves me well, and I have given him reasons;
Send him but hither, and I 'll fashion him.
Cas. The morning comes upon 's: we 'll leave you, Brutus,
And, friends, disperse yourselves; but all remember
What you have said, and show yourselves true Romans.
Bru. Good gentlemen, look fresh and merrily.
Let not our looks put on our purposes,
But bear it as our Roman actors do,
With untir'd spirits and formal constancy.
And so good morrow to you every one.
Exeunt all but Brutus.
Boy! Lucius! Fast asleep? It is no matter;
Enjoy the honey-heavy dew of slumber.
Thou hast no figures nor no fantasies
Which busy care draws in the brains of men;
Therefore thou sleep'st so sound.

Enter *Portia*

Por. Brutus, my lord!
Bru. Portia, what mean you? Wherefore rise you now?
It is not for your health thus to commit
Your weak condition to the raw cold morning.
Por. Nor for yours neither. You 've ungently, Brutus,
Stole from my bed; and yesternight, at supper,
You suddenly arose, and walk'd about,
Musing and sighing, with your arms across;
And when I ask'd you what the matter was,
You star'd upon me with ungentle looks.
I urg'd you further; then you scratch'd your head,
And too impatiently stamp'd with your foot.
Yet I insisted; yet you answer'd not,
But with an angry wafture of your hand
Gave sign for me to leave you. So I did,
Fearing to strengthen that impatience
Which seem'd too much enkindled, and withal
Hoping it was but an effect of humour,
Which sometime hath his hour with every man.
It will not let you eat, nor talk, nor sleep,
And could it work so much upon your shape
As it hath much prevail'd on your condition,
I should not know you, Brutus. Dear my lord,
Make me acquainted with your cause of grief.
Bru. I am not well in health, and that is all.
Por. Brutus is wise, and, were he not in health,
He would embrace the means to come by it.
Bru. Why, so I do. Good Portia, go to bed.
Por. Is Brutus sick? and is it physical
To walk unbraced and suck up the humours

186-8. If . . . should, if Antony loves Cæsar, he cannot do harm to any one but himself, in becoming despondent and committing suicide, and such a waster as Antony would probably not do that. **190. no fear,** nothing to be feared. **192. the clock,** an anachronism. **196. main,** general, or, strong. **198. apparent,** manifest. **200. augurers,** members of a priestly college whose duty it was to interpret omens. **204. unicorns,** a unicorn might be trapped by getting it to charge the tree which concealed the hunter and so imbed its horn in the trunk. **205. glasses,** a traditional way of capturing bears by scattering mirrors on the ground into which they would look. **holes,** pitfalls. **206. toils,** nets. **210. true bent,** right inclination. **216. rated,** rebuked. **218. by him,** by his house. **220. fashion him,** mould his sentiments.

225. put on, reveal. **227. formal constancy,** dignified firmness. **231. figures,** visions. **246. wafture,** waving. **250. humour,** physical condition. **254. condition,** disposition. **261. physical,** conducive to health.

Of the dank morning? What, is Brutus sick,
And will he steal out of his wholesome bed,
To dare the vile contagion of the night,
And tempt the rheumy and unpurged air
To add unto his sickness? No, my Brutus;
You have some sick offence within your mind,
Which, by the right and virtue of my place,
I ought to know of; and upon my knees
I charm you, by my once commended beauty,
By all your vows of love and that great vow
Which did incorporate and make us one,
That you unfold to me, yourself, your half,
Why you are heavy, and what men to-night
Have had resort to you; for here have been
Some six or seven, who did hide their faces
Even from darkness.

Bru. Kneel not, gentle Portia.

Por. I should not need, if you were gentle Brutus.
Within the bond of marriage, tell me, Brutus,
Is it excepted I should know no secrets
That appertain to you? Am I yourself
But, as it were, in sort or limitation,
To keep with you at meals, comfort your bed,
And talk to you sometimes? Dwell I but in the suburbs
Of your good pleasure? If it be no more,
Portia is Brutus' harlot, not his wife.

Bru. You are my true and honourable wife,
As dear to me as are the ruddy drops
That visit my sad heart.

Por. If this were true, then should I know this secret.
I grant I am a woman; but withal
A woman that Lord Brutus took to wife.
I grant I am a woman; but withal
A woman well-reputed, Cato's daughter.
Think you I am no stronger than my sex,
Being so father'd and so husbanded?
Tell me your counsels, I will not disclose 'em.
I have made strong proof of my constancy,
Giving myself a voluntary wound
Here, in the thigh; can I bear that with patience,
And not my husband's secrets?

Bru. O ye gods!
Render me worthy of this noble wife!
Knocking within.
Hark, hark! one knocks. Portia, go in a while,
And by and by thy bosom shall partake
The secrets of my heart.
All my engagements I will construe to thee,
All the charactery of my sad brows.
Leave me with haste. *Exit Portia.*
Lucius, who 's that knocks?

Re-enter *Lucius* with *Ligarius.*

Luc. Here is a sick man that would speak with you.

Bru. Caius Ligarius, that Metellus spake of.
Boy, stand aside. Caius Ligarius, how?

Lig. Vouchsafe good morrow from a feeble tongue.

Bru. O, what a time have you chose out, brave Caius,
To wear a kerchief! Would you were not sick!

Lig. I am not sick, if Brutus have in hand
Any exploit worthy the name of honour.

Bru. Such an exploit have I in hand, Ligarius,
Had you a healthful ear to hear of it.

Lig. By all the gods that Romans bow before,
I here discard my sickness! Soul of Rome!
Brave son, deriv'd from honourable loins!
Thou, like an exorcist, hast conjur'd up
My mortified spirit. Now bid me run,
And I will strive with things impossible;
Yea, get the better of them. What 's to do?

Bru. A piece of work that will make sick men whole.

Lig. But are not some whole that we must make sick?

Bru. That must we also. What it is, my Caius,
I shall unfold to thee, as we are going
To whom it must be done.

Lig. Set on your foot,
And with a heart new-fir'd I follow you,
To do I know not what; but it sufficeth
That Brutus leads me on. *Thunder.*

Bru. Follow me, then.
Exeunt.

Scene II. *Cæsar's house.*

Thunder and lightning. Enter *Cæsar,* in his night-gown.

Cæs. Nor heaven nor earth have been at peace to-night.
Thrice hath Calpurnia in her sleep cried out,
"Help! ho! they murder Cæsar!" Who 's within?

266. **rheumy,** causing colds. **unpurged,** not yet purified by the sun. 268. **sick offence,** disease, trouble. 271. **charm,** entreat. 283. **in . . . limitation,** in a partial or limited way. 292. **withal,** still. 295. **Cato's daughter,** Cato the younger, who fought against Cæsar, and committed suicide at Utica.

308. **All . . . of,** all that is written on. 313. **Vouchsafe,** deign to accept. 315. **wear a kerchief,** be ill. 323. **exorcist,** one who can summon or banish spirits. 324. **mortified,** deadened. **Scene ii: s. d. night-gown,** dressing gown.

Enter a *Servant*.

Serv. My lord?
Cæs. Go bid the priests do present sacrifice.
And bring me their opinions of success.
Serv. I will, my lord. *Exit.*

Enter *Calpurnia*.

Cal. What mean you, Cæsar? Think you to walk forth?
You shall not stir out of your house to-day.
Cæs. Cæsar shall forth. The things that threaten'd me
Ne'er look'd but on my back; when they shall see
The face of Cæsar, they are vanished.
Cal. Cæsar, I never stood on ceremonies,
Yet now they fright me. There is one within,
Besides the things that we have heard and seen,
Recounts most horrid sights seen by the watch.
A lioness hath whelped in the streets;
And graves have yawn'd, and yielded up their dead;
Fierce fiery warriors fight upon the clouds,
In ranks and squadrons and right form of war,
Which drizzled blood upon the Capitol;
The noise of battle hurtled in the air,
Horses did neigh, and dying men did groan,
And ghosts did shriek and squeal about the streets.
O Cæsar! these things are beyond all use,
And I do fear them.
Cæs. What can be avoided
Whose end is purpos'd by the mighty gods?
Yet Cæsar shall go forth; for these predictions
Are to the world in general as to Cæsar.
Cal. When beggars die there are no comets seen;
The heavens themselves blaze forth the death of princes.
Cæs. Cowards die many times before their deaths;
The valiant never taste of death but once.
Of all the wonders that I yet have heard,
It seems to me most strange that men should fear,
Seeing that death, a necessary end,
Will come when it will come.

Re-enter *Servant*.

What say the augurers?
Serv. They would not have you to stir forth to-day.
Plucking the entrails of an offering forth,
They could not find a heart within the beast.
Cæs. The gods do this in shame of cowardice;
Cæsar should be a beast without a heart,
If he should stay at home to-day for fear.
No, Cæsar shall not; Danger knows full well
That Cæsar is more dangerous than he.
We are two lions litter'd in one day,
And I the elder and more terrible;
And Cæsar shall go forth.
Cal. Alas, my lord,
Your wisdom is consum'd in confidence
Do not go forth to-day; call it my fear
That keeps you in the house, and not your own.
We 'll send Mark Antony to the senate-house,
And he shall say you are not well to-day.
Let me, upon my knee, prevail in this.
Cæs. Mark Antony shall say I am not well;
And, for thy humour, I will stay at home.

Enter *Decius*.

Here's Decius Brutus, he shall tell them so.
Dec. Cæsar, all hail! good morrow, worthy Cæsar;
I come to fetch you to the senate-house.
Cæs. And you are come in very happy time
To bear my greetings to the senators
And tell them that I will not come to-day.
Cannot, is false, and that I dare not, falser;
I will not come to-day. Tell them so, Decius.
Cal. Say he is sick.
Cæs. Shall Cæsar send a lie?
Have I in conquest stretch'd mine arm so far,
To be afeard to tell greybeards the truth?
Decius, go tell them Cæsar will not come.
Dec. Most mighty Cæsar, let me know some cause,
Lest I be laugh'd at when I tell them so.
Cæs. The cause is in my will; I will not come;
That is enough to satisfy the senate.
But for your private satisfaction,
Because I love you, I will let you know.
Calpurnia here, my wife, stays me at home.
She dreamt to-night she saw my statuë,
Which, like a fountain with an hundred spouts,
Did run pure blood; and many lusty Romans
Came smiling and did bathe their hands in it;
And these does she apply for warnings and portents
And evils imminent, and on her knee
Hath begg'd that I will stay at home to-day.

5. present, immediate. **6. success,** the result, i.e., good or bad omens. **13. stood on ceremonies,** gave heed to omens. **20. right form,** regular formation. **22. hurtled,** clashed. **25. use,** experience. **29. Are,** apply.

49. confidence, over-confidence. **56. humour,** whim. **75. stays,** keeps. **76. to-night,** last night.

Dec. This dream is all amiss interpreted;
It was a vision fair and fortunate.
Your statue spouting blood in many pipes,
In which so many smiling Romans bath'd
Signifies that from you great Rome shall suck
Reviving blood, and that great men shall press
For tinctures, stains, relics, and cognizance.
This by Calpurnia's dream is signified.

Cæs. And this way have you well expounded it.

Dec. I have, when you have heard what I can say;
And know it now: the senate have concluded
To give this day a crown to mighty Cæsar.
If you shall send them word you will not come,
Their minds may change. Besides, it were a mock
Apt to be render'd, for some one to say,
"Break up the senate till another time,
When Cæsar's wife shall meet with better dreams."
If Cæsar hide himself, shall they not whisper,
"Lo, Cæsar is afraid"?
Pardon me, Cæsar; for my dear dear love
To your proceeding bids me tell you this;
And reason to my love is liable.

Cæs. How foolish do your fears seem now, Calpurnia!
I am ashamed I did yield to them.
Give me my robe, for I will go.

Enter *Brutus, Ligarius, Metellus, Casca, Trebonius, Cinna* and *Publius.*

And look where Publius is come to fetch me.

Pub. Good morrow, Cæsar.

Cæs. Welcome, Publius.
What, Brutus, are you stirr'd so early too?
Good morrow, Casca. Caius Ligarius,
Cæsar was ne'er so much your enemy
As that same ague which hath made you lean.
What is 't o'clock?

Bru. Cæsar, 't is strucken eight.

Cæs. I thank you for your pains and courtesy.

Enter *Antony.*

See! Antony, that revels long a-nights,
Is notwithstanding up. Good morrow, Antony.

Ant. So to most noble Cæsar.

Cæs. Bid them prepare within;
I am to blame to be thus waited for.
Now, Cinna; now, Metellus; what, Trebonius!
I have an hour's talk in store for you;
Remember that you call on me to-day.
Be near me, that I may remember you.

Treb. Cæsar, I will; [*aside*] and so near will I be,
That your best friends shall wish I had been further.

Cæs. Good friends, go in, and taste some wine with me;
And we, like friends, will straightway go together.

Bru. [*Aside.*] That every like is not the same, O Cæsar,
The heart of Brutus earns to think upon!

Exeunt.

Scene III. *A street near the Capitol.*

Enter *Artemidorus* reading a paper.

"Cæsar, beware of Brutus; take heed of Cassius; come not near Casca; have an eye to Cinna; trust not Trebonius; mark well Metellus Cimber: Decius Brutus loves thee not: thou hast wronged Caius Ligarius. There is but one mind in all these men, and it is bent against Cæsar. If thou beest not immortal, look about you; security gives way to conspiracy. The mighty gods defend thee! Thy lover,

ARTEMIDORUS.

Here will I stand till Cæsar pass along,
And as a suitor will I give him this.
My heart laments that virtue cannot live
Out of the teeth of emulation.
If thou read this, O Cæsar, thou mayest live;
If not, the Fates with traitors do contrive.

Exit.

Scene IV. *Before the house of Brutus.*

Enter *Portia* and *Lucius.*

Por. I prithee, boy, run to the senate-house;
Stay not to answer me, but get thee gone.
Why dost thou stay?

Luc. To know my errand, madam.

Por. I would have had thee there, and here again.
Ere I can tell thee what thou shouldst do there.
O constancy, be strong upon my side.
Set a huge mountain 'tween my heart and tongue!
I have a man's mind, but a woman's might.
How hard it is for women to keep counsel!
Art thou here yet?

89. tinctures . . . cognizance, an allusion both to the practice of dipping handkerchiefs in the blood of martyrs; and to heraldic colors (tinctures) and devices (cognizances). **96. mock.** gibe. **103. proceeding,** career. **104. liable,** under the sway of.

128. That . . . same, alas that many apparent friends are not true ones. Brutus recoils from the part he has to play. **129. earns,** grieves. **Scene iii: 7. security gives,** over-confidence opens the. **10. lover,** friend. **14. Out . . . emulation,** unassailed by envy.

Luc. Madam, what should I do?
Run to the Capitol, and nothing else?
And so return to you, and nothing else?
Por. Yes, bring me word, boy, if thy lord look well,
For he went sickly forth; and take good note
What Cæsar doth, what suitors press to him.
Hark, boy! what noise is that?
Luc. I hear none, madam.
Por. Prithee, listen well;
I heard a bustling rumour, like a fray,
And the wind brings it from the Capitol.
Luc. Sooth, madam, I hear nothing.

Enter the *Soothsayer.*

Por. Come hither, fellow; which way hast thou been?
Sooth. At mine own house, good lady.
Por. What is 't o'clock?
Sooth. About the ninth hour, lady.
Por. Is Cæsar yet gone to the Capitol?
Sooth. Madam, not yet; I go to take my stand,
To see him pass on to the Capitol.
Por. Thou hast some suit to Cæsar, hast thou not?
Sooth. That I have, lady; if it will please Cæsar
To be so good to Cæsar as to hear me,
I shall beseech him to befriend himself.
Por. Why, know'st thou any harm 's intended towards him?
Sooth. None that I know will be, much that I fear may chance.
Good morrow to you. Here the street is narrow;
The throng that follows Cæsar at the heels,
Of senators, of prætors, common suitors,
Will crowd a feeble man almost to death:
I 'll get me to a place more void, and there
Speak to great Cæsar as he comes along.
Exit.
Por. I must go in. Ay me, how weak a thing
The heart of woman is! O Brutus,
The heavens speed thee in thine enterprise!
[*To herself.*] Sure the boy heard me. [*To Lucius.*] Brutus hath a suit
That Cæsar will not grant. O, I grow faint.
Run, Lucius, and commend me to my lord;
Say I am merry. Come to me again,
And bring me word what he doth say to thee.
Exeunt.

ACT III. SCENE I. *Rome. Before the Capitol.*

Flourish. Enter *Cæsar, Brutus, Cassius, Casca, Decius, Metellus, Trebonius, Cinna, Antony, Lepidus, Publius, Popilius, Artemidorus* and the *Soothsayer.*

Cæs. [*To the Soothsayer.*] The ides of March are come.
Sooth. Ay, Cæsar, but not gone.
Art. Hail, Cæsar! read this schedule.
Dec. Trebonius doth desire you to o'er-read,
At your best leisure, this his humble suit.
Art. O Cæsar, read mine first; for mine 's a suit
That touches Cæsar nearer. Read it, great Cæsar.
Cæs. What touches us ourself shall be last serv'd.
Art. Delay not, Cæsar; read it instantly.
Cæs. What, is the fellow mad?
Pub. Sirrah, give place.
Cas. What, urge you your petitions in the street?
Come to the Capitol.
Cæsar goes up to the Senate-House, the rest following.
Pop. I wish your enterprise to-day may thrive.
Cas. What enterprise, Popilius?
Pop. Fare you well.
Advances to Cæsar.
Bru. What said Popilius Lena?
Cas. He wish'd to-day our enterprise might thrive.
I fear our purpose is discovered.
Bru. Look, how he makes to Cæsar; mark him.
Cas. Casca, be sudden, for we fear prevention.
Brutus, what shall be done? If this be known,
Cassius or Cæsar never shall turn back,
For I will slay myself.
Bru. Cassius, be constant;
Popilius Lena speaks not of our purposes,
For, look, he smiles, and Cæsar doth not change.
Cas. Trebonius knows his time; for, look you, Brutus,
He draws Mark Antony out of the way.
Exeunt Antony and Trebonius.

Scene iv: 20. Sooth, in truth. **Act III, Scene i: 3. schedule,** written scroll. **37. void,** free from the crowd. **Act III, Scene i: 18. makes to,** approaches. **22. be constant,** do not be disturbed.

Dec. Where is Metellus Cimber? Let him go
And presently prefer his suit to Cæsar.
Bru. He is address'd; press near and second him.
Cin. Casca, you are the first that rears your hand.
Cæs. Are we all ready? What is now amiss
That Cæsar and his senate must redress?
Met. Most high, most mighty, and most puissant Cæsar,
Metellus Cimber throws before thy seat
An humble heart,— [*Kneeling*]
Cæs. I must prevent thee, Cimber.
These couchings and these lowly curtesies
Might fire the blood of ordinary men,
And turn pre-ordinance and first decree
Into the law of children. Be not fond
To think that Cæsar bears such rebel blood
That will be thaw'd from the true quality
With that which melteth fools; I mean, sweet words,
Low-crooked curtsies and base spaniel-fawning.
Thy brother by decree is banished;
If thou dost bend and pray and fawn for him,
I spurn thee like a cur out of my way.
Know, Cæsar doth not wrong, nor without cause
Will he be satisfied.
Met. Is there no voice more worthy than my own,
To sound more sweetly in great Cæsar's ear
For the repealing of my banish'd brother?
Bru. I kiss thy hand, but not in flattery, Cæsar;
Desiring thee that Publius Cimber may
Have an immediate freedom of repeal.
Cæs. What, Brutus!
Cas. Pardon, Cæsar; Cæsar, pardon!
As low as to thy foot doth Cassius fall,
To beg enfranchisement for Publius Cimber.
Cæs. I would be well mov'd, if I were as you;
If I could pray to move, prayers would move me;
But I am constant as the northern star,
Of whose true-fix'd and resting quality
There is no fellow in the firmament.
The skies are painted with unnumber'd sparks,
They are all fire and every one doth shine;
But there 's but one in all doth hold his place.
So in the world; 't is furnish'd well with men,
And men are flesh and blood, and apprehensive;
Yet in the number I do know but one
That unassailable holds on his rank,
Unshak'd of motion; and that I am he,
Let me a little show it, even in this:
That I was constant Cimber should be banish'd,
And constant do remain to keep him so.
Cin. O Cæsar,—
Cæs. Hence! wilt thou lift up Olympus?
Dec. Great Cæsar,—
Cæs. Doth not Brutus bootless kneel?
Casca. Speak, hands, for me!
They stab Cæsar.
Cæs. *Et tu Brute!* Then fall, Cæsar!
Dies.
Cin. Liberty! Freedom! Tyranny is dead!
Run hence, proclaim, cry it about the streets.
Cas. Some to the common pulpits, and cry out,
"Liberty, freedom, and enfranchisement!"
Bru. People and senators, be not affrighted;
Fly not; stand still; ambition's debt is paid.
Casca. Go to the pulpit, Brutus.
Dec. And Cassius too.
Bru. Where 's Publius?
Cin. Here, quite confounded with this mutiny.
Met. Stand fast together, lest some friend of Cæsar's
Should chance—
Bru. Talk not of standing. Publius, good cheer;
There is no harm intended to your person,
Nor to no Roman else. So tell them, Publius.
Cas. And leave us, Publius; lest that the people,
Rushing on us, should do your age some mischief.
Bru. Do so: and let no man abide this deed,
But we the doers.

Re-enter *Trebonius.*

Cas. Where is Antony?
Treb. Fled to his house amaz'd.
Men, wives, and children stare, cry out, and run,
As it were doomsday.
Bru. Fates, we will know your pleasures.
That we shall die, we know; 't is but the time
And drawing days out, that men stand upon.
Cas. Why, he that cuts off twenty years of life
Cuts off so many years of fearing death.

28. **presently . . . suit,** at once present his petition. 29. **address'd,** ready. 36. **couchings,** prostrations. 38. **pre-ordinance,** established law. 39. **fond,** foolish. 54. **freedom of repeal,** pardon and recall. 61. **resting,** stationary. 67. **apprehensive,** intelligent.

69. **holds . . . rank,** maintains his position. 75. **bootless,** unavailingly. 77. **Et tu, Brute,** this exclamation is given in the words supposed to have been spoken by Cæsar. 80. **common pulpits,** public rostra. 89. **good cheer,** be calm. 94. **abide,** pay the penalty for. 97. **wives,** women. 100. **drawing days out,** prolonging their lives. **stand upon,** make much of.

Bru. Grant that, and then is death a benefit;
So are we Cæsar's friends, that have abridg'd
His time of fearing death. Stoop, Romans, stoop,
And let us bathe our hands in Cæsar's blood
Up to the elbows, and besmear our swords;
Then walk we forth, even to the market-place,
And, waving our red weapons o'er our heads,
Let 's all cry, "Peace, freedom, and liberty!"
Cas. Stoop, then, and wash. How many ages hence
Shall this our lofty scene be acted over
In states unborn and accents yet unknown!
Bru. How many times shall Cæsar bleed in sport,
That now on Pompey's basis lies along
No worthier than the dust!
Cas. So oft as that shall be,
So often shall the knot of us be call'd
The men that gave their country liberty.
Dec. What, shall we forth?
Cas. Ay, every man away.
Brutus shall lead; and we will grace his heels
With the most boldest and best hearts of Rome.

Enter a *Servant*.

Bru. Soft! who comes here? A friend of Antony's.
Serv. Thus, Brutus, did my master bid me kneel,
Thus did Mark Antony bid me fall down;
And, being prostrate, thus he bade me say:
Brutus is noble, wise, valiant, and honest;
Cæsar was mighty, bold, royal, and loving;
Say I love Brutus, and I honour him;
Say I fear'd Cæsar, honour'd him, and lov'd him.
If Brutus will vouchsafe that Antony
May safely come to him, and be resolv'd
How Cæsar hath deserv'd to lie in death,
Mark Antony shall not love Cæsar dead
So well as Brutus living; but will follow
The fortunes and affairs of noble Brutus
Thorough the hazards of this untrod state
With all true faith. So says my master Antony.
Bru. Thy master is a wise and valiant Roman;
I never thought him worse.
Tell him, so please him come unto this place,
He shall be satisfied; and, by my honour,
Depart untouch'd.
Serv. I 'll fetch him presently.
Exit Servant.
Bru. I know that we shall have him well to friend.
Cas. I wish we may; but yet have I a mind
That fears him much, and my misgiving still
Falls shrewdly to the purpose.

Re-enter *Antony*.

Bru. But here comes Antony. Welcome, Mark Antony!
Ant. O mighty Cæsar! dost thou lie so low?
Are all thy conquests, glories, triumphs, spoils,
Shrunk to this little measure? Fare thee well!
I know not, gentlemen, what you intend,
Who else must be let blood, who else is rank;
If I myself, there is no hour so fit
As Cæsar's death's hour, nor no instrument
Of half that worth as those your swords, made rich
With the most noble blood of all this world.
I do beseech ye, if you bear me hard,
Now, whilst your purpled hands do reek and smoke,
Fulfil your pleasure. Live a thousand years,
I shall not find myself so apt to die;
No place will please me so, no mean of death,
As here by Cæsar, and by you cut off,
The choice and master spirits of this age.
Bru. O Antony, beg not your death of us.
Though now we must appear bloody and cruel,
As, by our hands and this our present act,
You see we do, yet see you but our hands
And this the bleeding business they have done.
Our hearts you see not; they are pitiful;
And pity to the general wrong of Rome—
As fire drives out fire, so pity pity—
Hath done this deed on Cæsar. For your part,
To you our swords have leaden points, Mark Antony;
Our arms no strength of malice, and our hearts
Of brothers' temper, do receive you in
With all kind love, good thoughts, and reverence.
Cas. Your voice shall be as strong as any man's
In the disposing of new dignities.
Bru. Only be patient till we have appeas'd
The multitude, beside themselves with fear,
And then we will deliver you the cause
Why I, that did love Cæsar when I struck him,
Have thus proceeded.
Ant. I doubt not of your wisdom.
Let each man render me his bloody hand.
First, Marcus Brutus, will I shake with you;
Next, Caius Cassius, do I take your hand;

115. Pompey's basis, base of Pompey's statue. **along,** prostrate. **117. knot,** band. **131. resolv'd,** convinced. **136. Thorough,** throughout. **140. so please him,** if he will. **143. well to friend,** as a loyal friend.

146. Falls . . . purpose, is wont to prove correct. **152. let blood,** bled, i.e., killed. **rank,** plethoric, in need of being bled. **159. Live,** if I live. **160. apt,** ready. **161. mean,** means. **162. by Cæsar,** beside Cæsar. **174. arms . . . malice,** our arms have no violent malice toward you. **178. dignities,** offices.

Now, Decius Brutus, yours; now yours, Metellus;
Yours, Cinna; and, my valiant Casca, yours;
Though last, not least in love, yours good Trebonius.
Gentlemen all—alas, what shall I say?
My credit now stands on such slippery ground
That one of two bad ways you must conceit me,
Either a coward or a flatterer.
That I did love thee, Cæsar, O, 't is true;
If then thy spirit look upon us now,
Shall it not grieve thee dearer than thy death,
To see thy Antony making his peace,
Shaking the bloody fingers of thy foes,
Most noble! in the presence of thy corse?
Had I as many eyes as thou hast wounds,
Weeping as fast as they stream forth thy blood,
It would become me better than to close
In terms of friendship with thine enemies.
Pardon me, Julius! Here wast thou bay'd, brave hart;
Here didst thou fall; and here thy hunters stand,
Sign'd in thy spoil, and crimson'd in thy lethe.
O world, thou wast the forest to this hart;
And this, indeed, O world, the heart of thee.
How like a deer, strucken by many princes,
Dost thou here lie!

Cas. Mark Antony,—

Ant. Pardon me, Caius Cassius!
The enemies of Cæsar shall say this;
Then, in a friend, it is cold modesty.

Cas. I blame you not for praising Cæsar so;
But what compact mean you to have with us?
Will you be prick'd in number of our friends;
Or shall we on, and not depend on you?

Ant. Therefore I took your hands, but was, indeed,
Sway'd from the point, by looking down on Cæsar.
Friends am I with you all and love you all,
Upon this hope, that you shall give me reasons
Why and wherein Cæsar was dangerous.

Bru. Or else were this a savage spectacle.
Our reasons are so full of good regard
That were you, Antony, the son of Cæsar,
You should be satisfied.

Ant. That 's all I seek;
And am, moreover, suitor that I may
Produce his body to the market-place;
And in the pulpit, as becomes a friend,
Speak in the order of his funeral.

Bru. You shall, Mark Antony.

Cas. Brutus, a word with you.
[*Aside to Bru.*] You know not what you do: do not consent
That Antony speak in his funeral.
Know you how much the people may be mov'd
By that which he will utter?

Bru. By your pardon.
I will myself into the pulpit first,
And show the reason of our Cæsar's death.
What Antony shall speak, I will protest
He speaks by leave and by permission,
And that we are contented Cæsar shall
Have all true rites and lawful ceremonies.
It shall advantage more than do us wrong.

Cas. I know not what may fall; I like it not.

Bru. Mark Antony, here, take you Cæsar's body.
You shall not in your funeral speech blame us,
But speak all good you can devise of Cæsar,
And say you do 't by our permission;
Else shall you not have any hand at all
About his funeral. And you shall speak
In the same pulpit whereto I am going,
After my speech is ended.

Ant. Be it so;
I do desire no more.

Bru. Prepare the body then, and follow us.

Exeunt all but Antony.

Ant. O, pardon me, thou bleeding piece of earth,
That I am meek and gentle with these butchers!
Thou art the ruins of the noblest man
That ever lived in the tide of times.
Woe to the hand that shed this costly blood!
Over thy wounds now do I prophesy,
(Which, like dumb mouths, do ope their ruby lips,
To beg the voice and utterance of my tongue)
A curse shall light upon the limbs of men;
Domestic fury and fierce civil strife
Shall cumber all the parts of Italy;
Blood and destruction shall be so in use
And dreadful objects so familiar
That mothers shall but smile when they behold
Their infants quartered with the hands of war;
All pity chok'd with custom of fell deeds;
And Cæsar's spirit, ranging for revenge,
With Ate by his side come hot from hell,
Shall in these confines with a monarch's voice

192. **conceit,** consider. 199. **corse,** corpse. 204. **bay'd,** brought to bay. **hart,** stag (with play on "heart"). 206. **Sign'd in,** marked with the signs of. **lethe,** death. 213. **modesty,** moderation. 216. **prick'd,** marked in the list. 224. **full . . . regard,** deserving of approval. 228. **Produce,** carry forth.

230. **order,** course. 238. **protest,** announce. 243. **fall,** befall. 257. **tide of times,** ebb and flow of human history. 268. **quartered,** slaughtered. 269. **fell,** cruel. 271. **Ate,** goddess of discord. 272. **confines,** regions.

Cry "Havoc," and let slip the dogs of war;
That this foul deed shall smell above the earth
With carrion men, groaning for burial.

Enter Octavius' *Servant.*

You serve Octavius Cæsar, do you not?
Serv. I do, Mark Antony.
Ant. Cæsar did write for him to come to Rome.
Serv. He did receive his letters, and is coming;
And bid me say to you by word of mouth—
O Cæsar!—
Ant. Thy heart is big; get thee apart and weep.
Passion, I see, is catching; for mine eyes,
Seeing those beads of sorrow stand in thine,
Began to water. Is thy master coming?
Serv. He lies to-night within seven leagues of Rome.
Ant. Post back with speed and tell him what hath chanc'd:
Here is a mourning Rome, a dangerous Rome,
No Rome of safety for Octavius yet;
Hie hence, and tell him so. Yet, stay awhile;
Thou shalt not back till I have borne this corse
Into the market-place: there shall I try,
In my oration, how the people take
The cruel issue of these bloody men;
According to the which, thou shalt discourse
To young Octavius of the state of things.
Lend me your hand.
Exeunt with Cæsar's body.

Scene II. *The Forum.*

Enter *Brutus* and *Cassius,* with the *Plebeians.*

Pleb. We will be satisfied! Let us be satisfied!
Bru. Then follow me, and give me audience, friends.
Cassius, go you into the other street,
And part the numbers.
Those that will hear me speak, let 'em stay here;
Those that will follow Cassius, go with him;
And public reasons shall be render'd
Of Cæsar's death.
First Pleb. I will hear Brutus speak.
Second Pleb. I will hear Cassius; and compare their reasons,
When severally we hear them render'd.
Exit Cassius, with some of the Plebeians.
Brutus goes into the pulpit.

Third Pleb. The noble Brutus is ascended; silence!
Bru. Be patient till the last.

Romans, countrymen, and lovers! hear me for my cause, and be silent, that you may hear. Believe me for mine honour, and have respect to mine honour, that you may believe. Censure me in your wisdom, and awake your senses, that you may the better judge. If there be any in this assembly, any dear friend of Cæsar's, to him I say, that Brutus' love to Cæsar was no less than his. If then that friend demand why Brutus rose against Cæsar, this is my answer: Not that I loved Cæsar less, but that I loved Rome more. Had you rather Cæsar were living and die all slaves, than that Cæsar was dead, to live all freemen? As Cæsar loved me, I weep for him; as he was fortunate, I rejoice at it; as he was valiant, I honour him; but, as he was ambitious, I slew him. There is tears for his love; joy for his fortune; honour for his valour; and death for his ambition. Who is here so base that would be a bondman? If any, speak; for him have I offended. Who is here so rude that would not be a Roman? If any, speak; for him have I offended. Who is here so vile that will not love his country? If any, speak; for him have I offended. I pause for a reply.

All. None, Brutus, none.

Bru. Then none have I offended. I have done no more to Cæsar than you shall do to Brutus. The question of his death is enrolled in the Capitol; his glory not extenuated, wherein he was worthy, nor his offences enforced, for which he suffered death.

Enter *Antony* and others, with *Cæsar's* body.

Here comes his body, mourned by Mark Antony; who, though he had no hand in his death, shall receive the benefit of his dying, a place in the commonwealth; as which of you shall not? With this I depart, that, as I slew my best lover for the good of Rome, I have the same dagger for myself, when it shall please my country to need my death.

All. Live, Brutus! live, live!
First Pleb. Bring him with triumph home unto his house.
Second Pleb. Give him a statue with his ancestors.
Third Pleb. Let him be Cæsar
Fourth Pleb. Cæsar's better parts
Shall be crown'd in Brutus.
First Pleb. We 'll bring him to his house
With shouts and clamours.

273. **Havoc,** signal for killing without quarter. **let slip,** unleash. 283. **Passion,** emotion. 294. **issue,** act. 295. **the which,** i.e., popular sentiment. **Scene ii:** 4. **part the numbers,** divide the crowd. 10. **severally,** individually. **S. d. pulpit,** rostrum, the stage balcony.

12. **till the last,** until I finish. 16. **Censure,** judge. 33. **so rude,** such a barbarian. 41. **question of,** reasons for. **enrolled,** recorded. 42. **extenuated,** belittled. 43. **enforced,** exaggerated.

Bru. My countrymen,—
Second Pleb. Peace, silence! Brutus speaks.
First Pleb. Peace, ho!
Bru. Good countrymen, let me depart alone,
And, for my sake, stay here with Antony.
Do grace to Cæsar's corpse, and grace his speech
Tending to Cæsar's glories, which Mark Antony,
By our permission, is allow'd to make.
I do entreat you, not a man depart
Save I alone, till Antony have spoke. *Exit.*
First Pleb. Stay, ho! and let us hear Mark Antony.
Third Pleb. Let him go up into the public chair;
We 'll hear him. Noble Antony, go up.
Ant. For Brutus' sake, I am beholding to you. *Goes into the pulpit.*
Fourth Pleb. What does he say of Brutus?
Third Pleb. He says, for Brutus' sake,
He finds himself beholding to us all.
Fourth Pleb. 'T were best he speak no harm of Brutus here.
First Pleb. This Cæsar was a tyrant.
Third Pleb. Nay, that 's certain:
We are blest that Rome is rid of him.
Second Pleb. Peace! let us hear what Antony can say.
Ant. You gentle Romans,—
All. Peace, ho! let us hear him.
Ant. Friends, Romans, countrymen, lend me your ears!
I come to bury Cæsar, not to praise him.
The evil that men do lives after them,
The good is oft interred with their bones;
So let it be with Cæsar. The noble Brutus
Hath told you Cæsar was ambitious;
If it were so, it was a grievous fault,
And grievously hath Cæsar answer'd it.
Here, under leave of Brutus and the rest—
For Brutus is an honourable man;
So are they all, all honourable men—
Come I to speak in Cæsar's funeral.
He was my friend, faithful and just to me;
But Brutus says he was ambitious,
And Brutus is an honourable man.
He hath brought many captives home to Rome,
Whose ransoms did the general coffers fill;
Did this in Cæsar seem ambitious?
When that the poor have cried, Cæsar hath wept;
Ambition should be made of sterner stuff:
Yet Brutus says he was ambitious,
And Brutus is an honourable man.
You all did see that on the Lupercal
I thrice presented him a kingly crown,
Which he did thrice refuse. Was this ambition?
Yet Brutus says he was ambitious,
And, sure, he is an honourable man.
I speak not to disprove what Brutus spoke,
But here I am to speak what I do know.
You all did love him once, not without cause;
What cause withholds you then to mourn for him?
O judgement! thou art fled to brutish beasts,
And men have lost their reason. Bear with me;
My heart is in the coffin there with Cæsar,
And I must pause till it come back to me.
First Pleb. Methinks there is much reason in his sayings.
Second Pleb. If thou consider rightly of the matter,
Cæsar has had great wrong.
Third Pleb. Has he, masters?
I fear there will a worse come in his place.
Fourth Pleb. Mark'd ye his words? He would not take the crown;
Therefore 't is certain he was not ambitious.
First Pleb. If it be found so, some will dear abide it.
Second Pleb. Poor soul! his eyes are red as fire with weeping.
Third Pleb. There 's not a nobler man in Rome than Antony.
Fourth Pleb. Now mark him, he begins again to speak.
Ant. But yesterday the word of Cæsar might
Have stood against the world; now lies he there,
And none so poor to do him reverence.
O masters, if I were dispos'd to stir
Your hearts and minds to mutiny and rage,
I should do Brutus wrong, and Cassius wrong,
Who, you all know, are honourable men.
I will not do them wrong; I rather choose
To wrong the dead, to wrong myself and you,
Than I will wrong such honourable men.
But here 's a parchment with the seal of Cæsar;
I found it in his closet; 't is his will.
Let but the commons hear this testament—
Which, pardon me, I do not mean to read—
And they would go and kiss dead Cæsar's wounds
And dip their napkins in his sacred blood,
Yea, beg a hair of him for memory,
And, dying, mention it within their wills,
Bequeathing it as a rich legacy
Unto their issue.

70. beholding, indebted. **85. answer'd,** atoned for. **94. general coffers,** public treasury.

125. And . . . reverence, there are none so humble as to show respect for him. **135. commons,** common people. **138. napkins,** handkerchiefs.

Fourth Pleb. We 'll hear the will. Read it, Mark Antony.
All. The will, the will! we will hear Cæsar's will.
Ant. Have patience, gentle friends, I must not read it;
It is not meet you know how Cæsar lov'd you.
You are not wood, you are not stones, but men;
And, being men, hearing the will of Cæsar,
It will inflame you, it will make you mad.
'T is good you know not that you are his heirs;
For, if you should, O, what would come of it?
Fourth Pleb. Read the will; we 'll hear it, Antony.
You shall read us the will, Cæsar's will.
Ant. Will you be patient? Will you stay a while?
I have o'ershot myself to tell you of it.
I fear I wrong the honourable men
Whose daggers have stabb'd Cæsar; I do fear it.
Fourth Pleb. They were traitors; honourable men!
All. The will! the testament!
Second Pleb. They were villains, murderers. The will! read the will.
Ant. You will compel me, then, to read the will?
Then make a ring about the corpse of Cæsar,
And let me show you him that made the will.
Shall I descend? and will you give me leave?
All. Come down.
Second Pleb. Descend.
Third Pleb. You shall have leave.
Antony comes down from the pulpit.
Fourth Pleb. A ring; stand round.
First Pleb. Stand from the hearse, stand from the body.
Second Pleb. Room for Antony, most noble Antony.
Ant. Nay, press not so upon me; stand far off.
All. Stand back; room; bear back!
Ant. If you have tears, prepare to shed them now.
You all do know this mantle; I remember
The first time ever Cæsar put it on.
'T was on a summer's evening in his tent,
That day he overcame the Nervii.
Look, in this place ran Cassius' dagger through;
See what a rent the envious Casca made;
Through this the well-beloved Brutus stabb'd,
And as he pluck'd his cursed steel away,
Mark how the blood of Cæsar followed it,
As rushing out of doors, to be resolv'd
If Brutus so unkindly knock'd, or no;
For Brutus, as you know, was Cæsar's angel.
Judge, O you gods, how dearly Cæsar lov'd him!
This was the most unkindest cut of all;
For when the noble Cæsar saw him stab,
Ingratitude, more strong than traitors' arms,
Quite vanquish'd him: then burst his mighty heart;
And, in his mantle muffling up his face,
Even at the base of Pompey's statuë,
Which all the while ran blood, great Cæsar fell.
O, what a fall was there, my countrymen!
Then I, and you, and all of us fell down,
Whilst bloody treason flourish'd over us.
O, now you weep, and I perceive you feel
The dint of pity: these are gracious drops.
Kind souls, what, weep you when you but behold
Our Cæsar's vesture wounded? Look you here:
Here is himself, marr'd, as you see, with traitors.
First Pleb. O piteous spectacle!
Second Pleb. O noble Cæsar!
Third Pleb. O woeful day!
Fourth Pleb. O traitors, villains!
First Pleb. O most bloody sight!
Second Pleb. We will be revenged!
All. Revenge! About!
Seek! Burn! Fire! Kill! Slay!
Let not a traitor live!
Ant. Stay, countrymen.
First Pleb. Peace there! hear the noble Antony.
Second Pleb. We 'll hear him, we 'll follow him, we 'll die with him.
Ant. Good friends, sweet friends, let me not stir you up
To such a sudden flood of mutiny.
They that have done this deed are honourable.
What private griefs they have, alas, I know not,
That made them do it; they are wise and honourable,
And will, no doubt, with reasons answer you.
I come not, friends, to steal away your hearts.
I am no orator, as Brutus is;
But, as you know me all, a plain blunt man
That love my friend; and that they know full well
That gave me public leave to speak of him;
For I have neither wit, nor words, nor worth,
Action, nor utterance, nor the power of speech
To stir men's blood; I only speak right on.

169. hearse, bier. **177. Nervii,** a Belgian tribe defeated by Cæsar in a desperate battle. **183. resolv'd,** assured.

185. angel, guardian spirit. **198. dint,** impression. **225. wit,** intelligence. **226. Action,** gesture. **utterance,** elocution. **227. right on,** as a plain man.

I tell you that which you yourselves do know;
Show you sweet Cæsar's wounds, poor, poor, dumb mouths,
And bid them speak for me: but were I Brutus,
And Brutus Antony, there were an Antony
Would ruffle up your spirits, and put a tongue
In every wound of Cæsar, that should move
The stones of Rome to rise and mutiny.

All. We 'll mutiny.

First Pleb. We 'll burn the house of Brutus.

Third Pleb. Away, then! come, seek the conspirators.

Ant. Yet hear me, countrymen; yet hear me speak.

All. Peace, ho! hear Antony, most noble Antony!

Ant. Why, friends, you go to do you know not what.
Wherein hath Cæsar thus deserv'd your loves?
Alas, you know not; I must tell you, then.
You have forgot the will I told you of.

All. Most true. The will! Let 's stay and hear the will.

Ant. Here is the will, and under Cæsar's seal.
To every Roman citizen he gives,
To every several man, seventy-five drachmas.

Second Pleb. O noble Cæsar! We 'll revenge his death.

Third Pleb. O royal Cæsar!

Ant. Hear me with patience.

All. Peace, ho!

Ant. Moreover, he hath left you all his walks,
His private arbours and new-planted orchards,
On this side Tiber; he hath left them you,
And to your heirs forever, common pleasures,
To walk abroad, and recreate yourselves.
Here was a Cæsar! When comes such another?

First Pleb. Never, never! Come, away, away!
We 'll burn his body in the holy place,
And with the brands fire the traitors' houses.
Take up the body.

Second Pleb. Go fetch fire.

Third Pleb. Pluck down benches.

Fourth Pleb. Pluck down forms, windows, anything.

Exeunt Plebeians with the body.

Ant. Now let it work. Mischief, thou art afoot,
Take thou what course thou wilt!

Enter a *Servant.*

How now, fellow?

Serv. Sir, Octavius is already come to Rome.

Ant. Where is he?

Serv. He and Lepidus are at Cæsar's house.

Ant. And thither will I straight to visit him;
He comes upon a wish. Fortune is merry,
And in this mood will give us anything.

Serv. I heard him say, Brutus and Cassius
Are rid like madmen through the gates of Rome.

Ant. Belike they had some notice of the people,
How I had moved them. Bring me to Octavius. *Exeunt.*

Scene III. *Rome. A street.*

Enter *Cinna* the poet, and after him the *Plebeians.*

Cin. I dreamt to-night that I did feast with Cæsar,
And things unluckily charge my fantasy.
I have no will to wander forth of doors,
Yet something leads me forth.

First Pleb. What is your name?

Second Pleb. Whither are you going?

Third Pleb. Where do you dwell?

Fourth Pleb. Are you a married man or a bachelor?

Second Pleb. Answer every man directly.

First Pleb. Ay, and briefly.

Fourth Pleb. Ay, and wisely.

Third Pleb. Ay, and truly, you were best.

Cin. What is my name? Whither am I going? Where do I dwell? Am I a married man or a bachelor? Then, to answer every man directly and briefly, wisely and truly: wisely I say, I am a bachelor.

Second Pleb. That 's as much as to say, they are fools that marry: you 'll bear me a bang for that, I fear. Proceed; directly.

Cin. Directly, I am going to Cæsar's funeral.

First Pleb. As a friend or an enemy?

Cin. As a friend.

Second Pleb. That matter is answered directly.

Fourth Pleb. For your dwelling,—briefly.

232. ruffle, stir. **247. drachmas,** Greek coins probably equivalent to Roman *denarii;* the modern value is about twenty cents. **255. pleasures,** pleasure grounds. **264. forms,** benches.

271. upon, in answer to. **274. Are rid,** have ridden. **275. Belike,** no doubt. **Scene iii: 2. And . . . fantasy,** my mind is full of ominous fancies. **13. you were best,** it would be best for you. **20. bear me a bang,** give me a blow. **26. For,** as for.

Cin. Briefly, I dwell by the Capitol.

Third Pleb. Your name, sir, truly.

Cin. Truly, my name is Cinna.

First Pleb. Tear him to pieces; he 's a conspirator.

Cin. I am Cinna the poet, I am Cinna the poet.

Fourth Pleb. Tear him for his bad verses, tear him for his bad verses.

Cin. I am not Cinna the conspirator.

Fourth Pleb. It is no matter, his name 's Cinna: pluck but his name out of his heart, and turn him going.

Third Pleb. Tear him, tear him! Come, brands, ho! fire-brands! To Brutus', to Cassius'; burn all! Some to Decius' house, and some to Casca's; some to Ligarius'. Away, go! *Exeunt.*

ACT IV. Scene I. *Rome. Antony's house.*

Antony, Octavius, and *Lepidus.*

Ant. These many, then, shall die; their names are prick'd.
Oct. Your brother too must die; consent you, Lepidus?
Lep. I do consent,—
Oct. Prick him down, Antony.
Lep. Upon condition Publius shall not live,
Who is your sister's son, Mark Antony.
Ant. He shall not live; look, with a spot I damn him.
But, Lepidus, go you to Cæsar's house;
Fetch the will hither, and we shall determine
How to cut off some charge in legacies.
Lep. What, shall I find you here?
Oct. Or here, or at the Capitol.
Exit Lepidus.
Ant. This is a slight unmeritable man,
Meet to be sent on errands; is it fit,
The threefold world divided, he should stand
One of the three to share it?
Oct. So you thought him;
And took his voice who should be prick'd to die,
In our black sentence and proscription.
Ant. Octavius, I have seen more days than you;
And though we lay these honours on this man
To ease ourselves of divers sland'rous loads,
He shall but bear them as the ass bears gold,
To groan and sweat under the business,
Either led or driven, as we point the way;
And having brought our treasure where we will,
Then take we down his load, and turn him off,
Like to the empty ass, to shake his ears
And graze in commons.
Oct. You may do your will;
But he 's a tried and valiant soldier.
Ant. So is my horse, Octavius; and for that
I do appoint him store of provender.
It is a creature that I teach to fight,
To wind, to stop, to run directly on,
His corporal motion govern'd by my spirit.
And, in some taste, is Lepidus but so;
He must be taught and train'd and bid go forth;
A barren-spirited fellow; one that feeds
On objects, arts, and imitations,
Which, out of use and stal'd by other men,
Begin his fashion. Do not talk of him
But as a property. And now, Octavius,
Listen great things. Brutus and Cassius
Are levying powers; we must straight make head;
Therefore let our alliance be combin'd,
Our best friends made, our means stretch'd;
And let us presently go sit in council
How covert matters may be best disclos'd
And open perils surest answered.
Oct. Let us do so; for we are at the stake,
And bay'd about with many enemies;
And some that smile have in their hearts, I fear,
Millions of mischiefs. *Exeunt.*

Scene II. *Camp near Sardis. Before Brutus's tent.*

Drum. Enter *Brutus, Lucilius, Lucius,* and the army. *Titinius* and *Pindarus* meet them.

Bru. Stand, ho!
Lucil. Give the word, ho! and stand.

Act IV, Scene i: 1. prick'd, marked. **9. cut . . . legacies,** avoid paying part of Cæsar's legacies. **15. One of the three,** this alliance of Antony, Octavius, and Lepidus is known as the second triumvirate. **26. empty,** unladen, useless. **27. commons,** common pasture.

Scene i: 32. wind, turn. **34. taste,** degree. **37. objects,** material things. **arts,** things acquired by study. **38-9. Which . . . fashion,** which, when made cheap and stale by others, serve as a new fashion for him. **40. property,** tool. **42. make head,** raise troops. **43. combin'd,** consolidated. **44. made,** secured. **46. covert,** hidden. **47. answered,** met. **48. at the stake,** i.e.. like a bear to be baited.

Bru. What now, Lucilius! is Cassius near?
Lucil. He is at hand; and Pindarus is come
To do you salutation from his master.
Bru. He greets me well. Your master, Pindarus,
In his own change, or by ill officers,
Hath given me some worthy cause to wish
Things done undone; but, if he be at hand,
I shall be satisfied.
Pin. I do not doubt
But that my noble master will appear
Such as he is, full of regard and honour.
Bru. He is not doubted. A word, Lucilius:
How he receiv'd you let me be resolv'd.
Lucil. With courtesy and with respect enough;
But not with such familiar instances,
Nor with such free and friendly conference,
As he hath us'd of old.
Bru. Thou hast describ'd
A hot friend cooling. Ever note, Lucilius,
When love begins to sicken and decay,
It useth an enforced ceremony.
There are no tricks in plain and simple faith;
But hollow men, like horses hot at hand,
Make gallant show and promise of their mettle; *Low march within.*
But when they should endure the bloody spur
They fall their crests, and, like deceitful jades,
Sink in the trial. Comes his army on?
Lucil. They mean this night in Sardis to be quarter'd.
The greater part, the horse in general,
Are come with Cassius.

Enter *Cassius* and his Powers.

Bru. Hark! he is arriv'd.
March gently on to meet him.
Cas. Stand, ho!
Bru. Stand, ho! Speak the word along.
First Sol. Stand!
Second Sol. Stand!
Third Sol. Stand!
Cas. Most noble brother, you have done me wrong.
Bru. Judge me, you gods! wrong I mine enemies?
And, if not so, how should I wrong a brother?
Cas. Brutus, this sober form of yours hides wrongs;
And when you do them—
Bru. Cassius, be content;
Speak your griefs softly; I do know you well.
Before the eyes of both our armies here,
(Which should perceive nothing but love from us)
Let us not wrangle. Bid them move away;
Then in my tent, Cassius, enlarge your griefs,
And I will give you audience.
Cas. Pindarus,
Bid our commanders lead their charges off
A little from this ground.
Bru. Lucilius, do you the like; and let no man
Come to our tent till we have done our conference.
Let Lucius and Titinius guard our door.
Exeunt.

Scene III. *In the tent of Brutus.*

Enter *Brutus* and *Cassius.*

Cas. That you have wrong'd me doth appear in this:
You have condemn'd and noted Lucius Pella
For taking bribes here of the Sardians;
Wherein my letters, praying on his side,
Because I knew the man was slighted off,—
Bru. You wrong'd yourself to write in such a case.
Cas. In such a time as this it is not meet
That every nice offence should bear his comment.
Bru. Let me tell you, Cassius, you yourself
Are much condemn'd to have an itching palm,
To sell and mart your offices for gold
To undeservers.
Cas. I an itching palm!
You know that you are Brutus that speaks this,
Or, by the gods, this speech were else your last.
Bru. The name of Cassius honours this corruption,
And chastisement doth therefore hide his head.
Cas. Chastisement!
Bru. Remember March, the ides of March remember:
Did not great Julius bleed for justice' sake?
What villain touch'd his body, that did stab
And not for justice? What, shall one of us,
That struck the foremost man of all this world
But for supporting robbers, shall we now
Contaminate our fingers with base bribes,
And sell the mighty space of our large honours

Scene ii: **6. greets me well,** does me honor. **7. his own change,** change in himself. **by,** through. **10. be satisfied,** be given an explanation. **12. full . . . honour,** full of, or, worthy of, honorable respect. **16. familiar instances,** easy cordiality. **17. conference,** talk. **23. hollow,** insincere. **hot at hand,** fiery when led by the hand, or, when held in. **26. fall,** lower. **jades,** nags. **27. Sink,** fail. **31. gently,** slowly. **40. form,** manner.

46. enlarge, set forth. **Scene iii: 2. noted,** branded with disgrace. **4. on his side,** on his behalf. **8. nice,** trivial. **bear his comment,** be examined. **10. to have,** for having. **11. mart,** market. **15. honours,** protects, sanctions

For so much trash as may be grasped thus?
I had rather be a dog and bay the moon,
Than such a Roman.

Cas. Brutus, bait not me;
I 'll not endure it: you forget yourself
To hedge me in. I am a soldier, I,
Older in practice, abler than yourself
To make conditions.

Bru. Go to; you are not, Cassius.

Cas. I am.

Bru. I say you are not.

Cas. Urge me no more, I shall forget myself;
Have mind upon your health, tempt me no farther.

Bru. Away, slight man!

Cas. Is 't possible?

Bru. Hear me, for I will speak.
Must I give way and room to your rash choler?
Shall I be frighted when a madman stares?

Cas. O ye gods, ye gods! must I endure all this?

Bru. All this! ay, more. Fret till your proud heart break;
Go show your slaves how choleric you are,
And make your bondmen tremble. Must I budge?
Must I observe you? Must I stand and crouch
Under your testy humour? By the gods,
You shall digest the venom of your spleen,
Though it do split you; for, from this day forth,
I 'll use you for my mirth, yea, for my laughter,
When you are waspish.

Cas. Is it come to this?

Bru. You say you are a better soldier:
Let it appear so; make your vaunting true,
And it shall please me well. For mine own part,
I shall be glad to learn of noble men.

Cas. You wrong me every way; you wrong me, Brutus;
I said an elder soldier, not a better.
Did I say "better"?

Bru. If you did, I care not.

Cas. When Cæsar liv'd, he durst not thus have mov'd me.

Bru. Peace, peace! you durst not so have tempted him.

Cas. I durst not!

Bru. No.

Cas. What, durst not tempt him!

Bru. For your life you durst not.

Cas. Do not presume too much upon my love;
I may do that I shall be sorry for.

Bru. You have done that you should be sorry for.
There is no terror, Cassius, in your threats,
For I am arm'd so strong in honesty
That they pass by me as the idle wind,
Which I respect not. I did send to you
For certain sums of gold, which you denied me;
For I can raise no money by vile means.—
By heaven, I had rather coin my heart,
And drop my blood for drachmas, than to wring
From the hard hands of peasants their vile trash
By any indirection.—I did send
To you for gold to pay my legions,
Which you denied me. Was that done like Cassius?
Should I have answer'd Caius Cassius so?
When Marcus Brutus grows so covetous
To lock such rascal counters from his friends,
Be ready, gods, with all your thunderbolts;
Dash him to pieces!

Cas. I denied you not.

Bru. You did.

Cas. I did not. He was but a fool that brought
My answer back. Brutus hath riv'd my heart.
A friend should bear his friend's infirmities,
But Brutus makes mine greater than they are.

Bru. I do not, till you practise them on me.

Cas. You love me not.

Bru. I do not like your faults.

Cas. A friendly eye could never see such faults.

Bru. A flatterer's would not, though they do appear
As huge as high Olympus.

Cas. Come, Antony, and young Octavius, come,
Revenge yourselves alone on Cassius,
For Cassius is aweary of the world;
Hated by one he loves; brav'd by his brother;
Check'd like a bondman; all his faults observ'd,
Set in a note-book, learn'd and conn'd by rote
To cast into my teeth. O, I could weep
My spirit from mine eyes! There is my dagger,
And here my naked breast; within, a heart
Dearer than Pluto's mine, richer than gold.

28. **bait,** provoke, worry. 30. **hedge me in,** control me. 32. **make conditions,** administer my office. 43. **choleric,** hot-tempered. 44. **budge,** flinch. 45. **observe,** be obsequious to. 50. **waspish,** in a passion. 54. **of,** from.

75. **indirection,** crookedness. 80. **rascal counters,** worthless coins. 85. **riv'd,** broken. 92. **Olympus,** mountain in Greece. 97. **Check'd,** reprimanded. 102. **Pluto's,** as lord of the underworld, Pluto was god of mineral wealth.

If that thou be'st a Roman, take it forth;
I, that denied thee gold, will give my heart.
Strike as thou didst at Cæsar; for, I know,
When thou didst hate him worst, thou lov'dst him better
Than ever thou lov'dst Cassius.

Bru. Sheathe your dagger.
Be angry when you will, it shall have scope.
Do what you will, dishonour shall be humour.
O Cassius, you are yoked with a lamb
That carries anger as the flint bears fire;
Who, much enforced, shows a hasty spark,
And straight is cold again.

Cas. Hath Cassius liv'd
To be but mirth and laughter to his Brutus,
When grief and blood ill-temper'd vexeth him?

Bru. When I spoke that, I was ill-temper'd too.

Cas. Do you confess so much? Give me your hand.

Bru. And my heart too.

Cas. O Brutus!

Bru. What 's the matter?

Cas. Have not you love enough to bear with me,
When that rash humour which my mother gave me
Makes me forgetful?

Bru. Yes, Cassius; and, from henceforth,
When you are over earnest with your Brutus,
He 'll think your mother chides, and leave you so.

Enter *Poet* followed by *Lucilius, Titinius,* and *Lucius.*

Poet. Let me go in to see the generals;
There is some grudge between 'em, 't is not meet
They be alone.

Lucil. You shall not come to them.

Poet. Nothing but death shall stay me.

Cas. How now! what 's the matter?

Poet. For shame, you generals! what do you mean?
Love, and be friends, as two such men should be;
For I have seen more years, I 'm sure, than ye.

Cas. Ha, ha! how vilely doth this cynic rhyme!

Bru. Get you hence, sirrah; saucy fellow, hence!

Cas. Bear with him, Brutus; 't is his fashion.

Bru. I 'll know his humour, when he knows his time.

108. scope, free expression. **109. dishonour . . . humour,** I shall call unworthy conduct a caprice. **115. blood ill-temper'd,** with a bad mixture of humors. **133. cynic,** rude fellow. **136. know . . . time,** recognize it as his way when he chooses the proper time.

What should the wars do with these jigging fools?
Companion, hence!

Cas. Away, away, be gone!

Exit Poet.

Bru. Lucilius and Titinius, bid the commanders
Prepare to lodge their companies to-night.

Cas. And come yourselves, and bring Messala with you
Immediately to us.

Exeunt Lucilius and Titinius.

Bru. Lucius, a bowl of wine!

Exit Lucius.

Cas. I did not think you could have been so angry.

Bru. O Cassius, I am sick of many griefs.

Cas. Of your philosophy you make no use
If you give place to accidental evils.

Bru. No man bears sorrow better. Portia is dead.

Cas. Ha! Portia?

Bru. She is dead.

Cas. How scap'd I killing when I cross'd you so?
O insupportable and touching loss!
Upon what sickness?

Bru. Impatient of my absence,
And grief that young Octavius with Mark Antony
Have made themselves so strong,—for with her death
That tidings came,—with this she fell distract,
And, her attendants absent, swallow'd fire.

Cas. And died so?

Bru. Even so.

Cas. O ye immortal gods!

Re-enter the Boy *Lucius,* with wine and tapers.

Bru. Speak no more of her. Give me a bowl of wine.
In this I bury all unkindness, Cassius.

Drinks.

Cas. My heart is thirsty for that noble pledge.
Fill, Lucius, till the wine o'erswell the cup;
I cannot drink too much of Brutus' love.

Drinks.

Re-enter *Titinius,* and *Messala.*

Bru. Come in, Titinius! *Exit Lucius.*
Welcome, good Messala.
Now sit we close about this taper here,
And call in question our necessities.

Cas. Portia, art thou gone?

138. Companion, fellow. **146. give . . . evils,** are upset by accidents. **154. with,** with the tidings of. **156. fire,** according to Plutarch, burning coals. **165. call in question,** discuss.

Bru. No more, I pray you.
Messala, I have here received letters
That young Octavius and Mark Antony
Come down upon us with a mighty power,
Bending their expedition toward Philippi.

Mes. Myself have letters of the self-same tenour.

Bru. With what addition?

Mes. That by proscription and bills of outlawry,
Octavius, Antony, and Lepidus
Have put to death an hundred senators.

Bru. Therein our letters do not well agree;
Mine speak of seventy senators that died
By their proscriptions, Cicero being one.

Cas. Cicero one?

Mes. Cicero is dead,
And by that order of proscription,
Had you your letters from your wife, my lord?

Bru. No, Messala.

Mes. Nor nothing in your letters writ of her?

Bru. Nothing, Messala.

Mes. That, methinks, is strange.

Bru. Why ask you? Hear you aught of her in yours?

Mes. No, my lord.

Bru. Now, as you are a Roman, tell me true.

Mes. Then like a Roman bear the truth I tell:
For certain she is dead, and by strange manner.

Bru. Why, farewell, Portia. We must die, Messala.
With meditating that she must die once,
I have the patience to endure it now.

Mes. Even so great men great losses should endure.

Cas. I have as much of this in art as you,
But yet my nature could not bear it so.

Bru. Well, to our work alive. What do you think
Of marching to Philippi presently?

Cas. I do not think it good.

Bru. Your reason?

Cas. This it is:
'T is better that the enemy seek us.
So shall he waste his means, weary his soldiers,
Doing himself offence; whilst we, lying still,
Are full of rest, defence, and nimbleness.

Bru. Good reasons must of force give place to better.
The people 'twixt Philippi and this ground
Do stand but in a forc'd affection,
For they have grudg'd us contribution.
The enemy, marching along by them,
By them shall make a fuller number up,
Come on refresh'd, new-added, and encourag'd;
From which advantage shall we cut him off
If at Philippi we do face him there,
These people at our back.

Cas. Hear me, good brother.

Bru. Under your pardon. You must note beside,
That we have tried the utmost of our friends;
Our legions are brim-full, our cause is ripe.
The enemy increaseth every day;
We, at the height, are ready to decline.
There is a tide in the affairs of men,
Which, taken at the flood, leads on to fortune;
Omitted, all the voyage of their life
Is bound in shallows and in miseries.
On such a full sea are we now afloat;
And we must take the current when it serves,
Or lose our ventures.

Cas. Then, with your will, go on.
We 'll along ourselves, and meet them at Philippi.

Bru. The deep of night is crept upon our talk,
And nature must obey necessity;
Which we will niggard with a little rest.
There is no more to say?

Cas. No more. Good-night.
Early to-morrow will we rise, and hence.

Bru. Lucius! [*Re-enter Lucius*] My gown. [*Exit Lucius.*] Farewell, good Messala;
Good-night, Titinius. Noble, noble Cassius,
Good-night, and good repose.

Cas. O my dear brother!
This was an ill beginning of the night.
Never come such division 'tween our souls!
Let it not, Brutus.

Re-enter *Lucius,* with the gown.

Bru. Everything is well.

Cas. Good-night, my lord.

Bru. Good-night, good brother.

Tit., Mes. Good-night, Lord Brutus.

Bru. Farewell, every one.

Exeunt all but Brutus and Lucius.

Give me the gown. Where is thy instrument?

Luc. Here in the tent.

Bru. What, thou speak'st drowsily?
Poor knave, I blame thee not; thou are o'er-watch'd.

170. **Bending their expedition,** directing their march. **Philippi,** in the eastern corner of Macedonia, near the sea. 191. **once,** some time. 194. **art,** philosophic discipline. 196. **work alive,** work that concerns us who live. 203. **force,** necessity.

205. **affection,** respect. 209. **new-added,** newly increased. 221. **bound in,** confined within. 224. **ventures,** investments. **with your will,** as you wish. 228. **Which . . . with,** to necessity we will allow. 241. **knave.** boy. **o'erwatch'd,** worn out by want of sleep.

Call Claudius and some other of my men;
I 'll have them sleep on cushions in my tent.
Luc. Varro and Claudius!

Enter *Varro* and *Claudius.*

Var. Calls my lord?
Bru. I pray you, sirs, lie in my tent and sleep;
It may be I shall raise you by and by
On business to my brother Cassius.
Var. So please you, we will stand and watch your pleasure.
Bru. I will not have it so: lie down, good sirs;
It may be I shall otherwise bethink me.
Varro and Claudius lie down.
Look, Lucius, here 's the book I sought for so;
I put it in the pocket of my gown.
Luc. I was sure your lordship did not give it me.
Bru. Bear with me, good boy, I am much forgetful.
Canst thou hold up thy heavy eyes a while,
And touch thy instrument a strain or two?
Luc. Ay, my lord, an 't please you.
Bru. It does, my boy.
I trouble thee too much, but thou art willing.
Luc. It is my duty, sir.
Bru. I should not urge thy duty past thy might;
I know young bloods look for a time of rest.
Luc. I have slept, my lord, already.
Bru. It was well done; and thou shalt sleep again;
I will not hold thee long. If I do live,
I will be good to thee. *Music, and a song.*
This is a sleepy tune. O murd'rous slumber,
Layest thou thy leaden mace upon my boy,
That plays thee music? Gentle knave, good-night;
I will not do thee so much wrong to wake thee.
If thou dost nod, thou break'st thy instrument.
I 'll take it from thee; and, good boy, good-night.
Let me see, let me see; is not the leaf turn'd down
Where I left reading? Here it is, I think.

Enter the *Ghost* of Cæsar.

How ill this taper burns! Ha! who comes here?
I think it is the weakness of mine eyes
That shapes this monstrous apparition.
It comes upon me. Art thou anything?
Art thou some god, some angel, or some devil,
That mak'st my blood cold and my hair to stare?
Speak to me what thou art.
Ghost. Thy evil spirit, Brutus.
Bru. Why com'st thou?
Ghost. To tell thee thou shalt see me at Philippi.
Bru. Well; then I shall see thee again?
Ghost. Ay, at Philippi.
Bru. Why, I will see thee at Philippi, then.
Exit Ghost.
Now I have taken heart thou vanishest.
Ill spirit, I would hold more talk with thee.
Boy, Lucius! Varro! Claudius! Sirs, awake!
Claudius!
Luc. The strings, my lord, are false.
Bru. He thinks he still is at his instrument.
Lucius, awake!
Luc. My lord?
Bru. Didst thou dream, Lucius, that thou so criedst out?
Luc. My lord, I do not know that I did cry.
Bru. Yes, that thou didst. Didst thou see anything?
Luc. Nothing, my lord.
Bru. Sleep again, Lucius. Sirrah Claudius!
Fellow thou, awake!
Var. My lord?
Clau. My lord?
Bru. Why did you so cry out, sirs, in your sleep?
Var., Clau. Did we, my lord?
Bru. Ay. Saw you anything?
Var. No, my lord, I saw nothing.
Clau. Nor I, my lord.
Bru. Go and commend me to my brother Cassius;
Bid him set on his powers betimes before,
And we will follow.
Var., Clau. It shall be done, my lord.
Exeunt.

247. raise, rouse. **257. instrument,** lute. **258. an 't,** an (if) it. **267. murd'rous slumber,** see *Macbeth,* II, ii, 38; II, iii, 81. **268. mace,** staff.

275. How . . . burns, a sign of a ghost's presence. **278. upon,** toward. **280. stare,** stand on end.

ACT V. Scene I. *The plains of Philippi.*

Enter *Octavius, Antony,* and their army.

Oct. Now, Antony, our hopes are answered.
You said the enemy would not come down,
But keep the hills and upper regions:
It proves not so: their battles are at hand;
They mean to warn us at Philippi here,
Answering before we do demand of them.

Ant. Tut, I am in their bosoms, and I know
Wherefore they do it. They could be content
To visit other places, and come down
With fearful bravery, thinking by this face
To fasten in our thoughts that they have courage;
But 't is not so.

Enter a *Messenger.*

Mess. Prepare you, generals.
The enemy comes on in gallant show;
Their bloody sign of battle is hung out,
And something to be done immediately.

Ant. Octavius, lead your battle softly on,
Upon the left hand of the even field.

Oct. Upon the right hand I; keep thou the left.

Ant. Why do you cross me in this exigent?

Oct. I do not cross you; but I will do so. *March.*

Drum. Enter *Brutus, Cassius,* and their army; *Lucilius, Titinius, Messala,* and others.

Bru. They stand, and would have parley.

Cas. Stand fast, Titinius; we must out and talk.

Oct. Mark Antony, shall we give sign of battle?

Ant. No, Cæsar, we will answer on their charge.
Make forth; the generals would have some words.

Oct. Stir not until the signal.

Bru. Words before blows; is it so, countrymen?

Oct. Not that we love words better, as you do.

Bru. Good words are better than bad strokes, Octavius.

Ant. In your bad strokes, Brutus, you give good words;
Witness the hole you made in Cæsar's heart,
Crying, "Long live! hail, Cæsar!"

Cas. Antony,
The posture of your blows are yet unknown;
But for your words, they rob the Hybla bees,
And leave them honeyless.

Ant. Not stingless too?

Bru. O, yes, and soundless too;
For you have stolen their buzzing, Antony,
And very wisely threat before you sting.

Ant. Villains, you did not so, when your vile daggers
Hack'd one another in the sides of Cæsar.
You show'd your teeth like apes, and fawn'd like hounds,
And bow'd like bondmen, kissing Cæsar's feet;
Whilst damned Casca, like a cur, behind
Struck Cæsar on the neck. O you flatterers!

Cas. Flatterers! Now, Brutus, thank yourself;
This tongue had not offended so to-day,
If Cassius might have rul'd.

Oct. Come, come, the cause! If arguing make us sweat,
The proof of it will turn to redder drops.
Look!
I draw a sword against conspirators;
When think you that the sword goes up again?
Never, till Cæsar's three and thirty wounds
Be well aveng'd; or till another Cæsar
Have added slaughter to the sword of traitors.

Bru. Cæsar, thou canst not die by traitors' hands,
Unless thou bring'st them with thee.

Oct. So I hope;
I was not born to die on Brutus' sword.

Bru. O, if thou wert the noblest of thy strain,
Young man, thou couldst not die more honourable.

Cas. A peevish schoolboy, worthless of such honour,
Join'd with a masker and a reveller!

Ant. Old Cassius still!

Oct. Come, Antony, away!
Defiance, traitors, hurl we in your teeth.
If you dare fight to-day, come to the field;
If not, when you have stomachs.

Exeunt Octavius, Antony, and army.

Act V, Scene i: 4. battles, armies. **5. warn,** challenge. **7. am . . . bosoms,** know their secrets. **10. With fearful bravery,** making a brave show. **face,** pretence. **17. even,** evenly divided, or, level. **19. exigent,** emergency. **20. do so,** as I said, or (as an aside), I will cross you in future. **24. answer . . . charge,** attack when they do. **25. Make,** step.

33. The posture . . . unknown, we do not yet know your method of dealing blows. Cassius is taunting Antony with not having been man enough to fight at the time of Cæsar's death; he had only seduced the mob with words. **34. Hybla,** a town in Sicily famous for honey. **41. show'd your teeth,** smiled. **48. the cause,** the business in hand. **49. proof of it,** i.e., fighting. **52. goes up again,** returns to its sheath. **54-5. or . . . traitors,** until I too have been killed by you traitors. **59. strain,** race. **61. peevish,** childish. **66. stomachs,** courage.

Cas. Why, now blow wind, swell billow, and swim bark!
The storm is up, and all is on the hazard.
Bru. Ho, Lucilius! hark, a word with you.
Lucil. *Standing forth.* My lord?
Brutus and Lucilius converse apart.
Cas. Messala!
Mes. *Standing forth.* What says my general?
Cas. Messala,
This is my birthday; as this very day
Was Cassius born. Give me thy hand, Messala.
Be thou my witness that against my will,
As Pompey was, am I compell'd to set
Upon one battle all our liberties.
You know that I held Epicurus strong
And his opinion; now I change my mind,
And partly credit things that do presage.
Coming from Sardis, on our former ensign
Two mighty eagles fell, and there they perch'd,
Gorging and feeding from our soldiers' hands;
Who to Philippi here consorted us.
This morning are they fled away and gone;
And in their steads do ravens, crows, and kites
Fly o'er our heads and downward look on us,
As we were sickly prey: their shadows seem
A canopy most fatal under which
Our army lies ready to give up the ghost.
Mes. Believe not so.
Cas. I but believe it partly;
For I am fresh of spirit and resolv'd
To meet all perils very constantly.
Bru. Even so Lucilius.
Cas. Now most noble Brutus,
The gods to-day stand friendly, that we may,
Lovers in peace, lead on our days to age!
But since the affairs of men rests still incertain,
Let 's reason with the worst that may befall.
If we do lose this battle, then is this
The very last time we shall speak together.
What are you then determined to do?
Bru. Even by the rule of that philosophy
By which I did blame Cato for the death
Which he did give himself,—I know not how,
But I do find it cowardly and vile,
For fear of what might fall, so to prevent
The time of life:—arming myself with patience
To stay the providence of some high powers
That govern us below.
Cas. Then, if we lose this battle,
You are contented to be led in triumph
Thorough the streets of Rome?
Bru. No, Cassius, no: think not, thou noble Roman,
That ever Brutus will go bound to Rome;
He bears too great a mind. But this same day
Must end that work the ides of March begun;
And whether we shall meet again I know not,
Therefore our everlasting farewell take.
For ever, and for ever, farewell, Cassius!
If we do meet again, why, we shall smile;
If not, why then this parting was well made.
Cas. For ever, and for ever, farewell, Brutus!
If we do meet again, we 'll smile indeed;
If not, 't is true this parting was well made.
Bru. Why, then, lead on. O, that a man might know
The end of this day's business ere it come!
But it sufficeth that the day will end,
And then the end is known. Come, ho! away!
Exeunt.

Scene II. *The field of battle.*

Alarum. Enter *Brutus* and *Messala.*

Bru. Ride, ride, Messala, ride, and give these bills
Unto the legions on the other side.
Loud alarum.
Let them set on at once; for I perceive
But cold demeanour in Octavius' wing,
And sudden push gives them the overthrow.
Ride, ride, Messala: let them all come down.
Exeunt.

Scene III. *Another part of the field.*

Alarums. Enter *Cassius* and *Titinius.*

Cas. O, look, Titinius, look, the villains fly!
Myself have to mine own turn'd enemy.
This ensign here of mine was turning back;
I slew the coward, and did take it from him.
Tit. O Cassius, Brutus gave the word too early;
Who, having some advantage on Octavius,
Took it too eagerly: his soldiers fell to spoil,
Whilst we by Antony are all enclos'd.

Enter *Pindarus.*

Pin. Fly further off, my lord, fly further off;

72. as, redundant particle. **75. As Pompey was,** at Pharsalia, where he was persuaded to fight against his own judgment. **77. Epicurus,** Cassius had agreed with Epicurus in disregarding omens. **80. former,** foremost. **83. consorted,** accompanied. **87. As,** as if. **92. constantly,** firmly. **97. reason with,** face. **102. Cato,** see above, note on II, ii, 295. **105. prevent,** anticipate. **106. time,** end, full period. **107. stay,** await.

Scene ii: 1. bills, orders. **2. side,** wing. **4. cold demeanour,** lack of ardor. **Scene iii: 3. ensign,** standard-bearer. **7. spoil,** looting.

Mark Antony is in your tents, my lord;
Fly, therefore, noble Cassius, fly far off.
Cas. This hill is far enough. Look, look, Titinius;
Are those my tents where I perceive the fire?
Tit. They are my lord.
Cas. Titinius, if thou lovest me,
Mount thou my horse, and hide thy spurs in him,
Till he have brought thee up to yonder troops,
And here again; that I may rest assur'd
Whether yond troops are friend or enemy.
Tit. I will be here again, even with a thought. *Exit.*
Cas. Go, Pindarus, get higher on that hill;
My sight was ever thick; regard Titinius,
And tell me what thou not'st about the field.
Pindarus ascends the hill.
This day I breathed first; time is come round,
And where I did begin, there shall I end;
My life is run his compass. Sirrah, what news?
Pin. [*Above.*] O my lord!
Cas. What news?
Pin. Titinius is enclosed round about
With horsemen, that make to him on the spur;
Yet he spurs on. Now they are almost on him.
Now, Titinius! Now some light. O, he lights too.
He 's ta'en. [*Shout.*] And, hark! they shout for joy.
Cas. Come down, behold no more.
O, coward that I am, to live so long,
To see my best friend ta'en before my face!
Pindarus descends.
Come hither, sirrah.
In Parthia did I take thee prisoner;
And then I swore thee, saving of thy life,
That whatsoever I did bid thee do,
Thou shouldst attempt it. Come now, keep thine oath;
Now be a freeman; and with this good sword,
That ran through Cæsar's bowels, search this bosom.
Stand not to answer; here, take thou the hilts,
And, when my face is cover'd, as 't is now,
Guide thou the sword. *Pindarus stabs him.*
Cæsar, thou art reveng'd,
Even with the sword that kill'd thee. *Dies.*
Pin. So, I am free; yet would not so have been,
Durst I have done my will. O Cassius,
Far from this country Pindarus shall run,
Where never Roman shall take note of him.
Exit.

Re-enter *Titinius* with *Messala.*

Mes. It is but change, Titinius; for Octavius
Is overthrown by noble Brutus' power,
As Cassius' legions are by Antony.
Tit. These tidings will well comfort Cassius.
Mes. Where did you leave him?
Tit. All disconsolate,
With Pindarus his bondman, on this hill.
Mes. Is not that he that lies upon the ground?
Tit. He lies not like the living. O my heart!
Mes. Is not that he?
Tit. No, this was he, Messala,
But Cassius is no more. O setting sun,
As in thy red rays thou dost sink tonight,
So in his red blood Cassius' day is set;
The sun of Rome is set! Our day is gone;
Clouds, dews, and dangers come; our deeds are done!
Mistrust of my success hath done this deed.
Mes. Mistrust of good success hath done this deed.
O hateful error, melancholy's child,
Why dost thou show to the apt thoughts of men
The things that are not? O error, soon conceiv'd,
Thou never com'st unto a happy birth,
But kill'st the mother that engender'd thee!
Tit. What, Pindarus! Where art thou, Pindarus?
Mes. Seek him, Titinius, whilst I go to meet
The noble Brutus, thrusting this report
Into his ears; I may say, "thrusting" it;
For piercing steel and darts envenomed
Shall be as welcome to the ears of Brutus
As tidings of this sight.
Tit. Hie you, Messala,
And I will seek for Pindarus the while.
Exit Messala.
Why didst thou send me forth, brave Cassius?
Did I not meet thy friends? and did not they
Put on my brows this wreath of victory,
And bid me give it thee? Didst thou not hear their shouts?
Alas, thou hast misconstrued everything!
But, hold thee, take this garland on thy brow;
Thy Brutus bid me give it thee, and I
Will do his bidding. Brutus, come apace,

19. even with, quick as. **21. thick,** dim. **22. S. d.,** i.e., he goes up on the balcony, see s. d. after l. 35. **25. compass,** cycle. **31. light,** dismount. **38. swore thee,** made thee swear.

51. change, exchange. **65. Mistrust,** i.e., Cassius' mistrust. **68. apt,** impressionable. **71. the mother,** as the viper causes the death of its mother, so the man in whose mind error is conceived is ruined by it. **87. apace,** quickly.

And see how I regarded Caius Cassius.
By your leave, gods! This is a Roman's part.
Come, Cassius' sword, and find Titinius' heart. *Kills himself.*

Alarum. Re-enter *Messala,* with *Brutus,* young *Cato, Strato, Volumnius, Lucilius* and others.

Bru. Where, where, Messala, doth his body lie?
Mes. Lo, yonder, and Titinius mourning it.
Bru. Titinius' face is upward.
Cato. He is slain.
Bru. O Julius Cæsar, thou art mighty yet!
Thy spirit walks abroad, and turns our swords
In our own proper entrails. *Low alarums.*
Cato. Brave Titinius!
Look, whe'er he have not crown'd dead Cassius!
Bru. Are yet two Romans living such as these?
The last of all the Romans, fare thee well!
It is impossible that ever Rome
Should breed thy fellow. Friends, I owe moe tears
To this dead man than you shall see me pay.
I shall find time, Cassius: I shall find time.
Come, therefore, and to Thassos send his body;
His funerals shall not be in our camp,
Lest it discomfort us. Lucilius, come;
And come, young Cato; let us to the field.
Labeo and Flavius, set our battles on.
'T is three o'clock; and, Romans, yet ere night
We shall try fortune in a second fight.
Exeunt.

Scene IV. *Another part of the field.*

Alarum. Enter *Brutus, Messala,* young *Cato, Lucilius,* and *Flavius.*

Bru. Yet countrymen, O, yet hold up your heads! *Exit Brutus.*
Cato. What bastard doth not? Who will go with me?
I will proclaim my name about the field.
I am the son of Marcus Cato, ho!
A foe to tyrants, and my country's friend;
I am the son of Marcus Cato, ho!

97. whe'er, whether. **101. fellow,** equal. **104. Thassos,** island near Philippi. **106. discomfort,** dishearten.

Enter *Soldiers,* and fight.

Lucil. And I am Brutus, Marcus Brutus, I;
Brutus, my country's friend; know me for Brutus! *Young Cato falls.*
O young and noble Cato, art thou down?
Why, now thou diest as bravely as Titinius,
And mayst be honour'd, being Cato's son.
1. Sol. Yield, or thou diest.
Lucil. Only I yield to die:
There is so much that thou wilt kill me straight; *Offering money.*
Kill Brutus, and be honour'd in his death.
1. Sol. We must not. A noble prisoner!

Enter *Antony.*

2. Sol. Room, ho! Tell Antony, Brutus is ta'en.
1. Sol. I 'll tell the news. Here comes the general.
Brutus is ta'en. Brutus is ta'en, my lord!
Ant. Where is he?
Lucil. Safe, Antony; Brutus is safe enough.
I dare assure thee that no enemy
Shall ever take alive the noble Brutus;
The gods defend him from so great a shame!
When you do find him, or alive or dead,
He will be found like Brutus, like himself.
Ant. This is not Brutus, friend; but, I assure you,
A prize no less in worth. Keep this man safe,
Give him all kindness; I had rather have
Such men my friends than enemies. Go on,
And see whe'er Brutus be alive or dead;
And bring us word unto Octavius' tent
How everything is chanc'd. *Exeunt.*

Scene V. *Another part of the field.*

Enter *Brutus, Dardanius, Clitus, Strato,* and *Volumnius.*

Bru. Come poor remains of friends, rest on this rock.
Cli. Statilius show'd the torchlight, but, my lord,
He came not back: he is or ta'en or slain.
Bru. Sit thee down, Clitus; slaying is the word,
It is a deed in fashion. Hark thee, Clitus.
Whispers.

7ff. The Folios do not name the speaker for ll. 7-8, and they are commonly given to Brutus, but they seem rather to be the utterance of Lucilius in his attempt to pose as Brutus. The speech-heading, *Luc.*, stands in the text before l. 9. It seems to have been misplaced by the printer. **12. Only I yield,** I yield only.

Cli. What, I, my lord? No, not for all the world.
Bru. Peace then! no words.
Cli. I 'll rather kill myself.
Bru. Hark thee, Dardanius. *Whispers.*
Dar. Shall I do such a deed?
Cli. O Dardanius!
Dar. O Clitus!
Cli. What ill request did Brutus make to thee?
Dar. To kill him, Clitus. Look, he meditates.
Cli. Now is that noble vessel full of grief,
That it runs over even at his eyes.
Bru. Come hither, good Volumnius; list a word.
Vol. What says my lord?
Bru. Why, this, Volumnius:
The ghost of Cæsar hath appear'd to me
Two several times by night; at Sardis once,
And, this last night, here in Philippi fields.
I know my hour is come.
Vol. Not so, my lord.
Bru. Nay, I am sure it is, Volumnius.
Thou seest the world, Volumnius, how it goes;
Our enemies have beat us to the pit:
Low alarums.
It is more worthy to leap in ourselves
Than tarry till they push us. Good Volumnius,
Thou know'st that we two went to school together;
Even for that our love of old, I prithee,
Hold thou my sword-hilts, whilst I run on it.
Vol. That's not an office for a friend, my lord. *Alarum still.*
Cli. Fly, fly, my lord; there is no tarrying here.
Bru. Farewell to you, and you, and you, Volumnius.
Strato, thou hast been all this while asleep;
Farewell to thee too, Strato. Countrymen,
My heart doth joy that yet in all my life
I found no man but he was true to me.
I shall have glory by this losing day
More than Octavius and Mark Antony
By this vile conquest shall attain unto.
So fare you well at once; for Brutus' tongue
Hath almost ended his life's history.
Night hangs upon mine eyes; my bones would rest,
That have but labour'd to attain this hour.
Alarum. Cry within, "Fly, fly, fly!"
Cli. Fly, my lord, fly.
Bru. Hence! I will follow.
Exeunt Clitus, Dardanius, and Volumnius.

23. **pit,** of destruction. 39. **at once,** once for all, or, all of you.

I prithee, Strato, stay thou by thy lord.
Thou art a fellow of a good respect;
Thy life hath had some smatch of honour in it.
Hold then my sword, and turn away thy face,
While I do run upon it. Wilt thou, Strato?
Stra. Give me your hand first. Fare you well, my lord.
Bru. Farewell, good Strato. [*Runs on his sword.*] Cæsar, now be still;
I kill'd not thee with half so good a will.
Dies.

Alarum. Retreat. Enter *Octavius, Antony, Messala, Lucilius,* and the army.

Oct. What man is that?
Mes. My master's man. Strato, where is thy master?
Stra. Free from the bondage you are in, Messala;
The conquerors can but make a fire of him,
For Brutus only overcame himself,
And no man else hath honour by his death.
Lucil. So Brutus should be found. I thank thee, Brutus,
That thou hast prov'd Lucilius' saying true.
Oct. All that serv'd Brutus, I will entertain them.
Fellow, wilt thou bestow thy time with me?
Stra. Ay, if Messala will prefer me to you.
Oct. Do so, good Messala.
Mes. How died my master, Strato?
Stra. I held the sword, and he did run on it.
Mes. Octavius, then take him to follow thee,
That did the latest service to my master.
Ant. This was the noblest Roman of them all.
All the conspirators, save only he,
Did that they did in envy of great Cæsar;
He only, in a general honest thought
And common good to all, made one of them.
His life was gentle, and the elements
So mix'd in him that Nature might stand up
And say to all the world, "This was a man!"
Oct. According to his virtue let us use him,
With all respect and rites of burial.
Within my tent his bones tonight shall lie,
Most like a soldier, ordered honourably.
So call the field to rest; and let's away
To part the glories of this happy day.
Exeunt omnes.

46. **smatch,** smack. 56. **only,** alone. 60. **entertain,** take into service. 61. **bestow,** spend. 62. **prefer,** recommend. 70. **that,** what. 73. **gentle,** that of a true gentleman. **the elements,** the four elements, fire, air, earth, and water. From these elements rose the humours of the human body, and in Brutus they were mingled in due proportion. 79. **most like,** as best befits. 80. **field,** army. 81. **part,** share.

The Tragedy of Hamlet, Prince of Denmark

"Shakespeare is not our poet, but the world's"—so Landor wrote nearly a century ago. And if this is true of Shakespeare's work in general, it is true in a very special degree of the play of *Hamlet*. *Hamlet* is no peculiar possession of the English race, but belongs to the whole world; it is a piece—a very wonderful piece—of that world of pity and terror which we call tragedy. It has been translated into almost every European language; it has been played on every modern stage, and it has profoundly affected the literature of more than one great nation. Around this play, above all others, there has accumulated a mass of criticism, theatrical, historical, philosophic, aesthetic, medico-psychological, and sheerly nonsensical. Much of this mass of Hamlet-literature is today quite valueless. Not infrequently the play has been treated as if it were a piece of actual history and its protagonist an historical figure whose character could be analyzed, whose malady diagnosed like that of Napoleon or a shell-shocked veteran of the World War. Matter has been read into the play that is not to be found there by the sharpest scrutiny, and it is not a little difficult to strike out on a road that leads to an understanding of this play without sticking fast in the mire of irrelevant matter that clings like the Slough of Despond about the pilgrim's feet.

In recent years, however, the research of patient scholarship has made much clear that was formerly confused or quite unknown. We know far more now than was once known as to the first source and the development of the Hamlet story, the immediate background of Shakespeare's play, and the conditions under which it was composed. We understand, as earlier critics did not, the limitations under which Shakespeare worked and can appreciate more accurately the mastery of his genius working within and yet transcending these limitations. It is now definitely established that Shakespeare's *Hamlet* is not an outright creation of his own such as *Othello,* but his reworking and transformation—transfiguration, one might say—of an age-old tale which in the first days of his apprenticeship in London had been given dramatic form by one of his predecessors. On this transformation it is now known that he spent both time and pains, for he has left us three distinct versions of this play.

The Text.—*Hamlet* comes to us in three different texts. The first of these is known as the First Quarto, of which only two copies are now extant. It was published in 1603 and the title-page states that it was written by Shakespeare. There is, indeed, some reason to believe that it represents a version of Shakespeare's first and incomplete revision of an older play, cut down for performance by a company on tour.

But the First Quarto gives us a very poor idea of Shakespeare's first attempt to re-write *Hamlet.* It could hardly be otherwise considering the manner in which this version got into print. On July 26, 1602, Roberts, a printer on friendly terms with Shakespeare's company, entered in the Stationers' Register "a book called the Revenge of Hamlet Prince [of] Denmark as it was lately acted by the Lord Chamberlain his servants." It is probable that Roberts made this entry to forestall an anticipated and unauthorized publication of this successful play by any one else. If so, he failed in his purpose, for about a year later a version of *Hamlet* appeared in print. It was published by N. L. [Nicholas Ling] and John Trundell, who advertised it with a flourish of trumpets on the title-page as having been played by "his Highness Servants [Shakespeare's company had been taken under the direct protection of James I on May 19, 1603] in the City of London, as also in the two Universities of Oxford and Cambridge and elsewhere." Recent criticism has made it fairly certain that the copy which Ling and Trundell sent to their printer was a most extraordinary hodge-podge. Apparently a minor actor, a hired man in Shakespeare's company, had secured the prompter's copy of the *Hamlet* that had been played on tour—a copy discarded by the company in favor of Shakespeare's final revision. This copy the treacherous actor carried to Ling and Trundell and to heighten its value told them that he could add to it the parts in which he had acted—he seems to have played Marcellus, and possibly another minor role or two—and also passages that he remembered from the new version. They, no doubt, jumped at his offer, and copy for the printer was put together which contained three distinct layers or strata: first, the stolen copy in which Shakespeare's revising work was mingled with that of the older playwright; second, passages corresponding word for word with the new version then on the stage—these being the actor's parts so far as the thief possessed them —and finally the thief's contributions from memory. How very bad his memory was may be seen by contrasting the First Quarto version of "To be or not to be" with the true text as it appears in the Second Quarto. Only in some such fashion can we explain the peculiarities of the First Quarto, at times giving us true Shakespeare, at times passages that he could never at any period of his career have written, and at times a jumbled mass of unmetrical unsyntactical matter in which, none the less, we catch gleams of Shakespearean diction.

We may well believe that Shakespeare and his company were shocked at seeing this garbled version of his great play in print. So far as possible it was their practice to withhold plays from publication, but such an outrage called for speedy redress. Accordingly, at the very close of the year 1604, a new edition of *Hamlet* appeared with a title-page designed to tell the public that here was the genuine article: "The Tragicall Historie of Hamlet, Prince of Denmarke. By William Shakespeare. Newly imprinted and enlarged to almost as much againe as it was, according to the true and perfect copie.—Printed by I. R. [James Roberts] for N. L. [Nicholas Ling] and are to be sold at his shoppe, etc." This is the Second Quarto; in the opinion of most modern scholars its text rests directly, or at only one remove, upon Shakespeare's autograph manuscript of *Hamlet.* The statement that this version is enlarged to "almost as much againe" is literally true: the Second Quarto contains about 4,000 lines as against the 2,143 of the First. But this is not the only change, names are altered; Corambis and his man Montano of the First Quarto become Polonius and Reynaldo in the Second; speeches are shifted from one part of the play to another, a rather different slant is given to the character of the Queen, and the character of Hamlet himself is elaborated and perfected by numberless touches, including the fine soliloquy in Act IV, scene iv. Unfortunately Roberts or his journeymen printers did a very bad job; the Second Quarto is marred by misprints, careless omissions of words and phrases, sometimes of whole lines, patent misreadings of Shakespeare's manuscript, wrong assignment of speeches, and other printers' blunders. Moreover, Shakespeare himself, probably, cancelled two interesting passages, Act II, ii, that in which Hamlet calls Denmark a prison (ll. 244-277) and the attack on the rival company of child-actors (ll. 358-379), in order not to give offense at court. The new Queen was at once a Danish princess and the patroness of the Children of the Revels, then acting at Blackfriars. Yet with all its faults the Second Quarto text gives us the longest and best version of *Hamlet* as Shakespeare conceived his play.

The third text, that of the Folio of 1623, is based upon the acting version of Shakespeare's own theatre. The Second Quarto version, the longest of all Shakespeare's plays, could never have been acted in the two to three hours' space which was the customary playing-time of an Elizabethan drama. The Folio text cuts some 200 lines—moralizing, and philosophic passages in particular—and omits the last long soliloquy of Hamlet (IV, iv). It introduces a number of minor changes in the text, restores the two long passages that the Second Quarto had omitted, and adds more and fuller stage-directions. Modern texts are compiled by a collation of the Second Quarto and the First Folio and are thus longer than either of the original versions.

Date.—It would seem from what has already been said that it is impossible to fix the date of *Hamlet,* since the play as it stands is the result of repeated revision. But it seems clear that no revision in which Shakespeare's hand was visible could have been on the boards before 1598, when Meres in compiling his famous list of Shakespeare's plays made no mention of a *Hamlet.* It is hardly credible that Meres should have attributed *Titus Andronicus* to Shakespeare and failed to have named *Hamlet,* if he had known such a play by the master. We may assume then that the *Hamlet* played by Shakespeare's Company at the Rose in 1594, and the *Hamlet* produced by them at the Theatre in 1596 were versions, more or less revised perhaps, of the first dramatization of the story. On the other hand, a reference by Gabriel Harvey of Cambridge to *Hamlet* as the work of Shakespeare cannot be dated later than February, 1601, when Essex died on the scaffold, since Harvey in the same note speaks of that nobleman as still living. We may assume then that some time between 1598 and the end of 1600 Shakespeare began his revision of the old play and that this unfinished work was produced in London and on tour. Harvey may have seen it at Cambridge. The final version was probably composed some time before the appearance of the First Quarto in 1603.

Sources.—The story of Hamlet, the wise prince who feigned madness to gain his revenge, goes back to the pre-historic age of Scandinavia, and probably had its origin in one of the bloody family feuds so frequent in Northern history and saga. It passed with the Vikings from the North to Danish Ireland, where it took on various Celtic accretions and returned to Scandinavia to become part of the traditional history of Denmark. It was preserved by oral tradition until about 1185, when Saxo Grammaticus, a Danish scholar, embodied it in his Latin *Historia Danica.*

Briefly Saxo's story is as follows: There were once two brothers in Jutland, Horwendil and Feng. Horwendil was a famous warrior; he slew the King of Norway in single fight and married Gerutha, the King of Denmark's daughter. His jealous brother murdered him, married the widow, and became ruler of Jutland. The orphan son of Horwendil, Amleth, saved his life by feigning madness, grovelling in the dirt, and talking what seemed sheer nonsense, but had, really, a hidden meaning. It may be noted in passing that this feigned madness is a constant feature of the legend and that it is quite simply motivated by the need of self-preservation. Had Amleth not seemed a hopeless idiot his uncle would quickly have sent him to follow his father. Even as it was, Feng grew suspicious and tried to learn whether the youth was really mad or only feigning. His first agent was a young woman—the original of Ophelia. The story here is somewhat confused, but it is clear that Amleth's sagacity and the maid's love for him enable him to escape the snare. A second attempt is made by a friend of Feng, who concealed himself in the straw of Geruth's chamber—a striking proof of the antiquity of the tale—in order to overhear a conversation between Amleth and his mother. Amleth, however, detects and kills the spy, rebukes his mother for her incestuous marriage, and tells her of his desire for revenge. Shortly after this Feng, who dared not slay Amleth openly, sent him to England with two attendants bearing a letter carved on wood—doubtless in the old runic letters of the North—bidding the King of England put him to death. On the voyage Amleth found and read the letter, and altered it so as to bid the English King kill the bearers and marry his daughter to the Prince. So it was done and after a year in England Amleth returned to Denmark where he found Feng and his followers celebrating at a banquet a false report of his death. He plays his old part of a fool, gets the retainers drunk, fires the hall, and slays Feng with his own sword. On the morrow he makes a long speech to the people and becomes King of Jutland. His further adventures have no bearing on the play. He ruled as a wise and brave King and finally fell in battle against the King of Denmark.

Such is the old tale, a typical revenge story of the barbaric North, related with many eloquent Latin flourishes by Saxo. First printed in 1514 it passed from medieval Latin into modern literature in the hands of Belleforest, a French writer of the sixteenth century, who included a translation of Saxo's tale of *Hamlet* in the fifth volume of his *Histoires Tragiques,* 1582. To Saxo's story Belleforest added a good deal of moralizing, but only one material incident; he made Feng the adulterous lover of Geruth before the murder of her husband. This addition plays its part in later versions; there is no trace of it in Saxo. An English translation of Belleforest, *The Hystorie of Hamblet,* appeared in 1608. This work is later than the publication of Shakespeare's play, and in one or two places shows the influence of the stage-version. We may disregard it as a link in the chain of sources.

Some time in the 1580's, during the first great outburst of English drama, the French story was dramatized for the English stage. Nash, a contemporary man of letters, alludes to it in his preface to Greene's *Menaphon,* 1589, and from certain allusions in his reference and other bits of evidence this old play is now generally supposed to have been the work of Thomas Kyd, author of a famous early play, *The Spanish Tragedy.* Unfortunately this *Ur-Hamlet,* as it is called, was never printed, and the manuscript was probably thrown aside when Shakespeare's masterpiece drove it off the stage. We are, however, able to reconstruct it in its general outline from our knowledge of Kyd's dramatic technique, from some vestiges that seem to remain in the First Quarto, and from a German play, *Der Bestrafte Brudermord,* which, there is good reason to believe, represents a degraded version of Kyd's lost play.

Kyd, it seems clear, very materially altered the story, not only to fit it for the stage, but to give it the Senecan coloring which he so much admired. Three new features in particular he seems to have introduced which had important consequences. The first of these was the Ghost of the murdered king crying for revenge. This ghost, like that of Andrea in *The Spanish Tragedy,* comes straight from Seneca, and Kyd probably flattered himself that here he had introduced a genuine classical touch into the old barbaric tale. To render the ghost's appeal more effective on the stage Kyd makes him reveal to Hamlet the truth, hitherto unknown, of his secret murder. This was an effective dramatic point, but it involved consequences which Kyd may not have realized. It forced him, in the first place, to substitute secret poisoning for the open manslaughter of his source, and so to give a touch of the Italian Renaissance to a tale of the Teutonic North. More than this it removed entirely the original and natural reason for Hamlet's feigned madness—self-preservation. It would have been more reasonable for Kyd to have dropped the feigned madness when he cancelled the motive therefor, but madness, real or feigned, had a grim fascination for the Elizabethans. Kyd had already exploited madness in the ravings of Hieronimo in *The Spanish Tragedy,* and he could not bring himself to forego this effective stage-business. So far from dropping it, he proceeded to duplicate it by making Hamlet's lady-love go mad, like Isabel, the wife of Hieronimo. The reason for Shakespeare's hero feigning madness by putting "an antic disposition on" has been endlessly debated. The simple truth is that this feigned madness was at once an essential part of the old story and an effective point in the new play. Shakespeare could no more have dispensed with this than a modern playwright could compose a *St. Joan* without bringing in her "voices."

In the second place, Kyd changed altogether the close of the old tale. He retold it in the form of Elizabethan tragedy, and this form—following Seneca—demanded the death of the hero. And so Hamlet, who in the saga emerges triumphant from the contest with his uncle, in the play goes down to death along with him. And they do not die alone. Kyd seems to have felt that the more deaths he staged the more tragic he made his play. The last scene of *The Spanish Tragedy* is something like a general massacre, and the same is true of *Hamlet.* Not only the "mighty opposites," Claudius and Hamlet, but Laertes, the Queen, and apparently in Kyd's play the original of Osric, lie dead on the stage at the close. To bring about this catastrophe Kyd invented the character of Laertes, a figure unknown in earlier versions, the fencing-match with Hamlet, the poisoned rapier, and the poisoned bowl. All this is melodramatic enough, but as centuries of performance have shown, immensely effective on the stage. The bloody catastrophe, like the feigned madness, was a fixed point in the plot when Shakespeare took it over. He could not well have changed it if he would, and that he would is more than doubtful.

Finally, Kyd, impelled by his passion for striking stage situations, introduced another quite novel feature—the play within the play. Such a device he had already employed to precipitate the catastrophe of *The Spanish Tragedy.* In his *Hamlet* he shifted it to the center and climax of the play. Its effectiveness is undeniable. Why Hamlet should need further proof of his uncle's guilt, how a travelling company chanced to have in their repertoire a play that exactly paralleled the circumstances of the crime of Claudius, why the King endured the representation of this crime in the dumb-show only to break down at the words of the stage-murderer—all these are questions that have caused much throwing about of brains. A simple solution of the whole matter is that the play within a play was another fixed point in the plot and that Shakespeare neither could nor would sacrifice so effective a scene. He has used all his art to cover up the difficulties and, for his own end, he has succeeded. Such questions as these are asked only by students, never by spectators of the play, and it cannot be too often said that Shakespeare wrote for the stage and not for the study.

What after all is the result of the long evolution of the tale from its earliest form to its last in Shakespeare's finished play? The answer may be given in two words, Shakespeare's Prince. The Hamlet of Shakespeare's play is Shakespeare's own creation. His play still shows a likeness to the old story; the character of Hamlet is wholly new. This new creation was in a sense forced upon Shakespeare and at the same time appealed to his instinctive interest in character and to his genius for character creation. It was forced on him by the nature of the plot he took over from the old play. This was a tragedy of revenge, and such a tragedy must open with the call for revenge and close with its accomplishment. How is the interval between these two given points to be filled? There are two methods: it may be filled by action, in which case the drama becomes a play of intrigue. This seems to have been Kyd's way. The reconstruction of his lost play shows it to have been an exciting drama of plot and counter-plot. All this remains in Shakespeare's play and imparts to it a most effective response to the primitive desire of the audience for action on the stage.

The thoughtful spectator, however, asks for something more than lively action, and Shakespeare, we may well believe, sympathized with this desire and decided to employ the second method of solving the dramatic problem. He would fill up the interval between the call to revenge and the accomplishment by developing the character of the revenger and showing that his delay was not due to external obstacles but inherent in the character itself. If we compare Shakespeare's play with what we may conjecture of Kyd's we can see him stroke by stroke developing and elaborating this character. The idea of external obstacles has been cancelled; not only has Kyd's reference to the King's guards been effaced, but Shakespeare has shown by the rebellion of Laertes how easy it would have been for Hamlet, had he been other than he was, to have overthrown the King. He has made Hamlet reproach himself again and again for his delay without a single hint at any objective hindrance to his aim. And here Shakespeare was confronted with a very real danger. To make his hero incapable of action because of weakness of will would be to render him unsympathetic, perhaps even despicable, to an Elizabethan audience. It is to avoid this danger that Shakespeare elaborates with such care and such multiplicity of detail the character of Hamlet until he has made him the most interesting, perhaps the most appealing, figure in all dramatic literature.

The character of Hamlet is by far the most complex in all the splendid gallery of Shakespeare's creations. In it old elements and new are inextricably blended. It was impossible for Shakespeare to return to the primitive simplicity of the saga-hero. The story of Hamlet had been translated by Kyd into a play of the Renaissance set in an atmosphere of Renaissance decadence and intrigue. It was Shakespeare's task to harmonize as fully as possible the old tale and the new setting in the character of his protagonist. That he wholly succeeded no thoughtful student of Shakespeare will now admit without some reservation. Certainly Shakespeare's Hamlet has not the consistency of a character created by some formula; he is not a type character, no more the typical revenger than Falstaff is the typical Miles Gloriosus. He has not even the consistency of a character created by Shakespeare in one free gush of imagination as he created Othello, for instance, or Macbeth. Yet Hamlet is, none the less, a real and very living character; he has the consistency, or inconsistency, of life itself, and in the lively interpretation of this character by a great actor the inconsistencies revealed by critical analysis are blended into harmony by the actor's art.

What, then, did Shakespeare do to transform the melodramatic revenger of the old play into the noble and profoundly pathetic protagonist of this tragedy of the inner soul? The answer is threefold.

The Character of Hamlet.—In the first place, Shakespeare has made his hero a true prince of the Renaissance. The phrase in which Ophelia describes him as courtier, soldier, scholar, gives us in brief the Renaissance ideal of the gentleman, and the Prince is, or should be, the first gentleman of the land. Hamlet's behavior to friends and foes, except when he is feigning madness, is that of the Prince trained in perfect courtesy. He is, likewise, the scholar, a student at Wittenberg, who desires above all things to return there. He has the scholar's love of books, the scholar's turn for moralizing and generalizing; he is acquainted with "your philosophy." The plot offered no opportunity to show Hamlet as a soldier, but his skill in swordsmanship, his bravery in the encounter with the pirates, the testimony of the warlike Fortinbras, and the military funeral accorded to him, all show the poet's wish to emphasize this side of his character. Moreover, like the splendid courtiers whom Shakespeare knew, Hamlet was interested in the drama and a patron of players. It is worth a note, in passing, that the play which Hamlet praises so highly is exactly the sort that would have commended itself to a courtly and scholarly patron of the drama in Shakespeare's day—a classic theme couched in language "climbing to the height of Seneca his style."

Education and environment alike have formed a character ill-fitted to reply to the ancient call of blood for blood. The ideals of the Renaissance did not include the old obligation of blood revenge, and Shakespeare's Renaissance Prince has no desire to bathe his hands in the blood of his father's murderer. It is true that Laertes, a gentleman of Hamlet's court, is quick to take up the task of revenge and stoops to base treachery to attain his end. But Laertes has been purposely drawn as a foil to Hamlet; he is a type familiar to Shakespeare's age, a barbarian thinly veneered with Renaissance culture. It is plain, throughout the play, that Hamlet shrinks from the actual commission of the deed of blood. He rejects the one chance offered him to slay the King with an excuse which is hard, if not impossible, to reconcile with his character. When he kills Polonius, taking him for the King, he acts on the instinctive impulse of self-preservation—had the King been behind the arras, Hamlet was a dead man—and when at last he does strike down his enemy it is on the equally primitive impulse to return blow for blow. Never once does Hamlet deliberately plan the execution of the task the Ghost had imposed upon him.

Hamlet is the Renaissance Prince, but he is something more: a highly individualized personality, emotional, idealistic, and melancholy. He is a man of quick and warm emotions. He adored his heroic father, he loved his gentle, easy-tempered mother, he was charmed by the beauty and innocence of Ophelia, he lavished his friendship upon the stoical Horatio. There is no trace in his nature of fierce or selfish passions; he calls himself, to be sure, "very proud, revengeful, ambitious," but this is when he is raving at Ophelia. His one reference to the throne of which he had been tricked comes almost at the end of the play; there is no other evidence that Hamlet regretted his loss. There is something passive in his emotional nature; he seems satisfied with feeling and with the contemplation of feeling, "the thoughts of love," and has little desire to seek further gratification in action. The epithets that Shakespeare puts into the mouths of other actors in the drama to characterize Hamlet—"young, good, gentle, dear, noble"—all point to this unselfish nature; they are summed up in Horatio's farewell—"Goodnight, sweet Prince." This is not a nature to move swiftly and resolutely to a deed of violence.

This gentle prince was, moreover, by nature an idealist. His famous speech (II, ii, 316-321), "What a piece of work is a man! How noble in reason, how infinite in faculty!"—is an epitome of the idealist's outlook on life. It would appear that Hamlet in his love of the good and the beautiful tended, before the tragic blow that shattered him, to idealize the reflections of the good and beautiful in the world around him. He calls the vain Laertes "a very noble youth"; he enshrines in his heart's core Horatio, whose Roman virtue is mainly that of a passive endurance; he certainly idealized the marriage relation as he saw it embodied in the protective affection of his father and the clinging fondness of his mother. While Shakespeare was elaborating his conception of Hamlet his mind was full of the character of Brutus, the perfect idealist of ancient times, whom he had just portrayed in his *Julius Cæsar*. Unconsciously, perhaps, he gave to his new creation something of the fine confidence of Brutus in the goodness of human nature. But Hamlet at the very beginning of our play appears as the idealist who has been suddenly and rudely disillusioned. This disillusion sprang not from his father's mysterious death, much as that must have affected him, but rather from the speedy and shameful remarriage of his mother. It is hard for us today to realize the shame of such a marriage. The medieval church denounced the marriage of a widower with his sister-in-law or a widow with her brother-in-law as incest. A dispensation for such a marriage was at times obtained, but it was a grave question whether the dispensing power even of the Pope could reach so far. In the German play we are specifically told that the Pope had allowed the remarriage of Gertrude with Claudius; this is probably a trace of Kyd's hand which Shakespeare has effaced. In the sixteenth century eight Catholic universities pronounced invalid the marriage of Henry VIII to the widow of his brother Arthur.

The effect of this scandalous marriage upon such an emotional and idealistic character as Hamlet would be inconceivable if Shakespeare himself had not used all his power to depict it. The first soliloquy of Hamlet shows his deep revulsion against this outrage on his moral nature: "this goodly frame the earth" has become to him "an unweeded garden"; woman a synonym for fleshly frailty. And it is not merely his mother's shame, but the placid acquiescence therein of his whole world that destroys Hamlet's faith in humanity. The garden is possessed by things "rank and gross in nature"; the sage Polonius has apparently advised this marriage; the innocent Ophelia is a favorite maid of honor of the guilty queen; the courtiers spend their ducats for miniatures of the new king. All the world is happy except Hamlet whose sable suit and mournful countenance are the one blot in a gay court. The whole face of the world has changed to him and his misery is heightened by the fact that he must bear it alone—

> Break my heart, for I must hold my tongue

he cries at the close of his first soliloquy.

At the beginning of the play, then, we find Hamlet, the disillusioned idealist, sunk in a state of profound melancholy. There is no need to exaggerate this mood into a pathologic state of melancholia. Hamlet's madness, we know from the history of the tale, was not real, but feigned. But there is no doubt about the morbid melancholy; Shakespeare even went so far as to dress his Prince in the sable cloak that to the Elizabethans designated the melancholy man; and to the Elizabethans the melancholiac was incapable of prompt and resolute action. Hamlet's one desire when we meet him first is to fly from the world that surrounds him and to forget it among his books at Wittenberg; but even this is denied him. In his bitterness he longs for death and only his consciousness of a divine command restrains him from self-slaughter. It is in this depressed state that the revelation of the Ghost comes to him, a revelation that only increases his horror of the world in which he lives. His father, he learns, has not only been murdered, but poisoned, treacherously, in his sleep, by none other than the smiling, smooth-spoken villain who has just been caressing the murdered man's son. His beloved mother has not only "posted to incestuous sheets"; she has been the adulterous mistress of the murderer before his crime.

The charge which the Ghost lays upon Hamlet is imperative—

> Revenge my foul and most unnatural murder.

Here at least is the call to action. But the mere action of revenge is incapable of satisfying Hamlet, of purging his mind of its accumulated bitterness. He accepts the charge; he cannot do otherwise; but he might kill the King out of hand without putting a crooked world right or restoring his mother's lost innocence. Indeed concern for his mother, shame for her guilt, a wish to open her eyes and touch her heart, far outweigh Hamlet's desire for revenge; at the very climax of the play he passes by his one fair chance for revenge to hasten to his mother's chamber for that terrible scene in which he turns her eyes into her very soul to see its black and grainèd spots. And so the summons of the Ghost to action leaves Hamlet less capable of action than before. After the first excitement of his interview with the Ghost Hamlet sinks back into his melancholy and finds an outlet for the bitterness that fills his heart in the wild and whirling words of his feigned madness.

This incapacity for premeditated action remains with Hamlet to the end of the play, except in one most striking instance, the play before the King. Here, under the stimulus of the player's speech and with another task in hand than a bloody revenge, he rouses himself from his lethargy long enough to plan a scene and write a speech which will catch the conscience of the King and so dispel the doubts that have risen in his own mind as to the authority of the Ghost's command.

His complete success in this scene, however, does not encourage him to take further action against the King. He is satisfied with the confirmation of the Ghost's message and thinks now only of his mother. When he has converted her to a sense of her sin he is content to be exiled to England and leaves the outcome to the Divinity that shapes our ends. It is hardly too much to say that by the close of the third act Hamlet has drifted into a deadening fatalism, and, as a result, Fate takes charge of the action. The death of Polonius, the madness and death of Ophelia, the deaths of the Queen, Laertes, and Hamlet himself are the direct consequences of his shifting the charge imposed on him upon a Providence which accomplishes its ends only through the actions of men. And yet in spite of his evasion and delay Hamlet never loses our interest nor forfeits our sympathy.

There is a special reason for this, and this reason involves the third element in Shakespeare's transformation of the simple avenger of Kyd into the complex and subtle character of his own tragedy. Into the character of Hamlet as it grew beneath his shaping hands Shakespeare put a double portion of his own personality. When Shakespeare set himself to work upon the play of *Hamlet* he had turned away from men of action, villains like Richard III, or heroes like Henry V, and was absorbed in a study of the contemplative character, satirical like Jaques, pessimistic like Duke Vincentio, worldly-wise like Ulysses. Among these figures Hamlet stands supreme, and this because Hamlet incarnates so much of Shakespeare himself. Again and again in the play we seem to catch the very voice of Shakespeare. It is the poet rather than the Prince who criticizes the pretensions of the rival child-actors and imparts professional instruction to the players; it is the poet who in the most famous of the soliloquies reckons among the ills of life "the pangs of dispriz'd love, the law's delay, the insolence of office." These are ills of which the well-beloved Prince could hardly have had a personal experience, but which reappear in a sonnet (66) where the poet is speaking in his own person.

Shakespeare has done more, however, than to make Hamlet an occasional mouthpiece of his thought. He has embodied in Hamlet many of his own characteristics, his gentleness, his courtesy, his frank and open nature, his love of books, his keen insight into human nature. Above all, that melancholy of disillusioned idealism, so dominant a trait in Hamlet, was characteristic of Shakespeare himself in middle life when in his great series of tragedies he set himself to probe the darker recesses of the human soul. Explain it as we may, the fact remains that there appears in the work of Shakespeare in the first years of the seventeenth century, a note of skepticism, a distrust of life, and, in particular, a bitterness toward women amounting almost to a sex-obsession. The so-called "bitter comedies," *Measure for Measure* and *Troilus and Cressida,* are the by-products, so to speak, of this mood. The tragedy of *Hamlet* is its supreme expression, and in *Hamlet* it is the Prince who mirrors Shakespeare's mind. This is true especially of the passages where Hamlet playing the role of the malcontent breaks into satire against life in general and women in particular, but it is also true of other scenes. At times the mask seems to drop and we see the face and hear the voice of the poet. It is not the Hamlet who has seen and talked with a departed spirit, but Shakespeare who speaks of the "bourne from which no traveller returns"; it is not Hamlet, the believer in a guiding Divinity, but Shakespeare in a bitter mood who drifts into the hopeless materialism of the grave-yard scene and traces the dust of Alexander to its progress in a bung-hole. It is this potent infusion of the poet's own personality, alike in its happier and darker qualities, that completes the transformation of the primitive Hamlet and gives to Shakespeare's Prince his peculiar and perennial appeal.

Such, then, was the contribution of Shakespeare in the development of an old tale of the Scandinavian heroic age. Others had told the story; he created the character of the hero.

Final Appreciation.—The tragedy of Hamlet occupies a unique position in Shakespeare's work. Written midway in his career as poet-dramatist, it differs both from the one tragedy of his youth and the creations of his later genius. It is not a tragedy of Fate like *Romeo and Juliet;* it is not a tragedy of crime like *Macbeth.* It is, in a word, the tragedy of the individual at his highest and best in conflict with a debasing and crushing environment, of the individual broken and stained in the conflict and emerging at last in a victory that is little better than a defeat. It is, perhaps, for this very reason the most modern in spirit of Shakespeare's plays and appeals most strongly to the student of today. Nor is its appeal as acting drama less potent. Archaic as is the form of the tragedy of blood, Shakespeare's art has given to this form an enduring vitality. The dramatic situations inherited from the old play have been exploited with such power as to retain their thrill through centuries. The characters from the King to the two grave-diggers are living figures; some of them, Fortinbras, Laertes, and Horatio, have been skilfully designed as contrasts to the protagonist. And this protagonist, Shakespeare's Hamlet, the child of the Renaissance, the representative of noble man struggling against a corrupt world, the mouthpiece often of his creator's thought, will remain, while the world endures, not only the highest expression of the poet's genius, but the supreme tragic figure in the literature of the world.

Stage History.—To write the stage history of *Hamlet* would be to recount the history of the English stage from Shakespeare's day to the present time. More fortunate than other plays it has, with one exception to be noted later, held the stage in the form that Shakespeare wrote it—allowing always for certain cuts and alterations of language.

Frequent contemporary references attest the popularity of *Hamlet* in Shakespeare's day. The role of the Prince was created by Burbage and an old tradition states that Shakespeare himself played the Ghost. It was played at Court in the season of 1619-20.

After the Restoration *Hamlet* was assigned to Davenant, who produced it with scenery at his new theatre in 1661. It was the first Shakespeare play that Pepys saw and he is loud in his praise of Betterton, who played the title-role, "the best part that ever man acted." During his long career Betterton retained this part, playing it, indeed, on his farewell performance when he was over seventy. Praised by such different critics as Pepys, Steele, and Colley Cibber, Betterton set a standard that was not reached again until the time of Garrick.

Garrick, who began in 1741 by playing the Ghost, was the most famous Hamlet of the eighteenth century. Yet it was Garrick alone of all English actor-managers who dared to lay violent hands upon the structure of the play. Influenced perhaps by contemporary neo-classic criticism and French practice, he cut out the Grave-diggers, the quarrel at Ophelia's grave, and the foppery of Osric. Fortunately he refrained from clapping on a happy ending; his Hamlet kills the King and dies himself by the sword of Laertes. It is to the credit of the eighteenth century audiences that this violent distortion of Shakespeare's masterpiece did not long hold the stage.

After Garrick the stage history of *Hamlet* can be little more than a rehearsal of the names of famous actors. Kemble apparently was the first to present a melancholy, introspective Hamlet; his performance is said to have been marked by a "fixed and sullen gloom." His brother, Charles, played a Hamlet "essentially mad." Fechter broke with old tradition by presenting a Danish Hamlet in the setting of a Viking Court. Irving's Hamlet laid special stress on the Prince's love for Ophelia, played to perfection by Ellen Terry.

Forbes-Robertson took the lead in restoring the Fortinbras ending, thus according to Hamlet the military funeral which Shakespeare had devised. Edwin Booth, one of the greatest of all Hamlets, distinguished especially by his lovely voice and significant gesture, used a version very close to the original text.

Of recent performances mention should be made of the production of Hamlet in modern dress in London and New York, 1925–26. John Gielgud swept New York off its feet by his passionate, emotional interpretation of the part in 1937. The simultaneous Leslie Howard production was perhaps a better spectacle, but the talented actor seemed unable to rise to the height of Shakespeare's Hamlet.

THE TRAGEDY OF HAMLET, PRINCE OF DENMARK

Dramatis Personæ

Claudius, King of Denmark.
Hamlet, son to the late, and nephew to the present King.
Polonius, Lord Chamberlain.
Horatio, friend to *Hamlet.*
Laertes, son to *Polonius.*
Voltimand,
Cornelius,
Rosencrantz,
Guildenstern,
Osric,
A Gentleman, } courtiers.
Marcellus,
Bernardo, } officers.
Francisco, a soldier.
Reynaldo, servant to *Polonius.*
A Priest.
Players.
Two Clowns, grave-diggers.
Fortinbras, Prince of Norway.
A Captain.
English Ambassadors.

Gertrude, Queen of Denmark, and mother to *Hamlet.*
Ophelia, daughter to *Polonius.*

Ghost of *Hamlet's* Father.

Lords, Ladies, Officers, Soldiers, Sailors, Messengers, and other Attendants.

SCENE: *Elsinore, Denmark.*

ACT I. Scene I. *Elsinore. A platform before the castle.*

Francisco at his post. Enter to him *Bernardo.*

Ber. Who 's there?
Fran. Nay, answer me. Stand, and unfold yourself.
Ber. Long live the king!
Fran. Bernardo?
Ber. He.
Fran. You come most carefully upon your hour.
Ber. 'T is now struck twelve: get thee to bed, Francisco.
Fran. For this relief much thanks; 't is bitter cold,
And I am sick at heart.
Ber. Have you had quiet guard?
Fran. Not a mouse stirring.
Ber. Well, good-night.
If you do meet Horatio and Marcellus,
The rivals of my watch, bid them make haste.

Enter *Horatio* and *Marcellus.*

Fran. I think I hear them. Stand, ho! Who is there?
Hor. Friends to this ground.
Mar. And liegemen to the Dane.
Fran. Give you good-night.
Mar. O, farewell, honest soldier:
Who hath reliev'd you?
Fran. Bernardo has my place.
Give you good-night. *Exit.*
Mar. Holla! Bernardo!
Ber. Say—
What, is Horatio there?
Hor. A piece of him.
Ber. Welcome, Horatio; welcome, good Marcellus.
Hor. What, has this thing appear'd again to-night?
Ber. I have seen nothing.
Mar. Horatio says 't is but our fantasy,
And will not let belief take hold of him
Touching this dreaded sight, twice seen of us;
Therefore I have entreated him along
With us to watch the minutes of this night,
That if again this apparition come,
He may approve our eyes and speak to it.
Hor. Tush, tush, 't will not appear.
Ber. Sit down a while,
And let us once again assail your ears,
That are so fortified against our story,
What we have two nights seen.
Hor. Well, sit we down,
And let us hear Bernardo speak of this.
Ber. Last night of all,

3. Long live the king, a password. **13. rivals,** partners. **16. Give you,** God give you.

29. approve, confirm.

When yond same star that 's westward from the pole
Had made his course t' illume that part of heaven
Where now it burns, Marcellus and myself,
The bell then beating one,—

Enter the *Ghost*.

Mar. Peace, break thee off! Look, where it comes again!
Ber. In the same figure, like the King that 's dead.
Mar. Thou art a scholar; speak to it, Horatio.
Ber. Looks it not like the King? Mark it, Horatio.
Hor. Most like; it harrows me with fear and wonder.
Ber. It would be spoke to.
Mar. Question it, Horatio.
Hor. What art thou that usurp'st this time of night,
Together with that fair and warlike form
In which the majesty of buried Denmark
Did sometimes march? By heaven I charge thee, speak!
Mar. It is offended.
Ber. See, it stalks away!
Hor. Stay! Speak, speak! I charge thee, speak! *Exit Ghost.*
Mar. 'T is gone, and will not answer.
Ber. How now, Horatio? you tremble and look pale;
Is not this something more than fantasy?
What think you on 't?
Hor. Before my God, I might not this believe
Without the sensible and true avouch
Of mine own eyes.
Mar. Is it not like the King?
Hor. As thou art to thyself.
Such was the very armour he had on
When he the ambitious Norway combated;
So frown'd he once, when, in an angry parle,
He smote the sledded Polacks on the ice.
'T is strange.
Mar. Thus twice before, and jump at this dead hour,
With martial stalk hath he gone by our watch.
Hor. In what particular thought to work I know not;
But, in the gross and scope of my opinion,
This bodes some strange eruption to our state.
Mar. Good now, sit down, and tell me, he that knows,
Why this same strict and most observant watch
So nightly toils the subject of the land,
And why such daily cast of brazen cannon,
And foreign mart for implements of war;
Why such impress of shipwrights, whose sore task
Does not divide the Sunday from the week;
What might be toward, that this sweaty haste
Doth make the night joint-labourer with the day,
Who is 't that can inform me?
Hor. That can I;
At least, the whisper goes so. Our last king,
Whose image even but now appear'd to us,
Was, as you know, by Fortinbras of Norway,
Thereto prick'd on by a most emulate pride,
Dar'd to the combat; in which our valiant Hamlet—
For so this side of our known world esteem'd him—
Did slay this Fortinbras; who, by a seal'd compact,
Well ratified by law and heraldry,
Did forfeit, with his life, all those his lands
Which he stood seiz'd of, to the conqueror;
Against the which, a moiety competent
Was gaged by our king; which had return'd
To the inheritance of Fortinbras,
Had he been vanquisher; as, by the same comart,
And carriage of the article design'd,
His fell to Hamlet. Now, sir, young Fortinbras,
Of unimproved mettle hot and full,
Hath in the skirts of Norway here and there
Shark'd up a list of lawless resolutes,
For food and diet, to some enterprise
That hath a stomach in 't; which is no other—
As it doth well appear unto our state—
But to recover of us, by strong hand
And terms compulsatory, those foresaid lands
So by his father lost; and this, I take it,
Is the main motive of our preparations,
The source of this our watch, and the chief head
Of this post-haste and romage in the land.
Ber. I think it be no other but e'en so;
Well may it sort that this portentous figure
Comes armed through our watch, so like the King
That was and is the question of these wars.
Hor. A mote it is to trouble the mind's eye.
In the most high and palmy state of Rome,

42. **scholar**, evil spirits were exorcised in Latin. 57. **sensible**, of the senses. **avouch**, proof. 62. **parle**, parley. 63. **sledded**, using sleds. 65. **jump**, just. 68. **gross and scope**, general drift.

72. **toils**, makes to toil. **subject**, subjects. 74. **mart**, trade. 75. **impress**, forced service. 83. **emulate**, envious. 89. **seiz'd of**, possessed. 90. **moiety competent**, equal portion. 91. **gaged**, pledged. 93. **comart**, agreement. 94. **carriage . . . design'd**, import of the agreement drawn up. 96. **unimproved**, untried. 98. **Shark'd up**, collected hastily. 100. **hath . . . in 't**, requires courage. 106. **head**, origin. 107. **romage**, bustle. 109. **sort**, befit.

A little ere the mightiest Julius fell,
The graves stood tenantless and the sheeted dead
Did squeak and gibber in the Roman streets.
. . . .
As stars with trains of fire and dews of blood,
Disasters in the sun; and the moist star
Upon whose influence Neptune's empire stands
Was sick almost to doomsday with eclipse:
And even the like precurse of fear'd events,
As harbingers preceding still the fates
And prologue to the omen coming on,
Have heaven and earth together demonstrated
Unto our climatures and countrymen.

Re-enter *Ghost.*

But soft, behold! Lo, where it comes again!
I 'll cross it, though it blast me. Stay, illusion!
If thou hast any sound, or use of voice,
Speak to me; *It spreads his arms.*
If there be any good thing to be done
That may to thee do ease and grace to me,
Speak to me;
If thou art privy to thy country's fate,
Which, happily, foreknowing may avoid,
O speak!
Or if thou hast uphoarded in thy life
Extorted treasure in the womb of earth,
For which, they say, you spirits oft walk in death,
Speak of it; stay, and speak! *The cock crows.*
Stop it, Marcellus.
Mar. Shall I strike at it with my partisan?
Hor. Do, if it will not stand.
Ber. 'T is here!
Hor. 'T is here!
Mar. 'T is gone! *Exit Ghost.*
We do it wrong, being so majestical,
To offer it the show of violence;
For it is as the air, invulnerable,
And our vain blows malicious mockery.
Ber. It was about to speak, when the cock crew.
Hor. And then it started like a guilty thing
Upon a fearful summons. I have heard,
The cock, that is the trumpet to the morn,
Doth with his lofty and shrill-sounding throat
Awake the god of day; and, at his warning,
Whether in sea or fire, in earth or air,
Th' extravagant and erring spirit hies
To his confine; and of the truth herein
This present object made probation.

118. Disasters, unfavorable aspects, possibly sunspots. **moist star,** moon. The break between ll. 116 and 117 has led most editors to a belief that a line has dropped out. **121. precurse,** precursor. **125. climatures,** country. **127. cross,** confront. **129. s. d. It,** the Ghost. **140. partisan,** halberd. **154. extravagant,** vagrant. **erring,** wandering. **156. probation,** proof.

Mar. It faded on the crowing of the cock.
Some say that ever 'gainst that season comes
Wherein our Saviour's birth is celebrated,
This bird of dawning singeth all night long;
And then, they say, no spirit dare stir abroad;
The nights are wholesome; then no planets strike,
No fairy takes, nor witch hath power to charm,
So hallow'd and so gracious is that time.
Hor. So have I heard and do in part believe it.
But, look, the morn, in russet mantle clad,
Walks o'er the dew of yon high eastward hill:
Break we our watch up; and, by my advice,
Let us impart what we have seen to-night
Unto young Hamlet; for, upon my life,
This spirit, dumb to us, will speak to him.
Do you consent we shall acquaint him with it,
As needful in our loves, fitting our duty?
Mar. Let 's do 't, I pray; and I this morning know
Where we shall find him most convenient.
Exeunt.

Scene II. *A room of state in the castle.*

Flourish. Enter *Claudius,* King of Denmark, *Gertrude,* the Queen, *Councillors* (*Voltimand* and *Cornelius*), *Polonius,* and his son *Laertes, Hamlet, Lords Attendant.*

King. Though yet of Hamlet our dear brother's death
The memory be green, and that it us befitted
To bear our hearts in grief, and our whole kingdom
To be contracted in one brow of woe,
Yet so far hath discretion fought with nature
That we with wisest sorrow think on him
Together with remembrance of ourselves:
Therefore our sometimes sister, now our queen,
Th' imperial jointress to this warlike state,
Have we, as 't were with a defeated joy,—
With an auspicious and a dropping eye,
With mirth in funeral and with dirge in marriage,
In equal scale weighing delight and dole,—
Taken to wife; nor have we herein barr'd
Your better wisdoms, which have freely gone
With this affair along. For all, our thanks.
Now follows that you know: young Fortinbras,
Holding a weak supposal of our worth,
Or thinking by our late dear brother's death

163. takes, bewitches. **Scene ii: 13. dole,** grief. **18. weak supposal,** slight opinion.

Our state to be disjoint and out of frame,
Colleagued with this dream of his advantage,
He hath not fail'd to pester us with message
Importing the surrender of those lands
Lost by his father, with all bonds of law,
To our most valiant brother. So much for him.
Now for ourself and for this time of meeting,
Thus much the business is: we have here writ
To Norway, uncle of young Fortinbras,—
Who, impotent and bed-rid, scarcely hears
Of this his nephew's purpose,—to suppress
His further gait herein, in that the levies,
The lists and full proportions, are all made
Out of his subject; and we here dispatch
You, good Cornelius, and you, Voltimand,
For bearing of this greeting to old Norway;
Giving to you no further personal power
To business with the king, more than the scope
Of these delated articles allow.
Giving a paper.
Farewell, and let your haste commend your duty.

Cor. }
Vol. } In that and all things will we show our duty.

King. We doubt it nothing; heartily farewell. *Exeunt Voltimand and Cornelius.*
And now, Laertes, what 's the news with you?
You told us of some suit; what is 't, Laertes?
You cannot speak of reason to the Dane,
And lose your voice: what wouldst thou beg, Laertes,
That shall not be my offer, not thy asking?
The head is not more native to the heart,
The hand more instrumental to the mouth,
Than is the throne of Denmark to thy father.
What wouldst thou have, Laertes?

Laer. My dread lord,
Your leave and favour to return to France;
From whence though willingly I came to Denmark
To show my duty in your coronation,
Yet now, I must confess, that duty done,
My thoughts and wishes bend again towards France
And bow them to your gracious leave and pardon.

King. Have you your father's leave? What says Polonius?

Pol. He hath, my lord, wrung from me my slow leave
By laboursome petition, and at last
Upon his will I seal'd my hard consent:
I do beseech you, give him leave to go.

King. Take thy fair hour, Laertes: time be thine,
And thy best graces spend it at thy will!
But now, my cousin Hamlet, and my son,—

Ham. [*Aside.*] A little more than kin, and less than kind.

King. How is it that the clouds still hang on you?

Ham. Not so, my lord; I am too much in the sun.

Queen. Good Hamlet, cast thy nighted colour off,
And let thine eye look like a friend on Denmark;
Do not for ever with thy vailed lids
Seek for thy noble father in the dust;
Thou know'st 't is common; all that lives must die,
Passing through nature to eternity.

Ham. Ay, madam, it is common.

Queen. If it be,
Why seems it so particular with thee?

Ham. Seems, madam! Nay, it is; I know not "seems."
'T is not alone my inky cloak, good mother,
Nor customary suits of solemn black,
Nor windy suspiration of forc'd breath,
No, nor the fruitful river in the eye,
Nor the dejected haviour of the visage,
Together with all forms, moods, shapes of grief,
That can denote me truly: these indeed seem,
For they are actions that a man might play;
But I have that within which passeth show,
These but the trappings and the suits of woe.

King. 'T is sweet and commendable in your nature, Hamlet,
To give these mourning duties to your father:
But you must know, your father lost a father,
That father lost, lost his; and the survivor bound
In filial obligation for some term
To do obsequious sorrow; but to persever
In obstinate condolement is a course
Of impious stubbornness; 't is unmanly grief;
It shows a will most incorrect to heaven,
A heart unfortified, a mind impatient,
An understanding simple and unschool'd;
For what we know must be, and is as common
As any the most vulgar thing to sense,
Why should we in our peevish opposition
Take it to heart? Fie! 't is a fault to heaven,
A fault against the dead, a fault to nature,
To reason most absurd, whose common theme
Is death of fathers, and who still hath cried,
From the first corse till he that died today,

20. frame, order. **21. advantage,** superiority. **31. gait,** proceeding. **32. proportions,** levies. **38. delated,** specifically set forth. **45. lose your voice,** waste your breath. **47. native,** related.

65. kind, natural. **67. sun,** (1) in the glamour of the court, (2) son. **70. vailed,** lowered. **79. windy suspiration,** heavy sighing. **93. condolement,** mourning. **99. vulgar,** common.

"This must be so." We pray you, throw to earth
This unprevailing woe, and think of us
As of a father; for, let the world take note,
You are the most immediate to our throne,
And with no less nobility of love
Than that which dearest father bears his son,
Do I impart towards you. For your intent
In going back to school in Wittenberg,
It is most retrograde to our desire;
And we beseech you, bend you to remain
Here in the cheer and comfort of our eye,
Our chiefest courtier, cousin, and our son.

Queen. Let not thy mother lose her prayers, Hamlet:
I prithee, stay with us; go not to Wittenberg.

Ham. I shall in all my best obey you, madam.

King. Why, 't is a loving and a fair reply:
Be as ourself in Denmark. Madam, come;
This gentle and unforc'd accord of Hamlet
Sits smiling to my heart; in grace whereof,
No jocund health that Denmark drinks to-day,
But the great cannon to the clouds shall tell,
And the King's rouse the heaven shall bruit again,
Re-speaking earthly thunder. Come away.

Flourish. Exeunt all but Hamlet.

Ham. O, that this too too sullied flesh would melt,
Thaw, and resolve itself into a dew!
Or that the Everlasting had not fix'd
His canon 'gainst self-slaughter! O God! God!
How weary, stale, flat, and unprofitable,
Seem to me all the uses of this world!
Fie on 't! ah fie! 'T is an unweeded garden,
That grows to seed; things rank and gross in nature
Possess it merely. That it should come thus!
But two months dead: nay, not so much, not two,
So excellent a king; that was, to this,
Hyperion to a satyr; so loving to my mother
That he might not beteem the winds of heaven
Visit her face too roughly—heaven and earth!
Must I remember? Why, she would hang on him,
As if increase of appetite had grown
By what it fed on; and yet, within a month,—
Let me not think on 't!—Frailty, thy name is woman!—
A little month, or e'er those shoes were old
With which she followed my poor father's body,
Like Niobe, all tears,—why she, even she—
O God! a beast, that wants discourse of reason,
Would have mourn'd longer—married with my uncle,
My father's brother, but no more like my father
Than I to Hercules; within a month,
Ere yet the salt of most unrighteous tears
Had left the flushing in her galled eyes,
She married. O, most wicked speed, to post
With such dexterity to incestuous sheets!
It is not, nor it cannot come to good:
But break my heart, for I must hold my tongue.

Enter *Horatio, Marcellus,* and *Bernardo.*

Hor. Hail to your lordship!

Ham. I am glad to see you well.
Horatio!—or I do forget myself.

Hor. The same, my lord, and your poor servant ever.

Ham. Sir, my good friend; I 'll change that name with you;
And what make you from Wittenberg, Horatio?
Marcellus.

Mar. My good lord!

Ham. I am very glad to see you. [*To Ber.*] Good even, sir.—
But what, in faith, make you from Wittenberg?

Hor. A truant disposition, good my lord.

Ham. I would not hear your enemy say so,
Nor shall you do my ear that violence,
To make it truster of your own report
Against yourself: I know you are no truant;
But what is your affair in Elsinore?
We 'll teach you for to drink ere you depart.

Hor. My lord, I came to see your father's funeral.

Ham. I prithee, do not mock me, fellow-student;
I think it was to see my mother's wedding.

Hor. Indeed, my lord, it followed hard upon.

Ham. Thrift, thrift, Horatio! The funeral bak'd-meats
Did coldly furnish forth the marriage tables.
Would I had met my dearest foe in heaven
Or ever I had seen that day, Horatio!
My father!—methinks I see my father.

Hor. Where, my lord?

Ham. In my mind's eye, Horatio.

112. impart, offer myself. **113. Wittenberg**, a German university founded in 1502. **114. retrograde**, contrary. **115. bend**, incline. **127. rouse**, bumper. **bruit**, noisily announce. **132. canon**, law. **134. uses**, customary occupations. **137. merely**, entirely. **141. beteem**, allow.

150. discourse of reason, reasoning power. **155. left the flushing**, stopped reddening. **156. post**, hasten. **157. incestuous:** In Shakespeare's day marriage with a deceased husband's brother was considered incestuous. **163. change**, exchange. **172. truster**, believer.

Hor. I saw him once; 'a was a goodly king.
Ham. 'A was a man, take him for all in all,
I shall not look upon his like again.
Hor. My lord, I think I saw him yester-night.
Ham. Saw? Who?
Hor. My lord, the King your father.
Ham. The King my father!
Hor. Season your admiration for a while
With an attent ear, till I may deliver,
Upon the witness of these gentlemen,
This marvel to you.
Ham. For God's love, let me hear.
Hor. Two nights together had these gentlemen,
Marcellus and Bernardo, on their watch,
In the dead waste and middle of the night,
Been thus encounter'd. A figure like your father,
Armed at point exactly, cap-a-pe,
Appears before them, and with solemn march
Goes slow and stately by them: thrice he walk'd
By their oppress'd and fear-surprised eyes,
Within his truncheon's length; whilst they, distill'd
Almost to jelly with the act of fear,
Stand dumb and speak not to him. This to me
In dreadful secrecy impart they did,
And I with them the third night kept the watch.
Where, as they had deliver'd, both in time,
Form of the thing, each word made true and good,
The apparition comes: I knew your father;
These hands are not more like.
Ham. But where was this?
Mar. My lord upon the platform where we watch.
Ham. Did you not speak to it?
Hor. My lord, I did;
But answer made it none: yet once methought
It lifted up it head and did address
Itself to motion, like as it would speak;
But even then the morning cock crew loud,
And at the sound it shrunk in haste away,
And vanish'd from our sight.
Ham. 'T is very strange.
Hor. As I do live, my honour'd lord, 't is true,
And we did think it writ down in our duty
To let you know of it.
Ham. Indeed, indeed, sirs, but this troubles me.
Hold you the watch to-night?
All. We do, my lord.
Ham. Arm'd, say you?
All. Arm'd, my lord.
Ham. From top to toe?
All. My lord, from head to foot.
Ham. Then saw you not his face?
Hor. O, yes, my lord; he wore his beaver up.
Ham. What, look'd he frowningly?
Hor. A countenance more in sorrow than in anger.
Ham. Pale, or red?
Hor. Nay, very pale.
Ham. And fix'd his eyes upon you?
Hor. Most constantly.
Ham. I would I had been there.
Hor. It would have much amaz'd you.
Ham. Very like, very like. Stay'd it long?
Hor. While one with moderate haste might tell a hundred.
Mar., *Ber.* Longer, longer.
Hor. Not when I saw 't.
Ham. His beard was grizzled, no?
Hor. It was, as I have seen it in his life,
A sable silver'd.
Ham. I will watch to-night;
Perchance 't will walk again.
Hor. I war'nt it will.
Ham. If it assume my noble father's person,
I 'll speak to it, though hell itself should gape
And bid me hold my peace; I pray you all,
If you have hitherto conceal'd this sight,
Let it be tenable in your silence still;
And whatsomever else shall hap to-night,
Give it an understanding, but no tongue;
I will requite your loves. So, fare you well.
Upon the platform 'twixt eleven and twelve,
I 'll visit you.
All. Our duty to your honour.
Ham. Your loves, as mine to you; farewell. *Exeunt all but Hamlet.*
My father's spirit—in arms! all is not well;
I doubt some foul play; would the night were come!
Till then sit still, my soul: foul deeds will rise,
Though all the earth o'erwhelm them to men's eyes. *Exit*

Scene III. *A room in the house of Polonius.*

Enter *Laertes* and *Ophelia,* his sister.

Laer. My necessaries are embark'd, farewell;

192. Season, moderate. **admiration,** astonishment. **193. attent,** attentive. **200. cap-a-pe,** from head to foot. **204. distill'd,** melted. **205. act,** action. **207. dreadful,** terrified. **216. it,** its.

230. beaver, visor. **238. tell,** count. **248. tenable,** held.

And, sister, as the winds give benefit
And convoy is assistant, do not sleep,
But let me hear from you.
Oph. Do you doubt that?
Laer. For Hamlet and the trifling of his favour,
Hold it a fashion and a toy in blood,
A violet in the youth of primy nature,
Forward, not permanent, sweet, not lasting,
The perfume and suppliance of a minute;
No more.
Oph. No more but so?
Laer. Think it no more:
For nature crescent does not grow alone
In thews and bulk, but, as this temple waxes,
The inward service of the mind and soul
Grows wide withal. Perhaps he loves you now,
And now no soil nor cautel doth besmirch
The virtue of his will; but you must fear,
His greatness weigh'd, his will is not his own;
For he himself is subject to his birth.
He may not, as unvalued persons do,
Carve for himself, for on his choice depends
The sanity and health of this whole state;
And therefore must his choice be circumscrib'd
Unto the voice and yielding of that body
Whereof he is the head. Then, if he says he loves you,
It fits your wisdom so far to believe it
As he in his particular act and place
May give his saying deed; which is no further
Than the main voice of Denmark goes withal.
Then weigh what loss your honour may sustain
If with too credent ear you list his songs,
Or lose your heart, or your chaste treasure open
To his unmaster'd importunity.
Fear it, Ophelia, fear it, my dear sister,
And keep you in the rear of your affection,
Out of the shot and danger of desire.
The chariest maid is prodigal enough,
If she unmask her beauty to the moon:
Virtue itself scapes not calumnious strokes:
The canker galls the infants of the spring
Too oft before their buttons be disclos'd,
And in the morn and liquid dew of youth
Contagious blastments are most imminent.
Be wary then, best safety lies in fear;
Youth to itself rebels, though none else near.
Oph. I shall the effect of this good lesson keep,
As watchman to my heart: but, good my brother,
Do not, as some ungracious pastors do,
Show me the steep and thorny way to heaven,
Whiles, like a puff'd and reckless libertine,
Himself the primrose path of dalliance treads,
And recks not his own rede.
Laer. O, fear me not;

Enter *Polonius.*

I stay too long: but here my father comes.
A double blessing is a double grace,
Occasion smiles upon a second leave.
Pol. Yet here, Laertes? Aboard, aboard, for shame!
The wind sits in the shoulder of your sail,
And you are stay'd for. There; my blessing with thee!
And these few precepts in thy memory
Look thou character. Give thy thoughts no tongue,
Nor any unproportion'd thought his act;
Be thou familiar, but by no means vulgar;
Those friends thou hast, and their adoption tried,
Grapple them unto thy soul with hoops of steel;
But do not dull thy palm with entertainment
Of each new-hatch'd, unfledg'd courage. Beware
Of entrance to a quarrel; but being in,
Bear 't that th' opposed may beware of thee.
Give every man thy ear, but few thy voice;
Take each man's censure, but reserve thy judgement.
Costly thy habit as thy purse can buy,
But not express'd in fancy; rich, not gaudy;
For the apparel oft proclaims the man,
And they in France of the best rank and station
Are of a most select and generous chief in that.
Neither a borrower nor a lender be;
For loan oft loses both itself and friend,
And borrowing dulleth edge of husbandry;
This above all: to thine own self be true,
And it must follow, as the night the day,
Thou canst not then be false to any man.
Farewell; my blessing season this in thee!
Laer. Most humbly do I take my leave, my lord.
Pol. The time invites you; go, your servants tend.
Laer. Farewell, Ophelia, and remember well
What I have said to you.
Oph. 'T is in my memory lock'd,
And you yourself shall keep the key of it.
Laer. Farewell. *Exit Laertes.*

3. **convoy**, conveyance. 6. **toy**, idle fancy. 7. **primy**, springlike. 8. **Forward**, premature. 9. **suppliance**, diversion. 11. **crescent**, growing. 15. **cautel**, deceit. 19. **unvalued**, of low rank. 30. **credent**, credulous. 39. **canker**, canker-worm. 40. **buttons**, buds.

47. **ungracious**, graceless. 51. **recks**, heeds. **rede**, advice. 59. **character**, inscribe. 60. **unproportion'd**, unbalanced. 65. **courage**, gallant youth. 69. **censure**, opinion. 74. **chief**, eminence. 77. **husbandry**, thrift. 83. **tend**, attend.

Pol. What is 't, Ophelia, he hath said to you?
Oph. So please you, something touching the Lord Hamlet.
Pol. Marry, well bethought.
'T is told me, he hath very oft of late
Given private time to you, and you yourself
Have of your audience been most free and bounteous.
If it be so—as so 't is put on me,
And that in way of caution—I must tell you,
You do not understand yourself so clearly
As it behoves my daughter and your honour.
What is between you? Give me up the truth.
Oph. He hath, my lord, of late made many tenders
Of his affection to me.
Pol. Affection! pooh! You speak like a green girl,
Unsifted in such perilous circumstance.
Do you believe his tenders, as you call them?
Oph. I do not know, my lord, what I should think.
Pol. Marry, I will teach you: think yourself a baby
That you have ta'en these tenders for true pay,
Which are not sterling. Tender yourself more dearly,
Or—not to crack the wind of the poor phrase,
Running it thus—you 'll tender me a fool.
Oph. My lord, he hath importun'd me with love
In honourable fashion.
Pol. Ay, fashion you may call it: go to, go to!
Oph. And hath given countenance to his speech, my lord,
With almost all the holy vows of heaven.
Pol. Ay, springes to catch woodcocks. I do know,
When the blood burns, how prodigal the soul
Lends the tongue vows. These blazes, daughter,
Giving more light than heat, extinct in both
Even in their promise, as it is a-making,
You must not take for fire. From this time
Be somewhat scanter of your maiden presence,
Set your entreatments at a higher rate
Than a command to parley: for Lord Hamlet,
Believe so much in him, that he is young,
And with a larger tether may he walk
Than may be given you: in few, Ophelia,
Do not believe his vows, for they are brokers,
Not of that dye which their investments show,
But mere implorators of unholy suits,
Breathing like sanctified and pious bawds,
The better to beguile. This is for all:
I would not, in plain terms, from this time forth,
Have you so slander any moment leisure
As to give words or talk with the Lord Hamlet.
Look to 't, I charge you: come your ways.
Oph. I shall obey, my lord. *Exeunt.*

Scene IV. *The platform.*

Enter *Hamlet, Horatio,* and *Marcellus.*

Ham. The air bites shrewdly; it is very cold.
Hor. It is a nipping and an eager air.
Ham. What hour now?
Hor. I think it lacks of twelve.
Mar. No, it is struck.
Hor. Indeed? I heard it not; it then draws near the season
Wherein the spirit held his wont to walk.
A flourish of trumpets, and two pieces goes off within.
What does this mean, my lord?
Ham. The King doth wake to-night and takes his rouse,
Keeps wassails, and the swagg'ring up-spring reels;
And, as he drains his draughts of Rhenish down,
The kettle-drum and trumpet thus bray out
The triumph of his pledge.
Hor. Is it a custom?
Ham. Ay, marry, is 't,
But to my mind, though I am native here
And to the manner born, it is a custom
More honour'd in the breach than the observance.
This heavy-headed revel east and west
Makes us traduc'd and tax'd of other nations:
They clepe us drunkards, and with swinish phrase
Soil our addition; and indeed it takes
From our achievements, though perform'd at height,
The pith and marrow of our attribute.
So oft it chances in particular men,
That for some vicious mole of nature in them,
As, in their birth—wherein they are not guilty,
Since nature cannot choose his origin—
By their o'ergrowth of some complexion

99. tenders, offers. **102. Unsifted,** untried. **107. Tender,** hold. **109. tender,** offer. **115. springes,** snares. **woodcocks,** stupid birds. **122. entreatments,** interviews. **127. brokers,** procurers.

128. investments, vestments, dress. **129. implorators,** solicitors. **133. slander,** disgrace. **Scene iv: 2. eager,** sharp. **8. wake,** hold a revel by night. **9. wassails,** revelry. **up-spring,** a dance. **12. pledge,** toast. **18. traduc'd,** censured. **tax'd,** blamed. **19. clepe,** call. **20. addition,** title of honor. **22. attribute,** reputation. **27. complexion,** natural disposition or tendency.

Oft breaking down the pales and forts of reason,
Or by some habit that too much o'er-leavens
The form of plausive manners, that these men,
Carrying, I say, the stamp of one defect,
Being nature's livery or fortune's star,—
His virtues else—be they as pure as grace,
As infinite as man may undergo—
Shall in the general censure take corruption
From that particular fault: the dram of e'il
Doth all the noble substance often dout
To his own scandal.

Enter *Ghost*.

Hor. Look, my lord, it comes!
Ham. Angels and ministers of grace defend us!
Be thou a spirit of health or goblin damn'd,
Bring with thee airs from heaven or blasts from hell,
Be thy intents wicked or charitable,
Thou com'st in such a questionable shape
That I will speak to thee. I 'll call thee Hamlet,
King, father, royal Dane. O, answer me!
Let me not burst in ignorance, but tell
Why thy canoniz'd bones, hearsed in death,
Have burst their cerements; why the sepulchre,
Wherein we saw thee quietly interr'd,
Hath op'd his ponderous and marble jaws,
To cast thee up again. What may this mean,
That thou, dead corse, again in complete steel
Revisits thus the glimpses of the moon,
Making night hideous, and we fools of nature
So horridly to shake our disposition
With thoughts beyond the reaches of our souls?
Say, why is this? Wherefore? What should we do? *Ghost beckons Hamlet.*
Hor. It beckons you to go away with it,
As if it some impartment did desire
To you alone.
Mar. Look, with what courteous action
It waves you to a more removed ground.
But do not go with it.
Hor. No, by no means.
Ham. It will not speak; then will I follow it.
Hor. Do not, my lord.
Ham. Why, what should be the fear?
I do not set my life at a pin's fee,
And for my soul, what can it do to that,
Being a thing immortal as itself?
It waves me forth again; I 'll follow it.
Hor. What if it tempt you toward the flood, my lord,
Or to the dreadful summit of the cliff
That beetles o'er his base into the sea,
And there assume some other horrible form,
Which might deprive your sovereignty of reason
And draw you into madness? Think of it.
The very place puts toys of desperation,
Without more motive, into every brain
That looks so many fathoms to the sea
And hears it roar beneath.
Ham. It waves me still.
Go on, I 'll follow thee.
Mar. You shall not go, my lord.
Ham. Hold off your hands.
Hor. Be rul'd; you shall not go.
Ham. My fate cries out,
And makes each petty artery in this body
As hardy as the Nemean lion's nerve.
Still am I call'd: unhand me, gentlemen;
By heaven, I 'll make a ghost of him that lets me!
I say, away!—Go on, I 'll follow thee.
Exeunt Ghost and Hamlet.
Hor. He waxes desperate with imagination.
Mar. Let 's follow; 't is not fit thus to obey him.
Hor. Have after—to what issue will this come?
Mar. Something is rotten in the state of Denmark.
Hor. Heaven will direct it.
Mar. Nay, let 's follow him.
Exeunt

Scene V. *Another part of the platform.*

Enter *Ghost* and *Hamlet*.

Ham. Where wilt thou lead me? Speak, I 'll go no further.
Ghost. Mark me.
Ham. I will.
Ghost. My hour is almost come,
When I to sulph'rous and tormenting flames
Must render up myself.
Ham. Alas, poor ghost!
Ghost. Pity me not, but lend thy serious hearing
To what I shall unfold.
Ham. Speak; I am bound to hear.

28. **pales,** enclosures. 29. **o'er-leavens,** corrupts. 30. **plausive,** pleasing. 35. **general censure,** popular judgment. 36. **e'il,** evil. 37. **dout,** extinguish. 40. **spirit of health,** good spirit. 43. **questionable,** inviting question. 47. **canoniz'd,** buried according to church rules. 55. **shake our disposition,** disturb us. 59. **impartment,** communication.

71. **beetles,** hangs over. 73. **deprive . . . reason,** destroy the sovereignty of your reason. 75. **toys,** whims, fancies. 83. **Nemean lion's,** a mythical monster slain by Hercules. **nerve,** sinew. 85. **lets,** hinders.

Ghost. So art thou to revenge, when thou shalt hear.
Ham. What?
Ghost. I am thy father's spirit,
Doom'd for a certain term to walk the night,
And for the day confin'd to fast in fires,
Till the foul crimes done in my days of nature
Are burnt and purg'd away: but that I am forbid
To tell the secrets of my prison-house,
I could a tale unfold whose lightest word
Would harrow up thy soul, freeze thy young blood,
Make thy two eyes, like stars, start from their spheres,
Thy knotty and combined locks to part
And each particular hair to stand an end,
Like quills upon the fretful porpentine.
But this eternal blazon must not be
To ears of flesh and blood. List, list, O, list!
If thou didst ever thy dear father love—
Ham. O God!
Ghost. Revenge his foul and most unnatural murder.
Ham. Murder!
Ghost. Murder most foul, as in the best it is,
But this most foul, strange, and unnatural.
Ham. Haste me to know't, that I, with wings as swift
As meditation or the thoughts of love,
May sweep to my revenge.
Ghost. I find thee apt;
And duller shouldst thou be than the fat weed
That roots itself in ease on Lethe wharf,
Wouldst thou not stir in this. Now, Hamlet, hear:
'T is given out that, sleeping in my orchard,
A serpent stung me; so the whole ear of Denmark
Is by a forged process of my death
Rankly abus'd; but know, thou noble youth,
The serpent that did sting thy father's life
Now wears his crown.
Ham. O my prophetic soul!
My uncle!
Ghost. Ay, that incestuous, that adulterate beast,
With witchcraft of his wit, with traitorous gifts,—
O wicked wit and gifts, that have the power
So to seduce!—won to his shameful lust
The will of my most seeming-virtuous queen;
O Hamlet, what a falling-off was there!
From me, whose love was of that dignity
That it went hand in hand even with the vow
I made to her in marriage, and to decline
Upon a wretch whose natural gifts were poor
To those of mine!
But virtue, as it never will be moved,
Though lewdness court it in a shape of heaven,
So lust, though to a radiant angel link'd,
Will sate itself in a celestial bed
And prey on garbage.
But, soft! methinks I scent the morning air,
Brief let me be. Sleeping within mine orchard,
My custom always of the afternoon,
Upon my secure hour thy uncle stole,
With juice of cursed hebona in a vial,
And in the porches of mine ears did pour
The lep'rous distilment; whose effect
Holds such an enmity with blood of man
That swift as quicksilver it courses through
The natural gates and alleys of the body,
And with a sudden vigour it doth posset
And curd, like eager droppings into milk,
The thin and wholesome blood: so did it mine,
And a most instant tetter bark'd about,
Most lazar-like, with vile and loathsome crust,
All my smooth body.
Thus was I, sleeping, by a brother's hand
Of life, of crown, of queen, at once dispatch'd;
Cut off even in the blossoms of my sin,
Unhouseled, disappointed, unanel'd,
No reckoning made, but sent to my account
With all my imperfections on my head.
O, horrible! O, horrible! most horrible!
If thou hast nature in thee, bear it not;
Let not the royal bed of Denmark be
A couch for luxury and damned incest.
But, howsomever thou pursuest this act,
Taint not thy mind, nor let thy soul contrive
Against thy mother aught: leave her to heaven
And to those thorns that in her bosom lodge,
To prick and sting her. Fare thee well at once!
The glow-worm shows the matin to be near,
And 'gins to pale his uneffectual fire.
Adieu, adieu, adieu! remember me. *Exit.*
Ham. O all you host of heaven! O earth! What else?
And shall I couple hell? O, fie! Hold, hold, my heart,
And you, my sinews, grow not instant old,
But bear me stiffly up. Remember thee?
Ay, thou poor ghost, while memory holds a seat
In this distracted globe. Remember thee?

20. porpentine, porcupine. **21. eternal blazon,** revelation of eternity. **33. wharf,** bank. **38. abus'd,** deceived. **42. adulterate,** adulterous.

61. secure, unsuspicious. **62. hebona,** yew. **68. posset,** curdle. **69. eager,** acid. **71. tetter,** scab, scurf. **72. lazar-like,** like a leper. **75. dispatch'd,** bereft. **77. Unhouseled,** without the sacrament of communion. **disappointed,** unprepared (by confession). **unanel'd,** without extreme unction. **83. luxury,** lust. **97. globe,** i.e., his head.

Yea, from the table of my memory
I 'll wipe away all trivial fond records,
All saws of books, all forms, all pressures past,
That youth and observation copied there,
And thy commandment all alone shall live
Within the book and volume of my brain,
Unmix'd with baser matter; yes, by heaven!
O most pernicious woman!
O villain, villain, smiling, damned villain!
My tables!—Meet it is I set it down
That one may smile and smile, and be a villain,
At least I 'm sure it may be so in Denmark.
So, uncle, there you are. Now to my word;
It is "Adieu, adieu! remember me."
I have sworn 't.

Hor. [*Within.*] My lord, my lord!
Mar. [*Within.*] Lord Hamlet!
Hor. [*Within.*] Heaven secure him!
Ham. So be it!
Mar. [*Within.*] Illo, ho, ho, my lord!
Ham. Hillo, ho, ho, boy! Come, bird, come.

Enter *Horatio* and *Marcellus*.

Mar. How is 't my noble lord?
Hor. What news, my lord?
Ham. O, wonderful!
Hor. Good my lord, tell it.
Ham. No, you will reveal it.
Hor. Not I, my lord, by heaven.
Mar. Nor I, my lord.
Ham. How say you, then, would heart of man once think it?—
But you 'll be secret?
Hor. } *Mar.* } Ay, by heaven, my lord.
Ham. There 's ne'er a villain dwelling in all Denmark
But he 's an arrant knave.
Hor. There needs no ghost, my lord, come from the grave
To tell us this.
Ham. Why, right, you are in the right.
And so, without more circumstance at all,
I hold it fit that we shake hands and part;
You, as your business and desire shall point you,
For every man has business and desire,
Such as it is; and for mine own poor part,
I will go pray.
Hor. These are but wild and whirling words, my lord.
Ham. I 'm sorry they offend you, heartily;
Yes, faith, heartily.
Hor. There 's no offence, my lord.
Ham. Yes, by Saint Patrick, but there is, Horatio,
And much offence too—touching this vision here,
It is an honest ghost, that let me tell you—
For your desire to know what is between us,
O'ermaster 't as you may. And now, good friends,
As you are friends, scholars, and soldiers,
Give me one poor request.
Hor. What is 't, my lord? We will.
Ham. Never make known what you have seen to-night.
Both. My lord, we will not.
Ham. Nay, but swear 't.
Hor. In faith,
My lord, not I.
Mar. Nor I, my lord, in faith.
Ham. Upon my sword.
Mar. We have sworn, my lord, already.
Ham. Indeed, upon my sword, indeed.
Ghost. Swear!

Ghost cries under the stage.

Ham. Ha, ha, boy! say'st thou so? Art thou there, truepenny?
Come on; you hear this fellow in the cellarage;
Consent to swear.
Hor. Propose the oath, my lord.
Ham. Never to speak of this that you have seen.
Swear by my sword.
Ghost. [*Beneath.*] Swear.
Ham. *Hic et ubique?* Then we'll shift our ground.
Come hither, gentlemen,
And lay your hands again upon my sword:
Swear by my sword
Never to speak of this that you have heard.
Ghost. [*Beneath.*] Swear by his sword.
Ham. Well said, old mole! Canst work i' th' earth so fast?
A worthy pioner! Once more remove, good friends.
Hor. O day and night, but this is wondrous strange!
Ham. And therefore as a stranger give it welcome.
There are more things in heaven and earth, Horatio,
Than are dreamt of in your philosophy.

98. **table**, tablet. 99. **fond**, foolish. 100. **saws**, maxims. **pressures**, impressions. 115. **Illo, etc.**, Falconer's call to his hawk. 127. **without more circumstance**, without more details.

136. **Saint Patrick**, St. Patrick's Purgatory in Ireland was a famous resort for pilgrims. There is peculiar fitness in Hamlet's swearing by St. Patrick after he had seen a ghost from Purgatory. 138. **honest ghost**, there was always the fear that the devil or an evil spirit might be attempting to ensnare by assuming the likeness of an honest ghost. Hamlet himself expresses this fear, II, ii, 633. 150. **truepenny**, honest fellow. 156. *Hic et ubique*, here and everywhere. 163. **pioner**, pioneer, sapper.

But come;
Here, as before, never, so help you mercy,
How strange or odd some'er I bear myself,—
As I perchance hereafter shall think meet
To put an antic disposition on—
That you, at such times seeing me, never shall,
With arms encumber'd thus, or this head-shake,
Or by pronouncing of some doubtful phrase
As "Well, well we know," or "We could, an if we would,"
Or "If we list to speak," or "There be, an if they might,"
Or such ambiguous giving out, to note
That you know aught of me,—this do swear,
So grace and mercy at your most need help you.

Ghost. [*Beneath.*] Swear.

Ham. Rest, rest, perturbed spirit! [*They swear.*] So, gentlemen,
With all my love I do commend me to you;
And what so poor a man as Hamlet is
May do, t' express his love and friending to you,
God willing, shall not lack. Let us go in together;
And still your fingers on your lips, I pray.
The time is out of joint; O cursed spite,
That ever I was born to set it right!
Nay, come, let 's go together. *Exeunt.*

ACT II. Scene I. *A room in the house of Polonius.*

Enter *Polonius* and *Reynaldo.*

Pol. Give him this money and these notes, Reynaldo.

Rey. I will, my lord.

Pol. You shall do marvellous wisely, good Reynaldo,
Before you visit him, to make inquire
Of his behaviour.

Rey. My lord, I did intend it.

Pol. Marry, well said, very well said. Look you, sir,
Inquire me first what Danskers are in Paris,
And how, and who, what means, and where they keep,
What company, at what expense; and finding
By this encompassment and drift of question
That they do know my son, come you more nearer
Than your particular demands will touch it:
Take you, as 't were, some distant knowledge of him,
As thus, "I know his father and his friends,
And in part him." Do you mark this, Reynaldo?

Rey. Ay, very well, my lord.

Pol. "And in part him; but," you may say, "not well.
But, if 't be he I mean, he's very wild,
Addicted so and so;" and there put on him
What forgeries you please; marry, none so rank
As may dishonour him,—take heed of that;
But, sir, such wanton, wild, and usual slips
As are companions noted and most known
To youth and liberty.

Rey. As gaming, my lord?

Pol. Ay, or drinking, fencing, swearing, quarrelling,
Drabbing; you may go so far.

Rey. My lord, that would dishonour him.

Pol. Faith, no, as you may season it in the charge.
You must not put another scandal on him,
That he is open to incontinency,
That 's not my meaning; but breathe his faults so quaintly
That they may seem the taints of liberty,
The flash and outbreak of a fiery mind,
A savageness in unreclaimed blood,
Of general assault.

Rey. But, my good lord,—

Pol. Wherefore should you do this?

Rey. Ay, my lord,
I would know that.

Pol. Marry, sir, here 's my drift,
And, I believe, it is a fetch of warrant:
You laying these slight sullies on my son
As 't were a thing a little soil'd i' th' working,
Mark you,
Your party in converse, him you would sound,
Having ever seen in the prenominate crimes
The youth you breathe of guilty, be assur'd
He closes with you in this consequence;
"Good sir," or so, or "friend," or "gentleman,"
According to the phrase or the addition
Of man and country—

172. antic, fantastic. **174. encumber'd,** folded. **Act II, Scene i: 7. Danskers,** Danes. **8. keep,** dwell. **10. encompassment,** roundabout conversation. **12. demands,** questions. The sense is that by these indirect means he can come nearer to what he wants to learn than by direct questioning.

30. incontinency, habitual licentiousness. **35. of general assault,** common to all men. **38. fetch of warrant,** justifiable device. **43. prenominate,** before mentioned. **45.** He falls in with you in this conclusion.

Rey. Very good, my lord.
Pol. And then, sir, does 'a this—'a does—
What was I about to say? By the mass, I was about to say something. Where did I leave?
Rey. At "closes in the consequence," at "friend or so," and "gentleman."
Pol. At "closes in the consequence," ay, marry—
He closes thus: "I know the gentleman.
I saw him yesterday, or th' other day,
Or then, or then, with such and such; and, as you say,
There was 'a gaming; there o'ertook in 's rouse;
There falling out at tennis;" or, perchance,
"I saw him enter such a house of sale,"
Videlicet, a brothel, or so forth.
See you now—
Your bait of falsehood takes this carp of truth;
And thus do we of wisdom and of reach,
With windlasses and with assays of bias,
By indirections find directions out;
So by my former lecture and advice,
Shall you my son. You have me, have you not?
Rey. My lord, I have.
Pol. God buy you; fare you well.
Rey. Good my lord.
Pol. Observe his inclination in yourself.
Rey. I shall, my lord
Pol. And let him ply his music.
Rey. Well, my lord.
Pol. Farewell! *Exit Reynaldo.*

Enter *Ophelia.*

How now, Ophelia! what 's the matter?
Oph. O, my lord, my lord, I have been so affrighted!
Pol. With what: i' th' name of God?
Oph. My lord, as I was sewing in my closet,
Lord Hamlet, with his doublet all unbrac'd,
No hat upon his head, his stockings fouled,
Ungarter'd, and down-gyved to his ankle,
Pale as his shirt, his knees knocking each other,
And with a look so piteous in purport
As if he had been loosed out of hell
To speak of horrors,—he comes before me.
Pol. Mad for thy love?
Oph. My lord, I do not know,
But truly, I do fear it.
Pol. What said he?
Oph. He took me by the wrist and held me hard;
Then goes he to the length of all his arm,
And, with his other hand thus o'er his brow,
He falls to such perusal of my face
As 'a would draw it. Long stay'd he so.
At last, a little shaking of mine arm,
And thrice his head thus waving up and down,
He rais'd a sigh so piteous and profound
That it did seem to shatter all his bulk
And end his being; that done, he lets me go;
And, with his head over his shoulder turn'd,
He seem'd to find his way without his eyes,
For out o' doors he went without their help,
And, to the last, bended their light on me.
Pol. Come, go with me, I will go seek the King.
This is the very ecstasy of love,
Whose violent property fordoes itself
And leads the will to desperate undertakings
As oft as any passion under heaven
That does afflict our natures: I am sorry,—
What, have you given him any hard words of late?
Oph. No, my good lord, but, as you did command,
I did repel his letters and denied
His access to me.
Pol. That hath made him mad.
I am sorry that with better heed and judgement
I had not quoted him. I fear'd he did but trifle
And meant to wreck thee; but beshrew my jealousy!
By heaven, it is as proper to our age
To cast beyond ourselves in our opinions
As it is common for the younger sort
To lack discretion. Come, go we to the King.
This must be known, which, being kept close, might move
More grief to hide than hate to utter love.
Come. *Exeunt.*

Scene II. *A room in the castle.*

Flourish. Enter *King, Queen, Rosencrantz, Guildenstern,* with others.

King. Welcome, dear Rosencrantz and Guildenstern!
Moreover that we much did long to see you,
The need we have to use you did provoke
Our hasty sending. Something have you heard

64. **reach,** ability. 65. **windlasses,** circuitous courses. **assays of bias,** indirect attempts. 71. **in yourself,** yourself. 80. **down-gyved,** hanging down like fetters. 82. **purport,** expression.

102. **ecstasy,** madness. 103. **property,** quality. **fordoes,** destroys. 112. **quoted,** observed. 115. **cast beyond,** to be over-calculating. 118-9. This probably means: keeping Hamlet's love a secret may cause more grief (i.e., in the continuation of his madness) than publishing it will cause hate (either on Hamlet's part for having his love exposed or on the part of his royal parents). **Scene ii: 2. Moreover that,** besides the fact that.

Of Hamlet's transformation; so I call it,
Sith nor th' exterior nor the inward man
Resembles that it was. What it should be,
More than his father's death, that thus hath put him
So much from th' understanding of himself,
I cannot dream of: I entreat you both,
That, being of so young days brought up with him
And sith so neighbour'd to his youth and haviour,
That you vouchsafe your rest here in our court
Some little time; so by your companies
To draw him on to pleasures, and to gather
So much as from occasions you may glean,
Whether aught, to us unknown, afflicts him thus,
That, open'd, lies within our remedy.

Queen. Good gentlemen, he hath much talk'd of you;
And sure I am two men there is not living
To whom he more adheres. If it will please you
To show us so much gentry and good will
As to expend your time with us a while
For the supply and profit of our hope,
Your visitation shall receive such thanks
As fits a king's remembrance.

Ros. Both your Majesties
Might, by the sovereign power you have of us,
Put your dread pleasures more into command
Than to entreaty.

Guil. But we both obey,
And here give up ourselves, in the full bent
To lay our service freely at your feet,
To be commanded.

King. Thanks, Rosencrantz and gentle Guildenstern.

Queen. Thanks, Guildenstern and gentle Rosencrantz;
And I beseech you instantly to visit
My too much changed son. Go, some of you,
And bring these gentlemen where Hamlet is.

Guil. Heavens make our presence and our practices
Pleasant and helpful to him!

Queen. Ay, amen!

Exeunt Rosencrantz, Guildenstern, and some Attendants.

Enter *Polonius.*

Pol. Th' ambassadors from Norway, my good lord,
Are joyfully return'd.

King. Thou still hast been the father of good news.

Pol. Have I, my lord? I assure you, my good liege,
I hold my duty as I hold my soul,
Both to my God and to my gracious king;
And I do think, or else this brain of mine
Hunts not the trail of policy so sure
As it hath us'd to do, that I have found
The very cause of Hamlet's lunacy.

King. O, speak of that; that do I long to hear.

Pol. Give first admittance to th' ambassadors.
My news shall be the fruit to that great feast.

King. Thyself do grace to them, and bring them in. *Exit Polonius.*
He tells me, my dear Gertrude, he hath found
The head and source of all your son's distemper.

Queen. I doubt it is no other but the main,
His father's death and our o'erhasty marriage.

Re-enter *Polonius,* with *Voltimand* and *Cornelius.*

King. Well, we shall sift him.—Welcome, my good friends!
Say, Voltimand, what from our brother Norway?

Volt. Most fair return of greetings and desires.
Upon our first, he sent out to suppress
His nephew's levies, which to him appear'd
To be a preparation 'gainst the Polack,
But, better look'd into, he truly found
It was against your Highness; whereat griev'd,
That so his sickness, age, and impotence
Was falsely borne in hand, sends out arrests
On Fortinbras; which he, in brief, obeys,
Receives rebuke from Norway, and in fine
Makes vow before his uncle never more
To give th' assay of arms against your Majesty:
Whereon old Norway, overcome with joy,
Gives him threescore thousand crowns in annual fee,
And his commission to employ those soldiers,
So levied as before, against the Polack;
With an entreaty, herein further shown, *Giving a paper.*
That it might please you to give quiet pass
Through your dominions for this enterprise,
On such regards of safety and allowance
As therein are set down.

King. It likes us well;
And at our more considered time we 'll read,

11. **of so,** from such. 22. **gentry,** courtesy. 30. **bent,** inclination.

47. Does not follow a clue with such cunning. 52. **fruit,** dessert. 56. **main,** principal point. 61. **first,** first audience. 67. **borne in hand,** deceived. 81. **considered,** proper for considering.

Answer, and think upon this business:
Meantime we thank you for your well-took labour.
Go to your rest; at night we 'll feast together:
Most welcome home!
Exeunt Ambassadors.
Pol. This business is well ended.
My liege, and madam, to expostulate
What majesty should be, what duty is,
Why day is day, night night, and time is time,
Were nothing but to waste night, day, and time;
Therefore, since brevity is the soul of wit
And tediousness the limbs and outward flourishes,
I will be brief. Your noble son is mad.
Mad call I it; for, to define true madness,
What is 't but to be nothing else but mad?
But let that go.
Queen. More matter, with less art.
Pol. Madam, I swear I use no art at all.
That he is mad, 't is true; 't is true 't is pity,
And pity 't is 't is true—a foolish figure!
But farewell it, for I will use no art.
Mad let us grant him then; and now remains
That we find out the cause of this effect,
Or rather say, the cause of this defect,
For this effect defective comes by cause.
Thus it remains, and the remainder thus.
Perpend.
I have a daughter—have while she is mine—
Who, in her duty and obedience, mark,
Hath given me this; now gather, and surmise.
Reads the letter.

"To the celestial and my soul's idol, the most beautified Ophelia,—"

That 's an ill phrase, a vile phrase; "beautified" is a vile phrase. But you shall hear. Thus:

"In her excellent white bosom, these."

Queen. Came this from Hamlet to her?
Pol. Good madam, stay a while; I will be faithful. *Reads.*

"Doubt thou the stars are fire,
Doubt that the sun doth move,
Doubt truth to be a liar,
But never doubt I love.

O dear Ophelia, I am ill at these numbers, I have not art to reckon my groans; but that I love thee best, O most best, believe it. Adieu.

Thine evermore, most dear lady,
Whilst this machine is to him,
HAMLET."

This in obedience hath my daughter shown me,
And more above, hath his solicitings,
As they fell out by time, by means, and place,
All given to mine ear.
King. But how hath she
Receiv'd his love?
Pol. What do you think of me?
King. As of a man faithful and honourable.
Pol. I would fain prove so. But what might you think,
When I had seen this hot love on the wing,—
As I perceiv'd it, I must tell you that,
Before my daughter told me,—what might you,
Or my dear Majesty your queen here, think,
If I had play'd the desk or table-book,
Or given my heart a winking, mute and dumb,
Or look'd upon this love with idle sight,
What might you think? No, I went round to work,
And my young mistress thus I did bespeak:
"Lord Hamlet is a prince out of thy star.
This must not be;" and then I prescripts gave her,
That she should lock herself from his resort,
Admit no messengers, receive no tokens.
Which done, she took the fruits of my advice;
And he, repell'd,—a short tale to make—
Fell into a sadness, then into a fast,
Thence to a watch, thence into a weakness,
Thence to a lightness, and, by this declension,
Into the madness wherein now he raves,
And all we mourn for.
King. Do you think 't is this?
Queen. It may be, very like.
Pol. Hath there been such a time—I would fain know that—
That I have positively said, "'T is so,"
When it prov'd otherwise?
King. Not that I know.
Pol. Take this from this, if this be otherwise:
If circumstances lead me, I will find
Where truth is hid, though it were hid indeed
Within the centre.
King. How may we try it further?
Pol. You know, sometimes he walks four hours together
Here in the lobby.
Queen. So he does, indeed.
Pol. At such a time I 'll loose my daughter to him:
Be you and I behind an arras then;
Mark the encounter, if he love her not
And be not from his reason fall'n thereon,

86. expostulate, expound. **120. ill,** unskilled. **124. machine,** body.

126. more above, in addition. **139. round,** roundly. **148. watch,** wakefulness. **156. This from this,** my head from my shoulders. **159. centre,** i.e., of the earth. **163. arras,** tapestry.

Let me be no assistant for a state,
But keep a farm and carters.

King. We will try it.

Enter *Hamlet,* reading on a book.

Queen. But look where sadly the poor wretch comes reading.

Pol. Away, I do beseech you, both away.
I 'll board him presently. O, give me leave.

Exeunt King, Queen and Attendants.

How does my good Lord Hamlet?

Ham. Well, God-a-mercy.

Pol. Do you know me, my lord?

Ham. Excellent well; you are a fishmonger.

Pol. Not I, my lord.

Ham. Then I would you were so honest a man.

Pol. Honest, my lord?

Ham. Ay, sir; to be honest, as this world goes, is to be one man picked out of ten thousand.

Pol. That 's very true, my lord.

Ham. For if the sun breed maggots in a dead dog, being a good kissing carrion—Have you a daughter?

Pol. I have, my lord.

Ham. Let her not walk i' th' sun: conception is a blessing, but as your daughter may conceive—Friend, look to 't.

Pol. [*Aside.*] How say you by that? Still harping on my daughter: yet he knew me not at first; 'a said I was a fishmonger; 'a is far gone; and truly in my youth I suffered much extremity for love; very near this. I 'll speak to him again.—What do you read, my lord?

Ham. Words, words, words.

Pol. What is the matter, my lord?

Ham. Between who?

Pol. I mean, the matter that you read, my lord.

Ham. Slanders, sir; for the satirical rogue says here that old men have grey beards, that their faces are wrinkled, their eyes purging thick amber and plum-tree gum, and that they have a plentiful lack of wit, together with most weak hams: all which, sir, though I most powerfully and potently believe, yet I hold it not honesty to have it thus set down; for yourself, sir, shall grow old as I am, if like a crab you could go backward.

Pol. [*Aside.*] Though this be madness, yet there is method in 't.—Will you walk out of the air, my lord?

Ham. Into my grave?

Pol. Indeed, that is out of the air. [*Aside.*]

170. board, accost. **presently,** immediately. **174. fishmonger,** probably here "pander." **182. good kissing,** good to kiss. **185. Conception,** (1) understanding, (2) the condition of being pregnant. **204. honesty,** decency.

How pregnant sometimes his replies are! a happiness that often madness hits on, which reason and sanity could not so prosperously be delivered of. I will leave him, and suddenly contrive the means of meeting between him and my daughter.—My lord, I will take my leave of you.

Ham. You cannot, sir, take from me anything that I will not more willingly part withal,—except my life, except my life, except my life.

Pol. Fare you well, my lord.

Ham. These tedious old fools!

Enter *Rosencrantz* and *Guildenstern.*

Pol. You go to seek the Lord Hamlet? There he is.

Ros. [*To Polonius.*] God save you, sir!

Exit Polonius.

Guil. My honoured lord!

Ros. My most dear lord!

Ham. My excellent good friends! How dost thou, Guildenstern? Ah, Rosencrantz! Good lads, how do you both?

Ros. As the indifferent children of the earth.

Guil. Happy in that we are not overhappy.
On Fortune's cap we are not the very button.

Ham. Nor the soles of her shoe?

Ros. Neither, my lord.

Ham. Then you live about her waist, or in the middle of her favours?

Guil. Faith, her privates we.

Ham. In the secret parts of Fortune? Oh, most true; she is a strumpet. What news?

Ros. None, my lord, but that the world 's grown honest.

Ham. Then is doomsday near; but your news is not true. Let me question more in particular: what have you, my good friends, deserved at the hands of Fortune, that she sends you to prison hither?

Guil. Prison, my lord?

Ham. Denmark 's a prison.

Ros. Then is the world one.

Ham. A goodly one, in which there are many confines, wards, and dungeons, Denmark being one o' th' worst.

Ros. We think not so, my lord.

Ham. Why, then, 't is none to you; for there is nothing either good or bad, but thinking makes it so: to me it is a prison.

Ros. Why, then, your ambition makes it one: 't is too narrow for your mind.

Ham. O God, I could be bounded in a nutshell and count myself a king of infinite space, were it not that I have bad dreams.

231. indifferent, ordinary.

Guil. Which dreams indeed are ambition, for the very substance of the ambitious is merely the shadow of a dream.

Ham. A dream itself is but a shadow.

Ros. Truly, and I hold ambition of so airy and light a quality that it is but a shadow's shadow.

Ham. Then are our beggars bodies, and our monarchs and outstretched heroes the beggars' shadows. Shall we to th' court? for, by my fay, I cannot reason.

Both. We 'll wait upon you.

Ham. No such matter. I will not sort you with the rest of my servants, for, to speak to you like an honest man, I am most dreadfully attended. But in the beaten way of friendship, what make you at Elsinore?

Ros. To visit you, my lord; no other occasion.

Ham. Beggar that I am, I am even poor in thanks, but I thank you; and sure, dear friends, my thanks are too dear a halfpenny. Were you not sent for? Is it your own inclining? Is it a free visitation? Come, come, deal justly with me: come, come; nay, speak.

Guil. What should we say, my lord?

Ham. Why, anything, but to th' purpose. You were sent for; and there is a kind of confession in your looks which your modesties have not craft enough to colour. I know the good king and queen have sent for you.

Ros. To what end, my lord?

Ham. That you must teach me: but let me conjure you, by the rights of our fellowship, by the consonancy of our youth, by the obligation of our ever-preserved love, and by what more dear a better proposer can charge you withal, be even and direct with me, whether you were sent for or no!

Ros. [*Aside to Guil.*] What say you?

Ham. [*Aside.*] Nay, then, I have an eye of you.—If you love me, hold not off.

Guil. My lord, we were sent for.

Ham. I will tell you why; so shall my anticipation prevent your discovery, and your secrecy to the King and Queen moult no feather. I have of late—but wherefore I know not—lost all my mirth, forgone all custom of exercises; and indeed it goes so heavily with my disposition that this goodly frame, the earth, seems to me a sterile promontory, this most excellent canopy, the air, look you, this brave o'erhanging firmament, this majestical roof fretted with golden fire, why, it appeareth nothing to me but a foul and pestilent congregation of vapours. What a piece of work is a man! How noble in reason! How infinite in faculties! In form and moving how express and admirable! In action how like an angel! In apprehension how like a god! The beauty of the world! The paragon of animals! And yet, to me, what is this quintessence of dust? Man delights not me—nor woman neither, though by your smiling you seem to say so.

Ros. My lord, there was no such stuff in my thoughts.

Ham. Why did ye laugh then, when I said, "Man delights not me"?

Ros. To think, my lord, if you delight not in man, what lenten entertainment the players shall receive from you. We coted them on the way, and hither are they coming to offer you service.

Ham. He that plays the king shall be welcome; his majesty shall have tribute on me; the adventurous knight shall use his foil and target; the lover shall not sigh gratis; the humorous man shall end his part in peace; the clown shall make those laugh whose lungs are tickle o' th' sere; and the lady shall say her mind freely, or the blank verse shall halt for 't. What players are they?

Ros. Even those you were wont to take such delight in, the tragedians of the city.

Ham. How chances it they travel? Their residence, both in reputation and profit, was better both ways.

Ros. I think their inhibition comes by the means of the late innovation.

Ham. Do they hold the same estimation they did when I was in the city? Are they so followed?

Ros. No, indeed, they are not.

Ham. How comes it? Do they grow rusty?

Ros. Nay, their endeavour keeps in the wonted pace; but there is, sir, an aery of children, little eyases, that cry out on the top of question, and are most tyrannically clapped for 't: these are now the fashion, and so berattle the common stages—so they call them—that many wearing rapiers are afraid of goose-quills and dare scarce come thither.

Ham. What, are they children? Who main-

270. **outstretched**, puffed up. 274. **sort**, rank. 277. **beaten way**, familiar course. 295. **consonancy**, agreement (in age). 297. **proposer**, speaker. 305. **prevent**, anticipate. **discovery**, disclosure.

318. **express**, exact. 329. **lenten**, dull. 330. **coted**, overtook. 338. **tickle o' th' sere**, on a hair-trigger. 339. **or**, even if. **halt**, limp. 344. **residence**, i.e., in the city. 346-7. **inhibition . . . innovation**, the prohibition or hindrance to continued residence (inhibition) was probably due to the innovation, i.e., that companies of child actors had become very popular during the first few years of the 17th century and had almost driven adult actors from the theatre. 354. **aery**, nest. Another reference to the children's companies, The Choristers of St. Paul's and the Children of the Revels. 355. **eyases**, nestling hawks. **cry . . . question**, cry out in high, shrill tones on the question (matters of debate or discussion). 356. **tyrannically**, violently. 359. **goose-quills**, i.e., satiric poems.

tains 'em? How are they escoted? Will they pursue the quality no longer than they can sing? Will they not say afterwards, if they should grow themselves to common players,— as it is most like, if their means are no better— their writers do them wrong, to make them exclaim against their own succession?

Ros. Faith, there has been much to do on both sides, and the nation holds it no sin to tarre them to controversy. There was for a while no money bid for argument unless the poet and the player went to cuffs in the question.

Ham. Is 't possible?

Guil. O, there has been much throwing about of brains.

Ham. Do the boys carry it away?

Ros. Ay, that they do, my lord; Hercules and his load too.

Ham. It is not very strange; for my uncle is king of Denmark, and those that would make mouths at him while my father lived, give twenty, forty, fifty, a hundred ducats apiece for his picture in little. 'Sblood, there is something in this more than natural, if philosophy could find it out.

Flourish within.

Guil. There are the players.

Ham. Gentlemen, you are welcome to Elsinore. Your hands, come, then. Th' appurtenance of welcome is fashion and ceremony: let me comply with you in this garb, lest my extent to the players, which, I tell you, must show fairly outwards, should more appear like entertainment than yours. You are welcome; but my uncle-father and aunt-mother are deceived.

Guil. In what, my dear lord?

Ham. I am but mad north-north-west: when the wind is southerly I know a hawk from a handsaw.

Enter *Polonius.*

Pol. Well be with you, gentlemen!

Ham. [*Aside to them.*] Hark you, Guildenstern, and you too, at each ear a hearer: that great baby you see there is not yet out of his swaddling-clouts.

Ros. Happily he is the second time come to them, for they say an old man is twice a child.

Ham. I will prophesy he comes to tell me of the players; mark it. [*Aloud.*] You say right, sir; a Monday morning; 't was then indeed.

Pol. My lord, I have news to tell you.

Ham. My lord, I have news to tell you. When Roscius was an actor in Rome—

Pol. The actors are come hither, my lord.

Ham. Buzz, buzz!

Pol. Upon mine honour,—

Ham. "Then came each actor on his ass,"—

Pol. The best actors in the world, either for tragedy, comedy, history, pastoral, pastoral-comical, historical-pastoral, scene individable, or poem unlimited. Seneca cannot be too heavy, nor Plautus too light for the law of writ and the liberty. These are the only men.

Ham. O Jephthah, judge of Israel, what a treasure hadst thou!

Pol. What a treasure had he, my lord?

Ham. Why,

"One fair daughter, and no more,
The which he loved passing well."

Pol. [*Aside.*] Still on my daughter.

Ham. Am I not i' th' right, old Jephthah?

Pol. If you call me Jephthah, my lord, I have a daughter that I love passing well.

Ham. Nay, that follows not.

Pol. What follows, then, my lord?

Ham. Why,

"As by lot, God wot,"

and then, you know,

"It came to pass as most like it was,"—

the first row of the pious chanson will show you more, for look where my abridgement comes.

Enter four or five *Players.*

You are welcome, masters, welcome all. I am glad to see thee well. Welcome, good friends. O, old friend! Why, thy face is valanced since I saw thee last; com'st thou to beard me in Denmark? What, my young lady and mistress! By 'r Lady, your ladyship is nearer to heaven than when I saw you last, by the altitude of a chopine. Pray God, your voice, like a piece of uncurrent gold, be not cracked within the ring. Masters, you are all welcome. We 'll e'en to 't like French falconers—fly at

362. **escoted,** maintained. 363. **quality,** profession of acting. 368. **succession,** future. 371. **tarre,** incite. 372. **argument,** dramatic subject. 378. **Hercules and his load,** probably refers to the Globe Theatre and its sign: Hercules bearing the globe for Atlas. 389. **comply,** be courteous. **garb,** outward show. 390. **extent,** behavior. 397-8. **hawk . . . handsaw,** workman's tools, with a quibble on "hawk," i.e., falcon, and "heronshaw," i.e., heron.

410. **Roscius,** famous Roman actor. 418-9. **scene . . . unlimited,** plays observing the unities of time, place, and action, or ones disregarding them. 420-1. **law . . . liberty,** this may refer again to the unities or the disregard of them; or more probably to following the text exactly in the presentation or to improvising on it. 422. **O . . . Israel,** title of a ballad. 438. **row,** stanza. 442. **valanced,** fringed (with a beard). 447. **chopine,** thick-soled shoe. 448-9. **uncurrent . . . ring,** if a crack in a coin extended from the edge through the ring that enclosed the king's head, it was rendered unfit for legal tender (uncurrent). Hamlet is, of course, referring to the change of voice the boy actor will soon experience.

anything we see; we 'll have a speech straight. Come, give us a taste of your quality; come, a passionate speech.

First Play. What speech, my good lord?

Ham. I heard thee speak me a speech once, but it was never acted; or, if it was, not above once; for the play, I remember, pleased not the million; 't was caviare to the general; but it was—as I received it, and others, whose judgement in such matters cried in the top of mine—an excellent play, well digested in the scenes, set down with as much modesty as cunning. I remember one said there were no sallets in the lines to make the matter savoury, nor no matter in the phrase that might indict the author of affection; but called it an honest method, as wholesome as sweet, and by very much more handsome than fine. One speech in 't I chiefly loved; 't was Æneas' tale to Dido, and thereabout of it especially when he speaks of Priam's slaughter. If it live in your memory, begin at this line: let me see, let me see—
"The rugged Pyrrhus, like th' Hyrcanian beast,"
—'T is not so; it begins with Pyrrhus:—
"The rugged Pyrrhus, he whose sable arms,
Black as his purpose, did the night resemble
When he lay couched in th' ominous horse,
Hath now this dread and black complexion smear'd
With heraldry more dismal: head to foot
Now is he total gules, horribly trick'd
With blood of fathers, mothers, daughters, sons,
Bak'd and impasted with the parching streets,
That lend a tyrannous and a damned light
To their lords' murder. Roasted in wrath and fire.
And thus o'er-sized with coagulate gore,
With eyes like carbuncles, the hellish Pyrrhus
Old grandsire Priam seeks."
So, proceed you.

Pol. 'Fore God, my lord, well spoken, with good accent and good discretion.

First Play. "Anon he finds him
Striking too short at Greeks; his antique sword,
Rebellious to his arm, lies where it falls,
Repugnant to command; unequal match'd,
Pyrrhus at Priam drives, in rage strikes wide,
But with the whiff and wind of his fell sword
Th' unnerved father falls. Then senseless Ilium,
Seeming to feel this blow, with flaming top
Stoops to his base, and with a hideous crash
Takes prisoner Pyrrhus' ear; for, lo! his sword,
Which was declining on the milky head
Of reverend Priam, seem'd i' th' air to stick;
So, as a painted tyrant, Pyrrhus stood
And like a neutral to his will and matter,
Did nothing.
But, as we often see, against some storm,
A silence in the heavens, the rack stand still,
The bold winds speechless and the orb below
As hush as death, anon the dreadful thunder
Doth rend the region; so, after Pyrrhus' pause,
Aroused vengeance sets him new a-work;
And never did the Cyclops' hammers fall
On Mars's armour forg'd for proof eterne
With less remorse than Pyrrhus' bleeding sword
Now falls on Priam.
Out, out, thou strumpet Fortune! All you gods,
In general synod take away her power!
Break all the spokes and fellies from her wheel,
And bowl the round nave down the hill of heaven
As low as to the fiends!"

Pol. This is too long.

Ham. It shall to the barber's, with your beard. Prithee, say on; he 's for a jig or a tale of bawdry, or he sleeps: say on; come to Hecuba.

First Play. "But who, Ah, woe! had seen the mobled queen"—

Ham. "The mobled queen"?

Pol. That 's good; "mobled queen" is good.

First Play. "Run barefoot up and down, threat'ning the flames
With bisson rheum, a clout about that head
Where late the diadem stood, and for a robe,
About her lank and all o'er-teemed loins,
A blanket, in the alarm of fear caught up;—
Who this had seen, with tongue in venom steep'd,
'Gainst Fortune's state would treason have pronounc'd:
But if the gods themselves did see her then,
When she saw Pyrrhus make malicious sport
In mincing with his sword her husband's limbs,
The instant burst of clamour that she made,
Unless things mortal move them not at all,

456-7. **caviare . . . general,** caviare is sturgeon's roe, a Russian delicacy. The meaning is that the play was too great a delicacy for the multitude (general). 459. **in the top,** over-topped. 462. **sallets,** salads, spicy jests. 464. **affection,** affectation. 467. **handsome,** well proportioned. **fine,** ornamented. 472. **Hyrcanian beast,** the tiger. 476. **horse,** the wooden horse at the siege of Troy. 479. **gules,** red. **trick'd,** adorned. 481. **impasted,** clotted. 484. **o'er-sized,** smeared over.

502. **painted tyrant,** tyrant in a picture. 503. **matter,** task. 506. **rack,** cloud. 512. **proof eterne,** eternal endurance. 517. **fellies,** rims. 518. **nave,** hub. 525. **mobled,** muffled. 529. **bisson rheum,** blinding tears. 531. **o'er-teemed,** exhausted with child-bearing.

Would have made milch the burning eyes of heaven,
And passion in the gods."

Pol. Look, whe'er he has not turned his colour and has tears in 's eyes. Prithee, no more.

Ham. 'T is well; I 'll have thee speak out the rest of this soon. Good my lord, will you see the players well bestowed? Do you hear? Let them be well used, for they are the abstract and brief chronicles of the time; after your death you were better have a bad epitaph than their ill report while you live.

Pol. My lord, I will use them according to their desert.

Ham. God's bodykins, man, much better! Use every man after his desert, and who shall scape whipping? Use them after your own honour and dignity; the less they deserve, the more merit is in your bounty. Take them in.

Pol. Come, sirs. *Exit.*

Ham. Follow him, friends; we 'll hear a play to-morrow. [*Exeunt all the Players but the First.*] Dost thou hear me, old friend? Can you play "The Murder of Gonzago"?

First Play. Ay, my lord.

Ham. We 'll ha 't to-morrow night. You could, for a need, study a speech of some dozen lines or sixteen lines, which I would set down and insert in 't, could you not?

First Play. Ay, my lord.

Ham. Very well. Follow that lord, and look you mock him not. [*Exit First Player.*] My good friends, I 'll leave you till night: you are welcome to Elsinore.

Ros. Good my lord!

Exeunt Rosencrantz and Guildenstern.

Ham. Ay, so, God buy to you.—Now I am alone.
O, what a rogue and peasant slave am I!
Is it not monstrous that this player here,
But in a fiction, in a dream of passion,
Could force his soul so to his own conceit
That from her working all his visage wann'd,
Tears in his eyes, distraction in his aspect,
A broken voice, and his whole function suiting
With forms to his conceit? And all for nothing!
For Hecuba!
What 's Hecuba to him, or he to Hecuba,
That he should weep for her? What would he do,
Had he the motive and the cue for passion
That I have? He would drown the stage with tears
And cleave the general ear with horrid speech,
Make mad the guilty and appal the free,
Confound the ignorant, and amaze indeed
The very faculties of eyes and ears.
Yet I,
A dull and muddy-mettled rascal, peak
Like John-a-dreams, unpregnant of my cause,
And can say nothing; no, not for a king,
Upon whose property and most dear life
A damn'd defeat was made. Am I a coward?
Who calls me villain, breaks my pate across,
Plucks off my beard and blows it in my face,
Tweaks me by the nose, gives me the lie i' th' throat
As deep as to the lungs, who does me this?
Ha!
'Swounds, I should take it; for it cannot be
But I am pigeon-liver'd and lack gall
To make oppression bitter, or ere this
I should ha' fatted all the region kites
With this slave's offal. Bloody, bawdy villain!
Remorseless, treacherous, lecherous, kindless villain!
O, vengeance!
Why, what an ass am I! This is most brave,
That I, the son of a dear father murdered,
Prompted to my revenge by heaven and hell,
Must, like a whore, unpack my heart with words,
And fall a-cursing, like a very drab,
A stallion!
Fie upon 't! Foh! About, my braines! Hum, I have heard
That guilty creatures sitting at a play
Have by the very cunning of the scene
Been struck so to the soul that presently
They have proclaim'd their malefactions;
For murder, though it have no tongue, will speak
With most miraculous organ: I 'll have these players
Play something like the murder of my father
Before mine uncle, I 'll observe his looks,
I 'll tent him to the quick; if he but blench,
I know my course. The spirit that I have seen
May be a devil; and the devil hath power
T' assume a pleasing shape; yea, and perhaps
Out of my weakness and my melancholy,
As he is very potent with such spirits,
Abuses me to damn me; I 'll have grounds
More relative than this—the play 's the thing
Wherein I 'll catch the conscience of the King.

Exit.

540. **milch,** moist. 579. **conceit,** imagination. 582. **function,** action. 583. **forms,** bodily expression.

594. **muddy-mettled,** irresolute. **peak,** mope. 595. **John-a-dreams,** sleepy person. **unpregnant of,** unquickened by. 609. **kindless,** unnatural. 616. **stallion,** harlot. 617. **About,** to work. 626. **tent,** probe. 631. **spirits,** humors, moods. 633. **relative,** definite.

ACT III. SCENE I. *A room in the castle.*

Enter *King, Queen, Polonius, Ophelia, Rosencrantz, Guildenstern,* and *Lords.*

King. And can you, by no drift of conference,
Get from him why he puts on this confusion,
Grating so harshly all his days of quiet
With turbulent and dangerous lunacy?
Ros. He does confess he feels himself distracted;
But from what cause 'a will by no means speak.
Guil. Nor do we find him forward to be sounded,
But, with a crafty madness, keeps aloof
When we would bring him on to some confession
Of his true state.
Queen. Did he receive you well?
Ros. Most like a gentleman.
Guil. But with much forcing of his disposition.
Ros. Niggard of question; but, of our demands,
Most free in his reply.
Queen. Did you assay him
To any pastime?
Ros. Madam, it so fell out, that certain players
We o'er-raught on the way; of these we told him,
And there did seem in him a kind of joy
To hear of it: they are here about the court,
And, as I think, they have already order
This night to play before him.
Pol. 'T is most true.
And he beseech'd me to entreat your Majesties
To hear and see the matter.
King. With all my heart; and it doth much content me
To hear him so inclin'd.
Good gentlemen, give him a further edge,
And drive his purpose into these delights.
Ros. We shall, my lord.
Exeunt Rosencrantz and Guildenstern.
King. Sweet Gertrude, leave us two,
For we have closely sent for Hamlet hither,
That he, as 't were by accident, may here
Affront Ophelia.
Her father and myself—lawful espials—
We 'll so bestow ourselves that, seeing unseen,
We may of their encounter frankly judge,
And gather by him, as he is behav'd,
If 't be th' affliction of his love or no
That thus he suffers for.
Queen. I shall obey you.
And for your part, Ophelia, I do wish
That your good beauties be the happy cause
Of Hamlet's wildness; so shall I hope your virtues
Will bring him to his wonted way again,
To both your honours.
Oph. Madam, I wish it may.
Exit Queen.
Pol. Ophelia, walk you here. Gracious, so please you,
We will bestow ourselves. [*To Ophelia.*] Read on this book,
That show of such an exercise may colour
Your loneliness. We are oft to blame in this,—
'T is too much prov'd—that with devotion's visage
And pious action we do sugar o'er
The devil himself.
King. [*Aside.*] O, 't is true!
How smart a lash that speech doth give my conscience!
The harlot's cheek, beautied with plast'ring art,
Is not more ugly to the thing that helps it
Than is my deed to my most painted word:
O heavy burden!
Pol. I hear him coming; let 's withdraw, my lord. *Exeunt King and Polonius.*

Enter *Hamlet.*

Ham. To be, or not to be: that is the question:
Whether 't is nobler in the mind to suffer
The slings and arrows of outrageous fortune,
Or to take arms against a sea of troubles,
And by opposing end them. To die, to sleep—
No more; and by a sleep to say we end
The heart-ache and the thousand natural shocks
That flesh is heir to; 't is a consummation
Devoutly to be wish'd; to die; to sleep;
To sleep, perchance to dream; ay, there 's the rub;
For in that sleep of death what dreams may come,
When we have shuffled off this mortal coil,
Must give us pause; there 's the respect
That makes calamity of so long life:

1. drift of conference, management of conversation. **7. forward,** willing. **12. forcing of his disposition,** unwillingness. **14. assay,** tempt. **17. o'er-raught,** overtook. **26. edge,** incitement. **28. us two,** the King and Polonius who are to spy on Hamlet. **32. espials,** spies.

45. exercise, act of devotion. **67. shuffled,** slipped, cast. **coil,** turmoil, with a play upon "coil," a ring of rope, here the flesh encircling the soul. **68. respect,** consideration.

For who would bear the whips and scorns of time,
Th' oppressor's wrong, the proud man's contumely,
The pangs of dispriz'd love, the law's delay,
The insolence of office, and the spurns
That patient merit of th' unworthy takes,
When he himself might his quietus make
With a bare bodkin? Who would fardels bear,
To grunt and sweat under a weary life,
But that the dread of something after death,
The undiscover'd country from whose bourn
No traveller returns, puzzles the will
And makes us rather bear those ills we have
Than fly to others that we know not of?
Thus conscience does make cowards of us all;
And thus the native hue of resolution
Is sicklied o'er with the pale cast of thought,
And enterprises of great pitch and moment
With this regard their currents turn awry,
And lose the name of action.—Soft you now,
The fair Ophelia!—Nymph, in thy orisons
Be all my sins remember'd.

Oph. Good my lord,
How does your honour for this many a day?

Ham. I humbly thank you, well, well, well.

Oph. My lord, I have remembrances of yours
That I have longed long to re-deliver.
I pray you, now receive them.

Ham. No, not I;
I never gave you aught.

Oph. My honour'd lord, you know right well you did,
And, with them, words of so sweet breath compos'd
As made the things more rich. Their perfume lost,
Take these again; for to the noble mind
Rich gifts wax poor when givers prove unkind.
There, my lord.

Ham. Ha, ha! are you honest?

Oph. My lord!

Ham. Are you fair?

Oph. What means your lordship?

Ham. That if you be honest and fair, your honesty should admit no discourse to your beauty.

Oph. Could beauty, my lord, have better commerce than with honesty?

Ham. Ay, truly; for the power of beauty will sooner transform honesty from what it is to a bawd than the force of honesty can translate beauty into his likeness. This was sometime a paradox, but now the time gives it proof. I did love you once.

Oph. Indeed, my lord, you made me believe so.

Ham. You should not have believed me, for virtue cannot so inoculate our old stock but we shall relish of it. I loved you not.

Oph. I was the more deceived.

Ham. Get thee to a nunnery; why wouldst thou be a breeder of sinners? I am myself indifferent honest, but yet I could accuse me of such things that it were better my mother had not borne me: I am very proud, revengeful, ambitious, with more offences at my beck than I have thoughts to put them in, imagination to give them shape, or time to act them in. What should such fellows as I do crawling between earth and heaven? We are arrant knaves all; believe none of us, go thy ways to a nunnery. Where 's your father?

Oph. At home, my lord.

Ham. Let the doors be shut upon him, that he may play the fool nowhere but in 's own house. Farewell!

Oph. O, help him, you sweet heavens!

Ham. If thou dost marry, I 'll give thee this plague for thy dowry: be thou as chaste as ice, as pure as snow, thou shalt not escape calumny. Get thee to a nunnery, farewell! Or, if thou wilt needs marry, marry a fool; for wise men know well enough what monsters you make of them. To a nunnery, go, and quickly too, farewell!

Oph. Heavenly powers, restore him!

Ham. I have heard of your paintings, well enough. God hath given you one face, and you make yourselves another. You jig and amble, and you lisp and nick-name God's creatures and make your wantonness your ignorance. Go to, I 'll no more on 't; it hath made me mad. I say, we will have no moe marriage: those that are married already, all but one, shall live; the rest shall keep as they are. To a nunnery, go. *Exit.*

Oph. O, what a noble mind is here o'erthrown!
The courtier's, soldier's, scholar's, eye, tongue, sword;
Th' expectancy and rose of the fair state,
The glass of fashion and the mould of form,
The observ'd of all observers, quite quite down!
And I, of ladies most deject and wretched,
That suck'd the honey of his music vows,
Now see that noble and most sovereign reason,
Like sweet bells jangled out of time and harsh;
That unmatch'd form and feature of blown youth

72. **dispriz'd,** disparaged. 75. **quietus,** full discharge, a legal term. 76. **fardels,** burdens. 83. **conscience,** self-consciousness, introspection. 86. **pitch,** height, a term from falconry. 87. **regard,** consideration. 89. **orisons,** prayers. 103. **honest,** chaste.

119. **inoculate,** graft. 120. **relish of it,** smack of the old stock. 152-3. Excuse your wanton speech by pretending ignorance. 156. **one,** Claudius. 166. **time,** tune, rhythm. 167. **blown,** blooming.

Blasted with ecstasy. O, woe is me,
T' have seen what I have seen, see what I see!

Re-enter *King* and *Polonius*.

King. Love! his affections do not that way tend;
Nor what he spake, though it lack'd form a little,
Was not like madness. There 's something in his soul
O'er which his melancholy sits on brood,
And I do doubt the hatch and the disclose
Will be some danger; which for to prevent,
I have in quick determination
Thus set it down: he shall with speed to England
For the demand of our neglected tribute.
Haply the seas and countries different
With variable objects shall expel
This something-settled matter in his heart,
Whereon his brains still beating puts him thus
From fashion of himself. What think you on 't?

Pol. It shall do well; but yet do I believe
The origin and commencement of his grief
Sprung from neglected love. How now, Ophelia?
You need not tell us what Lord Hamlet said;
We heard it all. My lord, do as you please,
But, if you hold it fit, after the play
Let his queen mother all alone entreat him
To show his grief; let her be round with him,
And I 'll be plac'd, so please you, in the ear
Of all their conference. If she find him not,
To England send him, or confine him where
Your wisdom best shall think.

King. It shall be so.
Madness in great ones must not unwatch'd go.

Exeunt.

Scene II. *A hall in the castle.*

Enter *Hamlet* and three of the *Players*.

Ham. Speak the speech, I pray you, as I pronounced it to you, trippingly on the tongue; but if you mouth it, as many of our players do, I had as lief the town-crier spoke my lines. Nor do not saw the air too much with your hand thus, but use all gently, for in the very torrent, tempest, and, as I may say, the whirlwind of your passion, you must acquire and beget a temperance that may give it smoothness. O, it offends me to the soul to see a robustious periwig-pated fellow tear a passion to tatters, to very rags, to split the ears of the groundlings, who for the most part are capable of nothing but inexplicable dumb-shows and noise: I would have such a fellow whipped for o'erdoing Termagant; it out-herods Herod: pray you, avoid it.

First Play. I warrant your honour.

Ham. Be not too tame neither, but let your own discretion be your tutor; suit the action to the word, the word to the action; with this special observance, that you o'erstep not the modesty of nature: for anything so o'erdone is from the purpose of playing, whose end, both at the first and now, was and is, to hold, as 't were, the mirror up to nature; to show virtue her own feature, scorn her own image, and the very age and body of the time his form and pressure. Now this overdone, or come tardy off, though it makes the unskilful laugh, cannot but make the judicious grieve; the censure of the which one must, in your allowance, o'erweigh a whole theatre of others. O, there be players that I have seen play, and heard others praise, and that highly, not to speak it profanely, that, neither having th' accent of Christians nor the gait of Christian, pagan, nor man, have so strutted and bellowed that I have thought some of Nature's journeymen had made men and not made them well, they imitated humanity so abominably.

First Play. I hope we have reformed that indifferently with us.

Ham. O, reform it altogether; and let those that play your clowns speak no more than is set down for them; for there be of them that will themselves laugh to set on some quantity of barren spectators to laugh too, though in the mean time some necessary question of the play be then to be considered. That 's villanous, and shows a most pitiful ambition in the fool that uses it. Go, make you ready.

Exeunt Players.

Enter *Polonius, Rosencrantz,* and *Guildenstern.*

How now, my lord! Will the King hear this piece of work?

Pol. And the Queen too, and that presently.

Ham. Bid the players make haste.

Exit Polonius.

168. **ecstasy,** madness. 193. **find,** find out. **Scene ii:** 10. **periwig-pated,** wearing a wig.

12. **groundlings,** those who stood in the "ground," pit, of the theatre, i.e., the most ignorant of the audience. 13. **are capable of,** can appreciate. 14. **Termagant,** a boisterous character in the old mystery plays, supposed to represent a god of the Saracens. 15. **Herod,** a ranting tyrant in the mystery plays. 23. **from,** apart from, contrary to. 27. **pressure,** impressions. 28. **come tardy off,** poorly done. 38. **journeymen,** workmen not yet masters of their trade. 41. **indifferently,** tolerably.

Will you two help to hasten them?

Ros.
Guil. } Ay, my lord.

Exeunt Rosencrantz and Guildenstern.

Ham. What ho! Horatio!

Enter *Horatio.*

Hor. Here, sweet lord, at your service.

Ham. Horatio, thou art e'en as just a man
As e'er my conversation cop'd withal.

Hor. O, my dear lord,—

Ham. Nay, do not think I flatter,
For what advancement may I hope from thee
That no revenue hast but thy good spirits
To feed and clothe thee? Why should the poor be flatter'd?
No, let the candied tongue lick absurd pomp,
And crook the pregnant hinges of the knee
Where thrift may follow fawning. Dost thou hear?
Since my dear soul was mistress of my choice
And could of men distinguish her election,
S' hath seal'd thee for herself, for thou hast been
As one, in suffering all, that suffers nothing,
A man that Fortune's buffets and rewards
Hast ta'en with equal thanks; and blest are those
Whose blood and judgement are so well commedled,
That they are not a pipe for Fortune's finger
To sound what stop she please. Give me that man
That is not passion's slave, and I will wear him
In my heart's core, ay, in my heart of heart,
As I do thee.—Something too much of this.—
There is a play to-night before the King;
One scene of it comes near the circumstance
Which I have told thee of my father's death.
I prithee, when thou seest that act a-foot,
Even with the very comment of thy soul
Observe my uncle: if his occulted guilt
Do not itself unkennel in one speech,
It is a damned ghost that we have seen,
And my imaginations are as foul
As Vulcan's stithy. Give him heedful note;
For I mine eyes will rivet to his face,
And after we will both our judgements join
In censure of his seeming.

Hor. Well, my lord.
If 'a steal aught the whilst this play is playing,
And scape detecting, I will pay the theft.

60. cop'd withal, met with. **65. candied,** sugared, flattering. **66. pregnant,** full of promise of good fortune. **67. thrift,** profit. **70. S' hath,** she (the soul) hath. **74. blood,** passions. **commedled,** blended. **84. very comment,** truest attention. **85. occulted,** hidden. **89. stithy,** forge, smithy. **92. censure,** judgment.

Danish march. A flourish. Enter *King, Queen, Polonius, Ophelia, Rosencrantz, Guildenstern,* and other *Lords* attendant, with his guard carrying torches.

Ham. They are coming to the play. I must be idle;
Get you a place.

King. How fares our cousin Hamlet?

Ham. Excellent, i' faith, of the chameleon's dish: I eat the air, promise-crammed—You cannot feed capons so.

King. I have nothing with this answer, Hamlet; these words are not mine.

Ham. No, nor mine now. [*To Polonius.*] My lord, you played once i' th' university, you say?

Pol. That did I, my lord, and was accounted a good actor.

Ham. What did you enact?

Pol. I did enact Julius Cæsar; I was killed i' th' Capitol; Brutus killed me.

Ham. It was a brute part of him to kill so capital a calf there. Be the players ready?

Ros. Ay, my lord, they stay upon your patience.

Queen. Come hither, my dear Hamlet, sit by me.

Ham. No, good mother, here 's metal more attractive.

Lying down at Ophelia's feet.

Pol. [*To the King.*] O, ho! do you mark that?

Ham. Lady, shall I lie in your lap?

Oph. No, my lord.

Ham. I mean, my head upon your lap?

Oph. Ay, my lord.

Ham. Do you think I meant country matters?

Oph. I think nothing, my lord.

Ham. That 's a fair thought to lie between maid's legs.

Oph. What is, my lord?

Ham. Nothing.

Oph. You are merry, my lord.

Ham. Who, I?

Oph. Ay, my lord.

Ham. O God, your only jig-maker. What should a man do but be merry? for, look you, how cheerfully my mother looks, and my father died within 's two hours.

Oph. Nay, 't is twice two months, my lord.

Ham. So long? Nay then, let the devil wear black, for I 'll have a suit of sables. O heavens! die two months ago, and not forgotten yet? Then there 's hope a great man's memory may outlive his life half a year; [140

98-9. chameleon's dish, air on which chameleons were thought to live. **132. jig-maker,** composer of "jigs"—songs and dances, often composed by the Fool who performed them. **138. suit of sables,** fine furred suit.

but, by 'r Lady, 'a must build churches then, or else shall 'a suffer not thinking on, with the hobby-horse, whose epitaph is, "For, O, for, O, the hobby-horse is forgot."

The trumpets sounds. The dumb-show enters.

Enter a King and Queen, the Queen embracing him and he her. She kneels and makes show of protestation unto him; he takes her up and declines his head upon her neck. He lays him down upon a bank of flowers. She, seeing him asleep, leaves him. Anon comes in another man, takes off his crown, kisses it, pours poison in the sleeper's ears, and leaves him. The Queen returns, finds the King dead, makes passionate action. The poisoner, with some three or four, come in again, seem to condole with her. The dead body is carried away. The poisoner woos the Queen with gifts; she seems harsh a while, but in the end accepts his love. *Exeunt.*

Oph. What means this, my lord?

Ham. Marry, this is miching mallecho; it means mischief.

Oph. Belike this show imports the argument of the play?

Enter *Prologue.*

Ham. We shall know by this fellow. The players cannot keep counsel, they 'll tell all.

Oph. Will 'a tell us what this show meant?

Ham. Ay, or any show that you will show him: be not you ashamed to show, he 'll not shame to tell you what it means.

Oph. You are naught, you are naught; I 'll mark the play.

Pro.

For us, and for our tragedy,
Here stooping to your clemency,
We beg your hearing patiently.

Exit.

Ham. Is this a prologue, or the posy of a ring?

Oph. 'T is brief, my lord.

Ham. As woman's love.

Enter two Players, *King* and *Queen.*

P. King. Full thirty times hath Phœbus' cart gone round
Neptune's salt wash and Tellus' orbed ground,
And thirty dozen moons with borrowed sheen
About the world have times twelve thirties been,
Since love our hearts and Hymen did our hands
Unite commutual in most sacred bands.

P. Queen. So many journeys may the sun and moon
Make us again count o'er ere love be done!
But, woe is me, you are so sick of late,
So far from cheer and from your former state,
That I distrust you. Yet, though I distrust,
Discomfort you, my lord, it nothing must;
For women fear too much, even as they love,
And women's fear and love hold quantity,
In neither aught, or in extremity.
Now, what my love is, proof hath made you know;
And as my love is siz'd, my fear is so:
Where love is great, the littlest doubts are fear;
Where little fears grow great, great love grows there.

P. King. Faith, I must leave thee, love, and shortly too.
My operant powers their functions leave to do;
And thou shalt live in this fair world behind,
Honour'd, belov'd; and haply one as kind
For husband shalt thou—

P. Queen. O, confound the rest!
Such love must needs be treason in my breast:
In second husband let me be accurst,
None wed the second but who kill'd the first.

Ham. [*Aside.*] That 's wormwood!

P. Queen. The instances that second marriage move
Are base respects of thrift, but none of love:
A second time I kill my husband dead,
When second husband kisses me in bed.

P. King. I do believe you think what now you speak,
But what we do determine oft we break.
Purpose is but the slave to memory,
Of violent birth, but poor validity;
Which now, the fruit unripe, sticks on the tree,
But fall unshaken when they mellow be.
Most necessary 't is that we forget
To pay ourselves what to ourselves is debt:
What to ourselves in passion we propose,
The passion ending, doth the purpose lose.
The violence of either grief or joy
Their own enactures with themselves destroy:
Where joy most revels, grief doth most lament;
Grief joys, joy grieves, on slender accident.

144. hobby-horse, a figure in the Morris Dance. **147. miching mallecho,** sneaking mischief. **157. naught,** bad, wanton. **162. posy,** motto.

175. distrust, am anxious about you. **177-8. hold . . . extremity,** keep proportion, either in nothing, or in the intensest feeling. **184. operant,** active. **192. instances,** motives. **move,** induce. **199. validity,** strength. **207. enactures,** acts.

This world is not for aye, nor 't is not strange
That even our loves should with our fortunes change,
For 't is a question left us yet to prove,
Whether love lead fortune, or else fortune love.
The great man down, you mark his favourite flies;
The poor advanc'd makes friends of enemies:
And hitherto doth love on fortune tend,
For who not needs shall never lack a friend;
And who in want a hollow friend doth try,
Directly seasons him his enemy.
But, orderly to end where I begun,
Our wills and fates do so contrary run
That our devices still are overthrown;
Our thoughts are ours, their ends none of our own:
So think thou wilt no second husband wed;
But die thy thoughts when thy first lord is dead.

P. Queen. Nor earth to me give food, nor heaven light!
Sport and repose lock from me day and night!
To desperation turn my trust and hope,
An anchor's cheer in prison be my scope!
Each opposite that blanks the face of joy
Meet what I would have well and it destroy!
Both here and hence pursue me lasting strife,
If, once a widow, ever I be wife!

Ham. If she should break it now!

P. King. 'T is deeply sworn. Sweet, leave me here a while.
My spirits grow dull, and fain I would beguile
The tedious day with sleep. *Sleeps.*

P. Queen. Sleep rock thy brain,
And never come mischance between us twain! *Exit.*

Ham. Madam, how like you this play?

Queen. The lady doth protest too much, methinks.

Ham. O, but she 'll keep her word.

King. Have you heard the argument? Is there no offence in 't?

Ham. No, no, they do but jest, poison in jest; no offence i' th' world.

King. What do you call the play?

Ham. The Mouse-trap. Marry, how? Tropically. This play is the image of a murder done in Vienna; Gonzago is the duke's name; his wife, Baptista. You shall see anon, 't is a knavish piece of work, but what of that? Your Majesty and we that have free souls, it touches us not: let the galled jade wince, our withers are unwrung.

Enter *Lucianus.*

This is one Lucianus, nephew to the king.

Oph. You are as good as a chorus, my lord.

Ham. I could interpret between you and your love, if I could see the puppets dallying.

Oph. You are keen, my lord, you are keen.

Ham. It would cost you a groaning to take off mine edge.

Oph. Still better, and worse.

Ham. So you mistake your husbands. Begin, murderer; leave thy damnable faces and begin. Come, "the croaking raven doth bellow for revenge."

Luc. Thoughts black, hands apt, drugs fit, and time agreeing;
Confederate season, else no creature seeing.
Thou mixture rank, of midnight weeds collected,
With Hecate's ban thrice blasted, thrice infected,
Thy natural magic and dire property
On wholesome life usurps immediately.
Pours the poison into the sleeper's ears.

Ham. He poisons him i' th' garden for his estate, his name 's Gonzago; the story is extant, and writ in very choice Italian; you shall see anon how the murderer gets the love of Gonzago's wife.

Oph. The King rises.

Ham. What, frighted with false fire?

Queen. How fares my lord?

Pol. Give o'er the play.

King. Give me some light. Away!

Pol. Lights, lights, lights!
Exeunt all but Hamlet and Horatio.

Ham. Why, let the strucken deer go weep,
The hart ungalled play;
For some must watch, while some must sleep,—
Thus runs the world away.
Would not this, sir, and a forest of feathers—if the rest of my fortunes turn Turk with me—with two Provincial roses on my razed shoes, get me a fellowship in a cry of players, sir?

Hor. Half a share.

Ham. A whole one, I.
For thou dost know, O Damon dear,
This realm dismantled was
Of Jove himself; and now reigns here
A very, very—pacock.

Hor. You might have rhymed.

219. **seasons him**, turns him into. 229. **anchor's**, anchorite's, hermit's. 230. **opposite**, adverse thing. **blanks**, blanches. 247. **Tropically**, figuratively. 248. **image**, representation. 252. **galled jade**, chafed horse.

256. **interpret**, like a showman explaining the action of puppets. 262. **mistake**, err in taking. 286. **feathers**, the plumes worn by actors. 287. **turn Turk**, go bad. 288. **Provincial roses**, rosettes like the roses of Provence, or, perhaps of Provins, near Paris, famous for its roses. **razed**, slashed. 289. **cry**, pack, company. 295. **pacock**, peacock, the emblem of vanity and lechery.

Ham. O good Horatio, I'll take the ghost's word for a thousand pound. Didst perceive?

Hor. Very well, my lord.

Ham. Upon the talk of the poisoning?

Hor. I did very well note him.

Ham. Ah, ha! Come, some music! Come, the recorders!

For if the king like not the comedy,
Why then, belike, he likes it not, perdy.
Come, some music!

Re-enter *Rosencrantz* and *Guildenstern.*

Guil. Good my lord, vouchsafe me a word with you.

Ham. Sir, a whole history.

Guil. The King, sir,—

Ham. Ay, sir, what of him?

Guil. Is in his retirement marvellous distempered.

Ham. With drink, sir?

Guil. No, my lord, with choler.

Ham. Your wisdom should show itself more richer to signify this to the doctor; for, for me to put him to his purgation would perhaps plunge him into more choler.

Guil. Good my lord, put your discourse into some frame, and start not so wildly from my affair.

Ham. I am tame, sir; pronounce.

Guil. The Queen, your mother, in most great affliction of spirit, hath sent me to you.

Ham. You are welcome.

Guil. Nay, good my lord, this courtesy is not of the right breed. If it shall please you to make me a wholesome answer I will do your mother's commandment; if not, your pardon and my return shall be the end of my business.

Ham. Sir, I cannot.

Ros. What, my lord?

Ham. Make you a wholesome answer: my wit 's diseased. But, sir, such answer as I can make, you shall command, or, rather, as you say, my mother. Therefore no more, but to the matter. My mother, you say,—

Ros. Then thus she says: your behaviour hath struck her into amazement and admiration.

Ham. O wonderful son, that can so stonish a mother! But is there no sequel at the heels of this mother's admiration? Impart.

Ros. She desires to speak with you in her closet ere you go to bed.

Ham. We shall obey, were she ten times our mother. Have you any further trade with us?

Ros. My lord, you once did love me.

Ham. And do still, by these pickers and stealers.

Ros. Good my lord, what is your cause of distemper? You do surely bar the door upon your own liberty if you deny your griefs to your friend.

Ham. Sir, I lack advancement.

Ros. How can that be, when you have the voice of the King himself for your succession in Denmark?

Ham. Ay, but "While the grass grows,"—the proverb is something musty.

Re-enter the *Players* with recorders.

O, the recorders! Let me see one.—To withdraw with you:—why do you go about to recover the wind of me, as if you would drive me into a toil?

Guil. O, my lord, if my duty be too bold, my love is too unmannerly.

Ham. I do not well understand that. Will you play upon this pipe?

Guil. My lord, I cannot.

Ham. I pray you.

Guil. Believe me, I cannot.

Ham. I do beseech you.

Guil. I know no touch of it, my lord.

Ham. 'T is as easy as lying: govern these ventages with your finger and thumb, give it breath with your mouth, and it will discourse most eloquent music. Look you, these are the stops.

Guil. But these cannot I command to any utt'rance of harmony; I have not the skill.

Ham. Why, look you now, how unworthy a thing you make of me! You would play upon me, you would seem to know my stops, you would pluck out the heart of my mystery, you would sound me from my lowest note to the top of my compass; and there is much music, excellent voice, in this little organ, yet cannot you make it speak. 'Sblood, do you think that I am easier to be played on than a pipe? Call me what instrument you will, though you can fret me, yet you cannot play upon me.

Enter *Polonius.*

God bless you, sir.

Pol. My lord, the Queen would speak with you, and presently.

Ham. Do you see yonder cloud that 's almost in shape of a camel?

303. **recorders,** musical pipes. 321. **frame,** order. 328. **wholesome,** sane. 339. **admiration,** astonishment.

348-9. **pickers and stealers,** hands, with reference to the prayer: "Keep my hands from picking and stealing." 359. **proverb,** "While the grass groweth, the horse starveth." 360. **withdraw,** speak in private. 361-2. **recover the wind,** get on the windward side, as in hunting. 362. **toil,** snare. 373. **ventages,** stops on the recorder. 383. **compass,** extent of voice. 385. **organ,** instrument, the recorder. 388. **fret,** (1) finger the frets (i.e., bars on the recorder), (2) vex.

Pol. By th' mass and 't is like a camel indeed.

Ham. Methinks it is like a weasel.

Pol. It is backed like a weasel.

Ham. Or like a whale?

Pol. Very like a whale.

Ham. Then I will come to my mother by and by. [*Aside.*] They fool me to the top of my bent.—I will come by and by.

Pol. I will say so. *Exit.*

Ham. "By and by" is easily said. Leave me, friends. *Exeunt all but Hamlet.*
'T is now the very witching time of night
When churchyards yawn and hell itself breathes out
Contagion to this world: now could I drink hot blood,
And do such bitter business as the day
Would quake to look on. Soft! now to my mother.
O heart, lose not thy nature, let not ever
The soul of Nero enter this firm bosom;
Let me be cruel, not unnatural.
I will speak daggers to her, but use none.
My tongue and soul in this be hypocrites;
How in my words somever she be shent,
To give them seals never, my soul, consent!
Exit.

Scene III. *A room in the castle.*

Enter *King, Rosencrantz,* and *Guildenstern.*

King. I like him not, nor stands it safe with us
To let his madness range. Therefore prepare you:
I your commission will forthwith dispatch,
And he to England shall along with you.
The terms of our estate may not endure
Hazard so neer's as doth hourly grow
Out of his braves.

Guil. We will ourselves provide.
Most holy and religious fear it is
To keep those many many bodies safe
That live and feed upon your Majesty.

Ros. The single and peculiar life is bound
With all the strength and armour of the mind
To keep itself from noyance, but much more
That spirit upon whose weal depends and rests
The lives of many. The cease of majesty
Dies not alone, but, like a gulf, doth draw
What 's near it with it: or it is a massy wheel,
Fix'd on the summit of the highest mount,
To whose huge spokes ten thousand lesser things
Are mortis'd and adjoin'd; which, when it falls,
Each small annexment, petty consequence,
Attends the boisterous ruin. Never alone
Did the King sigh, but with a general groan.

King. Arm you, I pray you, to this speedy voyage,
For we will fetters put about this fear,
Which now goes too free-footed.

Ros. We will haste us.
Exeunt Rosencrantz and Guildenstern.

Enter *Polonius.*

Pol. My lord, he 's going to his mother's closet:
Behind the arras I 'll convey myself,
To hear the process.—I 'll warrant she 'll tax him home;
And, as you said, and wisely was it said,
'T is meet that some more audience than a mother,
Since nature makes them partial, should o'erhear
The speech of vantage. Fare you well, my liege.
I 'll call upon you ere you go to bed,
And tell you what I know.

King. Thanks, dear my lord.
Exit Polonius.
O, my offence is rank, it smells to heaven;
It hath the primal eldest curse upon 't,
A brother's murder. Pray can I not,
Though inclination be as sharp as will.
My stronger guilt defeats my strong intent,
And, like a man to double business bound,
I stand in pause where I shall first begin,
And both neglect. What if this cursed hand
Were thicker than itself with brother's blood,
Is there not rain enough in the sweet heavens
To wash it white as snow? Whereto serves mercy
But to confront the visage of offence?
And what 's in prayer but this twofold force,
To be forestalled ere we come to fall,
Or pardon'd being down? Then I 'll look up;
My fault is past. But, O, what form of prayer
Can serve my turn? "Forgive me my foul murder"?
That cannot be; since I am still possess'd
Of those effects for which I did the murder,
My crown, mine own ambition, and my queen.

412. **Nero**, who murdered his mother, Agrippina. 416. **shent**, rebuked. 417. **give them seals**, confirm them with deeds. **Scene iii:** 5. **terms**, condition. 6. **neer's**, near us. 7. **braves**, bravadoes, insolent speech and behavior, an emendation of the Quarto *browes.* 11. **peculiar**, individual, private. 15. **cease**, death. 16. **gulf**, whirlpool.

21. **annexment**, appendage. 24 **Arm**, prepare. 29. **process**, interview. **tax**, reproach. 33. **of vantage**, from an advantageous point. 37. **primal . . . curse**, the curse of Cain. 47. **confront**, oppose.

May one be pardon'd and retain th' offence?
In the corrupted currents of this world
Offence's gilded hand may shove by justice,
And oft 't is seen the wicked prize itself
Buys out the law: but 't is not so above;
There is no shuffling, there the action lies
In his true nature; and we ourselves compell'd,
Even to the teeth and forehead of our faults,
To give in evidence. What then? What rests?
Try what repentance can.—What can it not?
Yet what can it when one cannot repent?
O wretched state! O bosom black as death!
O limed soul, that, struggling to be free,
Art more engag'd! Help, angels! Make assay!
Bow, stubborn knees, and, heart with strings of steel,
Be soft as sinews of the new-born babe!
All may be well. *He kneels.*

Enter *Hamlet.*

Ham. Now might I do it pat, now 'a is a-praying,
And now I 'll do 't.—And so 'a goes to heaven;
And so am I reveng'd. That would be scann'd:
A villain kills my father, and for that,
I, his sole son, do this same villain send
To heaven.
Oh, this is base and silly, not revenge.
'A took my father grossly, full of bread,
With all his crimes broad blown, as flush as May;
And how his audit stands who knows save Heaven?
But in our circumstance and course of thought
'T is heavy with him: and am I then reveng'd,
To take him in the purging of his soul,
When he is fit and season'd for his passage?
No!
Up, sword, and know thou a more horrid hent,
When he is drunk asleep, or in his rage,
Or in th' incestuous pleasure of his bed,
At game a-swearing, or about some act
That has no relish of salvation in 't,
Then trip him, that his heels may kick at heaven,
And that his soul may be as damn'd and black
As hell, whereto it goes. My mother stays.
This physic but prolongs thy sickly days.
Exit.

61. **shuffling,** trickery. 64. **rests,** remains. 68. **limed,** caught as with bird-lime. 75. **would be scann'd,** ought to be looked into. 79. **base and silly,** low and foolish. 80. **full of bread,** "this was the iniquity . . . of Sodom, pride, fulness of bread"—*Ezekiel*, xvi, 49. 81. **broad blown,** full blown. **flush,** lusty. 88. **hent,** grasp, here occasion for seizing. 91. **at game a-swearing,** cursing his luck at gambling. 96. **physic,** purging by prayer, cf. l. 85 above.

King. [*Rising.*] My words fly up, my thoughts remain below:
Words without thoughts never to heaven go.
Exit.

Scene IV. *The Queen's closet.*

Enter *Queen* and *Polonius.*

Pol. 'A will come straight, look you lay home to him:
Tell him his pranks have been too broad to bear with,
And that your Grace hath screen'd and stood between
Much heat and him. I 'll silence me e'en here.
Pray you, be round with him.
Ham. [*Within.*] Mother, mother, mother!
Queen. I 'll warrant you, fear me not.
Withdraw, I hear him coming.
Polonius hides behind the arras.

Enter *Hamlet.*

Ham. Now, mother, what 's the matter?
Queen. Hamlet, thou hast thy father much offended.
Ham. Mother, you have my father much offended.
Queen. Come, come, you answer with an idle tongue.
Ham. Go, go, you question with a wicked tongue.
Queen. Why, how now, Hamlet!
Ham. What 's the matter now?
Queen. Have you forgot me?
Ham. No, by the rood, not so.
You are the Queen, your husband's brother's wife;
And would it were not so, you are my mother.
Queen. Nay, then, I 'll set those to you that can speak.
Ham. Come, come, and sit you down; you shall not budge;
You go not till I set you up a glass
Where you may see the inmost part of you.
Queen. What wilt thou do? Thou wilt not murder me?
Help, ho!
Pol. [*Behind.*] What, ho! help!
Ham. [*Drawing.*] How now! A rat? Dead, for a ducat, dead!
Kills Polonius through the arras.
Pol. [*Behind.*] O, I am slain!
Queen. O me, what hast thou done?
Ham. Nay, I know not.
Is it the King?

Scene iv: 1. **lay home,** talk straight. 2. **broad,** unrestrained. 14. **rood,** cross.

Queen. O, what a rash and bloody deed is this!
Ham. A bloody deed—almost as bad, good mother,
As kill a king, and marry with his brother.
Queen. As kill a king!
Ham. Ay, lady, it was my word.
Lifts up the arras and discovers Polonius.
Thou wretched, rash, intruding fool, farewell!
I took thee for thy better; take thy fortune;
Thou find'st to be too busy is some danger.
—Leave wringing of your hands; peace, sit you down,
And let me wring your heart; for so I shall,
If it be made of penetrable stuff,
If damned custom have not braz'd it so
That it be proof and bulwark against sense.
Queen. What have I done, that thou dar'st wag thy tongue
In noise so rude against me?
Ham. Such an act
That blurs the grace and blush of modesty,
Calls virtue hypocrite, takes off the rose
From the fair forehead of an innocent love
And sets a blister there, makes marriage-vows
As false as dicers' oaths; O, such a deed
As from the body of contraction plucks
The very soul, and sweet religion makes
A rhapsody of words. Heaven's face doth glow,
And this solidity and compound mass,
With heated visage, as against the doom,
Is thought-sick at the act.
Queen. Ay me, what act,
That roars so loud and thunders in the index?
Ham. Look here, upon this picture, and on this,
The counterfeit presentment of two brothers.
See, what a grace was seated on this brow:
Hyperion's curls, the front of Jove himself,
An eye like Mars, to threaten and command,
A station like the herald Mercury
New-lighted on a heaven-kissing hill,
A combination and a form indeed,
Where every god did seem to set his seal,
To give the world assurance of a man:
This was your husband.—Look you now what follows:
Here is your husband, like a mildew'd ear,
Blasting his wholesome brother. Have you eyes?
Could you on this fair mountain leave to feed,
And batten on this moor? Ha! have you eyes?
You cannot call it love, for at your age
The hey-day in the blood is tame, it 's humble,
And waits upon the judgement; and what judgement
Would step from this to this? Sense sure you have,
Else could you not have motion; but sure, that sense
Is apoplex'd; for madness would not err,
Nor sense to ecstasy was ne'er so thrall'd
But it reserv'd some quantity of choice,
To serve in such a difference. What devil was 't
That thus hath cozen'd you at hoodman-blind?
Eyes without feeling, feeling without sight,
Ears without hands or eyes, smelling sans all,
Or but a sickly part of one true sense
Could not so mope.
O shame! where is thy blush? Rebellious hell,
If thou canst mutine in a matron's bones,
To flaming youth let virtue be as wax,
And melt in her own fire. Proclaim no shame
When the compulsive ardour gives the charge,
Since frost itself as actively doth burn
And reason panders will.
Queen. O Hamlet, speak no more!
Thou turn'st mine eyes into my very soul,
And there I see such black and grained spots
As will leave there their tinct.
Ham. Nay, but to live
In the rank sweat of an enseamed bed,
Stew'd in corruption, honeying and making love
Over the nasty sty—
Queen. O, speak to me no more!
These words like daggers enter in mine ears.
No more, sweet Hamlet!
Ham. A murderer and a villain,
A slave that is not twentieth part the tithe
Of your precedent lord! A vice of kings,
A cutpurse of the empire and the rule,
That from a shelf the precious diadem stole,
And put it in his pocket!
Queen. No more!

Enter *Ghost* in his night-gown.

Ham. A king of shreds and patches—
Save me, and hover o'er me with your wings,
You heavenly guards! What would your gracious figure?
Queen. Alas, he 's mad!
Ham. Do you not come your tardy son to chide,
That, laps'd in time and passion, lets go by
Th' important acting of your dread command?
O, say!

37. braz'd, hardened. **38. proof,** proof armor. **sense,** feeling. **44. sets a blister,** brands as a harlot. **46. contraction,** marriage contract. **48. rhapsody,** senseless string. **49. solidity . . . mass,** the earth. **50. doom,** last Judgement. **52. index,** prologue. **58. station,** bearing. **64-5. mildew'd ear, Blasting,** a reference to Pharaoh's dream, *Genesis,* xli, 5-7. **67. batten,** feed gluttonously.

73. apoplex'd, paralyzed. **77. cozen'd,** cheated. **hoodman-blind,** blind-man's buff. **88. panders,** plays the pander to. **will,** desire. **92. enseamed,** greasy. **98. vice,** the Vice, fool and mischief-maker of the old Morality plays. **107. laps'd . . . passion,** having allowed time to pass and the passion of revenge to cool.

Ghost. Do not forget! This visitation
Is but to whet thy almost blunted purpose.
But, look, amazement on thy mother sits;
O, step between her and her fighting soul.
Conceit in weakest bodies strongest works.
Speak to her, Hamlet.

Ham. How is it with you, lady?

Queen. Alas, how is 't with you,
That you do bend your eye on vacancy
And with th' incorporal air do hold discourse?
Forth at your eyes your spirits wildly peep,
And, as the sleeping soldiers in th' alarm,
Your bedded hair, like life in excrements,
Start up and stand an end. O gentle son,
Upon the heat and flame of thy distemper
Sprinkle cool patience. Whereon do you look?

Ham. On him, on him! Look you, how pale he glares!
His form and cause conjoin'd, preaching to stones,
Would make them capable. Do not look upon me,
Lest with this piteous action you convert
My stern effects; then what I have to do
Will want true colour, tears perchance for blood.

Queen. To whom do you speak this?

Ham. Do you see nothing there?

Queen. Nothing at all, yet all that is I see.

Ham. Nor did you nothing hear?

Queen. No, nothing but ourselves.

Ham. Why, look you there! Look, how it steals away!
My father, in his habit as he lived!
Look, where he goes, even now, out at the portal! *Exit Ghost.*

Queen. This is the very coinage of your brain:
This bodiless creation ecstasy
Is very cunning in.

Ham. Ecstasy!
My pulse, as yours, doth temperately keep time,
And makes as healthful music: it is not madness
That I have utter'd: bring me to the test,
And I the matter will re-word, which madness
Would gambol from. Mother, for love of grace,
Lay not that flattering unction to your soul,
That not your trespass, but my madness speaks;
It will but skin and film the ulcerous place,
Whiles rank corruption, mining all within,
Infects unseen. Confess yourself to Heaven;

112. amazement, distraction. **114. Conceit**, imagination. **121. bedded**, laid flat. **excrements**, outgrowths, like the hair. **122. an end**, upright. **127. capable**, susceptible. **128. convert**, divert. **129. effects**, outward symptoms of his purpose. **145. unction**, ointment.

Repent what 's past, avoid what is to come,
And do not spread the compost on the weeds,
To make them ranker. Forgive me this my virtue,
For in the fatness of these pursy times
Virtue itself of vice must pardon beg,
Yea, curb and woo for leave to do him good.

Queen. O Hamlet, thou hast cleft my heart in twain.

Ham. O, throw away the worser part of it,
And live the purer with the other half.
Good-night; but go not to my uncle's bed.
Assume a virtue, if you have it not.
That monster, custom, who all sense doth eat
Of habits evil, is angel yet in this,
That to the use of actions fair and good
He likewise gives a frock or livery,
That aptly is put on. Refrain to-night,
And that shall lend a kind of easiness
To the next abstinence; the next more easy;
For use almost can change the stamp of nature,
And either curb the devil or throw him out,
With wondrous potency. Once more, good-night;
And when you are desirous to be blest,
I 'll blessing beg of you. For this same lord,
Pointing to Polonius.
I do repent; but Heaven hath pleas'd it so,
To punish me with this and this with me,
That I must be their scourge and minister.
I will bestow him, and will answer well
The death I gave him. So, again, good-night.
I must be cruel, only to be kind.
Thus bad begins and worse remains behind.
One word more, good lady.

Queen. What shall I do?

Ham. Not this, by no means, that I bid you do:
Let the bloat king tempt you again to bed,
Pinch wanton on your cheek, call you his mouse,
And let him, for a pair of reechy kisses,
Or paddling in your neck with his damn'd fingers,
Make you to ravel all this matter out,
That I essentially am not in madness,
But mad in craft. 'T were good you let him know;
For who, that 's but a queen, fair, sober, wise,
Would from a paddock, from a bat, a gib,
Such dear concernings hide? Who would do so?
No, in despite of sense and secrecy,
Unpeg the basket on the house's top,
Let the birds fly, and like the famous ape,

155. curb, bow. **161-2.** Custom which destroys all sense (i.e., recognition) of evil habits. **163. use**, practice. **169. curb**, restrain. **Cf. M. of V. IV**, i, 217. **175. their**, the Heavens'. **184. reechy**, foul. **190. paddock**, toad. **gib**, tom-cat.

To try conclusions, in the basket creep,
And break your own neck down.
Queen. Be thou assur'd, if words be made of breath,
And breath of life, I have no life to breathe
What thou hast said to me.
Ham. I must to England; you know that?
Queen. Alack,
I had forgot. 'T is so concluded on.
Ham. There 's letters seal'd, and my two school-fellows,
Whom I will trust as I will adders fang'd,
They bear the mandate; they must sweep my way,
And marshal me to knavery. Let it work;
For 't is the sport to have the enginer
Hoist with his own petar; and 't shall go hard
But I will delve one yard below their mines,
And blow them at the moon. O, 't is most sweet,
When in one line two crafts directly meet.
This man shall set me packing.
I 'll lug the guts into the neighbour room.
Mother, good-night indeed. This counsellor
Is now most still, most secret, and most grave,
Who was in life a foolish prating knave.
Come, sir, to draw toward an end with you.
Good-night, mother.
Exeunt severally, Hamlet tugging in Polonius.

ACT IV. Scene I. *A room in the castle.*

Enter *King, Queen, Rosencrantz,* and *Guildenstern.*

King. There 's matter in these sighs, these profound heaves;
You must translate, 't is fit we understand them.
Where is your son?
Queen. Bestow this place on us a little while.
Exeunt Rosencrantz and Guildenstern.
Ah, mine own lord, what have I seen to-night!
King. What, Gertrude? How does Hamlet?
Queen. Mad as the sea and wind, when both contend
Which is the mightier—in his lawless fit,
Behind the arras hearing something stir,
Whips out his rapier, cries, "A rat, a rat!"
And in this brainish apprehension kills
The unseen good old man.
King. O heavy deed!
It had been so with us, had we been there.
His liberty is full of threats to all,
To you yourself, to us, to every one.
Alas, how shall this bloody deed be answer'd?
It will be laid to us, whose providence
Should have kept short, restrain'd, and out of haunt,
This mad young man; but so much was our love,
We would not understand what was most fit,
But, like the owner of a foul disease,
To keep it from divulging, let it feed
Even on the pith of life. Where is he gone?
Queen. To draw apart the body he hath kill'd,
O'er whom his very madness, like some ore
Among a mineral of metals base,
Shows itself pure; 'a weeps for what is done.
King. O Gertrude, come away!
The sun no sooner shall the mountains touch,
But we will ship him hence, and this vile deed
We must, with all our majesty and skill,
Both countenance and excuse. Ho, Guildenstern!

Re-enter *Rosencrantz* and *Guildenstern.*

Friends both, go join you with some further aid;
Hamlet in madness hath Polonius slain,
And from his mother's closet hath he dragg'd him.
Go seek him out, speak fair, and bring the body
Into the chapel. I pray you, haste in this.
Exeunt Rosencrantz and Guildenstern.
Come, Gertrude, we 'll call up our wisest friends
To let them know both what we mean to do
And what 's untimely done; so, haply, slander
Whose whisper o'er the world's diameter,
As level as the cannon to his blank,
Transports his poison'd shot, may miss our name,

195. conclusions, experiments. **204. sweep,** clear. **Act IV, Scene i: 11. brainish,** brain-sick. **17. providence,** foresight. **18. kept short,** held on a short tether. **haunt,** company.

207. petar, bomb. **210. crafts,** (1) boats, (2) acts of guile, crafty schemes. **211. packing,** (1) hurrying, (2) plotting. **Act IV, Scene i: 26. mineral,** mine. **40. so, haply, slander,** a phrase devised by Capell to fill out a lost half-line in the original text. **42. blank,** white center of a target.

And hit the woundless air. O, come away!
My soul is full of discord and dismay.
Exeunt.

Scene II. *Another room in the castle.*

Enter *Hamlet.*

Ham. Safely stowed.

Gentlemen. [*Within.*] Hamlet! Lord Hamlet!

Ham. But soft, what noise? Who calls on Hamlet?
O, here they come.

Enter *Rosencrantz* and *Guildenstern.*

Ros. What have you done, my lord, with the dead body?

Ham. Compounded it with dust, whereto 't is kin.

Ros. Tell us where 't is, that we may take it thence
And bear it to the chapel.

Ham. Do not believe it.

Ros. Believe what?

Ham. That I can keep your counsel and not mine own. Besides, to be demanded of a sponge, what replication should be made by the son of a king?

Ros. Take you me for a sponge, my lord?

Ham. Ay, sir, that soaks up the King's countenance, his rewards, his authorities. But such officers do the King best service in the end: he keeps them, like an ape an apple, in the corner of his jaw; first mouthed, to be last swallowed: when he needs what you have gleaned, it is but squeezing you, and, sponge, you shall be dry again.

Ros. I understand you not, my lord.

Ham. I am glad of it: a knavish speech sleeps in a foolish ear.

Ros. My lord, you must tell us where the body is, and go with us to the King.

Ham. The body is with the King, but the King is not with the body. The King is a thing—

Guil. A thing, my lord!

Ham. Of nothing; bring me to him. Hide fox, and all after. *Exeunt.*

Scene III. *Another room in the castle.*

Enter *King* and two or three.

King. I have sent to seek him, and to find the body.
How dangerous is it that this man goes loose!
Yet must not we put the strong law on him;
He 's lov'd of the distracted multitude,
Who like not in their judgement, but their eyes,
And where 't is so, the offender's scourge is weigh'd,
But never the offence. To bear all smooth and even,
This sudden sending him away must seem
Deliberate pause. Diseases desperate grown
By desperate appliance are reliev'd,
Or not at all.

Enter *Rosencrantz* and others.

How now! What hath befall'n?

Ros. Where the dead body is bestow'd, my lord,
We cannot get from him.

King. But where is he?

Ros. Without, my lord, guarded, to know your pleasure.

King. Bring him before us.

Ros. Ho! bring in the lord.

Enter *Hamlet* guarded and *Guildenstern.*

King. Now, Hamlet, where 's Polonius?

Ham. At supper.

King. At supper! Where?

Ham. Not where he eats, but where 'a is eaten: a certain convocation of politic worms are e'en at him. Your worm is your only emperor for diet: we fat all creatures else to fat us, and we fat ourselves for maggots. Your fat king and your lean beggar is but variable service, two dishes, but to one table; that 's the end.

King. Alas, alas!

Ham. A man may fish with the worm that hath eat of a king, and eat of the fish that hath fed of that worm.

King. What dost thou mean by this?

Ham. Nothing but to show you how a king may go a progress through the guts of a beggar.

King. Where is Polonius?

Ham. In heaven; send thither to see: if your messenger find him not there, seek him i' th' other place yourself. But if indeed, you find him not within this month, you shall nose him as you go up the stairs into the lobby.

King. Go seek him there.
To some Attendants.

Ham. 'A will stay till you come.
Exeunt Attendants.

King. Hamlet, this deed, for thine especial safety,—
Which we do tender, as we dearly grieve

44. woundless, invulnerable. **Scene ii: 12. demanded of,** questioned by. **13. replication,** reply. **17. countenance,** favor. **32-3. Hide fox,** a game like hide-and-seek. Hamlet seems to have rushed away here.

Scene iii: 6. scourge, punishment. **7. bear,** carry out. **21. politic,** cunning. **24. variable service,** different courses. **33. progress,** royal journey. **43. tender,** hold dear.

For that which thou hast done,—must send thee hence
With fiery quickness; therefore prepare thyself.
The bark is ready, and the wind at help,
Th' associates tend, and everything is bent
For England.

Ham. For England?

King. Ay, Hamlet.

Ham. Good.

King. So is it, if thou knew'st our purposes.

Ham. I see a cherub that sees them. But, come, for England! Farewell, dear mother.

King. Thy loving father, Hamlet.

Ham. My mother: father and mother is man and wife, man and wife is one flesh, and so, my mother. Come, for England! *Exit.*

King. Follow him at foot, tempt him with speed aboard,
Delay it not; I 'll have him hence to-night.
Away! for everything is seal'd and done
That else leans on th' affair, pray you, make haste.

Exeunt Rosencrantz and Guildenstern.

And, England, if my love thou hold'st at aught,—
As my great power thereof may give thee sense,
Since yet thy cicatrice looks raw and red
After the Danish sword, and thy free awe
Pays homage to us—thou mayst not coldly set
Our sovereign process, which imports at full,
By letters congruing to that effect,
The present death of Hamlet. Do it, England;
For like the hectic in my blood he rages,
And thou must cure me: till I know 't is done,
Howe'er my haps, my joys were ne'er begun. *Exit.*

Scene IV. *A plain in Denmark.*

Enter *Fortinbras*, and a *Captain*, with his army over the stage.

For. Go, captain, from me greet the Danish king.
Tell him that, by his license, Fortinbras
Craves the conveyance of a promis'd march
Over his kingdom. You know the rendezvous.
If that his Majesty would aught with us,
We shall express our duty in his eye;
And let him know so.

Cap. I will do 't, my lord.

For. Go softly on.

Exeunt Fortinbras and army.

Enter *Hamlet, Rosencrantz, Guildenstern* and others.

Ham. Good sir, whose powers are these?

Cap. They are of Norway, sir.

Ham. How purpos'd, sir, I pray you?

Cap. Against some part of Poland.

Ham. Who commands them, sir?

Cap. The nephew to old Norway, Fortinbras.

Ham. Goes it against the main of Poland, sir,
Or for some frontier?

Cap. Truly to speak, and with no addition,
We go to gain a little patch of ground
That hath in it no profit but the name.
To pay five ducats, five, I would not farm it:
Nor will it yield to Norway or the Pole
A ranker rate, should it be sold in fee.

Ham. Why, then the Polack never will defend it.

Cap. Yes, it is already garrison'd.

Ham. Two thousand souls and twenty thousand ducats
Will not debate the question of this straw.
This is th' imposthume of much wealth and peace,
That inward breaks, and shows no cause without
Why the man dies. I humbly thank you, sir.

Cap. God buy you, sir. *Exit.*

Ros. Will 't please you go, my lord?

Ham. I 'll be with you straight; go a little before. *Exeunt all except Hamlet.*
How all occasions do inform against me,
And spur my dull revenge! What is a man,
If his chief good and market of his time
Be but to sleep and feed? A beast, no more.
Sure He that made us with such large discourse,
Looking before and after, gave us not
That capability and god-like reason
To fust in us unus'd. Now, whether it be
Bestial oblivion, or some craven scruple
Of thinking too precisely on th' event,—
A thought which, quarter'd, hath but one part wisdom
And ever three parts coward,—I do not know
Why yet I live to say, "This thing 's to do,"
Sith I have cause and will and strength and means
To do 't: examples gross as earth exhort me;

47. tend, wait. **50. cherub,** angel of knowledge. **56. at foot,** close. **59. leans,** depends. **62. cicatrice,** scar. **63. free,** uncompelled. **64. coldly set,** regard slightly. **65. process,** command. **68. hectic,** fever. **Scene iv: 3. conveyance,** convoy. **6. in his eye,** in his presence.

8. softly, slowly. **15. the main,** the whole. **22. ranker,** higher. **fee,** fee simple, outright. **26. debate,** settle. **27. imposthume,** abscess. **34. market,** purchase. **36. discourse,** understanding. **39. fust,** grow mouldy. **40. oblivion,** forgetfulness. **41. event,** result.

Witness this army of such mass and charge
Led by a delicate and tender prince,
Whose spirit with divine ambition puff'd
Makes mouths at the invisible event,
Exposing what is mortal and unsure
To all that fortune, death, and danger dare,
Even for an egg-shell. Rightly to be great
Is not to stir without great argument,
But greatly to find quarrel in a straw
When honour 's at the stake. How stand I then,
That have a father kill'd, a mother stain'd,
Excitements of my reason and my blood,
And let all sleep, while to my shame I see
The imminent death of twenty thousand men,
That for a fantasy and trick of fame
Go to their graves like beds, fight for a plot
Whereon the numbers cannot try the cause,
Which is not tomb enough and continent
To hide the slain? O, from this time forth,
My thoughts be bloody, or be nothing worth!
Exit.

Scene V. *Elsinore. A room in the castle.*

Enter *Queen, Horatio,* and a *Gentleman.*

Queen. I will not speak with her.
Gent. She is importunate, indeed distract;
Her mood will needs be pitied.
Queen. What would she have?
Gent. She speaks much of her father; says she hears
There 's tricks i' th' world, and hems, and beats her heart,
Spurns enviously at straws, speaks things in doubt
That carry but half sense. Her speech is nothing,
Yet the unshaped use of it doth move
The hearers to collection. They yawn at it
And botch the words up fit to their own thoughts;
Which, as her winks, and nods, and gestures yield them,
Indeed would make one think there would be thought,
Though nothing sure, yet much unhappily.
Hor. 'T were good she were spoken with, for she may strew
Dangerous conjectures in ill-breeding minds.
Let her come in. *Exit Gentleman.*
Queen. [*Aside.*] To my sick soul, as sin's true nature is,
Each toy seems prologue to some great amiss;
So full of artless jealousy is guilt,
It spills itself in fearing to be spilt.

Enter *Ophelia,* distracted.

Oph. Where is the beauteous majesty of Denmark?
Queen. How now, Ophelia!
Oph. [*Sings.*]

How should I your true love know
From another one?
By his cockle hat and staff,
And his sandal shoon.

Queen. Alas, sweet lady, what imports this song?
Oph. Say you? Nay, pray you, mark.
[*Sings.*]

He is dead and gone, lady,
He is dead and gone;
At his head a grass-green turf
At his heels a stone.

Enter *King.*

Queen. Nay, but, Ophelia,—
Oph. Pray you, mark.
[*Sings.*]

White his shroud as the mountain snow,—

Queen. Alas, look here, my lord.
Oph. [*Sings.*]

Larded all with sweet flowers;
Which bewept to the ground did not go
With true-love showers.

King. How do you, pretty lady?
Oph. Well, God 'ild you! They say the owl was a baker's daughter. Lord, we know what we are, but know not what we may be. God be at your table!
King. Conceit upon her father.
Oph. Pray let 's have no words of this, but when they ask you what it means, say you this:
[*Sings.*]

To-morrow is Saint Valentine's day,
All in the morning betime,
And I a maid at your window,
To be your Valentine.

Then up he rose and donn'd his clothes,
And dupp'd the chamber door;
Let in the maid, that out a maid
Never departed more.

47. charge, expense. **54. argument,** reason. **58. Excitements,** incentives. **64. continent,** receptacle. **Scene v: 6. spurns,** kicks. **in doubt,** uncertainly. **9. collection,** inference. **yawn,** gape, wonder. **13. much unhappily,** expressing much ill-fortune.

18. amiss, misfortune. **20. spills,** destroys. **25. cockle hat,** a cockle shell in the hat was the sign of a pilgrim; a pilgrim's garb was sometimes a disguise for lovers, as in *R. and J.* **26. shoon,** shoes. **37. Larded,** garnished. **41. 'ild,** reward. **the owl,** referring to a legend that a baker's daughter was turned into an owl for refusing bread to our Lord. **53. dupp'd,** did up, opened.

King. Pretty Ophelia!

Oph. Indeed, without an oath I 'll make an end on 't.

> By gis, and by Saint Charity,
> Alack, and fie for shame!
> Young men will do 't, if they come to 't;
> By Cock, they are to blame.
>
> Quoth she, "Before you tumbled me,
> You promis'd me to wed."
>
> He answers:
> "So would I ha' done, by yonder sun,
> An thou hadst not come to my bed."

King. How long hath she been thus?

Oph. I hope all will be well. We must be patient; but I cannot choose but weep, to think they should lay him i' th' cold ground. My brother shall know of it; and so I thank you for your good counsel. Come, my coach! Good-night, ladies; good-night, sweet ladies; good-night, good-night. *Exit.*

King. Follow her close; give her good watch, I pray you.
Exeunt Horatio and Gentleman.
O, this is the poison of deep grief; it springs
All from her father's death—and now behold!
O Gertrude, Gertrude,
When sorrows come, they come not single spies,
But in battalions. First, her father slain;
Next, your son gone; and he most violent author
Of his own just remove; the people muddied,
Thick and unwholesome in their thoughts and whispers,
For good Polonius' death; and we have done but greenly
In hugger-mugger to inter him; poor Ophelia
Divided from herself and her fair judgement,
Without the which we are pictures, or mere beasts;
Last, and as much containing as all these,
Her brother is in secret come from France,
Feeds on his wonder, keeps himself in clouds,
And wants not buzzers to infect his ear
With pestilent speeches of his father's death,
Wherein necessity, of matter beggar'd,
Will nothing stick our persons to arraign
In ear and ear. O my dear Gertrude, this,
Like to a murd'ring-piece, in many places
Gives me superfluous death. *A noise within.*

Queen. Alack, what noise is this?

King. Attend! *Enter a Messenger.*
Where is my Switzers? Let them guard the door.
What is the matter?

Mess. Save yourself, my lord!
The ocean, overpeering of his list,
Eats not the flats with more impiteous haste
Than young Laertes, in a riotous head,
O'erbears your officers: the rabble call him lord;
And, as the world were now but to begin,
Antiquity forgot, custom not known,
The ratifiers and props of every word,
They cry, "Choose we! Laertes shall be king!"
Caps, hands, and tongues applaud it to the clouds,
"Laertes shall be king, Laertes king!"

Queen. How cheerfully on the false trail they cry!
O, this is counter, you false Danish dogs!

Noise within. Enter *Laertes* with other Danes.

King. The doors are broke.

Laer. Where is this king? Sirs, stand you all without.

Danes. No, let 's come in.

Laer. I pray you, give me leave.

Danes. We will, we will.
They retire without the door.

Laer. I thank you; keep the door. O thou vile king,
Give me my father!

Queen. Calmly, good Laertes.

Laer. That drop of blood that 's calm proclaims me bastard,
Cries cuckold to my father, brands the harlot
Even here, between the chaste unsmirched brow
Of my true mother.

King. What is the cause, Laertes,
That thy rebellion looks so giant-like?
Let him go, Gertrude; do not fear our person:
There 's such divinity doth hedge a king,
That treason can but peep to what it would,
Acts little of his will. Tell me, Laertes,
Why thou art thus incens'd. Let him go, Gertrude.
Speak, man.

Laer. Where is my father?

King. Dead.

Queen. But not by him.

King. Let him demand his fill.

Laer. How came he dead? I 'll not be juggled with.
To hell allegiance! Vows to the blackest devil!
Conscience and grace to the profoundest pit!
I dare damnation. To this point I stand,

gis, a corruption of Jesus. **62. Cock,** God. **81. muddied,** muddled. **83. greenly,** foolishly. **84. in hugger-mugger,** in secret haste. **89. wonder,** doubt. **in clouds,** invisible. **90. buzzers,** tale-bearers. **95. murd'ring-piece,** cannon loaded with case-shot.

97. Switzers, Swiss Guards. **99. list,** shore. **101. head,** armed force. **110. counter,** on the wrong scent.

That both the worlds I give to negligence,
Let come what comes; only I 'll be reveng'd
Most throughly for my father.
King. Who shall stay you?
Laer. My will, not all the world's:
And for my means, I 'll husband them so well,
They shall go far with little.
King. Good Laertes,
If you desire to know the certainty
Of your dear father, is 't writ in your revenge
That, swoopstake, you will draw both friend and foe,
Winner and loser?
Laer. None but his enemies.
King. Will you know them then?
Laer. To his good friends thus wide I 'll ope my arms,
And like the kind life-rend'ring pelican,
Repast them with my blood.
King. Why, now you speak
Like a good child and a true gentleman.
That I am guiltless of your father's death,
And am most sensibly in grief for it,
It shall as level to your judgement 'pear,
As day does to your eye.
A noise within. "Let her come in!"
Laer. How now! what noise is that?

Re-enter *Ophelia.*

O heat, dry up my brains! Tears seven times salt
Burn out the sense and virtue of mine eye!
By heaven, thy madness shall be paid with weight
Till our scale turn the beam. O rose of May!
Dear maid, kind sister, sweet Ophelia!
O heavens! is 't possible, a young maid's wits
Should be as mortal as an old man's life?
Nature is fine in love, and where 't is fine,
It sends some precious instance of itself
After the thing it loves.
Oph. [*Sings.*]

They bore him barefac'd on the bier;
Hey non nonny, nonny, hey nonny;
And in his grave rain'd many a tear,—

Fare you well, my dove!
Laer. Hadst thou thy wits and didst persuade revenge,
It could not move thus.

Oph. You must sing, "A-down a-down, and you call him a-down-a." O, how the wheel becomes it! It is the false steward, that stole his master's daughter.

Laer. This nothing 's more than matter.

Oph. There 's rosemary, that 's for remembrance; pray you, love, remember; and there is pansies, that 's for thoughts.

Laer. A document in madness, thoughts and remembrance fitted.

Oph. There 's fennel for you, and columbines; there 's rue for you, and here 's some for me; we may call it herb of grace o' Sundays; O, you must wear your rue with a difference. There 's a daisy. I would give you some violets, but they withered all when my father died; they say 'a made a good end,—
[*Sings.*]

For bonny sweet Robin is all my joy.

Laer. Thought and affliction, passion, hell itself,
She turns to favour and to prettiness.
Oph. [*Sings.*]

And will 'a not come again?
And will 'a not come again?
No, no, he is dead;
Go to thy death-bed;
He never will come again.

His beard was as white as snow,
All flaxen was his poll.
He is gone, he is gone,
And we cast away moan.
God ha' mercy on his soul!

And of all Christian souls, I pray God. God buy ye. *Exit.*
Laer. Do you see this, O God?
King. Laertes, I must commune with your grief,
Or you deny me right. Go but apart,
Make choice of whom your wisest friends you will,
And they shall hear and judge 'twixt you and me.
If by direct or by collateral hand
They find us touch'd, we will our kingdom give,
Our crown, our life, and all that we call ours,
To you in satisfaction; but if not,
Be you content to lend your patience to us,
And we shall jointly labour with your soul
To give it due content.
Laer. Let this be so.
His means of death, his obscure burial,
No trophy, sword, nor hatchment o'er his bones,
No noble rite nor formal ostentation,

142. **swoopstake,** the whole stake at once, indiscriminately. 146. **pelican,** according to old legend the pelican fed its young with its own blood. 151. **'pear,** appear. 161. **fine,** delicate. 162. **instance of itself,** a precious sample of itself, i.e., Ophelia's wits, sent after Polonius. 172. **wheel,** refrain, perhaps reminiscent of the nurse's spinning wheel at which she had learned the song.

174. **more,** more touching. 175-85. There is a symbolic meaning in her distribution of the flowers: to Laertes **rosemary** and **pansies** (*pensées*); to Claudius **fennel,** flattery and **columbines,** ingratitude; to the Queen and herself **rue,** symbolic of sorrow. The **difference** (an heraldic term denoting a distinction between two like coats of arms) is that **rue** for the Queen meant repentence. for herself regret. Then she gives the Queen a **daisy** (unfaithfulness) and no **violets** (fidelity). 207. **touch'd,** implicated. 214. **hatchment,** tablet bearing the coat of arms of the dead.

Cry to be heard, as 't were from heaven to earth,
That I must call 't in question.

King. So you shall;
And where th' offence is let the great axe fall.
I pray you, go with me. *Exeunt.*

Scene VI. *Another room in the castle.*

Enter *Horatio* with an *Attendant.*

Hor. What are they that would speak with me?

Att. Sea-faring men, sir; they say they have letters for you.

Hor. Let them come in. *Exit Attendant.*
I do not know from what part of the world
I should be greeted, if not from Lord Hamlet.

Enter *Sailors.*

First Sail. God bless you, sir.

Hor. Let Him bless thee too.

First Sail. 'A shall, sir, an 't please Him. There 's a letter for you, sir—it came from th' ambassador that was bound for England—if your name be Horatio, as I am let to know it is.

Hor. [*Reads.*]

"Horatio, when thou shalt have overlooked this, give these fellows some means to the King; they have letters for him. Ere we were two days old at sea, a pirate of very warlike appointment gave us chase. Finding ourselves too slow of sail, we put on a compelled valour and in the grapple I boarded them. On the instant they got clear of our ship, so I alone became their prisoner. They have dealt with me like thieves of mercy, but they knew what they did: I am to do a good turn for them. Let the King have the letters I have sent, and repair thou to me with as much haste as thou wouldest fly death. I have words to speak in thine ear will make thee dumb, yet are they much too light for the bore of the matter. These good fellows will bring thee where I am. Rosencrantz and Guildenstern hold their course for England; of them I have much to tell thee. Farewell.

He that thou knowest thine,
HAMLET."

Come, I will give you way for these your letters;
And do 't the speedier, that you may direct me
To him from whom you brought them. *Exeunt.*

Scene VII. *Another room in the castle.*

Fnter *King* and *Laertes.*

King. Now must your conscience my acquittance seal;
And you must put me in your heart for friend,
Sith you have heard, and with a knowing ear,
That he which hath your noble father slain
Pursued my life.

Laer. It well appears: but tell me
Why you proceeded not against these feats,
So criminal and so capital in nature,
As by your safety, wisdom, all things else,
You mainly were stirr'd up.

King. O, for two special reasons,
Which may to you, perhaps, seem much unsinew'd,
And yet to me they are strong. The Queen his mother
Lives almost by his looks; and for myself—
My virtue or my plague, be it either which—
She is so conjunctive to my life and soul,
That, as the star moves not but in his sphere,
I could not but by her. The other motive
Why to a public count I might not go,
Is the great love the general gender bear him;
Who, dipping all his faults in their affection,
Would, like the spring that turneth wood to stone,
Convert his gyves to graces; so that my arrows,
Too slightly timber'd for so loud a wind,
Would have reverted to my bow again,
And not where I have aim'd them.

Laer. And so have I a noble father lost,
A sister driven into desp'rate terms,
Whose worth, if praises may go back again,
Stood challenger on mount of all the age
For her perfections. But my revenge will come.

King. Break not your sleeps for that; you must not think
That we are made of stuff so flat and dull
That we can let our beard be shook with danger
And think it pastime. You shortly shall hear more.
I lov'd your father, and we love ourself,
And that, I hope, will teach you to imagine—

Enter a *Messenger* with letters.

How now! What news?

Mess. Letters, my lord, from Hamlet.
These to your Majesty; this to the Queen.

King. From Hamlet! Who brought them?

Mess. Sailors, my lord, they say; I saw them not.

Scene vi: 14. appointment, equipment. **25. bore,** calibre; here, importance.

7. capital, deserving death. **10. unsinew'd,** weak. **14. conjunctive,** closely united. **15. sphere,** according to Ptolemy's astronomy stars were set in spheres which revolved about the earth. **17. count,** reckoning. **18. general gender,** common people. **20.** A spring in Shakespeare's county was so charged with lime that it would petrify a bit of wood placed in it. **21. gyves,** fetters. **27-9.** "Whose worth, if praise may revert to what is past and gone, stood challenger on high to the age to deny her perfection."

They were given me by Claudio. He received them
Of him that brought them.
King. Laertes, you shall hear them.
Leave us. *Exit Messenger.*
[*Reads.*]

"High and mighty, You shall know I am set naked on your kingdom. To-morrow shall I beg leave to see your kingly eyes, when I shall, first asking you pardon, thereunto recount the occasion of my sudden and more strange return.
HAMLET."

What should this mean? Are all the rest come back?
Or is it some abuse, and no such thing?
Laer. Know you the hand?
King. 'T is Hamlet's character. "Naked!"
And in a postscript here, he says, "alone."
Can you devise me?
Laer. I 'm lost in it, my lord; but let him come:
It warms the very sickness in my heart
That I shall live and tell him to his teeth,
"Thus didest thou."
King. If it be so, Laertes,—
And how should it be so? How otherwise?—
Will you be rul'd by me?
Laer. Ay, my lord,
So you will not o'errule me to a peace.
King. To thine own peace. If he be now return'd,
As checking at his voyage, and that he means
No more to undertake it, I will work him
To an exploit, now ripe in my device,
Under the which he shall not choose but fall;
And for his death no wind of blame shall breathe,
But even his mother shall uncharge the practice
And call it accident.
Laer. My lord, I will be rul'd;
That rather, if you could devise it so
That I might be the organ.
King. It falls right.
You have been talk'd of since your travel much,
And that in Hamlet's hearing, for a quality
Wherein, they say, you shine. Your sum of parts
Did not together pluck such envy from him
As did that one, and that, in my regard,
Of the unworthiest siege.
Laer. What part is that, my lord?
King. A very riband in the cap of youth,
Yet needful too; for youth no less becomes
The light and careless livery that it wears
Than settled age his sables and his weeds,
Importing health and graveness. Two months since,
Here was a gentleman of Normandy;—
I have seen myself, and serv'd against, the French,
And they can well on horseback; but this gallant
Had witchcraft in 't; he grew unto his seat,
And to such wondrous doing brought his horse,
As had he been incorps'd and demi-natur'd
With the brave beast. So far he topp'd my thought,
That I, in forgery of shapes and tricks,
Come short of what he did.
Laer. A Norman, was 't?
King. A Norman.
Laer. Upon my life, Lamound.
King. The very same.
Laer. I know him well: he is the brooch indeed
And gem of all their nation.
King. He made confession of you,
And gave you such a masterly report
For art and exercise in your defence,
And for your rapier most especial,
That he cried out, 't would be a sight indeed
If one could match you. The scrimers of their nation,
He swore, had neither motion, guard, nor eye,
If you oppos'd them. Sir, this report of his
Did Hamlet so envenom with his envy
That he could nothing do but wish and beg
Your sudden coming o'er to play with you.
Now, out of this—
Laer. What out of this, my lord?
King. Laertes, was your father dear to you?
Or are you like the painting of a sorrow,
A face without a heart?
Laer. Why ask you this?
King. Not that I think you did not love your father,
But that I know love is begun by time,
And that I see, in passages of proof,
Time qualifies the spark and fire of it.
There lives within the very flame of love
A kind of wick or snuff that will abate it,
And nothing is at a like goodness still;
For goodness, growing to a plurisy,
Dies in his own too much. That we would do,
We should do when we would; for this "would" changes,
And hath abatements and delays as many
As there are tongues, are hands, are accidents;

44. naked, destitute. **50. abuse,** deception. **52. character,** handwriting. **54. devise,** advise. **63. checking at,** turning away from, a term of falconry. **68. uncharge the practice,** not charge the device with treachery. **71. organ,** instrument. **77. siege,** rank.

90. forgery, invention. **93. Lamound,** possibly Pietro Monte (La Mont), a famous cavalier. **96. confession,** report. **101. scrimers,** fencers. **113. passages of proof,** proved cases. **117. still,** always. **118. plurisy,** excess.

And then this "should" is like a spendthrift sigh,
That hurts by easing. But, to the quick of th' ulcer—
Hamlet comes back. What would you undertake,
To show yourself in deed your father's son
More than in words?

Laer. To cut his throat i' th' church.

King. No place, indeed, should murder sanctuarize;
Revenge should have no bounds. But, good Laertes,
Will you do this, keep close within your chamber.
Hamlet return'd shall know you are come home:
We 'll put on those shall praise your excellence
And set a double varnish on the fame
The Frenchman gave you, bring you in fine together
And wager on your heads; he, being remiss,
Most generous and free from all contriving,
Will not peruse the foils, so that, with ease,
Or with a little shuffling, you may choose
A sword unbated, and in a pass of practice
Requite him for your father.

Laer. I will do 't;
And, for that purpose, I 'll anoint my sword.
I bought an unction of a mountebank,
So mortal that, but dip a knife in it,
Where it draws blood no cataplasm so rare,
Collected from all simples that have virtue
Under the moon, can save the thing from death
That is but scratch'd withal. I 'll touch my point
With this contagion, that, if I gall him slightly,
It may be death.

King. Let 's further think of this,
Weigh what convenience both of time and means
May fit us to our shape. If this should fail,
And that our drift look through our bad performance,
'T were better not assay'd; therefore this project
Should have a back or second, that might hold
If this did blast in proof. Soft! let me see:
We 'll make a solemn wager on your cunnings—
I ha 't!
When in your motion you are hot and dry—
As make your bouts more violent to that end—
And that he calls for drink, I 'll have preferr'd him
A chalice for the nonce, whereon but sipping,
If he by chance escape your venom'd stuck,
Our purpose may hold there. But stay, what noise?

Enter *Queen.*

Queen. One woe doth tread upon another's heel,
So fast they follow: your sister 's drown'd, Laertes.

Laer. Drown'd! O, where?

Queen. There is a willow grows askant the brook,
That shows his hoar leaves in the glassy stream,
Therewith fantastic garlands did she make
Of crow-flowers, nettles, daisies, and long purples
That liberal shepherds give a grosser name,
But our cold maids do dead men's fingers call them;
There, on the pendent boughs her cronet weeds
Clamb'ring to hang, an envious sliver broke,
When down her weedy trophies and herself
Fell in the weeping brook. Her clothes spread wide,
And, mermaid-like, awhile they bore her up;
Which time she chanted snatches of old lauds,
As one incapable of her own distress,
Or like a creature native and indued
Unto that element. But long it could not be
Till that her garments, heavy with their drink,
Pull'd the poor wretch from her melodious lay
To muddy death.

Laer. Alas, then, she is drown'd.

Queen. Drown'd, drown'd.

Laer. Too much of water hast thou, poor Ophelia,
And therefore I forbid my tears; but yet
It is our trick: nature her custom holds,
Let shame say what it will; when these are gone,
The woman will be out. Adieu, my lord;
I have a speech o' fire that fain would blaze,
But that this folly drowns it. *Exit.*

King. Let 's follow, Gertrude.
How much I had to do to calm his rage!
Now fear I this will give it start again,
Therefore let 's follow. *Exeunt.*

123. spendthrift sigh, sighing was supposed to thin the blood and so shorten life. **128. sanctuarize,** afford sanctuary (protection) to. **134. in fine,** finally. **139. unbated,** not blunted. **142. mountebank,** quack. **144. cataplasm,** poultice. **145. simples,** herbs. **virtue,** healing power. **151. shape,** role. **155. blast in proof,** burst in the testing (like a cannon).

160. preferr'd, offered. **161. nonce,** occasion. **162. stuck,** thrust. **168. hoar,** grey-white. **169. Therewith,** with willow twigs. **171. liberal,** free-spoken. **173. cronet,** coronet. **178. lauds,** psalms of praise. **179. incapable,** without understanding. **180. indued,** in harmony with. **188. trick,** way.

ACT V. SCENE I. *A churchyard.*

Enter two *Clowns* with spades and pickaxes.

First Clo. Is she to be buried in Christian burial when she wilfully seeks her own salvation?

Second Clo. I tell thee she is, therefore make her grave straight. The crowner hath sat on her, and finds it Christian burial.

First Clo. How can that be, unless she drowned herself in her own defence?

Second Clo. Why, 't is found so.

First Clo. It must be *"se offendendo,"* it cannot be else. For here lies the point: if I drown myself wittingly, it argues an act, and an act hath three branches; it is, to act, to do, and to perform; argal, she drowned herself wittingly.

Second Clo. Nay, but hear you, goodman delver,—

First Clo. Give me leave. Here lies the water; good. Here stands the man; good. If the man go to this water and drown himself, it is, will he, nill he, he goes,—mark you that? But if the water come to him and drown him, he drowns not himself; argal, he that is not guilty of his own death shortens not his own life.

Second Clo. But is this law?

First Clo. Ay, marry, is 't; crowner's quest law.

Second Clo. Will you ha' the truth on 't? If this had not been a gentlewoman, she should have been buried out o' Christian burial.

First Clo. Why, there thou say'st; and the more pity that great folk should have countenance in this world to drown or hang themselves, more than their even Christian. Come, my spade! There is no ancient gentlemen but gardeners, ditchers, and grave-makers; they hold up Adam's profession.

Second Clo. Was he a gentleman?

First Clo. 'A was the first that ever bore arms.

Second Clo. Why, he had none.

First Clo. What, art a heathen? How dost thou understand the Scripture? The Scripture says Adam digged; could he dig without arms? I 'll put another question to thee. If thou answerest me not to the purpose, confess thyself—

Second Clo. Go to.

First Clo. What is he that builds stronger than either the mason, the shipwright, or the carpenter?

Second Clo. The gallows-maker; for that frame outlives a thousand tenants.

First Clo. I like thy wit well, in good faith. The gallows does well; but how does it well? It does well to those that do ill. Now, thou dost ill to say the gallows is built stronger than the church, argal, the gallows may do well to thee. To 't again, come.

Second Clo. "Who builds stronger than a mason, a shipwright, or a carpenter?"

First Clo. Ay, tell me that, and unyoke.

Second Clo. Marry, now I can tell.

First Clo. To 't.

Second Clo. Mass, I cannot tell.

First Clo. Cudgel thy brains no more about it, for your dull ass will not mend his pace with beating; and, when you are asked this question next, say "a grave-maker"; the houses that he makes lasts till doomsday. Go, get thee in; and fetch me a stoup of liquor. *Exit Second Clown.*

He digs, and sings.

In youth, when I did love, did love,
Methought it was very sweet,
To contract, O, the time for-a-my behove,
O, methought, there-a-was nothing-a meet.

Enter *Hamlet* and *Horatio.*

Ham. Has this fellow no feeling of his business? 'A sings at grave-making.

Hor. Custom hath made it in him a property of easiness.

Ham. 'T is e'en so: the hand of little employment hath the daintier sense.

First Clo. [*Sings.*]

But age, with his stealing steps,
Hath clawed me in his clutch,
And hath shipped me into the land,
As if I had never been such.

Throws up a skull.

Ham. That skull had a tongue in it, and could sing once. How the knave jowls it to the ground, as if it were Cain's jaw-bone, that did the first murder! This might be the pate of a politician, which this ass now o'erreaches; one that would circumvent God, might it not?

Hor. It might, my lord.

Ham. Or of a courtier, which could say, "Good morrow, sweet lord! How dost thou,

4. crowner, coroner. **9.** *se offendendo,* for *se defendendo,* a legal term meaning "in self defence." **13. argal,** ergo. **24. quest,** inquest. **30. countenance,** privilege. **32. even,** fellow.

59. unyoke, knock off. **67. stoup,** flagon. **71. behove,** advantage. **75-6. in . . . easiness,** easy for him. **84. jowls,** hurls. **85. Cain's jaw-bone,** according to legend Cain slew Abel with the jaw-bone of an ass. **87. o'erreaches,** outwits.

Conjures the wand'ring stars and makes them stand
Like wonder-wounded hearers? This is I,
Hamlet, the Dane!

Laer. The devil take thy soul!

Grappling with him.

Ham. Thou pray'st not well.
I prithee, take thy fingers from my throat,
For, though I am not splenitive and rash,
Yet have I something in me dangerous,
Which let thy wiseness fear. Hold off thy hand!

King. Pluck them asunder.

Queen. Hamlet, Hamlet!

All. Gentlemen,—

Hor. Good my lord, be quiet.

The Attendants part them.

Ham. Why, I will fight with him upon this theme
Until my eyelids will no longer wag.

Queen. O my son, what theme?

Ham. I lov'd Ophelia: forty thousand brothers
Could not, with all their quantity of love,
Make up my sum. What wilt thou do for her?

King. O, he is mad, Laertes.

Queen. For love of God, forbear him.

Ham. 'Swounds, show me what thou 't do.
Woo 't weep? Woo 't fight? Woo 't fast? Woo 't tear thyself?
Woo 't drink up eisel? Eat a crocodile?
I 'll do 't. Dost come here to whine?
To outface me with leaping in her grave?
Be buried quick with her, and so will I;
And, if thou prate of mountains, let them throw
Millions of acres on us, till our ground,
Singeing his pate against the burning zone,
Make Ossa like a wart! Nay, an thou 'lt mouth,
I 'll rant as well as thou.

Queen. This is mere madness,
And thus a while the fit will work on him;
Anon, as patient as the female dove,
When that her golden couplets are disclos'd,
His silence will sit drooping.

Ham. Hear you, sir,
What is the reason that you use me thus?
I lov'd you ever. But it is no matter.
Let Hercules himself do what he may,
The cat will mew and dog will have his day.

Exit.

King. I pray thee, good Horatio, wait upon him. *Exit Horatio.*
[*To Laertes.*] Strengthen your patience in our last night's speech;
We 'll put the matter to the present push.
Good Gertrude, set some watch over your son.
This grave shall have a living monument.
An hour of quiet shortly shall we see;
Till then, in patience our proceeding be.

Exeunt.

Scene II. *A hall in the castle.*

Enter *Hamlet* and *Horatio.*

Ham. So much for this, sir; now you shall see the other—
You do remember all the circumstance?

Hor. Remember it, my lord!

Ham. Sir, in my heart there was a kind of fighting,
That would not let me sleep; methought I lay
Worse than the mutines in the bilboes. Rashly,—
And prais'd be rashness for it: let us know
Our indiscretion sometime serves us well
When our deep plots do pall; and that should learn us
There 's a divinity that shapes our ends,
Rough-hew them how we will—

Hor. That is most certain.

Ham. Up from my cabin,
My sea-gown scarf'd about me, in the dark
Grop'd I to find out them, had my desire,
Finger'd their packet; and in fine withdrew
To mine own room again, making so bold,
My fears forgetting manners, to unseal
Their grand commission; where I found, Horatio,—
Ah, royal knavery!—an exact command,
Larded with many several sorts of reasons
Importing Denmark's health and England's too,
With, ho! such bugs and goblins in my life,
That, on the supervise, no leisure bated,
No, not to stay the grinding of the axe,
My head should be struck off.

Hor. Is 't possible?

Ham. Here 's the commission; read it at more leisure.
But wilt thou hear now how I did proceed?

Hor. I beseech you.

Ham. Being thus be-netted round with villainies,—
Ere I could make a prologue to my brains,

279. wand'ring stars, planets. **281.** The s. d. **Leaps into the grave,** found in most editions, is not in the authentic texts. It is an old stage practice, recently abandoned. **284. splenitive,** the spleen was thought to be the seat of anger. **209. eisel,** vinegar, cf. *Sonnet, cxi.* It was used also of the bitter drink offered Christ on the cross. **305. burning zone,** sun's orbit. **310. golden couplets,** the dove lays two eggs and the newly hatched young are covered with golden down.

318. present push, immediate test. **320. living,** lasting. **Scene ii: 6. mutines,** mutineers. **bilboes,** fetters. **9. pall,** fail. **15. Finger'd,** stole. **22. such . . . life,** such bugbears and imagined terrors if I were allowed to live. **23. supervise,** reading. **leisure bated,** delay allowed.

They had begun the play,—I sat me down,
Devis'd a new commission, wrote it fair;
I once did hold it, as our statists do,
A baseness to write fair, and labour'd much
How to forget that learning; but, sir, now
It did me yeoman's service. Wilt thou know
Th' effect of what I wrote?

Hor. Ay, good my lord.

Ham. An earnest conjuration from the King,
As England was his faithful tributary,
As love between them like the palm might flourish,
As peace should still her wheaten garland wear
And stand a comma 'tween their amities,
And many such-like "As"-es of great charge,
That, on the view and knowing of these contents,
Without debatement further, more or less,
He should those bearers put to sudden death,
Not shriving time allow'd.

Hor. How was this seal'd?

Ham. Why, even in that was Heaven ordinant.
I had my father's signet in my purse,
Which was the model of that Danish seal;
Folded the writ up in the form of th' other,
Subscrib'd it, gave 't th' impression, plac'd it safely,
The changeling never known. Now, the next day
Was our sea-fight; and what to this was sequent
Thou knowest already.

Hor. So Guildenstern and Rosencrantz go to 't.

Ham. Why man, they did make love to this employment;
They are not near my conscience; their defeat
Does by their own insinuation grow:
'T is dangerous when the baser nature comes
Between the pass and fell incensed points
Of mighty opposites.

Hor. Why, what a king is this!

Ham. Does it not, think thee, stand me now upon—
He that hath kill'd my king and whor'd my mother,
Popp'd in between th' election and my hopes,
Thrown out his angle for my proper life,
And with such cozenage—is 't not perfect conscience,
To quit him with this arm? And is 't not to be damn'd,
To let this canker of our nature come
In further evil?

Hor. It must be shortly known to him from England
What is the issue of the business there.

Ham. It will be short; the interim is mine,
And a man's life 's no more than to say "One."
But I am very sorry, good Horatio,
That to Laertes I forgot myself;
For, by the image of my cause, I see
The portraiture of his. I 'll court his favours:
But, sure, the bravery of his grief did put me
Into a tow'ring passion.

Hor. Peace! who comes here?

Enter young *Osric*.

Osr. Your lordship is right welcome back to Denmark.

Ham. I humbly thank you, sir. [*To Hor.*]—Dost know this water-fly?

Hor. No, my good lord.

Ham. Thy state is the more gracious, for 't is a vice to know him. He hath much land, and fertile; let a beast be lord of beasts, and his crib shall stand at the King's mess. 'T is a chough, but, as I say, spacious in the possession of dirt.

Osr. Sweet lord, if your lordship were at leisure, I should impart a thing to you from his Majesty.

Ham. I will receive it, sir, with all diligence of spirit. Put your bonnet to his right use; 't is for the head.

Osr. I thank your lordship, it is very hot.

Ham. No, believe me, 't is very cold; the wind is northerly.

Osr. It is indifferent cold, my lord, indeed.

Ham. Methinks it is very sultry and hot for my complexion.

Osr. Exceedingly, my lord; it is very sultry,—as 't were—I cannot tell how. But, my lord, his Majesty bade me signify to you that 'a has laid a great wager on your head. Sir, this is the matter,—

Ham. I beseech you, remember—

Hamlet moves him to put on his hat.

Osr. Nay, good my lord; for my ease, in good faith. Sir, here is newly come to court Laertes, believe me, an absolute gentleman, full of most excellent differences, of very soft society and great showing; indeed, to speak feelingly of him, he is the card or calen-

33. **statists,** statesmen. 42. **comma,** the smallest break, used here as a connective 43. **"As"-es,** (1) the particle *as*, cf. preceding lines, (2) asses. 47. **shriving,** absolution. 48. **ordinant,** ruling. 59. **insinuation,** meddling. 61. **fell,** cruel. 65. **election,** the Danish monarchy was elective and Claudius had been elected instead of Hamlet.

79. **bravery,** bravado. 89. **crib . . . mess,** his dish shall be at the king's table. 89. **chough,** chattering jackdaw. 111. **absolute,** perfect. 112. **differences,** distinguishing qualities. 114. **feelingly,** with just perception. **card,** chart.

dar of gentry, for you shall find in him the continent of what parts a gentleman would see.

Ham. Sir, his definement suffers no perdition in you; though, I know, to divide him inventorially would dizzy th' arithmetic of memory, and yet but yaw neither, in respect of his quick sail. But, in the verity of extolment, I take him to be a soul of great article, and his infusion of such dearth and rareness, as, to make true diction of him, his semblable is his mirror; and who else would trace him, his umbrage, nothing more.

Osr. Your lordship speaks most infallibly of him.

Ham. The concernancy, sir? Why do we wrap the gentleman in our more rawer breath?

Osr. Sir?

Hor. Is 't not possible to understand in another tongue? You will to 't, sir, really.

Ham. What imports the nomination of this gentleman?

Osr. Of Laertes?

Hor. His purse is empty already; all 's golden words are spent.

Ham. Of him, sir.

Osr. I know you are not ignorant—

Ham. I would you did, sir; yet, in faith, if you did, it would not much approve me. Well, sir?

Osr. You are not ignorant of what excellence Laertes is—

Ham. I dare not confess that, lest I should compare with him in excellence; but to know a man well were to know himself.

Osr. I mean, sir, for his weapon; but in the imputation laid on him by them, in his meed he 's unfellowed.

Ham. What 's his weapon?

Osr. Rapier and dagger.

Ham. That 's two of his weapons; but well.

Osr. The King, sir, hath wagered with him six Barbary horses, against the which he has impawned, as I take it, six French rapiers and poniards, with their assigns, as girdle, hangers, and so. Three of the carriages, in faith, are very dear to fancy, very responsive to the hilts, most delicate carriages, and of very liberal conceit.

Ham. What call you the carriages?

Hor. I knew you must be edified by the margent ere you had done.

Osr. The carriages, sir, are the hangers.

Ham. The phrase would be more germane to the matter, if we could carry cannon by our sides; I would it might be hangers till then. But, on: six Barbary horses against six French swords, their assigns, and three liberal-conceited carriages; that 's the French bet against the Danish. Why is all this "impawned," as you call it?

Osr. The King, sir, hath laid, sir, that in a dozen passes between yourself and him, he shall not exceed you three hits; he hath laid on twelve for nine; and it would come to immediate trial, if your lordship would vouchsafe the answer.

Ham. How if I answer no?

Osr. I mean, my lord, the opposition of your person in trial.

Ham. Sir, I will walk here in the hall; if it please his Majesty, it is the breathing time of day with me. Let the foils be brought, the gentleman willing, and the King hold his purpose, I will win for him an I can; if not, I will gain nothing but my shame and the odd hits.

Osr. Shall I deliver you so?

Ham. To this effect, sir; after what flourish your nature will.

Osr. I commend my duty to your lordship.

Ham. Yours, yours. [*Exit Osric.*] He does well to commend it himself; there are no tongues else for 's turn.

Hor. This lapwing runs away with the shell on his head.

Ham. 'A did, sir, comply with his dug before 'a suck'd it. Thus has he—and many more of the same bevy that I know the drossy age dotes on—only got the tune of the time and, out of an habit of encounter, a kind of yeasty collection, which carries them through and through the most fanned and winnowed opinions; and do but blow them to their trial, the bubbles are out.

Enter a *Lord.*

Lord. My lord, his Majesty commended him to you by young Osric, who brings back to him, that you attend him in the hall. He sends to know if your pleasure hold to play with Laertes, or that you will take longer time.

Ham. I am constant to my purposes; they follow the King's pleasure. If his fitness speaks, mine is ready, now or whensoever, provided I be so able as now.

115. continent, summary. **117. definement,** description. **119-20.** And yet only stagger (**yaw**) in trying to overtake his virtues. **121. article,** importance. **122. infusion,** essential quality. **123. semblable,** likeness. **125. umbrage,** shadow. **128. concernancy,** meaning. **132. will to 't,** will get there. **141. approve,** commend. **149. imputation,** reputation. **meed,** merit. **156. impawned,** wagered. **157. assigns,** accompaniments. **158. hangers,** straps on the sword-belt. **159. responsive,** corresponding. **160. liberal conceit,** elaborate design.

163. margent, marginal comment. **193. lapwing,** the new-hatched peewit (**lapwing**) was supposed to run around with the shell on its head. **195. comply with,** was polite to. **197. bevy,** covey. **198. yeasty,** frothy. **200. fanned and winnowed,** very select, like wheat with the chaff fanned and winnowed away. **201. blow . . . trial,** put them to a test.

Lord. The King and Queen and all are coming down.

Ham. In happy time.

Lord. The Queen desires you to use some gentle entertainment to Laertes before you fall to play.

Ham. She well instructs me. *Exit Lord.*

Hor. You will lose, my lord.

Ham. I do not think so; since he went into France, I have been in continual practice. I shall win at the odds. But thou wouldst not think how ill all 's here about my heart; but it is no matter.

Hor. Nay, good my lord,—

Ham. It is but foolery; but it is such a kind of gain-giving, as would perhaps trouble a woman.

Hor. If your mind dislike anything, obey it. I will forestall their repair hither, and say you are not fit.

Ham. Not a whit; we defy augury; there is special providence in the fall of a sparrow. If it be now, 't is not to come; if it be not to come, it will be now; if it be not now, yet it will come; the readiness is all. Since no man of aught he leaves knows, what is 't to leave betimes? Let be.

Enter *King, Queen, Laertes, Osric,* and all the State and other Attendants, with foils and daggers; a table and flagons of wine on it. Trumpets, drums, and Officers with cushions.

King. Come, Hamlet, come, and take this hand from me.
The King puts Laertes' hand into Hamlet's.

Ham. Give me your pardon, sir. I have done you wrong,
But pardon 't, as you are a gentleman.
This presence knows, and you must needs have heard,
How I am punish'd with a sore distraction.
What I have done
That might your nature, honour, and exception
Roughly awake, I here proclaim was madness.
Was 't Hamlet wrong'd Laertes? Never Hamlet!
If Hamlet from himself be ta'en away,
And when he 's not himself does wrong Laertes,
Then Hamlet does it not, Hamlet denies it.
Who does it, then? His madness. If 't be so,
Hamlet is of the faction that is wrong'd;
His madness is poor Hamlet's enemy.
Sir, in this audience,
Let my disclaiming from a purpos'd evil
Free me so far in your most generous thoughts,
That I have shot my arrow o'er the house
And hurt my brother.

Laer. I am satisfied in nature,
Whose motive, in this case, should stir me most
To my revenge; but in my terms of honour
I stand aloof, and will no reconcilement,
Till by some elder masters of known honour
I have a voice and precedent of peace,
To keep my name ungor'd. But till that time,
I do receive your offer'd love like love,
And will not wrong it.

Ham. I embrace it freely,
And will this brother's wager frankly play.
Give us the foils.

Laer. Come, one for me.

Ham. I 'll be your foil, Laertes; in mine ignorance
Your skill shall, like a star i' th' darkest night,
Stick fiery off indeed.

Laer. You mock me, sir.

Ham. No, by this hand.

King. Give them the foils, young Osric. Cousin Hamlet,
You know the wager?

Ham. Very well, my lord.
Your Grace hath laid the odds o' th' weaker side.

King. I do not fear it, I have seen you both;
But since he is better'd, we have therefore odds.

Laer. This is too heavy; let me see another.

Ham. This likes me well. These foils have all a length? *They prepare to play.*

Osr. Ay, my good lord.

King. Set me the stoups of wine upon that table.
If Hamlet give the first or second hit,
Or quit in answer of the third exchange,
Let all the battlements their ordnance fire.
The King shall drink to Hamlet's better breath,
And in the cup an union shall he throw,
Richer than that which four successive kings
In Denmark's crown have worn. Give me the cups,
And let the kettle to the trumpet speak,
The trumpet to the cannoneer without,
The cannons to the heavens, the heaven to earth,
"Now the King drinks to Hamlet." Come, begin;

226. gain-giving, misgiving. **235. betimes,** early. **239. presence,** royal assembly. **242. exception,** disapproval.

260. voice and precedent, authoritative opinion justified by precedent. **266. foil,** (1) blunt sword, (2) background for a jewel. **274. better'd,** improved in France. **280. quit,** repay, hit back. **283. union,** pearl. **286. kettle,** kettle-drum.

And you, the judges, bear a wary eye.
Trumpets sound.
Ham. Come on, sir.
Laer. Come, my lord. *They play.*
Ham. One.
Laer. No.
Ham. Judgement.
Osr. A hit, a very palpable hit.
Laer. Well; again.
King. Stay, give me drink. Hamlet, this pearl is thine;
Here 's to thy health! Give him the cup.
Trumpets sound, and shot goes off within.
Ham. I 'll play this bout first; set it by a while.
Come. [*They play.*] Another hit; what say you?
Laer. A touch, a touch, I do confess 't.
King. Our son shall win.
Queen. He 's fat, and scant of breath.
Here, Hamlet, take my napkin, rub thy brows.
The Queen carouses to thy fortune, Hamlet.
Ham. Good madam!
King. Gertrude, do not drink.
Queen. I will, my lord; I pray you, pardon me.
King. [*Aside.*] It is the poison'd cup; it is too late.
Ham. I dare not drink yet, madam; by and by.
Queen. Come, let me wipe thy face.
Laer. My lord, I 'll hit him now.
King. I do not think 't.
Laer. [*Aside.*] And yet it is almost against my conscience.
Ham. Come, for the third, Laertes; you but dally.
I pray you, pass with your best violence.
I am afeard you make a wanton of me.
Laer. Say you so? Come on. *They play.*
Osr. Nothing, neither way.
Laer. Have at you now!
Laertes wounds Hamlet; then, in scuffling, they change rapiers.
King. Part them; they are incens'd.
Ham. Nay, come, again.
Hamlet wounds Laertes. The Queen falls.
Osr. Look to the Queen there! Ho!
Hor. They bleed on both sides. How is 't, my lord!
Osr. How is 't, Laertes?
Laer. Why, as a woodcock to mine own springe, Osric;
I am justly kill'd with mine own treachery.
Ham. How does the Queen?
King. She swounds to see them bleed.
Queen. No, no, the drink, the drink,—O my dear Hamlet,—
The drink, the drink! I am poison'd. *Dies.*
Ham. O villainy! Ho! let the door be lock'd:
Treachery! Seek it out.
Laer. It is here Hamlet. Hamlet, thou art slain.
No med'cine in the world can do thee good;
In thee there is not half an hours life;
The treacherous instrument is in thy hand,
Unbated and envenom'd: the foul practice
Hath turn'd itself on me; lo, here I lie,
Never to rise again. Thy mother 's poison'd.
I can no more:—the King, the King 's to blame.
Ham. The point envenom'd too!
Then, venom, to thy work.
Hurts the King.
All. Treason! treason!
King. O, yet defend me, friends; I am but hurt.
Ham. Here, thou incestuous, murd'rous, damned Dane,
Drink off this potion! Is thy union here?
Follow my mother! *King dies.*
Laer. He is justly serv'd;
It is a poison temper'd by himself.
Exchange forgiveness with me, noble Hamlet;
Mine and my father's death come not upon thee,
Nor thine on me! *Dies.*
Ham. Heaven make thee free of it! I follow thee.
I am dead, Horatio. Wretched queen, adieu!
You that look pale and tremble at this chance,
That are but mutes or audience to this act,
Had I but time—as this fell sergeant, Death,
Is strict in his arrest—O, I could tell you—
But let it be. Horatio, I am dead;
Thou livest; report me and my cause aright
To the unsatisfied.
Hor. Never believe it:
I am more an antique Roman than a Dane;
Here 's yet some liquor left.
Ham. As thou 'rt a man,
Give me the cup; let go, by heaven, I 'll have 't!
O God, Horatio, what a wounded name,
Things standing thus unknown, shall live behind me!
If thou didst ever hold me in thy heart,
Absent thee from felicity a while

298. fat, sweaty. **310. wanton,** spoiled child. **315. Ho,** a call to stop the fight. **317. woodcock . . . springe,** cf. **I, iv, 15** and note.

339. temper'd mixed. **346. mutes,** performers who have no words to speak. **347. sergeant,** sheriff's officer. **352. antique Roman,** with reference to the old Roman fashion of suicide.

And in this harsh world draw thy breath in pain
To tell my story.
March afar off, and shot within.
What warlike noise is this?
Osr. Young Fortinbras, with conquest come from Poland,
To th' ambassadors of England gives
This warlike volley.
Ham. O, I die, Horatio;
The potent poison quite o'er-crows my spirit:
I cannot live to hear the news from England,
But I do prophesy th' election lights
On Fortinbras; he has my dying voice.
So tell him, with th' occurrents, more and less,
Which have solicited—the rest is silence.
Dies.
Hor. Now cracks a noble heart. Good-night, sweet prince,
And flights of angels sing thee to thy rest!
Why does the drum come hither?

Enter *Fortinbras* and the English *Ambassadors,* with drum, colours, and Attendants.

Fort. Where is this sight?
Hor. What is it you would see?
If aught of woe or wonder, cease your search.
Fort. This quarry cries on havoc. O proud Death,
What feast is toward in thine eternal cell,
That thou so many princes at a shot
So bloodily hast struck?
First Amb. The sight is dismal,
And our affairs from England come too late:
The ears are senseless that should give us hearing,
To tell him his commandment is fulfill'd,
That Rosencrantz and Guildenstern are dead.
Where should we have our thanks?
Hor. Not from his mouth,
Had it th' ability of life to thank you.
He never gave commandment for their death:
But since, so jump upon this bloody question,
You from the Polack wars, and you from England,
Are here arrived, give order that these bodies
High on a stage be placed to the view;
And let me speak to th' yet unknowing world
How these things came about: so shall you hear
Of carnal, bloody, and unnatural acts,
Of accidental judgements, casual slaughters,
Of deaths put on by cunning and forc'd cause,
And, in this upshot, purposes mistook
Fall'n on th' inventors' heads: all this can I
Truly deliver.
Fort. Let us haste to hear it,
And call the noblest to the audience.
For me, with sorrow I embrace my fortune:
I have some rights of memory in this kingdom,
Which now to claim, my vantage doth invite me.
Hor. Of that I shall have also cause to speak,
And from his mouth whose voice will draw on more:
But let this same be presently perform'd
Even while men's minds are wild, lest more mischance,
On plots and errors, happen.
Fort. Let four captains
Bear Hamlet, like a soldier, to the stage,
For he was likely, had he been put on,
To have prov'd most royal; and, for his passage,
The soldiers' music and the rites of war
Speak loudly for him.
Take up the bodies: such a sight as this
Becomes the field, but here shows much amiss.
Go, bid the soldiers shoot.
Exeunt marching, after the which a peal of ordnance are shot off.

368. occurrents, occurrences. **369. solicited,** caused. **375. quarry,** heap of slain. **cries on havoc,** proclaims general slaughter. **376. toward,** in preparation. **383. his.** the king's.

389. stage, platform. **400. rights of memory,** remembered claims. **403. voice,** vote. **draw on,** influence. **408. put on,** tested. **409. passage,** departure. **413. field,** i.e., battle-field.

Othello, the Moor of Venice

Othello ranks with *Hamlet, King Lear,* and *Macbeth* as one of Shakespeare's great tragic masterpieces. Like the other three it is a study in dramatic form of the presence and the power of evil in the world. It differs from them in its superb dramatic concentration upon a single theme; in its unity of tone, absence of under-plot and comic relief; and in the passionate intensity of its characterization. It is the most vivid and realistic of Shakespeare's tragedies. No other tragedy in English literature makes so poignant an appeal to our sense of sympathy for human suffering as *Othello;* we turn from it to cry with the wronged and ruined hero: "the pity of it, Iago, oh, the pity of it."

Text.—*Othello* was published for the first time six years after Shakespeare's death with the following title-page:

The Tragœdy of Othello, The Moore of Venice. As it hath been diverse times acted at the Globe and at the Black-Friers, by his Maiesties Servants. Written by William Shakespeare. London, Printed by N. O. for Thomas Walkley, and are to be sold at his shop, at the Eagle and Child, in Brittans Bursse 1622.

This is the First Quarto to which Walkley prefixed a brief epistle to the reader speaking of the author's death and saying that his name was "sufficient to vent [sell] his work," an interesting testimony to Shakespeare's popularity just before the appearance of the First Folio. This edition is one of the "good quartos"; it was regularly entered in the Stationers' Register in 1621 and presents a fair text, shorter by some 160 lines than that of the Folio, but often affording a better reading, and containing a few lines missing in the latter text. The presence in the Quarto of numerous oaths and expletives which have been carefully expurgated in the Folio goes to show that Walkley's "copy" was based on a theatrical manuscript antedating the law of 1606 forbidding the profane use of the name of God in stage plays.

When Heminges and Condell were preparing "copy" of *Othello* for the Folio they did not follow their usual practice of sending in a copy of the latest Quarto, but transcribed a manuscript in their possession. It is well that they did, for the Folio restores many fine Shakespearean lines—notably III, iii, 453-460 and the Willow Song—absent in the Quarto. Like most Folio texts that of *Othello* shows signs of revision. The present text has been established by a careful collation of the Quarto and the Folio.

Date.—There is little doubt that *Othello* was written late in 1603 or early in 1604. It was played at Court by Shakespeare's company on November 1, 1604, which means that it had been successful on the stage before that date. It was certainly later than Holland's translation of Pliny, 1601, a book evidently familiar to Shakespeare, who draws on it more than once in *Othello.* Stylistic and metrical tests place it after *Julius Cæsar* and before *Lear.* In all probability it follows close upon Shakespeare's last revision of *Hamlet* in 1602-3.

Source.—Shakespeare derived the plot of *Othello* from the seventh novel of the third decade of the *Hecatommithi* of Giraldo Cinthio, 1565-6, the same collection of Italian tales which contains the story of *Measure for Measure.* He may have read it in the Italian —there is some slight proof in *Othello* that Shakespeare could at this time read Italian— or in a French translation of 1584. The original Italian and an English translation are printed in the *Variorum Othello* and will more than repay a careful reading, for there is hardly a parallel case in literature of the power of genius to transmute base metal into the gold of poetry. Briefly Cinthio's tale runs as follows:

A fair and virtuous Venetian lady named Disdemona fell in love with a valiant Moor in the service of Venice and married him in spite of the opposition of her family. He was appointed to command a garrison in Cyprus and took his wife along with him. In his company was a wicked ensign who lusted after the lady and on her refusal to listen to him began to hate her and to plot revenge. A captain in the garrison, the familiar friend of the Moor and his wife, was cashiered for striking a soldier. Disdemona interceded for him and this suggested to the ensign the idea of persuading the

Moor that the captain was too familiar with his wife. This was no hard task, for Moors are naturally jealous. The ensign first told him that the captain had bragged of his conquest of Disdemona, then managed to have him witness a conversation in which the captain supposedly confessed his intimacy with the lady, and finally showed him a handkerchief, the Moor's gift to his wife, in the possession of a woman in the captain's lodgings. This handkerchief the ensign had stolen from Disdemona while she was caressing his infant child and had dropped in the captain's bedroom. The Moor's angry jealousy became so apparent that Disdemona went in tears to her friend, the ensign's wife, and implored her help. But this woman, who knew of the plot, was so afraid of her husband that she dared say nothing and only advised Disdemona not to give her husband cause of suspicion. Bribed by the Moor, the ensign undertook to kill the captain; he attacked him in the dark but only cut off his leg. Then he and the Moor killed Disdemona, beating her to death with a stocking full of sand and pulling the ceiling of the room down on the body to make it appear that she had been killed by an accident. The Moor, however, conceived a bitter hatred of the ensign and discharged him from his office, whereupon the ensign denounced him to the wounded captain. The captain in turn denounced him to the Venetian Senate, who recalled him and put him to the torture to extract a confession. Refusing to confess, the Moor was banished from Venice and murdered in exile by Disdemona's relatives to revenge her death. Some time later the ensign was caught in another plot, and tortured so extremely that he died miserably. After his death his widow told the whole story.

It is plain that Shakespeare followed the main outlines of his source step by step, and there are enough minor correspondences to suggest that Cinthio's tale lay open before him while he was writing *Othello*. But his alterations are more interesting and more important than his borrowings. His main task, of course, was to recast the story in dramatic form and Cinthio's loose and straggling narrative forced him to concentrate his energy on this. He discarded completely the long-drawn-out conclusion of the tale and substituted for it the swift and piteous catastrophe of the drama. He treated the beginning of the story with equal freedom; the great first act of *Othello* —masterly alike in its exposition and its power to arouse interest and sympathy—is Shakespeare's invention. There is no hint in the story of Desdemona's elopement, her father's pursuit, and the defense of the wedded lovers before the Senate. Shakespeare wove the threads of the plot more closely together by revealing Iago's malicious hatred at the very opening of the play, by making Iago the instrument of Cassio's disgrace, and finally by causing Iago's wife to reveal the whole vile plot. In construction *Othello* is a tragedy of intrigue and the intrigue begins with, centers about, and crashes upon the figure of Iago.

Type.—Of all Shakespeare's plays *Othello* approaches most nearly to a well-defined and popular type of Elizabethan drama, the domestic tragedy. The distinguishing feature of this type of drama is a grim and somewhat sordid realism in the native tradition of the miracle play. It is, of course, inherently probable that Shakespeare, always alive to the popular taste, should at one time or another have turned his hand to domestic tragedy, and attempts have been made to ascribe to him the authorship of *Arden,* 1592, and of *The Yorkshire Tragedy,* 1608. The best answer to such attempts is a thoughtful reading of *Othello*. When Shakespeare touched domestic tragedy he lifted and glorified it, as he did the chronicle play and the tragedy of blood.

Superficially *Othello* has much in common with this type. Cinthio's play is supposed to be a true story. The tragedy is one of private life; the protagonist, unlike most Shakespearean heroes, is neither a king nor a nobleman. The fate of a kingdom is not involved in the ruin of the Moor nor is his tragedy interwoven with the feuds of noble houses or the destiny of an empire. Yet when we turn from the typical domestic tragedy to *Othello* we feel that we have entered another world. There is a dignity, a note of universality, a breath of romance in the foreign setting, and above all a sense of the pathos of things mortal, that makes Shakespeare's domestic tragedy a thing alone, apart, and above.

Nevertheless that which primarily distinguishes *Othello* from the other great Shakespearean tragedies is its atmosphere of realism. Here is no ghost come from the grave crying for revenge, no weird sisters to kindle into life the germs of evil; the scene is not laid in distant legendary times. By his choice of subject Shakespeare imposed upon himself a realistic treatment that set limitations upon his genius such as are not apparent in *Hamlet, Lear,* and *Macbeth.* Yet it is the characteristic of genius to work within and triumph over self-imposed limitations. *Othello* has excellencies of its own and these of the first order. Nowhere else is Shakespeare's skill in the architectonics of the drama so admirably shown; nowhere else is the dramatic tension so gripping as in the temptation scene; nowhere else is the power of evil so immediately and terribly revealed. There is nothing mysterious or awe-inspiring in this revelation, but it is to the last degree realistic and convincing. Characters and events alike in *Othello* are more human and credible than in any other of Shakespeare's tragedies.

Characters.—One character alone in this play has been too often misunderstood. Iago's villainy is such that he has been called a demi-devil, or an incarnation of evil, rather than a man. It is true that the motives for his plot rehearsed in his soliloquies seem at first sight inadequate to account for his actions. In the language of modern psychology they might be termed a rationalization of his desires. Probably they were meant by Shakespeare to give a clue to Iago's character to the groundlings of the Globe.

The true character, the real motives, of Iago deserve a word of explanation. In the first place he is a mercenary soldier of the late Renaissance; it is not without significance that Shakespeare has given him a specifically Spanish name, thus identifying him to his English audience with the treachery and cold-blooded cruelty for which the Spaniard was notorious. He has the manners of a soldier; he is blunt, outspoken, careless of etiquette, and humorously cynical—"hard-boiled" one might call him today. He has in the minds of those who know him best many of the soldier's virtues, a quick and practical intelligence, a comradely readiness to help a friend, and above all a sterling honesty. "Honest" is indeed Iago's standing epithet; it is applied to him by almost every one in the play—Shakespeare's device, of course, to show his reputation in the world about him—and he himself accepts it with a characteristic sneer. Now the term "honest" in Shakespeare's day carried a different implication from that it bears in our commercial age; it meant four-square, upright, and trustworthy. The trust reposed in Iago by all who knew him, even by his shrewd and worldly wife, shows how well he had imposed his mask upon the world. There is nothing of this in the source; it is Shakespeare's method of making the central action of the drama credible and convincing. It is only honest Iago who could have so deceived the Moor.

When this mask of soldierly honesty is dropped we see what his associates never perceived until too late, the real man, a complete egoist, a hard materialist, contemptuous of moral standards, and devoured by a sense of his own intellectual superiority. He does not seem to have been a man of strong passions or of high ambition. In Cinthio the prime motive of the plot is the lust turned to hate of the ensign for the Moor's wife; in the play Iago shows, except for a passing moment, neither lust after nor hatred of Desdemona. Against Othello on the other hand he cherishes positive malice. He has long despised him for the simplicity that lets him trust his fellow-men; he hates him for the scandalous rumor that has linked the name of Othello and his own wife; and the Moor's refusal to gratify his petty ambition with the promotion that he deserves makes his cup of hate boil over.

But the real motive for his action lies deeper, in his wounded sense of intellectual superiority and his craving to assuage this wound by making those who had inflicted it the puppets of his will. It must be remembered, moreover, that Iago begins his action without realizing its fatal consequence. There is no hint in the play that he originally contemplated the double murder of Cassio and Desdemona. When he aroused the Moor's suspicions he unloosed a storm whose course he was unable to control, and at last he is wrecked upon an obstacle whose existence he was incapable of suspecting, the heroic self-sacrifice of his own wife. When we sum up all these points, Iago's professional indifference to human suffering, his peculiar contempt of moral standards, his wounded pride and desire to demonstrate his power, we get, it would seem, an explanation of his conduct which reveals it as humanly credible without forcing us to attribute to him a superhuman and Satanic malignity.

The success of his intrigue, moreover, is made possible by the characters of the other principal figures of the drama. Othello and Desdemona are by reason of their natures mere clay in his hands. Of Desdemona little need be said. Shakespeare took over from his source the gentle Venetian lady who "saw Othello's visage in his mind" and did downright violence to her fortunes to love the Moor and live with him. She idealized the hero, surrounded by an atmosphere of mystery and romance, who broke into the quiet of her home, and threw herself into his arms without the slightest knowledge of the depth of his nature. When the storm burst upon her she was ignorant of its meaning, and unable to withstand it. She does not think Othello can be jealous; she knows herself incapable of giving him cause; she can hardly believe that there are women in the world guilty of the fault she is charged with. Her behavior from the beginning of her trial: her foolishly generous persistence in pleading for Cassio, her childish duplicity in the matter of the handkerchief, her cries of pity and fear upon her death-bed, all spring from her essential femininity and innocence. Only once does she show a flash of that proud [1] self-respect which might have forced the issue and cleared her name and that when it is too late (IV, iii). But what Desdemona lacks in clear vision and moral courage she more than atones for in devoted love. Most pathetic of Shakespeare's ladies, the wrongs she suffers in passive innocence breathe out a perfume of divine self-forgetfulness.

Shakespeare had a harder task in raising the Moor of his source to the dignity of a tragic hero. In Cinthio this character is a cruel and jealous barbarian; the tale is told as a warning to Italian ladies not to marry men of foreign races and strange manners. Shakespeare, it is plain, disdained this petty moral. Catching a hint from a phrase in the source as to the valor and the noble person of the Moor, he recast the character completely. Shakespeare's Othello is the most heroic of Shakespeare's heroes; he is of royal descent, he has fought through a life of strange adventure, and, though a born barbarian, he has attained high rank in the Christian state of Venice. Shakespeare devotes a great part of the first act to building up the character of Othello, laying special stress on his self-possession and his grave and noble charm. It is only the angry father and the cynical Iago who see anything unnatural in Desdemona's choice of such a husband: "I think this tale would win my daughter too," says the Duke after listening to Othello's speech.

Another side of Othello's character, however, is revealed in the comment of that shrewd observer, Iago: "the Moor is of a free and open nature that thinks men honest that but seem to be so." Moving about in the brave new world which he has entered, Othello takes all its appearances for realities. Incapable of deceit himself—"Oh hardness to dissemble"—he believes all men honest and all women chaste, and it is this ignorance which proves his undoing. It is worth noting that his first dawning suspicion of his wife follows immediately upon Iago's bitter comment on the morals of Venetian ladies: "they do let God see the pranks they dare not show their husbands." Iago should know; he has himself a Venetian wife. Moreover Iago is a fellow of "exceeding honesty," and has, Othello naturally thinks, no cause except his friendly concern for his master's good name to warn him, as he has done with such apparent reluctance, to watch his wife's behavior. The success of Iago's intrigue depends upon the faith Othello reposes in this trusted friend and in his own ignorance of the character of the lady, separated from him by a wide interval of years, of race, and of another civilization, who had so suddenly entrusted her life to him.

When Othello's eyes are opened, as he thinks, to the deceit that European life has practiced on him, he plunges back into barbarism. The cruelty of the Moors was a byword in Shakespeare's England, and in the fierce jealousy of Othello and in his wild cry for blood we see the reclaimed barbarian relapsing into his native savagery. The much-debated question of Othello's jealousy needs little discussion. That he exhibits in his fall all the degrading symptoms of sexual jealousy is quite plain; that he was not jealous by nature is clear not only from the text, but from a comparison with Shakespeare's picture of such a naturally jealous man as Leontes in *The Winter's Tale*. Shakespeare himself has said the last word on this matter when he makes Othello call himself "one not easily jealous, but being wrought [i.e. worked upon] perplex'd [i.e. distracted] in the extreme." The Othello who strikes his wife in public,

[1] Compare by way of contrast the behavior of Imogen when accused of adultery—*Cymbeline*, III, iv.

heaps upon her in private the most outrageous abuse, and fees her maid as if she were the servant in a brothel, is indeed "perplex'd," driven in fact to the very verge of madness.

That which drives him is not merely sexual jealousy. Shakespeare has added to the agony of Othello another and a nobler element, quite foreign to his source: the passion for the loss of an ideal. Othello's lady was the fountain from which the current of his being ran, and this fountain seemed to him defiled. It is the overthrow and ruin of his faith which impels Othello to murder. If Desdemona is not the flower of virtue that she seems but a weed whose perfume is sheer poison, there is no way but one: she must die, "else she'll betray more men." It is for this reason that Othello can speak of his deed as a sacrifice rather than a murder and declare that he did naught in hate but all in honor.

Othello's loss of his ideal was due to his lack of faith in its reality and permanence. He suffered his reason to be "perplex'd" and threw away his instinctive faith. To the materialist, to an Iago, such a faith was folly, but Shakespeare knew that such a seeming folly ensured salvation. In the end, indeed, it is through such an act of instinctive and unwavering faith that the clouds are dispelled. Emilia needed no proof of the heavenly truth of her mistress, and her prompt sacrifice of life for her faith opens Othello's eyes to the depth of his fall and the extent of his loss. It is worth noting that this self-sacrifice of Emilia is Shakespeare's invention—there is nothing like it in the source—and one of his noblest strokes. It at once establishes Desdemona's innocence and makes possible the return of Othello to his true self.

None of Shakespeare's heroes falls quite so low as Othello, but none of them makes such a superb recovery. There is nothing in our literature to match his amazement at his folly, his sorrow for his loss, and his remorse for his crime. Yet it is not any of these, nor all of them together, that strikes in the last scene the note of tragic grandeur. Rather it is the return of the true Othello, the noble and tender hero whom Desdemona loved. Shakespeare's Othello is not the man to be led in chains like Cinthio's Moor, to deny his guilt, and hide his head in exile. He frankly confesses his deed, and when its full significance bursts upon him, he feels that he alone can pronounce the due sentence. His atonement is instant and complete. With a flash of memory that carries him back to the days when in the cause of Venice he struck down the Turk, he executes judgment upon himself and falls on Desdemona's bed to die upon a kiss that asks for pardon. It is this note of return and reconciliation in a tragedy of the lost and regained ideal that gives *Othello* a unique place in Shakespeare's tragedies.

Stage History.—From the beginning *Othello* has been one of the most popular of Shakespeare's plays upon the stage. A German visitor saw it at the Globe in 1610, and we know of six performances at Court before the closing of the theatres. After the Restoration it was assigned to the King's Company and so escaped the refining hand of Davenant. Pepys saw a performance as early as October, 1660, and pronounced it well done. The part of Desdemona was the first ever played on the English public stage by a woman, Mrs. Hughes, the mistress of Prince Rupert. Betterton played Othello to the Desdemona of Mrs. Bracegirdle, and Steele (*Tatler,* 167) pays a fine tribute to his performance of the part. From the beginning of the eighteenth century the stage history of *Othello* is little more than a rehearsal of the names of the greatest English actors. Garrick is said to have failed in the title-role. Kemble played it to the Desdemona of his sister. It was one of Kean's great parts; he was acting Othello when he collapsed upon the stage in 1831 to die a few weeks later. In 1876 Irving and Booth alternated the roles of Othello and Iago at the Lyceum; later Booth used to alternate the roles with Lawrence Barrett. No one who ever saw Booth as Iago can forget his look of devilish malignity in the last scene as he glared upon the bodies of his victims. Probably the most passionate and powerful interpretation of Othello was that of the Italian tragedian Salvini.

OTHELLO, THE MOOR OF VENICE

The Names of the Actors

Duke of Venice.
Brabantio, father to *Desdemona.*
Gratiano, } two noble Venetians.
Ludovico, }
Othello, the Moor.
Cassio, an honourable lieutenant.
Iago, a villain.
Roderigo, a gulled gentleman.
Montano, governor of Cyprus.
Clown.

Desdemona, wife to *Othello.*
Emilia, wife to *Iago.*
Bianca, a courtezan.

Senators, Gentlemen of Cyprus, Sailors, Officers, Messenger, Herald, Musicians, and Attendants.

[This list appears at the end of the play in the Folio.]

SCENE: *Venice; Cyprus.*

ACT I. Scene I. *Venice. A street.*

Enter *Roderigo and Iago.*

Rod. Tush, never tell me! I take it much unkindly
That thou, Iago, who hast had my purse
As if the strings were thine, shouldst know of this.
Iago. 'Sblood, but you will not hear me.
If ever I did dream of such a matter,
Abhor me.
Rod. Thou told'st me thou didst hold him in thy hate.
Iago. Despise me, if I do not. Three great ones of the city,
In personal suit to make me his lieutenant,
Off-capp'd to him; and, by the faith of man,
I know my price; I am worth no worse a place.
But he, as loving his own pride and purposes,
Evades them with a bombast circumstance
Horribly stuff'd with epithets of war;
And, in conclusion,
Nonsuits my mediators; for, "Certes," says he,
"I have already chose my officer."
And what was he?
Forsooth, a great arithmetician,
One Michael Cassio, a Florentine,
(A fellow almost damn'd in a fair wife)
That never set a squadron in the field,
Nor the division of a battle knows
More than a spinster, unless the bookish theoric,
Wherein the toged consuls can propose
As masterly as he. Mere prattle without practice
Is all his soldiership. But he, sir, had the election;
And I, of whom his eyes had seen the proof
At Rhodes, at Cyprus, and on other grounds
Christian and heathen, must be be-lee'd and calm'd
By debitor and creditor; this counter-caster,
He, in good time, must his lieutenant be,
And I—God bless the mark!—his Moorship's ancient.
Rod. By heaven, I rather would have been his hangman.
Iago. Why, there 's no remedy. 'T is the curse of service,
Preferment goes by letter and affection,
And not by old gradation, where each second
Stood heir to the first. Now, sir, be judge yourself
Whether I in any just term am affin'd
To love the Moor.
Rod. I would not follow him then.
Iago. O, sir, content you;
I follow him to serve my turn upon him.
We cannot all be masters, nor all masters

3. this, Desdemona's elopement. **10. Off-capp'd,** doffed their caps. **13. bombast circumstance,** inflated circumlocution. **16. Nonsuits,** rejects the suit of. **21.** Cassio has no wife in the play. In the source he has a lady (*una donna*) in his house, who may or may not be his wife. Shakespeare may have planned to give Cassio a wife and later have changed his mind. Some editors read **life,** interpreting "fair life" as meaning a civilian's life. **23. division,** disposition of troops.

24. theoric, theory. **25. toged,** wearing the toga, a mark of civilian office. **consuls,** senators. **29. Rhodes, Cyprus,** islands in the Mediterranean, outposts in the wars between Venice and the Turks. **31. counter-caster,** contemptuous term for "accountant." **33. God bless the mark,** an ironical apology for mentioning so mean and profane a thing as himself. **ancient,** standard bearer. **36. letter,** i.e., of recommendation. **37. old gradation,** established seniority. **39. affin'd,** bound.

Cannot be truly follow'd. You shall mark
Many a duteous and knee-crooking knave,
That, doting on his own obsequious bondage,
Wears out his time, much like his master's ass,
For nought but provender, and when he 's old, cashier'd.
Whip me such honest knaves. Others there are
Who, trimm'd in forms and visages of duty,
Keep yet their hearts attending on themselves,
And, throwing but shows of service on their lords,
Do well thrive by 'em, and when they have lin'd their coats
Do themselves homage. These fellows have some soul;
And such a one do I profess myself. For, sir,
It is as sure as you are Roderigo,
Were I the Moor, I would not be Iago:
In following him, I follow but myself;
Heaven is my judge, not I for love and duty,
But seeming so, for my peculiar end;
For when my outward action does demonstrate
The native act and figure of my heart
In compliment extern, 't is not long after
But I will wear my heart upon my sleeve
For daws to peck at: I am not what I am.

Rod. What a full fortune does the thick-lips owe,
If he can carry 't thus!

Iago. Call up her father,
Rouse him; make after him, poison his delight,
Proclaim him in the streets. Incense her kinsmen,
And, though he in a fertile climate dwell,
Plague him with flies; though that his joy be joy,
Yet throw such changes of vexation on 't,
As it may lose some colour.

Rod. Here is her father's house; I 'll call aloud.

Iago. Do, with like timorous accent and dire yell
As when, by night and negligence, the fire
Is spied in populous cities.

Rod. What, ho, Brabantio! Signior Brabantio, ho!

Iago. Awake! what, ho, Brabantio! thieves! thieves!
Look to your house, your daughter, and your bags!
Thieves! thieves!

Enter *Brabantio* above, at a window.

Bra. What is the reason of this terrible summons?
What is the matter there?

Rod. Signior, is all your family within?

Iago. Are your doors lock'd?

Bra. Why, wherefore ask you this?

Iago. 'Zounds, sir, you 're robb'd! For shame, put on your gown;
Your heart is burst, you have lost half your soul;
Even now, now, very now, an old black ram
Is tupping your white ewe. Arise, arise!
Awake the snorting citizens with the bell,
Or else the devil will make a grandsire of you.
Arise, I say!

Bra. What, have you lost your wits?

Rod. Most reverend signior, do you know my voice?

Bra. Not I. What are you?

Rod. My name is Roderigo.

Bra. The worser welcome;
I have charg'd thee not to haunt about my doors:
In honest plainness thou hast heard me say
My daughter is not for thee; and now, in madness,
Being full of supper and distempering draughts,
Upon malicious bravery dost thou come
To start my quiet.

Rod. Sir, sir, sir,—

Bra. But thou must needs be sure
My spirits and my place have in them power
To make this bitter to thee.

Rod. Patience, good sir.

Bra. What tell'st thou me of robbing? This is Venice;
My house is not a grange.

Rod. Most grave Brabantio,
In simple and pure soul I come to you.

Iago. 'Zounds, sir, you are one of those that will not serve God, if the devil bid you. Because we come to do you service and you think we are ruffians, you 'll have your daughter covered with a Barbary horse; you 'll have your nephews neigh to you; you 'll have coursers for cousins, and gennets for germans.

Bra. What profane wretch art thou?

Iago. I am one, sir, that comes to tell you your daughter and the Moor are now making the beast with two backs.

Bra. Thou art a villain.

Iago. You are—a senator.

Bra. This thou shalt answer. I know thee, Roderigo.

48. cashier'd, dismissed. **50. visages,** outward semblances. **53. lin'd their coats,** filled their pockets. **60. peculiar,** private. **63. compliment extern,** outward civility. **66. thick-lips,** i.e., negro. **owe,** own. **75. timorous,** terrifying.

90. snorting, snoring. **99. distempering,** intoxicating. **100. bravery,** bravado. **101. start,** disturb. **106. grange,** remote farm-house. **112. nephews,** grandsons. **114. gennets,** Spanish horses. **germans,** near relatives.

Rod. Sir, I will answer anything. But, I beseech you,
If 't be your pleasure and most wise consent,
(As partly I find it is) that your fair daughter,
At this odd-even and dull watch o' th' night,
Transported, with no worse nor better guard
But with a knave of common hire, a gondolier,
To the gross clasps of a lascivious Moor,—
If this be known to you and your allowance,
We then have done you bold and saucy wrongs;
But if you know not this, my manners tell me
We have your wrong rebuke. Do not believe
That, from the sense of all civility,
I thus would play and trifle with your reverence.
Your daughter, if you have not given her leave,
I say again, hath made a gross revolt;
Tying her duty, beauty, wit, and fortunes
In an extravagant and wheeling stranger
Of here and everywhere. Straight satisfy yourself.
If she be in her chamber or your house,
Let loose on me the justice of the state
For thus deluding you.

Bra. Strike on the tinder, ho!
Give me a taper! Call up all my people!
This accident is not unlike my dream;
Belief of it oppresses me already.
Light, I say! light! *Exit.*

Iago. Farewell; for I must leave you.
It seems not meet, nor wholesome to my place,
To be produc'd—as, if I stay, I shall—
Against the Moor; for, I do know, the state,
However this may gall him with some check,
Cannot with safety cast him, for he 's embark'd
With such loud reason to the Cyprus wars,
Which even now stands in act, that, for their souls,
Another of his fathom they have none,
To lead their business; in which regard,
Though I do hate him as I do hell-pains,
Yet, for necessity of present life,
I must show out a flag and sign of love,
Which is indeed but sign. That you shall surely find him,
Lead to the Sagittary the raised search;
And there will I be with him. So, farewell. *Exit.*

Enter *Brabantio* in his night-gown, and Servants with torches.

Bra. It is too true an evil; gone she is;
And what 's to come of my despised time
Is nought but bitterness. Now, Roderigo,
Where didst thou see her? O unhappy girl!
With the Moor, say'st thou? Who would be a father!
How didst thou know 't was she? O, she deceives me
Past thought! What said she to you? Get moe tapers;
Raise all my kindred. Are they married, think you?

Rod. Truly, I think they are.

Bra. O heaven! How got she out? O treason of the blood!
Fathers, from hence trust not your daughters' minds
By what you see them act. Is there not charms
By which the property of youth and maidhood
May be abus'd? Have you not read, Roderigo,
Of some such thing?

Rod. Yes, sir, I have indeed.

Bra. Call up my brother. O, would you had had her!
Some one way, some another. Do you know
Where we may apprehend her and the Moor?

Rod. I think I can discover him, if you please
To get good guard and go along with me.

Bra. Pray you, lead on. At every house I 'll call;
I may command at most. Get weapons, ho!
And raise some special officers of night.
On, good Roderigo; I 'll deserve your pains. *Exeunt.*

Scene II. *Another street.*

Enter *Othello, Iago,* and Attendants with torches.

Iago. Though in the trade of war I have slain men,
Yet do I hold it very stuff o' th' conscience
To do no contriv'd murder: I lack iniquity
Sometimes to do me service. Nine or ten times
I had thought to have yerk'd him here under the ribs.

Oth. 'T is better as it is.

Iago. Nay, but he prated,
And spoke such scurvy and provoking terms
Against your honour
That, with the little godliness I have,
I did full hard forbear him. But, I pray you, sir,

124. odd-even, i.e., between twelve and one. **128. allowance,** what you approve. **132. from,** contrary to. **137. extravagant and wheeling,** itinerant and roving. **141. tinder,** scorched linen kept in a metal box and ignited as need arose by a flint and steel. **149. check,** rebuke. **150. cast,** dismiss. **153. fathom,** capacity. **159. the Sagittary,** probably an inn.

173. property, nature. **174. abus'd,** deceived. **Scene ii: 5. yerk'd,** stabbed.

Are you fast married? Be assur'd of this,
That the magnifico is much belov'd,
And hath in his effect a voice potential
As double as the Duke's: he will divorce you;
Or put upon you what restraint or grievance
The law, with all his might to enforce it on,
Will give him cable.
Oth. Let him do his spite;
My services which I have done the signiory
Shall out-tongue his complaints. 'T is yet to know,—
Which, when I know that boasting is an honour,
I shall promulgate—I fetch my life and being
From men of royal siege, and my demerits
May speak unbonneted to as proud a fortune
As this that I have reach'd; for know, Iago,
But that I love the gentle Desdemona,
I would not my unhoused free condition
Put into circumscription and confine
For the sea's worth. But, look! what lights come yond?

Enter *Cassio,* with lights, Officers, and torches.

Iago. Those are the raised father and his friends.
You were best go in.
Oth. Not I; I must be found.
My parts, my title, and my perfect soul
Shall manifest me rightly. Is it they?
Iago. By Janus, I think no.
Oth. The servants of the Duke, and my lieutenant!
The goodness of the night upon you, friends!
What is the news?
Cas. The Duke does greet you, general,
And he requires your haste-post-haste appearance,
Even on the instant.
Oth. What is the matter, think you?
Cas. Something from Cyprus, as I may divine;
It is a business of some heat. The galleys
Have sent a dozen sequent messengers
This very night at one another's heels,
And many of the consuls, rais'd and met,
Are at the Duke's already. You have been hotly call'd for;
When, being not at your lodging to be found,
The Senate hath sent about three several quests
To search you out.
Oth. 'T is well I am found by you.
I will but spend a word here in the house,
And go with you. *Exit.*
Cas. Ancient, what makes he here?
Iago. Faith, he to-night hath boarded a land carack:
If it proves lawful prize, he 's made for ever.
Cas. I do not understand.
Iago. He 's married.
Cas. To who?

Re-enter *Othello.*

Iago. Marry, to—Come, captain, will you go?
Oth. Have with you.
Cas. Here comes another troop tc seek for you.

Enter *Brabantio, Roderigo,* and Officers with torches and weapons.

Iago. It is Brabantio. General, be advis'd;
He comes to bad intent.
Oth. Holla! stand there!
Rod. Signior, it is the Moor.
Bra. Down with him, thief!
They draw on both sides.
Iago. You, Roderigo! come, sir, I am for you.
Oth. Keep up your bright swords, for the dew will rust them.
Good signior, you shall more command with years
Than with your weapons.
Bra. O thou foul thief, where hast thou stow'd my daughter?
Damn'd as thou art, thou hast enchanted her;
For I 'll refer me to all things of sense,
If she in chains of magic were not bound,
Whether a maid so tender, fair, and happy,
So opposite to marriage that she shunn'd
The wealthy curled darlings of our nation,
Would ever have, t' incur a general mock,
Run from her guardage to the sooty bosom
Of such a thing as thou—to fear, not to delight.
Judge me the world, if 't is not gross in sense
That thou hast practis'd on her with foul charms,
Abus'd her delicate youth with drugs or minerals
That weakens motion. I 'll have 't disputed on;
'T is probable, and palpable to thinking.
I therefore apprehend and do attach thee
For an abuser of the world, a practiser
Of arts inhibited and out of warrant.

12. **magnifico**, Venetian senator. 14. **double**, weighty. 17. **cable**, rope, i.e., power. 18. **signiory**, Venetian senate. 22. **siege**, rank, lit., seat. **demerits**, deserts. 23. **unbonneted**, with hat off, i.e., with all courtesy. 26. **unhoused**, unhampered. 40. **heat**, urgency. **galleys**, naval officers. 41. **sequent**, successive.

50. **carack**, large merchantman. 67. **opposite to**, averse to. 70. **guardage**, guardianship. 72. **gross in sense**, obvious. 75. **motion**, power of movement. **disputed on**, argued in court. 78. **abuser**, corrupter. 79. **inhibited**, prohibited.

Lay hold upon him; if he do resist,
Subdue him at his peril.
Oth. Hold your hands,
Both you of my inclining, and the rest.
Were it my cue to fight, I should have known it
Without a prompter. Where will you that I go
To answer this your charge?
Bra. To prison, till fit time
Of law and course of direct session
Call thee to answer.
Oth. What if I do obey?
How may the Duke be therewith satisfied,
Whose messengers are here about my side
Upon some present business of the state
To bring me to him?
Off. 'T is true, most worthy signior.
The Duke 's in council; and your noble self,
I am sure, is sent for.
Bra. How? the Duke in council?
In this time of the night? Bring him away;
Mine 's not an idle cause. The Duke himself,
Or any of my brothers of the state,
Cannot but feel this wrong as 't were their own;
For if such actions may have passage free,
Bond-slaves and pagans shall our statesmen be. *Exeunt.*

Scene III. *A council-chamber.*

The *Duke* and *Senators* set at a table, with lights, Officers and Attendants.

Duke. There is no composition in these news
That gives them credit.
1. Sen. Indeed, they are disproportioned;
My letters say a hundred and seven galleys.
Duke. And mine, a hundred forty.
2. Sen. And mine, two hundred!
But though they jump not on a just account,—
As in these cases, where the aim reports,
'T is oft with difference—yet do they all confirm
A Turkish fleet, and bearing up to Cyprus.
Duke. Nay, it is possible enough to judgement.
I do not so secure me in the error
But the main article I do approve
In fearful sense.
Sailor. [*Within.*] What, ho! what, ho! what, ho!

Enter a *Sailor.*

Off. A messenger from the galleys.
Duke. Now, what 's the business?
Sail. The Turkish preparation makes for Rhodes;
So was I bid report here to the state
By Signior Angelo.
Duke. How say you by this change?
1. Sen. This cannot be,
By no assay of reason. 'T is a pageant,
To keep us in false gaze. When we consider
Th' importancy of Cyprus to the Turk,
And let ourselves again but understand
That, as it more concerns the Turk than Rhodes,
So may he with more facile question bear it,
For that it stands not in such warlike brace,
But altogether lacks th' abilities
That Rhodes is dress'd in; if we make thought of this,
We must not think the Turk is so unskilful
To leave that latest which concerns him first,
Neglecting an attempt of ease and gain
To wake and wage a danger profitless.
Duke. Nay, in all confidence, he 's not for Rhodes.
Off. Here is more news.

Enter a *Messenger.*

Mess. The Ottomites, reverend and gracious,
Steering with due course toward the isle of Rhodes,
Have there injointed them with an after fleet.
1. Sen. Ay, so I thought. How many, as you guess?
Mess. Of thirty sail; and now they do re-stem
Their backward course, bearing with frank appearance
Their purposes toward Cyprus. Signior Montano,
Your trusty and most valiant servitor,
With his free duty recommends you thus,
And prays you to believe him.
Duke. 'T is certain, then, for Cyprus.
Marcus Luccicos, is not he in town?
1. Sen. He 's now in Florence.
Duke. Write from us to him; post-post-haste dispatch.
1. Sen. Here comes Brabantio and the valiant Moor.

Enter *Brabantio, Othello, Cassio, Iago, Roderigo,* and Officers.

Duke. Valiant Othello, we must straight employ you

86. **course . . . session,** regular legal procedure. **Scene iii: 1. composition,** consistency. **5. jump,** agree. **just,** exact. **6. the aim reports,** the report is based on conjecture. **10-12. I do not . . . sense,** I am not so much reassured by this discrepancy as not to believe and fear the essential fact, i.e., the threatened attack.

18. assay of reason, reasonable test. **pageant,** pretence. **23. more . . . it,** carry it with easier contest. **24. brace,** defense. **30. wage,** risk. **35. after,** sent after. **37. re-stem,** steer back.

Against the general enemy Ottoman.
[*To Brabantio.*] I did not see you; welcome, gentle signior;
We lack'd your counsel and your help to-night.
Bra. So did I yours. Good your Grace, pardon me;
Neither my place nor aught I heard of business
Hath rais'd me from my bed, nor doth the general care
Take hold on me; for my particular grief
Is of so flood-gate and o'erbearing nature
That it engluts and swallows other sorrows
And it is still itself.
Duke. Why, what 's the matter?
Bra. My daughter! O, my daughter!
Sen. Dead?
Bra. Ay, to me;
She is abus'd, stol'n from me, and corrupted
By spells and medicines bought of mountebanks;
For nature so preposterously to err,
Being not deficient, blind, or lame of sense,
Sans witchcraft could not.
Duke. Whoe'er he be that in this foul proceeding
Hath thus beguil'd your daughter of herself
And you of her, the bloody book of law
You shall yourself read in the bitter letter
After your own sense, yea, though our proper son
Stood in your action.
Bra. Humbly I thank your Grace.
Here is the man,—this Moor, whom now, it seems,
Your special mandate for the state affairs
Hath hither brought.
All. We are very sorry for 't.
Duke. [*To Othello.*] What, in your own part, can you say to this?
Bra. Nothing, but this is so.
Oth. Most potent, grave, and reverend signiors,
My very noble and approv'd good masters,
That I have ta'en away this old man's daughter,
It is most true; true, I have married her:
The very head and front of my offending
Hath this extent, no more. Rude am I in my speech,
And little bless'd with the soft phrase of peace;
For since these arms of mine had seven years' pith
Till now, some nine moons wasted, they have us'd
Their dearest action in the tented field,
And little of this great world can I speak
More than pertains to feats of broils and battle,
And therefore little shall I grace my cause
In speaking for myself. Yet, by your gracious patience,
I will a round unvarnish'd tale deliver
Of my whole course of love; what drugs, what charms,
What conjuration and what mighty magic,
(For such proceeding I am charg'd withal,)
I won his daughter.
Bra. A maiden never bold;
Of spirit so still and quiet, that her motion
Blush'd at herself; and she, in spite of nature,
Of years, of country, credit, everything,
To fall in love with what she fear'd to look on!
It is a judgement maim'd and most imperfect
That will confess perfection so could err
Against all rules of nature, and must be driven
To find out practices of cunning hell,
Why this should be. I therefore vouch again
That with some mixtures powerful o'er the blood,
Or with some dram conjur'd to this effect,
He wrought upon her.
Duke. To vouch this is no proof,
Without more wider and more overt test
Than these thin habits and poor likelihoods
Of modern seeming do prefer against him.
1. Sen. But, Othello, speak.
Did you by indirect and forced courses
Subdue and poison this young maid's affections?
Or came it by request and such fair question
As soul to soul affordeth?
Oth. I do beseech you,
Send for the lady to the Sagittary,
And let her speak of me before her father;
If you do find me foul in her report,
The trust, the office I do hold of you,
Not only take away, but let your sentence
Even fall upon my life.
Duke. Fetch Desdemona hither.
Exeunt two or three.
Oth. Ancient, conduct them; you best know the place. *Exit Iago.*
And, till she come, as truly as to heaven
I do confess the vices of my blood,
So justly to your grave ears I 'll present
How I did thrive in this fair lady's love,
And she in mine.
Duke. Say it, Othello.
Oth. Her father lov'd me; oft invited me;
Still question'd me the story of my life
From year to year, the battles, sieges, fortunes,
That I have pass'd.
I ran it through, even from my boyish days,

61. mountebanks, quacks **64. Sans,** without. **70. Stood in,** were the object of.

95. motion, inward impulse. **108. thin habits,** superficial appearances. **109. modern,** trivial.

To th' very moment that he bade me tell it.
Wherein I spoke of most disastrous chances,
Of moving accidents by flood and field,
Of hair-breadth scapes i' th' imminent deadly breach,
Of being taken by the insolent foe
And sold to slavery, of my redemption thence
And portance in my travellers' history;
Wherein of antres vast and deserts idle,
Rough quarries, rocks, and hills whose heads touch heaven,
It was my hint to speak,—such was my process,—
And of the Cannibals that each other eat,
The Anthropophagi, and men whose heads
Do grow beneath their shoulders. This to hear
Would Desdemona seriously incline;
But still the house-affairs would draw her thence,
Which ever as she could with haste dispatch,
She 'd come again, and with a greedy ear
Devour up my discourse: which I observing,
Took once a pliant hour, and found good means
To draw from her a prayer of earnest heart
That I would all my pilgrimage dilate,
Whereof by parcels she had something heard,
But not intentively. I did consent,
And often did beguile her of her tears
When I did speak of some distressful stroke
That my youth suffer'd. My story being done,
She gave me for my pains a world of sighs.
She swore, in faith, 't was strange, 't was passing strange,
'T was pitiful, 't was wondrous pitiful.
She wish'd she had not heard it; yet she wish'd
That Heaven had made her such a man. She thank'd me,
And bade me, if I had a friend that lov'd her,
I should but teach him how to tell my story,
And that would woo her. Upon this hint I spake:
She lov'd me for the dangers I had pass'd,
And I lov'd her that she did pity them.
This only is the witchcraft I have us'd.
Here comes the lady; let her witness it.

Enter *Desdemona, Iago,* and Attendants.

Duke. I think this tale would win my daughter too.
Good Brabantio,
Take up this mangled matter at the best;
Men do their broken weapons rather use
Than their bare hands.

Bra. I pray you, hear her speak.
If she confess that she was half the wooer,
Destruction on my head, if my bad blame
Light on the man! Come hither, gentle mistress.
Do you perceive in all this noble company
Where most you owe obedience?

Des. My noble father,
I do perceive here a divided duty.
To you I am bound for life and education;
My life and education both do learn me
How to respect you; you are lord of all my duty;
I am hitherto your daughter. But here 's my husband;
And so much duty as my mother show'd
To you, preferring you before her father,
So much I challenge that I may profess
Due to the Moor, my lord.

Bra. God be with you! I have done.
Please it your Grace, on to the state-affairs.
I had rather to adopt a child than get it.
Come hither, Moor.
I here do give thee that with all my heart
Which, but thou hast already, with all my heart
I would keep from thee. For your sake, jewel,
I am glad at soul I have no other child;
For thy escape would teach me tyranny,
To hang clogs on them. I have done, my lord.

Duke. Let me speak like yourself, and lay a sentence,
Which, as a grise or step, may help these lovers
Into your favour.
When remedies are past, the griefs are ended
By seeing the worst, which late on hopes depended.
To mourn a mischief that is past and gone
Is the next way to draw new mischief on.
What cannot be preserv'd when fortune takes,
Patience her injury a mockery makes.
The robb'd that smiles steals something from the thief;
He robs himself that spends a bootless grief.

Bra. So let the Turk of Cyprus us beguile;
We lose it not, so long as we can smile.
He bears the sentence well that nothing bears
But the free comfort which from thence he hears,
But he bears both the sentence and the sorrow
That, to pay grief, must of poor patience borrow.
These sentences, to sugar, or to gall,
Being strong on both sides, are equivocal:
But words are words; I never yet did hear

136. imminent, overhanging. **139. portance,** conduct. **140. antres,** caves. **idle,** barren. **142. hint,** occasion. **process,** order (of events). **144. Anthropophagi,** man-eaters. **151. pliant,** convenient. **153. dilate,** relate in full. **155. intentively,** attentively. **173. at the best,** as well as possible.

199. like yourself, as you should. **200. grise,** degree. **209. bootless,** useless. **213. free comfort,** freely-given consolation. **216. sentences,** moral aphorisms. **217. equivocal,** equivalent.

That the bruis'd heart was pierced through the ear.
I humbly beseech you, proceed to th' affairs of state.

Duke. The Turk with a most mighty preparation makes for Cyprus. Othello, the fortitude of the place is best known to you; and though we have there a substitute of most allowed sufficiency, yet opinion, a sovereign mistress of effects, throws a more safer voice on you: you must therefore be content to slubber the gloss of your new fortunes with this more stubborn and boisterous expedition.

Oth. The tyrant custom, most grave senators,
Hath made the flinty and steel couch of war
My thrice-driven bed of down. I do agnize
A natural and prompt alacrity
I find in hardness, and do undertake
These present wars against the Ottomites.
Most humbly therefore bending to your state,
I crave fit disposition for my wife,
Due reference of place and exhibition,
With such accommodation and besort
As levels with her breeding.

Duke. If you please,
Be 't at her father's.

Bra. I 'll not have it so.

Oth. Nor I.

Des. Nor I; I would not there reside,
To put my father in impatient thoughts
By being in his eye. Most gracious duke,
To my unfolding lend your prosperous ear;
And let me find a charter in your voice,
T' assist my simpleness.

Duke. What would you, Desdemona?

Des. That I did love the Moor to live with him,
My downright violence and storm of fortunes
May trumpet to the world. My heart 's subdued
Even to the very quality of my lord:
I saw Othello's visage in his mind,
And to his honours and his valiant parts
Did I my soul and fortunes consecrate.
So that, dear lords, if I be left behind,
A moth of peace, and he go to the war,
The rites for which I love him are bereft me,
And I a heavy interim shall support
By his dear absence. Let me go with him.

Oth. Let her have your voice.
Vouch with me, Heaven, I therefore beg it not
To please the palate of my appetite,
Nor to comply with heat, the young affects
In my defunct and proper satisfaction,
But to be free and bounteous to her mind;
And Heaven defend your good souls, that you think
I will your serious and great business scant
When she is with me. No, when light-wing'd toys
Of feather'd Cupid seel with wanton dullness
My speculative and offic'd instruments
That my disports corrupt and taint my business,
Let housewives make a skillet of my helm,
And all indign and base adversities
Make head against my estimation!

Duke. Be it as you shall privately determine,
Either for her stay or going: th' affair cries haste,
And speed must answer it.

1. Sen. You must away to-night.

Des. To-night, my lord?

Duke. This night.

Oth. With all my heart.

Duke. At nine i' th' morning here we 'll meet again.
Othello, leave some officer behind,
And he shall our commission bring to you,
And such things else of quality and respect
As doth import you.

Oth. So please your Grace, my ancient;
A man he is of honesty and trust:
To his conveyance I assign my wife,
With what else needful your good Grace shall think
To be sent after me.

Duke. Let it be so.
Good-night to every one. [*To Brabantio.*] And, noble signior,
If virtue no delighted beauty lack,
Your son-in-law is far more fair than black.

1. Sen. Adieu, brave Moor; use Desdemona well.

Bra. Look to her, Moor, if thou hast eyes to see;
She has deceiv'd her father, and may thee.

Exeunt Duke, Brabantio, Senators, Officers, etc.

Oth. My life upon her faith! Honest Iago,
My Desdemona must I leave to thee.
I prithee, let thy wife attend on her;
And bring them after in the best advantage.

222. **fortitude**, strength. 224. **allowed**, acknowledged. 225. **opinion**, reputation. 227. **slubber**, sully. 232. **thrice-driven**, thrice-winnowed. **agnize**, acknowledge. 234. **hardness**, hardship. 238. **exhibition**, allowance. 239. **besort**, attendance. 240. **levels with**, suits. 245. **prosperous**, propitious. 246. **charter**, privilege. 250. The headlong and violent way of taking my fortunes by storm. 260. **dear**, deeply felt.

264-5. **affects . . . satisfaction**, a difficult passage. The text may be corrupt; but the sense is plain: Othello wishes to take his wife with him not to gratify his sensual desires but to comply with her request. 267. **defend**, forbid. 269. **toys**, trifles. 270. **seel**, blind, a term in falconry. Hawks were partly blinded by sewing up their eyelids. 271. **speculative and offic'd instruments**, visual and active powers 274. **indign**, unworthy. 275. **estimation**, reputation. 284. **import**, concern. 290. **delighted**, delightful. 298. **advantage**, opportunity.

Come, Desdemona; I have but an hour
Of love, of worldly matters and direction,
To spend with thee. We must obey the time.
Exeunt Othello and Desdemona.

Rod. Iago,—

Iago. What say'st thou, noble heart?

Rod. What will I do, think'st thou?

Iago. Why, go to bed, and sleep.

Rod. I will incontinently drown myself.

Iago. If thou dost, I shall never love thee after. Why, thou silly gentleman!

Rod. It is silliness to live when to live is torment; and then have we a prescription to die when Death is our physician.

Iago. O villanous! I have looked upon the world for four times seven years; and since I could distinguish betwixt a benefit and an injury, I never found man that knew how to love himself. Ere I would say I would drown myself for the love of a guinea-hen, I would change my humanity with a baboon.

Rod. What should I do? I confess it is my shame to be so fond, but it is not in my virtue to amend it.

Iago. Virtue! a fig! 't is in ourselves that we are thus or thus. Our bodies are our gardens, to the which our wills are gardeners; so that if we will plant nettles, or sow lettuce, set hyssop and weed up thyme, supply it with one gender of herbs, or distract it with many, either to have it sterile with idleness, or manured with industry, why, the power and corrigible authority of this lies in our wills. If the balance of our lives had not one scale of reason to poise another of sensuality, the blood and baseness of our natures would conduct us to most preposterous conclusions. But we have reason to cool our raging motions, our carnal stings, our unbitted lusts, whereof I take this that you call love to be a sect or scion.

Rod. It cannot be.

Iago. It is merely a lust of the blood and a permission of the will. Come, be a man. Drown thyself? drown cats and blind puppies. I have professed me thy friend, and I confess me knit to thy deserving with cables of perdurable toughness; I could never better stead thee than now. Put money in thy purse; follow thou the wars; defeat thy favour with an usurped beard. I say, put money in thy purse. It cannot be long that Desdemona should continue her love to the Moor,—put money in thy purse,—nor he his to her. It was a violent commencement in her, and thou shalt see an answerable sequestration: put but money in thy purse. These Moors are changeable in their wills;—fill thy purse with money;—the food that to him now is as luscious as locusts, shall be to him shortly as bitter as coloquintida. She must change for youth; when she is sated with his body, she will find the error of her choice—she must have change, she must—therefore put money in thy purse. If thou wilt needs damn thyself, do it a more delicate way than drowning. Make all the money thou canst. If sanctimony and a frail vow betwixt an erring barbarian and a super-subtle Venetian be not too hard for my wits and all the tribe of hell, thou shalt enjoy her; therefore make money. A pox of drowning thyself! it is clean out of the way. Seek thou rather to be hanged in compassing thy joy than to be drowned and go without her.

Rod. Wilt thou be fast to my hopes, if I depend on the issue?

Iago. Thou art sure of me—go, make money—I have told thee often, and I re-tell thee again and again, I hate the Moor. My cause is hearted; thine hath no less reason. Let us be conjunctive in our revenge against him. If thou canst cuckold him, thou dost thyself a pleasure, me a sport. There are many events in the womb of time which will be delivered. Traverse! go, provide thy money. We will have more of this to-morrow. Adieu.

Rod. Where shall we meet i' th' morning?

Iago. At my lodging.

Rod. I 'll be with thee betimes.

Iago. Go to; farewell. Do you hear, Roderigo?

Rod. What say you?

Iago. No more of drowning, do you hear?

Rod. I am chang'd; I 'll go sell all my land.
Exit.

Iago. Thus do I ever make my fool my purse;
For I mine own gain'd knowledge should profane
If I would time expend with such a snipe
But for my sport and profit. I hate the Moor;
And it is thought abroad that 'twixt my sheets
He has done my office. I know not if 't be true;
But I, for mere suspicion in that kind,
Will do as if for surety. He holds me well;
The better shall my purpose work on him.
Cassio 's a proper man: let me see now:
To get his place and to plume up my will

306. incontinently, immediately. **326. gender,** kind. **328-9. corrigible authority,** correcting control. **334. motions,** sexual appetites. **337. sect or scion,** cutting or shoot. **343. stead,** help. **345. defeat thy favour,** disguise thy face.

351. answerable sequestration, corresponding rupture. **355. locusts,** thought to be eaten by Moors. **356. coloquintida,** colocynth, a bitter fruit. **362. erring,** vagrant. **374. hearted,** fixed in the heart. **374. conjunctive,** united. **379. Traverse,** forward march. **391. snipe,** woodcock, fool. **398. proper,** handsome. **399. plume up,** make triumph.

In double knavery—How, how?—Let 's see:—
After some time, to abuse Othello's ear
That he is too familiar with his wife.
He hath a person and a smooth dispose
To be suspected, fram'd to make women false.
The Moor is of a free and open nature,
That thinks men honest that but seem to be so,
And will as tenderly be led by th' nose
As asses are.
I have 't. It is engender'd. Hell and night
Must bring this monstrous birth to the world's light. *Exit.*

Act II. Scene I. *A sea-port in Cyprus. An open place.*

Enter *Montano* and two *Gentlemen.*

Mon. What from the cape can you discern at sea?

1. Gent. Nothing at all; it is a high-wrought flood.
I cannot, 'twixt the heaven and the main,
Descry a sail.

Mon. Methinks the wind hath spoke aloud at land;
A fuller blast ne'er shook our battlements:
If it hath ruffian'd so upon the sea,
What ribs of oak, when mountains melt on them,
Can hold the mortise? What shall we hear of this?

2. Gent. A segregation of the Turkish fleet:
For do but stand upon the foaming shore,
The chidden billow seems to pelt the clouds;
The wind-shak'd surge, with high and monstrous mane,
Seems to cast water on the burning bear
And quench the guards of th' ever-fixed pole:
I never did like molestation view
On the enchafed flood.

Mon. If that the Turkish fleet
Be not enshelter'd and embay'd, they are drown'd;
It is impossible to bear it out.

Enter a third *Gentleman.*

3. Gent. News, lads! our wars are done.
The desperate tempest hath so bang'd the Turks,
That their designment halts. A noble ship of Venice
Hath seen a grievous wreck and sufferance
On most part of their fleet.

Mon. How? is this true?

3. Gent. The ship is here put in,
A Veronesa; Michael Cassio,
Lieutenant to the warlike Moor Othello,
Is come on shore; the Moor himself at sea,
And is in full commission here for Cyprus.

Mon. I am glad on 't; 't is a worthy governor.

3. Gent. But this same Cassio, though he speak of comfort
Touching the Turkish loss, yet he looks sadly,
And prays the Moor be safe; for they were parted
With foul and violent tempest.

Mon. Pray heavens he be;
For I have serv'd him, and the man commands
Like a full soldier. Let 's to the seaside, ho!
As well to see the vessel that 's come in
As to throw out our eyes for brave Othello,
Even till we make the main and th' aerial blue
An indistinct regard.

3. Gent. Come, let 's do so;
For every minute is expectancy
Of more arrivance.

Enter *Cassio.*

Cas. Thanks, you the valiant of this warlike isle,
That so approve the Moor! O, let the heavens
Give him defence against the elements,
For I have lost him on a dangerous sea.

Mon. Is he well shipp'd?

Cas. His bark is stoutly timber'd, and his pilot
Of very expert and approv'd allowance;
Therefore my hopes, not surfeited to death,
Stand in bold cure.

Within, "A sail, a sail, a sail!"

Enter a *Messenger.*

Cas. What noise?

Mess. The town is empty; on the brow o' th' sea
Stand ranks of people, and they cry, "A sail!"

403. **dispose**, disposition. **Act II, Scene i: 9. hold the mortise**, remain jointed. **10. segregation**, dispersion. **15. guards**, two stars in the constellation of the Little Bear. **pole**, pole-star. **16. molestation**, disturbance. **22. designment**, enterprise. **23. sufferance**, disaster.

Act II, Scene i: 26. A Veronesa, a ship equipped by Verona, then a town subject to Venice. **36. full**, thorough. **40. regard**, view. **42. arrivance**, arrival. **49. approv'd allowance**, established skill. **50-1. not . . . cure**, not being overindulged stand in expectation of fulfilment.

Cas. My hopes do shape him for the governor. *A shot.*
2. Gent. They do discharge their shot of courtesy.
Our friends at least.
Cas. I pray you, sir, go forth,
And give us truth who 't is that is arriv'd.
2. Gent. I shall. *Exit.*
Mon. But, good lieutenant, is your general wiv'd?
Cas. Most fortunately: he hath achiev'd a maid
That paragons description and wild fame;
One that excels the quirks of blazoning pens,
And in th' essential vesture of creation
Does tire the ingener.

Re-enter second *Gentleman.*

How now? who has put in?
2. Gent. 'T is one Iago, ancient to the general.
Cas. Has had most favourable and happy speed:
Tempests themselves, high seas, and howling winds,
The gutter'd rocks and congregated sands,
Traitors ensteep'd to clog the guiltless keel,
As having sense of beauty do omit
Their mortal natures, letting go safely by
The divine Desdemona.
Mon. What is she?
Cas. She that I spake of, our great captain's captain,
Left in the conduct of the bold Iago,
Whose footing here anticipates our thoughts
A se'nnight's speed. Great Jove, Othello guard,
And swell his sail with thine own powerful breath,
That he may bless this bay with his tall ship,
Make love's quick pants in Desdemona's arms,
Give renew'd fire to our extincted spirits,
And bring all Cyprus comfort!

Enter *Desdemona, Emilia, Iago, Roderigo,* and Attendants.

O, behold,
The riches of the ship is come on shore!
You men of Cyprus, let her have your knees.
Hail to thee, lady! and the grace of heaven,
Before, behind thee, and on every hand,
Enwheel thee round!
Des. I thank you, valiant Cassio.
What tidings can you tell me of my lord?
Cas. He is not yet arriv'd; nor know I aught
But that he 's well and will be shortly here.
Des. O, but I fear—How lost you company?
Cas. The great contention of the sea and skies
Parted our fellowship.—But, hark! a sail.
Within, "A sail, a sail!" *Guns heard.*
2. Gent. They give their greeting to the citadel:
This likewise is a friend.
Cas. See for the news.
Exit Gentleman.
Good ancient, you are welcome. [*To Emilia.*] Welcome, mistress.
Let it not gall your patience, good Iago,
That I extend my manners; 't is my breeding
That gives me this bold show of courtesy.
Kissing her.
Iago. Sir, would she give you so much of her lips
As of her tongue she oft bestows on me,
You 'd have enough.
Des. Alas, she has no speech.
Iago. In faith, too much;
I find it still, when I have list to sleep.
Marry, before your ladyship, I grant,
She puts her tongue a little in her heart,
And chides with thinking.
Emil. You have little cause to say so.
Iago. Come on, come on; you are pictures out of doors,
Bells in your parlours, wild-cats in your kitchens,
Saints in your injuries, devils being offended,
Players in your housewifery, and housewives in your beds.
Des. O, fie upon thee, slanderer!
Iago. Nay, it is true, or else I am a Turk.
You rise to play and go to bed to work.
Emil. You shall not write my praise.
Iago. No, let me not.
Des. What wouldst thou write of me, if thou shouldst praise me?
Iago. O gentle lady, do not put me to 't;
For I am nothing, if not critical.
Des. Come on, assay.—There 's one gone to the harbour?
Iago. Ay, madam.
Des. I am not merry; but I do beguile
The thing I am, by seeming otherwise.—
Come, how wouldst thou praise me?
Iago. I am about it; but indeed my invention
Comes from my pate as birdlime does from frieze;

62. **paragons,** excels. 63. **quirks,** conceits. **blazoning,** praising. 64. **essential vesture of creation,** real endowments. 65. **ingener,** inventor (of praises). 69. **gutter'd,** jagged. 70. **ensteep'd,** submerged. 72. **mortal,** deadly. 87. **Enwheel,** encompass.

112. **Saints in your injuries,** say spiteful things with a sanctimonious air. 113. **Players,** triflers. **housewives,** hussies. 127. **birdlime,** sticky substance for catching birds. **frieze,** coarse woolen cloth.

It plucks out brains and all. But my Muse labours,
And thus she is deliver'd:

If she be fair and wise, fairness and wit,
The one 's for use, the other useth it.

Des. Well prais'd! How if she be black and witty?

Iago.

If she be black, and thereto have a wit,
She 'll find a white that shall her blackness fit.

Des. Worse and worse.

Emil. How if fair and foolish?

Iago.

She never yet was foolish that was fair;
For even her folly help'd her to an heir.

Des. These are old fond paradoxes to make fools laugh i' th' alehouse. What miserable praise hast thou for her that 's foul and foolish?

Iago.

There 's none so foul and foolish thereunto,
But does foul pranks which fair and wise ones do.

Des. O heavy ignorance! thou praisest the worst best. But what praise couldst thou bestow on a deserving woman indeed, one that, in the authority of her merit, did justly put on the vouch of very malice itself?

Iago.

She that was ever fair and never proud,
Had tongue at will and yet was never loud,
Never lack'd gold and yet went never gay,
Fled from her wish and yet said, "Now I may";
She that being anger'd, her revenge being nigh,
Bade her wrong stay and her displeasure fly;
She that in wisdom never was so frail
To change the cod's head for the salmon's tail;
She that could think and ne'er disclose her mind
See suitors following and not look behind,
She was a wight, if ever such wights were,—

Des. To do what?

Iago.

To suckle fools and chronicle small beer.

Des. O most lame and impotent conclusion! Do not learn of him, Emilia, though he be thy husband. How say you, Cassio? Is he not a most profane and liberal counsellor?

Cas. He speaks home, madam: you may relish him more in the soldier than in the scholar.

Iago. [*Aside.*] He takes her by the palm; ay, well said, whisper. With as little a web as this will I ensnare as great a fly as Cassio. Ay, smile upon her, do; I will gyve thee in thine own courtship.—You say true; 't is so, indeed.—If such tricks as these strip you out of your lieutenantry, it had been better you had not kissed your three fingers so oft, which now again you are most apt to play the sir in. Very good; well kissed! an excellent curtsy! 'T is so, indeed. Yet again your fingers to your lips? Would they were clyster-pipes for your sake! [*Trumpet within.*]—The Moor! I know his trumpet.

Cas. 'T is truly so.

Des. Let 's meet him and receive him.

Cas. Lo, where he comes!

Enter *Othello* and Attendants.

Oth. O my fair warrior!

Des. My dear Othello!

Oth. It gives me wonder great as my content
To see you here before me. O my soul's joy!
If after every tempest come such calms,
May the winds blow till they have waken'd death!
And let the labouring bark climb hills of seas
Olympus-high, and duck again as low
As hell 's from heaven! If it were now to die,
'T were now to be most happy; for, I fear,
My soul hath her content so absolute
That not another comfort like to this
Succeeds in unknown fate.

Des. The heavens forbid
But that our loves and comforts should increase,
Even as our days do grow!

Oth. Amen to that, sweet powers!
I cannot speak enough of this content;
It stops me here; it is too much of joy.
And this, and this, the greatest discords be *They kiss.*
That e'er our hearts shall make!

Iago. [*Aside.*] O, you are well tun'd now!
But I 'll set down the pegs that make this music,
As honest as I am.

Oth. Come, let us to the castle.
News, friends: our wars are done, the Turks are drown'd.
How does my old acquaintance of this isle?
Honey, you shall be well desir'd in Cyprus;
I have found great love amongst them. O my sweet,
I prattle out of fashion, and I dote
In mine own comforts. I prithee, good Iago,

134. white, (1) white, (2) wight, person. **139. fond,** foolish. **147-8. put on the vouch,** challenge the testimony. **161. chronicle small beer,** keep small household accounts. **165. liberal,** licentious.

170. gyve, fetter. **175. sir,** gallant. **178. clyster-pipes,** tubes used for medical injections. **202. set down the pegs,** loosen the pegs and so untune the strings. **206. desir'd,** loved.

Go to the bay and disembark my coffers:
Bring thou the master to the citadel;
He is a good one, and his worthiness
Does challenge much respect. Come, Desdemona,
Once more, well met at Cyprus.

Exeunt Othello, Desdemona and Attendants.

Iago. Do thou meet me presently at the harbour. Come hither. If thou be'st valiant,—as, they say, base men being in love have then a nobility in their natures more than is native to them,—list me. The lieutenant to-night watches on the court of guard;—first, I must tell thee this: Desdemona is directly in love with him.

Rod. With him? why, 't is not possible.

Iago. Lay thy finger thus, and let thy soul be instructed. Mark me with what violence she first loved the Moor, but for bragging and telling her fantastical lies. To love him still for prating,—let not thy discreet heart think it. Her eye must be fed; and what delight shall she have to look on the devil? When the blood is made dull with the act of sport, there should be, again to inflame it, and to give satiety a fresh appetite, loveliness in favour, sympathy in years, manners, and beauties; all which the Moor is defective in. Now, for want of these required conveniences, her delicate tenderness will find itself abused, begin to heave the gorge, disrelish and abhor the Moor; very nature will instruct her in it and compel her to some second choice. Now, sir, this granted,—as it is a most pregnant and unforced position—who stands so eminent in the degree of this fortune as Cassio does? a knave very voluble; no further conscionable than in putting on the mere form of civil and humane seeming, for the better compassing of his salt and most hidden loose affection? Why, none; why, none; a slipper and subtle knave, a finder of occasion, that has an eye can stamp and counterfeit advantages, though true advantage never present itself; a devilish knave. Besides, the knave is handsome, young, and hath all those requisites in him that folly and green minds look after; a pestilent complete knave, and the woman hath found him already.

Rod. I cannot believe that in her; she 's full of most blessed condition.

Iago. Blessed fig's-end! The wine she drinks is made of grapes. If she had been blessed, she would never have loved the Moor. Blessed pudding! Didst thou not see her paddle with the palm of his hand? Didst not mark that?

Rod. Yes, that I did; but that was but courtesy.

Iago. Lechery, by this hand; an index and obscure prologue to the history of lust and foul thoughts. They met so near with their lips that their breaths embraced together. Villanous thoughts, Roderigo! When these mutualities so marshal the way, hard at hand comes the master and main exercise, th' incorporate conclusion. Pish! But, sir, be you ruled by me; I have brought you from Venice. Watch you to-night; for the command, I 'll lay 't upon you. Cassio knows you not: I 'll not be far from you. Do you find some occasion to anger Cassio, either by speaking too loud, or tainting his discipline; or from what other course you please, which the time shall more favourably minister.

Rod. Well?

Iago. Sir, he 's rash and very sudden in choler, and haply may strike at you: provoke him, that he may; for even out of that will I cause these of Cyprus to mutiny, whose qualification shall come into no true taste again but by the displanting of Cassio. So shall you have a shorter journey to your desires by the means I shall then have to prefer them; and the impediment most profitably removed, without the which there were no expectation of our prosperity.

Rod. I will do this, if you can bring it to any opportunity.

Iago. I warrant thee. Meet me by and by at the citadel; I must fetch his necessaries ashore. Farewell.

Rod. Adieu. *Exit.*

Iago. That Cassio loves her, I do well believe 't;
That she loves him, 't is apt and of great credit;
The Moor, howbeit that I endure him not,
Is of a constant, loving, noble nature,
And I dare think he 'll prove to Desdemona
A most dear husband. Now, I do love her too;
Not out of absolute lust, though peradventure
I stand accountant for as great a sin,
But partly led to diet my revenge,
For that I do suspect the lusty Moor
Hath leap'd into my seat; the thought whereof
Doth, like a poisonous mineral, gnaw my inwards;
And nothing can or shall content my soul
Till I am even'd with him, wife for wife;
Or failing so, yet that I put the Moor

211. **master,** ship's master. 220. **court of guard,** main guard-house. 236. **heave the gorge,** be nauseated. 239. **pregnant,** evident. 242. **conscionable,** conscientious. 244. **salt,** lewd. 245. **slipper,** slippery. 255. **condition,** qualities.

275. **tainting,** discrediting. 282. **qualification,** appeasement. 296. **apt,** natural. **of great credit,** very credible.

At least into a jealousy so strong
That judgement cannot cure. Which thing to do,
If this poor trash of Venice, whom I trash
For his quick hunting, stand the putting on,
I 'll have our Michael Cassio on the hip,
Abuse him to the Moor in the rank garb—
For I fear Cassio with my night-cap too—
Make the Moor thank me, love me, and reward me,
For making him egregiously an ass
And practising upon his peace and quiet
Even to madness. 'T is here, but yet confus'd;
Knavery's plain face is never seen till us'd.
Exit.

Scene II. *A street.*

Enter Othello's *Herald*, with a proclamation. People following.

Her. It is Othello's pleasure, our noble and valiant general, that, upon certain tidings now arrived importing the mere perdition of the Turkish fleet, every man put himself into triumph; some to dance, some to make bonfires, each man to what sport and revels his addiction leads him; for, beside these beneficial news, it is the celebration of his nuptial. So much was his pleasure should be proclaimed. All offices are open, and there is full liberty of feasting from this present hour of five till the bell have told eleven. Heaven bless the isle of Cyprus and our noble general Othello! *Exeunt.*

Scene III. *A hall in the castle.*

Enter *Othello, Desdemona, Cassio,* and Attendants.

Oth. Good Michael, look you to the guard to-night:
Let 's teach ourselves that honourable stop,
Not to outsport discretion.
Cas. Iago hath direction what to do;
But, notwithstanding, with my personal eye
Will I look to 't.
Oth. Iago is most honest.
Michael, good-night; to-morrow with your earliest
Let me have speech with you. [*To Desdemona.*] Come, my dear love,
The purchase made, the fruits are to ensue;
That profit 's yet to come 'tween me and you.
Good-night.
Exeunt Othello, Desdemona, and Attendants.

Enter *Iago.*

Cas. Welcome, Iago; we must to the watch.

Iago. Not this hour, lieutenant; 't is not yet ten o' th' clock. Our general cast us thus early for the love of his Desdemona; who let us not therefore blame: he hath not yet made wanton the night with her; and she is sport for Jove.

Cas. She 's a most exquisite lady.

Iago. And, I 'll warrant her, full of game.

Cas. Indeed, she 's a most fresh and delicate creature.

Iago. What an eye she has! Methinks it sounds a parley to provocation.

Cas. An inviting eye; and yet methinks right modest.

Iago. And when she speaks, is it not an alarum to love?

Cas. She is indeed perfection.

Iago. Well, happiness to their sheets! Come, lieutenant, I have a stoup of wine; and here without are a brace of Cyprus gallants that would fain have a measure to the health of black Othello.

Cas. Not to-night, good Iago: I have very poor and unhappy brains for drinking; I could well wish courtesy would invent some other custom of entertainment.

Iago. O, they are our friends: but one cup; I 'll drink for you.

Cas. I have drunk but one cup to-night, and that was craftily qualified too, and, behold, what innovation it makes here. I am unfortunate in the infirmity, and dare not task my weakness with any more.

Iago. What, man! 't is a night of revels: the gallants desire it.

Cas. Where are they?

Iago. Here at the door; I pray you, call them in.

Cas. I 'll do 't; but it dislikes me. *Exit.*

Iago. If I can fasten but one cup upon him,
With that which he hath drunk to-night already,
He 'll be as full of quarrel and offence
As my young mistress' dog. Now, my sick fool Roderigo,
Whom love hath turn'd almost the wrong side out,
To Desdemona hath to-night carous'd
Potations pottle-deep; and he 's to watch:

312. trash, worthless fellow. **trash,** check, a hunting term. **315. rank garb,** coarse fashion. **Scene ii: 3. mere perdition,** complete loss. **9. offices,** storerooms and kitchens.

Scene iii: 14. cast, dismissed. **30. stoup,** large measure. **41. craftily qualified,** slyly diluted. **42. innovation,** change for the worst. **56. pottle-deep,** to the bottom of the tankard.

Three lads of Cyprus, noble swelling spirits
That hold their honours in a wary distance,
The very elements of this warlike isle,
Have I to-night fluster'd with flowing cups,
And they watch too. Now, 'mongst this flock of drunkards
Am I to put our Cassio in some action
That may offend the isle. But here they come.

Re-enter *Cassio,* with him *Montano* and *Gentlemen.* Servants follow with wine.

If consequence do but approve my dream,
My boat sails freely, both with wind and stream.

Cas. 'Fore God, they have given me a rouse already.

Mon. Good faith, a little one; not past a pint, as I am a soldier.

Iago. Some wine, ho!
Sings.

And let me the canakin clink, clink;
And let me the canakin clink.
A soldier 's a man;
O, man's life 's but a span;
Why, then, let a soldier drink.

Some wine, boys!

Cas. 'Fore God, an excellent song.

Iago. I learned it in England, where, indeed, they are most potent in potting; your Dane, your German, and your swag-bellied Hollander—Drink, ho!—are nothing to your English.

Cas. Is your Englishman so exquisite in his drinking?

Iago. Why, he drinks you, with facility, your Dane dead drunk; he sweats not to overthrow your Almain; he gives your Hollander a vomit ere the next pottle can be filled.

Cas. To the health of our general!

Mon. I am for it, lieutenant; and I 'll do you justice.

Iago. O sweet England!

King Stephen was and-a worthy peer,
His breeches cost him but a crown;
He held them sixpence all too dear,
With that he call'd the tailor lown.

He was a wight of high renown,
And thou art but of low degree.
'T is pride that pulls the country down;
And take thy auld cloak about thee.

Some wine, ho!

Cas. Why, this is a more exquisite song than the other.

Iago. Will you hear 't again?

Cas. No; for I hold him to be unworthy of his place that does those things. Well, God 's above all; and there be souls must be saved, and there be souls must not be saved.

Iago. It 's true, good lieutenant.

Cas. For mine own part,—no offence to the general, nor any man of quality—I hope to be saved.

Iago. And so do I too, lieutenant.

Cas. Ay, but, by your leave, not before me; the lieutenant is to be saved before the ancient. Let 's have no more of this; let 's to our affairs.—God forgive us our sins!— Gentlemen, let 's look to our business. Do not think, gentlemen, I am drunk. This is my ancient; this is my right hand, and this is my left. I am not drunk now; I can stand well enough, and I speak well enough.

Gent. Excellent well.

Cas. Why, very well then; you must not think then that I am drunk. *Exit.*

Mon. To th' platform, masters; come, let 's set the watch.

Iago. You see this fellow that is gone before:
He is a soldier fit to stand by Cæsar
And give direction; and do but see his vice.
'T is to his virtue a just equinox,
The one as long as the other; 't is pity of him.
I fear the trust Othello puts him in,
On some odd time of his infirmity,
Will shake this island.

Mon. But is he often thus?

Iago. 'T is evermore his prologue to his sleep.
He 'll watch the horologe a double set,
If drink rock not his cradle.

Mon. It were well
The general were put in mind of it.
Perhaps he sees it not; or his good nature
Prizes the virtue that appears in Cassio,
And looks not on his evils. Is not this true?

Enter *Roderigo.*

Iago. [*Aside to him.*] How now, Roderigo!
I pray you, after the lieutenant; go.
Exit Roderigo.

Mon. And 't is great pity that the noble Moor
Should hazard such a place as his own second
With one of an ingraft infirmity:
It were an honest action to say
So to the Moor.

Iago. Not I, for this fair island.
I do love Cassio well; and would do much
To cure him of this evil.—But, hark! what noise? *Cry within:* "Help! help!"

58. hold . . . distance, i.e., are easily provoked to a quarrel. **59. elements,** i.e., typical inhabitants. **66. rouse,** bumper. **86. Almain,** German. **95. lown,** lout.

129. just equinox, exact counterpart. **135. horologe a double set,** the clock twice around.

Re-enter *Cassio,* pursuing *Roderigo.*

Cas. 'Zounds, you rogue! you rascal!
Mon. What 's the matter, lieutenant?
Cas. A knave teach me my duty!
I 'll beat the knave into a twiggen bottle.
Rod. Beat me?
Cas. Dost thou prate, rogue? *Striking Roderigo.*
Mon. Nay, good lieutenant; *Staying him.*
I pray you, sir, hold your hand.
Cas. Let me go, sir,
Or I 'll knock you o'er the mazzard.
Mon. Come, come, you 're drunk.
Cas. Drunk! *They fight.*
Iago. [*Aside to Roderigo.*] Away, I say; go out, and cry a mutiny. *Exit Roderigo.*
Nay, good lieutenant,—God's will, gentlemen;—
Help, ho! — Lieutenant, — sir, — Montano, —sir;—
Help, masters!—Here 's a goodly watch indeed! *A bell rings.*
Who 's that which rings the bell?—Diablo, ho!
The town will rise. God's will, lieutenant, hold!
You will be sham'd for ever.

Re-enter *Othello* and Attendants.

Oth. What is the matter here?
Mon. 'Zounds, I bleed still; I am hurt to th' death. He dies!
Oth. Hold, for your lives!
Iago. Hold, ho! Lieutenant,—sir,—Montano,—gentlemen,—
Have you forgot all sense of place and duty?
Hold! the general speaks to you; hold, for shame!
Oth. Why, how now, ho! from whence ariseth this?
Are we turn'd Turks, and to ourselves do that
Which Heaven hath forbid the Ottomites?
For Christian shame, put by this barbarous brawl.
He that stirs next to carve for his own rage
Holds his soul light; he dies upon his motion.
Silence that dreadful bell; it frights the isle
From her propriety. What is the matter, masters?
Honest Iago, that looks dead with grieving,
Speak, who began this? On thy love, I charge thee.
Iago. I do not know: friends all but now, even now,
In quarter, and in terms like bride and groom
Devesting them for bed; and then, but now—
As if some planet had unwitted men—
Swords out, and tilting one at other's breast,
In opposition bloody. I cannot speak
Any beginning to this peevish odds;
And would in action glorious I had lost
Those legs that brought me to a part of it!
Oth. How comes it, Michael, you are thus forgot?
Cas. I pray you, pardon me; I cannot speak.
Oth. Worthy Montano, you were wont to be civil;
The gravity and stillness of your youth
The world hath noted, and your name is great
In mouths of wisest censure. What 's the matter,
That you unlace your reputation thus,
And spend your rich opinion for the name
Of a night-brawler? Give me answer to it.
Mon. Worthy Othello, I am hurt to danger.
Your officer, Iago, can inform you—
While I spare speech, which something now offends me—
Of all that I do know; nor know I aught
By me that 's said or done amiss this night,
Unless self-charity be sometimes a vice,
And to defend ourselves it be a sin
When violence assails us.
Oth. Now, by heaven,
My blood begins my safer guides to rule;
And passion, having my best judgement collied,
Assays to lead the way. If I once stir
Or do but lift this arm, the best of you
Shall sink in my rebuke. Give me to know
How this foul rout began, who set it on;
And he that is approv'd in this offence,
Though he had twinn'd with me, both at a birth,
Shall lose me. What! in a town of war,
Yet wild, the people's hearts brimful of fear,
To manage private and domestic quarrel,
In night, and on the court and guard of safety!
'T is monstrous. Iago, who began 't?
Mon. If partially affin'd, or leagued in office,
Thou dost deliver more or less than truth,
Thou art no soldier.
Iago. Touch me not so near.
I had rather have this tongue cut from my mouth
Than it should do offence to Michael Cassio;
Yet, I persuade myself, to speak the truth
Shall nothing wrong him. Thus it is, general:
Montano and myself being in speech,

152. **twiggen bottle**, bottle covered with wickerwork. 154. **mazzard**, head. 173. **to carve**, to indulge himself. 174. **upon his motion**, as soon as he moves. 180. **quarter**, concord.

185. **peevish odds**, silly quarrel. 193. **censure**, judgement. 195. **rich opinion**, valuable reputation. 199. **offends**, pains. 206. **collied**, obscured. 211. **approv'd**, implicated. 218. **partially affin'd**, made partial by any relationship.

There comes a fellow crying out for help;
And Cassio following him with determin'd sword
To execute upon him. Sir, this gentleman
Steps in to Cassio and entreats his pause;
Myself the crying fellow did pursue,
Lest by his clamour—as it so fell out—
The town might fall in fright. He, swift of foot,
Outran my purpose; and I return'd the rather
For that I heard the clink and fall of swords,
And Cassio high in oath; which till to-night
I ne'er might say before. When I came back—
For this was brief—I found them close together,
At blow and thrust; even as again they were
When you yourself did part them.
More of this matter cannot I report.
But men are men; the best sometimes forget.
Though Cassio did some little wrong to him,
As men in rage strike those that wish them best,
Yet surely Cassio, I believe, receiv'd
From him that fled some strange indignity
Which patience could not pass.

Oth. I know, Iago,
Thy honesty and love doth mince this matter,
Making it light to Cassio. Cassio, I love thee;
But never more be officer of mine.

Re-enter *Desdemona,* attended.

Look, if my gentle love be not rais'd up!
I 'll make thee an example.

Des. What 's the matter, dear?

Oth. All 's well now, sweeting; come away to bed.
Sir, for your hurts, myself will be your surgeon.—
Lead him off. *To Montano, who is led off.*
Iago, look with care about the town,
And silence those whom this vile brawl distracted.
Come, Desdemona; 't is the soldiers' life
To have their balmy slumbers wak'd with strife. *Exeunt all but Iago and Cassio.*

Iago. What, are you hurt, lieutenant?

Cas. Ay, past all surgery.

Iago. Marry, God forbid!

Cas. Reputation, reputation, reputation! O, I have lost my reputation! I have lost the immortal part of myself, and what remains is bestial. My reputation, Iago, my reputation!

Iago. As I am an honest man, I thought you had received some bodily wound; there is more sense in that than in reputation. Reputation is an idle and most false imposition; oft got without merit, and lost without deserving. You have lost no reputation at all, unless you repute yourself such a loser. What, man! there are more ways to recover the general again. You are but now cast in his mood, a punishment more in policy than in malice; even so as one would beat his offenceless dog to affright an imperious lion. Sue to him again, and he 's yours.

Cas. I will rather sue to be despised than to deceive so good a commander with so slight, so drunken, and so indiscreet an officer. Drunk? and speak parrot? and squabble? swagger? swear? and discourse fustian with one's own shadow? O thou invisible spirit of wine, if thou hast no name to be known by, let us call thee devil!

Iago. What was he that you followed with your sword? What had he done to you?

Cas. I know not.

Iago. Is 't possible?

Cas. I remember a mass of things, but nothing distinctly; a quarrel, but nothing wherefore. O God, that men should put an enemy in their mouths to steal away their brains! That we should, with joy, pleasance, revel, and applause, transform ourselves into beasts!

Iago. Why, but you are now well enough. How came you thus recovered?

Cas. It hath pleased the devil drunkenness to give place to the devil wrath: one unperfectness shows me another, to make me frankly despise myself.

Iago. Come, you are too severe a moraler. As the time, the place, and the condition of this country stands, I could heartily wish this had not befallen; but since it is as it is, mend it for your own good.

Cas. I will ask him for my place again; he shall tell me I am a drunkard! Had I as many mouths as Hydra, such an answer would stop them all. To be now a sensible man, by and by a fool, and presently a beast! O strange! Every inordinate cup is unblessed and the ingredient is a devil.

Iago. Come, come, good wine is a good familiar creature, if it be well used; exclaim no more against it. And, good lieutenant, I think you think I love you.

Cas. I have well approved it, sir. I drunk!

Iago. You or any man living may be drunk at a time, man. I 'll tell you what you shall do. Our general's wife is now the general;—I may say so in this respect, for that he hath devoted and given up himself to the contemplation, mark, and denotement of her parts and

268. sense, feeling.

281. speak parrot, talk nonsense. 282. fustian, high-sounding nonsense.

That, I being absent and my place suppli'd,
My general will forget my love and service.
Des. Do not doubt that; before Emilia here
I give thee warrant of thy place. Assure thee,
If I do vow a friendship, I 'll perform it
To the last article. My lord shall never rest;
I 'll watch him tame, and talk him out of patience;
His bed shall seem a school, his board a shrift;
I 'll intermingle everything he does
With Cassio's suit: therefore be merry, Cassio;
For thy solicitor shall rather die
Than give thy cause away.

Enter *Othello* and *Iago*.

Emil. Madam, here comes my lord.
Cas. Madam, I 'll take my leave.
Des. Why, stay, and hear me speak.
Cas. Madam, not now; I am very ill at ease,
Unfit for mine own purposes.
Des. Well, do your discretion. *Exit Cassio.*
Iago. Ha! I like not that.
Oth. What dost thou say?
Iago. Nothing, my lord; or if—I know not what.
Oth. Was not that Cassio parted from my wife?
Iago. Cassio, my lord! No, sure, I cannot think it,
That he would steal away so guilty-like,
Seeing your coming.
Oth. I do believe 't was he.
Des. How now, my lord!
I have been talking with a suitor here,
A man that languishes in your displeasure.
Oth. Who is 't you mean?
Des. Why, your lieutenant, Cassio. Good my lord,
If I have any grace or power to move you,
His present reconciliation take;
For if he be not one that truly loves you,
That errs in ignorance and not in cunning,
I have no judgement in an honest face.
I prithee, call him back.
Oth. Went he hence now?
Des. Yes, faith; so humbled
That he hath left part of his grief with me,
To suffer with him. Good love, call him back.
Oth. Not now, sweet Desdemon; some other time.
Des. But shall 't be shortly?
Oth. The sooner, sweet, for you.
Des. Shall 't be to-night at supper?
Oth. No, not to-night.
Des. To-morrow dinner, then?
Oth. I shall not dine at home;
I meet the captains at the citadel.
Des. Why, then, to-morrow night; on Tuesday morn;
On Tuesday morn, or night; on Wednesday morn.
I prithee, name the time, but let it not
Exceed three days. In faith, he 's penitent;
And yet his trespass, in our common reason—
Save that, they say, the wars must make example
Out of their best—is not almost a fault
T' incur a private check. When shall he come?
Tell me, Othello. I wonder in my soul,
What you would ask me, that I should deny,
Or stand so mamm'ring on. What! Michael Cassio,
That came a-wooing with you, and so many a time,
When I have spoke of you dispraisingly,
Hath ta'en your part,—to have so much to do
To bring him in! Trust me, I could do much,—
Oth. Prithee, no more; let him come when he will
I will deny thee nothing.
Des. Why, this is not a boon.
'T is as I should entreat you wear your gloves,
Or feed on nourishing dishes, or keep you warm,
Or sue to you to do a peculiar profit
To your own person. Nay, when I have a suit
Wherein I mean to touch your love indeed,
It shall be full of poise and difficult weight
And fearful to be granted.
Oth. I will deny thee nothing;
Whereon, I do beseech thee, grant me this,
To leave me but a little to myself.
Des. Shall I deny you? No. Farewell, my lord.
Oth. Farewell, my Desdemona; I 'll come to thee straight.
Des. Emilia, come.—Be as your fancies teach you;
Whate'er you be, I am obedient.
Exeunt Desdemona and Emilia.
Oth. Excellent wretch! Perdition catch my soul,
But I do love thee! and when I love thee not,
Chaos is come again.
Iago. My noble lord,—
Oth. What dost thou say, Iago?
Iago. Did Michael Cassio, when you woo'd my lady,
Know of your love?

23. **watch him tame,** keep him awake until he submits (method used in the training of hawks). 24. **shrift,** confessional.

66. **not almost,** scarcely. 67. **check,** rebuke. 70. **mamm'ring,** hesitating. 82. **poise,** counterpoise. 90. **wretch,** term of affection often mingled with pity.

Oth. He did, from first to last. Why dost thou ask?
Iago. But for a satisfaction of my thought;
No further harm.
Oth. Why of thy thought, Iago?
Iago. I did not think he had been acqainted with her.
Oth. O, yes; and went between us very oft.
Iago. Indeed!
Oth. Indeed! ay, indeed. Discern'st thou aught in that?
Is he not honest?
Iago. Honest, my lord?
Oth. Honest! ay, honest.
Iago. My lord, for aught I know.
Oth. What dost thou think?
Iago. Think, my lord?
Oth. Think, my lord!
By heaven, he echoes me,
As if there were some monster in his thought
Too hideous to be shown.—Thou dost mean something:
I heard thee say even now, thou lik'st not that,
When Cassio left my wife. What didst not like?
And when I told thee he was of my counsel,
Of my whole course of wooing, thou criedst, "Indeed!"
And didst contract and purse thy brow together,
As if thou then hadst shut up in thy brain
Some horrible conceit. If thou dost love me,
Show me thy thought.
Iago. My lord, you know I love you.
Oth. I think thou dost;
And, for I know thou 'rt full of love and honesty,
And weigh'st thy words before thou giv'st them breath,
Therefore these stops of thine fright me the more;
For such things in a false disloyal knave
Are tricks of custom; but in a man that 's just
They 're close delations, working from the heart
That passion cannot rule.
Iago. For Michael Cassio,
I dare be sworn I think that he is honest.
Oth. I think so too.
Iago. Men should be what they seem;
Or those that be not, would they might seem none!
Oth. Certain, men should be what they seem.
Iago. Why, then, I think Cassio 's an honest man.
Oth. Nay, yet there 's more in this.
I prithee, speak to me as to thy thinkings,
As thou dost ruminate, and give thy worst of thoughts
The worst of words.
Iago. Good my lord, pardon me.
Though I am bound to every act of duty,
I am not bound to that all slaves are free to.
Utter my thoughts? Why, say they are vile and false;
As where 's that palace whereinto foul things
Sometimes intrude not? Who has a breast so pure
But some uncleanly apprehensions
Keep leets and law-days and in sessions sit
With meditations lawful?
Oth. Thou dost conspire against thy friend, Iago,
If thou but think'st him wrong'd and mak'st his ear
A stranger to thy thoughts.
Iago. I do beseech you—
Though I perchance am vicious in my guess,
As, I confess, it is my nature's plague
To spy into abuses, and oft my jealousy
Shapes faults that are not—that your wisdom yet,
From one that so imperfectly conceits,
Would take no notice, nor build yourself a trouble
Out of his scattering and unsure observance.
It were not for your quiet nor your good,
Nor for my manhood, honesty, and wisdom,
To let you know my thoughts.
Oth. What dost thou mean?
Iago. Good name in man and woman, dear my lord,
Is the immediate jewel of their souls.
Who steals my purse steals trash; 't is something, nothing;
'T was mine, 't is his, and has been slave to thousands;
But he that filches from me my good name
Robs me of that which not enriches him,
And makes me poor indeed.
Oth. By heaven, I 'll know thy thoughts.
Iago. You cannot, if my heart were in your hand;
Nor shall not, whilst 't is in my custody.
Oth. Ha!
Iago. O, beware, my lord, of jealousy;
It is the green-ey'd monster which doth mock
The meat it feeds on. That cuckold lives in bliss
Who, certain of his fate, loves not his wronger;
But, O, what damned minutes tells he o'er

111. of my counsel, in my confidence. **123. close delations**, secret accusations.

131. as . . . thinkings, as frankly as to thine own thoughts. **140. leets**, days on which court is held. **145. vicious**, wrong. **147. jealousy**, suspicion. **149. conceits**, imagines. **151. scattering**, random.

Who dotes, yet doubts, suspects, yet strongly loves!
Oth. O misery!
Iago. Poor and content is rich and rich enough,
But riches fineless is as poor as winter
To him that ever fears he shall be poor.
Good heaven, the souls of all my tribe defend
From jealousy!
Oth. Why, why is this?
Think'st thou I 'd make a life of jealousy,
To follow still the changes of the moon
With fresh suspicions? No! to be once in doubt
Is once to be resolv'd: exchange me for a goat,
When I shall turn the business of my soul
To such exsufflicate and blown surmises,
Matching thy inference. 'T is not to make me jealous
To say my wife is fair, feeds well, loves company,
Is free of speech, sings, plays, and dances well;
Where virtue is, these are more virtuous;
Nor from mine own weak merits will I draw
The smallest fear or doubt of her revolt;
For she had eyes, and chose me. No, Iago;
I 'll see before I doubt; when I doubt, prove;
And on the proof, there is no more but this,—
Away at once with love or jealousy!
Iago. I am glad of this, for now I shall have reason
To show the love and duty that I bear you
With franker spirit; therefore, as I am bound,
Receive it from me. I speak not yet of proof.
Look to your wife; observe her well with Cassio;
Wear your eyes thus, not jealous nor secure:
I would not have your free and noble nature,
Out of self-bounty, be abus'd; look to 't.
I know our country disposition well;
In Venice they do let God see the pranks
They dare not show their husbands. Their best conscience
Is not to leave 't undone, but keep 't unknown.
Oth. Dost thou say so?
Iago. She did deceive her father, marrying you;
And when she seem'd to shake and fear your looks,
She lov'd them most.
Oth. And so she did.
Iago. Why, go to then.
She that, so young, could give out such a seeming,
To seel her father's eyes up close as oak—
He thought 't was witchcraft—but I am much to blame.
I humbly do beseech you of your pardon
For too much loving you.
Oth. I am bound to thee for ever.
Iago. I see this hath a little dash'd your spirits.
Oth. Not a jot, not a jot.
Iago. I' faith, I fear it has.
I hope you will consider what is spoke
Comes from my love. But I do see you 're mov'd.
I am to pray you not to strain my speech
To grosser issues nor to larger reach
Than to suspicion.
Oth. I will not.
Iago. Should you do so, my lord,
My speech should fall into such vile success
Which my thoughts aim'd not at. Cassio 's my worthy friend,—
My lord, I see you 're mov'd.
Oth. No, not much mov'd.
I do not think but Desdemona 's honest.
Iago. Long live she so; and long live you to think so!
Oth. And yet, how nature erring from itself,—
Iago. Ay, there 's the point; as—to be bold with you—
Not to affect many proposed matches
Of her own clime, complexion, and degree,
Whereto we see in all things nature tends—
Foh! one may smell in such, a will most rank,
Foul disproportions, thoughts unnatural.
But pardon me; I do not in position
Distinctly speak of her; though I may fear
Her will, recoiling to her better judgement,
May fall to match you with her country forms,
And happily repent.
Oth. Farewell, farewell!
If more thou dost perceive, let me know more;
Set on thy wife to observe. Leave me, Iago.
Iago. [*Going.*] My lord, I take my leave.
Oth. Why did I marry? This honest creature doubtless
Sees and knows more, much more, than he unfolds.
Iago. [*Returning.*] My lord, I would I might entreat your honour
To scan this thing no farther; leave it to time.
Although 't is fit that Cassio have his place,
For, sure, he fills it up with great ability,
Yet, if you please to hold him off a while,
You shall by that perceive him and his means:
Note if your lady strain his entertainment

173. **fineless**, boundless. 182. **exsufflicate and blown**, insubstantial and inflated, like a bubble. 198. **secure**, careless. 200. **self-bounty**, innate generosity.

222. **success**, results. 225. **honest**, chaste. 232. **will**, desire. **rank**, foul. 234. **position**, formal assertion. 250. **strain his entertainment**, over-urge his reinstatement.

With any strong or vehement importunity;
Much will be seen in that. In the mean time,
Let me be thought too busy in my fears—
As worthy cause I have to fear I am—
And hold her free, I do beseech your honour.
Oth. Fear not my government.
Iago. I once more take my leave. *Exit.*
Oth. This fellow 's of exceeding honesty,
And knows all qualities, with a learned spirit,
Of human dealings. If I do prove her haggard,
Though that her jesses were my dear heartstrings,
I 'd whistle her off and let her down the wind
To prey at fortune. Haply, for I am black
And have not those soft parts of conversation
That chamberers have, or for I am declin'd
Into the vale of years,—yet that 's not much—
She 's gone. I am abus'd; and my relief
Must be to loathe her. O curse of marriage,
That we can call these delicate creatures ours,
And not their appetites! I had rather be a toad
And live upon the vapour of a dungeon,
Than keep a corner in the thing I love
For others' uses. Yet, 't is the plague of great ones;
Prerogativ'd are they less than the base:
'T is destiny unshunnable, like death.
Even then this forked plague is fated to us
When we do quicken. Look where she comes.

Re-enter *Desdemona* and *Emilia*.

If she be false, O, then heaven mocks itself!
I 'll not believe 't.
Des. How now, my dear Othello!
Your dinner, and the generous islanders
By you invited, do attend your presence.
Oth. I am to blame.
Des. Why do you speak so faintly?
Are you not well?
Oth. I have a pain upon my forehead here.
Des. Faith, that 's with watching; 't will away again.
Let me but bind it hard, within this hour
It will be well.
Oth. Your napkin is too little;
He puts the handkerchief from him; and it drops.
Let it alone. Come, I 'll go in with you.
Des. I am very sorry that you are not well.
Exeunt Othello and Desdemona.

Emil. I am glad I have found this napkin;
This was her first remembrance from the Moor:
My wayward husband hath a hundred times
Woo'd me to steal it; but she so loves the token,
For he conjur'd her she should ever keep it,
That she reserves it evermore about her
To kiss and talk to. I 'll have the work ta'en out,
And give 't Iago. What he will do with it
Heaven knows, not I;
I nothing but to please his fantasy.

Re-enter *Iago*.

Iago. How now! what do you here alone?
Emil. Do not you chide; I have a thing for you.
Iago. A thing for me? It is a common thing—
Emil. Ha!
Iago. To have a foolish wife.
Emil. O, is that all? What will you give me now
For that same handkerchief?
Iago. What handkerchief?
Emil. What handkerchief!
Why, that the Moor first gave to Desdemona;
That which so often you did bid me steal.
Iago. Hast stol'n it from her?
Emil. No, faith; she let it drop by negligence,
And, to th' advantage, I, being here, took 't up.
Look, here it is.
Iago. A good wench; give it me.
Emil. What will you do with 't, that you have been so earnest
To have me filch it?
Iago. [*Snatching it.*] Why, what is that to you?
Emil. If it be not for some purpose of import,
Give 't me again. Poor lady, she 'll run mad
When she shall lack it.
Iago. Be not acknown on 't; I have use for it.
Go, leave me. *Exit Emilia.*
I will in Cassio's lodging lose this napkin,
And let him find it. Trifles light as air
Are to the jealous confirmations strong
As proofs of holy writ; this may do something.
The Moor already changes with my poison:
Dangerous conceits are, in their nature, poisons,
Which at the first are scarce found to distaste,

255. **free,** i.e., from guilt. 256. **government,** self-control. 260. **haggard,** wild, untamed (used of hawks). 261. **jesses,** strings by which hawks were held. 262. **down the wind,** i.e., go free (trained hawks flew against the wind). 264. **conversation,** social intercourse. 265. **chamberers,** courtiers. 276. **forked plague,** horns of a cuckold. 277. **quicken,** begin to live. 280. **generous,** well-born. 285. **watching,** lying awake. 287. **napkin,** handkerchief.

292. **wayward,** wilful. 295. **reserves,** keeps. 296. **work ta'en out,** embroidery copied. 299. **fantasy,** whim. 312. **to th' advantage,** opportunely. 319. **Be not acknown,** do not admit knowledge of it.

But with a little act upon the blood,
Burn like the mines of sulphur. I did say so.

Re-enter *Othello*.

Look, where he comes! Not poppy, nor mandragora,
Nor all the drowsy syrups of the world
Shall ever medicine thee to that sweet sleep
Which thou ow'dst yesterday.

Oth. Ha! ha! false to me?

Iago. Why, how now, General! no more of that.

Oth. Avaunt! be gone! thou hast set me on the rack.
I swear 't is better to be much abus'd
Than but to know 't a little.

Iago. How now, my lord!

Oth. What sense had I of her stol'n hours of lust?
I saw 't not, thought it not, it harm'd not me:
I slept the next night well, fed well, was free and merry;
I found not Cassio's kisses on her lips:
He that is robb'd, not wanting what is stol'n,
Let him not know 't, and he 's not robb'd at all.

Iago. I am sorry to hear this.

Oth. I had been happy, if the general camp,
Pioners and all, had tasted her sweet body,
So I had nothing known. O, now, for ever
Farewell the tranquil mind! farewell content!
Farewell the plumed troop, and the big wars,
That makes ambition virtue! O, farewell!
Farewell the neighing steed, and the shrill trump,
The spirit-stirring drum, th' ear-piercing fife,
The royal banner, and all quality,
Pride, pomp, and circumstance of glorious war!
And, O you mortal engines, whose rude throats
Th' immortal Jove's dread clamours counterfeit,
Farewell! Othello's occupation 's gone!

Iago. Is 't possible, my lord?

Oth. Villain, be sure thou prove my love a whore,
Be sure of it; give me the ocular proof;
Or, by the worth of mine eternal soul,
Thou hadst been better have been born a dog
Than answer my wak'd wrath!

Iago. Is 't come to this?

Oth. Make me to see 't; or, at the least, so prove it,
That the probation bear no hinge nor loop
To hang a doubt on; or woe upon thy life!

Iago. My noble lord,—

330. mandragora, a soporific drug. **333. ow'dst,** ownedst. **346. Pioners,** pioneers, sappers. **354. circumstance,** ceremony. **365. probation,** proof.

Oth. If thou dost slander her and torture me,
Never pray more; abandon all remorse;
On horror's head horrors accumulate;
Do deeds to make heaven weep, all earth amaz'd;
For nothing canst thou to damnation add
Greater than that.

Iago. O grace! O Heaven forgive me!
Are you a man? Have you a soul or sense?
God buy you; take mine office. O wretched fool,
That lov'st to make thine honesty a vice!
O monstrous world! Take note, take note, O world,
To be direct and honest is not safe.
I thank you for this profit; and from hence
I 'll love no friend, sith love breeds such offence.

Oth. Nay, stay. Thou shouldst be honest.

Iago. I should be wise, for honesty 's a fool
And loses that it works for.

Oth. By the world,
I think my wife be honest and think she is not;
I think that thou art just and think thou art not.
I 'll have some proof. Her name, that was as fresh
As Dian's visage, is now begrim'd and black
As mine own face. If there be cords, or knives,
Poison, or fire, or suffocating streams,
I 'll not endure it. Would I were satisfied!

Iago. I see, sir, you are eaten up with passion;
I do repent me that I put it to you.
You would be satisfied?

Oth. Would! nay, I will.

Iago. And may; but, how? How satisfied, my lord?
Would you, the supervisor, grossly gape on—
Behold her tupp'd?

Oth. Death and damnation! O!

Iago. It were a tedious difficulty, I think,
To bring them to that prospect; damn them then,
If ever mortal eyes do see them bolster
More than their own! What then? How then?
What shall I say? Where 's satisfaction?
It is impossible you should see this,
Were they as prime as goats, as hot as monkeys,
As salt as wolves in pride, and fools as gross
As ignorance made drunk. But yet, I say,
If imputation and strong circumstances,
Which lead directly to the door of truth,
Will give you satisfaction, you might have 't.

379. profit, profitable lesson. **403. prime,** lecherous.

Oth. Give me a living reason she 's disloyal.
Iago. I do not like the office;
But, sith I am enter'd in this cause so far,
Prick'd to 't by foolish honesty and love,
I will go on. I lay with Cassio lately;
And, being troubled with a raging tooth,
I could not sleep.
There are a kind of men so loose of soul,
That in their sleeps will mutter their affairs;
One of this kind is Cassio.
In sleep I heard him say, "Sweet Desdemona,
Let us be wary, let us hide our loves";
And then, sir, would he gripe and wring my hand,
Cry, "O sweet creature!" and then kiss me hard,
As if he pluck'd up kisses by the roots
That grew upon my lips; then laid his leg
Over my thigh, and sigh'd and kiss'd; and then
Cried, "Cursed fate that gave thee to the Moor!"
Oth. O monstrous! monstrous!
Iago. Nay, this was but his dream.
Oth. But this denoted a foregone conclusion.
'T is a shrewd doubt, though it be but a dream.
Iago. And this may help to thicken other proofs
That do demonstrate thinly.
Oth. I 'll tear her all to pieces.
Iago. Nay, but be wise; yet we see nothing done.
She may be honest yet. Tell me but this,
Have you not sometimes seen a handkerchief
Spotted with strawberries in your wife's hand?
Oth. I gave her such a one; 't was my first gift.
Iago. I know not that; but such a handkerchief—
I am sure it was your wife's—did I to-day
See Cassio wipe his beard with.
Oth. If it be that,—
Iago. If it be that, or any that was hers,
It speaks against her with the other proofs.
Oth. O, that the slave had forty thousand lives!
One is too poor, too weak for my revenge.
Now do I see 't is true. Look here, Iago;
All my fond love thus do I blow to heaven.
'T is gone.
Arise, black vengeance, from the hollow hell!
Yield up, O love, thy crown and hearted throne
To tyrannous hate! Swell, bosom, with thy fraught,
For 't is of aspics' tongues!
Iago. Yet be content.
Oth. O, blood, blood, blood!
Iago. Patience, I say; your mind perhaps may change.
Oth. Never, Iago. Like to the Pontic Sea,
Whose icy current and compulsive course
Ne'er feels retiring ebb, but keeps due on
To the Propontic and the Hellespont,
Even so my bloody thoughts, with violent pace,
Shall ne'er look back, ne'er ebb to humble love,
Till that a capable and wide revenge
Swallow them up. Now, by yond marble heaven,
In the due reverence of a sacred vow
I here engage my words. *Kneels.*
Iago. Do not rise yet.
Witness, you ever-burning lights above.
You elements that clip us round about, *Kneels.*
Witness that here Iago doth give up
The execution of his wit, hands, heart,
To wrong'd Othello's service! Let him command,
And to obey shall be in me remorse,
What bloody business ever. *They rise.*
Oth. I greet thy love,
Not with vain thanks, but with acceptance bounteous,
And will upon the instant put thee to 't:
Within these three days let me hear thee say
That Cassio 's not alive.
Iago. My friend is dead; 't is done at your request.
But let her live.
Oth. Damn her, lewd minx! O, damn her!
Come, go with me apart; I will withdraw
To furnish me with some swift means of death
For the fair devil. Now art thou my lieutenant.
Iago. I am your own for ever. *Exeunt.*

Scene IV. *Before the castle.*

Enter *Desdemona, Emilia,* and *Clown.*

Des. Do you know, sirrah, where Lieutenant Cassio lies?

Clo. I dare not say he lies anywhere.

Des. Why, man?

Clo. He 's a soldier, and for me to say a soldier lies, 't is stabbing.

Des. Go to! Where lodges he?

412. Prick'd, incited. **428. foregone conclusion,** a previous experience. **429. shrewd doubt,** strong ground for suspecting evil. **449. fraught,** freight. **450. aspics',** asps'.

453. Pontic sea, Black Sea. **459. capable,** capacious. **464. clip,** surround. **466. execution,** performance. **468. remorse,** matter of conscience. **Scene iv: 2. lies,** resides.

Clo. To tell you where he lodges, is to tell you where I lie.

Des. Can anything be made of this?

Clo. I know not where he lodges, and for me to devise a lodging and say he lies here or he lies there, were to lie in mine own throat.

Des. Can you inquire him out, and be edified by report?

Clo. I will catechize the world for him; that is, make questions, and by them answer.

Des. Seek him, bid him come hither. Tell him I have moved my lord on his behalf, and hope all will be well.

Clo. To do this is within the compass of man's wit; and therefore I will attempt the doing it. *Exit.*

Des. Where should I lose the handkerchief, Emilia?

Emil. I know not, madam.

Des. Believe me, I had rather have lost my purse
Full of crusadoes; and, but my noble Moor
Is true of mind and made of no such baseness
As jealous creatures are, it were enough
To put him to ill thinking.

Emil. Is he not jealous?

Des. Who, he? I think the sun where he was born
Drew all such humours from him.

Emil. Look, where he comes.

Enter *Othello.*

Des. I will not leave him now till Cassio
Be call'd to him.—How is 't with you, my lord?

Oth. Well, my good lady. [*Aside.*] O, hardness to dissemble!—
How do you, Desdemona?

Des. Well, my good lord.

Oth. Give me your hand. This hand is moist, my lady.

Des. It yet hath felt no age nor known no sorrow.

Oth. This argues fruitfulness and liberal heart;
Hot, hot, and moist. This hand of yours requires
A sequester from liberty, fasting and prayer,
Much castigation, exercise devout;
For here 's a young and sweating devil here,
That commonly rebels. 'T is a good hand,
A frank one.

Des. You may, indeed, say so;
For 't was that hand that gave away my heart.

Oth. A liberal hand. The hearts of old gave hands;
But our new heraldry is hands, not hearts.

Des. I cannot speak of this. Come now, your promise.

Oth. What promise, chuck?

Des. I have sent to bid Cassio come speak with you.

Oth. I have a salt and sorry rheum offends me;
Lend me thy handkerchief.

Des. Here, my lord.

Oth. That which I gave you.

Des. I have it not about me.

Oth. Not?

Des. No, faith, my lord.

Oth. That 's a fault. That handkerchief
Did an Egyptian to my mother give;
She was a charmer, and could almost read
The thoughts of people. She told her, while she kept it
'T would make her amiable and subdue my father
Entirely to her love, but if she lost it,
Or made a gift of it, my father's eye
Should hold her loathed and his spirits should hunt
After new fancies. She, dying, gave it me;
And bid me, when my fate would have me wiv'd,
To give it her. I did so; and take heed on 't;
Make it a darling like your precious eye.
To lose 't or give 't away were such perdition
As nothing else could match.

Des. Is 't possible?

Oth. 'T is true; there 's magic in the web of it.
A sibyl, that had number'd in the world
The sun to course two hundred compasses,
In her prophetic fury sew'd the work;
The worms were hallowed that did breed the silk;
And it was dy'd in mummy which the skilful
Conserv'd of maidens' hearts.

Des. Indeed! is 't true?

Oth. Most veritable; therefore look to 't well.

Des. Then would to God that I had never seen 't!

Oth. Ha! wherefore?

Des. Why do you speak so startingly and rash?

Oth. Is 't lost? Is 't gone? Speak, is 't out o' the way?

Des. Heaven bless us!

Oth. Say you?

Des. It is not lost; but what an if it were?

Oth. How?

Des. I say, it is not lost.

23. **should,** could. 26. **crusadoes,** Portuguese gold coins stamped with a cross. 38. **fruitfulness,** generosity. 40. **sequester,** sequestration.

51. **sorry,** painful. 56. **Egyptian,** gypsy. 57. **charmer,** sorceress. 59. **amiable,** lovable. 74. **in mummy,** embalming fluid that oozed from mummies. 75. **conserv'd,** preserved out of. 79. **startingly,** abruptly.

Oth. Fetch 't, let me see 't.
Des. Why, so I can, sir, but I will not now.
This is a trick to put me from my suit:
Pray you, let Cassio be receiv'd again.
Oth. Fetch me the handkerchief; my mind misgives.
Des. Come, come;
You 'll never meet a more sufficient man.
Oth. The handkerchief!
Des. I pray, talk me of Cassio.
Oth. The handkerchief!
Des. A man that all his time
Hath founded his good fortunes on your love,
Shar'd dangers with you,—
Oth. The handkerchief!
Des. I' faith, you are to blame.
Oth. 'Zounds! *Exit Othello.*
Emil. Is not this man jealous?
Des. I ne'er saw this before.
Sure, there 's some wonder in this handkerchief;
I am most unhappy in the loss of it.
Emil. 'T is not a year or two shows us a man:
They are all but stomachs, and we all but food;
They eat us hungerly, and when they are full
They belch us.

Enter *Cassio* and *Iago*.

Look you, Cassio and my husband!
Iago. There is no other way, 't is she must do 't;
And, lo, the happiness! Go, and importune her.
Des. How now, good Cassio! what 's the news with you?
Cas. Madam, my former suit. I do beseech you
That by your virtuous means I may again
Exist, and be a member of his love
Whom I with all the office of my heart
Entirely honour: I would not be delay'd.
If my offence be of such mortal kind
That nor my service past, nor present sorrows,
Nor purpos'd merit in futurity
Can ransom me into his love again,
But to know so must be my benefit;
So shall I clothe me in a forc'd content,
And shut myself up in some other course,
To fortune's alms.
Des. Alas, thrice-gentle Cassio!
My advocation is not now in tune;
My lord is not my lord, nor should I know him
Were he in favour as in humour alter'd.
So help me every spirit sanctified
As I have spoken for you all my best
And stood within the blank of his displeasure
For my free speech! You must a while be patient.
What I can do I will; and more I will
Than for myself I dare. Let that suffice you.
Iago. Is my lord angry?
Emil. He went hence but now,
And certainly in strange unquietness.
Iago. Can he be angry? I have seen the cannon
When it hath blown his ranks into the air,
And, like the devil, from his very arm
Puff'd his own brother—and can he be angry?
Something of moment then. I will go meet him.
There 's matter in 't indeed, if he be angry.
Exit Iago.
Des. I prithee, do so. Something, sure, of state,
Either from Venice, or some unhatch'd practice
Made demonstrable here in Cyprus to him,
Hath puddled his clear spirit; and in such cases
Men's natures wrangle with inferior things,
Though great ones are their object. 'T is even so;
For let our finger ache, and it indues
Our other healthful members even to a sense
Of pain. Nay, we must think men are not gods,
Nor of them look for such observancy
As fits the bridal. Beshrew me much, Emilia,
I was, unhandsome warrior as I am,
Arraigning his unkindness with my soul;
But now I find I had suborn'd the witness,
And he 's indicted falsely.
Emil. Pray Heaven it be state-matters, as you think,
And no conception nor no jealous toy
Concerning you.
Des. Alas the day! I never gave him cause.
Emil. But jealous souls will not be answer'd so;
They are not ever jealous for the cause,
But jealous for they 're jealous. It is a monster
Begot upon itself, born on itself.
Des. Heaven keep that monster from Othello's mind!
Emil. Lady, amen.
Des. I will go seek him. Cassio, walk hereabout;

108. happiness, lucky chance. **111. virtuous,** effective. **123. advocation,** advocacy.

128. blank, range, lit., white spot in the target. **141. unhatch'd practice,** undeveloped plot. **143. puddled,** made muddy, troubled. **146. indues,** endows. **149. observancy,** devoted attention. **151. unhandsome,** unfair. **156. toy,** whim.

If I do find him fit, I 'll move your suit
And seek to effect it to my uttermost.
Cas. I humbly thank your ladyship.
Exeunt Desdemona and Emilia.

Enter *Bianca.*

Bian. Save you, friend Cassio!
Cas. What make you from home?
How is it with you, my most fair Bianca?
I' faith, sweet love, I was coming to your house.
Bian. And I was going to your lodging, Cassio.
What, keep a week away? seven days and nights?
Eightscore eight hours? and lovers' absent hours,
More tedious than the dial eightscore times?
O weary reck'ning!
Cas. Pardon me, Bianca.
I have this while with leaden thoughts been press'd;
But I shall, in a more continuate time,
Strike off this score of absence. Sweet Bianca,
Giving her Desdemona's handkerchief.
Take me this work out.
Bian. O Cassio, whence came this?
This is some token from a newer friend;
To the felt absence now I feel a cause.
Is 't come to this? Well, well.
Cas. Go to, woman!
Throw your vile guesses in the devil's teeth,
From whence you have them. You are jealous now
That this is from some mistress, some remembrance.
No, by my faith, Bianca.
Bian. Why, whose is it?
Cas. I know not, sweet; I found it in my chamber.
I like the work well; ere it be demanded—
As like enough it will—I 'd have it copied.
Take it, and do 't; and leave me for this time.
Bian. Leave you! Wherefore?
Cas. I do attend here on the General;
And think it no addition, nor my wish,
To have him see me woman'd.
Bian. Why, I pray you?
Cas. Not that I love you not.
Bian. But that you do not love me.
I pray you, bring me on the way a little,
And say if I shall see you soon at night.
Cas. 'T is but a little way that I can bring you,
For I attend here; but I 'll see you soon.
Bian. 'T is very good; I must be circumstanc'd. *Exeunt.*

Act IV. Scene I. *Cyprus. Before the castle.*

Enter *Othello* and *Iago.*

Iago. Will you think so?
Oth. Think so, Iago!
Iago. What,
To kiss in private?
Oth. An unauthoriz'd kiss.
Iago. Or to be naked with her friend in bed
An hour or more, not meaning any harm?
Oth. Naked in bed, Iago, and not mean harm!
It is hypocrisy against the devil:
They that mean virtuously, and yet do so,
The devil their virtue tempts, and they tempt heaven.
Iago. If they do nothing, 't is a venial slip;
But if I give my wife a handkerchief,—
Oth. What then?
Iago. Why, then, 't is hers, my lord; and, being hers,
She may, I think, bestow 't on any man.
Oth. She is protectress of her honour too;
May she give that?
Iago. Her honour is an essence that 's not seen;
They have it very oft that have it not:
But, for the handkerchief,—
Oth. By heaven, I would most gladly have forgot it.
Thou said'st—O, it comes o'er my memory,
As doth the raven o'er the infected house,
Boding to all—he had my handkerchief.
Iago. Ay, what of that?
Oth. That 's not so good now.
Iago. What
If I had said I had seen him do you wrong?
Or heard him say,—as knaves be such abroad,
Who having, by their own importunate suit,
Or voluntary dotage of some mistress,
Convinced or supplied them, cannot choose
But they must blab—
Oth. Hath he said anything?
Iago. He hath, my lord; but be you well assur'd,
No more than he 'll unswear.

178. continuate, uninterrupted. **Act IV, Scene i: 6. hypocrisy**, i.e., so to appear to sin without sinning.

194. addition, mark of distinction. **201. be circumstanc'd**, yield to circumstances. **Act IV, Scene i: 28. Convinced or supplied**, overcome or satisfied.

Oth. What hath he said?
Iago. Faith, that he did—I know not what he did.
Oth. What? what?
Iago. Lie—
Oth. With her?
Iago. With her, on her; what you will.

Oth. Lie with her! lie on her! We say lie on her, when they belie her. Lie with her! 'Zounds, that 's fulsome!—Handkerchief—confessions—handkerchief!—To confess, and be hanged for his labour;—first, to be hanged, and then to confess.—I tremble at it. Nature would not invest herself in such shadowing passion without some instruction. It is not words that shakes me thus. Pish! Noses, ears, and lips.—Is 't possible?—Confess—handkerchief!—O devil! *Falls in a trance.*

Iago. Work on,
My medicine, work! Thus credulous fools are caught;
And many worthy and chaste dames even thus,
All guiltless, meet reproach.—What, ho! my lord!
My lord, I say! Othello!

Enter *Cassio.*

How now, Cassio!
Cas. What 's the matter?
Iago. My lord is fall'n into an epilepsy.
This is his second fit; he had one yesterday.
Cas. Rub him about the temples.
Iago. No, forbear;
The lethargy must have his quiet course;
If not, he foams at mouth and by and by
Breaks out to savage madness. Look, he stirs.
Do you withdraw yourself a little while,
He will recover straight: when he is gone,
I would on great occasion speak with you.
Exit Cassio.
How is it, general? Have you not hurt your head?
Oth. Dost thou mock me?
Iago. I mock you not, by heaven.
Would you would bear your fortune like a man!
Oth. A horned man 's a monster and a beast.
Iago. There 's many a beast then in a populous city,
And many a civil monster.
Oth. Did he confess it?
Iago. Good sir, be a man;
Think every bearded fellow that 's but yok'd
May draw with you. There 's millions now alive
That nightly lie in those unproper beds
Which they dare swear peculiar; your case is better.
O, 't is the spite of hell, the fiend's arch-mock,
To lip a wanton in a secure couch,
And to suppose her chaste! No, let me know;
And knowing what I am, I know what she shall be.
Oth. O, thou art wise; 't is certain.
Iago. Stand you a while apart;
Confine yourself but in a patient list.
Whilst you were here o'erwhelmed with your grief—
A passion most unsuiting such a man—
Cassio came hither. I shifted him away,
And laid good 'scuse upon your ecstasy;
Bade him anon return and here speak with me,
The which he promis'd. Do but encave yourself,
And mark the fleers, the gibes, and notable scorns,
That dwell in every region of his face;
For I will make him tell the tale anew,
Where, how, how oft, how long ago, and when
He hath, and is again to cope your wife.
I say, but mark his gesture. Marry, patience;
Or I shall say you 're all in all in spleen,
And nothing of a man.
Oth. Dost thou hear, Iago?
I will be found most cunning in my patience;
But—dost thou hear?—most bloody.
Iago. That 's not amiss;
But yet keep time in all. Will you withdraw?
Othello retires.
Now will I question Cassio of Bianca,
A housewife that by selling her desires
Buys herself bread and clothes. It is a creature
That dotes on Cassio;—as 't is the strumpet's plague
To beguile many and be beguil'd by one;—
He, when he hears of her, cannot refrain
From the excess of laughter. Here he comes:

Re-enter *Cassio.*

As he shall smile, Othello shall go mad;
And his unbookish jealousy must construe
Poor Cassio's smiles, gestures, and light behaviours
Quite in the wrong. How do you, lieutenant?
Cas. The worser that you give me the addition
Whose want even kills me.
Iago. Ply Desdemona well, and you are sure on 't.

39-41. Nature . . . instruction, passion would not fill my mind with so many images unless they represented not mere words but actual facts. **63. horned man,** a cuckold. **65. civil,** civilized.

69. unproper, not their own. **70. peculiar,** their very own. **76. patient list,** confines of patience. **80. ecstasy,** fainting fit. **82. encave,** hide. **89. spleen,** anger. **102. unbookish,** ignorant. **105. addition,** title.

Now, if this suit lay in Bianca's power,
How quickly should you speed!

Cas. Alas, poor caitiff!

Oth. Look, how he laughs already!

Iago. I never knew a woman love man so.

Cas. Alas, poor rogue! I think, i' faith, she loves me.

Oth. Now he denies it faintly, and laughs it out.

Iago. Do you hear, Cassio?

Oth. Now he importunes him
To tell it o'er. Go to; well said, well said.

Iago. She gives it out that you shall marry her.
Do you intend it?

Cas. Ha, ha, ha!

Oth. Do ye triumph, Roman? Do you triumph?

Cas. I marry her! What? a customer! Prithee, bear some charity to my wit; do not think it so unwholesome. Ha, ha, ha!

Oth. So, so, so, so; they laugh that wins.

Iago. Faith, the cry goes that you shall marry her.

Cas. Prithee, say true.

Iago. I am a very villain else.

Oth. Have you scor'd me? Well.

Cas. This is the monkey's own giving out. She is persuaded I will marry her, out of her own love and flattery, not out of my promise.

Oth. Iago beckons me; now he begins the story.

Cas. She was here even now; she haunts me in every place. I was the other day talking on the sea-bank with certain Venetians; and thither comes the bauble, and, by this hand, she falls me thus about my neck—

Oth. Crying, "O dear Cassio!" as it were; his gesture imports it.

Cas. So hangs, and lolls, and weeps upon me; so shakes and pulls me. Ha, ha, ha!

Oth. Now he tells how she plucked him to my chamber. O, I see that nose of yours, but not that dog I shall throw it to.

Cas. Well, I must leave her company.

Iago. Before me! look, where she comes.

Enter *Bianca.*

Cas. 'T is such another fitchew! Marry, a perfumed one.—What do you mean by this haunting of me?

Bian. Let the devil and his dam haunt you! What did you mean by that same handkerchief you gave me even now? I was a fine fool to take it. I must take out the work? —A likely piece of work, that you should find it in your chamber, and know not who left it there! This is some minx's token, and I must take out the work? There; give it your hobby-horse: wheresoever you had it, I 'll take out no work on 't.

Cas. How now, my sweet Bianca! how now! how now!

Oth. By heaven, that should be my handkerchief!

Bian. If you 'll come to supper to-night, you may; if you will not, come when you are next prepared for. *Exit.*

Iago. After her, after her.

Cas. Faith, I must; she 'll rail in the streets else.

Iago. Will you sup there?

Cas. Faith, I intend so.

Iago. Well, I may chance to see you; for I would very fain speak with you.

Cas. Prithee, come; will you?

Iago. Go to; say no more. *Exit Cassio.*

Oth. [*Advancing.*] How shall I murder him, Iago?

Iago. Did you perceive how he laughed at his vice?

Oth. O Iago!

Iago. And did you see the handkerchief?

Oth. Was that mine?

Iago. Yours, by this hand: and to see how he prizes the foolish woman your wife! She gave it him, and he hath given it his whore.

Oth. I would have him nine years a-killing. A fine woman! a fair woman! a sweet woman!

Iago. Nay, you must forget that.

Oth. Ay, let her rot, and perish, and be damned to-night; for she shall not live. No, my heart is turned to stone; I strike it, and it hurts my hand. O, the world hath not a sweeter creature! She might lie by an emperor's side and command him tasks.

Iago. Nay, that 's not your way.

Oth. Hang her! I do but say what she is. So delicate with her needle! an admirable musician! O! she will sing the savageness out of a bear: of so high and plenteous wit and invention!

Iago. She 's the worse for all this.

Oth. O, a thousand thousand times! And then, of so gentle a condition!

Iago. Ay, too gentle.

Oth. Nay, that 's certain. But yet the pity of it, Iago! O Iago, the pity of it, Iago!

Iago. If you are so fond over her iniquity, give her patent to offend; for, if it touch not you, it comes near nobody.

Oth. I will chop her into messes. Cuckold me!

Iago. O, 't is foul in her.

Oth. With mine officer!

121. Roman, suggested by "triumph." **123. customer,** harlot. **130. scor'd,** branded. **139. bauble,** plaything. **150. fitchew,** polecat.

160. hobby-horse, lover, used contemptuously. **204. condition,** disposition.

Iago. That 's fouler.

Oth. Get me some poison, Iago, this night. I 'll not expostulate with her, lest her body and beauty unprovide my mind again. This night, Iago.

Iago. Do it not with poison; strangle her in her bed, even the bed she hath contaminated.

Oth. Good, good; the justice of it pleases; very good.

Iago. And for Cassio, let me be his undertaker: you shall hear more by midnight.

Oth. Excellent good! *A trumpet.*
What trumpet is that same?

Iago. Something from Venice sure.

Enter *Lodovico, Desdemona,* and Attendants.

'T is Lodovico.
Come from the Duke; and, see, your wife is with him.

Lod. God save you, worthy General!

Oth. With all my heart, sir.

Lod. The Duke and senators of Venice greet you. *Gives him a letter.*

Oth. I kiss the instrument of their pleasures. *Opens the letter, and reads.*

Des. And what 's the news, good cousin Lodovico?

Iago. I am very glad to see you, signior;
Welcome to Cyprus.

Lod. I thank you. How does Lieutenant Cassio?

Iago. Lives, sir.

Des. Cousin, there 's fall'n between him and my lord
An unkind breach; but you shall make all well.

Oth. Are you sure of that?

Des. My lord!

Oth. [*Reads.*] "This fail you not to do, as you will"—

Lod. He did not call; he 's busy in the paper.
Is there division 'twixt my lord and Cassio?

Des. A most unhappy one. I would do much
T' atone them, for the love I bear to Cassio.

Oth. Fire and brimstone!

Des. My lord?

Oth. Are you wise?

Des. What, is he angry?

Lod. May be the letter mov'd him;
For, as I think, they do command him home,
Deputing Cassio in his government.

Des. Trust me, I am glad on 't.

Oth. Indeed!

Des. My lord?

Oth. I am glad to see you mad.

Des. Why, sweet Othello,—

Oth. [*Striking her.*] Devil!

Des. I have not deserv'd this.

Lod. My lord, this would not be believ'd in Venice
Though I should swear I saw 't. 'T is very much.
Make her amends: she weeps.

Oth. O devil, devil!
If that the earth could teem with woman's tears,
Each drop she falls would prove a crocodile.
Out of my sight!

Des. I will not stay to offend you. *Going.*

Lod. Truly, an obedient lady:
I do beseech your lordship, call her back.

Oth. Mistress!

Des. My lord?

Oth. What would you with her, sir?

Lod. Who, I, my lord?

Oth. Ay; you did wish that I would make her turn.
Sir, she can turn, and turn, and yet go on,
And turn again; and she can weep, sir, weep;
And she 's obedient, as you say, obedient,
Very obedient. Proceed you in your tears.
Concerning this, sir,—O well-painted passion!—
I am commanded home.—Get you away;
I 'll send for you anon.—Sir, I obey the mandate,
And will return to Venice.—Hence, avaunt!— *Exit Desdemona.*
Cassio shall have my place. And, sir, to-night,
I do entreat that we may sup together.
You are welcome, sir, to Cyprus.—Goats and monkeys! *Exit.*

Lod. Is this the noble Moor whom our full Senate
Call all in all sufficient? Is this the nature
Whom passion could not shake? whose solid virtue
The shot of accident nor dart of chance
Could neither graze nor pierce?

Iago. He is much chang'd.

Lod. Are his wits safe? Is he not light of brain?

Iago. He 's that he is; I may not breathe my censure
What he might be. If what he might he is not,
I would to heaven he were!

Lod. What, strike his wife!

218. **unprovide,** weaken. 224. **undertaker,** dispatcher. 244. **atone,** bring together. 248. **Deputing,** substituting.

256. **teem,** engender. Refers to belief that the crocodile wept hypocritical tears over its victims. 268. **well-painted,** well-simulated. 281. **censure,** judgment.

Iago. Faith, that was not so well; yet would I knew
That stroke would prove the worst!
Lod. Is it his use?
Or did the letters work upon his blood,
And new-create this fault?
Iago. Alas, alas!
It is not honesty in me to speak
What I have seen and known. You shall observe him,
And his own courses will denote him so
That I may save my speech: do but go after,
And mark how he continues.
Lod. I am sorry that I am deceiv'd in him.
Exeunt.

Scene II. *A room in the castle.*

Enter *Othello* and *Emilia.*

Oth. You have seen nothing then?
Emil. Nor ever heard, nor ever did suspect.
Oth. Yes, you have seen Cassio and she together.
Emil. But then I saw no harm, and then I heard
Each syllable that breath made up between them.
Oth. What, did they never whisper?
Emil. Never, my lord.
Oth. Nor send you out o' th' way?
Emil. Never.
Oth. To fetch her fan, her gloves, her mask, nor nothing?
Emil. Never, my lord.
Oth. That 's strange.
Emil. I durst, my lord, to wager she is honest,
Lay down my soul at stake: if you think other,
Remove your thought; it doth abuse your bosom.
If any wretch have put this in your head,
Let Heaven requite it with the serpent's curse!
For, if she be not honest, chaste, and true,
There 's no man happy; the purest of their wives
Is foul as slander.
Oth. Bid her come hither; go.
Exit Emilia.
She says enough; yet she 's a simple bawd
That cannot say as much. This is a subtle whore,
A closet lock and key of villanous secrets;
And yet she 'll kneel and pray; I have seen her do 't.

Enter *Desdemona* with *Emilia.*

Des. My lord, what is your will?
Oth. Pray, chuck, come hither.
Des. What is your pleasure?
Oth. Let me see your eyes;
Look in my face.
Des. What horrible fancy 's this?
Oth. [*To Emilia.*] Some of your function, mistress;
Leave procreants alone and shut the door;
Cough, or cry "hem," if anybody come.
Your mystery, your mystery; nay, dispatch.
Exit Emilia.
Des. Upon my knees, what doth your speech import?
I understand a fury in your words,
But not the words.
Oth. Why, what art thou?
Des. Your wife, my lord; your true and loyal wife.
Oth. Come, swear it, damn thyself,
Lest, being like one of heaven, the devils themselves
Should fear to seize thee; therefore be double damn'd,
Swear thou art honest.
Des. Heaven doth truly know it.
Oth. Heaven truly knows that thou art false as hell.
Des. To whom, my lord? With whom? How am I false?
Oth. Ah, Desdemon! Away! away! away!
Des. Alas the heavy day! Why do you weep?
Am I the motive of these tears, my lord?
If haply you my father do suspect
An instrument of this your calling back,
Lay not your blame on me: if you have lost him,
Why, I have lost him too.
Oth. Had it pleas'd Heaven
To try me with affliction; had they rain'd
All kinds of sores and shames on my bare head,
Steep'd me in poverty to the very lips,
Given to captivity me and my utmost hopes,
I should have found in some place of my soul
A drop of patience; but, alas, to make me
A fixed figure for the time of scorn
To point his slow unmoving finger at!
Yet could I bear that too, well, very well;
But there, where I have garner'd up my heart,
Where either I must live, or bear no life;
The fountain from the which my current runs,
Or else dries up; to be discarded thence!
Or keep it as a cistern for foul toads

Scene ii: 27. Some of your function, do your office, i.e., as bawd. **30. mystery,** trade. **54. time of scorn,** scorn of the age. **55. slow unmoving,** moving so slowly as not to be observed.

To knot and gender in! Turn thy complexion there,
Patience, thou young and rose-lipp'd cherubin,
Ay, there look grim as hell!
Des. I hope my noble lord esteems me honest.
Oth. O, ay; as summer flies are in the shambles,
That quicken even with blowing. O thou weed,
Who art so lovely fair and smell'st so sweet
That the sense aches at thee, would thou hadst ne'er been born!
Des. Alas, what ignorant sin have I committed?
Oth. Was this fair paper, this most goodly book,
Made to write "whore" upon? What committed?
Committed! O thou public commoner!
I should make very forges of my cheeks,
That would to cinders burn up modesty,
Did I but speak thy deeds. What committed?
Heaven stops the nose at it, and the moon winks,
The bawdy wind, that kisses all it meets,
Is hush'd within the hollow mine of earth,
And will not hear it. What committed!
Impudent strumpet!
Des. By heaven, you do me wrong.
Oth. Are not you a strumpet?
Des. No, as I am a Christian.
If to preserve this vessel for my lord
From any other foul unlawful touch
Be not to be a strumpet, I am none.
Oth. What, not a whore?
Des. No, as I shall be sav'd.
Oth. Is 't possible?
Des. O, Heaven forgive us!
Oth. I cry you mercy, then.
I took you for that cunning whore of Venice
That married with Othello.—You, mistress,

Re-enter *Emilia.*

That have the office opposite to Saint Peter,
And keeps the gate of hell! You, you, ay, you!
We have done our course; there 's money for your pains.
I pray you, turn the key and keep our counsel.
Exit.
Emil. Alas, what does this gentleman conceive?
How do you, madam? How do you, my good lady?
Des. Faith, half asleep.
Emil. Good madam, what 's the matter with my lord?
Des. With who?
Emil. Why, with my lord, madam.
Des. Who is thy lord?
Emil. He that is yours, sweet lady.
Des. I have none: do not talk to me, Emilia;
I cannot weep, nor answers have I none
But what should go by water. Prithee, to-night
Lay on my bed my wedding sheets, remember;
And call thy husband hither.
Emil. Here 's a change indeed!
Exit.
Des. 'T is meet I should be us'd so, very meet.
How have I been behav'd, that he might stick
The small'st opinion on my least misuse?

Re-enter *Emilia* with *Iago.*

Iago. What is your pleasure, madam? How is 't with you?
Des. I cannot tell. Those that do teach young babes
Do it with gentle means and easy tasks.
He might have chid me so; for, in good faith,
I am a child to chiding.
Iago. What 's the matter, lady?
Emil. Alas, Iago, my lord hath so bewhor'd her,
Thrown such despite and heavy terms upon her,
That true hearts cannot bear.
Des. Am I that name, Iago?
Iago. What name, fair lady?
Des. Such as she said my lord did say I was.
Emil. He call'd her whore: a beggar in his drink
Could not have laid such terms upon his callet.
Iago. Why did he so?
Des. I do not know; I am sure I am none such.
Iago. Do not weep, do not weep. Alas the day!
Emil. Hath she forsook so many noble matches,
Her father and her country and her friends,
To be call'd whore? Would it not make one weep?
Des. It is my wretched fortune.
Iago. Beshrew him for 't!
How comes this trick upon him?
Des. Nay, Heaven doth know.
Emil. I will be hang'd, if some eternal villain,

62. Turn thy complexion, change thy color. **67. quicken . . . blowing,** are impregnated again as soon as they lay their eggs. **73. commoner,** prostitute. **77. winks,** shuts her eyes. **83. this vessel,** this body of mine.

104. go by water, be expressed in tears. **109. small'st opinion on my least misuse,** the least censure on my slightest misdemeanor. **121. callet,** whore.

Some busy and insinuating rogue,
Some cogging, cozening slave, to get some office,
Have not devis'd this slander: I 'll be hang'd else.

Iago. Fie, there is no such man; it is impossible.

Des. If any such there be, Heaven pardon him!

Emil. A halter pardon him and hell gnaw his bones!
Why should he call her whore? Who keeps her company?
What place? what time? what form? what likelihood?
The Moor 's abus'd by some most villanous knave,
Some base notorious knave, some scurvy fellow.
O heaven, that such companions thou 'dst unfold,
And put in every honest hand a whip
To lash the rascals naked through the world
Even from the east to th' west!

Iago. Speak within door.

Emil. O, fie upon them! Some such squire he was
That turn'd your wit the seamy side without,
And made you to suspect me with the Moor.

Iago. You are a fool; go to.

Des. Alas, Iago,
What shall I do to win my lord again?
Good friend, go to him; for, by this light of heaven,
I know not how I lost him. Here I kneel:
If e'er my will did trespass 'gainst his love,
Either in discourse of thought or actual deed,
Or that mine eyes, mine ears, or any sense
Delighted them in any other form;
Or that I do not yet, and ever did,
And ever will—though he do shake me off
To beggarly divorcement—love him dearly,
Comfort forswear me! Unkindness may do much;
And his unkindness may defeat my life,
But never taint my love. I cannot say "whore."
It does abhor me now I speak the word;
To do the act that might the addition earn
Not the world's mass of vanity could make me.

Iago. I pray you, be content; 't is but his humour.
The business of the state does him offence,
And he does chide with you.

Des. If 't were no other,—

Iago. It is but so, I warrant.
Trumpets within.
Hark, how these instruments summon to supper!
The messengers of Venice stays the meat.
Go in, and weep not; all things shall be well.
Exeunt Desdemona and Emilia.

Enter *Roderigo.*

How now, Roderigo!

Rod. I do not find that thou deal'st justly with me.

Iago. What in the contrary?

Rod. Every day thou daff'st me with some device, Iago; and rather, as it seems to me now, keep'st from me all conveniency than suppliest me with the least advantage of hope. I will indeed no longer endure it, nor am I yet persuaded to put up in peace what already I have foolishly suffered.

Iago. Will you hear me, Roderigo?

Rod. Faith, I have heard too much, for your words and performances are no kin together.

Iago. You charge me most unjustly.

Rod. With nought but truth. I have wasted myself out of my means. The jewels you have had from me to deliver Desdemona would half have corrupted a votarist. You have told me she hath received them and returned me expectations and comforts of sudden respect and acquaintance, but I find none.

Iago. Well; go to; very well.

Rod. Very well! go to! I cannot go to, man; nor 't is not very well. By this hand, I say 't is scurvy, and begin to find myself fopped in it.

Iago. Very well.

Rod. I tell you 't is not very well. I will make myself known to Desdemona: if she will return me my jewels, I will give over my suit and repent my unlawful solicitation; if not, assure yourself I will seek satisfaction of you.

Iago. You have said now.

Rod. Ay, and said nothing but what I protest intendment of doing.

Iago. Why, now I see there 's mettle in thee, and even from this instant do build on thee a better opinion than ever before. Give me thy hand, Roderigo: thou hast taken against me a most just exception; but yet, I protest, I have dealt most directly in thy affair.

Rod. It hath not appeared.

Iago. I grant indeed it hath not appeared, and your suspicion is not without wit and

132. cogging, lying. **cozening,** cheating. **141. unfold,** expose. **144. within door,** not so loud. **153. discourse,** range. **160. defeat,** destroy. **163. addition,** title, name of whore. **164. vanity,** finery.

170. stays the meat, wait for supper. **176. daff'st me,** puttest me off. **178. conveniency,** opportunity. **190. votarist,** nun. **192-3. sudden respect,** immediate notice. **197. fopped,** duped. **212. directly,** in a straightforward manner.

judgement. But, Roderigo, if thou hast that in thee indeed, which I have greater reason to believe now than ever—I mean purpose, courage, and valour—this night show it. If thou the next night following enjoy not Desdemona, take me from this world with treachery and devise engines for my life.

Rod. Well, what is it? Is it within reason and compass?

Iago. Sir, there is especial commission come from Venice to depute Cassio in Othello's place.

Rod. Is that true? Why, then Othello and Desdemona return again to Venice.

Iago. O, no; he goes into Mauritania and takes away with him the fair Desdemona, unless his abode be lingered here by some accident; wherein none can be so determinate as the removing of Cassio.

Rod. How do you mean, removing him?

Iago. Why, by making him uncapable of Othello's place; knocking out his brains.

Rod. And that you would have me to do?

Iago. Ay, if you dare do yourself a profit and a right. He sups to-night with a harlotry, and thither will I go to him; he knows not yet of his honourable fortune. If you will watch his going thence, which I will fashion to fall out between twelve and one, you may take him at your pleasure. I will be near to second your attempt, and he shall fall between us. Come, stand not amazed at it, but go along with me; I will show you such a necessity in his death that you shall think yourself bound to put it on him. It is now high supper-time, and the night grows to waste. About it.

Rod. I will hear further reason for this.

Iago. And you shall be satisfied. *Exeunt.*

Scene III. *Another room in the castle.*

Enter *Othello, Lodovico, Desdemona, Emilia,* and Attendants.

Lod. I do beseech you, sir, trouble yourself no further.
Oth. O, pardon me; 't will do me good to walk.
Lod. Madam, good-night; I humbly thank your ladyship.
Des. Your honour is most welcome.
Oth. Will you walk, sir?
O, Desdemona,—
Des. My lord?
Oth. Get you to bed on th' instant; I will be returned forthwith. Dismiss your attendant there. Look 't be done.
Des. I will, my lord.
Exeunt Othello, Lodovico, and Attendants.
Emil. How goes it now? He looks gentler than he did.
Des. He says he will return incontinent;
And hath commanded me to go to bed,
And bade me to dismiss you.
Emil. Dismiss me?
Des. It was his bidding; therefore, good Emilia,
Give me my nightly wearing, and adieu.
We must not now displease him.
Emil. I would you had never seen him!
Des. So would not I: my love doth so approve him,
That even his stubbornness, his checks, his frowns,—
Prithee, unpin me,—have grace and favour in them.
Emil. I have laid those sheets you bade me on the bed.
Des. All 's one. Good faith, how foolish are our minds!
If I do die before thee, prithee, shroud me
In one of those same sheets.
Emil. Come, come, you talk.
Des. My mother had a maid call'd Barbara;
She was in love, and he she lov'd prov'd mad
And did forsake her. She had a song of "willow";
An old thing 't was, but it express'd her fortune,
And she died singing it. That song to-night
Will not go from my mind; I have much to do
But to go hang my head all at one side
And sing it like poor Barbara. Prithee, dispatch.
Emil. Shall I go fetch your night-gown?
Des. No, unpin me here.
This Lodovico is a proper man.
Emil. A very handsome man.
Des. He speaks well.

Emil. I know a lady in Venice would have walked barefoot to Palestine for a touch of his nether lip.

Des. [*Singing.*]

The poor soul sat sighing by a sycamore tree,
Sing all a green willow;
Her hand on her bosom, her head on her knee,
Sing willow, willow, willow.
The fresh streams ran by her, and murmur'd her moans;
Sing willow, willow, willow;

222. engines for, contrivances against. **232. determinate**, decisive. **238. harlotry**, harlot. **250. grows to waste**, is wasting away.

Scene iii: 12. incontinent, immediately. **20. stubbornness**, harshness. **27. prov'd mad**, turned wild, inconstant. **34. night-gown**, dressing gown. **41ff.** Desdemona's song is a popular ballad altered by Shakespeare to fit the situation.

Her salt tears fell from her, and soften'd the stones;
Sing willow, willow, willow;

Lay by these;—
[*Singing.*] "*Willow, willow;*"—
Prithee, hie thee; he 'll come anon;—
[*Singing.*]

Sing all a green willow must be my garland.
Let nobody blame him, his scorn I approve,—

Nay, that 's not next.—Hark! who is 't that knocks?

Emil. It 's the wind.

Des. [*Singing.*]

I call'd my love false love; but what said he then?
Sing willow, willow, willow.
If I court moe women, you'll couch with moe men.—

So, get thee gone; good-night. Mine eyes do itch;
Doth that bode weeping?

Emil. 'T is neither here nor there.

Des. I have heard it said so. O, these men, these men!
Dost thou in conscience think,—tell me, Emilia,—
That there be women do abuse their husbands
In such gross kind?

Emil. There be some such, no question.

Des. Wouldst thou do such a deed for all the world?

Emil. Why, would not you?

Des. No, by this heavenly light!

Emil. Nor I neither by this heavenly light;
I might do 't as well i' th' dark.

Des. Wouldst thou do such a deed for all the world?

Emil. The world 's a huge thing; it is a great price
For a small vice.

Des. In troth, I think thou wouldst not.

Emil. In troth, I think I should; and undo 't when I had done. Marry, I would not do such a thing for a joint-ring, nor for measures of lawn, nor for gowns, petticoats, nor caps, nor any petty exhibition; but, for all the whole world,—'ud's pity, who would not make her husband a cuckold to make him a monarch? I should venture purgatory for 't.

Des. Beshrew me, if I would do such a wrong
For the whole world.

Emil. Why, the wrong is but a wrong i' th' world; and having the world for your labour, 't is a wrong in your own world, and you might quickly make it right.

Des. I do not think there is any such woman.

Emil. Yes, a dozen; and as many to th' vantage as would store the world they play'd for.
But I do think it is their husbands' faults
If wives do fall. Say that they slack their duties
And pour our treasures into foreign laps,
Or else break out in peevish jealousies,
Throwing restraint upon us; or say they strike us,
Or scant our former having in despite;
Why, we have galls, and though we have some grace,
Yet have we some revenge. Let husbands know
Their wives have sense like them; they see and smell
And have their palates both for sweet and sour
As husbands have. What is it that they do
When they change us for others? Is it sport?
I think it is. And doth affection breed it?
I think it doth. Is 't frailty that thus errs?
It is so too. And have not we affections,
Desires for sport, and frailty, as men have?
Then let them use us well; else let them know,
The ills we do, their ills instruct us so.

Des. Good-night, good-night. Heaven me such uses send,
Not to pick bad from bad, but by bad mend.

Exeunt.

ACT V. SCENE I. *Cyprus. A street.*

Enter *Iago* and *Roderigo*.

Iago. Here, stand behind this bulk; straight will he come:
Wear thy good rapier bare, and put it home.
Quick, quick; fear nothing; I 'll be at thy elbow.
It makes us, or it mars us; think on that,
And fix most firm thy resolution.

Rod. Be near at hand; I may miscarry in 't.

Iago. Here, at thy hand; be bold, and take thy stand.

Retires.

73. **joint-ring,** ring made of interlocking halves, a favorite love-token. 75. **exhibition,** stipend. 85-6. **to th' vantage,** to boot. 90. **peevish,** foolish. 92. **having,** allowance. 93. **galls,** resentment. 95. **sense,** feeling.

Act V, Scene i: 1. bulk, projecting part of a building.

Rod. I have no great devotion to the deed,
And yet he hath given me satisfying reasons:
'T is but a man gone. Forth, my sword: he dies.
Iago. I have rubb'd this young quat almost to the sense,
And he grows angry. Now, whether he kill Cassio,
Or Cassio him, or each do kill the other,
Every way makes my gain. Live Roderigo,
He calls me to a restitution large
Of gold and jewels that I bobb'd from him,
As gifts to Desdemona;
It must not be. If Cassio do remain,
He hath a daily beauty in his life
That makes me ugly; and, besides, the Moor
May unfold me to him; there stand I in much peril.
No, he must die. Be 't so. I hear him coming.

Enter *Cassio.*

Rod. I know his gait, 't is he.—Villain, thou diest! *Makes a pass at Cassio.*
Cas. That thrust had been mine enemy indeed,
But that my coat is better than thou know'st.
I will make proof of thine.
Draws, and wounds Roderigo.
Rod. O, I am slain.
Iago from behind wounds Cassio in the leg, and exit.
Cas. I am maim'd for ever. Help, ho! murder! murder! *Falls.*

Enter *Othello.*

Oth. The voice of Cassio! Iago keeps his word.
Rod. O, villain that I am!
Oth. It is even so.
Cas. O, help, ho! light! a surgeon!
Oth. 'T is he!—O brave Iago, honest and just,
That hast such noble sense of thy friends' wrong!
Thou teachest me. Minion, your dear lies dead,
And your unblest fate hies; strumpet, I come.
Forth of my heart those charms, thine eyes, are blotted;
Thy bed, lust-stain'd, shall with lust's blood be spotted. *Exit.*

Enter *Lodovico* and *Gratiano.*

Cas. What, ho! no watch? no passage? Murder! murder!
Gra. 'T is some mischance; the voice is very direful.
Cas. O, help!
Lod. Hark!
Rod. O wretched villain!
Lod. Two or three groan. It is a heavy night,
These may be counterfeits; let 's think 't unsafe
To come in to the cry without more help.
Rod. Nobody come? Then shall I bleed to death.

Re-enter *Iago,* with a light.

Lod. Hark!
Gra. Here 's one comes in his shirt, with light and weapons.
Iago. Who 's there? Whose noise is this that cries on murder?
Lod. We do not know.
Iago. Do not you hear a cry?
Cas. Here, here! for Heaven's sake, help me!
Iago. What 's the matter?
Gra. This is Othello's ancient, as I take it.
Lod. The same indeed; a very valiant fellow.
Iago. What are you here that cry so grievously?
Cas. Iago? O, I am spoil'd, undone by villains!
Give me some help.
Iago. O me, lieutenant! what villains have done this?
Cas. I think that one of them is hereabout,
And cannot make away.
Iago. O treacherous villains!
What are you there?—Come in, and give some help. [*To Lodovico and Gratiano.*]
Rod. O, help me there!
Cas. That 's one of them.
Iago. O murderous slave! O villain!
Stabs Roderigo.
Rod. O damn'd Iago! O inhuman dog!
Iago. Kill men i' th' dark!—Where be these bloody thieves?—
How silent in this town!—Ho! murder! murder!—
What may you be? Are you of good or evil?
Lod. As you shall prove us, praise us.
Iago. Signior Lodovico?
Lod. He, sir.
Iago. I cry you mercy. Here 's Cassio hurt by villains.
Gra. Cassio!
Iago. How is 't, brother!
Cas. My leg is cut in two.
Iago. Marry, heaven forbid!
Light, gentlemen! I 'll bind it with my shirt.

11. quat, pimple. **sense,** quick. **16. bobb'd,** cheated. **25. coat,** i.e., of mail worn under outer garments. **33. Minion,** hussy. **37. passage,** passers-by.

42. heavy, thick, cloudy. **47. cries on,** cries out.

Enter *Bianca*.

Bian. What is the matter, ho? Who is 't that cried?
Iago. Who is 't that cried!
Bian. O my dear Cassio! my sweet Cassio!
O Cassio, Cassio, Cassio!
Iago. O notable strumpet! Cassio, may you suspect
Who they should be that have thus mangled you?
Cas. No.
Gra. I am sorry to find you thus; I have been to seek you.
Iago. Lend me a garter. So. O, for a chair,
To bear him easily hence!
Bian. Alas, he faints! O Cassio, Cassio, Cassio!
Iago. Gentlemen all, I do suspect this trash
To be a party in this injury.
Patience a while, good Cassio. Come, come;
Lend me a light. Know we this face or no?
Alas, my friend and my dear countryman
Roderigo! No:—yes, sure:—O heaven! Roderigo.
Gra. What, of Venice?
Iago. Even he, sir; did you know him?
Gra. Know him? ay.
Iago. Signior Gratiano? I cry your gentle pardon;
These bloody accidents must excuse my manners,
That so neglected you.
Gra. I am glad to see you.
Iago. How do you, Cassio? O, a chair, a chair!
Gra. Roderigo!
Iago. He, he, 't is he. *A chair brought in.*
O, that 's well said; the chair.
Some good man bear him carefully from hence;
I 'll fetch the General's surgeon. [*To Bianca.*] For you, mistress,
Save you your labour. He that lies slain here, Cassio,
Was my dear friend. What malice was between you?
Cas. None in the world; nor do I know the man.
Iago. [*To Bian.*] What, look you pale? O, bear him out o' th' air.
Cassio and Roderigo are borne off.
Stay you, good gentlemen. Look you pale, mistress?
Do you perceive the gastness of her eye?
Nay, if you stare, we shall hear more anon.
Behold her well; I pray you, look upon her.
Do you see, gentlemen? Nay, guiltiness will speak,
Though tongues were out of use.

Enter *Emilia*.

Emil. Alas, what 's the matter? What 's the matter, husband?
Iago. Cassio hath here been set on in the dark
By Roderigo and fellows that are scap'd.
He 's almost slain, and Roderigo dead.
Emil. Alas, good gentlemen! alas, good Cassio!
Iago. This is the fruits of whoring. Prithee, Emilia,
Go know of Cassio where he supp'd to-night.
[*To Bianca.*] What, do you shake at that?
Bian. He supp'd at my house; but I therefore shake not.
Iago. O, did he so? I charge you, go with me.
Emil. Oh, fie upon thee, strumpet!
Bian. I am no strumpet, but of life as honest
As you that thus abuse me.
Emil. As I? Fie upon thee!
Iago. Kind gentlemen, let 's go see poor Cassio dress'd.
Come, mistress, you must tell 's another tale.
Emilia, run you to the citadel,
And tell my lord and lady what hath happ'd.
Will you go on afore? [*Aside.*] This is the night
That either makes me or fordoes me quite.
Exeunt.

Scene II. *A bedchamber in the castle: Desdemona in bed asleep.*

Enter *Othello* with a light.

Oth. It is the cause, it is the cause, my soul,—
Let me not name it to you, you chaste stars!—
It is the cause. Yet I 'll not shed her blood,
Nor scar that whiter skin of hers than snow,
And smooth as monumental alabaster.
Yet she must die, else she 'll betray more men.
Put out the light, and then put out the light:
If I quench thee, thou flaming minister,
I can again thy former light restore,
Should I repent me; but once put out thy light,
Thou cunning'st pattern of excelling nature,
I know not where is that Promethean heat

82. **chair**, sedan chair. 85. **trash**, i.e., Bianca. 97. **said**, done. 106. **gastness**, ghastliness.

129. **fordoes**, destroys. **Scene ii**: 12. **Promethean heat**, divine fire (stolen by Prometheus from heaven).

That can thy light relume. When I have pluck'd the rose
I cannot give it vital growth again,
It needs must wither; I 'll smell it on the tree. *Kisses her.*
Oh, balmy breath, that dost almost persuade
Justice to break her sword! One more, one more.
Be thus when thou art dead, and I will kill thee
And love thee after. One more, and that 's the last;
So sweet was ne'er so fatal. I must weep,
But they are cruel tears: this sorrow 's heavenly;
It strikes where it doth love. She wakes.

Des. Who 's there? Othello?

Oth. Ay, Desdemona.

Des. Will you come to bed, my lord?

Oth. Have you pray'd to-night, Desdemon?

Des. Ay, my lord.

Oth. If you bethink yourself of any crime
Unreconcil'd as yet to heaven and grace,
Solicit for it straight.

Des. Alack, my lord, what may you mean by that?

Oth. Well, do it, and be brief; I will walk by.
I would not kill thy unprepared spirit;
No; heaven forfend! I would not kill thy soul.

Des. Talk you of killing?

Oth. Ay, I do.

Des. Then heaven
Have mercy on me!

Oth. Amen, with all my heart!

Des. If you say so, I hope you will not kill me.

Oth. Hum!

Des. And yet I fear you; for you 're fatal then
When your eyes roll so. Why I should fear I know not,
Since guiltiness I know not; but yet I feel I fear.

Oth. Think on thy sins.

Des. They are loves I bear to you.

Oth. Ay, and for that thou diest.

Des. That death 's unnatural that kills for loving.
Alas, why gnaw you so your nether lip?
Some bloody passion shakes your very frame.
These are portents; but yet I hope, I hope,
They do not point on me.

Oth. Peace, and be still!

Des. I will so. What 's the matter?

Oth. That handkerchief which I so lov'd and gave thee
Thou gav'st to Cassio.

Des. No, by my life and soul!
Send for the man, and ask him.

Oth. Sweet soul, take heed,
Take heed of perjury; thou art on thy death-bed.

Des. Ay, but not yet to die.

Oth. Yes, presently:
Therefore confess thee freely of thy sin;
For to deny each article with oath
Cannot remove nor choke the strong conception
That I do groan withal. Thou art to die.

Des. Then Lord have mercy on me!

Oth. I say, amen.

Des. And have you mercy too! I never did
Offend you in my life; never lov'd Cassio
But with such general warranty of heaven
As I might love; I never gave him token.

Oth. By heaven, I saw my handkerchief in 's hand.
O perjur'd woman! thou dost stone my heart,
And makes me call what I intend to do
A murder, which I thought a sacrifice.
I saw the handkerchief.

Des. He found it then;
I never gave it him: send for him hither;
Let him confess a truth.

Oth. He hath confess'd.

Des. What, my lord?

Oth. That he hath us'd thee.

Des. How? unlawfully?

Oth. Ay.

Des. He will not say so.

Oth. No, his mouth is stopp'd;
Honest Iago hath ta'en order for 't.

Des. O! my fear interprets. What, is he dead?

Oth. Had all his hairs been lives, my great revenge
Had stomach for them all.

Des. Alas! he is betray'd and I undone.

Oth. Out, strumpet! weep'st thou for him to my face?

Des. O, banish me, my lord, but kill me not!

Oth. Down, strumpet!

Des. Kill me to-morrow; let me live to-night!

Oth. Nay, if you strive,—

Des. But half an hour!

Oth. Being done, there is no pause.

Des. But while I say one prayer!

Oth. It is too late.
He smothers her.

13. relume, rekindle. **21. this sorrow's heavenly,** because it results from a punishment divine in its justice. **30. by,** aside. **32. forfend,** forbid.

55. conception, intention. **63. stone,** turn to stone. **72. ta'en order,** made arrangements. **75. stomach,** appetite. **82. Being . . . pause,** now that it is being done, there can be no delay.

Emil. [*At the door.*] My lord, my lord! What, ho! my lord, my lord!
Oth. What noise is this? Not dead? not yet quite dead?
I that am cruel am yet merciful;
I would not have thee linger in thy pain.
So, so.
Emil. [*Within.*] What, ho! my lord, my lord!
Oth. Who 's there?
Emil. [*Within.*] O, good my lord, I would speak a word with you!
Oth. Yes:—'t is Emilia.—By and by.—She 's dead.
'T is like she comes to speak of Cassio's death.
The noise was high. Ha! no more moving?
Still as the grave. Shall she come in? Were 't good?—
I think she stirs again:—no. What 's best to do?
If she come in, she 'll sure speak to my wife.
My wife! my wife! what wife? I have no wife.
O, insupportable! O heavy hour!
Methinks it should be now a huge eclipse
Of sun and moon, and that th' affrighted globe
Did yawn at alteration.
Emil. [*Within.*] I do beseech you
That I may speak with you, O, good my lord!
Oth. I had forgot thee. O, come in, Emilia.
Soft; by and by.—Let me the curtains draw.—
Where art thou? *Opens the door.*

Enter *Emilia.*

What 's the matter with thee now?
Emil. O, my good lord, yonder 's foul murders done!
Oth. What, now?
Emil. But now, my lord.
Oth. It is the very error of the moon;
She comes more nearer earth than she was wont,
And makes men mad.
Emil. Cassio, my lord, hath kill'd a young Venetian
Call'd Roderigo.
Oth. Roderigo kill'd!
And Cassio kill'd!
Emil. No, Cassio is not kill'd.
Oth. Not Cassio kill'd! Then murder 's out of tune,
And sweet revenge grows harsh.
Des. O, falsely, falsely murder'd!
Emil. O Lord, what cry is that?
Oth. That! what?
Emil. Out, and alas! that was my lady's voice.
Help! help, ho! help! O lady, speak again!
Sweet Desdemona! O sweet mistress, speak!
Des. A guiltless death I die.
Emil. O, who hath done this deed?
Des. Nobody; I myself. Farewell!
Commend me to my kind lord. O, farewell! *Dies.*
Oth. Why, how should she be murder'd?
Emil. Alas, who knows?
Oth. You hear her say herself, it was not I.
Emil. She said so; I must needs report the truth.
Oth. She 's, like a liar, gone to burning hell.
'T was I that kill'd her.
Emil. O, the more angel she,
And you the blacker devil!
Oth. She turn'd to folly, and she was a whore.
Emil. Thou dost belie her, and thou art a devil.
Oth. She was false as water.
Emil. Thou art rash as fire, to say
That she was false: O, she was heavenly true!
Oth. Cassio did tup her; ask thy husband else.
O, I were damn'd beneath all depth in hell
But that I did proceed upon just grounds
To this extremity. Thy husband knew it all.
Emil. My husband?
Oth. Thy husband.
Emil. That she was false to wedlock?
Oth. Ay, with Cassio. Nay, had she been true,
If Heaven would make me such another world
Of one entire and perfect chrysolite,
I 'd not have sold her for it.
Emil. My husband?
Oth. Ay, 't was he that told me on her first.
An honest man he is, and hates the slime
That sticks on filthy deeds.
Emil. My husband?
Oth. What needs this iterance, woman? I say thy husband.
Emil. O mistress, villainy hath made mocks with love!
My husband say that she was false?
Oth. He, woman;
I say thy husband; dost understand the word?
My friend, thy husband, honest, honest Iago.
Emil. If he say so, may his pernicious soul
Rot half a grain a day! He lies to th' heart:
She was too fond of her most filthy bargain.
Oth. Ha!
Emil. Do thy worst!
This deed of thine is no more worthy heaven
Than thou wast worthy her.

101. yawn at alteration, gape with amazement at the change. Earthquakes were supposed to accompany eclipses. **109. error,** aberration, wandering from her orbit.

132. folly, wantonness. **145. chrysolite,** precious stone; according to Pliny the largest and costliest of gems. **151. villainy . . . love,** villainy hath made sport of deceived love.

Oth. Peace, you were best.
Emil. Thou hast not half that power to do me harm
As I have to be hurt. O gull! O dolt!
As ignorant as dirt! Thou hast done a deed—
I care not for thy sword; I 'll make thee known,
Though I lost twenty lives.—Help! help, ho! help!
The Moor hath kill'd my mistress! Murder! murder!

Enter *Montano, Gratiano, Iago,* and others.

Mon. What is the matter? How now, General!
Emil. O, are you come, Iago? You have done well,
That men must lay their murders on your neck.
Gra. What is the matter?
Emil. Disprove this villain, if thou be'st a man.
He says thou told'st him that his wife was false:
I know thou didst not, thou 'rt not such a villain.
Speak, for my heart is full.
Iago. I told him what I thought, and told no more
Than what he found himself was apt and true.
Emil. But did you ever tell him she was false?
Iago. I did.
Emil. You told a lie, an odious, damned lie;
Upon my soul, a lie, a wicked lie.
She false with Cassio!—did you say with Cassio?
Iago. With Cassio, mistress. Go to, charm your tongue.
Emil. I will not charm my tongue; I am bound to speak.
My mistress here lies murdered in her bed,—
All. O heavens forfend!
Emil. And your reports have set the murderer on.
Oth. Nay, stare not, masters; it is true, indeed.
Gra. 'T is a strange truth.
Mon. O monstrous act!
Emil. Villainy, villainy, villainy!
I think upon 't, I think: I smell 't,—O villainy!
I thought so then,—I 'll kill myself for grief—
O villainy, villainy!
Iago. What, are you mad? I charge you, get you home.
Emil. Good gentlemen, let me have leave to speak;
'T is proper I obey him, but not now.
Perchance, Iago, I will ne'er go home.
Oth. O! O! O! *He falls on the bed.*
Emil. Nay, lay thee down and roar;
For thou hast kill'd the sweetest innocent
That e'er did lift up eye.
Oth. [*Rising.*] O, she was foul!
I scarce did know you, uncle; there lies your niece,
Whose breath, indeed, these hands have newly stopp'd.
I know this act shows horrible and grim.
Gra. Poor Desdemon! I am glad thy father 's dead:
Thy match was mortal to him, and pure grief
Shore his old thread in twain. Did he live now,
This sight would make him do a desperate turn,
Yea, curse his better angel from his side,
And fall to reprobance.
Oth. 'T is pitiful; but yet Iago knows
That she with Cassio hath the act of shame
A thousand times committed. Cassio confess'd it;
And she did gratify his amorous works
With that recognizance and pledge of love
Which I first gave her: I saw it in his hand;
It was a handkerchief, an antique token
My father gave my mother.
Emil. O God! O heavenly God!
Iago. 'Zounds, hold your peace.
Emil. 'T will out, 't will out! I peace!
No, I will speak as liberal as the north:
Let Heaven and men and devils, let them all,
All, all, cry shame against me, yet I 'll speak.
Iago. Be wise, and get you home.
Emil. I will not.
Iago offers to stab Emilia
Gra. Fie!
Your sword upon a woman?
Emil. O thou dull Moor! that handkerchief thou speak'st of
I found by fortune and did give my husband;
For often, with a solemn earnestness,
More than indeed belong'd to such a trifle,
He begg'd of me to steal it.
Iago. Villanous whore!
Emil. She give it Cassio! No, alas! I found it,
And I did give 't my husband.
Iago. Filth, thou liest!
Emil. By heaven, I do not, I do not, gentlemen.

177. apt, natural. **183. charm,** silence with a charm. **192. then,** see IV, ii, 130ff. above.

209. reprobance, eternal damnation. **214. recognizance,** token. **220. liberal as the north,** as unrestrainedly as the north-wind.

O murderous coxcomb! what should such a fool
Do with so good a wife?
Oth. Are there no stones in heaven
But what serves for the thunder?—Precious villain!
He runs at Iago: Iago kills his wife.
Gra. The woman falls; sure, he hath kill'd his wife.
Emil. Ay, ay! O, lay me by my mistress' side. *Exit Iago.*
Gra. He 's gone, but his wife 's kill'd.
Mon. 'T is a notorious villain. Take you this weapon
Which I have here recover'd from the Moor:
Come, guard the door without; let him not pass,
But kill him rather. I 'll after that same villain,
For 't is a damned slave.
Exeunt Montano and Gratiano.
Oth. I am not valiant neither,
But every puny whipster gets my sword.
But why should honour outlive honesty?
Let it go all.
Emil. What did thy song bode, lady?
Hark, canst thou hear me? I will play the swan,
And die in music. [*Singing.*] "Willow, willow, willow!"—
Moor, she was chaste; she lov'd thee, cruel Moor;
So come my soul to bliss, as I speak true;
So speaking as I think, alas, I die. *Dies.*
Oth. I have another weapon in this chamber;
It was a sword of Spain, the ice-brook's temper,—
O, here it is. Uncle, I must come forth.
Gra. [*Within.*] If thou attempt it, it will cost thee dear:
Thou hast no weapon, and perforce must suffer.
Oth. Look in upon me then and speak with me,
Or, naked as I am, I will assault thee.

Re-enter *Gratiano.*

Gra. What is the matter?
Oth. Behold, I have a weapon;
A better never did itself sustain
Upon a soldier's thigh. I have seen the day
That, with this little arm and this good sword,
I have made my way through more impediments
Than twenty times your stop. But, O vain boast!
Who can control his fate? 't is not so now.
Be not afraid though you do see me weapon'd;
Here is my journey's end, here is my butt
And very sea-mark of my utmost sail.
Do you go back dismay'd? 'T is a lost fear;
Man but a rush against Othello's breast
And he retires. Where should Othello go?
Now, how dost thou look now? O ill-starr'd wench!
Pale as thy smock! when we shall meet at compt,
This look of thine will hurl my soul from heaven,
And fiends will snatch at it. Cold, cold, my girl!
Even like thy chastity. O cursed, cursed slave!
Whip me, ye devils,
From the possession of this heavenly sight!
Blow me about in winds! roast me in sulphur!
Wash me in steep-down gulfs of liquid fire!
O Desdemona, Desdemona! dead!
Oh! Oh! Oh!

Enter *Lodovico, Montano, Cassio* carried in a chair, and Officers, with *Iago* prisoner.

Lod. Where is this rash and most unfortunate man?
Oth. That 's he that was Othello; here I am.
Lod. Where is that viper? Bring the villain forth.
Oth. I look down towards his feet; but that 's a fable.
If that thou be'st a devil, I cannot kill thee.
Wounds Iago.
Lod. Wrench his sword from him.
Iago. I bleed, sir; but not kill'd.
Oth. I am not sorry neither. I 'd have thee live;
For, in my sense, 't is happiness to die.
Lod. O thou Othello, that wert once so good,
Fallen in the practice of a cursed slave,
What shall be said to thee?
Oth. Why, anything.
An honourable murderer, if you will;
For nought did I in hate, but all in honour.
Lod. This wretch hath part confess'd his villainy.
Did you and he consent in Cassio's death?
Oth. Ay.

234. **stones**, it was thought that thunder was accompanied by a stone or bolt from heaven. 244. **whipster**, stripling, lit., boy who whips a top. 253. **ice-brook's temper**, tempered in icy water. 258. **naked**, unarmed.

264. **your stop**, your power to stop me. 267. **butt** goal. 268. **sea-mark**, beacon, limit. 273. **compt**, reckoning, i.e., the Day of Judgment. 286. **I look . . . feet**, i.e., to see if they are cloven like the Devil's. 292. **in the practice**, into the power of the stratagems. 297. **consent in**, conspire together.

Cas. Dear General, I never gave you cause.
Oth. I do believe it, and I ask your pardon.
Will you, I pray, demand that demi-devil
Why he hath thus ensnar'd my soul and body?
Iago. Demand me nothing; what you know, you know.
From this time forth I never will speak word.
Lod. What, not to pray?
Gra. Torments will ope your lips.
Oth. Well, thou dost best.
Lod. Sir, you shall understand what hath befall'n,
Which, as I think, you know not. Here is a letter
Found in the pocket of the slain Roderigo,
And here another. The one of them imports
The death of Cassio to be undertook
By Roderigo.
Oth. O villain!
Cas. Most heathenish and most gross!
Lod. Now here 's another discontented paper,
Found in his pocket too; and this, it seems,
Roderigo meant t' have sent this damned villain;
But that belike Iago in the interim
Came in and satisfi'd him.
Oth. O thou pernicious caitiff!—
How came you, Cassio, by that handkerchief
That was my wife's?
Cas. I found it in my chamber;
And he himself confess'd but even now
That there he dropp'd it for a special purpose
Which wrought to his desire.
Oth. O fool! fool! fool!
Cas. There is besides in Roderigo's letter,
How he upbraids Iago, that he made him
Brave me upon the watch, whereon it came
That I was cast; and even but now he spake,
After long seeming dead, Iago hurt him,
Iago set him on.
Lod. You must forsake this room, and go with us.
Your power and your command is taken off,
And Cassio rules in Cyprus. For this slave,
If there be any cunning cruelty
That can torment him much and hold him long,
It shall be his. You shall close prisoner rest,
Till that the nature of your fault be known
To the Venetian state. Come, bring away.
Oth. Soft you; a word or two before you go.
I have done the state some service, and they know 't.
No more of that. I pray you, in your letters,
When you shall these unlucky deeds relate,
Speak of me as I am; nothing extenuate,
Nor set down aught in malice. Then must you speak
Of one that lov'd not wisely but too well;
Of one not easily jealous, but being wrought
Perplex'd in the extreme; of one whose hand,
Like the base Indian, threw a pearl away
Richer than all his tribe; of one whose subdued eyes,
Albeit unused to the melting mood,
Drops tears as fast as the Arabian trees
Their medicinal gum. Set you down this;
And say besides, that in Aleppo once,
Where a malignant and a turban'd Turk
Beat a Venetian and traduc'd the state,
I took by th' throat the circumcised dog,
And smote him, thus. *Stabs himself.*
Lod. O bloody period!
Gra. All that 's spoke is marr'd.
Oth. I kiss'd thee ere I kill'd thee: no way but this,
Killing myself, to die upon a kiss.
Falls on the bed, and dies.
Cas. This did I fear, but thought he had no weapon;
For he was great of heart.
Lod. [*To Iago.*] O Spartan dog,
More fell than anguish, hunger, or the sea!
Look on the tragic loading of this bed;
This is thy work. The object poisons sight;
Let it be hid. Gratiano, keep the house,
And seize upon the fortunes of the Moor,
For they succeed on you. To you, lord governor,
Remains the censure of this hellish villain;
The time, the place, the torture. O, enforce it!
Myself will straight aboard; and to the state
This heavy act with heavy heart relate.
Exeunt.

314. **discontented,** expressing dissatisfaction. 331. **taken off,** removed.

346. **Perplex'd,** distraught. 347. **base Indian,** i.e., who through ignorance despises jewels. 352. **Aleppo,** a Syrian town where Venice had special trading privileges. 357. **period,** end. 361. **Spartan dog,** bloodhound. 366. **seize upon,** take legal possession of. 368. **censure,** legal sentence.

The Tragedy of King Lear

Shakespeare's *King Lear,* driven off the boards by Tate's adaptation, was rediscovered by the Romantic critics. Their chorus of praise has been summed up by Swinburne, who calls *King Lear* "the most elemental and primeval" of Shakespeare's works. It may not be his best play; it is in some ways his most tremendous work, "the greatest single achievement of Teutonic or Northern genius."

Text.—*King Lear* was first published in 1608 with the following descriptive title-page: *M. William Shak-speare: His True Chronicle Historie of the life and death of King Lear and his three daughters. With the unfortunate life of Edgar, sonne and heire to the Earle of Gloster, and his sullen and assumed humor of Tom of Bedlam: As it was played before the King's Maiestie at Whitehall upon S. Stephans night in Christmas Hollidayes. By his Maiesties servants playing usually at the Gloabe on the Bancke-side. London, Printed for Nathaniel Butter, and are to be sold at his shop in Paul's Church-yard at the signe of the Pide Bull neere St. Austins Gate, 1608.* This is the First Quarto, usually referred to as the Pied Bull Quarto. The publisher did a very poor job; some one in his office corrected the sheets as they were going through the press, and corrected and uncorrected pages were bound up together with a result that of the nine copies of this edition extant no two are exactly alike. Yet this Quarto remains invaluable since it contains about three hundred genuine Shakespearean lines that are omitted in the Folio.

Another Quarto bearing the same date also exists but it is now known that this was printed in 1619. It is a mere reprint of the First Quarto.

The Folio text omits some 300 lines found in the Quarto and adds over 100 new lines. Evidently it depends upon another source than the First Quarto. The present text has been established by a careful collation of the Quarto and the Folio.

Date.—The date of *Lear* can be fixed within comparatively narrow limits. It was entered in the Stationers' Register on November 26, 1607, and this entry states that it had been "played at Whitehall upon Saint Stephen's night at Christmas last," *i.e.,* on December 26, 1606. *Lear* was therefore on the boards in the winter of 1606. On the other hand Shakespeare is known to have borrowed a number of unusual names for devils from a curious book by Harsnet, *A Declaration of Popish Impostures,* which was registered in the spring of 1603. Between these dates, then, Shakespeare's play must have been composed.

The Old Play of King Leir.—We can probably date *King Lear* late in 1605 or early in 1606 because of its relation to another play on the same subject. In May, 1594, an entry on the Stationers' Register of *The most famous chronicle history of Leire King of England and his three daughters* points to an intention to publish this play; but no edition of that date is known. In 1605, however, the *Tragical history of King Leir—as it was lately acted* was entered and printed as the *True Chronicle History, etc.* The author is unknown; certainly he does not imitate Shakespeare's play. On the other hand certain verbal resemblances and the close correspondence of one character (Perillus in *Leir,* Kent in *King Lear*) unknown in other versions of the story lead one to suspect that Shakespeare had read or seen the old play, and caught from it the idea of a tragedy on the subject, and that he drew from the earlier work certain suggestions for his own.

Source.—The source of the Lear story goes back to dim antiquity. Its earliest form seems to be that of a widely diffused folk-tale which runs about as follows: An old king asks his three daughters how much they love him; the two elder girls flatter him by extravagant professions; the youngest says simply that she loves him like salt. The King drives her away in a fit of anger, but later comes to learn the value of salt and is reconciled to her. This story makes its appearance in literature in Geoffrey of Monmouth's *Historia Regum Britanniæ* (ca. 1135). Geoffrey, who proposed to tell the story of ancient Britain, apparently filled up the unchronicled centuries between the discovery of the isle by Brutus, great-grandson of Æneas, and the invasion of Julius Cæsar, by drawing on British folk-lore for all sorts of stories and all sorts of names which he attached to certain mythical successors of

Brutus. One of these names is Lear, apparently derived from Llyr or Ler, a Celtic sea-god. Geoffrey makes him King of Britain and tells his story in great detail. He gives us the tale essentially as it appears in Shakespeare except that the tragic ending is wanting. In Geoffrey, Cordelia and her husband replace Lear on his throne where he reigns in peace until his death. Shortly thereafter the sons of Cordelia's wicked sisters throw her into prison where she commits suicide.

There are in all some fifty versions of the story. It seems to have enjoyed especial popularity in the sixteenth century, when the Welsh descent of the reigning Tudor dynasty directed fresh attention to Geoffrey's fabulous tales. They were not regarded as fabulous by the uncritical historians of that age, and the story of Lear was retold by all the Tudor chroniclers. Finally it was dramatized in the old play of *King Leir.*

The unknown author of this play introduces numerous changes and additions. Leir devises the love-test in order to entrap the reluctant Cordelia into a marriage with the King of Ireland, and after rejecting her gives away all his kingdom to his other daughters. A wise councilor, Perillus, warns Leir against his folly and later accompanies him in his distress: the daughters employ a murderer to kill the king, but their design is thwarted by a storm of thunder and lightning which terrifies the assassin. Cordelia is wooed by the disguised King of France and is herself disguised when she meets the outcast Leir. The play ends happily with the restoration of Leir to his throne.

Shakespeare's Alterations.—What changes did Shakespeare make, what new features did he introduce into his version? In the first place he has made it a tragedy. Unlike any of his predecessors Shakespeare saw the essentially tragic nature of this tale of filial ingratitude. He alone makes Cordelia fail in her attempt to restore Lear and by connecting her death in prison with this failure and making it the direct cause of Lear's death, he has given the tale a tragic unity that it possesses in no other form. He is the first also to bring the wicked sisters to their violent deaths. This is not only in accordance with Elizabethan tragic convention, but serves to heighten the terror of the catastrophe. It is to add a deeper shade to the tragedy, moreover, that Shakespeare represents Lear as driven mad by the cruelty of his daughters; there is no trace of this in earlier versions. The character of the Fool, too, is original with Shakespeare. He may have created the character to afford a good part for his fellow, Armin; but the character and the bitter jests of the Fool add immensely to the tragic irony of the play.

Shakespeare's chief addition to the tale, however, was the story of Gloucester and his two sons. This tale he found in Sidney's *Arcadia.* Here a bastard son of an Asian king slanders his legitimate brother to their father, who decrees his death. The son escapes and later returns to aid his father, who has been driven from his throne and blinded by the bastard. The old man begs his son to lead him to a rock that he might throw himself down and end his wretched life. After this the story diverges widely from Shakespeare, except that the old king dies, "his heart broken with unkindness and affliction."

Why did Shakespeare, contrary to his practice in his other tragedies, import an underplot into the simple and unified story of Lear and his daughters? There would seem to be two reasons. In the first place he must have realized that this story lacked some necessary element of dramatic action; the crisis comes early; after the division of the kingdom in Act I Lear is merely a passive figure. Shakespeare felt, perhaps, that there was some danger of the tragic theme degenerating into the merely pathetic, as in the old play. Moreover if the two wicked sisters were to perish at the close of the play some agent must be invented for their taking off. Shakespeare found in Sidney's story this needed increment of action and a character exactly adapted to his purpose. He wove it into the original fabric of his play with such skill that we feel the two to be of one piece, not a divided main and minor plot.

There was, however, another and more significant reason for Shakespeare's use of a double plot. *Lear,* as he planned it, was to be a tragedy of universal significance. Beginning in a clash between individuals, it was to end in the ruin of a kingdom. For such a result it may well have seemed to him that the single conflict was insufficient. The filial ingratitude of Goneril and Regan was so horrible, so extraordinary, that it might have seemed an exceptional case, one not to be taken into account in the reckoning of the evil wrought in the world by ingratitude; but when the ruthless ambition of Edmund is added to the heartless ingratitude of the daughters, when Gloucester is blinded and driven out to join the maddened king, when at last Edgar takes his place beside Cordelia as the champion of the right, we seem to be spectators of a world war between the powers of Good and Evil. Nature herself seems to take part in the conflict, the storm that bursts upon the head of Lear is but another phase of a struggle that convulses the physical, as it does the moral world.

The Theme.—The central idea of the old tale was one of contrast between the ingratitude of the daughters whom their father had nobly endowed and the devotion of the child that he had cast adrift. Shakespeare retains the main outline of the story, but he seizes for his theme upon its first half, filial ingratitude. The contrast remains, of course, but it is not dwelt upon. Cordelia has, after all, only a slight part in the play; in the old *Leir* she has a larger role. On the other hand no earlier author has laid such stress on the deliberate malignity of her sisters. This, no doubt, is because Shakespeare realized as no one else had done the profound significance of their behavior. As Love was the greatest, so its opposite, Hate, was to him the most terrible and destructive thing; and when Hate lurked under the mask of Love and assumed such forms as treason, breach of faith, or ingratitude, it took on its darkest shade. In *Lear,* the daughter, grown strong, turns upon an old father who had stripped himself to strengthen her. She forgets the ties of blood, tramples upon the deep maternal instinct which leads the woman to protect the weak, and strikes the old man down with blow on blow to shame, to suffering, and at last to madness. We recoil before the spectacle as before some breach in the laws of nature. When such things happen, Shakespeare seems to say, Chaos is come again. It is this impression which gives to *Lear* its peculiar, its universal, one might say, its symbolical significance.

Characters.—Yet if the play taken as a whole has a symbolical significance, the characters are anything but types and symbols; they are sharply individualized and living persons. Lear himself is not simply the father; he is a king before he is a father, in fact it is not till he ceases to be the king that he becomes the father. Goneril and Regan might seem at first mere types of filial ingratitude, but a closer glance shows how carefully Shakespeare has discriminated between the cold determined ruthlessness of Goneril and the passionate savagery of the weaker Regan. And the hateful daughters stand in sharp contrast to the wicked son who hates nobody and walks lightheartedly along a path of treachery and blood. Cordelia herself is far from being merely the good daughter of the old tale; she is Cordelia, King Lear's own daughter, with something of her father's pride and obstinacy, and with more than her father's need of love and power of loving. Edgar is something more than the male counterpart of Cordelia; he has nothing of her pride and little of her emotional nature. It is only adversity that shakes him out of his ignorance of evil and drills him into an active stoicism. Kent, too, with his rough honesty, his quick and fearless temper, his dog-like devotion to his unjust master, and his adoration of Cordelia—"kind and good princess"—is one of Shakespeare's great creations. And so it is with all the persons in the play down to the wretched Oswald and the shuddering servants who dress the bleeding eyes of Gloucester; they are not types, but living people.

Character and Destiny.—Now all the action of the play, symbolic as it may be, springs from and is determined by the character of the persons involved. It is Lear himself who brings about the tragedy of *Lear.* His tragic fault, to use a well-worn phrase, lies in an absorbing self-will that blinds him to all the world but himself. He has been a king for half a century and more and has become so accustomed to the idea of prompt and terrified obedience—"When I do stare, see how the subject quakes"—that all opposition to his will seems to him a crime little short of treason. Hence the rejection of Cordelia and the banishment of Kent. Yet Lear is not bad at heart. His fatal scheme of a division of his kingdom following upon a public declaration of his daughters' love, sprang from folly rather than from pride. He had a genuine affection for his children and a real desire to be assured of their love and gratitude; but his absorption in self led him to demand a public parade of their feelings without a thought of how it might affect them. His blindness to the flattery of the elder sisters, and his misunderstanding of Cordelia are due to this self-centeredness which cut him off from all the outside world and his autocratic anger at opposition completes the tragic crash of the first scene, one of the greatest that Shakespeare ever wrote.

The Redemption of Lear.—So far as the main character is concerned the play might be called, not the tragedy, but the redemption of King Lear. It is not at once that the process begins. In the scene at Goneril's court Lear is still his arbitrary and choleric self. At Regan's the sight of his servant in the stocks completely confounds him and he tries to beat down the brutal reality by vehement asseveration of its impossibility. Yet it is in this scene that Lear for the first time begins to take account of others in his hesitating attempt to find some excuse for Cornwall's discourtesy. It is not until he is rejected by both daughters and driven out into the storm that the real change in Lear begins. Paradoxically it is only when he is drifting down to madness that he comes to know himself, since under the stress of mental and physical suffering the old self-will which had so long blinded him to reality is beginning to give way. Lear's redemption is not wholly accomplished until his reunion with Cordelia. Then at last he throws off forever the kingly robe of pride and self-will and appears the simple man, owning his weakness, begging forgiveness, and asking for nothing in the world but his daughter's love. Here in the mind of sentimentalists the play should end. But Shakespeare's tragedy is made of sterner stuff. Lear has learned his lesson, but too late for this life. The powers of evil which his pride and folly had unloosed exhaust themselves in a final effort, and Cordelia lies dead in his arms. There is an outburst of agony and Lear passes away.

Meanwhile the same determinant of character is driving the evil-doers to their doom. Goneril and Regan are the inheritors of their father's self-will and passionate temper. It may be that they did not contemplate at first the extremities to which they finally proceed. But when Lear's power passes into their hands, they use it in his own arbitrary fashion, and his amazed resistance only hardens their determination. It is not until they learn of Lear's intention to resume his power, and of the threatened intervention of France in his behalf that they break out into Lear's own furious anger, mixed in their case with a ferocity that he had never shown. This is due, perhaps, to fear, which he had never felt—no one is so cruel as a coward—and the difference between Lear's banishment of Kent and their blinding of Gloucester marks the depth to which they have sunk. Finally Shakespeare adds a touch not found in his sources. Each of the sisters lusts after her fitting mate; it is not love that they feel, but an instinctive apprehension of their affinity in evil with Edmund; and this corruption of the best leads them inevitably to the worst, to mutual distrust, murder and suicide.

Atmosphere.—In no other play of Shakespeare's is the power of evil shown as an element of such tremendous force and such utter ruthlessness. Evil in *King Lear* is naked and unashamed; it rages like some convulsion in nature. It is for this reason, no doubt, that Shakespeare has set the scene of this symbolic tragedy far back in a mythical age. *Lear* is a tale of old, unhappy, far-off things; there were giants, we are told, before the Flood, and the figures in this play are gigantic, at times monstrous. They are pagans who swear by Jove and Juno; there is reference enough to the gods, to fate, to overruling stars, but there is no trace of any real religious belief. It is as if Shakespeare had wished to show us here humanity in the raw, stripped of its veneer of civilization, unsoftened by the influence of a religion of pity.

Final Appreciation.—The final impression left by *King Lear* is that of a tremendous, awe-inspiring creation of genius. It is futile to dwell on the inconsistencies and improbabilities of such a work; it is equally vain to ask for the lesson of *King Lear*. Shakespeare had something better to do when he wrote this play than to preach a sermon; he was concerned with something more profound than the distribution of poetical justice. Yet there is in *Lear* a recurring note, an undertone, that seems to reveal Shakespeare's intention, his outlook on the world. What is this outlook?

A poet critic has called it one of tragic fatalism, "over a world full of death and life without resting place or guidance." If this were true *King Lear* would be the expression of a dark and hopeless pessimism; but is it true in fact? Certainly when Shakespeare wrote this play he was possessed, obsessed perhaps, with his conception of the monstrous power of evil. But, after all, this evil is a transient power; it rages, but it passes, like a storm. At the close of the play the wicked daughters and Edmund are gone; they have destroyed, not only others, but themselves. Shakespeare's conception of this power seems to be that it is not only transient, but in its very nature self-destructive. The lesson of *Lear,* if we must seek for a lesson, may be told in the words of Milton:

> Evil on itself shall back recoil,
> And mix no more with goodness, when at last
> Gather'd like scum, and settled to itself,
> It shall be in eternal restless change
> Self-fed, and self-consumed.

Not only so but in this great revelation of the roots and springs of human life, Evil actually begets and fosters Good. The hypocrisy of her sisters calls forth the sincerity of Cordelia; their cruelty, her redeeming love. Without the treachery of Edmund we could not have the fidelity and fortitude of Edgar. The pathetic devotion of the Fool to his master is most apparent when that master has been driven out into the storm by the evil rulers of his world. Kent's cry for justice is provoked by the blind injustice of the King. Even in the minor characters this holds good; the old servant of Cornwall dies in protest against the savage cruelty of his lord, and the weak Albany rises into manhood when he discerns the demon hidden beneath the face of the woman who had bewitched him. It is not pessimism, this outlook of Shakespeare's in *King Lear.* The night is black, but it is lit with stars which night alone reveals.

Stage History.—None of Shakespeare's tragedies has had so unfortunate a stage history as *King Lear.* It was not so at first; it had the honor of an early presentation at Court and was repeatedly acted at the Globe. Yet there are few references to it before the closing of the theatres.

After the Restoration we hear little of it until 1681, when Nahum Tate, a playwright of the day, hit upon a happy device for stringing together, to use his own words, "a heap of jewels dazzling in their disorder." This was to introduce a love-interest, an heroic passion in the manner of Dryden, between Cordelia and Edgar and to bring the tragedy to a happy conclusion by their marriage and the restoration of Lear to his throne. The part of the Fool was excised as sinning against the decorum of tragedy, and Tate filled up the holes that he knocked in Shakespeare's play with verse of incredible baldness. Yet at once and for something like a century and a half it drove Shakespeare's play from the stage. Even Garrick with all his enthusiasm for Shakespeare did little more than cut out portions of Tate and restore some lines of Shakespeare. Kemble, 1808-9, revived a version nearer to Tate's than even that of Garrick. It was not until 1823 that Kean dared to restore the catastrophe, yet even he retained Tate's heroic lovers.

Finally Macready presented in 1837 the true text. Yet even he had deep misgivings about the Fool's part and ended by giving it to a girl. His production put a final end to what has been called the Tateification of *Lear.* Yet it must be noted that since his day the play has never held the stage as it did in the eighteenth century. Irving produced it with great splendor, but was himself incapable of sustaining the chief role even when assisted by Terry as Cordelia. The Italian tragedian Salvini was a famous Lear, and it was one of Edwin Booth's great parts.

It has been the fashion to say that *Lear* is unsuited—too great perhaps—for the stage. Assuredly *Lear* is almost impossible to produce on the modern picture-frame stage. For a true appreciation of its essentially dramatic values the student should consult the invaluable preface of Granville-Barker.

THE TRAGEDY OF KING LEAR

Dramatis Personæ

Lear, King of Britain.
King of France.
Duke of Burgundy.
Duke of Cornwall.
Duke of Albany.
Earl of Kent.
Earl of Gloucester.
Edgar, son to *Gloucester.*
Edmund, bastard son to *Gloucester.*
Curan, a courtier.
Old Man, tenant to *Gloucester.*

Doctor.
Fool.
Oswald, steward to *Goneril.*
A Captain employed by *Edmund.*
Gentleman attendant on *Cordelia.*
A Herald.
Servants to *Cornwall.*

Goneril, *Regan,* *Cordelia,* } daughters to *Lear.*

Knights of Lear's train, Captains, Messengers, Soldiers, and Attendants.

SCENE: *Britain.*

ACT I. Scene I. *King Lear's palace.*

Enter *Kent, Gloucester,* and *Edmund.*

Kent. I thought the King had more affected the Duke of Albany than Cornwall.

Glou. It did always seem so to us; but now, in the division of the kingdom, it appears not which of the Dukes he values most; for equalities are so weigh'd, that curiosity in neither can make choice of either's moiety.

Kent. Is not this your son, my lord?

Glou. His breeding, sir, hath been at my charge. I have so often blushed to acknowledge him, that now I am brazed to 't.

Kent. I cannot conceive you.

Glou. Sir, this young fellow's mother could; whereupon she grew round-wombed, and had, indeed, sir, a son for her cradle ere she had a husband for her bed. Do you smell a fault?

Kent. I cannot wish the fault undone, the issue of it being so proper.

Glou. But I have a son, sir, by order of law, some year elder than this, who yet is no dearer in my account. Though this knave came something saucily into the world before he was sent for, yet was his mother fair; there was good sport at his making, and the whoreson must be acknowledged. Do you know this noble gentleman, Edmund?

Edm. No, my lord.

Glou. My Lord of Kent. Remember him hereafter as my honourable friend.

Edm. My services to your lordship.

Kent. I must love you, and sue to know you better.

Edm. Sir, I shall study deserving.

Glou. He hath been out nine years, and away he shall again. The King is coming.

Sennet. Enter one bearing a coronet, then *King Lear,* then the *Dukes of Albany* and *Cornwall,* next *Goneril, Regan, Cordelia,* with followers.

Lear. Attend the lords of France and Burgundy, Gloucester.

Glou. I shall, my liege.

Exeunt Gloucester and Edmund.

Lear. Meantime we shall express our darker purpose.
Give me the map there. Know that we have divided
In three our kingdom; and 't is our fast intent
To shake all cares and business from our age,
Conferring them on younger strengths, while we
Unburden'd crawl toward death. Our son of Cornwall,
And you, our no less loving son of Albany,
We have this hour a constant will to publish
Our daughters' several dowers, that future strife
May be prevented now. The Princes, France and Burgundy,
Great rivals in our youngest daughter's love,
Long in our court have made their amorous sojourn,
And here are to be answer'd. Tell me, my daughters,—
Since now we will divest us both of rule,
Interest of territory, cares of state,—

1. affected, favored. **6. equalities,** shares. **curiosity,** careful investigation. **7. moiety,** share. **11. brazed,** hardened.

33. out, out of the country. **37. darker,** more secret. **51. Interest,** possession.

Which of you shall we say doth love us most,
That we our largest bounty may extend
Where nature doth with merit challenge? Goneril,
Our eldest-born, speak first.
Gon. Sir, I do love you more than words can wield the matter;
Dearer than eye-sight, space, and liberty:
Beyond what can be valued, rich or rare;
No less than life, with grace, health, beauty, honour;
As much as child e'er lov'd, or father found;
A love that makes breath poor, and speech unable:
Beyond all manner of so much I love you.
Cor. [*Aside.*] What shall Cordelia speak? Love and be silent.
Lear. Of all these bounds, even from this line to this,
With shadowy forests and with champains rich'd,
With plenteous rivers and wide-skirted meads,
We make thee lady. To thine and Albany's issues
Be this perpetual. What says our second daughter,
Our dearest Regan, wife of Cornwall? Speak.
Reg. I am made of that self metal as my sister,
And prize me at her worth. In my true heart
I find she names my very deed of love;
Only she comes too short, that I profess
Myself an enemy to all other joys
Which the most precious square of sense possesses;
And find I am alone felicitate
In your dear Highness' love.
Cor. [*Aside.*] Then poor Cordelia!
And yet not so; since, I am sure, my love 's
More ponderous than my tongue.
Lear. To thee and thine hereditary ever
Remain this ample third of our fair kingdom;
No less in space, validity, and pleasure,
Than that conferr'd on Goneril. Now, our joy,
Although our last and least, to whose young love
The vines of France and milk of Burgundy
Strive to be interess'd, what can you say to draw
A third more opulent than your sisters? Speak.
Cor. Nothing, my lord.
Lear. Nothing!
Cor. Nothing.
Lear. Nothing will come of nothing. Speak again.

54. Probably means—where nature (birth) as well as merit challenges (lays claim to) his generosity. 65. **champains,** open country. 71. **self,** same. 72. **prize me,** estimate myself. 76. **square of sense,** sense in its perfection. 77. **felicitate,** made happy. 83. **validity,** value. 86. **milk,** pastures. 87. **interess'd,** have a claim to.

Cor. Unhappy that I am, I cannot heave
My heart into my mouth. I love your Majesty
According to my bond; nor more nor less.
Lear. How, how, Cordelia! Mend your speech a little,
Lest you may mar your fortunes.
Cor. Good my lord,
You have begot me, bred me, lov'd me: I
Return those duties back as are right fit;
Obey you, love you, and most honour you.
Why have my sisters husbands, if they say
They love you all? Haply, when I shall wed,
That lord whose hand must take my plight shall carry
Half my love with him, half my care and duty.
Sure, I shall never marry like my sisters
To love my father all.
Lear. But goes thy heart with this?
Cor. Ay, my good lord.
Lear. So young, and so untender?
Cor. So young, my lord, and true.
Lear. Let it be so; thy truth, then, be thy dower!
For, by the sacred radiance of the sun,
The mysteries of Hecate, and the night;
By all the operation of the orbs
From whom we do exist, and cease to be;
Here I disclaim all my paternal care,
Propinquity and property of blood,
And as a stranger to my heart and me
Hold thee, from this, for ever. The barbarous Scythian,
Or he that makes his generation messes
To gorge his appetite, shall to my bosom
Be as well neighbour'd, piti'd, and reliev'd,
As thou my sometime daughter.
Kent. Good my liege,—
Lear. Peace, Kent!
Come not between the dragon and his wrath.
I lov'd her most, and thought to set my rest
On her kind nursery. [*To Cor.*] Hence, and avoid my sight!—
So be my grave my peace, as here I give
Her father's heart from her! Call France.—Who stirs?
Call Burgundy. Cornwall and Albany,
With my two daughters' dowers digest this third;
Let pride, which she calls plainness, marry her.
I do invest you jointly in my power,
Pre-eminence, and all the large effects
That troop with majesty. Ourself, by monthly course,
With reservation of an hundred knights,
By you to be sustain'd, shall our abode
Make with you by due turn. Only we still retain

95. **bond,** obligation. 103. **plight,** pledge. 112. **Hecate,** goddess of the infernal regions. 113. **operation,** influence. 116. **property,** identity. 126. **nursery,** nursing, tender care. 131. **plainness,** frankness.

The name, and all th' additions to a king;
The sway, revenue, execution of the rest,
Beloved sons, be yours; which to confirm,
This coronet part betwixt you.
Kent. Royal Lear,
Whom I have ever honour'd as my king,
Lov'd as my father, as my master follow'd
As my great patron thought on in my prayers,—
Lear. The bow is bent and drawn; make from the shaft.
Kent. Let it fall rather, though the fork invade
The region of my heart: be Kent unmannerly
When Lear is mad. What wouldst thou do, old man?
Think'st thou that duty shall have dread to speak
When power to flattery bows? To plainness honour 's bound,
When majesty falls to folly. Reserve thy state;
And, in thy best consideration, check
This hideous rashness. Answer my life my judgement,
Thy youngest daughter does not love thee least;
Nor are those empty-hearted whose low sounds
Reverb no hollowness.
Lear. Kent, on thy life, no more.
Kent. My life I never held but as a pawn
To wage against thine enemies, nor fear to lose it,
Thy safety being the motive.
Lear. Out of my sight!
Kent. See better, Lear; and let me still remain
The true blank of thine eye.
Lear. Now, by Apollo,—
Kent. Now, by Apollo, king,
Thou swear'st thy gods in vain.
Lear. O, vassal! miscreant!
Laying his hand on his sword.
Alb. / *Corn.* Dear sir, forbear.
Kent. Kill thy physician, and thy fee bestow
Upon the foul disease. Revoke thy doom;
Or, whilst I can vent clamour from my throat,
I 'll tell thee thou dost evil.
Lear. Hear me, recreant!
On thine allegiance, hear me!
That thou hast sought to make us break our vows,
Which we durst never yet, and with strain'd pride
To come betwixt our sentence and our power,
Which nor our nature nor our place can bear,
Our potency made good, take thy reward.
Five days we do allot thee, for provision
To shield thee from diseases of the world;
And on the sixth to turn thy hated back
Upon our kingdom. If, on the tenth day following,
Thy banish'd trunk be found in our dominions,
The moment is thy death. Away! By Jupiter,
This shall not be revok'd.
Kent. Fare thee well, king! Sith thus thou wilt appear,
Freedom lives hence, and banishment is here.
[*To Cordelia.*] The gods to their dear shelter take thee, maid,
That justly think'st, and hast most rightly said!
[*To Regan and Goneril.*] And your large speeches may your deeds approve,
That good effects may spring from words of love.
Thus Kent, O princes, bids you all adieu;
He 'll shape his old course in a country new.
Exit.

Flourish. Enter *Gloucester,* with *France* and *Burgundy,* Attendants.

Glou. Here 's France and Burgundy, my noble lord.
Lear. My Lord of Burgundy,
We first address toward you, who with this king
Hath rivall'd for our daughter. What, in the least,
Will you require in present dower with her,
Or cease your quest of love?
Bur. Most royal Majesty,
I crave no more than hath your Highness offer'd,
Nor will you tender less.
Lear. Right noble Burgundy,
When she was dear to us, we did hold her so;
But now her price is fall'n. Sir, there she stands:
If aught within that little-seeming substance,
Or all of it, with our displeasure piec'd,
And nothing more, may fitly like your Grace,
She 's there, and she is yours.
Bur. I know no answer.
Lear. Will you, with those infirmities she owes,
Unfriended, new-adopted to our hate,
Dower'd with our curse, and stranger'd with our oath,
Take her, or leave her?
Bur. Pardon me, royal sir;
Election makes not up in such conditions.

138. additions, titles. **151. Reserve thy state,** retain thy power. **156. Reverb**, reverberate. **161. blank,** white center of target **172. strain'd,** excessive.

183. Sith, since. **187. approve,** justify. **198. tender,** offer. **202. piec'd,** increased. **205. owes,** owns. **209. Election . . . up,** I will not choose her.

Lear. Then leave her, sir; for, by the power that made me,
I tell you all her wealth. [*To France.*] For you, great king,
I would not from your love make such a stray,
To match you where I hate; therefore beseech you
T' avert your liking a more worthier way
Than on a wretch whom Nature is asham'd
Almost t' acknowledge hers.
France. This is most strange,
That she, that even but now was your best object,
The argument of your praise, balm of your age,
Most best, most dearest, should in this trice of time
Commit a thing so monstrous, to dismantle
So many folds of favour. Sure, her offence
Must be of such unnatural degree,
That monsters it, or your fore-vouch'd affection
Fall'n into taint; which to believe of her,
Must be a faith that reason without miracle
Should never plant in me.
Cor. I yet beseech your Majesty,—
If for I want that glib and oily art,
To speak and purpose not; since what I well intend,
I 'll do 't before I speak,—that you make known
It is no vicious blot, murder, or foulness,
No unchaste action, or dishonoured step,
That hath depriv'd me of your grace and favour;
But even for want of that for which I am richer,
A still-soliciting eye, and such a tongue
That I am glad I have not, though not to have it
Hath lost me in your liking.
Lear. Better thou
Hadst not been born than not to have pleas'd me better.
France. Is it but this,—a tardiness in nature
Which often leaves the history unspoke
That it intends to do? My Lord of Burgundy,
What say you to the lady? Love is not love
When it is mingled with regards that stands
Aloof from th' entire point. Will you have her?
She is herself a dowry.
Bur. Royal Lear,
Give but that portion which yourself propos'd,
And here I take Cordelia by the hand,
Duchess of Burgundy.

218. **argument**, subject. 223. **monsters**, makes monstrous. 224. **taint**, reproach. 242. **regards**, consideration. 243. **entire**, essential, pure.

Lear. Nothing. I have sworn; I am firm.
Bur. I am sorry, then, you have so lost a father
That you must lose a husband.
Cor. Peace be with Burgundy!
Since that respects of fortune are his love,
I shall not be his wife.
France. Fairest Cordelia, that art most rich being poor,
Most choice forsaken, and most lov'd despis'd!
Thee and thy virtues here I seize upon,
Be it lawful I take up what 's cast away.
Gods, gods! 't is strange that from their cold'st neglect
My love should kindle to inflam'd respect.
Thy dowerless daughter, king, thrown to my chance,
Is queen of us, of ours, and our fair France.
Not all the dukes of waterish Burgundy
Shall buy this unpriz'd precious maid of me.
Bid them farewell, Cordelia, though unkind;
Thou losest here, a better where to find.
Lear. Thou hast her, France. Let her be thine; for we
Have no such daughter, nor shall ever see
That face of hers again.—[*To Cor.*] Therefore be gone
Without our grace, our love, our benison.—
Come, noble Burgundy.
Flourish. Exeunt Lear and Burgundy.
France. Bid farewell to your sisters.
Cor. The jewels of our father, with wash'd eyes
Cordelia leaves you. I know you what you are;
And like a sister am most loath to call
Your faults as they are named. Use well our father,
To your professed bosoms I commit him;
But yet, alas, stood I within his grace,
I would prefer him to a better place.
So, farewell to you both.
Reg. Prescribe not us our duties.
Gon. Let your study
Be to content your lord, who hath receiv'd you
At fortune's alms. You have obedience scanted,
And well are worth the want that you have wanted.
Cor. Time shall unfold what plighted cunning hides;
Who covers faults, at last shame them derides.
Well may you prosper!
France. Come, my fair Cordelia.
Exeunt France and Cordelia.
Gon. Sister, it is not little I have to say of

262. **unpriz'd**, probably priceless. 264. **where**, place. 268. **benison**, blessing. 271. **wash'd**, tearful. 275. **bosoms**, affections. 281. **scanted**, begrudged. 282. You well deserve the lack (of that affection) which you yourself are lacking in. 283. **plighted**, folded.

what most nearly appertains to us both. I think our father will hence to-night.

Reg. That 's most certain, and with you; next month with us.

Gon. You see how full of changes his age is; the observation we have made of it hath not been little. He always loved our sister most; and with what poor judgement he hath now cast her off appears too gross.

Reg. 'T is the infirmity of his age; yet he hath ever but slenderly known himself.

Gon. The best and soundest of his time hath been but rash; then must we look to receive from his age not alone the imperfections of long-engraffed condition, but therewithal the unruly waywardness that infirm and choleric years bring with them.

Reg. Such unconstant starts are we like to have from him as this of Kent's banishment.

Gon. There is further compliment of leave-taking between France and him. Pray you, let 's hit together; if our father carry authority with such disposition as he bears, this last surrender of his will but offend us.

Reg. We shall further think on 't.

Gon. We must do something, and i' th' heat. *Exeunt.*

Scene II. *The Earl of Gloucester's castle.*

Enter *Edmund* with a letter.

Edm. Thou, Nature, art my goddess; to thy law
My services are bound. Wherefore should I
Stand in the plague of custom, and permit
The curiosity of nations to deprive me,
For that I am some twelve or fourteen moonshines
Lag of a brother? Why bastard? Wherefore base?
When my dimensions are as well compact,
My mind as generous, and my shape as true,
As honest madam's issue? Why brand they us
With base? with baseness? bastardy? base, base?
Who, in the lusty stealth of nature, take
More composition and fierce quality
Than doth, within a dull, stale, tired bed,
Go to th' creating a whole tribe of fops,
Got 'tween asleep and wake? Well then,
Legitimate Edgar, I must have your land.
Our father's love is to the bastard Edmund
As to th' legitimate. Fine word, "legitimate"!
Well, my legitimate, if this letter speed
And my invention thrive, Edmund the base
Shall to th' legitimate. I grow; I prosper.
Now, gods, stand up for bastards!

Enter *Gloucester.*

Glou. Kent banish'd thus! and France in choler parted!
And the King gone to-night! subscrib'd his power!
Confin'd to exhibition! All this done
Upon the gad! Edmund, how now! what news?

Edm. So please your lordship, none.
Putting up the letter.

Glou. Why so earnestly seek you to put up that letter?

Edm. I know no news, my lord.

Glou. What paper were you reading?

Edm. Nothing, my lord.

Glou. No? What needed, then, that terrible dispatch of it into your pocket? The quality of nothing hath not such need to hide itself. Let 's see. Come, if it be nothing, I shall not need spectacles.

Edm. I beseech you, sir, pardon me. It is a letter from my brother, that I have not all o'erread; and for so much as I have perused, I find it not fit for your o'erlooking.

Glou. Give me the letter, sir.

Edm. I shall offend, either to detain or give it. The contents, as in part I understand them, are to blame.

Glou. Let 's see, let 's see.

Edm. I hope, for my brother's justification, he wrote this but as an essay or taste of my virtue.

Glou. [*Reads.*]

"This policy and reverence of age makes the world bitter to the best of our times; keeps our fortunes from us till our oldness cannot relish them. I begin to find an idle and fond bondage in the oppression of aged tyranny; who sways, not as it hath power, but as it is suffered. Come to me, that of this I may speak more. If our father would sleep till I waked him, you should enjoy half his revenue for ever, and live the beloved of your brother,

EDGAR."

Hum—conspiracy!—"Sleep till I wake him, you should enjoy half his revenue!"—My son Edgar! Had he a hand to write this? a heart and brain to breed it in?—When came this to you? Who brought it?

Edm. It was not brought me, my lord; there 's the cunning of it. I found it thrown in at the casement of my closet.

298. **time,** life. 301. **condition,** disposition. 304. **starts,** sudden impulses. 308. **hit,** agree. **Scene ii:** 3. **plague,** calamity. 4. **curiosity,** scruples. 6. **Lag of,** behind. 12. **More composition,** a fuller blending. 19. **speed,** succeed.

21. **Shall to th' legitimate,** shall rise to, become, the legitimate. 24. **subscrib'd,** surrendered. 25. **exhibition,** allowance, pension. 26. **gad,** spur. 47. **essay** trial. 48. **policy and reverence,** policy of revering. 49 **times,** lives. 50. **fond,** foolish.

Glou. You know the character to be your brother's?

Edm. If the matter were good, my lord, I durst swear it were his; but, in respect of that, I would fain think it were not.

Glou. It is his.

Edm. It is his hand, my lord; but I hope his heart is not in the contents.

Glou. Hath he never heretofore sounded you in this business?

Edm. Never, my lord; but I have heard him oft maintain it to be fit that, sons at perfect age, and fathers declined, the father should be as ward to the son, and the son manage his revenue.

Glou. O villain, villain! His very opinion in the letter! Abhorred villain! Unnatural, detested, brutish villain! worse than brutish! Go, sirrah, seek him; I 'll apprehend him. Abominable villain! Where is he?

Edm. I do not well know, my lord. If it shall please you to suspend your indignation against my brother till you can derive from him better testimony of his intent, you should run a certain course; where, if you violently proceed against him, mistaking his purpose, it would make a great gap in your own honour, and shake in pieces the heart of his obedience. I dare pawn down my life for him, that he hath wrote this to feel my affection to your honour, and to no further pretence of danger.

Glou. Think you so?

Edm. If your honour judge it meet, I will place you where you shall hear us confer of this, and by an auricular assurance have your satisfaction; and that without any further delay than this very evening.

Glou. He cannot be such a monster—

Edm. Nor is not, sure.

Glou. To his father, that so tenderly and entirely loves him. Heaven and earth! Edmund, seek him out; wind me into him, I pray you. Frame the business after your own wisdom. I would unstate myself, to be in a due resolution.

Edm. I will seek him, sir, presently; convey the business as I shall find means, and acquaint you withal.

Glou. These late eclipses in the sun and moon portend no good to us. Though the wisdom of nature can reason it thus and thus, yet nature finds itself scourged by the sequent effects. Love cools, friendship falls off, brothers divide: in cities, mutinies; in countries, discord; in palaces, treason; and the bond cracked 'twixt son and father. This villain of mine comes under the prediction; there 's son against father: the King falls from bias of nature; there 's father against child. We have seen the best of our time; machinations, hollowness, treachery, and all ruinous disorders, follow us disquietly to our graves. Find out this villain, Edmund; it shall lose thee nothing; do it carefully. And the noble and true-hearted Kent banished! his offence, honesty! 'T is strange. *Exit.*

Edm. This is the excellent foppery of the world, that, when we are sick in fortune,—often the surfeit of our own behaviour,—we make guilty of our disasters the sun, the moon, and the stars, as if we were villains on necessity, fools by heavenly compulsion, knaves, thieves, and treachers by spherical predominance, drunkards, liars, and adulterers by an enforced obedience of planetary influence, and all that we are evil in, by a divine thrusting on. An admirable evasion of whoremaster man, to lay his goatish disposition on the charge of a star! My father compounded with my mother under the dragon's tail; and my nativity was under *Ursa major;* so that it follows, I am rough and lecherous. Fut, I should have been that I am, had the maidenliest star in the firmament twinkled on my bastardizing. Edgar—

Enter *Edgar.*

and pat he comes like the catastrophe of the old comedy. My cue is villanous melancholy, with a sigh like Tom o' Bedlam.—O, these eclipses do portend these divisions! *fa, sol, la, mi.*

Edg. How now, brother Edmund! what serious contemplation are you in?

Edm. I am thinking, brother, of a prediction I read this other day, what should follow these eclipses.

Edg. Do you busy yourself with that?

Edm. I promise you, the effects he writ of succeed unhappily; as of unnaturalness between the child and the parent; death, dearth, dissolutions of ancient amities; divisions in state, menaces and maledictions against king and nobles; needless diffidences, banishment of friends, dissipation of cohorts, nuptial breaches, and I know not what.

Edg. How long have you been a sectary astronomical?

Edm. Come, come; when saw you my father last?

Edg. Why, the night gone by.

Edm. Spake you with him?

67. **character**, handwriting. 89. **where**, whereas. 94. **feel**, test. 95. **pretence of danger**, dangerous intention. 106. **wind . . . him**, worm your way into his confidence. 108. **unstate**, dispossess. 109. **due resolution**, proper certainty. 113-4. **wisdom of nature**, physical science.

121. **bias of nature**, natural inclination. 133. **treachers**, traitors. **spherical predominance**, planetary influence. 148. **Bedlam**, Bethlehem hospital for lunatics. 161. **diffidences**, suspicions. 164-5. **sectary astronomical**, devotee of astrology.

Edg. Ay, two hours together.

Edm. Parted you in good terms? Found you no displeasure in him by word nor countenance?

Edg. None at all.

Edm. Bethink yourself wherein you may have offended him; and at my entreaty forbear his presence until some little time hath qualified the heat of his displeasure, which at this instant so rageth in him, that with the mischief of your person it would scarce allay.

Edg. Some villain hath done me wrong.

Edm. That 's my fear. I pray you, have a continent forbearance till the speed of his rage goes slower; and, as I say, retire with me to my lodging, from whence I will fitly bring you to hear my lord speak. Pray ye, go; there 's my key. If you do stir abroad, go armed.

Edg. Armed, brother!

Edm. Brother, I advise you to the best; I am no honest man if there be any good meaning towards you. I have told you what I have seen and heard; but faintly, nothing like the image and horror of it. Pray you, away.

Edg. Shall I hear from you anon?

Edm. I do serve you in this business.
Exit Edgar.

A credulous father, and a brother noble,
Whose nature is so far from doing harms
That he suspects none; on whose foolish honesty
My practices ride easy. I see the business.
Let me, if not by birth, have lands by wit:
All with me 's meet that I can fashion fit.
Exit.

Scene III. *The Duke of Albany's palace.*

Enter *Goneril,* and *Oswald,* her Steward.

Gon. Did my father strike my gentleman for chiding of his Fool?

Osw. Ay, madam.

Gon. By day and night he wrongs me; every hour
He flashes into one gross crime or other
That sets us all at odds. I 'll not endure it.
His knights grow riotous, and himself upbraids us
On every trifle. When he returns from hunting,
I will not speak with him; say I am sick.
If you come slack of former services,
You shall do well; the fault of it I 'll answer.

Osw. He 's coming, madam; I hear him.
Horns within.

Gon. Put on what weary negligence you please,
You and your fellows; I 'd have it come to question.
If he distaste it, let him to our sister,
Whose mind and mine, I know, in that are one,
Not to be over-rul'd. Idle old man,
That still would manage those authorities
That he hath given away! Now, by my life,
Old fools are babes again, and must be us'd
With checks as flatteries, when they are seen abus'd.
Remember what I have said.

Osw. Well, madam.

Gon. And let his knights have colder looks among you;
What grows of it, no matter. Advise your fellows so.
I would breed from hence occasions, and I shall,
That I may speak. I 'll write straight to my sister,
To hold my very course. Prepare for dinner.
Exeunt.

Scene IV. *A hall in the same.*

Enter *Kent* disguised.

Kent. If but as well I other accents borrow,
That can my speech defuse, my good intent
May carry through itself to that full issue
For which I raz'd my likeness. Now, banish'd Kent,
If thou canst serve where thou dost stand condemn'd,
So may it come, thy master, whom thou lov'st,
Shall find thee full of labours.

Horns within. Enter *Lear, Knights,* and Attendants.

Lear. Let me not stay a jot for dinner; go get it ready. [*Exit an attendant.*] How now! what art thou?

Kent. A man, sir.

Lear. What dost thou profess? What wouldst thou with us?

Kent. I do profess to be no less than I seem; to serve him truly that will put me in trust; to love him that is honest; to converse with him that is wise and says little; to fear

177. qualified, assuaged. **179. mischief,** harm. **182. continent,** temperate. **192. image and horror,** horrible image.

Scene iii: 13. question, discussion. **19-20.** Old fools must be checked as well as flattered, and especially when they are being deceived (by their followers). **Scene iv: 2. defuse,** disguise. **4. raz'd,** erased. **8. stay,** wait. **12. What . . . profess,** what is your profession.

judgement; to fight when I cannot choose; and to eat no fish.

Lear. What art thou?

Kent. A very honest-hearted fellow, and as poor as the King.

Lear. If thou be as poor for a subject as he is for a king, thou art poor enough. What wouldst thou?

Kent. Service.

Lear. Who wouldst thou serve?

Kent. You.

Lear. Dost thou know me, fellow?

Kent. No, sir; but you have that in your countenance which I would fain call master.

Lear. What 's that?

Kent. Authority.

Lear. What services canst thou do?

Kent. I can keep honest counsel, ride, run, mar a curious tale in telling it, and deliver a plain message bluntly. That which ordinary men are fit for, I am qualified in; and the best of me is diligence.

Lear. How old art thou?

Kent. Not so young, sir, to love a woman for singing, nor so old to dote on her for anything. I have years on my back forty-eight.

Lear. Follow me; thou shalt serve me. If I like thee no worse after dinner, I will not part from thee yet. Dinner, ho, dinner! Where 's my knave? my Fool? Go you, and call my Fool hither. *Exit an attendant.*

Enter the Steward, *Oswald.*

You, you, sirrah, where 's my daughter?

Osw. So please you,— *Exit.*

Lear. What says the fellow there? Call the clotpoll back. [*Exit a knight.*] Where 's my Fool, ho? I think the world 's asleep.

Enter *Knight.*

How now! where 's that mongrel?

Knight. He says, my lord, your daughter is not well.

Lear. Why came not the slave back to me when I called him?

Knight. Sir, he answered me in the roundest manner, he would not.

Lear. 'A would not!

Knight. My lord, I know not what the matter is; but, to my judgement, your Highness is not entertain'd with that ceremonious affection as you were wont. There 's a great abatement of kindness appears as well in the general dependants as in the Duke himself also and your daughter.

Lear. Ha! say'st thou so?

Knight. I beseech you, pardon me, my lord, if I be mistaken; for my duty cannot be silent when I think your Highness wronged.

Lear. Thou but rememb'rest me of mine own conception. I have perceived a most faint neglect of late, which I have rather blamed as mine own jealous curiosity than as a very pretence and purpose of unkindness. I will look further into 't. But where 's my Fool? I have not seen him this two days.

Knight. Since my young lady 's going into France, sir, the Fool hath much pined away.

Lear. No more of that; I have noted it well. Go you, and tell my daughter I would speak with her. [*Exit an attendant.*] Go you, call hither my Fool. [*Exit an attendant.*]

Enter *Oswald.*

O, you sir, you sir, come you hither. Who am I, sir?

Osw. My lady's father.

Lear. "My lady's father"! My lord's knave! You whoreson dog! you slave! you cur!

Osw. I am none of these, my lord; I beseech your pardon.

Lear. Do you bandy looks with me, you rascal? *Striking him.*

Osw. I 'll not be strucken, my lord.

Kent. Nor tripped neither, you base football player. *Tripping up his heels.*

Lear. I thank thee, fellow. Thou serv'st me, and I 'll love thee.

Kent. Come, sir, arise, away! I 'll teach you differences. Away, away! If you will measure your lubber's length again, tarry; but away! go to. Have you wisdom? So. *Pushes Oswald out.*

Lear. Now, my friendly knave, I thank thee. There 's earnest of thy service. *Giving Kent money.*

Enter *Fool.*

Fool. Let me hire him too; here 's my coxcomb. *Offering Kent his cap.*

Lear. How now, my pretty knave! how dost thou?

Fool. Sirrah, you were best take my coxcomb.

Kent. Why, Fool?

Fool. Why? For taking one's part that 's out of favour. Nay, an thou canst not smile as the wind sits, thou 'lt catch cold shortly. There, take my coxcomb. Why, this fellow hath banished two on 's daughters, and did the third a blessing against his will; if thou follow him, thou must needs wear my coxcomb.—

18. to eat no fish, to be a Protestant. **51. clotpoll,** blockhead.

75. jealous curiosity, suspicious attentiveness. **very pretence,** real flaw. **104. earnest,** advance wages. **115. on 's,** of his.

How now, nuncle! Would I had two coxcombs and two daughters!

Lear. Why, my boy?

Fool. If I gave them all my living, I 'd keep my coxcombs myself. There 's mine; beg another of thy daughters.

Lear. Take heed, sirrah; the whip.

Fool. Truth 's a dog must to kennel; he must be whipped out, when Lady the brach may stand by the fire and stink.

Lear. A pestilent gall to me!

Fool. Sirrah, I 'll teach thee a speech.

Lear. Do.

Fool. Mark it, nuncle:

Have more than thou showest,
Speak less than thou knowest,
Lend less than thou owest,
Ride more than thou goest,
Learn more than thou trowest,
Set less than thou throwest;
Leave thy drink and thy whore,
And keep in-a-door,
And thou shalt have more
Than two tens to a score.

Kent. This is nothing, Fool.

Fool. Then 't is like the breath of an unfeed lawyer; you gave me nothing for 't. Can you make no use of nothing, nuncle?

Lear. Why, no, boy; nothing can be made out of nothing.

Fool. [*To Kent.*] Prithee, tell him so much the rent of his land comes to. He will not believe a Fool.

Lear. A bitter fool!

Fool. Dost thou know the difference, my boy, between a bitter fool and a sweet fool?

Lear. No, lad; teach me.

Fool.

That lord that counsell'd thee
  To give away thy land,
Come place him here by me,
  Do thou for him stand:
The sweet and bitter fool
  Will presently appear;
The one in motley here,
  The other found out there.

Lear. Dost thou call me fool, boy?

Fool. All thy other titles thou hast given away; that thou wast born with.

Kent. This is not altogether fool, my lord.

Fool. No, faith, lords and great men will not let me; if I had a monopoly out, they would have part on 't. And ladies, too, they will not let me have all the fool to myself; they 'll be snatching. Nuncle, give me an egg, and I 'll give thee two crowns.

Lear. What two crowns shall they be?

Fool. Why, after I have cut the egg i' th' middle, and eat up the meat, the two crowns of the egg. When thou clovest thy crown i' th' middle, and gav'st away both parts, thou bor'st thine ass on thy back o'er the dirt. Thou hadst little wit in thy bald crown, when thou gav'st thy golden one away. If I speak like myself in this, let him be whipped that first finds it so.

Fools had ne'er less grace in a year;
  For wise men are grown foppish,
And know not how their wits to wear,
  Their manners are so apish.

Lear. When were you wont to be so full of songs, sirrah?

Fool. I have used it, nuncle, ever since thou mad'st thy daughters thy mother, for when thou gav'st them the rod, and puttest down thine own breeches,

Then they for sudden joy did weep,
  And I for sorrow sung,
That such a king should play bo-peep
  And go the fools among.

Prithee, nuncle, keep a schoolmaster that can teach thy Fool to lie. I would fain learn to lie.

Lear. An you lie, sirrah, we 'll have you whipped.

Fool. I marvel what kin thou and thy daughters are. They 'll have me whipped for speaking true, thou 'lt have me whipped for lying; and sometimes I am whipp'd for holding my peace. I had rather be any kind o' thing than a Fool; and yet I would not be thee, nuncle; thou hast pared thy wit o' both sides, and left nothing i' the middle. Here comes one o' the parings.

Enter *Goneril.*

Lear. How now, daughter! what makes that frontlet on? Methinks you are too much of late i' th' frown.

Fool. Thou wast a pretty fellow when thou hadst no need to care for her frowning; now thou art an O without a figure. I am better than thou art now; I am a Fool, thou art nothing. [*To Goneril.*] Yes, forsooth, I will hold my tongue; so your face bids me, though you say nothing.

Mum, mum,
He that keeps nor crust nor crumb,
Weary of all, shall want some.

[*Pointing to Lear.*] That 's a sheal'd peascod.

Gon. Not only, sir, this your all-licens'd Fool,
But other of your insolent retinue

117. nuncle, mine uncle. **125. brach,** bitch. **133. owest,** ownest. **135. trowest,** believest. **136. Set . . . throwest,** stake less than you win at a throw.

208. frontlet, frown. **219. sheal'd peascod,** a peapod with the peas taken out.

Do hourly carp and quarrel, breaking forth
In rank and not-to-be-endured riots. Sir,
I had thought, by making this well known unto you,
To have found a safe redress; but now grow fearful,
By what yourself, too, late have spoke and done,
That you protect this course, and put it on
By your allowance; which if you should, the fault
Would not scape censure, nor the redresses sleep,
Which, in the tender of a wholesome weal,
Might in their working do you that offence,
Which else were shame, that then necessity
Will call discreet proceeding.

Fool. For, you know, nuncle,
"The hedge-sparrow fed the cuckoo so long,
That it had it head bit off by it young."
So, out went the candle, and we were left darkling.

Lear. Are you our daughter?

Gon. Come, sir,
I would you would make use of that good wisdom,
Whereof I know you are fraught, and put away
These dispositions, which of late transport you
From what you rightly are.

Fool. May not an ass know when the cart draws the horse? "Whoop, Jug! I love thee."

Lear. Doth any here know me? This is not Lear.
Doth Lear walk thus? speak thus? Where are his eyes?
Either his notion weakens, or his discernings
Are lethargied—Ha! waking? 'T is not so.
Who is it that can tell me who I am?

Fool. Lear's shadow.

Lear. I would learn that; for, by the marks of sovereignty, knowledge, and reason, I should be false persuaded I had daughters.

Fool. Which they will make an obedient father.

Lear. Your name, fair gentlewoman?

Gon. This admiration, sir, is much o' th' savour
Of other your new pranks. I do beseech you
To understand my purposes aright.
As you are old and reverend, you should be wise.
Here do you keep a hundred knights and squires;
Men so disorder'd, so debosh'd and bold,
That this our court, infected with their manners,
Shows like a riotous inn. Epicurism and lust
Makes it more like a tavern or a brothel
Than a grac'd palace. The shame itself doth speak
For instant remedy. Be then desir'd
By her, that else will take the thing she begs,
A little to disquantity your train;
And the remainders, that shall still depend,
To be such men as may besort your age,
Which know themselves and you.

Lear. Darkness and devils!
Saddle my horses; call my train together!
Degenerate bastard! I 'll not trouble thee;
Yet have I left a daughter.

Gon. You strike my people; and your disorder'd rabble
Make servants of their betters.

Enter *Albany.*

Lear. Woe, that too late repents!—O, sir, are you come?
Is it your will? Speak, sir.—Prepare my horses.—
Ingratitude, thou marble-hearted fiend,
More hideous when thou show'st thee in a child
Than the sea-monster!

Alb. Pray, sir, be patient.

Lear. [*To Goneril.*] Detested kite! thou liest.
My train are men of choice and rarest parts,
That all particulars of duty know,
And in the most exact regard support
The worships of their name. O most small fault,
How ugly didst thou in Cordelia show!
Which, like an engine, wrench'd my frame of nature
From the fix'd place; drew from my heart all love,
And added to the gall. O Lear, Lear, Lear!
Beat at this gate, that let thy folly in,
Striking his head.
And thy dear judgement out! Go, go, my people.

Alb. My lord, I am guiltless as I am ignorant
Of what hath moved you.

Lear. It may be so, my lord.
Hear, Nature! hear, dear goddess, hear!
Suspend thy purpose, if thou didst intend
To make this creature fruitful!
Into her womb convey sterility!
Dry up in her the organs of increase,
And from her derogate body never spring
A babe to honour her! If she must teem,
Create her child of spleen, that it may live

227. **put it on**, encourage it. 228. **allowance**, approval. 230. **tender**, care. **weal**, commonwealth. 241. **fraught**, stored. 248. **notion**, mind. 258. **admiration**, astonishment. 263. **debosh'd**, debauched.

270. **disquantity**, cut down. 271. **depend**, be dependent. 272. **besort**, befit. 288. **worships**, honors. 290. **engine**, the rack. 302. **derogate**, corrupt.

And be a thwart disnatur'd torment to her!
Let it stamp wrinkles in her brow of youth,
With cadent tears fret channels in her cheeks,
Turn all her mother's pains and benefits
To laughter and contempt, that she may feel
How sharper than a serpent's tooth it is
To have a thankless child!—Away, away! *Exit.*

Alb. Now, gods that we adore, whereof comes this?

Gon. Never afflict yourself to know the cause;
But let his disposition have that scope
That dotage gives it.

Re-enter *Lear.*

Lear. What, fifty of my followers at a clap!
Within a fortnight!

Alb. What 's the matter, sir?

Lear. I 'll tell thee. [*To Goneril.*] Life and death! I am asham'd
That thou hast power to shake my manhood thus;
That these hot tears, which break from me perforce,
Should make thee worth them. Blasts and fogs upon thee!
The untented woundings of a father's curse
Pierce every sense about thee! Old fond eyes,
Beweep this cause again, I 'll pluck ye out,
And cast you, with the waters that you loose,
To temper clay. Ha! is 't come to this?
Let it be so: I have another daughter,
Who, I am sure, is kind and comfortable.
When she shall hear this of thee, with her nails
She 'll flay thy wolvish visage. Thou shalt find
That I 'll resume the shape which thou dost think
I have cast off for ever. Thou shalt, I warrant thee.

Exeunt Lear, Kent, and attendants.

Gon. Do you mark that, my lord?

Alb. I cannot be so partial, Goneril,
To the great love I bear you,—

Gon. Pray you, content.—What, Oswald, ho!
[*To the Fool.*] You, sir, more knave than fool, after your master.

Fool. Nuncle Lear, nuncle Lear! tarry and take the Fool with thee.

A fox, when one has caught her,
And such a daughter,
Should sure to the slaughter,
If my cap would buy a halter.
So the Fool follows after.

Exit.

Gon. This man hath had good counsel,—a hundred knights!
'T is politic and safe to let him keep
At point a hundred knights; yes, that, on every dream,
Each buzz, each fancy, each complaint, dislike,
He may enguard his dotage with their powers,
And hold our lives in mercy. Oswald, I say!

Alb. Well, you may fear too far.

Gon. Safer than trust too far.
Let me still take away the harms I fear,
Not fear still to be taken. I know his heart.
What he hath utter'd I have writ my sister.
If she sustain him and his hundred knights,
When I have show'd the unfitness,—

Enter *Oswald.*

How now, Oswald!
What, have you writ that letter to my sister?

Osw. Ay, madam.

Gon. Take you some company, and away to horse:
Inform her full of my particular fear;
And thereto add such reasons of your own
As may compact it more. Get you gone;
And hasten your return. [*Exit Oswald.*] No, no, my lord,
This milky gentleness and course of yours
Though I condemn not, yet, under pardon,
You are much more at task for want of wisdom
Than prais'd for harmful mildness.

Alb. How far your eyes may pierce I cannot tell.
Striving to better, oft we mar what 's well.

Gon. Nay, then—

Alb. Well, well; the event. *Exeunt.*

Scene V. *Court before the same.*

Enter *Lear, Kent,* and *Fool.*

Lear. Go you before to Gloucester with these letters. Acquaint my daughter no further with anything you know than comes from her demand out of the letter. If your diligence be not speedy, I shall be there afore you.

Kent. I will not sleep, my lord, till I have delivered your letter. *Exit.*

Fool. If a man's brains were in 's heels, were 't not in danger of kibes?

Lear. Ay, boy.

Fool. Then, I prithee, be merry; thy wit shall ne'er go slip-shod.

Lear. Ha, ha, ha!

305. thwart, perverse. **307. cadent**, falling. **322. untented**, incurable. **328. comfortable**, comforting.

347. At point, in readiness. **262. compact**, confirm. **366. at task**, blamed. **Scene v: 9. kibes**, chilblains.

Fool. Shalt see thy other daughter will use thee kindly; for though she 's as like this as a crab 's like an apple, yet I can tell what I can tell.

Lear. What canst tell, boy?

Fool. She will taste as like this as a crab does to a crab. Thou canst tell why one's nose stands i' th' middle on 's face?

Lear. No.

Fool. Why, to keep one's eyes of either side 's nose, that what a man cannot smell out, he may spy into.

Lear. I did her wrong—

Fool. Canst tell how an oyster makes his shell?

Lear. No.

Fool. Nor I neither; but I can tell why a snail has a house.

Lear. Why?

Fool. Why, to put 's head in; not to give it away to his daughters, and leave his horns without a case.

Lear. I will forget my nature. So kind a father! Be my horses ready?

Fool. Thy asses are gone about 'em. The reason why the seven stars are no moe than seven is a pretty reason.

Lear. Because they are not eight?

Fool. Yes, indeed: Thou wouldst make a good Fool.

Lear. To take 't again perforce! Monster ingratitude!

Fool. If thou wert my Fool, nuncle, I 'd have thee beaten for being old before thy time.

Lear. How 's that?

Fool. Thou shouldst not have been old till thou hadst been wise.

Lear. O, let me not be mad, not mad, sweet heaven!
Keep me in temper; I would not be mad!

Enter *Gentleman.*

How now! are the horses ready?

Gent. Ready, my lord.

Lear. Come, boy.

Fool. She that 's a maid now, and laughs at my departure,
Shall not be a maid long, unless things be cut shorter. *Exeunt.*

ACT II. Scene I. *The Earl of Gloucester's castle.*

Enter *Edmund* and *Curan,* severally.

Edm. Save thee, Curan.

Cur. And you, sir. I have been with your father, and given him notice that the Duke of Cornwall and Regan his duchess will be here with him this night.

Edm. How comes that?

Cur. Nay, I know not. You have heard of the news abroad; I mean the whispered ones, for they are yet but ear-kissing arguments?

Edm. Not I. Pray you, what are they?

Cur. Have you heard of no likely wars toward, 'twixt the Dukes of Cornwall and Albany?

Edm. Not a word.

Cur. You may, then, in time. Fare you well, sir. *Exit.*

Edm. The Duke be here to-night? The better! best!
This weaves itself perforce into my business.
My father hath set guard to take my brother;
And I have one thing, of a queasy question,
Which I must act. Briefness and fortune, work!

Enter *Edgar.*

Brother, a word; descend. Brother, I say!
My father watches; O sir, fly this place;
Intelligence is given where you are hid;
You have now the good advantage of the night.
Have you not spoken 'gainst the Duke of Cornwall?
He 's coming hither, now, i' th' night, i' th' haste,
And Regan with him. Have you nothing said
Upon his party 'gainst the Duke of Albany?
Advise yourself.

Edg. I am sure on 't, not a word.

Edm. I hear my father coming: pardon me;
In cunning I must draw my sword upon you.
Draw; seem to defend yourself; now quit you well.
Yield! Come before my father. Light, ho, here!
Fly, brother. Torches, torches! So, farewell. *Exit Edgar.*
Some blood drawn on me would beget opinion *Wounds his arm.*

15. kindly, after her kind, nature. **Act II, Scene i: 9. ear-kissing,** whispered. **12. toward,** in prospect. **19. of a queasy question,** to be treated with great care.

38. seven stars, Pleiades. **Act II, Scene i: 35. beget,** create.

Of my more fierce endeavour. I have seen drunkards
Do more than this in sport. Father! father!
Stop, stop! No help?

Enter *Gloucester*, and Servants with torches.

Glou. Now, Edmund, where 's the villain?
Edm. Here stood he in the dark, his sharp sword out,
Mumbling of wicked charms, conjuring the moon
To stand 's auspicious mistress,—
Glou. But where is he?
Edm. Look, sir, I bleed.
Glou. Where is the villain, Edmund?
Edm. Fled this way, sir. When by no means he could—
Glou. Pursue him, ho! Go after. [*Exeunt some Servants.*] "By no means" what?
Edm. Persuade me to the murder of your lordship;
But that I told him, the revenging gods
'Gainst parricides did all their thunders bend;
Spoke, with how manifold and strong a bond
The child was bound to the father; sir, in fine,
Seeing how loathly opposite I stood
To his unnatural purpose, in fell motion,
With his prepared sword he charges home
My unprovided body, lanc'd mine arm;
But when he saw my best alarum'd spirits,
Bold in the quarrel's right, rous'd to the encounter,
Or whether gasted by the noise I made,
Full suddenly he fled.
Glou. Let him fly far.
Not in this land shall he remain uncaught;
And found,—dispatch. The noble Duke my master,
My worthy arch and patron, comes to-night.
By his authority I will proclaim it,
That he which finds him shall deserve our thanks,
Bringing the murderous coward to the stake;
He that conceals him, death.
Edm. When I dissuaded him from his intent,
And found him pight to do it, with curst speech
I threaten'd to discover him; he replied,
"Thou unpossessing bastard! dost thou think,
If I would stand against thee, would the reposal
Of any trust, virtue, or worth in thee
Make thy words faith'd? No! what I should deny,—
As this I would; ay, though thou didst produce
My very character,—I 'd turn it all
To thy suggestion, plot, and damned practice;
And thou must make a dullard of the world
If they not thought the profits of my death
Were very pregnant and potential spurs
To make thee seek it."
Glou. O strong and fasten'd villain!
Would he deny his letter? I never got him.
Tucket within.
Hark, the Duke's trumpets! I know not why he comes.
All ports I 'll bar, the villain shall not scape;
The Duke must grant me that. Besides, his picture
I will send far and near, that all the kingdom
May have due note of him; and of my land,
Loyal and natural boy, I 'll work the means
To make thee capable.

Enter *Cornwall, Regan,* and Attendants.

Corn. How now, my noble friend! since I came hither,
Which I can call but now, I have heard strange news.
Reg. If it be true, all vengeance comes too short
Which can pursue the offender. How dost, my lord?
Glou. O, madam, my old heart is crack'd, is crack'd!
Reg. What, did my father's godson seek your life?
He whom my father nam'd? your Edgar?
Glou. O, lady, lady, shame would have it hid!
Reg. Was he not companion with the riotous knights
That tends upon my father?
Glou. I know not, madam. 'T is too bad, too bad.
Edm. Yes, madam, he was of that consort.
Reg. No marvel, then, though he were ill affected:
'T is they have put him on the old man's death,
To have th' expense and waste of his revenues.
I have this present evening from my sister
Been well inform'd of them; and with such cautions,
That if they come to sojourn at my house,
I 'll not be there.
Corn. Nor I, assure thee, Regan.

36. **drunkards, etc.**, it was not unusual for an Elizabethan lover, flustered with wine, to cut his arm and drink his lady's health in sport. 52. **in fell motion,** with a fierce thrust. 57. **gasted,** frightened. 61. **arch,** master. 67. **pight,** determined. 69. **unpossessing,** incapable of inheriting.

72. **faith'd,** credited. 79. **fasten'd,** hardened. 82. **ports,** gates. 87. **capable,** able to inherit. 99. **consort,** fellowship.

Edmund, I hear that you have shown your father
A child-like office.
Edm. 'T was my duty, sir.
Glou. He did bewray his practice; and receiv'd
This hurt you see, striving to apprehend him.
Corn. Is he pursued?
Glou. Ay, my good lord.
Corn. If he be taken, he shall never more
Be fear'd of doing harm. Make your own purpose,
How in my strength you please. For you, Edmund,
Whose virtue and obedience doth this instant
So much commend itself, you shall be ours.
Natures of such deep trust we shall much need;
You we first seize on.
Edm. I shall serve you, sir,
Truly, however else.
Glou. For him I thank your Grace.
Corn. You know not why we came to visit you,—
Reg. Thus out of season, threading darkey'd night?
Occasions, noble Gloucester, of some poise,
Wherein we must have use of your advice.
Our father he hath writ, so hath our sister,
Of differences, which I best thought it fit
To answer from our home; the several messengers
From hence attend dispatch. Our good old friend,
Lay comforts to your bosom; and bestow
Your needful counsel to our business,
Which craves the instant use.
Glou. I serve you, madam.
Your Graces are right welcome.
Exeunt. Flourish.

Scene II. *Before Gloucester's castle.*

Enter *Kent* and the Steward *Oswald,* severally.

Osw. Good dawning to thee, friend. Art of this house?

Kent. Ay.

Osw. Where may we set our horses?

Kent. I' th' mire.

Osw. Prithee, if you lov'st me, tell me.

Kent. I love thee not.

Osw. Why, then, I care not for thee.

Kent. If I had thee in Lipsbury pinfold, I would make thee care for me.

Osw. Why dost thou use me thus? I know thee not.

Kent. Fellow, I know thee.

Osw. What dost thou know me for?

Kent. A knave; a rascal; an eater of broken meats; a base, proud, shallow, beggarly, three-suited, hundred-pound, filthy, worsted-stocking knave; a lily-livered, action-taking knave; a whoreson, glass-gazing, superserviceable, finical rogue; one-trunk-inheriting slave; one that wouldst be a bawd, in way of good service, and art nothing but the composition of a knave, beggar, coward, pandar, and the son and heir of a mongrel bitch; one whom I will beat into clamorous whining, if thou deni'st the least syllable of thy addition.

Osw. Why, what a monstrous fellow art thou, thus to rail on one that is neither known of thee nor knows thee!

Kent. What a brazen-faced varlet art thou, to deny thou knowest me! Is it two days since I tripped up thy heels, and beat thee before the King? Draw, you rogue; for, though it be night, yet the moon shines. I 'll make a sop o' th' moonshine of you, you whoreson cullionly barber-monger! Draw! [*Drawing his sword.*]

Osw. Away! I have nothing to do with thee.

Kent. Draw, you rascal! You come with letters against the King; and take Vanity the puppet's part against the royalty of her father. Draw, you rogue, or I 'll so carbonado your shanks,—draw, you rascal! Come your ways.

Osw. Help, ho! murder! help!

Kent. Strike, you slave! Stand, rogue, stand! You neat slave, strike. *Beating him.*

Osw. Help, ho! murder! murder!

Enter *Edmund* with his rapier drawn, *Cornwall, Regan, Gloucester,* and Servants.

Edm. How now! What 's the matter?

Kent. With you, goodman boy, an you please: come, I 'll flesh ye; come on, young master.

Glou. Weapons! arms! What 's the matter here?

Corn. Keep peace, upon your lives!
He dies that strikes again. What is the matter?

Reg. The messengers from our sister and the King.

Corn. What is your difference? Speak.

Osw. I am scarce in breath, my lord.

Kent. No marvel, you have so bestirred

108. **child-like,** filial. 109. **bewray,** betray. 122. **poise,** weight, importance. 126. **from,** away from. **Scene ii:** 9. **Lipsbury pinfold,** probably a proverbial phrase, meaning unknown.

18. **action-taking,** given to law suits. 19. **glass-gazing,** vain. **superserviceable,** over-officious. 34. **sop o' the moonshine,** I 'll steep you in your blood by moonlight. 36. **barber-monger,** patron of the barber shops. 39. **Vanity,** the part of Vanity, a puppet or actor in some allegorical show. 41. **carbonado,** slash.

your valour. You cowardly rascal. Nature disclaims in thee. A tailor made thee.

Corn. Thou art a strange fellow: a tailor make a man?

Kent. A tailor, sir. A stone-cutter or a painter could not have made him so ill, though they had been but two hours at the trade.

Corn. Speak yet, how grew your quarrel?

Osw. This ancient ruffian, sir, whose life I have spared at suit of his grey beard,—

Kent. Thou whoreson zed! thou unnecessary letter! My lord, if you will give me leave, I will tread this unbolted villain into mortar, and daub the wall of a jakes with him. Spare my grey beard, you wagtail?

Corn. Peace, sirrah!
You beastly knave, know you no reverence?

Kent. Yes, sir; but anger hath a privilege.

Corn. Why art thou angry?

Kent. That such a slave as this should wear a sword,
Who wears no honesty. Such smiling rogues as these,
Like rats, oft bite the holy cords a-twain
Which are too intrinse t' unloose; smooth every passion
That in the natures of their lords rebel;
Bring oil to fire, snow to their colder moods;
Renege, affirm, and turn their halcyon beaks
With every gale and vary of their masters,
Knowing nought, like dogs, but following.
A plague upon your epileptic visage!
Smile you my speeches, as I were a fool?
Goose, an I had you upon Sarum Plain,
I 'd drive ye cackling home to Camelot.

Corn. What, art thou mad, old fellow?

Glou. How fell you out? Say that.

Kent. No contraries hold more antipathy
Than I and such a knave.

Corn. Why dost thou call him knave? What is his fault?

Kent. His countenance likes me not.

Corn. No more, perchance, does mine, nor his, nor hers.

Kent. Sir, 't is my occupation to be plain;
I have seen better faces in my time
Than stands on any shoulder that I see
Before me at this instant.

Corn. This is some fellow
Who, having been prais'd for bluntness, doth affect
A saucy roughness, and constrains the garb
Quite from his nature. He cannot flatter, he;
An honest mind and plain, he must speak truth!
An they will take it, so; if not, he 's plain.
These kind of knaves I know, which in this plainness
Harbour more craft and more corrupter ends
Than twenty silly ducking observants
That stretch their duties nicely.

Kent. Sir, in good sooth, in sincere verity,
Under th' allowance of your great aspect,
Whose influence, like the wreath of radiant fire
On flickering Phœbus' front,—

Corn. What mean'st by this?

Kent. To go out of my dialect, which you discommend so much. I know, sir, I am no flatterer. He that beguiled you in a plain accent was a plain knave; which for my part I will not be, though I should win your displeasure to entreat me to 't.

Corn. What was th' offence you gave him?

Osw. I never gave him any.
It pleas'd the King his master very late
To strike at me, upon his misconstruction;
When he, conjunct, and flattering his displeasure,
Tripp'd me behind; being down, insulted, rail'd,
And put upon him such a deal of man
That worthied him, got praises of the King
For him attempting who was self-subdued;
And, in the fleshment of this dread exploit,
Drew on me here again.

Kent. None of these rogues and cowards
But Ajax is their fool.

Corn. Fetch forth the stocks!
You stubborn ancient knave, you reverend braggart,
We 'll teach you—

Kent. Sir, I am too old to learn.
Call not your stocks for me; I serve the King,
On whose employment I was sent to you.
You shall do small respects, show too bold malice
Against the grace and person of my master,
Stocking his messenger.

Corn. Fetch forth the stocks! As I have life and honour,
There shall he sit till noon.

Reg. Till noon! Till night, my lord; and all night too.

Kent. Why, madam, if I were your father's dog,
You should not use me so.

Reg. Sir, being his knave, I will.

Stocks brought out.

Corn. This is a fellow of the self-same colour

60. disclaims in, disowns. **69. zed,** the letter z. **71. unbolted,** coarse. **72. jakes,** a privy. **81. intrinse,** intricate. **84. Renege,** deny. **halcyon,** king-fisher, supposed, if hung by the neck, to turn with the wind. **89. Sarum,** Salisbury. **103. constrains the garb,** forces the assumed manner.

109. observants, courtiers. **125. conjunct,** united with him, taking his part. **128. worthied,** made him appear worthy. **130. fleshment,** first excitement.

Our sister speaks of. Come, bring away the stocks!
Glou. Let me beseech your Grace not to do so.
His fault is much, and the good King his master
Will check him for 't. Your purpos'd low correction
Is such as basest and contemned'st wretches
For pilferings and most common trespasses
Are punish'd with. The King must take it ill
That he 's so slightly valued in his messenger,
Should have him thus restrained.
Corn. I 'll answer that.
Reg. My sister may receive it much more worse
To have her gentleman abus'd, assaulted,
For following her affairs. Put in his legs.
Kent is put in the stocks.
Come, my good lord, away.
Exeunt all but Gloucester and Kent.
Glou. I am sorry for thee, friend; 't is the Duke's pleasure,
Whose disposition, all the world well knows,
Will not be rubb'd nor stopp'd. I 'll entreat for thee.
Kent. Pray, do not, sir. I have watch'd and travell'd hard;
Some time I shall sleep out, the rest I 'll whistle.
A good man's fortune may grow out at heels.
Give you good morrow!
Glou. The Duke 's to blame in this; 't will be ill took. *Exit.*
Kent. Good King, that must approve the common saw,
Thou out of heaven's benediction com'st
To the warm sun!
Approach, thou beacon to this under globe,
That by thy comfortable beams I may
Peruse this letter! Nothing almost sees miracles
But misery. I know 't is from Cordelia,
Who hath most fortunately been inform'd
Of my obscured course; [*reads*] "—and shall find time
From this enormous state—seeking to give
Losses their remedies."—All weary and o'erwatch'd,
Take vantage, heavy eyes, not to behold
This shameful lodging.
Fortune, good-night! Smile once more; turn thy wheel! *Sleeps.*

167. approve, prove true. **saw,** proverb. **168-9. out . . . sun,** from better to worse. **175-7. and . . . remedies,** a difficult passage: the best interpretation is that Kent reads from Cordelia's letter the words inclosed in quotations. **176. enormous state,** disordered kingdom.

Scene III. *The same.*

Enter *Edgar.*

Edg. I heard myself proclaim'd;
And by the happy hollow of a tree
Escap'd the hunt. No port is free; no place
That guard and most unusual vigilance
Does not attend my taking. Whiles I may scape
I will preserve myself, and am bethought
To take the basest and most poorest shape
That ever penury, in contempt of man,
Brought near to beast. My face I 'll grime with filth,
Blanket my loins, elf all my hairs in knots,
And with presented nakedness out-face
The winds and persecutions of the sky.
The country gives me proof and precedent
Of Bedlam beggars, who, with roaring voices,
Strike in their numb'd and mortified bare arms
Pins, wooden pricks, nails, sprigs of rosemary;
And with this horrible object, from low farms,
Poor pelting villages, sheep-cotes, and mills,
Sometimes with lunatic bans, sometimes with prayers,
Enforce their charity. Poor Turlygod! poor Tom!
That 's something yet. Edgar I nothing am.
Exit.

Scene IV. *The same. Kent in the stocks.*

Enter *Lear, Fool,* and *Gentleman.*

Lear. 'T is strange that they should so depart from home,
And not send back my messenger.
Gent. As I learn'd,
The night before there was no purpose in them
Of this remove.
Kent. Hail to thee, noble master!
Lear. Ha!
Mak'st thou this shame thy pastime?
Kent. No, my lord.
Fool. Ha, ha! he wears cruel garters. Horses are tied by the heads, dogs and bears by the neck, monkeys by the loins, and men by the legs. When a man 's over-lusty at legs, then he wears wooden nether-stocks.
Lear. What 's he that hath so much thy place mistook
To set thee here?

Scene iii: 5. attend my taking, wait to seize me. **10. elf,** tangle. **17. object,** appearance. **18. pelting,** paltry. **19. bans,** curses. **Scene iv: 7. cruel,** pun on crewel, i.e., worsted. **11. nether-stocks,** stockings.

Kent. It is both he and she;
Your son and daughter.

Lear. No.

Kent. Yes.

Lear. No, I say.

Kent. I say, yea.

Lear. No, no, they would not.

Kent. Yes, they have.

Lear. By Jupiter, I swear, no.

Kent. By Juno, I swear, ay.

Lear. They durst not do 't;
They could not, would not do 't. 'T is worse than murder,
To do upon respect such violent outrage.
Resolve me, with all modest haste, which way
Thou mightst deserve, or they impose, this usage,
Coming from us.

Kent. My lord, when at their home
I did commend your Highness' letters to them,
Ere I was risen from the place that show'd
My duty kneeling, came there a reeking post,
Stew'd in his haste, half breathless, panting forth
From Goneril his mistress salutations;
Deliver'd letters, spite of intermission,
Which presently they read. On whose contents,
They summon'd up their meiny, straight took horse;
Commanded me to follow, and attend
The leisure of their answer; gave me cold looks:
And meeting here the other messenger,
Whose welcome, I perceiv'd, had poison'd mine,—
Being the very fellow which of late
Display'd so saucily against your Highness,—
Having more man than wit about me, drew:
He rais'd the house with loud and coward cries.
Your son and daughter found this trespass worth
The shame which here it suffers.

Fool. Winter 's not gone yet, if the wild geese fly that way.

> Fathers that wear rags
> Do make their children blind;
> But fathers that bear bags
> Shall see their children kind.
> Fortune, that arrant whore,
> Ne'er turns the key to the poor.

But, for all this, thou shalt have as many dolours for thy daughters as thou canst tell in a year.

Lear. O, how this mother swells up toward my heart!
Hysterica passio, down, thou climbing sorrow,
Thy element 's below!—Where is this daughter?

Kent. With the Earl, sir; here within.

Lear. Follow me not; stay here.
Exit.

Gent. Made you no more offence but what you speak of?

Kent. None.
How chance the King comes with so small a number?

Fool. An thou hadst been set i' th' stocks for that question, thou hadst well deserv'd it.

Kent. Why, Fool?

Fool. We 'll set thee to school to an ant, to teach thee there 's no labouring i' th' winter. All that follow their noses are led by their eyes but blind men; and there 's not a nose among twenty but can smell him that 's stinking. Let go thy hold when a great wheel runs down a hill, lest it break thy neck with following; but the great one that goes upward, let him draw thee after. When a wise man gives thee better counsel, give me mine again; I would have none but knaves follow it, since a fool gives it.

> That sir which serves and seeks for gain,
> And follows but for form,
> Will pack when it begins to rain,
> And leave thee in the storm.
> But I will tarry; the Fool will stay,
> And let the wise man fly.
> The knave turns fool that runs away;
> The Fool no knave, perdy.

Enter *Lear* and *Gloucester*.

Kent. Where learn'd you this, Fool?

Fool. Not i' th' stocks, fool.

Lear. Deny to speak with me! They are sick? They are weary?
They have travell'd all the night? Mere fetches,
The images of revolt and flying off.
Fetch me a better answer.

Glou. My dear lord,
You know the fiery quality of the Duke;
How unremovable and fix'd he is
In his own course.

Lear. Vengeance! plague! death! confusion!
Fiery! What quality? Why, Gloucester, Gloucester,
I 'd speak with the Duke of Cornwall and his wife.

Glou. Well, my good lord, I have inform'd them so.

24. **upon respect**, deliberately. 33. **spite of intermission**, in spite of interrupting me. 35. **meiny**, household. 56. **mother**, hysterical passion, a disease.

89. **Deny**, refuse. 90. **fetches**, tricks. 91. **images**, signs. **flying off**, desertion.

Lear. Inform'd them! Dost thou understand me, man?
Glou. Ay, my good lord.
Lear. The King would speak with Cornwall; the dear father
Would with his daughter speak, commands her service.
Are they inform'd of this? My breath and blood!
Fiery? The fiery duke? Tell the hot duke that—
No, but not yet; may be he is not well.
Infirmity doth still neglect all office
Whereto our health is bound; we are not ourselves
When nature, being oppress'd, commands the mind
To suffer with the body. I 'll forbear;
And am fallen out with my more headier will,
To take the indispos'd and sickly fit
For the sound man.—Death on my state! wherefore *Looking on Kent.*
Should he sit here? This act persuades me
That this remotion of the Duke and her
Is practice only. Give me my servant forth.
Go tell the Duke and 's wife I 'd speak with them,
Now, presently. Bid them come forth and hear me,
Or at their chamber-door I 'll beat the drum
Till it cry sleep to death.
Glou. I would have all well betwixt you. *Exit.*
Lear. O me, my heart, my rising heart! But, down!
Fool. Cry to it, nuncle, as the cockney did to the eels when she put 'em i' th' paste alive; she knapped 'em o' th' coxcombs with a stick, and cried, "Down, wantons, down!" 'T was her brother that, in pure kindness to his horse, buttered his hay.

Enter *Cornwall, Regan, Gloucester,* and Servants.

Lear. Good morrow to you both.
Corn. Hail to your Grace! *Kent here set at liberty.*
Reg. I am glad to see your Highness.
Lear. Regan, I think you are; I know what reason
I have to think so. If thou shouldst not be glad,
I would divorce me from thy mother's tomb,
Sepulchring an adulteress. [*To Kent.*] O, are you free?
Some other time for that. Beloved Regan,
Thy sister 's naught. O Regan, she hath tied
Sharp-tooth'd unkindness, like a vulture, here. *Points to his heart.*
I can scarce speak to thee; thou 'lt not believe
With how deprav'd a quality—O Regan!
Reg. I pray you, sir, take patience. I have hope
You less know how to value her desert
Than she to scant her duty.
Lear. Say, how is that?
Reg. I cannot think my sister in the least
Would fail her obligation. If, sir, perchance
She have restrain'd the riots of your followers,
'T is on such ground, and to such wholesome end,
As clears her from all blame.
Lear. My curses on her!
Reg. O, sir, you are old;
Nature in you stands on the very verge
Of her confine. You should be rul'd and led
By some discretion that discerns your state
Better than you yourself. Therefore, I pray you,
That to our sister you do make return;
Say you have wrong'd her, sir.
Lear. Ask her forgiveness?
Do you but mark how this becomes the house:
"Dear daughter, I confess that I am old; *Kneeling.*
Age is unnecessary, on my knees I beg
That you 'll vouchsafe me raiment, bed, and food."
Reg. Good sir, no more; these are unsightly tricks.
Return you to my sister.
Lear. [*Rising.*] Never, Regan:
She hath abated me of half my train;
Look'd black upon me; struck me with her tongue,
Most serpent-like, upon the very heart.
All the stor'd vengeances of heaven fall
On her ingrateful top! Strike her young bones,
You taking airs, with lameness!
Corn. Fie, sir, fie!
Lear. You nimble lightnings, dart your blinding flames
Into her scornful eyes! Infect her beauty,
You fen-suck'd fogs, drawn by the powerful sun,
To fall and blast her pride!
Reg. O the blest gods! so will you wish on me,
When the rash mood is on.
Lear. No, Regan, thou shalt never have my curse.
Thy tender-hefted nature shall not give

107. office, duty. **111. more headier,** over-impetuous. **115. remotion,** removal. **120. cry sleep to death,** murder sleep. **136. naught,** worthless.

139. quality, manner. **140-2. I have . . . duty,** you are more likely to underestimate her worth than she is likely to neglect her duties toward you. **150. confine,** assigned limit. **155. house,** royal family. **157. unnecessary,** not wanted. **165. top,** head. **young bones,** unborn progeny. **166. taking,** malignant. **170. fall,** cause to fall. **174. tender-hefted,** delicately framed.

Thee o'er to harshness. Her eyes are fierce; but thine
Do comfort and not burn. 'T is not in thee
To grudge my pleasures, to cut off my train,
To bandy hasty words, to scant my sizes,
And in conclusion to oppose the bolt
Against my coming in. Thou better know'st
The offices of nature, bond of childhood,
Effects of courtesy, dues of gratitude.
Thy half o' th' kingdom hast thou not forgot,
Wherein I thee endow'd.

Reg. Good sir, to the purpose.

Tucket within.

Lear. Who put my man i' th' stocks?

Enter *Oswald.*

Corn. What trumpet 's that?

Reg. I know 't; my sister's. This approves her letter,
That she would soon be here. [*To Oswald.*] Is your lady come?

Lear. This is a slave whose easy-borrowed pride
Dwells in the fickle grace of her he follows.
Out, varlet, from my sight!

Corn. What means your Grace?

Enter *Goneril.*

Lear. Who stock'd my servant? Regan, I have good hope
Thou didst not know on 't. Who comes here? O heavens,
If you do love old men, if your sweet sway
Allow obedience, if you yourselves are old,
Make it your cause; send down, and take my part!
[*To Gon.*] Art not asham'd to look upon this beard?
O Regan, wilt thou take her by the hand?

Gon. Why not by the hand, sir? How have I offended?
All 's not offence that indiscretion finds
And dotage terms so.

Lear. O sides, you are too tough;
Will you yet hold? How came my man i' th' stocks?

Corn. I set him there, sir; but his own disorders
Deserv'd much less advancement

Lear. You! did you?

Reg. I pray you, father, being weak, seem so.
If, till the expiration of your month,
You will return and sojourn with my sister,
Dismissing half your train, come then to me.
I am now from home, and out of that provision
Which shall be needful for your entertainment.

Lear. Return to her, and fifty men dismiss'd!
No, rather I abjure all roofs, and choose
To wage against the enmity o' th' air;
To be a comrade with the wolf and owl,—
Necessity's sharp pinch. Return with her?
Why, the hot-blooded France, that dowerless took
Our youngest born, I could as well be brought
To knee his throne, and, squire-like, pension beg
To keep base life afoot. Return with her?
Persuade me rather to be slave and sumpter
To this detested groom. [*Pointing at Oswald.*]

Gon. At your choice, sir.

Lear. I prithee, daughter, do not make me mad;
I will not trouble thee, my child; farewell!
We 'll no more meet, no more see one another.
But yet thou art my flesh, my blood, my daughter;
Or rather a disease that 's in my flesh,
Which I must needs call mine; thou art a boil,
A plague-sore, an embossed carbuncle,
In my corrupted blood. But I 'll not chide thee;
Let shame come when it will, I do not call it.
I do not bid the thunder-bearer shoot,
Nor tell tales of thee to high-judging Jove.
Mend when thou canst; be better at thy leisure.
I can be patient; I can stay with Regan,
I and my hundred knights.

Reg. Not altogether so;
I look'd not for you yet, nor am provided
For your fit welcome. Give ear, sir, to my sister;
For those that mingle reason with your passion
Must be content to think you old, and so—
But she knows what she does.

Lear. Is this well spoken?

Reg. I dare avouch it, sir. What, fifty followers!
Is it not well? What should you need of more?
Yea, or so many, sith that both charge and danger
Speak 'gainst so great a number? How, in one house,
Should many people, under two commands,
Hold amity? 'T is hard; almost impossible.

Gon. Why might not you, my lord, receive attendance
From those that she calls servants or from mine?

178. **sizes**, allowances. 182. **Effects**, manifestations. 194. **Allow**, approve of.

212. **wage**, contend. 219. **sumpter**, drudge (lit., pack horse driver). 227. **embossed**, swollen. 242. **charge**, expense.

Reg. Why not, my lord? If then they chanc'd to slack ye,
We could control them. If you will come to me,—
For now I spy a danger—I entreat you
To bring but five and twenty; to no more
Will I give place or notice.
Lear. I gave you all.
Reg. And in good time you gave it.
Lear. Made you my guardians, my depositaries;
But kept a reservation to be followed
With such a number. What, must I come to you
With five and twenty, Regan? Said you so?
Reg. And speak 't again, my lord; no more with me.
Lear. Those wicked creatures yet do look well-favour'd
When others are more wicked; not being the worst
Stands in some rank of praise. [*To Gon.*] I 'll go with thee.
Thy fifty yet doth double five and twenty,
And thou art twice her love.
Gon. Hear me, my lord:
What need you five and twenty, ten, or five,
To follow in a house where twice so many
Have a command to tend you?
Reg. What need one?
Lear. O, reason not the need! Our basest beggars
Are in the poorest thing superfluous.
Allow not nature more than nature needs,
Man's life is cheap as beast's. Thou art a lady;
If only to go warm were gorgeous,
Why, nature needs not what thou gorgeous wear'st,
Which scarcely keeps thee warm. But, for true need,—
You heavens, give me that patience, patience I need!
You see me here, you gods, a poor old man,
As full of grief as age; wretched in both!
If it be you that stirs these daughters' hearts
Against their father, fool me not so much
To bear it tamely; touch me with noble anger,
And let not women's weapons, water-drops,
Stain my man's cheeks! No, you unnatural hags,
I will have such revenges on you both
That all the world shall—I will do such things,—
What they are, yet I know not; but they shall be
The terrors of the earth. You think I 'll weep:
No, I 'll not weep.
I have full cause of weeping; but this heart
Storm and tempest.
Shall break into a hundred thousand flaws,
Or ere I 'll weep. O, Fool! I shall go mad!
Exeunt Lear, Gloucester, Kent, and Fool.

Corn. Let us withdraw, 't will be a storm.
Reg. This house is little: the old man and 's people
Cannot be well bestow'd.
Gon. 'T is his own blame; hath put himself from rest,
And must needs taste his folly.
Reg. For his particular, I 'll receive him gladly,
But not one follower.
Gon. So am I purpos'd.
Where is my Lord of Gloucester?

Enter *Gloucester.*

Corn. Followed the old man forth. He is return'd.
Glou. The King is in high rage.
Corn. Whither is he going?
Glou. He calls to horse; but will I know not whither.
Corn. 'T is best to give him way; he leads himself.
Gon. My lord, entreat him by no means to stay.
Glou. Alack, the night comes on, and the bleak winds
Do sorely ruffle; for many miles about
There 's scarce a bush.
Reg. O, sir, to wilful men,
The injuries that they themselves procure
Must be their schoolmasters. Shut up your doors.
He is attended with a desperate train;
And what they may incense him to, being apt
To have his ear abus'd, wisdom bids fear.
Corn. Shut up your doors, my lord; 't is a wild night:
My Regan counsels well: come out o' th' storm.
Exeunt.

248. slack, neglect. **268. Are . . . superfluous,** have more than is necessary for bare existence. **278. fool,** make a fool of.

288 flaws, fragments. **295. For his particular,** as to him alone. **304. ruffle,** bluster.

ACT III. Scene I. *A Heath.*

Storm still. Enter *Kent* and a *Gentleman*, severally.

Kent. Who 's there, besides foul weather?
Gent. One minded like the weather, most unquietly.
Kent. I know you. Where 's the King?
Gent. Contending with the fretful elements;
Bids the wind blow the earth into the sea,
Or swell the curled waters 'bove the main,
That things might change or cease; tears his white hair,
Which the impetuous blasts, with eyeless rage,
Catch in their fury, and make nothing of;
Strives in his little world of man to out-scorn
The to-and-fro-conflicting wind and rain.
This night, wherein the cub-drawn bear would couch,
The lion and the belly-pinched wolf
Keep their fur dry, unbonneted he runs,
And bids what will take all.
Kent. But who is with him?
Gent. None but the Fool; who labours to outjest
His heart-struck injuries.
Kent. Sir, I do know you;
And dare, upon the warrant of my note,
Commend a dear thing to you. There is division,
Although as yet the face of it be cover'd
With mutual cunning, 'twixt Albany and Cornwall;
Who have—as who have not, that their great stars
Thron'd and set high?—servants, who seem no less,
Which are to France the spies and speculations
Intelligent of our state; what hath been seen,
Either in snuffs and packings of the Dukes,
Or the hard rein which both of them have borne
Against the old kind king, or something deeper,
Whereof perchance these are but furnishings;
But, true it is, from France there comes a power
Into this scattered kingdom; who already,
Wise in our negligence, have secret feet
In some of our best ports, and are at point
To show their open banner. Now to you:
If on my credit you dare build so far
To make your speed to Dover, you shall find
Some that will thank you, making just report
Of how unnatural and bemadding sorrow
The King hath cause to plain.
I am a gentleman of blood and breeding;
And, from some knowledge and assurance, offer
This office to you.
Gent. I will talk further with you.
Kent. No, do not.
For confirmation that I am much more
Than my out-wall, open this purse, and take
What it contains. If you shall see Cordelia,—
As fear not but you shall,—show her this ring;
And she will tell you who your fellow is
That yet you do not know. Fie on this storm!
I will go seek the King.
Gent. Give me your hand. Have you no more to say?
Kent. Few words, but, to effect, more than all yet;
That, when we have found the King,—in which your pain
That way, I 'll this,—he that first lights on him
Holla the other. *Exeunt severally.*

Scene II. *Another part of the Heath. Storm still.*

Enter *Lear* and *Fool*.

Lear. Blow, winds, and crack your cheeks! Rage! Blow!
You cataracts and hurricanoes, spout
Till you have drench'd our steeples, drown'd the cocks!
You sulph'rous and thought-executing fires,
Vaunt-couriers to oak-cleaving thunderbolts,
Singe my white head! And thou, all-shaking thunder,
Smite flat the thick rotundity o' th' world!
Crack nature's moulds, all germens spill at once,
That makes ingrateful man!

Fool. O nuncle, court holy-water in a dry house is better than this rain-water out o' door. Good nuncle, in, and ask thy daughters' blessing. Here 's a night pities neither wise man nor fool.

Lear. Rumble thy bellyful! Spit, fire! Spout, rain!
Nor rain, wind, thunder, fire, are my daughters.

Act III, Scene i: 6. main, mainland. **12. cub-drawn bear,** a bear sucked dry by her cubs, ravenous. **18. note,** information. **19. dear,** important. **24. speculations,** observers. **26. snuffs,** quarrels. **packings,** plottings.

39. plain, complain. **45. out-wall,** exterior. **52. to effect,** in importance. **53. pain,** laborious search. **Scene ii: 3. cocks,** weather cocks. **4. thought-executing,** with the speed of thought. **5. Vaunt-couriers,** forerunners. **8. germens,** seeds. **10. court holy-water,** flattery.

I tax not you, you elements, with unkindness,
I never gave you kingdom, call'd you children;
You owe me no subscription: then let fall
Your horrible pleasure. Here I stand, your slave,
A poor, infirm, weak, and despis'd old man;
But yet I call you servile ministers,
That will with two pernicious daughters join
Your high engender'd battles 'gainst a head
So old and white as this. Oh! Oh! 't is foul!

Fool. He that has a house to put 's head in has a good head-piece.

The cod-piece that will house
Before the head has any,
The head and he shall louse;
So beggars marry many.
The man that makes his toe
What he his heart should make
Shall of a corn cry woe,
And turn his sleep to wake.

For there was never yet fair woman but she made mouths in a glass.

Enter *Kent.*

Lear. No, I will be the pattern of all patience;
I will say nothing.

Kent. Who 's there?

Fool. Marry, here 's grace and a cod-piece; that 's a wise man and a fool.

Kent. Alas, sir, are you here? Things that love night
Love not such nights as these; the wrathful skies
Gallow the very wanderers of the dark,
And make them keep their caves. Since I was man,
Such sheets of fire, such bursts of horrid thunder,
Such groans of roaring wind and rain, I never
Remember to have heard: man's nature cannot carry
Th' affliction nor the fear.

Lear. Let the great gods,
That keep this dreadful pudder o'er our heads,
Find out their enemies now. Tremble, thou wretch,
That hast within thee undivulged crimes,
Unwhipp'd of justice; hide thee, thou bloody hand;
Thou perjur'd, and thou simular of virtue
That art incestuous; caitiff, to pieces shake,
That under covert and convenient seeming
Has practis'd on man's life; close pent-up guilts,
Rive your concealing continents, and cry
These dreadful summoners grace. I am a man
More sinn'd against than sinning.

Kent. Alack, bare-headed!
Gracious my lord, hard by here is a hovel;
Some friendship will it lend you 'gainst the tempest.
Repose you there; whilst I to this hard house—
More harder than the stone whereof 't is rais'd;
Which even but now, demanding after you,
Deni'd me to come in—return, and force
Their scanted courtesy.

Lear. My wits begin to turn.
Come on, my boy. How dost, my boy? Art cold?
I am cold myself. Where is this straw, my fellow?
The art of our necessities is strange,
That can make vile things precious. Come, your hovel.
Poor Fool and knave, I have one part in my heart
That 's sorry yet for thee.

Fool. [*Singing.*]

He that has and a little tiny wit,—
With heigh-ho, the wind and the rain,—
Must make content with his fortunes fit,
For the rain it raineth every day.

Lear. True, boy. Come, bring us to this hovel. *Exeunt Lear and Kent.*

Fool. This is a brave night to cool a courtezan.
I 'll speak a prophecy ere I go:
When priests are more in word than matter;
When brewers mar their malt with water;
When nobles are their tailors' tutors;
No heretics burn'd, but wenches' suitors;
When every case in law is right;
No squire in debt, nor no poor knight;
When slanders do not live in tongues;
Nor cutpurses come not to throngs;
When usurers tell their gold i' th' field;
And bawds and whores do churches build;
Then shall the realm of Albion
Come to great confusion.
Then comes the time, who lives to see 't,
That going shall be us'd with feet.
This prophecy Merlin shall make; for I live before his time. *Exit.*

Scene III. *Gloucester's castle.*

Enter *Gloucester* and *Edmund.*

Glou. Alack, alack, Edmund, I like not this unnatural dealing. When I desired their

18. **subscription**, allegiance. 27. **cod-piece**, part of man's clothes, an appendage worn on the front of the trousers. 31-4. The man who promotes his toe to the place of his heart will be plagued with corns in that tenderest region. The reference is to Lear's promotion of Goneril and Regan over Cordelia. 44. **Gallow**, terrify. 50. **pudder**, turmoil. 54. **simular**, simulator

58. **Rive**, split. **continents**, covers.

leave that I might pity him, they took from me the use of mine own house; charged me, on pain of their perpetual displeasure, neither to speak of him, entreat for him, nor any way sustain him.

Edm. Most savage and unnatural!

Glou. Go to; say you nothing. There is division between the Dukes, and a worse matter than that. I have received a letter this night; 't is dangerous to be spoken; I have locked the letter in my closet. These injuries the King now bears will be revenged home; there is part of a power already footed; we must incline to the King. I will seek him, and privily relieve him. Go you and maintain talk with the Duke, that my charity be not of him perceived. If he ask for me, I am ill, and gone to bed. If I die for it, as no less is threatened me, the King my old master must be relieved. There is some strange thing toward, Edmund; pray you, be careful. *Exit.*

Edm. This courtesy, forbid thee, shall the Duke
Instantly know; and of that letter too.
This seems a fair deserving, and must draw me
That which my father loses; no less than all.
The younger rises when the old doth fall.
Exit.

Scene IV. *The Heath. Before a hovel.*

Enter *Lear, Kent,* and *Fool.*

Kent. Here is the place, my lord; good my lord, enter.
The tyranny of the open night 's too rough
For nature to endure. *Storm still.*
Lear. Let me alone.
Kent. Good my lord, enter here.
Lear. Wilt break my heart?
Kent. I had rather break mine own. Good my lord, enter.
Lear. Thou think'st 't is much that this contentious storm
Invades us to the skin; so 't is to thee;
But where the greater malady is fix'd,
The lesser is scarce felt. Thou 'dst shun a bear;
But if thy flight lay toward the roaring sea,
Thou 'dst meet the bear i' th' mouth. When the mind 's free,
The body 's delicate; the tempest in my mind
Doth from my senses take all feeling else
Save what beats there. Filial ingratitude!
Is it not as this mouth should tear this hand
For lifting food to 't? But I will punish home:
No, I will weep no more. In such a night
To shut me out! Pour on; I will endure.
In such a night as this! O Regan, Goneril!
Your old kind father, whose frank heart gave all,—
O, that way madness lies; let me shun that;
No more of that.
Kent. Good my lord, enter here.
Lear. Prithee, go in thyself; seek thine own ease.
This tempest will not give me leave to ponder
On things would hurt me more. But I 'll go in.
[*To the Fool.*] In, boy; go first. You houseless poverty,—
Nay, get thee in. I 'll pray, and then I 'll sleep.
Exit Fool.
Poor naked wretches, wheresoe'er you are,
That bide the pelting of this pitiless storm,
How shall your houseless heads and unfed sides,
Your loop'd and window'd raggedness, defend you
From seasons such as these? O, I have ta'en
Too little care of this! Take physic, pomp;
Expose thyself to feel what wretches feel,
That thou mayst shake the superflux to them,
And show the heavens more just.

Edg. [*Within.*] Fathom and half, fathom and half! Poor Tom!

The Fool runs out from the hovel.

Fool. Come not in here, nuncle, here 's a spirit. Help me, help me!

Kent. Give me thy hand. Who 's there?

Fool. A spirit, a spirit! He says his name 's poor Tom.

Kent. What art thou that dost grumble there i' th' straw? Come forth.

Enter *Edgar,* disguised as a madman.

Edg. Away! the foul fiend follows me! "Through the sharp hawthorn blow the winds." Hum! go to thy cold bed, and warm thee.

Lear. Did'st thou give all to thy two daughters, and art thou come to this?

Edg. Who gives anything to poor Tom? whom the foul fiend hath led through fire and through flame, and through ford and whirlpool, o'er bog and quagmire; that hath laid knives under his pillow, and halters in his pew; set ratsbane by his porridge; made him proud of heart, to ride on a bay trotting-horse over four-inched bridges, to course his own shadow for a traitor. Bless thy five wits! Tom 's a-cold,—O, do de, do de, do de. Bless thee from whirlwinds, star-blasting, and taking! Do poor Tom some charity, whom the

Scene iii: 12. footed, on foot. **Scene iv: 11. i' th' mouth,** face to face. **12. delicate,** hard to please.

31. loop'd, full of holes. **35. superflux,** superfluity. **57. course,** pursue. **61. taking,** infection.

foul fiend vexes. There could I have him now, and there, and there again, and there.

Storm still.

Lear. What, his daughters brought him to this pass?
Couldst thou save nothing? Wouldst thou give 'em all?

Fool. Nay, he reserved a blanket, else we had been all shamed.

Lear. Now, all the plagues that in the pendulous air
Hang fated o'er men's faults light on thy daughters!

Kent. He hath no daughters, sir.

Lear. Death, traitor! nothing could have subdu'd nature
To such a lowness but his unkind daughters.
Is it the fashion, that discarded fathers
Should have thus little mercy on their flesh?
Judicious punishment! 'T was this flesh begot
Those pelican daughters.

Edg. Pillicock sat on Pillicock-hill.
Alow, alow, loo, loo!

Fool. This cold night will turn us all to fools and madmen.

Edg. Take heed o' th' foul fiend. Obey thy parents; keep thy word justly; swear not; commit not with man's sworn spouse; set not thy sweet heart on proud array. Tom 's a-cold.

Lear. What hast thou been?

Edg. A serving-man, proud in heart and mind; that curled my hair; wore gloves in my cap; served the lust of my mistress' heart, and did the act of darkness with her; swore as many oaths as I spake words, and broke them in the sweet face of heaven: one that slept in the contriving of lust, and waked to do it. Wine loved I deeply, dice dearly, and in woman out-paramoured the Turk: false of heart, light of ear, bloody of hand; hog in sloth, fox in stealth, wolf in greediness, dog in madness, lion in prey. Let not the creaking of shoes nor the rustling of silks betray thy poor heart to woman. Keep thy foot out of brothels, thy hand out of plackets, thy pen from lenders' books, and defy the foul fiend. Still through the hawthorn blows the cold wind. Says suum, mun, nonny. Dolphin my boy, boy, sessa! let him trot by. *Storm still.*

Lear. Why, thou wert better in thy grave than to answer with thy uncovered body this extremity of the skies. Is man no more than this? Consider him well. Thou ow'st the worm no silk, the beast no hide, the sheep no wool, the cat no perfume. Ha! here 's three on 's are sophisticated! Thou art the thing itself; unaccommodated man is no more but such a poor, bare, forked animal as thou art. Off, off, you lendings! come, unbutton here.

Tearing off his clothes.

Enter *Gloucester,* with a torch.

Fool. Prithee, nuncle, be contented; 't is a naughty night to swim in. Now a little fire in a wild field were like an old lecher's heart; a small spark, all the rest on 's body cold. Look, here comes a walking fire.

Edg. This is the foul fiend Flibbertigibbet; he begins at curfew, and walks till the first cock; he gives the web and the pin, squints the eye, and makes the hare-lip; mildews the white wheat, and hurts the poor creature of earth.

> Swithold footed thrice the 'old;
> He met the night-mare, and her ninefold;
> Bid her alight,
> And her troth plight,
> And, aroint thee, witch, aroint thee!

Kent. How fares your Grace?

Lear. What 's he?

Kent. Who 's there? What is 't you seek?

Glou. What are you there? Your names?

Edg. Poor Tom, that eats the swimming frog, the toad, the tadpole, the wall-newt, and the water; that in the fury of his heart, when the foul fiend rages, eats cow-dung for salads; swallows the old rat and the ditch-dog; drinks the green mantle of the standing pool; who is whipp'd from tithing to tithing, and stocked, punished, and imprisoned; who hath had three suits to his back, six shirts to his body,

> Horse to ride, and weapon to wear;
> But mice and rats, and such small deer,
> Have been Tom's food for seven long year.

Beware my follower. Peace, Smulkin; peace, thou fiend!

Glou. What, hath your Grace no better company?

Edg. The prince of darkness is a gentleman. Modo he 's call'd, and Mahu.

Glou. Our flesh and blood, my lord, is grown so vile
That it doth hate what gets it.

Edg. Poor Tom 's a-cold.

69. **pendulous**, suspended. 77. **pelican**, young pelicans were supposed to feed on their mother's blood. 88. **gloves . . . cap**, the custom of wearing a lady's glove in a cap as a sign of her favor. 95. **light of ear**, credulous of evil. 100. **placket**, opening in a petticoat. 103. **Dolphin my boy**, the reference is to an old ballad ridiculing the Dolphin, i.e., the Dauphin of France.

109. **cat**, civet-cat. 111. **unaccommodated**, undressed. 122. **web and the pin**, disease of the eye, cataracts. 125. **Swithold**, Swithold was St. Vitalis, invoked against nightmares. **'old**, wold, open country. 126. **ninefold**, the nine familiar spirits or foals attendant on the nightmare. 129. **aroint thee**, be gone. 135. **water**, water-newt. 137. **ditch-dog**, dead and thrown in a ditch. 139. **tithing**, district. 143. **deer**, animals. 151. **gets**, begets.

Glou. Go in with me; my duty cannot suffer
T' obey in all your daughters' hard commands.
Though their injunction be to bar my doors
And let this tyrannous night take hold upon you,
Yet have I ventur'd to come seek you out,
And bring you where both fire and food is ready.

Lear. First let me talk with this philosopher.
What is the cause of thunder?

Kent. Good my lord, take his offer; go into the house.

Lear. I 'll talk a word with this same learned Theban.
What is your study?

Edg. How to prevent the fiend, and to kill vermin.

Lear. Let me ask you one word in private.

Kent. Importune him once more to go, my lord;
His wits begin to unsettle.

Glou. Canst thou blame him?
Storm still.
His daughters seek his death. Ah, that good Kent!
He said it would be thus, poor banish'd man!
Thou say'st the King grows mad; I 'll tell thee, friend,
I am almost mad myself. I had a son,
Now outlaw'd from my blood; 'a sought my life,
But lately, very late. I lov'd him, friend,
No father his son dearer; true to tell thee,
The grief hath craz'd my wits. What a night 's this!
I do beseech your Grace,—

Lear. O, cry you mercy, sir.
Noble philosopher, your company.

Edg. Tom 's a-cold.

Glou. In, fellow, there, into the hovel; keep thee warm.

Lear. Come, let 's in all.

Kent. This way, my lord.

Lear. With him;
I will keep still with my philosopher.

Kent. Good my lord, soothe him; let him take the fellow.

Glou. Take him you on.

Kent. Sirrah, come on; go along with us.

Lear. Come, good Athenian.

Glou. No words, no words: hush.

Edg.

Child Rowland to the dark tower came;
His word was still, Fie, foh, and fum,
I smell the blood of a British man.

Exeunt.

164. prevent, anticipate, frustrate. **176. cry you mercy**, I beg your pardon. **186. Child**, a title. **Child . . . British man**, a fragment of a ballad.

Scene V. *Gloucester's castle.*

Enter *Cornwall* and *Edmund.*

Corn. I will have my revenge ere I depart his house.

Edm. How, my lord, I may be censured that nature thus gives way to loyalty, something fears me to think of.

Corn. I now perceive, it was not altogether your brother's evil disposition made him seek his death; but a provoking merit, set a-work by a reproveable badness in himself.

Edm. How malicious is my fortune, that I must repent to be just! This is the letter he spoke of, which approves him an intelligent party to the advantages of France. O heavens! that this treason were not, or not I the detector!

Corn. Go with me to the Duchess.

Edm. If the matter of this paper be certain, you have mighty business in hand.

Corn. True or false, it hath made thee Earl of Gloucester. Seek out where thy father is, that he may be ready for our apprehension.

Edm. [*Aside.*] If I find him comforting the King, it will stuff his suspicion more fully.—I will persever in my course of loyalty, though the conflict be sore between that and my blood.

Corn. I will lay trust upon thee; and thou shalt find a dearer father in my love. *Exeunt.*

Scene VI. *A building attached to Gloucester's castle.*

Enter *Kent* and *Gloucester.*

Glou. Here is better than the open air; take it thankfully. I will piece out the comfort with what addition I can. I will not be long from you.

Kent. All the power of his wits have given way to his impatience. The gods reward your kindness! *Exit Gloucester.*

Enter *Lear, Edgar,* and *Fool.*

Edg. Frateretto calls me; and tells me Nero is an angler in the lake of darkness. Pray, innocent, and beware the foul fiend.

Fool. Prithee, nuncle, tell me whether a madman be a gentleman or a yeoman?

Lear. A king, a king!

Fool. No, he 's a yeoman that has a gentleman to his son; for he 's a mad yeoman that sees his son a gentleman before him.

Lear. To have a thousand with red burning spits
Come hissing in upon 'em,—

Scene v: 3. censured, judged. **5. fears**, frightens. **8. provoking**, inciting. **9. himself**, Gloucester.

Edg. The foul fiend bites my back.

Fool. He 's mad that trusts in the tameness of a wolf, a horse's health, a boy's love, or a whore's oath.

Lear. It shall be done; I will arraign them straight.
[*To Edgar.*] Come, sit thou here, most learned justicer;
[*To the Fool.*] Thou, sapient sir, sit here. Now, you she foxes!

Edg. Look, where he stands and glares!
Wantest thou eyes at trial, madam?

Come o'er the bourn, Bessy, to me,—

Fool. [*Sings.*]

Her boat hath a leak,
And she must not speak
Why she dares not come over to thee.

Edg. The foul fiend haunts poor Tom in the voice of a nightingale. Hoppedance cries in Tom's belly for two white herring. Croak not, black angel; I have no food for thee.

Kent. How do you, sir? Stand you not so amaz'd:
Will you lie down and rest upon the cushions?

Lear. I 'll see their trial first. Bring in their evidence.
[*To Edgar.*] Thou robed man of justice, take thy place;
[*To the Fool.*] And thou, his yoke-fellow of equity,
Bench by his side. [*To Kent.*] You are o' th' commission,
Sit you too.

Edg. Let us deal justly.

Sleepest or wakest thou, jolly shepherd?
Thy sheep be in the corn;
And for one blast of thy minikin mouth,
Thy sheep shall take no harm.

Purr! the cat is grey.

Lear. Arraign her first; 't is Goneril. I here take my oath before this honourable assembly, she kicked the poor king her father.

Fool. Come hither, mistress. Is your name Goneril?

Lear. She cannot deny it.

Fool. Cry you mercy, I took you for a joint-stool.

Lear. And here 's another, whose warp'd looks proclaim
What store her heart is made on. Stop her there!
Arms, arms, sword, fire! Corruption in the place!
False justicer, why hast thou let her scape?

Edg. Bless thy five wits!

Kent. O pity! Sir, where is the patience now
That you so oft have boasted to retain?

Edg. [*Aside.*] My tears begin to take his part so much,
They 'll mar my counterfeiting.

Lear. The little dogs and all,
Tray, Blanch, and Sweetheart, see, they bark at me.

Edg. Tom will throw his head at them. Avaunt, you curs!

Be thy mouth or black or white,
Tooth that poisons if it bite;
Mastiff, greyhound, mongrel grim,
Hound or spaniel, brach or lym,
Or bobtail tike or trundle-tail,
Tom will make him weep and wail;
For, with throwing thus my head,
Dogs leapt the hatch, and all are fled.

Do de, de, de. Sessa! Come, march to wakes and fairs and market-towns. Poor Tom, thy horn is dry.

Lear. Then let them anatomize Regan; see what breeds about her heart. Is there any cause in nature that make these hard hearts? [*To Edgar.*] You, sir, I entertain for one of my hundred; only I do not like the fashion of your garments. You will say they are Persian attire, but let them be changed.

Enter *Gloucester.*

Kent. Now, good my lord, lie here and rest a while.

Lear. Make no noise, make no noise; draw the curtains; so, so, so. We 'll go to supper i' th' morning; so, so, so.

Fool. And I 'll go to bed at noon.

Glou. Come hither, friend; where is the King my master?

Kent. Here, sir; but trouble him not, his wits are gone.

Glou. Good friend, I prithee, take him in thy arms;
I have o'erheard a plot of death upon him.
There is a litter ready; lay him in 't,
And drive toward Dover, friend, where thou shalt meet
Both welcome and protection. Take up thy master.
If thou shouldst dally half an hour, his life,
With thine, and all that offer to defend him,
Stand in assured loss. Take up, take up;
And follow me, that will to some provision
Give thee quick conduct.

Kent. Oppressed nature sleeps.
This rest might yet have balm'd thy broken sinews,

Scene vi: 27. **bourn**, brook. 33. **white herring**, fresh herring. 35. **amaz'd**, confused. 45. **minikin**, small, dainty.

72. **brach**, bitch. **lym**, bloodhound. 73. **tike**, cur. **trundle-tail**, curly-tail. 76. **hatch**, lower half of a door. 83. **entertain**, engage. 105. **broken sinews**, racked nerves.

Which, if convenience will not allow,
Stand in hard cure. [*To the Fool.*] Come, help to bear thy master;
Thou must not stay behind.
Glou. Come, come, away.
Exeunt all but Edgar.
Edg. When we our betters see bearing our woes,
We scarcely think our miseries our foes.
Who alone suffers, suffers most i' th' mind,
Leaving free things and happy shows behind;
But then the mind much sufferance doth o'er-skip,
When grief hath mates, and bearing fellowship.
How light and portable my pain seems now,
When that which makes me bend makes the King bow,
He childed as I fathered! Tom, away!
Mark the high noises; and thyself bewray
When false opinion, whose wrong thoughts defile thee,
In thy just proof repeals and reconciles thee.
What will hap more to-night, safe scape the King!
Lurk, lurk. *Exit.*

Scene VII. *Gloucester's castle.*

Enter *Cornwall, Regan, Goneril, Edmund,* and Servants.

Corn. [*To Goneril.*] Post speedily to my lord your husband; show him this letter. The army of France is landed.—Seek out the traitor Gloucester. *Exeunt some of the Servants.*
Reg. Hang him instantly.
Gon. Pluck out his eyes.
Corn. Leave him to my displeasure.—Edmund, keep you our sister company; the revenges we are bound to take upon your traitorous father are not fit for your beholding. Advise the Duke, where you are going, to a most festinate preparation; we are bound to the like. Our posts shall be swift and intelligent betwixt us. Farewell, dear sister; farewell, my lord of Gloucester.

Enter *Oswald.*

How now! where 's the King?
Osw. My Lord of Gloucester hath convey'd him hence.
Some five or six and thirty of his knights,
Hot questrists after him, met him at gate,
Who, with some other of the lords dependants,
Are gone with him towards Dover, where they boast
To have well-armed friends.
Corn. Get horses for your mistress.
Gon. Farewell, sweet lord, and sister.
Corn. Edmund, farewell.
Exeunt Goneril, Edmund, and Oswald.
Go seek the traitor Gloucester,
Pinion him like a thief, bring him before us.
Exeunt other Servants.
Though well we may not pass upon his life
Without the form of justice, yet our power
Shall do a courtesy to our wrath, which men
May blame, but not control.

Enter *Gloucester* brought in by two or three.

Who 's there? The traitor?
Reg. Ingrateful fox! 't is he.
Corn. Bind fast his corky arms.
Glou. What means your Graces? Good my friends, consider
You are my guests. Do me no foul play, friends.
Corn. Bind him, I say. *Servants bind him.*
Reg. Hard, hard. O filthy traitor!
Glou. Unmerciful lady as you are, I 'm none.
Corn. To this chair bind him. Villain, thou shalt find— *Regan plucks his beard.*
Glou. By the kind gods, 't is most ignobly done
To pluck me by the beard.
Reg. So white, and such a traitor!
Glou. Naughty lady,
These hairs, which thou dost ravish from my chin,
Will quicken, and accuse thee. I am your host:
With robber's hands my hospitable favours
You should not ruffle thus. What will you do?
Corn. Come, sir, what letters had you late from France?
Reg. Be simple-answer'd, for we know the truth.
Corn. And what confederacy have you with the traitors
Late footed in the kingdom?
Reg. To whose hands you have sent the lunatic king?
Speak.
Glou I have a letter guessingly set down,
Which came from one that 's of a neutral heart,
And not from one oppos'd.
Corn. Cunning.
Reg. And false.
Corn. Where hast thou sent the King?
Glou. To Dover.

107. **Stand in hard cure**, are in a very dangerous condition. 114. **bearing**, endurance. 118. **bewray**, reveal. 120. **repeals**, restores to honor. 121. **What . . . to-night**, whatever else may happen to-night. **Scene vii: 11. festinate** hasty. 17. **questrists**, searchers.

29. **corky**, withered. 39. **quicken**, come to life. 45. **footed**, established.

Reg. Wherefore to Dover? Wast thou not charg'd at peril—
Corn. Wherefore to Dover? Let him answer that.
Glou. I am tied to th' stake, and I must stand the course.
Reg. Wherefore to Dover?
Glou. Because I would not see thy cruel nails
Pluck out his poor old eyes; nor thy fierce sister
In his anointed flesh stick boarish fangs.
The sea, with such a storm as his bare head
In hell-black night endur'd, would have buoy'd up
And quench'd the stelled fires;
Yet, poor old heart, he holp the heavens to rain.
If wolves had at thy gate howl'd that dearn time,
Thou shouldst have said, "Good porter, turn the key."
All cruels else subscrib'd: but I shall see
The winged vengeance overtake such children.
Corn. See 't shalt thou never. Fellows, hold the chair.
Upon these eyes of thine I 'll set my foot.
Glou. He that will think to live till he be old,
Give me some help!—O cruel! O ye gods!
Reg. One side will mock another; th' other too.
Corn. If you see vengeance,—
1. Serv. Hold your hand, my lord!
I have serv'd you ever since I was a child;
But better service have I never done you
Than now to bid you hold.
Reg. How now, you dog!
1. Serv. If you did wear a beard upon your chin,
I 'd shake it on this quarrel. What do you mean?
Corn. My villain! *They draw and fight.*
1. Serv. Nay, then, come on, and take the chance of anger.
Reg. Give me thy sword. A peasant stand up thus?
She takes a sword, and runs at him behind.
1. Serv. Oh, I am slain! My lord, you have one eye left
To see some mischief on him. Oh! *Dies.*
Corn. Lest it see more, prevent it. Out, vile jelly!
Where is thy lustre now?
Glou. All dark and comfortless. Where 's my son Edmund?
Edmund, enkindle all the sparks of nature,
To quit this horrid act.
Reg. Out, treacherous villain!
Thou call'st on him that hates thee. It was he
That made the overture of thy treasons to us,
Who is too good to pity thee.
Glou. O my follies! then Edgar was abus'd.
Kind gods, forgive me that, and prosper him!
Reg. Go thrust him out at gates, and let him smell
His way to Dover. *Exit one with Gloucester.*
How is 't, my lord? How look you?
Corn. I have receiv'd a hurt; follow me, lady.
Turn out that eyeless villain; throw this slave
Upon the dunghill. Regan, I bleed apace;
Untimely comes this hurt. Give me your arm.
Exit Cornwall, led by Regan.
2. Serv. I'll never care what wickedness I do,
If this man come to good.
3. Serv. If she live long,
And in the end meet the old course of death,
Women will all turn monsters.
2. Serv. Let 's follow the old earl, and get the Bedlam
To lead him where he would: his roguish madness
Allows itself to anything.
3. Serv. Go thou: I 'll fetch some flax and whites of eggs
To apply to his bleeding face. Now, Heaven help him! *Exeunt severally.*

ACT IV. Scene I. *The open country near Gloucester's castle.*

Enter *Edgar.*

Edg. Yet better thus, and known to be contemn'd,
Than, still contemn'd and flatter'd, to be worst.
The lowest and most dejected thing of fortune
Stands still in esperance, lives not in fear.
The lamentable change is from the best;
The worst returns to laughter. Welcome, then,
Thou unsubstantial air that I embrace!
The wretch that thou hast blown unto the worst
Owes nothing to thy blasts.

54. course, attack of dogs in bear-baiting. **60. buoy'd,** heaved. **61. stelled fires**, fixed stars. **63. dearn,** dreadful. **65. All . . . subscrib'd,** all cruel creatures, except you are forgiven. **Act IV, Scene i: 1. contemn'd,** despised. **4. esperance**, hope.

87. quit, requite. **89. overture,** disclosure. **101. old**, natural, familiar. **104. roguish,** vagrant. **Act IV, Scene i: 6. laughter**, a happier condition.

Enter *Gloucester*, led by an *Old Man*.

But who comes here?
My father, poorly led? World, world, O world!
But that thy strange mutations make us hate thee,
Life would not yield to age.

Old Man. O, my good lord, I have been your tenant, and your father's tenant, these four-score years.

Glou. Away, get thee away! Good friend, be gone;
Thy comforts can do me no good at all;
Thee they may hurt.

Old Man. Alack, sir, you cannot see your way.

Glou. I have no way, and therefore want no eyes;
I stumbled when I saw. Full oft 't is seen,
Our means secure us, and our mere defects
Prove our commodities. Ah! dear son Edgar,
The food of thy abused father's wrath!
Might I but live to see thee in my touch,
I 'd say I had eyes again!

Old Man. How now! Who 's there?

Edg. [*Aside*.] O gods! Who is 't can say, "I am at the worst"?
I am worse than e'er I was.

Old Man. 'T is poor mad Tom.

Edg. [*Aside*.] And worse I may be yet; the worst is not
So long as we can say, "This is the worst."

Old Man. Fellow, where goest?

Glou. Is it a beggar-man?

Old Man. Madman and beggar too.

Glou. He has some reason, else he could not beg.
I' th' last night's storm I such a fellow saw,
Which made me think a man a worm. My son
Came then into my mind, and yet my mind
Was then scarce friends with him. I have heard more since.
As flies to wanton boys, are we to the gods,
They kill us for their sport.

Edg. [*Aside*.] How should this be?
Bad is the trade that must play fool to sorrow,
Ang'ring itself and others.—Bless thee, master!

Glou. Is that the naked fellow?

Old Man. Ay, my lord.

Glou. Then, prithee, get thee gone. If, for my sake,
Thou wilt o'ertake us, hence a mile or twain
I' th' way toward Dover, do it for ancient love;
And bring some covering for this naked soul,
Who I 'll entreat to lead me.

Old Man. Alack, sir, he is mad.

Glou. 'T is the time's plague, when madmen lead the blind.
Do as I bid thee, or rather do thy pleasure;
Above the rest, be gone.

Old Man. I 'll bring him the best 'parel that I have,
Come on 't what will. *Exit.*

Glou. Sirrah, naked fellow,—

Edg. Poor Tom 's a-cold. [*Aside*.] I cannot daub it further—

Glou. Come hither, fellow.

Edg. [*Aside*.] And yet I must.—Bless thy sweet eyes, they bleed.

Glou. Know'st thou the way to Dover?

Edg. Both stile and gate, horse-way and foot-path. Poor Tom hath been scared out of his good wits. Bless thee, good man's son, from the foul fiend! Five fiends have been in poor Tom at once; of lust, as Obidicut; Hobbididence, prince of dumbness; Mahu, of stealing; Modo, of murder; Flibbertigibbet, of mopping and mowing, who since possesses chambermaids and waiting-women. So, bless thee, master!

Glou. Here, take this purse, thou whom the heavens' plagues
Have humbled to all strokes: that I am wretched
Makes thee the happier; heavens, deal so still!
Let the superfluous and lust-dieted man,
That slaves your ordinance, that will not see
Because he does not feel, feel your power quickly;
So distribution should undo excess,
And each man have enough. Dost thou know Dover?

Edg. Ay, master.

Glou. There is a cliff, whose high and bending head
Looks fearfully in the confined deep.
Bring me but to the very brim of it,
And I 'll repair the misery thou dost bear
With something rich about me. From that place
I shall no leading need.

Edg. Give me thy arm;
Poor Tom shall lead thee. *Exeunt.*

Scene II. *Before the Duke of Albany's palace.*

Enter *Goneril, Edmund, and Oswald.*

Gon. Welcome, my lord! I marvel our mild husband
Not met us on the way.—Now, where 's your master?

22. **Our . . . us,** our resources make us careless and confident. 23. **commodities,** benefits. 24. **food,** object.

54. **daub,** dissemble. 64. **mopping and mowing,** making grimaces. 71. **slaves your ordinance,** makes your divine dispensation subservient to himself.

Osw. Madam, within; but never man so chang'd.
I told him of the army that was landed;
He smil'd at it: I told him you were coming;
His answer was, "The worse:" of Gloucester's treachery,
And of the loyal service of his son,
When I inform'd him, then he call'd me sot,
And told me I had turn'd the wrong side out.
What most he should dislike seems pleasant to him;
What like, offensive.
Gon. [*To Edmund.*] Then shall you go no further.
It is the cowish terror of his spirit,
That dares not undertake; he 'll not feel wrongs
Which tie him to an answer. Our wishes on the way
May prove effects. Back, Edmund, to my brother;
Hasten his musters and conduct his powers.
I must change arms at home, and give the distaff
Into my husband's hands. This trusty servant
Shall pass between us. Ere long you are like to hear,
If you dare venture in your own behalf,
A mistress's command. Wear this; spare speech;
Decline your head. This kiss, if it durst speak,
Would stretch thy spirits up into the air.
Conceive, and fare thee well.
Edm. Yours in the ranks of death. *Exit.*
Gon. My most dear Gloucester!
O, the difference of man and man!
To thee a woman's services are due;
My Fool usurps my body.
Osw. Madam, here comes my lord.
Exit.

Enter the *Duke of Albany.*

Gon. I have been worth the whistle.
Alb. O Goneril!
You are not worth the dust which the rude wind
Blows in your face. I fear your disposition.
That nature which contemns its origin
Cannot be border'd certain in itself.
She that herself will sliver and disbranch
From her material sap, perforce must wither
And come to deadly use.
Gon. No more; the text is foolish.

Alb. Wisdom and goodness to the vile seem vile;
Filths savour but themselves. What have you done?
Tigers, not daughters, what have you perform'd?
A father, and a gracious aged man,
Whose reverence even the head-lugg'd bear would lick,
Most barbarous, most degenerate! have you madded.
Could my good brother suffer you to do it?
A man, a prince, by him so benefited!
If that the heavens do not their visible spirits
Send quickly down to tame these vile offences,
It will come,
Humanity must perforce prey on itself,
Like monsters of the deep.
Gon. Milk-liver'd man!
That bear'st a cheek for blows, a head for wrongs,
Who hast not in thy brows an eye discerning
Thine honour from thy suffering, that not know'st
Fools do those villains pity who are punish'd
Ere they have done their mischief; where 's thy drum?
France spreads his banners in our noiseless land,
With plumed helm thy state begins to threat;
Whiles thou, a moral fool, sits still, and criest,
"Alack, why does he so?"
Alb. See thyself, devil!
Proper deformity seems not in the fiend
So horrid as in woman.
Gon. O vain fool!
Alb. Thou changed and self-cover'd thing, for shame!
Be-monster not thy feature. Were 't my fitness
To let these hands obey my blood,
They are apt enough to dislocate and tear
Thy flesh and bones; howe'er thou art a fiend,
A woman's shape doth shield thee.
Gon. Marry, your manhood—Mew!

Enter a *Messenger.*

Alb. What news?
Mess. O, my good lord, the Duke of Cornwall 's dead;
Slain by his servant, going to put out
The other eye of Gloucester.
Alb. Gloucester's eyes!
Mess. A servant that he bred, thrill'd with remorse,
Oppos'd against the act, bending his sword

Scene ii: **12. cowish,** cowardly. **14. Our wishes,** i.e., for Albany's death, on our journey here. **17-8. I . . . hands,** I must take the sword from my weak husband's hands and give the distaff to him. **29. worth the whistle,** worth more attention. **33. border'd certain,** confined. **35. material,** essential. **36. deadly,** death-dealing.

43. madded, driven mad. **56. noiseless,** peaceful. **60. Proper,** according with his nature. **62. self-cover'd,** her true self, i.e., her evil nature is covered with a woman's form. To let it show through would "be-monster her feature." **63. my fitness,** fit for me. **64. blood,** passion. **66. howe'er,** although.

To his great master; who, thereat enrag'd,
Flew on him, and amongst them fell'd him dead;
But not without that harmful stroke, which since
Hath pluck'd him after.

Alb. This shows you are above,
You justicers, that these our nether crimes
So speedily can venge! But, O poor Gloucester!
Lost he his other eye?

Mess. Both, both, my lord.
This letter, madam, craves a speedy answer:
'T is from your sister.

Gon. [*Aside.*] One way I like this well;
But being widow, and my Gloucester with her,
May all the building in my fancy pluck
Upon my hateful life: another way,
The news is not so tart. I 'll read, and answer. *Exit.*

Alb. Where was his son when they did take his eyes?

Mess. Come with my lady hither.

Alb. He is not here.

Mess. No, my good lord; I met him back again.

Alb. Knows he the wickedness?

Mess. Ay, my good lord; 't was he inform'd against him;
And quit the house on purpose, that their punishment
Might have the freer course.

Alb. Gloucester, I live
To thank thee for the love thou show'dst the King,
And to revenge thine eyes. Come hither, friend;
Tell me what more thou know'st. *Exeunt.*

Scene III. *The French camp near Dover.*

Enter *Kent* and a *Gentleman.*

Kent. Why the King of France is so suddenly gone back, know you no reason?

Gent. Something he left imperfect in the state, which since his coming forth is thought of; which imports to the kingdom so much fear and danger that his personal return was most required and necessary.

Kent. Who hath he left behind him General?

Gent. The Marshal of France, Monsieur La Far.

Kent. Did your letters pierce the Queen to any demonstration of grief?

Gent. Ay, sir; she took them, read them in my presence;
And now and then an ample tear trill'd down
Her delicate cheek. It seem'd she was a queen
Over her passion, who, most rebel-like,
Sought to be king o'er her.

Kent. O, then it mov'd her.

Gent. Not to a rage; patience and sorrow strove
Who should express her goodliest. You have seen
Sunshine and rain at once: her smiles and tears
Were like a better way; those happy smilets
That play'd on her ripe lip seem'd not to know
What guests were in her eyes, which, parted thence,
As pearls from diamonds dropp'd. In brief,
Sorrow would be a rarity most beloved,
If all could so become it.

Kent. Made she no verbal question?

Gent. Faith, once or twice she heav'd the name of "father"
Pantingly forth, as if it press'd her heart;
Cried, "Sisters! sisters! Shame of ladies! sisters!
Kent! father! sisters! What, i' th' storm? i' th' night?
Let pity not be believ'd!" There she shook
The holy water from her heavenly eyes;
And clamour-moisten'd, then away she started
To deal with grief alone.

Kent. It is the stars,
The stars above us, govern our conditions;
Else one self mate and make could not beget
Such different issues. You spoke not with her since?

Gent. No.

Kent. Was this before the King return'd?

Gent. No, since.

Kent. Well, sir, the poor distressed Lear 's i' th' town;
Who sometime, in his better tune, remembers
What we are come about, and by no means
Will yield to see his daughter.

Gent. Why, good sir?

Kent. A sovereign shame so elbows him. His own unkindness,
That stripp'd her from his benediction, turn'd her
To foreign casualties, gave her dear rights
To his dog-hearted daughters,—these things sting
His mind so venomously, that burning shame
Detains him from Cordelia.

86. pluck, pull down.

Scene iii: 21. like a better way, like sunshine and rain, but better. **25. rarity,** a precious thing. **33. clamour-moisten'd,** wet with weeping. **35. conditions,** characters. **36. mate and make,** husband and wife. **41. better tune,** more reasonable moments. **46. casualties,** hazards.

Gent. Alack, poor gentleman!
Kent. Of Albany's and Cornwall's powers you heard not?
Gent. 'T is so, they are afoot.
Kent. Well, sir, I 'll bring you to our master Lear,
And leave you to attend him. Some dear cause
Will in concealment wrap me up a while;
When I am known aright, you shall not grieve
Lending me this acquaintance. I pray you, go
Along with me. *Exeunt.*

Scene IV. *The same. A tent.*

Enter, with drum and colours, *Cordelia, Doctor,* and Soldiers.

Cor. Alack, 't is he! Why, he was met even now
As mad as the vex'd sea, singing aloud,
Crown'd with rank fumiter and furrow-weeds,
With hardocks, hemlock, nettles, cuckoo-flowers,
Darnel, and all the idle weeds that grow
In our sustaining corn. A century send forth;
Search every acre in the high-grown field,
And bring him to our eye. [*Exit an Officer.*]
What can man's wisdom
In the restoring his bereaved sense?
He that helps him take all my outward worth.
Doct. There is means, madam.
Our foster-nurse of nature is repose,
The which he lacks; that to provoke in him,
Are many simples operative, whose power
Will close the eye of anguish.
Cor. All blest secrets,
All you unpublish'd virtues of the earth,
Spring with my tears! be aidant and remediate
In the good man's distress! Seek, seek for him,
Lest his ungovern'd rage dissolve the life
That wants the means to lead it.

Enter *Messenger.*

Mess. News, madam!
The British powers are marching hitherward.
Cor. 'T is known before; our preparation stands
In expectation of them. O dear father,
It is thy business that I go about;
Therefore great France
My mourning and important tears hath pitied.
No blown ambition doth our arms incite,
But love, dear love, and our ag'd father's right.
Soon may I hear and see him! *Exeunt.*

53. **dear,** private. **Scene iv: 3. fumiter,** an unpleasant herb. **4. hardocks,** probably burdocks. **cuckoo-flowers,** cowslips. **5. Darnel,** a weed. **idle,** useless. **6. century,** sentry. **14. simples,** medicinal herbs. **16. unpublish'd virtues,** secret beneficient qualities. **17. aidant and remediate,** aiding and remedial.

Scene V. *Gloucester's castle.*

Enter *Regan* and *Oswald.*

Reg. But are my brother's powers set forth?
Osw. Ay, madam.
Reg. Himself in person there?
Osw. Madam, with much ado.
Your sister is the better soldier.
Reg. Lord Edmund spake not with your lord at home?
Osw. No, madam.
Reg. What might import my sister's letter to him?
Osw. I know not, lady.
Reg. Faith, he is posted hence on serious matter.
It was great ignorance, Gloucester's eyes being out,
To let him live; where he arrives he moves
All hearts against us. Edmund, I think, is gone,
In pity of his misery, to dispatch
His nighted life; moreover, to descry
The strength o' the enemy.
Osw. I must needs after him, madam, with my letter.
Reg. Our troops set forth to-morrow, stay with us;
The ways are dangerous.
Osw. I may not, madam:
My lady charg'd my duty in this business.
Reg. Why should she write to Edmund? Might not you
Transport her purposes by word? Belike
Some thing—I know not what. I 'll love thee much,
Let me unseal the letter.
Osw. Madam, I had rather—
Reg. I know your lady does not love her husband;
I am sure of that; and at her late being here
She gave strange eliads and most speaking looks
To noble Edmund. I know you are of her bosom.
Osw. I, madam?
Reg. I speak in understanding; y' are, I know 't.
Therefore I do advise you, take this note:
My lord is dead; Edmund and I have talk'd;
And more convenient is he for my hand
Than for your lady's. You may gather more.
If you do find him, pray you, give him this;
And when your mistress hears thus much from you,

Scene v: 13. nighted, darkened. **25. eliads,** amorous glances.

I pray, desire her call her wisdom to her:
So, fare you well.
If you do chance to hear of that blind traitor,
Preferment falls on him that cuts him off.
Osw. Would I could meet him, madam! I would show
What party I do follow.
Reg. Fare thee well.
Exeunt.

Scene VI. *The country near Dover.*

Enter *Gloucester,* and *Edgar* dressed like a peasant.

Glou. When shall we come to th' top of that same hill?
Edg. You do climb up it now; look, how we labour.
Glou. Methinks the ground is even.
Edg. Horrible steep.
Hark, do you hear the sea?
Glou. No, truly.
Edg. Why, then, your other senses grow imperfect
By your eyes' anguish.
Glou. So may it be, indeed.
Methinks thy voice is alter'd, and thou speak'st
In better phrase and matter than thou didst.
Edg. You 're much deceiv'd. In nothing am I chang'd
But in my garments.
Glou. Methinks you 're better spoken.
Edg. Come on, sir, here 's the place; stand still. How fearful
And dizzy 't is, to cast one's eyes so low!
The crows and choughs that wing the midway air
Show scarce so gross as beetles. Half way down
Hangs one that gathers sampire, dreadful trade!
Methinks he seems no bigger than his head.
The fishermen, that walk upon the beach,
Appear like mice; and yond tall anchoring bark,
Diminish'd to her cock, her cock, a buoy
Almost too small for sight. The murmuring surge,
That on th' unnumber'd idle pebbles chafes,
Cannot be heard so high. I 'll look no more,
Lest my brain turn, and the deficient sight
Topple down headlong.
Glou. Set me where you stand.
Edg. Give me your hand; you are now within a foot
Of th' extreme verge. For all beneath the moon
Would I not leap upright.
Glou. Let go my hand.
Here, friend, 's another purse; in it a jewel
Well worth a poor man's taking. Fairies and gods
Prosper it with thee! Go thou further off;
Bid me farewell, and let me hear thee going.
Edg. Now fare you well, good sir.
Glou. With all my heart.
Edg. Why I do trifle thus with his despair
Is done to cure it.
Glou. [*Kneeling.*] O you mighty gods!
This world I do renounce, and in your sights
Shake patiently my great affliction off.
If I could bear it longer, and not fall
To quarrel with your great opposeless wills,
My snuff and loathed part of nature should
Burn itself out. If Edgar live, O bless him!
Now, fellow, fare thee well.
Edg. Gone, sir; farewell!
—And yet I know not how conceit may rob
The treasury of life, when life itself
Yields to the theft. [*Gloucester throws himself forward and falls.*] Had he been where he thought,
By this had thought been past. Alive or dead?—
Ho, you sir! friend! Hear you, sir! speak!—
Thus might he pass indeed; yet he revives.—
What are you, sir?
Glou. Away, and let me die.
Edg. Hadst thou been aught but gossamer, feathers, air,
So many fathom down precipitating,
Thou 'dst shiver'd like an egg: but thou dost breathe;
Hast heavy substance; bleed'st not; speak'st; art sound.
Ten masts at each make not the altitude
Which thou hast perpendicularly fell.
Thy life 's a miracle. Speak yet again.
Glou. But have I fall'n, or no?
Edg. From the dread summit of this chalky bourn.
Look up a-height; the shrill-gorg'd lark so far
Cannot be seen or heard. Do but look up.
Glou. Alack, I have no eyes.
Is wretchedness depriv'd that benefit,
To end itself by death? 'T was yet some comfort,
When misery could beguile the tyrant's rage,
And frustrate his proud will.
Edg. Give me your arm.

Scene vi: 13. choughs, jackdaws. **15. sampire,** sea fennel, used in pickles. **19. cock,** cock-boat.

38. opposeless, irresistible. **39. snuff,** burnt out age. **42. conceit,** imagination. **51. shiver'd,** shattered. **53. at each,** end to end. **57. bourn,** boundary. **58. shrill-gorg'd,** shrill-voiced.

Up: so; How is 't? Feel you your legs? You stand.
Glou. Too well, too well.
Edg. This is above all strangeness.
Upon the crown o' th' cliff, what thing was that
Which parted from you?
Glou. A poor unfortunate beggar.
Edg. As I stood here below, methought his eyes
Were two full moons; he had a thousand noses,
Horns whelk'd and waved like the enridged sea.
It was some fiend; therefore, thou happy father,
Think that the clearest gods, who make them honours
Of men's impossibilities, have preserv'd thee.
Glou. I do remember now. Henceforth I 'll bear
Affliction till it do cry out itself,
"Enough, enough," and die. That thing you speak of,
I took it for a man; often would it say,
"The fiend, the fiend:" He led me to that place.
Edg. Bear free and patient thoughts.

Enter *Lear* mad.

But who comes here?
The safer sense will ne'er accommodate
His master thus.

Lear. No, they cannot touch me for coining; I am the King himself.

Edg. O thou side-piercing sight!

Lear. Nature 's above art in that respect. There 's your press-money. That fellow handles his bow like a crow-keeper; draw me a clothier's yard. Look, look, a mouse! Peace, peace; this piece of toasted cheese will do 't. There 's my gauntlet; I 'll prove it on a giant. Bring up the brown bills. O, well flown, bird! I' th' clout, i' th' clout! Hewgh! Give the word.

Edg. Sweet marjoram.

Lear. Pass.

Glou. I know that voice.

Lear. Ha! Goneril, with a white beard! They flattered me like a dog, and told me I had white hairs in my beard ere the black ones were there. To say "ay" and "no" to everything I said! "Ay" and "no" too was no good divinity. When the rain came to wet me once, and the wind to make me chatter; when the thunder would not peace at my bidding; there I found 'em, there I smelt 'em out. Go to, they are not men o' their words: they told me I was everything; 't is a lie, I am not ague-proof.

Glou. The trick of that voice I do well remember.
Is 't not the King?
Lear. Ay, every inch a king!
When I do stare, see how the subject quakes.
I pardon that man's life. What was thy cause?
Adultery?
Thou shalt not die. Die for adultery! No:
The wren goes to 't, and the small gilded fly
Does lecher in my sight.
Let copulation thrive; for Gloucester's bastard son
Was kinder to his father than my daughters
Got 'tween the lawful sheets.
To 't, luxury, pell-mell! for I lack soldiers.
Behold yond simp'ring dame,
Whose face between her forks presageth snow,
That minces virtue, and does shake the head
To hear of pleasure's name,—
The fitchew, nor the soiled horse, goes to 't
With a more riotous appetite.
Down from the waist they are Centaurs,
Though women all above;
But to the girdle do the gods inherit,
Beneath is all the fiends';
There 's hell, there 's darkness, there 's the sulphurous pit,
Burning, scalding, stench, consumption; fie, fie, fie! pah, pah! Give me an ounce of civet; good apothecary, to sweeten my imagination. There 's money for thee.

Glou. O, let me kiss that hand!

Lear. Let me wipe it first; it smells of mortality.

Glou. O ruin'd piece of nature! This great world
Shall so wear out to nought. Dost thou know me?

Lear. I remember thine eyes well enough. Dost thou squiny at me? No, do thy worst, blind Cupid; I 'll not love. Read thou this challenge; mark but the penning of it.

Glou. Were all thy letters suns, I could not see one.
Edg. [*Aside.*] I would not take this from report. It is;
And my heart breaks at it.
Lear. Read.
Glou. What, with the case of eyes?

Lear. O, ho, are you there with me? No eyes in your head, nor no money in your purse? Your eyes are in a heavy case, your

71. **whelk'd**, twisted. 73. **clearest**, purest. 81. **safer**, saner. **accommodate**, equip. 87. **press-money**, money given to men "pressed" into military service. 89. **clothier's yard**, an arrow a cloth-yard long. 92. **bills**, halberds. 93. **clout**, white center of a target. **word**, password.

119. **luxury**, lust. 121. **forks**, legs. **snow**, virtue. 122. **minces**, affects. 124. **fitchew**, polecat. **soiled**, high fed. 140. **squiny**, squint. 147. **case**, sockets.

purse in a light; yet you see how this world goes.

Glou. I see it feelingly.

Lear. What, art mad? A man may see how this world goes with no eyes. Look with thine ears; see how yond justice rails upon yond simple thief. Hark, in thine ear: change places, and, handy-dandy, which is the justice, which is the thief? Thou hast seen a farmer's dog bark at a beggar?

Glou. Ay, sir.

Lear. And the creature run from the cur?
There thou mightst behold the great image of authority: a dog's obeyed in office.
Thou rascal beadle, hold thy bloody hand!
Why dost thou lash that whore? Strip thine own back;
Thou hotly lusts to use her in that kind
For which thou whip'st her. The usurer hangs the cozener.
Through tatter'd clothes small vices do appear;
Robes and furr'd gowns hides all. Plate sins with gold,
And the strong lance of justice hurtless breaks;
Arm it in rags, a pigmy's straw does pierce it.
None does offend, none, I say, none; I 'll able 'em.
Take that of me, my friend, who have the power
To seal th' accuser's lips. Get thee glass eyes,
And, like a scurvy politician, seem
To see the things thou dost not. Now, now, now, now.
Pull off my boots; harder, harder: so.

Edg. O, matter and impertinency mix'd;
Reason in madness!

Lear. If thou wilt weep my fortune, take my eyes.
I know thee well enough; thy name is Gloucester.
Thou must be patient; we came crying hither.
Thou know'st, the first time that we smell the air,
We wawl and cry. I will preach to thee; mark.

Glou. Alack, alack the day!

Lear. When we are born, we cry that we are come
To this great stage of fools.—This a good block.
It were a delicate stratagem, to shoe
A troop of horse with felt. I 'll put 't in proof;
And when I have stol'n upon these son-in-laws,
Then, kill, kill, kill, kill, kill, kill!

Enter a *Gentleman* with Attendants.

Gent. O, here he is! Lay hand upon him. Sir,
Your most dear daughter—

Lear. No rescue? What, a prisoner? I am even
The natural fool of fortune. Use me well;
You shall have ransom. Let me have a surgeon;
I am cut to th' brains.

Gent. You shall have anything.

Lear. No seconds? All myself?
Why, this would make a man a man of salt,
To use his eyes for garden water-pots,
Ay, and laying autumn's dust.

Gent. Good sir,—

Lear. I will die bravely, like a smug bridegroom. What!
I will be jovial. Come, come; I am a king,
My masters, know you that?

Gent. You are a royal one, and we obey you.

Lear. Then there 's life in 't. Come, an you get it, you shall get it by running. Sa, sa, sa, sa. *Exit running; attendants follow.*

Gent. A sight most pitiful in the meanest wretch,
Past speaking of in a king! Thou hast one daughter
Who redeems Nature from the general curse
Which twain have brought her to.

Edg. Hail, gentle sir.

Gent. Sir, speed you: what 's your will?

Edg. Do you hear aught, sir, of a battle toward?

Gent. Most sure and vulgar; every one hears that,
That can distinguish sound.

Edg. But, by your favour,
How near 's the other army?

Gent. Near and on speedy foot; the main descry
Stands on the hourly thought.

Edg. I thank you, sir; that 's all.

Gent. Though that the Queen on special cause is here,
Her army is mov'd on. *Exit.*

Edg. I thank you, sir.

Glou. You ever-gentle gods, take my breath from me;
Let not my worser spirit tempt me again
To die before you please!

Edg. Well pray you, father.

Glou. Now, good sir, what are you?

Edg. A most poor man, made tame to fortune's blows;

167. cozener, petty cheater. **172. able,** vouch for. **178. impertinency,** nonsense. **187. block,** hat.

199. salt, salt tears. **214. vulgar,** commonly known. **217-8. the main . . . thought,** discovery of the main body is expected every hour.

Who, by the art of known and feeling sorrows,
Am pregnant to good pity. Give me your hand,
I 'll lead you to some biding.
Glou. Hearty thanks;
The bounty and the benison of Heaven
To boot, and boot!

Enter *Oswald*.

Osw. A proclaim'd prize! Most happy!
That eyeless head of thine was first fram'd flesh
To raise my fortunes. Thou old unhappy traitor,
Briefly thyself remember; the sword is out
That must destroy thee.
Glou. Now let thy friendly hand
Put strength enough to 't. *Edgar interposes.*
Osw. Wherefore, bold peasant,
Dar'st thou support a publish'd traitor? Hence;
Lest that th' infection of his fortune take
Like hold on thee. Let go his arm.
Edg. 'Chill not let go, zir, without vurther 'casion.
Osw. Let go, slave, or thou diest!
Edg. Good gentleman, go your gait, and let poor volk pass. An 'chud ha' bin zwaggered out of my life, 't would not ha' bin zo long as 't is by a vortnight. Nay, come not near th' old man; keep out, 'che vor ye, or Ise try whether your costard or my ballow be the harder. 'Chill be plain with you.
Osw. Out, dunghill!
Edg. 'Chill pick your teeth, zir. Come, no matter vor your foins.
They fight, and Edgar knocks him down.
Osw. Slave, thou hast slain me. Villain, take my purse.
If ever thou wilt thrive, bury my body;
And give the letters which thou find'st about me
To Edmund Earl of Gloucester; seek him out
Upon the English party. O, untimely death!
Death! *Dies.*
Edg. I know thee well; a serviceable villain,
As duteous to the vices of thy mistress
As badness would desire.
Glou. What, is he dead?
Edg. Sit you down, father; rest you.
Let 's see these pockets; the letters that he speaks of
May be my friends. He 's dead; I am only sorry
He had no other death's-man. Let us see.
Leave, gentle wax; and, manners, blame us not.
To know our enemies' minds, we 'd rip their hearts;
Their papers, is more lawful.
[*Reads the letter.*]

"Let our reciprocal vows be remembered. You have many opportunities to cut him off; if your will want not, time and place will be fruitfully offered. There is nothing done, if he return the conqueror; then am I the prisoner, and his bed my jail; from the loathed warmth whereof deliver me, and supply the place for your labour.
"Your—wife, so I would say—
Affectionate servant,
GONERIL."

O indistinguish'd space of woman's will!
A plot upon her virtuous husband's life;
And the exchange my brother! Here, in the sands,
Thee I 'll rake up, the post unsanctified
Of murderous lechers; and in the mature time
With this ungracious paper strike the sight
Of the death-practis'd duke. For him 't is well
That of thy death and business I can tell.
Glou. The King is mad; how stiff is my vile sense
That I stand up and have ingenious feeling
Of my huge sorrows! Better I were distract;
So should my thoughts be sever'd from my griefs, *Drum afar off.*
And woes by wrong imaginations lose
The knowledge of themselves.
Edg. Give me your hand.
Far off, methinks, I hear the beaten drum.
Come, father, I 'll bestow you with a friend.
Exeunt.

Scene VII. *A tent in the French camp.*

Enter *Cordelia, Kent,* and *Doctor,* and Gentlewoman.

Cor. O thou good Kent, how shall I live and work
To match thy goodness? My life will be too short,
And every measure fail me.
Kent. To be acknowledg'd, madam, is o'erpaid.
All my reports go with the modest truth;
Nor more nor clipp'd, but so.
Cor. Be better suited;
These weeds are memories of those worser hours.
I prithee, put them off.

226. **art**, experience. 227. **pregnant**, disposed. 228. **biding**, abode. 233. **thyself remember**, say thy prayers. 239ff. It was a convention to put the southern dialect into the mouths of rustics. Edgar here poses as a peasant. 240. **'Chill**, I will. 243. **An 'chud**, if I could. 246. **'che vor ye**, I warn you. 247. **costard**, head. **ballow**, cudgel. 251. **foins**, thrusts.

276. **servant**, lover. 278. **indistinguish'd space**, undefinable scope. 281. **rake up**, cover over, bury. 287. **ingenious**, keen, sensitive. **Scene vii: 7. weeds**, garments.

Kent. Pardon, dear madam;
Yet to be known shortens my made intent.
My boon I make it, that you know me not
Till time and I think meet.

Cor. Then be 't so, my good lord. [*To the Doctor.*] How does the King?

Doct. Madam, sleeps still.

Cor. O you kind gods,
Cure this great breach in his abused nature!
Th' untun'd and jarring senses, O, wind up
Of this child-changed father!

Doct. So please your Majesty
That we may wake the King? He hath slept long.

Cor. Be govern'd by your knowledge, and proceed
I' th' sway of your own will.

Enter *Lear* in a chair carried by Servants.

Is he array'd?

Doct. Ay, madam; in the heaviness of sleep
We put fresh garments on him.

Gent. Good madam, be by, when we do awake him;
I doubt not of his temperance. *Music.*

Cor. Very well.

Doct. Please you, draw near.—Louder the music there!

Cor. O my dear father! Restoration hang
Thy medicine on my lips; and let this kiss
Repair those violent harms that my two sisters
Have in thy reverence made!

Kent. Kind and dear princess!

Cor. Had you not been their father, these white flakes
Did challenge pity of them. Was this a face
To be oppos'd against the warring winds?
To stand against the deep dread-bolted thunder?
In the most terrible and nimble stroke
Of quick, cross lightning? to watch—poor perdu!—
With this thin helm? Mine enemy's dog,
Though he had bit me, should have stood that night
Against my fire; and wast thou fain, poor father,
To hovel thee with swine and rogues forlorn
In short and musty straw? Alack, alack!
'T is wonder that thy life and wits at once
Had not concluded all. He wakes; speak to him.

Doct. Madam, do you; 't is fittest.

Cor. How does my royal lord? How fares your Majesty?

Lear. You do me wrong to take me out o' th' grave.
Thou art a soul in bliss; but I am bound
Upon a wheel of fire, that mine own tears
Do scald like molten lead.

Cor. Sir, do you know me?

Lear. You are a spirit, I know; when did you die?

Cor. Still, still, far wide!

Doct. He 's scarce awake; let him alone a while.

Lear. Where have I been? Where am I? Fair daylight?
I am mightily abus'd. I should even die with pity,
To see another thus. I know not what to say.
I will not swear these are my hands. Let 's see;
I feel this pin prick. Would I were assur'd
Of my condition!

Cor. O, look upon me, sir,
And hold your hand in benediction o'er me.
No, sir, you must not kneel.

Lear. Pray, do not mock me.
I am a very foolish fond old man.
Fourscore and upward, not an hour more nor less;
And, to deal plainly,
I fear I am not in my perfect mind.
Methinks I should know you, and know this man;
Yet I am doubtful; for I am mainly ignorant
What place this is, and all the skill I have
Remembers not these garments; nor I know not
Where I did lodge last night. Do not laugh at me;
For, as I am a man, I think this lady
To be my child Cordelia.

Cor. And so I am, I am.

Lear. Be your tears wet? Yes, faith. I pray, weep not.
If you have poison for me, I will drink it.
I know you do not love me; for your sisters
Have, as I do remember, done me wrong:
You have some cause, they have not.

Cor. No cause, no cause.

Lear. Am I in France?

Kent. In your own kingdom, sir.

Lear. Do not abuse me.

Doct. Be comforted, good madam; the great rage,
You see, is kill'd in him: and yet it is danger
To make him even o'er the time he has lost.
Desire him to go in; trouble him no more
Till further settling.

Cor. Will 't please your Highness walk?

9. **made intent**, prearranged plan. 35. **perdu**, soldier put in dangerous position. 36. **helm**, hair. 38. **fain**, glad. 42. **all**, altogether.

Lear. You must bear with me.
Pray you now, forget and forgive; I am old and foolish.

Exeunt all but Kent and Gentleman.

Gent. Holds it true, sir, that the Duke of Cornwall was so slain?

Kent. Most certain, sir.

Gent. Who is conductor of his people?

Kent. As 't is said, the bastard son of Gloucester.

Gent. They say Edgar, his banished son, is with the Earl of Kent in Germany.

Kent. Report is changeable. 'T is time to look about; the powers of the kingdom approach apace.

Gent. The arbitrement is like to be bloody. Fare you well, sir. *Exit.*

Kent. My point and period will be throughly wrought,
Or well or ill, as this day's battle 's fought.
Exit.

ACT V. Scene I. *The British camp, near Dover.*

Enter, with drum and colours, *Edmund, Regan,* Gentlemen, and Soldiers.

Edm. Know of the Duke if his last purpose hold,
Or whether since he is advis'd by aught
To change the course. He 's full of alteration
And self-reproving; bring his constant pleasure. *To a Gentleman, who goes out.*

Reg. Our sister's man is certainly miscarried.

Edm. 'T is to be doubted, madam.

Reg. Now, sweet lord,
You know the goodness I intend upon you.
Tell me—but truly—but then speak the truth,
Do you not love my sister?

Edm. In honour'd love.

Reg. But have you never found my brother's way
To the forfended place?

Edm. That thought abuses you.

Reg. I am doubtful that you have been conjunct
And bosom'd with her,—as far as we call hers.

Edm. No, by mine honour, madam.

Reg. I never shall endure her. Dear my lord,
Be not familiar with her.

Edm. Fear me not.
She and the Duke her husband!

Enter, with drum and colours, *Albany, Goneril,* and Soldiers.

Gon. [*Aside.*] I had rather lose the battle than that sister
Should loosen him and me.

Alb. Our very loving sister, well be-met.
Sir, this I heard: the King is come to his daughter,
With others whom the rigour of our state
Forc'd to cry out. Where I could not be honest,
I never yet was valiant. For this business,
It toucheth us, as France invades our land,
Not bolds the King, with others, whom, I fear,
Most just and heavy causes make oppose.

Edm. Sir, you speak nobly.

Reg. Why is this reason'd?

Gon. Combine together 'gainst the enemy;
For these domestic and particular broils
Are not the question here.

Alb. Let 's then determine
With the ancient of war on our proceeding.

Edm. I shall attend you presently at your tent.

Reg. Sister, you 'll go with us?

Gon. No.

Reg. 'T is most convenient; pray you, go with us.

Gon. [*Aside.*] O, ho, I know the riddle. I will go. *Exeunt both the armies.*

As they are going out, enter *Edgar* disguised.

Edg. If e'er your Grace had speech with man so poor,
Hear me one word. *Albany remains.*

Alb. I 'll overtake you.—Speak.

Edg. Before you fight the battle, ope this letter.
If you have victory, let the trumpet sound
For him that brought it. Wretched though I seem,
I can produce a champion that will prove
What is avouched there. If you miscarry,
Your business of the world hath so an end,
And machination ceases. Fortune love you!

Alb. Stay till I have read the letter.

Edg. I was forbid it.

Act V, Scene i: 4. constant pleasure, fixed resolve. **6. doubted,** feared. **11. forfended,** forbidden. **13.** In her confidence (suggesting also her embrace) to the utmost extent.

22. rigour of our state, our severe rule. **26.** "Not because France encourages the King and others." **30. particular,** private. **32. ancient of war,** veteran soldiers. **36. convenient,** befitting. **46. machination,** intrigue.

When time shall serve, let but the herald cry,
And I 'll appear again. *Exit.*
Alb. Why, fare thee well; I will o'erlook thy paper.

Re-enter *Edmund.*

Edm. The enemy 's in view; draw up your powers.
Here is the guess of their true strength and forces
By diligent discovery; but your haste
Is now urg'd on you.
Alb. We will greet the time. *Exit.*
Edm. To both these sisters have I sworn my love;
Each jealous of the other, as the stung
Are of the adder. Which of them shall I take?
Both? one? or neither? Neither can be enjoy'd,
If both remain alive. To take the widow
Exasperates, makes mad her sister Goneril;
And hardly shall I carry out my side,
Her husband being alive. Now then we 'll use
His countenance for the battle; which being done,
Let her that would be rid of him devise
His speedy taking off. As for the mercy
Which he intends to Lear and to Cordelia,
The battle done, and they within our power,
Shall never see his pardon; for my state
Stands on me to defend, not to debate. *Exit.*

Scene II. *A field between the two camps.*

Alarum within. Enter, with drum and colours, *Lear, Cordelia,* and Soldiers, over the stage; and exeunt.

Enter *Edgar* and *Gloucester.*

Edg. Here, father, take the shadow of this tree
For your good host; pray that the right may thrive.
If ever I return to you again,
I 'll bring you comfort.
Glou. Grace go with you, sir! *Exit Edgar.*

Alarum and retreat within. Re-enter *Edgar.*

Edg. Away, old man; give me thy hand; away!
King Lear hath lost, he and his daughter ta'en.
Give me thy hand; come on.
Glou. No further, sir; a man may rot even here.
Edg. What, in ill thoughts again? Men must endure
Their going hence, even as their coming hither;
Ripeness is all. Come on.
Glou. And that 's true too. *Exeunt.*

Scene III. *The British camp near Dover.*

Enter in conquest, with drum and colours, *Edmund; Lear* and *Cordelia* as prisoners: *Captain,* Soldiers, etc.

Edm. Some officers take them away. Good guard,
Until their greater pleasures first be known
That are to censure them.
Cor. We are not the first
Who, with best meaning, have incurr'd the worst.
For thee, oppressed king, am I cast down;
Myself could else out-frown false Fortune's frown.
Shall we not see these daughters and these sisters?
Lear. No, no, no, no! Come, let 's away to prison;
We two alone will sing like birds i' th' cage.
When thou dost ask me blessing, I 'll kneel down
And ask of thee forgiveness. So we 'll live,
And pray, and sing, and tell old tales, and laugh
At gilded butterflies, and hear poor rogues
Talk of court news; and we 'll talk with them too,
Who loses and who wins; who 's in, who 's out;
And take upon 's the mystery of things
As if we were gods' spies; and we 'll wear out,
In a wall'd prison, packs and sects of great ones,
That ebb and flow by the moon.
Edm. Take them away.
Lear. Upon such sacrifices, my Cordelia,
The gods themselves throw incense. Have I caught thee?
He that parts us shall bring a brand from heaven,
And fire us hence like foxes. Wipe thine eyes;
The good-years shall devour them, flesh and fell,

53. **discovery,** scouting. 54. **greet the time,** meet the situation. 61. **carry out my side,** win my game. 69. **Stands on,** requires.

Scene ii: 11. Ripeness, readiness. **Scene iii: 2. their greater pleasures,** the pleasure of the greater persons. **17. gods',** the pagan gods. **23. fire . . . foxes,** foxes used to be driven from their holes by fire and smoke. **24. good-years,** a word of uncertain meaning, probably equivalent to the devil; see note on 2 *K. Henry IV,* II, iv, 64. **fell,** skin.

Ere they shall make us weep. We 'll see 'em starve first.
Come. *Exeunt Lear and Cordelia, guarded.*

Edm. Come hither, captain; hark.
Take thou this note [*giving a paper*]; go follow them to prison.
One step I have advanc'd thee; if thou dost
As this instructs thee, thou dost make thy way
To noble fortunes. Know thou this, that men
Are as the time is; to be tender-minded
Does not become a sword. Thy great employment
Will not bear question; either say thou 'lt do 't,
Or thrive by other means.

Capt. I 'll do 't, my lord.

Edm. About it; and write happy when thou hast done.
Mark, I say, instantly; and carry it so
As I have set it down.

Capt. I cannot draw a cart, nor eat dried oats;
If it be man's work, I 'll do 't. *Exit.*

Flourish. Enter *Albany, Goneril, Regan,* another *Captain,* and Soldiers.

Alb. Sir, you have show'd to-day your valiant strain,
And fortune led you well. You have the captives
Who were the opposites of this day's strife;
I do require them of you, so to use them
As we shall find their merits and our safety
May equally determine.

Edm. Sir, I thought it fit
To send the old and miserable king
To some retention and appointed guard;
Whose age has charms in it, whose title more,
To pluck the common bosom on his side,
And turn our impress'd lances in our eyes
Which do command them. With him I sent the Queen,
My reason all the same; and they are ready
To-morrow, or at further space, t' appear
Where you shall hold your session. At this time
We sweat and bleed: the friend hath lost his friend;
And the best quarrels, in the heat, are curs'd
By those that feel their sharpness:
The question of Cordelia and her father
Requires a fitter place.

Alb. Sir, by your patience,
I hold you but a subject of this war,
Not as a brother.

Reg. That 's as we list to grace him.
Methinks our pleasure might have been demanded,
Ere you had spoke so far. He led our powers,
Bore the commission of my place and person;
The which immediacy may well stand up,
And call itself your brother.

Gon. Not so hot.
In his own grace he doth exalt himself,
More than in your addition.

Reg. In my rights,
By me invested, he compeers the best.

Alb. That were the most, if he should husband you.

Reg. Jesters do oft prove prophets.

Gon. Holla, holla!
That eye that told you so look'd but a-squint.

Reg. Lady, I am not well; else I should answer
From a full-flowing stomach. General,
Take thou my soldiers, prisoners, patrimony;
Dispose of them, of me; the walls is thine.
Witness the world, that I create thee here
My lord and master.

Gon. Mean you to enjoy him then?

Alb. The let-alone lies not in your good will.

Edm. Nor in thine, lord.

Alb. Half-blooded fellow, yes.

Reg. [*To Edmund.*] Let the drum strike, and prove my title thine.

Alb. Stay yet; hear reason. Edmund, I arrest thee
On capital treason; and, in thine attaint,
This gilded serpent. [*Pointing to Gon.*] For your claim, fair sister,
I bar it in the interest of my wife.
'T is she is sub-contracted to this lord,
And I, her husband, contradict your bans.
If you will marry, make your loves to me,
My lady is bespoke.

Gon. An interlude!

Alb. Thou art armed, Gloucester; let the trumpet sound.
If none appear to prove upon thy person
Thy heinous, manifest, and many treasons,
There is my pledge *Throwing down a glove.*
I 'll prove it on thy heart,
Ere I taste bread, thou art in nothing less
Than I have here proclaim'd thee.

Reg. Sick, O sick!

Gon. [*Aside.*] If not, I 'll ne'er trust medicine.

Edm. There 's my exchange [*throwing down a glove*]. What in the world he is

35. **write happy**, call yourself fortunate. 47. **retention**, safe-keeping. 49. **common bosom**, affection of the people. 50. **impress'd**, pressed into service.

63. **spoke so far**, said so much. 65. **immediacy**, nearness in command. 68. **your addition**, the title you give him. 69. **compeers**, equals. 74. **stomach**, passion of anger. 76. **walls . . . thine**, all is yours, with reference perhaps to Regan's Dover castle. 80. **Half-blooded**, Edmund was of base birth on the mother's side. 83. **attaint**, impeachment. 89. **interlude**, comedy. 96. **medicine**, poison.

That names me traitor, villain-like he lies.
Call by the trumpet;—he that dares approach,
On him, on you, who not? I will maintain
My truth and honour firmly.

Alb. A herald, ho!

Edm. A herald, ho, a herald!

Alb. Trust to thy single virtue; for thy soldiers,
All levied in my name, have in my name
Took their discharge.

Reg. My sickness grows upon me.

Alb. She is not well; convey her to my tent. *Exit Regan, led.*

Enter a *Herald.*

Come hither, herald,—Let the trumpet sound—
And read out this.

Capt. Sound, trumpet! *A trumpet sounds.*

Her. [*Reads.*]
"If any man of quality or degree within the lists of the army will maintain upon Edmund, supposed Earl of Gloucester, that he is a manifold traitor, let him appear by the third sound of the trumpet. He is bold in his defence."

Edm. Sound! *First trumpet.*

Her. Again! *Second trumpet.*

Her. Again! *Third trumpet.*

Trumpet answers within.

Enter *Edgar,* at the third sound, armed, with a trumpet before him.

Alb. Ask him his purposes, why he appears
Upon this call o' th' trumpet.

Her. What are you?
Your name, your quality? and why you answer
This present summons?

Edg. Know, my name is lost,
By treason's tooth bare-gnawn and canker-bit;
Yet am I noble as the adversary
I come to cope.

Alb. Which is that adversary?

Edg. What 's he that speaks for Edmund Earl of Gloucester?

Edm. Himself; what say'st thou to him?

Edg. Draw thy sword,
That, if my speech offend a noble heart,
Thy arm may do thee justice; here is mine.
Behold, it is the privilege of mine honours,
My oath, and my profession. I protest,
Maugre thy strength, youth, place, and eminence,
Despite thy victor-sword and fire-new fortune,
Thy valour, and thy heart, thou art a traitor;
False to thy gods, thy brother, and thy father;
Conspirant 'gainst this high illustrious prince;
And from th' extremest upward of thy head
To the descent and dust beneath thy foot,
A most toad-spotted traitor. Say thou "No,"
This sword, this arm, and my best spirits are bent
To prove upon thy heart, whereto I speak,
Thou liest.

Edm. In wisdom I should ask thy name;
But, since thy outside looks so fair and warlike,
And that thy tongue some say of breeding breathes,
What safe and nicely I might well delay,
By rule of knighthood, I disdain and spurn.
Back do I toss these treasons to thy head,
With the hell-hated lie o'erwhelm thy heart,
Which, for they yet glance by and scarcely bruise,
This sword of mine shall give them instant way,
Where they shall rest for ever. Trumpets, speak!

Alarums. They fight. Edmund falls.

Alb. Save him, save him!

Gon. This is mere practice, Gloucester.
By the law of arms thou wast not bound to answer
An unknown opposite: thou art not vanquish'd,
But cozen'd and beguil'd.

Alb. Shut your mouth, dame,
Or with this paper shall I stop it. Hold, sir.—
Thou worse than any name, read thine own evil.
No tearing, lady; I perceive you know it.

Gon. Say, if I do, the laws are mine, not thine,
Who can arraign me for 't?

Alb. Most monstrous! oh!—
Know'st thou this paper?

Gon. Ask me not what I know. *Exit.*

Alb. Go after her; she 's desperate; govern her.

Edm. What you have charg'd me with, that have I done;
And more, much more; the time will bring it out.
'T is past, and so am I. But what art thou
That hast this fortune on me? If thou 'rt noble,
I do forgive thee.

Edg. Let 's exchange charity.
I am no less in blood than thou art, Edmund;
If more, the more thou 'st wrong'd me.
My name is Edgar, and thy father's son.

103. virtue, valor. **112. supposed,** pretended. **122. canker-bit,** worm-eaten. **131. Maugre,** in spite of. **135. Conspirant,** conspirator.

137. descent, lowest part. **143. say,** assay, proof. **144. safe and nicely,** safely by being nice, i.e., punctilious as to the rank of the challenger. **151. practice,** foul play. **155. this paper,** the love-letter which Edgar took from the dead Oswald. **161. govern,** restrain.

The gods are just, and of our pleasant vices
Make instruments to plague us.
The dark and vicious place where thee he got
Cost him his eyes.
Edm. Thou 'st spoken right, 't is true.
The wheel is come full circle; I am here.
Alb. Methought thy very gait did prophesy
A royal nobleness. I must embrace thee.
Let sorrow split my heart, if ever I
Did hate thee or thy father!
Edg. Worthy prince, I know 't.
Alb. Where have you hid yourself?
How have you known the miseries of your father?
Edg. By nursing them, my lord. List a brief tale;
And when 't is told, oh, that my heart would burst!
The bloody proclamation to escape,
That follow'd me so near,—oh, our lives' sweetness!
That we the pain of death would hourly die
Rather than die at once!—taught me to shift
Into a madman's rags, t' assume a semblance
That very dogs disdain'd; and in this habit
Met I my father with his bleeding rings,
Their precious stones new lost; became his guide,
Led him, begg'd for him, sav'd him from despair;
Never,—O fault!—reveal'd myself unto him,
Until some half-hour past, when I was arm'd.
Not sure, though hoping, of this good success,
I ask'd his blessing, and from first to last
Told him my pilgrimage; but his flaw'd heart,
Alack, too weak the conflict to support!
'Twixt two extremes of passion, joy and grief,
Burst smilingly.
Edm. This speech of yours hath mov'd me,
And shall perchance do good. But speak you on;
You look as you had something more to say.
Alb. If there be more, more woeful, hold it in;
For I am almost ready to dissolve,
Hearing of this.
Edg. This would have seem'd a period
To such as love not sorrow; but another,
To amplify too much, would make much more,
And top extremity.
Whilst I was big in clamour came there in a man,
Who, having seen me in my worst estate,
Shunn'd my abhorr'd society; but then, finding
Who 't was that so endur'd, with his strong arms
He fasten'd on my neck, and bellow'd out
As he 'd burst heaven; threw him on my father;
Told the most piteous tale of Lear and him
That ever ear received; which in recounting,
His grief grew puissant, and the strings of life
Began to crack. Twice then the trumpets sounded,
And there I left him tranc'd.
Alb. But who was this?
Edg. Kent, sir, the banish'd Kent; who in disguise
Follow'd his enemy king, and did him service
Improper for a slave.

Enter a *Gentleman* with a bloody knife.

Gent. Help, help, O, help!
Edg. What kind of help?
Alb. Speak, man.
Edg. What means this bloody knife?
Gent. 'T is hot, it smokes;
It came even from the heart of—O, she 's dead!
Alb. Who dead? Speak, man.
Gent. Your lady, sir, your lady; and her sister
By her is poison'd; she confesses it.
Edm. I was contracted to them both. All three
Now marry in an instant.
Edg. Here comes Kent.

Enter *Kent*.

Alb. Produce the bodies, be they alive or dead.
This judgement of the heavens, that makes us tremble,
Touches us not with pity. *Exit Gentleman.*
—O, is this he?
The time will not allow the compliment
Which very manners urges.
Kent. I am come
To bid my king and master aye good-night.
Is he not here?
Alb. Great thing of us forgot!
Speak, Edmund, where 's the King? and where 's Cordelia?
The bodies of Goneril and Regan are brought in.
See'st thou this object, Kent?
Kent. Alack, why thus?
Edm. Yet Edmund was belov'd!
The one the other poison'd for my sake,
And after slew herself.
Alb. Even so. Cover their faces.
Edm. I pant for life. Some good I mean to do,

174. **wheel**, i.e., of fortune. 175. **gait**, bearing. 196. **flaw'd**, cracked. 207. **top extremity**, exceed the extreme limit. 208. **big in clamour**, loud in grief.

218. **tranc'd**, senseless.

Despite of mine own nature. Quickly send,
Be brief in it, to the castle; for my writ
Is on the life of Lear and on Cordelia.
Nay, send in time.
Alb. Run, run, O, run!
Edg. To who, my lord? Who has the office? Send
Thy token of reprieve.
Edm. Well thought on. Take my sword,
Give it the captain.
Edg. Haste thee, for thy life.
Exit Gentleman.
Edm. He hath commission from thy wife and me
To hang Cordelia in the prison, and
To lay the blame upon her own despair,
That she fordid herself.
Alb. The gods defend her! Bear him hence a while. *Edmund is borne off.*

Enter *Lear* with *Cordelia* in his arms *Gentleman* following.

Lear. Howl, howl, howl! O, you are men of stones!
Had I your tongues and eyes, I 'd use them so
That heaven's vault should crack. She 's gone for ever!
I know when one is dead, and when one lives;
She 's dead as earth. Lend me a looking-glass;
If that her breath will mist or stain the stone,
Why, then she lives.
Kent. Is this the promis'd end?
Edg. Or image of that horror?
Alb. Fall, and cease!
Lear. This feather stirs; she lives! If it be so,
It is a chance which does redeem all sorrows
That ever I have felt.
Kent. [*Kneeling.*] O my good master!
Lear. Prithee, away.
Edg. 'T is noble Kent, your friend.
Lear. A plague upon you, murderous traitors all!
I might have sav'd her; now she 's gone for ever!
Cordelia, Cordelia! stay a little. Ha!
What is 't thou say'st? Her voice was ever soft,
Gentle, and low; an excellent thing in woman.
I kill'd the slave that was a-hanging thee.
Gent. 'T is true, my lords, he did.
Lear. Did I not, fellow?
I have seen the day, with my good biting falchion
I would have made them skip. I am old now,
And these same crosses spoil me. Who are you?
Mine eyes are not o' th' best. I 'll tell you straight.
Kent. If Fortune brag of two she lov'd and hated,
One of them we behold.
Lear. This is a dull sight. Are you not Kent?
Kent. The same,
Your servant Kent. Where is your servant Caius?
Lear. He 's a good fellow, I can tell you that;
He 'll strike and quickly too. He 's dead and rotten.
Kent. No, my good lord; I am the very man,—
Lear. I 'll see that straight.
Kent. —That, from your first of difference and decay,
Have follow'd your sad steps.
Lear. You 're welcome hither.
Kent. Nor no man else; all 's cheerless, dark, and deadly.
Your eldest daughters have fordone themselves,
And desperately are dead.
Lear. Ay, so I think.
Alb. He knows not what he says; and vain is it
That we present us to him.

Enter a *Messenger.*

Edg. Very bootless.
Mess. Edmund is dead, my lord.
Alb. That 's but a trifle here,—
You lords and noble friends, know our intent.
What comfort to this great decay may come
Shall be appli'd. For us, we will resign,
During the life of this old majesty,
To him our absolute power; [*to Edgar and Kent*] you, to your rights,
With boot, and such addition as your honours
Have more than merited. All friends shall taste
The wages of their virtue, and all foes
The cup of their deservings. O, see, see!
Lear. And my poor fool is hang'd! No, no, no life!
Why should a dog, a horse, a rat, have life,
And thou no breath at all? Thou 'lt come no more,
Never, never, never, never, never!
Pray you, undo this button. Thank you, sir.
Do you see this? Look on her, look, her lips,
Look there, look there! *Dies.*
Edg. He faints! My lord, my lord!
Kent. Break, heart; I prithee, break!

255. forbid, destroyed. **262. stone**, crystal mirror. **263. the promis'd end**, the Last Judgment. **265. feather**, cf. 2 *K. Henry IV*, IV, iv, 34. **278. crosses**, troubles.

288. difference, change of fortune. **290. Nor . . . else**, no, neither I nor anyone is welcome here. **292. desperately**, in despair. **305. my poor fool**, Cordelia; **fool** is used as a term of endearment, as in *Winter's Tale*, II, i, 118. **310-11.** The final touch of tragic pathos. Lear thinks he sees Cordelia's lips move and dies believing she has come back to him.

Edg. Look up, my lord.
Kent. Vex not his ghost; O, let him pass! He hates him
That would upon the rack of this tough world
Stretch him out longer.
Edg. He is gone, indeed.
Kent. The wonder is he hath endur'd so long;
He but usurp'd his life.
Alb. Bear them from hence. Our present business
Is general woe. [*To Kent and Edgar.*] Friends of my soul, you twain
Rule in this realm, and the gor'd state sustain.
Kent. I have a journey, sir, shortly to go:
My master calls me, I must not say no.
Edg. The weight of this sad time we must obey;
Speak what we feel, not what we ought to say.
The oldest hath borne most; we that are young
Shall never see so much, nor live so long.
Exeunt, with a dead march.

The Tragedy of Macbeth

Macbeth, the latest in date of Shakespeare's four tragic masterpieces, is in some respects the greatest of them all. "It stands first," said Hazlitt, "for wildness of imagination, and rapidity of action—it is done upon a stronger and more systematic principle of contrast than any other of Shakespeare's plays." Written almost immediately after *Lear, Macbeth* is another evidence of the range and flexibility of Shakespeare's dramatic genius. Terse and concentrated, clear and simple, where *Lear* is long, complex, and world-embracing, it has the air of a magnificent impromptu dashed off at headlong speed by a master of his craft. Yet it is more than a masterpiece of dramatic art; it is a great poetic tragedy, and it contains a profound moral lesson taught with stern directness and dreadful power.

Text.—Macbeth was printed for the first time in the 1623 Folio. The "copy" furnished the printers must have been a transcript of the company's prompt-book, as is shown by numerous stage-directions calling for torches and music. No doubt this prompt-copy differed to some extent from the original version. *Macbeth* is one of the shortest of Shakespeare's plays, a fact which suggests abridgment, but it is unlikely that any important scenes have been omitted. On the other hand it is certain that there have been interpolations of song and dance features borrowed from the fashionable Court masques of the day which were becoming more and more frequent in regular drama. As will be seen later this mistaken notion of enlivening the sombre tragedy clung like a plague to productions of *Macbeth* for a couple of centuries. There are many corrupt and difficult passages in the text, a result, probably, both of revision in the theatre and of careless transcription.

Date.—Macbeth may be dated with some degree of certainty in 1606. In August 1605 King James visited Oxford and was entertained with a show in which three youths costumed as Sybils greeted him with Latin verses founded on the prophecies of the weird sisters to his ancestor Banquo, supposed founder of the royal house of Stuart. The King was delighted with this pageant, and the report of his Majesty's pleasure no doubt lingered in Oxford when Shakespeare came there with his company some six weeks later. It is highly likely that Shakespeare caught the idea of a play about Macbeth and Banquo to be presented at Court from this Oxford show. The references in *Macbeth* (IV, i) to the many Kings descended from Banquo and to the miraculous gift of curing scrofúla by the royal touch, a practice resumed by James early in his reign, are very plainly Shakespeare's compliment to his master and point to a performance of the play at Court. Allusions to the appearance of Banquo's ghost at the banquet in two plays, *The Puritan* and *The Knight of the Burning Pestle,* which can be dated in 1606 and 1607, show that *Macbeth* was on the stage at that time and references in the Porter's speech to equivocation and to the low price of corn also point to 1606 as the date of the play's first production.

Source.—The source of *Macbeth* is Holinshed's *Chronicles* which Shakespeare had already exploited in the plays dealing with English kings. A brief summary of the Holinshed narrative will show how closely Shakespeare followed his source.

King Duncan was so soft and gentle that he was incapable of rule. Macdowald with an army of kerns and gallowglasses rebelled against him but was defeated by Macbeth and Banquo. Later Macbeth defeated both a Norwegian and a Danish invasion and forced the Danes to pay a vast sum for the burial of their dead at St. Colme's Inch. Not long after Macbeth and Banquo, while walking together in the fields, were met by three women in strange and wild apparel. They greeted Macbeth as thane of Glamis, thane of Cawdor, and future King of Scotland. When Banquo bade them speak to him they prophesied that he would be the father of a line of kings, and thereupon they vanished. Later it was thought that these women were the weird sisters, that is, the Goddesses of destiny, for all that they foretold came true. Soon after this the thane of Cawdor was condemned for treason and his title bestowed upon Macbeth. This encouraged Macbeth to aspire to the crown, but he took no active steps till Duncan proclaimed Malcolm his son Prince of Cumberland and heir to the kingdom. Then Macbeth began to plot in earnest, encouraged by his wife who burned "in unquenchable desire to bear the name of queen." Finally with the aid of Banquo Macbeth attacked and slew Duncan and was crowned King at Scone. Duncan's sons fled to England and Ireland and Macbeth ruled unopposed.

For ten years Macbeth ruled well and wisely, but at last he began to treat his people cruelly. Remembering the prophecy made to Banquo he invited him and his son Fleance to a banquet and set murderers upon them. Banquo was killed, but Fleance escaped. Thereafter nothing prospered with Macbeth. Certain wizards warned him against Macduff whom he would have slain at once but that a witch in whom he trusted assured him that no man born of woman could kill him and that he would not be vanquished till Birnam wood came to Dunsinane. But when Macduff fled to England to join Malcolm, Macbeth slew his wife and children and all his retainers.

In England Macduff urged Malcolm to overthrow Macbeth, but Malcolm feared that Macduff might be sent to betray him and tested him by accusing himself of many vices. When Macduff lamented the state of Scotland oppressed by a tyrant and deserted by an unworthy heir, Malcolm recognized his true patriotism. Together they invaded Scotland, assisted by Siward of Northumberland with ten thousand men. On the way to Dunsinane they passed through Birnam wood and Malcolm ordered every soldier to cut down and carry a bough to conceal their numbers. When Macbeth saw the moving wood he fled, but was overtaken by Macduff, who revealed himself as the destined slayer of the tyrant by declaring that he had not been born of woman but had been ripped from his mother's womb. Thereupon he cut off Macbeth's head and brought it on a pole to Malcolm. Malcolm was hailed as King and promoted his thanes to be earls, the first that ever were in Scotland.

Shakespeare, it is plain, not only followed the main outline of the *Chronicles,* but borrowed many details and even phrases from it which he wove with fine art into the texture of his play. On the other hand there are some important divergences. The opening matter, the rebellion, the invasion, the treason of Cawdor, are compressed into the events of one day. It was of course impossible for Shakespeare to present Banquo, the ancestor of his royal master, as a rebel and a regicide. Accordingly he calmly altered history and showed a loyal Banquo horrified at the murder. The circumstances, moreover, of the murder of Duncan differ in the history and in the play. Holinshed says quite simply that Macbeth slew the King at Inverness; he gives no details; but Shakespeare found a story in an earlier chapter of Holinshed that gave him what he needed.

A Scottish nobleman, Donwald, cherished a secret grudge against King Duff. Spurred on by his wife he took the opportunity of the King's visit to his castle to accomplish his revenge. He and his wife plied the grooms who guarded the King with food and drink till they fell into a drunken slumber. Then Donwald sent in servants who killed the King, carried away his body, and buried it in secret. In the morning when the murder was discovered Donwald slew the grooms with his own hand accusing them of the deed. For six months after the murder there appeared no sun by day or moon by night and such outrageous winds arose that the people were in great fear. Monstrous sights were also seen: horses of singular beauty did eat their own flesh and a sparrow hawk was strangled by an owl.

Every reader of *Macbeth* will recall the use that Shakespeare has made of these details.

The most significant change that Shakespeare made was in his treatment of the supernatural element. In Holinshed we hear of certain wizards and a witch as well as of the three women who hailed Macbeth as King hereafter. These women Holinshed calls "the weird sisters, that is, the Goddesses of destiny." Apparently an old form of the legend had identified them with the Norns of northern mythology, but Shakespeare knew nothing about the Norns and he simply combined the various figures of Holinshed into the three sisters of his play whom he presented as the witches of popular superstition. There was a good reason for this change. The age-old belief in witchcraft had broken out in England with fresh violence on the arrival of the witch-hating James, and it was clear that a play presenting the awful consequences of association with witches would be well received by the King.

But there was another and a deeper reason. Shakespeare found in the story of *Macbeth* a vehicle for a new and profounder treatment of the problem of evil, its presence, and its power in the world. He had dealt with this problem in his earlier tragedies, but the story of Macbeth presented it in a peculiar light. Shakespeare saw in the witches and wizards of the tale symbols and embodiments of the omnipresent power of evil. In the belief of the day the witch was a human being, one of God's creatures, who had deliberately renounced God and sworn allegiance to the Devil. And here was a hero, who listened to the words of witches, sought them out for aid in his distress, and was led to ruin body and soul by the equivocation of the fiend. The sin of Macbeth is the sin of witchcraft, the deliberate and conscious choice of evil for good. We must not think of the witches as if they were the Fates of Grecian legend whose doom none might escape. Shakespeare believed in man's free will; he might have said with Whitman:

If we are lost no victor else has destroy'd us;
It is by ourselves we go down to eternal night.

And the night into which Macbeth sinks is darker and more terrible than that which envelops any other of his tragic heroes, for no other of them had made his fatal choice.

Shakespeare's task in his dramatization of this theme was to raise the character of the protagonist to the true height of the tragic hero. Macbeth is a very wicked man; he murders his kinsman and guest, King Duncan, he sets assassins on his trusting friend, he tramples down a bleeding country. If he were only a wicked man he would not be a tragic hero, only a figure in melodrama; but Macbeth is something more than this; he is a brave defender of his country, and like all Shakespeare's tragic heroes he is a courteous gentleman. His wife, who knew him well, declares that he is "too full of the milk of human kindness." He is no Richard Crookback to walk rejoicing along a road of blood, no Iago to triumph in his victory over innocence. He is a loving husband; the tie that binds him to his wife has made them one, and the gradual loosing and final severance of this tie plunges him into an abyss of loneliness that finds expression in some of the saddest lines in Shakespeare. He was ambitious, of course, but so are other of Shakespeare's heroes.

The peculiar and distinguishing characteristic of Macbeth is an imagination which both in intensity and wildness surpasses that of any other Shakespearean figure. If Hamlet is Shakespeare's tragic thinker Macbeth is his tragic poet. It is this imaginative power that sweeps Macbeth away more than once. At the fulfilment of the witches' first prophecy it presents an image of murder that makes his heart knock at his ribs. Later when he has screwed his courage to the sticking place it offers him the dagger dashed with gouts of blood, which marshals him the way to Duncan's chamber. When the deed is done it becomes an infernal torture. It conjures up the voice that cried "sleep no more"; it shows him the frightful picture of his blood-stained hands dyeing the whole sea red. It does more than this; since it could not restrain him from his first crime, it becomes by way of revenge a spur to prick him on to others. It is his imagination that shows him Banquo turning on him to wrench a barren sceptre from his gripe; Banquo dies that Macbeth may live free from the affliction of the terrible dreams that shake him nightly. Yet no sooner is Banquo dispatched than Macbeth's imagination conjures up at the banquet the ghost of his old friend and the ghastly phantom shatters his self-control beyond concealment or repair.[1]

The banquet scene, the climax of the play, marks another stage in the development, or rather the degeneration, of the character of Macbeth. He turns from his wife to seek the counsel of the witches. Lulled into false security by their predictions, he loses all sense of fear, and with it vanishes the torturing power of his imagination. The cruel and senseless massacre of Macduff's family leaves him unmoved; he is no longer haunted by the ghosts of his victims. It is by a triumph of his art that Shakespeare regains in a last act some measure of our sympathy for this fallen man. He does it by showing with matchless power the bitter disillusion of Macbeth. The crown for which he forfeited his soul has brought him only curses; the news of his wife's death evokes no burst of grief, for life seems to him now as empty of meaning as the babble of an idiot. From this lethargy of misery he is roused by the report of the moving wood. His dream of victory is broken, but there is still a chance for life and to this he clings with the fierce instinct of a hunted beast. It is only

[1] Shakespeare, of course, meant the ghost of Banquo to appear on the stage; it was a stage effect that he could not reject; but it has none of the objective reality of the Ghost in *Hamlet*. It does not speak; it is seen by no one but Macbeth and it vanishes when by a fierce effort of will he turns his mind from it. It is assuredly the creature of Macbeth's imagination.

when he meets Macduff that a trace of humanity returns. Though confident of his charmed life he is unwilling to strike Macduff; "my soul," he says, "is too much charged with blood of thine already." It is a fine touch of Shakespeare's art that these revealing words are spoken immediately before Macbeth learns the story of the avenger's birth. Yet even then, though all the powers of hell have failed him, his self-will and his strength remain and he dies fighting. But he has tasted the bitterness of death before he died. Shakespeare's exposition of his theme—the progressive degradation and final ruin of the wilfully sinning soul—is triumphantly complete.

The whole interest of this play centers about the protagonist; all other characters are properly subordinated to his. Yet a few words must be said about his wife. Shakespeare has sketched her with a few swift and strong strokes, and as is sometimes the case with sketches, the significance of his work has often been misunderstood. Lady Macbeth is no monster of cruelty nor demon of ambition. It is plain that Shakespeare conceived her as a slight and delicate woman; we hear of her little hand; we learn that she needs the stimulus of wine to carry her through the night of murder; we see her swooning in the reaction that follows. She is ambitious, indeed, but solely for her husband. With the fine instinct of a great artist Shakespeare has departed from his source; to have stressed, like Holinshed, her "insatiable ambition" would have destroyed the unity of interest in the play.

The dominant note in her character is an imperious and masterful will. Intensely practical she has none of Macbeth's fears and scruples. Her final ruin is not due to remorse, but to a complete collapse of body and mind brought on by the strain which she had suffered and the crushing disappointment of her hopes. It is an evidence of her strongly realistic character that in the sleep-walking scene —one of Shakespeare's greatest inventions; there is no trace of it in his source—she shows no sign of Macbeth's terrifying imagination. It is the remembrance of facts, not fancies, that troubles her: the sight of Duncan's blood upon her hand, the knocking at the door, the collapse of her lord at the banquet, the shameful butchery of a helpless woman—"the thane of Fife had a wife." Unlike Macbeth she is not sustained by belief in oracles; she has not even his last resort of desperate combat. Nothing is left her but death, and Shakespeare tells us that she sought death by her own hands.

Most of the characters of this play are little more than puppets; but there are two that deserve a brief consideration; Banquo's role, of course, is that of a contrast to Macbeth. He fights against the temptation to which his friend succumbs, yet Banquo is not unaffected by the witches' prophecy. In spite of his well-founded suspicion of Macbeth's guilt he makes no attempt to avenge the murder; he swears allegiance to the usurper in the hope that he might thus reap the reward foretold to his house. And this passive acquiescence is the direct cause of his death.

Macduff, on the other hand, represents the simplicity and strength of a soul untouched by any dealing with the powers of evil. With the instinctive abhorrence of virtue to guilt he at once goes into opposition to Macbeth, declines to attend his coronation, and refuses the bidding to his solemn feast. His flight to England is not from fear but solely to rejoin and aid the true heir to the throne. His essential innocence appears in his wild outcry that his loved ones were punished for his sins.

Construction.—In some ways the dramatic construction of *Macbeth* represents a return to the earlier and simpler technique of the chronicle plays. There are many scenes—most of them short—and there is no complicated intrigue. The action up to the banquet scene runs at headlong speed. After the great climax of the third act the speed slackens; in the fourth the action plainly drags; the cauldron scene is spectacular rather than dramatic, and in the long dialogue of the third scene Shakespeare follows his source so closely as to suggest a certain weariness before he rallied for a final effort. The last act presents an interesting method of construction, unique in Shakespeare's tragedies. After the prologue of the Lady's sleep-walking it consists of a series of short scenes showing alternately the forces gathering for the outward overthrow of Macbeth and the inward ruin of the hero's soul. The act is practically incapable of performance on the modern stage and though it doubtless gained its effect in Shakespeare's simpler theatre, it seems to lack the tremendous dramatic power of the last acts of *Hamlet, Lear,* and above all of *Othello.* What Shakespeare wished, apparently, was to reveal in action the slow inevitable stages by which the catastrophe, outer and inner, broke upon Macbeth, and to do this he discarded his former method of the one great closing scene, the last action of the play, leading up to the final conflict and catastrophe. After all we would not have it otherwise; it would take as rash a meddler as Davenant to rewrite the last act of *Macbeth.*

Final Appreciation.—About this tragedy there clings an atmosphere that is peculiarly its own. It is not merely the supernatural that creates it—there is a ghost in *Hamlet*—nor is it the bloody business of the action—there are as many murders in *Richard III.* It has often been noted that darkness broods over this play, that its most characteristic scenes take place by night. But this is not a night of peace and rest: it is an evil night in which wicked dreams abuse the sleeper and murder steals upon his victim. Night and Evil are, so to speak, identified, and Macbeth, who fought well and loyally by day, allies himself at night with the Power of Darkness. This, Shakespeare seems to say, is against the course of nature, and perhaps the most profound impression left by this dark tragedy is that of the unnatural, the abnormal, character of evil. The portents that accompany the death of Duncan are symbolic of the horror aroused in the normal world by this unnatural deed. In *Othello* evil appears as something hidden, subtle and poisonous; in *Lear* it is open, ruthless, and dreadfully powerful; in *Macbeth* it is both by turns and has in addition a Satanic quality of its own. Macbeth, who listened to the devil-worshipping witches, might have chosen as his device the words of Milton's Satan—"Evil, be thou my Good." Nowhere do we feel so strongly Shakespeare's abhorrence of the Power of Evil that lies so near our little world as in this, the last of his great tragedies.

Stage History.—One would suppose that *Macbeth* with its rapid action, its witches, and its combats would have been a most successful play in Shakespeare's age. Curiously, however, there is not a single account of its performance before 1642 except an entry, 1611, by Dr. Forman, and this is suspected of being a modern forgery. After the Restoration Davenant laid violent hands upon it. He not only "refined" the language to an almost incredible extent, but wrote in several new scenes, especially for Lady Macduff, a virtuous wife as opposed to Lady Macbeth. He cut out the Porter as improper to tragedy, but added a dreadful parody of the sleep-walking scene showing Lady Macbeth pursued by the ghost of Duncan. He greatly enlarged the songs and dances of the witches who now flew through the air "on machines." This travesty of Shakespeare delighted the age; Pepys, who saw *Macbeth* oftener than any other play of Shakespeare's, calls Davenant's version "a most excellent play in all respects—but especially in divertisement . . . which is a strange perfection in a tragedy."

Sad to say this malformation of Shakespeare's play held the stage till the time of Garrick. He cut out many of the Davenant scenes but retained the singing and dancing witches and had the audacity to compose a dying speech for Macbeth:

> Hell drags me down. I sink
> I sink. Oh! my soul is lost forever.
> Oh! *Dies.*

Garrick was a better actor than a poet.

Garrick's version held the stage for a century or more. Kemble and Mrs. Siddons were famous in their roles of Macbeth and his wife. Among the horde of witches in his production was a fine lady in powdered hair, rouge, and point lace; Pepys would have loved her. It was not until the time of Phelps, 1847, that the singing witches disappeared and Shakespeare's weird sisters came once more upon the stage.

Irving's spectacular production, 1888, suffered from his strange conception of the hero as a neurasthenic criminal; even Terry's sympathetic Lady Macbeth could not redeem the play. A production in New York with scenery designed by Gordon Craig showed how effective straight Shakespeare sympathetically produced can be. The two chief characters, however, call for a tone of speech and tradition of acting that has well-nigh disappeared from the stage.

THE TRAGEDY OF MACBETH

Dramatis Personæ

Duncan, King of Scotland.
Malcolm, / *Donalbain,* — his sons.
Macbeth, / *Banquo,* — generals of the King's army.
Macduff, / *Lennox,* / *Ross,* / *Menteith,* / *Angus,* / *Caithness,* — noblemen of Scotland.
Fleance, son to *Banquo.*
Siward, earl of Northumberland.
Young *Siward,* his son.
Seyton, an officer attending on Macbeth.
Boy, son to *Macduff.*
An English Doctor.
A Scotch Doctor.
A Captain.
A Porter.
An Old Man.
Lady Macbeth.
Lady Macduff.
Gentlewoman attending on *Lady Macbeth.*
Hecate.
Three Witches.
The Ghost of *Banquo.*
Apparitions.

Lords, Gentlemen, Officers, Soldiers, Murderers, Attendants, and Messengers.

SCENE: *Scotland; England.*

ACT I. Scene I. *A heath.*

Thunder and lightning. Enter three *Witches.*

1. Witch. When shall we three meet again
In thunder, lightning, or in rain?
2. Witch. When the hurlyburly 's done,
When the battle 's lost and won.
3. Witch. That will be ere the set of sun.
1. Witch. Where the place?
2. Witch. Upon the heath.
3. Witch. There to meet with Macbeth.
1. Witch. I come, Graymalkin!
All. Paddock calls:—Anon!
Fair is foul, and foul is fair;
Hover through the fog and filthy air. *Exeunt.*

Scene II. *A camp near Forres.*

Alarum within. Enter *King Duncan, Malcolm, Donalbain, Lennox,* with Attendants, meeting a bleeding *Captain.*

Dun. What bloody man is that? He can report,
As seemeth by his plight, of the revolt
The newest state.
Mal. This is the sergeant
Who like a good and hardy soldier fought
'Gainst my captivity. Hail, brave friend!
Say to the King the knowledge of the broil
As thou didst leave it.
Cap. Doubtful it stood,
As two spent swimmers that do cling together
And choke their art. The merciless Macdonwald—
Worthy to be a rebel, for to that
The multiplying villainies of nature
Do swarm upon him—from the Western Isles
Of kerns and gallowglasses is suppli'd;
And Fortune, on his damned quarrel smiling,
Show'd like a rebel's whore: but all 's too weak;
For brave Macbeth—well he deserves that name—
Disdaining Fortune, with his brandish'd steel,
Which smok'd with bloody execution,
(Like Valour's minion) carv'd out his passage
Till he fac'd the slave;
Which ne'er shook hands, nor bade farewell to him,
Till he unseam'd him from the nave to th' chaps,
And fix'd his head upon our battlements.
Dun. O valiant cousin! worthy gentleman!

3. hurlyburly's, turmoil's. **9. Graymalkin,** gray cat, a common familiar spirit of the witch. **10. Paddock,** toad. **Anon,** immediately.

Scene ii: 6, broil, battle. **9. choke,** render useless. **10. for to that,** because. **13. kerns,** light-armed Irish foot-soldiers. **gallowglasses,** retainers of Irish chiefs heavily armed. **19. minion,** favorite. **21. Which,** who, i.e., Macbeth. **22. nave,** navel. **chaps,** jaws. **24. cousin,** a common form of address from a king to a noble, but Duncan and Macbeth were really first cousins.

Cap. As whence the sun gins his reflection
Shipwrecking storms and direful thunders break,
So from that spring whence comfort seem'd to come
Discomfort swells. Mark, King of Scotland, mark!
No sooner justice had, with valour arm'd,
Compell'd these skipping kerns to trust their heels,
But the Norweyan lord, surveying vantage,
With furbish'd arms and new supplies of men
Began a fresh assault.
Dun. Dismay'd not this
Our captains, Macbeth and Banquo?
Cap. Yes;
As sparrows eagles, or the hare the lion.
If I say sooth, I must report they were
As cannons overcharg'd with double cracks;
So they doubly redoubled strokes upon the foe.
Except they meant to bathe in reeking wounds,
Or memorize another Golgotha,
I cannot tell.
But I am faint, my gashes cry for help.
Dun. So well thy words become thee as thy wounds;
They smack of honour both. Go get him surgeons. *Exit Captain, attended.*

Enter *Ross* and *Angus.*

Who comes here?
Mal. The worthy thane of Ross.
Len. What a haste looks through his eyes!
So should he look that seems to speak things strange.
Ross. God save the King!
Dun. Whence cam'st thou, worthy thane?
Ross. From Fife, great king;
Where the Norweyan banners flout the sky
And fan our people cold.
Norway himself, with terrible numbers,
Assisted by that most disloyal traitor,
The thane of Cawdor, began a dismal conflict;
Till that Bellona's bridegroom, lapp'd in proof,
Confronted him with self-comparisons,
Point against point, rebellious arm 'gainst arm,
Curbing his lavish spirit; and, to conclude,
The victory fell on us;—
Dun. Great happiness!
Ross. That now
Sweno, the Norway's king, craves composition;
Nor would we deign him burial of his men
Till he disbursed at Saint Colme's inch
Ten thousand dollars to our general use.
Dun. No more that thane of Cawdor shall deceive
Our bosom interest. Go pronounce his present death,
And with his former title greet Macbeth.
Ross. I 'll see it done.
Dun. What he hath lost, noble Macbeth hath won. *Exeunt.*

Scene III. *A heath near Forres.*

Thunder. Enter the three *Witches.*

1. Witch. Where hast thou been, sister?
2. Witch. Killing swine.
3. Witch. Sister, where thou?
1. Witch. A sailor's wife had chestnuts in her lap,
And munch'd, and munch'd, and munch'd. "Give me!" quoth I.
"Aroint thee, witch!" the rump-fed ronyon cries.
Her husband 's to Aleppo gone, master o' th' Tiger;
But in a sieve I 'll thither sail,
And, like a rat without a tail,
I 'll do, I 'll do, and I 'll do.
2. Witch. I 'll give thee a wind.
1. Witch. Thou 'rt kind.
3. Witch. And I another.
1. Witch. I myself have all the other,
And the very ports they blow,
All the quarters that they know
I' th' shipman's card.
I 'll drain him dry as hay:
Sleep shall neither night nor day
Hang upon his pent-house lid;
He shall live a man forbid.
Weary sev'nights nine times nine
Shall he dwindle, peak, and pine.
Though his bark cannot be lost,
Yet it shall be tempest-tost.
Look what I have.
2. Witch. Show me, show me.
1. Witch. Here I have a pilot's thumb,
Wreck'd as homeward he did come.
Drum within.

25. **gins his reflection,** the new danger came from the East. 31. **surveying vantage,** seeing a good opportunity. 32. **furbish'd,** burnished, fresh. 37. **cracks,** charges. 40. **memorize,** make memorable. 45. **thane,** Scottish title equivalent to baron. 47. **seems,** seems about. 49. **flout,** mock. 54. **Bellona,** Roman goddess of war. **lapp'd in proof,** clad in armor. 55. **Confronted . . . self-comparisons,** showed prowess equal to his own. 57. **lavish,** arrogant. 59. **composition,** terms of peace.

61. **Saint Colme's inch,** Inchcolm, the Isle of St. Columba, in the Firth of Forth. 64. **bosom interest,** loving confidence. **Scene iii: 6, Aroint,** be gone. **rump-fed ronyon,** mangy creature fed on refuse. 7. **Aleppo,** city in Syria. 8. **sieve,** a traditional vehicle of witches. 9. **rat . . . tail,** witches could change themselves into the form of animals, but could sometimes be recognized by a physical defect, such as the lack of a tail. 14. **other,** others. 15. **blow,** blow upon. 17. **card,** compass card or chart. 20. **pent-house lid,** eyelid. 21. **forbid,** accursed.

3. Witch. A drum, a drum!
Macbeth doth come.
All. The weird sisters, hand in hand,
Posters of the sea and land,
Thus do go about, about;
Thrice to thine, and thrice to mine,
And thrice again, to make up nine.
Peace! the charm 's wound up.

Enter *Macbeth* and *Banquo.*

Macb. So foul and fair a day I have not seen.
Ban. How far is 't call'd to Forres? What are these
So wither'd and so wild in their attire,
That look not like th' inhabitants o' th' earth,
And yet are on 't? Live you? or are you aught
That man may question? You seem to understand me,
By each at once her choppy finger laying
Upon her skinny lips: you should be women,
And yet your beards forbid me to interpret
That you are so.
Macb. Speak, if you can. What are you?
1. Witch. All hail, Macbeth! hail to thee, thane of Glamis!
2. Witch. All hail, Macbeth! hail to thee, thane of Cawdor!
3. Witch. All hail, Macbeth, that shalt be King hereafter!
Ban. Good sir, why do you start, and seem to fear
Things that do sound so fair?—
I' th' name of truth,
Are ye fantastical, or that indeed
Which outwardly ye show? My noble partner
You greet with present grace and great prediction
Of noble having and of royal hope,
That he seems rapt withal; to me you speak not.
If you can look into the seeds of time,
And say which grain will grow and which will not,
Speak then to me, who neither beg nor fear
Your favours nor your hate.
1. Witch. Hail!
2. Witch. Hail!
3. Witch. Hail!
1. Witch. Lesser than Macbeth, and greater.
2. Witch. Not so happy, yet much happier.
3. Witch. Thou shalt get kings, though thou be none;
So all hail, Macbeth and Banquo!
1. Witch. Banquo and Macbeth, all hail!
Macb. Stay, you imperfect speakers, tell me more.
By Sinel's death I know I am thane of Glamis;
But how of Cawdor? The thane of Cawdor lives,
A prosperous gentleman; and to be king
Stands not within the prospect of belief
No more than to be Cawdor. Say from whence
You owe this strange intelligence, or why
Upon this blasted heath you stop our way
With such prophetic greeting. Speak, I charge you. *Witches vanish.*
Ban. The earth hath bubbles, as the water has,
And these are of them. Whither are they vanish'd?
Macb. Into the air; and what seem'd corporal melted
As breath into the wind. Would they had stay'd!
Ban. Were such things here as we do speak about,
Or have we eaten on the insane root
That takes the reason prisoner?
Macb. Your children shall be kings.
Ban. You shall be King.
Macb. And thane of Cawdor too; went it not so?
Ban. To th' self-same tune and words. Who 's here?

Enter *Ross* and *Angus.*

Ross. The King hath happily receiv'd, Macbeth,
The news of thy success; and when he reads
Thy personal venture in the rebels' fight,
His wonders and his praises do contend
Which should be thine or his. Silenc'd with that,
In viewing o'er the rest o' th' self-same day,
He finds thee in the stout Norweyan ranks,
Nothing afeard of what thyself didst make,
Strange images of death. As thick as hail
Came post with post; and every one did bear
Thy praises in his kingdom's great defence,
And pour'd them down before him.
Ang. We are sent
To give thee from our royal master thanks;
Only to herald thee into his sight,
Not pay thee.
Ross. And, for an earnest of a greater honour,
He bade me, from him, call thee thane of Cawdor;
In which addition, hail, most worthy thane!
For it is thine.

32. **weird sisters,** sisters of destiny. 33. **Posters of,** travelers over. 44. **choppy,** chapped. 53. **fantastical,** creatures of the imagination. 54. **show,** appear to be. 56. **having,** possessions, rank.

71. **Sinel's,** Macbeth's father. 76. **owe,** have. 84. **on,** of. **insane root,** root that causes insanity. 96. **Nothing afeard,** not at all afraid. 106. **In . . . addition,** under which title.

Ban. [*Aside.*] What, can the devil speak true?
Macb. The thane of Cawdor lives; why do you dress me
In borrowed robes?
Ang. Who was the thane lives yet;
But under heavy judgement bears that life
Which he deserves to lose. Whether he was combin'd
With those of Norway, or did line the rebel
With hidden help and vantage, or that with both
He labour'd in his country's wreck, I know not;
But treasons capital, confess'd and prov'd,
Have overthrown him.
Macb. [*Aside.*] Glamis, and thane of Cawdor!
The greatest is behind. [*To Ross and Angus.*] Thanks for your pains.
[*To Ban.*] Do you not hope your children shall be kings,
When those that gave the thane of Cawdor to me
Promis'd no less to them?
Ban. That trusted home
Might yet enkindle you unto the crown,
Besides the thane of Cawdor. But 't is strange;
And oftentimes, to win us to our harm,
The instruments of darkness tell us truths,
Win us with honest trifles, to betray 's
In deepest consequence.
Cousins, a word, I pray you.
Macb. [*Aside.*] Two truths are told,
As happy prologues to the swelling act
Of the imperial theme.—I thank you, gentlemen.
[*Aside.*] This supernatural soliciting
Cannot be ill, cannot be good. If ill,
Why hath it given me earnest of success,
Commencing in a truth? I 'm thane of Cawdor.
If good, why do I yield to that suggestion
Whose horrid image doth unfix my hair
And make my seated heart knock at my ribs,
Against the use of nature? Present fears
Are less than horrible imaginings.
My thought, whose murder yet is but fantastical,
Shakes so my single state of man that function
Is smother'd in surmise, and nothing is
But what is not.
Ban. Look, how our partner 's rapt.
Macb. [*Aside.*] If chance will have me King, why, chance may crown me,
Without my stir.
Ban. New honours come upon him,
Like our strange garments, cleave not to their mould
But with the aid of use.
Macb. [*Aside.*] Come what come may,
Time and the hour runs through the roughest day.
Ban. Worthy Macbeth, we stay upon your leisure.
Macb. Give me your favour; my dull brain was wrought
With things forgotten. Kind gentlemen, your pains
Are register'd where every day I turn
The leaf to read them. Let us toward the King.
[*To Banquo.*] Think upon what hath chanc'd, and, at more time,
The interim having weigh'd it, let us speak
Our free hearts each to other.
Ban. Very gladly.
Macb. Till then, enough. Come, friends.
Exeunt.

Scene IV. *Forres. The palace.*

Flourish. Enter *King Duncan, Malcolm, Donalbain, Lennox,* and Attendants.

Dun. Is execution done on Cawdor? Are not
Those in commission yet return'd?
Mal. My liege,
They are not yet come back. But I have spoke
With one that saw him die; who did report
That very frankly he confess'd his treasons,
Implor'd your Highness' pardon, and set forth
A deep repentance. Nothing in his life
Became him like the leaving it. He died
As one that had been studied in his death
To throw away the dearest thing he ow'd,
As 't were a careless trifle.
Dun. There 's no art
To find the mind's construction in the face.
He was a gentleman on whom I built
An absolute trust.

Enter *Macbeth, Banquo, Ross, and Angus.*

O worthiest cousin!
The sin of my ingratitude even now
Was heavy on me. Thou art so far before
That swiftest wing of recompense is slow

112. line, support. **120. home,** to the full. **129. imperial theme,** theme of sovereignty. **130. soliciting,** temptation. **140. single state of man,** the harmonious kingdom of my mind. **140-2. function . . . not,** the power to act is lost in one overpowering image, that of the crown, which is for me the only reality. **144. my stir,** action on my part.

145. strange, new. **149. favour,** pardon. **wrought,** disturbed. **153. at . . . time,** when we have more time. **155. Our free hearts,** our hearts freely. **Scene iv: 2. in commission,** deputed to carry it out. **11. careless,** not cared for. **12. construction,** interpretation.

To overtake thee. Would thou hadst less deserv'd,
That the proportion both of thanks and payment
Might have been mine! only I have left to say,
More is thy due than more than all can pay.

Macb. The service and the loyalty I owe,
In doing it, pays itself. Your Highness' part
Is to receive our duties; and our duties
Are to your throne and state children and servants,
Which do but what they should, by doing everything
Safe toward your love and honour.

Dun. Welcome hither!
I have begun to plant thee, and will labour
To make thee full of growing. Noble Banquo,
That hast no less deserv'd, nor must be known
No less to have done so, let me infold thee
And hold thee to my heart.

Ban. There if I grow,
The harvest is your own.

Dun. My plenteous joys,
Wanton in fulness, seek to hide themselves
In drops of sorrow. Sons, kinsmen, thanes,
And you whose places are the nearest, know
We will establish our estate upon
Our eldest, Malcolm, whom we name hereafter
The Prince of Cumberland; which honour must
Not unaccompanied invest him only,
But signs of nobleness, like stars, shall shine
On all deservers. From hence to Inverness,
And bind us further to you.

Macb. The rest is labour, which is not us'd for you.
I 'll be myself the harbinger and make joyful
The hearing of my wife with your approach;
So humbly take my leave.

Dun. My worthy Cawdor!

Macb. [*Aside.*] The Prince of Cumberland! That is a step
On which I must fall down, or else o'erleap,
For in my way it lies. Stars, hide your fires;
Let not light see my black and deep desires;
The eye wink at the hand; yet let that be
Which the eye fears, when it is done, to see. *Exit.*

Dun. True, worthy Banquo; he is full so valiant,
And in his commendations I am fed;
It is a banquet to me. Let 's after him,
Whose care is gone before to bid us welcome.
It is a peerless kinsman. *Flourish. Exeunt.*

27. Safe toward, with sure regard for. **37-9.** The Prince of Cumberland was the official title of the heir to the Scottish throne, like that of the Prince of Wales. This nomination of Malcolm blocks Macbeth's chance of succession. Cf. ll. 48-50. **45. harbinger,** officer who went ahead to arrange lodging for the king.

Scene V. *Inverness. Macbeth's castle.*

Enter *Macbeth's Wife,* alone, with a letter.

Lady M. [*Reads.*]

"They met me in the day of success; and I have learned by the perfect'st report, they have more in them than mortal knowledge. When I burned in desire to question them further, they made themselves air, into which they vanished. Whiles I stood rapt in the wonder of it, came missives from the King, who all-hailed me 'Thane of Cawdor'; by which title, before, these weird sisters saluted me, and referred me to the coming on of time, with 'Hail, King that shalt be!' This have I thought good to deliver thee, my dearest partner of greatness, that thou mightst not lose the dues of rejoicing by being ignorant of what greatness is promised thee. Lay it to thy heart, and farewell."

Glamis thou art, and Cawdor; and shalt be
What thou art promis'd. Yet do I fear thy nature;
It is too full o' th' milk of human kindness
To catch the nearest way. Thou wouldst be great,
Art not without ambition, but without
The illness should attend it. What thou wouldst highly,
That wouldst thou holily; wouldst not play false,
And yet wouldst wrongly win. Thou 'dst have, great Glamis,
That which cries, "Thus thou must do, if thou have it";
And that which rather thou dost fear to do
Than wishest should be undone. Hie thee hither
That I may pour my spirits in thine ear,
And chastise with the valour of my tongue
All that impedes thee from the golden round
Which fate and metaphysical aid doth seem
To have thee crown'd withal.

Enter a *Messenger.*

What is your tidings?

Mess. The King comes here to-night.

Lady M. Thou 'rt mad to say it!
Is not thy master with him? who, were 't so,
Would have inform'd for preparation.

Mess. So please you, it is true; our thane is coming.
One of my fellows had the speed of him,

Scene v: 7. missives, messengers. **17 fear,** fear for. **18. milk of human kindness,** gentleness of human nature. **21. illness,** evil. **29. golden round,** the crown. **30. metaphysical,** supernatural. **36. had . . . of,** outstripped.

Who, almost dead for breath, had scarcely more
Than would make up his message.
Lady M. Give him tending;
He brings great news. *Exit Messenger.*
The raven himself is hoarse
That croaks the fatal entrance of Duncan
Under my battlements. Come, you spirits
That tend on mortal thoughts, unsex me here,
And fill me from the crown to the toe top-full
Of direst cruelty! make thick my blood;
Stop up th' access and passage to remorse,
That no compunctious visitings of nature
Shake my fell purpose, nor keep peace between
Th' effect and it! Come to my woman's breasts
And take my milk for gall, you murd'ring ministers,
Wherever in your sightless substances
You wait on nature's mischief! Come, thick night,
And pall thee in the dunnest smoke of hell,
That my keen knife see not the wound it makes,
Nor heaven peep through the blanket of the dark
To cry, "Hold, hold!"

Enter *Macbeth.*

Great Glamis! worthy Cawdor!
Greater than both, by the all-hail hereafter!
Thy letters have transported me beyond
This ignorant present, and I feel now
The future in the instant.
Macb. My dearest love,
Duncan comes here to-night.
Lady M. And when goes hence?
Macb. To-morrow, as he purposes.
Lady M. O, never
Shall sun that morrow see!
Your face, my thane, is as a book where men
May read strange matters. To beguile the time,
Look like the time; bear welcome in your eye,
Your hand, your tongue; look like th' innocent flower,
But be the serpent under 't. He that 's coming
Must be provided for; and you shall put
This night's great business into my dispatch,
Which shall to all our nights and days to come
Give solely sovereign sway and masterdom.
Macb. We will speak further.
Lady M. Only look up clear;
To alter favour ever is to fear.
Leave all the rest to me. *Exeunt.*

41-2. spirits . . . thoughts, evil spirits that inspire murderous thoughts. **45. remorse,** pity. **46. compunctious . . . nature.** natural feelings of pity. **49. murd'ring ministers,** instruments of murder. **50. sightless,** invisible. **52. pall,** wrap. **72. clear,** untroubled. **73. alter favour,** change countenance.

Scene VI. *Before Macbeth's castle.*

Hautboys and torches. Enter *King Duncan, Malcolm, Donalbain, Banquo, Lennox, Macduff, Ross, Angus,* and Attendants.

Dun. This castle hath a pleasant seat; the air
Nimbly and sweetly recommends itself
Unto our gentle senses.
Ban. This guest of summer,
The temple-haunting martlet, does approve,
By his loved mansionry, that the heaven's breath
Smells wooingly here; no jutty, frieze,
Buttress, nor coign of vantage, but this bird
Hath made his pendent bed and procreant cradle:
Where they most breed and haunt, I have observ'd
The air is delicate.

Enter *Lady Macbeth.*

Dun. See, see, our honour'd hostess!
The love that follows us sometime is our trouble,
Which still we thank as love. Herein I teach you
How you shall bid God 'ield us for your pains,
And thank us for your trouble.
Lady M. All our service
In every point twice done and then done double
Were poor and single business to contend
Against those honours deep and broad wherewith
Your Majesty loads our house: for those of old,
And the late dignities heap'd up to them,
We rest your hermits.
Dun. Where 's the thane of Cawdor?
We cours'd him at the heels, and had a purpose
To be his purveyor; but he rides well,
And his great love, sharp as his spur, hath holp him
To his home before us. Fair and noble hostess,
We are your guest to-night.
Lady M. Your servants ever
Have theirs, themselves, and what is theirs, in compt,

Scene vi: S. d. Hautboys, wind instruments. **3. gentle senses,** senses made gentle. **4. martlet,** martin. **approve,** prove. **5. mansionry,** nest-building. **6. jutty,** projection. **7. coign of vantage,** convenient corner. **11-14. The love . . . trouble,** the love that attends us is troublesome sometimes, but we always thank it because it is prompted by love. **13. 'ield,** yield, reward. **16. single,** small. **16-7. to contend Against,** in comparison with. **20. rest . . . hermits,** will pray for you, like hermits or beadsmen. **22. purveyor,** officer who went ahead to provide food for the king. **26. in compt,** subject to account.

To make their audit at your Highness' pleasure,
Still to return your own.
Dun. Give me your hand;
Conduct me to mine host: we love him highly,
And shall continue our graces towards him.
By your leave, hostess. *Exeunt.*

Scene VII. *Within Macbeth's castle.*

Hautboys and torches. Enter a *Sewer,* and divers *Servants* with dishes and service, over the stage. Then enter *Macbeth.*

Macb. If it were done when 't is done, then 't were well
It were done quickly: if the assassination
Could trammel up the consequence, and catch
With his surcease success; that but this blow
Might be the be-all and the end-all here,
But here, upon this bank and shoal of time,
We 'd jump the life to come. But in these cases
We still have judgement here, that we but teach
Bloody instructions, which, being taught, return
To plague th' inventor. This even-handed justice
Commends th' ingredients of our poison'd chalice
To our own lips. He 's here in double trust:
First, as I am his kinsman and his subject,
Strong both against the deed; then, as his host,
Who should against his murderer shut the door,
Not bear the knife myself. Besides, this Duncan
Hath borne his faculties so meek, hath been
So clear in his great office, that his virtues
Will plead like angels, trumpet-tongued, against
The deep damnation of his taking-off;
And pity, like a naked new-born babe
Striding the blast, or heaven's cherubin hors'd
Upon the sightless couriers of the air,
Shall blow the horrid deed in every eye,
That tears shall drown the wind. I have no spur
To prick the sides of my intent, but only
Vaulting ambition, which o'erleaps itself
And falls on the other—

Enter *Lady Macbeth.*

How now! what news?

Lady M. He has almost supp'd. Why have you left the chamber?
Macb. Hath he ask'd for me?
Lady M. Know you not he has?
Macb. We will proceed no further in this business.
He hath honour'd me of late; and I have bought
Golden opinions from all sorts of people,
Which would be worn now in their newest gloss,
Not cast aside so soon.
Lady M. Was the hope drunk
Wherein you dress'd yourself? Hath it slept since?
And wakes it now, to look so green and pale
At what it did so freely? From this time
Such I account thy love. Art thou afeard
To be the same in thine own act and valour
As thou art in desire? Wouldst thou have that
Which thou esteem'st the ornament of life,
And live a coward in thine own esteem,
Letting "I dare not" wait upon "I would,"
Like the poor cat i' th' adage?
Macb. Prithee, peace!
I dare do all that may become a man;
Who dares do more is none.
Lady M. What beast was 't, then,
That made you break this enterprise to me?
When you durst do it, then you were a man;
And, to be more than what you were, you would
Be so much more the man. Nor time nor place
Did then adhere, and yet you would make both.
They have made themselves, and that their fitness now
Does unmake you. I have given suck, and know
How tender 't is to love the babe that milks me;
I would, while it was smiling in my face,
Have pluck'd my nipple from his boneless gums
And dash'd the brains out, had I so sworn as you
Have done to this.
Macb. If we should fail?
Lady M. We fail?
But screw your courage to the sticking-place,
And we 'll not fail. When Duncan is asleep—
Whereto the rather shall his day's hard journey
Soundly invite him—his two chamberlains
Will I with wine and wassail so convince

28. Still, always. **Scene vii: S. d. Sewer**, butler. **3. trammel up**, entangle, as in a net. **4. with his surcease**, with the cessation of consequences. **7. jump**, risk. **17. faculties**, royal authority. **20. taking-off**, murder. **28. the other**, the other side.

37. green, sick. **45. th' adage**: "The cat would eat fish, and would not wet her feet." **48. break**, propose. **52. Did then adhere**, were suitable. **60. But**, only. **64. wassail**, carousing, liquor. **convince**, overpower.

That memory, the warder of the brain,
Shall be a fume, and the receipt of reason
A limbeck only: when in swinish sleep
Their drenched natures lies as in a death,
What cannot you and I perform upon
Th' unguarded Duncan? what not put upon
His spongy officers, who shall bear the guilt
Of our great quell?

Macb. Bring forth men-children only;
For thy undaunted mettle should compose
Nothing but males. Will it not be receiv'd,
When we have mark'd with blood those sleepy two
Of his own chamber and us'd their very daggers,
That they have done 't?

Lady M. Who dares receive it other,
As we shall make our griefs and clamour roar
Upon his death?

Macb. I am settled, and bend up
Each corporal agent to this terrible feat.
Away, and mock the time with fairest show;
False face must hide what the false heart doth know.

Exeunt.

ACT II. SCENE I. *The Court of Macbeth's castle.*

Enter *Banquo,* and *Fleance* with a torch before him.

Ban. How goes the night, boy?

Fle. The moon is down; I have not heard the clock.

Ban. And she goes down at twelve.

Fle. I take 't, 't is later, sir.

Ban. Hold, take my sword. There 's husbandry in heaven;
Their candles are all out. Take thee that too.
A heavy summons lies like lead upon me,
And yet I would not sleep. Merciful powers,
Restrain in me the cursed thoughts that nature
Gives way to in repose!

Enter *Macbeth,* and a Servant with a torch.

Give me my sword.
Who 's there?

Macb. A friend.

Ban. What, sir, not yet at rest? The King 's a-bed.
He hath been in unusual pleasure, and
Sent forth great largess to your offices.
This diamond he greets your wife withal,
By the name of most kind hostess; and shut up
In measureless content.

Macb. Being unprepar'd,
Our will became the servant to defect;
Which else should free have wrought.

Ban. All 's well.
I dreamt last night of the three weird sisters:
To you they have show'd some truth.

Macb. I think not of them;
Yet, when we can entreat an hour to serve,
We would spend it in some words upon that business,
If you would grant the time.

Ban. At your kind'st leisure.

Macb. If you shall cleave to my consent, when 't is,
It shall make honour for you.

Ban. So I lose none
In seeking to augment it, but still keep
My bosom franchis'd and allegiance clear,
I shall be counsell'd.

Macb. Good repose the while!

Ban. Thanks, sir; the like to you!

Exeunt Banquo and Fleance.

Macb. Go bid thy mistress, when my drink is ready,
She strike upon the bell. Get thee to bed.

Exit Servant.

Is this a dagger which I see before me,
The handle toward my hand? Come, let me clutch thee.
I have thee not, and yet I see thee still.
Art thou not, fatal vision, sensible
To feeling as to sight? or art thou but
A dagger of the mind, a false creation,
Proceeding from the heat-oppressed brain?
I see thee yet, in form as palpable
As this which now I draw.
Thou marshall'st me the way that I was going,
And such an instrument I was to use.
Mine eyes are made the fools o' th' other senses,
Or else worth all the rest: I see thee still,

65-7. **That . . . only,** according to old anatomists memory was stationed in the back of the head, like a warder to the brain. Drunkenness turns memory into a fume or smoke which rises into the part of the brain (receptacle) where reason is placed, as vapor from a retort rises into the cap (limbeck) of a still. **71. spongy,** drunken. **72. quell,** murder. **74. receiv'd,** believed. **Act II, Scene i: 4. husbandry,** economy. **5. that,** his dagger. **14. largess,** gifts. **offices,** servants' quarters.

77. other, otherwise. **78. As,** since. **Act II, Scene i: 25. If . . . 't is,** if you are loyal to me when the time comes. **28. franchis'd,** free from guilt. **36. fatal,** prophetic. **sensible,** perceptible.

And on thy blade and dudgeon gouts of blood,
Which was not so before. There 's no such thing.
It is the bloody business which informs
Thus to mine eyes. Now o'er the one half-world
Nature seems dead, and wicked dreams abuse
The curtain'd sleep: witchcraft celebrates
Pale Hecate's offerings, and wither'd Murder,
Alarum'd by his sentinel, the wolf,
Whose howl 's his watch, thus with his stealthy pace,
With Tarquin's ravishing strides, towards his design
Moves like a ghost. Thou sure and firm set earth,
Hear not my steps, which way they walk, for fear
The very stones prate of my whereabout,
And take the present horror from the time,
Which now suits with it. Whiles I threat, he lives:
Words to the heat of deeds too cold breath gives. *A bell rings.*
I go, and it is done; the bell invites me.
Hear it not, Duncan; for it is a knell
That summons thee to heaven or to hell. *Exit.*

Scene II. *The hall of the castle.*

Enter *Lady Macbeth.*

Lady M. That which hath made them drunk hath made me bold;
What hath quench'd them hath given me fire. Hark! Peace!
It was the owl that shriek'd, the fatal bellman
Which gives the stern'st good-night. He is about it.
The doors are open; and the surfeited grooms
Do mock their charge with snores. I have drugg'd their possets,
That death and nature do contend about them,
Whether they live or die.

Enter *Macbeth.*

Macb. Who 's there? What, ho!
Lady M. Alack, I am afraid they have awak'd,
And 't is not done. Th' attempt and not the deed
Confounds us. Hark! I laid their daggers ready;
He could not miss 'em. Had he not resembled
My father as he slept, I had done 't.—My husband?
Macb. I have done the deed. Didst thou not hear a noise?
Lady M. I heard the owl scream and the crickets cry.
Did not you speak?
Macb. When?
Lady M. Now.
Macb. As I descended?
Lady M. Ay.
Macb. Hark!
Who lies i' th' second chamber?
Lady M. Donalbain.
Macb. This is a sorry sight. *Looking on his hands.*
Lady M. A foolish thought, to say a sorry sight.
Macb. There 's one did laugh in 's sleep, and one cried, "Murder!"
That they did wake each other: I stood and heard them;
But they did say their prayers, and address'd them
Again to sleep.
Lady M. There are two lodg'd together.
Macb. One cried, "God bless us!" and "Amen" the other,
As they had seen me with these hangman's hands.
List'ning their fear, I could not say "Amen,"
When they did say, "God bless us!"
Lady M. Consider it not so deeply.
Macb. But wherefore could not I pronounce "Amen"?
I had most need of blessing, and "Amen"
Stuck in my throat.
Lady M. These deeds must not be thought
After these ways; so, it will make us mad.
Macb. Methought I heard a voice cry, "Sleep no more!
Macbeth does murder sleep,"—the innocent sleep,
Sleep that knits up the ravell'd sleave of care,
The death of each day's life, sore labour's bath,
Balm of hurt minds, great nature's second course,
Chief nourisher in life's feast,—
Lady M. What do you mean?
Macb. Still it cried, "Sleep no more!" to all the house;

46. **dudgeon,** hilt. **gouts,** drops. 48. **informs,** takes this shape. 50. **abuse,** deceive. 52. **Hecate's,** Hecate (here a dissyllable) was goddess of the underworld, and hence of witchcraft. 54. **his watch,** murder's signal. 55. **Tarquin's,** Sextus Tarquin, who ravished Lucretia. **Scene ii:** 3. **bellman,** the night watchman sent to condemned persons the night before their execution. 5. **grooms,** servants. 6. **possets,** hot drink composed of wine, milk, etc.

12. **Confounds,** ruins. 21. **sorry,** wretched. 25. **address'd them,** composed themselves. 28. **hangman's hands,** the Elizabethan hangman was accustomed to cut up the bodies of traitors; hence "bloody hands." 29. **List'ning,** listening to. 37. **sleave,** coarse unwrought silk. 39. **second course,** main course of a dinner.

"Glamis hath murder'd sleep, and therefore Cawdor
Shall sleep no more; Macbeth shall sleep no more."

Lady M. Who was it that thus cried? Why, worthy thane,
You do unbend your noble strength, to think
So brainsickly of things. Go get some water,
And wash this filthy witness from your hand.
Why did you bring these daggers from the place?
They must lie there: go carry them; and smear
The sleepy grooms with blood.

Macb. I 'll go no more.
I am afraid to think what I have done;
Look on 't again I dare not.

Lady M. Infirm of purpose!
Give me the daggers. The sleeping and the dead
Are but as pictures; 't is the eye of childhood
That fears a painted devil. If he do bleed,
I 'll gild the faces of the grooms withal;
For it must seem their guilt.
Exit. Knocking within.

Macb. Whence is that knocking?
How is 't with me, when every noise appalls me?
What hands are here? Ha! they pluck out mine eyes.
Will all great Neptune's ocean wash this blood
Clean from my hand? No, this my hand will rather
The multitudinous seas incarnadine,
Making the green one red.

Re-enter *Lady Macbeth.*

Lady M. My hands are of your colour; but I shame
To wear a heart so white. [*Knocking.*] I hear a knocking
At the south entry: retire we to our chamber.
A little water clears us of this deed;
How easy is it then! Your constancy
Hath left you unattended. [*Knocking.*] Hark! more knocking.
Get on your nightgown, lest occasion call us
And show us to be watchers. Be not lost
So poorly in your thoughts.

Macb. To know my deed, 't were best not know myself. *Knocking.*
Wake Duncan with thy knocking! I would thou couldst! *Exeunt.*

46. brainsickly, madly. **62. incarnadine,** make red. **68-9. constancy . . . unattended,** your firmness has deserted you. **70. nightgown,** dressing gown. **73. To . . . myself,** it would be better to lose consciousness of my being than to realize what I have done.

Scene III. *The courtyard of the castle.*

Enter a *Porter.* Knocking within.

Porter. Here 's a knocking indeed! If a man were porter of hell-gate, he should have old turning the key. [*Knocking.*] Knock, knock, knock! Who 's there, i' th' name of Belzebub? Here 's a farmer, that hanged himself on the expectation of plenty. Come in time; have napkins enow about you; here you 'll sweat for 't. [*Knocking.*] Knock, knock! Who 's there, in th' other devil's name? Faith, here 's an equivocator, that could swear in both the scales against either scale; who committed treason enough for God's sake, yet could not equivocate to heaven. O, come in, equivocator. [*Knocking.*] Knock, knock, knock! Who 's there? Faith, here 's an English tailor come hither, for stealing out of a French hose. Come in, tailor; here you may roast your goose. [*Knocking.*] Knock, knock; never at quiet! What are you? But this place is too cold for hell. I 'll devil-porter it no further: I had thought to have let in some of all professions that go the primrose way to th' everlasting bonfire. [*Knocking.*] Anon, anon. I pray you, remember the porter. *Opens the gate.*

Enter *Macduff* and *Lennox.*

Macd. Was it so late, friend, ere you went to bed,
That you do lie so late?

Port. Faith, sir, we were carousing till the second cock; and drink, sir, is a great provoker of three things.

Macd. What three things does drink especially provoke?

Port. Marry, sir, nose-painting, sleep, and urine. Lechery, sir, it provokes, and unprovokes; it provokes the desire, but it takes away the performance. Therefore, much drink may be said to be an equivocator with lechery: it makes him, and it mars him; it sets him on, and it takes him off; it persuades him, and disheartens him; makes him stand to, and not stand to; in conclusion, equivocates him in a sleep, and, giving him the lie, leaves him.

Macd. I believe drink gave thee the lie last night.

Port. That it did, sir, i' the very throat on me. But I requited him for his lie; and, I think, being too strong for him, though he

Scene iii: 3. old, a colloquial intensive (cf. "high old time"). **4-5. farmer . . . plenty,** the farmer who hoarded his grain had been ruined by the prospect of a large harvest and low prices. **6. napkins,** handkerchiefs. **16. French hose,** short and tight, from the material of which it would be hard to steal anything. **17. goose,** pressing iron.

took up my legs sometime, yet I made a shift to cast him.

Enter *Macbeth.*

Macd. Is thy master stirring?
Our knocking has awak'd him; here he comes.
Len. Good morrow, noble sir.
Macb. Good morrow, both.
Macd. Is the King stirring, worthy thane?
Macb. Not yet.
Macd. He did command me to call timely on him.
I have almost slipp'd the hour.
Macb. I 'll bring you to him.
Macd. I know this is a joyful trouble to you;
But yet 't is one.
Macb. The labour we delight in physics pain.
This is the door.
Macd. I 'll make so bold to call.
For 't is my limited service. *Exit.*
Len. Goes the King hence to-day?
Macb. He does; he did appoint so.
Len. The night has been unruly: where we lay,
Our chimneys were blown down; and, as they say,
Lamentings heard i' th' air; strange screams of death,
And prophesying with accents terrible
Of dire combustion and confus'd events
New hatch'd to th' woeful time. The obscure bird
Clamour'd the livelong night; some say, the earth
Was feverous and did shake.
Macb. 'T was a rough night.
Len. My young remembrance cannot parallel
A fellow to it.

Re-enter *Macduff.*

Macd. O horror, horror, horror! Tongue nor heart
Cannot conceive nor name thee!
Macb. } *Len.* } What 's the matter?
Macd. Confusion now hath made his masterpiece!
Most sacrilegious murder hath broke ope
The Lord's anointed temple, and stole thence
The life o' th' building!
Macb. What is 't you say? The life?
Len. Mean you his Majesty?
Macd. Approach the chamber, and destroy your sight
With a new Gorgon. Do not bid me speak;
See, and then speak yourselves.
Exeunt Macbeth and Lennox.
Awake, awake!
Ring the alarum-bell. Murder and treason!
Banquo and Donalbain! Malcolm! awake!
Shake off this downy sleep, death's counterfeit,
And look on death itself! Up, up, and see
The great doom's image! Malcolm! Banquo!
As from your graves rise up, and walk like sprites,
To countenance this horror! Ring the bell!
Bell rings.

Enter *Lady Macbeth.*

Lady M. What 's the business,
That such a hideous trumpet calls to parley
The sleepers of the house? Speak, speak!
Macd. O gentle lady,
'T is not for you to hear what I can speak;
The repetition in a woman's ear
Would murder as it fell.

Enter *Banquo.*

O Banquo, Banquo,
Our royal master 's murder'd!
Lady M. Woe, alas!
What, in our house?
Ban. Too cruel anywhere.
Dear Duff, I prithee, contradict thyself,
And say it is not so.

Re-enter *Macbeth* and *Lennox,* with *Ross.*

Macb. Had I but died an hour before this chance,
I had liv'd a blessed time; for, from this instant,
There 's nothing serious in mortality.
All is but toys; renown and grace is dead;
The wine of life is drawn, and the mere lees
Is left this vault to brag of.

Enter *Malcolm* and *Donalbain.*

Don. What is amiss?
Macb. You are, and do not know 't.
The spring, the head, the fountain of your blood
Is stopp'd; the very source of it is stopp'd.
Macd. Your royal father 's murder'd.
Mal. O, by whom?
Len. Those of his chamber, as it seem'd, had done 't.
Their hands and faces were all badg'd with blood;

46. cast, throw, throw up. **51. timely,** early. **55. physics,** cures. **57. limited,** appointed. **63. combustion,** tumult. **64. obscure bird,** owl. **71. Confusion,** destruction.

77. Gorgon, Medusa, one of the three monstrous Gorgons, turned people who saw her face into stone. **83. great doom's image,** image of the Day of Judgment. **85. countenance,** be in keeping with. **98. mortality,** human life. **107. badg'd,** marked.

So were their daggers, which unwip'd we found
Upon their pillows.
They star'd, and were distracted; no man's life
Was to be trusted with them.
Macb. O, yet I do repent me of my fury,
That I did kill them.
Macd. Wherefore did you so?
Macb. Who can be wise, amaz'd, temp'rate and furious,
Loyal and neutral, in a moment? No man.
Th' expedition of my violent love
Outrun the pauser, reason. Here lay Duncan,
His silver skin lac'd with his golden blood,
And his gash'd stabs look'd like a breach in nature
For ruin's wasteful entrance; there, the murderers,
Steep'd in the colours of their trade, their daggers
Unmannerly breech'd with gore. Who could refrain,
That had a heart to love, and in that heart
Courage to make 's love known?
Lady M. Help me hence, ho!
Macd. Look to the lady.
Mal. [*Aside to Donalbain.*] Why do we hold our tongues,
That most may claim this argument for ours?
Don. [*Aside to Malcolm.*] What should be spoken here, where our fate,
Hid in an auger-hole, may rush and seize us?
Let 's away;
Our tears are not yet brew'd.
Mal. [*Aside to Donalbain.*] Nor our strong sorrow
Upon the foot of motion.
Ban. Look to the lady;
Lady Macbeth is carried out.
And when we have our naked frailties hid,
That suffer in exposure, let us meet
And question this most bloody piece of work,
To know it further. Fears and scruples shake us:
In the great hand of God I stand, and thence
Against the undivulg'd pretence I fight
Of treasonous malice.
Macd. And so do I.
All. So all.
Macb. Let 's briefly put on manly readiness,
And meet i' th' hall together.
All. Well contented.
Exeunt all but Malcolm and Donalbain.
Mal. What will you do? Let 's not consort with them;
To show an unfelt sorrow is an office
Which the false man does easy. I 'll to England.
Don. To Ireland, I; our separated fortune
Shall keep us both the safer: where we are,
There 's daggers in men's smiles; the near in blood,
The nearer bloody.
Mal. This murderous shaft that 's shot
Hath not yet lighted, and our safest way
Is to avoid the aim. Therefore, to horse;
And let us not be dainty of leave-taking,
But shift away. There 's warrant in that theft
Which steals itself, when there 's no mercy left.
Exeunt.

Scene IV. *Outside Macbeth's castle.*

Enter *Ross* and an *Old Man.*

Old M. Threescore and ten I can remember well;
Within the volume of which time I have seen
Hours dreadful and things strange; but this sore night
Hath trifled former knowings.
Ross. Ah, good father,
Thou seest the heavens, as troubled with man's act,
Threatens his bloody stage: by th' clock 't is day,
And yet dark night strangles the travelling lamp.
Is 't night's predominance or the day's shame
That darkness does the face of earth entomb,
When living light should kiss it?
Old M. 'T is unnatural,
Even like the deed that 's done. On Tuesday last,
A falcon, tow'ring in her pride of place,
Was by a mousing owl hawk'd at and kill'd.
Ross. And Duncan's horses—a thing most strange and certain—
Beauteous and swift, the minions of their race,
Turn'd wild in nature, broke their stalls, flung out,
Contending 'gainst obedience, as they would make
War with mankind.
Old M. 'T is said they eat each other.
Ross. They did so, to th' amazement of mine eyes
That look'd upon 't.

116. expedition, haste. **122. breech'd,** clothed. **126. argument,** subject. **128. an auger-hole,** obscure place. **131. Upon . . . motion,** ready to be translated into action. **139. manly readiness,** male equipment, armor.

146-7. the near . . . bloody, the nearer the relationship, the more danger. **148. lighted,** spent its force **150. dainty,** ceremonious. **Scene iv: 4. Hath . . . knowings,** has made former experiences seem trivial. **8. predominance,** astrological influence. **12. tow'ring . . . place,** circling upward to the highest point in her flight.

Enter *Macduff*.

Here comes the good Macduff.
How goes the world, sir, now?
Macd. Why, see you not?
Ross. Is 't known who did this more than bloody deed?
Macd. Those that Macbeth hath slain.
Ross. Alas, the day!
What good could they pretend?
Macd. They were suborned.
Malcolm and Donalbain, the King's two sons,
Are stolen away and fled; which puts upon them
Suspicion of the deed.
Ross. 'Gainst nature still!
Thriftless ambition, that will ravin up
Thine own life's means! Then 't is most like
The sovereignty will fall upon Macbeth.
Macd. He is already nam'd, and gone to Scone
To be invested.
Ross. Where is Duncan's body?
Macd. Carried to Colmekill,
The sacred storehouse of his predecessors,
And guardian of their bones.
Ross. Will you to Scone?
Macd. No, cousin, I 'll to Fife.
Ross. Well, I will thither.
Macd. Well, may you see things well done there,—adieu!—
Lest our old robes sit easier than our new!
Ross. Farewell, father.
Old M. God's benison go with you; and with those
That would make good of bad, and friends of foes! *Exeunt.*

Act III. Scene I. *Forres. The palace.*

Enter *Banquo*.

Ban. Thou hast it now: King, Cawdor, Glamis, all,
As the weird women promis'd, and, I fear,
Thou play'dst most foully for 't: yet it was said
It should not stand in thy posterity,
But that myself should be the root and father
Of many kings. If there come truth from them—
As upon thee, Macbeth, their speeches shine—
Why, by the verities on thee made good,
May they not be my oracles as well,
And set me up in hope? But hush! no more.

Sennet sounded. Enter *Macbeth*, as King, *Lady Macbeth, Lennox, Ross*, Lords, and Attendants.

Macb. Here 's our chief guest.
Lady M. If he had been forgotten,
It had been as a gap in our great feast,
And all-thing unbecoming.
Macb. To-night we hold a solemn supper, sir,
And I 'll request your presence.
Ban. Let your Highness
Command upon me; to the which my duties
Are with a most indissoluble tie
For ever knit.
Macb. Ride you this afternoon?
Ban. Ay, my good lord.
Macb. We should have else desir'd your good advice,
(Which still hath been both grave and prosperous)
In this day's council; but we 'll take to-morrow.
Is 't far you ride?
Ban. As far, my lord, as will fill up the time
'Twixt this and supper. Go not my horse the better,
I must become a borrower of the night
For a dark hour or twain.
Macb. Fail not our feast.
Ban. My lord, I will not.
Macb. We hear our bloody cousins are bestow'd
In England and in Ireland, not confessing
Their cruel parricide, filling their hearers
With strange invention. But of that to-morrow,
When therewithal we shall have cause of state
Craving us jointly. Hie you to horse; adieu,
Till you return at night. Goes Fleance with you?
Ban. Ay, my good lord. Our time does call upon 's.
Macb. I wish your horses swift and sure of foot;
And so I do commend you to their backs.
Farewell. *Exit Banquo.*

24. pretend, intend. **suborned,** set on by others. **28. ravin up,** devour ravenously. **Act III, Scene i: 7. shine,** are conspicuously verified. **10. S. d. Sennet,** signal on a trumpet. **13. all-thing,** altogether. **14. solemn,** formal.

31. Scone, the ancient royal town where Scottish kings were crowned. **33. Colmekill,** Iona, one of the western isles, the burial place of Scottish kings. **40. benison,** blessing. **Act III, Scene i: 30. are bestow'd,** have taken refuge.

Let every man be master of his time
Till seven at night. To make society
The sweeter welcome, we will keep ourself
Till supper-time alone; while then, God be with you.
Exeunt all but Macbeth and a Servant.
Sirrah,
A word with you. Attend those men our pleasure?
Serv. They are, my lord, without the palace gate.
Macb. Bring them before us.
Exit Servant.
To be thus is nothing;
But to be safely thus. Our fears in Banquo
Stick deep; and in his royalty of nature
Reigns that which would be fear'd. 'T is much he dares;
And, to that dauntless temper of his mind,
He hath a wisdom that doth guide his valour
To act in safety. There is none but he
Whose being I do fear; and, under him,
My Genius is rebuk'd, as, it is said,
Mark Antony's was by Cæsar. He chid the sisters
When first they put the name of king upon me,
And bade them speak to him; then prophet-like
They hail'd him father to a line of kings.
Upon my head they plac'd a fruitless crown,
And put a barren sceptre in my gripe,
Thence to be wrench'd with an unlineal hand,
No son of mine succeeding. If 't be so,
For Banquo's issue have I fil'd my mind;
For them the gracious Duncan have I murder'd;
Put rancours in the vessel of my peace
Only for them; and mine eternal jewel
Given to the common enemy of man,
To make them kings, the seeds of Banquo kings!
Rather than so, come fate into the list,
And champion me to th' utterance! Who 's there?

Re-enter Servant, and two *Murderers.*

Now go to the door, and stay there till we call.
Exit Servant.
Was it not yesterday we spoke together?
1. Mur. It was, so please your Highness.
Macb. Well then, now
Have you consider'd of my speeches? Know
That it was he in the times past which held you
So under fortune, which you thought had been
Our innocent self. This I made good to you
In our last conference, pass'd in probation with you,
How you were borne in hand, how cross'd, the instruments,
Who wrought with them, and all things else that might
To half a soul and to a notion craz'd
Say, "Thus did Banquo."
1. Mur. You made it known to us.
Macb. I did so, and went further, which is now
Our point of second meeting. Do you find
Your patience so predominant in your nature
That you can let this go? Are you so gospell'd
To pray for this good man and for his issue,
Whose heavy hand hath bow'd you to the grave
And beggar'd yours for ever?
1. Mur. We are men, my liege.
Macb. Ay, in the catalogue ye go for men,
As hounds and greyhounds, mongrels, spaniels, curs,
Shoughs, water-rugs, and demi-wolves, are clept
All by the name of dogs; the valued file
Distinguishes the swift, the slow, the subtle,
The housekeeper, the hunter, every one
According to the gift which bounteous nature
Hath in him clos'd; whereby he does receive
Particular addition, from the bill
That writes them all alike; and so of men.
Now, if you have a station in the file,
Not i' th' worst rank of manhood, say 't;
And I will put that business in your bosoms,
Whose execution takes your enemy off,
Grapples you to the heart and love of us,
Who wear our health but sickly in his life,
Which in his death were perfect.
2. Mur. I am one, my liege,
Whom the vile blows and buffets of the world
Hath so incens'd that I am reckless what
I do to spite the world.
1. Mur. And I another
So weary with disasters, tugg'd with fortune,
That I would set my life on any chance,
To mend it, or be rid on 't.
Macb. Both of you
Know Banquo was your enemy.
Both Mur. True, my lord.

48. thus, a king. **51. would,** should. **56. My Genius . . . Cæsar,** Shakespeare got this story from Plutarch; cf. *Antony and Cleopatra,* II, iii, 18-22. **62. gripe,** grasp. **65. fil'd,** defiled. **68-9. mine . . . man,** sold my soul to the devil. **71. list,** lists, place of combat. **72. champion me,** fight for me. **to th' utterance,** to the death.

80. pass'd in probation, proved clearly. **81. borne in hand,** led on by deceitful promises. **83. notion craz'd,** feeble mind. **88. gospell'd,** full of the spirit of the gospel. **94. Shoughs, water-rugs,** shaggy dogs, water-dogs. **demi-wolves,** half dog, half wolf. **clept,** called. **95. valued file,** list based on value. **97. housekeeper,** watch-dog. **100-1. Particular . . . alike,** special value apart from the generic qualities of dogs. **107. in his life,** while he lives. **112. tugg'd with,** pulled about by.

Macb. So is he mine; and in such bloody distance,
That every minute of his being thrusts
Against my near'st of life; and though I could
With barefac'd power sweep him from my sight
And bid my will avouch it, yet I must not,
For certain friends that are both his and mine,
Whose loves I may not drop, but wail his fall
Who I myself struck down; and thence it is,
That I to your assistance do make love,
Masking the business from the common eye
For sundry weighty reasons.

2. Mur. We shall, my lord,
Perform what you command us.

1. Mur. Though our lives—

Macb. Your spirits shine through you. Within this hour at most
I will advise you where to plant yourselves;
Acquaint you with the perfect spy o' th' time,
The moment on 't; for 't must be done to-night,
And something from the palace; always thought
That I require a clearness: and with him—
To leave no rubs nor botches in the work—
Fleance his son, that keeps him company,
Whose absence is no less material to me
Than is his father's, must embrace the fate
Of that dark hour. Resolve yourselves apart;
I 'll come to you anon.

Both Mur. We are resolv'd, my lord.

Macb. I 'll call upon you straight; abide within. *Exeunt Murderers.*
It is concluded. Banquo, thy soul's flight,
If it find heaven, must find it out to-night.
Exit.

Scene II. *The palace.*

Enter *Lady Macbeth* and a *Servant.*

Lady M. Is Banquo gone from court?

Serv. Ay, madam, but returns again to-night.

Lady M. Say to the King, I would attend his leisure
For a few words.

Serv. Madam, I will. *Exit.*

Lady M. Nought 's had, all 's spent,
Where our desire is got without content:
'T is safer to be that which we destroy
Than by destruction dwell in doubtful joy.

Enter *Macbeth.*

How now, my lord! why do you keep alone,
Of sorriest fancies your companions making,
Using those thoughts which should indeed have died
With them they think on? Things without all remedy
Should be without regard; what 's done is done.

Macb. We have scorch'd the snake, not kill'd it;
She 'll close and be herself, whilst our poor malice
Remains in danger of her former tooth.
But let the frame of things disjoint, both the worlds suffer,
Ere we will eat our meal in fear, and sleep
In the affliction of these terrible dreams
That shake us nightly. Better be with the dead
Whom we, to gain our peace, have sent to peace,
Than on the torture of the mind to lie
In restless ecstasy. Duncan is in his grave;
After life's fitful fever he sleeps well.
Treason has done his worst; nor steel, nor poison,
Malice domestic, foreign levy, nothing,
Can touch him further.

Lady M. Come on,
Gentle my lord, sleek o'er your rugged looks;
Be bright and jovial among your guests to-night.

Macb. So shall I, love; and so, I pray, be you.
Let your remembrance apply to Banquo;
Present him eminence, both with eye and tongue—
Unsafe the while, that we
Must lave our honours in these flattering streams,
And make our faces vizards to our hearts,
Disguising what they are.

Lady M. You must leave this.

Macb. O, full of scorpions is my mind, dear wife!
Thou know'st that Banquo and his Fleance lives.

Lady M. But in them nature's copy 's not eterne.

Macb. There 's comfort yet; they are assailable:
Then be thou jocund; ere the bat hath flown

116. distance, enmity. **118. near'st of life,** most vital parts. **120. avouch,** warrant, affirm. **130. perfect . . . time,** exact knowledge of Banquo's arrival. **132. something,** some distance. **thought,** it being remembered. **133. require a clearness,** am not to be suspected. **134. rubs,** hindrances, slips. **138. Resolve yourselves,** make up your minds.

Scene ii: 13. scorch'd, scored, gashed. **14. close,** reunite. **16. frame of things,** the universe. **both the worlds,** heaven and earth. **22. ecstasy,** frenzy. **31. Present him eminence,** show him special favor. **32. Unsafe . . . that,** we are unsafe so long as. **34. vizards,** masks. **38. nature's . . . eterne,** their lease (**copy**) of life is not everlasting.

His cloister'd flight, ere to black Hecate's summons
The shard-borne beetle with his drowsy hums
Hath rung night's yawning peal, there shall be done
A deed of dreadful note.
Lady M. What 's to be done?
Macb. Be innocent of the knowledge, dearest chuck,
Till thou applaud the deed. Come, seeling night,
Scarf up the tender eye of pitiful day,
And with thy bloody and invisible hand
Cancel and tear to pieces that great bond
Which keeps me pale! Light thickens, and the crow
Makes wing to th' rooky wood;
Good things of day begin to droop and drowse,
Whiles night's black agents to their preys do rouse.
Thou marvell'st at my words, but hold thee still;
Things bad begun make strong themselves by ill.
So, prithee, go with me. *Exeunt.*

Scene III. *A park near the palace.*

Enter three *Murderers.*

1. Mur. But who did bid thee join with us?
3. Mur. Macbeth.
2. Mur. He needs not our mistrust, since he delivers
Our offices and what we have to do
To the direction just.
1. Mur. Then stand with us;
The west yet glimmers with some streaks of day.
Now spurs the lated traveller apace
To gain the timely inn; and near approaches
The subject of our watch.
3. Mur. Hark! I hear horses.
Ban. [*Within.*] Give us a light there, ho!
2. Mur. Then 't is he; the rest
That are within the note of expectation
Already are i' th' court.
1. Mur. His horses go about.
3. Mur. Almost a mile; but he does usually,
So all men do, from hence to th' palace gate
Make it their walk.

Enter *Banquo,* and *Fleance* with a torch.

2. Mur. A light, a light!
3. Mur. 'T is he.
1. Mur. Stand to 't.
Ban. It will be rain to-night.
1. Mur. Let it come down.
They set upon Banquo.
Ban. O, treachery! Fly, good Fleance, fly, fly, fly!
Thou mayst revenge. O slave!
Dies. Fleance escapes.
3. Mur. Who did strike out the light?
1. Mur. Was 't not the way?
3. Mur. There 's but one down; the son is fled.
2. Mur. We have lost
Best half of our affair.
1. Mur. Well, let 's away, and say how much is done. *Exeunt.*

Scene IV. *A hall in the palace.*

A banquet prepared. Enter *Macbeth, Lady Macbeth, Ross, Lennox,* Lords, and Attendants.

Macb. You know your own degrees; sit down: at first
And last, the hearty welcome.
Lords. Thanks to your Majesty.
Macb. Ourself will mingle with society
And play the humble host.
Our hostess keeps her state, but in best time
We will require her welcome.
Lady M. Pronounce it for me, sir, to all our friends,
For my heart speaks they are welcome.

Enter First *Murderer* at the door.

Macb. See, they encounter thee with their hearts' thanks.
Both sides are even; here I 'll sit i' th' midst.
Be large in mirth; anon we 'll drink a measure
The table round. [*Approaching the door.*] —There 's blood upon thy face.
Mur. 'T is Banquo's then.
Macb. 'T is better thee without than he within.
Is he dispatch'd?
Mur. My lord, his throat is cut; that I did for him.
Macb. Thou art the best o' th' cut-throats; yet he 's good
That did the like for Fleance. If thou didst it,
Thou art the nonpareil.

42. **shard-borne,** borne on horny wings. 43. **yawning,** drowsy. 46. **seeling,** eye-closing. Hawks were tamed by having their eyelids "seeled" or sewn shut. 49. **great bond,** both Banquo's lease of life and the promise made to Banquo by the witches. 51. **rooky,** inhabited by rooks. **Scene iii:** 2. **He,** the third murderer. 3. **offices,** duties. 4. **To . . . just,** exactly as Macbeth directed us 6. **lated,** belated. 10. **within . . . expectation,** on the list of expected guests.

Scene iv: 1. **degrees,** rank, order of precedence. 1-2. **at . . . last,** once for all. 5. **state,** chair of state. 6. **require,** ask for. 11. **large,** free. 14. **thee . . . within,** on the outside of thee than inside him.

Mur. Most royal sir,
Fleance is scap'd.

Macb. Then comes my fit again. I had else been perfect,
Whole as the marble, founded as the rock,
As broad and general as the casing air;
But now I am cabin'd, cribb'd, confin'd, bound in
To saucy doubts and fears. But Banquo 's safe?

Mur. Ay, my good lord; safe in a ditch he bides,
With twenty trenched gashes on his head,
The least a death to nature.

Macb. Thanks for that;
There the grown serpent lies: the worm that 's fled
Hath nature that in time will venom breed,
No teeth for th' present. Get thee gone; to-morrow
We 'll hear ourselves again. *Exit Murderer.*

Lady M. My royal lord,
You do not give the cheer: the feast is sold
That is not often vouch'd, while 't is a-making,
'T is given with welcome. To feed were best at home;
From thence, the sauce to meat is ceremony;
Meeting were bare without it.

Enter the Ghost of *Banquo,* and sits in *Macbeth's* place.

Macb. Sweet remembrancer!
Now, good digestion wait on appetite,
And health on both!

Len. May 't please your Highness sit.

Macb. Here had we now our country's honour roof'd,
Were the grac'd person of our Banquo present,
Who may I rather challenge for unkindness
Than pity for mischance.

Ross. His absence, sir,
Lays blame upon his promise. Please 't your Highness
To grace us with your royal company?

Macb. The table 's full.

Len. Here is a place reserv'd, sir.

Macb. Where?

Len. Here, my good lord. What is 't that moves your Highness?

Macb. Which of you have done this?

Lords. What, my good lord?

Macb. Thou canst not say I did it; never shake
Thy gory locks at me.

Ross. Gentlemen, rise: his Highness is not well.

Lady M. Sit, worthy friends; my lord is often thus,
And hath been from his youth. Pray you, keep seat;
The fit is momentary; upon a thought
He will again be well. If much you note him,
You shall offend him and extend his passion.
Feed, and regard him not. [*Aside to Macbeth.*] Are you a man?

Macb. Ay, and a bold one, that dare look on that
Which might appal the devil.

Lady M. [*Aside to Macbeth.*] O proper stuff!
This is the very painting of your fear;
This is the air-drawn dagger which, you said,
Led you to Duncan. O, these flaws and starts,
(Impostors to true fear) would well become
A woman's story at a winter's fire,
Authoriz'd by her grandam. Shame itself!
Why do you make such faces? When all 's done,
You look but on a stool.

Macb. Prithee, see there! behold! look! lo! how say you?
Why, what care I? If thou canst nod, speak too.
If charnel-houses and our graves must send
Those that we bury back, our monuments
Shall be the maws of kites. *Ghost vanishes.*

Lady M. [*Aside to Macbeth.*] What, quite unmann'd in folly?

Macb. If I stand here, I saw him.

Lady M. [*Aside to Macbeth.*] Fie, for shame!

Macb. Blood hath been shed ere now, i' th' olden time,
Ere humane statute purg'd the gentle weal;
Ay, and since too, murders have been perform'd
Too terrible for the ear. The times has been,
That, when the brains were out, the man would die,
And there an end; but now they rise again,
With twenty mortal murders on their crowns,
And push us from our stools. This is more strange
Than such a murder is.

Lady M. My worthy lord,
Your noble friends do lack you.

Macb. I do forget.
Do not muse at me, my most worthy friends;

23. **casing**, surrounding. 24. **cribb'd,** hampered. 25. **saucy**, insolent. 32. **hear ourselves,** discuss the matter. 33. **give the cheer**, act as a proper host. **the feast is sold,** like a meal at an inn. 36. **From thence,** away from home. 40. **roof'd,** under one roof. 41. **grac'd,** gracious, honored.

55. **upon a thought,** in a moment. 57. **extend,** prolong. 60. **O proper stuff,** what utter nonsense. 63. **flaws,** gusts of passion. 72-3. **our . . . kites,** let us be buried in the stomachs of hawks in which case ghosts could not rise. 76. **purg'd . . . weal,** made the nation gentle by purging it of violence. 81. **mortal murders,** fatal wounds. 84. **lack,** miss. 85. **muse,** wonder.

I have a strange infirmity, which is nothing
To those that know me. Come, love and health to all;
Then I 'll sit down. Give me some wine; fill full.
I drink to th' general joy o' the whole table,
And to our dear friend Banquo, whom we miss;
Would he were here! to all and him we thirst,
And all to all.
Lords. Our duties, and the pledge.

Re-enter *Ghost.*

Macb. Avaunt! and quit my sight! let the earth hide thee!
Thy bones are marrowless, thy blood is cold;
Thou hast no speculation in those eyes
Which thou dost glare with!
Lady M. Think of this, good peers,
But as a thing of custom; 't is no other,
Only it spoils the pleasure of the time.
Macb. What man dare, I dare.
Approach thou like the rugged Russian bear,
The arm'd rhinoceros, or th' Hyrcan tiger;
Take any shape but that, and my firm nerves
Shall never tremble. Or be alive again,
And dare me to the desert with thy sword;
If trembling I inhabit then, protest me
The baby of a girl. Hence, horrible shadow!
Unreal mockery, hence! *Ghost vanishes.*
Why, so; being gone,
I am a man again. Pray you, sit still.
Lady M. You have displac'd the mirth, broke the good meeting,
With most admir'd disorder.
Macb. Can such things be,
And overcome us like a summer's cloud,
Without our special wonder? You make me strange
Even to the disposition that I owe,
When now I think you can behold such sights,
And keep the natural ruby of your cheeks,
When mine is blanch'd with fear.
Ross. What sights, my lord?
Lady M. I pray you, speak not; he grows worse and worse;
Question enrages him. At once, good-night.
Stand not upon the order of your going,
But go at once.
Len. Good-night; and better health
Attend his Majesty!
Lady M. A kind good-night to all!
Exeunt Lords.
Macb. It will have blood, they say; blood will have blood.
Stones have been known to move and trees to speak;
Augures and understood relations have
By maggot-pies and choughs and rooks brought forth
The secret'st man of blood. What is the night?
Lady M. Almost at odds with morning, which is which.
Macb. How say'st thou, that Macduff denies his person
At our great bidding?
Lady M. Did you send to him, sir?
Macb. I hear it by the way; but I will send.
There 's not a one of them but in his house
I keep a servant fee'd. I will to-morrow,
(And betimes I will) to the weird sisters.
More shall they speak; for now I am bent to know,
By the worst means, the worst. For mine own good
All causes shall give way. I am in blood
Stepp'd in so far that, should I wade no more,
Returning were as tedious as go o'er.
Strange things I have in head, that will to hand,
Which must be acted ere they may be scann'd.
Lady M. You lack the season of all natures, sleep.
Macb. Come, we 'll to sleep. My strange and self-abuse
Is the initiate fear that wants hard use;
We are yet but young in deed. *Exeunt.*

Scene V. *A heath.*

Thunder. Enter the three *Witches,* meeting *Hecate.*

1. Witch. Why, how now, Hecate! you look angerly.
Hec. Have I not reason, beldams as you are,
Saucy and overbold? How did you dare
To trade and traffic with Macbeth
In riddles and affairs of death;
And I, the mistress of your charms,
The close contriver of all harms,
Was never call'd to bear my part,
Or show the glory of our art?
And, which is worse, all you have done
Hath been but for a wayward son,
Spiteful and wrathful, who, as others do,

91. thirst, offer a toast. **92. all to all,** all good health to all. **95. speculation,** light of intelligence. **101. Hyrcan,** of Hyrcania, near the Caspian Sea. **105. trembling I inhabit,** dwell, continue, in a state of trembling. **106. baby of a girl,** a girl's doll. **110. admir'd,** causing wonder. **119. Stand . . . going,** do not take formal leave.

123. Stones . . . speak, possibly an allusion to the superstition that stones refused to cover the body of a murdered man. Speaking trees may be a reminiscence of a passage in Reginald Scot's *Discovery of Witchcraft,* or of the incident in the *Æneid,* where a tree reveals a murder. **124. Augures,** auguries, interpretation of omens. **understood relations,** a continuation of the idea of auguries, the perception of significance in omens. **125. maggot-pies,** magpies. **choughs,** jackdaws. **139. will to hand,** must be acted. **141. season,** seasoning, preservative. **142. self-abuse,** self-delusion. **143. initiate fear,** fear of a novice in crime.

Loves for his own ends, not for you.
But make amends now; get you gone,
And at the pit of Acheron
Meet me i' th' morning; thither he
Will come to know his destiny.
Your vessels and your spells provide,
Your charms and everything beside.
I am for the air; this night I 'll spend
Unto a dismal and a fatal end;
Great business must be wrought ere noon.
Upon the corner of the moon
There hangs a vaporous drop profound;
I 'll catch it ere it come to ground;
And that distill'd by magic sleights
Shall raise such artificial sprites
As by the strength of their illusion
Shall draw him on to his confusion.
He shall spurn fate, scorn death, and bear
His hopes 'bove wisdom, grace, and fear;
And, you all know, security
Is mortals' chiefest enemy.

Music, and a song.

Hark! I am call'd; my little spirit, see,
Sits in a foggy cloud, and stays for me. *Exit.*

Sing within: "Come away, come away," etc.

1. Witch. Come, let 's make haste; she 'll soon be back again. *Exeunt.*

Scene VI. *Forres. The palace.*

Enter *Lennox* and another *Lord.*

Len. My former speeches have but hit your thoughts,
Which can interpret farther; only, I say,
Things have been strangely borne. The gracious Duncan
Was pitied of Macbeth; marry, he was dead:
And the right-valiant Banquo walk'd too late;
Whom, you may say (if 't please you) Fleance kill'd,
For Fleance fled; men must not walk too late.
Who cannot want the thought how monstrous
It was for Malcolm and for Donalbain
To kill their gracious father? Damned fact!
How it did grieve Macbeth! Did he not straight
In pious rage the two delinquents tear,
That were the slaves of drink and thralls of sleep?
Was not that nobly done? Ay, and wisely too;
For 't would have anger'd any heart alive
To hear the men deny 't. So that, I say,
He has borne all things well; and I do think
That had he Duncan's sons under his key—
As, an 't please Heaven, he shall not—they should find
What 't were to kill a father; so should Fleance.
But, peace! for from broad words, and 'cause he fail'd
His presence at the tyrant's feast, I hear
Macduff lives in disgrace. Sir, can you tell
Where he bestows himself?

Lord. The son of Duncan
(From whom this tyrant holds the due of birth)
Lives in the English court, and is receiv'd
Of the most pious Edward with such grace
That the malevolence of Fortune nothing
Takes from his high respect. Thither Macduff
Is gone to pray the holy king, upon his aid
To wake Northumberland and warlike Siward;
That, by the help of these—with Him above
To ratify the work—we may again
Give to our tables meat, sleep to our nights,
Free from our feasts and banquets bloody knives,
Do faithful homage and receive free honours;
All which we pine for now: and this report
Hath so exasperate their king that he
Prepares for some attempt of war.

Len. Sent he to Macduff?

Lord. He did; and with an absolute "Sir, not I,"
The cloudy messenger turns me his back,
And hums, as who should say, "You 'll rue the time
That clogs me with this answer."

Len. And that well might
Advise him to a caution, t' hold what distance
His wisdom can provide. Some holy angel
Fly to the court of England and unfold
His message ere he come, that a swift blessing
May soon return to this our suffering country
Under a hand accurs'd!

Lord. I 'll send my prayers with him. *Exeunt.*

15. Acheron, river in Hades. **24. profound**, having deep and hidden qualities. **32. security**, overconfidence. **Scene vi: 8. cannot . . . thought**, can help thinking.

21. from, because of. **broad**, plain. **27. Edward**, Edward the Confessor. **30. upon his aid**, in aid of Malcolm. **38. their king**, the king of England. **40. absolute**, positive. **41. cloudy**, sullen.

ACT IV. Scene I. *A cavern. In the middle, a boiling cauldron.*

Thunder. Enter the three *Witches.*

1. Witch. Thrice the brinded cat hath mew'd.
2. Witch. Thrice, and once the hedge-pig whin'd.
3. Witch. Harpier cries; " 'T is time, 't is time."
1. Witch. Round about the cauldron go;
In the poison'd entrails throw.
Toad, that under cold stone
Days and nights has thirty-one
Swelter'd venom sleeping got,
Boil thou first i' th' charmed pot.
All. Double, double, toil and trouble;
Fire burn and cauldron bubble.
2. Witch. Fillet of a fenny snake,
In the cauldron boil and bake;
Eye of newt and toe of frog,
Wool of bat and tongue of dog,
Adder's fork and blind-worm's sting,
Lizard's leg and howlet's wing,
For a charm of powerful trouble,
Like a hell-broth boil and bubble.
All. Double, double, toil and trouble;
Fire burn and cauldron bubble.
3. Witch. Scale of dragon, tooth of wolf,
Witches' mummy, maw and gulf
Of the ravin'd salt-sea shark,
Root of hemlock digg'd i' th' dark,
Liver of blaspheming Jew,
Gall of goat, and slips of yew
Sliver'd in the moon's eclipse,
Nose of Turk and Tartar's lips,
Finger of birth-strangled babe
Ditch-deliver'd by a drab,
Make the gruel thick and slab.
Add thereto a tiger's chaudron,
For th' ingredients of our cauldron.
All. Double, double, toil and trouble;
Fire burn and cauldron bubble.
2. Witch. Cool it with a baboon's blood,
Then the charm is firm and good.

Enter *Hecate* and the other three Witches.

Hec. O, well done! I commend your pains;
And every one shall share i' th' gains.
And now about the cauldron sing,
Like elves and fairies in a ring,
Enchanting all that you put in. *Exit Hecate.*
Music and a song: "Black spirits," etc.

2. Witch. By the pricking of my thumbs,
Something wicked this way comes.
Open, locks,
Whoever knocks!

Enter *Macbeth.*

Macb. How now, you secret, black, and midnight hags!
What is 't you do?
All. A deed without a name.
Macb. I conjure you, by that which you profess,
Howe'er you come to know it, answer me!
Though you untie the winds and let them fight
Against the churches; though the yesty waves
Confound and swallow navigation up;
Though bladed corn be lodg'd and trees blown down;
Though castles topple on their warders' heads;
Though palaces and pyramids do slope
Their heads to their foundations; though the treasure
Of nature's germen tumble all together,
Even till destruction sicken; answer me
To what I ask you.
1. Witch. Speak.
2. Witch. Demand.
3. Witch. We 'll answer.
1. Witch. Say, if thou 'dst rather hear it from our mouths,
Or from our masters'?
Macb. Call 'em; let me see 'em.
1. Witch. Pour in sow's blood, that hath eaten
Her nine farrow; grease that 's sweaten
From the murderer's gibbet throw
Into the flame.
All. Come, high or low;
Thyself and office deftly show!

Thunder. First *Apparition,* an armed Head.

Macb. Tell me, thou unknown power,—
1. Witch. He knows thy thought.
Hear his speech, but say thou nought.
1. App. Macbeth! Macbeth! Macbeth! beware Macduff;
Beware the thane of Fife. Dismiss me. Enough. *He descends.*
Macb. Whate'er thou art, for thy good caution, thanks;

Act IV, Scene i: 3. Harpier, the familiar of the third witch, in the form of a harpy. **12. fenny,** inhabiting swamps. **16. fork,** forked tongue. **blind-worm's,** small lizard thought to be poisonous. **17. howlet's,** owl's. **23. mummy,** medicine made from mummies. **gulf,** gullet. **24. ravin'd,** ravenous. **32. slab,** sticky. **33. chaudron,** entrails.

53. yesty, foamy. **55. bladed,** in the blade, green. **lodg'd,** beaten down. **59. nature's germen,** seeds of matter. **60. sicken,** be surfeited. **65. farrow,** litter of pigs. **68. S. d. armed Head,** representing the severed head of Macbeth (cf. V, viii, 54-5). But it may also suggest the rising of Scotland, led by Macduff; cf. the warning "beware Macduff," and "Rebellious head" (l. 97 below). "Head" is frequent in Shakespeare for a rebellion.

Thou hast harp'd my fear aright. But one word more,—
1. Witch. He will not be commanded. Here 's another,
More potent than the first.

Thunder. Second *Apparition,* a bloody Child.

2. App. Macbeth! Macbeth! Macbeth!
Macb. Had I three ears, I 'd hear thee.
2. App. Be bloody, bold, and resolute; laugh to scorn
The power of man; for none of woman born
Shall harm Macbeth. *Descends.*
Macb. Then live, Macduff: what need I fear of thee?
But yet I 'll make assurance double sure,
And take a bond of fate: thou shalt not live;
That I may tell pale-hearted fear it lies,
And sleep in spite of thunder.

Thunder. Third *Apparition,* a Child crowned, with a tree in his hand.

What is this
That rises like the issue of a king,
And wears upon his baby-brow the round
And top of sovereignty?
All. Listen, but speak not to 't.
3. App. Be lion-mettled, proud, and take no care
Who chafes, who frets, or where conspirers are.
Macbeth shall never vanquish'd be until
Great Birnam wood to high Dunsinane hill
Shall come against him. *Descends.*
Macb. That will never be.
Who can impress the forest, bid the tree
Unfix his earth-bound root? Sweet bodements! good!
Rebellious head, rise never till the wood
Of Birnam rise, and our high-plac'd Macbeth
Shall live the lease of nature, pay his breath
To time and mortal custom. Yet my heart
Throbs to know one thing: tell me, if your art
Can tell so much, shall Banquo's issue ever
Reign in this kingdom?
All. Seek to know no more.
Macb. I will be satisfied! Deny me this,
And an eternal curse fall on you! Let me know.
Why sinks that cauldron? And what noise is this? *Hautboys.*
1. Witch. Show!
2. Witch. Show!
3. Witch. Show!
All. Show his eyes, and grieve his heart;
Come like shadows, so depart!

A show of Eight *Kings* and *Banquo,* the last with a glass in his hand.

Macb. Thou art too like the spirit of Banquo; down!
Thy crown does sear mine eye-balls. And thy hair,
Thou other gold-bound brow, is like the first.
A third is like the former. Filthy hags!
Why do you show me this? A fourth! Start, eyes!
What, will the line stretch out to th' crack of doom?
Another yet! A seventh! I 'll see no more.
And yet the eighth appears, who bears a glass
Which shows me many more; and some I see
That twofold balls and treble sceptres carry.
Horrible sight! Now, I see, 't is true;
For the blood-bolter'd Banquo smiles upon me,
And points at them for his. [*Apparitions vanish.*] What, is this so?
1. Witch. Ay, sir, all this is so; but why
Stands Macbeth thus amazedly?
Come, sisters, cheer we up his sprites,
And show the best of our delights.
I 'll charm the air to give a sound,
While you perform your antic round;
That this great king may kindly say,
Our duties did his welcome pay.
Music. The Witches dance, and vanish.
Macb. Where are they? Gone? Let this pernicious hour
Stand aye accursed in the calendar!
Come in, without there!

Enter *Lennox.*

Len. What 's your Grace's will?
Macb. Saw you the weird sisters?
Len. No, my lord.
Macb. Came they not by you?
Len. No, indeed, my lord.
Macb. Infected be the air whereon they ride;
And damn'd all those that trust them! I did hear
The galloping of horse; who was 't came by?
Len. 'T is two or three, my lord, that bring you word
Macduff is fled to England.

74. harp'd, touched. **76. S. d. bloody Child,** a glance at the manner of Macduff's birth (cf. V, viii, 15-16). **86. S. d. a Child crowned, with a tree in his hand,** Malcolm, whose device it was that his soldiers should carry boughs before them (cf. V, iv, 4ff.). **88. round,** crown. **95. impress,** force into military service. **96. bodements,** prophecies. **99. lease of nature,** natural term. **100. mortal custom,** human custom of dying. **106. noise,** music.

121. twofold balls and treble sceptres carry, a reference to King James's being crowned at Scone and at Westminster, and assuming the title of King of Great Britain, France and Ireland. **123. blood-bolter'd,** having hair matted with blood. **130. antic round,** grotesque circular dance.

Macb. Fled to England!
Len. Ay, my good lord.
Macb. Time, thou anticipat'st my dread exploits:
The flighty purpose never is o'ertook
Unless the deed go with it. From this moment
The very firstlings of my heart shall be
The firstlings of my hand. And even now,
To crown my thoughts with acts, be it thought and done:
The castle of Macduff I will surprise;
Seize upon Fife; give to th' edge o' th' sword
His wife, his babes, and all unfortunate souls
That trace him in his line. No boasting like a fool;
This deed I 'll do before this purpose cool.
But no more sights!—Where are these gentlemen?
Come, bring me where they are. *Exeunt.*

Scene II. *Fife. Macduff's castle.*

Enter *Lady Macduff,* her *Son,* and *Ross.*

L. Macd. What had he done, to make him fly the land?
Ross. You must have patience, madam.
L. Macd. He had none;
His flight was madness: when our actions do not,
Our fears do make us traitors.
Ross. You know not
Whether it was his wisdom or his fear.
L. Macd. Wisdom! to leave his wife, to leave his babes,
His mansion and his titles, in a place
From whence himself does fly? He loves us not,
He wants the natural touch; for the poor wren,
The most diminutive of birds, will fight,
Her young ones in her nest, against the owl.
All is the fear and nothing is the love;
As little is the wisdom, where the flight
So runs against all reason.
Ross. My dearest coz,
I pray you, school yourself; but for your husband,
He is noble, wise, judicious, and best knows
The fits o' th' season. I dare not speak much further;
But cruel are the times when we are traitors
And do not know ourselves; when we hold rumour
From what we fear, yet know not what we fear,
But float upon a wild and violent sea
Each way and move. I take my leave of you;
Shall not be long but I 'll be here again.
Things at the worst will cease, or else climb upward
To what they were before. My pretty cousin,
Blessing upon you!
L. Macd. Father'd he is, and yet he 's fatherless.
Ross. I am so much a fool, should I stay longer,
It would be my disgrace and your discomfort.
I take my leave at once. *Exit.*
L. Macd. Sirrah, your father 's dead;
And what will you do now? How will you live?
Son. As birds do, mother.
L. Macd. What, with worms and flies?
Son. With what I get, I mean; and so do they.
L. Macd. Poor bird! thou 'dst never fear the net nor lime,
The pitfall nor the gin.
Son. Why should I, mother? Poor birds they are not set for.
My father is not dead, for all your saying.
L. Macd. Yes, he is dead. How wilt thou do for a father?
Son. Nay, how will you do for a husband?
L. Macd. Why, I can buy me twenty at any market.
Son. Then you 'll buy 'em to sell again.
L. Macd. Thou speak'st with all thy wit; and yet, i' faith,
With wit enough for thee.
Son. Was my father a traitor, mother?
L. Macd. Ay, that he was.
Son. What is a traitor?
L. Macd. Why, one that swears and lies.
Son. And be all traitors that do so?
L. Macd. Every one that does so is a traitor, and must be hanged.
Son. And must they all be hanged that swear and lie?
L. Macd. Every one.
Son. Who must hang them?
L. Macd. Why, the honest men.
Son. Then the liars and swearers are fools; for there are liars and swearers enow to beat the honest men and hang up them.
L. Macd. Now, God help thee, poor monkey!
But how wilt thou do for a father?
Son. If he were dead, you 'd weep for him; if you would not, it were a good sign that I should quickly have a new father.
L. Macd. Poor prattler, how thou talk'st!

145. flighty, fleeting. **153. trace,** follow. **Scene ii: 7. titles,** estates. **9. touch,** affection. **17. fits . . . season,** disorders of the time. **19. hold,** accept.

22. Each . . . move, every way and toss to and fro. **29. It . . . discomfort,** i.e., I should weep. **34. lime,** lime used for catching birds. **35. gin,** snare. **47. swears and lies,** takes an oath and breaks it.

Enter a *Messenger*.

Mess. Bless you, fair dame! I am not to you known,
Though in your state of honour I am perfect.
I doubt some danger does approach you nearly.
If you will take a homely man's advice,
Be not found here; hence, with your little ones.
To fright you thus, methinks, I am too savage;
To do worse to you were fell cruelty,
Which is too nigh your person. Heaven preserve you!
I dare abide no longer. *Exit Messenger.*
L. Macd. Whither should I fly?
I have done no harm. But I remember now
I am in this earthly world, where to do harm
Is often laudable, to do good sometime
Accounted dangerous folly. Why then, alas,
Do I put up that womanly defence,
To say I have done no harm?

Enter *Murderers*.

What are these faces?
1. Mur. Where is your husband?
L. Macd. I hope, in no place so unsanctified
Where such as thou mayst find him.
1. Mur. He 's a traitor.
Son. Thou liest, thou shag-ear'd villain!
1. Mur. What, you egg! *Stabbing him.*
Young fry of treachery!
Son. He has kill'd me, mother:
Run away, I pray you! *Dies.*
Exit Lady Macduff crying "Murder!" *Exeunt Murderers, following her.*

Scene III. *England. Before the King's palace.*

Enter *Malcolm* and *Macduff*.

Mal. Let us seek out some desolate shade, and there
Weep our sad bosoms empty.
Macd. Let us rather
Hold fast the mortal sword, and like good men
Bestride our down-fall'n birthdom. Each new morn
New widows howl, new orphans cry, new sorrows
Strike heaven on the face, that it resounds
As if it felt with Scotland, and yell'd out
Like syllable of dolour.
Mal. What I believe I 'll wail,
What know believe, and what I can redress,
As I shall find the time to friend, I will.
What you have spoke, it may be so perchance.
This tyrant, whose sole name blisters our tongues,
Was once thought honest; you have lov'd him well.
He hath not touch'd you yet. I am young; but something
You may deserve of him through me, and wisdom
To offer up a weak poor innocent lamb
To appease an angry god.
Macd. I am not treacherous.
Mal. But Macbeth is.
A good and virtuous nature may recoil
In an imperial charge. But I shall crave your pardon;
That which you are my thoughts cannot transpose.
Angels are bright still, though the brightest fell.
Though all things foul would wear the brows of grace,
Yet grace must still look so.
Macd. I have lost my hopes.
Mal. Perchance even there where I did find my doubts.
Why in that rawness left you wife and child,
Those precious motives, those strong knots of love,
Without leave-taking? I pray you,
Let not my jealousies be your dishonours,
But mine own safeties. You may be rightly just,
Whatever I shall think.
Macd. Bleed, bleed, poor country!
Great tyranny! lay thou thy basis sure,
For goodness dare not check thee; wear thou thy wrongs;
The title is affeer'd! Fare thee well, lord:
I would not be the villain that thou think'st
For the whole space that 's in the tyrant's grasp,
And the rich East to boot.
Mal. Be not offended;
I speak not as in absolute fear of you.
I think our country sinks beneath the yoke;
It weeps, it bleeds; and each new day a gash
Is added to her wounds. I think withal
There would be hands uplifted in my right;
And here from gracious England have I offer
Of goodly thousands. But, for all this,
When I shall tread upon the tyrant's head,

66. in . . . perfect, know your rank. **84. fry of treachery,** child of a traitor. **Scene iii: 4. Bestride,** stand over as defenders. **birthdom,** native land. **8. syllable of dolour,** cry of anguish.

10. the time . . . friend, good occasion. **12. sole,** mere. **15. wisdom,** it were wisdom. **19-20. recoil . . . charge,** act dishonorably under a king's orders. **21. transpose,** alter. **25. doubts,** of your honor, doubts awakened by Macduff's leaving his family. **26. rawness,** haste. **29. jealousies,** suspicions. **34. affeer'd,** confirmed.

Or wear it on my sword, yet my poor country
Shall have more vices than it had before,
More suffer and more sundry ways than ever,
By him that shall succeed.
Macd. What should he be?
Mal. It is myself I mean; in whom I know
All the particulars of vice so grafted
That, when they shall be open'd, black Macbeth
Will seem as pure as snow, and the poor state
Esteem him as a lamb, being compar'd
With my confineless harms.
Macd. Not in the legions
Of horrid hell can come a devil more damn'd
In evils to top Macbeth.
Mal. I grant him bloody,
Luxurious, avaricious, false, deceitful,
Sudden, malicious, smacking of every sin
That has a name; but there 's no bottom, none,
In my voluptuousness: your wives, your daughters,
Your matrons, and your maids, could not fill up
The cistern of my lust, and my desire
All continent impediments would o'erbear
That did oppose my will. Better Macbeth
Than such an one to reign.
Macd. Boundless intemperance
In nature is a tyranny; it hath been
Th' untimely emptying of the happy throne
And fall of many kings. But fear not yet
To take upon you what is yours: you may
Convey your pleasures in a spacious plenty,
And yet seem cold, the time you may so hoodwink.
We have willing dames enough; there cannot be
That vulture in you, to devour so many
As will to greatness dedicate themselves,
Finding it so inclin'd.
Mal. With this there grows
In my most ill-compos'd affection such
A stanchless avarice that, were I King,
I should cut off the nobles for their lands,
Desire his jewels and this other's house;
And my more-having would be as a sauce
To make me hunger more, that I should forge
Quarrels unjust against the good and loyal,
Destroying them for wealth.
Macd. This avarice
Sticks deeper, grows with more pernicious root
Than summer-seeming lust, and it hath been
The sword of our slain kings: yet do not fear;
Scotland hath foisons to fill up your will,
Of your mere own. All these are portable,
With other graces weigh'd.
Mal. But I have none. The king-becoming graces,
As justice, verity, temp'rance, stableness,
Bounty, perseverance, mercy, lowliness,
Devotion, patience, courage, fortitude,
I have no relish of them, but abound
In the division of each several crime,
Acting it many ways. Nay, had I power, I should
Pour the sweet milk of concord into hell,
Uproar the universal peace, confound
All unity on earth.
Macd. O Scotland, Scotland!
Mal. If such an one be fit to govern, speak.
I am as I have spoken.
Macd. Fit to govern!
No, not to live. O nation miserable,
With an untitled tyrant bloody-sceptred,
When shalt thou see thy wholesome days again,
Since that the truest issue of thy throne
By his own interdiction stands accurs'd,
And does blaspheme his breed? Thy royal father
Was a most sainted king; the queen that bore thee,
Oftener upon her knees than on her feet,
Died every day she liv'd. Fare thee well!
These evils thou repeat'st upon thyself
Hath banish'd me from Scotland. O my breast,
Thy hope ends here!
Mal. Macduff, this noble passion,
Child of integrity, hath from my soul
Wip'd the black scruples, reconcil'd my thoughts
To thy good truth and honour. Devilish Macbeth
By many of these trains hath sought to win me
Into his power, and modest wisdom plucks me
From over-credulous haste: but God above
Deal between thee and me! for even now
I put myself to thy direction, and
Unspeak mine own detraction; here abjure
The taints and blames I laid upon myself,
For strangers to my nature. I am yet
Unknown to woman, never was forsworn,
Scarcely have coveted what was mine own,
At no time broke my faith, would not betray
The devil to his fellow, and delight
No less in truth than life; my first false speaking
Was this upon myself. What I am truly,
Is thine and my poor country's to command;
Whither indeed, before thy here-approach,
Old Siward, with ten thousand warlike men,
Already at a point, was setting forth.

55. **confineless harms,** unlimited evil-doing. 58. **Luxurious,** lustful. 59. **Sudden,** violent. 64. **continent,** restraining. 69. **yet,** however. 71. **Convey,** obtain secretly. 72. **cold,** chaste. 77. **affection,** disposition. 78. **stanchless,** insatiable. 86. **summer-seeming,** belonging only to early life. 88. **foisons,** plenty. 89. **mere own,** your absolute possessions. **portable,** endurable.

95. **relish,** savor, trace. 96. **division,** variation (musical term). 107. **interdiction,** decree of exclusion. 111. **Died . . . liv'd,** lived a life of daily mortification. 118. **trains,** plots. 135. **at a point,** ready.

Now we 'll together; and the chance of goodness
Be like our warranted quarrel! Why are you silent?
Macd. Such welcome and unwelcome things at once
'T is hard to reconcile.

Enter a *Doctor*.

Mal. Well; more anon.—Comes the King forth, I pray you?
Doct. Ay, sir; there are a crew of wretched souls
That stay his cure: their malady convinces
The great assay of art; but at his touch—
Such sanctity hath Heaven given his hand—
They presently amend.
Mal. I thank you, doctor.
Exit Doctor.
Macd. What 's the disease he means?
Mal. 'T is call'd the evil:
A most miraculous work in this good king;
Which often, since my here-remain in England,
I have seen him do. How he solicits Heaven,
Himself best knows; but strangely-visited people,
All swollen and ulcerous, pitiful to the eye,
The mere despair of surgery, he cures,
Hanging a golden stamp about their necks,
Put on with holy prayers; and 't is spoken,
To the succeeding royalty he leaves
The healing benediction. With this strange virtue,
He hath a heavenly gift of prophecy,
And sundry blessings hang about his throne,
That speak him full of grace.

Enter *Ross*.

Macd. See, who comes here?
Mal. My countryman; but yet I know him not.
Macd. My ever-gentle cousin, welcome hither.
Mal. I know him now. Good God, betimes remove
The means that makes us strangers!
Ross. Sir, amen.
Macd. Stands Scotland where it did?
Ross. Alas, poor country!
Almost afraid to know itself. It cannot
Be call'd our mother, but our grave; where nothing,
But who knows nothing, is once seen to smile;

136. goodness, success. **142. stay his cure**, wait to be cured by him. **convinces**, is proof against. **143. assay of art**, skill of doctors. **146. the evil**, Scrofula was called "the king's evil." Belief in the healing power of the royal touch lasted down into the 18th century. **153. stamp**, coin. **166. nothing**, no one. **167. once**, ever.

Where sighs and groans and shrieks that rend the air
Are made, not mark'd; where violent sorrow seems
A modern ecstasy: the dead man's knell
Is there scarce ask'd for who; and good men's lives
Expire before the flowers in their caps,
Dying or ere they sicken.
Macd. O, relation
Too nice, and yet too true!
Mal. What 's the newest grief?
Ross. That of an hour's age doth hiss the speaker;
Each minute teems a new one.
Macd. How does my wife?
Ross. Why, well.
Macd. And all my children?
Ross. Well too.
Macd. The tyrant has not batter'd at their peace?
Ross. No; they were well at peace when I did leave 'em.
Macd. Be not a niggard of your speech; how goes 't?
Ross. When I came hither to transport the tidings,
Which I have heavily borne, there ran a rumour
Of many worthy fellows that were out;
Which was to my belief witness'd the rather,
For that I saw the tyrant's power a-foot.
Now is the time of help; your eye in Scotland
Would create soldiers, make our women fight,
To doff their dire distresses.
Mal. Be 't their comfort
We 're coming thither. Gracious England hath
Lent us good Siward and ten thousand men;
An older and a better soldier none
That Christendom gives out.
Ross. Would I could answer
This comfort with the like! But I have words
That would be howl'd out in the desert air,
Where hearing should not latch them.
Macd. What concern they?
The general cause? Or is it a fee-grief
Due to some single breast?
Ross. No mind that 's honest
But in it shares some woe; though the main part
Pertains to you alone.
Macd. If it be mine,
Keep it not from me, quickly let me have it.
Ross. Let not your ears despise my tongue for ever,

170. modern ecstasy, commonplace emotion. **174. nice**, minute. **175. hiss**, bring hissing upon (for repeating an old story). **176. teems**, brings forth. **182. heavily**, sadly. **183. out**, in arms. **192. gives out**, tells of. **195. latch**, catch. **196. fee-grief**, private grief.

Which shall possess them with the heaviest sound
That ever yet they heard.
Macd. Hum! I guess at it.
Ross. Your castle is surpris'd; your wife and babes
Savagely slaughter'd. To relate the manner,
Were, on the quarry of these murder'd deer,
To add the death of you.
Mal. Merciful heaven!
What, man! ne'er pull your hat upon your brows;
Give sorrow words: the grief that does not speak
Whispers the o'er-fraught heart and bids it break.
Macd. My children too?
Ross. Wife, children, servants, all
That could be found.
Macd. And I must be from thence!
My wife kill'd too?
Ross. I have said.
Mal. Be comforted.
Let 's make us med'cines of our great revenge,
To cure this deadly grief.
Macd. He has no children.—All my pretty ones?
Did you say all? O hell-kite! All?
What, all my pretty chickens and their dam
At one fell swoop?
Mal. Dispute it like a man.
Macd. I shall do so;
But I must also feel it as a man.
I cannot but remember such things were,
That were most precious to me. Did heaven look on,
And would not take their part? Sinful Macduff,
They were all struck for thee! Naught that I am,
Not for their own demerits, but for mine,
Fell slaughter on their souls. Heaven rest them now!
Mal. Be this the whetstone of your sword; let grief
Convert to anger; blunt not the heart, enrage it.
Macd. O, I could play the woman with mine eyes
And braggart with my tongue! But, gentle heavens,
Cut short all intermission: front to front
Bring thou this fiend of Scotland and myself;
Within my sword's length set him; if he scape,
Heaven forgive him too!
Mal. This time goes manly.
Come, go we to the King; our power is ready;
Our lack is nothing but our leave. Macbeth
Is ripe for shaking, and the powers above
Put on their instruments. Receive what cheer you may;
The night is long that never finds the day.
Exeunt.

ACT V. SCENE I. *Dunsinane. A room in the castle.*

Enter a *Doctor* of Physic and a Waiting *Gentlewoman.*

Doct. I have two nights watched with you, but can perceive no truth in your report. When was it she last walked?

Gent. Since his Majesty went into the field, I have seen her rise from her bed, throw her nightgown upon her, unlock her closet, take forth paper, fold it, write upon 't, read it, afterwards seal it, and again return to bed; yet all this while in a most fast sleep.

Doct. A great perturbation in nature, to receive at once the benefit of sleep, and do the effects of watching! In this slumb'ry agitation, besides her walking and other actual performances, what, at any time, have you heard her say?

Gent. That, sir, which I will not report after her.

Doct. You may to me: and 't is most meet you should.

Gent. Neither to you nor any one; having no witness to confirm my speech.

Enter *Lady Macbeth,* with a taper.

Lo you, here she comes! This is her very guise; and, upon my life, fast asleep. Observe her; stand close.

Doct. How came she by that light?

Gent. Why, it stood by her: she has light by her continually; 't is her command.

Doct. You see, her eyes are open.

Gent. Ay, but their sense are shut.

Doct. What is it she does now? Look, how she rubs her hands.

Gent. It is an accustomed action with her,

202. **possess**, fill. 206. **quarry**, heap of dead game. 220. **Dispute**, fight. **Act V, Scene i: 11-12. do . . . watching**, act as if awake.

229. **Convert**, change. 232. **intermission**, delay. 235. **time**, tune. 237. **Our . . . leave**, we have only to take leave. 239. **Put . . . instruments**, urge us on as their agents.

to seem thus washing her hands. I have known her continue in this a quarter of an hour.

Lady M. Yet here 's a spot.

Doct. Hark! she speaks. I will set down what comes from her, to satisfy my remembrance the more strongly.

Lady M. Out, damned spot! out, I say!—One: two: why, then 't is time to do 't.—Hell is murky!—Fie, my lord, fie! a soldier, and afeard? What need we fear who knows it, when none can call our power to account?—Yet who would have thought the old man to have had so much blood in him?

Doct. Do you mark that?

Lady M. The thane of Fife had a wife; where is she now?—What, will these hands ne'er be clean?—No more o' that, my lord, no more o' that; you mar all with this starting.

Doct. Go to, go to; you have known what you should not.

Gent. She has spoke what she should not, I am sure of that; Heaven knows what she has known.

Lady M. Here 's the smell of the blood still; all the perfumes of Arabia will not sweeten this little hand. Oh, oh, oh!

Doct. What a sigh is there! The heart is sorely charged.

Gent. I would not have such a heart in my bosom for the dignity of the whole body.

Doct. Well, well, well,—

Gent. Pray God it be, sir.

Doct. This disease is beyond my practice; yet I have known those which have walked in their sleep who have died holily in their beds.

Lady M. Wash your hands, put on your nightgown; look not so pale.—I tell you yet again, Banquo 's buried; he cannot come out on 's grave.

Doct. Even so?

Lady M. To bed, to bed! there 's knocking at the gate. Come, come, come, come, give me your hand. What 's done cannot be undone.—To bed, to bed, to bed! *Exit.*

Doct. Will she go now to bed?

Gent. Directly.

Doct. Foul whisp'rings are abroad; unnatural deeds
Do breed unnatural troubles; infected minds
To their deaf pillows will discharge their secrets
More needs she the divine than the physician.
God, God, forgive us all! Look after her;
Remove from her the means of all annoyance,
And still keep eyes upon her. So, good-night!
My mind she has mated, and amaz'd my sight.
I think, but dare not speak.

Gent. Good-night, good doctor.

Exeunt.

84. annoyance, self-injury. **86. mated,** bewildered.

Scene II. *The country near Dunsinane.*

Drum and colours. Enter *Menteith, Caithness, Angus, Lennox,* and Soldiers.

Ment. The English power is near, led on by Malcolm,
His uncle Siward, and the good Macduff.
Revenges burn in them; for their dear causes
Would to the bleeding and the grim alarm
Excite the mortified man.

Ang. Near Birnam wood
Shall we well meet them; that way are they coming.

Caith. Who knows if Donalbain be with his brother?

Len. For certain, sir, he is not; I have a file
Of all the gentry: there is Siward's son,
And many unrough youth that even now
Protest their first of manhood.

Ment. What does the tyrant?

Caith. Great Dunsinane he strongly fortifies.
Some say he 's mad, others that lesser hate him
Do call it valiant fury; but, for certain,
He cannot buckle his distemper'd cause
Within the belt of rule.

Ang. Now does he feel
His secret murders sticking on his hands;
Now minutely revolts upbraid his faith-breach;
Those he commands move only in command,
Nothing in love. Now does he feel his title
Hang loose about him, like a giant's robe
Upon a dwarfish thief.

Ment. Who then shall blame
His pester'd senses to recoil and start,
When all that is within him does condemn
Itself for being there?

Caith. Well, march we on
To give obedience where 't is truly ow'd.
Meet we the med'cine of the sickly weal,
And with him pour we in our country's purge
Each drop of us.

Len. Or so much as it needs
To dew the sovereign flower and drown the weeds.
Make we our march towards Birnam.

Exeunt, marching.

Scene ii: 3. dear, deeply felt. **4. bleeding . . . alarm,** bloody battle. **5. mortified,** deadened, strengthless. **8. file,** list. **10. unrough,** beardless. **11. Protest,** assert. **15. distemper'd cause,** disordered party. **18. minutely,** occurring every minute. **27. med'cine,** i.e., Malcolm. **weal,** commonwealth.

Scene III. *Dunsinane. A room in the castle.*

Enter *Macbeth, Doctor,* and Attendants.

Macb. Bring me no more reports; let them fly all;
Till Birnam wood remove to Dunsinane
I cannot taint with fear. What 's the boy Malcolm?
Was he not born of woman? The spirits that know
All mortal consequences have pronounc'd me thus:
"Fear not, Macbeth; no man that 's born of woman
Shall e'er have power upon thee." Then fly, false thanes,
And mingle with the English epicures!
The mind I sway by and the heart I bear
Shall never sag with doubt nor shake with fear.

Enter a *Servant.*

The devil damn thee black, thou cream-fac'd loon!
Where got'st thou that goose look?
Serv. There is ten thousand—
Macb. Geese, villain?
Serv. Soldiers, sir.
Macb. Go prick thy face, and over-red thy fear,
Thou lily-liver'd boy. What soldiers, patch?
Death of thy soul! those linen cheeks of thine
Are counsellors to fear. What soldiers, whey-face?
Serv. The English force, so please you.
Macb. Take thy face hence. [*Exit Servant.*] Seyton!—I am sick at heart
When I behold—Seyton, I say!—This push
Will chair me ever, or disseat me now.
I have liv'd long enough: my way of life
Is fall'n into the sear, the yellow leaf;
And that which should accompany old age,
As honour, love, obedience, troops of friends,
I must not look to have; but, in their stead,
Curses, not loud but deep, mouth-honour, breath
Which the poor heart would fain deny, and dare not.
Seyton!

Enter *Seyton.*

Sey. What 's your gracious pleasure?
Macb. What news more?
Sey. All is confirm'd, my lord, which was reported.
Macb. I 'll fight till from my bones my flesh be hack'd.
Give me my armour.
Sey. 'T is not needed yet.
Macb. I 'll put it on.
Send out moe horses; skirr the country round;
Hang those that talk of fear. Give me mine armour.
How does your patient, doctor?
Doct. Not so sick, my lord,
As she is troubled with thick-coming fancies,
That keep her from her rest.
Macb. Cure her of that.
Canst thou not minister to a mind diseas'd,
Pluck from the memory a rooted sorrow,
Raze out the written troubles of the brain,
And with some sweet oblivious antidote
Cleanse the stuff'd bosom of that perilous stuff
Which weighs upon the heart?
Doct. Therein the patient
Must minister to himself.
Macb. Throw physic to the dogs; I 'll none of it.
Come, put mine armour on; give me my staff.
Seyton, send out. Doctor, the thanes fly from me.
Come, sir, dispatch. If thou couldst, doctor, cast
The water of my land, find her disease,
And purge it to a sound and pristine health,
I would applaud thee to the very echo,
That should applaud again.—Pull 't off, I say.—
What rhubarb, senna, or what purgative drug,
Would scour these English hence? Hear'st thou of them?
Doct. Ay, my good lord; your royal preparation
Makes us hear something.
Macb. Bring it after me.
I will not be afraid of death and bane,
Till Birnam forest come to Dunsinane.
Doct. Were I from Dunsinane away and clear,
Profit again should hardly draw me here.
Exeunt.

Scene IV. *Country near Birnam wood.*

Drum and colours. Enter *Malcolm,* old *Siward* and his Son, *Macduff, Menteith, Caithness, Angus,* and Soldiers, marching.

Mal. Cousins, I hope the days are near at hand
That chambers will be safe.

Scene iii: 1. them, cf. line 7. **3. taint,** be infected by. **5. mortal consequences,** human destinies. **8. epicures,** unwarlike gluttons. **9. sway by,** am swayed by. **14. over-red,** redden with blood. **17. Are . . . fear,** cause fear. **20. push,** test, crisis. **21. chair,** enthrone. **disseat,** dethrone.

35. skirr, scour. **43. oblivious,** causing forgetfulness. **48. staff,** lance. **50. dispatch,** hurry. **cast the water,** analyze the urine, a common medical method of diagnosis. **58. it,** the armor. **Scene iv: 2. chambers,** bed-rooms, such as Duncan's.

Ment. We doubt it nothing.
Siw. What wood is this before us?
Ment. The wood of Birnam.
Mal. Let every soldier hew him down a bough
And bear 't before him; thereby shall we shadow
The numbers of our host and make discovery
Err in report of us.
Soldiers. It shall be done.
Siw. We learn no other but the confident tyrant
Keeps still in Dunsinane, and will endure
Our setting down before 't.
Mal. 'T is his main hope;
For where there is advantage to be given,
Both more and less have given him the revolt,
And none serve with him but constrained things
Whose hearts are absent too.
Macd. Let our just censures
Attend the true event, and put we on
Industrious soldiership.
Siw. The time approaches
That will with due decision make us know
What we shall say we have and what we owe.
Thoughts speculative their unsure hopes relate,
But certain issue strokes must arbitrate;
Towards which advance the war.
Exeunt, marching.

Scene V. *Dunsinane. Within the castle.*

Enter *Macbeth, Seyton,* and Soldiers, with drum and colours.

Macb. Hang out our banners on the outward walls;
The cry is still, "They come!" Our castle's strength
Will laugh a siege to scorn; here let them lie
Till famine and the ague eat them up.
Were they not forc'd with those that should be ours,
We might have met them dareful, beard to beard,
And beat them backward home.
A cry within of women.
What is that noise?
Sey. It is the cry of women, my good lord.
Exit.
Macb. I have almost forgot the taste of fears.
The time has been, my senses would have cool'd
To hear a night-shriek, and my fell of hair
Would at a dismal treatise rouse and stir
As life were in 't. I have supp'd full with horrors;
Direness, familiar to my slaughterous thoughts,
Cannot once start me.

Re-enter *Seyton.*

Wherefore was that cry?
Sey. The Queen, my lord, is dead.
Macb. She should have died hereafter;
There would have been a time for such a word.
To-morrow, and to-morrow, and to-morrow,
Creeps in this petty pace from day to day
To the last syllable of recorded time;
And all our yesterdays have lighted fools
The way to dusty death. Out, out, brief candle!
Life 's but a walking shadow, a poor player
That struts and frets his hour upon the stage
And then is heard no more. It is a tale
Told by an idiot, full of sound and fury,
Signifying nothing.

Enter a *Messenger.*

Thou com'st to use thy tongue; thy story quickly.
Mess. Gracious my lord,
I should report that which I say I saw,
But know not how to do it.
Macb. Well, say, sir.
Mess. As I did stand my watch upon the hill,
I look'd toward Birnam, and anon, methought,
The wood began to move.
Macb. Liar and slave!
Mess. Let me endure your wrath, if 't be not so.
Within this three mile may you see it coming:
I say, a moving grove.
Macb. If thou speak'st false,
Upon the next tree shall thou hang alive,
Till famine cling thee; if thy speech be sooth,
I care not if thou dost for me as much.
I pull in resolution, and begin
To doubt the equivocation of the fiend
That lies like truth: "Fear not, till Birnam wood
Do come to Dunsinane;" and now a wood
Comes toward Dunsinane. Arm, arm, and out!
If this which he avouches does appear,
There is nor flying hence nor tarrying here.

6. discovery, Macbeth's scouts. **11. advantage to be given,** opportunity afforded, i.e., chance of desertion in the field. **12. more and less,** high and low. **14. censures,** verdicts. **15. Attend . . . event,** await the actual outcome. **Scene v: 5. forc'd,** reinforced.

11. fell of hair, hair of the scalp. **12. dismal treatise,** horrible story. **14. slaughterous,** murderous. **15. start,** startle. **18. such a word,** i.e., as death. **40. cling,** shrivel up. **sooth,** truth.

I gin to be aweary of the sun,
And wish th' estate o' th' world were now undone.
Ring the alarum-bell! Blow, wind! come, wrack!
At least we 'll die with harness on our back.
Exeunt.

Scene VI. *Dunsinane. Before the castle.*

Drum and colours. Enter *Malcolm,* old *Siward, Macduff,* and their Army, with boughs.

Mal. Now near enough; your leavy screens throw down,
And show like those you are. You, worthy uncle,
Shall, with my cousin, your right noble son,
Lead our first battle. Worthy Macduff and we
Shall take upon 's what else remains to do,
According to our order.
Siw. Fare you well.
Do we but find the tyrant's power to-night,
Let us be beaten, if we cannot fight.
Macd. Make all our trumpets speak; give them all breath,
Those clamorous harbingers of blood and death.
Exeunt. Alarums continued.

Scene VII. *Another part of the field.*

Enter *Macbeth.*

Macb. They have tied me to a stake; I cannot fly,
But, bear-like, I must fight the course. What 's he
That was not born of woman? Such a one
Am I to fear, or none.

Enter young *Siward.*

Y. Siw. What is thy name?
Macb. Thou 'lt be afraid to hear it.
Y. Siw. No; though thou call'st thyself a hotter name
Than any is in hell.
Macb. My name 's Macbeth.
Y. Siw. The devil himself could not pronounce a title
More hateful to mine ear.
Macb. No, nor more fearful.
Y. Siw. Thou liest, abhorred tyrant; with my sword
I 'll prove the lie thou speak'st.
They fight and young Siward is slain.

Macb. Thou wast born of woman.
But swords I smile at, weapons laugh to scorn,
Brandish'd by man that 's of a woman born.
Exit.

Alarums. Enter *Macduff.*

Macd. That way the noise is. Tyrant, show thy face!
If thou be'st slain and with no stroke of mine,
My wife and children's ghosts will haunt me still.
I cannot strike at wretched kerns, whose arms
Are hir'd to bear their staves; either thou, Macbeth,
Or else my sword with an unbattered edge
I sheathe again undeeded. There thou shouldst be;
By this great clatter, one of greatest note
Seems bruited. Let me find him, Fortune!
And more I beg not. *Exit. Alarums.*

Enter *Malcolm* and old *Siward.*

Siw. This way, my lord; the castle 's gently render'd:
The tyrant's people on both sides do fight;
The noble thanes do bravely in the war;
The day almost itself professes yours,
And little is to do.
Mal. We have met with foes
That strike beside us.
Siw. Enter, sir, the castle.
Exeunt. Alarums.

Scene VIII. *The same.*

Enter *Macbeth.*

Macb. Why should I play the Roman fool, and die
On mine own sword? Whiles I see lives, the gashes
Do better upon them.

Enter *Macduff.*

Macd. Turn, hell-hound, turn!
Macb. Of all men else I have avoided thee:
But get thee back; my soul is too much charg'd
With blood of thine already.
Macd. I have no words,
My voice is in my sword, thou bloodier villain
Than terms can give thee out!
They fight. Alarum.

51. **wrack,** wreck, destruction. **Scene vi: 4. battle,** division. **Scene vii: 2. course,** a round in bear-baiting.

22. **bruited,** announced with noise. **24. gently render'd,** tamely surrendered. **27. itself professes,** declares itself. **29. strike . . . us,** fight along with us, or, deliberately avoid striking us. **Scene viii: 1. Roman fool,** possibly Cato, the traditional example of Roman stoicism, but Shakespeare may be thinking also of Brutus, Cassius, and Antony.

Macb. Thou losest labour.
As easy mayst thou the intrenchant air
With thy keen sword impress as make me bleed.
Let fall thy blade on vulnerable crests;
I bear a charmed life, which must not yield
To one of woman born.

Macd. Despair thy charm;
And let the angel whom thou still hast serv'd
Tell thee, Macduff was from his mother's womb
Untimely ripp'd.

Macb. Accursed be that tongue that tells me so,
For it hath cow'd my better part of man!
And be these juggling fiends no more believ'd
That palter with us in a double sense,
That keep the word of promise to our ear,
And break it to our hope. I 'll not fight with thee.

Macd. Then yield thee, coward,
And live to be the show and gaze o' th' time.
We 'll have thee, as our rarer monsters are,
Painted upon a pole, and underwrit,
"Here may you see the tyrant."

Macb. I will not yield,
To kiss the ground before young Malcolm's feet
And to be baited with the rabble's curse.
Though Birnam wood be come to Dunsinane,
And thou oppos'd, being of no woman born,
Yet I will try the last. Before my body
I throw my warlike shield. Lay on, Macduff,
And damn'd be him that first cries, "Hold, enough!" *Exeunt fighting. Alarums.*

Retreat and Flourish. Enter, with drum and colours, *Malcolm*, old *Siward, Ross*, Thanes, and Soldiers.

Mal. I would the friends we miss were safe arriv'd.

Siw. Some must go off; and yet, by these I see,
So great a day as this is cheaply bought.

Mal. Macduff is missing, and your noble son.

Ross. Your son, my lord, has paid a soldier's debt.
He only liv'd but till he was a man;
The which no sooner had his prowess confirm'd
In the unshrinking station where he fought,
But like a man he died.

Siw. Then he is dead?

Ross. Ay, and brought off the field. Your cause of sorrow
Must not be measur'd by his worth, for then
It hath no end.

Siw. Had he his hurts before?

Ross. Ay, on the front.

Siw. Why then, God's soldier be he!
Had I as many sons as I have hairs,
I would not wish them to a fairer death.
And so, his knell is knoll'd.

Mal. He 's worth more sorrow,
And that I 'll spend for him.

Siw. He 's worth no more.
They say he parted well, and paid his score;
And so, God be with him! Here comes newer comfort.

Re-enter *Macduff* with Macbeth's head.

Macd. Hail, king! for so thou art. Behold, where stands
The usurper's cursed head: the time is free.
I see thee compass'd with thy kingdom's pearl,
That speak my salutation in their minds;
Whose voices I desire aloud with mine:
Hail, King of Scotland!

All. Hail, King of Scotland! *Flourish.*

Mal. We shall not spend a large expense of time
Before we reckon with your several loves,
And make us even with you. My thanes and kinsmen,
Henceforth be earls, the first that ever Scotland
In such an honour nam'd. What 's more to do,
Which would be planted newly with the time,
As calling home our exil'd friends abroad
That fled the snares of watchful tyranny;
Producing forth the cruel ministers
Of this dead butcher and his fiend-like queen,
Who, as 't is thought, by self and violent hands
Took off her life; this, and what needful else
That calls upon us, by the grace of Grace,
We will perform in measure, time, and place.
So, thanks to all at once and to each one,
Whom we invite to see us crown'd at Scone.

Flourish. Exeunt omnes.

9. **intrenchant**, that cannot be cut. 14. **angel**, evil genius. 18. **cow'd . . . man**, broken my spirit. 26. **Painted**, with your picture. 36. **go off**, be killed. 42. **unshrinking station**, the post he did not desert.

52. **parted**, died. 54-5. **stands . . . . head**, Macbeth's severed head fixed on a pole stands in the ground. 55. **the time**, the world. 56. **compass'd . . . pearl**, surrounded by the best men of your kingdom. 63. **earls**, an English title. 68. **Producing forth**, bringing to justice. 70. **self and violent**, her own violent.

The Tragedy of Antony and Cleopatra

The great tragedies from *Julius Cæsar* to *Macbeth* are, in a sense, psychological dramas; they deal with the inner strife and final ruin of the hero. In *Antony and Cleopatra* Shakespeare turns to the world of action, to the clash of opposing forces for the domination of the world, to the overthrow of the sensuous East by the hard efficiency of Rome. Antony, the greatest living Roman, falls a victim to the seductive East incarnate in Cleopatra, and loses the world for her; but there is little or nothing here of the inner struggle, the combat in the hero's soul with the power of evil, that marks the earlier and greater tragedies. And if Cleopatra embodies the power of evil, it is evil in another guise than in that of the weird sisters or the cold malignity of Iago. *Antony and Cleopatra* is one of the most magnificent of Shakespeare's plays; it is the least tragic of his tragedies.

Text.—Antony and Cleopatra was entered by Edward Blount in the Stationers' Register on May 20th, 1608, but was left unpublished until 1623 when Blount was associated with Jaggard and others in the publication of the Folio.

The "copy" sent to Jaggard for *Antony and Cleopatra* was either Shakespeare's own manuscript or a transcript thereof. It cannot have been the company's prompt-book since the play as printed is far too long, over 3,000 lines, for presentation on Shakespeare's stage. Apart from a number of evident misprints and some confusion in the lining the Folio presents a good text. The difficulties which have troubled editors are due rather to the author himself, to the crowded and highly figurative style of Shakespeare's later work, than to any errors of transcriber or printer.

Date.—The entry in the Stationers' Register fixes the latest date for this play. Stylistic and metrical characteristics mark it as later than *Macbeth,* 1606, and a fairly obvious borrowing of an image, that of the dragonish or lion-like cloud, from Chapman's *Bussy,* published in 1607, suggests that Shakespeare had read this play before he finished *Antony and Cleopatra.* We may, therefore, date it with some confidence as first produced in the winter season of 1607-8.

The source of *Antony and Cleopatra* is, of course, Plutarch's *Life of Antony* in North's translation. Shakespeare here follows his source even more closely than he had done in *Julius Cæsar.* Not only does he take over the whole action and a host of minor characters from North, but he often turns the very words of North's prose into verse. Yet even in such passages he often adds a splendid phrase of his own which seems to give life and elevation to the whole; thus, for example, to the last speech of Antony—versified almost verbally from North—Shakespeare adds the words "put off my helmet to my countryman"—how vivid and concrete an image in the mouth of the dying soldier! Even in the action Shakespeare does not follow Plutarch slavishly; he omits, for example, the long account of Antony's Parthian Campaign; he condenses, he even invents actions and creates characters to suit his dramatic purposes—there is nothing in Plutarch to suggest Cleopatra's violent attack on the Messenger—and the character of Enobarbus is Shakespeare's own creation.

Construction.—The romantic-tragic story of Antony and Cleopatra was an old familiar one, and Elizabethan dramatists had handled it long before Shakespeare. As early as 1590 the Countess of Pembroke, Sidney's sister, translated Garnier's tragedy, *Marc Antoine;* Samuel Daniel, a poet of her circle, published his *Cleopatra* in 1594, and Brandon's *Virtuous Octavia* appeared in 1598. Shakespeare certainly owed nothing to these earlier plays; they are Senecan tragedies, stiff and lifeless. Shakespeare, on the other hand, reverts in this play to something like the old chronicle-history type. In construction *Antony and Cleopatra* more nearly resembles such a play as *Henry V* than the closely woven dramatic texture of *Othello.* The action follows the sequence of historical events; it shifts from Egypt to Rome, to Parthia, and back again to Egypt; only in the last half of the play is there anything like unity of place. Frequent comment has been made on the excessive number of scenes into which the acts are divided—thirteen in Act III, fifteen in Act IV. It should be remembered, however, that these divisions are the work of Shakespeare's editors. There is no sign of them in the original. It is plain that Shakespeare conceived the play as one continuous action, broken, perhaps, for a brief interval during the two hours' traffic of his stage, but otherwise running its course unchecked. In Dr. Johnson's happy phrase, "the continual hurry of the action, the variety of incidents, and the quick succession of one personage to another, call the mind forward without intermission from the first act to the last." And this variety of incidents and succession of persons has been most artfully arranged by Shakespeare to reveal the causes of this world tragedy and to contrast the characters involved in it.

The action opens in Egypt and the very first words, "Nay, but this dotage of our general's," strike the keynote. The need of a world of men for the great triumvir is made at once apparent and he answers to the call, but leaves his heart behind him: "I go from hence," he says to Cleopatra, "thy soldier, servant." The scene shifts to Rome and the reluctant praise of Antony by his enemy and rival confirms our conception of his potential power. The last scene of the act takes us back to Egypt to show us not only Cleopatra's passion for Antony but his continued enslavement to her in the promise to piece her throne with kingdoms.

The second act shows Antony at his best and worst. He dominates and overrides Octavius; his mere appearance in arms halts the threatened overthrow of Rome by young Pompey; he consents to a marriage with his rival's sister which shall cement the bond between them. Yet the alliance has hardly been concluded when we learn of his resolve to return to Egypt. That we may not forget Egypt and all it means, Shakespeare inserts here the scene in which Cleopatra learns of Antony's marriage and breaks out into a savage fury in violent contrast with her voluptuous charm in the former act. Two concluding scenes picture the rottenness of the world for which the rivals are contending; the lives of the triumvirs are saved only by a reluctant scruple on the part of Pompey; what might have been a massacre turns into an Alexandrian revel, and the third part of the world in the person of Lepidus is carried off dead drunk.

By way of contrast, and one must remember that there was no pause in the action here, the third act opens with an exhibition of the pristine Roman valor—Ventidius in triumph over the Parthians. Here are the soldiers that Antony might have led to the conquest of the world. The scene shifts back to Egypt to show Cleopatra's second interview with the messenger. One would have expected it to follow hard upon the first, but Shakespeare has other matters in hand; he will show Antony at the height of his career before he lets us see Cleopatra laying her snare to capture him again. A swift succession of scenes portrays the final breach between the rivals for empire and leads up to the test of strength at Actium. There we find Antony completely in Cleopatra's power, resolving in spite of warning and his own best judgment to fight on sea, deserted in the battle by his enchantress, and himself deserting his still faithful soldiers to follow her. It is interesting to note that by this time Shakespeare has discarded all the battle scenes, the clash of armies and the single combats, that mark his earlier plays. Only the "noise of a sea fight" is heard from behind the stage to mark the overthrow of Antony.

From this point on the action hurries swiftly to the death of Antony. We see him reconciled to Cleopatra, furiously jealous of her reception of Cæsar's messenger, then melting again at her entreaties. His impending fall is prophesied by the solemn music which proclaims his abandonment by the god he loved. His fortunes have corrupted honest men; his old friend Enobarbus leaves him. A brief flash of victory in battle is nullified by the desertion of the whole Egyptian fleet. Deceived by a false report of Cleopatra's death, he stabs himself, only to learn that she still lives and to die, laying the last of many thousand kisses upon her lips. This is not the Antony of the earlier acts; his whole character has dissolved and broken under Cleopatra's spell, like a cloud that with a thought dislimns. Yet such is Shakespeare's art that these last scenes do more to rouse our sympathy for Antony than all that has gone before; his bravery in battle, his comradeship with his soldiers, his magnanimity to the deserter, above all the depth and sincerity of his passion, raise him to a tragic dignity.

The last act is wholly Cleopatra's. Resolved on death in the high Roman fashion, she yet hesitates and falters. She tries in vain to win

Octavius as she had won Antony before him. It is only when she learns her failure that she rises to the height of resolution. She can stoop to jest and rally with the clown who brings the asps, only to rise a moment later into the great queen who has immortal longings. She has been the mistress and the ruin of Antony, now she claims him as her husband by the title of her courage. Octavius comes in once more to find her dead, and to pronounce her funeral oration. Rome has triumphed in the outer world, but the victory of the great lovers over external circumstances is perfectly accomplished.

Characters.—Great lovers, for though the main theme of the play is, as has been said, the clash of Rome and the East, yet Antony and Cleopatra stand out in this conflict as two of the most famous lovers in history or legend. And the art with which Shakespeare reveals their characters is the art of the fully accomplished master. His characterization of these two figures is as superior to that of, say, Romeo and Juliet as the passion that linked and wrecked them was fiercer and more profound than the first love of boy and girl in the earlier play. Antony is no poetizing sentimentalist; he is a tried soldier, a leader of men, the triple pillar of the world. Shakespeare takes pains to show him in this phase, as well as in the abandonment of all his better self to passion. His bitter remorse after his flight at Actium is as real and human as the relapse into Cleopatra's arms that follows. The rapid alternations of jealousy, reconcilement, frenzied rage, and utter despair that mark the last stage of his career are all characteristic of the grown and experienced man, too clear-sighted to trust where he has placed his love, too passionately loving to abandon her whom he distrusts. It is Shakespeare's Antony that we see in this play, and not Plutarch's. All that was coarse and cruel and base in Plutarch has been refined by Shakespeare—all that was brave and generous and self-forgetful has been exalted. With all his faults and follies there is something magnificent about this Antony.

Of Shakespeare's Cleopatra it is hard to speak without breaking into sheer rhapsody of praise. Certain it is that she is his supreme portrayal of the eternal feminine. No other woman in all his gallery of portraits is so fully realized or approaches her infinite variety. Here too we have to do with Shakespeare's Cleopatra, not with Plutarch's. To the Greek biographer she was simply the evil genius of Antony; to Shakespeare she is that and more. She is the courtesan of genius and the Queen of Egypt. Cleopatra is herself throughout, complete and consistent from beginning to end. If she coquets with Antony in the first scene, she tries her charms—in vain—on Cæsar in the last. And yet she is the Queen always, from the moment when she taunts Antony:

I would I had thy inches: thou shouldst know
There were a heart in Egypt

to the last act when she dons her robe and crown to die. It is because she is a queen that she shrinks in horror from exposure to the rabble of Rome; it is because she is a sensuous woman that she chooses a form of death "as sweet as balm, as soft as air, as gentle." The strain that gives unity and consistency to her character is her passion for Antony. This splendid Roman, so strong, so male, so pleasure-loving like herself, is her man of men. She has had lovers before; she will have none after him. When Antony is gone why should she stay "in this vile world"? It is the desire for reunion with her lover that exalts and glorifies her last moments. And yet to end upon this note is to miss the many-colored facets of her character, her wit, her gaiety, her rowdiness even, her queenly condescension, her intimate familiarity with her maids, her feminine fear of the maddened Antony, and her exultant triumph over the outwitted Cæsar. She is Shakespeare's Cleopatra; there is none like her, none.

Compared with Antony and Cleopatra most of the other characters in the play fade into insignificance. The majority are mere names borrowed from Plutarch with no substance behind them. Now and then, however, Shakespeare deigns, as it were, to take an interest in them, and with a dash of his pen puts life into them. The hearty soldier, Scaurus, is alive; so is the feeble, friendly, and ineffective Lepidus, and the somewhat futile Pompey. So too are Cleopatra's maids, a compound of wanton gaiety and whole-hearted devotion to their mistress. The one figure, however, that stands out among them is that of Enobarbus. Out of a name and an incident in Plutarch Shakespeare created a character.

Enobarbus is the plain, blunt soldier, familiar in other plays of Shakespeare; he is a mocker and a realist; he plays at times the part of the chorus in commenting upon the action. But he is always a very human figure. He is fully aware of Cleopatra's charm; he is ready to dally with her maids and dance the Egyptian Bacchanals with the triumvirs, Pompey and his crew. His cold reason sees through the folly of his master and yet he breaks into tears at Antony's pathetic farewell to his servants. Shakespeare uses his desertion and his remorseful death to portray at once the hopeless ruin of Antony's cause, his noble generosity, and the devotion he inspired even in such a cynical realist as Enobarbus.

Final Appreciation.—The peculiar glory of *Antony and Cleopatra* is its poetry. Shakespeare has come by this time a long way from the theatrical declamation of *Richard III* and the lyrical flow of *Romeo and Juliet.* He is in command of a verse capable of every shade of dramatic expression. It can sink to as low a pitch as

> He words me, girls, he words me

and rise a moment later to

> Finish, good lady; the bright day is done
> And we are for the dark.

It can be as splendidly decorative as the description of the barge or as unadorned as Antony's

> As for my wife,
> I would you had her spirit in such another.

And this extraordinary power of expression is conferred by Shakespeare's liberal hand on nearly all the speakers in the play.

Yet such is Shakespeare's art that each speaker preserves his own identity of utterance. We could never mistake a phrase of Cæsar's for one of Antony's or interchange the words of Cleopatra and Octavia. It was of this range, this power, this starry beauty of expression, that Coleridge was thinking when he coined the phrase "the happy valiancy of Shakespeare's style" in *Antony and Cleopatra.* More, perhaps, than most of Shakespeare's plays this drama calls for oral expression; its unheard melodies cry for rendition.

Stage History.—The stage history of *Antony and Cleopatra* may be written very briefly. There is no record of a performance before 1642. After the Restoration its place was taken by Dryden's *All for Love,* 1677–8, which drove Shakespeare's play off the boards for nearly a century. Dryden's play is not an adaptation of Shakespeare's; it is a fresh treatment of the theme in accordance with the prevailing neo-classical theories of drama. It preserves the unities of time and place; the world tragedy of Shakespeare is reduced to a story of heroic love, and Shakespeare's poetry has been replaced by Dryden's workmanlike rhetoric. Yet, to be frank, it is by far a better acting play than Shakespeare's, at least for the modern stage. A careful comparison of the two will more than repay any student of English drama.

It was not till 1759 that Garrick brought Shakespeare's play back to the stage; he took the part of Antony himself, but this play, given only six times, was one of Garrick's conspicuous failures. Not until the nineteenth century is there anything like a continuous history of *Antony and Cleopatra* upon the stage, and then for the most part it is a record either of failure or of a production in which poetry was pared away to make place for pageantry. Kemble's production, 1813, actually stuck bits of Dryden into Shakespeare's text. Phelps, 1849, gave it with few cuts and fair success. Occasionally an actress has been tempted by the part of Cleopatra, usually to a pronounced failure. A performance in modern dress by amateurs at Vassar, December 15, 1924, gave, what few professionals seem to have done, a thrilling rendering of Shakespeare's poetry.

THE TRAGEDY OF ANTONY AND CLEOPATRA

Dramatis Personæ

Mark Antony, *Octavius Cæsar*, *M. Æmilius Lepidus*, triumvirs.
Sextus Pompeius.
Domitius Enobarbus, *Ventidius*, *Eros*, *Scarus*, *Dercetas*, *Demetrius*, *Philo*, friends to *Antony*.
Canidius, lieutenant-general to *Antony*.
Mæcenas, *Agrippa*, *Dolabella*, *Proculeius*, *Thyreus*, *Gallus*, friends to *Cæsar*.
Taurus, lieutenant-general to *Cæsar*.
Menas, *Menecrates*, *Varrius*, friends to *Pompey*.
Silius, an officer in *Ventidius's* army.
An ambassador from *Antony* to *Cæsar*.
Alexas, *Mardian*, a eunuch, *Seleucus*, *Diomedes*, attendants on *Cleopatra*.
A Soothsayer.
A Clown.

Cleopatra, Queen of Egypt.
Octavia, sister to *Cæsar* and wife to *Antony*.
Charmian, *Iras*, attendants on *Cleopatra*.

Officers, Soldiers, Messengers, and other Attendants.

SCENE: *In several parts of the Roman Empire.*

ACT I. Scene I. *Alexandria. A room in Cleopatra's palace.*

Enter *Demetrius* and *Philo*.

Phi. Nay, but this dotage of our general's
O'erflows the measure: those his goodly eyes,
That o'er the files and musters of the war
Have glow'd like plated Mars, now bend, now turn,
The office and devotion of their view
Upon a tawny front. His captain's heart,
Which in the scuffles of great fights hath burst
The buckles on his breast, reneges all temper,
And is become the bellows and the fan
To cool a gipsy's lust.

Flourish. Enter *Antony, Cleopatra,* her ladies, the train, with Eunuchs fanning her.

Look, where they come!
Take but good note, and you shall see in him
The triple pillar of the world transform'd
Into a strumpet's fool. Behold and see.

Cleo. If it be love indeed, tell me how much.

Ant. There 's beggary in the love that can be reckon'd.

Cleo. I 'll set a bourn how far to be belov'd.

Ant. Then must thou needs find out new heaven, new earth.

Enter a *Messenger*.

Mess. News, my good lord, from Rome.

Ant. Grates me: the sum.

Cleo. Nay, hear them, Antony.
Fulvia perchance is angry; or, who knows
If the scarce-bearded Cæsar have not sent
His powerful mandate to you: "Do this, or this;
Take in that kingdom, and enfranchise that;
Perform 't, or else we damn thee."

Ant. How, my love!

Cleo. Perchance? nay, and most like:
You must not stay here longer, your dismission
Is come from Cæsar; therefore hear it, Antony.
Where 's Fulvia's process?—Cæsar's, I would say. Both?
Call in the messengers. As I am Egypt's queen,
Thou blushest, Antony and that blood of thine

3. files and musters, troops in battle formation. **4. plated,** in armor. **8. reneges all temper,** renounces all his spirit. **12. triple pillar,** i.e., one of the triumvirs. **16. bourn,** limit, boundary.

18. Grates, vexes. **20. Fulvia,** Antony's wife. **21. scarce-bearded,** in 40 B.C. when the play opens, Octavius Cæsar was 23, Antony 43. **28. process,** summons,

Is Cæsar's homager; else so thy cheek pays shame
When shrill-tongu'd Fulvia scolds. The messengers!

Ant. Let Rome in Tiber melt, and the wide arch
Of the rang'd empire fall! Here is my space.
Kingdoms are clay; our dungy earth alike
Feeds beast as man; the nobleness of life
Is to do thus, when such a mutual pair
Embracing.
And such a twain can do 't, in which I bind,
On pain of punishment, the world to wit
We stand up peerless.

Cleo. Excellent falsehood!
Why did he marry Fulvia, and not love her?
I 'll seem the fool I am not; Antony
Will be himself.

Ant. But stirr'd by Cleopatra.
Now, for the love of Love and her soft hours,
Let 's not confound the time with conference harsh:
There 's not a minute of our lives should stretch
Without some pleasure now. What sport to-night?

Cleo. Hear the ambassadors.

Ant. Fie, wrangling queen!
Whom everything becomes, to chide, to laugh,
To weep; whose every passion fully strives
To make itself, in thee, fair and admir'd!
No messenger but thine; and all alone
To-night we 'll wander through the streets and note
The qualities of people. Come, my queen;
Last night you did desire it.—Speak not to us.
Exeunt Antony and Cleopatra with their train.

Dem. Is Cæsar with Antonius priz'd so slight?

Phi. Sir, sometimes, when he is not Antony,
He comes too short of that great property
Which still should go with Antony.

Dem. I am full sorry
That he approves the common liar, who
Thus speaks of him at Rome; but I will hope
Of better deeds to-morrow. Rest you happy!
Exeunt.

Scene II. *Another room in Cleopatra's palace.*

Enter *Enobarbus,* a *Soothsayer, Charmian, Iras, Mardian* the Eunuch, and *Alexas.*

Char. Lord Alexas, sweet Alexas, most anything Alexas, almost most absolute Alexas, where 's the soothsayer that you prais'd so to the Queen? O, that I knew this husband, which, you say, must charge his horns with garlands!

Alex. Soothsayer!

Sooth. Your will?

Char. Is this the man? Is 't you, sir, that know things?

Sooth. In nature's infinite book of secrecy
A little I can read.

Alex. Show him your hand.

Eno. Bring in the banquet quickly; wine enough
Cleopatra's health to drink.

Char. Good sir, give me good fortune.

Sooth. I make not, but foresee.

Char. Pray, then, foresee me one.

Sooth. You shall be yet far fairer than you are.

Char. He means in flesh.

Iras. No, you shall paint when you are old.

Char. Wrinkles forbid!

Alex. Vex not his prescience; be attentive.

Char. Hush!

Sooth. You shall be more beloving than beloved.

Char. I had rather heat my liver with drinking.

Alex. Nay, hear him.

Char. Good now, some excellent fortune! Let me be married to three kings in a forenoon, and widow them all: let me have a child at fifty, to whom Herod of Jewry may do homage: find me to marry me with Octavius Cæsar, and companion me with my mistress.

Sooth. You shall outlive the lady whom you serve.

Char. O excellent! I love long life better than figs.

Sooth. You have seen and proved a fairer former fortune
Than that which is to approach.

Char. Then belike my children shall have no names. Prithee, how many boys and wenches must I have?

Sooth. If every of your wishes had a womb,
And fertile every wish, a million.

Char. Out, fool! I forgive thee for a witch.

Alex. You think none but your sheets are privy to your wishes.

Char. Nay, come, tell Iras hers.

Alex. We 'll know all our fortunes.

Eno. Mine and most of our fortunes to-night shall be—drunk to bed.

Iras. There 's a palm presages chastity, if nothing else.

34. **rang'd**, well-ordered. 39. **wit**, know. 43. **himself**, noble. **stirr'd**, inspired.

5. **with garlands**, i.e., like a bull led to the sacrifice. 47. **presages chastity**, i.e., because it is dry and cool.

Char. E'en as the o'erflowing Nilus presageth famine.

Iras. Go, you wild bedfellow, you cannot soothsay.

Char. Nay, if an oily palm be not a fruitful prognostication, I cannot scratch mine ear. Prithee, tell her but a work-a-day fortune.

Sooth. Your fortunes are alike.

Iras. But how, but how? Give me particulars.

Sooth. I have said.

Iras. Am I not an inch of fortune better than she?

Char. Well, if you were but an inch of fortune better than I, where would you choose it?

Iras. Not in my husband's nose.

Char. Our worser thoughts heavens mend! Alexas,—come, his fortune, his fortune! O, let him marry a woman that cannot go, sweet Isis, I beseech thee! and let her die too, and give him a worse! and let worse follow worse, till the worst of all follow him laughing to his grave, fifty-fold a cuckold! Good Isis, hear me this prayer, though thou deny me a matter of more weight; good Isis, I beseech thee!

Iras. Amen. Dear goddess, hear that prayer of the people! for, as it is a heartbreaking to see a handsome man loose-wiv'd, so it is a deadly sorrow to behold a foul knave uncuckolded; therefore, dear Isis, keep decorum, and fortune him accordingly!

Char. Amen.

Alex. Lo, now, if it lay in their hands to make me a cuckold, they would make themselves whores, but they 'd do 't!

Enter *Cleopatra.*

Eno. Hush! here comes Antony.
Char. Not he; the Queen.
Cleo. Saw you my lord?
Eno. No, lady.
Cleo. Was he not here?
Char. No, madam.
Cleo. He was dispos'd to mirth, but on the sudden
A Roman thought hath struck him. Enobarbus!
Eno. Madam?
Cleo. Seek him, and bring him hither. Where 's Alexas?
Alex. Here, at your service. My lord approaches.
Cleo. We will not look upon him: go with us. *Exeunt.*

Enter *Antony* with a *Messenger* and *Attendants.*

Mess. Fulvia thy wife first came into the field.
Ant. Against my brother Lucius?
Mess. Ay;
But soon that war had end, and the time's state
Made friends of them, jointing their force 'gainst Cæsar;
Whose better issue in the war from Italy
Upon the first encounter drave them.
Ant. Well, what worst?
Mess. The nature of bad news infects the teller.
Ant. When it concerns the fool or coward. On:
Things that are past are done with me. 'T is thus;
Who tells me true, though in his tale lie death,
I hear him as he flatter'd.
Mess. Labienus—
This is stiff news—hath, with his Parthian force,
Extended Asia from Euphrates;
His conquering banner shook from Syria
To Lydia and to Ionia,
Whilst—
Ant. Antony, thou wouldst say,—
Mess. O, my lord!
Ant. Speak to me home, mince not the general tongue.
Name Cleopatra as she is call'd in Rome;
Rail thou in Fulvia's phrase; and taunt my faults
With such full license as both truth and malice
Have power to utter. O, then we bring forth weeds
When our quick minds lie still; and our ills told us
Is as our earing. Fare thee well a while.
Mess. At your noble pleasure. *Exit.*
Ant. From Sicyon, ho, the news! Speak there!
First Att. The man from Sicyon,—is there such an one?
Sec. Att. He stays upon your will.
Ant. Let him appear.
These strong Egyptian fetters I must break,
Or lose myself in dotage.

Enter another *Messenger* with a letter.

What are you?
Sec. Mess. Fulvia thy wife is dead.
Ant. Where died she?
Sec. Mess. In Sicyon:

55. **work-a-day,** ordinary. 65. **go,** bear children, or, can't walk, bedridden.

105. **Extended,** seized upon. 114. **quick,** pregnant. **lie still,** untouched by the plow. 115. **earing,** plowing.

Her length of sickness, with what else more serious
Importeth thee to know, this bears.
Gives the letter.

Ant. Forbear me.
Exit Second Messenger.

There 's a great spirit gone! Thus did I desire it:
What our contempts doth often hurl from us,
We wish it ours again; the present pleasure,
By revolution low'ring, does become
The opposite of itself: she 's good, being gone;
The hand could pluck her back that shov'd her on.
I must from this enchanting queen break off;
Ten thousand harms, more than the ills I know,
My idleness doth hatch.

Re-enter *Enobarbus.*

How now! Enobarbus!

Eno. What 's your pleasure, sir?

Ant. I must with haste from hence.

Eno. Why, then, we kill all our women. We see how mortal an unkindness is to them; if they suffer our departure, death 's the word.

Ant. I must be gone.

Eno. Under a compelling occasion, let women die. It were pity to cast them away for nothing; though, between them and a great cause, they should be esteemed nothing. Cleopatra, catching but the least noise of this, dies instantly; I have seen her die twenty times upon far poorer moment: I do think there is mettle in Death, which commits some loving act upon her, she hath such a celerity in dying.

Ant. She is cunning past man's thought.

Eno. Alack, sir, no; her passions are made of nothing but the finest part of pure love. We cannot call her winds and waters sighs and tears; they are greater storms and tempests than almanacs can report. This cannot be cunning in her; if it be, she makes a shower of rain as well as Jove.

Ant. Would I had never seen her!

Eno. O, sir, you had then left unseen a wonderful piece of work; which not to have been blest withal would have discredited your travel.

Ant. Fulvia is dead.

Eno. Sir?

Ant. Fulvia is dead.

Eno. Fulvia!

Ant. Dead.

Eno. Why, sir, give the gods a thankful sacrifice. When it pleaseth their deities to take the wife of a man from him, it shows to man the tailors of the earth; comforting therein, that when old robes are worn out, there are members to make new. If there were no more women but Fulvia, then had you indeed a cut, and the case to be lamented: this grief is crown'd with consolation; your old smock brings forth a new petticoat: and indeed the tears live in an onion that should water this sorrow.

Ant. The business she hath broached in the state
Cannot endure my absence.

Eno. And the business you have broach'd here cannot be without you; especially that of Cleopatra's, which wholly depends on your abode.

Ant. No more light answers. Let our officers
Have notice what we purpose. I shall break
The cause of our expedience to the Queen,
And get her leave to part. For not alone
The death of Fulvia, with more urgent touches,
Do strongly speak to us; but the letters too
Of many our contriving friends in Rome
Petition us at home. Sextus Pompeius
Hath given the dare to Cæsar, and commands
The empire of the sea. Our slippery people,
Whose love is never link'd to the deserver
Till his deserts are past, begin to throw
Pompey the Great and all his dignities
Upon his son; who, high in name and power,
Higher than both in blood and life, stands up
For the main soldier; whose quality, going on,
The sides o' th' world may danger. Much is breeding,
Which, like the courser's hair, hath yet but life,
And not a serpent's poison. Say, our pleasure,
To such whose place is under us, requires
Our quick remove from hence.

Eno. I shall do 't. *Exeunt.*

Scene III. *Another room in the palace.*

Enter *Cleopatra, Charmian, Iras,* and *Alexas.*

Cleo. Where is he?

Char. I did not see him since.

Cleo. See where he is, who 's with him, what he does.

125. Forbear me, leave me. **129. revolution,** change of circumstances. **147. poorer moment,** less cause.

169. the tailors of the earth, i.e., the gods, who can provide a new garment (wife). **171. members,** persons. **173. cut,** blow. **185. expedience,** haste. **190. Petition us at home,** beg us to come home. **194-6. throw . . . Upon,** transfer to. **197-8. stands up . . . soldier,** aspires to be the foremost soldier. **198. quality,** nature. **199. sides,** frame. **200. courser's hair, etc.,** the superstition is still current that a horse's hair, if put into water, will turn into a snake.

I did not send you. If you find him sad,
Say I am dancing; if in mirth, report
That I am sudden sick. Quick, and return.
Exit Alexas.
Char. Madam, methinks, if you did love him dearly,
You do not hold the method to enforce
The like from him.
Cleo. What should I do, I do not?
Char. In each thing give him way, cross him in nothing.
Cleo. Thou teachest like a fool. The way to lose him!
Char. Tempt him not so too far; I wish, forbear:
In time we hate that which we often fear.

Enter *Antony.*

But here comes Antony.
Cleo. I am sick and sullen.
Ant. I am sorry to give breathing to my purpose,—
Cleo. Help me away, dear Charmian; I shall fall.
It cannot be thus long, the sides of nature
Will not sustain it.
Ant. Now, my dearest queen,—
Cleo. Pray you, stand farther from me.
Ant. What 's the matter?
Cleo. I know, by that same eye, there 's some good news.
What says the married woman? You may go.
Would she had never given you leave to come!
Let her not say 't is I that keep you here;
I have no power upon you; hers you are.
Ant. The gods best know,—
Cleo. O, never was there queen
So mightily betrayed! Yet at the first
I saw the treasons planted.
Ant. Cleopatra,—
Cleo. Why should I think you can be mine and true,
Though you in swearing shake the throned gods,
Who have been false to Fulvia? Riotous madness,
To be entangled with those mouth-made vows,
Which break themselves in swearing!
Ant. Most sweet queen,—
Cleo. Nay, pray you, seek no colour for your going,
But bid farewell, and go. When you sued staying,
Then was the time for words; no going then;
Eternity was in our lips and eyes,
Bliss in our brows' bent; none our parts so poor,
But was a race of heaven. They are so still,
Or thou, the greatest soldier of the world,
Art turn'd the greatest liar.
Ant. How now, lady!
Cleo. I would I had thy inches; thou shouldst know
There were a heart in Egypt.
Ant. Hear me, Queen:
The strong necessity of time commands
Our services a while; but my full heart
Remains in use with you. Our Italy
Shines o'er with civil swords; Sextus Pompeius
Makes his approaches to the port of Rome;
Equality of two domestic powers
Breed scrupulous faction; the hated, grown to strength,
Are newly grown to love; the condemn'd Pompey,
Rich in his father's honour, creeps apace
Into the hearts of such as have not thrived
Upon the present state, whose numbers threaten;
And quietness, grown sick of rest, would purge
By any desperate change. My more particular,
And that which most with you should safe my going,
Is Fulvia's death.
Cleo. Though age from folly could not give me freedom,
It does from childishness. Can Fulvia die?
Ant. She 's dead, my queen.
Look here, and at thy sovereign leisure read
The garboils she awak'd: at the last, best;
See when and where she died.
Cleo. O most false love!
Where be the sacred vials thou shouldst fill
With sorrowful water? Now I see, I see,
In Fulvia's death, how mine receiv'd shall be.
Ant. Quarrel no more, but be prepar'd to know
The purposes I bear; which are, or cease,
As you shall give th' advice. By the fire
That quickens Nilus' slime, I go from hence
Thy soldier, servant; making peace or war
As thou affects.
Cleo. Cut my lace, Charmian, come!
But let it be; I am quickly ill and well,
So Antony loves.
Ant. My precious queen, forbear;
And give true evidence to his love, which stands
An honourable trial.
Cleo. So Fulvia told me.

11. **I wish, forbear,** I wish that you would forbear. 32. **colour,** pretext. 33. **sued staying,** begged to stay. 36. **our brow's bent,** the arching of our brows.

37. **a race of heaven,** a breed of divine origin. 45. **civil swords,** i.e., drawn in civil war. 48. **scrupulous,** captious, carping. **faction,** party strife. 54. **particular,** private concern. 55. **safe,** make safe. 61. **garboils,** disturbances. 63. **sacred vials,** bottles of tears sometimes put by the Romans in urns of dead friends. 71. **affects,** pleasest.

I prithee, turn aside and weep for her;
Then bid adieu to me, and say the tears
Belong to Egypt. Good now, play one scene
Of excellent dissembling; and let it look
Like perfect honour.

Ant. You 'll heat my blood. No more!

Cleo. You can do better yet; but this is meetly.

Ant. Now, by my sword,—

Cleo. And target.—Still he mends;
But this is not the best. Look, prithee, Charmian,
How this Herculean Roman does become
The carriage of his chafe.

Ant. I 'll leave you, lady.

Cleo. Courteous lord, one word.
Sir, you and I must part—but that 's not it—
Sir, you and I have lov'd—but there 's not it;
That you know well. Something it is I would—
O, my oblivion is a very Antony,
And I am all forgotten.

Ant. But that your royalty
Holds idleness your subject, I should take you
For idleness itself.

Cleo. 'T is sweating labour
To bear such idleness so near the heart
As Cleopatra this. But, sir, forgive me,
Since my becomings kill me when they do not
Eye well to you. Your honour calls you hence;
Therefore be deaf to my unpitied folly,
And all the gods go with you! Upon your sword
Sit laurell'd victory, and smooth success
Be strew'd before your feet!

Ant. Let us go.—Come;
Our separation so abides, and flies,
That thou, residing here, goes yet with me,
And I, hence fleeting, here remain with thee.
Away! *Exeunt.*

Scene IV. *Rome. Cæsar's house.*

Enter *Octavius Cæsar,* reading a letter, *Lepidus,* and their train.

Cæs. You may see, Lepidus, and henceforth know,
It is not Cæsar's natural vice to hate
Our great competitor. From Alexandria
This is the news: he fishes, drinks, and wastes
The lamps of night in revel; is not more manlike
Than Cleopatra; nor the queen of Ptolemy
More womanly than he; hardly gave audience, or
Vouchsaf'd to think he had partners. You shall find there
A man who is the abstract of all faults
That all men follow.

Lep. I must not think there are
Evils enow to darken all his goodness.
His faults in him seem as the spots of heaven,
More fiery by night's blackness; hereditary,
Rather than purchas'd; what he cannot change,
Than what he chooses.

Cæs. You are too indulgent. Let 's grant it is not
Amiss to tumble on the bed of Ptolemy;
To give a kingdom for a mirth; to sit
And keep the turn of tippling with a slave;
To reel the streets at noon, and stand the buffet
With knaves that smell of sweat: say this becomes him,—
(As his composure must be rare indeed
Whom these things cannot blemish) yet must Antony
No way excuse his soils, when we do bear
So great weight in his lightness. If he fill'd
His vacancy with his voluptuousness,
Full surfeits and the dryness of his bones
Call on him for 't; but to confound such time
That drums him from his sport and speaks as loud
As his own state and ours, 't is to be chid
As we rate boys, who, being mature in knowledge,
Pawn their experience to their present pleasure,
And so rebel to judgement.

Enter a *Messenger.*

Lep. Here 's more news.

Mess. Thy biddings have been done; and every hour,
Most noble Cæsar, shalt thou have report
How 't is abroad. Pompey is strong at sea;
And it appears he is belov'd of those
That only have fear'd Cæsar: to the ports
The discontents repair; and men's reports
Give him much wrong'd.

Cæs. I should have known no less.
It hath been taught us from the primal state,
That he which is was wish'd until he were;
And the ebb'd man, ne'er loved till ne'er worth love,
Comes dear'd by being lack'd. This common body,
Like to a vagabond flag upon the stream,

81. meetly, fairly good. **84-5. How . . . chafe,** how becoming to this Roman, who boasts descent from Hercules, is the bearing of anger. **90. oblivion,** forgetfulness. **92. idleness,** frivolousness, flippancy. **97. Eye,** appear

14. purchas'd, acquired. **25. in his lightness,** because of his levity. **28. Call on him,** demand payment from him. **confound,** waste. **31. rate,** berate. **40. Give him,** make him out. **42. wish'd,** wanted. **43. ebb'd,** declined. **44. Comes dear'd,** becomes endeared. **45. flag,** iris.

Goes to and back, lackeying the varying tide,
To rot itself with motion.
Mess. Cæsar, I bring thee word,
Menecrates and Menas, famous pirates,
Makes the sea serve them, which they ear and wound
With keels of every kind. Many hot inroads
They make in Italy; the borders maritime
Lack blood to think on 't, and flush youth revolt:
No vessel can peep forth, but 't is as soon
Taken as seen; for Pompey's name strikes more
Than could his war resisted.
Cæs. Antony,
Leave thy lascivious wassails. When thou once
Was beaten from Modena, where thou slew'st
Hirtius and Pansa, consuls, at thy heel
Did famine follow; whom thou fought'st against,
Though daintily brought up, with patience more
Than savages could suffer. Thou didst drink
The stale of horses, and the gilded puddle
Which beasts would cough at; thy palate then did deign
The roughest berry on the rudest hedge;
Yea, like the stag, when snow the pasture sheets,
The barks of trees thou brows'd; on the Alps
It is reported thou didst eat strange flesh,
Which some did die to look on; and all this—
It wounds thine honour that I speak it now—
Was borne so like a soldier, that thy cheek
So much as lank'd not.
Lep. 'T is pity of him.
Cæs. Let his shames quickly
Drive him to Rome: 't is time we twain
Did show ourselves i' th' field, and to that end
Assemble we immediate counsel: Pompey
Thrives in our idleness.
Lep. To-morrow, Cæsar,
I shall be furnish'd to inform you rightly
Both what by sea and land I can be able
To front this present time.
Cæs. Till which encounter,
It is my business too. Farewell.
Lep. Farewell, my lord: what you shall know meantime
Of stirs abroad, I shall beseech you, sir,
To let me be partaker.
Cæs. Doubt not, sir;
I knew it for my bond. *Exeunt.*

46. **lackeying,** following. 49. **ear,** plough. 52. **Lack blood,** turn pale. **flush youth,** youth approaching manhood. 54-5. **for . . . resisted,** for Pompey's name is more powerful than his actual warfare if it were opposed. 56. **wassails,** revels. 58. **Hirtius and Pansa,** consuls sent against Antony in 43 B.C. 62. **stale,** urine. **gilded,** covered with yellow scum. 71. **lank'd not,** became not thin. 84. **for my bond,** for my bounden duty.

Scene V. *Alexandria. Cleopatra's palace.*

Enter *Cleopatra, Charmian,* Iras, and *Mardian.*

Cleo. Charmian!
Char. Madam?
Cleo. Ha, ha!
Give me to drink mandragora.
Char. Why, madam?
Cleo. That I might sleep out this great gap of time
My Antony is away.
Char. You think of him too much.
Cleo. O, 't is treason!
Char. Madam, I trust not so.
Cleo. Thou, eunuch Mardian!
Mar. What 's your Highness' pleasure?
Cleo. Not now to hear thee sing; I take no pleasure
In aught an eunuch has. 'T is well for thee,
That, being unseminar'd, thy freer thoughts
May not fly forth of Egypt. Hast thou affections?
Mar. Yes, gracious madam.
Cleo. Indeed!
Mar. Not in deed, madam, for I can do nothing
But what indeed is honest to be done;
Yet have I fierce affections, and think
What Venus did with Mars.
Cleo. O Charmian,
Where think'st thou he is now? Stands he, or sits he?
Or does he walk? Or is he on his horse?
O happy horse, to bear the weight of Antony!
Do bravely, horse! for wot'st thou whom thou mov'st?
The demi-Atlas of this earth, the arm
And burgonet of men. He 's speaking now,
Or murmuring, "Where 's my serpent of old Nile?"
For so he calls me. Now I feed myself
With most delicious poison. Think on me,
That am with Phœbus' amorous pinches black,
And wrinkled deep in time? Broad-fronted Cæsar,
When thou wast here above the ground, I was
A morsel for a monarch; and great Pompey
Would stand and make his eyes grow in my brow;
There would he anchor his aspect and die
With looking on his life.

4. **mandragora,** juice of the mandrake, supposed to be a soporific. 11. **unseminar'd,** sterilized. 12. **affections,** sexual passion. 23. **demi-Atlas,** the supporter of half the world. 24. **burgonet,** helmet, here, defense. 28. **black,** swarthy. Cleopatra was by blood a Greek and not an Egyptian. 29. **wrinkled,** Cleopatra was only thirty at this time. **Cæsar,** Julius Cæsar.

Enter *Alexas* from Antony.

Alex. Sovereign of Egypt, hail!
Cleo. How much unlike art thou Mark Antony!
Yet, coming from him, that great med'cine hath
With his tinct gilded thee.
How goes it with my brave Mark Antony?
Alex. Last thing he did, dear queen,
He kiss'd,—the last of many doubled kisses,—
This orient pearl. His speech sticks in my heart.
Cleo. Mine ear must pluck it thence.
Alex. "Good friend," quoth he,
"Say, the firm Roman to great Egypt sends
This treasure of an oyster; at whose foot,
To mend the petty present, I will piece
Her opulent throne with kingdoms. All the East,
Say thou, shall call her mistress." So he nodded,
And soberly did mount an arm-gaunt steed,
Who neigh'd so high that what I would have spoke
Was beastly dumb'd by him.
Cleo. What, was he sad or merry?
Alex. Like to the time o' th' year between the extremes
Of hot and cold, he was nor sad nor merry.
Cleo. O well-divided disposition! Note him,
Note him, good Charmian, 't is the man; but note him:
He was not sad, for he would shine on those
That make their looks by his; he was not merry,
Which seem'd to tell them his remembrance lay
In Egypt with his joy; but between both.
O heavenly mingle! Be'st thou sad or merry,
The violence of either thee becomes,
So does it no man else. Met'st thou my posts?
Alex. Ay, madam, twenty several messengers:
Why do you send so thick?
Cleo. Who 's born that day
When I forget to send to Antony,
Shall die a beggar. Ink and paper, Charmian.
Welcome, my good Alexas. Did I, Charmian,
Ever love Cæsar so?
Char. O that brave Cæsar!
Cleo. Be chok'd with such another emphasis!
Say, the brave Antony!
Char. The valiant Cæsar!
Cleo. By Isis, I will give thee bloody teeth,
If thou with Cæsar paragon again
My man of men.
Char. By your most gracious pardon,
I sing but after you.
Cleo. My salad days,
When I was green in judgement, cold in blood,
To say as I said then! But, come, away;
Get me ink and paper.
He shall have every day a several greeting,
Or I 'll unpeople Egypt. *Exeunt.*

ACT II. Scene I. *Messina. Pompey's house.*

Enter *Pompey, Menecrates,* and *Menas,* in warlike manner.

Pom. If the great gods be just, they shall assist
The deeds of justest men.
Mene. Know, worthy Pompey,
That what they do delay, they not deny.
Pom. Whiles we are suitors to their throne, decays
The thing we sue for.
Mene. We, ignorant of ourselves,
Beg often our own harms, which the wise powers
Deny us for our good; so find we profit
By losing of our prayers.
Pom. I shall do well:
The people love me, and the sea is mine;
My powers are crescent, and my auguring hope
Says it will come to th' full. Mark Antony
In Egypt sits at dinner, and will make
No wars without-doors: Cæsar gets money where
He loses hearts: Lepidus flatters both,
Of both is flatter'd; but he neither loves,
Nor either cares for him.
Men. Cæsar and Lepidus
Are in the field; a mighty strength they carry.
Pom. Where have you this? 'T is false.
Men. From Silvius, sir.
Pom. He dreams: I know they are in Rome together,

36. med'cine, physician, or possibly the elixir which was supposed to turn base metals into gold. **37. tinct,** tincture. **48. arm-gaunt,** gaunt with service, a campaign horse. *arm-girt* has been suggested as a possible reading. **50. dumb'd,** silenced.

71. paragon, compare as model. **Act II, Scene i: 10. auguring,** prophesying.

Looking for Antony. But all the charms of love,
Salt Cleopatra, soften thy wan'd lip!
Let witchcraft join with beauty, lust with both!
Tie up the libertine in a field of feasts,
Keep his brain fuming; Epicurean cooks
Sharpen with cloyless sauce his appetite;
That sleep and feeding may prorogue his honour
Even till a Lethe'd dulness!

Enter *Varrius.*

How now, Varrius!

Var. This is most certain that I shall deliver:
Mark Antony is every hour in Rome
Expected; since he went from Egypt 't is
A space for farther travel.

Pom. I could have given less matter
A better ear. Menas, I did not think
This amorous surfeiter would have donn'd his helm
For such a petty war. His soldiership
Is twice the other twain; but let us rear
The higher our opinion, that our stirring
Can from the lap of Egypt's widow pluck
The ne'er lust-wearied Antony.

Men. I cannot hope
Cæsar and Antony shall well greet together.
His wife that 's dead did trespasses to Cæsar;
His brother warr'd upon him, although, I think,
Not mov'd by Antony.

Pom. I know not, Menas,
How lesser enmities may give way to greater.
Were 't not that we stand up against them all,
'T were pregnant they should square between themselves;
For they have entertained cause enough
To draw their swords; but how the fear of us
May cement their divisions and bind up
The petty difference, we yet not know.
Be 't as our gods will have 't! It only stands
Our lives upon to use our strongest hands.
Come, Menas. *Exeunt.*

Scene II. *Rome. The house of Lepidus.*

Enter *Enobarbus* and *Lepidus.*

Lep. Good Enobarbus, 't is a worthy deed,
And shall become you well, to entreat your captain
To soft and gentle speech.

Eno. I shall entreat him
To answer like himself. If Cæsar move him,
Let Antony look over Cæsar's head
And speak as loud as Mars. By Jupiter,
Were I the wearer of Antonius' beard,
I would not shave 't to-day.

Lep. 'T is not a time
For private stomaching.

Eno. Every time
Serves for the matter that is then born in 't.

Lep. But small to greater matters must give way.

Eno. Not if the small come first.

Lep. Your speech is passion;
But, pray you, stir no embers up. Here comes
The noble Antony.

Enter *Antony* and Ventidius.

Eno. And yonder, Cæsar.

Enter *Cæsar, Mæcenas,* and *Agrippa.*

Ant. If we compose well here, to Parthia!
Hark, Ventidius.

Cæs. I do not know,
Mæcenas; ask Agrippa.

Lep. Noble friends,
That which combin'd us was most great, and let not
A leaner action rend us. What 's amiss,
May it be gently heard; when we debate
Our trivial difference loud, we do commit
Murder in healing wounds; then, noble partners,
The rather, for I earnestly beseech,
Touch you the sourest points with sweetest terms,
Nor curstness grow to th' matter.

Ant. 'T is spoken well.
Were we before our armies, and to fight,
I should do thus. *Flourish.*

Cæs. Welcome to Rome.

Ant. Thank you.

Cæs. Sit.

Ant. Sit, sir.

Cæs. Nay, then.

Ant. I learn you take things ill which are not so,
Or being, concern you not.

Cæs. I must be laugh'd at,
If, or for nothing or a little, I
Should say myself offended, and with you
Chiefly i' th' world; more laugh'd at, that I should
Once name you derogately, when to sound your name
It not concern'd me.

21. Salt, wanton. **wan'd,** faded. **26. prorogue,** defer, suspend. **31. space,** time for. **37. widow,** Cleopatra had married her brother Ptolemy. **45. pregnant,** very probable. **square,** square off, fight. **50-1. It . . . upon,** our lives depend wholly upon.

9. stomaching, resentment. **15. compose,** agree. **25. Nor . . . matter,** nor let scolding have a part in the discussion. **34. derogately,** disparagingly.

Ant. My being in Egypt, Cæsar,
What was 't to you?
Cæs. No more than my residing here at Rome
Might be to you in Egypt; yet, if you there
Did practise on my state, your being in Egypt
Might be my question.
Ant. How intend you, practis'd?
Cæs. You may be pleas'd to catch at mine intent
By what did here befall me. Your wife and brother
Made wars upon me; and their contestation
Was theme for you, you were the word of war.
Ant. You do mistake your business; my brother never
Did urge me in his act: I did inquire it,
And have my learning from some true reports
That drew their swords with you. Did he not rather
Discredit my authority with yours,
And make the wars alike against my stomach,
Having alike your cause? Of this my letters
Before did satisfy you. If you 'll patch a quarrel,
As matter whole you have not to make it with,
It must not be with this.
Cæs. You praise yourself
By laying defects of judgement to me; but
You patch'd up your excuses.
Ant. Not so, not so.
I know you could not lack, I am certain on 't,
Very necessity of this thought, that I,
Your partner in the cause 'gainst which he fought,
Could not with graceful eyes attend those wars
Which fronted mine own peace. As for my wife,
I would you had her spirit in such another.
The third o' th' world is yours, which with a snaffle
You may pace easy, but not such a wife.
Eno. Would we had all such wives, that the men might go to wars with the women!
Ant. So much uncurbable her garboils, Cæsar,
Made out of her impatience, which not wanted
Shrewdness of policy too, I grieving grant
Did you too much disquiet. For that you must
But say, I could not help it.
Cæs. I wrote to you:
When rioting in Alexandria you
Did pocket up my letters, and with taunts
Did gibe my missive out of audience.
Ant. Sir,
He fell upon me ere admitted: then
Three kings I had newly feasted, and did want
Of what I was i' th' morning; but next day
I told him of myself, which was as much
As to have ask'd him pardon. Let this fellow
Be nothing of our strife; if we contend,
Out of our question wipe him.
Cæs. You have broken
The article of your oath; which you shall never
Have tongue to charge me with.
Lep. Soft, Cæsar!
Ant. No,
Lepidus, let him speak.
The honour is sacred which he talks on now,
Supposing that I lack'd it. But, on, Cæsar:
The article of my oath.
Cæs. To lend me arms and aid when I requir'd them;
The which you both denied.
Ant. Neglected, rather;
And then when poisoned hours had bound me up
From mine own knowledge. As nearly as I may,
I 'll play the penitent to you; but mine honesty
Shall not make poor my greatness, nor my power
Work without it. Truth is, that Fulvia,
To have me out of Egypt, made wars here;
For which myself, the ignorant motive, do
So far ask pardon as befits mine honour
To stoop in such a case.
Lep. 'T is noble spoken.
Mæc. If it might please you, to enforce no further
The griefs between ye: to forget them quite
Were to remember that the present need
Speaks to atone you.
Lep. Worthily spoken, Mæcenas.
Eno. Or, if you borrow one another's love for the instant, you may, when you hear no more words of Pompey, return it again: you shall have time to wrangle in when you have nothing else to do.
Ant. Thou art a soldier only; speak no more.
Eno. That truth should be silent I had almost forgot.
Ant. You wrong this presence; therefore speak no more.
Eno. Go to, then; your considerate stone.
Cæs. I do not much dislike the matter, but
The manner of his speech; for 't cannot be
We shall remain in friendship, our conditions

39. **practise on**, plot against. 40. **question**, business. 44. **Was theme for you**, was undertaken in your interest. 46. **Did urge me**, use my name. 50. **stomach**, desire. 58. **Very necessity of this thought**, this completely inevitable thought. 60. **graceful**, favorable. 61. **fronted**, opposed. 64. **pace**, train, control. 74. **missive**, messenger.

78. **of myself**, of my condition. 94. **it**, i.e., greatness (his parity with Cæsar in the state). 102. **Speaks to atone you**, suggests your reconciliation. 112. **considerate**, thinking. 115. **conditions**, dispositions.

So diff'ring in their acts. Yet, if I knew
What hoop should hold us stanch, from edge to edge
O' th' world I would pursue it.
Agr. Give me leave, Cæsar,—
Cæs. Speak, Agrippa.
Agr. Thou hast a sister by the mother's side,
Admir'd Octavia. Great Mark Antony
Is now a widower.
Cæs. Say not so, Agrippa.
If Cleopatra heard you, your reproof
Were well deserved of rashness.
Ant. I am not married, Cæsar; let me hear
Agrippa further speak.
Agr. To hold you in perpetual amity,
To make you brothers, and to knit your hearts
With an unslipping knot, take Antony
Octavia to his wife; whose beauty claims
No worse a husband than the best of men;
Whose virtue and whose general graces speak
That which none else can utter. By this marriage,
All little jealousies, which now seem great,
And all great fears, which now import their dangers,
Would then be nothing. Truths would be tales,
Where now half-tales be truths; her love to both
Would each to other and all loves to both
Draw after her. Pardon what I have spoke;
For 't is a studied, not a present thought,
By duty ruminated.
Ant. Will Cæsar speak?
Cæs. Not till he hears how Antony is touch'd
With what is spoke already.
Ant. What power is in Agrippa,
If I would say, "Agrippa, be it so,"
To make this good?
Cæs. The power of Cæsar, and
His power unto Octavia.
Ant. May I never
To this good purpose, that so fairly shows,
Dream of impediment! Let me have thy hand:
Further this act of grace; and from this hour
The heart of brothers govern in our loves
And sway our great designs!
Cæs. There 's my hand.
A sister I bequeath you, whom no brother
Did ever love so dearly. Let her live
To join our kingdoms and our hearts; and never
Fly off our loves again!
Lep. Happily, amen!
Ant. I did not think to draw my sword 'gainst Pompey;
For he hath laid strange courtesies and great
Of late upon me. I must thank him only,
Lest my remembrance suffer ill report;
At heel of that, defy him.
Lep. Time calls upon 's.
Of us must Pompey presently be sought,
Or else he seeks out us.
Ant. Where lies he?
Cæs. About the mount Misena.
Ant. What is his strength by land?
Cæs. Great and increasing; but by sea
He is an absolute master.
Ant. So is the fame.
Would we had spoke together! Haste we for it;
Yet, ere we put ourselves in arms, dispatch we
The business we have talk'd of.
Cæs. With most gladness;
And do invite you to my sister's view,
Whither straight I 'll lead you.
Ant. Let us, Lepidus,
Not lack your company.
Lep. Noble Antony,
Not sickness should detain me.
Flourish. Exeunt Cæsar, Antony, Lepidus, and Ventidius.

Mæc. Welcome from Egypt, sir.

Eno. Half the heart of Cæsar, worthy Mæcenas! My honourable friend, Agrippa!

Agr. Good Enobarbus!

Mæc. We have cause to be glad that matters are so well digested. You stay'd well by 't in Egypt.

Eno. Ay, sir; we did sleep day out of countenance, and made the night light with drinking.

Mæc. Eight wild boars roasted whole at a breakfast, and but twelve persons there; is this true?

Eno. This was but as a fly by an eagle: we had much more monstrous matter of feast, which worthily deserved noting.

Mæc. She 's a most triumphant lady, if report be square to her.

Eno. When she first met Mark Antony, she purs'd up his heart, upon the river of Cydnus.

Agr. There she appear'd indeed, or my reporter devis'd well for her.

Eno. I will tell you.
The barge she sat in, like a burnish'd throne,
Burn'd on the water: the poop was beaten gold;
Purple the sails, and so perfumed that
The winds were love-sick with them: the oars were silver,

135. **import**, carry with them. 137. **half-tales be truths**, rumors are accepted as truths.

163. **Misena**, Shakespeare found this spelling in his source. The usual form is Misenum, a harbor in southern Italy. 166. **fame**, rumor. 167. **spoke together**, fought. 179. **You . . . by 't**, you amused yourself well. 190. **square**, just.

Which to the tune of flutes kept stroke, and made
The water which they beat to follow faster,
As amorous of their strokes. For her own person,
It beggar'd all description: she did lie
In her pavilion—cloth-of-gold of tissue—
O'er-picturing that Venus where we see
The fancy outwork nature. On each side her
Stood pretty dimpled boys, like smiling Cupids,
With divers-colour'd fans, whose wind did seem
To glow the delicate cheeks which they did cool,
And what they undid did.

Agr. O, rare for Antony!

Eno. Her gentlewomen, like the Nereides,
So many mermaids, tended her i' th' eyes,
And made their bends adornings. At the helm
A seeming mermaid steers; the silken tackle
Swell with the touches of those flower-soft hands,
That yarely frame the office. From the barge
A strange invisible perfume hits the sense
Of the adjacent wharfs. The city cast
Her people out upon her; and Antony
Enthron'd i' th' market-place, did sit alone,
Whistling to th' air, which, but for vacancy,
Had gone to gaze on Cleopatra too
And made a gap in nature.

Agr. Rare Egyptian!

Eno. Upon her landing, Antony sent to her,
Invited her to supper: she replied,
It should be better he became her guest;
Which she entreated. Our courteous Antony,
Whom ne'er the word of "No" woman heard speak
Being barber'd ten times o'er, goes to the feast,
And for his ordinary pays his heart
For what his eyes eat only.

Agr. Royal wench!
She made great Cæsar lay his sword to bed.
He plough'd her, and she cropp'd.

Eno. I saw her once
Hop forty paces through the public street;
And having lost her breath, she spoke, and panted,
That she did make defect perfection.
And, breathless, power breathe forth.

Mæc. Now Antony must leave her utterly.

Eno. Never; he will not.
Age cannot wither her, nor custom stale
Her infinite variety: other women cloy
The appetites they feed, but she makes hungry
Where most she satisfies, for vilest things
Become themselves in her, that the holy priests
Bless her when she is riggish.

Mæc. If beauty, wisdom, modesty, can settle
The heart of Antony, Octavia is
A blessed lottery to him.

Agr. Let us go.
Good Enobarbus, make yourself my guest
Whilst you abide here.

Eno. Humbly, sir, I thank you. *Exeunt.*

204. **tissue,** cloth interwoven with gold or silver. 212. **i' th' eyes,** i.e., in her sight. 213. **bends,** may be, obeisances, or even their motions in serving her. 216. **yarely frame,** dextrously perform. 221. **but for vacancy,** but for fear of causing a vacuum. 230. **ordinary,** meal. 237. **power,** i.e., of her charm.

244. **Become themselves,** are becoming. 245. **riggish,** wanton. 248. **lottery,** allotment.

Scene III. *Rome. Cæsar's house.*

Enter *Antony, Cæsar, Octavia* between them.

Ant. The world and my great office will sometimes
Divide me from your bosom.

Octa. All which time
Before the gods my knee shall bow my prayers
To them for you.

Ant. Good-night, sir. My Octavia,
Read not my blemishes in the world's report:
I have not kept my square; but that to come
Shall all be done by th' rule. Good-night, dear lady.
Good-night, sir.

Cæs. Good-night.

Exeunt Cæsar and Octavia.

Enter *Soothsayer.*

Ant. Now, sirrah; you do wish yourself in Egypt?

Sooth. Would I had never come from thence, nor you
Thither!

Ant. If you can, your reason?

Sooth. I see it in
My motion, have it not in my tongue; but yet
Hie you to Egypt again.

Ant. Say to me,
Whose fortunes shall rise higher, Cæsar's or mine?

Sooth. Cæsar's.
Therefore, O Antony, stay not by his side.
Thy demon, that thy spirit which keeps thee, is
Noble, courageous, high, unmatchable,
Where Cæsar's is not; but, near him, thy angel
Becomes a fear, as being o'erpower'd: therefore
Make space between you.

Ant. Speak this no more.

Sooth. To none but thee; no more, but when to thee.

Scene iii: 6. **kept my square,** kept my proper position, i.e., done as I should. 14. **My motion,** intuitively. 22. **a fear,** a thing which fears.

If thou dost play with him at any game,
Thou art sure to lose; and, of that natural luck,
He beats thee 'gainst the odds. Thy lustre thickens
When he shines by. I say again, thy spirit
Is all afraid to govern thee near him;
But, he away, 't is noble.

Ant. Get thee gone.—
Say to Ventidius I would speak with him;

Exit Soothsayer.

He shall to Parthia. Be it art or hap,
He hath spoken true. The very dice obey him;
And in our sports my better cunning faints
Under his chance: if we draw lots, he speeds;
His cocks do win the battle still of mine,
When it is all to nought; and his quails ever
Beat mine, inhoop'd, at odds. I will to Egypt;
And though I make this marriage for my peace,
I' th' East my pleasure lies.

Enter *Ventidius.*

O, come, Ventidius,
You must to Parthia. Your commission 's ready;
Follow me, and receive 't. *Exeunt.*

Scene IV. *Rome. A street.*

Enter *Lepidus, Mæcenas,* and *Agrippa.*

Lep. Trouble yourselves no further; pray you, hasten
Your generals after.

Agr. Sir, Mark Antony
Will e'en but kiss Octavia, and we 'll follow.

Lep. Till I shall see you in your soldier's dress,
Which will become you both, farewell.

Mæc. We shall,
As I conceive the journey, be at the Mount
Before you, Lepidus.

Lep. Your way is shorter;
My purposes do draw me much about.
You 'll win two days upon me.

Mæc. }
Agr. } Sir, good success!

Lep. Farewell. *Exeunt.*

Scene V. *Alexandria. Cleopatra's palace.*

Enter *Cleopatra, Charmian, Iras* and *Alexas.*

Cleo. Give me some music; music, moody food
Of us that trade in love.

All. The music, ho!

Enter *Mardian* the Eunuch.

Cleo. Let it alone; let 's to billiards. Come, Charmian.

Char. My arm is sore; best play with Mardian.

Cleo. As well a woman with an eunuch play'd
As with a woman. Come, you 'll play with me, sir?

Mar. As well as I can, madam.

Cleo. And when good will is showed, though 't come too short,
The actor may plead pardon. I 'll none now.
Give me mine angle, we 'll to th' river; there,
My music playing far off, I will betray
Tawny-finn'd fishes; my bended hook shall pierce
Their slimy jaws; and, as I draw them up,
I 'll think them every one an Antony,
And say, "Ah, ha! you 're caught."

Char. 'T was merry when
You wager'd on your angling; when your diver
Did hang a salt-fish on his hook, which he
With fervency drew up.

Cleo. That time,—O times!—
I laugh'd him out of patience; and that night
I laugh'd him into patience; and next morn,
Ere the ninth hour, I drunk him to his bed;
Then put my tires and mantles on him, whilst
I wore his sword Philippan.

Enter a *Messenger.*

O, from Italy!
Ram thou thy fruitful tidings in mine ears,
That long time have been barren.

Mess. Madam, madam,—

Cleo. Antonio's dead!—If thou say so, villain,
Thou kill'st thy mistress; but well and free,
If thou so yield him, there is gold, and here
My bluest veins to kiss; a hand that kings
Have lipp'd, and trembled kissing.

Mess. First, madam, he is well.

Cleo. Why, there 's more gold.
But, sirrah, mark, we use
To say the dead are well. Bring it to that,
The gold I give thee will I melt and pour
Down thy ill-uttering throat.

Mess. Good madam, hear me.

Cleo. Well, go to, I will.
But there 's no goodness in thy face; if Antony
Be free and healthful,—so tart a favour
To trumpet such good tidings! If not well,
Thou shouldst come like a Fury crown'd with snakes,
Not like a formal man.

Mess. Will 't please you hear me?

26. of, because of. 27. **thickens**, grows dim. 37. **all to nought**, when the odds are all to nothing on my side. 38. **inhoop'd**, enclosed for fighting. **Scene iv:** 6. **Mount**, Mount Misena. **Cf. II, ii, 163.**

Scene v: 10. angle, rod and line. **22. tires**, headdresses. **23. Philippan**, named for the battle of Philippi. **41. formal**, ordinary.

Cleo. I have a mind to strike thee ere thou speak'st;
Yet, if thou say Antony lives, 't is well,
Or friends with Cæsar, or not captive to him,
I 'll set thee in a shower of gold, and hail
Rich pearls upon thee.
Mess. Madam, he 's well.
Cleo. Well said.
Mess. And friends with Cæsar.
Cleo. Thou 'rt an honest man.
Mess. Cæsar and he are greater friends than ever.
Cleo. Make thee a fortune from me.
Mess. But yet, madam,—
Cleo. I do not like "But yet," it does allay
The good precedence; fie upon "But yet"!
"But yet" is as a jailer to bring forth
Some monstrous malefactor. Prithee, friend,
Pour out the pack of matter to mine ear,
The good and bad together: he 's friends with Cæsar;
In state of health thou say'st; and thou say'st free.
Mess. Free, madam! no; I made no such report.
He 's bound unto Octavia.
Cleo. For what good turn?
Mess. For the best turn i' th' bed.
Cleo. I am pale, Charmian.
Mess. Madam, he 's married to Octavia.
Cleo. The most infectious pestilence upon thee! *Strikes him down.*
Mess. Good madam, patience.
Cleo. What say you? Hence, *Strikes him again.*
Horrible villain! or I 'll spurn thine eyes
Like balls before me; I 'll unhair thy head.
She hales him up and down.
Thou shalt be whipp'd with wire, and stew'd in brine,
Smarting in ling'ring pickle.
Mess. Gracious madam,
I that do bring the news made not the match.
Cleo. Say 't is not so, a province I will give thee,
And make thy fortunes proud; the blow thou hadst
Shall make thy peace for moving me to rage;
And I will boot thee with what gift beside
Thy modesty can beg.
Mess. He 's married, madam.
Cleo. Rogue, thou hast liv'd too long.
Draws a knife.
Mess. Nay, then I 'll run.
What mean you, madam? I have made no fault. *Exit.*
Char. Good madam, keep yourself within yourself:
The man is innocent.
Cleo. Some innocents scape not the thunderbolt.
Melt Egypt into Nile! and kindly creatures
Turn all to serpents! Call the slave again:
Though I am mad, I will not bite him; call!
Char. He is afeard to come.
Cleo. I will not hurt him.
Exit Charmian.
These hands do lack nobility that they strike
A meaner than myself, since I myself
Have given myself the cause.

Re-enter *Charmian* and *Messenger.*

Come hither, sir.
Though it be honest, it is never good
To bring bad news: give to a gracious message
An host of tongues; but let ill tidings tell
Themselves when they be felt.
Mess. I have done my duty.
Cleo. Is he married?
I cannot hate thee worser than I do,
If thou again say yes.
Mess. He 's married, madam.
Cleo. The gods confound thee! dost thou hold there still?
Mess. Should I lie, madam?
Cleo. O, I would thou didst,
So half my Egypt were submerg'd and made
A cistern for scal'd snakes! Go, get thee hence!
Hadst thou Narcissus in thy face, to me
Thou wouldst appear most ugly. He is married?
Mess. I crave your Highness' pardon.
Cleo. He is married?
Mess. Take no offence that I would not offend you.
To punish me for what you make me do
Seems much unequal: he 's married to Octavia.
Cleo. O, that his fault should make a knave of thee,
That art not what thou 'rt sure of. Get thee hence;
The merchandise which thou hast brought from Rome
Are all too dear for me: lie they upon thy hand,
And be undone by 'em! *Exit Messenger.*
Char. Good your Highness, patience.
Cleo. In praising Antony, I have disprais'd Cæsar.
Char. Many times, madam.
Cleo. I am paid for 't now.

50-1. allay The good precedence, nullify the good news that has preceded. **63. spurn,** kick. **65. wire,** metal chains with knobs on the end. **71. boot thee,** give thee to boot.

78. kindly, natural. **94. So,** even if. **103. That art . . . of,** who are not the same thing (this disagreeable news) of which you are so sure.

Lead me from hence;
I faint, O Iras, Charmian! 'T is no matter.
Go to the fellow, good Alexas; bid him
Report the feature of Octavia, her years,
Her inclination; let him not leave out
The colour of her hair. Bring me word quickly. *Exit Alexas.*
Let him for ever go;—let him not—Charmian,
Though he be painted one way like a Gorgon,
The other way 's a Mars. Bid you Alexas
To Mardian.
Bring me word how tall she is. Pity me, Charmian,
But do not speak to me. Lead me to my chamber. *Exeunt.*

Scene VI. *Near Misenum.*

Flourish. Enter *Pompey* and *Menas* at one door, with drum and trumpet: at another *Cæsar, Antony, Lepidus, Enobarbus, Mæcenas, Agrippa,* with Soldiers marching.

Pom. Your hostages I have, so have you mine;
And we shall talk before we fight.
Cæs. Most meet
That first we come to words, and therefore have we
Our written purposes before us sent;
Which, if thou hast considered, let us know
If 't will tie up thy discontented sword,
And carry back to Sicily much tall youth
That else must perish here.
Pom. To you all three,
The senators alone of this great world,
Chief factors for the gods, I do not know
Wherefore my father should revengers want,
Having a son and friends; since Julius Cæsar,
Who at Philippi the good Brutus ghosted,
There saw you labouring for him. What was 't
That mov'd pale Cassius to conspire; and what
Made the all-honour'd, honest Roman, Brutus,
With the arm'd rest, courtiers of beauteous freedom,
To drench the Capitol, but that they would
Have one man but a man? And that is it
Hath made me rig my navy, at whose burden
The anger'd ocean foams; with which I meant
To scourge th' ingratitude that despiteful Rome
Cast on my noble father.
Cæs. Take your time.
Ant. Thou canst not fear us, Pompey, with thy sails;
We 'll speak with thee at sea. At land, thou know'st
How much we do o'er-count thee.
Pom. At land, indeed,
Thou dost o'er-count me of my father's house;
But, since the cuckoo builds not for himself,
Remain in 't as thou mayst.
Lep. Be pleas'd to tell us—
For this is from the present—how you take
The offers we have sent you.
Cæs. There 's the point.
Ant. Which do not be entreated to, but weigh
What it is worth embrac'd.
Cæs. And what may follow,
To try a larger fortune.
Pom. You have made me offer
Of Sicily, Sardinia; and I must
Rid all the sea of pirates; then, to send
Measures of wheat to Rome. This 'greed upon,
To part with unhack'd edges, and bear back
Our targes undinted.
Cæs. Ant. Lep. That 's our offer.
Pom. Know, then,
I came before you here a man prepar'd
To take this offer; but Mark Antony
Put me to some impatience.—Though I lose
The praise of it by telling, you must know,
When Cæsar and your brother were at blows,
Your mother came to Sicily and did find
Her welcome friendly.
Ant. I have heard it, Pompey;
And am well studied for a liberal thanks
Which I do owe you.
Pom. Let me have your hand.
I did not think, sir, to have met you here.
Ant. The beds i' th' East are soft; and thanks to you,
That call'd me timelier than my purpose hither,
For I have gain'd by 't.
Cæs. Since I saw you last,
There is a change upon you.
Pom. Well, I know not
What counts harsh Fortune casts upon my face;
But in my bosom shall she never come,
To make my heart her vassal.
Lep. Well met here.
Pom. I hope so, Lepidus. Thus we are agreed:
I crave our composition may be written,
And seal'd between us.
Cæs. That 's the next to do.

112. **feature,** general appearance. 113. **inclination,** disposition. 116-7. **Though . . . Mars,** refers to "perspective" pictures, which from different points of view revealed different objects. **Scene vi: 7. tall,** stout. 19. **but a man,** i.e., not become a superman.

26. **o'er-count,** outnumber. 27. **o'er-count,** cheat. 30. **from the present,** irrelevant. 39. **targes,** shields. 48. **am well studied for,** well prepared for. 55. **casts,** a metaphor from drawing lines in casting accounts. 59. **composition,** agreement.

Pom. We 'll feast each other ere we part; and let 's
Draw lots who shall begin.
Ant. That will I, Pompey.
Pom. No, Antony, take the lot;
But, first or last, your fine Egyptian cookery
Shall have the fame. I have heard that Julius Cæsar
Grew fat with feasting there.
Ant. You have heard much.
Pom. I have fair meanings, sir.
Ant. And fair words to them.
Pom. Then so much have I heard;
And I have heard, Apollodorus carried—
Eno. No more of that; he did so.
Pom. What, I pray you?
Eno. A certain queen to Cæsar in a mattress.
Pom. I know thee now. How far'st thou, soldier?
Eno. Well;
And well am like to do; for, I perceive,
Four feasts are toward.
Pom. Let me shake thy hand;
I never hated thee: I have seen thee fight,
When I have envied thy behaviour.
Eno. Sir,
I never lov'd you much; but I ha' prais'd ye,
When you have well deserv'd ten times as much
As I have said you did.
Pom. Enjoy thy plainness,
It nothing ill becomes thee.
Aboard my galley I invite you all:
Will you lead, lords?
Cæs. Ant. Lep. Show 's the way, sir.
Pom. Come.

Exeunt all but Menas and Enobarbus.

Men. [*Aside.*] Thy father, Pompey, would ne'er have made this treaty.—You and I have known, sir.

Eno. At sea, I think.

Men. We have, sir.

Eno. You have done well by water.

Men. And you by land.

Eno. I will praise any man that will praise me; though it cannot be denied what I have done by land.

Men. Nor what I have done by water.

Eno. Yes, something you can deny for your own safety: you have been a great thief by sea.

Men. And you by land.

Eno. There I deny my land service. But give me your hand, Menas: if our eyes had authority, here they might take two thieves kissing.

Men. All men's faces are true, whatsome'er their hands are.

Eno. But there is never a fair woman has a true face.

Men. No slander; they steal hearts.

Eno. We came hither to fight with you.

Men. For my part, I am sorry it is turn'd to a drinking. Pompey doth this day laugh away his fortune.

Eno. If he do, sure, he cannot weep 't back again.

Men. You 've said, sir. We look'd not for Mark Antony here: pray you, is he married to Cleopatra?

Eno. Cæsar's sister is called Octavia.

Men. True, sir; she was the wife of Caius Marcellus.

Eno. But she is now the wife of Marcus Antonius.

Men. Pray ye, sir?

Eno. 'T is true.

Men. Then is Cæsar and he for ever knit together.

Eno. If I were bound to divine of this unity, I would not prophesy so.

Men. I think the policy of that purpose made more in the marriage than the love of the parties.

Eno. I think so too. But you shall find the band that seems to tie their friendship together will be the very strangler of their amity: Octavia is of a holy, cold, and still conversation.

Men. Who would not have his wife so?

Eno. Not he that himself is not so; which is Mark Antony. He will to his Egyptian dish again: then shall the sighs of Octavia blow the fire up in Cæsar; and, as I said before, that which is the strength of their amity shall prove the immediate author of their variance. Antony will use his affection where it is; he married but his occasion here.

Men. And thus it may be. Come, sir, will you aboard? I have a health for you.

Eno. I shall take it, sir; we have us'd our throats in Egypt.

Men. Come, let 's away. *Exeunt.*

Scene VII. *On board Pompey's galley.*

Music plays. Enter two or three *Servants* with a banquet.

First Serv. Here they 'll be, man. Some o' their plants are ill-rooted already; the least wind i' the world will blow them down.

Sec. Serv. Lepidus is high-colour'd.

First Serv. They have made him drink alms-drink.

75. toward, i.e., in preparation. **100. take,** arrest.

131. conversation, deportment. **140. occasion,** need (of political alliances). **Scene vii: 2. plants,** soles of their feet. **6. alms-drink,** probably the leavings, usually reserved for alms-people.

Sec. Serv. As they pinch one another by the disposition, he cries out, "No more"; reconciles them to his entreaty, and himself to th' drink.

First Serv. But it raises the greater war between him and his discretion.

Sec. Serv. Why, this it is to have a name in great men's fellowship: I had as lief have a reed that will do me no service as a partisan I could not heave.

First Serv. To be called into a huge sphere, and not to be seen to move in 't, are the holes where eyes should be, which pitifully disaster the cheeks.

A sennet sounded. Enter *Cæsar, Antony, Lepidus, Pompey, Agrippa, Mæcenas, Enobarbus, Menas,* with other captains.

Ant. [*To Cæsar.*] Thus do they, sir: they take the flow o' th' Nile
By certain scales i' th' pyramid; they know,
By the height, the lowness, or the mean, if dearth
Or foison follow. The higher Nilus swells,
The more it promises; as it ebbs, the seedsman
Upon the slime and ooze scatters his grain,
And shortly comes to harvest.

Lep. You 've strange serpents there?

Ant. Ay, Lepidus.

Lep. Your serpent of Egypt is bred now of your mud by the operation of your sun: so is your crocodile.

Ant. They are so.

Pom. Sit,—and some wine! A health to Lepidus!

Lep. I am not so well as I should be, but I 'll ne'er out.

Eno. Not till you have slept; I fear me you 'll be in till then.

Lep. Nay, certainly, I have heard the Ptolemies' pyramises are very goodly things; without contradiction, I have heard that.

Men. [*Aside to Pompey.*] Pompey, a word.

Pom. [*Aside to Menas.*] Say in mine ear: what is 't?

Men. [*Aside to Pompey.*] Forsake thy seat, I do beseech thee, captain,
And hear me speak a word.

Pom. [*Aside to Menas.*] Forbear me till anon.—
This wine for Lepidus! [*Whispers in 's ear.*]

Lep. What manner o' thing is your crocodile?

Ant. It is shap'd, sir, like itself; and it is as broad as it hath breadth: it is just so high as it is, and moves with it own organs: it lives by that which nourisheth it; and the elements once out of it, it transmigrates.

Lep. What colour is it of?

Ant. Of it own colour too.

Lep. 'T is a strange serpent.

Ant. 'T is so. And the tears of it are wet.

Cæs. Will this description satisfy him?

Ant. With the health that Pompey gives him, else he is a very epicure.

Pom. [*Aside to Menas.*] Go hang, sir, hang! Tell me of that? Away!
Do as I bid you.—Where 's this cup I call'd for?

Men. [*Aside to Pompey.*] If for the sake of merit thou wilt hear me,
Rise from thy stool.

Pom. [*Aside to Menas.*] I think thou 'rt mad. The matter?

Rises, and walks aside.

Men. I have ever held my cap off to thy fortunes.

Pom. Thou hast serv'd me with much faith. What 's else to say?
Be jolly, lords.

Ant. These quick-sands, Lepidus,
Keep off them, for you sink.

Men. Wilt thou be lord of all the world?

Pom. What say'st thou?

Men. Wilt thou be lord of the whole world? That 's twice.

Pom. How should that be?

Men. But entertain it,
And, though thou think me poor, I am the man
Will give thee all the world.

Pom. Hast thou drunk well?

Men. No, Pompey, I have kept me from the cup.
Thou art, if thou dar'st be, the earthly Jove.
Whate'er the ocean pales, or sky inclips,
Is thine, if thou wilt ha 't.

Pom. Show me which way.

Men. These three world-sharers, these competitors,
Are in thy vessel: let me cut the cable;
And, when we are put off, fall to their throats:
All there is thine.

Pom. Ah, this thou shouldst have done,
And not have spoke on 't! In me 't is villainy;
In thee 't had been good service. Thou must know,
'T is not my profit that does lead mine honour;
Mine honour, it. Repent that e'er thy tongue
Hath so betray'd thine act. Being done unknown,
I should have found it afterwards well done;
But must condemn it now. Desist, and drink.

7-8. pinch . . . disposition, fall to quarreling. **15. partisan**, halberd. **18. disaster**, disfigure. **23. foison**, plenty. **40. pyramises**, pyramids.

50. elements, fundamental constituents. **63. held my cap off**, been a respectful servant. **74. pales**, surrounds as with palings.

Men. [*Aside.*] For this,
I 'll never follow thy pall'd fortunes more.
Who seeks, and will not take when once 't is offer'd,
Shall never find it more.
Pom. This health to Lepidus!
Ant. Bear him ashore. I 'll pledge it for him, Pompey.
Eno. Here 's to thee, Menas!
Men. Enobarbus, welcome!
Pom. Fill till the cup be hid.
Eno. There 's a strong fellow, Menas.
Pointing to the Attendant who carries off Lepidus.
Men. Why?
Eno. 'A bears the third part of the world, man; see'st not?
Men. The third part, then, is drunk: would it were all,
That it might go on wheels!
Eno. Drink thou; increase the reels.
Men. Come.
Pom. This is not yet an Alexandrian feast.
Ant. It ripens towards it. Strike the vessels, ho!
Here 's to Cæsar!
Cæs. I could well forbear 't.
It 's monstrous labour when I wash my brain
And it grows fouler.
Ant. Be a child o' th' time.
Cæs. Possess it, I 'll make answer.
But I had rather fast from all, four days,
Than drink so much in one.
Eno. [*To Antony.*] Ha, my brave emperor!
Shall we dance now the Egyptian Bacchanals,
And celebrate our drink?
Pom. Let 's ha 't, good soldier.
Ant. Come, let 's all take hands,
Till that the conquering wine hath steep'd our sense
In soft and delicate Lethe.
Eno. All take hands.
Make battery to our ears with the loud music;
The while I 'll place you; then the boy shall sing.
The holding every man shall bear as loud
As his strong sides can volley.
Music plays, Enobarbus places them hand in hand.

THE SONG

Come, thou monarch of the vine,
Plumpy Bacchus with pink eyne!
In thy vats our cares be drown'd,
With thy grapes our hairs be crown'd!
Cup us, till the world go round,
Cup us, till the world go round!

Cæs. What would you more? Pompey, good-night. Good brother,
Let me request you off; our graver business
Frowns at this levity. Gentle lords, let 's part;
You see we have burnt our cheeks. Strong Enobarb
Is weaker than the wine, and mine own tongue
Splits what it speaks; the wild disguise hath almost
Antick'd us all. What needs more words? Good-night.
Good Antony, your hand.
Pom. I 'll try you on the shore.
Ant. And shall, sir; give 's your hand.
Pom. O Antony,
You have my father's house,—But, what? we are friends.
Come, down into the boat.
Eno. Take heed you fall not.
Exeunt all but Enobarbus and Menas.
Menas, I 'll not on shore.
Men. No, to my cabin.
These drums! these trumpets, flutes! what!
Let Neptune hear we bid a loud farewell
To these great fellows. Sound and be hang'd, sound out!
Sound a flourish, with drums.
Eno. Ho! says 'a. There 's my cap.
Men. Ho! Noble captain, come. *Exeunt.*

ACT III. Scene I. *A plain in Syria.*

Enter *Ventidius* as it were in triumph, with *Silius,* and other Romans, Officers, and Soldiers; the dead body of Pacorus borne before him.

Ven. Now, darting Parthia, art thou struck; and now
Pleas'd Fortune does of Marcus Crassus' death

88. pall'd, languishing. **99. go on wheels,** proverbial expression—run smoothly. **100. reels,** drunken staggers or perhaps a contraction of "revels." **103. Strike the vessels,** broach the casks or strike your cups together (for the toast). **107. Possess it,** be master of it.

118. holding, burden, chorus. **121. pink,** blinking, half-closed. **131. disguise,** drunkenness. **132. Antick'd,** made buffons of. **Act III, Scene i: 1. darting,** skilled in throwing darts. **2. Crassus' death,** defeated and killed by the army of Orodes, King of Parthia, in 53 B.C.

Make me revenger. Bear the King's son's body
Before our army. Thy Pacorus, Orodes,
Pays this for Marcus Crassus.
  Sil. Noble Ventidius,
Whilst yet with Parthian blood thy sword is warm,
The fugitive Parthians follow. Spur through Media,
Mesopotamia, and the shelters whither
The routed fly; so thy grand captain Antony
Shall set thee on triumphant chariots and
Put garlands on thy head.
  Ven. O Silius, Silius,
I have done enough; a lower place, note well,
May make too great an act: for learn this, Silius;
Better to leave undone, than by our deed
Acquire too high a fame when him we serve 's away.
Cæsar and Antony have ever won
More in their officer than person. Sossius,
One of my place in Syria, his lieutenant,
For quick accumulation of renown,
Which he achiev'd by th' minute, lost his favour.
Who does i' the wars more than his captain can
Becomes his captain's captain; and ambition,
The soldier's virtue, rather makes choice of loss,
Than gain which darkens him.
I could do more to do Antonius good,
But 't would offend him; and in his offence
Should my performance perish.
  Sil. Thou hast, Ventidius, that
Without the which a soldier and his sword
Grants scarce distinction. Thou wilt write to Antony?
  Ven. I 'll humbly signify what in his name,
That magical word of war, we have effected;
How, with his banners and his well-paid ranks,
The ne'er-yet-beaten horse of Parthia
We have jaded out o' th' field.
  Sil. Where is he now?
  Ven. He purposeth to Athens; whither, with what haste
The weight we must convey with 's will permit,
We shall appear before him. On, there; pass along! *Exeunt.*

Scene II. *Rome. An antechamber in Cæsar's house.*

Enter *Agrippa* at one door, *Enobarbus* at another.

  Agr. What, are the brothers parted?
  Eno. They have dispatch'd with Pompey, he is gone;
The other three are sealing. Octavia weeps
To part from Rome; Cæsar is sad; and Lepidus,
Since Pompey's feast, as Menas says, is troubled
With the green sickness.
  Agr. 'T is a noble Lepidus.
  Eno. A very fine one: O, how he loves Cæsar!
  Agr. Nay, but how dearly he adores Mark Antony!
  Eno. Cæsar? Why, he 's the Jupiter of men.
  Agr. What 's Antony? The god of Jupiter.
  Eno. Spake you of Cæsar? How! the nonpareil!
  Agr. O Antony! O thou Arabian bird!
  Eno. Would you praise Cæsar, say "Cæsar"; go no further.
  Agr. Indeed, he plied them both with excellent praises.
  Eno. But he loves Cæsar best; yet he loves Antony.
Ho! hearts, tongues, figures, scribes, bards, poets, cannot
Think, speak, cast, write, sing, number, ho!
His love to Antony. But as for Cæsar,
Kneel down, kneel down, and wonder.
  Agr. Both he loves.
  Eno. They are his shards, and he their beetle. [*Trumpet within.*] So;
This is to horse. Adieu, noble Agrippa.
  Agr. Good fortune, worthy soldier; and farewell.

Enter *Cæsar, Antony, Lepidus,* and *Octavia.*

  Ant. No further, sir.
  Cæs. You take from me a great part of myself;
Use me well in 't. Sister, prove such a wife
As my thoughts make thee, and as my farthest band
Shall pass on thy approof. Most noble Antony,
Let not the piece of virtue which is set
Betwixt us as the cement of our love,
To keep it builded, be the ram to batter
The fortress of it; for better might we
Have lov'd without this mean, if on both parts
This be not cherish'd.
  Ant. Make me not offended
In your distrust.
  Cæs. I have said.
  Ant. You shall not find,
Though you be therein curious, the least cause

27. **that,** i.e., quality, perhaps "judgment." 29. **Grants scarce distinction,** are scarcely to be distinguished. 34. **jaded,** spurned.

3. **sealing,** i.e., their agreement. 6. **green sickness,** a kind of anæmia common among young girls. 12. **Arabian bird,** the phoenix, unique of its kind. 20. **shards,** wing cases of beetles. 26. **band,** bond, pledge. 27. **approof,** approval.

For what you seem to fear. So, the gods keep you,
And make the hearts of Romans serve your ends!
We will here part.
Cæs. Farewell, my dearest sister, fare thee well!
The elements be kind to thee, and make
Thy spirits all of comfort! Fare thee well!
Oct. My noble brother!
Ant. The April 's in her eyes; it is love's spring,
And these the showers to bring it on. Be cheerful.
Oct. Sir, look well to my husband's house; and—
Cæs. What,
Octavia?
Oct. I 'll tell you in your ear.
Ant. Her tongue will not obey her heart, nor can
Her heart inform her tongue,—the swan's down-feather,
That stands upon the swell at the full of tide,
And neither way inclines.
Eno. [*Aside to Agrippa.*] Will Cæsar weep?
Agr. [*Aside to Enobarbus.*] He has a cloud in 's face.
Eno. [*Aside to Agrippa.*] He were the worse for that, were he a horse;
So is he, being a man.
Agr. [*Aside to Enobarbus.*] Why, Enobarbus,
When Antony found Julius Cæsar dead,
He cried almost to roaring; and he wept
When at Philippi he found Brutus slain.
Eno. [*Aside to Agrippa.*] That year, indeed, he was troubled with a rheum;
What willingly he did confound he wail'd,
Believe 't, till I wept too.
Cæs. No, sweet Octavia,
You shall hear from me still; the time shall not
Out-go my thinking on you.
Ant. Come, sir, come;
I 'll wrestle with you in my strength of love.
Look, here I have you; thus I let you go,
And give you to the gods.
Cæs. Adieu; be happy!
Lep. Let all the number of the stars give light
To thy fair way!
Cæs. Farewell, farewell!
Kisses Octavia.
Ant. Farewell! *Trumpets sound. Exeunt.*

40. **elements,** i.e., air and water; a wish for a calm voyage. 51. **cloud in 's face,** a horse with no white mark in his forehead was said to have "a cloud in his face"; regarded as a blemish. 57. **rheum,** a cold causing watering of the eyes.

Scene III. *Alexandria. Cleopatra's palace.*

Enter *Cleopatra, Charmian, Iras,* and *Alexas.*

Cleo. Where is the fellow?
Alex. Half afeard to come.
Cleo. Go to, go to. Come hither, sir.

Enter the *Messenger* as before.

Alex. Good Majesty,
Herod of Jewry dare not look upon you
But when you are well pleas'd.
Cleo. That Herod's head
I 'll have; but how, when Antony is gone
Through whom I might command it? Come thou near.
Mess. Most gracious Majesty,—
Cleo. Didst thou behold Octavia?
Mess. Ay, dread queen.
Cleo. Where?
Mess. Madam, in Rome;
I look'd her in the face, and saw her led
Between her brother and Mark Antony.
Cleo. Is she as tall as me?
Mess. She is not, madam.
Cleo. Didst hear her speak? Is she shrill-tongu'd or low?
Mess. Madam, I heard her speak; she is low-voic'd.
Cleo. That 's not so good: he cannot like her long?
Char. Like her! O Isis! 't is impossible.
Cleo. I think so, Charmian. Dull of tongue, and dwarfish!
What majesty is in her gait? Remember,
If e'er thou look'st on majesty.
Mess. She creeps;
Her motion and her station are as one;
She shows a body rather than a life,
A statue than a breather.
Cleo. Is this certain?
Mess. Or I have no observance.
Char. Three in Egypt
Cannot make better note.
Cleo. He 's very knowing;
I do perceive 't. There 's nothing in her yet.
The fellow has good judgement.
Char. Excellent.
Cleo. Guess at her years, I prithee.
Mess. Madam,
She was a widow,—
Cleo. Widow! Charmian, hark.
Mess. And I do think she 's thirty.

3. **Herod,** appeared in the Miracle Plays as a ranting tyrant. It may be to such a character that Alexas alludes, but Cleopatra is thinking of the historical Herod of her day. 22. **station,** standing still.

Cleo. Bear'st thou her face in mind? Is 't long or round?
Mess. Round even to faultiness.
Cleo. For the most part, too, they are foolish that are so.
Her hair, what colour?
Mess. Brown, madam; and her forehead
As low as she would wish it.
Cleo. There 's gold for thee.
Thou must not take my former sharpness ill:
I will employ thee back again; I find thee
Most fit for business. Go make thee ready;
Our letters are prepar'd. *Exit Messenger.*
Char. A proper man.
Cleo. Indeed, he is so; I repent me much
That so I harried him. Why, methinks, by him,
This creature 's no such thing.
Char. Nothing, madam.
Cleo. The man hath seen some majesty, and should know.
Char. Hath he seen majesty? Isis else defend,
And serving you so long!
Cleo. I have one thing more to ask him yet, good Charmian:
But 't is no matter; thou shalt bring him to me
Where I will write. All may be well enough.
Char. I warrant you, madam. *Exeunt.*

Scene IV. *Athens. A room in Antony's house.*

Enter *Antony* and *Octavia.*

Ant. Nay, nay, Octavia, not only that,—
That were excusable, that, and thousands more
Of semblable import,—but he hath wag'd
New wars 'gainst Pompey; made his will, and read it
To public ear;
Spoke scantly of me; when perforce he could not
But pay me terms of honour, cold and sickly
He vented them; most narrow measure lent me:
When the best hint was given him, he not took 't,
Or did it from his teeth.
Oct. O my good lord,
Believe not all; or, if you must believe,
Stomach not all. A more unhappy lady,
If this division chance, ne'er stood between,
Praying for both parts.
The good gods will mock me presently,
When I shall pray, "O, bless my lord and husband!"
Undo that prayer, by crying out as loud,
"O, bless my brother!" Husband win, win brother,
Prays, and destroys the prayer; no midway
'Twixt these extremes at all.
Ant. Gentle Octavia,
Let your best love draw to that point which seeks
Best to preserve it: if I lose mine honour,
I lose myself; better I were not yours
Than yours so branchless. But, as you requested,
Yourself shall go between 's. The meantime, lady,
I 'll raise the preparation of a war
Shall stain your brother: make your soonest haste;
So your desires are yours.
Oct. Thanks to my lord.
The Jove of power make me most weak, most weak,
Your reconciler! Wars 'twixt you twain would be
As if the world should cleave, and that slain men
Should solder up the rift.
Ant. When it appears to you where this begins,
Turn your displeasure that way; for our faults
Can never be so equal, that your love
Can equally move with them. Provide your going;
Choose your own company, and command what cost
Your heart has mind to. *Exeunt.*

Scene V. *The same. Another room in Antony's house.*

Enter *Enobarbus* and *Eros* meeting.

Eno. How now, friend Eros!
Eros. There 's strange news come, sir.
Eno. What, man?
Eros. Cæsar and Lepidus have made wars upon Pompey.
Eno. This is old; what is the success?
Eros. Cæsar, having made use of him in the wars 'gainst Pompey, presently denied him rivality, would not let him partake in the glory of the action; and not resting here, accuses him of letters he had formerly wrote to Pompey; upon his own appeal, seizes him: so the poor third is up, till death enlarge his confine.
Eno. Then, world, thou hast a pair of chaps, no more;

Scene iv: 3. semblable, like. **6. scantly,** slightingly. **10. from his teeth,** hollowly, perfunctorily. **12. Stomach,** resent. **27. stain,** eclipse. **Scene v: 6. success,** outcome. **12. his,** Cæsar's. **13. is up,** "shut up" or "done for." **14. chaps,** jaws.

And throw between them all the food thou hast,
They 'll grind the one the other. Where 's Antony?
Eros. He 's walking in the garden—thus; and spurns
The rush that lies before him; cries, "Fool Lepidus!"
And threats the throat of that his officer
That murder'd Pompey.
Eno. Our great navy 's rigg'd.
Eros. For Italy and Cæsar. More, Domitius;
My lord desires you presently; my news
I might have told hereafter.
Eno. 'T will be nought;
But let it be. Bring me to Antony.
Eros. Come, sir. *Exeunt.*

Scene VI. *Rome. Cæsar's house.*

Enter *Cæsar, Agrippa,* and *Mæcenas.*

Cæs. Contemning Rome, he has done all this, and more,
In Alexandria: here 's the manner of 't:
I' th' market-place, on a tribunal silver'd,
Cleopatra and himself in chairs of gold
Were publicly enthron'd. At the feet sat
Cæsarion, whom they call my father's son,
And all the unlawful issue that their lust
Since then hath made between them. Unto her
He gave the stablishment of Egypt; made her
Of lower Syria, Cyprus, Lydia,
Absolute queen.
Mæc. This in the public eye?
Cæs. I' th' common show-place, where they exercise.
His sons he there proclaimed the kings of kings:
Great Media, Parthia, and Armenia,
He gave to Alexander; to Ptolemy he assign'd
Syria, Cilicia, and Phœnicia. She
In th' habiliments of the goddess Isis
That day appear'd; and oft before gave audience,
As 't is reported, so.
Mæc. Let Rome be thus
Inform'd.
Agr. Who, queasy with his insolence
Already, will their good thoughts call from him.

19. officer, After his defeat at the hands of Cæsar, Pompey turned against Antony and is supposed to have been murdered by his order. **Scene vi: 3. tribunal,** platform. **6. my father's,** Octavius was the grandnephew and adopted son of Julius Cæsar. **20. queasy,** nauseated.

Cæs. The people knows it; and have now receiv'd
His accusations.
Agr. Who does he accuse?
Cæs. Cæsar; and that, having in Sicily
Sextus Pompeius spoil'd, we had not rated him
His part o' th' isle. Then does he say, he lent me
Some shipping unrestor'd. Lastly, he frets
That Lepidus of the triumvirate
Should be depos'd; and, being, that we detain
All his revenue.
Agr. Sir, this should be answer'd.
Cæs. 'T is done already, and the messenger gone.
I have told him Lepidus was grown too cruel;
That he his high authority abus'd,
And did deserve his change. For what I have conquer'd,
I grant him part; but then, in his Armenia
And other of his conquer'd kingdoms, I
Demand the like.
Mæc. He 'll never yield to that.
Cæs. Nor must not then be yielded to in this.

Enter *Octavia* with her train.

Oct. Hail, Cæsar, and my lord! Hail, most dear Cæsar!
Cæs. That ever I should call thee castaway!
Oct. You have not call'd me so, nor have you cause.
Cæs. Why have you stolen upon us thus? You come not
Like Cæsar's sister. The wife of Antony
Should have an army for an usher, and
The neighs of horse to tell of her approach
Long ere she did appear; the trees by the way
Should have borne men, and expectation fainted,
Longing for what it had not; nay, the dust
Should have ascended to the roof of heaven,
Rais'd by your populous troops. But you are come
A market-maid to Rome, and have prevented
The ostentation of our love, which, left unshown,
Is often left unlov'd. We should have met you
By sea and land; supplying every stage
With an augmented greeting.
Oct. Good my lord,
To come thus was I not constrain'd, but did
On my free will. My lord, Mark Antony,
Hearing that you prepar'd for war, acquainted
My grieved ear withal; whereon, I begg'd
His pardon for return.

25. spoil'd, plundered. **rated,** assigned. **52. ostentation,** display.

Cæs. Which soon he granted,
Being an obstruct 'tween his lust and him.
Oct. Do not say so, my lord.
Cæs. I have eyes upon him,
And his affairs come to me on the wind.
Where is he now?
Oct. My lord, in Athens.
Cæs. No, my most wronged sister; Cleopatra
Hath nodded him to her. He hath given his empire
Up to a whore; who now are levying
The kings o' th' earth for war. He hath assembled
Bocchus, the King of Libya; Archelaus,
Of Cappadocia; Philadelphos, King
Of Paphlagonia; the Thracian king, Adallas;
King Malchus of Arabia; King of Pont;
Herod of Jewry; Mithridates, King
Of Comagene; Polemon and Amyntas,
The Kings of Mede and Lycaonia,
With a more larger list of sceptres.
Oct. Ay me, most wretched,
That have my heart parted betwixt two friends
That does afflict each other!
Cæs. Welcome hither!
Your letters did withhold our breaking forth,
Till we perceiv'd both how you were wrong led
And we in negligent danger. Cheer your heart.
Be you not troubled with the time, which drives
O'er your content these strong necessities;
But let determin'd things to destiny
Hold unbewail'd their way. Welcome to Rome;
Nothing more dear to me. You are abus'd
Beyond the mark of thought; and the high gods,
To do you justice, makes his ministers
Of us and those that love you. Best of comfort,
And ever welcome to us.
Agr. Welcome, lady.
Mæc. Welcome, dear madam.
Each heart in Rome does love and pity you;
Only th' adulterous Antony, most large
In his abominations, turns you off,
And gives his potent regiment to a trull,
That noises it against us.
Oct. Is it so, sir?
Cæs. Most certain. Sister, welcome. Pray you,
Be ever known to patience. My dear'st sister! *Exeunt.*

61. obstruct, obstruction. **81. negligent danger,** danger through negligence. **82. time,** present state of affairs. **88. his,** referring to "justice." **95. potent regiment,** powerful government. **96. noises,** causes a disturbance.

Scene VII. *Near Actium. Antony's camp.*

Enter *Cleopatra* and *Enobarbus.*

Cleo. I will be even with thee, doubt it not.
Eno. But why, why, why?
Cleo. Thou hast forspoke my being in these wars,
And say'st it is not fit.
Eno. Well, is it, is it?
Cleo. If not denounc'd against us, why should not we
Be there in person?
Eno. Well, I could reply:
If we should serve with horse and mares together,
The horse were merely lost; the mares would bear
A soldier and his horse.
Cleo. What is 't you say?
Eno. Your presence needs must puzzle Antony;
Take from his heart, take from his brain, from 's time,
What should not then be spar'd. He is already
Traduc'd for levity; and 't is said in Rome
That Photinus an eunuch and your maids
Manage this war.
Cleo. Sink Rome, and their tongues rot
That speak against us! A charge we bear i' th' war,
And, as the president of my kingdom, will
Appear there for a man. Speak not against it;
I will not stay behind.

Enter *Antony* and *Canidius.*

Eno. Nay, I have done.
Here comes the Emperor.
Ant. Is it not strange, Canidius,
That from Tarentum and Brundusium
He could so quickly cut the Ionian Sea,
And take in Toryne? You have heard on 't, sweet?
Cleo. Celerity is never more admir'd
Than by the negligent.
Ant. A good rebuke,
Which might have well becom'd the best of men,
To taunt at slackness. Canidius, we
Will fight with him by sea.
Cleo. By sea! what else?
Can. Why will my lord do so?
Ant. For that he dares us to 't.
Eno. So hath my lord dar'd him to single fight.

3. forspoke, spoken against. **5. denounc'd,** declared. **11. puzzle,** embarrass. **17. charge,** expense. **24. take in,** occupy.

Can. Ay, and to wage this battle at Pharsalia,
Where Cæsar fought with Pompey; but these offers,
Which serve not for his vantage, he shakes off;
And so should you.
Eno. Your ships are not well mann'd;
Your mariners are muleters, reapers, people
Ingross'd by swift impress. In Cæsar's fleet
Are those that often have 'gainst Pompey fought.
Their ships are yare; yours, heavy: no disgrace
Shall fall you for refusing him at sea,
Being prepar'd for land.
Ant. By sea, by sea.
Eno. Most worthy sir, you therein throw away
The absolute soldiership you have by land;
Distract your army, which doth most consist
Of war-mark'd footmen; leave unexecuted
Your own renowned knowledge; quite forego
The way which promises assurance; and
Give up yourself merely to chance and hazard,
From firm security.
Ant. I 'll fight at sea.
Cleo. I have sixty sails, Cæsar none better.
Ant. Our overplus of shipping will we burn;
And, with the rest full-mann'd, from th' head of Actium
Beat the approaching Cæsar. But if we fail,
We then can do 't at land.

Enter a *Messenger.*

Thy business?
Mess. The news is true, my lord; he is descried;
Cæsar has taken Toryne.
Ant. Can he be there in person? 'T is impossible;
Strange that his power should be. Canidius,
Our nineteen legions thou shalt hold by land,
And our twelve thousand horse. We 'll to our ship;
Away, my Thetis!

Enter a *Soldier.*

How now, worthy soldier!
Sold. O noble emperor, do not fight by sea;
Trust not to rotten planks! Do you misdoubt
This sword and these my wounds? Let th' Egyptians
And the Phœnicians go a-ducking; we
Have us'd to conquer, standing on the earth,
And fighting foot to foot.
Ant. Well, well: away!
Exeunt Antony, Cleopatra, and Enobarbus.
Sold. By Hercules, I think I am i' th' right.
Can. Soldier, thou art; but his whole action grows
Not in the power on 't: so our leader 's led,
And we are women's men.
Sold. You keep by land
The legions and the horse whole, do you not?
Can. Marcus Octavius, Marcus Justeius,
Publicola, and Cælius, are for sea;
But we keep whole by land. This speed of Cæsar's
Carries beyond belief.
Sold. While he was yet in Rome,
His power went out in such distractions as
Beguil'd all spies.
Can. Who 's his lieutenant, hear you?
Sold. They say, one Taurus.
Can. Well I know the man.

Enter a *Messenger.*

Mess. The Emperor calls Canidius.
Can. With news the time 's with labour, and throes forth,
Each minute, some. *Exeunt.*

Scene VIII. *A plain near Actium.*

Enter *Cæsar* and *Taurus,* with his army, marching.

Cæs. Taurus!
Taur. My lord?
Cæs. Strike not by land; keep whole; provoke not battle
Till we have done at sea. Do not exceed
The prescript of this scroll: our fortune lies
Upon this jump. *Exeunt.*

Scene IX. *Another part of the plain.*

Enter *Antony* and *Enobarbus.*

Ant. Set we our squadrons on yond side o' th' hill,
In eye of Cæsar's battle; from which place
We may the number of the ships behold,
And so proceed accordingly. *Exeunt.*

37. Ingross'd, enrolled. **impress,** conscription. **39. yare,** easy to manage. **43. absolute,** perfect. **48. merely,** utterly. **61. Thetis,** a sea goddess.

69-70. but . . . on 't, but this conduct (action) is not the expression of his own will-power. **77. distractions,** small detachments. **81. throes forth,** gives painful birth to. **Scene viii: 5. prescript,** instructions. **6. jump,** risk. **Scene ix: 2. battle,** army.

Scene X. *Another part of the plain.*

Canidius marcheth with his land army one way over the stage; and Taurus, the lieutenant of Cæsar, the other way. After their going in, is heard the noise of a sea-fight.

Alarum. Enter *Enobarbus.*

Eno. Nought, nought, all nought! I can behold no longer:
Th' Antoniad, the Egyptian admiral,
With all their sixty, fly and turn the rudder.
To see 't mine eyes are blasted.

Enter *Scarus.*

Scar. Gods and goddesses,
All the whole synod of them!
Eno. What 's thy passion?
Scar. The greater cantle of the world is lost
With very ignorance; we have kiss'd away
Kingdoms and provinces.
Eno. How appears the fight?
Scar. On our side like the token'd pestilence,
Where death is sure. Yon ribaudred nag of Egypt,—
Whom leprosy o'ertake!—i' th' midst o' the fight,
When vantage like a pair of twins appear'd,
Both as the same, or rather ours the elder,
The breese upon her, like a cow in June,
Hoists sails and flies.
Eno. That I beheld.
Mine eyes did sicken at the sight, and could not
Endure a further view.
Scar. She once being loof'd,
The noble ruin of her magic, Antony,
Claps on his sea-wing, and, like a doting mallard,
Leaving the fight in height, flies after her:
I never saw an action of such shame;
Experience, manhood, honour, ne'er before
Did violate so itself.
Eno. Alack, alack!

Enter *Canidius.*

Can. Our fortune on the sea is out of breath,
And sinks most lamentably. Had our general
Been what he knew himself, it had gone well.
O, he has given example for our flight,
Most grossly, by his own!
Eno. Ay, are you thereabouts?
Why, then, good-night indeed.
Can. Toward Peloponnesus are they fled.
Scar. 'T is easy to 't; and there I will attend
What further comes.
Can. To Cæsar will I render
My legions and my horse: six kings already
Show me the way of yielding.
Eno. I 'll yet follow
The wounded chance of Antony, though my reason
Sits in the wind against me. *Exeunt.*

Scene XI. *Alexandria. Cleopatra's palace.*

Enter *Antony* with *Attendants.*

Ant. Hark! the land bids me tread no more upon 't;
It is asham'd to bear me! Friends, come hither.
I am so lated in the world, that I
Have lost my way for ever. I have a ship
Laden with gold; take that, divide it; fly,
And make your peace with Cæsar.
All. Fly! not we.
Ant. I have fled myself; and have instructed cowards
To run and show their shoulders. Friends, be gone;
I have myself resolv'd upon a course
Which has no need of you; be gone.
My treasure 's in the harbour, take it. O,
I follow'd that I blush to look upon.
My very hairs do mutiny; for the white
Reprove the brown for rashness, and they them
For fear and doting. Friends, be gone; you shall
Have letters from me to some friends that will
Sweep your way for you. Pray you, look not sad,
Nor make replies of loathness: take the hint
Which my despair proclaims; let them be left
Which leaves itself. To the sea-side straightway;
I will possess you of that ship and treasure.
Leave me, I pray, a little; pray you now.
Nay, do so; for, indeed, I have lost command,
Therefore I pray you. I 'll see you by and by.
Sits down.

Enter *Cleopatra,* led by *Charmian* and *Iras; Eros* following.

Eros. Nay, gentle madam, to him, comfort him.
Iras. Do, most dear queen.

2. Antoniad, Antony's flag-ship. **6. cantle,** a segment of a circle. **9. token'd,** spotted. **10. ribaudred,** lewd. **14. breese,** gadfly. **18. loof'd,** luffed. **29. are you thereabouts,** are you thinking of flight?

37. Sits in the wind against, is in opposition to. Scene xi: **3. lated,** benighted. **18. loathness,** unwillingness. **23. command,** power to command.

Char. Do! Why, what else?
Cleo. Let me sit down. O Juno!
Ant. No, no, no, no, no.
Eros. See you here, sir?
Ant. O fie, fie, fie!
Char. Madam!
Iras. Madam, O good empress!
Eros. Sir, sir,—
Ant. Yes, my lord, yes; he at Philippi kept
His sword e'en like a dancer, while I struck
The lean and wrinkled Cassius; and 't was I
That the mad Brutus ended: he alone
Dealt on lieutenantry, and no practice had
In the brave squares of war; yet now—No matter.
Cleo. Ah, stand by.
Eros. The Queen, my lord, the Queen.
Iras. Go to him, madam, speak to him;
He 's unqualitied with very shame.
Cleo. Well then, sustain me. Oh!
Eros. Most noble sir, arise; the Queen approaches.
Her head 's declin'd, and death will seize her, but
Your comfort makes the rescue.
Ant. I have offended reputation,
A most unnoble swerving.
Eros. Sir, the Queen.
Ant. O, whither hast thou led me, Egypt? See,
How I convey my shame out of thine eyes
By looking back what I have left behind
'Stroy'd in dishonour.
Cleo. O my lord, my lord,
Forgive my fearful sails! I little thought
You would have followed.
Ant. Egypt, thou knew'st too well
My heart was to thy rudder tied by th' strings,
And thou shouldst tow me after. O'er my spirit
Thy full supremacy thou knew'st, and that
Thy beck might from the bidding of the gods
Command me.
Cleo. O, my pardon!
Ant. Now I must
To the young man send humble treaties, dodge
And palter in the shifts of lowness; who
With half the bulk o' th' world play'd as I pleas'd,
Making and marring fortunes. You did know
How much you were my conqueror; and that
My sword, made weak by my affection, would
Obey it on all cause.
Cleo. Pardon, pardon!
Ant. Fall not a tear, I say; one of them rates
All that is won and lost: give me a kiss.
Even this repays me. We sent our schoolmaster;
Is 'a come back? Love, I am full of lead.
Some wine, within there, and our viands! Fortune knows
We scorn her most when most she offers blows. *Exeunt.*

Scene XII. *Egypt. Cæsar's camp.*

Enter *Cæsar, Agrippa, Dolabella, Thyreus,* with others.

Cæs. Let him appear that 's come from Antony.
Know you him?
Dol. Cæsar, 't is his schoolmaster;
An argument that he is pluck'd, when hither
He sends so poor a pinion of his wing,
Which had superfluous kings for messengers
Not many moons gone by.

Enter *Ambassador* from Antony.

Cæs. Approach, and speak.
Amb. Such as I am, I come from Antony.
I was of late as petty to his ends
As is the morn-dew on the myrtle-leaf
To his grand sea.
Cæs. Be 't so: declare thine office.
Amb. Lord of his fortunes he salutes thee, and
Requires to live in Egypt; which not granted,
He lessens his requests, and to thee sues
To let him breathe between the heavens and earth,
A private man in Athens: this for him.
Next, Cleopatra does confess thy greatness;
Submits her to thy might; and of thee craves
The circle of the Ptolemies for her heirs,
Now hazarded to thy grace.
Cæs. For Antony,
I have no ears to his request. The Queen
Of audience nor desire shall fail, so she
From Egypt drive her all-disgraced friend,
Or take his life there. This if she perform,
She shall not sue unheard. So to them both.
Amb. Fortune pursue thee!
Cæs. Bring him through the bands. *Exit Ambassador.*
[*To Thyreus.*] To try thy eloquence, now 't is time; dispatch;
From Antony win Cleopatra; promise,
And in our name, what she requires; add more,
From thine invention, offers. Women are not

35-6. kept His sword like a dancer, i.e., sheathed. **39. on lieutenantry,** through lieutenants. **40. squares,** squadrons. **44. unqualitied,** unmanned. **63. palter,** equivocate. **shifts of lowness,** mean stratagems.

72. full of lead, heavy, dull. **Scene xii: 12. Requires,** requests. **18. circle,** crown. **19. hazarded,** staked and lost.

In their best fortunes strong; but want will perjure
The ne'er-touched vestal. Try thy cunning, Thyreus;
Make thine own edict for thy pains, which we
Will answer as a law.
Thyr. Cæsar, I go.
Cæs. Observe how Antony becomes his flaw,
And what thou think'st his very action speaks
In every power that moves.
Thyr. Cæsar, I shall.
Exeunt.

Scene XIII. *Alexandria. Cleopatra's palace.*

Enter *Cleopatra, Enobarbus, Charmian,* and *Iras.*

Cleo. What shall we do, Enobarbus?
Eno. Think, and die.
Cleo. Is Antony or we in fault for this?
Eno. Antony only, that would make his will
Lord of his reason. What though you fled
From that great face of war, whose several ranges
Frighted each other? Why should he follow?
The itch of his affection should not then
Have nick'd his captainship, at such a point,
When half to half the world oppos'd, he being
The mered question. 'T was a shame no less
Than was his loss, to course your flying flags,
And leave his navy gazing.
Cleo. Prithee, peace.

Enter *Antony* with the *Ambassador.*

Ant. Is that his answer?
Amb. Ay, my lord.
Ant. The Queen shall then have courtesy, so she
Will yield us up.
Amb. He says so.
Ant. Let her know 't.
To the boy Cæsar send this grizzled head,
And he will fill thy wishes to the brim
With principalities.
Cleo. That head, my lord?
Ant. To him again. Tell him he wears the rose
Of youth upon him, from which the world should note
Something particular. His coin, ships, legions,
May be a coward's; whose ministers would prevail
Under the service of a child as soon
As i' th' command of Cæsar. I dare him therefore
To lay his gay comparisons apart,
And answer me declin'd, sword against sword,
Ourselves alone. I 'll write it. Follow me.
Exeunt Antony and Ambassador.
Eno. [*Aside.*] Yes, like enough high-battl'd Cæsar will
Unstate his happiness, and be stag'd to th' show,
Against a sworder! I see men's judgements are
A parcel of their fortunes; and things outward
Do draw the inward quality after them,
To suffer all alike. That he should dream,
Knowing all measures, the full Cæsar will
Answer his emptiness! Cæsar, thou hast subdu'd
His judgement too.

Enter a *Servant.*

Serv. A messenger from Cæsar.
Cleo. What, no more ceremony? See, my women!
Against the blown rose may they stop their nose
That kneel'd unto the buds. Admit him, sir.
Exit Servant.
Eno. [*Aside.*] Mine honesty and I begin to square.
The loyalty well held to fools does make
Our faith mere folly; yet he that can endure
To follow with allegiance a fallen lord
Does conquer him that did his master conquer,
And earns a place i' th' story.

Enter *Thyreus.*

Cleo. Cæsar's will?
Thyr. Hear it apart.
Cleo. None but friends: say boldly.
Thyr. So, haply, are they friends to Antony.
Eno. He needs as many, sir, as Cæsar has;
Or needs not us. If Cæsar please, our master
Will leap to be his friend; for us, you know
Whose he is we are, and that is, Cæsar's.
Thyr. So.
Thus then, thou most renown'd: Cæsar entreats
Not to consider in what case thou stand'st
Further than he is Cæsar.

32. **Make . . . pains,** decree the reward for your efforts. 35-6. **very action . . . moves,** his character speaks in every one of his movements. **Scene xiii:** 3. **will,** physical desire. 8. **nick'd,** clipped and so spoiled. 10. **mered question,** sole matter of dispute. 11. **course,** chase. 22. **particular,** of personal merit.

27. **declin'd,** i.e., in both fortunes and years. 30. **Unstate,** deprive of dignity. **stag'd,** exhibited publicly. 35. **Knowing all measures,** having experienced all kinds of fortunes. 41. **square,** quarrel. 55. **Further . . . Cæsar,** i.e., not an emperor but a man of generous impulses.

Cleo. Go on: right royal.
Thyr. He knows that you embrace not Antony
As you did love, but as you feared him.
Cleo. Oh!
Thyr. The scars upon your honour, therefore, he
Does pity, as constrained blemishes,
Not as deserved.
Cleo. He is a god, and knows
What is most right. Mine honour was not yielded,
But conquer'd merely.
Eno. [*Aside.*] To be sure of that,
I will ask Antony. Sir, sir, thou art so leaky,
That we must leave thee to thy sinking, for
Thy dearest quit thee. *Exit Enobarbus.*
Thyr. Shall I say to Cæsar
What you require of him? for he partly begs
To be desir'd to give. It much would please him,
That of his fortunes you should make a staff
To lean upon; but it would warm his spirits,
To hear from me you had left Antony,
And put yourself under his shroud,
The universal landlord.
Cleo. What 's your name?
Thyr. My name is Thyreus.
Cleo. Most kind messenger,
Say to great Cæsar this: in deputation
I kiss his conqu'ring hand. Tell him, I am prompt
To lay my crown at 's feet, and there to kneel.
Tell him, from his all-obeying breath I hear
The doom of Egypt.
Thyr. 'T is your noblest course.
Wisdom and fortune combating together,
If that the former dare but what it can,
No chance may shake it. Give me grace to lay
My duty on your hand.
Cleo. Your Cæsar's father oft,
When he hath mus'd of taking kingdoms in,
Bestow'd his lips on that unworthy place,
As it rain'd kisses.

Re-enter *Antony* and *Enobarbus.*

Ant. Favours, by Jove that thunders!
What art thou, fellow?
Thyr. One that but performs
The bidding of the fullest man, and worthiest
To have command obey'd.
Eno. [*Aside.*] You will be whipp'd.
Ant. Approach there! Ah, you kite! Now, gods and devils!
Authority melts from me: of late, when I cried "Ho!"
Like boys unto a muss, kings would start forth,
And cry, "Your will?" Have you no ears? I am
Antony yet.

Enter *Servants.*

Take hence this Jack, and whip him.
Eno. [*Aside.*] 'T is better playing with a lion's whelp
Than with an old one dying.
Ant. Moon and stars!
Whip him! Were 't twenty of the greatest tributaries
That do acknowledge Cæsar, should I find them
So saucy with the hand of she here,—what 's her name,
Since she was Cleopatra? Whip him, fellows,
Till, like a boy, you see him cringe his face,
And whine aloud for mercy. Take him hence.
Thyr. Mark Antony,—
Ant. Tug him away. Being whipp'd,
Bring him again; this Jack of Cæsar's shall
Bear us an errand to him.—
Exeunt Servants with Thyreus.
You were half blasted ere I knew you; ha!
Have I my pillow left unpress'd in Rome,
Forborne the getting of a lawful race,
And by a gem of women, to be abus'd
By one that looks on feeders?
Cleo. Good my lord,—
Ant. You have been a boggler ever:
And when we in our viciousness grow hard—
O misery on 't!—the wise gods seel our eyes;
In our own filth drop our clear judgements; make us
Adore our errors; laugh at 's, while we strut
To our confusion.
Cleo. O, is 't come to this?
Ant. I found you as a morsel cold upon
Dead Cæsar's trencher; nay, you were a fragment
Of Cneius Pompey's; besides what hotter hours,
Unregister'd in vulgar fame, you have
Luxuriously pick'd out; for, I am sure,
Though you can guess what temperance should be,
You know not what it is.
Cleo. Wherefore is this?
Ant. To let a fellow that will take rewards
And say, "God quit you!" be familiar with
My playfellow, your hand; this kingly seal
And plighter of high hearts! O, that I were
Upon the hill of Basan, to outroar
The horned herd! for I have savage cause;
And to proclaim it civilly, were like

71. shroud, shelter. **74. deputation,** by proxy. **77. all-obeying,** obeyed by all. **81. grace,** the favor. **91. muss,** scramble.

93. Jack, rogue, term of contempt. **100. cringe,** distort. **109. feeders,** menials. **110. boggler,** shifty one. **112. seel,** sew up (as was done to hawks). **124. quit,** repay.

A halter'd neck which does the hangman thank
For being yare about him.

Re-enter *Servants* with *Thyreus.*

Is he whipp'd?
Serv. Soundly, my lord.
Ant. Cried he? and begg'd a pardon?
Serv. He did ask favour.
Ant. If that thy father live, let him repent
Thou wast not made his daughter; and be thou sorry
To follow Cæsar in his triumph, since
Thou hast been whipp'd for following him. Henceforth
The white hand of a lady fever thee,
Shake thou to look on 't. Get thee back to Cæsar,
Tell him thy entertainment. Look thou say
He makes me angry with him; for he seems
Proud and disdainful, harping on what I am,
Not what he knew I was. He makes me angry;
And at this time most easy 't is to do 't,
When my good stars, that were my former guides,
Have empty left their orbs, and shot their fires
Into th' abysm of hell. If he mislike
My speech and what is done, tell him he has
Hipparchus, my enfranched bondman, whom
He may at pleasure whip, or hang, or torture,
As he shall like, to quit me. Urge it thou:
Hence with thy stripes, begone!

Exit Thyreus.

Cleo. Have you done yet?
Ant. Alack, our terrene moon
Is now eclips'd; and it portends alone
The fall of Antony!
Cleo. I must stay his time.
Ant. To flatter Cæsar, would you mingle eyes
With one that ties his points?
Cleo. Not know me yet?
Ant. Cold-hearted toward me?
Cleo. Ah, dear, if I be so,
From my cold heart let heaven engender hail
And poison it in the source, and the first stone
Drop in my neck; as it determines, so
Dissolve my life! The next Cæsarion smite!
Till by degrees the memory of my womb,
Together with my brave Egyptians all,
By the discandying of this pelleted storm,
Lie graveless, till the flies and gnats of Nile
Have buried them for prey!
Ant. I am satisfied.
Cæsar sits down in Alexandria; where
I will oppose his fate. Our force by land
Hath nobly held; our sever'd navy too
Have knit again, and fleet, threat'ning most sea-like.
Where hast thou been, my heart? Dost thou hear, lady?
If from the field I shall return once more
To kiss these lips, I will appear in blood;
I and my sword will earn our chronicle.
There 's hope in 't yet.
Cleo. That 's my brave lord!
Ant. I will be treble-sinewed, hearted, breath'd,
And fight maliciously; for when mine hours
Were nice and lucky, men did ransom lives
Of me for jests; but now I 'll set my teeth,
And send to darkness all that stop me. Come,
Let 's have one other gaudy night. Call to me
All my sad captains; fill our bowls once more;
Let 's mock the midnight bell.
Cleo. It is my birthday.
I had thought t' have held it poor; but, since my lord
Is Antony again, I will be Cleopatra.
Ant. We will yet do well.
Cleo. Call all his noble captains to my lord.
Ant. Do so, we 'll speak to them; and to-night I 'll force
The wine peep through their scars. Come on, my queen;
There 's sap in 't yet. The next time I do fight,
I 'll make Death love me; for I will contend
Even with his pestilent scythe.

Exeunt all but Enobarbus.

Eno. Now he 'll outstare the lightning. To be furious,
Is to be frighted out of fear; and in that mood
The dove will peck the estridge; and I see still,
A diminution in our captain's brain
Restores his heart: when valour preys on reason,
It eats the sword it fights with. I will seek
Some way to leave him. *Exit.*

146. orbs, spheres in which stars move. **149. enfranched,** freed. Hipparchus had already deserted Antony. **153. terrene,** earthly. **157. points,** laces of his clothes. **161. determines,** ends (by dissolving). **162. Cæsarion,** her son by Julius Cæsar. **163. memory,** memorials, i.e., her children.

165. discandying, thawing. **171. fleet,** is afloat. **178. breath'd,** to be construed with **treble. 183. gaudy,** festive. **193. contend,** compete. **194. pestilent,** i.e., in time of pestilence. **195. furious,** madly brave. **197. estridge,** falcon.

Act IV. Scene I. *Before Alexandria. Cæsar's camp.*

Enter *Cæsar, Agrippa,* and *Mæcenas,* with his Army; Cæsar reading a letter.

Cæs. He calls me boy; and chides as he had power
To beat me out of Egypt. My messenger
He hath whipp'd with rods; dares me to personal combat,
Cæsar to Antony. Let the old ruffian know
I have many other ways to die; meantime
Laugh at his challenge.
Mæc. Cæsar must think,
When one so great begins to rage, he 's hunted
Even to falling. Give him no breath, but now
Make boot of his distraction: never anger
Made good guard for itself.
Cæs. Let our best heads
Know that to-morrow the last of many battles
We mean to fight. Within our files there are,
Of those that serv'd Mark Antony but late,
Enough to fetch him in. See it done,
And feast the army; we have store to do 't.
And they have earn'd the waste. Poor Antony! *Exeunt.*

Scene II. *Alexandria. Cleopatra's palace.*

Enter *Antony, Cleopatra, Enobarbus, Charmian, Iras, Alexas,* with others.

Ant. He will not fight with me, Domitius.
Eno. No?
Ant. Why should he not?
Eno. He thinks, being twenty times of better fortune,
He is twenty men to one.
Ant. To-morrow, soldier,
By sea and land I 'll fight; or I will live,
Or bathe my dying honour in the blood
Shall make it live again. Woo 't thou fight well?
Eno. I 'll strike, and cry, "Take all!"
Ant. Well said; come on.
Call forth my household servants; let 's to-night
Be bounteous at our meal.

Enter three or four *Servitors.*

Give me thy hand,
Thou hast been rightly honest;—so hast thou;—
Thou,—and thou,—and thou. You have serv'd me well,
And kings have been your fellows.
Cleo. [*Aside to Enobarbus.*] What means this?
Eno. [*Aside to Cleopatra.*] 'T is one of those odd tricks which sorrow shoots
Out of the mind.
Ant. And thou art honest too.
I wish I could be made so many men,
And all of you clapp'd up together in
An Antony, that I might do you service
So good as you have done.
All. The gods forbid!
Ant. Well, my good fellows, wait on me to-night
Scant not my cups; and make as much of me
As when mine empire was your fellow too,
And suffer'd my command.
Cleo. [*Aside to Enobarbus.*] What does he mean?
Eno. [*Aside to Cleopatra.*] To make his followers weep.
Ant. Tend me to-night;
May be it is the period of your duty:
Haply you shall not see me more; or if,
A mangled shadow. Perchance to-morrow
You 'll serve another master. I look on you
As one that takes his leave. Mine honest friends,
I turn you not away; but, like a master
Married to your good service, stay till death.
Tend me to-night two hours, I ask no more,
And the gods yield you for 't!
Eno. What mean you, sir,
To give them this discomfort? Look, they weep;
And I, an ass, am onion-ey'd: for shame,
Transform us not to women.
Ant. Ho, ho, ho!
Now the witch take me, if I meant it thus!
Grace grow where those drops fall! My hearty friends,
You take me in too dolorous a sense;
For I spake to you for your comfort, did desire you
To burn this night with torches. Know, my hearts,
I hope well of to-morrow; and will lead you
Where rather I 'll expect victorious life
Than death and honour. Let 's to supper, come,
And drown consideration. *Exeunt.*

Act IV, Scene i: 9. Make boot, take advantage. **16. waste,** cost. **Scene ii: 7. Woo 't,** would'st thou. **8. "Take all,"** I will expect or give no quarter.

33. yield, reward.

Scene III. *Before the palace.*

Enter a company of *Soldiers.*

First Sold. Brother, good-night; to-morrow is the day.
Sec. Sold. It will determine one way; fare you well.
Heard you of nothing strange about the streets?
First Sold. Nothing. What news?
Sec. Sold. Belike 't is but a rumour. Good-night to you.
First Sold. Well, sir, good-night.

They meet other *Soldiers.*

Sec. Sold. Soldiers, have careful watch.
Third Sold. And you. Good-night, good-night.
They place themselves in every corner of the stage.
Fourth Sold. Here we. And if to-morrow
Our navy thrive, I have an absolute hope
Our landmen will stand up.
Third Sold. 'T is a brave army,
And full of purpose.
Music of the hautboys under the stage.
Sec. Sold. Peace! what noise?
First Sold. List, list!
Sec. Sold. Hark!
First Sold. Music i' th' air.
Third Sold. Under the earth.
Fourth Sold. It signs well, does it not?
Third Sold. No.
First Sold. Peace, I say!
What should this mean?
Sec. Sold. 'T is the god Hercules, whom Antony loved,
Now leaves him.
First Sold. Walk; let 's see if other watchmen
Do hear what we do.
Sec. Sold. How now, masters!
All. [*Speaking together.*] How now!
How now! do you hear this?
First Sold. Ay; is 't not strange?
Third Sold. Do you hear, masters? Do you hear?
First Sold. Follow the noise so far as we have quarter;
Let 's see how it will give off.
All. Content. 'T is strange.
Exeunt.

2. determine one way, decide one way or another. **10. absolute,** certain. **14. signs well,** is a good omen. **22. quarter,** an assigned beat. **23. give off,** terminate.

Scene IV. *A room in the palace.*

Enter *Antony* and *Cleopatra, Charmian,* and others attending.

Ant. Eros! mine armour, Eros!
Cleo. Sleep a little.
Ant. No, my chuck. Eros, come; mine armour, Eros!

Enter *Eros* with armour.

Come, good fellow, put mine iron on.
If Fortune be not ours to-day, it is
Because we brave her. Come.
Cleo. Nay, I 'll help too.
What 's this for?
Ant. Ah, let be, let be! thou art
The armourer of my heart. False, false; this, this.
Cleo. Sooth, la, I 'll help. Thus it must be.
Ant. Well, well;
We shall thrive now. Seest thou, my good fellow?
Go put on thy defences.
Eros. Briefly, sir.
Cleo. Is not this buckled well?
Ant. Rarely, rarely:
He that unbuckles this, till we do please
To daff 't for our repose, shall hear a storm.
Thou fumblest, Eros; and my queen 's a squire
More tight at this than thou. Dispatch. O love,
That thou couldst see my wars to-day, and knew'st
The royal occupation! Thou shouldst see
A workman in 't.

Enter an armed *Soldier.*

Good-morrow to thee; welcome.
Thou look'st like him that knows a warlike charge.
To business that we love we rise betime
And go to 't with delight.
Sold. A thousand, sir,
Early though 't be, have on their riveted trim,
And at the port expect you.
Shout. Trumpets. Flourish.

Enter *Captains* and *Soldiers.*

Capt. The morn is fair. Good-morrow, general.
All. Good-morrow, general.
Ant. 'T is well blown, lads.
This morning, like the spirit of a youth
That means to be of note, begins betimes.

5. brave, defy. **10. Briefly,** quickly. **15. tight,** adroit. **25. blown,** referring to the flourish of trumpets.

So, so; come, give me that. This way; well said.
Fare thee well, dame, whate'er becomes of me.
This is a soldier's kiss; rebukeable [*Kisses her.*]
And worthy shameful check it were, to stand
On more mechanic compliment. I 'll leave thee
Now, like a man of steel. You that will fight,
Follow me close; I 'll bring you to 't. Adieu.
Exeunt Antony, Eros, Captains, and Soldiers.

Char. Please you, retire to your chamber.
Cleo. Lead me.
He goes forth gallantly. That he and Cæsar might
Determine this great war in single fight!
Then, Antony,—but now—Well, on. *Exeunt.*

Scene V. *Antony's camp.*

Trumpets sound. Enter *Antony* and *Eros.* A *Soldier* meets them.

Sold. The gods make this a happy day to Antony!
Ant. Would thou and those thy scars had once prevail'd
To make me fight at land!
Sold. Hadst thou done so,
The kings that have revolted, and the soldier
That has this morning left thee, would have still
Followed thy heels.
Ant. Who 's gone this morning?
Sold. Who?
One ever near thee: call for Enobarbus,
He shall not hear thee; or from Cæsar's camp
Say, "I am none of thine."
Ant. What sayest thou?
Sold. Sir,
He is with Cæsar.
Eros. Sir, his chests and treasure
He has not with him.
Ant. Is he gone?
Sold. Most certain.
Ant. Go, Eros, send his treasure after; do it;
Detain no jot, I charge thee. Write to him—
I will subscribe—gentle adieus and greetings;
Say that I wish he never find more cause
To change a master. O, my fortunes have
Corrupted honest men! Dispatch.—Enobarbus! *Exeunt.*

Scene VI. *Cæsar's camp.*

Flourish. Enter *Cæsar, Agrippa,* with *Enobarbus,* and *Dolabella.*

Cæs. Go forth, Agrippa, and begin the fight.
Our will is Antony be took alive;
Make it so known.
Agr. Cæsar, I shall. *Exit.*
Cæs. The time of universal peace is near:
Prove this a prosperous day, the three-nook'd world
Shall bear the olive freely.

Enter a *Messenger.*

Mess. Antony
Is come into the field.
Cæs. Go charge Agrippa
Plant those that have revolted in the vant,
That Antony may seem to spend his fury
Upon himself.
Exeunt all but Enobarbus.
Eno. Alexas did revolt; and went to Jewry on
Affairs of Antony; there did persuade
Great Herod to incline himself to Cæsar,
And leave his master Antony: for this pains
Cæsar hath hang'd him. Canidius and the rest
That fell away have entertainment, but
No honourable trust. I have done ill;
Of which I do accuse myself so sorely
That I will joy no more.

Enter a *Soldier* of Cæsar's.

Sold. Enobarbus, Antony
Hath after thee sent all thy treasure, with
His bounty overplus. The messenger
Came on my guard; and at thy tent is now
Unloading of his mules.
Eno. I give it you.
Sold. Mock not, Enobarbus;
I tell you true. Best you saf'd the bringer
Out of the host; I must attend mine office,
Or would have done 't myself. Your emperor
Continues still a Jove. *Exit.*
Eno. I am alone the villain of the earth,
And feel I am so most. O Antony,
Thou mine of bounty, how wouldst thou have paid
My better service, when my turpitude
Thou dost so crown with gold! This blows my heart:
If swift thought break it not, a swifter mean
Shall outstrike thought; but thought will do 't, I feel.
I fight against thee! No! I will go seek
Some ditch wherein to die; the foul'st best fits
My latter part of life. *Exit.*

32. **mechanic compliment,** i.e., vulgar demonstration. Scene v: 14. **subscribe,** sign.

6. **three-nook'd,** three-cornered. 9. **vant,** van. 17. **entertainment,** employment. 22. **bounty overplus,** a liberal gift in addition. 23. **on my guard,** while I was on guard. 26. **saf'd,** safe-convoyed. 34. **blows,** swells.

Scene VII. *Field of battle between the camps.*

Alarum. Drums and trumpets. Enter *Agrippa* and others.

Agr. Retire, we have engag'd ourselves too far:
Cæsar himself has work, and our oppression
Exceeds what we expected. *Exeunt.*

Alarums. Enter *Antony,* and *Scarus* wounded.

Scar. O my brave emperor, this is fought indeed!
Had we done so at first, we had droven them home
With clouts about their heads. *Alarum far off.*
Ant. Thou bleed'st apace.
Scar. I have a wound here that was like a T,
But now 't is made an H.
Ant. They do retire.
Scar. We 'll beat 'em into bench-holes. I have yet
Room for six scotches more.

Enter *Eros.*

Eros. They are beaten, sir; and our advantage serves
For a fair victory.
Scar. Let us score their backs,
And snatch 'em up, as we take hares, behind.
'T is sport to maul a runner.
Ant. I will reward thee
Once for thy sprightly comfort, and tenfold
For thy good valour. Come thee on.
Scar. I 'll halt after.
Exeunt.

Scene VIII. *Under the walls of Alexandria.*

Alarum. Enter *Antony* again in a march; *Scarus,* with others.

Ant. We have beat him to his camp. Run one before,
And let the Queen know of our gests. To-morrow,
Before the sun shall see 's, we 'll spill the blood
That has to-day escap'd. I thank you all;
For doughty-handed are you, and have fought
Not as you serv'd the cause, but as 't had been
Each man's like mine; you have shown all Hectors.
Enter the city, clip your wives, your friends,
Tell them your feats; whilst they with joyful tears
Wash the congealment from your wounds, and kiss
The honour'd gashes whole.

Enter *Cleopatra* attended.

[*To Scarus.*] Give me thy hand;
To this great fairy I 'll commend thy acts,
Make her thanks bless thee.—O thou day o' the world,
Chain mine arm'd neck; leap thou, attire and all,
Through proof of harness to my heart, and there
Ride on the pants triumphing!
Cleo. Lord of lords!
O infinite virtue, com'st thou smiling from
The world's great snare uncaught?
Ant. My nightingale,
We have beat them to their beds. What, girl! though grey
Do something mingle with our younger brown, yet ha' we
A brain that nourishes our nerves, and can
Get goal for goal of youth. Behold this man;
Commend unto his lips thy favouring hand.
Kiss it, my warrior! He hath fought to-day
As if a god, in hate of mankind, had
Destroyed in such a shape.
Cleo. I 'll give thee, friend,
An armour all of gold; it was a king's.
Ant. He has deserv'd it, were it carbuncled
Like holy Phœbus' car. Give me thy hand.
Through Alexandria make a jolly march;
Bear our hack'd targets like the men that owe them.
Had our great palace the capacity
To camp this host, we all would sup together
And drink carouses to the next day's fate,
Which promises royal peril. Trumpeters,
With brazen din blast you the city's ear,
Make mingle with our rattling tabourines,
That heaven and earth may strike their sounds together,
Applauding our approach. *Exeunt.*

Scene IX. *Cæsar's camp.*

Enter a *Sentry,* and his Company. *Enobarbus* follows.

Sent. If we be not reliev'd within this hour,
We must return to the court of guard: the night

Scene vii: 2. our oppression, forces by which we are oppressed. **6. clouts,** bandages. **8. H,** was pronounced "ache." **10. scotches,** cuts. **Scene viii: 2. gests,** exploits. **8. clip,** embrace.

12. fairy, enchantress. **15. proof of harness,** armor that is proof against weapons. **31. owe,** own. **37. tabourines,** drums. **Scene ix: 2. court of guard,** guardhouse.

Is shiny; and they say we shall embattle
By th' second hour i' th' morn.
First Sold. This last day was
A shrewd one to 's.
Eno. O, bear me witness, night,—
Sec. Sold. What man is this?
First Sold. Stand close, and list him.
Eno. Be witness to me, O thou blessed moon,
When men revolted shall upon record
Bear hateful memory, poor Enobarbus did
Before thy face repent!
Sent. Enobarbus?
Sec. Sold. Peace!
Hark further.
Eno. O sovereign mistress of true melancholy,
The poisonous damp of night disponge upon me,
That life, a very rebel to my will,
May hang no longer on me. Throw my heart
Against the flint and hardness of my fault;
Which, being dried with grief, will break to powder,
And finish all foul thoughts. O Antony,
Nobler than my revolt is infamous,
Forgive me in thine own particular;
But let the world rank me in register
A master-leaver and a fugitive.
O Antony! O Antony! *Dies.*
First Sold. Let 's speak
To him.
Sent. Let 's hear him, for the things he speaks
May concern Cæsar.
Sec. Sold. Let 's do so. But he sleeps.
Sent. Swoons rather; for so bad a prayer as his
Was never yet for sleep.
First Sold. Go we to him.
Sec. Sold. Awake, sir, awake; speak to us.
First. Sold. Hear you, sir?
Sent. The hand of death hath raught him.
[*Drums afar off.*] Hark! the drums
Demurely wake the sleepers. Let us bear him
To the court of guard; he is of note. Our hour
Is fully out.
Sec. Sold. Come on, then;
He may recover yet. *Exeunt with the body.*

Scene X. *Between the two camps.*

Enter *Antony* and *Scarus,* with their Army.

Ant. Their preparation is to-day by sea;
We please them not by land.

5. shrewd, evil. **13. disponge,** pour down. **20. own particular,** personally. **29. raught,** reached. **31. Demurely,** quietly.

Scar. For both, my lord.
Ant. I would they 'd fight i' the fire or i' the air;
We 'd fight there too. But this it is: our foot
Upon the hills adjoining to the city
Shall stay with us.—Order for sea is given;
They have put forth the haven—
Where their appointment we may best discover,
And look on their endeavour. *Exeunt.*

Scene XI. *Between the camps.*

Enter *Cæsar,* and his Army.

Cæs. But being charg'd, we will be still by land,
Which, as I take 't, we shall; for his best force
Is forth to man his galleys. To the vales,
And hold our best advantage. *Exeunt.*

Scene XII. *On the hill near the city.*

Enter *Antony* and *Scarus.*

Ant. Yet they are not join'd. Where yond pine does stand,
I shall discover all; I 'll bring thee word
Straight, how 't is like to go. *Exit.*
Scar. Swallows have built
In Cleopatra's sails their nests. The augurers
Say they know not, they cannot tell; look grimly,
And dare not speak their knowledge. Antony
Is valiant, and dejected; and, by starts,
His fretted fortunes give him hope and fear,
Of what he has and has not.
Alarum afar off, as at a sea-fight.

Re-enter *Antony.*

Ant. All is lost!
This foul Egyptian hath betrayed me.
My fleet hath yielded to the foe, and yonder
They cast their caps up and carouse together
Like friends long lost. Triple-turn'd whore! 't is thou
Hast sold me to this novice; and my heart
Makes only wars on thee. Bid them all fly;
For when I am reveng'd upon my charm,
I have done all. Bid them all fly; begone.
Exit Scarus.
O sun, thy uprise shall I see no more:
Fortune and Antony part here; even here

Scene xi: 1. Unless we are charged, we will hold our land forces inactive. **Scene xii: 4. sails,** ships. **13. Triple-turn'd,** three times faithless. **16. charm,** charmer.

Do we shake hands. All come to this? The hearts
That spaniel'd me at heels, to whom I gave
Their wishes, do discandy, melt their sweets
On blossoming Cæsar; and this pine is bark'd,
That overtopp'd them all. Betray'd I am.
O this false soul of Egypt! this grave charm,—
Whose eye beck'd forth my wars, and call'd them home;
Whose bosom was my crownet, my chief end,—
Like a right gipsy, hath, at fast and loose,
Beguil'd me to the very heart of loss.
What, Eros, Eros!

Enter *Cleopatra.*

Ah, thou spell! Avaunt!

Cleo. Why is my lord enrag'd against his love?

Ant. Vanish, or I shall give thee thy deserving,
And blemish Cæsar's triumph. Let him take thee,
And hoist thee up to the shouting plebeians!
Follow his chariot, like the greatest spot
Of all thy sex; most monster-like, be shown
For poor'st diminutives, for dolts; and let
Patient Octavia plough thy visage up
With her prepared nails. *Exit Cleopatra.*
'T is well thou 'rt gone,
If it be well to live; but better 't were
Thou fell'st into my fury, for one death
Might have prevented many. Eros, ho!
The shirt of Nessus is upon me: teach me,
Alcides, thou mine ancestor, thy rage.
Let me lodge Lichas on the horns o' th' moon;
And with those hands, that grasp'd the heaviest club,
Subdue my worthiest self. The witch shall die.
To the young Roman boy she hath sold me, and I fall
Under this plot. She dies for 't. Eros, ho!
Exit.

Scene XIII. *Alexandria. Cleopatra's palace.*

Enter *Cleopatra, Charmian, Iras,* and *Mardian.*

Cleo. Help me, my women! O, he 's more mad
Than Telamon for his shield; the boar of Thessaly
Was never so emboss'd.

Char. To th' monument!
There lock yourself, and send him word you are dead.
The soul and body rive not more in parting
Than greatness going off.

Cleo. To th' monument!
Mardian, go tell him I have slain myself;
Say, that the last I spoke was "Antony,"
And word it, prithee, piteously. Hence, Mardian,
And bring me how he takes my death. To th' monument! *Exeunt.*

Scene XIV. *Another room in the palace.*

Enter *Antony* and *Eros.*

Ant. Eros, thou yet behold'st me?

Eros. Ay, noble lord.

Ant. Sometime we see a cloud that 's dragonish;
A vapour sometime like a bear or lion,
A tower'd citadel, a pendent rock,
A forked mountain, or blue promontory
With trees upon 't, that nod unto the world,
And mock our eyes with air. Thou hast seen these signs;
They are black vesper's pageants.

Eros. Ay, my lord.

Ant. That which is now a horse, even with a thought
The rack dislimns, and makes it indistinct,
As water is in water.

Eros. It does, my lord.

Ant. My good knave Eros, now thy captain is
Even such a body: here I am Antony;
Yet cannot hold this visible shape, my knave.
I made these wars for Egypt; and the Queen,—
Whose heart I thought I had, for she had mine,
Which whilst it was mine had annex'd unto 't
A million moe, now lost,—she, Eros, has
Pack'd cards with Cæsar, and false-play'd my glory
Unto an enemy's triumph.
Nay, weep not, gentle Eros; there is left us
Ourselves to end ourselves.

Enter *Mardian.*

O, thy vile lady!
She has robb'd me of my sword.

Mar. No, Antony;

25. **grave charm,** destructive piece of witchcraft. 26. **beck'd forth,** beckoned forth by a nod. 27. **crownet,** coronet. 28. **fast and loose,** a cheating game common among gypsies. It consisted of tying a deceptively hard knot, which could be easily loosened by the trick of pulling both ends at the same time. 37. **dolts,** idiots. 43. **Nessus,** a shirt steeped in the poisoned blood of Nessus, the centaur, was given Hercules by his wife, Dejanira, unwittingly as a love charm. In agony he hurled Lichas, who had brought him the shirt, so high in the air that he sprinkled the clouds with blood.

Scene xiii: 2. Telamon, Ajax Telamon, frenzied by the loss of Achilles's armor to Odysseus. **3. emboss'd,** covered with foam. **Scene xiv: 10. rack dislimns,** cloud blots itself out. **19. Pack'd,** stacked.

My mistress lov'd thee, and her fortunes mingled
With thine entirely.
Ant. Hence, saucy eunuch; peace!
She hath betray'd me and shall die the death.
Mar. Death of one person can be paid but once,
And that she has discharg'd. What thou wouldst do
Is done unto thy hand; the last she spake
Was "Antony! most noble Antony!"
Then in the midst a tearing groan did break
The name of Antony; it was divided
Between her heart and lips. She render'd life,
Thy name so buried in her.
Ant. Dead, then?
Mar. Dead.
Ant. Unarm, Eros; the long day's task is done,
And we must sleep. [*To Mardian.*] That thou depart'st hence safe,
Does pay thy labour richly; go.
Exit Mardian.
Off, pluck off!
The seven-fold shield of Ajax cannot keep
The battery from my heart. O, cleave, my sides!
Heart, once be stronger than thy continent,
Crack thy frail case! Apace, Eros, apace.
No more a soldier. Bruised pieces, go;
You have been nobly borne.—From me a while. *Exit Eros.*
I will o'ertake thee, Cleopatra, and
Weep for my pardon. So it must be, for now
All length is torture; since the torch is out,
Lie down, and stray no farther. Now all labour
Mars what it does; yea, very force entangles
Itself with strength. Seal then and all is done.
Eros!—I come, my queen!—Eros!—Stay for me!
Where souls do couch on flowers, we 'll hand in hand,
And with our sprightly port make the ghosts gaze.
Dido and her Æneas shall want troops,
And all the haunt be ours. Come, Eros, Eros!

Re-enter *Eros.*

Eros. What would my lord?
Ant. Since Cleopatra died,
I have liv'd in such dishonour, that the gods
Detest my baseness. I, that with my sword
Quarter'd the world, and o'er green Neptune's back
With ships made cities, condemn myself to lack
The courage of a woman; less noble mind
Than she which by her death our Cæsar tells,
"I am conqueror of myself." Thou art sworn, Eros,
That, when the exigent should come, which now
Is come indeed, when I should see behind me
The inevitable prosecution of
Disgrace and horror, that, on my command,
Thou then wouldst kill me. Do 't; the time is come.
Thou strik'st not me, 't is Cæsar thou defeat'st.
Put colour in thy cheek.
Eros. The gods withhold me!
Shall I do that which all the Parthian darts,
Though enemy, lost aim, and could not?
Ant. Eros,
Wouldst thou be window'd in great Rome and see
Thy master thus with pleach'd arms, bending down
His corrigible neck, his face subdu'd
To penetrative shame, whilst the wheel'd seat
Of fortunate Cæsar, drawn before him, branded
His baseness that ensued?
Eros. I would not see 't.
Ant. Come, then; for with a wound I must be cur'd.
Draw that thy honest sword, which thou hast worn
Most useful for thy country.
Eros. O, sir, pardon me!
Ant. When I did make thee free, swor'st thou not then
To do this when I bade thee? Do it at once;
Or thy precedent services are all
But accidents unpurpos'd. Draw, and come.
Eros. Turn from me, then, that noble countenance,
Wherein the worship of the whole world lies.
Ant. Lo thee! *Turning from him.*
Eros. My sword is drawn.
Ant. Then let it do at once
The thing why thou hast drawn it.
Eros. My dear master,
My captain, and my emperor, let me say,
Before I strike this bloody stroke, farewell.
Ant. 'T is said, man; and farewell.
Eros. Farewell, great chief. Shall I strike now?
Ant. Now, Eros.
Eros. Why, there then. *Kills himself.*
Thus I do escape the sorrow
Of Antony's death.

39. battery from, the assault (the beating) proceeding from. **40. thy continent,** what contains thee. **46. length,** i.e., of life. **49. Seal,** sealing was the final act of a transaction. **52. port,** bearing.

63. exigent, crisis. **73. pleach'd,** folded. **74. corrigible,** submissive to correction. **75. penetrative,** penetrating. **77. ensued,** followed.

Ant. Thrice-nobler than myself!
Thou teachest me, O valiant Eros, what
I should, and thou couldst not. My queen and Eros
Have by their brave instruction got upon me
A nobleness in record; but I will be
A bridegroom in my death, and run into 't
As to a lover's bed. Come, then; and, Eros,
Thy master dies thy scholar: to do thus
Falling on his sword.
I learn'd of thee. How! not dead? not dead?
The guard, ho! O, dispatch me!

Enter *Dercetas* and *Guard.*

First Guard. What 's the noise?
Ant. I have done my work ill, friends. O, make an end
Of what I have begun.
Sec. Guard. The star is fallen.
First Guard. And time is at his period.
All. Alas, and woe!
Ant. Let him that loves me strike me dead.
First Guard. Not I.
Sec. Guard. Nor I.
Third Guard. Nor any one. *Exeunt Guard.*
Der. Thy death and fortunes bid thy followers fly.
This sword but shown to Cæsar with this tidings,
Shall enter me with him.

Enter *Diomedes.*

Dio. Where 's Antony?
Der. There, Diomed, there.
Dio. Lives he?
Wilt thou not answer, man?
Exit Dercetas.
Ant. Art thou there, Diomed? Draw thy sword, and give me
Sufficing strokes for death.
Dio. Most absolute lord,
My mistress Cleopatra sent me to thee.
Ant. When did she send thee?
Dio. Now, my lord.
Ant. Where is she?
Dio. Lock'd in her monument. She had a prophesying fear
Of what hath come to pass; for when she saw—
Which never shall be found—you did suspect
She had dispos'd with Cæsar, and that your rage
Would not be purg'd, she sent you word she was dead;
But, fearing since how it might work, hath sent
Me to proclaim the truth; and I am come,
I dread, too late.
Ant. Too late, good Diomed. Call my guard, I prithee.
Dio. What, ho, the Emperor's guard! The guard, what ho!
Come, your lord calls!

Enter four or five of the *Guard* of *Antony.*

Ant. Bear me, good friends, where Cleopatra bides;
'T is the last service that I shall command you.
First Guard. Woe, woe are we, sir, you may not live to wear
All your true followers out.
All. Most heavy day!
Ant. Nay, good my fellows, do not please sharp fate
To grace it with your sorrows; bid that welcome
Which comes to punish us, and we punish it
Seeming to bear it lightly. Take me up.
I have led you oft; carry me now, good friends,
And have my thanks for all.
Exeunt, bearing Antony.

Scene XV. *The Monument.*

Enter *Cleopatra,* and her maids aloft, with *Charmian* and *Iras.*

Cleo. O Charmian, I will never go from hence.
Char. Be comforted, dear madam.
Cleo. No, I will not.
All strange and terrible events are welcome,
But comforts we despise; our size of sorrow,
Proportion'd to our cause, must be as great
As that which makes it.

Enter, below, *Diomedes.*

How now! is he dead?
Dio. His death 's upon him, but not dead.
Look out o' th' other side your monument;
His guard have brought him thither.

Enter below *Antony,* borne by the Guard.

Cleo. O sun,
Burn the great sphere thou mov'st in! Darkling stand
The varying shore o' th' world. O Antony,
Antony, Antony! Help, Charmian, help, Iras, help;
Help, friends below; let 's draw him hither.
Ant. Peace!
Not Cæsar's valour hath o'erthrown Antony,
But Antony's hath triumph'd on itself.

98-9. **Have . . . record,** obtained advantage over me in the record of noble deeds. **113. enter me,** introduce me into favor. **123. dispos'd,** made terms.

Scene xv: **10. great sphere,** the sun was supposed to be a planet fixed in a solid sphere which moved it around the earth. **Darkling,** in darkness.

Cleo. So it should be, that none but Antony
Should conquer Antony; but woe 't is so!
Ant. I am dying, Egypt, dying; only
I here importune death a while, until
Of many thousand kisses the poor last
I lay upon thy lips.
Cleo. I dare not, dear,—
Dear my lord, pardon,—I dare not,
Lest I be taken. Not th' imperious show
Of the full-fortun'd Cæsar ever shall
Be brooch'd with me; if knife, drugs, serpents, have
Edge, sting, or operation, I am safe.
Your wife Octavia, with her modest eyes
And still conclusion, shall acquire no honour
Demuring upon me. But come, come, Antony,—
Help me, my women,—we must draw thee up.
Assist, good friends.
Ant. O, quick, or I am gone.
Cleo. Here 's sport indeed! How heavy weighs my lord!
Our strength is all gone into heaviness,
That makes the weight. Had I great Juno's power,
The strong-wing'd Mercury should fetch thee up
And set thee by Jove's side. Yet come a little,—
Wishers were ever fools,—O, come, come, come;
They heave Antony aloft to Cleopatra.
And welcome, welcome! Die where thou hast liv'd;
Quicken with kissing: had my lips that power,
Thus would I wear them out.
All. A heavy sight!
Ant. I am dying, Egypt, dying.
Give me some wine, and let me speak a little.
Cleo. No, let me speak; and let me rail so high,
That the false housewife Fortune break her wheel,
Provok'd by my offence.
Ant. One word, sweet queen:
Of Cæsar seek your honour, with your safety. O!
Cleo. They do not go together.
Ant. Gentle, hear me:
None about Cæsar trust but Proculeius.
Cleo. My resolution and my hands I 'll trust;
None about Cæsar.
Ant. The miserable change now at my end
Lament nor sorrow at; but please your thoughts
In feeding them with those my former fortunes
Wherein I liv'd, the greatest prince o' th' world,
The noblest; and do now not basely die,
Not cowardly put off my helmet to
My countryman,—a Roman by a Roman
Valiantly vanquish'd. Now my spirit is going;
I can no more.
Cleo. Noblest of men, woo 't die?
Hast thou no care of me? Shall I abide
In this dull world, which in thy absence is
No better than a sty? O, see, my women,
Antony dies.
The crown o' the earth doth melt. My lord!
O, wither'd is the garland of the war,
The soldier's pole is fall'n! Young boys and girls
Are level now with men; the odds is gone,
And there is nothing left remarkable
Beneath the visiting moon. *Faints.*
Char. O, quietness, lady!
Iras. She is dead too, our sovereign.
Char. Lady!
Iras. Madam!
Char. O madam, madam, madam!
Iras. Royal Egypt,
Empress!
Char. Peace, peace, Iris!
Cleo. No more but e'en a woman, and commanded
By such poor passion as the maid that milks
And does the meanest chares. It were for me
To throw my sceptre at the injurious gods;
To tell them that this world did equal theirs
Till they had stolen our jewel. All 's but nought;
Patience is sottish, and impatience does
Become a dog that 's mad: then is it sin
To rush into the secret house of death,
Ere death dare come to us? How do you, women?
What, what! good cheer! Why, how now, Charmian!
My noble girls! Ah, women, women, look,
Our lamp is spent, it 's out! Good sirs, take heart.
We 'll bury him; and then, what 's brave, what 's noble,
Let 's do it after the high Roman fashion,
And make Death proud to take us. Come, away;
This case of that huge spirit now is cold.
Ah, women, women! come; we have no friend
But resolution and the briefest end.
Exeunt; those above bearing off Antony's body.

21. dare not, i.e., descend from the monument. **25. brooch'd**, ornamented. **28. still conclusion**, quiet inferences. **29. Demuring**, looking demurely. **33. heaviness**, (1) sorrow, (2) weight. **39. Quicken**, receive life.

59. woo 't, wouldst thou. **65. pole**, standard or perhaps "pole-star." **66. odds**, superiority. **75. chares**, chores. **It were for me**, it would be right for. **91. briefest**, quickest.

ACT V. Scene I. *Alexandria. Cæsar's camp.*

Enter *Cæsar, Agrippa, Dolabella, Mæcenas, Gallus, Proculeius,* and others, his council of war.

Cæs. Go to him, Dolabella, bid him yield;
Being so frustrate, tell him he mocks
The pauses that he makes.
Dol. Cæsar, I shall.
Exit.

Enter *Dercetas* with the sword of Antony.

Cæs. Wherefore is that? and what art thou that dar'st
Appear thus to us?
Der. I am call'd Dercetas;
Mark Antony I serv'd, who best was worthy
Best to be serv'd: whilst he stood up and spoke,
He was my master; and I wore my life
To spend upon his haters. If thou please
To take me to thee, as I was to him
I 'll be to Cæsar; if thou pleasest not,
I yield thee up my life.
Cæs. What is 't thou say'st?
Der. I say, O Cæsar, Antony is dead.
Cæs. The breaking of so great a thing should make
A greater crack. The round world
Should have shook lions into civil streets,
And citizens to their dens. The death of Antony
Is not a single doom; in the name lay
A moiety of the world.
Der. He is dead, Cæsar;
Not by a public minister of justice,
Nor by a hired knife; but that self hand
Which writ his honour in the acts it did
Hath, with the courage which the heart did lend it,
Splitted the heart. This is his sword;
I robb'd his wound of it; behold it stain'd
With his most noble blood.
Cæs. Look you sad, friends?
The gods rebuke me, but it is tidings
To wash the eyes of kings.
Agr. And strange it is
That nature must compel us to lament
Our most persisted deeds.
Mæc. His taints and honours
Wag'd equal with him.
Agr. A rarer spirit never
Did steer humanity; but you, gods, will give us
Some faults to make us men. Cæsar is touch'd.
Mæc. When such a spacious mirror 's set before him,
He needs must see himself.
Cæs. O Antony!
I have followed thee to this; but we do launch
Diseases in our bodies. I must perforce
Have shown to thee such a declining day,
Or look on thine; we could not stall together
In the whole world: but yet let me lament,
With tears as sovereign as the blood of hearts,
That thou, my brother, my competitor
In top of all design, my mate in empire,
Friend and companion in the front of war,
The arm of mine own body, and the heart
Where mine his thoughts did kindle,—that our stars,
Unreconciliable, should divide
Our equalness to this. Hear me, good friends,—

Enter an *Egyptian.*

But I will tell you at some meeter season.
The business of this man looks out of him;
We 'll hear him what he says.—Whence are you?
Egyp. A poor Egyptian yet. The Queen my mistress,
Confin'd in all she has, her monument,
Of thy intents desires instruction,
That she preparedly may frame herself
To th' way she 's forc'd to.
Cæs. Bid her have good heart.
She soon shall know of us, by some of ours,
How honourable and how kindly we
Determine for her; for Cæsar cannot live
To be ungentle.
Egyp. So the gods preserve thee!
Exit.
Cæs. Come hither, Proculeius. Go and say,
We purpose her no shame. Give her what comforts
The quality of her passion shall require,
Lest, in her greatness, by some mortal stroke
She do defeat us; for her life in Rome
Would be eternal in our triumph. Go,
And with your speediest bring us what she says,
And how you find of her.
Pro. Cæsar, I shall. *Exit.*
Cæs. Gallus, go you along. [*Exit Gallus.*] Where 's Dolabella,
To second Proculeius?
All. Dolabella!
Cæs. Let him alone, for I remember now
How he 's employ'd; he shall in time be ready.
Go with me to my tent, where you shall see
How hardly I was drawn into this war,

36. launch, lance. **41. sovereign,** supreme in importance. **43. top,** highest. **66. Would . . . triumph,** would give our triumph eternal glory.

How calm and gentle I proceeded still
In all my writings. Go with me, and see
What I can show in this. *Exeunt.*

Scene II. *A room in the Monument.*

Enter *Cleopatra, Charmian, Iras,* and *Mardian.*

Cleo. My desolation does begin to make
A better life. 'T is paltry to be Cæsar;
Not being Fortune, he 's but Fortune's knave,
A minister of her will: and it is great
To do that thing that ends all other deeds;
Which shackles accidents and bolts up change;
Which sleeps, and never palates more the dung,
The beggar's nurse and Cæsar's.

Enter to the gates of the monument *Proculeius* and Soldiers.

Pro. Cæsar sends greeting to the Queen of Egypt;
And bids thee study on what fair demands
Thou mean'st to have him grant thee.
Cleo. What 's thy name?
Pro. My name is Proculeius.
Cleo. Antony
Did tell me of you, bade me trust you; but
I do not greatly care to be deceiv'd,
That have no use for trusting. If your master
Would have a queen his beggar, you must tell him
That majesty, to keep decorum, must
No less beg than a kingdom: if he please
To give me conquer'd Egypt for my son,
He gives me so much of mine own as I
Will kneel to him with thanks.
Pro. Be of good cheer,
You 're fallen into a princely hand; fear nothing.
Make your full reference freely to my lord,
Who is so full of grace that it flows over
On all that need. Let me report to him
Your sweet dependency, and you shall find
A conqueror that will pray in aid for kindness
Where he for grace is kneel'd to.
Cleo. Pray you, tell him
I am his fortune's vassal, and I send him
The greatness he has got. I hourly learn
A doctrine of obedience, and would gladly
Look him i' th' face.
Pro. This I 'll report, dear lady.
Have comfort, for I know your plight is pitied
Of him that caus'd it.

Here Proculeius and two of the Guard go out below and reappear behind Cleopatra.

—You see how easily she may be surpris'd.
Guard her till Cæsar come.
Iras. Royal queen!
Char. O Cleopatra! thou art taken, queen.
Cleo. Quick, quick, good hands.
Drawing a dagger.
Pro. Hold, worthy lady, hold!
Seizes and disarms her.
Do not yourself such wrong, who are in this
Reliev'd, but not betray'd.
Cleo. What, of death too,
That rids our dogs of languish?
Pro. Cleopatra,
Do not abuse my master's bounty by
Th' undoing of yourself. Let the world see
His nobleness well acted, which your death
Will never let come forth.
Cleo. Where art thou, Death?
Come hither, come! Come, come, and take a queen
Worth many babes and beggars!
Pro. O, temperance, lady!
Cleo. Sir, I will eat no meat, I 'll not drink, sir;
If idle talk will once be necessary
I 'll not sleep neither; this mortal house I 'll ruin,
Do Cæsar what he can. Know, sir, that I
Will not wait pinion'd at your master's court;
Nor once be chastis'd with the sober eye
Of dull Octavia. Shall they hoist me up
And show me to the shouting varletry
Of censuring Rome? Rather a ditch in Egypt
Be gentle grave unto me! Rather on Nilus' mud
Lay me stark nak'd, and let the waterflies
Blow me into abhorring! Rather make
My country's high pyramides my gibbet,
And hang me up in chains!
Pro. You do extend
These thoughts of horror further than you shall
Find cause in Cæsar.

Enter *Dolabella.*

Dol. Proculeius,
What thou hast done thy master Cæsar knows,
And he hath sent for thee: for the Queen,
I 'll take her to my guard.
Pro. So, Dolabella,
It shall content me best: be gentle to her.

3. **knave**, servant. 7-8. **dung . . . Cæsar's**, gross food that nourishes alike the beggar and Cæsar. 23. **reference**, appeal. 27. **pray in aid**, legal term, to call in the aid of a person with interest in the case.

42. **languish**, a lingering illness. 53. **pinion'd**, bound. 60. **Blow**, make fly-blown. **abhorring**, abomination.

[*To Cleopatra.*] To Cæsar I will speak what you shall please,
If you 'll employ me to him.

Cleo. Say, I would die.

Exeunt Proculeius and Soldiers.

Dol. Most noble empress, you have heard of me?

Cleo. I cannot tell.

Dol. Assuredly you know me.

Cleo. No matter, sir, what I have heard or known.
You laugh when boys or women tell their dreams;
Is 't not your trick?

Dol. I understand not, madam.

Cleo. I dream'd there was an Emperor Antony.
O, such another sleep, that I might see
But such another man!

Dol. If it might please ye,—

Cleo. His face was as the heavens; and therein stuck
A sun and moon, which kept their course and lighted
The little O, the earth.

Dol. Most sovereign creature,—

Cleo. His legs bestrid the ocean; his rear'd arm
Crested the world; his voice was propertied
As all the tuned spheres, and that to friends;
But when he meant to quail and shake the orb,
He was as rattling thunder. For his bounty,
There was no winter in 't; an autumn 't was
That grew the more by reaping: his delights
Were dolphin-like, they show'd his back above
The element they liv'd in: in his livery
Walk'd crowns and crownets; realms and islands were
As plates dropp'd from his pocket.

Dol. Cleopatra!

Cleo. Think you there was or might be such a man
As this I dream'd of?

Dol. Gentle madam, no.

Cleo. You lie, up to the hearing of the gods!
But, if there be or ever were one such,
It 's past the size of dreaming: nature wants stuff
To vie strange forms with fancy; yet, t' imagine
An Antony, were nature's piece 'gainst fancy,
Condemning shadows quite.

Dol. Hear me, good madam.
Your loss is as yourself, great; and you bear it
As answering to the weight. Would I might never
O'ertake pursu'd success, but I do feel,
By the rebound of yours, a grief that smites
My very heart at root.

Cleo. I thank you, sir.
Know you what Cæsar means to do with me?

Dol. I am loath to tell you what I would you knew.

Cleo. Nay, pray you, sir,—

Dol. Though he be honourable,—

Cleo. He 'll lead me, then, in triumph?

Dol. Madam, he will; I know 't.

Flourish.

Enter *Cæsar, Gallus, Proculeius, Mæcenas, Seleucus,* and others of his train.

All. Make way there! Cæsar!

Cæs. Which is the Queen of Egypt?

Dol. It is the Emperor, madam.

Cleopatra kneels.

Cæs. Arise, you shall not kneel.
I pray you, rise; rise, Egypt.

Cleo. Sir, the gods
Will have it thus; my master and my lord
I must obey.

Cæs. Take to you no hard thoughts:
The record of what injuries you did us,
Though written in our flesh, we shall remember
As things but done by chance.

Cleo. Sole sir o' th' world,
I cannot project mine own cause so well
To make it clear; but do confess I have
Been laden with like frailties which before
Have often sham'd our sex.

Cæs. Cleopatra, know
We will extenuate rather than enforce:
If you apply yourself to our intents,
Which towards you are most gentle, you shall find
A benefit in this change; but if you seek
To lay on me a cruelty, by taking
Antony's course, you shall bereave yourself
Of my good purposes, and put your children
To that destruction which I 'll guard them from,
If thereon you rely. I 'll take my leave.

Cleo. And may, through all the world; 't is yours; and we,
Your scutcheons and your signs of conquest, shall
Hang in what place you please. Here, my good lord.

Cæs. You shall advise me in all for Cleopatra.

Cleo. This is the brief of money, plate, and jewels,

83. Crested, overtopped. **propertied . . . friends,** harmonious as the spheres in speaking to friends. **92. plates,** silver coins. **99. were nature's . . . fancy,** i.e., in her masterpiece (Antony) nature came closest to equalling the achievement of imagination.

103. but I do feel, if I do not feel. **121. project,** set forth. **125. enforce,** stress.

I am possess'd of: 't is exactly valued,
Not petty things admitted. Where 's Seleucus?
Sel. Here, madam.
Cleo. This is my treasurer; let him speak, my lord,
Upon his peril, that I have reserv'd
To myself nothing. Speak the truth, Seleucus.
Sel. Madam,
I had rather seal my lips, than, to my peril,
Speak that which is not.
Cleo. What have I kept back?
Sel. Enough to purchase what you have made known.
Cæs. Nay, blush not, Cleopatra; I approve
Your wisdom in the deed.
Cleo. See, Cæsar! O, behold,
How pomp is followed! Mine will now be yours;
And, should we shift estates, yours would be mine.
Th' ingratitude of this Seleucus does
Even make me wild. O slave, of no more trust
Than love that 's hir'd! What, goest thou back? Thou shalt
Go back, I warrant thee; but I 'll catch thine eyes,
Though they had wings. Slave, soulless villain, dog!
O rarely base!
Cæs. Good queen, let us entreat you.
Cleo. O Cæsar, what a wounding shame is this,
That thou, vouchsafing here to visit me,
Doing the honour of thy lordliness
To one so meek, that mine own servant should
Parcel the sum of my disgraces by
Addition of his envy! Say, good Cæsar,
That I some lady trifles have reserv'd,
Immoment toys, things of such dignity
As we greet modern friends withal: and say,
Some nobler token I have kept apart
For Livia and Octavia, to induce
Their mediation; must I be unfolded
With one that I have bred? The gods! it smites me
Beneath the fall I have. [*To Seleucus.*] Prithee, go hence;
Or I shall show the cinders of my spirits
Through the ashes of my chance. Wert thou a man,
Thou wouldst have mercy on me.
Cæs. Forbear, Seleucus.
Exit Seleucus.
Cleo. Be it known, that we, the greatest, are misthought
For things that others do; and, when we fall,
We answer others' merits in our name,
Are therefore to be pitied.
Cæs. Cleopatra,
Not what you have reserv'd, nor what acknowledg'd,
Put we i' th' roll of conquest: still be 't yours,
Bestow it at your pleasure; and believe,
Cæsar 's no merchant, to make prize with you
Of things that merchants sold. Therefore be cheer'd,
Make not your thoughts your prisons; no, dear queen;
For we intend so to dispose you as
Yourself shall give us counsel. Feed, and sleep.
Our care and pity is so much upon you,
That we remain your friend; and so, adieu.
Cleo. My master, and my lord!
Cæs. Not so. Adieu.
Flourish. Exeunt Cæsar and his train.
Cleo. He words me, girls, he words me, that I should not
Be noble to myself; but, hark thee, Charmian.
Whispers Charmian.
Iras. Finish, good lady; the bright day is done,
And we are for the dark.
Cleo. Hie thee again.
I have spoke already, and it is provided;
Go put it to the haste.
Char. Madam, I will.

Re-enter *Dolabella.*

Dol. Where is the Queen?
Char. Behold, sir. *Exit.*
Cleo. Dolabella!
Dol. Madam, as thereto sworn by your command,
Which my love makes religion to obey,
I tell you this: Cæsar through Syria
Intends his journey; and within three days
You with your children will he send before.
Make your best use of this. I have perform'd
Your pleasure and my promise.
Cleo. Dolabella,
I shall remain your debtor.
Dol. I your servant.
Adieu, good queen; I must attend on Cæsar.
Exit.
Cleo. Farewell, and thanks! Now, Iras, what think'st thou?
Thou, an Egyptian puppet, shall be shown
In Rome, as well as I. Mechanic slaves
With greasy aprons, rules, and hammers, shall
Uplift us to the view; in their thick breaths,
Rank of gross diet, shall we be enclouded,
And forc'd to drink their vapour.
Iras. The gods forbid!

140. Not . . . admitted, petty things excluded. **151. Mine,** my followers. **163. Parcel,** itemize. **164. envy,** malice. **166. Immoment,** insignificant. **167. modern,** ordinary. **170-1. unfolded With,** betrayed by. **174. chance,** ill-fortune. **176. misthought,** misjudged.

177. We suffer the penalty deserved by our agents. **185. Make . . . prisons,** do not imagine you are a prisoner.

Cleo. Nay, 't is most certain, Iras: saucy lictors
Will catch at us, like strumpets; and scald rhymers
Ballad us out o' tune. The quick comedians
Extemporally will stage us, and present
Our Alexandrian revels; Antony
Shall be brought drunken forth, and I shall see
Some squeaking Cleopatra boy my greatness
I' th' posture of a whore.
Iras. O the good gods!
Cleo. Nay, that 's certain.
Iras. I 'll never see 't; for, I am sure, my nails
Are stronger than mine eyes.
Cleo. Why, that 's the way
To fool their preparation, and to conquer
Their most absurd intents.

Re-enter *Charmian.*

Now, Charmian!
Show me, my women, like a queen: go fetch
My best attires; I am again for Cydnus
To meet Mark Antony. Sirrah Iras, go.
Now, noble Charmian, we 'll dispatch indeed;
And, when thou hast done this chare, I 'll give thee leave
To play till doomsday. Bring our crown and all.
Wherefore 's this noise?

Exit Iras. A noise within.

Enter a *Guardsman.*

Guard. Here is a rural fellow
That will not be deni'd your Highness' presence.
He brings you figs.
Cleo. Let him come in. *Exit Guardsman.*
What poor an instrument
May do a noble deed! He brings me liberty.
My resolution 's plac'd, and I have nothing
Of woman in me; now from head to foot
I am marble-constant; now the fleeting moon
No planet is of mine.

Re-enter *Guardsman,* with *Clown* bringing in a basket.

Guard. This is the man.
Cleo. Avoid, and leave him.

Exit Guardsman.

Hast thou the pretty worm of Nilus there,
That kills and pains not?

Clown. Truly, I have him; but I would not be the party that should desire you to touch him, for his biting is immortal; those that do die of it do seldom or never recover.

Cleo. Remember'st thou any that have died on 't?

Clown. Very many, men and women too. I heard of one of them no longer than yesterday; a very honest woman, but something given to lie, as a woman should not do, but in the way of honesty; how she died of the biting of it, what pain she felt; truly, she makes a very good report o' th' worm. But he that will believe all that they say, shall never be saved by half that they do: but this is most falliable, the worm 's an odd worm.

Cleo. Get thee hence; farewell.

Clown. I wish you all joy of the worm.

Setting down his basket.

Cleo. Farewell.

Clown. You must think this, look you, that the worm will do his kind.

Cleo. Ay, ay; farewell.

Clown. Look you, the worm is not to be trusted but in the keeping of wise people; for, indeed, there is no goodness in the worm.

Cleo. Take thou no care; it shall be heeded.

Clown. Very good. Give it nothing, I pray you, for it is not worth the feeding.

Cleo. Will it eat me?

Clown. You must not think I am so simple but I know the devil himself will not eat a woman. I know that a woman is a dish for the gods, if the devil dress her not. But, truly, these same whoreson devils do the gods great harm in their women; for in every ten that they make, the devils mar five.

Cleo. Well, get thee gone; farewell.

Clown. Yes, forsooth; I wish you joy o' the worm. *Exit.*

Re-enter *Iras* with a robe and crown.

Cleo. Give me my robe, put on my crown; I have
Immortal longings in me. Now no more
The juice of Egypt's grape shall moist this lip.
Yare, yare, good Iras; quick. Methinks I hear
Antony call; I see him rouse himself
To praise my noble act; I hear him mock
The luck of Cæsar, which the gods give men
To excuse their after wrath. Husband, I come!
Now to that name my courage prove my title!
I am fire and air; my other elements
I give to baser life. So; have you done?
Come then, and take the last warmth of my lips.
Farewell, kind Charmian; Iras, long farewell.

Kisses them. Iras falls and dies.

Have I the aspic in my lips? Dost fall?

215. scald, scabby. **216. quick,** quick-witted. **236. What,** how. **238. plac'd,** fixed. **240. fleeting,** changeable. **243. worm,** serpent.

264. do his kind, act according to his nature. **292. my other elements,** i.e., earth and water. **296. aspic,** asp.

If thou and nature can so gently part,
The stroke of death is as a lover's pinch,
Which hurts, and is desir'd. Dost thou lie still?
If thus thou vanishest, thou tell'st the world
It is not worth leave-taking.
Char. Dissolve, thick cloud, and rain; that I may say
The gods themselves do weep!
Cleo. This proves me base.
If she first meet the curled Antony,
He 'll make demand of her, and spend that kiss
Which is my heaven to have. Come, thou mortal wretch,
To an asp, which she applies to her breast.
With thy sharp teeth this knot intrinsicate
Of life at once untie. Poor venomous fool,
Be angry, and dispatch. O, couldst thou speak,
That I might hear thee call great Cæsar ass
Unpolicied!
Char. O eastern star!
Cleo. Peace, peace!
Dost thou not see my baby at my breast,
That sucks the nurse asleep?
Char. O, break! O, break!
Cleo. As sweet as balm, as soft as air, as gentle,—
O Antony!—Nay, I will take thee too·
Applying another asp to her arm.
What should I stay— *Dies.*
Char. In this vile world? So, fare thee well!
Now boast thee, death, in thy possession lies
A lass unparallel'd. Downy windows, close;
And golden Phœbus never be beheld
Of eyes again so royal! Your crown 's awry;
I 'll mend it, and then play—

Enter the *Guard,* rushing in.

First Guard. Where 's the Queen?
Char. Speak softly, wake her not.
First Guard. Cæsar hath sent—
Char. Too slow a messenger.
Applies an asp.
O, come apace, dispatch! I partly feel thee.
First Guard. Approach, ho! All 's not well; Cæsar 's beguil'd.
Sec. Guard. There 's Dolabella sent from Cæsar; call him.
First Guard. What work is here! Charmian, is this well done?
Char. It is well done, and fitting for a princess
Descended of so many royal kings.
Ah, soldier! *Charmian dies.*

Re-enter *Dolabella.*

Dol. How goes it here?
Sec. Guard All dead.
Dol. Cæsar, thy thoughts
Touch their effects in this; thyself art coming
To see perform'd the dreaded act which thou
So sought'st to hinder.

Re-enter *Cæsar* and all his train, marching.

All. A way there, a way for Cæsar!
Dol. O sir, you are too sure an augurer;
That you did fear is done.
Cæs. Bravest at the last,
She levell'd at our purposes, and, being royal,
Took her own way. The manner of their deaths?
I do not see them bleed.
Dol. Who was last with them?
First Guard. A simple countryman, that brought her figs.
This was his basket.
Cæs. Poison'd, then.
First Guard. O Cæsar,
This Charmian liv'd but now; she stood and spake.
I found her trimming up the diadem
On her dead mistress. Tremblingly she stood
And on the sudden dropp'd.
Cæs. O noble weakness!
If they had swallow'd poison, 't would appear
By external swelling; but she looks like sleep,
As she would catch another Antony
In her strong toil of grace.
Dol. Here, on her breast,
There is a vent of blood and something blown.
The like is on her arm.
First Guard. This is an aspic's trail; and these fig-leaves
Have slime upon them, such as th' aspic leaves
Upon the caves of Nile.
Cæs. Most probable
That so she died; for her physician tells me
She hath pursu'd conclusions infinite
Of easy ways to die. Take up her bed;
And bear her women from the monument.
She shall be buried by her Antony;
No grave upon the earth shall clip in it
A pair so famous. High events as these
Strike those that make them; and their story is
No less in pity than his glory which
Brought them to be lamented. Our army shall
In solemn show attend this funeral;
And then to Rome. Come, Dolabella, see
High order in this great solemnity.
Exeunt omnes.

306. **mortal,** deadly. 307. **intrinsicate,** intricate. 311. **Unpolicied,** devoid of cunning.

333. **Touch their effects,** realize their fears. 337. **augurer,** prophet. 339. **levell'd at,** aimed at, hence "hit." 352. **something blown,** somewhat swollen. 358. **pursu'd conclusions,** tried experiments.

The Tragedy of Coriolanus

Like the other tragedies, *Coriolanus* is a tragedy of passion, but it differs from the others in important respects. Only here is the catastrophe brought about entirely through the character of the hero. He is pitted against circumstances of his own making, and he struggles alone: he is not, like Macbeth, opposed by fate; his misfortune, unlike Lear's, is not set against a convulsion of nature to give it extension. The play lacks those passages of reflection which bind *Hamlet* to the heart of every spectator, and its hero has neither the warmth nor the imagination of Othello. Yet no one can watch it in the theatre without excitement and awe, and we have Swinburne's assurance that he did not know a "loftier or a more perfect piece of man's work." Whatever *Coriolanus* may lack, it has craftsmanship and nobility in abundance.

Text.—There is no record of a performance of *Coriolanus* in Shakespeare's lifetime, and there was no printed edition before the Folio of 1623. The Folio text is good, in that it was printed from an authentic copy, but there are many printer's errors, chiefly mislineations, which occur most often at the beginnings and ends of speeches. Many of these may result from the printer's misjudgment of Shakespeare's copy, for in his later plays he tended to begin and end his speeches in the middle of the line, and it is probable that the speech headings were not always clear. The chances are that the text was printed from Shakespeare's autograph; the fulness of the stage directions makes this the more likely.

Date.—We have no definite external evidence of the date of composition. Jonson's *The Silent Women,* first acted in 1609, V, iv, 227, may echo *Coriolanus,* II, ii, 105, and "the coal of fire upon the ice" (I, i, 177) may be a recollection of the great frost of 1607-8, when the Thames was frozen over for the first time in more than forty years and "pans of coals" were burnt upon it. This evidence, which would date the play in 1608 or early 1609, is of course indecisive, but it gains conclusiveness from its agreement with the evidence from style and meter, which places the play before *Cymbeline* (1609) and after *Antony and Cleopatra* (1607).

Source.—For this story of fifth century (B.C.) Rome, Shakespeare again turned to North's translation of Plutarch's *Lives,* first printed in English in 1579, and followed his source more closely than he had in *Julius Cæsar* and *Antony and Cleopatra.* In the great declamatory speeches, which are also crises in the play—Coriolanus's denunciation of the "rank-scented meiny," III, i, 63-161; his speech to Aufidius, IV, v, 71-107, quoted below; and Volumnia's appeal to her son, V, iii, 94-182 — Shakespeare transforms North's vivid narrative prose into living dramatic poetry with a minimum of change and, apparently, with that ease of composition which Heminge and Condell described in their epistle to the readers of the First Folio. A comparison of North's version of Coriolanus's address to Aufidius when he transfers his allegiance to the Volsces to lines IV, v, 71-107, will illustrate Shakespeare's complete mastery of his medium at the height of his career.

I am Caius Martius, who hath done to thyself particularly, and to all the Volsces generally, great hurte and mischief, which I cannot denie for my surname of Coriolanus that I beare. For I never had other benefit nor recompence, of all the true and paynefull service I have done and the extreme daunger I have bene in, but this only surname: a good memorie and witnes, of the malice and displeasure thou showldest beare me. In deede the name only remaineth with me: for the rest, the envie and crueltie of the people of Rome have taken from me, by the sufferance of the dastardly nobilitie and magistrates, who have forsaken me, and let me be banished by the people. This extremitie hath now driven me to come as a poore suter, to take thy chimney harthe, not of any hope I have to save my life thereby. For if I had feared death, I would not have come hither to put my life in hazard: but prickt forward with spite and desire I have to be revenged of them that thus have banished me, whom now I beginne to be avenged on, putting my persone betweene thy enemies. Wherefore, if thou hast any harte to be wrecked of the injuries thy enemies have done thee, speede thee now, and let my miserie serve thy turne, and so use it, as my service maye be a benefit to the Volsces: promising thee, that I will fight with a better good will for all you, then ever I dyd when I was against you, knowing that they fight more valiantly, who knowe the force of their enemie, then such as have never proved it. And if it be so that thou dare not, and that thou art wearie to prove fortune any more: then am I also weary to live any lenger. And it were no wisedome in thee, to save the life of him, who hath bene heretofore thy mortall enemie, and whose service now can nothing helpe nor pleasure thee.

What Shakespeare made of this passage is no less appropriate to his purpose than the lines which immediately follow, Aufidius's reply, yet the former is almost pure Plutarch and the latter are entirely his own. Seven scenes in the play have no counterpart in Plutarch. In other scenes Shakespeare has changed and rearranged Plutarch's material, but when his source was dramatic, he made as few changes as he could. No other play of his owes more to its source than *Coriolanus*. This is not because Shakespeare's creative powers were waning, but because he could build his play only upon a certain conception of his hero's character, and this conception made it necessary for him to forego much that is characteristic of his other tragedies.

Belonging to that class of people whom Shakespeare describes in his sonnets as the "lords and owners of their faces," Coriolanus is the most self-sufficient of the tragic heroes, and he cannot therefore command our sympathy to a like degree. His dominant passion is aristocratic pride, and his pride and self-confidence are in turn buoyed up by his relatively poor powers of imagination and introspection. He is the converse of Hamlet. He cannot treat people better than, or even according to, their deserts, for he can imagine no deserts other than those he shares. Being primarily a man of action, he is necessarily free from those inner conflicts which give rise to the poetic outbursts of passion and reflection in the other tragedies. He is, to be sure, eloquent, but since his certainty does not permit him to doubt the justice of his actions, he is most eloquent in scorn. He is none the less the heart of the drama, and the whole play is keyed to his character.

The dramatist's problem in writing *Coriolanus* was to maintain the spectator's sympathetic interest in a play whose hero through repellent pride plans the monstrous destruction of his native city. Denied many of the attractions of the other tragedies, such a play could succeed only by its dignity and the dramatic power of its action. Accordingly there is a single plot which once under way marches to its inevitable conclusion through scenes of Shakespeare's best theatre. Although the dialogue does not pause for reflection or decoration, it achieves an austere beauty of its own. The greater degree of universality which the other tragedies enjoy is achieved by many means—some of them those which Shakespeare has here deliberately foregone—including the spectator's greater opportunity for self-identification with the hero. The most unprincely person will feel that he shares at least something with Hamlet and Lear, the pain, for instance, of misplaced affection. In the presence of these tragedies we do not feel that we are watching only the doom of an individual—nor do we in *Coriolanus,* but it is a narrow escape. Although the passions depicted do not attract us, they are universal; and Shakespeare has been at pains to give his hero as much human warmth as his arrogance would permit.

In Plutarch, Coriolanus is "churlish, uncivil, and altogether unfit for man's conversation." This is not true of Shakespeare's hero. Contrary to his practice, Shakespeare is careful to tell us that Coriolanus's training from childhood has made him what he is. He is never rude to his fellow patricians, and he takes no satisfaction in having surpassed the ablest of them in battle. Courage, integrity, and the aristocratic ideal have been instilled into him. He tells Aufidius that he hates him "worse than a promise-breaker," and he is amazed when his mother tells him to assume a regard for the citizens he does not feel. Because he does not realize that he has achieved his ideal, he cannot bear to listen to his praises. When he is hailed as the conqueror, he replies, "I will go wash." He does not even know that he is proud.[1]

From a bare suggestion in Plutarch, Shakespeare has created Virgilia in order to show her steadfast devotion to her husband and his fidelity to her. Their love is almost wordless: she is his "gracious silence," and he cannot unpack his heart to her; yet their love is implicit in every scene in which she appears, creating for him a sympathy unfelt in Shakespeare's source. In the end it is the combined power of his affection and integrity which make him relent his purpose in the face of

[1] For a fuller discussion of his character, see A. C. Bradley, "Coriolanus," The British Academy Shakespeare Lecture, Oxford Press, 1912.

almost certain death. When his wife and mother plead with him for the delivery of Rome, he is moved both by their pleas and that they should plead. That they whom he has alone supremely honored should kneel to him is more than he can bear:

What have you done? Behold! the heavens do
ope,
The gods look down, and this unnatural scene
They laugh at. Oh my mother! mother! O!
You have won a happy victory to Rome;
But, for your son, believe it, O believe it,
Most dangerously you have with him prevail'd,
If not most mortal to him. But let it come.

It is only a short-sighted view of Shakespeare that can agree with Hazlitt that "The whole dramatic moral of *Coriolanus* is that those who have little shall have less, and that those who have much shall take all that the others have left." The play is not a study in "black and white." It is a play in which the erring hero, if he is to remain a hero, must be greatly provoked; but we are not asked to sympathize wholly with either of the contending forces. Coriolanus is neither an egotist nor a tyrant. He can no more permit those he honors to kneel to him than he can make himself bow to the "rank-scented many."

The character of the citizens, like that of the hero, is part of the dramatic plan, and the drama springs from the conflict between them. Shakespeare has made it clear that while Coriolanus neither can nor will understand the citizens, they have no means of understanding him. They never see him as his fellow patricians see him. They know only that he is a courageous hero and that he reviles them. Urged on by the tribunes, they are not permitted to see that Coriolanus in his pride scorns them the more because he needs their voices so much. The inevitability of the tragedy lies in each side's continued ignorance of the other. We are not asked to scorn the citizens. They are starving, and in their extremity they demand food; and they want to preserve their constitutional rights. They quite reasonably fear the election of Coriolanus, but they will elect him anyway if only he will conform to custom, or make a show of conforming, to indicate that he is not completely hostile to them.

They are a kindly group of men. Although one of them justifiably accuses him of pride, another says that "what he cannot help in his nature, you cannot account a vice in him." Their fault is that they do not have much mind. Like the Englishmen they are, they will elect him if only he will offer them the hope of muddling through. They cannot hold to any fixed purpose, and so they become the victims of their own kindly impetuosity and the rigidity and machinations of their superiors. It is not in hatred of them that Shakespeare makes them agree that "that we did, we did for the best." What they say is true. Like Coriolanus, they were dreadfully misguided, but in their simple way they did what it seemed to them they should do. A misguided citizen is not necessarily a subject for greater scorn than a misguided patrician. This should be—and is not—especially clear to all readers of Shakespeare. In his sonnets Shakespeare names some of the things that make him long for death; one of them is "simple truth miscalled simplicity."

It should be noticed that Shakespeare gives his strongest condemnation of the common people to the headstrong Coriolanus and not to Brutus, who had more justification. As it has often been observed, he does not place such a condemnation on the lips of any of his more attractive characters. And it is not reasonable that the creator of Dogberry and Verges, of Bottom, of the faithful servant in *Lear,* of Adam in *As You Like It,* and the whole army of lovable ne'er-do-wells that swarm through the history plays should condemn the common people out of hand. It is nothing to the point that he is forever noting the unpleasant odor of the rabble. There is such a thing as historic fact.

Living when he did, Shakespeare could no more be democratic or anti-democratic than he could be a motorist. He quite obviously believed in the monarchical form of government and in an ordered society in which the classes were divided and the divisions fixed. He feared the disturbance of this order, believing that "degree" was part of the divine plan. And so deep-rooted was this passion for order that he habitually conceived ultimate horror in terms of chaos:

Perdition catch my soul,
But I do love thee! and when I love thee not,
Chaos is come again.

To describe the social order he uses a simile

familiar to writers since the twelfth century: comparison to the parts of the body. It has not been noticed often enough that while this comparison (used by Menenius in the first scene) establishes the superior function of the senate, it also assigns a necessary function to the populace, and that these functions are interdependent. This underlying conception of a fixed social order as a human embodiment of the universal plan lends a degree of dignity to the populace and keeps Coriolanus well on this side of the insufferable when he says,

> What's the matter,
> That in these several places of the city
> You cry against the noble senate, who,
> *Under the gods,* keep you in awe, which else
> Would feed on one another?

It is his allegiance to his aristocratic ideal and his inadequate concept of "degree" which brings Coriolanus to his end. His death, as Bradley has observed, moves us with awe but not, as in the other tragedies, with pity. And this has necessarily arisen from the subject and the treatment it imposed upon the dramatist. But after all, Shakespeare *chose* the subject for this his last tragedy. No doubt it appealed to him at that time because the point of view in which the greater tragedies had been conceived was passing, and he was less inclined to interpret the actions of his men and women as the expression of all-embracing universal forces.

Stage History.—For the first two centuries of its history, *Coriolanus* was not a popular play, but although we have no record of a production before 1682, we need not conclude that it was never produced before that time. Its first recorded performance, an adaptation by Nahum Tate, *The Ingratitude of a Commonwealth: or, the Fall of Caius Martius Coriolanus,* follows Shakespeare's play rather closely for its first four acts. The fifth act degenerates into melodrama. Aufidius' Lieutenant (IV, vii) becomes the unsuccessful lover of Virgilia, Volumnia goes wildly mad, and there is a general slaughter. The play was not a success. Another adaptation made by John Dennis in 1719, *The Invader of His Country: or, The Fatal Resentment,* seems to have been acted only three times. It used fewer of Shakespeare's lines than Tate had used, but it did not indulge in his elaboration of the plot.

A new dramatic version owing little to Shakespeare's play was made by James Thomson, author of the *Seasons,* and acted at Covent Garden shortly after his death. It is in no way the equal of Shakespeare's version, and would have no part in this account if later versions had not mingled parts of it with Shakespeare's tragedy. Various blends of Shakespeare and Thomson were successfully acted in England and America throughout the eighteenth and early nineteenth centuries. The version used by Kemble and Mrs. Siddons followed Shakespeare for the first three acts but used a strong infusion of Thomson in the last two. In this play these great actors scored one of their greatest successes, repeating their performance on many occasions over a long period of years. In it, in 1817, Kemble took leave of the stage. In 1820, *Coriolanus,* with Shakespeare's text almost restored, was performed by Kean. Through the first half of the century, when the English theatre produced fine actors and no playwrights, the play was popular, there being productions by Kean, Macready, John Vanderhoff, Samuel Phelps, and others; but with the coming of the new drama, its popularity waned, although there were productions by Sir Henry Irving and Sir F. R. Benson. In America the most successful performances were by Booth and Edwin Forrest.

In the present century the play has been successfully acted many times in France and Germany. In 1937-38 a presentation by the New York Division of the Federal Theater Project clearly demonstrated how a vigorous drama can triumph over inadequate production.

THE TRAGEDY OF CORIOLANUS

Dramatis Personæ

Caius Marcius, afterwards *Caius Marcius Coriolanus.*
Titus Lartius, / *Cominius,* } generals against the Volscians.
Menenius Agrippa, friend to *Coriolanus.*
Sicinius Velutus, / *Junius Brutus,* } tribunes of the people.
Young *Marcius,* son to *Coriolanus.*
Nicanor, a Roman.
A Roman Herald.
Tullus Aufidius, general of the Volscians.
Lieutenant to *Aufidius.*
Adrian, a Volscian.
Conspirators with *Aufidius.*
A Citizen of Antium.
Two Volscian Guards.

Volumnia, mother to *Coriolanus.*
Virgilia, wife to *Coriolanus.*
Valeria, friend to *Virgilia.*
Gentlewoman, attending on *Virgilia.*

Roman and Volscian Senators, Patricians, Ædiles, Lictors, Soldiers, Citizens, Messengers, Servants to Aufidius, and other Attendants.

SCENE: *Rome and the neighbourhood; Corioli and the neighbourhood; Antium.*

ACT I. SCENE I. *Rome. A street.*

Enter a company of mutinous *Citizens,* with staves, clubs, and other weapons.

First Cit. Before we proceed any further, hear me speak.

All. Speak, speak.

First Cit. You are all resolved rather to die than to famish?

All. Resolved, resolved.

First Cit. First, you know Caius Marcius is chief enemy to the people.

All. We know 't, we know 't.

First Cit. Let us kill him, and we 'll have corn at our own price. Is 't a verdict?

All. No more talking on 't; let it be done. Away, away!

Sec. Cit. One word, good citizens.

First Cit. We are accounted poor citizens, the patricians good. What authority surfeits on would relieve us. If they would yield us but the superfluity while it were wholesome, we might guess they relieved us humanely; but they think we are too dear: the leanness that afflicts us, the object of our misery, is as an inventory to particularize their abundance; our sufferance is a gain to them. Let us revenge this with our pikes, ere we become rakes; for the gods know I speak this in hunger for bread, not in thirst for revenge.

Sec. Cit. Would you proceed especially against Caius Marcius?

All. Against him first; he 's a very dog to the commonalty.

Sec. Cit. Consider you what services he has done for his country?

First Cit. Very well; and could be content to give him good report for 't, but that he pays himself with being proud.

Sec. Cit. Nay, but speak not maliciously.

First Cit. I say unto you, what he hath done famously, he did it to that end. Though soft-conscienced men can be content to say it was for his country, he did it to please his mother, and to be partly proud; which he is, even to the altitude of his virtue.

Sec. Cit. What he cannot help in his nature, you account a vice in him. You must in no way say he is covetous.

First Cit. If I must not, I need not be barren of accusations; he hath faults, with surplus, to tire in repetition. [*Shouts within.*] What shouts are these? The other side o' th' city is risen; why stay we prating here? To the Capitol!

All. Come, come.

First Cit. Soft! who comes here?

Enter *Menenius Agrippa.*

Sec. Cit. Worthy Menenius Agrippa, one that hath always loved the people.

First Cit. He 's one honest enough; would all the rest were so!

19. guess, suppose. **20. dear,** expensive. **21. object,** spectacle. **22. particularize,** itemize. **23. sufferance,** suffering. **24. rakes,** i.e., lean.

40. partly proud, partly to be proud.

Men. What work 's, my countrymen, in hand? Where go you
With bats and clubs? The matter? Speak, I pray you.

Sec. Cit. Our business is not unknown to th' Senate: they have had inkling this fortnight what we intend to do, which now we 'll show 'em in deeds. They say poor suitors have strong breaths; they shall know we have strong arms too.

Men. Why, masters, my good friends, mine honest neighbours,
Will you undo yourselves?

Sec. Cit. We cannot, sir, we are undone already.

Men. I tell you, friends, most charitable care
Have the patricians of you. For your wants,
Your suffering in this dearth, you may as well
Strike at the heaven with your staves as lift them
Against the Roman state, whose course will on
The way it takes, cracking ten thousand curbs
Of more strong link asunder than can ever
Appear in your impediment. For the dearth,
The gods, not the patricians, make it, and
Your knees to them (not arms) must help. Alack,
You are transported by calamity
Thither where more attends you, and you slander
The helms o' th' state, who care for you like fathers
When you curse them as enemies.

Sec. Cit. Care for us? True, indeed! They ne'er car'd for us yet: suffer us to famish, and their store-houses crammed with grain; make edicts for usury, to support usurers; repeal daily any wholesome act established against the rich, and provide more piercing statutes daily, to chain up and restrain the poor. If the wars eat us not up, they will; and there 's all the love they bear us.

Men. Either you must
Confess yourselves wondrous malicious,
Or be accus'd of folly. I shall tell you
A pretty tale. It may be you have heard it;
But, since it serves my purpose, I will venture
To stale 't a little more.

Sec. Cit. Well, I 'll hear it, sir; yet you must not think to fob off our disgrace with a tale; but, an 't please you, deliver.

Men. There was a time when all the body's members
Rebell'd against the belly; thus accus'd it:
That only like a gulf it did remain
I' th' midst o' th' body, idle and unactive,
Still cupboarding the viand, never bearing
Like labour with the rest, where th' other instruments
Did see and hear, devise, instruct, walk, feel,
And, mutually participate, did minister
Unto the appetite and affection common
Of the whole body. The belly answer'd—

Sec. Cit. Well, sir, what answer made the belly?

Men. Sir, I shall tell you. With a kind of smile,
Which ne'er came from the lungs, but even thus—
For, look you, I may make the belly smile
As well as speak—it tauntingly replied
To th' discontented members, the mutinous parts
That envied his receipt; even so most fitly
As you malign our senators for that
They are not such as you.

Sec. Cit. Your belly's answer? What!
The kingly-crowned head, the vigilant eye,
The counsellor heart, the arm our soldier,
Our steed the leg, the tongue our trumpeter,
With other muniments and petty helps
In this our fabric, if that they—

Men. What then?
'Fore me, this fellow speaks! What then? what then?

Sec. Cit. Should by the cormorant belly be restrain'd,
Who is the sink o' th' body,—

Men. Well, what then?

Sec. Cit. The former agents, if they did complain,
What could the belly answer?

Men. I will tell you.
If you 'll bestow a small—of what you have little—
Patience a while, you 'st hear the belly's answer.

Sec. Cit. Y' are long about it.

Men. Note me this, good friend;
Your most grave belly was deliberate,
Not rash like his accusers, and thus answered:
"True is it, my incorporate friends," quoth he,
"That I receive the general food at first
Which you do live upon; and fit it is,
Because I am the store-house and the shop
Of the whole body. But, if you do remember,
I send it through the rivers of your blood,
Even to the court, the heart, to th' seat o' th' brain;

72. curbs, chains on bridles. **79. helms,** pilots. **95. stale,** make stale. **97. fob off our disgrace,** trick us out of our sense of being ill-treated. **101. gulf,** devouring whirlpool.

106. participate, co-operating. **107. affection,** inclination. **111. smile . . . lungs,** i.e., a smile, not a laugh. **116. his receipt,** what he received. **even so most fitly,** even as fitly. **122. muniments,** furnishings. **125. cormorant,** ravenous. **126. sink,** cesspool. **130. you 'st,** you shall. **134. incorporate,** joined in one body. **137. shop,** workshop.

And, through the cranks and offices of man,
The strongest nerves and small inferior veins
From me receive that natural competency
Whereby they live. And though that all at once,
You, my good friends,"—this says the belly, mark me,—

Sec. Cit. Ay, sir; well, well.

Men. "Though all at once cannot
See what I do deliver out to each,
Yet I can make my audit up, that all
From me do back receive the flour of all,
And leave me but the bran." What say you to 't?

Sec. Cit. It was an answer. How apply you this?

Men. The senators of Rome are this good belly,
And you the mutinous members; for examine
Their counsels and their cares, disgest things rightly
Touching the weal o' th' common, you shall find
No public benefit which you receive
But it proceeds or comes from them to you
And no way from yourselves. What do you think,
You, the great toe of this assembly?

Sec. Cit. I the great toe! Why the great toe?

Men. For that, being one o' th' lowest, basest, poorest,
Of this most wise rebellion, thou goest foremost;
Thou rascal, that art worst in blood to run,
Lead'st first to win some vantage.
But make you ready your stiff bats and clubs;
Rome and her rats are at the point of battle,
The one side must have bale.

Enter *Caius Marcius.*

Hail, noble Marcius!

Mar. Thanks. What 's the matter, you dissentious rogues,
That, rubbing the poor itch of your opinion,
Make yourselves scabs?

Sec. Cit. We have ever your good word.

Mar. He that will give good words to thee will flatter
Beneath abhorring. What would you have, you curs,
That like nor peace nor war? The one affrights you,
The other makes you proud. He that trusts to you,
Where he should find you lions, finds you hares;
Where foxes, geese. You are no surer, no,
Than is the coal of fire upon the ice,
Or hailstone in the sun. Your virtue is
To make him worthy whose offence subdues him,
And curse that justice did it. Who deserves greatness
Deserves your hate; and your affections are
A sick man's appetite, who desires most that
Which would increase his evil. He that depends
Upon your favours swims with fins of lead
And hews down oaks with rushes. Hang ye! Trust ye?
With every minute you do change a mind,
And call him noble that was now your hate,
Him vile that was your garland. What 's the matter,
That in these several places of the city
You cry against the noble Senate, who,
(Under the gods) keep you in awe, which else
Would feed on one another? What 's their seeking?

Men. For corn at their own rates; whereof, they say,
The city is well stor'd.

Mar. Hang 'em! They say!
They 'll sit by the fire, and presume to know
What 's done i' th' Capitol; who 's like to rise,
Who thrives, and who declines; side factions, and give out
Conjectural marriages; making parties strong,
And feebling such as stand not in their liking
Below their cobbled shoes. They say there 's grain enough!
Would the nobility lay aside their ruth
And let me use my sword, I 'd make a quarry
With thousands of these quarter'd slaves, as high
As I could pick my lance.

Men. Nay, these are almost thoroughly persuaded;
For though abundantly they lack discretion,
Yet are they passing cowardly. But, I beseech you,
What says the other troop?

Mar. They are dissolv'd, hang 'em!
They said they were an-hungry; sigh'd forth proverbs,
That hunger broke stone walls, that dogs must eat,

141. cranks, winding passages. **offices,** service rooms as opposed to living quarters. **143. competency,** sufficiency. **154. disgest,** digest. **155. weal . . . common,** common weal or welfare. **163. rascal,** lean deer. **worst in blood,** in poor condition. **167. bale,** disaster. **170. scabs,** (1) sores. (2) worthless fellows.

179. To take up the cause of the punished offender and curse the justice that punished him. **187. now,** just now. **197. side,** espouse. **give out . . . marriages,** proclaim conjectural political alliances. **198. parties,** factions favored by them. **201. ruth,** pity. **202. quarry,** heap of slaughtered game. **204. pick,** pitch.

That meat was made for mouths, that the gods sent not
Corn for the rich men only. With these shreds
They vented their complainings; which being answer'd,
And a petition granted them,—a strange one
To break the heart of generosity,
And make bold power look pale,—they threw their caps
As they would hang them on the horns o' th' moon,
Shouting their emulation.

Men. What is granted them?

Mar. Five tribunes to defend their vulgar wisdoms,
Of their own choice. One 's Junius Brutus,
Sicinius Velutus, and I know not—'Sdeath!
The rabble should have first unroof'd the city,
Ere so prevail'd with me: it will in time
Win upon power and throw forth greater themes
For insurrection's arguing.

Men. This is strange.

Mar. Go, get you home, you fragments!

Enter a *Mesenger,* hastily.

Mess. Where 's Caius Marcius?

Mar. Here. What 's the matter?

Mess. The news is, sir, the Volsces are in arms.

Mar. I am glad on 't. Then we shall ha' means to vent
Our musty superfluity. See, our best elders.

Enter *Cominius, Titus Lartius,* with other *Senators; Junius Brutus* and *Sicinius Velutus.*

First Sen. Marcius, 't is true that you have lately told us;
The Volsces are in arms.

Mar. They have a leader,
Tullus Aufidius, that will put you to 't.
I sin in envying his nobility,
And were I anything but what I am,
I would wish me only he.

Com. You have fought together?

Mar. Were half to half the world by th' ears and he
Upon my party, I 'd revolt, to make
Only my wars with him. He is a lion
That I am proud to hunt.

First Sen. Then, worthy Marcius,
Attend upon Cominius to these wars.

Com. It is your former promise.

Mar. Sir, it is;
And I am constant. Titus Lartius, thou
Shalt see me once more strike at Tullus' face.
What, art thou stiff? Stand'st out?

Lart. No, Caius Marcius;
I 'll lean upon one crutch and fight with t' other,
Ere stay behind this business.

Men. O, true-bred!

First Sen. Your company to th' Capitol; where, I know,
Our greatest friends attend us.

Lart. [*To Cominius.*] Lead you on.
[*To Marcius.*] Follow Cominius; we must follow you;
Right worthy you priority.

Com. Noble Marcius!

First Sen. [*To the Citizens.*] Hence to your homes; begone!

Mar. Nay, let them follow.
The Volsces have much corn; take these rats thither
To gnaw their garners. Worshipful mutiners,
Your valour puts well forth; pray, follow.

Citizens steal away. Exeunt all but Sicinius and Brutus.

Sic. Was ever man so proud as is this Marcius?

Bru. He has no equal.

Sic. When we were chosen tribunes for the people,—

Bru. Mark'd you his lip and eyes?

Sic. Nay, but his taunts.

Bru. Being mov'd, he will not spare to gird the gods.

Sic. Be-mock the modest moon.

Bru. The present wars devour him! He is grown
Too proud to be so valiant.

Sic. Such a nature,
Tickled with good success, disdains the shadow
Which he treads on at noon. But I do wonder
His insolence can brook to be commanded
Under Cominius.

Bru. Fame, at the which he aims,
In whom already he 's well grac'd, cannot
Better be held nor more attain'd than by
A place below the first; for what miscarries
Shall be the general's fault, though he perform
To th' utmost of a man, and giddy censure
Will then cry out of Marcius, "O, if he
Had borne the business!"

Sic. Besides, if things go well,
Opinion that so sticks on Marcius shall
Of his demerits rob Cominius.

Bru. Come.
Half all Cominius' honours are to Marcius,
Though Marcius earn'd them not, and all his faults

213. **answer'd,** satisfied. 215. **generosity,** the gentry. 224. **power,** constituted authority. 226. **fragments,** term of contempt. 228. **Volsces,** the Volsci, a Latin people. 229. **vent,** get rid of.

255. **puts well forth,** shows well. 260. **gird,** make fun of. 263. **to be,** of being. 264. **disdains . . . noon,** i.e., his own shadow. 272. **giddy censure,** fickle opinion. 276. **demerits,** deserts, merits.

To Marcius shall be honours, though indeed
In aught he merit not.
Sic. Let 's hence, and hear
How the dispatch is made, and in what fashion,
More than his singularity, he goes
Upon this present action.
Bru. Let 's along. *Exeunt.*

Scene II. *Corioli. The Senate-house.*

Enter *Tullus Aufidius* with *Senators* of Corioli.

First Sen. So, your opinion is, Aufidius,
That they of Rome are enter'd in our counsels
And know how we proceed.
Auf. Is it not yours?
What ever have been thought on in this state,
That could be brought to bodily act ere Rome
Had circumvention? 'T is not four days gone
Since I heard thence; these are the words:—I think
I have the letter here; yes, here it is:—
[*Reads.*] "They have press'd a power, but it is not known
Whether for east or west: the dearth is great;
The people mutinous; and it is rumour'd,
Cominius, Marcius your old enemy,
(Who is of Rome worse hated than of you)
And Titus Lartius, a most valiant Roman,
These three lead on this preparation
Whither 't is bent. Most likely 't is for you;
Consider of it."
First Sen. Our army 's in the field.
We never yet made doubt but Rome was ready
To answer us.
Auf. Nor did you think it folly
To keep your great pretences veil'd till when
They needs must show themselves; which in the hatching,
It seem'd, appear'd to Rome. By the discovery
We shall be shorten'd in our aim, which was
To take in many towns ere almost Rome
Should know we were afoot.
Sec. Sen. Noble Aufidius,
Take your commission; hie you to your bands;
Let us alone to guard Corioli
If they set down before 's: for the remove
Bring up your army; but, I think, you 'll find
Th'ave not prepar'd for us.
Auf. O, doubt not that;
I speak from certainties. Nay, more,
Some parcels of their power are forth already,
And only hitherward. I leave your honours.
If we and Caius Marcius chance to meet,
'T is sworn between us we shall ever strike
Till one can do no more.
All. The gods assist you!
Auf. And keep your honours safe!
First Sen. Farewell.
Sec. Sen. Farewell.
All. Farewell. *Exeunt omnes.*

Scene III. *Rome. A room in the house of Marcius.*

Enter *Volumnia* and *Virgilia:* they set them down on two low stools, and sew.

Vol. I pray you, daughter, sing; or express yourself in a more comfortable sort. If my son were my husband, I should freelier rejoice in that absence wherein he won honour than in the embracements of his bed where he would show most love. When yet he was but tender-bodied and the only son of my womb, when youth with comeliness plucked all gaze his way, when for a day of kings' entreaties a mother should not sell him an hour from her beholding, I, considering how honour would become such a person, that it was no better than picture-like to hang by th' wall, if renown made it not stir, was pleased to let him seek danger where he was like to find fame. To a cruel war I sent him; from whence he returned, his brows bound with oak. I tell thee, daughter, I sprang not more in joy at first hearing he was a man-child than now in first seeing he had proved himself a man.

Vir. But had he died in the business, madam; how then?

Vol. Then his good report should have been my son; I therein would have found issue. Hear me profess sincerely: had I a dozen sons, each in my love alike and none less dear than thine and my good Marcius, I had rather had eleven die nobly for their country than one voluptuously surfeit out of action.

Enter a *Gentlewoman.*

Gent. Madam, the Lady Valeria is come to visit you.

Vir. Beseech you, give me leave to retire myself.

Vol. Indeed, you shall not.
Methinks I hear hither your husband's drum,
See him pluck Aufidius down by th' hair,
As children from a bear, the Volsces shunning him.

282. **More . . . singularity,** aside from his peculiarity. **Scene ii:** 2. **enter'd in,** privy to. 6. **circumvention,** means to circumvent. 9. **press'd a power,** conscripted troops. 20. **pretences,** plans. 23. **be shorten'd in,** fall short of. 28. **remove,** raising the siege.

2. **comfortable sort,** cheerful manner. 11. **person,** beauty of body. 16. **oak,** oak-leaves, decoration for valor. 27. **out of action,** inactive. 32. **hither,** sounding as far as here.

Methinks I see him stamp thus, and call thus:
"Come on, you cowards! you were got in fear,
Though you were born in Rome." His bloody brow
With his mail'd hand then wiping, forth he goes,
Like to a harvest-man that 's task'd to mow
Or all or lose his hire.

Vir. His bloody brow! O Jupiter, no blood!

Vol. Away, you fool! it more becomes a man
Than gilt his trophy. The breasts of Hecuba,
When she did suckle Hector, look'd not lovelier
Than Hector's forehead when it spit forth blood
At Grecian sword, contemning. Tell Valeria,
We are fit to bid her welcome.

Exit Gentlewoman.

Vir. Heavens bless my lord from fell Aufidius!

Vol. He 'll beat Aufidius' head below his knee
And tread upon his neck.

Enter *Valeria,* with an Usher and Gentlewoman.

Val. My ladies both, good day to you.

Vol. Sweet madam.

Vir. I am glad to see your ladyship.

Val. How do you both? You are manifest house-keepers. What are you sewing here? A fine spot, in good faith. How does your little son?

Vir. I thank your ladyship; well, good madam.

Vol. He had rather see the swords and hear a drum than look upon his schoolmaster.

Val. O' my word, the father's son: I 'll swear, 't is a very pretty boy. O' my troth, I looked upon him o' Wednesday half an hour together; has such a confirmed countenance. I saw him run after a gilded butterfly; and when he caught it, he let it go again; and after it again; and over and over he comes, and up again; catched it again; or whether his fall enraged him, or how 't was, he did so set his teeth and tear it. O, I warrant, how he mammocked it!

Vol. One on 's father's moods.

Val. Indeed, la, 't is a noble child.

Vir. A crack, madam.

Val. Come, lay aside your stitchery; I must have you play the idle housewife with me this afternoon.

Vir. No, good madam; I will not out of doors.

Val. Not out of doors!

Vol. She shall, she shall.

Vir. Indeed, no, by your patience; I 'll not over the threshold till my lord return from the wars.

Val. Fie, you confine yourself most unreasonably. Come, you must go visit the good lady that lies in.

Vir. I will wish her speedy strength, and visit her with my prayers; but I cannot go thither.

Vol. Why, I pray you?

Vir. 'T is not to save labour, nor that I want love.

Val. You would be another Penelope: yet, they say, all the yarn she spun in Ulysses' absence did but fill Ithaca full of moths. Come; I would your cambric were sensible as your finger, that you might leave pricking it for pity. Come, you shall go with us.

Vir. No, good madam, pardon me; indeed, I will not forth.

Val. In truth, la, go with me; and I 'll tell you excellent news of your husband.

Vir. O, good madam, there can be none yet.

Val. Verily, I do not jest with you; there came news from him last night.

Vir. Indeed, madam?

Val. In earnest, it 's true; I heard a senator speak it. Thus it is: the Volsces have an army forth; against whom Cominius the general is gone, with one part of our Roman power. Your lord and Titus Lartius are set down before their city Corioli; they nothing doubt prevailing and to make it brief wars. This is true, on mine honour; and so, I pray, go with us.

Vir. Give me excuse, good madam; I will obey you in everything hereafter.

Vol. Let her alone, lady. As she is now, she will but disease our better mirth.

Val. In troth, I think she would. Fare you well, then. Come, good sweet lady. Prithee, Virgilia, turn thy solemness out o' door, and go along with us.

Vir. No, at a word, madam; indeed, I must not. I wish you much mirth.

Val. Well, then, farewell. *Exeunt Ladies.*

Scene IV. *Before Corioli.*

Enter, with drum and colours, *Marcius, Titus Lartius,* with Captains and Soldiers as before the city Corioli. To them a *Messenger.*

Mar. Yonder comes news. A wager they have met.

36. **got,** begot. 39. **task'd,** employed. 43. **gilt his trophy,** gilding becomes his monument. **Hecuba,** Queen of Troy. 46. **contemning,** showing defiance. 48. **fell,** cruel. 55. **house-keepers,** stay-at-homes. 56. **spot,** pattern for embroidery. 64. **confirmed,** determined. 71. **mammocked,** tore in pieces. 72. **on 's,** of his. 74. **crack,** imp.

91. **want,** am lacking in. 95. **sensible,** sensitive. 117. **disease,** make uneasy. 122. **at a word,** positively.

Lart. My horse to yours, no.
Mar. 'T is done.
Lart. Agreed.
Mar. Say, has our general met the enemy?
Mess. They lie in view; but have not spoke as yet.
Lart. So, the good horse is mine.
Mar. I 'll buy him of you.
Lart. No, I 'll nor sell nor give him; lend you him I will
For half a hundred years. Summon the town.
Mar. How far off lie these armies?
Mess. Within this mile and half.
Mar. Then shall we hear their 'larum, and they ours.
Now, Mars, I prithee, make us quick in work,
That we with smoking swords may march from hence
To help our fielded friends! Come, blow thy blast.

They sound a parley. Enter two *Senators* with others on the walls.

Tullus Aufidius, is he within your walls?
First Sen. No, nor a man that fears you less than he,
That 's lesser than a little. [*Drum afar off.*] Hark! our drums
Are bringing forth our youth. We 'll break our walls,
Rather than they shall pound us up. Our gates,
Which yet seem shut, we have but pinn'd with rushes;
They 'll open of themselves. [*Alarum afar off.*] Hark you, far off!
There is Aufidius; list, what work he makes
Amongst your cloven army.
Mar. O, they are at it!
Lart. Their noise be our instruction. Ladders, ho!

Enter the army of the Volsces.

Mar. They fear us not, but issue forth their city.
Now put your shields before your hearts, and fight
With hearts more proof than shields. Advance, brave Titus!
They do disdain us much beyond our thoughts,
Which makes me sweat with wrath. Come on, my fellows!
He that retires, I 'll take him for a Volsce,
And he shall feel mine edge.

Alarum. The Romans are beat back to their trenches. Re-enter *Marcius,* cursing.

Mar. All the contagion of the south light on you,
You shames of Rome! you herd of—Boils and plagues
Plaster you o'er, that you may be abhorr'd
Further than seen, and one infect another
Against the wind a mile! You souls of geese,
That bear the shapes of men, how have you run
From slaves that apes would beat! Pluto and hell!
All hurt behind! Backs red, and faces pale
With flight and agued fear! Mend and charge home,
Or, by the fires of heaven, I 'll leave the foe
And make my wars on you. Look to 't; come on!
If you 'll stand fast, we 'll beat them to their wives,
As they us to our trenches.

Another alarum. The Volsces fly and *Marcius* follows them to the gates.

So, now the gates are ope; now prove good seconds.
'T is for the followers fortune widens them,
Not for the fliers: mark me, and do the like.
First Sol. Fool-hardiness; not I.
Sec. Sol. Nor I.
Marcius enters the gates and is shut in.
First Sol. See, they have shut him in.
Alarum continues.
All. To th' pot, I warrant him.

Re-enter *Titus Lartius.*

Lart. What is become of Marcius?
All. Slain, sir, doubtless.
First Sol. Following the fliers at the very heels,
With them he enters; who, upon the sudden,
Clapp'd to their gates: he is himself alone,
To answer all the city.
Lart. O noble fellow!
Who sensibly outdares his senseless sword,
And, when it bows, stands up. Thou art left, Marcius;
A carbuncle entire, as big as thou art,
Were not so rich a jewel. Thou wast a soldier
Even to Cato's wish, not fierce and terrible
Only in strokes; but, with thy grim looks and
The thunder-like percussion of thy sounds,

4. **spoke,** i.e., fought. 12. **fielded,** encamped in the field. 14. **less,** sense requires **more.** 17. **pound . . . up,** impound. 25. **proof,** tough, impenetrable.

30. **south,** south wind (supposed to breed disease). 38. **Mend,** reform (your ranks). 43. **seconds,** assistants. 47. **To th' pot,** i.e., to destruction. 52. **answer,** withstand. 53. **sensibly,** though sensitive to pain. 57. **Cato's,** Cato the Censor.

Thou mad'st thine enemies shake, as if the world
Were feverous and did tremble.

Re-enter *Marcius,* bleeding, assaulted by the enemy.

First Sol. Look, sir.
Lart. O, 't is Marcius!
Let 's fetch him off, or make remain alike.
They fight, and all enter the city.

Scene V. *Corioli. A street.*

Enter certain *Romans,* with spoils.

First Rom. This will I carry to Rome.
Sec. Rom. And I this.
Third Rom. A murrain on 't! I took this for silver. *Exeunt. Alarum continues still afar off.*

Enter *Marcius* and *Titus Lartius* with a Trumpet.

Mar. See here these movers that do prize their hours
At a crack'd drachma! Cushions, leaden spoons,
Irons of a doit, doublets that hangmen would
Bury with those that wore them, these base slaves,
Ere yet the fight be done, pack up. Down with them!
And hark, what noise the general makes! To him!
There is the man of my soul's hate, Aufidius,
Piercing our Romans; then, valiant Titus, take
Convenient numbers to make good the city;
Whilst I, with those that have the spirit, will haste
To help Cominius.
Lart. Worthy sir, thou bleed'st.
Thy exercise hath been too violent for
A second course of fight.
Mar. Sir, praise me not,
My work hath yet not warm'd me; fare you well.
The blood I drop is rather physical
Than dangerous to me. To Aufidius thus
I will appear, and fight.
Lart. Now the fair goddess, Fortune,
Fall deep in love with thee; and her great charms
Misguide thy opposers' swords! Bold gentleman,
Prosperity be thy page!
Mar. Thy friend no less
Than those she placeth highest! So, farewell.
Lart. Thou worthiest Marcius!
Exit Marcius.
Go, sound thy trumpet in the market-place;
Call thither all the officers o' th' town,
Where they shall know our mind. Away!
Exeunt.

Scene VI. *Near the camp of Cominius.*

Enter *Cominius,* as it were in retire, with soldiers.

Com. Breathe you, my friends; well fought. We are come off
Like Romans, neither foolish in our stands,
Nor cowardly in retire. Believe me, sirs,
We shall be charg'd again. Whiles we have struck,
By interims and conveying gusts we have heard
The charges of our friends. Ye Roman gods!
Lead their successes as we wish our own,
That both our powers, with smiling fronts encount'ring,
May give you thankful sacrifice.

Enter a *Messenger.*

Thy news?
Mess. The citizens of Corioli have issued
And given to Lartius and to Marcius battle.
I saw our party to their trenches driven,
And then I came away.
Com. Though thou speak'st truth,
Methinks thou speak'st not well. How long is 't since?
Mess. Above an hour, my lord.
Com. 'T is not a mile; briefly we heard their drums.
How couldst thou in a mile confound an hour,
And bring thy news so late?
Mess. Spies of the Volsces
Held me in chase, that I was forc'd to wheel
Three or four miles about, else had I, sir,
Half an hour since brought my report.

Enter *Marcius.*

Com. Who 's yonder,
That does appear as he were flay'd? O gods!
He has the stamp of Marcius; and I have
Before-time seen him thus.
Mar. Come I too late?

62. **make remain alike,** make our stay (remain) like his, i.e., share his fate. **Scene v: 4. movers,** cowards. **6. drachma,** Grecian silver coin. **7. of a doit,** worth a doit (small coin). **doublets . . . them,** the hangman was allowed the clothes of the prisoner. **10. the general,** Cominius. **19. physical,** medicinal, beneficial to health.

24. Thy friend, may she (prosperity) be thy friend. **Scene vi: 5. By interims,** at intervals. **gusts, i.e., of** wind. **16. briefly,** recently. **17. confound,** waste.

Com. The shepherd knows not thunder from a tabor
More than I know the sound of Marcius' tongue
From every meaner man.
Mar. Come I too late?
Com. Ay, if you come not in the blood of others,
But mantled in your own.
Mar. O, let me clip ye
In arms as sound as when I woo'd, in heart
As merry as when our nuptial day was done,
And tapers burn'd to bedward!
Com. Flower of warriors,
How is 't with Titus Lartius?
Mar. As with a man busied about decrees:
Condemning some to death, and some to exile;
Ransoming him, or pitying, threat'ning th' other;
Holding Corioli in the name of Rome,
Even like a fawning greyhound in the leash,
To let him slip at will.
Com. Where is that slave
Which told me they had beat you to your trenches?
Where is he? Call him hither.
Mar. Let him alone;
He did inform the truth. But for our gentlemen,
The common file—a plague! tribunes for them!—
The mouse ne'er shunn'd the cat as they did budge
From rascals worse than they.
Com. But how prevail'd you?
Mar. Will the time serve to tell? I do not think.
Where is the enemy? Are you lords o' th' field?
If not, why cease you till you are so?
Com. Marcius,
We have at disadvantage fought, and did
Retire to win our purpose.
Mar. How lies their battle? Know you on which side
They have plac'd their men of trust?
Com. As I guess, Marcius,
Their bands i' th' vaward are the Antiates,
Of their best trust; o'er them Aufidius,
Their very heart of hope.
Mar. I do beseech you,
By all the battles wherein we have fought,
By th' blood we have shed together, by the vows
We have made to endure friends, that you directly
Set me against Aufidius and his Antiates;
And that you not delay the present, but,
Filling the air with swords advanc'd and darts,
We prove this very hour.
Com. Though I could wish
You were conducted to a gentle bath
And balms applied to you, yet dare I never
Deny your asking: take your choice of those
That best can aid your action.
Mar. Those are they
That most are willing. If any such be here—
As it were sin to doubt—that love this painting
Wherein you see me smear'd; if any fear
Lesser his person than an ill report;
If any think brave death outweighs bad life,
And that his country 's dearer than himself;
Let him alone, or so many so minded,
Wave thus, to express his disposition,
And follow Marcius.
They all shout and wave their swords, take him up in their arms, and cast up their caps.
O, me alone? make you a sword of me?
If these shows be not outward, which of you
But is four Volsces? None of you but is
Able to bear against the great Aufidius
A shield as hard as his. A certain number,
Though thanks to all, must I select from all; the rest
Shall bear the business in some other fight,
As cause will be obey'd. Please you to march;
And four shall quickly draw out my command,
Which men are best inclin'd.
Com. March on, my fellows!
Make good this ostentation, and you shall
Divide in all with us. *Exeunt.*

Scene VII. *The gates of Corioli.*

Titus Lartius, having set a guard upon Corioli, going with drum and trumpet toward *Cominius* and *Caius Marcius,* enters with a *Lieutenant,* other Soldiers, and a Scout.

Lart. So, let the ports be guarded; keep your duties,
As I have set them down. If I do send, dispatch
Those centuries to our aid; the rest will serve
For a short holding. If we lose the field,
We cannot keep the town.
Lieu. Fear not our care, sir.
Lart. Hence, and shut your gates upon 's.
Our guider, come; to th' Roman camp conduct us. *Exeunt.*

25. tabor, small drum. **29. clip,** embrace. **39. let . . . slip,** unleash (a hunting term). **44. budge,** flee. **51. battle,** army. **53. vaward,** vanguard. **58. endure,** remain.

60. present, matter in hand. **62. prove,** make trial of. **70. Lesser his person,** less personal injury. **83. As . . . obey'd,** as occasion demands. **86. ostentation,** show (of valor). **Scene vii: 3. centuries,** companies.

Scene VIII. *A field of battle.*

Alarum as in battle. Enter *Marcius* and *Aufidius* at several doors.

Mar. I 'll fight with none but thee, for I do hate thee
Worse than a promise-breaker.
Auf. We hate alike.
Not Afric owns a serpent I abhor
More than thy fame and envy. Fix thy foot.
Mar. Let the first budger die the other's slave,
And the gods doom him after!
Auf. If I fly, Marcius,
Holloa me like a hare.
Mar. Within these three hours, Tullus,
Alone I fought in your Corioli walls,
And made what work I pleas'd. 'T is not my blood
Wherein thou seest me mask'd; for thy revenge
Wrench up thy power to th' highest.
Auf. Wert thou the Hector
That was the whip of your bragg'd progeny,
Thou shouldst not scape me here.
Here they fight, and certain Volsces come in the aid of Aufidius. Marcius fights till they be driven in breathless.
Officious, and not valiant, you have sham'd me
In your condemned seconds. *Exeunt.*

Scene IX. *The Roman camp.*

Flourish. Alarum. A retreat is sounded. Enter, at one door, *Cominius* with the Romans; at another door, *Marcius,* with his arm in a scarf.

Com. If I should tell thee o'er this thy day's work,
Thou 'lt not believe thy deeds; but I 'll report it
Where senators shall mingle tears with smiles,
Where great patricians shall attend and shrug,
I' th' end admire, where ladies shall be frighted,
And, gladly quak'd, hear more; where the dull tribunes,
That with the fusty plebeians hate thine honours,
Shall say against their hearts, "We thank the gods
Our Rome hath such a soldier."
Yet cam'st thou to a morsel of this feast,
Having fully din'd before.

Enter *Titus Lartius,* with his power, from the pursuit.

Lart. O general,
Here is the steed, we the caparison.
Hadst thou beheld—
Mar. Pray now, no more: my mother,
Who has a charter to extol her blood,
When she does praise me grieves me. I have done
As you have done, that 's what I can; induc'd
As you have been, that 's for my country.
He that has but effected his good will
Hath overta'en mine act.
Com. You shall not be
The grave of your deserving; Rome must know
The value of her own: 't were a concealment
Worse than a theft, no less than a traducement,
To hide your doings, and to silence that
Which, to the spire and top of praises vouch'd,
Would seem but modest; therefore, I beseech you—
In sign of what you are, not to reward
What you have done—before our army hear me.
Mar. I have some wounds upon me, and they smart
To hear themselves remember'd.
Com. Should they not,
Well might they fester 'gainst ingratitude,
And tent themselves with death. Of all the horses,
Whereof we have ta'en good and good store, of all
The treasure in this field achiev'd and city,
We render you the tenth, to be ta'en forth,
Before the common distribution, at
Your only choice.
Mar. I thank you, general;
But cannot make my heart consent to take
A bribe to pay my sword: I do refuse it,
And stand upon my common part with those
That have beheld the doing.
A long flourish. They all cry, "Marcius! Marcius!" *cast up their caps and lances. Cominius and Lartius stand bare.*
May these same instruments, which you profane,

Scene viii: 4. fame and envy, envied fame (Schmidt), rivalry in fame (Brooke). **12.** Who was great warrior (whip or scourge) of your vaunted race. The Romans claimed descent from Troy. **15. condemned seconds,** inadequate (doomed to failure) assistance. **Scene ix: 4. attend,** listen. **5. admire,** be astonished. **6. quak'd,** trembling. **7. fusty,** mouldy.

12. caparison, trappings, accoutrements. **14. charter,** privilege. **18. effected,** shown in action. **20. grave,** i.e., the hiding place. **22. traducement,** defamation. **29. not,** refers to hear in the preceding speech. **31. tent,** purge, cure. **32. good store,** many.

Never sound more! When drums and trumpets shall
I' th' field prove flatterers, let courts and cities be
Made all of false-fac'd soothing! When steel grows
Soft as the parasite's silk, let him be made
An overture for th' wars! No more, I say!
For that I have not wash'd my nose that bled,
Or foil'd some debile wretch,—which, without note,
Here 's many else have done,—you shout me forth
In acclamations hyperbolical,
As if I lov'd my little should be dieted
In praises sauc'd with lies.

Com. Too modest are you;
More cruel to your good report than grateful
To us that give you truly. By your patience,
If 'gainst yourself you be incens'd, we 'll put you,
(Like one that means his proper harm) in manacles,
Then reason safely with you. Therefore be it known,
As to us, to all the world, that Caius Marcius
Wears this war's garland; in token of the which,
My noble steed, known to the camp, I give him,
With all his trim belonging; and from this time,
For what he did before Corioli, call him,
With all the applause and clamour of the host,
Caius Marcius Coriolanus! Bear
Th' addition nobly ever!

Flourish. Trumpets sound, and drums.

Omnes. Caius Marcius Coriolanus!

Cor. I will go wash;
And when my face is fair, you shall perceive
Whether I blush or no; howbeit, I thank you.
I mean to stride your steed, and at all times
To undercrest your good addition
To th' fairness of my power.

Com. So, to our tent;
Where, ere we do repose us, we will write
To Rome of our success. You, Titus Lartius,
Must to Corioli back, send us to Rome
The best, with whom we may articulate
For their own good and ours.

Lart. I shall, my lord.

Cor. The gods begin to mock me. I, that now
Refus'd most princely gifts, am bound to beg
Of my lord general.

Com. Take 't; 't is yours. What is 't?

Cor. I sometime lay here in Corioli
At a poor man's house; he us'd me kindly.
He cried to me,—I saw him prisoner,—
But then Aufidius was within my view,
And wrath o'erwhelm'd my pity. I request you
To give my poor host freedom.

Com. O, well begg'd!
Were he the butcher of my son, he should
Be free as is the wind. Deliver him, Titus.

Lart. Marcius, his name?

Cor. By Jupiter! forgot.
I am weary; yea, my memory is tir'd.
Have we no wine here?

Com. Go we to our tent.
The blood upon your visage dries; 't is time
It should be look'd to. Come. *Exeunt.*

Scene X. *The camp of the Volsces.*

A flourish. Cornets. Enter *Tullus Aufidius,* bloody, with two or three *Soldiers.*

Auf. The town is ta'en!

First Sol. 'T will be deliver'd back on good condition.

Auf. Condition!
I would I were a Roman; for I cannot,
Being a Volsce, be that I am. Condition!
What good condition can a treaty find
I' th' part that is at mercy? Five times, Marcius,
I have fought with thee; so often hast thou beat me,
And wouldst do so, I think, should we encounter
As often as we eat. By th' elements,
If e'er again I meet him beard to beard,
He 's mine, or I am his. Mine emulation
Hath not that honour in 't it had; for where
I thought to crush him in an equal force,
True sword to sword, I 'll potch at him some way;
Or wrath or craft may get him.

First Sol. He 's the devil.

Auf. Bolder, though not so subtle. My valour 's poison'd
With only suff'ring stain by him; for him
Shall fly out of itself. Nor sleep nor sanctuary,
Being naked, sick, nor fane nor Capitol,
The prayers of priests nor times of sacrifice,
Embargements all of fury, shall lift up

44. **soothing,** flattery. 46. **overture,** proposal, thing proposed, here the "parasite" of l. 45. 48. **foil'd,** defeated. **debile,** weak. **note,** special notice. 51. **dieted In,** fed on. 54. **give,** report. 56. **proper,** own. 61. **his trim belonging,** the trimmings that belong to him. 68. **fair,** clean. 71. **undercrest,** to wear as a crest. 76. **articulate,** discuss terms.

Scene x: 2. **condition,** terms. 5. **that,** what. 7. **I' th' part,** i.e., for the side. 12. **emulation,** rivalry. 15. **potch,** thrust, strike wildly. 20. **fane,** temple. 22. **Embargements,** impediments, restraints.

Their rotten privilege and custom 'gainst
My hate to Marcius. Where I find him, were it
At home, upon my brother's guard, even there,
Against the hospitable canon, would I
Wash my fierce hand in 's heart. Go you to th' city;
Learn how 't is held, and what they are that must
Be hostages for Rome.

First Sol. Will not you go?

Auf. I am attended at the cypress grove.
I pray you—
'T is south the city mills—bring me word thither
How the world goes, that to the pace of it
I may spur on my journey.

First Sol. I shall, sir.

Exeunt.

ACT II. SCENE I. *Rome. A public place.*

Enter *Menenius,* with the two Tribunes of the people, *Sicinius* and *Brutus.*

Men. The augurer tells me we shall have news to-night.

Bru. Good or bad?

Men. Not according to the prayer of the people, for they love not Marcius.

Sic. Nature teaches beasts to know their friends.

Men. Pray you, who does the wolf love?

Sic. The lamb.

Men. Ay, to devour him; as the hungry plebeians would the noble Marcius.

Bru. He 's a lamb indeed, that baes like a bear.

Men. He 's a bear indeed, that lives like a lamb. You two are old men: tell me one thing that I shall ask you.

Both. Well, sir.

Men. In what enormity is Marcius poor in, that you two have not in abundance?

Bru. He 's poor in no one fault, but stored with all.

Sic. Especially in pride.

Bru. And topping all others in boasting.

Men. This is strange now. Do you two know how you are censured here in the city, I mean of us o' th' right-hand file? Do you?

Both. Why, how are we censured?

Men. Because you talk of pride now,—will you not be angry?

Both. Well, well, sir, well.

Men. Why, 't is no great matter; for a very little thief of occasion will rob you of a great deal of patience. Give your dispositions the reins, and be angry at your pleasures; at the least, if you take it as a pleasure to you in being so. You blame Marcius for being proud?

Bru. We do it not alone, sir.

Men. I know you can do very little alone, for your helps are many, or else your actions would grow wondrous single; your abilities are too infant-like for doing much alone. You talk of pride: O that you could turn your eyes toward the napes of your necks, and make but an interior survey of your good selves! O that you could!

Both. What then, sir?

Men. Why, then you should discover a brace of unmeriting, proud, violent, testy magistrates, alias fools, as any in Rome.

Sic. Menenius, you are known well enough too.

Men. I am known to be a humorous patrician, and one that loves a cup of hot wine with not a drop of allaying Tiber in 't; said to be something imperfect in favouring the first complaint; hasty and tinder-like upon too trivial motion; one that converses more with the buttock of the night than with the forehead of the morning. What I think, I utter, and spend my malice in my breath. Meeting two such wealsmen as you are—I cannot call you Lycurguses—if the drink you give me touch my palate adversely, I make a crooked face at it. I cannot say your worships have delivered the matter well, when I find the ass in compound with the major part of your syllables; and though I must be content to bear with those that say you are reverend grave men, yet they lie deadly that tell you have good faces. If you see this in the map of my microcosm, follows it that I am known well enough too? What harm can your beesom conspectuities glean out of this character, if I be known well enough too?

Bru. Come, sir, come, we know you well enough.

25. **upon . . . guard,** in my brother's keeping. 26. **hospitable canon,** law of hospitality. **Act II, Scene i:** 25. **censured,** thought of. 26. **right-hand file,** conservatives, aristocrats. 32. **occasion,** cause, motive. A little occasion is a thief to rob, etc.

30. **attended,** waited for. **Act II, Scene i:** 39. **single,** silly. 51. **humorous,** impulsive. 53. **Tiber,** i.e., water. 54. **something . . . complaint,** injudicious. 56. **motion,** cause. 59. **wealsmen,** politicians. 60. **Lycurguses,** statesmen. 63-4. **the ass in compound,** asininity compounded. 68-9. **the . . . microcosm,** i.e., my face. 70-1. **beesom conspectuities,** blinded sight.

Men. You know neither me, yourselves, nor anything. You are ambitious for poor knaves' caps and legs: you wear out a good wholesome forenoon in hearing a cause between an orange-wife and a faucet-seller; and then rejourn the controversy of three pence to a second day of audience. When you are hearing a matter between party and party, if you chance to be pinched with the colic, you make faces like mummers; set up the bloody flag against all patience; and, in roaring for a chamber-pot, dismiss the controversy bleeding, the more entangled by your hearing: all the peace you make in their cause is calling both the parties knaves. You are a pair of strange ones.

Bru. Come, come, you are well understood to be a perfecter giber for the table than a necessary bencher in the Capitol.

Men. Our very priests must become mockers, if they shall encounter such ridiculous subjects as you are. When you speak best unto the purpose, it is not worth the wagging of your beards; and your beards deserve not so honourable a grave as to stuff a botcher's cushion, or to be entombed in an ass's pack-saddle. Yet you must be saying Marcius is proud; who, in a cheap estimation, is worth all your predecessors since Deucalion, though peradventure some of the best of 'em were hereditary hangmen. God-den to your worships. More of your conversation would infect my brain, being the herdsmen of the beastly plebeians. I will be bold to take my leave of you.

Brutus and Sicinius go aside.

Enter *Volumnia, Virgilia,* and *Valeria.*

How now, my as fair as noble ladies,—and the moon, were she earthly, no nobler,—whither do you follow your eyes so fast?

Vol. Honourable Menenius, my boy Marcius approaches: for the love of Juno, let 's go.

Men. Ha! Marcius coming home?

Vol. Ay, worthy Menenius; and with most prosperous approbation.

Men. Take my cap, Jupiter, and I thank thee. Hoo! Marcius coming home!

Two Ladies. Nay, 't is true.

Vol. Look, here 's a letter from him; the state hath another, his wife another, and, I think, there 's one at home for you.

Men. I will make my very house reel tonight. A letter for me?

Vir. Yes, certain, there 's a letter for you; I saw 't.

Men. A letter for me! it gives me an estate of seven years' health, in which time I will make a lip at the physician: the most sovereign prescription in Galen is but empiricutic, and, to this preservative, of no better report than a horse-drench. Is he not wounded? He was wont to come home wounded.

Vir. O, no, no, no.

Vol. O, he is wounded; I thank the gods for 't.

Men. So do I too, if it be not too much. Brings 'a victory in his pocket? The wounds become him.

Vol. On 's brows. Menenius, he comes the third time home with the oaken garland.

Men. Has he disciplined Aufidius soundly?

Vol. Titus Lartius writes, they fought together, but Aufidius got off.

Men. And 't was time for him too. I 'll warrant him that. An he had stayed by him, I would not have been so fidiused for all the chests in Corioli, and the gold that 's in them. Is the Senate possessed of this?

Vol. Good ladies, let 's go.—Yes, yes, yes; the Senate has letters from the general, wherein he gives my son the whole name of the war. He hath in this action outdone his former deeds doubly.

Val. In troth, there 's wondrous things spoke of him.

Men. Wondrous! ay, I warrant you, and not without his true purchasing.

Vir. The gods grant them true!

Vol. True! pow, wow.

Men. True? I 'll be sworn they are true. Where is he wounded? [*To the Tribunes.*] God save your good worships! Marcius is coming home; he has more cause to be proud. —Where is he wounded?

Vol. I' th' shoulder and i' th' left arm. There will be large cicatrices to show the people, when he shall stand for his place. He received in the repulse of Tarquin seven hurts i' th' body.

Men. One i' th' neck, and two i' th' thigh, —there 's nine that I know.

Vol. He had, before this last expedition, twenty-five wounds upon him.

Men. Now it 's twenty-seven; every gash was an enemy's grave. Hark! the trumpets.

A shout and flourish.

Vol. These are the ushers of Marcius; be-

77. **caps and legs,** i.e., deference. 80. **rejourn,** adjourn. 84. **mummers,** masked actors. **set . . . flag,** declare war. 86. **bleeding,** i.e., uncured. 91. **perfecter . . . Capitol,** i.e., better fitted to be a jester at dinner than a senator at the Capitol. 97. **botcher's,** mender of old clothes. 101. **Deucalion,** the Greek Noah. 103. **God-den,** good evening. 114. **prosperous approbation,** success, lit., approval of success.

127. **make a lip at,** flaunt. 128. **Galen,** second century Greek physician. **empiricutic,** quackish. 137. **on 's brows,** i.e., the victory. 144. **fidiused,** in Aufidius' place. 149. **name,** fame. 164. **cicatrices,** scars. 165. **stand . . . place,** seek office. 166. **Tarquin,** refers to one of his four attempts to regain the throne (499 B.C.).

fore him he carries noise, and behind him he leaves tears.
Death, that dark spirit, in 's nervy arm doth lie,
Which, being advanc'd, declines, and then men die.

A sennet. Trumpets sound. Enter *Cominius* the general, and *Titus Lartius;* between them, *Coriolanus,* crowned with an oaken garland; with Captains and Soldiers, and a *Herald.*

Her. Know, Rome, that all alone Marcius did fight
Within Corioli gates; where he hath won,
With fame, a name to Caius Marcius; these
In honour follows Coriolanus.
Welcome to Rome, renowned Coriolanus!
Sound. Flourish.

All. Welcome to Rome, renowned Coriolanus!

Cor. No more of this; it does offend my heart.
Pray now, no more.

Com. Look, sir, your mother!

Cor. O,
You have, I know, petition'd all the gods
For my prosperity! *Kneels.*

Vol. Nay, my good soldier, up;
My gentle Marcius, worthy Caius, and
By deed-achieving honour newly nam'd,—
What is it?—Coriolanus must I call thee?—
But, O, thy wife!

Cor. My gracious silence, hail!
Wouldst thou have laugh'd had I come coffin'd home,
That weep'st to see me triumph? Ah, my dear,
Such eyes the widows in Corioli wear,
And mothers that lack sons.

Men. Now, the gods crown thee!

Cor. And live you yet? [*To Valeria.*] O my sweet lady, pardon.

Vol. I know not where to turn. O, welcome home;
And welcome, general; and y' are welcome all.

Men. A hundred thousand welcomes! I could weep
And I could laugh, I am light and heavy. Welcome!
A curse begin at very root on 's heart,
That is not glad to see thee! You are three
That Rome should dote on; yet, by the faith of men,
We have some old crab-trees here at home that will not
Be grafted to your relish. Yet welcome, warriors;
We call a nettle but a nettle and
The faults of fools but folly.

Com. Ever right.

Cor. Menenius ever, ever.

Her. Give way there, and go on!

Cor. [*To Volumnia and Virgilia.*] Your hand, and yours.
Ere in our own house I do shade my head,
The good patricians must be visited;
From whom I have receiv'd not only greetings,
But with them charge of honours.

Vol. I have lived
To see inherited my very wishes
And the buildings of my fancy; only
There 's one thing wanting, which I doubt not but
Our Rome will cast upon thee.

Cor. Know, good mother,
I had rather be their servant in my way
Than sway with them in theirs.

Com. On, to the Capitol!
Flourish. Cornets. Exeunt in state, as before. Brutus and Sicinius come forward.

Bru. All tongues speak of him, and the bleared sights
Are spectacled to see him. Your prattling nurse
Into a rapture lets her baby cry
While she chats him; the kitchen Malkin pins
Her richest lockram 'bout her reechy neck,
Clamb'ring the walls to eye him; stalls, bulks, windows,
Are smother'd up, leads fill'd, and ridges hors'd
With variable complexions, all agreeing
In earnestness to see him: seld-shown flamens
Do press among the popular throngs and puff
To win a vulgar station; our veil'd dames
Commit the war of white and damask in
Their nicely-gawded cheeks to th' wanton spoil
Of Phœbus' burning kisses;—such a pother
As if that whatsoever god who leads him
Were slily crept into his human powers
And gave him graceful posture.

Sic. On the sudden,
I warrant him consul.

Bru. Then our office may,
During his power, go sleep.

Sic. He cannot temp'rately transport his honours
From where he should begin and end, but will
Lose those he hath won.

177. **nervy**, sinewy. 178. **advanc'd**, raised. S. d. **sennet**, a trumpet signal. 205. **crab-trees**, crab-apple trees.

215. **inherited**, realized. 220. **sway**, rule. 223. **rapture**, fit. 224. **chats**, talks about. **Malkin**, wench. 225. **lockram**, linen. **reechy**, filthy. 226. **bulks**, display shelves outside a shop. 227. **leads**, leaded roof. **hors'd**, bestridden. 228. **variable complexions**, all types of people. 229. **seld-shown flamens**, seldom-appearing priests. 230. **popular throngs**, crowds of populace. **puff**, breathe hard, i.e., struggle. 231. **vulgar station**, place in the mob. 232. **Commit**, surrender. 233. **nicely-gawded**, carefully colored. 241. **From . . . end**, from the beginning to the end.

Bru. In that there 's comfort.
Sic. Doubt not
The commoners, for whom we stand, but they
Upon their ancient malice will forget
With the least cause these his new honours, which
That he will give them make I as little question
As he is proud to do 't.
Bru. I heard him swear,
Were he to stand for consul, never would he
Appear i' th' market-place, nor on him put
The napless vesture of humility,
Nor, showing, as the manner is, his wounds
To th' people, beg their stinking breaths.
Sic. 'T is right.
Bru. It was his word. O, he would miss it rather
Than carry it but by the suit of the gentry to him
And the desire of the nobles.
Sic. I wish no better
Than have him hold that purpose and to put it
In execution.
Bru. 'T is most like he will.
Sic. It shall be to him then as our good wills,
A sure destruction.
Bru. So it must fall out
To him or our authorities for an end.
We must suggest the people in what hatred
He still hath held them; that to 's power he would
Have made them mules, silenc'd their pleaders and
Dispropertied their freedoms, holding them,
In human action and capacity,
Of no more soul nor fitness for the world
Than camels in the war, who have their provand
Only for bearing burdens, and sore blows
For sinking under them.
Sic. This, as you say, suggested
At some time when his soaring insolence
Shall touch the people—which time shall not want,
If he be put upon 't; and that 's as easy
As to set dogs on sheep—will be his fire
To kindle their dry stubble; and their blaze
Shall darken him for ever.

Enter a Messenger.

Bru. What 's the matter?
Mess. You are sent for to the Capitol. 'T is thought
That Marcius shall be consul.
I have seen the dumb men throng to see him, and
The blind to hear him speak: matrons flung gloves,
Ladies and maids their scarfs and handkerchers,
Upon him as he pass'd; the nobles bended,
As to Jove's statue, and the commons made
A shower and thunder with their caps and shouts.
I never saw the like.
Bru. Let 's to the Capitol;
And carry with us ears and eyes for th' time,
But hearts for the event.
Sic. Have with you.
Exeunt.

Scene II. *The same. The Capitol.*

Enter two *Officers,* to lay cushions as it were in the Capitol.

First Off. Come, come, they are almost here. How many stand for consulships?

Sec. Off. Three, they say; but 't is thought of every one Coriolanus will carry it.

First Off. That 's a brave fellow; but he 's vengeance proud, and loves not the common people.

Sec. Off. Faith, there hath been many great men that have flattered the people, who ne'er loved them; and there be many that they have loved, they know not wherefore; so that, if they love they know not why, they hate upon no better a ground. Therefore, for Coriolanus neither to care whether they love or hate him manifests the true knowledge he has in their disposition; and out of his noble carelessness lets them plainly see 't.

First Off. If he did not care whether he had their love or no, he waved indifferently 'twixt doing them neither good nor harm; but he seeks their hate with greater devotion than they can render it him; and leaves nothing undone that may fully discover him their opposite. Now, to seem to affect the malice and displeasure of the people is as bad as that which he dislikes, to flatter them for their love.

Sec. Off. He hath deserved worthily of his country; and his ascent is not by such easy degrees as those who, having been supple and courteous to the people, bonneted, without any further deed to have them at all into their estimation and report: but he hath so planted

245. **which,** refers to cause. 250. **napless,** threadbare. 258. **as . . . wills,** according to one's desires. 260. **for an end,** as an end, i.e., destruction. 261. **suggest,** remind by insinuation. 262. **still,** always. 264. **Dispropertied,** taken away. 267. **provand,** provender. 275. **darken,** tarnish.

285. **time,** present. 286. **hearts . . . event,** minds for what's to come. **Scene ii:** 6. **vengeance,** violently. 8. **who,** i.e., the people. 22. **discover,** show. **opposite,** opponent. 30. **bonneted,** doffed their hats.

his honours in their eyes, and his actions in their hearts, that for their tongues to be silent, and not confess so much, were a kind of ingrateful injury; to report otherwise were a malice, that, giving itself the lie, would pluck reproof and rebuke from every ear that heard it.

First Off. No more of him; he 's a worthy man. Make way, they are coming.

A sennet. Enter the Patricians and the Tribunes of the People, Lictors before them: *Cominius* the consul, *Menenius, Coriolanus: Sicinius* and *Brutus.* Tribunes take their places by themselves: *Coriolanus* stands.

Men. Having determin'd of the Volsces and
To send for Titus Lartius, it remains,
As the main point of this our after-meeting,
To gratify his noble service that
Hath thus stood for his country; therefore, please you,
Most reverend and grave elders, to desire
The present consul and last general
In our well-found successes, to report
A little of that worthy work perform'd
By Caius Marcius Coriolanus, whom
We met here both to thank and to remember
With honours like himself. *Coriolanus sits.*
First Sen. Speak, good Cominius:
Leave nothing out for length, and make us think
Rather our state 's defective for requital
Than we to stretch it out. [*To the Tribunes.*] Masters o' th' people,
We do request your kindest ears, and after,
Your loving motion toward the common body
To yield what passes here.
Sic. We are convented
Upon a pleasing treaty, and have hearts
Inclinable to honour and advance
The theme of our assembly.
Bru. Which the rather
We shall be blest to do, if he remember
A kinder value of the people than
He hath hereto priz'd them at.
Men. That 's off, that 's off;
I would you rather had been silent. Please you
To hear Cominius speak?
Bru. Most willingly;
But yet my caution was more pertinent
Than the rebuke you give it.
Men. He loves your people;
But tie him not to be their bedfellow.
Worthy Cominius, speak. [*Coriolanus rises and offers to go away.*] Nay, keep your place.
First Sen. Sit, Coriolanus; never shame to hear
What you have nobly done.
Cor. Your honours' pardon;
I had rather have my wounds to heal again
Than hear say how I got them.
Bru. Sir, I hope
My words disbench'd you not.
Cor. No, sir; yet oft,
When blows have made me stay, I fled from words.
You sooth'd not, therefore hurt not; but your people,
I love them as they weigh.
Men. Pray now, sit down.
Cor. I had rather have one scratch my head i' th' sun
When the alarum were struck, than idly sit
To hear my nothings monster'd. *Exit.*
Men. Masters of the people,
Your multiplying spawn how can he flatter—
That 's thousand to one good one—when you now see
He had rather venture all his limbs for honour
Than one on 's ears to hear it? Proceed, Cominius.
Com. I shall lack voice; the deeds of Coriolanus
Should not be utter'd feebly. It is held
That valour is the chiefest virtue, and
Most dignifies the haver; if it be,
The man I speak of cannot in the world
Be singly counterpois'd. At sixteen years,
When Tarquin made a head for Rome, he fought
Beyond the mark of others: our then dictator,
Whom with all praise I point at, saw him fight,
When with his Amazonian chin he drove
The bristled lips before him. He bestrid
An o'er-press'd Roman, and i' th' consul's view
Slew three opposers: Tarquin's self he met,
And struck him on his knee: in that day's feats,
When he might act the woman in the scene,
He prov'd best man i' th' field, and for his meed
Was brow-bound with the oak. His pupil age
Man-enter'd thus, he waxed like a sea,
And in the brunt of seventeen battles since

44. gratify, reward. **47. last,** late. **48. well-found,** well-established. **52. like himself,** according to his deserts. **54. Rather . . . out,** rather that our state is unable to repay than that we are unwilling to stretch its resources. **57. motion toward,** offer to. **58. convented,** convened. **59. treaty,** proposal. **61. theme,** i.e., Coriolanus. **62. blest,** happy. **63. kinder value,** more friendly opinion. **64. priz'd,** estimated. **off,** amiss.

77. sooth'd, flattered. **78. as they weigh,** according to their worth. **81. monster'd,** made extraordinary. **83. That's,** i.e., there are a. **85. on 's,** of his. **91. singly counterpois'd,** equalled by one man. **92. made a head for,** made war on. **he . . . others,** surpassed the others in fighting. **95. Amazonian,** i.e., beardless. **99. on,** to. **100. in the scene,** on the stage.

He lurch'd all swords of the garland. For this last,
Before and in Corioli, let me say,
I cannot speak him home. He stopp'd the fliers;
And by his rare example made the coward
Turn terror into sport; as weeds before
A vessel under sail, so men obey'd
And fell below his stem: his sword, death's stamp,
Where it did mark, it took; from face to foot
He was a thing of blood, whose every motion
Was tim'd with dying cries. Alone he enter'd
The mortal gate of th' city, which he painted
With shunless destiny; aidless came off,
And with a sudden reinforcement struck
Corioli like a planet; now all 's his:
When, by and by, the din of war 'gan pierce
His ready sense, then straight his doubled spirit
Re-quicken'd what in flesh was fatigate,
And to the battle came he, where he did
Run reeking o'er the lives of men, as if
'T were a perpetual spoil; and till we call'd
Both field and city ours, he never stood
To ease his breast with panting.

Men. Worthy man!

First Sen. He cannot but with measure fit the honours
Which we devise him.

Com. Our spoils he kick'd at,
And look'd upon things precious as they were
The common muck of the world: he covets less
Than misery itself would give, rewards
His deeds with doing them, and is content
To spend the time to end it.

Men. He 's right noble.
Let him be call'd for.

First Sen. Call Coriolanus.

Off. He doth appear.

Re-enter *Coriolanus.*

Men. The Senate, Coriolanus, are well pleas'd
To make thee consul.

Cor. I do owe them still
My life and services.

Men. It then remains
That you do speak to the people.

Cor. I do beseech you,
Let me o'erleap that custom; for I cannot
Put on the gown, stand naked and entreat them,
For my wounds' sake, to give their suffrage: please you
That I may pass this doing.

Sic. Sir, the people
Must have their voices; neither will they bate
One jot of ceremony.

Men. Put them not to 't.
Pray you, go fit you to the custom and
Take to you, as your predecessors have,
Your honour with your form.

Cor. It is a part
That I shall blush in acting, and might well
Be taken from the people.

Bru. Mark you that?

Cor. To brag unto them, thus I did, and thus;
Show them th' unaching scars which I should hide,
As if I had receiv'd them for the hire
Of their breath only!

Men. Do not stand upon 't.
We recommend to you, tribunes of the people,
Our purpose to them; and to our noble consul
Wish we all joy and honour.

Senators. To Coriolanus come all joy and honour!

Flourish. Cornets. Exeunt all but Sicinius and Brutus.

Bru. You see how he intends to use the people.

Sic. May they perceive 's intent! He will require them,
As if he did contemn what he requested
Should be in them to give.

Bru. Come, we 'll inform them
Of our proceedings here: on th' market-place,
I know, they do attend us. *Exeunt.*

Scene III. *The same. The Forum.*

Enter seven or eight *Citizens.*

First Cit. Once, if he do require our voices, we ought not to deny him.

Sec. Cit. We may, sir, if we will.

Third Cit. We have power in ourselves to do it, but it is a power that we have no power to do; for if he show us his wounds and tell us his deeds, we are to put our tongues into those wounds and speak for them; so, if he tell us his noble deeds, we must also tell him our noble acceptance of them. Ingratitude is monstrous, and for the multitude to be ingrateful, were to make a monster of the multitude; of the which we being members, should bring ourselves to be monstrous members.

105. lurch'd, robbed. **107. speak him home,** do him full justice. **112. took,** slew. **115. mortal,** deadly (to an enemy). **painted . . . destiny,** smeared with the blood of those who could not escape their doom. **121. fatigate,** fatigued. **124. spoil,** havoc. **127. with measure,** properly. **128. spoils . . . at,** booty he spurned. **133. to end it,** merely to kill time.

143. pass this doing, omit this ceremony. **144. voices,** votes. **148. with your form,** with the usual ceremony. **155. recommend,** deliver, commit. **160. require,** petition. **161. contemn,** scorn.

First Cit. And to make us no better thought of, a little help will serve; for once we stood up about the corn, he himself stuck not to call us the many-headed multitude.

Third Cit. We have been called so of many; not that our heads are some brown, some black, some abram, some bald, but that our wits are so diversely coloured; and truly I think if all our wits were to issue out of one skull, they would fly east, west, north, south, and their consent of one direct way should be at once to all the points o' th' compass.

Sec. Cit. Think you so? Which way do you judge my wit would fly?

Third Cit. Nay, your wit will not so soon out as another man's will, 't is strongly wedged up in a block-head; but if it were at liberty, 't would, sure, southward.

Sec. Cit. Why that way?

Third Cit. To lose itself in a fog, where being three parts melted away with rotten dews, the fourth would return for conscience' sake, to help to get thee a wife.

Sec. Cit. You are never without your tricks; you may, you may.

Third Cit. Are you all resolved to give your voices? But that 's no matter, the greater part carries it. I say, if he would incline to the people, there was never a worthier man.

Enter *Coriolanus* in a gown of humility,
with *Menenius.*

Here he comes, and in the gown of humility; mark his behaviour. We are not to stay all together, but to come by him where he stands, by ones, by twos, and by threes. He 's to make his requests by particulars, wherein every one of us has a single honour, in giving him our own voices with our own tongues; therefore follow me, and I 'll direct you how you shall go by him.

All. Content, content. *Exeunt citizens.*

Men. O sir, you are not right. Have you not known
The worthiest men have done 't?
Cor. What must I say?
"I pray, sir,"—Plague upon 't! I cannot bring
My tongue to such a pace,—"Look, sir, my wounds!
I got them in my country's service, when
Some certain of your brethren roar'd and ran
From th' noise of our own drums."
Men. O me, the gods!
You must not speak of that. You must desire them
To think upon you.
Cor. Think upon me! Hang 'em!
I would they would forget me, like the virtues
Which our divines lose by 'em.
Men. You 'll mar all.
I 'll leave you. Pray you, speak to 'em, I pray you,
In wholesome manner. *Exit.*

Re-enter three of the *Citizens.*

Cor. Bid them wash their faces
And keep their teeth clean. So, here comes a brace.
You know the cause, sir, of my standing here.

Third Cit. We do, sir; tell us what hath brought you to 't.

Cor. Mine own desert.

Sec. Cit. Your own desert!

Cor. Ay, not mine own desire.

Third Cit. How not your own desire?

Cor. No, sir, 't was never my desire yet to trouble the poor with begging.

Third Cit. You must think, if we give you anything, we hope to gain by you.

Cor. Well then, I pray, your price o' th' consulship?

First Cit. The price is to ask it kindly.

Cor. Kindly! Sir, I pray, let me ha 't. I have wounds to show you, which shall be yours in private. Your good voice, sir; what say you?

Sec. Cit. You shall ha' it, worthy sir.

Cor. A match, sir. There 's in all two worthy voices begg'd. I have your alms; adieu.

Third Cit. But this is something odd.

Sec. Cit. An 't were to give again,—but 't is no matter. *Exeunt the three Citizens.*

Re-enter two other *Citizens.*

Cor. Pray you now, if it may stand with the tune of your voices that I may be consul, I have here the customary gown.

Fourth Cit. You have deserved nobly of your country, and you have not deserved nobly.

Cor. Your enigma?

Fourth Cit. You have been a scourge to her enemies, you have been a rod to her friends; you have not indeed loved the common people.

Cor. You should account me the more virtuous that I have not been common in my love. I will, sir, flatter my sworn brother, the people, to earn a dearer estimation of them; 't is a condition they account gentle: and since the wisdom of their choice is rather to have

Scene iii: 21. abram, auburn. **25. consent of,** agreement with. **39. you may,** i.e., have your joke. **42. incline to,** be favorable toward. **48. by particulars,** to individuals. **49. single,** separate.

64. lose by 'em, waste on them. **66. wholesome,** suitable. **91. stand . . . tune,** accord—with reference to voices, (1) votes, (2) singing voices.

my hat than my heart, I will practise the insinuating nod and be off to them most counterfeitly; that is, sir, I will counterfeit the bewitchment of some popular man and give it bountiful to the desirers. Therefore, beseech you, I may be consul.

Fifth Cit. We hope to find you our friend; and therefore give you our voices heartily.

Fourth Cit. You have received many wounds for your country.

Cor. I will not seal your knowledge with showing them. I will make much of your voices, and so trouble you no further.

Both Cit. The gods give you joy, sir, heartily! *Exeunt.*

Cor. Most sweet voices!
Better it is to die, better to starve,
Than crave the hire which first we do deserve.
Why in this wolvish toge should I stand here,
To beg of Hob and Dick, that does appear,
Their needless vouches? Custom calls me to 't.
What custom wills, in all things should we do 't,
The dust on antique time would lie unswept,
And mountainous error be too highly heapt
For truth to o'er-peer. Rather than fool it so,
Let the high office and the honour go
To one that would do thus.—I am half through;
The one part suffered, the other will I do.

Re-enter three *Citizens* more.

Here come moe voices.—
Your voices! For your voices I have fought;
Watch'd for your voices; for your voices bear
Of wounds two dozen odd; battles thrice six
I have seen and heard of; for your voices have
Done many things, some less, some more. Your voices.
Indeed, I would be consul.

Sixth Cit. He has done nobly, and cannot go without any honest man's voice.

Seventh Cit. Therefore let him be consul. The gods give him joy, and make him good friend to the people!

All Cit. Amen, amen. God save thee, noble consul! *Exeunt.*

Cor. Worthy voices!

Re-enter *Menenius,* with *Brutus* and *Sicinius.*

Men. You have stood your limitation, and the tribunes
Endue you with the people's voice. Remains
That, in th' official marks invested, you
Anon do meet the Senate.

Cor. Is this done?

Sic. The custom of request you have discharg'd.
The people do admit you, and are summon'd
To meet anon upon your approbation.

Cor. Where? At the Senate-house?

Sic. There, Coriolanus.

Cor. May I change these garments?

Sic. You may, sir.

Cor. That I 'll straight do; and, knowing myself again,
Repair to th' Senate-house.

Men. I 'll keep you company. Will you along?

Bru. We stay here for the people.

Sic. Fare you well.

Exeunt Coriolanus and Menenius.

He has it now, and by his looks methinks
'T is warm at 's heart.

Bru. With a proud heart he wore his humble weeds.
Will you dismiss the people?

Enter the *Plebeians.*

Sic. How now, my masters! have you chose this man?

First Cit. He has our voices, sir.

Bru. We pray the gods he may deserve your loves.

Sec. Cit. Amen, sir. To my poor unworthy notice,
He mock'd us when he begg'd our voices.

Third Cit. Certainly
He flouted us downright.

First Cit. No, 't is his kind of speech; he did not mock us.

Sec. Cit. Not one amongst us, save yourself, but says
He us'd us scornfully: he should have show'd us
His marks of merit, wounds receiv'd for 's country.

Sic. Why, so he did, I am sure.

All. No, no; no man saw 'em.

Third Cit. He said he had wounds, which he could show in private;
And with his hat, thus waving it in scorn,
"I would be consul," says he; "aged custom,
But by your voices, will not so permit me;
Your voices therefore." When we granted that,
Here was "I thank you for your voices; thank you;

107. be off, i.e., with my hat. **counterfeitly,** hypocritically. **108. popular man,** politician. **109. bountiful,** bountifully. **115. seal,** confirm. **121. hire,** pay. **first,** before any other. **122. wolvish toge,** possible reference to the wolf in sheep's clothing. **Cf. napless vesture,** II, i, 253. **124. vouches,** votes, lit., confirmations. **128. fool,** play the fool. **134. Watch'd,** stood watch. **146. limitation,** time-limit.

147. Endue, endow. **148. marks,** emblems. **152. upon your approbation,** for the purpose of ratifying your election. **155. knowing,** i.e., being.

Your most sweet voices. Now you have left your voices,
I have no further with you." Was not this mockery?
Sic. Why either were you ignorant to see 't,
Or, seeing it, of such childish friendliness
To yield your voices?
Bru. Could you not have told him
As you were lesson'd: when he had no power,
But was a petty servant to the state,
He was your enemy, ever spake against
Your liberties and the charters that you bear
I' th' body of the weal; and now, arriving
A place of potency and sway o' th' state,
If he should still malignantly remain
Fast foe to the *plebeii,* your voices might
Be curses to yourselves? You should have said
That as his worthy deeds did claim no less
Than what he stood for, so his gracious nature
Would think upon you for your voices and
Translate his malice towards you into love,
Standing your friendly lord.
Sic. Thus to have said,
As you were fore-advis'd, had touch'd his spirit
And tried his inclination; from him pluck'd
Either his gracious promise, which you might,
As cause had call'd you up, have held him to;
Or else it would have gall'd his surly nature,
Which easily endures not article
Tying him to aught; so putting him to rage,
You should have ta'en th' advantage of his choler
And pass'd him unelected.
Bru. Did you perceive
He did solicit you in free contempt
When he did need your loves, and do you think
That his contempt shall not be bruising to you,
When he hath power to crush? Why, had your bodies
No heart among you? Or had you tongues to cry
Against the rectorship of judgement?
Sic. Have you
Ere now deni'd the asker, and now again
Of him that did not ask, but mock, bestow
Your sued-for tongues?
Third Cit. He 's not confirm'd; we may deny him yet.
Sec. Cit. And will deny him.
I 'll have five hundred voices of that sound.
First Cit. I twice five hundred and their friends to piece 'em.
Bru. Get you hence instantly, and tell those friends,
They have chose a consul that will from them take
Their liberties, make them of no more voice
Than dogs, that are as often beat for barking
As therefore kept to do so.
Sic. Let them assemble,
And on a safer judgement all revoke
Your ignorant election. Enforce his pride,
And his old hate unto you; besides, forget not
With what contempt he wore the humble weed,
How in his suit he scorn'd you; but your loves,
Thinking upon his services, took from you
Th' apprehension of his present portance,
Which most gibingly, ungravely, he did fashion
After the inveterate hate he bears you.
Bru. Lay
A fault on us, your tribunes, that we labour'd,
No impediment between, but that you must
Cast your election on him.
Sic. Say, you chose him
More after our commandment than as guided
By your own true affections, and that your minds,
Pre-occupied with what you rather must do
Than what you should, made you against the grain
To voice him consul. Lay the fault on us.
Bru. Ay, spare us not. Say we read lectures to you,
How youngly he began to serve his country,
How long continued, and what stock he springs of,—
The noble house o' th' Marcians, from whence came
That Ancus Marcius, Numa's daughter's son,
Who, after great Hostilius, here was king;
Of the same house Publius and Quintus were,
That our best water brought by conduits hither;
And Censorinus, nobly named so,
Twice being by the people chosen censor,
Was his great ancestor.
Sic. One thus descended,
That hath beside well in his person wrought
To be set high in place, we did commend
To your remembrances; but you have found,
Scaling his present bearing with his past,
That he 's your fixed enemy, and revoke
Your sudden approbation.
Bru. Say, you ne'er had done 't—
Harp on that still—but by our putting on;
And presently, when you have drawn your number,
Repair to th' Capitol.

182. ignorant to see 't, so dull as not to see it. **185. lesson'd,** instructed. **188. charters,** privileges. **189. weal,** commonwealth. **202. call'd,** roused. **204. article,** stipulation. **212. heart,** mind. **213. rectorship,** guidance. **215. Of,** on. **220. piece,** increase.

227. Enforce, stress. **232. apprehension,** perception. **portance,** conduct. **235. labour'd . . . between,** worked to remove all obstacles. **246ff.** This whole account of the genealogy of the **Marcii**, including their supposed descent from Ancus, the fourth king of the Romans, is taken from *Plutarch*. **257. Scaling,** weighing. **260. putting on,** instigation. **261. drawn,** collected.

All. We will so. Almost all
Repent in their election.
Exeunt Plebeians.
Bru. Let them go on;
This mutiny were better put in hazard,
Than stay, past doubt, for greater.
If, as his nature is, he fall in rage
With their refusal, both observe and answer
The vantage of his anger.
Sic. To th' Capitol, come:
We will be there before the stream o' th' people;
And this shall seem, as partly 't is, their own,
Which we have goaded onward. *Exeunt.*

ACT III. SCENE I. *Rome. A street.*

Cornets. Enter *Coriolanus, Menenius,* all the *Gentry, Cominius, Titus Lartius,* and other *Senators.*

Cor. Tullus Aufidius then had made new head?
Lart. He had, my lord; and that it was which caus'd
Our swifter composition.
Cor. So then the Volsces stand but as at first,
Ready, when time shall prompt them, to make road
Upon 's again.
Com. They are worn, Lord Consul, so,
That we shall hardly in our ages see
Their banners wave again.
Cor. Saw you Aufidius?
Lart. On safe-guard he came to me, and did curse
Against the Volsces, for they had so vilely
Yielded the town: he is retired to Antium.
Cor. Spoke he of me?
Lart. He did, my lord.
Cor. How? What?
Lart. How often he had met you, sword to sword;
That of all things upon the earth he hated
Your person most; that he would pawn his fortunes
To hopeless restitution, so he might
Be call'd your vanquisher.
Cor. At Antium lives he?
Lart. At Antium.
Cor. I wish I had a cause to seek him there,
To oppose his hatred fully. Welcome home.

Enter *Sicinius* and *Brutus.*

Behold, these are the tribunes of the people,
The tongues o' th' common mouth. I do despise them,
For they do prank them in authority,
Against all noble sufferance.
Sic. Pass no further.
Cor. Ha! what is that?
Bru. It will be dangerous to go on. No further.
Cor. What makes this change?
Men. The matter?
Com. Hath he not pass'd the noble and the common?
Bru. Cominius, no.
Cor. Have I had children's voices?
First Sen. Tribunes, give way; he shall to th' market-place.
Bru. The people are incens'd against him.
Sic. Stop,
Or all will fall in broil.
Cor. Are these your herd?
Must these have voices, that can yield them now
And straight disclaim their tongues? What are your offices?
You being their mouths, why rule you not their teeth?
Have you not set them on?
Men. Be calm, be calm.
Cor. It is a purpos'd thing, and grows by plot,
To curb the will of the nobility.
Suffer 't, and live with such as cannot rule
Nor ever will be ruled.
Bru. Call 't not a plot.
The people cry you mock'd them, and of late,
When corn was given them gratis, you repin'd,
Scandal'd the suppliants for the people, call'd them
Time-pleasers, flatterers, foes to nobleness.
Cor. Why, this was known before.
Bru. Not to them all.
Cor. Have you inform'd them sithence?
Bru. How! I inform them!
Com. You are like to do such business.

264. put in hazard, risked. **265. stay,** wait. **greater,** i.e., hazard or risk. **Act III, Scene i: 1. made new head,** recruited new army. **3. composition,** coming to terms. **16. To hopeless restitution,** beyond hope of redemption.

267. answer . . . anger, profit by the advantage given by his anger. **Act III, Scene i: 23. prank them,** preen themselves. **24. noble sufferance,** permission of the aristocracy. **47. sithence,** since.

Bru. Not unlike,
Each way, to better yours.
Cor. Why then should I be consul? By yond clouds,
Let me deserve so ill as you, and make me
Your fellow tribune.
Sic. You show too much of that
For which the people stir. If you will pass
To where you are bound, you must inquire your way,
Which you are out of, with a gentler spirit,
Or never be so noble as a consul,
Nor yoke with him for tribune.
Men. Let 's be calm.
Com. The people are abus'd; set on. This palt'ring
Becomes not Rome, nor has Coriolanus
Deserv'd this so dishonour'd rub, laid falsely
I' th' plain way of his merit.
Cor. Tell me of corn!
This was my speech, and I will speak 't again—
Men. Not now, not now.
First Sen. Not in this heat, sir, now.
Cor. Now, as I live, I will. My nobler friends,
I crave their pardons;
For the mutable, rank-scented many, let them
Regard me as I do not flatter, and
Therein behold themselves. I say again,
In soothing them we nourish 'gainst our Senate
The cockle of rebellion, insolence, sedition,
Which we ourselves have plough'd for, sow'd, and scatter'd,
By mingling them with us, the honour'd number,
Who lack not virtue, no, nor power, but that
Which they have given to beggars.
Men. Well, no more.
First Sen. No more words, we beseech you.
Cor. How! no more!
As for my country I have shed my blood,
Not fearing outward force, so shall my lungs
Coin words till their decay against those measles,
Which we disdain should tetter us, yet sought
The very way to catch them.
Bru. You speak o' th' people
As if you were a god to punish, not
A man of their infirmity.
Sic. 'T were well
We let the people know 't.
Men. What, what? his choler?
Cor. Choler!
Were I as patient as the midnight sleep,
By Jove, 't would be my mind!
Sic. It is a mind
That shall remain a poison where it is,
Not poison any further.
Cor. Shall remain!
Hear you this Triton of the minnows? Mark you
His absolute "shall"?
Com. 'T was from the canon.
Cor. "Shall"!
O good but most unwise patricians! why,
You grave but reckless senators, have you thus
Given Hydra here to choose an officer,
That with his peremptory "shall," being but
The horn and noise o' th' monster's, wants not spirit
To say he 'll turn your current in a ditch,
And make your channel his? If he have power,
Then vail your ignorance; if none, awake
Your dangerous lenity. If you are learn'd,
Be not as common fools; if you are not,
Let them have cushions by you. You are plebeians,
If they be senators; and they are no less,
When, both your voices blended, the great'st taste
Most palates theirs. They choose their magistrate,
And such a one as he, who puts his "shall,"
His popular "shall," against a graver bench
Than ever frown'd in Greece. By Jove himself!
It makes the consuls base; and my soul aches
To know, when two authorities are up,
Neither supreme, how soon confusion
May enter 'twixt the gap of both and take
The one by th' other.
Com. Well, on to th' market-place.
Cor. Whoever gave that counsel, to give forth
The corn o' th' storehouse gratis, as 't was us'd
Sometime in Greece,—
Men. Well, well, no more of that.
Cor. Though there the people had more absolute power—
I say, they nourish'd disobedience, fed
The ruin of the state.
Bru. Why, shall the people give
One that speaks thus their voice?
Cor. I 'll give my reasons,
More worthier than their voices. They know the corn
Was not our recompense, resting well assur'd

48. **Not . . . yours,** not unlikely in every way to better yours (business, doings). 58. **abus'd,** deceived. 60. **rub,** obstacle. 67. **Regard . . . flatter,** pay me attention to the extent that I do not flatter. 70. **cockle,** weed. 78. **measles,** leprosy.

89. **Triton,** this sea-god was generally pictured as riding sea-horses or other monsters. 90. **from the canon,** contrary to law. 93. **Hydra,** many-headed, i.e., the multitude. 95. **horn and noise,** noisy horn. 98. **vail . . . ignorance,** let your ineptitude knuckle under. 99. **lenity,** mildness. 101. **have cushions,** i.e., be seated in the Senate. 103. **great'st . . . theirs,** the predominate taste (of the compound) smacks of them. 111. **take . . . other,** cause one to throw the other down. 121. **recompense,** payment for service.

That ne'er did service for 't; being press'd to th' war,
Even when the navel of the state was touch'd,
They would not thread the gates: this kind of service
Did not deserve corn gratis. Being i' th' war,
Their mutinies and revolts, wherein they show'd
Most valour, spoke not for them. Th' accusation
Which they have often made against the Senate,
All cause unborn, could never be the motive
Of our so frank donation. Well, what then?
How shall this bosom-multiplied digest
The Senate's courtesy? Let deeds express
What 's like to be their words: "We did request it;
We are the greater poll, and in true fear
They gave us our demands." Thus we debase
The nature of our seats and make the rabble
Call our cares fears; which will in time
Break ope the locks o' th' Senate and bring in
The crows to peck the eagles.

Men. Come, enough.

Bru. Enough, with over-measure.

Cor. No, take more!
What may be sworn by, both divine and human,
Seal what I end withal! This double worship,
Where one part does disdain with cause, the other
Insult without all reason, where gentry, title, wisdom,
Cannot conclude but by the yea and no
Of general ignorance,—it must omit
Real necessities, and give way the while
To unstable slightness; purpose so barr'd, it follows
Nothing is done to purpose. Therefore, beseech you,—
You that will be less fearful than discreet,
That love the fundamental part of state
More than you doubt the change on 't, that prefer
A noble life before a long, and wish
To jump a body with a dangerous physic
That 's sure of death without it, at once pluck out
The multitudinous tongue; let them not lick
The sweet which is their poison. Your dishonour
Mangles true judgement and bereaves the state
Of that integrity which should become 't,
Not having the power to do the good it would,
For th' ill which doth control 't.

Bru. Has said enough.

Sic. Has spoken like a traitor, and shall answer
As traitors do.

Cor. Thou wretch, despite o'erwhelm thee!
What should the people do with these bald tribunes?
On whom depending, their obedience fails
To th' greater bench. In a rebellion,
When what 's not meet, but what must be, was law,
Then were they chosen; in a better hour,
Let what is meet be said it must be meet,
And throw their power i' th' dust.

Bru. Manifest treason!

Sic. This a consul? No!

Bru. The ædiles, ho!

Enter an *Ædile.*

—Let him be apprehended.

Sic. Go, call the people; [*Exit Ædile*] in whose name myself
Attach thee as a traitorous innovator,
A foe to th' public weal. Obey, I charge thee,
And follow to thine answer.

Cor. Hence, old goat!

All Senators. We'll surety him.

Com. Ag'd sir, hands off.

Cor. Hence, rotten thing! or I shall shake thy bones
Out of thy garments.

Sic. Help, ye citizens!

Enter a rabble of *Plebeians,* with the *Ædiles.*

Men. On both sides more respect.

Sic. Here 's he that would take from you all your power.

Bru. Seize him, ædiles!

All Plebeians. Down with him! down with him!

Sec. Sen. Weapons, weapons, weapons!
They all bustle about Coriolanus crying.
Tribunes! Patricians! Citizens! What, ho!
Sicinius! Brutus! Coriolanus! Citizens!

All. Peace, peace, peace! Stay, hold, peace!

Men. What is about to be? I am out of breath;
Confusion 's near; I cannot speak. You, tribunes

124. **thread,** pass through. 129. **All cause unborn,** without cause. 131. **bosom-multiplied,** multitudinous bosom, like "many headed populace," compare l. 156 below. 132. **deeds,** i.e., their deeds. 134. **poll,** number. 142. **withal,** with. 144. **Insult,** exult. 145. **conclude,** reach a decision. 148. **purpose,** planning. 152. **doubt . . . on 't,** fear changes in it. 154. **jump,** put in hazard. 156. **tongue,** another of the many punning references to votes.

164. **despite,** malice. 167. **greater bench,** i.e., the senate. 168. **meet,** fitting. 173. **ædiles,** here *policemen.* In reality they were officials in rank next to the tribunes. 175. **Attach,** arrest. **innovator,** revolutionary. 178. **surety,** be surety for.

To th' people! Coriolanus, patience!
Speak, good Sicinius.
Sic. Hear me, people; peace!
All Plebeians. Let 's hear our tribune; peace! Speak, speak, speak!
Sic. You are at point to lose your liberties.
Marcius would have all from you; Marcius,
Whom late you have nam'd for consul.
Men. Fie, fie, fie!
This is the way to kindle, not to quench.
First Sen. To unbuild the city and to lay all flat.
Sic. What is the city but the people?
Plebeians. True,
The people are the city.
Bru. By the consent of all, we were establish'd
The people's magistrates.
Plebeians. You so remain.
Men. And so are like to do.
Com. That is the way to lay the city flat,
To bring the roof to the foundation
And bury all, which yet distinctly ranges,
In heaps and piles of ruin.
Sic. This deserves death.
Bru. Or let us stand to our authority,
Or let us lose it. We do here pronounce,
Upon the part o' th' people, in whose power
We were elected theirs, Marcius is worthy
Of present death.
Sic. Therefore lay hold of him;
Bear him to th' rock Tarpeian, and from thence
Into destruction cast him.
Bru. Ædiles, seize him!
Plebeians. Yield, Marcius, yield!
Men. Hear me one word;
Beseech you, tribunes, hear me but a word.
Æd. Peace, peace!
Men. [*To Brutus.*] Be that you seem, truly your country's friend,
And temp'rately proceed to what you would
Thus violently redress.
Bru. Sir, those cold ways
That seem like prudent helps are very poisonous
Where the disease is violent. Lay hands upon him,
And bear him to the rock.
Cor. No, I 'll die here.
Coriolanus draws his sword.
There 's some among you have beheld me fighting;
Come, try upon yourselves what you have seen me.
Men. Down with that sword! Tribunes, withdraw a while.
Bru. Lay hands upon him.
Com. Help, Marcius, help;
You that be noble, help him, young and old!
Plebeians. Down with him, down with him!
In this mutiny, the Tribunes, the Ædiles, and the People, are beat in.
Men. Go, get you to your house; begone, away!
All will be nought else.
Sec. Sen. Get you gone.
Com. Stand fast;
We have as many friends as enemies.
Men. Shall it be put to that?
First Sen. The gods forbid!
I prithee, noble friend, home to thy house;
Leave us to cure this cause.
Men. For 't is a sore upon us,
You cannot tent yourself: begone, beseech you.
Com. Come, sir, along with us.
Cor. I would they were barbarians—as they are,
Though in Rome litter'd—not Romans—as they are not,
Though calved i' th' porch o' th' Capitol!
Men. Begone!
Put not your worthy rage into your tongue;
One time will owe another.
Cor. On fair ground
I could beat forty of them.
Men. I could myself
Take up a brace of th' best of them; yea, the two tribunes.
Com. But now 't is odds beyond arithmetic;
And manhood is call'd foolery, when it stands
Against a falling fabric. Will you hence
Before the tag return, whose rage doth rend
Like interrupted waters, and o'erbear
What they are us'd to bear?
Men. Pray you, begone.
I 'll try whether my old wit be in request
With those that have but little: this must be patch'd
With cloth of any colour.
Com. Nay, come away.
Exeunt Coriolanus, Cominius and others.
A Patrician. This man has marr'd his fortune.
Men. His nature is too noble for the world;
He would not flatter Neptune for his trident,

206. which yet distinctly ranges, which is still separately ranked. **211. theirs,** i.e., their officers. **213. Tarpeian,** a bluff on the Capitoline hill over which condemned criminals were cast to their death. **225. seen me,** i.e., do.

231. nought, lost. **236. tent,** probe, cure. **242. One . . . another,** one time will be bound to pay (owe) another, or, time will mend all. **247. fabric,** building. **248. tag,** rabble. **249. interrupted,** disturbed.

Or Jove for 's power to thunder. His heart 's his mouth;
What his breast forges, that his tongue must vent;
And, being angry, does forget that ever
He heard the name of death. *A noise within.*
Here 's goodly work!

A Patrician. I would they were a-bed!

Men. I would they were in Tiber! What the vengeance!
Could he not speak 'em fair?

Re-enter *Brutus* and *Sicinius,* with the rabble again.

Sic. Where is this viper
That would depopulate the city and
Be every man himself?

Men. You worthy tribunes,—

Sic. He shall be thrown down the Tarpeian rock
With rigorous hands: he hath resisted law,
And therefore law shall scorn him further trial
Than the severity of the public power
Which he so sets at nought.

First Cit. He shall well know
The noble tribunes are the people's mouths,
And we their hands.

Plebeians. He shall, sure on 't.

Men. Sir, sir,—

Sic. Peace!

Men. Do not cry havoc, where you should but hunt
With modest warrant.

Sic. Sir, how comes 't that you
Have holp to make this rescue?

Men. Hear me speak.
As I do know the consul's worthiness,
So can I name his faults,—

Sic. Consul! what consul?

Men. The consul Coriolanus.

Bru. He consul!

Plebeians. No, no, no, no, no.

Men. If, by the tribunes' leave, and yours, good people,
I may be heard, I would crave a word or two;
The which shall turn you to no further harm
Than so much loss of time.

Sic. Speak briefly then;
For we are peremptory to dispatch
This viperous traitor. To eject him hence
Were but one danger, and to keep him here
Our certain death; therefore it is decreed
He dies to-night.

Men. Now the good gods forbid
That our renowned Rome, whose gratitude
Towards her deserved children is enroll'd
In Jove's own book, like an unnatural dam
Should now eat up her own!

Sic. He 's a disease that must be cut away.

Men. O, he 's a limb that has but a disease;
Mortal, to cut it off; to cure it, easy.
What has he done to Rome that 's worthy death?
Killing our enemies, the blood he hath lost—
Which, I dare vouch, is more than that he hath,
By many an ounce—he dropp'd it for his country;
And what is left, to lose it by his country
Were to us all that do 't and suffer it
A brand to the end o' the world.

Sic. This is clean kam.

Bru. Merely awry. When he did love his country,
It honour'd him.

Men. The service of the foot
Being once gangren'd, is not then respected
For what before it was,—

Bru. We 'll hear no more.
Pursue him to his house and pluck him thence,
Lest his infection, being of catching nature,
Spread further.

Men. One word more, one word.
This tiger-footed rage, when it shall find
The harm of unscann'd swiftness, will too late
Tie leaden pounds to 's heels. Proceed by process,
Lest parties, as he is belov'd, break out,
And sack great Rome with Romans.

Bru. If it were so,—

Sic. What do ye talk?
Have we not had a taste of his obedience?
Our ædiles smote? ourselves resisted? Come.

Men. Consider this: he has been bred i' th' wars
Since a' could draw a sword, and is ill school'd
In bolted language; meal and bran together
He throws without distinction. Give me leave;
I 'll go to him, and undertake to bring him
Where he shall answer, by a lawful form,
In peace, to his utmost peril.

First Sen. Noble tribunes,
It is the humane way: the other course
Will prove too bloody, and the end of it
Unknown to the beginning.

Sic. Noble Menenius,
Be you then as the people's officer.
Masters, lay down your weapons.

Bru. Go not home.

Sic. Meet on the market-place. We 'll attend you there;

257. heart 's, mind is. **276. modest warrant,** moderate authority. **284. turn you to,** occasion you. **286. peremptory,** firmly resolved. **292. deserved,** deserving.

297. Mortal, fatal. **303. suffer,** permit. **304. clean kam,** completely off the point. **305. Merely,** quite. **313. unscann'd,** ill-considered. **314. pounds,** pound-weights. **process,** legal processes. **315. parties,** factions. **322. bolted,** sifted, refined (of flour).

Where, if you bring not Marcius, we 'll proceed
In our first way.
Men. I 'll bring him to you.
[*To the Senators.*] Let me desire your company. He must come,
Or what is worst will follow.
First Sen. Pray you, let 's to him.
Exeunt omnes.

Scene II. *A room in the house of Coriolanus.*

Enter *Coriolanus,* with *Nobles.*

Cor. Let them pull all about mine ears, present me
Death on the wheel or at wild horses' heels,
Or pile ten hills on the Tarpeian rock,
That the precipitation might down stretch
Below the beam of sight, yet will I still
Be thus to them.
Noble. You do the nobler.
Cor. I muse my mother
Does not approve me further, who was wont
To call them woollen vassals, things created
To buy and sell with groats, to show bare heads
In congregations, to yawn, be still and wonder,
When one but of my ordinance stood up
To speak of peace or war.

Enter *Volumnia.*

—I talk of you.
Why did you wish me milder? Would you have me
False to my nature? Rather say I play
The man I am.
Vol. O, sir, sir, sir,
I would have had you put your power well on,
Before you had worn it out.
Cor. Let go.
Vol. You might have been enough the man you are,
With striving less to be so. Lesser had been
The thwartings of your dispositions, if
You had not show'd them how ye were dispos'd,
Ere they lack'd power to cross you.
Cor. Let them hang!
Vol. Ay, and burn too.

Enter *Menenius* with the *Senators.*

Men. Come, come, you have been too rough, something too rough;
You must return and mend it.
First Sen. There 's no remedy;
Unless, by not so doing, our good city
Cleave in the midst, and perish.
Vol. Pray, be counsell'd.
I have a heart as little apt as yours,
But yet a brain that leads my use of anger
To better vantage.
Men. Well said, noble woman!
Before he should thus stoop to th' herd, but that
The violent fit o' th' time craves it as physic
For the whole state, I would put mine armour on,
Which I can scarcely bear.
Cor. What must I do?
Men. Return to th' tribunes.
Cor. Well, what then? what then?
Men. Repent what you have spoke.
Cor. For them! I cannot do it to the gods;
Must I then do 't to them?
Vol. You are too absolute;
Though therein you can never be too noble,
But when extremities speak. I have heard you say
Honour and policy, like unsever'd friends,
I' th' war do grow together. Grant that, and tell me
In peace what each of them by th' other lose
That they combine not there.
Cor. Tush, tush!
Men. A good demand.
Vol. If it be honour in your wars to seem
The same you are not, which, for your best ends,
You adopt your policy, how is it less or worse
That it shall hold companionship in peace
With honour, as in war, since that to both
It stands in like request?
Cor. Why force you this?
Vol. Because that now it lies you on to speak
To th' people; not by your own instruction,
Nor by th' matter which your heart prompts you,
But with such words that are but roted in
Your tongue, though but bastards and syllables
Of no allowance to your bosom's truth.
Now, this no more dishonours you at all
Than to take in a town with gentle words,
Which else would put you to your fortune and
The hazard of much blood.
I would dissemble with my nature where
My fortunes and my friends at stake requir'd
I should do so in honour. I am in this,

4. precipitation, steepness. **5. Below the beam of sight,** further than eye can see. **7. muse,** wonder. **9. woollen,** coarse. **10. groats,** coins worth 4d. **12. ordinance,** rank. **18. Let go,** enough of that.

29. apt, impressionable. **39. absolute,** down-right, positive. **48. adopt,** adopt as. **51. It stands in like request,** it is equally in demand. **force,** urge. **52. lies you on,** lies with you. **53. own instruction,** natural promptings. **55. roted,** memorized. **57. Of no allowance to,** unauthorized by. **59. take in,** gain possession of. **60. fortune,** i.e., of war. **64. I am,** i.e., at stake.

Your wife, your son, these senators, the nobles;
And you will rather show our general louts
How you can frown, than spend a fawn upon 'em
For the inheritance of their loves and safeguard
Of what that want might ruin.

Men. Noble lady!
Come, go with us; speak fair. You may salve so,
Not what is dangerous present, but the loss
Of what is past.

Vol. I prithee now, my son,
Go to them, with this bonnet in thy hand;
And thus far having stretch'd it—here be with them—
Thy knee bussing the stones—for in such business
Action is eloquence, and the eyes of th' ignorant
More learned than the ears—waving thy head,
Which often thus correcting thy stout heart,
Now humble as the ripest mulberry
That will not hold the handling:—or say to them,
Thou art their soldier, and being bred in broils
Hast not the soft way which, thou dost confess,
Were fit for thee to use as they to claim,
In asking their good loves, but thou wilt frame
Thyself, forsooth, hereafter theirs, so far
As thou hast power and person.

Men. This but done,
Even as she speaks, why, their hearts were yours;
For they have pardons, being ask'd, as free
As words to little purpose.

Vol. Prithee now,
Go, and be rul'd; although I know thou hadst rather
Follow thine enemy in a fiery gulf
Than flatter him in a bower.

Enter *Cominius.*

Here is Cominius.

Com. I have been i' the market-place; and, sir, 't is fit
You make strong party, or defend yourself
By calmness or by absence. All 's in anger.

Men. Only fair speech.

Com. I think 't will serve, if he
Can thereto frame his spirit.

Vol. He must, and will.
Prithee now, say you will, and go about it.

Cor. Must I go show them my unbarb'd sconce? Must I
With my base tongue give to my noble heart
A lie that it must bear? Well, I will do 't;
Yet, were there but this single plot to lose,
This mould of Marcius, they to dust should grind it
And throw 't against the wind. To th' market-place!
You have put me now to such a part which never
I shall discharge to th' life.

Com. Come, come, we 'll prompt you.

Vol. I prithee now, sweet son, as thou hast said
My praises made thee first a soldier, so,
To have my praise for this, perform a part
Thou hast not done before.

Cor. Well, I must do 't.
Away, my disposition, and possess me
Some harlot's spirit! My throat of war be turn'd,
Which choir'd with my drum, into a pipe
Small as an eunuch's, or the virgin voice
That babies lull asleep! The smiles of knaves
Tent in my cheeks, and schoolboys' tears take up
The glasses of my sight! A beggar's tongue
Make motion through my lips, and my arm'd knees,
Who bow'd but in my stirrup, bend like his
That hath receiv'd an alms!—I will not do 't,
Lest I surcease to honour mine own truth
And by my body's action teach my mind
A most inherent baseness.

Vol. At thy choice, then.
To beg of thee, it is my more dishonour
Than thou of them. Come all to ruin! Let
Thy mother rather feel thy pride than fear
Thy dangerous stoutness; for I mock at death
With as big heart as thou. Do as thou list.
Thy valiantness was mine, thou suck'dst it from me,
But owe thy pride thyself.

Cor. Pray, be content.
Mother, I am going to the market-place;
Chide me no more. I 'll mountebank their loves,
Cog their hearts from them, and come home belov'd

67. **fawn,** flattery. 68. **inheritance,** possession. 69. **that . . . ruin,** the lack of that (i.e., the fawn) might ruin. 70. **salve,** remedy. 71. **Not,** not only. 75. **bussing,** kissing. 77. **waving thy head,** bowing. 78. This gesture repeated often thus (she bows) will discipline thy stout heart. 80. **hold,** bear. 83. **as they,** as for them. 88. **free,** abundant. 91. **gulf,** whirlpool. 94. **make,** gather a.

99. **unbarb'd sconce,** uncovered head. 102. **single plot,** i.e., his own body. 103. **mould,** (1) bodily frame, (2) earth (reference to **plot** of preceding line). 106. **to th' life,** naturally. 113. **choir'd,** harmonized. 116. **Tent in,** camp, lodge. **take up,** fill. 117. **glasses of my sight,** eyes. 121. **surcease,** cease. 124. **To . . . them,** it is more to my dishonor to beg of you than for you to beg of them. 126. **feel,** suffer by. 127. **stoutness,** obstinacy. 130. **owe,** own. 132. **mountebank,** act the quack for. 133. **Cog,** cheat.

Of all the trades in Rome. Look, I am going;
Commend me to my wife. I 'll return consul;
Or never trust to what my tongue can do
I' th' way of flattery further.

Vol. Do your will.

Exit Volumnia.

Com. Away! the tribunes do attend you. Arm yourself
To answer mildly; for they are prepar'd
With accusations, as I hear, more strong
Than are upon you yet.

Cor. The word is "mildly." Pray you, let us go.
Let them accuse me by invention, I
Will answer in mine honour.

Men. Ay, but mildly.

Cor. Well, mildly be it then. Mildly!

Exeunt.

Scene III. *The Forum.*

Enter *Sicinius* and *Brutus.*

Bru. In this point charge him home, that he affects
Tyrannical power: if he evade us there,
Enforce him with his envy to the people,
And that the spoil got on the Antiates
Was ne'er distributed.

Enter an *Ædile.*

What, will he come?

Æd. He 's coming.

Bru. How accompanied?

Æd. With old Menenius, and those senators
That always favour'd him.

Sic. Have you a catalogue
Of all the voices that we have procur'd
Set down by the poll?

Æd. I have; 't is ready.

Sic. Have you collected them by tribes?

Æd. I have.

Sic. Assemble presently the people hither;
And when they hear me say, "It shall be so
I' th' right and strength o' th' commons," be it either
For death, for fine, or banishment, then let them,
If I say fine, cry "Fine!" if death, cry "Death!"
Insisting on the old prerogative
And power i' th' truth o' th' cause.

Æd. I shall inform them.

Bru. And when such time they have begun to cry,
Let them not cease, but with a din confus'd
Enforce the present execution
Of what we chance to sentence.

Æd. Very well.

Sic. Make them be strong and ready for this hint,
When we shall hap to give 't them.

Bru. Go about it.

Exit Ædile.

Put him to choler straight. He hath been us'd
Ever to conquer, and to have his worth
Of contradiction. Being once chaf'd, he cannot
Be rein'd again to temperance; then he speaks
What 's in his heart, and that is there which looks
With us to break his neck.

Enter *Coriolanus, Menenius,* and *Cominius,* with others.

Sic. Well, here he comes.

Men. Calmly, I do beseech you.

Cor. Ay, as an ostler, that for th' poorest piece
Will bear the knave by the volume. Th' honour'd gods
Keep Rome in safety, and the chairs of justice
Supplied with worthy men! plant love among 's!
Throng our large temples with the shows of peace,
And not our streets with war!

First Sen. Amen, amen.

Men. A noble wish.

Re-enter *Ædile,* with *Plebeians.*

Sic. Draw near, ye people.

Æd. List to your tribunes. Audience! peace, I say!

Cor. First, hear me speak.

Both Tri. Well, say. Peace, ho!

Cor. Shall I be charg'd no further than this present?
Must all determine here?

Sic. I do demand
If you submit you to the people's voices,
Allow their officers, and are content
To suffer lawful censure for such faults
As shall be prov'd upon you?

Cor. I am content.

Men. Lo, citizens, he says he is content.
The warlike service he has done, consider; think

138. Arm yourself, prepare. **142. invention,** falsehood. **Scene iii: 1. charge him home,** accuse him. **affects,** wants. **3. Enforce,** press. **envy to,** hatred toward. **4. got on,** won from. **10. by the poll,** by individual names. **11. tribes,** administrative divisions of ancient Rome.

21. present, immediate. **26. to . . . contradiction,** to gain his point by contention. **29. which . . . neck,** which is likely to break his neck. **32. piece,** coin. **33. Will . . . volume,** will bear a whole book full of insults. **42. this present,** i.e., occasion. **43. determine,** end. **45. Allow,** acknowledge.

Upon the wounds his body bears, which show
Like graves i' th' holy churchyard.
Cor. Scratches with briers,
Scars to move laughter only.
Men. Consider further,
That when he speaks not like a citizen,
You find him like a soldier: do not take
His rougher accents for malicious sounds,
But, as I say, such as become a soldier
Rather than envy you.
Com. Well, well, no more.
Cor. What is the matter
That being pass'd for consul with full voice,
I am so dishonour'd that the very hour
You take it off again?
Sic. Answer to us.
Cor. Say, then; 't is true, I ought so.
Sic. We charge you, that you have contriv'd to take
From Rome all season'd office and to wind
Yourself into a power tyrannical;
For which you are a traitor to the people.
Cor. How! traitor!
Men. Nay, temperately; your promise.
Cor. The fires i' th' lowest hell fold in the people!
Call me their traitor! Thou injurious tribune!
Within thine eyes sat twenty thousand deaths,
In thy hands clutch'd as many millions, in
Thy lying tongue both numbers, I would say
"Thou liest" unto thee with a voice as free
As I do pray the gods.
Sic. Mark you this, people?
Plebeians. To th' rock, to th' rock with him!
Sic. Peace!
We need not put new matter to his charge.
What you have seen him do and heard him speak,
Beating your officers, cursing yourselves,
Opposing laws with strokes and here defying
Those whose great power must try him; even this,
So criminal and in such capital kind,
Deserves th' extremest death.
Bru. But since he hath
Serv'd well for Rome,—
Cor. What do you prate of service?
Bru. I talk of that, that know it.
Cor. You?
Men. Is this the promise that you made your mother?
Com. Know, I pray you,—
Cor. I 'll know no further.
Let them pronounce the steep Tarpeian death,
Vagabond exile, flaying, pent to linger
But with a grain a day, I would not buy
Their mercy at the price of one fair word;
Nor check my courage for what they can give,
To have 't with saying "Good morrow."
Sic. For that he has,
As much as in him lies, from time to time
Envied against the people, seeking means
To pluck away their power, as now at last
Given hostile strokes, and that not in the presence
Of dreaded justice, but on the ministers
That doth distribute it; in the name o' th' people
And in the power of us the tribunes, we,
Ev'n from this instant, banish him our city,
In peril of precipitation
From off the rock Tarpeian never more
To enter our Rome gates. I' th' people's name,
I say it shall be so.
Plebeians. It shall be so, it shall be so. Let him away!
He 's banished, and it shall be so.
Com. Hear me, my masters, and my common friends,—
Sic. He 's sentenc'd; no more hearing.
Com. Let me speak.
I have been consul, and can show for Rome
Her enemies' marks upon me. I do love
My country's good with a respect more tender
More holy and profound, than mine own life,
My dear wife's estimate, her womb's increase
And treasure of my loins; then if I would
Speak that,—
Sic. We know your drift; speak what?
Bru. There 's no more to be said, but he is banish'd
As enemy to the people and his country.
It shall be so.
Plebeians. It shall be so, it shall be so.
Cor. You common cry of curs! whose breath I hate
As reek o' th' rotten fens, whose loves I prize
As the dead carcasses of unburied men
That do corrupt my air, I banish you!
And here remain with your uncertainty!
Let every feeble rumour shake your hearts!
Your enemies, with nodding of their plumes,
Fan you into despair! Have the power still
To banish your defenders; till at length
Your ignorance—which finds not till it feels,
Making not reservation of yourselves,
Still your own foes—deliver you as most
Abated captives to some nation
That won you without blows! Despising,

57. **envy,** hatred toward. 63. **contriv'd,** plotted. 64. **season'd,** old, established. 70. **Within,** if within. 81. **capital kind,** manner deserving of death. 89. **pent,** imprisoned. **linger,** starve.

93. **To have 't,** even if I could have it. 97. **not,** not merely. 114. **estimate,** worth. 120. **cry,** pack. 124. **uncertainty,** fickleness. 129. **which . . . feels,** which learns not until it suffers. 130. Protecting you not from yourselves. 132. **Abated,** crestfallen.

For you, the city, thus I turn my back;
There is a world elsewhere.
Exeunt Coriolanus, Cominius, Menenius with the other Patricians. They all shout, and throw up their caps.

Æd. The people's enemy is gone, is gone!
Plebeians. Our enemy is banish'd! he is gone! Hoo! hoo!
Sic. Go, see him out at gates, and follow him,
As he hath follow'd you, with all despite;
Give him deserv'd vexation. Let a guard
Attend us through the city.
Plebeians. Come, come; let 's see him out at gates; come.
The gods preserve our noble tribunes! Come.
Exeunt.

ACT IV. SCENE I. *Rome. Before a gate of the city.*

Enter *Coriolanus, Volumnia, Virgilia, Menenius, Cominius,* with the young Nobility of Rome.

Cor. Come, leave your tears: a brief farewell. The beast
With many heads butts me away. Nay, mother,
Where is your ancient courage? You were us'd
To say extremity was the trier of spirits;
That common chances common men could bear;
That when the sea was calm all boats alike
Show'd mastership in floating; fortune's blows,
When most struck home, being gentle, wounded, craves
A noble cunning. You were us'd to load me
With precepts that would make invincible
The heart that conn'd them.
Vir. O heavens! O heavens!
Cor. Nay, I prithee, woman,—
Vol. Now the red pestilence strike all trades in Rome,
And occupations perish!
Cor. What, what, what!
I shall be lov'd when I am lack'd. Nay, mother,
Resume that spirit, when you were wont to say,
If you had been the wife of Hercules,
Six of his labours you 'd have done, and sav'd
Your husband so much sweat. Cominius,
Droop not; adieu. Farewell, my wife, my mother;
I 'll do well yet. Thou old and true Menenius,
Thy tears are salter than a younger man's,
And venomous to thine eyes. My sometime general,
I have seen thee stern, and thou hast oft beheld
Heart-hard'ning spectacles; tell these sad women
'T is fond to wail inevitable strokes,
As 't is to laugh at 'em. My mother, you wot well
My hazards still have been your solace; and
Believe 't not lightly—though I go alone,
Like to a lonely dragon, that his fen
Makes fear'd and talk'd of more than seen—your son
Will or exceed the common or be caught
With cautelous baits and practice.
Vol. My first son,
Whither wilt thou go? Take good Cominius
With thee a while; determine on some course,
More than a wild exposture to each chance
That starts i' th' way before thee.
Cor. O the gods!
Com. I 'll follow thee a month, devise with thee
Where thou shalt rest, that thou mayst hear of us
And we of thee. So if the time thrust forth
A cause for thy repeal, we shall not send
O'er the vast world to seek a single man,
And lose advantage, which doth ever cool
I' th' absence of the needer.
Cor. Fare ye well!
Thou hast years upon thee, and thou art too full
Of the wars' surfeits, to go rove with one
That 's yet unbruis'd. Bring me but out at gate.
Come, my sweet wife, my dearest mother, and
My friends of noble touch, when I am forth,
Bid me farewell, and smile. I pray you, come.
While I remain above the ground, you shall
Hear from me still, and never of me aught
But what is like me formerly.

139. despite, malice. **Act IV, Scene i: 7. fortune's . . . cunning,** there is a break in the syntax after **home. Being gentle** is a new subject. When fortune's blows are hardest, being calm when wounded requires noble fortitude. **13. red pestilence,** the plague. **23. venomous,** harmful. **26. fond,** foolish. **32. exceed the common,** excel. **33. cautelous . . . practice,** deceitful snares or treachery. **36. exposture,** exposure. **37. starts,** rises. **44. needer,** i.e., of advantage. **46. wars' surfeits,** excesses incident on military service. **49. noble touch,** proved nobleness.

Men. That 's worthily
As any ear can hear. Come, let 's not weep.
If I could shake off but one seven years
From these old arms and legs, by the good gods,
I 'd with thee every foot.
Cor. Give me thy hand:
Come. *Exeunt.*

Scene II. *Rome. A street near the gate.*

Enter the two Tribunes, *Sicinius, Brutus,* with the Ædile.

Sic. Bid them all home; he 's gone, and we 'll no further.
The nobility are vexed, whom we see have sided
In his behalf.
Bru. Now we have shown our power,
Let us seem humbler after it is done
Than when it was a-doing.
Sic. Bid them home.
Say their great enemy is gone, and they
Stand in their ancient strength.
Bru. Dismiss them home.
Exit Ædile.
Here comes his mother.

Enter *Volumnia, Virgilia,* and *Menenius.*

Sic. Let 's not meet her,
Bru. Why?
Sic. They say she 's mad.
Bru. They have ta'en note of us; keep on your way.
Vol. O, you 're well met. Th' hoarded plague o' th' gods
Requite your love!
Men. Peace, peace; be not so loud.
Vol. If that I could for weeping, you should hear,—
Nay, and you shall hear some. [*To Brutus.*] Will you be gone?
Vir. [*To Sicinius.*] You shall stay too. I would I had the power
To say so to my husband.
Sic. Are you mankind?
Vol. Ay, fool; is that a shame? Note but this fool.
Was not a man my father? Hadst thou foxship
To banish him that struck more blows for Rome
Than thou hast spoken words?
Sic. O blessed heavens!
Vol. Moe noble blows than ever thou wise words,
And for Rome's good. I 'll tell thee what:—yet go.
Nay, but thou shalt stay too:—I would my son
Were in Arabia and thy tribe before him,
His good sword in his hand.
Sic. What then?
Vir. What then!
He 'd make an end of thy posterity.
Vol. Bastards and all!
Good man, the wounds that he does bear for Rome!
Men. Come, come, peace.
Sic. I would he had continued to his country
As he began, and not unknit himself
The noble knot he made.
Bru. I would he had.
Vol. "I would he had"! 'T was you incens'd the rabble;
Cats, that can judge as fitly of his worth
As I can of those mysteries which heaven
Will not have earth to know.
Bru. Pray, let 's go.
Vol. Now, pray, sir, get you gone;
You have done a brave deed. Ere you go, hear this:
As far as doth the Capitol exceed
The meanest house in Rome, so far my son—
This lady's husband here, this, do you see?—
Whom you have banish'd, does exceed you all.
Bru. Well, well, we 'll leave you.
Sic. Why stay we to be baited
With one that wants her wits?
Exeunt Tribunes.
Vol. Take my prayers with you.
I would the gods had nothing else to do
But to confirm my curses! Could I meet 'em
But once a-day, it would unclog my heart
Of what lies heavy to 't.
Men. You have told them home;
And, by my troth, you have cause. You 'll sup with me?
Vol. Anger 's my meat; I sup upon myself,
And so shall starve with feeding. Come, let 's go.
[*To Virgilia.*] Leave this faint puling and lament as I do,
In anger, Juno-like. Come, come, come.
Exeunt the Ladies.
Men. Fie, fie, fie! *Exit.*

53. worthily, said as worthily. **Scene ii: 13. could,** i.e., speak. **16. mankind,** (1) human, (2) fierce virago. In her reply Volumnia stresses her humanness as opposed to his **foxship** (l. 18).

32. noble knot, bond of faithful service. **46. confirm,** i.e., by executing. **48. told them home,** given them a tongue-lashing. **52. puling,** whimpering.

Scene III. *A highway between Rome and Antium.*

Enter a *Roman* and a *Volsce* meeting.

Rom. I know you well, sir, and you know me: your name, I think, is Adrian.

Vols. It is so, sir: truly, I have forgot you.

Rom. I am a Roman; and my services are, as you are, against 'em. Know you me yet?

Vols. Nicanor? No.

Rom. The same, sir.

Vols. You had more beard when I last saw you; but your favour is well appeared by your tongue. What 's the news in Rome? I have a note from the Volscian state, to find you out there. You have well saved me a day's journey.

Rom. There hath been in Rome strange insurrections; the people against the senators, patricians, and nobles.

Vols. Hath been! Is it ended, then? Our state thinks not so: they are in a most warlike preparation, and hope to come upon them in the heat of their division.

Rom. The main blaze of it is past, but a small thing would make it flame again. For the nobles receive so to heart the banishment of that worthy Coriolanus, that they are in a ripe aptness to take all power from the people and to pluck from them their tribunes for ever. This lies glowing, I can tell you, and is almost mature for the violent breaking out.

Vols. Coriolanus banished?

Rom. Banished, sir.

Vols. You will be welcome with this intelligence, Nicanor.

Rom. The day serves well for them now. I have heard it said, the fittest time to corrupt a man's wife is when she 's fall'n out with her husband. Your noble Tullus Aufidius will appear well in these wars, his great opposer, Coriolanus, being now in no request of his country.

Vols. He cannot choose. I am most fortunate thus accidentally to encounter you: you have ended my business, and I will merrily accompany you home.

Rom. I shall, between this and supper, tell you most strange things from Rome; all tending to the good of their adversaries. Have you an army ready, say you?

Vols. A most royal one; the centurions and their charges, distinctly billeted, already in th' entertainment, and to be on foot at an hour's warning.

Rom. I am joyful to hear of their readiness, and am the man, I think, that shall set them in present action. So, sir, heartily well met, and most glad of your company.

Vols. You take my part from me, sir; I have the most cause to be glad of yours.

Rom. Well, let us go together. *Exeunt.*

9. favour, face. **appeared,** revealed. **11. a note,** instructions. **19. division,** disunion. **37. in no request,** neglected. **39. choose,** i.e., but succeed. **48. distinctly billeted,** separately housed. **49. entertainment,** receipt of pay and rations. **55. part,** speech.

Scene IV. *Antium. Before the house of Aufidius.*

Enter *Coriolanus,* in mean apparel, disguised and muffled.

Cor. A goodly city is this Antium. City,
'T is I that made thy widows; many an heir
Of these fair edifices 'fore my wars
Have I heard groan and drop: then know me not,
Lest that thy wives with spits and boys with stones
In puny battle slay me.

Enter a *Citizen.*

Save you, sir.

Cit. And you.

Cor. Direct me, if it be your will,
Where great Aufidius lies. Is he in Antium?

Cit. He is, and feasts the nobles of the state
At his house this night.

Cor. Which is his house, beseech you?

Cit. This, here before you.

Cor. Thank you, sir: farewell.

Exit Citizen.

O world, thy slippery turns! Friends now fast sworn,
Whose double bosoms seems to wear one heart,
Whose hours, whose bed, whose meal and exercise
Are still together, who twin, as 't were, in love
Unseparable, shall within this hour,
On a dissension of a doit, break out
To bitterest enmity; so, fellest foes,
Whose passions and whose plots have broke their sleep
To take the one the other, by some chance,
Some trick not worth an egg, shall grow dear friends
And interjoin their issues. So with me;
My birthplace hate I, and my love 's upon
This enemy town. I 'll enter. If he slay me,
He does fair justice; if he give me way,
I 'll do his country service. *Exit.*

Scene iv: 3. 'fore my wars, before me in battle. **5. spits,** iron prongs used for roasting meat. **6. Save,** God save. **12. slippery turns,** vicissitudes. **17. dissension of a doit,** dispute over a trifle. **18. fellest,** fiercest. **22. interjoin their issues,** i.e., by marriage. **25. give me way,** i.e., is friendly.

Scene V. *A hall in the house of Aufidius.*

Music plays. Enter a *Servingman.*

First Serv. Wine, wine, wine! What service is here! I think our fellows are asleep. *Exit.*

Enter a second *Servingman.*

Sec. Serv. Where 's Cotus? my master calls for him. Cotus! *Exit.*

Enter *Coriolanus.*

Cor. A goodly house! The feast smells well, but I
Appear not like a guest.

Re-enter the first *Servingman.*

First Serv. What would you have, friend? Whence are you? Here 's no place for you; pray, go to the door. *Exit.*

Cor. I have deserv'd no better entertainment,
In being Coriolanus.

Re-enter second *Servingman.*

Sec. Serv. Whence are you, sir? Has the porter his eyes in his head, that he gives entrance to such companions? Pray, get you out.

Cor. Away!

Sec. Serv. Away? get you away.

Cor. Now th' art troublesome.

Sec. Serv. Are you so brave? I 'll have you talk'd with anon.

Enter a third *Servingman.* The first meets him.

Third Serv. What fellow 's this?

First Serv. A strange one as ever I looked on; I cannot get him out o' th' house. Prithee, call my master to him.

Third Serv. What have you to do here, fellow? Pray you, avoid the house.

Cor. Let me but stand; I will not hurt your hearth.

Third Serv. What are you?

Cor. A gentleman.

Third Serv. A marv'llous poor one.

Cor. True, so I am.

Third Serv. Pray you, poor gentleman, take up some other station; here 's no place for you: pray you, avoid: come.

Cor. Follow your function, go, and batten on cold bits. *Pushes him away from him.*

Third Serv. What, you will not? Prithee, tell my master what a strange guest he has here.

Sec. Serv. And I shall. *Exit Second Servingman.*

Third Serv. Where dwell'st thou?

Cor. Under the canopy.

Third Serv. Under the canopy?

Cor. Ay.

Third Serv. Where 's that?

Cor. I' the city of kites and crows.

Third Serv. I' the city of kites and crows! What an ass it is! Then thou dwell'st with daws too?

Cor. No, I serve not thy master.

Third Serv. How, sir! do you meddle with my master?

Cor. Ay; 't is an honester service than to meddle with thy mistress.
Thou prat'st and prat'st; serve with thy trencher, hence!
Beats him away from him.

Enter *Aufidius* with the second *Servingman.*

Auf. Where is this fellow?

Sec. Serv. Here, sir: I 'd have beaten him like a dog, but for disturbing the lords within. *Servants retire.*

Auf. Whence com'st thou? What wouldst thou? Thy name?
Why speak'st not? Speak, man: what 's thy name?

Cor. If, Tullus [*unmuffling*], not yet thou know'st me, and, seeing me, dost not think me for the man I am, necessity commands me name myself.

Auf. What is thy name?

Cor. A name unmusical to the Volscians' ears,
And harsh in sound to thine.

Auf. Say, what 's thy name?
Thou hast a grim appearance, and thy face
Bears a command in 't; though thy tackle 's torn,
Thou show'st a noble vessel. What 's thy name?

Cor. Prepare thy brow to frown. Know'st thou me yet?

Auf. I know thee not. Thy name?

Cor. My name is Caius Marcius, who hath done
To thee particularly and to all the Volsces
Great hurt and mischief; thereto witness may
My surname, Coriolanus. The painful service,
The extreme dangers, and the drops of blood
Shed for my thankless country are requited
But with that surname; a good memory,
And witness of the malice and displeasure

14. companions, scurvy fellows. **25. avoid,** get out of. **35. Follow your function,** go about your business. **batten,** fatten.

41. canopy, sky. **45. kites,** scavenger hawks. **47. daws,** (1) jackdaws, (2) fools. **67. tackle,** rigging (of a ship). **77. memory,** reminder.

Which thou shouldst bear me: only that name remains.
The cruelty and envy of the people,
Permitted by our dastard nobles, who
Have all forsook me, hath devour'd the rest;
And suffer'd me by th' voice of slaves to be
Whoop'd out of Rome. Now this extremity
Hath brought me to thy hearth; not out of hope—
Mistake me not—to save my life, for if
I had fear'd death, of all the men i' th' world
I would have 'voided thee, but in mere spite,
To be full quit of those my banishers,
Stand I before thee here. Then if thou hast
A heart of wreak in thee, that wilt revenge
Thine own particular wrongs and stop those maims
Of shame seen through thy country, speed thee straight,
And make my misery serve thy turn. So use it
That my revengeful services may prove
As benefits to thee, for I will fight
Against my canker'd country with the spleen
Of all the under fiends. But if so be
Thou dar'st not this, and that to prove more fortunes
Th' art tired, then, in a word, I also am
Longer to live most weary, and present
My throat to thee and to thy ancient malice;
Which not to cut would show thee but a fool,
Since I have ever followed thee with hate,
Drawn tuns of blood out of thy country's breast,
And cannot live but to thy shame, unless
It be to do thee service.

Auf. O Marcius, Marcius!
Each word thou hast spoke hath weeded from my heart
A root of ancient envy. If Jupiter
Should from yond cloud speak divine things,
And say "'T is true," I 'd not believe them more
Than thee, all noble Marcius. Let me twine
Mine arms about that body, whereagainst
My grained ash an hundred times hath broke,
And scarr'd the moon with splinters. Here I clip
The anvil of my sword, and do contest
As hotly and as nobly with thy love
As ever in ambitious strength I did
Contend against thy valour. Know thou first,
I lov'd the maid I married; never man
Sigh'd truer breath; but that I see thee here,
Thou noble thing! more dances my rapt heart
Than when I first my wedded mistress saw
Bestride my threshold. Why, thou Mars! I tell thee,
We have a power on foot; and I had purpose
Once more to hew thy target from thy brawn,
Or lose mine arm for 't. Thou hast beat me out
Twelve several times, and I have nightly since
Dreamt of encounters 'twixt thyself and me;
We have been down together in my sleep,
Unbuckling helms, fisting each other's throat,
And wak'd half dead with nothing. Worthy Marcius,
Had we no quarrel else to Rome, but that
Thou art thence banish'd, we would muster all
From twelve to seventy, and pouring war
Into the bowels of ungrateful Rome,
Like a bold flood o'er-beat. O, come, go in,
And take our friendly senators by the hands;
Who now are here, taking their leaves of me,
Who am prepar'd against your territories,
Though not for Rome itself.

Cor. You bless me, gods!

Auf. Therefore, most absolute sir, if thou wilt have
The leading of thine own revenges, take
Th' one half of my commission; and set down—
As best thou art experienc'd, since thou know'st
Thy country's strength and weakness,—thine own ways;
Whether to knock against the gates of Rome,
Or rudely visit them in parts remote,
To fright them, ere destroy. But come in;
Let me commend thee first to those that shall
Say yea to thy desires. A thousand welcomes!
And more a friend than e'er an enemy;
Yet, Marcius, that was much. Your hand; most welcome!

Exeunt Coriolanus and Aufidius. The two Servingmen come forward.

First Serv. Here 's a strange alteration!

Sec. Serv. By my hand, I had thought to have strucken him with a cudgel; and yet my mind gave me his clothes made a false report of him.

First Serv. What an arm he has! He turn'd me about with his finger and his thumb, as one would set up a top.

Sec. Serv. Nay, I knew by his face that there was something in him. He had, sir, a kind of face, methought,—I cannot tell how to term it.

First Serv. He had so; looking as it were —would I were hanged, but I thought there was more in him than I could think.

Sec. Serv. So did I, I 'll be sworn. He is simply the rarest man i' th' world.

84. **Whoop'd**, hooted. 89. **full quit of**, fully avenged on. 91. **wreak**, vengeance. 92. **maims Of shame**, shameful injuries (done by Rome). 98. **under**, infernal. 99. **prove . . . fortunes**, take more chances. 105. **tuns**, large casks. 114. **grained ash**, spear. 121. **breath**, vows. 122. **dances**, makes leap.

131. **fisting**, grasping. 137. **o'er-beat**, beat down all before us. 142. **absolute**, perfect. 144. **set down**, determine. 157. **my . . . me**, I suspected. 161. **set up**, spin.

First Serv. I think he is; but a greater soldier than he you wot one.

Sec. Serv. Who? My master?

First Serv. Nay, it 's no matter for that.

Sec. Serv. Worth six on him.

First Serv. Nay, not so neither; but I take him to be the greater soldier.

Sec. Serv. Faith, look you, one cannot tell how to say that: for the defence of a town, our general is excellent.

First Serv. Ay, and for an assault too.

Re-enter third *Servingman.*

Third Serv. O slaves, I can tell you news,—news, you rascals!

Both. What, what, what? Let 's partake.

Third Serv. I would not be a Roman, of all nations; I had as lieve be a condemned man.

Both. Wherefore? wherefore?

Third Serv. Why, here 's he that was wont to thwack our general, Caius Marcius.

First Serv. Why do you say, "thwack our general"?

Third Serv. I do not say, "thwack our general"; but he was always good enough for him.

Sec. Serv. Come, we are fellows and friends; he was ever too hard for him; I have heard him say so himself.

First Serv. He was too hard for him directly, to say the troth on 't. Before Corioli he scotcht him and notcht him like a carbonado.

Sec. Serv. And he had been cannibally given, he might have boil'd and eaten him too.

First Serv. But more of thy news.

Third Serv. Why, he is so made on here within, as if he were son and heir to Mars; set at upper end o' th' table; no question asked him by any of the senators, but they stand bald before him. Our general himself makes a mistress of him; sanctifies himself with 's hand and turns up the white o' th' eye to his discourse. But the bottom of the news is, our general is cut i' th' middle and but one half of what he was yesterday; for the other has half, by the entreaty and grant of the whole table. He 'll go, he says, and sowl the porter of Rome gates by th' ears. He will mow all down before him, and leave his passage polled.

Sec. Serv. And he 's as like to do 't as any man I can imagine.

Third Serv. Do 't! he will do 't; for, look you, sir, he has as many friends as enemies; which friends, sir, as it were, durst not, look you, sir, show themselves, as we term it, his friends whilst he 's in directitude.

First Serv. Directitude! What 's that?

Third Serv. But when they shall see, sir, his crest up again, and the man in blood, they will out of their burrows, like conies after rain, and revel all with him.

First Serv. But when goes this forward?

Third Serv. To-morrow; to-day; presently; you shall have the drum struck up this afternoon. 'T is, as it were, a parcel of their feast, and to be executed ere they wipe their lips.

Sec. Serv. Why, then we shall have a stirring world again. This peace is nothing, but to rust iron, increase tailors, and breed ballad-makers.

First Serv. Let me have war, say I; it exceeds peace as far as day does night; it 's spritely, waking, audible, and full of vent. Peace is a very apoplexy, lethargy; mulled, deaf, sleepy, insensible; a getter of more bastard children than war 's a destroyer of men.

Sec. Serv. 'T is so; and as wars, in some sort, may be said to be a ravisher, so it cannot be denied but peace is a great maker of cuckolds.

First Serv. Ay, and it makes men hate one another.

Third Serv. Reason; because they then less need one another. The wars for my money! I hope to see Romans as cheap as Volscians.—They are rising, they are rising.

Both. In, in, in, in! *Exeunt.*

Scene VI. *Rome. A public place.*

Enter the two Tribunes *Sicinius* and *Brutus.*

Sic. We hear not of him, neither need we fear him;
His remedies are tame. The present peace
And quietness of the people, which before
Were in wild hurry here, do make his friends
Blush that the world goes well, who rather had,
Though they themselves did suffer by 't, behold
Dissentious numbers pest'ring streets than see
Our tradesmen singing in their shops and going
About their functions friendly.

171. **wot one,** know to be one, i.e., Aufidius. 182. **partake,** i.e., of it. 199. **carbonado,** steak cut for broiling. 203. **made on,** made much of. 208. **sanctifies . . . hand,** blesses himself with his hand, i.e., holds his hand. 209. **bottom,** fundamental part. 213. **sowl,** pull. 215. **leave . . . poll'd,** have his course cleared.

222. **directitude,** perhaps for **discredit.** 225. **in blood,** in good condition (hunting term). 226. **conies,** rabbits. 229. **presently,** at once. 238. **audible,** capable of hearing. **vent,** opportunity for action. 239. **mulled,** lethargic. 247. **Reason,** that is reasonable. 250. **rising,** i.e., from the table. **Scene vi:** 2. **remedies,** means of redress. **tame,** harmless, ineffectual. 7. **pest'ring,** infesting, blocking.

Enter *Menenius.*

Bru. We stood to 't in good time. Is this Menenius?
Sic. 'T is he, 't is he. O, he is grown most kind of late.
Hail, sir!
Men. Hail to you both!
Sic. Your Coriolanus
Is not much miss'd, but with his friends:
The commonwealth doth stand, and so would do,
Were he more angry at it.
Men. All 's well; and might have been much better, if
He could have temporiz'd.
Sic. Where is he, hear you?
Men. Nay, I hear nothing; his mother and his wife
Hear nothing from him.

Enter three or four *Citizens.*

All Citizens. The gods preserve you both!
Sic. God-den, our neighbours.
Bru. God-den to you all, god-den to you all.
First Cit. Ourselves, our wives, and children, on our knees,
Are bound to pray for you both.
Sic. Live, and thrive!
Bru. Farewell, kind neighbours! We wish'd Coriolanus
Had lov'd you as we did.
All Citizens. Now the gods keep you!
Both Tri. Farewell, farewell.
Exeunt Citizens.
Sic. This is a happier and more comely time
Than when these fellows ran about the streets,
Crying confusion.
Bru. Caius Marcius was
A worthy officer i' th' war; but insolent,
O'ercome with pride, ambitious past all thinking,
Self-loving,—
Sic. And affecting one sole throne,
Without assistance.
Men. I think not so.
Sic. We should by this, to all our lamentation,
If he had gone forth consul, found it so.
Bru. The gods have well prevented it, and Rome
Sits safe and still without him.

Enter an *Ædile.*

Æd. Worthy tribunes,
There is a slave, whom we have put in prison,
Reports the Volsces with two several powers
Are enter'd in the Roman territories,
And with the deepest malice of the war
Destroy what lies before 'em.
Men. 'T is Aufidius,
Who, hearing of our Marcius' banishment,
Thrusts forth his horns again into the world;
Which were inshell'd when Marcius stood for Rome,
And durst not once peep out.
Sic. Come, what talk you
Of Marcius?
Bru. Go see this rumourer whipp'd. It cannot be
The Volsces dare break with us.
Men. Cannot be!
We have record that very well it can;
And three examples of the like hath been
Within my age. But reason with the fellow,
Before you punish him, where he heard this,
Lest you shall chance to whip your information
And beat the messenger who bids beware
Of what is to be dreaded.
Sic. Tell not me!
I know this cannot be.
Bru. Not possible.

Enter a *Messenger.*

Mess. The nobles in great earnestness are going
All to the Senate-house; some news is come
That turns their countenances.
Sic. 'T is this slave,—
Go whip him 'fore the people's eyes,—his raising;
Nothing but his report.
Mess. Yes, worthy sir,
The slave's report is seconded; and more,
More fearful, is deliver'd.
Sic. What more fearful?
Mess. It is spoke freely out of many mouths—
How probable I do not know—that Marcius,
Join'd with Aufidius, leads a power 'gainst Rome,
And vows revenge as spacious as between
The young'st and oldest thing.
Sic. This is most likely!
Bru. Rais'd only, that the weaker sort may wish
Good Marcius home again.
Sic. The very trick on 't.
Men. This is unlikely.

20. God-den, God give you good evening. **27. comely,** orderly. **32. affecting . . . throne,** wanting to rule alone. **34. this,** i.e., time. **35. gone forth,** become. **37. still,** quiet. **39. several powers,** separate armies. **44. Thrusts . . . horns,** i.e., like a snail. **45. inshell'd,** drawn back into his shell. **stood for,** championed. **46. what,** why. **51. reason,** speak. **59. turns their countenances,** i.e., startles, frightens them. **67. as spacious as between,** as all-embracing as to include. **69. Rais'd,** invented, i.e., the news. **70. trick on 't,** trickery of it.

He and Aufidius can no more atone
Than violent'st contrariety.

Enter a second *Messenger*.

Sec. Mess. You are sent for to the Senate.
A fearful army, led by Caius Marcius
Associated with Aufidius, rages
Upon our territories; and have already
O'erborne their way, consum'd with fire, and took
What lay before them.

Enter *Cominius*.

Com. O, you have made good work!
Men. What news? what news?
Com. You have holp to ravish your own daughters and
To melt the city leads upon your pates,
To see your wives dishonour'd to your noses,—
Men. What 's the news? what 's the news?
Com. Your temples burned in their cement, and
Your franchises, whereon you stood, confin'd
Into an auger's bore.
Men. Pray now, your news?—
You have made fair work, I fear me.—Pray, your news?
If Marcius should be join'd with Volscians,—
Com. If!
He is their god: he leads them like a thing
Made by some other deity than nature,
That shapes man better; and they follow him,
Against us brats, with no less confidence
Than boys pursuing summer butterflies,
Or butchers killing flies.
Men. You have made good work,
You and your apron-men; you that stood so much
Upon the voice of occupation and
The breath of garlic-eaters!
Com. He will shake
Your Rome about your ears.
Men. As Hercules
Did shake down mellow fruit. You have made fair work!
Bru. But is this true, sir?
Com. Ay; and you 'll look pale
Before you find it other. All the regions
Do smilingly revolt; and who resists
Are mock'd for valiant ignorance,
And perish constant fools. Who is 't can blame him?
Your enemies and his find something in him.
Men. We are all undone, unless
The noble man have mercy.
Com. Who shall ask it?
The tribunes cannot do 't for shame; the people
Deserve such pity of him as the wolf
Does of the shepherds: for his best friends, if they
Should say, "Be good to Rome," they charg'd him even
As those should do that had deserv'd his hate,
And therein show'd like enemies.
Men. 'T is true.
If he were putting to my house the brand
That should consume it, I have not the face
To say, "Beseech you, cease." You have made fair hands,
You and your crafts! You have crafted fair!
Com. You have brought
A trembling upon Rome, such as was never
So incapable of help.
Both Tri. Say not we brought it.
Men. How! Was 't we? We lov'd him; but, like beasts
And cowardly nobles, gave way unto your clusters,
Who did hoot him out o' th' city.
Com. But I fear
They 'll roar him in again. Tullus Aufidius,
The second name of men, obeys his points
As if he were his officer. Desperation
Is all the policy, strength, and defence,
That Rome can make against them.

Enter a troop of *Citizens*.

Men. Here comes the clusters.
And is Aufidius with him? You are they
That made the air unwholesome, when you cast
Your stinking greasy caps in hooting at
Coriolanus' exile. Now he 's coming;
And not a hair upon a soldier's head
Which will not prove a whip. As many coxcombs
As you threw caps up will he tumble down,
And pay you for your voices. 'T is no matter;
If he could burn us all into one coal,
We have deserv'd it.
All Citizens. Faith, we hear fearful news.
First Cit. For mine own part,
When I said, banish him, I said, 't was pity.
Sec. Cit. And so did I.
Third Cit. And so did I; and, to say the truth, so did very many of us. That we did, we did for the best; and though we willingly con-

72. atone, become reconciled. **73. contrariety,** opposites. **78. O'erborne . . . way,** swept over their path. **81. holp,** helped. **82. leads,** leaden roofs. **83. to,** before. **85. cement,** mortar-fire so hot that it will consume even the mortar. **86f.** Your rights, which you have asserted, reduced to nothingness. **96. apron-men,** artisans. **97. occupation,** workmen. **103. smilingly,** gladly. **105. constant,** confirmed.

112. charg'd, would be advising. **114. show'd,** would appear. **117. made fair hands,** done good work. **122. clusters,** mobs. **124. roar,** i.e., with pain. **125. second name,** i.e., after Coriolanus. **points,** directions. **134. coxcombs,** fools' heads.

sented to his banishment, yet it was against our will.

Com. You 're goodly things, you voices!

Men. You have made
Good work, you and your cry! Shall 's to the Capitol?

Com. O, ay, what else?

Exeunt Cominius and Menenius.

Sic. Go, masters, get you home; be not dismay'd.
These are a side that would be glad to have
This true which they so seem to fear. Go home,
And show no sign of fear.

First Cit. The gods be good to us! Come, masters, let 's home. I ever said we were i' th' wrong when we banished him.

Sec. Cit. So did we all. But, come, let 's home. *Exeunt Citizens.*

Bru. I do not like this news.

Sic. Nor I.

Bru. Let 's to the Capitol. Would half my wealth
Would buy this for a lie!

Sic. Pray, let 's go.

Exeunt.

Scene VII. *A camp, at a small distance from Rome.*

Enter *Aufidius* with his *Lieutenant.*

Auf. Do they still fly to th' Roman?

Lieu. I do not know what witchcraft 's in him, but
Your soldiers use him as the grace 'fore meat,
Their talk at table, and their thanks at end;
And you are darken'd in this action, sir,
Even by your own.

Auf. I cannot help it now,
Unless, by using means, I lame the foot
Of our design. He bears himself more proudlier,
Even to my person, than I thought he would
When first I did embrace him; yet his nature
In that 's no changeling; and I must excuse
What cannot be amended.

Lieu. Yet I wish, sir,—
I mean for your particular,—you had not
Join'd in commission with him; but either
Have borne the action of yourself, or else
To him had left it solely.

Auf. I understand thee well; and be thou sure,
When he shall come to his account, he knows not
What I can urge against him. Although it seems,
And so he thinks, and is no less apparent
To th' vulgar eye, that he bears all things fairly,
And shows good husbandry for the Volscian state,
Fights dragon-like, and does achieve as soon
As draw his sword; yet he hath left undone
That which shall break his neck or hazard mine,
Whene'er we come to our account.

Lieu. Sir, I beseech you, think you he 'll carry Rome?

Auf. All places yields to him ere he sits down,
And the nobility of Rome are his:
The senators and patricians love him too;
The tribunes are no soldiers, and their people
Will be as rash in the repeal as hasty
To expel him thence. I think he 'll be to Rome
As is the osprey to the fish, who takes it
By sovereignty of nature. First he was
A noble servant to them, but he could not
Carry his honours even: whether 't was pride,
Which out of daily fortune ever taints
The happy man; whether defect of judgement,
To fail in the disposing of those chances
Which he was lord of; or whether nature,
Not to be other than one thing, not moving
From the casque to th' cushion, but commanding peace
Even with the same austerity and garb
As he controll'd the war; but one of these,—
As he hath spices of them all—not all,—
For I dare so far free him,—made him fear'd;
So, hated; and so, banish'd: but he has a merit
To choke it in th' utterance. So our virtues
Lie in th' interpretation of the time;
And power, unto itself most commendable,
Hath not a tomb so evident as a chair
T' extol what it hath done.
One fire drives out one fire; one nail, one nail;
Rights by rights founder, strengths by strengths do fail.
Come, let 's away. When, Caius, Rome is thine,
Thou art poor'st of all; then shortly art thou mine. *Exeunt.*

148. **cry,** pack (of hounds). 151. **a side,** of the party. Scene vii: 5. **darken'd . . . action,** over-shadowed in this campaign. 6. **own,** i.e., troops. 7. **means,** i.e., of curbing him. 11. **In that 's no changeling,** has not changed. 13. **particular,** own good. 14. **commission,** authority. 15. **of yourself,** by yourself, alone.

23. **achieve,** conquer. 28. **sits down,** besieges. 34. **osprey,** fish-hawk, supposed to hypnotize fish. 37. **even,** steadily. 38. **daily fortune,** constant good fortune. 40. **disposing,** exploiting. 41. **nature,** his nature. 42. **Not to be,** not capable of being. 43. **casque,** helmet, i.e., battlefield. **cushion,** i.e., the Senate. 47. **free,** acquit. 49. **it,** i.e., condemnation. 51. **unto,** in. 52f. **Is near its end when the possessor, seated in authority, justifies the steps by which he attained it.**

Act V. Scene I. *Rome. A public place.*

Enter *Menenius, Cominius, Sicinius, Brutus,* the two *Tribunes,* with others.

Men. No, I 'll not go. You hear what he hath said
Which was sometime his general; who lov'd him
In a most dear particular. He call'd me father;
But what o' that? Go, you that banish'd him;
A mile before his tent fall down, and knee
The way into his mercy. Nay, if he coy'd
To hear Cominius speak, I 'll keep at home.
Com. He would not seem to know me.
Men. Do you hear?
Com. Yet one time he did call me by my name.
I urg'd our old acquaintance, and the drops
That we have bled together. Coriolanus
He would not answer to; forbade all names;
He was a kind of nothing, titleless,
Till he had forg'd himself a name o' th' fire
Of burning Rome.
Men. Why, so; you have made good work!
A pair of tribunes that have rack'd for Rome
To make coals cheap! A noble memory!
Com. I minded him how royal 't was to pardon
When it was less expected; he replied,
It was a bare petition of a state
To one whom they had punish'd.
Men. Very well;
Could he say less?
Com. I offered to awaken his regard
For 's private friends; his answer to me was,
He could not stay to pick them in a pile
Of noisome musty chaff. He said 't was folly,
For one poor grain or two, to leave unburnt
And still to nose th' offence.
Men. For one poor grain or two!
I am one of those; his mother, wife, his child,
And this brave fellow too, we are the grains.
You are the musty chaff, and you are smelt
Above the moon. We must be burnt for you.
Sic. Nay, pray, be patient: if you refuse your aid
In this so never-needed help, yet do not
Upbraid 's with our distress. But, sure, if you
Would be your country's pleader, your good tongue,
More than the instant army we can make,
Might stop our countryman.
Men. No, I 'll not meddle.
Sic. Pray you, go to him.
Men. What should I do?
Bru. Only make trial what your love can do
For Rome, towards Marcius.
Men. Well, and say that Marcius
Return me, as Cominius is return'd,
Unheard; what then?
But as a discontented friend, grief-shot
With his unkindness? Say 't be so?
Sic. Yet your good will
Must have that thanks from Rome, after the measure
As you intended well.
Men. I 'll undertake 't.
I think he 'll hear me. Yet, to bite his lip
And hum at good Cominius, much unhearts me.
He was not taken well; he had not din'd.
The veins unfill'd, our blood is cold, and then
We pout upon the morning, are unapt
To give or to forgive; but when we have stuff'd
These pipes and these conveyances of our blood
With wine and feeding, we have suppler souls
Than in our priest-like fasts: therefore I 'll watch him
Till he be dieted to my request,
And then I 'll set upon him.
Bru. You know the very road into his kindness,
And cannot lose your way.
Men. Good faith, I 'll prove him,
Speed how it will. I shall ere long have knowledge
Of my success. *Exit.*
Com. He 'll never hear him.
Sic. Not?
Com. I tell you, he does sit in gold, his eye
Red as 't would burn Rome; and his injury
The jailer to his pity. I kneel'd before him;
'T was very faintly he said, "Rise"; dismiss'd me
Thus, with his speechless hand. What he would do,
He sent in writing after me, what he would not,
Bound with an oath to yield to his conditions;
So that all hope is vain,
Unless his noble mother and his wife,—
Who, as I hear, mean to solicit him
For mercy to his country. Therefore, let 's hence,
And with our fair entreaties haste them on.
Exeunt.

3. particular, personal way. **5. knee,** go on your knees. **6. coy'd,** was reluctant. **16. rack'd for Rome,** strained themselves for the cause of Rome. **17. coals,** charcoal. **20. bare,** poor. **28. nose,** smell. **37. instant . . . make,** the army we can muster at the moment.

49. unhearts, disheartens. **50. taken well,** i e., at a proper time. **52. pout,** glare. **57. dieted to,** fed up for. **60. prove,** try. **63. in gold,** on a golden throne. **66. faintly,** distantly. **69.** Binding us with an oath to submit to his conditions.

Scene II. *The Volscian camp before Rome. The Watch on guard.*

Enter to them, *Menenius.*

First Watch. Stay! Whence are you?
Sec. Watch. Stand, and go back.
Men. You guard like men; 't is well; but, by your leave,
I am an officer of state, and come
To speak with Coriolanus.
First Watch. From whence?
Men. From Rome.
First Watch. You may not pass, you must return; our general
Will no more hear from thence.
Sec. Watch. You 'll see your Rome embrac'd with fire before
You 'll speak with Coriolanus.
Men. Good my friends,
If you have heard your general talk of Rome
And of his friends there, it is lots to blanks,
My name hath touch'd your ears; it is Menenius.
First Watch. Be it so; go back: the virtue of your name
Is not here passable.
Men. I tell thee, fellow,
Thy general is my lover: I have been
The book of his good acts, whence men have read
His fame unparallel'd, haply amplified;
For I have ever magnified my friends,
(Of whom he 's chief) with all the size that verity
Would without lapsing suffer; nay, sometimes,
Like to a bowl upon a subtle ground,
I have tumbled past the throw; and in his praise
Have almost stamp'd the leasing. Therefore, fellow,
I must have leave to pass.

First Watch. Faith, sir, if you had told as many lies in his behalf as you have uttered words in your own, you should not pass here; no, though it were as virtuous to lie as to live chastely. Therefore, go back.

Men. Prithee, fellow, remember my name is Menenius, always factionary on the party of your general.

Sec. Watch. Howsoever you have been his liar, as you say you have, I am one that, telling true under him, must say you cannot pass. Therefore, go back.

Men. Has he dined, canst thou tell? for I would not speak with him till after dinner.

First Watch. You are a Roman, are you?

Men. I am, as thy general is.

First Watch. Then you should hate Rome, as he does. Can you, when you have pushed out your gates the very defender of them, and, in a violent popular ignorance, given your enemy your shield, think to front his revenges with the easy groans of old women, the virginal palms of your daughters, or with the palsied intercession of such a decayed dotant as you seem to be? Can you think to blow out the intended fire your city is ready to flame in, with such weak breath as this? No, you are deceived; therefore, back to Rome, and prepare for your execution: you are condemned, our general has sworn you out of reprieve and pardon.

Men. Sirrah, if thy captain knew I were here, he would use me with estimation.

First Watch. Come, my captain knows you not.

Men. I mean, thy general.

First Watch. My general cares not for you. Back, I say, go; lest I let forth your half-pint of blood. Back, that 's the utmost of your having; back!

Men. Nay, but, fellow, fellow,—

Enter *Coriolanus* with *Aufidius.*

Cor. What 's the matter?

Men. Now, you companion, I 'll say an errand for you: you shall know now that I am in estimation; you shall perceive that a Jack guardant cannot office me from my son Coriolanus: guess but by my entertainment with him if thou stand'st not i' th' state of hanging, or of some death more long in spectatorship, and crueller in suffering; behold now presently, and swound for what 's to come upon thee. [*To Cor.*] The glorious gods sit in hourly synod about thy particular prosperity, and love thee no worse than thy old father Menenius does! O my son, my son! thou art preparing fire for us; look thee, here 's water to quench it. I was hardly moved to come to thee; but being assured none but myself could move thee, I have been blown out of our gates with sighs; and conjure thee to pardon Rome, and thy petitionary countrymen. The good gods assuage thy wrath, and turn the dregs of it upon this varlet here,—this, who, like a block, hath denied my access to thee.

10. **it is lots to blanks,** it is likely. In a lottery, lots called for prizes, blanks did not. 16. **haply,** perhaps. 18. **size,** exaggeration. 19. **lapsing,** i.e., into falsehood. 20. **subtle,** deceptive. 21. **throw,** point aimed at (in the game of bowls). 22. **stamp'd the leasing,** established what is falsehood. 30. **factionary . . . party,** participant on the side.

43. **popular ignorance,** mob-like stupidity. 44. **front,** oppose. 47. **dotant,** dotard. 53. **out of,** beyond hope of. 56. **estimation,** esteem. 62. **having,** advance, lit., possession (of ground). 65. **an errand,** a message. 67. **Jack guardant,** saucy sentry. 68. **office,** hold by virtue of his office. 70. **in spectatorship,** to be witnessed. 74. **synod,** conference. 78. **hardly,** with difficulty. 85. **block,** blockhead.

Cor. Away!
Men. How? away?
Cor. Wife, mother, child, I know not. My affairs
Are servanted to others; though I owe
My revenge properly, my remission lies
In Volscian breasts. That we have been familiar,
Ingrate forgetfulness shall poison rather
Than pity note how much. Therefore, begone.
Mine ears against your suits are stronger than
Your gates against my force. Yet, for I loved thee,
Take this along. I writ it for thy sake,
Gives him a letter.
And would have sent it. Another word, Menenius,
I will not hear thee speak. This man, Aufidius,
Was my belov'd in Rome; yet thou behold'st!
Auf. You keep a constant temper.
Exeunt Coriolanus and Aufidius.

First Watch. Now, sir, is your name Menenius?

Sec. Watch. 'T is a spell, you see, of much power. You know the way home again.

First Watch. Do you hear how we are shent for keeping your greatness back?

Sec. Watch. What cause do you think I have to swound?

Men. I neither care for th' world nor your general; for such things as you, I can scarce think there 's any, y' are so slight. He that hath a will to die by himself fears it not from another. Let your general do his worst. For you, be that you are, long; and your misery increase with your age! I say to you, as I was said to, Away! *Exit.*

First Watch. A noble fellow, I warrant him.

Sec. Watch. The worthy fellow is our general. He 's the rock, the oak not to be windshaken. *Exeunt.*

Scene III. *The tent of Coriolanus.*

Enter *Coriolanus, Aufidius,* and others.

Cor. We will before the walls of Rome tomorrow
Set down our host. My partner in this action,
You must report to th' Volscian lords, how plainly
I have borne this business.
Auf. Only their ends
You have respected; stopp'd your ears against
The general suit of Rome; never admitted
A private whisper, no, not with such friends
That thought them sure of you.
Cor. This last old man,
Whom with a crack'd heart I have sent to Rome,
Lov'd me above the measure of a father;
Nay, godded me, indeed. Their latest refuge
Was to send him; for whose old love I have,
(Though I show'd sourly to him) once more offer'd
The first conditions, which they did refuse
And cannot now accept, to grace him only
That thought he could do more. A very little
I have yielded to. Fresh embassies and suits,
Nor from the state nor private friends, hereafter
Will I lend ear to. Ha! what shout is this?
Shout within.
Shall I be tempted to infringe my vow
In the same time 't is made? I will not.

Enter *Virgilia, Volumnia,* young *Marcius, Valeria,* with Attendants.

My wife comes foremost; then the honour'd mould
Wherein this trunk was fram'd, and in her hand
The grandchild to her blood. But out, affection!
All bond and privilege of nature, break!
Let it be virtuous to be obstinate.
What is that curtsy worth? or those doves' eyes,
Which can make gods forsworn? I melt, and am not
Of stronger earth than others. My mother bows,
As if Olympus to a molehill should
In supplication nod; and my young boy
Hath an aspect of intercession which
Great nature cries, "Deny not." Let the Volsces
Plough Rome and harrow Italy, I 'll never
Be such a gosling to obey instinct, but stand
As if a man were author of himself
And knew no other kin.
Vir. My lord and husband!
Cor. These eyes are not the same I wore in Rome.
Vir. The sorrow that delivers us thus chang'd
Makes you think so.

89. servanted, subjected. **90. properly,** myself. **remission,** mercy. **91. That . . . much,** I had rather ingrate oblivion destroy the memory of our friendship than pity recall it (to sway me from my purpose). **95. for,** because. **105. shent,** berated. **110. by himself,** i.e., by his own hand. **Scene iii: 2. Set down,** i.e., as besiegers. **3. plainly,** honestly. **4. borne,** conducted.

8. them, themselves. **11. godded,** idolized. **13. show'd sourly,** acted sullenly. **35. gosling,** young goose—reference to swimming instinct. **39. that . . . chang'd,** that shows us thus changed, i.e., in mourning. Virgilia purposely misconstrues his speech as a reference to a change in them and not in himself.

Cor. Like a dull actor now
I have forgot my part, and I am out,
Even to a full disgrace. Best of my flesh,
Forgive my tyranny; but do not say
For that, "Forgive our Romans." O, a kiss
Long as my exile, sweet as my revenge!
Now, by the jealous queen of heaven, that kiss
I carried from thee, dear; and my true lip
Hath virgin'd it e'er since. You gods! I prate,
And the most noble mother of the world
Leave unsaluted. Sink, my knee, i' th' earth; *Kneels.*
Of thy deep duty more impression show
Than that of common sons.
Vol. O, stand up, bless'd!
Whilst, with no softer cushion than the flint,
I kneel before thee; and unproperly
Show duty, as mistaken all this while
Between the child and parent. *Kneels.*
Cor. [*Raising her.*] What 's this?
Your knees to me? to your corrected son?
Then let the pebbles on the hungry beach
Fillip the stars; then let the mutinous winds
Strike the proud cedars 'gainst the fiery sun,
Murd'ring impossibility, to make
What cannot be, slight work.
Vol. Thou art my warrior;
I holp to frame thee. Do you know this lady?
Cor. The noble sister of Publicola,
The moon of Rome, chaste as the icicle
That 's curded by the frost from purest snow
And hangs on Dian's temple. Dear Valeria!
Vol. This is a poor epitome of yours,
Which by th' interpretation of full time
May show like all yourself.
Cor. The god of soldiers,
With the consent of supreme Jove, inform
Thy thoughts with nobleness; that thou mayst prove
To shame unvulnerable, and stick i' th' wars
Like a great sea-mark, standing every flaw,
And saving those that eye thee!
Vol. Your knee, sirrah.
Cor. That 's my brave boy!
Vol. Even he, your wife, this lady, and myself,
Are suitors to you.
Cor. I beseech you, peace;
Or, if you 'd ask, remember this before:
The thing I have forsworn to grant may never
Be held by you denials. Do not bid me
Dismiss my soldiers, or capitulate
Again with Rome's mechanics; tell me not
Wherein I seem unnatural; desire not
T' allay my rages and revenges with
Your colder reasons.
Vol. O, no more, no more!
You have said you will not grant us anything;
For we have nothing else to ask, but that
Which you deny already: yet we will ask,
That, if you fail in our request, the blame
May hang upon your hardness; therefore hear us.
Cor. Aufidius, and you Volsces, mark; for we 'll
Hear nought from Rome in private. Your request?
Vol. Should we be silent and not speak, our raiment
And state of bodies would bewray what life
We have led since thy exile. Think with thyself
How more unfortunate than all living women
Are we come hither; since that thy sight, which should
Make our eyes flow with joy, hearts dance with comforts,
Constrains them weep and shake with fear and sorrow;
Making the mother, wife, and child to see
The son, the husband, and the father tearing
His country's bowels out. And to poor we
Thine enmity 's most capital: thou barr'st us
Our prayers to the gods, which is a comfort
That all but we enjoy; for how can we,
Alas, how can we for our country pray,
Whereto we are bound, together with thy victory,
Whereto we are bound? Alack, or we must lose
The country, our dear nurse, or else thy person,
Our comfort in the country. We must find
An evident calamity, though we had
Our wish, which side should win; for either thou
Must, as a foreign recreant, be led
With manacles through our streets, or else
Triumphantly tread on thy country's ruin,
And bear the palm for having bravely shed
Thy wife and children's blood. For myself, son,
I purpose not to wait on fortune till
These wars determine. If I cannot persuade thee
Rather to show a noble grace to both parts
Than seek the end of one, thou shalt no sooner
March to assault thy country than to tread—

41. out, i.e., of words. **51. duty,** respect. Addresses the earth. **54. unproperly,** unnaturally (ll. 55-56 explain the unnatural reversal—parent kneeling to child). **57. corrected,** submissive. **58. hungry,** barren. **59. Fillip,** strike at. **61. Murd'ring,** doing away with. **62. slight work,** an easy task. **66. curded,** congealed. **71. inform,** form. **73. stick,** stick out. **74. standing every flaw,** withstanding every squall. **75. eye thee,** look to thee. **80-1.** The refusal to do the impossible cannot be considered by you the denial of your petition. **82. capitulate,** make terms.

90. fail in, fail to accede to. **95. bewray,** disclose. **112. evident,** certain. **113. which,** concerning which. **120. determine,** end. **123. than to tread,** than thou shalt tread (she'll kill herself). The **not** (l. 124) refers back to **no sooner** (l. 122).

Trust to 't, thou shalt not—on thy mother's womb,
That brought thee to this world.
Vir. Ay, and on mine,
That brought you forth this boy, to keep your name
Living to time.
Young Mar. 'A shall not tread on me.
I 'll run away till I am bigger, but then I 'll fight.
Cor. Not of a woman's tenderness to be,
Requires nor child nor woman's face to see.
I have sat too long. *Rising.*
Vol. Nay, go not from us thus.
If it were so that our request did tend
To save the Romans, thereby to destroy
The Volsces whom you serve, you might condemn us,
As poisonous of your honour. No; our suit
Is, that you reconcile them: while the Volsces
May say, "This mercy we have show'd"; the Romans,
"This we receiv'd"; and each in either side
Give the all-hail to thee, and cry, "Be blest
For making up this peace!" Thou know'st, great son,
The end of war 's uncertain, but this certain,
That, if thou conquer Rome, the benefit
Which thou shalt thereby reap is such a name
Whose repetition will be dogg'd with curses;
Whose chronicle thus writ: "The man was noble,
But with his last attempt he wip'd it out;
Destroy'd his country; and his name remains
To th' ensuing age abhorr'd." Speak to me, son.
Thou hast affected the fine strains of honour,
To imitate the graces of the gods;
To tear with thunder the wide cheeks o' the air,
And yet to charge thy sulphur with a bolt
That should but rive an oak. Why dost not speak?
Think'st thou it honourable for a noble man
Still to remember wrongs? Daughter, speak you;
He cares not for your weeping. Speak thou, boy;
Perhaps thy childishness will move him more
Than can our reasons. There 's no man in the world
More bound to 's mother; yet here he lets me prate
Like one i' th' stocks.—Thou hast never in thy life
Show'd thy dear mother any courtesy,
When she, poor hen, fond of no second brood,
Has cluck'd thee to the wars and safely home,
Loaden with honour. Say my request 's unjust,
And spurn me back; but if it be not so,
Thou art not honest; and the gods will plague thee,
That thou restrain'st from me the duty which
To a mother's part belongs.—He turns away.
Down, ladies; let us shame him with our knees.
To his surname Coriolanus longs more pride
Than pity to our prayers. Down! an end;
This is the last. So we will home to Rome,
And die among our neighbours.—Nay, behold 's!
This boy, that cannot tell what he would have,
But kneels and holds up hands for fellowship,
Does reason our petition with more strength
Than thou hast to deny 't.—Come, let us go.
This fellow had a Volscian to his mother;
His wife is in Corioli, and his child
Like him by chance.—Yet give us our dispatch.
I am hush'd until our city be a-fire,
And then I 'll speak a little.
He holds her by the hand, silent.
Cor. O mother, mother!
What have you done? Behold, the heavens do ope,
The gods look down, and this unnatural scene
They laugh at. O my mother, mother! O!
You have won a happy victory to Rome;
But, for your son,—believe it, O, believe it,
Most dangerously you have with him prevail'd,
If not most mortal to him. But, let it come.
Aufidius, though I cannot make true wars,
I 'll frame convenient peace. Now, good Aufidius,
Were you in my stead, would you have heard
A mother less, or granted less, Aufidius?
Auf. I was mov'd withal.
Cor. I dare be sworn you were;
And, sir, it is no little thing to make
Mine eyes to sweat compassion. But, good sir,
What peace you 'll make, advise me. For my part,
I 'll not to Rome, I 'll back with you; and pray you,
Stand to me in this cause.—O mother! wife!
Speaks apart with them.
Auf. [*Aside.*] I am glad thou hast set thy mercy and thy honour

146. attempt, undertaking. **149. strains,** impulses. **152. sulphur,** brimstone; supposed to be contained in lightning. **153. That . . . oak,** that should but rend an oak, i.e., do no real harm. **160. Like . . . stocks,** i.e., like a prisoner bound hand and foot.

161. courtesy, particular favor. **170. longs,** belongs. **175. for fellowship,** to keep us company. **176. reason,** argue. **180. dispatch,** dismissal. **189. If . . . him,** if not with most fatal results to him. **191. convenient,** proper. **196. sweat compassion,** weep for pity. **199. Stand to me,** back me up.

At difference in thee: out of that I 'll work
Myself a former fortune.

Cor. Ay, by and by;
But we will drink together; and you shall bear
A better witness back than words, which we,
On like conditions, will have counter-seal'd.
Come, enter with us. Ladies, you deserve
To have a temple built you: all the swords
In Italy, and her confederate arms,
Could not have made this peace. *Exeunt.*

Scene IV. *Rome. A public place.*

Enter *Menenius* and *Sicinius*.

Men. See you yond coign o' th' Capitol, yond corner-stone?

Sic. Why, what of that?

Men. If it be possible for you to displace it with your little finger, there is some hope the ladies of Rome, especially his mother, may prevail with him. But I say there is no hope in 't; our throats are sentenced and stay upon execution.

Sic. Is 't possible that so short a time can alter the condition of a man?

Men. There is differency between a grub and a butterfly; yet your butterfly was a grub. This Marcius is grown from man to dragon; he has wings; he 's more than a creeping thing.

Sic. He loved his mother dearly.

Men. So did he me; and he no more remembers his mother now than an eight-year-old horse. The tartness of his face sours ripe grapes; when he walks, he moves like an engine, and the ground shrinks before his treading. He is able to pierce a corslet with his eye; talks like a knell, and his hum is a battery. He sits in his state, as a thing made for Alexander. What he bids be done is finished with his bidding. He wants nothing of a god but eternity and a heaven to throne in.

Sic. Yes, mercy, if you report him truly.

Men. I paint him in the character. Mark what mercy his mother shall bring from him: there is no more mercy in him than there is milk in a male tiger; that shall our poor city find: and all this is long of you.

Sic. The gods be good unto us!

Men. No, in such a case the gods will not be good unto us. When we banished him, we respected not them; and, he returning to break our necks, they respect not us.

Enter a *Messenger*.

Mess. Sir, if you 'd save your life, fly to your house.
The plebeians have got your fellow-tribune
And hale him up and down, all swearing, if
The Roman ladies bring not comfort home,
They 'll give him death by inches.

Enter a second *Messenger*.

Sic. What 's the news?

Sec. Mess. Good news, good news! The ladies have prevail'd,
The Volscians are dislodg'd, and Marcius gone.
A merrier day did never yet greet Rome,
No, not th' expulsion of the Tarquins.

Sic. Friend,
Art thou certain this is true? Is 't most certain?

Sec. Mess. As certain as I know the sun is fire.
Where have you lurk'd, that you make doubt of it?
Ne'er through an arch so hurried the blown tide,
As the recomforted through the gates. Why, hark you!

Trumpets; hautboys; drums beat, all together.

The trumpets, sackbuts, psalteries, and fifes,
Tabors and cymbals and the shouting Romans,
Make the sun dance. Hark you!

A shout within.

Men. This is good news;
I will go meet the ladies. This Volumnia
Is worth of consuls, senators, patricians,
A city full; of tribunes, such as you,
A sea and land full. You have pray'd well to-day:
This morning for ten thousand of your throats
I 'd not have given a doit. Hark, how they joy! *Sound still, with the shouts.*

Sic. First, the gods bless you for your tidings; next,
Accept my thankfulness.

Sec. Mess. Sir, we have all
Great cause to give great thanks.

Sic. They are near the city?

Sec. Mess. Almost at point to enter.

Sic. We will meet them,
And help the joy. *Exeunt.*

201. difference, odds. **202. a former fortune**, into my former position. **204. witness**, i.e., a treaty. **205.** He will have a treaty on similar terms counter-sealed by himself and Aufidius for them. **Scene iv: 1. coign**, corner. **8. stay upon**, await. **11. differency**, difference. **19. engine**, i.e., of war; cannon or siege machinery. **20. corslet**, breastplate. **21. talks . . . battery**, his conversation bodes death, and his exclamation of impatience is like the sound of cannon (Brooke). **22. state**, throne, seat of state. **thing made for**, statue. **26. eternity**, immortality. **throne**, enthrone himself. **28. in the character**, as he is. **32. long of**, owing to.

36. respected, considered, heeded. **44. dislodg'd**, decamped. **49. lurk'd**, hidden. **50. blown**, swollen. **52. sackbuts**, trombones. **psalteries**, stringed instruments. **53. Tabors**, small drums.

Scene V. *The same. A street near the gate.*

Enter two *Senators* with Ladies [*Volumnia, Virgilia, Valeria,*] passing over the stage, with other Lords.

First Sen. Behold our patroness, the life of Rome!
Call all your tribes together, praise the gods,
And make triumphant fires! Strew flowers before them!
Unshout the noise that banish'd Marcius!
Repeal him with the welcome of his mother;
Cry, "Welcome, ladies, welcome!"
All. Welcome, ladies,
Welcome!

A flourish with drums and trumpets.
Exeunt.

Scene VI. *Antium. A public place.*

Enter *Tullus Aufidius,* with Attendants.

Auf. Go tell the lords o' th' city I am here;
Deliver them this paper: having read it,
Bid them repair to th' market-place, where I,
Even in theirs and in the commons' ears,
Will vouch the truth of it. Him I accuse
The city ports by this hath enter'd, and
Intends t' appear before the people, hoping
To purge himself with words. Dispatch.
Exeunt Attendants.

Enter three or four *Conspirators* of Aufidius' faction.

Most welcome!
First Con. How is it with our general?
Auf. Even so
As with a man by his own alms empoison'd,
And with his charity slain.
Sec. Con. Most noble sir,
If you do hold the same intent wherein
You wish'd us parties, we 'll deliver you
Of your great danger.
Auf. Sir, I cannot tell.
We must proceed as we do find the people.
Third Con. The people will remain uncertain whilst
'Twixt you there 's difference; but the fall of either
Makes the survivor heir of all.
Auf. I know it;
And my pretext to strike at him admits
A good construction. I rais'd him, and I pawn'd
Mine honour for his truth; who being so heighten'd,
He watered his new plants with dews of flattery,
Seducing so my friends; and, to this end,
He bow'd his nature, never known before
But to be rough, unswayable, and free.
Third Con. Sir, his stoutness
When he did stand for consul, which he lost
By lack of stooping,—
Auf. That I would have spoke of.
Being banish'd for 't, he came unto my hearth,
Presented to my knife his throat. I took him;
Made him joint-servant with me; gave him way
In all his own desires; nay, let him choose
Out of my files, his projects to accomplish,
My best and freshest men; serv'd his designments
In mine own person; holp to reap the fame
Which he did end all his, and took some pride
To do myself this wrong; till, at the last,
I seem'd his follower, not partner, and
He wag'd me with his countenance, as if
I had been mercenary.
First Con. So he did, my lord.
The army marvell'd at it, and, in the last,
When he had carried Rome and that we look'd
For no less spoil than glory,—
Auf. There was it,
For which my sinews shall be stretch'd upon him.
At a few drops of women's rheum, which are
As cheap as lies, he sold the blood and labour
Of our great action. Therefore shall he die,
And I 'll renew me in his fall. But, hark!
Drums and trumpets sound, with great shouts of the People.
First Con. Your native town you enter'd like a post,
And had no welcomes home; but he returns,
Splitting the air with noise.
Sec. Con. And patient fools,
Whose children he hath slain, their base throats tear
With giving him glory.
Third Con. Therefore, at your vantage,
Ere he express himself, or move the people
With what he would say, let him feel your sword,
Which we will second. When he lies along,

Scene v: 4. Unshout, undo by shouts. **5. Repeal,** call back. **Scene vi: 14. parties,** partisans. **18. difference,** dispute. **20. pretext,** motive.

21. good construction, favorable interpretation. **23. watered his new plants,** cultivated his new-found authority. **34. files,** ranks. **35. designments,** designs. **37. end all his,** consummate, achieve as all his own. **40. wag'd . . . countenance,** paid me with his favor. **45. stretch'd upon,** exerted against. **46. rheum,** tears. **50. post,** messenger. **54. at your vantage,** at your best opportunity. **57. along,** at full length, i.e., dead.

After your way his tale pronounc'd shall bury
His reasons with his body.
Auf. Say no more.
Here come the lords.

Enter the *Lords* of the city.

All the Lords. You are most welcome home.
Auf. I have not deserv'd it.
But, worthy lords, have you with heed perused
What I have written to you?
Lords. We have.
First Lord. And grieve to hear 't.
What faults he made before the last, I think
Might have found easy fines; but there to end
Where he was to begin, and give away
The benefit of our levies, answering us
With our own charge, making a treaty where
There was a yielding,—this admits no excuse.
Auf. He approaches; you shall hear him.

Enter *Coriolanus,* marching with drum and colours; Commoners being with him.

Cor. Hail, lords! I am return'd your soldier,
No more infected with my country's love
Than when I parted hence, but still subsisting
Under your great command. You are to know
That prosperously I have attempted and
With bloody passage led your wars even to
The gates of Rome. Our spoils we have brought home
Do more than counterpoise a full third part
The charges of the action. We have made peace
With no less honour to the Antiates
Than shame to the Romans; and we here deliver,
Subscrib'd by the consuls and patricians,
Together with the seal o' th' Senate, what
We have compounded on.
Auf. Read it not, noble lords;
But tell the traitor, in the highest degree
He hath abus'd your powers.
Cor. "Traitor!" How now!
Auf. Ay, traitor, Marcius!
Cor. Marcius!
Auf. Ay, Marcius, Caius Marcius! Dost thou think
I 'll grace thee with that robbery, thy stolen name,
Coriolanus, in Corioli?
You lords and heads o' th' state, perfidiously
He has betray'd your business, and given up,
For certain drops of salt, your city Rome,
I say "your city," to his wife and mother;
Breaking his oath and resolution like
A twist of rotten silk, never admitting
Counsel o' th' war, but at his nurse's tears
He whin'd and roar'd away your victory,
That pages blush'd at him and men of heart
Look'd wond'ring each at others.
Cor. Hear'st thou, Mars?
Auf. Name not the god, thou boy of tears!
Cor. Ha!
Auf. No more.
Cor. Measureless liar, thou hast made my heart
Too great for what contains it. Boy! O slave!
Pardon me, lords, 't is the first time that ever
I was forc'd to scold. Your judgements, my grave lords,
Must give this cur the lie; and his own notion—
Who wears my stripes impress'd upon him, that
Must bear my beating to his grave—shall join
To thrust the lie unto him.
First Lord. Peace, both, and hear me speak.
Cor. Cut me to pieces, Volsces; men and lads,
Stain all your edges on me. Boy! False hound!
If you have writ your annals true, 't is there,
That, like an eagle in a dove-cote, I
Flutter'd your Volscians in Corioli;
Alone I did it. Boy!
Auf. Why, noble lords,
Will you be put in mind of his blind fortune,
Which was your shame, by this unholy braggart,
'Fore your own eyes and ears?
All Conspirators. Let him die for 't.
All the People. Tear him to pieces! Do it presently!—He killed my son!—My daughter!—He killed my cousin Marcus!—He killed my father!
Sec. Lord. Peace, ho! not outrage: peace!
The man is noble and his fame folds in
This orb o' th' earth. His last offences to us
Shall have judicious hearing. Stand, Aufidius,
And trouble not the peace.
Cor. O that I had him,
With six Aufidiuses or more, his tribe,
To use my lawful sword!
Auf. Insolent villain!
All Conspirators. Kill, kill, kill, kill, kill him!

The Conspirators draw, and kill Marcius, who falls: Aufidius stands on him.

58. **After . . . pronounc'd,** the tale told according to your version. 67. **answering . . . charge,** repaying only our expense (in the expedition). 69. **yielding,** surrender. 72. **infected,** tainted. 73. **subsisting,** living, continuing. 78. **counterpoise,** equal (in value). 84. **compounded,** agreed.

96. **twist,** thread. **admitting . . . war,** permitting council of war. 99. **heart,** courage. 104. **Too . . . it,** too swollen because of what it contains, i.e., wrath. 107. **notion,** intelligence. 116. **Flutter'd,** dispersed. 128. **judicious,** judicial.

Lords. Hold, hold, hold, hold!
Auf. My noble masters, hear me speak.
First Lord. O Tullus!
Sec. Lord. Thou hast done a deed whereat valour will weep.
Third Lord. Tread not upon him. Masters all, be quiet;
Put up your swords.
Auf. My lords, when you shall know—as in this rage,
Provok'd by him, you cannot—the great danger
Which this man's life did owe you, you 'll rejoice
That he is thus cut off. Please it your honours
To call me to your Senate, I 'll deliver 141
Myself your loyal servant, or endure
Your heaviest censure.

139. did owe you, possessed, had for you. **141. deliver,** show.

First Lord. Bear from hence his body;
And mourn you for him. Let him be regarded
As the most noble corse that ever herald
Did follow to his urn.
Sec. Lord. His own impatience.
Takes from Aufidius a great part of blame.
Let 's make the best of it.
Auf. My rage is gone,
And I am struck with sorrow. Take him up.
Help, three o' th' chiefest soldiers; I 'll be one.
Beat thou the drum, that it speak mournfully.
Trail your steel pikes. Though in this city he
Hath widowed and unchilded many a one,
Which to this hour bewail the injury,
Yet he shall have a noble memory.
Assist.

Exeunt, bearing the body of Coriolanus. A dead march sounded.

Cymbeline

To pass from *Coriolanus* to *Cymbeline* is to leave the clash of arms and the discord of patricians and plebeians in ancient Rome for a world of romance, a strangely compounded world of court intrigue and idyllic country scenes. It is one of the most delightful of Shakespeare's plays and at the same time one of the most provoking. In style and construction alike it is a singularly uneven play; at times the light of Shakespeare's genius burns at its brightest in the lovely verse; at times it is so obscured as to make us question whether the voice we hear is that of a weary poet or, perhaps, not his own voice, but another's.

Text.—*Cymbeline* was first published in the Folio of 1623 where it is grouped with the Tragedies, the last play in the collection. It is much to be regretted that there is no earlier version of the play, for there is fairly plain evidence that the text has been edited. The "copy" sent to Jaggard was not Shakespeare's manuscript nor a transcript of it; nor could it have been a transcript of the company's prompt-book since it is far too long (ca. 3340 ll.) for representation on Shakespeare's stage. It must have been transcribed from a manuscript which contained Shakespeare's original text plus later additions, with passages marked for omission in acting, which passages were, none the less, retained in the "copy." The transcript can hardly have been very accurate, since the Folio text abounds in errors and obscurities which have furnished many opportunities for emendation.

Date.—A consensus of opinion places *Cymbeline* in 1609–1610. Stylistic and metrical characteristics connect it with the latest group of Shakespeare's plays—the so-called Romances. Probably it was written in 1609 to be produced by his company at their newly acquired "private" theatre, the Blackfriars, a fact which goes far to explain the difference of *Cymbeline* from Shakespeare's earlier romantic comedies.

Source.—The main plot of *Cymbeline*, that of the wager and the slandered lady, is set in a semi-historical frame-work of early British history. This plot goes back to a medieval folk-tale of which there are many versions differing in detail, all agreeing on a wager upon the chastity of a wife. The fullest version occurs in the *Decameron* (the ninth novel of the second day). Briefly, it runs as follows:

> At an inn in Paris some Italian merchants agree in cynical aspersions of wifely virtue. Bernabo of Genoa, however, is firm in asserting the chastity of his wife, Ginevra. A certain Ambrogiuolo declares that he could win her as he has won others and provokes the husband into a wager on her virtue. The tempter goes to Genoa and at once discovers that it would be hopeless to try to seduce the lady. Unwilling to lose the wager, he contrives to gain admittance to her bed-chamber concealed in a chest. While she sleeps he steals forth, notes the furniture and pictures of the room, steals a ring, a purse, and a girdle, and observes on the sleeper's breast a mole with a group of golden hairs. Returning to Paris he convinces Bernabo that he has won the wager. The husband returns to Italy, sends a servant to bid his wife meet him outside the city, and orders the man to kill her on the way. Overcome by her tears and protestations of innocence the servant spares her, takes her dress to show his master as evidence of her death, and leaves her his hat and doublet.

From this point the story varies widely from Shakespeare's version. It may be summarized as follows:

> After many adventures the disguised Ginevra becomes a trusted servant of the Soldan of Egypt. She sees one day in the market-place her own purse and girdle on a merchant's stall. In conversation with the owner, Ambrogiuolo, she learns that they had been given him by his mistress, Bernabo's wife. Using her influence with the Soldan, she contrives to confront the two merchants. The slanderer confesses his trick, the husband admits the murder of his wife. Ginevra then reveals herself and pardons her husband. The wicked Ambrogiuolo is bound to a stake and stung to death by wasps and gad-flies.

It is easy to see what Shakespeare took from this tale, which he may have read either in the original or in a French translation. He discarded the long drawn out denouement and devised something much more complicated and exciting. Yet even in the beginning he made changes to fit the type of romantic drama that he was planning. Instead of a merchant's wife he made his heroine a princess, secretly married to a noble gentleman of the court, and separated from him by her father's wrath. He arranged to have the wager thrust upon the husband in such a manner that he was in knightly honor bound to accept it, and he invented a new and thrilling scene in which the would-be seducer makes impudent advances to the lady.

For a setting to this story Shakespeare turned to his favorite Holinshed, and drew from its pages an ancient British king, Cymbeline, with his sons Guiderius and Arviragus, and all the matter of the refusal of tribute and the war with Rome. He treats this history, to be sure, with no such scrupulous accuracy as he used when following Plutarch. The names of all the Britons in the play, Cadwal and Polidore, Morgan, Cloten, Posthumus, and Imogen, slightly altered from Innogen, occur at one point or another in Holinshed.

There is yet another strand of considerable importance in the construction for which no direct source is known: the matter of the stolen princes, their nurture by the banished Belisarius, and their kindly reception of their disguised sister. Shakespeare, it seems, planned from the beginning to have Imogen fall in with her brothers. He may have caught a hint for the setting of this scene from an old play, *The Rare Triumphs of Love and Fortune*, 1589. Here we find a cave inhabited by an old nobleman banished from court on false report. To the cave comes a Princess Fidelia in search of her lover, Hermione—a name that Shakespeare was to use in a later play. This lover, like Posthumus, had been exiled for raising his eyes to the Princess. Her brother, like Cloten, seeks to kill him, but he turns out to be the son of the old noble, and in the end by the interposition of the gods the lovers are united. The cave, the banished noble, and the name of the Princess, all reappear in *Cymbeline.*

Type of Play.—Cymbeline, it is plain, is a mosaic of materials drawn from many and varied sources. It is idle to pretend that these materials have been blended into a harmonious whole. Shakespeare is often careless of such anachronisms as would have shocked his scholarly contemporary Ben Jonson; but this play is crowded with them. In fact there is a sharp discord between the main plot and its setting. Instead of the atmosphere of a cultured Renaissance Court which pervades *Hamlet,* we have here a medieval tale set in the court life of pre-Christian Britain; and this court life is itself a complete anachronism, where a princess reads Ovid, a suitor greets his lady at morning with a concert of instruments, and a wicked Queen and her brutal son defy a foreigner in terms more becoming patriotic Elizabethans than barbaric Britons. The actual construction of the play, too, is apparently as careless as the setting is impossible. Posthumus, the main figure of the wager-story, drops out of the play for two long acts. By the time he reappears in the fifth we have lost interest in him; and the attempt to restore him to the center of interest by his bravery in battle and the vision in the prison is singularly unsuccessful. During this act, moreover, the heroine vanishes from the scene until the very end. Throughout the construction is jerky and episodic, as far removed as possible from the closely woven fabric of *Othello.*

But the truth is that *Cymbeline* is not to be judged by the standards we apply to the great tragedies. The editors of the Folio, indeed, grouped it with the tragedies, but it is nothing of the sort. It is a tragi-comedy specifically adapted to the latest Elizabethan fashion in plays. What the fashionable audience of Blackfriars wanted was primarily entertainment, an interesting and romantic story, packed with thrills, an intrigue verging upon the tragic, but happily averted, plenty of music, vocal and instrumental, and scenic spectacle resembling as nearly as possible the costly and elaborate Court masques. All this Shakespeare gave them in abundance in *Cymbeline.* The central theme, virtue in distress, was sure of its appeal to an audience wearied with the storm and stress of high tragedy, and this theme is presented in a series of situations each with its own peculiar thrill, the laying of the wager, the bed-chamber scene, the imminent murder of the heroine, and, most effective of all, her discovery, as she supposes, of her husband's headless corpse. Danger threatens her from the beginning, but we are assured she will escape all perils. The poison plot of the wicked Queen is thwarted at its inception by the prudence of Cornelius; we are quite sure that the faithful Pisanio will never kill his lady; we know, if the characters in the play do not, that Imogen is not dead, but sleeping, and that the headless corpse is that of the villain Cloten. All this, of course, is a tissue of improbabilities, but realism is uncalled for, is out of place, indeed, in tragicomic romance. It is the art with which the poet tells his tale that appeals to us rather than the intrinsic truth of the tale itself. And nowhere is Shakespeare's art in the solution of a tangled web more admirable than in the last scene of *Cymbeline* where situation after situation is crowded in and one discovery follows another until the final solution and general reconciliation. Even the villain Iachimo is spared the death that befell his prototype in the Italian story. It is interesting to compare this scene with the finale of *Measure for Measure* and see how skilfully here Shakespeare avoids the tangled tissue of false pretences, deceptions, and down-right lies, which mar that scene.

A word needs to be said in passing about the vision of the penultimate scene of the play. From the time of Pope a long succession of editors has denounced it as unworthy of Shakespeare and attributed its authorship to some hanger-on about the theatre. This, to be frank, is nonsense. In the first place the whole scene, the music, the apparitions, the descent of Jupiter, are of a piece with other spectacular and masque-like scenes in Shakespeare's latest plays. It represents a condescension on Shakespeare's part to the demand of his public for spectacle upon the stage, and his readiness to employ the elaborate machinery which the stage had taken over from the court masque. Moreover some *deus ex machina* is needed at just this point to assure the audience that the hero imprisoned under sentence of death will escape and be reunited to his wife. Yet it is hard, perhaps impossible, to conceive of Shakespeare's writing the dreary doggerel here put into the mouths of the ghosts. Probably the best explanation is that of Dowden, namely that Shakespeare planned a vision in dumb-show—that he was cognizant of the vision is plain from lines 114–119, lines which only Shakespeare could have written—and that some time later the choral songs of the ghosts were added to prolong the spectacle. One might even go further and elide the tablet laid upon the hero's breast, an elision which would carry with it the soothsayer's pedantic exposition which clutters up the final scene. There is more than a little, in fact, in the whole play which is suspect: the expository soliloquies, the rhyming tages embedded in blank verse, the hopelessly low level of some of the blank verse itself. Since we have reason to believe that this play was printed from a revised copy of Shakespeare's original we need not be too careful to defend and justify passages that seem unworthy of Shakespeare at this stage of his career.

Characters.—One reads Shakespeare's plays, after all, for the story, the characters and the poetry. The story of *Cymbeline* with all its improbabilities is a delightful romantic tale. Even if Shakespeare's hand faltered at times in the construction of the plot, it had lost none of its cunning in the creation of character. So slight a sketch, for example, as that of Lucius is instinct with the calm dignity of ancient Rome. Cloten, perhaps the most despicable villain in Shakespeare, is a fully realized character, a bully, a brute, so swollen with self-conceit that he is impervious to ridicule; he embodies all that is basest in a corrupt court and comes to a fitting end by the hand of the rustic mountaineer whom he despises. Iachimo is a villain of quite another sort. A cynical man of the world, he laughs at the folly of a Briton so simple as to believe in woman's virtue, and craftily maneuvers him into a wager which he is sure, he believes, to win. He is shrewd enough to suspect at the first sight of Imogen that he has lost, yet bold enough to make a trial by the approved method of appeal to beauty scorned. A less hardened villain would have been crushed by her outburst of contemptuous anger, but Iachimo is not to be beaten by a British lady and lose his bet to a British lord. His instant volte-face and his rhapsodic praises of her banished husband not only pacify Imogen, they win her over—"All's well, sir. Take my power i' the court for yours." In the famous bed-chamber scene it is hard to know which most to wonder at, his reckless daring or his sensuous enjoyment of the situation; he is no brutal ravisher, but a subtle Italian with the true Latin love of beauty. After the scene in which he convinces Posthumus, he drops out of the play until the last act and then, sad to say, he is not the same Iachimo—at least at first. If Shakespeare wrote the feeble lines that express his remorse it must have been at an hour when his hand was very weary.

The character of Posthumus has been rather generally misunderstood. He has been blamed for his folly in accepting the wager, for his credulity in believing Iachimo's report, and for his cruelty in ordering the death of Imogen. All this is beside the mark; the wager, the loss of faith, the purposed revenge, were all parts of the old story, accepted as credible by generations of listeners. Shakespeare could not dramatize the tale and leave them out; but he has done his best, and not a little, to ennoble the character of the deluded husband. First of all we hear the praise of Posthumus at Court, re-echoed by his host at Rome; then we see him slowly and reluctantly drawn into the snare of Iachimo; and here Shakespeare adds a touch wanting, it seems, in all earlier versions. Should the Italian fail, as Posthumus is sure he will, he must answer his ill opinion of the lady's virtue with the sword. In the same way his remorse, while still believing in her guilt, and his resolve to lay down his life in Imogen's land as a small atonement for his guilt, are Shakespeare's own invention. "For Imogen's dear life take mine," he prays the gods. Instead of judging the behavior of Posthumus by nineteenth century standards it would befit the honest student of Shakespeare to accept him as Shakespeare saw him, a simple, gallant, deceived, and repentant gentleman, secure at last in the embrace of the noblest of Shakespeare's women.

Of Imogen it is hard to speak with anything like restraint. With the possible exception of Cleopatra she is the most fully presented both in strength and weakness of all Shakespeare's women. Like Cleopatra she is at once a royal lady and a loving woman; unlike Cleopatra she is a good woman. Perhaps the hardest task a creative poet can set himself is to make a virtuous woman thoroughly human and everlastingly attractive, and in the character of Imogen Shakespeare has happily accomplished the well-nigh impossible. A full analysis of her character would involve the study of every scene in which she appears, for Shakespeare never loses interest in her as he seems at times to do in Posthumus. She is stronger than Desdemona, gentler and more loving than Hermione, two other women accused like her of infidelity. The little touch of feminine spite with which she bids Cloten go tell his mother is set off by the equally feminine timidity with which she accosts the unknown outlaws. She is first, last, and always the woman in love, as devoted as she is chaste.

If we are to enjoy *Cymbeline* as we should, we must abandon the rule of reason, and submit to the spell of romance. And this romance is clothed in some of Shakespeare's loveliest poetry. It lacks, of course, the stormy splendors of the great tragedies, but it has a charm of its own, compounded of sweetness, simplicity, sensuous imagery, and direct dramatic expression. For the student of Shakespeare's development both as a poet-dramatist and as an observer of life, *Cymbeline* has a very special interest. We see him here toward the close of his career turning to practice, a little uncertainly at first, a new form of dramatic art. What is more important we see him emerging from the dark shadows of his tragic period into the sunny spaces of his latest work. Evil has not been forgotten; it is not ignored in *Cymbeline*. The Queen and Cloten are there to testify to its presence, but its dreadful power is passing.

Apart from a suspected record by Forman we have but one notice of a performance of *Cymbeline* before 1642. It was played at Court on New Year's Day, 1633, and Herbert tells us, was "well liked by the King." There is no account of its performance in the early Restoration period, but in 1682 Tom D'Urfey brought out a revision of the play entitled *The Injured Princess or the Fatal Wager*. For a Restoration "improvement" of Shakespeare this is a rather workman-like job. In the main he follows the lines of Shakespeare's action. This adaptation held the stage intermittently till the middle of the next century. Garrick's version, produced in 1761–62, restored Shakespeare's play to the stage with certain necessary cuts. It was at once successful, and the role of Posthumus became one of Garrick's favorite parts. Since Garrick's day *Cymbeline* has been revived from time to time by Kemble, by Macready, and by Phelps, under whom the beautiful Helen Faucit played Imogen. That role has naturally been a favorite with actresses: Mrs. Barry, Mrs. Siddons, Adelaide Neilson, and others, have all played it. Perhaps the most memorable revival was that at the Lyceum in 1896, when Ellen Terry played Imogen—"a fragrant memory" writes an old theatre-goer—to Irving's Iachimo.

CYMBELINE

Dramatis Personæ

Cymbeline, king of Britain.
Cloten, son to the Queen by a former husband.
Posthumus Leonatus, a gentleman, husband to *Imogen.*
Belarius, a banished lord disguised under the name of *Morgan.*
Guiderius, } sons to *Cymbeline,* disguised under the names of *Polydore* and *Cadwal,* supposed sons to *Morgan.*
Arviragus, }
Philario, friend to *Posthumus,* } Italians.
Iachimo, friend to *Philario,* }
Caius Lucius, general of the Roman forces.
Pisanio, servant to *Posthumus.*
Cornelius, a physician.
A Roman Captain.
Two British Captains.
A Frenchman, friend to *Philario.*
Two Lords of *Cymbeline's* court.
Two Gentlemen of the same.
Two Jailers.

Queen, wife to *Cymbeline.*
Imogen, daughter to *Cymbeline* by a former Queen.
Helen, a lady attending on *Imogen.*

Lords, Ladies, Roman Senators, Tribunes, a Soothsayer, a Dutchman, a Spaniard, Musicians, Officers, Captains, Soldiers, Messengers, and other Attendants.

Apparitions.

SCENE: *Britain; Rome.*

ACT I. SCENE I. *Britain. The garden of Cymbeline's palace.*

Enter two *Gentlemen.*

First Gent. You do not meet a man but frowns. Our bloods
No more obey the heavens than our courtiers
Still seem as does the King.
Sec. Gent. But what 's the matter?
First Gent. His daughter, and the heir of 's kingdom, whom
He purpos'd to his wife's sole son—a widow
That late he married—hath referr'd herself
Unto a poor but worthy gentleman. She 's wedded,
Her husband banish'd, she imprison'd; all
Is outward sorrow; though I think the King
Be touch'd at very heart.
Sec. Gent. None but the King?
First Gent. He that hath lost her too; so is the Queen,
That most desir'd the match: but not a courtier,
Although they wear their faces to the bent
Of the King's looks, hath a heart that is not
Glad at the thing they scowl at.
Sec. Gent. And why so?
First Gent. He that hath miss'd the Princess is a thing
Too bad for bad report; and he that hath her—
I mean, that married her, alack, good man!
And therefore banish'd—is a creature such
As, to seek through the regions of the earth
For one his like, there would be something failing
In him that should compare. I do not think
So fair an outward and such stuff within
Endows a man but he.
Sec. Gent. You speak him far.
First Gent. I do extend him, sir, within himself,
Crush him together rather than unfold
His measure duly.
Sec. Gent. What 's his name and birth?
First Gent. I cannot delve him to the root. His father
Was call'd Sicilius, who did join his honour
Against the Romans with Cassibelan,
But had his titles by Tenantius whom
He serv'd with glory and admir'd success,
So gain'd the sur-addition Leonatus;
And had, besides this gentleman in question,
Two other sons, who in the wars o' th' time
Died with their swords in hand; for which their father,
Then old and fond of issue, took such sorrow
That he quit being, and his gentle lady,
Big of this gentleman our theme, deceas'd
As he was born. The King he takes the babe

1. bloods . . . heavens, dispositions were supposed to be ruled by the stars. **3. Still seem,** always appear. **6. referr'd,** given, i.e., in marriage. **13. bent,** inclination. **14. looks,** glances.

24. You . . . far, you exaggerate in praising him. **29. join his honour,** linked his soldierly virtue. **30. Cassibelan,** King Lud's younger brother and king after him. **31. Tenantius,** King Lud's son. **33. sur-addition,** surname. **37. fond,** desirous. **38. quit being,** died.

To his protection, calls him Posthumus Leonatus,
Breeds him and makes him of his bed-chamber,
Puts to him all the learnings that his time
Could make him the receiver of; which he took,
As we do air, fast as 't was minister'd,
And in 's spring became a harvest; liv'd in court—
Which rare it is to do—most prais'd, most lov'd,
A sample to the youngest, to th' more mature
A glass that feated them, and to the graver
A child that guided dotards; to his mistress,
For whom he now is banish'd,—her own price
Proclaims how she esteem'd him and his virtue;
By her election may be truly read
What kind of man he is.

Sec. Gent. I honour him
Even out of your report. But, pray you, tell me,
Is she sole child to th' King?

First Gent. His only child.
He had two sons,—if this be worth your hearing,
Mark it—the eldest of them at three years old,
I' th' swathing-clothes the other, from their nursery
Were stolen, and to this hour no guess in knowledge
Which way they went.

Sec. Gent. How long is this ago?

First Gent. Some twenty years.

Sec. Gent. That a king's children should be so convey'd,
So slackly guarded, and the search so slow,
That could not trace them!

First Gent. Howsoe'er 't is strange,
Or that the negligence may well be laugh'd at,
Yet is it true, sir.

Sec. Gent. I do well believe you.

First Gent. We must forbear; here comes the gentleman,
The Queen, and Princess. *Exeunt.*

Enter the *Queen, Posthumus,* and *Imogen.*

Queen. No, be assur'd you shall not find me, daughter,
After the slander of most stepmothers,
Evil-ey'd unto you. You 're my prisoner, but
Your jailer shall deliver you the keys
That lock up your restraint. For you, Posthumus,
So soon as I can win th' offended King,
I will be known your advocate: marry, yet
The fire of rage is in him, and 't were good
You lean'd unto his sentence with what patience
Your wisdom may inform you.

Post. Please your Highness,
I will from hence to-day.

Queen. You know the peril.
I 'll fetch a turn about the garden, pitying
The pangs of barr'd affections, though the King
Hath charg'd you should not speak together. *Exit.*

Imo. O
Dissembling courtesy! How fine this tyrant
Can tickle where she wounds! My dearest husband,
I something fear my father's wrath; but nothing—
Always reserv'd my holy duty—what
His rage can do on me. You must be gone;
And I shall here abide the hourly shot
Of angry eyes, not comforted to live,
But that there is this jewel in the world
That I may see again.

Post. My queen! my mistress!
O lady, weep no more, lest I give cause
To be suspected of more tenderness
Than doth become a man. I will remain
The loyal'st husband that did e'er plight troth.
My residence in Rome at one Philario's,
Who to my father was a friend, to me
Known but by letter; thither write, my queen,
And with mine eyes I 'll drink the words you send,
Though ink be made of gall.

Re-enter *Queen.*

Queen. Be brief, I pray you.
If the King come, I shall incur I know not
How much of his displeasure. [*Aside.*] Yet I 'll move him
To walk this way. I never do him wrong
But he does buy my injuries, to be friends;
Pays dear for my offences. *Exit.*

Post. Should we be taking leave
As long a term as yet we have to live,
The loathness to depart would grow. Adieu!

Imo. Nay, stay a little;
Were you but riding forth to air yourself,
Such parting were too petty. Look here, love;
This diamond was my mother's: take it, heart;
But keep it till you woo another wife,
When Imogen is dead.

Post. How, how! another?
You gentle gods, give me but this I have,
And cere up my embracements from a next

42. Breeds, rears. **43. time,** years. **48. sample,** example. **49. feated,** fashioned. **60. guess in knowledge,** well-informed guess, or guess resulting in knowledge.

78. lean'd unto, submitted to. **79. inform you,** dictate to you. **105. buy,** pay for, reward. **116. cere up,** cover with wax (for burial).

With bonds of death! *Putting on the ring.*
Remain, remain thou here
While sense can keep it on. And, sweetest, fairest,
As I my poor self did exchange for you,
To your so infinite loss, so in our trifles
I still win of you; for my sake wear this.
It is a manacle of love; I 'll place it
Upon this fairest prisoner.
Putting a bracelet upon her arm.
Imo. O the gods!
When shall we see again?

Enter *Cymbeline* and *Lords.*

Post. Alack, the King!
Cym. Thou basest thing, avoid! Hence, from my sight!
If after this command thou fraught the court
With thy unworthiness, thou diest. Away!
Thou 'rt poison to my blood.
Post. The gods protect you!
And bless the good remainders of the court!
I am gone. *Exit.*
Imo. There cannot be a pinch in death
More sharp than this is.
Cym. O disloyal thing,
That shouldst repair my youth, thou heap'st
A year's age on me.
Imo. I beseech you, sir,
Harm not yourself with your vexation.
I am senseless of your wrath; a touch more rare
Subdues all pangs, all fears.
Cym. Past grace? obedience?
Imo. Past hope, and in despair; that way, past grace.
Cym. That mightst have had the sole son of my queen!
Imo. O blest, that I might not! I chose an eagle,
And did avoid a puttock.
Cym. Thou took'st a beggar; wouldst have made my throne
A seat for baseness.
Imo. No; I rather added
A lustre to it.
Cym. O thou vile one!
Imo. Sir,
It is your fault that I have lov'd Posthumus:
You bred him as my playfellow, and he is
A man worth any woman; overbuys me
Almost the sum he pays.
Cym. What, art thou mad?
Imo. Almost, sir; heaven restore me! Would I were
A neat-herd's daughter, and my Leonatus
Our neighbour shepherd's son!
Cym. Thou foolish thing!

Re-enter *Queen.*

They were again together; you have done
Not after our command. Away with her,
And pen her up.
Queen. Beseech your patience. Peace,
Dear lady daughter, peace! Sweet sovereign,
Leave us to ourselves; and make yourself some comfort
Out of your best advice.
Cym. Nay, let her languish
A drop of blood a day; and, being aged,
Die of this folly!
Exeunt Cymbeline and Lords.

Enter *Pisanio.*

Queen. Fie! you must give way.
Here is your servant. How now, sir! What news?
Pis. My lord your son drew on my master.
Queen. Ha!
No harm, I trust, is done?
Pis. There might have been,
But that my master rather play'd than fought
And had no help of anger: they were parted
By gentlemen at hand.
Queen. I am very glad on 't.
Imo. Your son 's my father's friend; he takes his part
To draw upon an exile. O brave sir!
I would they were in Afric both together;
Myself by with a needle, that I might prick
The goer-back. Why came you from your master?
Pis. On his command. He would not suffer me
To bring him to the haven; left these notes
Of what commands I should be subject to,
When 't pleas'd you to employ me.
Queen. This hath been
Your faithful servant: I dare lay mine honour
He will remain so.
Pis. I humbly thank your Highness.
Queen. Pray, walk a while.
Imo. About some half-hour hence,
I pray you, speak with me; you shall at least
Go see my lord aboard. For this time leave me. *Exeunt.*

Scene II. *A public place.*

Enter *Cloten* and two *Lords.*

First Lord. Sir, I would advise you to shift a shirt; the violence of action hath made you

121. win, get the better of. **124. see,** i.e., each other. **125. avoid,** get out. **126. fraught,** burden. **129. remainders,** those who remain. **132. repair,** restore. **135. senseless,** insensible. **a touch more rare,** a feeling more poignant. **140. puttock,** kite.

149. neat-herd's, cowherd's. **156. advice,** consideration. **176. walk,** withdraw.

reek as a sacrifice: where air comes out, air comes in; there 's none abroad so wholesome as that you vent.

Clo. If my shirt were bloody, then to shift it. Have I hurt him?

Sec. Lord. [*Aside.*] No, faith; not so much as his patience.

First Lord. Hurt him! His body 's a passable carcass, if he be not hurt; it is a throughfare for steel, if it be not hurt.

Sec. Lord. [*Aside.*] His steel was in debt; it went o' th' backside the town.

Clo. The villain would not stand me.

Sec. Lord. [*Aside.*] No; but he fled forward still, toward your face.

First Lord. Stand you! You have land enough of your own; but he added to your having, gave you some ground.

Sec. Lord. [*Aside.*] As many inches as you have oceans. Puppies!

Clo. I would they had not come between us.

Sec. Lord. [*Aside.*] So would I, till you had measured how long a fool you were upon the ground.

Clo. And that she should love this fellow and refuse me!

Sec. Lord. [*Aside.*] If it be a sin to make a true election, she is damned.

First Lord. Sir, as I told you always, her beauty and her brain go not together. She 's a good sign, but I have seen small reflection of her wit.

Sec. Lord. [*Aside.*] She shines not upon fools, lest the reflection should hurt her.

Clo. Come, I 'll to my chamber. Would there had been some hurt done!

Sec. Lord. [*Aside.*] I wish not so; unless it had been the fall of an ass, which is no great hurt.

Clo. You 'll go with us?

First Lord. I 'll attend your lordship.

Clo. Nay, come, let 's go together.

Sec. Lord. Well, my lord. *Exeunt.*

Scene III. *A room in the palace.*

Enter *Imogen* and *Pisanio.*

Imo. I would thou grew'st unto the shores o' th' haven,
And question'dst every sail: if he should write
And I not have it, 't were a paper lost,
As offer'd mercy is. What was the last
That he spake to thee?

Pis. It was, his queen, his queen!

Imo. Then wav'd his handkerchief?

Pis. And kiss'd it, madam.

Imo. Senseless linen! happier therein than I
And that was all?

Pis. No, madam; for so long
As he could make me with this eye or ear
Distinguish him from others, he did keep
The deck, with glove, or hat, or handkerchief,
Still waving, as the fits and stirs of 's mind
Could best express how slow his soul sail'd on,
How swift his ship.

Imo. Thou shouldst have made him
As little as a crow, or less, ere left
To after-eye him.

Pis. Madam, so I did.

Imo. I would have broke mine eye-strings; crack'd them, but
To look upon him, till the diminution
Of space had pointed him sharp as my needle;
Nay, follow'd him, till he had melted from
The smallness of a gnat to air, and then
Have turn'd mine eye and wept. But, good Pisanio,
When shall we hear from him?

Pis. Be assur'd, madam,
With his next vantage.

Imo. I did not take my leave of him, but had
Most pretty things to say. Ere I could tell him
How I would think on him at certain hours
Such thoughts and such, or I could make him swear
The shes of Italy should not betray
Mine interest and his honour, or have charg'd him,
At the sixth hour of morn, at noon, at midnight,
To encounter me with orisons, for then
I am in heaven for him; or ere I could
Give him that parting kiss which I had set
Betwixt two charming words, comes in my father
And like the tyrannous breathing of the north
Shakes all our buds from growing.

Enter a *Lady.*

Lady. The Queen, madam,
Desires your Highness' company.

Imo. Those things I bid you do, get them dispatch'd.
I will attend the Queen.

Pis. Madam, I shall.

Exeunt.

Scene ii: 10. passable, affording free passage. **14. it . . . town,** his steel didn't want to be seen and went around rather than through the town, i.e., it missed. **20. having,** possession. **30. election,** choice. **33. sign,** appearance. **Scene iii: 4. offer'd mercy,** pardon offered to a condemned criminal.

12. fits and stirs, violent emotion and agitation. **15. left To after-eye,** stopped looking after. **24. vantage,** opportunity. **32. encounter . . . orisons,** meet me with prayers. **35. charming,** with charms or spells. **36. north,** i.e., wind.

Scene IV. *Rome. Philario's house.*

Enter *Philario, Iachimo,* a *Frenchman,* a *Dutchman,* and a *Spaniard.*

Iach. Believe it, sir, I have seen him in Britain: he was then of a crescent note, expected to prove so worthy as since he hath been allowed the name of; but I could then have looked on him without the help of admiration, though the catalogue of his endowments had been tabled by his side and I to peruse him by items.

Phi. You speak of him when he was less furnished than now he is with that which makes him both without and within.

French. I have seen him in France: we had very many there could behold the sun with as firm eyes as he.

Iach. This matter of marrying his king's daughter, wherein he must be weighed rather by her value than his own, words him, I doubt not, a great deal from the matter.

French. And then his banishment.

Iach. Ay, and the approbation of those that weep this lamentable divorce under her colours are wonderfully to extend him; be it but to fortify her judgement, which else an easy battery might lay flat, for taking a beggar without less quality. But how comes it he is to sojourn with you? How creeps acquaintance?

Phi. His father and I were soldiers together; to whom I have been often bound for no less than my life.

Enter *Posthumus.*

Here comes the Briton. Let him be so entertained amongst you as suits with gentlemen of your knowing to a stranger of his quality. —I beseech you all, be better known to this gentleman, whom I commend to you as a noble friend of mine. How worthy he is I will leave to appear hereafter, rather than story him in his own hearing.

French. Sir, we have known together in Orleans.

Post. Since when I have been debtor to you for courtesies, which I will be ever to pay and yet pay still.

French. Sir, you o'er-rate my poor kindness: I was glad I did atone my countryman and you: it had been pity you should have been put together with so mortal a purpose as then each bore, upon importance of so slight and trivial a nature.

Post. By your pardon, sir, I was then a young traveller; rather shunned to go even with what I heard than in my every action to be guided by others' experiences: but upon my mended judgement—if I offend not to say it is mended—my quarrel was not altogether slight.

French. Faith, yes, to be put to the arbitrement of swords, and by such two that would by all likelihood have confounded one the other, or have fallen both.

Iach. Can we, with manners, ask what was the difference?

French. Safely, I think; 't was a contention in public, which may, without contradiction, suffer the report. It was much like an argument that fell out last night, where each of us fell in praise of our country-mistresses; this gentleman at that time vouching —and upon warrant of bloody affirmation—his to be more fair, virtuous, wise, chaste, constant, qualified, and less attemptable than any the rarest of our ladies in France.

Iach. That lady is not now living, or this gentleman's opinion by this worn out.

Post. She holds her virtue still, and I my mind.

Iach. You must not so far prefer her 'fore ours of Italy.

Post. Being so far provoked, as I was in France, I would abate her nothing, though I profess myself her adorer, not her friend.

Iach. As fair and as good—a kind of hand-in-hand comparison—had been something too fair and too good for any lady in Britain. If she went before others I have seen, as that diamond of yours outlustres many I have beheld, I could not but believe she excelled many: but I have not seen the most precious diamond that is, nor you the lady.

Post. I praised her as I rated her; so do I my stone.

Iach. What do you esteem it at?

Post. More than the world enjoys.

Iach. Either your unparagoned mistress is dead, or she 's outprized by a trifle.

Post. You are mistaken: the one may be sold, or given, or if there were wealth enough for the purchase, or merit for the gift; the other is not a thing for sale, and only the gift of the gods.

Iach. Which the gods have given you?

2. crescent, growing reputation. **7. tabled,** set down. **10. makes,** enriches, endows. **16. words . . . matter,** describes him, sets him in a light very different from reality. **20. under her colours,** i.e., her friends. **21. extend,** over-praise. **23. without less,** with less. **quality,** rank. **30. knowing,** experience. **34. story,** give an account of. **36. known together,** been acquainted. **39. which . . . still,** for which I shall ever be in your debt although I pay always. **42. atone,** reconcile.

44. put together, i.e., allowed to fight. **45. importance,** matter. **47. go even,** agree. **54. confounded,** killed. **59. suffer the report,** be told. **63. warrant . . . affirmation,** pledge of affirming with his blood. **65. attemptable,** i.e., in virtue. **74. friend,** lover.

Post. Which, by their graces, I will keep.

Iach. You may wear her in title yours; but, you know, strange fowl light upon neighbouring ponds. Your ring may be stolen too; so your brace of unprizable estimations, the one is but frail and the other casual. A cunning thief, or a that-way-accomplished courtier, would hazard the winning both of first and last.

Post. Your Italy contains none so accomplished a courtier to convince the honour of my mistress, if, in the holding or loss of that, you term her frail. I do nothing doubt you have store of thieves; notwithstanding, I fear not my ring.

Phi. Let us leave here, gentlemen.

Post. Sir, with all my heart. This worthy signior, I thank him, makes no stranger of me; we are familiar at first.

Iach. With five times so much conversation, I should get ground of your fair mistress, make her go back, even to the yielding, had I admittance, and opportunity to friend.

Post. No, no.

Iach. I dare thereupon pawn the moiety of my estate to your ring; which, in my opinion, o'ervalues it something: but I make my wager rather against your confidence than her reputation; and, to bar your offence herein too, I durst attempt it against any lady in the world.

Post. You are a great deal abused in too bold a persuasion; and I doubt not you sustain what you 're worthy of by your attempt.

Iach. What 's that?

Post. A repulse; though your attempt, as you call it, deserve more,—a punishment too.

Phi. Gentlemen, enough of this; it came in too suddenly: let it die as it was born, and, I pray you, be better acquainted.

Iach. Would I had put my estate and my neighbour's on th' approbation of what I have spoke!

Post. What lady would you choose to assail?

Iach. Yours, whom in constancy you think stands so safe. I will lay you ten thousand ducats to your ring, that, commend me to the court where your lady is, with no more advantage than the opportunity of a second conference, and I will bring from thence that honour of hers which you imagine so reserved.

Post. I will wage against your gold, gold to it: my ring I hold dear as my finger; 't is part of it.

Iach. You are afraid, and therein the wiser. If you buy ladies' flesh at a million a dram, you cannot preserve it from tainting. But I see you have some religion in you—that you fear.

Post. This is but a custom in your tongue; you bear a graver purpose, I hope.

Iach. I am the master of my speeches, and would undergo what 's spoken, I swear.

Post. Will you? I shall but lend my diamond till your return: let there be covenants drawn between 's. My mistress exceeds in goodness the hugeness of your unworthy thinking. I dare you to this match; here 's my ring.

Phi. I will have it no lay.

Iach. By the gods, it is one. If I bring you no sufficient testimony that I have enjoyed the dearest bodily part of your mistress, my ten thousand ducats are yours; so is your diamond too: if I come off, and leave her in such honour as you have trust in, she your jewel, this your jewel, and my gold are yours; provided I have your commendation for my more free entertainment.

Post. I embrace these conditions; let us have articles betwixt us. Only, thus far you shall answer: if you make your voyage upon her and give me directly to understand you have prevailed, I am no further your enemy; she is not worth our debate. If she remain unseduced, you not making it appear otherwise, for your ill opinion and th' assault you have made to her chastity you shall answer me with your sword.

Iach. Your hand; a covenant: we will have these things set down by lawful counsel, and straight away for Britain, lest the bargain should catch cold and starve. I will fetch my gold and have our two wagers recorded.

Post. Agreed.

Exeunt Posthumus and Iachimo.

French. Will this hold, think you?

Phi. Signior Iachimo will not from it. Pray, let us follow 'em. *Exeunt.*

Scene V. *Britain. A room in the palace.*

Enter *Queen, Ladies,* and *Cornelius.*

Queen. Whiles yet the dew 's on ground, gather those flowers;
Make haste. Who has the note of them?

1. Lady. I, madam.

Queen. Dispatch. *Exeunt Ladies.*
Now, master doctor, have you brought those drugs?

99. unprizable, without price. **estimations,** values. **104. to convince,** as to overcome. **107. fear,** fear for. **109. leave,** stop. **114. get ground,** win ground. **116. to friend,** as friend. **118. moiety,** half. **124. abused,** deceived. **125. persuasion,** opinion. **134. approbation,** proof.

149. that you fear, in as much as you fear—fear being a prime quality in religion. **151. bear a graver purpose,** have a more serious meaning. **153. undergo,** perform. **159. lay,** bet. **180. starve,** freeze. **Scene v: 2. note,** list.

Cor. Pleaseth your Highness, ay. Here they are, madam.
Presenting a small box.
But I beseech your Grace, without offence,—
My conscience bids me ask—wherefore you have
Commanded of me these most poisonous compounds,
Which are the movers of a languishing death,
But though slow, deadly.
Queen. I wonder, doctor,
Thou ask'st me such a question. Have I not been
Thy pupil long? Hast thou not learn'd me how
To make perfumes? distil? preserve? yea, so
That our great king himself doth woo me oft
For my confections? Having thus far proceeded,—
Unless thou think'st me devilish—is 't not meet
That I did amplify my judgement in
Other conclusions? I will try the forces
Of these thy compounds on such creatures as
We count not worth the hanging,—but none human—
To try the vigour of them and apply
Allayments to their act, and by them gather
Their several virtues and effects.
Cor. Your Highness
Shall from this practice but make hard your heart.
Besides, the seeing these effects will be
Both noisome and infectious.
Queen. O, content thee.

Enter *Pisanio.*

[*Aside.*] Here comes a flattering rascal; upon him
Will I first work. He 's for his master,
And enemy to my son. How now, Pisanio!
Doctor, your service for this time is ended;
Take your own way.
Cor. [*Aside.*] I do suspect you, madam;
But you shall do no harm.
Queen. [*To Pisanio.*] Hark thee, a word.
Cor. [*Aside.*] I do not like her. She doth think she has
Strange ling'ring poisons: I do know her spirit,
And will not trust one of her malice with
A drug of such damn'd nature. Those she has
Will stupefy and dull the sense a while,
Which first, perchance, she 'll prove on cats and dogs,
Then afterward up higher; but there is
No danger in what show of death it makes,
More than the locking-up the spirits a time,
To be more fresh, reviving. She is fool'd
With a most false effect; and I the truer,
So to be false with her.
Queen. No further service, doctor,
Until I send for thee.
Cor. I humbly take my leave.
Exit.
Queen. Weeps she still, say'st thou? Dost thou think in time
She will not quench and let instructions enter
Where folly now possesses? Do thou work:
When thou shalt bring me word she loves my son,
I 'll tell thee on the instant thou art then
As great as is thy master,—greater, for
His fortunes all lie speechless and his name
Is at last gasp. Return he cannot, nor
Continue where he is: to shift his being
Is to exchange one misery with another,
And every day that comes comes to decay
A day's work in him. What shalt thou expect,
To be depender on a thing that leans,
Who cannot be new built, nor has no friends
So much as but to prop him? *The Queen drops the box: Pisanio takes it up.*
Thou tak'st up
Thou know'st not what; but take it for thy labour:
It is a thing I made, which hath the King
Five times redeem'd from death. I do not know
What is more cordial. Nay, I prithee, take it;
It is an earnest of a further good
That I mean to thee. Tell thy mistress how
The case stands with her; do 't as from thyself.
Think what a chance thou changest on, but think
Thou hast thy mistress still; to boot, my son,
Who shall take notice of thee. I 'll move the King
To any shape of thy preferment such
As thou 'lt desire; and then myself, I chiefly,
That set thee on to this desert, am bound
To load thy merit richly. Call my women.
Think on my words. *Exit Pisanio.*
A sly and constant knave,
Not to be shak'd; the agent for his master
And the remembrancer of her to hold
The hand-fast to her lord. I have given him that
Which, if he take, shall quite unpeople her
Of liegers for her sweet, and which she after,
Except she bend her humour, shall be assur'd
To taste of too.

15. **confections,** compounds. 18. **conclusions,** experiments. 22. **Allayments . . . act,** antidotes. 26. **noisome,** disgusting.

44. **So to be false,** for being false. 47. **quench,** become cool. **instructions,** advice. 54. **being,** i.e., residence. 56. **decay,** destroy. 58. **leans,** totters. 64. **cordial,** beneficial to health. 65. **earnest,** pledge. 68. **chance . . . on,** good chance thy shifting brings about. 77. **remembrancer of her,** one who reminds her. 78. **hand-fast,** marriage contract. 80. **liegers,** ambassadors.

Re-enter *Pisanio* and *Ladies.*

So, so; well done, well done.
The violets, cowslips, and the primroses,
Bear to my closet. Fare thee well, Pisanio;
Think on my words.
Exeunt Queen and Ladies.

Pis. And shall do;
But when to my good lord I prove untrue,
I 'll choke myself: there 's all I 'll do for you.
Exit.

Scene VI. *Another room in the palace.*

Enter *Imogen.*

Imo. A father cruel, and a step-dame false;
A foolish suitor to a wedded lady,
That hath her husband banish'd;—O, that husband!
My supreme crown of grief! and those repeated
Vexations of it! Had I been thief-stolen,
As my two brothers, happy! but most miserable
Is the desire that 's glorious. Blessed be those,
How mean soe'er, that have their honest wills,
Which seasons comfort. Who may this be? Fie!

Enter *Pisanio* and *Iachimo.*

Pis. Madam, a noble gentleman of Rome,
Comes from my lord with letters.

Iach. Change you, madam?
The worthy Leonatus is in safety
And greets your Highness dearly.
Presents a letter.

Imo. Thanks, good sir;
You 're kindly welcome.

Iach. [*Aside.*] All of her that is out of door most rich!
If she be furnish'd with a mind so rare,
She is alone, th' Arabian bird, and I
Have lost the wager. Boldness be my friend!
Arm me, audacity, from head to foot!
Or, like the Parthian, I shall flying fight;
Rather, directly fly.

Imo. [*Reads.*]

"He is one of the noblest note, to whose kindnesses I am most infinitely tied. Reflect upon him accordingly, as you value your trust—
"LEONATUS."

So far I read aloud—
But even the very middle of my heart
Is warm'd by th' rest—and take it thankfully.
You are as welcome, worthy sir, as I
Have words to bid you, and shall find it so
In all that I can do.

Iach. Thanks, fairest lady.
What, are men mad? Hath nature given them eyes
To see this vaulted arch, and the rich crop
Of sea and land, which can distinguish 'twixt
The fiery orbs above and the twinn'd stones
Upon the number'd beach, and can we not
Partition make with spectacles so precious
'Twixt fair and foul?

Imo. What makes your admiration?

Iach. It cannot be i' th' eye, for apes and monkeys
'Twixt two such shes would chatter this way and
Contemn with mows the other; nor i' th' judgement,
For idiots in this case of favour would
Be wisely definite; nor i' th' appetite;
Sluttery to such neat excellence oppos'd
Should make desire vomit emptiness,
Not so allur'd to feed.

Imo. What is the matter, trow?

Iach. The cloyed will,—
That satiate yet unsatisfied desire, that tub
Both fill'd and running,—ravening first the lamb,
Longs after for the garbage.

Imo. What, dear sir,
Thus raps you? Are you well?

Iach. Thanks, madam; well. [*To Pisanio.*] Beseech you, sir, desire
My man's abode where I did leave him. He
Is strange and peevish.

Pis. I was going, sir,
To give him welcome. *Exit.*

Imo. Continues well my lord? His health, beseech you?

Iach. Well, madam.

Imo. Is he dispos'd to mirth? I hope he is.

Iach. Exceeding pleasant; none a stranger there
So merry and so gamesome. He is call'd
The Briton reveller.

Imo. When he was here,
He did incline to sadness and oft-times
Not knowing why.

Iach. I never saw him sad.
There is a Frenchman his companion, one
An eminent monsieur, that, it seems, much loves

7. that's glorious, for glory. **9. seasons comfort,** gives spice to happiness. **11. Change,** i.e., color. **17. Arabian bird,** the phoenix; never but one alive at a time. **20. Parthian,** cavalry of the East, famous for their archery as they seemed to retreat.

35. twinn'd, exactly alike. **36. number'd,** numerous (stones), i.e., unnumbered. **37. spectacles so precious,** eyes. **38. admiration,** wonder. **41. mows,** grimaces. **42. case of favour,** question regarding beauty. **44. Sluttery,** pertaining to a slovenly woman. **49. ravening,** devouring. **51. raps you,** transports you **53. abode,** staying. **62. sadness,** sobriety.

A Gallian girl at home. He furnaces
The thick sighs from him, whiles the jolly Briton—
Your lord, I mean—laughs from 's free lungs, cries "O,
Can my sides hold, to think that man, who knows
By history, report, or his own proof,
What woman is, yea, what she cannot choose
But must be, will his free hours languish for
Assured bondage?"

Imo. Will my lord say so?

Iach. Ay, madam, with his eyes in flood with laughter.
It is a recreation to be by
And hear him mock the Frenchman. But, heavens know,
Some men are much to blame.

Imo. Not he, I hope.

Iach. Not he; but yet heaven's bounty towards him might
Be used more thankfully. In himself, 't is much;
In you—which I account his—beyond all talents.
Whilst I am bound to wonder, I am bound
To pity too.

Imo. What do you pity, sir?

Iach. Two creatures heartily.

Imo. Am I one, sir?
You look on me; what wreck discern you in me
Deserves your pity?

Iach. Lamentable! What,
To hide me from the radiant sun, and solace
I' th' dungeon by a snuff!

Imo. I pray you, sir,
Deliver with more openness your answers
To my demands. Why do you pity me?

Iach. That others do,
I was about to say, enjoy your—But
It is an office of the gods to venge it,
Not mine to speak on 't.

Imo. You do seem to know
Something of me, or what concerns me: pray you,—
Since doubting things go ill often hurts more
Than to be sure they do; for certainties
Either are past remedies, or, timely knowing.
The remedy then born—discover to me
What both you spur and stop.

Iach. Had I this cheek
To bathe my lips upon; this hand, whose touch,
Whose every touch, would force the feeler's soul
To th' oath of loyalty; this object, which
Takes prisoner the wild motion of mine eye,
Fixing it only here; should I, damn'd then,
Slaver with lips as common as the stairs
That mount the Capitol; join gripes with hands
Made hard with hourly falsehood—falsehood, as
With labour; then lie peeping in an eye
Base and illustrous as the smoky light
That 's fed with stinking tallow: it were fit
That all the plagues of hell should at one time
Encounter such revolt.

Imo. My lord, I fear,
Has forgot Britain.

Iach. And himself. Not I,
Inclin'd to this intelligence, pronounce
The beggary of his change; but 't is your graces
That from my mutest conscience to my tongue
Charms this report out.

Imo. Let me hear no more.

Iach. O dearest soul! your cause doth strike my heart
With pity, that doth make me sick. A lady
So fair, and fasten'd to an empery
Would make the great'st king double,—to be partner'd
With tomboys hir'd with that self-exhibition
Which your own coffers yield! with diseas'd ventures
That play with all infirmities for gold
Which rottenness can lend nature! such boil'd stuff
As well might poison poison! Be reveng'd;
Or she that bore you was no queen, and you
Recoil from your great stock.

Imo. Reveng'd?
How should I be reveng'd? If this be true,—
As I have such a heart that both mine ears
Must not in haste abuse—if it be true,
How should I be reveng'd?

Iach. Should he make me
Live, like Diana's priest, betwixt cold sheets,
Whiles he is vaulting variable ramps,
In your despite, upon your purse? Revenge it.
I dedicate myself to your sweet pleasure,
More noble than that runagate to your bed,
And will continue fast to your affection,
Still close as sure.

Imo What, ho, Pisanio!

Iach. Let me my service tender on your lips.

Imo. Away! I do condemn mine ears that have

66. Gallian, Gallic. **furnaces,** exhales like a furnace. **80. talents,** i.e., price. **87. snuff,** burning wick, i.e., candle. **95. doubting,** suspecting. **98. then born,** i.e., may be born. **99. spur and stop,** i.e., seem about to say and then conceal.

109. illustrous, lustreless. **112. Encounter . . . revolt,** befall such inconstancy. **120. empery,** empire. **122. tomboys,** strumpets. **self-exhibition,** selfsame allowance, pension. **123. ventures,** i.e., persons. **128. Recoil,** fall off, degenerate. **134. ramps,** prostitutes. **137. runagate,** renegade.

So long attended thee. If thou wert honourable,
Thou wouldst have told this tale for virtue, not
For such an end thou seek'st,—as base as strange.
Thou wrong'st a gentleman, who is as far
From thy report as thou from honour, and
Solicits here a lady that disdains
Thee and the devil alike. What ho, Pisanio!
The King my father shall be made acquainted
Of thy assault: if he shall think it fit
A saucy stranger in his court to mart
As in a Romish stew, and to expound
His beastly mind to us, he hath a court
He little cares for and a daughter who
He not respects at all. What, ho, Pisanio!
Iach. O happy Leonatus! I may say.
The credit that thy lady hath of thee
Deserves thy trust, and thy most perfect goodness
Her assur'd credit. Blessed live you long
A lady to the worthiest sir that ever
Country call'd his! and you his mistress, only
For the most worthiest fit! Give me your pardon.
I have spoke this, to know if your affiance
Were deeply rooted, and shall make your lord,
That which he is, new o'er; and he is one
The truest manner'd, such a holy witch
That he enchants societies into him;
Half all men's hearts are his.
Imo. You make amends.
Iach. He sits 'mongst men like a descended god:
He hath a kind of honour sets him off,
More than a mortal seeming. Be not angry,
Most mighty princess, that I have adventur'd
To try your taking of a false report; which hath
Honour'd with confirmation your great judgement
In the election of a sir so rare,
Which you know cannot err. The love I bear him
Made me to fan you thus; but the gods made you,
Unlike all others, chaffless. Pray, your pardon.
Imo. All 's well, sir. Take my power i' th' court for yours.
Iach. My humble thanks. I had almost forgot
To entreat your Grace but in a small request,
And yet of moment too, for it concerns
Your lord, myself, and other noble friends,
Are partners in the business.
Imo. Pray, what is 't?
Iach. Some dozen Romans of us and your lord—
The best feather of our wing—have mingled sums
To buy a present for the Emperor;
Which I, the factor for the rest, have done
In France: 't is plate of rare device, and jewels
Of rich and exquisite form, their values great;
And I am something curious, being strange,
To have them in safe stowage. May it please you
To take them in protection?
Imo. Willingly;
And pawn mine honour for their safety: since
My lord hath interest in them, I will keep them
In my bedchamber.
Iach. They are in a trunk,
Attended by my men: I will make bold
To send them to you, only for this night;
I must aboard to-morrow.
Imo. O, no, no.
Iach. Yes, I beseech; or I shall short my word
By length'ning my return. From Gallia
I cross'd the seas on purpose and on promise
To see your Grace.
Imo. I thank you for your pains:
But not away to-morrow!
Iach. O, I must, madam;
Therefore I shall beseech you, if you please
To greet your lord with writing; do 't to-night.
I have outstood my time; which is material
To th' tender of our present.
Imo. I will write.
Send your trunk to me; it shall safe be kept,
And truly yielded you. You 're very welcome. *Exeunt.*

ACT II. SCENE I. *Before the palace.*

Enter *Cloten* and two *Lords.*

Clo. Was there ever man had such luck! When I kissed the jack, upon an up-cast to be hit away! I had a hundred pound on 't; and then a whoreson jackanapes must take me up for swearing, as if I borrowed mine oaths of him and might not spend them at my pleasure.

First Lord. What got he by that? You have broke his pate with your bowl.

151. mart, bargain. **163. affiance,** fidelity. **171. seeming,** appearance. **177. fan you,** winnow you. **Act II, Scene i: 2. kissed the jack,** touched the small white ball used as the target in the game of bowls. **up-cast,** cast, or throw.

188. factor, agent. **191. curious,** careful. **200. short,** impair. **207. outstood,** outstayed. **208. tender,** offering. **Act II, Scene i: 4. take me up,** upbraid me.

Sec. Lord. [*Aside.*] If his wit had been like him that broke it, it would have run all out.

Clo. When a gentleman is disposed to swear, it is not for any standers-by to curtail his oaths, ha?

Sec. Lord. No, my lord; [*aside*] nor crop the ears of them.

Clo. Whoreson dog! I give him satisfaction? Would he had been one of my rank!

Sec. Lord. [*Aside.*] To have smelt like a fool.

Clo. I am not vexed more at anything in the earth; a pox on 't! I had rather not be so noble as I am: they dare not fight with me, because of the Queen my mother: every Jack-slave hath his bellyful of fighting, and I must go up and down like a cock that nobody can match.

Sec. Lord. [*Aside.*] You are cock and capon too; and you crow, cock, with your comb on.

Clo. Sayest thou?

Sec. Lord. It is not fit your lordship should undertake every companion that you give offence to.

Clo. No, I know that; but it is fit I should commit offence to my inferiors.

Sec. Lord. Ay, it is fit for your lordship only.

Clo. Why, so I say.

First Lord. Did you hear of a stranger that 's come to court to-night?

Clo. A stranger, and I not know on 't!

Sec. Lord. [*Aside.*] He 's a strange fellow himself, and knows it not.

First Lord. There 's an Italian come; and, 't is thought, one of Leonatus' friends.

Clo. Leonatus! a banished rascal; and he 's another, whatsoever he be. Who told you of this stranger?

First Lord. One of your lordship's pages.

Clo. Is it fit I went to look upon him? Is there no derogation in 't?

Sec. Lord. You cannot derogate, my lord.

Clo. Not easily, I think.

Sec. Lord. [*Aside.*] You are a fool granted; therefore your issues, being foolish, do not derogate.

Clo. Come, I 'll go see this Italian. What I have lost to-day at bowls I 'll win to-night of him. Come, go.

Sec. Lord. I 'll attend your lordship.

Exeunt Cloten and First Lord.

That such a crafty devil as is his mother
Should yield the world this ass! A woman that
Bears all down with her brain; and this her son
Cannot take two from twenty, for his heart,
And leave eighteen. Alas, poor princess,
Thou divine Imogen, what thou endur'st,
Betwixt a father by thy step-dame govern'd,
A mother hourly coining plots, a wooer
More hateful than the foul expulsion is
Of thy dear husband! Then that horrid act
Of the divorce he 'd make! The heavens hold firm
The walls of thy dear honour, keep unshak'd
That temple, thy fair mind, that thou mayst stand,
T' enjoy thy banish'd lord and this great land!

Exit.

Scene II. *Imogen's bed-chamber: a trunk in one corner of it.*

Imogen in bed; a *Lady* attending.

Imo. Who 's there? My woman Helen?
Lady. Please you, madam.
Imo. What hour is it?
Lady. Almost midnight, madam.
Imo. I have read three hours then. Mine eyes are weak.
Fold down the leaf where I have left. To bed:
Take not away the taper, leave it burning;
And if thou canst awake by four o' th' clock,
I prithee, call me. Sleep hath seiz'd me wholly.

Exit Lady.

To your protection I commend me, gods.
From fairies and the tempters of the night
Guard me, beseech ye.

Sleeps. Iachimo comes from the trunk.

Iach. The crickets sing, and man's o'er-labour'd sense
Repairs itself by rest. Our Tarquin thus
Did softly press the rushes, ere he waken'd
The chastity he wounded. Cytherea!
How bravely thou becom'st thy bed, fresh lily,
And whiter than the sheets! That I might touch!
But kiss: one kiss! Rubies unparagon'd,
How dearly they do 't! 'T is her breathing that
Perfumes the chamber thus: the flame o' th' taper
Bows toward her, and would under-peep her lids
To see th' enclosed lights, now canopied
Under these windows white and azure, lac'd
With blue of heaven's own tinct. But my design,
To note the chamber: I will write all down:
Such and such pictures; there the window; such
Th' adornment of her bed; the arras; figures,

22. Jack-slave, low-born fellow. **26. comb,** coxcomb, fool's cap. **47. derogation,** disparagement (of himself).

12. Our Tarquin, the Roman in the story of Lucrece. **13. press the rushes,** i.e., with his feet, walked. **14. Cytherea,** Venus. **17. unparagon'd,** unequalled.

Why, such and such; and the contents o' th' story.
Ah, but some natural notes about her body,
Above ten thousand meaner moveables
Would testify, t' enrich mine inventory.
O sleep, thou ape of death, lie dull upon her!
And be her sense but as a monument,
Thus in a chapel lying! Come off, come off!
Taking off her bracelet.
As slippery as the Gordian knot was hard!
'T is mine; and this will witness outwardly,
As strongly as the conscience does within,
To th' madding of her lord. On her left breast
A mole cinque-spotted, like the crimson drops
I' th' bottom of a cowslip. Here 's a voucher,
Stronger than ever law could make; this secret
Will force him think I have pick'd the lock and ta'en
The treasure of her honour. No more. To what end?
Why should I write this down, that 's riveted,
Screw'd to my memory? She hath been reading late
The tale of Tereus; here the leaf 's turn'd down
Where Philomel gave up. I have enough.
To th' trunk again, and shut the spring of it.
Swift, swift, you dragons of the night, that dawning
May bare the raven's eye! I lodge in fear;
Though this a heavenly angel, hell is here.
Clock strikes.
One, two, three; time, time!
Goes into the trunk

Scene III. *An ante-chamber adjoining Imogen's apartments.*

Enter *Cloten* and *Lords*.

First Lord. Your lordship is the most patient man in loss, the most coldest that ever turn'd up ace.

Clo. It would make any man cold to lose.

First Lord. But not every man patient after the noble temper of your lordship. You are most hot and furious when you win.

Clo. Winning will put any man into courage. If I could get this foolish Imogen, I should have gold enough. It 's almost morning, is 't not?

First Lord. Day, my lord.

Clo. I would this music would come: I am advised to give her music o' mornings; they say it will penetrate.

Enter *Musicians.*

Come on; tune. If you can penetrate her with your fingering, so; we 'll try with tongue too: if none will do, let her remain; but I 'll never give o'er. First, a very excellent good-conceited thing; after, a wonderful sweet air, with admirable rich words to it; and then let her consider.

Hark, hark! the lark at heaven's gate sings,
And Phœbus gins arise
His steeds to water at those springs
On chalic'd flowers that lies;
And winking Mary-buds begin
To ope their golden eyes;
With every thing that pretty is,
My lady sweet, arise,
Arise, arise.

Clo. So, get you gone. If this penetrate, I will consider your music the better; if it do not, it is a vice in her ears, which horse-hairs and calves'-guts, nor the voice of unpaved eunuch to boot, can never amend.
Exeunt Musicians.

Enter *Cymbeline* and *Queen.*

Sec. Lord. Here comes the King.

Clo. I am glad I was up so late, for that 's the reason I was up so early: he cannot choose but take this service I have done fatherly. —Good morrow to your Majesty and to my gracious mother!

Cym. Attend you here the door of our stern daughter?
Will she not forth?

Clo. I have assailed her with musics, but she vouchsafes no notice.

Cym. The exile of her minion is too new;
She hath not yet forgot him: some more time
Must wear the print of his remembrance on 't,
And then she 's yours.

Queen. You are most bound to th' King,
Who lets go by no vantages that may
Prefer you to his daughter. Frame yourself
To orderly soliciting, and be friended
With aptness of the season; make denials
Increase your services; so seem as if
You were inspir'd to do those duties which
You tender to her, that you in all obey her,

27. **story,** i.e., the picture in the tapestry; cf. 2.4.69 below. 34. **Gordian knot,** the knot binding the yoke to the pole of Gordian's chariot was proverbially difficult to untie. Alexander finally cut it with his sword. 37. **madding,** maddening. 38. **cinque-spotted,** with five spots. 45. **Tereus,** King of Thrace, dishonored his sister-in-law, Philomela, and cut out her tongue to prevent betrayal. She was later changed into a nightingale. **Scene iii: 2. coldest,** coolest.

14. **penetrate,** touch. 18. **good-conceited,** fanciful. 25. **winking Mary-buds,** closed marigold buds. 32. **consider,** pay for. 33. **horse hairs,** bow strings. 34. **calves'-guts,** violin strings. **unpaved,** castrated. 39. **fatherly,** as a father, i.e., will be pleased. 46. **minion,** favorite. 47. **time . . . on 't,** sometime still Posthumus must be remembered. 52. **be friended With,** be favored by, i.e., take advantage of.

Save when command to your dismission tends,
And therein you are senseless.
Clo. Senseless! not so.

Enter a *Messenger.*

Mess. So like you, sir, ambassadors from Rome;
The one is Caius Lucius.
Cym. A worthy fellow,
Albeit he comes on angry purpose now;
But that 's no fault of his. We must receive him
According to the honour of his sender;
And towards himself, his goodness forespent on us,
We must extend our notice. Our dear son,
When you have given good morning to your mistress,
Attend the Queen and us; we shall have need
T' employ you towards this Roman. Come, our queen. *Exeunt all but Cloten.*
Clo. If she be up, I 'll speak with her; if not,
Let her lie still and dream. [*Knocks.*] By your leave, ho!
I know her women are about her; what
If I do line one of their hands? 'T is gold
Which buys admittance; oft it doth; yea, and makes
Diana's rangers false themselves, yield up
Their deer to th' stand o' th' stealer; and 't is gold
Which makes the true man kill'd and saves the thief,
Nay, sometime hangs both thief and true man: what
Can it not do and undo? I will make
One of her women lawyer to me, for
I yet not understand the case myself.
By your leave. *Knocks.*

Enter a *Lady.*

Lady. Who 's there that knocks?
Clo. A gentleman.
Lady. No more?
Clo. Yes, and a gentlewoman's son.
Lady. That 's more
Than some, whose tailors are as dear as yours,
Can justly boast of. What 's your lordship's pleasure?
Clo. Your lady's person. Is she ready?
Lady. Ay,
To keep her chamber.
Clo. There is gold for you;
Sell me your good report.
Lady. How! my good name? Or to report of you
What I shall think is good?—The Princess!

Enter *Imogen.*

Clo. Good morrow, fairest. Sister, your sweet hand. *Exit Lady.*
Imo. Good morrow, sir. You lay out too much pains
For purchasing but trouble: the thanks I give
Is telling you that I am poor of thanks
And scarce can spare them.
Clo. Still, I swear I love you.
Imo. If you but said so, 't were as deep with me:
If you swear still, your recompense is still
That I regard it not.
Clo. This is no answer.
Imo. But that you shall not say I yield being silent,
I would not speak. I pray you, spare me: faith,
I shall unfold equal discourtesy
To your best kindness: one of your great knowing
Should learn, being taught, forbearance.
Clo. To leave you in your madness, 't were my sin.
I will not.
Imo. Fools are not mad folks.
Clo. Do you call me fool?
Imo. As I am mad, I do:
If you 'll be patient, I 'll no more be mad;
That cures us both. I am much sorry, sir,
You put me to forget a lady's manners,
By being so verbal; and learn now, for all,
That I, which know my heart, do here pronounce,
By th' very truth of it, I care not for you,
And am so near the lack of charity
To accuse myself I hate you; which I had rather
You felt than make 't my boast.
Clo. You sin against
Obedience, which you owe your father: for
The contract you pretend with that base wretch,
One bred of alms and foster'd with cold dishes,
With scraps o' th' court, it is no contract, none;
And though it be allow'd in meaner parties—
Yet who than he more mean?—to knit their souls—
On whom there is no more dependency
But brats and beggary,—in self-figur'd knot,
Yet you are curb'd from that enlargement by

58. **Senseless**, insensible. 64. **forespent**, formerly spent. 74. **rangers**, nymphs. **yield . . . stealer**, fig., yield up their chastity. 75. **Stand** is the station from which the game is killed. 88. **report**, (1) news, (2) reputation.

102. **knowing**, knowledge. 111. **verbal**, plain-spoken. 123. On whom no one depends or relies excepting their brats and the poor. 124. **self-figur'd knot**, self-contracted marriage. 125. **enlargement**, freedom.

The consequence o' th' crown, and must not foil
The precious note of it with a base slave,
A hilding for a livery, a squire's cloth,
A pantler, not so eminent.
Imo. Profane fellow!
Wert thou the son of Jupiter and no more
But what thou art besides, thou wert too base
To be his groom: thou wert dignified enough,
Even to the point of envy, if 't were made
Comparative for your virtues, to be styl'd
The under-hangman of his kingdom, and hated
For being preferr'd so well.
Clo. The south-fog rot him!
Imo. He never can meet more mischance than come
To be but nam'd of thee. His meanest garment
That ever hath but clipp'd his body, is dearer
In my respect than all the hairs above thee,
Were they all made such men. How now?
Missing the bracelet. Pisanio!

Enter *Pisanio.*

Clo. "His garment!" Now the devil—
Imo. To Dorothy my woman hie thee presently—
Clo. "His garment!"
Imo. I am sprited with a fool,
Frighted, and anger'd worse. Go bid my woman
Search for a jewel that too casually
Hath left mine arm: it was thy master's: shrew me,
If I would lose it for a revenue
Of any king's in Europe. I do think
I saw 't this morning: confident I am
Last night 't was on mine arm; I kiss'd it.
I hope it be not gone to tell my lord
That I kiss aught but he.
Pis. 'T will not be lost.
Imo. I hope so; go and search.
Exit Pisanio.
Clo. You have abus'd me.
"His meanest garment!"
Imo. Ay, I said so, sir.
If you ill make 't an action, call witness to 't.
Clo. I will inform your father.
Imo. Your mother too:
She 's my good lady, and will conceive, I hope,
But the worst of me. So, I leave you, sir,
To th' worst of discontent. *Exit.*
Clo. I 'll be reveng'd.
"His meanest garment!" Well. *Exit.*

126. **consequence**, succession. **foil**, mar. 127. **note**, distinction. 128. **hilding for a livery**, a wretch suited to a servant's dress. **cloth**, livery. 129. **pantler**, pantry servant. 134. **Comparative for**, comparable to. 136. **south-fog**, the south wind was supposed to be unhealthful. 139. **clipp'd**, enclosed. 144. **sprited**, haunted. 156. **action**, i.e., at law.

Scene IV. *Rome. Philario's house.*

Enter *Posthumus* and *Philario.*

Post. Fear it not, sir: I would I were so sure
To win the King as I am bold her honour
Will remain hers.
Phi. What means do you make to him?
Post. Not any, but abide the change of time,
Quake in the present winter's state, and wish
That warmer days would come. In these fear'd hopes,
I barely gratify your love; they failing,
I must die much your debtor.
Phi. Your very goodness and your company
O'erpays all I can do. By this, your king
Hath heard of great Augustus. Caius Lucius
Will do 's commission throughly; and I think
He 'll grant the tribute, send th' arrearages,
Or look upon our Romans, whose remembrance
Is yet fresh in their grief.
Post. I do believe,
Statist though I am none, nor like to be,
That this will prove a war; and you shall hear
The legion now in Gallia sooner landed
In our not-fearing Britain than have tidings
Of any penny tribute paid. Our countrymen
Are men more order'd than when Julius Cæsar
Smil'd at their lack of skill, but found their courage
Worthy his frowning at. Their discipline,
Now wing-led with their courages, will make known
To their approvers they are people such
That mend upon the world.

Enter *Iachimo.*

Phi. See! Iachimo!
Post. The swiftest harts have posted you by land;
And winds of all the corners kiss'd your sails,
To make your vessel nimble.
Phi. Welcome, sir.
Post. I hope the briefness of your answer made
The speediness of your return.
Iach. Your lady
Is one of the fairest that I have look'd upon.
Post. And therewithal the best; or let her beauty
Look through a casement to allure false hearts
And be false with them.

6. **fear'd**, i.e., uncertain. 16. **Statist**, statesman. 21. **more order'd**, better disciplined. 24. **wing-led**, i.e., soaring. **courages**, gallants; cf. *Hamlet*, 1. 3. 65. 25. **approvers**, those who test them.

Iach. Here are letters for you.
Post. Their tenour good, I trust.
Iach. 'T is very like.
Phi. Was Caius Lucius in the Britain court
When you were there?
Iach. He was expected then,
But not approach'd.
Post. All is well yet.
Sparkles this stone as it was wont, or is 't not
Too dull for your good wearing?
Iach. If I have lost it,
I should have lost the worth of it in gold.
I 'll make a journey twice as far, t' enjoy
A second night of such sweet shortness which
Was mine in Britain; for the ring is won.
Post. The stone 's too hard to come by.
Iach. Not a whit,
Your lady being so easy.
Post. Make not, sir,
Your loss your sport. I hope you know that we
Must not continue friends.
Iach. Good sir, we must,
If you keep covenant. Had I not brought
The knowledge of your mistress home, I grant
We were to question farther; but I now
Profess myself the winner of her honour,
Together with your ring; and not the wronger
Of her or you, having proceeded but
By both your wills.
Post. If you can make 't apparent
That you have tasted her in bed, my hand
And ring is yours. If not, the foul opinion
You had of her pure honour gains or loses
Your sword or mine, or masterless leaves both
To who shall find them.
Iach. Sir, my circumstances,
Being so near the truth as I will make them,
Must first induce you to believe; whose strength
I will confirm with oath, which, I doubt not,
You 'll give me leave to spare, when you shall find
You need it not.
Post. Proceed.
Iach. First, her bedchamber,—
Where, I confess, I slept not, but profess
Had that was well worth watching—it was hang'd
With tapestry of silk and silver; the story
Proud Cleopatra, when she met her Roman,
And Cydnus swell'd above the banks, or for
The press of boats or pride; a piece of work
So bravely done, so rich, that it did strive
In workmanship and value; which I wonder'd
Could be so rarely and exactly wrought,
Since the true life on 't was—
Post. This is true;
And this you might have heard of here, by me,
Or by some other.
Iach. More particulars
Must justify my knowledge.
Post. So they must,
Or do your honour injury.
Iach. The chimney
Is south the chamber, and the chimney-piece
Chaste Dian bathing: never saw I figures
So likely to report themselves: the cutter
Was as another Nature, dumb; outwent her,
Motion and breath left out.
Post. This is a thing
Which you might from relation likewise reap,
Being, as it is, much spoke of.
Iach. The roof o' th' chamber
With golden cherubins is fretted. Her andirons—
I had forgot them—were two winking Cupids
Of silver, each on one foot standing, nicely
Depending on their brands.
Post. This is her honour!
Let it be granted you have seen all this—and praise
Be given to your remembrance—the description
Of what is in her chamber nothing saves
The wager you have laid.
Iach. Then, if you can,
Showing the bracelet.
Be pale; I beg but leave to air this jewel; see!
And now 't is up again: it must be married
To that your diamond; I 'll keep them.
Post. Jove!
Once more let me behold it. Is it that
Which I left with her?
Iach. Sir—I thank her—that.
She stripp'd it from her arm: I see her yet.
Her pretty action did outsell her gift,
And yet enrich'd it too. She gave it me, and said
She priz'd it once.
Post. May be she pluck'd it off
To send it me.
Iach. She writes so to you, doth she?
Post. O, no, no, no! 't is true. Here, take this too; *Gives the ring.*
It is a basilisk unto mine eye,
Kills me to look on 't. Let there be no honour
Where there is beauty; truth, where semblance; love,
Where there 's another man. The vows of women

52. **question farther,** i.e., fight a duel. 61. **circumstances,** details, particulars. 68. **watching,** keep awake for. 71. **Cydnus,** river in Asia Minor.

84. Was like nature except in giving the figures the power of speech—he even surpassed her (nature). 91. **Depending,** leaning. **brands,** torches. 97. **up,** i.e., back in his pocket. 102. **outsell,** exceed in value. 107. **basilisk,** cockatrice, a fabled monster—a serpent with a cockscomb on its head—which was believed to kill with a glance. 109. **semblance,** outward show (of truth).

Of no more bondage be, to where they are made,
Than they are to their virtues, which is nothing.
O, above measure false!

Phi. Have patience, sir,
And take your ring again; 't is not yet won.
It may be probable she lost it; or
Who knows if one of her women, being corrupted,
Hath stol'n it from her?

Post. Very true;
And so, I hope, he came by 't. Back my ring!
Render to me some corporal sign about her,
More evident than this; for this was stol'n.

Iach. By Jupiter, I had it from her arm.

Post. Hark you, he swears; by Jupiter he swears.
'T is true,—nay, keep the ring—'t is true. I am sure
She would not lose it: her attendants are
All sworn and honourable—they induc'd to steal it!
And by a stranger! No, he hath enjoy'd her:
The cognizance of her incontinency
Is this: she hath bought the name of whore thus dearly.
There, take thy hire; and all the fiends of hell
Divide themselves between you!

Phi. Sir, be patient.
This is not strong enough to be believ'd
Of one persuaded well of—

Post. Never talk on 't;
She hath been colted by him.

Iach. If you seek
For further satisfying, under her breast—
Worthy the pressing—lies a mole, right proud
Of that most delicate lodging. By my life,
I kiss'd it; and it gave me present hunger
To feed again, though full. You do remember
This stain upon her?

Post. Ay, and it doth confirm
Another stain, as big as hell can hold,
Were there no more but it.

Iach. Will you hear more?

Post. Spare your arithmetic; never count the turns;
Once, and a million!

Iach. I 'll be sworn—

Post. No swearing.
If you will swear you have not done 't, you lie;
And I will kill thee, if thou dost deny
Thou 'st made me cuckold.

Iach. I 'll deny nothing.

Post. O, that I had her here, to tear her limbmeal!

111. **bondage**, obligation. **to where**, i.e., toward those to whom. 127. **cognizance**, recognized sign or token. 147. **limbmeal**, limb from limb.

I will go there and do 't, i' th' court, before
Her father. I 'll do something— *Exit.*

Phi. Quite besides
The government of patience! You have won.
Let 's follow him, and pervert the present wrath
He hath against himself.

Iach. With all my heart.
Exeunt.

Scene V. *Another room in Philario's house.*

Enter *Posthumus.*

Post. Is there no way for men to be, but women
Must be half-workers? We are all bastards;
And that most venerable man which I
Did call my father, was I know not where
When I was stamp'd. Some coiner with his tools
Made me a counterfeit; yet my mother seem'd
The Dian of that time: so doth my wife
The nonpareil of this. O, vengeance, vengeance!
Me of my lawful pleasure she restrain'd
And pray'd me oft forbearance; did it with
A pudency so rosy the sweet view on 't
Might well have warm'd old Saturn; that I thought her
As chaste as unsunn'd snow. O, all the devils!
This yellow Iachimo, in an hour,—was 't not?—
Or less,—at first?—perchance he spoke not, but,
Like a full-acorn'd boar, a German one,
Cried "O!" and mounted; found no opposition
But what he look'd for should oppose and she
Should from encounter guard. Could I find out
The woman's part in me! For there 's no motion
That tends to vice in man, but I affirm
It is the woman's part; be it lying, note it,
The woman's; flattering, hers; deceiving, hers;
Lust and rank thoughts, hers, hers; revenges, hers;
Ambitions, covetings, change of prides, disdain,
Nice longing, slanders, mutability,

151. **pervert**, divert. Scene v: 2. **half-workers**, i.e., in producing a child. 8. **nonpareil**, paragon. 11. **pudency**, modesty. 16. **full-acorn'd**, full of acorns. 20. **motion**, impulse. 25. **change of prides**, constant varying of fads (in dress and behavior). 26. **Nice**, capricious.

All faults that may be nam'd, nay, that hell knows,
Why, hers, in part or all; but rather, all.
For even to vice
They are not constant, but are changing still
One vice, but of a minute old, for one
Not half so old as that. I 'll write against them,
Detest them, curse them; yet 't is greater skill
In a true hate, to pray they have their will.
The very devils cannot plague them better.
Exit.

Act III. Scene I. *Britain. A hall in the palace.*

Enter in state, *Cymbeline, Queen, Cloten,* and *Lords* at one door, and at another, *Caius Lucius* and *Attendants.*

Cym. Now say, what would Augustus Cæsar with us?
Luc. When Julius Cæsar, whose remembrance yet
Lives in men's eyes and will to ears and tongues
Be theme and hearing ever, was in this Britain
And conquer'd it, Cassibelan, thine uncle,—
Famous in Cæsar's praises, no whit less
Than in his feats deserving it—for him
And his succession granted Rome a tribute,
Yearly three thousand pounds, which by thee lately
Is left untender'd.
Queen. And, to kill the marvel,
Shall be so ever.
Clo. There be many Cæsars,
Ere such another Julius. Britain is
A world by itself; and we will nothing pay
For wearing our own noses.
Queen. That opportunity
Which then they had to take from 's, to resume
We have again. Remember, sir, my liege,
The kings your ancestors, together with
The natural bravery of your isle, which stands
As Neptune's park, ribb'd and pal'd in
With rocks unscaleable and roaring waters,
With sands that will not bear your enemies' boats,
But suck them up to th' topmast. A kind of conquest
Cæsar made here, but made not here his brag
Of "Came and saw and overcame": with shame—
The first that ever touch'd him—he was carried
From off our coast, twice beaten; and his shipping—
Poor ignorant baubles!—on our terrible seas,
Like egg-shells mov'd upon their surges, crack'd
As easily 'gainst our rocks; for joy whereof
The famed Cassibelan, who was once at point—
O giglot fortune!—to master Cæsar's sword,
Made Lud's town with rejoicing fires bright
And Britons strut with courage.

Clo. Come, there 's no more tribute to be paid: our kingdom is stronger than it was at that time; and, as I said, there is no moe such Cæsars. Other of them may have crooked noses, but to owe such straight arms, none.

Cym. Son, let your mother end.

Clo. We have yet many among us can gripe as hard as Cassibelan: I do not say I am one, but I have a hand. Why tribute? Why should we pay tribute? If Cæsar can hide the sun from us with a blanket, or put the moon in his pocket, we will pay him tribute for light; else, sir, no more tribute, pray you now.

Cym. You must know,
Till the injurious Romans did extort
This tribute from us, we were free. Cæsar's ambition,
Which swell'd so much that it did almost stretch
The sides o' th' world, against all colour here
Did put the yoke upon 's; which to shake off
Becomes a warlike people, whom we reckon
Ourselves to be. We do! Say then to Cæsar,
Our ancestor was that Mulmutius which
Ordain'd our laws, whose use the sword of Cæsar
Hath too much mangled; whose repair and franchise
Shall, by the power we hold, be our good deed,
Though Rome be therefore angry. Mulmutius made our laws,
Who was the first of Britain which did put
His brows within a golden crown and call'd
Himself a king.
Luc. I am sorry, Cymbeline,

14. opportunity, the taking advantage of a situation, opportunism, i.e., the conquest of Britain. **15. resume,** take back. **19. pal'd in,** enclosed. **27. ignorant baubles,** silly playthings, i.e., unseaworthy craft badly handled.

32. write against, denounce. **Act III, Scene i: 31. giglot,** fickle. **32. Lud's town,** London. **38. owe,** own. **51. against all colour,** against all reason, or perhaps, against all opposition. **54. We do,** i.e., we do shake off the yoke. **57. franchise,** free exercise.

That I am to pronounce Augustus Cæsar—
Cæsar, that hath moe kings his servants than
Thyself domestic officers—thine enemy.
Receive it from me, then: War and confusion
In Cæsar's name pronounce I 'gainst thee; look
For fury not to be resisted. Thus defied,
I thank thee for myself.

Cym. Thou art welcome, Caius.
Thy Cæsar knighted me; my youth I spent
Much under him; of him I gather'd honour,
Which he to seek of me again, perforce,
Behoves me keep at utterance. I am perfect
That the Pannonians and Dalmatians for
Their liberties are now in arms, a precedent
Which not to read would show the Britons cold:
So Cæsar shall not find them.

Luc. Let proof speak.

Clo. His Majesty bids you welcome. Make pastime with us a day or two, or longer: if you seek us afterwards in other terms, you shall find us in our salt-water girdle; if you beat us out of it, it is yours; if you fall in the adventure, our crows shall fare the better for you; and there 's an end.

Luc. So, sir.

Cym. I know your master's pleasure and he mine:
All the remain is "Welcome!" *Exeunt.*

Scene II. *Another room in the palace.*

Enter *Pisanio,* reading of a letter.

Pis. How! of adultery? Wherefore write you not
What monster 's her accuser? Leonatus!
O master! what a strange infection
Is fall'n into thy ear! What false Italian,
As poisonous-tongued as handed, hath prevail'd
On thy too ready hearing? Disloyal? No!
She 's punish'd for her truth, and undergoes,
More goddess-like than wife-life, such assaults
As would take in some virtue. O my master!
Thy mind to her is now as low as were
Thy fortunes. How! that I should murder her?
Upon the love and truth and vows which I
Have made to thy command? I, her? Her blood?
If it be so to do good service, never
Let me be counted serviceable. How look I,
That I should seem to lack humanity
So much as this fact comes to? *Reading.*

"Do 't; the letter
That I have sent her, by her own command
Shall give thee opportunity."

O damn'd paper!
Black as the ink that 's on thee! Senseless bauble,
Art thou a fedary for this act, and look'st
So virgin-like without? Lo, here she comes.

Enter *Imogen.*

I am ignorant in what I am commanded.

Imo. How now, Pisanio!

Pis. Madam, here is a letter from my lord.

Imo. Who? Thy lord? That is my lord, Leonatus!
O, learn'd indeed were that astronomer
That knew the stars as I his characters;
He 'd lay the future open. You good gods,
Let what is here contain'd relish of love,
Of my lord's health, of his content,—yet not
That we two are asunder; let that grieve him:
Some griefs are med'cinable; that is one of them,
For it doth physic love: of his content,
All but in that! Good wax, thy leave. Blest be
You bees that make these locks of counsel! Lovers
And men in dangerous bonds pray not alike;
Though forfeiters you cast in prison, yet
You clasp young Cupid's tables. Good news, gods!
[*Reads.*]

"Justice, and your father's wrath, should he take me in his dominion, could not be so cruel to me, as you, O the dearest of creatures, would even renew me with your eyes. Take notice that I am in Cambria, at Milford-Haven; what your own love will out of this advise you, follow. So he wishes you all happiness, that remains loyal to his vow, and your increasing in love

"LEONATUS POSTHUMUS."

O, for a horse with wings! Hear'st thou, Pisanio?
He is at Milford-Haven. Read, and tell me
How far 't is thither. If one of mean affairs
May plod it in a week, why may not I
Glide thither in a day? Then, true Pisanio,—
Who long'st, like me, to see thy lord; who long'st,—
O, let me bate,—but not like me—yet long'st,
But in a fainter kind;—O, not like me,
For mine 's beyond beyond—say, and speak thick,—
Love's counsellor should fill the bores of hearing,

73. **at utterance,** to the last extreme. **perfect,** well informed. 76. **read,** understand. **cold,** insensible. 87. **remain,** remainder. Scene ii: 10. **to,** compared to.

21. **fedary,** accomplice. 23. I will feign ignorance of the command laid on me. 28. **characters,** handwriting. 30. **relish,** taste. 36. **locks,** i.e., of beeswax. 38. **forfeiters,** i.e, of bonds. 39. **tables,** tablets. 45. **Cambria,** Wales. 56. **bate,** deduct (his longing must be less than hers). 58. **thick,** quickly.

To th' smothering of the sense—how far it is
To this same blessed Milford; and by the way
Tell me how Wales was made so happy as
T' inherit such a haven; but first of all,
How we may steal from hence, and for the gap
That we shall make in time, from our hencegoing
And our return, to excuse. But first, how get hence?
Why should excuse be born or ere begot?
We 'll talk of that hereafter. Prithee, speak,
How many score of miles may we well ride
'Twixt hour and hour?

Pis. One score t'wixt sun and sun,
Madam, 's enough for you, and too much too.

Imo. Why, one that rode to 's execution, man,
Could never go so slow. I have heard of riding wagers,
Where horses have been nimbler than the sands
That run i' th' clock's behalf. But this is fool'ry.
Go bid my woman feign a sickness, say
She 'll home to her father; and provide me presently
A riding-suit, no costlier than would fit
A franklin's housewife.

Pis. Madam, you 're best consider.

Imo. I see before me, man: nor here, nor there,
Nor what ensues, but have a fog in them,
That I cannot look through. Away, I prithee;
Do as I bid thee. There 's no more to say.
Accessible is none but Milford way. *Exeunt.*

Scene III. *Wales: a mountainous country with a cave.*

Enter from the cave *Belarius, Guiderius,* and *Arviragus.*

Bel. A goodly day not to keep house, with such
Whose roof 's as low as ours! Stoop, boys; this gate
Instructs you how t' adore the heavens and bows you
To a morning's holy office. The gates of monarchs
Are arch'd so high that giants may jet through
And keep their impious turbans on, without
Good morrow to the sun. Hail, thou fair heaven!
We house i' th' rock, yet use thee not so hardly
As prouder livers do.

Gui. Hail, heaven!

Arv. Hail, heaven!

Bel. Now for our mountain sport. Up to yond hill!
Your legs are young; I 'll tread these flats. Consider,
When you above perceive me like a crow,
That it is place which lessens and sets off;
And you may then revolve what tales I have told you
Of courts of princes, of the tricks in war;
This service is not service, so being done,
But being so allowed. To apprehend thus,
Draws us a profit from all things we see;
And often, to our comfort, shall we find
The sharded beetle in a safer hold
Than is the full-wing'd eagle. O, this life
Is nobler than attending for a check,
Richer than doing nothing for a bauble,
Prouder than rustling in unpaid-for silk:
Such gains the cap of him that makes him fine,
Yet keeps his book uncross'd. No life to ours.

Gui. Out of your proof you speak; we, poor unfledg'd,
Have never wing'd from view o' th' nest, nor knows not
What air 's from home. Haply this life is best,
If quiet life be best; sweeter to you
That have a sharper known; well corresponding
With your stiff age; but unto us it is
A cell of ignorance, travelling a-bed,
A prison of a debtor that not dares
To stride a limit.

Arv. What should we speak of
When we are old as you? When we shall hear
The rain and wind beat dark December, how,
In this our pinching cave, shall we discourse
The freezing hours away? We have seen nothing.
We are beastly; subtle as the fox for prey,
Like warlike as the wolf for what we eat.
Our valour is to chase what flies: our cage
We make a choir, as doth the prison'd bird,
And sing our bondage freely.

Bel. How you speak!
Did you but know the city's usuries
And felt them knowingly; the art o' th' court,
As hard to leave as keep; whose top to climb
Is certain falling, or so slipp'ry that
The fear 's as bad as falling; the toil o' th' war,

67. **or ere,** before. 75. **i' th' clock's behalf,** i.e., do the service of a clock. 79. **franklin's,** well-to-do land owner. 80. **before . . . through,** I see straight ahead to Milford; all the rest is lost in fog. **Scene iii: 1. keep house,** stay in the house. 2. **this gate,** the low entrance to the cave. 5. **jet,** strut.

17. **allowed,** acknowledged. 20. **sharded,** with scaly wing cases. 22. **attending,** doing service. **check,** reproof. 25. **gains . . . him,** gains the bows of his tailor. 26. **book uncross'd,** account unpaid (not crossed out). 31. **sharper,** more bitter. 35. **stride a limit,** over-step a boundary.

A pain that only seems to seek out danger
I' th' name of fame and honour; which dies i' th' search,
And hath as oft a sland'rous epitaph
As record of fair act; nay, many times,
Doth ill deserve by doing well; what 's worse,
Must curtsy at the censure;—O boys, this story
The world may read in me: my body 's mark'd
With Roman swords, and my report was once
First with the best of note. Cymbeline lov'd me,
And when a soldier was the theme, my name
Was not far off. Then was I as a tree
Whose boughs did bend with fruit; but in one night,
A storm or robbery, call it what you will,
Shook down my mellow hangings, nay, my leaves,
And left me bare to weather.

Gui. Uncertain favour!

Bel. My fault being nothing—as I have told you oft—
But that two villains, whose false oaths prevail'd
Before my perfect honour, swore to Cymbeline
I was confederate with the Romans; so
Followed my banishment, and this twenty years
This rock and these demesnes have been my world,
Where I have liv'd at honest freedom, paid
More pious debts to heaven than in all
The fore-end of my time. But up to th' mountains!
This is not hunters' language: he that strikes
The venison first shall be the lord o' th' feast;
To him the other two shall minister;
And we will fear no poison, which attends
In place of greater state. I 'll meet you in the valleys.

Exeunt Guiderius and Arviragus.

How hard it is to hide the sparks of nature!
These boys know little they are sons to th' King,
Nor Cymbeline dreams that they are alive.
They think they are mine; and, though train'd up thus meanly,
I' th' cave wherein they bow, their thoughts do hit
The roofs of palaces, and nature prompts them
In simple and low things to prince it much
Beyond the trick of others. This Polydore,
The heir of Cymbeline and Britain, who
The King his father call'd Guiderius,—Jove!
When on my three-foot stool I sit and tell
The warlike feats I have done, his spirits fly out
Into my story; say, "Thus mine enemy fell,
And thus I set my foot on 's neck;" even then
The princely blood flows in his cheek, he sweats,
Strains his young nerves and puts himself in posture
That acts my words. The younger brother, Cadwal,
Once Arviragus, in as like a figure,
Strikes life into my speech and shows much more
His own conceiving.—Hark, the game is rous'd!—
O Cymbeline! heaven and my conscience knows
Thou didst unjustly banish me; whereon,
At three and two years old, I stole these babes;
Thinking to bar thee of succession, as
Thou refts me of my lands. Euriphile,
Thou wast their nurse; they took thee for their mother,
And every day do honour to her grave.
Myself, Belarius, that am Morgan call'd,
They take for natural father.—The game is up.

Exit.

Scene IV. *Country near Milford-Haven.*

Enter *Pisanio* and *Imogen.*

Imo. Thou told'st me, when we came from horse, the place
Was near at hand: ne'er long'd my mother so
To see me first, as I have now. Pisanio! man!
Where is Posthumus? What is in thy mind,
That makes thee stare thus? Wherefore breaks that sigh
From the inward of thee? One, but painted thus,
Would be interpreted a thing perplex'd
Beyond self-explication. Put thyself
Into a haviour of less fear, ere wildness
Vanquish my staider senses. What 's the matter?
Why tender'st thou that paper to me, with
A look untender? If 't be summer news,
Smile to 't before; if winterly, thou need'st
But keep that count'nance still. My husband's hand!
That drug-damn'd Italy hath out-craftied him,
And he 's at some hard point. Speak, man! Thy tongue
May take off some extremity, which to read
Would be even mortal to me.

64. weather, storm. **83. bow,** stoop on entering.

94. nerves, sinews. **Scene iv: 9. haviour . . . fear,** behavior less fearsome. **15. drug-damn'd,** Italy was famous for its poisoning. **out-craftied,** excelled in craft. **16. at some hard point,** in some difficult position. **17. extremity,** distress.

Pis. Please you, read;
And you shall find me, wretched man, a thing
The most disdain'd of fortune.

Imo. [*Reads.*]

"Thy mistress, Pisanio, hath played the strumpet in my bed; the testimonies whereof lies bleeding in me. I speak not out of weak surmises, but from proof as strong as my grief and as certain as I expect my revenge. That part thou, Pisanio, must act for me, if thy faith be not tainted with the breach of hers. Let thine own hands take away her life: I shall give thee opportunity at Milford-Haven: She hath my letter for the purpose; where, if thou fear to strike and to make me certain it is done, thou art the pander to her dishonour and equally to me disloyal."

Pis. What shall I need to draw my sword? The paper
Hath cut her throat already. No, 't is slander,
Whose edge is sharper than the sword, whose tongue
Outvenoms all the worms of Nile, whose breath
Rides on the posting winds and doth belie
All corners of the world. Kings, queens, and states,
Maids, matrons, nay, the secrets of the grave
This viperous slander enters. What cheer, madam?

Imo. False to his bed! What! is it to be false
To lie in watch there and to think on him;
To weep 'twixt clock and clock; if sleep charge nature,
To break it with a fearful dream of him
And cry myself awake? That 's false to 's bed, is it?

Pis. Alas, good lady!

Imo. I false! Thy conscience witness!—Iachimo,
Thou didst accuse him of incontinency;
Thou then look'dst like a villain; now methinks
Thy favour 's good enough. Some jay of Italy
Whose mother was her painting, hath betray'd him!
Poor I am stale, a garment out of fashion;
And, for I am richer than to hang by th' walls,
I must be ripp'd.—To pieces with me!—O,
Men's vows are women's traitors! All good seeming,
By thy revolt, O husband, shall be thought
Put on for villainy; not born where 't grows,
But worn a bait for ladies.

Pis. Good madam, hear me.

Imo. True honest men, being heard like false Æneas,
Were in his time thought false, and Sinon's weeping
Did scandal many a holy tear, took pity
From most true wretchedness; so thou, Posthumus,
Wilt lay the leaven on all proper men;
Goodly and gallant shall be false and perjur'd
From thy great fail.—Come, fellow, be thou honest!
Do thou thy master's bidding. When thou see'st him,
A little witness my obedience. Look!
I draw the sword myself. Take it, and hit
The innocent mansion of my love, my heart.
Fear not; 't is empty of all things but grief.
Thy master is not there, who was indeed
The riches of it. Do his bidding; strike.
Thou mayst be valiant in a better cause,
But now thou seem'st a coward.

Pis. Hence, vile instrument!
Thou shalt not damn my hand.

Imo. Why, I must die;
And if I do not by thy hand, thou art
No servant of thy master's. Against self-slaughter
There is a prohibition so divine
That cravens my weak hand. Come, here 's my heart,
(Something 's afore 't,—soft, soft! we 'll no defence,)
Obedient as the scabbard. What is here?

Draws the letters from her bosom.

The scriptures of the loyal Leonatus,
All turn'd to heresy? Away, away,
Corrupters of my faith! you shall no more
Be stomachers to my heart. Thus may poor fools
Believe false teachers: though those that are betray'd
Do feel the treason sharply, yet the traitor
Stands in worse case of woe.
And thou, Posthumus, thou that didst set up
My disobedience 'gainst the King my father,
And make me put into contempt the suits
Of princely fellows, shalt hereafter find
It is no act of common passage, but
A strain of rareness; and I grieve myself
To think, when thou shalt be disedg'd by her
That now thou tirest on, how thy memory
Will then be pang'd by me. Prithee, dispatch!
The lamb entreats the butcher. Where 's thy knife?

30 **pander,** go-between. 37. **worms,** serpents. 38. **posting,** speeding. **belie,** tell lies about. 39. **states,** officers of state. 44. **charge,** load, burden. 51. **favour's,** look is. **jay,** strumpet. 52. **Whose . . . painting,** born of the paint-pot or cosmetics, artificial.

60. **false,** i.e., to Dido. 61. **Sinon's,** the Greek whose feigned tears brought about the fall of Troy. 64. **lay the leaven on,** corrupt. 66. **fail,** offense. 80. **cravens,** makes cowardly. 83. **scriptures,** (1) writings, (2) sacred writings. 86. **stomachers,** part of dress covering the breast. 90. **set up,** incite. 94. **It,** i.e., her choice of him. **passage,** occurrence. 96. **disedg'd,** surfeited. 97. **tirest,** tearest, devourest.

Thou art too slow to do thy master's bidding,
When I desire it too.
Pis. O gracious lady,
Since I receiv'd command to do this business
I have not slept one wink.
Imo. Do 't, and to bed then.
Pis. I 'll wake mine eye-balls out first.
Imo. Wherefore then
Didst undertake it? Why hast thou abus'd
So many miles with a pretence? This place?
Mine action and thine own? Our horses' labour?
The time inviting thee? The perturb'd court,
For my being absent? whereunto I never
Purpose return. Why hast thou gone so far,
To be unbent when thou hast ta'en thy stand,
Th' elected deer before thee?
Pis. But to win time
To lose so bad employment; in the which
I have consider'd of a course. Good lady,
Hear me with patience.
Imo. Talk thy tongue weary; speak:
I have heard I am a strumpet, and mine ear,
Therein false struck, can take no greater wound,
Nor tent to bottom that. But speak.
Pis. Then, madam,
I thought you would not back again.
Imo. Most like;
Bringing me here to kill me.
Pis. Not so, neither;
But if I were as wise as honest, then
My purpose would prove well. It cannot be
But that my master is abus'd.
Some villain, ay, and singular in his art,
Hath done you both this cursed injury.
Imo. Some Roman courtezan!
Pis. No, on my life.
I 'll give but notice you are dead, and send him
Some bloody sign of it; for 't is commanded
I should do so: you shall be miss'd at court,
And that will well confirm it.
Imo. Why, good fellow,
What shall I do the while? Where bide? How live?
Or in my life what comfort, when I am
Dead to my husband?
Pis. If you 'll back to th' court—
Imo. No court, no father; nor no more ado
With that harsh, noble, simple nothing,
That Cloten, whose love-suit hath been to me
As fearful as a siege.
Pis. If not at court,
Then not in Britain must you bide.
Imo. Where then?
Hath Britain all the sun that shines? Day, night,
Are they not but in Britain? I' th' world's volume
Our Britain seems as of it, but not in 't;
In a great pool a swan's nest: prithee, think
There 's livers out of Britain.
Pis. I am most glad
You think of other place. Th' ambassador,
Lucius the Roman, comes to Milford-Haven
To-morrow. Now, if you could wear a mind
Dark as your fortune is, and but disguise
That which, t' appear itself, must not yet be
But by self-danger, you should tread a course
Pretty and full of view; yea, haply, near
The residence of Posthumus; so nigh at least
That though his actions were not visible, yet
Report should render him hourly to your ear
As truly as he moves.
Imo. O, for such means,
Though peril to my modesty, not death on 't,
I would adventure.
Pis. Well, then, here 's the point.
You must forget to be a woman; change
Command into obedience; fear and niceness—
The handmaids of all women, or, more truly,
Woman it pretty self—into a waggish courage;
Ready in gibes, quick-answer'd, saucy, and
As quarrelous as the weasel; nay, you must
Forget that rarest treasure of your cheek,
Exposing it—but, O, the harder heart!
Alack, no remedy!—to the greedy touch
Of common-kissing Titan, and forget
Your laboursome and dainty trims, wherein
You made great Juno angry.
Imo. Nay, be brief!
I see into thy end, and am almost
A man already.
Pis. First, make yourself but like one.
Fore-thinking this, I have already fit—
'T is in my cloak-bag—doublet, hat, hose, all
That answer to them. Would you in their serving,
And with what imitation you can borrow
From youth of such a season, 'fore noble Lucius
Present yourself, desire his service, tell him
Wherein you 're happy,—which will make him know
If that his head have ear in music,—doubtless
With joy he will embrace you, for he 's honourable,
And doubling that, most holy. Your means abroad,

111. **unbent**, i.e., with unbent bow. 118. **Nor . . . that**, nor probe deeper than that. 124. **singular**, unparalleled.

147. **Dark**, obscure, lowly. 150. **Pretty . . . view**, becoming to you and full of opportunity. 158. **niceness**, fastidiousness. 160. **it**, its. 164. **harder heart**, i.e., for asking such a great sacrifice. 166. **Titan**, the sun. 167. **trims**, finery. 168. **angry**, i.e., jealous. 171. **Fore-thinking**, anticipating. **fit**, prepared, ready. 173. **in their serving**, outfitted in them. 175. **season**, age. 177. **happy**, gifted.

You have me, rich; and I will never fail
Beginning nor supplyment.
Imo. Thou art all the comfort
The gods will diet me with. Prithee, away.
There 's more to be consider'd; but we 'll even
All that good time will give us. This attempt
I am soldier to, and will abide it with
A prince's courage. Away, I prithee.
Pis. Well, madam, we must take a short farewell,
Lest, being miss'd, I be suspected of
Your carriage from the court. My noble mistress,
Here is a box;—I had it from the Queen;—
What 's in 't is precious: if you are sick at sea,
Or stomach-qualm'd at land, a dram of this
Will drive away distemper. To some shade,
And fit you to your manhood: may the gods
Direct you to the best!
Imo. Amen! I thank thee. *Exeunt.*

Scene V. *A room in the palace.*

Enter *Cymbeline, Queen, Cloten, Lucius,* and *Attendants.*

Cym. Thus far; and so farewell.
Luc. Thanks, royal sir.
My emperor hath wrote, I must from hence;
And am right sorry that I must report ye
My master's enemy.
Cym. Our subjects, sir,
Will not endure his yoke; and for ourself
To show less sovereignty than they, must needs
Appear unkinglike.
Luc. So, sir. I desire of you
A conduct over-land to Milford-Haven.
Madam, all joy befall your Grace, and you!
Cym. My lords, you are appointed for that office;
The due of honour in no point omit.
So farewell, noble Lucius.
Luc. Your hand, my lord.
Clo. Receive it friendly; but from this time forth
I wear it as your enemy.
Luc. Sir, the event
Is yet to name the winner. Fare you well.
Cym. Leave not the worthy Lucius, good my lords,
Till he have cross'd the Severn. Happiness!
Exeunt Lucius and Lords.
Queen. He goes hence frowning; but it honours us
That we have given him cause.
Clo. 'T is all the better;
Your valiant Britons have their wishes in it.
Cym. Lucius hath wrote already to the Emperor
How it goes here. It fits us therefore ripely
Our chariots and our horsemen be in readiness.
The powers that he already hath in Gallia
Will soon be drawn to head, from whence he moves
His war for Britain.
Queen. 'T is not sleepy business,
But must be look'd to speedily and strongly.
Cym. Our expectation that it would be thus
Hath made us forward. But, my gentle queen,
Where is our daughter? She hath not appear'd
Before the Roman, nor to us hath tender'd
The duty of the day. She looks us like
A thing more made of malice than of duty;
We have noted it. Call her before us, for
We have been too slight in sufferance.
Exit an attendant.
Queen. Royal sir.
Since the exile of Posthumus, most retir'd
Hath her life been; the cure whereof, my lord,
'T is time must do. Beseech your Majesty,
Forbear sharp speeches to her; she 's a lady
So tender of rebukes that words are strokes
And strokes death to her.

Re-enter *Attendant.*

Cym. Where is she, sir? How
Can her contempt be answer'd?
Atten. Please you, sir,
Her chambers are all lock'd; and there 's no answer
That will be given to th' loud'st of noise we make.
Queen. My lord, when last I went to visit her,
She pray'd me to excuse her keeping close,
Whereto constrain'd by her infirmity,
She should that duty leave unpaid to you,
Which daily she was bound to proffer: this
She wish'd me to make known; but our great court
Made me to blame in memory.
Cym. Her doors lock'd?
Not seen of late? Grant, heavens, that which I fear
Prove false! *Exit.*
Queen. Son, I say, follow the King.
Clo. That man of hers, Pisanio, her old servant,
I have not seen these two days. *Exit.*

184. **even,** profit by. 186. **I am soldier to,** I am enlisted in. **Scene v: 14. event,** outcome.

22. **fits,** befits. **ripely,** urgently. 32. **looks us,** seems to us. 35. **slight in sufferance,** negligent in allowing this. 50. **great court,** i.e., the entertainment of Lucius.

Queen. [*To attendant.*] Go, look after.
Pisanio, thou, that stand'st so for Posthumus!
He hath a drug of mine; I pray his absence
Proceed by swallowing that, for he believes
It is a thing most precious. But for her,
Where is she gone? Haply, despair hath seiz'd her,
Or, wing'd with fervour of her love, she 's flown
To her desir'd Posthumus: gone she is
To death or to dishonour; and my end
Can make good use of either. She being down,
I have the placing of the British crown.

Re-enter *Cloten.*

How now, my son!
Clo. 'T is certain she is fled.
Go in and cheer the King: he rages; none
Dare come about him.
Queen. [*Aside.*] All the better: may
This night forestall him of the coming day!
Exit.
Clo. I love and hate her; for she 's fair and royal,
And that she hath all courtly parts more exquisite
Than lady, ladies, woman; from every one
The best she hath, and she, of all compounded,
Outsells them all. I love her therefore; but
Disdaining me and throwing favours on
The low Posthumus slanders so her judgement
That what 's else rare is chok'd; and in that point
I will conclude to hate her, nay, indeed,
To be reveng'd upon her. For when fools
Shall—

Enter *Pisanio.*

Who is here? What, are you packing, sirrah?
Come hither. Ah, you precious pandar! Villain,
Where is thy lady? In a word; or else
Thou art straightway with the fiends.
Pis. O, good my lord!
Clo. Where is thy lady? or, by Jupiter,
I will not ask again. Close villain,
I 'll have this secret from thy heart, or rip
Thy heart to find it. Is she with Posthumus,
From whose so many weights of baseness cannot
A dram of worth be drawn?
Pis. Alas, my lord,
How can she be with him? When was she miss'd?
He is in Rome.
Clo. Where is she, sir? Come nearer.
No further halting. Satisfy me home
What is become of her.

58. by, from. **69. forestall,** deprive. **80. packing,** leaving or plotting. **85. Close,** secretive. **92. home,** completely.

Pis. O, my all-worthy lord!
Clo. All-worthy villain!
Discover where thy mistress is at once,
At the next word. No more of worthy lord!
Speak, or thy silence on the instant is
Thy condemnation and thy death.
Pis. Then, sir,
This paper is the history of my knowledge
Touching her flight. *Presenting a letter.*
Clo. Let 's see 't. I will pursue her
Even to Augustus' throne.
Pis. [*Aside.*] Or this, or perish.
She 's far enough; and what he learns by this
May prove his travel, not her danger.
Clo. Hum!
Pis. [*Aside.*] I 'll write to my lord she 's dead. O Imogen,
Safe mayst thou wander, safe return again!
Clo. Sirrah, is this letter true?
Pis. Sir, as I think.

Clo. It is Posthumus' hand; I know 't. Sirrah, if thou wouldst not be a villain, but do me true service, undergo those employments wherein I should have cause to use thee with a serious industry, that is, what villainy soe'er I bid thee do, to perform it directly and truly, I would think thee an honest man: thou shouldst neither want my means for thy relief nor my voice for thy preferment.

Pis. Well, my good lord.

Clo. Wilt thou serve me? For since patiently and constantly thou hast stuck to the bare fortune of that beggar Posthumus, thou canst not, in the course of gratitude, but be a diligent follower of mine. Wilt thou serve me?

Pis. Sir, I will.

Clo. Give me thy hand; here 's my purse. Hast any of thy late master's garments in thy possession?

Pis. I have, my lord, at my lodging, the same suit he wore when he took leave of my lady and mistress.

Clo. The first service thou dost me, fetch that suit hither: let it be thy first service; go.

Pis. I shall, my lord. *Exit.*

Clo. Meet thee at Milford-Haven!—I forgot to ask him one thing; I 'll remember 't anon;—even there, thou villain Posthumus, will I kill thee. I would these garments were come. She said upon a time—the bitterness of it I now belch from my heart—that she held the very garment of Posthumus in more respect than my noble and natural person, together with the adornment of my qualities. With that suit upon my back, will I ravish her,—first kill him, and in her eyes; there shall she see my valour, which will then be a torment to her contempt,—he on the ground, my speech of insultment ended on his dead body; and when my lust hath dined,—which, as I say, to vex her I will execute in the clothes that she so praised,—to the court I 'll knock her back, foot her home again. She hath despised me rejoicingly, and I 'll be merry in my revenge.

Re-enter *Pisanio* with the clothes.

Be those the garments?

Pis. Ay, my noble lord.

Clo. How long is 't since she went to Milford-Haven?

Pis. She can scarce be there yet.

Clo. Bring this apparel to my chamber; that is the second thing that I have commanded thee; the third is, that thou wilt be a voluntary mute to my design. Be but duteous, and true preferment shall tender itself to thee. My revenge is now at Milford; would I had wings to follow it! Come, and be true. 162 *Exit.*

Pis. Thou bid'st me to my loss; for true to thee
Were to prove false, which I will never be,
To him that is most true. To Milford go,
And find not her whom thou pursuest. Flow, flow,
You heavenly blessings, on her! This fool's speed 167
Be cross'd with slowness; labour be his meed! *Exit.*

Scene VI. *Wales. Before the cave.*

Enter *Imogen,* alone in boy's clothes.

Imo. I see a man's life is a tedious one:
I have tir'd myself, and for two nights together
Have made the ground my bed. I should be sick,
But that my resolution helps me. Milford,
When from the mountain-top Pisanio show'd thee,
Thou wast within a ken. O Jove! I think
Foundations fly the wretched; such, I mean,
Where they should be reliev'd. Two beggars told me
I could not miss my way: will poor folks lie,
That have afflictions on them, knowing 't is
A punishment or trial? Yes; no wonder,
When rich ones scarce tell true. To lapse in fulness
Is sorer than to lie for need; and falsehood
Is worse in kings than beggars. My dear lord!
Thou art one o' th' false ones: now I think on thee,
My hunger 's gone; but even before, I was
At point to sink for food. But what is this?
Here is a path to 't. 'T is some savage hold:
I were best not call; I dare not call; yet famine,
Ere clean it o'erthrow nature, makes it valiant.
Plenty and peace breeds cowards; hardness ever
Of hardiness is mother. Ho! who 's here?
If anything that 's civil, speak; if savage,
Take or lend. Ho! No answer? Then I 'll enter.
Best draw my sword; and if mine enemy
But fear the sword like me, he 'll scarcely look on 't.
Such a foe, good heavens! *Exit to the cave.*

Enter *Belarius, Guiderius,* and *Arviragus.*

Bel. You, Polydore, have prov'd best woodman and
Are master of the feast. Cadwal and I
Will play the cook and servant; 't is our match:
The sweat of industry would dry and die,
But for the end it works to. Come; our stomachs
Will make what 's homely savoury; weariness
Can snore upon the flint, when resty sloth
Finds the down pillow hard. Now peace be here,
Poor house, that keep'st thyself!

Gui. I am throughly weary.

Arv. I am weak with toil, yet strong in appetite.

Gui. There is cold meat i' th' cave; we 'll browse on that,
Whilst what we have kill'd be cook'd.

Bel. [*Looking into the cave.*] Stay; come not in.
But that it eats our victuals, I should think
Here were a fairy.

Gui. What 's the matter, sir?

Bel. By Jupiter, an angel! or, if not,
An earthly paragon! Behold divineness
No elder than a boy!

Re-enter *Imogen.*

Imo. Good masters, harm me not.
Before I enter'd here I call'd, and thought
To have begg'd or bought what I have took. Good troth,

148. foot, kick. **168. cross'd,** thwarted. **Scene vi: 6. within a ken,** within view. **7. Foundations,** (1) fixed places, (2) almshouses.

16. even, just. **18. hold,** stronghold. **21. hardness,** hardship. **24. Take or lend,** take my life or lend me food. **28. woodman,** huntsman. **30. match,** agreement. **34. resty,** torpid, dull.

I have stolen nought, nor would not, though I had found
Gold strew'd i' th' floor. Here 's money for my meat.
I would have left it on the board so soon
As I had made my meal, and parted with
Prayers for the provider.
Gui. Money, youth?
Arv. All gold and silver rather turn to dirt!
As 't is no better reckon'd, but of those
Who worship dirty gods.
Imo. I see you 're angry.
Know, if you kill me for my fault, I should
Have died had I not made it.
Bel. Whither bound?
Imo. To Milford-Haven.
Bel. What 's your name?
Imo. Fidele, sir. I have a kinsman who
Is bound for Italy; he embark'd at Milford;
To whom being going, almost spent with hunger,
I am fall'n in this offence.
Bel. Prithee, fair youth,
Think us no churls, nor measure our good minds
By this rude place we live in. Well encounter'd!
'T is almost night: you shall have better cheer
Ere you depart; and thanks to stay and eat it.
Boys, bid him welcome.
Gui. Were you a woman, youth,
I should woo hard but be your groom: in honesty:
I bid for you as I do buy.
Arv. I 'll make 't my comfort
He is a man; I 'll love him as my brother;
And such a welcome as I 'd give to him
After long absence, such is yours. Most welcome!
Be sprightly, for you fall 'mongst friends.
Imo. 'Mongst friends,
If brothers. [*Aside.*] Would it had been so, that they
Had been my father's sons! Then had my prize
Been less, and so more equal ballasting
To thee, Posthumus.
Bel. He wrings at some distress.
Gui. Would I could free 't!
Arv. Or I, whate'er it be,
What pain it cost, what danger. Gods!
Bel. Hark, boys. *Whispering.*
Imo. Great men,
That had a court no bigger than this cave,
That did attend themselves and had the virtue
Which their own conscience seal'd them, laying by
That nothing-gift of differing multitudes,
Could not out-peer these twain. Pardon me, gods!
I 'd change my sex to be companion with them,
Since Leonatus false.
Bel. It shall be so.
Boys, we 'll go dress our hunt. Fair youth, come in.
Discourse is heavy, fasting; when we have supp'd,
We 'll mannerly demand thee of thy story,
So far as thou wilt speak it.
Gui. Pray, draw near.
Arv. The night to th' owl and morn to th' lark less welcome.
Imo. Thanks, sir.
Arv. I pray, draw near. *Exeunt.*

Scene VII. *Rome. A public place.*

Enter two Roman *Senators* and *Tribunes*.

First Sen. This is the tenour of the Emperor's writ:
That since the common men are now in action
'Gainst the Pannonians and Dalmatians,
And that the legions now in Gallia are
Full weak to undertake our wars against
The fall'n-off Britons, that we do incite
The gentry to this business. He creates
Lucius proconsul; and to you the tribunes,
For this immediate levy, he commends
His absolute commission. Long live Cæsar!
First Tri. Is Lucius general of the forces?
Sec. Sen. Ay.
First Tri. Remaining now in Gallia?
First Sen. With those legions
Which I have spoke of, whereunto your levy
Must be supplyant: the words of your commission
Will tie you to the numbers and the time
Of their dispatch.
First Tri. We will discharge our duty.
Exeunt.

70. but be, but to be. **71. buy,** pay. In other words, it is a bonafide bid. **77. prize,** value. **79. wrings,** writhes.

85. seal'd them, confirmed in them. **86. nothing-gift . . . multitudes,** worthless gift of ruling the contentious mobs. **87. out-peer,** surpass. **Scene vii: 6 fall'n-off,** rebel. **14. supplyant,** reinforcements. **15. tie you to,** bind you to. i.e., specify.

ACT IV. Scene I. *Wales. Near the cave of Belarius.*

Enter *Cloten.*

Clo. I am near to the place where they should meet, if Pisanio have mapped it truly. How fit his garments serve me! Why should his mistress, who was made by him that made the tailor, not be fit too? the rather—saving reverence of the word—for 't is said a woman's fitness comes by fits. Therein I must play the workman. I dare speak it to myself—for it is not vain-glory for a man and his glass to confer in his own chamber—I mean, the lines of my body are as well drawn as his; no less young, more strong, not beneath him in fortunes, beyond him in the advantage of the time, above him in birth, alike conversant in general services, and more remarkable in single oppositions; yet this imperceiverant thing loves him in my despite. What mortality is! Posthumus, thy head, which now is growing upon thy shoulders, shall within this hour be off; thy mistress enforced; thy garments cut to pieces before her face: and all this done, spurn her home to her father; who may haply be a little angry for my so rough usage; but my mother, having power of his testiness, shall turn all into my commendations. My horse is tied up safe. Out, sword, and to a sore purpose! Fortune, put them into my hand! This is the very description of their meeting-place; and the fellow dares not deceive me. *Exit.*

Scene II. *Before the cave of Belarius.*

Enter *Belarius, Guiderius, Arviragus,* and *Imogen,* from the cave.

Bel. [*To Imogen.*] You are not well: remain here in the cave;
We 'll come to you after hunting.
Arv. [*To Imogen.*] Brother, stay here.
Are we not brothers?
Imo. So man and man should be;
But clay and clay differs in dignity,
Whose dust is both alike. I am very sick.
Gui. Go you to hunting; I 'll abide with him.
Imo. So sick I am not, yet I am not well;
But not so citizen a wanton as
To seem to die ere sick. So please you, leave me;
Stick to your journal course: the breach of custom
Is breach of all. I am ill, but your being by me
Cannot amend me; society is no comfort
To one not sociable: I am not very sick,
Since I can reason of it. Pray you, trust me here.
I 'll rob none but myself; and let me die,
Stealing so poorly.
Gui. I love thee; I have spoke it;
How much the quantity, the weight as much,
As I do love my father.
Bel. What? how? how?
Arv. If it be sin to say so, sir, I yoke me
In my good brother's fault: I know not why
I love this youth; and I have heard you say,
Love's reason 's without reason: the bier at door,
And a demand who is 't shall die, I 'd say
My father, not this youth.
Bel. [*Aside.*] O noble strain!
O worthiness of nature! breed of greatness!
Cowards father cowards and base things sire base:
Nature hath meal and bran, contempt and grace.
I 'm not their father; yet who this should be,
Doth miracle itself, lov'd before me.—
'T is the ninth hour o' th' morn.
Arv. Brother, farewell.
Imo. I wish ye sport.
Arv. You health.—So please you, sir.
Imo. [*Aside.*] These are kind creatures. Gods, what lies I have heard!
Our courtiers say all 's savage but at court;
Experience, O, thou disprov'st report!
Th' imperious seas breeds monsters; for the dish
Poor tributary rivers as sweet fish.
I am sick still, heart-sick. Pisanio,
I 'll now taste of thy drug. *Swallows some.*
Gui. I could not stir him.
He said he was gentle, but unfortunate;
Dishonestly afflicted, but yet honest.
Arv. Thus did he answer me; yet said, hereafter
I might know more.
Bel. To the field, to the field!
We 'll leave you for this time. Go in and rest.
Arv. We 'll not be long away.
Bel. Pray, be not sick,
For you must be our housewife.
Imo. Well or ill,
I am bound to you. *Exit to the cave.*

3. **serve,** fit. 12-13. **advantage of the time,** present favorable circumstances. 13. **general services,** military service to the state. **single oppositions.** single combat. 14. **imperceiverant,** flighty. 15. **What,** what a thing. **Scene ii:** 8. **citizen a wanton,** effeminate a spoiled child.

10. **journal,** daily. 17. **How much,** however much. 29. **Doth miracle itself,** is incomprehensible. 35. **for the dish,** for eating. 36. **as sweet fish,** i.e., breed as sweet fish as the sea. 39. **gentle,** i.e., of birth.

Bel. And shalt be ever.
This youth, howe'er distress'd, appears he hath had
Good ancestors.
Arv. How angel-like he sings!
Gui. But his neat cookery! He cut our roots in characters,
And sauc'd our broths, as Juno had been sick
And he her dieter.
Arv. Nobly he yokes
A smiling with a sigh, as if the sigh
Was that it was, for not being such a smile;
The smile mocking the sigh, that it would fly
From so divine a temple, to commix
With winds that sailors rail at.
Gui. I do note
That grief and patience, rooted in him both,
Mingle their spurs together.
Arv. Grow, patience!
And let the stinking elder, grief, untwine
His perishing root with the increasing vine!
Bel. It is great morning. Come, away!—Who 's there?

Enter *Cloten.*

Clo. I cannot find those runagates; that villain
Hath mock'd me. I am faint.
Bel. Those runagates!
Means he not us? I partly know him. 'T is
Cloten, the son o' th' Queen. I fear some ambush.
I saw him not these many years, and yet
I know 't is he. We are held as outlaws; hence!
Gui. He is but one. You and my brother search
What companies are near. Pray you, away;
Let me alone with him.
Exeunt Belarius and Arviragus.
Clo. Soft! What are you
That fly me thus? Some villain mountaineers?
I have heard of such. What slave art thou?
Gui. A thing
More slavish did I ne'er than answering
A slave without a knock.
Clo. Thou art a robber,
A law-breaker, a villain. Yield thee, thief.
Gui. To who? To thee? What art thou? Have not I
An arm as big as thine? a heart as big?
Thy words, I grant, are bigger; for I wear not
My dagger in my mouth. Say what thou art,
Why I should yield to thee.
Clo. Thou villain base,
Know'st me not by my clothes?
Gui. No, nor thy tailor, rascal,
Who is thy grandfather. He made those clothes,
Which, as it seems, make thee.
Clo. Thou precious varlet,
My tailor made them not.
Gui. Hence, then, and thank
The man that gave them thee. Thou art some fool;
I am loath to beat thee.
Clo. Thou injurious thief,
Hear but my name, and tremble.
Gui. What 's thy name?
Clo. Cloten, thou villain.
Gui. Cloten, thou double villain, be thy name,
I cannot tremble at it: were it Toad, or Adder, Spider,
'T would move me sooner.
Clo. To thy further fear,
Nay, to thy mere confusion, thou shalt know
I am son to the Queen.
Gui. I am sorry for 't; not seeming
So worthy as thy birth.
Clo. Art not afeard?
Gui. Those that I reverence those I fear, the wise:
At fools I laugh, not fear them.
Clo. Die the death!
When I have slain thee with my proper hand,
I 'll follow those that even now fled hence,
And on the gates of Lud's town set your heads.
Yield, rustic mountaineer.
Fight and exeunt.

Re-enter *Belarius* and *Arviragus.*

Bel. No company 's abroad?
Arv. None in the world. You did mistake him, sure.
Bel. I cannot tell,—long is it since I saw him.
But time hath nothing blurr'd those lines of favour
Which then he wore: the snatches in his voice,
And burst of speaking, were as his: I am absolute
'T was very Cloten.
Arv. In this place we left them.
I wish my brother make good time with him,
You say he is so fell.
Bel. Being scarce made up,
I mean, to man, he had not apprehension
Of roaring terrors; for the defect of judgement
Is oft the cease of fear.

58. spurs, roots. **59. elder,** elder-tree. **untwine,** cease to twine. **61. great morning,** broad day. **74. a knock,** a blow.

86. injurious, insulting. **92. mere,** complete, absolute. **97. proper,** own. **104. favour,** appearance. **105. snatches,** breaks. **108. make good time,** be fortunate, come off well. **110. apprehension,** comprehension. **112. cease,** cessation, extinction.

Re-enter *Guiderius* with Cloten's head.

But, see, thy brother.
Gui. This Cloten was a fool, an empty purse;
There was no money in 't: not Hercules
Could have knock'd out his brains, for he had none.
Yet I not doing this, the fool had borne
My head as I do his.
Bel. What hast thou done?
Gui. I am perfect what: cut off one Cloten's head,
Son to the Queen, after his own report;
Who call'd me traitor, mountaineer, and swore
With his own single hand he 'd take us in,
Displace our heads where—thank the gods!—they grow,
And set them on Lud's town.
Bel. We are all undone.
Gui. Why, worthy father, what have we to lose,
But that he swore to take, our lives? The law
Protects not us; then why should we be tender
To let an arrogant piece of flesh threat us,
Play judge and executioner all himself,
For we do fear the law? What company
Discover you abroad?
Bel. No single soul
Can we set eye on; but in all safe reason
He must have some attendants. Though his humour
Was nothing but mutation, ay, and that
From one bad thing to worse, not frenzy, not
Absolute madness could so far have rav'd
To bring him here alone; although perhaps
It may be heard at court that such as we
Cave here, hunt here, are outlaws, and in time
May make some stronger head; the which he hearing -
As it is like him—might break out, and swear
He 'd fetch us in; yet is 't not probable
To come alone, either he so undertaking,
Or they so suffering. Then on good ground we fear,
If we do fear this body hath a tail
More perilous than the head.
Arv. Let ordinance
Come as the gods foresay it; howsoe'er,
My brother hath done well.
Bel. I had no mind
To hunt this day; the boy Fidele's sickness
Did make my way long forth.
Gui. With his own sword,
Which he did wave against my throat, I have ta'en
His head from him: I 'll throw 't into the creek
Behind our rock; and let it to the sea,
And tell the fishes he 's the Queen's son, Cloten.
That 's all I reck. *Exit.*
Bel. I fear 't will be reveng'd.
Would, Polydore, thou hadst not done 't! though valour
Becomes thee well enough.
Arv. Would I had done 't,
So the revenge alone pursu'd me! Polydore,
I love thee brotherly, but envy much
Thou hast robb'd me of this deed: I would revenges,
That possible strength might meet, would seek us through
And put us to our answer.
Bel. Well, 't is done.
We 'll hunt no more to-day, nor seek for danger
Where there 's no profit. I prithee, to our rock;
You and Fidele play the cooks: I 'll stay
Till hasty Polydore return, and bring him
To dinner presently.
Arv. Poor sick Fidele!
I 'll willingly to him: to gain his colour
I 'd let a parish of such Clotens blood,
And praise myself for charity. *Exit.*
Bel. O thou goddess,
Thou divine Nature, how thyself thou blazon'st
In these two princely boys! They are as gentle
As zephyrs blowing below the violet,
Not wagging his sweet head; and yet as rough,
Their royal blood enchaf'd, as the rud'st wind,
That by the top doth take the mountain pine,
And make him stoop to the vale. 'T is wonder
That an invisible instinct should frame them
To royalty unlearn'd, honour untaught,
Civility not seen from other, valour
That wildly grows in them, but yields a crop
As if it had been sow'd. Yet still it 's strange
What Cloten's being here to us portends,
Or what his death will bring us.

Re-enter *Guiderius.*

Gui. Where 's my brother?
I have sent Cloten's clotpoll down the stream,
In embassy to his mother. His body 's hostage
For his return. *Solemn music.*
Bel. My ingenious instrument!
Hark, Polydore, it sounds! But what occasion
Hath Cadwal now to give it motion? Hark!

118. I am perfect, I know. **125. that,** that which. **139. May . . . head,** draw together some stronger force. **145. ordinance,** what is ordained. **149. long forth,** (seem) a long time from home.

154. reck, care. **160. would seek us through,** seek us out. **167. to gain his colour,** to restore his health. **174. enchaf'd,** chafed, enraged. **184. clotpoll,** blockhead.

Gui. Is he at home?
Bel. He went hence even now.
Gui. What does he mean? Since death of my dear'st mother
It did not speak before. All solemn things
Should answer solemn accidents. The matter?
Triumphs for nothing and lamenting toys
Is jollity for apes and grief for boys.
Is Cadwal mad?

Re-enter *Arviragus,* with *Imogen* as dead, bearing her in his arms.

Bel. Look, here he comes,
And brings the dire occasion in his arms
Of what we blame him for.
Arv. The bird is dead
That we have made so much on. I had rather
Have skipp'd from sixteen years of age to sixty,
To have turn'd my leaping-time into a crutch,
Than have seen this.
Gui. O sweetest, fairest lily!
My brother wears thee not the one half so well
As when thou grew'st thyself.
Bel. O melancholy!
Who ever yet could sound thy bottom? find
The ooze, to show what coast thy sluggish care
Might easiliest harbour in? Thou blessed thing!
Jove knows what man thou mightst have made; but I,
Thou diedst, a most rare boy, of melancholy.
How found you him?
Arv. Stark, as you see;
Thus smiling, as some fly had tickled slumber,
Not as death's dart, being laugh'd at! his right cheek
Reposing on a cushion.
Gui. Where?
Arv. O' th' floor,
His arms thus leagu'd: I thought he slept, and put
My clouted brogues from off my feet, whose rudeness
Answer'd my steps too loud.
Gui. Why, he but sleeps!
If he be gone, he 'll make his grave a bed:
With female fairies will his tomb be haunted,
And worms will not come to thee.
Arv. With fairest flowers
Whilst summer lasts and I live here, Fidele,
I 'll sweeten thy sad grave: thou shalt not lack
The flower that 's like thy face, pale primrose, nor
The azur'd harebell, like thy veins, no, nor
The leaf of eglantine, whom not to slander,
Out-sweeten'd not thy breath: the ruddock would,
With charitable bill,—O bill, sore shaming
Those rich-left heirs that let their fathers lie
Without a monument!—bring thee all this;
Yea, and furr'd moss besides, when flowers are none,
To winter-ground thy corse.
Gui. Prithee, have done;
And do not play in wench-like words with that
Which is so serious. Let us bury him,
And not protract with admiration what
Is now due debt. To the grave!
Arv. Say, where shall 's lay him?
Gui. By good Euriphile, our mother.
Arv. Be 't so;
And let us, Polydore, though now our voices
Have got the mannish crack, sing him to the ground,
At once our mother; use like note and words,
Save that Euriphile must be Fidele.
Gui. Cadwal,
I cannot sing. I 'll weep, and word it with thee;
For notes of sorrow out of tune are worse
Than priests and fanes that lie.
Arv. We 'll speak it, then.
Bel. Great griefs, I see, med'cine the less; for Cloten
Is quite forgot. He was a queen's son, boys;
And though he came our enemy, remember
He was paid for that: though mean and mighty, rotting
Together, have one dust, yet reverence,
That angel of the world, doth make distinction
Of place 'tween high and low. Our foe was princely;
And though you took his life, as being our foe,
Yet bury him as a prince.
Gui. Pray you, fetch him hither.
Thersites' body is as good as Ajax',
When neither are alive.
Arv. If you 'll go fetch him,
We 'll say our song the whilst.—Brother, begin. *Exit Belarius.*
Gui. Nay, Cadwal, we must lay his head to the east;
My father hath a reason for 't.
Arv. 'T is true.
Gui. Come on then, and remove him.
Arv. So. Begin.

193. toys, trifles. **214. clouted,** hob-nailed.

224. ruddock, robin. **229. winter-ground,** cover (like ground protected from frost). **242. fanes,** temples. **243. med'cine,** cure. **252. Thersites' . . . Ajax',** a buffoon and a hero in the Trojan war.

SONG

Gui.

Fear no more the heat o' th' sun,
Nor the furious winter's rages;
Thou thy worldly task hast done,
Home art gone, and ta'en thy wages.
Golden lads and girls all must,
As chimney-sweepers, come to dust.

Arv.

Fear no more the frown o' th' great;
Thou art past the tyrant's stroke.
Care no more to clothe and eat;
To thee the reed is as the oak.
The sceptre, learning, physic, must
All follow this, and come to dust.

Gui.

Fear no more the lightning-flash,

Arv.

Nor th' all-dreaded thunder-stone;

Gui.

Fear not slander, censure rash;

Arv.

Thou hast finish'd joy and moan.

Both.

All lovers young, all lovers must
Consign to thee, and come to dust.

Gui.

No exorciser harm thee!

Arv.

Nor no witchcraft charm thee!

Gui.

Ghost unlaid forbear thee!

Arv.

Nothing ill come near thee!

Both.

Quiet consummation have,
And renowned be thy grave!

Re-enter *Belarius,* with the body of Cloten.

Gui. We have done our obsequies. Come, lay him down.

Bel. Here 's a few flowers; but 'bout midnight, more.
The herbs that have on them cold dew o' th' night
Are strewings fitt'st for graves. Upon their faces.
You were as flowers, now wither'd; even so
These herblets shall, which we upon you strew.
Come on, away; apart upon our knees.
The ground that gave them first has them again:
Their pleasures here are past, so is their pain.

Exeunt Belarius, Guiderius, and Arviragus.

Imo. [*Awaking.*] Yes, sir, to Milford-Haven; which is the way?—
I thank you.—By yond bush?—Pray, how far thither?
'Ods pittikins! can it be six mile yet?
I have gone all night. Faith, I 'll lie down and sleep.
But, soft! no bedfellow!—O gods and goddesses! [*Seeing the body of Cloten.*]
These flowers are like the pleasures of the world;
This bloody man, the care on 't. I hope I dream;
For so I thought I was a cave-keeper
And cook to honest creatures. But 't is not so:
'T was but a bolt of nothing, shot at nothing,
Which the brain makes of fumes. Our very eyes
Are sometimes like our judgements, blind. Good faith,
I tremble still with fear; but if there be
Yet left in heaven as small a drop of pity
As a wren's eye, fear'd gods, a part of it!
The dream 's here still, even when I wake. It is
Without me, as within me; not imagin'd, felt.
A headless man! The garments of Posthumus?
I know the shape of 's leg; this is his hand,
His foot Mercurial, his Martial thigh,
The brawns of Hercules; but his Jovial face—
Murder in heaven?—How!—'T is gone. Pisanio,
All curses madded Hecuba gave the Greeks,
And mine to boot, be darted on thee! Thou,
Conspir'd with that irregulous devil, Cloten,
Hath here cut off my lord. To write and read
Be henceforth treacherous! Damn'd Pisanio
Hath with his forged letters,—damn'd Pisanio—
From this most bravest vessel of the world
Struck the main-top! O Posthumus! alas,
Where is thy head? Where 's that? Ay me! where 's that?
Pisanio might have kill'd thee at the heart,
And left this head on. How should this be, Pisanio?
'T is he and Cloten: malice and lucre in them
Have laid this woe here. O, 't is pregnant, pregnant!

271. **thunder-stone,** thunderbolt—a stone was supposed to accompany the lightning flash. 276. **exorciser,** conjurer. 280. **consummation,** end.

293. **'Ods pittikins,** God's pity. 301. **fumes,** fantasms, delusions. 310. **Mercurial,** i.e., swift, like Mercury. **Martial,** like Mars, powerful. 311. **brawns,** muscles, tendons. **Jovial,** like Jove, benign. 313. **madded,** maddened. 315. **irregulous,** lawless. 325. **pregnant,** clear, evident.

The drug he gave me, which he said was precious
And cordial to me, have I not found it
Murd'rous to the senses? That confirms it home:
This is Pisanio's deed, and Cloten's. O!
Give colour to my pale cheek with thy blood,
That we the horrider may seem to those
Which chance to find us. O, my lord, my lord!
Falls on the body.

Enter *Lucius, Captains,* and a *Soothsayer.*

First Cap. To them the legions garrison'd in Gallia,
After your will, have cross'd the sea, attending
You here at Milford-Haven with your ships.
They are in readiness.
Luc. But what from Rome?
First Cap. The senate hath stirr'd up the confiners
And gentlemen of Italy, most willing spirits,
That promise noble service; and they come
Under the conduct of bold Iachimo,
Sienna's brother.
Luc. When expect you them?
First Cap. With the next benefit o' th' wind.
Luc. This forwardness
Makes our hopes fair. Command our present numbers
Be muster'd; bid the captains look to 't. Now, sir,
What have you dream'd of late of this war's purpose?
Sooth. Last night the very gods show'd me a vision—
I fast and pray'd for their intelligence—thus:
I saw Jove's bird, the Roman eagle, wing'd
From the spongy south to this part of the west,
There vanish'd in the sunbeams; which portends—
Unless my sins abuse my divination—
Success to the Roman host.
Luc. Dream often so,
And never false. Soft, ho! what trunk is here
Without his top? The ruin speaks that sometime
It was a worthy building. How! a page!
Or dead, or sleeping on him? But dead rather;
For nature doth abhor to make his bed
With the defunct, or sleep upon the dead.
Let 's see the boy's face.
First Cap. He 's alive, my lord.
Luc. He 'll then instruct us of this body. Young one,
Inform us of thy fortunes, for it seems
They crave to be demanded. Who is this
Thou mak'st thy bloody pillow? Or who was he
That, otherwise than noble nature did,
Hath alter'd that good picture? What 's thy interest
In this sad wreck? How came it? Who is it?
What art thou?
Imo. I am nothing: or if not,
Nothing to be were better. This was my master,
A very valiant Briton and a good,
That here by mountaineers lies slain. Alas!
There is no more such masters: I may wander
From east to occident, cry out for service,
Try many, all good, serve truly, never
Find such another master.
Luc. 'Lack, good youth!
Thou mov'st no less with thy complaining than
Thy master in bleeding: say his name, good friend.
Imo. Richard du Champ. [*Aside.*] If I do lie and do
No harm by it, though the gods hear, I hope
They 'll pardon it.—Say you, sir?
Luc. Thy name?
Imo. Fidele, sir.
Luc. Thou dost approve thyself the very same;
Thy name well fits thy faith, thy faith thy name.
Wilt take thy chance with me? I will not say
Thou shalt be so well master'd, but, be sure,
No less belov'd. The Roman Emperor's letters,
Sent by a consul to me, should not sooner
Than thine own worth prefer thee: go with me.
Imo. I 'll follow, sir. But first, an 't please the gods,
I 'll hide my master from the flies, as deep
As these poor pickaxes can dig; and when
With wild-wood leaves and weeds I ha' strew'd his grave,
And on it said a century of prayers,
Such as I can, twice o'er, I 'll weep and sigh;
And leaving so his service, follow you,
So please you entertain me.
Luc. Ay, good youth;
And rather father thee than master thee.
My friends,
The boy hath taught us manly duties: let us
Find out the prettiest daisied plot we can,
And make him with our pikes and partisans
A grave. Come, arm him.—Boy, he is preferr'd

333. **To,** in addition to. 337. **confiners,** borderers. 362. **demanded,** inquired into.

391. **century,** hundred. 399. **partisans,** halberds—long handled weapons with spear-like heads for thrusting and sharpened edges for hacking. 400. **arm him,** pick him up.

By thee to us, and he shall be interr'd
As soldiers can. Be cheerful; wipe thine eyes.
Some falls are means the happier to arise.
Exeunt.

Scene III. *A room in the palace.*

Enter *Cymbeline, Lords, Pisanio,* and *Attendants.*

Cym. Again; and bring me word how 't is with her. *Exit an attendant.*
A fever with the absence of her son,
A madness, of which her life 's in danger. Heavens,
How deeply you at once do touch me! Imogen,
The great part of my comfort, gone; my queen
Upon a desperate bed, and in a time
When fearful wars point at me; her son gone,
So needful for this present: it strikes me, past
The hope of comfort.—But for thee, fellow,
Who needs must know of her departure and
Dost seem so ignorant, we 'll enforce it from thee
By a sharp torture.
Pis. Sir, my life is yours;
I humbly set it at your will; but, for my mistress,
I nothing know where she remains, why gone,
Nor when she purposes return. Beseech your Highness,
Hold me your loyal servant.
First Lord. Good my liege,
The day that she was missing he was here:
I dare be bound he 's true and shall perform
All parts of his subjection loyally. For Cloten,
There wants no diligence in seeking him,
And will, no doubt, be found.
Cym. The time is troublesome.
[*To Pisanio.*] We 'll slip you for a season; but our jealousy
Does yet depend.
First Lord. So please your Majesty,
The Roman legions, all from Gallia drawn,
Are landed on your coast, with a supply
Of Roman gentlemen, by the senate sent.
Cym. Now for the counsel of my son and queen!
I am amaz'd with matter.
First Lord. Good my liege,
Your preparation can affront no less
Than what you hear of. Come more, for more you 're ready;
The want is but to put those powers in motion
That long to move.
Cym. I thank you. Let 's withdraw,
And meet the time as it seeks us. We fear not
What can from Italy annoy us; but
We grieve at chances here. Away!
Exeunt all but Pisanio.
Pis. I heard no letter from my master since
I wrote him Imogen was slain: 't is strange:
Nor hear I from my mistress, who did promise
To yield me often tidings; neither know I
What is betid to Cloten; but remain
Perplex'd in all. The heavens still must work.
Wherein I am false I am honest; not true, to be true.
These present wars shall find I love my country,
Even to the note o' th' King, or I 'll fall in them.
All other doubts, by time let them be clear'd.
Fortune brings in some boats that are not steer'd. *Exit.*

22. **slip you,** release you (hunting term). **jealousy,** suspicion. 23. **depend,** impend. 28. **amaz'd with matter,** confused by the pressure of affairs. 29. **affront,** confront.

44. **note,** notice.

Scene IV. *Wales. Before the cave of Belarius.*

Enter *Belarius, Guiderius,* and *Arviragus.*

Gui. The noise is round about us.
Bel. Let us from it.
Arv. What pleasure, sir, find we in life, to lock it
From action and adventure?
Gui. Nay, what hope
Have we in hiding us? This way, the Romans
Must or for Britons slay us, or receive us
For barbarous and unnatural revolts
During their use, and slay us after.
Bel. Sons,
We 'll higher to the mountains; there secure us.
To the King's party there 's no going: newness
Of Cloten's death—we being not known, not muster'd
Among the bands—may drive us to a render
Where we have liv'd, and so extort from 's that
Which we have done, whose answer would be death
Drawn on with torture.
Gui. This is, sir, a doubt
In such a time nothing becoming you,
Nor satisfying us.
Arv. It is not likely
That when they hear the Roman horses neigh,

Scene iv: 4. **This way,** i.e., by hiding ourselves. 6. **revolts,** deserters. 13. **answer,** punishment.

Behold their quarter'd fires, have both their eyes
And ears so cloy'd importantly as now,
That they will waste their time upon our note,
To know from whence we are.
Bel. O, I am known
Of many in the army: many years,
Though Cloten then but young, you see, not wore him
From my remembrance. And, besides, the King
Hath not deserv'd my service nor your loves,
Who find in my exile the want of breeding,
The certainty of this hard life; aye hopeless
To have the courtesy your cradle promis'd,
But to be still hot Summer's tanlings and
The shrinking slaves of Winter.
Gui. Than be so
Better to cease to be. Pray, sir, to th' army:
I and my brother are not known; yourself
So out of thought, and thereto so o'ergrown,
Cannot be question'd.
Arv. By this sun that shines,
I 'll thither! What thing is it that I never
Did see man die! scarce ever look'd on blood,
But that of coward hares, hot goats, and venison!
Never bestrid a horse, save one that had
A rider like myself, who ne'er wore rowel
Nor iron on his heel! I am asham'd
To look upon the holy sun, to have
The benefit of his blest beams, remaining
So long a poor unknown.
Gui. By heavens, I 'll go.
If you will bless me, sir, and give me leave,
I 'll take the better care; but if you will not,
The hazard therefore due fall on me by
The hands of Romans!
Arv. So say I; amen.
Bel. No reason I, since of your lives you set
So slight a valuation, should reserve
My crack'd one to more care. Have with you, boys!
If in your country wars you chance to die,
That is my bed too, lads, and there I 'll lie.
Lead, lead! [*Aside.*] The time seems long; their blood thinks scorn
Till it fly out and show them princes born.
Exeunt.

ACT V. SCENE I. *Britain. The Roman camp.*

Enter *Posthumus* alone with a bloody handkerchief.

Post. Yea, bloody cloth, I 'll keep thee, for I e'en wished
Thou shouldst be colour'd thus. You married ones,
If each of you should take this course, how many
Must murder wives much better than themselves
For wrying but a little! O Pisanio!
Every good servant does not all commands;
No bond but to do just ones. Gods! if you
Should have ta'en vengeance on my faults, I never
Had liv'd to put on this; so had you saved
The noble Imogen to repent, and struck
Me, wretch, more worth your vengeance. But, alack,
You snatch some hence for little faults; that 's love,
To have them fall no more: you some permit
To second ills with ills, each elder worse,
And make them dread it, to the doers' thrift.
But Imogen is your own; do your best wills,
And make me blest to obey! I am brought hither
Among th' Italian gentry, and to fight
Against my lady's kingdom: 't is enough
That, Britain, I have kill'd thy mistress; peace!
I 'll give no wound to thee. Therefore, good heavens,
Hear patiently my purpose; I 'll disrobe me
Of these Italian weeds and suit myself
As does a Briton peasant; so I 'll fight
Against the part I come with; so I 'll die
For thee, O Imogen, even for whom my life
Is every breath a death; and thus, unknown,
Pitied nor hated, to the face of peril
Myself I 'll dedicate. Let me make men know
More valour in me than my habits show.
Gods, put the strength o' th' Leonati in me!
To shame the guise o' th' world, I will begin
The fashion, less without and more within.
Exit.

18. **quarter'd fires**, fires in their camp or quarters. 19. **cloy'd importantly**, filled with important matters. 20. **our note**, noting us. 29. **tanlings**, those tanned by the sun. 33. **o'ergrown**, i.e., with hair. **Act V. Scene i:** 5. **wrying**, swerving. 9. **put on**, instigate.

15. **to the doers' thrift**, to the doers' advantage. The passage may mean that by committing a series of crimes each worse than the last, the sinner finally becomes fearful and repents. 23. **suit**, dress. 25. **part**, side. 30. **habits**, clothing. 32. **guise**, practice, i.e., much outward show.

Scene II. *Field of battle between the British and Roman camps.*

Enter *Lucius, Iachimo,* and the *Roman Army* at one door; and the *Briton Army* at another; *Leonatus Posthumus* following, like a poor soldier. They march over and go out. Then enter again, in skirmish, *Iachimo* and *Posthumus:* he vanquisheth and disarmeth *Iachimo,* and then leaves him.

Iach. The heaviness and guilt within my bosom
Takes off my manhood: I have belied a lady,
The Princess of this country, and the air on 't
Revengingly enfeebles me; or could this carl,
A very drudge of nature's, have subdued me
In my profession? Knighthoods and honours, borne
As I wear mine, are titles but of scorn.
If that thy gentry, Britain, go before
This lout as he exceeds our lords, the odds
Is that we scarce are men and you are gods.
Exit.

The battle continues; the *Britons* fly; *Cymbeline* is taken: then enter, to his rescue, *Belarius, Guiderius,* and *Arviragus.*

Bel. Stand, stand! We have th' advantage of the ground;
The lane is guarded. Nothing routs us but
The villainy of our fears.
Gui., *Arv.* Stand, stand, and fight!

Re-enter *Posthumus,* and seconds the *Britons.* They rescue *Cymbeline,* and exeunt. Then re-enter *Lucius, Iachimo,* and *Imogen.*

Luc. Away, boy, from the troops, and save thyself;
For friends kill friends, and the disorder 's such
As war were hoodwink'd.
Iach. 'T is their fresh supplies.
Luc. It is a day turn'd strangely. Or betimes
Let 's reinforce, or fly. *Exeunt.*

Scene III. *Another part of the field.*

Enter *Posthumus* and a *Briton Lord.*

Lord. Cam'st thou from where they made the stand?
Post. I did;
Though you, it seems, come from the fliers.
Lord. I did.
Post. No blame be to you, sir, for all was lost,
But that the heavens fought; the King himself
Of his wings destitute, the army broken,
And but the backs of Britons seen, all flying
Through a strait lane; the enemy full-hearted,
Lolling the tongue with slaught'ring, having work
More plentiful than tools to do 't, struck down
Some mortally, some slightly touch'd, some falling
Merely through fear; that the straight pass was damm'd
With dead men hurt behind, and cowards living
To die with lengthen'd shame.
Lord. Where was this lane?
Post. Close by the battle, ditch'd, and wall'd with turf;
Which gave advantage to an ancient soldier,
An honest one, I warrant; who deserv'd
So long a breeding as his white beard came to,
In doing this for 's country. Athwart the lane,
He, with two striplings—lads more like to run
The country base than to commit such slaughter,
With faces fit for masks, or rather fairer
Than those for preservation cas'd, or shame,—
Made good the passage; cried to those that fled,
"Our Britain's harts die flying, not our men.
To darkness fleet souls that fly backwards. Stand!
Or we are Romans and will give you that
Like beasts which you shun beastly, and may save
But to look back in frown. Stand, stand!" These three,
Three thousand confident, in act as many—
For three performers are the file when all
The rest do nothing—with this word "Stand, stand!"
Accommodated by the place, more charming
With their own nobleness, which could have turn'd
A distaff to a lance, gilded pale looks.
Part shame, part spirit renew'd; that some, turn'd coward
But by example—O, a sin in war,
Damn'd in the first beginners!—gan to look

3. **on 't,** of it. 4. **carl,** churl, peasant. 8. **go before,** exceed. 16. **hoodwink'd,** blindfolded.

7. **strait,** narrow. **full-hearted,** full of courage. 16-7. **who deserv'd . . . came to,** who deserved the nurture of his country for so many years as his white beard indicated. 20. **base,** prisoners' base, a running game. 22. **cas'd,** covered with masks. **shame,** modesty. 27-28. **may save . . . frown,** may avoid by at least casting back a look of defiance. 29. **confident,** in confidence. 30. **file,** rank of soldiers. 32. **more charming,** bewitching more men. 34. **gilded,** with color, the red badge of courage. 35. **Part . . . part,** some . . . some.

The way that they did, and to grin like lions
Upon the pikes o' th' hunters. Then began
A stop i' th' chaser, a retire, anon
A rout, confusion thick: forthwith they fly
Chickens, the way which they stoop'd eagles; slaves,
The strides they victors made: and now our cowards,
Like fragments in hard voyages, became
The life o' th' need. Having found the back-door open
Of the unguarded hearts, heavens, how they wound
Some slain before, some dying, some their friends
O'er-borne i' th' former wave; ten, chas'd by one,
Are now each one the slaughter-man of twenty.
Those that would die or ere resist are grown
The mortal bugs o' th' field.

Lord. This was strange chance.
A narrow lane, an old man, and two boys!

Post. Nay, do not wonder at it; you are made
Rather to wonder at the things you hear
Than to work any. Will you rhyme upon 't,
And vent it for a mock'ry? Here is one:
"Two boys, an old man twice a boy, a lane,
Preserv'd the Britons, was the Romans' bane."

Lord. Nay, be not angry, sir.

Post. 'Lack, to what end?
Who dares not stand his foe, I 'll be his friend;
For if he 'll do as he is made to do,
I know he 'll quickly fly my friendship too.
You have put me into rhyme.

Lord. Farewell; you 're angry.
Exit.

Post. Still going? This is a lord! O noble misery,
To be i' th' field, and ask "what news?" of me!
To-day how many would have given their honours
To have sav'd their carcases! took heel to do 't,
And yet died too! I, in mine own woe charm'd,
Could not find Death where I did hear him groan,
Nor feel him where he struck. Being an ugly monster,
'T is strange he hides him in fresh cups, soft beds,
Sweet words; or hath moe ministers than we
That draw his knives i' th' war. Well, I will find him;
For being now a favourer to the Briton,
No more a Briton, I have resum'd again
The part I came in. Fight I will no more,
But yield me to the veriest hind that shall
Once touch my shoulder. Great the slaughter is
Here made by th' Roman; great the answer be
Britons must take. For me, my ransom 's death:
On either side I come to spend my breath;
Which neither here I 'll keep nor bear again,
But end it by some means for Imogen.

Enter two *British Captains* and *Soldiers.*

First Cap. Great Jupiter be prais'd! Lucius is taken:
'T is thought the old man and his sons were angels.

Sec. Cap. There was a fourth man, in a silly habit,
That gave th' affront with them.

First Cap. So 't is reported;
But none of 'em can be found. Stand! who 's there?

Post. A Roman,
Who had not now been drooping here, if seconds
Had answer'd him.

Sec. Cap. Lay hands on him; a dog!
A leg of Rome shall not return to tell
What crows have peck'd them here. He brags his service
As if he were of note. Bring him to the King.

Enter *Cymbeline, Belarius, Guiderius, Arviragus, Pisanio,* and *Roman Captives.* The *Captains* present *Posthumus* to *Cymbeline,* who delivers him over to a *Jailer.* Exeunt omnes.

Scene IV. *A British prison.*

Enter *Posthumus* and two *Jailers.*

First Jail. You shall not now be stol'n, you have locks upon you;
So graze as you find pasture.

Sec. Jail. Ay, or a stomach.
Exeunt Jailers.

Post. Most welcome, bondage! for thou art a way,
I think, to liberty; yet am I better
Than one that 's sick o' th' gout; since he had rather
Groan so in perpetuity than be cur'd

38. **they**, i.e., the three. 42. **stoop'd**, swooped down. They fly back like chickens the road they came like eagles; retrace like slaves the steps they took as victors. 44. **fragments**, i.e., of food. 45. **The life . . . need**, food for life in time of need. 47. **Some . . . some . . . some**, the charging Britons wound some who were slain before, some already dying, and some overthrown in the first charge. 50. **or ere**, rather than. 51. **bugs**, bugbears, terrors. 64. **noble misery**, miserable titled nobility. 68. **charm'd**, made invulnerable.

77. **hind**, peasant. 79. **answer**, retaliation. 86. **silly**, plain, simple. 90. **seconds**, supporters. **Scene iv:** 2. **stomach**, appetite.

By th' sure physician, Death, who is the key
T' unbar these locks. My conscience, thou art fetter'd
More than my shanks and wrists: you good gods, give me
The penitent instrument to pick that bolt,
Then, free for ever! Is 't enough I am sorry?
So children temporal fathers do appease;
Gods are more full of mercy. Must I repent,
I cannot do it better than in gyves,
Desir'd more than constrain'd; to satisfy,
If of my freedom 't is the main part, take
No stricter render of me than my all.
I know you are more clement than vile men,
Who of their broken debtors take a third,
A sixth, a tenth, letting them thrive again
On their abatement: that 's not my desire.
For Imogen's dear life take mine; and though
'T is not so dear, yet 't is a life; you coin'd it:
'Tween man and man they weigh not every stamp;
Though light, take pieces for the figure's sake;
You rather mine, being yours; and so, great powers,
If you will take this audit, take this life,
And cancel these cold bonds. O Imogen!
I 'll speak to thee in silence. *Sleeps.*

Solemn music. Enter, as in an apparition, *Sicilius Leonatus,* father to *Posthumus*; an old man, attired like a warrior; leading in his hand an ancient matron, his wife, and mother to *Posthumus,* with music before them. Then, after other music, follows the two young *Leonati,* brothers to *Posthumus,* with wounds as they died in the wars. They circle *Posthumus* round, as he lies sleeping.

Sici.
No more, thou thunder-master, show
Thy spite on mortal flies:
With Mars fall out, with Juno chide,
That thy adulteries
Rates and revenges.
Hath my poor boy done aught but well,
Whose face I never saw?
I died whilst in the womb he stay'd
Attending Nature's law;
Whose father then, as men report
Thou orphans' father art,
Thou shouldst have been, and shielded him
From this earth-vexing smart.

Moth.
Lucina lent not me her aid,
But took me in my throes;
That from me was Posthumus ript,
Came crying 'mongst his foes,
A thing of pity!

Sici.
Great Nature, like his ancestry,
Moulded the stuff so fair,
That he deserv'd the praise o' the world,
As great Sicilius' heir.

First Bro.
When once he was mature for man,
In Britain where was he
That could stand up his parallel,
Or fruitful object be
In eye of Imogen, that best
Could deem his dignity?

Moth.
With marriage wherefore was he mock'd,
To be exil'd, and thrown
From Leonati seat, and cast
From her his dearest one,
Sweet Imogen?

Sici.
Why did you suffer Iachimo,
Slight thing of Italy,
To taint his nobler heart and brain
With needless jealousy;
And to become the geck and scorn
O' th' other's villainy?

Sec. Bro.
For this from stiller seats we came,
Our parents and us twain,
That striking in our country's cause
Fell bravely and were slain,
Our fealty and Tenantius' right
With honour to maintain.

First Bro.
Like hardiment Posthumus hath
To Cymbeline perform'd.
Then, Jupiter, thou king of gods,
Why hast thou thus adjourn'd
The graces for his merits due,
Being all to dolours turn'd?

Sici.
Thy crystal window ope; look out;
No longer exercise
Upon a valiant race thy harsh
And potent injuries.

Moth.
Since, Jupiter, our son is good,
Take off his miseries.

Sici.
Peep through thy marble mansion; help;
Or we poor ghosts will cry
To the shining synod of the rest
Against thy deity.

14. gyves, fetters. **15. constrain'd,** forced (upon me). **17. render,** surrender. **21. abatement,** diminished capital. **24. stamp,** coin. **25. figure's,** the image on the coin. **26. You . . . yours,** you gods should be the rather ready to take the light coin of my life, since it is yours; you coined it. **43. Lucina,** goddess who presided over births.

67. geck, dupe. **75. hardiment,** bold exploit. **78. adjourn'd,** delayed.

Both Bro.
Help, Jupiter; or we appeal,
And from thy justice fly.

Jupiter descends in thunder and lightning, sitting upon an eagle: he throws a thunderbolt. The Ghosts fall on their knees.

Jup. No more, you petty spirits of region low,
Offend our hearing; hush! How dare you ghosts
Accuse the thunderer, whose bolt, you know,
Sky-planted, batters all rebelling coasts?
Poor shadows of Elysium, hence, and rest
Upon your never-withering banks of flowers.
Be not with mortal accidents opprest;
No care of yours it is; you know 't is ours.
Whom best I love I cross; to make my gift,
The more delay'd, delighted. Be content;
Your low-laid son our godhead will uplift.
His comforts thrive, his trials well are spent.
Our jovial star reign'd at his birth, and in
Our temple was he married. Rise, and fade.
He shall be lord of Lady Imogen,
And happier much by his affliction made.
This tablet lay upon his breast, wherein
Our pleasure his full fortune doth confine.
And so, away! No farther with your din
Express impatience, lest you stir up mine.
Mount, eagle, to my palace crystalline.
Ascends.

Sici. He came in thunder; his celestial breath
Was sulphurous to smell. The holy eagle
Stoop'd, as to foot us: his ascension is
More sweet than our blest fields: his royal bird
Prunes the immortal wing and cloys his beak,
As when his god is pleas'd.

All. Thanks, Jupiter!

Sici. The marble pavement closes, he is enter'd
His radiant roof. Away! and, to be blest,
Let us with care perform his great behest.
The Ghosts vanish.

Post. [*Waking.*] Sleep, thou hast been a grandsire, and begot
A father to me, and thou hast created
A mother and two brothers; but, O scorn!
Gone! they went hence so soon as they were born.
And so I am awake. Poor wretches that depend
On greatness' favour dream as I have done,
Wake and find nothing. But, alas, I swerve:
Many dream not to find, neither deserve,
And yet are steep'd in favours; so am I,
That have this golden chance and know not why.
What fairies haunt this ground? A book? O rare one!
Be not, as is our fangled world, a garment
Nobler than that it covers! Let thy effects
So follow, to be most unlike our courtiers,
As good as promise!
[*Reads.*]

Whenas a lion's whelp shall, to himself unknown, without seeking find, and be embraced by a piece of tender air; and when from a stately cedar shall be lopp'd branches, which, being dead many years, shall after revive, be jointed to the old stock and freshly grow; then shall Posthumus end his miseries, Britain be fortunate and flourish in peace and plenty.

'T is still a dream, or else such stuff as madmen
Tongue and brain not; either both or nothing;
Or senseless speaking or a speaking such
As sense cannot untie. Be what it is,
The action of my life is like it, which
I 'll keep, if but for sympathy.

Re-enter *Jailer.*

Jail. Come, sir, are you ready for death?

Post. Over-roasted rather; ready long ago.

Jail. Hanging is the word, sir: if you be ready for that, you are well cooked.

Post. So, if I prove a good repast to the spectators, the dish pays the shot.

Jail. A heavy reckoning for you, sir. But the comfort is, you shall be called to no more payments, fear no more tavern-bills, which are often the sadness of parting, as the procuring of mirth. You come in faint for want of meat, depart reeling with too much drink; sorry that you have paid too much, and sorry that you are paid too much; purse and brain both empty; the brain the heavier for being too light, the purse too light, being drawn of heaviness. O, of this contradiction you shall now be quit. O, the charity of a penny cord! It sums up thousands in a trice. You have no true debitor and creditor but it; of what 's past, is, and to come, the discharge: your neck, sir, is pen, book, and counters; so the acquittance follows.

Post. I am merrier to die than thou art to live.

Jail. Indeed, sir, he that sleeps feels not the toothache; but a man that were to sleep your sleep, and a hangman to help him to bed, I think he would change places with his offi-

102. delighted, delightful. **105. jovial star,** Jupiter (favorable sign). **116. foot,** strike. **118. Prunes,** preens. **cloys,** strokes (with his claw). **125. scorn,** mockery. **129. swerve,** i.e., from the point.

134. fangled, showily decorated. **151. for sympathy,** because of the similarity. **158. shot,** reckoning. **172. debitor and creditor,** accounting book. **174. counters,** round pieces of metal used in calculations.

cer; for, look you, sir, you know not which way you shall go.

Post. Yes, indeed do I, fellow.

Jail. Your Death has eyes in 's head then; I have not seen him so pictured. You must either be directed by some that take upon them to know, or to take upon yourself that which I am sure you do not know, or jump the after inquiry on your own peril; and how you shall speed in your journey's end, I think you 'll never return to tell one.

Post. I tell thee, fellow, there are none want eyes to direct them the way I am going, but such as wink and will not use them.

Jail. What an infinite mock is this, that a man should have the best use of eyes to see the way of blindness! I am sure hanging 's the way of winking.

Enter a *Messenger.*

Mess. Knock off his manacles; bring your prisoner to the King.

Post. Thou bring'st good news; I am called to be made free.

Jail. I 'll be hanged then.

Post. Thou shalt be then freer than a jailer; no bolts for the dead.

Exeunt all but the Jailer.

Jail. Unless a man would marry a gallows and beget young gibbets, I never saw one so prone. Yet, on my conscience, there are verier knaves desire to live, for all he be a Roman; and there be some of them too that die against their wills: so should I, if I were one. I would we were all of one mind, and one mind good. O, there were desolation of jailers and gallowses! I speak against my present profit, but my wish hath a preferment in 't. *Exit.*

Scene V. *Cymbeline's tent.*

Enter *Cymbeline, Belarius, Guiderius, Arviragus, Pisanio, Lords, Officers,* and *Attendants.*

Cym. Stand by my side, you whom the gods have made
Preservers of my throne. Woe is my heart
That the poor soldier that so richly fought,
Whose rags sham'd gilded arms, whose naked breast
Stepp'd before targes of proof, cannot be found:
He shall be happy that can find him, if
Our grace can make him so.

Bel. I never saw
Such noble fury in so poor a thing;
Such precious deeds in one that promis'd nought
But beggary and poor looks.

Cym. No tidings of him?

Pis. He hath been search'd among the dead and living,
But no trace of him.

Cym. To my grief, I am
The heir of his reward; [*to Belarius, Guiderius, and Arviragus*] which I will add
To you, the liver, heart and brain of Britain,
By whom I grant she lives. 'T is now the time
To ask of whence you are. Report it.

Bel. Sir,
In Cambria are we born, and gentlemen.
Further to boast were neither true nor modest,
Unless I add, we are honest.

Cym. Bow your knees.
Arise my knights o' th' battle: I create you
Companions to our person and will fit you
With dignities becoming your estates.

Enter *Cornelius* and *Ladies.*

There 's business in these faces. Why so sadly
Greet you our victory? You look like Romans,
And not o' th' court of Britain.

Cor. Hail, great King!
To sour your happiness, I must report
The Queen is dead.

Cym. Who worse than a physician
Would this report become? But I consider,
By med'cine life may be prolong'd, yet death
Will seize the doctor too. How ended she?

Cor. With horror, madly dying, like her life,
Which, being cruel to the world, concluded
Most cruel to herself. What she confess'd
I will report, so please you. These her women
Can trip me, if I err; who with wet cheeks
Were present when she finish'd.

Cym. Prithee, say.

Cor. First, she confess'd she never lov'd you; only
Affected greatness got by you, not you;
Married your royalty, was wife to your place,
Abhorr'd your person.

Cym. She alone knew this;
And, but she spoke it dying, I would not
Believe her lips in opening it. Proceed.

Cor. Your daughter, whom she bore in hand to love
With much integrity, she did confess
Was as a scorpion to her sight; whose life,
But that her flight prevented it, she had
Ta'en off by poison.

188. jump, hazard. **194. wink,** close the eyes. **208. prone,** i.e., to die. **Scene v: 5. targes of proof,** shields tested (for hardness).

35. trip, refute. **38. Affected,** loved. **42. opening,** revealing. **43. bore in hand,** pretended.

Cym. O most delicate fiend!
Who is 't can read a woman? Is there more?
Cor. More, sir, and worse. She did confess she had
For you a mortal mineral, which, being took,
Should by the minute feed on life, and ling'ring
By inches waste you; in which time she purpos'd,
By watching, weeping, tendance, kissing, to
O'ercome you with her show, and, in time,
When she had fitted you with her craft, to work
Her son into th' adoption of the crown;
But, failing of her end by his strange absence,
Grew shameless-desperate; open'd, in despite
Of heaven and men, her purposes; repented
The evils she hatch'd were not effected; so
Despairing died.
Cym. Heard you all this, her women?
Lad. We did, so please your Highness.
Cym. Mine eyes
Were not in fault, for she was beautiful;
Mine ears, that heard her flattery; nor my heart,
That thought her like her seeming. It had been vicious
To have mistrusted her; yet, O my daughter!
That it was folly in me, thou mayst say,
And prove it in thy feeling. Heaven mend all!

Enter *Lucius, Iachimo,* the *Soothsayer* and other *Roman Prisoners* guarded; *Posthumus* behind, and *Imogen.*

Thou com'st not, Caius, now for tribute; that
The Britons have raz'd out, though with the loss
Of many a bold one, whose kinsmen have made suit
That their good souls may be appeas'd with slaughter
Of you their captives, which ourself have granted.
So think of your estate.
Luc. Consider, sir, the chance of war. The day
Was yours by accident. Had it gone with us,
We should not, when the blood was cool, have threaten'd
Our prisoners with the sword. But since the gods
Will have it thus, that nothing but our lives
May be call'd ransom, let it come. Sufficeth
A Roman, with a Roman's heart can suffer:
Augustus lives to think on 't; and so much
For my peculiar care. This one thing only
I will entreat: my boy, a Briton born,
Let him be ransom'd. Never master had
A page so kind, so duteous, diligent,
So tender over his occasions, true,
So feat, so nurse-like: let his virtue join
With my request, which I 'll make bold your Highness
Cannot deny: he hath done no Briton harm,
Though he have serv'd a Roman. Save him, sir,
And spare no blood beside.
Cym. I have surely seen him;
His favour is familiar to me.—Boy,
Thou hast look'd thyself into my grace,
And art mine own. I know not why, wherefore,
To say "Live, boy." Ne'er thank thy master; live,
And ask of Cymbeline what boon thou wilt,
Fitting my bounty and thy state, I 'll give it,
Yea, though thou do demand a prisoner,
The noblest ta'en.
Imo. I humbly thank your Highness.
Luc. I do not bid thee beg my life, good lad;
And yet I know thou wilt.
Imo. No, no, alack,
There 's other work in hand: I see a thing
Bitter to me as death; your life, good master,
Must shuffle for itself.
Luc. The boy disdains me,
He leaves me, scorns me: briefly die their joys
That place them on the truth of girls and boys.
Why stands he so perplex'd?
Cym. What wouldst thou, boy?
I love thee more and more; think more and more
What 's best to ask. Know'st him thou look'st on? Speak,
Wilt have him live? Is he thy kin? thy friend?
Imo. He is a Roman, no more kin to me
Than I to your Highness; who, being born your vassal,
Am something nearer.
Cym. Wherefore ey'st him so?
Imo. I 'll tell you, sir, in private, if you please
To give me hearing.
Cym. Ay, with all my heart,
And lend my best attention. What 's thy name?
Imo. Fidele, sir.
Cym. Thou 'rt my good youth, my page;
I 'll be thy master. Walk with me; speak freely.
Cymbeline and Imogen talk apart.
Bel. Is not this boy, reviv'd from death,—
Arv. One sand another
Not more resembles,—that sweet rosy lad
Who died, and was Fidele? What think you?
Gui. The same dead thing alive.

47. delicate, artful, ingenious. **55. fitted,** prepared. **56. adoption,** right by adoption. **83. peculiar,** particular, private.

87. tender . . . occasions, sensible of his master's needs. **88. feat,** neat, trim.

Bel. Peace, peace! see further: he eyes us not; forbear;
Creatures may be alike: were 't he, I am sure
He would have spoke to us.
Gui. But we see him dead.
Bel. Be silent; let 's see further.
Pis. [*Aside.*] It is my mistress.
Since she is living, let the time run on
To good or bad.

Cymbeline and Imogen come forward.

Cym. Come, stand thou by our side;
Make thy demand aloud. [*To Iachimo.*] Sir, step you forth;
Give answer to this boy, and do it freely;
Or, by our greatness and the grace of it,
Which is our honour, bitter torture shall
Winnow the truth from falsehood.—On, speak to him.
Imo. My boon is, that this gentleman may render
Of whom he had this ring.
Post. [*Aside.*] What 's that to him?
Cym. That diamond upon your finger, say
How came it yours?
Iach. Thou 'lt torture me to leave unspoken that
Which, to be spoke, would torture thee.
Cym. How? me?
Iach. I am glad to be constrain'd to utter that
Which torments me to conceal. By villainy
I got this ring. 'T was Leonatus' jewel,
Whom thou didst banish; and—which more may grieve thee,
As it doth me—a nobler sir ne'er lived
'Twixt sky and ground. Wilt thou hear more, my lord?
Cym. All that belongs to this.
Iach. That paragon, thy daughter,—
For whom my heart drops blood, and my false spirits
Quail to remember,—Give me leave; I faint.
Cym. My daughter! what of her? Renew thy strength.
I had rather thou shouldst live while Nature will
Than die ere I hear more. Strive, man, and speak.
Iach. Upon a time,—unhappy was the clock
That struck the hour!—it was in Rome,—accurs'd
The mansion where!—'t was at a feast,—O, would
Our viands had been poison'd, or at least
Those which I heav'd to head!—the good Posthumus—
What should I say? He was too good to be
Where ill men were; and was the best of all
Amongst the rar'st of good ones,—sitting sadly,
Hearing us praise our loves of Italy
For beauty that made barren the swell'd boast
Of him that best could speak, for feature, laming
The shrine of Venus, or straight-pight Minerva,
Postures beyond brief nature, for condition,
A shop of all the qualities that man
Loves woman for, besides that hook of wiving,
Fairness which strikes the eye—
Cym. I stand on fire:
Come to the matter.
Iach. All too soon I shall,
Unless thou wouldst grieve quickly. This Posthumus,
Most like a noble lord in love and one
That had a royal lover, took his hint;
And, not dispraising whom we prais'd,—therein
He was as calm as virtue,—he began
His mistress' picture; which by his tongue being made,
And then a mind put in 't, either our brags
Were crack'd of kitchen-trulls, or his description
Prov'd us unspeaking sots.
Cym. Nay, nay, to the purpose.
Iach. Your daughter's chastity—there it begins.
He spake of her, as Dian had hot dreams,
And she alone were cold; whereat I, wretch,
Made scruple of his praise; and wager'd with him
Pieces of gold 'gainst this which then he wore
Upon his honour'd finger, to attain
In suit the place of 's bed and win this ring
By hers and mine adultery. He, true knight,
No lesser of her honour confident
Than I did truly find her, stakes this ring;
And would so, had it been a carbuncle
Of Phœbus' wheel, and might so safely, had it
Been all the worth of 's car. Away to Britain
Post I in this design: well may you, sir,
Remember me at court, where I was taught
Of your chaste daughter the wide difference
'Twixt amorous and villanous. Being thus quench'd
Of hope, not longing, mine Italian brain
Gan in your duller Britain operate
Most vilely; for my vantage, excellent;
And, to be brief, my practice so prevail'd,

126. **see him dead,** see him like the ghost of one dead. 139. **to leave,** for leaving.

163. **feature,** bodily form, shape. **laming,** making to appear lame. 164. **straight-pight,** erect. 165. **beyond brief nature,** immortal. **condition,** temperament. 167. **besides . . . wiving,** in addition to that incentive to marriage. 177. **crack'd of kitchen-trulls,** vaunted of kitchen wenches. 178. **unspeaking,** speechless. 182. **Made scruple of,** doubted.

That I return'd with simular proof enough
To make the noble Leonatus mad,
By wounding his belief in her renown
With tokens thus, and thus; averring notes
Of chamber-hanging, pictures, this her bracelet,—
O cunning, how I got it!—nay, some marks
Of secret on her person, that he could not
But think her bond of chastity quite crack'd,
I having ta'en the forfeit. Whereupon—
Methinks, I see him now—

Post. [*Advancing.*] Ay, so thou dost,
Italian fiend! Ay me, most credulous fool,
Egregious murderer, thief, anything
That 's due to all the villains past, in being,
To come! O, give me cord, or knife, or poison,
Some upright justicer! Thou, King, send out
For torturers ingenious; it is I
That all th' abhorred things o' th' earth amend
By being worse than they. I am Posthumus,
That kill'd thy daughter:—villain-like, I lie—
That caused a lesser villain than myself
A sacrilegious thief, to do 't. The temple
Of Virtue was she; yea, and she herself.
Spit, and throw stones, cast mire upon me, set
The dogs o' th' street to bay me; every villain
Be call'd Posthumus Leonatus; and
Be villainy less than 't was! O Imogen!
My queen, my life, my wife! O Imogen,
Imogen, Imogen!

Imo. Peace, my lord; hear, hear—

Post. Shall 's have a play of this? Thou scornful page,
There lie thy part. *Striking her; she falls.*

Pis. O, gentlemen, help
Mine and your mistress! O, my Lord Posthumus!
You ne'er kill'd Imogen till now. Help, help!
Mine honour'd lady!

Cym. Does the world go round?

Post. How comes these staggers on me?

Pis. Wake, my mistress!

Cym. If this be so, the gods do mean to strike me
To death with mortal joy.

Pis. How fares my mistress?

Imo. O, get thee from my sight;
Thou gav'st me poison. Dangerous fellow, hence!
Breathe not where princes are.

Cym. The tune of Imogen!

Pis. Lady,
The gods throw stones of sulphur on me, if
That box I gave you was not thought by me
A precious thing. I had it from the Queen.

Cym. New matter still?

Imo. It poison'd me.

Cor. O gods!
I left out one thing which the Queen confess'd,
Which must approve thee honest. "If Pisanio
Have," said she, "given his mistress that confection
Which I gave him for cordial, she is serv'd
As I would serve a rat."

Cym. What 's this, Cornelius?

Cor. The Queen, sir, very oft importun'd me
To temper poisons for her, still pretending
The satisfaction of her knowledge only
In killing creatures vile, as cats and dogs,
Of no esteem. I, dreading that her purpose
Was of more danger, did compound for her
A certain stuff, which, being ta'en, would cease
The present power of life, but in short time
All offices of nature should again
Do their due functions. Have you ta'en of it?

Imo. Most like I did, for I was dead.

Bel. My boys,
There was our error.

Gui. This is, sure, Fidele.

Imo. Why did you throw your wedded lady from you?
Think that you are upon a lock, and now
Throw me again. *Embracing him.*

Post. Hang there like fruit, my soul,
Till the tree die!

Cym. How now, my flesh, my child!
What, mak'st thou me a dullard in this act?
Wilt thou not speak to me?

Imo. [*Kneeling.*] Your blessing, sir.

Bel. [*To Guiderius and Arviragus.*] Though you did love this youth, I blame ye not;
You had a motive for 't.

Cym. My tears that fall
Prove holy water on thee! Imogen,
Thy mother 's dead.

Imo. I am sorry for 't, my lord.

Cym. O, she was naught; and long of her it was
That we meet here so strangely; but her son
Is gone, we know not how nor where.

Pis. My lord,
Now fear is from me, I 'll speak troth. Lord Cloten,
Upon my lady's missing, came to me
With his sword drawn; foam'd at the mouth, and swore,
If I discover'd not which way she was gone,
It was my instant death. By accident,
I had a feigned letter of my master's
Then in my pocket, which directed him
To seek her on the mountains near to Milford;
Where, in a frenzy, in my master's garments,

200. simular, simulated, counterfeit. **221. she,** Virtue. **233. staggers,** dizziness, confusion. **239. tune,** i.e., voice.

262. lock, wrestling hold. **265. dullard,** bystander. **271. naught,** wicked. **long of,** owing to. **274. troth,** truth.

Which he enforc'd from me, away he posts
With unchaste purpose and with oath to violate
My lady's honour. What became of him
I further know not.
Gui. Let me end the story:
I slew him there.
Cym. Marry, the gods forfend!
I would not thy good deeds should from my lips
Pluck a hard sentence. Prithee, valiant youth,
Deny 't again.
Gui. I have spoke it, and I did it.
Cym. He was a prince.
Gui. A most incivil one. The wrongs he did me
Were nothing prince-like; for he did provoke me
With language that would make me spurn the sea,
If it could so roar to me. I cut off 's head;
And am right glad he is not standing here
To tell this tale of mine.
Cym. I am sorry for thee.
By thine own tongue thou art condemn'd, and must
Endure our law. Thou 'rt dead.
Imo. That headless man
I thought had been my lord.
Cym. Bind the offender,
And take him from our presence.
Bel. Stay, sir King;
This man is better than the man he slew,
As well descended as thyself; and hath
More of thee merited than a band of Clotens
Had ever scar for. [*To the Guard.*] Let his arms alone;
They were not born for bondage.
Cym. Why, old soldier,
Wilt thou undo the worth thou art unpaid for,
By tasting of our wrath? How of descent
As good as we?
Arv. In that he spake too far.
Cym. And thou shalt die for 't.
Bel. We will die all three
But I will prove that two on 's are as good
As I have given out him. My sons, I must
For mine own part unfold a dangerous speech,
Though, haply, well for you.
Arv. Your danger 's ours.
Gui. And our good his.
Bel. Have at it then, by leave.
Thou hadst, great King, a subject who
Was call'd Belarius.
Cym. What of him? He is
A banish'd traitor.
Bel. He it is that hath
Assum'd this age, indeed a banish'd man;
I know not how a traitor.

319. **Assum'd,** put on, reached.

Cym. Take him hence.
The whole world shall not save him.
Bel. Not too hot.
First pay me for the nursing of thy sons;
And let it be confiscate all so soon
As I have receiv'd it.
Cym. Nursing of my sons?
Bel. I am too blunt and saucy; here 's my knee.
Ere I arise, I will prefer my sons;
Then spare not the old father. Mighty sir,
These two young gentlemen, that call me father
And think they are my sons, are none of mine;
They are the issue of your loins, my liege,
And blood of your begetting.
Cym. How! my issue?
Bel. So sure as you your father's. I, old Morgan,
Am that Belarius whom you sometime banish'd.
Your pleasure was my mere offence, my punishment
Itself, and all my treason; that I suffer'd
Was all the harm I did. These gentle princes—
For such and so they are—these twenty years
Have I train'd up: those arts they have as I
Could put into them; my breeding was, sir, as
Your Highness knows. Their nurse, Euriphile,
Whom for the theft I wedded, stole these children
Upon my banishment: I mov'd her to 't,
Having receiv'd the punishment before,
For that which I did then. Beaten for loyalty
Excited me to treason. Their dear loss,
The more of you 't was felt, the more it shap'd
Unto my end of stealing them. But, gracious sir,
Here are your sons again; and I must lose
Two of the sweet'st companions in the world.
The benediction of these covering heavens
Fall on their heads like dew! for they are worthy
To inlay heaven with stars.
Cym. Thou weep'st, and speak'st.
The service that you three have done is more
Unlike than this thou tell'st. I lost my children;
If these be they, I know not how to wish
A pair of worthier sons.
Bel. Be pleas'd awhile.
This gentleman, whom I call Polydore,
Most worthy prince, as yours, is true Guiderius;
This gentleman, my Cadwal, Arviragus,
Your younger princely son. He, sir, was lapp'd
In a most curious mantle, wrought by th' hand

334. **pleasure,** will, decision in the matter. **mere,** only. 344. **Beaten,** my being beaten. 354. **Unlike,** unlikely.

Of his queen mother, which for more probation
I can with ease produce.
Cym. Guiderius had
Upon his neck a mole, a sanguine star;
It was a mark of wonder.
Bel. This is he,
Who hath upon him still that natural stamp.
It was wise Nature's end in the donation,
To be his evidence now.
Cym. O, what am I?
A mother to the birth of three? Ne'er mother
Rejoic'd deliverance more. Blest pray you be,
That, after this strange starting from your orbs,
You may reign in them now! O Imogen,
Thou hast lost by this a kingdom.
Imo. No, my lord;
I have got two worlds by 't. O my gentle brothers,
Have we thus met? O, never say hereafter
But I am truest speaker. You call'd me brother,
When I was but your sister; I you brothers,
When ye were so indeed.
Cym. Did you e'er meet?
Arv. Ay, my good lord.
Gui. And at first meeting lov'd;
Continu'd so, until we thought he died.
Cor. By the Queen's dram she swallow'd.
Cym. O rare instinct!
When shall I hear all through? This fierce abridgement
Hath to it circumstantial branches, which
Distinction should be rich in. Where, how liv'd you?
And when came you to serve our Roman captive?
How parted with your brothers? How first met them?
Why fled you from the court? and whither? These
And your three motives to the battle, with
I know not how much more, should be demanded;
And all the other by-dependencies,
From chance to chance; but nor the time nor place
Will serve our long inter'gatories. See,
Posthumus anchors upon Imogen,
And she, like harmless lightning, throws her eye
On him, her brothers, me, her master, hitting
Each object with a joy; the counterchange
Is severally in all. Let 's quit this ground,
And smoke the temple with our sacrifices.
[*To Belarius.*] Thou art my brother; so we 'll hold thee ever.
Imo. You are my father too, and did relieve me,
To see this gracious season.
Cym. All o'erjoy'd,
Save these in bonds. Let them be joyful too,
For they shall taste our comfort.
Imo. My good master,
I will yet do you service.
Luc. Happy be you!
Cym. The forlorn soldier, that so nobly fought,
He would have well becom'd this place, and grac'd
The thankings of a king.
Post. I am, sir,
The soldier that did company these three
In poor beseeming; 't was a fitment for
The purpose I then follow'd. That I was he,
Speak, Iachimo: I had you down and might
Have made you finish.
Iach. [*Kneeling.*] I am down again;
But now my heavy conscience sinks my knee,
As then your force did. Take that life, beseech you,
Which I so often owe; but your ring first,
And here the bracelet of the truest princess
That ever swore her faith.
Post. Kneel not to me.
The power that I have on you is to spare you,
The malice towards you to forgive you. Live,
And deal with others better.
Cym. Nobly doom'd!
We 'll learn our freeness of a son-in-law;
Pardon 's the word to all.
Arv. You holp us, sir,
As you did mean indeed to be our brother;
Joy'd are we that you are.
Post. Your servant, Princes. Good my lord of Rome,
Call forth your soothsayer. As I slept, methought
Great Jupiter, upon his eagle back'd,
Appear'd to me, with other spritely shows
Of mine own kindred. When I wak'd, I found
This label on my bosom, whose containing
Is so from sense in hardness, that I can
Make no collection of it. Let him show
His skill in the construction.

362. **probation**, proof. 364. **sanguine**, red. 367. **donation**, gift. 371. **orbs**, orbits, spheres of action. 383. **circumstantial . . . in**, attendant offshoots or stories (**circumstantial branches**) which should be rich in details (**distinction**). 388. **your three motives**, the motives of you three. 390. **by-dependencies**, attendant circumstances. 391. **chance to chance**, event to event.

396. **counterchange . . . all**, the exchange (of glances) is mutual and peculiar to each. In other words, each looks at her and loves her in a manner proper to his relationship. 400. **relieve**, rescue. 405. **forlorn**, lost, missing. 409. **beseeming**, appearance. **fitment**, dress, equipment. 415. **often**, many times. 420. **doom'd**, adjudged. 421. **freeness**, generosity. 428. **spritely**, ghostly. 430. **label**, writing, lit., seal. 432. **collection**, inference, conclusion. 433. **construction**, interpretation.

Luc. Philarmonus!
Sooth. Here, my good lord.
Luc. Read, and declare the meaning.
Sooth. [*Reads.*]

Whenas a lion's whelp shall, to himself unknown, without seeking find, and be embraced by a piece of tender air; and when from a stately cedar shall be lopped branches, which, being dead many years, shall after revive, be jointed to the old stock, and freshly grow; then shall Posthumus end his miseries, Britain be fortunate and flourish in peace and plenty.

Thou, Leonatus, art the lion's whelp;
The fit and apt construction of thy name,
Being *leo-natus,* doth import so much.
[*To Cymbeline.*] The piece of tender air, thy virtuous daughter,
Which we call *mollis aer;* and *mollis aer*
We term it *mulier;* which *mulier* I divine
Is this most constant wife, who, even now,
Answering the letter of the oracle,
Unknown to you, unsought, were clipp'd about
With this most tender air.
Cym. This hath some seeming.
Sooth. The lofty cedar, royal Cymbeline,
Personates thee; and thy lopp'd branches point
Thy two sons forth; who, by Belarius stol'n,
For many years thought dead, are now reviv'd,
To the majestic cedar join'd, whose issue
Promises Britain peace and plenty.
Cym. Well;

445. leo-natus, born of the lion. 452. seeming, likelihood.

My peace we will begin. And, Caius Lucius,
Although the victor, we submit to Cæsar,
And to the Roman empire, promising
To pay our wonted tribute, from the which
We were dissuaded by our wicked queen;
Whom heavens, in justice, both on her and hers,
Have laid most heavy hand.
Sooth. The fingers of the powers above do tune
The harmony of this peace. The vision
Which I made known to Lucius, ere the stroke
Of this yet scarce-cold battle, at this instant
Is full accomplish'd; for the Roman eagle,
From south to west on wing soaring aloft,
Lessen'd herself, and in the beams o' th' sun
So vanish'd; which foreshow'd our princely eagle,
Th' imperial Cæsar, should again unite
His favour with the radiant Cymbeline,
Which shines here in the west.
Cym. Laud we the gods;
And let our crooked smokes climb to their nostrils
From our bless'd altars. Publish we this peace
To all our subjects. Set we forward: let
A Roman and a British ensign wave
Friendly together: so through Lud's town march;
And in the temple of great Jupiter
Our peace we 'll ratify; seal it with feasts.
Set on there! Never was a war did cease,
Ere bloody hands were wash'd, with such a peace. *Exeunt.*

484. did cease, that did cease.

The Winter's Tale

The title of this play, rightly understood, is the best introduction to an appreciation of its character. The phrase "a winter's tale" was a catch-word in Elizabethan England. Peele's delightful play, *The Old Wives' Tale,* was "a winter's tale to drive away the time" and Marlowe's Jew remembers old women who told him "winter's tales and spoke of spirits and ghosts." Shakespeare's Mamillius, in this very play, declares

> A sad tale 's best for winter: I have one
> Of spirits and goblins.

A "winter's tale" then is a story told to pass away the hours on long winter's nights; it makes no pretence to being a true story; it may be "sad," that is, serious, but hardly tragic. When Shakespeare baptized the play he was about to offer his audience at the Blackfriars *The Winter's Tale,* he meant that he was offering them a pastime, an old story, improbable, fantastic even, but with a certain otherworldly charm. He could not have taken very seriously the romance that he was dramatizing; he was as conscious as we can be of its essential unreality; but it was an entertaining tale of approved popularity. And as he settled to his task of remaking it into the new form of tragi-comedy something in it stirred him; he caught fire, and created out of the lifeless figures of the tale characters instinct with his own creative genius. It is this blend of romance and realism that gives to *The Winter's Tale* its own peculiar character and charm.

Text.—The Winter's Tale was printed for the first time in the Folio where it is the last of the fourteen comedies. There is reason to believe that when Jaggard began to print the Folio the players were unable to furnish him "copy" for this play. Typographical evidence makes it fairly certain that *The Winter's Tale* was inserted between the thirteenth comedy, *Twelfth Night,* and the first of the histories, *King John,* after that play and several others had been set up in type.

An interesting entry in the *Office Book* of Sir Henry Herbert, Master of the Revels, on August 19, 1623, proves that the official prompt-book was lost at that time:

> For the King's players. An olde playe called Winter's Tale, formerly allowed of by Sir George Bucke and likewise by me on Mr Hemmings his word that there was nothing profane added or reformed, thogh the allowed booke was missing; and therefore I returned it without a fee.

This means that in anticipation of a revival, Heminges, acting for Shakespeare's company, called on Sir Henry and told him that the prompt-book licensed by his predecessor in office, Buck, was lost, but assured him that what they wished to play did not differ from the lost book. Sir Herbert took his word for it and passed the book without exacting his usual fee. How was it possible, then, for the company to furnish "copy" to Jaggard some time in 1623 and to stage a performance at Court on January 18, 1624, and what was it that Sir Henry "returned"? In all probability a transcript compiled by the company's regular scrivener from the "parts" of the actors which would still be in existence. This would explain some of the peculiarities of the Folio text: its careful division into acts and scenes, its notable absence of stage-directions, and its trick of printing at the head of each scene the names of all the characters who are "on" in that scene, often failing to provide the proper entrances and exits for them. The scanty stage-directions of the Folio must have been supplied by the scribe from his remembrance of the play as acted. The transcript seems to have been a careful one, for the text of the play is unusually accurate.

Date.—In the suspected entries of Dr. Forman there is a record of a performance of *The Winter's Tale* on May 15, 1611. We do not need this notice, however, to assure us that the play was on the stage in that year, for there is an undoubted record of a Court performance on November 5, 1611. It is possible, indeed, that it was written and acted in 1610. The startling stage-direction, *Exit pursued by a beare,* certainly points to the presence of a bear on the stage, and it is an interesting fact that in the popular play, *Mucedorus,* produced by Shakespeare's company shortly before 1610, there are two scenes in which a bear appears, in one of which the clown falls over the beast—to the huge delight, no doubt, of the groundlings—in the other a lady is chased off the stage by the bear. Evidently in 1610-11 Shakespeare's company could command the service of a bear tame enough to appear on the stage. It has been argued that *The Winter's Tale* must come after Jonson's *Masque of Oberon,* presented at Court, January 1, 1611, since the dance of twelve satyrs in the play (IV, iv), three of whom are said to have danced before the King, is plainly a transference to the play of the grotesque dance of the masque. Yet this does not prove the priority of the Masque, since the dance in the play is not an essential: it is preceded by a more appropriate dance of shepherds and shepherdesses, and may have been inserted into *The Winter's Tale* any time after January 1, 1611. We may safely date the play then late in 1610 or early in the following year.

Source.—The source of *The Winter's Tale* is Robert Greene's pastoral romance, *Pandosto or the Triumph of Time,* one of the most popular novels of Shakespeare's day. The first edition, apparently the one that Shakespeare used, appeared in 1588. A brief outline of the plot will show what use Shakespeare made of it.

Pandosto, King of Bohemia, entertains at his Court his boyhood friend Egistus, King of Sicily. Pandosto's wife, Bellaria, treats his guest with such courtesy that she arouses her husband's jealousy. He orders his cup-bearer, Franion, to poison Egistus, and when Franion remonstrates, he threatens him with death. The cup-bearer reveals the plot to Egistus and together they escape to Sicily. Thereupon Pandosto accuses his wife of adultery, and throws her into prison where she gives birth to a girl baby. Pandosto declares the child a bastard and has it put alone into a boat and turned adrift on the sea. Bellaria is brought to trial charged not only with adultery, but with a plot to poison the King. She appeals to the oracle on the isle of Delphos. The oracle replies: "Bellaria is chaste: Egistus blameless: Franion a true subject: Pandosto treacherous: his babe an innocent; and the King shall live without an heir if that which is lost be not found." When the oracle is read in the court, the King is overcome with remorse, confesses his guilt, and asks for pardon. At this moment news is brought in that Garinter, his son by Bellaria, has suddenly died. The shock is such that the Queen dies on the spot and Pandosto has to be forcibly restrained from suicide. He buries the Queen and the Prince in a splendid tomb and visits it every day to mourn for them.

Meanwhile the boat with the baby has drifted to the shore of Sicily where the child is discovered by a poor shepherd, Porrus, who brings her up as his own, giving her the name of Fawnia. She grows up a girl lovely as the Goddess Flora. Dorastus, the only son of Egistus, falls in love with her, and they plan to escape to Italy. Porrus, alarmed by the gossip about the Prince and Fawnia, sets out to inform the King that she is not his child but a foundling. On his way, however, he is lured on to the Prince's ship and the whole party are driven by storm to the coast of Bohemia. Here Pandosto throws Dorastus into prison and makes violent love to his unknown daughter. He presses his unwelcome suit upon her until an embassy arrives from Egistus asking him to free the Prince and put Fawnia and Porrus to death. At this point the shepherd tells how he found Fawnia and displays a mantle, chain, and jewels that were with her in the boat. Pandosto recognizes her as his daughter, and consents to her marriage with Dorastus. Shortly thereafter Pandosto falls into a fit of melancholy and kills himself.

Shakespeare, it is clear, followed the main outline of Greene's romance, but he allowed himself considerable freedom in his dramatization. He changed all the names, shifted the scenes in Bohemia to Sicily and *vice versa,* and eliminated the more unpleasant features of the tale, the death of the slandered Queen, Pandosto's unnatural passion for his own daughter, and his final suicide. He does more than this, however, he recasts the euphuistic style of Greene into his own vigorous prose and lovely verse, cuts out the tedious soliloquies with which the tale abounds, and substitutes for them striking dramatic situations. He introduces a whole group of new characters such as Paulina, the shepherd's clownish son, and the rogue Autolycus. For the artificial pastoralism of the romance he gives us, when the scene shifts to Bohemia, a lively realistic picture of country life in Merry England. Above all he devises an entirely new denouement in which the Queen returns to life and is reunited to her husband and her long-lost daughter. As in the other plays of this period, *The Winter's Tale* ends with reunion and reconciliation.

Type.—The Winter's Tale is a tragi-comedy, probably the best that Shakespeare ever wrote. In spite of the passage of sixteen years between two acts of the play the action is more closely woven and better sustained than in *Cymbeline* and there is more, and more interesting, action than in the almost plotless *Tempest.* One does not look for real life realistically presented in such plays, but for lively action abounding in surprise and sensation, and there is plenty of this in *The Winter's Tale*. The sudden and quite unmotivated jealousy of Leontes is the first surprise—compare the slow development of jealousy in *Othello;* the apparent death of Hermione just when her innocence has been established is another. Polixenes' angry denunciation of his son's love for the fair shepherdess gives a new and unexpected turn to the action—there is no scene at all resembling this in the source—and the return of Hermione as the statue come to life caps the climax. The whole last act is a skilful building up to this scene. Shakespeare even refuses to stage the recognition between father and daughter lest it should detract from the effect at which he is aiming, an effect that must have been doubly striking in the soft candlelight of the Blackfriars theatre, for which the play was first designed. The conclusion imposes a happy ending upon the grave tragic foundation of the first three acts, but there is no wresting of the plot or violation of character to bring about this conclusion. The tragic action ends with the trial scene; the fourth act is a joyous interlude that points to a happy ending—we feel sure that no adverse fate can mar the idyllic love of such a pair as Florizel and Perdita. There is less music and masque-like spectacle in *The Winter's Tale* than in its related plays, but to atone for this we have the dances at the shepherd's feast and the songs of Autolycus, songs aptly fitted to the singer and his surroundings.

Characters.—Surprise, sensation, and spectacle are for the spectator of this rarely presented play; what is there for the reader? There is, for one thing, the pleasure that arises from observing Shakespeare's mastery of characterization, from meeting another living group of Shakespeare's people. Unreal as the action of *The Winter's Tale* is, the characters that move through that action are very much alive. It has been said that in tragi-comedy the plot makes the characters, not the characters the plot. This may be true elsewhere; it is not so in this play. Leontes, for example, once we accept, as Shakespeare would have us, the existence of his causeless jealousy, is a powerfully realistic portrait of a man possessed by the evil spirit of this basest of passions. It is interesting to compare his case with that of Othello. While Othello's anguish springs in great part from the loss of his ideal, the jealousy of Leontes is purely selfish; there is no thought in him of the pity of it. He suffers like Othello: "nor night nor day no rest," he cries; but his one hope to cure his anguish is by the torture of the Queen. His self-imposed delusion is only heightened by opposition; even against the word of the god he breaks out in rebellion, "There is no truth at all i' th' oracle . . . this is mere falsehood." It takes the shock of the Prince's death, followed at once, as he believes, by that of his wife to whip the offending demon out of him. It is as though a sleeper had been suddenly and rudely wakened from a fearful dream.

The insane nature of the King's jealousy is made clear by the unanimous and unshaken belief of all his courtiers in the Queen's innocence. This belief is embodied and most daringly expressed in the character of Paulina. Like Emilia in Othello she is constant in her faith and fearless in asserting it, but while Emilia is a mere serving-woman, Paulina is a great lady who dares confront even a tyrant in his rage. And when his rage is past she watches over him like a guardian angel, keeping alive his repentance and repelling the weaker minds who would have him tamely forget his evil and forgive himself. It is to her that Shakespeare rightly entrusts the guarding of the hidden Queen, and we may perhaps be allowed a passing regret that he yields to the conventions of comedy and pairs her off at the last with Camillo. Paulina needs no second husband; her satisfaction is complete in the restoration of Hermione to her husband's arms and the return of the lost child, Perdita. Hermione, too, is a fully realized character. Every inch a Queen she is at once the most dignified and most gracious of Shakespeare's noble ladies. Secure in her virtue she can jest playfully with her husband's friend or repel with calm scorn her husband's frantic accusations. In the great trial scene she fights, not for her life—"I prize it not a straw"—but for her honor. There is no trace of fear nor of self-pity in her; her plea is for the justice that slandered innocence demands. Her long silence of sixteen years has been blamed as the behavior of an unforgiving chastity and defended as heroic submission to the will of the gods. So to consider is to turn Shakespeare's play into veritable history and to judge his characters like historic personages.

Her silence is Shakespeare's device to bring about her revelation at the end; he was as unwilling to kill Hermione as to sacrifice the chastity of Isabella, and to restore her to her husband before the lost child was found would be to wreck his play. It is with fine art that Shakespeare preserves this silence when she comes to life. She has no words for Leontes, only the embrace that betokens forgiveness, and then she turns to Perdita,

> Tell me, mine own,
> Where hast thou been preserv'd? Where liv'd? how found
> Thy father's court?

Of Perdita herself there is little need to speak. Her part in the action is merely passive; she is the fair shepherdess of an old story beloved by a Prince Charming, and found to be the daughter of a King. Yet we seem to know Perdita better, perhaps, than many of Shakespeare's heroines, and this is because all that she says and all that is said of her is couched in Shakespeare's loveliest and most memorable verse. One little touch, indeed, reveals her as the true daughter of Hermione with all her mother's courage. After the savage abuse of Polixenes and his threat of a death as cruel as she is tender she says simply and quietly

> I was not much afeard; for once or twice
> I was about to speak and tell him plainly
> The self-same sun that shines upon his court
> Hides not his visage from our cottage.

Strongly contrasting with these courtly characters are the country folk: the honest shepherd, his foolish son, and the rival rustic beauties, who gather at the sheep-shearing to taste Perdita's warden pies and hear a puritan sing psalms to horn pipes. These are characters from Shakespeare's own countryside. Perhaps on his return to Stratford he met at some country festival such a jovial hostess as the shepherd's old wife who "welcom'd all, serv'd all, would sing her song and dance her turn." And if these are drawn from life, so to be sure is Autolycus, the gayest, most impudent, and most delightful rogue in Shakespeare. His part in the action is small enough; another than he might have lured the shepherd and the clown on board the Prince's ship, but we could not do without Autolycus. Shakespeare introduces him just at the right moment to let us know that the tragic action is over and that the fun is about to begin. And how Autolycus enjoys the fun; whether he is picking pockets, peddling catch-penny ballads, or in his character of haughty courtier browbeating the shepherd and threatening the clown with death by torture! It is happy evidence of Shakespeare's lasting delight in the humors of his fellow men and of his unquenchable gayety that in his declining years he could catch in action and create for the stage such a character as Autolycus.

Stage History.—All the performances of *The Winter's Tale* of which we have record before the closing of the theatres—with the exception of the suspected Forman note—were given at Court. Apparently this play exactly met the taste of an audience that preferred tragi-comedy to tragedy. It was performed at the time of the Princess Elizabeth's marriage, more than once before King James, and lastly before Charles I in 1634—six times in all. Then it went into retirement for over a century. Its violation of the unities was too startling, its rustic mirth too simple for Restoration standards. In 1741 it was revived at the little theatre in Goodman's Fields with some success. Garrick's adaptation, *Florizel and Perdita,* 1756, which cut out nearly all the first three acts, was very successful and held the stage with some intermission for the rest of the century. In the Romantic age Shakespeare's play returned to the stage more or less in its original form. Kemble produced it in 1802, playing Leontes to the Hermione of Mrs. Siddons. In 1856 there was a superb spectacular production by Charles Kean in which the poetry was rather overlaid by scenery and costume, Bacchic revels and Pyrrhic dances. Ellen Terry made her first appearance on the stage at this time as the boy, Mamillius. Half a century later she played Hermione in Tree's revival at His Majesty's. Perhaps the most famous production of the century was that of Mary Anderson at the Lyceum in 1887 in which she doubled the roles of Hermione and Perdita and won all hearts by her grave dignity as the Queen and her youthful charm as the daughter.

THE WINTER'S TALE

The Names of the Actors

Leontes, king of Sicilia.
Mamillius, young prince of Sicilia.
Camillo, / *Antigonus,* / *Cleomenes,* / *Dion,* } Four Lords of Sicilia.
Polixenes, king of Bohemia.
Florizel, prince of Bohemia.
Archidamus, a lord of Bohemia.
Old Shepherd, reputed father of *Perdita.*
Clown, his son.
Autolycus, a rogue.
A Mariner.
A Jailer.

Hermione, queen to *Leontes.*
Perdita, daughter to *Leontes* and *Hermione.*
Paulina, wife to *Antigonus.*
Emilia, a lady.
Other Ladies attending on the Queen.
Mopsa, / *Dorcas,* } shepherdesses.

Time, as Chorus.

Other Lords and Gentlemen, Ladies, Officers, Servants, Shepherds, and Shepherdesses.

[This list appears at the end of the play in the Folio]

SCENE: *Sicilia and Bohemia.*

ACT I. Scene I. *Sicilia. In the palace of Leontes.*

Enter *Camillo* and *Archidamus.*

Arch. If you shall chance, Camillo, to visit Bohemia on the like occasion whereon my services are now on foot, you shall see, as I have said, great difference betwixt our Bohemia and your Sicilia.

Cam. I think, this coming summer, the King of Sicilia means to pay Bohemia the visitation which he justly owes him.

Arch. Wherein our entertainment shall shame us: we will be justified in our loves; for indeed—

Cam. Beseech you,—

Arch. Verily, I speak it in the freedom of my knowledge: we cannot with such magnificence—in so rare—I know not what to say. We will give you sleepy drinks, that your senses (unintelligent of our insufficience) may, though they cannot praise us, as little accuse us.

Cam. You pay a great deal too dear for what 's given freely.

Arch. Believe me, I speak as my understanding instructs me and as mine honesty puts it to utterance.

Cam. Sicilia cannot show himself overkind to Bohemia. They were trained together in their childhoods; and there rooted betwixt them then such an affection, which cannot choose but branch now. Since their more mature dignities and royal necessities made separation of their society, their encounters, (though not personal) hath been royally attorneyed with interchange of gifts, letters, loving embassies; that they have seemed to be together, though absent; shook hands, as over a vast; and embraced, as it were, from the ends of opposed winds. The heavens continue their loves!

Arch. I think there is not in the world either malice or matter to alter it. You have an unspeakable comfort of your young prince Mamillius: it is a gentleman of the greatest promise that ever came into my note.

Cam. I very well agree with you in the hopes of him: it is a gallant child; one that indeed physics the subject, makes old hearts fresh. They that went on crutches ere he was born desire yet their life to see him a man.

Arch. Would they else be content to die?

Cam. Yes; if there were no other excuse why they should desire to live.

Arch. If the King had no son, they would desire to live on crutches till he had one.

Exeunt.

Scene II. *In the palace.*

Enter *Leontes, Hermione, Mamillius, Polixenes, Camillo* and *Attendants.*

Pol. Nine changes of the wat'ry star hath been

10. **be . . . loves,** make amends with a warm welcome.

29-30. **attorneyed,** performed by proxy. 31. **that,** so that. 33. **vast,** vast expanse. 40. **note,** observation. 43. **physics the subject,** does good to the people. Scene ii: 1. **wat'ry star,** the moon, "the governess of floods."

The shepherd's note since we have left our throne
Without a burden; time as long again
Would be fill'd up, my brother, with our thanks,
And yet we should, for perpetuity,
Go hence in debt; and therefore, like a cipher,
Yet standing in rich place, I multiply
With one "We thank you" many thousands moe
That go before it.
Leon. Stay your thanks a while.
And pay them when you part.
Pol. Sir, that 's to-morrow
I am question'd by my fears, of what may chance
Or breed upon our absence; that may blow
No sneaping winds at home, to make us say,
"This is put forth too truly." Besides, I have stay'd
To tire your Royalty.
Leon. We are tougher, brother,
Than you can put us to 't.
Pol. No longer stay.
Leon. One sen-night longer.
Pol. Very sooth, to-morrow.
Leon. We 'll part the time between 's then; and in that
I 'll no gainsaying.
Pol. Press me not (beseech you) so.
There is no tongue that moves, none, none i' th' world,
So soon as yours could win me: so it should now,
Were there necessity in your request, although
'T were needful I denied it. My affairs
Do even drag me homeward; which to hinder
Were, in your love, a whip to me; my stay
To you a charge and trouble: to save both,
Farewell, our brother.
Leon. Tongue-tied our Queen? Speak you.
Her. I had thought, sir, to have held my peace until
You had drawn oaths from him not to stay. You, sir,
Charge him too coldly. Tell him, you are sure
All in Bohemia 's well; this satisfaction
The by-gone day proclaim'd. Say this to him,
He 's beat from his best ward.
Leon. Well said, Hermione.
Her. To tell, he longs to see his son, were strong;
But let him say so then, and let him go;
But let him swear so, and he shall not stay;
We 'll thwack him hence with distaffs.
Yet of your royal presence I 'll adventure
The borrow of a week. When at Bohemia
You take my lord, I 'll give him my commission
To let him there a month behind the gest
Prefix'd for 's parting; yet, good deed, Leontes,
I love thee not a jar o' the clock behind
What lady she her lord. You 'll stay?
Pol. No, madam.
Her. Nay, but you will?
Pol. I may not, verily.
Her. Verily!
You put me off with limber vows; but I,
Though you would seek t' unsphere the stars with oaths,
Should yet say, "Sir, no going." Verily,
You shall not go; a lady's "Verily" is
As potent as a lord's. Will you go yet?
Force me to keep you as a prisoner,
Not like a guest; so you shall pay your fees
When you depart, and save your thanks. How say you?
My prisoner? or my guest? By your dread "Verily,"
One of them you shall be.
Pol. Your guest, then, madam.
To be your prisoner should import offending,
Which is for me less easy to commit
Than you to punish.
Her. Not your jailer, then,
But your kind hostess. Come, I 'll question you
Of my lord's tricks and yours when you were boys.
You were pretty lordings then?
Pol. We were, fair Queen,
Two lads that thought there was no more behind
But such a day to-morrow as to-day,
And to be boy eternal.
Her. Was not my lord
The verier wag o' th' two?
Pol. We were as twinn'd lambs that did frisk i' th' sun,
And bleat the one at th' other. What we chang'd
Was innocence for innocence; we knew not
The doctrine of ill-doing, nor dream'd
That any did. Had we pursued that life,
And our weak spirits ne'er been higher rear'd
With stronger blood, we should have answer'd Heaven

6-7. like . . . place, as a cipher, when put in the right place, may, though worthless in itself, change a small number into a large one. **8. moe,** more. **9. Stay,** postpone. **11-14.** I fear what may happen in my absence. May no nipping winds blow at home to make me say my fears were true. **13. sneaping,** nipping. **15-16. are . . . to 't,** are too tough for any test of that kind. **19. I 'll . . . gainsaying,** I will have no refusal. **25. Were . . . me,** would make your love an injury to me. **33. beat . . . ward,** deprived of his best argument (a fencing term).

39. borrow, borrowing. **40. take,** charm. **41. let him,** detain him. **gest,** time allowed for a halt. **42. good deed,** indeed. **43. jar,** tick. **44. What lady she,** any woman whatever. **53. fees,** fees paid by prisoners on leaving jail. **57. import,** imply.

Boldly, "Not guilty"; the imposition clear'd
Hereditary ours.
Her. By this we gather
You have tripp'd since.
Pol. O my most sacred lady!
Temptations have since then been born to 's; for
In those unfledg'd days was my wife a girl;
Your precious self had then not cross'd the eyes
Of my young play-fellow.
Her. Grace to boot!
Of this make no conclusion, lest you say
Your Queen and I are devils: yet go on;
The offences we have made you do we 'll answer,
If you first sinn'd with us, and that with us
You did continue fault, and that you slipp'd not
With any but with us.
Leon. Is he won yet?
Her. He 'll stay, my lord.
Leon. At my request he would not.
Hermione, my dearest, thou never spok'st
To better purpose.
Her. Never?
Leon. Never, but once.
Her. What! have I twice said well? When was 't before?
I prithee tell me; cram 's with praise, and make 's
As fat as tame things. One good deed dying tongueless
Slaughters a thousand waiting upon that.
Our praises are our wages; you may ride 's
With one soft kiss a thousand furlongs ere
With spur we heat an acre. But to the goal:
My last good deed was to entreat his stay;
What was my first? It has an elder sister,
Or I mistake you. O, would her name were Grace!
But once before I spoke to the purpose; when?
Nay, let me have 't; I long.
Leon. Why, that was when
Three crabbed months had sour'd themselves to death,
Ere I could make thee open thy white hand
And clap thyself my love; then didst thou utter,
"I am yours for ever."
Her. 'T is grace indeed.
Why, lo you now, I have spoke to the purpose twice:
The one for ever earn'd a royal husband;
The other for some while a friend.
Leon. [*Aside.*] Too hot, too hot!
To mingle friendship far is mingling bloods.
I have *tremor cordis* on me; my heart dances,
But not for joy; not joy. This entertainment
May a free face put on, derive a liberty
From heartiness, from bounty, fertile bosom,
And well become the agent; 't may, I grant;
But to be paddling palms and pinching fingers,
As now they are, and making practis'd smiles,
As in a looking-glass; and then to sigh, as 't were
The mort o' th' deer;—O, that is entertainment
My bosom likes not, nor my brows! Mamillius,
Art thou my boy?
Mam. Ay, my good lord.
Leon. I' fecks!
Why, that 's my bawcock. What, hast smutch'd thy nose?
They say it is a copy out of mine. Come, captain,
We must be neat; not neat, but cleanly, captain:
And yet the steer, the heifer, and the calf
Are all call'd neat.—Still virginalling
Upon his palm!—How now, you wanton calf!
Art thou my calf?
Mam. Yes, if you will, my lord.
Leon. Thou want'st a rough pash and the shoots that I have,
To be full like me; yet they say we are
Almost as like as eggs; women say so,
That will say anything. But were they false
As o'er-dyed blacks, as wind, as waters, false
As dice are to be wish'd by one that fixes
No bourn 'twixt his and mine, yet were it true
To say this boy were like me. Come, sir page,
Look on me with your welkin eye. Sweet villain!
Most dear'st! my collop! Can thy dam?—may 't be?—
Affection! thy intention stabs the centre.
Thou dost make possible things not so held,

74-5. **the . . . ours**, we would have been free from the original sin entailed upon the human race. 80. **Grace to boot**, Heaven's grace help me, a playful ejaculation. 92. **tongueless**, unpraised. 96. **heat**, traverse swiftly. 99. **would . . . Grace**, would that that deed might be called a gracious one. 104. **clap**, clasp hands.

110. *tremor cordis*, fluttering of the heart. 112. **free**, open, innocent. 113. **fertile**, generous. 118. **mort**, blast on the horn announcing the death of the deer. 119. **brows**, an allusion to the horns of the cuckold. 120. **I' fecks**, in faith. 121. **bawcock** (*beau coq*), fine fellow. 123. **neat**, the other meaning of "neat" ("cattle") suggests horns. 125. **virginalling**, fingering, as if playing the virginals, a primitive kind of piano. 128. **pash**, head. **shoots**, horns. 132. **o'er-dyed blacks**, black clothes rotted by too much dye. 136. **welkin**, sky-blue. 137. **my collop**, piece of my flesh. 138-46. **Affection . . . brows**, amorous passion, thou dost penetrate the very soul; things thought impossible thou dost make possible; thou hast to do with the world of dreams, dost link thyself with the unreal and nonexistent. In the world of reality, then, it is very credible that thou mayest have a definite object; in this case thou hast one, an unlawful one, and the thought of it drives me mad with jealousy.

Communicat'st with dreams;—how can this be?—
With what 's unreal thou coactive art,
And fellow'st nothing. Then 't is very credent
Thou mayst co-join with something; and thou dost,
And that beyond commission, and I find it,
And that to the infection of my brains
And hardening of my brows.

Pol. What means Sicilia?

Her. He something seems unsettled.

Pol. How, my lord!

Leon. What cheer? How is 't with you, best brother?

Her. You look
As if you held a brow of much distraction.
Are you mov'd, my lord?

Leon. No, in good earnest.
How sometimes nature will betray its folly,
Its tenderness, and make itself a pastime
To harder bosoms! Looking on the lines
Of my boy's face, methoughts I did recoil
Twenty-three years, and saw myself unbreech'd
In my green velvet coat, my dagger muzzl'd,
Lest it should bite its master, and so prove,
As ornaments oft do, too dangerous.
How like, methought, I then was to this kernel,
This squash, this gentleman. Mine honest friend,
Will you take eggs for money?

Mam. No, my lord, I 'll fight.

Leon. You will! Why, happy man be 's dole! My brother,
Are so fond of your young prince as we
Do seem to be of ours?

Pol. If at home, sir,
He 's all my exercise, my mirth, my matter,
Now my sworn friend and then mine enemy,
My parasite, my soldier, statesman, all:
He makes a July's day short as December,
And with his varying childness cures in me
Thoughts that would thick my blood.

Leon. So stands this squire
Offic'd with me. We two will walk, my lord,
And leave you to your graver steps. Hermione,
How thou lov'st us, show in our brother's welcome;
Let what is dear in Sicily be cheap.
Next to thyself and my young rover, he 's
Apparent to my heart.

Her. If you would seek us,
We are yours i' th' garden. Shall 's attend you there?

Leon. To your own bents dispose you; you 'll be found,
Be you beneath the sky. [*Aside.*] I am angling now,
Though you perceive me not how I give line.
Go to, go to!
How she holds up the neb, the bill to him!
And arms her with the boldness of a wife
To her allowing husband!

Exeunt Polixenes, Hermione, and attendants.

Gone already!
Inch-thick, knee-deep, o'er head and ears a fork'd one!
Go, play, boy, play: thy mother plays, and I
Play too, but so disgrac'd a part, whose issue
Will hiss me to my grave; contempt and clamour
Will be my knell. Go, play, boy, play. There have been,
(Or I am much deceiv'd) cuckolds ere now;
And many a man there is (even at this present,
Now while I speak this) holds his wife by th' arm,
That little thinks she has been sluic'd in 's absence
And his pond fish'd by his next neighbour, by
Sir Smile, his neighbour: nay, there 's comfort in 't
Whiles other men have gates, and those gates open'd,
As mine, against their will. Should all despair
That have revolted wives, the tenth of mankind
Would hang themselves. Physic for 't there 's none:
It is a bawdy planet, that will strike
Where 't is predominant; and 't is powerful, think it,
From east, west, north, and south: be it concluded,
No barricado for a belly; know 't;
It will let in and out the enemy
With bag and baggage. Many thousand on 's
Have the disease, and feel 't not. How now, boy!

Mam. I am like you, they say.

Leon. Why, that 's some comfort.
What, Camillo there?

Cam. Ay, my good lord.

Leon. Go play, Mamillius; thou 'rt an honest man. *Exit Mamillius.*
Camillo, this great sir will yet stay longer.

Cam. You had much ado to make his anchor hold.
When you cast out, it still came home.

Leon. Didst note it?

144. commission, lawful limits. **160. squash,** unripe pea-pod. **161. take . . . money,** let yourself be cheated. **163. happy . . . dole,** may happiness be his lot. **171-2. So . . . me,** this boy performs a like service for me. **177. Apparent,** heir apparent.

183. neb, beak, nose. **184. arms her with,** puts on. **185. allowing,** approving. **186. fork'd,** horned. **188. issue,** outcome. **201. strike,** blast. **202. predominant,** in the ascendant.

Cam. He would not stay at your petitions; made
His business more material.
Leon. Didst perceive it?
Aside. They 're here with me already, whisp'ring, rounding,
"Sicilia is a so-forth:" 't is far gone,
When I shall gust it last. How came 't, Camillo,
That he did stay?
Cam. At the good Queen's entreaty.
Leon. At the Queen's be 't; "good" should be pertinent;
But, so it is, it is not. Was this taken
By any understanding pate but thine?
For thy conceit is soaking,—will draw in
More than the common blocks. Not noted, is 't,
But of the finer natures? By some severals
Of head-piece extraordinary? Lower messes
Perchance are to this business purblind? Say.
Cam. Business, my lord? I think most understand
Bohemia stays here longer.
Leon. Ha!
Cam. Stays here longer.
Leon. Ay, but why?
Cam. To satisfy your Highness and the entreaties
Of our most gracious mistress.
Leon. Satisfy!
Th' entreaties of your mistress! Satisfy!
Let that suffice. I have trusted thee, Camillo,
With all the nearest things to my heart, as well
My chamber-councils, wherein, priest-like, thou
Hast cleans'd my bosom, I from thee departed
Thy penitent reform'd; but we have been
Deceiv'd in thy integrity, deceiv'd
In that which seems so.
Cam. Be it forbid, my lord!
Leon. To bide upon 't, thou art not honest, or,
If thou inclin'st that way, thou art a coward,
Which hoxes honesty behind, restraining
From course requir'd; or else thou must be counted
A servant grafted in my serious trust
And therein negligent; or else a fool
That seest a game play'd home, the rich stake drawn,
And tak'st it all for jest.
Cam. My gracious lord,
I may be negligent, foolish, and fearful;
In every one of these no man is free
But that his negligence, his folly, fear,
Among the infinite doings of the world,
Sometime puts forth. In your affairs, my lord,
If ever I were wilful-negligent,
It was my folly; if industriously
I play'd the fool, it was my negligence,
Not weighing well the end; if ever fearful
To do a thing, where I the issue doubted,
Whereof the execution did cry out
Against the non-performance, 't was a fear
Which oft infects the wisest: these, my lord,
Are such allow'd infirmities that honesty
Is never free of. But, beseech your Grace,
Be plainer with me; let me know my trespass
By its own visage. If I then deny it,
'T is none of mine.
Leon. Ha' not you seen, Camillo,—
But that 's past doubt, you have, or your eye-glass
Is thicker than a cuckold's horn,—or heard,—
For to a vision so apparent rumour
Cannot be mute—or thought,—for cogitation
Resides not in that man that does not think,—
My wife is slippery? If thou wilt confess,
Or else be impudently negative,
To have nor eyes nor ears nor thought, then say
My wife 's a hobby-horse,—deserves a name
As rank as any flax-wench that puts to
Before her troth-plight: say 't and justify 't.
Cam. I would not be a stander-by to hear
My sovereign mistress clouded so, without
My present vengeance taken. Shrew my heart,
You never spoke what did become you less
Than this; which to reiterate were sin
As deep as that, though true.
Leon. Is whispering nothing?
Is leaning cheek to cheek? Is meeting noses?
Kissing with inside lip? stopping the career
Of laughter with a sigh?—a note infallible
Of breaking honesty;—horsing foot on foot?
Skulking in corners? wishing clocks more swift?
Hours, minutes? noon, midnight? and all eyes
Blind with the pin-and-web but theirs, theirs only,
That would unseen be wicked? Is this nothing?
Why, then the world and all that 's in 't is nothing;
The covering sky is nothing; Bohemia nothing;

216. **material**, important. 217. **They 're . . . me**, people are mocking me, with a gesture toward his forehead. **rounding**, whispering. 219. **gust**, taste, perceive. 221. **pertinent**, appropriate. 222. **taken**, perceived. 224. **conceit**, intelligence. **soaking**, receptive. 225. **blocks**, blockheads. 226. **severals**, individuals. 227. **Lower messes**, persons having inferior place at table. 237. **chamber-councils**, private affairs. 242. **bide**, dwell, insist. 244. **hoxes**, hamstrings.

254. **puts forth**, appears. 256. **industriously**, purposely. 268. **eye-glass**, crystalline lens of the eye. 270. **vision so apparent**, sight so plain. 277. **puts to**, sins. 288. **horsing**, setting. 291. **pin-and-web**, cataract.

My wife is nothing; nor nothing have these nothings,
If this be nothing.
Cam. Good my lord, be cur'd
Of this diseas'd opinion, and betimes;
For 't is most dangerous.
Leon. Say it be, 't is true.
Cam. No, no, my lord.
Leon. It is; you lie, you lie!
I say thou liest, Camillo, and I hate thee,
Pronounce thee a gross lout, a mindless slave,
Or else a hovering temporizer, that
Canst with thine eyes at once see good and evil,
Inclining to them both. Were my wife's liver
Infected as her life, she would not live
The running of one glass.
Cam. Who does infect her?
Leon. Why, he that wears her like her medal, hanging
About his neck, Bohemia; who, if I
Had servants true about me, that bare eyes
To see alike mine honour as their profits,
Their own particular thrifts, they would do that
Which should undo more doing; ay, and thou,
His cup-bearer,—whom I from meaner form
Have bench'd and rear'd to worship, who mayst see
Plainly as heaven sees earth and earth sees heaven,
How I am gall'd,—mightst bespice a cup,
To give mine enemy a lasting wink;
Which draught to me were cordial.
Cam. Sir, my lord,
I could do this, and that with no rash potion,
But with a lingering dram that should not work
Maliciously like poison; but I cannot
Believe this crack to be in my dread mistress,
So sovereignly being honourable.
I have lov'd thee,—
Leon. Make that thy question, and go rot!
Dost think I am so muddy, so unsettled,
To appoint myself in this vexation, sully
The purity and whiteness of my sheets—
Which to preserve is sleep, which being spotted
Is goads, thorns, nettles, tails of wasps—
Give scandal to the blood o' th' Prince my son,
(Who I do think is mine and love as mine)
Without ripe moving to 't? Would I do this?
Could man so blench?
Cam. I must believe you, sir;
I do; and will fetch off Bohemia for 't;
Provided that, when he 's removed, your Highness
Will take again your queen as yours at first,
Even for your son's sake; and thereby forsealing
The injury of tongues in courts and kingdoms
Known and allied to yours.
Leon. Thou dost advise me
Even so as I mine own course have set down.
I 'll give no blemish to her honour, none.
Cam. My lord,
Go then; and with a countenance as clear
As friendship wears at feasts, keep with Bohemia
And with your queen. I am his cupbearer:
If from me he have wholesome beverage,
Account me not your servant.
Leon. This is all:
Do 't and thou hast the one half of my heart;
Do 't not, thou split'st thine own.
Cam. I 'll do 't, my lord.
Leon. I will seem friendly, as thou hast advis'd me. *Exit.*
Cam. O miserable lady! But, for me,
What case stand I in? I must be the poisoner
Of good Polixenes; and my ground to do 't
Is the obedience to a master, one
Who in rebellion with himself will have
All that are his so too. To do this deed,
Promotion follows. If I could find example
Of thousands that had struck anointed kings
And flourish'd after, I 'd not do 't; but since
Nor brass nor stone nor parchment bears not one,
Let villainy itself forswear 't. I must
Forsake the court. To do 't, or no, is certain
To me a break-neck. Happy star reign now!
Here comes Bohemia.

Re-enter *Polixenes.*

Pol. This is strange; methinks
My favour here begins to warp. Not speak!
Good day, Camillo.
Cam. Hail, most royal sir!
Pol. What is the news i' th' court?
Cam. None rare, my lord.
Pol. The King hath on him such a countenance
As he had lost some province and a region
Lov'd as he loves himself. Even now I met him
With customary compliment; when he,
Wafting his eyes to th' contrary and falling
A lip of much contempt, speeds from me, and
So leaves me to consider what is breeding
That changeth thus his manners.

302. **hovering**, wavering. 306. **glass**, hour-glass. 311. **particular thrifts**, private gains. 313. **meaner form**, a lower seat. 314. **bench'd**, given high office. **worship**, dignity. 316. **bespice**, spice, with poison. 317. **lasting wink**, sleep of death. 324. **question**, theme. 326. **appoint . . . in**, put myself into. 332. **ripe moving**, adequate reason. 333. **blench**, swerve from the road.

334. **fetch off**, make away with. 337. **forsealing**, sealing up, silencing. 372. **falling**, letting fall, curling.

Cam. I dare not know, my lord.
Pol. How! dare not? Do not! Do you know, and dare not?
Be intelligent to me: 't is thereabouts;
For, to yourself, what you do know, you must,
And cannot say, you dare not. Good Camillo,
Your chang'd complexions are to me a mirror
Which shows me mine chang'd too; for I must be
A party in this alteration, finding
Myself thus alter'd with 't.
Cam. There is a sickness
Which puts some of us in distemper, but
I cannot name the disease; and it is caught
Of you that yet are well.
Pol. How! caught of me?
Make me not sighted like the basilisk.
I have look'd on thousands, who have sped the better
By my regard, but kill'd none so. Camillo,—
As you are certainly a gentleman, thereto
Clerk-like experienc'd, which no less adorns
Our gentry than our parents' noble names,
In whose success we are gentle,—I beseech you,
If you know aught which does behove my knowledge
Thereof to be inform'd, imprison 't not
In ignorant concealment.
Cam. I may not answer.
Pol. A sickness caught of me, and yet I well!
I must be answer'd. Dost thou hear, Camillo?
I conjure thee, by all the parts of man
Which honour does acknowledge, whereof the least
Is not this suit of mine, that thou declare
What incidency thou dost guess of harm
Is creeping toward me; how far off, how near;
Which way to be prevented, if to be;
If not, how best to bear it.
Cam. Sir, I will tell you,
Since I am charg'd in honour and by him
That I think honourable; therefore mark my counsel,
Which must be ev'n as swiftly follow'd as
I mean to utter it, or both yourself and me
Cry lost, and so good night!
Pol. On, good Camillo.
Cam. I am appointed him to murder you.
Pol. By whom, Camillo?
Cam. By the King.
Pol. For what?
Cam. He thinks, nay, with all confidence he swears,
As he had seen 't or been an instrument
To vice you to 't, that you have touch'd his queen
Forbiddenly.
Pol. O, then my best blood turn
To an infected jelly, and my name
Be yok'd with his that did betray the Best!
Turn then my freshest reputation to
A savour that may strike the dullest nostril
Where I arrive, and my approach be shunn'd,
Nay, hated too, worse than the great'st infection
That e'er was heard or read!
Cam. Swear his thought over
By each particular star in heaven and
By all their influences, you may as well
Forbid the sea for to obey the moon
As or by oath remove or counsel shake
The fabric of his folly, whose foundation
Is pil'd upon his faith and will continue
The standing of his body.
Pol. How should this grow?
Cam. I know not; but I am sure 't is safer to
Avoid what 's grown than question how 't is born.
If therefore you dare trust my honesty,
That lies enclosed in this trunk which you
Shall bear along impawn'd, away to-night!
Your followers I will whisper to the business,
And will by twos and threes at several posterns
Clear them o' th' city. For myself, I 'll put
My fortunes to your service, which are here
By this discovery lost. Be not uncertain;
For, by the honour of my parents, I
Have utter'd truth, which if you seek to prove,
I dare not stand by; nor shall you be safer
Than one condemn'd by the King's own mouth, thereon
His execution sworn.
Pol. I do believe thee;
I saw his heart in 's face. Give me thy hand:
Be pilot to me, and thy places shall
Still neighbour mine. My ships are ready and
My people did expect my hence departure
Two days ago. This jealousy
Is for a precious creature: as she 's rare,
Must it be great; and as his person 's mighty,
Must it be violent; and as he does conceive
He is dishonour'd by a man which ever

378. **Be intelligent**, speak out. **thereabouts**, something of this kind. 388. **Make . . . sighted**, do not say I have eyes. **basilisk**, fabulous reptile whose look caused death. 394. **In . . . gentle**, by inheritance from whom we derive our high rank. 397. **ignorant**, that keeps me ignorant. 403. **incidency**, happening. 412. **him**, the one.

416. **vice**, force. 419. **his**, Judas'. 424. **Swear . . . over**, try to overpower his thoughts by swearing. 431. **The . . . body**, while his body endures. 435. **trunk**, body. 436. **impawn'd**, as a pledge of my good faith. 438. **posterns**, small gates. 441. **this discovery**, my disclosure to you. 444. **stand by**, await the outcome. 448-9. **thy . . . mine**, you shall always have an office beside me.

Profess'd to him, why, his revenges must
In that be made more bitter. Fear o'ershades me.
Good expedition be my friend, and comfort
The gracious queen;—part of his theme, but nothing
Of his ill-ta'en suspicion! Come, Camillo;
I will respect thee as a father if
Thou bear'st my life off hence. Let us avoid.

Cam. It is in mine authority to command
The keys of all the posterns. Please your Highness
To take the urgent hour. Come, sir, away.

Exeunt.

ACT II. Scene I. *A room in the palace.*

Enter *Hermione, Mamillius,* and *Ladies.*

Her. Take the boy to you; he so troubles me,
'T is past enduring.

First Lady. Come, my gracious lord,
Shall I be your playfellow?

Mam. No, I 'll none of you.

First Lady. Why, my sweet lord?

Mam. You 'll kiss me hard and speak to me as if
I were a baby still.—I love you better.

Sec. Lady. And why so, my lord?

Mam. Not for because
Your brows are blacker; yet black brows, they say,
Become some women best, so that there be not
Too much hair there, but in a semicircle,
Or a half-moon made with a pen.

Sec. Lady. Who taught this?

Mam. I learn'd it out of women's faces. Pray now
What colour are your eyebrows?

First Lady. Blue, my lord.

Mam. Nay, that 's a mock. I have seen a lady's nose
That has been blue, but not her eyebrows.

First Lady. Hark ye;
The Queen your mother rounds apace. We shall
Present our services to a fine new prince
One of these days; and then you 'd wanton with us,
If we would have you.

Sec. Lady. She is spread of late
Into a goodly bulk: good time encounter her!

Her. What wisdom stirs amongst you? Come, sir, now
I am for you again. Pray you, sit by us,
And tell 's a tale.

Mam. Merry or sad shall 't be?

Her. As merry as you will.

Mam. A sad tale 's best for winter. I have one
Of sprites and goblins.

Her. Let 's have that, good sir.
Come on, sit down; come on, and do your best
To fright me with your sprites; you 're powerful at it.

Mam. There was a man—

Her. Nay, come, sit down; then on.

Mam. Dwelt by a churchyard. I will tell it softly;
Yond crickets shall not hear it.

Her. Come on, then,
And give 't me in mine ear.

Enter *Leontes,* with *Antigonus, Lords,* and others.

Leon. Was he met there? his train? Camillo with him?

First Lord. Behind the tuft of pines I met them; never
Saw I men scour so on their way. I eyed
Them even to their ships.

Leon. How blest am I
In my just censure, in my true opinion!
Alack, for lesser knowledge! How accurs'd
In being so blest! There may be in the cup
A spider steep'd, and one may drink, depart,
And yet partake no venom, for his knowledge
Is not infected; but if one present
Th' abhorr'd ingredient to his eye, make known
How he hath drunk, he cracks his gorge, his sides,
With violent hefts. I have drunk, and seen the spider.
Camillo was his help in this, his pander.
There is a plot against my life, my crown.

456. Profess'd, professed friendship. **458-60. Good . . . suspicion,** may my hasty departure befriend me and bring some comfort to the good queen, who is linked with me in the king's thoughts, but is without reason the object of his ill-founded suspicion. **Act II, Scene i: 18. wanton,** play.

31. crickets, chattering ladies of the court. **37. censure,** judgment. **38. Alack . . . knowledge,** alas, would that I knew less. **41. partake no venom,** there was a popular belief that a spider in one's drink was poisonous only if observed. **45. hefts,** retchings.

All 's true that is mistrusted: that false villain
Whom I employ'd was pre-employ'd by him.
He has discover'd my design, and I
Remain a pinch'd thing; yea, a very trick
For them to play at will. How came the posterns
So easily open?

First Lord. By his great authority;
Which often hath no less prevail'd than so
On your command.

Leon. I know 't too well.
Give me the boy. I am glad you did not nurse him.
Though he does bear some signs of me, yet you
Have too much blood in him.

Her. What is this? Sport?

Leon. Bear the boy hence; he shall not come about her.
Away with him! and let her sport herself
With that she 's big with; for 't is Polixenes
Has made thee swell thus.

Her. But I 'd say he had not,
And I 'll be sworn you would believe my saying,
Howe'er you lean to the nayward.

Leon. You, my lords,
Look on her, mark her well; be but about
To say she is a goodly lady, and
The justice of your hearts will thereto add
'T is pity she 's not honest, honourable.
Praise her but for this her without-door form
(Which on my faith deserves high speech) and straight
The shrug, the hum or ha, these petty brands
That calumny doth use—O, I am out—
That mercy does, for calumny will sear
Virtue itself; these shrugs, these hums and ha's,
When you have said she 's goodly, come between
Ere you can say she 's honest: but be 't known,
From him that has most cause to grieve it should be,
She 's an adulteress.

Her. Should a villain say so,
The most replenish'd villain in the world,
He were as much more villain: you, my lord,
Do but mistake.

Leon. You have mistook, my lady,
Polixenes for Leontes. O thou thing!
Which I 'll not call a creature of thy place,
Lest barbarism, making me the precedent,
Should a like language use to all degrees,
And mannerly distinguishment leave out
Betwixt the prince and beggar; I have said
She 's an adulteress; I have said with whom;
More, she 's a traitor, and Camillo is
A fedary with her, and one that knows
What she should shame to know herself
But with her most vile principal, that she 's
A bed-swerver, even as bad as those
That vulgars give bold'st titles; ay, and privy
To this their late escape.

Her. No, by my life,
Privy to none of this. How will this grieve you,
When you shall come to clearer knowledge, that
You thus have publish'd me! Gentle, my lord,
You scarce can right me throughly then to say
You did mistake.

Leon. No; if I mistake
In those foundations which I build upon,
The centre is not big enough to bear
A school-boy's top. Away with her, to prison!
He who shall speak for her is afar off guilty
But that he speaks.

Her. There 's some ill planet reigns;
I must be patient till the heavens look
With an aspect more favourable. Good my lords,
I am not prone to weeping, as our sex
Commonly are, the want of which vain dew
Perchance shall dry your pities; but I have
That honourable grief lodg'd here which burns
Worse than tears drown. Beseech you all, my lords,
With thoughts so qualified as your charities
Shall best instruct you, measure me; and so
The King's will be perform'd!

Leon. Shall I be heard?

Her. Who is 't that goes with me? Beseech your Highness,
My women may be with me; for you see
My plight requires it. Do not weep, good fools;
There is no cause. When you shall know your mistress
Has deserv'd prison, then abound in tears
As I come out; this action I now go on
Is for my better grace. Adieu, my lord.
I never wish'd to see you sorry; now
I trust I shall. My women, come; you have leave.

Leon. Go, do our bidding; hence!

Exit Queen guarded, with Ladies.

First Lord. Beseech your Highness, call the Queen again.

Ant. Be certain what you do, sir, lest your justice

51. **pinch'd,** tortured. 64. **the nayward,** denial. 69. **without-door form,** outward appearance. 83. **place,** rank. 86. **mannerly distinguishment,** proper distinctions.

90. **fedary,** confederate. 98. **publish'd,** publicly accused. 102. **centre,** of the earth. 104-5. **is . . . speaks,** acquires some guilt in merely defending her. 115. **heard,** obeyed. 121. **action,** campaign.

Prove violence; in the which three great ones suffer,
Yourself, your queen, your son.

First Lord. For her, my lord,
I dare my life lay down and will do 't, sir,
Please you t' accept it, that the Queen is spotless
I' th' eyes of Heaven and to you; I mean,
In this which you accuse her.

Ant. If it prove
She 's otherwise, I 'll keep my stables where
I lodge my wife; I 'll go in couples with her;
Than when I feel and see her no farther trust her;
For every inch of woman in the world,
Ay, every dram of woman's flesh is false,
If she be.

Leon. Hold your peaces.

First Lord. Good my lord,—

Ant. It is for you we speak, not for ourselves.
You are abus'd, and by some putter-on
That will be damn'd for 't; would I knew the villain,
I would land-damn him. Be she honour-flaw'd,
I have three daughters; the eldest is eleven;
The second and the third, nine, and some five;
If this prove true, they 'll pay for 't. By mine honour,
I 'll geld 'em all; fourteen they shall not see
To bring false generations: they are co-heirs;
And I had rather glib myself than they
Should not produce fair issue.

Leon. Cease; no more.
You smell this business with a sense as cold
As is a dead man's nose; but I do see 't and feel 't,
As you feel doing thus; and see withal
The instruments that feel.

Ant. If it be so,
We need no grave to bury honesty.
There 's not a grain of it the face to sweeten
Of the whole dungy earth.

Leon. What! lack I credit?

First Lord. I had rather you did lack than I, my lord,
Upon this ground; and more it would content me
To have her honour true than your suspicion,
Be blam'd for 't how you might.

Leon. Why, what need we
Commune with you of this, but rather follow
Our forceful instigation? Our prerogative
Calls not your counsels, but our natural goodness
Imparts this; which if you, or stupefied
Or seeming so in skill, cannot or will not
Relish a truth like us, inform yourselves
We need no more of your advice: the matter,
The loss, the gain, the ord'ring on 't, is all
Properly ours.

Ant. And I wish, my liege,
You had only in your silent judgement tried it,
Without more overture.

Leon. How could that be?
Either thou art most ignorant by age,
Or thou wert born a fool. Camillo's flight,
Added to their familiarity
(Which was as gross as ever touch'd conjecture,
That lack'd sight only, nought for approbation
But only seeing, all other circumstances
Made up to th' deed) doth push on this proceeding.
Yet, for a greater confirmation
(For in an act of this importance 't were
Most piteous to be wild) I have dispatch'd in post
To sacred Delphos, to Apollo's temple,
Cleomenes and Dion, whom you know
Of stuff'd sufficiency; now from the oracle
They will bring all; whose spiritual counsel had,
Shall stop or spur me. Have I done well?

First Lord. Well done, my lord.

Leon. Though I am satisfied and need no more
Than what I know, yet shall the oracle
Give rest to th' minds of others, such as he
Whose ignorant credulity will not
Come up to th' truth. So have we thought it good
From our free person she should be confin'd,
Lest that the treachery of the two fled hence
Be left her to perform. Come, follow us;
We are to speak in public, for this business
Will raise us all.

Ant. [*Aside.*] To laughter, as I take it,
If the good truth were known. *Exeunt.*

Scene II. *A prison.*

Enter *Paulina*, a *Gentleman*, and *Attendants*.

Paul. The keeper of the prison, call to him;
Let him have knowledge who I am.

Exit Gentleman.

134-5. I 'll . . . wife, I will lock up my wife as I lock up mares in the stable. **141. putter-on,** plotter. **143. land-damn,** the general sense of punishment is obvious, but the precise meaning of the word is conjectural. **148. bring false,** bring forth illegitimate. **149. glib,** geld. **153-4. As . . . feel,** as you feel my pulling of your nose or beard, and see my fingers doing it. **159. Upon this ground,** in this matter. **163. forceful instigation,** strong impulse.

164. Calls not, does not call for. **166. in skill,** by design. **172. overture,** disclosure. **176. touch'd conjecture,** conjecture reached to. **177. approbation,** proof. **185. stuff'd sufficiency,** entire competence. **186. had,** when obtained. **194. free,** easily accessible. **198. raise,** rouse.

Good lady,
No court in Europe is too good for thee;
What dost thou then in prison?

Re-enter *Gentleman,* with the *Jailer.*

Now, good sir,
You know me, do you not?
Jail. For a worthy lady,
And one who much I honour.
Paul. Pray you then,
Conduct me to the Queen.
Jail. I may not, madam.
To the contrary I have express commandment.
Paul. Here 's ado,
To lock up honesty and honour from
Th' access of gentle visitors! Is 't lawful, pray you,
To see her women? Any of them? Emilia?
Jail. So please you, madam,
To put apart these your attendants, I
Shall bring Emilia forth.
Paul. I pray now, call her.
Withdraw yourselves.
Exeunt Gentleman and attendants.
Jail. And, madam,
I must be present at your conference.
Paul. Well, be 't so, prithee. *Exit Jailer.*
Here 's such ado to make no stain a stain
As passes colouring.

Re-enter *Jailer,* with *Emilia.*

Dear gentlewoman,
How fares our gracious lady?
Emil. As well as one so great and so forlorn
May hold together: on her frights and griefs,
(Which never tender lady hath borne greater)
She is something before her time deliver'd.
Paul. A boy?
Emil. A daughter, and a goodly babe,
Lusty and like to live: the Queen receives
Much comfort in 't; says, "My poor prisoner,
I am innocent as you."
Paul. I dare be sworn.
These dangerous unsafe lunes i' th' King, beshrew them!
He must be told on 't, and he shall. The office
Becomes a woman best; I 'll take 't upon me.
If I prove honey-mouth'd, let my tongue blister
And never to my red-look'd anger be
The trumpet any more. Pray you, Emilia,
Commend my best obedience to the Queen.
If she dares trust me with her little babe,
I 'll show 't the King and undertake to be
Her advocate to the loud'st. We do not know
How he may soften at the sight o' th' child.
The silence often of pure innocence
Persuades when speaking fails.
Emil. Most worthy madam,
Your honour and your goodness is so evident
That your free undertaking cannot miss
A thriving issue: there is no lady living
So meet for this great errand. Please your ladyship
To visit the next room, I 'll presently
Acquaint the Queen of your most noble offer;
Who but to-day hammer'd of this design,
But durst not tempt a minister of honour,
Lest she should be denied.
Paul. Tell her, Emilia,
I 'll use that tongue I have. If wit flow from 't
As boldness from my bosom, let 't not be doubted
I shall do good.
Emil. Now be you blest for it!
I 'll to the Queen. Please you, come something nearer.
Jail. Madam, if 't please the Queen to send the babe,
I know not what I shall incur to pass it,
Having no warrant.
Paul. You need not fear it, sir.
This child was prisoner to the womb and is
By law and process of great Nature thence
Freed and enfranchis'd, not a party to
The anger of the King nor guilty of,
(If any be) the trespass of the Queen.
Jail. I do believe it.
Paul. Do not you fear. Upon mine honour, I
Will stand betwixt you and danger. *Exeunt.*

Scene III. *A room in the palace.*

Enter *Leontes, Antigonus, Lords,* and *Servants.*

Leon. Nor night nor day no rest. It is but weakness
To bear the matter thus; mere weakness. If
The cause were not in being,—part o' th' cause,
She th' adulteress; for the harlot king
Is quite beyond mine arm, out of the blank
And level of my brain, plot-proof; but she
I can hook to me: say that she were gone,
Given to the fire, a moiety of my rest
Might come to me again. Who 's there?
First Serv. My lord?
Leon. How does the boy?
First Serv. He took good rest to-night;
'T is hop'd his sickness is discharg'd.

20. passes colouring, exceeds all painting. **30. lunes,** fits of lunacy.

44. free, generous. **45. thriving issue,** happy result. **49. hammer'd of,** pondered on. **50. tempt,** attempt, ask. **Scene iii: 4. harlot,** licentious. **5. blank,** white spot in the center of a target. **6. level,** aim.

Leon. To see his nobleness!
Conceiving the dishonour of his mother,
He straight declin'd, droop'd, took it deeply,
Fasten'd and fix'd the shame on 't in himself,
Threw off his spirit, his appetite, his sleep,
And downright languish'd. Leave me solely; go,
See how he fares. [*Exit Servant.*] Fie, fie! no thought of him;
The very thought of my revenges that way
Recoil upon me: in himself too mighty,
And in his parties, his alliance. Let him be
Until a time may serve; for present vengeance,
Take it on her. Camillo and Polixenes
Laugh at me, make their pastime at my sorrow:
They should not laugh if I could reach them, nor
Shall she within my power.

Enter *Paulina* with a babe.

First Lord. You must not enter.
Paul. Nay, rather, good my lords, be second to me.
Fear you his tyrannous passion more, alas,
Than the Queen's life? A gracious innocent soul,
More free than he is jealous.
Ant. That 's enough.
Sec. Serv. Madam, he hath not slept tonight; commanded
None should come at him.
Paul. Not so hot, good sir;
I come to bring him sleep. 'T is such as you,
That creep like shadows by him and do sigh
At each his needless heavings, such as you
Nourish the cause of his awaking. I
Do come with words as medicinal as true,
Honest as either, to purge him of that humour
That presses him from sleep.
Leon. What noise there, ho?
Paul. No noise, my lord; but needful conference
About some gossips for your Highness.
Leon. How!
Away with that audacious lady! Antigonus,
I charg'd thee that she should not come about me:
I knew she would.
Ant. I told her so, my lord,
On your displeasure's peril and on mine,
She should not visit you.
Leon. What, canst not rule her?
Paul. From all dishonesty he can. In this—
Unless he take the course that you have done,
Commit me for committing honour—trust it,
He shall not rule me.
Ant. La you now, you hear.
When she will take the rein I let her run;
But she 'll not stumble.
Paul. Good my liege, I come—
And, I beseech you, hear me, who professes
Myself your loyal servant, your physician,
Your most obedient counsellor, yet that dares
Less appear so in comforting your evils,
Than such as most seem yours—I say, I come
From your good queen.
Leon. Good queen!
Paul. Good queen, my lord,
Good queen; I say good queen;
And would by combat make her good, so were I
A man, the worst about you.
Leon. Force her hence.
Paul. Let him that makes but trifles of his eyes
First hand me: on mine own accord I 'll off,
But first I 'll do my errand. The good queen,
(For she is good) hath brought you forth a daughter;
Here 't is; commends it to your blessing.
Laying down the child.
Leon. Out!
A mankind witch! Hence with her, out o' door!
A most intelligencing bawd!
Paul. Not so.
I am as ignorant in that as you
In so entitling me, and no less honest
Than you are mad; which is enough, I 'll warrant,
As this world goes, to pass for honest.
Leon. Traitors!
Will you not push her out? Give her the bastard.
Thou dotard! thou art woman-tir'd, unroosted
By thy dame Partlet here. Take up the bastard;
Take 't up, I say; give 't to thy crone.
Paul. For ever
Unvenerable be thy hands, if thou
Tak'st up the Princess by that forced baseness
Which he has put upon 't!
Leon. He dreads his wife.
Paul. So I would you did; then 't were past all doubt
You 'd call your children yours.
Leon. A nest of traitors!
Ant. I am none, by this good light.
Paul. Nor I, nor any
But one that 's here, and that 's himself; for he

18. him, Polixenes. **27. be . . . to,** help. **30. free,** innocent. **41. gossips,** baptismal sponsors. **49. Commit,** imprison.

56. comforting, encouraging. **57. Than . . . yours,** than those who seem most loyal to you. **67. mankind,** masculine, violent. **68. intelligencing bawd,** go-between for lovers. **74. woman-tir'd,** henpecked. **unroosted,** put off the perch. **75. dame Partlet,** the name of the hen in the old beast fable. **78. by . . . baseness,** under that false name of bastard.

The sacred honour of himself, his queen's,
His hopeful son's, his babe's, betrays to slander,
Whose sting is sharper than the sword's, and will not—
For, as the case now stands, it is a curse
He cannot be compell'd to 't—once remove
The root of his opinion, which is rotten
As ever oak or stone was sound.
Leon. A callat
Of boundless tongue, who late hath beat her husband
And now baits me! This brat is none of mine;
It is the issue of Polixenes.
Hence with it, and together with the dam
Commit them to the fire!
Paul. It is yours;
And, might we lay th' old proverb to your charge,
So like you, 't is the worse. Behold, my lords,
Although the print be little, the whole matter
And copy of the father, eye, nose, lip.
The trick of 's frown, his forehead, nay, the valley,
The pretty dimples of his chin and cheek, his smiles,
The very mould and frame of hand, nail, finger;
And thou, good goddess Nature, which hast made it
So like to him that got it, if thou hast
The ordering of the mind too, 'mongst all colours
No yellow in 't, lest she suspect, as he does,
Her children not her husband's!
Leon. A gross hag!
And, lozel, thou art worthy to be hang'd,
That wilt not stay her tongue.
Ant. Hang all the husbands
That cannot do that feat, you 'll leave yourself
Hardly one subject.
Leon. Once more, take her hence.
Paul. A most unworthy and unnatural lord
Can do no more.
Leon. I 'll ha' thee burnt.
Paul. I care not;
It is an heretic that makes the fire,
Not she which burns in 't. I 'll not call you tyrant;
But this most cruel usage of your queen,
(Not able to produce more accusation
Than your own weak-hing'd fancy) something savours
Of tyranny and will ignoble make you,
Yea, scandalous to the world.
Leon. On your allegiance,
Out of the chamber with her! Were I a tyrant,
Where were her life? She durst not call me so,
If she did know me one. Away with her!
Paul. I pray you, do not push me; I 'll be gone.
Look to your babe, my lord; 't is yours. Jove send her
A better guiding spirit! What needs these hands?
You, that are thus so tender o'er his follies,
Will never do him good, not one of you.
So, so; farewell; we are gone. *Exit.*
Leon. Thou, traitor, hast set on thy wife to this.
My child? Away with 't! Even thou, that hast
A heart so tender o'er it, take it hence
And see it instantly consum'd with fire;
Even thou and none but thou. Take it up straight.
Within this hour bring me word 't is done,
And by good testimony, or I 'll seize thy life,
With what thou else call'st thine. If thou refuse
And wilt encounter with my wrath, say so;
The bastard brains with these my proper hands
Shall I dash out. Go, take it to the fire;
For thou set'st on thy wife.
Ant. I did not, sir.
These lords, my noble fellows, if they please,
Can clear me in 't.
Lords. We can. My royal liege,
He is not guilty of her coming hither.
Leon. You 're liars all.
First Lord. Beseech your Highness, give us better credit.
We have always truly serv'd you, and beseech
So to esteem of us, and on our knees we beg,
(As recompense of our dear services
Past and to come) that you do change this purpose,
Which being so horrible, so bloody, must
Lead on to some foul issue. We all kneel.
Leon. I am a feather for each wind that blows.
Shall I live on to see this bastard kneel
And call me father? Better burn it now
Than curse it then. But be it; let it live.
It shall not neither. You, sir, come you hither;
You that have been so tenderly officious
With Lady Margery, your midwife there,
To save this bastard's life,—for 't is a bastard,
So sure as this beard 's gray,—what will you adventure
To save this brat's life?
Ant. Anything, my lord,

90. **callat**, scold. 96-7. **proverb . . . worse**, "the devil calls him his white son; he is so like him that he is the worse for it." 107. **yellow**, color of jealousy. 109. **lozel**, rascal.

127. **What . . . hands**, why need I be pushed out? 160. **Lady Margery**, "Lady Margery," a variant on "Dame Partlet," a cackling hen. 162. **this**, Antigonus'.

That my ability may undergo
And nobleness impose; at least thus much:
I 'll pawn the little blood which I have left
To save the innocent: anything possible.

Leon. It shall be possible. Swear by this sword
Thou wilt perform my bidding.

Ant. I will, my lord.

Leon. Mark and perform it; see'st thou? for the fail
Of any point in 't shall not only be
Death to thyself but to thy lewd-tongued wife,
Whom for this time we pardon. We enjoin thee,
As thou art liege-man to us, that thou carry
This female bastard hence, and that thou bear it
To some remote and desert place quite out
Of our dominions, and that there thou leave it,
Without more mercy, to it own protection
And favour of the climate. As by strange fortune
It came to us, I do in justice charge thee,
On thy soul's peril and thy body's torture,
That thou commend it strangely to some place
Where chance may nurse or end it. Take it up.

Ant. I swear to do this, though a present death
Had been more merciful. Come on, poor babe.
Some powerful spirit instruct the kites and ravens
To be thy nurses! Wolves and bears, they say,
Casting their savageness aside, have done
Like offices of pity. Sir, be prosperous
In more than this deed does require! And blessing
Against this cruelty fight on thy side,
Poor thing, condemn'd to loss!

Exit with the babe.

Leon. No, I 'll not rear
Another's issue.

Enter a *Servant.*

Serv. Please your Highness, posts
From those you sent to th' oracle are come
An hour since. Cleomenes and Dion,
Being well arriv'd from Delphos, are both landed,
Hasting to the court.

First Lord. So please you, sir, their speed
Hath been beyond accompt.

Leon. Twenty-three days
They have been absent; 't is good speed; foretells
The great Apollo suddenly will have
The truth of this appear. Prepare you, lords;
Summon a session, that we may arraign
Our most disloyal lady; for, as she hath
Been publicly accus'd, so shall she have
A just and open trial. While she lives
My heart will be a burden to me. Leave me,
And think upon my bidding.

Exeunt.

ACT III. Scene I. *Sicilia. On the road.*

Enter *Cleomenes* and *Dion.*

Cleo. The climate 's delicate, the air most sweet,
Fertile the isle, the temple much surpassing
The common praise it bears.

Dion. I shall report,
For most it caught me, the celestial habits,
(Methinks I so should term them) and the reverence
Of the grave wearers. O, the sacrifice!
How ceremonious, solemn, and unearthly
It was i' th' offering!

Cleo. But of all, the burst
And the ear-deaf'ning voice o' th' oracle,
Kin to Jove's thunder, so surpris'd my sense,
That I was nothing.

Dion. If th' event o' th' journey
Prove as successful to the Queen,—O be 't so!—
As it hath been to us rare, pleasant, speedy,
The time is worth the use on 't.

Cleo. Great Apollo
Turn all to th' best! These proclamations,
So forcing faults upon Hermione,
I little like.

Dion. The violent carriage of it
Will clear or end the business. When the oracle,
(Thus by Apollo's great divine seal'd up)
Shall the contents discover, something rare
Even then will rush to knowledge. Go; fresh horses!
And gracious be the issue!

Exeunt.

164. undergo, undertake. **170. fail**, failure. **182. commend**, entrust. **strangely**, as of alien birth. **Act III. Scene i: 2. isle**, Shakespeare follows Pandosto in confusing Delos, the island of Apollo, with Delphi, the seat of Apollo's oracle. **4. habits**, robes.

192. loss, perdition. **198. accompt**, calculation. **Act III. Scene i: 14. worth . . . on 't**, well spent. **17. carriage**, handling. **19. great divine**, high priest.

Scene II. *Sicilia. A court of justice.*

Enter *Leontes, Lords,* and *Officers.*

Leon. This sessions (to our great grief we pronounce)
Even pushes 'gainst our heart,—the party tried
The daughter of a king, our wife, and one
Of us too much belov'd. Let us be clear'd
Of being tyrannous, since we so openly
Proceed in justice, which shall have due course
Even to the guilt or the purgation.
Produce the prisoner.

Off. It is his Highness' pleasure that the Queen
Appear in person here in court. Silence!

Enter *Hermione* as to her trial; *Paulina* and *Ladies* attending.

Leon. Read the indictment.

Off. [*Reads.*]

"Hermione, Queen to the worthy Leontes, King of Sicilia, thou art here accused and arraigned of high treason, in committing adultery with Polixenes, King of Bohemia, and conspiring with Camillo to take away the life of our sovereign lord the King, thy royal husband: the pretence whereof being by circumstances partly laid open, thou, Hermione, contrary to the faith and allegiance of a true subject, didst counsel and aid them, for their better safety, to fly away by night."

Her. Since what I am to say must be but that
Which contradicts my accusation, and
The testimony on my part no other
But what comes from myself, it shall scarce boot me
To say "Not guilty": mine integrity
Being counted falsehood, shall, as I express it,
Be so receiv'd. But thus:—If powers divine
Behold our human actions (as they do)
I doubt not then but innocence shall make
False accusation blush, and tyranny
Tremble at patience. You, my lord, best know,
(Whom least will seem to do so,) my past life
Hath been as continent, as chaste, as true,
As I am now unhappy; which is more
Than history can pattern, though devis'd
And play'd to take spectators. For behold me,
A fellow of the royal bed, which owe
A moiety of the throne, a great king's daughter,
The mother to a hopeful prince, here standing
To prate and talk for life and honour 'fore
Who please to come and hear. For life, I prize it
As I weigh grief, which I would spare; for honour,
'T is a derivative from me to mine,
And only that I stand for. I appeal
To your own conscience, sir, before Polixenes
Came to your court, how I was in your grace,
How merited to be so; since he came,
With what encounter so uncurrent I
Have strain'd t' appear thus; if one jot beyond
The bound of honour, or in act or will
That way inclining, harden'd be the hearts
Of all that hear me, and my near'st of kin
Cry fie upon my grave!

Leon. I ne'er heard yet
That any of these bolder vices wanted
Less impudence to gainsay what they did
Than to perform it first.

Her. That 's true enough;
Though 't is a saying, sir, not due to me.

Leon. You will not own it.

Her. More than mistress of
Which comes to me in name of fault, I must not
At all acknowledge. For Polixenes,
With whom I am accus'd, I do confess
I lov'd him as in honour he requir'd,
With such a kind of love as might become
A lady like me, with a love even such,
So and no other, as yourself commanded;
Which not to have done I think had been in me
Both disobedience and ingratitude
To you and toward your friend, whose love had spoke,
Even since it could speak, from an infant, freely
That it was yours. Now, for conspiracy,
I know not how it tastes; though it be dish'd
For me to try how. All I know of it
Is that Camillo was an honest man;
And why he left your court, the gods themselves,
(Wotting no more than I) are ignorant.

Leon. You knew of his departure, as you know
What you have underta'en to do in 's absence.

Her. Sir,
You speak a language that I understand not.
My life stands in the level of your dreams,
Which I 'll lay down.

1. sessions, trial. **pronounce,** declare. **7. purgation,** acquittal. **16. pretence,** design. **38. take,** charm.

43-4. For . . . spare, life and grief are one and the same to me; I would glady be rid of (spare) both. **50. encounter,** behavior. **uncurrent,** unusual. **51. strain'd,** gone beyond proper limits. **56. wanted,** lacked. **59. due,** applicable. **60-1. More . . . Which,** guilty of more than what. **64. requir'd,** deserved. **82. in . . . of,** at the mercy of your delusions.

Leon. Your actions are my dreams;
You had a bastard by Polixenes,
And I but dream'd it. As you were past all shame,—
Those of your fact are so,—so past all truth,
Which to deny concerns more than avails; for as
Thy brat hath been cast out, like to itself,
No father owning it,—which is, indeed,
More criminal in thee than it,—so thou
Shalt feel our justice, in whose easiest passage
Look for no less than death.

Her. Sir, spare your threats.
The bug which you would fright me with I seek;
To me can life be no commodity.
The crown and comfort of my life, your favour,
I do give lost; for I do feel it gone,
But know not how it went. My second joy
And first-fruits of my body, from his presence
I am barr'd, like one infectious. My third comfort,
Starr'd most unluckily, is from my breast,—
The innocent milk in it most innocent mouth
Hal'd out to murder; myself on every post
Proclaim'd a strumpet; with immodest hatred
The child-bed privilege denied, which longs
To women of all fashion; lastly, hurried
Here to this place, i' th' open air, before
I have got strength of limit. Now, my liege,
Tell me what blessings I have here alive,
That I should fear to die? Therefore proceed.
But yet hear this: mistake me not; no life,
I prize it not a straw, but for mine honour,
Which I would free,—if I shall be condemn'd
Upon surmises (all proofs sleeping else
But what your jealousies awake) I tell you
'T is rigour and not law. Your honours all,
I do refer me to the oracle:
Apollo be my judge!

First Lord. This your request
Is altogether just; therefore bring forth,
And in Apollo's name, his oracle.

Exeunt certain Officers.

Her. The Emperor of Russia was my father:
O that he were alive, and here beholding
His daughter's trial! that he did but see
The flatness of my misery, yet with eyes
Of pity, not revenge!

86. **of your fact**, who do such evil deeds. 87. **Which . . . avails**, denial costs you more trouble than it is worth. 88. **like to itself**, as an outcast should be. 93. **bug**, bogey. 94. **commodity**, profit. 100. **Starr'd . . . unluckily**, born under most unlucky stars. 103. **immodest**, immoderate. 105. **fashion**, kinds, degrees. 107. **limit**, period of convalescence after childbirth. 110. **no life**. I do not plead for life. 115. **rigour**, tyranny. 123. **flatness**, completeness.

Re-enter *Officers*, with *Cleomenes* and *Dion.*

Off. You here shall swear upon this sword of justice,
That you, Cleomenes and Dion, have
Been both at Delphos, and from thence have brought
This seal'd-up oracle, by the hand deliver'd
Of great Apollo's priest, and that since then
You have not dar'd to break the holy seal
Nor read the secrets in 't.

Cleo. Dion. All this we swear.

Leon. Break up the seals and read.

Off. [*Reads.*]

"Hermione is chaste; Polixenes blameless; Camillo a true subject; Leontes a jealous tyrant; his innocent babe truly begotten; and the King shall live without an heir, if that which is lost be not found."

Lords. Now blessed be the great Apollo!

Her. Praised!

Leon. Hast thou read truth?

Off. Ay, my lord; even so
As it is here set down.

Leon. There is no truth at all i' th' oracle.
The sessions shall proceed; this is mere falsehood.

Enter a *Servant.*

Serv. My lord the King, the King!

Leon. What is the business?

Serv. O sir, I shall be hated to report it!
The Prince your son, with mere conceit and fear
Of the Queen's speed, is gone.

Leon. How! gone?

Serv. Is dead.

Leon. Apollo 's angry; and the heavens themselves
Do strike at my injustice. *Hermione swoons.*
How now there!

Paul. This news is mortal to the Queen. Look down
And see what Death is doing.

Leon. Take her hence;
Her heart is but o'ercharg'd; she will recover.
I have too much believ'd mine own suspicion.
Beseech you, tenderly apply to her
Some remedies for life.

Exeunt Paulina and Ladies, with Hermione.

Apollo, pardon
My great profaneness 'gainst thine oracle!
I 'll reconcile me to Polixenes,
New woo my queen, recall the good Camillo,
Whom I proclaim a man of truth, of mercy;
For, being transported by my jealousies
To bloody thoughts and to revenge, I chose

145. **conceit**, imagining. 146. **speed**, fortunes.

Camillo for the minister to poison
My friend Polixenes; which had been done,
But that the good mind of Camillo tardied
My swift command, though I with death and with
Reward did threaten and encourage him,
Not doing 't and being done. He, most humane
And fill'd with honour, to my kingly guest
Unclasp'd my practice, quit his fortunes here,
Which you knew great, and to the hazard
Of all incertainties himself commended,
No richer than his honour. How he glisters
Through my dark rust! And how his piety
Does my deeds make the blacker!

Re-enter *Paulina*.

Paul. Woe the while!
O, cut my lace, lest my heart, cracking it,
Break too!

First Lord. What fit is this, good lady?

Paul. What studied torments, tyrant, hast for me?
What wheels? racks? fires? What flaying? boiling
In leads or oils? What old or newer torture
Must I receive, whose every word deserves
To taste of thy most worst? Thy tyranny
Together working with thy jealousies,
Fancies too weak for boys, too green and idle
For girls of nine, O, think what they have done
And then run mad indeed, stark mad! for all
Thy by-gone fooleries were but spices of it.
That thou betray'dst Polixenes, 't was nothing;
That did but show thee of a fool, inconstant
And damnable ingrateful: nor was 't much,
Thou wouldst have poison'd good Camillo's honour,
To have him kill a king; poor trespasses,
More monstrous standing by; whereof I reckon
The casting forth to crows thy baby-daughter
To be or none or little, though a devil
Would have shed water out of fire ere done 't:
Nor is 't directly laid to thee, the death
Of the young Prince, whose honourable thoughts,
(Thoughts high for one so tender) cleft the heart
That could conceive a gross and foolish sire
Blemish'd his gracious dam; this is not, no,
Laid to thy answer: but the last,—O lords,
When I have said, cry "Woe!"—the Queen, the Queen,
The sweet'st, dear'st creature 's dead, and vengeance for 't
Not dropp'd down yet.

First Lord. The higher powers forbid!

Paul. I say she 's dead; I 'll swear 't. If word nor oath
Prevail not, go and see: if you can bring
Tincture or lustre in her lip, her eye,
Heat outwardly or breath within, I 'll serve you
As I would do the gods. But, O thou tyrant!
Do not repent these things, for they are heavier
Than all thy woes can stir; therefore betake thee
To nothing but despair. A thousand knees
Ten thousand years together, naked, fasting,
Upon a barren mountain, and still winter
In storm perpetual, could not move the gods
To look that way thou wert.

Leon. Go on, go on;
Thou canst not speak too much. I have deserv'd
All tongues to talk their bitt'rest.

First Lord. Say no more.
Howe'er the business goes, you have made fault
I' th' boldness of your speech.

Paul. I am sorry for 't.
All faults I make, when I shall come to know them,
I do repent. Alas! I have show'd too much
The rashness of a woman; he is touch'd
To the noble heart. What 's gone and what 's past help
Should be past grief. Do not receive affliction
At my petition; I beseech you, rather
Let me be punish'd, that have minded you
Of what you should forget. Now, good my liege,
Sir, royal sir, forgive a foolish woman.
The love I bore your queen—lo, fool again!—
I 'll speak of her no more, nor of your children;
I 'll not remember you of my own lord,
Who is lost too. Take your patience to you,
And I 'll say nothing.

Leon. Thou didst speak but well
When most the truth; which I receive much better
Than to be pitied of thee. Prithee, bring me
To the dead bodies of my queen and son.
One grave shall be for both; upon them shall
The causes of their death appear, unto
Our shame perpetual. Once a day I 'll visit
The chapel where they lie, and tears shed there
Shall be my recreation. So long as nature
Will bear up with this exercise, so long
I daily vow to use it. Come and lead me
To these sorrows. *Exeunt.*

168. Unclasp'd my practice, revealed my design. **171. No . . . honour,** with no riches but. **185. spices,** foretastes. **201. said,** reported it.

210. stir, remove. **225. my petition,** cf. ll. 210-11. **231. remember,** remind. **241. recreation,** means of restoration of mind.

Scene III. *Bohemia. A desert country near the sea.*

Enter *Antigonus,* with the *Babe,* and a *Mariner.*

Ant. Thou art perfect then, our ship hath touch'd upon
The deserts of Bohemia?
Mar. Ay, my lord; and fear
We have landed in ill time: the skies look grimly
And threaten present blusters. In my conscience,
The heavens with that we have in hand are angry
And frown upon 's.
Ant. Their sacred wills be done! Go, get aboard;
Look to thy bark. I 'll not be long before
I call upon thee.
Mar. Make your best haste, and go not
Too far i' th' land; 't is like to be loud weather.
Besides, this place is famous for the creatures
Of prey that keep upon 't.
Ant. Go thou away;
I 'll follow instantly.
Mar. I am glad at heart
To be so rid o' th' business. *Exit.*
Ant. Come, poor babe.
I have heard, but not believ'd, the spirits o' the dead
May walk again. If such thing be, thy mother
Appear'd to me last night, for ne'er was dream
So like a waking. To me comes a creature,
Sometimes her head on one side, some another;
I never saw a vessel of like sorrow,
So fill'd and so becoming; in pure white robes,
Like very sanctity, she did approach
My cabin where I lay; thrice bow'd before me,
And, gasping to begin some speech, her eyes
Became two spouts; the fury spent, anon
Did this break from her: "Good Antigonus,
Since fate, against thy better disposition,
Hath made thy person for the thrower-out
Of my poor babe, according to thine oath,
Places remote enough are in Bohemia,
There weep and leave it crying; and, for the babe
Is counted lost for ever, Perdita,
I prithee, call 't. For this ungentle business,
Put on thee by my lord, thou ne'er shalt see
Thy wife Paulina more." And so, with shrieks,
She melted into air. Affrighted much,
I did in time collect myself and thought
This was so, and no slumber. Dreams are toys;
Yet for this once, yea, superstitiously,
I will be squar'd by this. I do believe
Hermione hath suffer'd death, and that
Apollo would (this being indeed the issue
Of King Polixenes) it should here be laid,
Either for life or death, upon the earth
Of its right father. Blossom, speed thee well!
There lie, and there thy character; there these,
Which may, if Fortune please, both breed thee, pretty,
Laying down the babe, with a paper and a bundle.
And still rest thine. The storm begins, poor wretch,
That for thy mother's fault art thus expos'd
To loss and what may follow! Weep I cannot,
But my heart bleeds; and most accurs'd am I
To be by oath enjoin'd to this. Farewell!
The day frowns more and more; thou 'rt like to have
A lullaby too rough. I never saw
The heavens so dim by day. A savage clamour!
Well may I get aboard! This is the chase;
I am gone for ever. *Exit, pursued by a bear.*

Enter a *Shepherd.*

Shep. I would there were no age between ten and three-and-twenty, or that youth would sleep out the rest; for there is nothing in the between but getting wenches with child, wronging the ancientry, stealing, fighting. Hark you now! Would any but these boiled brains of nineteen and two-and-twenty hunt this weather? They have scared away two of my best sheep, which I fear the wolf will sooner find than the master. If anywhere I have them, 't is by the seaside, browsing of ivy. Good luck, an 't be thy will! what have we here? Mercy on 's, a barne; a very pretty barne! A boy or a child, I wonder? A pretty one; a very pretty one: sure, some scape. Though I am not bookish, yet I can read waiting-gentlewoman in the scape. This has been some stair-work, some trunk-work, some behind-door-work; they were warmer that got this than the poor thing is here. I 'll take it up for pity: yet I 'll tarry till my son come; he hallooed but even now. Whoa, ho, hoa!

1. **perfect**, certain. 2. **Bohemia**, Shakespeare follows Greene in bestowing a sea-coast upon Bohemia. 21. **vessel**, creature. 22. **So . . . becoming**, the phrase refers both to the person and the vessel, and means so complete and so beautiful. 33. **lost**, i.e., *perdita.*

41. **squar'd**, ruled. 47. **character**, written record of the child's identity. **these**, jewels. 48-9. **Which . . . thine**, may the gold and jewels pay for thy upbringing and leave a residue for thee. 57. **chase**, hunted animal (cf. ll. 65-7). 63. **ancientry**, old people. 64. **boiled**, hot. 70. **barne**, child. 71. **child**, girl. 72. **some scape**, the result of some misdemeanor.

Enter *Clown.*

Clo. Hilloa, loa!

Shep. What, art so near? If thou 'lt see a thing to talk on when thou art dead and rotten, come hither. What ail'st thou, man?

Clo. I have seen two such sights, by sea and by land! But I am not to say it is a sea, for it is now the sky; betwixt the firmament and it you cannot thrust a bodkin's point.

Shep. Why, boy, how is it?

Clo. I would you did but see how it chafes, how it rages, how it takes up the shore! But that 's not to the point. O, the most piteous cry of the poor souls! Sometimes to see 'em, and not to see 'em; now the ship boring the moon with her mainmast, and anon swallowed with yest and froth, as you 'd thrust a cork into a hogshead. And then for the land-service, to see how the bear tore out his shoulder-bone; how he cried to me for help and said his name was Antigonus, a nobleman. But to make an end of the ship, to see how the sea flap-dragoned it; but, first, how the poor souls roared, and the sea mocked them; and how the poor gentleman roared and the bear mocked him, both roaring louder than the sea or weather.

Shep. Name of mercy, when was this, boy?

Clo. Now, now; I have not winked since I saw these sights. The men are not yet cold under water, nor the bear half dined on the gentleman. He 's at it now.

Shep. Would I had been by, to have helped the old man!

Clo. I would you had been by the ship side, to have helped her; there your charity would have lacked footing.

Shep. Heavy matters! heavy matters! But look thee here, boy. Now bless thyself; thou met'st with things dying, I with things new-born. Here 's a sight for thee; look thee, a bearing-cloth for a squire's child! Look thee here; take up, take up, boy; open 't. So, let 's see: it was told me I should be rich by the fairies. This is some changeling; open 't. What 's within, boy?

Clo. You 're a made old man; if the sins of your youth are forgiven you, you 're well to live. Gold! all gold!

Shep. This is fairy gold, boy, and 't will prove so: up with 't, keep it close: home, home, the next way. We are lucky, boy; and to be so still requires nothing but secrecy. Let my sheep go: come, good boy, the next way home.

Clo. Go you the next way with your findings. I 'll go see if the bear be gone from the gentleman and how much he hath eaten: they are never curst but when they are hungry: if there be any of him left, I 'll bury it.

Shep. That 's a good deed. If thou mayest discern by that which is left of him what he is, fetch me to th' sight of him.

Clo. Marry, will I; and you shall help to put him i' th' ground.

Shep. 'T is a lucky day, boy, and we 'll do good deeds on 't. *Exeunt.*

ACT IV. Scene I.

Enter *Time,* the *Chorus.*

Time. I, that please some, try all, both joy and terror
Of good and bad, that makes and unfolds error,
Now take upon me, in the name of Time,
To use my wings. Impute it not a crime
To me or my swift passage, that I slide
O'er sixteen years and leave the growth untried
Of that wide gap, since it is in my power
To o'erthrow law and in one self-born hour
To plant and o'erwhelm custom. Let me pass
The same I am, ere ancient'st order was
Or what is now receiv'd. I witness to
The times that brought them in; so shall I do
To the freshest things now reigning, and make stale
The glistering of this present, as my tale
Now seems to it. Your patience this allowing,
I turn my glass and give my scene such growing
As you had slept between. Leontes leaving,
The effects of his fond jealousies so grieving

90. takes up, devours. **94. yest,** foam. **95-6. land-service,** military as opposed to naval service, i.e., the business on land. **100. flap-dragoned,** swallowed it as one would a snap-dragon, i.e., a raisin in a bowl of burning brandy. **Act IV, Scene i: S. d. Time, the Chorus,** may have been suggested by the sub-title of *Pandosto,* "the Triumph of Time." **2. makes . . . error,** cause and reveal mistakes. **6. growth untried,** events unknown.

119. bearing-cloth, christening robe. **122. changeling,** see note on *Midsummer Night's Dream,* 2. 1. 23. **125-6. well to live,** well off. **135. curst,** fierce. **Act IV, Scene i: 8. self-born,** selfsame.

That he shuts up himself, imagine me,
Gentle spectators, that I now may be
In fair Bohemia; and remember well,
I mentioned a son o' th' King's, which Florizel
I now name to you; and with speed so pace
To speak of Perdita, now grown in grace
Equal with wond'ring. What of her ensues
I list not prophesy; but let Time's news
Be known when 't is brought forth. A shepherd's daughter,
And what to her adheres, which follows after,
Is th' argument of Time. Of this allow,
If ever you have spent time worse ere now;
If never, yet that Time himself doth say
He wishes earnestly you never may. *Exit.*

Scene II. *Bohemia. The palace of Polixenes.*

Enter *Polixenes* and *Camillo.*

Pol. I pray thee, good Camillo, be no more importunate: 't is a sickness denying thee anything; a death to grant this.

Cam. It is fifteen years since I saw my country; though I have for the most part been aired abroad, I desire to lay my bones there. Besides, the penitent king, my master, hath sent for me; to whose feeling sorrows I might be some allay, or I o'erween to think so, which is another spur to my departure.

Pol. As thou lov'st me, Camillo, wipe not out the rest of thy services by leaving me now: the need I have of thee thine own goodness hath made: better not to have had thee than thus to want thee: thou, having made me businesses which none without thee can sufficiently manage, must either stay to execute them thyself or take away with thee the very services thou hast done; which if I have not enough considered, (as too much I cannot,) to be more thankful to thee shall be my study, and my profit therein the heaping friendships. Of that fatal country, Sicilia, prithee speak no more; whose very naming punishes me with the remembrance of that penitent, as thou call'st him, and reconciled king, my brother; whose loss of his most precious queen and children are even now to be afresh lamented. Say to me, when saw'st thou the Prince Florizel, my son? Kings are no less unhappy, their issue not being gracious, than they are in losing them when they have approved their virtues.

Cam. Sir, it is three days since I saw the Prince. What his happier affairs may be, are to me unknown: but I have missingly noted, he is of late much retired from court and is less frequent to his princely exercises than formerly he hath appeared.

Pol. I have considered so much, Camillo, and with some care; so far that I have eyes under my service which look upon his removedness; from whom I have this intelligence, that he is seldom from the house of a most homely shepherd, a man, they say, that from very nothing, and beyond the imagination of his neighbours, is grown into an unspeakable estate.

Cam. I have heard, sir, of such a man, who hath a daughter of most rare note: the report of her is extended more than can be thought to begin from such a cottage.

Pol. That 's likewise part of my intelligence; but, I fear, the angle that plucks our son thither. Thou shalt accompany us to the place; where we will (not appearing what we are) have some question with the shepherd; from whose simplicity I think it not uneasy to get the cause of my son's resort thither. Prithee, be my present partner in this business, and lay aside the thoughts of Sicilia.

Cam. I willingly obey your command.

Pol. My best Camillo! We must disguise ourselves. *Exeunt.*

Scene III. *A road near the Shepherd's cottage.*

Enter *Autolycus,* singing.

When daffodils begin to peer,
  With heigh! the doxy over the dale,
Why, then comes in the sweet o' the year;
  For the red blood reigns in the winter's pale.

The white sheet bleaching on the hedge,
  With heigh! the sweet birds, O, how they sing!
Doth set my pugging tooth on edge;
  For a quart of ale is a dish for a king.

The lark, that tirra-lyra chants,
  With heigh! with heigh! the thrush and the jay,
Are summer songs for me and my aunts,
  While we lie tumbling in the hay.

I have served Prince Florizel, and in my time wore three-pile; but now I am out of service.

5-6. **been aired,** lived. 8. **feeling,** keenly felt. 9. **allay,** alleviation. **or I o'erween,** unless I presume too much. 21. **heaping friendships,** heaping up of friendly acts. 32. **approved,** proved.

35. **missingly,** regretfully. 40-2. **eyes . . . removedness,** servants directed to observe his absences. **Scene iii:** 2. **doxy,** beggar's wench. 4. **pale,** the word means both "pale" and "enclosure," and either sense is possible here—the red blood of spring reigns in the pale blood of winter, or in what had been the domain of winter. The latter sense seems the better. 7. **pugging,** thievish. 11. **aunts,** wenches. 14. **three-pile,** thick expensive velvet.

But shall I go mourn for that, my dear?
The pale moon shines by night;
And when I wander here and there,
I then do most go right.

If tinkers may have leave to live,
And bear the sow-skin budget,
Then my account I well may give,
And in the stocks avouch it.

My traffic is sheets; when the kite builds, look to lesser linen. My father named me Autolycus, who being, as I am, littered under Mercury, was likewise a snapper-up of unconsidered trifles. With die and drab I purchased this caparison, and my revenue is the silly cheat. Gallows and knock are too powerful on the highway; beating and hanging are terrors to me; for the life to come, I sleep out the thought of it. A prize! a prize!

Enter *Clown.*

Clo. Let me see: every 'leven wether tods; every tod yields pound and odd shilling; fifteen hundred shorn, what comes the wool to?

Aut. [*Aside.*] If the springe hold, the cock 's mine.

Clo. I cannot do 't without counters. Let me see: what am I to buy for our sheep-shearing feast? Three pound of sugar, five pound of currants, rice,—what will this sister of mine do with rice? But my father hath made her mistress of the feast, and she lays it on. She hath made me four-and-twenty nosegays for the shearers, three-man song-men all, and very good ones; but they are most of them means and bases; but one puritan amongst them, and he sings psalms to hornpipes. I must have saffron to colour the warden pies; mace; dates—none, that 's out of my note; nutmegs, seven; a race or two of ginger, but that I may beg; four pounds of prunes, and as many of raisins o' the sun.

Aut. O that ever I was born!

Grovelling on the ground.

Clo. I' th' name of me—

Aut. O, help me, help me! pluck but off these rags, and then, death, death!

Clo. Alack, poor soul! thou hast need of more rags to lay on thee, rather than have these off.

Aut. O sir, the loathsomeness of them offend me more than the stripes I have received, which are mighty ones and millions.

Clo. Alas, poor man! a million of beating may come to a great matter.

Aut. I am robbed, sir, and beaten; my money and apparel ta'en from me, and these detestable things put upon me.

Clo. What, by a horseman, or a footman?

Aut. A footman, sweet sir, a footman.

Clo. Indeed, he should be a footman by the garments he has left with thee. If this be a horseman's coat, it hath seen very hot service. Lend me thy hand, I 'll help thee. Come, lend me thy hand.

Aut. O, good sir, tenderly, O!

Clo. Alas, poor soul!

Aut. O, good sir, softly, good sir! I fear, sir, my shoulder-blade is out.

Clo. How now! canst stand?

Aut. Softly, dear sir; [*picking his pocket*] good sir, softly. You ha' done me a charitable office.

Clo. Dost lack any money? I have a little money for thee.

Aut. No, good sweet sir; no, I beseech you, sir. I have a kinsman not past three quarters of a mile hence, unto whom I was going. I shall there have money, or anything I want. Offer me no money, I pray you; that kills my heart.

Clo. What manner of fellow was he that robbed you?

Aut. A fellow, sir, that I have known to go about with troll-my-dames. I knew him once a servant of the Prince. I cannot tell, good sir, for which of his virtues it was, but he was certainly whipped out of the court.

Clo. His vices, you would say; there 's no virtue whipp'd out of the court: they cherish it to make it stay there; and yet it will no more but abide.

Aut. Vices, I would say, sir. I know this man well: he hath been since an ape-bearer; then a process-server, a bailiff; then he compassed a motion of the Prodigal Son, and married a tinker's wife within a mile where my land and living lies; and, having flown over many knavish professions, he settled only in rogue. Some call him Autolycus.

Clo. Out upon him! prig, for my life, prig: he haunts wakes, fairs, and bear-baitings.

Aut. Very true, sir; he, sir, he: that 's the rogue that put me into this apparel.

20. budget, wallet. **23-4. My . . . linen,** I steal large sheets; when the kite is building its nest, keep an eye on your smaller pieces of linen, which it is fond of. **24. under Mercury,** the mythological Autolycus, was the son of Mercury, god of thieves, and was a thief himself. So the modern Autolycus was born when the planet Mercury was in the ascendant. **26-7. With . . . caparison,** through dice and disreputable women I acquired this outfit, i.e., his rags. **27. is . . . cheat,** is derived from petty thieving. **28. knock,** blows of travelers. **33. every . . . tods,** every eleven sheep yield a tod (28 lbs.) of wool. **36. springe,** snare. **cock's,** woodcock's (a proverbially stupid bird). **38. counters,** imitation coins used for reckoning. **44. three-man song-men,** singers of catches. **46. means,** tenors. **47. hornpipes,** i.e., gay tunes. **48. saffron,** orange-red coloring. **warden,** made of warden pears. **49. note,** list. **50. race,** root. **52. o' the sun,** sun-dried.

92. troll-my-dames, a game in which balls were "trolled" through arches set on a board. **99. abide,** stay but a short time. **101. ape-bearer,** showman with a trained monkey. **102-3. compassed a motion,** got possession of a puppet show. **108. prig,** thief.

Clo. Not a more cowardly rogue in all Bohemia: if you had but looked big and spit at him, he 'd have run.

Aut. I must confess to you, sir, I am no fighter: I am false of heart that way; and that he knew, I warrant him.

Clo. How do you now?

Aut. Sweet sir, much better than I was; I can stand and walk. I will even take my leave of you, and pace softly towards my kinsman's.

Clo. Shall I bring thee on the way?

Aut. No, good-faced sir; no, sweet sir.

Clo. Then fare thee well. I must go buy spices for our sheep-shearing. *Exit.*

Aut. Prosper you, sweet sir!—Your purse is not hot enough to purchase your spice. I 'll be with you at your sheep-shearing too: if I make not this cheat bring out another and the shearers prove sheep, let me be unrolled and my name put in the book of virtue!

Song

Jog on, jog on, the foot-path way,
And merrily hent the stile-a;
A merry heart goes all the day
Your sad tires in a mile-a. *Exit.*

Scene IV. *Bohemia. The Shepherd's cottage.*

Enter *Florizel* and *Perdita.*

Flo. These your unusual weeds to each part of you
Does give a life; no shepherdess, but Flora,
Peering in April's front. This your sheep-shearing
Is as a meeting of the petty gods,
And you the queen on 't.

Per. Sir, my gracious lord,
To chide at your extremes it not becomes me.
O, pardon, that I name them! Your high self,
The gracious mark o' th' land, you have obscur'd
With a swain's wearing, and me, poor lowly maid,
Most goddess-like prank'd up. But that our feasts
In every mess have folly, and the feeders
Digest it with a custom, I should blush
To see you so attir'd; sworn, I think,
To show myself a glass.

Flo. I bless the time
When my good falcon made her flight across
Thy father's ground.

Per. Now Jove afford you cause!
To me the difference forges dread; your greatness
Hath not been us'd to fear. Even now I tremble
To think your father, by some accident,
Should pass this way as you did. O, the Fates!
How would he look, to see his work so noble
Vilely bound up? What would he say? Or how
Should I, in these my borrowed flaunts, behold
The sternness of his presence?

Flo. Apprehend
Nothing but jollity. The gods themselves,
Humbling their deities to love, have taken
The shapes of beasts upon them. Jupiter
Became a bull, and bellow'd; the green Neptune
A ram, and bleated; and the fire-rob'd god,
Golden Apollo, a poor humble swain,
As I seem now. Their transformations
Were never for a piece of beauty rarer,
Nor in a way so chaste, since my desires
Run not before mine honour, nor my lusts
Burn hotter than my faith.

Per. O, but, sir,
Your resolution cannot hold, when 't is
Oppos'd, as it must be, by th' power of the King.
One of these two must be necessities,
Which then will speak, that you must change this purpose,
Or I my life.

Flo. Thou dearest Perdita,
With these forc'd thoughts, I prithee, darken not
The mirth o' th' feast. Or I 'll be thine, my fair,
Or not my father's. For I cannot be
Mine own, nor anything to any, if
I be not thine. To this I am most constant,
Though destiny say no. Be merry, gentle!
Strangle such thoughts as these with anything
That you behold the while. Your guests are coming.
Lift up your countenance, as it were the day
Of celebration of that nuptial which
We two have sworn shall come.

Per. O lady Fortune,
Stand you auspicious!

Flo. See, your guests approach.
Address yourself to entertain them sprightly,
And let 's be red with mirth.

130. unrolled, struck off the roll of thieves. **133. hent,** take. **Scene iv: 1. unusual weeds,** Perdita is in a fancy dress designed by Florizel; cf. ll. 9-10 below. **3. Peering . . . front,** appearing, peeping at the beginning of April. **6. extremes,** extravagant compliments. **11. mess,** course. **12. with a custom,** from habit. **13-14. sworn . . . glass,** as if you were sworn to show me, as in a glass, my true station.

17. difference, i.e., in rank. **22. bound up,** like a book, i.e., dressed. **23. flaunts,** finery.

Enter *Shepherd, Clown, Mopsa, Dorcas,* and others, with *Polixenes* and *Camillo* disguised.

Shep. Fie, daughter! when my old wife liv'd, upon
This day she was both pantler, butler, cook,
Both dame and servant; welcom'd all, serv'd all;
Would sing her song and dance her turn; now here,
At upper end o' th' table, now i' th' middle;
On his shoulder, and his; her face o' fire
With labour; and the thing she took to quench it,
She would to each one sip. You are retired,
As if you were a feasted one and not
The hostess of the meeting: pray you, bid
These unknown friends to 's welcome, for it is
A way to make us better friends, more known.
Come, quench your blushes, and present yourself
That which you are, mistress o' the feast. Come on,
And bid us welcome to your sheep-shearing,
As your good flock shall prosper.
Per. [*To Polixenes.*] Sir, welcome.
It is my father's will I should take on me
The hostess-ship o' the day. [*To Camillo.*] You 're welcome, sir.
Give me those flowers there, Dorcas. Reverend sirs,
For you there 's rosemary and rue; these keep
Seeming and savour all the winter long.
Grace and remembrance be to you both,
And welcome to our shearing!
Pol. Shepherdess,—
A fair one are you—well you fit our ages
With flowers of winter.
Per. Sir, the year growing ancient,
Not yet on summer's death, nor on the birth
Of trembling winter, the fairest flowers o' th' season
Are our carnations and streak'd gillyflowers,
Which some call Nature's bastards: of that kind
Our rustic garden 's barren; and I care not
To get slips of them.
Pol. Wherefore, gentle maiden,
Do you neglect them?
Per. For I have heard it said
There is an art which in their piedness shares
With great creating Nature.
Pol. Say there be;
Yet Nature is made better by no mean
But Nature makes that mean; so, over that art
Which you say adds to Nature, is an art
That Nature makes. You see, sweet maid, we marry
A gentler scion to the wildest stock,
And make conceive a bark of baser kind
By bud of nobler race. This is an art
Which does mend Nature, change it rather, but
The art itself is Nature.
Per. So it is.
Pol. Then make your garden rich in gillyflowers,
And do not call them bastards.
Per. I 'll not put
The dibble in earth to set one slip of them;
No more than were I painted I would wish
This youth should say 't were well, and only therefore
Desire to breed by me. Here 's flowers for you;
Hot lavender, mints, savory, marjoram;
The marigold, that goes to bed wi' th' sun
And with him rises weeping. These are flowers
Of middle summer, and I think they are given
To men of middle age. You 're very welcome.
Cam. I should leave grazing, were I of your flock,
And only live by gazing.
Per. Out, alas!
You 'd be so lean, that blasts of January
Would blow you through and through. Now, my fair'st friend,
I would I had some flowers o' th' spring that might
Become your time of day; and yours, and yours,
That wear upon your virgin branches yet
Your maidenheads growing. O Proserpina,
For the flowers now, that frighted thou let'st fall
From Dis's waggon! daffodils,
That come before the swallow dares, and take
The winds of March with beauty; violets dim,
But sweeter than the lids of Juno's eyes
Or Cytherea's breath; pale primroses,
That die unmarried, ere they can behold
Bright Phœbus in his strength—a malady
Most incident to maids; bold oxlips and
The crown imperial; lilies of all kinds,
The flower-de-luce being one! O, these I lack,

56. **pantler,** servant in charge of pantry. 75. **Seeming and savour,** appearance and perfume. 82. **gillyflowers,** clove-scented pinks. 83. **Nature's bastards,** because grown artificially (cf. ll. 87-88). 89. **mean,** instrument.

100. **dibble,** tool for making holes. 104. **Hot,** aromatic. 116-18. **Proserpina . . . waggon,** while Proserpina was gathering flowers in the vale of Enna, Pluto or Dis, god of the underworld, came up in his chariot and carried her down with him to share his throne. 119. **take,** charm. 122. **Cytherea's,** Venus. 123-4. **That . . . strength,** that die in spring, before the full heat of summer. 126. **crown imperial,** a flower recently imported into England (*fritillaria imperialis*). 127. **flower-de-luce,** iris.

To make you garlands of, and my sweet friend,
To strew him o'er and o'er!
Flo. What, like a corse?
Per. No, like a bank for love to lie and play on;
Not like a corse; or if, not to be buried
But quick and in mine arms. Come, take your flowers.
Methinks I play as I have seen them do
In Whitsun pastorals. Sure this robe of mine
Does change my disposition.
Flo. What you do
Still betters what is done. When you speak, sweet,
I'd have you do it ever; when you sing,
I 'd have you buy and sell so, so give alms,
Pray so; and for the ord'ring your affairs,
To sing them too. When you do dance, I wish you
A wave o' th' sea, that you might ever do
Nothing but that; move still, still so,
And own no other function. Each your doing,
So singular in each particular,
Crowns what you are doing in the present deeds,
That all your acts are queens.
Per. O Doricles,
Your praises are too large. But that your youth,
And the true blood which peeps so fairly through 't,
Do plainly give you out an unstain'd shepherd,
With wisdom I might fear, my Doricles,
You woo'd me the false way.
Flo. I think you have
As little skill to fear as I have purpose
To put you to 't. But come; our dance, I pray.
Your hand, my Perdita: so turtles pair,
That never mean to part.
Per. I 'll swear for 'em.
Pol. This is the prettiest low-born lass that ever
Ran on the green-sward. Nothing she does or seems
But smacks of something greater than herself,
Too noble for this place.
Cam. He tells her something
That makes her blood look out. Good sooth, she is
The queen of curds and cream.
Clo. Come on, strike up!
Dor. Mopsa must be your mistress; marry, garlic,
To mend her kissing with!
Mop. Now, in good time!
Clo. Not a word, a word; we stand upon our manners.
Come, strike up!

Music. Here a dance of Shepherds and Shepherdesses.

Pol. Pray, good shepherd, what fair swain is this
Which dances with your daughter?
Shep. They call him Doricles; and boasts himself
To have a worthy feeding; but I have it
Upon his own report, and I believe it.
He looks like sooth. He says he loves my daughter.
I think so too; for never gaz'd the moon
Upon the water as he 'll stand and read,
As 't were, my daughter's eyes; and, to be plain,
I think there is not half a kiss to choose
Who loves another best.
Pol. She dances featly.
Shep. So she does anything, though I report it,
That should be silent. If young Doricles
Do light upon her, she shall bring him that
Which he not dreams of.

Enter a *Servant.*

Serv. O master, if you did but hear the pedlar at the door, you would never dance again after a tabor and pipe; no, the bagpipe could not move you: he sings several tunes faster than you 'll tell money: he utters them as he had eaten ballads and all men's ears grew to his tunes.

Clo. He could never come better; he shall come in. I love a ballad but even too well, if it be doleful matter merrily set down, or a very pleasant thing indeed and sung lamentably.

Serv. He hath songs for man or woman, of all sizes; no milliner can so fit his customers with gloves: he has the prettiest love-songs for maids; so without bawdry, which is strange; with such delicate burdens of dildos and fadings, "jump her and thump her;" and where some stretch-mouthed rascal would, as it were, mean mischief and break a foul gap into the matter, he makes the maid to answer, "Whoop, do me no harm, good man;" puts him off, slights him, with "Whoop, do me no harm, good man."

Pol. This is a brave fellow.

132. quick, alive. **134. Whitsun pastorals**, morris dances at Whitsuntide. **143. Each your doing**, everything you do. **144. singular**, peculiar to you. **145. what . . . deeds**, what you are now doing. **152. skill**, reason. **154. turtles**, turtle-doves. **163. in good time**, indignant expression such as "I like that."

169. feeding, pasture land. **176. featly**, gracefully. **183. tabor**, small drum. **187. better**, at a better time. **192. milliner**, dealer in women's goods. **194-5. dildos and fadings**, words occurring in ballad refrains. **196. stretch-mouthed**, foul-mouthed. **197-8. break . . . matter**, interject a coarse phrase.

Clo. Believe me, thou talkest of an admirable conceited fellow. Has he any unbraided wares?

Serv. He hath ribbons of all the colours i' th' rainbow; points more than all the lawyers in Bohemia can learnedly handle, though they come to him by th' gross; inkles, caddises, cambrics, lawns: why, he sings 'em over as they were gods or goddesses; you would think a smock were a she-angel, he so chants to the sleeve-hand and the work about the square on 't.

Clo. Prithee bring him in; and let him approach singing.

Per. Forewarn him that he use no scurrilous words in 's tunes. *Exit Servant.*

Clo. You have of these pedlars, that have more in them than you 'd think, sister.

Per. Ay, good brother, or go about to think.

Enter *Autolycus,* singing.

Lawn as white as driven snow;
Cypress black as e'er was crow;
Gloves as sweet as damask roses;
Masks for faces and for noses;
Bugle bracelet, necklace amber,
Perfume for a lady's chamber;
Golden quoifs and stomachers
For my lads to give their dears;
Pins and poking-sticks of steel;
What maids lack from head to heel.
Come buy of me, come; come buy,
come buy;
Buy, lads, or else your lasses cry.
Come buy.

Clo. If I were not in love with Mopsa, thou shouldst take no money of me; but being enthralled as I am, it will also be the bondage of certain ribbons and gloves.

Mop. I was promised them against the feast; but they come not too late now.

Dor. He hath promised you more than that, or there be liars.

Mop. He hath paid you all he promised you. May be he has paid you more, which will shame you to give him again.

Clo. Is there no manners left among maids? Will they wear their plackets where they should bear their faces? Is there not milking-time, when you are going to bed, or kiln-hole, to whistle off these secrets, but you must be tittle-tattling before all our guests? 'T is well they are whisp'ring: clamour your tongues, and not a word more.

Mop. I have done. Come, you promised me a tawdry-lace and a pair of sweet gloves.

Clo. Have I not told thee how I was cozened by the way and lost all my money?

Aut. And indeed, sir, there are cozeners abroad; therefore it behoves men to be wary.

Clo. Fear not thou, man, thou shalt lose nothing here.

Aut. I hope so, sir; for I have about me many parcels of charge.

Clo. What hast here? Ballads?

Mop. Pray now, buy some: I love a ballad in print, o' life, for then we are sure they are true.

Aut. Here 's one to a very doleful tune, how a usurer's wife was brought to bed of twenty money-bags at a burden, and how she longed to eat adders' heads and toads carbonadoed.

Mop. Is it true, think you?

Aut. Very true, and but a month old.

Dor. Bless me from marrying a usurer!

Aut. Here 's the midwife's name to 't, one Mistress Tale-porter, and five or six honest wives that were present. Why should I carry lies abroad?

Mop. Pray you now, buy it.

Clo. Come on, lay it by, and let 's first see moe ballads: we 'll buy the other things anon.

Aut. Here 's another ballad of a fish that appeared upon the coast on Wednesday the four-score of April, forty thousand fathom above water, and sung this ballad against the hard hearts of maids: it was thought she was a woman and was turned into a cold fish for she would not exchange flesh with one that loved her. The ballad is very pitiful and as true.

Dor. Is it true too, think you?

Aut. Five justices' hands at it, and witnesses more than my pack will hold.

Clo. Lay it by too. Another.

Aut. This is a merry ballad, but a very pretty one.

Mop. Let 's have some merry ones.

Aut. Why, this is a passing merry one and goes to the tune of "Two maids wooing a man." There 's scarce a maid westward but she sings it; 't is in request, I can tell you.

Mop. We can both sing it. If thou 'lt bear a part, thou shalt hear. 'T is in three parts.

203-4. **admirable conceited**, very clever. 204. **unbraided**, unfaded. 206. **points**, (1) laces for fastening clothes, (2) arguments. 208. **inkles**, linen tape. **caddises**, worsted tape for garters. 212. **work . . . square**, embroidery on the yoke. 217. **You have**, there are some. 221. **Cypress**, crape. 224. **Bugle bracelet**, bracelet of black beads. 226. **quoifs**, tight-fitting caps. **stomachers**, ornamental covering for the chest. 228. **poking-sticks**, metal rods used in arranging the plaits of ruffs. 235. **it . . . of**, I shall be slave enough to buy. 245. **plackets**, petticoats. 247. **kiln-hole**, fire-place for making malt, hence a place for gossip.

250. **clamour**, silence. 253. **tawdry-lace**, a silk neckerchief called after St. Audrey. They were sold at the fair on St. Audrey's day at Ely. 261. **charge**, value. 268. **carbonadoed**, hacked for broiling.

Dor. We had the tune on 't a month ago.

Aut. I can bear my part; you must know 't is my occupation. Have at it with you.

Song

Aut. Get you hence, for I must go
Where it fits not you to know.

Dor. Whither? *Mop.* O, whither? *Dor.* Whither?

Mop. It becomes thy oath full well,
Thou to me thy secrets tell,

Dor. Me too, let me go thither.

Mop. Or thou goest to th' grange or mill.

Dor. If to either, thou dost ill.

Aut. Neither. *Dor.* What, neither? *Aut.* Neither.

Dor. Thou hast sworn my love to be.

Mop. Thou hast sworn it more to me.
Then whither goest? Say, whither?

Clo. We 'll have this song out anon by ourselves. My father and the gentlemen are in sad talk, and we 'll not trouble them. Come, bring away thy pack after me. Wenches, I 'll buy for you both. Pedlar, let 's have the first choice. Follow me, girls.

Exit with Dorcas and Mopsa.

Aut. And you shall pay well for 'em.

Song

Will you buy any tape,
Or lace for your cape,
My dainty duck, my dear-a?
Any silk, any thread,
Any toys for your head,
Of the new'st and fin'st, fin'st wear-a?
Come to the pedlar;
Money 's a meddler,
That doth utter all men's ware-a.

Exit.

Re-enter *Servant.*

Serv. Master, there is three carters, three shepherds, three neat-herds, three swine-herds, that have made themselves all men of hair. They call themselves Saltiers; and they have a dance which the wenches say is a gallimaufry of gambols, because they are not in 't; but they themselves are o' th' mind, if it be not too rough for some that know little but bowling, it will please plentifully.

Shep. Away! we 'll none on 't. Here has been too much homely foolery already. I know, sir, we weary you.

Pol. You weary those that refresh us: pray, let 's see these four threes of herdsmen.

Serv. One three of them, by their own report, sir, hath danced before the King; and not the worst of the three but jumps twelve foot and a half by th' squire.

Shep. Leave your prating: since these good men are pleased, let them come in; but quickly now.

Serv. Why, they stay at door, sir. *Exit.*

Here a dance of twelve Satyrs.

Pol. O, father, you 'll know more of that hereafter.
[*To Camillo.*] Is it not too far gone? 'T is time to part them.
He 's simple and tells much. [*To Florizel.*] How now, fair shepherd!
Your heart is full of something that does take
Your mind from feasting. Sooth, when I was young
And handed love as you do, I was wont
To load my she with knacks: I would have ransack'd
The pedlar's silken treasury and have pour'd it
To her acceptance; you have let him go
And nothing marted with him. If your lass
Interpretation should abuse and call this
Your lack of love or bounty, you were straited
For a reply; at least if you make a care
Of happy holding her.

Flo. Old sir, I know
She prizes not such trifles as these are:
The gifts she looks from me are pack'd and lock'd
Up in my heart; which I have given already,
But not deliver'd. O, hear me breathe my life
Before this ancient sir, whom it should seem,
Hath sometime lov'd! I take thy hand, this hand,
As soft as dove's down and as white as it,
Or Ethiopian's tooth, or the fann'd snow that 's bolted
By the northern blasts twice o'er.

Pol. What follows this?
How prettily the young swain seems to wash
The hand was fair before! I have put you out.
But to your protestation; let me hear
What you profess.

Flo. Do, and be witness to 't.

Pol. And this my neighbour too?

Flo. And he, and more
Than he, and men, the earth, the heavens, and all:
That, were I crown'd the most imperial monarch,
Thereof most worthy, were I the fairest youth

330. **utter**, bring out for sale. 333. **men of hair**, dressed in skins. 334. **Saltiers**, satyrs. 335. **gallimaufry**, medley. 339. **bowling**, a quiet, aristocratic game. 346. **danced . . . King**, this satyr-dance is thought to be an imitation of Jonson's masque, *Oberon*, produced at Court on January 1, 1611.

348. **squire**, foot rule. 358. **handed**, handled, was in 359. **knacks**, knickknacks. 362. **marted with**, bought from. 363. **Interpretation . . . abuse**, misinterpret. 364. **straited**, at a loss. 374. **bolted**, sifted. 377. **put you out**, interrupted you.

That ever made eye swerve, had force and knowledge
More than was ever man's, I would not prize them
Without her love; for her employ them all;
Commend them and condemn them to her service
Or to their own perdition.

Pol. Fairly offer'd.

Cam. This shows a sound affection.

Shep. But, my daughter,
Say you the like to him?

Per. I cannot speak
So well, nothing so well; no, nor mean better.
By th' pattern of mine own thoughts I cut out
The purity of his.

Shep. Take hands, a bargain!
And, friends unknown, you shall bear witness to 't:
I give my daughter to him, and will make
Her portion equal his.

Flo. O, that must be
I' th' virtue of your daughter: one being dead,
I shall have more than you can dream of yet.
Enough then for your wonder. But, come on,
Contract us 'fore these witnesses.

Shep. Come, your hand;
And, daughter, yours.

Pol. Soft, swain, a while, beseech you.
Have you a father?

Flo. I have; but what of him?

Pol. Knows he of this?

Flo. He neither does nor shall.

Pol. Methinks a father
Is at the nuptial of his son a guest
That best becomes the table. Pray you once more,
Is not your father grown incapable
Of reasonable affairs? Is he not stupid
With age and alt'ring rheums? Can he speak? hear?
Know man from man? dispute his own estate?
Lies he not bed-rid? and again does nothing
But what he did being childish?

Flo. No, good sir;
He has his health, and ampler strength indeed
Than most have of his age.

Pol. By my white beard,
You offer him, if this be so, a wrong
Something unfilial. Reason my son
Should choose himself a wife, but as good reason
The father, all whose joy is nothing else
But fair posterity, should hold some counsel
In such a business.

Flo. I yield all this;
But for some other reasons, my grave sir,
Which 't is not fit you know, I not acquaint
My father of this business.

Pol. Let him know 't.

Flo. He shall not.

Pol. Prithee, let him.

Flo. No, he must not.

Shep. Let him, my son. He shall not need to grieve
At knowing of thy choice.

Flo. Come, come, he must not.
Mark our contract.

Pol. Mark your divorce, young sir, *Discovering himself.*
Whom son I dare not call. Thou art too base
To be acknowledg'd. Thou a sceptre's heir,
That thus affects a sheep-hook! Thou old traitor,
I am sorry that by hanging thee I can
But shorten thy life one week. And thou, fresh piece
Of excellent witchcraft, whom of force must know
The royal fool thou cop'st with,—

Shep. O, my heart!

Pol. I 'll have thy beauty scratch'd with briers, and made
More homely than thy state. For thee, fond boy,
If I may ever know thou dost but sigh
That thou no more shalt see this knack (as never
I mean thou shalt) we 'll bar thee from succession,
Not hold thee of our blood, no, not our kin,
Farre than Deucalion off: mark thou my words.
Follow us to the court. Thou churl, for this time,
Though full of our displeasure, yet we free thee
From the dead blow of it. And you, enchantment,—
Worthy enough a herdsman, yea, him too,
That makes himself, but for our honour therein,
Unworthy thee,—if ever henceforth thou
These rural latches to his entrance open,
Or hoop his body more with thy embraces,
I will devise a death as cruel for thee
As thou art tender to 't. *Exit.*

Per. Even here undone!
I was not much afeard; for once or twice
I was about to speak, and tell him plainly
The self-same sun that shines upon his court
Hides not his visage from our cottage, but

384. made eye swerve, attracted eyes. **409. alt'ring rheums,** weakening rheumatism. **410. dispute,** discuss. **416. Reason,** it is reasonable.

434. cop'st, hast to do. **441. Farre,** farther. **Deucalion,** see note on *Julius Cæsar,* I, ii, 152. **444. dead,** deadly. **enchantment,** i.e., Perdita. **445. him,** i.e., worthy of him. **446. but . . . therein,** apart from his royal rank.

Looks on alike. Will 't please you, sir, be gone?
I told you what would come of this: beseech you,
Of your own state take care: this dream of mine,—
Being now awake, I 'll queen it no inch farther,
But milk my ewes and weep.
Cam. Why, how now, father!
Speak ere thou diest.
Shep. I cannot speak, nor think,
Nor dare to know that which I know. O sir!
You have undone a man of fourscore three,
That thought to fill his grave in quiet, yea,
To die upon the bed my father died,
To lie close by his honest bones; but now
Some hangman must put on my shroud and lay me
Where no priest shovels in dust. O cursed wretch,
That knew'st this was the Prince, and wouldst adventure
To mingle faith with him! Undone! undone!
If I might die within this hour, I have liv'd
To die when I desire. *Exit.*
Flo. Why look you so upon me?
I am but sorry, not afeard; delay'd,
But nothing alter'd. What I was, I am;
More straining on for plucking back, not following
My leash unwillingly.
Cam. Gracious my lord,
You know your father's temper: at this time
He will allow no speech, which I do guess
You do not purpose to him; and as hardly
Will he endure your sight as yet, I fear:
Then, till the fury of his Highness settle,
Come not before him.
Flo. I not purpose it.
I think, Camillo?
Cam. Even he, my lord.
Per. How often have I told you 't would be thus!
How often said, my dignity would last
But till 't were known!
Flo. It cannot fail but by
The violation of my faith; and then
Let Nature crush the sides o' th' earth together
And mar the seeds within! Lift up thy looks.
From my succession wipe me, father; I
Am heir to my affection.
Cam. Be advis'd.
Flo. I am, and by my fancy: if my reason
Will thereto be obedient, I have reason;
If not, my senses, better pleas'd with madness,
Do bid it welcome.
Cam. This is desperate, sir.
Flo. So call it, but it does fulfil my vow;
I needs must think it honesty. Camillo,
Not for Bohemia, nor the pomp that may
Be thereat gleaned, for all the sun sees or
The close earth wombs or the profound seas hides
In unknown fathoms, will I break my oath
To this my fair belov'd; therefore, I pray you,
As you have ever been my father's honour'd friend,
When he shall miss me,—as, in faith, I mean not
To see him any more,—cast your good counsels
Upon his passion; let myself and Fortune
Tug for the time to come. This you may know
And so deliver: I am put to sea
With her who here I cannot hold on shore;
And most opportune to our need I have
A vessel rides fast by, but not prepar'd
For this design. What course I mean to hold
Shall nothing benefit your knowledge, nor
Concern me the reporting.
Cam. O my lord!
I would your spirit were easier for advice,
Or stronger for your need.
Flo. Hark, Perdita! *Drawing her aside.*
I 'll hear you [*To Camillo.*] by and by.
Cam. He 's irremoveable,
Resolv'd for flight. Now were I happy, if
His going I could frame to serve my turn,
Save him from danger, do him love and honour,
Purchase the sight again of dear Sicilia
And that unhappy king, my master, whom
I so much thirst to see.
Flo. Now, good Camillo;
I am so fraught with curious business that
I leave out ceremony.
Cam. Sir, I think
You have heard of my poor services, i' th' love
That I have borne your father?
Flo. Very nobly
Have you deserv'd: it is my father's music
To speak your deeds, not little of his care
To have them recompens'd as thought on.
Cam. Well, my lord,
If you may please to think I love the King
And through him what 's nearest to him, which is
Your gracious self, embrace but my direction,
If your more ponderous and settled project
May suffer alteration. On mine honour,
I 'll point you where you shall have such receiving

456. on alike, on all alike. **468. Where . . . dust,** at the foot of the gallows, without having earth cast on his body by the priest. **489. seeds,** of matter (cf. *Macbeth,* 4, i, 59). **492. fancy,** love.

513-4. Shall . . . reporting, it shall not profit you to know nor is it my business to tell you. **524. curious,** anxious.

As shall become your Highness; where you may
Enjoy your mistress, from the whom, I see,
There 's no disjunction to be made, but by—
As heavens forefend!—your ruin; marry her,
And, with my best endeavours in your absence,
Your discontenting father strive to qualify
And bring him up to liking.

Flo. How, Camillo,
May this, almost a miracle, be done?
That I may call thee something more than man
And after that trust to thee.

Cam. Have you thought on
A place whereto you 'll go?

Flo. Not any yet:
But as th' unthought-on accident is guilty
To what we wildly do, so we profess
Ourselves to be the slaves of chance, and flies
Of every wind that blows.

Cam. Then list to me.
This follows: if you will not change your purpose
But undergo this flight, make for Sicilia,
And there present yourself and your fair princess,
(For so I see she must be) 'fore Leontes.
She shall be habited as it becomes
The partner of your bed. Methinks I see
Leontes opening his free arms and weeping
His welcomes forth; asks thee, the son, forgiveness,
As 't were i' th' father's person; kisses the hands
Of your fresh princess; o'er and o'er divides him
'Twixt his unkindness and his kindness; the one
He chides to hell and bids the other grow
Faster than thought or time.

Flo. Worthy Camillo,
What colour for my visitation shall I
Hold up before him?

Cam. Sent by the King your father
To greet him and to give him comforts. Sir,
The manner of your bearing towards him, with
What you as from your father shall deliver,
Things known betwixt us three, I 'll write you down;
The which shall point you forth at every sitting
What you must say; that he shall not perceive
But that you have your father's bosom there
And speak his very heart.

Flo. I am bound to you.
There is some sap in this.

Cam. A cause more promising
Than a wild dedication of yourselves
To unpath'd waters, undream'd shores, most certain
To miseries enough; no hope to help you,
But as you shake off one to take another;
Nothing so certain as your anchors, who
Do their best office, if they can but stay you
Where you 'll be loath to be: besides, you know,
Prosperity 's the very bond of love,
Whose fresh complexion and whose heart together
Affliction alters.

Per. One of these is true.
I think affliction may subdue the cheek,
But not take in the mind.

Cam. Yea, say you so?
There shall not at your father's house these seven years
Be born another such.

Flo. My good Camillo,
She 's as forward of her breeding as
She is i' th' rear o' our birth.

Cam. I cannot say 't is pity
She lacks instructions, for she seems a mistress
To most that teach.

Per. Your pardon, sir; for this
I 'll blush you thanks.

Flo. My prettiest Perdita!
But O, the thorns we stand upon! Camillo,
Preserver of my father, now of me,
The medicine of our house, how shall we do?
We are not furnish'd like Bohemia's son,
Nor shall appear in Sicilia.

Cam. My lord,
Fear none of this: I think you know my fortunes
Do all lie there: it shall be so my care
To have you royally appointed as if
The scene you play were mine. For instance, sir,
That you may know you shall not want, one word. *They talk aside.*

Re-enter *Autolycus.*

Aut. Ha, ha! what a fool Honesty is! and Trust, his sworn brother, a very simple gentleman! I have sold all my trumpery; not a counterfeit stone, not a ribbon, glass, pomander, brooch, table-book, ballad, knife, tape, glove, shoe-tie, bracelet, horn-ring, to keep my pack from fasting. They throng who

542. qualify, soften. **543. bring . . . liking,** persuade him to accept your choice. **558. free,** generous. **561. him,** i.e., his talk. **565. colour,** excuse. **571. point you forth,** guide you. **sitting,** interview.

586. subdue the cheek, i.e., with tears. **587. take in,** overcome. **599. appear,** i.e., as a prince. **603. instance,** proof. **608. pomander,** scent-ball. **609. table-book,** notebook.

should buy first, as if my trinkets had been hallowed, and brought a benediction to the buyer; by which means I saw whose purse was best in picture, and what I saw, to my good use I remembered. My clown, who wants but something to be a reasonable man, grew so in love with the wenches' song, that he would not stir his pettitoes till he had both tune and words; which so drew the rest of the herd to me that all their other senses stuck in ears: you might have pinched a placket, it was senseless; 't was nothing to geld a codpiece of a purse; I would have filed keys off that hung in chains: no hearing, no feeling, but my sir's song, and admiring the nothing of it. So that in this time of lethargy I picked and cut most of their festival purses; and had not the old man come in with a whoo-bub against his daughter and the King's son and scared my choughs from the chaff, I had not left a purse alive in the whole army.

Camillo, Florizel, and Perdita come forward.

Cam. Nay, but my letters, by this means being there
So soon as you arrive, shall clear that doubt.

Flo. And those that you 'll procure from King Leontes?

Cam. Shall satisfy your father.

Per. Happy be you!
All that you speak shows fair.

Cam. Who have we here?

Seeing Autolycus.

We 'll make an instrument of this, omit
Nothing may give us aid.

Aut. [*Aside.*] If they have overheard me now, why, hanging.

Cam. How now, good fellow! why shak'st thou so? Fear not, man; here 's no harm intended to thee.

Aut. I am a poor fellow, sir.

Cam. Why, be so still; here 's nobody will steal that from thee: yet for the outside of thy poverty we must make an exchange; therefore discase thee instantly,—thou must think there 's a necessity in 't,—and change garments with this gentleman. Though the pennyworth on his side be the worst, yet hold thee, there 's some boot.

Aut. I am a poor fellow, sir. [*Aside.*] I know ye well enough.

Cam. Nay, prithee, dispatch. The gentleman is half flayed already.

Aut. Are you in earnest, sir? [*Aside.*] I smell the trick on 't.

Flo. Dispatch, I prithee.

Aut. Indeed, I have had earnest; but I cannot with conscience take it.

Cam. Unbuckle, unbuckle.

Florizel and Autolycus exchange garments.

Fortunate mistress,—let my prophecy
Come home to ye!—you must retire yourself
Into some covert. Take your sweetheart's hat
And pluck it o'er your brows, muffle your face,
Dismantle you, and, as you can, disliken
The truth of your own seeming; that you may—
For I do fear eyes over—to shipboard
Get undescried.

Per. I see the play so lies
That I must bear a part.

Cam. No remedy.
Have you done there?

Flo. Should I now meet my father,
He would not call me son.

Cam. Nay, you shall have no hat.

Giving it to Perdita.

Come, lady, come. Farewell, my friend.

Aut. Adieu, sir.

Flo. O Perdita, what have we twain forgot!
Pray you, a word.

Cam. [*Aside.*] What I do next, shall be to tell the King
Of this escape and whither they are bound;
Wherein my hope is I shall so prevail
To force him after; in whose company
I shall re-view Sicilia, for whose sight
I have a woman's longing.

Flo. Fortune speed us!
Thus we set on, Camillo, to the sea-side.

Cam. The swifter speed the better.

Exeunt Florizel, Perdita, and Camillo.

Aut. I understand the business, I hear it: to have an open ear, a quick eye, and a nimble hand, is necessary for a cut-purse; a good nose is requisite also, to smell out work for the other senses. I see this is the time that the unjust man doth thrive. What an exchange had this been without boot! What a boot is here with this exchange! Sure the gods do this year connive at us, and we may do anything extempore. The Prince himself is about a piece of iniquity, stealing away from his father with his clog at his heels. If I thought it were a piece of honesty to acquaint the King withal, I would not do 't. I hold it the more knavery to conceal it; and therein am I constant to my profession.

614. picture, appearance. **618. pettitoes,** pig's feet. **620. stuck in ears,** were concentrated in their ears. **621. pinched a placket,** stolen a petticoat. **622. geld a codpiece,** rob a breeches' pocket. **624. my sir's,** i.e., the clown's. **627. whoo-bub,** hubbub. **629. choughs,** jackdaws. **646. discase,** undress. **648-9. the . . . worst,** he has the worst of the bargain.

658. earnest, payment to bind a bargain. **665-6. disliken . . . seeming,** disguise yourself. **667. eyes over,** observing eyes. **694. clog,** encumbrance, i.e., Perdita.

Shepherd decides to tell Polixenes Perdita is not his to save himself.

Re-enter *Clown* and *Shepherd*.

Aside, aside; here is more matter for a hot brain: every lane's end, every shop, church, session, hanging, yields a careful man work.

Clo. See, see; what a man you are now! There is no other way but to tell the King she 's a changeling and none of your flesh and blood.

Shep. Nay, but hear me.

Clo. Nay, but hear me.

Shep. Go to, then.

Clo. She being none of your flesh and blood, your flesh and blood has not offended the King; and so your flesh and blood is not to be punished by him. Show those things you found about her, those secret things, all but what she has with her: this being done, let the law go whistle: I warrant you.

Shep. I will tell the King all, every word, yea, and his son's pranks too; who, I may say, is no honest man, neither to his father nor to me, to go about to make me the King's brother-in-law.

Clo. Indeed, brother-in-law was the farthest off you could have been to him, and then your blood had been the dearer by I know how much an ounce.

Aut. [*Aside.*] Very wisely, puppies!

Shep. Well, let us to the King: there is that in this fardel will make him scratch his beard.

Aut. [*Aside.*] I know not what impediment this complaint may be to the flight of my master.

Clo. Pray heartily he be at palace.

Aut. [*Aside.*] Though I am not naturally honest, I am so sometimes by chance. Let me pocket up my pedlar's excrement. [*Takes off his false beard.*] How now, rustics! whither are you bound?

Shep. To the palace, an it like your worship.

Aut. Your affairs there? What, with whom, the condition of that fardel, the place of your dwelling, your names, your ages, of what having, breeding, and anything that is fitting to be known, discover?

Clo. We are but plain fellows, sir.

Aut. A lie; you are rough and hairy. Let me have no lying. It becomes none but tradesmen, and they often give us soldiers the lie; but we pay them for it with stamped coin, not stabbing steel; therefore they do not give us the lie.

Clo. Your worship had like to have given us one, if you had not taken yourself with the manner.

Shep. Are you a courtier, an 't like you, sir?

Aut. Whether it like me or no, I am a courtier. Seest thou not the air of the court in these enfoldings? Hath not my gait in it the measure of the court? Receives not thy nose court-odour from me? Reflect I not on thy baseness court-contempt? Think'st thou, for that I insinuate, or touse from thee thy business, I am therefore no courtier? I am courtier cap-a-pie, and one that will either push on or pluck back thy business there; whereupon I command thee to open thy affair.

Shep. My business, sir, is to the King.

Aut. What advocate hast thou to him?

Shep. I know not, an 't like you.

Clo. Advocate 's the court-word for a pheasant. Say you have none.

Shep. None, sir; I have no pheasant, cock nor hen.

Aut. How blessed are we that are not simple men!
Yet Nature might have made me as these are,
Therefore I will not disdain.

Clo. This cannot be but a great courtier.

Shep. His garments are rich, but he wears them not handsomely.

Clo. He seems to be the more noble in being fantastical. A great man, I 'll warrant; I know by the picking on 's teeth.

Aut. The fardel there? What 's i' th' fardel? Wherefore that box?

Shep. Sir, there lies such secrets in this fardel and box, which none must know but the King; and which he shall know within this hour, if I may come to th' speech of him.

Aut. Age, thou hast lost thy labour.

Shep. Why, sir?

Aut. The King is not at the palace. He is gone aboard a new ship to purge melancholy and air himself; for, if thou be'st capable of things serious, thou must know the King is full of grief.

Shep. So 't is said, sir; about his son, that should have married a shepherd's daughter.

Aut. If that shepherd be not in hand-fast, let him fly: the curses he shall have, the tortures he shall feel, will break the back of man, the heart of monster.

Clo. Think you so, sir?

Aut. Not he alone shall suffer what wit can

727. fardel, bundle. **733. excrement,** outgrowth, beard. **739-40. having,** estate. **744-8.** Tradesmen give the lie by cheating honest soldiers, who pay them good money, so the tradesmen do not give the lie, they sell it.

750. taken . . . manner, caught yourself in the act. **755. enfoldings,** clothes. **756. measure,** dignified walk. **759. insinuate,** wheedle. **touse,** extract. **761. cap-a-pie,** from head to foot. **768. pheasant,** i.e., as a bribe to a judge in a court of justice. **779. the . . . teeth,** the mark of an Elizabethan man about town. **794. hand-fast,** custody.

make heavy and vengeance bitter, but those that are germane to him, though removed fifty times, shall all come under the hangman; which though it be great pity; yet it is necessary. An old sheep-whistling rogue, a ram-tender, to offer to have his daughter come into grace! Some say he shall be stoned; but that death is too soft for him, say I. Draw our throne into a sheep-cote! All deaths are too few, the sharpest too easy.

Clo. Has the old man e'er a son, sir, do you hear, an 't like you, sir?

Aut. He has a son, who shall be flayed alive; then 'nointed over with honey, set on the head of a wasp's nest; then stand till he be three quarters and a dram dead; then recovered again with aqua-vitæ or some other hot infusion; then, raw as he is, and in the hottest day prognostication proclaims, shall he be set against a brick-wall, the sun looking with a southward eye upon him, where he is to behold him with flies blown to death. But what talk we of these traitorly rascals, whose miseries are to be smiled at, their offences being so capital? Tell me, for you seem to be honest plain men, what you have to the King: being something gently considered, I 'll bring you where he is aboard, tender your persons to his presence, whisper him in your behalfs; and if it be in man, besides the King, to effect your suits, here is man shall do it.

Clo. He seems to be of great authority: close with him, give him gold; and though authority be a stubborn bear, yet he is oft led by the nose with gold: show the inside of your purse to the outside of his hand, and no more ado. Remember "stoned," and "flayed alive."

Shep. An 't please you, sir, to undertake the business for us, here is that gold I have: I 'll make it as much more, and leave this young man in pawn till I bring it you.

Aut. After I have done what I promised?

Shep. Ay, sir.

Aut. Well, give me the moiety. Are you a party in this business?

Clo. In some sort, sir; but though my case be a pitiful one, I hope I shall not be flayed out of it.

Aut. O, that 's the case of the shepherd's son: hang him, he 'll be made an example.

Clo. Comfort, good comfort! We must to the King and show our strange sights: he must know 't is none of your daughter nor my sister; we are gone else. Sir, I will give you as much as this old man does when the business is performed, and remain, as he says, your pawn till it be brought you.

Aut. I will trust you. Walk before toward the sea-side; go on the right hand. I will but look upon the hedge and follow you.

Clo. We are blest in this man, as I may say, even blest.

Shep. Let 's before as he bids us. He was provided to do us good.

Exeunt Shepherd and Clown.

Aut. If I had a mind to be honest, I see Fortune would not suffer me; she drops booties in my mouth. I am courted now with a double occasion, gold and a means to do the Prince my master good; which who knows how that may turn back to my advancement? I will bring these two moles, these blind ones, aboard him: if he think it fit to shore them again, and that the complaint they have to the King concerns him nothing, let him call me rogue for being so far officious; for I am proof against that title and what shame else belongs to 't. To him will I present them: there may be matter in it. *Exit.*

ACT V. SCENE I. *In Leontes' palace.*

Enter *Leontes, Cleomenes, Dion, Paulina,* and Servants.

Cleo. Sir, you have done enough, and have perform'd
A saint-like sorrow: no fault could you make,
Which you have not redeem'd; indeed, paid down
More penitence than done trespass: at the last
Do as the heavens have done, forget your evil;
With them forgive yourself.

Leon. Whilst I remember
Her and her virtues, I cannot forget
My blemishes in them, and so still think of
The wrong I did myself; which was so much
That heirless it hath made my kingdom, and
Destroy'd the sweet'st companion that e'er man
Bred his hopes out of.

Paul. True, too true, my lord:

800. germane, related. **814. aqua-vitæ,** ardent spirits. **816. prognostication,** the almanac. **824. gently considered,** given a gentlemanly present. **825. tender,** introduce. **830. close with him,** take his offer.

843. case, situation, skin.

If, one by one, you wedded all the world,
Or, from the all that are, took something good
To make a perfect woman, she you kill'd
Would be unparallel'd.
Leon. I think so. Kill'd!
She I kill'd! I did so; but thou strik'st me
Sorely, to say I did: it is as bitter
Upon thy tongue as in my thought. Now, good, now,
Say so but seldom.
Cleo. Not at all, good lady.
You might have spoken a thousand things that would
Have done the time more benefit and grac'd
Your kindness better.
Paul. You are one of those
Would have him wed again.
Dion. If you would not so,
You pity not the state, nor the remembrance
Of his most sovereign name; consider little
What dangers, by his Highness' fail of issue,
May drop upon his kingdom and devour
Incertain lookers on. What were more holy
Than to rejoice the former queen is well?
What holier than, for royalty's repair,
For present comfort and for future good,
To bless the bed of majesty again
With a sweet fellow to 't?
Paul. There is none worthy,
Respecting her that 's gone. Besides, the gods
Will have fulfill'd their secret purposes;
For has not the divine Apollo said,
Is 't not the tenour of his oracle,
That King Leontes shall not have an heir
Till his lost child be found? which that it shall,
Is all as monstrous to our human reason
As my Antigonus to break his grave
And come again to me; who, on my life,
Did perish with the infant. 'T is your counsel
My lord should to the heavens be contrary,
Oppose against their wills. [*To Leontes.*] Care not for issue;
The crown will find an heir. Great Alexander
Left his to th' worthiest; so his successor
Was like to be the best.
Leon. Good Paulina,
Who hast the memory of Hermione,
I know, in honour, O, that ever I
Had squar'd me to thy counsel! then, even now,
I might have look'd upon my queen's full eyes,
Have taken treasure from her lips—
Paul. And left them
More rich for what they yielded.
Leon. Thou speak'st truth.
No more such wives; therefore, no wife. One worse,
And better us'd, would make her sainted spirit
Again possess her corpse, and on this stage,
(Where we offenders now appear) soul-vex'd,
Begin, "And why to me—?"
Paul. Had she such power,
She had just cause.
Leon. She had; and would incense me
To murder her I married.
Paul I should so.
Were I the ghost that walk'd, I 'd bid you mark
Her eye, and tell me for what dull part in 't
You chose her; then I 'd shriek, that even your ears
Should rift to hear me; and the words that follow'd
Should be "Remember mine."
Leon. Stars, stars,
And all eyes else dead coals! Fear thou no wife;
I 'll have no wife, Paulina.
Paul. Will you swear
Never to marry but by my free leave?
Leon. Never, Paulina; so be blest my spirit!
Paul. Then, good my lords, bear witness to his oath.
Cleo. You tempt him over-much.
Paul. Unless another,
As like Hermione as is her picture,
Affront his eye.
Cleo. Good madam,—
Paul. I have done.
Yet, if my lord will marry,—if you will, sir,
No remedy, but you will,—give me the office
To choose you a queen: she shall not be so young
As was your former; but she shall be such
As, walk'd your first queen's ghost, it should take joy
To see her in your arms.
Leon. My true Paulina,
We shall not marry till thou bid'st us.
Paul. That
Shall be when your first queen 's again in breath;
Never till then.

Enter a *Gentleman.*

Gent. One that gives out himself Prince Florizel,
Son of Polixenes, with his princess (she
The fairest I have yet beheld) desires access
To your high presence.
Leon. What with him? He comes not
Like to his father's greatness: his approach,

22. **time,** occasion. 27. **fail,** lack. 29. **Incertain,** irresolute. 35. **Respecting,** compared with. 52. **squar'd me,** adjusted myself.

60. **why to me,** why this insult to me. 66. **rift,** burst. 75. **Affront,** confront. 89. **Like . . . greatness,** in the royal style of his father.

Florizel says his father sent him & that Perdita is a Libyan princess

So out of circumstance and sudden, tells us
'T is not a visitation fram'd, but forc'd
By need and accident. What train?
Gent. But few,
And those but mean.
Leon. His princess, say you, with him?
Gent. Ay, the most peerless piece of earth, I think,
That e'er the sun shone bright on.
Paul. O Hermione,
As every present time doth boast itself
Above a better gone, so must thy grave
Give way to what 's seen now! Sir, you yourself
Have said and writ so, but your writing now
Is colder than that theme, "She had not been,
Nor was not to be equall'd;"—thus your verse
Flow'd with her beauty once: 't is shrewdly ebb'd,
To say you have seen a better.
Gent. Pardon, madam:
The one I have almost forgot,—your pardon,—
The other, when she has obtain'd your eye,
Will have your tongue too. This is a creature,
Would she begin a sect, might quench the zeal
Of all professors else, make proselytes
Of who she but bid follow.
Paul. How? Not women?
Gent. Women will love her, that she is a woman
More worth than any man; men, that she is
The rarest of all women.
Leon. Go, Cleomenes;
Yourself, assisted with your honour'd friends,
Bring them to our embracement. Still, 't is strange
Exeunt Cleomenes and others.
He thus should steal upon us.
Paul. Had our prince,
Jewel of children, seen this hour, he had pair'd
Well with this lord. There was not full a month
Between their births.
Leon. Prithee, no more; cease: thou know'st
He dies to me again when talk'd of. Sure,
When I shall see this gentleman, thy speeches
Will bring me to consider that which may
Unfurnish me of reason. They are come.

Re-enter *Cleomenes* and others, with *Florizel* and *Perdita*.

Your mother was most true to wedlock, Prince,
For she did print your royal father off,
Conceiving you. Were I but twenty-one,
Your father's image is so hit in you,
His very air, that I should call you brother,
As I did him, and speak of something wildly
By us perform'd before. Most dearly welcome!
And your fair princess,—goddess!—O, alas!
I lost a couple, that 'twixt heaven and earth
Might thus have stood begetting wonder as
You, gracious couple, do; and then I lost—
All mine own folly—the society,
Amity too, of your brave father, whom,
Though bearing misery, I desire my life
Once more to look on him.
Flo. By his command
Have I here touch'd Sicilia, and from him
Give you all greetings that a king, at friend,
Can send his brother; and, but infirmity
Which waits upon worn times hath something seiz'd
His wish'd ability, he had himself
The lands and waters 'twixt your throne and his
Measur'd to look upon you; whom he loves—
He bade me say so—more than all the sceptres
And those that bear them living.
Leon. O my brother,
Good gentleman! the wrongs I have done thee stir
Afresh within me, and these thy offices,
So rarely kind, are as interpreters
Of my behind-hand slackness. Welcome hither,
As is the spring to the earth. And hath he too
Expos'd this paragon to th' fearful usage,
(At least ungentle,) of the dreadful Neptune,
To greet a man not worth her pains, much less
Th' adventure of her person?
Flo. Good my lord,
She came from Libya.
Leon. Where the warlike Smalus,
That noble honour'd lord, is fear'd and lov'd?
Flo. Most royal sir, from thence; from him, whose daughter
His tears proclaim'd his, parting with her; thence,
(A prosperous south-wind friendly) we have cross'd,
To execute the charge my father gave me
For visiting your Highness: my best train
I have from your Sicilian shores dismiss'd;
Who for Bohemia bend, to signify

90. **out of circumstance**, unceremonious. 102. **shrewdly**, greatly. 103. **To**, if you now. 108. **professors else**, professing members of other sects. 113. **assisted with**, accompanied by. 114. **to our embracement**, to be welcomed. 123. **Unfurnish**, deprive.

129-30. **something . . . before**, some youthful frolic. 137-8. **desire . . . him**, wish during my life, or, wish to live in order to see him again. 140. **at friend**, on friendly relations. 142. **worn times**, old age. **something**, somewhat. 149. **offices**, gracious words. 156. **adventure**, risk. 163. **my best train**, most of my retinue. 165. **bend**, make.

Not only my success in Libya, sir,
But my arrival and my wife's in safety
Here where we are.
Leon. The blessed gods
Purge all infection from our air whilst you
Do climate here! You have a holy father,
A graceful gentleman, against whose person,
So sacred as it is, I have done sin;
For which the heavens, taking angry note,
Have left me issueless; and your father 's blest,
As he from heaven merits it, with you
Worthy his goodness. What might I have been,
Might I a son and daughter now have look'd on,
Such goodly things as you?

Enter a *Lord.*

Lord. Most noble sir,
That which I shall report will bear no credit,
Were not the proof so nigh. Please you, great sir,
Bohemia greets you from himself by me;
Desires you to attach his son, who has—
His dignity and duty both cast off—
Fled from his father, from his hopes, and with
A shepherd's daughter.
Leon. Where 's Bohemia? Speak.
Lord. Here in your city; I now came from him.
I speak amazedly; and it becomes
My marvel and my message. To your court
Whiles he was hast'ning, in the chase, it seems,
Of this fair couple, meets he on the way
The father of this seeming lady, and
Her brother, having both their country quitted
With this young prince.
Flo. Camillo has betray'd me;
Whose honour and whose honesty till now
Endur'd all weathers.
Lord. Lay 't so to his charge:
He 's with the King your father.
Leon. Who? Camillo?
Lord. Camillo, sir; I spake with him; who now
Has these poor men in question. Never saw I
Wretches so quake. They kneel, they kiss the earth,
Forswear themselves as often as they speak:
Bohemia stops his ears, and threatens them
With divers deaths in death.
Per. O my poor father!
The heaven sets spies upon us, will not have
Our contract celebrated.
Leon. You are married?
Flo. We are not, sir, nor are we like to be.
The stars, I see, will kiss the valleys first;
The odds for high and low 's alike.
Leon. My lord,
Is this the daughter of a king?
Flo. She is,
When once she is my wife.
Leon. That "once," I see, by your good father's speed,
Will come on very slowly. I am sorry,
Most sorry, you have broken from his liking
Where you were tied in duty, and as sorry
Your choice is not so rich in worth as beauty,
That you might well enjoy her.
Flo. Dear, look up.
Though Fortune, visible an enemy,
Should chase us with my father, power no jot
Hath she to change our loves. Beseech you, sir,
Remember since you ow'd no more to time
Than I do now: with thought of such affections,
Step forth mine advocate: at your request
My father will grant precious things as trifles.
Leon. Would he do so, I 'd beg your precious mistress,
Which he counts but a trifle.
Paul. Sir, my liege,
Your eye hath too much youth in 't. Not a month
'Fore your queen died, she was more worth such gazes
Than what you look on now.
Leon. I thought of her,
Even in these looks I made. [*To Florizel.*] But your petition
Is yet unanswer'd. I will to your father.
Your honour not o'erthrown by your desires,
I am friend to them and you; upon which errand
I now go toward him; therefore follow me
And mark what way I make: come, good my lord.
Exeunt.

Scene II: *Before Leontes' palace.*

Enter *Autolycus* and a *Gentleman.*

Aut. Beseech you, sir, were you present at this relation?

First Gent. I was by at the opening of the fardel, heard the old shepherd deliver the manner how he found it; whereupon, after a little amazedness, we were all commanded out of the chamber; only this, methought, I heard the shepherd say, he found the child.

170. climate, sojourn in our climate. **182. attach,** arrest. **187. amazedly,** confusedly. **187-8. it . . . marvel,** as befits my wonder. **202. deaths,** severe tortures.

207. The . . . alike, fortune cheats high and low alike, perhaps with an allusion to false dice. **219. since,** when. **230. Your . . . not,** provided your honor be not. **233. way I make,** success I have.

Aut. I would most gladly know the issue of it.

First Gent. I make a broken delivery of the business; but the changes I perceived in the King and Camillo were very notes of admiration. They seemed almost, with staring on one another, to tear the cases of their eyes. There was speech in their dumbness, language in their very gesture; they looked as they had heard of a world ransom'd, or one destroyed: a notable passion of wonder appeared in them; but the wisest beholder, that knew no more but seeing, could not say if th' importance were joy or sorrow; but in the extremity of the one, it must needs be.

Enter another *Gentleman.*

Here comes a gentleman that haply knows more. The news, Rogero?

Sec. Gent. Nothing but bonfires: the oracle is fulfilled; the King's daughter is found; such a deal of wonder is broken out within this hour that ballad-makers cannot be able to express it.

Enter a third *Gentleman.*

Here comes the Lady Paulina's steward: he can deliver you more. How goes it now, sir? This news which is called true is so like an old tale, that the verity of it is in strong suspicion: has the King found his heir?

Third Gent. Most true, if ever truth were pregnant by circumstance: that which you hear you 'll swear you see, there is such unity in the proofs. The mantle of Queen Hermione's, her jewel about the neck of it, the letters of Antigonus found with it, which they know to be his character, the majesty of the creature in resemblance of the mother, the affection of nobleness which nature shows above her breeding, and many other evidences proclaim her with all certainty to be the King's daughter. Did you see the meeting of the two kings?

Sec. Gent. No.

Third Gent. Then have you lost a sight which was to be seen, cannot be spoken of. There might you have beheld one joy crown another, so in and such manner that it seemed sorrow wept to take leave of them, for their joy waded in tears. There was casting up of eyes, holding up of hands, with countenance of such distraction that they were to be known by garment, not by favour. Our king, being ready to leap out of himself for joy of his found daughter, as if that joy were now become a loss, cries, "O, thy mother, thy mother!" then asks Bohemia forgiveness; then embraces his son-in-law; then again worries he his daughter with clipping her; now he thanks the old shepherd, which stands by like a weatherbitten conduit of many kings' reigns. I never heard of such another encounter, which lames report to follow it and undoes description to do it.

Sec. Gent. What, pray you, became of Antigonus, that carried hence the child?

Third Gent. Like an old tale still, which will have matter to rehearse, though credit be asleep and not an ear open. He was torn to pieces with a bear; this avouches the shepherd's son, who has not only his innocence, which seems much, to justify him, but a handkerchief and rings of his that Paulina knows.

First Gent. What became of his bark and his followers?

Third Gent. Wrecked the same instant of their master's death and in the view of the shepherd; so that all the instruments which aided to expose the child were even then lost when it was found. But O, the noble combat that 'twixt joy and sorrow was fought in Paulina! She had one eye declined for the loss of her husband, another elevated that the oracle was fulfilled. She lifted the Princess from the earth, and so locks her in embracing, as if she would pin her to her heart that she might no more be in danger of losing.

First Gent. The dignity of this act was worth the audience of kings and princes; for by such was it acted.

Third Gent. One of the prettiest touches of all, and that which angled for mine eyes, (caught the water though not the fish) was when, at the relation of the Queen's death, with the manner how she came to 't bravely confessed and lamented by the King, how attentiveness wounded his daughter; till, from one sign of dolour to another, she did, with an "Alas," I would fain say, bleed tears, for I am sure my heart wept blood. Who was most marble there changed colour; some swooned, all sorrowed. If all the world could have seen 't, the woe had been universal.

First Gent. Are they returned to the court?

Third Gent. No. The Princess hearing of her mother's statue, which is in the keeping of Paulina,—a piece many years in doing and now newly performed by that rare Italian

10. make . . . delivery, give an incoherent account. **12-13. notes of admiration**, exclamation marks. **14. cases**, sockets. **19. no . . . seeing**, no more than he could see. **20. importance**, import. **34. pregnant by circumstance**, made convincing by circumstantial evidence. **38. character**, handwriting. **40. affection**, instinct. **50. countenance**, appearance.

53. favour, face. **58. clipping**, embracing. **60. weatherbitten**, weather-beaten. **conduit**, fountain, in the form of a statue. **63. do**, describe. **70. innocence**, stupidity. **91. water**, i.e., tears. **98. marble**, hardhearted. **105. performed**, completed.

master, Julio Romano, who, had he himself eternity and could put breath into his work, would beguile Nature of her custom, so perfectly he is her ape: he so near to Hermione hath done Hermione that they say one would speak to her and stand in hope of answer. Thither with all greediness of affection are they gone, and there they intend to sup.

Sec. Gent. I thought she had some great matter there in hand; for she hath privately twice or thrice a day, ever since the death of Hermione, visited that removed house. Shall we thither and with our company piece the rejoicing?

First Gent. Who would be thence that has the benefit of access? Every wink of an eye some new grace will be born: our absence makes us unthrifty to our knowledge. Let 's along.

Exeunt Gentlemen.

Aut. Now, had I not the dash of my former life in me, would preferment drop on my head. I brought the old man and his son aboard the Prince, told him I heard them talk of a fardel and I know not what; but he at that time, overfond of the shepherd's daughter (so he then took her to be) who began to be much sea-sick, and himself little better, extremity of weather continuing, this mystery remained undiscovered. But 't is all one to me; for had I been the finder out of this secret, it would not have relished among my other discredits.

Enter *Shepherd* and *Clown.*

Here come those I have done good to against my will, and already appearing in the blossoms of their fortune.

Shep. Come, boy; I am past moe children, but thy sons and daughters will be all gentlemen born.

Clo. You are well met, sir. You denied to fight with me this other day, because I was no gentleman born. See you these clothes? Say you see them not and think me still no gentleman born. You were best say these robes are not gentlemen born. Give me the lie, do, and try whether I am not now a gentleman born.

Aut. I know you are now, sir, a gentleman born.

Clo. Ay, and have been so any time these four hours.

Shep. And so have I, boy.

Clo. So you have; but I was a gentleman born before my father; for the King's son took me by the hand, and called me brother; and then the two kings called my father brother; and then the Prince, my brother, and the Princess, my sister, called my father father; and so we wept, and there was the first gentleman-like tears that ever we shed.

Shep. We may live, son, to shed many more.

Clo. Ay; or else 't were hard luck, being in so preposterous estate as we are.

Aut. I humbly beseech you, sir, to pardon me all the faults I have committed to your worship, and to give me your good report to the Prince my master.

Shep. Prithee, son, do; for we must be gentle, now we are gentlemen.

Clo. Thou wilt amend thy life?

Aut. Ay, an it like your good worship.

Clo. Give me thy hand: I will swear to the Prince thou art as honest a true fellow as any is in Bohemia.

Shep. You may say it, but not swear it.

Clo. Not swear it, now I am a gentleman? Let boors and franklins say it, I 'll swear it.

Shep. How if it be false, son?

Clo. If it be ne'er so false, a true gentleman may swear it in the behalf of his friend; and I 'll swear to the Prince thou art a tall fellow of thy hands and that thou wilt not be drunk; but I know thou art no tall fellow of thy hands and that thou wilt be drunk; but I 'll swear it, and I would thou wouldst be a tall fellow of thy hands.

Aut. I will prove so, sir, to my power.

Clo. Ay, by any means prove a tall fellow. If I do not wonder how thou dar'st venture to be drunk, not being a tall fellow, trust me not. Hark! the kings and the princes, our kindred, are going to see the Queen's picture. Come, follow us; we 'll be thy good masters.

Exeunt.

Scene III. *A chapel in Paulina's house.*

Enter *Leontes, Polixenes, Florizel, Perdita, Camillo, Paulina, Lords,* etc.

Leon. O grave and good Paulina, the great comfort
That I have had of thee!

Paul. What, sovereign sir,
I did not well I meant well. All my services
You have paid home; but that you have vouchsaf'd,
With your crown'd brother and these your contracted

105. Julio Romano, Italian artist of the 16th century. **106. eternity,** eternal life. **107. custom,** trade. **108. ape,** imitator. **116. removed,** remote. **117. piece,** add to. **120-1. our . . . to,** in being absent we are not increasing. **133. relished,** been appreciated.

174. boors, peasants. **franklins,** small landowners. **178-9. tall . . . hands,** brave fellow in action. **189. be . . . masters,** look after you. **Scene iii: 4. home,** in full.

Heirs of your kingdoms, my poor house to visit,
It is a surplus of your grace, which never
My life may last to answer.

Leon. O Paulina,
We honour you with trouble: but we came
To see the statue of our queen. Your gallery
Have we pass'd through, not without much content
In many singularities; but we saw not
That which my daughter came to look upon,
The statue of her mother.

Paul. As she liv'd peerless,
So her dead likeness, I do well believe,
Excels whatever yet you look'd upon
Or hand of man hath done; therefore I keep it
Lonely, apart. But here it is. Prepare
To see the life as lively mock'd as ever
Still sleep mock'd death. Behold, and say 't is well.

Paulina draws a curtain, and discovers Hermione standing like a statue.

I like your silence; it the more shows off
Your wonder; but yet speak: first, you, my liege;
Comes it not something near?

Leon. Her natural posture!
Chide me, dear stone, that I may say indeed
Thou art Hermione; or rather, thou art she
In thy not chiding, for she was as tender
As infancy and grace. But yet, Paulina,
Hermione was not so much wrinkled, nothing
So aged as this seems.

Pol. O, not by much.

Paul. So much the more our carver's excellence,
Which lets go by some sixteen years and makes her
As she liv'd now.

Leon. As now she might have done,
So much to my good comfort, as it is
Now piercing to my soul. O, thus she stood,
Even with such life of majesty, warm life,
As now it coldly stands, when first I woo'd her!
I am asham'd; does not the stone rebuke me
For being more stone than it? O royal piece
There 's magic in thy majesty, which has
My evils conjur'd to remembrance, and
From thy admiring daughter took the spirits,
Standing like stone with thee.

Per. And give me leave,
And do not say 't is superstition, that
I kneel and then implore her blessing. Lady,
Dear queen, that ended when I but began,
Give me that hand of yours to kiss.

Paul. O, patience!
The statue is but newly fix'd, the colour 's
Not dry.

Cam. My lord, your sorrow was too sore laid on,
Which sixteen winters cannot blow away,
So many summers dry: scarce any joy
Did ever so long live; no sorrow
But kill'd itself much sooner.

Pol. Dear my brother,
Let him that was the cause of this have power
To take off so much grief from you as he
Will piece up in himself.

Paul. Indeed, my lord,
If I had thought the sight of my poor image
Would thus have wrought you,—for the stone is mine—
I 'd not have show'd it.

Leon. Do not draw the curtain.

Paul. No longer shall you gaze on 't, lest your fancy
May think anon it moves.

Leon. Let be, let be.
Would I were dead, but that, methinks, already—
What was he that did make it? See, my lord,
Would you not deem it breath'd, and that those veins
Did verily bear blood?

Pol. Masterly done!
The very life seems warm upon her lip.

Leon. The fixure of her eye has motion in 't,
As we are mock'd with art.

Paul. I 'll draw the curtain.
My lord 's almost so far transported that
He 'll think anon it lives.

Leon. O sweet Paulina,
Make me to think so twenty years together!
No settled senses of the world can match
The pleasure of that madness. Let 't alone.

Paul. I am sorry, sir, I have thus far stirr'd you; but
I could afflict you farther.

Leon. Do, Paulina;
For this affliction has a taste as sweet
As any cordial comfort. Still, methinks,
There is an air comes from her. What fine chisel
Could ever yet cut breath? Let no man mock me,
For I will kiss her.

Paul. Good my lord, forbear.
The ruddiness upon her lip is wet;
You 'll mar it if you kiss it, stain your own
With oily painting. Shall I draw the curtain?

11. content, pleasure. **12. singularities,** rarities. **19. as lively,** in as lifelike a way. **28. nothing,** by no means.

54. him, i.e., Polixenes. **56. Will . . . himself,** will add to his own sorrow. **58. wrought,** moved. **62. Would . . . already,** may I die if it is not moving now. **67. fixure,** fixedness. **68. As,** for so.

Leon. No, not these twenty years.
Per. So long could I
Stand by, a looker on.
Paul. Either forbear,
Quit presently the chapel, or resolve you
For more amazement. If you can behold it,
I 'll make the statue move indeed, descend
And take you by the hand; but then you 'll think—
Which I protest against—I am assisted
By wicked powers.
Leon. What you can make her do,
I am content to look on; what to speak,
I am content to hear; for 't is as easy
To make her speak as move.
Paul. It is requir'd
You do awake your faith. Then all stand still,
On: those that think it is unlawful business
I am about, let them depart.
Leon. Proceed;
No foot shall stir.
Paul. Music, awake her; strike! *Music.*
'T is time; descend; be stone no more; approach.
Strike all that look upon with marvel. Come,
I 'll fill your grave up: stir, nay, come away,
Bequeath to death your numbness; for from him
Dear life redeems you. You perceive she stirs.
Hermione comes down.
Start not; her actions shall be holy as
You hear my spell is lawful: do not shun her
Until you see her die again, for then
You kill her double. Nay, present your hand.
When she was young you woo'd her; now in age
Is she become the suitor?
Leon. O, she 's warm!
If this be magic, let it be an art
Lawful as eating.
Pol. She embraces him.
Cam. She hangs about his neck.
If she pertain to life let her speak too.
Pol. Ay, and make 't manifest where she has liv'd,
Or how stolen from the dead.
Paul. That she is living,
Were it but told you, should be hooted at
Like an old tale; but it appears she lives,
Though yet she speak not. Mark a little while.
Please you to interpose, fair madam; kneel
And pray your mother's blessing. Turn, good lady;
Our Perdita is found.
Her. You gods, look down
And from your sacred vials pour your graces
Upon my daughter's head! Tell me, mine own,
Where hast thou been preserv'd? where liv'd? how found
Thy father's court? for thou shalt hear that I,
Knowing by Paulina that the oracle
Gave hope thou wast in being, have preserv'd
Myself to see the issue.
Paul. There 's time enough for that;
Lest they desire upon this push to trouble
Your joys with like relation. Go together,
You precious winners all; your exultation
Partake to every one. I, an old turtle,
Will wing me to some wither'd bough and there
My mate, that 's never to be found again,
Lament till I am lost.
Leon. O peace, Paulina!
Thou shouldst a husband take by my consent,
As I by thine a wife; this is a match,
And made between 's by vows. Thou hast found mine;
But how, is to be question'd; for I saw her,
As I thought, dead, and have, in vain, said many
A prayer upon her grave. I 'll not seek far—
For him, I partly know his mind—to find thee
An honourable husband. Come, Camillo,
And take her by the hand, whose worth and honesty
Is richly noted and here justified
By us, a pair of kings. Let 's from this place.
[*To Hermione.*] What! look upon my brother. Both your pardons,
That e'er I put between your holy looks
My ill suspicion. This your son-in-law
And son unto the King, whom heavens directing,
Is troth-plight to your daughter. Good Paulina,
Lead us from hence, where we may leisurely
Each one demand and answer to his part
Perform'd in this wide gap of time since first
We were dissever'd. Hastily lead away.
Exeunt.

96. **On**, forward, on with what we have to do.

129. **push**, exciting occasion. 130. **like relation**, a similar story. 132. **Partake to**, share with. **turtle**, turtle-dove. 145. **richly noted**, well known. **justified**, confirmed. 147. **What . . . brother**, Hermione has avoided looking at Polixenes. 149. **This**, this is.

The Tempest

Text.—*The Tempest* stands first in the famous First Folio edition of Shakespeare's plays, 1623. It may have been given this place of honor because of its success at Court where it was performed during the festivities that followed the marriage of the Princess Elizabeth to the Prince Palatine on February 19, 1613. This Folio version is the only text we have; fortunately it seems to have been printed from a good clean copy, and the text is remarkably free from misprints or corruptions. There is some reason to believe, however, that the original version may have been cut down for this performance at Court. The stage directions in the Folio are remarkably full and precise. It has been suggested that they are Shakespeare's own, written at Stratford for a play which he did not expect to direct himself upon the stage in London.

Date.—It is possible to fix the date of *The Tempest* fairly closely. We have first a record of its performance at Court in the late winter of 1613. Another record, long supposed to be a forgery, but now generally accepted, tells of an earlier Court performance on Hallowmas night, November 1, 1611. Inasmuch as only plays that had been successful on the public stage were commanded for Court performances, we may assume that *The Tempest* had achieved such success not later than the Autumn of this year. Some interesting evidence exists to show that it cannot have been written before the Autumn of 1610.

The Virginia Voyage.—During the first years of King James's reign public interest had been rapidly increasing in the first English colony beyond the seas. In the year 1609 great preparations were made for sending additional settlers and provisions to the infant settlement at Jamestown, Virginia, and on June 2 of that year a fleet of nine ships set sail from Plymouth to cross the Atlantic. In mid-ocean they encountered a terrific storm, the fleet was scattered, and the flag-ship, the *Sea Venture,* disappeared from sight. One by one the other vessels struggled into port at Jamestown, but the flag-ship, bearing the leaders of the expedition, Sir George Somers and Sir Thomas Gates, was never seen again. The ship and her crew were given up for lost and mourned in England and Virginia. One can imagine, then, the joyous excitement when in the Autumn of 1610 the news reached England that while the *Sea Venture* had been wrecked, not a life had been lost, and that Somers, Gates, and their companions were safe ashore in Virginia. What had happened was one of the strangest stories in that age of seafaring and adventure. Driven south from her escorts, the vessel had run before the wind and finally crashed on a coral reef half a mile or so from one of the islands of the "still-vexed Bermoothes." By the luckiest of chances she was wedged fast and did not founder and the entire crew got safely to shore. For nine months or more they remained in that "dangerous and dreaded island or rather islands of the Bermudas . . . so terrible to all that ever touched on them, and such tempest, thunders, and other fearful objects are seen and heard about them, that they be commonly called *The Devil's Islands* . . . it being counted of most that they can be no habitation of men, but rather given over to Devils and wicked spirits." [1]

The shipwrecked crew, however, found that this terrible reputation was but ill-deserved. On the contrary the islands proved to be "the richest, healthfullest, and pleasing land." The air was temperate and the country fruitful. The fairies of the rocks proved to be flocks of birds and the devils that haunted the woods only herds of swine. The mariners made a pleasant drink out of cedar berries and found gushings of fresh water by digging. So they lived in comfort through the Autumn and Winter till in the Spring of 1610 they plucked up heart, built a pair of tiny pinnaces from the timbers of the *Sea Venture* and the cedar wood of the islands, launched them safely on May 10, and slipped across a calm sea to Jamestown, where they were welcomed like men risen from the dead.

The good news was carried to England later in the Summer, and in October of 1610 Silvester Jourdan, one of the crew of the *Sea Venture,* published a pamphlet entitled, *A Discovery of the Bermudas, otherwise called the Isle of Divels.* Later in the year there ap-

[1] Quoted from Strachey's *Repertory.*

peared *A True Declaration of the Estate of the Colony in Virginia.* This may have been written by William Strachey, another member of the *Sea Venture's* party. Certainly he did write *A True Repertory of the Wracke and Redemption of Sir Thomas Gates Knight, etc., etc.* It did not appear in print until 1625, when it was included in *Purchas his Pilgrimes,* but there is little doubt that Shakespeare saw it in manuscript, as there is no doubt whatever that he read both the pamphlets mentioned above. A host of verbal parallels between the pamphlets, the letter, and his play, dealing with the storm, the wreck, and the island, show that he had not only read them carefully, but had so steeped his mind in them that again and again he borrowed their very words.

Earlier than the late Autumn of 1610, then, Shakespeare cannot have begun to write *The Tempest.* But there is every reason to believe that he began his work promptly, while the story was still fresh news and he may well have completed it, and turned it over to his company to be produced in the Autumn of the following year, 1611, as, if we may believe Malone and the disputed *Accounts of the Revels,* it was played at Court on Hallowmas night.

Source.—As we have seen, it was the story of the wreck of the *Sea Venture* and the stay of her crew in the Isle of Devils which set Shakespeare to writing a play which would exploit the popular interest in this event. But this story had nothing dramatic in it; background, atmosphere, some few realistic touches it could give him, but little else. Something more was needed, a tale to furnish a definite plot, to give backbone to his projected play. And this tale Shakespeare found. It was an old story of a banished prince who was a magician and had one fair daughter. After years of exile the son of the prince who had dispossessed him comes into his hands, but instead of wreaking revenge on him the enchanter marries him off to his daughter and so heals the ancient feud. There is a Spanish tale something to this effect, but it is unlikely that Shakespeare knew it. A German play, *Die Schöne Sidea,* written by Jacob Ayrer, who died in 1605, has some interesting parallels to *The Tempest,* but on the whole it seems more likely that the Spanish tale, the German play, and Shakespeare's *Tempest,* all derive from a common source, some fairy-tale of banishment, enchantment, and young love, that has been lost to us in the "dark backward and abysm of time." Whatever this source was, we may be sure that Shakespeare dealt with it freely, choosing and rejecting as he saw fit, and shaping its incidents to suit his purpose.

Shakespeare's purpose, we may well believe, when he sat down to write *The Tempest,* was to amuse and delight his audience with a good show. How good a show it is, no one can tell who has not had the fortune to see it acted as Shakespeare meant it to be, upon a stage that in some measure at least resembles the stage for which he wrote. Those who were lucky enough to see it some dozen years ago upon such a stage, produced and directed by lovers of Shakespeare whose one thought was to revive its ancient magic, can testify to its charm. Here was something for all tastes; music, song, and dance, spectacle and pageant, rollicking fun and grotesque shapes, a tale of true love, crossed, but only briefly crossed, and happily concluded, and over all and about all the magic of Shakespeare's verse at its loveliest and sweetest. The laughter and applause of an audience of children at a matinée bore hearty witness to their delight; but no outward sign was adequate to express the joy of a true lover of Shakespeare in seeing a play so long familiar in the closet in lively action upon the stage. *The Tempest* is not, perhaps, great drama, but it is distinctly what Shakespeare meant it to be, a good show, a delightful theatrical entertainment.

Plot and characters.—The story itself, this tale of the wise and good enchanter, his innocent and lovely daughter, the Prince brought to her feet by her father's magic, and the conclusion in which old enmities are forgotten and old wrongs pardoned, is told in the simplest and most straightforward fashion. Here, for once, Shakespeare has observed the famous Unities of Time and Place. Perhaps he did so laughingly to show Jonson and the classicists of his day how easy it was to do; more likely he was wise enough to see how such an observance simplified and speeded up the plot. All the action except the first scene takes place upon the enchanted island, and it all is confined within the brief space of an afternoon. This gives time for the introduction of the masque-like elements, the songs, the dances, spectacles like the disappearance of the banquet "with a quaint device," or the vanishing of the nymphs and reapers "to a strange, hollow, and confused noise"—devices which must have taxed the machinery of Shakespeare's theatre to its utmost. And it is just these masque-like elements that give its special and peculiar charm to *The Tempest.*

The characters, too, are simple and attractive. Here is no Hamlet to baffle the scrutiny of centuries of critics, no Cleopatra to present the eternal riddle of a woman's will. Ferdinand is the Prince Charming of old fairy tales and little more; Miranda is guileless youth and innocence; Prospero is wisdom and benevolence combined; Stephano and Trinculo furnish the fooling demanded by the pit. Ariel is, as his name shows, a spirit of air, the genius or attendant spirit of Eastern magic. Only in the character of Caliban do we find a certain complexity. He is in the first place a monster, the offspring of a witch and a devil; as such he stands at the opposite pole from Ariel. He is of the earth earthy and serves his master with fear and hatred. Prospero's rule, it would seem, extends over all the elements, from the genius of the air to the gnome of earth. There is, however, something more than this in Caliban. His very name, an anagram for Cannibal, would at once suggest to the audience a thought of the American savage, the Carib of the Western Isles. Already the idea of the noble savage, the unspoilt child of nature, had begun to haunt the brains of European thinkers. Shakespeare, we may well believe, had no such idealized conception. What he had heard from voyagers of the "noble savage" led him to believe that this child of nature was almost sub-human, apter to imitate European vices than virtues, treacherous and bloody. Something of all this he put into Caliban, with his bitter hatred of the master who had dispossessed him of his island, his joyful acceptance of the drunken Stephano with his "celestial liquor" as a new and better master, and his treacherous plot to murder Prospero in his sleep. Yet with all this there is a freshness and nearness to nature in Caliban that raises him above the merely brutal. Some of the loveliest lines of the play —"be not afeard; the isle is full of noises"— are put into his mouth, and one can imagine him after the departure of Prospero returning to his old life of indolent freedom with a certain simple happiness.

Theme.—Primarily *The Tempest* is a stage-play to entertain and amuse an audience, but as in all of Shakespeare's work there is something more than this included. It is a commonplace of criticism that the later plays of Shakespeare, *Pericles, Cymbeline, The Winter's Tale, The Tempest,* all deal with the reunion of separated friends and families, with the reconciliation of enemies, and the forgiveness of wrongs. And this dominant theme is most strongly sounded in *The Tempest.* Prospero, the protagonist, has been deeply wronged; the hour has come for his revenge and his enemies are powerless in his hands; but his "nobler reason" overcomes his anger, he knows that "the rarer action is in virtue than in vengeance," and the "sole drift of his purpose" is to lead the evil-doers to confession and repentance. And when this is accomplished he heals the old feud between Milan and Naples by the marriage of Ferdinand and Miranda, heirs respectively of these two states, and prepares for a retirement where "every third thought shall be my grave." In *The Tempest* vengeance yields to mercy, and Evil, represented on the one hand by the shipwrecked lords, on the other by Caliban and his confederates, is impotent, and even ridiculous, in the presence of an all-powerful and benevolent Providence.

Allegory and Autobiography.—Various attempts have been made to read an allegorical significance into *The Tempest.* In Lowell's interpretation, for example, Prospero represents the creative poet, and his attendant ministers the phases of his art; Ariel, the lyric fancy, Caliban, realistic and grotesque comedy. Miranda stands for "pure poetry," Ferdinand for young love; and their union represents the romantic achievement of the poet. It is, of course, impossible to imagine that Shakespeare had any such formulated scheme in his mind, but any reader is at liberty to draw from the play what allegorical significance he can.

What seems more certain is that Shakespeare consciously or unconsciously put more of himself and his outlook on life into *The Tempest* than into any other of his plays, with the possible exception of *Hamlet.* When he wrote *The Tempest* he had already retired to Stratford, coming up to London at infrequent intervals to turn over a manuscript or supervise a production. The thought must have been ever present in his mind that his career, crowded with so many achievements, was fast drawing to a close. It is impossible not to catch the voice of the poet himself when Prospero recounts his deeds of magic (V, i, 40-50), abjures his art, and in the *Epilogue* begs for the indulgence and kind prayers of the spectators. We may well believe that the most famous lines of the play (IV, i, 148-158) represent Shakespeare's final outlook on life, his realization of the transitory nature of all things, "the great globe itself, yea, all which it inherit." But in this final outlook there is none of the bitterness that marks the tragedies. The wisdom of Prospero-Shakespeare is grave, but ripe and kindly. Life for him is over, but life renews itself in the union of Ferdinand and Miranda, "our dear-beloved." *The Tempest* opens with a storm; it closes with "calm seas, auspicious gales." It is a serene sunset after a troubled but glorious day.

Stage history.—The history of *The Tempest* on the stage is almost entirely a story of its increasing and changing embellishments as a spectacle. From the beginning it was a "show" rather than a drama proper, a "show" whose spectacular effects must have taxed all the resources of Shakespeare's theatre, but one adorned, as later versions ceased to be, with much of Shakespeare's loveliest verse.

It was acted at Court in 1611 and again in the series of plays presented in 1613 in honor of the wedding of the Princess Elizabeth. Then it disappears from our ken until the Restoration—unless, indeed, we find an imitation of it in Fletcher's *Sea Voyage,* a play with less spectacle and more varied, if confusing, action than *The Tempest.*

It was one of the plays allotted to Davenant and in 1667 he and Dryden rewrote it in such a way as to shock all lovers of Shakespeare, but one which delighted theatre-goers for over a century. They doubled most of the parts, gave Miranda a wanton sister, invented a youth, prisoner on the island, as ignorant of women as Miranda of men, and provided both Ariel and Caliban with female counterparts. Much of Shakespeare's finest poetry was struck out and its place supplied by indecent Restoration wit. This travesty was at once extremely successful on the stage. Pepys saw it more than once and always with fresh pleasure, "the most innocent play I ever saw" and "full of good variety." He regularly records full houses and at his first attendance notes the presence of the King and the Court.

Encouraged by this success Shadwell a few years later turned the Dryden-Davenant play into an opera, retaining most of their additions and adding very elaborate scenic effects, such as the sinking of the ship in the first scene, a Masque of Furies and a Masque of Neptune. Music vocal and instrumental largely supplanted Shakespeare's poetry and proved vastly attractive to the age; "no succeeding opera" says on old historian "got more money."

In alternating Davenant and Shadwell forms this alteration held the stage till the time of Garrick. After producing, 1756, an operatic version, an improvement on Shadwell's by eliminating much of the Restoration "wit," he had the courage in the following year to produce the play in its original form with some success but not enough to restore it permanently to the stage. As late as 1789 Kemble restored much of the Davenant matter that Garrick had dropped and even in a performance of 1806 he kept the two pairs of lovers.

It was left for Macready, who had rescued *King Lear,* to redeem *The Tempest* from its long degradation. His first production, 1838, running fifty-five nights, definitely established Shakespeare's text as the true acting version.

Repeated performances in the last hundred years have shown the charm and the beauty of Shakespeare's play upon the stage. As a rule it has been presented more or less as a spectacle; in 1857 as a gorgeous show with floating fairies and dissolving scenes; in 1871 with music by Arne and Purcell. Tree staged it splendidly in 1904, playing himself the part of Caliban. That such accessories are not needed was proved to some minds at least by the simple and delightful performance in New York already referred to above, and again by a beautiful amateur production at Princeton in the Spring of 1937.

THE TEMPEST

Names of the Actors

Alonso, King of Naples.
Sebastian, his brother.
Prospero, the right Duke of Milan.
Antonio, his brother, the usurping Duke of Milan.
Ferdinand, son to the King of Naples.
Gonzalo, an honest old counsellor.
Adrian, } Lords.
Francisco, }
Caliban, a savage and deformed slave.
Trinculo, a jester.
Stephano, a drunken butler.
Master of a ship, Boatswain, Mariners.
Miranda, daughter to *Prospero.*
Ariel, an airy spirit.
Iris, }
Ceres, }
Juno, } Spirits.
Nymphs, }
Reapers, }

Other Spirits attending on *Prospero.*

[This list appears at the end of the play in the Folio]

SCENE: *On board a ship at sea; afterwards an uninhabited island.*

ACT I. Scene I. *On board a ship at sea.*

A tempestuous noise of thunder and lightning heard. Enter a *Shipmaster* and a *Boatswain.*

Mast. Boatswain!

Boats. Here, master; what cheer?

Mast. Good; speak to the mariners: fall to 't, yarely, or we run ourselves aground; bestir, bestir. *Exit.*

Enter *Mariners.*

Boats. Heigh, my hearts! Cheerly, cheerly, my hearts! Yare, yare! Take in the topsail. Tend to th' master's whistle.—Blow till thou burst thy wind, if room enough!

Enter *Alonso, Sebastian, Antonio, Ferdinand, Gonzalo,* and others.

Alon. Good boatswain, have care. Where 's the master? Play the men.

Boats. I pray now, keep below.

Ant. Where is the master, boatswain?

Boats. Do you not hear him? You mar our labour. Keep your cabins; you do assist the storm.

Gon. Nay, good, be patient.

Boats. When the sea is. Hence! What cares these roarers for the name of king? To cabin! Silence! Trouble us not.

Gon. Good, yet remember whom thou hast aboard.

Boats. None that I more love than myself. You are a counsellor; if you can command these elements to silence, and work the peace of the present, we will not hand a rope more; use your authority. If you cannot, give thanks you have lived so long, and make yourself ready in your cabin for the mischance of the hour, if it so hap.—Cheerly, good hearts!—Out of our way, I say. *Exit.*

Gon. I have great comfort from this fellow. Methinks he hath no drowning mark upon him; his complexion is perfect gallows. Stand fast, good Fate, to his hanging; make the rope of his destiny our cable, for our own doth little advantage. If he be not born to be hanged, our case is miserable. *Exeunt.*

Re-enter *Boatswain.*

Boats. Down with the topmast! Yare! Lower, lower! Bring her to try wi' the main-course. [*A cry within.*] A plague upon this howling! They are louder than the weather or our office.

Enter *Sebastian, Antonio,* and *Gonzalo.*

Yet again! What do you here? Shall we give o'er and drown? Have you a mind to sink?

Seb. A pox o' your throat, you bawling, blasphemous, incharitable dog!

Boats. Work you, then.

Ant. Hang, cur! hang, you whoreson, insolent noisemaker! We are less afraid to be drowned than thou art.

Gon. I 'll warrant him for drowning though the ship were no stronger than a nutshell and as leaky as an unstanched wench.

Boats. Lay her a-hold, a-hold! Set her two courses off to sea again; lay her off.

Enter *Mariners* wet.

Mariners. All lost! To prayers, to prayers! All lost!

Boats. What, must our mouths be cold?

4. yarely, nimbly. **9. room,** sea-room.

32. complexion, appearance. **38. Bring her to try,** bring her close to the wind. **main-course,** mainsail. **52. a-hold,** close to the wind.

Gon. The King and Prince at prayers!
Let 's assist them,
For our case is as theirs.
Seb. I 'm out of patience.
Ant. We are merely cheated of our lives by drunkards.
This wide-chapp'd rascal—would thou mightst lie drowning
The washing of ten tides!
Gon. He 'll be hang'd yet,
Though every drop of water swear against it
And gape at wid'st to glut him.
A confused noise within: Mercy on us!
We split, we split! Farewell, my wife and children!
Farewell, brother! We split, we split, we split!
Ant. Let 's all sink wi' th' King.
Seb. Let 's take leave of him. *Exit.*
Gon. Now would I give a thousand furlongs of sea for an acre of barren ground, long heath, brown furze, anything. The wills above be done! but I would fain die a dry death. *Exeunt.*

Scene II. *The island. Before Prospero's cell.*

Enter *Prospero* and *Miranda.*

Mir. If by your art, my dearest father, you have
Put the wild waters in this roar, allay them.
The sky, it seems, would pour down stinking pitch,
But that the sea, mounting to th' welkin's cheek,
Dashes the fire out. O, I have suffered
With those that I saw suffer! a brave vessel
(Who had, no doubt, some noble creature in her)
Dash'd all to pieces! O, the cry did knock
Against my very heart. Poor souls, they perish'd.
Had I been any god of power, I would
Have sunk the sea within the earth or ere
It should the good ship so have swallow'd and
The fraughting souls within her.
Pros. Be collected;
No more amazement. Tell your piteous heart
There 's no harm done.
Mir. O, woe the day!
Pros. No harm.
I have done nothing but in care of thee,
Of thee, my dear one, thee my daughter, who
Art ignorant of what thou art, naught knowing
Of whence I am, nor that I am more better
Than Prospero, master of a full poor cell,
And thy no greater father.
Mir. More to know
Did never meddle with my thoughts.
Pros. 'T is time
I should inform thee farther. Lend thy hand,
And pluck my magic garment from me. So,
Lays down his mantle.
Lie there, my art. Wipe thou thine eyes; have comfort.
The direful spectacle of the wreck, which touch'd
The very virtue of compassion in thee,
I have with such provision in mine art
So safely ordered that there is no soul—
No, not so much perdition as an hair
Betid to any creature in the vessel
Which thou heard'st cry, which thou saw'st sink. Sit down;
For thou must now know farther.
Mir. You have often
Begun to tell me what I am; but stopp'd
And left me to a bootless inquisition,
Concluding, "Stay, not yet."
Pros. The hour 's now come;
The very minute bids thee ope thine ear.
Obey and be attentive. Canst thou remember
A time before we came unto this cell?
I do not think thou canst, for then thou wast not
Out three years old.
Mir. Certainly, sir, I can.
Pros. By what? By any other house or person?
Of anything the image tell me, that
Hath kept with thy remembrance.
Mir. 'T is far off
And rather like a dream than an assurance
That my remembrance warrants. Had I not
Four or five women once that tended me?
Pros. Thou hadst, and more, Miranda. But how is it
That this lives in thy mind? What seest thou else
In the dark backward and abysm of time?
If thou remember'st aught ere thou cam'st here,
How thou cam'st here thou may'st.
Mir. But that I do not.
Pros. Twelve year since, Miranda, twelve year since,
Thy father was the Duke of Milan and
A prince of power.
Mir. Sir, are not you my father?
Pros. Thy mother was a piece of virtue, and
She said thou wast my daughter; and thy father
Was Duke of Milan, and his only heir

59. merely, absolutely. **60. wide-chapp'd,** wide-mouthed. **63. glut,** swallow. **Scene ii. 4. welkin's,** sky's. **13. fraughting,** constituting the freight or cargo. **14. amazement,** fear.

27. virtue, quality. **30. perdition,** loss. **31. Betid,** betided, happened. **35. bootless inquisition,** profitless questioning. **41. Out,** quite. **56. piece,** masterpiece.

And princess no worse issued.
Mir. O the heavens!
What foul play had we, that we came from thence?
Or blessed was 't we did?
Pros. Both, both, my girl.
By foul play, as thou say'st, were we heav'd thence,
But blessedly holp hither.
Mir. O, my heart bleeds
To think o' th' teen that I have turn'd you to,
Which is from my remembrance! Please you, farther.
Pros. My brother and thy uncle, call'd Antonio—
I pray thee, mark me—that a brother should
Be so perfidious!—he whom next thyself
Of all the world I lov'd, and to him put
The manage of my state; as at that time
Through all the signories it was the first,
And Prospero the prime duke, being so reputed
In dignity, and for the liberal arts
Without a parallel; those being all my study,
The government I cast upon my brother
And to my state grew stranger, being transported
And rapt in secret studies. Thy false uncle—
Dost thou attend me?
Mir. Sir, most heedfully.
Pros. Being once perfected how to grant suits,
How to deny them, who t' advance and who
To trash for overtopping, new created
The creatures that were mine, I say, or chang'd 'em,
Or else new form'd 'em; having both the key
Of officer and office, set all hearts i' th' state
To what tune pleas'd his ear; that now he was
The ivy which had hid my princely trunk,
And suck'd my verdure out on 't. Thou attend'st not.
Mir. O, good sir, I do.
Pros. I pray thee, mark me.
I, thus neglecting worldly ends, all dedicated
To closeness and the bettering of my mind
With that which, but by being so retir'd,
O'er-priz'd all popular rate, in my false brother
Awak'd an evil nature; and my trust,
Like a good parent, did beget of him
A falsehood, in its contrary as great
As my trust was; which had indeed no limit,
A confidence sans bound. He being thus lorded,
Not only with what my revenue yielded,
But what my power might else exact,—like one
Who having into truth, by telling of it,
Made such a sinner of his memory
To credit his own lie,—he did believe
He was indeed the Duke: out o' th' substitution,
And executing the outward face of royalty,
With all prerogative, hence his ambition growing—
Dost thou hear?
Mir. Your tale, sir, would cure deafness.
Pros. To have no screen between this part he play'd
And him he play'd it for, he needs will be
Absolute Milan. Me, poor man!—my library
Was dukedom large enough—of temporal royalties
He thinks me now incapable; confederates—
So dry he was for sway—wi' th' King of Naples
To give him annual tribute, do him homage,
Subject his coronet to his crown, and bend
The dukedom yet unbow'd—alas, poor Milan!—
To most ignoble stooping.
Mir. O the heavens!
Pros. Mark his condition and th' event, then tell me
If this might be a brother.
Mir. I should sin
To think but nobly of my grandmother.
Good wombs have borne bad sons.
Pros. Now the condition.
This King of Naples, being an enemy
To me inveterate, hearkens my brother's suit;
Which was, that he, in lieu o' th' premises,
Of homage and I know not how much tribute,
Should presently extirpate me and mine
Out of the dukedom, and confer fair Milan
With all the honours on my brother; whereon,
A treacherous army levied, one midnight
Fated to th' purpose did Antonio open
The gates of Milan; and i' th' dead of darkness,
The ministers for the purpose hurried thence
Me and thy crying self.
Mir. Alack, for pity!
I, not rememb'ring how I cried out then,
Will cry it o'er again: it is a hint

59. issued, descended. **64. teen,** grief. **71. signories,** principalities of Italy. **77. secret,** magical, occult. **81. trash for overtopping,** check for rising too high. **83. key,** (1) key to office, (2) tuning key. **91-2.** with that learning which, save for involving retirement, should be valued more highly than it is in popular estimation.

97. sans, without. **100. into,** unto. **100-2.** The meaning seems to be that he had told the lie so often that his memory had betrayed him into believing it. **103. substitution,** deputyship. **112. dry,** thirsty. **117. condition,** agreement. **123. in lieu o' th' premises,** in return for his promises. **134. hint,** occasion.

That wrings mine eyes to 't.
Pros. Hear a little further,
And then I 'll bring thee to the present business
Which now 's upon 's, without the which this story
Were most impertinent.
Mir. Wherefore did they not
That hour destroy us?
Pros. Well demanded, wench;
My tale provokes that question. Dear, they durst not,
(So dear the love my people bore me) nor set
A mark so bloody on the business; but
With colours fairer painted their foul ends.
In few, they hurried us aboard a bark,
Bore us some leagues to sea; where they prepared
A rotten carcass of a butt, not rigg'd,
Nor tackle, sail, nor mast; the very rats
Instinctively have quit it. There they hoist us,
To cry to th' sea that roar'd to us, to sigh
To the winds whose pity, sighing back again,
Did us but loving wrong.
Mir. Alack, what trouble
Was I then to you!
Pros. O, a cherubin
Thou wast that did preserve me. Thou didst smile,
Infused with a fortitude from heaven,
When I have deck'd the sea with drops full salt,
Under my burden groan'd; which rais'd in me
An undergoing stomach, to bear up
Against what should ensue.
Mir. How came we ashore?
Pros. By Providence divine.
Some food we had and some fresh water that
A noble Neapolitan, Gonzalo,
Out of his charity, who being then appointed
Master of this design, did give us, with
Rich garments, linens, stuffs, and necessaries,
Which since have steaded much; so, of his gentleness,
Knowing I lov'd my books, he furnish'd me
From mine own library with volumes that
I prize above my dukedom.
Mir. Would I might
But ever see that man!
Pros. Now I arise.
Puts on his robe.
Sit still, and hear the last of our sea-sorrow.
Here in this island we arriv'd; and here
Have I, thy schoolmaster, made thee more profit
Than other princess can that have more time
For vainer hours, and tutors not so careful.
Mir. Heavens thank you for 't! And now, I pray you, sir,
For still 't is beating in my mind, your reason
For raising this sea-storm?
Pros. Know thus far forth.
By accident most strange, bountiful Fortune,
Now my dear lady, hath mine enemies
Brought to this shore; and by my prescience
I find my zenith doth depend upon
A most auspicious star, whose influence
If now I court not but omit, my fortunes
Will ever after droop. Here cease more questions.
Thou art inclin'd to sleep; 't is a good dulness,
And give it way. I know thou canst not choose. *Miranda sleeps.*
Come away, servant, come; I am ready now.
Approach, my Ariel; come.

Enter *Ariel.*

Ari. All hail, great master! grave sir, hail! I come
To answer thy best pleasure, be 't to fly,
To swim, to dive into the fire, to ride
On the curl'd clouds. To thy strong bidding task
Ariel and all his quality.
Pros. Hast thou, spirit,
Perform'd to point the tempest that I bade thee?
Ari. To every article.
I boarded the king's ship; now on the beak,
Now in the waist, the deck, in every cabin,
I flam'd amazement. Sometime I 'd divide,
And burn in many places: on the topmast,
The yards and bowsprit, would I flame distinctly,
Then meet and join. Jove's lightning, the precursors
O' th' dreadful thunder-claps, more momentary
And sight-outrunning were not; the fire and cracks
Of sulphurous roaring the most mighty Neptune
Seem to besiege, and make his bold waves tremble,
Yea, his dread trident shake.
Pros. My brave spirit!
Who was so firm, so constant, that this coil
Would not infect his reason?
Ari. Not a soul
But felt a fever of the mad, and play'd

146. butt, tub. **155. deck'd,** sprinkled. **157. undergoing stomach,** enduring courage. **165. steaded,** helped.

179. dear, kind. **181. zenith,** high point of fortune. **183. omit,** ignore. **193. quality,** skill. **194. to point,** in every detail. **198. amazement,** terror. **202. momentary,** instantaneous. **207. coil,** turmoil.

Some tricks of desperation. All but mariners
Plung'd in the foaming brine and quit the vessel;
Then all afire with me, the King's son, Ferdinand,
With hair up-staring,—then like reeds, not hair,—
Was the first man that leap'd; cried, "Hell is empty,
And all the devils are here."
Pros. Why, that 's my spirit!
But was not this nigh shore?
Ari. Close by, my master.
Pros. But are they, Ariel, safe?
Ari. Not a hair perish'd;
On their sustaining garments not a blemish,
But fresher than before; and, as thou bad'st me,
In troops I have dispers'd them 'bout the isle.
The King's son have I landed by himself,
Whom I left cooling of the air with sighs
In an odd angle of the isle, and sitting,
His arms in this sad knot.
Pros. Of the King's ship
The mariners say how thou hast dispos'd,
And all the rest o' th' fleet.
Ari. Safely in harbour
Is the King's ship; in the deep nook, where once
Thou call'dst me up at midnight to fetch dew
From the still-vex'd Bermoothes, there she's hid;
The mariners all under hatches stow'd,
Who, with a charm join'd to their suffer'd labour,
I have left asleep; and for the rest o' th' fleet,
Which I dispers'd, they all have met again,
And are upon the Mediterranean float
Bound sadly home for Naples,
Supposing that they saw the King's ship wreck'd
And his great person perish.
Pros. Ariel, thy charge
Exactly is perform'd; but there 's more work.
What is the time o' th' day?
Ari. Past the mid season.
Pros. At least two glasses. The time 'twixt six and now
Must by us both be spent most preciously.
Ari. Is there more toil? Since thou dost give me pains,
Let me remember thee what thou hast promis'd,
Which is not yet perform'd me.
Pros. How now? moody?
What is 't thou canst demand?
Ari. My liberty.
Pros. Before the time be out? No more!
Ari. I prithee,
Remember I have done thee worthy service,
Told thee no lies, made thee no mistakings, serv'd
Without or grudge or grumblings. Thou did promise
To bate me a full year.
Pros. Dost thou forget
From what a torment I did free thee?
Ari. No.
Pros. Thou dost, and think'st it much to tread the ooze
Of the salt deep,
To run upon the sharp wind of the north,
To do me business in the veins o' th' earth
When it is bak'd with frost.
Ari. I do not, sir.
Pros. Thou liest, malignant thing! Hast thou forgot
The foul witch Sycorax, who with age and envy
Was grown into a hoop? Hast thou forgot her?
Ari. No, sir.
Pros. Thou hast. Where was she born? Speak; tell me.
Ari. Sir, in Argier.
Pros. O, was she so? I must
Once in a month recount what thou hast been,
Which thou forget'st. This damn'd witch Sycorax,
For mischiefs manifold and sorceries terrible
To enter human hearing, from Argier,
Thou know'st, was banish'd; for one thing she did
They would not take her life. Is not this true?
Ari. Ay, sir.
Pros. This blue-ey'd hag was hither brought with child,
And here was left by th' sailors. Thou, my slave,
As thou report'st thyself, was then her servant;
And, for thou wast a spirit too delicate
To act her earthy and abhorr'd commands,
Refusing her grand hests, she did confine thee,
By help of her more potent ministers
And in her most unmitigable rage,
Into a cloven pine; within which rift
Imprison'd thou didst painfully remain
A dozen years; within which space she died
And left thee there, where thou didst vent thy groans
As fast as mill-wheels strike. Then was this island—
Save for the son that she did litter here,

218. **sustaining,** upholding (in the water). 229. **still-vex'd Bermoothes,** ever-stormy Bermudas. 234. **float,** sea. 240. **glasses,** hour-glasses. 242. **pains,** tasks. 243. **remember,** remind.

261. **Argier,** Algiers. 266-7. **for one thing she did They would not take her life.** This may refer to some service done to the state. 269. **blue-ey'd,** blear-eyed. 272. **for,** because. 274. **hests,** behests.

A freckl'd whelp, hag-born,—not honour'd with
A human shape.
Ari. Yes, Caliban her son.
Pros. Dull thing, I say so; he, that Caliban
Whom now I keep in service. Thou best know'st
What torment I did find thee in; thy groans
Did make wolves howl, and penetrate the breasts
Of ever-angry bears. It was a torment
To lay upon the damn'd, which Sycorax
Could not again undo. It was mine art,
When I arriv'd and heard thee, that made gape
The pine, and let thee out.
Ari. I thank thee, master.
Pros. If thou more murmur'st, I will rend an oak
And peg thee in his knotty entrails till
Thou hast howl'd away twelve winters.
Ari. Pardon, master;
I will be correspondent to command
And do my spriting gently.
Pros. Do so, and after two days
I will discharge thee.
Ari. That 's my noble master!
What shall I do? say what. What shall I do?
Pros. Go make thyself like a nymph o' th' sea; be subject
To no sight but thine and mine, invisible
To every eyeball else. Go take this shape
And hither come in 't. Go, hence with diligence!
Exit Ariel.
Awake, dear heart, awake! Thou hast slept well;
Awake!
Mir. The strangeness of your story put
Heaviness in me.
Pros. Shake it off. Come on,
We 'll visit Caliban my slave, who never
Yields us kind answer.
Mir. 'T is a villain, sir,
I do not love to look on.
Pros. But, as 't is,
We cannot miss him: he does make our fire,
Fetch in our wood, and serves in offices
That profit us. What, ho! slave! Caliban!
Thou earth, thou! speak.
Cal. [*Within.*] There 's wood enough within.
Pros. Come forth, I say! there 's other business for thee.
Come, thou tortoise! when?

Re-enter *Ariel* like a water-nymph.

Fine apparition! My quaint Ariel,
Hark in thine ear.
Ari. My lord, it shall be done.
Exit.
Pros. Thou poisonous slave, got by the devil himself
Upon thy wicked dam, come forth!

Enter *Caliban.*

Cal. As wicked dew as e'er my mother brush'd
With raven's feather from unwholesome fen
Drop on you both! A south-west blow on ye
And blister you all o'er!
Pros. For this, be sure, to-night thou shalt have cramps,
Side-stitches that shall pen thy breath up; urchins
Shall, for that vast of night that they may work,
All exercise on thee; thou shalt be pinch'd
As thick as honeycomb, each pinch more stinging
Than bees that made 'em.
Cal. I must eat my dinner.
This island 's mine, by Sycorax my mother,
Which thou tak'st from me. When thou cam'st first,
Thou strok'st me and made much of me, wouldst give me
Water with berries in 't, and teach me how
To name the bigger light, and how the less,
That burn by day and night; and then I lov'd thee
And show'd thee all the qualities o' th' isle,
The fresh springs, brine-pits, barren place and fertile.
Curs'd be I that did so! All the charms
Of Sycorax, toads, beetles, bats, light on you!
For I am all the subjects that you have,
Which first was mine own king; and here you sty me
In this hard rock, whiles you do keep from me
The rest o' th' island.
Pros. Thou most lying slave,
Whom stripes may move, not kindness! I have us'd thee,
Filth as thou art, with human care, and lodg'd thee
In mine own cell, till thou didst seek to violate
The honour of my child.
Cal. O ho, O ho! would 't had been done!
Thou didst prevent me; I had peopl'd else
This isle with Calibans.
Pros. Abhorred slave,
Which any print of goodness wilt not take,

297. **correspondent,** obedient. 311. **miss,** do without. 316. **when,** impatient exclamation.

317. **quaint,** fine, dainty. 326. **urchins,** hobgoblins. 327. **vast,** dead void.

Being capable of all ill! I pitied thee,
Took pains to make thee speak, taught thee each hour
One thing or other: when thou didst not, savage,
Know thine own meaning, but wouldst gabble like
A thing most brutish, I endow'd thy purposes
With words that made them known. But thy vile race,
Though thou didst learn, had that in 't which good natures
Could not abide to be with; therefore wast thou
Deservedly confin'd into this rock, who hadst
Deserv'd more than a prison.
Cal. You taught me language; and my profit on 't
Is, I know how to curse. The red plague rid you
For learning me your language!
Pros. Hag-seed, hence!
Fetch us in fuel; and be quick, thou 'rt best,
To answer other business. Shrug'st thou, malice?
If thou neglect'st or dost unwillingly
What I command, I 'll rack thee with old cramps,
Fill all thy bones with aches, make thee roar
That beasts shall tremble at thy din.
Cal. No, pray thee.
[*Aside.*] I must obey. His art is of such power
It would control my dam's god, Setebos,
And make a vassal of him.
Pros. So, slave; hence!
Exit Caliban.

Enter *Ferdinand;* and *Ariel,* invisible, playing and singing.

ARIEL'S SONG

Come unto these yellow sands,
And then take hands.
Curtsied when you have, and kiss'd
The wild waves whist,
Foot it featly here and there,
And, sweet sprites, bear
The burthen.

Burthen dispersedly

Hark, hark! bow-wow,
The watch dogs bark! Bow-wow!
Ari. Hark, Hark! I hear
The strain of strutting chanticleer
Cry, "Cock-a-diddle-dow."

Fer. Where should this music be? I' th' air or th' earth?

358. **race**, inherited nature. 374. **Setebos**, a name known to Elizabethan voyagers as a god or devil worshipped by American savages. Used with great effect by Browning in *Caliban on Setebos*. 379. **whist**, hushed. 380. **featly**, nimbly. 382. **burthen**, refrain. 383. **dispersedly**, i.e.—hummed in the bass throughout the song.

It sounds no more; and, sure, it waits upon
Some god o' th' island. Sitting on a bank,
Weeping again the King my father's wreck,
This music crept by me upon the waters,
Allaying both their fury and my passion
With its sweet air; thence I have follow'd it,
Or it hath drawn me rather. But 't is gone.
No, it begins again.

ARIEL'S SONG

Full fathom five thy father lies;
Of his bones are coral made;
Those are pearls that were his eyes:
Nothing of him that doth fade
But doth suffer a sea-change
Into something rich and strange.
Sea-nymphs hourly ring his knell:

Burden. Ding-dong.
Ari. Hark! now I hear them,—ding-dong, bell.
Fer. The ditty does remember my drown'd father.
This is no mortal business, nor no sound
That the earth owes. I hear it now above me.
Pros. The fringed curtains of thine eye advance
And say what thou seest yond.
Mir. What is 't? A spirit?
Lord, how it looks about! Believe me, sir,
It carries a brave form. But 't is a spirit.
Pros. No, wench; it eats and sleeps and hath such senses
As we have, such. This gallant which thou seest
Was in the wreck; and, but he 's something stain'd
With grief, that 's beauty's canker, thou mightst call him
A goodly person. He hath lost his fellows
And strays about to find 'em.
Mir. I might call him
A thing divine; for nothing natural
I ever saw so noble.
Pros. [*Aside.*] It goes on, I see,
As my soul prompts it. Spirit, fine spirit! I'll free thee
Within two days for this.
Fer. Most sure, the goddess
On whom these airs attend! Vouchsafe my prayer
May know if you remain upon this island,
And that you will some good instruction give
How I may bear me here: my prime request,
Which I do last pronounce, is, O you wonder!
If you be maid or no?
Mir. No wonder, sir,
But certainly a maid.
Fer. My language! heavens!

405. **remember**, commemorate. 407. **owes**, owns. 408. **advance**, raise. 415. **canker**, destructive worm.

I am the best of them that speak this speech,
Were I but where 't is spoken.
Pros. How? the best?
What wert thou, if the King of Naples heard thee?
Fer. A single thing, as I am now, that wonders
To hear thee speak of Naples. He does hear me;
And that he does I weep. Myself am Naples,
Who with mine eyes, never since at ebb, beheld
The King my father wreck'd.
Mir. Alack, for mercy!
Fer. Yes, faith, and all his lords; the Duke of Milan
And his brave son being twain.
Pros. [*Aside.*] The Duke of Milan
And his more braver daughter could control thee,
If now 't were fit to do 't. At the first sight
They have chang'd eyes. Delicate Ariel,
I 'll set thee free for this. [*To Ferdinand.*] A word, good sir;
I fear you have done yourself some wrong; a word.
Mir. Why speaks my father so ungently? This
Is the third man that e'er I saw, the first
That e'er I sigh'd for. Pity move my father
To be inclin'd my way!
Fer. O, if a virgin,
And your affection not gone forth, I 'll make you
The Queen of Naples.
Pros. Soft, sir! one word more.
[*Aside.*] They are both in either's powers; but this swift business
I must uneasy make, lest too light winning
Make the prize light.—One word more; I charge thee
That thou attend me. Thou dost here usurp
The name thou ow'st not; and hast put thyself
Upon this island as a spy, to win it
From me, the lord on 't.
Fer. No, as I am a man.
Mir. There's nothing ill can dwell in such a temple.
If the ill spirit have so fair a house,
Good things will strive to dwell with 't.
Pros. Follow me.
Speak not you for him; he 's a traitor. Come.
I 'll manacle thy neck and feet together.
Sea-water shalt thou drink; thy food shall be
The fresh-brook mussels, wither'd roots and husks
Wherein the acorn cradled. Follow.
Fer. No;
I will resist such entertainment till
Mine enemy has more power.
He draws, and is charmed from moving.
Mir. O dear father,
Make not too rash a trial of him, for
He 's gentle and not fearful.
Pros. What! I say;
My foot my tutor? Put thy sword up, traitor,
Who mak'st a show but dar'st not strike, thy conscience
Is so possess'd with guilt. Come from thy ward,
For I can here disarm thee with this stick
And make thy weapon drop.
Mir. Beseech you, father.
Pros. Hence! hang not on my garments.
Mir. Sir, have pity;
I 'll be his surety.
Pros. Silence! one word more
Shall make me chide thee, if not hate thee. What!
An advocate for an impostor! hush!
Thou think'st there is no more such shapes as he,
Having seen but him and Caliban. Foolish wench!
To th' most of men this is a Caliban,
And they to him are angels.
Mir. My affections
Are then most humble; I have no ambition
To see a goodlier man.
Pros. Come on; obey.
Thy nerves are in their infancy again
And have no vigour in them.
Fer. So they are.
My spirits, as in a dream, are all bound up.
My father's loss, the weakness which I feel,
The wreck of all my friends, nor this man's threats,
To whom I am subdu'd, are but light to me,
Might I but through my prison once a day
Behold this maid: all corners else o' th' earth
Let liberty make use of; space enough
Have I in such a prison.
Pros. [*Aside.*] It works. [*To Ferdinand.*] Come on.
—Thou hast done well, fine Ariel!—Follow me.
[*To Ariel.*] Hark what thou else shalt do me.
Mir. Be of comfort;
My father 's of a better nature, sir,
Than he appears by speech. This is unwonted
Which now came from him.
Pros. [*To Ariel.*] Thou shalt be as free
As mountain winds; but then exactly do
All points of my command.
Ari. To th' syllable.
Pros. Come, follow.—
Speak not for him. *Exeunt.*

432. single, solitary. **439. control,** contradict. **443. you . . . wrong,** you have misrepresented yourself.

468. fearful, to be feared. **469. foot,** inferior, here Miranda. **471. ward,** posture of defense. **484. nerves,** muscles.

Act II. Scene I. *Another part of the island.*

Enter *Alonso, Sebastian, Antonio, Gonzalo, Adrian, Francisco,* and others.

Gon. Beseech you, sir, be merry; you have cause,
So have we all, of joy; for our escape
Is much beyond our loss. Our hint of woe
Is common; every day some sailor's wife,
The masters of some merchant, and the merchant
Have just our theme of woe; but for the miracle,
I mean our preservation, few in millions
Can speak like us. Then wisely, good sir, weigh
Our sorrow with our comfort.

Alon. Prithee, peace.

Seb. He receives comfort like cold porridge.

Ant. The visitor will not give him o'er so.

Seb. Look, he's winding up the watch of his wit; by and by it will strike.

Gon. Sir,—

Seb. One. Tell.

Gon. When every grief is entertain'd that 's offer'd,
Comes to the entertainer—

Seb. A dollar.

Gon. Dolour comes to him, indeed; you have spoken truer than you purposed.

Seb. You have taken it wiselier than I meant you should.

Gon. Therefore, my lord,—

Ant. Fie, what a spendthrift is he of his tongue!

Alon. I prithee, spare.

Gon. Well, I have done. But yet,—

Seb. He will be talking.

Ant. Which, of he or Adrian, for a good wager, first begins to crow?

Seb. The old cock.

Ant. The cockerel.

Seb. Done. The wager?

Ant. A laughter.

Seb. A match!

Adr. Though this island seem to be desert,—

Seb. Ha, ha, ha! Antonio! So you 're paid.

Adr. Uninhabitable and almost inaccessible,—

Seb. Yet,—

Adr. Yet,—

Ant. He could not miss 't.

Adr. It must needs be of subtle, tender, and delicate temperance.

Ant. Temperance was a delicate wench.

Seb. Ay, and a subtle; as he most learnedly delivered.

Adr. The air breathes upon us here most sweetly.

Seb. As if it had lungs and rotten ones.

Ant. Or as 't were perfumed by a fen.

Gon. Here is everything advantageous to life.

Ant. True; save means to live.

Seb. Of that there 's none, or little.

Gon. How lush and lusty the grass looks! How green!

Ant. The ground indeed is tawny.

Seb. With an eye of green in 't.

Ant. He misses not much.

Seb. No; he doth but mistake the truth totally.

Gon. But the rarity of it is,—which is indeed almost beyond credit,—

Seb. As many vouched rarities are.

Gon. That our garments, being, as they were, drenched in the sea, hold notwithstanding their freshness and glosses, being rather new-dyed than stained with salt water.

Ant. If but one of his pockets could speak, would it not say he lies?

Seb. Ay, or very falsely pocket up his report.

Gon. Methinks our garments are now as fresh as when we put them on first in Afric, at the marriage of the King's fair daughter Claribel to the King of Tunis.

Seb. 'T was a sweet marriage, and we prosper well in our return.

Adr. Tunis was never graced before with such a paragon to their queen.

Gon. Not since widow Dido's time.

Ant. Widow! a pox o' that! How came that widow in? Widow Dido!

Seb. What if he had said "widower Æneas" too? Good Lord, how you take it!

Adr. "Widow Dido" said you? You make me study of that. She was of Carthage, not of Tunis.

Gon. This Tunis, sir, was Carthage.

Adr. Carthage?

Gon. I assure you, Carthage.

Ant. His word is more than the miraculous harp.

Seb. He hath raised the wall and houses too.

Ant. What impossible matter will he make easy next?

Seb. I think he will carry this island home in his pocket and give it his son for an apple.

Ant. And, sowing the kernels of it in the sea, bring forth more islands.

5. merchant, merchant ship. **11. visitor,** visitor to the sick, here Gonzalo. **15. Tell,** count. **33. laughter,** (1) a laugh, (2) a setting of eggs. **40. miss 't,** miss the word "yet." **42. temperance,** temperature, in l. 43 reference to character in morality play or to a character in Chapman's *May-Day.*

55. eye, tinge. **56. misses not much,** is not far wrong. **60. vouched,** asserted. **86-7.** The harp of Amphion, which raised the walls of Thebes.

Gon. Ay.
Ant. Why, in good time.
Gon. Sir, we were talking that our garments seem now as fresh as when we were at Tunis at the marriage of your daughter, who is now Queen.
Ant. And the rarest that e'er came there.
Seb. Bate, I beseech you, widow Dido.
Ant. O, widow Dido! ay, widow Dido.
Gon. Is not, sir, my doublet as fresh as the first day I wore it? I mean, in a sort.
Ant. That "sort" was well fished for.
Gon. When I wore it at your daughter's marriage?
Alon. You cram these words into mine ears against
The stomach of my sense. Would I had never
Married my daughter there! for, coming thence,
My son is lost and, in my rate, she too,
Who is so far from Italy removed
I ne'er again shall see her. O thou mine heir
Of Naples and of Milan, what strange fish
Hath made his meal on thee?
Fran. Sir, he may live.
I saw him beat the surges under him,
And ride upon their backs: he trod the water,
Whose enmity he flung aside, and breasted
The surge most swoln that met him: his bold head
'Bove the contentious waves he kept, and oared
Himself with his good arms in lusty stroke
To th' shore, that o'er his wave-worn basis bowed,
As stooping to relieve him: I not doubt
He came alive to land.
Alon. No, no, he 's gone.
Seb. Sir, you may thank yourself for this great loss,
That would not bless our Europe with your daughter,
But rather loose her to an African;
Where she at least is banish'd from your eye,
Who hath cause to wet the grief on 't.
Alon. Prithee, peace.
Seb. You were kneel'd to and importun'd otherwise
By all of us, and the fair soul herself
Weigh'd between loathness and obedience, at
Which end o' th' beam should bow. We have lost your son,
I fear, for ever: Milan and Naples have
Moe widows in them of this business' making
Than we bring men to comfort them.
The fault 's your own.
Alon. So is the dear'st o' th' loss.
Gon. My lord Sebastian,
The truth you speak doth lack some gentleness
And time to speak it in. You rub the sore,
When you should bring the plaster.
Seb. Very well.
Ant. And most chirurgeonly.
Gon. It is foul weather in us all, good sir,
When you are cloudy.
Seb. Foul weather?
Ant. Very foul.
Gon. Had I plantation of this isle, my lord,—
Ant. He 'd sow 't with nettle-seed.
Seb. Or docks, or mallows.
Gon. And were the king on 't, what would I do?
Seb. Scape being drunk for want of wine.
Gon. I' th' commonwealth I would by contraries
Execute all things; for no kind of traffic
Would I admit; no name of magistrate;
Letters should not be known; riches, poverty,
And use of service, none; contract, succession,
Bourn, bound of land, tilth, vineyard, none;
No use of metal, corn, or wine, or oil;
No occupation; all men idle, all;
And women too, but innocent and pure;
No sovereignty;—
Seb. Yet he would be king on 't.
Ant. The latter end of his commonwealth forgets the beginning.
Gon. All things in common nature should produce
Without sweat or endeavour: treason, felony,
Sword, pike, knife, gun, or need of any engine,
Would I not have; but nature should bring forth,
Of it own kind, all foison, all abundance,
To feed my innocent people.
Seb. No marrying 'mong his subjects?
Ant. None, man; all idle; whores and knaves.
Gon. I would with such perfection govern, sir,
T' excel the golden age.
Seb. Save his Majesty!
Ant. Long live Gonzalo!
Gon. And,—do you mark me, sir?
Alon. Prithee, no more; thou dost talk nothing to me.

103. in a sort, to a certain extent. **104. sort,** the word "sort" used in l. 103. **107. stomach,** inclination. **109. rate,** judgment. **125. loose her,** turn her loose. **127. Who,** which (refers to eye). **130. Weigh'd,** balanced. **loathness,** unwillingness. **130-1. at Which end o' th' beam should bow,** although the syntax is confused, the meaning is clear enough: the girl is torn between her own desires and the wishes of her father. The figure of the balanced scales is clear. The syntax requires a "she" before "should."

133. Moe, more. **140. chirurgeonly,** like a surgeon. **143. plantation,** colonization. **147-168.** This passage follows closely Montaigne's picture of an ideal commonwealth in his essay "Of the Caniballes." Shakespeare read it in Florio's English translation of 1603. **150. Letters,** learning. **152. Bourn,** boundary. **tilth,** tillage. **161. engine,** instrument of war. **163. it,** its. **foison,** plenty. **171. nothing.** nonsense.

Gon. I do well believe your Highness; and did it to minister occasion to these gentlemen, who are of such sensible and nimble lungs that they always use to laugh at nothing.

Ant. 'T was you we laughed at.

Gon. Who in this kind of merry fooling am nothing to you: so you may continue and laugh at nothing still.

Ant. What a blow was there given!

Seb. An it had not fallen flatlong.

Gon. You are gentlemen of brave mettle; you would lift the moon out of her sphere, if she would continue in it five weeks without changing.

Enter *Ariel* invisible, playing solemn music.

Seb. We would so, and then go a bat-fowling.

Ant. Nay, good my lord, be not angry.

Gon. No, I warrant you; I will not adventure my discretion so weakly. Will you laugh me asleep, for I am very heavy?

Ant. Go sleep, and hear us.

All sleep except Alon., Seb., and Ant.

Alon. What, all so soon asleep! I wish mine eyes
Would, with themselves, shut up my thoughts. I find
They are inclin'd to do so.
Seb. Please you, sir,
Do not omit the heavy offer of it.
It seldom visits sorrow; when it doth,
It is a comforter.
Ant. We two, my lord,
Will guard your person while you take your rest,
And watch your safety.
Alon. Thank you. Wondrous heavy.
Alonso sleeps. Exit Ariel.
Seb. What a strange drowsiness possesses them!
Ant. It is the quality o' th' climate.
Seb. Why
Doth it not then our eyelids sink? I find not
Myself dispos'd to sleep.
Ant. Nor I; my spirits are nimble.
They fell together all, as by consent;
They dropp'd, as by a thunder-stroke. What might,
Worthy Sebastian, O, what might—? No more:—
And yet methinks I see it in thy face,
What thou shouldst be: the occasion speaks thee, and
My strong imagination sees a crown
Dropping upon thy head.
Seb. What, art thou waking?
Ant. Do you not hear me speak?
Seb. I do; and surely
It is a sleepy language, and thou speak'st
Out of thy sleep. What is it thou didst say?
This is a strange repose, to be asleep
With eyes wide open; standing, speaking, moving,
And yet so fast asleep.
Ant. Noble Sebastian,
Thou let'st thy fortune sleep—die, rather; wink'st
Whiles thou art waking.
Seb. Thou dost snore distinctly;
There 's meaning in thy snores.
Ant. I am more serious than my custom; you
Must be so too, if heed me; which to do
Trebles thee o'er.
Seb. Well, I am standing water.
Ant. I 'll teach you how to flow.
Seb. Do so. To ebb
Hereditary sloth instructs me.
Ant. O,
If you but knew how you the purpose cherish
Whiles thus you mock it! how, in stripping it.
You more invest it! Ebbing men, indeed,
Most often do so near the bottom run
By their own fear or sloth.
Seb. Prithee, say on.
The setting of thine eye and cheek proclaim
A matter from thee, and a birth indeed
Which throes thee much to yield.
Ant. Thus, sir:
Although this lord of weak remembrance, this,
Who shall be of as little memory
When he is earth'd, hath here almost persuaded—
For he 's a spirit of persuasion, only
Professes to persuade—the King his son 's alive,
'T is as impossible that he 's undrown'd
As he that sleeps here swims.
Seb. I have no hope
That he 's undrown'd.
Ant. O, out of that no hope
What great hope have you! No hope that way is

173. minister occasion, offer an opportunity. **174. sensible,** sensitive. **181. flatlong,** with the flat of the sword. **185. a bat-fowling,** hunting birds at night. **187-88. adventure,** risk. **188. discretion,** reputation for discretion. **189. heavy,** drowsy. **194. omit,** ignore. **203. consent,** concerted action. **207. speaks,** proclaims.

216. wink'st, closest thine eyes. **221. Trebles,** makes three times as great. **standing,** quiet. **224-28.** If you but knew how you cherish the notion of being King even while you mock at it, how in stripping it bare of pretense you clothe it in reality. Men whose fortunes are at the ebb often lose themselves in shallows because of fear and sloth. **230. matter,** important business. **231. throes,** pains. **232. remembrance,** memory. **234. earth'd,** buried. **236. Professes,** practices as a profession. **240-44.** No hope of Ferdinand's life means for you so great a hope (i.e., the crown) that ambition itself cannot rise beyond it without hesitating to believe what it may discover there; "but doubt" means "but must doubt."

Another way so high a hope that even
Ambition cannot pierce a wink beyond,
But doubt discovery there. Will you grant with me
That Ferdinand is drown'd?
Seb. He 's gone.
Ant. Then, tell me,
Who 's the next heir of Naples?
Seb. Claribel.
Ant. She that is Queen of Tunis; she that dwells
Ten leagues beyond man's life; she that from Naples
Can have no note, unless the sun were post—
The man i' th' moon 's too slow—till new-born chins
Be rough and razorable; she that—from whom
We all were sea-swallow'd, though some cast again,
And by that destiny to perform an act
Whereof what 's past is prologue, what to come
In yours and my discharge.
Seb. What stuff is this! How say you?
'T is true, my brother's daughter 's Queen of Tunis;
So is she heir of Naples; 'twixt which regions
There is some space.
Ant. A space whose every cubit
Seems to cry out, "How shall that Claribel
Measure us back to Naples? Keep in Tunis,
And let Sebastian wake." Say, this were death
That now hath seiz'd them; why, they were no worse
Than now they are. There be that can rule Naples
As well as he that sleeps; lords that can prate
As amply and unnecessarily
As this Gonzalo; I myself could make
A chough of as deep chat. O, that you bore
The mind that I do! what a sleep were this
For your advancement! Do you understand me?
Seb. Methinks I do.
Ant. And how does your content
Tender your own good fortune?
Seb. I remember
You did supplant your brother Prospero.
Ant. True.
And look how well my garments sit upon me;
Much feater than before: my brother's servants
Were then my fellows; now they are my men.

248. **note**, information. 250. **from whom**, coming from whom. 251. **cast**, (1) cast ashore; (2) cast as actors. 254. **discharge**, performance. 266. **chough**, jackdaw. **deep chat**, profound chatter. 269. **content**, desire, wish. 270. **Tender**, regard. 273. **feater**, more trimly.

Seb. But, for your conscience?
Ant. Ay, sir, where lies that? If 't were a kibe,
'T would put me to my slipper; but I feel not
This deity in my bosom. Twenty consciences,
That stand 'twixt me and Milan, candied be they
And melt ere they molest! Here lies your brother,
No better than the earth he lies upon
If he were that which now he 's like, that 's dead;
Whom I, with this obedient steel, three inches of it,
Can lay to bed for ever; whiles you, doing thus,
To the perpetual wink for aye might put
This ancient morsel, this Sir Prudence, who
Should not upbraid our course. For all the rest,
They 'll take suggestion as a cat laps milk;
They 'll tell the clock to any business that
We say befits the hour.
Seb. Thy case, dear friend,
Shall be my precedent; as thou got'st Milan,
I 'll come by Naples. Draw thy sword. One stroke
Shall free thee from the tribute which thou payest,
And I the King shall love thee.
Ant. Draw together;
And when I rear my hand, do you the like,
To fall it on Gonzalo.
Seb. O, but one word.
They talk apart

Re-enter *Ariel* invisible, with music and song.

Ari. My master through his art foresees the danger
That you, his friend, are in; and sends me forth—
For else his project dies—to keep them living.
Sings in Gonzalo's ear.

While you here do snoring lie,
Open-ey'd Conspiracy
His time doth take.
If of life you keep a care,
Shake off slumber, and beware;
Awake, awake!

Ant. Then let us both be sudden.
Gon. Now, good angels
Preserve the King. *Wakes Alonso.*
Alon. Why, how now? Ho, awake! Why are you drawn?
Wherefore this ghastly looking?
Gon. What 's the matter?

276. **kibe**, chilblain. 279. **candied**, congealed. 285. **perpetual wink**, everlasting sleep. 288. **suggestion**, our promptings. 289. **tell the clock**, count the strokes, agree with us. 296. **To fall**, to let it fall.

Seb. Whiles we stood here securing your repose,
Even now, we heard a hollow burst of bellowing
Like bulls, or rather lions: did 't not wake you?
It struck mine ear most terribly.
Alon. I heard nothing.
Ant. O, 't was a din to fright a monster's ear,
To make an earthquake! Sure, it was the roar
Of a whole herd of lions.
Alon. Heard you this, Gonzalo?
Gon. Upon mine honour, sir, I heard a humming,
And that a strange one too, which did awake me.
I shak'd you, sir, and cried: as mine eyes open'd,
I saw their weapons drawn: there was a noise,
That 's verily. 'T is best we stand upon our guard,
Or that we quit this place. Let 's draw our weapons.
Alon. Lead off this ground; and let 's make further search
For my poor son.
Gon. Heavens keep him from these beasts!
For he is, sure, i' th' island.
Alon. Lead away.
Ari. Prospero my lord shall know what I have done.
So, King, go safely on to seek thy son. *Exeunt.*

Scene II. *Another part of the island.*

Enter *Caliban* with a burden of wood. A noise of thunder heard.

Cal. All the infections that the sun sucks up.
From bogs, fens, flats, on Prosper fall and make him
By inch-meal a disease! His spirits hear me
And yet I needs must curse. But they 'll nor pinch,
Fright me with urchin-shows, pitch me i' th' mire,
Nor lead me, like a firebrand, in the dark
Out of my way, unless he bid 'em; but
For every trifle are they set upon me,
Sometime like apes that mow and chatter at me
And after bite me, then like hedgehogs which
Lie tumbling in my barefoot way and mount
Their pricks at my footfall; sometime am I
All wound with adders who with cloven tongues
Do hiss me into madness.

Enter *Trinculo.*

Lo, now lo!
Here comes a spirit of his, and to torment me
For bringing wood in slowly. I 'll fall flat;
Perchance he will not mind me.

Trin. Here 's neither bush nor shrub, to bear off any weather at all, and another storm brewing; I hear it sing i' th' wind: yond same black cloud, yond huge one, looks like a foul bombard that would shed his liquor. If it should thunder as it did before, I know not where to hide my head; yond same cloud cannot choose but fall by pailfuls. What have we here? A man or a fish? Dead or alive? A fish; he smells like a fish; a very ancient and fish-like smell; a kind of not-of-the-newest Poor-John. A strange fish! Were I in England now, as once I was, and had but this fish painted, not a holiday fool there but would give a piece of silver: there would this monster make a man; any strange beast there makes a man: when they will not give a doit to relieve a lame beggar, they will lay out ten to see a dead Indian. Legged like a man! and his fins like arms! Warm o' my troth! I do now let loose my opinion, hold it no longer: this is no fish, but an islander, that hath lately suffered by a thunderbolt. [*Thunder.*] Alas, the storm is come again! My best way is to creep under his gaberdine; there is no other shelter hereabout: misery acquaints a man with strange bedfellows. I will here shroud till the dregs of the storm be past.

Enter *Stephano,* singing: a bottle in his hand.

Ste. "I shall no more to sea, to sea,
Here shall I die ashore—"

This is a very scurvy tune to sing at a man's funeral. Well, here 's my comfort. *Drinks. Sings.*

"The master, the swabber, the boatswain, and I,
The gunner and his mate
Lov'd Moll, Meg, and Marian, and Margery,
But none of us car'd for Kate;
For she had a tongue with a tang,
Would cry to a sailor, Go hang!
She lov'd not the savour of tar nor of pitch,
Yet a tailor might scratch her where'er she did itch;
Then to sea, boys, and let her go hang!"

3. inch-meal, inch by inch. **5. urchin-shows,** apparitions of goblins. **9. mow,** make faces.

19. bear off, keep off. **21. bombard,** leather wine vessel. **28. Poor-John,** salted hake. **32. make a man,** make a man's fortune. **33. doit,** the smallest coin. **40. gaberdine,** cloak. **42. shroud,** hide.

This is a scurvy tune too; but here 's my comfort. *Drinks.*

Cal. Do not torment me! Oh!

Ste. What 's the matter? Have we devils here? Do you put tricks upon 's with savages and men of Ind, ha? I have not scaped drowning to be afeard now of your four legs; for it hath been said, "As proper a man as ever went on four legs cannot make him give ground"; and it shall be said so again while Stephano breathes at nostrils.

Cal. The spirit torments me! Oh!

Ste. This is some monster of the isle with four legs who hath got, as I take it, an ague. Where the devil should he learn our language? I will give him some relief, if it be but for that. If I can recover him and keep him tame and get to Naples with him, he 's a present for any emperor that ever trod on neat's-leather.

Cal. Do not torment me, prithee; I 'll bring my wood home faster.

Ste. He 's in his fit now and does not talk after the wisest. He shall taste of my bottle; if he have never drunk wine afore, it will go near to remove his fit. If I can recover him and keep him tame, I will not take too much for him; he shall pay for him that hath him, and that soundly.

Cal. Thou dost me yet but little hurt; thou wilt anon, I know it by thy trembling. Now Prosper works upon thee.

Ste. Come on your ways: open your mouth; here is that which will give language to you, cat: open your mouth; this will shake your shaking, I can tell you, and that soundly: you cannot tell who 's your friend: open your chaps again.

Trin. I should know that voice; it should be—but he is drowned; and these are devils. O defend me!

Ste. Four legs and two voices; a most delicate monster! His forward voice now is to speak well of his friend; his backward voice is to utter foul speeches and to detract. If all the wine in my bottle will recover him, I will help his ague. Come. Amen! I will pour some in thy other mouth.

Trin. Stephano!

Ste. Doth thy other mouth call me? Mercy, mercy! This is a devil, and no monster. I will leave him; I have no long spoon.

Trin. Stephano! If thou beest Stephano, touch me and speak to me; for I am Trinculo,—be not afeard—thy good friend Trinculo.

Ste. If thou beest Trinculo, come forth. I 'll pull thee by the lesser legs. If any be Trinculo's legs, these are they. Thou art very Trinculo indeed! How cam'st thou to be the siege of this moon-calf? Can he vent Trinculos?

Trin. I took him to be killed with a thunder-stroke. But art thou not drowned, Stephano? I hope now thou art not drowned. Is the storm over-blown? I hid me under the dead moon-calf's gaberdine for fear of the storm. And art thou living, Stephano? O Stephano, two Neapolitans scaped!

Ste. Prithee, do not turn me about; my stomach is not constant.

Cal. [*Aside.*] These be fine things, an if they be not sprites.
That 's a brave god and bears celestial liquor.
I will kneel to him.

Ste. How didst thou scape? How cam'st thou hither? Swear by this bottle how thou cam'st hither,—I escaped upon a butt of sack which the sailors heaved o'erboard—by this bottle, which I made of the bark of a tree with mine own hands since I was cast ashore.

Cal. I 'll swear upon that bottle to be thy true subject; for the liquor is not earthly.

Ste. Here; swear then how thou escap'dst.

Trin. Swom ashore, man, like a duck. I can swim like a duck, I 'll be sworn.

Ste. Here, kiss the book. Though thou canst swim like a duck, thou art made like a goose.

Trin. O Stephano, hast any more of this?

Ste. The whole butt, man: my cellar is in a rock by th' seaside where my wine is hid. How now, moon-calf! how does thine ague?

Cal. Hast thou not dropp'd from heaven?

Ste. Out o' th' moon, I do assure thee. I was the man i' th' moon when time was.

Cal. I have seen thee in her and I do adore thee.
My mistress show'd me thee and thy dog and thy bush.

Ste. Come, swear to that, kiss the book: I will furnish it anon with new contents. Swear.

Trin. By this good light, this is a very shallow monster! I afeard of him! A very weak monster! The man i' th' moon! A most poor credulous monster! Well drawn, monster, in good sooth!

Cal. I 'll show thee every fertile inch o' th' island;
And I will kiss thy foot. I prithee, be my god.

Trin. By this light, a most perfidious and drunken monster! When 's god 's asleep, he 'll rob his bottle.

Cal. I 'll kiss thy foot. I 'll swear myself thy subject.

71. recover, restore. **73. neat's leather,** cow-hide. **83. trembling,** a sign of being possessed by the devil. **86-7.** "Good liquor will make a cat speak." **93. delicate,** lovely. **103.** "He must have a long spoon that must eat with the devil."

111. siege, excrement. **moon-calf,** monster. **vent,** emit. **150. drawn,** drunk.

Ste. Come on then; down, and swear.

Trin. I shall laugh myself to death at this puppy-headed monster. A most scurvy monster! I could find in my heart to beat him—

Ste. Come, kiss.

Trin. But that the poor monster 's in drink. An abominable monster!

Cal. I 'll show thee the best springs; I 'll pluck thee berries;
I 'll fish for thee and get thee wood enough.
A plague upon the tyrant that I serve!
I 'll bear him no more sticks, but follow thee,
Thou wondrous man.

Trin. A most ridiculous monster, to make a wonder of a poor drunkard!

Cal. I prithee, let me bring thee where crabs grow;
And I with my long nails will dig thee pig-nuts;
Show thee a jay's nest and instruct thee how
To snare the nimble marmoset. I 'll bring thee
To clust'ring filberts and sometimes I 'll get thee
Young scamels from the rock. Wilt thou go with me?

Ste. I prithee now, lead the way without any more talking. Trinculo, the King and all our company else being drowned, we will inherit here. Here! bear my bottle. Fellow Trinculo, we 'll fill him by and by again.

Caliban sings drunkenly.

Farewell, master; farewell, farewell!

Trin. A howling monster; a drunken monster!

Cal.

No more dams I 'll make for fish;
Nor fetch in firing
At requiring;
Nor scrape trenchering, nor wash dish.
'Ban, 'Ban, Cacaliban
Has a new master, get a new man.

Freedom, hey-day! hey-day, freedom! freedom, hey-dey, freedom!

Ste. O brave monster! Lead the way.

Exeunt.

ACT III. Scene I. *Before Prospero's cell.*

Enter *Ferdinand,* bearing a log.

Fer. There be some sports are painful, and their labour
Delight in them sets off; some kinds of baseness
Are nobly undergone, and most poor matters
Point to rich ends. This my mean task
Would be as heavy to me as odious, but
The mistress which I serve quickens what 's dead
And makes my labours pleasures. O, she is
Ten times more gentle than her father 's crabbed,
And he 's compos'd of harshness. I must remove
Some thousands of these logs and pile them up,
Upon a sore injunction. My sweet mistress
Weeps when she sees me work, and says such baseness
Had never like executor. I forget;
But these sweet thoughts do even refresh my labours,
Most busy least, when I do it.

Enter *Miranda;* and *Prospero* at a distance, unseen.

Mir. Alas, now, pray you,
Work not so hard. I would the lightning had
Burnt up those logs that you are enjoin'd to pile!
Pray, set it down and rest you. When this burns,
'T will weep for having wearied you. My father
Is hard at study; pray now, rest yourself;
He 's safe for these three hours.

Fer. O most dear mistress,
The sun will set before I shall discharge
What I must strive to do.

Mir. If you 'll sit down,
I 'll bear your logs the while: pray, give me that;
I 'll carry it to the pile.

Fer. No, precious creature;
I had rather crack my sinews, break my back,
Than you should such dishonour undergo,
While I sit lazy by.

Mir. It would become me
As well as it does you; and I should do it
With much more ease, for my good will is to it,
And yours it is against.

Pros. Poor worm, thou art infected!
This visitation shows it.

171. crabs, crab-apples. **Act III, Scene i: 2. sets off,** makes up for. **15. Most busy least when I do it:** This is one of the most disputed passages in Shakespeare. There seems, however, to be general agreement that it means that Ferdinand is most busy with thoughts of Miranda when he appears least occupied, and that his musings refresh him for further work.

176. scamels: This word has never been explained with certainty. The most plausible explanation is that it means sea-malls, sea-gulls whose young, caught before they could fly, were considered a delicacy. **179-80. inherit,** take possession. **187. trenchering,** trenchers. **Act III, Scene i: 32. visitation,** (1) visit to Ferdinand, (2) affliction with plague.

Mir. You look wearily.
Fer. No, noble mistress; 't is fresh morning with me
When you are by at night. I do beseech you—
Chiefly that I might set it in my prayers—
What is your name?
Mir. Miranda.—O my father,
I have broke your hest to say so!
Fer. Admir'd Miranda!
Indeed the top of admiration! worth
What 's dearest to the world! Full many a lady
I have ey'd with best regard, and many a time
Th' harmony of their tongues hath into bondage
Brought my too diligent ear; for several virtues
Have I lik'd several women, never any
With so full soul, but some defect in her
Did quarrel with the noblest grace she ow'd
And put it to the foil; but you, O you,
So perfect and so peerless, are created
Of every creature's best!
Mir. I do not know
One of my sex; no woman's face remember,
Save, from my glass, mine own; nor have I seen
More that I may call men than you, good friend,
And my dear father: how features are abroad,
I am skilless of; but, by my modesty,
The jewel in my dower, I would not wish
Any companion in the world but you;
Nor can imagination form a shape,
Besides yourself, to like of. But I prattle
Something too wildly, and my father's precepts
I therein do forget.
Fer. I am in my condition
A prince, Miranda; I do think, a king;
I would, not so!—and would no more endure
This wooden slavery than to suffer
The flesh-fly blow my mouth. Hear my soul speak.
The very instant that I saw you, did
My heart fly to your service; there resides,
To make me slave to it; and for your sake
Am I this patient log-man.
Mir. Do you love me?
Fer. O heaven, O earth, bear witness to this sound,
And crown what I profess with kind event
If I speak true! if hollowly, invert
What best is boded me to mischief! I
Beyond all limit of what else i' th' world
Do love, prize, honour you.
Mir. I am a fool
To weep at what I am glad of.
Pros. Fair encounter
Of two most rare affections! Heavens rain grace
On that which breeds between 'em!
Fer. Wherefore weep you?
Mir. At mine unworthiness, that dare not offer
What I desire to give, and much less take
What I shall die to want. But this is trifling;
And all the more it seeks to hide itself,
The bigger bulk it shows. Hence, bashful cunning!
And prompt me, plain and holy innocence!
I am your wife, if you will marry me;
If not, I 'll die your maid: to be your fellow
You may deny me; but I 'll be your servant,
Whether you will or no.
Fer. My mistress, dearest;
And I thus humble ever.
Mir. My husband, then?
Fer. Ay, with a heart as willing
As bondage e'er of freedom: here 's my hand.
Mir. And mine, with my heart in 't: and now farewell
Till half an hour hence.
Fer. A thousand thousand!
Exeunt Fer. and Mir. severally.
Pros. So glad of this as they I cannot be,
Who are surpris'd withal; but my rejoicing
At nothing can be more. I 'll to my book,
For yet ere supper-time must I perform
Much business appertaining. *Exit.*

Scene II. *Another part of the island.*

Enter *Caliban, Stephano,* and *Trinculo.*

Ste. Tell not me: when the butt is out, we will drink water; not a drop before; therefore bear up, and board 'em. Servant-monster, drink to me.

Trin. Servant-monster! the folly of this island! They say there 's but five upon this isle: we are three of them; if th' other two be brained like us, the state totters.

Ste. Drink, servant-monster, when I bid thee. Thy eyes are almost set in thy head.

Trin. Where should they be set else? He were a brave monster indeed, if they were set in his tail.

Ste. My man-monster hath drowned his tongue in sack: for my part, the sea cannot drown me; I swam, ere I could recover the shore, five and thirty leagues off and on. By this light, thou shalt be my lieutenant, monster, or my standard.

46. And . . . foil, defeated, marred it. **53. skilless,** ignorant. **70. invert,** convert. **71. boded,** destined. **79. die to want,** die if I miss. **Scene ii: 10. set,** fixed by drinking. **18. standard,** standard-bearer.

Trin. Your lieutenant, if you list; he 's no standard.

Ste. We 'll not run, Monsieur Monster.

Trin. Nor go neither; but you 'll lie like dogs and yet say nothing neither.

Ste. Moon-calf, speak once in thy life, if thou beest a good moon-calf.

Cal. How does thy honour? Let me lick thy shoe.
I 'll not serve him; he is not valiant.

Trin. Thou liest, most ignorant monster! I am in case to justle a constable. Why, thou deboshed fish, thou, was there ever man a coward that hath drunk so much sack as I to-day? Wilt thou tell a monstrous lie, being but half a fish and half a monster?

Cal. Lo, how he mocks me! Wilt thou let him, my lord?

Trin. "Lord" quoth he! That a monster should be such a natural!

Cal. Lo, lo, again! Bite him to death, I prithee.

Ste. Trinculo, keep a good tongue in your head. If you prove a mutineer,—the next tree! The poor monster 's my subject and he shall not suffer indignity.

Call. I thank my noble lord. Wilt thou be pleas'd
To hearken once again to the suit I made to thee?

Ste. Marry, will I; kneel and repeat it. I will stand, and so shall Trinculo.

Enter *Ariel,* invisible.

Cal. As I told thee before, I am subject to a tyrant, a sorcerer, that by his cunning hath cheated me of the island.

Ari. Thou liest.

Cal. Thou liest, thou jesting monkey, thou.
I would my valiant master would destroy thee!
I do not lie.

Ste. Trinculo, if you trouble him any more in 's tale, by this hand, I will supplant some of your teeth.

Trin. Why, I said nothing.

Ste. Mum, then, and no more. Proceed.

Cal. I say, by sorcery he got this isle;
From me he got it. If thy greatness will
Revenge it on him,—for I know thou dar'st,
But this thing dare not,—

Ste. That 's most certain.

Cal. Thou shalt be lord of it and I 'll serve thee.

Ste. How now shall this be compassed? Canst thou bring me to the party?

Cal. Yea, yea, my lord. I 'll yield him thee asleep,
Where thou mayst knock a nail into his head.

Ari. Thou liest; thou canst not.

Cal. What a pied ninny 's this! Thou scurvy patch!
I do beseech thy greatness, give him blows
And take his bottle from him. When that 's gone
He shall drink nought but brine; for I 'll not show him
Where the quick freshes are.

Ste. Trinculo, run into no further danger. Interrupt the monster one word further, and, by this hand, I 'll turn my mercy out o' doors and make a stock-fish of thee.

Trin. Why, what did I? I did nothing. I 'll go farther off.

Ste. Didst thou not say he lied?

Ari. Thou liest.

Ste. Do I so? Take thou that. [*Beats him.*] As you like this, give me the lie another time.

Trin. I did not give the lie. Out o' your wits and hearing too? A pox o' your bottle! this can sack and drinking do. A murrain on your monster, and the devil take your fingers!

Cal. Ha, ha, ha!

Ste. Now, forward with your tale. Prithee, stand farther off.

Cal. Beat him enough: after a little time
I 'll beat him too.

Ste. Stand farther. Come, proceed.

Cal. Why, as I told thee, 't is a custom with him,
I' th' afternoon to sleep. There thou mayst brain him,
Having first seiz'd his books, or with a log
Batter his skull, or paunch him with a stake,
Or cut his wezand with thy knife. Remember
First to possess his books; for without them
He 's but a sot, as I am, nor hath not
One spirit to command: they all do hate him
As rootedly as I. Burn but his books.
He has brave utensils,—for so he calls them,—
Which, when he has a house, he 'll deck withal.
And that most deeply to consider is
The beauty of his daughter: he himself
Calls her a nonpareil: I never saw a woman
But only Sycorax my dam and she;
But she as far surpasseth Sycorax
As great'st does least.

Ste. Is it so brave a lass?

Cal. Ay, lord; she will become thy bed, I warrant,
And bring thee forth brave brood.

19-20. he's no standard, he's not capable of standing. **22. go,** walk. **29. case,** condition. **30. deboshed,** debauched. **37. natural,** idiot.

71. pied ninny, fool in motley. **patch,** fool, jester. **75. quick freshes,** springs of fresh water. **79. stock-fish,** dried cod. **88. murrain,** plague. **98. paunch,** stab him in the belly. **99. wezand,** wind-pipe. **101. sot,** blockhead.

Ste. Monster, I will kill this man: his daughter and I will be king and queen,—save our Graces!—and Trinculo and thyself shall be viceroys. Dost thou like the plot, Trinculo?

Trin. Excellent.

Ste. Give me thy hand: I am sorry I beat thee; but, while thou liv'st, keep a good tongue in thy head.

Cal. Within this half hour will he be asleep.
Wilt thou destroy him then?

Ste. Ay, on mine honour.

Ari. This will I tell my master.

Cal. Thou mak'st me merry; I am full of pleasure.
Let us be jocund. Will you troll the catch
You taught me but while-ere?

Ste. At thy request, monster, I will do reason, any reason. Come on, Trinculo, let us sing. *Sings.*

Flout 'em and cout 'em
And scout 'em and flout 'em;
Thought is free.

Cal. That 's not the tune.

Ariel plays the tune on a tabor and pipe.

Ste. What is this same?

Trin. This is the tune of our catch, played by the picture of Nobody.

Ste. If thou beest a man, show thyself in thy likeness. If thou beest a devil, take 't as thou list.

Trin. O, forgive me my sins!

Ste. He that dies pays all debts. I defy thee. Mercy upon us!

Cal. Art thou afeard?

Ste. No, monster, not I.

Cal. Be not afeard. The isle is full of noises,
Sounds and sweet airs, that give delight and hurt not.
Sometimes a thousand twangling instruments
Will hum about mine ears, and sometime voices
That, if I then had wak'd after long sleep,
Will make me sleep again; and then, in dreaming,
The clouds methought would open and show riches
Ready to drop upon me, that, when I wak'd,
I cried to dream again.

Ste. This will prove a brave kingdom to me, where I shall have my music for nothing.

Cal. When Prospero is destroyed.

Ste. That shall be by and by. I remember the story.

Trin. The sound is going away. Let's follow it, and after do our work.

Ste. Lead, monster; we 'll follow. I would I could see this taborer; he lays it on.

Trin. Wilt come? I 'll follow Stephano.
Exeunt.

Scene III. *Another part of the island.*

Enter *Alonso, Sebastian, Antonio, Gonzalo, Adrian, Francisco,* etc.

Gon. By 'r lakin, I can go no further, sir;
My old bones aches. Here 's a maze trod indeed
Through forth-rights and meanders! By your patience,
I needs must rest me.

Alon. Old lord, I cannot blame thee,
Who am myself attach'd with weariness
To th' dulling of my spirits. Sit down, and rest.
Even here I will put off my hope and keep it
No longer for my flatterer: he is drown'd
Whom thus we stray to find, and the sea mocks
Our frustrate search on land. Well, let him go.

Ant. [*Aside to Seb.*] I am right glad that he 's so out of hope.
Do not, for one repulse, forego the purpose
That you resolv'd t' effect.

Seb. [*Aside to Ant.*] The next advantage
Will we take throughly.

Ant. [*Aside to Seb.*] Let it be to-night;
For, now they are oppress'd with travel, they
Will not, nor cannot, use such vigilance
As when they are fresh.

Seb. [*Aside to Ant.*] I say, to-night. No more.

Solemn and strange music; and Prospero on the top invisible. Enter several strange shapes, bringing in a banquet; and dance about it with gentle actions of salutation; and, inviting the King, etc., to eat, they depart.

Alon. What harmony is this? My good friends, hark!

Gon. Marvellous sweet music!

Alon. Give us kind keepers, heavens! What were these?

Seb. A living drollery. Now I will believe
That there are unicorns, that in Arabia
There is one tree, the phœnix' throne, one phœnix
At this hour reigning there.

Ant. I 'll believe both;

126. troll, sing. **catch,** part-song. **130. cout,** colt, i.e., make fools of. **133. S. d. tabor,** small drum, usually accompanying a pipe.

1. By'r lakin, by our Lady. **3. forth-rights,** straight paths. **meanders,** winding paths. **5. attach'd,** seized. **17. S. d. top,** Prospero appears on balcony at back of stage. **21. drollery,** puppet-show.

And what does else want credit, come to me,
And I 'll be sworn 't is true. Travellers ne'er did lie,
Though fools at home condemn 'em.
Gon. If in Naples
I should report this now, would they believe me?
If I should say, I saw such islanders—
For, certes, these are people of the island—
Who, though they are of monstrous shape, yet, note,
Their manners are more gentle-kind, than of
Our human generation you shall find
Many, nay, almost any.
Pros. [*Aside.*] Honest lord,
Thou hast said well; for some of you there present
Are worse than devils.
Alon. I cannot too much muse
Such shapes, such gesture, and such sound, expressing,
Although they want the use of tongue, a kind
Of excellent dumb discourse.
Pros. [*Aside.*] Praise in departing.
Fran. They vanish'd strangely.
Seb. No matter, since
They have left their viands behind, for we have stomachs.
Will 't please you taste of what is here?
Alon. Not I.
Gon. Faith, sir, you need not fear. When we were boys,
Who would believe that there were mountaineers
Dew-lapp'd like bulls, whose throats had hanging at 'em
Wallets of flesh? or that there were such men
Whose heads stood in their breasts? which now we find
Each putter-out of five for one will bring us
Good warrant of.
Alon. I will stand to and feed,
Although my last: no matter, since I feel
The best is past. Brother, my lord the Duke,
Stand to and do as we.

Thunder and lightning. Enter Ariel, like a harpy; claps his wings upon the table; and, with a quaint device, the banquet vanishes.

Ari. You are three men of sin, whom Destiny,
That hath to instrument this lower world
And what is in 't, the never-surfeited sea
Hath caus'd to belch up you; and on this island
Where man doth not inhabit; you 'mongst men
Being most unfit to live. I have made you mad;
And even with such-like valour men hang and drown
Their proper selves.
Alonso, Sebastian, etc., draw.
You fools! I and my fellows
Are ministers of Fate: the elements,
Of whom your swords are temper'd, may as well
Wound the loud winds, or with bemock'd-at stabs
Kill the still-closing waters, as diminish
One dowle that 's in my plume: my fellow-ministers
Are like invulnerable. If you could hurt,
Your swords are now too massy for your strengths
And will not be uplifted. But remember—
For that 's my business to you—that you three
From Milan did supplant good Prospero;
Expos'd unto the sea, which hath requit it,
Him and his innocent child; for which foul deed
The powers, delaying, not forgetting, have
Incens'd the seas and shores, yea, all the creatures,
Against your peace. Thee of thy son, Alonso,
They have bereft; and do pronounce by me
Ling'ring perdition, worse than any death
Can be at once, shall step by step attend
You and your ways; whose wraths to guard you from—
Which here, in this most desolate isle, else falls
Upon your heads—is nothing but heart's sorrow
And a clear life ensuing.

He vanishes in thunder; then, to soft music, enter the shapes again, and dance, with mocks and mows, and carrying out the table.

Pros. Bravely the figure of this harpy hast thou
Perform'd, my Ariel; a grace it had, devouring.
Of my instruction hast thou nothing bated
In what thou hadst to say; so, with good life
And observation strange, my meaner ministers

36. **muse,** marvel at. 39. **Praise in departing,** Proverbial—Hold your praise until you see the outcome. 41. **stomachs,** appetites. 44ff. The passage refers to the wild tales brought back by Elizabethan travellers of monstrous men dewlapped like bulls or without heads and with eyes in their breasts. Now Gonzalo says, every traveller who insures his safe return at a premium of 1 to 5 will assure us these tales are true. 52. S. d. The harpy was a fabled monster with the face of a woman and the body of a bird of prey. 54. **to,** for.

60. **proper,** own. 65. **dowle,** downy feather. 71. **requit,** requited. 84. **devouring,** absorbing, completely fulfilling my commands. 86. **good life,** life likeness. 87. **observation strange,** usually careful attention.

Their several kinds have done. My high charms work,
And these mine enemies are all knit up
In their distractions: they now are in my power;
And in these fits I leave them, while I visit
Young Ferdinand, whom they suppose is drown'd,
And his and mine lov'd darling. *Exit.*
Gon. I' th' name of something holy, sir, why stand you
In this strange stare?
Alon. O, it is monstrous, monstrous!
Methought the billows spoke and told me of it;
The winds did sing it to me, and the thunder,
That deep and dreadful organ-pipe, pronounc'd
The name of Prosper; it did bass my trespass.
Therefore my son i' th' ooze is bedded, and
I 'll seek him deeper than e'er plummet sounded
And with him there lie mudded. *Exit.*
Seb. But one fiend at a time,
I 'll fight their legions o'er.
Ant. I 'll be thy second.
Exeunt Sebastian and Antonio.
Gon. All three of them are desperate: their great guilt,
Like poison given to work a great time after,
Now gins to bite the spirits. I do beseech you
That are of suppler joints, follow them swiftly
And hinder them from what this ecstasy
May now provoke them to.
Adr. Follow, I pray you.
Exeunt omnes.

ACT IV. Scene I. *Before Prospero's cell.*

Enter *Prospero, Ferdinand,* and *Miranda.*

Pros. If I have too austerely punish'd you,
Your compensation makes amends, for I
Have given you here a third of mine own life,
Or that for which I live; who once again
I tender to thy hand. All thy vexations
Were but my trials of thy love, and thou
Hast strangely stood the test. Here, afore Heaven,
I ratify this my rich gift. O Ferdinand,
Do not smile at me that I boast her off,
For thou shalt find she will outstrip all praise
And make it halt behind her.
Fer. I do believe it
Against an oracle.
Pros. Then, as my gift and thine own acquisition
Worthily purchas'd, take my daughter: but
If thou dost break her virgin-knot before
All sanctimonious ceremonies may
With full and holy rite be minister'd,
No sweet aspersion shall the heavens let fall
To make this contract grow; but barren Hate,
Sour-eyed Disdain and Discord shall bestrew
The union of your bed with weeds so loathly
That you shall hate it both. Therefore take heed,
As Hymen's lamps shall light you.
Fer. As I hope
For quiet days, fair issue, and long life,
With such love as 't is now, the murkiest den,
The most opportune place, the strong'st suggestion
Our worser genius can, shall never melt
Mine honour into lust, to take away
The edge of that day's celebration
When I shall think or Phœbus' steeds are founder'd
Or Night kept chain'd below.
Pros. Fairly spoke.
Sit then and talk with her; she is thine own.
What, Ariel! my industrious servant, Ariel!

Enter *Ariel.*

Ari. What would my potent master? Here I am.
Pros. Thou and thy meaner fellows your last service
Did worthily perform; and I must use you
In such another trick. Go bring the rabble,
O'er whom I give thee power, here to this place.
Incite them to quick motion; for I must
Bestow upon the eyes of this young couple
Some vanity of mine art. It is my promise,
And they expect it from me.
Ari. Presently?
Pros. Ay, with a twink.
Ari.
Before you can say "come" and "go."
And breathe twice and cry "so, so,"
Each one, tripping on his toe,
Will be here with mop and mow.
Do you love me, master? No?

Pros. Dearly, my delicate Ariel. Do not approach
Till thou dost hear me call.

88. kinds, rôles. **Act IV, Scene 1: 3. a third of mine own life:** Best interpreted to mean that Miranda shared his interest with himself and his dukedom. **7. strangely,** uncommonly well. **18. aspersion,** sprinkling of holy water.

99. bass, to utter in deep tones. **108. ecstasy,** frenzy. **Act IV, Scene i: 37. rabble,** crowd. **41. vanity,** illusion. **43. twink,** twinkling. **47. mop,** grimace.

Ari. Well, I conceive. *Exit.*

Pros. Look thou be true; do not give dalliance
Too much the rein: the strongest oaths are straw
To the fire i' th' blood. Be more abstemious,
Or else, good night your vow!

Fer. I warrant you, sir;
The white cold virgin snow upon my heart
Abates the ardour of my liver.

Pros. Well.
Now come, my Ariel! bring a corollary,
Rather than want a spirit. Appear and pertly!
No tongue! all eyes! Be silent. *Soft music.*

Enter *Iris.*

Iris. Ceres, most bounteous lady, thy rich leas
Of wheat, rye, barley, vetches, oats, and pease;
Thy turfy mountains, where live nibbling sheep,
And flat meads thatch'd with stover, them to keep;
Thy banks with pioned and twilled brims,
Which spongy April at thy hest betrims
To make cold nymphs chaste crowns; and thy broom-groves,
Whose shadow the dismissed bachelor loves,
Being lass-lorn; thy pole-clipp'd vineyard;
And thy sea-marge, sterile and rocky-hard,
Where thou thyself dost air;—the queen o' th' sky,
Whose watery arch and messenger am I,
Bids thee leave these, and with her sovereign grace, *Juno descends.*
Here on this grass-plot, in this very place,
To come and sport; her peacocks fly amain.
Approach, rich Ceres, her to entertain.

Enter *Ceres.*

Cer. Hail, many-coloured messenger, that ne'er
Dost disobey the wife of Jupiter;
Who with thy saffron wings upon my flowers
Diffusest honey-drops, refreshing showers,
And with each end of thy blue bow dost crown
My bosky acres and my unshrubb'd down,
Rich scarf to my proud earth; why hath thy queen
Summon'd me hither, to this short-grass'd green?

Iris. A contract of true love to celebrate;
And some donation freely to estate
On the blest lovers.

Cer. Tell me, heavenly bow,
If Venus or her son, as thou dost know,
Do now attend the Queen? Since they did plot
The means that dusky Dis my daughter got,
Her and her blind boy's scandal'd company
I have forsworn.

Iris. Of her society
Be not afraid: I met her deity
Cutting the clouds towards Paphos, and her son
Dove-drawn with her. Here thought they to have done
Some wanton charm upon this man and maid,
Whose vows are, that no bed-right shall be paid
Till Hymen's torch be lighted; but in vain.
Mars's hot minion is return'd again;
Her waspish-headed son has broke his arrows,
Swears he will shoot no more, but play with sparrows
And be a boy right out.

Cer. Highest queen of state,
Great Juno, comes; I know her by her gait.

Juno. How does my bounteous sister? Go with me
To bless this twain, that they may prosperous be
And honour'd in their issue. *They sing.*

Juno.
Honour, riches, marriage-blessing,
Long continuance, and increasing,
Hourly joys be still upon you!
Juno sings her blessings on you.

Cer.
Earth's increase foison plenty,
Barns and garners never empty,
Vines with clustering bunches growing,
Plants with goodly burden bowing.
Spring come to you at the farthest
In the very end of harvest!
Scarcity and want shall shun you;
Ceres' blessing so is on you.

Fer. This is a most majestic vision, and
Harmonious charmingly. May I be bold
To think these spirits?

Pros. Spirits, which by mine art

56. liver, supposed seat of the passions. **57. corollary,** surplus. **59. S. d. Enter Iris.** The passage, 60-138, is in the form of a conventional Court Masque, which relied more on the costuming, music and dancing for effectiveness than upon the poetry. This masque is set to rhymed couplets of so little grace that some contend that it is an interpolation and no work of Shakespeare's. There is no proof of this. **60. leas,** fields. **61. vetches,** forage plants. **63. stover,** fodder. **64. pioned and twilled brims.** No satisfactory explanation of this passage has been found. It has been suggested that "pioned" means dug or trenched and "twilled" may refer to refacing the edges of the bank with mud. **66. broom-groves,** thickets of broom, a plant used to bind vines. **68. pole-clipp'd vineyard,** with vines clinging to the poles. **71. watery arch,** rainbow. **74. amain,** swiftly.

85. estate, bestow. **89. Dis,** Pluto. **90. scandal'd,** scandalous. **98. minion,** darling. **99. waspish-headed,** irritable.

I have from their confines call'd to enact
My present fancies.

Fer. Let me live here ever;
So rare a wonder'd father and a wise
Makes this place Paradise.

Pros. Sweet, now, silence!
Juno and Ceres whisper seriously.
There 's something else to do; hush, and be mute,
Or else our spell is marr'd.

Juno and Ceres whisper, and send Iris on employment.

Iris. You nymphs, call'd Naiads, of the windring brooks,
With your sedg'd crowns and ever-harmless looks,
Leave your crisp channels, and on this green land
Answer your summons; Juno does command.
Come, temperate nymphs, and help to celebrate
A contract of true love; be not too late.

Enter certain *Nymphs.*

You sunburnt sicklemen, of August weary,
Come hither from the furrow and be merry.
Make holiday; your rye-straw hats put on
And these fresh nymphs encounter every one
In country footing.

Enter certain *Reapers,* properly habited: *they join with the Nymphs in a graceful dance; towards the end whereof Prospero starts suddenly, and speaks; after which, to a strange, hollow, and confused noise, they heavily vanish.*

Pros. [*Aside.*] I had forgot that foul conspiracy
Of the beast Caliban and his confederates
Against my life. The minute of their plot
Is almost come. [*To the Spirits.*] Well done! avoid; no more!

Fer. This is strange. Your father 's in some passion.
That works him strongly.

Mir. Never till this day
Saw I him touch'd with anger, so distemper'd.

Pros. You do look, my son, in a mov'd sort,
As if you were dismay'd: be cheerful, sir,
Our revels now are ended. These our actors,
As I foretold you, were all spirits, and
Are melted into air, into thin air;
And, like the baseless fabric of this vision,
The cloud-capp'd towers, the gorgeous palaces,
The solemn temples, the great globe itself,
Yea, all which it inherit, shall dissolve
And, like this insubstantial pageant faded,
Leave not a rack behind. We are such stuff
As dreams are made on, and our little life
Is rounded with a sleep. Sir, I am vex'd,—
Bear with my weakness—my old brain is troubled.
Be not disturb'd with my infirmity.
If you be pleas'd, retire into my cell
And there repose: a turn or two I 'll walk,
To still my beating mind.

Fer. Mir. We wish your peace.
Exeunt.

Pros. Come with a thought. I thank thee, Ariel; come.

Enter *Ariel.*

Ari. Thy thoughts I cleave to. What's thy pleasure?

Pros. Spirit,
We must prepare to meet with Caliban.

Ari. Ay, my commander. When I presented Ceres,
I thought to have told thee of it, but I fear'd
Lest I might anger thee.

Pros. Say again, where didst thou leave these varlets?

Ari. I told you, sir, they were red-hot with drinking;
So full of valour that they smote the air
For breathing in their faces; beat the ground
For kissing of their feet; yet always bending
Towards their project. Then I beat my tabor;
At which, like unback'd colts, they prick'd their ears,
Advanc'd their eyelids, lifted up their noses
As they smelt music. So I charm'd their ears
That calf-like they my lowing follow'd through
Tooth'd briers, sharp furzes, pricking gorse, and thorns,
Which enter'd their frail shins. At last I left them
I' th' filthy-mantled pool beyond your cell,
There dancing up to th' chins, that the foul lake
O'erstunk their feet.

Pros. This was well done, my bird.
Thy shape invisible retain thou still.
The trumpery in my house, go bring it hither,
For stale to catch these thieves.

Ari. I go, I go.
Exit.

Pros. A devil, a born devil, on whose nature
Nurture can never stick; on whom my pains,
Humanely taken, all, all lost, quite lost;
And as with age his body uglier grows,
So his mind cankers. I will plague them all,
Even to roaring.

123. wonder'd, wonder-working. **130. crisp,** rippling. **138. footing,** dancing. **142. avoid,** begone.

156. rack, cloud. **167. presented,** represented. **187. stale,** decoy.

Re-enter *Ariel,* loaden with glittering apparel, etc.

Come, hang them on this line.

Prospero and *Ariel* remain, invisible. Enter *Caliban, Stephano,* and *Trinculo,* all wet.

Cal. Pray you, tread softly, that the blind mole may not
Hear a foot fall; we now are near his cell.

Ste. Monster, your fairy, which you say is a harmless fairy, has done little better than played the Jack with us.

Trin. Monster, I do smell all horse-piss, at which my nose is in great indignation.

Ste. So is mine. Do you hear, monster? If I should take a displeasure against you, look you,—

Trin. Thou wert but a lost monster.

Cal. Good my lord, give me thy favour still.
Be patient, for the prize I'll bring thee to
Shall hoodwink this mischance; therefore speak softly.
All 's hush'd as midnight yet.

Trin. Ay, but to lose our bottles in the pool,—

Ste. There is not only disgrace and dishonour in that, monster, but an infinite loss.

Trin. That 's more to me than my wetting; yet this is your harmless fairy, monster!

Ste. I will fetch off my bottle, though I be o'er ears for my labour.

Cal. Prithee, my king, be quiet. See'st thou here,
This is the mouth o' th' cell. No noise, and enter.
Do that good mischief which may make this island
Thine own for ever, and I, thy Caliban,
For aye thy foot-licker.

Ste. Give me thy hand. I do begin to have bloody thoughts.

Trin. O King Stephano! O peer! O worthy Stephano! look what a wardrobe here is for thee!

Cal. Let it alone, thou fool; it is but trash.

Trin. O, ho, monster! we know what belongs to a frippery. O King Stephano!

Ste. Put off that gown, Trinculo; by this hand, I 'll have that gown.

Trin. Thy Grace shall have it.

Cal. The dropsy drown this fool! what do you mean
To dote thus on such luggage? Let 't alone
And do the murder first. If he awake,
From toe to crown he 'll fill our skins with pinches,
Make us strange stuff.

Ste. Be you quiet, monster. Mistress line, is not this my jerkin? Now is the jerkin under the line: now, jerkin, you are like to lose your hair and prove a bald jerkin.

Trin. Do, do; we steal by line and level, an 't like your Grace.

Ste. I thank thee for that jest; here 's a garment for 't. Wit shall not go unrewarded while I am king of this country. "Steal by line and level" is an excellent pass of pate; there 's another garment for 't.

Trin. Monster, come, put some lime upon your fingers, and away with the rest.

Cal. I will have none on 't. We shall lose our time,
And all be turn'd to barnacles, or to apes
With foreheads villanous low.

Ste. Monster, lay-to your fingers. Help to bear this away where my hogshead of wine is, or I 'll turn you out of my kingdom. Go to, carry this.

Trin. And this.

Ste. Ay, and this.

A noise of hunters heard. Enter divers Spirits, in shape of dogs and hounds, hunting them about, Prospero and Ariel setting them on.

Pros Hey, Mountain, hey!

Ari. Silver! there it goes, Silver!

Pros. Fury, Fury! there, Tyrant, there! hark! hark!

Caliban, Stephano, and Trinculo are driven out.

Go charge my goblins that they grind their joints
With dry convulsions, shorten up their sinews
With aged cramps, and more pinch-spotted make them
Than pard or cat o' mountain.

Ari. Hark, they roar!

Pros. Let them be hunted soundly. At this hour
Lies at my mercy all mine enemies.
Shortly shall all my labours end, and thou
Shalt have the air at freedom. For a little
Follow, and do me service. *Exeunt.*

193. **line,** linden tree. 198. **Jack,** knave. 206. **hoodwink,** cover up. 222. From a ballad, a version of which Shakespeare used in *Othello II,* iii, 93 ff:

King Stephen was a worthy peer,
His breeches cost him but a crown,
He held them sixpence all too dear,
With that he called the tailor lown.
Cf. *Othello* II, iii, 93.

226. **frippery,** old-clothes shop.

235 ff.: The punning of this passage is complicated. **Under the line** may refer to hanging; or it may refer to the equator, and the losing of the hair may refer to the fevers contracted in the tropics. On the other hand, the jerkin may lose its hair or nap by being worn. 244. **pass of pate,** sally of wit. 246. **lime,** bird-lime. 249. **barnacles:** There was a strange belief in Shakespeare's day that a certain kind of shell-fish (barnacle) produced wild geese.

Act V. Scene I. *Before Prospero's cell.*

Enter *Prospero in his magic robes, and Ariel.*

Pros. Now does my project gather to a head.
My charms crack not; my spirits obey; and Time
Goes upright with his carriage. How 's the day?
Ari. On the sixth hour; at which time, my lord,
You said our work should cease.
Pros. I did say so,
When first I rais'd the tempest. Say, my spirit,
How fares the King and 's followers?
Ari. Confin'd together
In the same fashion as you gave in charge,
Just as you left them; all prisoners, sir,
In the line-grove which weather-fends your cell;
They cannot budge till your release. The King,
His brother, and yours, abide all three distracted,
And the remainder mourning over them,
Brimful of sorrow and dismay; but chiefly
Him that you term'd, sir, "The good old lord Gonzalo,"
His tears runs down his beard, like winter's drops
From eaves of reeds. Your charm so strongly works 'em
That if you now beheld them, your affections
Would become tender.
Pros. Dost thou think so, spirit?
Ari. Mine would, sir, were I human.
Pros. And mine shall.
Hast thou, which art but air, a touch, a feeling
Of their afflictions, and shall not myself,
One of their kind, that relish all as sharply
Passion as they, be kindlier mov'd than thou art?
Though with their high wrongs I am struck to the quick,
Yet with my nobler reason 'gainst my fury
Do I take part: the rarer action is
In virtue than in vengeance: they being penitent,
The sole drift of my purpose doth extend
Not a frown further. Go release them, Ariel.
My charms I 'll break, their senses I 'll restore,
And they shall be themselves.
Ari. I 'll fetch them, sir. *Exit.*

Pros. Ye elves of hills, brooks, standing lakes, and groves,
And ye that on the sands with printless foot
Do chase the ebbing Neptune, and do fly him
When he comes back; you demi-puppets that
By moonshine do the green sour ringlets make,
Whereof the ewe not bites; and you whose pastime
Is to make midnight mushrooms, that rejoice
To hear the solemn curfew; by whose aid,
Weak masters though ye be, I have bedimm'd
The noontide sun, call'd forth the mutinous winds,
And 'twixt the green sea and the azur'd vault
Set roaring war; to the dread rattling thunder
Have I given fire, and rifted Jove's stout oak
With his own bolt; the strong-bas'd promontory
Have I made shake, and by the spurs pluck'd up
The pine and cedar; graves at my command
Have wak'd their sleepers, op'd, and let 'em forth
By my so potent art. But this rough magic
I here abjure, and, when I have requir'd
Some heavenly music, which even now I do,
To work mine end upon their senses that
This airy charm is for, I 'll break my staff,
Bury it certain fathoms in the earth,
And deeper than did ever plummet sound
I 'll drown my book. *Solemn music.*

Here enters *Ariel* before: *then Alonso, with a frantic gesture, attended by Gonzalo; Sebastian and Antonio in like manner, attended by Adrian and Francisco. They all enter the circle which Prospero had made, and there stand charmed; which Prospero observing, speaks.*

A solemn air and the best comforter
To an unsettled fancy cure thy brains,
Now useless, boil'd within thy skull! There stand,
For you are spell-stopp'd.
Holy Gonzalo, honourable man,
Mine eyes, ev'n sociable to the shew of thine,
Fall fellowly drops. The charm dissolves apace,
And as the morning steals upon the night,
Melting the darkness, so their rising senses
Begin to chase the ignorant fumes that mantle
Their clearer reason. O good Gonzalo,

3. carriage, burden. **10. line-grove,** linden-grove.

37. green sour ringlets, dark green grass-circles, supposed to be made by fairies dancing in a ring. **45. given fire,** set off, discharged. **63. sociable,** in sympathy with.

My true preserver, and a loyal sir
To him thou follow'st! I will pay thy graces
Home both in word and deed. Most cruelly
Did thou, Alonso, use me and my daughter.
Thy brother was a furtherer in the act.
Thou art pinch'd for 't now, Sebastian. Flesh and blood,
You, brother mine, that entertain'd ambition,
Expell'd remorse and nature, whom, with Sebastian,
Whose inward pinches therefore are most strong,
Would here have kill'd your king, I do forgive thee,
Unnatural though thou art. Their understanding
Begins to swell, and the approaching tide
Will shortly fill the reasonable shore
That now lie foul and muddy. Not one of them
That yet looks on me, or would know me! Ariel,
Fetch me the hat and rapier in my cell;
I will discase me, and myself present
As I was sometime Milan: quickly, spirit;
Thou shalt ere long be free.

Ariel sings and helps to attire him.

Ari.

"Where the bee sucks, there suck I.
In a cowslip's bell I lie;
There I couch when owls do cry.
On the bat's back I do fly
After summer merrily.
Merrily, merrily shall I live now
Under the blossom that hangs on the bough."

Pros. Why, that 's my dainty Ariel! I shall miss thee;
But yet thou shalt have freedom. So, so, so.
To the King's ship, invisible as thou art;
There shalt thou find the mariners asleep
Under the hatches. The master and the boatswain
Being awake, enforce them to this place,
And presently, I prithee.

Ari. I drink the air before me, and return
Or ere your pulse twice beat. *Exit.*

Gon. All torment, trouble, wonder, and amazement
Inhabits here. Some heavenly power guide us
Out of this fearful country!

Pros. Behold, sir King,
The wronged Duke of Milan, Prospero.
For more assurance that a living prince
Does now speak to thee, I embrace thy body;
And to thee and thy company I bid
A hearty welcome.

Alon. Whe'er thou be'st he or no,
Or some enchanted trifle to abuse me,
As late I have been, I not know. Thy pulse
Beats as of flesh and blood; and, since I saw thee,
Th' affliction of my mind amends, with which,
I fear, a madness held me: this must crave,
An if this be at all, a most strange story.
Thy dukedom I resign and do entreat
Thou pardon me my wrongs. But how should Prospero
Be living and be here?

Pros. First, noble friend,
Let me embrace thine age, whose honour cannot
Be measur'd or confin'd.

Gon. Whether this be
Or be not, I 'll not swear.

Pros. You do yet taste
Some subtleties o' the isle, that will not let you
Believe things certain. Welcome, my friends all!
[*Aside to Sebastian and Antonio.*] But you, my brace of lords, were I so minded,
I here could pluck his Highness' frown upon you
And justify you traitors. At this time
I will tell no tales.

Seb. [*Aside.*] The devil speaks in him.

Pros. No.
For you, most wicked sir, whom to call brother
Would even infect my mouth, I do forgive
Thy rankest fault; all of them; and require
My dukedom of thee, which perforce, I know,
Thou must restore.

Alon. If thou be'st Prospero,
Give us particulars of thy preservation,
How thou hast met us here, whom three hours since
Were wreck'd upon this shore, where I have lost—
How sharp the point of this remembrance is!—
My dear son Ferdinand.

Pros. I am woe for 't, sir.

Alon. Irreparable is the loss, and Patience
Says it is past her cure.

Pros. I rather think
You have not sought her help, of whose soft grace
For the like loss I have her sovereign aid
And rest myself content.

Alon. You the like loss!

Pros. As great to me as late; and, supportable
To make the dear loss, have I means much weaker
Than you may call to comfort you, for I
Have lost my daughter.

71. Home, fully. **81. reasonable shore,** shore of reason. **85. discase me,** change my clothes.

112. trifle, mockery. **abuse,** deceive. **124. subtleties,** illusions. **128. justify,** prove. **139. woe,** sorry

Alon. A daughter?
O heavens, that they were living both in Naples,
The King and Queen there! That they were, I wish
Myself were mudded in that oozy bed
Where my son lies. When did you lose your daughter?
Pros. In this last tempest. I perceive, these lords
At this encounter do so much admire
That they devour their reason and scarce think
Their eyes do offices of truth, their words
Are natural breath; but, howsoe'er you have
Been justled from your senses, know for certain
That I am Prospero and that very duke
Which was thrust forth of Milan, who most strangely
Upon this shore, where you were wreck'd, was landed,
To be the lord on 't. No more yet of this;
For 't is a chronicle of day by day,
Not a relation for a breakfast nor
Befitting this first meeting. Welcome, sir;
This cell 's my court. Here have I few attendants,
And subjects none abroad: pray you, look in.
My dukedom since you have given me again,
I will requite you with as good a thing;
At least bring forth a wonder, to content ye
As much as me my dukedom.

Here Prospero discovers Ferdinand and Miranda playing at chess.

Mir. Sweet lord, you play me false.
Fer. No, my dearest love,
I would not for the world.
Mir. Yes, for a score of kingdoms you should wrangle,
And I would call it fair play.
Alon. If this prove
A vision of the island, one dear son
Shall I twice lose.
Seb. A most high miracle!
Fer. Though the seas threaten, they are merciful;
I have curs'd them without cause. *Kneels.*
Alon. Now all the blessings
Of a glad father compass thee about!
Arise, and say how thou cam'st here.
Mir. O, wonder!
How many goodly creatures are there here!
How beauteous mankind is! O brave new world,
That has such people in 't!
Pros. 'T is new to thee.
Alon. What is this maid with whom thou wast at play?
Your eld'st acquaintance cannot be three hours.
Is she the goddess that hath sever'd us,
And brought us thus together?
Fer. Sir, she is mortal,
But by immortal Providence she 's mine.
I chose her when I could not ask my father
For his advice, nor thought I had one. She
Is daughter to this famous Duke of Milan,
Of whom so often I have heard renown,
But never saw before; of whom I have
Receiv'd a second life; and second father
This lady makes him to me.
Alon. I am hers.
But, O, how oddly will it sound that I
Must ask my child forgiveness!
Pros. There, sir, stop.
Let us not burden our remembrances with
A heaviness that 's gone.
Gon. I have inly wept,
Or should have spoke ere this. Look down, you gods,
And on this couple drop a blessed crown!
For it is you that have chalk'd forth the way
Which brought us hither.
Alon. I say, Amen, Gonzalo!
Gon. Was Milan thrust from Milan, that his issue
Should become Kings of Naples? O, rejoice
Beyond a common joy, and set it down
With gold on lasting pillars: in one voyage
Did Claribel her husband find at Tunis,
And Ferdinand, her brother, found a wife
Where he himself was lost, Prospero his dukedom
In a poor isle, and all of us ourselves
When no man was his own.
Alon. [*To Ferdinand and Miranda*] Give me your hands.
Let grief and sorrow still embrace his heart
That doth not wish you joy!
Gon. Be it so! Amen!

Re-enter *Ariel,* with the Master and Boatswain amazedly following.

O, look, sir, look, sir! here is more of us.
I prophesied, if a gallows were on land,
This fellow could not drown. Now, blasphemy,
That swear'st grace o'erboard, not an oath on shore?
Hast thou no mouth by land? What is the news?
Boats. The best news is, that we have safely found
Our king and company; the next, our ship—
Which, but three glasses since, we gave out split—
Is tight and yare and bravely rigg'd as when
We first put out to sea.

154. admire, wonder. 155. devour, destroy.

186. eld'st, longest possible. 224. yare, ready.

Ari. [*Aside to Prospero.*] Sir, all this service
Have I done since I went.
Pros. [*Aside to Ariel.*] My tricksy spirit!
Alon. These are not natural events; they strengthen
From strange to stranger. Say, how came you hither?
Boats. If I did think, sir, I were well awake,
I 'd strive to tell you. We were dead of sleep,
And—how we know not—all clapp'd under hatches;
Where but even now with strange and several noises
Of roaring, shrieking, howling, jingling chains,
And moe diversity of sounds, all horrible,
We were awak'd; straightway, at liberty;
Where we, in all our trim, freshly beheld
Our royal, good, and gallant ship, our master
Cap'ring to eye her. On a trice, so please you,
Even in a dream, were we divided from them
And were brought moping hither.
Ari. [*Aside to Prospero.*] Was 't well done?
Pros. [*Aside to Ariel.*] Bravely, my diligence. Thou shalt be free.
Alon. This is as strange a maze as e'er men trod;
And there is in this business more than nature
Was ever conduct of: some oracle
Must rectify our knowledge.
Pros. Sir, my liege,
Do not infest your mind with beating on
The strangeness of this business: at pick'd leisure,
Which shall be shortly, single I 'll resolve you,
Which to you shall seem probable, of every
These happen'd accidents; till when, be cheerful
And think of each thing well. [*Aside to Ariel.*] Come hither, spirit.
Set Caliban and his companions free;
Untie the spell. [*Exit Ariel.*] How fares my gracious sir?
There are yet missing of your company
Some few odd lads that you remember not.

Re-enter *Ariel,* driving in *Caliban, Stephano,* and *Trinculo,* in their stolen apparel.

Ste. Every man shift for all the rest, and let no man take care for himself; for all is but fortune. Coragio, bully-monster, coragio!
Trin. If these be true spies which I wear in my head, here 's a goodly sight.
Cal. O Setebos, these be brave spirits indeed!
How fine my master is! I am afraid
He will chastise me.
Seb. Ha, ha!
What things are these, my lord Antonio?
Will money buy 'em?
Ant. Very like; one of them
Is a plain fish, and, no doubt, marketable.
Pros. Mark but the badges of these men, my lords,
Then say if they be true. This mis-shapen knave,
His mother was a witch, and one so strong
That could control the moon, make flows and ebbs,
And deal in her command without her power.
These three have robb'd me; and this demi-devil—
For he 's a bastard one—had plotted with them
To take my life. Two of these fellows you
Must know and own; this thing of darkness I
Acknowledge mine.
Cal. I shall be pinch'd to death.
Alon. Is not this Stephano, my drunken butler?
Seb. He is drunk now. Where had he wine?
Alon. And Trinculo is reeling ripe. Where should they
Find this grand liquor that hath gilded 'em?
How cam'st thou in this pickle?
Trin. I have been in such a pickle since I saw you last that, I fear me, will never out of my bones. I shall not fear fly-blowing.
Seb. Why, how now, Stephano!
Ste. O, touch me not; I am not Stephano, but a cramp.
Pros. You 'd be king o' the isle, sirrah?
Ste. I should have been a sore one then.
Alon. This is a strange thing as e'er I look'd on. *Pointing to Caliban.*
Pros. He is as disproportion'd in his manners
As in his shape. Go, sirrah, to my cell;
Take with you your companions: as you look
To have my pardon, trim it handsomely.
Cal. Ay, that I will; and I 'll be wise hereafter
And seek for grace. What a thrice-double ass
Was I, to take this drunkard for a god
And worship this dull fool!
Pros. Go to; away!
Alon. Hence, and bestow your luggage where you found it.

230. **of sleep,** asleep. 236. **our trim,** our holiday suits. The sailors, like all other characters in this last scene, are in fine clothes to make a brave show. 240. **moping,** in a daze. 244. **conduct,** instigator, conductor. 246. **infest,** harass.

267. **badges,** (1) servants' arm-badges, (2) The stolen apparel they are wearing. 271. **deal in her command,** exert her (the moon's) influence; **without her power,** beyond her sphere. 280. **gilded,** flushed, intoxicated.

Seb. Or stole it, rather.
Pros. Sir, I invite your Highness and your train
To my poor cell, where you shall take your rest
For this one night; which, part of it, I 'll waste
With such discourse as, I not doubt, shall make it
Go quick away,—the story of my life
And the particular accidents gone by
Since I came to this isle: and in the morn
I 'll bring you to your ship and so to Naples,
Where I have hope to see the nuptial
Of these our dear-belov'd solemnized;
And thence retire me to my Milan, where
Every third thought shall be my grave.
Alon. I long
To hear the story of your life, which must
Take the ear strangely.
Pros. I 'll deliver all;
And promise you calm seas, auspicious gales,
And sail so expeditious that shall catch
Your royal fleet far off. [*Aside to Ariel.*] My Ariel, chick,
That is thy charge. Then to the elements
Be free, and fare thou well! Please you, draw near. *Exeunt omnes.*

Epilogue

SPOKEN BY PROSPERO.

Now my charms are all o'erthrown,
And what strength I have 's mine own,
Which is most faint: now, 't is true,
I must be here confin'd by you,
Or sent to Naples. Let me not,
Since I have my dukedom got
And pardon'd the deceiver, dwell
In this bare island by your spell;
But release me from my bands
With the help of your good hands.
Gentle breath of yours my sails
Must fill, or else my project fails,
Which was to please. Now I want
Spirits to enforce, art to enchant,
And my ending is despair,
Unless I be reliev'd by prayer,
Which pierces so that it assaults
Mercy itself and frees all faults.
As you from crimes would pardon'd be.
Let your indulgence set me free. *Exit.*

10. hands, applause. **18. Mercy,** God, the All-Merciful.

Sonnets

In the Renaissance the ability to compose poetry was regarded as a part of every gentleman's cultural equipment. To be sure, not every gentleman wrote well, but he might be expected to turn a verse now and then, as a modern man might be expected to take a hand at cards. Of course he would not write for pay or publication, and he might even pretend that he wrote with no intention of achieving any public whatever. This state of affairs led to the custom of writing verse epistles and presenting poems in manuscript to one's friends. If the friend were proud of the poems, he would permit *his* friends to copy them, and so the writer might, without ever regularly publishing his poems, achieve a reputation and a public. In aristocratic Elizabethan society, professional writers, like Shakespeare, could not hope to achieve true gentility, but they could and did write verse letters; they could write poems to their friends, and if these poems were widely circulated, they had nothing to lose. We know from Francis Meres' *Palladis Tamia* that Shakespeare's "sugared sonnets" were circulating in manuscript "among his private friends" as early as 1598, but they were not published until eleven years later when, by means known only to himself, Thomas Thorpe, a not very reputable publisher, acquired a manuscript copy of the sonnets and published them in an unauthorized edition. They appeared in print without Shakespeare's knowledge and, of course, entirely without his corrections. Thorpe arranged them in what seemed to him their proper order, and had them printed by George Eld.

Presumably all the sonnets are not in their proper order; only in some instances is there a logical progression from one sonnet to the next. It may be that Thorpe inadvertently disarranged them, and thereby increased the disorder, but it is certain that they never were intended to be an ordered sequence telling a coherent story. There is no invented narrative, nothing that can be called a plot. They tell a story only by implication. In their larger divisions they are without doubt properly arranged, falling into three distinct groups: 1-126, 127-152, and 153-154. The first two groups are addressed to, or concern themselves with, respectively, a young man, the poet's friend, and a young woman, the poet's mistress. The last two sonnets, free translations of a Greek poem by Marianus, a Byzantine writer of about the fifth century, bear no relation to the rest of the sonnets and were included in the volume because Thorpe wanted as many of Shakespeare's sonnets as he could lay his hands on. The worst of the sonnets are wretched; but the best are poems such as have never been surpassed, and they speak the speech of genuine and deep emotion which no one with the slightest feeling for poetry can fail to recognize.

Date.—We cannot say with certainty when the sonnets were written, but it seems clear that they were composed early in Shakespeare's career. Meres did not say how many sonnets were circulating in manuscript in 1598, but in the following year corrupt versions of two of the sonnets were published in a volume of poems called *The Passionate Pilgrim.* Both these sonnets, numbers 138 and 144, are about the poet's mistress ("the dark lady," as she has come to be known), and we learn from them that both the poet's friendship with the young man and his affair with the lady were well advanced, that the friend and the lady had met, and that the poet thinks, but is not sure, that they have betrayed him. It follows that most of the events reflected in the sonnets had occurred by 1599 at the very latest. The sonnets in his plays attest Shakespeare's early interest in that poetic form. In *Romeo and Juliet* (1596), lines I, v, 96–110 and the prologues to the first and second acts are sonnets, and the sonnets in *Love's Labours Lost* (I, i, 80–93; I, i, 161–174; V, ii, 344–357; and V, ii, 403–416) were probably worked into the dialogue when Shakespeare first composed the play in 1593 rather than during his later revision of it. Besides, most of the verbal parallels between the sonnets and his other works are to his poems, *Venus and Adonis* and *Lucrece,* and his earlier plays. Then too, during the years 1591–1596, there was a veritable epidemic of sonneteering, and Shakespeare was not a man to ignore fashion. It must be admitted that all the evidence for dating the sonnets does not point to an early date, but since none of the evidence is altogether conclusive, we must base our decision on the preponderance of it. The years 1592–1596 seem to be the most likely time. And if, allowing for the poet's use of metaphor and exaggeration, we assume that the sonnets mean what they say, we must conclude that they were written early in his career, for they tell of a young poet whose success was not yet assured. We may conclude that the sonnets were composed over a period of years (at least three, as we learn from sonnet 104) and dispatched as letters to the young man and the dark lady. They refer to successive events and describe successive emotional states. We learn of Shakespeare's admiration and deep affection for a young man of gentle birth, of his love for his mistress, of their betrayal of him, and how, when he had to choose between them, he chose the friend.

In one of the wisest passages in modern literature, Thoreau observes that it takes two to tell the truth, one to speak and another to hear. If we are to hear the voice of the poet in these sonnets, we must do our part. We must understand that he was not speaking to us but to contemporaries who were familiar with the events to which he refers. We must remember that the meaning of words shifts with the centuries and that although it may be true that human emotion does not change, it is undoubtedly true that concepts in which emotion is verbally embodied do change, and that a comparison which seems inevitably apt to the men of one century seems forced and distorted to a later age. Now, to Shakespeare and his contemporaries the words "love" and "lover" as applied by one man to another could and did mean "friendship" and "friend," and were so used throughout Shakespeare's works. "I tell thee, fellow, thy general is my lover," says Menenius speaking of his chief friend, Coriolanus. John Donne, poet and Dean of St. Paul's, concludes many of his letters to other men with the words, "Your lover." This was the usage of the day. There was also the Renaissance concept of the superiority of the friendship of man for man over the affection of man for woman. This was part of the intellectual inheritance of the age, and people heard it with no sense of strangeness. When the warrior Aufidius welcomes his late enemy Coriolanus to the ranks of the Volsces, he says,

> Know thou first,
> I lov'd the maid I married; never man
> Sigh'd truer breath; but that I see thee here,
> Thou noble thing! more dances my rapt heart
> Than when I first my wedded mistress saw
> Bestride my threshold.

This is the concept behind the sonnets, and such are the terms in which the young man is addressed. Although on first hearing they are strange to the modern ear, it is immediately clear that Shakespeare's devotion to the young man was profound and that their friendship was bound by ties of admiration and deep regard. On the other hand he respected neither the dark lady nor his love for her. His attraction to her was primarily erotic. It is quite idle to imagine him a man with Victorian standards of propriety. In this matter, too, he was of his age.

His attitude toward the lady is a completely earthy one, utterly lacking in romance; and she is the antithesis of the heroines of all the other contemporary sonnet sequences, Spenser's *Amoretti,* for instance, and Sir Philip Sidney's *Astrophel and Stella.* They were chaste, cool, aloof; their lovers protested passion; they answered in disdain—and were taken at their word. They all looked alike. Following the Elizabethan ideal of beauty, their hair was gold, their eyes suns, their skin milk. As we learn from sonnet 130, Shakespeare's mistress was unlike them in every respect. No one knows who the woman was, but she was something of a lady. She played the spinet and had a taste for verse. Her taste in men was splendid. She was a married woman, probably quite young. Shakespeare was almost thirty and feeling older. His first child was now almost a young woman, and he himself had been buffeting the world for years. Sometimes, thinking of his mistress, it seemed to him that his days were "past the best." This will seem strange only to people old enough to have forgotten that the passing of youth may be as poignant an experience as the passing of middle age. So he played the game of love and said nothing about his age:

> When my love swears that she is made of truth,
> I do believe her, though I know she lies,
> That she might think me some untutor'd youth
> Unlearned in the world's false subtleties.

But the game did not last; she was better at it than he. She found the young friend attractive, her own fortitude negligible; and she played her poet false.

He seems not to have been made for philandering. He became increasingly troubled by the realization that in their love they were "forsworn." In sonnet 66 he lists the wrongs which make him long for death; they include "faith unhappily forsworn," and "honour wrongfully misplaced." Yet he still loved her, and, restive because neither his reason nor his wits could "dissuade one foolish heart from serving" her, he came to think of his love as

a fever, longing still
For that which longer nurseth the disease . . .

And in the end he turned from her with revulsion:

For I have sworn thee fair, and thought thee bright,
Who art as black as hell, as dark as night.

Sonnet 146 is his testament of remorse. Although the sonnets do not tell a story, we may discern a story behind them. It is an old story, and not at all of the kind a poet is likely to have invented about himself. At first it may even seem a little naive, but it is not naive. There is a frank acceptance of emotional experience, of joy in the emotion—and there is a subsequent realization of guilt. It is chiefly in this last respect that the modern reader of the implied story of the sonnets finds it strange; remorse, at the moment, is out of fashion. The sonnets are not sophisticated. There is no distrust of the emotion before the emotion, and there is no diminution of it by subjecting it to the play of the intellect.

Standing in sharp contrast to Shakespeare's love for the dark lady is his friendship for the young man. With her there was always the spectre of her light reputation and their infidelity to bar him from contentment. With the friend, although he was separated from him by age and social station, there was an association on terms of moral equality which matured into a "marriage of true minds." The friend was a young man of gentle birth. He was handsome, charming, and, at the time of their meeting, quite unspoiled. It was his fresh youthfulness that most impressed Shakespeare:

Shall I compare thee to a summer's day?
Thou art more lovely and more temperate . . .

The first sonnets urge the young man to marry in order that his beauty may be perpetuated in children. He is a very eligible youth, but for some reason he is reluctant to marry. It may simply have been that he was not in love. In any case, Shakespeare is advising him to marry, and the advice is given earnestly but deferentially. As Shakespeare's poems go, these are minor compositions, very pretty compliments with some lines of exquisite beauty—but on the whole they are formal. As one reads on, however, he discovers passages in which the formality drops away and the poet speaks with conviction, and he soon observes that these passages are all on the same theme—"Time's thievish progress to eternity":

For never-resting Time leads summer on
To hideous winter and confounds him there;
Sap check'd with frost and lusty leaves quite gone,
Beauty o'er-snowed and bareness everywhere.

The antiquity of this theme made it no less impressive to Shakespeare. There is small consolation in reflecting that beauty has faded and men have died since the beginning of time. From Shakespeare's earliest poems to his latest plays he speaks of beauty, and it continually brings to his mind the melancholy reflection that beauty fades. In his last play, *The Tempest,* he mentions grief, and adds parenthetically, "That's beauty's canker."

The early sonnets urging the young man to marry lose their strangeness to modern ears when we remember the poet's love of beauty and his fear of mutability, two qualities of his nature which, acting together, intensify each other and create in his early poems the rich emotion of his maturer work. It is no accident that the first sonnet (No. 12) to rise to the estate of major poetry—"When I do count the clock that tells the time"—devotes its first twelve lines to a description of the havoc wrought by time.

With the fifteenth sonnet he introduces a new theme. There is another immortality than that bestowed by children; there is the immortality of enduring poetry. Shakespeare promises so to celebrate his friend's virtues in verse that, as long as the poems shall last, he will be remembered as he was in his youth:

And all in war with Time for love of you
As he takes from you, I engraft you new.

At first Shakespeare makes the promise humbly and somewhat tentatively. He was then a new poet, confident of his powers but uncertain of his success. He speaks of his "barren rhyme" and "pupil pen," and he thinks of his sonnets as the work of a beginner which will be outshone by other writers. It was in this frame of mind that, at about the same time, he wrote his dedication to *Venus and Adonis* and referred to the poem as "my unpolished lines." But his progress was swift, and, having won some recognition as a poet, he realized that his "slight muse" might "please these curious days." Further recognition bringing greater self-confidence, he writes with passionate assurance that his poetry *will* endure and carry with it the splendid memory of his friend:

Not marble nor the gilded monuments
Of princes shall outlive this powerful rhyme,
But you shall shine more bright in these contents
Than unswept stone besmeared with sluttish
 time . . .

Although his first notable success convinced Shakespeare that his poetry would resist the triumph of time, he was not at all certain that his name would endure. Later, toward the end of the 1590's, he was of course aware of his fame. But in 1595 his greatest plays were all unwritten. He was then the author of some unpublished sonnets and his two poems. Such plays as he had written were not his to publish, and besides, the reputation of plays was not as great as their popularity. He had little fame to expect from them. He was not only a playwright, he was an actor, and actors suffered from an even lower public esteem than playwrights. In the eyes of the law, actors, rogues, and vagabonds were the same sort of people. This opprobrium was new to him; he had had a better social station in Stratford. Now as an actor and playwright in London he was anxious to better his position. It is natural enough that he was uneasy over the light reputation of his mistress, and that, although he had no doubt of his poetry's worth, he was uncertain of his reputation as a poet. The sonnets which say that he expects to be forgotten after his death express the dreadful and honest fears of the young writer:

O, if, I say, you look upon this verse
When I perhaps compounded am with clay,
Do not so much as my poor name rehearse,
But let your love even with my life decay . . .

It is obvious from the volume of his work that Shakespeare's days in London were very full, and it is impossible to believe that he was altogether unhappy. Still, he was not entirely at home in the life he led. After all, he was a player, barred from "public honour," feeling the injustice of a fortune

That did not better for my life provide
Than public means which public manners breeds.
Thence comes it that my name receives a brand,
And almost thence my nature is subdued
To what it works in, like the dyer's hand:
Pity me then, and wish I were renew'd . . .

This discontentment found release in his friendship with the young gentleman. It is no wonder that it seemed to him a compensation for all his misfortunes and that he should express his satisfaction in such a sonnet as "When in disgrace with fortune and men's eyes."

Shakespeare then, at about thirty, was a promising writer in London. He had his work, his mistress, and his friend; and of the three his friend gave him the least cause for self-reproach. When the friend and mistress met and he had to decide between them, he did not hesitate. It may be he was over-generous in his estimate of his friend. Perhaps the young man was a little too pliant. But in the affairs of the heart Shakespeare expected (see Sonnet 41) a certain compliance of all young men, and, alas! he expected even less restraint from his lady. But although she was untrue to both her husband and her lover, it cannot be said that she deceived anyone. It is her eternal charm that, Cressida-like, she did not even deceive herself.

Not all students of Shakespeare will agree to the historicity of the events reflected in the sonnets, and the reader who finds himself in disagreement with the convictions of the present editors need only to come to his own conclusions. There is no possibility that the vast body of conflicting opinions about Shakespeare's sonnets can be considerably increased. The speculations as to the identity of the young man and the dark lady have been discussed in the General Introduction.

SONNETS

1

From fairest creatures we desire increase,
That thereby beauty's rose might never die,
But as the riper should by time decease,
His tender heir might bear his memory:
But thou, contracted to thine own bright eyes,
Feed'st thy light's flame with self-substantial fuel,
Making a famine where abundance lies,
Thyself thy foe, to thy sweet self too cruel.
Thou that art now the world's fresh ornament
And only herald to the gaudy spring,
Within thine own bud buriest thy content
And, tender churl, mak'st waste in niggarding.
  Pity the world, or else this glutton be,
  To eat the world's due, by the grave and thee.

5. **contracted,** betrothed. 6. **self-substantial fuel,** fuel composed of the same substance as the flame. 11. **content,** potential fatherhood. 13-14. The meaning is that by selfishly refusing to marry and have children the friend cheats the world of the posterity he owes it.

2

When forty winters shall besiege thy brow,
And dig deep trenches in thy beauty's field,
Thy youth's proud livery, so gaz'd on now,
Will be a tatter'd weed, of small worth held..
Then being ask'd where all thy beauty lies,
Where all the treasure of thy lusty days,
To say, within thine own deep-sunken eyes,
Were an all-eating shame and thriftless praise.
How much more praise deserv'd thy beauty's use
If thou couldst answer, "This fair child of mine
Shall sum my count and make my old excuse,"
Proving his beauty by succession thine!
  This were to be new made when thou art old,
  And see thy blood warm when thou feel'st it cold.

3

Look in thy glass, and tell the face thou viewest
Now is the time that face should form another;
Whose fresh repair if now thou not renewest,
Thou dost beguile the world, unbless some mother.
For where is she so fair whose unear'd womb
Disdains the tillage of thy husbandry?
Or who is he so fond will be the tomb,
Of his self-love to stop posterity?
Thou art thy mother's glass, and she in thee
Calls back the lovely April of her prime;
So thou through windows of thine age shalt see
Despite of wrinkles this thy golden time.
  But if thou live, remember'd not to be,
  Die single, and thine image dies with thee.

5. **unear'd,** unploughed. 7. **fond,** foolish.

4

Unthrifty loveliness, why dost thou spend
Upon thyself thy beauty's legacy?
Nature's bequest gives nothing, but doth lend,
And being frank she lends to those are free.
Then, beauteous niggard, why dost thou abuse
The bounteous largess given thee to give?
Profitless usurer, why dost thou use
So great a sum of sums, yet canst not live?
For having traffic with thyself alone,
Thou of thyself thy sweet self dost deceive.
Then how, when Nature calls thee to be gone,
What acceptable audit canst thou leave?
  Thy unus'd beauty must be tomb'd with thee,
  Which, used, lives the executor to be.

4. **frank,** liberal. **free,** generous.

5

Those hours that with gentle work did frame
The lovely gaze where every eye doth dwell,
Will play the tyrants to the very same
And that unfair which fairly doth excel;
For never-resting time leads summer on
To hideous winter and confounds him there,
Sap check'd with frost and lusty leaves quite gone,
Beauty o'ersnow'd and bareness everywhere;
Then, were not summer's distillation left,
A liquid prisoner pent in walls of glass,
Beauty's effect with beauty were bereft,
Nor it nor no remembrance what it was:
  But flowers distill'd, though they with winter meet,
  Leese but their show; their substance still lives sweet.

2. **gaze,** sight. 4. **unfair,** make unfair.

6

Then let not winter's ragged hand deface
In thee thy summer, ere thou be distill'd:
Make sweet some vial; treasure thou some place

With beauty's treasure, ere it be self-kill'd.
That use is not forbidden usury
Which happies those that pay the willing loan;
That's for thyself to breed another thee,
Or ten times happier, be it ten for one;
Ten times thyself were happier than thou art,
If ten of thine ten times refigur'd thee:
Then what could death do, if thou shouldst depart,
Leaving thee living in posterity?
Be not self-will'd, for thou art much too fair
To be death's conquest and make worms thine heir.

1. ragged, rugged. 3. treasure, enrich.

7

Lo! in the orient when the gracious light
Lifts up his burning head, each under eye
Doth homage to his new-appearing sight,
Serving with looks his sacred majesty;
And having climb'd the steep-up heavenly hill,
Resembling strong youth in his middle age,
Yet mortal looks adore his beauty still,
Attending on his golden pilgrimage;
But when from highmost pitch, with weary car,
Like feeble age, he reeleth from the day,
The eyes, 'fore duteous, now converted are
From his low tract and look another way:
So thou, thyself out-going in thy noon,
Unlook'd on diest, unless thou get a son.

8

Music to hear, why hear'st thou music sadly?
Sweets with sweets war not, joy delights in joy.
Why lov'st thou that which thou receiv'st not gladly,
Or else receiv'st with pleasure thine annoy?
If the true concord of well-tuned sounds,
By unions married, do offend thine ear,
They do but sweetly chide thee, who confounds
In singleness the parts that thou shouldst bear.
Mark how one string, sweet husband to another,
Strikes each in each by mutual ordering,
Resembling sire and child and happy mother,
Who, all in one, one pleasing note do sing;
Whose speechless song, being many, seeming one,
Sings this to thee: "Thou single wilt prove none."

10. mutual ordering, ordered harmony.

9

Is it for fear to wet a widow's eye
That thou consum'st thyself in single life?
Ah! if thou issueless shalt hap to die,
The world will wail thee, like a makeless wife;
The world will be thy widow and still weep
That thou no form of thee hast left behind,
When every private widow well may keep
By children's eyes her husband's shape in mind.
Look, what an unthrift in the world doth spend
Shifts but his place, for still the world enjoys it;
But beauty's waste hath in the world an end,
And kept unus'd, the user so destroys it.
No love toward others in that bosom sits
That on himself such murderous shame commits.

4. makeless, mateless. 5. still, continually.

10

For shame! deny that thou bear'st love to any,
Who for thyself art so unprovident.
Grant, if thou wilt, thou art belov'd of many,
But that thou none lov'st is most evident;
For thou art so possess'd with murderous hate
That 'gainst thyself thou stick'st not to conspire,
Seeking that beauteous roof to ruinate
Which to repair should be thy chief desire.
O, change thy thought, that I may change my mind:
Shall hate be fairer lodg'd than gentle love?
Be as thy presence is, gracious and kind,
Or to thyself at least kind-hearted prove:
Make thee another self, for love of me,
That beauty still may live in thine or thee.

6. stick'st, hesitatest. 7. roof, body.

11

As fast as thou shalt wane, so fast thou grow'st
In one of thine, from that which thou departest;
And that fresh blood which youngly thou bestow'st
Thou mayst call thine when thou from youth convertest.
Herein lives wisdom, beauty, and increase;
Without this, folly, age, and cold decay.
If all were minded so, the times should cease
And threescore year would make the world away.
Let those whom Nature hath not made for store,
Harsh, featureless, and rude, barrenly perish:
Look, whom she best endow'd she gave the more;

Which bounteous gift thou shouldst in bounty cherish.
She carv'd thee for her seal, and meant thereby
Thou shouldst print more, not let that copy die.

4. convertest, changest. **9. store,** breeding.

12

When I do count the clock that tells the time,
And see the brave day sunk in hideous night;
When I behold the violet past prime,
And sable curls all silver'd o'er with white;
When lofty trees I see barren of leaves
Which erst from heat did canopy the herd,
And summer's green, all girded up in sheaves,
Borne on the bier with white and bristly beard;
Then of thy beauty do I question make,
That thou among the wastes of time must go,
Since sweets and beauties do themselves forsake
And die as fast as they see others grow;
And nothing 'gainst Time's scythe can make defence
Save breed, to brave him when he takes thee hence.

2. brave, beautiful. **14. breed,** progeny.

13

O that you were yourself! but, love, you are
No longer yours than you yourself here live:
Against this coming end you should prepare,
And your sweet semblance to some other give.
So should that beauty which you hold in lease
Find no determination; then you were
Yourself again after yourself's decease,
When your sweet issue your sweet form should bear.
Who lets so fair a house fall to decay,
Which husbandry in honour might uphold
Against the stormy gusts of winter's day
And barren rage of death's eternal cold?
O, none but unthrifts. Dear my love, you know
You had a father: let your son say so.

6. determination, end.

14

Not from the stars do I my judgement pluck;
And yet methinks I have astronomy,
But not to tell of good or evil luck,
Of plagues, of dearths, or seasons' quality;
Nor can I fortune to brief minutes tell,
'Pointing to each his thunder, rain, and wind,
Or say with princes if it shall go well,
By oft predict that I in heaven find:
But from thine eyes my knowledge I derive,
And, constant stars, in them I read such art
As "Truth and beauty shall together thrive,
If from thyself to store thou wouldst convert;"
Or else of thee this I prognosticate:
Thy end is truth's and beauty's doom and date.

2. astronomy, astrology. **5. tell,** allot. **8. oft predict,** frequent predictions. **10. art,** knowledge.

15

When I consider everything that grows
Holds in perfection but a little moment,
That this huge stage presenteth nought but shows
Whereon the stars in secret influence comment;
When I perceive that men as plants increase,
Cheered and check'd even by the self-same sky,
Vaunt in their youthful sap, at height decrease,
And wear their brave state out of memory;
Then the conceit of this inconstant stay
Sets you most rich in youth before my sight,
Where wasteful Time debateth with Decay,
To change your day of youth to sullied night;
And, all in war with Time for love of you,
As he takes from you, I engraft you new.

4. influence, Astrologers believed that a power emanating from the stars helped form the character and fortune of men. **7. Vaunt,** exult. **9. conceit,** idea. **14. I . . . new,** This is the first of the poet's promises of immortality in verse.

16

But wherefore do not you a mightier way
Make war upon this bloody tyrant, Time?
And fortify yourself in your decay
With means more blessed than my barren rhyme?
Now stand you on the top of happy hours,
And many maiden gardens, yet unset,
With virtuous wish would bear your living flowers,
Much liker than your painted counterfeit:
So should the lines of life that life repair,
Which this time's pencil, or my pupil pen,
Neither in inward worth nor outward fair,
Can make you live yourself in eyes of men.
To give away yourself keeps yourself still,
And you must live, drawn by your own sweet skill.

9. lines of life, children. **10. this time's pencil** portraiture, see l. 8. **11. fair,** beauty. **13. give away yourself,** beget children.

17

Who will believe my verse in time to come,
If it were fill'd with your most high deserts?

Though yet, heaven knows, it is but as a tomb
Which hides your life and shows not half your parts.
If I could write the beauty of your eyes
And in fresh numbers number all your graces,
The age to come would say, "This poet lies;
Such heavenly touches ne'er touch'd earthly faces."
So should my papers, yellowed with their age,
Be scorn'd like old men of less truth than tongue,
And your true rights be term'd a poet's rage
And stretched metre of an antique song:
But were some child of yours alive that time,
You should live twice, in it and in my rhyme.

6. numbers, verses. 11. rage, exaggeration.

18

Shall I compare thee to a summer's day?
Thou art more lovely and more temperate:
Rough winds do shake the darling buds of May,
And summer's lease hath all too short a date:
Sometime too hot the eye of heaven shines,
And often is his gold complexion dimm'd;
And every fair from fair sometime declines,
By chance or nature's changing course untrimm'd:
But thy eternal summer shall not fade
Nor lose possession of that fair thou ow'st,
Nor shall Death brag thou wand'rest in his shade,
When in eternal lines to time thou grow'st;
So long as men can breathe or eyes can see,
So long lives this and this gives life to thee.

7. Every beautiful object loses its beauty. 8. untrimm'd, deprived of beauty. 10. ow'st, ownest.

19

Devouring Time, blunt thou the lion's paws,
And make the earth devour her own sweet brood;
Pluck the keen teeth from the fierce tiger's jaws,
And burn the long-liv'd phœnix in her blood;
Make glad and sorry seasons as thou fleets,
And do whate'er thou wilt, swift-footed Time,
To the wide world and all her fading sweets;
But I forbid thee one most heinous crime:
O, carve not with thy hours my love's fair brow,
Nor draw no lines there with thine antique pen;
Him in thy course untainted do allow
For beauty's pattern to succeeding men.
Yet, do thy worst, old Time: despite thy wrong,
My love shall in my verse ever live young.

20

A woman's face with Nature's own hand painted
Hast thou, the master-mistress of my passion;
A woman's gentle heart, but not acquainted
With shifting change, as is false women's fashion;
An eye more bright than theirs, less false in rolling,
Gilding the object whereupon it gazeth;
A man in hue all hues in his controlling,
Which steals men's eyes and women's souls amazeth.
And for a woman wert thou first created;
Till Nature, as she wrought thee, fell a-doting,
And by addition me of thee defeated
By adding one thing to my purpose nothing.
But since she prick'd thee out for women's pleasure,
Mine be thy love, and thy love's use their treasure.

7-8. The passage has been widely and variously explained, although its primary meaning is clear. Shakespeare has just described the man as surpassing the beauty of woman. He now continues by giving him a complexion surpassing all others.

21

So is it not with me as with that Muse,
Stirr'd by a painted beauty to his verse,
Who heaven itself for ornament doth use
And every fair with his fair doth rehearse,
Making a couplement of proud compare
With sun and moon, with earth and sea's rich gems,
With April's first-born flowers, and all things rare
That heaven's air in this huge rondure hems.
O let me, true in love, but truly write,
And then believe me, my love is as fair
As any mother's child, though not so bright
As those gold candles fix'd in heaven's air:
Let them say more that like of hearsay well;
I will not praise that purpose not to sell.

1. Muse, poet. 5. couplement . . . compare, proud comparison. 8. rondure, circle, world. 13. like . . . well, like exaggerated rumor.

22

My glass shall not persuade me I am old,
So long as youth and thou are of one date;
But when in thee time's furrows I behold,
Then look I death my days should expiate.
For all that beauty that doth cover thee

Is but the seemly raiment of my heart,
Which in thy breast doth live, as thine in me:
How can I then be elder than thou art?
O therefore, love, be of thyself so wary
As I, not for myself but for thee will;
Bearing thy heart, which I will keep so chary
As tender nurse her babe from faring ill.
Presume not on thy heart when mine is slain;
Thou gav'st me thine, not to give back again.

4. expiate, end. **13. Presume not on,** do not expect to regain.

23

As an unperfect actor on the stage
Who with his fear is put besides his part,
Or some fierce thing replete with too much rage,
Whose strength's abundance weakens his own heart,
So I, for fear of trust, forget to say
The perfect ceremony of love's rite,
And in mine own love's strength seem to decay,
O'ercharg'd with burden of mine own love's might.
O, let my looks be then the eloquence
And dumb presagers of my speaking breast,
Who plead for love and look for recompense
More than that tongue that more hath more express'd.
O, learn to read what silent love hath writ:
To hear with eyes belongs to love's fine wit.

2. besides, out of. **5. for fear of trust,** fearful that I may not be trusted. **10. presagers,** indicators.

24

Mine eye hath play'd the painter and hath stell'd
Thy beauty's form in table of my heart;
My body is the frame wherein 'tis held,
And perspective it is best painter's art.
For through the painter must you see his skill
To find where your true image pictur'd lies;
Which in my bosom's shop is hanging still,
That hath his windows glazed with thine eyes.
Now see what good turns eyes for eyes have done:
Mine eyes have drawn thy shape, and thine for me
Are windows to my breast, wherethrough the sun
Delights to peep, to gaze therein on thee;
Yet eyes this cunning want to grace their art;
They draw but what they see, know not the heart.

1. stell'd, fixed. **2. table,** surface on which a picture is drawn. **4. perspective,** An essential part of a picture, the frame (See l. 3), completes perspective, which, Shakespeare says, is the "best painter's art."

25

Let those who are in favour with their stars
Of public honour and proud titles boast,
Whilst I, whom fortune of such triumph bars,
Unlook'd for joy in that I honour most.
Great princes' favourites their fair leaves spread
But as the marigold at the sun's eye,
And in themselves their pride lies buried,
For at a frown they in their glory die.
The painful warrior famoused for worth,
After a thousand victories once foil'd,
Is from the book of honour razed forth,
And all the rest forgot for which he toil'd:
Then happy I, that love and am beloved
Where I may not remove nor be removed.

4. Unlook'd for, unexpectedly. **6. But,** only. **9. painful warrior,** a warrior who endures much. **famoused,** renowned.

26

Lord of my love, to whom in vassalage
Thy merit hath my duty strongly knit,
To thee I send this written ambassage,
To witness duty, not to show my wit;
Duty so great, which wit so poor as mine
May make seem bare, in wanting words to show it,
But that I hope some good conceit of thine
In thy soul's thought, all naked, will bestow it;
Till whatsoever star that guides my moving
Points on me graciously with fair aspect,
And puts apparel on my tattered loving,
To show me worthy of thy sweet respect:
Then may I dare to boast how I do love thee;
Till then not show my head where thou mayst prove me.

3. this written ambassage, It is clear that this sonnet was sent as a verse epistle to the friend. **8. bestow,** dignify, clothe.

27

Weary with toil, I haste me to my bed,
The dear repose for limbs with travel tired;
But then begins a journey in my head
To work my mind, when body's work's expired;
For then my thoughts—from far where I abide—
Intend a zealous pilgrimage to thee,
And keep my drooping eyelids open wide,
Looking on darkness which the blind do see;
Save that my soul's imaginary sight
Presents thy shadow to my sightless view,
Which, like a jewel hung in ghastly night,
Makes black night beauteous and her old face new.

Lo! thus, by day my limbs, by night my mind,
For thee and for myself no quiet find.

6. **Intend**, plan. 10. **shadow**, image.

28

How can I then return in happy plight,
That am debarr'd the benefit of rest?
When day's oppression is not eas'd by night,
But day by night, and night by day, oppress'd,
And each, though enemies to either's reign,
Do in consent shake hands to torture me,
The one by toil, the other to complain
How far I toil, still farther off from thee.
I tell the day, to please him, thou art bright
And dost him grace when clouds do blot the heaven;
So flatter I the swart-complexion'd night,
When sparkling stars twire not, thou gild'st the even:
But day doth daily draw my sorrows longer,
And night doth nightly make grief's length seem stronger.

12. **twire**, twinkle.

29

When in disgrace with Fortune and men's eyes,
I all alone beweep my out-cast state,
And trouble deaf heaven with my bootless cries,
And look upon myself, and curse my fate,
Wishing me like to one more rich in hope,
Featured like him, like him with friends possess'd,
Desiring this man's art, and that man's scope,
With what I most enjoy contented least;
Yet in these thoughts myself almost despising,
Haply, I think on thee,—and then my state,
Like to the lark at break of day arising
From sullen earth, sings hymns at heaven's gate;
For thy sweet love remembered such wealth brings
That then I scorn to change my state with kings.

3. **bootless**, futile. 7. **art**, skill. **scope**, range of opportunity.

30

When to the sessions of sweet silent thought
I summon up remembrance of things past,
I sigh the lack of many a thing I sought,
And with old woes new wail my dear time's waste:
Then can I drown an eye, unus'd to flow,
For precious friends hid in death's dateless night,
And weep afresh love's long since cancell'd woe,
And moan the expense of many a vanish'd sight:
Then can I grieve at grievances foregone,
And heavily from woe to woe tell o'er
The sad account of fore-bemoaned moan,
Which I new pay as if not paid before.
But if the while I think on thee, dear friend,
All losses are restor'd and sorrows end.

4. **time's waste**, time wasted in seeking what he did not find. See line 3. 6. **dateless**, without end. 8. Lament what many an object or past experience has cost me. 9. **foregone**, past.

31

Thy bosom is endeared with all hearts
Which I by lacking have supposed dead;
And there reigns love and all love's loving parts,
And all those friends which I thought buried.
How many a holy and obsequious tear
Hath dear religious love stolen from mine eye,
As interest of the dead, which now appear
But things remov'd that hidden in thee lie!
Thou art the grave where buried love doth live,
Hung with the trophies of my lovers gone,
Who all their parts of me to thee did give,
That due of many now is thine alone.
Their images I lov'd I view in thee,
And thou, all they, hast all the all of me.

5. **obsequious**, funereal.

32

If thou survive my well-contented day
When that churl Death my bones with dust shall cover,
And shalt by fortune once more re-survey
These poor rude lines of thy deceased lover,
Compare them with the bett'ring of the time,
And though they be outstripp'd by every pen,
Reserve them for my love, not for their rhyme,
Exceeded by the height of happier men.
O, then vouchsafe me but this loving thought:
"Had my friend's Muse grown with this growing age,
A dearer birth than this his love had brought,
To march in ranks of better equipage;
But since he died and poets better prove,
Theirs for their style I'll read, his for his love."

33

Full many a glorious morning have I seen
Flatter the mountain-tops with sovereign eye,
Kissing with golden face the meadows green,
Gilding pale streams with heavenly alchemy;
Anon permit the basest clouds to ride

With ugly rack on his celestial face,
And from the forlorn world his visage hide,
Stealing unseen to west with this disgrace:
Even so my sun one early morn did shine
With all-triumphant splendour on my brow;
But out, alack! he was but one hour mine;
The region-cloud hath mask'd him from me now.
  Yet him for this my love no whit disdaineth;
  Suns of the world may stain when heaven's sun staineth.

2. **Flatter,** The morning light is compared to the glance of the Sovereign's eye, and is therefore said to flatter. 6. **rack,** clouds. 12. **region-cloud,** Shakespeare sometimes uses region to mean the upper air. 14. **stain,** be obscured.

34

Why didst thou promise such a beauteous day
And make me travel forth without my cloak,
To let base clouds o'ertake me in my way,
Hiding thy bravery in their rotten smoke?
'Tis not enough that through the cloud thou break,
To dry the rain on my storm-beaten face,
For no man well of such a salve can speak
That heals the wound and cures not the disgrace.
Nor can thy shame give physic to my grief;
Though thou repent, yet I have still the loss:
The offender's sorrow lends but weak relief
To him that bears the strong offence's cross.
  Ah! but those tears are pearl which thy love sheds,
  And they are rich, and ransom all ill deeds.

4. **bravery,** splendor. **smoke,** mist.

35

No more be griev'd at that which thou hast done:
Roses have thorns, and silver fountains mud;
Clouds and eclipses stain both moon and sun,
And loathsome canker lives in sweetest bud.
All men make faults, and even I in this,
Authorizing thy trespass with compare,
Myself corrupting, salving thy amiss,
Excusing thy sins more than thy sins are;
For to thy sensual fault I bring in sense—
Thy adverse party is thy advocate—
And 'gainst myself a lawful plea commence.
Such civil war is in my love and hate
  That I an accessary needs must be
  To that sweet thief which sourly robs from me.

3. **stain,** obscure. 6. **Authorizing,** sanctioning.

36

Let me confess that we two must be twain,
Although our undivided loves are one:
So shall those blots that do with me remain,
Without thy help by me be borne alone.
In our two loves there is but one respect,
Though in our lives a separable spite,
Which though it alter not love's sole effect,
Yet doth it steal sweet hours from love's delight.
I may not evermore acknowledge thee,
Lest my bewailed guilt should do thee shame,
Nor thou with public kindness honour me,
Unless thou take that honour from thy name:
  But do not so; I love thee in such sort
  As, thou being mine, mine is thy good report.

5. **respect,** consideration. 6. **separable,** separating.

37

As a decrepit father takes delight
To see his active child do deeds of youth,
So I, made lame by fortune's dearest spite,
Take all my comfort of thy worth and truth.
For whether beauty, birth, or wealth, or wit,
Or any of these all, or all, or more,
Entitled in thy parts do crowned sit,
I make my love engrafted to this store:
So then I am not lame, poor, not despis'd,
Whilst that this shadow doth such substance give
That I in thy abundance am suffic'd
And by a part of all thy glory live.
  Look, what is best, that best I wish in thee:
  This wish I have; then ten times happy me!

3. **dearest,** greatest. 7. **Entitled,** rightfully. 10. **shadow,** Often used by Shakespeare in contrast with reality. Here it is the poet's imaginary possession of the excellences of the friend.

38

How can my Muse want subject to invent,
While thou dost breathe, that pour'st into my verse
Thine own sweet argument, too excellent
For every vulgar paper to rehearse?
O, give thyself the thanks, if aught in me
Worthy perusal stand against thy sight;
For who's so dumb that cannot write to thee,
When thou thyself dost give invention light?
Be thou the tenth Muse, ten times more in worth
Than those old nine which rhymers invocate;
And he that calls on thee, let him bring forth
Eternal numbers to outlive long date.
  If my slight Muse do please these curious days,
  The pain be mine, but thine shall be the praise.

4. **rehearse,** relate. 12. **numbers,** verses.

39

O, how thy worth with manners may I sing,
When thou art all the better part of me?
What can mine own praise to mine own self bring?
And what is't but mine own when I praise thee?
Even for this let us divided live,
And our dear love lose name of single one,
That by this separation I may give
That due to thee which thou deserv'st alone.
O absence, what a torment wouldst thou prove,
Were it not thy sour leisure gave sweet leave
To entertain the time with thoughts of love,
Which time and thoughts so sweetly doth deceive,
And that thou teachest how to make one twain,
By praising him here who doth hence remain!

1. with manners, fittingly. **13-14.** "Absence teaches how to make two persons of one—one absent in reality, the other present in imagination."

40

Take all my loves, my love, yea, take them all;
What hast thou then more than thou hadst before?
No love, my love, that thou mayst true love call;
All mine was thine before thou hadst this more.
Then if for my love thou my love receivest,
I cannot blame thee for my love thou usest;
But yet be blam'd, if thou this self deceivest
By wilful taste of what thyself refusest.
I do forgive thy robbery, gentle thief,
Although thou steal thee all my poverty;
And yet, love knows, it is a greater grief
To bear love's wrong than hate's known injury.
Lascivious grace, in whom all ill well shows,
Kill me with spites; yet we must not be foes.

5. my love receivest, receive her whom I love. **6. for,** because. **14. spites,** injuries.

41

Those pretty wrongs that liberty commits,
When I am sometime absent from thy heart,
Thy beauty and thy years full well befits,
For still temptation follows where thou art.
Gentle thou art and therefore to be won;
Beauteous thou art, therefore to be assailed;
And when a woman woos, what woman's son
Will sourly leave her till she have prevailed?
Ay me! but yet thou mightst my seat forbear,
And chide thy beauty and thy straying youth,
Who lead thee in their riot even there
Where thou art forc'd to break a twofold truth:
Hers, by thy beauty tempting her to thee,
Thine, by thy beauty being false to me.

42

That thou hast her, it is not all my grief,
And yet it may be said I lov'd her dearly;
That she hath thee, is of my wailing chief,
A loss in love that touches me more nearly.
Loving offenders, thus I will excuse ye:
Thou dost love her, because thou know'st I love her:
And for my sake even so doth she abuse me,
Suff'ring my friend for my sake to approve her.
If I lose thee, my loss is my love's gain,
And losing her, my friend hath found that loss;
Both find each other, and I lose both twain,
And both for my sake lay on me this cross.
But here's the joy; my friend and I are one;
Sweet flattery! then she loves but me alone.

8. approve, make trial of. **9. love's,** mistress's.

43

When most I wink, then do mine eyes best see,
For all the day they view things unrespected;
But when I sleep, in dreams they look on thee,
And darkly bright are bright in dark directed.
Then thou, whose shadow shadows doth make bright,
How would thy shadow's form form happy show
To the clear day with thy much clearer light,
When to unseeing eyes thy shade shines so!
How would, I say, mine eyes be blessed made
By looking on thee in the living day,
When in dead night thy fair imperfect shade
Through heavy sleep on sightless eyes doth stay!
All days are nights to see till I see thee,
And nights bright days when dreams do show thee me.

1. wink, close my eyes. **2. unrespected,** unregarded. **4.** And although it is dark, they see, and, in the darkness, are clearly directed. **5. shadow,** image. **shadows,** darkness. **11. imperfect,** Imperfect because it is only a shadow of the friend who is perfect.

44

If the dull substance of my flesh were thought,
Injurious distance should not stop my way;
For then, despite of space, I would be brought,
From limits far remote, where thou dost stay.
No matter then although my foot did stand
Upon the farthest earth remov'd from thee;
For nimble thought can jump both sea and land

As soon as think the place where he would be.
But, ah! thought kills me that I am not thought,
To leap large lengths of miles when thou art gone,
But that, so much of earth and water wrought,
I must attend time's leisure with my moan,
  Receiving nought by elements so slow
  But heavy tears, badges of either's woe.

4. where, to the place where. **11. So much** composed of these, the duller elements.

45

The other two, slight air and purging fire,
Are both with thee, wherever I abide;
The first my thought, the other my desire,
These present-absent with swift motion slide.
For when these quicker elements are gone
In tender embassy of love to thee,
My life, being made of four, with two alone
Sinks down to death, oppress'd with melanch'ly;
Until life's composition be recured
By those swift messengers return'd from thee,
Who even but now come back again, assured
Of thy fair health, recounting it to me:
  This told, I joy; but then no longer glad,
  I send them back again and straight grow sad.

1. two, i.e., elements. See sonnet 44. **9. composition,** union of the four elements. **recured,** restored.

46

Mine eye and heart are at a mortal war,
How to divide the conquest of thy sight;
Mine eye my heart thy picture's sight would bar,
My heart mine eye the freedom of that right.
My heart doth plead that thou in him dost lie,—
A closet never pierc'd with crystal eyes—
But the defendant doth that plea deny
And says in him thy fair appearance lies.
To 'cide this title is impanneled
A quest of thoughts, all tenants to the heart,
And by their verdict is determined
The clear eye's moiety and the dear heart's part;
  As thus: mine eye's due is thy outward part,
  And my heart's right thy inward love of heart.

9. 'cide, decide. **10. quest,** inquest, jury. **12. moiety,** share.

47

Betwixt mine eye and heart a league is took,
And each doth good turns now unto the other.
When that mine eye is famish'd for a look,
Or heart in love with sighs himself doth smother,
With my love's picture then my eye doth feast
And to the painted banquet bids my heart;
Another time mine eye is my heart's guest
And in his thoughts of love doth share a part.
So, either by thy picture or my love,
Thyself away art present still with me,
For thou not farther than my thoughts canst move,
And I am still with them and they with thee;
  Or, if they sleep, thy picture in my sight
  Awakes my heart to heart's and eye's delight.

6. the painted banquet, "my love's picture," line 5.

48

How careful was I, when I took my way,
Each trifle under truest bars to thrust,
That to my use it might unused stay
From hands of falsehood, in sure wards of trust!
But thou, to whom my jewels trifles are,
Most worthy comfort, now my greatest grief,
Thou, best of dearest and mine only care,
Art left the prey of every vulgar thief.
Thee have I not lock'd up in any chest,
Save where thou art not, though I feel thou art,
Within the gentle closure of my breast,
From whence at pleasure thou mayst come and part;
  And even thence thou wilt be stolen, I fear,
  For truth proves thievish for a prize so dear.

49

Against that time, if ever that time come,
When I shall see thee frown on my defects,
Whenas thy love hath cast his utmost sum,
Call'd to that audit by advis'd respects;
Against that time when thou shalt strangely pass
And scarcely greet me with that sun, thine eye,
When love, converted from the thing it was,
Shall reasons find of settled gravity;
Against that time do I ensconce me here
Within the knowledge of mine own desert,
And this my hand against myself uprear,
To guard the lawful reasons on thy part:
  To leave poor me thou hast the strength of laws,
  Since why to love I can allege no cause.

3. cast . . . sum, closed his account. **4. advis'd respects,** prudent considerations.

50

How heavy do I journey on the way,
When what I seek, my weary travel's end,
Doth teach that ease and that repose to say,
"Thus far the miles are measur'd from thy friend!"
The beast that bears me, tired with my woe,
Plods dully on, to bear that weight in me,
As if by some instinct the wretch did know
His rider lov'd not speed, being made from thee.
The bloody spur cannot provoke him on
That sometimes anger thrusts into his hide,
Which heavily he answers with a groan,
More sharp to me than spurring to his side;
For that same groan doth put this in my mind:
My grief lies onward and my joy behind.

8. made, directed.

51

Thus can my love excuse the slow offence
Of my dull bearer when from thee I speed:
From where thou art why should I haste me thence?
Till I return, of posting is no need.
O, what excuse will my poor beast then find,
When swift extremity can seem but slow?
Then should I spur, though mounted on the wind,
In winged speed no motion shall I know:
Then can no horse with my desire keep pace;
Therefore desire, of perfect'st love being made,
Shall neigh—no dull flesh—in his fiery race;
But love, for love, thus shall excuse my jade:
Since from thee going he went wilful-slow,
Towards thee I'll run and give him leave to go.

1. slow offence, the offence of slowness. **6. swift extremity,** great speed. **8.** The greatest speed will seem no motion at all. **14. go,** walk.

52

So am I as the rich, whose blessed key
Can bring him to his sweet up-locked treasure,
The which he will not every hour survey,
For blunting the fine point of seldom pleasure.
Therefore are feasts so solemn and so rare,
Since, seldom coming, in the long year set,
Like stones of worth they thinly placed are,
Or captain jewels in the carconet.
So is the time that keeps you as my chest,
Or as the wardrobe which the robe doth hide,
To make some special instant special blest
By new unfolding his imprison'd pride.
Blessed are you, whose worthiness gives scope,
Being had, to triumph, being lack'd, to hope.

4. For, for fear of. **8. carconet,** necklace.

53

What is your substance, whereof are you made,
That millions of strange shadows on you tend?
Since every one hath, every one, one shade,
And you, but one, can every shadow lend.
Describe Adonis, and the counterfeit
Is poorly imitated after you;
On Helen's cheek all art of beauty set,
And you in Grecian tires are painted new:
Speak of the spring and foison of the year,
The one doth shadow of your beauty show,
The other as your bounty doth appear;
And you in every blessed shape we know.
In all external grace you have some part,
But you like none, none you, for constant heart.

3. Every other person has only one shadow. **8. tires,** attire. **14. like none,** are like none. **none you,** none is like you.

54

O, how much more doth beauty beauteous seem
By that sweet ornament which truth doth give!
The rose looks fair, but fairer we it deem
For that sweet odour which doth in it live.
The canker-blooms have full as deep a dye
As the perfumed tincture of the roses,
Hang on such thorns, and play as wantonly
When summer's breath their masked buds discloses:
But, for their virtue only is their show,
They live unwoo'd and unrespected fade;
Die to themselves. Sweet roses do not so;
Of their sweet deaths are sweetest odours made:
And so of you, beauteous and lovely youth,
When that shall fade, my verse distils your truth.

55

Not marble, nor the gilded monuments
Of princes shall outlive this powerful rhyme,
But you shall shine more bright in these contents
Than unswept stone besmear'd with sluttish time.
When wasteful war shall statues overturn,
And broils root out the work of masonry,
Nor Mars his sword nor war's quick fire shall burn

The living record of your memory.
'Gainst death and all-oblivious enmity
Shall you pace forth; your praise shall still find room,
Even in the eyes of all posterity
That wear this world out to the ending doom.
So, till the judgement that yourself arise,
You live in this, and dwell in lovers' eyes.

4. unswept stone, The reference is to a horizontal grave stone, as in the floor of a church. **13. judgement that,** Judgement Day when.

56

Sweet love, renew thy force; be it not said
Thy edge should blunter be than appetite,
Which but to-day by feeding is allay'd,
To-morrow sharpen'd in his former might.
So, love, be thou; although to-day thou fill
Thy hungry eyes even till they wink with fulness,
To-morrow see again, and do not kill
The spirit of love with a perpetual dullness.
Let this sad interim like the ocean be
Which parts the shore, where two contracted new
Come daily to the banks, that, when they see
Return of love, more blest may be the view;
Else call it winter, which being full of care
Makes summer's welcome thrice more wish'd, more rare.

6. wink, close. **10. contracted,** betrothed.

57

Being your slave, what should I do but tend
Upon the hours and times of your desire?
I have no precious time at all to spend,
Nor services to do, till you require.
Nor dare I chide the world-without-end hour
Whilst I, my sovereign, watch the clock for you,
Nor think the bitterness of absence sour
When you have bid your servant once adieu.
Nor dare I question with my jealous thought
Where you may be, or your affairs suppose,
But, like a sad slave, stay and think of nought
Save, where you are how happy you make those.
So true a fool is love that in your will
Though you do anything, he thinks no ill.

58

That god forbid that made me first your slave,
I should in thought control your times of pleasure,
Or at your hand th' account of hours to crave,
Being your vassal, bound to stay your leisure!
O, let me suffer, being at your beck,
The imprison'd absence of your liberty;
And patience, tame to sufferance, bide each check,
Without accusing you of injury.
Be where you list, your charter is so strong
That you yourself may privilege your time
To what you will; to you it doth belong
Yourself to pardon of self-doing crime.
I am to wait, though waiting so be hell,
Not blame your pleasure, be it ill or well.

6. imprison'd absence, Absence from the friend is thought of as imprisonment. **12. self-doing,** done by yourself.

59

If there be nothing new, but that which is
Hath been before, how are our brains beguil'd,
Which, labouring for invention, bear amiss
The second burden of a former child!
O that record could with a backward look,
Even of five hundred courses of the sun,
Show me your image in some antique book,
Since mind at first in character was done!
That I might see what the old world could say
To this composed wonder of your frame;
Whether we are mended, or where better they,
Or whether revolution be the same.
O, sure I am, the wits of former days
To subjects worse have given admiring praise.

3. invention, originality. **8. character,** writing. **10. composed wonder,** wonderful composition. **11. where,** whether.

60

Like as the waves make towards the pebbled shore,
So do our minutes hasten to their end,
Each changing place with that which goes before,
In sequent toil all forwards do contend.
Nativity, once in the main of light,
Crawls to maturity, wherewith being crown'd,
Crooked eclipses 'gainst his glory fight,
And Time that gave, doth now his gift confound.
Time doth transfix the flourish set on youth
And delves the parallels in beauty's brow,
Feeds on the rarities of nature's truth,
And nothing stands but for his scythe to mow;
And yet to times in hope my verse shall stand
Praising thy worth, despite his cruel hand.

5. main of light, the immensity of light; i.e. the firmament. **13. times in hope,** the future.

61

Is it thy will thy image should keep open
My heavy eyelids to the weary night?
Dost thou desire my slumbers should be broken,
While shadows like to thee do mock my sight?
Is it thy spirit that thou send'st from thee
So far from home into my deeds to pry,
To find out shames and idle hours in me,
The scope and tenour of thy jealousy?
O, no! thy love, though much, is not so great:
It is my love that keeps mine eye awake;
Mine own true love that doth my rest defeat,
To play the watchman ever for thy sake:
For thee watch I whilst thou dost wake elsewhere,
From me far off, with others all too near.

62

Sin of self-love possesseth all mine eye
And all my soul and all my every part;
And for this sin there is no remedy,
It is so grounded inward in my heart.
Methinks no face so gracious is as mine,
No shape so true, no truth of such account;
And so myself mine own worth do define,
As I all other in all words surmount.
But when my glass shows me myself indeed,
Beated and chopp'd with tann'd antiquity,
Mine own self-love quite contrary I read;
Self so self-loving were iniquity.
'Tis thee, myself, that for myself I praise,
Painting my age with beauty of thy days.

63

Against my love shall be, as I am now,
With Time's injurious hand crush'd and o'erworn;
When hours have drain'd his blood and fill'd his brow
With lines and wrinkles; when his youthful morn
Hath travell'd on to age's steepy night,
And all those beauties whereof now he's king
Are vanishing or vanish'd out of sight,
Stealing away the treasure of his spring:
For such a time do I now fortify
Against confounding age's cruel knife,
That he shall never cut from memory
My sweet love's beauty, though my lover's life.
His beauty shall in these black lines be seen,
And they shall live, and he in them still green.

64

When I have seen by Time's fell hand defaced
The rich proud cost of outworn buried age;
When sometime lofty towers I see down-razed,
And brass eternal slave to mortal rage:
When I have seen the hungry ocean gain
Advantage on the kingdom of the shore,
And the firm soil win of the watery main,
Increasing store with loss and loss with store:
When I have seen such interchange of state,
Or state itself confounded to decay;
Ruin hath taught me thus to ruminate—
That Time will come and take my love away.
This thought is as a death, which cannot choose
But weep to have that which it fears to lose.

65

Since brass, nor stone, nor earth, nor boundless sea,
But sad mortality o'er-sways their power,
How with this rage shall beauty hold a plea,
Whose action is no stronger than a flower?
O, how shall summer's honey breath hold out
Against the wrackful siege of batt'ring days,
When rocks impregnable are not so stout,
Nor gates of steel so strong, but Time decays?
O fearful meditation! where, alack,
Shall Time's best jewel from Time's chest lie hid?
Or what strong hand can hold his swift foot back?
Or who his spoil of beauty can forbid?
O, none, unless this miracle have might,
That in black ink my love may still shine bright.

6. wrackful, destructive. **12. spoil,** plundering.

66

Tir'd with all these, for restful death I cry:
As, to behold desert a beggar born,
And needy nothing trimm'd in jollity,
And purest faith unhappily forsworn,
And gilded honour shamefully misplac'd,
And maiden virtue rudely strumpeted,
And right perfection wrongfully disgrac'd,
And strength by limping sway disabled,
And art made tongue-tied by authority,
And folly, doctor-like, controlling skill,
And simple truth miscall'd simplicity,
And captive good attending captain ill:
Tir'd with all these, from these would I be gone,
Save that to die, I leave my love alone.

10. doctor-like, with an assured and learned air

67

Ah! wherefore with infection should he live,
And with his presence grace impiety,
That sin by him advantage should achieve
And lace itself with his society?
Why should false painting imitate his cheek
And steal dead seeming of his living hue?
Why should poor beauty indirectly seek
Roses of shadow, since his rose is true?
Why should he live, now Nature bankrupt is,
Beggar'd of blood to blush through lively veins?
For she hath no exchequer now but his,
And, proud of many, lives upon his gains.
O, him she stores, to show what wealth she had
In days long since, before these last so bad.

1. with infection, in this infected world. **4. lace,** decorate. **13. stores,** treasures.

68

Thus is his cheek the map of days outworn,
When beauty liv'd and died as flowers do now,
Before these bastard signs of fair were born,
Or durst inhabit on a living brow;
Before the golden tresses of the dead,
The right of sepulchres, were shorn away,
To live a second life on second head;
Ere beauty's dead fleece made another gay:
In him those holy antique hours are seen,
Without all ornament, itself and true,
Making no summer of another's green,
Robbing no old to dress his beauty new;
And him as for a map doth Nature store,
To show false Art what beauty was of yore.

3. signs of fair, imitations of beauty, here specifically, wigs.

69

Those parts of thee that the world's eye doth view
Want nothing that the thought of hearts can mend;
All tongues, the voice of souls, give thee that due,
Utt'ring bare truth, even so as foes commend.
Thy outward thus with outward praise is crown'd;
But those same tongues that give thee so thine own,
In other accents do this praise confound
By seeing farther than the eye hath shown.
They look into the beauty of thy mind,
And that, in guess, they measure by thy deeds;
Then, churls, their thoughts, although their eyes were kind,
To thy fair flower add the rank smell of weeds:
But why thy odour matcheth not thy show,
The soil is this, that thou dost common grow.

14. soil, ground, cause.

70

That thou art blam'd shall not be thy defect,
For slander's mark was ever yet the fair;
The ornament of beauty is suspect,
A crow that flies in heaven's sweetest air.
So thou be good, slander doth but approve
Thy worth the greater, being woo'd of Time;
For canker vice the sweetest buds doth love,
And thou present'st a pure unstained prime.
Thou hast pass'd by the ambush of young days,
Either not assail'd, or victor being charg'd;
Yet this thy praise cannot be so thy praise,
To tie up envy evermore enlarg'd:
If some suspect of ill mask'd not thy show,
Then thou alone kingdoms of hearts shouldst owe.

3. suspect, suspicion. **5-8.** The meaning is that since the admirable qualities which make a young man popular also make him more subject to temptation, scandal is but testimony of worth. **14. owe,** own.

71

No longer mourn for me when I am dead
Than you shall hear the surly sullen bell
Give warning to the world that I am fled
From this vile world with vilest worms to dwell.
Nay, if you read this line, remember not
The hand that writ it, for I love you so
That I in your sweet thoughts would be forgot
If thinking on me then should make you woe.
O if, I say, you look upon this verse
When I perhaps compounded am with clay,
Do not so much as my poor name rehearse,
But let your love even with my life decay,
Lest the wise world should look into your moan
And mock you with me after I am gone.

72

O, lest the world should task you to recite
What merit liv'd in me that you should love
After my death, dear love, forget me quite,
For you in me can nothing worthy prove;
Unless you would devise some virtuous lie,
To do more for me than mine own desert,
And hang more praise upon deceased I
Than niggard truth would willingly impart:
O, lest your true love may seem false in this,
That you for love speak well of me untrue,
My name be buried where my body is,
And live no more to shame nor me nor you.

For I am sham'd by that which I bring forth,
And so should you, to love things nothing worth.

4. **prove**, discover. 10. **untrue**, untruly.

73

That time of year thou mayst in me behold
When yellow leaves, or none, or few, do hang
Upon those boughs which shake against the cold,
Bare ruin'd choirs where late the sweet birds sang.
In me thou see'st the twilight of such day
As after sunset fadeth in the west,
Which by and by black night doth take away,
Death's second self, that seals up all in rest.
In me thou see'st the glowing of such fire
That on the ashes of his youth doth lie,
As the death-bed whereon it must expire,
Consum'd with that which it was nourish'd by.
This thou perceiv'st, which makes thy love more strong,
To love that well which thou must leave ere long.

74

But be contented: when that fell arrest
Without all bail shall carry me away,
My life hath in this line some interest,
Which for memorial still with thee shall stay.
When thou reviewest this, thou dost review
The very part was consecrate to thee:
The earth can have but earth, which is his due;
My spirit is thine, the better part of me:
So then thou hast but lost the dregs of life,
The prey of worms, my body being dead,
The coward conquest of a wretch's knife,
Too base of thee to be remembered.
The worth of that is that which it contains,
And that is this, and this with thee remains.

9. **dregs of life**, the physical as opposed to the spiritual. 13. **of that**, of anything. 14. My chief worth is my spirit which, embodied in these poems, remains with you after my death.

75

So are you to my thoughts as food to life,
Or as sweet-season'd showers are to the ground;
And for the peace of you I hold such strife
As 'twixt a miser and his wealth is found;
Now proud as an enjoyer, and anon
Doubting the filching age will steal his treasure;
Now counting best to be with you alone,
Then better'd that the world may see my pleasure;
Sometime all full with feasting on your sight,
And by and by clean starved for a look;
Possessing or pursuing no delight,
Save what is had or must from you be took.
Thus do I pine and surfeit day by day,
Or gluttoning on all, or all away.

3. **peace**, contentment to be found in you. 8. **better'd that**, being happier because. 14. **Or**, either. **Or all away**, or, you being away, having no pleasure.

76

Why is my verse so barren of new pride,
So far from variation or quick change?
Why with the time do I not glance aside
To new-found methods and to compounds strange?
Why write I still all one, ever the same,
And keep invention in a noted weed,
That every word doth almost tell my name,
Showing their birth and where they did proceed?
O, know, sweet love, I always write of you,
And you and love are still my argument;
So all my best is dressing old words new,
Spending again what is already spent:
For as the sun is daily new and old,
So is my love still telling what is told.

1. **new pride**, novelty. 6. Write new poems in a manner already familiar.

77

Thy glass will show thee how thy beauties wear,
Thy dial how thy precious minutes waste;
The vacant leaves thy mind's imprint will bear,
And of this book this learning mayst thou taste.
The wrinkles which thy glass will truly show
Of mouthed graves will give thee memory;
Thou by the dial's shady stealth mayst know
Time's thievish progress to eternity.
Look, what thy memory cannot contain
Commit to these waste blanks, and thou shalt find
Those children nurs'd, deliver'd from thy brain,
To take a new acquaintance of thy mind.
These offices, so oft as thou wilt look,
Shall profit thee and much enrich thy book.

3. **vacant leaves**, The leaves of a blank book sent as a gift with this sonnet. 13. **offices**, practices.

78

So oft have I invok'd thee for my Muse
And found such fair assistance in my verse
As every alien pen hath got my use
And under thee their poesy disperse.
Thine eyes, that taught the dumb on high to sing
And heavy ignorance aloft to fly,
Have added feathers to the learned's wing
And given grace a double majesty.
Yet be most proud of that which I compile,
Whose influence is thine and born of thee:
In others' works thou dost but mend the style,
And arts with thy sweet graces graced be;
But thou art all my art and dost advance
As high as learning my rude ignorance.

3. As, that. **hath . . . use,** follows my custom. **4. under thee,** under thy patronage. **9. compile,** compose. **10. influence,** inspiration.

79

Whilst I alone did call upon thy aid,
My verse alone had all thy gentle grace,
But now my gracious numbers are decay'd
And my sick Muse doth give another place.
I grant, sweet love, thy lovely argument
Deserves the travail of a worthier pen;
Yet what of thee thy poet doth invent
He robs thee of and pays it thee again.
He lends thee virtue and he stole that word
From thy behaviour; beauty doth he give
And found it in thy cheek; he can afford
No praise to thee but what in thee doth live.
Then thank him not for that which he doth say,
Since what he owes thee thou thyself dost pay.

4. give another place, give place to another. **5. thy lovely argument,** the theme of thy beauty.

80

O, how I faint when I of you do write,
Knowing a better spirit doth use your name,
And in the praise thereof spends all his might,
To make me tongue-tied, speaking of your fame!
But since your worth—wide as the ocean is,—
The humble as the proudest sail doth bear,
My saucy bark, inferior far to his,
On your broad main doth wilfully appear.
Your shallowest help will hold me up afloat,
Whilst he upon your soundless deep doth ride;
Or, being wrack'd, I am a worthless boat,
He of tall building and of goodly pride.
Then if he thrive and I be cast away,
The worst was this—my love was my decay.

2. a better spirit. No one knows who this other, the rival poet, was. The best guess is Chapman. **8. wilfully,** venturously.

81

Or I shall live your epitaph to make,
Or you survive when I in earth am rotten;
From hence your memory death cannot take,
Although in me each part will be forgotten.
Your name from hence immortal life shall have,
Though I, once gone, to all the world must die:
The earth can yield me but a common grave,
When you entombed in men's eyes shall lie.
Your monument shall be my gentle verse,
Which eyes not yet created shall o'er-read,
And tongues to be your being shall rehearse
When all the breathers of this world are dead;
You still shall live—such virtue hath my pen—
Where breath most breathes, even in the mouths of men.

82

I grant thou wert not married to my Muse,
And therefore mayst without attaint o'erlook
The dedicated words which writers use
Of their fair subject, blessing every book.
Thou art as fair in knowledge as in hue,
Finding thy worth a limit past my praise,
And therefore art enforc'd to seek anew
Some fresher stamp of the time-bettering days.
And do so, love; yet when they have devis'd
What strained touches rhetoric can lend,
Thou truly fair wert truly sympathiz'd
In true plain words by thy true-telling friend;
And their gross painting might be better us'd
Where cheeks need blood; in thee it is abus'd.

2. attaint, disgrace. **o'erlook,** read. **5. hue,** beauty. **11. sympathiz'd,** matched.

83

I never saw that you did painting need,
And therefore to your fair no painting set;
I found, or thought I found, you did exceed
The barren tender of a poet's debt:
And therefore have I slept in your report,
That you yourself being extant well might show
How far a modern quill doth come too short,
Speaking of worth, what worth in you doth grow.
This silence for my sin you did impute,
Which shall be most my glory, being dumb;
For I impair not beauty being mute,
When others would give life and bring a tomb.
There lives more life in one of your fair eyes
Than both your poets can in praise devise.

4. tender, offering. **5. in your report,** in describing you. **7. modern,** ordinary.

84

Who is it that says most, which can say more
Than this rich praise, that you alone are you?
In whose confine immured is the store
Which should example where your equal grew.
Lean penury within that pen doth dwell
That to his subject lends not some small glory;
But he that writes of you, if he can tell
That you are you, so dignifies his story.
Let him but copy what in you is writ,
Not making worse what nature made so clear,
And such a counterpart shall fame his wit,
Making his style admired everywhere.
You to your beauteous blessings add a curse,
Being fond on praise, which makes your praises worse.

3-4. None but yourself can be your parallel. 10. clear, glorious. **11. fame his wit,** make his poem famous.

85

My tongue-tied Muse in manners holds her still,
While comments of your praise, richly compil'd,
Reserve their character with golden quill
And precious phrase by all the Muses fil'd.
I think good thoughts whilst other write good words,
And, like unlettered clerk, still cry "Amen"
To every hymn that able spirit affords
In polish'd form of well-refined pen.
Hearing you prais'd, I say, " 'Tis so, 'tis true,"
And to the most of praise add something more;
But that is in my thought, whose love to you,
Though words come hindmost, holds his rank before.
Then others for the breath of words respect,
Me for my dumb thoughts, speaking in effect.

1. in manners, modestly. **2. compil'd,** composed. **3. Reserve,** preserve; cf. Sonnet 32. l. 7. Or it may be a misprint for "receive." **4. fil'd,** polished. **7. that able spirit,** the rival poet. **11. in my thought,** i.e., silently.

86

Was it the proud full sail of his great verse,
Bound for the prize of all too precious you,
That did my ripe thoughts in my brain inhearse,
Making their tomb the womb wherein they grew?
Was it his spirit, by spirits taught to write
Above a mortal pitch, that struck me dead?
No, neither he, nor his compeers by night
Giving him aid, my verse astonished.
He, nor that affable familiar ghost
Which nightly gulls him with intelligence,
As victors of my silence cannot boast;
I was not sick of any fear from thence:
But when your countenance fill'd up his line
Then lack'd I matter; that enfeebled mine.

3. inhearse, bury. **8. astonished,** dismayed. **10. gulls,** cheats.

87

Farewell! thou art too dear for my possessing,
And like enough thou know'st thy estimate.
The charter of thy worth gives thee releasing;
My bonds in thee are all determinate.
For how do I hold thee but by thy granting?
And for that riches where is my deserving?
The cause of this fair gift in me is wanting,
And so my patent back again is swerving.
Thyself thou gav'st, thy own worth then not knowing,
Or me, to whom thou gav'st it, else mistaking;
So thy great gift, upon misprision growing,
Comes home again, on better judgement making.
Thus have I had thee, as a dream doth flatter,
In sleep a king, but waking no such matter.

2. estimate, value. **4. determinate,** ended. **8. patent,** privilege. **11. upon misprision growing,** having its origin in a mistake.

88

When thou shalt be dispos'd to set me light,
And place my merit in the eye of scorn,
Upon thy side against myself I'll fight
And prove thee virtuous, though thou art forsworn.
With mine own weakness being best acquainted,
Upon thy part I can set down a story
Of faults conceal'd, wherein I am attainted,
That thou in losing me shall win much glory:
And I by this will be a gainer too;
For bending all my loving thoughts on thee,
The injuries that to myself I do,
Doing thee vantage, double-vantage me.
Such is my love, to thee I so belong,
That for thy right myself will bear all wrong.

1. set me light, hold a light estimate of me. **6. Upon thy part,** in your behalf.

89

Say that thou didst forsake me for some fault,
And I will comment upon that offence;
Speak of my lameness, and I straight will halt,
Against thy reasons making no defence.
Thou canst not, love, disgrace me half so ill,
To set a form upon desired change,
As I'll myself disgrace: knowing thy will,

I will acquaintance strangle and look strange;
Be absent from thy walks; and in my tongue
Thy sweet beloved name no more shall dwell,
Lest I, too much profane, should do it wrong,
And haply of our old acquaintance tell.
For thee, against myself I'll vow debate,
For I must ne'er love him whom thou dost hate.

2. comment, discourse. 6. To give a becoming appearance to the change you desire.

90

Then hate me when thou wilt; if ever, now;
Now, while the world is bent my deeds to cross,
Join with the spite of fortune, make me bow,
And do not drop in for an after-loss:
Ah! do not, when my heart hath scap'd this sorrow,
Come in the rearward of a conquer'd woe;
Give not a windy night a rainy morrow,
To linger out a purpos'd overthrow.
If thou wilt leave me, do not leave me last,
When other petty griefs have done their spite,
But in the onset come: so shall I taste
At first the very worst of fortune's might;
And other strains of woe, which now seem woe,
Compar'd with loss of thee will not seem so.

2. cross, thwart. 4. And not unexpectedly find grief at a later time.

91

Some glory in their birth, some in their skill,
Some in their wealth, some in their bodies' force;
Some in their garments, though new-fangled ill,
Some in their hawks and hounds, some in their horse;
And every humour hath his adjunct pleasure,
Wherein it finds a joy above the rest:
But these particulars are not my measure;
All these I better in one general best.
Thy love is better than high birth to me,
Richer than wealth, prouder than garments' cost,
Of more delight than hawks or horses be;
And having thee, of all men's pride I boast:
Wretched in this alone, that thou mayst take
All this away, and me most wretched make.

3. new-fangled ill, fashionable but ugly. **5. humour,** disposition. **adjunct,** connected. **7. measure,** measure of joy.

92

But do thy worst to steal thyself away,
For term of life thou art assured mine,
And life no longer than thy love will stay,
For it depends upon that love of thine.
Then need I not to fear the worst of wrongs,
When in the least of them my life hath end.
I see a better state to me belongs
Than that which on thy humour doth depend;
Thou canst not vex me with inconstant mind,
Since that my life on thy revolt doth lie.
O, what a happy title do I find,
Happy to have thy love, happy to die!
But what's so blessed-fair that fears no blot?
Thou mayst be false, and yet I know it not.

5-6. "The worst of wrongs" would be to live without the affection of the friend, but this is impossible because the ending of the friendship would bring death.

93

So shall I live, supposing thou art true,
Like a deceived husband; so love's face
May still seem love to me, though alter'd new;
Thy looks with me, thy heart in other place:
For there can live no hatred in thine eye,
Therefore in that I cannot know thy change.
In many's looks the false heart's history
Is writ in moods and frowns and wrinkles strange;
But heaven in thy creation did decree
That in thy face sweet love should ever dwell;
Whate'er thy thoughts or thy heart's workings be,
Thy looks should nothing thence but sweetness tell.
How like Eve's apple doth thy beauty grow,
If thy sweet virtue answer not thy show!

94

They that have power to hurt and will do none,
That do not do the thing they most do show,
Who, moving others, are themselves as stone,
Unmoved, cold, and to temptation slow;
They rightly do inherit heaven's graces,
And husband nature's riches from expense;
They are the lords and owners of their faces,
Others but stewards of their excellence.
The summer's flower is to the summer sweet,
Though to itself it only live and die,
But if that flower with base infection meet,
The basest weed outbraves his dignity:
For sweetest things turn sourest by their deeds;
Lilies that fester smell far worse than weeds.

6. husband, hoard. **expense,** expenditure, waste.

95

How sweet and lovely dost thou make the shame
Which, like a canker in the fragrant rose,

Doth spot the beauty of thy budding name!
O, in what sweets dost thou thy sins enclose.
That tongue that tells the story of thy days,
Making lascivious comments on thy sport,
Cannot dispraise but in a kind of praise;
Naming thy name blesses an ill report.
O, what a mansion have those vices got
Which for their habitation chose out thee,
Where beauty's veil doth cover every blot
And all things turns to fair that eyes can see!
  Take heed, dear heart, of this large privilege;
  The hardest knife ill-us'd doth lose his edge.

2. canker, cankerworm. **8.** The naming of your name, like making the sign of the cross, counteracts the evil said of you. **13. privilege,** license.

96

Some say thy fault is youth, some wantonness;
Some say thy grace is youth and gentle sport;
Both grace and faults are lov'd of more and less;
Thou mak'st faults graces that to thee resort.
As on the finger of a throned queen
The basest jewel will be well esteem'd,
So are those errors that in thee are seen
To truths translated and for true things deem'd.
How many lambs might the stern wolf betray
If like a lamb he could his looks translate!
How many gazers mightst thou lead away,
If thou wouldst use the strength of all thy state!
  But do not so; I love thee in such sort
  As, thou being mine, mine is thy good report.

3. more and less, persons of all ranks. **8. translated,** transformed.

97

How like a winter hath my absence been
From thee, the pleasure of the fleeting year!
What freezings have I felt, what dark days seen!
What old December's bareness everywhere!
And yet this time remov'd was summer's time;
The teeming autumn, big with rich increase,
Bearing the wanton burthen of the prime,
Like widowed wombs after their lords' decease.
Yet this abundant issue seem'd to me
But hope of orphans and unfathered fruit;
For summer and his pleasures wait on thee,
And, thou away, the very birds are mute;
  Or, if they sing, 'tis with so dull a cheer
  That leaves look pale, dreading the winter's near.

5. remov'd, of absence. **7. prime,** spring.

98

From you have I been absent in the spring,
When proud-pied April, dress'd in all his trim,
Hath put a spirit of youth in everything,
That heavy Saturn laugh'd and leap'd with him.
Yet nor the lays of birds, nor the sweet smell
Of different flowers in odour and in hue,
Could make me any summer's story tell,
Or from their proud lap pluck them where they grew;
Nor did I wonder at the lily's white,
Nor praise the deep vermilion in the rose;
They were but sweet, but figures of delight
Drawn after you, you pattern of all those.
  Yet seem'd it winter still, and, you away,
  As with your shadow I with these did play.

2. proud-pied, magnificent in many colors. **4. heavy Saturn,** The god Saturn was cold, austere, melancholy.

99

The forward violet thus did I chide:
Sweet thief, whence didst thou steal thy sweet that smells,
If not from my love's breath? The purple pride
Which on thy soft cheek for complexion dwells
In my love's veins thou hast too grossly dy'd.
The lily I condemned for thy hand,
And buds of marjoram had stolen thy hair;
The roses fearfully on thorns did stand,
One blushing shame, another white despair;
A third, nor red nor white, had stol'n of both
And to his robbery had annex'd thy breath;
But, for his theft, in pride of all his growth
A vengeful canker eat him up to death.
  More flowers I noted, yet I none could see
  But sweet or colour it had stol'n from thee.

1-15. This is the only one of Shakespeare's sonnets having fifteen lines. **1. forward,** early. **6. for thy hand,** for stealing thy hand.

100

Where art thou, Muse, that thou forget'st so long
To speak of that which gives thee all thy might?
Spend'st thou thy fury on some worthless song,
Dark'ning thy power to lend base subjects light?
Return, forgetful Muse, and straight redeem
In gentle numbers time so idly spent;
Sing to the ear that doth thy lays esteem
And gives thy pen both skill and argument.
Rise, resty Muse, my love's sweet face survey,
If Time have any wrinkle graven there;

If any, be a satire to decay,
And make Time's spoils despised everywhere.
Give my love fame faster than Time wastes life;
So thou prevent'st his scythe and crooked knife.

3. fury, inspiration. **9. resty,** sluggish. **11. be . . . decay,** satirize the destructive power of time. **14. prevent'st,** forestall'st.

101

O truant Muse, what shall be thy amends
For thy neglect of truth in beauty dy'd?
Both truth and beauty on my love depends;
So dost thou too, and therein dignifi'd.
Make answer, Muse: wilt thou not haply say,
"Truth needs no colour, with his colour fix'd;
Beauty no pencil, beauty's truth to lay;
But best is best, if never intermix'd"?
Because he needs no praise, wilt thou be dumb?
Excuse not silence so; for 't lies in thee
To make him much outlive a gilded tomb
And to be prais'd of ages yet to be.
Then do thy office, Muse; I teach thee how
To make him seem long hence as he shows now.

4. dignified, art dignified.

102

My love is strengthen'd, though more weak in seeming;
I love not less, though less the show appear:
That love is merchandiz'd whose rich esteeming
The owner's tongue doth publish everywhere.
Our love was new and then but in the spring,
When I was wont to greet it with my lays;
As Philomel in summer's front doth sing
And stops her pipe in growth of riper days:
Not that the summer is less pleasant now
Than when her mournful hymns did hush the night,
But that wild music burdens every bough,
And sweets grown common lose their dear delight.
Therefore like her I sometime hold my tongue,
Because I would not dull you with my song.

3. esteeming, worth. **7. Philomel,** the nightingale.

103

Alack, what poverty my Muse brings forth,
That having such a scope to show her pride,
The argument, all bare, is of more worth
Than when it hath my added praise beside!
O, blame me not, if I no more can write!
Look in your glass, and there appears a face
That over-goes my blunt invention quite,
Dulling my lines and doing me disgrace.
Were it not sinful then, striving to mend,
To mar the subject that before was well?
For to no other pass my verses tend
Than of your graces and your gifts to tell;
And more, much more, than in my verse can sit
Your own glass shows you when you look in it.

11. pass, end. **13. sit,** be contained.

104

To me, fair friend, you never can be old,
For as you were when first your eye I ey'd,
Such seems your beauty still. Three winters cold
Have from the forests shook three summers' pride,
Three beauteous springs to yellow autumn turn'd
In process of the seasons have I seen,
Three April perfumes in three hot Junes burn'd,
Since first I saw you fresh, which yet are green.
Ah! yet doth beauty, like a dial-hand,
Steal from his figure and no pace perceiv'd;
So your sweet hue, which methinks still doth stand,
Hath motion, and mine eye may be deceiv'd:
For fear of which, hear this, thou age unbred:
Ere you were born was beauty's summer dead.

105

Let not my love be call'd idolatry,
Nor my beloved as an idol show,
Since all alike my songs and praises be
To one, of one, still such, and ever so.
Kind is my love to-day, to-morrow kind,
Still constant in a wondrous excellence;
Therefore my verse, to constancy confin'd,
One thing expressing, leaves out difference.
"Fair, kind, and true" is all my argument,
"Fair, kind, and true" varying to other words;
And in this change is my invention spent,
Three themes in one, which wondrous scope affords.
"Fair," "kind," and "true," have often liv'd alone,
Which three till now never kept seat in one.

2. show, appear. **8. difference,** variety.

106

When in the chronicle of wasted time
I see descriptions of the fairest wights,

And beauty making beautiful old rhyme
In praise of ladies dead and lovely knights;
Then, in the blazon of sweet beauty's best,
Of hand, of foot, of lip, of eye, of brow,
I see their antique pen would have express'd
Even such a beauty as you master now.
So all their praises are but prophecies
Of this our time, all you prefiguring,
And, for they look'd but with divining eyes,
They had not skill enough your worth to sing:
For we, which now behold these present days,
Have eyes to wonder, but lack tongues to praise.

1. chronicle of wasted time: history of olden days. **2. wights,** men. **11. for,** because. **divining eyes,** prophesying eyes, i.e., seeing from a distance and not face to face.

107

Not mine own fears, nor the prophetic soul
Of the wide world, dreaming on things to come,
Can yet the lease of my true love control,
Suppos'd as forfeit to a confin'd doom.
The mortal moon hath her eclipse endur'd,
And the sad augurs mock their own presage;
Incertainties now crown themselves assur'd,
And peace proclaims olives of endless age.
Now with the drops of this most balmy time
My love looks fresh, and Death to me subscribes,
Since, spite of him, I'll live in this poor rhyme,
While he insults o'er dull and speechless tribes:
And thou in this shalt find thy monument,
When tyrants' crests and tombs of brass are spent.

3. lease, duration. **4. Wrongly thought to be doomed to forfeiture. 5. The mortal moon,** Queen Elizabeth. **her eclipse endur'd,** Sometimes taken to refer to the queen's death, and sometimes to her "climacteric" year, the sixty-third, which she passed out of on September 6, 1596. **10. subscribes,** submits.

108

What's in the brain that ink may character,
Which hath not figur'd to thee my true spirit?
What's new to speak, what new to register,
That may express my love or thy dear merit?
Nothing, sweet boy; but yet, like prayers divine,
I must each day say o'er the very same,
Counting no old thing old, thou mine, I thine,
Even as when first I hallowed thy fair name.
So that eternal love in love's fresh case
Weighs not the dust and injury of age,
Nor gives to necessary wrinkles place,
But makes antiquity for aye his page;
Finding the first conceit of love there bred
Where time and outward form would show it dead.

1. character, write. **9. in love's fresh case,** given new expression. **13. the first conceit of love,** love's earliest bloom.

109

O never say that I was false of heart,
Though absence seem'd my flame to qualify.
As easy might I from myself depart
As from my soul, which in thy breast doth lie.
That is my home of love; if I have rang'd,
Like him that travels I return again,
Just to the time, not with the time exchang'd,
So that myself bring water for my stain.
Never believe, though in my nature reign'd
All frailties that besiege all kinds of blood,
That it could so preposterously be stain'd,
To leave for nothing all thy sum of good;
For nothing this wide universe I call,
Save thou, my rose; in it thou art my all.

2. qualify, moderate. **7. Just to the time,** punctually. **exchang'd,** changed. **8. myself . . . stain,** justify my fault of absence.

110

Alas, 'tis true I have gone here and there
And made myself a motley to the view,
Gor'd mine own thoughts, sold cheap what is most dear,
Made old offences of affections new.
Most true it is that I have look'd on truth
Askance and strangely; but, by all above,
These blenches gave my heart another youth,
And worse essays prov'd thee my best of love.
Now all is done, have what shall have no end:
Mine appetite I never more will grind
On newer proof, to try an older friend,
A god in love, to whom I am confin'd.
Then give me welcome, next my heaven the best,
Even to thy pure and most most loving breast.

2. motley . . . view, a public jester. **4. Made new friends and neglected older ones. 7. blenches,** glances aside. **10. grind,** whet.

111

O, for my sake do you with Fortune chide,
The guilty goddess of my harmful deeds,
That did not better for my life provide
Than public means which public manners breeds.
Thence comes it that my name receives a brand,

And almost thence my nature is subdu'd
To what it works in, like the dyer's hand.
Pity me, then, and wish I were renew'd;
Whilst, like a willing patient, I will drink
Potions of eisel 'gainst my strong infection;
No bitterness that I will bitter think,
Nor double penance, to correct correction.
  Pity me then, dear friend, and I assure ye
  Even that your pity is enough to cure me.

4. public means, A way of livelihood dependent on public favor. **public,** vulgar. **8. renew'd,** restored. **10. eisel,** vinegar. **12.** I will not refuse a double penance to make my correction doubly sure.

112

Your love and pity doth th' impression fill
Which vulgar scandal stamp'd upon my brow;
For what care I who calls me well or ill,
So you o'er-green my bad, my good allow?
You are my all-the-world, and I must strive
To know my shames and praises from your tongue;
None else to me, nor I to none alive,
That my steel'd sense or changes right or wrong.
In so profound abysm I throw all care
Of others' voices, that my adder's sense
To critic and to flatterer stopped are.
Mark how with my neglect I do dispense:
  You are so strongly in my purpose bred
  That all the world besides, methinks, are dead.

4. o'er-green, cover as grass covers the bare earth. **7-8.** There is no one but us, and only you can influence my opinion of right or wrong. **10. adder's sense,** the adder was thought deaf. See Psalm 58.4. **12.** Notice my indifference to the neglect of others.

113

Since I left you, mine eye is in my mind;
And that which governs me to go about
Doth part his function and is partly blind,
Seems seeing, but effectually is out:
For it no form delivers to the heart
Of bird, of flower, or shape, which it doth latch:
Of his quick objects hath the mind no part,
Nor his own vision holds what it doth catch;
For if it see the rud'st or gentlest sight,
The most sweet favour or deformed'st creature,
The mountain or the sea, the day or night,
The crow or dove, it shapes them to your feature:
  Incapable of more, replete with you,
  My most true mind thus maketh mine eye untrue.

1. mine . . . mind, I see the remembered image of you. **3. part,** divide. **6. latch,** lay hold of. **7. quick,** presented in swift succession.

114

Or whether doth my mind, being crown'd with you,
Drink up the monarch's plague, this flattery?
Or whether shall I say, mine eye saith true,
And that your love taught it this alchemy,
To make of monsters and things indigest
Such cherubins as your sweet self resemble,
Creating every bad a perfect best,
As fast as objects to his beams assemble?
O, 'tis the first; 'tis flattery in my seeing,
And my great mind most kingly drinks it up:
Mine eye well knows what with his gust is 'greeing,
And to his palate doth prepare the cup.
  If it be poison'd, 'tis the lesser sin
  That mine eye loves it and doth first begin.

1 and 3. Or whether, Is it true that? The phrase is used to introduce alternative statements. **1. crown'd with,** intoxicated with thoughts of. **5. indigest,** formless. **11. gust,** taste.

115

Those lines that I before have writ do lie,
Even those that said I could not love you dearer;
Yet then my judgement knew no reason why
My most full flame should afterwards burn clearer.
But reckoning time, whose million'd accidents
Creep in 'twixt vows and change decrees of kings,
Tan sacred beauty, blunt the sharp'st intents,
Divert strong minds to the course of alt'ring things;
Alas, why, fearing of time's tyranny,
Might I not then say, "Now I love you best,"
When I was certain o'er incertainty,
Crowning the present, doubting of the rest?
  Love is a babe; then might I not say so,
  To give full growth to that which still doth grow.

116

Let me not to the marriage of true minds
Admit impediments. Love is not love
Which alters when it alteration finds,
Or bends with the remover to remove.
O no, it is an ever-fixed mark
That looks on tempests and is never shaken;
It is the star to every wand'ring bark,
Whose worth's unknown, although his height be taken.
Love's not Time's fool, though rosy lips and cheeks
Within his bending sickle's compass come;

Love alters not with his brief hours and weeks,
But bears it out even to the edge of doom.
If this be error and upon me proved,
I never writ, nor no man ever loved.

4. **remover**, inconstant one. **to remove**, depart from one's abiding place. 8. The altitude of a star is known, but the riches it contains are unknowable.

117

Accuse me thus: that I have scanted all
Wherein I should your great deserts repay,
Forgot upon your dearest love to call,
Whereto all bonds do tie me day by day;
That I have frequent been with unknown minds,
And given to time your own dear-purchas'd right;
That I have hoisted sail to all the winds
Which should transport me farthest from your sight.
Book both my wilfulness and errors down,
And on just proof surmise accumulate;
Bring me within the level of your frown,
But shoot not at me in your wakened hate,
Since my appeal says I did strive to prove
The constancy and virtue of your love.

5. **been . . . minds**, been familiar with nonentities. 10. Add what you suspect to what you know.

118

Like as, to make our appetites more keen,
With eager compounds we our palate urge,
As, to prevent our maladies unseen,
We sicken to shun sickness when we purge;
Even so, being full of your ne'er-cloying sweetness,
To bitter sauces did I frame my feeding,
And, sick of welfare, found a kind of meetness
To be diseas'd, ere that there was true needing.
Thus policy in love, t' anticipate
The ills that were not, grew to faults assured,
And brought to medicine a healthful state
Which, rank of goodness, would by ill be cured:
But thence I learn, and find the lesson true,
Drugs poison him that so fell sick of you.

7. **sick of welfare**, sated with happiness. 10. **faults assured**, positive faults. 11. **brought to medicine**, prescribed drugs for.

119

What potions have I drunk of Siren tears,
Distill'd from limbecks foul as hell within,
Applying fears to hopes and hopes to fears,
Still losing when I saw myself to win!
What wretched errors hath my heart committed,
Whilst it hath thought itself so blessed never!
How have mine eyes out of their spheres been fitted,
In the distraction of this madding fever!
O benefit of ill! now I find true
That better is by evil still made better;
And ruin'd love, when it is built anew,
Grows fairer than at first, more strong, far greater.
So I return rebuk'd to my content,
And gain by ills thrice more than I have spent.

2. **limbecks**, alembics. 4. Winning new loves but losing the old. 7. **fitted**, convulsed. 8. A probable reference to the affair with the dark lady.

120

That you were once unkind befriends me now,
And for that sorrow, which I then did feel,
Needs must I under my transgression bow,
Unless my nerves were brass or hammered steel.
For if you were by my unkindness shaken
As I by yours, you've pass'd a hell of time;
And I, a tyrant, have no leisure taken
To weigh how once I suffered in your crime.
O, that our night of woe might have remember'd
My deepest sense, how hard true sorrow hits,
And soon to you, as you to me, then tender'd
The humble salve which wounded bosoms fits!
But that your trespass now becomes a fee;
Mine ransoms yours, and yours must ransom me.

8. **weigh**, consider. **your crime**, offense against me. 13. **fee**, recompense.

121

'Tis better to be vile than vile esteemed,
When not to be receives reproach of being;
And the just pleasure lost which is so deemed
Not by our feeling but by others' seeing.
For why should others' false adulterate eyes
Give salutation to my sportive blood?
Or on my frailties why are frailer spies,
Which in their wills count bad what I think good?
No, I am that I am, and they that level
At my abuses reckon up their own;
I may be straight, though they themselves be bevel;
By their rank thoughts my deeds must not be shown;
Unless this general evil they maintain,
All men are bad, and in their badness reign.

5-6. Why should vicious (**adulterate**) people greet me as one of their kind because of my **sportive blood**. 11. **bevel**, slanting, therefore not upright.

122

Thy gift, thy tables, are within my brain
Full character'd with lasting memory,
Which shall above that idle rank remain,
Beyond all date, even to eternity:
Or at the least, so long as brain and heart
Have faculty by nature to subsist;
Till each to raz'd oblivion yield his part
Of thee, thy record never can be miss'd.
That poor retention could not so much hold,
Nor need I tallies thy dear love to score;
Therefore to give them from me was I bold,
To trust those tables that receive thee more.
  To keep an adjunct to remember thee
  Were to import forgetfulness in me.

1. tables, memorandum book. **3. idle rank,** useless series of leaves. **7. raz'd oblivion,** the oblivion of complete destruction. **9. poor retention,** thy tables.

123

No, Time, thou shalt not boast that I do change.
Thy pyramids build up with newer might
To me are nothing novel, nothing strange;
They are but dressings of a former sight.
Our dates are brief, and therefore we admire
What thou dost foist upon us that is old,
And rather make them born to our desire
Than think that we before have heard them told.
Thy registers and thee I both defy,
Not wond'ring at the present nor the past,
For thy records and what we see doth lie,
Made more or less by thy continual haste.
  This I do vow and this shall ever be;
  I will be true, despite thy scythe and thee.

2. pyramids, structures in general. **newer,** more recent. **4. dressings,** refashionings. **5. dates,** years. **12. Made more or less,** are in false focus.

124

If my dear love were but the child of state,
It might for Fortune's bastard be unfather'd,
As subject to Time's love or to Time's hate,
Weeds among weeds, or flowers with flowers gather'd.
No, it was builded far from accident;
It suffers not in smiling pomp, nor falls
Under the blow of thralled discontent,
Whereto th' inviting time our fashion calls:
It fears not policy, that heretic,
Which works on leases of short-number'd hours,
But all alone stands hugely politic,
That it nor grows with heat nor drowns with showers.
  To this I witness call the fools of Time,
  Which die for goodness, who have liv'd for crime.

1. state, somewhat accidental (See l. 5) circumstances. **7. thralled discontent,** discontent held in subjection. **9. policy,** self-interest. **heretic,** heretic because it has no true faith. **11. politic,** wise.

125

Were't aught to me I bore the canopy,
With my extern the outward honouring,
Or laid great bases for eternity,
Which proves more short than waste or ruining?
Have I not seen dwellers on form and favour
Lose all and more by paying too much rent,
For compound sweet forgoing simple savour,
Pitiful thrivers, in their gazing spent?
No, let me be obsequious in thy heart,
And take thou my oblation, poor but free,
Which is not mix'd with seconds, knows no art,
But mutual render, only me for thee.
  Hence, thou suborn'd informer! A true soul
  When most impeach'd stands least in thy control.

1. bore the canopy, rendered outward homage. **3.** Made great plans for the future. **8. Pitiful thrivers,** wasters pitiable even in their prosperity. **11. seconds,** inferior matter. **12. mutual render,** fair exchange. **13. suborn'd informer,** jealousy or suspicion.

126

O thou, my lovely boy, who in thy power
Dost hold Time's fickle glass, his sickle, hour;
Who hast by waning grown, and therein show'st
Thy lovers withering as thy sweet self grow'st;
If Nature, sovereign mistress over wrack,
As thou goest onwards, still will pluck thee back,
She keeps thee to this purpose, that her skill
May Time disgrace and wretched minutes kill.
Yet fear her, O thou minion of her pleasure!
She may detain, but not still keep, her treasure;
Her audit, though delay'd, answer'd must be,
And her quietus is to render thee.

1-12. This, the last poem in the series addressed to the friend, consists of six rhymed couplets. **1-2.** The second line is variously interpreted, but the fundamental meaning of the passage is clear: the young man seemingly has the power to defy time. **3. Who . . . grown,** He grows more beautiful as he grows older. **6. pluck thee back,** keep you young. **12. quietus,** acquittance of the account.

127

In the old age black was not counted fair,
Or if it were, it bore not beauty's name;
But now is black beauty's successive heir,
And beauty slander'd with a bastard shame:

For since each hand hath put on nature's power,
Fairing the foul with art's false borrow'd face,
Sweet beauty hath no name, no holy bower,
But is profan'd, if not lives in disgrace.
Therefore my mistress' brows are raven black,
Her eyes so suited, and they mourners seem
At such who, not born fair, no beauty lack,
Sland'ring creation with a false esteem:
Yet so they mourn, becoming of their woe,
That every tongue says beauty should look so.

1. fair, (1) beautiful, (2) light-colored. 4. Blonde beauty is supposed produced by artificial means. 11. no beauty lack, i.e., because their beauty is artificial.

128

How oft, when thou, my music, music play'st,
Upon that blessed wood whose motion sounds
With thy sweet fingers, when thou gently sway'st
The wiry concord that mine ear confounds,
Do I envy those jacks that nimble leap
To kiss the tender inward of thy hand,
Whilst my poor lips, which should that harvest reap,
At the wood's boldness by thee blushing stand!
To be so tickled, they would change their state
And situation with those dancing chips,
O'er whom thy fingers walk with gentle gait,
Making dead wood more blest than living lips.
Since saucy jacks so happy are in this,
Give them thy fingers, me thy lips to kiss.

2. blessed wood, keys of the spinet or the virginal. 5. jacks, keys.

129

The expense of spirit in a waste of shame
Is lust in action; and till action, lust
Is perjur'd, murd'rous, bloody, full of blame,
Savage, extreme, rude, cruel, not to trust:
Enjoy'd no sooner but despised straight,
Past reason hunted, and no sooner had,
Past reason hated, as a swallowed bait
On purpose laid to make the taker mad;
Mad in pursuit and in possession so;
Had, having, and in quest to have, extreme;
A bliss in proof, and prov'd, a very woe;
Before, a joy propos'd; behind a dream.
All this the world well knows; yet none knows well
To shun the heaven that leads men to this hell.

1. expense, expenditure. 2. till action, until expressed in deeds.

130

My mistress' eyes are nothing like the sun;
Coral is far more red than her lips' red;
If snow be white, why then her breasts are dun;
If hairs be wires, black wires grow on her head.
I have seen roses damask'd, red and white,
But no such roses see I in her cheeks;
And in some perfumes is there more delight
Than in the breath that from my mistress reeks.
I love to hear her speak, yet well I know
That music hath a far more pleasing sound;
I grant I never saw a goddess go;
My mistress, when she walks, treads on the ground:
And yet, by heaven, I think my love as rare
As any she belied with false compare.

131

Thou art as tyrannous, so as thou art,
As those whose beauties proudly make them cruel;
For well thou know'st to my dear doting heart
Thou art the fairest and most precious jewel.
Yet, in good faith, some say that thee behold
Thy face hath not the power to make love groan:
To say they err I dare not be so bold,
Although I swear it to myself alone.
And, to be sure that is not false I swear,
A thousand groans, but thinking on thy face,
One on another's neck, do witness bear
Thy black is fairest in my judgement's place.
In nothing art thou black save in thy deeds,
And thence this slander, as I think, proceeds.

11. One on another's neck, in rapid succession.

132

Thine eyes I love, and they, as pitying me,
Knowing thy heart torments me with disdain,
Have put on black and loving mourners be,
Looking with pretty ruth upon my pain.
And truly not the morning sun of heaven
Better becomes the grey cheeks of the east,
Nor that full star that ushers in the eyen
Doth half that glory to the sober west,
As those two mourning eyes become thy face.
O, let it then as well beseem thy heart
To mourn for me, since mourning doth thee grace,
And suit thy pity like in every part.
Then will I swear beauty herself is black
And all they foul that thy complexion lack.

4. ruth, pity. 12. suit, dress. like, alike.

133

Beshrew that heart that makes my heart to groan
For that deep wound it gives my friend and me!
Is't not enough to torture me alone,
But slave to slavery my sweet'st friend must be?
Me from myself thy cruel eye hath taken,
And my next self thou harder hast engrossed:
Of him, myself, and thee, I am forsaken;
A torment thrice threefold thus to be crossed.
Prison my heart in thy steel bosom's ward,
But then my friend's heart let my poor heart bail;
Whoe'er keeps me, let my heart be his guard;
Thou canst not then use rigour in my gaol:
  And yet thou wilt; for I, being pent in thee,
  Perforce am thine, and all that is in me.

6. next self, *alter ego,* **the friend. 10. Let my poor heart secure the freedom of my friend's heart.**

134

So, now I have confess'd that he is thine,
And I myself am mortgag'd to thy will,
Myself I'll forfeit, so that other mine
Thou wilt restore, to be my comfort still:
But thou wilt not, nor he will not be free,
For thou art covetous and he is kind;
He learn'd but surety-like to write for me
Under that bond that him as fast doth bind.
The statute of thy beauty thou wilt take,
Thou usurer, that put'st forth all to use,
And sue a friend came debtor for my sake;
So him I lose through my unkind abuse.
  Him have I lost; thou hast both him and me:
  He pays the whole, and yet am I not free.

7. surety-like, as a man endorses a bond. The terminology of the sonnet is legal. The meaning is that the friend, to whom Shakespeare is indebted, has unwittingly been led into the betrayal of his friendship.

135

Whoever hath her wish, thou hast thy *Will,*
And *Will* to boot, and *Will* in overplus;
More than enough am I that vex thee still,
To thy sweet will making addition thus.
Wilt thou, whose will is large and spacious,
Not once vouchsafe to hide my will in thine?
Shall will in others seem right gracious,
And in my will no fair acceptance shine?
The sea, all water, yet receives rain still
And in abundance addeth to his store;
So thou, being rich in *Will,* add to thy *Will*
One will of mine, to make thy large *Will* more.
  Let no unkind no fair beseechers kill;
  Think all but one, and me in that one *Will.*

Sonnets 135-6 are distinguished chiefly by their four-way puns. (1) Will is the poet's name. (2) The friend is here called Will. The word means (3) volition and (4) desire. 13. unkind, perhaps means "unkindness."

136

If thy soul check thee that I come so near,
Swear to thy blind soul that I was thy *Will,*
And will, thy soul knows, is admitted there;
Thus far for love, my love-suit, sweet, fulfil.
Will will fulfil the treasure of thy love,
Ay, fill it full with wills, and my will one.
In things of great receipt with ease we prove
Among a number one is reckon'd none:
Then in the number let me pass untold,
Though in thy store's account I one must be;
For nothing hold me, so it please thee hold
That nothing me, a something sweet to thee.
  Make but my name thy love and love that still,
  And then thou lov'st me, for my name is *Will.*

137

Thou blind fool, Love, what dost thou to mine eyes,
That they behold, and see not what they see?
They know what beauty is, see where it lies,
Yet what the best is take the worst to be.
If eyes, corrupt by over-partial looks
Be anchor'd in the bay where all men ride,
Why of eyes' falsehood hast thou forged hooks,
Whereto the judgement of my heart is tied?
Why should my heart think that a several plot
Which my heart knows the wide world's common place?
Or mine eyes seeing this, say this is not,
To put fair truth upon so foul a face?
  In things right true my heart and eyes have erred,
  And to this false plague are they now transferred.

6. bay . . . ride, a roadstead open to any man's ship. 9. several, private.

138

When my love swears that she is made of truth,
I do believe her, though I know she lies,
That she might think me some untutor'd youth,
Unlearned in the world's false subtleties.
Thus vainly thinking that she thinks me young,
Although she knows my days are past the best,

Simply I credit her false-speaking tongue:
On both sides thus is simple truth suppress'd.
But wherefore says she not she is unjust?
And wherefore say not I that I am old?
O, love's best habit is in seeming trust,
And age in love loves not to have years told:
  Therefore I lie with her and she with me,
  And in our faults by lies we flattered be.

139

O, call not me to justify the wrong
That thy unkindness lays upon my heart;
Wound me not with thine eye, but with thy tongue;
Use power with power, and slay me not by art.
Tell me thou lov'st elsewhere, but in my sight,
Dear heart, forbear to glance thine eye aside:
What need'st thou wound with cunning when thy might
Is more than my o'er-press'd defence can bide?
Let me excuse thee: ah! my love well knows
Her pretty looks have been mine enemies,
And therefore from my face she turns my foes,
That they elsewhere might dart their injuries.
  Yet do not so; but since I am near slain,
  Kill me outright with looks and rid my pain.

11. my foes, her pretty looks (l. 10).

140

Be wise as thou art cruel; do not press
My tongue-tied patience with too much disdain,
Lest sorrow lend me words, and words express
The manner of my pity-wanting pain.
If I might teach thee wit, better it were,
Though not to love, yet, love, to tell me so;
As testy sick men, when their deaths be near,
No news but health from their physicians know;
For, if I should despair, I should grow mad,
And in my madness might speak ill of thee;
Now this ill-wresting world is grown so bad,
Mad slanderers by mad ears believed be.
  That I may not be so, nor thou belied,
  Bear thine eyes straight, though thy proud heart go wide.

6. Though not to love, even if you do not love me. 11. ill-wresting, putting the worst interpretation on everything.

141

In faith, I do not love thee with mine eyes,
For they in thee a thousand errors note;
But 'tis my heart that loves what they despise,
Who in despite of view is pleas'd to dote;
Nor are mine ears with thy tongue's tune delighted,
Nor tender feeling, to base touches prone,
Nor taste, nor smell, desire to be invited
To any sensual feast with thee alone:
But my five wits nor my five senses can
Dissuade one foolish heart from serving thee,
Who leaves unsway'd the likeness of a man,
Thy proud heart's slave and vassal wretch to be:
  Only my plague thus far I count my gain,
  That she that makes me sin awards me pain.

9. five wits, common wit, imagination, fantasy, estimation, and memory.

142

Love is my sin, and thy dear virtue hate,
Hate of my sin, grounded on sinful loving:
O, but with mine compare thou thine own state,
And thou shalt find it merits not reproving;
Or, if it do, not from those lips of thine,
That have profan'd their scarlet ornaments
And seal'd false bonds of love as oft as mine,
Robb'd others' beds' revenues of their rents.
Be it lawful I love thee, as thou lov'st those
Whom thine eyes woo as mine importune thee:
Root pity in thy heart, that when it grows
Thy pity may deserve to pitied be.
  If thou dost seek to have what thou dost hide,
  By self-example mayst thou be denied.

1. dear, especial. 13. hide, hide from me, refuse.

143

Lo! as a careful housewife runs to catch
One of her feathered creatures broke away,
Sets down her babe, and makes all swift dispatch
In pursuit of the thing she would have stay;
Whilst her neglected childs holds her in chase,
Cries to catch her whose busy care is bent
To follow that which flies before her face,
Not prizing her poor infant's discontent:
So runn'st thou after that which flies from thee,
Whilst I, thy babe, chase thee afar behind;
But if thou catch thy hope, turn back to me,
And play the mother's part, kiss me, be kind:
  So will I pray that thou mayst have thy *Will*,
  If thou turn back, and my loud crying still.

13. Will, see note on Sonnets 135-136.

144

Two loves I have, of comfort and despair,
Which like two spirits do suggest me still:

The better angel is a man right fair,
The worser spirit a woman colour'd ill.
To win me soon to hell, my female evil
Tempteth my better angel from my side,
And would corrupt my saint to be a devil,
Wooing his purity with her foul pride.
And whether that my angel be turn'd fiend
Suspect I may, yet not directly tell;
But being both from me, both to each friend,
I guess one angel in another's hell:
  Yet this shall I ne'er know, but live in doubt,
  Till my bad angel fire my good one out.

2. suggest, prompt, tempt. **11. from,** absent from. **both to each friend,** each friendly to the other.

145

Those lips that Love's own hand did make
Breath'd forth the sound that said, "I hate,"
To me that languish'd for her sake;
But when she saw my woeful state,
Straight in her heart did mercy come,
Chiding that tongue that ever sweet
Was us'd in giving gentle doom,
And taught it thus anew to greet:
"I hate," she alter'd with an end,
That follow'd it as gentle day
Doth follow night, who like a fiend
From heaven to hell is flown away;
  "I hate" from hate away she threw,
  And saved my life, saying "not you."

The only one of the sonnets in tetrameter lines.

146

Poor soul, the centre of my sinful earth,
Thrall to these rebel powers that thee array,
Why dost thou pine within and suffer dearth,
Painting thy outward walls so costly gay?
Why so large cost, having so short a lease,
Dost thou upon thy fading mansion spend?
Shall worms, inheritors of this excess,
Eat up thy charge? Is this thy body's end?
Then, soul, live thou upon thy servant's loss,
And let that pine to aggravate thy store;
Buy terms divine in selling hours of dross
Within be fed, without be rich no more:
  So shalt thou feed on Death, that feeds on men,
  And Death once dead, there's no more dying then.

10. aggravate, increase. **11. terms divine,** eternity in heaven.

147

My love is as a fever, longing still
For that which longer nurseth the disease;
Feeding on that which doth preserve the ill,
Th' uncertain sickly appetite to please.
My reason, the physician to my love,
Angry that his prescriptions are not kept,
Hath left me, and I desperate now approve
Desire is death, which physic did except.
Past cure I am, now reason is past care,
And frantic-mad with evermore unrest;
My thoughts and my discourse as madmen's are,
At random from the truth vainly express'd;
  For I have sworn thee fair and thought thee bright,
  Who art as black as hell, as dark as night.

6. kept, followed. **7-8. and . . . except,** I, whose condition is desperate, discover that for desire to refuse the physic of reason is death.

148

O me, what eyes hath Love put in my head,
Which have no correspondence with true sight;
Or, if they have, where is my judgment fled,
That censures falsely what they see aright?
If that be fair whereon my false eyes dote,
What means the world to say it is not so?
If it be not, then love doth well denote
Love's eye is not so true as all men's: no,
How can it? O, how can Love's eye be true,
That is so vex'd with watching and with tears?
No marvel then, though I mistake my view;
The sun itself sees not till heaven clears.
  O cunning Love! with tears thou keep'st me blind,
  Lest eyes well-seeing thy foul faults should find.

4. censures, judges. **10. watching,** wakefulness.

149

Canst thou, O cruel! say I love thee not,
When I against myself with thee partake?
Do I not think on thee, when I forgot
Am of myself, all tyrant, for thy sake?
Who hateth thee that I do call my friend?
On whom frown'st thou that I do fawn upon?
Nay, if thou lour'st on me, do I not spend
Revenge upon myself with present moan?
What merit do I in myself respect,
That is so proud thy service to despise,
When all my best doth worship thy defect,
Commanded by the motion of thine eyes?
  But, love, hate on, for now I know thy mind;
  Those that can see thou lov'st, and I am blind.

2. partake, take part. **4. all tyrant,** thou complete tyrant.

150

O, from what power hast thou this powerful might,
With insufficiency my heart to sway?
To make me give the lie to my true sight,
And swear that brightness doth not grace the day?
Whence hast thou this becoming of things ill,
That in the very refuse of thy deeds
There is such strength and warrantise of skill
That, in my mind, thy worst all best exceeds?
Who taught thee how to make me love thee more
The more I hear and see just cause of hate?
O, though I love what others do abhor,
With others thou shouldst not abhor my state:
If thy unworthiness rais'd love in me,
More worthy I to be belov'd of thee.

7. warrantise, assurance.

151

Love is too young to know what conscience is;
Yet who knows not conscience is born of love?
Then, gentle cheater, urge not my amiss,
Lest guilty of my faults thy sweet self prove:
For, thou betraying me, I do betray
My nobler part to my gross body's treason;
My soul doth tell my body that he may
Triumph in love; flesh stays no farther reason,
But, rising at thy name, doth point out thee
As his triumphant prize. Proud of this pride,
He is contented thy poor drudge to be,
To stand in thy affairs, fall by thy side.
No want of conscience hold it that I call
Her "love" for whose dear love I rise and fall.

3. urge, stress. **amiss,** sinfulness.

152

In loving thee thou know'st I am forsworn,
But thou art twice forsworn, to me love swearing;
In act thy bed-vow broke, and new faith torn,
In vowing new hate after new love bearing.
But why of two oaths' breach do I accuse thee,
When I break twenty? I am perjur'd most;
For all my vows are oaths but to misuse thee,
And all my honest faith in thee is lost.
For I have sworn deep oaths of thy deep kindness,
Oaths of thy love, thy truth, thy constancy;
And, to enlighten thee, gave eyes to blindness,
Or made them swear against the thing they see;
For I have sworn thee fair; more perjur'd I,
To swear against the truth so foul a lie!

1. I am forsworn, presumably towards his own wife. **2. twice,** see l. 3. **7. oaths . . . thee,** deceptive oaths. **8. honest faith,** sincerity. **11. enlighten,** shed lustre upon.

153

Cupid laid by his brand, and fell asleep.
A maid of Dian's this advantage found,
And his love-kindling fire did quickly steep
In a cold valley-fountain of that ground;
Which borrow'd from this holy fire of Love
A dateless lively heat, still to endure,
And grew a seething bath, which yet men prove
Against strange maladies a sovereign cure.
But at my mistress' eye Love's brand new-fired,
The boy for trial needs would touch my breast;
I, sick withal, the help of bath desired,
And thither hied, a sad distemper'd guest,
But found no cure: the bath for my help lies
Where Cupid got new fire—my mistress' eyes.

Sonnets 153 and 154 were possibly written to be given to a lady who was going to stay at Bath. **6. dateless,** endless.

154

The little Love-god lying once asleep
Laid by his side his heart-inflaming brand,
Whilst many nymphs that vow'd chaste life to keep
Came tripping by; but in her maiden hand
The fairest votary took up that fire
Which many legions of true hearts had warm'd;
And so the general of hot desire
Was, sleeping, by a virgin hand disarm'd.
This brand she quenched in a cool well by,
Which from Love's fire took heat perpetual,
Growing a bath and healthful remedy
For men diseas'd; but I, my mistress' thrall,
Came there for cure, and this by that I prove:
Love's fire heats water, water cools not love.